# SOCIAL SYSTEMS AND FAMILY PATTERNS

## A Propositional Inventory

# SOCIAL SYSTEMS AND FAMILY PATTERNS

## A Propositional Inventory

**WILLIAM J. GOODE**

**ELIZABETH HOPKINS**

**HELEN M. McCLURE**

The Bobbs-Merrill Company, Inc.
Indianapolis • New York

# CONTENTS

# INTRODUCTION

## I.

This compilation of research findings on the family as a social institution contains most of the major correlations among factors internal to the family unit—for example, "In a society that has permissive attitudes toward premarital pregnancy, there is a lower correlation between divorce and premarital pregnancy than in a society which is less permissive"; or, "A society that requires a long period of sexual abstinence after the birth of a child is also more likely to have ritual patterns of initiation at puberty and to extrude the adolescent boy from his family at puberty than is the society with no postpartum sex taboo."

This compendium also contains most of the major propositions relating family variables to *other* institutions—for example, "Because war is likely to create a higher sex ratio (through either a shortage of men or the capture of women), there is an association between warfare as a social pattern and polygyny"; or, "The introduction of a cash economy leads to the breakdown of elders' control over the mate choices made by the younger generation." Of course, a fairly high percentage of less important propositions relating to the family are also stated here.

For the most part, these relations apply not merely to the twentieth-century urban United States, but to most family systems. Moreover, although the sociology of the family has been rightly criticized for its low level of research sophistication, most of these propositions can be viewed as at least crude approximations of empirical reality.

Within the limitations to be sketched later, such an inventory has a wide array of uses and raises several important theoretical questions in the field of sociology. These limitations are discussed most appropriately in Section IV, which is devoted to the construction of this compendium. Its uses are briefly listed here and are discussed in the succeeding section. The place of such a compilation in contemporary theory is a more fundamental question and will be outlined in greater detail in Section III.

## II. THE USES OF A PROPOSITIONAL INVENTORY

The various uses of this inventory apply to four main areas of social science activity: (1) social engineering, such as family counseling and community planning; (2) family research; (3) sociological theory; and (4) social science, the strategy of development.

Although Western social analysts have never doubted the pragmatic importance of the family as an institution and although the family is one of the most popular topics in contemporary social research, as a field its progress has been hampered by failure in systematization, in organization, and even in simple compilation. Scattered research has often remained unintegrated. Findings that apply to the United States have not been systematically confronted by those from other nations and cultures. Relevant materials are to be found in journals that are accessible or known only to few. Research has remained on a fairly concrete level, with few attempts to develop such theoretical patterns, although considerable progress has been made in the past five years in the development of more rigorous theoretical frameworks for analyzing relations either

(a) internal to family systems or (b) between family variables and those of other institutions.

The social engineer who does not reject the general goals of the society and who wishes to help individuals or groups to adjust better within that system may be little concerned with the theoretical problems of a field, but he is highly interested in its specific descriptive findings. He wishes to utilize the hard data resulting from good research but cannot, in his devotion to solving the problems of his clients, spend much of his energy or attention in reanalyzing an entire field. He needs to have data presented to him in an easily accessible and usable form. Although he learns a great deal from his own practice by advising others and watching the results, he may not have the facilities or the time to conduct research himself. Therefore, he needs to have some source which will contain, in an organized if simple form, most of the findings of the field. Since he cannot, without an elaborate library study, even locate all the possible sources of useful information, a compendium that brings together materials from a wide variety of publications should be of some service to him.

The family counselor is perhaps most concerned with two main family relationships: the adjustment between husband and wife, and the consequences of various child-rearing practices or parent-child relations for the development of the child. In this compendium, the research findings relating to these areas are presented in hundreds of propositions describing the effects of such adjustment variables as mother's employment, dominance of the mother, egalitarianism or authoritarianism, rank and education differences, religiosity, etc., on marital adjustment and child development. Of course, the community planner who wishes to develop a better school system, to reduce juvenile delinquency in a given neighborhood, or to increase the achievement motivation of deprived youngsters will already know many or most of these patterns, just as the well-trained family counselor will know most of the findings that are presented here. On the other hand, it is always of some use to the planner or advisor to have at hand a body of information that will remind him from time to time of materials that he may know but has forgotten for the moment. And, of course, while using some of the findings presented here as a kind of checklist, it may be that even the well-informed practitioner will locate relevant data that he has not come across in his reading.

Since this inventory organizes the main body of family research into related propositions grouped under large categories, the family researcher should find it especially useful. He can look under a category such as "age" or "economic patterns," and find immediately a substantial number of hypotheses that have interested researchers in the past. He will be able to see that many of these remain unsettled, since a proposition may be both affirmed and denied.

Certain groups of propositions seem to emerge as challenging questions, since they suggest somewhat contradictory patterns or, at least, confused ones. For example, a long list of researches has depicted a wide array of consequences from success to dependency that flows from being an eldest son; but the more closely one looks at the findings, the more complex and qualified they become.[1] Similarly, when the mother has somewhat greater power in family decisions and has a relatively close relation with her son, the likelihood is greater that the boy will acquire the psychological patterns now called "high need for achievement." However, the exact conditions under which these results occur are not clear, and some of the mother-dominant patterns are also associated with dependency, alcoholism, and homosexuality.

Consequently, a review of sections in this inventory or a comparison of the consequences of several variables often discloses gaps in our knowledge, or contrary relations, and thus suggests points at which research might be useful to resolve important issues.

At the same time, of course, such a compilation helps a researcher to avoid wasting his time in "discovering" a relationship that has been described many times before. Because the materials in this field as in other sociological fields are rarely well organized and are published in a wide array of journals, this danger is always present. To utilize his time more effectively, the researcher should be able to begin with hypotheses that have been already stated and use his talents to move beyond that point in his own research. Any substantial compilation of research findings should, therefore, be of utility to the family researcher.

Since Section IV will be largely devoted to the problems of social theory that are raised by such a compilation, only a brief comment is necessary here. However, some of these problems may be listed at this point:

*The utility of general sociological theory for the analysis of a specific institution such as the family*

*Functionalism*

[1] Eleanor Singer, *Birth Order, Educational Aspirations, and Educational Attainment* (Columbia University Ph.D. dissertation, 1966).

*The problems of quantification*

*Sociological and nonsociological variables: models for sociology*

*Boundaries and exchanges between social units*

Because this compendium does not confine itself only to sociological findings, but extends also to data from other fields such as economics, psychology and psychiatry, social work, anthropology, and political science, fundamental questions are raised as to the *form* that sociological theory should take. Should it confine itself to sociological variables when much of social behavior is clearly shaped by nonsociological factors? The findings in this compilation are *hypotheses,* but at what point does a set of hypotheses become transformed into something like a *theory?* Is it possible to rework some of the subsections of this compilation and to develop from it a more integrated and systematic set of relations that would both sum up those findings and suggest still others?

The lack of theoretical rigor in sociology is evident. Do such compendia as this one help us to achieve greater rigor? At the very least such a compilation does present a challenge to the social theorist, whether his aim is a unified and general social science or a rigorous sociological theory. Indeed, even those who believe that social theory is more appropriately a wise commentary on social behavior may be moved to that form of theorizing by a perusal of this array of family behavior.

Finally, this inventory should be of some use in the strategy of social science development. In addition to the tasks of applying findings to concrete situations and creating specific research investigations, some social scientists have the responsibility of thinking about long-term strategy in sociology or social science in general. Although grants may be made for specific investigations, the criteria for such decisions will not only be whether a given idea has been tested before, but also whether it seems worthwhile to do so as part of a broader program in understanding human behavior. Foundation executives who wish to support social science must concern themselves with the training of young graduate students now, in the light of the future of the field.

A perusal of this compendium should then be useful, for it indicates some areas in which a great amount of work has been done and others in which relatively little has been done (e.g., the exchanges of resources among some segments of the society, institutions, agencies, and organizations). Foundations, both private and governmental, have been reluctant to support men who wish to achieve theoretical integrations of the findings in their field and, by contrast, have been far more generous in supporting concrete investigations, especially when the researchers promise to interview several hundred people about a given topic and produce thousands of cross-tabulations from a set of IBM cards or computer tapes. A study of this compilation may suggest the desirability of a research strategy that will spend far more time on theoretical work, specifically, the more rigorous integration of research findings and the development of more systematic hypotheses from them, and somewhat less time on the traditional survey. Perhaps sociology might progress if somewhat less emphasis were placed on the "practical applications" section that figures so largely in requests for research grants.

In any event, it seems likely that those who concern themselves with social science strategy will find some merit in this compilation, since it sums up a considerable part of one subfield in social science. By directing attention to what has in fact been accomplished, perhaps we may see better what ought to be our aims in the future.

This inventory also raises a question that figures largely in current discussions of social science strategy: the problem of archives and information retrieval. This compendium has all the uses noted above because it basically is a *source book,* a crude information retrieval system. If all these data were on tape, if a location, coding, and flow procedure were continuously augmenting the archives, *and* if every concerned social scientist or engineer could elicit those data by pushing a button on his desk or by telephoning, this monograph would be redundant.

However, in contrast to the popular conception of the computerized present, in which machines happily and swiftly translate from the Chinese, engage in intimate midnight conversations about the idiosyncrasies of the scientists who serve them, or quietly pulsate while waiting to disgorge data, most social scientists live in this century, not the next. In this one, they must do their own observing, reading, translating, and coding. In order to look up information, a human being must go to the library. The information is still in books and often not easily accessible even there: the book is not available, its data are not organized to answer easily the researcher's purposes, or (more likely) the scientist has only a vague notion of just which book or books he needs.

As General Marshall commented drily after

World War II when asked whether the United States was girded for the new system, i.e., pushbutton warfare, "Well, we do have the button." Many systems of information retrieval are under way and present social science strategy takes for granted the expenditure of large amounts for still more complex plans, but the social scientist cannot live in the future. Even those few who have the button learn, when they press it, that it is not connected with anything. We all have the ability to call spirits from the vasty deep, but as Hotspur implied several centuries ago, very likely they will not come when called.

Primitive as this present information retrieval system is, it should be useful in the several areas noted above: family counseling and community planning, family research and social theory, and social science strategy. We hope, too, that the scholar who looks at this archival form will be better able to see how improvements can be made so as to serve all of these ends much more effectively.

## III. PROBLEMS OF THEORY

Although it is as a source book that this compendium will be useful to most, its more fundamental aim is theoretical. It can serve as a point of departure for theory, and it raises some broader theoretical questions in the general field of sociology.

At the simplest level, when a good many propositions are brought together that center on a general variable such as the *size* of the kin unit or a somewhat more restricted one such as incest taboos, the theorist may also see how such a set might be integrated into a more fruitful interpretation or idea. Theory is after all a *structure* of empirical findings; it is easier to search out such a structure if the findings are brought together.

At a deeper level, however, this inventory raises still more basic theoretical questions and thus may serve as a stimulus to a broader integrative effort in the field of sociology. The more important of these questions are discussed below.

### GENERAL THEORY AND SPECIAL THEORIES

What is the relation between the general theory of sociology and the special theories that have been evolved in such subfields as bureaucracy, the professions, religion, and the family? One obvious exchange between the two is that the sociologist begins with general theory as an orientation and as a set of more or less standard hypotheses. On the one hand, he infers that these are also correct when applied to a particular area of social behavior and tests their correctness there. Reciprocally, and typically, the special relations in a given social institution force him to reformulate those general ideas and sometimes to generate new ones.

Thus, general theories suggest that if we encounter a continuing group anywhere, in the Ituri Forest or in a computerized factory, we expect also to observe that its members will define the appropriate requirements for entrance and the kinds of acts that should be punished by ostracism or expulsion; that new members undergo a period of socialization in order to learn the proper values and skills of the group; that its members evaluate and rank one another; that leadership activities include both the maintenance of harmonious social relations and the solution of environmental problems; that the group has a continued interaction pattern with other groups; and so on.

On the other hand, such general hypotheses must be tested anew with each particular group and in the process may well be qualified or specified further. Indeed, one of the important but relatively overlooked problems of sociological theory is precisely the difficulty in translating general theory into more specific formulations, for example, "middle range" or institutional theory. These problems especially illustrate the lack of rigor in the field of sociology.

Consideration of a few examples will not solve these problems but will help to locate some of the difficulties. One may be taken from the process of adjustment to divorce. Our general notions of exchange theory would suggest that since the divorced mother with several children is worth less on the marriage market than the woman with only one child, she should therefore need a longer time to find a second husband. At the present time, the data suggest the contrary, since the mother with several children will waste far less of her courtship energy on men who are not interested in children and since at least a few men are attracted by the woman who has already demonstrated her dedication to home and family.

A second example may be drawn from one of the general notions that sociologists hold with reference to social change: the formation of the state or the still-later process of industrialization typically undermines or dissolves large kin structures such as lineages and clans. Since these are most strongly developed and are typically led by members of the higher-ranking families in any society, industrialization should have the most destructive impact on the family patterns of the upper social strata. However, present data suggest otherwise, in part because the closer links of exchange and support among kin toward the upper social strata permit such families to utilize more effectively the new opportunities in the industrializing process. More specifically, sons in the lower social strata have relatively little to lose if they rebel against their elders, since the latter do not usually control the new resources and opportunities that are made available in a period of economic growth. By contrast, family elders in the upper social strata are more likely to be in charge of these new opportunities and can command some obedience by withholding or granting them to members of their kin network.

The general advantages in power and freedom the husband enjoys in our society and the greater temptations to become involved in activities outside the home might lead one to infer that husbands would ask for divorce before wives. However, a more detailed examination of this process suggests that the husband can enjoy social acceptability outside the home while failing substantially in his familial obligations; in effect, he can make himself thoroughly obnoxious to his wife while appearing respectable to outsiders. One consequence is that he can follow a strategy that will impel his wife to ask for a divorce first, even though he may himself have first become alienated from the marriage relationship.[2]

It is not certain that from general sociological theory one could predict the *existence* of the common incest taboos in all societies, though one could perhaps predict some of their *patterns* once their existence has been postulated at all (e.g., they are most severe for relatives defined as being the closest in blood relationship; they extend furthest in the direction that is defined as genealogically most important, etc.). However, if we move one step toward greater specificity and ask what are the common incest behaviors, when the taboos have in fact been violated, again general theory is a relatively weak reed. We might be able to infer that the most common pattern would be father-daughter

incest and the least common, mother-son incest, but the prediction of other specific relations might be extremely weak.

Finally, to take an example worked out independently by both Davis and Merton some 25 years ago, we might suppose from our general knowledge of caste and the relative evaluations of different personal traits in the society that one of the least likely marriage combinations would be that of a white woman and a Negro man. As is well known, however, this has been the most common type of legal interracial union. Here, in effect, the white woman can trade her caste advantages for the economic advantages of the successful Negro man.[3]

These examples do not illustrate a single principle, except perhaps the obvious one, that at the present time in sociology there is a small or large gap between the general principles used to explain how a society operates and the somewhat more specific patterns of behavior to be found in subareas of social action such as work, religion, or the family. General theory suggests a checklist of important variables and some predicted relationships, but they seem insufficient except as a general *approach*. In some instances, the general theory suggests the wrong variables or gives too great weight to them, for example, the predictive weight of *values* as against the resources that individuals can use in their bargaining processes. Sometimes, as in the case of incest taboos generally, it is not clear that general theory would be capable of making an adequate prediction. Perhaps in all of these cases general theory simply cannot *specify* with sufficient detail; it is like a large vise that cannot close far enough to seize upon small objects.

This failure in specification can be illustrated by reference to one of the oldest of social science conceptions, the distinction variously called rural-urban, Gemeinschaft-Gesellschaft, immigrant-native born, innerdirected-otherdirected, Negro-white, and further specified fruitfully by Parsons' pattern variables. Although sociologists have been able to apply the pattern variables to a wide range of social relations, they are of relatively little use in the analysis of family behavior since almost all family-role definitions fall on the same side of these five dichotomies. That is to say, they are all collectivity oriented, ascriptive, particularistic, affective, and diffuse. Similarly, while much of general the-

---

[2]See the more extended analysis of this process in "The Strategy of Divorce," in *Women in Divorce,* 2nd ed. (New York: The Free Press, 1964), Chapter 15.

[3]On this point, see the articles by Kingsley Davis, "Intermarriage in Caste Societies," *American Anthropology* 43 (1941): 388–395; and Robert K. Merton, "Intermarriage and the Social Structure," *Psychiatry* 4 (1941): 361–374.

ory is concerned with the way in which a group maintains its collective character and boundaries, it has paid relatively less attention to social units such as the family that are under strong social pressures to remain intact.

By considering where and how our general theory fails to serve as an adequate guide, we may be better able to improve it. The present inventory suggests especially some of the following difficulties.

*Areas of inquiry that are relatively less developed.* We are especially able to locate substantive areas that have been less well developed (e.g., particular combinations of pattern variables or the dissolution of groups under high pressure to stay together) when we constantly attempt to confront our most general formulations with the somewhat more detailed behavior patterns in specific institutions.

*Precision.* Our most general formulations have not been phrased with sufficient specificity and precision; therefore, when we attempt to apply them to more concrete areas of behavior, we find that we can reason to quite contradictory conclusions. Our formulations are too vague to guide us toward precise predictions. We find this out most notably when we attempt to make those predictions and then to test them against the data to be observed in specific institutional areas such as a corporation, a church, or a family.

*Explicitness.* In spite of the continued efforts of our best theorists, few have attempted to formulate more than small theory fragments or to expound more than a general orientation toward social behavior. A general theory of sociology cannot merely be a list of a set of variables or a checklist of phenomena and types of behavior, but it must state specific predictions of relations between variables and also show how these are linked to other such predictions. This is risky and, of course, open to attack; but the structure can only be improved by stating explicitly which relationships are guiding our theorizing and then by testing them against specific behaviors.

*The lack of connection between subsets of variables.* Sociology now contains many subtheories, such as those relating to role bargaining, small groups, organizations, stratification, etc. All of these overlap and to some extent they draw upon some common sociological principle. However, those who wish to use any of these as a guide or a more general theory as a guide cannot easily decide when to apply *one* of these in analyzing a given pattern of social behavior or when to borrow variables from several of these simultaneously.

This is a simple way of stating that we have not specified our phenomena adequately and that we have not looked closely enough to see which of our general principles can be illustrated by any of these subtheories.

Because of these gaps and the advantages that would flow from bridging them, this inventory should be of some merit to general theory. It should be possible, except when our theory is inadequate in some respect, to predict almost all of the *sociological* relationships in this inventory. Where such a prediction seems to be difficult or impossible, the general theory would seem to be somewhat inadequate. It is precisely *at those points* that we should attempt to improve it.

## FUNCTIONALISM

In this inventory, the functionalist vocabulary—e.g., "the function of the incest taboo is to integrate the society"—is not used because it no longer serves any purpose in contemporary family theory. Fortunately, the intellectual debate as to the theoretical correctness of functionalism has ended. Contemporary attacks on functionalism are now of relevance only to the sociology of science, as an example of a controversy that has outlived its issues.

Ralf Dahrendorf, attacker of functionalism but wiser than many who agree with his critiques, has concluded that, "the structural-functional theory is no longer to be discarded from sociology. Its problems are those of every sociologist, and critiques against it betray the intention of refining it and extending it, not of rejecting it."

An adequate analysis of the present controversy would be out of place here, where we are concerned only with its importance for the sociology of the family. Essentially, functionalism had considerable importance a generation ago. It was never a *theory* but a theoretical *orientation* that called the theorist's attention to a range of data which had not been overlooked by previous sociologists, but had not been viewed as systematically necessary. I suggested some years ago that the first functionalist was the first man who thought wisely and systematically about social behavior.[4] As an emerging way of thinking, it is evident in the work of Emile Durkheim; the classicists Gilbert Murray, Jane Ellen Harrison, and Frances Cornford; Charles Beard; Thorstein Veblen and Lincoln Steffens; and many

[4]See the more extended discussion in my *Religion Among the Primitives* (Glencoe, Ill.: The Free Press, 1951), Chapter 2.

others who wrote in the first decades of this century.

It embodied a new set of theoretical and observational *emphases,* not a set of hypotheses. These may be listed briefly:

*Less emphasis on history or technology and more on social relations: explanations for social behavior must be found in the social structure.*

*More emphasis on the interconnections between different areas of social action in this society, even when participants do not recognize those connections: a greater attempt to analyze social behavior by taking the point of view of the participant and thus a greater emphasis on informal social behavior and structures.*

Phrased this way, however, it is clear that Kingsley Davis is correct in his assertion that functionalism *is* sociology or, at least, that the controversy is over because whatever was fruitful in functionalism has now been absorbed into the main body of sociology.[5] Even those who attack functionalism become functionalists when they carry out sociological analysis.

Perhaps the best index of the intellectual emptiness of that controversy is that functionalism no longer has any *defenders.* Those who attack it assert that functionalism postulates changelessness and, therefore, cannot analyze social change; that it claims the existing society is harmoniously equilibrated; and that all the parts of the society support one another. However, since no sociologist can be found who admits holding such absurd notions, these attacks remain largely unanswered.

The controversy has lost its relevance not only because whatever was significant in early functionalist work has been absorbed, but also because sociologists have gradually come to see that the apparent difficulties it seemed to pose were largely matters of rhetoric and vocabulary. A consideration of these verbal obscurities will clarify the content of this compendium as well as the process of stating hypotheses.

Without doubt, some early functionalists sought to avoid the risk of causal and correlational statements by using a more obscure vocabulary, but we can no longer escape that responsibility. Moreover, once we have seen clearly that the term "function" contains no *mystique* at all, any significant proposition in the functionalist rhetoric can

easily be translated into an ordinary hypothesis of social science.

For example, let us consider the following proposition: "The bride-price system functions to increase marital stability by giving both the husband's and the bride's kin a material interest in maintaining the union." Or, "Boarding schools have the function of limiting the social relations of well-to-do youngsters to those who belong to the same class and thus the function of maintaining the pattern of class homogamy in the society." All such propositions that have the form "X has the function of Y," or "X functions to perform Y" mean no more than "X has the following effect." This propositional form sometimes suggests erroneously that Y is the *only* consequence of X, but its primary meaning is that Y is *a* consequence of X. In more cautious language, we would now say "one of the effects of X is Y." In more technical terms, we would simply expect to find a correlation or association between X and Y, whether or not we implied by that correlation a causal relation. Such a translation from an old-fashioned, functionalist rhetoric to the vocabulary of causality and correlation is complete; there is *no meaning left over,* no penumbra of denotation that requires any additional theoretical or methodological detail. To say "X is a function of Y" is simply to say that X is caused by Y, nothing more.

An apparent additional complexity enters with a variant phrasing, "The function of rules against illegitimacy is to guarantee that each child shall have a mother and father who will assume the responsibility of nurturing and socializing the child." Or, in a more skeletonic form, "The function of X is Y." Again, this statement does assert that the rules against illegitimacy have certain consequences. However, it also contains a further implicit assertion. Properly understood, this additional content also propounds no mystery and does not require the ingenious, though superfluous, formalization that Hempel has given to it.[6] The above proposition does *not* contain an assertion that the rules against illegitimacy are *necessary.* The phrase "the function of" means: the *theoretically most important* consequences of X are Y. Thus, among the various consequences of the rules against illegitimacy, the greatest impact is to be found in the area of responsibility for children. The statement,

[5]Kingsley Davis, "The Myth of Functional Analysis as a Special Method in Sociology and Anthropology," *American Sociological Review* 24 (1959): 757–773.

[6]Karl G. Hempel, "The Logic of Functional Analysis," in *Aspects of Scientific Explanation* (New York: The Free Press, 1965), pp. 305 ff. It is indicative of the obsolescent character of such formulations that almost all of Hempel's examples derive from works written a generation ago.

then, contains an implicit quantitative estimate of the various consequences of the rules against illegitimacy.

Although such a statement is technically somewhat difficult to test, as are all statements of quantitative effect in social relations, it contains no logical meaning other than causal or correlational. It is not necessary to invoke some such factor as the "necessity of rules against illegitimacy in order to guarantee the continued existence of the society," though that type of rhetoric was once common.

On the other hand, we must not forget that careless practitioners can distort and muddle any mode of thought. To take an example from the literature: "Since identification with the male-role model is necessary for healthy psychological development, the father is given that function," or "Since the function of the mother is emotional and expressive in her relations with her children, social structures insure that she carries out such activities." Although doubtless some sociologists have made statements like these, they are not so much examples of "functionalist thinking" as simply poor theory. They are both muddled, while both contain an empirical statement.

Both also, however, contain a *non sequitur*. The logic is wrong even if, in fact, males and females do carry out such activities in most societies. Specifically, even though mothers and fathers are generally given such role obligations in most societies, *why* role allocations are so made is an empirical question to be investigated. To use the word "function" explains as little as the word "instinct" and both have been used widely as substitutes for explanation.

Indeed, it is precisely when we make a habit of translating functional rhetoric into a causal or correlational vocabulary that we can perceive quickly when a social analyst is invoking the term "function" in some mystical sense instead of the causal explanation that is required for an empirical phenomenon.

A further consequence of this view is that once we become adept at this kind of translation no *special* problems of proof or research design are required by a functionalist orientation. As social scientists have found to their sorrow, to demonstrate a close causal link between any two variables in social behavior is difficult, and even more difficult when we are speaking of larger social patterns such as the influence of religious behavior on, say, family patterns or warfare; but these problems are simply the harsh lot of all analysts who wish to move from intuition and speculation toward empirical proof.

Philosophers of science can find special problems of logic and method in functionalist formulations only by failing to see how simple most of the formulations are and how easily some of the more muddled ones can be discarded without loss. If we say, for example, that "avoidance patterns function to reduce conflict between affinal kin," we are asserting no more than that if a mother-in-law and a son-in-law who live in the same household are required to have little social interaction and perhaps are even forbidden to be alone together in the same hut, they will quarrel less than they otherwise would. Such a proposition is commonsensical, though the difficulty of creating a research design by which we could control for all other relevant variables (e.g., how much *potential* conflict between the two exists in each society) and demonstrate that there is more or less conflict where avoidance patterns are found is rather great. However, the logic of demonstration and design is the same as in any other attempt to show the linkage between two variables.

Of course, the problem of proof would become nearly insurmountable if we were instead attempting to prove that the avoidance rules were *created* in order to prevent conflict among affinal kin, but almost no contemporary sociologist would make such an assertion.

It is for these reasons, then, that this inventory does not utilize the functionalist vocabulary. Perhaps sociologists once resorted to that rhetoric as a kind of halfway house between armchair speculation about social processes and a more risky causal and correlational analysis. However, we have passed that point and it is now necessary to accept the responsibility for observing and demonstrating how certain social variables affect each other.

## QUANTIFICATION

In the generation that ended with World War II, sociologists debated the issue of quantification bitterly. It arouses little emotion among contemporary sociologists, though some European and English analysts continue to write about it. However, the debate faded in the United States, but not because sociologists worked out an adequate solution to the problem or because one side convinced the other. As so often happens in the history of science, a basic methodological problem was simply bypassed as being no longer of interest, and the debate died down in part because the most active proponents of either side retired from the scene. Sociologists commonly believe that this debate was a conflict between generations—the older generation espousing intuition and the younger generation proclaiming the superiority of statistics and quantification. In fact, however, the major polemicists were by and large age peers who simply represented somewhat different modes of analysis or took different epistemological positions. If a Lynd, Lundberg, Burgess, or Reed Bain represented the younger generation who espoused quantification, Blumer, Howard Becker, Willard Waller, and others represented the same generation but found quantification much less appealing. If one looks to a slightly older group, MacIver's lack of interest in quantification can be matched by the enthusiasm of, say, a Stuart Rice or Chapin *for* quantification.

Nevertheless, the gradually emerging consensus that sociology must measure and quantify has not solved one fundamental issue: which are the central variables in sociology? It has, however, ended the debate as to *whether* quantification is desirable. Generally sociologists have agreed that the goal of empirical research is powerful and precise propositions, with the hope and assumption that moving in that direction would inevitably yield hypotheses containing precise numbers. Perhaps the skeptics would turn this assertion around and claim that sociologists decided to speak in numbers, with the hope that the process of seeking quantification would inevitably yield powerful, precise propositions.

Understandably enough, many sociologists still doubt that the fruitfulness of our hypotheses has justified all the energy that went into the process of quantification. That skeptical interpretation is partly a literary criticism, asserting that intellectually sociology is not sufficiently elegant. It also grows from the much more fundamental problem noted above, which has many ramifications, not all of which can be dealt with in this introductory essay. This problem inevitably links with a question to be discussed later: which *model of science* ought sociology to imitate and what role ought nonsociological variables to play in the development of sociology?

To restate this problem: after several decades of an increasing devotion to, and technical sophistication in, quantification, sociologists have not yet come to any agreement that they should focus on the measurement of any *particular* set of *variables;* and the measurements which they have obtained of the many thousands of variables they have utilized do not represent any gradual approximation to a "true value" or a precise *numerical prediction* (e.g., the valence of carbon, the atomic weight of oxygen).

In the sense of empirical order and regularity, all our *numerical* results are "accidental." Sociologists do expect to find the same general *relationship* (e.g., a higher percentage of girls who marry very young will be pregnant before marriage than will those who marry at later ages) in successive samples or populations, but they would be astounded rather than elated if they found exactly the same correlations between these variables.

Somewhat less briefly, but more concretely, as against the gradual historical agreement on the true temperature at which ice freezes under standard conditions, even though measured by different kinds of thermometers, sociology can show no such successive approximations. If we measure marital adjustment or anomie, we cannot state the value of the numerical point at which a marriage or a society will dissolve. Even if it is urged that the achievement of such relative constants as the freezing temperature of water or the earth's gravity was a long, slow process in the history of physical science, it must be conceded that we do not even have a list of such candidates in view.

If the goal of quantification is the statement of *relationships,* we should gradually be approaching some precise numerical *predictions.* Again, our aims should be modest. It would be presumptuous to hope for so elegant a formulation as a sociological parallel to the gas law, asserting precisely how much a volume of gas will expand with increasing heat or will rise in temperature with compression. Still, our efforts at quantification seem so far to have moved us little toward even any *approximations* to such formulations.

Our fundamental failure (assuming that there is as much order in human relations as some of us suppose) is in the selection of *what to measure.* We cannot decide *which* variables are the significant ones. It is in this sense that the numerical results of our investigations may be called "accidental." After two decades of work on various scales of anomie, we are no closer than before to an agreement on precisely what we are measuring or which instrument we are to use. For various reasons, some of them to be noted later, our efforts toward precise, numerical formulations may be as frustrated in the future as they have been in the recent past.

These critical remarks explain why the exact correlations have been omitted from the hypotheses recorded in this compendium. Of course, the vast majority of these authors did not calculate a coefficient or association or correlation. However, even where such a figure has been given, it is largely irrelevant because it has no enduring quality. It is worth knowing that there is a generally inverse relationship between the divorce rate and class position or between class and marital stability, but the exact correlation will vary from country to country and from time to time. It is, of course, interesting to know, for some purposes, whether the correlation is high or low; and we are always interested in whether that correlation is reliable, that is, will always be found in any society or sample. Nevertheless, the exact figure is historically idiosyncratic, often accidental, and has little relevance for the development of theory.

It is not merely that we have been unable to agree on a limited set of variables whose precise measurement we intend to master in the field as a whole, but that we have failed to locate *smaller* subsystems of family (or more generally, sociological) variables which are so linked that we can use them to account for almost all of their variance in that system. We can ascertain that horticulture is associated generally with a matrilineal system and that the matrilineal structure creates certain types of tensions between a woman's brother (who is a member of her lineage) and her husband (who is not a member). However, we have not been able to locate any subset of variables relating to matriliny that would explain most of the variance in the behavior of people with such systems. Formally, we have not been able to locate subsystems of social variables such that if we obtain the numerical values of the first and the second variables, we could then state with some precision the numerical value of the third.

These comments do not aim, however, at criticizing contemporary sociology or urging that we abandon quantification. Such an exhortation would be both futile and unwise. We lose little by attempting to measure more accurately, and perhaps the vision of precise numerical predictions may become a reality in some distant future.

Although my personal hope has always been that we would achieve such formulations, these comments are not to be viewed as a general denunciation of sociology for its failure, but simply as a clarification of the theoretical difficulty in quantifying hypotheses relating to the family or to social processes generally. Perhaps if we can specify more adequately what our theoretical and technical problems in *measurement* are and why formulation of exact numerical hypotheses is so difficult, we shall either be able to see a better way of achieving the elegance many sociologists have sought or, instead, decide to take a different road altogether, with very different types of formulation as our scientific goal.

## SOCIOLOGICAL AND NONSOCIOLOGICAL VARIABLES

Since Emile Durkheim expounded the dictum that social phenomena should be explained by social factors, an increasing percentage of sociologists have tried to follow that rule and to understand better how to distinguish sociological variables from economic, psychological, or even political ones. Durkheim's rejection, at times cavalier, of psychological, racial, and climatological factors as explanations of suicide rates in favor of sociological ones showed at least that the sociological variables have an independent existence, an independent impact on human behavior. A comparison of the sociological articles of the 1920's with those of the present decade shows that though his dictum is not always followed, far more reports now conform to his rule than they did 50 years ago.

However, this apparent triumph of a sociological conception of human behavior has only transformed the issue without solving it. It must now be reconsidered in a somewhat different form. With the publication in 1937 of Talcott Parsons' *The Structure of Social Action* and Ralph Linton's *The Study of Man,* both an explication and an example of the sociological position became available. Of course, sociologists paid far more attention to Linton's work at first, but both have educated a generation of sociologists to be more sensitive to the distinction among different kinds of social variables. Now, the well-trained sociologist at least knows *when* he has abandoned a sociological interpretation and adduced economic, political, or psychodynamic factors to complete the solution.

It is now clear that sociological explanations are *possible.* That theoretical problem has been solved, but now the question is: When should we be *satisfied* with a purely sociological interpretation? Parsons has also raised this question implicitly, not only by his essays in the fields of psychodynamics, political science, and economics, but also by his continued attempt to create an integrated body of theory for all the social sciences. Homans has also raised the question by flatly asserting that all the sociological interpretations of any importance are basically psychological or economic.[7] In addition, many younger sociolo-

[7]Talcott Parsons, Edward A. Shils, and Edward C. Tolman, *Toward a General Theory of Action* (Cambridge, Mass.: Harvard University, 1951); with Robert F. Bales, *Family Socialization and Interaction Process* (Glencoe, Ill.: The Free Press, 1955); "On the Concept of Influence," *Public Opinion Quarterly* 27 (1963): 37–62; "On the Concept of Political Power," *Proceedings of the*

gists have little patience with the ideal of a "pure" sociology or the importance of departmental labels. And, of course, the field has always included some social scientists who object to so sharp a theoretical division, as professionals generally object to newly emerging specialties which may challenge their competence in the field.

Consequently, in a period when sociology has become increasingly successful both among laymen and among colleagues in sister disciplines, as evidenced by the frequent use of sociology as a source for interpretations and ideas, sociologists themselves continue to wonder whether any theoretical line can be drawn between sociology as a theoretical system and other social sciences. If we cannot solve the question here, perhaps we can at least clarify it somewhat.

The notion that an independent science of society might be possible is ancient, and so are most of the philosophical arguments in its favor. Aristotle certainly knew he was analyzing different phenomena when he lectured on political structures or on the anatomy of the porpoise. Moreover, he understood that a system has very different qualities, viewed as a unity, than its parts. Perhaps no one actually proclaimed the new "science" of sociology until Ibn Khaldun, but the general notion was not lost to the Western intellectual tradition. However, it was not until the nineteenth century that a clarification of the theoretical position of such a hypothetical science seemed to be possible. By that time, a "ladder of sciences" had begun to emerge. Pleasingly enough, their chronological order followed their philosophical and logical order: first physics, then chemistry (appropriately, physical chemistry before organic), and then biology. A science of society was developing and, naturally, economics came first. In the evolutionist thought of the time, sociology surely would follow, as Comte's somewhat premature announcement asserted.

Certain theoretical matters were clear enough. One is simply that though in every century the problems of physics, chemistry, biology, and sociology were being pursued, the intellectual breakthroughs in different fields occurred in orderly succession, thus suggesting that the problems were qualitatively different. The brilliant *physicists* of the

seventeenth century could not, for example, solve the *chemical* problem of combustion.

Second, although many investigators did pursue several fields simultaneously, a division of labor was gradually recognized. Consequently, of course, men in one field became less and less likely to create or even to be competent in another: the fields were theoretically distinct. The same conception ought, then, to be applicable to the newly emerging social sciences.

In that view, each science is on an "emergent level" of its own, not in a chronological or evolutionary but a *qualitative* sense. Problems at one level cannot be explained by the variables of another. The factors used to explain the motions of the heavenly bodies can also explain those of a pendulum or a falling body, but not combustion or gestation. The biological facts of anatomy cannot explain the social phenomenon of language. Economic theory is of little use in interpreting most of family behavior.

This view rests on both the pragmatic and the philosophical idea that any concrete object or process is infinitely complex and may be viewed from very different perspectives. An automobile is a physical mass, but it is also a product of technology, as well as a piece of merchandise in economic transactions. It has a cultural meaning, and its social definition is important in the interaction among members of a family. Thus, each science focuses on a particular slice of the totality of any phenomenon. Our task in sociology has been to learn how to isolate our slice better and to study it more effectively.

True enough, such distinctions do change over time and, at least in the great sciences, adjacent fields may eventually link. In the twentieth century, the Second Law of Thermodynamics can be used to interpret some chemical processes, and organic chemistry can be used to explain problems in intracellular physiology. Nevertheless, when these sciences first took form, the variables and problems were qualitatively distinct.

However, the ladder of *social* sciences has always been somewhat shaky, or at least of an uncertain form; the theoretical relations of each social science to the other remained unclear. Economics is more advanced than sociology, but it would be difficult to demonstrate that experimental psychology is less advanced than economics. It is safe to say, however, that neither of these latter two looks to the other for solutions to its problems. Political science has made only limited progress toward a separate set of problems and variables, an independent theoretical system, and

*American Philosophical Society* 107 (1963): 232–262; with Neil J. Smelser, *Economy and Society* (Glencoe, Ill.: The Free Press, 1956). George C. Homans, *Social Behavior: Its Elementary Forms* (New York: Harcourt, Brace and World, 1961), p. 12. More recently, however, Homans has stated a more qualified view in his "Reply to Rezak," *American Sociological Review* 31 (1966): 543.

as a science often seems to be indistinguishable from political sociology. Sociologists have discarded physical variables such as climate, and biological variables such as race, but are frequently tempted by psychological factors such as motivation or personality, or economic variables such as resources in the bargaining process.

They give way to that temptation because as scientists they wish to explain more of the *variance* in their phenomena than purely sociological variables can. For example, we can hardly explain fully the relatively high rates of illegitimacy in eighteenth- and nineteenth-century Sweden (compared to that of other Western nations) by describing the social customs that encouraged dalliance among young men and women in farming regions.[8] Their long courtship process took place in an atmosphere of considerable sexual freedom (though organized by many social definitions of appropriate behavior) and marriage was relatively late. On the other hand, we would have to move outside of sociological variables to biological variables in order to explain why the illegitimacy rates were not still higher. There, too, we would expect to find that social customs linked with such biological factors to keep the rate relatively modest, but without question, our full explanation would need nonsociological factors. Or, if we wanted to explain why Swedish (but not Italian) farmers developed this courtship pattern most elaborately, we would very likely have to include both political and economic variables.

The fact is, as noted before, that most of our correlations in sociology are relatively low and, thus, our explanations *need* other variables to be complete. In fact, when we achieve a correlation of 0.6 or higher, we begin to suspect that our variables are contaminated with one another if they are not simple tautologies. As noted earlier, we do not find smaller subsystems of sociological variables such that the value of one is a function of the values of others. As a consequence, when we develop a "formula" its values are somewhat accidental and idiosyncratic. We do not expect to find the same values in other but similar samples.

Partly we solve the question by learning how to "translate" other types of variables into a sociological form. Thus, "race" is not a biological variable but is rather defined by its social meaning. Physical handicaps, similarly, are not treated as biological factors but are given a social definition. If we oc-

cupy ourselves with the economic process, we attempt to locate sociological variables within that process.

We also escape embarrassment somewhat by lowering our aspirations and trying to avoid comparison with the more developed physical sciences. It is consoling to remember in this connection that it took chemists nearly the whole of the eighteenth century to work out the simple facts of combustion that any high-school pupil learns quickly.

In addition, sociologists sometimes assert that we should expect less success in our aim at elegance because our phenomena are more *complex*. We would probably evoke very little assent or sympathy from physical scientists on this point. On the other hand, it does seem reasonable to assert that however complex the problem of the physicist, he can at least solve it without concerning himself much with whether the nuclear reactions under investigation are being shaped by biological or psychological factors. The organic chemist who first synthesized urea or who worked out the structure of the benzene ring did not wonder whether economic or political variables needed to be taken into account. By contrast, the sociologist of the family knows very well that some part of the phenomena he is trying to explain is affected by political, economic, or psychological factors, and even physical variables such as space and energy. He may not be competent to analyze them adequately, but he cannot shrug them off as being inconsequential.

Two alternative strategies can be followed in coping with this theoretical problem if the sociologist maintains his hope of developing a science of sociology. One of these is simply to follow the variance wherever it may lead. That is, if the sociological factors that have been adduced explain relatively little of the problem, and correlations are correspondingly low, then this strategy would dictate a search for *any* factors of *any* kind whatsoever that would help to explain the phenomenon further. The argument in its favor is crudely pragmatic. The working scientist in the developed fields does not ordinarily concern himself with whether he is working on one emergent level or another or where he finds his variables. Having selected a problem, he wishes to make as elegant a formulation as he can; and whether it seems to "fit" some prior definition of the field is of little consequence to him. Similarly, then, the sociologist of the family who finds that he must utilize biological or economic variables in order to explain the socialization process, or psychological ones to explain courtship behavior or conflict between in-laws,

[8]See my article, "The Theoretical Importance of Love," *American Sociological Review* 24 (1959): 38–47; and Karl Robert V. Wikman, *Die Einleitung der Ehe. Acta Academiae Aboensis (Humahiora)* 11 (1937).

should feel no embarrassment at moving outside his limited range of sociological variables. Instead, he would aim at explaining his phenomenon as fully as possible, with the hope that eventually some greater orderliness would emerge. That is, from many such investigations we would ultimately begin to learn better which variables hang together. At some distant future, moreover, presumably those variables that hung most closely together, that were in fact functions of one another, could be stated as far more elegant formulas than is now possible.

The alternative strategy would continue to postulate stubbornly the existence of a real world of sociological variables and would aim at an increasingly clear statement of both the variables and the *problems* that are to be solved. Under this view, the problems that we have selected cannot be fully explained by *sociological* variables because they *themselves* are not purely *sociological* problems: They are so concrete as to include a wide range of other factors. To hope to "explain" so concrete a phenomenon as the family is as visionary as trying to explain so concrete a phenomenon as a "rock." Our more successful elder brothers have rather chosen highly refined, abstract problems to investigate. They have not simply studied "planets," but certain aspects of their *motion*.

The history of every science is studded with thousands of failures that were due to an inability to separate out an abstract variable or *phenomenon to study* or were due to focusing on a concrete and many-faceted problem which the investigative tools of the period were too imprecise to handle. We shall advance as little in understanding conflict as a *sociological* phenomenon, explained by sociological variables, as medicine did in explaining the phenomenon of "fever" until we have made greater progress in *defining* the problem itself sociologically. That is to say, we must move toward a conceptually more rigorous definition of the phenomenon to be explained; and thereby we will find that our analytic sociological variables will have far more interpretative power.

This inventory illustrates these larger issues, and its selective criteria may help a modicum in clarifying them. Thus, in the initial stages of collecting hypotheses, we concentrated entirely on the sociological literature, with no distinction being made between sociology and anthropology.

However, not every event that happened *within* the family can be called a family phenomenon or variable. After all, we did not propose to record all the biological data on human beings, even though such processes do take place within the family cir-

cle. We wished to concentrate on *family roles*. Family interaction *exemplifies* most psychodynamic processes and doubtless these processes underlie much of family behavior, but the phenomenon we have chosen is the family as a sociological entity.

By and large, we want to record all the hypotheses that related one family pattern to another—divorce rates and marital adjustment of parents; parent-child relations and learning how to play a male role; prostitution and marriage patterns; and so on.

However, precisely because we did not intend to record the exact correlations (even when they had been calculated) and because we knew the correlations were small in any event, it seemed wise to include in the inventory any other kinds of variables *when they affect family-role patterns* or when family patterns affect these other variables. Polygyny is affected by many family patterns, but it is also affected by warfare. Kinship structures are affected by economic as well as by political variables. Many factors in parent-child relations, both sociological and psychological, increase or reduce the chances of schizophrenia in a child. That is, after the initial period in which we focused only on the sociological literature, we began to include any hypothesis that seemed to affect the sociological phenomenon of the family, whether those variables were economic, political, psychological, or whatever.

If the first of the two alternative strategies outlined above were followed (i.e., following the variance wherever it leads), this inventory would be useful in mapping the linkages between family and other kinds of phenomena and thus would help in the preliminary stages of attempting to account for as much variance as possible. Perhaps the thorough mapping of even one concrete institution such as the family would indicate whether one could indeed explain most of the variance of any important family phenomena and thus eventually move toward more elegant formulations of social behavior.

Alternatively, perhaps a perusal of the variegated factors that have been used to explain family phenomena, and the wide range of phenomena to be explained, may instead suggest to the acute student just how we might develop more purely *sociological* definitions of such apparently concrete phenomena. Perhaps the very number of such variables will suggest the advantages of parsimony and thus stimulate the investigator to work out different variables, more rigorously sociological, to explain a more analytically defined socio-

logical process. Perhaps the weakness of our formulations in family sociology stems precisely from
our inability so far to discard "the family" as a
sociological phenomenon and to locate within it
the important abstract variables and processes to
be observed and explained.

## MODELS FOR SOCIOLOGY

In the fields of family and religion my own work
has concentrated on sociological factors, primarily
because I have supposed that the institutions of
family and religion are the more purely sociological
in character, that is, sociological factors explain far
more of the variance in religious and family behavior than in the human behavior within other great
social institutions. Nevertheless, I view both strategies as defensible. Properly pursued, either ought
to clarify a question that was raised earlier in this
discussion: which science ought sociology to imitate?

In most methodological and theoretical discussions, sociologists have tended to look toward the
case of physics, with its high mathematical development and its hundreds of years of systematic
experimentation. However, it should not be forgotten that as each great science has taken form, each
has developed a very *different* intellectual style:
*none* is like the others. The science-minded sociologist admires the deductive character of physics
and supposes that "real theory" consists in a small
group of definitions, empirical observations, and
mathematical formulations, from which hundreds
of specific formulas can be deduced, each applying to a wide range of concrete physical phenomena. But physics is *sui generic*. By contrast,
chemistry has a far less developed propensity
toward deductive logic and mathematical formulation. Indeed, organic chemistry, which in sheer
bulk has come to dominate chemistry, is precisely
quantitative, but structural far more than mathematical.

In contrast to both of these, biology has utilized
mathematics very little and only recently at that. It
has also developed no great overarching body of
theory, though it has created several subsegments
of theory. Only one of these is highly rigorous,
quantitative, and structural: genetics. Our most rigorously developed sister discipline, economics,
has become highly mathematical, but has utilized
empirical data in its theoretical development less
than any other social science, and of course far less
than any of the physical sciences.

These comments are not criticisms of any of
these fields or of sociology itself. They rather suggest that we ought at least to be alert to the possible

*substantive* differences in different types of
phenomena, which might force us to develop very
different theoretical *styles*. Perhaps sociology will
be much more like biology, a congeries of small
theory fragments, with the emergence from time to
time of somewhat larger advances such as Dar-
win's theory of evolution or Mendel's laws of genetics that will integrate some of these fragments,
without ever culminating in a great logicomath-
ematical theoretical pattern.

At this stage, in any event, we are much closer
to early nineteenth-century biology. We are gathering immense quantities of rather detailed descriptive data and locating many low-order correlations among these phenomena. If we are
successful in abstracting analytical variables and
problems, perhaps we may move toward a more
intellectually satisfying set of formulations. On the
other hand, the example of biology should remind
us that there are other forms of achievement
than the mathematical and that the accumulation
of many small descriptive relations may still
yield a fundamental understanding of social behavior.

## BOUNDARIES AND EXCHANGES BETWEEN SOCIAL UNITS

Even if the modern sociologist lays greater emphasis on conflict than on harmony, on contin-
gency than on stability, or on change than on
maintenance, he cannot avoid perceiving or assuming that this society is made up of many persisting social subsystems such as kin networks,
friendship circles, colleges, corporations, or clubs.
People, roles, activities, and values are linked together. Ordinarily, both sociologists and laymen
take these subsystems for granted and often label
them distinctly. Each subsystem is partly distinguished from others by the special rights and obligations its members feel toward one another:
Members of one family are linked by role obligations they do not owe to outsiders; family rights
link family members differently than job duties link
employees of a corporation.

However, since all members of any subsystem
or group are also members of *other* groups or
subsystems, boundaries are sometimes empirically
and definitionally unclear.[9] Research seems not to
have foundered on these difficulties, in part because the sociologist has pragmatically viewed as

[9]For some of the complexities in defining "groups," see
the extended discussion by Robert K. Merton, "The Prob-
lematics of Reference Group Theory," in *Social Theory
and Social Structure,* 2nd ed. (Glencoe, Ill.: The Free
Press, 1957), pp. 284ff.

subsystems primarily those groups whose members interact rather frequently with one another. When a boundary is defined at all, it may be viewed as a point at which members at a periphery seem to be interacting with "outsiders" as much as with "insiders."

Even if the sociologist is skeptical of some epistemologists' claims that such subsystems are created by arbitrary conceptualizations and are not simply "there" to be uncovered by search, he knows that there are *many* possible subsystems that *could* become the focus of his attention. In nature, the scientist is able ultimately to locate systems of *variables* (rather than simply systems of concrete objects) such that the value of one variable is a function of the values of others in the system: energy and mass; volume, temperature, and pressure; mass, distance, and gravitational attraction; and so on.

No set of variables has been found in social relations such that a very small number of variables determine one another rather completely. On the other hand, animal groupings are also to be found in nature, just as family units are found in societies; and these require analyses of both intragroup and intergroup interactions. A forest or tundra may be viewed as a subsystem. A hurricane may be seen as a system or as one element of a much larger system of meteorological forces.

Sociologists have recognized that all social subsystems are in interaction with one another—eventually each circle of friendship links up with all others; members of one corporation are linked indirectly with members of other corporations. Utilizing this fact might yield more powerful analyses of social behavior, but the sociologists have wrestled little with the problem.

Perhaps they have sensed that progress would be unlikely without more precise techniques of *measurement*. For example, even if we assert that the religious and familial subsystems of a society are in interaction; that one familial "output" is socializing the child to believe in and contribute to his church; and that reciprocally the church supports family values, we have then stated no more than what any adult member of the society already knows, without gaining any additional hypotheses or data about that exchange. We have no techniques for measuring how *much* weight to give to each input or exchange or how much the behavior of individuals in one subsystem is affected by their role obligations in another.

Although such exchanges of outputs or inputs between *concrete subunits of the society* are in principle measurable, for the most part they have been asserted rather than counted or weighed.

They can also be observed crudely, by taking note of the occasions when the role obligations in one subsystem require performances in the other: as father or head of the kin unit, for example, I may be obligated to bring my kin to a religious ceremony.[10]

However, the problems of both measurement and theory become much more subtle and difficult if one or both of the subsystems under focus are not concrete but abstract, that is, *variables* rather than specific *groups*. Unfortunately, in the strict sense, all variables and subsystems are to some degree abstract, so that the obscurity is often troubling. For example, how do the economy and family systems affect one another? A purchase can be observed more easily than an "economy." Any interaction between people can be viewed *abstractly* as an economic transaction or even a power transaction, but measuring the input and output between all such economic behavior *within* family patterns seems rather unlikely at present, however fruitful theoretically such data might be.

This problem is not reduced much if we move from so grandiose a problem as "economy-kinship system" exchanges to asking how much of the variance of a given social act is attributable to economic variables and how much to family variables. The two are, to begin with, on different theoretical levels. In addition, although respondents can doubtless be persuaded to estimate that percentage ("When you knocked your boss down, would you say this was caused fifty, forty, or thirty percent by economic variables?"), we have no basis for supposing that such guesses are valid. It is not even certain they make any sense.

Without at least crude measures of *how much* is exchanged between subsystems, we can do little more than Parsons or Smelser has done, that is, diagram speculatively a set of hypothetical "boxes" or subsystems and label the *kinds* of outputs and inputs each gives or receives from the others. Such reminders indicate how little we know, but as yet they have not evoked either empirical measurement or a fruitful set of hypotheses.[11]

For these reasons, even the crude relations of

[10]This is the form of analysis I used in *Religion Among the Primitives,* in which I noted the points at which religious rights and duties intersected with those in the economic, political, and familial spheres.

[11]Talcott Parsons, Edward A. Shils, and Edward C. Tolman, *Toward a General Theory of Action;* Talcott Parsons and Neil J. Smelser, *Economy and Society,* Chapter 2; Neil J. Smelser, *Social Change in the Industrial Revolution* (Chicago: University of Chicago Press, 1959). Also see Talcott Parson *et al.* (eds.), *The Theories of Society* (New York: The Free Press, 1961), pp. 60ff.

this inventory may be stimulating. Perhaps, as so often happens in science, we shall bypass most of the epistemological and conceptual problems noted above. The question of "theoretical level" may turn out to be irrelevant. Still more important, we may find that we need not, at first, measure "how much" is exchanged between subsystems or units. Instead, we may be able to reduce the problem by ascertaining how much variance in one variable is accounted for by another: how well can we "predict" the divorce rate, the fertility values, the lineage structure, or husband–wife-role definitions in a sample of societies, from one or more economic variables? At present, economic variables do not predict such behavior well, but they have not yet been developed for cross-cultural application. Most can be used only for economic transactions in an industrial society. In any event, perhaps the appropriate first step is the development of statistical relations in which we attempt to ascertain how *much* of the total variation we can account for by the variables of one subsystem or another.

In this inventory, as stated earlier, the associations between various traits of family systems and those of other subsystems (e.g., warfare, political integration, money) have been recorded, but no quantitative values of correlations are given. Of course, sociologists in the future will more often make such calculations, as they will also make a greater effort to ascertain how much each variable seems to account for others. Thus, the associations presented here are at least a first step.

Such future steps will yield a more precise understanding of how much the subsystems of a society exchange with one another, or support or undermine one another. Thereby, we shall also better understand how and by how *much* a society manages to maintain itself from one year to the next. Here, at least, is a useful set of first steps, a wide range of points at which family patterns are linked with one another and with other nonfamily patterns. These should be good junctures at which to attempt to see the processes by which each subsystem feeds into the others.

## HYPOTHESES, THEORIES, AND AXIOMATIZATION

As is clear, this inventory is made up of propositions or hypotheses, not *theories*. First, a theory is a *structure* of empirical propositions, not a mere aggregation of facts. Second, a theory has at its core one, or at most few, relations from which a wide range of related propositions can be inferred. Thus, for all its crudity, the Darwinian theory of evolution yields testable inferences about specific paleontological sequences (*eohippus* to *equus hippus*), the proliferation of subspecies from a species on the Galapagos Islands, the disappearance of a species, practical techniques for creating new varieties of plants and animals, and so on. Few theories come to be dignified as "laws" or "rules" (the Second Law of Thermodynamics, the Phase Rule); but these do summarize many observations and propositions and thus can be used to predict a wide range of concrete physical processes. More important, once such a theory has been propounded, researchers can deduce from it still other relationships, as yet untested and hitherto unknown, so that the range of application of the theory is expanded, or at least specified. When scientists validate these further inferences about the unknown, they give more credence to the larger theory. Philosophers have pointed out for centuries that this is an error in logic, but it is not a pragmatic misstep.

Since few of even those who believe sociology is a science claim that we have achieved any theories in this strict sense, and since by any standards the sociology of the family is less vigorously developed than most subfields, it is therefore to be expected that this inventory is not a body of theories. However, can such a compilation of discrete findings serve the goal of theory development?

In the development of rigorous theory, more is needed than the statement of a set of presumably related propositions. The most crucial missing element is *closure.* Have we included all the major variables that affect one another, that somehow form a small "system"? To select a well-worn example, almost any social trait is correlated to some degree with any rough definition of "class." However, some of these (e.g., income and education) are really part of the definition. Most of them are only weakly associated with *one another*. We cannot be sure that any of them are *determinants,* whether the elements in "class" actually cause such traits, or whether possibly both "class" and those traits are caused by something else.

To find subsets of variables that are determinants of one another requires both a set of causal findings and some imagination. Often an important determinant is hidden or missing. More commonly the nodules or fragments of rigorous theory are difficult to create because in social behavior a wide range of variables is related—if only indirectly—one to another, and we do not see how to carve out the crucial ones and eliminate the mass of less significant data.

The process of *final* elimination of extraneous

variables and propositions, the achievement of an elegant and parsimonious set of statements, is aided by axiomatization; but preliminary steps can be taken by deciding on the qualities of each proposition. Zetterberg's explication of propositions suggests one such classification of sociological assertions.[12] For example, some are *reversible,* others not (e.g., aggressiveness in the parent arouses aggressiveness in the child and vice versa; but the statement that mother absence increases the chances of psychological problems in the child is not reversible to the same degree). *Deterministic* statements in sociology (if X, then always Y) are rare and upon scrutiny often turn out to be definitions. Sociology has far more *stochastic* propositions, expressing instead a *probability* (e.g., calculations of the chances of remarriage if various traits of a divorcée or widow are high or low: age, income, beauty, number of children, etc.).

Propositions may also be classified as to whether they assert *sequential* or simultaneous or *coextensive* relationships; whether the relationship is *sufficient* or *contingent* (i.e., it holds only under specified conditions); and whether it is *necessary* (without motherly affection, a child always grows up to be abnormal) or *substitutable.*

Although these are important judgments in examining any set of findings in this compilation, most of them can be reached without deep inquiry. The reader will likely err only occasionally in supposing a relationship to be reversible when it is not; or necessary when it is not; or sequential when it is really simultaneous. In any event, when we do select a set of propositions for more rigorous systematization, we are then forced to make such judgments about them. If we are careful, we shall also examine how strongly they are correlated, for otherwise it is less likely that they can be determinants of one another.

Some sociologists have attempted axiomatizations, especially in small groups and organizational theory, in the hope of deducing relations other than those contained in their initial fund of data and with perhaps also the esthetic aim of elegance as well. Essentially, the scientist seeks to bound and encompass his subuniverse by *defining* which items he will include; by expressing certain *postulates* that he will leave unproved (but which seem both necessary for the axiomatization and unassailable). These are drawn from his empirical findings, as few as possible, although they may be no more than reasonable assumptions. If he wishes to be very rigorous, he may also specify for which kinds

of *operations* his mode of logic calls. Many such problems of judgments must be solved in transforming a set of empirical correlations into near-syllogisms or deductions.[13]

*If* he has selected the key propositions in an array of findings, he may be able to deduce not only the original array, but also some new hypotheses that in strict logic are implicit in the crucial set chosen. Indeed, a good number of such attempts have been successful, although to my knowledge none has been in family sociology.[14]

This inventory can supply the foundations for more rigorous structures of hypotheses, but it does not, as presented, suggest the junctures at which axiomatization might be most profitable. Such points are clearest when a set of related variables has emerged or intuition has seized upon them. Most of these hypotheses are arranged here in sets in which *one* variable is linked with *many* others, but their interrelations with each other are not to be found in the same place. Those further links must be sought under their appropriate headings. By systematically searching out all those interlinkages, a *matrix* or a set of interrelations could be constructed; but only through such a process could one begin to guess at or find a fruitful set of variables from which to construct a sequence of axiomatizing steps.

In addition to these uses in theorizing, it is possible, as noted earlier, to locate *gaps* in sets of hypotheses, where few relations have been recorded. Inconsistencies have also been noted here and there, which may also suggest possible new hypotheses or variables to account for contrary findings.

Thus, although this inventory is not a theory, or even a set of theories, and although it is but the crudest part of a foundation for rigorous theorizing, it can be used directly to build small-scale theories and its simple formulations can at least help the theorist to create the more parsimonious and precise hypotheses that are necessary for more systematic transformations of these findings.

[13]For some of the technical problems of axiomatization, see the careful exposition by Herbert L. Cestner and Robert K. Leik, "Deductions from 'Axiomatic Theory,'" *American Sociological Review* 29 (1964): 819–835. See also Gerald Hage, "An Axiomatic Theory of Organizations," *Administrative Science Quarterly* 10 (1965): 289–420, and Allen H. Barton's strictures on its logic in "Comments on Hage's 'An Axiomatic Theory of Organizations,'" *ibid.* 11 (1966): 134–139.
[14]See examples in Hans L. Zetterberg, *On Theory and Verification,* Chapter 5; Herbert A. Simon, *Models of Man* (New York: Wiley, 1957); and Joseph Berger, Morris Zelditch, and Bo Anderson, *Sociological Theories in Progress,* vol. I (New York: Houghton Mifflin, 1966).

[12]Hans L. Zetterberg, *On Theory and Verification in Sociology,* 3rd ed. (Totowa, New Jersey: Bedminster Press, 1965), pp. 69ff., and Chapter 5.

# IV. PROCEDURES AND LIMITATIONS

In compiling these propositions, we followed a simple general plan which inevitably became more complex in its specific applications. Going through the standard literature on the family, we simply abstracted all the propositions in which at least one of the variables was a family variable. If the research report asserted that there is a correlation or association between a family variable (divorce rate, fertility, paternal absence) and another variable, whether or not related to the family (parent-child conflict, class, voting, matrilineage), we recorded it twice, once under each variable. We began with the literature of sociology and anthropology, but eventually added that of psychology as well. Since we covered the main sources in which family research appears, we can suppose that we have recorded most of the relations now published.

So simple a statement omits many minor procedural decisions and three definitions of the task. Each of these coped with a problem, but the solution was not always ideal. The most troublesome question is: what is a proposition?

All scientific propositions are stated as a simple or complex correlation between two or more variables. Therefore, one type of assertion to be rejected is the *definition:* "In a matrilineal society, property is inherited through the mother's side of the family." In such a statement, an association is *implicit:* type of kinship system x inheritance pattern, but the relationship is so by definition.

Some propositions *are* empirical, but are correct by *factual* definition, and those are to be rejected: "The higher the mortality rate in the adult years, the shorter the duration of marriage." Essentially, such a statement asserts that if people die early, their marriages end sooner.

Within this same category are propositions that seem at first to be ambiguous: "Where residence is avunculocal and factors favoring the development of an extended family are present, the avunculocal extended family will develop." Again this is so by at least empirical definition. The proposition essentially says: "When factors press toward direction Y (and if counterpressures are weak), there will be a movement toward Y."

The next category of rejected propositions is that of simple descriptions without a correlation: "In every decade since the Civil War, the United States divorce rate has risen"; "German fathers are more authoritarian than Dutch fathers"; "Middle-class fathers project their present status into the future

for their children." Aside from the error and ambiguity in this last assertion, it states merely that all X do Y, no matter what the circumstances. Such descriptions are necessary in scientific work, as are definitions, and may even report the outcome of considerable work, but they do not embody relations between variables.

A third type of statement that has been excluded relates in part to styles of rhetoric in the social sciences (to be discussed below in somewhat greater detail): the failure to specify what the relationship *is.* Here are some examples: "Variations in power structures within the family have *marked effects* on personality"; "Power distribution within the family will *condition* the way a boy expects power to be distributed in the outside world"; "The failure to achieve in school has a simultaneously *negative significance* for the child within the family"; "Changes in social institutions and economic production may be the *functional consequence* of the organization of family units in the society." Doubtless, social scientists who avoid the risk of error by using such phrases as "involved with," "reflection of," or "related to" feel they have reported a prediction or fact, but it is not clear precisely what it is.

A fourth type of excluded assertion simply contains no family variable, though it may have been derived from a study of the family: "The more severe the emotional disturbances in the child, the less related are dependency and oral behavior in the child"; "There is a correlation between dependency and achievement striving"; "The more permissive are parents about their child's aggression, the less the child's anticipation of punishment"; or "The higher the social class of a family, the lower percentage of the family income will be spent on food and rent." Note that the behavior recorded here occurs *in* the family, but the fundamental variables are not *family* roles and obligations. The family is a site of much interaction, as any concrete social unit must be. However, we cannot, merely because power and economic variables affect one another *within* the family, record all such relations as *family patterns.* In our editorial revisions, we have therefore tried to exclude such relationships.

A fifth type asserts a relationship, but confines it to a particular society: "In Alorese society, poor parental care leads to a lack of self-confidence in the children"; "In France, the legal structure gives power to the husband and therefore he is more dominant in family relations."

This form may also be found in many reports which contain no such specific national label, but where the proposition clearly applies to only one country: "With increasing age of the wife and duration of marriage, there is an increased use of contraception." This may apply to the United States and to some other countries at this time in history, but it is hardly to be accepted as a general prediction about family behavior.

A sixth type, like the third, avoids risk by a rhetorical device, though in this instance the relationship *is* specified: "Fathers of artistic children are *very often* obsessive, detached, humorless individuals"; "Fathers of artistic children are *often* intelligent, but seldom original, creative thinkers"; "*Many* lower-class fathers fail to give their sons emotional support." The qualifications "sometimes," "often," or "many" achieve safety; otherwise the relationship between the variables is stated clearly. On the other hand, such rhetorical devices fail as propositions because the statement can be made about almost any set of variables or any set of people. Thus, for example, the above proposition about the fathers of artistic children may be asserted about any set of fathers. It is not so much that the proposition cannot be weighed against empirical observations, but rather that it would be difficult to prove that it is incorrect.

Finally, how trivial or accidental may a correlation be without being excluded? Even in a modest inquiry, the modern researcher may ask the computer to calculate hundreds of correlations in the hope that some may yield information. The docile machine cares little whether its mentor has any clear hypotheses in mind. Since many factors *are* associated, if weakly or distantly, the yield of non-zero correlations may be astonishing. A census volume contains many implicit correlations in its tables. Should a propositional inventory simply re-record all the published literature or at least all its tables? At the other end of this extreme, should the sociologist refuse to publish any findings unless he can develop a set of hypotheses rigorously deduced from some central theoretical formulation; and should we avoid summarizing findings unless we can locate the central theoretical formula that sums up all of them neatly? Or, as a procedural matter, should we delay publication of this inventory until we can select only those relationships that sum up all the subsidiary ones?

We decided that there was no *logical* solution to this problem and no *theoretical* solution short of an elaborate—and at this stage of sociological development wasteful—attempt at a pseudoaxiomat-

ization. We simply retained all propositions that seemed to state a relationship which is expected to hold in a wide range of societies and historical epochs, but we preferred to err on the side of *inclusion*. The trivial can be passed over quickly, and it does add something to the richness of a given phenomenon or process. Indeed, we suppose that by casting so wide a net more precise theoretical integration may be facilitated.

However, selection inevitably means editing and requires some decision about the different rhetorics of different fields. These change: as a field becomes more rigorous it moves toward a more specific statement of relationships in quantitative terms.

Sociology, for example, is gradually discarding a functionalist rhetoric ("Initiation ceremonies function to integrate the child into the adult male sex role") in favor of correlational assertions ("There is a correlation between a long *postpartum* sex taboo and a close physical association between mother and son, and severe puberty initiation ceremonies"). Increasingly, some type of coefficient of correlation is actually calculated. In a growing minority of research reports, some kind of variance or regression analysis is presented, and occasionally even a mathematical formulation is presented (for example, the Zipf-Stauffer law of intervening opportunities).

By contrast, psychodynamic reports *conceal* an implicit correlation within clinical descriptions and typological assertions and (more frequently than sociological ones) use the safety device of "often," "some," or "there is a tendency" to avoid the intellectual risk of a plain correlational or causal assertion. Instead of flatly claiming that the chances of schizophrenia in the child are increased Y percent if the mother is cold and the father weak, the psychologist is more likely to state that "The schizophrenic mother is cold, etc.," or "Fathers of artistic children often have children not because they want them, but because children are part of the formal pattern of marriage."

The relevant psychological literature also poses a problem of *coding* or classification, although this issue is not relevant for abstracting or locating the proposition itself. It is much easier to place sociological propositions under an appropriate category such as "class," "role definition," etc., than it is to find a small number of appropriate headings for the psychological literature. The psychodynamicist is much more prone to use quasi-literary descriptions of parental behavior; for example, "The father is autocratic, cold, and childish." We have, in the main, placed such patterns under very general categories such as ''parent-child relations'' for lack of generally accepted variables.

Anthropologists are more likely now than they were in the past to report precise counts and cause cross-tabulations, but are still far less likely than either sociologists or psychologists to assume or imply that their results have cross-cultural validity. This difference of style arises from the anthropologist's skepticism toward grand theory and his contempt for slovenly field data. Its historical roots are to be found both in the past failures of general hypotheses and the vast amount of work that was required over many decades to pierce the cobwebs of false or distorted stories told by missionaries, hunters, explorers, and district commissioners about primitive societies. Thus, even when the anthropologist *believes* that a high bride price increases marital stability because it gives both families a stake in the union—if the wife behaves badly, her family may have to return the goods or cattle; if the husband is cruel, her family may refuse —he may nevertheless confine himself to the modest claim that ''among the Bahima. . . .''

Our choices are not simple, because the strict exclusion of all propositions that do not *explicitly* claim cross-cultural validity would ignore hundreds of worthwhile findings. On the other hand, to abstract the *implicit* correlation is to do some violence to the author's statement and his scientific modesty.

A defensible rule cannot be formulated easily. Doubtless, we have erred on both ends of these two extremes, but in general we have again been more inclusive than exclusive. That is, where we could lay bare the underlying proposition without much editing, we have taken on ourselves the responsibility of claiming a wider validity than the psychologist's handful of clinical cases, the anthropologist's single society, or the sociologist's small sample in a midwestern city. At the worst, the result will be that some of these propositions will be refuted by future research work.

This last point raises the inevitable question: how correct are these findings? Should we not have included under each proposition an assessment of its validity?[15]

In fact, at the early stages of our abstracting, we did record the research plan and the tables that were the factual bases for the proposition, just as we recorded both the actual words of the author and our somewhat more laconic version of his

proposition. Several factors ultimately argued against this procedure. First, as we moved back in time from the most recent literature in sociology and as we began to cover the fields of anthropology and psychology, tables occurred less frequently. But though figures may represent more precise data, they are not necessarily more valid or *correct* data. Without tables, we would need an elaborate set of criteria (not yet formulated explicitly in any of these fields) for assessing the worth of each correlation.

Second, within all fields many decades elapse before a relatively simple ''finding'' is definitively pinned down; for example, whether in fact the chances of schizophrenia are really higher toward the lower classes seems to be as uncertain now as a generation ago.[16] The correlations between marital happiness and dozens of personal and impersonal traits are still shaky after more than one hundred research studies on this problem. The data supporting the theory of complementary needs have been neither definitively confirmed nor disconfirmed.

Social phenomena are complex and often seem disorderly. Our measuring instruments are crude and our research designs frequently not rigorous. It would therefore be a triumph of faith over modesty to proclaim that we are certain of *this* relationship, but *know* the data supporting *that* one are not to be trusted. We would, in effect, be claiming that we know for certain whether or not a given finding is definitely correct or incorrect decades before adequate research has pinned down that fact.

Nevertheless, all scientists do just that in their day-to-day thinking and reading. They recognize the sampling bias of one study or the poor questionnaire of another. At a deeper level, the sociologist, like any other scientist, responds to new data by matching them against his own vision of social relations and social structure, intuitively rejecting some while accepting others. At some level of articulateness every scientist may accept some data from a poor study and reject others from a seemingly better designed one because they fit or fail to fit some of his own hypotheses and observations. Of course, everyone makes errors in these judgments. Presumably he will eventually change his opinion as the weight of good evidence changes. In short, at any given time the scientist must weigh

[15]The propositional inventory that has been directed by Reuben Hill at the University of Minnesota, to be discussed later, has recorded the research design as well as the results of the studies in its sample.

[16]See the recent work by H. Warren Dunham, *Community and Schizophrenia: An Epidemiological Analysis* (Detroit: Wayne State University Press, 1965), as well as his earlier work with Robert E. L. Faris, *Mental Disorders in Urban Areas* (Chicago: University of Chicago Press, 1939).

evidence before he can be certain of his judgment. Consequently, though the propositions in this inventory have not been labeled as more or less correct, we have in fact weighed them. With few exceptions (those marked by the phrase "this proposition is also denied" to indicate that contrary data have also been reported), further evidence (we suppose) will very likely confirm the hypotheses.

It may, however, be worth repeating that a goodly percentage of these are not *causal* relationships since the correlation may be caused by still another variable not expressed in the hypotheses; that the correlation is often low; and that often one or both variables are vague. For example, as noted earlier, almost any social trait is correlated with "class," but sociologists have not succeeded in dissecting just which factors in that complex variable are the causal ones. When such a dissection has been adequately made, doubtless we shall find that many correlations between class and some family variable will turn out to be caused by some specific subvariable which is now included unknowingly in the broader term.

In the initial abstracting the author's words were recorded, but almost all the propositions were eventually edited for reasons noted above or to achieve clarity or brevity. This poses an interesting bibliographical problem. Indeed, the difficulties seemed so troubling that for a long while we held to the decision *not* to include the sources from which the hypotheses were taken.

First, any given proposition may have been found in many sources, no one of which was the first to "discover" it. In eliminating repetitions we did not concern ourselves with the delicate and often unanswerable question of priority. It is mainly an accident if the surviving proposition was extracted from the first publication ever to enunciate it. Nevertheless to give a specific bibliographical source is to suggest—here, erroneously—that the author enjoys priority.

Second, contemporary social science is still discursive. The author first outlines a *framework* for presenting his hypothesis. He offers many qualifications that limit the application of his data, for example, the data may refer only to a student sample, to one primitive society, to a clinical sample, and so on. He might protest in dismay at the elimination of his qualifications, as well as at the vulnerable bareness of the resulting hypothesis.

Next, the relations abstracted may not have been at all the central focus of the original article, but a subsidiary idea or even a dependent clause. For example, an author may have commented "because a money economy weakens kin obligations, the Manus. . . ." Whatever the main theme of his report, this clause asserts a causal relationship between an economic variable and kin obligations, and that correlation is recorded. Although almost every research report utilizes such implicit hypotheses without further analysis, some authors might object that they have been held responsible for a "finding" which was only incidental to their investigation.

As against these possible criticisms, we have nevertheless included the source of the proposition used in the inventory. By each hypothesis is a number which refers to a specific item in the bibliography. It is to be hoped that the usefulness of sources will outweigh the slight dismay that some authors will feel. Of course, in a search extending over a decade, and covering thousands of articles and books, we have committed errors of citation and recording. Some we could correct. One set that we could not correct because our resources were inadequate was the occasional failure to record the source of the proposition. In some cases, memory could lead us back to the article or book, but all too often the cost of finding the source persuaded us that we should not attempt it. We hope that this failure will not prove annoying to the reader, since the focus of the inventory is, after all, on the content of the proposition rather than which author enunciated it.

A final note on other inventories will place this one in a clearer perspective. Sociologists began to feel increasingly inundated by data after World War II and have since that time evolved many schemes for the organization and retrieval of data. An entire volume would now be needed to describe all of these efforts, some of them costing hundreds of thousands of dollars, at transforming the raw data of studies into some type of "library" of computer tapes that can be easily used. The development of computerized archives is moving forward in many subfields.

But data archives form only one method for dealing with the increased volume of data. Rigorous theory may sometimes be created (e.g., by the axiomatizing process), and thus a great mass of data can be expressed parsimoniously. In the period after World War II sociologists expended more effort in creating small bodies of at least approximations to rigorous sets of theories, notably in what has come to be called small groups theory.

A third movement, midway between the tightly reasoned set of organized hypotheses and the mass of archival data on tapes, aimed at propositional inventories, for example, in the subfields of social change, family, and political behavior.[17]

Most of these were abandoned or curtailed as the researchers saw how much tedious work each required. In view of the sheer manpower poured into the task, it is unfortunate that the only two that were carried out on a large scale were in the field of the family. However, these have a somewhat different form and serve different purposes. Over the longer run, the family inventory that has been developed by the Institute of Family Research at the University of Minnesota under the direction of Reuben Hill will be of great utility because it will be maintained as a *continuing* process by an *organization*. Even with a fair amount of research assistance, the individual scholar cannot develop a steady procedure for monitoring the vast flow of new materials, abstracting them, coding them, and storing them in a computer.

Even if he could carry out so formidable a task, such an inventory would be a personal nuisance to the individual scholar since it must be easily available to visiting researchers, students, planners, social workers, etc. The scholar would not be able to get his own work done if he were to respond personally to all such appropriate demands. By contrast an organization is able without great added cost not only to be accessible to such potential users, but also to expand its inventory to include an adequate control over new publications and to publish occasional bibliographies.[18]

On the other hand, although the organization can, through computerization, create such a massive product, the sheer bulk makes the information available to individual researchers and practical workers only through a computer link or through a visit to such a center. Consequently there is still a place for such an ordinary bound volume as this one, with a somewhat more skeletonic summing up of the field.

The great number of relationships presented in this inventory should not obscure the question of *coverage*. The topic of the family is popular among laymen and social scientists; thousands of articles are published in this field every year, in hundreds of languages. No practicable staff could be certain of obtaining, much less abstracting, all of it.

At best, such an inventory can aim at only an approximation of completeness. We abstracted systematically all the main journals (through the year 1964 and extending back in some cases to a generation ago) in which research in this field is published and a goodly segment of the monographs and textbook summaries. Although we did utilize foreign sources somewhat, for the most part these were ignored. At the present time most sociological *research* (as contrasted with essays) on the family is carried out by scholars in the United States, and since most of the research in other countries parallels the findings of research in the English language, we believe the loss is not great.

A more substantial loss occurs because each person who abstracts varies in his perception of propositions, both from one time to another and from others who might read the same report. On the other hand, since the same relationship is likely to appear in dozens of sources we can hope that this gap is eventually narrowed as the search continues in many sources.

There is, however, no simple technique by which one can *demonstrate* that, at some point, the cost of still more extensive reading is much greater than the increment of additional propositions. The process is potentially endless if the aim is a completely exhaustive coverage. Consequently, the decision to cease abstracting was, finally, arbitrary.

Of course, this compilation would not have been possible without the help of both foundations and dedicated people. The money was always insufficient, and we have, like other researchers who believe their project worthwhile, shamelessly exploited whatever resources we could command or cajole. The National Institutes of Mental Health was a major patron, but at crucial points both the Russell Sage Foundation and the Social Science Research Council were helpful, especially at a time when our spirits were low and to continue seemed impossible. William H. Y. Hackett, Jr., Director of the College Division of The Bobbs-Merrill Company, was generous, too, because of his belief that a propositional inventory in several fields of sociology would advance our discipline.

In addition, the Council for Research in the Social Sciences of Columbia University and the Department of Sociology through the Work Study Program were both willing, especially at the point when a final push seemed fruitful, to contribute to this project. And, as in other work we have done, the Bureau of Applied Social Research continued

---

[17]A few inventories have appeared in one form or another. See, for example, Herbert Hyman, *Political Socialization* (New York: The Free Press, 1959); Bernard Berelson and Gary A. Steiner, *Human Behavior* (New York: Harcourt, Brace and World, 1964); and Leon Festinger notes in *A Theory of Cognitive Dissonance* (Stanford: Stanford University Press, 1957), p. vii, that he and others began one in "Communication and Social Influence" but gave it up.

[18]Jean Aldous, *International Bibliography of Research in Marriage and the Family, 1900–1964* (Minneapolis: University of Minnesota Press, Family Study Center, 1967).

to take from our shoulders many administrative tasks that would otherwise have reduced our efficiency. It is in order, finally, to express our gratefulness to the many friends and co-workers who have at some phase or another given their time and energy to this huge and often tedious task. Unfortunately some may be overlooked after so many years. Without these contributions of self, this work could not have been done. To these people, we express our thanks: Peter Berliant, Peter S. Brooks, Herbert Bynder, Joni M. Cherbo, Harry Davidow, Marquita Fredette, Lawrence H. Geiger, Samuel Gross, Maria Morfoupolou, Kay P. Moseley, John Quitter, Nicholas Tavuchis, Sidney R. Waldron.

WILLIAM J. GOODE

# SOCIAL SYSTEMS AND FAMILY PATTERNS

## A Propositional Inventory

## ABDUCTION        X   Class

In societies in which abduction is a social pattern, it is more likely to occur when a man lacks the economic means for a legitimate marriage and does not have the personal attractiveness or seductive skill needed to persuade a girl to elope with him. (L026)

## ABORTION      X   Abortion, Attitude Toward

The use of socially obligatory abortion as a punitive measure is always found in association with the attitude that voluntary abortion is illicit and to be penalized. (D071)

### Adult-Child Role Definition

The greater the emphasis on the status disparity between adult and child, the more likely is abortion of the firstborn. (D071)

### Fertility Values

When a society places a high value on children, the rate of abortion is low. (S064)

### Illegitimacy, Attitude Toward

Abortion will be less common if illegitimate children and their parents are less stigmatized. The contrary is also asserted.

### Independence of Women

The abortion rate will rise with the increasing independence of women. (H111)

### Marital Adjustment

There is an inverse relation between abortion and the marital adjustment of wives. (K161)

### Marital Status

Abortions are as likely to be performed upon married as upon unmarried women. (E092)

### Mental Illness of Child (Schizophrenia)

The frequency of previous still births and abortions is much higher among mothers of schizophrenic children than among mothers of nonschizophrenics. (T108)

### Parental-Role Adjustment

There is a low correlation between the abortion of the first child and the parents' reluctance to grow up. (D071)

### Premarital Pregnancy

Premarital pregnancy that ends before marriage is much more likely to result in abortion than in miscarriage or birth. (E092)

### Premarital Sex Relations

Where premarital sex relations are relatively institutionalized, it is more likely that the unwed mother aborts; where such relations are informally accepted, abortion of a resultant pregnancy is less likely. (D071)

### Race

Premarital pregnancy is much more likely to be terminated by induced abortion among white than it is among Negro females. (E092)

### Rank of Women

The abortion rate will rise with the increasing independence of women. (H111)

### Sex Taboo (Postpregnancy)

Married women are more likely to give the sex drive priority over the maternal impulse and thus resort to abortion in societies where there are taboos on coitus during pregnancy and lactation and where monogamy prevails. (D071)

### Sex Taboo (Postpregnancy) X   Parent-Child Relations (Hostility)

There is a relationship between unconscious parental hostility toward the unborn child (as a motive for abortion) and taboo on coitus during pregnancy and lactation in monogamous societies. (D071)

### Social Structure

Societies in which abortion is culturally imposed, especially punitively, tend to be those which lack alternative outlets for neurotic tensions and anxieties. (D071)

## ABORTION, ATTITUDE TOWARD    X   Abortion

The use of socially obligatory abortion as a punitive measure is always found in association with the attitude that voluntary abortion is illicit and to be penalized. (D071)

## ABORTION (COMPULSORY)    X   Incest Anxiety

There is a correlation between the unconscious belief that an unborn child is the offspring of a socially improper father, such as the paternal or maternal grandfather, and the custom of compulsory abortion. (D071)

## ACADEMIC MOTIVATION OF CHILD BY CLASS    X   Child-Rearing Practices (Dependency)

High independence training has a greater effect on high academic motivation among middle-class than among lower-class youths. (E102)

### Size of Family

Among high achieving adolescents, small family size has a greater effect on high academic motivation among lower-class than among middle-class adolescents. (E102)

## ACCIDENT-PRONENESS OF CHILD    X   Authoritarianism

Children who grow up in an authoritarian home environment in which feelings of rejection and resulting hostility are fostered are more likely to become accident-prone than those who are raised in a permissive home (the manifestation of an inward turning of aggression). (K122)

### Broken Homes

Children who are accident-prone are more likely than normal children to come from broken homes. (K122)

### Ordinal Position

Later-born children are more likely than earlier-born children to be accident-prone. (K122)

### Size of Family
Children who are accident-prone come from larger families than normal children. (K122)

## ACCULTURATION         X   Adultery
Under situations of European contact, extramarital relations tend to increase. (B148)

### Authority Structure of Family
The authority of the father deteriorates as children become increasingly oriented toward the donor culture. (S051)

### Avoidance Relationship
Traditional avoidance relationships tend to deteriorate with increasing acculturation. (B166)

### Clan
As the degree of acculturation increases, clan organization tends to diminish in importance. (B093)

### Class
Ethnic groups with high social status tend to be the most acculturated. (S051)

### Cohesion of Community
The relationship between acculturated families and unacculturated families is characterized by hostility and a low frequency of social interaction. (B034)

Well-integrated communities tend to be resistant to changes which might alter their distinctive cultural identity. (S053)

### Cohesion of Culture
When the society is not well-integrated culturally, acculturation will occur on the familial or individual level. (S046)

### Cohesion of Family
When family bonds are strong, the rate of acculturation is retarded. (S051)

### Cohesion of Kin Network
When interfamilial ties are strong, the society will tend to be resistant to acculturative changes. (A023)

### Community
Acculturation tends to break down the correspondence between the kin unit and the community. (K049)

### Conflict in Family
The chances of marital and familial conflict are greatest whenever an individual member of a family enters a new social environment while other members remain in the old cultural area or whenever a family moves to a different place and its members vary in the degree to which they assimilate the new culture. (B033)

When the value orientation of the family is conservative, acculturation will be accompanied by conflict. (B042)

### Conformity
Children in more acculturated families are less frequently responsive to parental proposals or interference. (B040)

### Descent (Matrilineal)
A matrilineal-descent organization tends to be abandoned under acculturative pressures. (C068)

### Divorce
The divorce rate tends to increase under acculturative conditions. The contrary is also asserted. (M069)

### Economic Role of Joint Family
The joint family under pressures of acculturation is more likely to lose its economic than its social functions. (M081)

### Educational System
Day schools have greater influence in promoting changes within the Indian community than do boarding schools. (P010)

### Endogamy
Resistance to acculturation is facilitated by the pattern of community endogamy. (F014)

### Endogamy (Ethnic)
Where the pattern of ethnic endogamy is strong, the ethnic group will tend to be resistant to acculturation. (S051)

### Exogamy
Rules of clan exogamy tend to deteriorate in situations of European contact. (R056)

### Father-Son Relations
Under Western acculturation the father-son tie in a matrilineal society emerges into greater importance. (F073)

### Fecundity
Sociocultural stress (acting on the reproductive mechanism of women) reduces fecundity. (H024)

### Fertility
The birthrate tends to decline in stituations of culture contact. (H135)

### Geographic Mobility
Those who migrate individually become acculturated more rapidly than do those who migrate with families. (S051)

### Illegitimacy
Under conditions of European contact, the rate of illegitimacy will tend to increase. (B148)

### Inheritance
Inheritance will tend to shift from matrilineal to patrilineal under the pressures of colonial administrators. (M082)

### Inheritance (Matrilineal)
In the acculturative situation, patterns of matrilineal inheritance weaken. (F055)

### Intergenerational Relations
Intergenerational conflict tends to occur wherever a situation of acculturation exists. (S052)

### Intermarriage (Ethnic)
The rate of acculturation is accelerated when there is ethnic or racial intermarriage with the donor culture. (B049)

Children of ethnic intermarriages will participate less in the indigenous culture if the parent who represents the donor culture has little interest or sympathy with the social organization or culture of the indigenous group. (L031)

Intermarriage increases cultural assimilation, particularly when the woman belongs to the dominant culture. (P052)

Intermarriage increases cultural breakdown or cultural assimilation, particularly when the woman belongs to the dominant culture. (P052)

### Kin-Role Definition
Kinship obligations tend to weaken under conditions of acculturation. (E067)

### Kinship
Absorption of cultural traits is more likely if the kin structure is complex and each unit has a separate cultural identity. (M233)

### Kinship, Importance of
Kinship ties beyond those of closest kin tend to be unimportant where much social and cultural assimilation occurs. (E104)

### Marital Stability
There is no correlation between the degree of individual acculturation and marital instability. The contrary is also asserted. (F062)

### Mate Selection (Free Choice)
With acculturation the choice of a mate becomes increasingly independent of family opinion. (A034)

### Monogamy/Polyandry
Wherever modern European culture has penetrated and modified indigenous culture, polyandry is giving way to monogamy. (M048)

### Nonkin Relations
When there is a differential participation of the members of a family in the dominant institutions, members will vary greatly from one another in their degree of acculturation. (B042)

### Parent-Child Relations (Control)
An increase in acculturation correlates with the weakening of parental control. (S135)

### Parent-Child Relations (Interaction)
The greater the degree of acculturation, the less frequent and less intense is the interaction initiated by the parents. (B040)

### Personality Problems of Child
If parents attempt to assimilate new cultural values too rapidly, they will project their role conflicts onto the child in an attempt to work out the discrepancies between new and old roles, resulting in emotional disturbance of the child. (B242)

### Political Role of Clan
The political functions of the clan tend to be lost with acculturation. (W080)

### Political Structure
Societies in which tensions exist between a state political structure and a corporate lineage organization will tend to be more susceptible to acculturation. (F073)

### Polygyny
Acculturation is accompanied by less approval of polygyny. (J009)

Polygyny tends to be abandoned with the adoption of Christianity. (V021)

### Population
Apathy, due to loss of old customs in the process of acculturation, leads to extension of the practice of abortion and to a decrease in population. (B081)

When social disintegration characterizes a cultural contact situation, depopulation tends to occur. (E080)

### Power Structure of Family
The acculturation of matrilineal tribes tends to result in an increase in the power of the father within the family. (E046)

### Preferential Marriage
Marriage regulations tend to deteriorate under conditions of acculturation. (E067)

### Rank of Men
The status of the male will tend to be accorded greater importance under European acculturative pressures. (S120)

### Rank of Wife
As the group becomes acculturated, the status of the wife becomes more egalitarian. (S051)

### Rank of Women
When the woman commands the control position and authority in the family, the ethnic group will tend to be resistant toward acculturation. (B055)

### Residence
A sedentary, localized, village settlement pattern permits greater resistance to acculturation than does one of a seminomadic food-gathering character. (E021)

When families live in small, scattered, unstable settlements, the degree of acculturation tends to be low. (S046)

### Residence (Matrilocal)
The deterioration of patterns of matrilocal residence tends to be directly correlated with the degree of acculturation. (B093)

### Residence (Neolocal)
The adoption of patterns of neolocal residence tends to accompany acculturation. (N030)

### Role Conflict
When one spouse is more acculturated than the other, role conflict is greater for the husband. (S039)

### Sex Relations
When a pattern of sexual relations is established between indigenous people and members of the donor culture, the rate of acculturation is accelerated. (S046)

### Sex Status
Boys are more likely than girls to identify with Europeans and to emulate them. (P009)

### Size of Family
A reduction in the size of the family tends to accompany acculturation. (M081)

### Social Mobility
There is a positive relationship between the acculturation of an ethnic group and its social mobility. (S051)

### Stability of Extended Family
The disintegration of the extended family is directly correlated with the degree of acculturation. (B093)

### Stability of Family
Families which are marginal to both unacculturated and acculturated groups tend to be restless, unsatisfied, unpredictable, and psychologically unstable. (B034)

### Stability of Family Structure
Cultural assimilation tends to be accelerated when familial institutions are changed. (S046)

Cultural features which are associated with the family tend to be more resistant to acculturation. (S111)

### Stability of Family System
The disintegration of the family system is accelerated by the adoption of external cultural values. (B043)

Acculturation tends to result in the breakdown of the traditional family system. (S135)

Cultural assimilation tends to be accelerated when familial institutions are changed. (S046)

### Stability of Joint Family
The joint family structure tends to deteriorate with increasing acculturation. (M081)

### Stability of Kinship System
The kinship structure tends to disintegrate with increasing acculturation. (P044)

### Values
When the orientation of the parents toward the donor culture is positive, the degree of acculturation will be higher. (B043)

## ACCULTURATION ANXIETY
### X   Cohesion of Family
When strong familial ties are maintained, the emotional disturbances that frequently accompany culture contact are reduced. (S051)

### Sex-Role Definition
Acculturative anxiety is less likely to occur if there is a continuity of sex role between the traditional and acculturated situation (e.g., women are likely to play the same roles even in a situation of acculturation). (S039)

### Sex Status
Men tend to exhibit greater acculturative anxiety (than women) since the disruption created in rapid culture change affects them more directly. (S039)

### Stability of Family
Acculturative anxiety resulting from the contact situation tends to result in an unstable family structure. (S090)

## ACHIEVEMENT
### X   Child-Rearing Practices (Achievement)
Mothers of high-achieving sons are more likely to give emotional support for their sons' achievements. (G156)

### Child-Rearing Practices (Creativity)
Mothers of high-achieving sons are more likely to reward them for trying something new. (G156)

### Child-Rearing Practices (Dependency)
Children's achievement behavior outside the home does not correlate with independence training by mother. (C118)

Early training in mastery increases higher achievement, *provided* independence does not mean generalized restrictiveness, authoritarianism, or "rejection" by the parents. (M246)

In Brazil, Germany, and Japan, sons whose mothers expected them to care for themselves at an early age performed better at arithmetic, were more optimistic toward life, and were less spontaneous in a graphic expression test. (M246)

### Child-Rearing Practices (Favoritism)
Children who have learning problems are likely to have mothers who show marked preference for the child's sibling. (R113)

### Dependency on Lineage
The minimization of individual achievement within the lineage is correlated with a greater psychological dependence on the lineage and residence group and a greater physical dependence on them for subsistence needs. (F015)

### Employment
Employed parents tend to evaluate more highly the occupational success of their children than do retired parents. (S220)

### Employment of Mother
Regardless of whether the mother likes to work, young children (third to sixth graders) of working mothers show a lower performance level. (G156)

### Husband-Wife Relations (Power)
An equalitarian spousal relationship is associated with boys who are high achievers in systems (e.g., the school) external to the family. (S205)

### Juvenile Delinquency
There is a correlation between low family occupational-educational achievement and delinquency in the son. (W152)

### Marital Adjustment
If (as in the lower class) the husband is not expected to be an economic success, marital satisfaction is not affected by his failure to achieve it. (G014)

### Mother-Son Relations (Affection)
Among mothers with strong achievement needs, the greater the son's achievement, the greater the affectional warmth displayed by the mother. (B275)

### Ordinal Position
There is no relationship between the child's ordinal position and his level of achievement. (S218)

Under really frightening conditions firstborn individuals will be less effective than later-born individuals. (S263)

Later-born flyers tend to be more effective fighter pilots than firstborn flyers. (S263)

### Parent-Child Relations (Financial Help)
Children who have been successful in their occupations tend to give their retired parents more financial assistance than do less successful children. (S220)

### Power Structure of Family
In joint family systems, when a man has made a fortune by his own skill and has invested it in property other than farming land, he will tend to be reluctant to allow other members of the family to interfere in its management. (M021)

The more responsible and skillful the man is in extrafamilial roles, the greater is the effective superiority of the husband in family decision making. (P083)

Families with a conflict in the power structure have sons with low levels of performance, and with low achievement motivation. (S205)

The equalitarian family is associated with ineffective socialization for achievement roles. (S205)

### Sibling Structure (Age Difference)
There is no relationship between age intervals between siblings and their level of achievement. (S218)

### Sibling Structure (Sex)
Children with male siblings are more likely to be high in achievement than are those with female siblings. (S218)

### Size of Family
Proportionally more of the most effective fighter pilots (aces) are from large families; more pilots from small families are nonaces. (S263)

### Values (Egalitarianism)
Because there is more egalitarian bias in American than in British values, it has been more difficult for American upper-class families to claim a superiority of breed that would give them a recognized quasi-monopoly on high achievement (something that the English gentry has maintained). (P083)

## ACHIEVEMENT ASPIRATION
### X   Parent-Child Relations (Rejection)
Persons having high achievement orientation tend to perceive their childhoods as unhappy and their relationships with their parents as involving emotional rejection. (S205)

## ACHIEVEMENT ASPIRATIONS
### X   Surrogate Mother
When their infants are six months of age, mothers who have been the only caretaking figure for their infants have higher achievement aspirations for their children than do mothers who have provided other maternal figures for their infants. (C107)

When the child is six months of age, mothers who have reared the child themselves have higher achievement expectations for the child than do mothers of children who have been reared by more than one mother figure (i.e., nurse, grandparent, friend of mother, older sister of child). (C124)

## ACHIEVEMENT ASPIRATIONS OF MOTHER
### X   Maternal Overprotectiveness
Maternal overprotectiveness is likely to occur if the mother has been thwarted in her educational or career ambitions. (L163)

## ACHIEVEMENT DEMANDS
### X   Cognitive Development
The mother's excessive ambition for the child is likely to foster learning problems for the child. (R113)

### Mental Illness (Schizophrenia/Neurosis)
Schizophrenics are under greater parental pressure to become successful than are neurotics. (M197)

### Paternal/Maternal Role
Adolescents are more likely to view the mother as demanding achievement than the father. (B250)

### Peer Relations
The mother's concern with the child's achievement is related to the child's being victimized or teased in his relationships with peers. (R113)

### Personality of Child (Withdrawal)
Children whose mothers are very concerned with the children's achievement tend to be withdrawn and seclusive and are likely to indulge in daydreaming to a great degree. (R113)

## ACHIEVEMENT (MATHEMATICS)
### X   Child-Rearing Practices (Achievement Demands)
High-school students who are high achievers in mathematics are more likely than the average student to give a negative and autocratic characterization of their family relationships, indicating stress on achievement, discipline, control, and regimen. (K148)

## ACHIEVEMENT MOTIVATION
### X   Achievement Motivation of Mother
The relationship between the achievement motivation of mothers and sons is curvilinear; a very high level of achievement motivation in mothers is related to low achievement motivation in their sons. (M246)

### Age of Mother
In small, middle-class families, sons of young mothers tend to have higher achievement motivation than do sons of older mothers. (R106)

### Authoritarianism
The more permissive the familial atmosphere, the greater the achievement motivation of the child. (D074)

The more restrictive and authoritarian the familial atmosphere, the greater the achievement motivation of the child. (D074)

### Authoritarianism of Father
Authoritarian fathers tend to have children with lower achievement motivation than do less authoritarian fathers. (R097)

### Broken Homes
In the United States, men coming from broken homes tend to have lower achievement motivation than those from intact homes. (M246)

### Child-Rearing Attitudes (Competitiveness)
Mothers of boys with high achievement motivation tend to expect their sons to be more competitive than do mothers of sons with low achievement motivation. (R097)

### Child-Rearing Practices (Achievement)
Within cultures high in rigidity, the greater the stress on achievement training, the higher the level of folktale achievement imagery. (M246)

Parents of boys with high achievement motivation tend to react to good performance with more warmth and approval, or with disapproval at poor performance, than do parents of boys with low achievement motivation. (R106)

### Child-Rearing Practices (Achievement Demands)
"Excessive" parental achievement demands are associated with low achievement motivation in the child. (B275)

Mothers who consistently tend to demand excellence tend to have high achievement motivation. (G156)

Mothers of sons with high achievement motivation are more likely to insist that they master certain skills in both school and home. (G156)

Middle-class mothers of sons with high achievement motivation are likely to expect achievement in their sons at earlier ages than are mothers of sons with low achievement motivation. (M246)

Fathers of boys with high achievement motivation make fewer statements which urge their sons to work hard than do the fathers of sons with low achievement motivation. (R098)

Strong achievement motivation tends to develop when parents set high goals for their children. (R106)

### Child-Rearing Practices (Achievement/Dependency)
Mothers of boys with high achievement motivation tend to stress the achievement training of their sons rather than independence training. (R097)

### Child-Rearing Practices (Authoritarianism)
Authoritarianism, restrictiveness, and/or rejection in child-rearing practices are associated with low achievement motivation in the son. (M246)

### Child-Rearing Practices (Collective)
Kibbutz children have lower achievement motivation than non kibbutz children. (R096)

### Child-Rearing Practices (Demands)
If a mother makes more demands of her child before the age of eight, the child will develop a stronger achievement motivation than if she does not make such demands. (W139)

### Child-Rearing Practices (Demands/Restrictions)
A child will develop a strong achievement motivation if, by the time the child is seven, the number of demands placed upon the child by the mother exceeds the number of restrictions. (W139)

### Child-Rearing Practices (Dependency)
A dominant mother may aid the development of achievement motivation if she is strong and does not achieve overprotectiveness. An authoritarian and indulgent mother will keep the son from developing the skills for mastering tasks on his own and will prevent him from developing autonomy while encouraging an exaggerated opinion of his own achievements. (M246)

Stress on independence training is highly correlated with the amount of achievement imagery in the folktales current in a culture. (M246)

The more stress placed on independence training during early childhood, the higher the achievement motivation of the children. (M246)

The more severe the parental training in independence, the higher the level of achievement motivation. (C101)

Mothers of sons with high achievement motivation are more likely to insist that they make decisions for themselves. (G156)

There is a correlation between the extent of early independence training of the child and the amount of need achievement present in the myths of the society. (K111)

In lower-class families, the later the independence mastery training, the higher the boy's achievement motivation. (M246)

In cultures which expect independence mastery quite late, if at all, earlier stress on achievement leads to higher achievement motivation. (M246)

There is no relationship between expecting the child to

care for himself at an early age and achievement motivation in Brazil, Germany, or Japan. (M246)

Fathers of sons with high achievement motivation tend to grant their sons more autonomy in decision-making situations than do fathers with low achievement motivation. (R096)

Mothers of sons with low achievement motivation tend to grant their sons more autonomy than do mothers of sons with high achievement motivation. (R096)

Parents of children with high achievement motivation tend to expect their children to be self-reliant when competing against standards of excellence. (R097)

Parents of children with high achievement motivation tend to grant their children autonomy in problem solving and decision making in situations where the children have freedom of action and responsibility for success or failure. (R097)

Mothers of boys with high levels of achievement motivation tend to expect less self-reliance from their sons than do mothers of boys with low achievement motivation. (R106)

### Child-Rearing Practices (Guilt)
An emphasis on achievement drive is likely to be correlated with the inculcation by the mother of a sense of guilt in childhood. (V029)

### Child-Rearing Practices (Permissiveness)
Mothers of sons with high achievement motivation are more likely to be permissive regarding their taking care of themselves. (G156)

### Child-Rearing Practices (Permissiveness/Restrictiveness)
Permissive child-rearing practices are no more related to achievement motivation in sons than are restrictive child-rearing practices. (G156)

### Child-Rearing Practices (Punishment)
Mothers of children with strong achievement motivation do not differ from mothers of children with weak achievement motivation in the number and intensity of punishments for demands not fulfilled by the child and restrictions not obeyed by the child. (W139)

### Child-Rearing Practices (Restrictiveness)
Although mothers of sons with high achievement motivation placed fewer restrictions on their sons than did mothers of those with low achievement motivation, the restrictions they did make were imposed at an earlier age. (M246)

### Child-Rearing Practices (Rewards)
The more highly a mother evaluates her child's accomplishments and the more she rewards them, the stronger her child's achievement motivation will be. (W139)

### Child-Rearing Practices (Setting Standards)
Parents of boys with high achievement motivation set higher standards of excellence for the son's performance than do parents of boys low in achievement motivation. (M246)

Parents of children with high achievement motivation set high performance goals for their children. (R097)

Strong achievement motivation tends to develop when parents impose standards of excellence upon problem-solving tasks, even in situations where such standards are not explicit. (R106)

### Chores

The greater the extent of the child's participation in household tasks, the higher his level of achievement motivation. (C101)

### Class

When the wife is dominant (v. husband-dominant, autonomic, or conflcit-type), the highest average active-future orientation of sons is found in the low socioeconomic status group. (S205)

### Cohesion of Family

Family structures which are effective in training boys for achievement tend to do so at the cost of heightened intrapsychic tension and lowered familial integration. (S205)

### Dependency

Boys with high achievement motivation are less likely to ask for parental aid in a problem-solving situation than are boys with low achievement motivation. (R098)

### Divorce

There is a direct relation between achievement motivation (competition, individualism, status striving) and divorce. (K161)

### Father Absence

Father-absent or mother-child households are associated with low achievement motivation. (M246)

In cultures where fathers tend to be very authoritarian, separation of the son from the father is likely to promote high achievement motivation if it does not occur so early as to promote the development of strong mother-son ties associated with a mother-child household. (M246)

In Turkey high achievement motivation is related to separation from the father. (M246)

### Father-Son Relations (Affection)

Sons who have received insufficient paternal affection are lower in achievement needs than sons who have received adequate paternal affection. (M204)

### Father-Son Relations (Control)

Strong paternal control allowing little autonomy of investigation inhibits high achievement motivation in the son. (B275)

### Handicapped Child (Deafness)

There is a correlation between achievement motivation in the normal child and independence-training attitudes in the mother, but not if the child is deaf. (G129)

### Identification with Father

Strong father identification is associated with high achievement motivation in the son. (M204)

### Institutional Care

There is a correlation between institutionalization of the child and lack of achievement motivation. (Y045)

### Interaction in Family

Family structures which optimize a smooth internal functioning of the family system are relatively less successful in socializing children for achievement motivation. (S205)

### Joint Family

Where earnings are shared among members of a joint family in India, a family member is less likely than in other types of families to show initiative. (N069)

### Marriage, Attitude Toward

The higher the individual's achievement motivation, the less likely is he to place a high priority on marriage. (B245)

### Maternal Overprotectiveness

Overprotective mothers tend to have fewer children with high achievement motivation than do dominant mothers. (R097)

### Mother-Son Relations (Indulgence)

Indulgent and ever-forgiving mothers are not associated with high achievement motivation. (G156)

### Mother-Son Relations (Rejection)

Mothers of boys with high achievement motivation tend to be more rejecting than do mothers of boys with low achievement motivation. (R098)

### Mother-Son Relations (Warmth)

Warm mother-son relations are not associated with high achievement motivation. (G156)

The relationship between mothers and sons with high achievement motivation tends to be warmer than is the relationship between mothers and sons with low achievement motivation. (R098)

### Occupation of Father

There is no association between the father's occupation and the child's level of achievement motivation. (C101)

### Occupational Aspirations

Mothers of sons with high achievement motivation have higher occupational aspirations for their sons than do mothers of those low in achievement motivation. (M246)

### Ordinal Position

In the United States, firstborn children are likely to have higher achievement motivation than later-born children. (M246)

In India and Japan later-born children tend to have higher achievement motivation than firstborn children. (M246)

Last-born children in large families tend to have lower achievement motivation than do earlier-born children in large families. (R106)

Last-born children in small families tend to have higher achievement motivation than do earlier-born children. (R106)

### Parent-Child Relations (Authoritarianism)

Mothers of boys high in achievement motivation display more authoritarianism toward their sons than do mothers of those low in achievement motivation. (M246)

Fathers of boys high in achievement motivation show less dominating or authoritarian behavior toward the son than do fathers of those low in achievement motivation. (M246)

### Parent-Child Relations (Closeness)
Close emotional ties between parent and child produce lower achievement motivation (college students) than does the suppression of immediate emotional response. (D065)

### Parent-Child Relations (Dominance)
Fathers of sons with low achievement motivation more frequently made decisions pertaining to the sons' expected activities and performance than did fathers of boys high in achievement motivation. (M246)

Dominating behavior does not inhibit the development of achievement motivation if it comes from the mother, but only if it comes from the father. (M246)

### Parent-Child Relations (Evaluation)
Among male college students, the higher the achievement score (measured by T.A.T.), the more likely they are to view their parents as unfriendly, unhelpful, and unsuccessful. (M060)

Striving for achievement is more frequent among boys who perceive their relationship with their parents as unsatisfying. (M060)

Strong achievement motivation tends to develop when parents indicate a high evaluation of their child's competence to do a task well. (R106)

### Parent-Child Relations (Rejection)
Among male college students, the higher the achievement score (measured by T.A.T.), the more likely they are to perceive their parents, particularly their father, as rejecting.

The more rejected the child is by his parents (accompanied by a reduction in self-esteem and a turning to extrinsic sources for a sense of self-accomplishment), the greater will the child's desire for achievement be ego-motivated. (A059)

Persons having high achievement orientation tend to perceive their childhood as unhappy and their relationships with their parents as involving emotional rejection. (S205)

### Parent-Child Relations (Warmth)
Parents of sons with high achievement motivation give more psychological support and display more warmth or generally positive affection toward the sons in an achievement situation than do parents of boys with low achievement motivation. (M246)

### Paternal-Role Model
Having a highly successful father as a role model is negatively related to high achievement motivation in the son. (G156)

### Personality of Child (Anal Character)
The greater the mother's need for achievement, the more likely she is to have children with an anal character.

### Personality of Mother (Competitiveness)
Mothers of boys with high achievement motivation tend to be more competitive than mothers of boys with low achievement motivation. (R097)

### Personality of Mother (Dominance)
Mothers of boys with high achievement motivation tend to stress the achievement training of their sons rather than independence training. (R097)

Mothers of boys with high achievement motivation tend to be more dominant and demanding than mothers of boys with low achievement motivation. (R097)

### Personality of Parents (Competitiveness)
Parents of boys with a high achievement motivation tend to be more competitive than do parents of boys with low achievement motivation. (R106)

### Polygyny
Low achievement motivation is more likely in cultures characterized by some form of polygyny than it is in monogamous cultures. (M246)

### Power Structure of Family
Families where the father tends to dominate are not associated with high achievement motivation. (G156)

In families where the authority structure is more evenly dispersed, granting the mother considerable power, the sons are more likely to be high achievement seekers. (G156)

Mothers of boys with high achievement motivation tend to be more dominant than do mothers of boys with low achievement motivation. (R106)

In societies that have institutionalized male dominance, fathers whose dominance is so great that a son generalizes from his low intrafamilial potency to the world at large may have a low achievement orientation. (S205)

### Residence
There is no association between family residence (inner and outer industrial and inner and outer residential suburbs) and the child's level of achievement orientation. (C101)

### Scholastic Adjustment
Children who drop out from high school are more likely to have parents who are indifferent to their school attendance than are those who do not drop out. (H189)

### Sex-Role Definition
In societies which institutionalize male dominance, a male role model is necessary for achievement orientation. (S205)

### Sibling Structure (Sex)
There is no relationship between the individual's achievement motivation and the sex of his siblings, holding family size constant. (T095)

### Sibling Structure (Twins)
### X Personality Problems (Anality)
Twinship decreases the correlation between achievement strivings and anal behavior manifestations. (B224)

### Size of Family
Family size is negatively related to achievement motivation in the child. (E102)

The larger the size of the family, the lower the achievement motivation of the sons. (R083)

In lower-class families, achievement motivation decreases as family size increases. (R106)

### Size of Family by Class
Small family size is more important in determining high achievement motivation in youngest males than is high social class. (R106)

### Surrogate Mother
Mothers who rear their children themselves are less likely to have achievement fantasies characterized by personal failure than are mothers who provide maternal substitutes for their children (nurses, grandparents, older sister of the child, and friends). (C124)

## ACHIEVEMENT MOTIVATION OF MOTHER
### X   Achievement Motivation
The relationship between the achievement motivation of mothers and sons is curvilinear; a very high level of achievement motivation in mothers is related to low achievement motivation in their sons. (M246)

### Child-Rearing Attitudes (Dependency)
There is a curvilinear relationship between achievement motivation of mothers and their independence-training attitudes toward the child. (G129)

## ACHIEVEMENT VALUES        X   Age of Mother
Sons of older mothers (40 years or older) are more likely to have values similar to their mothers' regarding achievement than are sons with younger mothers (20–39 years); this is not true in the middle class. (R097)

### Child-Rearing Practices (Dependency)
The earlier the child receives independence training, the greater the similarity between mother and son on values regarding achievement. (R097)

### Child-Rearing Practices (Punishment)
The use of physical punishment as a child-rearing practice is positively associated with low value consensus between mother and son regarding achievement values. (R097)

### Class
The higher the social class (lower to upper middle class), the greater the value similarity between mother and son regarding achievement. (R097)

### Ordinal Position
Only and oldest sons are more likely than are intermediate and youngest sons to have values similar to their mothers' regarding achievement. (R097)

### Personality of Child (Aggression)
There is a positive association between high achievement-oriented homes and resulting aggressive, tense, domineering, and cruel personality traits in children. (B252)

### Power Structure of Family
The more the father believes in achievement values, the less his son's power is. (M060)

### Sex-Role Definition
In achievement-oriented cultures, there is greater role differentiation between men and women. (M060)

### Size of Family
There is a curvilinear relationship between family size and value similarity between mother and son regarding achievement; value similarity is highest in medium-sized families and lowest in small and large families. (R097)

## ACHIEVEMENT VALUES OF MOTHER
### X   Achievement Values of Son
Mothers with strong achievement orientations are no more successful in transmitting their values to their sons than are mothers with weak achievement values. (R097)

## ACHIEVEMENT VALUES OF SON
### X   Achievement Values of Mother
Mothers with strong achievement orientations are no more successful in transmitting their values to their sons than are mothers with weak achievement values. (R097)

## ACQUAINTANCESHIP, TYPE OF
### X   Mate Selection
Marriage is more likely for couples who meet at one or the other's home than for those who meet at work. (C002)

More couples marry who meet through their parents or relatives (while living close by) than couples who meet through school or college acquaintances. (C002)

## ACTIVITY LEVEL OF CHILD
### X   Child-Rearing Practices (Giving Reasons)
Children from homes characterized by a high level of explanation by the parents of family decisions have a higher activity level than children from homes where there is not a great amount of explanation. (B266)

## ADJUSTMENT        X   Interaction in Family
Joint recreation and joint participation in activities by all family members brings a high degree of satisfaction with family life.

## ADJUSTMENT OF CHILD   X   Divorce/Separation
Children of discord or separation suffer greater disadvantages than those whose parents actually divorce. (G134)

### Employment of Mother
Daughters of working mothers are less likely to be well adjusted than those of nonworking mothers. (S265)

Employment/nonemployment of the mother is not related to adjustment of children. (S265)

### Geographic Mobility
The child who is not given ample time to react to a notice of his family's change of residence is more likely to develop fantasy and ambivalence concerning the change than the child who is allowed time for adjustment. (S222)

### Institutional Care
The process of intellectual, physical, and emotional deterioration of the child, attendant upon institutionalization, may be arrested if he is reunited with his mother within three months, but not after five months. (Y045)

### Institutional Care, Duration of
The adverse effects of institutionalization upon babies are more likely to disappear when the babies are restored to their mothers before three months of institutionalization have elapsed. (B270)

### Marital Adjustment
A correlation exists between marriage adjustment and the child's adjustment. (F094)

### Mother Absence
In children under five years of age, children who had intimate and happy relations with their mothers and

were then deprived of them suffered more from the loss than did children who never knew their mothers. (B270)

### Remarriage

Regarding their children's adjustment, divorcées who are remarried are more likely to claim satisfaction with the "way things are" than are those who are not remarried. (G157)

The longer the child has been in an intact family the more difficult it is for him to adjust to a new marriage after the former has been dissolved. (R129)

### Stepparent/Natural Parent

The adjustment of a stepchild to stepparents is more difficult than the adjustment of a child to his real parents. (B286)

### Surrogate Mother

The adverse effects of institutionalization on babies are lessened if there is a mother surrogate in the institution. (B270)

### Surrogate Parent

A child tends to adjust better to a parental surrogate when the surrogate's behavior is similar to that of his real parent. (M058)

The successful adjustment of the adopted child to a new home is less likely if one or both of the foster-parents are emotionally disturbed. (T086)

### Surrogate Siblings

Foster-home care is likely to succeed if a child is placed with a child of the same age but opposite sex as the foster-child. (B270)

Foster-home care is more likely to be successful if there are other children in the home, especially if these are the siblings of the foster-child. (B270)

Foster-home care is more likely to be successful if there is a difference of four years or more in either direction between the foster-child and the foster-parents' own child of the same sex. (B270)

## ADJUSTMENT OF CHILD (SOCIAL AND PHYSICAL)
### X    Mother-Child Relations (Consistency)

Mood shifts in mothers characterized by alternating moods of hostility-overprotectiveness toward their children are positively associated with a diminished capacity on the part of the children to relate themselves to humans or to manipulate inanimate objects. (S209)

## ADJUSTMENT OF MOTHER
### X    Illegitimacy (Adoption)

Unwed mothers who keep their children have more problems and are less secure in their ability to handle future problems than are unwed mothers who give up their children. (J020)

## ADJUSTMENT TO PARENTS
### X    Age of Adult Child

Older mothers are better adjusted to their own parents than are younger mothers; but younger wives without children are better adjusted to their parents than are older wives without children. (S011)

## ADOLESCENT ROLE, DEFINITION OF
### X    Social Adjustment

If the transition from childhood to adult status is con-

trolled, adolescent problem behavior will be absent. (B033)

## ADOPTION    X    Adoption, Attitudes of Parents

More parents adopt children because of a general love of children and the factor of infertility than because of other psychological factors (fear of pregnancy, desire for companionship, etc.). (F117)

### Death Rate

In societies in which the survival rate for the population is low, adoption is more likely to occur than in societies with a high survival rate. (D080)

### Descent

Daughters are less frequently adopted in matrilocal and matrilineal societies than in patrilocal and patrilineal societies. (D057)

The incidence of adoption will be high in societies which stress the importance of continuity in the descent line. (S122)

### Descent (Matrilineal)

In matrilineal societies girls will tend to be adopted more frequently than boys. (F040)

### Education of Parents

Couples of higher educational level are more likely to withdraw their application for adoption than couples of lower educational level. (F117)

### Emotional Problems of Child

Since the adopted child is likely to realize that he does not belong (fear of loss of self), he is more likely than the child reared at home to have aggravated difficulty in resolving the Oedipal complex (castration fear, loss of penis). (B253)

### Employment of Parents

The more stable the employment of the parents, the more likely it is that they will adopt a child. (F117)

### Fecundity

Women who have not been able to have children and who then adopt a child are no more likely to become pregnant than are presumably "infertile" women who do not adopt a child.

### Fertility

Adoption of children is more likely to occur when the couple has no children of their own. (B059)

There is a correlation between the decision to adopt a child and the occurrence of pregnancy in a previously sterile woman. This hypothesis is also denied. (B309)

### Heirs, Absence of

Adoption tends to occur most frequently when there are no legal heirs within the family.

### Kin-Role Definition

Adoption is less common where the transmission of lineage obligations is less important. (G028)

### Kin Ties

In societies in which the survival rate is low, adoption reinforces existing kinship bonds by "filling the gap" within the extended family. (D082)

### Parenthood

Negro parents who have already had a child of their own through means other than the social agency are less likely to complete the adoption process than Negro parents who never had a child before. (This does not hold true for white parents.) (F117)

**Property**
Patterns of adoption are not likely to occur in marginal hunting and gathering societies where there is little property. (M085)

**Race**
Negro parents who apply for adoption are more likely to prefer a child of their own coloring than a child who is much darker or much lighter. (F117)

Negro couples are less likely to adopt a child than white couples, with the exception of the lower classes where the Negro adoption rate exceeds that of whites. (F118)

**Religion (Ancestor Worship)**
Adoption will tend to be stressed in societies which have ancestor worship. (L088)

**Sex-Role Adjustment**
Reduction in the level of anxiety concerning the female role and motherhood is a causal factor in the woman's decision to adopt a child. (B309)

**Stability of Lineage**
When the maintenance of lineal continuity is stressed, the rate of adoption will tend to be higher. (W043)

**Sterility**
Adoption is most likely to occur when the married couple is sterile. (D025)

**Sterility, Adjustment to**
The success of adoption among infertile couples depends mainly on their having adjusted to their infertility. (L153)

## ADOPTION (ACCEPTANCE BY AGENCY)
**X Divorce**
If a person has been previously divorced, it is more likely that an adoption agency will reject his application to adopt a child. (F117)

**Education of Parents**
Couples of lower educational level are more likely than couples of higher educational level to be rejected by adoption agencies. (F117)

## ADOPTION, ADJUSTMENT TO
**X Sibling Structure**
The successful adjustment of the adopted child to a new home is less likely when children of the foster-parents are present, but is more likely if his own siblings or another foster-child is present. (T086)

## ADOPTION, AGE AT     X Adoption, Success of
Parents who adopt a child under two years of age are more likely to succeed in rearing the child than parents who adopt a child two years of age or older. (F117)

**Behavior Problems**
There is a higher frequency of behavior problems, (e.g., stealing, lying, cruelty to animals, and destructiveness of property) among late adoptees than among those placed early. (H242)

**I.Q.**
Children with I.Q.'s of 110 or above are more likely to have been adopted before the age of six months than those with lower I.Q.'s. (H242)

**Race**
Negro couples tend to apply for adoption at a later age than white couples. (F118)

## ADOPTION, ATTITUDES OF PARENTS
**X Adoption**
More parents adopt children because of a general love of children and the factor of infertility than because of other psychological factors (fear of pregnancy, desire for companionship, etc.). (F117)

## ADOPTION (HUSBAND)     X Heirs, Absence of
The adoption of the husband by the wife's family tends to occur when the wife is without male siblings. (H082)

**Rank of Husband**
Men who are adopted into the families of their wives tend to be of lower status. (H082)

## ADOPTION OF OUTSIDERS
**X Authority Structure**
Avuncular authority in matrilineal society is weakened with the institution of adopting slave children. (S069)

## ADOPTION (SEX PREFERENCE)
**X Adoption, Success of**
Parents who adopt boys are more likely to be ready for parenthood and therefore more likely to succeed in rearing the child than are parents who adopt girls. (F117)

**Race**
White couples indicate a high preference for a male child when applying for adoption; Negro couples indicate a high preference for a female child. (F117)

## ADOPTION, SUCCESS OF     X Adoption, Age at
Parents who adopt a child under two years of age are more likely to succeed in rearing the child than parents who adopt a child two years of age or older. (F117)

**X Adoption (Sex Preference)**
Parents who adopt boys are more likely to be ready for parenthood and therefore more likely to succeed in rearing the child than are parents who adopt girls. (F117)

**Sterility**
The success of adoption is higher among infertile couples to the degree they have adjusted to their infertility. (L153)

## ADOPTION (URBAN/RURAL)     X I.Q.
Urban adoptive parents are more insistent that the child to be adopted be of average intelligence or above than are rural adoptive parents. (M192)

## ADULT-CHILD RELATIONS     X Ordinal Position
Early-born children tend to be more adult oriented than later-born children. (R106)

**Sibling Structure (Age Difference)**
Firstborn children with a brother two to four years younger are less friendly, less obedient, and less responsive to adults than those with a brother four to six years younger. (K098)

The greater the age difference between siblings, the more adult-oriented is the firstborn child. (K149)

The less the age difference between siblings the more likely the firstborn child is to be more adult-oriented than his younger sibling. (K149)

### Sibling Structure (Sex)

Firstborn girls tend to be more adult-oriented than boys, regardless of the sex of their younger sibling. (K149)

## ADULT-CHILD RELATIONS (AFFECT)
### X    Institutional Care

If a baby is institutionalized for a long period, he will show, as an aftereffect, a cheerful but shallow attachment to any adult within his orbit. (B270)

## ADULT-CHILD RELATIONS (APPROVAL)
### X    Ordinal Position

Second-born children are more responsive to adult approval than are firstborns, only if there is a two- to four-year difference in age between siblings. (K098)

## ADULT-CHILD RELATIONS (CONTROL)
### X    Identification

A child tends to identify with the person or persons having closest control over his destiny. (M058)

## ADULT-CHILD RELATIONS (FRIENDLINESS)
### X    Sibling Structure

Girls having a sibling two years older or younger were more friendly to adults than were a parallel group of boys. (K098)

### Sibling Structure (Age and Sex)

Among boys with siblings close to them in age, those with an older sister are more friendly to adults than those with an older brother. When the sibling is younger the pattern is reversed. (K098)

### Sibling Structure (Age Difference)

Second-born males are likely to be low in friendliness to adults if they have a sibling who is less than two years older but are likely to be more friendly to adults if the sibling is more than two years older. (K098)

### Sibling Structure (Sex)

Girls with a younger brother are more friendly to adults than girls with a younger sister. (K098)

Girls with a younger brother (up to six years younger) are more friendly to adults and more responsive to adult sympathy and approval than are boys with a younger brother. (K098)

## ADULT-CHILD RELATIONS (INDULGENCE)
### X    Role of Mother

In societies where mothers have few economic responsibilities and are little involved in the ceremonial life of the tribe, there tends to be more indulgence with infants. (W127)

## ADULT-CHILD RELATIONS (INTERACTION)
### X    Child-Rearing Attitudes (Dominance)

Children of parents who reflect large differences in dominance attitudes (measured by the USC Parent Attitude Survey) will avoid adult contacts in free-activity settings to a greater degree than children of parents who reflect small differences in dominance attitudes. (T101)

## ADULT-CHILD RELATIONS (ISOLATION)
### X    Class

The extent to which children are isolated from adults' experience varies with social class (more strongly in upper, much less in lower). (S076)

## ADULT-CHILD ROLE DEFINITION    X    Abortion

The greater the emphasis on the status disparity between adult and child, the more likely is abortion of the firstborn. (D071)

### Parental-Role Adjustment

The greater the emphasis on the status disparity between adult and child, the more difficult will be the adjustment to adult status upon entering the status of parent. (D071)

## ADULT-PEER RELATIONS    X    Ordinal Position

The first child in a family is more commonly adult-oriented, while the second child is more likely to be peer-oriented. (F084)

## ADULT ROLE    X    Class

Among Negroes, lower-class children are more likely than middle-class children to perceive the transition from dependency to an independent attitude toward the world as traumatic.

### Dependency

In Western society reduction of the child's dependence on the nuclear family is necessary for the assumption of adult roles. (G156)

### Personality of Parents (Stability)

Physical and emotional steadiness of the parents is necessary for preparing the child for reciprocal adult relationships. (C093)

## ADULT ROLE BEHAVIOR
### X    Child-Rearing Practices (Control)

The rate of practice of adult roles increases with the degree of control exercised by the parents. (M179)

### Child-Rearing Practices (Strictness)

The stricter the rule enforcing behavior of the parents during early childhood (age 0–6), the greater the likelihood that a child (age 6–12) will sanction an age-mate whom he observes breaking a rule. (M179)

### Parent-Child Relations (Affection)

The response patterns of relationships established in childhood appear to determine the expression of affection in adult life. (B270)

### Parent-Child Relations (Warmth)

The greater the degree of parental warmth, the more likely it is that the rule-enforcing behavior (either restrictive or permissive) of an individual will resemble that of his parents. (M179)

## ADULT STATUS, BARRIERS TO    X    Age-Groups

Age-groups arise when the roles inculcated within the family and kinship situation are incompatible with those of the total social structure and therefore prevent the individual from achieving a mature status. (E086)

### Conflict Between Generations

To the degree that impediments to the attainment of full social status within the family or kin group exist, harmonious interaction between generations is less likely. (E086)

## ADULTERY    X    Acculturation

Under situations of European contact, extramarital relations tend to increase. (B148)

### Adultery, Attitude Toward

When sanctions against adultery are severe, the incidence of adultery will tend to be low. (F065)

Adultery is most apt to be widely prevalent where there are no severe restrictions against extramarital relations. (H074)

## Age
Of single persons, the older and more experienced they are, the higher they think the incidence of adultery is. (C124)

## Age at Marriage
The rate of adultery will increase as the age of men at marriage rises. (H110)

The younger the age at marriage, the higher the incidence of extramarital relations among women. (T054)

## Age of Husband
In Western countries, extramarital sexual intercourse increases in frequency with increasing age among upper-class husbands, while decreasing in frequency with age among lower-class husbands. (G156)

## Authority Structure of Family
The weakening of parental authority is directly correlated with an increase in extramarital relations. (G058)

## Divorce
Divorce will be a consequence of adultery only when the wife has frequently had extramarital relations. (H074)

## Divorce, Attitude Toward
With an increase in extramarital relations, the attitude toward divorce becomes more tolerant. (T054)

## Economic Pattern (Mercantile)
Marital relations among traveling merchants are loose; the men are thought to have wives along their routes and the women are thought to be unfaithful. (T072)

## Economic Pattern (Migrant Labor)
The introduction of patterns of migratory labor results in an increase in extramarital relations among women. (S121)

The adoption of patterns of migratory labor will tend to result in an increase in extramarital relations. (S134)

## Economic Role of Women
There will be an increase in the incidence of extramarital relations with the decreasing economic importance of the woman's role. (B166)

## Exogamy
Where there are exogamic restrictions against marriage, restrictions against extramarital intercourse tend to be established also. (L056)

## Frigidity
There is a correlation between frigidity in women and adulterous and promiscuous behavior of their husbands.

## Geographic Mobility
The rate of extramarital relations tends to increase with an increase in geographical mobility. (G093)

## Marital Adjustment
Marital conflict is likely to characterize most relationships when extramarital relations are prevalent. (H074)

There is a direct relation between fidelity and marital adjustment. (K161)

There is no difference between those who are highly satisfied with their marriage and those who are not, regarding whether or not they have been involved in extramarital sexual and/or emotional relationships. (N062)

## Marital Status
Belief in the prevalence of adultery is greater among single persons than among married persons. (C132)

## Marital Status (Male)
Seduction of wives of polygynists is frequent where there is a scarcity of unmarried girls in relation to the number of bachelors. (W128)

## Personality of Parents (Aggression)
Among parents of children who are severely abused (beaten, tortured, etc.), it is the aggressive parent who is most likely to be also sexually promiscuous and unfaithful to his or her spouse. (Y043)

## Personality Problems
Infidelity and promiscuity tend to be an "acting-out" of neurotic conflict.

## Polygyny
Extramarital intercourse is more frequent in polygynous households. (D055)

## Polygyny, Number of Wives
Under polygyny, wives are more likely to commit adultery if they are in a household with many wives. (C057)

## Preferential Marriage (Exchange)
Extramarital relations are likely to occur when the marriage has been contracted as the second phase of an exchange of women. (T064)

## Preferential Marriage, Restrictiveness of
When the preferential marriage pattern is highly restricted, the incidence of extramarital relationships will tend to be high. (K062)

## Premarital Sex Relations
Extramarital relations are more likely to occur if sexual relations are practiced before marriage. (B191)

## Premarital Sex Relations, Attitude Toward
Adultery is less frequent where premarital sexual relations are freely accepted. (H074)

## Privacy
Extramarital relations are less likely to occur if the social situation does not permit privacy. (M085)

## Sex Ratio
The scarcity of women in towns militates against the fidelity of a town wife. (M170)

## Sex Taboo
Among monogamous unions, the observance of periods of restrictions against sexual relations will tend to result in males having extramarital relations. (V021)

## Sex Taboo (Postpartum)
In monogamous marriages the custom of abstention from sexual intercourse during pregnancy and before weaning tends to result in greater promiscuity. (L113)

## Sex Taboo (Pregnancy)
Restrictions against intercourse during pregnancy is likely to lead to extramarital relations when the union is monogamous. (A034)

## Sexual Adjustment
Married women who are least satisfied sexually by their husbands are most likely to desire extramarital sexual relations. (C132)

### Superego Formation

Low strength of conscience (as measured by the Psychopathic Deviate Scale of the Minnesota Multiphasic Personality Inventory) is positively associated with extramarital sexual involvements. (N062)

There are no significant differences between persons having high strength of conscience and those having low conscience strength (measured by the Psychopathic Deviate scale of the Minnesota Multiphasic Personality Inventory) with regard to either emotional (nonsexual) or fantasy extramarital involvements. (N062)

### Urban/Rural

Belief in the prevalence of adultery is greater among those living in urban areas than in rural areas (France). (C124)

The rate of extramarital relations tends to be higher in urban rather than in rural areas. (E026)

### Urbanization

Urban conditions tend to increase the incidence of extramarital relations. (G058)

### Wife Inheritance

The possibility of seduction is increased by the custom by which a son may inherit his father's wives. (E102)

### ADULTERY, ATTITUDE TOWARD     X   Adultery

When sanctions against adultery are severe, the incidence of adultery will tend to be low. (F065)

Adultery is most apt to be widely prevalent where there are no severe restrictions against extramarital relations. (H074)

### Adultery, Type of

Marital infidelity is less likely to be disapproved when it is termed a temporary expedient when spouses are separated; more disapproved when the adultery is a love relationship; and most disapproved when this love relationship is with another married person. (C124)

### Adultery, Value of

The value placed upon extramarital relations tends to be directly correlated with the severity of the sanctions against relations outside marriage. (F092)

### Age Difference

Extramarital relations are more likely to be tolerated if the husband is considerably older than the wife. (S153)

### Authority Structure of Family

Tolerance toward extramarital relations will increase with a weakening of the family authority structure. (S158)

### Class

Restrictions against extramarital relations tend to be more severe among members of the upper class. (M063)

Members of the upper class will tend to have stronger expectations of marital fidelity. (R062)

### Class of Wife

Extramarital relations of a wife, if the husband is sterile, is less likely to be censured if the woman is of the upper class. (F045)

### Courtship Status

Persons engaged or going steady are more likely to disapprove of adultery than are other single persons. (C124)

### Descent (Patrilineal)

In societies with a strong emphasis on patrilineal descent, there is a greater emphasis upon the chastity and fidelity of women. (B086)

### Divorce, Attitude Toward

The greater the spouse's fear of the consequences of divorce, the greater the willingness to tolerate the adulterous behavior of one's partner. (B033)

### Exogamy

Under exogamy, and in villages with high solidarity, intravillage adultery is defined as incest, but is admired by the native members of the village, since adultery is against the in-marrying spouse. (F076)

### Fertility

Extramarital relations are less likely to be censured if the wife is barren. (B191)

### Impotence

If the husband is impotent, he is more likely to condone the extramarital relations of his wife. (W082)

### Kin/Nonkin

Censure of adultery will tend to be stronger when it involves members of the same clan. The contrary is also asserted. (H074)

When a husband and an adulterer are members of the same clan, the husband is less likely to be permitted to take action against the offender. (H074)

When the husband and adulterer are of the same clan, the act is not likely to be punished. (H138)

### Marital Adjustment of Husband

Happy husbands, more often than the unhappy, believe that it is essential for an ideal marriage that both husband and wife be absolutely faithful to each other in sex matters. (T074)

### Marital Adjustment of Parents

The more happily married a person's parents were, the more highly he disapproves of extramarital relations. (C124)

### Personality (Permissiveness)

The less permissive an individual is, the less likely he is to approve of adultery. (C124)

### Premarital Sex Relations, Attitude Toward

There is no correlation between cultural permissiveness toward premarital sexual intercourse and permissiveness toward adulterous relations after marriage. (E092)

### Rank

Extramarital relations are more likely to be tolerated if the status of the man is high. (W104)

### Rank of Husband

Reprisals against adultery are more severe if the husband's social rank is high. (B201)

### Rank of Husband/Adulterer

The action taken by a husband against the adulterer will vary with the relative rank of the individuals concerned. (T069)

### Residence

Adultery is viewed as a more serious offense when the offender lives close by. (W128)

### Sex Education
Persons indicating "friends" as their source of sex education are more likely to approve of adultery than those obtaining their sex education from other sources. (C124)

### Sterility
When a man is impotent or sterile, he is more likely to condone or even encourage the extramarital relations of his wife. (H066)

## ADULTERY, DIFFICULTY OF
### X   Adultery, Value of
Extramarital relations will tend to be more highly valued if the couple experiences difficulty or danger in establishing a relationship of this character. (G050)

## ADULTERY (FANTASY)     X   Marital Adjustment
The lower a person's marital satisfaction (as measured by Anselm Strauss's marital satisfaction scale), the more likely is he to have fantasy involvements in extramarital relationships. (N062)

## ADULTERY OF FATHER     X   Sexual Deviance
Fathers of sexually deviant (perverted) boys are more likely to have sexual relations outside their marriage than are fathers of "normal" boys. (M209)

## ADULTERY/PREMARITAL SEX RELATIONS
### X   Social Control
Adultery is punished more by primitive societies than is intercourse with one's own betrothed. (B006)

## ADULTERY, TYPE OF
### X   Adultery, Attitude Toward
Marital infidelity is less likely to be disapproved when it is termed a temporary expedient when spouses are separated; more disapproved when the adultery is a love relationship; and most disapproved when this love relationship is with another married person. (C124)

## ADULTERY, VALUE OF
### X   Adultery, Attitude Toward
The value placed upon extramarital relations tends to be directly correlated with the severity of the sanctions against relations outside marriage. (F092)

### Adultery, Difficulty of
Extramarital relations will tend to be more highly valued if the couple experiences difficulty or danger in establishing a relationship of this character. (G050)

## AFFINAL/CONSANGUINEAL TIES
### X   Descent (Unilineal)
Matrilineal societies are more likely to fuse the obligational ties inherent in consanguineal and affinal forms of relationship than are patrilineal societies. (G147)

### Exogamy (Village)
Patterns of village exogamy are directly correlated with the tendency to regard affinal and consanguineal kin ties as mutually exclusive. (B302)

## AFFINAL RELATIONS
### X   Affinal Role Obligations
A husband is more likely to be exempt from some of the formal obligations to his affines if his relationship with these relatives is good. (C060)

### Age at Marriage
The younger their age at marriage, the more likely are the couples to have in-law problems (interference or rejection). (I005)

When marriage is patrilinear and patrilocal, the younger the woman is when she is married, the more complete her integration with the husband's family is likely to be. (P083)

### Cohesion of Lineage
Where the solidarity of the lineages of the husband and wife is so strong as to minimize the demands one can make on the other, one marriage partner will be unable to become a full participant in the descent group of his or her spouse. (Z003)

### Dependency of Wife
The more emotionally dependent a wife is upon her mother, the more likely it is that her husband will have strained relations with his in-laws. (K089)

The husband's adjustment to his mother-in-law is inversely related to his wife's dependence on her mother. (S011)

The husband's adjustment to his father-in-law is directly related to his wife's dependence on her father. (S011)

The impact of the wife's dependency on her husband's adjustment to his in-laws is specific to the parent on whom the wife is dependent. (S011)

### Divorce, Ease of
When divorce is easy and frequent, affection "is usually weak or even completely absent" between affinal kinsmen. (P087)

### Economic Cooperation
When a series of reciprocal economic obligations characterizes the relationship between affines, a greater attempt will be made to maintain a peaceful relationship. (W062)

### Economic Rank
As the economic standing of their in-laws increases, so does the cordiality of the relations of interracial couples with their in-laws. (K019)

### Education of Husband
The higher the education of the husband, the better are his relations with his in-laws. (K089)

### Education of Wife
Men married to better-educated wives are more likely to have poor relations with their in-laws than are men married to similarly or poorly educated wives. (K089)

### Intermarriage (Racial)
Of those wives in interracial marriages who have strained relations with their in-laws, it is more likely that the strained relations will be with the mother-in-law than with any other in-law. (K019)

### Marital Adjustment
Marital adjustment is more likely when the engaged couple likes their future fathers-in-law and mothers-in-law very much. (B033)

There is a direct relation between favorable relation with in-laws and marital adjustment. (K161)

Couples who are approved by the respective in-laws before marriage are more likely to be adjusted in marriage than couples who are not approved. (L004)

### Marital Stability

Marital stability in patrilineal societies is directly correlated with the degree of identification of the wife to her husband's lineage. (F073)

### Mother-Daughter Relations

The greater the emphasis on the tie between the mother and daughter, the more likely there is to be tension between the husband and his mother-in-law. (P062)

### Mother-Son Relations

The more a mother-in-law is like a man's loved mother or unlike a disliked mother, the closer are relations between husband and mother-in-law likely to be. (K161)

### Parent-Child Relations (Attachment)

Strong attachment between an adult son and his mother is rarer than attachment between an adult daughter and her mother: hence, structural protection against mother-in-law trouble from the groom's side is not as strong as it is in dealing with the wife's mother. (P083)

### Parent-Child Relations (Evaluation)

In disturbed families, where the spouse is critical of his own parents, his marital partner tends to be friendly toward them. (B204)

### Parent-Daughter Relations

The husband's adjustment to in-laws is independent of the wife's adjustment to her parents. (S011)

### Residence

Parents-in-law and children-in-law are emotionally closer if the children-in-law's own parents have died or if they live at some distance away. (T087)

### Sex Status

People have a closer relationship with their children-in-law if they have no child of the same sex. (T087)

### Witchcraft

Suspicion of the use of witchcraft by wives is directly correlated with a negative attitude toward affinal relations. (L109)

## AFFINAL RELATIONS (COHESION)
### X   Affinal Ties

The degree of solidarity achieved by the union of families by marriage is directly correlated with the closeness of the social relationship before marriage. (W131)

## AFFINAL RELATIONS (CONFLICT)
### X   Dependency

In-law problems in marriage will more frequently involve the wife's parents than the husband's parents since females are more likely to be attached to and dependent on families of orientation than are males. A corollary of this is that the likelihood of a husband having in-law difficulties increases with the degree of the wife's attachment to and dependency on her parents. (S011)

### Descent/Residence

Affinal conflict will tend to be more severe under conditions of patrilocal residence if the descent pattern is matrilineal. (M050)

### Education

When there is a marked degree of difference in the education of the mother-in-law and daughter-in-law, serious conflicts are likely to occur. (H032)

### Husband/Wife

In-law problems in marriage more frequently involve the wife's parents than the husband's parents. The contrary of this proposition is also asserted (U.S.). (K014)

### Marriage Payment

Affinal conflict will be particularly intense if the husband has failed to pay the bride price. (S090)

### Maternal-Role Definition

Conflicts between mother-in-law and daughter-in-law are more frequent than between mother-in-law and son-in-law. (B033)

### Preferential Marriage (Cross-Cousin)

In patrilineal system, when the cross-cousin marriage is between father's sister's son and mother's brother's daughter (v. father's sister's daughter), there is less friction between mother-in-law and daughter-in-law. (H043)

The institution of cross-cousin marriage as a preferential pattern will tend to reduce affinal conflicts. (G056)

### Residence (Patrilocal)

Under uxorilocal residence, the friction and conflict inherent in affinal relationships will, if the society is patrilineal, tend to result in virilocal residence. (D008)

### Sex Status

Females are more likely to complain about their in-laws than are males. (C023)

### Sibling Status

Conflicts between parents-in-law and children-in-law are more likely when the husband or wife is an only child. (B033)

## AFFINAL RELATIONS (INTERACTION)
### X   Kin Terminology

Failure to differentiate terminologically between the husband and wife may reflect an ambilateral pattern of residence and the high frequency of interaction with both groups of affinals. (F046)

## AFFINAL RELATIONS (RESPECT)
### X   Genealogical Proximity

Affinal affection and respect increase inversely with the strength of social ties based on blood relationship. (Q001)

### Preferential Marriage (Cross-Cousin)

Under a patrilineal system, respect is paid to affines who have married a female relative, so that matrilateral rather than patrilateral cross-cousin marriage is preferred (Brahman). (G028)

## AFFINAL ROLE DEFINITION
### X   Kin Terminology

The formal character of the relationship between affinals is reflected in the selection of kin terms of address. (B083)

The terminological equation of affinals with consanguineals may be directly correlated with their acceptance of consanguineal roles upon marriage. (F046)

## AFFINAL ROLE OBLIGATIONS
### X   Affinal Relations

A husband is more likely to be exempt from some of the formal obligations to his affines if his relationship with these relatives is good. (C060)

### Class
Affinal obligations are more elaborate among the upper social strata. (K045)

### Polygyny (Sororal)
The institutionalization of sororal polygyny may be manipulated by parents to induce their son-in-law to observe his affinal obligations, (i.e., rewarding him for good behavior by letting him marry the second sister). (H049)

### AFFINAL TIES     X   Affinal Relations (Cohesion)
The degree of solidarity achieved by the union of families by marriage is directly correlated with the closeness of the social relationship before marriage. (W131)

### Avoidance Relationship
The relationship between affinals of adjacent generations tends to be characterized by avoidance or respect. (E064)

### Children
The birth of children will tend to strengthen the relationship between affinal kinsmen. (M128)

### Community Solidarity
In the absence of political machinery, community solidarity is maintained by affirming ties of marriage and uterine kinship (The Iatmul). (B303)

### Descent
Bilateral societies are more likely than lineal societies to de-emphasize affinal ties. (D084)

While lineal societies are able to de-emphasize affinal relationships, a bilateral society cannot do this for the affines become cognates to ego's offspring. (D084)

### Endogamy (Community)
When patterns of community endogamy are violated, marriages will tend to be into kinship units with preexisting affinal ties. (B111)

Affinal ties are less likely to link members of various communities together in extensive interaction or to complement agnation in societies where the primary emphasis is upon local endogamy. (H222)

### Incest Taboo
The extension of incest taboos tends to be inhibited to the extent that any given person is linked with the same consanguineal kin-group as ego's spouse; and is extended to the extent that the person is linked by blood with ego. (M019)

### Inheritance
Affinal relations are more likely to be kept distinct from cognatic relations when the wife is not entitled to inherit land. (F122)

### Joking Relationship
Joking relationships between affinals tend to be between those who are members of the same generation. (R021)

### Marital Stability
Marital stability is directly correlated with the strength of the bonds between affinal kinsmen. (K065)

### Marriage Payment
The institution of bride-wealth at marriage strengthens the affinal relationship. (S081)

### Mate Selection
When affinal bonds are important, marriages subsequent to the initial marriage will tend to be contracted with the same family. (S068)

When marriages are contracted between people who live in different villages, they will tend to occur between communities which are already related by existing marriage alliances. (T039)

### Preferential Marriage
When one or more marriage alliances have been established with a certain clan, there is a preference for further marriages with the same clan. (C039)

### Preferential Marriage (Levirate/Sororate)
The levirate and sororate will tend to occur in a society which stresses the importance of retaining affinal bonds. (L039)

### Premarital Sex Relations, Attitude Toward
Where affinal ties confer important rights to land and other resources, premarital sexual freedom is more likely to be restricted. (V036)

### Residence
Affinal obligations are more likely to be maintained if the affines live nearby. (M129)

### AGE     X   Adultery
Of single persons, the older and more experienced they are, the higher they think the incidence of adultery is. (C124)

### Authority Structure of Family
The older the woman, the more likely she is to be head of the household. (S211)

### Avoidance Relationship
Both the very young and the aged are more likely to be excepted from much of the typical avoidance behavior. (S153)

An avoidance relationship between siblings is more likely to be enforced after puberty. (V020)

### Dating Frequency
The younger the divorcée, the more likely is she to date frequently. (G157)

### Disorganization of Family
Among preadolescents, there is a stronger relationship between family disorganization and delinquency than among adolescents. (T002)

### Divorce
The difference in rates of divorce between homogamous Catholic and Protestant marriages (lower rate of divorce) and interreligious marriages between Catholics and Protestants (higher rate of divorce) is less among older couples than it is among younger couples. (B314)

### Divorce, Adjustment
Adjustment to divorce is easier for the young than for the old. (B033)

### Employment of Mother
The older the child, the more likely it is that he will adjust satisfactorily to the mother's employment outside the home. (R108)

### Employment of Women, Attitude Toward
The older the child (range: 5–11 years) the more likely he is to attribute discomfort to the mother at leaving her children to go to work. (S265)

### Fertility Values
The older the wife is (and therefore less able to bear children), the higher she values fertility.

### Genealogical Ties, Knowledge of
Older persons tend to have a better knowledge of the genealogy of their family than younger members of the family. (B065)

### Homosexuality
Homosexuality is most likely to occur in early adolescence when fear of sexuality is greatest. (H219)

### Husband-Wife Relations (Companionship)
Older wives (past the age of 50) value the companionship with their husbands more highly than do young wives.

### Husband-Wife Relations (Evaluation)
Older husbands tend to have a more positive evaluation of their wives than do younger husbands. (B232)

### Husband-Wife Relations (Intimacy)
The intimacy of the relationship between husband and wife is directly correlated with their age. The contrary is also asserted. (W082)

### Kin Relations (Interaction)
Among older persons (50 years and up), there is no relationship between age and amount of contact with intimate kin. (C116)

### Kin Relations (Sibling/Children)
Persons between the ages of 50 and 70 are more likely to identify siblings and other collateral kin as intimates, those over 70 are more likely to choose their children as intimates. (C116)

### Kin Terminology
Informal variants of kinship terms tend to be used more by children than by adults. (B083)

Where relative age is of significance in structuring social relations, this distinction will be found in the kinship terminology. (B111)

Formal variants of the kinship term tend to be used more as the individual becomes older. (S050)

### Kin Ties (Fictive)
The establishment of fictive kin bonds of brotherhood tends to be between men of the same age level. (O018)

### Marital Adjustment
Marital problems as well as feelings of inadequacy progressively decrease with age. (G126)

There is no relationship between age and the reported level of marital happiness. (G126)

There is no relationship between age and the types of problems reported in the marital relationship. (G126)

### Marriage, Attitude Toward
Pressures toward marriage increase with a person's increasing age. This relationship is also asserted to be curvilinear. (G015)

### Mate Selection
Mate selection tends to occur between individuals of the same generation and of similar age. (E055)

### Mate Selection (Free Choice)
Marriages are more likely to be arranged by the parents when the couple is young. (M085)

### Mate Selection (Residence)
Residential propinquity as a factor in mate selection is greater among the very young and the very old than among the middle age groups. (C023)

### Neurosis
Older unmarried mothers are generally more neurotic than young unmarried mothers. (Y048)

### Parent-Child Relations
There is no relationship between age of married offspring and their adjustment to their parents. (S011)

### Parent-Child Relations (Affection)
The younger problem son is likely to perceive both parents to be more loving and controlling than the older problem son perceives them to be. (V038)

### Parental-Role Adjustment
The older the person, the less likely is he to report feelings of inadequacy in the parental role. (G126)

### Polygyny
In polygynous societies there is a positive correlation between increasing age and a higher percentage of men in polygynous marriages. (B012)

### Pregnancy, Attitude Toward
Age of mother and her attitude toward pregnancy are not associated (U.S.). (S191)

### Sex Relations
Sexual intercourse in marriage decreases in frequency with age. (C023)

### Sex-Role Adjustment
The older the person is, the less likely is he or she to feel inadequate as provider or housekeeper. (G126)

### Stepparent-Child Relations
The younger the children and parents, the more readily they will adjust to step-relationships. (B286)

### Surrogate Parent, Adjustment to
The younger the child, the more likely it is that he will make a satisfactory adjustment to living with stepparents and guardians. (R108)

The younger the child, the more likely is discontinuity of parent surrogates to result in feelings of insecurity on the part of the child. (S214)

### Values (Authority)
During adolescence, increasing age correlates with increasingly similar attitudes toward authority in the home and authority outside it (school and peer situations). (T100)

### Witchcraft
Accusations of witchcraft are more likely to be directed against persons likely to feel the resentment and anxieties of mature ages and the frustrations springing from envy of youth. (N015)

## AGE AND EDUCATION OF MOTHER

### X   Child-Rearing Practices (Authoritarianism)
The older and less educated the mother, the more authoritarian she will be in child rearing. (S229)

## AGE AT BETROTHAL                              X   Polygyny
Where polygyny is widely practiced, women will tend to be betrothed at an earlier age. (T058)

## AGE AT MARRIAGE                              X   Adultery
The rate of adultery will increase as the age of men at marriage rises. (H110)

The younger the age at marriage, the higher is the incidence of extramarital relations among women. (T054)

### Affinal Relations
The younger their age at marriage, the more likely are the couples to have in-law problems (interference or rejection). (I005)

When marriage is patrilinear and patrilocal, the younger the woman is when she is married, the more complete her integration with the husband's family is likely to be. (P083)

### Aspiration Level
Girls who marry in their teens are less likely to have a high aspiration level (further education or training) than those who do not. (M231)

### Birth Control
Early female marriage and premarital conception are associated with ignorance of birth control. (P083)

### Birth Spacing
The average time interval between marriage of a couple and the birth of their first child increases with the average age at marriage of the couple. (C019)

### Broken Home
Persons who come from homes broken by death, desertion, or divorce tend to marry at an earlier age than those from intact homes. (H189)

### Class
Higher-class men tend to marry later than do lower-class men.

There is a correlation between expected deferment of marriage after high-school graduation and social status level. (B248)

Marriage is likely to come earlier for the unskilled laboring groups and higher for the more skilled, professional and upper-income groups. (C023)

The nobility of Western countries tend to marry at younger ages than persons in other classes. (G156)

### Cohesion of Family
The more distant the female college student's ties to her parents, the later the age at which she plans to marry; the relationship is curvilinear for men. (R116)

### Dating
There is no relationship between age of initial or steady dating and age at marriage. (B248)

Girls who marry in their teens are more likely to start dating at an earlier age than those who do not. (M231)

The final institutionalization of steady dating is likely to increase the average age at marriage and decrease the range of marriage age, especially regarding teen-age marriages. (P083)

### Death of Parent
Children are more likely not to marry, or marry late, if one parent (especially the father) dies when the child is between ten and twenty years of age. (T087)

### Divorce
The divorce rate will be lower when marriage is early. (B191)

Among marriages where premarital illegitimacy has occurred, divorce is more likely to occur among very early and very late marriages than among the middle age groups (Denmark). (C124)

Among both fertile and childless marriages, the divorce rate varies inversely with the wife's age at marriage (Denmark). (C129)

The later a woman marries (and hence the less chance she feels she has of remarriage), the less likely divorce is. (D083)

Women who marry at an extremely young age are more likely than those who marry at a more mature age to have their marriages dissolved by divorce. (G012)

The earlier is the age of marriage in a system of free mate choice, the more likely is the failure of conjugal integration at first marriage. (P083)

An increase in the average age at marriage, and especially a reduction in the incidence of teen-age marriages, is likely to result in a decline in the type of divorce which results from premature commitment. (P083)

### Economic Dependence
The age at marriage tends to increase with the introduction of an economy which permits economic independence. (W082)

### Education
Among American men and women the median age at first marriage is higher for both the well-educated and those with little education than it is for those with average amounts of education. (H203)

There is a correlation between interrupted schooling and early female marriage. (P083)

### Employment of Mother
Earlier marriages increase the tendency for mothers to seek employment outside the home. (Y047)

### Fertility
Fertility decreases as the age of the woman at marriage increases. (B012)

### Fertility Values
When fertility is emphasized the age of marriage for women will tend to be lower. (H164)

### Husband-Wife Relations (Economic)
There is no correlation between the age at marriage and reports of financial difficulties. (I005)

### Husband-Wife Relations (Jealousy)
The younger the age at marriage, the more likely are wives to complain of jealousy and outside activities of the husband (his not settling down and running around too much). (I005)

### Illegitimacy
A high rate of illegitimacy tends to be correlated with a delay in the age at marriage. (F060)

The rate of illegitimacy tends to be directly correlated with the age at marriage. (H164)

The illegitimacy rate tends to be inversely correlated with age at marriage. (T035)

### Income
The younger the age at marriage, the less likely are couples to have adequate finances to conduct their marital life. (I005)

### Industrialization
Women in industrial societies have a higher average age at marriage and have a greater probability of never being married than women in nonindustrial societies. (N054)

### Intermarriage (Racial and Ethnic)
Children of intermarriages (racial and ethnic) marry earlier than children of homogamous marriages. (B311)

Children of intermarriages who also intermarry themselves are apt to be younger than those who marry members of their own ethnic or racial group. (B311)

In ethnic or racial intermarriage the partners are more likely to be older than in the case of marriages within the racial or ethnic group. (B311)

### Intermarriage (Religious)
Religious endogamy is inversely related to the couple's ages at marriage. (C128)

### Juvenile Delinquency
There is no relationship between age at marriage of parents and the development of delinquency. (G123)

### Land
When there is frontier land available, farmers tend to marry earlier. (G156)

### Love
The younger the individual when marriage is arranged, the lower the likelihood of a love relationship developing outside of the marriage bond. (G156)

### Martial Adjustment
An early age at marriage is predictive of marital unhappiness. (B033)

Marital happiness is directly related to early age at marriage. (B033)

### Marriage Ceremony, Expense of
A higher age at marriage is observed in societies in which the expense of the marriage ceremony is high. (F121)

### Marriage Chances
The younger the average age at marriage, the higher the proportion of the population who will eventually marry. (K161)

### Marriage Payment
The age at marriage varies in direct relationship to the price of bride wealth. (B035)

The age of males at marriage tends to rise with the inflation of bride-wealth rates. (L026)

Men will tend to marry later in societies in which marriage payment is institutionalized. (O030)

With an increase in the amount of the marriage payment, there will be a corresponding decrease in the age of women at marriage. (T054)

### Mate Selection (Complementarity/Homogamy)
The younger the person, the less likely is mate selection to be based mainly on complementary needs, but rather on similar sociopsychological background factors, resulting from his more limited associations. (B293)

### Mate Selection (Free Choice)
Men are more likely to marry late in order to maximize their position in the marriage market when families rather than peer groups control unmarried girls (thus assuring the man in his late twenties or early thirties access to desirable girls). (P083)

### Maternal Role, Attitude Toward
Mothers who enjoy looking after their babies tend to have married younger than mothers who do not enjoy caring for their babies. (N051)

### Mental Illness
Mental illness is more likely to occur among those who have had an early marriage. (L122)

### Occupation
In general, the men in occupations requiring the acquisition of more financial resources or the pursuit of more specialized training tend to delay their first marriage more than men in most other occupations. (G012)

### Ordinal Position
There is no relation between a man's age at marriage and his sibling position. (T092)

### Parent-Child Relations (Financial Help)
The younger the age at marital contraction, the more likely are couples to seek financial assistance from their parents. (I005)

### Parent-Child Relations (Rejection)
Girls who marry in their teens are more likely to have had unsatisfactory family relations (i.e., see their parents as nonloving, nonaccepting, find little satisfaction in their roles at home, rebel against their parents, etc.) than those who do not marry in their teens. (M231)

### Personality (Ego Strength)
People with feelings of ego deficiency marry earlier than those who feel more adequate. (B293)

### Personality (Emotional Stability)
Girls who marry in their teens are more emotionally unstable than those who do not. (M231)

### Polygyny
Early marriages for females and late marriages for males are associated with societies where polygyny is the ideal. (G156)

### Premarital Pregnancy
Premarital illegitimacy and conception are more apt to occur among very early and very late marriages. (C129)

### Premarital Sex Relations
When marriage regulations force most men to remain bachelors until well into their thirties, the rate of seduction will be high. (H034)

The later the age of marriage, the higher the incidence of premarital sexual relations. (P052)

A decline in the incidence and risks of sex relations is likely to increase the average age at marriage and decrease the range of marriage age, especially reducing teen-age marriages. (P083)

### Prostitution
Postponement of men's marriage is more likely to occur where some form of prostitution or common-law arrangement with lower-class girls is possible. (P083)

### Race
A larger percentage of Negro brides than white brides are below 19 years of age. (C010)

There is no significant difference between white and Negro grooms and the proportion marrying under 20 years of age. (C010)

Between the ages of 20 and 30 there is a smaller proportion of Negro grooms than of white grooms (U.S.). (C010)

### Religiosity
Persons who marry at an early age (under 18 years) are less likely to be active in religious activities than are those who marry later.

### Remarriage
Because norms regarding the age range of a potential spouse grant men more liberty in marrying someone younger, widowers are more likely to remarry than are widows. (G156)

The percentage of marriages that are remarriages varies directly with age. (H013)

### Residence (Segregation of Sexes)
In societies with separate residences for girls, the age of marriage will be later. (W128)

### Sex Norms
A decline in the double standard is likely to increase the average age at marriage and decrease the range of marriage age, especially reducing teen-age marriages. (P083)

### Sex Norms (Premarital Chastity)
The earlier the age at marriage in a society, the greater is the value placed on premarital chastity. (O031)

### Sex Ratio
When the ratio of men to women is proportionately high, the age at marriage of men will increase while that of women will decrease. (H116)

### Sexual Adjustment
There is no correlation between age at marriage and sexual adjustment. (I005)

### Sexual Aggression
A high frequency of rape will tend to occur in societies where there is a strong economic or other barrier to marriage which prolongs the bachelorhood of some males into their late twenties. (L026)

### Sibling Relations (Conflict)
Girls who marry in their teens are more likely to report extensive quarreling with their siblings than are those who do not. (M231)

### Sibling Status
Only sons tend to marry early. (H165)

### Slavery (Pawnship)
The institution of pawnship is likely to be associated with a later age of marriage for men and an earlier age of marriage for women. (D081)

### Social Adjustment
There is a correlation between social maladjustment and early marriage (under 18 years of age). (H189)

### Social Mobility
The upwardly mobile tend to defer marriage (in Sweden until about age 30); those who marry before 25 have a lower chance of an ascending career.

Those who marry into a higher social class are likely to marry late, while early marriage is associated with marrying into a lower status group (England).

### Stability of Kinship Structure
Changes in the kinship structure tend to be retarded if there is a long span between generations (i.e., men marry late). (T058)

### Urban/Rural
Rural men and women marry at an earlier age than do city young people. The contrary is also asserted. (B033)

### Urbanization
The more urbanized the society, the later the average age at marriage. (S219)

### Warfare
Men will tend to marry later in societies where warfare is an institutionalized pattern. (O030)

### Work Adjustment
Those who marry at an early age (under 18 years) are less likely to make a successful adjustment to their work than are those who marry later.

## AGE AT MARRIAGE /PREMARITAL SEX RELATIONS    X    Sexual Interest
Institutionalized preoccupation with sex is more likely to occur in societies in which the age at marriage is late and premarital sexual relations are discouraged. (S262)

## AGE AT PREGNANCY    X    Maternal Overprotectiveness
Maternal overprotectiveness tends to be directly correlated with the age of the mother at the birth of the first child. (L162)

## AGE AT REMARRIAGE    X    Marital Status
Age at remarriage is associated with previous marital status: the divorced marry earlier, the widowed later. (C010)

## AGE AT WEANING    X    Class
Lower-class children have a significantly higher median age at completion of weaning than do middle-class children. This hypothesis is also denied. (H011)

## AGE DIFFERENCE    X    Adultery, Attitude Toward
Extramarital relations are more likely to be tolerated if the husband is considerably older than the wife. (S153)

### Age of Husband/Wife
Age differences between spouses tend to be smaller when the husband is older than the wife than they do when the wife is older than the husband. The contrary is also asserted. (D083)

### Avoidance Relationship
Avoidance relationships are more likely to exist between individuals of different ages than between people of similar ages. (B085)

### Cohesion of Family
Family solidarity will be increased if the age differential between parent and child is reduced. (I007)

### Conflict Between Wives
There is less likely to be friction between co-wives if there is a disparity in age. (O031)

### Descent (Matrilineal)
As matrilineal groups become weaker, there tends to be less disapproval of marriages between generations. (C090)

### Divorce
The greater the age differential between mates, the greater is the likelihood of divorce. (C005)

Divorce is more frequent among couples where the wife is much older than the husband than where she is slightly older or younger. (D083)

### Generation
When there is a generational discrepancy between the husband and wife there will generally be found to be no significant discrepancy between their ages. (F037)

### Husband-Wife Relations (Intimacy)
"Paternalization" of the husband-wife relationship through a high age differential at marriage is likely to make intimacy between spouses more difficult. (P083)

The relationship between a husband and a wife will be more intimate if they are of the same age. (T058)

### Intermarriage (Racial and Ethnic)
There is less likely to be an age difference between husband and wife (with the husband older) in homogamous marriages than in intermarriages (racial and ethnic). (B311)

### Marital Adjustment
The greater the age differences between spouses, the more likely it is that serious conflict will develop within the marriage. (T109)

### Marital Stability
Marital stability tends to be greater when husband and wife are of approximately the same age. (T058)

### Marital Status
A greater age difference is found between individuals who marry individuals of a different marital status than themselves and individuals who marry people of their own marital status (except when both have married before). (H013)

Husbands are older than wives (by more years) when one or both have been married before than when neither has been married before. (H013)

### Marriage Order
In polygyny the difference in age between a man and each successive wife increases. (S174)

### Mate Selection (Economic Motives)
When there is a significant disparity between the ages of the husband and wife, economic factors tend to be dominant in the selection of a mate. (T069)

### Mental Illness (Schizophrenia)
Mothers of schizophrenics are more likely than mothers of neurotics or normals to have married men considerably older than themselves. (M218)

### Mental Retardation
Among disturbed children, the older their parents are, the greater the mental deficiency, especially for mothers 30 years of age or older at the time of conception. (H198)

### Neurosis (Gastric)
Gastric neurosis in married men is directly correlated with a higher-than-average proportion of marriages to older women. (F113)

### Occupational Rank
Age differences between husbands and wives show no definite pattern in relation to level of occupation. (G012)

### Role Definition in Family
Cognitive discrepancy in role behavior between family members is a function of age discrepancy. (S075)

### Sibling Relations
A large age disparity between marriage partners may offset their lack of experience in complementary sibling statuses when they were young, thereby allowing a successful marriage relationship. (T089)

### Sibling Rivalry
The greater the age difference, the less the rivalry between siblings. (C090)

## AGE-GROUP IDENTIFICATION
### X   Marital Status
Identification as being old is greater among widowed people than among married people. This hypothesis is also denied. (P002)

## AGE-GROUPS          X   Adult Status, Barriers to
Age-groups arise when the roles inculcated within the family and kinship situation are incompatible with those of the total social structure and therefore prevent the individual from achieving a mature status. (E086)

### Community
Age-group organizations are more likely to be adopted and retained in societies in which the community pattern is multiclan and endogamous, rather than single-clan and exogamous, for descent groups are the central focus of loyalty in the latter. (L175)

### Descent (Matrilineal/Patrilineal)
An institutionalized age-grade system is more likely to occur in patrilineal than in matrilineal societies. (Y001)

### Incest
There is an association between the existence of age-villages and the fear of incest between father-in-law and daughter-in-law. (W128)

### Isolation of Nuclear Family
Youth movements are likely to be stronger and to exert more political pressure on parents in isolated nuclear families of urban centers than in families deeply embedded in a network of extended kin. (P083)

### Kin-Group, Importance of
When families and kin-groups are almost self-sufficient social units (as in segmentary societies) age-groups do not occur. (E086)

### Kin-Role Definition
The conflict between kinship and age-grade allegiances will be more intense in societies where the age-grade is the major determinant of status. (E037)

### Kinship, Importance of
Age-grading into a corporate, integrated hierarchal organization is inversely correlated with the extent to which kinship principles and groups serve as focal points of social integration. (E102)

### Personality Adjustment
The age-grade, by providing the adolescent with a well-ordered, predictable scheme of roles and relationships, lessens adolescent tension. (N008)

### Political Role of Clan
The political importance of the clan structure is inversely correlated with the political importance of the age-set system. (B126)

## Political Role of Kin-Group

The extent of corporate organization of age-groups is negatively correlated with the performance by kinship groups of basic political and ritual tasks. (E086)

The greater the exclusion of kinship groups from basic political and ritual tasks and from territorial rights, the greater the degree of age-group hierarchy. (E086)

The greater the exclusion of kinship groups from basic political and ritual tasks and from territorial rights, the greater the degree of regulation of behavior by age-groups. (E086)

Where kinship groups do not perform basic political and ritual tasks and do not have territorial rights, there is a greater degree of corporate organization of the age-groups. (E086)

## Political Structure (Segmentary)

Within segmentary societies, age-groups are not likely to occur. (E086)

## Rank of Women

The low status of women relative to men is partly a result of the age-village organization. (W128)

## Religious Role of Kin-Group

The degree of corporate organization of age-groups is negatively correlated with the performance by kinship groups of basic political and ritual tasks. (E086)

## Residence

The importance of the age-grade system is inversely correlated with the localization of kin-groups. (E037)

Age-group organizations are more likely to be adopted and retained in societies in which the community pattern is multiclan and endogamous rather than single-clan and exogamous for descent groups are the central focus of loyalty in the latter. (L175)

## Role Conflict

Age-groups arise when the role dispositions of the family are incompatible with those of the total social structure. (E102)

## Social Mobility Within Family

Age-groups occur when the structure of the family or descent group blocks the younger members from attaining social status within the family. (E102)

## Stratification

Age-groups arise where social status depends to some extent on individual achievement and is not entirely based on membership in kinship or other hereditary groups. (E086)

## Stratification, Basis of

Age-groups occur in those societies in which social status depends on individual achievement and is not entirely based on membership in kinship or other hereditary groups. (E102)

## Urbanization

The extent of urbanization is inversely correlated with the persistence of the traditional age-grade system. (N016)

## Values

In any society in which the larger societal norms are very different from those within the family, some type of age-group (e.g., adolescent peer groups) will arise to bridge the necessary transition between the two. (G156)

# AGE OF ADULT CHILD

## X    Adjustment to Parents

Older mothers are better adjusted to their own parents than are younger mothers; but younger wives without children are better adjusted to their parents than are older wives without children. (S011)

# AGE OF BETROTHAL        X    Stratification

Given a relatively homogeneous level of riches or poverty in a society, there will be an absence of child betrothal practices. (F076)

# AGE OF CHILD        X    Child-Rearing Practices (Achievement)

Mother-son relations that are related to high achievement in sons are most effective if they begin when the son is about six to eight years of age. (G156)

## Child-Rearing Practices (Aggression)

There is no relationship between the age of the child and the severity of mother's punishment for mother-directed aggression. (M216)

Mothers are no more likely to punish older children than younger children for peer-directed aggression (cross-cultural). (M216)

## Child-Rearing Practices (Authoritarianism)

No relationship exists between authoritarian child control and the age of the child. (H200)

## Child-Rearing Practices (Authoritarianism of Mother/Father)

Fathers are likely to be just as authoritarian and autocratic when directing the behavior of their older adolescents as they are when directing their younger children. Mothers are likely to be seen as less autocratic or authoritarian in child rearing by their older than by their younger children. (E100)

## Child-Rearing Practices, Evaluation of

In accord with Homans' theory of distributive justice, it is predicted that, since younger adolescents are likely to expect less freedom in decision making than older youths, they are less likely to approve parental policy which allows them considerable leeway in self-direction. (E100)

Older and younger adolescents are equally likely to favorably evaluate child-rearing policies of dominant parents. Younger adolescents (junior-high-school age) are less likely than older youths to favor democratic, equalitarian, and permissive child-rearing practices. (E100)

## Child-Rearing Practices (Indulgence)

The younger the child (2–4 years v. 5–7 years), the more indulgent (giving in, bribing, compromising, etc.) the parents. (I006)

## Child-Rearing Practices (Permissiveness)

Both mothers and fathers are more likely to treat their older offspring permissively than they are their younger children. (E100)

## Child-Rearing Practices (Punishment)

The older the boy, the lower the proportion of punishments received from the mother; for girls, the proportion of punishments received from the mother remains constant regardless of age. (J026)

### Child-Rearing Practices (Sex Role)
Parental demands for appropriate sex-role behavior are made at an earlier age for boys than for girls. (L141)

### Conformity
The younger the child (7–16 years, inclusive), the greater his concern with being the "good child" his parents want him to be. (W138)

### Divorce Process
The older the children, the longer the interval between a serious consideration of divorce and the actual filing of the suit. (G157)

### Emotional Problems (Parental Conflicts)
The older the child (2–4 years v. 5–7 years), the less likely is he to exhibit emotional behavior (i.e., vocal, withdrawal, overt physical aggression against self, passive reactions) when in conflict with his parents. (I006)

### Employment of Mother
The older the children, the more likely it is that the mother is employed. (S265)

If a woman's children are of school age, she is more likely either to take outside employment or to consider it. (W150)

### Employment of Mother, Attitude Toward
The younger the children, the greater the likelihood that men will disapprove of the mother's employment. (S257)

### Employment of Parents, Attitude Toward
The older the child, the more likely is he to perceive his working parent or parents as possibly unhappy with work. (H222)

### Father Absence
Due to increased domestic responsibility and lack of supervision, the lack of an adult male in the home is likely to have more negative effects as the age of the girl increases. (R108)

The younger the boy, the more likely it is that he will be negatively affected by the absence of an adult male in the home. (R108)

### Father-Child Relations (Control)
During the elementary-school years, the father's control over the child declines and that of outside political authority increases. (H180)

### Friendship
The younger the children in the family, the more likely is the divorcée to maintain marriage friends during the separation and divorce period. (G157)

### Identification with Kin
Older children name fewer family members as their ego-ideals than do younger children. (H244)

### Identification with Like-Sex Parent
There is no correlation between chronological age in children and the degree of imitation of the like-sex parent. (H210)

### Identification with Parents
Identification with both parents is stronger among younger boys than among older boys. (E098)

The individual's perceived similarity to his father and mother varies inversely with age. (F111)

### Identification with Parents/Nonfamily Members
Younger children (7 and 8 years old) desire to be like someone in their families more so than older children (11 and 12 years old), who prefer to be like nonfamily members such as movie stars and athletic heroes. (W138)

### Income, Attitude Toward
At the (later) ages during which the children in a family require high material expenses, the husband/wife's satisfaction with their income is very low.

### I.Q. of Parent/Child
The older the child, the higher the correlation between the I.Q. of a child and that of his parents. (H173)

### Juvenile Delinquency
There is no relationship between delinquency and the age of the child at the time his family is disrupted. (N057)

### Maternal-Role Behavior
There is no relationship between age of the infant and maternal behavior (sensitivity, consistency or frequency of maternal acts). (B272)

### Mental Illness of Parent
Delayed parental reaction to a trauma in his childhood is more likely to occur when the child of the disturbed parent reaches the age at which the parent had the traumatic episode. (H246)

### Mother Absence
Since the child is able to differentiate an object from the love afforded by that object (because of developed ego), he will react to separation from the mother with grief and mourning; the infant whose ego is undifferentiated from the mother, will react with anxiety. (B255)

### Mother-Child Relations (Affection)
There is a positive and significant relationship between the degree of love that mothers show their infants and the degree of love shown to the same child during preadolescence. (S273)

### Mother-Child Relations (Control)
There is a positive, though not significant, relationship between the amount of autonomy or control mothers exhibit toward their infants and the amount of autonomy or control exhibited toward the same child during preadolescence. (S273)

### Parent-Child Relations (Affection)
The younger the children, the higher their affection for their parents. (B286)

### Parent-Child Relations (Ambivalence)
Preadolescents display more ambivalence toward their parents than do younger children. (W135)

### Parent-Child Relations (Conflict)
Conflict of daughter with father increases through adolescence, but her conflict with the mother decreases. (S219)

### Parent-Child Relations (Democratic)
In families of older (high-school) youths, adolescents are more apt to view their parents' relations with them as democratic than as autocratic or permissive. (B323)

### Parent-Child Relations (Dominance)
Older children are more likely than younger children to view the parent of the same sex as more dominant and punitive. (K116)

### Parent-Child Relations (Permissiveness)
In families of older (high-school) youths, adolescents are more apt to view their parents' relations with them as democratic than as autocratic or permissive. (B323)

### Parent-Child Relations (Preference)
The older the child, the more likely he will be to prefer one parent to the other. (B286)

As children grow older (five to nine years of age) there is an increase in mother preference, and a decrease in father preference. (G117)

Children of all ages prefer their mothers to their fathers, except five-year-old girls, who prefer their fathers. (G117)

### Parent-Child Relations (Rejection)
Parents are more likely to reject their boys when they become adolescent than to reject them when they are small children. (M217)

### Parent-Child Relations (Support)
In adolescence, the child is less likely to turn to his parents for help and support than to other adults or peers. (J023)

### Parental-Role Behavior
The older the child, the more likely are the parents to share the responsibility of disciplining the child and in guiding the child's play activities. (G133)

### Paternal Role
With increasing age, children increasingly attribute dominance and punitive characteristics to the same-sex parent. (H180)

### Paternal Role (Discipline)
The older the child, the greater is the importance of discipline by the father. (H208)

### Political Attitudes
Parental influence on their children's political sentiments is less as the children grow older and influences from other agencies (school, peers) assume more relative importance. (H244)

### Power Structure of Family
Older (high-school) adolescents are more likely to perceive father as dominant in family matters; younger (junior-high) are more likely to say there is equality between parents. (B323)

The perception of father or mother as dominant will decrease with age for both sexes; there will be a shift from seeing a single parent as dominant to seeing both parents as equal (U.S.). (H180)

### Rank of Wife
As the wife grows old and becomes the mother of adult sons and daughters, her social position improves. (W082)

### Self-Conception
There is no clear relationship between the age of the child at time of divorce and his present level of self-esteem. (R129)

Among children who were very young at the time of divorce, those who had older mothers are more likely to have high self-esteem than those who had very young mothers. (R129)

### Sex-Role Definition
The younger the children in a family where the mother works, the more likely it is that she will be faced with role conflict over working. (K089)

### Sex-Role Definition (Power)
The older the child is, the more he tends to discriminate male, but not female, sex and age roles by reference to their power. (E090)

The older the child, the less is the father's sex role perceived as more powerful than the mother's sex role. (E090)

### Sex-Role Identification
Within the younger ages, identification with the controlling role of the father becomes stronger among boys, but a similar sex-typed age trend is not found among girls. (E098)

Compared with younger subjects, older subjects have stronger tendencies to imitate the like-sex, rather than the opposite-sex, parent. (H179)

Frequency of like-sex imitation is not significantly greater with older children. (H179)

### Surrogate Mother, Evaluation of
The divorcée is more likely to claim that substitute child care is excellent if the children are younger than if they are older. (G157)

### Surrogate Parent, Adjustment to
Very young and grown children assimilate a new parent more easily than do adolescent children. (B286)

The younger the adopted child is when he enters his new home, the more likely it is that he will successfully adjust to the situation. (T086)

### Voting
Agreement between the voting patterns of parents and child decreases as the age of the child increases. (H244)

### AGE OF CHILDREN          X    Cohesion of Family
The relationship between the age of children in the home and family solidarity is inverse. (J001)

### Custody
The mother is more likely to be given custody of the children if they are young. (C060)

### Husband-Wife Relations (Dependency)
There is an inverse relationship between the degree of dependence of a woman on her husband and the age of her children. (S080)

### AGE OF DIVORCÉE
#### X    Remarriage, Comparison with First
Age of the divorcée does not affect the general pattern of greater satisfaction with the second marriage. (G157)

### AGE OF FAMILY HEAD    X    Cohesion of Family
The integration of the family varies by age of the family head. Other tests have shown no significant correlation between age of parents and family integration. (S217)

## AGE OF FATHER
### X    Illegitimacy (Place of Delivery)
Fathers of illegitimate children born at institutions tend to be younger than those of illegitimate children born in private practice. (V002)

## AGE OF HUSBAND                          X    Adultery
In Western countries, extramarital sexual intercourse increases in frequency with increasing age among upper-class husbands, while decreasing in frequency with age among lower-class husbands. (G156)

### Authority Structure of Family
The husband's authority in the household is reinforced when he is the oldest person within it. (C090)

### Husband-Wife Relations (Evaluation)
Older husbands tend to have a more positive evaluation of their wives than do younger husbands. (B232)

### Marital Stability
The stability of the marriage is directly correlated with the age of the husband. (F073)

## AGE OF HUSBAND/WIFE         X    Age Difference
Age differences between spouses tend to be smaller when the husband is older than the wife than they do when the wife is older than the husband. The contrary is also asserted. (D083)

### Income, Attitude Toward
When the husband is younger than the wife, the wife tends to be less satisfied with the family's standard of living.

### Marital Adjustment
Marriage is most likely to be successful if the spouses are of the same age or if the wife is younger than the husband. (S244)

## AGE OF KIN    X    Mental Illness, Attitude Toward
The younger the relatives of a mental patient are, the more likely they are to consider mental illness an acquired, curable sickness, which is treatable by hospitalization. (F109)

## AGE OF KIN-GROUP                X    Incest Taboo
The distance to which incest taboos are extended appears primarily a function of the time which has elapsed since the establishment of the kin-groups that have channeled them. (M019)

## AGE OF LINEAGE          X    Cohesion of Lineage
Lineage cohesiveness tends to be directly correlated with the age of the lineage. (L066)

### Residence
Patrilineages of recent origin are more often confined to a particular locality than others are. (G022)

## AGE OF MALE                          X    Mate Selection
The range of eligible women is greater, the older the male. (S153)

## AGE OF MALE CHILD          X    Rank of Women
In patrilineal societies, the status of a woman tends to be directly correlated with the age of her son. (F073)

## AGE OF MARRIED PERSONS          X    Residence
Young couples are more likely to live with one set of parents for a while than are older couples. (G156)

## AGE OF MOTHER    X    Achievement Motivation
In small, middle-class families, sons of young mothers tend to have higher achievement motivation than do sons of older mothers. (R106)

### Achievement Values
Sons of older mothers (40 years or older) are more likely to have values similar to their mothers' regarding achievement than sons with younger mothers (20–39 years); this is not true in the middle class. (R097)

### Breast Feeding, Duration of
There is no necessary correlation between the length of time a child is nursed and the age of the mother. (G148)

### Child-Rearing Attitudes (Authoritarianism)
There is an inverse curvilinear relationship between a mother's age and authoritarian maternal attitudes. (Z011)

### Child-Rearing Practices (Aggression)
The younger the mother, the more likely is she to urge her child to fight back when attacked by other children (U.S.). (S191)

### Child-Rearing Practices (Authoritarianism)
No relationship exists between authoritarian child control and the age of the mother. (H200)

### Child-Rearing Practices (Criticism)
The younger the mother, the more likely is she to use ridicule as a technique of child rearing (U.S.). (S191)

### Child-Rearing Practices (Dependency)
Younger mothers (20–39 years) are more likely than older mothers (40 years or older) to train their sons at an earlier age to be independent. (R097)

### Child-Rearing Practices (Punishment)
Older mothers (40 years or older) are more likely than younger mothers (20–39 years) to use psychological punishment-rewards in child rearing. (R097)

Younger mothers tend to be more irritable, quicker to punish, and more severe with their children than older mothers. (S191)

The younger the mother, the more likely is she to use physical punishment in child rearing (U.S.). (S191)

The younger the mother, the more likely is she to use withdrawal of privileges as a technique of control (U.S.). (S191)

### Emotional Problems of Child
The younger the mother and the child at the time of divorce, the more likely it is that the child will be emotionally disturbed. (R129)

### Fertility (Real/Ideal)
Among wives planning to have more children, the older the wife, the more likely that her ideal family size is smaller than she intended. Among those undecided, the amount of disparity tends to be inversely related with age. (Y046)

### Fertility Values
The older the mother, the smaller the ideal family size she reports. (Y049)

### Husband-Wife Relations (Conflict)
Younger mothers are more likely than older mothers to quarrel with their husbands. (S191)

#### Illegitimacy (Adoption)
The younger the unwed mother, the more likely is she to surrender the baby for adoption. (J020)

#### Illegitimacy (Place of Delivery)
A greater percentage of unwed mothers, 21 years of age or younger, had their babies delivered in institutions rather than through private practice. (V002)

#### Maternal-Role Behavior
There is no direct correlation between maternal behavior and the age of the mother. (L165)

#### Mother-Child Relations (Affection)
There is no difference between younger (20–39 years old) and older (40 years old or older) mothers regarding their willingness to display affection to their children. (R097)

#### Mother-Child Relations (Hostility)
Younger mothers are more likely than older mothers to express an underlying feeling of hostility toward children. (S191)

#### Mother-Child Relations (Warmth)
The older the mother, the warmer she is toward her infant child, except when the child is a first one. (S191)

#### Parent-Child Relations
Of wives with children, the older wives tend to be better adjusted to their own parents; while among wives without children, the younger tend to be better adjusted to their own parents. (S011)

#### Personality of Child (Self-Esteem)
Children whose mothers were relatively young when they were widowed are less likely to have high self-esteem than those whose mothers were older when widowed. (R129)

#### Psychosomatic Illness of Child
The younger the mother at the time of divorce, the more likely the children are to have many psychosomatic symptoms. (R129)

Children whose mothers were relatively young when they were widowed are more likely to show psychosomatic symptoms of anxiety. (R129)

#### Self-Conception of Child
Children whose mothers were relatively young when they were widowed are less likely to have high self-esteem than those whose mothers were older when widowed. (R129)

### AGE OF PARENTS
#### X   Authority Structure of Family
Older parents are less able than younger parents to enforce their socialization demands. (R106)

#### Child-Rearing Attitudes
For both parents, concern with obedience and discipline problems decreases with age (education-controlled). (G126)

#### Child-Rearing Practices (Achievement)
Older parents tend to place less emphasis on achievement in child rearing than do younger parents. (R106)

#### Child-Rearing Practices (Dependency)
Older parents tend to place less emphasis on self-reliance of their children than do younger parents. (R106)

#### Child-Rearing Practices (Indulgence)
Older parents tend to be more indulgent and solicitous toward their children than do younger parents. (R106)

#### Child-Rearing Practices (Punishment)
Older mothers tend to be less hostile and to use less physical punishment than do younger ones; older fathers tend to be more lax in discipline and to use less physical punishment. (B232)

#### Child-Rearing Problems
The older the parent, the less likely is he to report having problems in child rearing. (G126)

Older parents are more concerned with inadequacies and problems in physical and material care; younger parents are more concerned with interpersonal difficulties (their own lack of tolerance for the child's behavior, or obedience and discipline problems). (G126)

#### Juvenile Delinquency
There is no relationship between age of parents and the development of delinquency. (G123)

### AGE OF PATRILINEAL DESCENT
#### X   Kin Terminology (Omaha)
The occurrence of Omaha systems of terminology indicates that the pattern of patrilineal descent is of great age. (L061)

### AGE OF PROBLEM CHILD
#### X   Neurosis Personality of Parents
Compared to mothers of younger maladjusted children, mothers of maladjusted adolescents are more likely to have the characteristics of authoritarianism, strictness, approval of activity, inconsiderateness of husband, ascendance; fathers are likely to have the characteristics of marital conflict, seclusiveness, inconsiderateness of wife (PARI). (Z011)

### AGE OF SONS   X   Authority Structure of Family
The authority of the father is inversely correlated with the age of his sons. (F073)

### AGE OF SURROGATE MOTHER
#### X   Identification with Surrogate Mother
The younger the foster-mother, the more likely that the child will identify with her. (W149)

### AGE OF UNILINEAL DESCENT
#### X   Kin Terminology
The proportion of unilineal features found in the terminology will be directly correlated with the age of the unilineal descent pattern. (L061)

### AGE OF WIFE   X   Divorce Adjustment
The older the divorcée, the more likely is she to experience difficult emotional problems. (G157)

When the marriage is short, there is no relationship between age of the divorcée and difficulty of the emotional problems experienced in divorce. (G157)

#### Divorce, Attitude Toward
The younger the divorcée, the more likely is she to claim that persons discriminated against her because of being divorced. (G157)

#### Divorce Decision
Stability of the final decision to divorce is unrelated to the age of the wife. (G157)

### Divorce, Initiation of
The wife is slightly more likely to be the first to suggest divorce if she is in a young age bracket, and the husband to be the first to suggest divorce if she is older. (G157)

### Divorce Process
The older the wife, the longer the interval between a serious consideration to divorce and the actual filing of the suit. (G157)

Controlling for duration of the marriage, the older the wife, the longer the interval between a serious consideration of divorce and actually filing suit. (G157)

### Husband-Wife Relations (Affection)
The older the wife at the time of marriage, the higher is her satisfaction with the husband's expression of affection. (G157)

### Marriage Ceremony
Civil ceremonies are more frequent among younger than among older brides. (C128)

### Preferential Marriage (Levirate)
Remarriage of the widow under the levirate is less likely to occur if the wife is at an advanced age. (S158)

### Role Behavior of Wife
Young wives are apt to play a strong encouraging role for their husbands, as compared with the wives in their forties who are more "collaborators" with their husbands, and the older wives who concentrate mainly on housework.

### AGE OF WOMEN          X   Rank of Women
The status of women is directly correlated with their age. (L079)

### AGE-ROLE DEFINITION          X   Incest
There is a correlation between violation of generational boundaries (confusion in age roles) and sexual deviance in the family, particularly incest.

### AGE/SEX STATUS     X   Identification with Parents
Boys show a decline in identification with parents with age, but girls are more likely to continue to idealize their parents. (H244)

### AGGRESSION          X   Aggression of Parent
When both parents are low in aggressiveness, then the child is also low in aggressiveness. (E091)

The level of aggression of the like-sex parent will be most influential in determining frequency of aggression in doll play by the child. (L157)

### Anxiety of Mother
The greater the child-rearing anxiety of the mother (anxiety about child, conflict with child, maladjustment, dissatisfaction, low self-esteem), the greater the aggressive behavior of the child. (B232)

Mothers who are highly anxious concerning child rearing report more aggressive children than mothers who are not as anxious (U.S.). (S191)

### Authority Structure of Family
Children who are bullying, domineering, and aggressive tend to come from families in which there are conflicting authority figures. (R113)

### Child-Rearing Anxiety of Father
The greater the child-rearing anxiety of the father, the lower the incidence of aggression in school by daughters with hostile mothers, and the higher the incidence at home. (B232)

### Child-Rearing Practices (Achievement Demands)
Parents of aggressive boys are less likely to have higher academic achievement demands than are parents of normals. (B243)

### Child-Rearing Practices (Aggression)
The more permissive the parents are toward the child's aggressive behavior, the more likely is the child to anticipate a reward for aggressive behavior and consequently to exhibit aggression.

In the aggressive boys' families, one or the other of the parents almost invariably encourages aggression by the boy toward outside adults (teachers) and peers. (B213)

There is a curvilinear relationship between the severity of punishment for aggression shown toward the mother and the incidence of aggressive behavior in preschool children. (B243)

Mothers of aggressive boys tend to be more permissive of aggression toward themselves than do mothers of normals; the fathers do not differ with respect to the two groups. (B243)

Parents of aggressive children are more likely to reward and encourage aggressive behavior than parents of nonaggressive children. (C120)

If the father does not tolerate aggression at home, which is mostly the case with fathers of foreign ethnicity, the child is likely to exhibit aggressive behavior in environments outside the home (e.g., school). (E091)

When the father is low in punishment for aggression, regardless of mother's score, the child tends to be low in aggression. (E091)

There is a positive relationship between parental punishment for aggression and aggressive behavior in school. (E093)

Maternal punishment is more positively related than is paternal punishment to the child's aggressive behavior in the school setting. (E093)

For both boys and girls, high-status children who are severely punished for aggression are more aggressive than children from other classes who are subjected to lesser degrees of aggression punishment. (E093)

Punishment for aggression by parents increases the likelihood that the child will manifest aggressive behavior; this relationship is strongest among upper-class families. (E097)

The relationship between punishment by mothers for aggression and aggressive behavior is curvilinear. Medium punishment is associated with less aggression than either high or low punishment. (E097)

A mother's punishment of her child's aggression is positively related to the amount of aggression the child displayed. Permissiveness of aggression is positively related to the child's expression of aggression. (L169)

High permissiveness for aggression toward parents is associated with high aggression toward parents. (S191)

Parents' permissiveness toward aggression is not associated with strength of child's fantasy aggression (projective aggression) (U.S.). (S191)

Permissiveness of expression of aggression by the parents is positively related to the development of aggressive behavior in children. (S246)

Among five-year olds, both high permissiveness and high punishment of aggressive behavior are associated with the development of aggressive behavior in the child at home, although permissiveness and punishment are negatively correlated with each other (among five-year olds). (S246)

Greater amounts of punishment of aggressive behavior lead eventually to lesser amounts of such behavior (by age 12). (S246)

The suppression of the early expression of aggression in the home increases the strength of self-aggression (as opposed to antisocial aggression against others) in later years. (S246)

### Child-Rearing Practices (Chores)
Parents of aggressive or nonaggressive boys do not vary with regard to the amount of household responsibilities they assign to their sons. (B243)

### Child-Rearing Practices (Clarity)
Among homes characterized by a high level of explanation by the parents, the more explicit the behavior restrictions, the less aggressive the child. (B266)

### Child-Rearing Practices (Consensus)
Fathers of aggressive boys are less likely to report agreement with their wives about the child-rearing process than are fathers of normals. (B243)

Parents who frequently disagree about child-rearing matters report more aggressive children than do parents who disagree less frequently (U.S.). (S191)

### Child-Rearing Practices (Consistency)
Where one parent is lax about discipline and the other is punitive, the child is more likely to be aggressive (than if parents are consistent). (B259)

Since aggressive action not only satisfies a primary drive (i.e., of aggression or the primary drive whose frustration produced the aggressive drive) but may also become a source of pleasure in itself, if rewarded, then mothers who are not firm (unable to disapprove consistently) are more likely than those who are firm to produce children who are hostile, with high (overt) aggressive drives. (F103)

### Child-Rearing Practices (Democratic)
Children from democratic homes (parents who encourage free experimentation by their children and are less controlling (aggression being defined by psychosocial factors such as fearlessness, cruelty, disobedience, etc.) than children from nondemocratic homes. (M224)

### Child-Rearing Practices (Dependency)
The parents of aggressive adolescent boys more often stress the need for the boy to be independent than those of control group. (B213)

Parents of aggressive boys are more likely to reject or punish dependent behavior than are parents of normals. (B243)

Frustration of a child's dependency needs is a continual initiator of hostile and aggressive behavior. (B246)

### Child-Rearing Practices (Favoritism)
Individuals with falling dreams were more likely to express direct aggression against their mothers when they were the favored sibling than when some other sibling was favored. (H216)

Children who tend toward bullying, aggressive, and domineering behavior are likely to have mothers who show marked preference for the child's sibling. (R113)

### Child-Rearing Practices (Frustration)
Children who are severely frustrated by their mothers are more aggressive (doll play) than children who are mildly frustrated by their mothers.

Frustration of the infant's desires is not related to later aggression. (S238)

### Child-Rearing Practices (Giving Reasons)
Parents of nonaggressive adolescent boys use reasoning as a method of training and control to a much greater extent than do parents of the aggressive boys. (B213)

Children from homes characterized by a high level of explanation by the parents are more aggressive than children from homes where there is not much explanation of family decisions. (B266)

### Child-Rearing Practices (Maturity Demands)
There is a positive relationship between fathers' expecting overly mature behavior from their children and aggression, bullying, and domineering on the part of the child. (R100)

### Child-Rearing Practices (Neglect)
The greater the neglect of the child, the more likely that it will be aggressive. (M203)

### Child-Rearing Practices (Nurturance)
There is a correlation between a lack of maternal nurturance and the incidence of aggressive behavior in boys. (B243)

Mothers who are not nurturant are more likely to produce children high in hostility or aggression drive than mothers who satisfy their children's needs. (F103)

### Child-Rearing Practices (Obedience)
Mothers of aggressive boys impose fewer demands for obedience and are less consistent in these demands than are mothers of normals. (B243)

### Child-Rearing Practices (Permissiveness)
Children who are bullying, domineering, and aggressive are likely to have mothers who are more permissive. (R113)

### Child-Rearing Practices (Punishment)
Fathers of aggressive adolescent boys are more prone to use physical punishment than are control fathers. (B213)

Parents of aggressive adolescent boys tend to deprive their sons of certain possessions and privileges (as a form of discipline) more often than parents of the control group. (B213)

Physical punishment increases the amount of aggression in the child. (B232)

Boys' aggression at school is directly related to the mother's hostility and use of physical punishment; girls' is not. The reverse situation holds when the father is hostile and punitive, although the differences in the correlations for boys and girls are then less marked. (B232)

Since punitiveness by the mother causes both coun-teraggression and aggression anxiety, the further the distance from the mother and the home, the less the child inhibits his aggression. (B232)

Within the schoolroom, girls with either high- or low-punitive mothers exhibited the least aggression (a curvi-linear relation), but aggression by boys increased linearly with punitiveness of the mother. (B232)

In a doll-play diagnostic situation the number of aggres-sive acts by both sexes is linearly related to the punitive-ness of the mothers. (B232)

The more the mother punishes, the more aggressive are both boys and girls at home; aggressiveness of boys at school has a curvilinear relation with punishment by the father and tends to occur particularly when the father is low-punitive and the mother is highly punitive. (B232)

Both hostility and physical punishment by one or both parents tend to summate, producing more severe con-duct problems in the home; this is also true for boys in the schoolroom (but not for girls). (B232)

When mothers are highly punitive, girls are more likely to develop controls over their aggressive feelings than are boys, or than are girls who are highly punished by their fathers; but boys whose fathers punish them mod-erately are more likely to develop such controls. (B232)

Parents of aggressive boys tend to use ridicule, depriva-tion of privileges, and physical punishment as discipline more often than do parents of normal boys. (B246)

Aggressive boys are as likely as nonaggressive boys to perceive their parents as inflicting punishment. (K103)

With boys, there is a linear correlation between severity of punishment by parents and the amount of overt social aggression exhibited in preschool; for girls, the relation is curvilinear. (L157)

Severity of punishment by like-sex parent correlates with frequency of aggression in doll play of girls, but not of boys. (L157)

Children whose mothers are very punitive tend to ex-hibit bullying, domineering, and generally aggressive behavior. (R113)

The more severe the punishment, the more aggression the child is likely to show. (S191)

For boys, the relationship between the amount of ag-gression and the severity of maternal punitiveness is positive. (S246)

For girls, there is a curvilinear relationship between ma-ternal punitiveness and the development of aggression. Both the severely punished and the least severely pun-ished girls are less aggressive than those with an inter-mediate amount of punishment. (S246)

If boys are punished in such a way that socialization is increased, they are likely to develop self-aggression. (S246)

Due to the mechanism of displacement, the more severe the punishment of the child, the more likely that he will inhibit overt, interpersonal aggression and will be more aggressive in fantasy. (S248)

### Child-Rearing Practices (Restrictiveness)
Insofar as restrictions frustrate the child, the parent's restrictiveness encourages aggression in the child. (B232)

The severity of the parental restrictions imposed upon the boy outside the home does not covary with his aggressiveness. (B243)

Parents of "normal" adolescents, particularly the moth-ers, impose stronger restrictions and demands on their sons than do parents of hyperaggressive adolescents. (B275)

### Child-Rearing Practices (Rewards)
Boys who receive tangible rewards are more likely to be self-aggressive than those who do not. (S246)

### Child-Rearing Practices (Sex)
Parents of aggressive and normal sons do not vary with respect to their handling of the son's early sex behavior, both being nonpermissive but nonpunitive. (B243)

Fathers of aggressive boys are more likely to be permis-sive toward adolescent heterosexual behavior than are fathers of normals. (B243)

### Child-Rearing Practices (Sex Role)
Fathers of aggressive boys are less likely to make de-mands for masculine behavior than are fathers of nor-mals. (B243)

### Child-Rearing Practices (Strictness)
When the child has a very severe father and an indulgent mother, his aggression is likely to be directed outwardly rather than against himself. (S078)

### Conformity
Aggressive boys are more resistant to the socialization demands of their parents than are normals. (B243)

### Dependency
In comparison to control adolescent boys, aggressive boys make fewer dependency demands upon their par-ents. (B213)

Aggressive boys are less likely to show emotional de-pendency on their fathers and, to a lesser extent, on their mothers, than are normals. (B243)

Aggressive boys are more likely to manifest dependency anxiety concerning their relationship with their parents, as measured by avoidance and secretiveness, than are normals. (B243)

The more aggressive the child, the less dependent his behavior toward his parents. (K103)

The greater the child's dependency on his parents, the more likely he will be to learn and practice control of aggressive behavior. (K103)

### Economic Dependence
There is no relationship between the aggressiveness of the boy and his degree of economic dependence upon his parents. (B243)

### Father Absence
Father-present boys are more likely to give aggressive (doll play) responses to playmates than are father-pre-sent girls; among father-absent children, sex is not related to age-mate aggression.

Boys whose fathers are absent from home are less ag-gressive than boys whose fathers are not absent. (H197)

When the father is absent from the home, there is a greater likelihood that boys will develop aggressive behavior. (M181)

Boys whose fathers are absent from the home are less likely to show doll-play aggression than boys whose fathers are present. Absence of father is unrelated to aggression in girls. (S228)

When the father is absent from the home, the boy is more likely to direct aggression against the parent dolls as opposed to the child dolls than when the father is present. (S228)

Absence of the father from the home is not related to the content of the aggression shown by girls or boys. (S228)

When the father is absent from the home, the daughter is less likely to direct aggression against the baby doll than she is when the father is present. (S228)

### Father-Child Relations (Hostility)
There is a correlation between the degree of father's hostility toward the son and the degree of son's aggression toward teachers, peers, and parents. (B243)

### Father-Son Relations (Affection)
There is a negative correlation between aggressiveness of the son and the amount of time spent in affectionate interaction with the father. (B243)

### Father-Son Relations (Hostility)
Aggressive adolescent boys feel more hostility toward their fathers than do control boys. (B213)

### Father-Son Relations (Interaction)
Fathers of aggressive male adolescents spend less time with their sons than do fathers of control groups. (No difference between mothers of both groups.) (B213)

### Father-Son Relations (Rejection)
Fathers of aggressive male adolescents are more distant and cold toward their sons, as compared with fathers of control groups, who are more friendly and pleasant toward their sons. (B213)

### Foster-Home/Institutional Care
Children who are reared during the first three years of infancy in institutions are more likely to manifest aggressive disorders in adolescence than are children reared in foster homes; the latter are more likely to be timid and withdrawn. (B243)

### Household Composition
The composite household tends to reduce overt expression of intrafamilial aggression. (C035)

### Husband-Wife Relations (Evaluation)
Mothers who have low esteem for their husbands report more aggressive children than do mothers who are more admiring and commendatory of their spouses (U.S.). (S191)

### Husband-Wife Relations (Warmth)
The parents of aggressive boys demonstrate less warmth and regard for each other than do the parents of normal boys. (B246)

### Identification
In doll play, the child tends to identify with the doll that represents his most important source of conflict relating to aggression and aggression control in the family. (S228)

### Identification with Father
Adolescent control boys are more inclined to identify with their fathers than aggressive boys are. (B213)

Identification with an aggressive and/or antisocial father is a cause of aggression in the son. (B243)

### Identification with Like-Sex Parent
Expressed aggression toward the father by the daughter is associated with negative feelings toward similarity with the mother. (L136)

### Identification with Parents
Aggressive boys are less likely to identify with their parents, particularly the father, than are normals. (B243)

The stronger the child's identification with the parent, the more his level of aggression in doll play will approximate his perception of the level of aggression of the parent. (L157)

### Immigrant/Nonimmigrant
Children with fathers of foreign origin tend to be more aggressive than children with American fathers. (E091)

### Institutional Care
Orphaned children who spend their early years in institutions are more likely to manifest aggressive traits when later placed in foster homes than those who are not institutionalized. (T086)

### I.Q. of Parents
There is no relationship between a parent's intelligence and the aggression of the son. (M210)

### Juvenile Delinquency (Running Away)
Delinquent children who run away are more likely to have parents who display physical aggression in the home than are delinquent children who do not run away. (F093)

### Marital Adjustment of Parents
Parents of aggressive boys are more likely to have a disrupted marital relationship than are parents of normals. (B243)

### Maternal Overprotectiveness
Overindulgence on the part of the mother is correlated with aggressive and egocentric behavior in the child. (B033)

### Mother-Child Relations
Fantasy aggression by children (measured by doll play) is increased when the mother is present. (L147)

### Mother-Child Relations (Rejection)
Children having mothers who are cold, distant, and neglectful tend to be aggressive, acting out behavior such as lying and general destructiveness. (R113)

### Mother-Child Relations (Warmth)
The less warm the mother is to the child, the more likely it is that the child will be aggressive. (B243)

### Mother-Son Relations (Affection)
There is no relationship between aggression in the boy and the amount of affection shown him by his mother. (B243)

Aggressive boys (perhaps due to dependency anxiety) are more likely than normals to avoid demonstrations of affection by the mother by the time they are adolescents. (B243)

### Occupational Rank of Father
The higher the rank of the father's occupation, the higher is the rate of aggression in the child. (E097)

### Ordinal Position
Older siblings are less likely than younger or only children to display (doll play) aggressive actions. (S228)

Frequency of use of parents as agents of aggression in doll play does not vary with ordinal position of the boy; only male children are more likely to use the boy doll, and younger brothers the girl doll, as agents of aggression than are the older brothers. (S228)

The mother, boy, and baby dolls are less likely to be used as objects of aggression by older brothers than they are by younger or only boys. (S228)

There is no correlation between dolls used as objects or agents of aggression and ordinal position of the girl. (S228)

### Parent-Child Relations (Affection)
Parents of aggressive boys demonstrate less warmth and affection toward their sons than do the parents of normal children. (B246)

The more the child perceives his parents as being nurturing and gratifying, the more likely he will be to learn and practice control of aggressive behavior. (K103)

### Parent-Child Relations (Aggression)
Aggressive boys are more likely than normals to manifest indirect aggression against their fathers, but the two groups do not differ with respect to their mothers. (B243)

Aggressive boys are slightly more likely to be physically aggressive toward their mothers than are normals, but there is no difference between the two groups with respect to their fathers. (B243)

There is no relationship between the aggressiveness of the boy and the amount of verbal aggression he displays toward his parents. (B243)

### Parent-Child Relations (Anger)
Aggressive boys are more likely than nonaggressive boys to perceive parent-child interaction as characterized by anger. (K103)

### Parent-Child Relations (Evaluation)
Aggressive adolescent boys give more unfavorable pictures of their fathers than of their mothers. (B213)

### Parent-Child Relations (Frustration)
The more frustrated the child in his relations with his parents, the greater his need to display some form of aggression.

### Parent-Child Relations (Harshness)
The harsher the parents are in their relations with their children, the more likely the children are to aggress in return against the parents themselves.

### Parent-Child Relations (Hostility)
Children are more likely to express aggression when parental behavior toward them has been hostile and to express submissive behavior when the parental relationship has been protective and warm. (B243)

Aggressive boys do not differ from normals with respect to amount of hostility felt toward their mothers, but they tend to feel more hostility toward their fathers than do normals. (B243)

Aggressive boys are more likely to have feelings of hostility (as measured by the TAT) toward their fathers than are normals, but the two groups do not differ with respect to their mothers. (B243)

The more aggressive the child, the more hostile and less gratifying he will perceive his parents to be. (K103)

### Parent-Child Relations (Interaction)
In democratic homes, high parent-child interaction produces more aggression in the child than low parent-child interaction. (B266)

### Parent-Child Relations (Obedience)
Parents of aggressive adolescent boys report much more resistance to their discipline than do parents of control boys. (B213)

Nonaggressive boys are more likely than aggressive boys to obey their mothers rather than their fathers. (K103)

### Parent-Child Relations (Physical Abuse)
Parents who severely abuse their children are more likely than others to react with hostility and with either physical or emotional attacks toward outsiders who are viewed as causing a family crisis. (Y043)

### Parent-Child Relations (Rejection)
(Reputed) aggression in boys is correlated with their rejection of one or both parent figures. (C098)

Children's aggression, in which the child shows violence, cruelty, malicious mischief, and open defiance of authority, correlates with parental rejection. (S183)

### Parent-Child Relations (Resentment)
Hyperaggressive adolescents are more likely than "normals" to resent whatever demands their parents make on them. (B275)

### Paternal/Maternal Role
Nonaggressive boys are more likely than aggressive boys to perceive their mothers, rather than their fathers, as punishing them. (K103)

In middle-class families, mothers tend to be more frequent targets of aggression by children than do fathers. (N049)

### Paternal Role (Discipline)
If the father is the chief disciplinarian of a five-year-old boy, the boy is more likely to exhibit self-aggression at age 12. (S246)

### Personality of Child (Guilt)
The less able the child is to display aggression against his parents, the more likely is he to become intropunitive.

### Personality of Father
A child who is judged by his parents as aggressive, uncontrolled, and hard to discipline is likely to have a father (as judged by either the father *himself* or by the mother) who is cold and aloof, severe and authoritarian, tense, immature, prone to anger, disorganized, and unsuccessful. (B237)

### Personality of Mother (Hostility)
Since resentment is easily converted into aggressive action, particularly when encouraged (frequently hostile mothers direct a child's aggression toward other adults), mothers who are hostile are more likely to produce children who are overtly aggressive than are those who are not hostile. (F103)

### Personality of Mother (Satisfaction)
Mothers who are not satisfied with their present situation (frequency of mention of things they would rather be doing) report more aggressive children than mothers who are satisfied with their present situation (U.S.). (S191)

### Power Structure of Family
Nonaggressive boys are more likely than aggressive boys to perceive the mother as being the boss of the family. (K103)

### Pregnancy, Attitude Toward
There is no relationship between the mother's attitude on becoming pregnant and the amount of reported aggression from her children. (S191)

### Premarital Sex Relations
Aggressive boys are more likely to engage in premarital intercourse than are normals. (B243)

### Religion
There is no relationship between a parent's religious affiliation and antisocial or socialized aggression of the son. (M210)

### Scholastic Achievement Demands
Parents of normal children have higher expectations for their sons' school achievement than parents of aggressive boys. (Both groups of boys matched for I.Q.). (B213)

### Self-Conception
Mothers perceive themselves to be more intropunitive than their children perceive them to be. (M177)

### Self-Conception of Mother
Mothers who have less self-esteem report more aggressive children than mothers who have self-confidence (U.S.). (S191)

### Sex Status
Among preschool-aged children, boys exhibit more (doll play) aggression than girls toward the father; while there is no difference between boys and girls regarding the amount of aggression displayed toward the mother. (J026)

Boys rate higher in aggression toward father and in self-rated aggression than girls do. (L136)

The frequency of aggression in doll play is greater for boys than for girls. (L157)

Since girls retain their initial mother identification, while boys usually shift to their father, girls at age five are more likely to display prosocial aggression; boys to display antisocial aggression. There is an increase in both sexes of prosocial behavior during the ages five to eight (U.S.). (S191)

Boys are more likely than girls to make the father and boy child the objects of aggression in doll play; girls are more likely to employ the girl and baby doll as objects of aggression. (S228)

Boys and girls do not differ in the amount of aggression directed against the mother doll. (S228)

Girls are more likely to direct aggression against the boy doll than are boys against the girl doll. (S228)

Boys are more aggressive than girls in doll play, being more likely to use physical violence, aggression involving imaginary figures, and aggression against impersonal objects. They do not differ from girls with respect to the amount of aggression involving no bodily injury. (S228)

### Sexual Adjustment
The degree of satisfaction found in a sexual relationship is related to the opportunities it offers for the expression of aggression. (S037)

### Sibling Status
Aggressive children are more likely to be only children than are nonaggressive children. (S229)

### Size of Kin-Group
The smaller the kin-group, the greater the tendency for the aggressor alone to be held responsible for his act. (S086)

## AGGRESSION ANXIETY
### X   Child-Rearing Practices (Aggression)
Punishment for aggression against the parents in early childhood increases aggression anxiety in girls in later years. (S246)

Nonpermissiveness of aggression toward parents increases aggression anxiety in both boys and girls. (S246)

If aggression is allowed in the home and conscience is not highly developed, both girls and boys are likely to develop aggression anxiety in later years. (S246)

### Child-Rearing Practices (Dependency)
Punishment of dependency and physical punishment in early childhood do not increase aggression anxiety in girls in later years. (S246)

### Child-Rearing Practices (Punishment)
No form of punishment, except the withdrawal of love, is associated with the development of aggression anxiety in boys. (S246)

For boys, both aggression anxiety and self-aggression are preceded by a nonpermissive background. (S246)

### Child-Rearing Practices (Sex Role)
If parents allow girls to act in ways which are inappropriate for sex-typing (aggression against other children, fighting back when attacked, etc.) aggression anxiety increases. (S246)

### Mother-Child Relations (Communication)
Inadequate verbal communication between mother and child produces, in the stuttering child, displaced aggression anxiety upon siblings or other relatives, and fear of losing mother. (W136)

### Parent-Child Relations (Affection)
Since a mutually affectionate relationship between parent and child fosters the development of conscience in the child, parents who are affectionate are more likely than those who are not to produce adolescents with high fantasy-aggression anxiety. (C113)

### Paternal-Role Definition
The greater the amount of the father's participation in

child rearing, the greater the aggression anxiety which develops in girls. (S246)

### Therapeutic Practices

The degree of anxiety generated by the socialization of aggression in the child is inversely correlated with the degree to which a society utilizes punitive measures against the child. (K111)

The degree of anxiety generated by the socialization of aggression in the child (the degree to which punishment for aggression has led to inhibitions of aggression responses and consequent intropunitive or self-aggression) is correlated with the extent to which the society employs sacrifice as a therapeutic practice. (K111)

The degree of anxiety generated by the socialization of aggression in the child is correlated with the extent to which the society employs bloodletting as a therapeutic practice. (K111)

## AGGRESSION ANXIETY BY SEX STATUS
### X   Child-Rearing Practices (Aggression)

Permissiveness toward aggression against other children increases aggression anxiety in both boys and girls, but affects girls much more than boys. (S246)

### Identification with Like-Sex Parent

Identification with like-sex parent correlates with frequency of aggression in doll play for boys, but not for girls, unless the mother is atypically aggressive. (L157)

## AGGRESSION (FANTASY)
### X   Child-Rearing Practices (Punishment)

Children of more severely punishing mothers display more fantasy aggression than do other children. (S191)

## AGGRESSION/GUILT   X   Paternal/Maternal Role

Families where the mother is the main source of love and the father the primary disciplinary agent are associated with aggressiveness in the child; families in which the mother is the primary agent of both discipline and love are associated with repression and intrapunitiveness in the child. (H201)

## AGGRESSION OF MOTHER
### X   Mental Illness (Schizophrenia)

Schizophrenia tends to be directly correlated with a pattern of concealed maternal aggressiveness. (N061)

### Mother-Child Relations (Affection)

Due to a process of sublimation, there is a correlation between the mother's aggressive instincts and the extent of her tenderness for her infant. (B272)

### Mother-Child Relations (Protectiveness)

By a process of sublimation, there is a correlation between the mother's aggressive instincts and the extent of her protective activity on behalf of her infant. (B272)

## AGGRESSION OF PARENT          X   Aggression

When both parents are low in aggressiveness, then the child is also low in aggressiveness. (E091)

The level of aggression of the like-sex parent will be most influential in determining frequency of aggression in doll play by the child. (L157)

## ALCOHOLISM
### X   Child-Rearing Practices (Consistency)

Alcoholism is correlated with an erratic pattern of severity and indulgence on the part of the father. (C122)

When the parental authority pattern is severe yet erratic, alcoholism is likely to occur; when it is consistently severe, schizophrenia is a more likely consequence. (C122)

If an adult nonkin member of the household imposes demands counter to those of the parents, the son is more likely to become alcoholic. (M195)

### Child-Rearing Practices (Control)

The more that the father exerts a controlling and punitive discipline over the son, the more likely the son is to become alcoholic. (M195)

The less the parental supervision of the boy, the more likely he is to become an alcoholic. (M195)

### Child-Rearing Practices (Demands)

The higher the parental demands made on the son, the less likely is he to become an alcoholic. (M195)

### Child-Rearing Practices (Dependency)

The greater the family's satisfaction of the child's dependency needs, the less likely is he to become alcoholic. (M195)

The more conflict the family creates in the son concerning his dependency needs, the more likely he is to become alcoholic. (M195)

### Child-Rearing Practices (Restrictiveness)

There is a negative correlation between the degree of restrictiveness which the mother exerts over the son and the development of alcoholism in the son. (M195)

### Child-Rearing Practices (Sex Role)

There is no correlation between the mother's discouragement of independent or masculine behavior in the son and the son's alcoholism. (M195)

### Death of Father

Alcoholic women are likely to have experienced the deaths of their fathers at an earlier age than are nonalcoholic women. (H222)

There is no difference between alcoholic and nonalcoholic males and the age at which they experienced the death of their fathers. (H222)

### Dependency/Sex-Role Identification

Boys reared in family situations which create in them both dependency conflicts and role confusion are more likely to become alcoholics. (M195)

### Descent (Bilateral)

Heavy drinking is associated with bilateral descent. (W127)

### Deviance of Mother/Father

Social deviance (criminality, alcoholism, adultery) on the part of the mother is correlated with alcoholism in the son; paternal deviance is not. (M195)

### Drinking

Alcoholics are more likely to have had parents with inconsistent attitudes toward drinking than are nonalcoholics. (D078)

### Extended Family

Alcoholism is less likely to occur in the extended family system. (T110)

### Father-Child Relations (Affection)

Alcoholism tends to be correlated with a father whose attitude is cold and dominating. (C122)

### Father-Child Relations (Rejection)
The more rejecting the father is of the son, the more likely that the latter will become an alcoholic. (M195)

Alcoholic fathers are more likely than nonalcoholic fathers to reject their sons. (M195)

### Husband-Wife Relations (Dominance-Mothering)
Wives of alcoholics are more likely to be domineering and mothering than wives of nonalcoholics. (D078)

### Marital Adjustment
The more a husband's alcoholism provides unconscious gratification for both partners, the more resistant to change are both the alcoholism and the marital conflict which it generates. (B225)

### Maternal Overprotectiveness
Maternal overprotection and pampering of the child are causes of alcoholism in later life. (M195)

Maternal overprotection of the child is not related to alcoholism in later life. (M195)

### Maternal-Role Behavior
Mothers who resent their role in the family, as expressed by assuming the role of a martyr or by neglecting the home, are more likely to have alcoholic sons than are mothers who play passive, active, or dictatorial roles in the home. (M195)

### Mother-Child Relations (Affection)
Alcoholism is associated with the child's having a definitely expressed and disproportionately greater love for his mother than for his father. (D078)

### Mother-Child Relations (Consistency)
The more alternating and inconsistent the mother is in her affections, the more likely it is that alcoholism will develop in the son. (M195)

### Mother-Child Relations (Rejection)
There is a correlation between maternal rejection and alcoholism in the son, when the father is present. (M195)

### Mother-Son Relations (Hostility)
Alcoholism tends to be correlated with a pattern of masked hostility on the part of the mother. (C122)

### Neurosis of Mother
The mother of the alcoholic is likely to be neurotic—the unsatisfied, masochistic woman escaping the feminine role and exhibiting martyred or shrewish attitudes. (C122)

### Oral Problems
Oral fixation, produced by overindulgence or frustration during the oral stage of development, is associated with alcoholism. (M195)

### Ordinal Position
In families where the parents are alcoholics, younger siblings are more likely than older siblings to become alcoholics. (G125)

The relationship between birth order and alcoholism disappears when parental loss is controlled; hence, birth rank as an independent variable has no place in the etiology of alcoholism. (L159)

There are significantly more last-born, than first- or middle-born, children among alcoholics. (L159)

### Parent-Child Relations (Dominance)
Alcoholism is associated with a domineering but idealized mother and a stern, autocratic father whom one fears as a child. (D078)

### Parent-Child Relations (Rejection)
Alcoholics are more likely than nonalcoholics to have rejected their parents, particularly their mothers, during childhood. (M195)

### Parent Loss
Loss of a parent in early childhood is more frequently a factor in the history of female than of male alcoholics. (L159)

Since female alcoholics are more likely than males to have lost a parent in early childhood and are, thus, more prone to psychotic disturbance, their prognosis is less favorable than that for male alcoholics. (L159)

### Personality of Mother
Alcoholism tends to be correlated with a serious frustration of ego needs on the part of the mother. (C122)

### Personality of Mother (Insecurity)
Alcoholism tends to be associated with a high degree of maternal insecurity. (C122)

### Personality of Parents
Alcoholism is more likely among people who had a stern, autocratic father and an overprotective mother.

Among upper-class parents of alcoholics, mothers are more likely to be overindulgent and overprotective and fathers to lack affection, be domineering, and overly severe than are parents of nonalcoholic offspring. (B261)

### Personality of Parents (Maturity)
Parents of alcoholics are more likely to be emotionally immature than are parents of nonalcoholics. (B261)

### Personality Problems of Husband/Wife
Alcoholic husbands are more poorly adjusted than their wives (MMPI), particularly tending to act out in an antisocial manner. In nonalcoholic but conflicting couples, the reverse is true, but to a lesser extent. (B225)

### Personality Problems of Parents
Parents whose reactions to crises are escapist, rather than realistic or aggressive, are more likely to have sons who become alcoholics. (M195)

### Personality Problems of Wife
Alcoholism in the husband is correlated with feelings of inadequacy and a need for dominance in the wife.

### Power Structure of Family
Alcoholics are more likely than others to have indulgent, overprotective mothers and domineering, inconsistently severe fathers.

The alcoholic father is more likely to play a passive and dependent role in his family than a dominant one. (M195)

### Religiosity
Strong adherance to Catholicism by the mother correlates negatively with alcoholism in the son. (M195)

### Sex Anxiety of Mother
There is no correlation between the mother's sexual anxiety and alcoholism in the son. (M195)

### Sex-Role Identification
There is a correlation between alcoholism in men and their earlier rejection of their paternal model. (M195)

### Sex Status
### X   Dependency Sex-Role Conflict
Among alcoholics, females are more likely than males to have a background of role confusion (rather than of dependency conflict). (M195)

### Sexual Deviance
There is a correlation between sexual deviance in the family, as expressed in incest or illegitimacy, and later alcoholism in the child. (M195)

### Sibling Relations (Affection)
Alcoholics are more likely than nonalcoholics to have been cool or indifferent toward their siblings during childhood. (M195)

### Size of Family
Since later-born children tend to be less welcome and less often breast-fed (and both patterns frustrate their dependency needs), large families (i.e. with more later-borns) are likely to produce a greater number of alcoholics than are small families. (S236)

### Weaning
Alcoholism is associated with a pattern of indulgence in feeding followed by a traumatic period at weaning. (C122)

## ALCOHOLISM, ATTITUDE TOWARD
### X   Sex Status
Women are more likely to be sympathetic to an alcoholic husband than are men to an alcoholic wife.

## ALCOHOLISM/CRIMINALITY
### X   Immigrant/Nonimmigrant
Parental immigration is negatively related to alcoholism, but is unrelated to criminality. (M195)

### Power Structure of Family
Boys from families in which the father is dominant are more likely to become criminal than alcoholic. (M195)

## ALCOHOLISM IN FAMILY
### X   Alcoholism of Child
Children from alcoholic families are more likely to go to extremes regarding their drinking behavior than are children from nonalcoholic families; that is, they tend to become alcoholics or they do not drink at all. (D078)

### Psychosomatic Illness of Child
Children from alcoholic families have more psychosomatic illnesses than do children from nonalcoholic families. (D078)

## ALCOHOLISM OF CHILD
### X   Alcoholism in Family
Children from alcoholic families are more likely to go to extremes regarding their drinking behavior than are children from nonalcoholic families; that is, they tend to become alcoholics or they do not drink at all. (D078)

### Child-Rearing Practices (Protection)
Alcoholism is more likely to occur when parents lack confidence in the child's ability and fear that they must shield him. (C122)

### Child-Rearing Practices (Strictness)
Alcoholics are more likely to have been reared in exceedingly strict homes where obedience was unquestioned and little freedom was allowed. (D078)

### Marital Adjustment
The greater the degree of parental conflict, the more likely it is that the child will become an alcoholic. (M195)

## ALCOHOLISM OF FATHER
### X   Behavior Problems of Son/Daughter
Sons of alcoholic fathers are more likely to develop behavior problems than are daughters. (B285)

### Incest
Fathers who have had sexual relations with their daughters are also more likely to be alcoholic. (K119)

### Juvenile Delinquency
Alcoholism of father contributes indirectly to delinquency of child by contributing to the development of the traits of hostility and unconventionality. (W152)

Boys who have the feeling of not being appreciated, the feeling of isolation and introversiveness, are more likely to develop into delinquents if they have alcoholic fathers.

Fathers of delinquents are more likely to drink than are fathers of nondelinquents. (W152)

## ALCOHOLISM OF HUSBAND
### X   Marital Adjustment
There is a correlation between alcoholism of the husband and intense marital conflict. (M195)

### Personality Problems of Wife
When the husband stops drinking (alcoholism) the wife is apt to develop a more severe personal pathology than she had while the husband was an alcoholic. (B225)

Wives of alcoholics showed fewer symptoms of mental disturbance when their husbands were sober than when they were drinking. (H238)

## ALCOHOLISM OF MOTHER
### X   Juvenile Delinquency
Alcoholism of the mother is associated more with delinquents than with nondelinquents and may contribute indirectly to the delinquency of the son through development of the trait of unconventionality. (W152)

## ALCOHOLISM OF PARENT
### X   Identification with Parents
Alcoholism in a parent impedes adequate identification by the child with a parent figure.

### Neurosis of Child
Children of alcoholics are more likely to be neurotic and alcoholics themselves.

### Neurosis/Psychopathy
Children from families with an alcoholic parent are more likely to be neurotic than psychotic. (B285)

## ALCOHOLISM OF SON
### X   Husband-Wife Relations (Conflict)
Overtly antagonistic parents are more likely to produce an alcoholic son than are parents who are indifferent or affectionate. (M195)

### Husband-Wife Relations (Evaluation)
The lower the esteem of the father for the mother, the more likely it is that the son will become an alcoholic. (M195)

### Marital Adjustment of Parents
Alcoholism is more likely to occur if the mother manipulates the son in response to a perceived indifference of her husband toward her marriage. (C122)

### Mother-Son Relations (Achievement)
Alcoholism is correlated with a compulsive concern with ambition for the son on the part of the mother. (C122)

### Remarriage
There is no correlation between the number of the mother's marriages and alcoholism in the son. (M195)

## ALIMONY    X    Class
The lower the socioeconomic status of the male, the greater the likelihood of his being able to escape child support and alimony expenditures. (G134)

## ANALOGY    X    Incest Taboo
To the extent that any secondary or more remote relative resembles a sexually tabooed member of the nuclear family, avoidance behavior will tend to be extended to him. (M019)

### Joking Relationship
When joking relationships between particular relations are prescribed, those in analogous relationships are treated in the same way. (L111)

### Kin-Role Definition
Kin roles tend to be extended to all individuals who stand in a comparable relationship to classificatory kinsmen. (R069)

### Kin Terminology (Classificatory)
When ego's classificatory kinsmen stand in a given relationship to one another, ego is more likely to use a classificatory terminology for them which is comparable to their relationship to one another (e.g., if he calls his father's brothers "father," he calls their children "brother and sister"). (H104)

## ANCESTORS    X    Kin-Role Definition
The character of relations (e.g., resentment, fear) between kinsmen will tend to be projected onto the society's conception of dead ancestors. (K050)

### Property
When there are no family property holdings to inherit or defend, there is no pattern of binding new family unity to an ancestral tradition. (O002)

## ANXIETY    X    Achievement
## X    Ordinal Position
Under really frightening conditions firstborn individuals will be less effective than later-born individuals. (S263)

### Child-Rearing Practices (Consistency)
Sleep disturbances and nightmares of the child are associated with lack of consistency in the mother's child-rearing practices. (R113)

### Child-Rearing Practices (Dependency)
The greater the number of dependency needs that are not met by the parents, the greater the anxiety produced in the child. (S202)

### Child-Rearing Practices (Sex Role)
Resulting from sex-typed child-rearing practices, girls tend to be more anxious than boys. (B252)

### Dependency
The less dependent the child is on the parents, the less anxiety he will feel over the anticipation of loss of their love. (K103)

### Father Absence
When the father is absent from the home, there is a greater likelihood that anxiety will develop in the child. (M181)

### Identification of Mother with Daughter
A high degree of anxiety and anxious dependence in regard to the mother is inversely correlated with the mother's degree of indentification with the daughter. (H218)

A high degree of anxiety in regard to the mother's safety is inversely correlated with the mother's degree of identification with the daughter. (H218)

A high degree of general anxiety is inversely correlated with the mother's degree of identification with the daughter. (H218)

### Identification with Like-Sex Parent
In therapy situations, low-anxiety subjects describe their like-sexed parents as more like themselves than do high-anxiety subjects. (L145)

### Maternal Overprotectiveness
Overprotective and infantilizing behavior on the part of the mother toward the child tends to foster chronic anxiety in the child. (R113)

### Mother Absence
Since the death instinct operates in the child as the fear of annihilation, the separation of the child from his mother induces neurotic anxiety as the expression of this instinct in addition to the apprehension that the infant has destroyed (by his sadistic impulses) his mother (the persecutory object). (B255)

### Mother-Child Relations (Rejection)
If the mother consistently reacts with disapproval to the infant's need for tenderness, he will react with anxiety. (B255)

### Neurosis in Family
Within neurotic families, members tend to exhibit similar kinds of anxieties. (F077)

### Occupation of Father
Children whose fathers are of professional status have lower anxiety scores (as measured by the Test Anxiety Scale) than children whose fathers are nonprofessionals. (A062)

### Ordinal Position
The later born the child, the less anxious and fearful he is likely to become in an anxiety-producing situation. (S263)

Communicating with others has less effect on the anxiety level of later-born subjects than on firstborns. This proposition is also denied. (S263)

The simple physical presence of others is more likely to reduce the anxiety level of firstborn and only children than is the case for later-born children. (S263)

Firstborn children are more anxious than later-born children. (T095)

### Ordinal Position
### X    Personality (Affiliative Need)
In an anxiety-producing situation, firstborn and only

children are much more likely than later-born individuals to seek the company of others. (S263)

The later born the child, the less likely he is to respond to anxiety by seeking company. (S263)

When anxiety level is held constant (when only truly anxious subjects are considered), firstborn and only children are more likely than later-born subjects to seek the company of others. (S263)

Firstborn subjects from both small and large families are more likely than later-born persons to respond to anxiety by seeking company. (S263)

### Parent-Child Relations
The greater the anxiety in the child (provoked by the confusion of his parents), the more likely it is to be displaced away from the disturbed relationship and into a phobia of an object. (C119)

### Parent-Child Relations (Affection)
A rise in affectional frustration will be accompanied by a corresponding anxiety toward frustration from this source. (T106)

### Parent-Child Relations (Evaluation)
Parents of children with low anxiety view their children more favorably (based on personality ratings) than do parents of children with high anxiety. (D072)

Mothers do not evaluate their children any differently on personality checklists, whether the children have high or low anxiety. (D072)

Fathers of low-anxiety children evaluate them more favorably (on personality checklists) than do fathers of high-anxiety children. (D072)

Parents of boys with low anxiety are more likely to evaluate them as more mature, better leaders, and more generous and affectionate than do parents of boys with high anxiety. (D072)

Parents of girls with low anxiety are more likely to evaluate them as relaxed and adaptable than are parents of girls with high anxiety. (D072)

Parents of high-anxiety girls are more likely to see them as more ambitious than are parents of low-anxiety girls. (D072)

### Parent-Child Relations (Hostility)
Anxiety in the child may lead to hostile behavior toward the parents. (T086)

### Parent-Child Relations (Rejection)
There is a correlation between parental rejection and anxiety in the child. (T086)

### Personality (Fear)
There is a correlation between the degree of fear of others (persons and spirits), typical for a culture, and the degree of anxiety typically produced by socialization in that culture. (W142)

### Religion, Role of Deities
Societies with predominantly aggressive deities (accompanied by more hurt and pain and less nurturance in infancy) are more likely to produce anxiety in the child than are societies with predominantly benevolent deities (accompanied by considerable nurturance and less pain in infancy). (L141)

### Remarriage
Children of broken homes are likely to show more anxiety if the parent remarries than if he (she) does not. (R129)

### Sex-Role Identification
Because boys experience greater anxiety than girls, due to their transition from mother tie to father identification, boys are less likely to emulate their fathers directly than are girls to emulate their mothers directly.

### Sibling Status
Only children tend to be less fearful and anxious than firstborn children. (S263)

### Sibling Structure
In three-child families, firstborn girls and nonfirstborn boys are least likely to be anxious and to have sex identification conflicts; in a two-child family the second-born child with a sibling of the same sex is least likely to have such problems. (R114)

### Sibling Structure (Sex)
Only male children are more anxious; only female children are less anxious than are children with other sibling sets. (R114)

In two-child families, the older child with a younger sibling of the same sex is more anxious, and the older child with a younger sibling of the opposite sex is less anxious than the norm. (R114)

In three-child families, firstborn children with siblings of the opposite sex are highly anxious; those with siblings of the same sex are low on anxiety. (R114)

### Size of Family
The larger the family, the less anxious the children are likely to be. (R114)

Subjects from large families are less anxious than subjects from small families. (S263)

The difference in anxiety level between first- and later-born children is greater in small families than it is in large families. (S263)

### Socialization, Severity of
There is a correlation between the severity of socialization imposed upon the child in any system of behavior and the degree of anxiety and concern regarding that system in later life (negative fixation). (W142)

### Surrogate Mother
Children who are cared for by someone other than the mother for a significant proportion of the time are likely to have neurotic anxiety symptoms such as phobias and to tend to act peculiarly. (R113)

### ANXIETY DREAMS          X   Dependency
Individuals with falling dreams are far more likely to be overdependent on their mothers than are individuals with attack dreams. (H216)

### Maternal Overprotectiveness
Falling dreams will tend to occur in cases of marked maternal overprotectiveness. (H216)

### ANXIETY (NIGHTMARES)
### X   Mother-Child Relations (Seductiveness)
Children whose mothers are overly seductive in their behavior toward the child are likely to have frequent nightmares. (R113)

## ANXIETY OF CHILD        X   Anxiety of Parents
Children's anxiety scores on the TAS, LPS, and MAS tests are more highly correlated with the mother's anxiety scores than the father's. (A057)

Anxiety scores of both boys and girls are positively related more so to mother's than father's anxiety scores as measured by four anxiety scales (Test Anxiety Scale, Need for Achievement Scale, Lack of Protection Scale, and Taylor's Manifest Anxiety Scale). (A062)

There is a correlation between conflicting anxieties in the parent and anxiety in the child. (C119)

## ANXIETY OF FATHER          X   Anxiety of Son
There is a slight tendency for anxiety scores of boys to be positively related to the anxiety scores of their fathers (measured by Test Anxiety Scale, Need for Achievement Scale, Lack of Protection Scale, and Taylor's Manifest Anxiety Scale). (A062)

## ANXIETY OF MOTHER          X   Aggression
The greater the child-rearing anxiety of the mother (anxiety about child, conflict with child, maladjustment, dissatisfaction, low self-esteem), the greater the aggressive behavior of the child. (B232)

Mothers who are highly anxious concerning child rearing report more aggressive children than mothers who are not as anxious (U.S.). (S191)

### Emotional Adjustment of Child
The higher the anxiety level of the mother, the lower the rate of development in early childhood and the lower the child's emotional adjustment. (D075)

### Health of Child
Infants of less anxious mothers (as measured by MMPI protocols) show as high or higher incidence of gastrointestinal disturbances (frequency of regurgitation and burping) than infants of more anxious mothers. (P072)

### Illness of Child
There is no evidence that mothers of cerebral-palsied children exhibit more anxiety than mothers of normal children. (B320)

### Mental Illness (Schizophrenia)
Schizophrenia tends to be associated with a pattern of concealed tension and anxiety in the mother. (T105)

### Sex-Role Adjustment
The higher the anxiety level in the woman, the greater the tendency for her to experience conflict with her husband and manifest irritability toward her children. (D075)

### Size of Family
The smaller the number of children born to the mother, the higher her anxiety about their health. (R112)

## ANXIETY OF PARENTS         X   Anxiety of Child
Children's anxiety scores on the TAS, NAS, LPS, and MAS tests are more highly correlated with the mother's anxiety scores than the father's. (A057)

Anxiety scores of both boys and girls are positively related more so to mother's than father's anxiety scores, as measured by four anxiety scales (Test Anxiety Scale, Need for Achievement Scale, Lack of Protection Scale, and Taylor's Manifest Anxiety Scale). (A062)

There is a correlation between conflicting anxieties in the parent and anxiety in the child. (C119)

### Identification with Parents
Identification is positively associated with moderate parental anxiety over impulse expression, particularly in the areas of aggression and sexuality. (R098)

### Juvenile Delinquency
Severe delinquency is frequently associated with acute parental anxieties of inadequacy. (B291)

### Mental Illness (Schizophrenia)
Schizophrenic patients will tend to have parents who are afraid of any intense emotions, whether of love, anger, envy, or jealousy. (S259)

### Personality Problems of Child
Parental anxiety about certain developmental stages in the child overstimulates or understimulates the child and may produce the same problem in the child as the parents have. (A069)

## ANXIETY OF SON            X   Anxiety of Father
There is a slight tendency for anxiety scores of boys to be positively related to the anxiety scores of their fathers (measured by Test Anxiety Scale, Need for Achievement Scale, Lack of Protection Scale, and Taylor's Manifest Anxiety Scale). (A062)

### Mother-Son Relations (Self-Ideal)
There is a correlation between the degree of discrepancy between the boy's self-perception and his mother's ideal for him and the degree of his manifest anxiety. (S225)

## ANXIETY /SELF-CONCEPTION          X   Divorce
Divorce may have more influence upon level of anxiety in the child than upon level of self-esteem. (R129)

## ANXIETY (WEANING)         X   Ordinal Position
Older children are more likely to experience anxiety in the weaning and nursing situations than are middle or younger children. (S202)

## ART        X   Child-Rearing Practices (Severity)
Decorative art forms are more likely to be complex in societies that are generally severe in training their children. (W127)

### Socialization Anxiety
There is a correlation between the degree of socialization anxiety characteristic of a society and the complexity of design of that society's art. (K111)

## ART (DESIGN MOTIFS)
        X   Kin Terminology (Generation)
Kinship systems which merge alternate generations (Crow) will tend to use alternating patterns as design motifs. (B304)

Kinship systems with generational terminology (Hawaiian) will tend to use horizontal segmentary patterns as design motifs. (B304)

## ARTIFICIAL INSEMINATION, ATTITUDE
## TOWARD                      X   Religion
Roman Catholics are more likely to disapprove of artificial insemination, regardless of whether the donor is the husband or anonymous, than are persons with other religious affiliations. (V035)

### Scholastic Achievement
The greater the academic achievement of the college student, the more likely he is to accept artificial insemination. (V035)

The greater the academic achievement of the college student, the less likely he is to accept artificial insemination. (V035)

### Sex Status
Women are more likely than men to accept artificial insemination in cases where the husband is the donor. (V035)

Women are less likely than men to accept artificial insemination in cases when the donor is other than the husband. (V035)

## ASCRIPTION/ACHIEVEMENT
### X    Parent-Child Relations (Conflict)
The less the choices of life (e.g., education, occupation, marriage) are settled beforehand by ascription, the greater the degree of parent-youth conflict. (D058)

## ASPIRATION LEVEL          X    Age at Marriage
Girls who marry in their teens are less likely to have a high aspiration level (further education or training) than those who do not. (M231)

### Authoritarianism
Parents who score high on authoritarianism (on the California F–scale) are likely to have higher expectations for their children than are parents who are not authoritarian. (K117)

### Disorganization of Family
Incomplete families inhibit the child's ambition only in families where middle-class values are most fully entrenched. (T095)

### Education of Parents
High parental education is associated with high ambition in the child. (T095)

### Father-Child Relations (Closeness)
The higher a person's level of aspiration, the less frequently he confided in his father in childhood. (D001)

### Father-Child Relations (Punishment)
People with high levels of aspiration were more fearful of punishment from their fathers in childhood than were those with low levels of aspiration. (D001)

### Fertility
White collar men with several children have higher levels of aspiration than those with few children. (L115)

### Happiness in Childhood
People who experienced a lesser degree of happiness in their childhood had higher levels of aspiration than those who had experienced a greater degree of happiness. (D001)

Students who have high ambitions (as measured by the Reissman Scale of Ambition) are more likely to feel they have had an unhappy childhood than those who do not have high ambitions. (T095)

### Interaction in Family
Satisfaction with interpersonal relationships in the family of orientation is inversely correlated with high aspirational level of the individual. (D001)

### Interaction in Family (Affection)
Females with high aspirations are more likely to perceive their family milieu as depriving than are females with lower aspirations. (R117)

Males with high aspirations are more likely to perceive their milieu as depriving than are males with lower aspirations. (R117)

### Mental Illness (Schizophrenia)
Parents of normals have higher aspiration levels than do parents of neurotics or schizophrenics. (F110)

Schizophrenia tends to be correlated with strong feelings of ambition on the part of the mother for the patient and her tendency to live vicariously through the patient. (N061)

### Ordinal Position
There is no relationship between ambition level and sibling position when family size is held constant. (T095)

### Parent-Child Relations
Young people with high occupational aspirations are more likely to have experienced unsatisfactory interpersonal relationships with their parents than are students with lower levels of aspiration. (R117)

### Parent-Child Relations (Attachment)
Students who have high ambitions (as measured by the Reissman Scale of Ambition) express less attachment to their parents than do those who do not have high ambitions. (T095)

### Parent-Child Relations (Evaluation)
If the child is overvalued by his parents, his aspirational level will be above realistic expectations of success. (A059)

### Parent-Child Relations (Favoritism)
"High" aspirers define their parents as showing more favoritism toward some child in the family than do "low" aspirers. (D001)

### Parent-Child Relations (Harshness)
Adolescent boys with high aspirations are less apt to perceive their parents as harsh than are those with lower aspirations. (R117)

### Parent-Child Relations (Interaction)
Boys with high aspirations are more likely to have participated in shared activities with their parents than are boys with lower aspirations. (R117)

### Parent-Child Relations (Rejection)
The more the child is rejected by his parents (consequently, suffering a reduction in self-esteem), the more likely is his development of an aspirational level that is far in excess of realistic considerations. (A059)

People with high levels of aspiration are more likely to have had feelings of not being wanted by their parents when they were children than are people with low levels of aspiration. (D001)

Students who are high aspirers (as measured by Reissman Ambition Scale) are more likely to feel rejected by their parents than are those who are not high aspirers. (T095)

### Parent-Child Relations (Support)
Male adolescents who are given high aspirational encouragement from parents are more apt to possess higher levels of ambition than are those given low parental motivation. (B313)

### Scholastic Achievement
Children who drop out of high school are more likely to have parents who are indifferent to their school attendance than are those who do not drop out. (H189)

### Sibling Relations (Conflict)
There is no significant difference in the degree of sibling conflict between people who have high levels of aspiration and those who have low levels of aspiration. (D001)

There is no significant relationship between the level of aspiration and the degree of sibling conflict in childhood. (D001)

### Size of Family
Parents in small families are more likely to have higher aspirations for their children than are parents in large families. (R106)

Boys from large families are less likely to have high ambitions than are boys from smaller families. This relationship does not apply for females. (T095)

Students from small families are more likely to have higher educational than material ambitions; students from large families, higher material than educational ambitions. (T095)

### Surrogate Mother
When their infants are six months of age, mothers who have been the only caretaking figure for their infants have higher achievement aspirations for their children than have mothers who have provided other maternal figures for their infants. (C107)

When the child is six months of age, mothers who have reared the child themselves have higher achievement expectations for the child than have mothers of children who have been reared by more than one mother figure, i.e., a nurse, grandparent, friend of mother, older sister of child. (C124)

## ASPIRATION LEVEL OF MOTHER
### X   Maternal Overprotectiveness
Maternal overprotectiveness is likely to occur if the mother has been thwarted in her educational or career ambitions. (L163)

## ASPIRATIONS (CLARITY OF GOALS)
### X   Child-Rearing Practices (Clarity)
Adults from more structured homes with clear standards have more clearly perceived goals than those from less structured homes. (L172)

## ASSIMILATION
### X   Intermarriage (Racial and Ethnic)
The greater the rate of assimilation, the higher the rate of interracial and interethnic marriages. (B311)

## ATHLETICS                              X   Peer Relations
The fathers of adolescent boys who are accepted by their peers are more likely to be interested in athletic activities than are the fathers of boys who are rejected by their peers. (F108)

## AUTHORITARIANISM
### X   Accident-Proneness of Child
Children who grow up in an authoritarian home environment in which feelings of rejection and resulting hostility are fostered are more likely to become accident-prone than those who are raised in a permissive home (the manifestation of an inward turning of aggression). (K122)

### Achievement Motivation
The more permissive the familial atmosphere, the greater the achievement motivation of the child. (D074)

The more restrictive and authoritarian the familial atmosphere, the greater the achievement motivation of the child. (D074)

### Aspiration Level
Parents who score high on authoritarianism (on the California F–scale) are likely to have higher expectations for their children than are parents who are not authoritarian. (K117)

### Child-Rearing Practices (Control)
Use of the threat that God will punish the child's deviant behavior as a means of controlling the child is associated with parents who have authoritarian personality structures. (N055)

### Child-Rearing Practices (Rigidity)
Authoritarianism of parents is correlated with parental rigidity and intolerance concerning children's noise, antics, etc. (H209)

### Class
Middle-class adolescents are more likely to view their parents as democratic, equalitarian, or permissive, whereas their lower-class counterparts are more likely to consider their parents to be autocratic or authoritarian. (E100)

Authoritarianism is less likely to be translated directly into power assertion over the children in the middle class than in the lower class because of the middle-class child-rearing norms which inhibit direct expressions of power. (H213)

### Class Anxiety of Parents
Authoritarian parents are more likely to feel threatened in their social and economic status than are normal parents. (M203)

### Cohesion of Family
### X   Interaction in Family (Affection/Duty)
Among democratic families, voluntary exchange of emotions, (i.e., affection, happiness, and satisfaction between family members) leads to family solidarity; among authoritarian families, a greater sense of duty and responsibility lead to increased family solidarity. (K113)

### Conformity
The more authoritarian the male adolescent, the more likely he is to follow the motivational directives of his parents concerning academic matters. (B297)

### Creativity of Child
The punitive and intimidating atmosphere of the authoritarian home is likely to result in a diminishing of the creativity and imagination of the child. (M203)

### Education of Mother
The degree to which the mother is possessive or authoritarian is inversely related to the amount of education she has received. (S187)

### Employment of Mother
Working mothers tend to be less authoritarian and more equalitarian than nonworking mothers. (G128)

### Father-Son Relations
Poor father-son relations tend to produce an authoritarian orientation in the son. (L179)

### Interaction with Peer/Parent
Children are likely to be democratic in their social behavior if they spend more time with peers who have

the same power, rather than with parents who are of superior power. (G136)

### Marital Adjustment

There is a greater marital maladjustment (measured by the Burgess–Cottrell marriage adjustment schedule) among authoritarian than among democratic families. (K113)

### Marital Adjustment
### X   Parent-Child Relations

Satisfactory parent-child relations is a more important factor in the marital adjustment of democratic families than of authoritarian families. (K113)

### Marital Adjustment
### X   Peer Relations

There is no relationship between marital adjustment and the child's relations with his peers for either authoritarian or democratic families. (K113)

### Moral Beliefs of Child

Authoritarian families are more likely than others to have children who exhibit immature moral judgment, especially in the areas of immanent justice and belief in the efficacy of extreme punishment. (B275)

### Parent-Child Relations (Affection)

Authoritarianism of parents does not correlate with the intensity of affection between parents and child. (H209)

### Parent-Child Relations (Dominance)

Preschool children who exhibit authoritarian behavior tend to have parents who are dominant and possessive toward their children.

### Parent-Child Relations (Evaluation)

The greater the person's authoritarianism, the lower his evaluation of his parents. (C107)

### Paternal/Maternal Role

Fathers of disturbed children are likely to be more authoritarian than mothers. (P067)

### Peer Relations

Children from democratic homes tend to be more popular among their peers than children from authoritarian homes. (K113)

### Personality Adjustment

Democratic parents are no more likely to have better-adjusted children than are authoritarian parents.

### Personality Problems of Child

Parents who have an authoritarian ideology tend to be dominant and possessive of their children and these traits are associated with the development of social and psychological problems (criminality, neuroses, psychoses). (K117)

### Religion

In small families, Catholic parents are more likely to be either autocratic or authoritarian. (E100)

### Scholastic/Creative Achievement

Parents of academic achievers are more authoritarian in their values and attitudes than are parents of creative adolescents. (E102)

### Sex Composition of Family

If females, rather than males, are predominant among the children in the family, the mother is likely to score higher on authoritarianism, fostering dependency, breaking the will, martyrdom, deification, inconsiderateness of husband, suppression of sex, ascendence of

mother, intrusiveness, and dependency of mother. (PARI) (Z011)

### Social Adjustment

Children from democratic homes tend to be socially more outgoing than those from authoritarian homes. (K113)

### Speech Problems

Children with articulation problems are more likely to view their parents as authoritarian than are children without articulation problems. (F095)

## AUTHORITARIANISM OF CHILD
### X   Child-Rearing Practices (Discipline)

Children who are very authoritarian and ethnocentric are likely to have parents who use rigid and harsh forms of discipline. (L149)

## AUTHORITARIANISM OF FATHER
### X   Achievement Motivation

Authoritarian fathers tend to have children with lower achievement motivation than do less authoritarian fathers. (R097)

### Child-Rearing Attitudes

Democratic attitudes in the father significantly correlate with the attitudes of equalitarian treatment of children and the encouragement of their independence and affection as a means of control. (N053)

### Criminality

Normal persons are more likely than habitual criminals to have authoritarian fathers. (C105)

### Size of Family

Fathers in small families, particularly in the middle class, tend to be less authoritarian than fathers in large families. (R106)

## AUTHORITARIANISM OF MOTHER
### X   Child-Rearing Practices (Discipline)

Mothers who score high in authoritarianism (on the basis of interviews and a modified F–scale) tend to prefer nonlove-oriented discipline techniques. (H200)

### Employment of Mother

Working mothers tend to be less authoritarian and more equalitarian than nonworking mothers. (G127)

### Ethnic Attitudes of Child

If a mother has authoritarian attitudes her children tend to share her ethnic bias. (M222)

### Occupation of Mother

If a mother holds an entrepreneurial job she is more likely to be authoritarian than if she holds a bureaucratic job. (J022)

### Sex Education

The more authoritarian the mother, the less likely it is that the mother will communicate with the daughter, particularly on sexual matters. (B245)

### Sexual Deviance

If the mother is authoritarian, the son is more likely to become a sexual deviant. (M209)

## AUTHORITARIANISM OF MOTHER/FATHER
### X   Child-Rearing Practices (Control)

The father's authoritarianism and power needs correlate with both his and his wife's claim to unqualified power relative to the child, but the mother's authoritarianism is not related to her claim to power. (H182)

### Child-Rearing Values

Women who are very authoritarian (as measured by the F–scale) are more likely than men who are very authoritarian to view their children in subordinate and restricted roles. (K117)

## AUTHORITY          X   Economic Role

The authority of a kinsman will be directly correlated with his control of the kin-group's economic resources. (W082)

## AUTHORITY, ATTITUDE TOWARD
### X   Father-Child Relations (Authority)

There is a correlation between the individual's attitude toward the authority of the father and his attitude toward impersonal sources of authority, such as the state, teachers, etc. (M214)

There is no relationship between the individual's attitude toward paternal authority and his attitude toward more impersonal, nonparental sources of authority. (M214)

### Homosexuality

Overt homosexuality may develop as a method of expressing defiance of authority. (T104)

## AUTHORITY STRUCTURE
### X   Adoption of Outsiders

Avuncular authority in matrilineal society is weakened with the institution of adopting slave children. (S069)

### Cohesion of Joint Family

The more efficiency and technical knowledge, rather than seniority, become the basis for decision making, the greater the threat to the solidarity of the joint family system. (G156)

### Legal Status

The more closely associated a person (e.g., father) is to the status possessing the most jural authority (e.g., grandfather) in a hierarchy, the less likely he is to have an informal and equal relationship with his own subordinates in the hierarchy. (A009)

### Preferential Marriage (Cross-Cousin)

The type of cross-cousin marriage which occurs will be directly correlated with the relative who exercises control over the allocation of a female as a wife (i.e., patrilateral—father's sister's husband; matrilateral—mother's brother; avuncular—mother's brother's wife's brother). (C126)

## AUTHORITY STRUCTURE OF CLAN   X   Divorce

The incidence of divorce will tend to increase with the weakening of the clan authority structure. (S158)

## AUTHORITY STRUCTURE OF FAMILY
### X   Acculturation

The authority of the father deteriorates as children become increasingly oriented toward the donor culture. (S051)

### Adultery

The weakening of parental authority is directly correlated with an increase in extramarital relations. (G068)

### Adultery, Attitude Toward

Tolerance toward extramarital relations will increase with a weakening of the family authority structure. (S158)

### Age

The older the woman, the more likely she is to be head of the household. (S211)

### Age of Husband

The husband's authority in the household is reinforced when he is the oldest person within it. (C090)

### Age of Parents

Older parents are less able than younger parents to enforce their socialization demands. (R106)

### Age of Sons

The authority of the father is inversely correlated with the age of his sons. (F073)

### Aggression

Children who are bullying, domineering, and aggressive tend to come from families in which there are conflicting authority figures. (R113)

### Authority Structure of Family Orientation

Mothers who remember their mothers as having had much authority tend to act similarly in their own families. (B260)

### Avoidance Relationship

When there is potential conflict and hostility between men who hold hierarchical positions in the family authority structure, avoidance patterns tend to characterize their relationship (e.g., a matrilineal system, a man and his sister's son). (G055)

### Behavior Problems (Acting Out)

Children who are prone to temper tantrums tend to come from families in which the mother is in conflict with another authority figure. (R113)

### Behavior Problems (Stealing, Lying)

Children who lie and steal tend to come from families in which there are conflicting authority figures. (R113)

### Clan

The institutionalization of a clan structure tends to reinforce parental authority. (W082)

### Clan, Importance of

The legitimacy of the father's authority is questioned as the father becomes less a representation of the clan and of tradition due to the decreasing importance of the clan for the family and the increasing power of the state. (T016)

### Class

The lower the class, the more likely is the husband to claim authority. (G156)

The higher the social class, the greater the authority of the elder persons in the family. (G156)

There is no correlation between class and views of equal or unequal distribution of family authority between parents. (H180)

People from a lower-class background are more likely to view their mothers as the principal authority figures than persons from upper-class backgrounds, who are more likely to view their fathers as the principal authority figures. (K114)

Schizophrenics at all class levels tend to see their mothers, rather than their fathers, as the dominant authority figure in the family. (K114)

Patterns of parental authority do not vary with socioeconomic factors in families of schizophrenic children. (S187)

### Cohesion of Family

In families favoring authority equally distributed between husband and wife and in families tending to favor dominance by the husband, family solidarity is significantly greater than in families which tend to favor dominance by the wife. (J001)

### Descent (Matrilineal)

Avuncular authority is greater when the matrilineage is strong. (S192)

### Descent (Patrilineal)

A shift in the emphasis in lineality from maternal to paternal ancestry will tend to occur when the authority of the mother's brother, within the family, is weakened. (E016)

### Descent (Unilineal)

Kinsmen invested with disciplinary authority will be members of the lineage group. (W065)

### Division of Labor by Sex

When there is little difference between men and women in prestige, the authority of the male in the family is reinforced by a sharp division of labor that restricts the woman's role to matters concerning the training of daughters or the management of the home. (P083)

### Ecological Conditions

The more severe the conditions for survival are for a family, the more authority the husband/father has.

### Economic Dependence

With increasing economic independence, authority within the extended family tends to shift from the head of this kin unit to the husband in the nuclear family. (O023)

The development of patterns of economic independence tends to undermine the family authority structure. (T068)

### Economic Pattern (Migrant Labor)

The family authority structure will tend to be weakened under conditions of migrant labor. (L093)

In situations of migratory labor, the wife enjoys greater independence and is less likely to submit to her husband's authority. (S171)

### Economic Pattern (Money)

The authority of the father in the peasant family decreases as the family becomes less of a production unit and more of an income-earning unit. (B031)

With the development of a money economy in matrilineal societies, the father tends to supersede the mother's brother in legal and moral importance. (G056)

### Education (Western)

The family authority structure is weakened by the education of younger members in western schools. (R040)

### Employment of Women

The greater the decline of the traditional authority of the family, the more likely it is that the wife may seek security through an independent career and/or through reinforcing her personal ties with her husband by a companionate form of marriage. (M198)

### Extended/Nuclear Family

Parental control will tend to be stronger in extended families than in nuclear families. (F073)

### Father-Child Relations (Affection)

When the father is remembered as a strong authority figure, daughters more than sons, tend to recall him less often as being highly affectionate. (B297)

### Father-Son Relations (Closeness)

The loss of paternal authority, especially in the allocation of work, increases the closeness between father and son in the modern era. (T087)

### Father-Son Relations (Conflict)

When the father has great authority over his children, tension and conflict will tend to characterize the father-son relationship. (B107)

### Functions of Family

The abdication of some of their former educational, economic, and recreational roles has led to a serious diminution in parental authority. (S051)

### Grandfather-Grandchild Relations

The greater the authority position of the grandfather within the household, the less permissive the grandfather-grandchild relationship. (G156)

### Identification

The weaker members in a family authority structure (i.e., children) tend to adopt more characteristics of the more powerful, rather than of the less powerful, other person. (B216)

### Illegitimacy

When the distinction between legitimacy and illegitimacy decreases, parental authority is diminished. (T073)

### Incest (Mother-Son)

In the few cases in which mother-son incest occurred, no restraining agent was at home (e.g., father, siblings). (W123)

### Industrialization

The greater the degree of industrialization, the greater the likelihood that the patriarchal family structure will disappear. (K100)

### Inheritance

When the amount of land inherited by sons is adequate, the traditional patterns of authority are no longer acknowledged. (A013)

Children who are to inherit a greater portion of the property have greater authority. (B193)

The authority of the father will tend to be stronger if he has exclusive control over the choice of his heir. (F073)

There is less parental authority under conditions in which inheritance is not permitted. (T073)

### Inheritance (Matrilineal)

A matriarchal authority structure is associated with matrilineal inheritance of property and matrilocal residence. (S098)

### Inheritance (Patrilineal)

Control by the father is more likely to be powerful if the inheritance pattern is patrilineal. (F073)

### Kin Terminology
A tendency to use personal names rather than kinship terms reflects the weakening of the hierarchical structure of the family. (B083)

Asymmetrical relations of authority between the male members of an extended family creates asymmetry in the kinship terminological system. (G028)

### Kinship, Importance of
In societies where kinship provides the basis for practically all the differentiation within the social system, males have the principal rights of authority. (S080)

### Marital Adjustment
Marital adjustment is positively associated with equality of authority in family. (C023)

### Marital Stability
Where there is a lack of marital stability, parental authority is weakened. (T073)

### Marital Status (Male)
The authority of the wife in the family increases upon the death of her husband. (C022)

### Marriage Order
In the polygamous family, the greater the seniority of the wife, the greater her authority in the family. (M198)

### Mate Selection (Free Choice)
Increased freedom in mate selection is associated with reduced control by family elders. (G156)

The more powerful the older persons are in a society, the more likely they are to have a voice in mate selection. (K152)

When there are strong patterns of authority within an extended family structure, the choice of marriage partner tends to be arranged by the parents. (S043)

### Mental Illness (Manic-Depressive)
Manic-depressives are likely to come from families in which there are a number of authority figures. (C092)

### Mental Illness (Paranoia)
Paranoid tendencies are more likely to develop when parental authority is erratic. (S187)

### Mental Illness (Schizophrenia)
The family of the schizophrenic is more likely than others to have a continuous flow of denials of its members' statements. (H187)

### Mother-Child Relations (Affection)
When the mother is remembered as a strong authority figure, her grown children, when parents themselves, tend to recall her less often as being highly affectionate. (B297)

### Mother-Child Relations (Closeness)
When the mother stands in a relationship of intimacy and confidence to her children, it is difficult for her to perform disciplinary functions. (R030)

### Occupation
The professional group is more favorable to the notion of equal authority for husband and wife within the family than any other occupational group. (F009)

### Occupational Choice
Secular contact is positively associated with the increase in the son's freedom to choose an occupation. (T001)

### Occupational Rank
The amount of paternal authority is greater among the higher occupational groups than among the lower occupational groups. (K030)

### Parent-Child Relations (Closeness)
When there is a great discrepancy in the relative authority in the husband and wife, the relationship of the wife to the children will be more intimate than that of the authoritarian father to the child, which is one of respect and avoidance. (L064)

### Parent-Child Relations (Conflict)
There is no relationship between the degree of parent-child conflict and the type of family authority pattern. (B249)

The degree of friction which characterizes the parent-child relationship is directly correlated with the degree of authority of the parent over the child. (W098)

### Parent-Child Relations (Formality)
Parental authority tends to be greater if the relationship, between the parent and child is of a formal character. (R030)

### Parent-Child Relations (Hostility)
The greater the authority of the parents, the more likely they are to repress their hostility and project it onto the child. (M203)

The less the authority of the parents, the more likely that the child will project his hostility onto the parents. (M203)

### Parental Role Adjustment
Fathers tend to be less secure in their role as disciplinarian as mothers take on greater responsibility and authority in the family. (M201)

### Personality of Child (Competitiveness)
Children who are overly competitive with siblings tend to come from families in which there are conflicting authority figures. (R113)

### Personality of Child (Nightmares)
Children who have nightmares are likely to come from families in which there are conflicting authority figures. (R113)

### Personality of Child (Responsibility)
The more equal the parental authority, the lower the child's ratings for responsible behavior. (B250)

### Personality of Child (Restless, Excitable)
Children who are restless and excitable tend to come from families in which there are conflicting authority figures. (R113)

### Political Structure
Patterns of authority within the family structure tend to be extended into the political sphere. (B107)

The relationship of the child and father will tend to reflect the pattern of authority found in the political structure. (M029)

Where the state is democratic or nonexistent, kin relations are fairly nondeferential and "democratic." Where the state has been autocratic for a long period of time, kin relationships tend to be autocratic too. (S189)

    

### Polygyny
The husband in the polygynous family tends to be more aloof and surrounded by greater authority than the husband of the monogamous family. (M041)

### Power Structure of Family
The greater the importance of the decision to be made, the greater the correspondence between the authority structure of the family and the amount of power actually exercised. (S190)

### Preferential Marriage (Cross-Cousin)
When marriage is allowed or preferred with mother's brother's daughter but forbidden or disapproved with father's sister's daughter the jural authority over a young man will be vested in his father or his father's lineage. (M023)

### Property
If adult married children remain in their parents' homes, one of the parents is more likely to be considered head of the household than the son or son-in-law; if they start their own households and invite the parents in, they are most likely to be the household heads. (B312)

When land is owned jointly by patrilineal extended families, the authority of men over their wives, younger brothers, and sons is strengthened. (G028)

A high correlation exists between ownership or direct tenancy of the homestead and its headship. This control tends also to be vested in the dominant and senior member of the group. (S211)

### Race
In the middle and upper class in America, there is no relationship between racial origin and the structure of authority in the family. (M215)

Negro professors are less likely to be dominant in the family as regards decisions about purchases and living standards, than are white professors. (M215)

### Religion
Protestant children are more likely than Catholic children to see authority as residing in either father or mother rather than being equally distributed between the parents. (H180)

The amount of paternal authority does not vary significantly between Catholic and Protestant families. (K030)

### Religion (Ancestor Worship)
Ancestor worship serves to reinforce authority of elders and the oldest male. (H164)

### Religion (Christianity)
With the adoption of Christianity, a family authority structure becomes increasingly egalitarian. (B122)

Christianity will tend to weaken the authority of the extended family leader inasmuch as his office rests upon supernatural sanction. (O023)

### Religion (Role of Deities)
The role of the deity will tend to parallel that of the father in the family authority structure. (H084)

### Residence
The missionary compound system is apt to undermine the family, more especially the respect for and authority of parents. (E080)

### Residence (Men's House)
When men are residentially separated from their wives, their control over women is less. (M067)

### Residence (Neolocal)
With the establishment of neolocal residence, it is difficult for the older members of the family to exercise authority. (C035)

### Role Definition in Family
Decisions are more likely to be made jointly by both husband and wife when the activity concerned is within the household than when the activity is outside the household.

Loss of autocracy in the family structure leads to an increase in comradeship within the family group.

### Sex Ratio
The sex ratio does not determine the sex to which family headship is assigned. (S211)

### Sex Status
Both sons and daughters perceive mothers more often than fathers as exercising strong authority in the home. (B260)

More sons than daughters perceive their fathers as having a strong role of authority in the family. (B260)

Among teen-agers, sons are more likely than daughters to feel they have little or no voice in family affairs. (D079)

Men are more likely to view their fathers as having exercised moderate authority over them and women are more likely to view their fathers as having exercised little or no authority. (K114)

Female, as compared with male, heads of families are more preoccupied with household affairs and are less influential in the unit's external relations. (S211)

### Sexual Adjustment
The greater the stress the couple places on joint decision making, the greater is the importance they attach to successful sexual relations. (B267)

### Sibling Rank
A distinction will be made between siblings in terms of their order of birth if the family authority structure expresses a hierarchy of privilege and responsibility. (K045)

### Sibling Relations (Solidarity)
When the relationship of men within the family is one of authority and subordination, little emphasis is placed upon the solidarity of peers. (G028)

### Size of Household
The larger the household, the greater the differentiation of formal authority. (G156)

The larger the household, the more likely it is that it will have a male head. (S211)

### Slavery
Household slavery is more likely to occur among groups where autocratic control is generalized to family (or extended family) organization. (S069)

### Social Network
The more dispersed a couple's network of social contacts, the more likely they are to stress the importance of joint decision making by husband and wife. (B268)

### Stability of Family

An authoritarian family structure is more likely to be stable when the children and the wife accept the authority position of the father than when they do not accept paternal authority as legitimate. (K030)

### Stability of Family Structure

The greater the structural stability of the family, the more likely it is that headship and dominance (formal and real leadership) coincide. (S211)

### Stratification, Basis of

Where the stratification system is based on individual achievement, high authority of the elders is difficult to maintain. (G156)

A job-based stratification system greatly reduces the authority of family elders, while a land-based stratification system is associated with the maintenance of both real and symbolic authority of the elders. (G156)

### Suicide

Suicide in young people is more likely to be associated with extreme subordination to the authority of the older generation than with any other cause. (S025)

### Urban/Rural

Decisions concerning family activities are more often made jointly by both spouses in an urban environment than in a rural environment.

### Urbanization

There is a correlation between increasing urbanism and the decline of paternal authority. (C134)

Under urban conditions, with an expanding universe of social contacts, a shift of authority will occur from hereditary elders to new income-getting elites and from mother's brother to father. (F029)

Under urban pressures, there is a tendency for the father's authority and responsibility in matrilineal societies to increase rapidly over that of the mother's brother. (M050)

Urbanization is correlated with a decline in manifestations of both patriarchal and matriarchal authority. (R088)

### Values

Lack of consistent authority in the home tends to result in serious disturbance in the (manic-depressive) child's value system. (C092)

## AUTHORITY STRUCTURE OF FAMILY (ASYMMETRICAL)
### X  Husband-Wife Relations (Emotion)

An asymmetrical relationship within the authority structure of the family tends to be associated with a partial repudiation of emotional ties with women. (G028)

### Sibling Relations (Hostility)

When asymmetrical relationships characterize the authority structure of the family, brothers near in age and of similar status in the extended family tend to be covertly hostile to each other. (G028)

## AUTHORITY STRUCTURE OF FAMILY (DAUGHTER'S)
### X  Authority Structure of Family (Mother's)

Mothers are more likely to exercise authority in their own homes when they remember their mothers doing so. (B297)

## AUTHORITY STRUCTURE OF FAMILY (DEMOCRACY)    X  Cognitive Development

Democratic homes are associated with a favorable rate of intellectual growth in the child. (B257)

## AUTHORITY STRUCTURE OF FAMILY (MATRILINEAL)    X  Sibling Relations (Solidarity)

In matrilineal societies men are less likely to quarrel with their sisters since this weakens their authority over the next generation. (C090)

## AUTHORITY STRUCTURE OF FAMILY (MOTHER'S)
### X  Authority Structure of Family (Daughter's)

Mothers are more likely to exercise authority in their own homes when they remember their mothers doing so. (B297)

## AUTHORITY STRUCTURE OF FAMILY ORIENTATION    X  Authority Structure of Family

Mothers who remember their mothers as having had much authority tend to act similarly in their own families. (B260)

## AUTHORITY STRUCTURE OF FAMILY (PATERNALISTIC)    X  Personality Problems

Loss of paternalistic family (with its emphasis on authority, responsibility, and emotional attachments), accompanied by increased freedom for the individual and lack of adequate substitution of new structures and values that were provided for by the paternalistic homes, is a major cause of neurotic personality disorders. (B244)

## AUTHORITY STRUCTURE OF FAMILY (PATRIARCHAL)    X  Religion

Indigenous patterns of patriarchical authority facilitates a conversion to Christianity. (F060)

## AUTHORITY STRUCTURE OF FAMILY (PERCEPTION OF)    X  Sex Status

Both sons and daughters perceive mothers, more often than fathers, as exercising strong authority in the home. (B260)

More sons than daughters perceive their fathers as having a strong role of authority in the family. (B260)

## AUTHORITY STRUCTURE OF LINEAGE
### X  Cohesion of Lineage

When internally exercised authority within agnatic sections is weak, the group will be characterized by a high degree of fluidity. (M023)

### Exogamy

The existence of exogamous restrictions against affines prevents ambiguities within the lineage authority structure. (T039)

### Property (Individual)

The authority of the lineage head is undermined with the increasing importance of individually owned property. (W090)

## AUTHORITY STRUCTURE OF MARRIAGE
### X  Resources of Wife

When the wife gains increasing resources in the family, patriarchal role definitions will weaken. (P083)

## AUTHORITY STRUCTURE OF SOCIETY
### X  Mate Selection

The more powerful the older persons are in a society, the more likely they are to have a voice in mate selection. (K152)

# AUTOEROTICISM

### X Child-Rearing Practices (Discipline)

There is a positive correlation between boys' masturbation and the extent to which their parents use threats of withdrawal of love as a means of discipline. (B213)

### Class

Lower-class adolescent boys go through a briefer period of masturbation than do middle-class boys. (B244)

Middle-class children masturbate more, and to a later age, than lower-class children. (R127)

### Dependency Anxiety

There is a correlation between the extent to which a boy masturbates and the degree of his anxiety about dependency on his parents. (B243)

### Homosexuality

Overt homosexuality may develop (as a method of withdrawing from reality) as an alternative to autoeroticism. (T104)

### Institutional Care

If the child is institutionalized he is more likely to indulge in a high level of autoerotic activity. (Y045)

If the child is institutionalized he is less likely to engage in autoerotic activity. (Y045)

### Marital Adjustment

There is no evidence that restraints against female masturbation are favorable to marital adjustment. (K161)

### Maternal Overprotectiveness

Maternal overprotection does not affect patterns of masturbation in the child. (L161)

### Mother-Child Relations (Affection)

Autoerotic activity tends to be positively correlated with positive maternal affect. (H216)

Infants of ambivalent mothers tend to have characteristic rocking movements; infants of warm, consistent, and emotionally balanced mothers tend to have more frequently genital-oriented motor activity. (H216)

### Mother-Child Relations (Warmth)

Children of warm and loving mothers are more likely to engage in masturbation than are children of cold and rejecting mothers. (S079)

### Parent Absence

Children faced with the absence of parents may turn, for alternate satisfaction, to autoerotic devices. (H239)

### Parent-Child Relations (Anxiety)

Masturbation appears to be an attempt to flood the body with pleasurable stimulation in order to ward off the painful anxieties of the child-parent relationship. (C088)

### Parent-Child Relations (Hostility)

There is a correlation between the extent to which a boy masturbates and his hostility toward his parents. (B243)

### Parent-Child Relations (Rejection)

There is a correlation between parental rejection of the son and the extent to which the boy masturbates. (B243)

### Sexual Restrictions, Postpubertal

When there is sexual freedom of childhood, and the more or less enforced repression after puberty, masturbation is fairly common. (H223)

# AVOIDANCE RELATIONSHIP    X Acculturation

Traditional avoidance relationships tend to deteriorate with increasing acculturation. (B166)

### Affinal Ties

The relationship between affinals of adjacent generations tends to be characterized by avoidance or respect. (E064)

### Age

Both the very young and the aged are more likely to be excepted from much of the typical avoidance behavior. (S153)

An avoidance relationship between siblings is more likely to be enforced after puberty. (V020)

### Age Difference

Avoidance relationships are more likely to exist between individuals of different ages than between people of similar ages. (B085)

### Authority Structure of Family

When there is potential conflict and hostility between men who hold hierarchical positions in the family authority structure, avoidance patterns tend to characterize their relationship (e.g., in a matrilineal system, a man and his sister's son). (G055)

### Avoidance Relationship (Extension)

The most common "focal" avoidance relationships (brother-sister, man to mother-in-law, and man to son's wife) usually carry a number of symmetrical extensions. For example, in a society where a man must avoid his sister, he must also avoid female cousins. Where he avoids his mother-in-law, he also avoids others of his wife's blood kin. (S189)

### Community

Avoidance relationships tend to be abandoned with an increase in the heterogeneity of community composition. (E068)

### Competition

Avoidance patterns are more likely to occur between kinsmen in direct competition for social rank. (M235)

### Conflict Between Kin

Avoidance or respect relationships tend to suppress or control conflict between relatives who have a close kinship bond. (S080)

### Descent (Unilineal)

There is a correlation between the severity of kin avoidance and the presence of unilineal kin-groups. (S079)

Unilineal kin-groups are strongly correlated with the presence of avoidance relationships and also with joking relationships. (S189)

### Endogamy (Class)

When class endogamy is common, affinal avoidance is not strictly observed. (C094)

### Exogamy

Where patterns of avoidance exist between affinals, marriage with certain kinsmen will tend to be avoided because of its disruptive character. (E078)

### Exogamy (Village)

There is a weak, but positive, correlation between the presence of exogamous communities and the severity of kin avoidance. (S079)

## Generation

Avoidance restraint between relatives of the opposite sex tends to become heightened between relatives of the opposite sex of the same generation. (O027)

Avoidance relationships are more likely to obtain between kinsmen of adjacent generation. (R052)

## Housing

Avoidance relationships will tend to be modified with a change toward Western housing arrangements. (B118)

## Incest

Avoidance and formality tend to characterize the relationship between siblings when the incestuous attraction between them is strong. (G055)

## Incest Taboo

When kinsmen are prohibited as marriage partners, their relationships will tend to be characterized by avoidance or respect. (H090)

Incest prohibitions require external support from a rule of avoidance when they have not been strongly internalized in the individual conscience. (M019)

Avoidance relationships are more likely to be established with kinsmen who are subject to the incest taboo. (M085)

One determinant of the severity of kin avoidance is a strong incest fear in the society. (S079)

## Joking Relationship

The institutionalization of patterns of joking behavior tends to be accompanied by the institutionalization of avoidance with other kinsmen. (R039)

When a joking relationship is established with siblings of the wife, an avoidance relationship tends also to obtain between the husband and the wife's parents. (R052)

## Kin-Group, Importance of

The establishment of an avoidance relationship with certain kinsmen tends to reinforce the importance of the kin-group. (K076)

## Kin-Role Definition

Societies with a high degree of structuring of kinship patterns (unilineality, unilocality, exogamy) are more prone to kin avoidance. (S079)

## Kin Ties (Consanguineal/Affinal)

Very few consanguineal kin relationships are characterized by avoidance. Where they do occur they are between same-generation cross-sex kin. (S189)

## Legal Responsibility

In societies where children are subjected to extrusion from the household or brother-sister avoidance during the first stage of puberty (8–10 years), the concept of joint liability is found (i.e., liability falls on the members of an individual's descent group if the offender cannot be apprehended or meet his legal liability); in societies where neither extrusion nor brother-sister avoidance is found during the first stage of puberty, the concept of individual liability is found (i.e., the individual alone is held responsible and punished for his acts). (C093)

## Marital Stability

Rules of avoidance between kinsmen tend to be relaxed with the persistence of the marriage and the advent of children. (E039)

## Marital Status

The avoidance relationship between siblings of the opposite sex is relaxed after the marriage of the girl. (G055)

## Preferential Marriage (Cross-Cousin)

Avoidance relations form part of the cross-cousin marriage and sib complex. (L039)

## Property Rights

Avoidance patterns between siblings are more likely to occur when property rights are fluid. (M235)

## Puberty

The activation of an avoidance relationship between siblings tends to occur at adolescence. (S098)

## Rank

Avoidance patterns are more likely to occur between kinsmen in direct competition for social rank. (M235)

## Rank of Affines

Avoidance relationships tend to be established between affinals who are of unequal status. (S153)

## Religion (Christianity)

Avoidance taboos are less likely to be respected among Christians. (H164)

## Residence

When a strong avoidance relationship is established between relatives, the kinsmen involved are more likely to avoid common residence. (H062)

## Residence (Bilocal)

Societies with a bilocal rule of residence have a low severity of kin avoidance. (S079)

## Residence (Matrilocal)

An association exists between the parent-in-law taboo and matrilocal residence. (L128)

## Residence (Patrilocal)

There is a close association between the patrilocal rule of residence and the avoidance of the son's wife. (S079)

## Sex of Kinsmen

Emotional involvement appears to be greater in cross- than in like-sex sibling avoidance. (M235)

## Sex Status

Avoidance relationships will tend to be more severe if the affinal kinsman is of the opposite sex. (H165)

Like-sex sibling avoidance seems to break down more rapidly than does cross-sex avoidance. (M235)

Men seldom avoid other men and women rarely avoid women. Avoidance is, first of all, characteristic of cross-sex kin relationships. (S189)

Avoidance relationships tend to characterize affinals of adjacent generations and of the opposite sex. (T065)

## Sex Taboo (Postpartum)

In societies with long durations of the postpartum sex taboo, avoidance of kin is common. (S079)

In societies with long durations of the postpartum sex taboo, the severity of kin avoidance will be greater (this includes mother-in-law avoidance, son's wife avoidance, brother-sister avoidance, etc.). (S079)

## Sexual Restrictions

Avoidance relationships will tend to obtain between kinsmen who are prohibited as sexual partners. (M120)

### Sibling Relations (Solidarity)

A mild avoidance relationship between brother and sister will tend to enhance the solidarity of the pair. (S060)

### Subsistence Pattern

Avoidance patterns are more likely to occur in marginal societies where people must live in small and isolated groups for long periods of time under conditions of extreme hardship. (M235)

## AVOIDANCE RELATIONSHIP (AFFINES)
### X  Avoidance Relationship (Consanguineal)

There is an association between son's wife avoidance and brother-sister avoidance; between mother-in-law avoidance and brother-sister avoidance; between cousin and brother-sister avoidance; between father-in-law and mother-in-law avoidance; between mother-in-law avoidance and avoidance of son's wife. (S079)

## AVOIDANCE RELATIONSHIP (CONSANGUINEAL)
### X  Avoidance Relationship (Affinal)

There is an association between son's wife avoidance and brother-sister avoidance; between mother-in-law avoidance and brother-sister avoidance; between cousin and brother-sister avoidance; between father-in-law and mother-in-law avoidance; between mother-in-law avoidance and avoidance of son's wife. (S079)

## AVOIDANCE RELATIONSHIP (EXTENSION)
### X  Avoidance Relationship

The most common "focal" avoidance relationships (brother-sister, man to mother-in-law, and man to son's wife) usually carry a number of symmetrical extensions. For example, in a society where a man must avoid his sister, he must also avoid female cousins. Where he avoids his mother-in-law, he also avoids others of his wife's blood kin. (S189)

## AVUNCULAR RELATIONSHIP
### X  Descent (Matrilineal)

The avuncular relationship tends to be emphasized in societies in which matrilineal descent is well-developed. (S106)

### Descent (Matrilineal/Patrilineal)

The avuncular relationship in a matrilineal society tends to be characterized by greater hostility and rivalry than does the comparable relationship in a patrilineal society. (G055)

### Residence

An avuncular relationship between ego and the maternal uncle tends to be correlated with physical proximity between the intermarrying lineages. (F010)

### Residence (Virilocal)

When residence is virilocal in a matrilineal society, the transference of hostile wishes on the part of the male from the father to the mother's brother is less completely carried out. (G055)

## AVUNCULATE  X  Kin Terminology (Omaha)

The development of the avunculate in patrilineal societies is associated with the development of Omaha terminology. (L061)

## AVUNCULATE/UXORILOCAL RESIDENCE
### X  Endogamy (Community)

Patterns of uxorilocal residence and avuncular guardianship produce a strong pressure toward community endogamy. (B111)

# B

**BACHELORHOOD**  **X  Prostitution**
The demand for prostitutes' services declines with a decline in the bachelor population. (P083)

**BEAUTY OF WOMEN**  **X  Marital Adjustment**
There is a direct relation between the physical attractiveness of women and marital adjustment. (K161)

**BED WETTING**
**X  Child-Rearing Practices (Consistency)**
Regressive enuresis of the child is unlikely to be due to inconsistent child-rearing practices of the mother. (R113)

**Child-Rearing Practices (Criticism)**
Enuresis fixation in the child is related to excessively critical and depreciative behavior of the mother. (R113)

**Child-Rearing Practices (Rejection)**
Regressive enuresis of the child is related to cold, distant, and neglectful treatment by the mother. (R113)

**Feeding (Demand)**
There is no relationship between whether the infant was fed on a schedule or by self-demand and his duration of bed wetting (U.S.). (S191)

**Feeding Problems**
Among children who have been severely toilet trained, those who have feeding problems are less likely to be bed wetters (U.S.). (S191)

**Mother-Child Relations (Responsiveness)**
There is no relationship between degree of responsiveness of the mother to the child's crying and duration of bed wetting (U.S.). (S191)

**Mother-Child Relations (Warmth)**
Severe training leads to late bed wetting if the mother is cold, but not if she is warm. (S191)

**Parent-Child Relations (Hostility)**
Prolonged years of enuresis in childhood indicates hostility toward parents. (B283)

**Parent-Child Relations (Rejection)**
Neglected and/or rejected children are more likely than overprotected children to become enuretic. (B238)

**Sex Anxiety of Mother**
High sexual anxiety of the mother is associated with late persistence of bed wetting of the child. (S191)

**Sibling Status**
Prolonged bed wetting is no more common in families where the child has younger brothers and sisters than where the child does not (U.S.). (S191)

**Weaning**
There is no relationship between the duration of bed wetting and severity of weaning (U.S.). (S191)

**BEHAVIOR DEVELOPMENT**
**X  Mother-Child Relations (Affection)**
Affectional interchange between mother and child is positively related to the infant's development of exploratory and manipulative behavior. (Y042)

**BEHAVIOR DEVELOPMENT OF CHILD (SOCIAL BEHAVIOR)**
**X  Child-Rearing Practices (Consistency)**
There is a low, but positive, relationship between maternal consistency and development in the infant of outgoing social behavior. (Y042)

**BEHAVIOR OF CHILD**  **X  Breast Feeding**
Breast feeding and later child behavior are not associated. (S191)

**Child-Rearing Attitudes**
Behavior of middle-class children does not correlate with parental attitudes toward child rearing. (Z010)

**BEHAVIOR PROBLEMS**  **X  Adoption, Age at**
There is a higher frequency of behavior problems (e.g., stealing, lying, cruelty to animals, and destructiveness of property) among late adoptees than among those placed early. (H242)

**Broken Homes**
The relationship between parental loss during early childhood and subsequent psychopathology in the child is most firmly established in the case of personalities prone to delinquent and psychopathic behavior. (B269)

Delinquent girls from unbroken homes are less likely than delinquent girls from broken homes to have social problems, such as alcoholism, sexual irregularities, or mental disabilities. (S210)

**Child-Rearing Attitudes**
Maternal child-rearing attitudes are not related to the behavioral or mental problems of the child. (M208)

**Child Rearing (Collective)**
Children reared collectively (on kibbutzim) exhibit more enuresis and thumb-sucking than children reared within the family. (G124)

Children who are reared collectively (mother surrogate for each group) are more likely than children raised at home by their own mothers to develop behavior problems enuresis, thumb-sucking, nail-biting, aggression). (R094)

**Child-Rearing Practices (Consensus)**
There is a positive association between parental conflict about authority over the child and antisocial behavior in the child (e.g., lying, stealing, bullying, aggression, domineering, and excessive competition with siblings). (R100)

**Child-Rearing Practices (Consistency)**
The more contradictory the demands placed upon the child by adults in the home, the more likely he is to show maladjusted behavior both at home and at school. (C117)

Mothers who are consistently rigid or overpermissive in the child's second or third year are more likely to have child problems in the areas of sleeping, feeding, and toilet training than are mothers who are consistent in child-rearing practices that are neither exceedingly rigid nor permissive. This does not hold for children during their first year. (K113)

There is no relationship between the mother's inconsistency or consistency and child problems in the areas of sleeping, feeding, and toilet training. (K113)

Disobediency, stealing, truancy from school, and disobedience with a hostile component in the child are correlated with inconsistent discipline on the part of the mother. (R081)

Inconsistent discipline by the mother causes the child to test the limits of tolerance by others via his misbehavior, thus provoking others to set up limits for him. (R091)

### Child-Rearing Practices (Control)
Controlling and inflexible child rearing on the part of the father is positively associated with antisocial behavior (stealing, lying, truancy from school, overtly competitive children) in the child. (R100)

### Child-Rearing Practices (Illness)
Where parents are integrated, realistic, and accepting of their child's illness, behavioral disturbance is minimal. (F081)

### Child-Rearing Practices (Permissiveness)
There is no statistical support for the hypothesis that mothers of children with primary behavior disorders are more lax and overindulgent than are mothers of normal children.

Unconscious parental permission is associated with antisocial behavior in the child; this includes truancy as well as other behavior expressing forbidden impulses.

### Child-Rearing Practices (Punishment)
The use of physical punishment on the part of the parents is positively associated with antisocial behavior in the child, (e.g., lying, stealing, temper tantrums, disobedience with accompanying hostility, destructiveness, aggression, domineering, and bullying). (R100)

### Class
Children of better-educated parents are more likely to have problems (e.g., thumb-sucking, crying, obsessional habits, etc.) than are children of rural parents or urban working-class parents (France). (F097)

### Criminality and Mental Illness/Broken Home
It is criminal or psychotic behavior on the part of the parent rather than the broken home which causes delinquency and other behavioral problems in the child. (B285)

### Employment of Mother
Regardless of whether the mother likes to work, young children (third to sixth graders) of working mothers are more likely to respond to a frustrating problem with nonadaptive behavior, such as crying or blaming themselves. (G156)

"Problem children" of working mothers tend to be younger than problem children of nonworking mothers. (M058)

### Employment of Mother, Attitude Toward
Due to the mechanism of displacement, frustration of mothers whose marriage prohibits their return to work correlates with behavioral problems in the child. (S265)

### Father Absence
When the father is absent for long periods of time, his children more often develop behavior problems, such as dependence on the mother.

### Father-Child Relations (Hostility)
Father-child relations that are characterized by hostility on the part of the father are positively associated with antisocial behavior (e.g., stealing, truancy, temper tantrums, etc.) in the child. (R100)

### Father-Son Relations (Rejection)
"Problem" sons are more likely than normal sons to perceive their fathers to be more harsh and rejecting than their mothers. (V038)

### Identification with Parents
The internalization of a powerful but hostile parental image may lead the individual to project these introjected attributes upon other figures in his environment (acting out). (B278)

### Institutional Care
Babies who have been institutionalized from birth to six months are consistently less vocal than those in families, the difference being discernible from age two months. (B270)

If a baby is institutionalized for a long period, he will demonstrate a monotonous rocking of the body and sometimes head-banging. (B270)

Children who are raised from early infancy in institutions without an adequate parent surrogate develop aggressive, distractible, and uncontrolled behavior. (B270)

### Marital Adjustment
Unsatisfactory relations between adults in the home is correlated with maladjusted behavior of the child, both at home and at school. (C117)

### Maternal Overprotectiveness
Overprotected children are more likely to be disobedient, impudent, to exhibit temper tantrums, and to make excessive demands on others. (B033)

### Maternal-Role Behavior
Children who have been frustrated in early suckling and "mothering" give up sucking later and less spontaneously.

### Mental Illness of Parents (Schizophrenia)
Schizophrenia in the parent may be a cause of behavior problems in the child where there is a close mother-child relationship when the child is under the age of ten or a close father-son relationship when the son is in the Oedipal phase or is under the age of six. (B285)

Schizophrenia in the mother is more likely than schizophrenia in the father to produce behavior problems in the child. (B285)

Parents with psychoses other than schizophrenia are less likely to have children who suffer from behavior problems than are schizophrenic parents. (B285)

The child of schizophrenic parents is more likely than the child of parents with other mental or behavioral disturbances to develop behavior problems before puberty. (B285)

### Mother Absence

Children who are separated from their mothers or adequate mother substitutes are likely to develop such autoerotic habits as finger-sucking, other sucking activities with tongue, lips, and mouth, rocking and other rhythmical movements, head-knocking, and (among older children) masturbation.

Children who are deprived of mothers before they are six months old demonstrate behavior which is characterized, generally, by unresponsiveness: they are immobile, quiet, and listless. (B270)

Children separated from their mothers are more likely to exhibit regressive tendencies than are children not separated. (B270)

### Mother-Child Relations

Genital play by the infant is related to satisfactory relationship with the mother.

### Mother-Child Relations (Consistency)

Inconsistency in maternal emotions toward the child is a cause of the infant's turning back upon himself, as manifested by his rocking himself, playing with his feces, etc. (B272)

### Mother-Son Relations (Affection)

Adolescent boys showing behavior problems are more likely than normal boys to perceive their mothers to be more permissive and loving than their fathers. (V038)

### Ordinal Position

Habit disorder among disturbed children is found among only and oldest children, but not among middle children. (H198)

### Parent Absence

Children faced with the absence of parents may develop regressive patterns, such as loss of sphincter control. (H239)

### Parent-Child Relations

If the mother is maladjusted and the father adopts ineffectual disciplinary methods, the child is likely to develop social-conduct problems. (P070)

### Parent-Child Relations (Affection)

If the child fails to obtain favorable attention (affection) from his parents, he will engage in destructive activity. (B033)

### Parent-Child Relations (Hostility)

Children who exhibit conduct problems are more likely to have parents who exhibit more hostility toward them than are children who do not have such problems. (S242)

### Parent-Child Relations (Interaction)

If interaction between children and their parents is frustrated by the parents, maladaptive behavior (aggression, overdemanding, withdrawal, etc.) is likely to develop. (W137)

### Parent-Child Relations (Preference)

Problem children are more likely to like parents of the opposite sex than nonproblem children. (G117)

### Parent-Child Relations (Rejection)

Those who are rejected by their parents show excessive activity and restlessness, make trouble in school, lack sustained application, often show delinquent behavior.

Children who exhibit conduct problems are more likely to have parents who reject them more than do parents of nonproblem children. (S242)

### Parent Loss

Children suddenly faced with the absence of parents will try to rectify the situation by seeking the return of the parents by finding an adult substitute. (H239)

### Parental Attitudes (Consensus)

Adolescent boys who show behavior problems are more likely than normal boys to perceive disparities between the attitudes and behavior of their two parents. (V038)

### Personality of Mother

A child who is a conduct problem is likely to have a mother whose personality (as estimated by her or her husband) demonstrates rejection, withdrawal, nervousness, inconsistency, and irritable aggressiveness. (B237)

### Personality of Mother (Oral)

The male children of mothers who attempt to resolve oral conflicts by acting seductively and demanding with them develop greatly exacerbated Oedipal tensions which, in turn, are compensated for by aggressive and destructive acting out. (R099)

### Pregnancy, Attitude Toward

Mothers who are greatly concerned about hurting their unborn children during pregnancy tend to have babies who behave abnormally (in terms of crying, sleeping, fussing, etc.) during the first five days after birth. (F096)

Mothers whose babies behave abnormally in the first five days after birth either wanted their pregnancy very much or very much did not want the pregnancy. (F096)

### Pregnancy (Planned/Unplanned)

There is no relationship between abnormal behavior among newborn babies and whether or not the pregnancy had been planned. (F096)

### Scapegoating

If parents relieve their conflict by having a child perform the scapegoat role, the child is socialized to the role by the use of inconsistent pressures and will not learn the role of a well-behaved child. (B204)

### Surrogate Mother

The older the infant (3–7 months), the more severe the disturbances (sleeping, eating, apathy, loss of abilities, excessive crying, and blunted social responsiveness) resulting from a change in mother figures. (Y042)

### Surrogate/Natural Parents

Children adopted after the age of six months are more likely to exhibit antisocial tendencies than are children raised by their own parents. (H243)

## BEHAVIOR PROBLEMS (ACTING OUT)
### X   Authority Structure of Family

Children who are prone to temper tantrums tend to come from families in which the mother is in conflict with another authority figure. (R113)

### Child-Rearing Practices (Consistency)

Temper tantrums of the child are associated with lack of consistency in the child-rearing practices of the mother. (R113)

### Child-Rearing Practices (Permissiveness)

Children having mothers who are overly permissive are prone to temper tantrums. (R113)

### Child-Rearing Practices (Punishment)
Children whose mothers are excessively punitive are prone to temper tantrums. (R113)

Children whose mothers are excessively punitive tend to be destructive, restless, and excitable. (R113)

Children whose mothers are excessively critical and depreciative tend to be prone to temper tantrums. (R113)

### Education of Parents
Parents with better education are more likely to have problems with their children regarding temper tantrums.

### Personality Problems of Parents
There is a correlation between parents' unresolved unconscious needs and the behavior of their acting-out children (K151)

## BEHAVIOR PROBLEMS (BY SEX)
### X   Mental Illness of Parent (Psychosis)
Daughters of parents with affective (other than schizophrenia) psychoses are more likely to develop behavior problems than are sons. (B285)

## BEHAVIOR PROBLEMS (CHEATING)
### X   Ordinal Position
Cheating is more common among firstborn children than among any other sibling position. (H215)

## BEHAVIOR PROBLEMS (CRYING)
### X   Mother-Child Relations (Consistency)
The amount of crying by the infant is positively related to maternal anxiety and inconsistency in attention to the infant. (B272)

### Weaning
Mothers whose babies cry a good deal are gentler in their weaning methods than are mothers of placid babies (U.S.). (S191)

## BEHAVIOR PROBLEMS (FEEDING)
### X   Personality Problems
Unsatisfied tension in the mother or infant is a primary cause of feeding disturbance. (B272)

The greater the anxiety of the mother, the more likely it is that her flow of milk for the infant is established slowly or not at all. (B272)

## BEHAVIOR PROBLEMS (FINGER-SUCKING)
### X   Class
Children of the better-educated parents are more likely to suck their fingers than are children of comfortable country parents and working-class urban parents (France). (F097)

### Weaning
Too-early weaning may lead to finger-sucking. (F097)

## BEHAVIOR PROBLEMS (LYING)
### X   Parent-Child Relations (Closeness)
There is a positive relationship between parents who are cold, distant, and neglectful and lying in the child. (R100)

## BEHAVIOR PROBLEMS (LYING, STEALING)
### X   Child-Rearing Practices (Favoritism)
Children who lie and steal tend to have mothers who show marked preference for the child's sibling. (R113)

### Child-Rearing Practices (Punishment)
The mothers' excessively punitive behavior toward the child is related to lying and solitary stealing by the child. (R113)

Excessively critical and depreciative behavior of the mother toward the child is related to lying and solitary stealing by the child. (R113)

### Mother-Child Relations (Rejection)
Children whose mothers overtly reject and dislike them are more likely to lie and engage in solitary stealing. (R113)

## BEHAVIOR PROBLEMS (NAIL-BITING)
### X   Child-Rearing Practices (Consistency)
Excessive nail-biting of the child is not likely to be due to lack of consistency in the mother's child-rearing practices. (R113)

### Child-Rearing Practices (Punishment)
Use of physical punishment by the father is positively associated with nail-biting in the child. (R100)

### Employment of Mother
Children whose mothers worked full time before the children were two years of age tend to bite their nails significantly more than children whose mothers did not begin full-time employment until the children were three years of age. (Y047)

### Mother–Child Relations (Seductiveness)
Children whose mothers are overly seductive in their behavior toward them are likely to have a nail-biting problem. (R113)

## BEHAVIOR PROBLEMS (NONORAL EROTICISM)
### X   Mother Absence
Separation from the mother is a cause of rocking, fecal play, and other nonoral autoeroticism in the infant. (B272)

## BEHAVIOR PROBLEMS (OBEDIENCE)
### X   Father–Child Relations (Closeness)
There is a positive relationship between fathers who are cold, distant, and neglectful, and mild disobedience in the child. (R100)

## BEHAVIOR PROBLEMS (OBEDIENCE-HOSTILITY)
### X   Child-Rearing Practices (Maturity Demands)
There is a positive relationship between the father's expecting overly mature behavior on the part of the child and the child's disobedience accompanied by hostility. (R100)

## BEHAVIOR PROBLEMS OF FAMILY
### X   Juvenile Delinquency/Neurosis
Unfavorable conditions (alcoholism, epilepsy, psychosis, criminality) occur more frequently in the family histories of delinquents than in those of neurotics. (B238)

## BEHAVIOR PROBLEMS OF PARENTS
### X   Juvenile Delinquency
Among children of families where one parent was a juvenile problem and where the child himself now is having behavior adjustment problems in school, there is a decisive correlation between the behavior of the preadolescent child and that of his parent at the time he or she was a youthful offender. (K151)

Parental behavior characterized by dishonesty, untruthfulness, scapegoating, and lack of consideration for neighbors is related to delinquent behavior. (N052)

## BEHAVIOR PROBLEMS OF SON/DAUGHTER
### X   Alcoholism of Father
Sons of alcoholic fathers are more likely to develop behavior problems than are daughters. (B285)

## BEHAVIOR PROBLEMS (PASSIVITY, HYPERACTIVITY)          X   Mother Absence
Separation from the mother is a cause of the infant's loss of interest in the outside world, manifested in either passivity or hyperactivity. (B272)

## BEHAVIOR PROBLEMS (RUNNING AWAY)
### X   Marital Adjustment
Disturbed marital relations are associated with running away from home in girls. (R102)

### Mother-Daughter Relations (Affection)
Among girls, deprivation of maternal love is associated with running away from home. (R102)

### Mother-Daughter Relations (Maternal Role)
Subtle pressure by the mother on the daughter to take over the maternal role is associated with the daughter's running away from home. (R102)

## BEHAVIOR PROBLEMS (STEALING)
### X   Broken Homes
Conduct disorder (e.g., stealing) is significantly related to broken homes, especially among older children, only children, and children with three or more siblings. (H198)

### Child-Rearing Practices (Maturity Demands)
There is a positive relationship between fathers who expect overly mature behavior from their children and stealing by children. (R100)

### Father-Child Relations (Closeness)
There is a positive relationship between fathers who are cold, distant, and neglectful and children who steal. (R100)

## BEHAVIOR PROBLEMS (STEALING, LYING)
### X   Authority Structure of Family
Children who lie and steal tend to come from families in which there are conflicting authority figures. (R113)

### Child-Rearing Practices (Permissiveness)
Children who lie and steal tend to have mothers who are overly permissive. (R113)

## BEHAVIOR PROBLEMS (TASK WITHDRAWAL)
### X   Child-Rearing Practices (Acceleration)
Adolescent withdrawal from tasks is negatively related to maternal acceleration of the child during his early years (2–7). (K115)

### Child-Rearing Practices (Discipline)
Maternal justification of disciplinary measures during the child's early years (2–7) is negatively related to the tendency to withdraw from tasks when the child is an adolescent. (K115)

## BEHAVIOR PROBLEMS (THUMB-SUCKING)
### X   Breast Feeding, Duration of
Infants who are breast fed for a reasonably long period of time are less likely to become thumb-suckers than infants who had little or no breast-feeding experience. (Y042)

There is no difference between infants who have had no breast feeding and those who have been breast fed for a longer-than-"average" period of time regarding the duration and severity of thumb-sucking. (Y042)

The sucking drive is strengthened by prolonged gratification. (Y042)

### Class
The incidence of thumb-sucking is much greater among middle-class children than among lower-class children.

Middle-class white children show the same proportion of thumb-sucking as do middle-class Negro children.

Among middle-class children there is significantly more thumb-sucking than among working-class children. (W002)

### Father-Child Relations (Closeness)
There is a negative relationship between fathers who are cold, distant, and neglectful and thumb-sucking in the children. (R100)

### Feeding
The severity of thumb-sucking is in proportion to the insufficiency of sucking time during feeding. (Y042)

### Parent-Child Relations (Frustration)
Thumb-sucking is the result of frustration in general rather than of frustration in the area of feeding.

### Weaning
There is no significant difference between early-and late-weaned children regarding the duration and severity of thumb-sucking. (Y042)

### Weaning/Feeding
The earlier the child is weaned and the less frequently the child is fed, the more likely is he to suck his thumb.

## BEHAVIOR PROBLEMS (TRUANCY)
### X   Child-Rearing Practices (Consistency)
Truancy on the part of the child is related to lack of consistency in the mother's child-rearing practices. (R113)

### Child-Rearing Practices (Punishment)
The use of physical punishment by the father is positively associated with truancy of children from school. (R100)

## BEHAVIORAL DEVELOPMENT
### X   Mother-Child Relations (Affect)
The mother's emotional involvement with the child is positively related to the infant's development of exploratory and manipulative behavior. (Y042)

## BEREAVEMENT          Age of Mother
### Personality of Child (Self-Esteem)
Children whose mothers were relatively young when they were widowed are less likely to have high self-esteem than those whose mothers were older when widowed. (R129)

### Age of Mother
### X   Psychosomatic Illness of Child
Children whose mothers were relatively young when they were widowed are more likely to show psychosomatic symptoms of anxiety. (R129)

### Cohesion of Family
The acuteness of the sorrow at the death of a member will increase the emotional interdependence and unity of the family. (B033)

### Friendship
Among large families of low socioeconomic status, adolescents from homes where one parent is deceased have fewer friends than do adolescents from homes where both parents are living and there are fewer siblings.

### Marital Adjustment
Orphans are less likely to have favorable marital adjustments than are people from backgrounds with one or both parents living. (K161)

### Preferential Marriage (Levirate)
The levirate tends to minimize the disruptive consequences of the death of a husband. (R069)

### Self-Conception/Religion
Among children whose families have been broken by death there is no relationship between religion and low self-esteem. (R129)

## BEREAVEMENT/DIVORCE
### X   Emotional Problems
Widowhood is associated with greater emotional problems following the loss of a spouse than is divorce. (G157)

## BEREAVEMENT/REMARRIAGE
### X   Personality of Child (Self-Esteem)
Children whose parents were separated by death are likely to have as high self-esteem as those from intact families if the widowed parent does not remarry. (R129)

## BIGOTRY
### X   Child-Rearing Practices (Consistency)
There is a direct correlation between bigotry in a child and neglectful and inconsistent child-rearing practices by the parents. (M247)

### Child-Rearing Practices (Punishment)
Parents of bigoted people tend to be more stern and punitive in their child-rearing practices than are parents of normal children. (M247)

### Parent-Child Relations (Ambivalence)
Bigoted people tend to show more ambivalence toward their parents than do nonbigoted people. (M247)

### Personality of Parents
Parents of bigoted children do not exhibit any specific personality characteristics to differentiate them from the parents of nonbigoted children. (M247)

## BILATERAL ORGANIZATION
### X   Descent (Asymetrical)
Asymetrical descent may develop from a unilineal pattern as a consequence of the increasing importance of the bilateral family. (S097)

## BIRTH CONTROL        X   Age at Marriage
Early female marriage and premarital conception are associated with ignorance of birth control. (P083)

### Class
Lower-status groups adopt methods of contraception at a slower rate than do upper-status groups. (F101)

Although religious differentials persist within each class,

generally the higher the class, the greater the use of contraception. (F101)

Among Catholics (only) there is no consistent relationship between background characteristics (education, income, occupation) and attitudes expressed toward family limitation. (F101)

Members of lower classes are more likely than others to use withdrawal as a method of family limitation. (F101)

Among Protestants higher-status groups are more likely than others to choose the diaphragm as a contraceptive, while lower-status groups are more likely than others to choose the douche. (F101)

Among Catholics there is no relationship between class and the method of contraception used. (F101)

When contraceptives are introduced, the upper social strata are more likely to begin using them than are the lower social strata. (G156)

Couples in the lower-lower class who are not middle-class-oriented are less likely than couples in other classes to use contraception and planning. (P083)

There is an inverse relationship between the number of unplanned pregnancies and social class. (W022)

### Education
There is a direct correlation between approval of birth control and educational level. (B033)

### Employment of Wife
Wives who avoid pregnancy are more likely to be employed or in school than confined to homemaking alone. (P003)

### Fecundity
Couples who regulate conception are more likely to be fecund than those who do not. (F101)

Fecund couples are more likely to regulate conception effectively than subfecund couples. (F101)

### Fertility
When birth control methods become available to all socioeconomic groups, fertility differences by class are reduced. (W022)

### Fertility Values
When fertility is stressed, methods of birth control are less likely to be employed. (V020)

### Income
There is an increase in family planning with an increase in income. (F101)

### Intermarriage
Parents in intermarriages exercise greater birth control and thus have fewer children than do parents in homogamous marriages in order to prevent the lack of identification and status of marginality which children of intermarriages tend to have. (B012)

### Marital Adjustment
Couples who are able to control fertility according to their desires have a higher marital adjustment. (F002)

Marital-role tension is not related to the ability to estimate successfully future family size. (F002)

### Mental Illness (Schizophrenia/Neurosis)
There is no correlation between schizophrenic, neurotic, or normal women with regard to planning or not planning pregnancy or to the number of unfavorable symptoms during pregnancy. (P080)

### • Mental Retardation
The more severe the retardation, the less able is the individual to carry out effective contraception. (B307)

### Occupational Rank
The lower the occupational status, the less common is the use of contraception. (F101)

### Pregnancy, Timing of
Couples who are early postmarital conceivers tend to have a higher number of unplanned pregnancies than those who conceive later in the marriage. (C125)

### Premarital Sex Relations
As birth-control knowledge becomes more generalized, exploitive premarital sex behavior as a late adolescent pattern is likely to decline. (P083)

### Prostitution
When the pattern of marriage is monogamous, extended restriction against sexual relations between husband and wife as a method of birth control will tend to lead to prostitution. (P034)

### Religion
The use of contraceptives is lower for Catholics than for Protestants, and lower for Protestants than for Jews (F101)

There is no correlation between religious affiliation and the planning of pregnancy. (P080)

### Religion/Education
When the rhythm method is the only method of family limitation used, it is inversely related to education for Catholics and directly related for Protestants. (F101)

### Religiosity
The closer the attachment to the Catholic Church, the greater the tendency to avoid contraception, while the closer attachment of Protestants to the church results in a greater use of contraception. (F101)

### Religious Affiliation
Catholic women married to Protestant men practice birth control more than Protestant women married to Catholic men, and both types practice birth control more than when both spouses are Catholic or Protestant. (L010)

### Residence (Urban/Rural)
People with farm backgrounds are less likely than others to control fertility. (F101)

People living in metropolitan areas are more likely than others to adopt appliance methods of family limitation and less likely to adopt either rhythm or withdrawal methods. (F101)

### Sex Status
There is little difference between the families of male university graduates and female university graduates in the spacing of the birth of the first child after marriage. (A003)

Of those couples who indicated that they were using contraceptives since the birth of their first child, significantly more wives distrusted the contraceptive method than did husbands. (L013)

### Sexual Adjustment
Wives who have confidence in the contraceptive being used experience better sexual adjustment following the birth of the first child than do wives who mistrust the contraceptive being used. On the other hand, there is no significant difference in sexual adjustment between husbands who trust the contraceptive they use and those who mistrust it. (L013)

### Sibling Rivalry
There is a correlation between parental identification with the child and regression to early attitudes of sibling rivalry and the practice of the spacing of births by abortion. (D071)

### Size of Family
The smaller the family, the more likely it is to have been planned. (F101)

## BIRTH (PREMATURE), ADJUSTMENT TO
### X  Conflict in Family
Parents who seek a reality-based understanding of the implications of a premature birth are more likely than those who have avoided external information (external to self-fantasy) to retain healthy family relationships throughout (and after) the crisis (i.e., of premature birth). (C108)

Parents who express negative feelings (aggression, guilt) about a premature birth are more likely than those who suppress these feelings to retain healthy family relationships throughout (and after) the crisis (i.e., of premature birth). (C108)

### Independence of Family
Parents who seek help (medical, familial, religious) are more likely than those who are reluctant to accept assistance (assuming it is available) to retain healthy family relationships throughout (and after) the crisis of a premature birth. (C108)

## BIRTH RATE       X  Economic Role of Family
The lower the economic usefulness of the large family, the lower the fertility. (W022)

## BIRTH SPACING              X  Age at Marriage
The average time interval between marriage of a couple and the birth of their first child increases with the average age at marriage of the couple. (C019)

### Children, Number of
There is an inverse relationship between the interval from marriage to birth of the first child and the number of children eventually born (i.e., the larger the number of children in the family, the smaller is the interval between marriage and the birth of the first child). (U.S. university graduates). (L018)

### Marriage Ceremony
The time interval between marriage and the birth of the first child is longer for couples having religious wedding ceremonies than for couples having civil wedding ceremonies. (C019)

### Occupation
The interval from marriage to the birth of the first child varies directly with position on the occupational scale; laborers and farmers have a shorter interval than do professional groups. (C019)

### Pregnancy, Attitude Toward
The greater the time between the previous and the new pregnancy, the greater was the proportion of mothers who were "delighted." (S191)

### Premarital Pregnancy
Where there is premarital conception, the interval between the first and second child is greater than when the first child is conceived after marriage (Denmark). (C124)

### BIRTH STATUS OF CHILD          X   Child Support
Men are less likely to support their wives' children by other unions than their own children from the same women. (B245)

### BODY IMAGE
#### X   Mother-Child Relations (Physical Contact)
A disturbance of the body image will result from a deficiency in the physical contact (touching, looking, kinesthetic experience) between mother and child. (B241)

### BREAST FEEDING          X   Behavior of Child
Breast feeding and later child behavior are not associated. (S191)

### Breast Feeding, Attitude Toward
The experience of having nursed will not affect the mother's desire to continue nursing. (P063)

### Class
A significantly higher percentage of lower-class (Chicago) children were breast-fed only than were middle-class (Chicago) children. (H011)

There is no significant difference in the use of breast feeding between the middle class and the working class. (W002)

Breast feeding is more prevalent in the lower class. (W002)

There is no significant difference in the duration of breast feeding between the middle class and the working class. (W002)

### Dependency
Feeding practice (breast v. bottle feeding) and dependency of child are not associated. (S191)

### Dependency of Mother
Women who prefer to bottle feed their children are more likely than those who prefer to breast feed to show dependent personality traits. (A063)

### Emotional and Behavioral Adjustment
At ten days after birth, breast-fed infants are more likely to show emotional disturbance and nonnutritional sucking than are cup-fed infants. (B272)

### Father Absence
When the father is absent for long periods of time, children are more often breast fed.

### Feeding Problems
There is no relationship between whether or not the infant was breast fed and his having feeding problems (e.g., prolonged periods of appetite loss, etc.) (U.S.). (S191)

### Guilt
Women who choose to bottle feed their children are more likely to manifest guilt feelings than are those who prefer breast feeding. (A063)

### Health of Child
Children who are breast fed tend to be physically superior to those who are not. (B272)

### I.Q.
Given the same environment, breast-fed infants are more advanced mentally than are bottle-fed infants.

### Juvenile Delinquency/Neurosis
A greater number of delinquent children than neurotic children have not been breast fed. (B214)

### Maternal-Role Behavior
Whether or not breast feeding is continued is directly related to the amount of maternalness exhibited in the first few days of breast feeding. (P063)

### Mental Illness of Child (Schizophrenia/Neurosis)
Mothers of schizophrenic children are more likely to breast feed (the patients) than are mothers of neurotics.

### Mother-Child Relations
The more sensitive, consistent, and attentive the mother is relative to the child, the more likely she is to breast feed the infant. (B272)

### Mother-Child Relations (Affection)
Because of the physical closeness with the mother, breast feeding is more conducive than is bottle feeding to satisfying the child's affective needs. (Y042)

### Mother-Child Relations (Rejection)
There is a correlation between maternal rejection of the child and the practice of bottle feeding the child. (A063)

There is no correlation between maternal rejection and the practice of bottle feeding the infant. (A063)

### Mother-Child Relations (Warmth)
There is no relationship between degree of warmth displayed toward the child in infancy and the mother's decision to breast feed or not to breast feed her child (U.S.). (S191)

### Motor Development
Given the same environment, breast-fed infants are slightly less advanced in body development than are bottle-fed infants.

### Obesity
Obesity in the child is correlated with inadequate breast feeding and prolonged bottle feeding. (B272)

### Ordinal Position
Among families that have more than two children, older children are more likely to have been breast fed than are younger children (U.S.). (S191)

The later the birth rank of a child, the less likely it is that he will be breast fed, and if he is, the period of breast feeding will be shorter. (S263)

### Personality Adjustment (Nervousness)
There is no relationship between bottle or breast feeding and the degree of nervousness in the child. (S200)

### Personality Development
Generous suckling and later weaning lead to generosity, optimism, and cooperative peaceful behavior; ungenerous suckling and early weaning lead to arrogance, aggression, impatience, suspicion, competitiveness, quarrelsomeness, and nostalgic sadness.

### Personality (Motherliness)
The psychosomatic state of motherliness is correlated with and depends upon the mother's breast feeding of the child. (B272)

### Personality Problems
There is no relationship between the type or the degree of mental disturbance which a child develops and the fact of having been breast or bottle fed. (B239)

### Personality Problems of Child
Maternal anxiety about breast feeding is a cause of irritability and excitability in the child. (B272)

### Personality Problems of Mother (Oral/Anal)
Women who prefer to bottle feed their children are more likely to show oral eroticism, oral sadism, and anal expulsiveness than are those who prefer breast feeding. (A063)

### Personality Problems of Mother (Penis Envy)
Women who choose to breast feed rather than bottle feed their children are more likely to manifest penis envy. (A063)

### Personality (Security)
There is no relationship between breast feeding in infancy and security in college students.

### Pregnancy, Attitude Toward
There is no relationship between how happy the mother was on becoming pregnant and her decision to breast feed or not to breast feed the child (U.S.). (S191)

### Premarital Pregnancy
Premarital pregnancy is more likely among those who prefer to bottle feed their children than among those who prefer breast feeding. (A063)

### Self-Conception of Mother
There is no relation between the practice of bottle feeding and a lack of self-esteem on the part of the mother. (A063)

### Sex Anxiety of Mother
There is a negative correlation between the mother's sex anxiety and the practice of breast feeding the child. (A063)

### Sex-Role Adjustment of Mother
There is a correlation between maternal psychosexual and sex-role adjustment and the desire and ability to breast feed the child. (A063)

Women who prefer bottle feeding are more likely than those who prefer breast feeding to manifest sex-role dissatisfaction. (A063)

### Sibling Rivalry
Women who choose to bottle feed their children are more likely to report sibling rivalry than are those who breast feed. (A063)

### Speech Development
There is no relationship between the age at which a child learns to talk and bottle or breast feeding. (S200)

### Values
There is a correlation between the practice of unlimited breast feeding of the infant and the norm of generosity in the larger society. (K111)

## BREAST FEEDING, ATTITUDE TOWARD
### X   Breast Feeding
The experience of having nursed will not affect the mother's desire to continue nursing. (P063)

### Breast Feeding Problems
The more positive the mother's attitude toward breast feeding her child, the more milk she will produce. (B272)

The infants of mothers with positive attitudes toward breast feeding tend to have less difficulty in sucking, to refuse the breast less and the bottle more, than do those of negative mothers. (B272)

## BREAST FEEDING, DURATION OF
### X   Age of Mother
There is no necessary correlation between the length of time a child is nursed and the age of the mother. (G148)

### Behavior Problems (Thumb-Sucking)
Infants who are breast fed for a reasonably long period of time are less likely to become thumb-suckers than infants who have had little or no breast-feeding experience. (Y042)

There is no difference between infants who have had no breast feeding and those who have been breast fed for a longer-than-"average" period of time regarding the duration and severity of thumb-sucking. (Y042)

The sucking drive is strengthened by prolonged gratification. (Y042)

### Class
Breast feeding is more prevalent and of longer duration among lower-class than among upper-class Negro families. (W133)

### Class/Child-Rearing Attitudes
Extended durations of breast feeding are a function of irregular maternal behavior arising from poor socioeconomic conditions, rather than of a positive supportive attitude toward child rearing. (B272)

### Emotional Adjustment of Child
There is no relationship between duration of breast feeding and emotional maladjustment of the child. (K113)

### Fertility
An extended lactation period will tend to reduce the fertility rate. (F028)

### I.Q.
After nine months, there is a negative correlation between duration of breast feeding of the infant and his intelligence level. (B272)

### Juvenile Delinquency/Neurosis
Neurotic children tend to have been breast fed for longer periods than delinquent children. (B214)

Neurotic children tend to have been breast fed for longer periods than delinquent children. (B238)

### Maternal Overprotectiveness
There is a correlation between maternal overprotection and length of time the infant is breast fed. (A063)

Overprotected children had a significantly longer breast-feeding time than did nonoverprotected children. (L117)

If maternal overprotection is the result of a compensatory reaction to feelings of rejection, it will not result in extended breast feeding. (L162)

#### Maternal-Role Behavior
Maternal behavior is positively correlated with a preference for breast feeding for five months or longer. (L165)

#### Mental Illness (Schizophrenia/Neurosis)
Mothers of schizophrenics are more likely to breast feed for a short period (six weeks or less) than are mothers of neurotics.

#### Mother-Child Relations (Rejection)
Mothers who breast feed the infant for one month or less tend to be rejecting; those who breast feed for 12 months or more tend to be overprotective. (B272)

#### Ordinal Position
There is no significant correlation between the length of breast feeding and the ordinal position of the child. (L162)

Only children tend to be weaned earlier than first children of multichildren families. (L162)

Midchildren tend to be breast-fed longer than either younger or older children. (L162)

Among larger families (more than two children) where the children have been breast fed, the duration of breast feeding is shorter for older children than for younger children (U.S.). (S191)

#### Personality Development
There is no association between the duration of breast feeding and childhood personality development. (S200)

#### Personality of Child (Emotional Maturity)
There is a correlation between months of breast feeding and the emotional maturity of the child. (B272)

#### Personality of Child (Security)
Persons who were never breast fed, or who were breast fed for over one year, show more security than those breast fed for intermediate periods. (B272)

#### Pregnancy, Attitude Toward
Children who are "wanted" tend to be nursed longer than children who are not wanted. (L162)

#### Sex Status of Child
There is no direct association between the length of breast feeding and the sex of the child. (L162)

#### Subsistence Pattern (Hunting and Gathering)
The wild food products collected by women (in societies with hunting and gathering economies) do not provide sufficient suitable food for young children; so thus the time of nursing is prolonged and consequently intervals between births become greater. (T082)

### BREAST-FEEDING PROBLEMS
#### X   Breast Feeding, Attitude Toward
The more positive the mother's attitude toward breast feeding her child, the more milk she will produce. (B272)

The infants of mothers with positive attitudes toward breast feeding tend to have less difficulty in sucking, to refuse the breast less and the bottle more, than do those of negative mothers. (B272)

### BREASTS          X   Sex Taboo (Postpartum)
In societies with a long duration of the postpartum sex taboo, a woman's breasts are less likely to be considered sexual stimuli and feeling of breasts is not part of the sexual interaction. (S079)

### BROKEN HOME
#### X   Accident-Proneness of Child
Children who are accident-prone are more likely than normal children to come from broken homes. (K122)

#### Achievement Motivation
In the United States, men coming from broken homes tend to have lower achievement motivation than those from intact homes. (M246)

#### Age at Marriage
Persons who come from homes broken by death, desertion, or divorce tend to marry at an earlier age than those from intact homes. (H189)

#### Behavior Problems
The relationship between parental loss during early childhood and subsequent psychopathology in the child is most firmly established in the case of personalities prone to delinquent and psychopathic behavior. (B269)

Delinquent girls from unbroken homes are less likely than delinquent girls from broken homes to have social problems, such as alcoholism, sexual irregularities, or mental disabilities. (S210)

#### Behavior Problems (Stealing)
Conduct disorder (e.g., stealing) is significantly related to broken homes, especially among older children, only children, and children with three or more siblings. (H198)

#### Child-Rearing Practices (Punishment)
Children from broken homes are more likely to receive more severe punishment for their delinquency than children who are not from broken homes. (T002)

#### Childhood (Emotional Security)
There is no relationship between divorce, separation, or illegitimate parenthood and remembering an emotionally insecure childhood. (P086)

#### Class
Low socioeconomic status is associated with a high percentage of broken homes. (M181)

#### Criminality
Habitual criminals are much more likely to come from broken homes than are noncriminals. (C105)

#### Dependency
Mother and child are more likely to be more dependent on each other in a broken family than in an intact family. (R129)

#### Deviance
Parents are much more likely to be social deviants (alcoholics, criminals, promiscuous) if they are in broken homes rather than united homes. (M181)

#### Divorce
Among those who have been divorced and remarried, more are likely to come from divorced homes, fewer are likely to come from homes in which one or both parents have died, and still fewer from families that remained intact. (G126)

#### Emotional Problems of Child
Estrangement of the child from the family environment in the early years leads to severe emotional problems in later years. (B283)

### Friendship Choice
Intact families tend to avoid close friendship with broken families, regardless of whether they have been broken by death, divorce, desertion, one remarriage, or both persons being remarried. (Z008)

### Illegitimacy
Girls from homes broken by death or divorce are more likely to have illegitimate children than are those from intact homes. (N055)

### Immigrant/Nonimmigrant
There is a higher percentage of broken homes among native-born than among foreign-born individuals (U.S.). (S210)

### Income
The lower the economic class of the family, the higher the death and divorce rate. (B286)

### Juvenile Delinquency
Regardless of class, delinquency rates are higher for broken than for unbroken homes. (G156)

Regardless of class, delinquency rates are highest for children of homes broken by separation or divorce than by death of a parent (U.S.). (G156)

Children from homes that are intact, but unhappily so, are twice as likely to become delinquents as are those from intact, happy homes (U.S.). (G156)

Children from widowed or widowered homes are 50 per cent more likely to be delinquents than are those from intact homes (U.S.). (G156)

Delinquents are slightly more likely to come from divorced than from intact homes. (U.S.). (G156)

Juvenile delinquents who are Negro are more likely to come from broken homes than are juvenile delinquents who are white. (M009)

The proportion of broken homes among juvenile delinquents who are Negro is greater than the proportion of broken homes among juvenile delinquents who are white. (M009)

The longer the home remains broken, the more likely is the child to become delinquent. (M196)

Delinquent girls are more likely to come from broken homes than nondelinquent girls, broken homes do not distinguish delinquent from nondelinquent boys. (M205)

There is no correlation between the age of the child when the home is broken and the incidence of delinquent behavior by the child. (N063)

There is a correlation between broken homes and delinquency in the higher classes, but not in the lower classes (S219)

### Juvenile Delinquency by (Sex Status)
Female juvenile delinquents are more likely than male juvenile delinquents to come from broken homes. (M009)

### Juvenile Delinquency/Neurosis
A greater number of delinquent than neurotic children come from broken homes. (B214)

### Juvenile Delinquency (Recidivism)
Broken homes are more characteristic of repeated juvenile offenders than of first offenders. (M009)

### Marital Adjustment
Among married persons, those who were reared in divorced homes are more likely to feel inadequacies in their present marital relationship and to admit to problems in their marriages than are those from families in which one or both parents have died or families that remained intact. (G126)

### Maternal Role, Attitude Toward
Broken homes are associated with unwillingness on the part of the mother to accept the responsibility of the child. (K120)

### Mental Deficiency
Among disturbed children, mental deficiency is associated with normal, rather than broken homes. (H198)

### Mental Illness (Schizophrenia)
Mothers of schizophrenics are more likely than those of neurotics or normals to come from homes broken by separation, divorce, or death. (M218)

There is a higher incidence of divorce, separation, and desertion among parents of schizophrenics than among those of the control group ("normals"). (O034)

### Mother-Child Relations (Rejection)
Broken homes are associated with mothers who are likely to resent and reject their children. (K120)

### Neurosis
Divorce, separation, and desertion as causes of deprivation occur more frequently in the parents of psychopathic personalities and psychoneurotics than among parents of psychotics or "normals." (O034)

### Parent-Child Relations
The success of the parent-child relations is not necessarily contingent upon whether the home is broken or unbroken (but rather on the degree of adjustment between the child and parents). (B286)

The adjustment of adolescents to parents is likely to be poorer in broken homes than in unbroken homes. (N010)

### Parental-Role Adjustment
Among those who are married, persons coming from families in which there has been divorce, separation, or a death of one or both parents are more likely to mention their children as the most positive aspect of their marriage than those who were raised in families that remained intact. (G126)

### Peer Relations
Adolescent girls from reconstituted families are more likely than those from broken and unbroken families to maintain better relations with their classmates. (B276)

There is no difference between adolescents from unbroken homes and those from broken and reconstituted homes regarding their popularity among classmates. (B276)

Adolescent boys from unbroken families are more likely to report a greater number of school friends than adolescent boys from broken and reconstituted families. (B276)

### Personality Adjustment
Adolescents from unbroken homes are no more likely to show personality maladjustments (Minnesota Personality Test) than are adolescents from broken and reconstituted families. (B276)

### Personality Adjustment (Happiness)
Persons reared in divorced or separated homes are more likely to report feeling greater present unhappiness than are persons who were reared in homes where both or one parent died or persons from homes where the family was intact. (G126)

Among married persons, those who have come from divorced families are more likely to report unhappiness than are those who are from either families that remained intact or families in which one or both parents died. (G126)

### Personality of Mother (Insecurity)
Broken homes are associated with insecurity in the mother. (K120)

### Personality Problems (Anxiety)
Women reared in families where one or both parents have died or in divorced families show greater physical and psychological anxiety than do women from families that have remained intact. (G126)

### Personality Problems (Nervous Breakdown)
Persons reared in divorced homes are more likely to report having felt at some time that they were about to have a nervous breakdown than are persons from intact families or families where one parent has died. (G126)

### Psychosomatic Illness
There is no relationship between the severity and frequency of psychosomatic symptoms of children from broken and those from unbroken homes. (N057)

Among children whose families have been broken by death, there is no relationship between religion and the likelihood of the child to have many psychosomatic symptoms. Catholics and Jews are no more likely than Protestants to have many psychosomatic symptoms. (R129)

### Race
There is a higher percentage of broken homes among Negroes than among whites. (S210)

### Scholastic Achievement
There is no difference between adolescents from unbroken homes and those from broken and reconstituted homes regarding their mean school-grade point average. (B276)

### Scholastic Adjustment
Adolescent girls from reconstituted families are more likely than those from broken and unbroken families to have positive attitudes regarding school. (B276)

Adolescent girls from reconstituted families are more likely than those from broken and unbroken families to maintain better relationships with their teachers. (B276)

There is no difference between adolescents from unbroken homes and those from broken and reconstituted homes regarding their degree of participation in school activities. (B276)

There is no difference between adolescents from unbroken homes and those from broken and reconstituted homes regarding their attitudes toward school. (B276)

Adolescents from unbroken homes are less likely to be absent from school than are those from broken and reconstituted homes. (B276)

### Self-Conception
Children of divorced or separated parents are more likely than children of intact families to have low self-esteem. (R129)

Children whose parents are separated are as likely as children of intact families to have high self-esteem, but they are less likely to have medium self-esteem and more likely to have low self-esteem. (R129)

Children whose parents had been separated by death do not differ from those of intact families in terms of self-esteem. (R129)

### Self-Conception of Child
The child's self-esteem (as measured by Q-Sort Personality Tests) is greater among families where both natural parents are living and together than among homes broken by divorce or death of the father. (S264)

### Social Adjustment
Men from broken homes are less likely to show successful social adaptation than are those from intact homes. (H206)

Asocial behavior is more likely on the part of men from broken homes than men from intact homes. (H206)

## BROKEN HOME, AGE AT
### X   Juvenile Delinquency
Among children from broken homes, delinquents are more likely to have experienced the break at an earlier age than are nondelinquent children. (M196)

Prisoners are more likely to have been separated from their parents at an earlier age than are persons from the general population. (M196)

Among delinquents separated from their parents, the earlier the age of separation the larger the number of court offenses (Court Offense Score). (S182)

## BROKEN HOME (DEATH/DIVORCE)
### X   Emotional Problems of Child
It is divorce in particular, rather than family breakup in general, that is most closely associated with signs of emotional disturbances among Catholics and Jews. (R129)

### Personality Adjustment of Child
Children whose mothers were widowed when they were relatively young tend to be somewhat better adjusted than children whose mothers were divorced when they were young. (R129)

### Stepparent-Child Relations
Children who have lost a parent by death will adjust better to a stepparent than will children from divorced homes. (B286)

## BROKEN HOME (STEPCHILDREN)
### X   Juvenile Delinquency
There is no correlation between the number of stepchildren in the broken home and delinquency in the child. (N063)

# C

**CANNIBALISM   X   Religion (Maternal Deities)**
Cannibalism tends to be associated with matrilineal fertility cults. (W154)

**CAR OWNERSHIP             Juvenile Delinquency**
**X   Child-Rearing Practices (Control)**
Because of the freedom from family control which the ownership of a car allows the adolescent, the youngster who owns a car is more likely to become delinquent than the one who does not. (N057)

**CASTRATION ANXIETY      X   Menstrual Taboo**
Extensiveness of menstrual taboos in a society is associated with intensity and frequency of castration anxiety among men. (S079)

**Mother–Son Relations (Sex)**
The intensity and frequency of castration anxiety is associated with an intense sexual tie of the boy with the mother. (S079)

**CASTRATION COMPLEX   X   Dependency of Son**
The castration complex is directly associated with a high degree of dependence on the mother. (W154)

**CELIBACY                          X   Remarriage**
Because norms approving celibacy are never strict for men, widowers are more likely to remarry than are widows. (G156)

**CHILD DEVELOPMENT        X   Size of Family**
There is no relationship between family size and mothers' correct recollection of their children's developmental record, i.e., age of weaning, walking, toilet training, health record. (M236)

**CHILD PSYCHOLOGY, TRAINING IN**
**X   Child-Rearing Attitudes**
Parents who have taken courses in child psychology are less likely to manifest harsh, punitive, or excessively demanding and overpossessive child-rearing attitudes. (C097)

**CHILD REARING                          X   Class**
Middle-class parents are more likely than working-class parents to discuss child rearing with friends, neighbors, and experts. (K089)

**CHILD-REARING ANXIETY**
**X   Child-Rearing Practices (Punishment)**
The greater the parent's child-rearing anxiety, the greater his hostility and use of physical punishment. (B232)

**Dependency**
To the degree that the mother shows child-rearing anxiety, the more likely it is that her daughter will show attention-seeking behavior and dependence. (B232)

**Ordinal Position**
Early-born children are treated with more anxiety than are later-born children. (R106)

**Toilet Training**
The more severe the mother is in toilet training the child, the more likely is she to be highly anxious concerning child rearing (U.S.). (S191)

**CHILD-REARING ANXIETY OF FATHER**
**X   Aggression**
The greater the child-rearing anxiety of the father, the lower the incidence of aggression in school by daughters with hostile mothers and the higher the incidence at home. (B232)

**CHILD-REARING ANXIETY OF MOTHER**
**X   Feeding (Demand)**
High child-rearing anxiety of the mother is associated with the use of scheduled feeding. (S191)

**CHILD-REARING ATTITUDES   X   Age of Parents**
For both parents, concern with obedience and discipline problems decreases with age (education-controlled). (G126)

**Authoritarianism of Father**
Democratic attitudes in the father significantly correlate with the attitudes of equalitarian treatment of children and the encouragement of their independence and affection as a means of control. (N053)

**Behavior of Child**
Behavior of middle-class children does not correlate with parental attitudes toward child rearing. (Z010)

**Behavior Problems**
Maternal child-rearing attitudes are not related to the behavioral or mental problems of the child. (M208)

**Child Psychology, Training in**
Parents who have taken courses in child psychology are less likely to manifest harsh, punitive, or excessively demanding and overpossessive child-rearing attitudes. (C097)

**Education of Mother**
The higher the educational level of the mother, the more likely is she to justify her disciplinary measures. (K115)

**Mental Illness of Child**
Girls with incipient psychopathology are more likely to attribute deviant child-rearing attitudes to their mothers than are normal girls. (H185)

**Mental Illness of Child (Schizophrenia)**
Although the mothers of schizophrenic and normal children do not differ in their attitudes toward child-rearing practices, schizophrenic children perceive their mothers as holding more deviant attitudes than do normal children. (G127)

The pathological child-rearing attitudes of mothers of schizophrenic children are a reaction to the child's disorder rather than a cause of it. (K096)

The more pathological the parental attitudes, the more severe the type of schizophrenia in the child. (W147)

### Mental Problems

Mothers of schizophrenic children showed less pathological child-rearing attitudes than did the mothers of brain-damaged and retarded children. Mothers of both groups of ill children manifest more pathological child-rearing attitudes than do mothers of normal children. (K096)

Mothers of "normals" are less certain regarding their attitudes toward various child-rearing practices than are mothers of mongols and psychotic children. (P075)

### Parent-Child Relations (Acceptance)

As measured by the PARI, Stanford-Binet, and Q-Sort Personality Tests, there is little relationship between various parental attitudes toward child rearing and parental acceptance of the child.

### Parent-Child Relations (Conflict)

There is no relationship between parental child-rearing attitudes and the degree of conflict they had experienced with their parents during their adolescence. (B249)

### Parental-Role Adjustment

Parents who report greater feelings of adequacy in the parental role are more likely than parents who feel more inadequate to identify physical care or material problems as sources of concern in child rearing. (G126)

### Personality Problems of Child (Acting Out)

Attitudes of mothers of disturbed children do not correlate with the child's being an "acting out" or an "internalizing" symptom type. Fathers of "internalizers" are more likely to favor nonpunishment and express affection. (Z011)

### Pregnancy, Attitude Toward

Pregnant women who regard their condition as an illness are more likely to express retaliatory child-rearing attitudes than those women who accept pregnancy as a natural development, regardless of social status. (R107)

### Pregnancy, Attitude Toward/Class

Parental attitudes toward pregnancy are more closely related to child-rearing attitudes than is class. (R107)

### Religion

Catholic parents are more likely than Protestant parents to value filial obedience. (E102)

### Scholastic Achievement

Mothers of high achieving students are more likely to have dominating child-rearing attitudes than are mothers of low achievers. (D074)

Mothers of high achieving students are more likely to have ignoring attitudes toward the child than are mothers of low achievers, attitudes which imply high restrictions on the child in the home. (D074)

Mothers of high achieving students tend to have more punitive attitudes with respect to child rearing than do those of low achievers. (D074)

### Size of Family

The disparity between parental attitudes (discipline, control) toward psychotic children and normal siblings decreases with increasing size of family. (D064)

## CHILD-REARING ATTITUDES (AGGRESSION)
### X    Child-Rearing Practices (Permissiveness)

The more permissive the mother regarding aggression, the less severe she will be in punishing aggressive behavior (U.S.). (S191)

## CHILD-REARING ATTITUDES (AUTHORITARIANISM)    X    Age of Mother

There is an inverse curvilinear relationship between the mother's age and authoritarian maternal attitudes. (Z011)

### Education

The more education the mother has, the less likely she is to be authoritarian and controlling in her maternal attitudes. (Z011)

### Juvenile Delinquency

Mothers of delinquent children are more likely than mothers of normal children to have punitive, controlling, and authoritarian attitudes toward the child. (M208)

### Mental Illness

Mothers of psychiatric patients are more likely to have authoritarian and controlling attitudes than are mothers of normals. (T097)

### Mental Illness (Schizophrenia/Neurosis)

Mothers of schizophrenics are more likely than mothers of neurotics or normals to have controlling and authoritarian attitudes toward rearing the child. (M218)

### Occupational Rank

The higher the occupational level of the husband, the less authoritarian and controlling the maternal attitudes. (Z011)

### Pregnancy Anxiety

Mothers who were highly anxious during pregnancy have more authoritarian attitudes toward child rearing than do mothers who were not as anxious during pregnancy. (D067)

### Sex-Role Identification of Child

The more authoritarian the mother's attitudes relative to children, the greater their imitation of like-sex parent. (H179)

## CHILD-REARING ATTITUDES (COMPETITIVENESS)
### X    Achievement Motivation

Mothers of boys with high achievement motivation tend to expect their sons to be more competitive than do mothers of sons with low achievement motivation. (R097)

## CHILD-REARING ATTITUDES (CONSENSUS)
### X    Homogamy

The greater the similarity of the parents' backgrounds, the higher their agreement regarding child-rearing practices. (G156)

### Personality Adjustment of Child

There is a curvilinear relationship between the amount of discrepancy between the parents in their role prescriptions for the child and the child's consequent conflict and maladjustment.

### Personality of Mother (Anomie)

Anomic mothers tend significantly to be in disagreement with their husbands' views on discipline; nonanomic mothers report that they and their husbands were agreed. (A069)

## CHILD-REARING ATTITUDES (DEMOCRATIC)
### X    Juvenile Delinquency
Mothers of delinquents do not differ from mothers of normal children in the extent to which they hold democratic child-rearing attitudes. (M208)

### Mental Illness of Child
There is no correlation between the extent to which the mother has democratic child-rearing attitudes and the mental health of the child. (T097)

### Personality Problems of Child
There is no tendency for young daughters with incipient psychopathology to attribute more democratic attitudes that are viewed as deviant to their mothers than normal daughters do. (H177)

## CHILD-REARING ATTITUDES (DEPENDENCY)
### X    Achievement Motivation of Mother
There is a curvilinear relationship between achievement motivation of mothers and their independence-training attitudes toward the child. (G129)

### Mental Illness (Schizophrenia)
Mental illness is directly correlated with the hostility of the mother toward any initiative or independence on the part of the daughter. (L118)

### Occupation of Husband
Mothers whose husbands have entrepreneurial jobs are more likely than mothers whose husbands have bureaucratic jobs to say that children should be put on their own as soon as possible to solve their own problems. (M062)

### Religion
There is no significant difference between Protestant and Catholic mothers' attitudes toward independence training in social settings where Catholics have moved away from more traditional Catholic attitudes. (M246)

## CHILD-REARING ATTITUDES (DISCIPLINE)
### X    Child-Rearing Practices (Strictness)
The advocacy of firm discipline by the father correlates with the attitudes of strictness, forcing independence upon the child, and the use of harsh punishment. (N053)

### Marital Adjustment of Wife
Happy wives more often consider it essential that children be held to a strict discipline than do unhappy wives. (T074)

## CHILD-REARING ATTITUDES (DOMINANCE)
### X    Adult-Child Relations (Interaction)
Children of parents who reflect large differences in dominance attitudes (measured by the USC Parent Attitude Survey) will avoid adult contacts in free-activity setting to a greater degree than children of parents who reflect small differences in dominance attitudes. (T101)

## CHILD-REARING ATTITUDES (EVALUATION)
### X    Mental Illness (Schizophrenia)
"Poor" premorbid schizophrenics (those with poor general functioning before the onset of illness) perceive their parents' child-rearing attitudes as being more deviant than do "good" premorbid schizophrenics, who in turn perceive these attitudes as being more deviant than do normal subjects. (G127)

## CHILD-REARING ATTITUDES (FLEXIBILITY)
### X    Power Structure of Family
Parents reared in families in which the mother had more control than the father are more likely to show flexibility in their child-rearing attitudes than are those from families with other control patterns. (B249)

## CHILD-REARING ATTITUDES (NEED GRATIFICATION)
### X    Mental Illness (Schizophrenia)
Mothers of schizophrenic children are more likely than others to have restrictive attitudes regarding the gratification of the child's physical and psychological needs. (B284)

## CHILD-REARING ATTITUDES (OVERPOSSESSIVENESS)
### X    Mental Illness of Child (Schizophrenia)
Mothers of schizophrenic children tend to be more "overpossessive" (as measured by the PARI) in their child-rearing attitudes than do mothers of normal children. (S249)

## CHILD-REARING ATTITUDES (PATHOLOGICAL)
### X    Personality Problems
Mothers are more likely to be pathological in the child-rearing attitudes if the child is not normal. (S187)

## CHILD-REARING ATTITUDES (PERMISSIVENESS)
### X    I.Q. of Father
Fathers who express permissive child-rearing attitudes are more intelligent (Terman Concept Mastery Test) than those who express restrictive child-rearing attitudes. (B227)

### Personality of Father
Fathers who express permissive child-rearing attitudes are more likely to be self-reliant, ascendant, rebellious toward authority figures, persuasive, counteractive, and sarcastic. (B227)

## CHILD-REARING ATTITUDES (RESTRICTIVENESS)
### X    Conformity
Fathers who express restrictive child-rearing attitudes have higher scores on a test of conforming behavior (Crutchfield). (B227)

### Ethnocentrism
Fathers who express restrictive child-rearing attitudes have higher scores on the Ethnocentrism Scale than fathers who express permissive attitudes. (B227)

### Mental Illness (Schizophrenia)
If the mother expresses restrictive attitudes about child rearing, it is more likely that her son will become a schizophrenic. (B227)

### Personality of Father
Fathers who are more restrictive in their attitudes toward child rearing tend to be constricted, submissive, suggestible individuals with little self-assurance; fathers who are more permissive tend to be more self-reliant, ascendant, and to function effectively (Q-Sort Personality Evaluations). (S249)

### Political Attitudes (Conservatism)
If the family has restrictive child-rearing attitudes, the child is more likely to develop conservative political opinions. (B227)

## CHILD-REARING ATTITUDES (RIGIDITY)
### X   Mental Illness of Child (Schizophrenia)
Parents of schizophrenics tend to have rigid attitudes regarding acceptable behavior. (K093)

### Urban/Rural
Parents who were reared on farms are more likely to be rigid in their child-rearing attitudes than are others. (B249)

## CHILD-REARING ATTITUDES (SEX)
### X   Premarital Sex Relations (Dalliance)
Exploitive premarital sex behavior, as a late adolescent pattern, is likely to decline as parental opposition to premarital sex relations declines. (P083)

## CHILD-REARING ATTITUDES (SEX ROLE)
### X   Employment of Mother
Working and nonworking mothers do not express differing points of view on sex-role training. (Y051)

### Occupation
Mothers whose husbands have entrepreneurial jobs (as opposed to mothers whose husbands have bureaucratic jobs) more often state that, among adolescents, males should perform activities traditionally associated with their sex (washing the family car) and girls should also perform activities traditionally associated with their sex (making beds). (M062)

## CHILD-REARING ATTITUDES (STRICTNESS)
### X   Child-Rearing Practices
There is a correlation between parental child-rearing practices and the child-rearing attitudes of the adolescent, with a tendency for those coming from less strict homes to be more strict in their attitudes than their parents were. (B249)

### Mental Illness
Mothers of psychiatric patients are less likely to have strict child-rearing attitudes than are mothers of normals. (T097)

## CHILD REARING (COLLECTIVE)
### Achievement Motivation
### X   Child-Rearing Practices (Collective)
Kibbutz children have lower achievement motivation than do nonkibbutz children. (R096)

### Behavior Problems
Children reared collectively (in kibbutzim) exhibit more enuresis and thumb-sucking than children reared within the family. (G124)

Children who are reared collectively (mother surrogate for each group) are more likely than children raised at home by their own mothers to develop behavior problems (enuresis, thumb-sucking, nail-biting, aggression). (R094)

### Economic Pattern (Collective)
Where the economic pattern is collective, the socialization of children becomes the responsibility of the group. (E087)

### I.Q.
Children reared collectively (in kibbutzim) have higher I.Q.'s (after 10 years of age) than do children reared at home, despite early retardation in ego development due to inconsistent mothering. (R095)

Kibbutz children have a higher level of intellectual de-

velopment than do nonkibbutz children (as measured by interpretations of Rorschach and TAT tests). (R096)

### Motor Development
There is no relationship between the development of motor processes and communal rearing of children. (S214)

### Neurosis
Among collectively reared (on kibbutzim) children, neurosis is a result of specific parent-child interaction rather than of the conditions of collective education. (G124)

### Occupational Aspirations
Kibbutz children identify fewer long-range occupational goals than do nonkibbutz children (on Rorschach tests). (R096)

### Parent-Child Relations (Ambivalence)
The reduction in the socializing duties of the Israeli parents on the collectives has reduced the ambivalence (hostility-love) of the parent-child relationship by permitting the parent to give love without thwarting the child as much as in the standard type of family. (T087)

### Sexual Problems (of Adolescents)
Adolescents raised in kibbutzim have fewer problems concerning heterosexual activities and sexual problems have generally less salience for them than adolescents raised in families. (R096)

### Social Adjustment of Child
Rorschach tests show no difference between kibbutz-reared and nonkibbutz-reared children in overall social adjustment. (R096)

## CHILD-REARING PRACTICES
### X   Child-Rearing Attitudes (Strictness)
There is a correlation between parental child-rearing practices and the child-rearing attitudes of the adolescent, with a tendency for those coming from less strict homes to be more strict in their attitudes than their parents were. (B249)

### Child-Rearing Values of Daughter
There is no correlation betweet the child-rearing values of the daughter and the practices of the mother, except concerning frequent punishment for disobedience. (W153)

### Class
Upper-class mothers are more likely than middle-class mothers to justify their demands on children by asserting their authority, while middle-class mothers are more likely to appeal to a general moral principle or a rule originating outside the family. (G156)

Middle-class parents have not changed the values they have tried to inculcate in their children; but because they have been more responsive to the experts, they have quickly changed their techniques in the service of the same values, while working-class parents have lagged behind. (K089)

Middle-class mothers want their husbands to be supportive of the children, especially of sons, and do not ask for the imposition of much constraint; middle-class fathers play a role in accordance with this demand, but working-class mothers want their husbands to give restraints and working-class fathers often refuse to take this responsibility. (K089)

The lower the social class, the more likely a mother is to

use traditional methods of infant rearing (breast feeding demand feeding, late weaning, and pacifiers) as opposed to more formalized methods derived from psychological literature. (K160)

Social class of parents generally does not correlate with child-rearing practices. (M180)

### Class (Modal Personality)
There is no correlation between child-rearing techniques and the modal personality of a social class. (M180)

### Creativity
Children whose mothers encourage their maturation are higher in intellecutal originality than are children whose mothers encourage infantile behavior. (A071)

### Economic Role
The emphasis in child training will be toward the kinds of behavior especially useful for the adult economy. (B037)

### Education of Mother/Father
The mother's child-rearing behavior is more closely related to her husband's rather than to her own educational level. (B250)

### Employment of Mother
Mothers with jobs tend to discipline their children in order to acquaint them with frustration more than do mothers with no employment. (G127)

Mothers with jobs tend to be more prescriptive concerning rules of their children's behavior than do mothers with no outside employment. (G127)

Mothers with no employment outside the home are more likely to use personalistic appeals as the justification for the rules of behavior to their children than are mothers with jobs. (G127)

There is no difference between married working and nonworking mothers regarding various child-rearing practices (measured by the Schoben Scale). (G127)

Working and nonworking mothers do not differ significantly in their child-rearing practices and attitudes. (S257)

The classification of mothers by whether or not they are employed is almost unrelated to child-rearing patterns. (Y051)

### Employment of Mother, Attitude Toward
If mothers are in their *preferred* work or nonwork *roles,* working or not working makes little difference in their child rearing. (Y050)

### Employment of Mother/Education
Education of mother is more highly correlated with differences in child-rearing practices than whether or not the mother is employed. (Y051)

In *nonworking* groups, college mothers are significantly more often rated high in independence training, in sensitivity, in consistency between principles and practice, and in clarity in limit setting; thus having higher mean scores on "adequacy of mothering." (Y051)

However, *working* groups differ only on ratings of sensitivity to child's needs (high-school lower) and father's being the stricter parent (college lower). (Y051)

### Isolation of Nuclear Family
Children who are being brought up for "sociological interdependence" (i.e., anchorage and identification in the wider kin-group rather than the nuclear family) will be taught and brought up by members of the child's descent group as well as by the parents; children who are being brought up for "sociological independence" (i.e., anchorage and identification in the nuclear family) will be brought up by nonmembers of the descent group as well as by their parents. (C093)

### Moral Beliefs
Parental possessiveness and dominance are positively correlated with the child's acceptance of beliefs in immanent justice, moral realism, retribution, and severe punishment; the tendency of parents to ignore the child is negatively correlated with such beliefs. (J021)

The tendency of the parents to ignore the child should be positively correlated with the child's acceptance of belief in communicable responsibility (guilt by association); parental possessiveness and dominance should be negatively correlated with the child's acceptance of such beliefs. (J021)

### Motor Development
Among Negroes, the less the parents push the child to develop motor functions (sitting, creeping, standing, walking), the more quickly will the child develop them. (W133)

### Neurosis
Children whose parents are indulgent, repressive, or inconsistent toward them are more likely to develop emotional disturbances.

There is no statistical support for the hypothesis that mothers of neurotic children are more restrictive than mothers of normal children.

### Occupation of Father
The occupation of the father does not correlate with the mother's child-rearing practices. (S265)

### Ordinal Position
Mothers tend to show greater relaxation in their child-rearing behavior, especially in their feeding practices, with their second and later children than with the first. (B272)

Parents discipline the firstborn child more and are less consistent and more permissive in their behavior toward him than is the case for later-born children. (S263)

Firstborn children are more likely to be overprotected than later-born children. (S263)

### Parent-Child Relations, Perception of
The behavior of parents toward their children is not significantly correlated with their remembered relationship with their own parents. (B297)

### Peer Relations
Peer-dependent children (who seek dependent rewards from their peers but avoid close relationships with adults) tend to be raised in family environments characterized by lack of supervision and restriction, low parental demands, emotionally indifferent parents, punitive or lax discipline, and encouragement of masculine behavior. (M221)

### Personality Development
No significant and consistent one-to-one relationships have been found between child-care practices in the first and second year and later personality development. (C124)

### Political Integration
The use of bogeymen to scare children into conformity is more likely where physical punishment is little used and where there is a low level of political integration. (A053)

### Religiosity
There is no relationship between strong religious belief and the kinds of child-rearing practices to which a child has been subjected. (B254)

### Sex Status
Boys receive somewhat more physical punishment than girls (except for aggressive girls). (S191)

Girls are more often disciplined by love-oriented techniques. (S191)

Girls receive somewhat more praise for "good" behavior than boys. (S191)

Girls are more often subject to withdrawal for "bad" behavior than boys. (S191)

### Sibling Structure (Age Difference)
The greater the age difference between siblings, the more the firstborn child is "stimulated and instructed" by adults, regardless of the sex of the child. (K149)

### Size of Family
Child neglect is no greater in large families than in small.

Parents in small families spend more time and effort on each child than is the case for large families. (R106)

### Social Network of Parents
The more dispersed a couple's network of social contacts, the more likely they are to be self-conscious about methods of bringing up their children. (B268)

### Socialization, Effectiveness of
The greater the use of the socializing techniques which appeal to forces internal to the child's need system, the greater the internalization of moral standards. (H208)

The more frequent the use of external coercive devices, the more likely the child is to develop a moral orientation based upon fear of authority. (H208)

### Values
Child-rearing practices are related less to general cultural attitudes toward children than to values specific to each system or area of behavior. (W142)

### Work Attitudes of Mother
If mothers work and prefer to do so, or do not work and prefer not to work, working or not working makes little difference in their child-rearing behavior. (Y050)

## CHILD-REARING PRACTICES (ACCELERATION)
### X Behavior Problems (Task Withdrawal)
Adolescent withdrawal from tasks is negatively related to maternal acceleration of the child during his early years (2–7). (K115)

### I.Q.
There is a positive relationship between maternal acceleration of the 2–7-year-old son and his intelligence scores when an adolescent. (K115)

### Mental Illness (Schizophrenia)
A significantly greater number of schizophrenic daughters than of normal ones believed that their mothers tried to accelerate their development during their childhood. (H186)

### Ordinal Position
Mothers tend to accelerate the socialization training of the last-born child to the level of the elder siblings in order to be finished with child care. (R106)

## CHILD-REARING PRACTICES (ACHIEVEMENT)
### X Achievement
Mothers of high achieving sons are more likely to give emotional support for their sons' achievements. (G156)

### Achievement Motivation
Within cultures high in rigidity, the greater the stress on achievement training, the higher the level of folktale achievement imagery. (M246)

Parents of boys with high achievement motivation tend to react to good performance with more warmth and approval, or with disapproval at poor performance, than do parents of boys with low achievement motivation. (R106)

### Age of Child
Mother-son relations that are related to high achievement in sons are most effective if they begin when the son is about six to eight years of age. (G156)

### Age of Parents
Older parents tend to place less emphasis on achievement in child rearing than do younger parents. (R106)

### Child-Rearing Practices (Approval)
Maternal rewarding of achievement efforts of child correlated with rewarding of approval-seeking behavior. (C118)

### Child-Rearing Practices (Dependency)
Mothers who reward achievement efforts of children are less likely to be nurturant or acceptant of dependency. (Maternal rewarding of achievement correlates with independence training.) (C118)

### Class
Lower-class parents place less emphasis on instilling achievement goals in their children than do middle-class parents. (E102)

Middle-class parents place greater emphasis on early training for individual achievement than do lower-class parents. (E102)

### Cognitive Development (Verbal)
Discipline emphasizing academic achievement is associated with a favorable development of verbal activity in the child. (B257)

Rewarding good and criticizing poor academic achievement is positively associated with high verbal ability in children. (B257)

### Mother-Child Relations (Affection)
Maternal rewards for children's achievement efforts do not correlate with expression of maternal affection. (C118)

### Sex Status
Boys are more likely to be socialized to achieve than are girls. (G156)

Fathers are more concerned about how well their sons achieve than about how well their daughters achieve. (J026)

### Surrogate Mother

When their infants are one year of age, mothers who have provided other care-taking figures for their babies are more concerned with their achievement than are mothers who have been the only maternal figure for their infants. (C107)

### CHILD-REARING PRACTICES (ACHIEVEMENT/CONFORMITY)     X   Sex Status

Mothers tend to stress avoidance of undesirable qualities and/or conditions for girls and to stress development and achievement for boys.

### Subsistence Pattern

Compliance training is associated with high-food-accumulation economies (e.g., herding); achievement training is associated with low food-accumulation economies (e.g., hunting and fishing). (M246)

### CHILD-REARING PRACTICES (ACHIEVEMENT DEMANDS)     X   Achievement (Mathematics)

High-school students who are high achievers in mathematics are more likely than the average student to give a negative and autocratic characterization of their family relationships, indicating stress on achievement, discipline, control, and regimen. (K148)

### Achievement Motivation

"Excessive" parental achievement demands are associated with low achievement motivation in the child. (B275)

Mothers who consistently tend to demand excellence tend to have sons with high achievement motivation. (G156)

Mothers of sons with high achievement motivation are more likely to insist that they master certain skills in both school and home. (G156)

Middle-class mothers of sons with high achievement motivation are likely to expect achievement in their sons at earlier ages than are mothers of sons with low achievement motivation. (M246)

Fathers of boys with high achievement motivation make fewer statements which urge their sons to work hard than do the fathers of sons with low achievement motivation. (R098)

Strong achievement motivation tends to develop when parents set high goals for their children. (R106)

### Aggression

Parents of aggressive boys are less likely to have higher academic achievement demands than are parents of normals. (B243)

### Class

Middle- and lower-class parents are equally likely to make achievement demands on high achieving adolescents. (E102)

Middle-class parents are much more likely to make achievement demands of low achieving adolescents than are lower-class parents. (E102)

Middle-class families tend to demand higher achievement in the areas of skill, knowledge, and initiative than do lower-class families. (G156)

More of the working-class mothers than of the middle-class mothers place high pressures on their children to do well in school. (S191)

Fewer working-class mothers than middle-class mothers have any real expectation that their children will go to college. (S191)

### Cognitive Development (Verbal)

Mothers of children with high verbal ability are more likely to pressure their children for improvement than are mothers of children with low verbal ability. (B257)

### Educational Aspirations

Among adolescents whose parents have college expectations for them, those who are uncertain about college are more likely to receive frequent achievement demands than are those who are certain regarding their college plans. (E102)

### Employment of Mother

Mothers with a job tend to expect more of their children than do nonworking mothers.

### Mental Illness

Mental illness tends to be directly correlated with maternal emphasis on high performance for the child. (L126)

### Paternal/Maternal Role

Mothers are more likely than fathers to pressure children for achievement. (B273)

### Scholastic Achievement

Low scholastic achievers are more likely than high scholastic achievers to report strong parental demands for achievement. (E102)

Parental achievement demands are not related to the child's scholastic performance, regardless of the parents' social class. (E102)

Regardless of the child's academic motivation, parental achievement demands are negatively related to the child's scholastic attainment. (E102)

Parental scholastic achievement demands have little effect in keeping the child in school. (E102)

### Scholastic Motivation

Parental achievement demands have a greater effect on increasing the child's academic motivation among low scholastic achievers than among high scholastic achievers. (E102)

### Sex Status

Girls are less likely than boys to receive strong parental demands for achievement. (E102)

### Size of Family

Parents in small families tend to place a greater stress upon the personal achievement of their children than do parents in large families. (R106)

### Surrogate Parent, Adjustment to

A child of low intelligence is more likely to become adjusted to a foster home if the parents do not have high expectations concerning the intellectual achievement of the child. (T086)

### CHILD-REARING PRACTICES (ACHIEVEMENT/DEPENDENCY)     X   Class

Parents in lower-middle-class families are more likely to teach their sons to accept their social status and to conform; upper-middle-class parents are more likely to stress achievement, mobility, and independence. (T100)

## CHILD-REARING PRACTICES (ACHIEVEMENT/INDEPENDENCE)
### X   Achievement Motivation
Mothers of boys with high achievement motivation tend to stress the achievement training of their sons rather than independence training. (R097)

## CHILD-REARING PRACTICES (ADAPTATION)
### X   Cognitive Development
The extent to which the mother adapts the experiences and materials to the infant's individual capacities is positively related to the infant's intellectual development. (Y042)

### Dependency
The extent to which the mother adapts to the infant's individual capacities is unrelated to the development of autonomy in the infant. (Y042)

### Personality of Child (Stress)
The extent to which the mother adapts the experiences and materials to the infant's individual capacities is positively related to the infant's capacity to cope with stress. (Y042)

## CHILD-REARING PRACTICES (ADJUSTMENT/ACHIEVEMENT)
### X   Economic Cooperation
The greater the stress on cooperation rather than production in the economy, the more likely it is that parents concern themselves with the social adjustment of the child as opposed to his achievement. (M203)

## CHILD-REARING PRACTICES (ADVICE)
### X   Juvenile Delinquency
There is a negative relationship between the amount of parental advice and information given a youngster and delinquent behavior in adolescents, particularly in girls. (N057)

## CHILD-REARING PRACTICES (ADVICE/OVERPROTECTION)   X   Dependency
Frequent advice by mothers to adolescent boys is related to overdependency and overprotection. (N057)

## CHILD-REARING PRACTICES (AFFECTION)
### X   Oedipus Complex
The Oedipus complex is less likely to occur in societies in which the infant is treated gently and affectionately. (D057)

### Ordinal Position
There is more disciplinary friction between the mother and the first child than with his sibling(s). (L160)

### Parent-Child Relations (Rejection)
In the later years of childhood, the use of withdrawal of love as a method of discipline is correlated with parental rejection of the boy. (B243)

### Sex Status
Girls are exposed to more parental affection than are boys. (B252)

### Superego Formation
Parents' use of withdrawal of love as a method of discipline is correlated with the degree of the child's conscience development *only when* the mother is relatively warm and affectionate. (B243)

The positive relationship between maternal use of withdrawal of love and internalization of moral standards in the child holds only if the mother-child relationship is characterized by warmth. (B275)

Love-oriented techniques of discipline and "high conscience" in five-year-old children are associated. (S191)

### Values (Achievement)
There is a positive relationship between the mother's use of love-oriented discipline techniques and similar achievement values in mother and son. (R097)

## CHILD-REARING PRACTICES (AFFECTION/CONTROL)      X   Mental Illness (Schizophrenia/Neurosis)
More parents of schizophrenics than of neurotics withheld their affection to control the patients' behavior. (M061)

## CHILD-REARING PRACTICES (AGGRESSION)
### X   Age of Child
There is no relationship between the age of the child and the severity of the mother's punishment for mother-directed aggression. (M216)

Mothers are no more likely to punish older children than younger children for peer-directed aggression (cross-cultural). (M216)

### Age of Mother
The younger the mother, the more likely is she to urge her child to fight back when attacked by other children (U.S.). (S191)

### Aggression
The more permissive the parents are toward the child's aggressive behavior, the more likely is the child to anticipate a reward for aggressive behavior and consequently to exhibit aggression.

In the aggressive boys' families, one or the other of the parents almost invariably encourages aggression by the boy toward outside adults (teachers) and peers. (B213)

There is a curvilinear relationship between the severity of punishment for aggression shown toward the mother and the incidence of aggressive behavior in preschool children. (B243)

Mothers of aggressive boys tend to be more permissive of aggression toward themselves than do mothers of normals; the fathers do not differ with respect to the two groups. (B243)

Parents of aggressive children are more likely to reward and encourage aggressive behavior than parents of nonaggressive children. (C120)

If the father does not tolerate aggression at home, which is mostly the case with fathers of foreign ethnicity, the child is likely to exhibit aggressive behavior in environments outside the home (e.g., school). (E091)

When the father is low in punishment for aggression, regardless of mother's score, the child tends to be low in aggression. (E091)

There is a positive relationship between parental punishment for aggression and aggressive behavior in school. (E093)

Maternal punishment is more positively related than is paternal punishment to the child's aggressive behavior in the school setting. (E093)

For both boys and girls, high-status children who are

severely punished for aggression are more aggressive than are children from other classes who are subjected to lesser degrees of aggression punishment. (E093)

Punishment for aggression by parents increases the likelihood that the child will manifest aggressive behavior; this relationship is strongest among upper-class families. (E097)

The relationship between punishment by mothers for aggression and aggressive behavior is curvilinear. Medium punishment is associated with less aggression than either high or low punishment. (E097)

A mother's punishment of her child's aggression is positively related to the amount of aggression the child displayed. Permissiveness of aggression is positively related to the child's expression of aggression. (L169)

High permissiveness for aggression toward parents is associated with high aggression toward parents. (S191)

Parents' permissiveness toward aggression is not associated with strength of child's fantasy aggression (projective aggression) (U.S.). (S191)

Permissiveness of expression of aggression by the parents is positively related to the development of aggressive behavior in children. (S246)

Among five-year-olds, both high permissiveness and high punishment of aggressive behavior are associated with the development of aggressive behavior in the child at home, although permissiveness and punishment are negatively correlated with each other (among five-year-olds). (S246)

Greater amounts of punishment of aggressive behavior lead eventually to less amounts of such behavior (by age 12). (S246)

The suppression of the early expression of aggression in the home increases the strength of self-aggression (as opposed to antisocial aggression against others) in later years. (S246)

### Aggression Anxiety
Nonpermissiveness of aggression toward parents increases aggression anxiety in both boys and girls. (S246)

Punishment for aggression against the parents in early childhood increases aggression anxiety in girls in later years. (S246)

If aggression is allowed in the home and conscience is not highly developed, both girls and boys are likely to develop aggression anxiety in later years. (S246)

### Aggression Anxiety by Sex Status
Permissiveness toward aggression against other children increases aggression anxiety in both boys and girls, but affects girls much more than boys. (S246)

### Child-Rearing Practices (Chores)
Mothers who are high in responsibility training (variety and frequency of chores assigned) are more severe in punishing mother-directed aggression in the child. (M216)

### Child-Rearing Practices (Dependency)
Mothers who are accepting of the child's dependency are less likely to punish the child for aggression directed toward the parents than are mothers who are not accepting of their child's dependent behavior. (S191)

### Child-Rearing Practices (Discipline)
Mothers who punish their children for mother-directed aggression tend to use physical punishment and manipulation of gifts as means of child discipline. (M216)

### Child-Rearing Practices (Giving Reasons)
There is a negative relationship between the mother's use of reasoning in child rearing and severity of punishment for parent-directed aggression (U.S.). (S191)

### Child-Rearing Practices (Household Rules)
Mothers who are permissive regarding the child's parent-directed aggression are less restrictive about noise in the house, cleanliness, and care of household property (U.S.). (S191)

### Child-Rearing Practices (Punishment)
The more permissive the parents are toward the child's aggressive behavior, the less the child's anticipation of punishment.

Parents who use punishment as a means of control tend to encourage aggression by their children toward others, but will not tolerate aggression toward themselves. (M186)

Mothers who are permissive regarding the child's parent-directed aggression are less likely to use physical punishment as a disciplinary technique than are nonpermissive mothers (U.S.). (S191)

### Child-Rearing Practices (Sex)
Mothers who are nonpermissive regarding sexual behavior demand more self-control regarding aggression from their children than do mothers who are more permissive regarding sexual behavior. (M186)

There is a positive relationship between permissiveness regarding the child's aggression directed toward the parent and permissiveness regarding sex activity among children (U.S.). (S191)

### Child-Rearing Values (Self-Control)
Mothers who place a high value on their children's acquiring self-control are more likely to punish their children for temper tantrums than are mothers who do not value self-control as highly. (K110)

### Class
Working-class parents emphasize the teaching of responding to acts of aggression (fighting back) more than do upper-middle-class parents. (B235)

For both boys and girls, there is no relationship between social class and the severity of maternal punishment for aggression. (E093)

High-status girls are punished by both parents less severely for peer-directed aggression than are low-status girls. Middle-class boys are punished more severely by their mothers, but not by their fathers, for peer-directed aggression than are lower- and upper-status boys. (E093)

Lower-status girls are punished more severely by their fathers for aggression than are girls from high-status families. For sons, there is no relationship between social class and the severity of paternal punishment for aggression. (E093)

There is no relationship between social class and the severity of parental punishment for parent-directed aggression. (E093)

There is no relationship between social class and parental use of psychological *v.* physical punishment for aggressive behavior in the child. (E093)

The lower class is less tolerant of aggression by children than is the middle class (U.S.). (L003)

There is no significant difference between the middle class and the lower class in the toleration of aggression by children. (L003)

Lower-class mothers are no more encouraging of aggressive behavior directed toward other children than are middle-class mothers (U.S.). (S191)

Middle-class mothers are more permissive than lower-class mothers toward children's aggression against their parents (U.S.). (S191)

Middle-class mothers and better-educated working-class mothers permit their children to express aggression toward parents somewhat more freely and punish such aggressive outbursts less severely than do lesser-educated working-class mothers. (S191)

Middle-class (British) families are somewhat less inclined to allow children to show aggression toward their parents than are working-class (British) families. (S191)

There is no difference between lower- and middle-class mothers in relation to permissiveness regarding aggression against siblings (U.S.). (S191)

There is no significant differences between middle-class parents and working-class parents in their demands for aggression by their children against other children. (W002)

There is no significant difference between middle-class and working-class parents in the extent to which they encourage their children to fight back. (W002)

There is no significant difference between middle-class children and working-class children in the amount of aggression in the home. (W002)

Middle-class parents are more permissive toward aggression against them than are working-class parents. (W002)

### Cohesion of Community
The more intimate and interdependent the social and economic bonds are among members of a community, the more likely are the children to be punished for peer-directed aggression. (M216)

### Education/Class
Mother's education is more strongly associated with mother's permissiveness toward aggression than is socioeconomic status of family (U.S.). (S191)

### Ethnic Attitudes
Maternal punitiveness toward aggressive behavior is positively related to anti-Semitism in daughters. (W146)

### Ethnicity (Jewish/Italian)
Italians are less permissive of aggression toward parents than are Jews. (M060)

### Extended/Nuclear Family
Children living in extended families are slightly more likely to be punished for peer-directed aggression than are those living in nuclear isolated families. (M216)

Children living in extended families are more likely to be punished for mother-directed aggression than are those who reside in nuclear isolated families. (M216)

### Feeding Problems
There is a positive relationship between prohibition of expressions of aggression toward the parents and feeding problems (e.g., prolonged periods of appetite loss, etc.) in the child (U.S.). (S191)

### Household Structure
There is a correlation between the punishment for aggression and household structure; nuclear households are least severe, then polygynous and mother-child households, and most severe are extended family households. (W127)

### Identification of Mother with Daughter
Mothers with a high degree of identification with their daughters are more likely to tolerate expressions of anger in their children than are mothers who do not identify. (H218)

### Illness, Explanation of
The severity of aggression training in the society (temper tantrums, verbal aggression, damage to property, and disobedience) is related to a tendency to explain illness as being caused by aggression (e.g., disobedience to spirits, injected poison, magical weapons). (W127)

### Income, Mother's Contribution
Mothers who make economic contributions to the family finances are more severe in their punishment of mother-directed aggression in the child. (M216)

### Maternal-Role Behavior
The greater the proportion of time the mother spends in child care (children aged 7–10), the more likely is she to reward the child for peer-directed aggression. (M216)

### Mental Illness (Schizophrenia)
A significantly greater number of schizophrenic daughters than of normal ones believed that their mothers attempted to suppress the daughters' aggression during their childhood. (H186)

Schizophrenia tends to be directly correlated with a maternal pattern of ignoring the patient's anger. (N061)

### Mother-Child Relations (Warmth)
Mother's warmth and her permissiveness toward aggression are not associated (U.S.). (S191)

### Occupation of Parents
There is no difference among occupational classes regarding punishment of children for aggression against parents. (E097)

### Ordinal Position
Older children are given more freedom in quarreling with siblings than are later children. In two-child families the older child is also permitted more leeway in fighting with neighborhood children (U.S.). (S191)

There is no association between the ordinal position of siblings and permissiveness for parent-directed aggression (U.S.). (S191)

### Paternal/Maternal Role
Mothers are more permissive of the son's aggression toward themselves than are fathers. (B243)

Middle-class mothers are more likely to place strong prohibitions on overt aggression than are fathers (U.S.). (K103)

### Scholastic Adjustment (Reading)
If a child has not been allowed the expression of aggression, he is more likely than the child who has been allowed such expression to develop a reading disability. (S225)

### Sex Composition of Family
The greater the number of women residing in the extended family household, the more likely is the child to be punished for peer-directed aggression. (M216)

There is no relationship between the number of men residing in the extended family household and the severity of punishment the child receives for peer-directed aggression. (M216)

### Sex Status
Middle-class boys are taught to respond to acts of aggression, while middle-class girls are taught to avoid such situations. (B235)

There is no relationship between the sex of the child and the severity of the mother's punishment for mother-directed aggression. (M216)

Mothers are less permissive toward aggression in girls than in boys; but only regarding aggression toward parents and toward children outside the family, not toward siblings. (S191)

Sex of child and severity of punishment for aggression are not associated, though girls get much less encouragement to fight back in their outside quarrels (U.S.). (S191)

Boys are allowed more aggression in their relations with neighborhood children than are girls (U.S.). (S191)

Boys are allowed no more freedom than girls in relation to aggression toward siblings (U.S.). (S191)

Parents are more permissive with boys than with girls regarding parent-directed aggression (U.S.). (S191)

There is no difference between boys and girls with respect to the severity of punishment for parent-directed aggression (U.S.). (S191)

### Sibling Structure
There is no relationship between the number of siblings in the family and the severity of punishment for mother-directed aggression by the child. (M216)

The greater the number of siblings in the family, the more severe the punishment for peer-directed aggression. (M216)

### Social Mobility of Mother
Upwardly mobile mothers are more punitive with regard to aggression by their children than are nonmobile mothers. (S014)

### Socialization, Effectiveness of
Resistance to temptation by the child is not correlated with severity toward control of aggression by parents. (G120)

### Spiritual Beings
Societies with severe training in the control of aggression and which also believe spirits cause illness are more likely to classify the spirits as animal rather than human. (W127)

### Superego Formation
High guilt in the child correlates with severity toward control of aggression by parents. (G120)

The longer parents inhibit a child from expressing his aggression, the greater the severity of the child's superego. (G145)

### Therapeutic Practices
Cultures that permit little aggressive behavior in small children tend to be more concerned with health matters, e.g., the use of various therapies and explanations for illness. (P084)

### Toilet Training
The more severe the parents are in toilet training the child, the less likely are they to tolerate aggressive behavior by the child directed against them, an the more likely are they to punish parent-directed aggression (U.S.). (S191)

Mothers who are permissive regarding the child's parent-directed aggression are less severe in toilet training than are nonpermissive mothers (U.S.). (S191)

## CHILD-REARING PRACTICES (AGGRESSION/FEEDING)   X   Class
Middle-class mothers who are permissive in relation to the infant's feeding schedules tend to be more punitive toward aggression than do lower-class mothers. (B272)

## CHILD-REARING PRACTICES (AGGRESSION/SEX)   X   Witchcraft
Sorcery is used to explain illness more often in societies where children are punished severely, either for sex or aggression, than in other societies. (W127)

## CHILD-REARING PRACTICES (APPROVAL)   X   Child-Rearing Practices (Achievement)
Maternal rewarding of achievement efforts of child correlates with rewarding of approval-seeking behavior. (C118)

## CHILD-REARING PRACTICES (ATTENTION)   X   Ordinal Position
First children receive greater attention than do later children. (B252)

## CHILD-REARING PRACTICES (AUTHORITARIANISM)   X   Achievement Motivation
Authoritarianism, restrictiveness, and/or rejection in child-rearing practices are associated with low achievement motivation in the son. (M246)

### Age and Education of Mother
The older and less educated the mother, the more authoritarian she will be in child rearing. (S229)

### Age of Child
No relationship exists between authoritarian child control and the age of the child. (H200)

### Age of Mother
No relationship exists between authoritarian child control and the age of the mother. (H200)

### Class
Lower-class parents are more autocratic or authoritarian in handling their younger sons and daughters than are middle-class parents. Moving from younger females to younger males, older females and older males, successively smaller class differences in parent-adolescent decision making are observed. (E100)

### Creativity (Mathematics)
Highly creative and productive mathematically ori-

ented adolescents tend to view their parents as more autocratic than do normal college students. (K148)

### Dependency
Authoritarian discipline increases the dependency of the child and his acceptance of punishment. (M203)

### Ethnocentrism of Child
Due to the mechanism of displacement, the more authoritarian the child-rearing practices of the parents, the more likely it is that the child will be ethnocentric. (M222)

### Ethnocentrism of Child, by Age
Ethnocentrism in children correlates with the mother's authoritarian child-rearing practices more in adult life than in childhood. (M222)

### Ethnocentrism of Mother
The more authoritarian the child-rearing practices of the mother, the more likely she is to be ethnocentric. (M222)

### Identification
Authoritarian discipline increases the child's identification with the punishing authority. (M203)

### Ordinal Position
No relationship exists between maternal authoritarian child control and the birth order of the children. (H200)

### Personality Adjustment of Parents
Authoritarian discipline correlates less with the developmental needs of the child than with the insecurity and irrationality of the parents. (M203)

### Personality of Child (Authoritarianism)
Authoritarian control by the father correlates with the child's attitudes of deification of the parent, devotion to the father role, child's adjustment to the present situation, father's suppression of aggression and sex, fostering of dependency, and the use of punishment. (N053)

### Personality of Child (Hostility)
Parents who control their children in an authoritarian manner are more likely than those who rationally discipline their children to produce adolescents with high fantasy hostility. (C113)

If parents are affectionate toward their children, then the degree of overt hostility expressed by adolescents will be positively related to the authoritarian control by their parents. (C113)

### Pregnancy Anxiety
The higher the anxiety level of the mother during pregnancy, the greater the likelihood that she will be overcontrolling and authoritarian in her child-rearing practices. (D075)

### Premarital Sex Relations
The more authoritarian the parents in rearing the girl, particularly in regard to her sex behavior, the more likely it is that she may indulge in premarital sex out of rebellion and hostility against the parents. (B245)

If the parents impose authoritarian restrictions upon the girl but fail to make her aware of their reasons for doing so, it is more likely that the girl's restraint against premarital intercourse will break down when she is not under direct supervision. (B245)

### Sex Status of Child
No relationship exists between authoritarian child control and the sex of the child. (H200)

### Size of Family
No relationship exists between maternal authoritarian child control and the number of children in the family. (H200)

### Socialization, Effectiveness of
The rigidity and superficiality of authoritarian rules of discipline make less likely their internalization by the child. (M203)

## CHILD-REARING PRACTICES (AUTHORITARIANISM/DEMOCRATIC)
### X    Religion
Catholic and Protestant parents are similar in the control they exercise over their younger sons and daughters; only Catholic and Protestant fathers (not mothers) differ in relating to their older adolescents. Protestant fathers tend to be democratic, equalitarian, or permissive in rearing their older children, and proportionally more Catholic fathers tend to be either autocratic or authoritarian. (E100)

## CHILD-REARING PRACTICES (AUTHORITARIANISM OF MOTHER/FATHER)
### X    Age of Child
Fathers are likely to be just as authoritarian and autocratic when directing the behavior of their older adolescents as they are when directing their younger children. Mothers are likely to be seen as less autocratic or authoritarian in child rearing by their older than their younger children. (E100)

## CHILD-REARING PRACTICES (AUTHORITARIANISM/RESTRICTIVENESS)
### X    Scholastic Achievement of Child
Mothers of high achievers are more authoritarian and restrictive in the handling of their children than are mothers of low achievers. (E102)

## CHILD-REARING PRACTICES (AUTHORITY)
### X    Class
There is no significant difference between working-class and middle-class parents regarding the teaching of authority dependence and ingratiation of authority. (B235)

### Mental Illness (Manic Depressive)
Manic depressives tend to come from families in which standards of authority are poorly expressed, yet in which strict and conventional behavior is stressed. (C092)

### Neurosis
Arbitrary imposition of authority within the family of orientation correlates with neurosis in the child. (G020)

## CHILD-REARING PRACTICES (AUTOEROTICISM)
### X    Mental Illness (Schizophrenia)
Schizophrenia is directly associated with a punitive and prohibitive attitude toward masturbation on the part of the mother. (T105)

### Sex Status of Child
Among mothers who were most strongly inclined to differntiate sex roles, boys' mothers were more permissive about masturbation than were girls' mothers. (S191)

## CHILD-REARING PRACTICES (BEHAVIOR PROBLEMS)    X    Sex Status of Parent
There is no relationship between the sex of the parent and the measure suggested (punishment, verbal persuasion, building confidence, diverting child, obtaining out-

side help) for the correction of children who lie and fight. (M223)

## CHILD-REARING PRACTICES (BODY CONTACT)
### X Class
Lower-class Negro babies have more body contact (being held, carried, actively played with) than do upper-class Negro babies. (W133)

## CHILD-REARING PRACTICES BY SEX STATUS
### X Class
There are greater social-class differences in the rearing of girls than in the rearing of boys. (E100)

## CHILD-REARING PRACTICES (CHANGE)
### X Race
Child-rearing practices change more slowly among Negroes than among whites (U.S.). (L124)

## CHILD-REARING PRACTICES, CHILD'S
## PERCEPTION OF     X Child-Rearing Practices, Mother's Perception of
Children perceive their mothers as more punishing than mothers perceive themselves. (M177)

## CHILD-REARING PRACTICES (CHORES)
### X Aggression
Parents of aggressive or nonaggressive boys do not vary with regard to the amount of household responsibilities they assign to their sons. (B243)

### Child-Rearing Practices (Aggression)
Mothers who are high in responsibility training (variety and frequency of chores assigned) are more severe in punishing mother-directed aggression in the child. (M216)

### Child-Rearing Practices (Permissiveness)
There is a positive relationship between the mother's general permissiveness and the number of chores allocated to the child. (M216)

### Class
Middle-class parents train their children at a younger age in tasks such as sewing, cooking, helping around the house; lower-class parents train their children for these tasks when the child is old enough to be able to use the skills to help the parents.

### Education of Mother
The more educated the mother is, the more likely is she to assign regular tasks to the child. (S191)

Regardless of socioeconomic level, better-educated mothers gave their children more regular household chores to perform. (S191)

### Employment of Mother
Mothers with a job tend to encourage their children to perform household tasks more than do nonworking mothers. (S191)

### Employment of Mother, Evaluation of
Mothers who enjoy their jobs are less likely to give additional responsibilities to their children than are mothers who are not as fond of their work. (Y047)

### Income, Mother's Contribution to
There is a positive relationship between the degree to which mothers contribute to the family income and the severity of their responsibility training (variety and frequency of chores assigned to the child). (M216)

### Ordinal Position
Older and middle children are assigned more tasks than younger children. (S191)

### Sex Status
There is no relationship between the sex of the child and degree of responsibility training received (frequency of chore performance and number of chores assigned). (M216)

### Sibling Structure
The greater the number of younger siblings a child has, the more likely is the mother to emphasize his responsibility training (frequency and variety of chores assigned). (M216)

There is no relationship between the number of siblings in the family and the degree of emphasis the mother places on responsibility training (frequency and variety of chores assigned). (M216)

### Work Attitudes of Mother
Mothers who enjoy their jobs are less likely to give additional responsibilities to their children than are mothers who are not as fond of their work. (Y047)

## CHILD-REARING PRACTICES (CLARITY)
### X Aggression
Among homes characterized by a high level of explanation by the parents, the more explicit the behavior restrictions, the less aggressive the child. (B266)

### Aspirations (Clarity of Goals)
Adults from more-structured homes with clear standards have more clearly perceived future goals than those from less-structured homes. (L172)

### Conformity
Among homes characterized by a high level of explanation of family decisions by the parents, the more explicit the behavior restrictions, the more obedient the children. (B266)

### Creativity
Among homes characterized by a high level of parental explanation of family decisions, explicit behavior restrictions are correlated negatively with the ability to be original. (B266)

### Identification with Parents
High identification is associated with the clarity, explicitness, and immediacy of goals and sanctions communicated to the child. (R098)

### Maternal-Role Behavior
The greater the proportion of time the mother spends in child care (children aged 7–10), the more likely is she to communicate rules clearly to the child. (M216)

### Personality of Child (Curiosity)
Among homes characterized by a high level of parental explanation of family decisions, explicit behavior restrictions produce a child who has restricted curiosity. (B266)

### Personality of Child (Fear)
Among homes where there is a high level of parental explanation of family decisions, the more explicit the behavioral restrictions, the more fearful the child. (B266)

### Personality of Child (Negativism)
Among homes characterized by a high level of parental explanation of family decisions, the more explicit the behavior restrictions, the less negative the children are. (B266)

### Personality of Child (Planfulness)
Among homes characterized by a high level of explanation by the parents of family decisions, the more explicit the behavior restrictions, the less planful the child. (B266)

### Personality of Child (Quietness)
Among homes characterized by a high level of parental explanation of family decisions, explicit behavioral restrictions produce a quiet child. (B266)

### Personality of Child (Tenacity)
Among homes characterized by a high level of explanation by the parents of family decisions, the more explicit the behavior restrictions, the less tenacious the child. (B266)

### Personality (Self-Confidence)
Adults who came from more-structured homes with clear standards have greater self-confidence than those from less-structured homes. (L172)

### Sibling Relations (Conflict)
Among homes characterized by high levels of parental explanation of family decisions, the more explicit the behavior restrictions, the less quarrelsome the children. (B266)

### Socialization, Effectiveness of
The more explicit the standards, the more likely it is that the child will internalize the values of the socializing agent. (A058)

## CHILD-REARING PRACTICES (CLEANLINESS)
### X Class
Middle-class parents are more rigorous than are lower-class parents in teaching their children cleanliness habits (France). (F097)

Children of working-class parents acquire cleanliness habits at an earlier age than do country children or children of better-educated families (France). (F097)

### Toilet Training
Early toilet training is no more effective in teaching the child cleanliness than is later toilet training.

## CHILD-REARING PRACTICES (COLLECTIVE)
### X Achievement Motivation
Kibbutz children have lower achievement motivation than nonkibbutz children. (R096)

## CHILD-REARING PRACTICES (COMPETENCE)
### X Urban/Rural
Mothers from urban areas are more likely to be knowledgable in infant care and in their interpretation of infant behavior than are mothers from rural areas. (B272)

## CHILD-REARING PRACTICES (CONFORMITY)
### X Class
Middle-class parents are more likely to encourage the child to act on the basis of internalized norms; lower-class parents, to stress compliance with parental authority. (T100)

### Conformity
Women who were isolated from their mothers' attentions in childhood will tend to encourage deviant behavior in one child, in order to participate as an adult in a relationship denied the mother in childhood. (H217)

### Creativity/Intelligence of Children
The parents of highly intelligent children limit individual divergence, while parents of highly creative children encourage it. (G114) .

### Religion (Beliefs)
The greater the extent to which rewards are contingent upon conformity to parental demands, the greater the degree to which supernatural nurturance is thought to be contingent upon obedience to supernatural demands. (S036)

## CHILD-REARING PRACTICES (CONSENSUS)
### X Aggression
Fathers of aggressive boys are less likely to report agreement with their wives about the child-rearing process than are fathers of normals. (B243)

Parents who frequently disagree about child-rearing matters report more aggressive children than do parents who disagree less frequently (U.S.). (S191)

### Behavior Problems
There is a positive association between parental conflict about authority over the child and antisocial behavior in the child (e.g., lying, stealing, bullying, aggression, domineering, excessive competition with siblings). (R100)

### Child-Rearing Practices (Consistency)
Inconsistent discipline is associated with a lack of agreement between parents. (K120)

### Class
In middle-class families, parents tend to exhibit a more unified front in enforcing rules and making demands on children than in lower-class families. (N049)

### Conformity
There is a positive relationship between parental conflict about authority over the child and the child's being disobedient with accompanying hostility. (R100)

### Husband-Wife Relations (Warmth)
Parents who report agreement with the spouse about child-rearing practices are more likely to have warm and affectionate feelings toward the spouse than are those who report disagreement. (B243)

### Mother-Child Relations (Warmth)
Mothers who report agreement with spouse about child-rearing practices are more likely to be warm, accepting, and nonpunitive toward their sons than are those who report disagreement. (B243)

### Personality Problems
There is a positive relationship between parental conflict about authority over the child and children who are frequently discouraged, depressed, restless, and excitable. (R100)

### Race Attitudes
The greater the perceived discrepancy between the parents in discouraging the child from playing with Negroes, the more prejudiced is the child. (B226)

### Scholastic Adjustment
There is no relationship between discrepancy between parental attitudes (measured by the PARI, ATE and Q Sort Personality Tests) and the child's first-grade school adjustment and popularity.

## CHILD-REARING PRACTICES (CONSISTENCY)
### X Aggression
Where one parent is lax about discipline and the other is punitive, the child is more likely to be aggressive (than if parents are consistent). (B259)

Since aggressive action not only satisfies a primary drive (i.e., of aggression or the primary drive whose frustration produced the aggressive drive) but may also become a source of pleasure in itself, if rewarded, then mothers who are not firm (unable to disapprove consistently) are more likely than those who are firm to produce children who are hostile, with high (overt) aggressive drives. (F103)

### Alcoholism
Alcoholism is correlated with an erratic pattern of severity and indulgence on the part of the father. (C122)

When the parental authority pattern is severe yet erratic, alcoholism is likely to occur; when it is consistently severe, schizophrenia is a more likely consequence. (C122)

If an adult nonkin member of the household imposes demands counter to those of the parents, the son is more likely to become alcoholic. (M195)

### Anxiety
Sleep disturbances and nightmares of the child are associated with lack of consistency in the mother's child-rearing practices. (R113)

### Bed Wetting
Regressive enuresis of the child is unlikely to be due to inconsistent child-rearing practices of the mother. (R113)

### Behavior Development of Child (Social Behavior)
There is a low but positive relationship between maternal consistency and development in the infant of outgoing social behavior. (Y042)

### Behavior Problems
The more contradictory the demands placed upon the child by adults in the home, the more likely he is to show maladjusted behavior both at home and at school. (C117)

Mothers who are consistently rigid or overpermissive in the child's second or third year are more likely to have child problems in the areas of sleeping, feeding, and toilet training than are mothers who are consistent in child-rearing practices that are neither exceedingly rigid nor permissive. This does not hold for children during their first year. (K113)

There is no relationship between the mother's inconsistency or consistency and child problems in the areas of sleeping, feeding, and toilet training. (K113)

Disobediency, stealing, truancy from school, and disobedience with a hostile component in a child are correlated with inconsistent discipline on the part of the mother. (R081)

Inconsistent discipline by the mother causes the child to test the limits of tolerance by others via his misbehavior, thus provoking others to set up limits for him. (R091)

### Behavior Problems (Acting Out)
Temper tantrums of the child are associated with lack of consistency in the child-rearing practices of the mother. (R113)

### Behavior Problems (Nail-Biting)
Excessive nail-biting of the child is not likely to be due to lack of consistency in the mother's child-rearing practices. (R113)

### Behavior Problems (Truancy)
Truancy on the part of the child is related to lack of consistency in the mother's child-rearing practices. (R113)

### Bigotry
There is a direct correlation between bigotry in a child and neglectful and inconsistent child-rearing practices by the parents. (M247)

### Child-Rearing Practices (Consensus)
Inconsistent discipline is associated with lack of agreement between parents. (K120)

### Class
Middle-class parents are more consistent in their child supervision than are lower-class parents. (R127)

### Cognitive Development
There is a low but positive relationship between maternal consistency and the intellectual development of the infant. (Y042)

### Conformity
If a child is not exposed to contradictory goals and practices, he is then, as a result of reinforcement, more apt to be receptive to those accepted by his parents. (C086)

Inconsistent child-rearing practices are not likely to result in overly conforming or submissive behavior in the child. (R113)

### Criminality
Boys whose fathers have been criminals, but who are disciplined consistently, tend not to become criminals. (M199)

### Emotional Problems of Child
The more inconsistent and contradictory the mother's behavior during her offspring's early childhood, the more psychologically unstable the child will be in later years. (B283)

### Employment of Mother
Among working mothers there is more inconsistency in child rearing among mothers who do not enjoy their work than among the satisfied. (Y051)

### Employment of Mother, Evaluation of
Among working mothers there is more inconsistency in child rearing among mothers who are dissatisfied with their employment than among the satisfied mothers. (Y050)

### Employment of Mother (Satisfaction)
Among nonworking mothers clarity on limit setting is more characteristic of the mothers satisfied with not working. Dissatisfied mothers show more inconsistency between principles and practices. Control is an "issue" between mother and child for dissatisfied mothers. Lack of emotional satisfaction in relationships with the child

is more frequent among dissatisfied than among satisfied mothers. High confidence in the mother role is more common among satisfied mothers. In general, mothering is inferior. (Y051)

### Husband-Wife Relations (Conflict)
The greater the conflict between the parents, the greater the inconsistency in their treatment of the child and the greater the impediment to his socialization. (B232)

### Husband-Wife Relations (Evaluation)
Mothers who are consistent in their discipline think more highly of their husbands than do mothers who are inconsistent (U.S.). (S191)

### Husband-Wife Relations (Identification)
High identification is associated with similarity or consistency between the parents regarding various child-rearing practices. (R098)

### Identification with Kin
When the character of the discipline is inconsistent, little internalized identification with adult relatives takes place. (G044)

### Juvenile Delinquency
The juvenile delinquent is more likely to have had a parent whose gratification of the child's wishes was inconsistent. (M194)

Consistent discipline of whatever type decreases the chances of delinquency of the child, while erratic discipline increases the chances. (M194)

### Juvenile Delinquency by Sex Status
There is a correlation between inconsistency of discipline by mothers and delinquent behavior in girls but not in boys. (N063)

### Juvenile Delinquency/Neurosis
A greater number of delinquent than of neurotic children experience inconsistent discipline in the home. (B214)

### Maternal Role
Mothers who are the primary caretakers of their babies tend to be inconsistent concerning rules about aggressive behavior and other rules. (M216)

### Mental Illness (Catatonia)
Catatonia is more likely to occur in a family environment in which the dominant parent exercises authority inconsistently and regards the children as responsible. (S187)

### Mental Illness of Child
There is a correlation between the consistency of the parents' expectations of the behavior of the child and the child's mental health. (F116)

Inconsistency of demands and prohibitions, inconsistency in rewards and punishments, and overrigidity tend to break a child's defenses, weaken the ego or superego structure, or bring about fixation at a narcissistic level. (L120)

Alternation between understimulation and overstimulation may be directly correlated with mental illness in the child. (S188)

### Mental Illness (Paranoia)
Paranoia is more likely to occur in families in which the dominant parent expects complete obedience, yet exercises authority erratically. (S187)

### Mental Illness (Schizophrenia/Neurosis)
In the lower class, more parents of schizophrenics than of neurotics are inconsistent in their use of discipline. (M197)

### Mother-Child Relations (Acceptance)
Mothers who are consistent in their discipline are more accepting of their children than are mothers who are inconsistent (U.S.). (S191)

### Mother-Child Relations (Affection)
Mothers who are consistent in their discipline are more affectionate in their relations with their child than are mothers who are inconsistent (U.S.). (S191)

### Mother-Child Relations (Hostility)
Disobedience and hostility of the child are associated with lack of consistency in the child-rearing practices of the mother. (R113)

### Mother-Child Relations (Warmth)
Mothers who are inconsistent in their discipline because of concern for the child (e.g., child is sick, mother doesn't want to hurt the child, etc.) are warmer with their children than are mothers who are inconsistent because of self-concern (e.g., mother is too busy, too tired, forgets to punish the child, the situation is too public, etc.) (U.S.). (S191)

### Parent-Child Relations (Conflict)
Where discipline is inconsistent, parent-child conflict is more likely. (B249)

### Parent-Child Relations (Rejection)
In broken homes inconsistent discipline is associated with rejection of the child. (K120)

### Personality (Distrust)
Inconsistent maternal behavior and communication lead to a basic feeling of mistrust in the child.

### Personality of Child (Dependency)
Mothers of overdependent children tend to be less consistent in their interaction with their children than do mothers in the control group. (S204)

Consistency of mother-child interactions is unrelated to the development of autonomy in the infant. (Y042)

### Personality of Child (Stress)
There is a low but positive relationship between maternal consistency and the infant's ability to cope with stress situations. (Y042)

### Personality of Mother
Inconsistent disciplining of the child is correlated with the mother's view of discipline as a proof of her hostility (accompanied by guilt). (R091)

### Personality of Mother (Anomie)
Anomic mothers tend significantly to be inconsistent in their child-rearing practices, whereas nonanomic mothers tend to be consistent. (A069)

### Personality Problems
Inconsistent disciplining on the part of the mother is significantly associated with the following problems evidenced in the child: 1) disobedience, with hostile component; 2) temper; 3) overly competitive with siblings; 4) restless, excitable; 5) bullying, aggressive, domineer-

ing; 6) sleep disturbance; 7) disobedience, milder; 8) stealing; 9) frequent nightmares; 10) truancy from school (possible trend). (R091)

### Personality Problems of Child (Acting Out)
Extreme inconsistency, with "periods of overgratification of early instinctual drives alternated with severe frustration of these drives" is the cause of antisocial acting out in the child. (A069)

### Personality Problems of Child (Masochism)
Mothers who not only overstimulate aggressive and sexual drives in their children, but who give promises of acceptance (love) when severely disciplining them (pain), are more likely than mothers who discipline normally to produce children who have morally masochistic egos. (B281)

### Pregnancy, Attitude Toward
Mothers who are inconsistent in their discipline because of concern for the child (e.g., child is sick, mother doesn't want to hurt the child, etc.) were happier on becoming pregnant than were mothers who are inconsistent because of self-concern (e.g., mother is too busy, too tired, forgets to punish the child, the situation is too public, etc.) (U.S.). (S191)

### Psychotherapy of Mother
Therapy that focuses on alleviating guilt in mothers in regard to placing and enforcing reasonable restrictions on their children is the most effective measure of producing more consistent disciplinary measures by mothers. (R091)

### Religion (Role of Deities)
The greater the inconsistency in socialization (that is, the same behavior may be both rewarded and punished), the greater the degree to which supernatural punishment is viewed as occurring arbitrarily, not contingent on good or bad behavior. (S036)

### Scholastic Adjustment
Children with school phobia are likely to have parents who discipline inconsistently, being sometimes lenient and other times punitive. (C115)

### Self-Conception of Mother
Mothers who are consistent in their discipline have greater self-esteem than do mothers who are inconsistent (U.S.). (S191)

### Sibling Rivalry
The outstanding cause of sibling rivalry is the lack of consistency in discipline. (B033)

The child who is overly competitive with siblings is likely to have a mother who is inconsistent in her child-rearing practices. (R113)

### Socialization, Effectiveness of
Child training is more easily attained when parental demands toward children are consistent. (M058)

Effective socialization of the child is correlated with orderly, consistent, patient behavior on the part of the parent. (M203)

### Superego Formation
Mothers who are not firm (unable to disapprove consistently) are more likely than those who are firm to produce children lacking in conscience development. (F103)

### Surrogate/Natural Parents
Since parent substitutes (nurses, teachers) are more objective toward the child than the parents are, they are more likely to institute basic disciplines with less frustration on the part of the child. (S214)

## CHILD-REARING PRACTICES (CONTROL)
### X    Adult Role Behavior
The rate of practice of adult roles increases with the degree of control exercised by the parents. (M179)

### Alcoholism
The more the father exerts a controlling and punitive discipline over the son, the more likely the son is to become alcoholic. (M195)

The less the parental supervision of the boy, the more likely he is to become an alcoholic. (M195)

### Authoritarianism
Use of the threat that God will punish the child's deviant behavior as a means of controlling the child is associated with parents who have authoritarian personality structures. (N055)

### Authoritarianism of Mother/Father
The father's authoritarianism and power need correlate with both his and his wife's claim to unqualified power relative to the child, but the mother's authoritarianism is not related to her claims to power. (H182)

### Behavior Problems
Controlling and inflexible child rearing on the part of the father is positively associated with antisocial behavior (stealing, lying, truancy from school, overtly competitive children) in the child. (R100)

### Child-Rearing Practices (Punishment)
As perceived by daughters, there is no relationship between maternal control and degree of verbal punishment attributed to the mother; as perceived by sons, there is a positive relationship between maternal control and degree of verbal punishment attributed to the mother. (H196)

### Class
Lower-class parents of mental patients are more likely than middle-class parents of mental patients to use physically harsh and inconsistent means of control. (M061)

### Cognitive Development (Verbal)
Parental overlimitation and excessive control are associated with a favorable rate of verbal development in the child. (B257)

### Conformity
The greater the affection and control exercised by the parents, the greater is the likelihood that the child will submit to adult standards. The less restricting the parent is, the greater the likelihood the child will conform to peer standards. (D063)

The greater the frequency of control attempts by parents, the higher will be the relationship between firmness of control and the child's conformity with the opinions of others. (J024)

The more rigid the control which the parents attempt to exercise over adolescents, the more they feel the impulse to rebel and reject parental values when in a position to do so. (M056)

### Dependency

The longer the parent maintains strong control over the child, the greater the postponement in the development of motives for self-directed achievement. (D063)

### Disorganization of Family

There is little difference between a well-integrated family and a disorganized one in relation to supervision of male children. (T002)

There is a great difference between the supervision of female children in a well-integrated family and in a disorganized one. (T002)

### Economic Level

Societies with a high accumulation of food resources put more stress on compliance, whereas societies with a low accumulation push children toward assertiveness. (B037)

### Education of Mother

Whereas extreme control over a young daughter's behavior is almost entirely a lower-class phenomenon, highly educated mothers are as likely as those who never entered high school to exercise such control over a young son. (E100)

### Employment of Mother

Mothers who are employed outside of the home are more likely to use the threat that God will punish the child for deviant behavior as a means of control than are mothers who are unemployed. (N055)

### Identification with Parents

Identification is correlated with moderate-to-low parental control over the child's behavior and the consistency of that control. (R098)

### Income

Adolescents from families of higher-income strata who are accepted by their peers are granted more personal freedom by their families than are those at the middle and low economic levels. (F108)

Mothers of low-income families are more likely than those of higher-income families to use the threat that God will punish the child for deviant behavior as a means of control. (N055)

### Juvenile Delinquency

To the extent that social control of the child is reduced in the broken home or the unbroken home (where there is poor marital adjustment), the child is likely to become delinquent. (N057)

Because of the freedom from family control which the ownership of a car allows the adolescent, the youngster who owns a car is more likely to become delinquent than the one who does not. (N057)

Mothers of delinquent children tend to show excessive control but little awareness of their children's feelings. (S183)

### Love

The greater the freedom allotted to adolescents, the greater the likelihood they will fall in love. (G156)

### Maternal Role Behavior

The more time the mother allocates to the care of older children (10    years), the less likely is she to use manipulative gifts and privileges to control the child. (M216)

### Mental Illness (Schizophrenia)

Schizophrenics report having been subjected to greater parental control than do nonschizophrenics. (L155)

### Parent-Child Relations (Affection)

Parental use of the threat that God will punish the child for deviant behavior is associated with low affectivity between parents and child. (N055)

### Paternal/Maternal Role

Mothers are seen by both boys and girls to be more indirect in their control of children than are fathers. (D069)

Mothers tend to show much greater concern with the child's television viewing than do fathers. (H178)

### Personality of Child (Shyness)

Children whose mothers are rigidly dominating and controlling tend to be shy. (R113)

### Personality of Father

The more the father tends to internalize conflict (MMPI IR Score), the more likely the son is to perceive the mother to be "controlling" and "hostile controlling." (V038)

### Personality of Son

The higher the son's psychopathology (MMPI), the more likely he is to perceive the mother to be "controlling" and "physically controlling." (V038)

### Personality Problems (Inhibition)

Overinhibited behavior, characterized by seclusiveness, shyness, and apathy in children, correlates with repressive overcontrol in the parents. (S183)

### Personality Problems of Child (Depression)

Controlling and inflexible child rearing on the part of fathers is positively associated with frequent depression and discouragement in children. (R100)

### Personality Problems of Child (Masochism)

The mothers of morally masochistic children are more likely to be overcontrolling (directly or indirectly through attacks of family members aimed at lowering self-esteem) than are the mothers of normal children. (B281)

### Political Affiliation of Child

The relationship between degree of parental control and conformity to the parents' politics is curvilinear; highest conformity occurs where control was moderate, less conformity where control was weak, and least among those subject to the strictest parental control. (H244)

### Pregnancy Anxiety

High anxiety during pregnancy is related to high maternal control in child rearing. (D067)

### Race (Class)

Middle-class Negro girls are expected to remain closer to home than are middle-class white girls.

### Religion

Parental affiliation with traditional churches (i.e., those that deny the competence of the actor and exalt the direct control of man's affairs by God) is associated with use of the threat, as a means of control, that God will punish the child. (N055)

### Sex Composition of Family
Fathers are more likely to control boys with brothers and no sisters more strictly than boys with sisters and no brothers. (B322)

### Sex Status
Girls tend to be under more strict adult supervision than boys. (P069)

### Sibling Structure (Sex)
Girls with brothers are more apt to experience external behavior-control methods than are girls with sisters and no brothers. (B322)

In middle-class families the high-school-aged girl with brothers, but no sisters, has greatest influence in self-direction; the girl with all sisters has the least. (E100)

### Size of Family
The larger the family, the more likely the parents are to use external rather than internal controls. (B322)

Middle-class parents with boys and lower-class parents with girls are more likely to use strict controls of their children as family size increases than are middle-class parents with no boys and lower-class parents with no girls. (B322)

### Social Mobility Aspirations
Parental leniency is associated with children who are upward aspirers. (E102)

### Socialization, Effectiveness of
Closer supervision and home ties in girls produce a greater consciousness of the status and values held by the family than is found in boys. (P069)

### Urban/Rural
Rural parents tend to exert greater control over their children than do urban parents. (W144)

### Values
There is only a low association between mothers' concern about television program content (relative to their children) and their exercise of control over programs viewed. (H178)

## CHILD-REARING PRACTICES (CONTROL, AWARENESS)
### X   Mother-Child Relations (Conflict)
Low awareness and high control of the child are associated with greater conflict between mother and child. (C114)

## CHILD-REARING PRACTICES (CONTROL-GIVING REASONS)   X   Scholastic Motivation of Daughter
High parental power (parents who are either autocratic or authoritarian), combined with parental explanation of rules and discipline, is associated with low academic motivation in girls. (E102)

### Scholastic Motivation of Son
High parental control (parents who are either autocratic or authoritarian) combined with parental explanation of rules and discipline, is associated with high academic motivation in sons. (E102)

## CHILD-REARING PRACTICES (CONTROL-NURTURANCE)
### X   Maternal Role, Attitude Toward
Mothers who are high in control and low in nurturance are perceived by both sons and daughters as more rejecting of the homemaking role. (H196)

## CHILD-REARING PRACTICES (CREATIVITY)
### X   Achievement
Mothers of high achieving sons are more likely to reward them for trying something new. (G156)

## CHILD-REARING PRACTICES (CRITICISM)
### X   Age of Mother
The younger the mother, the more likely is she to use ridicule as a technique of child rearing (U.S.). (S191)

### Bed Wetting
Enuresis fixation in the child is related to excessively critical and depreciative behavior of the mother. (R113)

### Education of Mother
There is a positive relationship between the mother's educational level and the amount of maternal criticism of daughters. (K115)

### I.Q.
Maternal criticism is related to high intelligence in girls but not in boys (ages 4–7). (K115)

With maternal educational level held constant, there is a positive relationship between maternal criticism and intelligence scores for daughters (3½ and 5½ years old). (K115)

### Mother-Child Relations (Hostility)
Children whose mothers are excessively critical and depreciative are likely to be disobedient and hostile. (R113)

### Personality of Child (Restless, Excitable)
Children whose mothers are excessively critical and depreciative of them tend to be restless and excitable. (R113)

### Personality of Child (Withdrawal)
Children whose mothers are excessively critical and depreciative tend to be shy, seclusive, and withdrawn, and to daydream a great deal. (R113)

### Scholastic Adjustment
Children whose mothers are excessively critical and depreciative of them tend to be reluctant or fearful toward school. (R113)

### Sibling Rivalry
Children whose mothers are excessively critical and depreciative tend to be overly competitive with siblings. (R113)

### Superego Formation
The greater the effectiveness of parental criticism, the more complete the formation of an ego ideal and of conscience in the child. (B234)

## CHILD-REARING PRACTICES (CURIOSITY-AUTONOMY)   X   Religion
Protestant parents are more likely than Catholic parents to encourage curiosity and personal autonomy on the part of their children. (E102)

## CHILD-REARING PRACTICES (DECEPTION)
### X   Parent-Child Relations (Affect)
When lying and deception play an important role in child training, the child will tend to withdraw psychologically from his parents. (L064)

## CHILD-REARING PRACTICES (DEMANDS)
### X   Achievement Motivation
If a mother makes more demands of her child before the age of eight, the child will develop a stronger achieve-

ment motivation than if she does not make such demands. (W139)

**Alcoholism**

The higher the parental demands made on the son, the less likely is he to become an alcoholic. (M195)

**Class**

More working-class mothers than middle-class mothers place high pressures on their children to do well in school. (S191)

Fewer working-class mothers than middle-class mothers have any real expectation that their children will go to college. (S191)

**Criminality**

The lower the parental demands placed on the son, the more likely he is to become a criminal. (M195)

**Identification with Mother**

(In the older child) the more severe the demands placed upon the child by the mother, the stronger the child's identification with the mother. (A060)

**I.Q. (Verbal/Nonverbal)**

The I.Q. combination of high verbal and low nonverbal ability is more likely among children whose mothers are highly demanding and intrusive. (B289)

**Mental Illness (Manic Depressive)**

Excessively high parental demands (which lead to resentment of the parents, introjection of a conflicting parent- and self-image, and dependence on external sources of self-esteem) are a cause of manic-depression in the child. (P078)

**Personality (Introversion)**

Inhibitory demands and discipline by the parents are negatively correlated with introversion in the child. (S221)

**Personality of Child (Ego-Strength)**

Inhibitory demands and discipline by the parents are correlated with ego weakness in the child. (S221)

**Personality of Child (Impulsiveness)**

Inhibitory parental demands and discipline are correlated with impulsivity in the child. (S221)

**Scholastic Achievement**

Parents of children with high academic achievement make more specific and more clearly defined demands upon their children than do parents of under-achievers. (S256)

**Socialization, Effectiveness of**

The higher the level of demands and restrictions imposed by parents upon children, the more likely it is that the children will resist temptation. (G120)

**Superego Formation**

Parents or parental surrogates who care enough to set limits and make demands are necessary for the development of conscience in the child. (C093)

## CHILD-REARING PRACTICES (DEMANDS/RESTRICTIONS)
### X Achievement Motivation

A child will develop a strong achievement motivation if, by the time the child is seven, the number of demands placed upon the child by the mother exceeds the number of restrictions she places upon him. (W139)

## CHILD-REARING PRACTICES (DEMOCRATIC)
### X Aggression

Children from democratic homes (parents who encourage free experimentation by their children and are less controlling) are more aggressive (aggression being defined by psychosocial factors such as fearlessness, cruelty, disobedience, etc.) than are children from nondemocratic homes. (M224)

**Creativity**

Children from democratic homes (parents who encourage free experimentation by their children) are more likely to be involved in and more able to contribute to group activities that demand intellectual curiosity, originality, and constructiveness. (B287)

**Education of Parents**

Parents who are college educated are most likely to be democratic and equalitarian. (E100)

**I.Q.**

Children and parents of democratic homes (homes in which the parents encourage free experimentation by their children) have a higher I.Q. than do children and parents of nondemocratic homes. (B287)

**Juvenile Delinquency**

Children from democratically managed families are less likely to become delinquents than are children from undemocratically managed families. (B287)

**Peer Relations**

Children from democratic homes (parents who encourage free experimentation by their children) are more involved in peer-centered activities than are children from nondemocratic families. (B287)

Children from democratic homes (parents who encourage free experimentation by their children) are more likely to be in a favored position (successful in bossing and having high group status) in the peer groups to which they belong. (B287)

**Personality of Child (Self-Confidence)**

When parents seldom explain their rules to children, children of democratic parents are more apt to express self-confidence than are children of autocratic or permissive parents. (E105)

**Personality of Parents**

A democratic approach to child rearing by the mother is correlated with her inactivity and masculinity of interests. (B259)

A democratic approach to child rearing in the father has a greater element of permissiveness than does such an approach in the mother. (B259)

**Sibling Structure (Age Difference)**

The closer the children in age, the more likely it is that the mother will treat them more rationally, democratically, and with more understanding. (L160)

## CHILD-REARING PRACTICES (DEPENDENCY)
### X Academic Motivation of Child by Class

High independence training has a greater effect on high academic motivation among middle-class than among lower-class youths. (E102)

**Achievement**

Children's achievement behavior outside the home does not correlate with independence training by the mother. (C118)

Early training in mastery increases higher achievement, *provided* independence does not mean generalized restrictiveness, authoritarianism, or "rejection" by the parents. (M246)

In Brazil, Germany, and Japan, sons whose mothers expected them to care for themselves at an early age performed better at arithmetic, were more optimistic toward life, and were less spontaneous in a graphic expression test. (M246)

### Achievement Motivation

A dominant mother may aid the development of achievement motivation if she is strong and does not achieve overprotectiveness. An authoritarian and indulgent mother will keep the son from developing the skills for mastering tasks on his own and will prevent him from developing autonomy while encouraging an exaggerated opinion of his own achievements. (M246)

Stress on independence training is highly correlated with the amount of achievement imagery in the folktales current in a culture. (M246)

The more stress placed on independence training during early childhood, the higher the achievement motivation of the children. (M246)

The more severe the parental training in independence, the higher the level of achievement motivation. (C101)

Mothers of sons with high achievement motivation are more likely to insist that they make decisions for themselves. (G156)

There is a correlation between the extent of early independence training of the child and the amount of need achievement present in the myths of the society. (K111)

In lower-class families, the later the independence mastery training, the higher the boy's achievement motivation. (M246)

In cultures which expect independence mastery quite late, if at all, earlier stress on achievement leads to higher achievement motivation. (M246)

There is no relationship between expecting the child to care for himself at an early age and achievement motivation in Brazil, Germany, or Japan. (M246)

Fathers of sons with high achievement motivation tend to grant their sons more autonomy in decision-making situations than do fathers of sons with low achievement motivation. (R096)

Mothers of sons with low achievement motivation tend to grant their sons more autonomy than do mothers of sons with high achievement motivation. (R096)

Parents of children with high achievement motivation tend to expect their children to be self-reliant when competing against standards of excellence. (R097)

Parents of children with high achievement motivation tend to grant their children autonomy in problem solving and decision making in situations where the children have freedom of action and responsibility for success or failure. (R097)

Mothers of boys with high levels of achievement motivation tend to expect less self-reliance from their sons than do mothers of boys with low achievement motivation. (R106)

### Achievement Values

The earlier the child receives independence training, the greater the similarity between mother and son on values regarding achievement. (R097)

### Age of Mother

Younger mothers (20–39 years) are more likely than older mothers (40 years or older) to train their sons at an earlier age to be independent. (R097)

### Age of Parents

Older parents tend to place less emphasis on self-reliance of their children than do younger parents. (R106)

### Aggression

The parents of aggressive adolescent boys more often stress the need for the boy to be independent than do those of control group. (B213)

Parents of aggressive boys are more likely to reject or punish dependent behavior than are parents of normals. (B243)

Frustration of a child's dependency needs is a continual initiator of hostile and aggressive behavior. (B246)

### Aggression Anxiety

Punishment of dependency and physical punishment in early childhood do not increase aggression anxiety in girls in later years. (S246)

### Alcoholism

The greater the family's satisfaction of the child's dependency needs, the less likely he is to become alcoholic. (M195)

The more conflict the family creates in the son concerning his dependency needs, the more likely he is to become alcoholic. (M195)

### Anxiety

The greater the number of dependency needs that are not met by the parents, the greater the anxiety produced in the child. (S202)

### Child-Rearing Practices (Achievement)

Mothers who reward achievement efforts of children are less likely to be nurturant or acceptant of dependency (maternal rewarding of achievement correlates with independence training). (C118)

### Child-Rearing Practices (Aggression)

Mothers who are accepting of the child's dependency are less likely to punish the child for aggression directed toward the parents than are mothers who are not accepting of their child's dependent behavior. (S191)

### Child-Rearing Practices (Giving Reasons)

Low independence training is associated with infrequent use of explanation and reasoning by parents. (E102)

### Child-Rearing Practices (Punishment)

Mothers who are accepting of their child's dependent behavior are less likely to use physical punishment than are mothers who are not accepting (U.S.). (S191)

### Child-Rearing Practices (Sex)

Mothers who are not permissive regarding their children's sexual behavior are more negative in their response to dependency than are mothers who are permissive (U.S.). (S191)

### Class

There is no significant difference between middle class and working class in how much mothers keep track of their children. (H011)

The age at which boys and girls might go to the movies alone is earlier for the lower class than for the middle class. (H011)

The time at which boys and girls are expected to be in at night is earlier for the middle class than for the lower class. (H011)

The age at which boys and girls go downtown alone is earlier in the middle class than in the lower class. (H011)

Children are allowed to go farther away from the house during the day if they come from the middle class than if they come from the lower class. (H011)

Middle-class mothers whose husbands have entre-preneurial jobs are more likely than those of lower-class entrepreneurial status to stop close supervision of a youngster by the time he is 12 years old or even earlier. (M062)

Lower-class families are more likely than families of other social statuses to stress caretaking earlier than in-dependence and mastery in childrearing. (M246)

Lower-class families grant a greater degree of indepen-dence to their adolescents than do middle-class families. (P001)

Middle-class parents place more emphasis on indepen-dence training than do lower-class parents. (R098)

Middle-class parents expect their children to assume responsibility earlier. (S187)

Working-class mothers were less permissive, more ir-ritated, more rejecting, and had a more punishing atti-tude toward dependency of child than did middle-class mothers. (S191)

### Cognitive Development (Nonverbal)

For boys, but not for girls, there is a tendency for mater-nal behavior fostering independence to be positively associated with nonverbal (spatial and numerical) ability. (B257)

### Cognitive Development (Verbal)

There is no relationship between verbal ability in chil-dren and maternal behavior that fosters dependency. (B257)

### Criminality

The greater the family's frustration (and extinction) of the son's dependency needs, the more likely he is to become a criminal. (M195)

### Dependency

There is a curvilinear relationship between the severity of the mother's frustration or punishment of depend-ency and the amount of overt dependency shown by the child. (B243)

Tendencies toward dependency in the child are likely to be increased by parental punishment specifically di-rected against dependent behavior. (M221)

Mothers of dependent children do not significantly tend to punish the child's dependent behavior. (M221)

Fathers of boys with high levels of independence tend to give their sons a higher degree of autonomy in mak-ing their own decisions than do fathers of boys with low levels of independence. (R106)

Reward for dependency of child increased dependency only when it was superimposed upon punishment for the same behavior. (S191)

Permissiveness for dependent behavior of the child was not associated with dependent behavior of the child. (S191)

The greater the child's understanding of where his par-ents expect him to be independent or dependent, the more able is the child to become independent. (S202)

### Dependency of Son

Fathers of boys with a high level of independence ex-pect their sons to be more self-reliant in problem solving than do fathers of boys with low levels of independence. (R106)

### Education of Mother

Regardless of socioeconomic status, better-educated mothers were more permissive toward the child's de-pendency. (S191)

### Educational Aspiration

Independence training is positively related to the child's desire to further his education. (E102)

Adolescents who are college oriented are more likely than those who are indifferent or undecided to have experienced active paternal independence training. (E102)

Youths with parents who are very active in indepen-dence training are more likely than those with inactive parents to desire to complete high school. (E102)

### Emotional Adjustment of Child

The more gradual the steps from dependence to inde-pendence, the greater the likelihood that the child will be emotionally healthy. (L134)

### Employment of Mother

Working mothers of high-school education are more likely than nonworking mothers to stress independence training. (Y050)

Working mothers of college education are less likely than nonworking mothers to stress independence train-ing. (Y050)

### Father Absence

In societies with a high percentage of mother-child households, the child is more indulged and rewarded in his dependency demands by the mother. (S079)

### Feeding Problems

There is a positive relationship between parents' nega-tive reactions to acts of dependency by the child and child-feeding problems (e.g., prolonged appetite loss, etc.). (U.S.). (S191)

### Handicapped Child (Deafness)

Mothers with high achievement motivation are more likely to have later independence-training attitudes to-ward the deaf child than toward the normal child. (G129)

### Husband-Wife Relations (Evaluation)

Mothers who are accepting of their child's dependent behavior have greater esteem for their husbands than do mothers who are not accepting (U.S.). (S191)

### Illness, Explanation of
The severity of independence training is associated with dependency explanations for illness (e.g., soul stealing, spirit possession). (W127)

### Mental Illness of Child
There is a greater possibility of mental illness if the child is encouraged to be excessively dependent on his mother. (M164)

### Mental Illness (Schizophrenia)
The failure of the parents to educate toward and facilitate emancipation of the children from the family is a cause of schizophrenia in the child. (F097)

A significantly larger number of schizophrenic daughters than of normal ones believe their mothers attempted to break their wills during childhood. (H186)

More schizophrenic daughters than normal ones believe that their mothers fostered the daughter's dependency on them during childhood. (H186)

Schizophrenia tends to be correlated with a continuing expectation on the part of the mother of obedience and dependence during adolescence. (L126)

### Mother-Child Relations (Consistency)
Mothers who unwillingly accede to their children'd demands for excessive dependency will be more inconsistent in the treatment of their children than will mothers who willingly accede or do not accede to their children's excessive dependency demands. (S202)

### Mother-Child Relations (Warmth)
Mothers who are accepting of dependency behavior in their children are more likely to be warmer to their children than are mothers who are not accepting. (S191)

### Neurosis (Gastric)
Gastric neurosis is directly correlated with a premature emphasis by the parents on independence. (F113)

### Occupation
Middle-class mothers whose husbands' occupations are in the enterpreneurial category are more likely to train their children to take a more active and independent approach to the world than are mothers whose husbands' occupations are in the bureaucratic category. (B273)

Homes in which the husband is self-employed are more likely to emphasize the development of independence and mastery in their children than are homes in which the husband is employed in a large organization, particularly within the middle class. (B273)

### Occupation of Father
Among blue collar boys, there is a slight positive relationship between the degree of dissatisfaction expressed by the son concerning his father's occupation and paternal independence training. (E102)

Among white collar boys, there is a slight negative relationship between the son's dissatisfaction with his father's occupation and paternal independence training. (E102)

### Parent-Child Relations (Interaction)
### X  Child-Rearing Practices (Permissiveness)
Promoting the child's independence is a characteristic of parents who participate in much activity with the child. Such parents also tend to be permissive in early feeding and toilet-training procedures, but punish for misbehavior. (S010)

### Parental Role
Children are likely to report their cross-sex parent as allowing more autonomy than their same-sex parent. (D069)

### Personality Adjustment
Fathers of maladjusted children are less likely to report marital conflict and to force independence in the child than are fathers of normal children. (Z011)

### Personality Problems
Children who are denied the autonomy of free choice are more likely to become obsessed by repetitive acts or to become sticklers for exactness.

### Polygyny
In societies with a higher percentage of polygynous households, the young child's dependency demands are indulged and rewarded. (S079)

### Power Structure of Family
Low independence training is associated with parental autocracy. (E102)

### Religion
Catholic parents tend to begin independence training at a later date in the development of their children than do Protestant parents. (E100)

Protestant mothers stress independence and mastery in child rearing earlier than do Catholic mothers. (M246)

### Religion (Ritual)
Where infant dependency needs are anticipated and satisfied *prior* to their expression, supernatural nurturance is more likely to be believed to be contingent upon, and evoked by, compulsive rituals. (S036)

The greater the initial satisfaction of dependency, the greater the degree to which supernatural nurturance is thought to be contingent upon the employment of compulsive ritual. (S036)

### Religion, Role of Deities
Where child-rearing practices emphasize independence training, deities are likely to be aggressive rather than benevolent. (L141)

The greater the initial satisfaction of infant dependency needs as soon as they are manifested and the lower the socialization anxiety of dependence, the greater the degree to which supernatural nurturance is contingent upon propitiatory rituals (i.e., the gods give help even if not solicited and help is not contingent on obedience). (S036)

Gods are thought to be more aggressive in societies where boys are subject to strong pressure for self-reliance and independence. (W127)

The belief in aggressive gods requires child training which stresses independence and self-reliance to prepare the child for coping with a hostile world as an adult. (W127)

### Scholastic Achievement
There is a positive relationship between the severity of independence training and high achievement among college students. (D065)

Parents of children with high academic-achievement records showed significantly more interest in fostering the independence of their children than did parents of under-achievers. (S256)

### Scholastic Achievement by Sex Status of Child
High independence training by parents is associated with high scholastic achievement in adolescents; the relationship is stronger for boys than for girls. (E102)

### Scholastic Adjustment
Youths with parents very active in independence training are much more likely than those with inactive parents to have positive attitudes concerning school. (E102)

### Scholastic Aspirations
Adolescent college orientation is more related to parental independence training than to parental expectations concerning posthigh-school education. (E102)

### Scholastic Motivation of Child
Participation of both parents in independence training is associated with high academic motivation in the child. (E102)

### Scholastic Motivation of Child by Class
High independence training has a greater effect on high academic motivation among middle-class than among lower-class youths. (E102)

### Sex Composition of Family
Among large families, parents are less active in independence training if all their offspring are boys. (E102)

### Sex Status
Boys are pushed toward self-reliance more than girls. (G156)

### Sexual Deviance
The mothers of sexually deviant boys foster more dependency than do mothers of "normal" boys. (M209)

### Size of Family
In general, parents who have larger numbers of children living at home are more likely to prevent their adolescents from making their own decisions. This is more frequently the case among parents of younger boys and least frequent among mothers and fathers of high-school-aged boys. (E100)

Parents with large families are less active in independence training than are parents with small families. (E102)

There is a curvilinear relationship between age of independence training and family size: mothers of medium-sized families train their children earlier than those of large or small families. (R097)

Parents in small families tend to place greater emphasis on urging their children to be self-reliant in situations where they compete with standards of excellence. (R106)

### Therapeutic Practices
The age of socialization of independence behavior is correlated with the amount of patient acitvity during illness. (K111)

Initial indulgence of the drive for dependence on the mother, a child-training antecedent of guilt, is not related to the extent to which a society employs intropunitive therapy (blood letting, sacrifice) for illness. (K111)

### Toilet Training
Cultures that begin toilet training early begin independence training later; cultures that begin independence training early are late in toilet training. (P084)

### Values (Individualism/Cooperation)
A society emphasizing individualistic achievement would begin by inculcating in the children a belief in their own competence, while a society emphasizing group cooperation and authority of leaders or parents would inculcate in the children a belief in their own dependence on more competent seniors. (F069)

## CHILD-REARING PRACTICES (DEPENDENCY/ ACHIEVEMENT DEMANDS)
### X Scholastic Motivation of Child
Independence training has a much greater effect than parental achievement demands on the child's academic motivation. (E102)

Among children with low scholastic records, parental achievement demands are more important than is independence training in leading to high academic motivation. (E102)

Among children with high scholastic records, parental achievement demands lead to high academic motivation only when accompanied by active independence training. (E102)

## CHILD-REARING PRACTICES (DEPENDENCY ANXIETY)      X Illness
The degree of anxiety generated by the socialization of dependence in the child is correlated with the amount of activity the child engaged in when he was ill. (K111)

## CHILD-REARING PRACTICES (DEPENDENCY)/EDUCATION OF PARENTS
### X Scholastic Motivation of Child
High independence training has as great or greater an effect than does parental educational level on academic motivation in the adolescent. (E102)

## CHILD-REARING PRACTICES (DEPENDENCY)/PARENTAL EXPECTATIONS
### X Educational Aspirations
Adolescent college orientation is more related to parental independence training than to parental expectations concerning posthigh-school education. (E102)

## CHILD-REARING PRACTICES (DEPRIVATION OF PRIVILEGES)
### X Child-Rearing Practices (Rewards)
Use of tangible rewards is associated with use of deprivation of privileges as a method of punishment (U.S.). (S191)

## CHILD-REARING PRACTICES (DIFFERENTIAL TREATMENT)      X Class
The higher the social class the more likely it is that children of either sex will be disciplined the same. (B236)

### Identification with Like/Cross-Sex Parent
Identification with like- or opposite-sex parent is associated with differential treatment of sons and daughters regarding permissiveness, rewards, and punishment. (R098)

## CHILD-REARING PRACTICES (DISCIPLINE)
### X Authoritarianism of Child
Children who are very authoritarian and ethnocentric

are likely to have parents who use rigid and harsh forms of discipline. (L149)

### Authoritarianism of Mother
Mothers who score high in authoritarianism (on the basis of interviews and a modified F–scale) tend to prefer nonlove-oriented discipline techniques. (H200)

### Autoeroticism
There is a positive correlation between boys' masturbation and the extent to which their parents use threats of withdrawal of love as a means of discipline. (B213)

### Behavior Problems (Task Withdrawal)
Maternal justification of disciplinary measures during the child's early years (2–7) is negatively related to the tendency to withdraw from tasks when the child is an adolescent. (K115)

### Child-Rearing Practices (Aggression)
Mothers who punish their children for mother-directed aggression tend to use physical punishment and manipulation of gifts as means of child discipline. (M216)

### Class
The lower the class, the more likely it is that boys will receive inadequate discipline and support and that girls will be overprotected. (B236)

Children from high socioeconomic class families suggest more constructive and amicable solutions to discipline situations; children from middle-class families suggest appealing to authority as a solution for discipline. (G117)

The standard of behavior demanded of noble children is higher than that expected from commoners. (W098)

### Cognitive Development (Nonverbal)
Overanxious disciplinary measures are associated with low development of nonverbal, especially spatial, ability in the child. (B257)

### Conformity
Children raised in homes in which discipline was perceived to be just are more likely to be conformists than are children who perceived discipline to be unjust.

There is a positive correlation between firmness of parental discipline and a child's conformity with the opinions of others. (J024)

### Dependency
In the early years of childhood, the use of withdrawal of love as a method of discipline is correlated with dependency of the boy on the parents. (B243)

There is a negative correlation between parental discipline by means of deprivation of privileges and dependency of the boy on the parents. (B243)

For girls there is a positive relationship between severity of maternal discipline during ages 2–7 and dependency upon mother during adolescent years. (K115)

### Dependency Anxiety
The greater the degree of anxiety typically generated in the society by the socialization of dependence, the earlier the age at which the child is subjected to the socialization of dependence (i.e., greater the degree, earlier the age). (K111)

### Employment of Mother
Mothers with jobs tend to discipline their children more often than do mothers with no employment. (G156)

Working mothers who like to work are more likely to use mild discipline. (G156)

Working mothers in lower-class families use the same techniques of discipline as do nonworking mothers. (M211)

### Ethnocentrism
If the child is ethnocentric, he is more likely to view discipline as threatening, traumatic, overwhelming, and unintelligible. (B227)

### Ethnocentrism of Parents
Parents who are ethnocentric (as measured by Adorno's E–Scale) tend to stress discipline and obedience, while those who are less ethnocentric stress love and understanding in child rearing. (K117)

### Food Value
There is a correlation between the use of water as a disciplinary agent in childhood and an institutionalized fear of water as manifested in eating habits. (K111)

### Illegitimacy
Unwed mothers, as contrasted with single, never-pregnant girls, were not disciplined as much by their parents. (V027)

As opposed to single, never-pregnant girls, unwed mothers more frequently felt that they should have received more discipline from their parents and more religious training. (V027)

### I.Q.
When maternal educational level is controlled, there is a positive relationship between maternal justification for disciplinary measures and intelligence scores of 4–7-year-old boys and girls. (K115)

There is a positive relationship between maternal justification of disciplinary measures during the child's early years (2–7) and adolescent intelligence scores in sons. (K115)

### Juvenile Delinquency
Poor maternal disciplinary practices (extreme permissiveness, overstrictness, or inconsistency) are correlated with delinquency.

### Juvenile Delinquency/Neurosis
A greater number of neurotic children than of delinquent children experience normal discipline. (B214)

Neurotic children (neurosis measured by phobias, anxiety, obsessions) are more likely than delinquent children to have experienced normal discipline, but are also more likely to have received overstrict discipline, while delinquent children are more likely to have received inconsistent discipline. (B238)

### Marital Adjustment
There is a direct relation between mild, firm childhood discipline and marital adjustment. (K161)

The type of home discipline which most tends to be associated with marital happiness is that which is described as "firm," not "harsh." (T079)

### Mental Illness
There is no correlation between psychosis and the father's methods of discipline. (M164)

### Mental Illness of Child
Parents tend to discipline normal siblings more rationally than psychotic children. (D064)

Mothers of prepsychotics are likely to be either punitive or entirely lax in their discipline. (M164)

### Ordinal Position
First children are more likely than later children to be exposed to psychological discipline. (B252)

### Parent-Child Relations (Conflict)
If discipline is consistent and fair, teen-agers are less likely to describe their adolescence as conflictual. (B249)

### Religion
Protestant mothers are more likely to use symbolic sanctions for discipline as opposed to physical punishment, while Catholic mothers are more likely to use physical sanctions. (V037)

### Religion, Role of Deities
The type of punishment by the deity for a breach of religious norms will be similar to discipline patterns within the family system of the society. (H060)

### Size of Family
Children in large families are more likely to be disciplined for the sake of family harmony than are children in small families. (R106)

### Superego Formation
The child's sense of guilt about agression correlates with parents' use of psychological discipline. (A054)

## CHILD-REARING PRACTICES (DISCIPLINE/CHORES)
### X   Work Attitude of Mother
Mothers with positive attitudes toward their work are more likely to use milder discipline and to demand less sharing of household tasks than are mothers who dislike their work. (S265)

## CHILD-REARING PRACTICES (DISCIPLINE/OVERPROTECTIVENESS)
### X   Sex Status of Child
In the lower middle class, boys are most susceptible to the ill effects of insufficient parental discipline; girls, to the detrimental influence of parental overprotection. (B273)

## CHILD-REARING PRACTICES (DISCIPLINE/RELIGION)     X   Illegitimacy
As opposed to single, never-pregnant girls, unwed mothers more frequently felt that they should have received more discipline from their parents and more religious training. (V027)

## CHILD-REARING PRACTICES (ECONOMICS)
### X   Money, Child's Knowledge of
Children's knowledge of the use of money correlates with the parents' permitting them to experience the use of money and with the parents' wise handling of the family income. (M182)

Children's knowledge of the use of money does not correlate with their parents' giving them an allowance, permitting them to earn money, or using money to reward or punish their behavior. (M182)

## CHILD-REARING PRACTICES (EDUCATION)
### X   Class
At lower middle-class and lower-class levels, parental emphasis on attending college is more likely to appear only after the child has shown good performance at school than it is at higher-class levels, where parental stress is more likely to precede performance. (B291)

### Class/Religion
Catholic families are less likely to stress education of girls beyond high school than are Protestant families. This difference increases with class ranking. (E102)

### Education of Parents
College-educated parents are much more likely to support the desires of their children concerning going to college than are noncollege-educated parents. (E102)

### Employment of Mother
It is not the case that the mother's employment outside the family leads to the educational neglect of the children. (R093)

### Paternal/Maternal-Role Behavior
Among both lower and middle classes, mothers are much more directive than fathers in specifying the kind of school their children should attend. This holds for both Negroes and whites. (B256)

Fathers tend to be more nondirective in their advice on education than mothers are. B297)

## CHILD-REARING PRACTICES, EVALUATION OF
### X   Age of Child
In accord with Homans' theory of distributive justice, it is predicted that, since younger adolescents are likely to expect less freedom in decision making than older youths, they are less likely to approve parental policy which allows them considerable leeway in self-direction. (E100)

Older and younger adolescents are equally likely to favorably evaluate child-rearing policies of dominant parents. Younger adolescents (junior-high-school age) are less likely than older youths to favor democratic, equalitarian, and permissive child-rearing practices. (E100)

### Child-Rearing Practices (Permissiveness)
Adolescents whose parents are democratic are more likely to be satisfied with the child-rearing policy of their parents than those whose parents are highly dominant or permissive. (E100)

### Child-Rearing Values (Punishment)
Among mothers who spanked their children frequently, those who thought it effective had greater confidence in their child rearing than did those who thought it ineffective (U.S.). (S191)

### Parent-Child Relations
The more favorable the adolescent's attitude toward the freedom and responsibility allotted him by the parents, the more likely it is that he will have a positive attitude toward other areas of family adjustment. (N063)

### Parent-Child Relations (Hostility)
The greater the hostility of the child to parental discipline, the more likely he is to be hostile in other areas of parent-child interaction. (N063)

## CHILD-REARING PRACTICES (EXPLORATION)
### X   Class
Upper-class Negro parents more often discourage their babies from reaching out toward objects and persons than do lower-class Negro parents. (W133)

### Creativity of Child
High creativity in adolescents is associated with parents who emphasize the importance of values, openness to experience, and varied interests. (E102)

### Motor Development
Among Negroes, children who are discouraged from reaching out toward objects and other persons have a lower rate of motor development (sitting, creeping, standing, walking) than do children who are encouraged to do so. (W133)

## CHILD-REARING PRACTICES (FAVORITISM)
### X  Achievement
Children who have learning problems are likely to have mothers who show marked preference for the child's sibling. (R113)

### Aggression
Individuals with falling dreams were more likely to express direct aggression against their mothers when they were the favored sibling than when some other sibling was favored. (H216)

Children who tend toward bullying, aggressive, and domineering behavior are likely to have mothers who show marked preference for the child's sibling. (R113)

### Behavior Problems (Lying, Stealing)
Children who lie and steal tend to have mothers who show marked preference for the child's sibling. (R113)

### Criminality
Parents of habitual criminals are more likely to have shown differential treatment to one or more of their children than are the parents of normal persons. (C105)

### Mother-Child Relations (Hostility)
Children whose mothers show marked preference for the child's sibling tend to be hostile and disobedient. (R113)

### Personality of Child (Competitiveness)
A child whose mother shows a marked preference for a sibling tends to be overly competitive with siblings and with other children. (R113)

### Personality of Child (Depression)
A child who is depressed and discouraged tends to have a mother who shows preference for the child's sibling. (R113)

### Personality of Child (Restless, Excitable)
Children whose mothers show marked preference for a sibling are likely to be restless and excitable. (R113)

## CHILD-REARING PRACTICES (FINGER-SUCKING)
### X  Neurosis
Harsh preventative measures for finger-sucking are correlated with neurosis in children (France). (F097)

## CHILD-REARING PRACTICES (FLEXIBILITY)
### X  Social Adjustment of Child
If parents are more flexible in problematic child-rearing situations (if they can change behavior, roles, and attitudes), children are more likely to be socially competent. (T102)

## CHILD-REARING PRACTICES (FRIENDSHIP)
### X  Mental Illness (Schizophrenia)
Schizophrenia is directly correlated with the inhibition of friendships by the mother. (L118)

### Race Attitudes
The less the parents discourage their children from playing with Negro children, while not finding pleasure in letting them choose their own friends, the more ambivalent the parents are in their own racial attitudes. (B226)

Children who say that their parents have prohibited them from playing with Negroes have a higher prejudice rating than do children who say their parents did not discourage them from playing with Negroes. (B226)

Parents who are pleased with their children playing with Negroes have children who are less prejudiced than do parents who discourage interracial playmates. (B226)

Parents who have used spoken prohibitions against their children playing with Negroes produce greater racial prejudice in their children than do parents who use more subtle forms of discouragement. (B226)

### Race Attitudes
### X  Sex Status
Among children who say their parents have not discouraged them from playing with Negro children, boys are less prejudiced than girls. (B226)

Among children who say their parents have prohibited them from playing with Negroes, there is no association between sex and degree of prejudice. (B226)

## CHILD-REARING PRACTICES (FRUSTRATION)
### X  Aggression
Children who are severely frustrated by their mothers are more aggressive (doll play) than are children who are mildly frustrated by their mothers.

Frustration of the infant's desires is not related to later aggression. (S238)

### Class
Lower-class parents tend to subject their children to less frustration of impulse than do middle-class parents. (M178)

### Identification with Parents
Maximum identification is a function of the parents' withholding resources the child desires. (B251)

### Personality (Drive)
Frustration in the child resulting from child-rearing practices increases the child's general drive level.

## CHILD-REARING PRACTICES (GENEROSITY)
### X  Juvenile Delinquency
Delinquents are more likely than nondelinquents to have parents who are not generous. (N057)

There is no relationship between high generosity of parents and low delinquent behavior in their children. (N057)

Adolescents (particularly boys) are more likely to become delinquent if they have large sums of money available than if they have a moderate amount. (N057)

## CHILD-REARING PRACTICES (GENITAL MANIPULATION)   X  Personality Development
A focus on the genital stage of development is more likely to occur when genital manipulation is used as a means of quieting the infant. (S261)

## CHILD-REARING PRACTICES (GIVING REASONS)
### X  Activity Level of Child
Children from homes characterized by a high level of

explanation by the parents of family decisions have a higher activity level than children from homes where there is not a great amount of explanation. (B266)

### Aggression

Parents of nonaggressive adolescent boys use reasoning as a method of training and control to a much greater extent than do parents of the aggressive boys. (B213)

Children from homes characterized by a high level of explanation by the parents are more aggressive than children from homes where there is not much explanation of family decisions. (B266)

### Child-Rearing Practices (Aggression)

There is a negative relationship between the mother's use of reasoning in child rearing and severity of punishment for parent-directed aggression (U.S.) (S191)

### Child-Rearing Practices (Clarity) X Aggression

Among homes characterized by a high level of explanation by the parents, the more explicit the behavior restrictions, the less aggressive the child. (B266)

### Child-Rearing Practices (Clarity) X Creativity

Among homes characterized by a high level of parental explanation of family decisions, explicit behavior restrictions are correlated negatively with the ability to be original. (B266)

### Child-Rearing Practices (Clarity) X Personality of Child (Curiosity)

Among homes characterized by a high level of parental explanation of family decisions, explicit behavior restrictions produce a child who has restricted curiosity. (B266)

### Child-Rearing Practices (Clarity) X Personality of Child (Fear)

Among homes where there is a high level of parental explanation of family decisions, the more explicit the behavioral restrictions, the more fearful the child. (B266)

### Child-Rearing Practices (Clarity) X Personality of Child (Negativism)

Among homes characterized by a high level of parental explanation of family decisions, the more explicit the behavior restrictions, the less negative the children are. (B266)

### Child-Rearing Practices (Clarity) X Personality of Child (Planfulness)

Among homes characterized by a high level of explanation by the parents of family decisions, the more explicit the behavior restrictions, the less planful the child. (B266)

### Child-Rearing Practices (Clarity) X Personality of Child (Quietness)

Among homes characterized by a high level of parental explanation of family decisions, explicit behavioral restrictions produce a quiet child. (B266)

### Child-Rearing Practices (Clarity) X Personality of Child (Tenacity)

Among homes characterized by a high level of explanation by the parents of family decisions, the more explicit the behavior restrictions, the less tenacious the child. (B266)

### Child-Rearing Practices (Clarity) X Sibling Relations (Conflict)

Among homes characterized by high levels of parental explanation of family decisions, the more explicit the behavior restrictions, the less quarrelsome the children. (B266)

### Child-Rearing Practices (Dependency)

Low independence training is associated with infrequent use of explanation and reasoning by parents. (E102)

### Child-Rearing Practices (Household Rules)

There is no difference between parents who use reasoning frequently and those who do not regarding strictness in household matters (neatness, orderliness, helping around the home, and being quiet) (U.S.). (S191)

### Child-Rearing Practices (Punishment)

The use of reasoning as a technique of control is correlated with avoidance of the techniques of physical punishment and of withdrawal of love for mothers as well as for fathers of normals (nonaggressive boys), but not for fathers of aggressive boys. (B243)

Use of reasoning is negatively associated with the use of physical punishment in child rearing (U.S.). (S191)

Parents who use reason frequently are more likely to follow through on threats of punishment than are parents who do not use reasoning (U.S.). (S191)

### Child-Rearing Practices (Sex)

There is a positive relationship between the parents' use of reasoning in child rearing and permissiveness regarding the child's sexual behavior (U.S.). (S191)

### Class

Lower-class autocratic mothers and middle-class democratic and permissive mothers and fathers are more likely to give explanations for their policies than are other parents. (E105)

### Conformity

Children from families where there is a high level of explanation by the parents of family decisions are less conforming than children from homes where there is not as much explanation of family decisions. (B266)

### Conformity X Child-Rearing Practices (Clarity)

Among homes characterized by a high level of explanation of family decisions by the parents, the more explicit the behavior restrictions, the more obedient the children. (B266)

### Creativity

The child raised in a home in which the parents consult with the child about regulations and attempt to explain discipline is more intellectually curious, original, and constructive than the child raised in an authoritarian home. (L146)

### Dependency

As the level of power decreases, parents' explanations of their policies are more likely to create a sense of self-confidence and independence. (E105)

### Educational Aspiration

Among adolescents whose parents have college expectations for them, those who are uncertain about college receive less reasoning and explanation in child rearing than do those who are certain regarding their college plans. (E102)

### I.Q.
Arbitrary maternal discipline is associated with low I.Q. scores, whereas explained maternal discipline is associated with high I.Q. scores. (K127)

### Juvenile Delinquency
Parents who explain punishment are less likely than those who do not to produce delinquent children. (N057)

Children who are allowed to explain their behavior are less likely to become delinquent than those who are not permitted to do so. (N057)

### Leadership
There is a positive relationship for boys and a negative relationship for girls between principled discipline by parents (reasoning with child and apologizing for unfair treatment) and leadership abilities in the child (based on teachers' ratings of influence in group activities). (B250)

### Mother-Child Relations (Warmth)
Mothers who have a warm relationship with their children are more likely to use praise and reasoning rather than punishment as a means of control than are mothers who do not have warm mother-child relations. (M186)

### Parent-Child Relations (Affection)
The more likely parents are to provide explanations for their rules, the more likely their adolescents are to have a strong attraction for their parents. (E105)

### Parent-Child Relations (Interaction) X Conformity
In homes characterized by a high level of parental explanation of family decisions, high parent-child interaction produces greater non-conformity in the child than does low parent-child interaction. (B266)

### Parent-Child Relations (Warmth)
There is a correlation between parental use of reasoning as a technique of control and parental attitudes of warmth, nurturance, and acceptance. (B243)

### Paternal/Maternal-Role Behavior
Fathers of psychotic children are more likely than mothers to explain the rationale of parental discipline. (D064)

### Peer Relations
The child raised in a home in which parents consult with the child about regulations and attempt to explain discipline is more successful in leadership than is the child raised in an authoritarian home. (L146)

### Personality of Child (Curiosity)
Children from families characterized by a high level of explanation by the parents of family decisions are more curious than children from homes where there is not much explanation of family decisions. (B266)

### Personality of Child (Fear)
Children from homes where there is a high level of explanation by the parents of family decisions are more fearless than are children from homes where there is not much explanation of family decisions. (B266)

### Personality of Child (Planfulness)
Children from homes characterized by a high level of explanation by the parents of family decisions are more planful than are children from homes where there is not much explanation of family decisions. (B266)

### Scholastic Achievement
Parental explanation of policies, when accompanied by autocratic control, is more apt to produce low academic achievement than high achievement. (E105)

### Social Adjustment of Child
Children raised in a home in which parents consult with them about regulations and attempt to explain discipline are more socially outgoing and active in both a hostile and friendly way than children raised in an authoritarian home. (L146)

### Superego Formation
The use of reasoning as a technique of control is associated with the development of conscience in the son as indicated by guilt feelings about aggression toward parents, teachers, and peers. (B243)

### CHILD-REARING PRACTICES (GIVING REASONS/POWER)    X   Conformity
The frequency with which a parent explains his rules to his children is more effective in inducing conformity to the rules than are the different levels of power exerted (autocratic, democratic, and permissive). (E105)

### CHILD-REARING PRACTICES (GIVING REASONS)/POWER STRUCTURE OF FAMILY    X   Scholastic Motivation
Which parent has greater power in child rearing has less effect than use of explanation and reasoning on high academic motivation in the child. (E102)

### CHILD-REARING PRACTICES (GUILT)    X   Achievement Motivation
An emphasis on achievement drive is likely to be correlated with the inculcation by the mother of a sense of guilt in childhood. (V029)

### CHILD-REARING PRACTICES (HANDICRAFTS)    X   Cognitive Development (Nonverbal)
For children of both sexes, the amount of time either parent spends with the child in arts, crafts, and hobbies is not related to the child's nonverbal (spatial and numerical) ability. (B257)

### CHILD-REARING PRACTICES (HELP-GIVING)    X   Cognitive Development (Verbal)
Mothers of children with high verbal ability are more likely to give both verbal and physical help to their children than are mothers of children with low verbal ability. (B257)

### CHILD-REARING PRACTICES (HOUSEHOLD RULES)    X   Child-Rearing Practices (Aggression)
Mothers who are permissive regarding the child's parent-directed aggression are less restrictive about noise in the house, cleanliness, and care of household property (U.S.). (S191)

### Child-Rearing Practices (Giving Reasons)
There is no difference between parents who use reasoning frequently and those who do not regarding strictness in household matters (neatness, orderliness, helping around the home, and being quiet) (U.S.). (S191)

### Child-Rearing Practices (Sex)

Mothers who are not permissive regarding their children's sexual behavior are stricter about noise, table manners, and care of household property than are mothers who are permissive regarding their children's sexual behavior (U.S.). (S191)

### Toilet Training

The more severe the mother is in toilet training the child, the greater the demands on the child for conformity with household rules (table manners, neatness, orderliness, and care of house and furniture) (U.S.). (S191)

## CHILD-REARING PRACTICES (ILLNESS)
### X    Behavior Problems

Where parents are integrated, realistic and accepting of their child's illness, behavioral disturbance is minimal. (F081)

## CHILD-REARING PRACTICES (IMPULSE CONTROL)
### X    Class

Middle-class parents permit less free play of the impulses of their children than do lower-class parents.

## CHILD-REARING PRACTICES (INDULGENCE)
### X    Age of Child

The younger the child (2–4 years v. 5–7 years), the more indulgent (giving in, bribing, compromising, etc.) the parents. (I006)

### Age of Parents

Older parents tend to be more indulgent and solicitous toward their children than do younger parents. (R106)

### Employment of Mother, Evaluation of

Mothers who like their jobs are more likely to be indulgent toward their children than are mothers who are not as satisfied with their jobs. (Y047)

### Household Composition

The degree of infant indulgence is roughly proportional to the number of adults living in the household; extended and polygynous families tend to be predominantly indulgent, nuclear families are unpredictable, and in mother-child households the probability of indulgence is slight. (W127)

### Mental Illness (Manic-Depressive)

Manic-depressives tend to have been over-indulged in childhood. (C092)

### Ordinal Position

Last-born children in large families are more likely to be pampered and overindulged than are earlier-born children. (R106)

### Polygyny (Sororal)

Societies with sororal polygyny (in which co-wives customarily are sisters), as compared with other forms of marriage, are more likely to be indulgent in the initial care of the infant and less severe in subsequent socialization. (W142)

### Religion, Role of Deities

Societies with indulgent child-rearing practices have more benevolent deities in the cultural belief system; societies having less indulgent child-rearing practices have more aggressive deities. (L141)

Societies in which infants are treated indulgently will perceive gods as benevolent; where indulgence is low, gods will be perceived as aggressive. (W127)

### Scholastic Achievement

The indulgence of children by their kinsmen tends to retard the process of education. (B075)

### Sibling Structure (Age Difference)

The wider the spacing between siblings, the more relaxed the mother is and the more attention she devotes to the second-born child as compared to the firstborn; the second-born male with an older sister is the most indulged. (K149)

### Size of Family

The larger the family, the more likely is the younger child to be indulged (U.S.). (S191)

The infant is likely to be treated more indulgently in large extended families where there are many persons to care for the infant. (W127)

### Theft

A high frequency of theft is found in societies with severe weaning and low indulgence of infants. (W127)

### Toilet Training

When parents are particularly fond of and indulgent toward children, training in sphincter control will occur at a late age. (D025)

### Work Attitudes of Mother

Mothers who like their jobs are more likely to be indulgent toward their children than are mothers who are not as satisfied with their jobs. (Y047)

## CHILD-REARING PRACTICES (INDULGENCE AND ANXIETY)
### X    Sibling Status

Regardless of the sex of the child, the longer the child remains the only child in the family, probably the more indulged and possibly the more anxiously reared he will be. (K149)

## CHILD-REARING PRACTICES (INDULGENCE IN CHILDHOOD)
### X    Child-Rearing Practices (Indulgence in Infancy)

There is a negative correlation between the degree of initial indulgence of the infant and the severity of the socialization which is later imposed on the child. (W142)

## CHILD-REARING PRACTICES (INDULGENCE IN INFANCY)
### X    Child-Rearing Practices (Indulgence in Childhood)

There is a negative correlation between the degree of initial indulgence of the infant and the severity of the socialization which is later imposed on the child. (W142)

## CHILD-REARING PRACTICES (ISOLATION)
### X    Child-Rearing Practices (Physical Abuse)

Children who are severely abused (beaten, tortured, etc.) by their parents are also likely to be denied normal social and recreational contacts with their peers. (Y043)

### Child-Rearing Practices (Praise)

Use of praise is associated with use of isolation as methods of punishment (U.S.). (S191)

### Class

Middle-class and upper-class parents are both observed to utilize consistent, as distinct from idiosyncratic, isolation to avert the child's adoption of deviant goals and practices. (C086)

### Education

Better-educated parents are more likely to use physical isolation of the child as a means of punishment than are rural or urban working-class parents.

### Mental Illness (Schizophrenia)

A significantly greater number of schizophrenic daughters than of normal ones believed their mothers attempted to exclude outside influences during their childhood. (H186)

## CHILD-REARING PRACTICES (KIN)
### X  Child-Rearing Practices (Punishment)

Adults (generally, maternal grandmother) other than parents are more likely to use severe punishment upon the child than are the parents. (C117)

### Cohesion of Extended Family

The greater the strength of the extended family as a whole, the more likely it is that children will be reared not only by their own parents but by other kin as well. (M198)

### Kin Relations (Dependency)

When the discipline and control of the child are in the hands of other relatives as well as the parents, the pattern of interaction among kinsmen will be characterized by mutual dependence. (H021)

### Parent-Child Relations (Obedience)

The greater the control of adults other than parents over the child (especially, maternal grandmother), the less amenable is the child likely to be. (C117)

### Paternal Role (Discipline)

The greater the control of adults other than parents (particularly the maternal grandmother) over the child, the more likely it is that the father will use severe punishment in handling the child. (C117)

### Superego Formation

There is a low positive correlation between the importance of relatives (other than parents), as opposed to unrelated persons, as agents of socialization of the child and the development of guilt feelings as measured by the patient's feeling of responsibility for his illness. (W142)

## CHILD-REARING PRACTICES (LEADERSHIP)
### X  Education

The higher the parents' educational level, the more marked are the differences between boys and girls regarding prenatal nurturance, companionship, and praise as they affect leadership abilities in the child (i.e., enhancing the relationship for boys and reducing it for girls). (B250)

## CHILD-REARING PRACTICES (LYING)   X  Class

There is no significant difference between working-class and middle-class families regarding the teaching of attitudes towards lying. (B235)

## CHILD-REARING PRACTICES (MATERIAL VALUES)   X  Class

Working-class families tend to instill in their children greater concern for material objects than do upper middle-class families. (B235)

## CHILD-REARING PRACTICES (MATURITY DEMANDS)   X  Aggression

There is a positive relationship between fathers' expecting overly mature behavior from their children and aggression, bullying, and domineering on the part of the child. (R100)

### Behavior Problems (Obedience/Hostility)

There is a positive relationship between the father's expecting overly mature behavior on the part of the child and the child's disobedience accompanied by hostility. (R100)

### Behavior Problems (Stealing)

There is a positive relationship between fathers who expect overly mature behavior from their children and stealing by children. (R100)

### Motor Adjustment

There is a negative relationship between the father's expecting overly mature behavior on the part of the child and the child's motor development. (R100)

### Personality Development (Maturity)

There is no relationship between mothers who expect overly mature behavior from their children and the child's remaining immature (as measured by general immaturity, enuresis, and reluctance to go to school). (R100)

### Personality Development of Child

Children whose mothers encourage their maturation are higher in emotional stability, total emotional freedom, group identification, and freedom from conflict than are children whose mothers encourage infantile behavior. (A071)

### Personality Problems

There is a negative relationship between fathers who expect overly mature behavior on the part of the child and child-personality problems characterized by delusions, obsessions, and withdrawal. (R100)

## CHILD-REARING PRACTICES (MECHANICAL RESTRICTIONS)   X  Class

Mechanical restrictions (playpen, crib, or baby tender) are used more frequently by upper-class than by lower-class Negro parents. (W133)

## CHILD-REARING PRACTICES (MOTHER'S PERCEPTION OF)
### X  Child-Rearing Practices, Child's Perception of

Children perceive their mothers as more punishing than mothers perceive themselves. (M177)

## CHILD-REARING PRACTICES (MOTOR FREEDOM)   X  Class

Lower-class Negro parents allow their babies more freedom to experiment (exercise their motor functions and experiment with motion) than do upper-class Negro parents. (W133)

## CHILD-REARING PRACTICES (NEATNESS)
### X  Child-Rearing Practices (Sex)

Mothers who are nonpermissive regarding sexual behavior require more neatness, orderliness, and cleanliness of their children than do mothers who are more permissive regarding sexual behavior. (M186)

## CHILD-REARING PRACTICES (NEGLECT)
### X  Aggression

The greater the neglect of the child, the more likely that it will be aggressive. (M203)

### Death Rate

The greater the neglect of the child, the less likely that it will survive. (M203)

### Employment of Mother
When the mother works, conditions of child neglect are created. (Y051)

### Household Management
Families which are marked by their severe neglect of children are more likely to have little routine in the management of daily household tasks and little assignment of responsibility for these tasks than are other types of families. (Y043)

### Housing
Bad housing, as such, is not the cause of a parent's neglecting his child. (B270)

### Juvenile Delinquency
Parental negligence and exposure to delinquent behavior are predisposing factors toward socialized delinquency (which is defined as having bad companions, engaging in cooperative stealing, habitual truancy from school and home, etc.). (J024)

If the parents both neglect the child and provide poor role models for the child, the child is more likely to become a delinquent than if only one of these factors is present. (M194)

If both parents have a neglecting attitude toward the child, it is more likely that the child will commit property crimes than any other kinds of crimes. (M194)

Delinquents are more likely than normal persons to suffer from non-support and negligence of parents. (O033)

### Juvenile Delinquency, Age at
The more neglecting the attitude of parents toward the child, the more likely it is that he will become delinquent at an early age rather than at a late age. (M194)

### Juvenile Delinquency, by Class
There is a correlation between parental neglect and delinquency, but less so in the lower classes than in the higher. (S219)

### Maternal Deprivation
Children who suffered early maternal deprivation are likely to grow up to subject their own children to similar neglect. (B270)

### Personality of Parent
In families where the children are seriously neglected, either parent—but most usually the mother—has a personality which is characterized by temperamental instability and incapability to adopt an abstract attitude. (B270)

### Sex-Role Definition
The ambiguity of the roles of the adult male and female is likely to result in the neglect of the children. (B040)

### Size of Family
Child neglect is no greater in large families than in small. (B270)

## CHILD-REARING PRACTICES (NONVERBAL STIMULATION)
### X Cognitive Development (Nonverbal)
For boys, nonverbal stimulation (permissiveness regarding object experimentation, availability of toys and gadgets, and lack of physical restrictions) is positively associated with spatial and numerical ability. (B257)

## CHILD-REARING PRACTICES (NURTURANCE)
### X Aggression
There is a correlation between a lack of maternal nurturance and the incidence of aggressive behavior in boys. (B243)

Mothers who are not nurturant are more likely to produce children high in hostility or aggression drive than are mothers who satisfy their children's needs. (F103)

### Dependency
There is *no* association between dependency behavior in the preschool situation and nurturance of child at bedtime. (S014)

The more non-nurturant (punitive) the mothers of preschool boys, the more dependent they are. (S238)

The more nonnurturant (punitive) the mothers of preschool girls, the less dependent they are. (S238)

### Education
There is no relationship between parental educational level and degree of nurturance shown in child rearing. (B250)

### Ordinal Position
Second and later children receive less nurturance at bedtime from mothers than do first and only children. (S014)

### Personality Development of Parent
If a person suffers from an oral character disorder (is childish, impulse-ridden) he will give inconsistent nurture to his children when they are young and will be unable to help them with their problems of development. (R110)

### Personality of Child (Pessimism)
Mothers who are not nurturant are more likely to produce pessimistic children than are mothers who respond helpfully and fulfill children's needs. (F103)

### Personality of Child (Submissiveness)
The less nurturant the mother, the more submissive the child.

### Sex Status
Socialization of girls is more likely to emphasize nurturance than the socialization of boys (cross-cultural). (G156)

### Superego Formation
There is no relationship between degree of initial nurturance of the child and development of guilt feelings as measured by the patient's feeling of responsibility for his illness. (W142)

## CHILD-REARING PRACTICES (NURTURANCE AND CONTROL)
### X Sex Status
With respect to nurturance and control, the mother is likely to treat children of both sexes equally, whereas the father is more likely to be more nurturing toward the daughter and more controlling toward the son. (J031)

## CHILD-REARING PRACTICES (NURTURANCE/CLARITY)
### X Socialization, Effectiveness of
Given a minimal level of nurturance, effectiveness of socialization is not increased by additional nurturance but is produced by increasing explicitness of standards. (M183)

## CHILD-REARING PRACTICES (NURTURANCE/ DEPENDENCY)                    X    Recreation
Games of physical skill seem to be positively associated with low permissiveness and high conflict over nurturance and self-reliant behavior. (R003)

## CHILD-REARING PRACTICES (OBEDIENCE)
### X    Aggression
Mothers of aggressive boys impose fewer demands for obedience and are less consistent in these demands than are mothers of normals. (B243)

### Child-Rearing Practices (Sex)
Mothers who are nonpermissive regarding sexual behavior (modesty, masturbation, sex-play permissiveness) require greater obedience from their children than permissive mothers do. (M186)

### Ethnocentrism
Parents of ethnocentric persons tend to emphasize the submission of the child to the demands of dominating parents. (M222)

### Homicide
Where strict obedience is emphasized in socialization, the rate of homicide is likely to be high. (S187)

### Menstrual Taboos
When menstrual taboos are extensive in the society there is severe punishment for disobedience and very strict obedience demands are made on children. (S079)

### Mental Illness (Schizophrenia)
Where strict obedience is emphasized in socialization, mental illness will tend to be manifest in paranoid schizophrenia. (S187)

### Political Structure
Severity of obedience training is associated with the number of levels of political organization above the community level. (A053)

### Sex Status
Obedience is more likely to be stressed for girls than for boys. (G156)

### Slavery
The institution of slavery tends to promote child-rearing practices stressing obedience and responsibility rather than achievement. (M246)

### Socialization, Effectiveness of
The higher the level of obedience enforced by parents upon children, the more likely that the children will resist temptation. (G120)

Effective socialization of the child is more likely if automatic obedience, rather than positive rewards or reasoning is stressed by parents. (M203)

## CHILD-REARING PRACTICES (OBEDIENCE/DEPENDENCY)
### X    Economic Level
Preliterate societies with large stores of food put much pressure upon children for responsibility and obedience and little stress upon achievement and independence. (W127)

### Theft
Theft is more frequent in societies which severely punish older children for disobedience, irresponsibility, lack of self-reliance, and lack of achievement. (W127)

## CHILD-REARING PRACTICES (OCCUPATIONAL CHOICE)            X    Paternal/Maternal Role
Middle-class mothers, white and Negro, are more likely to attempt to influence their children's occupational choice than are middle-class fathers. This does not hold for lower-class parents, white or Negro. (B256)

## CHILD-REARING PRACTICES OF FATHER
### X    Personality of Son (Responsibility)
There is a positive relationship between responsibility in the son (based on teachers' ratings of dependability in fulfilling obligations) and discipline and authority from the father. (B250)

## CHILD-REARING PRACTICES OF FATHER (AUTOCRATIC/DEMOCRATIC)
### X    Scholastic Motivation of Child
Academic motivation in the child increases as paternal power in child rearing decreases from autocratic to more democratic in form. (E102)

## CHILD-REARING PRACTICES OF FATHER (DEMOCRATIC)
### X    Scholastic Motivation of Child
High academic motivation in the child is strongly related to democratic child-rearing practices by the father. (E102)

## CHILD-REARING PRACTICES OF FATHER (DEPENDENCY)
### X    Occupational Aspirations of Son
High paternal independence training is associated with high occupational aspirations on the part of the son regardless of the father's occupation. (E102)

### Scholastic Motivation of Child
High paternal involvement in independence training is associated with high academic motivation in adolescents of both sexes. (E102)

## CHILD-REARING PRACTICES OF FATHER (PUNISHMENT)                    X    Class
The fathers of lower-class mentally ill patients tend to be physically violent at times, more than do fathers of middle-class patients. (M061)

### Occupational Aspirations of Child
Students with high occupational aspirations are more fearful of paternal punishment than are students with lower occupational aspirations. (E102)

## CHILD-REARING PRACTICES OF FATHER (STRICTNESS)            X    Employment of Mother
Among nondelinquents, overstrictness on the part of fathers is more likely in families where the mother is employed. (S265)

## CHILD-REARING PRACTICES (ORAL)
### X    Dependency
The greater the mother's over indulgence of oral and other needs of her infant, the greater the dependency strivings in her children. (B224)

The more the mother frustrates the oral needs of the infant, the greater the dependency striving of the child. (B224)

## CHILD-REARING PRACTICES (ORAL AND DEPENDENCY NEEDS)        X    Child-Rearing Practices (Sex)
Cultures that are permissive regarding the infant's oral needs and dependency needs tend to be nonpermissive in sex training; cultures that are nonpermissive regarding

the infant's oral and dependency needs tend to be permissive in sex training. (P084)

## CHILD-REARING PRACTICES (ORAL FRUSTRATION)    X    Personality Problems (Oral)
The greater the amount of oral frustration in infancy, the more likely the incidence of oral fixation in later years. (B224)

## CHILD-REARING PRACTICES (ORDERLINESS)    X    Toilet Training
Mothers who are severe in toilet training are more demanding regarding orderliness (U.S.). (S191)

## CHILD-REARING PRACTICES (OVERSTIMULATION)    X    Personality Development
Maternal overstimulation of the sensory organs of the child contributes to inadequate ego growth and possibly psychosis. (B324)

## CHILD-REARING PRACTICES (PERFECTIONISM/COMPLIANCE)    X    Mental Illness (Schizophrenia/Neurosis)
Mothers of schizophrenics are more likely to be rigid perfectionists who stress disciplinary compliance than are mothers of neurotics. (M061)

## CHILD-REARING PRACTICES (PERMISSIVENESS)    X    Achievement Motivation
Mothers of sons with high achievement motivation are more likely to be permissive regarding their taking care of themselves. (G156)

### Age of Child
Both mothers and fathers are more likely to treat their older offspring permissively than they are their younger children. (E100)

### Aggression
Children who are bullying, domineering, and aggressive are likely to have mothers who are more permissive. (R113)

### Behavior Problems
There is no statistical support for the hypothesis that mothers of children with primary behavior disorders are more lax and overindulgent than are mothers of normal children.

Unconscious parental permission is associated with antisocial behavior in the child; this includes truancy as well as other behavior expressing forbidden impulses.

### Behavior Problems (Acting Out)
Children having mothers who are overly permissive are prone to temper tantrums. (R113)

### Behavior Problems (Stealing, Lying)
Children who lie and steal tend to have mothers who are overly permissive. (R113)

### Child-Rearing Attitudes (Aggression)
The more permissive the mother regarding aggression, the less severe she will be in punishing aggressive behavior (U.S.). (S191)

### Child-Rearing Practices (Chores)
There is a positive relationship between the mother's general permissiveness and the number of chores allocated to the child. (M216)

### Child-Rearing Practices, Evaluation of
Adolescents whose parents are democratic are more likely to be satisfied with the child-rearing policy of their

parents than those whose parents are highly dominant or permissive. (E100)

### Child-Rearing Values
Parents who are permissive with their children are more likely to hold values that emphasize the child's development than to have traditional conceptions of what is a "good" child. (B007)

### Class
Lower-class Negro mothers are more likely to be permissive in their handling of their children than are middle-class Negro mothers. (B272)

Lower-class families are more likely to be easy going and permissive in child-rearing practices than are middle-class families. (C023)

Middle-class families are more permissive in child rearing than are lower-class families. (G156)

Middle-class parents were more restrictive than working-class parents 25 years ago, but now they are more permissive and the gap between them is narrowing. (K089)

Child rearing in the lower classes tends to be more punitive and less permissive than in upper-class families. (M058)

Parents of lower-class children are more likely to permit fuller gratification of organically based drives than are parents of middle-class children. (R127)

### Cohesion of Family
Family solidarity and interpersonal harmony seem to be more likely in families in which parents allow the adolescent some involvement in running his own life than in families in which parents tend to exclude the adolescent from choosing his own behavior and goals. (E100)

### Education of Father
Fathers having a high-school education or less are more likely to be permissive toward their older children than are fathers having a year or so of college. (E100)

### Education of Parents
Autocratic mothers of young daughters, autocratic fathers of young sons and daughters, and permissive fathers of older youths are most likely to have less than a tenth-grade education. Autocratic mothers of boys and older girls, autocratic fathers of high-school-aged children, permissive mothers and fathers of younger adolescents are most likely to have one or more years of college. (E100)

Both mothers and fathers who are permissive in rearing their younger rather than their older children are more likely to have acquired some college education. (E100)

Parents with least education tend to be most domineering since they have limited insight into the developmental needs of their adolescent children; this is supported by the finding of a strong negative relationship between the authoritarian-control factor on the PARI and educational level in a sample of 60 mothers in a psychiatric hospital. (E100)

### Ethnic Attitudes
If a mother's relations with her children are characterized as permissive, then there will be no correlation between her attitudes toward other ethnic groups and those of her children. (W146)

There is a negative relationship between a mother's permissiveness and her daughter's anti-Semitism. (W146)

### Feeding
Parents in the sample who tend to treat the child casually also tend to be permissive in early feeding training, not to punish for misbehavior, and not to promote his independence. (S010)

### Housing
Permissiveness in child rearing varies directly with the amount of space within the home. (B007)

### Income, Mother's Contribution to
The greater the importance of the mother's economic contribution to the family, the less permissive she will be with her children. (M216)

### Inheritance
Rules of succession are more likely to be violated by the individual headman if he is permitted an undisciplined childhood. (M124)

### Juvenile Delinquency
Permissiveness by the father contributes to the development of the delinquency-linked trait of social assertiveness and thus indirectly to delinquency.

Parents who are extremely uncritical or permissive or extremely critical or nonpermissive are more likely to produce delinquent children than are those who are selectively critical. (N057)

### Moral Beliefs of Child
As parental constraint decreases, the child's belief in immanent justice, moral realism, retribution, and severe punishment tends to decline. (J021)

### Motor Development
Among Negroes, children from homes that are more permissive rather than punishing about non-approved habits (thumb-sucking, hair-pulling, etc.) show more advanced motor development (sitting, creeping, standing, walking). (W133)

### Occupation
Mothers whose husbands have bureaucratic jobs are more likely to be permissive in their child-rearing practices than those whose husbands have entrepreneurial jobs. (J030)

### Ordinal Position
Parents tend to be more permissive and relaxed in their treatment of second children than they are in relation to the firstborn child. (F084)

### Parent-Child Relations (Interaction)
Promoting the child's independence is a characteristic of parents who participate in much activity with the child. Such parents also tend to be permissive in early feeding and toilet-training procedures but to punish for misbehavior. (S010)

### Parent-Child Relations (Rejection)
Adolescents who have autocratic or laissez-faire and ignoring parents are more likely to report that they have felt unwanted. (E100)

Child-rearing structures which permit considerable participation in self-direction are least likely to provoke feelings of rejection in the adolescent. (E100)

### Paternal/Maternal Role
Children at all ages perceive mothers as more permissive or equalitarian in the child-rearing realtionship than are fathers, while fathers are more likely to be thought of as dominant. (E100)

### Peer Relations
The more permissively the child is raised, the more likely it is that he will be responsive to the *mores* of his peers rather than of adults. (M188)

### Personality (Ego Strength)
There is a correlation between early permissiveness and susceptibility to external social sanctions. (V029)

### Personality of Child (Ego Strength)
There is a correlation between parental tolerance and ego strength in the child. (S221)

### Personality of Child (Hostility)
Children having mothers who are overly permissive are likely to be hostile and disobedient. (R113)

### Personality of Mother
Permissive mothers tend to be extroverted and nonneurotic. Punitive mothers tend to be introverted and neurotic.

### Recreation
The presence of games of strategy is positively associated with low permissiveness in child training, high severity of bowel training, and high reward for obedient behavior. (R003)

### School Attendance
There is a positive relationship between the mother's general permissiveness and the regularity with which the child attends school. (M216)

### Sex-Role Identification
The more permissive the parents, the more likely it is that the boy will develop strong masculine identification. (M183)

### Sex Status
Mothers of young children tend to be more lenient with their sons than with their daughters. (K098)

### Size of Family
The larger the family, the more permissive are the parents in child rearing. (B007)

### Social Network
Parents whose chief source of guidance is their relations with their contemporaries will be much more permissive in their child-rearing practices than parents whose chief identifications are not with other people.

### Technology
There is a negative correlation between the level of technological development of a society and permissiveness of the child-rearing practices. (L168)

## CHILD-REARING PRACTICES (PERMISSIVENESS/GIVING REASONS)
### X Dependency
Adolescents whose parents are permissive in their authority and explain their rules are most likely to be autonomous; adolescents whose parents are autocratic and who seldom give explanations for their rules of conduct are least apt to be autonomous. (E105)

## CHILD-REARING PRACTICES (PERMISSIVENESS/RESTRICTIVENESS)     X Achievement Motivation
Permissive child-rearing practices are no more related to

achievement motivation in sons than are restrictive child-rearing practices. (G156)

## CHILD-REARING PRACTICES (PHYSICAL ABUSE)
### X    Child-Rearing Practices (Isolation)
Children who are severely abused (beaten, tortured, etc.) by their parents are also likely to be denied normal social and recreational contacts with their peers. (Y043)

## CHILD-REARING PRACTICES (PHYSICAL CONTACT)                    X    Dependency
Amount and quality of physical contact between mother and infant are not related to the development of autonomy in the infant. (Y042)

### I.Q.
The amount and quality of physical contact between mother and child are positively related to intelligence in the child. (Y042)

### Personality of Child (Stress)
The amount and quality ⌐f physical contact between mother and child are positively related to the infant's capacity to handle stress. (Y042)

## CHILD-REARING PRACTICES (PHYSICAL NEGLECT)                    X    Class
Physically neglected (underfed, dirty, etc.) children are more likely to be found in the lower classes than in the upper classes. (Y043)

## CHILD-REARING PRACTICES (POLITICAL INDOCTRINATION)               X    Class
At higher-class levels, mothers are more likely to be attuned to cultural change and innovation and, therefore, less likely to indoctrinate children in the parental views on politics. (H244)

## CHILD-REARING PRACTICES (POWER)    X    Class
Working-class parents are more likely to use unqualified power assertions over their children than are middle-class parents, and working-class mothers are less likely than working-class fathers to do so. (H182)

### Conformity
The assertion by mothers of unqualified power in reaction to the child's noncompliance correlates with hostility, power assertiveness, and resistance to influence in the child. Such a correlation does not exist, however, with respect to power assertion by the mother prior to any response by the child, nor to power assertion of either type by fathers. (H182)

### Mother-Child Relations (Hostility)
The mother's assertion of unqualified power in reaction to the child's noncompliance is not caused by the hostility and rebelliousness of the child, but, rather, produces these characteristics. (H182)

### Ordinal Position of Mother
Mothers who have been younger children tend to find it difficult to set limits to the power of an older child. (H217)

### Personality of Child (Aggression/Guilt)
Direct power-assertive disciplinary techniques are associated with aggression in the child; "softer" discipline techniques with repression and guilt. (H201)

### Personality of Child (Consideration for Others)
In a high power-assertive context, the child is likely to develop consideration for others based solely on fear of punishment. (H212)

Children raised in a home in which power was not used arbitrarily are likely to develop consideration for others if either love-oriented or other-oriented discipline is used. (H212)

The development of consideration for others by children raised in a home in which power was not used arbitrarily is independent of the type of discipline used. (H212)

### Personality of Child (Hostility)
As the child's dependence on his parents decreases, the parents' unqualified power assertion is less likely to result in hostility, power assertiveness, and resistance to influence on the part of the child. (H182)

### Socialization, Effectiveness of
The greater the use of unqualified power by the parent, the less likely the child's internalization of controls and the more likely his compliance on the basis of expediency or fear. (H182)

## CHILD-REARING PRACTICES (PRAISE)
### X    Child-Rearing Practices (Isolation)
Use of praise is associated with use of isolation as methods of punishment (U.S.). (S191)

### Child-Rearing Practices (Punishment)
Use of praise is negatively associated with use of physical punishment as a method of punishment (U.S.). (S191)

## CHILD-REARING PRACTICES (PRAISE/PUNISHMENT)                    X    Residence
Mothers who raise their children in multiple-family dwellings are more sparing in their use of both praise and punishment than are mothers who raise their children in single-family dwellings. (M216)

## CHILD-REARING PRACTICES (PROTECTION)
### X    Alcoholism of Child
Alcoholism is more likely to occur when parents lack confidence in the child's ability and fear they must shield him. (C122)

## CHILD-REARING PRACTICES (PUNISHMENT)
### X    Achievement Motivation
Mothers of children with strong achievement motivation do not differ from mothers of children with weak achievement motivation in the number and intensity of punishments for demands not fulfilled by the child and restrictions not obeyed by the child. (W139)

### Achievement Values
The use of physical punishment as a child-rearing practice is positively associated with low consensus between mother and son regarding achievement values. (R097)

### Age of Child
The older the boy, the lower the proportion of punishments received from the mother; for girls the proportion of punishments received from the mother remains constant regardless of age. (J026)

### Age of Mother
Older mothers (40 years or older) are more likely than younger mothers (20–39 years) to use psychological punishment-rewards in child rearing. (R097)

Younger mothers tend to be more irritable, quicker to punish, and more severe with their children than do older mothers. (S191)

The younger the mother, the more likely is she to

use physical punishment in child rearing (U.S.). (S191)

The younger the mother, the more likely is she to use withdrawal of privileges as a technique of control (U.S.). (S191)

### Age of Parents
Older mothers tend to be less hostile and to use less physical punishment than do younger ones; older fathers tend to be more lax in discipline and to use less physical punishment. (B232)

### Aggression
Fathers of aggressive adolescent boys are more prone to use physical punishment than control fathers. (B213)

Parents of aggressive adolescent boys tend to deprive their sons of certain possessions and privileges (as a form of discipline) more often than do parents of the control group. (B213)

Physical punishment increases the amount of aggression in the child. (B232)

Boys' aggression at school is directly related to the mother's hostility and use of physical punishment; girls' is not. The reverse situation holds when the father is hostile and punitive, although the differences in the correlations for boys and girls are then less marked. (B232)

Since punitiveness by the mother causes both counteragression and aggression anxiety, the further the distance from the mother and home, the less the child inhibits his aggression. (B232)

Within the schoolroom, girls with either high- or low-punitive mothers exhibited the least aggression (a curvilinear relation), but aggression by boys increased linearly with punitiveness of the mother. (B232)

In a doll-play diagnostic situation, the number of aggressive acts by both sexes is linearly related to the punitiveness of mothers. (B232)

The more the mother punishes, the more aggressive are both boys and girls at home; aggressiveness of boys at school has a curvilinear relation with punishment by the father and tends to occur particularly when the father is low-punitive and the mother is high-punitive. (B232)

When mothers are highly punitive, girls are more likely to develop controls over their aggressive feelings than are boys or than girls who are highly punished by their fathers; but boys whose fathers punish them moderately are more likely to develop such controls. (B232)

Both hostility and physical punishment by one or both parents tend to summate, producing more severe conduct problems in the home; this is also true for boys in the schoolroom (but not for girls). (B232)

Parents of aggressive boys tend to use ridicule, deprivation of privileges, and physical punishment as discipline more often than do parents of normal boys. (B246)

Aggressive boys are as likely as nonaggressive boys to perceive their parents as inflicting punishment. (K103)

With boys, there is a linear correlation between severity of punishment by parents and the amount of overt social aggression exhibited in preschool; for girls, the relation is curvilinear. (L157)

Severity of punishment by like-sex parent correlates with frequency of aggression in doll play of girls, but not of boys. (L157)

Children whose mothers are very punitive tend toward bullying, domineering, and generally aggressive behavior. (R113)

The more severe the punishment, the more aggression the child is likely to show. (S191)

For boys, the relationship between the amount of aggression and the severity of maternal punitiveness is positive. (S246)

For girls, there is a curvilinear relationship between maternal punitiveness and the development of aggression. Both the severely punished and the least severely punished girls are less aggressive than those with an intermediate amount of punishment. (S246)

If boys are punished in such a way that socialization is increased, they are likely to develop self-aggression. (S246)

Due to the mechanism of displacement, the more severe the punishment of the child, the more likely that he will inhibit overt, interpersonal aggression and will be more aggressive in fantasy. (S248)

### Aggression Anxiety
No form of punishment, except the withdrawal of love, is associated with the development of aggression anxiety in boys. (S246)

For boys, both aggression anxiety and self-aggression are preceded by a nonpermissive background. (S246)

### Aggression (Fantasy)
Children of more severely punishing mothers display more fantasy aggression than do other children. (S191)

### Behavior Problems
The use of physical punishment on the part of the parents is positively associated with antisocial behavior in the child (e.g., lying, stealing, temper tantrums, disobedience with accompanying hostility, destructiveness, aggression, domineering, and bullying). (R100)

### Behavior Problems (Acting Out)
Children whose mothers are excessively punitive are prone to temper tantrums. (R113)

Children whose mothers are excessively punitive tend to be destructive, restless, and excitable. (R113)

Children whose mothers are excessively critical and depreciative tend to be prone to temper tantrums. (R113)

### Behavior Problems (Lying, Stealing)
The mother's excessively punitive behavior toward the child is related to lying and solitary stealing by the child. (R113)

Excessively critical and depreciative behavior of the mother toward the child is related to lying and solitary stealing by the child. (R113)

### Behavior Problems (Nailbiting)
Use of physical punishment by the father is positively associated with nail-biting in the child. (R100)

### Behavior Problems (Truancy)
The use of physical punishment by the father is positively associated with truancy of children from school. (R100)

### Bigotry
Parents of bigoted people tend to be more stern and

punitive in their child-rearing practices than are parents of normal children. (M247)

**Broken Homes**
Children from broken homes are more likely to receive more severe punishment for their delinquency than children who are not from broken homes. (T002)

**Child-Rearing Anxiety**
The greater the parent's child-rearing anxiety, the greater his hostility and use of physical punishment. (B232)

**Child-Rearing Practices (Aggression)**
The more permissive the parents are toward the child's aggressive behavior, the less the child's anticipation of punishment.

Parents who use punishment as a means of control tend to encourage aggression by their children toward others, but will not tolerate aggression toward themselves. (M186)

Mothers who are permissive regarding the child's parent-directed aggression are less likely to use physical punishment as a disciplinary technique than are nonpermissive mothers (U.S.). (S191)

**Child-Rearing Practices (Control)**
As perceived by daughters, there is no relationship between maternal control and degree of verbal punishment attributed to the mother; as perceived by sons, there is a positive relationship between maternal control and degree of verbal punishment attributed to the mother. (H196)

**Child-Rearing Practices (Dependency)**
Mothers who are accepting of their child's dependent behavior are less likely to use physical punishment than are mothers who are not accepting (U.S.). (S191)

**Child-Rearing Practices (Giving Reasons)**
The use of reasoning as a technique of control is correlated with avoidance of the techniques of physical punishment and of withdrawal of love for mothers as well as for fathers of normals (nonaggressive boys), but not for fathers of aggressive boys. (B243)

Use of reasoning is negatively associated with the use of physical punishment in child rearing (U.S.). (S191)

Parents who use reason frequently are more likely to follow through on threats of punishment than are parents who do not use reasoning (U.S.). (S191)

**Child-Rearing Practices (Kin)**
Adults (generally, maternal grandmother) other than parents are more likely to use severe punishment upon the child than are the parents. (C117)

**Child-Rearing Practices (Praise)**
Use of praise is negatively associated with use of physical punishment as a method of punishment (U.S.). (S191)

**Child-Rearing Practices (Rewards)**
Use of tangible rewards is associated with use of physical punishment as a discipline method (U.S.). (S191)

**Class**
The higher the class, the greater the preference for "psychological" punishment (i.e., discipline that addresses itself to the child as a personality) rather than physical punishment (Indonesia). (D065)

Middle-class parents tend to use less physical punishment than lower-class parents and rely more on appeals to guilt and the threat of the withdrawal of love. (L169)

Middle-class mothers whose husbands have entrepreneurial jobs are more likely than lower-class mothers (entrepreneurial) to favor symbolic punishments instead of spanking and slapping. (M062)

The higher the socioeconomic status of the parents, the less punitive and controlling are their child-rearing practices. (R090)

Social rank is negatively related to the extent of retaliatory child-rearing practices (e.g., rejection, rigidity, and punitiveness). (R107)

Lower-class parents tend to punish their children physically much more than do middle-class parents. (R127)

More punishment is applied to children of working-class families than of middle-class families, but the difference is greater with respect to object-oriented than to love-oriented techniques (U.S.). (S191)

Regardless of educational level, middle-class mothers use ridicule as a technique of discipline less than working-class mothers do. (S191)

Regardless of educational level, middle-class mothers use isolation as a technique of discipline more than working-class mothers do. (S191)

Middle-class mothers and better-educated working-class mothers punish their children less often physically or by depriving them of privileges than do lesser-educated working-class mothers. (U.S.). (S191)

**Criminality**
There is a correlation between aggression in the home environment, as measured by parental use of threats, punitive punishment, or unfavorable comparisons to others as techniques of discipline, and criminal behavior in the son. (M195)

Parents of recidivist prisoners are more likely to have used physical methods of punishment and are generally more irrational in their punishment methods. (S187)

**Criminality/Alcoholism**
Punitive methods of discipline correlate with criminality, but not alcoholism, in the son. (M195)

**Dependency**
There is no relationship between parental use of physical punishment and the degree of dependency of the child on the parent. (B243)

Nonaggressive boys whose parents use physical punishment are more likely to show anxiety about dependency on their teachers and peers than are those whose parents do not use such discipline. (B243)

Maternal punitiveness is inversely correlated with dependency behavior. (K111)

The more severely punished the child, the more likely he (or she) is to be dependent upon other children rather than upon a teacher. (S238)

**Dependency of Child**
Withdrawal of love as a method of punishment and increased emotional dependency of child are associated. (S191)

### Deviance
Children whose parents are both punitive and emotionally ambivalent toward the child are more likely to become social deviants than are children with more lenient, more consistent parents. (W137)

### Education
The lower the educational level of the parents, the more punitive the parents. (B250)

There is no relationship between parental education and degree of affective reward and/or affective punishment in child rearing. (B250)

### Employment of Mother
Among stable homes (homes without parental conflict, criminality, or other social deviance), nonworking mothers are more likely to use physical punishment on their boys than are working mothers. (M211)

### Ethnocentrism
If a child's parents discipline him by physical punishment, the child is more likely to be ethnocentric.

### Feeding
Punishing children for misbehavior is a characteristic of parents who are permissive in early feeding practices. Such parents also tend to participate in much activity with the child and to treat him casually. (S010)

### Feeding Problems
There is a positive relationship between use of physical punishment and feeding problems (e.g., prolonged periods of appetite loss, etc.) in the child (U.S.). (S191)

### Foster Home, Adjustment to
Children who failed to establish stable relationships in foster homes give more accounts of severe punishment meted out to children (as measured by the Children Apperception Test) than do children who did develop them. (W145)

### Homosexuality
Mothers of homosexuals are apt to have been harder on their sons in matters of discipline (been angrier, bawled them out more, and given more physical punishment) than other mothers. (U004)

Homosexuality may occur as a response to severe punishment at the hands of the mother. (W126)

### Husband-Wife Relations (Hostility)
Mothers of aggressive boys who had frequently spanked their sons tended to be hostile to their husbands. (B213)

### Husband-Wife Relations (Warmth)
Mothers who use nagging and scolding as means of disciplining the son are more likely to lack warmth for their husbands and to disagree with them over disciplinary policies than are mothers who do not. (B243)

### Husband-Wife Relations (Warmth/Hostility)
Mothers who use physical punishment are likely to have less warmth for and more hostility toward their husbands than mothers who do not. (B243)

### Identification with Mother
The more often the mother uses the withdrawal of love as a disciplinary method, the stronger will be the child's identification with his mother. (A060)

### Identification with Parents
There is a positive relationship between a moderate degree of punishment by the parents and the strength of identification with either or both parents.

### Incest (Father-Daughter)
The incestuous father is more likely than the typical father to use punishment sadistically or with hostility rather than for disciplinary purposes. (W123)

### I.Q.
Maternal coercion is associated with low intelligence scores for boys and girls aged 2–4. (K115)

There is no relationship between maternal coercion and intelligence scores of preschool-aged children when maternal educational level is controlled. (K115)

There is no relationship between the child's intelligence and his perception of his parents as either punitive or not. (L149)

### Juvenile Delinquency
Parents of boys who are frequent juvenile offenders are more likely to show a punitive attitude toward the boys regarding their offenses than are parents of boys who are first offenders.

A negative curvilinear relationship exists between the severity of punishment and delinquency in the son. (B243)

More children who have been disciplined punitively or with laxity go to a penal institution than those children who have been controlled by love-oriented methods. (M194)

There is no relationship between parental use of physical punishment and delinquent behavior by the child. (N063)

Children who feel their fathers punish them unfairly are more likely to show delinquent behavior than are those who do not. (N063)

There is a correlation between strict discipline by the mother and delinquency in the daughter. (N063)

Delinquency in the child correlates with nagging by the parents. (N063)

There is a correlation between delinquency in the child and parental use of withdrawal of love as a method of discipline. (N063)

There is a curvilinear relationship between delinquency in the child and parental scolding. (N063)

### Juvenile Delinquency (Crime Against a Person)
If the parents use punitive or lax means of discipline, the child is more likely to commit crimes against a person than if the parents use love-oriented techniques without punitiveness. (M194)

### Juvenile Delinquency (Reform)
If the parents use erratic and nonpunitive disciplinary methods, the delinquent child will reform earlier (before his twenty-third year) than if the parents use punitive methods. (M194)

### Juvenile Delinquency (Sex Offenses and Drunkenness)
It is more likely that lax or erratically punitive methods of discipline will result in sex crimes and drunkenness by the child than any other kinds of crimes. (M194)

### Juvenile Delinquency (Traffic Offenses)
If the parents use punitive methods of discipline rather than other methods, the child is more likely to commit traffic offenses than other types of crimes. (M194)

### Leadership
Children who perceive themselves as autonomous and their parents as coercive (punishing) tend to be more active as leaders in their peer groups than others do. (H235)

### Marital Adjustment
Parents who employ ridicule as a means of discipline are less likely to be well-adjusted to each other than are those who do not. (B243)

### Menstrual Taboos
In a society that gives great importance to physical punishment as a technique of child discipline, menstrual taboos are likely to be extensive. (S079)

### Mental Illness
Excessive maternal control and punishment after puberty tends to be directly correlated with mental illness. (S187)

### Mental Illness of Child
Parents tend to discipline psychotic children more severely than they do normal children. (D064)

### Mental Illness of Child (Schizophrenia)
Fathers of schizophrenics and schizoids are more likely to use punishment than are fathers of children with adjustment reactions, conduct disturbances, and sociopathic symptoms. (Z011)

### Mental Illness (Schizophrenia)
Fathers of white schizophrenics are more likely than fathers of normals to administer brutal and erratic discipline and may also encourage the development of aim-inhibited hostility and a masochistic orientation toward father symbols in later life. (B221)

Persons who have been subjected to parental trauma are more likely than others to become schizophrenic. (J019)

### Mental Illness (Schizophrenia/Neurosis)
In the middle class, more parents of schizophrenics than of neurotics use the technique of withdrawal of affection to control the child's behavior. (M197)

### Mother-Child Relations (Affection)
If a child acquired his original affection for his mother under conditions which contained considerable punishment, then the child's love for his mother will persist, despite much discouragement, punishment, evidence of dislike, etc. (M187)

### Mother-Child Relations (Hostility)
Children whose mothers are excessively punitive are more likely to be disobedient with hostility. (R113)

### Mother-Child Relations (Rejection)
Mothers who show signs of rejection are more likely to use physical punishment even though they consider it ineffective than are mothers who fully accept their children. (S191)

### Mother-Son Relations (Hostility)
Mothers of aggressive boys who had frequently spanked their sons tended to be hostile toward their sons. (B213)

### Mother-Son Relations (Ridicule)
Mothers of aggressive boys who had frequently spanked their sons tended to ridicule them. (B213)

### Nationality
American mothers tend to be more permissive and less punitive than English mothers. (L169)

### Occupation
Middle-class mothers whose husbands have enterpreneurial jobs are significantly more likely than mothers of similar social status whose husbands have bureaucratic jobs to use symbolic rather than direct punishments in disciplining their children. (M062)

Middle-class mothers whose husbands have enterpreneurial jobs are more likely than middle-class mothers whose husbands have bureaucratic jobs to use harsh means to stop a child from sucking a part of his body. (M062)

### Occupation of Parents
The relative frequency of physical and psychological punishment is not related to parent's occupation. (E097)

### Ordinal Position
In two-child families, there is no association between ordinal position and the use of physical punishment. (S191)

Only and oldest children have suffered significantly more physical punishment and deprivation of privileges. (S191)

### Parent-Child Relations
Parents who treat their children casually punish their children less for misdemeanors than do parents who do not treat their children casually. (S010)

### Parent-Child Relations (Control)
Corporal punishment in the discipline of children will tend to be used more when the parents can exercise a high degree of control over their children. (S064)

### Parent-Child Relations (Evaluation)
The more gratifying to the child is his relationship with his parents, the more likely it is that he will respond to psychological techniques of discipline. (B236)

### Parent-Child Relations (Fear)
Children are more likely to fear punishment by parents who have a preconceived notion of the amount of punishment that is needed and proceed to administer it without much regard for the child's protestations than by parents who spank the child until he cries.

Physical punishment increases the child's fear of and decreases his love of the parent. (B232)

### Parent-Child Relations (Interaction)
Punishing children for misbehavior is a characteristic of parents who are permissive in early feeding practices. Such parents also tend to participate in much activity with the child and to treat him casually. (S010)

### Parent-Child Relations (Interaction)
### X Child-Rearing Practices (Permissiveness)
Promoting the child's independence is a characteristic of parents who participate in much activity wih the child. Such parents tend to be permissive in early feeding and toilet-training procedures, but to punish for misbehavior. (S010)

### Parent-Child Relations (Rejection)

There is a correlation between the use of deprivation of privileges as a method of discipline and an attitude of rejection and punitiveness toward the child on the part of the parents. (B243)

Parents who use ridicule as a technique of discipline are more likely to be rejecting of their sons than are those who do not. (B243)

Parents who use nagging and scolding as a means of discipline are more likely to be rejecting of the son than are those who do not. (B243)

### Parent-Child Relations (Warmth)

Spanking is most effective if applied by the parent who is warmer toward the child. (S191)

### Parental Role (Discipline)

Whichever parent is stricter tends to be the chief disciplinarian in the family. (S246)

### Paternal/Maternal Role

Mothers tend to employ "love-oriented" techniques (i.e., threat of withdrawal of affection); fathers rely on more direct methods (e.g., physical punishment) but only in relation to the boy. (B273)

### Paternal/Maternal-Role Behavior

The child feels punishment by the like-sex parent (as opposed to cross-sex parent) to be more severe. (B232)

### Paternal/Maternal-Role Definition

In families where both parents are warm to the child, spanking is more effective where the father, rather than the mother, is the disciplinarian (U.S.). (S191)

### Peer Relations

Children who perceive themselves as autonomous and their parents as coercive (punishing) are more actively friendly with their peers than are others. (H205)

Children who perceive themselves as autonomous and their parents as coercive (punishing) tend to be more active than others as leaders in their peer groups. (H205)

### Personality (Excitability)

The use of physical punishment by the parents is positively associated with children who are restless and excitable. (R100)

### Personality (Guilt)

The greater the punishment (and inhibition) of extrapunitive aggression, the more likely is self-aggression or intropunitive behavior. (K111)

### Personality (Inhibition)

There is a correlation between maternal punitiveness and generalized inhibition in the child. (K111)

### Personality of Child (Punitiveness)

Parents who are punitive are likely to have children who are also punitive [children's punitiveness measured by the Problem Situations Test (PST)]. (L149)

### Personality of Child (Sociability)

Girls who received a great deal of "interaction type of discipline" (parental reasoning, being spanked, punished by having to aid in household tasks) develop a greater interest in being with people when they become adults than do girls who received noninteraction discipline (told to leave the room, prevented from being with friends, etc.) during childhood; this is not true for boys. (H191)

### Personality of Mother (Anomie)

There is a significant tendency for anomic mothers to be lenient in the child-rearing practices and for nonanomic mothers to be harsh. (A069)

Anomic mothers reported that they tended to discipline their children according to their own moods, tempers, or whims, whereas nonanomic mothers tended not to let their moods influence their punishment practices. (A069)

### Personality of Mother (Extroversion)

Extroverted mothers are less punitive toward their children than are introverted mothers. (L169)

### Personality of Son (Guilt)

Mothers of "high guilt" boys more frequently use love-oriented techniques of punishment, while mothers of "low guilt" boys are more likely to use physical punishment. (S078)

### Personality Problems

There is a curvilinear relationship between parental hostility and physical punishment and personality problems in the child (in the home). (B232)

Father's hostility and physical punishment are positively related to hostile withdrawal by girls at both home and school; by boys only at home. (B232)

The more that psychological "love-oriented" techniques of discipline are used upon the child, the more likely he is to become anxious, dependent, and sensitive to rejection. (B236)

### Personality Problems (Antisocial/Aggression)

The parents of aggressive antisocial boys discipline more punitively than do the parents of aggressive "social" boys. (M210)

### Personality Problems (Depression)

The use of physical punishment by the father is positively associated with a child who is frequently depressed and discouraged. (R100)

### Personality Problems (Neurosis/Acting Out)

Mothers or parents of neurotic children had a tendency to repress their children's developmental instinctual drives, whereas mothers of acting-out children did not; mothers or parents of neurotic children had a tendency to punish their children socially, whereas anomic mothers did not. (A069)

### Property

The nurturing person is less likely to inflict pain on the infant in societies where the property is owned by the women than in societies where it is not. (L141)

### Race

Among lower-class families, fathers of Negro children tend to discipline their children more than do white fathers. (G117)

### Race Attitudes

Prejudiced persons are more likely than unprejudiced persons to report harsh and threatening parental discipline during their childhood caused by infringement of rules rather than of principles. (A061)

### Religion, Role of Deities

If the nurturing agents (parents, etc.) of the society do not use pain as a control stimulus during infancy, benevolent deities are more common in the belief system. (L141)

Societies with aggressive deities and high pain in the treatment of infants are more likely to have capricious gods than are societies with benevolent deities and low pain in the treatment of infants. (L141)

The severity of parental punishment for disobedience is paralleled by supernatural punishment for disobedience of supernatural demands. (S036)

### Scholastic Achievement
Children who perceive themselves as autonomous and their parents as coercive (punishing) tend to do better academically than others. (H205)

### Sex-Role Identification of Daughter
Low sex-role identification in daughters is associated with maternal use of withdrawal of love as a disciplinary technique. (M206)

### Sex Status
Physical punishment is more frequently used by parents of boys than by parents of girls. (B232)

Fathers physically punish girls less than boys. (B232)

Children are more likely to receive punishment from the parent of the same sex. (B250)

Girls are more often disciplined by "love-oriented" techniques (praise, withdrawal of love, etc.) than boys are (U.S.). (S191)

### Sex Status of Child
Girls are exposed to more love-oriented discipline and less punishment than boys are. (B252)

### Sexual Deviance
Fathers of sexual deviants are more likely to use physical punishment than are fathers of "normal" boys. (M209)

### Size of Family
There is a curvilinear relationship between use of psychological punishment and family size; mothers of medium-sized families are more likely to use psychological punishment than are mothers of small or large families. (R097)

### Social Mobility Aspirations
Adolescents who have upward mobility aspirations are more likely than those with downward aspirations to have received psychological rather than physical punishment as children. (D077)

Parental leniency is associated with children who are upward aspirers. (E102)

Parents of upward aspirers use more verbal and less physical discipline than do parents of children who do not have mobility aspirations. (E102)

### Socialization, Effectiveness of
The disciplinary technique of denying love is more likely than physical punishment to keep the child oriented toward parental socialization goals. (G120)

Nonphysical discipline tends to be less effective in child training than physical discipline. (M058)

### Sociopathic Personality
Parents of those with sociopathic personalities use harsh discipline significantly *less* frequently than do parents of normals, but parents of the former do not differ from parents of individuals with other disorders. (O032)

### Superego Formation
Mothers who use less authority and less strictness are more likely to have children who have low degrees of guilt, but the 24-hour-day disciplinarian supported by the father develops a high guilt pattern.

The parent who produces a high level of guilt uses scolding, deprivation, ostracism, and creates hurt feelings in the child; parents who produce fear in the child use spanking and hitting more.

Children with low guilt are more likely to have parents who use a less love-oriented child-rearing technique (reasoning, praise, or deprivation).

Less indulgence or greater severity of weaning is associated with high guilt in the child.

Guilt in children correlates with psychological discipline in the middle class but not in the working class. (G120)

Resistance to temptation and reactions of guilt are correlated with psychological (v. physical) techniques of discipline. (G120)

There is no relationship between parental use of withdrawal of love as a method of discipline and the development of conscience in the child. (N063)

There is a low positive correlation between the use of love-oriented techniques of punishment by parents and the development of guilt feelings as measured by the patient's feeling of responsibility for his own physical illness. (W142)

### Therapeutic Practices
The degree of importance of love-oriented techniques of punishment is not related to the extent to which a society employs intropunitive therapy (bloodletting, sacrifice) for illness. (K111)

### Toilet Training
The more severe the mother is in toilet training, the more likely is she (in other areas of child training) to use physical punishment, deprive the child of privileges, and avoid using reason in handling the child (U.S.). (S191)

## CHILD-REARING PRACTICES (PUNISHMENT/ GIVING REASONS)     X  Juvenile Delinquency
Parents of delinquents are more likely than parents of nondelinquents to use physical punishment rather than reasoning in disciplining the child. (B243)

## CHILD-REARING PRACTICES (PUNISHMENT/REWARDS)     X  Conformity
Rewarding, rather than punishing, the child is more influential in developing social compliance (frequency and alacrity with which the child accedes to the demands and suggestions of other persons). (C102)

### Identification with Mother
Given dependency upon the mother by the child, the more stable a balance between denial of reciprocity and positive reward she establishes regarding the demands of the child, the more likely is the child to develop a stable expectation system and to identify with the mother as an object and as a set of standards. (B234)

### Superego Formation
Children whose parents employ both rewards and punishments have a more greatly developed sense of con-

science than do children whose parents employ only rewards. (R106)

## CHILD-REARING PRACTICES (READING)
### X   Cognitive Development (Verbal)
The amount of time the father spends reading to the child is positively associated with high verbal ability in daughters, but not in sons. (B257)

The amount of time the mother spends reading to the child is not related to either the son's or the daughter's verbal ability. (B257)

## CHILD-REARING PRACTICES (READING HABITS)
### X   I.Q./Creativity
Families of highly intelligent children (Binet) are more likely to subscribe to several children's magazines than are the families of highly creative children (Guilford–Cattell). (G132)

## CHILD-REARING PRACTICES (RECREATION)
### X   Juvenile Delinquency
Parents of juvenile delinquents provide fewer recreational outlets, both in and outside the home, than do parents of nondelinquents. (S210)

## CHILD-REARING PRACTICES (REJECTION)
### X   Bedwetting
Regressive enuresis of the child is related to cold, distant, and neglectful treatment by the mother. (R113)

## CHILD-REARING PRACTICES (RESPONSIBILITY)
### X   Class
Middle-class parents place more emphasis on an early assumption of responsibility than do lower-class parents.

### Emotional Stability of Parents
Physical and emotional steadiness of the parents is necessary for developing a sense of responsibility in the child. (C093)

### Employment of Mother
Mothers with professions tend to justify the rules of discipline applied to their children as encouraging responsibility; mothers without outside employment do not.

### Identification with Mother
The more the child is required to substitute for the mother, the greater his identification with the mother. (A060)

### Juvenile Delinquency
The amount of responsibility delegated to an adolescent (particularly boys) is inversely related to the delinquent behavior he manifests. (N057)

### Maternal Overprotectiveness
The mother's experience of premature responsibilities early in life is a cause of overprotection of her child. (B272)

### Mental Retardation
If one child in a family is mentally retarded, the oldest child is often made to play the role of parental surrogate.

### Ordinal Position
The firstborn child is given more responsibility than the younger child regardless of sex, but firstborn girls are given more responsibility than firstborn boys. (K149)

### Personality of Child (Speech Defects)
Children who are given too many responsibilities by the mother are more likely to develop speech defects. (R113)

### Race (Class)
In both middle and lower classes, Negro parents train their girls for responsibility in household tasks at an earlier age than do white parents.

### Sex Status
Socialization of girls stresses responsibility, "being dutiful," more so than the socialization of boys (cross-cultural). (G156)

### Sibling Rivalry
Children who are given too many responsibilities at home by the mother (household chores, caring for younger siblings) tend to be overly competitive with siblings and to display bullying, domineering, and aggressive behavior. (R113)

### Sibling Structure (Age Difference)
The boy with a younger brother is given more responsibility than the younger sibling when the spacing is close than is the boy with a younger sister. (K149)

As the age difference between siblings increases, girls have much more responsibility relative to the younger sibling than boys do. (K149)

## CHILD-REARING PRACTICES (RESPONSIVENESS)
### X   Dependency
The extent to which the mother responds to the infant's vocal and physical communications is unrelated to the development of autonomy in the infant. (Y042)

## CHILD-REARING PRACTICES (RESTRICTIVENESS)
### X   Achievement Motivation
Although mothers of sons with high achievement motivation placed fewer restrictions on their sons than did mothers of those with low achievement motivation, the restrictions they did make were imposed at an earlier age. (M246)

### Aggression
Insofar as restrictions frustrate the child, the parent's restrictiveness encourages aggression in the child. (B232)

The severity of parental restrictions imposed upon the boy outside the home does not covary with his aggressiveness. (B243)

Parents of "normal" adolescents, particularly the mothers, impose stronger restrictions and demands on their sons than do parents of hyperaggressive adolescents. (B275)

### Alcoholism
There is a negative correlation between the degree of restrictiveness which the mother exerts over the son and the development of alcoholism in the son. (M195)

### Child-Rearing Values
If the mother believes in unconditional love for her children, the extent to which her child-rearing ideology stresses the middle-class values of diligence, thrift, and achievement will not correlate with the extent to which her daughter perceives her as overcircumscribing her freedom. (K101)

The more the mother's child-rearing ideology stresses the middle-class values of diligence, thrift, and achievement, the more likely it is that the daughter will perceive her as overcircumscribing her freedom. (K101)

## Class

Middle-class mothers impose fewer restrictions and demands on children than do working-class mothers (U.S.). (S191)

Middle-class mothers are less restricting of free-range exploration by the child than are lower-class mothers (U.S.). (S191)

Middle-class mothers are less restrictive regarding activity in the home than are lower-class mothers (U.S.). (S191)

Middle-class British families were more inclined to impose restrictions on the children with respect to neatness in the house, being quiet, going to bed promptly, etc., than were the working-class families of British origin. (S191)

Discipline is more restrictive among upper-class than among lower-class Negro families. (W133)

## Conformity

For girls, there is a positive relationship between excessive maternal restrictiveness between ages 4–7 and their conformity to parental demands during adolescence. (K115)

## Dependency

A curvilinear relationship exists between the severity of demands and restrictions made by parents and the development of autonomy in the child. (M203)

The more restrictive the parent, the greater the likelihood that the child will become overly dependent. (S204)

## Education of Mother

Regardless of socioeconomic level, better-educated mothers were less restrictive in the child's use of fingers for eating, less restrictive about his treatment of house and furniture, and applied less pressure for neatness and orderliness. (S191)

## Extended/Nuclear Family

Societies with extended families are more likely to be severe in their control over dependent, aggressive, and sexual behavior than are societies with nuclear families. (W142)

## I.Q.

Maternal restrictiveness is associated with low intelligence scores for boys and girls aged 2–4. (K115)

There is no relationship between maternal restrictiveness and intelligence scores of preschool-aged children when maternal educational level is controlled. (K115)

Maternal restrictiveness and coerciveness are associated with low I.Q. scores, whereas maternal justification of discipline is related to high I.Q. scores. (K127)

There is a correlation between paternal overrestriction and a low performance of the child on the Picture Completion Test (WISC). (M213)

## I.Q. (Verbal/Nonverbal)

The I.Q. combination of low verbal and high nonverbal abilities is more likely among children whose mothers allow them considerable freedom to experiment. (B289)

## Juvenile Delinquency

There is a curvilinear relationship between the degree to which the child is scolded and restricted and the child's delinquent behavior. (N063)

There is a curvilinear relationship between the amount of freedom allowed by parents and delinquency in the child. (N063)

## Mental Illness (Schizophrenia)

Mothers of schizophrenics are more restrictive than mothers of normals. (H186)

## Motor Development

Among Negroes, children who are not restricted to a specific area, but are allowed to move freely around the home, are more advanced in motor development (creeping, sitting, standing, walking) than are children who are restricted to a particular area. (W133)

## Occupational Achievement of Child

Occupational failure is more likely to occur where there has been interference with the child's techniques for satisfaction and crippling restraints or disapproval. (H220)

## Parent-Child Relations (Conflict)

The more severe the parental restriction upon the child, the more likely is parent-child conflict. (B249)

## Personality of Father

Restrictive fathers are more likely to be submissive, suggestible, conforming, indecisive, ineffectual, and overcontrolled. (B227)

## Personality of Father (Self-Confidence)

Restrictive child rearing by the father is positively associated with his being submissive and having little self-assurance in situations outside of the home. (R100)

## Personality Problems

Overinhibited behavior, characterized by seclusiveness, shyness, and apathy in children, correlates with repressive overcontrol in the parents. (S182)

## Political Opinion

Parents who are less restrictive in their child-rearing practices (approving of free expression of a child's desires) are more radical in their political opinions. (S249)

## Premarital Sex Relations

The more fully the parents insulate the girl from social contacts, the less likely it is that the contacts she does have with men will lead to an orderly courtship and marriage. (B245)

## Religion

Catholic fathers, but not Catholic mothers, tend to increase their control and restrictiveness as their children become older; this tendency is reversed among Protestant fathers. (E100)

Catholic mothers are more likely to be restrictive than are Protestant mothers. (V037)

## Scholastic Motivation of Child

Among children with high scholastic records, those with low academic motivation are more apt to be reared restrictively and punitively than are those with high academic motivation. (E102)

### Social Adjustment of Child
The less autocratic, restrictive, and severe the parents, the greater is the likelihood that the child will be socially well adjusted in his peer group. (M178)

### Socialization, Effectiveness of
If the parents are restrictive, the child is more likely to internalize parental values and more likely to resist temptation. (G118)

## CHILD-REARING PRACTICES (RESTRICTIVENESS/DEMANDS)    X Dependency
Adult-dependent boys (who rejected any interaction with their peers, but strongly sought dependent relationships with adults) tend to be raised in a family environment characterized by high parental demands and strict parental supervision and restriction. (M221)

## CHILD-REARING PRACTICES (RESTRICTIVENESS/WARMTH)    X Ordinal Position
Parents tend to handle first children with more interference, more restrictiveness, and less warmth than they handle second children. (D064)

## CHILD-REARING PRACTICES (REWARDS)    X Achievement Motivation
The more highly a mother evaluates her child's accomplishments and the more she rewards them, the stronger her child's achievement motivation will be. (W139)

### Aggression
Boys who receive tangible rewards are more likely to be self-aggressive than are those who do not. (S246)

### Child-Rearing Practices (Deprivation of Privileges)
Use of tangible rewards is associated with use of deprivation of privileges as a method of punishment (U.S.). (S191)

### Child-Rearing Practices (Punishment)
Use of tangible rewards is associated with use of physical punishment as a discipline method (U.S.). (S191)

### Child-Rearing Practices (Sex)
Mothers who frequently use praise or reward in child rearing are more permissive regarding their children's sexual behavior than are mothers who employ these techniques less frequently (U.S.). (S191)

### Class
Socioeconomic rank and the use of rewards in socialization are not associated.

### Conformity
With younger children, mothers who reward compliance (child's acceding to her demands and suggestions) are no more or less prone to punish their children for noncompliance than are mothers who do not reward their children for compliance. (C102)

With older children, mothers who reward compliance also punish for noncompliance; mothers who do not reward for compliance, ignore noncompliant behavior. (C102)

### Father-Son Relations (Affection)
Among aggressive boys, the use of tangible rewards by the father is positively correlated with the amount of affectionate interaction with the father in early childhood; among normals, these factors are negatively related. (B243)

### Husband-Wife Relations (Evaluation)
Mothers who frequently use praise or tangible rewards in child rearing have greater esteem for their husbands than do mothers who do not employ these techniques as frequently (U.S.). (S191)

### Husband-Wife Relations (Warmth)
There is a correlation between the amount of parental praise for the son and degree of warmth between spouses. (B243)

### Maternal Role, Attitude Toward
Mothers who frequently use praise or tangible rewards in child rearing express greater satisfaction with being mothers and wives than do those who use these techniques less frequently (U.S.). (S191)

### Mother-Child Relations (Affection)
Mothers who frequently use praise or tangible rewards in child rearing are warm and more affectionate with their children than mothers who do not use these techniques (so frequently) (U.S.). (S191)

### Mother-Son Relations (Affection)
Mothers who provide material rewards for their sons are more likely to show warmth for them. (B243)

### Peer Relations
There is a positive relationship for boys and a negative relationship for girls between affective rewards for good behavior and leadership abilities in the child (based on teachers' ratings of influence in group activities). (B250)

### Religion
Catholic mothers are more likely to use material rewards for good behavior than are Protestant mothers. (V037)

## CHILD-REARING PRACTICES (REWARDS AND PUNISHMENT)    X Class
More middle-class parents than lower-class parents use reward or praise as a successful technique of discipline. (L003)

More middle-class mothers than lower-class mothers use withdrawl of love as a technique of discipline. (L003)

More middle-class parents than lower-class parents deprive children of privileges as a technique of discipline (Boston). (L003)

More lower-class parents than middle-class parents use physical punishment as a technique of discipline (Boston). (L003)

There is no significant difference between the middle-class parents and lower-class parents in the techniques of discipline used. (L003)

### Personality Development of Parent
Parents who have anal character disorders (fixation at toilet training and language-learning stage of development) are more likely than others to use the giving and withholding of favors as a way of training their children. (R110)

## CHILD-REARING PRACTICES (RIGIDITY)    X Authoritarianism
Authoritarianism of parents is correlated with parental rigidity and intolerance concerning children's noise, antics, etc. (H209)

### Creativity
Children whose mothers are flexible in their use of authority are higher in intellectual originality, intellectual

vigor, and total intellectual freedom than are children whose mothers are rigid in their use of authority. (A071)

### Personality Development of Child
Children whose mothers are flexible in their use of authority are higher in assertiveness and high frustration tolerance than are children whose mothers are rigid in their use of authority. (A071)

### Personality of Child (Anal Character)
Anal character in the child is positively related to the rigidity of the mother in child rearing.

### Personality of Child (Stubbornness)
There is no relationship between the mother's rigidity in child rearing and stubbornness in the child.

### Personality of Child (Submissiveness)
There is no relationship between the mother's rigidity in child rearing and submissiveness in the child.

### Surrogate/Natural Parents
Surrogate parents are more likely to be rigid in their attitudes and expectations toward children than are natural parents. (H243)

## CHILD-REARING PRACTICES (RISK)
### X  I.Q./Creativity
The parents of highly intelligent children encourage the minimization of risk, while those of highly creative children accept risks. (G114)

## CHILD-REARING PRACTICES (ROLE MODELS)
### X  Juvenile Delinquency
If the parents both neglect the child and provide poor role models for the child, the child is more likely to become a delinquent than if only one of these factors is present. (M194)

## CHILD-REARING PRACTICES (RULES)
### X  Personality (Obsessions)
Parents who follow fixed rules for living, thus developing a sense of ritual in the child, are more likely to have children who develop obsessional habits (an attachment to a particular object, insistence on certain ways of doing things, etc.). (F097)

## CHILD-REARING PRACTICES (SAFETY)
### X  Employment of Mother
Mothers with professions tend to invoke more rules of behavior designed to protect their children's physical safety than do nonprofessional mothers.

## CHILD-REARING PRACTICES (SCHEDULES)
### X  Cognitive Development (Nonverbal)
Parental strictness regarding time schedules is not associated with nonverbal (spatial and numerical) ability in children. (B257)

## CHILD-REARING PRACTICES (SCHEDULING)
### X  Class
Middle-class parents are stricter in dealing with their children than are lower-class parents with respect to age at which the child takes a nap and time the child must be home at night.

### Personality of Mother (Anomie)
Nonanomic mothers tend significantly to schedule their children; anomic mothers seldom maintain scheduling. (A069)

## CHILD-REARING PRACTICES (SCHOLASTIC ACHIEVEMENT)      X  Self-Conception of Child
Students who report only supportive responses on the part of the parents to school grades do not differ in level of self-esteem from those who report both supportive and punitive responses. (R129)

Students who report only supportive responses as well as those who report supportive and punitive responses to school grades by the parents have higher self-esteem than those who reported only punitive responses. (R129)

Students who said that their mothers were satisfied even when their grades were average or below average had higher self-esteem than did those who reported that their mothers were dissatisfied. (R129)

Students with lowest self-esteem were not those who reported their mothers to be dissatisfied, but those who said that the mother never commented on their marks. (R129)

## CHILD-REARING PRACTICES (SCHOOL WORK)
### X  Scholastic Achievement of Child
High scholastic achievement in adolescents is associated with parents who emphasize the importance of being studious and with their being more vigilant and critical regarding the adolescent's schoolwork. (E102)

## CHILD-REARING PRACTICES (SELF-CONTROL)
### X  Occupation
Middle-class mothers whose husbands' occupations are of an entrepreneurial nature are more likely than mothers whose husbands' occupations are of a bureaucratic nature to emphasize their children's development of strong self-control. (B273)

## CHILD-REARING PRACTICES (SETTING STANDARDS)      X  Achievement Motivation
Parents of boys with high achievement motivation set higher standards of excellence for the son's performance than do parents of boys low in achievement motivation. (M246)

Parents of children with high achievement motivation set high performance goals for their children. (R097)

Strong achievement motivation tends to develop when parents impose standards of excellence upon problem-solving tasks, even in situations where such standards are not explicit. (R106)

### Father Absence
Mother-son families tend to lower stress on high standards of achievement for the son. (M246)

## CHILD-REARING PRACTICES (SEVERITY)  X  Art
Decorative art forms are more likely to be complex in societies that are generally severe in training their children. (W127)

### Class
The lower the social class, the more severe child-training methods are likely to be. (K160)

### Conformity
Either excessive severity or excessive caution in parental child-rearing practices is a cause of rebelliousness in the child against parents and other adult authorities.

### Mental Illness (Schizothymia)
Severe child-rearing practices in the oral, sex, dependence, and aggression areas are associated with schizothymia.

### Scholastic Achievement
Among college students, perceived severity of upbringing is associated with high achievement. (D065)

### Socialization, Effectiveness of
A curvilinear relationship exists between the severity of demands and restrictions made by the parents upon the child and the adequacy of socialization of the child. (M203)

## CHILD-REARING PRACTICES (SEVERITY/CONSISTENCY)     X     Class/Race
The degree of severity and consistency of child rearing is correlated more with class than with race. (B272)

## CHILD-REARING PRACTICES (SEX)
### X     Aggression
Parents of aggressive and normal sons do not vary with respect to their handling of the son's early sex behavior, both being nonpermissive but nonpunitive. (B243)

Fathers of aggressive boys are more likely to be permissive toward adolescent heterosexual behavior than are fathers of normals. (B243)

### Child-Rearing Practices (Aggression)
Mothers who are nonpermissive regarding sexual behavior demand more self-control regarding aggression from their children than do mothers who are more permissive regarding sexual behavior. (M186)

There is a positive relationship between permissiveness regarding the child's aggression toward the parents and permissiveness regarding sex activity among children (U.S.). (S191)

### Child-Rearing Practices (Dependency)
Mothers who are not permissive regarding their children's sexual behavior are more negative in their response to dependency than are mothers who are permissive (U.S.). (S191)

### Child-Rearing Practices (Giving Reasons)
There is a positive relationship between the parents' use of reasoning in child rearing and permissiveness regarding the child's sexual behavior (U.S.). (S191)

### Child-Rearing Practices (Household Rules)
Mothers who are not permissive regarding their children's sexual behavior are stricter about noise, table manners, and care of household property than are mothers who are permissive regarding their children's sexual behavior (U.S.). (S191)

### Child-Rearing Practices (Neatness)
Mothers who are nonpermissive regarding sexual behavior require more neatness, orderliness, and cleanliness of their children than do mothers who are more permissive regarding sexual behavior. (M186)

### Child-Rearing Practices (Obedience)
Mothers who are nonpermissive regarding sexual behavior (modesty, masturbation, sex-play permissiveness) require greater obedience from their children than permissive mothers do. (M186)

### Child-Rearing Practices (Oral and Dependency Needs)
Cultures that are permissive regarding the infant's oral needs and dependency needs tend to be nonpermissive in sex training; cultures that are nonpermissive regarding the infant's oral and dependency needs tend to be permissive in sex training. (P084)

### Child-Rearing Practices (Rewards)
Mothers who frequently use praise or reward in child rearing are more permissive regarding their children's sexual behavior than are mothers who employ these techniques less frequently (U.S.). (S191)

### Child-Rearing Practices (Sex Role)
Mothers who are not permissive regarding their children's sexual behavior are more likely to emphasize that their daughters should be "feminine" and their sons "masculine" than are mothers who are permissive regarding sexual behavior (U.S.). (S191)

### Child-Rearing Practices (Supervision)
Mothers who are not permissive regarding their children's sexual behavior check their child's whereabouts more frequently than do mothers who are permissive (U.S.). (S191)

### Class
The lower class is less permissive of the sexual activities of their children than are middle-class parents. (L003)

Working-class mothers are far less permissive and more punitive than are middle-class mothers toward sex exploration, and their sex training is much more severe. (S191)

Middle-class mothers and better-educated working-class mothers are more permissive about sex behavior in their children than are lesser-educated working-class mothers (U.S.). (S191)

### Illness, Explanation of
There seems to be no correlation between severity of sexual training and sexual explanations of illness. (W127)

### Incest Taboo
Close physical contact between brother and sister in childhood leads to a strong sexual aversion between the two and to lax prohibitions against incest in the society. (F079)

Separation of brother and sister in childhood or low degree of physical contact leads to a strong desire between the two and to strong prohibitions against incest within the society. (F079)

Physical nearness with no physical interaction generates highest incest anxiety among these three conditions. (F079)

Lack of alternative sexual outlets, under the condition of low physical contact between brother and sister, generates high incest anxiety. (F079)

### Love Magic
Love magic is associated with a high sexual socialization anxiety (that is, childhood training emphasizes deprivation and punishment with respect to sex, producing adult anxieties). (H222)

### Marital Adjustment of Husband
Favorable parental attitudes in response to the child's curiosity about sex are associated with marital adjustment of husbands. (T079)

### Menstrual Taboos
Severe sexual training is associated with elaborate menstrual taboos. (S079)

### Mental Illness (Schizophrenia)
Parents of normals are more likely to be acceptant of sexual expression than are parents of schizophrenics. (F110)

A significantly greater number of schizophrenic daughters than of normal ones believed that their mothers attempted to suppress the daughters' sex life during their childhood. (H186)

Mental illness is correlated with the instillation by the mother of an attitude of fear and hatred toward the opposite sex. (L118)

Mothers of schizophrenics tend to discourage interest in the opposite sex. (M218)

Parents of schizophrenics are more likely than others to instill deep feelings of guilt concerning masturbation and relationships with the opposite sex. (W143)

### Mother-Child Relations (Warmth)
Mothers who are not permissive regarding their children's sexual behavior tend to be more emotionally cold toward their children than do mothers who are permissive in the area of sexual behavior (U.S.). (S191)

### Neurosis
There is a positive relationship between the severity and punitiveness of her family and group's attitudes toward sex and the degree to which the unwed mother reacts neurotically to herself and her baby. (Y048)

### Occupation
Middle-class mothers whose husbands have entrepreneurial jobs are more likely than mothers of the same class whose husbands have bureaucratic jobs to say that they took measures to stop a child who touched his sex organs. (M062)

### Paternal/Maternal Role
Fathers are more permissive toward adolescent heterosexual behavior than are mothers. (B243)

Middle-class mothers are more permissive of the sexual activities of their children than are middle-class fathers. (L003)

Lower-class fathers are more permissive of the sexual activities of their children than are lower-class mothers. (L003)

### Polygyny
Severity of sex training is greater in polygynous societies. (W127)

### Scholastic Achievement
Mothers who are nonpermissive regarding sexual behavior expect their children to do better in school than do mothers who are more permissive in this area. (M186)

### Sex Anxiety of Parent
There is a correlation between the level of the parents'
sex anxiety and their punitiveness against the son's sex behavior. (B243)

### Sex Taboo (Postpartum)
Societies with long durations of postpartum sex taboo are likely also to have a rather severe sex training. (S079)

### Sex Taboo (Pregnancy)
Severe sex training in a society is associated with prolonged sex taboo during pregnancy.

### Sexual Fantasies
When sex training in the society is severe, unconscious sexual fantasies will be numerous. (S079)

### Sexual Interest of Child
The mother's own sexual stimulation of her children is one determinant of the degree and intensity of the child's preoccupation with sex. (S079)

### Socialization, Effectiveness of
The higher the pressure by parents on children against overt sexual behavior, the more likely it is that the children will resist temptation. (G120)

### Superego Formation
Societies with early training in modesty and the inhibition of heterosexual play tend to have a high guilt orientation. (W127)

### Therapeutic Practices
Societies with severe sex training tend to believe that abstention from sexual intercourse by the patient would have a therapeutic effect on his illness. (W127)

### Toilet Training
The more severe the parents are in toilet training the child, the less permissive they are about the child's sex behavior (i.e., modesty, masturbation, social sex play) (U.S.). (S191)

Mothers who are not permissive regarding their children's sexual behavior are more severe in their toilet training than are mothers who are permissive regarding sex (U.S.). (S191)

## CHILD-REARING PRACTICES (SEX/AGGRESSION)
### X    Child-Rearing Values (Punishment)
The father's approval of the use of physical punishment correlates negatively with suppression of sex and aggression in the child. (N053)

### Personality of Child
Children from homes in which sexuality and aggression are denied are more likely than children from homes in which these realities are recognized to have distortions of and uncertainties about their own perceptions of family situations. (S212)

## CHILD-REARING PRACTICES (SEX/ DEPENDENCY/AGGRESSION)
### X    Sex Status of Child
Compared to those of maladjusted males, mothers of maladjusted females score higher on suppression of sex and ascendance of mother; fathers score higher on fostering dependency, deception suppression of aggression, and suppression of sex (PARI). (Z011)

## CHILD-REARING PRACTICES (SEX ROLE)
### X    Age of Child
Parental demands for appropriate sex-role behavior are made at an earlier age for boys than for girls. (L141)

### Aggression

Fathers of aggressive boys are less likely to make demands for masculine behavior than are fathers of normals. (B243)

### Aggression Anxiety

If parents allow girls to act in ways which are inappropriate for sex typing (aggression against other children, fighting back when attacked, etc.), aggression anxiety increases. (S246)

### Alcoholism

There is no correlation between the mother's discouragement of independent or masculine behavior in the son and the son's alcoholism. (M195)

### Anxiety

Resulting from sex-typed child-rearing practices, girls tend to be more anxious than boys. (B252)

### Child-Rearing Practices (Sex)

Mothers who are not permissive regarding their children's sexual behavior are more likely to emphasize that their daughters should be "feminine" and their sons "masculine" than are mothers who are permissive regarding sexual behavior (U.S.). (S191)

### Class

There is a decrease in the differential treatment of boys and girls by parents with an increase in socioeconomic status. (B273)

### Cognitive Development (Nonverbal)

Maternal emphasis on the son's adopting a masculine role and sex-appropriate behavior is not related to the son's nonverbal (spatial and numerical) ability. (B257)

### Cognitive Development (Verbal)

There is no relationship between the mother's emphasis on her daughter's femininity and sex-appropriate behavior and the daughter's verbal ability. (B257)

### Cohesion of Kin-Group

Societies will be characterized by greater differentiation of socialization by sex if they are also characterized by large family groups with cooperative interaction. (B264)

### Dependency

Resulting from sex-typed child-rearing practices, girls tend to be more dependent than boys. (B252)

### Education of Mother

Regardless of socioeconomic level, better-educated mothers are less inclined to insist that a boy be masculine and a girl feminine. (S191)

### Education of Parents

The higher the educational level of the parents, the less likely is there to be differential child rearing for daughters and sons. (B250)

The higher the parents' educational level, the less does sex-differential treatment of sons and daughters affect the child's capacity for responsible behavior (i.e., paternal power and affection increases responsibility in sons and lowers responsibility in daughters). At the graduate level, maternal effect becomes more influential for both sexes (i.e., maternal power and affection being more likely to foster responsibility in boys and impede it in girls). (B250)

### Husband-Wife Relations (Warmth)

Parents of aggressive boys who stress masculine behavior are less likely to be warm and acceptant of their spouses than are those who do not stress such behavior. (B243)

### Identification with Like/Cross-Sex Parents

Identification with like- or opposite-sex parent is associated with the explicitness of the parents' sex-role expectations and their investment in them. (R098)

### Identification with Parents

Identification with like- or opposite-sex parent is associated with differential treatment of sons and daughters regarding permissiveness, rewards, punishment. (R098)

### Marital Adjustment

The child is more likely to learn, and be rewarded for, sex-appropriate behavior in families characterized by interparental harmony. (P064)

### Maternal-Role Behavior

To the degree that the social-emotional leader (the mother) upholds the family value system, she can socialize her daugher in the sex role considered appropriate to that system. (F094)

### Paternal/Maternal Role

Fathers are more likely than mothers to treat children of the two sexes differently. (B273)

### Peer Relations

Greater parental punishment for boys than for girls for opposite sex behavior leads to stronger feelings of hostility among boys toward girls than among girls toward boys. (L141)

### Personality of Child (Obedience)

Because of sex-typed child-rearing practices, girls tend to be more obedient and cooperative than boys. (B252)

### Personality of Child (Timidity)

Because of sex-typed child-rearing practices, girls tend to be more timid and sensitive to rejection than boys. (B252)

### Polygyny

Polygynous societies tend to have larger sex differences in socialization practices than do monogamous societies. (B264)

### Sex-Role Definition

Mothers who are most strongly inclined to differentiate sex roles place higher demands upon girls than upon boys for table manners, being neat and orderly, and instant obedience. (S191)

### Sex-Role Identification

Greater parental punishment for boys than for girls for incorrect sex-role behavior leads to greater anxiety among males than among females regarding sex-role identification. (L141)

Boys' being more likely to be punished for and to repress opposite-sex-role behavior leads to the following types of identifications where there exists a discrepancy between sex-role preference and sex-role identification: boys are more likely to show same-sex preference, while having underlying opposite-sex-role identifications; females will show opposite-sex preference, while having underlying same-sex-role identification. (L141)

Greater parental punishment for boys than for girls for opposite-sex behavior may lead to repression rather than an unlearning of opposite-sex-role behavior in boys. (L141)

### Sex-Role Identification of Daughter
Strong sex-role identification in the daughter is not associated with maternal encouragement of participation in feminine activities. (M206)

Strong sex-role identification in the daughter is positively associated with paternal encouragement of the daughter's participation in feminine activities. (M206)

### Sex-Role Identification of Son
Parental encouragement of the son's participation in masculine activities is not related to the son's sex-role identification. (M206)

### Subsistence Pattern
In societies where large animals are hunted, where grain rather than root crops are grown, where large or milking animals are kept, where fishing is unimportant or absent, or where settlement is nomadic rather than sedentary, large differences in training of the sexes is likely to occur. (W127)

### Superego Formation
Because of sex-typed child-rearing practices, at comparable age levels, girls tend to be "better socialized" than boys. (B252)

### Technology
Societies will be characterized by greater differentiation of socialization by sex if their economies value strength and motor skills which are typically masculine. (B264)

## CHILD-REARING PRACTICES (SIBLING CONFLICTS)  X  Ordinal Position
Mothers are more permissive of oldest than of middle or younger children's quarreling with siblings. (S191)

## CHILD-REARING PRACTICES (SLEEPING)  X  Class
Upper-class Negro parents enforce more rigid sleeping schedules than do lower-class Negro parents. (W133)

### Maternal Role, Attitude Toward
Rejection of the mother role is associated with rigid practices regarding the sleeping patterns of children; over absorption in the mother role being associated with overpermissive practices regarding sleeping patterns of the child. (K113)

### Toilet Training
There is no relationship between the mother's severity in toilet training and her strictness regarding the child's bedtime rules (U.S.). (S191)

## CHILD-REARING PRACTICES (SOCIAL BEHAVIOR)  X  Social Adjustment
If the parents evaluate unfavorably the social behavior and achievements of the child and often punish him for failure to meet parental standards, the child is likely to develop anxiety in confronting social situations (e.g., in front of an audience, in performing a test); this is not true if the parents evaluate favorably, but punish the child infrequently. (P066)

## CHILD-REARING PRACTICES (SOCIAL MOBILITY)  X  Educational Aspirations
Parents of college-oriented sons are more likely than parents of non-college-oriented sons to encourage upward mobility. (E102)

## CHILD-REARING PRACTICES (SOCIAL STIMULATION)  X  Cognitive Development
Amount of stimulation by the mother oriented to eliciting social responses in the infant is positively related to intellectual development in the infant. (Y042)

### Social Development
Direct efforts by the mother to elicit social responses in the infant are moderately related to actual outgoing social behavior in the infant. (Y042)

## CHILD-REARING PRACTICES (STRICTNESS)  X  Adult Role Behavior
The stricter the rule enforcing behavior of the parents during early childhood (aged 0–6), the greater the likelihood that a child (aged 6–12) will sanction an age-mate whom he observes breaking a rule. (M179)

### Aggression
When the child has a very severe father and an indulgent mother his aggression is likely to be directed outwardly rather than against himself. (S078)

### Alcoholism of Child
Alcoholics are more likely to have been reared in exceedingly strict homes where obedience was unquestioned and little freedom was allowed. (D078)

### Child-Rearing Practices (Discipline)
The advocacy of firm discipline by the father correlates with the attitudes of strictness, forcing independence upon the child, and the use of harsh punishment. (N053)

### Class
Middle-class parents place their children under a stricter regimen than do lower-class parents. (D065)

Parents of high socioeconomic status use more strict child-rearing methods than do parents of lower socioeconomic status (Chicago Negroes). (F117)

There is no significant difference between the middle class and the working class in which parent is stricter with the child. (W002)

Fathers are reported to be stricter with the child in both the middle class and the working class. (W002)

There is no significant difference between the middle class and the working class in the strictness of parents in requiring obedience. (W002)

Middle-class mothers are more inclined to drop the subject occasionally if the child does not do what was asked than are working-class mothers. (W002)

### Cognitive Development (Verbal)
There is no relationship between the degree of paternal, as against maternal, strictness and verbal ability in the daughter. (B257)

Among girls with low ability in spatial perception, paternal strictness is positively associated with high verbal ability. (B257)

### Conformity
For girls, there is a positive relationship between an excessive severity of discipline between ages 4–7 years and their conformity to parental demands during adolescence. (K115)

Children whose mothers are rigidly dominating and controlling in their behavior toward the child tend to be submissive and overly conforming. (R113)

### Criminality
Habitual criminals are likely to characterize their fathers as having been too strict or too lenient in terms of discipine than are normal persons, who tend to avoid both extremes of characterization. (C105)

### Dependency
For girls, the more severe the discipline administered by the mother, the greater is the dependency upon the mother. (K127)

### Employment of Mother
Mothers with a college background less often report the father as the stricter parent when these mothers work than when they do not work. (Y051)

Among nondelinquents, overstrictness on the part of fathers is more likely in families where the mother is employed. (S265)

### I.Q./Creativity
Mothers of highly intelligent (Binet) children are more likely to be morally strict in the upbringing of their children than are the mothers of highly creative (Guilford–Cattell) children. (G132)

### Juvenile Delinquency
There is a positive relationship between strict discipline by the mother and delinquent behavior in girls. (N057)

Strict discipline by parents and delinquent behavior in boys are not related. (N057)

Strict discipline by the father and delinquent behavior in girls are related. (N057)

### Juvenile Delinquency/Neurosis
More neurotic children than delinquent (acting out) children have received overly strict discipline. (A069)

### Mental Problems
Mothers of mongoloids are stricter than are mothers of psychotics, who are less strict than mothers of normal children. (P075)

### Paternal/Maternal Role
Subjects who say the father is strict also claim the father is the principal disciplinarian in the family. Those who report the father as mild in discipline say that the mother is the principal disciplinarian. (S078)

### Scholastic Achievement
Mothers of children who are high achievers (in junior high school) are stricter disciplinarians than others of low achievers. (T090)

### Sex Status of Child
Parents are more lenient in disciplining children of the opposite sex than of the same sex. (B273)

### Sex Status of Parent
Regardless of social class or education, husbands are inclined to believe that their wives are not strict enough with the children, while the wives tend to believe that their husbands are too strict. (S191)

## CHILD-REARING PRACTICES (SUBMISSION)
### X   Scholastic Achievement
If a child is called on consistently to submit or to sacrifice for others his scholastic problems will be greater than those of children reared in a normal home. (S212)

## CHILD-REARING PRACTICES (SUPERVISION)
### X   Child-Rearing Practices (Sex)
Mothers who are not permissive regarding their children's sexual behavior check their child's whereabouts more frequently than do mothers who are permissive (U.S.). (S191)

### Class
A greater part of the activity of the upper-class child comes under the purview of adults—kin, functionaries and others—than is true of the middle-class child. (C086)

### I.Q./Creativity of Children
Parents of highly intelligent children exercise more supervision over the behavior and academic performance of their children than do the parents of highly creative children. (G114)

### Juvenile Delinquency
If the mother tends to shift her responsibility of supervising the child to an irresponsible child or adult, the child is more likely to become delinquent. (M058)

Unsuitable supervision by the mother is more associated with juvenile delinquency. (M058)

Whether the mother works or not, the quality of the supervision her child receives determines his delinquency pattern. (M058)

Juvenile delinquents are less supervised than are nondelinquents. (S210)

### Juvenile Delinquency/Mental Illness
The parents of delinquents are more likely than the parents of psychotics and normals to fail to supervise their children or to repudiate them. (O033)

### Sociopathic Personality
There is a correlation between lack of maternal supervision and the development of sociopathic personality in the child. (O032)

## CHILD-REARING PRACTICES (TELEVISION)
### X   Class
The higher the status group to which the mother belongs, the more likely she is to set restrictions on the television programs watched by her children. (H178)

## CHILD-REARING PRACTICES (TOYS)
### X   Cognitive Development (Nonverbal)
The number of toys a child is given during preschool years is not related to his nonverbal (spatial and numerical) ability. (B257)

## CHILD-REARING PRACTICES (TRAUMA)
### X   Myths
There is a correlation between those aspects of child rearing which are typically traumatic for the infant in a given society and the sort of problem situations which recur in the myths of that people. (K111)

## CHILD-REARING PRACTICES (VERBAL FREEDOM)   X   Cognitive Development (Verbal)
Parental verbal permissiveness (e.g., permissiveness for verbal aggression, participation in meal conversation, adult conversation and topics, etc.) is positively associated with high verbal ability in children. (B257)

## CHILD-REARING PRACTICES (VERBAL STIMULATION)
### X   Cognitive Development (Verbal)
Verbal stimulation and interest shown by the mother

(e.g., reading storybooks to child, interest shown in child's speech habits, importance shown to verbal accomplishments) during early childhood and school years is positively associated with high verbal ability in the child. (B257)

## CHILD-REARING PRACTICES (VERBALIZATION)
### X   Child-Rearing Values (Punishment)
The father's approval of the use of physical punishment correlates with the encouragement of verbalization in the child. (N053)

## CHILD-REARING PROBLEMS   X   Age of Parents
The older the parent, the less likely is he to report having problems in child rearing. (G126)

Older parents are more concerned with inadequacies and problems in physical and material care; younger parents are more concerned with interpersonal difficulties (their own lack of tolerance for the child's behavior, or obedience and discipline problems). (G126)

### Divorce Adjustment
The greater the emotional difficulties experienced by the divorcée, the more likely is she to claim that there was some period during the divorce when the children had been harder to handle. This relationship does not change with increasing time since the divorce. (G157)

### Education
There is no relationship between individual educational level and the admission of problems in child rearing. (G126)

### Father-Child Relations
There is an association between the divorcée's claim that her children were too young to know or remember their father and her claim that there had never been any period where the children had been more difficult to handle. (G157)

### Father-Child Relations (Visitation After Divorce)
When the divorcée claims that the children were easier to handle after the ex-husband's visits, she is more likely to say that he should visit more frequently; if they were harder to handle, she is more likely to want the ex-husband's visits to be less frequent. (G157)

### Sex Status
There is no relationship between the sex of parents and the types of child-rearing problems they name as important. (G126)

### Sex Status of Parent
Women are more likely to mention having difficulties in rearing their children than are men. (G126)

### Size of Family
The larger the family, the more likely are parents to mention having child-rearing problems. (G126)

## CHILD-REARING PROBLEMS (GENERAL)
### X   Child-Rearing Problems (Obedience)
Parents who admit to problems in child rearing are more likely than parents who do not admit to problems to identify obedience as a major problem rather than other types of difficulties. (G126)

## CHILD-REARING PROBLEMS (OBEDIENCE)
### X   Child-Rearing Problems (General)
Parents who admit to problems in child rearing are more likely than parents who do not admit to problems to identify obedience as a major problem rather than other types of difficulties. (G126)

### Education
The higher the educational level, the more likely are parents to be concerned with obedience problems. (G126)

## CHILD-REARING VALUES
### X   Authoritarianism of Mother/Father
Women who are very authoritarian (as measured by the F–scale) are more likely than men who are very authoritarian to view their children in subordinate and restricted roles. (K117)

### Child-Rearing Practices (Permissiveness)
Parents who are permissive with their children are more likely to hold values that emphasize the child's development than to have traditional conceptions of what is a "good" child. (B007)

### Child-Rearing Practices (Restrictiveness)
If the mother believes in unconditional love for her children, the extent to which her child-rearing ideology stresses the middle-class values of diligence, thrift, and achievement will not correlate with the extent to which her daughter perceives her as overcircumscribing her freedom. (K101)

The more the mother's child-rearing ideology stresses the middle-class values of diligence, thrift, and achievement, the more likely it is that the daughter will perceive her as overcircumscribing her freedom. (K101)

### Class
Working-class parents are concerned more about the act and its consequences; middle-class parents far more about the motive for the act. (K089)

Working-class parents value obedience, neatness, and cleanliness more than do middle-class parents. Middle-class parents value curiosity, happiness, consideration, and self-control more highly than do working-class parents. (K089)

Middle-class values about child rearing are about the same whether parents read expert advice, or popular newspapers and magazines, or nothing at all; but working-class parents who read books have middle-class values, as against the working-class parents who do not read; the latter have lower-class values. (K089)

Middle-class parents feel obliged to be supportive of their children, while working-class values emphasize constraints which the children must accept. (K089)

Middle-class parental values are more acceptant and equalitarian, while working-class parental values are oriented toward maintaining order and obedience. (K089)

There is no significant difference in the reading of magazines and newspapers as sources of ideas about child rearing between middle-class mothers and working-class mothers. (W002)

Expert books as a source of ideas about child rearing are mentioned more by middle-class mothers than by working-class mothers. (W002)

People or friends as sources of ideas about child rearing are mentioned more by middle-class mothers than by working-class mothers (U.S.). (W002)

There is no significant difference in the use of child-rearing authorities as sources of ideas about child rearing between middle-class mothers and working-class mothers. (W002)

### Economic Level

Variables which rank higher in societies with a high accumulation of food resources (obedience and responsibility) are emphasized more strongly in the training of girls than of boys, whereas the variables which rank higher in societies with a low accumulation of food resources (achievement, self-reliance, and independence) are emphasized more strongly in the training of boys than of girls. (B037)

### Father Absence

When the father is away for long periods, the mother tends to demand from her children obedience and politeness rather than happiness and self-realization. (L156)

### I.Q./Creativity

Mothers of highly creative children (Binet) are more likely to favor internal values in friends of their children than are the parents of highly intelligent children (Guilford–Cattell). (G132)

Mothers of highly intelligent children (Binet) are more likely to favor such external values as good family and good manners in friends of their children than are the parents of highly creative children (Guilford–Cattell). (G132)

### Mother-Child Relations

The attitude of the mother toward her mentally ill child (babying, indulgence) will directly reflect the cultural definition of the mother-child relationship. (S187)

### Personality of Parents (Tolerance of Ambiguity)

Parents who are intolerant of ambiguity (as measured by Adorno's E–Scale) tend to view their children in subordinate and restricted roles. (K117)

### Religion

Protestant parents are more likely than Catholic parents to stress the importance of knowledge. (M246)

### Values

A transition in the larger culture from repression to tolerance of basic impulses results in a similar transition in child-rearing values. (M203)

## CHILD-REARING VALUES (ADJUSTMENT/ INDEPENDENCE)    X    Occupation

Mothers whose husbands have bureaucratic jobs are more likely to aim for the adjustment of their children to their social groups, whereas mothers whose husbands have entrepreneurial jobs are more likely to endeavor to foster independence in their children. (J030)

## CHILD-REARING VALUES (AGGRESSION)
### X    Class

Working-class fathers are more likely than middle-class fathers to regard the child's ability to defend himself as important. (K110)

## CHILD-REARING VALUES (AGREEMENT)
### X    Juvenile Delinquency

The higher the parental consensus concerning child rearing, the less likely is the child to become a delinquent.

### Scholastic Achievement

If the parents disagree between themselves on the behavior standards of the child, the child is likely to be an unsuccessful student. (H174)

### Self-Conception of Child

If the parents disagree as to the desired characteristics of the child, then the child's self-concept will also be unstable. (W158)

## CHILD-REARING VALUES (CLEANLINESS)
### X    Class

Working-class mothers value cleanliness and neatness in their children more than do middle-class mothers. (K110)

## CHILD-REARING VALUES (CONFORMITY)
### X    Class

Working-class parents are more concerned than middle-class parents with actions and qualities in their children that assure respectability, thus emphasizing socially prescribed patterns. (B275)

Working-class parental values center on conformity to external prescriptions; middle-class parental values on self-direction. (K089)

Working-class parents want the child to conform to externally imposed standards, while middle-class parents are more attentive to the child's internal dynamics. (K089)

### Occupation

If the father has an entrepreneurial position, the parents try to inculcate self-reliance; if the father's position is bureaucratic, the parents attempt to inculcate accommodative values. (B273)

## CHILD-REARING VALUES (CONSISTENCY)
### X    Personality of Parents (Other-Directedness)

Parents whose character structures are "other-directed" are more likely than "inner-directed" parents to have contradictory sets of beliefs about the requirements of child rearing. (C096)

## CHILD-REARING VALUES (CONTROL)
### X    Paternal/Maternal Role

Mothers are more likely to suggest coercive methods of control of children than are fathers. (J029)

Mothers are more likely to vacillate between mild and severe methods of control than are fathers. (J029)

## CHILD-REARING VALUES (CURIOSITY)    X    Class

Middle-class mothers are more likely than working-class mothers to regard curiosity as desirable in their children. (K110)

## CHILD-REARING VALUES (DEMOCRATIC)
### X    Parent-Child Relations (Affection)

The child from the democratic, egalitarian home is more likely to have a genuine, personalized love for his parents and less repressed hostility and aggression. (M203)

## CHILD-REARING VALUES (DEPENDABILITY)
### X    Class

Middle-class fathers are more likely than working-class fathers to value dependability in their children. (K110)

## CHILD-REARING VALUES (DEPENDENCY)
### X    Class

Working-class parents are more likely to want their children to conform to externally imposed standards (as opposed to self-direction) than are middle-class parents. (K089)

#### Ethnicity
Jewish parents are more apt to stress early independence training of children than are Italian parents. (M060)

#### Kin-Role Definition
Individuals are not expected to assume responsibility for the actions of other persons in societies organized around the value of "sociological independence" (i.e., in which the individuals are anchored in and identify with the nuclear family); individuals are required to assume the responsibility for their lineage or clan-mates in societies organized around the value of "sociological interdependence" (i.e., in societies in which individuals are anchored in and identify with the wider kin-group. (C093)

#### Occupation of Mother
Mothers with a profession tend to stress the importance of self-sufficiency for their children more than do non-professional mothers.

#### Personality of Parents (Other-Directedness)
Other-directedness in parents (measured by Kassarjian's I-Q Social Preference Scale) is positively correlated with beliefs fostering dependency in the child. (C111)

#### Religion
Protestant parents are more likely than Catholic parents to believe that children should be by themselves, away from their parents, and are often better when they are on their own. (M246)

Protestant parents are more likely than Catholic parents to stress the importance of an individual's finding out things on his own. (M246)

There is no significant difference between Protestant and Catholic mothers' attitudes toward independence training in social settings where Catholics have moved away from more traditional Catholic attitudes. (M246)

#### Residence (Extrusion)
Children who are being brought up for "sociological interdependence," anchorage, and identification in the *wider kin-group* will experience physical disruption or discontinuity in their relations with the nuclear family through extrusion or brother-sister avoidance during the first stage of puberty (8–10 years); whereas children who are brought up for "sociological independence," anchorage, and identification in the *nuclear* family will experience physical continuity without disruption in their nuclear-family relations during the first stage of puberty. (C093)

### CHILD-REARING VALUES (HAPPINESS)  X  Class
Working-class mothers are less likely than are middle-class mothers to regard happiness as highly desirable for their boys. (K110)

Middle-class mothers are more likely to view happiness for their children as comprising curiosity and ambition, while working-class mothers relate happiness to honesty and popularity. (K110)

### CHILD-REARING VALUES (HONESTY)    X  Class
Parents of both working and middle class tend to regard honesty as of primary importance in the child. (K110)

### CHILD-REARING VALUES (HONESTY/POPULARITY)      X  Class
If working-class mothers value honesty, they are less likely to value popularity in their children; among middle-class mothers, evaluation of these two traits is associated positively (U.S.). (K110)

### CHILD-REARING VALUES (MATE SELECTION AND OCCUPATION)      X  Values
The greater a culture's emphasis on scholarship and learning, the more likely it is that parents will guide their children into intellectual careers or marriages with intellectuals. (M203)

### CHILD-REARING VALUES (OBEDIENCE)      X  Class
Working-class parents put more stress on obedience to parental commands than do middle-class parents. (K089)

Working-class parents are more likely than middle-class parents to value obedience to parental authority. (K110)

### CHILD-REARING VALUES OF DAUGHTER      X  Child-Rearing Practices
There is no correlation between the child-rearing values of the daughter and the practices of the mother except concerning frequent punishment for disobedience. (W153)

### CHILD-REARING VALUES OF FATHER      X  Child-Rearing Values of Mother
A high correlation exists between the structure of attitudes toward child rearing of mothers and fathers. (N053)

### CHILD-REARING VALUES OF MOTHER      X  Child Rearing Values of Father
A high correlation exists between the structure of attitudes toward child rearing of mothers and fathers. (N053)

### CHILD-REARING VALUES (PERMISSIVENESS)      X  Occupation
When couples are classed as "bureaucratic" (the breadwinner works in a large bureaucracy) or "entrepreneurial" (the breadwinner has a business of his own), the former are more permissive in their child-rearing values. (A053)

#### Personality of Parents (Other-Directedness)
Other-directedness in parents (measured by Kassarjian's I-Q Social Preference Scale) is positively correlated with the tendency to believe in permissive child rearing. (C111)

### CHILD-REARING VALUES (POPULARITY)      X  Social Network
Parents whose chief source of guidance is their relations with their contemporaries will place a much greater emphasis on their child's popularity within his peer group than will parents whose chief indentifications are with other people.

### CHILD-REARING VALUES (PUNISHMENT)      X  Child-Rearing Practices, Evaluation of
Among mothers who spanked their children frequently, those who thought it effective had greater confidence in their child rearing than did those who thought it ineffective (U.S.). (S191)

#### Child-Rearing Practices (Sex/Aggression)
The father's approval of the use of physical punishment correlates negatively with suppression of sex and aggression in the child. (N053)

### Child-Rearing Practices (Verbalization)
The father's approval of the use of physical punishment correlates with the encouragement of verbalization in the child. (N053)

### Marital Adjustment
The father's approval of the use of physical punishment correlates with marital conflict. (N053)

### Mother-Child Relations (Rejection)
Among mothers who spank their children frequently, those who consider it ineffective are more rejecting than those who consider it effective (U.S.). (S191)

### Self-Conception of Mother
Among mothers who spanked their children frequently, those who thought it effective had greater self-esteem than did those who thought it ineffective (U.S.). (S191)

## CHILD-REARING VALUES (RESTRICTIVENESS)
### X  Ethnocentrism of Parents
Ethnocentric parents are likely to hold attitudes which place their children in subordinate and restricted roles. (K117)

## CHILD-REARING VALUES (RIGIDITY)
### X  Urban/Rural
Girls raised in rural areas are more likely to face inflexible rules about adolescent behavior and parental control than are girls raised in urban environments.

## CHILD-REARING VALUES/ROLE MODEL
### X  Self-Conception of Child
The child's perception of himself correlates not with the model of his parents but with the parents' ideals for the child. (B234)

## CHILD-REARING VALUES (SELF-CONTROL)
### X  Child-Rearing Practices (Aggression)
Mothers who place a high value on their children's acquiring self-control are more likely to punish their children for temper tantrums than are mothers who do not value self-control as highly. (K110)

### Class
Middle-class parents are more likely than working-class parents to value self-control in their children. (K110)

## CHILD-REARING VALUES (SOCIAL ADJUSTMENT)
### X  Class
Middle-class parents are more concerned with the child's ability to get along with others (e.g., his friendliness and cooperativeness) than are working-class parents. (K110)

## CHILD-REARING VALUES (STRICTNESS)
### X  Personality of Parents (Other-Directedness)
Other-directedness in parents (measured by Kassarjian's I-Q Social Preference Scale) is positively correlated with the belief in strictness in child rearing. (C111)

## CHILD-REARING VALUES (SYMPATHY)  X  Class
Middle-class parents are more likely than working-class parents to value the development of sympathetic concern for other people in their children. (K110)

## CHILD SUPPORT    X  Birth Status of Child
Men are less likely to support their wives' children by other unions than their own children from the same women. (B245)

### Child Support, Attitude Toward
The ex-husband's resentment of support payments is associated with his payments being less regular. (G157)

### Divorce Arrangements
When the wife thinks that the property settlement is fair, the husband is slightly less likely to think the child-support payments are unfair or to resent them. (G157)

### Divorce Complaints
The divorcée's complaint that nonsupport was a cause of the divorce is associated with the husband who never or rarely makes his child-support payments. (G157)

### Divorce, Initiation of
The husband is most likely to make regular child-support payments when the first suggestion to divorce was mutual, less likely to pay regularly when the first suggested divorce, and least likely when his wife first suggested divorce. (G157)

If the husband resents the child-support payments, which spouse made the first suggestion to divorce does not affect his lack of continuity in child support. When he does not resent the child-support payments, a mutual suggestion to divorce is more highly associated with regular child-support payments than when either the wife or the husband was the first to suggest divorce. (G157)

### Employment (Regularity)
The more regular the husband's employment record during marriage, the more likely is he to make his child-support payments. (G157)

### Income of Husband
Among divorced couples, the amount of income is unrelated to the continuity of child-support payments. (G157)

Regardless of the number of children in the family, the husband's income is only slightly related to the amount of child-support payments ordered by the court. (G157)

### Remarriage
Divorcées who are remarried are slightly more likely than those who are not remarried to report that their husbands resented child-support payments. (G157)

If the husband does not resent the child-support payments, the remarriage of his ex-wife does not affect the continuity of his payments. If the husband does resent the child-support payments, remarriage of his ex-wife is associated with less continuity of child-support payments. (G157)

Remarriage of the divorcée is associated with less continuity of child-support payments by the ex-husband. (G157)

## CHILD SUPPORT, ATTITUDE TOWARD
### X  Child Support
The ex-husband's resentment of support payments is associated with his payments being less regular. (G157)

## CHILD SUPPORT (EVALUATION)
### X  Husband-Wife Relations
When the divorcée's attitudes toward her ex-husband are held constant, there is no relationship between his attitudes toward her (positive or negative) and the regularity of his child-support payments. (G157)

## CHILDBIRTH                    X   Dependency
Mothers who have psychopathic reactions to childbirth are similar in most psychological traits to those who have no such reactions, but they do manifest much greater dependence on their own mothers. (M193)

### Ego Development of Mother
Mothers who have psychopathic reactions to childbirth have less well-developed ego resources (measured by Rorschach responses) than do mothers who react without such pathologies. (M193)

### Marital Stability
Marital stability is likely to increase with the birth of the first child. (E042)

### Mental Illness
There is no positive correlation between psychosis and the conditions of the child's birth. (M164)

### Personality Adjustment
Mothers of prematurely born infants are more likely than others to react to birth in a disordered manner. (K108)

## CHILDBIRTH (ANXIETY)              X   Mental Illness
Mental illness in the child is associated with maternal anxiety at the time of birth. (L126)

## CHILDBIRTH ATTITUDE
### X   Mother-Child Relations (Affection)
Women who feel that childbirth is hard are less likely to express physical affection for their child. (N051)

### Sexual Adjustment
Those who fear another childbirth and labor after the first pregnancy have a poorer sexual adjustment than do those who have no such fear (U.S.). (L013)

## CHILDBIRTH PROBLEMS
### X   Mental Illness (Schizophrenia/Neurosis)
Mothers of schizophrenics are more likely to have had difficulties associated with parturition than are mothers of neurotics.

### Mother-Child Relations (Rejection)
There is a correlation between birth difficulties and rejection of the child by the mother.

## CHILDHOOD        X   Maternal Overprotectiveness
Extreme deprivation in the mother's childhood is a cause of later overprotectiveness toward her own child. (B272)

The mother's experience of harsh realities early in life is associated with her later overprotectiveness toward her child. (B272)

### Neurosis of Spouse
There is an association between the childhood emotional experience of one spouse and the C.M.I. (Cornell Medical Index of Neurosis) score of the other. (P086)

## CHILDHOOD (EMOTIONAL SECURITY)
### X   Broken Homes
There is no relationship between divorce, separation, or illegitimate parenthood and remembering an emotionally insecure childhood. (P086)

### Marital Adjustment
Satisfactory marital adjustment is more likely when both partners experienced emotionally secure childhoods than it is when one or both partners recall an insecure childhood. (P086)

### Power Structure of Family
Men who dominate in the marriage relationship are more likely to have experienced an emotionally insecure childhood. (P086)

### Premarital Pregnancy
There is no relationship between premarital conception and recall of an emotionally insecure childhood. (P086)

## CHILDHOOD EXPERIENCE
### X   Maternal Overprotectiveness
The mother's experience of harsh realities early in life is a cause of her later overprotectiveness toward her child. (B272)

## CHILDREN                        X   Affinal Ties
The birth of children will tend to strengthen the relationship between affinal kinsmen. (M128)

### Desertion/Divorce
Families where divorce occurs have children less often than do families where desertion occurs (for comparable durations of marriage). (M011)

### Divorce
The alleged association between divorce and childlessness has been a statistically spurious one and may not exist at all. (M011)

Couples who have children are more likely to stay together than are childless couples, even though they may have been previously married and divorced. (P062)

### Divorce, Attitude Toward
Divorce tends to be more censured by society when children are involved. (G015)

### Divorce Process
The anticipated effect of the divorce on the children is not related to the time interval between serious consideration of divorce and filing suit. (G157)

### Employment of Wife
Wives with no children are much more likely to work than are those who have young children. (L002)

### Marital Adjustment
The number of children in the family does *not* affect marital tension. (F002)

### Marital Stability
Marriage is more likely to be stable if there are children. (B191)

Among those who have been divorced, there is an association between marital stability and having children. (P059)

### Recreation
Recreational activities of married couples tend to become more differentiated after the birth of children. (B209)

### Remarriage
Widowed or divorced women with children are more likely than those with no children to remarry quickly or not at all. (G011)

### Separation
Separation is less likely to occur if there are children. (B111)

## CHILDREN, DESIRE FOR            X   Sibling Status
Only children are more likely than others to want no children. (T089)

## CHILDREN, EVALUATION OF    X    Concubinage
The institutionalization of concubinage is directly correlated with the desire for numerous children. (S122)

### Infant Mortality
A high value tends to be placed upon children when the rate of infant mortality is high. (E030)

### Marital Adjustment
Husbands who feel that children are an aid to college achievement have higher marital adjustment scores than husbands who feel that children disturb college achievement (U.S.). (C003)

### Marital Stability
Marital stability will tend to be greater if children are valued. (H164)

### Rank of Wife
Where children are highly valued the status of the wife is directly correlated with her fertility. (D040)

### Religion (Ancestor Cult)
The importance of children will tend to be stressed in societies which have institutionalized an ancestor cult. (F058)

## CHILDREN, NUMBER OF    X    Birth Spacing
There is an inverse relationship between the interval from marriage to the birth of the first child and the number of children eventually born (i.e., the larger the number of children in the family, the smaller is the interval between marriage and the birth of the first child) (U.S. university graduates). (L018)

### Marital Adjustment
There is no direct correlation between the presence or absence of children or the number of children and marital happiness. (I007)

### Mother-Child Relations (Affection)
Greater concern and affection during nursing are more common among mothers who have had more than one child. (P063)

## CHORES    X    Achievement Motivation
The greater the extent of the child's participation in household tasks, the higher his level of achievement motivation. (C101)

### Class
There is a positive correlation between class and sharing of household duties when the wife is working. (G134)

### Division of Labor by Sex
The less the household-task training before the marriage for both partners, the more diffuse the division of labor will be at the beginning of marital life.

### Employment of Mother
Mothers with jobs tend to encourage their children to perform household tasks more than do non-working mothers.

### Employment of Wife
On the average, husbands of working wives do a greater proportion of housework than do husbands of housewives. (B208)

Couples are more likely to share a greater number of household tasks when the wife is employed full time, or attending school, than if she is employed part time. (G133)

Husbands and children of working wives are more likely to take an active role in household chores than are families of nonworking wives. (S257)

### Power Structure of Family
Couples who stress the importance of joint decision making also share child care and housework. (B209)

### Pregnancy, Attitude Toward
The mothers who feel most tied down by their household duties tend to be the ones who were unhappy over pregnancy. (S191)

### Size of Family
Couples with no children share a greater number of household tasks than do those with children. (G133)

### Social Mobility Aspirations
The higher the occupational mobility desired by the husband, the less the time spent in household-task performance.

### Work Attitudes of Mother
Working mothers who like to work are less likely to shoulder their children with household tasks. (G156)

## CHORES, BY CLASS    X    Employment of Mother
Adolescent daughters of lower-class working mothers report greater household responsibilities than do those of middle-class working mothers. (G156)

## CLAN    X    Acculturation
As the degree of acculturation increases, clan organization tends to diminish in importance. (B093)

### Authority Structure of Family
The institutionalization of a clan structure tends to reinforce parental authority. (W082)

### Descent/Residence, Consistency of
Clans can only develop in the presence of consistent rules of descent and residence. (M171)

### Generational Emphasis
The degree to which the generation principle is violated is directly correlated with the maturity of the clan system. (G046)

### Inheritance
In societies with a clan organization, the inheritance pattern will tend to insure the retention of clan property. (W082)

### Kin Terminology
Crow and Omaha terminologies are associated with unilineal societies and a well-developed clan system. (L061)

Members of the same marriage clan will tend to address each other by sibling terminology. (S095)

### Kin Terminology (Bifurcate Merging)
Clans, whether patrilocal, matrilocal, or avunculocal in type, tend to be associated with bifurcate merging terminology. (M019)

### Kin Terminology (Classificatory)
The classificatory system of relationship is connected with the social divisions known as "clans." (R123)

Classificatory terminology and the clan system tend to evolve together. (S098)

### Kin Ties
The range of acknowledged kinship ties will tend to be extended by institutions such as clans. (M137)

### Kin Ties (Fictive)
The institutionalization of fictive kin ties will be inhibited by the existence of the clan system. (F049)

### Population
The appearance of the clan organization tends to be correlated with an increase in the density and the size of the population. (G045)

### Residence
The emergence of a clan structure tends to occur with an increase in the regularity of the residence pattern. (S120)

Clan formation requires some factor (such as war or tribal movements) which makes for dislocation of bands and concentration of them in large, multiband communities. (S194)

### Social Evolution
Clan organization occurs in societies which represent an intermediate level of social evolution. (W076)

### Subsistence Pattern
A society based upon a clan structure is better adapted to subsistence than to a money economy. (H064)

### Subsistence Pattern (Horticultural)
Clan systems are associated with an economy based on horticulture. (G045)

### CLAN AFFILIATION X Marriage Chances
More nonagnatic clan members tend to marry only once, and later, than agnatic clan members. (R054)

### Mate Selection (Remarriage)
In remarriage, men are more likely to select a wife who is of the same clan as the first wife. (C039)

### CLAN AFFILIATION OF WIVES X Conflict Between Wives
Where a man marries women from different clans, there is more likely to be friction among them. (M137)

### CLAN, IMPORTANCE OF X Authority Structure of Family
The legitimacy of the father's authority is questioned as the father becomes less a representation of the clan and of tradition due to the decreasing importance of the clan for the family and the increasing power of the state. (T016)

### Exogamy
Exogamic restrictions tend to be relaxed with a decrease in the importance of the clan. (N030)

### Genealogical Depth
The depth of the genealogy is directly correlated with the importance of the clan as a social unit. (M051)

### Genealogical Ties, Knowledge of
The accuracy of genealogy will be directly correlated with the importance of the clan as a social unit. (M051)

### Husband-Wife Relations (Dependency)
The dependence of a wife on her husband is inversely correlated with the importance of clan affiliations. (W082)

### Kin Relations (Interaction)
The importance of clan membership is directly correlated with the frequency of contact with clan members. (H088)

### Religion (Ancestor Worship)
Ancestor worship tends to reinforce the importance of clan affiliation. (H164)

### CLAN (MATRILINEAL) X Descent (Double)
The creation, *ab initio,* of a distributed, unorganized, matrilineal clan is not likely in the absence of an overt or covert double descent system. (A048)

### Inheritance (Matrilineal)
Where a clan organization is matrilineal, the inheritance of property tends also to be matrilineal. (W103)

### CLAN, NUMBER OF X Descent (Bilateral)
The adoption of bilateral descent can occur in a unilineal system only when there is an indefinite number of intermarrying clans. (S098)

### CLAN (PATRILINEAL) X Inheritance (Patrilineal)
The patrilineal clan will tend to emerge when there is a greater emphasis on patrilineal inheritance. (S120)

### CLAN (PATRILINEAL/MATRILINEAL) X Kin Terminology (Bifurcate Merging)
Bifurcate merging terminology tends to be associated with clan systems of either a patrilineal or matrilineal character. (W050)

### CLAN-ROLE OBLIGATIONS X Cohesion of Clan
The cohesion of the clan tends to be reinforced by a norm which specifies that the relationship of an individual to a member of a clan determines his relation with all members of the clan. (R026)

### CLAN STRUCTURE X Division of Labor
When the structure of the clan is hierarchical in its patterns, the development of occupational specialization and social differentiation is facilitated. (F039)

### Geographical Mobility
The proliferation of unilineal kin and the formation of large and segmented clans require physical mobility and territorial expansion. (B327)

### Political Centralization
Centralized political authority tends to inhibit or curtail extensive development of a segmentary clan system. (F089)

### Subsistence Pattern (Pastoral/Agricultural)
The clan structure will be of an egalitarian character in societies whose economic pattern is that of migratory agriculture or pastoralism. (F039)

### CLASS X Abduction
In societies in which abduction is a social pattern, it is more likely to occur when a man lacks the economic means for a legitimate marriage and does not have the personal attractiveness or seductive skill needed to persuade a girl to elope with him. (L026)

### Acculturation
Ethnic groups with high social rank tend to be the most acculturated. (S051)

### Achievement Motivation
When the wife is dominant (*v.* husband-dominant, autonomic, or conflict-type), the highest average active-

future orientation of sons is found in the low socioeconomic status group. (S205)

### Achievement Values
The higher the social class (lower to upper middle class), the greater the value similarity between mother and son regarding achievement. (R097)

### Adult-Child Relations (Isolation)
The extent to which children are isolated from adults' experience varies with social class (more strongly in upper and much less in lower). (S076)

### Adult Role
Among Negroes, lower-class children are more likely than middle-class children to perceive the transition from dependency to an independent attitude toward the world as traumatic.

### Adultery, Attitude Toward
Restrictions against extramarital relations tend to be more severe among members of the upper class. (M063)

Members of the upper class will tend to have stronger expectations of marital fidelity. (R062)

### Affinal Role Obligations
Affinal obligations are more elaborate among the upper social strata. (K045)

### Age at Marriage
Higher-class men tend to marry later than do lower-class men.

There is a correlation between expected deferment of marriage after high-school graduation and social status level. (B248)

Marriage is likely to come earlier for the unskilled laboring groups and higher for the more skilled, professional, and upper-income groups. (C023)

The nobility of Western countries tend to marry at younger ages than do persons in other classes. (G156)

### Age at Weaning
Lower-class children have a significantly higher median age at completion of weaning than do middle-class children. This hypothesis is also denied. (H011)

### Alimony
The lower the socioeconomic status of the male, the greater the likelihood of his being able to escape child support and alimony expenditures. (G134)

### Authoritarianism
Middle-class adolescents are more likely to view their parents as democratic, equalitarian or permissive; their lower-class counterparts are more likely to consider their parents to be autocratic or authoritarian. (E100)

Authoritarianism is less likely to be translated directly into power assertion over the children in the middle class than in the lower class because of the middle-class child-rearing norms which inhibit direct expression of power. (H213)

### Authority Structure of Family
The lower the class, the more likely is the husband to claim authority. (G156)

The higher the social class, the greater the authority of the elder persons in the family. (G156)

There is no correlation between class and views of equal or unequal distribution of family authority between parents. (H180)

People from a lower-class background are more likely to view their mothers as the principal authority figure than are persons from upper-class backgrounds, who are more likely to view their fathers as the principal authority figure. (K114)

Schizophrenics at all class levels tend to see their mothers, rather than their fathers, as the dominant authority figure in the family. (K114)

Patterns of parental authority do not vary with socioeconomic factors in families of schizophrenic children. (S187)

### Autoeroticism
Lower-class adolescent boys go through a briefer period of masturbation than do middle-class boys. (B244)

Middle-class children masturbate more, and to a later age, than do lower-class children. (R127)

### Behavior Problems
Children of better-educated parents are more likely to have problems (e.g., thumb-sucking, crying, obsessional habits, etc.) than are children of rural parents or urban working-class parents (France). (F097)

### Behavior Problems (Finger-Sucking)
Children of the better-educated parents are more likely to suck their fingers than are children of comfortable country parents and working-class urban parents (France). (F097)

### Behavior Problems (Thumb-Sucking)
The incidence of thumb-sucking is much greater among middle-class children than among lower-class children.

Middle-class white children show the same proportion of thumb-sucking as do middle-class Negro children.

Among middle-class children there is significantly more thumb-sucking than among working-class children. (W002)

### Birth Control
Lower-status groups adopt methods of contraception at a slower rate than do upper-status groups. (F101)

Although religious differentials persist within each class, generally the higher the class, the greater the use of contraception. (F101)

Members of lower classes are more likely than others to use withdrawal as a method of family limitation. (F101)

Among Catholics (only) there is no consistent relationship between background characteristics (education, income, occupation) and attitudes expressed toward family limitation. (F101)

Among Protestants higher-status groups are more likely than others to choose the diaphragm as a contraceptive, while lower-status groups are more likely than others to choose the douche. (F101)

Among Catholics there is no relationship between class and the method of contraception used. (F101)

When contraceptives are introduced, the upper social strata are more likely to begin using them than are the lower social strata. (G156)

Couples in the lower-lower class who are not middle-class-oriented are less likely than couples in other classes to use contraceptives and planning. (P083)

There is an inverse relationship between the number of unplanned pregnancies and social class. (W022)

### Breast Feeding
A significantly higher percentage of lower-class (Chicago) children were breast-fed only than were middle-class (Chicago) children. (H011)

There is no significant difference in the use of breast feeding between the middle class and the working class (U.S.). (W002)

Breast feeding is more prevalent in the lower class. (W002)

There is no significant difference in the duration of breast feeding between the middle class and the working class (U.S.). (W002)

### Breast Feeding, Duration of
Breast feeding is more prevalent and of longer duration among lower-class than among upper-class Negro families. (W133)

### Broken Homes
Low socioeconomic status is associated with a high percentage of broken homes. (M181)

### Broken Home
### X   Juvenile Delinquency
There is a correlation between broken homes and delinquency in the higher classes, but not in the lower classes. (S219)

### Child Rearing
Middle-class parents are more likely than working-class parents to discuss child rearing with friends, neighbors, and experts. (K089)

### Child-Rearing Practices
Upper-class mothers are more likely than middle-class mothers to justify their demands on children by asserting their authority, while middle-class mothers are more likely to appeal to a general moral principle or a rule originating outside the family. (G156)

Middle-class parents have not changed the values they have tried to inculcate in their children; but because they have been more responsive to the experts, they have quickly changed their techniques in the service of the same values, while working-class parents have lagged behind. (K089)

Middle-class mothers want their husbands to be supportive of the children, especially of sons, and do not ask for the imposition of much constraint; middle-class fathers play a role in accordance with this demand, but working-class mothers want their husbands to give restraints and working-class fathers often refuse to take this responsibility. (K089)

The lower the social class, the more likely a mother is to use traditional methods of infant rearing (breast feeding, demand feeding, late weaning, and pacifiers), as opposed to more formalized methods derived from psychological literature. (K160)

Social class of parents generally does not correlate with child-rearing practices. (M180)

### Child-Rearing Practices (Achievement)
Middle-class parents place greater emphasis on early training for individual achievement than do lower-class parents. (E102)

Lower-class parents place less emphasis on instilling achievement goals in their children than do middle-class parents. (E102)

### Child-Rearing Practices (Achievement Demands)
Middle- and lower-class parents are equally likely to make achievement demands on high achieving adolescents. (E102)

Middle-class parents are much more likely to make achievement demands of low achieving adolescents than are lower-class parents. (E102)

Middle-class families tend to demand higher achievement in the areas of skill, knowledge, and initiative than do lower-class families. (G156)

More of the working-class mothers than of the middle-class mothers place high pressures on their children to do well in school. (S191)

Fewer working-class mothers than middle-class mothers have any real expectation that their children will go to college. (S191)

### Child-Rearing Practices (Achievement/Dependency)
Parents in lower-middle-class families are more likely to teach their sons to accept their social status and to conform; upper-middle-class parents are more likely to stress achievement, mobility, and independence. (T100)

### Child-Rearing Practices (Aggression)
Working-class parents emphasize the teaching of responding to acts of aggression (fighting back) more than do upper-middle-class parents. (B235)

For both boys and girls, there is no relationship between social class and the severity of maternal punishment for aggression. (E093)

High-status girls are punished by both parents less severely for peer-directed aggression than are low-status girls. Middle-class boys are punished more severely by their mothers, but not by their fathers, for peer-directed aggression than are lower- and upper-status boys. (E093)

Lower-status girls are punished more severely by their fathers for aggression than are girls from high-status families. For sons, there is no relationship between social class and the severity of paternal punishment for aggression. (E093)

There is no relationship between social class and the severity of parental punishment for parent-directed aggression. (E093)

There is no relationship between social class and parental use of psychological v. physical punishment for aggressive behavior in the child. (E093)

The lower class is less tolerant of aggression by children than is the middle class (U.S.). (L003)

There is no significant difference between the middle class and the lower class in the toleration of aggression by children. (L003)

Lower-class mothers are no more encouraging of aggressive behavior directed toward other children than are middle-class mothers (U.S.). (S191)

There is no difference between lower- and middle-class mothers in relation to permissiveness regarding aggression between siblings (U.S.). (S191)

Middle-class mothers are more permissive than are lower-class mothers toward children's aggression against their parents (U.S.). (S191)

Middle-class mothers and better-educated working-class mothers permit their children to express aggression toward parents somewhat more freely and punish such aggressive outbursts less severely than do lesser-educated working-class mothers (U.S.). (S191)

Middle-class (British) families are somewhat less inclined to allow children to show aggression toward their parents than are working-class (British) families. (S191)

There is no significant difference between middle-class parents and working-class parents in their demands for aggression by their children against other children. (W002)

There is no significant difference between middle-class and working-class parents in the extent to which they encourage their children to fight back. (W002)

There is no significant difference between middle-class children and working-class children in the amount of aggression in the home. (W002)

Middle-class parents are more permissive toward aggression against them than are working-class parents. (W002)

### Child-Rearing Practices (Aggression/Feeding)
Middle-class mothers who are permissive in relation to the infant's feeding schedules tend to be more punitive toward aggression than do lower-class mothers. (B272)

### Child-Rearing Practices (Authoritarianism)
Lower-class parents are more autocratic or authoritarian in handling their younger sons and daughters than are middle-class parents. Moving from younger females to younger males, older females and older males, successively smaller class differences in parent-adolescent decision making are observed. (E100)

### Child-Rearing Practices (Authority)
There is no significant difference between working-class and middle-class parents regarding the teaching of authority dependence and ingratiation of authority. (B235)

### Child-Rearing Practices (Body Contact)
Lower-class Negro babies have more body contact (being held, carried, actively played with) than do upper-class Negro babies. (W133)

### Child-Rearing Practices by Sex Status
There are greater social-class differences in the rearing of girls than in the rearing of boys. (E100)

### Child-Rearing Practices (Chores)
Middle-class parents train their children at a younger age in tasks such as sewing, cooking, helping around the house; lower-class parents train their children for these tasks when the child is old enough to be able to use the skills to help the parents.

### Child-Rearing Practices (Cleanliness)
Middle-class parents are more rigorous than are lower-class parents in teaching their children cleanliness habits (France). (F097)

Children of working-class parents acquire cleanliness habits at an earlier age than do country children or children of better-educated families (France). (F097)

### Child-Rearing Practices (Conformity)
Middle-class parents are more likely to encourage the child to act on the basis of internalized norms; lower-class parents, to stress compliance with parental authority. (T100)

### Child-Rearing Practices (Consensus)
In middle-class families, parents tend to exhibit a more unified front in enforcing rules and making demands on children than in lower-class families. (N049)

### Child-Rearing Practices (Consistency)
Middle-class parents are more consistent in their child supervision than are lower-class parents. (R127)

### Child-Rearing Practices (Control)
Lower-class parents of mental patients are more likely than middle-class parents of mental patients to use physically harsh and inconsistent means of control. (M061)

### Child-Rearing Practices (Demands)
More working-class mothers than middle-class mothers place high pressures on their children to do well in school. (S191)

Fewer working-class mothers than middle-class mothers have any real expectation that their children will go to college. (S191)

### Child-Rearing Practices (Dependency)
There is no significant difference between middle class and working class in how much mothers keep track of their children. (H011)

The age at which boys and girls might go to the movies alone is earlier for the lower class than for the middle class. (H011)

The time at which boys and girls are expected in at night is earlier for the middle class than for the lower class. (H011)

The age at which boys and girls go downtown alone is earlier in the middle class than in the lower class. (H011)

Children are allowed to go farther away from the house during the day if they come from the middle class than if they come from the lower class. (H011)

Middle-class mothers whose husbands have entrepreneurial jobs are more likely than those of lower-class entrepreneurial status to stop close supervision of a youngster by the time he is 12 years old or even earlier. (M062)

Lower-class families are more likely than families of other social statuses to stress caretaking earlier than independence and mastery in child rearing. (M246)

Lower-class families grant a greater degree of independence to their adolescents than do middle-class families. (P001)

Middle-class parents place more emphasis on independence training than do lower-class parents. (R098)

Middle-class parents expect their children to assume responsibility earlier. (S187)

Working-class mothers were less permissive, more ir-ritated, more rejecting, and had a more punishing atti-tude toward dependency of child than did middle-class mothers. (S191)

### Child-Rearing Practices (Dependency) X  Academic Motivation of Child by Class

High independence training has a greater effect on high academic motivation among middle-class than among lower-class youths. (E102)

### Child-Rearing Practices (Differential Treatment)

The higher the social class the more likely it is that chil-dren of either sex will be disciplined the same. (B236)

### Child-Rearing Practices (Discipline)

The lower the class, the more likely it is that boys will receive inadequate discipline and support and that girls will be overprotected. (B236)

Children from the high socioeconomic class suggest more constructive and amicable solutions to discipline situations; children from middle-class families suggest appealing to authority as a solution for discipline. (G117)

The standard of behavior demanded of noble children is higher than that expected from commoners. (W098)

### Child-Rearing Practices (Education)

At lower middle-class and lower-class levels, parental emphasis on attending college is more likely to appear only after the child has shown good performance at school than it is at higher-class levels, where parental stress is more likely to precede performance. (B291)

### Child-Rearing Practices (Exploration)

Upper-class Negro parents more often discourage their babies from reaching out toward objects and persons than do lower-class Negro parents. (W133)

### Child-Rearing Practices (Frustration)

Lower-class parents tend to subject their children to less frustration of impulse than do middle-class parents. (M178)

### Child-Rearing Practices (Giving Reasons)

Lower-class autocratic mothers and middle-class demo-cratic and permissive mothers and fathers are more likely to give explanations for their policies than are other parents. (E105)

### Child-Rearing Practices (Impulse Control)

Middle-class parents permit less free play of the impulses of their children than do lower-class parents.

### Child-Rearing Practices (Isolation)

Middle-class and upper-class parents are both observed to utilize consistent, as distinct from idiosyncratic, isola-tion to avert the child's adoption of deviant goals and practices. (C086)

### Child-Rearing Practices (Lying)

There is no significant difference between working-class and middle-class families regarding the teaching of atti-tudes toward lying. (B235)

### Child-Rearing Practices (Material Values)

Working-class families tend to instill in their children greater concern for material objects than do upper mid-dle-class families. (B235)

### Child-Rearing Practices (Mechanical Restrictions)

Mechanical restrictions (playpen, crib, or baby tender) are used more frequently by upper-class than by lower-class Negro parents. (W133)

### Child-Rearing Practices (Motor Freedom)

Lower-class Negro parents allow their babies more free-dom to experiment (exercise their motor functions and experiment with motion) than do upper-class Negro parents. (W133)

### Child-Rearing Practices (Permissiveness)

Lower-class Negro mothers are more likely to be per-missive in their handling of their children than are mid-dle-class Negro mothers. (B272)

Lower-class families are more likely to be easygoing and permissive in child-rearing practices than are middle-class families. (C023)

Middle-class families are more permissive in child rear-ing than are lower-class families. (G156)

Middle-class parents were more restrictive than work-ing-class parents 25 years ago, but now they are more permissive and the gap between them is narrowing. (K089)

Child rearing in the lower classes tends to be more puni-tive, less permissive than in upper-class families. (M058)

Parents of lower-class children are more likely to permit fuller gratification of organically based drives than are parents of middle-class children. (R127)

### Child-Rearing Practices of Father (Punishment)

The fathers of lower-class mentally ill patients tend to be physically violent at times, more than do fathers of mid-dle-class patients. (M061)

### Child-Rearing Practices (Physical Neglect)

Physically neglected (underfed, dirty, etc.) children are more likely to be found in the lower classes than in the upper classes. (Y043)

### Child-Rearing Practices (Political Indoctrination)

At higher-class levels, mothers are more likely to be attuned to cultural change and innovation and, there-fore, less likely to indoctrinate children in the parental views on politics. (H244)

### Child-Rearing Practices (Power)

Working-class parents are more likely to use unqualified power assertion over their children than are middle-class parents, and working-class mothers are less likely than working-class fathers to do so. (H182)

### Child-Rearing Practices (Punishment)

The higher the class, the greater the preference for "psychological" punishment (i.e., discipline that ad-dresses itself to the child as a personality) rather than physical punishment (Indonesia). (D065)

Middle-class parents tend to use less physical punish-ment than lower-class parents and rely more on appeals to guilt and the threat of the withdrawal of love. (L169)

Middle-class mothers whose husbands have entrepre-neurial jobs are more likely than lower-class mothers (entrepreneurial) to favor symbolic punishments instead of spanking and slapping. (M062)

The higher the socioeconomic status of the parents, the less punitive and controlling are their child-rearing prac-tices. (R090)

Social rank is negatively related to the extent of retaliatory child-rearing practices (e.g., rejection, rigidity, and punitiveness). (R107)

Lower-class parents tend to punish their children physically much more than do middle-class parents. (R127)

More punishment is applied to children of working-class families than of middle-class families, but the difference is greater with respect to object-oriented than to love-oriented techniques (U.S.). (S191)

Regardless of educational level, middle-class mothers use ridicule as a technique of discipline less than working-class mothers do. (S191)

Regardless of educational level, middle-class mothers use isolation as a technique of discipline more than working-class mothers do. (S191)

Middle-class mothers and better-educated working-class mothers punish their children less often physically or by depriving them of privileges than do lesser-educated working-class mothers (U.S.). (S191)

### Child-Rearing Practices (Responsibility)
Middle-class parents place more emphasis on an early assumption of responsibility than do lower-class parents.

### Child-Rearing Practices (Restrictiveness)
Middle-class mothers impose fewer restrictions and demands on children than do working-class mothers (U.S.). (S191)

Middle-class mothers are less restrictive of free-range exploration by their children than are lower-class mothers (U.S.). (S191)

Middle-class mothers are less restrictive regarding activity in the home than are lower-class mothers (U.S.). (S191)

Middle-class British families were more inclined to impose restrictions on the children with respect to neatness in the house, being quiet, going to bed promptly, etc., than were the working-class families of British origin. (S191)

Discipline is more restrictive among upper-class than among lower-class Negro families. (W133)

### Child-Rearing Practices (Rewards)
Socioeconomic rank and the use of rewards in socialization are not associated.

### Child-Rearing Practices (Rewards and Punishment)
More middle-class parents than lower-class parents used reward or praise as a successful technique of discipline. (L003)

More middle-class mothers than lower-class mothers use withdrawal of love as a technique of discipline. (L003)

More middle-class parents than lower-class parents deprive children of privileges as a technique of discipline (Boston). (L003)

More lower-class parents than middle-class parents use physical punishment as a technique of discipline (Boston). (L003)

There is no significant difference between the middle-class parents and lower-class parents in the techniques of discipline used. (L003)

### Child-Rearing Practices (Scheduling)
Middle-class parents are stricter in dealing with their children than are lower-class parents with respect to age at which the child takes a nap and time when the child must be home at night.

### Child-Rearing Practices (Severity)
The lower the social class, the more severe child-training methods are likely to be. (K160)

### Child-Rearing Practices (Sex)
The lower class is less permissive of the sexual activities of their children than are middle-class parents. (L003)

Working-class mothers are far less permissive and more punitive than middle-class mothers toward sex exploration, and their sex training is much more severe. (S191)

Middle-class mothers and better-educated working-class mothers are more permissive about sex behavior in their children than are lesser-educated working-class mothers (U.S.). (S191)

### Child-Rearing Practices (Sex Role)
There is a decrease in the differential treatment of boys and girls by parents with an increase in socioeconomic status. (B273)

### Child-Rearing Practices (Sleeping)
Upper-class Negro parents enforce more rigid sleeping schedules than do lower-class Negro parents. (W133)

### Child-Rearing Practices (Strictness)
Middle-class parents place their children under a stricter regimen than do lower-class parents. (D065)

Parents of high socioeconomic status use more strict child-rearing methods than do parents of lower socioeconomic status (Chicago Negroes). (F117)

There is no significant difference between the middle class and the working class in which parent is stricter with the child. (W002)

Fathers are reported to be stricter with the child in both the middle class and the working class. (W002)

There is no significant difference between the middle class and the working class in the strictness of parents in requiring obedience. (W002)

Middle-class mothers are more inclined to drop the subject occasionally if the child does not do what was asked than are working-class mothers. (W002)

### Child-Rearing Practices (Supervision)
A greater part of the activity of the upper-class child comes under the purview of adults—kin, functionaries, and others—than is true of the middle-class child. (C086)

### Child-Rearing Practices (Television)
The higher the status group to which the mother belongs, the more likely she is to set restrictions on the television programs watched by her children. (H178)

### Child-Rearing Values
Working-class parents are concerned more about the act and its consequences; middle-class parents far more about the motive for the act. (K089)

Working-class parents value obedience, neatness, and cleanliness more than do middle-class parents. Middle-class parents value curiosity, happiness, consideration, and self-control more highly than do working-class parents. (K089)

Middle-class values about child rearing are about the same, whether parents read expert advice, or popular newspapers and magazines, or nothing at all; but working-class parents who read books have middle-class values, as against the working-class parents who do not read; the latter have lower-class values. (K089)

Middle-class parents feel obliged to be supportive of their children, while working-class values emphasize constraints which the children must accept. (K089)

Middle-class parental values are more acceptant and equalitarian, while working-class parental values are oriented toward maintaining order and obedience. (K089) There is no significant difference in the reading of magazines and newspapers as sources of ideas about child rearing between middle-class mothers and working-class mothers. (W002)

Expert books as a source of ideas about child rearing are mentioned more by middle-class mothers than by working-class mothers. (W002)

People or friends as sources of ideas about child rearing are mentioned more by middle-class mothers than by working-class mothers (U.S.). (W002)

There is no significant difference in the use of child-rearing authorities as sources of ideas for child rearing between middle-class mothers and working-class mothers (U.S.). (W002)

### Child-Rearing Values (Aggression)
Working-class fathers are more likely than are middle-class fathers to regard the child's ability to defend himself as important. (K110)

### Child-Rearing Values (Cleanliness)
Working-class mothers value cleanliness and neatness in their children more than do middle-class mothers. (K110)

### Child-Rearing Values (Conformity)
Working-class parents are more concerned than are middle-class parents with actions and qualities in their children that assure respectability, thus emphasizing socially prescribed patterns. (B275)

Working-class parental values center on conformity to external prescriptions; middle-class parental values on self-direction. (K089)

Working-class parents want the child to conform to externally imposed standards, while middle-class parents are more attentive to the child's internal dynamics. (K089)

### Child-Rearing Values (Curiosity)
Middle-class mothers are more likely than are working-class mothers to regard curiosity as desirable in their children. (K110)

### Child-Rearing Values (Dependability)
Middle-class fathers are more likely than are working-class fathers to value dependability in their chidren. (K110)

### Child-Rearing Values (Dependency)
Working-class parents are more likely to want their children to conform to externally imposed standards (as opposed to self-direction) than are middle-class parents. (K089)

### Child-Rearing Values (Happiness)
Working-class mothers are less likely than are middle-class mothers to regard happiness as highly desirable for their boys. (K110)

Middle-class mothers are more likely to view happiness for their children as comprising curiosity and ambition, while working-class mothers relate happiness to honesty and popularity. (K110)

### Child-Rearing Values (Honesty)
Parents of both working and middle class tend to regard honesty as of primary importance in the child. (K110)

### Child-Rearing Values (Honesty/Popularity)
If working-class mothers value honesty, they are less likely to value popularity in their children; among middle-class mothers, evaluation of these two traits is associated positively (U.S.). (K110)

### Child-Rearing Values (Obedience)
Working-class parents put more stress on obedience to parental commands than do middle-class parents. (K089)

Working-class parents are more likely than are middle-class parents to value obedience to parental authority. (K110)

### Child-Rearing Values (Self-Control)
Middle-class parents are more likely than are working-class parents to value self-control in their children. (K110)

### Child-Rearing Values (Social Adjustment)
Middle-class parents are more concerned with the child's ability to get along with others (e.g., his friendliness, cooperativeness) than are working-class parents. (K110)

### Child-Rearing Values (Sympathy)
Middle-class parents are more likely than are working-class parents to value the development of sympathetic concern for other people in their children. (K110)

### Chores
There is a positive correlation between class and sharing of household duties when the wife is working. (G134)

### Cognitive Development
The degree of intellectual growth is directly correlated with the position of the family in the class structure. (B033)

### Cohesion of Extended Kin
The kinship ties of people from upper-upper economic brackets tend to be closer than those of people from average-income backgrounds. (C134)

### Cohesion of Kin-Group
Members of the upper class will make a greater effort to preserve the solidarity of the kin-group. (W098)

### Conformity
Toward the higher social strata, there is greater conformity with ideal family patterns. (B033)

Members of the upper class are expected to conform more rigorously to the norms of the community. (F014)

### Consensus in Family
The higher the social status of the family, the higher the degree of consensus among the family members. (D061)

### Dating
There is a curvilinear relationship between social-status levels and number of steady dates for men; an inverse relationship obtains for women. (B248)

There is no relationship between social-class level and the tendency to date/not date persons not attending school. (B248)

### Dependency
Lower-class paranoid schizophrenics show more dependence on their mothers, but less dependence on the family as a whole, than do middle-class paranoid schizophrenics. (L155)

Middle-class children are more dependent on displays of warmth and love for a sense of security and belonging than are lower-class children. (M061)

There is no correlation between adolescents' degree of felt emancipation from their parents and the socioeconomic status of their families. (T100)

The lower the social class, the more likely it is that the adolescent perceives himself as independent from his parents. (T100)

There is no significant difference in the dependence of the child between the middle class and the working class. (W002)

There is no significant difference in the amount of attention the child wants between the middle class and the working class. (W002)

### Descent (Patrilineal)
The upper class, inasmuch as it tends to stress the status of ancestors, will give greater importance to the patrilineal line of descent (U.S.). (P012)

### Desertion
Because of the growing system of bureaucratic records, marital desertion remains possible only for lower-class persons. (G156)

### Deviance, Visibility of
The lower the social class, the more visible to the community is the deviant social behavior of a family (child abuse, separation, nonsupport, etc.). (Y043)

### Disorganization of Family
Psychologically disturbed children from the lower class are more likely to come from a family atmosphere of physical tension and disorganization than are those from middle-class homes. (M197)

Disorganized families (either broken homes or those with poor authority patterns) are more likely to be found in the lower classes than in the upper. (Y043)

### Division of Labor by Sex
Low-income families with both husband and wife working show a greater deviation from the traditional division of labor as compared with high-income families with both husband and wife working.

### Divorce
Being divorced is more characteristic of tenant families than of owner families. (C009)

As the upper-class wives' economic needs are granted better legal protection, creating dependence upon their husbands, upper-class women are "freer" to leave their spouses. (G156)

Prior to the late nineteenth century, the divorce rate was highest in the upper classes (U.S.). (G156)

In societies where equal access to divorce is granted to all classes, the divorce rates will be higher among the lower classes. (G156)

Structural hindrances to divorce are fewer among families of low socioeconomic status than among high-ranking lineages. (P083)

Divorce among commoners is more frequent than among aristocrats. (W108)

### Divorce, Age at
A woman is more likely to initiate divorce when she reaches old age if she is of the upper class, for by returning to her kinsmen she maximizes status by reassociating with kin in positions of power. (G142)

### Divorce, Attitude Toward
The higher the class, the more liberal the attitudes toward divorce. (G156)

### Duration of Marriage
The lower the class, the shorter the average duration of marriage. (G157)

### Economic Dependence of Women
The economic independence of women is more likely to occur among the lower economic groups in urban areas. (G056)

### Education Difference Between Husband-Wife
A great difference in formal education between husband and wife is less likely to occur between spouses in the lower than in the middle or upper classes, because husbands in the latter cases are likely to have received considerable formal education, but in the lower stratas neither husbands nor wives have had much education. (P083)

### Education of Parents/Class X Scholastic Motivation of Child
Educational level of parents has a greater effect on high academic motivation in the child than does social class. (E102)

### Educational Aspirations
There is a high correlation between socioeconomic class and parental stress on college, this largely accounts for the relationship between class and the desire of the child to attend college. (B291)

### Educational Aspirations of Child
The family's feeling about whether the child should be expected to go to college is more strongly related to socioeconomic status than to the mother's education, although both make a difference. (S191)

### Educational Aspirations of Parents
Middle-class parents place greater emphasis on their children going to college than do lower-class parents. (E102)

### Emotional Problems of Child (Toilet Training)
There is no difference between lower- and middle-class children in the emotional disturbances caused by toilet training (U.S.). (S191)

### Employment of Mother
Lower-class mothers are more likely to have to work than are middle-class mothers. (G156)

Mothers in lower socioeconomic classes are more likely than those in the upper socioeconomic classes to be employed. (N057)

### Employment of Mother, Attitude Toward
Negative attitudes toward mothers who work tend to be strongest in those classes where the work is not an economic necessity. (G015)

Poorer-class mothers are more concerned about the effects of their working on their children than are better-off mothers. (Y047)

### Employment of Wife, Attitude Toward
More lower-class husbands object to their wives' working than do husbands from other classes. (K150)

### Endogamy
Endogamy is more common in the lowest and the highest social strata. (B013)

Patterns of community endogamy are more likely to be violated by members of the upper class. (W117)

### Engagement, Duration of
The period of engagement or betrothal is longer toward the upper strata. (G156)

### Extended Kin Relations (Interaction)
The greater the disparity in social class between kin, the less contact is likely between them.

### Extended Kin Ties
The extended family appears to have a better chance of resistance to the forces of industrialization among the wealthy and official classes than among the poor. (B033)

The mobility of a lower-class family member is less encumbered than that of family members in other classes by a commitment to an extended family system. (G156)

### Father Absence
Lower-class families are more likely to have women as the heads of households than are middle-class or upper-class families. (F003)

The mother-centered type of family structure is more common in Negro and white populations of the lower class. (P012)

### Father-Child Relations
Lower-class fathers are less affectionate than middle-class fathers. (H011)

Lower-class fathers "play with" their children more than do middle-class fathers, but middle-class fathers teach and read to their children more than lower-class fathers. (H011)

There is no class difference in the amount of caretaking by fathers. (H011)

Lower-class fathers of mentally ill children tend to be cruel and rejecting, while middle-class fathers are passive and ineffectual. (S187)

### Father-Child Relations (Supportive)
Middle-class fathers are more likely than working-class fathers to be supportive of their children. (R129)

Middle-class boys are considerably more likely than working-class boys to have supportive fathers, but middle-class girls are only slightly, if at all, more likely than working-class girls to have supportive fathers; the same relationship exists when father-child relationships are compared between upper- and lower-class boys and girls. (R129)

### Father-Son Relations
Middle-class men are more likely to be work-oriented and to reject both strong family ties in general and strong ties with their fathers; this is in contrast with men from upper-class families, who are less oriented toward work as a field of accomplishment, have stronger positive family feelings, and respect their fathers more. (L115)

### Fecundity
There is no consistent difference in fecundity between major social and economic strata. (F101)

### Feeding
Socioeconomic status and feeding practices are not associated (U.S.). (S191)

Upper-class Negro parents enforce more rigid feeding schedules than do lower-class Negro parents. (W133)

### Feeding (Demand)
A greater percentage of lower-class children than of middle-class children are fed whenever they are hungry (U.S.). (L003)

### Fertility
Although there is a negative correlation between socioeconomic level and fertility, this relationship tends to change from negative to positive at the highest levels. (A065)

In the areas occupied by middle-class families, there are more children than in areas of extreme poverty and family disorganization (U.S. Negro). (F078)

Before the introduction of effective contraceptives, the upper classes were more likely to have a higher birth rate. (G156)

The lower the class, the higher the birth rate. This relationship does not hold. (G156)

There is no correlation between fertility and class. (I007)

Increase in fertility is directly related to socioeconomic class. (K004)

Fertility rates are likely to be higher in the upper middle and upper classes than in the middle middle and lower middle classes, particularly where the societal value system fosters pride in lineage, because the upper classes have more resources for hiring mother surrogates and the middle classes are more concerned with concentrating more limited resources on fewer children and greater success. (P083)

Among couples who have planned their fertility most completely, a positive relationship exists between fertility and socioeconomic status. (R119)

### Fertility (Real/Ideal)
Socioeconomic position is directly correlated with both actual and ideal size of family, the latter always being higher than the average actual number of children. (Y046)

Lower-class mothers tend to express ideals of family size smaller than the intended size; this discrepancy is reversed among average and high-status mothers. (Y046)

### Fertility Values
The higher the class (measured by income, education, and occupation), the larger the desired family size. (Y049)

### Genealogical Depth
The generational depth of the genealogies of the aristocratic class will tend to be greater than that of the lower classes. (K045)

### Geographic Mobility
Upper upper-class families are more likely to be residentially stable than are other classes. (C134)

### Happiness in Childhood
Middle-class children are more likely to perceive their homes as pleasant places to live than are lower-class children. (R127)

### Homogamy
Among women, those who marry into a different class are more likely to marry upward. (G156)

Girls from high social origins are more likely to marry homogamously than those from lower social backgrounds. (K150)

### Household Composition
Middle-class households are more likely to contain aged parents and their children and grandchildren than are lower-class families. (B312)

### Husband-Wife Relations (Affection)
The higher the social rank of the married partners, the greater the expression of love and affection. (G157)

Romantic attachment and emotional involvement are lower among married couples in the lower strata. (G157)

### Husband-Wife Relations (Authority)
Husbands in the lower strata are more likely to be authoritarian. (G157)

Wives in lower-class families are less likely to object to husband dominance. (G157)

### Husband-Wife Relations (Closeness)
The higher the married couple's social rank, the more likely they are to turn to each other for help in trouble and the less likely they are to turn their negative feelings against each other. (G157)

### Husband-Wife Relations (Communication)
Married couples of high social rank communicate their emotional problems more often than do couples of lower social rank. (G157)

### Husband-Wife Relations (Dependency)
As the potential for the woman to earn as much as her husband decreases with class, the higher the class, the more financially dependent the woman is upon her husband. (G156)

### Husband-Wife Relations, Evaluation of
Regardless of educational level, middle-class mothers admire their husbands more and quarrel less with them over the way children should be raised than do working-class mothers (U.S.). (S191)

### Husband-Wife Relations (Interaction)
White collar families report more husband-wife interaction than do blue collar families. (H201)

### Husband-Wife Relations (Intimacy)
Lower-class couples are less willing to share confidences. (G157)

The higher the social class, the greater the social and psychological resources to maintain role complementarity and emotional compatibility or to minimize marital contact when contact is frustrating. (P083)

### Husband-Wife Relations (Power)
Regardless of the sex of the spouse, the more dominant tends to come from the family of higher socioeconomic status. (W148)

### Identification
Middle-class parents are more likely than lower-class parents to provide effective identification figures for their children during childhood. (M197)

### Illegitimacy
Lower-class unions are more likely to be common-law and have illegitimate children than are unions in other classes. (C134)

The lower the social class, the less commitment there is to the family norm of legitimacy. (G151)

The lower the social stratum, the higher the illegitimacy rate. (G156)

### Illegitimacy (Adoption)
There is no correlation between social class and the Catholic mother's tendency to keep her illegitimate child. (J020)

Unwed mothers who kept their children came from families of lower socioeconomic status than did those who released their children for adoption. (V027)

### Illegitimacy, Attitude Toward
A society disapproves less of illegitimacy when it occurs in the lower social ranks. (G156)

### Illegitimacy Rate
The lower the social stratum, the higher the illegitimacy rate. (G156)

### Incest
Violation of incest taboos is more likely to be characteristic of the upper or ruling class. (Q001)

### Income of Husband/Wife
The higher the socioeconomic stratum, the greater is the difference between the income of the husband and wife. (G134)

### Intermarriage (Religious)
The percentage of Catholic marriages which are mixed marriages varies directly with social class, as reflected in graded rental areas. (T010)

### I.Q.
### X  Size of Family by Class
The larger the family (number of siblings), the lower the intelligence level of the child; this relationship declines at the higher socioeconomic levels and may even be reversed. (A065)

### Joint Family
Joint families in India are more common among upper-class families than among lower-class families. (M081)

### Juvenile Delinquency
Boys who are frequent juvenile offenders are more

likely to be from low socioeconomic classes than are boys who have one offense. (G144)

The lower the socioeconomic status of the parents, the more likely it is that the child will become delinquent. (G144)

If the child belongs to a noncohesive home in a higher-class neighborhood, he is less likely to become delinquent than is a child who belongs to a noncohesive home in a poor neighborhood. (M194)

Mobile lower-class families are more likely than mobile upper-class families to produce delinquent children. (N057)

There is no correlation between social class of the family and delinquent behavior in the child. (N063)

Among residentially mobile families, there is no correlation between class and delinquency in the child. (N063)

### Kin Network
The higher the socioeconomic stratum, the more extended and tightly organized is the network of kin relations. (G134)

### Kin/Nonkin Interaction
In the United States, lower-middle and middle-middle classes, the frequency of relations with the collateral and affinal network is lower than is the frequency of relations with the occupational peer group and the neighborhood. (P083)

### Kin Relations
Controlling for family size, there appears to be no significant correlation between social class and active maintenance of kin relations. (R084)

### Kin Relations (Interaction)
Blue collar migrants have more contact with their relatives than do white collar migrants. (J033)

Upper-class persons tend to visit their extended family more often than do lower-class persons. (S265)

### Kin Terminology
Members of the lower class tend to use informal variants more frequently than do members of higher social classes. (B083)

The restriction of kin ties to encompass only members of the immediate nuclear family tends to occur among members of the lowest classes in urban areas. (G056)

### Kin Ties
Kinship ties are geographically more extended toward the higher social strata. (Q001)

Family ties tend to persist more among peasant and lower-class groups than among upper classes in a situation of social change (family reforms). (T073)

### Kin Ties (Fictive)
Among members of the upper class, the establishment of fictive kin ties tends to occur with kinsmen rather than with nonkinsmen. (F049)

Deterioration of patterns of fictive kinship is most likely to occur among the economically mobile upper and middle classes and the industrial wage-earning working class. (M080)

The higher one's social class, the smaller the likelihood of being addressed by a stranger as a kinsman. (N012)

### Kinship, Importance of
A deterioration of the importance of kinship is most likely to occur in the economically mobile upper and middle classes and in the industrial wage-earning working class. (M080)

### Legal Status of Wife
The higher the class, the greater is the legal protection of the wife's financial needs. (G156)

### Love
The role of romantic love in originating marriage is less in the upper classes. (P083)

### Marital Adjustment
There is a positive correlation between socioeconomic class and marital satisfaction scores. (G134)

Lower-class paranoid schizophrenics see their parents as more ill-suited for each other than do middle-class paranoid schizophrenics. (L155)

Marital adjustment of spouses varies directly with their social class. (R011)

Marital adjustment does not have any association with the social class of the spouse's parents, except that the lower-lower class has poorer adjustment than the other classes. (R011)

### Marital Adjustment of Wife
The higher the husband's social status, the more likely is the wife to value the marriage as highly satisfactory. (R011)

### Marital Stability
Marital stability is lower among the lower classes. (G156)

### Marital Status
Consensual and casual unions are more common toward the lower social strata. (C024)

Remarried persons are more likely to be found in somewhat lower-class strata than are those who stay married. (G157)

### Marriage, Attitude Toward
Middle-class and upper-class marriages are likely to be more oriented toward the child or family as a whole than are lower-class marriages, which tend to be more oriented toward the compatibility of the husband and wife, with less concern for responsibility for the children. (C121)

### Marriage Chances
The higher the social rank of the woman, the more likely she is to remain unmarried. (H222)

### Marriage, Goals of
The higher the class, the more willing the family is to subordinate tension reduction to other functions of marriage (such as representation and socialization) and to duties to uphold the dominant mores concerning the "sanctity" of marriage. (P083)

### Marriage Payment
In societies where there are marriage exchanges (e.g., bride price or dowry systems), the economic exchanges between the bride's family and the groom's family are more likely to approach equality toward the upper strata than toward the lower strata. (G156)

### Mate Selection
Similar social backgrounds increase the likelihood that a couple will marry one another. (G134)

Where marriage is viewed as an exchange, equivalence of social rank is likely to be the rule between contracting families. (P083)

### Mate Selection (Free Choice)
Where parents are in control of marriage arrangement, social standing, economic status, and financial return are the major considerations in mate selection. (B033)

European patterns of individual choice in marriage tend to be more common among the poorer groups. (G056)

The higher the social rank of the family, the less freedom allowed in courtship. (G156)

Parental influence tends to be greater in the selection of a mate toward the upper classes. (R062)

### Mate Selection (Near Kin)
Among the upper classes, marriage with near kin is more likely than among the lower classes. (S140)

### Maternal Overprotectiveness
The higher the social status of the mother, the more likely she is to be overprotective toward the child. (H183)

Male schizophrenics from the middle class are more likely to have overprotective mothers than are those from the lower class. (M197)

### Maternal Role
Mothers of lower-class mental patients are more likely than mothers of middle-class mental patients to have almost sole responsibility for family affairs, have little time for the patients, and have difficulty maintaining order in the household. (M061)

Working-class mothers are more likely to have sole responsibility for family affairs, have less time for their children, and have more difficulty in maintaining order in the home than middle-class mothers. (M197)

### Maternal Role, Attitude Toward
Middle-class mothers are less sure about the adequacy of their maternal-role performance than are upper- or lower-class mothers. (S280)

### Maternal-Role Definition
The higher the socioeconomic class, the more likely it is that the wife will stress the activity of maintaining personal relationships over that of routine housekeeping. (S243)

Upper- and middle-class mothers are less likely to accept the "service" aspects of the maternal role than are lower-class mothers. (S280)

The aspect of the maternal role most likely stressed among lower-class mothers is caring for physical needs; among middle-class mothers, it is development of character and morality; and among upper-class mothers, it is handling social and emotional needs. (S280)

### Mental Deficiency, Attitude Toward
The class of the family is directly correlated with the degree to which the mental defective is defined as abnormal. (P065)

### Mental Illness
The psychopathological processes of antisocial character disorders appear to be the same regardless of the economic or social status of the family. (B310)

The severity and frequency of any particular type of psychopathology are greater in the lower classes than in the upper. (B310)

Social status is negatively correlated with mental illness, regardless of a person's marital status (single, married, divorced, etc.). (H222)

### Mental Illness (Hospitalization)
Families of low social status are likely to leave a psychotic member of the family in a mental institution for a longer period of years than are families of high social status. (H222)

### Mental Illness, Mother's Response to
Lower-class mothers of mentally ill children tend to be more overprotective, whereas upper- and middle-class mothers tend to reject the schizophrenic child. (S187)

### Mental Illness of Child (Schizophrenia) X Mother-Child Relations (Affection)
In the lower class, there is a correlation between lack of maternal affection and schizophrenia in the child; in the middle class, the correlation is between schizophrenia and maternal overprotectiveness and overambitiousness for the child. (P078)

### Mental Illness (Schizophrenia)/Aggression
Lower-class paranoid schizophrenics are less likely to verbalize their symptoms and are more likely to manifest them through hostile acts than are middle-class paranoid schizophrenics. (L155)

### Mental Illness (Social Adjustment)
The higher the social class of his family, the higher the level of posthospital social and work performance of the mental patient. (F124)

There is no relationship between social class of the family and the patient's success or failure in remaining in the community. (F124)

Lower-class patients are less likely to return to their families after discharge from psychiatric institutions than are those from middle-class families. (R083)

### Mental Problems
Family members of low social status are less likely to be aware of psychological problems of self and others than are family members of higher social status. (H222)

### Mother-Child Relations (Affection)
Middle-class mothers are more responsive to their babies' crying than are working-class mothers. (W002)

There is no significant difference between middle-class and working-class mothers in the amount of fun they have in taking care of their babies. (W002)

There is no significant difference between the middle-class and working-class mothers in their warmth of demonstrativeness. (W002)

### Mother-Child Relations (Closeness)
Middle-class mental patients show a greater involvement with their mothers than do lower-class mental patients. (R127)

### Mother-Child Relations (Favoritism)
Girls from upper middle-class homes are more likely to attribute preference for a male child to the mother than are girls from the lower classes. (H181)

### Mother-Child Relations (Idealization)
Lower-class paranoid schizophrenics express greater idealization of their mothers than do middle-class paranoid schizophrenics. (L155)

### Mother-Child Relations (Interaction)
Lower-class working mothers are less likely to allocate particular time periods to spend with their children or to organize activities with them than are middle-class working mothers. (G156)

The mothers of lower-class mentally ill patients tend to spend less time with them than do those of middle-class patients. (M061)

### Mother-Child Relations (Interest)
The mothers of lower-class mentally ill patients tend to show less concern for their children's personality development than do mothers of middle-class patients. (M061)

### Mother-Child Relations (Succorance)
As opposed to lower-class mothers whose husbands have entrepreneurial jobs, middle-class mothers (entrepreneurial) are less likely to give immediate attention to babies who cry when nothing serious is wrong with them. (M062)

### Mother-Child Relations (Warmth)
When mothers of the same educational level but of different socioeconomic rank are compared, we find that middle-class mothers are more affectionately warm toward their children and less likely to display rejection (U.S.). (S191)

Among Irish families, social class and warmth of mother toward the child are not associated. (S191)

### Mother-Daughter Relations
The urban lower class is more likely than other segments of the population to stress the kinship tie between mother and daughter. (P062)

### Mother-Son Relations (Possessiveness)
The higher the family's socioeconomic class, the less likely it is that the mother will be overly possessive. (F119)

### Neurosis
The higher the unmarried mother's socioeconomic status, the more disturbed she is. (Y048)

### Ordinal Position X Occupational Aspirations of Son
Firstborn middle-class sons are slightly more likely than those born later to have high occupational aspirations. The reverse is true for lower-class boys. (E102)

### Parent-Child Relations
The higher the class, the more likely are the parents to treat the child as an individual rather than as a part of a collectivity (Indonesia). (D065)

Adjustment of adolescents to parents varies directly with socioeconomic level when the fact that the home is broken or unbroken is held constant. The association, however, is stronger in unbroken homes. This relationship also holds when farm-nonfarm residence is held constant. (N010)

In an achievement-oriented society, the lower classes give less support to the family socialization functions; in lower-class families, extrafamilial-role participations by the children are likely to lead to disenchantment with their parents. (P083)

### Parent-Child Relations (Affection)
Parent-child relations are more ambilvalent (greater threat of withdrawal of affection) in middle than in lower classes. (W143)

Middle-class children are more likely to identify success with parental affection than are lower-class children. (W143)

### Parent-Child Relations (Conflict)
Tension between parents and children in the lower-middle class is expressed more mildly between parents and children in the lower class. (M061)

The expression of tension between parents and children in the lower-middle class is more verbal, with violence being condemned, while in the lower class, tension is less verbally expressed. (M061)

### Parent-Child Relations (Control)
The more social benefits a family has to offer, the more able they will be to control the actions of their children. (G156)

Parental affection is a more powerful instrument of control in mental patients of the middle classes than of the lower classes. (M061)

### Parent-Child Relations (Egalitarianism)
The higher the class of the parents, the more equalitarian and acceptant they are with their children. (M180)

### Parent-Child Relations (Employment)
Upper middle-class children are more likely than lower middle- and working-class children to judge the work of their parents as pleasant. (H222)

### Parent-Child Relations (Help)
Parental financial assistance is more likely to be given to middle-class than to working-class children. (A066)

Parental assistance (babysitting, help in sickness, and childbirth, etc.) are more likely to be given to working-class children than to middle-class children. (A066)

### Parent-Child Relations (Hostility)
Lower-class paranoids are more likely to deny any hostility toward their parents than are middle-class paranoids. (S187)

### Parent-Child Relations (Interaction)
Social withdrawal of adolescents from their families, as measured by leisure time spent away from the home, is greater in the lower class than in the middle class. (S219)

### Parent-Child Relations (Obedience)
Middle-class children are more obedient of parental authority than are lower-class children. (S210)

### Parent-Child Relations (Rebellion)
Lower-class mentally ill patients and their siblings tend to rebel against parental control more than do middle-class patients. (M061)

### Parent-Child Relations (Rejection)
Lower-class paranoid schizophrenics experience more feelings of rejection from their parents, particularly from

their fathers, than do middle-class paranoid schizophrenics. (L155)

Children from lower-status families are more likely to reject their families than are children from higher-status backgrounds. (S274)

### Parental-Role Definition
Upper-class parents tend to assert their absolute rank vis-à-vis their children more than do middle-class parents. (C086)

### Paternal-Role Behavior
Fathers of lower-class mental patients are more likely than fathers of middle-class patients to have been feared; generally, however, they were uninvolved in family affairs. (M061)

The fathers of mentally ill lower-class patients tend to display less interest in household affairs than do fathers of middle-class patients. (M061)

### Paternal-Role Definition
Fathers are more apt to hold a position of marginality of role in the family in the lower classes than in the middle classes. (S080)

### Personality Adjustment
Middle-class child-rearing practices are more likely than are lower-class child-rearing practices to cause frustration and anxiety that inhibit good mental health in later years.

### Personality Problems
The lower the social class of the unwed mother, the more likely she is to be psychologically disturbed. The contrary hypothesis is also asserted. (S224)

### Political Attitudes
Since overtly expressed opposition to political regimes by parents varies *inversely* with class level, parent-youth solidarity in terms of political conflict also varies inversely with social-class level. (G019)

### Polygyny
In societies where polygyny is practiced, the higher the man's social or economic position, the more likely is he to have more than one wife. (G156)

### Power Structure of Families with Mentally Ill Members
Three clusters of interpersonal relations and child-rearing practices were found among *middle-class* parents more than among lower-class parents of mental patients: 1) the mother played a more dominant role in family power structure as well as in child-rearing process; 2) the father participated more in family life than in the lower class, but the children questioned his masculinity; 3) parental control of children was primarily verbal, but was more effective than that in the lower class. (M061)

### Power Structure of Family
Familial relations between members of the lower class tend to be both more egalitarian and more intimate. (B083)

Middle-class adolescents are more apt to report their fathers as dominant in conjugal and child-rearing relations than are lower-class adolescents, while lower-class adolescents are more apt to report their mothers as dominant in these areas. (B323)

Lower-class families are more likely to be matriarchies than are families of other classes. (C134)

Lower-class families are more likely to be patriarchal than are families of other classes. (C134)

The higher the social class, the greater the man's influence in the family. (G156)

Middle-class children are more likely to view the father as more powerful than are children from lower socio-economic strata. (H180)

The higher the social rank of families, the less the power of the sons and the greater the power of the fathers. (M060)

The mother's power in decision making does seem to be influenced by class status. (M060)

### Preferential Marriage
A preferential marriage pattern is more likely to be adopted if it is associated with a group which is prestigious. (C060)

### Preferential Marriage (Cross-Cousin)
The decline in the adherence to preferential marriage patterns tends to occur more commonly among the middle class than among members of the lower class. (P023)

### Pregnancy, Attitude Toward
There is an inverse relationship between a woman's social status and her perception of pregnancy as an illness. (R107)

Middle-class mothers tend to be more pleased about the advent of a new child than do lower-class mothers (U.S.). (S191)

### Premarital Sex Relations
Premarital intercourse is more likely to occur between people of the same social class than across class lines; when class lines are crossed, premarital intercourse is most likely between males of a higher and females of a lower social class. (E092)

In Western countries, premarital sexual intercourse begins at an earlier age among men in the lower strata. (G156)

The preservation of premarital chastity will tend to be of greater concern to members of the upper class. (R040)

There is an inverse correlation between class and premarital sexual activity for men, but not for women. (S219)

### Psychotherapy, Attitude Toward
Middle-class families are more likely to acknowledge mental illness in their members and to support therapeutic treatment than are lower-class families. (M197)

### Recreation
Family and kinship play a more important role in providing for companionship and recreational needs among urban working-class people than among urban people at a higher social rank. (D010)

Children of middle-class parents take out physical and sexual drives in ritualized forms (e.g., sports competition) more than lower-class children do. (R127)

## Religion
Religion is a more potent factor in the family life of the working-class family than in the business-class or university family. (B033)

## Residence
The tendency for residential propinquity to operate in mate selection is greater among the lower socioeconomic groups than among the higher ones. (C023)

Old people are more apt to live with other generations of their family when they are of the middle class than when they are of other classes (Vienna). (R120)

## Residence with Parents
There is no significant relationship between the social class of the children and living with their aged parents or in independent households. (G119)

## Rituals in Family
As one moves upward in the social scale, family rituals increase in number, variety, richness, and willing cooperation by individual family members. (B004)

## Role Behavior
Socialization processes operate so that those socialized in upper-class families will tend to assume more "parental" roles toward most others, whereas those socialized in families at lower levels tend to assume more "child" roles. (P062)

## Role Definition in Family
Considering the family as a triad of roles—High Status Authority (HSA), Low Status Subordinate (LSS), and High Status Friend (HSF)—the lower-class parent is more likely to play the role of HSA to a child of the same sex than is a middle-class parent, while in the middle class, a parent is more apt to play both roles, regardless of child's sex.

## Role Definition of Husband-Wife
Lower-class husbands are less likely than middle-class husbands to share housekeeping tasks. (G157)

The higher the social class, the more likely the husband and wife are to agree on the importance of social-emotional behavior. (L173)

## Role Definition of Wife
The higher the socioeconomic class, the higher the social rewards for wives' participation in voluntary organizations. (S276)

The higher the socioeconomic class, the less likely is the role of "wife" defined in such a way as to conflict with membership in voluntary organizations. (S276)

The higher the socioeconomic class, the less the importance attached by the wife to her familial roles. (S276)

## Sex Relations
Frequency of sexual intercourse in marriage varies inversely with socioeconomic status. (C023)

The upper strata have a higher proportion of women who derive sexual satisfaction in marriage (U.S.). (G156)

College men who date girls of lower social class are more likely to be sexually aggressive than when they date girls from the same or upper classes. (K161)

In contrast with neurotic girls from the lower class, the sexual promiscuity of those from the middle class tends

to decrease with age due to their desire for social mobility and marriage. (M197)

Male neurotics from the middle class are more likely to be passive in their approach toward women than are those from the lower class. (M197)

## Sex Restrictions
The premarital behavior of girls of higher social rank tends to be more strictly controlled than that of daughters of lower social rank. (T069)

## Sex-Role Definition
In families of high socioeconomic rank, both sexes participate together in leisure-time activities more, while in families of low socioeconomic status, sex-segregated patterns are more common. (G157)

Marital roles are more likely to be allocated by "traditional" sex standards among the lower class. (G157)

Children (5–11 years old) from lower middle-class and working-class homes are more likely to perceive the male role as involving nontraditional domestic activity than are children from upper middle-class homes. This is more so for boys than for girls. (H236)

Among lower occupational groups, children appear to differentiate sex roles earlier and to a greater extent, leaving a smaller area of behavior permissible to both sexes than among middle socioeconomic groups. (J022)

In middle-class families, mothers' and fathers' roles are not as sharply differentiated as in the working-class families. (K089)

The lower the social class, the less likely a woman is to feel any role conflict between her position as housewife and the possible position as career woman. (K089)

Middle-class mothers have generally the same conceptions for their boys as for their girls regarding traits they consider desirable; working-class mothers are more likely to regard dependability, being a good student, and ambition as desirable for boys, but happiness, good manners, cleanliness, and neatness as more desirable for girls. (K110)

Boys from the lower classes are more likely to attribute nontraditional domestic roles to men than are boys from upper middle-class homes. (S265)

## Sex-Role Identification
Lower-class children develop strong preference patterns for sex-role differentiation at an earlier age than do middle-class children. (H197)

## Sexual Aggression
Sexual aggressors when compared with the sexually offended are more likely to be still lower in rank than are nonaggressors when compared with the nonoffended. (K018)

## Sexual Behavior
Men from lower educational and occupational levels find sexual outlets with members of the opposite sex at earlier ages than do those from higher socioeconomic levels. (K102)

## Sibling Relations
Lower-class mental patients are less likely than middle-class mental patients to have had rewarding relationships with their siblings. (M061)

Lower-class children are more likely to have negative

feelings toward their siblings than are those from the middle class. (M197)

### Sibling Relations (Authority)
Lower-class mentally ill patients tend to have resented their siblings' supervision and authority during childhood more than middle-class patients did. (M061)

### Sibling Relations (Warmth)
Lower-class mentally ill patients tend to have had fewer positive relationships with their brothers and sisters than did middle-class patients. (M061)

### Size of Extended Family
The size of the extended family tends to vary directly with its economic position and status. (H052)

The extended family tends to be small in the lower classes and large in the higher classes. (H172)

### Size of Family
The frequency of the large family decreases with rising rental or educational status. (B033)

The higher the social class, the smaller the size of the family is likely to be. The contrary is also asserted for some non-Western countries. (C134)

Among couples with no unplanned pregnancies, there is a direct relationship between socioeconomic status and family size. (W022)

There is little difference in the average family size between the various social classes. The contrary is also asserted. (W023)

### Size of Family
### X   Academic Motivation of Child by Class
Among high achieving adolescents, small family size has a greater effect on high academic motivation among lower-class than among middle-class adolescents. (E102)

### Size of Kin Network
The higher the social class, the more extended the family structure. (P083)

### Sleeping Arrangements
There is an inverse correlation between the closeness of sleeping arrangements and class. (M230)

### Social Interaction
The lower the social class of a family, the less likely it is that it will entertain friends at home. (K089)

### Social Isolation of Women
The economic importance of women of the lower class inhibits the pattern of social isolation that is found among members of the upper class. (G072)

### Social Network
The lower the couple's social class, the more likely it is that they have a relatively interconnected set of social contacts (i.e., their friends are in social relations with one another). (B267)

### Stability of Family Structure
Changes in family norms and behavior are less prevalent in the elite than in the rank and file. (T013)

### Sterilization
Operations for sterilization are more frequent among the lower-income groups than among the higher-income groups. (F101)

### Superego Formation
There is no correlation between social class and the guilt of the child about disobedience or aggression. (A054)

### Toilet Training
Lower-class mothers are more severe in toilet training than are middle-class mothers. This hypothesis is also denied. (H011)

Toilet training is begun earlier in the middle class than in the lower class (Chicago). (L003)

Toilet training is completed earlier in the lower class than in the middle class (Boston). (L003)

There is no significant difference between the middle class and the lower class in the time when toilet training is begun or completed. (L003)

Middle-class mothers whose husbands have entrepreneurial jobs are more likely than lower-class mothers (entrepreneurial) to begin bowel training when the infant is nine months old or even earlier. (M062)

Working-class mothers are quicker and more severe in toilet training than are middle-class mothers (but begin training no earlier) (U.S.). (S191)

Lower-class Negro parents are more likely to toilet train their babies after 12 months; upper-class Negro parents to toilet train their babies before 12 months. (W133)

### Values (Familism)
Middle-class and upper-class marriages are likely to be more oriented toward the child or family as a whole than are lower-class marriages; the latter tend to be more oriented toward the compatibility of the husband and wife and show less concern about responsibility for the children. (C121)

Middle-class men are more likely to be work-oriented and to reject both strong family ties in general and strong ties with their fathers; this is in contrast with men from upper-class families, who are less oriented toward work as a field of accomplishment, have stronger positive family feelings, and respect their fathers more. (L115)

### Values (Family)
The difference in familial attitudes between lower-class normals and paranoid schizophrenics is less than that between middle-class normals and paranoid schizophrenics. (L155)

### Voluntary Organizations
The higher the socioeconomic class, the higher the social rewards for wives' participation in voluntary organizations. (S243)

The higher the socioeconomic class, the less likely is the role of "wife" defined in such a way as to conflict with membership in voluntary organizations. (S243)

The higher the socioeconomic class, the less importance attached by the wife to her familial roles for purpose of her self-definition (compared with outside activity). (S243)

### Weaning
Lower-class children have a significantly higher median age at completion of weaning than do middle-class children. This hypothesis is also denied. (H011)

Upper middle-class mothers excpect their children to be

weaned at an earlier age than do lower-class mothers (Indonesia). (T084)

Lower-class Negro parents are more likely to bottle wean their babies after 12 months; upper-class Negro parents are more likely to bottle wean their babies before 12 months. (W133)

**Work Attitudes**

The higher the class, the greater the personal satisfaction derived by the mother from working. (G156)

## CLASS AND EMPLOYMENT
### X Marital Adjustment

Working-class–working-wife group has more husband-wife disagreements than do the other groups. (H175)

## CLASS ANXIETY OF PARENTS
### X Authoritarianism

Authoritarian parents are more likely to feel threatened in their social and economic status than are normal parents. (M203)

## CLASS, ATTITUDE TOWARD
### X Pregnancy, Attitude Toward

The socially unstable woman (dissatisfied with her social position) is more likely than the socially stable woman to view pregnancy as an illness, as troubling, and as dangerous. (R107)

## CLASS/CHILD-REARING ATTITUDES
### X Breast Feeding, Duration of

Extended durations of breast feeding are a function of irregular maternal behavior arising from poor socioeconomic conditions rather than of a positive supportive attitude toward child rearing. (B272)

## CLASS CONSCIOUSNESS OF CHILD
### X Parent-Child Relations (Rejection)

Among working-class elementary-school children, those who exhibit concern about their social status are more likely to reject their parents than are those who are not status conscious. (E102)

## CLASS/EDUCATION      X Toilet Training

Better-educated mothers, regardless of socioeconomic level, and middle-class mothers, regardless of educational level, are somewhat less severe in toilet training than are lesser-educated working-class mothers (U.S.). (S191)

## CLASS/EXTENDED FAMILY MEMBERSHIP
### X Cohesion of Society

Class membership is more effective than extended family membership in resolving the tension between competition and solidarity: a nuclear family unit need not limit its achievement as much in order to remain in its class as it must in order to remain integrated in the extended family of which it is a unit. (P083)

## CLASS (MODAL PERSONALITY)
### X Child-Rearing Practices

There is no correlation between child-rearing techniques and the modal personality of a social class. (M180)

## CLASS (MOTHER'S AWARENESS OF)
### X Creativity of Child/I.Q.

Mothers of highly intelligent children (Binet) are more likely to be conscious of their parents' social class than are the parents of highly creative children (Guilford–Cattell). (G132)

## CLASS OF HUSBAND      X Cohesion of Family

Family solidarity is likely to be greater if the rank of the family derives solely from the husband's rank. (T106)

**Employment of Mother**

Employed mothers are more likely to have husbands in low socioeconomic categories. (S265)

**Intermarriage (Religious)**

Religious endogamy is inversely related to the status level of the groom. (C128)

**Marriage Ceremony**

Civil marriages are inversely related to the status levels of the grooms. (C128)

## CLASS OF WIFE      X Adultery, Attitude Toward

Extramarital relations of a wife, if the husband is sterile, is less likely to be censured if the woman is of the upper class. (F045)

## CLASS/RACE
### X Child-Rearing Practices (Severity/Consistency)

The degree of severity and consistency of child rearing is correlated more with class than with race. (B272)

## CLASS/RELIGION
### X Child-Rearing Practices (Education)

Catholic families are less likely to stress education of girls beyond high school than are Protestant families. This difference increases with class ranking. (E102)

## CLASS VALUES      X Sex Relations

Where the pains of low status are very high, irresponsible mating behavior and primitive masculine values are more likely to predominate. (P083)

## CLIMATE      X Father Absence

Mother-child households tend to occur more frequently in tropical regions than in areas farther from the equator. (M246)

**Polygyny**

Some form of polygyny is more likely to be found in hot climates than in more temperate climates. (M246)

## COGNITIVE BELIEFS
### X Power Structure of Family

The less the mother and son are dominated by the father in the power area, the greater the disposition of both to believe that the world can be rationally mastered and that a son should risk separation from his family. (M060)

## COGNITIVE DEVELOPMENT
### X Achievement Demands

The mother's excessive ambition for the child is likely to foster learning problems for the child. (R113)

**Authority Structure of Family (Democracy)**

Democratic homes are associated with a favorable rate of intellectual growth in the child. (B257)

**Child-Rearing Practices (Adaptation)**

The extent to which the mother adapts the experiences and materials to the infant's individual capacities is positively related to the infant's intellectual development. (Y042)

**Child-Rearing Practices (Consistency)**

There is a low but positive relationship between maternal consistency and the intellectual development of the infant. (Y042)

## Child-Rearing Practices (Social Stimulation)
Amount of stimulation by the mother oriented to eliciting social responses in the infant is positively related to intellectual development in the infant. (Y042)

## Class
The degree of intellectual growth is directly correlated with the position of the family in the class structure. (B033)

## Disorganization of Family
Children whose cognitive structures have become differentiated are more likely to be "insulated from role experience" (e.g., hurt by broken homes, unhappily married parents, etc.) than they were before the cognitive structures were differentiated. (P083)

## Foster Home/Institutional Care
Children raised in institutions are less able to conceptualize and have lower intelligence scores and poorer speech than do children raised in foster homes. (P068)

## Institutional Care
Children who have been reared in institutions, without ever having had parental care of adequate parental surrogates, are more intellectually retarded and have poorer conceptual ability than do children reared in normal homes. (G128)

## Institutional Care/Foster Home
Children who are reared from early infancy in institutions and then are placed in foster homes are less able to conceptualize than are children who are placed directly in foster homes in early infancy. (B270)

## Interaction in Family (Warmth)
A warm family atmosphere is associated with a favorable rate of intellectual growth in the child. (B257)

## Marital Adjustment of Mother
Children whose mothers have had happy childhoods and are satisfied with marriage rate higher on Rorschach tests in intellectual vigor and energy than do children whose mothers had unhappy childhoods and are not satisfied with marriage. (A071)

## Maternal Deprivation
Children deprived of their mothers have an impaired ability to relate to other people and to think abstractly, and generally have an impaired ego and superego development. (B270)

## Maternal Overprotection
Maternal overprotection is associated with acceleration and interest in reading and with arithmetic retardation.

## Mother Absence
Children deprived of their mothers at birth are consistently less vocal from the age of six months than are children not so deprived. (B270)

Children separated from their mothers show less interest and reactivity as early as the eighth to twelfth weeks than do children not separated from their mothers. (B270)

The longer a child is deprived of mother or mother surrogate, the lower his intelligence level becomes (as measured on the Development Quotient Scale). (B270)

## Mother-Child Relations
A strong mother-child or mother-surrogate relationship established through a certain rhythm of stimulation, gratification, and deprivation is correlated with the capacity of the child to differentiate the environment and with the manipulation of symbols in order to secure ends valued by the mother-child relationship. (P083)

## Mother-Child Relations (Affection)
The development of a sense of time in the child is dependent upon his experiencing time directly, in relation to maternal love and gratification. (Y045)

## Mother-Child Relations (Warmth)
Children whose mothers are highly accepting and show great warmth toward the children are higher in intellectual originality than are children whose mothers are rejecting. (A071)

## Parent-Child Relations (Nurturance)
Withdrawal of nurturance (support and affection) has greater association with effective performance on learning tasks than does consistent nurturance, because the child is motivated to gain the assurance of the parents. (H184)

## Parent Loss
Children reared without normal parental relationships demonstrate a deficient time sense. (G128)

Children reared without normal parental relationships demonstrate a meagerness of imagination. (G128)

## Pregnancy Anxiety
Infants of mothers who were highly anxious during pregnancy have lower scores on the Bayley Mental Scale than do infants of mothers who were not as anxious during pregnancy. (D067)

## Scapegoating
Where family anxiety and problems require the use of a scapegoat for relief and no child is an appropriate symbol, the child's cognitive distortion ensues to permit the scapegoating. (B204)

## Sibling Structure (Age Difference)
The number of interests of a child increases as the age difference between himself and his siblings increases. (K126)

## Surrogate Mother
Whether the infant is cared for predominantly by the mother or by other persons is not related to his intellectual development. (Y042)

## Surrogate Mother-Child Relations (Attention)
Children receiving all the attention of a foster mother are significantly accelerated in mental development compared with those children who have to share the attention of the surrogate mother with others. (B270)

## COGNITIVE DEVELOPMENT (ABSTRACT THINKING)   X   Mother Absence
Children who have been deprived of their mothers during their early years exhibit a deficiency or a lag in the capacity for abstract thinking. (C106)

## COGNITIVE DEVELOPMENT (NONVERBAL)   X   Child-Rearing Practices (Dependency)
For boys, but not for girls, there is a tendency for maternal behavior fostering independence to be positively associated with nonverbal (spatial and numerical) ability. (B257)

### Child-Rearing Practices (Discipline)
Overanxious disciplinary measures are associated with low development of nonverbal, especially spatial, ability in the child. (B257)

### Child-Rearing Practices (Handicrafts)
For children of both sexes, the amount of time either parent spends with the child in arts, crafts, and hobbies is not related to the child's nonverbal (spatial and numerical) ability. (B257)

### Child-Rearing Practices (Nonverbal Stimulation)
For boys, nonverbal stimulation (permissiveness regarding object experimentation, availability of toys and gadgets, and lack of physical restriction) is positively associated with spatial and numerical ability. (B257)

### Child-Rearing Practices (Schedules)
Parental strictness regarding time schedules is not associated with nonverbal (spatial and numerical) ability in children. (B257)

### Child-Rearing Practices (Sex Role)
Maternal emphasis on the son's adopting a masculine role and sex-appropriate behavior is not related to the son's nonverbal (spatial and numerical) ability. (B257)

### Child-Rearing Practices (Toys)
The number of toys a child is given during preschool years is not related to his nonverbal (spatial and numerical) ability. (B257)

## COGNITIVE DEVELOPMENT (READING)
### X   Parent-Child Relations (Rejection)
Rejected children are more likely to score low on reading ability.

## COGNITIVE DEVELOPMENT (TIME)
### X   Mother Absence
Maternally deprived children are less advanced or mature in their concept of time than are maternally nondeprived children. (C106)

## COGNITIVE DEVELOPMENT (VERBAL)
### X   Child-Rearing Practices (Achievement)
Discipline emphasizing academic achievement is associated with a favorable development of verbal ability in the child. (B257)

Rewarding good and criticizing poor academic achievement is positively associated with high verbal ability in children. (B257)

### Child-Rearing Practices (Achievement Demands)
Mothers of children with high verbal ability are more likely to pressure their children for improvement than are mothers of children with low verbal ability. (B257)

### Child-Rearing Practices (Control)
Parental overlimitation and excessive control are associated with a favorable rate of verbal development in the child. (B257)

### Child-Rearing Practices (Dependency)
There is no relationship between verbal ability in children and maternal behavior that fosters dependency. (B257)

### Child-Rearing Practices (Help-Giving)
Mothers of children with high verbal ability are more likely to give both verbal and physical help to their children than are mothers of children with low verbal ability. (B257)

### Child-Rearing Practices (Reading)
The amount of time the father spends reading to the child is positively associated with high verbal ability in daughters, but not in sons. (B257)

The amount of time the mother spends reading to the child is not related to either the son's or the daughter's verbal ability. (B257)

### Child-Rearing Practices (Sex Role)
There is no relationship between the mother's emphasis on her daughter's femininity and sex-appropriate behavior and the daughter's verbal ability. (B257)

### Child-Rearing Practices (Strictness)
There is no relationship between the degree of paternal, as against maternal, strictness and verbal ability in the daughter. (B257)

Among girls with low ability in spatial perception, paternal strictness is positively associated with high verbal ability. (B257)

### Child-Rearing Practices (Verbal Freedom)
Parental verbal permissiveness (e.g., permissiveness for verbal aggression, participation in meal conversation, adult conversation and topics, etc.) is positively associated with high verbal ability in children. (B257)

### Child-Rearing Practices (Verbal Stimulation)
Verbal stimulation and interest shown by the mother (e.g., reading storybooks to child, interest shown in child's speech habits, importance shown to verbal accomplishments) during early childhood and school years is positively associated with high verbal ability in the child. (B257)

### Maternal Overprotectiveness
Maternal overprotection is associated with a favorable rate of verbal development in the child. (B257)

## COHESION       X   Conflict
When trouble arises between consanguineally related males, it tends to be displaced to affinal females. (G012)

## COHESION BETWEEN LINEAGES     X   Land
The granting of land to individuals who are members of other lineages strengthens relations between lineages. (W056)

### Lineage Rights
The solidarity of bonds between lineages tends to be strengthened if the prerogatives which they possess are similar. (L070)

## COHESION OF CASTE    X   Geographic Mobility
The solidarity of the caste is strengthened if the caste segments of the community are predisposed toward special immobility. (B013)

## COHESION OF CLAN    X   Clan-Role Obligations
The cohesion of the clan tends to be reinforced by a norm which specifies that the relationship of an individual to a member of a clan determines his relationship with all members of the clan. (R026)

### Conflict
Interclan hostility tends to reinforce the solidarity of the clan. (W049)

### Descent (Bilateral)
The adoption of bilateral descent will result in the breakdown of the clan system unless there is an indefinite number of intermarrying clans. (S098)

### Economic Dependence

The clan structure will be weakened with the introduction of individual economic independence. (C056)

### Economic Importance of Clan

The strength of the clan structure tends to be directly correlated with its economic importance. (D034)

The disintegration of the clan structure is directly correlated with its loss of traditional political, judicial, and economic functions. (W082)

### Exogamy

A relaxation in exogamic restrictions is associated with a deterioration of clan organization. (S115)

### Husband-Wife Relations (Closeness)

The importance of clan solidarity is inversely correlated with the strength of the relationship between husband and wife. (H103)

With the deterioration of the clan system, the relationship between husband and wife becomes more personal. (W082)

### Intermarriage

Intermarriage with members of the donor culture will tend to result in a decline in the indigenous clan or lineage system. (L031)

### Kin Terminology

Paralleling the decline of the clan system is the decline in knowledge and use of kinship terminology. (L031)

### Kin Terminology (Generation)

When the clan organization of a society is strong, generational distinctions will tend to be overridden in the kinship terminology. (M042)

### Political Importance of Clan

The disintegration of the clan structure is directly correlated with its loss of traditional political, judicial, and economic functions. (W082)

### Preferential Marriage (Parallel-Cousin)

Preferential marriage patterns which entail clan endogamy will tend to decline with the deterioration of the clan organization. (H165)

### Religion (Ancestor Cult)

Clan unity will tend to be reinforced by the institutionalization of an ancestoral cult. (B111)

### Religion (Christianity)

When a matrilineal society is subjected to Christian missionary pressures toward patrilineality, the clan structure disintegrates. (E016)

### Religion (Clan Ceremonies)

The occurrence of ceremonies on the clan level will function to reinforce the unity of the clan. (M046)

### Religion (Conversion)

Clan cohesion tends to deteriorate with the conversion of its members to nonindigenous religions. (S099)

### Residence

A greater emphasis on territorial ties is associated with the breakdown of the clan structure. (E016)

The solidarity of the clan structure is inversely correlated with emphasis on territorial ties. (E016)

The strength of ties between clan members is directly correlated with the residential localization of the clan. (F039)

### Stratification

Clan structure tends to disintegrate with the emergence of class stratification. (B098)

### Warfare

Warfare is associated with the deterioration of the clan structure. (R054)

Localized warfare tends to reinforce the cohesion of the clan. (S099)

## COHESION OF COMMUNITY       X    Acculturation

The relationship between acculturated families and unacculturated families is characterized by hostility and a low frequency of social interaction. (B034)

Well-integrated communities tend to be resistant to changes which might alter their distinctive cultural identities. (S053)

### Child-Rearing Practices (Aggression)

The more intimate and interdependent the social and economic bonds are among members of a community, the more likely are the children to be punished for peer-directed aggression. (M216)

### Cohesion of Family

There is a negative correlation between intense collective identification and family solidarity. (T013)

The transition from an extremely cohesive community to a less cohesive one (i.e., from "bund" to "commune") is associated with an increased importance of the individual family (Israel). (T013)

The relationship between internal family solidarity and community cohesiveness is curvilinear. At the optimum range, both are high. At one extreme, family solidarity is increased at the expense of community cohesiveness. At the other extreme, community cohesiveness increases at the expense of internal family solidarity. (T099)

### Corporate Kin-Group

A social structure based on an association of exogamous corporate patrilineal-descent groups is not likely to hold together unless it is knit together by a web of kinship ties that counterbalance the centrifugal tendencies of the descent groups.

### Economic Cooperation

In the absence of pressures toward interfamilial cooperation in the economic sphere, the bond between families within the community tends to weaken. (G027)

### Endogamy (Community)

Community endogamy tends to be associated with a belief that the members of the village should constitute a strong in-group vis-à-vis all outsiders. (G034)

### Exogamy

When community solidarity is strong, exogamic restrictions tend to arise. (E078)

Exogamic restrictions reinforce community solidarity. (R069)

### Genealogy, Importance of

Stress on ancestry will serve to divide the community if its origins are diverse. (G150)

### Kin Ties

The solidarity of a community tends to be reinforced if the members of the village are bound by kinship ties. (G056)

### Kin Ties (Fictive)

Community solidarity will be enhanced by the extension of fictive kin ties to nonkinsmen within this area. (M080)

### Nuclear Family

The formation of families of procreation is likely to weaken the primary group characteristics of the "bund" type of collective and disrupt its unity (Israel). (T013)

### Residence

When the pattern of settlement is dispersed, there is a low social articulation of families within the settlement. (M025)

### Sibling Group

Under conditions of conflict, the independence of the uterine sibling group tends to jeopardize the cohesion and continuity of villages. (T080)

### COHESION OF CULTURE          X   Acculturation

When the society is not well-integrated culturally, acculturation will occur on the familial or individual level. (S046)

### Parent-Child Relations (Interaction)

The frequency and intensity of interaction between parents and children tends to be reduced with cultural disintegration. (B040)

### COHESION OF ETHNIC GROUP
####          X   Initiation Rites

The institution of puberty rites serves to reinforce the cohesion of the ethnic group. (J007)

### Intermarriage (Ethnic)

The cohesion of the group tends to disintegrate as its members marry individuals of other ethnic groups. (A010)

### COHESION OF EXTENDED FAMILY
####          X   Child-Rearing Practices (Kin)

The greater the strength of the extended family as a whole, the more likely it is that children will be reared not only by their own parents but by other kin as well. (M198)

### Economic Rank

The cohesiveness of the extended family will be directly correlated with its wealth. (G101)

### Kin Ties (Fictive)

The extension of the kinship unit by fictive ties with nonkinsmen tends to occur in societies where the extended family is weak. (L064)

### Political Role of Extended Family

As extended family relationships have begun to lose their political and career meanings the possibility of family ties based more upon affection and less upon obligation is increased. (P083)

### Values (Cooperation)

Extended family kinship relations will be reinforced by an emphasis on cooperation in the value system of the society. (V016)

### Warfare

Bonds of the extended family tend to weaken under conditions of general peace. (L093)

### COHESION OF EXTENDED FAMILY (PATRILINEAL)          X   Polyandry (Fraternal)

Fraternal polyandry functions to reinforce the solidarity of the patrilineal extended family. (G056)

### COHESION OF EXTENDED KIN          X   Class

The kinship ties of people from upper-upper economic brackets tend to be closer than those of people from average-income backgrounds. (C134)

### COHESION OF FAMILY          X   Acculturation

When family bonds are strong, the rate of acculturation is retarded. (S051)

### Acculturation Anxiety

When strong familial ties are maintained, the emotional disturbances that frequently accompany culture contact are reduced. (S051)

### Achievement Motivation

Family structures which are effective in training boys for achievement tend to do so at the cost of heightened intrapsychic tension and lowered familial integration. (S205)

### Age at Marriage

The more distant the female college student's ties to her parents, the later the age at which she plans to marry; the relationship is curvilinear for men. (R116)

### Age Difference

Family solidarity will be increased if the age differential between parent and child is reduced. (I007)

### Age of Children

The relationship between the age of children in the home and family solidarity is inverse. (J001)

### Age of Family Head

The integration of the family varies by age of the family head. Other tests have shown no significant correlation between age of parents and family integration. (S217)

### Authority Structure of Family

In families favoring authority equally distributed between the husband and wife and in families tending to favor dominance by the husband, family solidarity is significantly greater than in families which tend to favor dominance by the wife. (J001)

### Bereavement

The acuteness of the sorrow at the death of a member will increase the emotional interdependence and unity of the family. (B033)

### Child-Rearing Practices (Permissiveness)

Family solidarity and interpersonal harmony seem to be more likely in families in which parents allow the adolescent some involvement in running his own life than in families in which parents tend to exclude the adolescent from choosing his own behavior and goals. (E100)

### Class of Husband

Family solidarity is likely to be greater if the rank of the family derives solely from the husband's rank. (T106)

### Cohesion of Community

There is a negative correlation between intense collective identification and family solidarity. (T013)

The transition from an extremely cohesive community to a less cohesive one (i.e., from "bund" to "commune") is associated with an increased importance of the individual family (Israel). (T013)

The relationship between internal family solidarity and community cohesiveness is curvilinear. At the optimum range, both are high. At one extreme, family solidarity is increased at the expense of community cohesiveness. At the other extreme, community cohesiveness increases at the expense of internal family soldarity. (T099)

### Collateral Ties
There is a direct correlation between family disorganization and a breakdown in collateral relational ties among kin. (K087)

### Community, Family Participation in
The more satisfied a family with its locale and the more active it is in it, the more likely it is that the family will be adjusted and integrated internally. (S217)

### Community Organization
The more undifferentiated and cohesive the community, the weaker the internal family solidarity. (T099)

### Community Orientation
The more integrated the nuclear family, the greater its general community concern. (S217)

### Community Satisfaction
The more integrated the nonfarm nuclear family of a fringe area, the greater its satisfaction with the community. (S217)

### Consensus in Family
Family adjustment is more likely to occur when its members have common interests, ideas, and ideals. (B033)

Parents of poorly adjusted families show less agreement in their descriptions of family situations than do parents of well-adjusted families. (V032)

### Crisis
When the family group is threatened by severe tensions, there tends to be a sudden rallying of forces toward uniting the family. (B202)

The disorganizing effects of crises are resisted better by families with a high degree of solidarity than are those with a low degree of solidarity. (J001)

### Dependency
Overt dependency of the child is heightened by lack of cohesion within the family and parental rejection. (M221)

College students with relatively distant ties to their families, compared with those who are relatively close, are more likely to prefer individual-oriented activities and less likely to prefer group-oriented activities. (R116)

### Descent
Loyalty and obligation are more likely to correlate with gratification and interaction in bilineal-descent systems than in other descent systems, especially when marriage does not involve a change in community for either spouse. (P083)

### Deviance
The greater the degree of unity and intimate association in a family, the less is the likelihood of a member participating in behavior which will bring disgrace to the family. (B033)

### Deviance, Isolation from
A high degree of family unity is associated with isolation from deviant and destructive patterns of behavior. (B033)

### Deviance of Family Member, Attitude Toward
Families with a high degree of unity are likely to feel disgraced by delinquent or criminal behavior of a member. (B033)

### Division of Labor
Occupational differentiation tends to weaken the traditional familial ties of the peasant social structure. (G027)

### Economic Attitudes of Husband-Wife
Family integration is directly related to the congruence of economic expectations of the couples. (B033)

### Economic Conditions
The vulnerability of the family to the depression appeared to vary inversely with its integration and adaptability. (B033)

### Economic Cooperation
When economic cooperation exists between related families of orientation and procreation, closer emotional relationships develop between them than if there is no economic cooperation. (S002)

### Economic Dependence
Family ties tend to be strengthened by the increase of intrafamilial debts. (V010)

Family cohesion tends to deteriorate with the development of patterns of economic independence. (W082)

The cohesiveness of the family is directly correlated with the economic interdependence of its members. (W082)

### Economic Level
Consumer credit, the easy mortgage, social security, and the family doctor have made it possible for many working-class families and most middle-class families to use kinship ties more as a potential source of friendship and less as the source of (more or less mandatory) advice and of ascriptive solidarity obligations. (P083)

### Economic Pattern (Migrant Labor)
The cohesion of the family is weakened by the adoption of patterns of migrant labor. (S121)

### Economic Rank
Among poor people, sons are more likely to separate from their families and to seek a new fortune; poor people are less concerned with ties of relationship. (B223)

When kinsmen have about the same amount of wealth, members of a given family are forced to be self-reliant since there are no wealthy individuals on whom they can be dependent. (H021)

### Economic Role of Wife
The cohesion of the family will tend to be weakened if a wife's services are no longer of economic importance. (W082)

### Education
The more integrated the family, the less the amount of formal education it is likely to have. (S217)

The more integrated the family, the greater the amount of formal education. (S217)

### Education Differences Between Husband and Wife
The education and maturity differential that existed between the wife and her husband in the classical bour-

geois marriage reduces the solidarity and nurturance of the family. (P083)

### Emotional Adjustment
The greater the emotional involvement of the members of the family with one another, the greater the need for freedom from extreme emotional and physical stimulation. (C093)

### Ethnocentrism
When most or all of the emotional and cultural values of the individual person are derived from those of his family exclusively and conditioned largely within the solidarity of one family setting only, there is more likely to be an overevaluation of the in-group and a sense of arbitrary superiority over the out-group. (L167)

### Extended Kin Ties
The more the culture utilizes the extended family as a basic social unit, the greater the identification of the individual with the family group. (M166)

### Father-Son Relations (Emotional Attachment)
When the son fails to establish a common emotional bond with the father, it is almost impossible for the family to continue as a functioning and perpetuate unit after the death of the father. (C024)

### Fertility
The greater the internal family solidarity, the higher the birth rate. (T099)

### Fertility Values
The more distant the female college student's ties with her family, the fewer children she is likely to expect to have. (R116)

### Generation
Patterns of equality between alternate generations of kinsmen tend to be associated with a weak family organization. (D034)

### Geographic Mobility
The tendency toward disruption where family members are separated is especially likely where a previous intercommunication has been insufficient to provide the sharing of experiences and the common understanding of feelings, attitudes, and ideals essential to a durable relationship. (B033)

Family members will invest less emotional energy in those members who may be expected to move away than in those members who are expected to remain in the group permanently. (C093)

The less intimate the family life, the more likely that the child plans to leave the community when adult. (R111)

Family solidarity is weakened by geographical mobility. (S076)

The more mobile geographically the nuclear family, the less likely it is to be integrated. (S217)

### Identification with Community
The more intense the individual's identification with the collective, the lower the solidarity of the family. (T098)

### Identification with Parents
When the social structure emphasizes family solidarity, the degree of identification with the parents will tend to be high. (F058)

### Illegitimacy (Adoption)
Unwed mothers who keep their children have significantly less positive intrafamily relationships and home situations than do those who release their children for adoption. (V027)

### Illness
By isolating the medical deviant from his family, the hospital prevents secondary gains and reduces the emotional burden on the nuclear family. (P083)

The trust and confiding character of the doctor-patient relationship preserves more of the autonomy of the nuclear family than would be the case if this function were transferred to the extended family network. (P083)

### Incest Taboos
In any boundary-maintaining system (e.g., family), the closer the emotional involvement of the members, the more likely is it to give rise to incest taboos. (C093)

### Industrialization
There is a negative correlation between industrialization and family integration. (K024)

### Inheritance
The cohesiveness of the family is directly correlated with a pattern of inheritance which promises an equal share of property among the children. (L064)

### Initiation Rites
Initiation rites are more likely to occur when tribal ties are stronger than family ties. (W154)

### Institutional Care of Retarded Child
Institutionalizing a retarded child, rather than rearing him at home, is inversely related to family cohesiveness. (J027)

### Interaction in Family
A family is more likely to perceive itself as self-sufficient if each member is preoccupied with peacefully maintaining intrafamily relations. (W124)

### Interaction in Family (Affection)
The more cohesive and integrated the nuclear family, the greater its satisfaction of members' emotional and affectional needs. (S217)

### Interaction in Family (Affection/Duty)
Among democratic families, voluntary exchange of emotions (i.e., affection, happiness, and satisfaction between family members) leads to family solidarity; among authoritarian families, greater sense of duty and responsibility leads to family solidarity. (K113)

### Intermarriage
The weaker the child's ties to his immediate and extended families, the more likely he is to marry outside his group. (H240)

### Juvenile Delinquency
Juvenile delinquency will be less likely when the solidarity of the family is high. (B055)

Among families which are cohesive, the child is more likely to commit traffic crimes than other kinds of crimes. (M194)

Among residentially mobile families, there is no correlation between degree of family integration, as measured by attitudes of the child toward the parents, and delinquency in the child. (N063)

In families which have maintained love and affection between their members, children are less likely to become delinquents than in families in which these affectional bonds have broken down. (S210)

### Kin/Nonkin Relations
The cohesiveness of the family is directly correlated with the exclusiveness of its role as a unit of mutual aid. (L064)

### Kin Ties
Widespread sets of relationships with relatives are correlated with splitting of the elementary family. (G012)

There is no demonstrated relation between family closeness and number of consanguineal relatives. (R084)

### Leadership
Members of integrated families are more likely to hold formal leadership positions in outside groups than are members from nonintegrated families. (S217)

### Legal Structure
Strong family relations are more likely to occur where the family is strongly supported by law. (F092)

### Marital Stability
The cohesiveness of the family is directly correlated with the stability of the marriage pattern. (L064)

### Maternal-Role Definition
When no other adult woman has a role similar to that of the mother, the average intensity of affective involvement in relations within the family is likely to be high. (P012)

### Mental Illness
Where there is mental disorganization within a family based on a pattern of pseudomutuality, family members attempt to preserve the family's autonomy. (W021)

### Mental Illness/Neurosis
The families of neurotic patients are more likely than those of mentally ill patients to be closely knit. (M061)

### Mental Illness (Schizophrenia)
The more cohesive and centripetal the family structure, the more likely is the schizophrenic to manifest a symbiotic rather than an isolate pattern of interaction. (P077)

Schizophrenics tend to come from families in which the maintenance of intense intrafamily relationships assumes greater importance than the preservation of individual identity. (W124)

### Monogamy
Ties of affection within the nuclear family will tend to be stronger in monogamous than in polygamous unions. (A034)

### Nonkin Activities
The higher the degree of family cohesion, the greater the participation in organized activity outside the family. The reverse is also asserted. (S217)

### Nonkin Relations
As marriage becomes a more effective source of solidarity and tension reduction, there is less demand for such experiences in extrafamilial-role participations; hence, the primary character of kin networks and of other peer groups declines and they become relations of entertainment, rather than of mutual support, and can be left or entered into more easily. (P083)

### Nonkin Relations (Conflict)
The solidarity of the family will be reinforced by conflict in extrafamilial relations. (S064)

### Occupational Aspirations
Students who have high occupational aspirations are less concerned with maintaining family ties via physical closeness (i.e., they are more likely to leave family for some time, moving around the country to facilitate occupational advancement) than are students who have lower occupational aspirations. (E102)

### Parent-Child Relations (Affection)
There is a correlation between closeness of family life and fondness for both parents on the part of the child, particularly fondness for the mother on the part of sons. (R116)

### Parent-Child Relations (Conflict)
Conflict and tensions between the adolescent and family are correlated with the intensity of the bonds between family members. (W113)

### Peer Relations
Family solidarity is weakened as the peer group gains in importance in the life of the child. (C087)

### Personality Adjustment of Child
A complete home, mother, father, children are necessary for the development of a balanced and socially adjusted personality in the child. (S210)

### Personality of Child (Introversion)
The greater the familial involvement of the parents, the less likely is introversion in the child. (S221)

### Personality of Child (Responsibility)
There is a correlation between the strength of family ties of the child (college student) and the extent to which he assumes responsible adult roles. (R116)

### Personality of Mother (Satisfaction)
There is a correlation between the closeness of family life (as reported by college students) and the degree to which the mother is satisfied with her life. (R116)

### Personality Problems of Child
If a child is not allowed to develop a sense of belonging to the family because of the lack of affection among members, he is more likely than the child who is accepted to become psychopathic. (S226)

### Power Structure of Family
Strong ties between parents and children tend to reduce effective leadership in the family. (B202)

### Preferential Marriage (Cross-Cousin)
Cross-cousin marriage to the mother's brother's daughter reinforces the cohesion of the families of these siblings. (L046)

### Property
The unity of the extended family tends to be maintained if the father retains control of all property possessed by the group as long as he lives. (G013)

### Race Attitudes
Prejudiced persons are more likely than unprejudiced persons to have an "ingroup orientation" toward their family, manifested in a preoccupation with the family's status and prestige. (A061)

### Reference Group
Conflicting reference groups for various members of the family tend to lead to mutual alienation from the family. (B202)

### Religion
Catholic families are more strongly integrated than are non-Catholic families. (Z006)

### Religion (Ancestor Worship)
With the weakening of ancestor worship, family solidarity tends to deteriorate. (H103)

### Residence
Family networks are more closely knit when relatives and friends live in close proximity. (B210)

Stronger sibling and parental family roles are found in the urban-fringe family than in the central-city family. (J003)

### Residential Stability
The more integrated the family, the longer its residence in the tribal community. (S217)

### Rituals in Family
Family ritual increases pride in family. (B206)

### Role Definitions of Husband and Wife
Family adjustment is more likely to occur when the husband and wife have a congruence of economic expectations and roles. (B033)

### Scapegoating
The greater the extent to which the parents displace their difficulties onto the child, the more likely it is that the stability and solidarity of the family will be maintained. (V033)

### Scapegoating (Intrafamily)
Scapegoating within a family system tends to reinforce its solidarity. (B204)

### Scholastic Adjustment of Child
The closer the student's ties to his family, the better his adjustment to the campus community. (R116)

### Sex-Role Definition
The greater the integration of the family, the greater the encouragement of role specialization by sex of child. (F094)

Parental-role differentiation is associated with decreased emotional intensity and increased psychological distance among family members. (S216)

### Sex-Role Identification
The lower the family's integration, the more likely it is that girls will react to criticism about the performance of social-emotional, but not instrumental, behavior. (F094)

The lower the integration of the family, the greater the possibility that boys are aware of parental criticism of their performance of instrumental behavior but perceive no definite pattern with respect to socioemotional activities. (F094)

### Size of Family
The larger the family, the greater the emphasis on the group rather than on the individual. (I007)

Emotional relationships among family members will tend to be more diffuse and stable with an increase in family size. (I007)

Affective relationships between family members are more likely to persist when the family is small in size. (I007)

Members of large families tend to be more interdependent with each other than do members of small families. The reverse is also asserted. (R106)

The larger the size of the nuclear family, the greater the amount of time and effort given to the family. (S217)

### Sleeping Arrangements
It seems highly probable that affection and degree of integration with the family are greatest among the lower class where there is a greater intimacy of sleeping arrangements. (M230)

### Social Mobility
The strengthening of the family results in a restriction of social mobility and the reinforcement of social-class lines. (B033)

The general effect of upward or downward social mobility of a family member is the weakening of kinship and family ties (especially for males). (B033)

Families that are socially mobile, upward or downward, are more likely to exhibit signs of disunity than are families that are socially stable in their class patterns. (C134)

Social mobility is facilitated by weakened affective bonds between family members. (T106)

### Social Mobility of Children
Family solidarity is not adversely affected by upward social mobility of the children. (S220)

### Socialization, Agents of
Collective responsibility for education and socialization welds the various relationships of the family firmly together. (M019)

### Stepmother, Attitude Toward
Prejudice against the entrance of a stepmother into the family produces tension in the family. (B286)

### Subsistence Pattern (Nomadic)
Nomadic tribes are more likely to develop strong family and family-group ties. (B223)

### Technology
With the existence of modern means of communication, relations between kin are likely to be stronger and more frequent than they were in the past. (P083)

### Urban/Rural
Rural background is correlated with family integration. There is no correlation between these two variables. (S217)

### Urbanization
There is no evidence that increased urbanization of a family leads to the disintegration of the family. (C134)

### Value Consensus
If family members accept the legitimacy of external institutions and have a differential commitment to them, family solidarity is reduced. (B202)

### Values (Familism)
The preservation of traditional family values increases family unity. (B033)

### Values (Individualism)

Individualism serves to separate the individual from his family and to weaken the relationship between family members. (B033)

Where the societal value system stresses individualism, family solidarity will be weakened. (S076)

### Values (Traditional)

The more a society's values and institutions are based on obedience to tradition, the more dependent are its members on the family and kin-groups.

### Warfare

Warfare will tend to accentuate the importance of the family as a unit and to strengthen among its members a sense of family responsibility. (G139)

## COHESION OF FAMILY/ACHIEVEMENT VALUES
### X  Sex Status

Where there are strains between family solidarity and pressures to achieve, boys in a family are more apt to feel them than are girls. (C086)

## COHESION OF FAMILY AND COMMUNITY
### , X  Family-Community Relations

Internal family solidarity and community cohesiveness increase to the degree that a balance is struck between the family's involvement in and isolation from the community. (T099)

## COHESION OF FAMILY, CHANGE IN
### X  Personalty (Stress)

When strong affective ties have been formed between members of the family, situational pressures which force their modification will impose important strains upon the individual. (P012)

## COHESION OF GROUP    X  Kin/Nonkin

Solidarity among kin is more easily maintained than in other groups (i.e., occupational or neighborhood peer groups) since the boundaries are clearer. (P083)

## COHESION OF JOINT FAMILY
### X  Authority Structure

The more efficiency and technical knowledge, rather than seniority, become the basis for decision making, the greater is the threat to the solidarity of the joint family system. (G156)

### Economic Dependence

The cohesion of the joint family is weakened by the development of patterns of economic individualism. (M081)

### Social Mobility

Social mobility of one of the males, if accompanied by a reluctance to share his greater wealth, leads to a decrease in the solidarity of the joint family. (G156)

## COHESION OF KIN-GROUP
### X  Child-Rearing Practices (Sex Role)

Societies will be characterized by greater differentiation of socialization by sex if they are also characterized by large family groups with cooperative interaction. (B264)

### Class

Members of the upper class will make a greater effort to preserve the solidarity of the kin-group. (W098)

### Community Ceremonials

Community ceremonies tend to reinforce close kinship ties between members of the community. (D013)

### Conflict

When trouble arises between consanguineally related males it tends to be displaced to affinal females. (G012)

### Crisis (Epidemic)

The fragmentation of larger kin and local residential units into households tends to occur with the increase in local migration which accompanies an epidemic plague. (B041)

### Death

The cohesion of the kin-group is higher at the death of one of its members. (S096)

### Descent (Ambilateral)

The cohesiveness of the descent group tends to be undermined when descent is ambilateral. (F068)

### Descent (Unilineal)

The cohesion of the kin-group will be greater if a pattern of unilineal descent is instituted. (S098)

### Economic and Legal Role of Kin-Group

The cohesion of a kin unit is directly correlated with its importance as a unit of economic and jural obligations. (E048)

### Economic Cooperation

The strength of the relationship between kinsmen will be directly correlated with the extent to which the relationship involves economic cooperation. (O023)

### Economic Dependence

The kin structure tends to weaken with the development of opportunity for economic independence. (F059)

### Economic Level

In societies where conditions of food insecurity and hunger frustrations exist, kin-groups will be more cohesive than other social groups and will perform a greater number of significant functions. (N026)

### Exogamy

The sense of identification with a kin-group will be stronger if marriage is prohibited between its members. (W115)

### Functions of Kin-Group

The retention of kin ties after fission can only occur if the kin-group is multifunctional in character. (G111)

### Geographic Mobility

The solidarity of the ties of kinship is inversely correlated with the degree of mobility of the members of the kin unit. (H165)

### Homicide

When exaction of proper retribution for homicide would disrupt a solidarity that is important to maintain, the crime goes unpunished. Murder of the family head by a member of the nuclear family does not create a feud. (L112)

### Incest Taboo

The prohibition of marriage within the kin-group or family tends to increase its solidarity. (E069)

The extension of incest taboos functions to increase the solidarity of the social group through an expansion of the sphere of kinship ties. (L060)

### Kin/Nonkin

Boundary-maintaining systems composed of consanguineal kinsmen lead to stronger feelings of closeness among members than boundary-maintaining systems composed of nonconsanguineal kinsmen. (C093)

### Kin-Role Definition

The more obligations there are among kinsmen, the greater the solidarity there is between kinsmen. (B209)

### Kin Ties (Fictive)

When fictive kinship ties are established between individuals who are already consanguineal kinsmen, the alliance serves to reinforce preexisting bonds. (A029)

The institutionalization of fictive kin ties tends to occur in societies where kin units are weak or absent. (F049)

### Marital Stability

A lack of solidarity among members of a unilateral group appears to be correlated with easy divorces, remarriages, and frequent extramarital liaisons. (H021)

### Marriage Payment

Marriage payment serves to reinforce the bonds between kinsmen. (H107)

### Mate Selection

When the continuity of the kinship unit is stressed, marriage will tend to be arranged by the family head and to be based on economic and social rank. (B033)

### Population

A decline in population will tend to encourage the consolidation of kinship segments which have previously separated. (W031)

### Preferential Marriage

The solidarity of the kin structure is directly correlated with the specificity of the relationship which is designated as the preferred marriage form. (N023)

### Preferential Marriage (Cross-Cousin)

The institutionalization of cross-cousin marriage strengthens the integration of the kin-group. (H062)

Matrilineal cross-cousin marriage tends to destroy the solidarity of the patrilineal group. (W065)

Patrilineal cross-cousin marriage tends to reinforce the solidarity of a patrilineal group. (W065)

### Preferential Marriage (Exchange)

The institutionalization of exchange marriage functions to strengthen the kin ties between families. (G053)

### Preferential Marriage (Father's Sister's Daughter)

Preferential marriage with the father's sister's daughter reinforces the solidarity of the kin-group inasmuch as the cycle of exchange involves only two generations. (N023)

### Preferential Marriage (First-Cousin)

The establishment of patterns of preferential marriage with the first cousin functions to reinforce the solidarity of the kin-group. (W098)

### Preferential Marriage (Parallel-Cousin)

Parallel-cousin marriage is an effective factor in inhibiting the formation of corporate kin-group on higher levels of segmentation. (M023)

### Property

The greater the control of disposable wealth, the greater is the tendency for the kin unit to maintain its cohesion. (F029)

### Protection

When individuals are no longer dependent upon their kinsmen for personal security, the kin unit will tend to break down. (O013)

### Rank

The higher the rank, the greater the tendency of the larger kin unit to maintain its cohesion. (F029)

### Rank of Kin

Allegiance to specific sections of the kin-group will tend to be directly correlated with their social rank. (G038)

More distant kin bonds will be remembered and exercised if they are links to important kin-groups and outstanding individuals. (K045)

### Religion

Kin bonds tend to be weaker if members of the family do not share the same religious affiliation. (H164)

### Religion (Ancestor Worship)

Ancestor worship reinforces the solidarity of the kin-group. (R023)

### Religion (Ritual)

The persistence of the kin-group tends to be associated with its continued importance as a ritual unit. (K045)

### Residence

Common residence will reinforce the cohesion of the kin-group. (F030)

Kinship bonds tend to be weakened if kinsmen are not residentially propinquitous. (H164)

The solidarity of a kin-group is directly correlated with its degree of localization. (H165)

### Residence (Neolocal)

The disintegration of ethnic and extended family bonds will be manifest in a trend toward single-family households. (S090)

### Ritual in Kin-Group

Common ritual will tend to reinforce the cohesiveness of the kin-group. (F026)

### Role Definition of Husband-Wife

Couples with closely-knit kin networks (its members are all in interaction with one another) tend to define more rigorously the roles of husbands and wives than do couples with loosely-knit kin networks. (B210)

### Segmentation

When migrating kin-groups maintain cohesion through patterns of continued interaction, the establishment of a segmentary structure is to be expected. (F033)

### Siblings, Number of

The incidence of partition exhibits a tendency to a progressive decrease as the size of the sibling group increases. (F075)

### Size of Kin-Group

The cohesion of the kin-group is inversely correlated with its size. (H074)

### Stability of Extended Family

With the break up of the extended family, a weakening of kinship ties in general will occur. (G072)

### Urbanization

Where urban populations are ethnically homogeneous, there is no evidence that city life tends to weaken kinship bonds. (B036)

## COHESION OF KIN NETWORK
### X    Acculturation

When interfamilial ties are strong, the society will tend to be resistant to acculturative changes. (A023)

### Economic Cooperation

The primary extension of family sentiment to members of the wider kinship group largely depends upon how much the latter fulfills the family task of distributing and consuming food. (R087)

### Husband-Wife Relations (Closeness)

When ties with extended kin network are strong, emotional relationships between spouses tend to diminish. (G012)

## COHESION OF LINEAGE    X    Affinal Relations

Where the solidarity of the lineages of the husband and wife is so strong as to minimize the demands one can make on the other, one marriage partner will be unable to become a full participant in the descent group of his or her spouse. (Z003)

### Age of Lineage

Lineage cohesiveness tends to be directly correlated with the age of the lineage. (L066)

### Authority Structure of Lineage

When internally exercised authority within agnatic sections is weak, the group will be characterized by a high degree of fluidity. (M023)

### Conflict in Nuclear Family

When the solidarity of exogamous patrilineages is strong, nuclear families tend to be split by the conflicting loyalties of the spouses. (L027)

### Descent/Residence

When the residence rule conflicts with the unilinear descent pattern, the strength of unilinear alignments is weakened. (M027)

### Divorce

When the solidarity of exogamous patrilineages is strong, divorce, as a consequence of the conflicting loyalties of the spouses, is very common. (L027)

### Economic Cooperation

Lineage solidarity is reinforced by a pattern of economic cooperation between lineage members. (W056)

### Economic Level

Lineage solidarity will become increasingly undermined as pressure on economic resources increases. (W056)

### Economic Stability

The stability of the kin-structured agricultural system is reflected in the importance of lineage unity in the value system. (W056)

### Endogamy

Lineage endogamy tends to occur in situations where it is imperative to maintain lineage solidarity. (B087)

### Geographic Mobility

The persistence of unilinear group solidarity is inhibited by the migration of segments to other settlements. (F033)

### Inheritance

If the lineage is strong, it is more likely to be the social unit through which property is transmitted. (S192)

### Kin Terminology (Iroquois)

Weak unilineal descent groups are associated with Iroquois terminology. (C126)

### Kin Ties of Husband-Wife

Where the solidarity of the lineages of the husband and wife is so strong as to lower the demands each spouse could make on the other, one marriage partner (usually the wife) must sever connections with his or her natal group. (Z003)

### Land

When the lineage has control over land, it will have greater generational depth and, therefore, greater unity and strength than those lineages which have only movables to inherit. (G028)

### Marital Stability

The corporateness of lineages fostered the stability of endogamous unions. (S158)

### Monogamy

The predominance of monogamous marriages in matrilineal societies which have previously been polygynous and polyandrous will tend to result in the weakening of matrilineal bonds. (G056)

### Parent-Child Relations (Closeness)

The relationship between the child and his parent who is not relevant to the lineage structure will be weaker if lineage affiliation is stressed. (G056)

### Political Succession

When political offices are established as achieved statuses, lineage solidarity is weakened. (S123)

### Religion (Ancestor Worship)

The ancestor cult increases the sense of group identification and group solidarity among members of the lineage. (W115)

### Residence

Unilineal units will be weakened if the residence pattern fails to reinforce their membership. (D034)

### Residence (Bilocal)

Anything which lessens the strength of unilinear bonds favors bilocal residence, provided that the factors that militate against neolocal residence are also present (e.g., large, multifamily dwellings and collective rather than individual enterprise). (M019)

### Ritual

Lineage solidarity tends to be reinforced by the institution of specific ceremonies or rituals which involve all members of the social unit. (M072)

### Size of Kin-Group

The ambiguity of the lineage unit is inversely correlated with the size of the exogamic unit. (L065)

### Size of Lineage

The degree of lineage cohesiveness tends to be directly correlated with its size. (L066)

### Subsistence Pattern (Agricultural)

The importance of unilineal affiliation tends to be stressed more strongly in agricultural societies. (W056)

### Warfare

When patterns of interlineage warfare are abandoned, the solidarity of the lineage is diminished. (W056)

## COHESION OF MOIETY          X   Size of Moiety

An increase in size of prosperous moieties leads to a weakening of kinship feelings among its members. (L110)

## COHESION OF PATRILINEAL GROUP
### X   Polygyny (Non-Sororal)

Nonsororal polygyny tends to reinforce the solidarity of the male members of the patrilineal group. (G028)

## COHESION OF SOCIETY
### X   Class/Extended Family Membership

Class membership is more effective than extended family membership in resolving the tension between competition and solidarity; a nuclear family unit need not limit its achievement as much in order to remain integrated in its class as it must in order to remain integrated in the extended family of which it is a unit. (P083)

### Father-Son Relations (Loyalty)

The moral disintegration of society is correlated with expressions of son-father disloyalty. (G012)

### Kin Ties (Fictive)

The institutionalization of patterns of fictive kinship strengthens intercommunity relations. (M080)

In a society marked by ethnic and linguistic diversity, the extension of kinship bonds to nonkinsmen serves as an important cohesive factor. (O018)

### Marriage Class System

A shift from a four-section to a six-section system creates a wider sphere of social solidarity by expanding the sphere of kinship relations. (L060)

### Witchcraft

The moral disintegration of society is indexed by accusation of witchcraft against fathers by sons. (G012)

## COINCIDENCE          X   Kin Terminology

When marriage to a cross-cousin is the preferential form, a woman's husband's father and her father's sister's husband will tend to be terminologically equated. (E018)

### Kin Terminology (Classificatory)

Mother's sister's husband and mother's brother's daughter's husband will be terminologically equated with father or father's brother when the levirate and cross-generational marriage with wife's brother occurs. (F010)

When ego can trace a kinship connection to some relative in two different ways, the two types of bonds tend to be ignored and the relative tends to be called by the same term. (M019)

The equivalence of mother's brother and father's sister's son is a function of their possible identity under conditions of avuncular marriage. (M020)

When avuncular marriage operates in conjunction with a cross-cousin marriage, mother's mother and father's sister tend to be subsumed under the same term. (M020)

Under conditions of fraternal polyandry, brothers of a husband will tend to be called father by the children. (S068)

When two kin roles coincide in the same individual, classificatory terminology tends to occur. (S093)

Father's sister's daughter will tend to be terminologically equated with her mother in a dual organization, since they may both be considered potential wives. (S097)

### Preferential Marriage

When the preferential marriage patterns of the levirate and of a woman to her husband's sister's son are practiced simultaneously, husband's brother and husband's sister's son will tend to be terminologically equated. (A020)

## COLLATERAL TIES          X   Cohesion of Family

There is a direct correlation between family disorganization and a breakdown in collateral relational ties among kin. (K087)

## COMMUNICATION (INTERCOMMUNITY)
### X   Marriage Rate

A decline in the marriage rate tends to be correlated with decreased inter-village communication; the latter reduces the number of potential mates available to those of a marriageable age. (B043)

## COMMUNICATION (INTERPERSONAL)
### X   Disorganization of Family

There is a direct correlation between poor interpersonal communication (within the family and between family members and outsiders) and family disorganization. (K087)

## COMMUNITY          X   Acculturation

Acculturation tends to break down the correspondence between the kin unit and the community. (K049)

### Age-Groups

Age-group organizations are more likely to be adopted and retained in societies in which the community pattern is multiclan and endogamous rather than single-clan and exogamous, for descent groups are the central focus of loyalty in the latter. (L175)

### Avoidance Relationship

Avoidance relationships tend to be abandoned with an increase in the heterogeneity of community composition. (E068)

### Corporate Kin-Group

Corporate descent groups can exist only in more or less homogeneous societies. (F020)

The degree of congruence of a unilineal kin-group and the community and the extent of its corporate function are directly correlated. (F039)

### Economic Pattern (Migrant Labor)

If the lineage forms the basis of the village structure, the effects of migratory labor will be less disruptive for the village. (W132)

### Inheritance

With the socioeconomic stabilization of community organization, a formalization of rules about inheritance tends to occur. (L063)

### Lineage Depth

Where the frequency of fissioning is such as to produce lineages of shallow depth and narrow span, the tendency for the village to become a kin-group is inhibited. (S283)

### Mate Selection
Mate selection tends to occur between members of the same community. (M080)

### Mate Selection (Residence)
Residentially propinquitous mate selection is higher if the neighborhood is self-sufficient (i.e., in terms of shopping areas, schools, churches, recreation centers, and places of work). (K020)

Segregation of an identifiable group of people increases the likelihood of residentially propinquitous marriages. (K020)

### Residence
An unplanned settlement pattern will tend to occur only where there is no localization of the lineage. (H147)

## COMMUNITY CEREMONIALS
### X   Cohesion of Kin-Group
Community ceremonies tend to reinforce close kinship ties between members of the community. (D013)

## COMMUNITY, FAMILY PARTICIPATION IN
### X   Cohesion of Family
The more satisfied a family with its locale and the more active it is in it, the more likely the family will be adjusted and integrated internally. (S217)

## COMMUNITY HOMOGENEITY
### X   Social Network
Tightly knit family friendship networks (i.e., a high frequency of interaction among family units) are more often found in communities that are homogeneous. (G156)

## COMMUNITY ISOLATION
### X   Endogamy (Community)
Isolated communities are more likely to be endogamous. (H139)

### Kinship, Importance of
The importance of kin ties is directly correlated with the degree of isolation and size of a community. (S111)

### Segmentary Structure
The development of a segmentary structure tends to be inhibited by a settlement pattern of self-sufficient communities. (F033)

### Size of Clan
Compact settlement in autonomous communities is associated with restriction on the increase in the size of the clan and the number of its component basic lineages. (F089)

## COMMUNITY (MULTILINEAGE)
### X   Economic Pattern
A multilineage structure occurs only in those communities whose economy permits large numbers of people to live together. (S001)

### Warfare
Under the pressure of warfare multilineage settlements tend to break up into the several lineages of which they are composed. (F010)

## COMMUNITY ORGANIZATION
### X   Cohesion of Family
The more undifferentiated and cohesive the community, the weaker the internal family solidarity. (T099)

## COMMUNITY ORIENTATION
### X   Cohesion of Family
The more integrated the nuclear family, the greater its general community concern. (S217)

## COMMUNITY SATISFACTION
### X   Cohesion of Family
The more integrated the nonfarm nuclear family of a fringe area, the greater its satisfaction with the community. (S217)

## COMMUNITY SOLIDARITY          X   Affinal Ties
In the absence of political machinery, community solidarity is maintained by affirming ties of marriage and uterine kinship (the Iatmul). (B303)

## COMMUNITY STABILITY
### X   Endogamy (Community)
Community endogamy tends to be correlated with the stabilization of community membership. (L063)

### Social Network
Tightly knit family friendship networks (i.e., a high frequency of interaction among family units) are more often found in neighborhoods exhibiting a great deal of stability. (G156)

## COMMUNITY (UNILINEAGE)
### X   Residence (Unilocal)
Unilocal residence rules will tend to be more rigid in unilineal communities. (F010)

## COMPETITION          X   Avoidance Relationship
Avoidance patterns are more likely to occur between kinsmen in direct competition for social rank. (M235)

### Size of Family
Life in a small family is more competitive than life in a large family. (R106)

### Social Mobility
Intraclass competition among upper-class families lessens the likelihood that any given family will maintain its status over the generation. (G156)

## COMPETITION AMONG WIVES
### X   Rank of Women
In polygynous societies the acute competition among a man's various wives for the position of favorite decreases the status of women in relation to men. (W128)

## COMPETITION FOR WOMEN          X   Polygyny
Where polygyny is stressed, competition for women will be high. (O023)

## COMPETITION WITHIN LINEAGE
### X   Honorary Titles
The existence of honorary titles tends to stimulate intralineage competition. (F015)

## COMPOSITION OF FAMILY
### X   Preferential Marriage (Cross-Cousin)
Patrilateral cross-cousin marriage is most likely to occur in a matrilineal society if the father has no nephews. (G055)

## CONCUBINAGE          X   Children, Evaluation of
The institutionalization of concubinage is directly correlated with the desire for numerous children. (S122)

### Descent
Concubinage is more likely to be institutionalized in societies where the importance of maintaining the descent line is stressed. (F035)

### Fecundity
Concubinage is more likely to occur when the wife is without children. (S134)

### Marital Stability
Marriages will tend to be more stable if concubinage is institutionalized. (B191)

### Polygyny
An increase in the number of concubines is directly correlated with the decrease in the number of polygynous unions. (S135)

## CONFLICT         X   Cohesion
When trouble arises between consanguineally related males, it tends to be displaced to affinal females. (G012)

### Cohesion of Clan
Interclan hostility tends to reinforce the solidarity of the clan. (W049)

### Cohesion of Kin Group
When trouble rises between consanguineally related males it tends to be displaced to affinal females. (G012)

### Descent/Residence
Matrilocality can occur in a patrilineal society only when intrasocietal hostilities are repressed and latent antagonism channeled into intense warfare. (M027)

### Descent (Unilineal)
When unilineal ties are emphasized for residence, inheritance, and succession, quarrels will be more frequent. (S284)

### Economic Cooperation
There is more likely to be tension between relatives when their relationship implies economic responsibilities. (F087)

### Endogamy (Community)
Hostility between villages will increase as marriage patterns become increasingly endogamous. (P008)

### Exogamy (Community)
The establishment of bonds of intermarriage between villages will tend to inhibit hostile relations between the communities. (E015)

The rate of intermarriage will tend to be higher if intervillage relations are not characterized by hostility. (K045)

### Kin Ties (Fictive)
The extension of fictive kin ties will increase the potentiality of friction in intergroup relations. (W075)

### Land
Intracommunity conflict occurs when lineages have unequal holdings in land (unless devices are developed to redistribute land rights to persons outside the owning group). (G029)

### Land Consolidation
Conflicts between larger kin units are less likely to occur if the landholdings of these units are not consolidated. (B299)

### Residence
Conflict within a village or between villages is more likely to occur where the village is composed of a few localized lineages than where lineage members are dispersed throughout the village. (H234)

### Size of Household
The larger the household, the greater the potential for conflict among its peers. (G156)

### Size of Kin Sub-Groups
Smaller segments of unilineal kin-groups are more likely to be the feuding units than are larger groups. (S189)

## CONFLICT AMONG KIN      X   Legal Ties
There is more likely to be tension between relatives when their relationship implies jural responsibilities. (F087)

## CONFLICT BETWEEN CLANS
### X   Intermarriage (Clan)
There is a direct correlation between the degree of hostility between clans and the extent to which their members intermarry. (B187)

### Residence
Conflict between clans is more likely to occur if the clans live nearby. (M129)

## CONFLICT BETWEEN GENERATIONS
### X   Adult Status, Barriers to
To the degree that impediments to the attainment of full social status within the family or kin-group exist, harmonious interaction between generations is unlikely. (E086)

### Polygyny
Where polygyny is the ideal, there is a strong potential conflict between different generations. (E086)

### Values
The adoption of new standards and definitions of behavior by the younger generation will be a source of intergenerational conflict in the family and community. (B042)

## CONFLICT BETWEEN KIN
### X   Avoidance Relationship
Avoidance or respect relationships tend to suppress or control conflict between relatives who have a close kinship bond. (S080)

## CONFLICT BETWEEN KIN-GROUPS
### X   Kin Ties (Fictive)
The extension of kin bonds to nonkinsmen increases the instability and potentialities for conflict between kin-groups. (W075)

## CONFLICT BETWEEN LINEAGES    X   Residence
Hostility tends to be more intense between lineages if they are of different territorial affiliation. (L070)

## CONFLICT BETWEEN WIVES    X   Age Difference
There is less likely to be friction between co-wives if there is a disparity in age. (O031)

### Clan Affiliation of Wives
Where a man marries women from different clans, there is more likely to be friction among them. (M137)

### Economic Dependence of Wives
There will be a greater adjustment of conflict between wives in a polygynous family if the wives are economically interdependent. (A030)

### Economic Rank
A first wife is more likely to accept a second wife if the economic status of the original couple is high. (S158)

### Polygyny
The relationship between co-wives will tend to be more amicable, the more closely related they are. (H128)

### Polygyny, Number of Wives
The amount of friction in a polygynous family is directly correlated with the number of wives. (A030)

### Polygyny (Sororal)
There is likely to be less conflict between co-wives when polygyny is sororal. (H139)

### Rank of Wives
Overt conflict between wives will tend to occur between wives who are of the same age and level of seniority. (B054)

### Sibling Rivalry
There is an association between sibling rivalry and rivalry between co-wives. (L133)

### Witchcraft
Sorcery is more likely to occur in societies which maximize jealousy between co-wives. (W127)

## CONFLICT IN ADOLESCENCE
### X   Social Structure (Differentiation)
The extent to which adolescence is a period of tension and conflict is directly correlated with the structural complexity of the society. (W113)

## CONFLICT IN CLAN    X   Residence
The geographical separation of subclans tends to indicate the pressure of friction between the groups. (M129)

### Segmentation
Clan fission is associated with intraclan hostility. (R054)

## CONFLICT IN FAMILY    X   Acculturation
The chances of marital and familial conflict are greatest whenever an individual member of a family enters a new social environment while other members remain in the old cultural area or whenever a family moves to a different place and its members vary in the degree to which they assimilate the new culture. (B033)

When the value orientation of the family is conservative, acculturation will be accompanied by conflict. (B042)

### Birth (Premature), Adjustment to
Parents who seek a reality-based understanding of the implications of a premature birth are more likely than those who have avoided external information (external to self-fantasy) to retain healthy family relationships throughout (and after) the crisis (i.e., of premature birth). (C108)

Parents who express negative feelings (aggression, guilt) about a premature birth are more likely than those who suppress these feelings to retain healthy family relationships throughout (and after) the crisis (i.e., of premature birth). (C108)

### Division of Labor
Given the intensity of feeling between the members of the small nuclear family, the dispersion of their activities outside the home increases the probability and intensity of conflict. (D058)

### Economic Dependence
When members of the joint family are economically dependent upon one another, friction is likely to characterize their relationship. (N014)

### Economic Role
Economic conflicts, when they do arise in families, seem to be related to differences in attitudes of family members toward economic goals and differences in the members' conceptions of their economic roles. (B033)

### Education
Differences in education are an important source of conflict between generations of a family as well as between members of a single generation. (H032)

### Emotional Adjustment of Child
There is a correlation between emotional disturbances in the child and familial disunity and conflict. (M200)

### Husband-Wife Relations (Economic)
When there is a divergent interest between a husband and wife in regard to expenditures for consumer goods, intrafamilial conflict will occur. (H028)

### Income
Increasing income and the increasing desire for purchase goods means increasing occasions for family conflict over how wages will be used. (H032)

### Inheritance
Tension within the extended family will be directly correlated with unequal distribution of the inheritance. (H086)

### Intermarriage (Cultural)
The discrepancy of value orientations of persons who intermarry is a basis of family conflict. (S075)

### Juvenile Delinquency
Boys who are frequent juvenile offenders are more likely to report family tensions than are those who have one offense.

### Mental Illness of Child
Mentally disturbed children tend to appear in families in which they are involved in conflict or disequilibrium between the parents. (S075)

### Mental Illness (Schizophrenia)
Female schizophrenics are more likely to conflict with their mothers and to participate in intrafamilial conflict than are schizophrenic males. (B279)

Conflict in the home of female schizophrenics tends to center around parental disapproval of her extrafamilial interests and behavior; in the case of male schizophrenics, it is more likely to center around instrumental problems, such as his failure to find regular employment. (B279)

### Mother-Child Relations
The mother is more likely to attempt to shield the child from the effects of conflict in the home than are other adults in the home. (C117)

### Occupational Choice (Migrant Labor)
The selection of migrant labor as an occupation is indicative of tensions and conflicts within the family. (F060)

### Parent-Child Relations (Allegiance)
In case of conflict, the child tends to show more alle-

giance to the mother, the father, and the other adult resident in the home, in that order. (C117)

### Personality Problems of Child
Emotionally disturbed children are more likely to be involved in parental conflicts than are "normal" children. (S185)

### Residence
Separation of family members, one from another, is more likely to lead to family conflict than if the family remains together. (C023)

### Ritual in Family
Family tension and discord result from different attitudes about ritual among members of a family. (B206)

Rituals in family living reduce stress and strain in the family. (B206)

### Role Behavior
Instrumental discrepancy (i.e., the lack of the physical and practical prerequisites necessary for role performance), whether fortuitous or consciously or unconsciously motivated, is a cause of conflict in the family.

### Role Definition
Inadequate familiarity with required roles is a cause of conflict in the family, as, for instance, is common between adolescents and parents, between parents after the birth of the first child, and so on.

The segmentalization of an individual's activity in the urban situation increases the tension within the family. (B033)

### Scapegoating
Where anxiety and problems exist in a family, the child with physical pecularities is most apt to become the focus of family problems. (B204)

### Scholastic Adjustment
The greater the conflict between family members, especially if one (father, mother, or child) is dominant, the greater the likelihood that the child will refuse to go to school. (K106)

### Segmentation of Joint Family
Hostility between wives of siblings is a major factor in the fission of the joint family. (M081)

### Size of Family
The smaller the family size, the more intense the feeling between its members and, hence, the more conflict between them. (D058)

### Social Adjustment of Child
The less the tension in family relationships (parent-parent and parent-child), the greater the likelihood that the child will be socially well adjusted within his peer group. (M178)

### Social Adjustment, Premorbid
There is more interpersonal conflict in families of schizophrenic patients with poor premorbid adjustment than in families of patients with good adjustment (Phillips Scale). (F115)

A greater proportion of the conflict that arises in families of schizophrenics with poor, as compared to good, premorbid adjustment is due to conflict between the parents, rather than between parents and son (Phillips Scale). (F115)

Schizophrenics with good premorbid adjustment have less conflict with their parents than do patients with poor adjustment (Phillips Scale). (F115)

Schizophrenics with poor premorbid adjustment have more difficulty with mother cues than with father cues on visual discrimination tests, whereas patients with good premorbid adjustment are more disturbed by father cues. (F115)

### Suicide
Suicide may be resorted to because of acute conflict with the family or because it is the only symptom which will be recognized as such by the family. (P078)

### Values
When differential and contradictory values prevail in a culture, family conflict will tend to arise where family members have internalized this conflict. (S075)

## CONFLICT IN KIN-GROUP          X   Exogamy
In an exogamous lineage system, the tensions resulting from a conflicting allegiance to the families of procreation and orientation are intensified. (F020)

### Joking Relationship
The establishment of a joking relationship tends to suppress or control potential conflict between relatives who have a close kinship bond. (S080)

### Kin Ties
A failure to sever the wife's ties to her natal group in a patrilineal and patrilocal society will engender serious tensions both within and between kin-groups. (N008)

### Preferential Marriage, Violation of
Patrilineal cross-cousin marriage in a matrilineal society is more likely to occur if the man has quarreled with the leader of his matrilineage. (G055, G057)

### Residence (Neolocal)
Neolocal residence in a society which is characterized by unilocal patterns will tend to be the result of conflict within the kin unit. (M070)

### Size of Kin-Group
In the process of expansion, conflict among the members increases. (F121)

### Stability of Extended Family
Conflict within the extended family will tend to lead to its fission. (P029)

### Stability of Kin-Group
Fission within the kin-group tends to result as a consequence of internal conflict. (P020)

## CONFLICT IN KIN NETWORK
### X   Disorganization of Family
Family disorganization correlates with troubled relations between husbands' and wives' kin and themselves. (K087)

### Economic Dependence
The greater the economic self-sufficiency of the individual, the more likely he is to conflict with and/or withdraw from the extended family. (M198)

## CONFLICT IN LINEAGE
### X   Geographical Mobility
Where kinship obligations are bilateral in character, migration in response to intralineage conflict is facilitated. (S092)

Conflicts over claims within the lineage tend to increase with an increase in the mobility of lineage members. (W082)

**Religion (Totemism)**
There is a positive correlation between sib totemism and intralineage conflict. (F015)

**Segmentation**
Lineage segmentation tends to be directly correlated with internal dissension within the lineage group. (G056)

## CONFLICT IN NUCLEAR FAMILY
**X Cohesion of Lineage**
When the solidarity of exogamous patrilineages is strong, nuclear families tend to be split by the conflicting loyalties of the spouses. (L027)

## CONFORMITY          **X Acculturation**
Children in more acculturated families are less frequently responsive to parental proposals or interference. (B040)

**Age of Child**
The younger the child (7–16 years, inclusive), the greater his concern with being the "good child" his parents want him to be. (W138)

**Aggression**
Aggressive boys are more resistant to the socialization demands of their parents than are normals. (B243)

**Authoritarianism**
The more authoritarian the male adolescent, the more likely he is to follow the motivational directives of his parents concerning academic matters. (B297)

**Child-Rearing Attitudes (Restrictiveness)**
Fathers who express restrictive child-rearing attitudes have higher scores on a test of conforming behavior (Crutchfield). (B227)

**Child-Rearing Practices (Clarity)**
Among homes characterized by a high level of explanation of family decision by the parents, the more explicit the behavior restrictions, the more obedient the children. (B266)

**Child-Rearing Practices (Conformity)**
Women who were isolated from their mother's attentions in childhood will tend to encourage deviant behavior in one child in order to participate as an adult in a relationship denied the mother in childhood. (H217)

**Child-Rearing Practices (Consensus)**
There is a positive relationship between parental conflict about authority over the child and the child's being disobedient with accompanying hostility. (R100)

**Child-Rearing Practices (Consistency)**
If a child is not exposed to contradictory goals and practices, he is then, as a result of reinforcement, more apt to be receptive to those accepted by his parents. (C086)

Inconsistent child-rearing practices are not likely to result in overly conforming or submissive behavior in the child. (R113)

**Child-Rearing Practices (Control)**
The greater the affection and control exercised by the parents, the greater is the likelihood that the child will submit to adult standards. The less restricting the parent

is, the greater the likelihood that the child will conform to peer standards. (D063)

The greater the frequency of control attempts by parents, the higher will be the relationship between firmness of control and the child's conformity with the opinions of others. (J024)

The more rigid the control which the parents attempt to exercise over adolescents, the more they feel the impulse to rebel and reject parental values when in a position to do so. (M056)

**Child-Rearing Practices (Discipline)**
Children raised in homes in which discipline was perceived to be just are more likely to be conformists than are children who perceived discipline to be unjust.

There is a positive correlation between firmness of parental discipline and a child's conformity with the opinions of others. (J024)

**Child-Rearing Practices (Giving Reasons)**
Children from families where there is a high level of explanation by the parents of family decisions are less conforming than are children from homes where there is not as much explanation of family decisions. (B266)

**Child-Rearing Practices (Giving Reasons/Power)**
The frequency with which a parent explains his rules to his children is more effective in inducing conformity to the rules than are the different levels of power exerted (autocratic, democratic, and permissive). (E105)

**Child-Rearing Practices (Power)**
The assertion by mothers of unqualified power in reaction to the child's noncompliance correlates with hostility, power assertiveness, and resistance to influence in the child. Such a correlation does not exist, however, with respect to power assertion by the mother prior to any noncompliant response by the child nor to power assertion of either type by fathers. (H182)

**Child-Rearing Practices (Punishment/Reward)**
Rewarding, rather than punishing, the child is more influential in developing social compliance (frequency and alacrity with which the child accedes to the demands and suggestions of other persons). (C102)

**Child-Rearing Practices (Restrictiveness)**
For girls, there is a positive relationship between excessive maternal restrictiveness between ages 4–7 and their conformity to parental demands during adolescence. (K115)

**Child-Rearing Practices (Rewards)**
With younger children, mothers who reward compliance (child's acceding to her demands and suggestions) are no more or less prone to punish their children for noncompliance than are mothers who do not reward their children for compliance. (C102)

With older children, mothers who reward compliance also punish for noncompliance; mothers who do not reward for compliance ignore noncompliant behavior. (C102)

**Child-Rearing Practices (Severity)**
Either excessive severity or excessive caution in parental child-rearing practices is a cause of rebelliousness in the child against parents and other adult authorities.

### Child-Rearing Practices (Strictness)
For girls, there is a positive relationship between an excessive severity of discipline between ages 4–7 years and their conformity to parental demands during adolescence. (K115)

Children whose mothers are rigidly dominating and controlling in their behavior toward the child tend to be submissive and overly conforming. (R113)

### Class
Toward the higher social strata, there is greater conformity with ideal family patterns. (B033)

Members of the upper class are expected to conform more rigorously to the norms of the community. (F014)

### Dependency
There is a correlation between the son's dependency on the parents and his conformity to parental prohibitions. (B243)

The more a child is dependent upon parents rather than peers for approval the more likely his behavior will be similar to that of his parents rather than that of his peers. (M179)

### Dependency Anxiety
Boys who are anxious about their dependency on their parents are more likely to resist parental restrictions than are boys with low anxiety. (B243)

### Education of Mother
Maternal educational level is unrelated to adolescent conformity in children. (K115)

### Father-Daughter Relations (Aggression)
Expressed aggression toward the father by the daughter is associated with nonconformity to authority patterns. (L136)

### Identification of Mother with Daughter
Daughters who are the objects of maternal identification tend to conform more to their mother's wishes than do daughters who are not. (H218)

### Juvenile Delinquency
If the child revolts against the values of the father he is more likely to become a delinquent. (M194)

### Kin Relations (Interaction)
The upper-class child has more contacts with extended kin; this prevents him from accepting deviant peergroup goals. (C086)

### Marital Adjustment
Marital adjustment is associated with a high degree of conventional behavior. (B033)

### Maternal Overprotectiveness
For boys, maternal overprotection during ages 4–7 is positively related to their conformity to parental demands during adolescence. (K115)

### Mental Illness of Child (Schizophrenia/Neurosis)
Schizophrenics are more likely than neurotic children to submit to the demands of their parents and community. (M197)

### Mental Illness (Schizophrenia/Neurosis)
Schizophrenics rebel less against the authority of their parents than do neurotics. Schizophrenics are more likely to have complied with their parents' demands, not only in childhood, but even during adolescence, when neurotics (in both middle and lower classes) were attempting to establish their independence. (M061)

Significantly more schizophrenics than neurotics (holding class constant) tend to have had lifelong patterns of submissive behavior—conformity to standards of home and community. (M061)

### Mother-Child Relations (Compliance)
Social compliance (frequency and alacrity with which children accede to demands and suggestions) of the child with his mother is associated with social compliance with his peers. (C102)

### Mother-Child Relations (Conformity)
Within various age levels, social compliance (frequency and alacrity with which children accede to demands and suggestions) of the child with his mother is associated with social compliance with his peers. (C102)

Social compliance (frequency and alacrity with which children accede to demands and suggestions) of the child with his mother is associated with the child's compliance toward other adults. (C102)

### Mother-Child Relations (Interaction)
The degree of attention a child receives from its mother tends to be inversely correlated with the degree of conformity of the child. (H217)

### Mother-Son Relations (Affection)
There is a positive relationship between maternal affection during the son's early years (2–7) and his conformity to parental demands during adolescence. (K115)

### Occupation
The more that the individual's occupation puts him in a position of public prominence, the greater the conformity demanded of him in his family life. (F106)

### Occupation of Father
Children whose fathers are in white collar occupations are more likely to be conformists than are children whose fathers are in blue collar occupations.

### Ordinal Position
There is no relationship between sibling birth order and the child's tendency to conform (measured by Davis' Compliant-Defiant Instrument). (S233)

Firstborn and only children are more influencible or more likely to conform than are those born later. (S263)

### Parent-Child Relations
Children who are opposite-sex allied (i.e., join parent in family conflict) are more conforming to what is expected of them than are children who are same-sex allied. (B263)

### Parent-Child Relations (Affection)
There is a correlation between the degree of affection the child has for the parent and the degree to which the child conforms to parental values. (N063)

The need to retain whatever warmth may exist in situations of affective insecurity will tend to lead—in the child—to an attempt to exercise control and to conform to the ideals of the parents. (T106)

### Parent-Child Relations (Closeness)
More detached parent-child relations may produce a child who has less concern for social conformity. (Y047)

### Parent-Child Relations (Control)

When the parental conception of the child's role in the community is widely different from that approved by the adolescent's group, rebellious behavior will result in direct proportion to the degree to which the parents intervene. (B033)

### Parent-Child Relations (Evaluation)

The more conforming the child to group opinion, the more likely is he to have an idealized perception of his parents; the more able the child is to make independent judgments, the more balanced (praise and criticism) is his perception of his parents. (M184)

### Parent-Child Relations (Interaction)

In homes characterized by a high level of parental explanation of family decisions, high parent-child interaction produces greater nonconformity in the child than does low parent-child interaction. (B266)

### Parent-Child Relations (Power)

Adolescents who feel that their parents use coercive rather than legitimate measures in exerting their power are less likely to conform to rules of conduct when their parents are absent than are other adolescents. (E105)

### Parental Role

When the mother is nurturant and nondisciplining and the father is disciplinarian and nonnurturant, the child will be likely to violate cultural norms when authority forces are absent. (S216)

### Parents/Peer Group

A significant correlation exists between the attitude of the adolescent toward the use of kosher meat and the attitude of his membership groups (i.e., the parents and peer group). (R010)

There is a tendency for adolescents to agree more closely with their peer group than with their parents in their attitudes toward the use of kosher meat. (R010)

### Paternal/Maternal Role

Those viewing the mother as a disciplinarian are more likely to reveal a discrepancy between what they think they should do and what they say they actually do than are those viewing the father as a disciplinarian. (H067)

### Peer Relations

The rejection of familial authority is more likely to occur if the child finds support for his rebellion in his peer group. (A013)

The greater the strength of the adolescent clique or gang, the greater the possibility of opposition to or evasion of parental authority and sanctions. (S219)

### Personality of Child (Authoritarianism)

The more authoritarian and "self-rejecting" the Jewish individual is, the less is his deviation from parents' ethnocentric ideology, despite exposure to the liberalizing atmosphere of college. (H244)

### Personality Problems (Hostility)

The more automatic and unquestioning the child's acceptance of parental authority, the more likely is the unconscious accumulation of repressed resentment and hostility. (M203)

### Physical Development

In the upper and middle classes, the later the maturation of the boy, the less likely he is to conform; in the lower classes, the later the maturation, the greater the conformity. With girls from the upper classes, the earlier the maturation, the greater the conformity. (T100)

### Power Structure of Family

As structural asymmetry increases in parent-child relations toward either autocratic or permissive control, parents' efforts at explanation of their rules are more necessary to make children obey. (E105)

### Sibling Structure (Sex)

Children with male siblings have a greater tendency to conform than do children with female siblings (measured by Davis' Compliant-Defiant Instrument). (S233)

### Social Isolation

A home which isolates a child socially is more likely than others to produce a child who conforms with the opinions of others. (J024)

### Social v. Economic Rank

The "social" component of socioeconomic status (i.e., parental education) shows a stronger inverse correlation with boys' compliance with authority than does the economic component (Berkeley Social Rating Scale). (T100)

## CONFORMITY (PEERS/PARENTS)    X   Values

Adolescent girls are more inclined to follow peers' advice than parents' advice in choices deriving meaning from the peer society and more likely to favor parents' opinion than peers' in choices deriving meaning from the larger society in which there are status positions to which one can aspire as an adult. (B292)

Adolescents are more given to peer conformity in making choices in areas where social values are changing rapidly and parental conformity where social values are relatively stable. (B292)

Adolescents are more disposed to peer conformity in making choices with immediate consequences and parental conformity for choices with emphasis on long-term effect. (B292)

## CONFORMITY WITH KIN ROLE  X  Urban/Rural

Obligations toward kinsmen are more likely to be neglected in urban areas. (G083)

## CONFORMITY WITH KIN RULE
### X   Genealogical Proximity

Behavior conforms more closely with kin rules, the closer the kin ties between individuals. (G053)

## CONSENSUAL UNION
### X   Marriage, Attitude Toward

Where consensual unions are common, the punishments for entering them are less severe and the rewards for marrying are not as great. (G151)

## CONSENSUAL UNION, APPROVAL OF
### X   Consensual Union, Reasons for Entering

Where the ranking of consensual cohabitation is low, women are more likely to enter it because of pressing economic needs rather than out of a hope for eventual marriage. (B245)

## CONSENSUAL UNION, REASONS FOR ENTERING
### X   Consensual Union, Approval of

Where the ranking of consensual cohabitation is low, women are more likely to enter it because of pressing economic needs rather than out of a hope for eventual marriage. (B245)

## CONSENSUS          X  Dyadic Relationships
The rate of interaction is correlated with the amount of agreement between two family members (i.e., willingness to accept information). (C124)

The rate of interaction is related to the rate of agreement between two family members (i.e., willingness to accept information). (C124)

The interaction rate between two family members is related to the agreement by the older dyad member. (C124)

### Kin/Nonkin Interaction
The members of a family show higher consensus on attitudes than do the members of any artificially composed group. (D061)

There is no difference in the degree of consensus between family, on the one hand, and artificially composed groups, on the other. (D061)

Emotional interaction is less likely to lead to agreement in the family setting than in groups of strangers, and instrumental interaction is more likely to produce agreement in a family setting than it is among strangers. (L180)

## CONSENSUS IN FAMILY          X  Class
The higher the social status of the family, the higher the degree of consensus among the family members. (D061)

### Cohesion of Family
Family adjustment is more likely to occur when its members have common interests, ideas, and ideals. (B033)

Parents of poorly adjusted families show less agreement in their descriptions of family situations than do parents of well-adjusted families. (V032)

### Size of Family
The larger the family, the greater the degree of consensus. (I007)

## COOPERATION          X  Residence
Since the ties among male residents under uxorilocality are not based on kinship but on propinquity, they cooperate less among themselves than do males under vivilocality. (T080)

## CORPORATE KIN-GROUP
### X  Cohesion of Community
A social structure based on an association of exogamous corporate patrilineal-descent groups is not likely to hold together unless it is knit together by a web of kinship ties that counterbalance the centrifugal tendencies of the descent groups.

### Community
Corporate descent groups can exist only in more or less homogenous societies. (F020)

The degree of congruence of a unilineal kin-group and the community and the extent of its corporate function are directly correlated. (F039)

### Descent (Bilateral)
Bilateral descent and the resulting personal and stem kindred tend to occur where collective and corporate kin control is absent or minimal. (D011)

The corporate character of the clan structure tends to deteriorate with an increase in an emphasis on both maternal and paternal kinsmen. (W103)

### Economic Pattern (Money)
The collapse of the unilineal descent group as a corporate landholding group accompanies an adjustment to a money economy. (G056)

### Fertility Values
Fertility will tend to be stressed in societies where the major corporate groups are kinship groups. (M127)

### Geographic Mobility
The development of strongly corporate unilineal descent groups is contingent upon the stabilization of population in a fairly small area. (B301)

### Industrialization
The corporate control of property by a kin-group is rare in industrialized societies. (B082)

### Inheritance
A shift from brother-brother to father-son inheritance would seem likely generally to weaken the solidarity of the corporate lineage. (F073)

### Kin/Nonkin
Where kinship is extended and becomes the basis for corporate group membership, it will drastically limit the degree to which major roles may be successfully assigned on nonkinship bases. (F073)

### Kindred/Lineage
Kindreds are less able than lineages to act as a collectivity regarding either internal activities (e.g., owning land, administering justice) or external conflicts. (G156)

### Land
Corporate kin landholding maintains kin ties. (F017)

### Political Stability
The coexistence in a society of corporate lineages with political institutions of the state type makes for strains and instability. (F073)

### Political Structure
With the development of a state organization, the corporate function of unilinear kin-groups tends to diminish. (F039)

The emergence of the state structure is inhibited by the principle of group corporateness which is manifest in the lineage group structure. (S087)

### Political Structure (Bureaucratic)
One of the major obstacles to the establishment of a bureaucratic structure is the kinship system with corporate patrilineages. (F073)

### Population
With an increase in the size of the population aggregate, it becomes necessary to identify and classify groups rather than individuals, so that corporate descent groups are formed. (O006)

### Preferential Marriage (Cross-Cousin)
Since the central figure of any patrilateral system must be the alternation of exchange, the descent group cannot be a corporate group, because its solidarity is destroyed by the separation of successive generations by opposed interests and statuses. (N072)

### Property
Individual ownership tends to increase with the deterioration of the corporate character of the clan structure. (W013)

### Residence
The corporate character of a clan or large-scale lineage is directly correlated with the localization of the group. (L051)

### Size of Kin-Groups
Smaller segments of unilineal kin-groups are more likely to engage in continuous corporate enterprise than are larger groups. (S189)

### Slavery (Pawnship)
The development of a system of property in pawns and slaves tends to encourage the development of corporate descent groups. (D081)

## CORPORATE KIN GROUPINGS    X Descent
A unilinear descent system can more easily develop into a corporate group with leadership and capacity to act as a unified body than can a bilateral descent system. (P083)

## CORPORATE KIN TIES
### X Economic Pattern (Money)
Cash economy tends to destroy corporate kinship bonds with villages. (T080)

## COURTSHIP    X Honeymoon
Where there are more peer relationships during courtship and the couple to be married are better acquainted, the function of the honeymoon as a bridge over role discontinuity (from courtship to marriage) is not as crucial. (P083)

### Husband-Wife Relations (Conflict)
For men there is a slight relationship between marital disagreements and the extent of premarital courtship. (P071)

### Marital Adjustment
There is a direct relation between conflict-free engagement and marital adjustment. (K161)

### Mate Selection (Free Choice)
With the decline of parental control over marriage, courtship on the part of young people becomes the approved preliminary to engagement and marriage. (B033)

When there is free mate choice, it is usually preceded by courtship. (S189)

### Parent-Child Relations (Closeness)
Close attachment between mother and son is related to slow courtship progress in the son. The closer the female to her father, the more advanced she is in courtship progress. (J026)

### Personality (Complementary Needs)
Need complementarity is more operative at a late than at an early stage of a romantic relationship. (K109)

### Premarital Sex Relations
A preoccupation with premarital sexual relations tends to occur when the demographic situation limits the availability of eligible persons. (S037)

### Value Consensus
Value consensus is more crucial at an early stage than at a later stage in a romantic relationship. (K109)

## COURTSHIP AND DATING STATUS
### X Parent-Child Relations (Criticism)
Married or engaged males are more critical of their parents than are men dating one particular girl more than others; there is no difference in how much girls criticize their parents according to whether they are dating, or married, or engaged. (H228)

## COURTSHIP (CHAPERONAGE)    X Love
The stricter the chaperonage system, the more able is the society to prevent love relationships from developing. (G156)

## COURTSHIP, DURATION OF
### X Marital Adjustment
The longer the courtship and engagement, the more likely it is that the marriage will be well adjusted. (C134)

### Residence
Throughout the period of the courtship, the degree of residential propinquity remains for the most part unaltered. (C002)

## COURTSHIP (INTERRACIAL)
### X Courtship (Secrecy)
Interracial courtship is characterized by secrecy. (G001)

### Parent-Child Relations (Approval)
Among interracial couples, the usual courtship activities do not take place in the home because of certain disapproval of their parents. (G001)

## COURTSHIP (SECRECY)
### X Courtship (Interracial)
Interracial courtship is characterized by secrecy. (G001)

## COURTSHIP STATUS
### X Adultery, Attitude Toward
Persons engaged or going steady are more likely to disapprove of adultery than are other single persons. (C124)

### Empathy
Empathy will increase as love develops from dating through marriage stages. (C023)

Dating girls report equal amounts of disagreement with their parents and dates; engaged girls see less disagreement with partners and a constant amount with parents; married girls estimate an increased disagreement with partners (when actually it declines). (H229)

Sons report more disagreement with parents than with partners during dating and courtship periods; after marriage, sons feel an increase in disagreement with partners. (H229)

### Identification with Cross-Sex Parent
With advancing courtship children are more apt to pair off with partners who bear similarities to their opposite-sex parents. (H229)

### Parent-Child Relations (Criticism)
Age held constant, males who have been engaged (excluding those who are married) are more independent (are more critical) of their parents than are those who have not; while for girls, there is no difference in their independence, engaged or not. (H228)

## COUVADE    X Descent (Matrilineal)
The custom of couvade is more likely to occur in matrilineal societies. (W154)

### Sleeping Arrangements
There is a strong association between the practice of couvade and exclusive mother-child sleeping arrangements. (B251)

## CREATIVE/SCHOLASTIC ACHIEVEMENT
### Authoritarianism
#### X   Scholastic/Creative Achievement

Parents of academic achievers are more authoritarian in their values and attitudes than are parents of creative adolescents. (E102)

## CREATIVITY        X   Child-Rearing Practices

Children whose mothers encourage their maturation are higher in intellectual originality than are children whose mothers encourage infantile behavior. (A071)

### Child-Rearing Practices (Clarity)

Among homes characterized by a high level of parental explanation of family decisions, explicit behavior restrictions are correlated negatively with the ability to be original. (B266)

### Child-Rearing Practices (Democratic)

Children from democratic homes (parents who encourage free experimentation by their children) are more likely to be involved in and more able to contribute to group activities that demand intellectual curiosity, originality, and constructiveness. (B287)

### Child-Rearing Practices (Giving Reasons)

The child raised in a home in which the parents consult with the child about regulations and attempt to explain discipline is more intellectually curious, original, and constructive than is the child raised in an authoritarian home. (L146)

### Child-Rearing Practices (Rigidity)

Children whose mothers are flexible in their use of authority are higher in intellectual originality, intellectual vigor, and total intellectual freedom than are children whose mothers are rigid in their use of authority. (A071)

### Parent-Child Relations (Closeness)

The more creative research chemists tend to report a greater isolation from parents in early adolescence. (M060)

## CREATIVITY/INTELLIGENCE OF CHILDREN
### X   Child-Rearing Practices (Conformity)

The parents of highly intelligent children limit individual divergence, while parents of highly creative children encourage it. (G114)

### Parent-Child Relations (Criticism)

The parents of highly intelligent children are more critical of their children and of the school than are parents of highly creative children. (G114)

## CREATIVITY/I.Q. OF CHILD
### X   Class (Mother's Awareness of)

Mothers of highly intelligent children (Binet) are more likely to be conscious of their parents' social class than are the parents of highly creative children (Guilford-Cattell). (G132)

### Occupation of Mother

The mothers of highly intelligent (Binet) children are more likely to be full-time housewives than are the mothers of highly creative (Guilford-Cattell) children. (G132)

### Personality of Parents (Insecurity)

Parents of highly intelligent children (Binet) are more likely to have feelings of insecurity than are the parents of highly creative children (Guilford-Cattell). (G132)

### Reading Habits of Family

Families of highly intelligent children (Binet) are more likely to subscribe to many magazines than are the families of highly creative children (Guilford-Cattell). (G132)

## CREATIVITY (MATHEMATICS)
### X   Child-Rearing Practices (Authoritarianism)

Highly creative and productive mathematically oriented adolescents tend to view their parents as more autocratic than do normal college students. (K148)

## CREATIVITY OF CHILD        X   Authoritarianism

The punitive and intimidating atmosphere of the authoritarian home is likely to result in a diminishing of the creativity and imagination of the child. (M203)

### Child-Rearing Practices (Exploration)

High creativity in adolescents is associated with parents who emphasize the importance of values, openness to experience, and varied interests. (E102)

### Education of Parents

There is a correlation between the educational level of the parents and the degree of creativity of the child. (R109)

### Occupational Rank of Parent

There is no relationship between parental occupational level and the degree of creativity of the child. (R109)

## CRIMINALITY        X   Authoritarianism of Father

Normal persons are more likely than are habitual criminals to have authoritarian fathers. (C105)

### Broken Homes

Habitual criminals are much more likely to come from broken homes than are noncriminals. (C105)

### Child-Rearing Practices (Consistency)

Boys whose fathers have been criminals but who are disciplined consistently tend not to become criminals. (M199)

### Child-Rearing Practices (Demands)

The lower the parental demands placed on the son, the more likely he is to become a criminal. (M195)

### Child-Rearing Practices (Dependency)

The greater the family's frustration (and extinction) of the son's dependency needs, the more likely he is to become a criminal. (M195)

### Child-Rearing Practices (Favoritism)

Parents of habitual criminals are more likely to have shown differential treatment to one or more of their children than are the parents of normal persons. (C105)

### Child-Rearing Practices (Punishment)

There is a correlation between aggression in the home environment, as measured by parental use of threats, punitive punishment, or unfavorable comparisons to others as techniques of discipline, and criminal behavior in the son. (M195)

Parents of recidivist prisoners are more likely to have used physical methods of punishment and are generally more irrational in their punishment methods. (S187)

### Child-Rearing Practices (Strictness)

Habitual criminals are likely to characterize their fathers as having been too strict or too lenient in terms of discipline than are normal persons, who tend to avoid both extremes of characterization. (C105)

### Criminality of Sibling
Habitual criminals are more likely than are normal persons to have a brother who is or has been a delinquent. (C105)

### Deviance of Parents
There is a correlation between deviance by either parent (alcoholism, or criminal or promiscuous behavior) and criminal behavior in the son. (M195)

### Employment of Mother
In the lower class, if the mother of an unstable family (open parental conflict, criminality, and other varieties of social deviance are considered to be indices of instability) is employed, the son is more likely to become an adult delinquent than if she is not employed. (M211)

### Father-Child Relations (Rejection)
The more rejecting the father is of the son, the more likely it is that the latter will become a criminal. (M195)

### Father-Son Relations (Rejection)
Boys whose fathers are criminals are less likely to become criminals if accepted by their fathers than if rejected by them. (H208)

Crime rates are highest among boys whose fathers have rejected them. (M199)

### Identification with Parents
Identification of the son with a deviant paternal model is strongly correlated with criminal behavior. (M195)

### Marital Adjustment
There is a correlation between parental conflict and criminal behavior of the son. (M195)

### Maternal Deprivation
There is a significant correlation between a childhood history of early maternal deprivation (below the age of six and for at least six months' duration) and a criminal record in later life. (E093)

### Maternal Overprotectiveness
There is a negative correlation between maternal overprotection and criminality. (M164)

### Maternal Role, Attitude Toward
There is a correlation between the mother's ambivalence toward her familial role and criminal behavior in the son. (M195)

### Mother-Child Relations (Warmth)
Normal persons are more likely to characterize their mothers as being warm and understanding than are habitual criminals. (C105)

### Mother-Son Relations (Rejection)
There is a correlation between maternal rejection and criminality in the son, particularly when the father is absent. (M195)

### Mother-Son Relations (Warmth)
Criminal rates tend to be higher among boys whose mothers do not display maternal warmth. (M199)

### Ordinal Position
Habitual criminals are less likely than normal persons to have been the oldest child. (C105)

### Parent-Child Relations (Affection)
Among adult criminals, more have had nonloving parents than any other type. (M194)

Boys whose parents are loving tend not to become criminals. (M199)

### Parent-Child Relations (Rejection)
There is a direct correlation between criminality and a family background in which the mother is rejecting and neglecting and the father aggressive. (M164)

### Personality of Father
Normal persons are more likely than habitual criminals to have fathers characterized as successful and respected, strict, strong, and demonstrating leadership. (C105)

### Personality Problems of Father
Deviant reactions to crises (aggressive or escapist) by the father are correlated with criminality in the son. (M195)

### Personality Problems of Mother
Habitual criminals are much more likely to have suspicious and neurotic mothers than are normal persons. (C105)

Mothers who react unrealistically to crises through aggression, desertion, or escapism are more likely to have criminal sons than are those who respond realistically. (M195)

### Sexual Deviance
There is a correlation between sexual deviance in the family (illegitimacy or incest) and later criminal behavior in the son. (M195)

### Sibling Relations
There is significantly less interaction and support among the brothers and sisters of the family of a habitual criminal than among those of a normal person. (C105)

## CRIMINALITY/ALCOHOLISM
### X    Child-Rearing Practices (Punishment)
Punitive methods of discipline by the mother correlate with criminality, but not alcoholism, in the son. (M195)

### Marital Adjustment
An attitude of indifference (rather than of either affection or conflict) between the parents is most likely to produce criminal behavior in the son, but is least likely to create alcoholism. (M195)

## CRIMINALITY AND MENTAL ILLNESS/BROKEN HOME    X    Behavior Problems
It is criminal or psychotic behavior on the part of the parent rather than the broken home which causes delinquency and other behavior problems in the child. (B285)

## CRIMINALITY OF FATHER
### X    Juvenile Delinquency
Fathers of delinquents are more likely than those of nondelinquents to have trouble with the law. (W152)

## CRIMINALITY OF PARENTS
### X    Juvenile Delinquency
If either of the parents has a criminal record, it is more likely that the child will become a delinquent. (M194)

## CRIMINALITY OF SIBLING    X    Criminality
The habitual criminal is more likely than the normal person to have a brother who is or has been a delinquent. (C105)

## CRISIS    X    Cohesion of Family
When the family group is threatened by severe tensions there tends to be a sudden rallying of forces toward uniting the family. (B202)

The disorganizing effects of crises are resisted better by families with a high degree of solidarity than by those with a low degree of solidarity. (J001)

### CRISIS, ADJUSTMENT TO          X    Dependency
Extreme emotional reaction to crisis is less frequent in families where the members have developed self-sufficiency and more frequent in those where there is great emotional dependency on one another. (B033)

### CRISIS (EPIDEMIC)    X    Cohesion of Kin-Group
The fragmentation of larger kin and local residential units into households tends to occur with the increase in local migration which accompanies an epidemic plague. (B041)

### CRISIS (SOCIAL)    X    Disorganization of Family
Disturbances in the family structure tend to be associated with widespread social and economic disintegration. (K065)

#### Illegitimacy Rate
Illegitimacy is directly correlated with social disintegration and economic disorder. (K065)

#### Marriage Rate
Great social disturbance or upheaval will cause a drop in the marriage rate. (C001)

### CULTURAL EVOLUTION
#### X    Descent (Matrilineal/Patrilineal)
Simpler cultures tend to be matrilineal; more advanced ones, patrilineal. (L110)

#### Family, Institutionalization of
A shift from dependence on biological patterns (instincts or drives) to cultural patterns (socialization) is associated with greater human involvement in the formation and operation of the family unit. (G156)

### CUSTODY          X    Age of Children
The mother is more likely to be given custody of the children if they are young. (C060)

### CUSTODY OF CHILDREN
#### X    Divorce, Adjustment to
The parent who retains the children after divorce experiences less of a crisis than the one who is cut off from both the former mate and the children. (B033)

# D

**DATING**

**X   Age at Marriage**
There is no relationship between age of initial or steady dating and age at marriage. (B248)

Girls who marry in their teens are more likely to start dating at an earlier age than are those who do not. (M231)

The final institutionalization of steady dating is likely to increase the average age at marriage and decrease the range of marriage age, especially reducing teen-age marriages. (P083)

**Class**
There is a curvilinear relationship between social-status levels and number of steady dates for men; an inverse relationship obtains for women. (B248)

There is no relationship between social-class level and the tendency to date/not to date persons not attending school. (B248)

**Dating During Marriage**
Dating during marriage (with husband) is positively associated with the frequency with which the divorcée dates after the divorce. (G157)

Regardless of whether the divorcée dated with her husband during the marriage, those who begin dating during the separation period exhibit a high frequency of dating after the divorce. (G157)

When dating during the separation period is controlled, there is no relationship between dating during the marriage (with husband) and the frequency with which the divorcée dates after the divorce. (G157)

**Divorce**
Longer periods of acquaintanceship prior to engagement and marriage are associated with a lower proneness to divorce. (G157)

The greater the time lapse since the granting of the decree, the more likely is the divorcée to become a frequent dater; but the proportion of divorcées who never date is not affected by the time lapse since the granting of the decree. (G157)

**Divorce Adjustment**
The greater the emotional problems experienced by the divorcée, the lower her dating frequency after the divorce. (G157)

**Divorce/Bereavement, Adjustment to**
Ability to take part in a new relationship is related to better adjustment whether the loss of a spouse was by death or by divorce. (G156)

**Divorce Complaints**
Those who complain of value conflicts have the highest post divorce dating frequency. (G157)

**Divorce, Initiation of**
Among divorcées who rarely or never date, the highest proportion is formed among those whose husbands first suggested the divorce, followed by those who themselves suggested the divorce, and lastly by those who claim the suggestion to divorce was mutual. (G157)

**Divorcée's Attitude Toward Ex-Husband**
Divorcées who claim negative or loving attitudes toward their ex-spouses are less likely than those who feel friendly or indifferent toward them to be steady daters. (G157)

**Education of Divorcée**
The higher the educational level, the greater the frequency of dating for the divorcée. (G157)

**Empathy**
The greater the accuracy in role-taking of dating pairs, the greater the satisfaction in dating behavior and the greater the degree of dating involvement. (S279)

**Employment of Mother**
Adolescent daughters of lower-class working mothers are more likely to seek in steady dating a substitute for family security or companionship than are adolescent daughters of middle-class working mothers. (G156)

**Engagement, Duration of**
A long period of acquaintanceship prior to engagement is associated with a longer period of engagement. (G157)

**Extramarital Relations**
Among the various complaints made by the divorcées, those who complain that their husbands were involved with other women have the lowest postdivorce dating frequency. (G157)

**Friendship**
Divorcées who date before the separation are less likely to keep their marriage friends than are those who do not date before separating. (G157)

**Husband-Wife Relations**
Among divorcées who are unattached (not remarried or steady daters), frequent daters are less likely to feel antagonistic toward their ex-spouses than are those who date less frequently. (G157)

**Marital Adjustment**
Cultures that approve of dating do not necessarily produce young people that are better adjusted socially or able to make more satisfactory choices of their marriage partners. (M185)

The more successful youth are in the competitive area of dating, the less prepared they may be for marital adjustment. (S219)

**Marriage, Attitude Toward**
Divorcées with positive attitudes toward love and marriage are more likely to claim they have dating opportunities to meet people than are those with negative attitudes. (G157)

### Mate Selection
College students tend to stress the same factors in selecting dates as in selecting mates. (C023)

### Mother-Child Relations
Divorcées who give more attention to their children are less likely to become steady daters. (G157)

Mothers are more likely to encourage their daughters to date than they are their sons. (K161)

### Parent-Child Relations (Criticism)
Males who are dating are more likely to criticize their parents than are nondating males; girls not dating are just as likely to criticize their parents as are girls who are dating. (H228)

Age held constant, males who have gone steady are more independent of (criticize more) their parents than do those who have not; there is no such difference for females. (H228)

### Premarital Sex Relations
Early steady dating is associated with a decline in the dalliance pattern (i.e., exploitative premarital sex behavior). (P083)

### Religion
Catholic divorcées are less likely to date than are Protestant divorcées. (G157)

### Remarriage
There is a positive relationship between the divorcée's desire to remarry and her dating frequency. (G157)

When the divorcée desires to remarry, there is a high positive relationship between opportunities to meet people and dating frequency; when the divorcée does not wish to remarry, a low positive relationship is found between social opportunities and dating frequency. (G157)

When there are no social opportunities reported, the relationship between the divorcée's desire to remarry and the frequency with which she dates is positive, but low. (G157)

Controlling for the time lapse since the divorce, there is a positive relationship between the divorcée's having a steady date and her claims that there is someone among her male friends that she would consider a potential spouse. (G157)

### Residence
Dating partners, like marriage partners, are more likely to live nearby than farther away. (C002)

### Sex-Role Adjustment
The more insecure the parents in their sex roles, the more likely they are to encourage the child to engage in heterosexual social activity at an early age. (R104)

### Sex-Role Definition
Adolescents believe mothers know more about dating than fathers. (N057)

Adolescents believe that parents of the opposite sex know less about dating than parents of the same sex (as the adolescent). (N057)

### Sexual Aggression
A correlation exists between the degree of involvement in dating relationship and the level of erotic intimacy offense. (K001)

### Social Opportunities
Divorcées who receive help from both friends and family in meeting people have a higher dating frequency than do those who receive help from either friends or family, followed by those who receive help from neither group. (G157)

When the divorcée both wishes to remarry and claims many opportunities to meet people, her frequency of dating is maximized. (G157)

### Surrogate Mother, Evaluation of
Whether or not the divorcée is dating frequently, she is likely to believe that substitute child care is excellent. (G157)

### Values
There is a parallelism between the norms of competition and success prevalent in the larger American society and the norms which govern dating behavior. (S219)

## DATING DURING MARRIAGE          X  Dating
Dating during marriage (with husband) is positively associated with the frequency with which the divorcée dates after the divorce. (G157)

Regardless of whether the divorcée dated with her husband during the marriage, those who begin dating during the separation period exhibit a high frequency of dating after the divorce. (G157)

When dating during the separation period is controlled, there is no relationship between dating during the marriage (with husband) and the frequency with which the divorcée dates after the divorce. (G157)

### Divorce Decision
The frequency with which the husband and wife dated one another during the marriage is not related to the stability of the final decision to divorce. (G157)

### Duration of Marriage
Among divorced couples, there is a low inverse relationship between the frequency with which the couple went out together during their marriage and the length of their marriage. (G157)

The relationship between low frequency of "dating" during the marriage and longer duration of marriage is greater among those with higher income. (G157)

### Income
Among divorced couples, higher income is associated with a higher frequency of dating during marriage. (G157)

### Size of Family
Among divorced couples, the greater the number of children, the lower the frequency with which the couple "dated" during the marriage. (G157)

## DATING FREQUENCY                    X  Age
The younger the divorcée, the more likely is she to date frequently. (G157)

### Sexual Aggression
Dating frequency is not significantly related to proneness to sexual aggression. (K108)

## DATING GOAL                        X  Sex Status
Men are less interested in marriage as a consideration in dating than women are. (B244)

## DATING, PARENTAL APPROVAL OF
### X    Marital Adjustment of Parents
The happier the parents are in their marriage, the less likely it is that they will oppose dating by their children. (S219)

### Sex Status of Child
The parent is more likely to oppose dating by the cross-sex rather than by the same-sex child. (S219)

## DATING (PARENT'S KNOWLEDGE OF)
### X    Juvenile Delinquency
There is a negative relationship between parent's knowledge of dating behavior and delinquent adjustment. (N057)

## DATING RELATIONSHIP    X    Sexual Aggression
Sexual aggression, preceded by mutually acceptable sex play, is more likely to occur among couples with a durable and involved dating relationship than among couples who have just begun to date. (K018)

### Sexual Permissiveness
The more permissive the society regarding premarital sex relations, the more likely it is that those who experience premarital coitus with their steady or fiancé(e) will be satisfied with the relationship.

## DAUGHTER/WIFE
### X    Sex-Role Definition (Egalitarianism)
Men are likely to hold more egalitarian views about the role of their daughters in society than about the role of their wives. (K099)

## DEATH    X    Cohesion of Kin-Group
The cohesion of the kin-group is higher at the death of one of its members. (S096)

### Mental Illness
Psychologically disturbed patients have in common an appreciably greater incidence of bereavement in childhood than that obtaining among Americans in general. (A070)

### Scholastic Adjustment
School phobics are more likely than are normal children to have experienced death or the threat of death (relative to self or family) prior to school attendance. (D065)

### Stability of Polygynous Family
The polygynous household in a matrilineal society is likely to disperse after the death of the husband since wives and children never become part of the husband's descent group nor are there common property interests to hold them together over time. (C090)

## DEATH (FATHER/MOTHER)
### X    Emotional Problems of Women
Women are more likely to have emotional problems later in life after the loss of a mother rather than of a father. (H188)

## DEATH OF FATHER    X    Alcoholism
Alcoholic women are likely to have experienced the deaths of their fathers at earlier ages than are nonalcoholic women. (H222)

There is no difference between alcoholic and nonalcoholic males and the ages at which they experienced the deaths of their fathers. (H222)

### Neurosis
There is no difference between male psychoneurotics and normals or between women psychoneurotics and normals and the ages at which they have experienced the deaths of their fathers. (H226)

### Sex-Role Identification
Men who have lost their fathers in childhood have difficulties in masculine identification. (A070)

When the father dies and the mother is unaffectionate and deviant in her behavior toward her sons, sex-role identification instability (both feminine and aggressive tendencies) is much more common than when the mother is affectionate and nondeviant. (M181)

### Stability of Extended Family
Fission of the extended family is not likely to occur until the death of the father. (G072)

## DEATH OF GRANDMOTHER
### X    Identification of Mother with Daughter
Mothers who have high degrees of identification with their daughters were more likely to have lost their own mothers before the age of 16 than were mothers who did not identify with their daughters. (H218) ·

## DEATH OF LIKE-SEX PARENT    X    Mental Illness
Mental illness tends to be directly correlated with the death of the parent of the same sex. (S187)

## DEATH OF MATERNAL GRANDFATHER
### X    Mental Illness (Schizophrenia)
Mental illness tends to be correlated with an early death of the maternal grandfather. (L118)

## DEATH OF MOTHER    X    Marital Adjustment
Men who have lost mothers have oral problems and express in their marital relationships unusual dependency and hostility. (A070)

### Mental Illness (Schizophrenia)
Schizophrenic women who are more seriously ill are more likely to have experienced the deaths of their mothers at an early age (1–5 years) than are schizophrenic women who are not as seriously ill. (H226)

### Neurosis
Psychoneurotics are more likely than are normal children to have experienced the deaths of their mothers while they were between the ages of one and five. (H226)

## DEATH OF MOTHER/FATHER    X    Self-Conception
Self-esteem of the child whose parents have been separated by death is somewhat lower if the mother has died than if the father has died. (R129)

## DEATH OF PARENT    X    Age at Marriage
Children are more likely not to marry, or marry late, if one parent (especially the father) dies when the child is between 10 and 20 years of age. (T087)

### Dependency
The child who grows up with one parent (after the death of the other) is more likely than others to have difficulty in making a normal separation from his parent when he becomes an adult. (H188)

### Emotional Problems of Child
Children who lose a parent by death are less likely to

become emotionally disturbed if the remaining parent keeps the home intact than if he does not. (H188)

### Guilt
If a child is prepared for a parent's death, he is less likely to experience excessive guilt and responsibility in the future. (H188)

### Maternal Overprotectiveness
Death of the mother's parents during childhood is a cause of her later overprotectiveness toward her child. (B272)

### Mental Illness
There is no relationship between losing the parent by death and mental disorders in the child. (P072)

There is a definite correlation between the death of a parent and mental illness. (S187)

### Mental Illness (Schizophrenia)
There is a correlation between the loss of one or both parents and the development of schizophrenia in the child. (B308)

Schizophrenic women are more likely to have lost either or both of their parents by death at an earlier age than are normals. (H226)

There is no difference between schizophrenic and non-schizophrenic males and the age at which they experienced the deaths of one or both parents. (H226)

### DEATH OF SIBLING X Mental Illness
Mental illness appears to be correlated with the death of a sibling of the patient. (S187)

### DEATH OF SPOUSE X Sex Status
Among older persons (those over 65), women are more able successfully to adjust to widowhood than are men to widowerhood. (C116)

### DEATH RATE X Adoption
In societies in which the survival rate for the population is low, adoption is more likely to occur than in societies with a high survival rate. (D080)

### Child-Rearing Practices (Neglect)
The greater the neglect of the child, the less likely it is that it will survive. (M203)

### Divorce
The lower the death rate in a society, the greater the rate of divorce. This proposition is also denied.

### Employment of Mother
(In England and Scotland prior to 1914) children of working mothers had a higher death rate than those of nonworking mothers. (S265)

The sooner the mother resumes work after the birth of a child, the higher the rate of infant mortality. (S265)

### Isolation of Nuclear Family
Where there is a strong likelihood that a child might be deprived of one or both of his biological parents before outgrowing his dependency on them (e.g., where living is "harsh"), the isolated nuclear family is less likely to occur (because of the need for substitute parents to complete the socialization process). (P083)

### Kin Ties
Where the mortality rate is high, the importance of consanguineal relationships tends to be less. (L063)

### Mother-Child Relations (Affect)
Child mortality rates are positively associated with absence of emotional interchange with the mother. (S209)

### Nuclear/Extended Family
Nuclear families are more common in societies with low mortality; joint households, in societies with high mortality. (C090)

### Occupational Rank of Mother
The higher the occupational level of the mother, the lower the death rate of their children. (S265)

### Sibling Rivalry
If the death rate is low, strong competition between sons of a polygynous father (which can degenerate into fratricidal warfare) is likely to occur. (P083)

### DEATH RATE OF CHILDREN X Mother-Child Relations (Affect)
Child mortality rates are positively associated with absence of emotional interchange with the mother. (S209)

### DEATH RITUAL X Sex Status
As the loss of the husband is usually considered to have a greater impact on the family structure, elaborate death rituals are more likely to exist for the husband than for the wife. (G156)

### DELINQUENCY OF FAMILY MEMBERS X Juvenile Delinquency
There is a positive correlation between becoming a juvenile delinquent and having a family in which there are other delinquent members. (S210)

### DELINQUENCY OF MOTHER X Employment of Mother (Regularity)
Irregularly employed mothers of delinquent sons are more likely to have once been juvenile delinquents themselves than are either regularly employed or nonemployed mothers of delinquents. (S265)

### Juvenile Delinquency
Delinquency of the mother contributes indirectly to the son's delinquency by contributing to traits of a defensive attitude, a feeling of inadequacy, and a lack of self-criticism.

Delinquency of the mother contributes directly to the delinquency of the child.

A child having a tendency to fantasy or receptive trends is more likely to become delinquent if his mother is delinquent.

### DELINQUENCY OF PARENTS X Juvenile Delinquency
Parents with histories of severe delinquency tend to have children who are also delinquent. (B291)

### DEPENDENCY X Achievement Motivation
Boys with high achievement motivation are less likely to ask for parental aid in a problem-solving situation than are boys with low achievement motivation. (R098)

### Adult Role
In Western society reduction of the child's dependence on the nuclear family is necessary for the assumption of adult roles. (G156)

### Affinal Relations (Conflict)
In-law problems in marriage will more frequently involve the wife's parents than the husband's parents since females are more likely to be attached to and

depend on families of orientation than are males. A corollary of this is that the likelihood of a husband having in-law difficulties increases with the degree of the wife's attachment to and dependency on her parents. (S011)

### Aggression
In comparison to control adolescent boys, aggressive boys make fewer dependency demands upon their parents. (B213)

Aggressive boys are less likely to show emotional dependency on their fathers and, to a lesser extent, on their mothers than are normals. (B243)

Aggressive boys are more likely to manifest dependency anxiety concerning their relationships with their parents, as measured by avoidance and secretiveness, than are normals. (B243)

The more aggressive the child, the less dependent his behavior toward his parents. (K103)

The greater the child's dependency on his parents, the more likely he will be to learn and practice control of aggressive behavior. (K103)

### Anxiety
The less dependent the child is on the parents, the less anxiety he will feel over the anticipation of loss of their love. (K103)

### Anxiety Dreams
Individuals with falling dreams are far more likely to be overdependent on their mothers than are individuals with attack dreams. (H216)

### Breast Feeding
Feeding practice (breast *v.* bottle feeding) and dependency of child are not associated. (S191)

### Broken Home
Mother and child are more likely to be more dependent on each other in a broken family than in an intact family. (R129)

### Child-Rearing Anxiety
To the degree that the mother shows child-rearing anxiety, the more likely it is that her daughter will show attention-seeking behavior, and dependence. (B232)

### Child-Rearing Practices (Adaptation)
The extent to which the mother adapts to the infant's individual capacities is unrelated to the development of autonomy in the infant. (Y042)

### Child-Rearing Practices (Advice/Overprotection)
Frequent advice by mothers to adolescent boys is related to overdependency and overprotection. (N057)

### Child-Rearing Practices (Authoritarianism)
Authoritarian discipline increases the dependency of the child and his acceptance of punishment. (M203)

### Child-Rearing Practices (Control)
The longer the parent maintains strong control over the child, the greater the postponement in the development of motives for self-directed achievement. (D063)

### Child-Rearing Practices (Dependency)
There is a curvilinear relationship between the severity of the mother's frustration or punishment of dependency and the amount of overt dependency shown by the child. (B243)

Tendencies toward dependency in the child are likely to be increased by parental punishment specifically directed against dependent behavior. (M221)

Mothers of dependent children do not significantly tend to punish the child's dependent behavior. (M221)

Fathers of boys with high levels of independence tend to give their sons a higher degree of autonomy in making their own decisions than do fathers of boys with low levels of independence. (R106)

Reward for dependency of child increased dependency only when it was superimposed upon punishment for the same behavior. (S191)

Permissiveness for dependent behavior of the child was not associated with dependent behavior of the child. (S191)

The greater the child's understanding of where his parents expect him to be independent or dependent, the more able is the child to become independent. (S202)

### Child-Rearing Practices (Discipline)
In the early years of childhood, the use of withdrawal of love as a method of discipline is correlated with dependency of the boy on the parents. (B243)

There is a negative correlation between parental discipline by means of deprivation of privileges and dependency of the boy on the parents. (B243)

For girls, there is a positive relationship between severity of maternal discipline during ages 2–7, and dependency upon the mother during the adolescent years. (K115)

### Child-Rearing Practices (Giving Reasons)
As the level of power decreases, parents' explanations of their policies are more likely to create a sense of self-confidence and independence. (E105)

### Child-Rearing Practices (Nurturance)
There is *no* association between dependency behavior in the preschool situation and nurturance of the child at bedtime. (S014)

The more nonnurturant (punitive) the mothers of preschool boys, the more dependent they are. (S238)

The more nonnurturant (punitive) the mothers of preschool girls, the less dependent they are. (S238)

### Child-Rearing Practices (Oral)
The greater the mother's overindulgence of oral and other needs of her infant, the greater the dependency strivings in her children. (B224)

The more the mother frustrates the oral needs of the infant, the greater the dependency striving of the child. (B224)

### Child-Rearing Practices (Permissiveness/Giving Reasons)
Adolescents whose parents are permissive in their authority and explain their rules are most likely to be autonomous; adolescents whose parents are autocratic and who seldom give explanations for their rules of conduct are least apt to be autonomous. (E105)

### Child-Rearing Practices (Physical Contact)
Amount and quality of physical contact between mother and infant are not related to the development of autonomy in the infant. (Y042)

### Child-Rearing Practices (Punishment)

There is no relationship between parental use of physical punishment and the degree of dependency of the child on the parent. (B243)

Nonaggressive boys whose parents use physical punishment are more likely to show anxiety about dependency on their teachers and peers than are those whose parents do not use such discipline. (B243)

Maternal punitiveness is inversely correlated with dependency behavior. (K111)

The more severely punished the child, the more likely he (or she) is to be dependent upon other children, rather than upon a teacher. (S238)

### Child-Rearing Practices (Punishment) X Dependency of Child

Withdrawal of love as a method of punishment and increased emotional dependency of the child are associated. (S191)

### Child-Rearing Practices (Punishment) X Peer Relations

Children who perceive themselves as autonomous and their parents as coercive (punishing) are more actively friendly with their peers than are others. (H205)

Children who perceive themselves as autonomous and their parents as coercive (punishing) tend to be more active than others as leaders in their peer groups. (H205)

### Child-Rearing Practices (Punishment) X Scholastic Achievement

Children who perceive themselves as autonomous and their parents as coercive (punishing) tend to do better academically than others. (H205)

### Child-Rearing Practices (Responsiveness)

The extent to which the mother responds to the infant's vocal and physical communications is unrelated to the development of autonomy in the infant. (Y042)

### Child-Rearing Practices (Restrictiveness)

A curvilinear relationship exists between the severity of demands and restrictions made by parents and the development of autonomy in the child. (M203)

The more restrictive the parent, the greater the likelihood that the child will become overly dependent. (S204)

### Child-Rearing Practices (Restrictiveness/Demands)

Adult-dependent boys (who rejected any interaction with their peers, but strongly sought dependent relationships with adults) tend to be raised in a family environment characterized by high parental demands and strict parental supervision and restriction. (M221)

### Child-Rearing Practices (Sex Role)

Resulting from sex-typed child-rearing practices, girls tend to be more dependent than boys. (B252)

### Child-Rearing Practices (Strictness)

For girls, the more severe the discipline administered by the mother, the greater is the dependency upon the mother. (K127)

### Childbirth

Mothers who have psychopathic reactions to childbirth are similar in most psychological traits to those who have no such reactions, but they do manifest much greater dependence on their own mothers. (M193)

### Class

Lower-class paranoid schizophrenics show more dependence on their mothers, but less dependence on the family as a whole, then do middle-class paranoid schizophrenics. (L155)

Middle-class children are more dependent on displays of warmth and love for a sense of security and belonging than are lower-class children. (M061)

There is no correlation between adolescents' degree of felt emancipation from their parents and the socioeconomic status of their families. (T100)

The lower the social class, the more likely it is that the adolescent perceives himself as independent from his parents. (T100)

There is no significant difference in the dependence of the child between the middle class and the working class. (W002)

There is no significant difference in the amount of attention the child wants between middle class and working class. (W002)

### Cohesion of Family

Overt dependency of the child is heightened by lack of cohesion within the family and parental rejection. (M221)

College students with relatively distant ties to their families, compared with those who are relatively close, are more likely to prefer individual-oriented activities and are less likely to prefer group-oriented activiities. (R116)

### Conformity

There is a correlation between the son's dependency on the parents and his conformity to parental prohibitions. (B243)

The more a child is dependent upon parents rather than peers for approval, the more likely his behavior will be similar to that of his parents rather than to that of his peers. (M179)

### Crisis, Adjustment to

Extreme emotional reaction to crisis is less frequent in families where the members have developed self-sufficiency and more frequent in those where there is great emotional dependency on one another. (B033)

### Death of Parent

The child who grows up with one parent (after the death of the other) is more likely than others to have difficulty in making a normal separation from his parent when he becomes an adult. (H188)

### Disorganization of Family

There is a correlation between the occurrence of major discontinuities (severe illness, changes in the physical or social environment) between the ages of nine months and three years and dependency in the child. (B272)

Extremely dependent boys are more likely to have been raised in families characterized by parental conflict and deviant behavior (e.g., dictatorial or passive mothers, neurotic mothers, incest, etc.). (M221)

### Education

The higher the education of the wife, the less dependent she is on her children.

### Employment of Mother
When the mother works, the child's dependency needs are increased. (Y050)

Children of mothers who are employed are no more dependent than are children of mothers who are not employed. (Y047)

### Extended/Nuclear Family
The extended family is better able to care for the aged, ill, crippled, or infirm than is the nuclear family. (G156)

### Father Absence
There is a correlation between the lack of the continuous presence of the father in the home and dependency in the child. (B272)

No significant relationship exists between absence of the father from the home and dependency. (M181)

The absence of the father from the home increases the son's dependence on the mother. (M195)

If the father is frequently absent from the home for extended periods of time during the first three years of the child's life, it is more likely that the child will be overdependent. (S204)

### Father-Child Relations (Interest)
The greater the paternal interest in the child, the more self-reliant the child. (L150)

### Feeding
Dependent behavior of the child in the preschool period is positively associated with degree of frustration of the child during the nursing and weaning periods. (S014)

If an infant's feeding schedule is frustrating, the child is likely to be dependent. (S238)

### Feeding (Demand)
Among girls there is no relationship between feeding practices and dependency on the mother; among boys those fed by self-demand are more dependent on their mothers than are those fed on a schedule (U.S.). (S191)

### Homosexuality
Overt homosexuality may develop in response to a fear of adult responsibility. (T104)

### Husband-Wife Relations (Conflict)
The greater the conflict between the parents, the more likely it is that the period of dependency of the child on the mother will be prolonged.

### Identification with Mother
The more the infant is dependent upon the mother for satisfaction of primary needs, the more likely he will be to develop a *generalized dependency* upon, and subsequent identification with, her. (A049)

The greater the extent of the child's identification with the mother, the more independent he is and the more he resents the mother's restrictions. (B272)

### Identification with Non-Family Members
The greater the child's emotional dependency on his parents, the more likely is he in his relations with others to identify with the person rather than with the person's values and goals. (A059)

### Identification with Parent
The greater the dependence of the child on the parent, whether the latter is aggressive and/or loving, the greater his identification with that parent. (B234)

There is a correlation between dependency on the parents and identification with parents and internalization of their values. (B243)

### Initiation Rites
Societies in which early childhood-training practices foster a very close dependency relationship between the mother and her young son tend to provide drastic puberty rites to break this bond. (M058)

### I.Q.
Children's intellectual achievement behavior (I.Q.) correlates with their emotional independence from their parents. (C118)

### Juvenile Delinquency
Juvenile delinquents are far more independent from their parents than are nondelinquents.

The greater the child's acceptance of the freedom allowed him by his parents, the less likely he is to show delinquent behavior. (N063)

### Juvenile Delinquency (Aggressive)
Aggressive delinquency is caused primarily by the disruption of the child's dependency relationship with his parents. (B246)

### Love
Love relationships during adolescence or young-adult years help to reduce dependence on the family. (G156)

### Marital Adjustment
Couples who plan to be independent of their parents have a greater chance for marital success. (B244)

### Marriage Chances
Where dependence of both male and female children upon the mother is encouraged, it is more likely that both men and women will prefer relying upon residing with their families of origin to the responsibilities of marriage. (B245)

### Maternal Overprotectiveness
Maternal overprotection tends to be directly correlated with an inhibition of patterns of independence in the child. (L163)

Maternal overprotectiveness tends to be correlated with an early/premature assumption of family responsibility (whether through death of parent or poverty). (L163)

### Maternal-Role Behavior
The emotional dependence of the children on the mother will be increased if she serves as an intermediary between father and children. (H082)

### Mental Illness
An exclusive emotional dependency on the mother tends to be directly correlated with mental illness. (L118)

### Mental Illness of Child (Schizophrenia)
The relationship between the schizophrenic child and his parents tends to be one of intense emotional dependency. (G022)

The mother of the schizophrenic is more likely than the mother of the neurotic (and the normal) to describe the child as being dependent upon her, but is less likely to disapprove of such behavior. (M218)

### Mental Illness (Schizophrenia)
Fathers of schizophrenics are more likely to be dependent on their mothers than are fathers of normals. (K125)

Schizophrenia tends to be directly correlated with an intense emotional relationship and strong dependency with the mother. (L126)

Schizophrenics reveal greater dependency upon parents than do nonschizophrenics. (L155)

Schizophrenia is correlated with dependency of the patient on her mother. (N061)

### Mother-Child Relations (Affection)
There is no relationship between whether or not the child has been frustrated in his affective relationship with the mother during infancy and his later dependency (at age five) (U.S.). (S191)

### Mother-Child Relations (Permissiveness)
The greater the permissiveness and support on the part of the mother in relation to the child, the greater the child's dependency upon and diffuse attachment to the mother. (B234)

### Mother-Child Relations (Possessiveness)
Overpossessiveness on the part of the mother, characteristic of schizophrenogenic mothers, may actually be only the manifestation of her dependency on the child as her surrogate-mother figure. (S213)

### Mother-Child Relations (Rejection)
Mothers showing some child rejection had more dependent children than did those who showed no rejection. (S191)

### Mother-Child Relations (Responsiveness)
There is no relationship between how responsive the mother is to her child's crying and the child's dependency on the mother (U.S.). (S191)

### Mother-Child Relations (Warmth)
There is no relationship between the warmth shown by the mother toward the infant and later (age five) dependent behavior by the child. (S191)

### Mother-Son Relations (Acceptance)
There is a positive relationship between maternal acceptance during ages 2–7 and dependency upon the mother during the son's adolescent years. (K115)

### Mother-Son Relations (Affection)
Maternal affection during the son's early years (2–7) is positively associated with his dependency upon the mother during the adolescent years. (K115)

### Mother-Son Relations (Closeness)
The greater boys' attachment to "mother figures," the higher their (reputed) dependence. (C098)

### Ordinal Position
First children are more likely to end up anxious and dependent than are later children, who tend to be more aggressive and self-confident. (B252)

A firstborn child is more vulnerable to the loss of his parent's love than are subsequently born children. (C104)

The correlation between being a first or only child and dependency behavior in the preschool situation is caused by the less permissive scheduling of feeding, nursing, and weaning received by the first and only children. (S014)

Older children are more dependent on their parents than are middle or younger children. (S202)

Only children are more dependent than firstborn children. (S263)

In an ambiguous situation early-born persons are more likely than later-born persons to seek other people as a means of evaluation and when with others are more likely to rely on others in evaluating their own opinions and emotional states. (S263)

### Parent-Child Relations
The adjustment of married offspring to their parents is directly related to the dependence of married offspring on their parents. (S011)

### Parent-Child Relations (Control)
The greater the child's need for parental approval, the greater his acceptance of parental limitation upon the free exercise of his will. (A059)

### Parent-Child Relations (Evaluation)
The more overvalued is the child by his parents, the greater will be the child's dependency on external rather than intrinsic criteria as sources for his self-esteem. (A059)

### Parent-Child Relations (Guilt)
The greater the guilt felt by the child when he is striving for independence in conflict with his parental allegiances, the less likely he is to emancipate himself from dependency on his parents. (A059)

### Parental Roles
There is a correlation between the degree of parental independence from family life and the degree of independence of the child from the family. (F106)

### Peer Relations
Adolescent peer groups, by representing nonfamily norms, aid in reducing the child's dependence on his family. (G156)

The more involved an adolescent becomes with his peer group, the more he is emancipated from his parents. (H228)

Children who perceive themselves as autonomous and their parents as coercive (punishing) are more actively friendly with their peers than are others. (H205)

The higher the popularity of the child among peers, the less dependent he is on his parents. (M176)

The greater the commitment of the adolescent to the peer group, the less dependent he/she is likely to be upon his/her family. (P083)

### Personality (Emotion)
The more that the child's dependence is extended to the family as a whole, as opposed to his parents, the less emotional commitment he is likely to have to his marriage (when adult) or to any other single individual. (M198)

### Personality of Father
Pervasively dependent boys (who seek dependent relationships in an indiscriminate manner) tend to be raised in family environments characterized by dominant fathers, by paternal neuroses, grandiosity, feelings of vic-

timization, aggressiveness, and excessive drinking. (M221)

### Personality of Mother (Warmth)
Warmth of mother and dependency of child are not associated. (S191)

### Personality Problems (Emotional Insecurity)
The more that a child's dependence is extended to his family as a whole, as opposed to his parents, the more likely he is to be emotionally insecure. (M198)

### Personality (Stress)
The greater a man's emotional dependence on his mother, the lower his resistance to psychological stress. (S191)

### Psychopathy of Child
Disruption of the dependency relationship with the mother is a cause of psychopathic behavior in the child. (B243)

### Race Attitudes
Prejudiced persons are more likely than unprejudiced persons to perceive their dependencies on their parents as materialistic and utilitarian rather than as based on the need for love and affection. (A061)

### Religion (Totemism)
An intense childhood conflict over dependence on the mother appears to be a predisposing, but not sufficient, cause for the development of totemism in a society. (F015)

### Religiosity
There is no relationship between strong religious beliefs and dependence on the father. (B254)

### Scholastic Achievement
High-school dropouts are more likely to be dependent children who are unwilling to assume any self-responsibility than are those who remain in school. This is more so for boys than for girls. (E102)

Children who perceive themselves as autonomous and their parents as coercive (punishing) tend to do better academically than others. (H205)

Mothers of daughters who are poor academic achievers are more likely to need the dependency of their daughters (as measured by the PARI) than are mothers of academic achievers. (S230)

### Scholastic Adjustment
School phobics are less likely than normal children to be socially mature and relatively independent from their mothers. (D065)

### School System
An impersonal school system, by representing norms that are different from those found in the family, helps to reduce the child's dependence on his family. (G156)

### Sex Status
Women tend to have a greater dependency upon the family than men do. (G153)

Women are handicapped in making the psychosocial shift to the family of procreation which our culture demands because they do not become emancipated from their families of orientation to the same degree as men. (K014)

Women do not become emancipated from their families to the same degree or in the same manner as men. (K014)

Girls are more highly dependent on their parents than boys are when both rate low in popularity among their peers. (M176)

More male than female emotionally disturbed children have intense and dependent relationships with their mothers. (M197)

Dependence on mothers is more likely among females than among males. (S011)

The finding that there are no sex differences in summary ratings of dependency is contrary to the popular belief that girls are more dependent on their mothers than boys. (S191)

Wives are more likely to be homesick for their parents than are husbands. (W006)

### Sibling Structure (Sex)
A boy with a much older sister is likely to be more withdrawn and dependent than is a boy with a much older brother. (K149)

### Size of Family
Children in large families tend to be more self-reliant than children in small families. (R106)

### Social Mobility Aspirations
Children who are upward aspirers are more independent of their parents regarding judgments and behavior than are children who are not upward aspirers. (E102)

### Surrogate Mother
When their infants are one year of age, mothers who have been the only caretaking agent for their infants are more dependent on the child for their own need gratification than are mothers who have provided other maternal figures for their infants. (C107)

At one year of age children are more emotionally dependent on their mothers in families where the mothering is provided by one person than in families where it is provided by more than one person (i.e., nurse, grandparent, mother's friend, and older sister of child). (C124)

Among children of mothers who work, those whose mothers have provided a succession of different mother substitutes are more dependent than are those whose mothers have provided more stable arrangements. (Y047)

### Toilet Training
Severity of toilet training is not related to dependency in the child. (B224)

### Weaning
There is no relationship between the age at which the child begins weaning, the duration of weaning, or the age at which weaning is completed and the child's dependency on his mother (at age 5). (S191)

The more severe the infant's weaning, the more likely it is that he will be dependent as a child. (S238)

### Weaning/Toilet Training
There is no relationship between severity or age at onset of weaning and toilet training and dependency in the child. (B272)

## DEPENDENCY/AGGRESSION
### X   Mother-Child Relations (Consistency)
Children whose mothers vacillate between nurturance

and rejection are more likely to become overdependent rather than aggressive. (B243)

## DEPENDENCY ANXIETY          X   Autoeroticism
There is a correlation between the extent to which a boy masturbates and the degree of his anxiety about dependency on his parents. (B243)

### Child-Rearing Practices (Discipline)
The greater the degree of anxiety typically generated in the society by the socialization of dependence, the earlier the age at which the child is subjected to the socialization of dependence (i.e., greater the degree, earlier the age). (K111)

### Conformity
Boys who are anxious about their dependency on their parents are more likely to resist parental restrictions than are boys with low anxiety. (B243)

### Parent-Child Relations (Hostility)
Dependency anxiety in girls correlates with parental hostility, especially the father's, but parallel relations for boys are largely insignificant. (B232)

## DEPENDENCY OF CHILD
### X   Child-Rearing Practices (Punishment)
Withdrawal of love as a method of punishment and increased emotional dependency of child are associated. (S191)

### Sibling Status
The mothers of only children reported more dependent behavior than did the mothers of children with siblings. (S191)

### Weaning
Severity of weaning and dependency of child are not associated. (S191)

## DEPENDENCY OF DAUGHTER
### X   Employment of Mother
Among middle-class adolescent daughters, those whose mothers work tend to be more independent. (G156)

## DEPENDENCY OF FATHER
### X   Scholastic Adjustment
Girls with school phobia, are likely to have fathers with strong dependency needs. (C115)

## DEPENDENCY OF HUSBAND
### X   Neurosis of Wife (Invalidism)
When the dependency of the husband is expressed in a pattern of sadistic domination, the wife will frequently adopt symptoms of neurotic invalidism as an escape. (R115)

## DEPENDENCY OF MOTHER   X   Breast Feeding
Women who prefer to bottle feed their children are more likely than those who prefer to breast feed to show dependent personality traits. (A063)

### Mental Illness (Schizophrenia)
The ego-weakness of a schizophrenic tends to be correlated with a parent-child relationship in which the mother is dependent upon the child for fulfillment. (L114)

Schizophrenia tends to be directly correlated with patterns of dependence of the patient's mother on the patient's maternal grandmother. (N061)

### Mother-Child Relations (Gratification)
There is a negative relationship between the mother's

prenatal dependency needs and postnatal dependency on her infant for need gratification. (C124)

## DEPENDENCY OF PARENTS          X   Role Conflict
When aged parents experience the role reversal of moving from independency to material dependency on their children, both parents and children experience role conflict. (G119)

## DEPENDENCY OF SON     X   Castration Complex
The castration complex is directly associated with a high degree of dependence on the mother. (W154)

### Child-Rearing Practices (Dependency)
Fathers of boys with a high level of independence expect their sons to be more self-reliant in problem solving than do fathers of boys with low levels of independence. (R106)

### Employment of Mother
Sons of working mothers are more likely to be dependent than are sons of non-working mothers. (S265)

### Power Structure of Family
The less the mother and son are dominated by the father in the power area, the greater the disposition of both to believe that the world can be rationally mastered and that a son should risk separation from his family. (M060)

## DEPENDENCY OF WIFE     X   Affinal Relations
The more emotionally dependent a wife is upon her mother, the more likely it is that her husband will have strained relations with his in-laws.

The husband's adjustment to his mother-in-law is inversely related to his wife's dependence on her mother. (S011)

The husband's adjustment to his father-in-law is directly related to his wife's dependence on her father. (S011)

The impact of the wife's dependency on her husband's adjustment to his in-laws is specific to the parent on whom the wife is dependent. (S011)

## DEPENDENCY OF WOMEN   X   Marital Stability
The stability of the marriage tends to decrease with an increase in the independence of women. (D031)

## DEPENDENCY ON FATHER          X   Mental Illness
Mental illness in women is directly correlated with a strong dependency and preoccupation with the father during the early years. (F085)

## DEPENDENCY ON LINEAGE       X   Achievement
The minimization of individual achievement within the lineage is correlated with a greater psychological dependence on the lineage and residence group and a greater physical dependence on them for subsistence needs. (F015)

## DEPENDENCY/SEX-ROLE CONFLICT
### X   Sex Status
Among alcoholics, females are more likely than males to have a background of sex-role confusion (rather than of dependency conflict). (M195)

## DEPENDENCY/SEX-ROLE IDENTIFICATION
### X   Alcoholism
Boys reared in family situations which create in them both dependency conflicts and role confusion are more likely to become alcoholics. (M195)

# DEPENDENCY (SOCIAL/ECONOMIC)
### X   Parent-Child Relations (Conflict)
The more that adolescents withdraw socially from their families, but remain physically dependent, the more likely is parent-youth conflict. (S219)

# DESCENT                              X Adoption
Daughters are less frequently adopted in matrilocal and matrilineal societies than in patrilocal and patrilineal societies. (D057)

The incidence of adoption will be high in societies which stress the importance of a continuity in the descent line. (S122)

### Affinal Ties
Bilateral societies are more likely than lineal societies to de-emphasize affinal ties. (D084)

While lineal societies are able to de-emphasize affinal relationships, a bilateral society cannot do this for the affines become cognates to ego's offspring. (D084)

### Cohesion of Family
Loyalty and obligation are more likely to correlate with gratification and interaction in bilineal-descent systems than in other descent systems, especially when marriage does not involve a change in community for either spouse. (P083)

### Concubinage
Concubinage is more likely to be institutionalized in societies where the importance of maintaining the descent line is stressed. (F035)

### Corporate Kin Groupings
A unilinear descent system can more easily develop into a corporate group with leadership and capacity to act as a unified body than can a bilateral descent system. (P083)

### Division of Labor By Sex
Bilocal residence, bilateral descent, and Hawaiian terminology are more likely in societies in which subsistence activities of men and women are balanced. (D057)

### Economic Cooperation
The descent group will be more strictly delineated if there are patterns of economic cooperation between its members. (M131)

### Economic Role of Men
Men are less important in the agricultural pursuits and more important in fishing activity in patrilocal than in matrilocal societies. (A072)

### Economic Role of Men/Women
The development of a matrilineal or patrilineal descent system will be affected by the emphasis on male or female production and control of resources. (F033)

### Exogamy
As the control of the descent group over its members decreases, there is a narrowing of the range within which an effective prohibition on intermarriage operates. (C090)

Exogamic restrictions will tend to conform to the pattern of descent. (O023)

### Exogamy (Village)
Patrilineal kinship systems, which purposefully exclude overlapping obligational ties between affinal and consanguineal kinsmen, have a higher correlation than do matrilineal systems with patterns of village exogamy. (G147)

### Extended Kin Relations
The larger kinship group is more likely to support the individual family (i.e., financial aid, settling political disputes, etc.) in a society where a strong organized descent system exists. (G156)

### Father-Son Relations
Kinship systems where the father-son tie is dominant are patrilineal, patrilocal, and, by and large, patriarchal. (H172)

### Father-Son Relations (Warmth/Hospitality)
Among patrilineal peoples, father–son hostility or avoidance is pronounced; among matrilineal peoples, there is a warm and affectionate father-son relationship. (L133)

### Geographic Mobility
Mixed patterns of unilineal and bilateral descent are more likely to occur in societies in which geographic mobility of the population is fairly great. (B301)

The descent group will tend to be ambiguously defined under conditions of high physical mobility. (M131)

### Husband-Wife Relations
High importance of the husband-wife tie is associated with a kinship structure that is patrilineal, patrilocal, or neolocal. (H172)

### Husband-Wife Relations (Closeness)
In matrilineal societies, the bond between a woman and her brother is stronger than her bond to her husband. (G116)

### Illegitimacy
Commitment to the norm of legitimacy will be greater among the strata or kin relations where the concern with the kin line is higher. (G151)

### Incest Taboo
The extension of incest taboos will tend to follow the structure of the descent pattern. (S098)

### Incest Taboo (Brother-Sister)
Brother-sister incest is a more serious offense in a matrilineal society than in a patrilineal or bilateral society. (C093)

### Infanticide (Female)
Female infanticide is less common if descent is traced through the female line. (F121)

### Inheritance
Rules of inheritance are dependent on the form of descent which prevails in a given society. (S095)

### Kin Terminology (Merging)
Matrilineal systems are more likely than patrilineal ones to have a merging rather than a collateralizing terminology. (A048)

### Lineage Communities
Monolineage communities are likely to be rarer in matrilineal than in patrilineal systems. Monolineage includes demes, agamous communities, exogamous barrios, wards, hamlets, and localized lineages. (A048)

### Marital Stability
Societies in which the system of descent is matrilineal tend to be characterized by greater marital instability than do patrilineal societies. (L039)

## Marriage Class System

The development of a six-class marriage system from a simple dual organization tends to occur as a result of the recognition of patrilineal, as well as matrilineal, descent. (S095)

## Marriage Payment

Bride price will be higher in patrilineal than in matrilineal societies. (G156)

## Mate Selection

The more important the descent system for social placement, the more likely is mate selection to be regulated and not left to the whims of young people. (G156)

## Menstrual Taboos

There is no correlation between the extensiveness of menstrual taboos and the various rules of descent and residence (e.g., matrilineality–patrilineality, etc.). (S079)

## Political Succession

There is a highly significant association between lateral succession to the headman's position and matriliny and lineal succession and patriliny. (A048)

## Preferential Marriage

Asymmetrical patterns of marriage require neither unilinear descent groups nor any particular rule of lineal descent. (N067)

## Preferential Marriage (Cross-Cousin)

Matrilineal societies have a higher incidence of symmetrical cross-cousin marriage than do patrilineal societies. (C124)

Where the preferential marriage pattern is that of cross-cousin marriage, descent will be traced in two lines. (E065)

Prefential unilateral cross-cousin marriage can only arise in unilateral societies. (N067)

Cross-cousin marriage is the result of the conflict between patrilineal and matrilineal principles. (S093)

There is no association between the rule of descent and laterality of prescription. (N072)

## Property

As property becomes more movable and more easily transformed into money terms, the importance of the unilinear descent system declines. (P083)

As the individual's physical control over property is more protected by law and the state rather than by relatives, the importance of the unilinear descent system declines. (P083)

## Rank of Men/Women

The rule of descent is only indirectly correlated with the ranked status of the sexes (insofar as the rule is connected with the mode of residence). (L110)

## Religion (Christianity)

Matrilineal societies will tend to be more resistant to the acceptance of Christianity than will patrilineal societies. (H060)

## Religion (Ritual Objects)

The custodianship or control of sacred objects by either men or women is correlated with a corresponding male or female descent line. (M037)

## Residence

Localized lineages appear to be stronger among matrilocal than among patrilocal societies. (A072)

When a choice of descent may be made among alternatives, residence with a group frequently serves as either a contingent or final factor in fixing present affiliation and that of descendents. (D011)

Variation in residence is closely related to descent group affiliation. (F029)

When the settlement pattern is that of the scattered band, the development of a lineage organization tends to be inhibited. (S046)

## Sex Preference

In unilineal societies the child whose sex insures the continuity of the lineage will tend to be preferred. (W082)

## Sex-Role Definition

Patrilineal societies usually exaggerate the physiological importance of the father; matrilineal societies, the role of the mother. (H233)

## Size of Community

When the community is small, the development of a larger consanguineal unit is inhibited. (S120)

## Stability of Kin-Group

The importance of descent is directly correlated with the stability of the kin-group. (S098)

## Stratification

Matrilineal systems tend to have hereditary, rather than complex, stratification systems to a greater degree than is the case for patrilineal and bilateral systems. (A048)

## Subsistence Pattern

The descent pattern of a society is unrelated to the means of subsistence. (G056)

# DESCENT (AMBILATERAL)

## X  Cohesion of Kin-Group

The cohesiveness of the descent group tends to be undermined when descent is ambilateral. (F068)

## Subsistence Pattern (Hunting)

In societies with simple hunting economies descent tends to be ambilateral. (N027)

# DESCENT (ASYMMETRICAL)

## X  Bilateral Organization

Asymmetrical descent may develop from a unilineal pattern as a consequence of the increasing importance of the bilateral family. (S097)

## Kinship (Bilateral)

Asymmetrical descent may develop from a unilineal pattern as a consequence of the increasing importance of the bilateral family. (S097)

## Marriage Class System

The adoption of asymmetrical descent will divide a society with a moiety organization into a six-class marriage system. (S098)

## Moiety System

Asymmetrical descent is associated frequently with moiety organization. (S097)

## Preferential Marriage

When a descent pattern is asymmetrical, patterns of cross-cousin marriage must also be asymmetrical. (S097)

### Preferential Marriage (Exchange)
Exchange of sisters as wives is prohibited by a descent system which is bilateral for one sex and unilateral for the other. (S097)

## DESCENT (BILATERAL)          X   Alcoholism
Heavy drinking is associated with bilateral descent. (W127)

### Clans, Number of
The adoption of bilateral descent can occur in a unilineal system only when there is an indefinite number of intermarrying clans. (S098)

### Cohesion of Clan
The adoption of bilateral descent will result in the breakdown of the clan system unless there is an indefinite number of intermarrying clans. (S098)

### Corporate Kin-Group
Bilateral descent and the resulting personal and stem kindred tend to occur where collective and corporate kin control is absent or minimal. (D011)

The corporate character of the clan structure tends to deteriorate with an increase in an emphais on both maternal and paternal kinsmen. (W103)

### Descent (Patrilineal)
Where a matrilineal society is subjected to patrilineal pressures, a bilateral descent system tends to develop. (S095)

### Descent (Unilineal)
The stronger the unilineal descent groups are in a society, the weaker the bilateral descent groups tend to be. (C124)

### Divorce
The divorce rate is higher when the descent pattern is bilateral. (S265)

### Economic Rights of Women
Bilateral organizations tend to occur in societies which have rankings and considerable material wealth if the women are permitted equal access to strategic resources. (B060)

### Employment of Women
The employment of women reinforces the trend toward bilateralism. (P083)

### Endogamy
Continuity can be maintained through bilateral descent only if the kin-group is endogamous. (F068)

### Geographic Mobility
Ecological exigencies favoring a high degree of geographical mobility correlate with reliance by people on bilateral kin in finding new places to settle, consequently favoring a village composed of bilateral kin. (B301)

### Husband-Wife Relations (Egalitarianism)
The equality of status between husband and wife tends to be associated with bilateral patterns of descent. (S123)

### Incest Taboo
When descent is bilateral marriage tends to be forbidden between cross-, as well as parallel-, cousins. (F051)

Bilateral extension of incest taboos follows inevitably the establishment of bilateral kin-group. (M019)

### Independence of Nuclear Family
In bilateral societies the nuclear family tends to have greater autonomy than is usual among societies where the clan is the important social unit. (B060)

### Joking-Avoidance Relationship
There appears to be a correlation between the presence of the original bilateral family and the absence or weakness of certain forms of ceremonial behavior, especially joking and avoidance relationships. (L039)

### Kin Terminology
There is a positive correlation between lineal terminology and bilateral descent. (D057)

The extension of sibling terms to both cross- and parallel-cousins indicates a change in the direction of bilaterality. (M077)

### Kin Terminology (Generation)
When the emphasis is on bilateral descent, terminology will be generational. (O023)

### Kindred
A characteristic of bilateral societies is the formation of temporary kindred-based action groups. (F127)

### Marriage-Class System
A marriage class system is more likely to arise with the adoption of bilateral descent. (S097)

### Mother-Daughter Relations
The mother-daughter relation tends to be especially close in bilateral descent systems. (P062)

### Political Structure
The flexibility of the bilateral structure mitigates against the development of extensive sociopolitical groupings of kin, since, as circumstances change, alliances are dissolved. (P082)

There is an association between the political division of the nation into nonlocalized, widely dispersed sectors and strong bilateral emphasis. (S195)

### Preferential Marriage (Cross-Cousin)
When descent is bilateral, marriage with cross-cousins tends to be prohibited. (O023)

### Preferential Marriage (Symmetrical Cross-Cousin)
Symmetrical cross-cousin marriage is more likely to be found in bilateral societies. (C124)

### Rank of Women
The status of women tends to be higher in bilateral than in patrilineal societies. (K060)

### Residence
Where residence patterns are flexible, bilateral descent tends to occur. (O030)

Dispersion of the town, village, or settlement and a scattering of households are associated with the development of bilaterality. (S192)

### Residence (Neolocal)
A change to neolocal residence from any form of unilocal residence will ultimately result in bilateral descent. (M019)

Neolocal residence is normally associated with bilateral descent. (M019)

#### Social Mobility
Bilateral descent is more likely to characterize societies with high degrees of social mobility. (G101)

#### Stability of Kin Group
In bilateral descent systems, there is no enduring kinship-group structure. (S080)

#### Stability of Lineage
Bilateral descent undermines lineage stability. (G013)

#### Subsistence Pattern (Hunting and Gathering)
Societies with marginal techniques of hunting and gathering tend to be characterized by bilateral descent. (S119)

#### Technology
Bilateral organizations may also occur in societies which have rankings and considerable material wealth if the women are permitted equal access to strategic resources. (B060)

#### Warfare
A bilateral society has better opportunities for the formation of large-scale fighting forces than does a society with a highly segmented unilineal descent system and no form of centralized authority. (F127)

### DESCENT (BILATERAL FILIATION)
#### X    Intermarriage
Interclass caste marriages are more likely to be prohibited when membership in the superior caste is derived from bilateral filiation. (F117)

### DESCENT (BILINEAL)    X    Peer Relations
More intense adolescent peer-group life is likely to be found in societies having bilineal descent and neolocal residence than in a patrilineal, patrilocal system. (P083)

### DESCENT (CLAN)    X    Incest Taboo
Clan organizations develop with the extension of incest taboos from the nuclear family to other members of the mother's kin-group. (S098)

### DESCENT (DOUBLE)    X    Clan (Matrilineal)
The creation, *ab initio,* of a distributed, unorganized, matrilineal clan is not likely in the absence of an overt or covert double descent system. (A048)

#### Endogamy
In double unilineal societies the desire to keep the property inherited from both lines tends to encourage endogamy within the settlement. (H245)

#### Endogamy (Caste)
Caste endogamy must always be associated with systems in which the person is affiliated with both parents. (Y053)

#### Genealogical Depth
Societies with a double descent pattern tend to be characterized by shallow genealogies (two to four generations). (H245)

#### Moiety System (Matrilineal)
Given a system based on exogamous matrimoieties, if residence becomes patrilocal, a double descent system of matrimoieties and patrisibs will occur. (L178)

#### Political Integration
A system of double descent is conducive to a pattern of politically independent villages (H245)

Double descent functions to increase the degree of political integration between communities. (R069)

#### Political Structure
In societies characterized by dual descent, the political significance of one descent group will tend to be undercut by the fact that in many contexts affiliation with the other group will be relevant. (H245)

#### Segmentary Structure
Double descent inhibits the emergence of segmentary lineages. (S087)

#### Segmentation
Double descent patterns appear to be incompatible with the recognition of many levels of lineage segmentation. (H245)

#### Size of Village
A system of double descent tends to result in villages of very large size. (H245)

### DESCENT (DUAL)    X    Lineage Depth
A limited depth of the unilineal descent group tends to occur in systems of dual descent. (G062)

### DESCENT (FICTIVE)    X    Descent (Unilineal)
When a unilinear kin-group is faced with extinction, some fiction of descent will be resorted to in order to provide a member through whom the group can maintain its continuity. (D011)

### DESCENT (FOUR LINES)
#### X    Preferential Marriage (Second-Cousin)
When the preferential marriage pattern is that of second-cousin, descent will be traced through four lines. (E065)

### DESCENT (LINEAGE)    X    Segmentation
The lines of fission within a clan will follow the lineage affiliations of the clan members. (R054)

### DESCENT (MATRILINEAL)    X    Acculturation
A matrilineal-descent organization tends to be abandoned under acculturative pressures. (C068)

#### Adoption
In matrilineal societies girls will tend to be adopted more frequently than boys. (F040)

#### Age Difference
As matrilineal groups become weaker, there tends to be less disapproval of marriage between generations. (C090)

#### Authority Structure of Family
Avuncular authority is greater when the matrilineage is strong. (S192)

#### Avuncular Relationship
The avuncular relationship tends to be emphasized in societies in which matrilineal descent is well-developed. (S106)

#### Couvade
The custom of couvade is more likely to occur in matrilineal societies. (W154)

#### Descent (Patrilineal)
Matrilineal clan organization does not precede the patrilineal. (W078)

Matrilineal clan organization is a precondition for the mergence of the patrilineal clan. (W078)

### Division of Labor
When the small household becomes the primary work unit for each occupation, matriliny tends to disappear. (A048)

### Divorce
Divorce is less likely to occur in societies with patterns of matrilineal rather than bilateral descent. (S267)

Divorce is less likely to occur in matrilineal societies since the husband must leave his children and property and return to his own kin as an unmarried son. (S267)

### Ecological Conditions
Within the world's horticultural zones matrilineal peoples seem to be found, in the main, outside of or bordering on the tropical forest and outside those zones where cattle can be raised in numbers. (A048)

### Economic Cooperation
Matrilineages are not likely to be found in societies which demand large-scale cooperation among males. (G156)

### Economic Level (Productivity)
Matriliny is most likely to disappear in the face of the increased importance of large-scale coordination of male labor; increased importance of property such as domesticates in the hands of males (property, that is, which is divisible and which can multiply), and the regulation of economic and political life through nonkinship ties. Most, if not all, of these features are likely to be associated with increased productivity. (A048)

### Economic Pattern
Matrilineages are not found in societies where central economic organization is not based on kinship. (G156)

Abundance of land, individualism in production, and lack of investment in valuable fixed resources do not provide favorable conditions for the formation of widespan localized matrilineages. (T080)

### Economic Pattern (Market)
When a matrilineal system enters a market economy, matriliny disappears. (A048)

### Economic Role of Women
Matrilineal descent groups arise when women's work groups control the resource bases. (A048)

When the control of strategic resources is in the hands of the women, the stability of the matrilineal descent system is reinforced. (L039)

### Father-Child Relations
Matrilineal descent patterns tend to weaken with the strengthening of the relationships between the father and his children. (E016)

### Father-Son Relations (Affection)
The relationship between father and son in matrilineal societies is more likely to be characterized by affection and less tension than in patrilineal societies. (F074)

### Father-Son Relations (Closeness)
The intensity of the affective relationship between father and son is inversely associated with a matrilineal system. (F092)

### Father-Son Relations (Conflict)
Tension between father and son will be lower in societies with matrilineal descent. (M226)

### Father-Son Relations (Hostility)
In a matrilineal system ego is more likely to feel hostility toward the mother's brother than toward the father. (G055)

### Geographical Mobility of Women
Women in matrilineal societies are less likely than women in other societies to settle permanently in a foreign area. (C090)

### Housing
There is a correlation between large community houses and matriarchal institutions. (T082)

### Husband-Wife Relations
Where the woman bears children for her own blood line, the wifely bond tends to be weak. (G012)

### Husband-Wife Relations (Intimacy)
When descent, inheritance, and succession are matrilineal, the role of the father is negligible and the significance of marriage as both an intimate union and an alliance is mitigated. (D018)

### Incest Taboo
Matrilineal extension of incest taboos follows inevitably after the introduction of matrilineal descent. (M019)

### Industrialization
Matrilineages are not found in societies that are very little or highly industrialized. (G156)

### Initiation Rites
Initiation ceremonies for girls are correlated with matriliny. (L133)

### Kin Terminology (Bifurcate Merging)
Over 70 per cent of all matrilineal systems for which there is information have either Crow or Iroquois cousin terms. (A048)

### Kin Terminology (Generation)
In the presence of exogamous matrilineages, matrisibs or matrimoieties, kinship terms for father's sister tend to be extended to father's sister's daughter and those for brother's daughter to mother's brother's daughter. (M019)

### Moiety System
The moiety system tends to occur in association with matrilineal descent. (G060)

Matrimoieties are found to occur in societies which have had matrilineal descent for a long time. (M019)

### Oedipal Complex
The Oedipus complex is less likely to occur in societies with matrilocal residence and matrilineal descent. (D057)

### Mother-Son Relations
Where the mother-son tie is given prominence, the kinship structure tends to be patrilineal, patrilocal, and generally, patriarchal. (H172)

### Paternal Role
In matrilineal societies the father is more likely to share in the care of the children. (W154)

Because the status of father is unstable in matrilineal societies, he must validate his position through his contribution to the everyday life of the household group. (Z001)

### Paternity, Ignorance of
Ignorance about the role of the male in procreation is more likely to occur in matrilineal societies. (W154)

### Political Centralization
Matrilineages are not found in societies where central political organizations are not based on kinship. (G156)

### Political Role of Descent Group
The matrilineal descent group tends to disintegrate upon the loss of its political functions. (G056)

### Political Structure
When bureaucratic political structures arise, matriliny tends to disappear. (A048)

### Polyandry
Polyandry is associated with matrilineality. (B205)

### Polyandry/Polygyny
The combined custom of polyandrous and polygynous unions are consistent with a strong matrilineal system. (G055)

### Preferential Marriage (Granddaughter)
Marriage with the granddaughter is incompatible with matrilineal descent. (S093)

### Rank of Husband
When the descent system is matrilineal, the status of the husband tends to be subordinate. (Y001)

### Rank of Women
In matrilineal societies women tend to occupy a relatively high, if unofficial, status in the society. (M069)

### Religion (Role of Deities)
Cults of the Great Mother are more likely to be found in societies with a strong matrilineal emphasis. (W154)

### Residence (Avunculocal)
The pattern of avunculocal residence requires a prior rule of matrilineal descent. (G052)

### Residence/Inheritance
Consistent matrilocal residence and matrilineal property interests tend to produce a matrilineal descent group. (L110)

### Residence (Matrilocal)
Matrilineal descent tends to occur in societies in which the pattern of residence is matrilocal. (H043)

### Residence (Patrilocal)
If local circumstances do not favor avunculocal residence, a matrilineal society under strong patrilocal pressure is likely to adopt patrilocal residence without giving up its matrilineal lineages, sibs, or moieties. (M019)

Matrilineal kin-groups tend to disappear or cease to be exogamous when patrilocal residence is adopted. (M019)

### Sex-Role Definition
The extension of female behavior into sectors commonly defined as male is more likely to occur in matrilineal societies. (W154)

### Stability of Family
In matrilineal systems wives and children belong to another descent group than that of the husband-father and this leads to some degree of instability in the household, for a woman is not bound to her husband by his control over her children. (C090)

### Subsistence Pattern
Matriliny disappears when the subsistence base shifts to one primarily dependent on movable property (e.g., domesticates) which can be controlled by individual men. (A048)

matrilineal systems are strikingly infrequent in those areas of the world where the plough is used, where there is intensive wet-rice agriculture, or where there are extensive irrigation works coordinated and maintained by supracommunity organizations. (A048)

### Subsistence Pattern (Agricultural)
The matriarchate is closely linked with a subsistence system in which a hunting or shepherd people passes over to a stage of more intensive agriculture. (L108)

Matrilineal descent tends to be correlated with an economy based on intensive farming. (N017)

Matrilineal descent is not exclusively associated with an agricultural economy. (N017)

### Subsistence Pattern (Horticultural)
Matrilineal systems are overrepresented in the horticultural areas. (A048)

Matrilineages are most likely to be found in societies where women play important roles in food production (e.g., societies based upon gardening). (G156)

### Values (Paternity)
In a matrilineal system there is less concern (than in a patrilineal system) with the identity of the biological father as long as the mother is married. (G156)

## DESCENT (MATRILINEAL)/PATERNITY, IGNORANCE OF          X  Oedipal Complex
In societies characterized by both matrilineal descent and an ignorance of physiological paternity, the Oedipal complex will not occur. (M226)

## DESCENT (MATRILINEAL/PATRILINEAL)
### X  Age-Groups
An institutionalized age-grade system is more likely to occur in patrilineal than in matrilineal societies. (Y001)

### Avuncular Relationship
The avuncular relationship in a matrilineal society tends to be characterized by greater hostility and rivalry than does the comparable relationship in a patrilineal society. (G055)

### Cultural Evolution
Simpler cultures tend to be matrilineal; more advanced ones, patrilineal. (L110)

### Divorce
As the position of the male is subject to greater strain, the divorce rate is likely to be higher in a matrilineage than in a patrilineage. (G156)

### Father-Son Relations (Aid)
The father in a patrilineage is more able to help his sons (offering gifts and bequeathing some possessions) than he is in a matrilineage. (G156)

### Father-Son Relations (Closeness)
The father is more able to have close emotional ties with his son in a patrilineage than in a matrilineage. (G156)

### Father-Son Relations (Conflict)
There is greater potential for strain in the father-son relationship in a matrilineage than in a patrilineage since the father's daily interaction is with his sons while his property goes to his sister's sons. (G156)

### Father-Son Relations (Obedience)
The father in a matrilineage is less able to command obedience from his sons than the father in a patrilineage. (G156)

### Husband-Wife Tie
The bond of a sister with her brother is stronger and the bond with her husband is weaker in matrilineal than in patrilineal societies. (G012)

### Kin Terminology (Merging)
Matrilineal systems are more likely than patrilineal ones to have merging, rather than collateralizing, terminology. (A048)

### Marriage Payment
The amount of the marriage payment tends to be higher in patrilineal than in matrilineal societies. (L101)

### Oedipal Complex
The Oedipus complex develops in early infancy in matrilineal, as well as in patrilineal, societies. (G055)

In a patriarchal society the Oedipal conflict involves the desire of the son to murder the father and marry the mother, whereas in matrilineal society it is the wish to murder the maternal uncle and to marry the sister. (M173)

### Power Structure of Family
Control over the husband's authority is of greater importance for the matrilineage than for the patrilineage. (G156)

### Preferential Marriage (Cross-Cousin)
Matrilateral cross-cousin marriage is more likely to take place in patrilineal societies; patrilateral cross-cousin marriage is more likely to take place in matrilineal societies. (C093)

### Religion (Ancestor Worship)
Ancestor worship serves to reinforce the distinction between paternal and maternal kin-groups. (H164)

### DESCENT (PARALLEL)    X  Descent (Unilineal)
Parallel descent is likely to occur only in societies with strong unilinear patterns. (M234)

### DESCENT (PATRIARCHY)
### X  Kin Terminology (Classificatory)
The emergence of a patriarchal family will result in the abandonment of a classificatory system of relationships. (R034)

### DESCENT (PATRILINEAL)
### X  Adultery, Attitude Toward
In societies with a strong emphasis on patrilineal descent, there is a greater emphasis upon the chastity and fidelity of women. (B086)

### Authority Structure of Family
A shift in the emphasis in lineality from maternal to paternal ancestry will tend to occur when the authority of the mother's brother within the family is weakened. (E016)

### Class
The upper class, inasmuch as it tends to stress the status of ancestors, will give greater importance to the patrilineal line of descent (U.S.). (P012)

### Descent (Bilateral)
Where a matrilineal society is subjected to patrilineal pressures, a bilateral descent system tends to develop. (S095)

### Descent (Matrilineal)
Matrilineal clan organization does not precede the patrilineal. (W078)

Matrilineal clan organization is a precondition for the emergence of the patrilineal clan. (W078)

### Divorce
The divorce rate is low in patrilineal systems where the bonds which tie a woman to her husband are extremely strong. (G116)

### Divorce, Ease of
In societies where the patrilineal organization is strong, divorce can only be obtained at the will of the husband. (L041)

### Economic Rank
The depth of the patrilineal structure tends to be greater when the family has permanent agricultural land. (G028)

### Endogamy (Community)
As village endogamy increases, the emphasis on the male line is lessened and the situation appears to be favorable to change from patrilineality to bilateral social organization. (P008)

### Exogamy (Clan)
Decreased emphasis on paternal descent may be associated with breakdown of clan exogamy. (S192)

### Father-Child Relations
Filial piety is correlated with patrilineal descent. (F087)

### Father-Child Relations (Intimacy)
In a society with a strong patrilineal emphasis, the relationship between mother and child tends to be intimate, whereas the relationship between father and child tends to be restrained. (H105)

### Father-Son Relations (Conflict)
There will be greater tension in the father-son relationship in patrilineal than in matrilineal society. (F074)

### Husband-Wife Relations
Where women bear children for their husband's group, the wifely bond tends to be strong. (G012)

### Incest Taboo
With an increasing importance in patrilineal affiliation, incest taboos will tend to extend to the patrisib of the mother. (L060)

Patrilineal extension of incest taboos follows inevitably after the introduction of patrilineal descent. (M019)

### Kin Terminology
When a patrilineal culture exerts strong pressures on a society which is matrilineal in its organization, terminological groupings will tend to break down. (A021)

With the growing importance of the patriarchal family, sibling terminology tends to be extended to cross-cousins. (R034)

### Kin Terminology (Generation)
In the presence of exogamous patrilineages, patrisibs, or patrimoieties, kinship terms for mother's sister tend to be extended to mother's brother's daughter and those for sister's daughter to father's sister's daughter. (M019)

### Kin Terminology (Siblings)
Terminological distinctions between half and full siblings will not occur when the patrilineal principle is strong. (R054)

### Marital Stability
Marital stability is directly correlated with patrilineal descent. (F062)

### Mother-Son Relations
Where the mother–son tie is given prominence, the kinship structure is patrilineal, patrilocal, and, generally, patriarchal. (H172)

### Penis Envy
Penis envy is associated with patterns of patrilineal descent and will not occur in matrilineal societies (F112)

### Political Structure (Centralization)
A social structure based on an association of exogamous corporate patrilineal descent groups is not likely to remain organized in a permanent political system unless it is subject to some form of overriding, centralized government. (F120)

### Polygyny
Polygyny tends to be associated with patrilineal organization. (F010)

### Preferential Marriage (Levirate)
The institution of the levirate is an indication of the strength of the patrilineal organization. (K049)

### Premarital Sex Relations, Attitude Toward
Premarital relations are less likely to be tolerated in patrilineal societies. (F073)

### Rank of Women
The status of women in a society with a strong patrilineal organization tends to be low. (K049)

### Residence (Amitalocal)
Amitalocal residence patterns require prior rules of patrilineal descent. (G052)

### Residence (Patrilocal)
When a society shifts to regular patrilocal residence, the group automatically becomes patrilineal. (G029)

### Secret Societies
Secret societies will tend to be of greater importance when the social structure is patrilineal. (C077)

### Sex Norms
There is an association between patrilineage and an emphasis on sexual fidelity in marriage. (F087)

### Sex Preference
The emphasis on male children is directly correlated with the strength of the patrilineal organization. (K049)

### Sex-Role Definition
The belief that women are dangerous as peers, either because of their excessive sexuality or because of their inherent perversity, is associated with patrilinear descent patterns. (P083)

The conception of women as property tends to be associated with a patrilineal descent system. (S093)

### Sibling Relations
When residence and inheritance patterns are patrilocal and patrilineal, the relationship between male siblings will be the strongest tie in and the dominant element of the kinship structure. (G053)

### Sterility, Attribution of
Patrilineal tribes tend to attribute sterility to the man rather than to the woman. (T081)

### Stratification
Stratification tends to result in the development of patrilineal descent. (T068)

### Subsistence Pattern (Pastoral)
Societies with pastoral economies tend to be patrilineal. (R045)

### Warfare
Warfare and the enhancement of the male role in regard to warfare tends to strengthen the patrilineal organization of the society. (F010)

## DESCENT (PATRILINEAL/MATRILINEAL)
### X   Economic Pattern (Migratory Labor)
Patrilineal peoples adjust themselves more readily than do matrilineal peoples to the absence of a large number of men created by a situation of migratory labor. (W132)

### Lineage, Importance of
When family and lineages are about equal as principles of local organization, the merging of patrilineal and matrilineal kin as joint members of a single genealogical generation is more likely. (T080)

### Residence
When there is a simultaneous occurrence of both patrilineal and matrilineal kin-groups, one will tend to be localized and the other nonlocalized. (M045)

## DESCENT/RESIDENCE
### X   Affinal Relations (Conflict)
Affinal conflict will tend to be more severe under conditions of patrilocal residence if the descent pattern is matrilineal. (M050)

### Cohesion of Lineage
When the residence rule conflicts with the unilinear descent pattern the strength of unilinear alignments is weakened. (M027)

### Conflict
Matrilocality can occur in a patrilineal society only when intrasocietal hostilities are repressed and latent antagonism is channeled into intense warfare. (M027)

### Economic Role of Women
Matrilocal residence and matrilineal descent tend to be practiced when agriculture is in the hands of the women. (B033)

### Endogamy (Community)
When residence is patrilocal, yet important obligations exist among matrilineal kinsmen, the resultant conflict of (residential) interest may lead to village endogamy. (S092)

### Inheritance
Descent and inheritance rules are more highly correlated with the prevalent residence practice among matrilocal cultures than among patrilocal groups. (A072)

Matrilineal inheritance is normally associated with matrilocal or avunuculocal residence and with matrilineal descent. (M019)

### Property
There is a correlation between the sex which will own the house and the type of descent and residence pattern. (L043)

### Stability of Community
In unilineally organized societies in which the mode of postmarital residence is not the same as the mode of reckoning descent, local groupings in such societies will be unstable. (T080)

### Stability of Extended Family
When residence and descent patterns are not congruent the extended family will tend to break up upon the death of the head. (M050)

## DESCENT/RESIDENCE, CONSISTENCY OF
### X    Clan
Clans can only develop in the presence of consistent rules of descent and residence. (M171)

### Stability of Kin Structure
The degree of social stability is directly correlated with the congruity between descent and residence patterns. (H112)

## DESCENT/RESIDENCE (MATRILINEAL/VIRILOCAL)    X   Endogamy
When matrilineal descent is combined with patterns of virilocal residence, community endogamy tends to occur. (S144)

## DESCENT/RESIDENCE (PATRILINEAL/PATRILOCAL)
### X   Economic Role of Men
Patrilineal and patrilocal tendencies are strengthened with an increase in the importance of the man's economic role. (L063)

## DESCENT (SEGMENTARY LINEAGE)
### X   Sibling Rank
The segmentary lineage system rests upon the fundamental postulate of the equivalence of male siblings. (L076)

## DESCENT (SYMMETRICAL)
### X   Stability of Lineage
In societies which possess a segmented lineage system, the possibility of one of the segments decreasing in size is guarded against by rules of some form of symmetry; the symmetrical arrangement insures at least a social permanence as great for one segment as for another. (H037)

## DESCENT (UNILATERAL)
### X   Kin Terminology (Bifurcate Merging)
Bifurcate merging terminology tends to be found in societies which have rigid groupings of kinsmen based on unilateral descent. (S106)

## DESCENT (UNILINEAL)
### X   Affinal/Consanguineal Ties
Matrilineal societies are more likely to fuse the obligational ties inherent in consanguineal and affinal forms of relationship than are patrilineal societies. (G147)

### Authority Structure of Family
Kinsmen invested with disciplinary authority will be members of the lineage group. (W065)

### Avoidance Relationship
There is a correlation between the severity of kin avoidance and the presence of unilineal kin-groups. (S079)

Unilineal kin-groups are strongly correlated with the presence of avoidance relationships and also with joking relationships. (S189)

### Cohesion of Kin-Group
The cohesion of the kin-group will be greater if a pattern of unilineal descent is instituted. (S098)

### Conflict
When unilineal ties are emphasized for residence, inheritance, and succession, quarrels will be more frequent. (S284)

### Descent (Bilateral)
The stronger the unilineal descent groups are in a society, the weaker the bilateral descent groups tend to be. (C126)

### Descent (Fictive)
When a unilinear kin-group is faced with extinction, some fiction of descent will be resorted to in order to provide a member through whom the group can maintain its continuity. (D011)

### Descent (Parallel)
Parallel descent is likely to occur only in societies with strong unilinear patterns. (M234)

### Division of Labor
Unilineal descent groups break down when a modern economic framework with occupational differentiation is introduced. (F020)

The range of effective organization of unilineal kin-groups tends to be limited in societies which have a high degree of economic specialization. (F033)

### Ecological Conditions
Nonunilineal descent groups are more likely to occur than are unilinear descent groups in situations where the environment is hostile. (B327)

### Economic Pattern
Unilineal descent groups tend to occur most frequently in relatively homogeneous precapitalistic economies in which there is some degree of technological sophistication and value is attached to rights in endurable property. (F020)

### Economic Security
The unilinear structure tends to be elaborated under conditions of economic security. (F010)

### Exogamy
When the unilineage begins to dissolve, so does the rule of lineage exogamy. (H157)

### Genealogical Depth
A restriction of genealogical data indicates the disintegration of a unilineal system. (M077)

### Genealogical Ties
The genealogical unity of the kin-group is directly correlated with linearity of descent. (G101)

### Genealogy
The manipulation of genealogy tends to occur in societies where unilineal descent is emphasized. (S116)

### Isolation of Nuclear Family
Absence of emphasis on one line of descent increases the structural isolation of conjugal family. (P012)

### Kin Terminology (Bifurcate Merging)
Bifurcate merging terminology develops with the introduction of the sib system. (L039)

Bifurcate merging terminology tends to be associated with exogamous unilineal groups. (M047)

When the emphasis is upon unilineal descent, kinship terminology will tend to distinguish between the lineal and collateral kinsmen. (O023)

Bifurcate merging terminology is generally associated with a pattern of unilinear descent. (W067)

### Kin Terminology (Classification)
When unilineal kin structure is strong, members of the same clan may be terminologically equated. (M042)

### Kin Terminology (Generation)
When a society tries to combine patrilineal and matrilineal terminologies, a generational system is likely to emerge. (B201)

Generation- or Polynesian-type kinship systems tend to occur in societies which are without unilineal descent groups. (L039)

When unilineal kin-groups are highly developed, generational distinctions will tend to be omitted in the kinship terminology. (P016)

### Long House
Long houses tend to be associated with a social organization which is unilineal in character. (L049)

### Marriage Class System
A marriage class system can only emerge if one of the lines recognized in bilateral descent is dominant. (S098)

### Moiety System
The unilineal affiliation of the moiety structure will tend to be consonant with patterns of affiliation on the lineage level. (E032)

A moiety system precedes the development of unilineal kin-groups or sibs. (L040)

### Nonkin Relations
A weak form of unilineal system and economic, political, and religious institutions not based on kinship are correlated. (B301)

### Political Structure
The development of a unilineal kin structure tends to be inhibited by the establishment of centralized political authority. (F033)

Unilateral descent groups tend to be eliminated when political organization is highly developed. (L110)

### Population
Nonunilineal descent groups are more likely to occur than are unilinear descent groups where the population fluctuates and expands irregularly. (B327)

### Preferential Marriage
Ethnographic reports indicate a high correlation of the matrilateral preference in patrilineal societies; the patrilateral preference is usually recorded in societies following matrilineal descent. (L176)

### Preferential Marriage (Asymmetrical Cross-Cousin)
Cross-cousin marriage, if it is to be instituted in a unilineal kinship system, must be asymmetrical in its character. (T018)

### Preferential Marriage (Cross-Cousin)
Matrilateral cross-cousin marriage in association with matrilineages or patrilineal cross-cousin marriages with patrilineages do not appear to produce symmetric exchanges of women. (L176)

Cross-cousin marriage tends to be associated with systems of unilineal descent. (S098)

### Religion (Ancestor Cult)
The composition of the ancestor cult group will reflect the patterns of unilineal descent. (R023)

### Residence
The development of a unilinear kin-group is contingent upon the consistency of residence patterns. (G049)

Post-nuptial residence patterns will generally conform to clan descent. (L049)

Clans and extended families disappear with all residence changes except that of avunculocal rule. (M019)

When the residence pattern is consistently matrilocal or patrilocal there will be a tendency for unilineal kin-groups to form. (S065)

### Residence (Bilocal)
Where bilocal residence persists or where tendencies to unilocality do not go too far descent remains nonunilinear. (G029)

The unilinear kin-group tends to disappear as a consequence of the adoption of bilocal or neolocal residence. (M019)

### Residence (Unilocal)
Unilocal residential groupings tend to give rise to unilineal descent groups based on the same principle. (L061)

A fixed rule of residence whereby all men or all women after marriage continue to reside with or near their own linear relatives of the same sex is conducive to a unilinear rather than bilateral descent. (M019)

A stable unilocal residence pattern is especially influential in the development of unilineal descent groups. (M045)

### Section System
Two-section systems do not require descent groups or a particular rule of lineal descent. (N067)

### Segmentation
When patterns of unilinear descent are associated with lineage endogamy, the production of discrete kin-groups will not occur. (M023)

### Size of Community
Unilineal kin-groups emerge with a minimal threshold of population size and stability. (F033)

The formation of unilineal kin-groups is directly correlated with the size of the community. (W056)

### Size of Lineage
Conformity with the rules of lineality is more likely to occur if the lineage is large in size. (B147)

### Stratification
The appearance of social stratification in a sib-structured tribe tends to weaken the social importance of the sib structure. (O006)

Unilineal computation of status tends to blur lines of stratification. (T069)

### Subsistence Pattern
Poverty of habitat and of productive technology tend to inhibit the development of unilineal descent groups. (F020)

There is a universal tendency under conditions of small-scale production by domestic units for the development of unilineal kin-groups. (F033)

### Technology
Unilineal descent groups are not of significance among peoples who live in small groups, depend upon a rudimentary technology, and have little durable property. (B045)

### Values (Individualism)
Individualism may become an increasingly important value in situations where two patterns of unilinear descent are in conflict. (F069)

## DESCENT (UNILINEAL) EXTENDED FAMILY
### X   Mate Selection (Free Choice)
There is a decided, though imperfect, tendency for marriage to be either arranged or by parents' consent when either unilineal kin-groups or frequent extended family households are present. (S189)

## DESERTION                                           X   Class
Because of the growing system of bureaucratic records, marital desertion remains possible only for lower-class persons. (G156)

### Divorce, Ease of
The greater the institutionalized difficulty in obtaining divorce, the greater the incidence of disintegration of families by physical separation (e.g., desertion). (K161)

### Economic Pattern (Migrant Labor)
Desertion is more likely to occur in situations of labor migration where there is a "sexually differentiated enculturative experience." (S266)

### Incest (Father-Daughter)
Families in which father-daughter incest occurs tend to be characterized by desertion by the maternal grandfather. (K091)

In families where father-daughter incest occurs the parents are more likely than are typical parents to desert the family at some time. (K091)

### Intermarriage (Ethnic)
Marital conflict stemming from differing nationality backgrounds may be one factor in the overrepresentation of Catholics in desertion cases. (K010)

### Marriage Ceremony
Couples involved in desertion cases are more likely to have had a civil wedding ceremony. (K010)

### Occupational Rank
Desertion cases among nonwhites are concentrated in the lower occupational classes, but are not concentrated in the lower occupational classes among whites (i.e., there is no substantial justification for referring to desertion as the "poor man's divorce"). (K010)

Comparing the occupational distribution of males in the general population and of deserting husbands broken down by race, the following occurs: among both whites and Negroes, the upper occupational classes are under-represented in desertions; for the whites the *bottom three* occupational classes (when combined) are slightly *over*represented in desertions, while among Negroes these classes are slightly *under*represented. (K010)

### Race
Desertion is more likely to occur among Negroes than among whites. (M001)

### Rank of Women
Desertion is more likely to occur where women are regarded by wives as occupying subordinate status. (S266)

### Religion
Desertion cases are more likely to be among Catholics than among other religious groups. (G156)

The fact that in desertion cases Catholics are overrepresented may be due to differential reporting rates between Catholics and non-Catholics. (K010)

The fact that the Catholic Church does not recognize divorce may be one factor in the overrepresentation of Catholics in desertion cases. (K010)

The overrepresentation of Catholics in desertion cases is only partially explained by the fact that a greater proportion of Catholics are found in the lower occupational classes than are other religious groups. (K010)

The overrepresentation of Catholics in desertion cases may be due to marital conflicts which stem from differing nationality backgrounds. (K010)

## DESERTION, AS GROUNDS FOR DIVORCE
### X   Husband/Wife
When desertion is the grounds for divorce in primary marriages, it is more likely that the wife will get the divorce rather than the husband. (K003)

## DESERTION BY FATHER
### X   Sociopathic Personality of Son
There is a correlation between desertion by the father and sociopathic personality in the son. (O032)

## DESERTION BY PREVIOUSLY DIVORCED
### X   Occupational Rank
The proportion of desertion cases which involve previous divorce experience varies directly with occupational level among native white persons. (K010)

## DESERTION BY WIVES
### X   Preferential Marriage, Restrictiveness of
When the preferential marriage pattern is highly restrictive in character, the incidence of desertion by wives will tend to be high. (K062)

## DESERTION BY WOMEN                    X   Polygyny
Desertion by women is more likely to occur when a husband acquires a second wife. (W108)

## DESERTION/DIVORCE                     X   Children
Families where divorce occurs have children less often than do families where desertion occurs (for comparable durations of marriage). (M011)

## DEVIANCE                              X   Broken Homes
Parents are much more likely to be social deviants (al-

coholics, criminals, promiscuous) if they are in broken homes rather than united homes. (M181)

### Child-Rearing Practices (Punishment)
Children whose parents are both punitive and emotionally ambivalent toward the child are more likely to become social deviants than are children with more lenient, more consistent parents. (W137)

### Cohesion of Family
The greater the degree of unity and intimate association in a family, the less is the likelihood of a member participating in behavior which will bring disgrace to the family. (B033)

### Father-Son Relations (Approval)
Fathers whose sons are not deviant are more likely to approve their sons' behavior than are fathers whose sons are deviant. (W137)

### Self-Conception of Mother
Children whose mothers have low self-esteem are more likely to become social deviants than are those whose mothers have higher self-esteem. (W137)

## DEVIANCE, ISOLATION FROM
### X Cohesion of Family
The degree of family unity is correlated with the degree of isolation from deviant and destructive patterns of behavior. (B033)

## DEVIANCE OF FAMILY MEMBER, ATTITUDE TOWARD      X Cohesion of Family
Families with a high degree of unity are likely to feel disgraced by delinquent or criminal behavior of a member. (B033)

## DEVIANCE OF FATHER      X Deviance of Son
Sons of men who are criminals, sexually promiscuous, or alcoholics tend to become social deviants themselves. (M199)

## DEVIANCE OF MOTHER/FATHER
### X Alcoholism
Social deviance (criminality, alcoholism, adultery) on the part of the mother is correlated with alcoholism in the son; paternal deviance is not. (M195)

## DEVIANCE OF PARENTS      X Criminality
There is a correlation between deviance by either parent (alcoholism, or criminal or promiscuous behavior) and criminal behavior in the son. (M195)

## DEVIANCE OF SON      X Deviance of Father
Sons of men who are criminals, sexually promiscuous, or alcoholics tend to become social deviants themselves. (M199)

### Marital Adjustment of Parents
Mothers of nondeviant boys, as compared with mothers of deviant boys, report a higher degree of spousal adjustment. (W137)

### Occupation of Father
The father's occupation (white or blue collar) is not related to whether or not the boy exhibits deviant behavior. (W151)

## DEVIANCE, TOLERANCE OF      X Size of Family
Larger families can accommodate a problem child or a psychotic with less disruption than can the small nuclear family. (A047)

## DEVIANCE, VISIBILITY OF      X Class
The lower the social class, the more visible to the community is the deviant social behavior of a family (child abuse, separation, nonsupport, etc.). (Y043)

## DISINTEGRATION OF KIN-GROUP
### X Residence (Neolocal)
Any influence which tends to undermine or inhibit large local aggregations of kinsmen will create conditions favorable to neolocal residence. (M019)

## DISORGANIZATION OF FAMILY      X Age
Among preadolescents there is a stronger relationship between family disorganization and delinquency than among adolescents. (T002)

### Aspiration Level
Incomplete families inhibit the child's ambition only in families where middle-class values are most fully entrenched. (T095)

### Child-Rearing Practices (Control)
There is little difference between a well-integrated family and a disorganized one in relation to supervision of male children. (T002)

There is a great difference between the supervision of female children in a well-integrated family and in a disorganized one. (T002)

### Class
Psychologically disturbed children from the lower class are more likely to come from a family atmosphere of physical tension and disorganization than are those from middle-class homes. (M197)

Disorganized families (either broken homes or those with poor authority patterns) are more likely to be found in the lower classes than in the upper. (Y043)

### Cognitive Development
Children whose cognitive structures have become differentiated are more likely to be "insulated from role experience" (e.g., hurt by broken home, unhappily married parents, etc.) than they were before the cognitive structures were differentiated. (P083)

### Communication (Interpersonal)
There is a direct correlation between poor interpersonal communication (within the family and between family members and outsiders) and family disorganization.

### Conflict in Kin Network
Family disorganization correlates with troubled relations between husbands' and wives' kin and themselves. (K087)

### Crisis (Social)
Disturbances in the family structure tend to be associated with widespread social and economic disintegration. (K065)

### Dependency
There is a correlation between the occurrence of major discontinuities (severe illness, changes in the physical or social environment) between the ages of nine months and three years and dependency in the child. (B272)

Extremely dependent boys are more likely to have been raised in families characterized by parental conflict and deviant behavior (e.g., dictatorial or passive mothers, neurotic mothers, incest, etc.). (M221)

### Economic Pattern (Migrant Labor)
Family structure tends to deteriorate with the adoption of patterns of migrant labor. (K066)

### Emotional Problems of Child
Disturbed children are likely to come from homes characterized by an atmosphere of confusion and disorganization. (S187)

### Employment of Mother
Employment of the mother is correlated with a disorganized family life. (Y050)

### Friendship (Closeness)
The more intimate are the family friends, the less likely is the family to experience desertion and divorce. (Z008)

### Geographical Mobility
The disorganization of the Negro family is correlated with mobility and urbanization. (B033)

The shortage of land in rural areas results in a high rate of internal and external migration with correlated repercussions on the degree of family organization. (S032)

### Health of Child
In children under one year of age, separation from family and familiar surroundings causes physical upsets such as colds, sore throats, and feeding, sleeping, and digestive upsets.

### Incest (Father-Daughter)
Fathers who have had sexual relations with their daughters come from families characterized by a high degree of disorganization. (K119)

### Incest (Sibling/Father-Daughter)
In general, sibling incest did not have as disturbing an effect on the other family members as did father-daughter incest. The mother, especially, was less disturbed and agitated. (W123)

### Intermarriage
Intermarriage is more likely to take place among individuals who come from families that are disorganized, than from stable families. (H008)

### I.Q. of Child
There is a correlation between disturbance in family relationships and the child's low performance on the block design and object assembly tests (WISC). (M213)

### Juvenile Delinquency
There is a correlation between the seriousness of the boy's delinquency and the degree of instability and disturbance of his family life. (N059)

There is a correlation between marital disruption and the severity of delinquency in the son. (W152)

### Juvenile Delinquency/Neurosis
Delinquent children are more likely than neurotics to have undergone a series of changes of home and maternal care (neurosis measured by phobias, anxiety level, obsessions, etc.). (B238)

### Mate Selection
Individuals from emotionally disturbed childhood homes do not necessarily tend to marry persons with similar backgrounds. (P086)

### Mental Illness (Autism)
Autism is more likely to occur as a reaction to a disturbed family environment when the disturbance occurs during the period in which the mother is the primary object to the child (i.e., from six months to three years). (S188)

### Mental Illness of Child (Schizophrenia/Neurosis)
In the lower class, more schizophrenic than neurotic children were reared in a family atmosphere of physical tension and disorganization. (M197)

### Mental Illness (Schizophrenia)
Schizophrenics tend to be from a disturbed family environment. (L123)

A high proportion of schizophrenics come from disorganized family environments (death, divorce, separation, psychosis, neurosis, alcoholism). (S187)

### Personality of Parents
Parents (of schizophrenic children) who lack direction and organization are less likely than are parents who are well ordered to function adequately (with respect to communication between marital partners, the mother's decisiveness, her appropriate satisfaction with self and children, interest in physical environment). (B240)

### Race
Family disorganization is more likely to occur among Negroes than among whites. (T002)

### Scholastic Achievement
High-school dropouts are more likely than graduates to come from unstable, impoverished home environments. (E102)

### Sex Status
More women than men recall disturbed childhood homes. (P086)

Disturbances in the home are likely to have greater effect on girls than on boys since the degree and length of exposure to disturbed family situations is greater for girls. (P086)

### Social Adjustment
Disorganization in the family (malfunctioning of its expressive roles, i.e., interpersonal relations) causes malfunctioning in roles outside of the family system. (G122)

### Social Control
Family disintegration occurs when there is a tolerance of individual variation. (B033)

Family disintegration occurs where there is an absence of techniques to compel an erring member to abide by the norms of public opinion. (B033)

### Urban/Rural
Family disorganization is more likely to occur among urban families than among rural families. (T002)

### Warfare
Family disorganization increases with the acceleration of social changes during wartime or preparation for war. (B033)

## DISORGANIZATION OF FAMILY/BROKEN HOMES    X   Emotional Adjustment
Adolescents from homes that remain intact, but unhappily so, have greater adjustment problems than do those whose homes are broken by divorce or death (U.S.). (G156)

## DIVISION OF LABOR     X   Clan Structure

When the structure of the clan is hierarchical in its patterns, the development of occupational specialization and social differentiation is facilitated. (F039)

#### Cohesion of Family

Occupational differentiation tends to weaken the traditional familial ties of the peasant social structure. (G027)

#### Conflict in Family

Given the intensity of feeling between the members of the small nuclear family, the dispersion of their activities outside the home increases the probability and intensity of conflict. (D058)

#### Descent (Matrilineal)

When the small household becomes the primary work unit for each occupation, matriliny tends to disappear. (A048)

#### Descent (Unilineal)

Unilineal descent groups break down when a modern economic framework with occupational differentiation is introduced. (F020)

The range of effective organization of unilineal kingroups tends to be limited in societies which have a high degree of economic specialization. (F033)

#### Economic Cooperation

When the division of labor is rudimentary and there is sufficient land available the economic pattern tends to consist of cooperation between close relatives. (W056)

#### Kin Ties

Kin ties tend to be of greatest importance in societies which lack patterns of economic specialization. (L072)

#### Resources

Task allocation is determined by whether or not the family member is already skillful at a certain task.

#### Values (Marriage)

The more differentiated are jobs in the society in the economic sphere, the more important is mutual emotional support between spouses. (D080)

The more differentiated are jobs in the society, the more emphasis is placed on marriage for love and the less emphasis on economic advancement and social standing. (D080)

## DIVISION OF LABOR BY SEX
### X   Authority Structure of Family

When there is little difference between men and women in prestige, the authority of the male in the family is reinforced by a sharp division of labor that restricts the woman's role to matters concerning the training of daughters or the management of the home. (P083)

#### Chores

The less the household-task training before the marriage for both partners, the more diffused the division of labor will be at the beginning of marital life.

#### Class

Low-income families with both husband and wife working show a greater deviation from the traditional division of labor as compared with high-income families with both husband and wife working.

#### Descent

Bilocal residence, bilateral descent, and Hawaiian terminology are more likely in societies in which subsistence activities of men and women are balanced. (D057)

#### Independence of Women

The sexual division of labor of desert (nomadic) life permits a higher degree of freedom to women than does that of urban living. (S116)

#### Inheritance

When the division of labor by sex is sharp, the inheritance of personal possessions will tend to be between members of the same sex. (T053)

#### Polyandry

Polyandry is associated with the sexual division of labor in which the woman makes a very small contribution to family subsistence. (B205)

#### Power Structure of Family

When the wife is the one who has the greater power in the family, she is also the one who carries most of the household labor.

#### Rank of Women

The status of women is more likely to be high where there is not a rigid sexual division of labor. (W081)

#### Residence

The sexual division of labor is not correlated with residence after marriage. (A071)

#### Sex-Role Identification

The stronger the masculine identification of the boy, the more likely it is that his home is marked by a flexible division of labor between mother and father and fewer rules regarding duties. (M183)

#### Social Network

Husband and wife are more likely to divide responsibilities according to traditional sex roles when they reside in a tightly knit friendship network (i.e., a high frequency of interaction among family units) than in a loosely knit friendship network. (G156)

#### Technology

Division of labor by sex is greater in agriculture, merchandising, and laboring specialties than in industrial communities where women often work along with men. (T072)

## DIVISION OF LABOR IN FAMILY
### X   Sibling Relations (Conflict)

Status differentials in the type of labor will frequently be a source of conflict between siblings. (R012)

## DIVORCE      X   Acculturation

The divorce rate tends to increase under acculturative conditions. The contrary is also asserted. (M069)

#### Achievement Motivation

There is a direct relation between achievement motivation (competition, individualism, status striving) and divorce. (K161)

#### Adoption (Acceptance by Agency)

If a person has been previously divorced, it is more likely that an adoption agency will reject his application to adopt a child. (F117)

#### Adultery

Divorce will be a consequence of adultery only when the wife has frequently had extramarital relations. (H074)

## Age

The difference in rates of divorce between homogamous Catholic and Protestant marriages (lower rate of divorce) and interreligious marriages between Catholics and Protestants (higher rate of divorce) is less among older couples than it is among younger couples. (B314)

## Age at Marriage

The divorce rate will be lower when marriage is early. (B191)

Among marriages where premarital illegitimacy has occurred, divorce is more likely to occur among very early and very late marriages than among the middle age groups (Denmark). (C124)

Among both fertile and childless marriages, the divorce rate varies inversely with the wife's age at marriage (Denmark). (C129)

The later a woman marries (and hence the less chance she feels she has of remarriage), the less likely divorce is. (D083)

Women who marry at an extremely young age are more likely than those who marry at a more mature age to have their marriages dissolved by divorce. (G012)

The earlier is the age of marriage in a system of free mate choice, the more likely is the failure of conjugal integration at first marriage. (P083)

An increase in the average age at marriage, and especially a reduction in the incidence of teen-age marriages, is likely to result in a decline in the type of divorce which results from premature commitment. (P083)

## Age Difference

The greater the age differential between mates, the greater is the likelihood of divorce. (C005)

Divorce is more frequent among couples where the wife is much older than the husband than where she is slightly older or younger. (D083)

## Anxiety/Self-Conception

Divorce may have more influence upon level of anxiety in the child than upon level of self-esteem. (R129)

## Authority Structure of Clan

The incidence of divorce will tend to increase with the weakening of the clan authority structure. (S158)

## Broken Home

Among those who have been divorced and remarried, more are likely to come from divorced homes, fewer are likely to come from homes in which one or both parents have died, and still fewer from families that remained intact. (G126)

## Children

The alleged association between divorce and childlessness has been a statistically spurious one and may not exist at all. (M011)

Couples who have children are more likely to stay together than are childless couples, even though they may have been previously married and divorced. (P062)

## Class

Being divorced is more characteristic of tenant families than of owner families. (C009)

As the upper-class wives' economic needs are granted better legal protection, creating less dependence upon their husbands, upper-class women are "freer" to leave their spouses. (G156)

Prior to the late nineteenth century, the divorce rate was highest in the upper classes (U.S.). (G156)

In societies where equal access to divorce is granted to all classes, the divorce rates will be higher among the lower classes. (G156)

Structural hindrances to divorce are fewer among families of low socioeconomic status than among high-ranking lineages. (P083)

Divorce among commoners is more frequent than among aristocrats. (W108)

## Cohesion of Lineage

When the solidarity of exogamous patrilineages is strong, divorce, as a consequence of the conflicting loyalties of the spouses, is very common. (L027)

## Dating

Longer periods of acquaintanceship prior to engagement and marriage are associated with a lower proneness to divorce. (G157)

The greater the time lapse since the granting of the decree, the more likely is the divorcée to become a frequent dater; however, the proportion of divorcées who never date is not affected by the time lapse since the granting of the decree. (G157)

## Death Rate

The lower the death rate in a society, the greater the rate of divorce. This proposition is also denied.

## Descent (Bilateral)

The divorce rate is higher when the descent pattern is bilateral. (S265)

## Descent (Matrilineal)

Divorce is less likely to occur in societies with patterns of matrilineal rather than bilateral descent. (S265)

Divorce is less likely to occur in matrilineal societies since the husband must leave his children and property and return to his own kin as an unmarried son. (S267)

As the position of the male is subject to greater strain, the divorce rate is likely to be higher in a matrilineage than in a patrilineage. (G156)

## Descent (Patrilineal)

The divorce rate is low in patrilineal systems where the bonds which tie a woman to her husband are extremely strong. (G116)

## Divorce Adjustment

When divorce will result in economic and social dislocation, the rate of divorce tends to be low. (S037)

## Divorce, Attitude Toward

The high toleration for divorce in the United States is directly related to the high actual number of divorces. (C134)

Lessened disapproval of divorce is associated with higher divorce rates. (G156)

## Divorce, Cost of

The greater the expenses of a divorce, the higher the divorce rate. (D083)

### Divorce, Ease of
The rate of divorce will be related to the cost of the action and the severity of legal impediments. (B033)

The easier it is to divorce, the higher is the divorce rate. (G134)

### Divorce in Family History
The likelihood of divorce increases with the rate of divorce in the family line. (L019)

### Divorce of Parents
Individuals whose parents were divorced are more likely to become divorced themselves than are individuals whose parents were not divorced. (K161)

### Duration of Marriage
The higher the frequency of divorce, the earlier in marriage divorce will take place. (D083)

The "divorce percentage" decreases after the third year of marriage. (K002)

Divorce is more frequent among couples who have been married for a short period of time than it is among those who have been married longer. (P062)

### Economic Conditions
Divorces are likely to decrease during depressions at a greater rate than during nondepressions at a greater rate than during nondepression periods. (C023)

### Economic Dependence of Wife
Increased divorce rates are related to increased social provisions for the economic independence of the wife. (G156)

### Economic Dependence of Women
Women are more likely to seek a divorce as a solution for an unsatisfactory marriage if they are economically independent of their husbands than if they are economically dependent upon them. (L024)

### Economic Rank
There is a rough inverse correlation between economic status and rate of divorce. (G002)

### Education
Divorce declines with higher educational level.

There is a curvilinear relationship between education and divorce: divorce rates being low for persons of the lowest and the highest educational levels, but higher for those who have completed grammar school and high school.

Unhappily married couples with a high-school or college education are more likely to be divorced than are those with a grammar-school education.

The higher the educational level, the lower the divorce rates. (G156)

Proneness to divorce decreases slightly with higher education for whites and increases for Negroes. (G157)

The higher the educational level of the couple, the greater the likelihood that the suggestion to divorce will be mutual. (G157)

### Education Difference Between Husband-Wife
Differences between husband and wife in the number of years of formal education are unrelated to whether or not a couple will divorce. (B244)

### Education of Women
There is a direct relation between the educational level of women and divorce. (K161)

### Emotional Adjustment/Religion
The experience of divorce is more strongly related to signs of psychic and emotional disturbance among Catholic and Jewish children than among Protestant children. (R129)

### Employment of Wife
Divorcées are more likely than not to have always or usually held a full-time job during their marriages. (G157)

### Employment of Women
The fewer the economic opportunities for women, the less likely the woman will seek divorce if divorce means supporting herself and/or her children. (D083)

The greater economic and social independence associated with employment of women is directly related to an increase in divorce. (K161)

### Employment (Regularity)
Divorced couples are more likely to report an unsteady employment record on the part of the husband. (G157)

### Ethnicity
Jewish females have a lower divorce rate than do non-Jewish females. (B010)

### Extended Kin Relations
Since upper-class families are more likely to have extensive and stable kinship networks, marital disruption within their ranks would be more likely to create problems in extended kin relations. (G156)

Divorce is less likely where it would threaten kinship relations. (G156)

Marital expectations that tend to focus on the larger extended family, rather than on the relationship between husband and wife, tend to reduce tension between spouses and, consequently, lower the likelihood of divorce. (G156)

### Fecundity
Sterility is more likely to be an important cause of divorce in societies which highly value fertility in women. (P083)

### Fertility
Divorced women as a group are relatively less fertile than are women who marry only once. (B012)

Childless marriages and those where illegitimacy occurs (where the wife bears a child prior to marriage) are more likely to end in divorce than are fertile marriages (Denmark). (C129)

The higher the divorce rate, the closer the rate of fertility of those obtaining divorces will approximate the normal. (D083)

Married couples who are not well adjusted, who for many reasons may be prone to divorce, are less likely to have children. (G156)

Divorce is more likely to occur in cases of marital infidelity when there are no children. (H074)

There is a direct relation between low fertility and divorce. (K161)

The greater proneness to divorce of remarried persons than of persons who have been married only once leads to a spurious overemphasis of childlessness in divorce. (M011)

### Friendship
In cities where there is a lower divorce rate, families are more likely to associate with remarried families than in cities where the divorce rates are higher. (Z008)

Families with friends who have traits in common are more likely to have lower rates for desertion and divorce than families with friends who are unlike themselves. (Z008)

### Geographic Mobility
Areas with the highest residential mobility, such as the rooming-house and apartment-house districts, have the highest divorce rate. (B033)

There is a positive relationship between the amount of residential mobility and divorce. (B033)

There is a lower proportion of divorced people among migrants than among nonmigrants. (F008)

Divorced persons tend to be more mobile than the general urban population. (G157)

Divorce is much more likely in urban areas, where there is much geographical mobility. (L024)

### Geographic Mobility by Sex Status
Migration to a village, town, or city is more likely among farm women than among farm men when their marriages have been broken. (G011)

### Homogamy
Homogamy, by eliminating many areas of potential disagreement, tends to reduce proneness to divorce. (G156)

Divorced persons are less likely to have homogamous marriages than are persons who stay married. (G157)

The highest proportion of divorced persons have had hypogamous marriages, then hypergamous marriages, and lastly homogamous marriages. (G157)

Divorced persons are less likely to have occupationally homogamous marriages than are those who remain married. (G157)

Divorced persons are more likely to have occupationally hypogamous marriages than are those who remain married. (G157)

Divorced persons are no more likely to have occupationally hypergamous marriages than are those who remain married. (G157)

### Homogamy (Education)
Divorced persons are most likely to have had educationally homogamous marriages, then educationally hypogamous marriages, and lastly educationally hypergamous marriages. (G157)

### Homogamy (Religious)
Denominationally homogamous Protestant married couples are less likely to divorce than are Protestant marriages where the spouses are of different denominations. (B314)

Marriages between two unaffiliated Protestants are less apt to end in divorce than are marriages where one partner is affiliated and the other is not. (B314)

### Husband/Wife
The husband more frequently than the wife is the first to desire a divorce. (G157)

The husband is more often than the wife the party who adopts a line of behavior which forces the other spouse to suggest a divorce. (G157)

The wife is more likely than the husband, even under unpleasant marital conditions, to feel disposed to stay in the marriage. (G157)

### Husband-Wife Relations (Evaluation)
When there is a disparity between the real husband or wife and the image of the ideal mate the probability of divorce is high. (B033)

### Husband-Wife Relations (Intensity)
The divorce rate is higher in societies with a high affective intensity in the husband-wife relationship. (P057)

### Husband-Wife Relations (Shared Activities)
A higher proportion of divorced than of happily married persons report mutual enjoyment in sharing such "non-home-centered" activities as dancing and drinking. (G157)

### Identification with Parents
Divorce or separation of parents makes less likely the adequate identification of the child with a parent figure.

### Illegitimacy
Among marriages where premarital illegitimacy has occurred, divorce is more likely to occur among very early and very late marriages than among the middle age groups (Denmark). (C124)

### Income
There is an inverse correlation between income and divorce rate. (G134)

### Income
### X   Sexual Disability of Husband (Divorce)
Among men who have been physically disabled, those who have remained married are more likely to have higher incomes than are those who are divorced or separated. (N060)

### Infant Betrothal
The incidence of divorce will tend to be lower where infant betrothal is common. (B191)

### Intermarriage (Religious)
Mixed marriages between Catholics and Protestants are more likely to end when the Protestant partner belongs to no particular denomination than when he does. (B314)

Divorce is less likely to occur among all-Catholic marriages than among mixed marriages of Catholics. (C006)

Spouses who marry outside their own faiths are more likely to become divorced than are couples who marry intrafaith. (C134)

Of the three religious types of marriage, nonmixed ones have the lowest divorce rate, mixed the next highest rate, and marriages in which there is no religious faith the highest. (L010)

In mixed marriages the divorce rate is higher when a Catholic man marries a Protestant woman than when a Protestant man marries a Catholic woman. (L010)

The divorce rate is low, compared to other types of mixed marriages, in marriages in which a Catholic woman marries a man with no religious faith. (L010)

In mixed marriages the highest divorce rate was in marriages in which the largest percentage of husbands and wives were church members (i.e., the Catholic father-Protestant mother combinations). (L010)

Mixed marriages are less likely to end in divorce if one spouse changes to the faith of the other, but the percentage of mixed marriages ending in divorce is higher when the Catholic wife has changed to the Protestant faith and when the Protestant husband has changed to the Catholic faith than in the other two possibilities (i.e., Protestant wives changing to Catholicism and Catholic husbands changing to Protestantism). (L010)

Among cross-faith marriages, divorce rates are highest for Jews, lower for Protestants, and lowest for Catholics. (Z008)

### Isolation of Nuclear Family
Sterility and failure to integrate with the matrilinear or patrilinear line are likely to be more important causes of divorce where the conjugal family is integrated with the extended family; where the nuclear family is isolated, failure of tension reduction is likely to be the more important cause of divorce. (P083)

Divorce is more likely to result from problems associated with the husband's failure to support the wife properly or with his behaving dishonorably in situations where the nuclear family is isolated, than where extended family ties are strong and failure of the husband can be more easily compensated by the efforts of relatives. (P083)

### Juvenile Delinquency
Among delinquents, white children are more likely to have experienced disorganization of the home by divorce than are Negro children. (M196)

Among delinquents, Negro boys are no more likely than Negro girls to have come from divorced homes; white girls are no more likely to have come from divorced homes than are white boys. (M196)

The higher a country's divorce rate, the higher its delinquency rate. (Z008)

### Kinship
Divorce is less likely to occur in societies with a wide web of imputed kinship. (S267)

### Legal Status of Wife
Greater legal protection of the wife's financial needs increases the likelihood that she will seek a divorce. (G156)

### Legal Structure
Greater access to the legal agencies of the society that grant divorces is associated with higher divorce rates. (G156)

### Lineage
Divorce becomes even more frequent in areas where lineages are weak or absent. (F073)

### Marital Adjustment
Divorced men are more likely to have had better marital adjustment during the early years of marriage than are men who remain married. (P071)

Divorced women have less satisfactory marital adjustment during the early years of marriage than do women who remain married. (P071)

### Marital Status
The probability of divorce rises with each successive marriage. (M013)

### Marriage, Approval of
Disapproval of the marriage by friends of kin is associated with a higher propensity for divorce. (G156)

### Marriage, Attitude Toward
Where the possession of a household is fundamental to status, men and women are less likely to divorce unless provocation is great. (C090)

### Marriage Ceremony
Couples having a nonreligious wedding ceremony are more likely to get divorced than are couples who have a religious wedding. (C005)

Among fertile marriages, the divorce rate is higher for the civil marriages than for the church marriages (Denmark). (C124)

### Marriage, Goal of
When the major function of marriage is alliance of two lineages, the husband is likely to be more hesitant about initiating divorce for fear of alienating his wife's lineage. (P083)

### Marriage Payment
There is an inverse correlation between the divorce rate in a society and the prevalence of dowry or marriage payment. (G134)

The higher the divorce rate in a society, the smaller the size of the bride price or dowry. (G156)

The possibility of divorce is inversely correlated with the amount of the marriage payment. (S158)

### Mate Selection
Divorce is infrequent in the extended Chinese family since romance is sacrificed to prudential consideration and social status. (B033)

The more important are emotional relationships in themselves as the grounds for mate selection in marriage, the higher the divorce rate will be. (D080)

### Mate Selection (Free Choice)
As the elders and kin lose their control over marriage, the divorce rate increases. (H062)

### Nuclear Family, Importance of
High divorce rates are more likely in social systems in which the strains attributable to the relative importance of the nuclear family and the marital relationship are great. (P062)

### Occupation
There is no relationship between the occupation of the husband and the likelihood of divorce among unhappily married couples.

Unskilled occupational groups have a higher divorce rate than do skilled or professional groups. (C005)

Divorce is more prevalent among unskilled or semi-skilled occupational groups than among professional, proprietary, clerical, and sales occupational groups. (G002)

Within any given class position, specific occupations may have high or low divorce rates. (G134)

Actors, musicians, commercial travelers, and doctors have the greatest overrepresentation in divorce, although no discernible socioeconomic pattern emerges when the divorce ratios are arranged by major occupational categories. (K010)

### Occupation
### X  Sexual Disability of Husband (Divorce)
Among men who have been physically disabled, those who have remained married are more likely to be in managerial-professional occupations than are those who are divorced or separated. (N060)

### Occupation (Husband Absence)
There is a higher rate of divorce and marital unhappiness in occupations requiring travel away from home. (B033)

### Occupational Rank
There is a rough inverse association between frequency of divorce and occupational level. (K010)

### Parenthood
The shorter the interval between marriage and birth of the first child, the less likely it is that the marriage will end in divorce. This assertion is also denied. (D083)

### Polygyny
The rate of divorce tends to be higher in polygynous marriages. (B012)

When divorce is easy the stimulus to polygyny, which might otherwise come from the desire for issue, is not great. (B298)

### Preferential Marriage (Cross-Cousin)
Matrilineal cross-cousin marriage in a matrilineal society will tend to occur if the parents of the man are divorced. (G055)

### Preferential Marriage (Levirate/Sororate)
Divorce is less likely to occur in societies where the levirate and sororate have been instituted. (S158)

### Pregnancy, Timing of
The longer the couple waits after pregnancy to marry, the greater the chances they will divorce. (C125)

Of the premaritally pregnant who do divorce, divorce occurs earlier than among the couples who were not premaritally pregnant. (C125)

Within marriage, those who conceive very early have a higher divorce rate than those who conceive later. (C125)

Divorce rates and interval to first birth are negatively related. (C125)

### Premarital Pregnancy
In marriages where the first child is conceived premaritally (and born in wedlock) the length of the interval between conception and marriage is negatively related to divorce rate. (C124)

Proneness to divorce among couples who are in love when premarital pregnancy occurs is lower than when premarital pregnancy is not associated with a love relationship. (C124)

Marriages with premarital conception are more likely to end in divorce than are marriages with postmarital con-

ception of the first child, except where both spouses married young (Denmark). (C129)

### Prostitution
The greater the institutionalized bonds against divorce, the higher the incidence of prostitution. (K161)

### Psychosomatic Illness
Children whose parents are divorced are more likely than those from intact families to report psychosomatic symptoms. (R129)

Catholics and Jews whose parents are divorced are more likely than those from intact families to have psychosomatic symptoms, but this is less true of Protestants. (R129)

### Race
Divorce rates have been and currently are higher among nonwhites than among whites (U.S.). (G156)

Among people who are charged with desertion, divorce rates are higher for whites than for Negroes. (K010)

### Rank of Wife
Divorce is less likely to occur if the status of the wife is high. (R040)

### Recreation
Divorce is less apt to occur where the husband has the alternative companionship of male friends in recreational activities. (D083)

Where there are opportunities for outdoor recreation, the divorce rate will be lower. (D083)

### Religion
Catholics are less likely to get divorced than non-Catholics. (C023)

Among marriages of mixed faiths, the divorce rate is highest when the husband is Catholic and the wife Protestant. (G156)

Marriage between persons without religious affiliations have the highest divorce rates, followed by persons of interfaith marriages. (G156)

When both husband and wife are of the same religion, few differences in divorce rates exist among Catholics, Protestants, and Jews. (G156)

When both spouses are of the same religious affiliation, their proneness to divorce is lower. (G156)

Divorce is more likely among Protestants than Jews and among Jews more than Catholics. (M001)

### Religion
### X  Sexual Disability of Husband (Divorce)
In marriages where the husband has been physically disabled, Catholics are no more likely than are Protestants to be divorced or separated and Jews are less likely to be divorced than are Gentiles. (N060)

### Religion of Husband–Wife
Divorce is more likely to occur among Catholic husbands married to Protestant wives than among Catholic wives married to Protestant husbands. (C006)

### Religiosity
Catholic divorcées who attend church infrequently following the divorce are likely to claim that they attended more frequently during the marriage. (G157)

Unhappily married couples who are not very religious

are more likely to be divorced than are those who are devout. (G157)

### Remarriage
Divorced persons are more likely to remarry than to remain not married. (C023)

A high divorce rate in any culture will be accompanied by a high remarriage rate. (G015)

The divorce rate increases with successive marriages. (L024)

### Residence
Areas where lineages have been dispersed have higher divorce rates than do those where lineages are intact. (F073)

Where there is alternating residence by brother-sister solidarity, the divorce rate between spouses is high. (F076)

### Residence (Matrilocal)
Where a woman remains in her natal home (after marriage), the marriage bond is fragile and the divorce rate is high. (G012)

### Residence (Patrilocal)
In matrilineal societies, where the woman moves out of her natal family in order to produce children for her husband's line, the woman's bonds to her husband tend to be strong and the divorce rate is low. (G012)

### Role Definition of Husband/Wife
Differing opinions between husband and wife regarding their marital-role obligations are associated with a greater proneness to divorce. (G156)

### Self-Conception of Child
Catholic children of divorced parents are more likely than Catholics and Jews from intact families to have low self-esteem, but divorce makes no difference in level of self-esteem among Protestant families. (R129)

### Sexual Adjustment
Sexual problems in marriage are usually related to other marital tensions and consequently are not a direct cause of divorce. (G156)

Complaints of sexual problems are reported by those who divorce. (G156)

### Sexual Disability of Husband, Age at
The earlier the age (25 years or younger) at which the spouse is physically disabled, the more likely is he to be divorced or separated. (N060)

### Sexual Disability of Husband (Divorce) X Education
Among men who have been physically disabled, the proportion of those who remain married exceeds those who are divorced or separated at all educational levels. (N060)

### Sexual Permissiveness
The more permissive the sex norms of a culture, the lower the divorce rate differential between premarital and postmarital pregnancies. (C125)

### Sexual Restrictions
The more restrictive the sex norms of a culture, the lower the divorce rate differential between early and late postmarital conceivers. (C125)

### Sibling Relations (Solidarity)
When the sibling group constitutes a unity, the divorce rate is high. (T080)

### Size of Family
Marriages with few or no children have a higher divorce rate than others. (F101)

### Size of Family X Sexual Disability of Husband (Divorce)
Among men who have been physically disabled, those who are married have a greater number of children than those who are divorced or separated. (N060)

### Sleeping Arrangements of Husband-Wife
The divorce rate in the various social classes is highest in the separate-bedroom class and lowest in the double-bed class. (M230)

### Social Mobility
An increase in the divorce rate is correlated with a higher rate of social mobility. (T106)

### Social Structure (Homogeneity)
Cultural homogeneity of the population appears to be correlated with a low divorce rate, while heterogeneity seems to be associated with a high rate. (B033)

### Sociopathic Personality
It is more likely that boys with sociopathic personalities have parents who are divorced (or have been divorced before marrying) than boys with no mental problems or boys with other mental problems. (O032)

### Status of Divorcée
The divorce rate is likely to be higher in a society in which there is social recognition of the role of divorced women. (G142)

### Status of Women
Divorce will be rare if the women are believed to be invested with special supernatural powers. (M069)

### Sterility
Divorce is more likely to occur if the wife is barren. (S090)

### Urban/Rural
Countries that are rural typically have lower divorce rates than do those that are predominately urban. (B033)

Divorce is positively related to urban residence. (C005)

In Western countries, rural people tend to have lower divorce rates than do urban dwellers. (G156)

### Urbanization
There is a direct relation between urbanization and divorce. (K161)

### Urbanization/Industrialization
Urbanization and industrialization do not necessarily increase the divorce rates. (G134)

### Values (Secular)
There is a direct relation between societal secularization and divorce. (K161)

### Warfare
In wartime divorces are likely to increase at a greater rate than in peacetime. (C023)

Countries that were mobilized during the war show a

greater increase in divorce rate than do neighboring countries that did not mobilize. (Z008)

### Widowhood
Divorces among remarried persons who have been widowed are no more likely than are divorces among primary marriages. (M242)

## DIVORCE ADJUSTMENT          X   Age
Adjustment to divorce is easier for the young than for the old. (B033)

### Age of Wife
The older the divorcée, the more likely is she to experience difficult emotional problems. (G157)

When the marriage is short, there is no relationship between age of the divorcée and difficulty of the emotional problems experienced in divorce. (G157)

### Child-Rearing Problems
The greater the emotional difficulties experienced by the divorcée, the more likely is she to claim that there was some period during the divorce when the children had been harder to handle. This relationship does not change with increasing time since the divorce. (G157)

### Custody of Children
The parent who retains the children after divorce experiences less of a crisis than the one who is cut off from both the former mate and the children. (B033)

### Dating
The greater the emotional problems experienced by the divorcée, the lower her dating frequency after the divorce. (G157)

### Divorce
When divorce will result in economic and social dislocation, the rate of divorce tends to be low. (S037)

### Divorce, Attitude Toward
Divorce is an extreme crisis for family members when there is strong community opinion against it. (B033)

The more ambivalent the divorcée about obtaining the divorce, the greater the emotional problems she experiences. (G157)

Divorcées who experience some discrimination are more likely to have difficult emotional problems in divorce than are those who experience no discrimination. (G157)

Indifference by friends and kin regarding the divorce is associated with the fewest emotional problems being experienced by the divorcée and definite disapproval or approval with difficult emotional problems. (G157)

Among divorcées who are not remarried, those who claim they would be willing to wipe out the divorce are most likely to have experienced difficult emotional problems in the divorce, followed by those who experienced medium emotional problems, and lastly by those who had few emotional problems. (G157)

### Divorce Decision
The more stable the divorce decision, the fewer the emotional problems experienced by the divorcée. (G157)

### Divorce, Initiation of
Divorcées who experience the least emotional problems in divorce are most likely to report that the sugges-

tion to divorce was mutual and less likely to report that they first suggested the divorce. (G157)

### Divorce, Institutionalization of
Structural disruptions are created by lack of institutionalized post-divorce institutions. (G015)

The fewer and less explicit the institutional norms and patterns surrounding the postdivorce status, the greater the likelihood of guilt. (G156)

The fewer and less explicit the structural support for divorced persons (e.g., responsibility for child, support of wife), the more difficult will be the postdivorce period for the individual. (G156)

### Divorce Process
There is no relationship between the time interval between a serious consideration of divorce and obtaining the decree and the severity of emotional problems experienced by the divorcée during the divorce period. (G157)

### Duration of Marriage
For younger divorcées a long-lasting marriage is associated with difficult emotional problems in divorce. (G157)

For older divorcées a long-lasting marriage is associated with few emotional problems in divorce. (G157)

### Extended Family Ties
Divorce is less disruptive socially and personally when an extended family pattern exists. (E083)

### Husband-Wife Relations (Affect)
Divorcées who are positively emotionally involved with their husbands after the divorce are more likely than those who are less emotionally involved to experience difficult emotional problems in divorce. (G157)

### Husband-Wife Relations (Interdependence)
When emotional involvement is relatively weak, persons in these families may change from the situation of marriage to that of divorce without experiencing a crisis. (B033)

### Husband-Wife Relations (Punishment)
Divorcées who experience a great deal of emotional turmoil during the divorce are more likely to claim a desire to punish their husbands than are those who had fewer emotional problems. (G157)

### Kin Terminology (Classificatory)
Divorce will be less disruptive in societies with classificatory terminology. (R071)

### Marital Status
Divorcées who have some friends divorced or divorcing are slightly more likely to have few emotional problems in divorce than are those who have no friends divorced or divorcing. (G157)

### Nuclear Family, Importance of
Divorce tends to be more disruptive with an increase in the structural importance of the nuclear family. (G015)

### Occupational Rank of Husband
Divorcées, whose husbands have middle- or upper-class occupations are slightly more likely than those of husbands with lower-class occupations to experience difficult emotional problems in divorce. (G157)

### Religion

Catholic divorcées are slightly more likely to experience difficult emotional problems during divorce than are Protestant divorcées. (G157)

### Remarriage

Divorcées who experience their greatest periods of loneliness during either the separation period or when the decree is granted are more likely than those who experience loneliness during other periods of the divorce procedure to remarry soon after the divorce. (G157)

### Sex Status

Divorce affects the general adjustment of women more than that of men. (G126)

The husband is more likely to feel guilty about demanding a divorce than is the wife. (G156)

### Size of Family

Divorcées experiencing difficult emotional problems are more likely to have two or more children than one child. (G157)

### Size of Kin Network

Divorce will have a less disruptive effect when the number of the child's kin is large. (H141)

### Surrogate Parents

The consequences of divorce will be less disruptive if the kinship is classificatory in character. (G093)

### Urban/Rural

Divorcées from rural backgrounds are more likely to experience difficult emotional problems during the divorce than are divorcées from urban backgrounds. (G157)

## DIVORCE, AGE AT          X     Class

A woman is more likely to initiate divorce when she reaches old age if she is of the upper class, for by returning to her kinsmen she maximizes status by reassociating with kin in positions of power. (G142)

### Rank of Women

A woman is more likely to initiate divorce when she reaches old age when her status as an elderly woman independent of her marital status is high. (G142)

## DIVORCE AGREEMENTS

### X     Divorce Discussions

Couples are least likely to agree with regard to the matter of the children, more likely to agree on support payments, and most likely to agree regarding property division. (G157)

### Education of Husband

Husbands with some college education are slightly more likely than are those with no college education to keep all or some of their divorce agreements. (G157)

### Employment (Regularity)

There is a positive relationship between the steadiness of the husband's work and his keeping the divorce agreements. (G157)

### Religion

There is no difference between Protestant and Catholic husbands regarding the keeping of divorce agreements, although husbands with no religious affiliation are less likely to keep their agreements. (G157)

## DIVORCE ARRANGEMENTS     X    Child Support

When the wife thinks that the property settlement is fair, the husband is slightly less likely to think the child-support payments are unfair or to resent them. (G157)

### Duration of Marriage

Holding constant to the amount of property owned by the divorcing couple, there is no association between the length of time the marriage lasted and whether the couple split their property. (G157)

### Property

For all occupational classes, the divorcing couple is much more likely to split the property when there is more of it. (G157)

### Size of Family

There is no relationship between the number of children and the type of property division (split of property, all property going to either husband or wife) made by divorcing couples. (G157)

## DIVORCE, ATTITUDE TOWARD     X    Adultery

With an increase in extramarital relations, the attitude toward divorce becomes more tolerant. (T054)

### Adultery, Attitude Toward

The greater the spouse's fear of the consequences of divorce, the greater the willingness to tolerate the adulterous behavior of one's partner. (B033)

### Age of Wife

The younger the divorcée, the more likely is she to claim that persons discriminated against her because of being divorced. (G157)

### Children

Divorce tends to be more censured by society when children are involved. (G015)

### Class

The higher the class, the more liberal the attitudes toward divorce. (G156)

### Divorce

The high toleration for divorce in the United States is directly related to the high actual number of divorces. (C134)

Lessened disapproval of divorce is associated with higher divorce rates. (G156)

### Divorce Adjustment

Divorce is an extreme crisis for family members when there is strong community opinion against it. (B033)

The more ambivalent the divorcée about obtaining the divorce, the greater the emotional problems she experiences. (G156)

Divorcées who experience some discrimination are more likely to have difficult emotional problems in divorce than are those who experience no discrimination. (G157)

Indifference by friends and kin regarding the divorce is associated with the fewest emotional problems being experienced by the divorcée and definite disapproval or approval with difficult emotional problems. (G157)

Among divorcées who are not remarried, those who claim they would be willing to wipe out the divorce are most likely to have experienced difficult emotional problems in the divorce, followed by those who experienced medium emotional problems, and lastly by those who had few emotional problems. (G157)

### Divorce, Initiation of
When the first suggestion of and insistence upon divorce are from the wife, her friends and kin are more likely than his to approve of the divorce than when the initiation and insistence come from the husband. (G157)

### Education of Wife
Divorced women with grammar-school education are more likely to report social discrimination against them because of their divorced status. (G157)

### Friends of Husband/Wife
Shared friends of the couple are more likely than friends of the husband alone to express approval and less likely to express disapproval of the divorce. (G157)

### Kin/Friends
For both the husband and wife, their family members are more likely to disapprove of the divorce than are their respective friends. (G157)

Both the husband's and wife's kin are less likely to be indifferent about the divorce than are friends. (G157)

### Occupation
The professional group is more liberal than any other occupational strata in its attitudes toward divorce laws. (F009)

### Religion
The wife's and husband's religious affiliation is unrelated to the degree of approval/disapproval expressed by her or his kin and friends. (G157)

### Remarriage
Censure expressed toward the status of the divorced woman acts to push her toward remarriage. (G015)

The ambiguity of status of the divorced woman and her lesser social approval push her toward remarriage. (G015)

Divorcées who remarried earlier are slightly more likely to report social discrimination against them because of their status as divorced. (G157)

A larger proportion of divorcées is likely to claim that there is someone among their male friends that they might consider marrying if their friends or kin approved or felt indifferent toward the divorce than if they originally disapproved of the divorce. (G157)

### Social Network of Husband/Wife
The wife's friends and family are much more likely to feel strong approval of the divorce than are the husband's friends, but this does not hold for mild approval. (G157)

## DIVORCE/BEREAVEMENT, ADJUSTMENT TO
### X   Dating
Ability to take part in a new relationship is related to higher adjustment whether the loss of a spouse was by death or by divorce. (G156)

## DIVORCE COMPLAINTS      X   Child Support
The divorcee's complaint that non-support was a cause of the divorce is associated with the husband who never or rarely makes his child support payments. (G157)

### Dating
Those who complain of value conflicts have the highest post divorce dating frequency. (G157)

### Divorce Complaints
Complaints by divorcées that their husbands' drinking was a cause of divorce are positively associated with complaints that the complex of staying away, drinking, gambling, and being "out with the boys" was a cause of divorce. (G157)

Divorcées who claim that the complex of staying away, drinking, gambling, and being with the boys was a cause of divorce are also likely to claim that their husbands' neglect of home life was a cause of divorce. (G157)

Divorcées who complain that their husbands' overspending was a cause of divorce are highly likely to complain that their husbands' time spent away from home was also a cause of divorce. (G157)

Divorcées who claim that their husbands' drinking was a cause of divorce are as likely to claim that his overspending also was a cause of divorce. (G157)

### Divorce Decision
The stability of the final divorce decision is not related to various kinds of divorce complaints. (G157)

### Divorce, Initiation of
Of the various complaints of the divorcée, the husband's drinking, overspending, nonsupport, and the complex of drinking, gambling, and staying out with the boys are highly correlated with the wife being the first to suggest a divorce. (G157)

Of the various complaints of the divorcée, a conflict in values and dominance by the husband are associated with a mutual suggestion to divorce. (G157)

### Divorce Process
Of the complaints made by divorcées, dominance by the husband is associated with a longer-than-average time interval between a serious consideration of divorce and filing suit. (G157)

### Duration of Marriage
Complaints of personality conflicts by divorcées are associated with a short duration of marriage. (G157)

The frequency of complaints by the divorcée that the husband neglected his homelife increases among marriages of a longer duration. (G157)

The frequency of complaints by the divorcée regarding value conflicts decreases among marriages of a longer duration. (G157)

The frequency of complaints by the divorcée that the husband's drinking was a cause of divorce increases among marriages of a longer duration. (G157)

The frequency of complaints by divorcées regarding the complex of staying away, drinking, gambling, and being out with the boys increases among marriages of a longer duration. (G157)

### Employment (Regularity)
Among husbands in the same income group, job instability increases the claims by the ex-wife that nonsupport was a cause of divorce. (G157)

### Extramarital Relations

Divorcées who claim that their husbands' overspending was a cause of divorce are not likely to claim that another woman was also a cause of the divorce. (G157)

Divorcées who claim that another woman was a cause of divorce are not likely to claim that their husbands' drinking was also a cause of divorce. (G157)

Divorcées who claim that their husbands' neglect of homelife was a cause of divorce are not likely to claim that another woman was also a cause of divorce. (G157)

The divorcée who complains that "another woman" was a cause of divorce is also likely to claim desertion as a cause of the divorce. (G157)

### Homogamy (Education)

Divorcées who marry downward educationally are least likely to complain that their husbands' neglect of home-life was a cause of divorce, then divorcées who marry at the same educational level, and lastly divorcées who marry upward educationally. (G157)

Divorcées who married upward educationally are slightly more likely to claim that their husbands' over-spending was a cause of divorce than are those who married at the same educational level, followed by divorcées who married downward educationally. (G157)

### Homogamy (Occupation)

Divorcées who were occupationally hypergamous are more likely than those who were occupationally hypogamous to claim that value conflicts were a cause of divorce. (G157)

### Income

The higher the husband's income, the less likely is his ex-wife to claim that nonsupport was a cause of their divorce. (G157)

Among divorcées, there is a low positive association between complaints of the husband's overspending and his failure to provide an adequate income. (G157)

Among husbands who worked steadily, the higher his income, the more likely is the ex-wife to complain that nonsupport is a cause of divorce. (G157)

The higher the husband's income, the more likely is his ex-wife to complain that his overspending was a cause of divorce. (G157)

### Race

Negro divorcées are no more likely than white divor-cées to charge that personality conflicts were a cause of divorce. (G157)

Negro divorcées are more likely than white divorcées to claim that value conflicts were a cause of divorce. (G157)

### Religion

Divorcées of Protestant husbands are more likely than divorcées of Catholic husbands to complain that person-ality conflicts were a cause of divorce. (G157)

Protestant divorcées are no more likely than Catholic divorcées to claim that personality conflicts were a cause of divorce. (G157)

Divorcées from mixed-faith marriages are no more likely than those from like-faith marriages to claim that personality conflicts were a cause of divorce. (G157)

Divorcées of Protestant husbands are more likely than are divorcées of Catholic husbands to claim that value conflicts were a cause of divorce. (G157)

Protestant divorcées are more likely than Catholic divor-cées to claim that value conflicts were a cause of di-vorce. (G157)

### Remarriage

The divorcée's complaints of the husband's staying away, drinking, being with "the boys," and gambling are associated with claims that the experience of the first marriage had made the second easier. (G157)

### Urban/Rural

Divorcées from urban backgrounds are more likely to complain about their husbands' personalities as causes of divorce than are divorcées from rural backgrounds. (G157)

Divorcées from rural backgrounds are slightly more likely to complain that their husbands were too authori-tarian than are those from urban backgrounds. (G157)

Among divorcées, urban wives married to urban hus-bands are most likely to complain that personality con-flicts were the cause of divorce, followed by rural-urban marriage combinations, and lastly by rural wives who were married to rural husbands. (G157)

Divorcées from rural backgrounds are slightly more likely to claim nonsupport as a cause of divorce than are divorcées from urban backgrounds. (G157)

Husbands of rural background are slightly more likely than those of urban background to have their ex-wives claim nonsupport as a cause of divorce. (G157)

Rural divorcées who were married to urban husbands are least likely to complain that nonsupport was a cause of their divorces, followed by urban divorcées who were married to urban husbands, next by urban divor-cées who were married to rural husbands, and lastly by rural divorcées who were married to rural husbands. (G157)

Divorcées from rural backgrounds are slightly more likely to complain that their husbands' neglect of home-life was a cause of their divorces. (G157)

Rural divorcées who were married to urban husbands are most likely to complain that their husbands' neglect of homelife was a cause of divorces, followed by the urban divorcées who were married to urban husbands, and lastly by both the urban divorcées married to rural husbands and the rural divorcées married to rural hus-bands. (G157)

Rural divorcées who were married to rural husbands are most likely to claim that value conflicts were a cause of divorce, followed by rural divorcées married to urban husbands, next by urban divorcées married to rural hus-bands, and lastly by urban divorcées married to rural husbands. (G157)

## DIVORCE, COST OF          X   Divorce

The greater the expenses of a divorce, the higher the divorce rate. (D083)

## DIVORCE DECISION          X   Age of Wife

Stability of the final decision to divorce is unrelated to the age of the wife. (G157)

### Dating During Marriage
The frequency with which the husband and wife dated one another during the marriage is not related to the stability of the final decision to divorce. (G157)

### Divorce Adjustment
The more stable the divorce decision, the fewer the emotional problems experienced by the divorcée. (G157)

### Divorce Complaints
The stability of the final divorce decision is not related to various kinds of divorce complaints. (G157)

### Divorce, Initiation of
Among Catholics, when the wife is the first to suggest the divorce, the divorce decision is less stable. (G157)

### Duration of Marriage
The stability of the final decision to divorce is not related to the duration of the marriage. (G157)

### Extramarital Relations
The stability of the final divorce decision is not related to whether either spouse was in love with another. (G157)

### Religion
The stability of the final decision to divorce is not associated with either the husband's or the wife's religious affiliation. (G157)

### Religiosity
For both Protestants and Catholics, stable divorce decisions are found among those who are the most devout. (G157)

Among devout divorcées, the devout Catholic is highly stable in her decision to divorce whether or not the husband first suggested the divorce, while the devout Protestant is unstable in her divorce decision if it was not the husband who first suggested the divorce. (G157)

The stability of the divorce decision is lowest for those Catholics who attended church most frequently during the marriage and began attending infrequently after the divorce. (G157)

### Size of Family
The stability of the final decision to divorce is not related to the number of children in the family. (G157)

### Urban/Rural
Stability of the final decision to divorce is unrelated to whether the couples are from rural or urban background. (G157)

## DIVORCE/DESERTION    X    Occupational Rank
When the occupational distribution of Philadelphia desertion cases is compared to that of the Philadelphia divorce sample, a surprising degree of similarity is evident. (K010)

## DIVORCE DISCUSSIONS
### X    Divorce Agreements
Couples are least likely to agree with regard to the matter of the children, more likely to agree on support payments, and most likely to agree regarding property division. (G157)

### Economic Rank
There is a positive relationship between the amount of property and discussions of property as a part of the divorce arrangements. This holds only when the husband has a high-school education or more. (G157)

### Education of Husband
The higher the husband's educational level, the higher the frequency with which the couple will talk over divorce arrangements. (G157)

When the couple's property is of little or no value, there is no relationship between the husband's education and the frequency with which the couple talked about divorce arrangements; with increasing amounts of property, a positive relationship exists between the husband's education and frequency of talks. (G157)

## DIVORCE, EASE OF    X    Affinal Relations
When divorce is easy and frequent, affection "is usually weak or even completely absent" between affinal kinsmen. (P087)

### Descent (Patrilineal)
In societies where the patrilineal organization is strong, divorce can only be obtained at the will of the husband. (L041)

### Desertion
The greater the institutionalized difficulty in obtaining divorce, the greater the incidence of disintegration of families by physical separation (e.g., desertion). (K161)

### Divorce
The rate of divorce will be related to the cost of the action and the severity of legal impediment. (B033)

The easier it is to divorce, the higher is the divorce rate. (G134)

### Mate Selection
When subjective factors are culturally prescribed as the basis of mate selection, a correlated easy system of divorce tends to occur. (S076)

## DIVORCE, GROUNDS FOR    X    Husband/Wife
The husband is more likely than the wife, in *remarriages*, to seek a divorce on the grounds of desertion. (K003)

### Warfare
In societies in which the emphasis is upon warfare, sterility is likely to be a ground for divorce. (T107)

In societies in which the emphasis is upon warfare, the failure to have male children is likely to be grounds for divorce. (T107)

## DIVORCE IN FAMILY HISTORY    X    Divorce
The likelihood of divorce increases with the rate of divorce in the family line. (L019)

## DIVORCE, INITIATION OF    X    Age of Wife
The wife is slightly more likely to be the first to suggest divorce if she is in a young age bracket, and the husband to be the first to suggest divorce if she is older. (G157)

### Child Support
The husband is most likely to make regular child-support payments when the first suggestion to divorce was mutual, less likely to pay regularly when he first suggested divorce, and least likely when his wife first suggested divorce. (G157)

If the husband resents the child-support payments, which spouse made the first suggestion to divorce does not affect his lack of continuity in child support. When he does not resent the child-support payments, a mutual suggestion to divorce is more highly associated with regular child-support payments than when either the wife or the husband was the first to suggest divorce. (G157)

### Dating
Among divorcées who rarely or never date, the highest proportion is found among those whose husbands first suggested the divorce, followed by those who themselves suggested the divorce, and lastly by those who claim the suggestion to divorce was mutual. (G157)

### Divorce Adjustment
Divorcées who experience the least emotional problems in divorce are most likely to report that the suggestion to divorce was mutual and less likely to report that they first suggested the divorce. (G157)

### Divorce, Attitude Toward
When the first suggestion of and insistence upon divorce are from the wife, her friends and kin are more likely than his to approve of the divorce than when the initiation and insistence come from the husband. (G157)

### Divorce Complaints
Of the various complaints of the divorcée, the husband's drinking, overspending, nonsupport, and the complex of drinking, gambling, and staying out with the boys are highly correlated with the wife being the first to suggest a divorce. (G157)

Of the various complaints of the divorcée, a conflict in values and dominance by the husband are associated with a mutual suggestion to divorce. (G157)

### Divorce Decision
Among Catholics, when the wife is the first to suggest the divorce, the divorce decision is less stable. (G157)

### Divorce, Insistence on
The highest percentage of divorcées claims that they both suggested and insisted upon the divorce; the smallest proportion claims that their husbands both suggested and insisted upon the divorce. (G157)

### Divorce Process
The time interval between a serious consideration of divorce and filing suit is longest when the suggestion to divorce is mutual, shorter when the wife first suggests a divorce, and shortest when the husband is the first to suggest a divorce. (G157)

The time interval between a serious consideration to divorce and filing suit is longer when the wife first suggests and continues to insist upon the divorce than when the husband both suggests and insists. (G157)

### Education of Wife
The education of the wife is unrelated to who made the first suggestion to divorce. (G157)

### Employment of Wife
Wives who held jobs during their marriages are slightly more likely to be the first to suggest and insist on the divorce than are those who did not work. (G157)

### Employment (Regularity)
When the husband was not a steady worker, there is a greater likelihood that the wife both first suggested and continued to insist upon the divorce than when he was a steady worker. (G157)

### Extramarital Relations
The wife is most likely both to suggest first and later insist upon the divorce when she is in love with another and her husband is not, and she is least likely to suggest first and later insist when she is not in love but her husband is. (G157)

The husband is most likely to both first suggest and later insist upon divorce when he is in love with another and his wife is not; and he is least likely to suggest and insist when he is not in love with another and his wife is. (G157)

### Friendship
When the husband was the first to make the decision to divorce, the divorcée is slightly more likely to keep her marriage friends than when the suggestion was mutual; she is least likely to keep her marriage friends when she was the one who first suggested the divorce. (G157)

### Homogamy (Education)
In educationally hypogamous marriages, the wife is no more likely to be the first to suggest divorce than in educationally homogamous marriages where education is high-school or less. (G157)

### Husband/Wife
Holding religion constant, the wife is more likely to claim that she both suggested first and continued to insist on the divorce and is least likely to claim that her husband both suggested the divorce first and insisted upon it. (G157)

It is generally easier for a man to initiate divorce than for a woman. (S158)

### Income
Wives are less likely to make the first suggestion to divorce if they are married to husbands with steady income. (G157)

### Occupational Rank of Husband
Wives of men in high-status occupations are slightly less likely to make the first suggestion to divorce; the husbands are slightly more likely to make the first suggestion. (G157)

### Rank of Divorcée
The lower the social status of the (female) divorcée in the society, the less likely are women to initiate divorce. (S115)

### Religion
The religious affiliation of the wife is unrelated to who first suggests a divorce. (G157)

Among Catholic and Protestant divorcées, Catholic divorcées who rarely attend church are most likely to claim that they were the first to suggest a divorce. (G157)

### Religiosity
Those Catholics who attend church less frequently are more likely than those who attend with greater frequency to be the first to suggest a divorce. (G157)

### Remarriage
Controlling for the time lapse since the divorce, divorcées who claim that their husbands were the first to suggest divorce are less likely to be remarried than when the suggestion was the divorcées or mutual. (G157)

### Sex Status
Since the husband is more involved outside of the home environment and consequently less dependent upon the marriage as his only source of personal satisfaction, he is more likely to be the one who initiates the breakup of the marriage. (G156)

## DIVORCE, INSISTENCE ON
### X   Divorce, Initiation of
The highest percentage of divorcées claims that they both suggested and insisted upon the divorce; the smallest proportion claims that their husbands both suggested and insisted upon the divorce. (G157)

## DIVORCE, INSTITUTIONALIZATION OF
### X   Divorce Adjustment
Structural disruptions are created by lack of institutionalized postdivorce institutions. (G015)

The fewer and less explicit the institutional norms and patterns surrounding the postdivorce status, the greater the likelihood of guilt. (G156)

The fewer and less explicit the structural supports for divorced persons (e.g., responsibility for child, support of wife), the more difficult will be the postdivorce period for the individual. (G156)

## DIVORCE OF BARREN WIFE
### X   Fecundity of Wives
A barren wife is less likely to be divorced if the other wives are fertile. (S174)

## DIVORCE OF PARENTS                 X   Divorce
Individuals whose parents were divorced are more likely to become divorced themselves than are individuals whose parents were not divorced. (K161)

### Marriage, Attitude Toward
The attitude of women toward marriage is favorable even if their parents were divorced. (W003)

## DIVORCE PROCESS           X   Age of Child
The older the children, the longer the interval between a serious consideration of divorce and the actual filing of the suit. (G157)

### Age of Wife
The older the wife, the longer the interval between a serious consideration to divorce and the actual filing of the suit. (G157)

Controlling for duration of the marriage, the older the wife, the longer the interval between a serious consideration of divorce and actually filing suit. (G157)

### Children
The anticipated effects of the divorce on the children are not related to the time interval between serious consideration to divorce and filing suit. (G157)

### Divorce Adjustment
There is no relationship between the time interval between a serious consideration of divorce and obtaining the decree and the severity of emotional problems experienced by the divorcée during the divorce period. (G157)

### Divorce Complaints
Of the complaints made by divorcées, dominance by the husband is associated with a longer-than-average time interval between a serious consideration of divorce and filing suit. (G157)

### Divorce, Initiation of
The time interval between a serious consideration of divorce and filing suit is longest when the suggestion to divorce is mutual, shorter when the wife first suggests a divorce, and shortest when the husband is the first to suggest a divorce. (G157)

The time interval between a serious consideration to divorce and filing suit is longer when the wife first suggests and continues to insist upon the divorce than when the husband both suggests and insists. (G157)

### Duration of Marriage
The longer the duration of the marriage, the greater the time between a serious consideration of divorce and the filing of the suit. (G157)

Controlling for age of the wife, the longer the duration of the marriage, the longer the interval between a serious consideration to divorce and filing suit. (G157)

Controlling for rural/urban background of the wife, the longer the duration of marriage, the longer the interval between a serious consideration of divorce and filing suit. (G157)

### Education of Husband
The husband's educational level is unrelated to the length of time taken between a serious consideration of divorce and the filing of the suit. (G157)

### Employment of Wife
Job holding by the wife during the marriage is not associated with a shorter period between a serious consideration to divorce and the actual filing of the suit. (G157)

### Extramarital Relations
When the wife is in love with someone prior to the divorce, the time interval between a serious consideration to divorce and the actual filing of the suit is lengthened. (G157)

Among the complaints made by the divorcée, the husband's involvement with another woman is associated with a shorter-than-average time interval between a serious consideration of divorce and filing suit. (G157)

### Friendship
When the time between the decision to divorce and filing suit is short, the divorcée is more likely to maintain her marriage friends than when the time is long. (G157)

### Income of Divorcée
The longer the time lapse since the divorce, the more likely is the divorcée to claim that she is "best off" economically at present than she was during the marriage or any time during the divorce process. (G157)

### Income of Husband
The husband's income is unrelated to the length of time taken between a serious consideration of divorce and the filing of the suit. (G157)

### Marriage, Approval of
Prior approval or disapproval of the marriage by friends or kin is unrelated to the length of time taken by the couple between a serious consideration to divorce and filing suit. (G157)

### Marriage Counseling
Couples who take a longer time between a serious consideration to divorce and filing suit are more likely to seek marriage counseling. (G157)

### Occupation of Husband
The occupation of the husband is unrelated to the length of time taken between a serious consideration of divorce and the filing of the suit. (G157)

### Race
Whites from rural backgrounds take slightly more time between decisions to divorce and filing suits than do Negroes from the same backgrounds. (G157)

Negroes from small towns take considerably longer than do whites between decisions to divorce and filing suits. (G157)

Urban Negroes take about the same amount of time as do urban whites from serious decisions to divorce to the actual filings of the suits. (G157)

### Religion
The wife's or husband's religious affiliation is unrelated to the time taken between a serious consideration of divorce and filing suit. (G157)

Frequency of church attendance by the wife is unrelated to the length of time taken between a serious consideration to divorce and filing suit. (G157)

### Remarriage
Divorcées who take a longer time between a serious consideration to divorce and filing suit are more likely to remarry soon after the divorce. (G157)

### Residence
When marriage duration is over 15 years, there is no difference between rural, small-town, and urban wives regarding the time taken between a serious consideration of divorce and the filing of suit. (G157)

### Size of Family
The larger the family (up to three children), the longer the interval between a serious consideration of divorce and filing suit. (G157)

### Urban/Rural
Couples from rural backgrounds take a longer time between a serious consideration of divorce and the actual filings of the suits than do couples from urban backgrounds. (G157)

## DIVORCE/SEPARATION
### X    Adjustment of Child
Children of discord or separation suffer greater disadvantages than those whose parents actually divorce. (G134)

## DIVORCE/WIDOWHOOD    X    Remarriage
Divorced persons are much more likely to remarry than are those who have been widowed. (M242)

## DIVORCÉE'S ATTITUDE TOWARD EX-HUSBAND
### X    Dating
Divorcées who claim negative or loving attitudes toward their ex-spouses are less likely than those who feel friendly or indifferent toward them to be steady daters. (G157)

## DRINKING    X    Alcoholism
Alcoholics are more likely to have had parents with inconsistent attitudes toward drinking than are nonalcoholics. (D078)

### Premarital Sex Relations, Attitude Toward
Excessive drinking in a society and premarital sexual freedom tend to be associated. (K046)

### Sex Anxiety
Sexual anxiety is inversely correlated with an excessive use of alcohol. (K046)

## DRUG ADDICTION
### X    Father-Son Relations (Dominance)
Where fathers are prominent members of a family, they will tend, in the case of the drug addict, to be severe and dominating. (F090)

### Maternal Overprotectiveness
Mothers of drug addicts tend to be overprotective, controlling, and indulgent. (F090)

### Sex-Role Model
Most heroin addicts come from families where there is a lack of model for the male role. (F090)

## DURATION OF MARRIAGE    X    Class
The lower the class, the shorter the average duration of marriage. (G157)

### Dating During Marriage
Among divorced couples, there is a low inverse relationship between the frequency with which the couple went out together during their marriage and the length of their marriage. (G157)

The relationship between low frequency of "dating" during the marriage and longer duration of marriage is greater among those with higher income. (G157)

### Divorce
The higher the frequency of divorce, the earlier in marriage divorce will take place. (D083)

The "divorce percentage" decreases after the third year of marriage. (K002)

Divorce is more frequent among couples who have been married for a short period of time than it is among those who have been married longer. (P062)

### Divorce Adjustment
For younger divorcées a long-lasting marriage is associated with difficult emotional problems in divorce. (G157)

For older divorcées a long-lasting marriage is associated with few emotional problems in divorce. (G157)

### Divorce Arrangements
Holding constant to the amount of property owned by the divorcing couple, there is no association between the length of time the marriage lasted and whether the couple split their property. (G157)

### Divorce Complaints
Complaints of personality conflicts by divorcées are associated with a short duration of marriage. (G157)

The frequency of complaints by the divorcée that the husband neglected his homelife increases among marriages of longer duration. (G157)

The frequency of complaints by the divorcée regarding value conflicts decreases among marriages of a longer duration. (G157)

The frequency of complaints by the divorcée that the husband's drinking was a cause of divorce increases among marriages of a longer duration. (G157)

The frequency of complaints by divorcées regarding the complex of staying away, drinking, gambling, and being out with the boys increases among marriages of longer duration. (G157)

### Divorce Decision
The stability of the final decision to divorce is not related to the duration of the marriage. (G157)

### Divorce Process
The longer the duration of the marriage, the greater the time between a serious consideration of divorce and the filing of the suit. (G157)

Controlling for age of the wife, the longer the duration of the marriage, the longer the interval between a serious consideration of divorce and filing suit. (G157)

Controlling for rural/urban background of the wife, the longer the duration of marriage, the longer the interval between a serious consideration of divorce and filing suit. (G157)

### Education
Grammar-school educated persons divorce earlier than persons with a college education. (G157)

### Engagement, Duration of
The longer the engagement period, the higher the average duration of marriage. (G157)

In the upper strata, a longer engagement period is more likely to increase the average length of marriage. (G157)

### Extramarital Relations
The frequency of complaints by divorcées of other women as causes of divorce increases among marriages of longer duration. (G157)

### Fertility Values
The longer the duration of the marriage, the smaller the number of additional children preferred.

### Husband-Wife Relations
The marriage tie gradually becomes firmer as the marriage endures. (G111)

### Husband-Wife Relations (Communication)
The longer the duration of the marriage, the less is the communication of emotional problems between the two partners. (K089)

### Illegitimacy
In the Caribbean, common-law marriages endure as long as those initiated in the church. (G151)

### Juvenile Delinquency
The younger the child when his parents' marriage ends, the more likely he will become a delinquent.

### Marital Adjustment
The better the marital adjustment during the early stages of marriage, the greater the chance for marital success. (M185)

The longer the length of the marriage, the poorer the marital adjustment. (P086)

### Marriage Order of Wife
The duration of marriage for divorced women is shorter for secondary wives. (B012)

### Mental Illness of Spouse
Mental illness among spouses of chronically ill mental patients increases with the number of years of marriage. (K159)

### Neurosis
There is no association between duration of marriage and degree of complementarity of neurosis among married couples. (P086)

### Parent-Child Relations
The longer the marriage, the greater the convergence of parental attitudes and behaviors toward the children. (B232)

There is no correlation between the adjustment of married offspring to their parents and number of years married. (S011)

### Parent-Child Relations (Aid)
The longer a child is married, the less likely are the parents to give financial assistance. (A066)

### Parent-Child Relations (Interaction)
The longer a wife has been married, the less frequently she will see her parents. (K089)

### Personality (Complementary Needs)
Couples who are married longer (at least 10 years) are more likely than are couples married for shorter periods of time to have complementary need patterns. (M190)

### Personality of Husband/Wife
There is a correlation between degree of similarity in psychological complexity of marital partners, as measured by the number of "human movement" responses to Rorschach tests, and the duration of the marriage.

There is a correlation between complementarity of personality traits of marital partners, as measured by the quality of "human movement" responses to Rorschach tests, and the duration of marriage.

Interaction between husbands and wives leads to assimilation of roles and both tend to grow more alike through time. (B216)

There is no evidence that spouses grow more alike in terms of interests, attitudes, temperament, and intellectual abilities as the length of marriage increases. (N073)

### Race
Negroes are slightly more likely to have a longer duration of marriage than are whites. (G157)

Among urban populations, Negrores are more likely to have shorter durations of marriage than are whites. (G157)

Negro marriages ending in divorce are more likely to have lasted longer than are white marriages ending in divorce. (K003)

### Religiosity
For Catholics, a higher frequency of church attendance increases the mean duration of marriage; for Protestants, a higher frequency of church attendance slightly decreases the duration of marriage. (G157)

### Role Behavior of Husband-Wife
The greater the length of the marriage, the more accurately can one marital partner assume the role of the other. (T092)

### Role Definition of Husband/Wife
Consensus of couples regarding marital roles is correlated with length of marriage. (T092)

### Sex-Role Definition
With the passage of years after the marriage, there is an increasing role differentiation between husband and wife.

### Size of Family
The number of children involved in a divorce is less likely to alter the average duration of marriage among urban marriages than among rural marriages. (G157)

### Urban/Nonurban
Among couples who have divorced, those with nonurban backgrounds have longer marriage durations than do those with urban backgrounds, (G157)

### Urban/Rural
Of those marriages which are terminated, urban couples have a shorter duration of marriage. (M167)

## DYADIC RELATIONS    X    Consensus
The rate of interaction is correlated with the amount of agreement between two family members (i.e., willingness to accept information). (C124)

The rate of interaction is related to the rate of agreement between two family members (i.e., willingness to accept information). (C124)

The interaction rate between two family members is related to the agreement by the older dyad member. (C124)

### Interaction in Family
If time is not scarce, a high interaction rate on the part of one family member toward another elicits a high interaction rate from the latter toward the former. (C124)

If time is not scarce, all the dyadic relationships in a family tend to have the same interaction rate. (C124)

### Interaction in Family (Affection)
The more affectionate two family members are to each other, the more affectionate they will be to other family members and the more affection the others will show to one another. (C124)

All the dyadic relationships in a family tend to have the same degree of affection rather than disparate degrees of affection. (C124)

### Power Structure of Family
If two family members have a relation of high dominance-high submission, each will be more apt to be either highly dominant or highly submissive to other group members than less so; and dyadic relationships among these other family members will also be characterized by high dominance-high submissiveness. (C124)

If an older family member has a low dominance toward a younger family member, the younger member will have a low submission score. (C124)

If an older family member has high dominance toward a younger family member, the younger family member will have a high submissiveness toward the older family member (the exception is where the older family member is the mother and the younger member is the child). (C124)

All the dyadic relationships in a family tend to have the same, rather than varying, ratios of dominance to submission. (C124)

## DYADIC RELATIONS (AFFECTION)
### X    Interaction in Family
The greater the affection between two family members, the higher the interaction rate. (C124)

## DYADIC RELATIONS IN FAMILY
### X    Mental Illness of Child (Schizophrenia)
Family "skews," where one dyadic relationship within it dominates family life at the expense of the needs of other members, are a cause of schizophrenia in the child. (F097)

## DYADIC RELATIONS (INTERACTION)
### X    Size of Family
Dyads in a large family are more likely to have a low rate of interaction than are dyads in a small family. (C124)

# E

## ECOLOGICAL CONDITIONS
### X   Authority Structure of Family
The more severe the conditions for survival are for a family, the more authority the husband/father has.

### Descent (Matrilineal)
Within the world's horticultural zones matrilineal peoples seem to be found, in the main, outside of or bordering on the tropical forest and outside those zones where cattle can be raised in numbers. (A048)

### Descent (Unilineal)
Nonunilineal descent groups are more likely to occur than unilinear descent groups in situations where the environment is hostile. (B327)

### Endogamy (Lineage)
Lineage endogamy tends to arise under specific ecological conditions. (S158)

### Independence of Family
Seasonal variations and irregular natural hazards in the subsistence environment encourage a high degree of autonomy in the smallest social unit, the family. (S174)

### Stability of Family Structure
The patrilineal family structure tends to deteriorate when the geographical environment permits family self-sufficiency. (N014)

## ECONOMIC AND CEREMONIAL ROLE OF MOTHER   X   Adult-Child Relations (Indulgence)
### X   Role of Mother
In societies where mothers have few economic responsibilities and are little involved in the ceremonial life of the tribe, there tends to be more indulgence with infants. (W127)

## ECONOMIC AND LEGAL ROLE OF KIN-GROUP
### X   Cohesion of Kin-Group
The cohesion of a kin unit is directly correlated with its importance as a unit of economic and jural obligations. (E048)

## ECONOMIC ATTITUDES
### X   Marital Adjustment of Wife
Unhappy wives more often regard it as essential for an ideal marriage that the wife should be allowed a definite budget, more often insist that the wife should not be financially dependent on her husband, and more often believe that marriage should be postponed until income is comfortable. (T074)

### Occupational Rank
Where social contact among wives and families of members cuts across occupational rank of a corporation, the pressures from families are more likely to support the attitudes of management than where such contact occurs primarily "horizontally" in the hierarchy. (M166)

## ECONOMIC ATTITUDES OF CHILD
### X   Economic Attitudes of Parents
Children's attitudes toward money and other material things do not correlate with the parents' attitudes. (M182)

## ECONOMIC ATTITUDES OF HUSBAND/WIFE
### X   Cohesion of Family
Family integration is directly related to the congruence of economic expectations of the couples. (B033)

## ECONOMIC ATTITUDES OF PARENTS
### X   Economic Attitudes of Child
Children's attitudes toward money and other material things do not correlate with the parents' attitudes. (M182)

## ECONOMIC/CEREMONIAL ROLE OF EXTENDED FAMILY   X   Extended Family, Importance of
The role of the extended family will tend to be a minor one when it lacks ceremonial or economic functions. (N017)

## ECONOMIC CONDITIONS
### X   Cohesion of Family
The vulnerability of the family to the depression appeared to vary inversely with its integration and adaptability. (B033)

### Divorce
Divorces are likely to decrease during depressions at a greater rate than during nondepression periods. (C023)

### Extended Family
Where no one source of livelihood provides enough for a family to subsist, some form of extended family is likely to be found. (S090)

The persistence of extended families may be the result of poverty rather than of any cohesive force within the family. (S090)

### Fertility
Peace and prosperity are more conducive to higher birth rates than are war and economic depression. (B244)

Change from favorable to unfavorable economic conditions produces a decline in annual birth rates, long-run trends remaining stable. (F101)

Fertility varies directly with the general level of economic activity of the society. (K004)

### Illegitimacy
During depressions, illegitimacy is likely to increase at a greater rate than during nondepression periods. (C023)

### Infanticide
Infanticide occurs more frequently in time of famine. (D057)

### Marital Stability (Polygyny/Monogamy)
Economic pressures are more likely to lead to marital instability in the polygynous family than in the monogamous family. (M198)

### Marital Status
### X   Suicide
Suicide rate of married persons correlates more highly

with business cycles than does the suicide rate of single persons. (S078)

### Marriage Rate

During depressions marriages are likely to decrease at a greater rate than during nondepression periods. (C023)

There is a direct relation between the marriage rate and prosperity and an inverse relation between marriage rate and economic decline. (K161)

Marriages tend to occur during periods when the food supply is abundant. (S099)

### Paternal Role

Where there is insecurity in jobs for men, the father is apt to hold a position of marginality in the family. (S080)

### Premarital Pregnancy

A higher percentage of first births is conceived before marriage during a depression. (C023)

### Property, Division of

Fission of family land is more likely to occur during periods of economic pressure. (L066)

### Residence

In societies governed by matrilineal descent, wide-span local matrilineages are more likely to exist where access to land or to other valuable natural resources is limited. (T080)

### Sex Relations

The frequency of sexual relations tends to be directly correlated with the abundance of the food supply. (H139)

### Sex-Role Behavior

A depression in our society changes the role of the father more than that of any other member, for his status and position in the family rests more on his occupational level and income than that of other members. (B033)

### Size of Family

The small patriarchal family will supercede the large patriarchal family when economic conditions make it a more efficient industrial instrument. (B033)

Couples who start their families early in periods of prosperity do not necessarily have a much larger completed family, especially if the period of prosperity is shortly followed by a period of depression. Conversely, couples who, in periods of depression, postpone starting their families have some tendency to make up this deficit later in life if economic conditions change before they are too old. Thus, periods of depression or prosperity have to extend over a number of years before they materially affect the total reproduction of a generation. (W012)

### Stability of Extended Family

The fission of an extended family tends to be directly correlated with economic pressures. (B086)

Adverse economic conditions will tend to hasten the fissioning of extended family groups. (W031)

### Stability of Lineage

Adverse economic pressures will tend to undermine the persistence of a lineage system. (W056)

### Structure of Family

The family structure will change in response to changes in economic conditions. (W082)

## ECONOMIC CONDITIONS, ADJUSTMENT TO
### X   Marital Status

Family groups meet economic crisis more effectively than do single, unattached, or widowed men and women. (F078)

## ECONOMIC CONDITIONS (LABOR)
### X   Fertility Values

The greater the community's immediate need for labor and production, the less likely it is that large families will be considered desirable. (T098)

## ECONOMIC COOPERATION
### X   Affinal Relations

When a series of reciprocal economic obligations characterizes the relationship between affines, a greater attempt will be made to maintain a peaceful relationship. (W062)

### Child-Rearing Practices
### (Adjustment/Achievement)

The greater the stress on cooperation rather than production in the economy, the more likely it is that parents concern themselves with the social adjustment of the child as opposed to achievement. (M203)

### Cohesion of Community

In the absence of pressures toward interfamilial cooperation in the economic sphere, the bond between families within the community tends to weaken. (G027)

### Cohesion of Family

When economic cooperation exists between related families of orientation and procreation, closer emotional relationships develop between them than if there is no economic cooperation. (S002)

### Cohesion of Kin-Group

The strength of the relationship between kinsmen will be directly correlated with the extent to which the relationship involves economic cooperation. (O023)

### Cohesion of Kin Network

The primary extension of family sentiment to members of the wider kinship group largely depends upon how much the latter fulfills the family task of distributing and consuming food. (R087)

### Cohesion of Lineage

Lineage solidarity is reinforced by a pattern of economic cooperation between lineage members. (W056)

### Conflict

There is more likely to be tension between relatives when their relationship implies economic responsibilities. (F087)

### Descent

The descent group will be more strictly delineated if there are patterns of economic cooperation between its members. (M131)

### Descent (Matrilineal)

Matrilineages are not likely to be found in societies which demand large-scale cooperation among males. (G156)

### Division of Labor

When the division of labor is rudimentary and there is sufficient land available the economic pattern tends to consist of cooperation between close relatives. (W056)

### Economic Pattern (Money)
The entrance into a money economy has the effect of breaking down extended family patterns of pooling goods and services. (S041)

### Extended/Nuclear Family
The extended family is better able to amass capital for an economic venture than is the nuclear family. (G156)

### Homosexuality
The absence of homosexuality is correlated with an economic pattern that requires cooperative work between groups of males. (V025)

### Intergenerational Relations
Economic cooperation between related families of different generations creates closer emotional ties between the families. (S002)

### Intermarriage
Patterns of intermarriage between two groups tend to occur with the establishment of patterns of economic reciprocity. (B058)

### Kin Relations (Interaction)
Frequency of contact is closely correlated with frequency of help between relatives. (G033)

### Kin Ties
The extension or maintenance of kinship ties between spatially separated units is directly correlated with the presence of patterns of economic interdependence. (S159)

### Men's Societies
Men's societies tend to occur in communities of moderate size where economic cooperation is a stable pattern. (M067)

### Parent-Child Relations (Conflict)
Parent-child conflict is at a minimum in rural areas because farming requires the common cooperation of all members of the family and there is a common interest in family property. (B033)

### Polyandry
Polyandry often occurs where some economic advantage accrues to the participating males (e.g., land shortage, mutual help in hunting or fishing). (S189)

### Residence
Where there is no need for families to consolidate for economic cooperation, the localization of lineages tends to be inhibited. (P026)

### Size of Kin-Group
Patterns of economic cooperation between kinsmen tend to be correlated with the size of the kin-group. (W056)

### Stability of Extended Family
The differentials in labor power that each nuclear family supplies to the household are a major cause of fission of the extended family household. (R012)

### Values (Familism)
When the system of land tenure requires the economic cooperation of the family, the values which unify the family will be of a familial nature. (B033)

Familism is reinforced by the rural labor pattern when farming is a common occupation of the family with all members participating in it cooperatively. (B033)

## ECONOMIC DEPENDENCE     X     Age at Marriage
The age at marriage tends to increase with the introduction of an economy which permits economic independence. (W082)

### Aggression
There is no relationship between the aggressiveness of the boy and his degree of economic dependence upon his parents. (B243)

### Authority Structure of Family
With increasing economic independence, authority within the extended family tends to shift from the head of this kin unit to the husband in the nuclear family. (O023)

The development of patterns of economic independence tends to undermine the family authority structure. (T068)

### Cohesion of Clan
The clan structure will be weakened with the introduction of individual economic independence. (C056)

### Cohesion of Family
Family ties tend to be strengthened by the increase of intrafamilial debts. (V010)

The cohesiveness of the family is directly correlated with the economic interdependence of its members. (W082)

Family cohesion tends to deteriorate with the development of patterns of economic independence. (W082)

### Cohesion of Joint Family
The cohesion of the joint family is weakened by the development of patterns of economic individualism. (M081)

### Cohesion of Kin-Groups
The kin structure tends to weaken with the development of opportunity for economic independence. (F059)

### Conflict in Family
When members of the joint family are economically dependent upon one another, friction is likely to characterize their relationship. (N014)

### Conflict in Kin Network
The greater the economic self-sufficiency of the individual, the more likely he is to conflict with and/or withdraw from the extended family. (M198)

### Economic Pattern (Money)
Where cash crops have been introduced, householders depend less on a wider circle of their kinfolk. (H222)

### Emotional Adjustment
Among elderly persons (75 years of age or older) living with their children, the more financially independent they are, the higher their morale. (C116)

### Kin-Role Behavior
Kin obligations tend to be increasingly evaded with the introduction of an economy which permits economic independence. (F059)

### Kin Ties
Kinship ties will tend to disintegrate with the development of patterns of economic independence. (N046)

### Kinship, Importance of
Where the community is economically self-sufficient, role relationships are defined by kinship. (L072)

#### Marriage Payment
Economic independence is inhibited by the familial debt which the bride-price system creates. (V010)

#### Mate Selection (Free Choice)
With increasing economic independence of the individual, the selection of the mate tends to be an individual rather than a family decision. (R038)

#### Parent-Child Relations (Authority)
The authority of parents tends to be directly correlated with the continuing economic dependence of their children. (L064)

#### Parent-Child Relations (Control)
The degree of effective discipline over a boy decreases as his earnings increase. (C024)

#### Polygyny
With the introduction of an economy which permits economic independence, the age at which a male may contract a polygynous union is younger. (W082)

#### Power Structure of Family
The more economically independent children and parents are of each other when children grow up, the more dominant the child becomes in the family. (B311)

Independence from parental control will tend to accompany economic independence. (H103)

#### Religion (Ancestor Cult)
The ancestor cult tends to deteriorate under conditions of economic independence. (W092)

#### Residence, Change in
A modification of residence patterns may occur when the deviant desires to establish a pattern of economic dependency with more affluent members of his kin-group. (G039)

#### Residence (Neolocal)
Economic individualism in its various manifestations (e.g., private property or individual enterprise in the economic sphere) facilitates the establishment of independent households by married couples. (M019)

As the productivity of the male has increased and as he has been able to include his own family in his work arrangement, the neolocal trend has been greatly stimulated. (V017)

#### Sibling Relations (Solidarity)
When siblings are economically independent of the extended family, the equivalence and solidarity of peers is stressed. (G028)

#### Size of Kin-Group
When the size of the kin-group is small, economic independence is fostered. (H164)

#### Stability of Extended Family
The disintegration of the extended family is directly correlated with the increasing economic independence of the individual. (O023)

#### Urban/Rural
Farm families are economically self-sufficient to a much greater extent than are urban families. (B033)

#### Urbanization
With the dispersion of the children to the city for education and non-farm occupations, the farm family declines as a self-sustaining unit. (B033)

#### Values (Familism)
When the family is a self-sufficient unit family solidarity and the values of stability, continuity, and security are stressed. (B033)

### ECONOMIC DEPENDENCE OF CHILD
#### X   Size of Family Unit
When the size of the family unit of consumption is small, economic independence tends to be fostered in the child. (H164)

### ECONOMIC DEPENDENCE OF CHILDREN
#### X   Mate Selection (Free Choice)
When children become economically independent, an increasing percentage of marriages are contracted without parental consent. (H032)

#### Stability of Extended Family
Division of the extended family is more likely if the son is financially independent. (H052)

### ECONOMIC DEPENDENCE OF FAMILY
#### X   Juvenile Delinquency
The families of juvenile delinquents are more dependent upon relief agencies or relatives for financial aid than are the families of nondelinquents. (G123)

### ECONOMIC DEPENDENCE OF LINEAGE
#### X   Genealogical Depth
Genealogical depth is dependent on the range of economic and social self-sufficiency. (M168)

### ECONOMIC DEPENDENCE OF SIBLINGS
#### X   Sibling Relations (Solidarity)
The solidarity of siblings will be directly correlated with their degree of economic interdependence. (W082)

### ECONOMIC DEPENDENCE OF WIFE
#### X   Divorce
Increased divorce rates are related to increased social provisions for the economic independence of the wife. (G156)

#### Economic Pattern (Wage Labor)
With the adoption of wage labor, the economic status of the wife tends to be lowered. (H103)

With the adoption of wage labor, the dependence of the wife on her husband increases. (O023)

#### Power Structure of Family
The control of the husband over the wife will tend to be weakened if the wife is economically independent. (F073)

### ECONOMIC DEPENDENCE OF WIVES
#### X   Conflict Between Wives
There will be a greater adjustment of conflict between wives in a polygynous family if the wives are economically interdependent. (A030)

### ECONOMIC DEPENDENCE OF WOMEN
#### X   Class
The economic independence of women is more likely to occur among the lower economic groups in urban areas. (G156)

#### Divorce
Women are more likely to seek a divorce as a solution for an unsatisfactory marriage if they are economically independent of their husbands than if they are economically dependent upon them. (L024)

### Kinship, Importance of
Where property relations are male-dominated, women place a higher emphasis on kinship ties. (R118)

### Legal Status of Women
An increase in the economic independence of women will tend to be accompanied by an increase in their legal prerogatives. (O023)

### Marital Stability
Marital instability increases with an increasing economic independence of women. (B110)

### Marriage Payment
Marriage without bride price is associated with the increasing economic independence of women. (L129)

### Rank of Women
When women are economically independent their rank will tend to be equal to that of men. (G028)

### Urbanization
The economic independence of Negro women is highest in the city, second in the rural nonfarm, and least in the rural farm. (B033)

## ECONOMIC EXCHANGE
### X   Premarital Pregnancy, Attitude Toward
The greater the disruption of the socioeconomic system of reciprocal gifts and services caused by illegitimate births, the more likely it is that premarital pregnancy will be condemned. (D071)

## ECONOMIC IMPORTANCE OF CLAN
### X   Cohesion of Clan
The strength of the clan structure tends to be directly correlated with its economic importance. (D034)

The disintegration of the clan structure is directly correlated with its loss of traditional political, judicial, and economic functions. (W082)

### Rank of Clan
The persistence of economic function is greatest in clans with a higher ranking in the hierarchy of power and prestige. (F039)

## ECONOMIC IMPORTANCE OF FAMILY
### X   Subsistence Pattern (Horticultural)
When the economic pattern is that of horticulture, the family will tend to be the major unit of economic activity. (O023)

## ECONOMIC IMPORTANCE OF PARENTS
### X   Parent-Child Relations (Affection)
The affection of children varies directly with their parents' effectiveness as good providers. (W056)

## ECONOMIC IMPORTANCE OF WOMEN
### Polygyny
Polygynous unions tend to be more highly valued as a marriage form if the role of the woman has more economic importance. (W056)

### Subsistence Pattern (Pastoral)
In societies with pastoral economies, women assume little importance in the economic structure. (P024)

## ECONOMIC LEVEL
### X   Child-Rearing Practices (Control)
Societies with a high accumulation of food resources put more stress on compliance, whereas societies with a low accumulation push children toward assertiveness. (B037)

### Child-Rearing Practices (Obedience/Dependency)
Preliterate societies with large stores of food put much pressure upon children for responsibility and obedience and little stress upon achievement and independence. (W127)

### Child-Rearing Values
Variables which rank higher in societies with a high accumulation of food resources (obedience and responsibility) are emphasized more strongly in the training of girls than of boys, whereas the variables which rank higher in societies with a low accumulation of food resources (achievement, self-reliance, and independence) are emphasized more strongly in the training of boys than of girls. (B037)

### Cohesion of Family
Consumer credit, the easy mortgage, social security, and the family doctor have made it possible for many working-class families and most middle-class families to use kinship ties more as a potential source of friendship and less as the source of (more or less mandatory) advice and of ascriptive solidarity obligations. (P083)

### Cohesion of Kin-Group
In societies where conditions of food insecurity and hunger frustrations exist, kin-groups will be more cohesive than will other social groups and will perform a greater number of significant functions. (N026)

### Cohesion of Lineage
Lineage solidarity will become increasingly undermined as pressure on economic resources increases. (W056)

### Fertility
Fertility tends to be inversely correlated with the standard of living. (T011)

### Kin Ties, Importance of
When a family is marginal economically, kin ties are important for the survival of the group. (O006)

### Kinship
A kinship structure which permits a broad definition of potential kinship will correlate with societies with marginal economies and a wide range of interareal interaction. (H225)

### Kinship, Importance of
In societies with marginal economies and simple technology, kinship bonds tend to be of primary importance in defining social relations. (B075)

### Marriage Payment
Where the economy does not permit the accumulation of property, the marriage payments will be in service rather than in goods. (W080)

### Polyandry
Polyandry is associated with low economic production, forcing brothers to work cooperatively for survival. (B205)

Polyandry is more likely to occur in societies where poverty is so great that a single man cannot support a wife and children with any degree of reliability. (P083)

### Polygyny
Polygyny tends to be encouraged when other opportunities for investment are limited. (G013)

A higher incidence of polygyny tends to accompany an increase in the economic level. (S096)

### Polygyny, Attitude Toward

Unless the food supply is precarious, the first wife may consider the presence of another wife to be of advantage. (S098)

### Population Density

Improvement in the resource base or improvement in the method of exploitation usually means an increase in population density and the appearance of larger bands or villages. (O006)

### Residence

Above a minimal level of economic adjustment, a greater degree of variance in the relationship between residence rule and economic organization occurs. (A072)

### Segmentation

The segmentation of local groups and lineages is, in part, a response to the pressure of the presence of heritable wealth. (M168)

Lineage segmentation will tend to occur when economic resources of the area are inadequate to support the population. (T020)

### Sexual Permissiveness

Sexual restrictions will tend to be minimal in societies where the food supply is inadequate. (H139)

### Slavery/Marriage of War Captives

With the development of an economic surplus sufficient to support specialized groups, war captives can be incorporated into the tribe as slaves rather than as husbands and wives. (O006)

### Social Structure

When the economic pattern is not sufficiently productive or permanent of locale to support large concentrations of population, or stable settlement, the sociopolitical organization will remain basically along kinship lines. (M033)

### Social Structure (Differentiation)

Where a stable food supply permits the establishment of good-sized permanent communities, an elaboration of the social structure occurs. (M033)

### Stability of Matrilineal Organization

The most unstable type of matrilineal system may be found in neolocal or avunculocal peasant societies with an economic surplus that can be converted either into permanent wealth or differential living standards. (C090)

## ECONOMIC LEVEL (OPPORTUNITIES)
### X   Father-Son Relations (Competition)

The open expression of competition between father and son is more likely to occur when economic and political opportunities are scarce in subsistence societies. (G116)

## ECONOMIC LEVEL (PRODUCTIVITY)
### X   Descent (Matrilineal)

Matriliny is most likely to disappear in the face of the increased importance of large-scale coordination of male labor; increased importance of property such as domesticates in the hands of males (property, that is, which is divisible and which can multiply); and the regulation of economic and political life through nonkinship ties. Most, if not all, of these features are likely to be associated with increased productivity. (A048)

## ECONOMIC PATTERN
### X   Community (Multilineage)

A multilineage structure occurs only in those communities whose economy permits large numbers of people to live together. (S001)

### Descent (Matrilineal)

Matrilineages are not found in societies where central economic organization is not based on kinship. (G156)

Abundance of land, individualism in production, and lack of investment in valuable fixed resources do not provide favorable conditions for the formation of widespan localized matrilineages. (T080)

### Descent (Unilineal)

Unilineal descent groups tend to occur most frequently in relatively homogeneous precapitalistic economies in which there is some degree of technological sophistication and value is attached to rights in endurable property. (F020)

### Exogamy (Community)

When it is economically advantageous to establish relationships in other regions or with other ethnic groups, community exogamy will tend to occur. (H076)

### Fertility Values

The desire for children is directly correlated with the advantageousness of a large family in the economic organization. (W082)

### Inheritance

The decline in the power of property, as compared with the purchasing power gained by work, reduces the importance of expectation of inheritance as a factor in relationships between married children, their siblings, and their parents. (P083)

### Kinship

Complexity of kinship structure tends to be correlated with the complexity of the economic organization. (F039)

### Kinship, Importance of

If production in a society is based on the recruitment of labor through a kinship system, production organizations tend to be permanent and diffuse in nature. (U003)

### Monogamy

Monogamy tends to occur where simple economic patterns characterize a society. (K090)

### Polygyny

Polygyny among the rich and powerful is more likely to occur in societies in which economic institutions allow high economic rewards for executive capacity (if agriculture or husbandry is extensive and private property well institutionalized). (P083)

### Residence (Matrilocal)

Seasonal wage work reinforces a matrilocal residence pattern. (P083)

### Residence (Patrilocal)

Patrilocal residence rules are more likely to occur in any system in which the status of men is greatly superior to that of women (e.g., where there is a pastoral economy, polygyny, the development of movable property which can be accumulated in quantity—herds, slaves, money). (P083)

### Size of Kin-Group
The scale of the kin-group is related to the ecological situation and the form of economic cooperation involved. (F033)

### Social Structure
The organization of a society on a suprafamilial level occurs as a direct response to a change in the economic pattern. (S111)

### Stability of Lineage
The persistence of the lineage structure tends to be directly correlated with the stability and retention of the traditional economic pattern. (G056)

## ECONOMIC PATTERN (COLLECTIVE)
### X  Child-Rearing (Collective)
Where the economic pattern is collective, the socialization of children becomes the responsibility of the group. (E087)

### Lineage Ties
With a change from a collective economy to one based on individual activity, there is a loosening of the lineal and collateral bonds within the society. (H062)

## ECONOMIC PATTERN (FEUDAL)   X  Exogamy
The development of a feudal system tends to result in the extension of exogamic regulations. (M080)

### Kin Ties (Fictive)
The economic organization of a feudal society tends to be conducive to the institutionalization of fictive kin relations. (F049)

## ECONOMIC PATTERN (HOUSEHOLD)
### X  Social Change
When the major unit of economic production and consumption is the household, receptivity to innovation is limited. (N013)

## ECONOMIC PATTERN (LABOR)
### X  Premarital Sex Relations
When the pattern of economic activity permits the women and young unmarried men to work singly in the same general area, the rate of seduction will be high. (H034)

## ECONOMIC PATTERN (LAND USE)
### X  Endogamy (Community)
Where a premium is placed on maintaining potential access to as much land as possible, the value of marrying within the local community is enhanced. (H222)

## ECONOMIC PATTERN (LOCAL DOMESTIC INDUSTRY)   X  Inheritance
A system of equal division of inheritance favors the development of local industry. (H066)

## ECONOMIC PATTERN (MARKET)
### X  Descent (Matrilineal)
When a matrilineal system enters a market economy, matriliny disappears. (A048)

### Kinship, Importance of
The part played by kinship in a mechanism for ordering social life diminishes as the economic relations which are critically important for maintaining the kinship system are replaced by the impersonal relations of the market. (W056)

## ECONOMIC PATTERN (MERCANTILE)
### X  Adultery
Marital relations among traveling merchants are loose; the men are thought to have wives along their routes and the women are thought to be unfaithful. (T072)

### Size of Family Unit
Merchant communities are likely to have larger family units than others. (T072)

### Stability of Extended Family
Under the impact of change from a feudal to a mercantile economic system, the patrilocal extended family is disintegrating as a permanent residential unit. (G028)

## ECONOMIC PATTERN (MIGRANT LABOR)
### X  Adultery
The introduction of patterns of migratory labor results in an increase in extramarital relations among women. (S121)

The adoption of patterns of migratory labor will tend to result in an increase in extramarital relations. (S134)

### Authority Structure of Family
The family authority structure will tend to be weakened under conditions of migrant labor. (L093)

In situations of migratory labor, the wife enjoys greater independence and is less likely to submit to her husband's authority. (S171)

### Cohesion of Family
The cohesion of the family is weakened by the adoption of patterns of migrant labor. (S121)

### Community
If the lineage forms the basis of the village structure, the effects of migratory labor will be less disruptive for the village. (W132)

### Descent (Patrilineal/Matrilineal)
Patrilineal peoples adjust themselves more readily than do matrilineal peoples to the absence of a large number of men created by a situation of migratory labor. (W132)

### Desertion
Desertion is more likely to occur in situations of labor migration where there is a "sexually differentiated enculturative experience." (S266)

### Disorganization of Family
Family structure tends to deteriorate with the adoption of patterns of migrant labor. (K066)

### Fertility
A decrease in the birth rate will tend to accompany the establishment of patterns of migratory labor. (H135)

### Homosexuality
Homosexuality tends to arise when the economic pattern is that of migratory labor. (T071)

### Mate Selection (Free Choice)
Under conditions of labor migration, women have far greater power and independence in marriage negotiations. (K065)

### Prostitution
The separation of husbands from their wives and families, as migrants to urban areas, tends to be associated with a high incidence of prostitution in the urban areas. (I004)

# ECONOMIC PATTERN (MONEY)
### X   Authority Structure of Family
The authority of the father in the peasant family decreases as the family becomes less of a production unit and more of an income-earning unit. (B031)

With the development of a money economy in matrilineal societies, the father tends to supersede the mother's brother in legal and moral importance. (G056)

### Corporate Kin-Group
The collapse of the unilineal descent group as a corporate landholding group accompanies an adjustment to a money economy. (G056)

### Corporate Kin Ties
Cash economy tends to destroy corporate kinship bonds with villages. (T080)

### Economic Cooperation
The entrance into a money economy has the effect of breaking down extended family patterns of pooling goods and services. (S041)

### Economic Dependence
Where cash crops have been introduced, householders depend less on a wider circle of their kinfolk. (H222)

### Economic Role of Extended Family
The development of a money economy has resulted in the deterioration of the basic economic function and division of labor of the extended family. (R012)

### Inheritance (Bilateral)
With the institution of a money economy in a matrilineal society, inheritance patterns tend to shift from a matrilineal to a bilateral orientation. (G056)

### Kin Ties
The adoption of a cash economy will tend to narrow the range of kinship relationship to a smaller number of close bilateral kin. (G056)

### Nuclear Family, Importance of
With the adoption of a money economy, the conjugal relationship in matrilineal tribes has been strengthened and the conjugal or parental family has emerged as the key group. (G056)

### Polygyny
Polygyny tends to be abandoned with the institution of a money economy and wage labor. (W056)

### Power Structure of Family
With the introduction of a money economy and the subsequent financial independence of sons, the position of the father is weakened by the removal of the special economic control. (R005)

### Residence (Matrilocal)
With the adoption of a cash economy there is a strong tendency away from matrilocality. (H032)

### Stability of Lineage
The extent of the disintegration of the traditional lineage system depends on the degree of absorption of the inhabitants into the modern economy of cash crops, cash wages, and urban occupations. (G056)

# ECONOMIC PATTERN (PRIVATE PROPERTY)
### X   Monogamy
Where the economic pattern is one in which property is held privately, the mode of marriage tends to be monogamy. (E087)

# ECONOMIC PATTERN (TRADE)
### X   Kinship, Importance of
The deterioration of the importance of kin ties as a framework for social relations tends to occur with the extension of economic ties through trade. (W075)

### Religion (Kin-Based)
The abandonment of religious elements that relate directly to kinship or kin units is directly correlated with an extension and centralization of trade. (W075)

# ECONOMIC PATTERN (WAGE LABOR)
### X   Economic Dependence of Wife
With the adoption of wage labor, the economic status of the wife tends to be lowered. (H103)

With the adoption of wage labor, the dependence of the wife on her husband increases. (O023)

### Nuclear Family
The system of wage labor and the existence of a small nuclear family are associated. (G112)

### Remarriage
With the introduction of a wage economy, a man is no longer compelled to remarry after the death of his wife, since the wife's services are no longer indispensible. (W082)

### Social Control
When men become more dependent on income from labor abroad and less on lineage land, they free themselves more from lineage control. (F088)

### Stability of Extended Family
Wage labor and opportunity for work outside the village may in themselves cause the breakdown of the extended family. (R012)

# ECONOMIC RANK          X   Affinal Relations
As the economic standing of their in-laws increases, so does the cordiality of the relations of interracial couples with their in-laws. (K019)

### Cohesion of Extended Family
The cohesiveness of the extended family will be directly correlated with its wealth. (G101)

### Cohesion of Family
Among poor people, sons are more likely to separate from their families and seek a new fortune; poor people are less concerned with ties of relationship. (B223)

When kinsmen have about the same amount of wealth, members of a given family are forced to be self-reliant since there are no wealthy individuals on whom they can be dependent. (H021)

### Conflict Between Wives
A first wife is more likely to accept a second wife if the economic status of the original couple is high. (S158)

### Descent (Patrilineal)
The depth of the patrilineal structure tends to be greater when the family has permanent agricultural land. (G028)

### Divorce
There is a rough inverse correlation between economic status and rate of divorce. (G002)

### Divorce Discussions
There is a positive relationship between the amount of property and discussions of property as a part of the

divorce arrangements. This holds only when the husband has a high-school education or more. (G157)

### Extended Family
The extended family pattern tends to be more characteristic of groups with higher economic status. (L066)

### Fertility
There is a negative correlation between fertility and economic level of the family. (I007)

There is a positive correlation between fertility and economic level of the family. (I007)

Fertility rates vary inversely with level of living in the rural population, both farm and nonfarm, both white and nonwhite. (T011)

### Isolation of Nuclear Family
The greater the opportunity for consumption of wealth on the part of the individual family, the greater is its tendency to become independent of the larger kin unit. (F029)

### Joint Family
Joint families are more likely to occur in the upper economic rank than in the lower economic rank (Bengal). (M012)

### Kin Roles
When alternate kin roles present themselves, the selection will tend to be determined by the economic rank of the kinsmen. (F037)

### Kin Ties
A vertical extension of kinship ties tends to be directly correlated with the economic status of the lineage. (T039)

### Marital Stability
The stability of the marriage is directly correlated with the economic status of the husband and wife. (M086)

### Marriage Chances
Since the married state requires a particular minimum standard of living, the poorer the male is, the less likely is he to marry. (B245)

### Marriage Payment
The number of relatives involved in an exchange of gifts at marriage will be directly correlated with the status of the families of the bride and groom. (H134)

### Marriage Payment (Groom Service)
If a man is of lower economic status, he is more likely to substitute groom service for bride price. (B107)

### Mate Selection (Free Choice)
The marriages of the more wealthy families tend to be arranged by the parental groups. (E015)

### Nuclear Family
The nuclear family pattern tends to be associated with a lower socioeconomic status. (L066)

### Occupational Aspirations of Son
▸ Economic responsibility forcing the oldest son of lower-class families into an early entrance into the labor market, effectively indoctrinating him into manual-type jobs, is a factor contributing to low occupational aspirations of oldest sons of lower-class families. (E102)

### Peer Relations
Adolescents at the middle economic level whose mothers work are more likely to be rejected by their peers than are those at low or high economic levels. (F108)

### Polygyny
Where economic power is less effectively secured by political power, polygyny will make the consolidation of large family estates more difficult because of fragmentation caused by the large numbers of heirs. (P083)

Polygyny is generally confined to men of high economic status. (T041)

The number of wives a man acquires in a polygynous union is directly correlated with his wealth. (W081)

### Power Structure of Family
Paternal power increases with an increase in the income level of the family. (K030)

### Preferential Marriage (Exchange)
Exchange marriage is more likely to occur between members of families which are of low economic status. (H105)

### Rank of Lineage
The rank of a lineage will be directly correlated with its economic status. (S158)

### Residence
When husband's wife's family is poor, residence is more likely to be matrilocal; if both are wealthy, it is likely to be bilocal. (G013)

Patterns of matrilocal residence will be violated if the husband's lineage has greater holdings in land. (G065)

Violation of normal residence prescriptions is more likely when it may improve economic status. (L110)

### Residence (Uxorilocal)
Uxorilocal residence tends to occur when the husband is of low economic status. (T039)

### Size of Family
The size of the joint family will depend upon the size of the family estate. (M021)

### Stability of Extended Family
The larger the amount of land or other wealth to support it, the greater the stability of the extended family household. (G156)

When the father of an extended family is landless or extremely poor, fission of the extended family is more likely to occur. (R012)

### Stability of Kin-Group
The stability of the kin-group is directly correlated with its economic status. (H165)

## ECONOMIC RANK/EDUCATION    X    Fertility
The direct association of number of births per married woman with size of farm operated by the husband is independent of the number of years of schooling completed by the wife. (H010)

## ECONOMIC RANK (HOUSING STANDARDS)
## X    Illegitimacy
Illegitimacy is inversely related to the standards of housing. (S003)

## ECONOMIC RANK OF CLAN    X    Rank of Clan
The status of a clan will be directly correlated with its economic position. (T065)

## ECONOMIC RANK OF FAMILY    X    Incest Taboo
The reaction to incest is more severe if the individuals involved belong to wealthy families. (H052)

# ECONOMIC RANK OF FATHER
### X   Incest (Father-Daughter)
Where father-daughter incest occurs, the father is likely to come from a background characterized by poverty and inadequate housing. (K091)

### Power Structure of Family
In matrilineal societies the degree of control of the father over his sons is directly correlated with his wealth. (W132)

# ECONOMIC RANK OF HUSBAND          X   Fertility
Fertility of Negro manual laborers is inversely related to the economic position of the husband. (G020)

### Marriage Payment (Groom Service)
The duration of groom service is likely to be shortened if the prospective bridegroom is rich and the prospective bride comes from a poor family. (B223)

# ECONOMIC RANK OF HUSBAND-WIFE
### X   Marital Stability
Marital stability is more likely to characterize marriages in which both the family of the husband and wife are of high economic status. (B108)

# ECONOMIC RANK OF KIN-GROUP
### X   Size of Kin-Group
The size of the kin-group will be directly correlated with its economic status. (M131)

# ECONOMIC RANK OF LINEAGE
### X   Political Rank of Lineage
The political importance of a lineage tends to be directly correlated with its economic status. (L070)

# ECONOMIC RANK OF MEN AND WOMEN
### X   Marital Stability
Changes in the relative economic positions of men and women contribute to the instability of relations between husbands and wives. (O029)

# ECONOMIC RANK OF PARENTAL GROUP
### X   Residence (Patrilocal/Matrilocal)
Residential affiliation will tend to be with the parental group which has the largest landholding. (G029)

# ECONOMIC RANK OF PARENTS
### X   Marriage Payment (Bride Service)
Bride service as a substitute for bride payment is most commonly contracted by men whose parents are dead, separated, or unwilling to shoulder the financial burden of the bride price. (S090)

### Residence (Bilocal)
Residential affiliation under patterns of bilocal residence tend to be based upon the relative economic status of the parents of the husband and wife. (B111)

# ECONOMIC RANK OF WIFE
### X   Residence (Matrilocal)
In a patrilocal society, matrilocal residence is more likely to occur if the family of the wife is wealthy. (L074)

# ECONOMIC RELATIONS     X   Sexual Aggression
When the assertion of individual aggression is rigidly tabooed in the sexual sphere, the hostilities generated by sexual jealousy will find their outlets in the economic relations of the group. (M048)

# ECONOMIC RIGHTS OF WOMEN
### X   Descent (Bilateral)
Bilateral organizations tend to occur in societies which have rankings and considerable material wealth if the women are permitted equal access to strategic resources. (B060)

# ECONOMIC ROLE          X   Authority
The authority of a kinsman will be directly correlated with his control of the kin-group's economic resources. (W082)

### Child-Rearing Practices
The emphasis in child training will be toward the kinds of behavior especially useful for the adult economy. (B037)

### Conflict in Family
Economic conflicts, when they do arise in families, seem to be related to differences in attitudes of family members toward economic goals and differences in the members' conceptions of their economic roles. (B033)

### Kin Terminology (Merging)
The terminological merging of son and daughter under a single term for child will be favored by conditions of economic equality in their obligation. (F046)

### Power Structure of Family
When the economic position of the father is insecure (e.g., in times of unemployment), he loses the legitimation of his authority and tends to become increasingly arbitrary. (B207)

### Role Conflict in Family
Where the economic activities of the individual are not important, conflicting claims within the family for his services will be minimal. (S037)

# ECONOMIC ROLE OF CHILD
### X   Parent-Child Relations (Preference)
Each parent will tend to prefer among his or her children those who may later be expected to relieve his or her economic burden. (A030)

### Sex Preference
Parents will tend to prefer children of the sex which has the economically more productive role. (L064)

# ECONOMIC ROLE OF CHILDREN
### X   Paternal Role, Attitude Toward
Male attitudes are more favorable toward fatherhood when the economic utility of children in the society is high. (D071)

# ECONOMIC ROLE OF EXTENDED FAMILY
### X   Economic Pattern (Money)
The development of a money economy has resulted in the deterioration of the basic economic function and division of labor in the extended family. (R012)

# ECONOMIC ROLE OF FAMILY     X   Birth Rate
The lower the economic usefulness of the large family, the lower the fertility. (W022)

### Kin Ties (Fictive)
The deterioration of patterns of fictive kinship are most extreme in areas where the family no longer forms the primary unit of production. (M080)

### Power Structure of Family
The influence of the mother in the family increases as the family becomes less of a production unit and more of an income-earning unit. (B031)

## ECONOMIC ROLE OF HUSBAND
### X   Employment of Wife, Attitude Toward
When the dominance of the husband in large part depends upon the economic importance of his role, he will tend to inhibit the development of his wife's economic potential. (L064)

### Independence of Nuclear Family
The economic status of the husband will be more important if the nuclear family is economically independent. (H165)

### Marital Adjustment
The husband's economic role (e.g., a combination of length of time in position, regularity of employment, amount of income, and amount of savings) is not related to his marital happiness rating. (G157)

## ECONOMIC ROLE OF HUSBAND-WIFE
### X   Marital Stability
Marital stability is directly correlated with the stability of the economic role of the husband and wife. (W082)

### Role Behavior in Family
Where both husband and wife work and are financially independent, there is much less familism and much more individualism in the members of the family. (B033)

## ECONOMIC ROLE OF JOINT FAMILY
### X   Acculturation
The joint family under pressures of acculturation is more likely to lose its economic than its social functions. (M081)

## ECONOMIC ROLE OF KIN
### X   Identification with Extended Kin
The extension of family sentiment to members of the wider kinship group depends upon the role of the latter in fulfilling the original family functions of distributing and consuming food. (R087)

## ECONOMIC ROLE OF KIN-GROUP
### X   Residence
Where dispersed homesteads and localized lineages occur, there is a tendency for work groups to be made up of consanguineal relatives; where the pattern is that of the concentrated village, lineages are of less importance and mutual assistance groups are as often composed of friends, neighbors, or affinal relatives as of consanguineal kin. (A072)

### Stratification
There is a corresponding relation between the decline of economic function of the kin-group and the rise of stratification. (F039)

## ECONOMIC ROLE OF MEN        X   Descent
Men are less important in the agricultural pursuits and more important in fishing activity in patrilocal than in matrilocal societies. (A072)

### Descent/Residence (Patrilineal/Patrilocal)
Patrilineal and patrilocal tendencies are strengthened with an increase in the importance of the man's economic role. (L063)

### Residence (Patrilocal)
Patrilocal residence is promoted by any modification in the basic economy whereby masculine activity in the sex division of labor comes to yield the principle means of a subsistence. (M019)

### Residence (Virilocal)
When men play the major role in agricultural activities, the residence patterns tend to be virilocal. (G055)

## ECONOMIC ROLE OF MEN/WOMEN
### X   Descent
The development of a matrilineal or patrilineal descent system will be affected by the emphasis on male or female production and control of resources. (F033)

### Sex Preference
The preferred sex of the child will be the one that is viewed as more important economically. (W157)

### Sex Ratio
The sex ratio in marginal societies will reflect any differential economic value of the sex roles. (G149)

### Stability of Family
Instability of the family is likely to occur when either the male or the female plays a disproportionate role in the economy. (W154)

## ECONOMIC ROLE OF MENTAL PATIENT
### X   Social Adjustment (After Hospitalization)
Formerly hospitalized mental patients who live with parents and are neither steadily employed nor active socially are not the only potential economic heads of the household, while those who are steadily employed and do have social activities are usually the only potential sources of economic support in the family. (F098)

## ECONOMIC ROLE OF NUCLEAR FAMILY
### X   Role Definition in Family
With the diminishing importance of the nuclear household as a producing unit, it becomes more important emotionally. (C090)

## ECONOMIC ROLE OF WIFE
### X   Cohesion of Family
The cohesion of the family will tend to be weakened if a wife's services are no longer of economic importance. (W082)

### Husband-Wife Relations (Closeness)
The relationship between husband and wife will be stronger if the wife is of economic importance. (O023)

### Marital Status
The percentage of unmarried adults will tend to be higher if the role of wife is not of economic importance. (H164)

### Power Structure of Family
When women control strategic resources they will tend to have, within the nuclear family, more influence than will their husbands. (H032)

When the wife is of economic importance, the relationship between husband and wife will tend to be more equal. (O023)

## ECONOMIC ROLE OF WOMEN        X   Adultery
There will be an increase in the incidence of extramarital relations with the decreasing economic importance of the woman's role. (B166)

### Descent (Matrilineal)
Matrilineal descent groups arise when women's work groups control the resource bases. (A048)

When the control of strategic resources is in the hands of the women, the stability of the matrilineal descent system is reinforced. (L039)

### Descent/Residence

Matrilocal residence and matrilineal descent tend to be practiced when agriculture is in the hands of women. (B033)

### Headhunting

Headhunting is likely to develop in matrilineal societies in which women have the major economic role. (W154)

### Infanticide

Female infanticide will be less frequent if the economic contribution of females is thought to be great. (W156)

### Menstrual Taboo

There is no correlation between extensiveness of menstrual taboos and the importance of the woman's contribution to the subsistence of the economy. (S079)

### Polyandry

Conditions in which women play a role of equal importance in the economy and have equal rights to property are conducive to polyandry. (S068)

### Polygyny

Polygyny is more likely to occur where the role of the woman is of greater economic importance. (S153)

### Property

When women have the exclusive agricultural role, property rights to land tend to be matrilineal. (B133)

### Residence (Matrilocal)

Matrilocal residence tends to be associated with the woman's control of production and the ownership of land. (M019)

When economic pressures increase the importance of maintaining the integrity and continuity of the female household work crew, matrilocal residence will tend to occur. (M020)

Among sedentary groups where property is significant and women are the prime cultivators, matrilocal residence is favored. (O006)

### Secret Societies

Men's secret societies are more likely to occur in matrilineal societies in response to the woman's position of economic dominance. (W154)

### Sexual Interest of Women

With a decrease in the importance of the economic duties of women, they will tend to become increasingly preoccupied with sex. (B171)

### Social Isolation of Women

The social isolation of women tends to be directly correlated with the lack of importance of their economic role. (G072)

## ECONOMIC SECURITY    X  Descent (Unilineal)

The unilinear structure tends to be elaborated under conditions of economic security. (F010)

### Fertility

Economic security is positively correlated with increase in fertility. (W022)

### Marital Adjustment

There is a greater degree of marital adjustment among couples with security as indicated by savings, lack of indebtedness, and insurance than among couples without this security. (W004)

### Mother-Child Relations

Financial stress is negatively associated with positive mother-child interaction during preadolescence. (S273)

### Preferential Marriage (Levirate)

Claims to the widow of a deceased brother will not necessarily be activated if the woman has a grown son old enough to support her. (S096)

## ECONOMIC STABILITY    X  Cohesion of Lineage

The stability of the kin-structured agricultural system is reflected in the importance of lineage unity in the value system. (W056)

## ECONOMIC STRUCTURE OF FAMILY
### X  Size of Household

The larger the household, the greater the differentiation of economic roles. (G156)

## ECONOMIC STRUCTURE OF SOCIETY
### Geographical Mobility

Approval of geographical mobility of family members is associated with a society whose economy is based on talent rather than on birthright. (G156)

## ECONOMIC SUCCESS
### X  Husband-Wife Relations (Communication)

When the husband is economically successful he shares more of his work experience with his wife as compared with a relative estrangement if he is not economically successful. (K089)

## ECONOMIC VALUE OF CHILDREN    X  Fertility

An emphasis on fertility is directly correlated with the economic value of children. (H164)

## ECONOMY                     X  Residence

Neolocal rules of residence are associated with systems that tend to isolate or emphasize the individual or the nuclear family: monogamy, the growth of territorial states, the development of private property, individual enterprise in the economic sphere, personal freedom in choice of marital partners, and individual migration. (P083)

## EDUCATION        X  Affinal Relations (Conflict)

When there is a marked degree of difference in the education of the mother-in-law and the daughter-in-law, serious conflicts are likely to occur. (H032)

### Age at Marriage

Among American men and women the median age at first marriage is higher for both the well educated and for those with little education than it is for those with average amounts of education. (H203)

There is a correlation between interrupted schooling and early female marriage. (P083)

### Birth Control

There is a direct correlation between approval of birth control and educational level. (B033)

### Child-Rearing Attitudes (Authoritarianism)

The more education the mother has, the less likely she is to be authoritarian and controlling in her maternal attitudes. (Z011)

### Child-Rearing Practices (Isolation)

Better-educated parents are more likely to use physical isolation of the child as a means of punishment than are rural or urban working-class parents.

### Child-Rearing Practices (Leadership)

The higher the parents' educational level, the more marked are the differences between boys and girls regarding parental nurturance, companionship, and praise as they affect leadership abilities in the child (i.e., enhancing the relationship for boys and reducing it for girls). (B250)

### Child-Rearing Practices (Nurturance)

There is no relationship between parental educational level and degree of nurturance shown in child rearing. (B250)

### Child-Rearing Practices (Punishment)

The lower the educational level of the parents, the more punitive the parents. (B250)

There is no relationship between parental education and degree of affective reward and/or affective punishment in child rearing. (B250)

### Child-Rearing Problems

There is no relationship between individual educational level and the admission of problems in child rearing. (G126)

### Child-Rearing Problems (Obedience)

The higher the educational level, the more likely are parents to be concerned with obedience problems. (G126)

### Cohesion of Family

The more integrated the family, the less the amount of formal education it is likely to have. (S217)

The more integrated the family, the greater the amount of formal education. (S217)

### Conflict in Family

Differences in education are an important source of conflict between generations of a family as well as between members of a single generation. (H032)

### Dependency

The higher the education of the wife, the less dependent she is on her children.

### Divorce

Divorce declines with higher educational level.

There is a curvilinear relationship between education and divorce: divorce rates being low for persons of the lowest and the highest educational levels, but higher for those who have completed grammar school and high school.

Unhappily married couples with a high-school or college education are more likely to be divorced than are those with a grammar-school education.

The higher the educational level, the lower the divorce rates. (G156)

Proneness to divorce decreases slightly with higher education for whites and increases for Negroes. (G157)

The higher the educational level of the couple, the greater the likelihood that the suggestion to divorce will be mutual. (G157)

### Duration of Marriage

Grammar-school educated persons divorce earlier than do persons with a college education. (G157)

### Employment of Mother, Attitude Toward

The likelihood of favorable attitudes toward working mothers increases with educational level. (S257)

### Employment of Wife

Women with more education are more in favor of working after marriage than are women with less education. (S257)

### Husband-Wife Relations (Communication)

The higher the educational level (blue collar marriages), the more likely the person is to feel the need for verbal communication in marriage. (K089)

The higher the educational level, the more communication there is likely to be in a marriage. (K089)

The higher the educational background of a husband, the less discontent his wife is likely to have over communication. (K089)

### Husband-Wife Relations (Complaints)

The higher the educational level, the more likely are persons to refer to "relationship difficulties" (i.e., consideration, bossing, intimacy, etc.) as the source of marital problems than to such other difficulties as financial and material (more so for women than for men). (G126)

### Husband-Wife Relations (Intimacy)

The higher the educational level, the more likely the person is to consider all communications between spouses as private and not subject to discussion, even with other relatives. (K089)

### Husband-Wife Relations (Shared Activities)

The higher the educational level, the more time spouses are likely to spend together in recreational activities. (K089)

The higher the educational level the more communication there is likely to be in marriage. (K089)

### Illegitimacy

Unwed pregnant women have significantly more education than (married) multigravida. (C099)

Amount of education is inversely related to illegitimacy. (S003)

### Marital Adjustment

The higher the educational level, the greater the individual's chance for marital success. (B244)

College-educated husbands who feel that college attendance aids marital adjustment have a higher marital adjustment score than do husbands who feel that it disturbs marital adjustment. (C003)

The higher the educational level, the more likely are persons to report feelings of inadequacies and marital problems. (G126)

When age is controlled, the relationship between high educational level and greater marital problems reported does not exist. (G126)

A positive relationship exists between the education level of husband and wife and marital happiness. (G157)

Wives, but not husbands, are less happy if they have more education than their spouses. (G157)

Men tend to be happier if they are more educated than their wives; while wives are slightly less happy if they have equal education. (G157)

The higher the educational backgrounds of blue collar workers, the more involved they are emotionally in their marriages. (K089)

### Marital Status (Male)
Among American men 35 to 64 years old, those with either low or high educational levels are more likely to be married or to have been married than are those with average levels of education. (H203)

### Marriage, Attitude Toward
The higher the educational level, the more likely a person will consider "psychic congeniality" and similar traits as important in marital adjustment. (K089)

### Marriage Chances
Females with a lower educational level are more likely to marry than are females with a higher educational level. (H001)

### Mate Selection
The educational level of the groom varies directly with the educational level of the bride when religion is controlled for. (H014)

### Mother-Child Relations (Possessiveness)
Maternal possessiveness is negatively correlated with education of the mother. (S187)

### Ordinal Position
Firstborn children in two-child families are more likely than their siblings to attend college, regardless of the sex of the second-born child. (A073)

### Parent-Child Relations (Affection)
There is no relationship between parental education and degree of affection shown to the children. (B250)

### Parent-Child Relations (Authority)
Both mother and father lose influence as the children undertake school education. (H032)

### Parent-Child Relations (Concern)
The higher the educational level of the parents, the more concern they are likely to feel about their relationships with their children. (K089)

### Parent-Child Relations (Conflict)
There is no relationship between parental education and the degree of parent-child conflict. (B249)

### Parent-Child Relations (Consensus)
The more formal education required by specialization, the greater the conflict in values between parents and youth. (D058)

### Parent-Child Relations (Indulgence)
The lower the parents' educational level, the more indulgent they are of their children. (B250)

### Parent-Child Relations (Interaction)
The lower the educational level of the parents, the less time they spend with their children. (B250)

### Parent-Child Relations (Overprotectiveness)
The lower the parents' educational level, the more overprotective they are of their children. (B250)

### Parent-Child Relations (Rebellion)
The more highly educated the parents, the more likely are their children to express opposition to parental authority. (B250)

### Parent-Child Relations (Rejection)
The lower the educational level of the parents, the more rejecting they are of their children. (B250)

### Parental-Role Adjustment
The higher the educational level, the more likely are persons to feel inadequate concerning their lack of tolerance for the children's behavior; women are more likely to express this inadequacy than are men. (G126)

The higher the educational level, the more likely are persons to feel inadequate in the affective child-parent relationship; men are more likely to express these affective difficulties than are women. (G126)

### Power Structure of Family
The greater the education of the spouse, the larger his share in marital decision making will be.

### Pregnancy, Planned/Unplanned
There is no correlation between college attendance and the planning of pregnancy. This hypothesis is also denied. (P080)

### Premarital Sex Relations
The higher the educational level, the less likely is premarital sexual intercourse. (E092)

The lower the education, the earlier a male is likely to begin acquiring sexual experience. (K160)

The lower the education of males, the more frequently they are likely to have premarital sexual relations. (K160)

### Remarriage
Remarriage is more likely to take place among highly educated men than among poorly educated men. (O001)

### Sex-Role Definition
The lower the educational level, the more traditional are couples' ideas about sex concerns and about the rights of men to silence and to protection from women's affairs. (K089)

The higher the educational level, the less clear is the role differentiation of spouses in marriage. (K089)

### Sexual Activity
Among males there is an inverse relationship between educational level and sexual activity. (C023)

### Sexual Behavior
Men with a grade-school education are more likely to have had premarital sexual experiences, to have extramarital relations after marriage, and around the age of 40 to limit their sexual relations to their spouses; men with a college education are more likely to be virginal when married, to refrain from extramarital contacts in the early years of marriage, and to have extramarital relations around the age of 35–40. (B244)

### Sexual Disability of Husband (Divorce)
Among men who have been physically disabled, the proportion of those who remain married exceeds those who are divorced or separated at all educational levels. (N060)

### Sibling Structure (Sex)
Second-born children are more likely to attend college if the first born child is male. (A073)

### Social Network
The higher the level of education of the family, the more likely it is that it has a relatively dispersed set of social contacts. (B267)

The higher the education of a couple, the less likely it is that social contacts with friends and neighbors will decrease as the marriage progresses. (K089)

### Sterilization
There is an inverse relationship between the educational level and frequency of operations for sterilization. (F101)

### Toilet Training
The more highly educated the parents, the more likely are they to have toilet-training problems with their children.

### Value Conflict (Family/Economic)
Low educational level is likely to accompany greater conflict between family values and values of economic success, while higher educational level is more apt to be found in conjunction with less conflict between family values and values of economic success. (J033)

### Values
The lower the educational background, the more likely a person is to believe patriarchy is the proper power structure for the family. (K089)

### Values (Extended/Nuclear Family)
Those highly educated are more apt to prefer the nuclear family, while those less highly educated prefer the extended family. (J033)

## EDUCATION, ATTITUDE TOWARD
### X Employment of Women
There is no relationship between the daughter's decision to spend a good portion of her life in paid employment and the parents' attitudes about the purpose of college or the importance of education for their daughter. (S231)

## EDUCATION/CLASS
### X Child-Rearing Practices (Aggression)
Mother's education is more strongly associated with mother's permissiveness toward aggression than is socioeconomic status of the family (U.S.). (S191)

## EDUCATION DIFFERENCE BETWEEN HUSBAND-WIFE
### X Class
A great difference in formal education between husband and wife is less likely to occur between spouses in the lower than in the middle or upper classes, because husbands in the latter cases are likely to have received considerable formal education, but in the lower stratas neither husbands nor wives have had much education. (P083)

### X Cohesion of Family
The education and maturity differential that existed between the wife and her husband in the classical bourgeois marriage reduces the solidarity and nurturance of the family. (P083)

### Divorce
Differences between husband and wife in the number of years of formal education are unrelated to whether or not a couple will divorce. (B244)

### Husband-Wife Relations (Power)
The husband is more likely than not to be more dominant in the marriage where the husband has at least three years more education than the wife or the wife has one or two years more education than the husband. (L014)

The relationship between husband and wife is more likely than not to be egalitarian where the husband and wife have an equal number of years of education. (L014)

### Marital Adjustment
Wives with husbands who have superior education make higher happiness scores than wives who are superior to their husbands in education. (C023)

## EDUCATION/EMPLOYMENT OF MOTHER
### X Child-Rearing Practices
### X Employment of Mother/Education
Education of the mother is more highly correlated with differences in child-rearing practices than whether or not the mother is employed. (Y051)

In *nonworking* groups college mothers are significantly more often rated high in independence training, in sensitivity, in consistency between principles and practice, and in clarity in limit setting, thus having higher mean scores on "adequacy of mothering."

However, *working* groups differ only on ratings of sensitivity to child's needs (high-school lower) and father's being stricter parent (college lower). (Y051)

## EDUCATION (FAMILY/NON-FAMILY)
### X Parent-Child Relations (Conflict)
The more education is in the hands of extrafamilial authorities, the greater is the parent-youth conflict. (D058)

## EDUCATION/OCCUPATION OF FATHER
### X Educational Aspiration
High educational ambition in the child is associated with the father's educational level being high relative to his occupation. (T095)

## EDUCATION/OCCUPATION OF PARENTS
### X Educational Aspiration
Parental educational-cultural attainment is a more significant factor than is the father's occupation in determining the educational aspirations of adolescent sons. (E102)

## EDUCATION OF CHILD
### X Educational Aspiration
Parents of school dropouts are more likely to lack understanding and concern with the development of their children's interests in school than are parents of in-school students. (E102)

### Husband-Wife Relations (Conflict)
Families where the child has graduated from high school are less likely to have husband-wife conflicts than are families that have not produced high-school graduates. (Z008)

### Illegitimacy
Illegitimate children are less likely to receive adequate education. (G156)

### Parent-Child Relations (Authority)
Among children from the dominant social group, the lower their educational level, the less likely it is that they will be acceptant of parental authority. Among children from subordinate groups, the greater the extent of their

education, the more likely they are to reject parental authority. (K121)

### Power Structure of Family
Maternal authority is a more frequent factor in the education of the children in the family than is paternal authority. (K030)

### Religion/Size of Family
As family size increases, Catholic parents are more likely than are Protestant parents to insist on college education for their children. (E102)

## EDUCATION OF DIVORCÉE          X    Dating
The higher the educational level, the greater the frequency of dating for the divorcée. (G157)

### Friendship
The higher the educational level of the divorcée, the more likely is she to maintain marriage friends during the separation and divorce period. (G157)

The higher the educational level of the divorcée, the more likely is she to have a circle of friends. (G157)

### Remarriage
College-educated divorcées move into a new marriage more slowly than do those divorcées with a high-school or grammar-school education. (G157)

### Size of Family
Among divorcées, the lower the education level, the larger the family size. (G157)

## EDUCATION OF FATHER
### X    Child-Rearing Practices (Permissiveness)
Fathers having a high-school education or less are more likely to be permissive toward their older children than are fathers having a year or so of college. (E100)

### Illegitimacy (Place of Delivery)
Illegitimate babies, born in private practice, have fathers with higher educational attainments than do babies born in institutions. (V002)

### Incest (Father-Daughter)
Where father-daughter incest occurs, the father is likely to have had little education. (K091)

### I.Q.
A positive correlation exists between the child's I.Q. and the father's educational level. (H173)

### I.Q. of Natural/Adopted Child
The correlation between the I.Q. of the child and his father's educational level is about the same, whether or not his own father or his foster father rears him. (H173)

### Occupational Aspirations of Son
Boys with fathers who have less than a high-school education are more likely to aspire to occupations that are higher than to occupations that are lower than those of their fathers. (E102)

Occupational aspirations of the son are positively related to the father's educational level, regardless of the father's occupation (unskilled labor to professional-managerial work). (E102)

### Occupational Aspirations of Son/Occupational Rank of Father
The strength of the positive relationship between the father's educational level and the son's occupational aspirations weakens as the level of the father's occupa-

tion decreases (professional-managerial to unskilled labor). (E102)

### Scholastic Achievement of Child
College students whose fathers did not obtain a college degree are more likely to drop out of college than are students whose fathers did obtain a degree. (A067)

### Social Mobility Aspirations of Child
The higher the level of education of the father, the higher the level of mobility aspiration in the child. (T095)

## EDUCATION OF FATHER/MOTHER
### X    Scholastic Motivation
The father's educational level has a stronger effect on the adolescent's academic motivation than the mother's educational attainment. (E102)

## EDUCATION OF HUSBAND    X    Affinal Relations
The higher the education of the husband, the better are his relations with his in-laws. (K089)

### Divorce Agreements
Husbands with some college education are slightly more likely than are those with no college education to keep all or some of their divorce agreements. (G157)

### Divorce Discussions
The higher the husband's educational level, the higher the frequency with which the couple will talk over divorce arrangements. (G157)

When the couple's property is of little or no value, there is no relationship between the husband's education and the frequency with which the couple talked about divorce arrangements; with increasing amounts of property, a positive relationship exists between the husband's education and the frequency of talks. (G157)

### Divorce Process
The husband's educational level is unrelated to the length of time taken between a serious consideration of divorce and the filing of the suit. (G157)

### Father-Son Relations
The higher the educational level of a man, the more likely it is that his relations with his father are good. (K089)

### Fertility (Real/Ideal)
If the husband's educational level is eight years or less, the wife tends to consider as ideal fewer children than she actually intends to have; this relationship is reversed at higher educational levels. (Y046)

### Marriage Payment
The desirability of an education in the husband produces a pattern of marriage payments by the bride's family. (M081)

### Mate Selection (Residence)
There is *no* relationship between educational level of prospective husbands and their choice of a mate living near their homes. (C002)

### Power Structure of Family
The amount of paternal power is greater among husbands with medium educational levels than among husbands with either low or high educational levels. (K030)

The higher the educational level of the husband, the less power he exerts in the family. (K089)

### Power Structure of Family (Violence)
The lower the educational level of the husband, the more likely he is to resort to physical punishment in order to impose his will in the family. (K089)

## EDUCATION OF HUSBAND/WIFE     X Fertility
The number of years of schooling completed, by either the wife or the husband, varies inversely with fertility. (H010)

### Husband-Wife Relations (Intimacy)
A great differential in formal education between husband and wife is likely to make intimacy between spouses more difficult. (P083)

### Intermarriage (Racial)
Japanese-American couples are likely to be more educated than the general American population. (S004)

### Marital Adjustment
Marital adjustment is more likely when both the husband and wife are college graduates and have had postgraduate or professional training. (B033)

Equality in education is conducive to better marital adjustment. (G157)

The higher the education, the better the marital adjustment. (O001)

## EDUCATION OF MOTHER     X Authoritarianism
The degree to which the mother is possessive or authoritarian is inversely related to the amount of education she has received. (S187)

### Child-Rearing Attitudes
The higher the educational level of the mother, the more likely is she to justify her disciplinary measures. (K115)

### Child-Rearing Practices (Chores)
The more educated the mother is, the more likely is she to assign regular tasks to the child. (S191)

Regardless of socioeconomic level, better-educated mothers gave their children more regular household chores to perform. (S191)

### Child-Rearing Practices (Control)
Whereas extreme control over a young daughter's behavior is almost entirely a lower-class phenomenon, highly educated mothers are as likely as those who never entered high school to exercise such control over a young son. (E100)

### Child-Rearing Practices (Criticism)
There is a positive relationship between the mother's educational level and the amount of maternal criticism of daughters. (K115)

### Child-Rearing Practices (Dependency)
Regardless of socioeconomic status, better-educated mothers were more permissive toward the child's dependency. (S191)

### Child-Rearing Practices (Restrictiveness)
Regardless of socioeconomic level, better-educated mothers were less restrictive on the child's use of fingers for eating, less restrictive about his treatment of house and furniture, and applied less pressure for neatness and orderliness. (S191)

### Child-Rearing Practices (Sex Role)
Regardless of socioeconomic level, better-educated mothers are less inclined to insist that a boy be masculine and a girl feminine. (S191)

### Conformity
Maternal educational level is unrelated to adolescent conformity in children. (K115)

### Emotional Problems of Child
Children with emotional problems are more likely to have mothers with low education. (B283)

### Employment of Mother
Mothers with more education are more likely to be employed than are mothers with less education. (N057)

### Fertility
The higher the educational level of the mother, the lower the number of children she will bear. (C134)

### Illegitimacy (Adoption)
The more educated the unwed mother, the more likely is she to give up the illegitimate child. (J020)

### Illegitimacy (Place of Delivery)
The lower the educational attainment of the unwed mother, the more likely it is that she will have her baby in the county in which she resides. (V002)

Unwed mothers whose babies are delivered in private practice have a higher educational attainment than do unwed mothers whose babies are born in institutions. (V002)

### Juvenile Delinquency
Children of less-educated employed mothers are more likely to become delinquent than are children of more-educated employed mothers. (N057)

### Maternal Overprotectiveness
There is no relationship between maternal overprotection and the educational level of the mother. (K115)

### Mother-Child Relations (Acceptance)
The mother's educational level is not related to maternal acceptance. (K115)

### Mother-Child Relations (Hostility)
The older and less educated the mother, the more severely hostile she will be toward her children. (S229)

### X Mother-Child Relations (Possessiveness)
Maternal possessiveness is negatively correlated with education of the mother. (S187)

### Mother-Son Relations (Possessiveness)
If the mother of a schizophrenic son has been educated beyond grammar school, she is likely to feel less possessive toward her son than if she is less well educated. (F099)

The more educated the mother of a schizophrenic boy, the less likely it is that she will be overly possessive. (F119)

### Scholastic Achievement of Child
College students whose mothers did not obtain a college degree are more likely to drop out of college than are students whose mothers did attain a degree. (A067)

### Toilet Training
Regardless of socioeconomic level, better-educated mothers toilet trained their children earlier. (S191)

## EDUCATION OF MOTHER/FATHER
### X   Child-Rearing Practices
The mother's child-rearing behavior is more closely related to her husband's than to her own educational level. (B250)

### Educational Aspiration
Children whose mothers have had more schooling than their fathers are more likely to have high educational ambitions than are children whose parents have had equivalent schooling. (T095)

The mother's education is as important as the father's education in predicting the child's ambition when the father's occupation is held constant. (T095)

### Mobility Aspiration of Child
The child is more likely to have mobility ambitions if the mother's educational level is higher than the father's than if her educational level is less than or equal to his. (T096)

If the mother's educational level is higher than that of the father, the child's mobility aspirational level is higher. (T096)

### Size of Family
Family size shows a greater negative correlation with the educational level of the mother than with that of the father. (A065)

## EDUCATION OF PARENTS        X   Adoption
Couples of higher educational level are more likely to withdraw their application for adoption than couples of lower educational level. (F117)

### Adoption (Acceptance by Agency)
Couples of lower educational level are more likely than couples of higher educational level to be rejected by adoption agencies. (F117)

### Aspiration Level
High parental education is associated with high ambition in the child. (T095)

### Behavior Problems (Acting Out)
Parents with better education are more likely to have problems with their children regarding temper tantrums.

### Child-Rearing Practices (Democratic)
Parents who are college educated are most likely to be democratic and equalitarian. (E100)

### Child-Rearing Practices (Dependency)/Education of Parents
### X   Scholastic Motivation of Child
High independence training has as great or greater an effect than does parental educational level on academic motivation in the adolescent. (E102)

### Child-Rearing Practices (Education)
College-educated parents are much more likely to support the desires of their children regarding going to college than are noncollege-educated parents. (E102)

### Child-Rearing Practices (Permissiveness)
Parent with least education tend to be most domineering since they have limited insight into the developmental needs of their adolescent children; this is supported by the finding of a strong negative relationship between the authoritarian-control factor on the PARI and educational level in a sample of 60 mothers in a psychiatric hospital. (E100)

Autocratic mothers of young daughters, autocratic fathers of young sons and daughters, and permissive fathers of older youths are most likely to have less than a tenth-grade education. Autocratic mothers of boys and older girls, autocratic fathers of high-school-aged children, and permissive mothers and fathers of younger adolescents are most likely to have one or more years of college. (E100)

Both mothers and fathers who are permissive in rearing their younger rather than their older children are more likely to have acquired some college education. (E100)

### Child-Rearing Practices (Sex Role)
The higher the educational level of the parents, the less likely is there to be differential child rearing for the daughters and sons. (B250)

The higher the parents' educational level, the less does sex-differential treatment of sons and daughters affect the child's capacity for responsible behavior (i.e., paternal power and affection increases responsibility in sons and lowers responsibility in daughters). At the graduate level, maternal effect becomes more influential for both sexes (i.e., maternal power and affection being more likely to foster responsibility in boys and impede it in girls). (B250)

### Creativity of Child
There is a correlation between the educational level of the parents and the degree of creativity of the child. (R109)

### Educational Aspiration
The child's motivations to further his education are positively related to the educational level of the mother and father. (E102)

The child's uncertainty regarding completion of high school is negatively related to parental educational level. (E102)

### Employment of Women
There is no relationship between the daughter's decision to spend a good portion of her life in paid employment and the educational level of her parents. (S231)

### I.Q.
There is no relationship between the educational level of the parents and the intelligence of the child. (B282)

There is a correlation between the level of parental education and the mental ability of three-year-old Negro children. (H191)

### I.Q./Creativity
Parents of highly intelligent (Binet) children are more likely to have had more specialized educational training than are the parents of highly creative (Guilford-Cattell) children. (G132)

### Juvenile Delinquency
Neither the education of the father nor the education of the mother had any significant influence on the child's delinquent behavior (Cambridge-Somerville Study). (M194)

### Personality Adjustment of Child
There is a low correlation between low personality adjustment in the child (as measured by the Rogers Test of Personality Adjustment) and the mother's and father's

educational level, but those whose fathers have had postgraduate education have the lowest scores. (B251)

### Personality Adjustment of Daughter
The level of parental education is not significantly related to the personality adjustment of daughters. (B247)

### Scholastic Motivation
The greater the parents' educational attainment, the higher the adolescent's academic motivation, regardless of social class. (E102)

There is a positive relationship between parents' educational level and academic motivation in the adolescent, regardless of the degree of parental independence training. (E102)

### Sex Anxiety
Education is positively correlated with less sex anxiety in both parents. (B232)

## EDUCATION OF PARENTS/CLASS
### X  Scholastic Motivation of Child
Educational level of parents has a greater effect on high academic motivation in the child than does social class. (E102)

## EDUCATION OF SON    X  Occupation of Father
Among blue collar boys, there is a slight positive relationship between the degree of their dissatisfaction about their fathers' occupations and their parents' insistence on a college education. (E102)

Among white collar sons, there is a slight negative relationship between the son's dissatisfaction with his father's occupation and parental insistence on college. (E102)

### Occupational Aspiration of Son
Boys who have college-oriented parents are more likely to have high occupational aspirations than are those who do not, regardless of their evaluation of their fathers' occupations. (E102)·

## EDUCATION OF SPOUSES
### X  Marital Adjustment
Equality in education is conducive to better marital adjustment. (G157)

## EDUCATION OF SURROGATE FATHER
### X  I.Q. of Adopted Child
There is no correlation between the educational level of the foster father and the I.Q. of his adopted child. (H173)

## EDUCATION OF WIFE      X  Affinal Relations
Men married to better-educated wives are more likely to have poor relations with their in-laws than are men married to similarly or poorly educated wives. (K089)

### Divorce, Attitude Toward
Divorced women with grammar-school education are more likely to report social discrimination against them because of their divorced status. (G157)

### Divorce, Initiation of
The education of the wife is unrelated to who made the first suggestion to divorce. (G157)

### Extended Kin Relations
Men married to better-educated wives are more likely to have poor relations with their in-laws than are men married to similarly or poorly educated wives. (K089)

### Fertility
Whether the husband has a farm or nonfarm occupation is a less important factor than the number of years of schooling completed by the wife in determining fertility. Occupation of husband, however, exerts an appreciable differentiating effect among women with more than five years of schooling. (H010)

The inverse relationship of number of live births with educational level of the rural wife holds even when the size of the farm operated by the husband is controlled. (H010)

### Fertility Values
Wives with a high level of education prefer a very large number of children or no children at all as compared with wives of middle or no education who want an average number of children. (V046)

Wives with an education beyond high school express an ideal somewhat smaller than the intended number of children; this relationship is reversed at the lower educational levels. (Y046)

### Husband-Wife Relations (Companionship)
The higher education level of women brought them to a more equal level with men and thus increased the companionship between husband and wife.

### Husband-Wife Relations (Dependency)
Literate women are more maritally dependent than are illiterate women. (L079)

### Husband-Wife Relations (Evaluation)
The higher the educational level of the wife, the more likely she is to blame her husband for economic failure. (K089)

Among lower-class families, the less educated the woman, the more critical is she of her husband (U.S.). (S191)

### Husband-Wife Relations (Friendship)
The higher the educational level of a woman, the more likely it is that her husband is also her most intimate friend. (K089)

### Marital Adjustment
If the wife's education exceeds that of the husband's by three or more years, a great amount of conflict is apt to arise in the family. (B033)

Marital happiness is greater among couples where the wife has more than a high-school education than where the wife has less than a high-school education. (B033)

### Marriage Payment
The size of the marriage payment is directly correlated with the educational level of the wife. (W082)

### Mother-Child Relations (Acceptance)
Mothers who are highly educated tend to be more accepting of their children than do mothers with less education. (K115)

### Mother-Child Relations (Dependency)
The higher the education of the wife, the less dependent she is on her children.

### Sex Relations
The lower the educational level of a blue collar wife, the more likely it is that she will find sexual satisfaction in an unhappy marriage. (K089)

### Sex-Role Definition
The higher the educational level of wives, the less favorably they look upon housework. (K089)

The higher the educational level of wives, the greater their satisfaction with the position of homemaker. (K089)

The higher the educational level of wives, the more likely they are to be defensive about their desire to work. (K089)

### Size of Family
Farm families in which the wife's schooling was from none to six years have fewer children than do farm families in which the wife had seven or more years of schooling. (K016)

## EDUCATION OF WOMEN          X   Divorce
There is a direct relation between the educational level of women and divorce. (K161)

### Marriage, Attitude Toward
There is an inverse relation between the educational level of women and their desire for marriage. (K161)

### Residence (Neolocal)
The self-sufficiency fostered by a higher level of education in the wife tends to produce pressures toward neolocal residence. (M081)

### Sex Relations
Women with more education (married to blue collar husbands) are more likely to react to marital unhappiness with deviant sexual needs than are women of low educational backgrounds. (K089)

## EDUCATION (WESTERN)
### X   Authority Structure of Family
The family authority structure is weakened by the education of younger members in western schools. (R040)

## EDUCATIONAL ASPIRATION
### X   Child-Rearing Practices (Achievement Demands)
Among adolescents whose parents have college expectations for them, those who are uncertain about college are more likely to receive frequent achievement demands than are those who are certain regarding their college plans. (E102)

### Child-Rearing Practices (Dependency)
Independence training is positively related to the child's desire to further his education. (E102)

Adolescents who are college oriented are more likely than those who are indifferent or undecided to have experienced active paternal independence training. (E102)

Youths with parents who are very active in independence training are more likely than those with inactive parents to desire to complete high school. (E102)

### Child-Rearing Practices (Dependency)/Parental Expectations
Adolescent college orientation is more related to parental independence training than to parental expectations concerning posthigh-school education. (E102)

### Child-Rearing Practices (Giving Reasons)
Among adolescents whose parents have college expectations for them, those who are uncertain about college receive less reasoning and explanation in child rearing

than do those who are certain regarding their college plans. (E102)

### Child-Rearing Practices (Social Mobility)
Parents of college-oriented sons are more likely than parents of noncollege-oriented sons to encourage upward mobility. (E102)

### Class
There is a high correlation between socioeconomic class and parental stress on college; this largely accounts for the relationship between class and the desire of the child to attend college. (B291)

### Education/Occupation of Father
High educational ambition in the child is associated with the father's educational level being high relative to his occupation. (T095)

### Education/Occupation of Parents
Parental educational–cultural attainment is a more significant factor than is the father's occupation in determining the educational aspirations of adolescent sons. (E102)

### Education of Child
Parents of school dropouts are more likely to lack understanding and concern with the development of their children's interests in school than are parents of in-school students. (E102)

### Education of Mother/Father
Children whose mothers have had more schooling than their fathers are more likely to have high educational ambitions than are children whose parents have had equivalent schooling. (T095)

The mother's education is as important as the father's education in predicting the child's ambition when the father's occupation is held constant. (T095)

### Education of Parents
The child's motivations to further his education are positively related to the educational level of the mother and father. (E102)

The child's uncertainty regarding completion of high school is negatively related to parental educational level. (E102)

### Educational Aspiration of Parents
The greater the parental stress on attending college, the more likely it is that the child will wish to go. When stress is low, boys are more likely to wish to attend than girls, but this relationship is reversed at the higher stress levels. (B291)

### Homogamy (Occupation)
Working-class parents are more likely to prefer better education for their children when the mother's occupation before marriage was nonmanual rather than manual. (L115)

### Occupation of Father
Among blue collar boys there is a strong positive relationship between the degree of dissatisfaction about their fathers' occupations and their parents' insistence on a college education. (E102)

### Occupational Aspiration of Parents
Parents of college-oriented sons are more likely to hold middle-class occupational aspirations for their sons than are parents of noncollege-oriented sons. (E102)

### Ordinal Position
Parents are more likely to insist that their oldest child attend college, holding class constant. (E102)

First-born children are more likely than later-born children to have college aspirations. (E102)

Among lower-class adolescents, those who have no siblings are much more likely to be college oriented than are those who are the oldest child in large families. (E102)

### Premarital Sex Relations
The higher the educational aspirations of boys, the older they are likely to be before first engaging in sexual intercourse. (C134)

### Race
Negro mothers are more likely to have unrealistic educational goals for their children than are white mothers. (L124)

### Religion
The importance of parental stress on college for the educational aspirations of their children reduces, but does not destroy, the effect of religious affiliation on college plans. Jews remain, at every stress level, the highest, followed by Protestants and then Catholics. (B291)

Jewish parents, followed by Protestant and Catholic parents, place the greatest emphasis on a college education for their children. (E102)

In the lower class, Protestant youths are more likely to have positive attitudes regarding school and to feel certain about completing high school than are Catholic youths, regardless of the size of their families. (E102)

Among college-oriented youths, Catholic youths are less likely to have parents who insist on college than are Protestant youths. (E102)

Among large lower-class families, Catholic parents are more likely to stress college for older sons than are Protestant parents. (E102)

### Scholastic Achievement
Low achieving adolescents who are exposed to conditions that generate and facilitate upward mobility (middle-class status, college-educated fathers who are active in independence training, and parents who insist on their children going to college) are as likely as high achieving adolescents who are not exposed to such conditions to plan definitely to attend college. (E102)

### Sex Status
Boys who desire to go to college are more likely to have parents who insist on such a course of action than are college-oriented girls, regardless of family class position. (E102)

College-educated parents are much less likely to insist on college for their daughters than for their sons. (E102)

Parents expect boys to go further in school than they do girls. (S191)

### Size of Family
Only children are more likely to anticipate education beyond the high-school level than are adolescents from families with six or more children. (E102)

Insofar as the chances of attending college are concerned, a larger number of children in the family is a greater hindrance for lower-class than for middle-class youths. (E102)

## EDUCATIONAL ASPIRATION OF CHILD
### X    Class
The family's feeling about whether the child should be expected to go to college is more strongly related to socioeconomic status than to the mother's education, although both make a difference. (S191)

## EDUCATIONAL ASPIRATION OF PARENTS
### X    Class
Middle-class parents place greater emphasis on their children's going to college than do lower-class parents. (E102)

### Educational Aspiration
The greater the parental stress on attending college, the more likely it is that the child will wish to go. When stress is low, boys are more likely to wish to attend than girls, but this relationship is reversed at the higher stress levels. (B291)

### Scholastic Motivation of Child
Parental expectations regarding the adolescent's continuing his posthigh-school education has little influence on the adolescent's academic motivation. (E102)

Among adolescents who are not college oriented, those whose parents have college ambitions for them are higher in academic motivation than are those whose parents do not. (E102)

## EDUCATIONAL SYSTEM    X    Acculturation
Day schools have greater influence in promoting changes within the Indian community than do boarding schools. (P010)

## EDUCATIONAL VALUES
### X    Employment of Women, Attitude Toward
There is no correlation between the job orientation of college girls and their parents' perception of the importance of an education. (S255)

## EGO DEVELOPMENT OF CHILD
### X    Mother-Child Relations (Affection)
The infant who is exposed to a mother whose emotional investment is ambivalent and/or unpredictable will be more likely to have an arrested ego development. (H216)

### Mother-Child Relations (Anxiety)
When the dominant feeling of the parent toward the child is one of anxiety, empathized anxiety for the parent will keep the child from advancing beyond the infantile sense of union with the mother to a mature awareness of the self as a separate individual. (S259)

## EGO DEVELOPMENT OF MOTHER
### X    Childbirth
Mothers who have psychopathic reactions to childbirth have less well-developed ego resources (measured by Rorschach responses) than do mothers who react without such pathologies. (M193)

## ELOPEMENT    X    Marital Adjustment
Marital adjustment is negatively correlated with elopement. (C023)

### Mate Selection (Free Choice)
Elopement is likely to occur when parents disregard the wishes of the child in choice of a spouse. (B181)

Elopement tends to occur when there is a serious discrepancy between the criteria of the parents and of the child for mate selection. (S043)

When mate selection is largely the consequence of parental decision, patterns of elopement are likely to occur. (T107)

### Parent-Child Relations (Control)
The rate of elopement tends to increase with a reduction in the strength of family control. (H062)

### Polygyny
In polygynous societies, where it is difficult for a man to marry at an early age, the incidence of elopement is high. (W056)

### Preferential Marriage, Restrictiveness of
When a preferential marriage pattern is severely restrictive, the incidence of elopement will tend to be high. (K062)

### Urbanization
The incidence of elopement tends to be directly correlated with the degree of urbanization. (L064)

## EMOTIONAL ADJUSTMENT
### X  Cohesion of Family
The greater the emotional involvement of the members of the family with one another, the greater the need for freedom from extreme emotional and physical stimulation. (C093)

### Disorganization of Family/Broken Home
Adolescents from homes that remain intact, but unhappily so, have greater adjustment problems than do those whose homes are broken by divorce or death (U.S.). (G156)

### Economic Dependence
Among elderly persons (75 years of age or older) living with their children, the more financially independent they are, the higher their morale. (C116)

### Employment of Mother
There is no difference between married working and nonworking mothers regarding their emotional stability as measured by the Gordon Personal Profile. (G127)

Health status; marital, sexual, and emotional adjustment; and number and seriousness of child problems do not correlate with employment or nonemployment of the mother. (S265)

### Illegitimacy
There is no correlation between emotional immaturity and having illegitimate children. (N055)

### Loss of Family Member
The greater the number of losses that have occurred before, the more likely it is that the loss of a member of the immediate family will be severely felt. (T091)

The longer it takes to secure a substitute, the more likely it is that the loss of a member of the immediate family will be severely felt. (T091)

The more recent the loss of a member of a person's immediate family, the more severe will be its psychological effects. (T091)

The older the member of the immediate family who has been lost, the more severe the psychological effects will be for the survivors. (T091)

The younger the person, the more severely will he be affected by the loss of a member of the immediate family. (T091)

### Marital Adjustment
Marital adjustment is more likely when the husband and wife are emotionally stable. (B033)

### Marital Status
Among young adults, those who are single tend to be better adjusted emotionally than those who are married; this difference evens out, however, with age. (M232)

### Parent-Child Relations (Evaluation)
Parents of emotionally disturbed children are more likely to devaluate their children than are parents of normals. (M200)

### Self-Conception
Parents of emotionally disturbed children are more likely to emphasize aggressive, distrustful, or dependent behavioral traits in describing self, spouse, and child than are parents of normals, who tend to emphasize managerial, competitive behavior. (M200)

Parents of emotionally disturbed children are more likely to show rejection of themselves and their interpersonal behavior than are parents of normals. (M200)

### Weaning
Children who are weaned late have more severe reactions to weaning than do children who are weaned early. (Y042)

## EMOTIONAL ADJUSTMENT OF CHILD
### X  Anxiety of Mother
The higher the anxiety level of the mother, the lower the rate of development in early childhood and the lower the child's emotional adjustment. (D075)

### Breast Feeding, Duration of
There is no relationship between duration of breast feeding and emotional maladjustment of the child. (K113)

### Child-Rearing Practices (Dependency)
The more gradual the steps from dependence to independence, the greater the likelihood that the child will be emotionally healthy. (L134)

### Conflict in Family
There is a correlation between emotional disturbances in the child and familial disunity and conflict. (M200)

### Husband-Wife Relations (Consensus)
Parental agreement/disagreement on descriptions of the child's behavior does not vary with the emotional adjustment of the child. (M200)

### Personality Problems of Parent
There is a correlation between emotional problems in the child and psychopathology in the parent. (M200)

### Pregnancy Anxiety
Infants whose mothers were highly anxious during pregnancy exhibit lower emotional adjustment than do infants of mothers who were not as anxious during pregnancy. (D067)

### Self-Conception of Husband/Wife
Agreement/disagreement between a parent's self-description and the spouse's description is not related to the emotional adjustment/maladjustment of their children.

### Sex-Role Definition
In nuclear families, the greater the degree of parental-role differentiation, the poorer the emotional adjustment of the child. (S216)

### Sibling Structure
There is a positive relationship between birth of a sibling while the child is in his second year and greater emotional maladjustment of the child. (K113)

### Weaning
Late-weaned infants show more weaning frustration than do early-weaned infants. (B272)

The child's frustration by weaning is associated with late weaning (longer practice in sucking), severe methods, indecisiveness during weaning. (S191)

## EMOTIONAL ADJUSTMENT OF MOTHER
### X   Employment of Mother
Employment/nonemployment of the mother does not correlate with her emotional adjustment. (S265)

### Maternal-Role Behavior
The amount of time spent in care of younger children (3–6 years of age) is not related to the emotional stability of the mother. (M216)

The greater the amount of time spent in care of older children (7–10 years of age), the higher the emotional instability of the mother. (M216)

### Personality Problems of Child
Child problems correlate more with the mother's emotional adjustment than with her occupational status. (S265)

The number and seriousness of child problems do not correlate with employment/nonemployment of the mother, but with the mother's emotional adjustment. (S265)

## EMOTIONAL ADJUSTMENT OF ORPHAN
### X   Identification with Parents
If an orphan's early childhood years were spent in a home with two parents who had well-defined roles (i.e., early identifications were good), he is more likely to show a high degree of stability later on. (H188)

## EMOTIONAL ADJUSTMENT OF PARENTS
### X   Mental Illness (Schizophrenia/Neurosis)
Parents of normals are more likely to be well adjusted emotionally than are parents of neurotics or schizophrenics. (F110)

Parents of normals are less likely to be rigid than are the parents of schizophrenics or neurotics. (F110)

### Neurosis
The greater the emotional maladjustment of the individual parent, the more likely it is that the child will be neurotic. (F110)

## EMOTIONAL ADJUSTMENT/RELIGION
### X   Divorce
The experience of divorce is more strongly related to signs of psychic and emotional disturbance among Catholic and Jewish children than among Protestant children. (R129)

## EMOTIONAL AND BEHAVIORAL ADJUSTMENT
### X   Breast Feeding
At ten days after birth, breast-fed infants are more likely to show emotional disturbance and nonnutritional sucking than are cup-fed infants. (B272)

## EMOTIONAL BEHAVIOR OF INFANT
### X   Emotional Behavior of Mother
There is a correlation between the *form* of expressive behavior of the mother and that of the child, but the reaction of the infant to the *intensity* of the mother's expressive behavior is more varied, approaching an inverse relationship. (B272)

## EMOTIONAL BEHAVIOR OR MOTHER
### X   Emotional Behavior of Infant
There is a correlation between the *form* of expressive behavior of the mother and that of the child, but the reaction of the infant to the *intensity* of the mother's expressive behavior is more varied, approaching an inverse relationship. (B272)

## EMOTIONAL/INSTRUMENTAL BEHAVIOR
### X   Kin/Nonkin Interaction
Emotionality further increases satisfaction among family members and decreases satisfaction in stranger interaction, while instrumentality increases satisfaction in stranger interaction and decreases it in family interaction. (L180)

## EMOTIONAL PROBLEMS
### X   Bereavement/Divorce
Widowhood is associated with greater emotional problems following the loss of a spouse than is divorce. (G157)

### Husband-Wife Relations (Power)
The higher equality of modern marital partners brings a greater relief from their emotional problems by creating greater interdependence.

### Marital Adjustment
Emotional disturbance of married couples tends to be directly correlated with an attitude of severe disappointment of each partner with the other and with the marriage. (V028)

### Parent-Child Relations (Conflict)
There is a correlation between emotional disturbance in the child and his involvement in a conflict situation between his parents; the former never occurs without the latter.

### Parent-Child Relations (Rejection)
Dissociative behavior is more likely to result from conformity as an attempt to avoid parental rejection than from other types of internalization of parental attitudes. (W143)

### Scapegoating
The greater the extent to which the parents displace their difficulties onto the child, the more likely it is that the child will become emotionally maladjusted. (V033)

### Weaning
Early weaning is likely to be more traumatic for the child than is later weaning. (B272)

There is no relationship between age of weaning and emotional disturbances in the child. (B272)

## EMOTIONAL PROBLEMS OF CHILD
### X   Adoption
Since the adopted child is likely to realize that he does not belong (fear of loss of self), he is more likely than the child reared at home to have aggravated difficulty in

resolving the Oedipal complex (castration fear, loss of penis). (B253)

### Age of Mother
The younger the mother and the child at the time of divorce, the more likely it is that the child will be emotionally disturbed. (R129)

### Broken Home
Estrangement of the child from the family environment in the early years leads to severe emotional problems in later years. (B283)

### Broken Home (Divorce V. Death)
It is divorce in particular, rather than family breakup in general, that is most closely associated with signs of emotional disturbances among children of Catholics and Jews. (R129)

### Child-Rearing Practices (Consistency)
The more inconsistent and contradictory the mother's behavior during her offspring's early childhood, the more psychologically unstable the child will be in later years. (B283)

### Death of Parent
Children who lose a parent by death are less likely to become emotionally disturbed if the remaining parent keeps the home intact than if he does not. (H188)

### Disorganization of Family
Disturbed children are likely to come from homes characterized by an atmosphere of confusion and disorganization. (S187)

### Education of Mother
Children with emotional problems are more likely to have mothers with low education. (B283)

### Emotional Problems of Mother
If the mother has emotional problems, the children are likely to develop emotional problems. (B283)

### Husband-Wife Relations (Communication)
Parents (Italian- and Irish-American backgrounds) of emotionally disturbed children are less likely than those of normal children to discuss sensitive and important issues. (V031)

### Husband-Wife Relations (Evaluation)
Parents of emotionally disturbed children are more likely to devaluate their spouses than are parents of normals. (M200)

### Identification of Mother with Daughter
When the degree of identification of the mother with her daughter is too encompassing, emotional instability in the daughter is likely to result. (H218)

### Identification with Child
Parents of emotionally disturbed children are less likely than are parents of normals to identify with the child. (M200)

### Identification with Spouse
Spouses who identify with each other are less likely to have children who are emotionally disturbed, than are spouses who do not identify with each other. (M200)

### Income
Children whose fathers have high incomes are less likely to have emotional problems (it is usually a more stable work history of the father which accounts for the higher income). (B290)

### Institutional Care
If a baby is institutionalized for a long period, it will show an apathetic withdrawal from all emotional entanglements. (B270)

### Kin Relations (Dependency)
Parents of emotionally disturbed children (of Italian- and Irish-American backgrounds) are more likely than are parents of normal children to have conflicts concerning independence from the extended family. (V031)

### Marital Adjustment
Spouses who devaluate one another are more likely to have emotionally disturbed children than are parents of normals. (M200)

Emotionally disturbed children are more likely than relatively healthy children to come from families in which the marriage relationship of the parents is disturbed. (V028)

### Mother Absence
If the mother is absent during infancy and, consequently, the child receives care from numerous persons instead of from mainly one, the child develops problems of personal adjustment. (G121)

### Mother-Child Relations (Consistency)
The mother who alternates in overindulgence and rejection of her child is more likely than the mother who is consistent in her attitudes to produce a child who is unhappy at home and intensely homesick when away from it. (S226)

### Ordinal Position
Middle children, ranging from next to oldest to next to youngest, tend to have more emotional problems than do children who are oldest or youngest. (B283)

### Parent-Child Relations (Separation)
The more intensive the separation of child from parent (as in a residential as opposed to a day nursery), the greater the emotional imbalance of the child. (S265)

Parents (of Italian- and Irish-American backgrounds) of emotionally disturbed children are more likely* than those of normal children to contrive physical separations through family routines (working hours, recreation). (V031)

### Parent Loss
In children over one year of age, separation from family members causes physical as well as emotional problems, particularly increased dependency needs and regression in learned skills (e.g., feeding self, walking, speaking, and bladder control).

### Religiosity
In families with regular church attendance, children are less likely to develop emotional problems. (B290)

### Size of Family
Children from large families tend to have more emotional problems than do children from small families. (B283)

### Social Welfare
Children with emotional problems are more likely to belong to families which receive public financial assistance. (B290)

### Value Conflict
Although the parents (of Italian- and Irish-American backgrounds) of emotionally disturbed children have congruent unconscious value orientations, they are more likely than are the parents of normal children to have severe conflicts concerning new and old values, the mother appearing to be more progressive. (V.031)

### Weaning
The greater the preparation for weaning and the more gradually the mother makes the shift, the lower the frustration experienced by the child during the transition. (S191)

The more consistent the mother in her weaning practices, the less uncertainty produced in the child and, consequently, the lower his frustration experienced during the transition. (S191)

The longer the duration of weaning, the greater the frustration produced in the child. (S191)

### EMOTIONAL PROBLEMS OF CHILD (DREAMING)    X    Employment of Mother
Children of mothers who worked full time before their children were two years old are more likely to have bad dreams than are children of mothers who did not begin full employment until their children were three years old. (Y047)

### EMOTIONAL PROBLEMS OF CHILD (FEAR OF ANIMALS)    X    Employment of Mother
Children whose mothers worked full time before the children were two years old are less afraid of animals than are children whose mothers did not begin full-time employment until the children were three years old. (Y047)

### EMOTIONAL PROBLEMS OF CHILD (TOILET TRAINING)    X    Class
There is no difference between lower- and middle-class children in the emotional disturbances caused by toilet training (U.S.). (S191)

### EMOTIONAL PROBLEMS OF CHILD (WEANING)    X    Feeding Problems
There is no relationship between whether or not the child was emotionally upset over weaning and his having later feeding problems (e.g., prolonged loss of appetite) (U.S.). (S191)

### EMOTIONAL PROBLEMS OF FATHER    X    Juvenile Delinquency
Emotional disturbance of the father contributes indirectly to delinquency of the child by contributing to the development of the child's tendency toward fantasy.

A child having a feeling of inadequacy is more likely to become delinquent if his father is emotionally disturbed.

### EMOTIONAL PROBLEMS OF MOTHER    X    Emotional Problems of Child
If the mother has emotional problems, the children are likely to develop emotional problems. (B283)

### Junvenile Delinquency
Delinquents, more than nondelinquents, tend to have emotionally disturbed mothers.

The mother's employment, per se, is not a cause of juvenile delinquency. (G127)

### Maternal Overprotectiveness
There is a correlation between affect hunger in the mother and her overprotection of the child. (B272)

### Mental Illness
Mental illness is directly correlated with a family environment in which the mother is emotionally disturbed. (F085)

### Mother-Child Relations
Negative emotional states (dullness, gloominess, unresponsiveness) in the mother are negatively associated with positive mother-child interaction during preadolescence. (S273)

### EMOTIONAL PROBLEMS OF PARENTS    X    Juvenile Delinquency
If the parents have shown emotional or behavioral disturbances, the child is likely to display delinquent behavior.

### Mental Illness/Personality Problems of Child
Parents of schizophrenic and neurotic children tend to show less emotional disturbance than do parents of acting-out and psychosomatic children. (L144)

### EMOTIONAL PROBLEMS OF SPOUSE    X    Mental Illness, Recovery from
A patient is less likely to respond to therapy if his or her spouse is also subject to serious emotional problems. (M228)

### EMOTIONAL PROBLEMS OF WOMEN    X    Death (Father/Mother)
Women are more likely to have emotional problems later in life after the loss of a mother rather than of a father. (H188)

### EMOTIONAL PROBLEMS (PARENTAL CONFLICTS)    X    Age of Child
The older the child (2–4 years v. 5–7 years), the less likely is he to exhibit emotional behavior (i.e., vocal, withdrawal, overt physical aggression against self, passive reactions) when in conflict with his parents. (I006)

### EMOTIONAL STABILITY OF PARENTS    X    Child-Rearing Practices (Responsibility)
Physical and emotional steadiness of the parents is necessary for developing a sense of responsibility in the child. (C093)

### EMOTIONAL TIES    X    Extended/Nuclear Family
The emotional ties between family members will be less intense in the extended family than in the nuclear family. (G156)

### EMPATHY    X    Courtship Status
Empathy will increase as love develops from dating through marriage stages. (C023)

Dating girls report equal amounts of disagreement with their parents and dates; engaged girls see less disagreement with partner and a constant amount with parents; married girls estimate an increased disagreement with partners (when actually it declines). (H229)

Sons report more disagreement with parents than with partners during dating and engagement periods; after marriage, sons feel an increase in disagreement with partners. (H229)

### Dating

The greater the accuracy in role-taking of dating pairs, the greater the satisfaction in dating behavior and the greater the degree of dating involvement. (S279)

### Interaction in Family (Emotional)

The more emotional the family interaction, the more accurately will participants perceive the satisfaction of other participants. (L180)

### Marital Adjustment

The more empathy from her husband the wife receives in her emotional problems, the more successful is the marriage. (S279)

When confronted with hypothetical family situations in which husband and wife must deal with role conflict, couples whose marriages were "in trouble" were less likely than those whose marriages were "not in trouble" to choose solutions which involved taking the role of the other and were characterized by less sympathy and agreement on a course of action to take. (S279)

There is no significant relationship between empathy (defined as "taking the role of another with sufficient accuracy so that one can predict his responses") and marital adjustment (Locke, Sabagh, and Thomes). (S279)

Couples who deal with conflict by remaining ignorant of each other's plans tend to be better adjusted than those who do not. (S279)

Marital happiness increases with an individual's ability to predict accurately the spouse's reactions to situations. (T092)

Marital happiness increases when self-perception and the spouse's perception are congruent. (T092)

### Marital Status

There is more empathy between married pairs than between favorite dates. (S279)

### Parent-Child Relations

The greater the role-taking accuracy of adult children vis-à-vis (in relation to) their parents, the better the adjustment to these parents. (S279)

For tradition-oriented, dependent parents whose attitudes conflict with those of their children role-taking accuracy vis-à-vis their children is inveresely related to adjustment. (S279)

### Parent-Child Relations (Affect)

A child with parents who differ in the amount and kind of affect they display is likely to be more sensitive to parental affect than is a child whose parents are similar in these characteristics. (R098)

### Parenthood

Married offspring with children are more likely to appreciate the problems and difficulties of their parents than are those without children. (S011)

### Status in Family

Following marriage, sons have better insight into their fathers' attitudes than daughters have into their mothers' attitudes; while before marriage, daughters have better insight into their mothers' attitudes than sons have into their fathers'. (H229)

At the dating, engagement, and courtship stages, mothers are more apt to have better insight (i.e., better able to predict responses) into their daughters' attitudes than fathers have into their sons' attitudes. (H229)

Boys' insights into partners' attitudes during the engagement and marriage periods are better than their insights into their parents' attitudes. (H229)

Dating girls have more insight into their mothers' attitudes than they do into those of their partners, but engaged and married girls understand their partners' attitudes better than they do their mothers'. (H229)

Engaged and married girls are better understood by fiancés and husbands than by parents. (H229)

Parental insight into boys' attitudes is never, in any stage of courtship, as acute as that of their sons' partners. (H229)

## EMPLOYMENT                    X   Achievement

Employed parents tend to evaluate more highly the occupational success of their children than do retired parents. (S220)

### Income, Attitude Toward

If the husband's working hours are longer than the wife's working hours, the wife tends to be satisfied with the family income level.

### Marital Stability

In the initiation of economic crisis (unemployment), the necessity of considering the children first and of facing new problems increases the stability between the husband and wife. (B207)

### Power Structure of Family

The partner who works more has more power. This is true not only for working wives v. nonworking wives, but also even reflects the number of hours the husband works.

### Size of Family

Employed men have more children than unemployed men; employed women have fewer children than unemployed women. (B244)

## EMPLOYMENT, ATTITUDE TOWARD
### X   Employment of Mother (Regularity)

The irregularly employed mother is motivated to work less for economic reasons than to escape domestic and maternal responsibilities. (S265)

### Employment of Women, Attitude Toward

There is a direct correlation between attitude of college girls toward future employment and that of their mothers. (S255)

## EMPLOYMENT OF CHILD
### X   Mental Illness of Child (Schizophrenia/Neurosis)

In the lower class, schizophrenic children are more likely to be required to contribute to the family than are neurotics. (M197)

## EMPLOYMENT OF DAUGHTER
### X   Employment of Mother

Daughters of working mothers are more likely to intend to continue working after marriage than are those of nonworking mothers. (S265)

## EMPLOYMENT OF DIVORCÉE          X   Friendship

Divorcées who had jobs at some time during the marriage, but not during the separation and immediate post-divorce period, are most likely to maintain their marriage friends, followed by divorcées who did not have a job at any time, next by divorcées who had jobs during the marriage and the separation and immediate postdivorce period, and last by those divorcées who did not have jobs during the marriage but did have jobs during the separation and postdivorce period. (G157)

### Income of Divorcée
Among remarried divorcées, job holding is not associated with having enough income to meet expenses; among the not-remarried, those who claim they have enough are slightly more likely to have a job than are those who claim they do not have enough. (G157)

### EMPLOYMENT OF MOTHER    X Achievement
Regardless of whether the mother likes to work, young children (third to sixth graders) of working mothers show a lower performance level. (G156)

### Adjustment of Child
Daughters of working mothers are less likely to be well adjusted than are those of nonworking mothers. (S265)

Employment/nonemployment of the mother is not related to adjustment of children. (S265)

### Age
The older the child, the more likely it is that he will adjust satisfactorily to the mother's employment outside the home. (R108)

### Age at Marriage
Earlier marriages increase the tendency for mothers to seek employment outside the home. (Y047)

### Age of Child
The older the children, the more likely it is that the mother is employed. (S265)

If a woman's children are of school age, she is more likely either to take outside employment or to consider it. (W150)

### Authoritarianism
Working mothers tend to be less authoritarian and more equalitarian than nonworking mothers. (G127)

### Authoritarianism of Mother
Working mothers tend to be less authoritarian and more equalitarian than nonworking mothers. (G127)

### Behavior Problems
Regardless of whether the mother likes to work, young children (third to sixth graders) of working mothers are more likely to respond to a frustrating problem with nonadaptive behavior such as crying or blaming themselves. (G156)

"Problem children" of working mothers tend to be younger than do problem children of nonworking mothers. (M058)

### Behavior Problems (Nail-Biting)
Children whose mothers worked full time before the children were two years of age tend to bite their nails significantly more than do children whose mothers did not begin full-time employment until the children were three years of age. (Y047)

### Child-Rearing Attitudes (Sex Role)
Working and nonworking mothers do not express differing points of view on sex-role training. (Y051)

### Child-Rearing Practices
Mothers with jobs tend to discipline their children in order to acquaint them with frustration more than do mothers with no employment.

Mothers with jobs tend to be more prescriptive concerning rules of their children's behavior than do mothers with no outside employment.

Mothers with no employment outside the home are more likely to use personalistic appeals as the justification for the rules of behavior applied to their children than are mothers with jobs. (G127)

There is no difference between married working and nonworking mothers regarding various child-rearing practices (measured by the Schoben Scale). (G127)

Working and nonworking mothers do not differ significantly in their child-rearing practices and attitudes. (S257)

The classification of mothers by whether or not they are employed is almost unrelated to child-rearing patterns. (Y051)

### Child-Rearing Practices (Achievement Demands)
Mothers with a job tend to expect more of their children than do nonworking mothers.

### Child-Rearing Practices (Chores)
Mothers with a job tend to encourage their children to perform household tasks more than do nonworking mothers. (S191)

### Child-Rearing Practices (Consistency)
Among working mothers there is more inconsistency in child rearing among mothers who do not enjoy their work than among the satisfied. (Y051)

### Child-Rearing Practices (Control)
Mothers who are employed outside of the home are more likely to use the threat that God will punish the child for deviant behavior as a means of control than are mothers who are unemployed. (N055)

### Child-Rearing Practices (Dependency)
Working mothers of high-school education are more likely than nonworking mothers to stress independence training. (Y050)

Working mothers of college education are less likely than nonworking mothers to stress independence training. (Y050)

### Child-Rearing Practices (Discipline)
Mothers with jobs tend to discipline their children more often than do mothers with no employment. (G156)

Working mothers who like to work are more likely to use mild discipline. (G156)

Working mothers in lower-class families use the same techniques of discipline as do nonworking mothers. (M211)

### Child-Rearing Practices (Education)
It is not the case that the mother's employment outside the family leads to the educational neglect of the children. (R093)

### Child-Rearing Practices (Neglect)
When the mother works, conditions of child neglect are created. (Y051)

### Child-Rearing Practices (Punishment)
Among stable homes (homes without parental conflict, criminality, or other social deviance), nonworking mothers are more likely to use physical punishment on their boys than are working mothers. (M211)

### Child-Rearing Practices (Responsibility)
Mothers with professions tend to justify the rules of discipline applied to their children as encouraging responsibility, mothers without outside employment do not.

### Child-Rearing Practices (Safety)
Mothers with professions tend to invoke more rules of behavior designed to protect their children's physical safety than do nonprofessional mothers.

### Child-Rearing Practices (Strictness)
Mothers with college backgrounds less often report the father as the stricter parent when these mothers work than when they do not work. (Y051)

Among nondelinquents, overstrictness on the part of fathers is more likely in families where the mother is employed. (S265)

### Chores
Mothers with jobs tend to encourage their children to perform household tasks more than do nonworking mothers.

### Chores, by Class
Adolescent daughters of lower-class working mothers report greater household responsibilities than do those of middle-class working mothers. (G156)

### Class
Lower-class mothers are more likely to have to work than are middle-class mothers. (G156)

Mothers in lower socioeconomic classes are more likely than those in the upper socioeconomic classes to be employed. (N057)

### Class of Husband
Employed mothers are more likely to have husbands in low socioeconomic categories. (S265)

### Criminality
In the lower class, if the mother of an unstable family (open parental conflict, criminality, and other varieties of social deviances are considered to be indices of instability) is employed, the son is more likely to become an adult delinquent than if she is not employed. (M211)

### Dating
Adolescent daughters of lower-class working mothers are more likely to seek in steady dating a substitute for family security or companionship than are adolescent daughters of middle-class working mothers. (G156)

### Death Rate
(In England and Scotland prior to 1914) children of working mothers had a higher death rate than did those of nonworking mothers. (S265)

The sooner the mother resumes work after the birth of a child, the higher the rate of infant mortality. (S265)

### Dependency
Children of mothers who are employed are no more dependent than are children of mothers who are not employed. (Y047)

When the mother works, the child's dependency needs are increased. (Y050)

### Dependency of Daughter
Among middle-class adolescent daughters, those whose mothers work tend to be more independent. (G156)

### Dependency of Son
Sons of working mothers are more likely to be dependent than are sons of nonworking mothers. (S265)

### Disorganization of Family
Employment of the mother is correlated with a disorganized family life. (Y050)

### Education of Mother
Mothers with more education are more likely to be employed than are mothers with less education. (N057)

### Emotional Adjustment
There is no difference between married working and nonworking mothers regarding their emotional stability as measured by the Gordon Personal Profile. (G127)

Health status, marital, sexual, and emotional adjustment, and number and seriousness of child problems do not correlate with employment or nonemployment of the mother. (S265)

### Emotional Adjustment of Mother
Employment/nonemployment of the mother does not correlate with her emotional adjustment. (S265)

### Emotional Problems of Child (Dreaming)
Children of mothers who worked full time before their children were two years old are more likely to have bad dreams than are children of mothers who did not begin full employment until the children were three years old. (Y047)

### Emotional Problems of Child (Fear of Animals)
Children whose mothers worked full time before the children were two years old are less afraid of animals than are children whose mothers did not begin full-time employment until the children were three years old. (Y047)

### Employment of Daughter
Daughters of working mothers are more likely to intend to continue working after marriage than are those of nonworking mothers. (S265)

### Employment of Mother, Attitude Toward
The children of working mothers are more likely to approve of their mothers' working than are children of nonworking mothers. (S265)

### Father Absence
In families where the father's occupation takes him away from the home for extended periods of time, the mother is less likely to work outside the home. (G156)

### Father-Daughter Relations (Evaluation)
Where the mother is employed, the daughter's evaluation of the father tends to be diminished. (M058)

### Father-Daughter Relations (Favoritism)
Daughters of working mothers are more likely to attribute preference for a female child to the father than are daughters of nonworking mothers. (H181)

### Father-Son Relations (Evaluation)
In lower-class families, it is more likely that the father-son relationship will be viewed unfavorably by the son if the mother is employed than if she is not. (M211)

### Fertility

Working mothers have a lower birth rate than do non-working mothers. (S265)

### Health

Health status, marital, sexual, and emotional adjustment, and number and seriousness of child problems do not correlate with employment or nonemployment of the mother. (S265)

### Health of Mother

Employment/nonemployment of the mother does not correlate with her health status. (S265)

### Household Composition

A joint household with three generations is more likely when a young mother is working than when she is unemployed. (R120)

### Husband-Wife Relations (Egalitarianism)

Greater marital equality increases the tendency for mothers to seek outside employment. (Y047)

### Income

The higher the income of the family, the less likely it is that the mother is employed. (C134)

The lower the income of the husband, the greater the likelihood that the mother's outside employment will be an extension of her family role. (R093)

### I.Q.

There is no relationship between the employment status of the mother and the mental ability of the three-year-old Negro child. (H191)

### I.Q./Creativity

The mothers of highly intelligent (Binet) children are more likely to be full-time housewives than are the mothers of highly creative (Guilford-Chattell) children. (G132)

### Juvenile Delinquency

The mother's employment, per se, is not a cause of juvenile delinquency. (G127)

If the mother is employed outside the home, the child is more likely to become a juvenile delinquent. (H183)

There is more delinquent behavior in families where mothers are employed. (N052)

Working mothers are more likely than are nonworking mothers to produce delinquent children, particularly in rural areas. (N057)

There is a correlation between employment of the mother and delinquency of the child in the middle class, but only to an insignificant extent in the lower and upper classes. (N063)

Juvenile delinquents are more likely to come from homes where the mother is the sole supporter than are nondelinquents. (S210)

In intact homes, delinquency is more likely if the mother is employed; but it is not related to the mother's employment in broken homes. (S265)

### Juvenile Delinquency by Sex Status

Since direct control is more effective over girls than over boys, there is a closer relationship between employment of the mother and delinquent behavior in girls than in boys. (N057)

### Marital Adjustment

Employment of the mother does not change the general level of happiness in the marriage. (G156)

Employment of the mother increases the frequency of marital conflict. (G156)

There is no relationship in lower-class families between the employment of the mother and conflict between husband and wife. (M211)

Regardless of class, nonemployed mothers are more likely than employed mothers to have well-adjusted marriage relations. (N063, N058)

Employment/nonemployment of the mother does not correlate with the extent of her sexual and marital adjustment. (S265)

Health status, marital, sexual, and emotional adjustment, and number and seriousness of child problems do not correlate with employment or nonemployment of the mother. (S265)

Employed mothers are more likely to report quarrelling in the family, to have lived apart from their husbands, and to have considered divorce. (S265)

### Marital Status (Female)

Compared with mothers who do not work, employed mothers are more likely to be widowed, divorced, or separated. (S265)

### Maternal Role

Women with children are most likely to be in the labor force when all the children are in school. (G156)

### Maternal-Role Adjustment

Employment or nonemployment of the mother does not correlate with adjustment to children; however, unemployed mothers were more likely to desire more children and to feel nervous due to their children. (S265)

Working mothers, more frequently than nonworking mothers, express anxiety about their role as mother (significant at 5 per cent level). (Y050)

Among dissatisfied (with role) mothers, those who work are less likely to have problems of control of child, emotional satisfaction, or adequacy of mothering. (Y050)

### Maternal-Role Adjustment/Size of Family

Employed mothers are more likely than nonemployed mothers to be well adjusted to children in small, but not in large, families. (S265)

### Maternal-Role Behavior

Lower-class working mothers are less likely to feel the need to compensate for their absence from the home than are middle-class mothers. (G156)

Employment of the mother is related to undue impatience on her part, neglect of the children, loss of discipline, loneliness of the children, and their inadequate socialization. (S265)

The working mother is less motherly than the nonworking mother. (Y050)

### Mental Illness

Mothers who are not employed are more likely to be psychotic than are mothers who are employed. (S275)

### Mother-Child Relations

Employment that serves ego needs of the mother improves the parent-child relationship. (G127)

If the mother is employed outside the home, she is likely to develop a strenuous and irritable relationship with the child. (H183)

Full-time employment of mothers of children under three years of age leads to an inadequate development of the mother-child relationship. (Y047)

### Mother-Child Relations (Affection)

The degree of affection of the adolescent for the mother does not correlate with employment/nonemployment of the mother. (S265)

### Mother-Child Relations (Interaction)

Working lowers the interaction of the mother with the child. (Y050)

### Mother-Child Relations (Understanding)

Mothers who have had jobs in the past are more likely to devote more effort to the understanding of their children's problems than are either presently working or unemployed mothers.

### Mother-Child Relations (Warmth)

If the mother is employed outside the home, she is likely to be less frustrated and more capable of warm interaction with the child. (H183)

### Mother-Daughter Relations (Interest/Control)

Daughters of mothers who are employed are no more likely to feel that their mothers have less control over or interest in them than do daughters of mothers who are not employed. (Y047)

### Mother-Son Relations (Affection)

Working mothers in lower-class families do not differ from nonworking mothers in the affection given their sons. (M211)

### Mother-Son Relations (Evaluation)

There is no relationship, in lower-class families, between the employment of the mother and the evaluation by her son of the mother-son relationship. (M211)

### Mother-Son Relations (Protectiveness)

Among stable homes (no conflict, criminality, or social deviance), nonworking mothers are more likely to be protective of their sons than are working mothers. (M211)

### Neurosis

Mothers who are employed are more likely to be neurotic than are mothers who are not employed. (S275)

### Occupation of Husband X Marital Adjustment of Working Mothers

The difference in marital adjustment scores between working and nonworking mothers tends to be smallest among women whose husbands are in professional and managerial occupations. (S257)

### Parent-Child Relations (Closeness)

Children of working mothers who provide substitute care have more detached parent-child relations than do those of mothers who do not work and remain with the child. (Y047)

### Parent-Child Relations (Communication/Rejection)

Daughters of working mothers are more likely than those of nonworking mothers to feel that their parents disapproved of them, that their fathers rejected them and that they disapproved of their fathers, that there was a lack of communication with their parents, and that homelife was not happy. (S265)

### Parent-Child Relations (Employment)

Girls with working mothers are more likely to feel that their mothers like to work than do those whose mothers do not work. (H222)

Children of working mothers are more likely to perceive their fathers as feeling unhappy or uncomfortable about going to work and leaving the children behind than are children of nonworking mothers. (H222)

### Parent-Child Relations (Interaction)

When mothers work, the contact between older parents and grown children is greater. (B312)

### Parent-Child Relations (Rebellion)

Children are less likely to be reported as rebellious by working mothers (of high-school background) than by nonworking mothers. (Y050)

### Parent-Daughter Relations (Closeness)

Daughters of working mothers do not feel as close to their parents as do daughters of mothers who do not work. (Y047)

### Parental-Role Behavior

Entertaining the child in the late afternoon is more likely to be shared by both parents when the wife is employed full time than if she is a full-time homemaker. (G133)

Staying home with the children during part of the weekend is more likely to be shared when the wife is a full-time homemaker than if she is employed full time. (G133)

### Paternal Role

There is a greater opportunity for the father to play a strong role with his children where the mother in the family also works. (M058)

### Paternal Role (Strictness)

Mothers with college backgrounds more often report the father as the less strict parent when these mothers work than when they do not. (Y051)

Mothers with a high-school background more often report the father as the stricter parent when these mothers work than when they do not. (Y051)

### Peer Relations

Adolescents at the middle economic level whose mothers work are more likely to be rejected by their peers than are those at low or high economic levels. (F108)

As regards peer-groups adjustment, adolescents whose mothers have worked when they were young show no difference from adolescents whose mothers did not work. (Y047)

### Personality Adjustment of Child

Maternal employment during various periods of the child's life (less than 4 years, 4 to 6 years, less than 7 years) has no relationship to the child's personality adjustment (as measured by the Minnesota Test of Personality). (B294)

### Personality of Mother

There is no difference between married working and nonworking mothers with respect to sociability (as measured by the Gordon Personal Profile), responsibility, or ascendancy. (G127)

### Personality Problems of Child
Health status, marital, sexual, and emotional adjustment, and number and seriousness of child problems do not correlate with employment or nonemployment of the mother. (S265)

### Personality Problems of Child (Defensiveness)
Sons of employed mothers are more likely to be defensive than are those of nonemployed mothers. (S265)

### Personality Problems of Child (Withdrawal)
There is a correlation between the employment of the mother and withdrawing behavior in the child. (R108)

### Power Structure of Family
The husband is more likely to be dominant in decision making if the wife is employed than if she is not. The contrary is also reported. (M215)

### Pregnancy, Attitude Toward
Mothers who do not work are not more pleased over pregnancy than are mothers who work (no matter whether they work only before marriage, before and after marriage, or after the birth of the child). (S191)

Previous work experience of the mother does not correlate with her acceptance of pregnancy or the mother role. (S265)

### Race
More Negro mothers than white mothers are in the labor force. (H018)

### Recreation of Daughter
Adolescent daughters of lower-class working mothers report fewer leisure-time activities than do those of middle-class working mothers. (G156)

Among middle-class adolescent daughters, those whose mothers work tend to engage in a great deal of organized and unorganized leisure activity. (G156)

### Remarriage
Remarriage is negatively associated with job holding of the divorcée-mother. (G157)

Remarried divorcées are less likely to expect to work than are those who have not remarried. (G157)

### Scholastic Achievement of Child
There is no correlation between maternal employment and educational competence (grade average) of the child. (S265)

Children of working mothers are likely to have lower intellectual performance in school than are children whose mothers do not work. (S265)

### Scholastic Adjustment
Sons of working mothers are no more likely than are sons of nonworking mothers to exhibit deviant behavior in school, to be leaders in school, or to conform to school expectations. (W151)

### Scholastic Adjustment of Child
Maternal employment during various periods of the child's life (less than 4 years, 4 to 6 years, less than 7 years) is unrelated to the child's adjustment in school (as measured by the Otis Quick-Scoring Form, the Stanford Achievement Test, and the Iowa Test of Educational Development). (B294)

### Sex Anxiety of Son
In lower-class families, if the mother is employed, the son is more likely to have sex anxieties. (M211)

### Sex-Role Behavior
Working mothers participate less in household tasks and their husbands participate more; they have less control over household activities and are less likely to endorse the traditional sex-role ideology than are mothers who stay at home. (S265)

### Sex-Role Definition of Daughter
Daughters of nonworking mothers are more likely to perceive themselves as "housewives" when they grow up than are daughters of working mothers. (H222)

Daughters of working mothers are more likely than are daughters of nonworking mothers to say that they plan to continue working after marriage. (H222)

Girls whose mothers do not work are more likely to sex-type various behaviors than are girls whose mothers are employed. (H224)

Girls whose mothers are employed are less likely to sex-type various behaviors than are adults; those whose mothers do not work are more likely to sex-type behaviors than are adults. (H224)

The mother's working outside the home or not working has no influence on the daughter's concept of the feminine role. (S252)

### Sex Status X Sex-Role Definition
(Among children 5–11 years of age) sons of working mothers are more likely than are daughters of working mothers to perceive the woman's role as involving employment outside of the home. (H236)

### Sexual Adjustment
Health status, marital, sexual, and emotional adjustment, and number and seriousness of child problems do not correlate with employment or nonemployment of the mother. (S265)

### Sibling Rivalry
If, in lower-class families, the mother is employed, sibling rivalry is less likely to be evident. (M211)

### Size of Family
Mothers in large families are more likely to be employed than are mothers in small families. (N057)

Employed mothers are more likely to have smaller families. (S265)

### Urban/Rural
Employed mothers are more likely to have urban residence than are mothers who do not work. (S265)

### Values
Mothers with jobs tend to believe that frustration is a basic part of life more than mothers without employment.

### Work Attitudes of Child
Children of nonworking mothers are more likely to perceive work as having unpleasant connotations for women than are children of working mothers. (H236)

Children of working mothers are more likely than are children of nonworking mothers to perceive work as having unpleasant connotations for men. (H236)

## EMPLOYMENT OF MOTHER, ADJUSTMENT TO
### X    Ordinal Position
The last-born child is more likely to suffer maladjustment as a result of the employment of his mother than are the children at other age spacings. (R108)

## EMPLOYMENT OF MOTHER, ATTITUDE TOWARD
### X    Age of Child
The younger the children, the greater the likelihood that men will disapprove of the mother's employment. (S257)

### Behavior Problems
Due to the mechanism of displacement, frustrations of mothers whose marriage prohibits their return to work correlate with behavioral problems in the child. (S265)

### Child-Rearing Practices
If mothers are in their *preferred* work or nonwork roles, working or not working makes little difference in their child rearing. (Y050)

### Class
Negative attitudes toward mothers who work tend to be strongest in those classes where the work is not an economic necessity. (G015)

Poorer-class mothers are more concerned about the effects of their working on their children than are better-off mothers. (Y047)

### Education
The likelihood of favorable attitudes towards working mothers increases with educational level. (S257)

### Employment of Mother
The children of working mothers are more likely to approve of their mothers' working than are children of nonworking mothers. (S265)

### Income
The more the mother's employment is based on economic necessity, the greater the likelihood that men will approve. (S257)

### Maternal-Role Adjustment
Mothers who do not work and do not wish to do so are more likely to be satisfied mothers and to be more successful in child-rearing practices than are mothers who are nonworking because of a "duty to mothering." (Y050)

### Mother-Child Relations
The greater the mother's guilt concerning her employment (feeling she is neglecting the child), the less satisfactory will the parent-child relationship be. (G127)

### Sex Status of Child
Girls are more likely than boys to approve of their mother's working. (S265)

### Size of Family
The more children a woman has, the more she sees her job as simply an economic necessity. (R117)

## EMPLOYMENT OF MOTHER/BROKEN HOME
### X    Juvenile Delinquency
Delinquency in girls correlates more with the variable of broken homes than with employment or nonemployment of the mother. (S265)

In intact homes delinquency is more likely if the mother is employed, but is not related to the mother's employment in broken homes. (S265)

## EMPLOYMENT OF MOTHER, DURATION OF
### X    Maternal-Role Adjustment
While employment of the mother initially produces poorer adjustment to children, the longer the duration of employment, the better the adjustment. (S265)

## EMPLOYMENT OF MOTHER/EDUCATION
### X    Child-Rearing Practices
Education of the mother is more highly correlated with differences in child-rearing practices than whether or not the mother is employed. (Y051)

In *nonworking* groups, college mothers are significantly more often rated high in independence training, in sensitivity, in consistency between principles and practice, and in clarity in limit setting; thus having higher mean scores on "adequacy of mothering." (Y051)

However, *working* groups differ only on ratings of sensitivity to child's needs (high school lower) and the father's being the stricter parent (college lower). (Y051)

## EMPLOYMENT OF MOTHER, EVALUATION OF
### X    Child-Rearing Practices (Chores)
Mothers who enjoy their jobs are less likely to give additional responsibilities to their children than are mothers who are not as fond of their work. (Y047)

### Child-Rearing Practices (Consistency)
Among working mothers there is more inconsistency in child rearing among mothers who are dissatisfied with their employment than among the satisfied mothers. (Y050)

### Child-Rearing Practices (Indulgence)
Mothers who like their jobs are more likely to be indulgent toward their children than are mothers who are not as satisfied with their jobs. (Y047)

## EMPLOYMENT OF MOTHER, POSTMARITAL
### X    Employment, Premarital
Premarital job experiences increase the tendency for mothers to seek employment after marriage. (Y047)

## EMPLOYMENT OF MOTHER (REGULARITY)
### X    Delinquency of Mother
Irregularly employed mothers of delinquent sons are more likely to have once been juvenile delinquents themselves than are either regularly employed or nonemployed mothers of delinquents. (S265)

### Employment, Attitude Toward
The irregularly employed mother is motivated to work less for economic reasons than to escape domestic and maternal responsibilities. (S265)

### Juvenile Delinquency
Delinquency in boys does not correlate with employment/nonemployment of the mother, but with irregular, as opposed to regular, employment on the part of mothers who work. (S265)

Children of mothers who are sporadically employed are more likely to be delinquents than are children of mothers who are regularly employed or who do not work at all. (Y047)

### Maternal Overprotectiveness
Women who are overprotective tend to have stable patterns of employment. (L163)

### Personality Problems/Delinquency

Delinquent sons of irregularly employed mothers are more likely to have emotional conflicts and are more likely to be truants at ten years of age or younger; nondelinquent sons of regularly employed mothers are more likely to manifest hostility. (S265)

### Personality Problems of Parents

A son's delinquency and a mother's sporadic employment both correlate with, and are caused by, the emotionally disturbed and antisocial characteristics of the parents. (S265)

## EMPLOYMENT OF MOTHER (SATISFACTION)
### X  Child-Rearing Practices (Consistency)

Among nonworking mothers clarity on limit setting is more characteristic of the mothers satisfied with not working. Dissatisfied mothers show more inconsistency between principles and practices. Control is an "issue" between mother and child for dissatisfied mothers. Lack of emotional satisfaction in relationships with the child is more frequent among dissatisfied than among satisfied mothers. High confidence in the mother role is more common among satisfied mothers. In general, mothering is inferior. (Y051)

## EMPLOYMENT OF PARENTS        X  Adoption

The more stable the employment of the parents, the more likely it is that they will adopt a child. (F117)

## EMPLOYMENT OF PARENTS, ATTITUDE TOWARD        X  Age of Child

The older the child, the more likely is he to perceive his working parent or parents as possibly unhappy with work. (H222)

## EMPLOYMENT OF WIFE        X  Birth Control

Wives who avoid pregnancy are more likely to be employed or in school than confined to homemaking alone. (P003)

### Children

Wives with no children are much more likely to work than are those who have young children. (L002)

### Chores

On the average, husbands of working wives do a greater proportion of housework than do husbands of housewives. (B208)

Couples are more likely to share a greater number of household tasks when the wife is employed full time or attending school than if she is employed part time. (G133)

Husbands and children of working wives are more likely to take an active role in household chores than are families of nonworking wives. (S257)

### Divorce

Divorcées are more likely than not to have always or usually held a full-time job during their marriages. (G157)

### Divorce, Initiation of

Wives who held jobs during their marriages are slightly more likely to be the first to suggest and insist on the divorce than are those who did not work. (G157)

### Divorce Process

Job holding by the wife during the marriage is not associated with a shorter period between a serious consideration to divorce and the actual filing of the suit. (G157)

### Education

Women with more education are more in favor of working after marriage than are women with less education. (S257)

### Employment of Wife, Attitude Toward

If the husband's attitude toward his wife's outside employment is positive, she is likely either to take outside employment or to consider it. (W150)

### Employment, Premarital

If a woman had a job before she married and continued working after marriage, she is likely either to take a job in the future or to consider it. (W150)

### Fecundity

Wives who work are more likely to be subfecund than are those who do not work. (F101)

Wives who have worked longest since marriage are most likely to be subfecund. (F101)

### Husband-Wife Relations (Companionship)

Husbands of nonworking wives are more likely than are husbands of working wives to believe that employment of the wife will lead to decreased companionship on her part.

Wives employed outside the home enjoy less companionship with their husbands than do wives who spend most of their time around the home.

### Husband-Wife Relations (Dependency)

When the wife works at a job away from her husband, she attains greater independence from her husband.

### Husband-Wife Relations (Hostility)

Wives who are employed outside the home are more apt to express their hostilities against their husbands than are wives who are not employed.

### Income

The lower the economic contribution of the husband to the family, the more likely the wife is to become employed outside the home.

When the husband's family of orientation is higher in income level than his own, the wife is more likely to become employed outside the home.

### Life Cycle

Family life cycle correlates more closely with the variations in wives' working than does age. (L002)

### Marital Adjustment

Couples in which the wife does not work or only works part time are likely to be better adjusted than are couples in which the wife works full time.

If the wife wants to work but does not, her level of marital adjustment will be lower. (G156)

Size of family does not affect the fact that nonemployed women have better-adjusted marriages than employed women. (N058, N063)

Women who have remarried after divorce, annulment, or widowhood are likely to have more successful marriages if they are employed than if they are not. (N058, N063)

The failure to segregate lines of achievement will result in competition between husband and wife which may be disruptive of the solidarity of the marriage. (P012)

Marital satisfaction is independent of whether or not the wife works. (S257)

### Marital Status (Female)
Women married once and living with their husbands are less likely to be in the labor force than are women who have remarried. (G011)

The proportion of women married for the first time in the labor force declines with the duration of marriage, while there is little difference between the labor-force participation rates for the several durations of marriage up to ten years for those living with the second or subsequent husband. (G011)

### Occupational Rank, Premarital
If a woman performed in an occupation previous to her marriage which required high educational achievement or specialized training, she is likely either to take outside employment or to consider it. (W150)

### Power Structure of Family
No significant differences appear in the dominance in family decisions as between the employed wife and the nonemployed wife. (B208)

"Husband-dominated" families tend to become more egalitarian as a result of the wife's working outside the home. (B208)

The wife's ability to influence family decisions increases more when she works among the lower than among the upper strata. (G156)

### Race
Negro wives are more often employed outside the home than are white wives.

### Role Behavior of Husband-Wife
The task of managing the family's money matters is less likely to be shared if the wife is employed full time than if she is not—the wife being more likely to take over financial matters. (G133)

### Role Definition of Wife
When wives work, they change toward equalitarian authority expectations. (B208)

On the average, husbands of working wives change toward equalitarian authority expectations. (B208)

### Values
Employment of the wife-mother increases the likelihood that both husband and wife will have an egalitarian rather than a patriarchal ideology about family life. (B231)

## EMPLOYMENT OF WIFE, ATTITUDE TOWARD
### X   Class
More lower-class husbands object to their wives' working than do husbands from other classes. (K150)

### Economic Role of Husband
When the dominance of the husband in large part depends upon the economic importance of his role, he will tend to inhibit the development of his wife's economic potential. (L064)

### Employment of Wife
If the husband's attitude toward his wife's outside employment is positive, she is likely either to take outside employment or to consider it. (W150)

### Income of Husband
As the income and occupational stability of the lower-class man increase, he is increasingly likely to insist that only he, and not his wife, work for gain. (P083)

### Marital Adjustment
In families where the wife works, the husband's disapproval of her working is related to a lower level of marital adjustment. (G156)

### Mate Selection (Intelligence)
Men who prefer women of equal intelligence are less likely to object to a woman having a career than are men who prefer women of lower intelligence than themselves. (H190)

## EMPLOYMENT OF WOMEN
### X   Authority Structure of Family
The greater the decline of the traditional authority of the family, the more likely it is that the wife may seek security through an independent career and/or through reinforcing her personal ties with her husband by a companionate form of marriage. (M198)

### Descent (Bilateral)
The employment of women reinforces the trend toward bilateralism. (P083)

### Divorce
The fewer the economic opportunities for women, the less likely the woman will seek divorce if divorce means supporting herself and/or her children. (D083)

The greater economic and social independence associated with employment of women is directly related to an increase in divorce. (K161)

### Education, Attitude Toward
There is no relationship between the daughter's decision to spend a good portion of her life in paid employment and the parents' attitudes about the purpose of college or the importance of education for their daughter. (S231)

### Education of Parents
There is no relalationship between the daughter's decision to spend a good portion of her life in paid employment and the educational level of her parents. (S231)

### Employment of Women, Attitude Toward
More husbands of nonworking wives oppose the employment of women than do husbands of working wives.

Husbands of working wives are less likely than husbands of nonworking wives to believe that children should be finished with school before the wife is employed outside the home.

### Fertility Values
Women who work are less apt to be seriously considering having more children than are women who are not working. (R121)

### Husband-Wife Relations (Companionship)
Husbands of nonworking wives are more likely than are husbands of working wives to believe that employment of the wife will lead to decreased companionship on her part.

### Husband-Wife Relations (Neglect)
Husbands of nonworking wives are more likely than are husbands of working wives to believe that if the wife is employed she will neglect him.

### Isolation of Nuclear Family
Salaried employment of women is likely to promote the isolation of the nuclear family from the patrilineage. (P083)

### Kin Ties (Bilateral)
The employment of women reinforces the trend toward bilateralism. (P083)

### Marital Status (Female)
Divorced and widowed women are more likely to work than are married women. (Y074)

### Power Structure of Family
As women seek employment outside the family, a shift in the authority pattern from one single dominant head to control by consensus occurs. (B033)

### Sex Relations
Husbands of women who work are more likely than are husbands of nonworking wives to admit equality of control in sexual relations.

### Sex-Role Definition
In lower-class groups where women are also gainfully employed, male authority is more likely to be based upon superiority in strength. (P083)

Children of working mothers are more likely to attribute work roles to women than are those of non-working mothers. (S265)

If a woman's husband accepts an obligation for child care and household chores, then she is likely either to take outside employment or to consider it. (W150)

### Tension Management
As competition pressures increase and the need for women employed in "expressive" occupations (secretaries, nurses, teachers, etc.), where their function is partly that of tension reduction, increases, the tension-reduction burden on the nuclear family is likely to decrease. (P083)

### Work Attitude of Mother
There is a significant relationship between the mother's work orientation (i.e., attitudes toward work and work history) and the daughter's decision to spend a good portion of her life in paid employment. (S231)

### EMPLOYMENT OF WOMEN, ATTITUDE TOWARD          X   Age
The older the child (range: 5–11 years), the more likely he is to attribute discomfort to the mother at leaving her children to go to work. (S265)

### Educational Values
There is no correlation between the job orientation of college girls and their parents' perception of the importance of an education. (S255)

### Employment, Attitude Toward
There is a direct correlation between the attitude of college girls toward future employment and that of their mothers. (S255)

### Employment of Women
More husbands of nonworking wives oppose the employment of women than do husbands of working wives.

Husbands of working wives are less likely than are husbands of nonworking wives to believe that children should be finished with school before the wife is employed outside the home.

### Homemaker Role, Substitutes for
The husband's opposition to employment for women outside the home increases to the degree that the work requires disruption of family role obligations for which adequate substitutes cannot conveniently be supplied. In the working class, it is more difficult to provide substitutes. (D060)

### Marital Status (Female)
Favorable attitudes toward women working tend to change to unfavorable attitudes when women are married and have children. (G015)

Single women are less likely than married women to see their employment as important for their sense of self-worth. (S257)

### Occupational Rank
The professional group is more equalitarian in its views on the propriety of employment of married women than is any other occupational stratum. (F009)

### Sex Status
Women are more likely than men to favor employment for women outside the home. (D060)

### Size of Family
As the number of children increases, the economic need for the mother to be employed outside the family increases; at the same time, however, the necessity that she stay at home becomes more acute. (R093)

### EMPLOYMENT, PREMARITAL          X   Employment of Mother, Postmarital
Premarital job experiences increase the tendency for mothers to seek employment after marriage. (Y047)

### Employment of Wife
If a woman had a job before she married and continued working after marriage, she is likely either to take a job in the future or to consider it. (W150)

### EMPLOYMENT (REGULARITY)   X   Child Support
The more regular the husband's employment record during marriage, the more likely is he to make his child-support payments. (G157)

### Divorce
Divorced couples are more likely to report an unsteady employment record on the part of the husband. (G157)

### Divorce Agreements
There is a positive relationship between the steadiness of the husband's work and his keeping the divorce agreements. (G157)

### Divorce Complaints
Among husbands in the same income group, job instability increases the claims by the ex-wife that nonsupport was a cause of divorce. (G157)

### Divorce, Initiation of
When the husband was not a steady worker, there is a greater likelihood that the wife both first suggested and continued to insist upon the divorce than when he was a steady worker. (G157)

### Marital Adjustment
Regularity of the husband's employment is positively related to marital adjustment. (G157)

## ENDOGAMOUS DEMES
**X   Kin Terminology (Structure)**
When the community structure is that of an endogamous deme, sibling terms tend to be extended to both
cross- and parallel-cousins. (M019)

## ENDOGAMY                              **X   Acculturation**
Resistence to acculturation is facilitated by the pattern
of community endogamy. (F014)

**Class**
Endogamy is more common in the lowest and the highest social strata. (B013)

Patterns of community endogamy are more likely to be
violated by members of the upper class. (W117)

**Cohesion of Lineage**
Lineage endogamy tends to occur in situations where it
is imperative to maintain lineage solidarity. (B087)

**Descent (Bilateral)**
Continuity can be maintained through bilateral descent
only if the kin-group is endogamous. (F068)

**Descent (Double)**
In double unilineal societies, the desire to keep the property inherited from both lines tends to encourage endogamy within the settlement. (H245)

**Descent/Residence (Matrilineal/Virilocal)**
When matrilineal descent is combined with patterns of
virilocal residence, community endogamy tends to occur. (S144)

**Headhunting**
Where community endogamy inhibits the development
of external kinship ties, headhunting is more likely to
occur. (H245)

**Inheritance (Bilateral)**
Bilateral inheritance leads to local endogamy. (H171)

**Kindred Systems**
Kindred groupings are more likely to be endogamous
than exogamous. (G156)

**Marital Stability**
The selection of a mate from within the kin-group is
conducive to marital stability. (H165)

**Property**
Disputes over property reinforce endogamy within the
kin-group. (R034)

**Rank of Husband**
The censure of the wife by the community at the infringement of rules of caste endogamy will be less
severe if the husband is of a higher status. (P020)

**Size of Lineage**
The unilineal group will be larger when the boundaries
of the endogamous unit are wide. (G056)

## ENDOGAMY (CASTE)          **X   Descent (Double)**
Caste endogamy must always be associated with sys-
tems in which the person is affiliated with both parents.
(Y053)

**Exogamy (Village)**
Village exogamy is the consequence of caste endogamy.
(G149)

## ENDOGAMY (CLAN)          **X   Marriage Payment**
With a breakdown in the pattern of endogamous marriage in the clan, the size of the marriage payment will
increase. (H165)

**Property**
Marriage to a man of an appropriate lineage will tend to
be instituted if the desire is to retain control over valuable properties within that lineage. (B108)

**Residence**
Clan endogamy tends to be directly correlated with the
localization of the kinship unit. (H165)

## ENDOGAMY (CLASS)   **X   Avoidance Relationship**
When class endogamy is common, affinal avoidance is
not strictly observed. (C094)

**Stratification**
The more rigid the stratification, the more stringent the
restrictions enforcing class endogamy. (D018)

## ENDOGAMY (COMMUNITY)          **X   Affinal Ties**
When patterns of community endogamy are violated,
marriages will tend to be into kinship units with preexisting affinal ties. (B111)

Affinal ties are less likely to link members of various
communities together in extensive interaction or to
complement agnation in societies where the primary
emphasis is upon local endogamy. (H222)

**Avunculate/Uxorilocal Residence**
Patterns of uxorilocal residence and avuncular guardianship produce a strong pressure toward community endogamy. (B111)

**Cohesion of Community**
Community endogamy tends to be associated with a
belief that the members of the village should constitute
a strong in-group vis-à-vis all outsiders. (G034)

**Community Isolation**
Isolated communities are more likely to be endogamous. (H139)

**Community Stability**
Community endogamy tends to be correlated with the
stabilization of community membership. (L063)

**Conflict**
Hostility between villages will increase as marriage patterns become increasingly endogamous. (P008)

**Descent (Patrilineal)**
As village endogamy increases, the emphasis on the
male line is lessened and the situation appears to be
favorable to change from patrilineality to bilateral social
organization. (P008)

**Descent/Residence**
When residence is patrilocal, yet important obligations
exist among matrilineal kinsmen, the resultant conflict
of (residential) interest may lead to village endogamy.
(S092)

**Economic Pattern (Land Use)**
Where a premium is placed on maintaining potential
access to as much land as possible, the value of marrying
within the local community is enhanced. (H222)

**Lineages, Number of**
When the village is composed of two or more lineages

or clans, marriage is usually endogamous as to village. (W054)

### Marital Stability
Marital stability is more likely to occur where shifts at marriage occur only within the community and do not dislocate the husband and wife from relatives and friends. (A072)

### Mate Selection
Unless there are specific rules of local exogamy, most marriages will take place between members of the same community. (M071)

### Moiety System
A moiety system tends to encourage community endogamy. (O005)

### Political Ties, Strength of
Political alliances beyond the community deteriorate as marriages are increasingly concluded within the same sib or village. (P008)

### Rank of Women
Village endogamy strengthens the status of women. (P008)

### Residence (Matrilocal)
There is an association between matrilocal residence in sedentary communities and local endogamy. (M019)

### Residence (Unilocal)
Conformity to patterns of unilocal residence tends to be directly correlated with the stability of patterns of community endogamy. (L063)

### Residence (Uxorilocal)
When residence is uxorilocal, the community will tend to be endogamous. (H147)

### Size of Community
Community endogamy tends to be correlated with the stabilization of community membership. (L063)

### Stratification
Community endogamy tends to support an egalitarian social structure. (F014)

### Subsistence Pattern
Patterns of community endogamy tend to be correlated with a marginal subsistence economy and a scarcity of land. (W069)

### Warfare
Under conditions of continuous intervillage warfare communities will tend to be endogamous. (W031)

## ENDOGAMY (ETHNIC)   X   Acculturation
Where the pattern of ethnic endogamy is strong, the ethnic group will tend to be resistant to acculturation. (S051)

### Ethnocentrism
The preservation of ethnic identity will be facilitated if there are restrictions against interethnic marriages. (D024)

Ethnic endogamy tends to occur when the members of an ethnic group regard themselves as culturally and racially superior. (H077)

A community which is conscious of its ethnic uniqueness will tend to be endogamous. (W073)

### Rank of Ethnic Group
The rate of ethnic endogamy tends to be high when the status of the ethnic group is low. (S102)

## ENDOGAMY (LINEAGE)   X   Ecological Conditions
Lineage endogamy tends to arise under specific ecological conditions. (S158)

## ENDOGAMY (TRIBAL)   X   Residence (Uxorilocal)
When the residential pattern is uxorilocal, marriage will tend to be within the political unit. (M032)

## ENDOGAMY (VILLAGE)   X   Marital Stability
Marital stability is more likely to occur when marriages are arranged within the village. (B302)

## ENGAGEMENT, AGE AT   X   Sex Ratio
Engagement age of women will tend to be earlier if there is a scarcity of women. (J008)

## ENGAGEMENT, DURATION OF   X   Class
The period of engagement or betrothal is longer toward the upper strata. (G156)

### Dating
A long period of acquaintanceship prior to engagement is associated with a longer period of engagement. (G157)

### Duration of Marriage
The longer the engagement period, the higher the average duration of marriage. (G157)

In the upper strata, a longer engagement period is more likely to increase the average length of marriage. (G157)

### Marital Adjustment
The longer the period of acquaintance in courtship and engagement, the higher the probability of a successful marriage. (B033)

Long engagement periods are correlated with reports of marital happiness. (G156)

### Marriage, Approval of
Among couples who divorce, the proportion of family members who expressed approval prior to the marriage (both the husband's and wife's family members) increases among those with a longer engagement period. (G157)

Among divorced couples, the proportion of friends (of both the husband and wife) who approved prior to the marriage increases among those who had a longer engagement. (G157)

### Marriage, Attitude Toward
Long engagement periods are associated with a complex of attitudes indicative of a more serious commitment to marriage in general. (G157)

### Premarital Pregnancy
Premarital pregnancy cases are associated with a short or nonexistent engagement period. (M243)

### Rank
The length of engagement is directly correlated with the status of the engaged couple. (H128)

### Warfare
Length of betrothal is likely to be sharply reduced during periods of warfare. (G139)

## ENGAGEMENT, STABILITY OF
### X    Geographical Mobility
Engagements are more frequently broken when the two persons are separated geographically. (B033)

### Homogamy (Culture)
Engagement is more frequently broken when the couple is culturally divergent. (B033)

### Premarital Sex Relations
Premarital sexual intercourse strengthens the relations of the engaged couple. (C023)

### Rank
Engagements between individuals of high status will tend to be more stable. (B181)

### Religion
Engagements between persons of different religious affiliations are more likely to be broken than are those of persons of like faith. (G157)

### Sex Status
Men are more likely to break an engagement if they have any doubts than are women. (P071)

## ENVIRONMENTAL PROBLEMS
### X    Parent-Child Relations (Affect)
When the family moves from a home context to a less familiar one, the social-emotional response of the father will become more negative; conversely, the social-emotional response of the mother will become more positive. (O035)

When the family moves from a home context to a less familiar one, there will be proportionally fewer positive social-emotional responses between father and son than between father and daughter; and, conversely, there will be a higher proportion of positive social-emotional responses between mothers and male children than between mothers and their daughters. (O035)

### Parent-Child Relations (Competition)
When the external situation is unfamiliar, so that the adaptive role of the family takes primacy, an adolescent son will be more apt to compete with his father than when the family is operating under familiar conditions and integrative behavior is more characteristic; conversely, in a familiar context (integrative), an adolescent daughter is more apt to compete with her mother than she is in an unfamiliar (adaptive) setting. (O035)

### Paternal/Maternal-Role Behavior
In an unfamiliar context where adaptive behavior is most characteristic of the family, the father's role will be more highly activated than will be the mother's; the converse is true in the familiar setting of the home, where integrative behavior predominates. (O035)

## ESTHETIC DEVELOPMENT
### X    Parent-Child Relations (Affect)
In Alorese society, a stifled emotional capacity resulting from lack of emotional ties between parents and child during childhood lessens esthetic development. (M202)

## ETHNIC ATTITUDES
### X    Child-Rearing Practices (Aggression)
Maternal punitiveness toward aggressive behavior is positively related to anti-Semitism in daughters. (W146)

### Child-Rearing Practices (Permissiveness)
If a mother's relations with her children are characterized as permissive, then there will be no correlation between her attitudes toward other ethnic groups and those of her children. (W146)

There is a negative relationship between a mother's permissiveness and her daughter's anti-Semitism. (W146)

### Intermarriage (Ethnic)
Intermarriage is more likely to take place among self-hating minority-group members than among minority-group members who take pride in their status. (B012)

## ETHNIC ATTITUDES/CHILD-REARING PRACTICES (AUTHORITARIANISM)
### X    Ethnic Attitudes of Child
Ethnic attitudes of children correlate with ethnic attitudes of mothers and do not correlate with authoritarian child-rearing practices of their mothers. (M222)

## ETHNIC ATTITUDES OF CHILD
### X    Authoritarianism of Mother
If a mother has authoritarian attitudes, her children tend to share her ethnic bias. (M222)

### Ethnic Attitudes/Child-Rearing Practices (Authoritarianism)
Ethnic attitudes of children correlate with ethnic attitudes of mothers and do not correlate with authoritarian child-rearing practices of their mothers. (M222)

## ETHNIC GROUP, SOCIAL VISIBILITY OF
### X    Intermarriage (Ethnic)
The likelihood of intermarriage increases as the social visibility of a group decreases. (M015)

## ETHNIC SUB GROUPS
### X    Intermarriage (Religious)
The intermarriage rate between Catholics and non-Catholics tends to be reduced by the presence of closely knit ethnic subgroups among the Catholics of a community. (T010)

## ETHNICITY
### X    Child-Rearing Values (Dependency)
Jewish parents are more apt to stress early independence training of children than are Italian parents. (M060)

### Divorce
Jewish females have a lower divorce rate than do non-Jewish females. (B010)

### Mental Illness
More siblings of Jewish than of Protestant background are likely to be mentally ill if it is the mother who is mentally disturbed, suggesting that Jewish mothers have more effect on their children. (S187)

### Name Changing
A greater proportion of Jewish females than of non-Jewish females may retain their husbands' names after divorce (U.S.). (B010)

### Parent-Child Relations (Ambivalence)
Jewish patients are likely to have affiliative tendencies toward their fathers and withdrawal and ambivalent hostile-affiliative tendencies toward their mothers; Italian patients are likely to withdraw from both their fathers and mothers; among the Irish, the males tend to withdraw from their fathers and have ambivalent attitudes toward their mothers, but the girls, on the other hand,

have affiliative tendencies toward their fathers, and, like the males, have ambivalent attitudes toward their mothers. (S187)

## ETHNICITY (JEWISH/ITALIAN)
### X    Child-Rearing Practices (Aggression)
Italians are less permissive of aggression toward parents than are Jews. (M060)

### Toilet Training
Italian mothers tend to be more severe than Jewish mothers in toilet training their children. (M060)

## ETHNICITY OF MOTHER/FATHER
### X    Sex-Role Model of Son
The father's ethnic background has greater significance in the formation of the son's role model than the mother's ethnic background. (E091)

## ETHNICITY/RELIGION/RACE    X    Intermarriage
Intermarriage is more likely to take place between ethnic groups than between religious groups and between religious groups than between racially defined groups. (B012)

Interethnic marriage is more likely to take place within the same religion than between different religions. (B012)

## ETHNOCENTRISM
### X    Child-Rearing Attitudes (Restrictiveness)
Fathers who express restrictive child-rearing attitudes have higher scores on the Ethnocentrism Scale than fathers who express permissive attitudes. (B227)

### Child-Rearing Practices (Discipline)
If the child is ethnocentric, he is more likely to view discipline as threatening, traumatic, overwhelming, and unintelligible. (B227)

### Child-Rearing Practices (Obedience)
Parents of ethnocentric persons tend to emphasize the submission of the child to the demands of dominating parents. (M222)

### Child-Rearing Practices (Punishment)
If a child's parents discipline him by physical punishment, the child is more likely to be ethnocentric.

### Cohesion of Family
When most or all of the emotional and cultural values of the individual person are derived from those of his family exclusively and conditioned largely within the solidarity of one family setting only, there is more likely to be an overevaluation of the in-group and a sense of arbitrary superiority over the out-group. (L167)

### Endogamy (Ethnic)
The preservation of ethnic identity will be facilitated if there are restrictions against interethnic marriages. (D024)

Ethnic endogamy tends to occur when the members of an ethnic group regard themselves as culturally and racially superior. (H077)

A community which is conscious of its ethnic uniqueness is more likely to be endogamous. (W073)

### Parent-Child Relations (Rejection)
Ethnocentric children are more likely to have parents who ignore them.

### Preferential Marriage (Parallel-Cousin)
Parallel-cousin marriage tends to be instituted in societies which emphasize ethnic exclusiveness. (G072)

## ETHNOCENTRISM OF CHILD
### X    Child-Rearing Practices (Authoritarianism)
Due to the mechanism of displacement, the more authoritarian the child-rearing practices of the parents, the more likely it is that the child will be ethnocentric. (M222)

## ETHNOCENTRISM OF CHILD, BY AGE
### X    Child-Rearing Practices (Authoritarianism)
Ethnocentrism in children correlates with the mother's authoritarian child-rearing practices more in adult life than in childhood. (M222)

## ETHNOCENTRISM OF MOTHER
### X    Child-Rearing Practices (Authoritarianism)
The more authoritarian the child-rearing practices of the mother, the more likely she is to be ethnocentric. (M222)

## ETHNOCENTRISM OF PARENTS
### X    Child-Rearing Practices (Discipline)
Parents who are ethnocentric (as measured by Adorno's E-Scale) tend to stress discipline and obedience, while those who are less ethnocentric stress love and understanding in child rearing. (K117)

### Child-Rearing Values (Restrictiveness)
Ethnocentric parents are likely to hold attitudes which place their children in subordinate and restricted roles. (K117)

## EVALUATION OF FAMILY MEMBERS
### X    Self-Conception
If a father rates himself favorably on several family attitude variables, he also rates his wife and child favorably. (B237)

## EXOGAMY    X    Acculturation
Rules of clan exogamy tend to deteriorate in situations of European contact. (R056)

### Adultery
Where there are exogamic restrictions against marriage, restrictions against extramarital intercourse tend to be established also. (L056)

### Adultery, Attitude Toward
Under exogamy, and in villages with high solidarity, intra-village adultery is defined as incest, but is admired by the native members of the village since adultery is against the in-marrying spouse. (F076)

### Authority Structure of Lineage
The existence of exogamous restrictions against affines prevents ambiguities within the lineage authority structure. (T039)

### Avoidance Relationship
Where patterns of avoidance exist between affinals, marriage with certain kinsmen will tend to be avoided because of its disruptive character. (E078)

### Clan, Importance of
Exogamic restrictions tend to be relaxed with a decrease in the importance of the clan. (N030)

### Cohesion of Clan
A relaxation in exogamic restrictions is associated with a deterioration of clan organization. (S115)

### Cohesion of Community
When community solidarity is strong, exogamic restrictions tend to arise. (E078)

Exogamic restrictions reinforce community solidarity. (R069)

### Cohesion of Kin-Group
The sense of identification with a kin-group will be stronger if sexual relations are prohibited between its members. (W115)

### Conflict in Kin-Group
In an exogamous lineage system, the tensions resulting from a conflicting allegiance to the families of procreation and orientation are intensified. (F020)

### Descent
As the control of the descent group over its members decreases, there is a narrowing of the range within which an effective prohibition on intermarriage operates. (C090)

Exogamic restrictions will tend to conform to the pattern of descent. (O023)

### Descent (Unilineal)
When the unilineage begins to dissolve, so does the rule of lineage exogamy. (H157)

### Economic Pattern (Feudal)
The development of a feudal system tends to result in the extension of exogamic regulations. (M080)

### Fecundity
Rules of exogamy are likely to increase the likelihood of female fecundity. (P083)

### Genealogical Proximity
The strength of exogamic restrictions will vary directly with the proximity of the relationship of the kinsmen. (C075)

The severity of the reaction to an exogamic violation will vary directly with the proximity of the relationship between kinsmen. (S081)

### Genealogy
When exogamic or preferential marriage restrictions are violated, kinship affiliations tend to be adjusted. (K082)

When exogamic restrictions are violated, the genealogy of the children will tend to be adjusted. (S156)

### Incest, Attitude Toward
The degree of censure of incest will tend to be higher in societies which have exogamic kinship units. (H133)

### Incest Taboo, Range of
Where there is a very large number of relationships which carry the incest taboo, violations of it are frequent. (E084)

### Kin Relations (Interaction)
The greater the intensity and frequency of interaction with relatives, the more likely are exogamous prohibitions (U.S.). (C131)

### Kin Terminology
With an increasing violation of exogamic restrictions, kin terminology tends to be abandoned. (R064)

### Kin Terminology (Bifurcate Merging)
Bifurcate merging terminology tends to be associated with exogamous unilinear groups. (M047)

### Lineage
In societies where lineages are found, marriage patterns will tend to be exogamous rather than endogamous. (G156)

### Marriage Payment
The violation of exogamic restrictions will tend to be severely censured if the marriage results in an inequitable adjustment in the marriage payment. (W097)

### Political Importance of Clan
When clans are politically important, exogamy is customary. (M168)

### Political Rank
Exogamic restrictions are more likely to be violated if the individual is of high political status. (L109)

### Population
Exogamic restrictions tend to be violated with a decrease in population. (E068)

### Preferential Marriage (Marriage Group)
Where marriage groups are precisely defined, the reaction to the violation of exogamic restrictions will be more severe. (C079)

### Religion (Totemism)
Totemic belief is associated with groups that are not specifically exogamous. (G045)

### Residence
Doubt about the correctness of a union tends to be reduced if the bride and bridegroom do not belong to the same residential group. (E084)

Exogamic restrictions are more likely to be infringed if the families concerned are not residentially propinquitous. (G097)

Adherence to exogamic restrictions is of greater importance when the kinsmen are of the same community. (H128)

### Residence (Neolocal)
When a marriage infringes exogamic restrictions, the couple will tend to establish neolocal residence. (C075)

### Segmentation
The violation of regulations of clan exogamy serves as an index of impending clan fission. (M129)

The clan tends to lose its exogamous character with successive divisions within the unit. (R034)

The violation of exogamic restrictions within the lineage is indicative of an approaching lineage segmentation. (T059)

### Size of Clan
Breaches of clan exogamy tend to occur in the clan of the greatest numerical strength. (B031)

### Size of Group
Out-marriages increase as the percentage of the population in each group decreases. (G156)

### Size of Kin-Group
Exogamous restrictions tend to relax as the kin unit increases in size. (A033)

The smaller the kinship group, the more likely it is to be exogamous. (G156)

Proscriptions against marriage with certain kinsmen are more likely to be violated if the size of the group is small. (L041)

The degree to which exogamic restrictions are extended is inversely correlated with the size of the kin-group. (M131)

### Size of Lineage
The ability to enforce exogamic restrictions is inversely correlated with the size of the lineage. (A032)

When the lineage is large, exogamous restrictions will be confined more to preventing the actual marriage of individuals than to attempting to prohibit illicit sexual relations. (A032)

### Social Disorganization
With the development of a situation of social disorganization, exogamic restrictions will tend to be violated. (M137)

### Stability of Kin-Group
The stability of the kin-group tends to be reinforced by patterns of group exogamy. (M137)

### Stability of Kinship Structure
The kinship structure tends to disintegrate with the violation of exogamic restrictions. (R067)

### Stability of Society
Exogamy leads to social stability under these conditions: when there is an accepted mode of regulating descent and a classificatory system of kinship.

### Subsistence Pattern (Pastoral)
Societies with pastoral economies tend to develop an exogamous clan structure. (M069)

### Urbanization
Traditional prohibition against marriage between individuals with the same surname tends to be infringed more in urban areas. (F035)

### EXOGAMY (CLAN)    X    Descent (Patrilineal)
Decreased emphasis on paternal descent may be associated with a breakdown of clan exogamy. (S192)

### Exogamy (Village)
Patterns of village exogamy are directly correlated with the institution of clan exogamy. (B302)

### EXOGAMY (COMMUNITY)    X    Conflict
The establishment of bonds of intermarriage between villages will tend to inhibit hostile relations between the communities. (E015)

The rate of intermarriage will tend to be higher if inter-village relations are not characterized by hostility. (K045)

### Economic Pattern
When it is economically advantageous to establish relationships in other regions or with other ethnic groups, community exogamy will tend to occur. (H076)

### Residence
When community exogamy prohibits marriage between residents of the same community, preferred sex and marriage partners will be found to be residents of nearby communities. (M019)

### Size of Community
In general, the smaller the residential, ethnic, or religious group unit, the greater the proportion of marriages contracted with spouses outside the unit. (B073)

Community exogamy is usually found in small communities, most of whose members are genetically related. (D057)

### X    Values
When the marriage pattern is that of community exogamy, cultural variation between villages tends to be reduced. (L066)

### EXOGAMY/DESCENT (PATRILINEAL)
### X    Kin Terminology
A change from merging to bifurcate merging terminology indicates the establishment of exogamous patrilineal organizations. (F010)

### EXOGAMY (INFORMAL)    X    Kin Ties
Exogamy is more apt to be extended further by people who identify relatives as their best friends than by people who report nonrelatives as their best friends. (C131)

### Sex Status
Women tend to try to extend informal rules of exogamy further than men do. (C131)

### EXOGAMY (LINEAGE)    X    Exogamy (Village)
Village exogamy is the consequence of lineage exogamy. (G149)

### Stability of Lineage
When a lineage lacks exogamy and has a bilateral kinship system of the Hawaiian type, it is less likely to endure. (G013)

### EXOGAMY/RESIDENCE    X    Kin Terminology
The importance of residence patterns as determinants of kin terminology is inversely correlated with the presence and strength of exogamic kin groups. (L061)

### EXOGAMY (VILLAGE)
### X    Affinal/Consanguineal Ties
Patterns of village exogamy are directly correlated with the tendency to regard affinal and consanguineal kin ties as mutually exclusive. (B302)

### Avoidance Relationship
There is a weak, but positive, correlation between the presence of exogamous communities and the severity of kin avoidance. (S079)

### Descent
Patrilineal kinship systems, which exclude overlapping obligational ties between affinal and consanguineal kinsmen, have a higher correlation than do matrilineal systems with patterns of village exogamy. (G147)

### Endogamy (Caste)
Village exogamy is the consequence of caste endogamy. (G149)

### Exogamy (Clan)
Patterns of village exogamy are directly correlated with the institution of clan exogamy. (B302)

### Exogamy (Lineage)
Village exogamy is the consequence if lineage exogamy. (G149)

### Geographic Mobility
Village exogamy is the consequence of territorial stabilization of kin-groups. (G142)

##### Residence

Patterns of village exogamy are directly correlated with territorial stabilization of kin-groups. (B302)

Village exogamy is the consequence of territorial stabilization of kin-groups. (G149)

## EXTENDED FAMILY         X   Alcoholism

Alcoholism is less likely to occur in the extended family system. (T110)

##### Economic Conditions

Where no one source of livelihood provides enough for a family to subsist, some form of extended family is likely to be found. (S090)

The persistence of extended families may be the result of poverty rather than of any cohesive force within the family. (S090)

##### Economic Rank

The extended family pattern tends to be more characteristic of groups with higher economic status. (L066)

##### Kin Relations (Security)

Highly structured, rigid, tradition-determined personal communities, such as the joint family of India and China or the rigid patrilineal systems of Africa, offer a high degree of reliance or security for their members. (H026)

##### Marriage Chances

When the extended family is the most important source of support and solidarity in a society, it is more likely that all family members are interdependent in regard to their marriage chances. (P083)

##### Oedipal Complex

The Oedipal complex is less likely to occur in societies in which there is an extended family pattern. (D057)

##### Property

The extended family tends to develop where immovable property constitutes a major form of wealth. (M019)

##### Social Mobility

Extended family systems tend to restrict the geographical and occupational mobility of males. (P083)

##### Subsistence Pattern (Agriculture)

The persistence of the extended family depends upon the population being rooted to the soil and isolated from divergent patterns of behavior. (B033)

##### Subsistence Pattern (Pastoral)

Pastoral economies are more likely to be characterized by an extended family structure. (M069)

The extended family structure tends to be associated with pastoral economies. (P024)

##### Urban/Rural

Rural families have a wider generational span than do urban families. (B033)

## EXTENDED FAMILY (BILATERAL)
#### X   Kin-Role Definition

With an increasing importance of the bilateral extended family in the economic sphere, other functions formerly assumed by clan members will tend also to be transferred to members of this unit. (L031)

## EXTENDED FAMILY, DISINTEGRATION OF
#### X   Sibling Ties

Fission of the extended family tends to be resisted if the brothers are uterine rather than half-siblings. (W056)

## EXTENDED FAMILY, IMPORTANCE OF
#### X   Economic/Ceremonial Role of Extended Family

The role of the extended family will tend to be a minor one when it lacks ceremonial or economic functions. (N017)

##### Subsistence Pattern (Agriculture)

When the economy is that of sedentary agriculture, the extended family tends to be emphasized. (E008)

## EXTENDED FAMILY TIES    X   Divorce Adjustment

Divorce is less disruptive socially and personally when an extended family pattern exists. (E083)

##### Neighborhood Relations

Extensive family connections are relatively incompatible with integration of the nuclear family into the neighborhood. (P083)

##### Residence

The greater the dispersal of the extended family, the more likely is a conflict between the ties of kinship and marriage. (M198)

There is no correlation between the dispersal of the extended family and the strengthening of the ties of marriage. (M198)

##### Social Mobility

Mobile persons have patterns of extended family relations more closely correlated to their former status than to that of the class they move toward. (S272)

The degree of extended family orientation tends to increase as the head of the household engages more and more in higher-status occupations. (S272)

##### Social Mobility of Women

Mobile women have a weaker orientation to their extended family than do stable ones. (S272)

## EXTENDED KIN RELATIONS     X   Descent

The larger kinship group is more likely to support the individual family (i.e., financial aid, settling political disputes, etc.) in a society where a strong organized descent system exists. (G156)

##### Divorce

Since upper-class families are more likely to have extensive and stable kinship networks, marital disruption within their ranks would be more likely to create problems in extended kin relations. (G156)

Divorce is less likely where it would threaten kinship relations. (G156)

Marital expectations that tend to focus on the larger extended family rather than on the relationship between husband and wife tend to reduce tension between spouses and, consequently, lower the likelihood of divorce. (G156)

##### Education of Wife

Men married to better-educated wives are more likely to have poor relations with their in-laws than are men married to similarly or poorly educated wives.

### Sex-Role Definition
The more segregated the family's conjugal roles, the more likely it is that each spouse can call on practical help from same-sex kin. (F106)

## EXTENDED KIN RELATIONS (INTERACTION)
### X Class
The greater the disparity in social class between kin, the less contact is likely between them.

## EXTENDED KIN TIES          X Class
The extended family appears to have a better chance of resistance to the forces of industrialization among the wealthy and official classes than among the poor. (B033)

The mobility of a lower-class family member is less encumbered than that of family members in other classes by a commitment to an extended family system. (G156)

### Cohesion of Family
The more the culture utilizes the extended family as a basic social unit, the greater the identification of the individual with the family group. (M166)

### Geographic Mobility
If the ideal of consanguinity is strong, the extended family will persist in spite of physical dispersion. (A013)

The less important kinship ties become, the more able are family members to be geographically mobile. (G156)

### Parent-Child Relations (Conflict)
In Western society, a small number of kin present who can act as buffers increases the potential for conflict between parents and children. (G156)

### Parent-Child Relations (Help)
Among working-class families, parental assistance (especially in the form of such services as babysitting and help during illness and childbirth) is more likely to be given by the wife's parents than by the husband's parents. (A066)

Among middle-class families, parental assistance to married children is as likely to be given by the wife's parents as by the husband's. (A066)

The wife's parents are more likely to give indirect financial aid (nonreciprocal gifts) rather than cash loans (so as not to usurp the son-in-law's position as provider) than are the son's parents. (A066)

## EXTENDED/NUCLEAR FAMILY
### X Authority Structure of Family
Parental control will tend to be stronger in extended families than in nuclear families. (F073)

### Child-Rearing Practices (Aggression)
Children living in extended families are slightly more likely to be punished for peer-directed aggression than are those living in nuclear isolated families. (M216)

Children living in extended families are more likely to be punished for mother-directed aggression than are those who reside in nuclear isolated families. (M216)

### Child-Rearing Practices (Restrictiveness)
Societies with extended families are more likely to be severe in their control over dependent, aggressive, and

sexual behavior than are societies with nuclear families. (W142)

### Dependency
The extended family is better able to care for the aged, ill, crippled, or infirm than is the nuclear family. (G156)

### Economic Cooperation
The extended family is better able to amass capital for an economic venture than is the nuclear family. (G156)

### Emotional Ties
The emotional ties between family members will be less intense in the extended family than in the nuclear family. (G156)

### Incest Taboo
Societies whose institutions are arranged around the anchorage and identification of individuals in the wider kin-group will make the final inculcation of the core (prohibition of sexual relations among nuclear family members) incest taboo at the early stage of puberty (8 to 10 years) by means of extrusion or brother-sister avoidance or both; societies whose institutions are arranged around anchorage and identification of individuals in the nuclear family will make the final inculcation of the core incest taboo by means of *verbal-symbolic* instruction, leaving the child within the boundaries of the nuclear family during the first stage of puberty. (C093)

### Industrialization
Populations that have shifted from the extended family structure to the nuclear family structure are more likely to have become adjusted to industrialization than are populations that have attempted to keep alive the old extended family. (K024)

The effects of industrialization on the family are more intensely felt when the shift from the extended family to the nuclear family takes place before the main period of industrialization than when it takes place after the main period of industrialization. (K024)

### Loss of Family Member
Death or absence of one of the adults more seriously impairs the effectiveness of the nuclear family than of the extended family. (G156)

### Political Influence
The extended family has a greater potential for commanding political influence than has the nuclear family. (G156)

### Population
Family autonomy tends to increase with an increase in population pressure. (S158)

### Socialization, Effectiveness of
The Western family, particularly the American (nuclear) family, should be more effective in the functions of early socialization and tension reduction than classical Western families or families found in preindustrial and/or nonliterate societies. (P083)

### Socialization of Child
The socialization of children takes longer in a nuclear family system than in an extended kin network system. (P062)

### Subsistence Pattern (Agriculture)
Extended families are associated with areas of spatially separated agriculture, while nuclear families tend to be associated with areas of localized agricultural systems. (A072)

## EXTENDED/NUCLEAR FAMILY TIES
### X   Social Change
With social class held constant, men who most accept the value of change are also most likely to support the nuclear form of intergeneration relationship (i.e., no necessary geographical propinquity, occupational involvement, nepotism, or hierarchical authority structure). (J033)

## EXTRAMARITAL RELATIONS          X   Dating
Among the various complaints made by divorcées, those who complain that their husbands were involved with other women have the lowest postdivorce dating frequency. (G157)

### Divorce Complaints
Divorcées who claim that their husbands' overspending was a cause of divorce are not likely to claim that another woman was also a cause of the divorce. (G157)

Divorcées who claim that another woman was a cause of divorce are not likely to claim that their husbands' drinking was also a cause of divorce. (G157)

Divorcées who claim that their husbands' neglect of homelife was a cause of divorce are not likely to claim that another woman was also a cause of divorce. (G157)

The divorcée who complains that "another woman" was a cause of divorce is also likely to claim desertion as a cause of the divorce. (G157)

### Divorce Decision
The stability of the final divorce decision is not related to whether either spouse was in love with another. (G157)

### Divorce, Initiation of
The wife is most likely both to suggest first and later insist upon the divorce when she is in love with another and her husband is not; she is least likely to suggest first and later insist when she is not in love but her husband is. (G157)

The husband is most likely to both first suggest and later insist upon divorce when he is in love with another and his wife is not; he is least likely to suggest and insist when he is not in love with another and his wife is. (G157)

### Divorce Process
When the wife is in love with someone prior to the divorce, the time interval between a serious consideration to divorce and the actual filing of the suit is lengthened. (G157)

Among the complaints made by the divorcée, the husband's involvement with another woman is associated with a shorter-than-average time interval between a serious consideration of divorce and filing suit. (G157)

### Duration of Marriage
The frequency of complaints by divorcées of other women as a cause of divorce increases among marriages of longer duration. (G157)

### Friendship
When the divorcée is in love with another man, she is less likely to keep her marriage friends during the separation and divorce period than when she is not in love with another man. (G157)

Whether the husband was in love with another woman is not related to the divorcée's maintenance of marriage friends during the separation and divorce period. (G157)

### Husband-Wife Relations (Punishment)
The divorcée is more likely to desire to punish her husband if he was involved with another woman than if he was not. (G157)

### Remarriage
Divorcées who are in love with another man during the marriage are more likely to remarry soon after the divorce than are those who are not in love with another man. (G157)

## EXTRAMARITAL RELATIONS, ATTITUDE
## TOWARD          X   Marital Adjustment of Wife
More happy wives than unhappy wives believe it undesirable for husband and wife to have had sex relations with each other before marriage, consider it essential that the wife be a virgin at marriage, and consider it essential that both spouses be faithful after marriage. (T074)

# F

## FAMILY-COMMUNITY RELATIONS
### X  Cohesion of Family and Community
Internal family solidarity and community cohesiveness increase to the degree that a balance is struck between the family's involvement in and isolation from the community. (T099)

### Personality Problems of Child
When there is a sufficient integration of the family into community organizations, the children are less likely to develop emotional problems. (B290)

## FAMILY/FRIENDS  X  Social Adjustment
Aid from friends is more highly associated with the divorcée's claims of having many or some opportunities to meet people than is aid from family members. (G157)

Divorcées who have help from both friends and family claim the most opportunities to meet people, followed by those who had help from either friends or family members, and lastly by those who had no help from either. (G157)

## FAMILY, INSTITUTIONALIZATION OF
### X  Cultural Evolution
A shift from dependence on biological patterns (instincts or drives) to cultural patterns (socialization) is associated with greater human involvement in the formation and operation of the family unit. (G156)

## FAMILY/NONFAMILY
### X  Political Attitudes of Child
The political atmosphere in an area is more likely to reduce parental influence on the political attitudes and behavior of the child when parents have deviant or minority opinions. (H244)

## FAMILY-SCHOOL RELATIONS
### X  Scholastic Achievement
Families who support the school are more likely to facilitate the performance of their children. (P083)

### Values (Familism)
Families are less likely to support the school if the inner culture of the family is very divergent from the culture of the school. (P083)

## FATHER ABSENCE  X  Achievement Motivation
Father-absent or mother-child households are associated with low achievement motivation. (M246)

In cultures where fathers tend to be very authoritarian, separation of the son from the father is likely to promote high achievement motivation if it does not occur so early as to promote the development of strong mother-son ties associated with a mother-child household. (M246)

In Turkey high achievement motivation is related to separation from the father. (M246)

### Age of Child
Due to increased domestic responsibility and lack of supervision, the lack of an adult male in the home is likely to have more negative effects as the age of the girl increases. (R108)

The younger the boy, the more likely it is that he will be negatively affected by the absence of an adult male in the home. (R108)

### Aggression
Father-present boys are more likely to give aggressive (doll play) responses to playmates than are father-present girls; among father-absent children, sex is not related to age-mate aggression.

Boys whose fathers are absent from home are less aggressive than are boys whose fathers are not absent. (H197)

When the father is absent from the home, there is a greater likelihood that boys will develop aggressive behavior. (M181)

Boys whose fathers are absent from the home are less likely to show doll-play aggression than boys whose fathers are present. Absence of father is unrelated to aggression in girls. (S228)

When the father is absent from the home, the boy is more likely to direct aggression against the parent dolls as opposed to the child dolls than when the father is present. (S228)

Absence of the father from the home is not related to the content of the aggression shown by girls or boys. (S228)

When the father is absent from the home, the daughter is less likely to direct aggression against the baby doll than she is when the father is present. (S228)

### Anxiety
When the father is absent from the home, there is a greater likelihood that anxiety will develop in the child. (M181)

### Behavior Problems
When the father is absent for long periods of time, his children more often develop behavior problems such as dependence on the mother.

### Breast Feeding
When the father is absent for long periods of time, children are more often breast fed.

### Child-Rearing Practices (Dependency)
In societies with a high percentage of mother-child households, the child is more indulged and rewarded in his dependency demands by the mother. (S079)

### Child-Rearing Practices (Setting Standards)
Mother-son families tend to lower stress on high standards of achievement for the son. (M246)

### Child-Rearing Values
When the father is away for long periods, the mother tends to demand from her children obedience and po-

liteness rather than happiness and self-realization. (L156)

## Class
Lower-class families are more likely to have women as the heads of households than are middle-class or upper-class families. (F003)

The mother-centered type of family structure is more common in Negro and white populations of the lower class. (P012)

## Climate
Mother-child households tend to occur more frequently in tropical regions than in areas farther from the equator. (M246)

## Dependency
There is a correlation between the lack of the continuous presence of the father in the home and dependency in the child. (B272)

No significant relationship exists between absence of the father from the home and dependency. (M181)

The absence of the father from the home increases the son's dependence on the mother. (M195)

If the father is frequently absent from the home for extended periods of time during the first three years of the child's life, it is more likely that the child will be overdependent. (S204)

## Employment of Mother
In families where the father's occupation takes him away from the home for extended periods of time, the mother is less likely to work outside the home. (G156)

## Father-Child Relations (Idealization)
If the father is away for long periods, the child will tend to idealize the father. (L156)

## Homosexuality
No significant relationship exists between homosexuality and the absence of the father from the family. (M181)

The fathers of sexually deviant homosexual boys are more likely to have been absent for extended periods of time than are the fathers of "normal" boys. (M209)

## Household Composition
Mothers who were raised in households in which there were no men for the first six years of their lives are more likely to develop households of their own in which there is no man present for the first six years of their children's lives.

## Identification with Father
Sons who have been separated from their fathers during the Oedipal period show weaker identification with their fathers during early adult years than do sons who were not separated. (L170)

The absence of the father from the home (separation or divorce) is associated with insecurity on the part of the son in his identification with his father. (L171)

## I.Q.
Children in families without a male head tend to have lower levels of intelligence than do children with fathers. (A065)

There is a negative correlation between paternal absence after the age of five and the ability (WISC) of the child. (M213)

## Juvenile Delinquency/Neurosis
Interruptions in the father-child relationship occur more frequently in delinquent than in neurotic children. (B214)

## Marriage Chances
Sons reared in homes where the father is absent are less likely to move toward courtship and marriage than are sons from intact families, except where the father's absence occurred after the boy reached the eighth grade. (S219)

## Maternal Overprotectiveness
In families where the father is away from the home for extended periods of time, the mother is more likely to overprotect her children. (G156)

Wives (of Norwegian sailors) whose husbands were absent for extended periods of time exceeded matched mothers whose husbands were not absent in being overprotective and stressing obedience and politeness (not happiness or self-realization). (M181)

## Mental Illness
Mental illness among females is more likely to occur if the father is absent from the family. (S187)

## Mental Illness of Child
The absence of the father may be less detrimental than his presence to the mental health of the child if he is too aloof or despised by the mother. (L123)

## Mental Illness of Child (Schizophrenia)
There is no relationship between the incidence of schizophrenic reactions in the child and the absence of the father during the child's first 20 years. (L144)

## Mental Illness (Schizophrenia)
Most fathers of aggressive, acting-out, "childish" schizophrenic adolescents began their participation in the life of the family after the mother-child relationship had developed during the father's absence (and, hence, were treated by the children as intruders). (S208)

## Mental Illness (Schizophrenia/Neurosis)
Schizophrenic and neurotic persons are more likely to have suffered the loss of their fathers during childhood than are normals. (M218)

## Mother-Child Relations (Hostility)
When the father is absent for long periods of time, the children are more likely to express hostility toward the mother.

## Mother-Child Relations (Sex)
Children who are raised in homes in which there is no father or father surrogate during the first six years of their lives tend to have mothers who are more sexually attached to them than do children in normal homes. (S079)

## Oedipal Complex
The fantasy image of an absent father (both idealized and sadistic) reinforces the inverted Oedipal complex in boys. (L170)

Sons who are separated from their fathers during the Oedipal period show greater Oedipal intensity during early adult years than do sons who did not experience separation. (L170)

### Peer Relations

Compared with girls and with boys whose fathers are absent from home, only boys whose fathers are present choose same-sex playmates more often.

Boys whose fathers are away from home for a length of time are less well adjusted among peers than are boys whose fathers are present regularly. This is not so for girls. (G156)

### Personality of Child

When the father is absent (as in sailor families), the mother is the source of the male child's main frustrations and his personality is likely to be either passive-feminine or phallic-narcissistic.

### Personality of Child (Maturity)

The absence of the father from the home (separation or divorce) is associated with greater immaturity in the son. (L171)

There is a direct relationship between the absence of a father from the home and a child's preference for immediate, rather than delayed, gratification (an indicator of level of maturity). (M207)

The absence of the father will not affect the maturity of the children of a delayed-reward culture such as Grenada (characterized by trust in economic affairs, i.e., long-term payments) as it does the children of an "immediate reward culture." (M207)

Norwegian girls maintain greater maturity than boys do after the absence of the father from the home; this difference is not manifest in the Caribbean culture. (M207)

Absence of the father leads to immaturity in the young child, but not in the child over 11. (M207)

### Personality of Child (Needs)

Boys whose fathers are absent from the family are less inclined to postpone gratification of their needs than are those whose fathers are at home. (B275)

### Personality of Child (Pseudomaturity)

When the father is absent for long periods of time, children are likely to develop a facade of maturity.

### Personality Problems of Child

When the father is absent from the home, there is greater likelihood that the child will become alcoholic, homosexual, or totalitarian. (M181)

### Personality Problems of Child (Oral)

When the father is absent from the home, boys are more apt to exhibit oral regression (thumb-sucking, nail-biting, smoking). (M181)

### Residence (Extrusion)

In societies with a high proportion of mother-child households, boys are more likely to move away from home at or before puberty. (S189)

### Scholastic Adjustment of Child

Absence of an adult male in the home is correlated with academic failure in the child. (R108)

### Self-Conception of Child

There is a correlation between the absence of an adult male in the home and lack of self-esteem in the child. (R108)

### Sex-Role Behavior

Boys who are reared in homes in which there is no father or father surrogate for the first six years of their lives tend to be more effeminate than do boys raised in normal homes. (B216)

In families where the father is absent, male children are slower to develop sex-role patterns than in families where the father is present. (B216)

There is a strong association between father absence and sons who behave like girls both in fantasy and overt behavior. (B251)

Father absence is associated with exaggerated masculine behavior on the part of the son. (B251)

When the father is absent from the home, resources for dependency are limited and therefore the child is both more dependent on the limited resources and more resentful of the dependency because of the limited satisfaction involved. He is thus both feminine in his dependency and aggressive in his reaction against this dependency. (M181)

### Sex-Role Definition

Absence of the father from the home is a cause of delay or distortion in the sex-typing process in the son. (S228)

### Sex-Role Identification

When the father is absent for long periods of time, the boy is more likely to develop a feminine sex identification.

Father absence is associated with cross-sex identification. (B251)

When the father is absent from the home, there is a greater likelihood that boys will have an unstable sex-role identification (by manifesting both feminine and aggressive behavior). (M181)

When the father is absent, male children are more likely to develop feminine components in their personalities. (M181)

When the father dies, greater sex-role identification instability (manifestation of both feminine and aggressive tendencies) develops in boys than when the father absents himself from the family. (M181)

## FATHER ABSENCE, ADJUSTMENT TO
### X  Sex Status

Boys are more likely to show maladjustment as a result of the absence of the father than are girls. (R108)

## FATHER ABSENCE, AGE AT
### X  Juvenile Delinquency

The older a boy at the time of the father's first (lengthy) absence from home, the more likely it is that he will become a gang member. (M181)

## FATHER ABSENCE, AGE OF CHILD
### X  Sex-Role Identification

When the father is absent from the home and the mother is affectionate and nondeviant in her behavior toward the son, the middle childhood period (ages 6–12) is most susceptible to the development of sex-role identification instability (both feminine and aggressive tendencies). (M181)

When the father is absent from the home and the mother is deviant in her behavior and not affectionate to her son, the age of the child at the time of father absence is not important in the development of sex-role identification instability (both feminine and aggressive tendencies). (M181)

## FATHER ABSENCE/PERSONALITY (PASSIVITY)
### X  Mental Illness of Child
Fathers of prepsychotic children tend to be passive or absent from the home. (M164)

## FATHER-CHILD RELATIONS
### X  Child-Rearing Problems
There is an association between the divorcée's claim that her children were too young to know or remember their father and her claim that there had never been any period where the children had been more difficult to handle. (G157)

### Class
Lower-class fathers are found to be less affectionate than middle-class fathers. (H011)

Lower-class fathers play with their children more than middle-class fathers, but middle-class fathers teach and read to their children more than lower-class fathers. (H011)

There is no class difference in the amount of caretaking by fathers. (H011)

Lower-class fathers of mentally ill children tend to be cruel and rejecting, while middle-class fathers are passive and ineffectual. (S187)

### Descent (Matrilineal)
Matrilineal descent patterns tend to weaken with the strengthening of the relationships between the father and his children. (E016)

### Descent (Patrilineal)
Filial piety is correlated with patrilineal descent. (F087)

### Juvenile Delinquency
Recidivists are less likely to have fathers who were comrades, and recidivists are less likely to pattern themselves after their own fathers.

### Juvenile Delinquency/Neurosis
Disturbed emotional relationships between father and child occur more frequently in delinquent than in neurotic children. (B214)

### Maternal-Role Behavior
Maternal mediation is more disruptive of father-child relationships in a nuclear than in a paternalistic society. (S216)

### Mental Illness
Mental illness is more likely to occur if the father resents the intrusion of the child. (L123)

### Mental Illness of Child (Schizophrenia)
Schizophrenic children are less likely to view their fathers as dominating than are normal children. There is no difference between normal and schizophrenic children and their perceived paternal strictness and restrictiveness of children's behavior. (K114)

### Moiety System (Matrilineal)
Bonds linking the individual with his father are more important in matrilineal societies which lack a moiety structure. (L070)

### Mother-Child Relations (Rejection)
Maternal rejection in early life is directly correlated with subsequent attitudes of disappointment toward the father. (N061)

### Remarriage
With remarriage or with increasing time since divorce, the proportion of divorcées wanting the children to see their father more decreases, while the proportion wanting them to see him less increases. (G157)

### Socialization, Agents of
Girls are more likely to show positive attitudes toward the father when the parents are the main socializing agents than when they are not. Boys show no differences in this respect. (R089)

## FATHER-CHILD RELATIONS (AFFECTION)
### X  Alcoholism
Alcoholism tends to be correlated with a father whose attitude is cold and dominating. (C122)

### Authority Structure of Family
When the father is remembered as a strong authority figure, daughters more than sons tend to recall him less often as being highly affectionate. (B297)

### Identification with Father
Fathers are more likely to be highly affectionate if they remember their own fathers as being so. (B297)

### Race Attitudes
Prejudiced males are more likely than unprejudiced males to perceive their fathers as being remote and stern as opposed to mild and affectionate. (A061)

### Sex Status
Boys are more likely than girls to attribute affective qualities to their fathers. (H201)

## FATHER–CHILD RELATIONS (APPRECIATION)
### X  Sex Status of Child
Fathers show more appreciation of their daughters than of their sons. (J026)

## FATHER-CHILD RELATIONS (AUTHORITARIANISM)
### X  Religion
Autocratic and authoritarian fathers are most likely to be found in large Catholic families, particularly in relation to older adolescents. (E100)

### Size of Family
Lower-class fathers are likely to establish autocratic or authoritarian relationships with their sons and daughters regardless of the size of the family. (E100)

## FATHER-CHILD RELATIONS (AUTHORITY)
### X  Authority, Attitude Toward
There is a correlation between the individual's attitude toward the authority of the father and his attitude toward impersonal sources of authority, such as the state, teachers, etc. (M214)

There is no relationship between the individual's attitude toward paternal authority and his attitude toward more impersonal, nonparental sources of authority. (M214)

### Paternal-Role Definition
The greater the child's conception of an ideal father approximates his actual father, the more successful will the father be in establishing authority.

## FATHER-CHILD RELATIONS (AUTHORITY/SEX ROLE)

### X   Mental Illness (Schizophrenia/Neurosis)

More schizophrenic than neurotic patients questioned their fathers' masculinity and authority. (M061)

## FATHER-CHILD RELATIONS (CLOSENESS)

### X   Aspiration Level

The higher a person's level of aspiration, the less frequently he confided in his father in childhood. (D001)

### Behavior Problems (Obedience)

There is a positive relationship between fathers who are cold, distant, and neglectful and mild disobedience in the child. (R100)

### Behavior Problems (Stealing)

There is a positive relationship between fathers who are cold, distant, and neglectful and children who steal. (R100)

### Behavior Problems (Thumb-Sucking)

There is a negative relationship between fathers who are cold, distant, and neglectful and thumb-sucking in children. (R100)

### Marriage, Attitude Toward

The closer the child with the father (and correspondingly distant with the mother), the greater is his doubt about his chances for a successful marriage. (L137)

### Mental Illness (Schizophrenia/Neurosis)

Fathers of lower-class schizophrenics tend to be regarded as more distant and punitive persons than do fathers of neurotics. (M061)

### Occupational Aspirations of Child

Students who have high occupational aspirations confide less in their fathers than do students with lower occupational aspirations. (E102)

### Personality of Child (Shyness)

There is a positive relationship between fathers who are cold, distant, and neglectful and shyness in the child. (R100)

### Personality of Daughter (Expressiveness/Instrumental)

Expressive personality traits in the daughter are associated with perception of the father as attentive and protective; instrumental personality traits are associated with perception of the father as cold, distant, and critical. (J026)

### Self-Conception of Child

Adolescents who report close relationships with their fathers are more likely to have high self-esteem and stable self-images than are those who describe these relationships as more distant. (R129)

When father-son closeness is controlled, upper-class boys are more likely to have higher self-esteem than are lower-class boys but the difference between them is reduced. (R129)

## FATHER-CHILD RELATIONS (CONCERN)

### X   Sex Status of Child

Fathers show less concern for their daughters than for their sons. (J026)

## FATHER-CHILD RELATIONS (CONTROL)

### X   Age of Child

During the elementary-school years, the father's control over the child declines and that of outside political authority increases. (H180)

## FATHER-CHILD RELATIONS (DATING)

### X   Sex Status

Fathers are more likely to oppose dating by their daughters than by their sons. (K161)

## FATHER-CHILD RELATIONS (DOMINANCE)

### X   Mental Illness (Schizophrenia)

Schizophrenia tends to be associated with a pattern of sadistic domination in the father's relationship with the child. (R115)

## FATHER-CHILD RELATIONS (EVALUATION)

### X   Mental Illness (Paranoia)

Paranoia is directly correlated with a perception of the father as weak and ineffectual. (N050)

### Personality of Father (Hostility)

The father's perceived negative feelings toward others (hostility, etc.) are correlated with his perception of the child as hostile toward others, even though the actual hostility of the child is not so related.

## FATHER-CHILD RELATIONS (HOSTILITY)

### X   Aggression

There is a correlation between degree of the father's hostility toward the son and the degree of the son's aggression toward teachers, peers, and parents. (B243)

### Behavior Problems

Father-child relations that are characterized by hostility on the part of the father are positively associated with antisocial behavior (e.g., stealing, truancy, temper tantrums, etc.) in the child. (R100)

### Father-Child Relations (Privileges)

Fathers who frequently deprived their sons of privileges tended to lack warmth for them, to be rejecting, and to be hostile toward them. (B213)

### I.Q.

Girls' intelligence (at school) is negatively related to their fathers' hostility. (B232)

### Personality Problems of Child

The greater the hostility of the father, the greater the incidence of personality problems (shy, anxious, withdrawn) in the child. (B232)

### Polygyny

There is a correlation between polygyny and the reduction of hostile paternal feelings toward the unborn. (D071)

### Sex Status

More male than female emotionally disturbed children have distant and hostile relationships with their fathers. (M197)

### Sex Status of Child

Girls see their fathers as more punitive and hostile than do boys. (H180)

### Sex Taboo, Postpregnancy

The unconscious hostility of the father toward the unborn child is a cause of taboo against coitus during pregnancy. (D071)

## FATHER-CHILD RELATIONS (IDEALIZATION)

### X   Father Absence

If the father is away for long periods, the child will tend to idealize the father. (L156)

## FATHER-CHILD RELATIONS (INTENSITY)
**X   Polygyny**
The father-child relationship will be less intense in polygynous families. (K061)

## FATHER-CHILD RELATIONS (INTERACTION)
**X   Homosexuality**
Fathers of homosexuals are likely to have given less than the usual amount of care (attention, love, training, friendship, affection, praise, and play) than are other fathers. (U004)

**Race**
Among the lower class, fathers of Negro children spend less time teaching and playing with their children than do white fathers. (G117)

## FATHER-CHILD RELATIONS (INTEREST)
**X   Dependency**
The greater the paternal interest in the child, the more self-reliant the child. (L150)

**Parent-Child Relations (Preference)**
The less interest the father has in the children, the more likely they are to prefer the mother. (L150)

**Self-Conception**
Paternal interest is not strongly related to self-esteem in children, except for the extreme group who reported that the father knew none of their friends; this group is distinctly more likely to have low self-esteem than those whose fathers knew most of their friends. (R129)

**Sibling Relations**
The greater the paternal interest in the children, the more likely they are to express ambivalent feelings toward their siblings. (L150)

## FATHER-CHILD RELATIONS (INTIMACY)
**X   Descent (Patrilineal)**
In a society with a strong patrilineal emphasis, the relationship between mother and child tends to be intimate, whereas the relationship between father and child tends to be restrained. (H105)

**Polygyny, Number of Wives**
The greater the number of wives the father has, the less likely he is to be intimate with his children. (M198)

## FATHER-CHILD RELATIONS (JEALOUSY)
**X   Mental Illness (Schizophrenia)**
Schizophrenia is likely to be associated with a paternal pattern of dependency on the mother which manifests itself as aggressiveness and jealousy toward the children as competitors for her attention. (R115)

## FATHER-CHILD RELATIONS (PERMISSIVENESS)
**X   Power Structure of Family**
Where the father is seen as dominant in family and child-rearing decisions, adolescents are more likely to view their fathers as autocratic than they are to view them as permissive or equalitarian. (B323)

## FATHER-CHILD RELATIONS (POWER)
**X   Sex Status**
Sons tend to be the objects of fathers' power assertion more than daughters. (H180)

## FATHER-CHILD RELATIONS (PRIVILEGES)
**X   Father-Child Relations (Hostility)**
Fathers who frequently deprived their sons of privileges tended to lack warmth for them, to be rejecting, and to be hostile toward them. (B213)

## FATHER-CHILD RELATIONS (PROTECTIVENESS)
**X   Identification with Father**
Lack of the father's concern with protection of his children leads to lack of identification by the children with their father. (M202)

## FATHER-CHILD RELATIONS (PUNISHMENT)
**X   Aspiration Level**
People with high levels of aspiration were more fearful of punishment from their fathers in childhood than were those with low levels of aspiration. (D001)

## FATHER-CHILD RELATIONS (REJECTION)
**X   Alcoholism**
The more rejecting the father is of the son, the more likely that the latter will become an alcoholic. (M195)

Alcoholic fathers are more likely than nonalcoholic fathers to reject their sons. (M195)

**Criminality**
The more rejecting the father is of the son, the more likely it is that the latter will become a criminal. (M195)

**Homosexuality**
Homosexuality is more likely to occur where the father is perceived to have abandoned the child and there is a consequent identification with the mother. (F085)

**Mental Illness**
Mental illness tends to be associated with a cruel and rejecting father. (S187)

**Mental Illness of Child**
Fathers of prepsychotics tend to be rejecting toward the child. (M164)

**Mental Illness (Schizophrenia)**
Fathers of schizophrenics are more likely to be rejecting than are fathers of normals. (K125)

Schizophrenia tends to be directly correlated with a father who is cruel and rejecting. (L123)

**Self-Conception of Child**
If a father has expressed feelings of rejection for his child, the child will not manifest a corresponding feeling of self-rejection. (C104)

**Self-Conception of Father**
A father with strong feelings of self-rejection will tend to regard his son as a model of himself and reject him proportionately. (C104)

## FATHER-CHILD RELATIONS (SEX)
**X   Mental Illness (Schizophrenia)**
Schizophrenia tends to be correlated with a fear of erotic interest in the father. (N061)

## FATHER-CHILD RELATIONS (SUPPORTIVE)
**X   Class**
Middle-class fathers are more likely than working-class fathers to be supportive of their children. (R129)

Middle-class boys are considerably more likely than working-class boys to have supportive fathers, but middle-class girls are only slightly, if at all, more likely than working-class girls to have supportive fathers; the same relationship exists when father-child relationships are compared between upper- and lower-class boys and girls. (R129)

## FATHER-CHILD RELATIONS (VISITATION AFTER DIVORCE)        X    Child-Rearing Problems
When the divorcée claims that the children were easier to handle after the ex-husband's visits, she is more likely to say that he should visit more frequently; if they were harder to handle, she is more likely to want the ex-husband's visits to be less frequent. (G157)

## FATHER-CHILD RELATIONS (WARMTH)
### X    Identification with Father
The stronger the identification of adolescent boys with their fathers, the more likely it is that they view their fathers as highly nurturant and rewarding. (M183)

### Mental Illness (Schizophrenia/Neurosis)
In the lower class, more fathers of schizophrenics than of neurotics were regarded by the child as distant and punitive persons. (M197)

### Personality Problems of Child
If the father adopts an autocratic attitude and lacks a warm parental concern, the child develops personality problems. (P070)

## FATHER-DAUGHTER RELATIONS
### X    Social Mobility Aspirations of Daughter
Female mobility aspirants are more likely than female nonaspirants to perceive their relationship with their fathers as depriving. (R101)

## FATHER-DAUGHTER RELATIONS (ADVICE)
### X    Juvenile Delinquency
Girls who always consult their fathers on sexual problems are more likely than those who turn to both parents to be delinquents. (N057)

## FATHER-DAUGHTER RELATIONS (AFFECTION)
### X    Scholastic Achievement
As measured by the PARI, fathers of daughters who are poor academically are more likely to avoid expressions of affection than are fathers of daughters who do well academically. (S230)

## FATHER-DAUGHTER RELATIONS (AGGRESSION)
### X    Conformity
Expressed aggression toward the father by the daughter is associated with nonconformity to authority patterns. (L136)

## FATHER-DAUGHTER RELATIONS (ALIENATION)
### X    Paternal Role (Authority)
Abdication of the father from his authority role results in his daughter's emotional alienation. (B297)

## FATHER-DAUGHTER RELATIONS (AUTHORITY)
### X    Mother-Daughter Relations (Authority)
When one parent is highly authoritative toward the daughter, the other parent is not. (B260)

## FATHER-DAUGHTER RELATIONS (CONFLICT)
### X    Mother-Daughter Relations (Conflict)
At puberty mother-daughter conflicts are more likely than are father-daughter conflicts in the family. (L148)

From the ages of 11 to 17 the amount of conflict or disharmony between the mother and the daughter is almost exactly complementary to that between father and daughter (i.e., an increase in one will be accompanied by a decrease in the other). (L148)

## FATHER-DAUGHTER RELATIONS (CONSISTENCY)
### X    Mental Illness
Mental illness is more likely to occur when the allegiance of the daughter is with the father, particularly if inconsistent, rather than with the mother. (L123)

## FATHER-DAUGHTER RELATIONS (EVALUATION)
### X    Employment of Mother
Where the mother is employed, the daughter's evaluation of the father tends to be diminished. (M058)

## FATHER-DAUGHTER RELATIONS (FAVORITISM)
### X    Employment of Mother
Daughters of working mothers are more likely to attribute preference for a female child to the father than are daughters of nonworking mothers. (H181)

## FATHER-DAUGHTER RELATIONS (INTERACTION)
### X    Mother-Daughter Relations (Interaction)
At puberty there is more interaction, both harmonious and disharmonious, between mothers and daughters than between fathers and daughters. (L148)

## FATHER-DAUGHTER RELATIONS (REJECTION)
### X    Superego Formation
There is no association between the father's rejection or acceptance of his daughter and the daughter's level of conscience development (U.S.). (S191)

## FATHER-DAUGHTER RELATIONS (SEX)
### X    Frigidity
Frigidity in women is associated with a defense mechanism against unresolved sexual feelings about the father.

### Incest (Father-Daughter)
Incestuous fathers are more likely than typical fathers to play with their daughters sexually; they do this long before incest occurs. (W123)

## FATHER/MOTHER ABSENCE        X    Illegitimacy
Absence of the father is more closely associated with illegitimacy than is the absence of the mother. (G156)

## FATHER-SON RELATIONS        X    Acculturation
Under (Western) acculturation the father-son tie in a matrilineal society emerges into greater importance. (F073)

### Authoritarianism
Poor father-son relations tend to produce an authoritarian orientation in the son. (L179)

### Class
Middle-class men are more likely to be work oriented and to reject both strong family ties in general and strong ties with their fathers; this is in contrast with men from upper-class families, who are less oriented toward work as a field of accomplishment, have stronger positive family feelings, and respect their fathers more. (L115)

### Descent
Kinship systems where the father-son tie is dominant are patrilineal, patrilocal, and, by and large, patriarchal. (H172)

### Education of Husband
The higher the educational level of a man, the more likely it is that his relations with his father are good. (K089)

### Identification with Father
The degree of identification with the father is positively related to the son's perception of his father as a gratifying individual. (P076)

### Maternal Overprotectiveness
In families characterized by maternal overprotection, the father-son relationship is one of indifference or impatience, though not overtly one of hostility. (L163)

### Personality of Son (Optimism)
Poor father-son relations tend to produce in the son a pessimistic outlook on the future of the social order. (L179)

### Political Interest of Son
Poor father-son relations tend to produce low political information and interest in the son. (L179)

### Scholastic Achievement
Boys with primary neurotic learning inhibitions (poor learning not associated with other behavior or personality problems) are likely to have fathers who see them as competitors for the mothers' affection and who, therefore, deprecate their achievements. (G143)

### Sex-Role Definition
The more masculine the sex typing of the adolescent boy, the more likely it is that he will perceive his relationship with his father as favorable. (M220)

There is no correlation between the degree of masculinity of the adolescent boy and the nature of his relationship with his father. (M220)

### Structure of Family
Where the father-son axis is emphasized, the basic kin unit is the patrilineal extended family. (H172)

## FATHER-SON RELATIONS (ACCEPTANCE)
### X   Sex Anxiety of Father
Fathers who are highly anxious about sex are less likely to be acceptant of their sons than are fathers who are low in sex anxiety. (B213)

## FATHER-SON RELATIONS (AFFECTION)
### X   Achievement Motivation
Sons who have received insufficient paternal affection are lower in achievement needs than are sons who have received adequate paternal affection. (M204)

### Aggression
There is a negative correlation between aggressiveness of the son and the amount of time spent in affectionate interaction with the father. (B243)

### Child-Rearing Practices (Rewards)
Among aggressive boys, the use of tangible rewards by the father is positively correlated with the amount of affectionate interaction with the father in early childhood; among normals, these factors are negatively related. (B243)

### Descent (Matrilineal)
The relationship between father and son in matrilineal societies is more likely to be characterized by affection and less tension than in patrilineal societies. (F074)

### Father-Son Relations (Closeness)
Sons who have received insufficient paternal affection are less likely than sons who have received adequate paternal affection to prefer their fathers as spare-time companions and persons to whom they would confide secrets. (M204)

### Father-Son Relations of Father
Fathers who remember their fathers as having been affectionate tend to act in a similar way toward their own children. (B260)

### Friendship
Sons who have received insufficient paternal affection desire a greater number of friends than do sons who have received adequate paternal affection. (M204)

Sons whose relations with their fathers are characterized by insufficient paternal affection have fewer friends than do those who have received adequate paternal affection. (M204)

### Identification with Father
The more warm and affectionate the father, the more likely the son's identification with him. (M183)

### Juvenile Delinquency
Lack of paternal affection contributes indirectly to juvenile delinquency.

If an affectionate relationship is lacking between the father and the son, it is more likely that the child will become delinquent. (M194)

### Marital Adjustment
Marriages generally need less dominant-submissive adjustment when the male has had close affectionate ties with his own father. (T092)

### Mother-Son Relations (Affection)
The strength of the transferred attachment to the father is in direct proportion to the strength of the earlier attachment to the mother. (D076)

### Occupational Aspirations of Son
Among boys who are independent in decision making, there is no relationship between paternal love and occupational aspirations of the sons. (E102)

Among boys who are reared permissively by their fathers, high paternal love is more likely than low paternal love to be associated with high occupational aspirations in the sons. (E102)

### Parent-Son Relations
Sons who have received insufficient paternal affection are more likely to feel unjustly treated by their parents than are sons who have received adequate paternal affection. (M204)

### Parent-Son Relations (Affection)
Sons who have received insufficient paternal affection are less likely to feel loved by their parents than are sons who have received adequate paternal affection. (M204)

### Personality of Father (Antisocial)
Insufficient paternal affection is associated with the son's perception of his father as unsocial or antisocial. (M204)

### Personality of Son
Sons who have received insufficient paternal affection are more unhappy and less calm than are those who have received adequate paternal affection. (M204)

Sons who have received insufficient paternal affection are more likely to feel dominated by a hostile, unfriendly, and controlling environment than are sons who have received adequate paternal affection. (M204)

### Personality of Son (Hostility)
Sons who have received insufficient paternal affection have more hostile attitudes toward others than do sons who have received adequate paternal affection. (M204)

### Personality of Son (Power)
Sons who have received insufficient paternal affection have a greater need to control and manipulate others than do sons who have received adequate paternal affection. (M204)

### Role in Family
Sons who have received insufficient paternal affection are less likely to give affection and support to their families than are sons who have received adequate paternal affection. (M204)

### Sex-Role Identification
If a father is warm, affectionate, and rewarding, the son is likely to develop strong masculine attitudes and to identify with his father. (M204)

### Sexual Interest
Sons who have received sufficient paternal affection are more able to extend affection to members of the opposite sex than are sons who have received insufficient paternal affection. (M204)

Sons who have received sufficient paternal affection show a greater interest in the opposite sex than do sons who have received insufficient paternal affection. (M204)

### Social Adjustment of Son
Sons whose relations with their fathers are characterized by insufficient paternal affection are less adjusted socially than are sons who have received adequate paternal affection. (M204)

## FATHER-SON RELATIONS (AFFECTION/POWER)
### X Occupational Aspirations of Son
Among boys who are dependent in decision making, high paternal love is associated with high occupational aspirations, more so under the condition of permissive paternal power than of autocratic paternal power. (E102)

## FATHER-SON RELATIONS (AID)
### X Descent (Matrilineal/Patrilineal)
The father in a patrilineage is more able to help his sons (offering gifts and bequeathing some possessions) than he is in a matrilineage. (G156)

## FATHER-SON RELATIONS (AMBIVALENCE)
### X Sex-Role Definition (Inconsistency)
A changing male image in which the child is adored yet the image of the father is despotic and godlike will tend to result in an ambivalent attitude of love and hatred, submissiveness and defiance on the part of the male child toward his father. (T107)

## FATHER-SON RELATIONS (APPROVAL)
### X Deviance
Fathers whose sons are not deviant are more likely to approve their sons' behavior than are fathers whose sons are deviant. (W137)

## FATHER-SON RELATIONS (CLOSENESS)
### X Authority Structure of Family
The loss of paternal authority, especially in the allocation of work, increases the closeness between father and son in the modern era. (T087)

### Descent (Matrilineal)
The intensity of the affective relationship between father and son is inversely associated with a matrilineal system. (F092)

### Descent (Matrilineal/Patrilineal)
The father is more able to have close emotional ties with his son in a patrilineage than in a matrilineage. (G156)

### Father-Son Relations (Affection)
Sons who have received insufficient paternal affection are less likely than sons who have received adequate paternal affection to prefer their fathers as spare-time companions and persons to whom they would confide secrets. (M204)

### Marital Adjustment
The husband's close attachment to his father in family orientation is correlated with reports of marital happiness in the family of procreation. (G156)

### Occupational Choice
The closer the emotional bond between the father and son, the closer the correspondence between the son's vocational interests and the father's occupation. (C110)

## FATHER-SON RELATIONS (COMPETITION)
### X Economic Level (Opportunities)
The open expression of competition between father and son is more likely to occur when economic and political opportunities are scarce in subsistence societies. (G116)

## FATHER-SON RELATIONS (CONFLICT)
### X Authority Structure of Family
When the father has absolute authority over his children, tension and conflict will tend to characterize the father-son relationship. (B107)

### Descent (Matrilineal)
Tension between father and son will be lower in societies with matrilineal descent. (M226)

### Descent (Matrilineal/Patrilineal)
There is greater potential for strain in the father-son relationship in a matrilineage than in a patrilineage since the father's daily interaction is with his sons while his property goes to his sister's sons. (G156)

### Descent (Patrilineal)
There will be greater tension in the father-son relationship in patrilineal than in matrilineal societies. (F074)

### Inheritance (Dual)
In the community in which property is divided between the patriclan and the matriclan, the relationship of a man with his father is less marked by conflict. (G111)

### Juvenile Delinquency
Juvenile delinquency in the boy is associated with conflicts with the father figure and an unconscious wish to displace him with the mother, resulting from unresolved disturbances with the mother during childhood. (B233)

### Status in Family
When the status of the married son within the extended family is ambiguous, the father-son relationship tends to be characterized by conflict and tension. (B107)

## FATHER-SON RELATIONS (CONTROL)
### X Achievement Motivation
Strong paternal control, allowing little autonomy of investigation, inhibits high achievement motivation in the son. (B275)

## FATHER-SON RELATIONS (DEFERENCE)
### X Husband-Wife Relations (Deference)
When the father receives marked deference from the

son, he also tends to receive marked deference from the mother. (S189)

## FATHER-SON RELATIONS (DEPENDENCY)
### X    Occupational Aspirations of Son
Sons of autocratic fathers are less likely than those whose fathers allow and encourage independent decision making to have high occupational aspirations. (E102)

## FATHER-SON RELATIONS (DOMINANCE)
### X    Drug Addiction
Where fathers are prominent members of a family, they will tend, in the case of the drug addict, to be severe and dominating. (F090)

### Personality of Son (Realism)
Sons who view themselves as highly dependent on and dominated by their fathers have a more realistic view of the world; those who do not feel dominated or dependent are more likely to be afraid of or to avoid facing reality. (M204)

## FATHER-SON RELATIONS (EMOTIONAL ATTACHMENT)    X    Cohesion of Family
When the son fails to establish a common emotional bond with the father, it is almost impossible for the family to continue as a functioning and perpetuate unit after the death of the father. (C024)

## FATHER-SON RELATIONS (EVALUATION)
### X    Employment of Mother
In lower-class families, it is more likely that the father-son relationship will be viewed unfavorably by the son if the mother is employed than if she is not. (M211)

### Marital Adjustment
Marital happiness is directly related to the congruence between the husband's self-perception and his perception of his father. (T092)

## FATHER-SON RELATIONS (HOSTILITY)
### X    Aggression
Aggressive adolescent boys feel more hostility toward their fathers than do control boys. (B213)

### Descent (Matrilineal)
In a matrilineal system ego is more likely to feel hostility toward the mother's brother than toward the father. (G055)

### Juvenile Delinquency
Juvenile delinquent boys are more likely to be critical and resentful of their fathers than are nondelinquents. (S229)

### Mental Illness of Child
Mental illness is more likely to occur in males when the hostility of the father is turned against the child. (L123)

### Personality Adjustment of Son
Normal subjects (soldiers) are likely to regard their fathers' behavior toward them more favorably than are neuropsychiatric subjects, who tend to recall their fathers as hostile and rejecting (Schaefer's Report of Parental Behavior Inventory—RPBI). (V034)

## FATHER-SON RELATIONS, IMPORTANCE OF
### X    Political Structure
Where the father-son tie is central, overall national states with centralized governments exist; submission to parental authority is consistent with similar ties with the wider government. (H172)

### Religion
Societies in which the father-son relationship is stressed will tend to be polytheistic. (H172)

## FATHER-SON RELATIONS (INTERACTION)
### X    Aggression
Fathers of aggressive male adolescents spend less time with their sons than do fathers of control groups. (No difference between mothers of both groups.) (B213)

### Sex-Role Identification
The greater the interaction between father and son and the more active the role taken by the father in his son's upbringing, the stronger the masculine identification of the boy. (M183)

## FATHER-SON RELATIONS (LOYALTY)
### X    Cohesion of Society
The moral disintegration of society is correlated with expressions of son-father disloyalty. (G012)

## FATHER-SON RELATIONS (OBEDIENCE)
### X    Descent (Matrilineal/Patrilineal)
The father in a matrilineage is less able to command obedience from his sons than is the father in a patrilineage. (G156)

## FATHER-SON RELATIONS OF FATHER
### X    Father-Son Relations (Affection)
Fathers who remember their fathers as having been affectionate tend to act in a similar way toward their own children. (B260)

## FATHER-SON RELATIONS (PHYSICAL ABUSE)
### X    Sociopathic Personality
Physical abuse by the father is not related to the development of sociopathic personality in the son. (O032)

## FATHER-SON RELATIONS (PUNISHMENT)
### X    Identification with Father
The more punitive and threatening the father, the more likely is the son to identify with him. (M183)

## FATHER-SON RELATIONS (PUNISHMENT/REWARD)
### X    Sex-Role Identification
The more masculine and father-identified the boy, the more likely he is to perceive the father as both highly rewarding and highly punitive. (M183)

## FATHER-SON RELATIONS (REJECTION)
### X    Aggression
Fathers of aggressive male adolescents are more distant and cold toward their sons as compared with fathers of control groups, who are more friendly and pleasant toward their sons. (B213)

### Behavior Problems
"Problem" sons are more likely than normal sons to perceive their fathers to be more harsh and rejecting than their mothers. (V038)

### Criminality
Boys whose fathers are criminals are less likely to become criminals if accepted by their fathers than if rejected by them. (H208)

Crime rates are highest among boys whose fathers have rejected them. (M199)

### Homosexuality
Fathers of sexually deviant (homosexual) boys are more likely to have rejected their sons than are fathers of "normal" boys. (M209)

### Mental Illness (Schizophrenia)

Good premorbid schizophrenics (good general functioning before onset of illness) perceive their fathers as having been more rejecting than do poor premorbid schizophrenics or normal subjects. (G127)

### Sex Anxiety

There is a correlation between the father's sex anxiety and his rejection of the son. (B243)

### Superego Formation

Boys who have fathers who are rejecting have lower conscience development then do boys of accepting fathers (U.S.). (S191)

## FATHER-SON RELATIONS (REWARD/PUNISHMENT)
### X    Identification with Father

The stronger the boy's identification with his father, the more likely is he to perceive him as both rewarding and punitive. (A060)

## FATHER-SON RELATIONS (STRICTNESS)
### X    Personality Adjustment of Son

Withdrawal from an extremely punitive and harsh father may favor, rather than retard, personality adjustment in the son. (M204)

## FATHER-SON RELATIONS (SUBORDINATION)
### X    Sibling Rivalry

Explicit and almost institutionalized sibling rivalry is, in a sense, a corollary to the stern subordination-superordination relationship which obtains between fathers and sons. (F073)

## FATHER-SON RELATIONS (WARMTH)
### X    Identification with Father

A father-son relationship characterized by warmth is more conducive to son-father identification than one not so characterized. (P064)

Degree of father-son identification is positively correlated more with the warmth of the relationship than with the masculinity of the father. (P064)

### Sex-Role Behavior

Acquisition of male sex-role traits (father-role playing, identification with the father, and masculinity of attitudes) are positively correlated with a warm and rewarding father-son relationship. (B216)

### Socialization, Effectiveness of

The warmer and more rewarding the total father-son relationship, the greater the likelihood of internalization and acceptance of parental values. (S216)

### Sociopathic Personality of Son

There is a negative correlation between coldness on the part of the father and sociopathic personality in the son. (O032)

## FATHER-SON RELATIONS (WARMTH/HOSTILITY)
### X    Descent

Among patrilineal peoples, father-son hostility or avoidance is pronounced; among matrilineal peoples, there is a warm and affectionate father-son relationship. (L133)

## FECUNDITY                           X    Acculturation

Sociocultural stress (acting on the reproductive mechanism of women) reduces fecundity. (H024)

### Adoption

Women who have not been able to have children and who then adopt a child are no more likely to become pregnant than are presumably "infertile" women who do not adopt a child.

### Birth Control

Couples who regulate conception are more likely to be fecund than are those who do not. (F101)

Fecund couples are more likely to regulate conception effectively than are subfecund couples. (F101)

### Class

There is no consistent difference in fecundity between major social and economic strata. (F101)

### Concubinage

Concubinage is more likely to occur when the wife is without children. (S134)

### Divorce

Sterility is more likely to be an important cause of divorce in societies which highly value fertility in women. (P083)

### Divorce of Barren Wife

A barren wife is less likely to be divorced if the other wives are fertile. (S174)

### Employment of Wife

Wives who work are more likely to be subfecund than are those who do not work. (F101)

Wives who have worked longest since marriage are most likely to be subfecund. (F101)

### Exogamy

Rules of exogamy are likely to increase the likelihood of female fecundity. (P083)

### Mate Selection

Men are less likely to wish to marry a sterile woman than a fecund one. (B245)

### Maternal-Role Behavior

Maternal behavior (e.g., following adoption of a child) may induce physiological changes favorable to conception in women previously sterile. This proposition is also denied. (P083)

### Personality Problems of Women (Socio-Cultural Stress)

Amenorrhea, spontaneous abortion, and infertility have been shown to be associated with personal disorder that originates in sociocultural stress. (H024)

### Premarital Sex Relations

Prepubertal sexual relations may result in sterility. (W109)

### Religion

Catholics are more likely to have impairments to fecundity than are Protestants. (F101)

## FEEDING
### X    Behavior Problems (Thumb-Sucking)

The severity of thumb-sucking is in proportion to the insufficiency of sucking time during feeding. (Y042)

### Child-Rearing Practices (Permissiveness)

Parents in the sample who tend to treat the child casually also tend to be permissive in early feeding training, not to punish for misbehavior, and not to promote independence. (S010)

**Child-Rearing Practices (Punishment)**
Punishing children for misbehavior is a characteristic of parents who are permissive in early feeding practices. Such parents also tend to participate in much activity with the child and to treat him casually. (S010)

**Class**
Socioeconomic status and feeding practices are not associated (U.S.). (S191)

Upper-class Negro parents enforce more rigid feeding schedules than do lower-class Negro parents. (W133)

**Dependency**
Dependent behavior of the child in the preschool period is positively associated with degree of frustration of the child during the nursing and weaning periods. (S014)

If an infant's feeding schedule is frustrating, the child is likely to be dependent. (S238)

**Feeding Problems**
There is no relationship between infant-feeding practices and later feeding problems (U.S.). (S191)

**Health of Child**
There is no relationship between the flexibility/rigidity of the feeding schedule and the health of the infant. (B272)

**Health of Child, Anxiety About**
The more anxious the mother about the child's health (concerning a balanced diet), the more likely is she to be inconsistent (punishing, forcing, taking food away from child) in her feeding practices (U.S.). (S191)

**Mother-Child Relations (Interest)**
There is a correlation between the mother's interest in the child and the amount of affection and concern displayed during nursing. (P063)

**Motor Development of Child**
The more satisfactory the feeding experience for the infant, the greater his confidence in bodily movement is likely to be. (B272)

**Personality Adjustment of Child**
Children who were not held by the mother during feedings tend to show lower personal and social adjustment than do those who were. (B272)

**Personality of Mother**
The feeding techniques employed by the mother are determined by her own personality rather than by the activity level or other characteristics of the infant. (B272)

**Race**
Negro parents are more permissive than are white parents in feeding their children. This proposition is also denied.

## FEEDING, ATTITUDE TOWARD
**X   Feeding (Demand)**
There is no relationship between maternal approval of self-demand feeding schedules and a satisfactory feeding experience for either mother or infant. (B272)

**Social Adjustment of Child**
The more satisfactory the feeding experience for the infant, the more mature his social responsiveness is likely to be. (B272)

## FEEDING (DEMAND)          X   Bed Wetting
There is no relationship between whether the infant was fed on a schedule or by self-demand and his duration of bed wetting (U.S.). (S191)

**Child-Rearing Anxiety of Mother**
High child-rearing anxiety of the mother is associated with the use of scheduled feeding. (S191)

**Class**
A greater percentage of lower-class children than of middle-class children are fed whenever they are hungry (U.S.). (L003)

**Dependency**
Among girls there is no relationship between feeding practices and dependency on the mother; among boys those fed by self-demand are more dependent on their mothers than are those fed on a schedule (U.S.). (S191)

**Feeding, Attitude Toward**
There is no relationship between maternal approval of self-demand feeding schedules and a satisfactory feeding experience for either mother or infant. (B272)

**Feeding Problems**
There is no relationship between whether the infant was fed by schedule or self-demand and his having feeding problems (e.g., prolonged periods of appetite loss, etc.) (U.S.) (S191)

**Mental Illness (Schizophrenia)**
There is a direct correlation between the rigidity of the mother in establishing a feeding schedule and the subsequent appearance of schizophrenia. (T105)

**Mother-Child Relations (Warmth)**
The mother's lack of warmth and scheduled feeding are associated. (S191)

**Occupation of Husband**
Middle-class mothers whose husbands have entrepreneurial jobs are significantly more likely than are mothers of similar social status whose husbands have bureaucratic jobs to feed babies on schedule. (M062)

**Ordinal Position**
Second and later children are treated more permissively in scheduling of feeding than are first or only children and also more permissively in aspects of infant nursing and weaning. (S014)

**Personality Adjustment of Child**
There is no relationship between different types of feeding, demand schedules, and weaning and the personal and social adjustment of the child. (B272)

There is no relationship between the feeding of infants on a regular or a demand schedule and their level of personality adjustment (as measured by the California Test of Personality or the Ford Modification of the Haggerty-Olson-Wickman Behavior Rating Scale). (S200)

**Personality Adjustment of Child (Belonging)**
Children who are fed on a demand schedule rather than on a regular feeding schedule have stronger feelings of not belonging (as measured by the California Test of Personality). (S200)

**Personality Adjustment of Child (Oral)**
Children fed on a demand schedule have no more "oral symptoms" (i.e., finger-sucking, nail-biting, stuttering, eating difficulties, bashfulness, or slowness in talking)

than do children fed on a regular feeding schedule. (S200)

### Personality of Child (Emotional Maturity)
There is a correlation between degree of self-regulation of food intake and the emotional maturity of the child. (B272)

### Social Adjustment of Child
There is no relationship between the feeding of infants on a regular or a demand schedule and their level of social adjustment (as measured by the California Test of Personality or the Ford Modification of the Haggerty-Olson-Wickman Behavior Rating Scale). (S200)

### Social Mobility of Mother
There is an association between the use of self-demand feeding by mothers and upward mobility of mothers. (S014)

## FEEDING PROBLEMS                  X   Bed Wetting
Among children who have been severely toilet trained, those who have feeding problems are less likely to be bed wetters (U.S.). (S191)

### Breast Feeding
There is no relationship between whether or not the infant was breast-fed and his having feeding problems (e.g., prolonged periods of appetite loss, etc.) (U.S.). (S191)

### Child-Rearing Practices (Aggression)
There is a positive relationship between prohibition of expressions of aggression toward the parents and feeding problems (e.g., prolonged periods of appetite loss, etc.) in the child (U.S.). (S191)

### Child-Rearing Practices (Dependency)
There is a positive relationship between parents' negative reactions to acts of dependency by the child and child-feeding problems (e.g., prolonged appetite loss, etc.) (U.S.). (S191)

### Child-Rearing Practices (Punishment)
There is a positive relationship between the use of physical punishment and feeding problems (e.g., prolonged periods of appetite loss, etc.) in the child (U.S.). (S191)

### Emotional Problems of Child (Weaning)
There is no relationship between whether or not the child was emotionally upset over weaning and his having later feeding problems (e.g., prolonged loss of appetite) (U.S.). (S191)

### Feeding
There is no relationship between infant-feeding practices and later feeding problems. (U.S.). (S191)

### Feeding (Demand)
There is no relationship between whether the infant was fed by schedule or self-demand and his having feeding problems (e.g., prolonged periods of appetite loss, etc.) (U.S.). (S191)

### Mother-Child Relations (Warmth)
There is a positive relationship between mothers who display little warmth toward their children and child-feeding problems (e.g., prolonged periods of appetite loss, etc.) (U.S.). (S191)

### Scholastic Adjustment (Reading)
Children with reading disabilities are more likely than children who have no difficulty reading to have had uncomfortable experiences in the oral stage of development (particularly when being fed). (S225)

### Toilet Training
There is a positive relationship between severe toilet training and feeding problems (e.g., prolonged periods of appetite loss, etc.) in the child (U.S.). (S191)

### Weaning
There is no relationship between the age at which weaning was started and feeding problems (e.g., prolonged periods of appetite loss, etc.) (U.S.). (S191)

## FEEDING/TOILET TRAINING                X   Race
White mothers are more likely to be rigorous in the handling of feeding and weaning of their infants; Negro mothers, in the handling of toilet training. (B272)

## FERTILITY                          X   Acculturation
The birthrate tends to decline in situations of culture contact. (H135)

### Adoption
Adoption of children is more likely to occur when the couple has no children of its own. (B059)

There is a correlation between the decision to adopt a child and the occurrence of pregnancy in a previously sterile woman. This hypothesis is also denied. (B309)

### Adultery, Attitude Toward
Extramarital relations are less likely to be censured if the wife is barren. (B191)

### Age at Marriage
Fertility decreases as the age of the woman at marriage increases. (B012)

### Aspiration Level
White collar men with several children have higher levels of aspiration than do those with few children. (L115)

### Birth Control
When birth control methods become available to all socioeconomic groups, fertility differences by class are reduced. (W022)

### Breast Feeding, Duration of
An extended lactation period will tend to reduce the fertility rate. (F028)

### Class
Although there is a negative correlation between socioeconomic level and fertility, this relationship tends to change from negative to positive at the highest levels. (A065)

In the areas occupied by middle-class families, there are more children than in areas of extreme poverty and family disorganization (U.S. Negro). (F078)

Before the introduction of effective contraceptives, the upper classes were more likely to have a higher birth rate. (G156)

The lower the class, the higher the birth rate. This relationship does not hold. (G156)

There is no correlation between fertility and class. (I007)

Increase in fertility is directly related to socioeconomic class. (K004)

Fertility rates are likely to be higher in the upper-middle and upper classes than in the middle-middle and lower-middle classes, particularly where the societal value system fosters pride in lineage, because the upper classes have more resources for hiring mother surrogates and the middle classes are more concerned with concentrating more limited resources on fewer children and greater success. (P083)

Among couples who have planned their fertility most completely, a positive relationship exists between fertility and socioeconomic status. (R119)

### Cohesion of Family
The greater the internal family solidarity, the higher the birth rate. (T099)

### Divorce
Divorced woman as a group are relatively less fertile than are women who marry only once. (B012)

Childless marriages and those where illegitimacy occurs (where the wife bears a child prior to marriage) are more likely to end in divorce than are fertile marriages (Denmark). (C129)

The higher the divorce rate, the closer the rate of fertility of those obtaining divorces will approximate the normal. (D083)

Married couples who are not well adjusted, who for many reasons may be prone to divorce, are less likely to have children. (G156)

Divorce is more likely to occur in cases of marital infidelity when there are no children. (H074)

There is a direct relation between low fertility and divorce. (K161)

The greater proneness to divorce of remarried persons than of persons who have been married only once leads to a spurious overemphasis of childlessness in divorce. (M011)

### Economic Conditions
Peace and prosperity are more conducive to higher birth rates than are war and economic depression. (B244)

Changes from favorable to unfavorable economic conditions produce a decline in annual birth rates, long-run trends remaining stable. (F101)

Fertility varies directly with the general level of economic activity of the society. (K004)

### Economic Level
Fertility tends to be inversely correlated with the standard of living. (T011)

### Economic Pattern (Migrant Labor)
A decrease in the birth rate will tend to accompany the establishment of patterns of migratory labor. (H135)

### Economic Rank
There is a negative correlation between fertility and economic level of the family. (I007)

There is a positive correlation between fertility and economic level of the family. (I007)

Fertility rates vary inversely with level of living in the rural population, both farm and nonfarm, both white and nonwhite. (T011)

### Economic Rank/Education
The direct association of number of births per married woman with size of farm operated by the husband is independent of the number of years of schooling completed by the wife. (H010)

### Economic Rank of Husband
Fertility of Negro manual laborers is inversely related to the economic position of the husband. (G020)

### Economic Security
Economic security is positively correlated with increase in fertility. (W022)

### Education of Husband-Wife
The number of years of schooling completed, by either the wife or the husband, varies inversely with fertility. (H010)

### Education of Mother
The higher the educational level of the mother, the lower the number of children she will bear. (C134)

### Education of Wife
Whether the husband has a farm or nonfarm occupation is a less important factor than the number of years of schooling completed by the wife in determining fertility. Occupation of husband, however, exerts an appreciable differentiating effect among women with more than five years of schooling. (H010)

The inverse relationship of number of live births with educational level of the rural wife holds even when the size of the farm operated by the husband is controlled. (H010)

### Employment of Mother
Working mothers have a lower birth rate than nonworking mothers. (S265)

### Geographic Mobility
An increase in the rate of fertility in areas where the land resources are limited will tend to accelerate the rate of migration. (A014)

### Homogamy (Nationality)
Marriages between United States-born and foreign-born individuals are associated with lower fertility than are marriages between two United States-born or two foreign-born individuals. (B300)

### Homogamy (Religion)
Fertility rates are highest among couples whose marriages and parents' marriages were homogamous according to religious affiliation; lower among couples who have unifaith marriages, but whose parents had mixed-faith marriages; and lowest among those who have mixed-faith marriages and whose parents had mixed-faith marriages. (B300)

### Husband-Wife Relations
The wife who is fertile (and thus more assured of the stability of her marriage) will identify more fully with the interests of her husband. (H165)

### Husband-Wife Relations (Egalitarianism)
The relation between husband and wife will be more egalitarian in character if the wife has borne children. (H165)

### Immigrant/Nonimmigrant
The average number of children born to foreign-born

wives is significantly greater than is the average number born to native white women. (G020)

### Income
Within each class, families with higher income tend to have more children. (G156)

The higher the gross income of a family, the larger the number of live births per married woman. (H010)

### Income/Education
Excess fertility (unwanted children) is inversely related to education more closely and consistently than it is to income. (F101)

### Infant Mortality
A lower infant mortality rate in a society is associated with a trend toward a low birth rate. (G156)

### Inheritance (Single-Heir)
The single-heir system of inheritance tends to retard the birth rate. (H066)

### Intermarriage (Ethnic)
Regardless of religious affiliation, marriages between persons of different national origins tend to show lower fertility rates. (B300)

### Intermarriage (Racial)
The number of children of interracial families is smaller than the number of children in single-racial samples. This propostion is also denied. (G001)

### I.Q. of Parents
There is no relationship between the intelligence of the parents and the number of children they have or their ages at birth of their first child. (A065)

### Lineage
The emphasis upon a high birth rate will be directly correlated with the strength of the lineage system. (F069)

### Marital Adjustment
Doubts concerning marital adjustment may lead to not having children. (B244)

### Marital Stability
The stability of a marriage is directly correlated with the fertility of the wife. (H165)

Women married once have more children than do women married two or more times. (N051)

A low birth rate is directly correlated with marital insta-bility. (W091)

### Marital Status (Female)
Divorced women who remarry bear fewer children than do those who were never divorced. (F101)

### Marriage Payment
The size of marriage payment is directly correlated with the number of years of potential fertility in the woman. (H165)

### Mental Illness (Schizophrenia)
Married schizophrenic individuals tend to have fewer children than do normals. (B285)

### Mental Retardation
The more severe the retardation, the lower the birth rates among mentally retarded persons. This proposition is also denied. (B307)

### Monogamy
The birth rate tends to be higher among monogamous than among polygamous unions. (P034)

### Occupational Rank
While there was an inverse relationship between fertility and occupational status during the early part of the twentieth century, it seems that in the future there will be a direct relationship between fertility and occupa-tional status. (W022)

### Polygyny
Polygyny has the effect of lowering reproduction. (D055)

A decrease in the birth rate tends to accompany the repression of polygyny. The contrary is also asserted. (H135)

Husbands of barren women are more likely than others to take additional wives. (L110)

Polygyny yields greater fertility in societies in which there are more marriageable women than men; where the sex ratio is nearly 1:1, the marriage form more likely to assure the greatest fertility is monogamy. (P083)

### Preferential Marriage (Levirate)
The levirate is less likely to be enforced if the wife has borne children. (T054)

### Pregnancy, Accidental
The proportion of accidental pregnancies increases with the number of children the mother has. (F101)

### Premarital Sex Relations
The more unstable are premarital sexual unions, the less fertile is the woman likely to be. (B245)

### Premarital Sex Relations, Age at
The earlier the age at which the woman is first exposed to intercourse, the more fertile she is likely to be. (B245)

### Property
Fertility rates are higher among couples who own their own homes than among those who rent. (R119)

### Race
More Negro families than white families are childless. This proposition is also denied. (H018)

### Rank
Social prestige and authority in societies based on kin-ship principles are correlated with the relative fertility of individuals and families. (T080)

### Rank of Women
The rank of women tends to be directly correlated with their fertility. (H139)

### Religion
Protestants are more likely than Catholics to have no children and Catholics are more likely to have a larger number of children than are Protestants. This proposi-tion is also denied. (B033)

The proportion of childless couples is highest for Pro-testant-Catholic mixed marriages and lowest for the Catholic couple. (B033)

### Rent
Average monthly rent is inversely related to fertility. (D006)

### Residence
The percentage of poor housing is directly related to fertility. (D006)

Fertility is likely to be higher among families living in the urban fringe areas than among urban families. (J003)

### Residence (Urban)
Among Protestants (only) there is an inverse relationship between city size and fertility rate. (F101)

### Residence (Urban/Rural)
The birth rate is higher on farms than elsewhere. (F101)

### Sex Composition of Family
Parents whose first two children are both of the same sex are more likely to have a third child than are parents who have two children of opposite sexes. (F123)

### Sex Status of Schizophrenics
Married schizophrenic females tend to have more children than do their male counterparts. (R103)

### Sex Taboo (Postpartum)
The longer the period of postpartum abstinence, the lower the fertility. (N054)

### Sex Taboo (Postpregnancy)
Laxity in the adherence to pregnancy taboos is directly correlated with the number of children which have preceded the pregnancy. (H122)

### Size of Community
As village size increases, fertility decreases. (D006)

### Social Mobility
Very low or high fertility in an upper-class family contributes to loss of rank. (G156)

In the suburbs, upwardly mobile men do not have fewer children than do nonmobile men; there may be a slight inverse association. (L115)

Rapid social mobility in a society is associated with low fertility. (R119)

### Social Mobility Aspirations
Lowered social mobility aspirations lead to higher fertility. (W022)

### Stability of Family
Fertility decreases as family instability increases. (D055)

### Subsistence Pattern
The more sedentary life associated with gardening or fishing economies causes an increase in fertility. (T082)

### Urban/Rural
Fertility rates tend to be higher in rural areas. (I007)

### Urbanization
Fertility is inversely related to degree of urbanization. (D006)

### Values (Individualism)
The birth rate tends to be inversely correlated with the emphasis of the society on individualism. (F069)

### FERTILITY-DEATH RATES                    X Values
In a society whose values are based upon individual initiative in coping with problems, the birth and death rates tend to be more balanced than in societies characterized by other types of individual adaptation.

In societies characterized by individuals whose actions are guided by their relations with their contemporaries, both birth and death rates are more likely to decline than in societies characterized by other types of individual adaptation.

### FERTILITY(REAL/IDEAL)          X Age of Mother
Among wives planning to have more children, the older the wife, the more likely it is that her ideal family size is smaller than the intended. Among those undecided, the amount of disparity tends to be inversely related with age. (Y046)

### Class
Socioeconomic position is directly correlated with both actual and ideal size of the family, the latter always being higher than the average actual number of children. (Y046)

Lower-class mothers tend to express ideals of family size smaller than the intended size; this discrepancy is reversed among average and high-status mothers. (Y046)

### Education of Husband
If the husband's educational level is eight years or less, the wife tends to consider as ideal fewer children than she actually intends to have; this relationship is reversed at higher educational levels. (Y046)

### Income
Lower-income groups express an ideal family size smaller than that intended, the discrepancy becoming minimal in the middle- and upper-income groups. (Y046)

### Occupational Rank of Husband
If the husband's occupational level is craftsman or higher, the wife tends to consider as ideal more children than she intends to have; at the lower occupational levels this relationship is reversed. (Y046)

### FERTILITY VALUES                    X Abortion
When a society places a high value on children, the rate of abortion is low. (S064)

### Age
The older the wife is (and therefore less able to bear children), the higher she values fertility.

### Age at Marriage
When fertility is emphasized, the age of marriage for women will tend to be lower. (H164)

### Age of Mother
The older the mother, the smaller the ideal family size she reports. (Y049)

### Birth Control
When fertility is stressed, methods of birth control are less likely to be employed. (V020)

### Class
The higher the class (measured by income, education, and occupation), the larger the desired family size. (Y049)

### Cohesion of Family
The more distant the female college student's ties with her family, the fewer children she is likely to expect to have. (R116)

### Corporate Kin-Group
Fertility will tend to be stressed in societies where the major corporate groups are kinship groups. (M127)

### Duration of Marriage
The longer the duration of the marriage, the smaller the number of additional children preferred.

### Economic Conditions (Labor)
The greater the community's immediate need for labor and production, the less likely it is that large families will be considered desirable. (T098)

### Economic Pattern
The desire for children is directly correlated with the advantageousness of a large family in the economic organization. (W082)

### Economic Value of Children
An emphasis on fertility is directly correlated with the economic value of children. (H164)

### Education of Wife
Wives with a high level of education prefer a very large number of children or no children at all as compared with wives of middle or no education who want an average number of children. (Y046)

Wives with an education beyond high school express an ideal somewhat smaller than the intended number of children; this relationship is reversed at the lower educational levels. (Y046)

### Employment of Women
Women who work are less apt to be seriously considering having more children than are women who are not working. (R121)

### Husband-Wife Relations
The greater the emphasis placed on the husband-wife relationship, the less likely it is that large families will be considered desirable. (T098)

### Identification with Community
The more intense the individual's identification with the collectivity, the less likely he is to desire children. (T098)

### Illegitimacy, Attitude Toward
When the importance of fertility is stressed, the birth of a child before marriage will be less detrimental to the status of the girl. (V020)

### Intermarriage (Religious)
Couples of mixed-faith marriages tend to desire about the same number of children as those of nonmixed marriages. (B300)

### Marital Adjustment
The higher the marital satisfaction of the two partners, the larger the number of children preferred.

### Marriage Chances
A higher percentage of all women will eventually marry in societies in which fertility is stressed. (M127)

### Mortality Rates
Greater effort is expended to inculcate fertility values in high mortality societies. (G156)

### Polygyny
Polygyny tends to be associated with a strong emphasis upon a large number of children. (O023)

### Remarriage
There will be a high rate of remarriage in societies which stress the importance of fertility. (M127)

### Self-Conception of Mother
The higher the mother's self-evaluation, the more likely is she to want children. (M186)

### Sex Status
Males tend to stress economic motives more than do females as reasons for desiring limitations in the size of their families of procreation. (C007)

The desire for smaller families than the parents had is more likely among males than among females. (C007)

### Sibling Status
Single children are less likely than are persons with siblings to be content without children of their own. (T091)

### Size of Family
Students are more likely to want smaller families than the families from which they came. (C007)

The difference in the desired size of students' families of procreation and their families of orientation increases as the actual size of the family of orientation increases. (C007)

The more children they already have, the less delighted the parents are likely to be with the prospect of having another child. (S263)

### Social Mobility
When a major shift takes place in the prestige level of the husband's job, the wife wants fewer children.

### Urban/Rural
Urban wives value the chance to have children as one of the most valuable parts of marriage, while rural wives tend to do so less.

### Urbanization
The more urbanized the population, the smaller number of children it prefers.

### Values (Individualism)
The greater the concern for the future growth and continuity of the collectivity, the more likely it is that large families will be considered desirable. (T098)

The greater the emphasis put on the value of individualism, the less likely it is that large families will be considered desirable. (T098)

### Values (Sex Role)
The more egalitarian the ideology with respect to sex differentiation, the less likely it is that large families will be considered desirable. (T098)

### Warfare
Children are more greatly desired when warfare is common. (F092)

## FILICIDE    X    Maternal-Role Adjustment
Conscious feelings on the part of the mother of inability to bring up the child may lead to filicide. (T085)

### Paternal/Maternal Role
Mothers are more likely to commit filicide than fathers are. (T085)

## FOOD VALUE
### X    Child-Rearing Practices (Discipline)
There is a correlation between the use of water as a disciplinary agent in childhood and an institutionalized fear of water, as manifested in eating habits. (K111)

## FOSTER HOME, ADJUSTMENT TO
### X   Child-Rearing Practices (Punishment)
Children who failed to establish stable relationships in foster homes give more accounts of severe punishment meted out to children (as measured by the Children Apperception Test) than do children who did develop them. (W145)

### Marital Adjustment of Parents
Children who fail to establish stable relationships in foster homes are more likely than are children who do to have had parents whose relationship was tense, causing emotional rejection of the child. (W145)

### Parent-Child Relations (Rejection)
Children who fail to establish stable relationships in foster homes relate more stories of loneliness, rejection, and desertion of the child than those who did establish them. They also lack a sense of family relationship. (W145)

## FOSTER HOME/INSTITUTIONAL CARE
### X   Aggression
Children who are reared during the first three years of infancy in institutions are more likely to manifest aggressive disorders in adolescence than are children reared in foster homes; the latter are more likely to be timid and withdrawn. (B243)

### Cognitive Development
Children raised in insititutions are less able to conceptualize and have lower intelligence scores and poorer speech than do children raised in foster homes. (P068)

### Scholastic Achievement
Children raised in foster homes achieve better in school than do children raised in institutions. (P068)

### Social Adjustment of Child
Children raised in foster homes are socially more mature and better able to establish relationships than are children raised in institutions. (P068)

## FRIENDS OF HUSBAND/WIFE
### X   Divorce, Attitude Toward
Shared friends of the couple are more likely than friends of the husband alone to express approval and less likely to express disapproval of the divorce. (G157)

## FRIENDSHIP                  X   Age of Child
The younger the children in the family, the more likely is the divorcée to maintain marriage friends during the separation and divorce period. (G157)

### Bereavement
Among large families of low socioeconomic status, adolescents from homes where one parent is deceased have fewer friends than do adolescents from homes where both parents are living and there are fewer siblings.

### Dating
Divorcées who date before the separation are less likely to keep their marriage friends than are those who do not date before separating. (G157)

### Divorce
In cities where there is a lower divorce rate, families are more likely to associate with remarried families than in cities where the divorce rates are higher. (Z008)

Families with friends who have traits in common are more likely to have lower rates for desertion and divorce than families with friends who are unlike themselves. (Z008)

### Divorce, Initiation of
When the husband was the first to make the decision to divorce, the divorcée is slightly more likely to keep her marriage friends than when the suggestion was mutual; she is least likely to keep her marriage friends when she was the one who first suggested the divorce. (G157)

### Divorce Process
When the time between the decision to divorce and filing suit is short, the divorcée is more likely to maintain her marriage friends than when the time is long. (G157)

### Education of Divorcée
The higher the educational level of the divorcée, the more likely is she to maintain marriage friends during the separation and divorce period. (G157)

The higher the educational level of the divorcée, the more likely is she to have a circle of friends. (G157)

### Employment of Divorcée
Divorcées who had jobs at some time during the marriage, but not during the separation and immediate postdivorce period, are most likely to maintain their marriage friends, followed by divorcées who did not have a job at any time, next by divorcées who had jobs during the marriage and the separation and immediate postdivorce period, and last by those divorcées who did not have jobs during the marriage but did have jobs during the separation and postdivorce period. (G157)

### Extramarital Relations
When the divorcée is in love with another man she is less likely to keep her marriage friends during the separation and divorce period than when she is not in love with another man. (G157)

Whether the husband was in love with another woman is not related to the divorcée's maintenance of marriage friends during the separation and divorce period. (G157)

### Father-Son Relations (Affection)
Sons who have received insufficient paternal affection desire a greater number of friends than do sons who have received adequate paternal affection. (M204)

Sons whose relations with their fathers are characterized by insufficient paternal affection have fewer friends than do those who have received adequate paternal affection. (M204)

### Husband/Wife
In middle-class families, the husband will initiate a greater number of the shared primary friendships which the couple have in common than will his wife. (B317)

A middle-class couple is more apt to visit friends shared by both partners when the friendships were initiated by the husband. (B317)

In middle-class families, husband-initiated friendships shared by husband and wife involve a wider range of activities in which he and his wife participate with their friends than do friendships which the wife initiates. (B317)

In middle-class families, the shared friendships initiated by the husband will be characterized by a stronger positive affect than those initiated by the wife. (B317)

In middle-class families, a husband shares confidences

with an unmarried friend (disregarding sex) who is the couple's shared friend more often than his wife does. (B317)

Of a middle-class couple's *shared* friends, both spouses are more likely to list three closest men friends than women; and of these, they are both more likely to list men secured as friends by the husband. He will also list an unmarried female friend more often than his wife will list an unmarried male friend. (B317)

### Income of Husband
When the husband's income bracket is higher, the divorcée is slightly more likely to maintain marriage friends during the separation and divorce period than when his income is lower. (G157)

### Interaction in Family
The greater the extent to which a social relationship (friendship, etc.) duplicates for the partners their earliest intrafamilial relationships, the more likely is it to succeed. (T094)

### Interaction with Family
Persons become isolated from their families when they enter into interracial friendships. (G001)

### Juvenile Delinquency
Families whose friends have traits similar to their own (income, faith, origin, and kin) are more likely to have lower rates for delinquency arrests than are families whose friends have less in common. (Z008)

### Marital Adjustment
Marital adjustment is more likely to occur when the husband and wife have many friends in common. (B033)

Persons who have had many friends, both male and female, are more likely to have marital success. (B244)

### Marital Status
Middle-class couples are less likely to establish close shared friendships subsequent to marriage than they are to establish friendships separately prior to marriage. (B317)

Married men and women are more likely to turn to other people in times of unhappiness or for help than are nonmarried people. (G126)

The intensity of friendship is a function of age and marital status. (R006)

Remarried people are more likely to have family friends with whom they do not have as much in common (income, faith, origin, and kin) than are people who have intact families. (Z008)

### Marital Status (Female)
Divorcées who have different friends during the separation and divorce period than those during the marriage are more likely to rate their new friends as better or the same as their marriage friends. (G157)

Divorcées who keep their marriage friends during the separation and divorce period are slightly more likely than those with different friends to have no divorced friends but one or more divorcing friends. (G157)

### Occupational Rank of Divorcée
The higher the occupational group of the divorcée, the more likely is she to maintain marriage friends during the separation and divorce period. (G157)

### Religion
Protestant divorcées are as likely as Catholic divorcées and those of other religious faiths to maintain the friends they had during the marriage while the separation and divorce are taking place. (G157)

### Remarriage
Divorcées who have a circle of close friends are more likely to claim that there is someone among their male friends that they would consider marrying than are divorcées who do not have friends and those who are not finding friends. (G157)

### Separation
The longer the time lapse since the separation, the greater the proportion of divorcées who claim they presently have a circle of friends. (G157)

### Sex Status
A husband is more apt to exchange confidences with the female in another couple unit (husband-initiated friends) than his wife is with the other male. (B317)

With friends of a middle-class couple (both couple and single units), husbands are more likely to exchange confidences with men than with women and wives with women than with men. (B317)

### Sibling Status
Older persons (in their seventies) with siblings are more likely to describe their friends in terms of specific activities undertaken together while those without siblings use diffuse descriptions of their friends: friendship is a quasi-kinship relation for many older people. (C116)

### Size of Family
The more children in the family, the more likely is the divorcée to maintain marriage friends during the separation and divorce period. (G157)

### Social Adjustment
Divorcées who have new sets of friends are slightly more likely to have more opportunities to meet people than are those who maintain their marriage friends. (G157)

Divorcées who receive help from married friends are more likely to have social opportunities than are those who receive help from a new circle of friends. (G157)

**FRIENDSHIP CHOICE          X   Broken Home**
Intact families tend to avoid close friendship with broken families regardless of whether they have been broken by death, divorce, desertion, one remarriage, or both persons being remarried. (Z008)

### Juvenile Delinquency
Both families in which there are juvenile arrest records and families with no arrest records tend to avoid friendships with families which have juvenile arrest records. (Z008)

In cities where the delinquency rate is higher, families are more likely to avoid friendship with families in which there is a child who has been arrested for delinquency than in cities where the delinquency rate is lower. (Z008)

#### Marital Status
Families are more likely to avoid social relations with remarried families in which both parents have remarried or in which the woman only has remarried; when fathers only have remarried, avoidance is not as great. (Z008)

#### Ordinal Position
Firstborns are more likely to concentrate their choice of interpersonal preferences on fewer persons than are later borns. (S232)

As firstborns are more dependent than later-born children, they are more likely to choose their friends on the basis of what other persons will think of them rather than according to their own personal needs. (S232)

Firstborns are more likely to choose popular persons for friends than are later-born children. (S232)

#### Peer Relations
#### X   Sibling Structure (Sex)
When their sibling is male, firstborns are more likely to prefer male friends than are second borns; when their sibling is female, the reverse obtains as to male preference. (K094)

#### Residence
People in newer cities are more likely to avoid friendships with broken families than are those from older cities. (Z008)

### FRIENDSHIP CHOICE (AGE)   X   Ordinal Position
Firstborns are more likely to prefer playmates younger than themselves than are second-born children, but this is less true, the greater the age disparity between siblings. (K094)

#### Sibling Structure (Sex)
A child with a sister is more likely to prefer a younger child as a playmate than is a child with a brother. (K094)

When spacing is over four years, children from cross-sex pairs are more likely to prefer younger friends than are those from like-sex pairs. (K094)

### FRIENDSHIP CHOICE (SEX)
#### X   Power Structure of Family
Among schizophrenics, those from father-dominated families are more likely to have friends of both sexes than are those from mother-dominated families, who are more likely to be social isolates. (F117)

#### Sibling Structure (Sex)
The greater the age disparity between siblings, the more likely it is that the child prefers friends of the same sex. (K094)

Children from cross-sex pairs are more likely to prefer friends of the opposite sex or to be indifferent to sex of a friend than are children of same-sex pairs. (K094)

When the age disparity between siblings is over two years, firstborns with a sister are more likely to be indifferent to sex of playmate than are those with a brother; for second born children, the reverse obtains. (K094)

### FRIENDSHIP (CLOSENESS)
#### X   Disorganization of Family
The more intimate the family friends, the less likely is the family to experience desertion and divorce. (Z008)

#### Juvenile Delinquency
The more intimate the family friends, the less likely are the families to have children with arrest records. (Z008)

#### Kin/Nonkin
The closer the families' friends, the more likely they are to be kin members than nonkin members. (Z008)

#### Kin Terminology (Fictive)
Use or nonuse of kin terms when addressing friends and acquaintances is correlated with the degree of intimacy of the relationship. (N012)

#### Marital Status
Remarried friends are more likely to be reported as being less intimate family friends than are friends with nondisrupted families. (Z008)

### FRIGIDITY          X   Adultery
There is a correlation between frigidity in women and adulterous and promiscuous behavior of their husbands.

#### Father-Daughter Relations (Sex)
Frigidity in women is associated with a defense mechanism against unresolved sexual feelings about the father.

### FUNCTIONS OF CLAN          X   Stability of Clan
The disintegration of the clan structure is directly correlated with its loss of traditional political, judicial, and economic functions. (W082)

### FUNCTIONS OF FAMILY
#### X   Authority Structure of Family
The abdication of some of their former educational, economic, and recreational roles has led to a serious diminution in parental authority. (S051)

#### Industrialization
The social functions of the family decrease with increasing industrialization. (K100)

#### Interaction in Family
With the loss of subsistence roles and the removal of most other roles from the home, the amount of interaction within the family is reduced. (B040)

#### Social Structure (Differentiation)
The loss of the family's function is correlated with the increased specialization of the roles and functions in the society at large. (A047)

### FUNCTIONS OF KIN-GROUP
#### X   Cohesion of Kin-Group
The retention of kin ties after fission can only occur if the kin-group is multifunctional in character. (G111)

#### Stratification
Although other functions are lost with the rise of stratification, unilineal kin-groups tend to retain those which are associated with religious ritual. (F039)

#### Territorial Expansion
As territorial units grow larger and stronger, kinship groupings will become more simple, more vague, and increasingly limited in function. (B064)

# G

**GENEALOGICAL DEPTH   X   Clan, Importance of**
The depth of the genealogy is directly correlated with the importance of the clan of a social unit. (M051)

**Class**
The generational depth of the genealogies of the aristocratic class will tend to be greater than that of the lower classes. (K045)

**Descent (Double)**
Societies with a double descent pattern tend to be characterized by shallow genealogies (two to four generations). (H245)

**Descent (Unilineal)**
A restriction of genealogical data indicates the disintegration of a unilineal system. (M077)

**Economic Dependence of Lineage**
Genealogical depth is dependent on the range of economic and social self-sufficiency. (M168)

**Political Role of Lineage**
Long genealogies are more likely to be found in those systems where corporate lineages provide the central political framework of the total structure and where there is no specialized authority outside the lineage. (M168)

**Political Structure (Band)**
Shallow depth lineages may be found in societies in which the political unit is a wandering band or horde composed of only a few families. (M168)

**Population**
With a decrease in population, the depth of genealogies is reduced. (K081)

**Rank of Descent Group**
The genealogical depth of the lineage (which is significant to ego) will be greater than that of the lineages of other relatives. (N012)

**Rank of Lineage**
The rank of the lineage will be directly correlated with the depth of its genealogy. (F039)

**Residence**
Where lineages are tied with specific land tracts, they are likely to have genealogies of great depth. (T080)

**GENEALOGICAL POSITION   X   Kin Terminology**
If a given relative does not fall within the range of attributes of his genealogical placement, the kin term of address directed toward him tends to reflect his deviation, that is, to reflect his actual status in the household or in a hypothetical normative household. (N012)

**GENEALOGICAL PROXIMITY**
**X   Affinal Relations (Respect)**
Affinal affection and respect increase inversely with the strength of social ties based on blood relationship. (Q001)

**Conformity with Kin Rule**
Behavior conforms more closely with kin rules, the closer the kin ties between individuals. (G053)

**Exogamy**
The strength of exogamic restrictions will vary directly with the proximity of the relationship of the kinsmen. (C075)

The severity of the reaction to an exogamic violation will vary directly with the proximity of the relationship between kinsmen. (S081)

**Incest Taboo**
The seriousness of incest is directly correlated with the genealogical proximity of the kinsmen who are involved. (W100)

**Kin Relations (Interaction)**
The frequency of visits between family members will be directly proportional to the closeness of kinship. (B033)

**Kin-Role Behavior**
Adherence to a kin role is directly correlated with the genealogical proximity of the kinsmen. (H137)

Behavior toward classificatory kinsmen will conform more closely with the rules for that term, the closer the genealogical proximity between the individuals in the relationship. (H138)

**Legal Responsibility**
When the clan as a collectivity is responsible for the actions of its members, retaliatory action will also tend to be taken against kinsmen who are most closely related to the defendant. (G039)

**Mate Selection**
People tend to select sex and marriage partners in direct proportion to the nearness of their actual or conventional kinship. (M019)

**Residence**
There is a relationship between neighborhoods and kinship; the closer the kinship relation, the closer the proximity to each other in residence. (K050)

Residential propinquity tends to be directly correlated with the consanguineal proximity of the kinsmen. (L077)

**GENEALOGICAL PROXIMITY/INTERACTION**
**X   Kin Relations (Closeness)**
The strength of children's affective ties with kin varies more directly with frequency of interaction than with genealogical proximity. (M054)

**GENEALOGICAL PROXIMITY OF HUSBAND/WIFE          X   Marriage Payment**
The amount paid as marriage payment is inversely correlated with the closeness of the kin relationship between husband and wife. (B032)

**GENEALOGICAL TIES      X   Descent (Unilineal)**
The genealogical unity of the kin-group is directly correlated with linearity of descent. (G101)

### Political Solidarity
The political solidarity between communities will be increased if they share a common genealogical history. (R063)

### GENEALOGICAL TIES, KNOWLEDGE OF    X   Age
Older persons tend to have a better knowledge of the genealogy of their family than younger members of the family. (B065)

### Clan, Importance of
The accuracy of genealogy will be directly correlated with the importance of the clan as a social unit. (M051)

### Marital Status
Married persons tend to have a greater depth and breadth than the unmarried in the range of their known genealogical ties. (G033)

### Political Role of Clan
There is a positive correlation between the political function of a clan system and the occurrence of a genealogical structure. (E043)

### Property Rights
Ancestral connections are more likely to be remembered if rights in property or in offices that are valued are attached to the lineage. (M168)

### Rank
The range of genealogical knowledge will be directly correlated with the social status of the individual. (D125)

### Residence
When the kinship system is of a bilateral character, the child's knowledge of his father's or his mother's branch will depend upon his place of residence. (H062)

### Sex Status
The informant will tend to have a wider knowledge of the genealogical ties of his parent of the same sex. (G033)

Women tend to have a wider knowledge of genealogical ties than men do. (G033)

### Size of Kin-Group
Although the depth and breadth of genealogical knowledge increases with age, this increase is greater the larger the size of ego's kin-group during adolescence. (G033)

### GENEALOGY    X   Descent (Unilineal)
The manipulation of genealogy tends to occur in societies where unilineal descent is emphasized. (S116)

### Exogamy
When exogamic or preferential marriage restrictions are violated, kinship affiliations tend to be adjusted. (K082)

When exogamic restrictions are violated, the genealogy of the children will tend to be adjusted. (S156)

### Political Importance of Lineage
The absence of political functions in a lineage correlates with the absence of genealogical structure. (S087)

### GENEALOGY, ADJUSTMENT OF
### X   Ranking of Lineages
The manipulation of genealogy tends to occur in societies with a ranked lineage system. (E028)

### GENEALOGY, IMPORTANCE OF
### X   Cohesion of Community
Stress on ancestry will serve to divide the community if its origins are diverse. (G150)

### Ordinal Position, Importance of
The existence of this mechanism (i.e., genealogy) is correlated with a form of social structure where the attainment or possession of rank, power, and religious privilege is bound up with the fact of seniority by birth. (F086)

### Political Structure (Egalitarianism)
Stress on ancestry will serve to divide the community if its political values are egalitarian. (G150)

### Property Rights
Genealogy is more important when kin ties confer land rights. (G150)

### Rank
Genealogies are more likely to be stressed among individuals of high status. (T069)

### Rank of Lineage
When the relative collateral rank of a lineage defines the social status of the individual, genealogies will assume a place of great importance in the society. (K049)

### Residence
A lack of interest in genealogical relations is associated with the settlement pattern of dispersal and recongregation. (D056)

### Stability of Kin-Group
Genealogies will tend to have greater importance when the group is mobile and expanding. (B147)

### GENERATION    X   Age Difference
When there is a generational discrepancy between the husband and wife there will generally be found to be no significant discrepancy between their ages. (F037)

### Avoidance Relationship
Avoidance restraint between relatives of the opposite sex tends to become heightened between relatives of the opposite sex of the same generation. (O027)

Avoidance relationships are more likely to obtain between kinsmen of adjacent generations. (R052)

### Cohesion of Family
Patterns of equality between alternate generations of kinsmen tend to be associated with a weak family organization. (D034)

### Joking Relationship
Joking relationships tend to occur between individuals of the same or alternating generations. (S106)

The degree of license permitted in the joking relationship tends to be greater as the generation span between the kinsmen increases. (T026)

### Joking Relationship, Asymmetrical
When a joking relationship exists between kinsmen of adjacent generations, the relationship will tend to be asymmetrical in character. (R039)

### Kin Relations (Closeness)
The relationship between kinsmen of widely separated generations such as grandparents-grandchildren tends to be characterized by affection and indulgence. (N030)

### Kin Relations (Interaction)
When older persons (50 years and up) do not have children living close to them and thus available social interaction, they are more likely to substitute as inti-

mates collateral kin (i.e., of their own age) rather than ascending or descending kin. (C116)

### Kin Terminology
The omission of kin terms is more likely to occur with relatives of a younger generation. (C049)

### Mate Selection
When there is a significant discrepancy in the generational level of the husband and wife, the factors in mate selection will tend to be of an economic character. (E069)

Mate selection tends to occur between two individuals who are of the same generation. (F037)

## GENERATIONAL EMPHASIS    X  Clan
The degree to which the generation principle is violated is directly correlated with the maturity of the clan system. (G046)

### Marriage Class System
The marriage class system tends to be correlated with an emphasis on generational levels. (E066)

### Residence (Virilocal)
Virilocal residence in a matrilocal society is associated with organization by genealogical generation within the village. (T080)

### Self-Conception
Institutionally imposed generational separateness is necessary for the child to develop a sense of identity. (C093)

### Socialization, Effectiveness of
The adequate learning of social roles requires that there not be a confusion of the generations between parents and children (e.g., a father who acts as the son of his wife). (L123)

### Stability of Lineage
Where genealogical generation is stressed as a principle of local organization, lineage structure is likely to be unstable. (T080)

## GEOGRAPHIC MOBILITY    X  Acculturation
Those who migrate individually become acculturated more rapidly than do those who migrate with families. (S051)

### Adjustment of Child
The child who is not given ample time to react to a notice of his family's change of residence is more likely to develop fantasy and ambivalence concerning the change than the child who is allowed time for adjustment. (S222)

### Adultery
The rate of extramarital relations tends to increase with an increase in geographical mobility. (G093)

### Clan Structure
The proliferation of unilineal kin and the formation of large and segmented clans requires physical mobility and territorial expansion. (B327)

### Class
Upper upper-class families are more likely to be residentially stable than are other classes. (C134)

### Cohesion of Caste
The solidarity of the caste is strengthened if the caste segments of the community are predisposed toward spatial immobility. (D013)

### Cohesion of Family
The tendency toward disruption where family members are separated is especially likely where a previous intercommunication has been insufficient to provide the sharing of experiences and the common understanding of feelings, attitudes, and ideals essential to a durable relationship. (B033)

Family members will invest less emotional energy in those members who may be expected to move away than in those members who are expected to remain in the group permanently. (C093)

The less intimate the family life, the more likely it is that the child plans to leave the community when adult. (R111)

Family solidarity is weakened by geographical mobility. (S076)

The more mobile geographically the nuclear family, the less likely it is to be integrated. (S217)

### Cohesion of Kin-Group
The solidarity of the ties of kinship is inversely correlated with the degree of mobility of the members of the kin unit. (H165)

### Cohesion of Lineage
The persistence of unilinear group solidarity is inhibited by the migration of segments to other settlements. (F033)

### Conflict in Lineage
Where kinship obligations are bilateral in character, migration in response to intralineage conflict is facilitated. (S092)

Conflicts over claims within the lineage tend to increase with an increase in the mobility of lineage members. (W082)

### Corporate Kin-Group
The development of strongly corporate unilineal descent groups are contingent upon the stabilization of population in a fairly small area. (B301)

### Descent
Mixed patterns of unilineal and bilateral descent are more likely to occur in societies in which geographical mobility of the population is fairly great. (B301)

The descent group will tend to be ambiguously defined under conditions of high physical mobility. (M131)

### Descent (Bilateral)
Ecological exigencies favoring a high degree of geographical mobility correlate with reliance by people on bilateral kin in finding new places to settle, consequently favoring a village composed of bilateral kin. (B301)

### Disorganization of Family
The disorganization of the Negro family is correlated with mobility and urbanization. (B033)

The shortage of land in rural areas results in a high rate of internal and external migration with correlated repercussions on the degree of family organization. (S032)

### Divorce
Areas with the highest residential mobility, such as the rooming-house and apartment-house districts, have the highest divorce rate. (B033)

There is a positive relationship between the amount of residential mobility and divorce. (B033)

There is a lower proportion of divorced people among migrants than among nonmigrants. (F008)

Divorced persons tend to be more mobile than the general urban population. (G157)

Divorce is much more likely in urban areas, where there is much geographical mobility. (L024)

### Economic Structure of Society
Approval of geographical mobility of family members is associated with a society whose economy is based on talent rather than on birthright. (G156)

### Engagement, Stability of
Engagements are more frequently broken when the two persons are separated geographically. (B033)

### Exogamy (Village)
Village exogamy is the consequence of territorial stabilization of kin-groups. (G142)

### Extended Kin Ties
If the ideal of consanguinity is strong, the extended family will persist in spite of physical dispersion. (A013)

The less important kinship ties become, the more able are family members to be geographicallly mobile. (G156)

### Fertility
An increase in the rate of fertility in areas where the land resources are limited will tend to accelerate the rate of migration. (A014)

### Homogamy
Girls who are geographically mobile are less apt to marry homogamously than are those who have lived in the same location all their lives. (K150)

### Identification with Extended Family
Lack of interaction with the extended family caused by geographical mobility does not lead to the lessening of extended family identification. (L181)

High identification with the extended family does not limit the geographical mobility of a nuclear family. (L181)

### Identification with Family
The greater the residential mobility of the individual, the weaker his identification with family groups. (M166)

### Inheritance
When the system of land inheritance is relatively inflexible, population increase will tend to result in urban migration. (B082)

Siblings who do not inherit are more likely to move geographically. (T039)

### Inheritance (Single-Heir)
People in single-heir inheritance systems are residentially more mobile than are people in other types of inheritance systems. (H066)

### Interaction with Extended/Nuclear Family
Residential mobility breaks down contact with the extended family and tends to limit frequent interaction to the marital family unit. (M166)

### Intermarriage (Religious)
Women who married within their own religion are more likely than those of interfaith marriages to have been married within their own state of residence. (C128)

### Juvenile Delinquency
Delinquent girls are more likely to have fathers who were born in another state than are normal girls. (N057)

There is no relationship between birthplace of the father and delinquency in boys. (N057)

Adolescents in mobile families are more likely to be involved in delinquent behavior than are those in nonmobile families. (N057)

There is a correlation between residential mobility and delinquency in the child. (N063)

### Juvenile Delinquency by Sex Status
The greater the geographic mobility of the father, the more likely is delinquency in the girl, but not in the boy. (N063)

### Kin Relations (Interaction)
Migrants show no fewer kinship contacts than natives do. (J034)

The greater the geographical mobility of a family, the less contact it will have with its extended kin. (L181)

Kin who have moved are less apt to visit extended family than are those who have not. (S265)

### Kin Ties
Migratory patterns tend to be determined by where affinal and consanguineal kin outside the village are located. (G063)

Ties with relatives outside the immediate nuclear family are more affected by geographical separation in the lower than in the middle class. (R084)

### Kin Ties (Fictive)
The establishment of fictive kin ties with individuals in other districts facilitates physical mobility. (F049)

### Kinship, Importance of
Kin affiliations will decrease in importance with an increase in geographical mobility. (B142)

### Marital Stability
When geographical mobility is high, so is marital instability. (C090)

Patterns of labor migration tend to undermine the stability of marriage. (K065)

Marital breakup is more likely to occur among refugees than among nonrefugees. (L001)

Wife stealing tends to increase in situations of labor migration. (S266)

Women are less likely to be tolerant of marital unhappiness in situations where patterns of labor migration provide options for mobility. (S266)

### Marital Status
The widowed and divorced are more migratory than are the married. (F008)

In-migrants have a higher proportion married than has the total population. (F008)

Negro out-migrants have a lower percentage married

than the Negro population of the cities from which they come. Immigrants have a higher proportion married than the total population. (F008)

A higher proportion of out-migrants are married than of the population in the cities they left. (F008)

### Marriage Rate
The emigration of a large number of people of marriageable age will cause a drop in the marriage rate. (C001)

Once they have migrated, migrants have an especially high marriage rate. (H001)

### Mental Illness
There is no relationship between residential mobility and mental illness in a family member. (F107)

If a member of the family is mentally ill, particularly if he is a husband, the family is more likely to move to a new residence. (F107)

There is no relationship between having a former mental patient in the home and residential mobility of families. (F124)

### Mental Illness, Attitude Toward
Among homeowners, relatives' feelings of stigma due to a family member being a mental patient are correlated with residential mobility. Among renters, this association holds only for the middle class (as opposed to the lower class). This correlation among middle-class renters is increased if the patient occupies the kin role of "son" and if his posthospital occupational and social performance is poor. (F107)

Families who feel stigma due to a relative's being a mental patient are less likely to be satisfied with their present dwelling unit. (F107)

### Nuclear Family
The nuclear family is common where geographical mobility and individual independence are found. (C090)

### Occupation (Nonagricultural)
The geographical dispersion of kinsmen tends to be directly correlated with nonagricultural occupations. (T039)

### Ordinal Position
The individuals who migrate tend to be younger sons within the family. (A022)

### Personality Problems of Child
There is no relationship between the number of residences of families of disturbed children and those of normal children. (P074)

### Personality Problems of Father
There is no difference between fathers of disturbed children and fathers of normal children regarding their acceptance of residential change. (P074)

### Personality Problems of Mother
Mothers of normal children are more likely to accept residential change than are mothers of disturbed children. (P074)

### Political Structure
A lineage structure which constitutes a single pyramidal system will be associated with a continual migration and spatial movement of the component groups. (M168)

### Polygyny
There seems to be no direct correlation between polygyny and labor migration. (S266)

### Power Structure of Family
Urban migration tends to weaken parental control. (F060)

When the younger members of the family are absent because of migration to town for work, there tends to be a shift in the balance of power from the oldest to the middle generation. (G028)

### Preferential Marriage
Preferential marriage patterns will tend to be modified under conditions of high physical mobility. (E060)

### Property
Where property rights exist mainly in agricultural land and hereditary occupations, mobility will tend to be minimized. (G149)

### Residence (Bilocal)
The adoption of a migratory life in unstable bands seems particularly conducive to a bilocal rule of residence. (M019)

### Residence (Matrilocal)
Matrilocal residence tends to occur only among the larger, more stable, tribes. (O006)

### Residence (Neolocal)
Individual migration, as a consequence of overpopulation or developing organization, facilitates the establishment of independent households by married couples. (M019)

### Residence (Virilocal)
There is a relationship between virilocal residence in a matrilocal society and a high rate of individual mobility. (T080)

### Scholastic Adjustment
Among sons, low geographical mobility of the family is significantly related to leadership in school and conformity to school expectations. (W151)

### Segmentation
Migration, as a consequence of land shortage, is an important stimulus to fission. (W056)

### Sex Ratio
The sex ratio tends to reflect the permanency of the movement of migrant laborers to industrial areas. (S127)

### Sex Status
There is a greater likelihood that widowed and divorced men will migrate away from big cities than will widowed and divorced women. (F008)

### Size of Family
The larger the family, the more likely it is to move. (F107)

### Social Network
Where there has been residential stability and husbands and wives continue to live in the same local areas in which they have grown up, women tend to associate with women and men tend to associate with men. (B209)

The greater the family's physical mobility, the more likely it is that its network of social contacts is dispersed. (B267)

#### Stability of Family
The family tends to be extremely unstable where the population is mobile (in the sense that it has no roots more than a generation deep in a given place). (A015)

#### Stability of Joint Family
The breakdown of joint families tends to occur in the urban context as a consequence of the demands of physical mobility in an industrial labor force. (M021)

The joint family tends to break down when migration and settlement in a new area is by individuals and not by large blocks of patrilineal relatives. (M021)

#### Stability of Kin-Group
The disintegration of the kinship groupings tends to be accelerated with migration. (B064)

#### Stability of Kinship Structure
The structure of the kinship system will be weakened by the migration of men to other areas as laborers. (W056)

#### Stability of Lineage
Residential mobility will tend to result in the disintegration of the lineage structure. (F062)

#### Stratification
Geographical mobility is a major factor in the disruption of a stable class system. (F014)

The cleavage of lineages into social classes tends to occur with migration. (K049)

#### Structure of Family
With an increase in physical mobility, the matrilineal family structure will tend to revise into a small bilateral family. (G156)

#### Urban/Rural
Farm families are more stable in residence than urban families. (B033)

#### Values (Extended/Nuclear Family)
Those living further from the location of their homes during their early teen years are more likely to espouse nuclear family norms, while those who live near to their early homes are more likely to espouse extended family norms. (J033)

### GEOGRAPHIC MOBILITY BY SEX STATUS
#### X   Divorce
Migration to a village, town, or city is more likely among farm women than among farm men when their marriages have been broken. (G011)

### GEOGRAPHIC MOBILITY/COHESION OF FAMILY          X   Juvenile Delinquency
The positive relationship between mobility and delinquency increases as family integration decreases (i.e., geographical mobility does not increase juvenile delinquency as much if the family integration is lower). (N057)

### GEOGRAPHIC MOBILITY OF WOMEN
#### X   Descent (Matrilineal)
Women in matrilineal societies are less likely than are women in other societies to settle permanently in a foreign area. (C090)

### GEOGRAPHIC MOBILITY (URBAN/RURAL)
#### X   Kin Relations (Interaction)
Rural migrants interact more with kin than do urban migrants. (J034)

### GERONTOCRACY
#### X   Inheritance (Brother-Brother)
A gerontocratic political structure is more likely to develop if the inheritance pattern is from brother to brother. (F073)

#### Lineage, Importance of
One aspect of the declining influence of the lineage would appear to be a decline in the authority and respect granted older men. (F073)

#### Moiety System
Matrilineal moiety systems tend to occur in association with a pattern of gerontocracy. (S097)

#### Polygyny
When the political structure is gerontocratic in nature, polygyny tends to be concentrated among older men. (F073)

#### Residence
The greater frequency of elderly men living alone is an aspect of the general decline in their prestige and authority. (F073)

The position of older men appears to decline where local lineages have been physically dispersed. (F073)

### GRANDFATHER-GRANDCHILD RELATIONS
#### X   Authority Structure of Family
The greater the authority position of the grandfather within the household, the less permissive the grandfather-grandchild relationship. (G156)

### GRANDMOTHER-GRANDCHILD RELATIONS (INDULGENCE)   X   Maternal Overprotectiveness
Overprotective mothers tend to be reinforced by the indulgent attitudes of grandmothers. (L163)

### GRANDPARENT-GRANDCHILD RELATIONS
#### X   Parent-Child Relations (Affect)
The more ego is emotionally involved in his own family of orientation, the more likely he is to extend this involvement to the family of orientation of his parents. (R084)

### GRANDPARENT-GRANDCHILD RELATIONS (CLOSENESS)          X   Parental Role
Closeness between grandparent and grandchild can occur only when the grandparent has given up his or her parental role, thus being disassociated from family and authority. (C116)

### GRANDPARENTS          X   Kin Relations
The maintenance of the link with the different branches of the male line is more likely if the paternal grandfather is still alive. (H233)

### GROOM SERVICE          X   Marriage Payment
If groom service is given, the amount of the bride price will tend to be reduced. (H130)

### GROUP MARRIAGE          X   Polyandry
Polyandry is usually associated with group marriage and vice versa. (S189)

### GUILT          X   Breast Feeding
Women who choose to bottle feed their children are more likely to manifest guilt feelings than are those who prefer breast feeding. (A063)

#### Death of Parent
If a child is prepared for a parent's death, he is less likely to experience excessive guilt and responsibility in the future. (H188)

### Illness of Child

Mothers of cerebral-palsied children exhibit no more guilt feelings than do mothers of nonhandicapped children. (B320)

### Mental Retardation

The more guilty the mother feels for bearing a retarded child, the less she accepts the child. (Z006)

# H

## HANDICAPPED CHILD (DEAFNESS)
### X   Achievement Motivation
There is a correlation between achievement motivation in the normal child and independence-training attitudes in the mother, but not if the child is deaf. (G129)

### Child-Rearing Practices (Dependency)
Mothers with high achievement motivation are more likely to have later independence-training attitudes toward the deaf child than toward the normal child. (G129)

## HANDICAPPED CHILD, RESPONSE TO
### X   Religion
Among mothers of cerebral-palsied children, Catholic mothers are more guilty, unrealistic, and withdrawn than are Protestant and Jewish mothers. (J027)

Catholic mothers of handicapped children have more pathological attitudes than Protestant and Jewish mothers. (J027)

Among mothers of cerebral-palsied children, Protestant mothers are less anxious than Catholic or Jewish mothers. (J027)

## HAPPINESS
### X   Husband-Wife Relations (Communication)
Communicativeness in marriage was more related to general happiness for women than for men. (L173)

### Marital Adjustment
A spouse's general happiness is more closely related to satisfaction with the social-emotional aspects of a marriage relationship than with the tasks and decisions in marriage or with the husband's work. (L173)

### Sexual Adjustment
Sexual satisfaction is more related to general happiness for men than for women. (L173)

## HAPPINESS IN CHILDHOOD
### X   Aspiration Level
People who experienced a lesser degree of happiness in their childhood had higher levels of aspiration than did those who had experienced a greater degree of happiness. (D001)

Students who have high ambitions (as measured by the Reissman Scale of Ambition) are more likely to feel they have had an unhappy childhood than those who do not have high ambitions. (T095)

### Class
Middle-class children are more likely to perceive their homes as pleasant places to live than are lower-class children. (R127)

### Marital Adjustment
There is a direct correlation between marital adjustment and the spouse's degree of happiness in childhood. (B033)

### Maternal-Role Behavior
There is no direct correlation between maternal behavior and the mother's happiness in childhood. (L165)

### Social Mobility
The upward mobile business leader tends to come from an impoverished home with a spiritually bleak and physically depressed family atmosphere and an inadequate, unreliable father.

## HEADHUNTING   X   Economic Role of Women
Headhunting is likely to develop in matrilineal societies in which women have the major economic role. (W154)

### Endogamy
Where community endogamy inhibits the development of external kinship ties, headhunting is more likely to occur. (H245)

## HEALTH   X   Employment of Mother
Health status, marital, sexual, and emotional adjustment, and number and seriousness of child problems do not correlate with employment or nonemployment of the mother. (S265)

### Illegitimacy
Illegitimacy is inversely related to the state of health. (S003)

### Marital Adjustment
Marital adjustment is associated with good health in the husband and wife. (B033)

### Mother-Child Relations (Interaction)
Babies who have not had adequate contact with their mothers exhibit a refusal to breast feed, loss of appetite, failure to assimilate food, and rigidity of body muscles.

### Sibling Structure
Health estimates for firstborns from opposite-sibling pairs tend to be better than those for second-born children; the reverse obtains for children from same-sex sibling pairs. (K104)

When spacing is under four years, the health estimates for firstborns with a cross-sex sibling are better than those for firstborns with a same-sex sibling; when spacing is under two years, second-born children with a same-sex sibling are judged healthier than those with cross-sex sibling. (K104)

## HEALTH AND PERSONALITY ADJUSTMENT
### X   Marital Status
There is a correlation between mental and physical health and marriage. (M219)

## HEALTH OF CHILD   X   Anxiety of Mother
Infants of less anxious mothers (as measured by MMPI protocols) show as high or higher an incidence of gastrointestinal disturbances (frequency of regurgitation and burping) than infants of more anxious mothers. (P072)

### Breast Feeding

Children who are breast fed tend to be physically superior to those who are not. (B272)

### Disorganization of Family

In children under one year of age, separation from family and familiar surroundings causes physical upsets such as colds, sore throats, and feeding, sleeping, and digestive upsets.

### Feeding

There is no relationship between the flexibility/rigidity of the feeding schedule and the health of the infant. (B272)

### Illegitimacy

Illegitimate children are more likely to experience a higher disease and death rate. (G156)

### Institutional Care/Family

Children who have the psychological support of a family atmosphere (v. children institutionalized in a physically sterile setting) are less susceptible to colds and epidemics of infectious diseases. (P068)

### Maternal-Role Behavior

Absence of sufficient mothering is associated with gastrointestinal disorders in the child. (P072)

### Mother-Child Relations

There is a correlation between three-month colic in the infant and anxious overpermissiveness on the part of the mother. (B272)

Neurodermatitis in the infant is related to maternal hostility in the garb of anxiety. (B272)

Hypermotility in the infant is related to the mother's oscillation between pampering and hostility. (B272)

### Pregnancy (Emotional Problems)

Emotional disturbance in the mother during pregnancy is associated with gastrointestinal disorders in the infant. This hypothesis is also denied. (P072)

## HEALTH OF CHILD, ANXIETY ABOUT
### X  Feeding

The more anxious the mother about the child's health (concerning a balanced diet), the more likely is she to be inconsistent (punishing, forcing, taking food away from the child) in her feeding practices (U.S.). (S191)

## HEALTH OF MOTHER
### X  Employment of Mother

Employment/nonemployment of the mother does not correlate with her health status. (S265)

### Mother-Child Relations

Poor physical health of the mother is negatively associated with positive mother-child relations during preadolescence. (S273)

## HEIRS, ABSENCE OF          X  Adoption

Adoption tends to occur most frequently when there are no legal heirs within the family.

### Adoption (Husband)

The adoption of the husband by the wife's family tends to occur when the wife is without male siblings. (H082)

### Marriage Pattern (Woman)

Woman-marriage (a woman marrying a woman) is more likely to occur when there is no male heir in a household. (L091)

### Preferential Marriage (Parallel-Cousin)

In patrilineal societies in which there is no direct male heir, daughters are more likely to be married to male kinsmen of their lineage. (R118)

### Residence (Matrilocal)

In a patrilocal society, when the family of the bride is without male heirs, the residence after marriage is more likely to be matrilocal. (S059)

## HOMEMAKER ROLE, SUBSTITUTES FOR
### X  Employment of Women, Attitude Toward

The husband's opposition to employment for women outside the home increases to the degree that the work requires disruption of family role-obligations for which adequate substitutes cannot conveniently be supplied. In the working class it is more difficult to provide substitutes. (D060)

## HOMICIDE
### X  Child-Rearing Practices (Obedience)

Where strict obedience is emphasized in socialization, the rate of homicide is likely to be high. (S187)

### Cohesion of Kin-Group

When exaction of proper retribution for homicide would disrupt a solidarity that is important to maintain, the crime goes unpunished. Murder of the family head by a member of the nuclear family does not create a feud. (L112)

### Marital Status

The married are more likely to commit murder than are the single. (S078)

### Sex Status

The rate of homicide among males is higher than among females. (S078)

## HOMOGAMY
### X  Child-Rearing Attitudes (Consensus)

The greater the similarity of the parents' backgrounds, the higher their agreement regarding child-rearing practices. (G156)

### Class

Among women, those who marry into a different class are more likely to marry upward. (G156)

Girls from high school origins are more likely to marry homogamously than are those from lower social backgrounds. (K150)

### Divorce

Homogamy, by eliminating many areas of potential disagreement, tends to reduce proneness to divorce. (G156)

Divorced persons are less likely to have homogamous marriages than are persons who stay married. (G157)

The highest proportion of divorced persons have had hypogamous marriages, then hypergamous marriages, and lastly homogamous marriages. (G157)

Divorced persons are less likely to have occupationally homogamous marriages than are those who remain married. (G157)

Divorced persons are more likely to have occupationally hypogamous marriages than are those who remain married. (G157)

Divorced persons are no more likely to have occupationally hypergamous marriages than are those who remain married. (G157)

### Geographic Mobility
Girls who are geographically mobile are less apt to marry homogamously than are those who have lived in the same location all their lives. (K150)

### Husband-Wife Relations (Empathy)
There is no relationship between understanding the marital partner and similarity between self and mate. (T092)

### Husband-Wife Relations (Evaluation)
The wife's perceived similarity between self and husband is not related to how favorably she evaluates her husband. (K124)

### Illegitimacy
If the mates of unwed mothers differ from them in education or age, it is more likely that lesser-educated women will choose men of the same age but more education, while better-educated women will choose men of the same or higher education, but older age. (V002)

### Marital Adjustment
There is a positive association between marital adjustment and a similarity in the family backgrounds of the husband and wife. (B033)

### Occupation
Homogamous marriages are less prevalent in professional strata than in any other strata. (F009)

### Personality of Husband-Wife (Similarity)
Psychological similarity between marital partners is less likely than is sociocultural similarity. (T092)

### Political Solidarity
Political unity tends to be solidified by a system of hypergamous marriages. (M032)

### Political Structure (Feudalism)
Patterns of hypogamy tend to occur in feudal societies. (L101)

### Polygyny
A class sytem associates hypergamy with polygyny. (V030)

### Religion
Jews are most likely to marry endogamously, followed by Catholics and lastly by Protestants. (G156)

Persons who marry outside of their own religions are less convinced believers in the religion to which they ostensibly belong. (G156)

### Residence
The smaller the hometown, the less likely girls are to marry heterogamously. (K150)

### Sex Ratio by Class
The more hypergamy in the society, the greater the likelihood of a surplus of females at the top of the status hierarchy and a scarcity at the bottom. (V030)

### Sex Ratio Within Caste
Hypergamous marriages tend to occur when there is an insufficient number of marriageable women within the caste. (N030)

### Sex Role Definition
In hypergamous marriages where women marry men of inferior status, they will tend to reject the usual subordinate position. (H079)

### Social Mobility Aspirations (Occupation)
When the wife's family occupies a higher occupational level than does the husband's, he adopts high mobility aspirations in order to reach that same level.

### Social Network
The more opportunities a girl has to meet eligible marriage partners, the more likely she is to make a homogamous marriage. (K150)

### Urban/Rural
For a girl, urban origins are more likely to result in a heterogamous marriage than are nonurban origins. (K150)

## HOMOGAMY (CASTE)          X  Homogamy (Class)
Caste-heterogamous marriages are most likely to be between persons of the same class, usually middle class or higher (U.S.). (G156)

### Occupational Achievement
Women who marry into a lower caste usually marry occupationally successful males (U.S.). (G156)

### Stratification, Basis of
Hypergamy may be found in caste systems only when the basis of stratification is nonracial. (D018)

## HOMOGAMY (CLASS)          X  Homogamy (Caste)
Caste-heterogamous marriages are most likely to be between persons of the same class, usually middle class or higher (U.S.). (G156)

### Husband-Wife Relations (Companionship)
When there is a great difference between the socioeconomic rank of the husband and the wife, the feeling of companionship between the two is lower. (R011)

### Intermarriage (Racial)
Intermarriage is more likely to take place among people of the same social status than of different social statuses. (H008)

### I.Q.
A higher proportion of women who marry upward socially receive over-average I.Q. test scores than of those who marry within the same class. (L115)

A higher proportion of women who marry within their class make high I.Q. scores than do those who move down the social scale at marriage. (L115)

### Marital Adjustment
Marital adjustment is higher in same-class than in cross-class marriages. (C023)

Marital adjustment tends to vary directly with the closeness of the social class of one spouse to the social class of the other spouse. (R011)

There is no association between marital adjustment and the closeness of the social class of the parents of one spouse to the social class of the parents of the other spouse. (R011)

Marital adjustment varies directly with the closeness of the social class of the parents of one spouse to the social class of the parents of the other spouse. (R011)

### Marriage Order
Class endogamy is less likely to be observed in second marriages. (T054)

### Mate Selection
When religion is controlled for, the class of the residential area in which the bride lives varies directly with the class of the residential area in which the groom lives. (H014)

### Occupational Rank
The higher the occupational stratum of the male, the more commonly he marries down; the lower the occupational level of the male, the more frequently he marries up. (C008)

### Occupational Rank of Father
Sons of upper occupational-level fathers are more likely to marry down than up; sons of lower-level fathers are more likely to marry up than down. (C008)

### Sex Status
Among the upper strata, a greater proportion of men marry downward than do women. (G157)

Men are more likely to marry below their social status than women are. (J035)

There is a greater emphasis upon women of high status marrying endogamously than upon men. (W098)

## HOMOGAMY (CULTURAL)
### X    Engagement, Stability of
Engagment is more frequently broken when the couple is culturally divergent. (B033)

### Marital Adjustment
People with similar cultural backgrounds have fewer marital-adjustment problems than do people with different cultural backgrounds. (B033)

### Values
In most societies preferred mates are found to be fellow citizens who do not exhibit significant cultural differences. (M019)

## HOMOGAMY (EDUCATION)    X    Divorce
Divorced persons are most likely to have had educationally homogamous marriages, then educationally hypogamous marriages, and lastly educationally hypergamous marriages. (G157)

### Divorce Complaints
Divorcées who marry downward educationally are least likely to complain that their husbands' neglect of home-life was a cause of divorce, then divorcées who marry at the same education level, and lastly divorcées who marry upward educationally. (G157)

Divorcées who married upward educationally are slightly more likely to claim that their husbands' overspending was a cause of divorce than are those who married at the same educational level, followed by divorcées who married downward educationally. (G157)

### Divorce, Initiation of
In educationally hypogamous marriages, the wife is no more likely to be the first to suggest divorce than in educationally homogamous marriages where education is high school or less. (G157)

### Sex Status
Men are more apt to marry women of lower educational attainment than women are to marry men of lower educational attainment. (J035)

## HOMOGAMY (ETHNIC-RELIGIOUS)
### X    Marital Adjustment
There is a direct relation between ethnic and religious similarity and marital adjustment. (K161)

## HOMOGAMY (I.Q.)    X    Sex Status
People who marry are more likely to be of the same I.Q. than not; and if they are not, men are more likely to be the more intelligent. (J035)

## HOMOGAMY (NATIONALITY)    X    Fertility
Marriages between United States-born and foreign-born individuals are associated with lower fertility than are marriages between two United States-born or two foreign-born individuals. (B300)

## HOMOGAMY (OCCUPATION)
### X    Divorce Complaints
Divorcées who were occupationally hypergamous are more likely than those who were occupationally hypogamous to claim that value conflicts were a cause of divorce. (G157)

### Educational Aspirations
Working-class parents are more likely to prefer a better education for their children when the mother's occupation before marriage was nonmanual rather than manual. (L115)

### Occupational Rank
Intraoccupational endogamy is greater in the lower occupational strata than among the higher occupational strata. (C008)

### Social Mobility Aspirations
When the wife's family occupies a higher occupational level than the husband's, he adopts high mobility aspirations in order to reach that same level.

## HOMOGAMY (PERSONALITY)
### X    Marital Adjustment
Marital happiness is a function of similarity in personality. (C023)

### Mental Illness of Child (Schizophrenia)
The parents of schizophrenic children tend to marry individuals with a defense structure that is similar to their own. (K107)

## HOMOGAMY (RELIGION)    X    Fertility
Fertility rates are highest among couples whose marriages and parents' marriages were homogamous according to religious affiliation; lower among couples who have unifaith marriages, but whose parents had mixed-faith marriages; and lowest among those who have mixed-faith marriages and whose parents had mixed-faith marriages. (B300)

### Husband-Wife Relations (Companionship)
Married couples with different religious affiliations are less able to maintain companionship relations than are couples with the same religious affiliation.

### Intermarriage (Religious)
The children of mixed marriages tend to marry those outside their religious group more often than do the offspring of marriages in which both spouses are of the same religion. (T010)

## HOMOGAMY (RELIGIOUS)          X   Divorce
Denominationally homogamous Protestant married couples are less likely to divorce than are Protestant marriages where the spouses are of different denominations. (B314)

Marriages between two unaffiliated Protestants are less apt to end in divorce than are marriages where one partner is affiliated and the other is not. (B314)

### Social Mobility
The socially mobile become increasingly heterogamous in selection of boyfriends in terms of religion, while the socially nonmobile become increasingly homogamous in terms of religion. (K150)

## HOMOGAMY (VALUES)
### X   Parent-Child Relations (Communication)
The higher the degree of contact (living with and communication among) between children and parents, the more likely are the children to select mates who have the same values found in their parental home. (C103)

## HOMOSEXUALITY          X   Age
Homosexuality is most likely to occur in early adolescence when fear of sexuality is greatest. (H219)

### Authority, Attitude Toward
Overt homosexuality may develop as a method of expressing defiance of authority. (T104)

### Autoeroticism
Overt homosexuality may develop (as a method of withdrawing from reality) as an alternative to autoeroticism. (T104)

### Child-Rearing Practices (Punishment)
Mothers of homosexuals are apt to have been harder on their sons in matters of discipline (been angrier, bawled them out more, and given more physical punishment) than other mothers. (U004)

Homosexuality may occur as a response to severe punishment at the hands of the mother. (W126)

### Dependency
Overt homosexuality may develop in response to a fear of adult responsibility. (T104)

### Economic Cooperation
The absence of homosexuality is correlated with an economic pattern that requires cooperative work between groups of males. (V025)

### Economic Pattern (Migrant Labor)
Homosexuality tends to arise when the economic pattern is that of migratory labor. (T071)

### Father Absence
No significant relationship exists between homosexuality and the absence of the father from the family. (M181)

The fathers of sexually deviant homosexual boys are more likely to have been absent for extended periods of time than are the fathers of "normal" boys. (M209)

### Father-Child Relations (Interaction)
Fathers of homosexuals are likely to have given less than the usual amount of care (attention, love, training, friendship, affection, praise, and play) than are other fathers. (U004)

### Father-Child Relations (Rejection)
Homosexuality is more likely to occur where the father is perceived to have abandoned the child and there is a consequent identification with the mother. (F085)

### Father-Son Relations (Rejection)
Fathers of sexually deviant (homosexual) boys are more likely to have rejected their sons than are fathers of "normal" boys. (M209)

### Identification with Cross-Sex Parent
Male homosexuals tend to have an exaggerated identification with their mothers. (R126)

### Mental Illness
There is no positive correlation between psychosis and homosexual tendencies. (M164)

### Mental Illness (Paranoia)
Patients who are paranoid tend also to have homosexual tendencies. (N050)

### Mother-Child Relations (Affection)
There is a correlation between lack of maternal affection and lesbianism in the daughter. (R104)

Mothers of male homosexuals are more likely to have withheld love, friendliness, and affection than are other mothers. (U004)

### Mother-Son Relations
Male homosexuals are more likely than heterosexual males to have suitor-like relationships with their mothers (i.e., bringing them gifts, taking them out as one would a girl friend). (W140)

### Mother-Son Relations (Idealization)
Homosexuality is more common among boys who overidealize their mothers. (W140)

### Mother-Son Relations (Possessiveness)
The more possessive the mother, the more likely is homosexuality in the son. (R104)

### Mother-Son Relations (Sex)
Concern with homosexuality may be a defense against strong erotic attachment to the mother. (N050)

### Occupational Rank of Mother/Father
The greater the occupational prestige of the wife outside the home, relative to the man, the more likely is homosexuality in the son. (R104)

### Parent-Child Relations
Neurotic homosexual males are more likely to have had unsatisfactory father-son relations and overintense mother-son relations than are heterosexual neurotic males. (W140)

### Parent-Child Relations (Anxiety)
Homosexuality is more likely to occur where the anxiety-inducing parent is of the opposite sex. (S258)

### Parent-Child Relations (Rejection)
Homosexuality is more likely to develop if the child perceives that his sex was a disappointment to his parents. (T104)

### Paternal Role
Homosexuality is less likely to occur if the father has a strong position in the family. (W126)

### Power Structure of Family
Men who were reared in families where the father was

weak (or absent) and the mother was the dominant figure are more inclined toward homosexuality. (W140)

### Power Structure of Family (Wife Dominance)
The greater the authority of the mother in the home, relative to the father, the more likely is homosexuality in the son. (R104)

### Self-Conception (Social Relations)
Homosexuality is more likely to occur if the individual has little self-esteem and difficulty in establishing relationships with others. (T104)

### Sex Ratio
Homosexual practices are more frequent where bachelors greatly outnumber unmarried girls. (W128)

### Sex- Role Definition
Homosexuality is to be expected in a society in which the relations between men and women are placed in a sharp contrast (in which men, from their early childhood are almost exclusively in the company of men and women in the company of women). (T107)

### Sex- Role Model
The less adequate the father as a masculine sex model, the more likely is homosexuality in the son. (R104)

### Sibling Structure (Monozygotic/Dizygotic Twins)
Homosexuality of both twins is more likely among monozygotic than among dizygotic twins. (M212)

### Superego Formation
Homosexuality is likely to be repressed or overt to the extent that the superego is stern or weak. (T104)

## HOMOSEXUALITY, ATTITUDE TOWARD
### X   Rank of Women
Societies in which homosexuality is less disapproved are more likely to hold women in low esteem. (C091)

## HOMOSEXUALITY, OVERTNESS OF
### X   Sexual Permissiveness
Overtones of homosexuality will be directly correlated with overtness of general sexual expression. (S187)

## HONEYMOON     X   Courtship
Where there are more peer relationships during courtship and the couple to be married is better acquainted, the function of the honeymoon as a bridge over role discontinuity (from courtship to marriage) is not as crucial. (P083)

### Premarital Sex Relations
Couples who have had premarital sex relations are less likely to take a wedding trip than are those who have not. (P083)

## HONORARY TITLES
### X   Competition Within Lineage
The existence of honorary titles tends to stimulate intra-lineage competition. (F015)

## HOSPITALIZATION   X   Role Definition in Family
Among mental patients whose posthospital social and vocational performance was low, those whose primary role in the family was that of child were more likely to stay out of the hospital than were those whose primary role was that of spouse. (F124)

Family members influence instrumental performance; married men must meet higher levels of instrumental performance than must single men living with parents because wives have higher expectations than parents

do. This factor does not, however, explain rates of rehospitalization. (F124)

Differential demands of family account for the fact that patients from conjugal families return to the hospital more frequently than do those from parental families. (F124)

## HOUSEHOLD COMPOSITION     X   Aggression
The composite household tends to reduce overt expression of intrafamilial aggression. (C035)

### Child-Rearing Practices (Indulgence)
The degree of infant indulgence is roughly proportional to the number of adults living in the household; extended and polygynous families tend to be predominantly indulgent, nuclear families are unpredictable, and in mother-child households the probability of indulgence is slight. (W127)

### Class
Middle-class households are more likely to contain aged parents and their children and grandchildren than are lower-class families. (B312)

### Employment of Mother
A joint household with three generations is more likely when a young mother is working than when she is unemployed. (R120)

### Father Absence
Mothers who were raised in households in which there were no men for the first six years of their lives are more likely to develop households of their own in which there is no man present for the first six years of their children's lives.

### Husband-Wife Relations (Closeness)
The personal relations of the husband and wife will be less important when the family structure is that of an extended household. (L079)

### Inheritance (Equal Division)
The typical family in the equal-division inheritance pattern tends to consist of man and wife with a smaller number of children but fewer celibates. (H066)

### Marital Adjustment
The greater the number of adults other than husband and wife residing in the home, the more likely is disharmony between the marital partners. (C117)

When other adults than the parents live in the home, the fewer the outside interests of the former, the greater the conflict between the latter. (C117)

### Mate Selection (Disorganization)
The greater the disorganization of mating relations, the greater the incidence of domestic units consisting of single mothers with their children and/or their grandchildren. (S211)

### Mental Illness
Mental illness is less likely to occur where the residential unit is the extended family. (T110)

### Mental Illness (Hospitalization)
There is no significant difference in the type of family setting of mental patients with low levels of social and vocational performance who succeed in remaining in the community and those who return to the hospital. (F124)

### Mental Illness (Social Adjustment)
The greater the extent to which the family is of the same, rather than of ascending or descending generation, the lower the level of posthospital performance of the mental patient. (S245)

### Mother-Child Relations (Warmth)
There is a curvilinear relationship between the number of adults residing in the family and the maternal warmth displayed toward the child, a few additional adults tending to produce conditions favorable to warmth and a larger number tending to produce less emotional expressiveness (cross-cultural). (M216)

### Personality of Mother (Emotional Stability)
The mother tends to be more emotionally unstable when the only man living in the household is her husband than when other men are present. (M216)

### Race (Urbanization)
Urban Negro families are more likely than the rest of the population to have women as heads (U.S.). (L124)

### Sex Status
Male heads of households are more likely to accommodate their daughters' than their sons' children and are more likely to accommodate their daughters' illegitimate than their legitimate children. (S211)

### Sex Status of Household Head
Households under male heads are more likely to have a higher proportion of nonlineage to lineage kin among male members than are households under female heads. (F072)

Men are more willing to accommodate unrelated persons in their homes than their own illegitimate children. With women, the reverse is true. (S211)

Domestic units under female heads are more likely to contain three (or more) generations than are units under male heads. (S211)

### Superego Formation
There is more guilt orientation in nuclear households than in mother–child households. (W127)

## HOUSEHOLD MANAGEMENT
### X   Child-Rearing Practices (Neglect)
Families which are marked by their severe neglect of children are more likely to have little routine in the management of daily household tasks and little assignment of responsibility for these tasks than are other types of families. (Y043)

### Juvenile Delinquency
Families of juvenile delinquents have a less-planned household routine than do families of nondelinquents. (G123)

## HOUSEHOLD STRUCTURE
### X   Child-Rearing Practices (Aggression)
There is a correlation between the punishment for aggression and household structure; nuclear households are least severe, then polygynous and mother-child households, and most severe are extended family households. (W127)

## HOUSING          X   Avoidance Relationship
Avoidance relationships will tend to be modified with a change toward Western housing arrangements. (B118)

### Child-Rearing Practices (Neglect)
Bad housing, as such, is not the cause of a parent's neglecting his child. (B270)

### Child-Rearing Practices (Permissiveness)
Permissiveness in child rearing varies directly with the amount of space within the home. (B007)

### Descent (Matrilineal)
There is a correlation between large community houses and matriarchal institutions. (T082)

### Incest
Overcrowded homes are more likely than others to produce incestuous behavior. (W143)

### Juvenile Delinquency
Delinquents are more likely to come from families that reside in crowded living conditions than are nondelinquents. (S210)

### Occupational Choice
Where children grow up in crowded living space (family), they are less likely to want to follow in the occupations of their fathers. (P061)

### Polyandry
The appearance of polyandry may be correlated with heavy demands for housing construction. (V025)

### Residence
The more available housing is, the less frequently will aged parents live with any of their grown children. (B312)

## HOUSING (URBAN)
### X   Stability of Extended Family
The housing facilities of the urban community tend to result in the physical dislocation of the extended family. (A013)

### Stability of Joint Family
The joint family tends to disappear in urban areas as a consequence of housing conditions. (M021)

## HUMAN SACRIFICE
### X   Parent-Child Relations (Ambivalence)
Human sacrifice is more likely to occur in societies in which there is an ambivalence in the parent-child relationship. (W154)

### Religion (Maternal Deities)
Human sacrifice tends to be associated with matrilineal fertility cults. (W154)

## HUSBAND/WIFE     X   Affinal Relations (Conflict)
In-law problems in marriage more frequently involve the wife's parents than the husband's parents. The contrary of this proposition is also asserted (U.S.). (K014)

### Desertion as Grounds for Divorce
When desertion is the grounds for divorce in primary marriages, it is more likely that the wife will get the divorce rather than the husband. (K003)

### Divorce
The husband more frequently than the wife is the first to desire a divorce. (G157)

The husband is more often than the wife the party who adopts a line of behavior which forces the other spouse to suggest a divorce. (G157)

The wife is more likely than the husband, even under unpleasant marital conditions, to feel disposed to stay in the marriage. (G157)

### Divorce, Grounds for
The husband is more likely than the wife, in *remarriages,* to seek a divorce on the grounds of desertion. (K003)

### Divorce, Initiation of
Holding religion constant, the wife is more likely to claim that she both suggested first and continued to insist on divorce and is least likely to claim that her husband both suggested the divorce first and insisted upon it. (G157)

It is generally easier for a man to initiate divorce than for a woman. (S158)

### Friendship
In middle-class families, the husband will initiate a greater number of the shared primary friendships which the couple have in common than will his wife. (B317)

A middle-class couple is more apt to visit friends shared by both partners when the friendships were initiated by the husband. (B317)

In middle-class families, husband-initiated friendships shared by husband and wife involve a wider range of activities in which he and his wife participate with their friends than do friendships which the wife initiates. (B317)

In middle-class families, the shared friendships initiated by the husband will be characterized by a stronger positive effect than those initiated by the wife. (B317)

In middle-class families, a husband shares confidences with an unmarried friend (disregarding sex) who is the couple's shared friend more often than his wife does. (B317)

Of a middle-class couple's *shared* friends, both spouses are more likely to list three closest men friends rather than women; and of these, they are both more likely to list men secured as friends by the husband. He will also list an unmarried female friend more often than his wife will list an unmarried male friend. (B317)

### Husband-Wife Relations (Communication)
A wife is more apt than her husband to communicate her feelings to her spouse when she is upset. (L173)

### Husband-Wife Relations (Interaction)
Wives are more likely than husbands to see their parents two or three times a week; husbands are more likely to see their parents weekly or monthly. (W006)

### Political Attitudes
Husband and wife are likely to have similar political attitudes. (B265)

The correlation between one spouse's political attitudes and his or her perception of the other spouse's attitudes is greater than the actual attitude correlation. (B265)

### Political Attitudes (Consensus)
Husbands and wives tend to share the same political preferences and attitudes. (W148)

### Political Discussions
The wife is more likely than the husband to discuss political matters with her spouse and to be aware of his opinions. (H244)

### Residence
When it is necessary for either the husband or wife to change his or her residential community at marriage, it is more usually the woman rather than the man who changes domicile. (M019)

### Role Behavior
The husband is more likely than the wife to be less interested in the home and to be more easily attracted to activities outside of it. (G157)

The husband is more likely than the wife to be involved in activities outside of the home that have an emotional overtone (e.g., drinking, club behavior with "the boys," extreme dedication to an occupational task, etc.). (G157)

### Sex-Role Definition (Instrumental/Expressive)
Husbands tend to have the instrumental ideal role, and wives the expressive ideal role when spouses are asked to describe the "ideal mate." (K153)

## HUSBAND-WIFE RELATIONS    X    Dating
Among divorcées who are unattached (not remarried or steady daters), frequent daters are less likely to feel antagonistic toward their ex-spouses than are those who date less frequently. (G157)

### Descent
High importance of the husband-wife tie is associated with a kinship structure that is patrilineal, patrilocal, or neolocal. (H172)

### Descent (Matrilineal)
Where the woman bears children for her own blood line, the wifely bond tends to be weak. (G012)

### Descent (Patrilineal)
Where women bear children for their husbands' group, the wifely bond tends to be strong. (G012)

### Duration of Marriage
The marriage tie gradually becomes firmer as the marriage endures. (G111)

### Fertility
The wife who is fertile (and thus more assured of the stability of her marriage) will identify more fully with the interests of her husband. (H165)

### Fertility Values
The greater the emphasis placed on the husband-wife relationship, the less likely it is that large families will be considered desirable. (T098)

### Income of Divorcée
Divorcées who feel they have enough with which to meet expenses are less likely to have antagonistic feelings toward their ex-husbands than are those who do not feel they have enough. This difference increases over time. (G157)

### Juvenile Delinquency
There is no relationship between the degree of interest taken in the activities of the spouse and delinquent behavior in the children. (N057)

There is no relationship between the frequency of requests by the mother for assistance by the father with housework and delinquent behavior in the children. (N057)

#### Lineage Ties
When ties between lineage members are emphasized, bonds between the husband and wife are correspondingly of minimal importance. (H043)

#### Marital Adjustment
The success of the marriage will depend upon the satisfaction of the fundamental personality needs like love, affection, self-fulfillment, and prestige. (B033)

#### Mental Illness of Child (Schizophrenia)
Schizophrenia in children correlates with family situations where one spouse gratifies rather than combats the other's narcissistic needs. (L114)

#### Prostitution
A relationship between the need for a peer type of interaction with women and the development of a class of sophisticated prostitutes of the geisha variety occurs when the wives are made incapable of such interaction by the limitation of their experience and their formal education. (P083)

The demand for prostitutes' services has declined with the inclusion of the beauty parlor in the working-class wife's budget. (P083)

#### Remarriage
Divorcées who feel negative or loving attitudes toward their ex-husbands are less likely to claim there is a potential spouse among their male friends than are those who feel friendly or indifferent toward their ex-husbands. (G157)

#### Residence (Virilocal)
Other things being equal, a wife will reside with her husband if he (or whoever has jural authority over him) has unrestricted rights over her sexual and economic services. (F074)

#### Role Model
There is a positive association between daughters who perceive their parents as actively concerned with one another and the daughters' choice of their mothers as their adult-role models. (H201)

#### Sex-Role Behavior
In social-emotional behavior, husband and wife within the same marriage tend to be more alike than they are like other husbands and wives (across marriages). (L173)

#### Social Network
The husband is more likely to see his friends independently of his wife when they reside in a closely knit friendship network (i.e., a high frequency of interaction among family units) than in a loosely knit friendship network. (G156)

The more married couples can count on an outside network of friends for aid, the less often they will have to turn to one another for help. (G156)

## HUSBAND-WIFE RELATIONS (AFFECT)
#### X    Divorce, Adjustment to
Divorcées who are positively emotionally involved with their husbands after the divorce are more likely than those who are less emotionally involved to experience difficult emotional problems in divorce. (G157)

## HUSBAND-WIFE RELATIONS (AFFECTION)
#### X    Age of Wife
The older the wife at the time of marriage, the higher is her satisfaction with the husband's expression of affection. (G157)

#### Class
The higher the social rank of the married partners, the greater the expression of love and affection. (G157)

Romantic attachment and emotional involvement is lower among married couples in the lower strata. (G157)

#### Husband-Wife Relations (Companionship)
The higher the degree of companionship between marital partners, the more likely they are to express love openly.

#### Husband-Wife Relations (Egalitarianism)
When the character of the marriage relationship rests primarily on an affective attachment for the other person, mutuality and equality are more likely to occur. (P012)

#### Marital Adjustment
There is a direct relation between expressions of affection and marital adjustment. (K161)

Decline of agreement on affectional activity in the marital relationship is highly associated with a decline in marital adjustment. (P071)

#### Marital Stability
In societies in which there are no expectations of emotional attachments between husband and wife, marriages will tend to be more stable. (G138)

#### Parent-Child Relations (Affection)
Feelings of inadequacy and insecurity and inferiority on the part of either parent or frustration in the affectional relationship may lead to compensation through a struggle for attention and affection from the child. (B033)

A child can love both parents if his parents love one another; a child is forced to side with one parent against the other if the parents hate one another. (L134)

#### Pregnancy, Attitude Toward
The stronger the wife's esteem and affection for her husband, the happier she is about pregnancy. (S191)

## HUSBAND-WIFE RELATIONS (AGGRESSION)
#### X    Preferential Marriage (Exchange)
The exchange of siblings in marriage acts as a deterrent to mistreatment by the husband or wife. (C035)

#### Property Exchange at Marriage
The exchange of property between families at the time of marriage acts as a deterrent to subsequent injury of either spouse. (C035)

#### Sex Status
Among middle-class Americans, wives are likely to show more verbal aggression than are husbands. (W148)

## HUSBAND-WIFE RELATIONS (AUTHORITARIANISM)
**X   Class**

Husbands in the lower strata are more likely to be authoritarian. (G157)

Wives in lower-class families are less likely to object to husband dominance. (G157)

## HUSBAND-WIFE RELATIONS (AUTHORITY)
**X   Husband-Wife Relations (Punishment)**

The authority of the husband over the wife tends to be greater if he is socially permitted to administer corporal punishment to her. (H164)

### Sex-Role Definition
When there is a pronounced polarity of roles between the husband and wife, most marriages will tend to show some conflict over the question of authority. (L064)

## HUSBAND-WIFE RELATIONS (CLOSENESS)
**X   Class**

The higher the married couple's social rank, the more likely they are to turn to each other for help in trouble and the less likely they are to turn their negative feelings against each other. (G157)

### Cohesion of Clan
The importance of clan solidarity is inversely correlated with the strength of the relationship between husband and wife. (H103)

With the deterioration of the clan system, the relationship between husband and wife becomes more personal. (W082)

### Cohesion of Kin Network
When ties with extended kin network are strong, emotional relationships between spouses tend to diminish. (G012)

### Descent
In matrilineal societies, the bond between a woman and her brother is stronger than her bond to her husband. (G116)

### Economic Role of Wife
The relationship between husband and wife will be stronger if the wife is of economic importance. (O023)

### Household Composition
The personal relations of the husband and wife will be less important when the family structure is that of an extended household. (L079)

### Identification
The less intense the relationship of the parents appears to the child, the more likely it is that he will transfer his Oedipal jealousy and his object of identification to persons outside the family. (M203)

### Identification with Father
The closer the marital relationship, the higher the son's identification with his father. (R098)

### Isolation of Nuclear Family
The more isolated the nuclear family is in the social structure, the more dependent spouses are upon each other and the weaker their ties with their own parents and adult siblings. (P062)

### Lineage, Importance of
The weakness of the husband-wife bond correlates with a strong lineage principle. (E101)

### Marriage Payment
The greater the extent to which marriage becomes a personal bond between the partners rather than an expression of the wider kinship network, the less the amount which will be paid as the bride price or dowry. (G134)

### Mental Illness
When the parents are close and have a high emotional investment in each other, the patient improves; conversely, when the parents are "emotionally divorced," the patient regresses. (B315)

### Mother-Child Relations (Closeness)
The more "husband centered" the mother is, the less child centered she is, as indicated by physical closeness, sleeping together with the children, etc. (S079)

### Parental Role
Marital ties that result from mutual dependency are strongest during the time of child rearing; marital ties that result from similarity are strongest when there are no children or after the children are grown. (C116)

### Polygyny
The ties between husband and wife are less strong in a polygamous family. (K157)

### Sex-Role Definition
Lack of husband-wife-role differentiation is positively associated with conjugal solidarity. (S216)

### Size of Household
The strength of the relationship between husband and wife is inversely correlated with the size of the household. (H164)

When the household size in the society becomes smaller, the relationship between a man and wife becomes closer. (H227)

### Sleeping Arrangements
It would seem highly probably that a husband and wife occupying the same bed are, on the whole, likely to be in every way closer to each other than are a husband and wife who occupy separate beds or separate bedrooms. (M230)

## HUSBAND-WIFE RELATIONS (COMMUNICATION)
**X   Class**

Married couples of higher social rank communicate their emotional problems more often than do couples of lower social rank. (G157)

### Duration of Marriage
The longer the duration of the marriage, the less communication of emotional problems between the two partners. (K089)

### Economic Success
When the husband is economically successful, he shares more of his work experiences with his wife as compared with a relative estrangement if he is not economically successful. (K089)

### Education
The higher the educational level (blue collar marriages), the more likely the person is to feel the need for verbal communication in marriage. (K089)

The higher the educational level, the more communication there is likely to be in a marriage. (K089)

The higher the educational background of a husband,

the less discontent his wife is likely to have over communication. (K089)

### Emotional Problems of Child
Parents (Italian- and Irish-American backgrounds) of emotionally disturbed children are less likely than those of normal children to discuss sensitive and important issues. (V031)

### Happiness
Communicativeness in marriage was more related to general happiness for women than for men. (L173)

### Husband/Wife
A wife is more apt than her husband to communicate her feelings to her spouse when she is upset. (L173)

### Husband-Wife Relations (Companionship)
Companionship between married partners is associated with communication. (L173)

### Mental Illness (Schizophrenia/Neurosis)
Parents of normals are more likely than are parents of neurotics or schizophrenics to be high in the clarity and quantity of their communication with each other. (F110)

Parents of neurotics are more likely than are parents of schizophrenics to be communicative and unambiguous with each other. (F110)

### Personality of Wife (Emotional Stability)
The higher the communication between the married couple, the more stable the emotional equilibrium of the wife. (L173)

### Social Mobility Aspirations
Husbands with high mobility aspirations as compared with non-mobile husbands, communicate more extensively with their wives about their work experiences.

### Socialization, Effectiveness of
Defective communication between mother and father is likely to lessen the child's opportunity to learn or internalize the respective role systems in the family. (L121)

### Urban/Rural
Wives in urban areas tend to communicate their emotional problems with their husbands less than do wives in rural areas.

## HUSBAND-WIFE RELATIONS (COMPANIONSHIP)
### X   Age
Older wives (past the age of 50) value the companionship with their husbands more highly than do young wives.

### Education of Wife
The higher educational level of women brought them to a more equal level with men and thus increased the companionship between husband and wife.

### Employment of Wife
Husbands of nonworking wives are more likely than are husbands of working wives to believe that employment of the wife will lead to decreased companionship on her part.

Wives employed outside the home enjoy less companionship with their husbands than do wives who spend most of their time around the home.

### Homogamy (Class)
When there is a great difference between the socioeconomic rank of the husband and the wife, the feeling of companionship between the two is lower. (R011)

### Homogamy (Religion)
Married couples with different religious affiliations are less able to maintain companionship relations than are couples with the same religious affiliation.

### Husband-Wife Relations (Affection)
The higher the degree of companionship between marital partners, the more likely they are to express love openly.

### Husband-Wife Relations (Communication)
Companionship between married partners is associated with communication. (L173)

### Income
With a higher standard of living, the husband has more leisure time available; thus an intimate companionship develops between husband and wife which was hard to achieve when no free time was available.

### Independence of Women
The readjustment of familial patterns in terms of companionship and mutual affection between husband and wife is correlated with women's actual or potential economic independence and their educational and social equality. (B033)

### Religiosity of Wife
The more constant is the religious attendance by the wife (especially if it is more frequent than the husband's), the higher she values companionship with the husband.

### Urban/Rural
Rural wives rate higher the companionship with their husbands (being deprived of close contact with other women) than do urban wives.

### Voluntary Organizations
When both husband and wife participate jointly in organizations, the companionship experienced is greater than that of joint participation in leisure-time activities.

## HUSBAND-WIFE RELATIONS (COMPATIBILITY)
### X   Social Network
When a high value is put on the compatibility of husband and wife, their extrafamilial contacts are more likely to be shared. (B209)

## HUSBAND-WIFE RELATIONS (COMPLAINTS)
### X   Education
The higher the educational level, the more likely are persons to refer to "relationship difficulties" (i.e., consideration, bossing, intimacy, etc.) as the source of marital problems than to such other difficulties as financial and material (more so for women than for men). (G126)

### Urban/Rural
Divorcées from urban backgrounds are more likely to complain about their husbands' personalities as causes of divorce than are divorcées from rural backgrounds. (G157)

Divorcées from rural backgrounds are slightly more likely to complain that their husbands were too authoritarian than are those from urban backgrounds. (G157)

Among divorcées, urban wives married to urban husbands are most likely to complain that personality conflicts were the cause of divorce, followed by rural-urban marriage combinations, and lastly by rural wives married to rural husbands. (G157)

Divorcées from rural backgrounds are slightly more likely to claim nonsupport as a cause of divorce than are divorcées from urban backgrounds. (G157)

Husbands of rural background are slightly more likely than are those of urban background to have their ex-wives claim nonsupport as a cause of divorce. (G157)

## HUSBAND-WIFE RELATIONS (CONFLICT)
### X  Age of Mother
Younger mothers are more likely than older mothers to quarrel with their husbands. (S191)

### Alcoholism of Son
Overtly antagonistic parents are more likely to produce an alcoholic son than are parents who are indifferent or affectionate. (M195)

### Child-Rearing Practices (Consistency)
The greater the conflict between the parents, the greater the inconsistency in their treatment of the child and the greater the impediment to his socialization. (B232)

### Courtship
For men there is a slight relationship between marital disagreements and the extent of premarital courtship. (P071)

### Dependency
The greater the conflict between the parents, the more likely it is that the period of dependency of the child on the mother will be prolonged.

### Education of Child
Families where the child has graduated from high school are less likely to have husband-wife conflicts than are families that have not produced high-school graduates. (Z008)

### Juvenile Delinquency
There is a correlation between frequency of parental quarrels and delinquent behavior in the girl. (N063)

There is a curvilinear relationship between frequency of parental quarrels and delinquent behavior in the son. (N063)

### Mental Illness
Mental illness tends to be correlated with conflict between parents. (L119)

### Mental Illness of Child
Mental illness of offspring is associated with a family environment in which there is open conflict between the parents. (F085)

### Mental Illness of Child (Schizophrenia)
Parents of schizophrenic children who have made good premorbid adjustment show less conflict (lack of cooperation and compromise) than do parents of schizophrenics who have made poor premorbid adjustment. (F117)

### Mental Illness (Schizophrenia)
There is more likely to be a high degree of marital conflict between the parents of the male schizophrenic than there is between the parents of the female. (B279)

Parents of schizophrenics are more likely to relate to each other with greater conflict and hostility than are parents of nonschizophrenics. (F117)

### Mental Illness (Schizophrenia/Neurosis)
Fathers of lower-class schizophrenics tend to quarrel and fight more with their wives than do fathers of neurotics. (M061)

In the lower class, more fathers of schizophrenics quarrel and fight with their wives than do fathers of neurotics. (M197)

### Power Structure of Family
Where there is a shift in the marital authority pattern, domestic quarrels are more frequent. (S171)

### Religion
In marriages of mixed faiths, a Catholic wife is likely to tolerate more conflict than a Protestant wife before initiating a divorce. (G156)

### Role Conflict
Conflict in the parent between his familial and outside roles is correlated with discord between the parents, each trying to coerce and dominate the other and increase his own personal freedom. (F106)

### Role Model
Children who report high parental disagreement are more likely to avoid choosing either parent as a role model, more often choosing peers. (H201)

### Scapegoating
The child selected as the object of parental hostility in a disturbed family is the one that best symbolizes the conflicts between the parents. (B204)

### Sex-Role Definition
Marital conflict will be reduced by specialization of sex role and activity. (S216)

### Value Conflict
Conflict in cultural value orientation is a cause of marital conflict. (V033)

## HUSBAND-WIFE RELATIONS (CONSENSUS)
### X  Emotional Adjustment of Child
Parental agreement/disagreement on descriptions of the child's behavior does not vary with the emotional adjustment of the child. (M200)

### Marital Adjustment
The greater the disagreement on domestic values, the lower the marital integration of the couple. (F116)

Marital satisfaction tends to be directly correlated with a common definition of interest between the husband and wife. (G050)

Couples who have shared attitudes toward activities are more likely to have better marital adjustment than are couples who do not have shared attitudes toward activities. (L004)

Couples who are well adjusted are more likely to have congruent perceptions of each other than are maladjusted couples. (L152)

### Marital Stability
Where husband and wife do not share the same values, there is a higher probability of breakup than among those who share the same values. (L116)

### Mental Illness (Schizophrenia/Neurosis)
Parents of normals and neurotics are more likely than are parents of schizophrenics to be in agreement in their views. (F110)

### Self-Conception of Wife
The higher the mother's self-esteem, the more likely is there to be general agreement between mother and father. (M186)

### Sexual Adjustment
The greater the stress the couple places on shared interests, the greater the importance they attach to successful sexual relations. (B267)

### Social Network
The more interconnected a couple's social network, the more likely it is that there will be consensus on family norms. (B268)

## HUSBAND-WIFE RELATIONS (COOPERATION)
### X   Marital Adjustment of Husband
Husbands who express a high level of need satisfaction are better able to cooperate with their wives in problem solving than are husbands who express a low level of need satisfaction.

## HUSBAND-WIFE RELATIONS (DECISIONS)
### X   Personality (Complementary Needs)
The husband is more likely to accept the decisions of his wife if there is a high degree of similarity between the husband's need for succorance and the wife's need to be nurturant (nurturance and succorance measured by a forced-choice questionnaire constructed by the author).

## HUSBAND-WIFE RELATIONS (DEFERENCE)
### X   Father-Son Relations (Deference)
When the father receives marked deference from his son, he also tends to receive marked deference from the mother. (S189)

## HUSBAND-WIFE RELATIONS (DEPENDENCY)
### X   Age of Children
There is an inverse relationship between the degree of dependence of a woman on her husband and the age of her children. (S080)

### Clan, Importance of
The dependence of a wife on her husband is inversely correlated with the importance of clan affiliation. (W082)

### Class
As the potential for the women to earn as much as her husband decreases with class, the higher the class, the more financially dependent the woman is upon her husband. (G156)

### Education of Wife
Literate women are more maritally dependent than are illiterate women. (L079)

### Employment of Wife
When the wife works at a job away from her husband, she attains greater independence from her husband.

### Marital Adjustment
Marital adjustment is better where the wife feels greater dependency on the husband than the husband does on the wife. (P071)

### Marital Stability
The less the husband and wife depend on each other, the greater are their chances of splitting up. (L116)

### Mate Selection (Love)
As men become potentially less dependent upon women for home management and cooking (due to the availability of services such as restaurants, laundries, etc.), affectional ties become a more important factor in the decision to marry. (P083)

### Mental Illness of Child (Schizophrenia)
Schizophrenia in children correlates with family situations in which the husband-wife relationship is one of neurotic dependency. (L114)

## HUSBAND-WIFE RELATIONS (DISAGREEMENTS)
### X   Marital Adjustment
Couples who settle disagreements by compromise rather than by one or the other giving in have a better chance for marital success. (B244)

## HUSBAND-WIFE RELATIONS (DOMINANCE)
### X   Mental Illness of Child (Schizophrenia)
Schizophrenia in children correlates with family situations in which wives are dominant and castrating in their relationships with their husbands. (L114)

## HUSBAND-WIFE RELATIONS (DOMINANCE/MOTHERING)   X   Alcoholism
Wives of alcoholics are more likely to be domineering and mothering than are wives of nonalcoholics. (D078)

## HUSBAND-WIFE RELATIONS (ECONOMIC)
### X   Age at Marriage
There is no correlation between the age at marriage and reports of financial difficulties. (I005)

### Conflict in Family
When there is a divergent interest between a husband and wife in regard to expenditures for consumer goods, intrafamilial conflict will occur. (H028)

### Income, Allocation of
The wife's knowledge of the amount of her husband's income is directly related to the proportion of the income the husband gives as a family allowance to the wife. (Y003)

## HUSBAND-WIFE RELATIONS (EGALITARIANISM)
### X   Descent (Bilateral)
The equality of status between husband and wife tends to be associated with bilateral patterns of descent. (S123)

### Employment of Mother
Greater marital equality increases the tendency for mothers to seek outside employment. (Y047)

### Fertility
The relation between husband and wife will be more egalitarian in character if the wife has borne children. (H165)

### Husband-Wife Relations (Affection)
When the character of the marriage relationship rests primarily on an affective attachment for the other person, mutuality and equality are more likely to occur. (P012)

### Husband-Wife Relations (Interaction)
When the rate of interaction between husband and wife is high, the relationship between spouses will tend to be egalitarian in character. (H165)

### Kin/Nonkin Relations

There is more equality of relationship between husband and wife (shared interests, joint organization) with a low degree of extrafamilial social contacts. (B209)

### Marital Adjustment

The relationship between well-adjusted mates is more likely than that between poorly adjusted mates to be one of equality. (L004)

### Marital Adjustment of Husbands

More unhappy than happy husbands believe it essential or very desirable that the husband "wear the pants" and that he be as old as the wife. They stress the importance of the husband's being the intellectual superior and dislike women who are more clever than themselves. (T074)

### Mother-Child Relations (Closeness)

Where both husband and wife were attached to their respective mothers, the relationship between husband and wife is more likely to be equalitarian than not. (L014)

### Personality Adjustment

Egalitarian spousal relationship is associated with boys who are well integrated into the family system and are relatively free of anxiety. (S205)

### Values

In societies which emphasize vertical superordination-subordination relationships, egalitarian relationships between husband and wife are less common. (P083)

## HUSBAND-WIFE RELATIONS (EMOTION)
### X   Authority Structure of Family (Asymmetrical)

An asymmetrical relationship within the authority structure of the family tends to be associated with a partial repudiation of emotional ties with women. (G028)

## HUSBAND-WIFE RELATIONS (EMOTIONAL INTENSITY)                 X   Social Network

The more interconnected the couple's network of social contacts, the less intense their emotional investment in the conjugal relationship. (B267)

## HUSBAND-WIFE RELATIONS (EMOTIONAL INTERDEPENDENCE)        X   Divorce Adjustment

When emotional involvement is relatively weak, persons in these families may change from the situation of marriage to that of divorce without experiencing a crisis. (B033)

### Marital Adjustment

Happily married couples have a higher degree of emotional interdependence than unhappily married couples do. (B033)

## HUSBAND-WIFE RELATIONS (EMOTIONAL SUPPORT)           X   Pregnancy, Attitude Toward

The greater the amount of emotional support on the part of the husband, the less is the wife disturbed psychologically during pregnancy. (L135)

## HUSBAND-WIFE RELATIONS (EMPATHY)
### X   Homogamy

There is no relationship between understanding the marital partner and similarity between self and mate. (T092)

## HUSBAND-WIFE RELATIONS (EVALUATION)
### X   Age

Older husbands tend to have more positive evaluation of their wives than do younger husbands. (B232)

### Age of Husband

Older husbands tend to have a more positive evaluation of their wives than do younger husbands. (B232)

### Aggression

Mothers who have low esteem for their husbands report more aggressive children than do mothers who are more admiring and commendatory of their spouses (U.S.). (S191)

### Alcoholism of Son

The lower the esteem of the father for the mother, the more likely that the son will become an alcoholic. (M195)

### Child-Rearing Practices (Consistency)

Mothers who are consistent in their discipline think more highly of their husbands than do mothers who are inconsistent (U.S.). (S191)

### Child-Rearing Practices (Dependency)

Mothers who are accepting of their child's dependent behavior have greater esteem for their husbands than do mothers who are not accepting (U.S.). (S191)

### Child-Rearing Practices (Reward)

Mothers who frequently use praise or tangible rewards in child rearing have greater esteem for their husbands than do mothers who do not employ these techniques as frequently (U.S.). (S191)

### Child Support

When the divorcée's attitudes toward her ex-husband are held constant, there is no relationship between his attitudes toward her (positive or negative) and the regularity of his child-support payments. (G157)

### Class

Regardless of educational level, middle-class mothers admire their husbands more and quarrel less with them over the way children should be raised than do working-class mothers (U.S.). (S191)

### Divorce

When there is a disparity between the real husband or wife and the image of the ideal mate the probability of divorce is high. (B033)

### Education of Wife

The higher the educational level of the wife, the more likely she is to blame her husband for economic failure. (K089)

Among lower-class families, the less educated the woman, the more critical is she of her husband. (S191)

### Emotional Problems of Child

Parents of emotionally disturbed children are more likely to devaluate their spouses than are parents of normals. (M200)

### Homogamy

The wife's perceived similarity between self and husband is not related to how favorably she evaluates her husband. (K124)

### Identification with Father

The more that the mother approves of the father as a model for the child, the more likely it is that the boy will identify with the father. (B234)

The more positive the mother's evaluation of the father, the higher the son's identification with his father. (R098)

### Marital Adjustment

Couples who are well adjusted are more likely to have congruent perceptions of each other than are maladjusted couples. (L152)

Happily married couples exhibit less realism in their personality appraisals than do unhappily married couples. (T092)

Marital happiness increases with the perceived similarity between self and spouse. (T092)

Marital happiness is not directly related to the wife's self-perception and the husband's perception of the wife. (T092)

### Marital Adjustment of Wife

Wives who express a high satisfaction of their needs in marriage tend to describe their husbands in more favorable terms than do wives whose need satisfaction is low.

### Mental Illness of Child (Schizophrenia)

The ego weakness of a schizophrenic child is correlated with the depreciated images for identification presented by the devaluation of one parent by the other. (L114)

Schizophrenia in the child correlates with the mother's distrust and lack of confidence in her husband. (L114)

### Mental Illness (Schizophrenia)

Mothers of schizophrenic sons more often deprecate their husbands as desirable models for their sons than do mothers of normals. (K093)

Mothers of schizophrenics are more likely than are mothers of neurotics or normals to regard their husbands as having been weak, ineffectual, or remote. (M218)

Mothers of schizophrenics are more likely than are those of neurotics or normals to regard their husbands as weak, lacking ambition and drive, and avoiding responsibility in the home. (M218)

Schizophrenia in daughters is directly correlated with the constant deprecation of the patient's father by her mother. (N061)

### Mother-Child Relations (Rejection)

Maternal rejection in early life is directly correlated with a perception of the husband as inadequate. (N061)

### Personality of Husband (Similarity)

Wives who perceive a high degree of similarity between themselves and their husbands and those who do not are equally likely to see their husbands as having desirable social traits. (K124)

### Self-Conception

The higher the approval by the one marriage partner, the higher the self-confidence created in the other partner. (T092)

Persons tend to rate themselves less favorably than they rate their spouses and less favorably than they are rated by their spouses. (T092)

### Self-Conception of Wife

The higher the wife's evaluation of herself (self-esteem ratings), the higher her evaluation of her husband. (M186)

### Toilet Training

The more severe the mother is in toilet training the child, the lower her esteem for her husband (U.S.). (S191)

## HUSBAND-WIFE RELATIONS (FINANCES)
### X Juvenile Delinquency

The home in which there is financial generosity toward the mother is less likely to produce delinquent children than is the home in which the mother has insufficient funds.

## HUSBAND-WIFE RELATIONS (FRIENDSHIP)
### X Education of Wife

The higher the educational level of a woman, the more likely it is that her husband is also her most intimate friend. (K089)

## HUSBAND-WIFE RELATIONS (HOSTILITY)
### X Child-Rearing Practices (Punishment)

Mothers of aggressive boys who had frequently spanked their sons tended to be hostile to their husbands. (B213)

### Employment of Wife

Wives who are employed outside the home are more apt to express their hostilities against their husbands than are wives who are not employed.

### Mental Illness (Schizophrenia/Neurosis)

Parents of schizophrenics are more likely to report hostility toward their spouses than are parents of normals or neurotics. (F110)

## HUSBAND-WIFE RELATIONS (IDENTIFICATION)
### X Child-Rearing Practices (Consistency)

High identification is associated with similarity or consistency between the parents regarding various child-rearing practices. (R098)

## HUSBAND-WIFE RELATIONS, IMPORTANCE OF
### X Polygyny

Polygyny of any variety is negatively associated with an emphasis on the husband-wife tie. (H172)

### Residence

High importance of the husband-wife tie is associated with a kinship structure that is patrilineal, patrilocal, or neolocal. (H172)

### Social Network

The more dispersed the couple's network of social contacts (i.e., its members do not see one another independently of the couple), the greater the stress placed upon conjugal privacy and the primacy of the conjugal relationship over all external ties. (B267)

### Values (Individualism)

Marital relationships tend to be more important and more highly valued in societies which are individualistic in their orientation. (F069)

When the husband-wife relationship is dominant, self-reliance will be stressed. (H172)

## HUSBAND-WIFE RELATIONS (INTENSITY)
### X Divorce

The divorce rate is higher in societies with a high affective intensity in the husband-wife relationship. (P057)

### Mother-Child Household

Where a high percentage of the households in the society is made up of mother and child, the husband-wife relationship is less intense. (S079)

### Mother-Child Relations (Intensity)
The more "husband centered" the mother is, the less child centered she is, as indicated by physical closeness, sleeping with the children, etc. (S079)

### Sex Taboo (Postpartum)
In societies having long periods of taboo against sex relations after childbirth, the intensity of the husband and wife relationship is lower. (S079)

### Urbanization
When families move to towns (away from kin), the conjugal bond tends to become more intense. (G012)

## HUSBAND-WIFE RELATIONS (INTERACTION)
### X Class
White collar families report more husband-wife interaction than do blue collar families. (H201)

### Husband/Wife
Wives are more likely than husbands to see their parents two or three times a week; husbands are more likely to see their parents weekly or monthly. (W006)

### Husband-Wife Relations (Egalitarianism)
When the rate of interaction between husband and wife is high, the relationship between spouses will tend to be egalitarian in character. (H165)

### Marital Adjustment
The degree of physical separation between husband and wife is directly correlated with emotional disturbance. (V028)

### Size of Community
The rate of interaction between husbands and wives will tend to be higher if the community is small in size. (H165)

### Social Network
Husband and wife tend to spend more time apart when residing in a family friendship network which is tightly knit (i.e., a high frequency of interaction among family units) than in one which is loosely knit. (G156)

## HUSBAND-WIFE RELATIONS (INTIMACY)
### X Age
The intimacy of the relationship between husband and wife is directly correlated with their age. The contrary is also asserted. (W082)

### Age Difference
"Paternalization" of the husband-wife relationship through a high age differential at marriage is likely to make intimacy between spouses more difficult. (P083)

The relationship between a husband and wife will be more intimate if they are of the same age. (T058)

### Class
Lower-class couples are less willing to share confidences. (G157)

The higher the social class, the greater the social and psychological resources to maintain role complementarity and emotional compatibility or to minimize marital contact when contact is frustrating. (P083)

### Descent (Matrilineal)
When descent, inheritance, and succession are matrilineal, the role of the father is negligible and the significance of marriage as both an intimate union and an alliance is mitigated. (D018)

### Education
The higher the educational level, the more likely the person is to consider all communications between spouses as private and not subject to discussions even with other relatives. (K089)

### Education of Husband-Wife
A great differential in formal education between husband and wife is likely to make intimacy between spouses more difficult. (P083)

### Isolation of Nuclear Family
The more isolated the nuclear family in a society is, the more dependent the husband will be on a high level of intimacy in a monogamous marriage. (P083)

### Kin-Group, Importance of
When kin-groups play an important role in a social system, objective status and obligations to other kin, not subjective sentiments, tend to characterize the marriage relationship. (P012)

### Kin Ties
The husband-wife relationship will tend to be characterized by an attitude of reserve if the allegiance of the husband lies primarily with his extended family. (S115)

### Monogamy
Monogamy through personal choice is likely to permit a higher level of intimacy in marriage than does polygyny. (P083)

### Scapegoating
In disturbed families, solidarity of the marriage increases with scapegoating of a child. (B204)

### Sex-Role Definition
Where there is segregation of sexes in everyday life and interests, the husband-wife relationship is likely to be less intimate. (K157)

### Sibling Relations (Solidarity)
When there is sister-brother solidarity, husband-wife solidarity is low. (F076)

### Social Isolation of Women
Isolation of women from the community, by reducing the value of their conversation, is likely to make intimacy between husband and wife more difficult. (P083)

### Structure of Family
The lower the level of interaction and intimacy between husband and wife, the less likely is the development of a strong conjugal system. (P083)

## HUSBAND-WIFE RELATIONS (JEALOUSY)
### X Age at Marriage
The younger the age at marriage, the more likely are wives to complain of jealousy and outside activities of the husband (his not settling down and running around too much). (I005)

### Parent-Child Relations (Rejection)
The aversion of the husband or wife to children is more likely when the spouse wishes to maintain the monopoly of the love of the spouse or fears that a rival may displace him (or her). (B033)

## HUSBAND-WIFE RELATIONS (NEGLECT)
### X Employment of Women
Husbands of nonworking wives are more likely than husbands of working wives to believe that if the wife is employed she will neglect him.

# HUSBAND-WIFE RELATIONS (POWER)
## X Achievement
An equalitarian spousal relationship is associated with boys who are high achievers in systems (e.g., the school) external to the family. (S205)

## Class
Regardless of the sex of the spouse, the more dominant tends to come from the family of higher socioeconomic status. (W148)

## Education Difference Between Husband-Wife
The husband is more likely than not to be dominant in the marriage where the husband has at least three years more education than the wife or the wife has one or two years more education than the husband. (L014)

The relationship between husband and wife is more likely than not to be egalitarian where the husband and wife have an equal number of years of education. (L014)

## Emotional Problems
The higher equality of modern marital partners brings a greater relief of their emotional problems by creating greater interdependence.

## Intelligence
The husband is more likely than not to be dominant in the marriage if he rates himself as superior or inferior to his wife in mental ability. (L014)

The wife is more likely than not to be dominant if the husband rates her as equal to himself in mental ability. (L014)

The wife is more likely than not to be dominant if she rates herself as superior to her husband in mental ability. (L014)

## Interaction in Family (Affection)
Affectional interaction is more likely to occur in families where the spouses share equal statuses rather than where one is dominant over the other (Midwestern Mennonites). (K113)

## Marital Adjustment
Husbands are more likely to be adjusted to the marriage if they submit to the domination of the wife and grant her deference and respect. Wives are more likely to be adjusted if they defer to the husband's judgment and expect less deference and respect from their husbands. (T092)

## Marriage Payment
The dowry gives a woman economic leverage in her relations vis-à-vis the husband. (K154)

## Mental Illness (Schizophrenia)
There is more vying for dominance between the parents of poor premorbid schizophrenics (poor general functioning before onset of illness) than in the interaction of parents of normal subjects. (G127)

## Parent-Child Relations
When there is dominance of one spouse rather than equalitarian relations in marital situations, the father and mother are equally likely to be dominant in parental relations. (B323)

## Parent-Child Relations (Conflict)
The husband is more likely than not to be dominant over the wife where the husband had conflict with his father and the wife did not have conflict with her father. (L014)

The husband is more likely than not to be dominant over the wife where the husband had conflict with his mother and the wife did not have conflict with her mother. (L014)

The relationship between husband and wife is more likely than not to be equalitarian where neither the husband nor the wife had conflict with their mothers and where *their* parents did not conflict with one another. (L014)

The wife is more likely than not to be dominant over the husband where the wife had conflict with her mother and the husband did not have conflict with his mother. (L014)

## Parent-Child Relations (Discipline)
The husband is more likely than not to be dominant over the wife where the husband disliked the discipline given to him by his parents and the wife did not mind discipline given to her by her parents. (L014)

The wife is more likely than not to be dominant over the husband where the husband did not mind the discipline given to him by his parents and the wife disliked the discipline given to her by her parents. (L014)

The wife is more likely than not to be dominant over the husband where the discipline given to the wife by her parents was such that she had her own way. (L014)

## Parent-Child Relations (Power)
The greater the spouse's residue of resentment from a power struggle, the greater is the likelihood that it will be expressed by the assertion of power over the children. (H213)

## Personality of Husband/Wife (Authority)
Where the husband is not rebellious toward authority and the wife is rebellious toward authority, the wife is more likely than not to be more dominant than the husband. (L014)

## Personality of Spouse (Hostility)
The more dominant spouse is usually the more overtly hostile spouse. (W148)

## Rank of Women
In an informal decision-making situation in which the husband and wife initially disagree on a number of decisions, the proportion of decisions finally won by the wife will vary directly with the power position of the wife vis-à-vis the husband as defined by the culture. (S013)

## Residence (Patrilocal/Neolocal)
The dominant position of a husband over his wife is easier to maintain when the residence pattern is patrilocal rather than neolocal. (L064)

## Urban/Rural
Urban wives are less submissive to their husbands than are rural wives. (H164)

# HUSBAND-WIFE RELATIONS (PUNISHMENT)
## X Divorce Adjustment
Divorcées who experience a great deal of emotional turmoil during the divorce are more likely to claim a desire to punish their husbands than are those who had fewer emotional problems. (G157)

## Extramarital Relations
The divorcée is more likely to desire to punish her husband if he was involved with another woman than if he was not. (G157)

### Husband-Wife Relations (Authority)
The authority of the husband over the wife tends to be greater if he is socially permitted to administer corporal punishment to her. (H164)

## HUSBAND-WIFE RELATIONS (RESPECT)
### X  Identification with Father
Middle-class mentally ill patients tend to have had identification problems toward the father as a result of the double-bind behavior of mothers (i.e., most mothers taught patients to respect their fathers, but their behavior suggested that they did not respect their husbands as much as they claimed). (M061)

## HUSBAND-WIFE RELATIONS (ROLE CONFLICT)
### X  Parent-Child Relations (Closeness)
The stronger the ties of a husband to his parents, the greater is the likelihood that role conflicts will develop over his position as son-in-law and husband. (K089)

### Parent-Child Relations (Evaluation)
In families where the degree of consensus between husband and wife on domestic values is low, there is no relationship between the extent of role tension in the marriage and the amount of disagreement between the parents as to whether they are satisfied with specific activities of the child. (F116)

### Parent-Child Relations (Satisfaction)
In families in which the degree of consensus between husband and wife on domestic values is high, the extent of role tension in the marriage varies directly with the amount of disagreement between the parents on satisfaction with specific activities of the child. (F116)

## HUSBAND-WIFE RELATIONS (ROLE STRAIN)
### X  Role Definition of Husband-Wife
Deviation of husband or wife from the modal rank order of role performances in their subculture is correlated with the degree of role strain (nonfulfillment of role expectations of spouse) they experience. (H204)

The degree to which the husband's or wife's rank ordering of role expectations of the other spouse corresponds with the modal rank order of role expectations of the other spouse in their subculture is not related to the degree of role strain in their relationship. (H204)

The degree of the husband's deviation from the modal rank order of role performance in that subculture is correlated with the degree of role strain experienced by the wife; a similar association is not found for deviation by the wife. (H204)

The degree of role strain experienced by the husband or wife is correlated with the degree of deviation of the other spouse from his or her modal rank ordering of role expectations of him (her). (H204)

## HUSBAND-WIFE RELATIONS (SHARED ACTIVITIES)
### X  Divorce
A higher proportion of divorced than of happily married persons reports mutual enjoyment in sharing such "non-home-centered" activities as dancing and drinking. (G157)

### Education
The higher the educational level the more communication there is likely to be in a marriage. (K089)

The higher the educational level the more time spouses are likely to spend together in recreational activities. (K089)

### Juvenile Delinquency
The home in which there is shared mother-father recreation is less likely to produce delinquent children than is the home in which activities are separate. (N057)

### Kin/Nonkin Relations
Where statuses of relative-friend-workmate are filled by the same people, the activities of the spouses tend to become separated. (G012)

### Marital Adjustment
Couples who enjoy sharing the same activities have a greater chance of marital success. (B244)

The degree of leisure activities shared after marriage is not highly related to the degree of disenchantment felt in the marital relationship. (P071)

### Marital Adjustment of Husband
Happy husbands more often think it is essential or very desirable that mates take their vacations together; the unhappy more often think it is undesirable. (T074)

### Marital Adjustment of Wife
Unhappy wives more often say that it is undesirable for spouses to take their vacations together; happy wives think it is desirable. (T074)

### Maternal Overprotectiveness
Parents of overprotected children share significantly fewer social activities together than do those of nonoverprotected children. (L117)

Overprotective mothers tend to share little common social life with their husbands. (L163)

### Social Network
Couples who belong to highly connected social networks (i.e., its members see one another independently of the couple) are less likely to stress shared interests and joint recreation. (B268)

Where relatives, neighbors, friends, and workmates tend to be the same people the activities of spouses become separated. (G116)

## HUSBAND-WIFE RELATIONS (SHARED INTERESTS)
### Marital Adjustment
There is a direct relationship between a community of interest (in terms of joint participation in outside activities, mutual friends, agreement on social values, and agreement on family values) and marital adjustment. (K161)

## HUSBAND-WIFE RELATIONS (SPEAKING PATTERNS)
### X  Marital Adjustment
If one spouse needs little social stimulus to begin talking, while the other needs a greater stimulus and also perceives the former spouse's voice as irritating, the happiness score of the couple is likely to be low.

## HUSBAND-WIFE RELATIONS (SUPPORT)
### X  Interaction in Family (Support)
The support patterns (solidarity, contending, dominant, conflicting) of all pairs in a nuclear family tend to be similar to those of the husband and wife, even when the husband and wife are not involved in those other pairs. (S207)

### Size of Family
As family groups increase in size from three, to four, to five, there is decreasing likelihood that there will be mutual support in the husband-wife dyad. (S207)

## HUSBAND-WIFE RELATIONS (UNDERSTANDING)
### X   Marital Adjustment
The more responding and understanding the husband is about his wife's emotional problems, the higher is the wife's satisfaction with the marriage life.

## HUSBAND-WIFE RELATIONS (WARMTH)
### X   Aggression
The parents of aggressive boys demonstrate less warmth and regard for each other than do the parents of normal boys. (B246)

### Child-Rearing Practices (Consensus)
Parents who report agreement with the spouse about child-rearing practices are more likely to have warm and affectionate feelings toward the spouse than are those who report disagreement. (B243)

### Child-Rearing Practices (Punishment)
Mothers who use nagging and scolding as means of disciplining the son are more likely to lack warmth for their husbands and to disagree with them over disciplinary policies than are mothers who do not. (B243)

### Child-Rearing Practices (Reward)
There is a correlation between the amount of parental praise for the son and degree of warmth between spouses. (B243)

### Child-Rearing Practices (Sex Role)
Parents of agressive boys who stress masculine behavior are less likely to be warm and acceptant of their spouses than are those who do not stress such behavior. (B243)

### Mother-Son Relations (Rejection)
Aggressive boys whose mothers lack warmth for their husbands are more likely to feel rejected by their mothers than are those whose mothers have more positive attitudes toward their husbands. (B243)

### Mother-Son Relations (Reward)
Mothers who praised their sons tended to display a high degree of warmth for their husbands. (B213)

### Sex Anxiety of Father
There is a correlation between the level of the father's sex anxiety and his lack of warmth toward his wife. (B243)

Fathers who were highly anxious about sex tended to be less warm toward their wives than did fathers who were low in sex anxiety. (B213)

### Toilet Training
The more severe the mother in toilet training, the lower the warmth felt for her husband (U.S.). (S191)

## HUSBAND-WIFE RELATIONS (WARMTH/HOSTILITY)
### X   Child-Rearing Practices (Punishment)
Mothers who use physical punishment are likely to have less warmth for and more hostility toward their husbands than mothers who do not. (B243)

## HUSBAND-WIFE RELATIONS (WIFE BEATING)
### X   Personality of Husband
Husbands who beat their wives tend to be more passive, indecisive, and sexually inadequate than are other husbands. (S253)

### Personality of Wife
Wives whose husbands beat them are likely to be more aggressive, masculine, frigid, and masochistic than are other wives. (S253)

### Sex Composition of Family
Wives are less likely to tolerate beating by the husband when they have an adolescent son. (S253)

## HUSBAND-WIFE TIE
### X   Descent (Matrilineal/Patrilineal)
The bond of a sister with her brother is stronger and the bond with her husband is weaker in matrilineal than in patrilineal societies. (G012)

# IDENTIFICATION

### X  Adult-Child Relations (Control)
A child tends to identify with the person or persons having closest control over his destiny. (M058)

### Aggression
In doll play, the child tends to identify with the doll that represents his most important source of conflict relating to aggression and aggression control in the family. (S228)

### Authority Structure of Family
The weaker members in a family authority structure (i.e., children) tend to adopt more characteristics of the more powerful, rather than the less powerful, other person. (B216)

### Child-Rearing Practices (Authoritarianism)
Authoritarian discipline increases the child's identification with the punishing authority. (M203)

### Class
Middle-class parents are more likely than lower-class parents to provide effective identification figures for their children during childhood. (M197)

### Husband-Wife Relations (Closeness)
The less intense the relationship of the parents appears to the child, the more likely it is that he will transfer his Oedipal jealousy and his object of identification to persons outside the family. (M203)

### Lineage/Nuclear Family
Since a lineage is an indissoluble unit, it provides a more permanent sense of identification for the individual than does the nuclear family, which is dissoluble. (C093)

### Mental Illness of Child (Schizophrenia)
Presentation to the child of irreconcilable role models for identification is a cause of schizophrenia in the child. (F097)

### Mental Illness (Schizophrenia)
For men there is a *negative* correlation between identification with the father, mother, and "most people," in that order, and a tendency to schizophrenia. (R103)

Among females there is a correlation between identification with the mother and all types of abnormal trends. (R103)

### Mother-Child Relations (Affection)
The more emotionally remote the mother (and the weaker the daughter's attachment to her), the less likely it is that the daughter will be able to identify with a strong maternal figure who can both love and educate the child. (B272)

Identification is positively associated with the spontaneity with which the mother expresses affection. (R098)

### Mother-Child Relations (Empathy)
The mother who is better able to state correctly her child's preferences, ambitions, and fears is also more likely to feel the same way herself. This correlation between awareness and identification is higher between girl and mother than between boy and mother.

### Mother-Daughter Relations (Control)
High maternal identification in daughters is associated with perception of the mother as high in control. (H196)

### Neurosis
Where children do not identify with parents as a result of cultural and class differences between them, they do not feel guilt or hostility at their negative feelings toward the parents and thus do not develop neuroses as a result. (G020)

### Ordinal Position
In general, children are more likely to identify with or be more involved with those in the family above them in the age hierarchy than with those below them (firstborn children with parents, second born children with older siblings. etc.). (K149)

Firstborn and only children have less of a tendency to identify with other people having similar character traits than do later-born children. (S278)

### Parent-Child Relations (Interaction)
The degree to which the foster child identifies with his natural parents is correlated with, and dependent upon, the extent of his contact with them. (W149)

### Parental Role
The child identifies with the parent who is the source of its most severe frustrations. (A060)

### Power Structure of Family
The child is more likely to identify with the person he conceives as most powerful (i.e., the parent who most effectively controls his rewards and punishments). (A060)

### Sex Status
Girls tend to identify with people they know personally, either inside or outside of the family; boys identify with general societal roles or with well-known persons epitomizing these roles. (W138)

### Sibling Structure (Age and Sex)
As the age difference between siblings increases, identification of the older with the younger is highest and decreases most slowly among girls with younger sisters; it is not quite as high among boys with younger brothers and decreases slowly; it decreases more rapidly with spacing among boys with younger sisters and most rapidly of all among girls with younger brothers. (K149)

Among like-sex siblings, the greater the age difference between siblings, the greater the desire of the younger to have the assets and advantages of the older; the conscious desire of the younger to become the older sibling decreases more slowly with spacing among girls with an older brother than among boys with an older sister. (K149)

### Speech Development
There is a correlation between the presence of an adult identification model and the development of language in the child. (Y045)

## IDENTIFICATION/CHILD-REARING PRACTICES
### X Socialization, Effectiveness of
The child's imitation of the parental model correlates, not with identification with (internalization of) parents' attitudes, but with the process differential reinforcement of his behavior. (B234)

## IDENTIFICATION OF MOTHER WITH CHILD
### X Mental Illness
There is a high degree of correlation between mental illness and the failure of the mother of the patient to identify with the patient. (H218)

### Mental Illness of Child
Mental disturbances in the child are more likely to occur when the mother identifies the child exclusively with herself than when she identifies the child with both parents. (H218)

## IDENTIFICATION OF MOTHER WITH DAUGHTER
### X Anxiety
A high degree of anxiety and anxious dependence in regard to the mother is inversely correlated with the mother's degree of identification with the daughter. (H218)

A high degree of anxiety in regard to the mother's safety is inversely correlated with the mother's degree of identification with the daughter. (H218)

A high degree of general anxiety is inversely correlated with the mother's degree of identification with the daughter. (H218)

### Child-Rearing Practices (Aggression)
Mothers with a high degree of identification with their daughters are more likely to tolerate expressions of anger in their children than are mothers who do not identify. (H218)

### Conformity
Daughters who are the objects of maternal identification tend to conform more to their mothers' wishes than do daughters who are not. (H218)

### Death of Grandmother
Mothers who have high degrees of identification with their daughters were more likely to have lost their own mothers before the age of 16 than were mothers who did not identify with their daughters. (H218)

### Emotional Problems of Child
When the degree of identification of the mother with her daughter is too encompassing, emotional instability in the daughter is likely to result. (H218)

### Marital Adjustment
Mothers who have a high degree of identification with their daughters tend to view their marriages more positively than do mothers who fail to identify with their daughters. (H218)

### Mother-Daughter Relations
Mothers who have a high degree of identification with their daughters tended themselves to have a better relationship with their own mothers. (H218)

### Mother-Daughter Relations (Communication)
A high degree of identification of the mother with the daughter is directly correlated with ease on the part of the daughter of communicating emotions, fantasies, and dreams. (H218)

A high degree of identification of the mother with the daughter is directly correlated with an ease, on the part of the daughter, of communicating anger toward her mother. (H218)

### Personality Adjustment
There is a direct correlation between the degree of identification with the daughter and the perception of the daughter as well adjusted. (H218)

Mothers are more likely to rate daughters with whom they identify as better adjusted than other siblings. (H218)

### Personality (Ego-Strength)
A high degree of emotional security or ego strength is directly correlated with a conscious acknowledgment on the part of the mother of a personality resemblance with her daughter. (H218)

### Self-Conception of Mother
Mothers with low evaluations of self will tend to reject identifications with their daughters if they see these undesirable traits mirrored in their daughters' activities. (H218)

### Sexual Adjustment
Mothers who have a high degree of identification with their daughters tend to be better adjusted sexually than are mothers who do not. (H218)

## IDENTIFICATION OF PARENTS
### X Mental Illness of Child (Schizophrenia)
Schizophrenia in children is more likely to appear in families where parents still identify with their own parental homes. (L114)

## IDENTIFICATION WITH ADULT KIN
### X Socialization, Effectiveness of
The more the child identifies with adult relatives, the more the child acquires the desired roles and goals of his society. (G044)

## IDENTIFICATION WITH CHILD
### X Emotional Problems of Child
Parents of emotionally disturbed children are less likely than are parents of normals to identify with the child. (M200)

### Maternal Role
The less that the mother has developed the passive aims essential to the maternal role, the less likely it is that she will be able to identify with the child's needs or to respond to his demands without feeling a threat to her own ego. (B272)

### Sex Status
Parents tend to identify more closely with babies of the same sex as themselves.

## IDENTIFICATION WITH COMMUNITY
### X Cohesion of Family
The more intense the individual's identification with the collective, the lower the solidarity of the family. (T098)

### Fertility Values
The more intense the individual's identification with the collectivity, the less likely he is to desire children. (T098)

## IDENTIFICATION WITH CROSS-SEX PARENT
### X   Courtship Status
With advancing courtship, children are more apt to pair off with partners who bear similarities to their opposite-sex parents. (H229)

### Homosexuality
Male homosexuals tend to have an exaggerated identification with their mothers. (R126)

### Juvenile Delinquency
Juvenile delinquents are more likely to like parents of the opposite sex than are nondelinquents; but juvenile delinquent boys are more likely to prefer their mothers than juvenile delinquent girls are to prefer their fathers. (G117)

### Mother-Son Relations (Control)
The more the mother is perceived as controlling, the greater the son's maternal identification. (H196)

### Neurosis
Persons with neuroses tend to identify themselves with the parent of the opposite sex. (L145)

### Peer Relations
Boys who perceive themselves as more like their fathers than their mothers are perceived more favorably by their peers; girls who see themselves as more like their mothers than their fathers are viewed less favorably by their peers. (J026)

### Personality of Daughter (Dominance)
Girls who rank high in dominance show stronger identification with their fathers than with their mothers. (R126)

### Sex-Role Definition
Cross-sex parental identification facilitates the adoption of appropriate sex role in the child. (S240)

### Sex Status
College-educated males identify with their mothers; college-educated females identify with their fathers (similarity of responses to California F-Scale). (W144)

### Sibling Structure (Sex)
Having a favored sibling of the opposite sex may often aid cross-sex parental identification. (R126)

## IDENTIFICATION WITH EXTENDED FAMILY
### X   Geographical Mobility
Lack of interaction with the extended family caused by geographical mobility does not lead to the lessening of extended family identification. (L181)

High identification with the extended family does not limit the geographical mobility of a nuclear family. (L181)

## IDENTIFICATION WITH EXTENDED KIN
### X   Economic Role of Kin
The extension of family sentiment to members of the wider kinship group depends upon the role of the latter in fulfilling the original family functions of distributing and consuming food. (R087)

## IDENTIFICATION WITH FAMILY
### X   Geographic Mobility
The greater the residential mobility of the individual, the weaker his identification with family groups. (M166)

### Illegitimacy (Adoption)
Unwed mothers who release their children for adoption are more likely to identify positively with, and be accepted by, parents, adults, peers, or social groups that communicate and maintain a meaningful awareness of the stigma attached to illegitimacy. (V027)

### Initiation Rites
In societies where the children are to be anchored in and are to identify with the wider kin-group, there is more likely to be a disruption of the child's relations with his parents in the form of initiation rites than in societies in which the children are brought up to be anchored in and to identify with the nuclear family. (C093)

### Social Mobility Aspirations
Children who are upward aspirers are more conscious of the differences between themselves and their families than are children who are not upward aspirers. (E102)

### Surrogate Parent
There is no relationship between identification with mainly one family and the age at which the child enters foster placement. (W149)

The greater the proportion of the child's lifetime spent in the present foster home, the more likely is the child to identify with his foster parents. (W149)

## IDENTIFICATION WITH FAMILY/NON-FAMILY
## MEMBER          X   Social Mobility Aspirations
Adolescents with upward mobility aspirations are less likely than others to choose an "ideal" adult to emulate from within their own families. (D077)

## IDENTIFICATION WITH FAMILY ROLES
### X   Parent-Child Relations (Rebellion)
The less the parents identify with the cardinal role of family membership, the more likely is a revolt by the children during adolescence. (F106)

### Parent-Child Relations (Rejection)
The less the parents identify with the cardinal role of family membership, the more likely it is that they will be rejected by their children. (F106)

### Role Behavior in Family
The greater the extent to which the parents identify with the cardinal role of family membership, the more likely they are to be able to exchange roles occasionally without confusion. (F106)

### Sex-Role Adjustment
The greater the extent to which the parents identify with the cardinal role of family membership, the more likely they are to tolerate status differences between them. (F106)

## IDENTIFICATION WITH FATHER
### X   Achievement Motivation
Strong father identification is associated with high achievement motivation in the son. (M204)

### Aggression
Adolescent control boys are more inclined to identify with their fathers than aggressive boys are. (B213)

Identification with an aggressive and/or antisocial father is a cause of aggression in the son. (B243)

### Father Absence
Sons who have been separated from their fathers during the Oedipal period show weaker identification with their fathers during early adult years than do sons who were not separated. (L170)

The absence of the father from the home (separation or divorce) is associated with insecurity on the part of the son in his identification with his father. (L171)

### Father-Child Relations (Affection)
Fathers are more likely to be highly affectionate if they remember their own fathers as being so. (B297)

### Father-Child Relations (Protectiveness)
Lack of the father's concern with protection of his children leads to lack of identification by the children with their father. (M202)

### Father-Child Relations (Warmth)
The stronger the identification of adolescent boys with their fathers, the more likely it is that they view their fathers as highly nurturant and rewarding. (M183)

### Father-Son Relations
The degree of identification with the father is positively related to the son's perception of his father as a gratifying individual. (P076)

### Father-Son Relations (Affection)
The more warm and affectionate the father, the more likely the son's identification with him. (M183)

### Father-Son Relations (Punishment)
The more punitive and threatening the father, the more likely is the son to identify with him. (M183)

### Father-Son Relations (Reward/Punishment)
The stronger the boy's identification with his father, the more likely is he to perceive him as both rewarding and punitive. (A060)

### Father-Son Relations (Warmth)
A father-son relationship characterized by warmth is more conducive to son-father identification than one not so characterized. (P064)

Degree of father-son identification is positively correlated more with the warmth of the relationship than with the masculinity of the father. (P064)

### Husband-Wife Relations (Closeness)
The closer the marital relationship, the higher the son's identification with his father. (R098)

### Husband-Wife Relations (Evaluation)
The more that the mother approves of the father as a model for the child, the more likely it is that the boy will identify with the father. (B234)

The more positive the mother's evaluation of the father, the higher the son's identification with his father. (R098)

### Husband-Wife Relations (Respect)
Middle-class mentally ill patients tend to have had identification problems toward the father as a result of the double-bind behavior of mothers (i.e., most mothers taught patients to respect their fathers, but their behavior suggested that they did not respect their husbands as much as they claimed).(M061)

### Identification with Mother
The more the boy's identification with his mother develops into sexual object cathexis, the more hostile and jealous becomes his identification with his father. (B234)

Personal identification with the mother (precedes and) facilitates identification with the father. (S240)

### Juvenile Delinquency
A lower proportion of delinquents than of nondelinquents regard their fathers as acceptable patterns for emulation. (S210)

Juvenile delinquents are less likely to identify with their fathers than are nondelinquents. (S210)

### Mother-Son Relations (Affection)
If the mother remains the focus of affection and reward-giving, father-son identification will be seriously retarded. (P064)

### Parent-Child Relations (Gratification)
Boys who are highly identified with their fathers perceive a greater differential between their parents' reward value than do boys who are less identified with their fathers. (P076)

### Paternal Role
For sons, high father identification is associated with high involvement by the father in child-rearing activities. (R098)

### Paternal-Role Model
The more available the father is as a role model, the higher the son's identification with his father. (R098)

### Personality Adjustment
Boys who identify with their fathers are more likely to make better social and emotional adjustment (as measured by teacher ratings) than those who do not. (P076)

### Personality of Mother (Dominance)
The more dominant the mother, the less strongly the boy tends to identify with the father. (P064)

### Personality of Mother (Masculinity)
There is a negative relationship between a mother's masculinity and a son's identification with his father. (P076)

### Personality of Son (Masculinity)
The degree of father identification is correlated with masculinity of attitude (P064)

### Sex-Role Behavior of Father
Boys whose fathers stress masculine behavior are more likely to identify with the father than are those whose fathers do not stress such behavior. (B243)

### Sex-Role Identification
The more the child (male and female) internalizes a reciprocal role relationship with the father, the more likely he or she is to develop an appropriate sex-role orientation. (J031)

### Sexual Interest
High paternal identification is associated with strong heterosexual interests in the son. (M204)

## IDENTIFICATION WITH FATHER BY SEX STATUS
### X    Parent-Child Relations (Fear)
The greater the young boy's fear of the punitive, castrating father, the more complete the resolution of the Oedipal complex and the development of identification. With girls, however, since they are already "castrated," there is low fear of the "aggressor" and thus low iden-

tification with the father and low superego formation. (B234)

## IDENTIFICATION WITH FATHER/MOTHER
### X   Superego Formation
Children who identify with their fathers are more likely to be guilt oriented than are children who identify with their mothers. (W127)

## IDENTIFICATION WITH KIN     X   Age of Child
Older children name fewer family members as their ego ideals than do younger children. (H244)

### Child-Rearing Practices (Consistency)
When the character of the discipline is inconsistent, little internalized identification with adult relatives takes place. (G044)

## IDENTIFICATION WITH LIKE/CROSS-SEX PARENT   X   Child-Rearing Practices (Differential Treatment)
Identification with like- or opposite-sex parent is associated with differential treatment of sons and daughters regarding permissiveness, rewards, and punishment. (R098)

### Child-Rearing Practices (Sex Role)
Identification with like- or opposite-sex parent is associated with the explicitness of the parents' sex-role expectations and their investment in them. (R098)

### Personality Adjustment
In boys, a high degree of self-concept modeling after the father is associated with high personality adjustment; in girls, a high degree of self-concept modeling after the mother is not associated with high personality adjustment. (J026)

For both males and females, failure to identify with the father is more closely associated with trends toward abnormality than is failure to identify with the mother. (J026)

### Sex-Role Behavior
Identification with the same-sex parent is correlated with normal adult sex-role behavior. (B277)

Identification with the cross-sex parent is a cause of inverted adult sex-role behavior. (B277)

A confused identification with both parents is a cause of neurotic adult sex-role behavior. (B277)

Excessive identification with the cross-sex parent in childhood is a cause of homosexuality in the adult. (B277)

### Sex Status
Girls are less likely to choose mothers as the principal role model than boys are to choose fathers. (E098)

### Sex Status of Child
Males identify more with their fathers than with their mothers; females identify equally with both parents. (J026)

### Sexual Adjustment
Among twins, the one closer to, and more identified with, the cross-sex parent is more likely to become homosexual; the one closer to the same-sex parent is more likely to be heterosexual. (M212)

## IDENTIFICATION WITH LIKE-SEX PARENT
### X   Age of Child
There is no correlation between chronological age in children and the degree of imitation of the like-sex parent. (H210)

### Aggression
Expressed aggression toward the father by the daughter is associated with negative feelings toward similarity with the mother. (L136)

### Aggression Anxiety By Sex Status
Identification with like-sex parent correlates with frequency of aggression in doll play for boys, but not for girls, unless the mother is atypically aggressive. (L157)

### Anxiety
In therapy situations, low anxiety subjects describe their like-sex parents as more like themselves than do high anxiety subjects. (L145)

### Marital Adjustment
Men who are satisfied with their marriages are likely to identify more strongly with their fathers than are men who are unsatisfied with their marriages. (L140)

### Parent-Child Relations (Affection)
The higher the affection of girls for their mothers, the closer both real and perceived identification will be. (G153)

There is no evidence that higher affection of boys for their fathers leads to closer perceived or real identification. (G153)

### Parent-Child Relations (Rejection)
Rejection by the parent of the opposite sex tends to result in a strong identification with the parent of the same sex. (F085)

### Peer Relations
Children who have established a sex identification with the like-sex parent tend to prefer the company of members of their own sex. (R126)

### Personality of Child (Self-Control)
The more a girl takes her mother as a role model, the greater is the degree of impulse control that she will manifest. (B288)

### Sex-Role Behavior
Feminine behavior is more closely related to imitation of the mother than masculine behavior is to imitation of the father. (H210)

### Sex-Role Identification
Children learn their proper sex-roles through identification with their like-sex parents, if these parents represent the appropriate sex-role models. (R126)

### Sex-Role Identification of Child
Imitation of the like-sex parent is more important to the development of feminity in girls than it is to the development of masculinity in boys. (H179)

### Sex Status
Girls are more likely than boys to identify with the same-sex parent.

Boys identify with their fathers much less than girls identify with their mothers. (H193)

### Socialization, Effectiveness of
Conscience development effectiveness of socialization) in the child is not necessarily associated with intensity of identification with the same-sex parent. (K103)

### Superego Formation
The development of conscience in the child correlates with the extent to which the like-sex parent is available as an object of identification. (G120)

## IDENTIFICATION WITH MOTHER
### X   Child-Rearing Practices (Demands)
(In the older child) the more severe the demands placed upon the child by the mother, the stronger the child's identification with the mother. (A060)

### Child-Rearing Practices (Punishment)
The more often the mother uses the withdrawal of love as a disciplinary method, the stronger will be the child's identification with his mother. (A060)

### Child-Rearing Practices (Punishment/Rewards)
Given dependency upon the mother by the child, the more stable a balance between denial of reciprocity and positive reward she establishes regarding the demands of the child, the more likely is the child to develop a stable expectation system and to identify with the mother as an object and as a set of standards. (B234)

### Child-Rearing Practices (Responsibility)
The more the child is required to substitute for the mother, the greater his identification with the mother. (A060)

### Dependency
The more the infant is dependent upon the mother for satisfaction of primary needs, the more likely he will be to develop a *generalized dependency* upon, and subsequent identification with, her. (A049)

The greater the extent of the child's identification with the mother, the more independent he is and the more he resents the mother's restrictions. (B272)

### Identification with Father
The more the boy's identification with his mother develops into sexual object cathexis, the more hostile and jealous becomes his identification with his father. (B234)

Personal identification with the mother (precedes and) facilitates identification with the father. (S240)

### Mental Illness
Mental illness is directly correlated with a primary emphasis upon the mother and her family rather than upon the father. (F085)

### Mental Illness of Mother/Daughter
The greater the extent to which the daughter identifies with her mother, the more likely it is that psychosis in the mother will lead to psychosis in the daughter. (H192)

### Mother-Child Relations
There is a negative relationship between a mother's projection of fears and preferences onto the child and the child's identification with the mother. (C114)

### Mother-Child Relations (Awareness)
There is a positive relationship between the mother's awareness of the child and identification of the child with the mother (higher for girls than for boys). (C114)

### Mother-Child Relations (Oedipal)
The greater the identification of the woman with a psychotic mother, the more likely she is to project onto the child her former relationship with her mother, unconsciously reversing the Oedipal situation. (H192)

### Mother-Daughter Relations (Affection)
Daughters are more likely to identify strongly with their mothers if they perceive them as nurturant, affectional, rewarding, and warm. (M206)

### Mother-Daughter Relations (Control)
Perception of the mother as high in control and low in nurturance is associated with high maternal identification in daughters. (H196)

### Mother-Daughter Relations (Restrictiveness)
Girls who perceived their mothers as overcircumscribing their freedom are less likely to identify with their mothers than are those who did not so perceive their mothers. (A060)

### Mother-Son Relations (Control)
There is no relationship between the son's perception of the degree of control his mother exerts on his freedom and the strength of his identification with her. (A060)

### Mother-Son Relations (Nurturance/Control)
Perception of the mother as both high in control and nurturance is associated with high maternal identification in sons. (H196)

### Occupational Interests
The more closely the boy identifies with his mother, the more mature his vocational interests are likely to be (Strong Vocational Interest Blank). (S254)

The hypothesis that the higher the identification between mother and son the higher the son's scores on the occupational level was not supported by the results (Strong Vocational Interest Blank). (S254)

The more completely the son identifies with his mother, the more likely he is to develop strong primary interest patterns. (S254)

There is apparently no relationship between congruence of the son's interests and his occupational preference and the degree of mother–son identification. (S254)

The more closely the boy identifies with his mother, the more masculine his interests tend to be. (S254)

Boys who rejected interests in masculine areas were likely to accept more fully their mothers' perceptions of them as their own perceptions than were boys who rejected interests in feminine areas. (S254)

### Personality (Ego Control)
Among college females, degree of ego control (containment of impulse) is positively related to degree of maternal identification, overcontrollers manifesting stronger identification than undercontrollers. (B258)

### Personality (Ego Resiliency)
Among college females, degree of ego resiliency (capacity to adapt under the strain of new environmental demands) is unrelated to degree of maternal identification. (B258)

### Self-Conception of Mother
The more that the mother approves of herself as a model for her children, the more likely it is that the

children will emulate characteristics of the mother. (B234)

### Sleeping Arrangements
Exclusive mother-child sleeping arrangements coupled with matrilocal residence are strongly associated with maximum feminine identification in the child. (B251)

There is a strong association between exclusive mother-child sleeping arrangements and primary feminine identification during infancy. (B251)

### Urban/Rural
Children from rural homes are more likely to identify with their mothers than are those from urban homes. (A060)

## IDENTIFICATION WITH MOTHER/FATHER
### X   Illegitimacy
Unwed mothers tended to identify with their mothers during childhood, but with their fathers during adolescence. (V027)

## IDENTIFICATION WITH NONFAMILY MEMBERS
### X   Dependency
The greater the child's emotional dependency on his parents, the more likely is he in his relations with others to identify with the person rather than with the person's values and goals. (A059)

## IDENTIFICATION WITH PARENTS
### X   Age of Child
Identification with both parents is stronger among younger boys than among older boys. (E098)

The individual's perceived similarity to his father and mother varies inversely with age. (F111)

### Age/Sex Status
Boys show a decline in identification with parents with age, but girls are more likely to continue to idealize their parents. (H244)

### Aggression
Aggressive boys are less likely to identify with their parents, particularly the father, than are normals. (B243)

The stronger the child's identification with the parent, the more his level of aggression in doll play will approximate his perception of the level of aggression of the parent. (L157)

### Alcoholism of Parent
Alcoholism in a parent impedes adequate identification by the child with a parent figure.

### Anxiety of Parents
Identification is positively associated with moderate parental anxiety over impulse expression, particularly in the areas of aggression and sexuality. (R098)

### Behavior Problems
The internalization of a powerful but hostile parental image may lead the individual to project these introjected attributes upon other figures in his environment (acting out). (B278)

### Child-Rearing Practices (Clarity)
High identification is associated with the clarity, explicitness, and immediacy of goals and sanctions communicated to the child. (R098)

### Child-Rearing Practices (Control)
Identification is correlated with moderate-to-low parental control over the child's behavior and the consistency of that control. (R098)

### Child-Rearing Practices (Frustration)
Maximum identification is a function of the parents' withholding resources the child desires. (B251)

### Child-Rearing Practices (Punishment)
There is a positive relationship between a moderate degree of punishment by the parents and the strength of identification with either or both parents.

### Child-Rearing Practices (Sex Role)
Identification with like- or opposite-sex parent is associated with differential treatment of sons and daughters regarding permissiveness, rewards, punishment. (R098)

### Cohesion of Family
When the social structure emphasizes family solidarity, the degree of identification with the parents will tend to be high. (F058)

### Criminality
Identification of the son with a deviant paternal model is strongly correlated with criminal behavior. (M195)

### Dependency
The greater the dependence of the child on the parent, whether the latter is aggressive and/or loving, the greater his identification with that parent. (B234)

There is a correlation between dependency on the parents and identification with parents and internalization of their values. (B243)

### Divorce
Divorce or separation of parents makes less likely the adequate identification of the child with a parent figure.

### Emotional Adjustment of Orphan
If an orphan's early childhood was spent in a home with two parents who had well-defined roles (i.e., early identifications were good), he is more likely to show a high degree of stability later on. (H188)

### Juvenile Delinquency
There is an inverse correlation between extent of the child's identification with the parents and delinquency in the child. (N063)

### Marital Adjustment
The greater the conflict between the parents, the more likely that the resolution of the Oedipal conflict through identification with the same-sex parent will be impeded.

### Maternal Role
The degree to which females feel they are like their mothers is more dependent on the extent to which the mother meets the child's concept of ideal mother than is the case among males. (J032)

### Maternal Role, Attitude Toward
Identification is positively related to the mother's commitment to her parental role. (R098)

### Mental Illness of Child (Psychosis)
The prevention of normal ego development and identification processes through the Oedipal complex (due to maladjustment on the part of the parent) causes psychosis in the child. (B285)

### Mental Illness (Schizophrenia/Neurosis)
Schizophrenics have greater problems of identification with a parental figure than do neurotics. (M197)

### Mother Absence
Identification is related to the length, timing, and predictability of the mother's separations from the child. (R098)

### Mother-Child Relations (Empathy)
Identification is associated with the mother's ability to empathize with the child or her capacity for direct sensitivity to his needs. (R098)

### Occupational Choice
The greater the degree of identification with either or both parents, the more likely is the child to develop vocational interests which are appropriately sex typed (according to popular stereotype), depending on the parent with whom the child identifies. (C110)

The degree of the son's identification with the father significantly corresponds with the similarity of vocational interests of the son and the father's occupation. This relationship holds for mothers and daughters, but not significantly. (C110)

### Parent-Child Relations
The more the parents meet the needs of the child and teach him the things he wants to learn, the more likely is the child to attempt to emulate the parents. (C093)

### Parent-Child Relations (Affection)
In single-parent situations, one condition for being loved by the parent who is present is some type (actual or fantasy) of identification with the absent parent.

The identification of the child with the parents correlates with his love for them, not with the degree to which they are sexual objects for him (this object choice follows only as a secondary result). (B234)

The degree of identification of the child with the parent correlates with the degree to which the parent is a loved or prestigeful person. (B234)

The more frequent the expression of warmth and affection, the greater is the identification of the child with the parent. (H208)

The more positive the attitudes and feelings of the child toward the parents, the more likely he is to consider himself to be similar to his parents. (J032)

### Parent-Child Relations (Authority)
High identification is associated with fairly strong assumption and enactment of authority by one or both parents. (R098)

### Parent-Child Relations (Complementarity)
The greater the complementarity of relations between parent and child, the less likely the child's identification with parent as a role model. (G120)

### Parent-Child Relations (Frustration)
A child is more apt to identify with the parent with whom he has experienced more serious frustration. (U004)

### Parent-Child Relations (Nurturance)
The greater the degree of affectional nurturance and indulgence received by the child, the less likely it is that he will identify with the parent and internalize his values. (B243)

### Parent-Child Relations (Warmth)
There is a curvilinear relationship between parental warmth and the extent of the child's identification. (B243)

Identification of preschool children with parents correlates with the mother's warmth and acceptance and her use of loss of love as a means of control and, for boys, with acceptance by the father. (M183)

Frustration resulting from absence of parental love, warmth, and support is associated with positional identification (identification without adoption of specific characteristics of the model) as against personal identification. (S240)

### Parental-Role Adjustment
Failure of the parents to provide adequately for the child leads to serious problems of satisfactory identification of the child with a parental figure. (M197)

Identification is positively related to the parent's self-esteem and confidence in child rearing. (R098)

### Parental-Role Definition
The larger the discrepancy between subjects' rating of actual *v.* ideal traits of their parents, the less similar to the parents the subjects rate themselves to be; subjects tend to identify only with those parental traits which they admire or wish to emulate. (J032)

### Peer Relations
If the child's identification with his parent is based upon the support given by the parent, he will be less dependent upon peer-group approval than if the identification is with nonsupporting parents. (C114)

### Personality Adjustment
Nonneurotic persons do not usually identify with one parent rather than with the other. (L145)

Personal identification with both parents is associated with general psychological health. (S240)

### Personality of Child (Activity Drive)
The greater the strength of an exploratory or activity drive in the child, the more likely that he will emulate the behavior of a parent who is active in the manipulation of the environment, even without direct reinforcement. (B234)

### Personality of Child (Ego Strength)
The weaker the child's ego, the more it resorts to identification with parents and other adult figures in its adjustment to the adult world.

### Personality of Parents (Dominance)
American boys tend to identify with the more aggressive and dominant parent, whether it be the father or the mother. (H211)

American girls tend to identify with the mother, regardless of the personality traits of the parents. (H211)

### Power Structure of Family
The similarity of a child's behavior to that of his parents is independent of the sex of the parent exercising power in the family. (M179)

### Puberty
During the first stage of puberty (8 to 10 years of age), society is more able to interfere with and weaken the child's identification with his parents, thus implanting its

values and attitudes, than during the later stage of puberty. (C093)

### Rank of Ethnic Group
In a society committed to the principle of status achievement, a child tends to identify less with parents who are in a less-esteemed ethnic group. (C086)

### Self-Conception of Child
If the child's identification with his parents is based upon the support given by the parents, he will have more self-esteem than if the identification is with nonsupporting parents. (C114)

### Sex-Role Definition
Appropriate sex typing and high conscience development correlate with each other and correlate with (and result from) the process of parental identification. (M183)

### Sex Status
The child usually identifies with the parent of the same sex as the child.

### Sibling Status
The "only" child is likely to be more strongly identified with his parents than are children of other sibling statuses. (L157)

### Social Change, Rate of
The more rapid the rate of social change, the less likely that the child will perceive his parents as appropriate models of behavior. (M188)

### Social Mobility
Children who identify with and accept the values of their parents tend to continue in the parents' trend of social mobility; children who rebel against their parents' values and have accompanying ambivalent parental identification are more likely to exhibit a reversal from their parents' social mobility pattern.

### Social Mobility Pressures
Parental pressure for social mobility on the part of the child tends later to disrupt the identification of the child with parental figures and to produce a basic emotional insecurity in the child. (M197)

### Socialization, Effectiveness of
Children who identify with the parent are more likely to accept the parent's moral, cognitive, and expressive standards, and thus the standards of the larger society. (B234)

### Stepparent/Natural Parent
Children living with natural parents are more likely to emulate their parents than are children living with a stepparent. (B286)

### Stratification, Basis of
A child tends to identify less with parents who are in a subordinate class position, in a society committed to the principle of upward mobility. (C086)

### Superego Formation
The greater the extent to which a child identifies with an aggressive, punitive parent, the greater his hostility toward himself and toward his environment at large and the less likely is the formation of superego and guilt feelings. (B234)

The greater the identification of the child with the parent, the more he imitates, not the model of his parent, but that of the parent's superego. (B234)

Since early socialization tends to produce stronger identification, it also results in guilt over contravening parental values. (W127)

### IDENTIFICATION WITH PARENTS/NONFAMILY MEMBERS    X    Age of Child
Younger children (7–8 years old) desire to be like someone in their families more so than do older children (11 and 12 years old), who prefer to be like nonfamily members, such as movie stars and athletic heroes. (W138)

### IDENTIFICATION WITH PARENTS OR STEPPARENTS    X    Illegitimacy
Unwed mothers were more ashamed of and embarrassed by their parents and stepparents than were the single, never-pregnant females. (V027)

### IDENTIFICATION WITH SIBLINGS    X    Polygyny
There is likely to be more mutual identification between sons of a monogamous couple than between sons of different mothers. (P083)

### Sibling Structure (Age and Sex)
Among like-sex siblings, the greater the age difference between siblings, the greater the desire of the younger to have the assets and advantages of the older; the conscious desire of the younger to become the older sibling decreases more slowly with spacing among girls with an older brother than among boys with an older sister. (K149)

### Sibling Structure (Age Difference)
Among second-born children, the closer the spacing between siblings, the stronger the identification with the older sibling. (K149)

### Sibling Structure (Sex)
Among second-born children, identification with the older sibling is stronger when siblings are the same sex than it is when they are of opposite sexes (probably strongest for the girl with an older sister and weakest for the boy with an older sister). (K149)

### IDENTIFICATION WITH SPOUSE    X    Emotional Problems of Child
Spouses who identify with each other are less likely to have children who are emotionally disturbed than are spouses who do not identify with each other. (M200)

### IDENTIFICATION WITH SURROGATE MOTHER    X    Age of Surrogate Mother
The younger the foster-mother, the more likely that the child will identify with her. (W149)

### IDENTIFICATION WITH WIFE    X    Pregnancy, Attitude Toward
It is more likely that husbands whose sexual desires lessen during the pregnancy of their wives identify with their wives and their wives' experiences more than do husbands whose sexual desires do not lessen. (L013)

### ILLEGITIMACY    X    Acculturation
Under conditions of European contact, the rate of illegitimacy will tend to increase. (B148)

### Age    X    Neurosis
Older unmarried mothers are generally more neurotic than are young unmarried mothers. (Y048)

### Age at Marriage
A high rate of illegitimacy tends to be correlated with a delay in the age at marriage. (F060)

The rate of illegitimacy tends to be directly correlated with age at marriage. (H164)

The illegitimacy rate tends to be inversely correlated with age at marriage. (T035)

### Age at Marriage
### X   Divorce
Among marriages where premarital illegitimacy has occurred, divorce is more likely to occur among very early and very late marriages than among the middle age groups (Denmark). (C124)

### Authority Structure of Family
When the distinction between legitimacy and illegitimacy decreases, parental authority is diminished. (T073)

### Broken Home
Girls from homes broken by death or divorce are more likely to have illegitimate children than are those from intact homes. (N055)

### Child-Rearing Practices (Discipline)
Unwed mothers, as contrasted with single, never-pregnant girls, were not disciplined as much by their parents. (V027)

As opposed to a single, never-pregnant girls, unwed mothers more frequently felt that they should have received more discipline from their parents and more religious training. (V027)

### Class
Lower-class unions are more likely to be common-law and to have illegitimate children than are unions in other classes. (C134)

The lower the social class, the less commitment there is to the family norm of legitimacy. (G151)

The lower the social stratum, the higher the illegitimacy rate. (G156)

### Class
### X   Personality Problems
The lower the social class of the unwed mother, the more likely she is to be psychologically disturbed. The contrary hypothesis is also asserted. (S224)

### Crisis (Social)
Illegitimacy is directly correlated with social disintegration and economic disorder. (K065)

### Descent
Commitment to the norm of legitimacy will be greater among the strata or kin relations where the concern with the kin line is higher. (G151)

### Divorce
### X   Age at Marriage
Among marriages where premarital illegitimacy has occurred, divorce is more likely to occur among very early and very late marriages than among the middle age groups (Denmark). (C124)

### Duration of Marriage
In the Caribbean, common-law marriages endure as long as those initiated in the church. (G151)

### Economic Conditions
During depressions, illegitimacy is likely to increase at a greater rate than during nondepression periods. (C023)

### Economic Rank (Housing Standards)
Illegitimacy is inversely related to the standards of housing. (S003)

### Education
Unwed pregnant women have significantly more education than (married) multigravida. (C099)

Amount of education is inversely related to illegitimacy. (S003)

### Education of Child
Illegitimate children are less likely to receive adequate education. (G156)

### Emotional Adjustment
There is no correlation between emotional immaturity and having illegitimate children. (N055)

### Father/Mother Absence
Absence of the father is more closely associated with illegitimacy than is the absence of the mother. (G156)

### Health
Illegitimacy is inversely related to the state of health. (S003)

### Health of Child
Illegitimate children are more likely to experience a higher disease and death rate. (G156)

### Homogamy
If the mates of unwed mothers differ from them in education or age, it is more likely that lesser-educated women will choose men of the same age but more education, while better-educated women will choose men of the same or higher education but older in age. (V002)

### Identification with Mother/Father
Unwed mothers tended to identify with their mothers during childhood, but with their fathers during adolescence. (V027)

### Identification with Parents or Stepparents
Unwed mothers were more ashamed of and embarrassed by their parents and stepparents than were the single, never-pregnant females. (V027)

### Illegitimacy, Attitude Toward
Illegitimacy is correlated with a relatively permissive attitude of the community toward illegitimacy. (K065)

The rate of illegitimacy is inversely correlated with the strength of the sanctions against premarital pregnancy. (S134)

As illegitimate births become more frequent, societal attitudes toward premarital pregnancy tend to become less severe. (S171)

### Illegitimacy of Parents
Illegitimate children are more likely to produce illegitimate children when they become adults. (G156)

### I.Q.
There is no correlation between low intelligence and having illegitimate children. (N055)

### Marital Status (Female)
Divorced women are more likely to have illegitimate children than are the unmarried. (O027)

### Maternal Role, Attitude Toward
Unwed pregnant women express less desire for pregnancy and less maternal feeling than married pregnant women do. (C099)

Unwed pregnant women exhibit more depression and withdrawal and see the maternal role as being less important than (married) primigravida do. (C099)

### Mental Illness
Unwed mothers are more likely to have psychopathological problems prior to pregnancy than married mothers are. (L135)

### Neurosis
### X   Child-Rearing Practices (Sex)
There is a positive relationship between the severity and punitiveness of her family and group's attitudes toward sex and the degree to which the unwed mother reacts neurotically to herself and her baby. (Y048)

### Neurosis
### X   Class
The higher the unmarried mother's socioeconomic status, the more disturbed she is. (Y048)

### Occupation
Illegitimate children are less likely to obtain satisfactory jobs. (G156)

Girls who are employed in the field of housework are more likely to have illegitimate children than are those in other occupations. (N055)

### Parent-Child Relations (Closeness)
Unwed mothers tended to be closer to their parents during the childhood and more distant from them during adolescence than did single, never-pregnant females. (V027)

### Parent-Child Relations (Control)
The rate of illegitimate birth is directly correlated with the weakening of parental control. (K065)

### Parent-Child Relations (Favoritism)
Unwed mothers tended to be favored more by their fathers than by their mothers. (V027)

### Parent-Peer Relations
As compared with single, never-pregnant females, all the unwed mothers reported that they were influenced more favorably by their mothers during childhood and by their peers during high school. (V027)

### Personality of Father/Mother
The personalities of the unmarried mother and father are more likely to be of similar neurotic structure than of different neurotic structure (i.e., equally irresponsible, dependent, and hostile to the opposite sex). (Y048)

### Personality of Mother (Masculinity)
There is no correlation between the female's masculine personality traits and having illegitimate children. (N055)

### Personality Problems
Unmarried mothers tend to be more neurotic and more extroverted than do married mothers (as measured by the Maudsley Personality Inventory). (E094)

### Personality Problems of Adolescents
The unwed adolescent mother is more likely to have become pregnant as a result of the emotional problems in her life rather than because of ignorance or lack of adult self-control. (Y048)

### Power Structure of Family
Unwed mothers are more likely to have been raised in homes in which one parent, particularly the mother, dominated than in one in which both parents were active participants. (Y048)

Unwed mothers are more likely than married mothers to have had possessive mothers and passive fathers. (Y048)

### Pregnancy
Unwed mothers conceive in a shorter period of time than married mothers do. This hypothesis is also denied. (Y048)

Unwed mothers are less likely to miscarry than married mothers are. This hypothesis is also denied. (Y048)

Unwed mothers are less likely to experience prenatal nausea than married mothers are. This hypothesis is also denied. (Y048)

Unwed mothers have fewer complications and difficulties in giving birth than married mothers do. This hypothesis is also denied. (Y048)

### Pregnancy Anxiety (Psychosomatic)
Unwed pregnant women express less psychosomatic anxiety than do multigravida (married). (C099)

### Premarital Sex Relations, Attitude Toward
The rate of the illegitimate births tends to be inversely correlated with the severity of censure of premarital relations. (L053)

Premarital relations are more likely to be condoned if the girl does not become pregnant. (W105)

### Race (Urbanization)
Illegitimacy is more likely among urban Negro families than among the rest of the population (U.S.). (L124)

### Rank
Commitment to the norm of legitimacy will be greater among the strata or kin lines which enjoy a higher prestige. (G151)

### Religiosity
Unwed mothers and their parents are less likely to attend church as frequently as the single, never-pregnant girls and their parents. (V027)

### Residence
Illegitimate children are more likely to remain in the care of their mothers, their mothers' kin, or to live with their siblings; legitimate children are more likely to remain in their fathers' care. (S211)

### Sibling Rivalry
Children within the family who are illegitimate are subject to even greater sibling rivalry pressures. (C024)

### Social Disorganization
Illegitimacy is directly related to social disorganization. (S003)

### Social Network
The unwed mother is more likely than the average mother to have lacked normal social and romantic contacts. (Y048)

### Unemployment
Illegitimacy is directly related to unemployment. (S003)

**Urban/Rural**

The rate of illegitimacy is higher in urban than in rural areas. (K065)

**Urbanization**

The rate of illegitimacy is directly correlated with the degree of urbanization. (H164)

**Warfare**

In wartime illegitimacy is likely to increase at a greater rate than during peacetime. (C023)

## ILLEGITIMACY (ADOPTION)

**X   Adjustment of Mother**

Unwed mothers who keep their children have more problems and are less secure in their ability to handle future problems than are unwed mothers who give up their children. (J020)

**Age of Mother**

The younger the unwed mother, the more likely is she to surrender the baby for adoption. (J020)

**Class**

There is no correlation between social class and the Catholic mother's tendency to keep her illegitimate child. (J020)

Unwed mothers who kept their children came from families of lower socioeconomic status than did those who released their children for adoption. (V027)

**Cohesion of Family**

Unwed mothers who keep their children have significantly less positive intrafamily relationships and home situations than do those who release their children for adoption. (V027)

**Education of Mother**

The more educated the unwed mother, the more likely is she to give up the illegitimate child. (J020)

**Identification with Family**

Unwed mothers who released their children for adoption are more likely to identify positively with, and to be accepted by, parents, adults, peers, or social groups that communicate and maintain a meaningful awareness of the stigma attached to illegitimacy. (V027)

**Illegitimacy, Attitude Toward**

The greater the identification of unwed mothers with individuals or social groups which communicate and maintain an awareness of the stigma attached to illegitimacy, the more likely is the mother to give up the child. (J020)

**I.Q. of Mother**

Unwed mothers who keep their children are lower in intelligence than are unwed mothers who surrender their children. (J020)

**Marital Status (Male)**

The unwed mother whose child is by a man who is married rather than unmarried is more likely to keep her child. (J020)

**Mental Illness (Psychosis/Neurosis)**

Psychotic unwed mothers are more possessive of their babies than are neurotic unwed mothers. (Y048)

**Parent-Child Relations**

Unwed mothers who give up their children have better relations with their parents than do unwed mothers who keep their children. (J020)

**Personality (Ego Strength)**

Unmarried mothers who keep their children in comparison with those who surrender their children tend to be lower in ego strength or stability and more submissive. (J020)

**Personality of Mother (Hostility)**

Controlling for father domination in the parental home, the unwed mother with strong hostile feelings toward the father of her child is more likely than the less hostile unwed mother to keep her baby as a weapon against the man. (Y048)

**Power Structure of Family**

As compared with unwed mothers who released their children for adoption, unwed mothers who kept their children came from unhappy and mother-dominated homes. (V027)

Unwed mothers from mother-dominated homes are more likely to have stronger attachments to their babies (i.e., desire to take them home) than are unwed mothers from father-dominated homes. (Y048)

**Race**

Negro unmarried mothers tend to keep their babies more than do white unmarried mothers. (J020)

**Religion**

Catholic unmarried mothers are less likely to give up their children than are mothers with other religious affiliations. (J020)

**Sex Attitudes**

Unwed mothers who kept their children had less self-confidence and experience in heterosexual relations and more negative attitudes concerning sex than did those who released their children for adoption. (V027)

**Size of Family**

Unwed mothers who keep their children have a higher mean number of siblings and half-siblings than do unwed mothers who release their children for adoption. (V027)

**Social Adjustment**

Unwed mothers who give up their children get along better with their friends than do unwed mothers who keep their children. (J020)

**Values**

The greater the recognition by the unwed mother that surrendering the child is the norm, the more likely is she to conform and thus give up the child. (J020)

## ILLEGITIMACY AND PREMARITAL CONCEPTION

**X   Marriage Ceremony**

Premarital conception and illegitimacy are more likely to occur among couples having a civil wedding ceremony than among those who have a church ceremony (Denmark). (C129)

**Occupation**

Premarital illegitimacy and conception are more likely to occur among laborers than among other occupational groups. (C129)

## ILLEGITIMACY, ATTITUDE TOWARD

**X   Abortion**

Abortion will be less common if illegitimate children and their parents are less stigmatized. The contrary is also asserted. (T041)

### Class

A society disapproves less of illegitimacy when it occurs in the lower social ranks. (G156)

### Fertility Values

When the importance of fertility is stressed, the birth of a child before marriage will not be detrimental to the status of the girl. (V020)

### Illegitimacy

Illegitimacy is correlated with a relatively permissive attitude of the community toward illegitimacy. (K065)

The rate of illegitimacy is inversely correlated with the strength of the sanctions against premarital pregnancy. (S134)

As illegitimate births become more frequent, societal attitudes toward premarital pregnancy tend to become less severe. (S171)

### Illegitimacy (Adoption)

The greater the identification of unwed mothers with individuals or social groups which communicate and maintain an awareness of the stigma attached to illegitimacy, the more likely is the mother to give up the child. (J020)

### Occupation

Pastors and physicians are more likely and social workers and public health nurses are less likely to favor marriage as opposed to adoption as a solution to premarital pregnancy. (S224)

### Polygyny

With the prohibition of polygyny, the attitude toward illegitimacy becomes more lenient. (S134)

### Race

Negroes, as compared with other segments of American society, do not as strongly disapprove the having of children out of wedlock. (J020)

### Sexual Permissiveness

With the increasing acceptance of illegitimate births, restrictions on adolescent girls after puberty tend to be relaxed. (C055)

### Social Disorganization

The amount of social disruption caused by illegitimacy is related to the degree of social disapproval of illegitimacy. (G156)

### Values (Paternity)

Societal attitudes toward illegitimacy of children from adulterous unions vary with societal value on physiological and/or sociological paternity. (D054)

## ILLEGITIMACY OF PARENTS       X   Illegitimacy

Illegitimate children are more likely to produce illegitimate children when they become adults. (G156)

## ILLEGITIMACY (PLACE OF DELIVERY)
### X   Age of Father

Fathers of illegitimate children born at institutions tend to be younger than do those of illegitimate children born in private practice. (V002)

### Age of Mother

A greater percentage of unwed mothers, 21 years of age or younger, had their babies delivered in institutions rather than through private practice. (V002)

### Education of Father

Illegitimate babies born in private practice have fathers with higher educational attainments than do babies born in institutions. (V002)

### Education of Mother

The lower the educational attainment of the unwed mother the more likely it is that she will have her baby in the county in which she resides. (V002)

Unwed mothers whose babies are delivered in private practice have a higher educational attainment than do unwed mothers whose babies are born in institutions. (V002)

## ILLEGITIMACY RATE                         X   Class

The lower the social stratum, the higher the illegitimacy rate. (G156)

### Social Disorganization Rate

Social disorganization is directly correlated with illegitimacy. (S003)

## ILLNESS
### X   Child-Rearing Practices (Dependence Anxiety)

The degree of anxiety generated by the socialization of dependence in the child is correlated with the amount of activity the child engaged in when he was ill. (K111)

### Cohesion of Family

By isolating the medical deviant from his family, the hospital prevents secondary gains and reduces the emotional burden on the nuclear family. (P083)

The trust and confiding character of the doctor-patient relationship preserve more of the autonomy of the nuclear family than would be the case if his function were transferred to the extended family network. (P083)

### Juvenile Delinquency

If the family of orientation of the parents was affected by physical diseases such as cancer, tuberculosis, drunkenness, venereal diseases, etc., then the child is more likely to become a juvenile delinquent. (G144)

## ILLNESS, EXPLANATION OF
### X   Child-Rearing Practices (Aggression)

The severity of aggression training in the society (temper tantrums, verbal aggression, damage to property, and disobedience) is related to a tendency to explain illness as being caused by aggression (e.g., disobedience to spirits, injected poison, magical weapons). (W127)

### Child-Rearing Practices (Dependency)

The severity of independence training is associated with dependency explanations of illness (e.g., soul stealing, spirit possession). (W127)

### Child-Rearing Practices (Sex)

There seems to be no correlation between severity of sexual training and sexual explanations of illness. (W127)

### Socialization Anxiety

In any society, the greater the customary anxiety concerning socialization in any area of behavior, the more likely it is that illness will be thought to be associated with that area. (W142)

### Toilet Training

There does not seem to be any correlation between severity of toilet training and anal explanations of illness. (W127)

### Weaning
The severity of weaning is correlated with oral explanations of illness (e.g., poisoned food or magic spells). (W127)

### ILLNESS OF CHILD          X   Anxiety of Mother
There is no evidence that mothers of cerebral-palsied children exhibit more anxiety than do mothers of normal children. (B320)

### Guilt
Mothers of cerebral-palsied children exhibit no more guilt feelings than do mothers of nonhandicapped children. (B320)

### Maternal Overprotectiveness
Death-threatening illness in the child is a cause of maternal overprotection. (B272)

### Personality Problems of Mother (Unrealistic Attitudes)
Mothers of cerebral-palsied children do not exhibit less realistic attitudes than do mothers of normal children. (B320)

### Social Adjustment of Mother
Mothers of cerebral-palsied children do not exhibit any greater tendency to withdraw from social contact than do mothers of normal children. (B320)

### ILLNESS OF FAMILY MEMBERS          X   Juvenile Delinquency
Families of juvenile delinquents are more likely to include members who have physical ailments than are families of nondelinquents. (G123)

### ILLNESS OF FATHER      X   Juvenile Delinquency
Serious physical ailment of the father contributes indirectly to delinquency of the child by contributing to the development of hostility and lack of conscientiousness.

### ILLNESS OF MOTHER     X   Juvenile Delinquency
Serious physical ailment of the mother may contribute indirectly to delinquency in the son by contributing to a tendency toward fantasy.

Boys who are ambivalent to authority or unconventional in attitudes are more likely to become delinquent if their mothers are seriously ill.

### ILLNESS OF PARENTS     X   Juvenile Delinquency
The parents of delinquent children suffer from some form of illness or deformity more frequently than do the parents of other children. (B238)

### Mental Illness of Child (Autism)
Autism is more likely to occur if a parent becomes ill during the vulnerable developmental period. (S188)

### ILLNESS OF PARENTS (DYSPEPSIA)          X   Psychosomatic Illness of Child
Gastric neurosis in the child tends to be correlated with patterns of dyspepsia in the parents. (F113)

### IMMIGRANT/NONIMMIGRANT     X   Aggression
Children with fathers of foreign origin tend to be more aggressive than do children with American fathers. (E091)

### Alcoholism/Criminality
Parental immigration is negatively related to alcoholism, but is unrelated to criminality. (M195)

### Broken Home
There is a higher percentage of broken homes among native-born than among foreign-born individuals (U.S.). (S210)

### Fertility
The average number of children born to foreign-born wives is significantly greater than the average number born to native white women. (G020)

### Intermarriage (Religious)
The percentage of mixed-faith marriages is higher among immigrants than among the native-born (U.S.). (B300)

### Juvenile Delinquency
If the father is an immigrant to the United States, the child is less likely to become a delinquent than if the father is a citizen of the United States. The reverse is also asserted. (M194)

### Parent-Child Relations (Conflict)
The immigrant family undergoes the most rapid rate of social change in any society and therefore has the greatest amount of parent-youth conflict. (D058)

### IMPOTENCE     •     X   Adultery, Attitude Toward
If the husband is impotent, he is more likely to condone the extramarital relations of his wife. (W082)

### INCEST                              X   Age Group
There is an association between the existence of age-villages and the fear of incest between father-in-law and daughter-in-law. (W128)

### Age-Role Definition
There is a correlation between violation of generational boundaries (confusion in age roles) and sexual deviance in the family, particularly incest.

### Alcoholism of Father
Fathers who have had sexual relations with their daughters are also more likely to be alcoholic. (K119)

### Avoidance Relationship
Avoidance and formality tend to characterize the relationship between siblings when the incestuous attraction between them is strong. (G055)

### Class
Violation of incest taboos is more likely to be characteristic of the upper or ruling class. (Q001)

### Housing
Overcrowded homes are more likely than others to produce incestuous behavior. (W143)

### Isolation of Family
There is a correlation between incest and the isolation of the family from its larger social and cultural environment.

### Joking Relationship
When marriage occurs between kinsmen who are not permitted to marry, the discrepancy is adjusted by establishing a joking relationship between the husband and wife. (M085)

### Kin Terminology          X   Incest Taboo
When marriages between prohibited (but distant) kinsmen occur, there tends to be an adjustment of kinship terminology to make the union socially acceptable. (T039)

### Mental Illness of Child (Schizophrenia)
There is a correlation between a fear of, or preoccupation with, incest and schizophrenia in the child.

### Moiety
When the community is divided into two exogamous groups, the rate of incest will be high. (O011)

### Parental-Role Behavior
The failure of a parent to fulfill his normal role may cause an incestuous link to develop between the child of his own sex and the other parent or cause homosexuality in the child.

### Personality Problems of Child
The severity of reaction (psychopathology) to incest is of the same intensity whether girls have relations with a father or with a father substitute. (K091)

### Scapegoating
In the father-daughter and brother-sister type of incest, the female participant is usually estranged from the family. The mother tends to condone, at least outwardly, the behavior of the husband and son. (W123)

### Sex Attitudes
In families where sibling incest occurs, the sex attitudes between the siblings are less inhibited than in families where father-daughter incest occurs. (W123)

### Sexual Permissiveness
Incest is less likely to occur if sexual relations are only minimally restricted. (H139)

### Wife Inheritance
The likelihood that a man will seduce his father's wives is increased by the custom of permitting a son to inherit his father's wives. (E086)

### INCEST ANXIETY       X   Abortion (Compulsory)
There is a correlation between the unconscious belief than an unborn child is the offspring of a socially improper father, such as the paternal or maternal grandfather, and the custom of compulsory abortion. (D071)

### INCEST, ATTITUDE TOWARD       X   Exogamy
The degree of censure of incest will tend to be higher in societies which have exogamic kinship units. (H133)

### Incest Taboo
The inhibition or termination of an incestuous relationship is more likely to occur if the punishment for such an offense is severe. (B076)

### INCEST (BROTHER-SISTER)       X   Ordinal Position
Brother participants in incestuous relations are usually older than their sisters. (W123)

### Paternal-Role Behavior
At the onset of brother-sister incest, the father was absent from, subordinate in, or indifferent to the family; or he was incapacitated, old and weak, overworked, or concerned with earning a living; or he may have been completely concerned with nonfamily matters. (W123)

### Power Structure of Family
In families where there was brother-sister incest, the father did not have the dominant position that he had in father-daughter incest families. (W123)

### INCEST (FATHER-DAUGHTER)
### X   Child-Rearing Practices (Punishment)
The incestuous father is more likely than the typical father to use punishment sadistically or with hostility rather than for disciplinary purposes. (W123)

### Desertion
Families in which father-daughter incest occurs tend to be characterized by desertion by the maternal grandmother. (K091)

In families where father-daughter incest occurs the parents are more likely than are typical parents to desert the family at some time. (K091)

### Disorganization of Family
Fathers who have had sexual relations with their daughters come from families characterized by a high degree of disorganization. (K119)

### Economic Rank of Father
Where father-daughter incest occurs, the father is likely to come from a background characterized by poverty and inadequate housing. (K091)

### Education of Father
Where father-daughter incest occurs, the father is likely to have had little education. (K091)

### Father-Daughter Relations (Sex)
Incestuous fathers are more likely than typical fathers to play with their daughters sexually; they do this long before incest occurs. (W123)

### Juvenile Delinquency
Girls who practice incest are likely to be delinquent in other ways. (K091)

### Maternal Role
Families in which father-daughter incest occurs are apt to be characterized by the daughters' assumptions of the mother role when the mothers have deserted the family. (K091)

### Mother-Daughter Relations (Rejection)
Girls who have had sexual relations with their fathers tend to view their mothers as cruel, unjust, and depriving. (K119)

### Occupation of Maternal Grandmother
In families where father-daughter incest occurs, the maternal grandmothers are apt to be employed in menial positions (domestics, waitresses). (K091)

### Occupational Stability of Father
Fathers who have had sexual relations with their daughters have histories of occupational instability and irresponsibility. (K119)

### Ordinal Position
In the cases of father-daughter incest, the father usually selected the eldest daughter in the home as his first incest partner, but also tried to initiate incest with the other accessible daughters. (W123)

### Parent-Child Relations (Warmth)
Where father-daughter incest occurs, the father is apt to have had little warmth or understanding from his own parents. (K091)

### Paternal-Role Behavior
The incestuous father is more likely than the typical father to maintain his power by threats rather than by his financial contribution. (W123)

The incestuous father is more likely than the typical father to exploit his family by retaining authority but shifting responsibilities to family members. (W123)

### Personality of Maternal Grandmother
In families where father-daughter incest occurs, the maternal grandmothers were apt to be stern, demanding, controlling, cold, and hostile, rejecting their daughters and pampering their sons. (K091)

### Sex-Role Identification of Daughter
Girls who have had sexual relations with their fathers indicate poor sexual identification when tested on the Draw-A-Man Test. (K119)

### Sexual Permissiveness
When father-daughter incest is tolerated or not restricted in the family, the sexual norms of the family are permissive. (W123)

### INCEST (FATHER-SON)
#### X Mother-Son Relations (Hostility)
When father-son incest occurs, it is usually looked upon with a dim view on the part of the mother and sometimes with an attitude of hostility. (Z008)

### INCEST (MOTHER-SON)
#### X Authority Structure of Family
In the few cases in which mother-son incest occurred, no restraining agent was at home (e.g., father, siblings). (W123)

#### Power Structure of Family
In families where mother-son incest occurs, the mother was dominant, while the father was absent or subordinate. (W123)

#### Self-Conception
The more developed the sense of self (in mother, son, or both), the less likely is mother-son incest to occur. (C093)

### INCEST (SIBLING/FATHER-DAUGHTER)
#### X Disorganization of Family
In general, sibling incest did not have as disturbing an effect on the other family members as did father-daughter incest. The mother, especially, was less disturbed and agitated. (W123)

### INCEST TABOO
#### X Affinal Ties
The extension of incest taboos tends to be inhibited to the extent that any given person is linked with the same consanguineal kin-group as ego's spouse and is extended to the extent that the person is linked by blood with ego. (M019)

#### Age of Kin-Group
The distance to which incest taboos are extended appears primarily a function of the time which has elapsed since the establishment of the kin-groups that have channeled them. (M019)

#### Analogy
To the extent that any secondary or more remote relative resembles a sexually tabooed member of the nuclear family, avoidance behavior will tend to be extended to him. (M019)

#### Avoidance Relationship
When kinsmen are prohibited as marriage partners, their relationships will tend to be characterized by avoidance or respect. (H090)

Incest prohibitions require external support from a rule of avoidance when they have not been strongly internalized in the individual conscience. (M019)

Avoidance relationships are more likely to be established with kinsmen who are subject to the incest taboo. (M085)

One determinant of the severity of kin avoidance is a strong incest fear in the society. (S079)

### Child-Rearing Practices (Sex)
Close physical contact between brother and sister in childhood leads to a strong sexual aversion between the two and to lax prohibitions against incest in the society. (F079)

Separation of brother and sister in childhood or low degree of physical contact leads to a strong desire between the two and to strong prohibitions against incest within the society. (F079)

Physical nearness with no physical interaction generates highest incest anxiety among these three conditions. (F079)

Lack of alternative sexual outlets, under the condition of low physical contact between brother and sister, generates high incest anxiety. (F079)

### Cohesion of Family
In any boundary-maintaining system (e.g., family), the closer the emotional involvement of the members, the more likely is it to give rise to incest taboos. (C093)

### Cohesion of Kin-Group
The prohibition of marriage within the kin-group or family tends to increase its solidarity. (E069)

The extension of incest taboos functions to increase the solidarity of the social group through an expansion of the sphere of kinship ties. (L060)

### Descent
The extension of incest taboos will tend to follow the structure of the descent pattern. (S098)

### Descent (Bilateral)
When descent is bilateral, marriage tends to be forbidden between cross-, as well as parallel-, cousins. (F051)

Bilateral extension of incest taboos follows inevitably the establishment of bilateral kin-group. (M019)

### Descent (Clan)
Clan organizations develop with the extension of incest taboos from the nuclear family to other members of the mother's kin-group. (S098)

### Descent (Matrilineal)
Matrilineal extension of incest taboos follows inevitably after the introduction of matrilineal descent. (M019)

### Descent (Patrilineal)
With an increasing importance in patrilineal affiliation, incest taboos will tend to extend to the patrisib of the mother. (L060)

Patrilineal extension of incest taboos follows inevitably after the introduction of patrilineal descent. (M019)

### Economic Rank of Family
The reaction to incest is more severe if the individuals involved belong to wealthy families. (H052)

### Extended/Nuclear Family
Societies whose institutions are arranged around the anchorage and identification of individuals in the wider kin group will make the final inculcation of the core

(prohibition of sexual relations among nuclear family members) incest taboo at the early stage of puberty (8 to 10 years) by means of extrusion or brother-sister avoidance or both; societies whose institutions are arranged around anchorage and identification of individuals in the nuclear family will make the final inculcation of the core incest taboo by means of *verbal-symbolic* instruction, leaving the child within the boundaries of the nuclear family during the first stage of puberty. (C093)

### Genealogical Proximity
The seriousness of incest is directly correlated with the genealogical proximity of the kinsmen who are involved. (W100)

### Incest, Attitude Toward
The inhibition or termination of an incestuous relationship is more likely to occur if the punishment for such an offense is severe. (B076)

### Joking Relationship
If a joking relationship obtains between two kinsmen who are prohibited from marriage, the censure which normally attends the breaking of this rule is lessened. (M085)

### Kin-Group
In the absence of any type of consanguineal kin-group, either unilinear or bilateral, there is little tendency to extend primary incest taboos beyond secondary relatives. (M019)

### Kin-Group, Importance of
The distance to which incest taboos are extended to kin-groups is correlated with the social importance of those kin-groups. (M019)

### Kin Terminology
Kinship terms which apply to members of the nuclear family tend to be extended to all kinsmen who fall under the incest taboo. (L058)

The asymmetrical extension of incest taboos fosters the development of Crow-Omaha terminology. (L061)

Restrictions against sexual relations will tend to be extended to kinsmen who are terminologically equated with actual siblings. (T039)

When marriages between prohibited (but distant) kinsmen occur, there tends to be an adjustment of kinship terminology to make the union socially acceptable. (T039)

### Kin Terminology (Classificatory)
Incest taboos tend to be extended to all kinsmen who are terminologically equated with members of the nuclear family. (O016)

### Kin Ties
Incest taboos are more likely to be extended to consanguineal than to affinal kin. (M019)

If kinship affiliation is realigned, incest taboos will be altered in harmony with this change. (V017)

### Kin Ties (Fictive)
Incest taboos tend to be extended to individuals with whom a bond of fictive kinship has been established. (L064)

### Marital Status
The reaction to incest will be far more severe if either of the individuals are married. (H052)

### Marriage Class System (Eight)
The eight-class marriage system develops when incest taboos are extended to both cross-cousins. (L060)

### Marriage Class System (Six)
The development of a six-class system tends to result from an asymmetrical extension of incest taboos to only one of the first cross-cousins. (L060)

### Polygyny
The emphasis on the incest taboo is stronger where older men are permitted to take another young wife (instead of helping their younger brothers or sons to marry). (E086)

### Population
A population decrease tends to result in the diminution of exogamy and incest taboos. (P008)

### Preferential Marriage (Asymmetrical Cross-Cousin)
The transformation of systems of bilateral first cross-cousin marriage into systems of asymmetrical first cross-cousin marriage tends to be associated with an extension of incest taboos. (L061)

### Preferential Marriage (Cross-Cousin)
Cross-cousin marriage will not occur if there is an extension of incest taboos to members of the father's lineage as well as to the matrilineal sib. (M082)

### Rank
The reaction to incest may be less severe if the offending couple is of high status. (C079)

### Residence
The modification of incest rules will tend to be followed by changes in the residence pattern. (P008)

The extension of incest taboos to other kinsmen beyond the nuclear family is most likely to occur among those who share a common residence with the nuclear group. (S098)

### Sexual Behavior of Women
The low sexual excitability of women is probably a factor in permitting the incest taboo to be elaborated. (P083)

### Social Control
Incest which violates the strongest group norms is subject to stronger sanctions than is other incest. (F076)

### Social Structure
The extension of incest taboos is correlated either with an increase in complexity of social structure or with a higher degree of integration. (L130)

### INCEST TABOO (BROTHER-SISTER)   X   Descent
Brother-sister incest is a more serious offense in a matrilineal society than in a patrilineal or a bilateral society. (C093)

### INCEST TABOO, RANGE OF   X   Exogamy
Where there is a very large number of relationships which carry the incest taboo, violations of it are frequent. (E084)

## INCOME                          X Age at Marriage

The younger the age at marriage, the less likely are couples to have adequate finances to conduct their marital life. (I005)

### Birth Control

There is an increase in family planning with an increase in income. (F101)

### Broken Home

The lower the economic class of the family, the higher the death and divorce rate. (B286)

### Child-Rearing Practices (Control)

Adolescents from families of higher income strata who are accepted by their peers are granted more personal freedom by their families than are those at the middle and low economic levels. (F108)

Mothers of low-income families are more likely than those of higher-income families to use the threat that God will punish the child for deviant behavior as a means of control. (N055)

### Conflict in Family

Increasing income and the increasing desire for purchase goods means increasing occasions for family conflict over how wages will be used. (H032)

### Dating During Marriage

Among divorced couples, higher income is associated with a higher frequency of dating during marriage. (G157)

### Divorce

There is an inverse correlation between income and divorce rate. (G134)

### Divorce Complaints

The higher the husband's income, the less likely is his ex-wife to claim that nonsupport was a cause of their divorce. (G157)

Among divorcées there is a low positive association between complaints of the husband's overspending and his failure to provide an adequate income. (G157)

Among husbands who worked steadily, the higher his income, the more likely is the ex-wife to complain that nonsupport was a cause of divorce. (G157)

The higher the husband's income, the more likely is his ex-wife to complain that his overspending was a cause of divorce. (G157)

### Divorce, Initiation of

Wives are less likely to make the first suggestion to divorce if they are married to husbands with steady income. (G157)

### Emotional Problems of Child

Children whose fathers have high incomes are less likely to have emotional problems (it is usually a more stable work history of the father which accounts for the higher income). (B290)

### Employment of Mother

The higher the income of the family, the less likely it is that the mother is employed. (C134)

The lower the income of the husband, the greater the likelihood that the mother's outside employment will be an extension of her family role. (R093)

### Employment of Mother, Attitude Toward

The more the mother's employment is based on economic necessity, the greater the likelihood that men will approve. (S257)

### Employment of Wife

The lower the economic contribution of the husband to the family, the more likely the wife is to become employed outside the home.

When the husband's family of orientation is higher in income level than his own, the wife is more likely to become employed outside the home.

### Fertility

Within each class, families with higher income tend to have more children. (G156)

The higher the gross income of a family, the larger the number of live births per married woman. (H010)

### Fertility (Real/Ideal)

Lower-income groups express an ideal family size smaller than that intended, the discrepancy becoming minimal in the middle- and upper-income groups. (Y046)

### Husband-Wife Relations (Companionship)

With a higher standard of living, the husband has more leisure time available and thus an intimate companionship develops between husband and wife which was hard to achieve when no free time was available.

### Income, Attitude Toward

The higher the family income, the greater the satisfaction with the standard of living (other things being equal).

### Marital Adjustment

Marital adjustment is associated with a moderate income at marriage rather than with a low or high income. (B033)

Wives from very-low-income families or from very-high-income families tend to be more satisfied with their marriages as compared with wives from middle-income families. (B033)

Insufficient income is the most frequent source of marital conflict among both husbands and wives. (B033)

Excluding wives who hold professional jobs, there is no relationship between income and marital happiness for either spouse. (G157)

Feeling that one's income is adequate is positively related to marital adjustment. (G157)

The lower the income of a family, the more likely it is that the marriage will be unhappy. (K089)

### Marital Status (Male)

Married men living with their first wives have a slightly higher median income than do those living with their second or subsequent wives. (G011)

During the initial ten years of first marriage, there is a gradual increase in income of the husband. There is also an increase for husbands married more than once, but the increase is not as appreciable. (G011)

### Marriage Chances

Among American males 35 to 64 years old, the higher the present income, the more likely the man is to be married or to have been married. (H203)

### Mate Selection (Residence)
Individuals with low income are likely to be more propinquitous in their mate selection than are individuals with high income. (K020)

### Mental Illness (Social Adjustment)
The greater the income of the family, the higher the posthospital performance of the mental patient. (S245)

### Occupational Heterogeneity of Households
The function of occupational heterogeneity of agricultural households in Yugoslavia is to cover the deficit in income of the agricultural holding. (B031)

### Parent-Child Relations (Financial Help)
As the income of parents increases, the amount of financial assistance given to children increases. (S220)

### Personality (Aggression)
Poor management of family income is associated with the delinquency-linked traits of destructiveness-sadistic trends, extroversion of action, lack of conscientiousness, and receptive trends.

### Power Structure of Family
The higher the husband's income, the less power he exerts in his family. (K089)

### Residence
The larger the older parents' income is, the more willing are grown children to have them in the same household. (B312)

### Sexual Disability of Husband (Divorce)
Among men who have been physically disabled, those who have remained married are more likely to have higher incomes than are those who are divorced or separated. (N060)

### Size of Family
There is a positive correlation between amount of income and number of children in the family. (B244)

Farm families with low incomes have fewer children than do farm families with high incomes. (K016)

## INCOME, ALLOCATION OF
### X   Husband-Wife Relations (Economic)
The wife's knowledge of the amount of her husband's income is directly related to the proportion of the income the husband gives as a family allowance to the wife. (Y003)

### Size of Family
Family size is inversely related to the proportion of income spent for rent. (C009)

### Urban/Rural
In rural families, personal appearance is sacrificed for other needs and wants to a greater extent than with the city family. (B033)

## INCOME, ATTITUDE TOWARD   X   Age of Child
At the (later) ages during which the children in a family require high material expenses, the husband/wife's satisfaction with their income is very low.

### Age of Husband/Wife
When the husband is younger than the wife, the wife tends to be less satisfied with the family's standard of living.

### Employment
If the husband's working hours are longer than the wife's working hours, the wife tends to be satisfied with the family income level.

### Income
The higher the family income, the greater the satisfaction with the standard of living (other things being equal).

### Income of Divorcée
Divorcées who have not remarried are more likely to claim they have an adequate income, even when they do not receive an objectively adequate income. (G157)

Regardless of whether the not-remarried divorcée is employed, a lower percentage receives an objectively adequate income than the percentage who feel that they have enough to meet expenses. (G157)

When the remarried divorcées hold jobs, a higher proportion receives an objectively adequate income than admit that they have adequate finances to meet expenses; among those who do not have jobs, fewer have an objectively adequate income than admit that they have enough. (G157)

### I.Q./Creativity
Parents of highly intelligent children (Binet) are more likely to be aware of financial difficulties in their own childhoods than are the parents of highly creative children (Guilford-Cattell). (G132)

### Marital Adjustment
Unhappy men more often consider it essential or desirable that the wife be financially indpendent of the husband and more often believe that marriage should be postponed until income is adequate to prevent serious skimping. (T074)

### Size of Family
When there is a large number of children born in a family, the satisfaction with the standard of living tends to be lower; when the children number from one to three, the satisfaction with the family standard of living tends to be higher.

## INCOME/EDUCATION         X   Fertility
Excess fertility (unwanted children) is inversely related to education more closely and consistently than it is to income. (F101)

## INCOME, MOTHER'S CONTRIBUTION TO
### X   Child-Rearing Practices (Aggression)
Mothers who make economic contributions to the family finances are more severe in their punishment of mother-directed aggression in the child. (M216)

### Child-Rearing Practices (Chores)
There is a positive relationship between the degree to which mothers contribute to the family income and the severity of their responsibility training (variety and frequency of chores assigned to the child). (M216)

### Child-Rearing Practices (Permissiveness)
The greater the importance of the mother's economic contribution to the family, the less permissiive she will be with her children. (M216)

## INCOME OF DIVORCÉE        X   Divorce Process
The longer the time lapse since the divorce, the more likely is the divorcée to claim that she is "best off"

economically at present than she was during the marriage or at any time during the divorce process. (G157)

### Employment of Divorcée

Among remarried divorcées, job holding is not associated with having enough of an income to meet expenses; among the not-remarried, those who claim they have enough are slightly more likely to have a job than are those who claim they do not have enough. (G157)

### Husband-Wife Relations

Divorcées who feel they have enough with which to meet expenses are less likely to have antagonistic feelings toward their ex-husbands than are those who do not feel they have enough. This difference increases over time. (G157)

### Income, Attitude Toward

Divorcées who have not remarried are more likely to claim they have an adequate income even when they do not receive an objectively adequate income. (G157)

Regardless of whether the not-remarried divorcée is employed, a lower percentage receives an objectively adequate income than the percentage who feel that they have enough to meet expenses. (G157)

When the remarried divorcées hold jobs, a higher proportion receives an objectively adequate income than admits that they have adequate finances to meet expenses; among those who do not have jobs, fewer have an objectively adequate income than admit that they have enough. (G157)

### Race

There is no difference between white and Negro divorcées who have remarried in the amount of income available for weekly expenses; while among the not-remarried, white divorcées have a good deal more money for expenses than Negro divorcées. (G157)

### Remarriage

Remarried divorcées are more likely to claim they have enough money with which to meet expenses than are those who are not remarried. (G157)

The difference between divorcées with one or two children being more likely to claim enough to meet expenses than those with three or more children declines among those who have remarried. (G157)

Remarried divorcées have higher income expectations than do those not remarried. (G157)

Remarriage is negatively associated with the divorcée's feeling that she is economically worse off at present than during the marriage. (G157)

Remarried divorcées are more likely than those who have not remarried to feel that at present they are economically better off than during the marriage. (G157)

Remarried divorcées who have stayed at the same income level are more likely than are those who have not remarried to report that they have enough with which to meet expenses. (G157)

Remarried divorcées are much more likely than are those who are not remarried to claim that one area of improvement since the divorce is the economic. (G157)

Divorcées who are not married are much more likely than those who are married to claim that they wish their

income might be steadier, or both steadier and larger. (G157)

## INCOME OF HUSBAND      X    Child Support

Among divorced couples, the amount of income is unrelated to the continuity of child-support payments. (G157)

Regardless of the number of children in the family, the husband's income is only slightly related to the amount of child-support payments ordered by the court. (G157)

### Divorce Process

The husband's income is unrelated to the length of time taken between a serious consideration of divorce and the filing of the suit. (G157)

### Employment of Wife, Attitude Toward

As the income and occupational stability of the lower-class man increase, he is increasingly likely to insist that only he, and not his wife, work for gain. (P083)

### Friendship

When the husband's income bracket is higher, the divorcée is slightly more likely to maintain marriage friends during the separation and divorce period than when his income is lower. (G157)

## INCOME OF HUSBAND/WIFE      X    Class

The higher the socioeconomic stratum, the greater is the difference between the income of the husband and wife. (G134)

## INCOME (SAVINGS)      X    Marital Status (Male)

Men who are married and separated from their wives tend to save more of their income than do unmarried men or men whose wives are with them. (W079)

## INDEPENDENCE OF FAMILY
### X   Birth (Premature), Adjustment to

Parents who seek help (medical, familial, religious) are more likely than those who are reluctant to accept assistance (assuming it is available) to retain healthy relationships throughout (and after) the crisis of a premature birth. (C108)

### Ecological Conditions

Seasonal variations and irregular natural hazards in the subsistence environment encourage a high degree of autonomy in the smallest social unit, the family. (S174)

## INDEPENDENCE OF NUCLEAR FAMILY
### X   Descent (Bilateral)

In bilateral societies, the nuclear family tends to have greater autonomy than is usual among societies where the clan is the important social unit. (B060)

### Economic Role of Husband

The economic status of the husband will be more important if the nuclear family is economically independent. (H165)

### Kin Terminology (Collateral)

With the emergence of the nuclear family as the basic subsistence unit, a trend toward collaterality will develop and the basic Eskimo system will arise. (V017)

### Mate Selection (Love)

Love as an essential factor in mate selection is most likely to be found in societies where the nuclear unit is relatively independent of the larger kinship group. (G156)

### Occupation
The independence of the nuclear family is directly correlated with the independence of occupation from the kin roles. (G112)

### Property (Individual)
The development of patterns of individual ownership of land is directly correlated with the emergence of the parental family as a domestic group and an economically autonomous unit. (G156)

### Role Conflict
Where the society approves the independence of the conjugal unit but does not make this possible for the aged, role conflict for both the aged parents and their children is likely to occur. (G119)

### Social Control
The greater the independence of the nuclear family from the wider kinship network, the less able are both to exert control over one another. (G156)

### Urban/Rural
Urban families tend to be more highly individuated (differentiated, autonomous) than do rural families. (B267)

## INDEPENDENCE OF WIFE
### X   Power Structure of Family
The legal protection of women's property rights, the capacity to mobilize kin for assistance, and decreasing pressures against adultery make the wife under 45 a "potential prize in the seduction game" and thus decrease her dependency upon her husband for status. (P083)

## INDEPENDENCE OF WOMEN          X   Abortion
The abortion rate will rise with the increasing independence of women. (H111)

### Division of Labor by Sex
The sexual division of labor of desert (nomadic) life permits a higher degree of freedom to women than does that of urban living. (S116)

### Husband-Wife Relations (Companionship)
The readjustment of familial patterns in terms of companionship and mutual affection between husband and wife is correlated with women's actual or potential economic independence and their educational and social equality. (B033)

### Marital Stability
The stability of marriage tends to decrease with an increase in the independence of women. (D031)

### Religion
Women will tend to become more independent with the adoption of Christianity. (H103)

### Size of Family
A restriction of family size tends to be associated with a position of greater freedom and independence for women. (S064)

## INDUSTRIALIZATION          X   Age at Marriage
Women in industrial societies have a higher average age at marriage and have a greater probability of never being married than do women in nonindustrial societies. (N054)

### Authority Structure of Family
The greater the degree of industrialization, the greater the likelihood that the patriarchal family structure will disappear. (K100)

### Cohesion of Family
There is a negative correlation between industrialization and family integration. (K024)

### Corporate Kin-Group
The corporate control of property by a kin-group is rare in industrialized societies. (B082)

### Descent (Matrilineal)
Matrilineages are not found in societies that are very little, or highly, industrialized. (G156)

### Extended/Nuclear Family
Populations that have shifted from the extended family structure to the nuclear family are more likely to have become adjusted to industrialization than are populations that have attempted to keep alive the old extended family. (K024)

The effects of industrialization on the family are more intensely felt when the shift from the extended family to the nuclear family takes place before the main period of industrialization than when it takes place after the main period of industrialization. (K024)

### Functions of Family
The social functions of the family decrease with increasing industrialization. (K100)

### Inheritance (Single-Heir)
Inhabitants of single-heir regions respond more to a demand for permanent industrial labor since more people are free to leave for industrial jobs. (H066)

### Kin Terminology (Fictive)
The fictive use of kinship terminology tends to be abandoned in the context of industrialization. (B083)

### Kin Ties
The range of kin ties is inversely correlated with the degree of industrialization. (B082)

### Kin Ties (Fictive)
With the development of industrialization, formalized fictive kin-groups have declined in number, size, and importance. (N012)

### Marital Stability
Marital stability tends to be inversely correlated with the degree of industrialization. (D031)

### Nuclear Family
The restriction of kinship obligations to the nuclear family tends to accompany industrialization. (F055)

There is no relationship between industrialization and the percentage of nuclear families. (G113)

With the rise of industrialization, the nuclear family is displacing the extended family and has come to be the dominant form in urban areas. (N012)

### Population Control
"Primitive" societies are more likely to use abortion and infanticide, as methods of controlling the population; industrial societies use postponement of marriage, denial of marriage, and birth control. (P083)

### Power Structure of Family
Rebellion of women against their subordinate position in marriage accompanies industrialization and the actual or potential economic independence of women. (B033)

### Role Definition
Increased concern with the definition and enactment of family obligations is associated with societies undergoing industrialization. (G156)

### Size of Family
Increasing industrialization is correlated with decreasing family size. (K100)

### Social Structure (Kin-Based)
Family-centered social organizations tend to disintegrate with industrialization and mobility and with the economic independence of women. (B033)

### Stem Family
As industrialization advances, conjugal family organization replaces the stem family organization. (G112)

## INDUSTRIALIZATION/URBANIZATION
### X  Role Definition of Husband/Wife
Industrialization and urbanization do not lead to a reduction in marital role specialization. (S205)

## INFANT BETROTHAL    X  Divorce
The incidence of divorce will tend to be lower where infant betrothal is common. (B191)

### Preferential Marriage
Infant betrothal is likely to exist where preferential marriage patterns occur. (G097)

### Preferential Marriage (Cross-Cousin)
Infant betrothal is correlated with cross-cousin marriage. (M241)

### Premarital Sex Relations, Attitude Toward
There is a greater control over the premarital sexual activity of a girl if she has been betrothed in infancy. (E080)

### Rank of Family
Infant betrothal is more likely to occur among families of high status. (H138)

## INFANT MORTALITY  X  Children, Evaluation of
A high value tends to be placed upon children when the rate of infant mortality is high. (E030)

### Fertility
A lower infant mortality rate in a society is associated with a trend toward a low birth rate. (G156)

### Mother Absence
The absence of the mother during the first year is directly related to the increase in infant mortality. (S277)

## INFANTICIDE    X  Economic Conditions
Infanticide occurs more frequently in times of famine. (D057)

### Economic Role of Women
Female infanticide will be less frequent if the economic contribution of females is thought to be great. (W156)

### Sex Ratio
The sex ratio in favor of females is not likely to be brought about by male infanticide, but usually through warfare or other hazardous masculine occupations. (L110)

### Subsistence Pattern (Nomadic)
Deformed infants are more frequently killed in nomadic areas. (D057)

## INFANTICIDE (FEMALE)    X  Descent
Female infanticide is less common if descent is traced through the female line. (F121)

### Polyandry
Polyandry may be the result of a scarcity of women due to the practice of female infanticide. (M019)

## INHERITANCE    X  Acculturation
Inheritance will tend to shift from matrilineal to patrilineal under the pressures of colonial administrators. (M082)

### Affinal Ties
Affinal relations are more likely to be kept distinct from cognatic relations when the wife is not entitled to inherit land. (F122)

### Authority Structure of Family
When the amount of land inherited by sons is inadequate, the traditional patterns of authority are no longer acknowledged. (A013)

Children who are to inherit a greater portion of the property have greater authority. (B193)

The authority of the father will tend to be stronger if he has exclusive control over the choice of his heir. (F073)

There is less parental authority under conditions in which inheritance is not permitted. (T073)

### Child-Rearing Practices (Permissiveness)
Rules of succession are more likely to be violated by the individual headman if he is permitted an undisciplined childhood. (H124)

### Clan
In societies with a clan organization, the inheritance pattern will tend to insure the retention of clan property. (W082)

### Cohesion of Family
The cohesiveness of the family is directly correlated with a pattern of inheritance which promises an equal share of property among the children. (L064)

### Cohesion of Lineage
If the lineage is strong, it is the social unit through which property is transmitted. (S192)

### Community
With the socioeconomic stabilization of community organization, a formalization of rules about inheritance tends to occur. (L063)

### Conflict in Family
Tension within the extended family will be directly correlated with unequal distribution of the inheritance. (H086)

### Corporate Kin-Group
A shift from brother-brother to father-son inheritance would seem likely generally to weaken the solidarity of the corporate lineage. (F073)

### Descent
Rules of inheritance are dependent on the form of descent which prevails in a given society. (S095)

### Descent/Residence
Descent and inheritance rules are more highly correlated with the prevalent residence practice among matrilocal cultures than among patrilocal groups. (A072)

Matrilineal inheritance is normally associated with matrilocal or avunculocal residence and with matrilineal descent. (M019)

### Division of Labor by Sex
When the division of labor by sex is sharp, the inheritance of personal possessions will tend to be between members of the same sex. (T053)

### Economic Pattern
The decline in the power of property, as compared with the purchasing power gained by work, reduces the importance of expectation of inheritance as a factor in relationships among married children, their siblings, and their parents. (P083)

### Economic Pattern (Local Domestic Industry)
A system of equal division of inheritance favors the development of local industry. (H066)

### Geographic Mobility
When the system of land inheritance is relatively inflexible, population increase will tend to result in urban migration. (B082)

Siblings who do not inherit are more likely to move geographically. (T039)

### Kin Relations (Closeness)
The relationship between kinsmen who are not involved in the same line of inheritance tends to be warm and indulgent. (F073)

### Kin Terminology
Inheritance rules will be reflected in the kinship terminology. (M058)

### Political Structure
A monopolistic extension of political control will be facilitated by instituting political offices of a hereditary character. (W075)

### Power Structure of Family
The maintenance of parental control tends to be correlated with patterns of delayed inheritance. (L064)

Maiden aunts, bachelor uncles, and childless couples have special powers within the family where the inheritance pattern allows for testamentary freedom. (P060)

### Rank
Inheritance rights will be more clearly defined among families of higher status. (B183)

### Rank of Child
The rank of the child in the family will be directly correlated with his or her eligibility for the inheritance of family property. (W082)

### Rank of Women
Where women inherit and transmit property equally with men their status will tend to be equal to that of men. (P011)

### Residence
When residence is patrilocal, the inheritance of economic privileges will tend to be patrilineal. (G038)

Patterns of residence will tend to be consonant with the prevailing inheritance pattern. (H129)

Avuncular inheritance will tend to be resented if the nephew does not reside with his uncle. (K049)

Patterns of descent and inheritance tend to reflect residence patterns. (T039)

The grouping of kinsmen tends to correlate with patterns of land inheritance. (T039)

Inheritance of land tends to be directly correlated with residential propinquity of the land-owning group. (T039)

### Residence (Neolocal)
A modification in inheritance rules, such as the replacement of primogeniture by the division of an estate among a number of heirs, will tend to favor neolocal residence. (M019)

### Sibling Rank
The equality of status of siblings will tend to be reflected in the inheritance pattern. (F073)

### Sibling Relations (Conflict)
Conflict arises among male siblings when only one gets the inheritance (magic) and where primogeniture may be set aside. (F076)

### Sibling Rivalry
The character of the inheritance pattern may create a situation of intense rivalry between siblings. (S090)

### Social Structure
Differences in inheritance systems tend to cause changes in social and economic structures. (H066)

### Stability of Extended Family
Where siblings receive an unequal proportion of family estate, there is a greater tendency for the extended family to divide. (A033)

When the system of inheritance designates an equal share for all sons, fission of the extended family is inevitable when the holdings in land are too small to support each of the sons independently. (R012)

### Stability of Family
The stability of the family is more likely to be preserved if the father is not permitted to leave his property to his favorite. (H124)

### Stability of Kin-Group
The rigidity or stability of inheritance patterns tends to be contingent upon the stability of the social groupings. (G038)

### Stratification
An inheritance pattern which involves the subdivision of the estate facilitates the economic differentiation of descent lines. (S123)

### INHERITANCE (BILATERAL)
#### X  Economic Pattern (Money)
With the institution of a money economy in a matrilineal society, inheritance patterns tend to shift from a matrilineal to a bilateral orientation. (G156)

#### Endogamy
Bilateral inheritance leads to strict local endogamy. (H171)

## INHERITANCE (BROTHER-BROTHER)
### X Gerontocracy
A gerontocratic political structure is more likely to develop if the inheritance pattern is from brother to brother. (F073)

## INHERITANCE, CONFLICT OVER
### X Polygyny (Ranking of Wives)
Owing to polygyny and the associated practice of ranking wives, disputes about the succession are almost inevitable. (S196)

## INHERITANCE (DUAL)
### X Father-Son Relations (Conflict)
In the community in which property is divided between the patrician and the matrician, the relationship of a man with his father is less marked by conflict. (G111)

## INHERITANCE (EQUAL DIVISION)
### X Household Composition
The typical family in the equal-division inheritance pattern tends to consist of man and wife with a smaller number of children but fewer celibates. (H066)

### Population
Equal division of inheritance tends to increase population growth. (H066)

Any given increase in productivity under a system of equal division of inheritance tends to exhaust itself in an increase in population and to accelerate the process of division. (H066)

## INHERITANCE (MATRILINEAL) X Acculturation
In the acculturative situation, patterns of matrilineal inheritance weaken. (F055)

### Authority Structure of Family
A matriarchal authority structure is associated with matrilineal inheritance of property and matrilocal residence. (S098)

### Clan (Matrilineal)
Where a clan organization is matrilineal, the inheritance of property tends also to be matrilineal. (W103)

### Monogamy
Where matrilineal descent and matrilocal residence are coupled with female ownership and control of agricultural land and houses, exclusive monogamy is likely to occur. (D057)

### Religion (Christianity)
Under missionary pressure, patterns of inheritance will tend to shift from matrilineal to patrilineal. (M031)

### Residence (Matrilocal)
Matrilineal inheritance of land will tend to produce a change in residence rules toward matrilocality (unless the village is composed of several lineages). (W054)

### Residence (Patrilocal)
When there are several lineages within the village, it is possible to maintain patterns of patrilocal residence, although the inheritance of the land is matrilineal. (W054)

## INHERITANCE (PATRILINEAL)
### X Authority Structure of Family
Control by the father is more likely to be powerful if the inheritance pattern is patrilineal. (F073)

### Clan (Patrilineal)
The patrilineal clan will tend to emerge with a greater emphasis on patrilineal inheritance. (S120)

### Sex Preference
When the inheritance pattern is patrilineal, boys will be more highly valued than girls. (R035)

## INHERITANCE (PRIMOGENITURE)
### X Occupational Choice
When primogeniture is the established pattern of inheritance, other children will tend to seek nonagricultural occupations. (B082)

### Sibling Rivalry
Where primogeniture is the basis for inheritance but where it may be set aside, jealousy among brothers is likely to result. (F092)

### Stability of Extended Family
Primogeniture as a mode of inheritance tends to produce fission within the extended family. (S090)

## INHERITANCE RULES, COMPLEXITY OF
### X Inheritance Rules, Manipulation of
Complicated rules of succession make their manipulation particularly easy. (L174)

## INHERITANCE RULES, MANIPULATION OF
### X Inheritance Rules, Complexity of
Complicated rules of succession make their manipulation particularly easy. (L174)

## INHERITANCE (SINGLE HEIR)      X Fertility
The single-heir system of inheritance tends to retard the birth rate. (H066)

### Geographical Mobility
People in single-heir inheritance systems are residentially more mobile than are people in other types of inheritance systems. (H066)

### Industrialization
Inhabitants of single-heir regions respond more to a demand for permanent industrial labor since more people are free to leave for industrial jobs. (H066)

### Marriage Chances
In single-heir inheritance systems, the brothers and sisters of the owner tended to remain unmarried. (H066)

## INHERITANCE (UNILINEAL)      X Land Allocation
When the allocation of land under patterns of unilinear inheritance is no longer viewed as equitable, nonunilinear inheritance patterns will be adopted. (G029)

### Residence
The emergence of unilineal rules of inheritance tends to be directly correlated with the stabilization of the residence pattern. (L063)

## INITIATION RITES   X Cohesion of Ethnic Group
The institution of puberty rites serves to reinforce the cohesion of the ethnic group. (J007)

### Cohesion of Family
Initiation rites are more likely to occur when tribal ties are stronger than family ties. (W154)

### Dependency
Societies in which early childhood-training practices foster a very close dependency relationship between the mother and her young son tend to provide drastic puberty rites to break this bond. (M058)

### Descent (Matrilineal)
Initiation ceremonies for girls are correlated with matriliny. (L133)

### Identification with Family
In societies in which the children are to be anchored in and to identify with the wider kin-group, there is more likely to be a disruption of the child's relations with his parents in the form of initiation rites than in societies in which the children are brought up to be anchored in and to identify with the nuclear family. (C093)

### Mother-Son Relations (Closeness)
There is a strong correlation between tribal initiations and cultures having strong mother-son ties (i.e., long nursing, common sleeping). (D057)

### Parent-Child Relations (Conflict)
The absence of transitional rituals and the prolongation of dependence of youth are causes of (American) parent-youth conflicts. (S219)

### Parent-Child Relations (Control)
The age at which male initiation rites are undertaken is directly correlated with the strength of parental control over their offspring. (C045)

### Premarital Sex Relations
In societies that bring up their children for anchorage and identification in the wider kin-group, there is no relationship between the presence or absence of initiation ceremonies and prohibition or permission of premarital sexual relations. (C093)

### Puberty
Initiation ceremonies will be more severe and, consequently, effective when observed during the first stage of puberty (8 to 10 years of age) than during the second stage (after 10), as the child is more susceptible to societal influences. (C093)

More societies will take formal and explicit steps (e.g., initiation ceremonies) during the first stage of puberty (8 to 10 years of age) than during the second stage of puberty (emergence of secondary sex traits). (C093)

### Rank of Women
When the status of women is inferior to that of men, they will tend to be excluded from the initiation rites of the males and fail to have initiation rites of their own. (J007)

### Residence (Matrilocal/Other)
In matrilocal societies, female initiation rites announce the change in status when a girl marries; in other societies her moving away from home announces the change in status. (C093)

### Sex-Role Definition
Puberty rites for girls will tend to occur only in those societies in which the women play an important overt part in the society. (M038)

### Sex Taboo (Postpartum)
A long duration of the postpartum sex taboo is associated with initiation ceremonies for boys. (S079)

In societies with long durations of postpartum sex taboo, initiation ceremonies for girls are also found. (S079)

There is a strong correlation between prolonged postpartum sex taboo and male initiation rites at puberty. (W127)

### Sleeping Arrangements (Mother-Infant)
Male initiation rites at puberty are correlated with exclusive mother-infant sleeping arrangements. (W127)

### INITIATION RITES/COUVADE    X    Residence
Initiation rites are more frequently found in societies with exclusive mother-infant sleeping arrangements and patrilocal residence; the couvade is more frequent in societies with exclusive sleeping and matrilocal residence. (W127)

### INSTITUTIONAL CARE
#### X    Achievement Motivation
There is a correlation between institutionalization of the child and lack of achievement motivation. (Y045)

#### Adjustment of Child
The process of intellectual, physical, and emotional deterioration of the child, attendant upon institutionalization, may be arrested if he is reunited with his mother within three months, but not after five months. (Y045)

#### Adult-Child Relations (Affect)
If a baby is institutionalized for a long period, he will show, as an aftereffect, a cheerful but shallow attachment to any adult within his orbit. (B270)

#### Aggression
Orphaned children who spend their early years in institutions are more likely to manifest aggressive traits when later placed in foster homes than are those who are not institutionalized. (T086)

#### Autoeroticism
If the child is institutionalized he is more likely to indulge in a high level of autoerotic activity. (Y045)

If the child is institutionalized he is less likely to engage in autoerotic activity. (Y045)

#### Behavior Problems
Babies who have been institutionalized from birth to six months are consistently less vocal than those in families, the difference being discernible from age two months. (B270)

If a baby is institutionalized for a long period, he will demonstrate a monotonous rocking of the body and sometimes head-banging. (B270)

Children who are raised from early infancy in institutions without an adequate parent surrogate develop aggressive, distractible, and uncontrolled behavior. (B270)

#### Cognitive Development
Children who have been reared in institutions, without ever having had parental care or adequate parental surrogates, are more intellectually retarded and have poorer conceptual ability than do children reared in normal homes. (G128)

#### Emotional Problems of Child
If a baby is institutionalized for a long period, it will show an apathetic withdrawal from all emotional entanglements. (B270)

#### Interaction in Family (Warmth)
Institutionalizing a retarded child, rather than having him remain at home, is inversely related to warmth among family members. (J027)

#### Juvenile Delinquency/Neurosis
Delinquents are more likely than neurotics (measured by

phobias, anxiety, obsessions) to have lived part of their lives in institutions, children's homes, etc. (B238)

### Marital Adjustment
Among Catholic parents, marital adjustment is not related to whether the retarded child is living at home or is institutionalized. (J027)

Among Protestant and Jewish families, lower level of marital adjustment is related to the retarded child's living at home rather than being institutionalized. (J027)

### Mental Problems
Institutionalized children are more likely than those raised in a family to develop psychiatric disturbances and to become asocial, delinquent, feeble-minded, psychotic, or problem children. (S201)

### Mother-Child Relations (Hostility)
If a baby is institutionalized for long periods, he will show a hostile reaction to the mother on his return to her. (B270)

### Motor Development
There is a correlation between institutionalization and retardation and disturbance in the motor functions of the child. (Y045)

There is a correlation between institutionalization and a lower activity level in the child. (Y045)

Institutionalization of the child results in initial hyperactivity, followed by a depression in the level of activity. (Y045)

### Parent-Child Relations (Punishment)
Children who are deprived from their parents and taken to institutions tend to regard the motive for this deprivation as being a punishment. (B270)

### Personality Problems
Children who are raised from early infancy in institutions without adequate parent surrogates and who consequently develop personality disorders will not have these disorders cured by later community and foster-family experiences. (B270)

Children who are raised from early infancy in institutions without adequate parent surrogates do not develop normal patterns of anxiety and self-inhibition. (B270)

### Personality Problems (Depression)
The behavior of babies which are taken from their mothers and institutionalized at the age of six to nine months is very often a deep unresponsive depression. (B270)

### Personality Problems of Child
If a baby is institutionalized for a long period, when he is returned to his mother he will show an excessive demandingness toward the mother or substitute mother, in which intense possessiveness is combined with intolerance of frustration, acute jealousy, and violent temper tantrums. (B270)

The personality disorders developed by a child who has been raised from early infancy in an institution cannot be ameliorated by providing a parent surrogate if the surrogate is not provided before age two and one-half years. (B270)

Children who are raised in institutions for the first three years of their lives, without parental care or adequate parental surrogates, are hyperactive, restless, unable to concentrate, unmanageable, and generally demonstrate

lack of normal capacity for inhibition, as compared with normal children. (G128)

### Personality Problems (Speech)
Children who are reared from early infancy in institutions and then placed in foster homes are much more likely to develop speech disabilities than are children who are placed in foster homes directly in early infancy. (B270)

### Physical Development
The longer an infant is institutionalized, the lower his development quotient, as measured by the Hetzer-Wolf Baby Test, becomes. (B270)

### Pregnancy (Stress)
Mothers who experience emotional stress during pregnancy are more likely than others to give birth to infants who are later placed in institutions (thus compounding the effect of physical and mental impairment from being born of such mothers). (S227)

### Sibling Relations
Living arrangements (home or institutional) for retarded children are not related to sibling adjustment. (J027)

### Social Adjustment
Children who are reared in institutions from early infancy and then placed in foster homes are much less able to establish social relationships than are children who are placed in foster homes directly in early infancy. (B270)

A higher percentage of children raised from early infancy in institutions and then placed in foster homes is socially maladjusted than children raised in their own homes in infancy and later placed in foster homes. (B270)

Children who are raised in institutions without parental care or adequate parental surrogates are less socially mature than are normal children. (G128)

### Social Adjustment of Child
Institutionalization of the child may cause him to seek affection insatiably and to be indiscriminately sociable. (Y045)

Institutionalization of the child may be a cause of inadequate social discrimination on his part, with regard to both different persons and different kinds of emotional expression. (Y045)

### Speech Development
The aspect of behavior of institutionalized babies which is most adversely affected is speech, with the ability to express being more retarded than the ability to understand. (B270)

## INSTITUTIONAL CARE, AGE AT          X I.Q.
Intellectual damage to the child, due to institutionalization, is most likely between three and twelve months of age. (Y045)

## INSTITUTIONAL CARE, DURATION OF
### X Adjustment of Child
The adverse effects of institutionalization upon babies are more likely to disappear when the babies are restored to their mothers before three months of institutionalization have elapsed. (B270)

## INSTITUTIONAL CARE/FAMILY
### X Health of Child
Children who have the psychological support of a family

setting (v. children institutionalized in a physically sterile setting) are less susceptible to colds and epidemics of infectious diseases. (P068)

## INSTITUTIONAL CARE/FOSTER HOME
### X   Cognitive Development
Children who are reared from early infancy in institutions and then placed in foster homes are less able to conceptualize than are children who are placed directly in foster homes in early infancy. (B270)

## INSTITUTIONAL CARE OF RETARDED CHILD
### X   Cohesion of Family
Institutionalizing a retarded child, rather than rearing him at home, is inversely related to family cohesiveness. (J027)

## INTELLIGENCE
### X   Husband-Wife Relations (Power)
The husband is more likely than not to be dominant in the marriage if he rates himself as superior or inferior to his wife, in mental ability. (L014)

The wife is more likely than not to be dominant if the husband rates her as equal to himself in mental ability. (L014)

The wife is more likely than not to be dominant if she rates herself as superior to her husband in mental ability. (L014)

## INTELLIGENCE/CREATIVITY OF CHILDREN
### X   Child-Rearing Practices (Supervision)
Parents of highly intelligent children exercise more supervision over the behavior and academic performance of their children than do the parents of highly creative children. (G114)

## INTERACTION          X   Intermarriage (Ethnic)
The opportunity for unmarried young people to associate with members of another ethnic group will directly affect the rate of intermarriage. (H036)

## INTERACTION AMONG KIN        X   Residence
Only when the degree of kinship is remote does geographical distance influence contact. (G033)

## INTERACTION IN FAMILY
### X   Achievement Motivation of Child
Family structures which optimize a smooth internal functioning of the family system are relatively less successful in socializing children for achievement motivation. (S205)

### Adjustment
Joint recreation and joint participation in activities by all family members bring a high degree of satisfaction with family life.

### Aspiration Level
Satisfaction with interpersonal relationships in the family of orientation is inversely correlated with high aspirational level of the individual. (D001)

### Cohesion of Family
A family is more likely to perceive itself as self-sufficient if each member is preoccupied with peacefully maintaining intrafamily relations. (W124)

### Dyadic Relations
If time is not scarce, a high interaction rate on the part of one family member toward another elicits a high interaction rate from the latter toward the former. (C124)

If time is not scarce, all the dyadic relationships in a family tend to have the same interaction rate. (C124)

### Dyadic Relations (Affection)
The greater the affection between two family members, the higher the interaction rate. (C124)

### Friendship
The greater the extent to which a social relationship (friendship, etc.) duplicates for the partners their earliest intrafamilial relationships, the more likely is it to succeed. (T094)

### Functions of Family
With the loss of subsistence roles and the renewal of most other roles from the home, the amount of interaction within the family is reduced. (B040)

### Marital Adjustment
Marital success is more likely when the couple have grown up in a harmonious and understanding family environment. (C023)

### Mental Illness, Recovery from
Any improvement attained by the mental patient during therapy would be temporary unless his family also changed in a constructive direction. (F083)

### Mental Illness (Schizophrenia)
There is no relationship between the voluntary choice of living away from one's family and the development of schizophrenia, but there is an association between involuntary lack of family life (because of death, sterility, etc.) and schizophrenia. (H202)

There is no correlation between family environment and schizophrenia. (M164)

Within the families of persons who later develop acute schizophrenic episodes, those relations which are openly acknowledged as acceptable have a quality of intense and enduring pseudomutuality. (W021)

Family disorganization (schizophrenic) correlates with an absence of spontaneity, novelty, humor, and zest in participation together. (W021)

Members of schizophrenic families tend to use intermediaries in interacting with other family members. (W021)

### Personality Development
Reciprocal exchange between family members (both nuclear and extended) and the child is responsible for the child's development of a sense of self. (C093)

### Personality Problems
When one member of a family suffers from a chronic symptomatology, the patterns of interaction within the family become stereotyped and communication impoverished. (B242)

### Role Definition
The greater the parental commitment to the family, the more likely it is that each person's role outside the home will be shared with the others in the family and the less likely that outside roles will be allowed to compete with family obligations. (F106)

### Role Definition in Family
Disruption of usual family activity and continuity is as-

sociated with a tendency toward role de-differentiation within the family. (S216)

### Sex-Role Identification
The more harmonious the *total* family relationship, the more likely it is that the appropriate sex modeling will occur. (P064)

### Sibling Relations (Interaction)
If other family members interact frequently with the children, the children will not interact as often with each other; if they are ignored by other family members, they will interact more often. (C124)

### Size of Family
Dyads with low interaction rates are more frequent in large families than in small families. (C124)

In large families with low dominance rates, time will be scarce and it is therefore less likely that all dyads will have the same interaction rate; but in small families and in high dominance large families, the rate is more likely to be the same. (C124)

### Social Mobility Aspirations
Lower satisfaction with family relationships is positively and significantly related to the willingness to sacrifice to attain a higher-level occupation. (M060)

### Social Network
The more intraconjugal interaction is idealized and stressed, the more tense are relations between conjugal units likely to be. (C134)

## INTERACTION IN FAMILY (AFFECTION)
### X   Aspiration Level
Females with high aspirations are more likely to perceive their family milieu as depriving than are females with lower aspirations. (R117)

Males with high aspirations are more likely to perceive their family milieu as depriving than are males with lower aspirations. (R117)

### Cohesion of Family
The more cohesive and integrated the nuclear family, the greater its satisfaction of members' emotional and affectional needs. (S217)

### Dyadic Relations
The more affectionate two family members are to each other, the more affectionate they will be to other family members, and the more affection the others will show to one another. (C124)

All the dyadic relationships in a family tend to have the same degree of affection rather than disparate degrees of affection. (C124)

### Husband-Wife Relations (Power)
Affectional interaction is more likely to occur in families where the spouses share equal statuses rather than where one is dominant over the other (Midwestern Mennonites). (K113)

### Mate Selection (Love)
Patterns of marriage based on romantic love are more likely to occur in societies in which the family pattern is characterized by affectional frustration than in societies in which the family relationship is a warm one. (T106)

### Maternal Role
When no other adult woman in the household has a role similar to that of the mother, the average intensity of affective involvement in family relations is likely to be high (U.S.). (P102)

## INTERACTION IN FAMILY (AFFECTION/DUTY)
### X   Cohesion of Family
Among democratic families, voluntary exchange of emotions (i.e., affection, happiness, and satisfaction between family members) leads to family solidarity; among authoritarian families, greater sense of duty and responsibility leads to family solidarity. (K113)

## INTERACTION IN FAMILY (CLOSENESS)
### X   Size of Family
Adolescents from small families have better relations with their parents and other siblings than do those from larger families. (I008)

## INTERACTION IN FAMILY (EMOTIONAL)
### X   Empathy
The more emotional the family interaction, the more accurately will participants perceive the satisfaction of other participants. (L180)

## INTERACTION IN FAMILY (EMOTIONAL INTENSITY)
### X   Mental Illness (Manic-Depressive)
Manic depressives tend to come from families in which the internal relations are intense and in which there is a sense of isolation from the world. (S181)

### Social Network
The more dispersed the activities of the family outside the home, the more intense the feelings between the members of the family. (D058)

## INTERACTION IN FAMILY (INCONSISTENCY)
### X   Personality (Identity)
Since strong identification is primary for the development of a child's identity, families with inconsistencies in intrafamilial relationships are more likely than others to produce children with disturbances of identity. (B241)

## INTERACTION IN FAMILY (INTERESTS)
### X   Ritual in Family
Families in which the members share common interests tend to develop family rituals. (B206)

## INTERACTION IN FAMILY (INTIMACY)
### X   Juvenile Delinquency
Severe delinquency is frequently associated with a lack of durable intimate relationships with relatives. (B291)

### Marital Adjustment
Marital adjustment is positively associated with intimacy of association within the family. (C023)

### Peer Relations
The less intimate the family life, the less likely is the child to be popular among his peers. (R111)

### Size of Family
An inverse curvilinear relationship exists between size of family and intimacy of family life. (R111)

## INTERACTION IN FAMILY (SUPPORT)
### X   Husband-Wife Relations (Support)
The support patterns (solidarity, contending, dominant, conflicting) of all pairs in a nuclear family tend to be similar to those of the husband and wife, even when the husband and wife are not involved in those other pairs. (S207)

## INTERACTION IN FAMILY (WARMTH)
### X   Cognitive Development
A warm family atmosphere is associated with a favorable rate of intellectual growth in the child. (B257)

### Institutional Care
Institutionalizing a retarded child, rather than having him remain at home, is inversely related to warmth among family members. (J027)

## INTERACTION WITH EXTENDED/NUCLEAR
## FAMILY          X   Geographic Mobility
Residential mobility breaks down contact with the extended family and tends to limit frequent interaction to the marital family unit. (M166)

## INTERACTION WITH FAMILY      X   Friendship
Persons become isolated from their families when they enter into interracial friendships. (G001)

### Juvenile Delinquency
Isolation from the family physically or mentally is likely to increase the association of the child with delinquency. (B033)

## INTERACTION WITH FAMILY (INTIMACY)
### X   Residence
The desire to avoid intimate family relationships is a cause of the tendency of schizophrenics to move into the central areas of big cities. (H202)

## INTERACTION WITH FAMILY (LEISURE)
### X   Social Mobility Aspirations
Adolescents with upward mobility aspirations are likely to spend more time than are other adolescents in leisure activities with their families. (D077)

## INTERACTION WITH PEER/PARENT
### X   Authoritarianism
Children are likely to be democratic in their social behavior if they spend more time with peers who have the same power rather than with parents who are of superior power. (G136)

## INTERGENERATIONAL RELATIONS
### X   Acculturation
Intergenerational conflict tends to occur wherever a situation of acculturation exists. (S052)

### Economic Cooperation
Economic cooperation between related families of different generations creates closer emotional ties between the families. (S002)

## INTERGENERATIONAL RELATIONS (AUTHORITY)
### X   Intragenerational Relations (Warmth)
When there is a rigorous pattern of authority between generations, relationships among individuals of the same generation tend to be characterized by warmth and intimacy. (K049)

## INTRAGENERATIONAL RELATIONS (AUTHORITY)
### X   Intergenerational Relations (Warmth)
When there is a rigorous pattern of authority between generations, relationships among individuals of the same generation tend to be characterized by warmth and intimacy. (K049)

## INTERMARRIAGE          X   Birth Control
Parents in intermarriages exercise greater birth control and thus have fewer children than do parents in homogamous marriages in order to prevent the lack of identification and status of marginality which children of intermarriages tend to have. (B012)

### Cohesion of Clan
Intermarriage with members of the donor culture will tend to result in a decline in the indigenous clan or lineage system. (L031)

### Cohesion of Family
The weaker the child's ties to his immediate and extended families, the more likely he is to marry outside his group. (H240)

### Descent (Bilateral Filiation)
Interclass caste marriages are more likely to be prohibited when membership in the superior caste is derived from bilateral filiation. (F117)

### Disorganization of Family
Intermarriage is more likely to take place among individuals who come from families that are disorganized than from stable families. (H008)

### Economic Cooperation
Patterns of intermarriage between two groups tend to occur with the establishment of patterns of economic reciprocity. (B058)

### Ethnicity/Religion/Race
Intermarriage is more likely to take place between ethnic groups than between religious groups and between religious groups than between racially defined groups. (B012)

Interethnic marriage is more likely to take place within the same religion than between different religions. (B012)

### Marginal Status of Child
The children of intermarriages are more likely to lack adequate identification and to have marginal status than are the children of homogamous parents. (B012)

### Mate Selection (Free Choice)
A culture which has the concept of individualism in mate choice as embedded in a "romantic complex" is more likely to have more intermarriage than is a culture without such a concept. (B012)

### Parent-Child Relations
The poorer the parent-child relations, the more likely the child will intermarry. (H240)

### Parent-Child Relations (Help)
It is just as likely that parental help will be extended to children who have intermarried (religion, class, educational level, ethnic descent) as to those who have married people of their own cultural background. (S002)

### Political Relations
Peaceful relations between adjacent tribes are more likely to be maintained if there is a pattern of intermarriage between the groups. (E080)

Intermarriage between different tribal groups tends to strengthen their political relations. (K060)

### Polygyny
Intertribal marriage may be correlated with the practice of polygyny. (B167)

### Rank of Lineage
The rank of a lineage will be affected by the extent to which it intermarries with superior groups. (S158)

### Religion
Intermarriage is most frequent among Protestants, less among Catholics, and least among Jews. (B244)

### Religion/Class
Class intermarriage is as likely to take place as is religious intermarriage. (M015)

### Religiosity of Parents
The weaker the ties of parents to religion, the more likely the child is to intermarry. (H240)

### Sex Ratio
The rate of intermarriage will be correlated with the sex ratio of the group. (M227)

### Sex Status
Among members of the upper caste, men are more likely to violate patterns of racial endogamy than women are; but upper-caste women are more likely than men to marry downward in caste. (M227)

### Size of Group
The rate of intermarriage with other groups will be negatively correlated with the size of the group. (M227)

### Social Distance
The following exogamous marriages are ranked in the amount of social disapproval they incur (from greatest to least) as follows: (1) interracial marriages, (2) internationality, interclass, and interfaith marriages, (3) intereducational group marriages, and (4) interregional marriages (U.S.). (J035)

### Social Interaction
Intermarriage between groups will be directly correlated with the frequency of intergroup interaction. (M227)

### Social Mobility
Intermarriage is less likely to be disruptive in societies where patterns of mobility permit a movement from the families of orientation. (M227)

### Social Mobility Aspirations
Intermarriage is more likely to take place where a drive toward upward social mobility is present than where it is absent. (B012)

### Structure of Family, Changes in
Intermarriage tends to intensify changes in family organization in a culture-contact situation. (S053)

### Urban/Rural
The partners in intermarriages are more likely to be of urban background than of rural background. (G033)

## INTERMARRIAGE (CLAN)
### X   Conflict Between Clans
There is a direct correlation between the degree of hostility between clans and the extent to which their members intermarry. (B187)

### Joking Relationship
The joking relationship is basically associated with clans that generally intermarry. (B111)

### Political Power
The consolidation of political power will be implemented by the intermarriage of ranking clans. (R034)

## INTERMARRIAGE (CLASS)        X   Property
When intermarriage of localized lineages of different social class occurs, the general tendency is the transfer of economic wealth from the lower class to the upper (i.e., hypergamy is more likely). (L051)

### Social Mobility
Interclass unions are more likely to occur in societies in which social mobility is stressed. (M227)

### Values (Democratic)
Interclass marriages are more likely to occur in societies which stress democratic values. (M227)

### Values (Marriage)
Interclass marriages are more likely to occur in societies in which romantic love is emphasized as a basis for marriage. (M227)

## INTERMARRIAGE (COMMUNITY)
### X   Political Relations
Political relations between communities are more likely to be hostile if there is no pattern of intermarriage between the villages. (T069)

The incidence of intermarriages will tend to be high between communities which maintain peaceful political relations. (T069)

## INTERMARRIAGE (CULTURAL)
### X   Conflict in Family
The discrepancy of value orientations of persons who intermarry is a basis of family conflict. (S075)

## INTERMARRIAGE (ETHNIC)        X   Acculturation
The rate of acculturation is accelerated when there is ethnic or racial intermarriage with the donor culture. (B049)

Children of ethnic intermarriages will participate less in their indigenous culture if the parent who represents the donor culture has little interest or sympathy with the social organization or culture of the indigenous group. (L031)

Intermarriage increases cultural assimilation, particularly when the woman belongs to the dominant culture. (P052)

Intermarriage increases cultural breakdown or cultural assimilation, particularly when the woman belongs to the dominant culture. (P052)

### Cohesion of Ethnic Group
The cohesion of the group tends to disintegrate as its members marry individuals of other ethnic groups. (A010)

### Desertion
Marital conflict stemming from differing nationality backgrounds may be one factor in the overrepresentation of Catholics in desertion cases. (K010)

### Ethnic Attitudes
Intermarriage is more likely to take place among self-hating minority-group members than among minority-group members who take pride in their status. (B012)

### Ethnic Group, Social Visibility of
The likelihood of intermarriage increases as the social visibility of a group decreases. (M015)

### Fertility
Regardless of religious affiliation, marriages between persons of different national origins tend to show lower fertility rates. (B300)

### Interaction
The opportunity for unmarried young people to associate with members of another ethnic opposite group will directly affect the rate of intermarriage. (H036)

### Intermarriage (Religious)
Marriages across major religious denominational lines more often involve spouses of different ethnic stock than spouses of the same ethnic stock. (H014)

### Language
The rate of intermarriage tends to be higher when the ethnic groups in question share a common language. (L045)

### Political Relations
When patterns of intermarriage exist between two tribes, the character of their political relationship will tend to be cooperative. (B058)

### Rank of Ethnic Group
When there is a discrepancy in the social status of two ethnic groups, the rate of intermarriage will be low. (T013)

### Religion
It is more likely that interethnic intermarriage will take place among Protestants than among Catholics and among Catholics than among Jews. (H014)

### Residence
The rate of intermarriage will be higher among members of the ethnic groups who reside at the periphery of the group's territory. (M046)

### Social Mobility
Ethnic intermarriage will increase as the amount of social mobility of an ethnic group increases. (B029)

### Stability of Kinship Structure
The disintegration of the traditional kinship system is directly correlated with an increase in the rate of intermarriage. (H062)

The adoption of elements of the kinship structure of another group is more likely to occur when there is a high incidence of intermarriage between ethnic groups. (H080)

### Technology
The rate of intermarriage will tend to be restricted if the technological pattern of cultures in contact is diverse. (H036)

### Values
Intermarriage is more likely to take place among heterogeneous groups that have developed social proximity (i.e., similar standards of living, similar social-class position, etc.) than among heterogeneous groups that have not developed social proximity. (B012)

The rate of intermarriage will be higher when the cultures of the ethnic groups are similar. (L045)

## INTERMARRIAGE OF CHILD
### X   Intermarriage of Parent
Children of parents from different religious backgrounds are more likely to intermarry than are children of parents with identical religious backgrounds. (H240)

## INTERMARRIAGE OF PARENT
### X   Intermarriage of Child
Children of parents from different religious backgrounds are more likely to intermarry than are children of parents with identical religious backgrounds. (H240)

## INTERMARRIAGE (POLITICAL)      X   Warfare
A tribe which is not sure of its martial standing and general security may seek alliances through intermarriage with stronger tribes. (C091)

## INTERMARRIAGE (RACIAL)   X   Affinal Relations
Of those wives in interracial marriages who have strained relations with their in-laws, it is more likely that the strained relations will be with the mother-in-law than with any other in-law. (K019)

### Education of Husband-Wife
Japanese-American couples are likely to be more educated than the general American population. (S004)

### Fertility
The number of children of interracial families is smaller than the number of children in single-racial families. This proposition is also denied. (G001)

### Homogamy (Class)
Intermarriage is more likely to take place among people of the same social status than of different social statuses. (H008)

### Intermarriage (Religious)
Racial intermarriages are also more likely to be religious intermarriages than to be between members of the same religion. (G003)

### Marital Adjustment
Marital happiness is lower for intermarriages than for marriages of the same race and/or religion. (B033)

### Marriage Ceremony
Civil, rather than religious, wedding ceremonies are more frequent in interracial marriages. (G001)

### Occupational Discrimination
In interracial marriages, the Negro spouse seems to be less subject to economic sanctions in his occupation than is the white spouse. (G001)

### Occupational Rank of Wife
Negro men marrying white women tend to marry white women with low occupational status rather than high occupational status. (G003)

### Race
The initial acceptance of racial intermarriage tends to be correlated with the presence of more than two racial types. (D018)

### Sex Ratio
Intermarriage is more likely to take place between different racial groups where there exists an unbalanced sex ratio than among groups where there is a balanced sex ratio. (B012)

The initial acceptance of racial intermarriage tends to be correlated with the scarcity of women of the upper castes. (D018)

### Sex Status
Interracial marriages tend to be between aboriginal women and white men. (F063)

Negro men and white women are more likely to intermarry than are white men and Negro women. (G003)

Marriages between Negroes and whites are most likely to be caste-hypogamous, the white women marrying a Negro man (U.S.). (G156)

## INTERMARRIAGE (RACIAL AND ETHNIC)
### X    Age at Marriage
Children of intermarriages (racial and ethnic) marry earlier than do children of homogamous marriages. (B311)

Children of intermarriages who also intermarry themselves are apt to be younger than those who marry members of their own ethnic or racial group. (B311)

In ethnic or racial intermarriage the partners are more likely to be older than in the case of marriages within the racial or ethnic group. (B311)

### Age Difference
There is less likely to be an age difference between husband and wife (with the husband older) in homogamous marriages than in intermarriages (racial and ethnic). (B311)

### Assimilation
The greater the rate of assimilation, the higher the rate of interracial and interethnic marriages. (B311)

### Intolerance
The greater the decrease in intolerance, the higher the rate of intermarriage. (B311)

### Marital Status
Those intermarrying are more likely to have been previously divorced than are couples intramarrying. (B311)

### Rank of Minorities
The greater the rise in social rank of a minority, the greater the rate of racial and ethnic intermarriage. (B311)

### Social Distance
The greater the rate of decreasing social distance between racial and ethnic groups, the greater the rate of their intermarriage. (B311)

## INTERMARRIAGE (RACIAL), ATTITUDE TOWARD
### X    Personality of Wife
The Negro community tends to accept the white wife if her personal qualities are such as would make a Negro acceptable. (G001)

## INTERMARRIAGE (RELIGIOUS)
### X    Age at Marriage
Religious endogamy is inversely related to the couple's ages at marriage. (C128)

### Class
The percentage of Catholic marriages which are mixed marriages varies directly with social class, as reflected in graded rental areas. (T010)

### Class of Husband
Religious endogamy is inversely related to the status level of the groom. (C128)

### Divorce
Mixed marriages between Catholics and Protestants are more likely to end when the Protestant partner belongs to no particular denomination than when he does. (B314)

Divorce is less likely to occur among all-Catholic marriages than among mixed marriages of Catholics. (C006)

Spouses who marry outside their own faiths are more likely to become divorced than are couples who marry interfaith. (C134)

Of the three religious types of marriage, nonmixed ones have the lowest divorce rate, mixed the next highest rate, and marriages in which there is no religious faith the highest. (L010)

In mixed marriages, the divorce rate is higher when a Catholic man marries a Protestant woman than when a Protestant man marries a Catholic woman. (L010)

The divorce rate is low, compared to other types of mixed marriages, in marriages in which a Catholic woman marries a man with no religious faith. (L010)

In mixed marriages, the highest divorce rate was in marriages in which the largest percentage of husbands and wives were church members (i.e., the Catholic father-Protestant mother combinations). (L010)

Mixed marriages are less likely to end in divorce if one spouse changes to the faith of the other. But the percentage of mixed marriages ending in divorce is higher when the Catholic wife has changed to the Protestant faith and when the Protestant husband has changed to the Catholic faith than in the other two possibilities (i.e., Protestant wives changing to Catholicism and Catholic husbands changing to Protestantism). (L010)

Among cross-faith marriages, divorce rates are highest for Jews, lower for Protestants, and lowest for Catholics. (Z008)

### Ethnic Subgroups
The intermarriage rate between Catholics and non-Catholics tends to be reduced by the presence of closely-knit ethnic subgroups among the Catholics of a community. (T010)

### Fertility Values
Couples of mixed-faith marriages tend to desire about the same number of children as those of nonmixed marriages. (B300)

### Geographic Mobility
Women who married within their own religion are more likely than those of interfaith marriages to have been married within their own state of residence. (C128)

### Homogamy (Religion)
The children of mixed marriages tend to marry those outside their religious group more often than do the offspring of marriages in which both spouses are of the same religion. (T010)

### Immigrant/Nonimmigrant
The percentage of mixed-faith marriages is higher among immigrants than among the native-born (U.S.). (B300)

### Intermarriage (Ethnic)
Marriages across major religious denominational lines more often involve spouses of different ethnic stock than of the same ethnic stock. (H014)

### Intermarriage (Racial)
Racial intermarriages are also more likely to be religious intermarriages than to be marriages between members of the same religion. (G003)

### Marital Adjustment
Mixed-faith marriages are associated with a slightly lower level of marital satisfaction than are nonmixed marriages. (B300)

## Marriage Ceremony

Civil ceremonies are more frequent among interfaith marriages than among religiously endogamous marriages. (C128)

## Mate Selection (Residence)

A higher proportion of Catholic men who marry non-Catholic women marry propinquitously than do Catholic women who marry non-Catholic men. (Propinquitous marriage: bride and groom live within a radius of 20 blocks.) (S016)

## Premarital Pregnancy

Higher premarital pregnancy rates are found among mixed marriages than among homogamous religious marriages. (M243)

## Religion

Intermarriage is more likely to take place among Catholics than among Protestants. (C006)

In interfaith marriages, the child is more likely to be brought up in the faith of the mother than of the father. This is less true of Catholics and Jews than of Protestants. (C134)

In mixed marriages, the most common tendency seems to be that the children, especially the daughters, follow the faith of the mother. (L010)

## Religion (Change)

Spouses are as likely in mixed marriages to change from Catholicism to Protestantism as from Protestantism to Catholicism. (L010)

## Religious Beliefs X Sex Status

In cross-faith marriages, men abandon their faiths more readily than women. (Z008)

## Residence with Parents

Single people, living with their parents, tend to marry someone of their own religion more often than do single people living away from their parents. (C134)

## Size of Religious Group

The rate of intermarriage between Catholics and non-Catholics varies inversely with the proportion of Catholics in the total population (provided that ethnic and/or social rank differences do not prevent occupational and social contacts). (T010)

## Urban/Rural

There is no relation between urban or rural background and interfaith marriage. (H240)

## INTOLERANCE                    X Intermarriage

The greater the decrease in intolerance, the higher the rate of intermarriage. (B311)

## I.Q.                          X Adoption, Age at

Children with I.Q.'s of 110 or above are more likely to have been adopted before the age of six months than are those with lower I.Q.'s. (H242)

## Adoption (Urban/Rural)

Urban adoptive parents are more insistent that the child to be adopted be of average intelligence or above than are rural adoptive parents. (M192)

## Breast Feeding

Given the same environment, breast-fed infants are more advanced mentally than are bottle-fed infants.

## Breast Feeding, Duration of

After nine months, there is a negative correlation between duration of breast feeding of the infant and his intelligence level. (B272)

## Child-Rearing (Collective)

Children reared collectively (on kibbutzim) have higher I.Q.'s (after 10 years of age) than do children reared at home, despite early retardation in ego development due to inconsistent mothering. (R095)

Kibbutz children have a higher level of intellectual development than do nonkibbutz children (as measured by interpretations of Rorschach and TAT tests). (R096)

## Child-Rearing Practices (Acceleration)

There is a positive relationship between maternal acceleration of the 2–7-year-old son and his intelligence scores when an adolescent. (K115)

## Child-Rearing Practices (Criticism)

Maternal criticism is related to high intelligence in girls, but not in boys (ages 4–7). (K115)

With maternal educational level held constant, there is a positive relationship between materal criticism and intelligence scores for daughters 3½ and 5½ years old. (K115)

## Child-Rearing Practices (Democratic)

Children and parents of democratic homes (homes in which the parents encourage free experimentation by their children) have a higher I.Q. than do children and parents of nondemocratic homes. (B287)

## Child-Rearing Practices (Discipline)

When maternal educational level is controlled, there is a positive relationship between maternal justification for disciplinary measures and intelligence scores of 4–7-year-old boys and girls. (K115)

There is a positive relationship between maternal justification of disciplinary measures during the child's early years (2–7) and adolescent intelligence scores in sons. (K115)

## Child-Rearing Practices (Giving Reasons)

Arbitrary maternal discipline is associated with low I.Q. scores, whereas explained maternal discipline is associated with high I.Q. scores. (K127)

## Child-Rearing Practices (Physical Contact)

The amount and quality of physical contact between mother and child is positively related to intelligence in the child. (Y042)

## Child-Rearing Practices (Punishment)

Maternal coercion is associated with low intelligence scores for boys and girls aged 2–4. (K115)

There is no relationship between maternal coercion and intelligence scores of preschool-aged children when maternal educational level is controlled. (K115)

There is no relationship between the child's intelligence and his perception of his parents as either punitive or not. (L149)

## Child-Rearing Practices (Restrictiveness)

Maternal restrictiveness is associated with low intelligence scores for boys and girls aged 2–4. (K115)

There is no relationship between maternal restrictiveness and intelligence scores of preschool-aged children when maternal educational level is controlled. (K115)

Maternal restrictiveness and coerciveness are associated with low I.Q. scores, whereas maternal justification of discipline is related to high I.Q. scores. (K127)

There is a correlation between paternal overrestriction and a low performance of the child on the Picture Completion Test (WISC). (M213)

### Dependency
Children's intellectual achievement behavior (I.Q.) correlates with their emotional independence from their parents. (C118)

### Education of Father
A positive correlation exists between the child's I.Q. and the father's educational level. (H173)

### Education of Parents
There is no relationship between the educational level of the parents and the intelligence of the child. (B282)

There is a correlation between level of parental education and the mental ability of three-year-old Negro children. (H191)

### Employment of Mother
There is no relationship between the employment status of the mother and the mental ability of the three-year-old Negro child. (H191)

### Father Absence
Children in families without a male head tend to have lower levels of intelligence than do children with fathers. (A065)

There is a negative correlation between paternal absence after the age of five and the ability (WISC) of the child. (M213)

### Father-Child Relations (Hostility)
Girls' intelligence (at school) is negatively related to their fathers' hostility. (B232)

### Homogamy (Class)
A higher proportion of women who marry upward socially receive over-average I.Q. test scores than of those who marry within the same class. (L115)

A higher proportion of women who marry within their class make high I.Q. scores than of those who move down the social scale at marriage. (L115)

### Illegitimacy
There is no correlation between low intelligence and having illegitimate children. (N055)

### Institutional Care, Age at
Intellectual damage to the child due to institutionalization is most likely between three and twelve months of age. (Y045)

### Marital Adjustment
Marital adjustment is higher when one spouse perceives the other's mental ability as equal to that of his or her own. (B033)

### Marriage Chances
Persons with lower intelligence ratings are less likely to get married. (H222)

The offspring of parents with low intelligence ratings are less likely to marry or to produce children than are those of parents with average or high intelligence ratings. (H231)

### Mate Selection
Husbands and wives tend to be of the same intelligence level. (W148)

### Mother Absence
Children deprived of their mothers during the first year experience a large drop in intelligence (as measured by the Development Quotient Scale) between the ages of four and twelve months. (B270)

### Mother-Child Relations
Mothers of children of average intelligence tend to be more dominating, more ignoring, and more possessive than do the mothers of gifted children. (H199)

### Mother-Child Relations (Democracy)
Democratic attitudes are more characteristic of mothers of children with high, rather than low, I.Q.'s. (E102)

### Mother-Child Relations (Interest)
Lack of maternal interest is negatively correlated with the child's performance on the Picture Completion Test and the Picture Arrangement Test (WISC). (M213)

### Mother-Child Relations (Warmth)
Positive, warm attitudes are more characteristic of mothers of children with high, rather than low, I.Q.'s. (E102)

### Occupation of Father
There is no relationship between the mental development of the preschool Negro child and the occupation of the father. (H191)

### Occupational Rank of Father
There is a correlation between the occupational level of the father and the intelligence of the child. (B282)

### Occupational Rank of Surrogate Father
Children with higher I.Q. are more likely to have been adopted by fathers in higher-ranking occupations than are those with lower I.Q. (H242)

### Ordinal Position
Firstborn children are more likely to be high in intelligence than are children in other ordinal positions. (B282)

The oldest child and the "baby of the family" receive disproportionate amounts of parental attention and both have average higher I.Q. scores than do middle-born siblings. (L115)

There is no relationship between the ordinal position of the child and his intelligence. (S218)

### Parent-Child Relations (Protective/Democratic)
The lower the I.Q. of the child, the more likely that the parents will be protective in their attitude toward him; the higher the I.Q., the more likely that the mother will have democratic attitudes. (B259)

### Parent Loss
Children who are raised without parents or adequate parent surrogates yield a significantly lower score on the Stanford-Binet I.Q. Test than do normal children. (B270)

### Sibling Structure
There is a slight tendency for Negro preschool children with high mental abilities to have relatively fewer siblings. (H191)

### Sibling Structure (Age Difference)
The greater the age interval between siblings, the greater their intelligence is likely to be. (A065)

There is no relationship between age intervals between siblings and their levels of I.Q. (S218)

### Sibling Structure (Sex)
Children with male siblings are more likely to be high in intelligence than are those with female siblings. (S218)

### Sibling Structure (Twins)
Twins tend to have a lower average intelligence than does the total population (A065)

### Size of Family
The fewer the number of children, the greater the intelligence of the child. (B282)

The intelligence of an individual is positively correlated with the number of offspring he produces. (B305)

The intelligence of an individual is negatively correlated with the size of the family from which the individual comes. (B305)

Within each occupational class, children from smaller families have higher I.Q. scores, on the average, than do children from larger families. (L115)

### Size of Family by Class
The larger the family (number of siblings), the lower the intelligence level of the child; this relationship declines at the higher socioeconomic levels and may even be reversed. (A065)

## I.Q./CREATIVITY
### X    Child-Rearing Practices (Reading Habits)
Families of highly intelligent children (Binet) are more likely to subscribe to several children's magazines than are the families of highly creative children (Guilford-Cattell). (G132)

### Child-Rearing Practices (Risk)
The parents of highly intelligent children encourage the minimization of risks, while those of highly creative children accept risks. (G114)

### Child-Rearing Practices (Strictness)
Mothers of highly intelligent (Binet) children are more likely to be morally strict in the upbringing of their children than are the mothers of highly creative (Guilford-Cattell) children. (G132)

### Child-Rearing Values
Mothers of highly creative children (Binet) are more likely to favor internal values in friends of their children than are the parents of highly intelligent children (Guilford-Cattell). (G132)

Mothers of highly intelligent children (Binet) are more likely to favor such external values as good family and good manners in friends of their children than are the parents of highly creative children (Guilford-Cattell). (G132)

### Class (Mother's Awareness of)
Mothers of highly intelligent children (Binet) are more likely to be conscious of their parents' social class than are the parents of highly creative children (Guilford-Cattell). (G132)

### Education of Parents
Parents of highly intelligent (Binet) children are more likely to have had more specialized educational training than are the parents of highly creative (Guilford-Cattell) children. (G132)

### Employment of Mother
The mothers of highly intelligent (Binet) children are more likely to be full-time housewives than are the mothers of highly creative (Guilford-Cattell) children. (G132)

### Income, Attitude Toward
Parents of highly intelligent children (Binet) are more likely to be aware of financial difficulties in their own childhoods than are the parents of highly creative children (Guilford-Cattell). (G132)

### Parent-Child Relations (Criticism)
Parents of highly intelligent children (Binet) are more likely to be critical of reports concerning their child's performance in school than are the parents of highly creative children (Guilford-Cattell). (G132)

### Parental-Role Adjustment
Parents of highly intelligent children (Binet) are more likely to be satisfied with their own child-rearing practices than are the parents of highly creative children (Guilford-Cattell). (G132)

### Personality of Parents (Insecurity)
The parents of highly intelligent children have experienced more insecurity than have the parents of highly creative children. (G114)

Parents of highly intelligent children (Binet) are more likely to have feelings of insecurity than are the parents of highly creative children (Guilford-Cattell). (G132)

### Reading Habits of Family
### X    Creativity/I.Q. of Child
Families of highly intelligent children (Binet) are more likely to subscribe to many magazines than are the families of highly creative children (Guilford-Cattell). (G132)

## I.Q./CREATIVITY OF CHILDREN
### Child-Rearing Practices (Supervision)
Parents of highly intelligent children exercise more supervision over the behavior and academic performances of their children than do the parents of highly creative children. (G114)

## I.Q. DIFFERENCES BETWEEN DATING PARTNERS
### X    Sexual Aggression
The intelligence difference between sexually aggressive males and sexually offended females is more likely to be greater than the intelligence difference between nonaggressive males and nonoffended females. (K018)

## I.Q. OF ADOPTED CHILD
### X    Education of Surrogate Father
There is no correlation between the educational level of the foster father and the I.Q. of his adopted child. (H173)

## I.Q. OF CHILD    X    Disorganization of Family
There is a correlation between disturbance in family relationships and the child's low performance on the Block Design and Object Assembly Tests (WISC). (M213)

### I.Q. of Natural/Surrogate Parent

After the adopted child is four years of age, his I.Q. correlates with that of his natural mother, but not with that of his foster mother. (H173)

### I.Q. of Parents

Parent-child intelligence levels resemble each other at an earlier age for girls than for boys. (H214)

### I.Q. OF CHILD, BY AGE          X    I.Q. of Parents

Before two years of age, the I.Q. of the child is not related to parental ability; at later ages, however, there is a correlation between the two. (H173)

### I.Q. OF FATHER
####          X    Child-Rearing Attitudes (Permissiveness)

Fathers who express permissive child-rearing attitudes are more intelligent (Terman Concept Mastery Test) than those who express restrictive child-rearing attitudes. (B227)

### I.Q. OF KIN
####          X    Mental Illness (Social Adjustment)

There is no relationship between intelligence (as measured by the Borgatta-Corsini "Quick Word Test") of the mental patient's family and the patient's success or failure in remaining in the community. (F124)

The higher the relatives' intelligence (Borgatta-Corsini "Quick Word Test"), the higher the former mental patient's level of social and occupational performance is likely to be. (F124)

Patients with low levels of social and vocational performance who succeed in remaining in the community have family members with significantly lower intelligence scores (Borgatta-Corsini "Quick Work Test") than do patients who were rehospitalized. (F124)

### I.Q. OF MOTHER      X    Illegitimacy (Adoption)

Unwed mothers who keep their children are lower in intelligence than are unwed mothers who surrender their children. (J020)

####          I.Q. of Natural/Adopted Child

The correlation between the I.Q. of the child and the I.Q. of his natural mother is higher if they live together than if the child lives with a foster mother. (H173)

####          Mother-Child Relations

There is a positive correlation between the mother's intelligence and a positive preadolescent mother-child interaction. (S273)

### I.Q. OF NATURAL/ADOPTED CHILD
####          X    Education of Father

The correlation between the I.Q. of the child and his father's educational level is about the same, whether or not his own father or his foster father rears him. (H173)

####          I.Q. of Mother

The correlation between the I.Q. of the child and the I.Q. of his natural mother is higher if they live together than if the child lives with a foster mother. (H173)

### I.Q. OF NATURAL/SURROGATE PARENT
####          X    I.Q. of Child

After the adopted child is four years of age, his I.Q. correlates with that of his natural mother, but not with that of his foster mother. (H173)

### I.Q. OF PARENT/CHILD          X    Age of Child

The older the child, the higher the correlation between the I.Q. of a child and that of his parents. (H173)

### I.Q. OF PARENTS          X    Aggression

There is no relationship between a parent's intelligence and aggression of the son. (M210)

####          Fertility

There is no relationship between the intelligence of the parents and the number of children they have or their ages at birth of the first child. (A065)

####          I.Q. of Child

Parent-child intelligence levels resemble each other at an earlier age for girls than for boys. (H214)

####          I.Q. of Child, by Age

Before two years of age, the I.Q. of the child is not related to parental ability; at later ages, however, there is a correlation between the two. (H173)

####          Size of Family

The lower the intelligence of the parents, the larger the average family size. (H231)

There is a curvilinear relationship between intelligence of parents and family size; parents with the highest and lowest intelligence ratings have the highest reproductive rates. (H231)

### I.Q. (VERBAL/NONVERBAL)
####          X    Child-Rearing Practices (Demands)

The I.Q. combination of high verbal and low nonverbal abilities is more likely among children whose mothers are highly demanding and intrusive. (B289)

####          Child-Rearing Practices (Restrictiveness)

The I.Q. combination of low verbal and high nonverbal abilities is more likely among children whose mothers allow them considerable freedom to experiment. (B289)

### ISOLATION OF FAMILY          X    Incest

There is a correlation between incest and the isolation of the family from its larger social and cultural environment.

####          Oedipal Complex

The appearance of the Oedipal complex is correlated with the degree of isolation of the family unit. (M226)

####          Value Conflict

Where there is a conflict between familial and community values, the parents may keep the children isolated from all but formal contact with the social environment outside the home. (B033)

### ISOLATION OF NUCLEAR FAMILY
####          X    Age Groups

Youth movements are likely to be stronger and to exert more political pressure on parents in isolated nuclear families of urban centers than in families deeply embedded in a network of extended kin. (P083)

####          Child-Rearing Practices

Children who are being brought up for "sociological interdependence" (i.e., anchorage and identification in the wider kin-group rather than in the nuclear family) will be taught and brought up by members of the child's descent group, as well as by the parents; children who are being brought up for "sociological independence (i.e., anchorage and identification in the nuclear family) will be brought up by nonmembers of the descent group, as well as by their parents. (C093)

### Death Rate
Where there is a strong likelihood that a child might be deprived of one or both of his biological parents before outgrowing his dependency on them (e.g., where living is "harsh"), the isolated nuclear family is less likely to occur (because of the need for substitute parents to complete the socialization process). (P083)

### Descent (Unilineal)
Absence of emphasis on one line of descent increases the structural isolation of the conjugal family. (P012)

### Divorce
Sterility and failure to integrate with the matrilinear or patrilinear line are likely to be more important causes of divorce where the conjugal family is integrated with the extended family; where the nuclear family is isolated, failure of tension reduction is likely to be the more important cause of divorce. (P083)

Divorce is more likely to result from problems associated with the husband's failure to support the wife properly or with his behaving dishonorably if the nuclear family is isolated, than where extended family ties are strong and failure of the husband can be more easily compensated by the efforts of relatives. (P083)

### Economic Rank
The greater the opportunity for consumption of wealth on the part of the individual family, the greater is its tendency to become independent of the larger kin unit. (F029)

### Employment of Women
Salaried employment of women is likely to promote the isolation of the nuclear family from the patrilineage. (P083)

### Husband-Wife Relations (Closeness)
The more isolated the nuclear family is in the social structure, the more dependent spouses are upon each other and the weaker their ties with their own parents and adult siblings. (P062)

### Husband-Wife Relations (Intimacy)
The more isolated the nuclear family in a society is, the more dependent the husband will be on a high level of intimacy in a monogamous marriage. (P083)

### Kin/Nonkin
The greater the isolation of the nuclear family in society, the greater the sharpness of status differences between family members and nonfamily members. (P062)

### Kin Terminology
The isolated nuclear family tends to be associated with kinship terminology of the lineal type. (M019)

### Kin Terminology (Bifurcate Collateral)
Bifurcate collateral terminology functions to reinforce the isolation of the nuclear family from collateral nuclear family. (S060)

### Marital Stability
The emergence of a nuclear family which is independent of a larger kin unit tends to be conducive to great marital stability. (L064)

### Nationalism
There is a correlation between the rise of nationalism and the isolation of the nuclear family. (P083)

### Parental-Role Definition
Parenthood assumes more significance for the emotional balance of the parents themselves, as well as for the socialization of their children, in social structures in which the nuclear family is relatively isolated than is the case in systems in which solidarity with extended kin is more pronounced. (P062)

### Power Structure of Family
When the nuclear family is isolated, there is a concomitant shift in the mother's status within the family to a position of centrality. (C024)

### Residence (Neolocal)
Neolocal rules of residence are associated with systems that tend to isolate or emphasize the individual or the nuclear family (monogamy, the growth of territorial states, the development of private property, individual enterprise in the economic sphere, personal freedom in choice of marital partners, and individual migration). (P083)

### Role Behavior in Family
The isolation of the nuclear family is conditional upon the capacity of the marriage to provide stimulation and tension reduction on the peer level rather than merely on the more regressive levels of husband's omnipotence and mother-child symbiosis. (P083)

### Role Definition in Family
The greater the isolation of the conjugal unit, the greater the number of functions (such as care for the sick and aged) which are taken over by nonfamily institutions. (C134)

### Role Definitions, Flexibility of
A greater flexibility of kin role is tolerated when residence pattern is that of the isolated nuclear family. (F050)

### Sex-Role Definition
Differentiation between the roles of the parents on the basis of sex becomes more significant for the socialization process and the complementarity of roles within marriage accentuated in social systems characterized by comparative isolation of the nuclear family than is the case in systems in which solidarity with extended kin is more pronounced. (P062)

### Social Mobility
Where the nuclear family is a relatively isolated unit, occupational mobility is normal. (S080)

### Urbanization
The degree of urbanization is directly correlated with an increasing proportion of independent nuclear families. (L064)

### Values (Individualism)
There is a relationship between value systems oriented to achievement and individualism and the growing isolation of the nuclear family. (P083)

## ISOLATION OF SOCIETY
### X   Kinship, Importance of
When the society is small and isolated, the family will play a large part in societal institutions. (F021)

# J

## JOINT FAMILY      X Achievement Motivation
Where earnings are shared among members of a joint family in India, a family member is less likely than in other types of families to show initiative. (M081)

### Class
Joint families (in India) are more common among upper-class families than among lower-class families. (N069)

### Economic Rank
Joint families are more likely to occur in the upper economic rank than in the lower economic rank (Bengal). (M012)

### Mate Selection
Arranged marriages, preventing the conjugal bond from becoming too strong and threatening to break the household into nuclear family units, are associated with joint family systems. (G156)

### Property Ownership (Corporate)
The corporate ownership of landed estates tends to stabilize and strengthen the joint family. (M021)

### Sex-Role Definition
Segregation of the sexes before and after marriage is associated with the joint family system due to the fact that it prevents the possibility of strong male-female liaisons from forming that would threaten the solidarity of the male lineage. (G156)

### Urban/Rural
The joint family structure is today more characteristic of rural than of urban families. (M081)

## JOINT FAMILY/NUCLEAR FAMILY
###      X Kin-Role Definition
There will be more nepotism in an industrialized social system where the joint family, rather than the nuclear family, prevails. (N069)

## JOKING-AVOIDANCE RELATIONSHIPS
###      X Descent (Bilateral)
There appears to be a correlation between the presence of the original bilateral family and the absence or weakness of certain forms of ceremonial behavior, especially joking and avoidance relationships. (L039)

## JOKING RELATIONSHIP      X Affinal Ties
Joking relationships between affinals tend to be between those who are members of the same generation. (R021)

### Analogy
When joking relationships between particular relations are prescribed, those in analogous relationships are treated in the same way. (L111)

### Avoidance Relationship
The institutionalization of patterns of joking behavior tends to be accompanied by the institutionalization of avoidance with other kinsmen. (R039)

When a joking relationship is established with siblings of the wife, an avoidance relationship tends also to obtain between the husband and the wife's parents. (R052)

### Conflict in Kin-Group
The establishment of a joking relationship tends to suppress or control potential conflict between relatives who have a close kinship bond. (S080)

### Generation
Joking relationships tend to occur between individuals of the same or alternating generation. (S106)

The degree of license permitted in the joking relationship tends to be greater as the generation span between the kinsmen increases. (T026)

### Incest
When marriage occurs between kinsmen who are not permitted to marry, the discrepancy is adjusted by establishing a joking relationship between the husband and wife. (M085)

### Incest Taboo
If a joking relationship obtains between two kinsmen who are prohibited from marriage, the censure which normally attends the breaking of this rule is lessened. (M085)

### Intermarriage (Clan)
The joking relationship is basically associated with clans that generally intermarry. (B111)

### Kin Terminology (Classificatory)
Joking relationships tend to be extended to all classificatory kinsmen of the relatives in question. (R052)

### Paternal Role (Discipline)
The joking relationship between alternate generations will occur only in the absence of a joint family organization and in systems where the father is the disciplinarian of the family. (D034)

### Preferential Marriage (Secondary Marriage)
When preferential mating with siblings-in-law of the opposite sex is prescribed, the patterned behavior toward such relatives tends to be characterized by license. (M019)

### Rank of Kinsmen
The joking relationship tends to obtain between kinsmen who are not in a superordinate-subordinate relationship. (D034)

A joking relationship is more likely between kinsmen who are of equal status. (L070)

### Residence
Joking relationships will tend to be abandoned if the relatives in question are coresidents. (W115)

### Sexual Relationship (Potential)
The joking relationship tends to obtain between relatives standing in a potential sexual relationship to each other. (M019)

### Witchcraft
Accusations of witchcraft as manifestations of aggression are unlikely to occur between kinsmen who stand in a joking relationship. (T059)

## JOKING RELATIONSHIP, ASYMMETRICAL
### X  Generation
When a joking relationship exists between kinsmen of adjacent generations, the relationship will tend to be asymmetrical in character. (R039)

## JUVENILE DELINQUENCY    X  Achievement
There is a correlation between low family occupational-educational achievement and delinquency in the son. (W152)

### Age at Marriage
There is no relationship between age at marriage of parents and the development of delinquency. (G123)

### Age of Child
There is no relationship between delinquency and the age of the child at the time his family is disrupted. (N057)

### Age of Parents
There is no relationship between age of parents and the development of delinquency. (G123)

### Alcoholism of Father
Alcoholism of father contributes indirectly to delinquency of child by contributing to the development of the traits of hostility and unconventionality. (W152)

Boys who have the feeling of not being appreciated, the feeling of isolation, and introversiveness are more likely to develop into delinquents if they have alcoholic fathers.

Fathers of delinquents are more likely to drink than are fathers of nondelinquents. (W152)

### Alcoholism of Mother
Alcoholism of the mother is associated more with delinquents than with nondelinquents and may contribute indirectly to the delinquency of the son through development of the trait of unconventionality. (W152)

### Anxiety of Parents
Severe delinquency is frequently associated with acute parental anxieties of inadequacy. (B291)

### Behavior Problems of Parents
Among children of families where one parent was a juvenile problem and where the child himself now is having behavior adjustment problems in school, there is a decisive correlation between the behavior of the preadolescent child and that of his parent at the time he or she was a youthful offender. (K151)

Parental behavior characterized by dishonesty, untruthfulness, scapegoating, and lack of consideration for neighbors is related to delinquent behavior. (N052)

### Broken Home
Regardless of class, delinquency rates are higher for broken than for unbroken homes. (G156)

Regardless of class, delinquency rates are highest for children of homes broken by separation or divorce than by death of a parent (U.S.). (G156)

Children from homes that are intact, but unhappily so, are twice as likely to become delinquents as are those from intact, happy homes (U.S.). (G156)

Children from widowed or widowered homes are 50 per cent more likely to be delinquents than are those from intact homes (U.S.). (G156)

Delinquents are slightly more likely to come from divorced than from intact homes (U.S.). (G156)

Juvenile delinquents who are Negro are more likely to come from broken homes than are juvenile delinquents who are white. (M009)

The proportion of broken homes among juvenile delinquents who are Negro is greater than the proportion of broken homes among juvenile delinquents who are white. (M009)

The longer the home remains broken, the more likely is the child to become delinquent. (M196)

Among delinquents separated from their parents, the earlier the age of separation, the larger the number of court offenses (Court Offense Score). (S182)

Delinquent girls are more likely to come from broken homes than are nondelinquent girls; broken homes do not distinguish delinquent from nondelinquent boys. (M205)

There is no correlation between the age of the child when the home is broken and the incidence of delinquent behavior by the child. (N063)

There is a correlation between broken homes and delinquency in the higher classes, but not in the lower classes. (S219)

### Broken Home, Age At
Among children from broken homes, delinquents are more likely to have experienced the break at an earlier age than are nondelinquent children. (M196)

Prisoners are more likely to have been separated from their parents at an earlier age than are persons from the general population. (M196)

### Broken Home (Stepchildren)
There is no correlation between the number of stepchildren in the broken home and delinquency in the child. (N063)

### Child-Rearing Attitudes (Authoritarianism)
Mothers of delinquent children are more likely than are mothers of normal children to have punitive, controlling, and authoritarian attitudes toward the child. (M208)

### Child-Rearing Attitudes (Democratic)
Mothers of delinquents do not differ from mothers of normal children in the extent to which they hold democratic child-rearing attitudes. (M208)

### Child-Rearing Practices (Advice)
There is a negative relationship between the amount of parental advice and information given a youngster and delinquent behavior in adolescents, particularly in girls. (N057)

### Child-Rearing Practices (Consistency)
The juvenile delinquent is more likely to have had a parent whose gratification of the child's wishes was inconsistent. (M194)

Consistent discipline, of whatever type, decreases the chances of delinquency of the child, while erratic discipline increases the chances. (M194)

### Child-Rearing Practices (Control)
To the extent that social control of the child is reduced in the broken home or the unbroken home (where there

is poor marital adjustment), the child is likely to become delinquent. (N057)

Because of the freedom from family control which the ownership of a car allows the adolescent, the youngster who owns a car is more likely to become delinquent than the one who does not. (N057)

Mothers of delinquent children tend to show excessive control but little awareness of their children's feelings. (S183)

### Child-Rearing Practices (Democratic)
Children from democratically managed families are less likely to become delinquents than are children from undemocratically managed families. (B287)

### Child-Rearing Practices (Discipline)
Poor maternal disciplinary practices (extreme permissiveness, overstrictness, or inconsistency) are correlated with delinquency.

### Child-Rearing Practices (Generosity)
Delinquents are more likely than nondelinquents to have parents who are not generous. (N057)

There is no relationship between high generosity of parents and low delinquent behavior in their children. (N057)

Adolescents (particularly boys) are more likely to become delinquent if they have large sums of money available than if they have a moderate amount. (N057)

### Child-Rearing Practices (Giving Reasons)
Parents who explain punishment are less likely than those who do not to produce delinquent children. (N057)

Children who are allowed to explain their behavior are less likely to become delinquent than are those who are not permitted to do so. (N057)

### Child-Rearing Practices (Neglect)
Parental negligence and exposure to delinquent behavior are predisposing factors toward socialized delinquency (which is defined as having bad companions, engaging in cooperative stealing, habitual truancy from school and home, etc.). (J024)

If the parents both neglect the child and provide poor role models for the child, the child is more likely to become a delinquent than if only one of these factors is present. (M194)

If both parents have a neglecting attitude toward the child, it is more likely that the child will commit property crimes than any other kinds of crimes. (M194)

Delinquents are more likely than normal persons to suffer from nonsupport and negligence of parents. (O033)

### Child-Rearing Practices (Permissiveness)
Permissiveness by the father contributes to the development of the delinquency-linked trait of social assertiveness and, thus, indirectly to delinquency.

Parents who are extremely uncritical or permissive or extremely critical or nonpermissive are more likely to produce delinquent children than are those who are selectively critical. (N057)

### Child-Rearing Practices (Punishment)
Parents of boys who are frequent juvenile offenders are more likely to show a punitive attitude toward the boys regarding their offenses than are parents of boys who are first offenders.

A negative curvilinear relationship exists between the severity of punishment and delinquency in the son. (B243)

More children who have been disciplined punitively or with laxity go to a penal institution than do those children who have been controlled by love-oriented methods. (M194)

There is no relationship between parental use of physical punishment and delinquent behavior by the child. (N063)

Children who feel that their fathers punish them unfairly are more likely to show delinquent behavior than are those who do not. (N063)

There is a correlation between strict discipline by the mother and delinquency in the daughter. (N063)

Delinquency in the child correlates with nagging by the parents. (N063)

There is a correlation between delinquency in the child and parental use of withdrawal of love as a method of discipline. (N063)

There is a curvilinear relationship between delinquency in the child and parental scolding. (N063)

### Child-Rearing Practices (Punishment/Giving Reasons)
Parents of delinquents are more likely than parents of nondelinquents to use physical punishment rather than reasoning in disciplining the child. (B243)

### Child-Rearing Practices (Recreation)
Parents of juvenile delinquents provide fewer recreational outlets, both in and outside of the home, than do parents of nondelinquents. (S210)

### Child-Rearing Practices (Responsibility)
The amount of responsibility delegated to an adolescent (particularly boys) is inversely related to the delinquent behavior he manifests. (N057)

### Child-Rearing Practices (Restrictiveness)
There is a curvilinear relationship between the degree to which the child is scolded and restricted and the child's delinquent behavior. (N063)

There is a curvilinear relationship between the amount of freedom allowed by parents and delinquency in the child. (N063)

### Child-Rearing Practices (Role Models)
If the parents both neglect the child and provide poor role models for the child, the child is more likely to become a delinquent than if only one of these factors is present. (M194)

### Child-Rearing Practices (Strictness)
There is a positive relationship between strict discipline by the mother and delinquent behavior in girls. (N057)

Strict discipline by parents and delinquent behavior in boys are not related. (N057)

Strict discipline by the father and delinquent behavior in girls are related. (N057)

### Child-Rearing Practices (Supervision)
If the mother tends to shift her responsibility of supervising the child to an irresponsible child or adult, the child is more likely to become delinquent. (M058)

Unsuitable supervision by the mother is more closely associated with juvenile delinquency. (M058)

Whether the mother works or not, the quality of the supervision her child receives determines his delinquency pattern. (M058)

Juvenile delinquents are less supervised than are nondelinquents. (S210)

### Child-Rearing Values (Agreement)
The higher the parental consensus concerning child rearing, the less likely is the child to become a delinquent.

### Class
Boys who are frequent juvenile offenders are more likely to be from low socioeconomic classes than are boys who have one offense. (G144)

The lower the socioeconomic status of the parents, the more likely it is that the child will become delinquent. (G144)

If the child belongs to a noncohesive home in a higher-class neighborhood, he is less likely to become delinquent than is a child who belongs to a noncohesive home in a poor neighborhood. (M194)

Mobile lower-class families are more likely than mobile upper-class families to produce delinquent children. (N057)

There is no correlation between the social class of the family and delinquent behavior in the child. (N063)

Among residentially mobile families, there is no correlation between class and delinquency in the child. (N063)

### Cohesion of Family
Juvenile delinquency will be less likely when the solidarity of the family is high. (B055)

Among families which are cohesive, the child is more likely to commit traffic crimes than other kinds of crimes. (M194)

Among residentially mobile families, there is no correlation between degree of family integration, as measured by attitudes of the child toward the parents, and delinquency in the child. (N063)

In families which have maintained love and affection between their members, children are less likely to become delinquents than in families in which these affectional bonds have broken down. (S210)

### Conflict in Family
Boys who are frequent juvenile offenders are more likely to report family tensions than are those who have one offense.

### Conformity
If the child revolts against the values of the father he is more likely to become a delinquent. (M194)

### Criminality of Father
Fathers of delinquents are more likely than are those of nondelinquents to have trouble with the law. (W152)

### Criminality of Parents
If either of the parents has a criminal record, it is more likely that the child will become a delinquent. (M194)

### Dating (Parents' Knowledge of)
There is a negative relationship between parents' knowledge of dating behavior and delinquent adjustment. (N057)

### Delinquency of Family Members
There is a positive correlation between becoming a juvenile delinquent and having a family in which there are other delinquent members. (S210)

### Delinquency of Mother
Delinquency of the mother contributes indirectly to the son's delinquency by contributing to traits of a defensive attitude, a feeling of inadequacy, and a lack of self-criticism.

Delinquency of the mother contributes directly to the delinquency of the child.

A child having a tendency to fantasy or receptive trends is more likely to become delinquent if his mother is delinquent.

### Delinquency of Parents
Parents with histories of severe delinquency tend to have children who are also delinquent. (B291)

### Dependency
Juvenile delinquents are far more independent from their parents than are nondelinquents.

The greater the child's acceptance of the freedom allowed him by his parents, the less likely he is to show delinquent behavior. (N063)

### Disorganization of Family
There is a correlation between the seriousness of the boy's delinquency and the degree of instability and disturbance of his family life. (N059)

There is a correlation between marital disruption and the severity of delinquency in the son. (W152)

### Divorce
Among delinquents, white children are more likely to have experienced disorganization of the home by divorce than are Negro children. (M196)

Among delinquents, Negro boys are no more likely than Negro girls to have come from divorced homes; white girls are more likely to have come from divorced homes than are white boys. (M196)

The higher a country's divorce rate, the higher its delinquency rate. (Z008)

### Duration of Marriage
The younger the child when his parents' marriage ends, the more likely he will become a delinquent.

### Economic Dependence of Family
The families of juvenile delinquents are more dependent upon relief agencies or relatives for financial aid than are families of nondelinquents. (G123)

### Education of Mother

Children of less-educated employed mothers are more likely to become delinquent than are children of more-educated employed mothers. (N057)

### Education of Parents

Neither the education of the father nor the education of the mother had any significant influence on the child's delinquent behavior (Cambridge-Somerville Study). (M194)

### Emotional Problems of Father

Emotional disturbance of the father contributes indirectly to delinquency of the child by contributing to the development of the child's tendency toward fantasy.

A child having a feeling of inadequacy is more likely to become delinquent if his father is emotionally disturbed.

### Emotional Problems of Mother

Delinquents more than nondelinquents tend to have emotionally disturbed mothers.

The mother's employment, per se, is not a cause of juvenile delinquency. (G127)

### Emotional Problems of Parents

If the parents have shown emotional or behavioral disturbances, the child is likely to display delinquent behavior.

### Employment of Mother

The mother's employment, per se, is not a cause of juvenile delinquency.

If the mother is employed outside the home, the child is more likely to become a juvenile delinquent. (H183)

There is more delinquent behavior in families where mothers are employed. (N052)

Working mothers are more likely than nonworking mothers to produce delinquent children, particularly in rural areas. (N057)

There is a correlation between employment of the mother and delinquency of the child in the middle class, but only to an insignificant extent in the lower and upper classes. (N063)

Juvenile delinquents are more likely to come from homes where the mother is the sole supporter than are nondelinquents. (S210)

In intact homes, delinquency is more likely if the mother is employed, but is not related to the mother's employment in broken homes. (S265)

### Employment of Mother/Broken Home

Delinquency in girls correlates more with the variable of broken homes than with employment or nonemployment of the mother. (S265)

In intact homes, delinquency is more likely if the mother is employed, but is not related to the mother's employment in broken homes. (S265)

### Employment of Mother (Regularity)

Delinquency in boys does not correlate with employment/nonemployment of the mother, but with irregular, as opposed to regular, employment on the part of mothers who work. (S265)

Children of mothers who are sporadically employed are more likely to be delinquents than are children of mothers who are regularly employed or do not work at all. (Y047)

### Father Absence, Age at

The older a boy at the time of the father's first (lengthy) absence from home, the more likely it is that he will become a gang member. (M181)

### Father-Child Relations

Recidivists are less likely to have fathers who are comrades, and recidivists are less likely to pattern themselves after their own fathers.

### Father-Daughter Relations (Advice)

Girls who always consult their fathers on sexual problems are more likely than those who turn to both parents to be delinquents. (N057)

### Father-Son Relations (Affection)

Lack of paternal affection contributes indirectly to juvenile delinquency.

If an affectionate relationship is lacking between the father and the son, it is more likely that the child will become delinquent. (M194)

### Father-Son Relations (Conflict)

Juvenile delinquency in the boy is associated with conflicts with the father figure and an unconscious wish to displace him with the mother, resulting from unresolved disturbances with the mother during childhood. (B233)

### Father-Son Relations (Hostility)

Juvenile delinquent boys are more likely to be critical and resentful of their fathers than are nondelinquents. (S229)

### Friendship

Families whose friends have traits similar to their own (income, faith, origin, and kin) are more likely to have lower rates for delinquency arrests than are families whose friends have less in common. (Z008)

### Friendship Choice

Both families in which there are juvenile arrest records and families with no arrest records tend to avoid friendships with families which have juvenile arrest records. (Z008)

In cities where the delinquency rate is higher, families are more likely to avoid friendship with families in which there is a child who has been arrested for delinquency than in cities where the delinquency rate is lower. (Z008)

### Friendship (Closeness)

The more intimate the family friends, the less likely are the families to have children with arrest records. (Z008)

### Geographic Mobility

Delinquent girls are more likely to have fathers who were born in another state than are normal girls. (N057)

There is no relationship between birthplace of the father and delinquency in boys. (N057)

Adolescents in mobile families are more likely to be involved in delinquent behavior than are those in nonmobile families. (N057)

There is a correlation between residential mobility and delinquency in the child. (N063)

### Geographic Mobility/Cohesion of Family

The positive relationship between mobility and delinquency increases as family integration decreases (i.e., geographical mobility does not increase juvenile delinquency as much if the family integration is lower). (N057)

### Household Routine

Families of juvenile delinquents have a less-planned household routine than do families of nondelinquents. (G123)

### Housing

Delinquents are more likely to come from families that reside in crowded living conditions than are nondelinquents. (S210)

### Husband-Wife Relations

There is no relationship between the degree of interest taken in the activities of the spouse and delinquent behavior in the children. (N057)

There is no relationship between the frequency of request by the mother for assistance by the father with housework and delinquent behavior in the children. (N057)

### Husband-Wife Relations (Conflict)

There is a correlation between frequency of parental quarrels and delinquent behavior in the girl. (N063)

There is a curvilinear relationship between frequency of parental quarrels and delinquent behavior in the son. (N063)

### Husband-Wife Relations (Finances)

The home in which there is financial generosity toward the mother is less likely to produce delinquent children than is the home in which the mother has insufficient funds.

### Husband-Wife Relations (Shared Activities)

The home in which there is shared mother-father recreation is less likely to produce delinquent children than is the home in which activities are separate. (N057)

### Identification with Cross-Sex Parent

Juvenile delinquents are more likely to like parents of the opposite sex than are nondelinquents, but juvenile delinquent boys are more likely to prefer their mothers than juvenile delinquent girls are to prefer their fathers. (G117)

### Identification with Father

A lower proportion of delinquents than of nondelinquents regard their fathers as acceptable patterns for emulation. (S210)

Juvenile delinquents are less likely to identify with their fathers than are nondelinquents. (S210)

### Identification with Parents

There is an inverse correlation between extent of the child's identification with the parents and delinquency in the child. (N063)

### Illness

If the family of orientation of the parents was affected by physical diseases such as cancer, tuberculosis, drunkenness, venereal diseases, etc., then the child is more likely to become a juvenile delinquent. (G144)

### Illness of Family Members

Families of juvenile delinquents are more likely to include members who have physical ailments than are families of nondelinquents. (G123)

### Illness of Father

Serious physical ailment of the father contributes indirectly to delinquency of the child by contributing to the development of hostility and lack of conscientiousness.

### Illness of Mother

Serious physical ailment of the mother may contribute indirectly to delinquency in the son by contributing to a tendency toward fantasy.

Boys who are ambivalent to authority or unconventional in attitudes are more likely to become delinquent if their mothers are seriously ill.

### Illness of Parents

The parents of delinquent children suffer from some form of illness or deformity more frequently than do parents of other children. (B238)

### Immigrant/Nonimmigrant

If the father is an immigrant to the United States, the child is less likely to become a delinquent than if the father is a citizen of the United States. The reverse is also asserted. (M194)

### Incest (Father-Daughter)

Girls who practice incest are likely to be delinquent in other ways. (K091)

### Interaction in Family (Intimacy)

Severe delinquency is frequently associated with a lack of durable intimate relationships with relatives. (B291)

### Interaction with Family

Isolation from the family physically or mentally is likely to increase the association of the child with delinquency. (B033)

### Marital Adjustment

If the husband and the wife have an incompatible marriage relationship, the child is more likely to become delinquent.

Among the predictors of nondelinquent behavior, the happiness of the marriage has greater predictive power than whether the parents have remarried or whether the child is living with both parents or only one. (N057)

A home in which the insecurities of the parents cause them to quarrel severely is more likely to produce delinquent children than the home in which normal disagreements are worked out among the members. (S226)

### Maternal-Role Behavior

There is no relationship between excessively clean housekeeping (or the reverse) by the mother and delinquent behavior of the children. (N057)

### Mental Illness in Parents' Families

If the family of orientation of the parents has been affected by such mental diseases as psychoses, psychoneuroses, epilepsies, sex inversions, etc., the child is more likely to become a juvenile delinquent. (G144)

If the family of orientation of the mother has been affected by more mental diseases than has the family of orientation of the father, then the child is more likely to become a juvenile delinquent. (G144)

### Mental Illness of Parents

Although the mothers of delinquents do not differ (with respect to psychiatric diagnosis) from the mothers of psychotics and of normals, the fathers of delinquents are more likely to be sociopathic than are those of the other two groups. (O033)

### Mother Absence

There is no correlation between frequency and length of separation from the mother and delinquency in the son. (N059)

Prolonged separation of a child from his mother in the first five years of life is a cause of delinquency in later life. (N059)

Juvenile delinquents who have spent part of their childhood separated from their families are more likely to commit further offenses than are those who were reared at home. (N059)

There is a correlation between the frequency of separation from the mother in early childhood and the seriousness of delinquency in the boy. (N059)

The child who has been separated from his mother (during the first three years of life) is more likely to become delinquent than are children of the same family who were not separated. (S226)

Mothers of delinquents tend to spend less time in the home than do mothers of nondelinquents. (W152)

Separation from the mother during the first five years of the infant's life is a major cause of delinquency. (Y047)

### Mother-Child Relations (Affection)

If the child has a nonaffectionate relationship with his mother and is consulted frequently by a social worker, he will less often become delinquent than will a child with an affectionate mother. (M194)

### Mother-Child Relations (Closeness)

Nondelinquent girls are more likely to talk over problems with their mothers than are delinquent girls; this distinction does not hold for delinquent and nondelinquent boys. (M205)

### Mother-Child Relations (Consistency)

Delinquents are more likely than others to have had inconsistent interaction with their mothers. (B238)

### Mother-Child Relations (Rejection)

Mothers of delinquents do not differ from mothers of normal children with respect to hostility toward or rejection of the child. (M208)

### Mother-Son Relations (Neglect)

The more neglecting is the behavior of the mother toward the son, the more likely it is that the child will exhibit more severe delinquent behavior. (M194)

### Occupation of Father

More delinquents come from families where the father is unskilled or has slight skills than from families where the father is semiskilled or skilled. (S210)

### Occupational Rank of Mother

Mothers of delinquents tend to hold lower-level jobs than do mothers of nondelinquents. (W152)

### Ordinal Position

Only children and youngest children (supposedly the spoiled or favored ones) are less likely to be delinquent than are children of other birth ranks. (B238)

Only children are less likely than children who have siblings to be recidivists. (B238)

There is no correlation between birth order and delinquency. (B238)

If the child holds a middle ordinal position among the children of the family, it is more likely that he will become delinquent than if he holds any other ordinal position. (M194)

Oldest and only children show less delinquent behavior than do intermediate and youngest children. (N052)

Since intermediate sons (as opposed to eldest) prefer achievement through leadership of a group (peers) rather than through individual activity, they are more prone to delinquency than are their older brothers. (S226)

### Parent-Child Relations

Delinquent boys of preadolescent age (modal age 11) are more likely to have poor family relations than are older boys (modal age 15). (F093)

Of two siblings who grew up within the same environment, the one who had a good relationship with one of the parents is less likely to become delinquent than is the other. (B238)

Juvenile delinquency is more closely linked with disturbed parent-child relationships than with more remote environmental factors. (F093)

The data provide some support for the belief that, during adolescence, juvenile-delinquent behavior is more closely related to the attitude of the child toward the parent than that of the parent toward the child. (N052)

### Parent-Child Relations (Acceptance)

Juvenile delinquents have stronger feelings of not being recognized and appreciated and are more resentful toward their parents than are nondelinquents.

Where the parents have an accepting attitude toward the child, there is no correlation between parental scolding and withdrawal of love and delinquent behavior in the child. (N063)

### Parent-Child Relations (Advice)

There is a negative relationship between delinquent behavior and the frequency with which adolescents consult their parents as to future occupations (this is particularly significant for girls). (N057)

There is a negative correlation between the amount of parental advice received and delinquency in the girl and between advice from the father and delinquency in the boy. There is an inverse curvilinear relationship between the amount of advice received from the mother and the son's delinquency. (N063)

There is a curvilinear relationship between the frequency with which girls consult their fathers about sex and their degree of rapport about dating and delinquent behavior in the girl. (N063)

The amount of parental help and rapport with the child concerning scholastic problems of the future occupation reduces delinquent behavior in the girl, but not in the boy. (N063)

### Parent-Child Relations (Affect)

Severe delinquency tends to occur where the parent is withdrawn emotionally in his relationships with his children. (B291)

Juvenile delinquents are more likely to be emotionally deprived than are nondelinquents since they experience greater indifference, more actual hostility, less affection, and greater feelings of not being cared for by their parents. (S210)

### Parent-Child Relations (Affection)

A lower proportion of mothers than of fathers of delinquents are not closely attached to their sons. (B243)

The closer and more affectionate the relationship between parents and child, the less likely it is that the child will become delinquent. (B243)

Lack of adequate affectional dependency relationships with parents is a cause of delinquency in the child. (B243)

The more the parents provide affection and a feeling of belongingness and establish rapport with the child, the less is the likelihood that the child will engage in delinquent behavior. (M178)

### Parent-Child Relations (Affection/Neglect)

If both parents are neglecting in their behavior toward the child, the child is more likely to become delinquent than if only one parent is neglecting and the other loving. (M194)

If the mother is neglecting toward the child and the father is loving, the child is more likely to become delinquent than if the mother is loving and the father is neglecting. (M194)

### Parent-Child Relations (Approval)

Delinquent adolescents are more likely to have difficulty in pleasing their fathers than their mothers. (N057)

### Parent-Child Relations (Communication)

Recurring sequences of conflicting messages ("split double-binds") proceeding from mother and father, (respectively) are a cause of delinquent behavior in the child. (F100)

### Parent-Child Relations (Conflict)

Delinquents tend to have less conflict with their parents than do nondelinquents since their parents, although concerned, are permissive. (W152)

Conflict with parents and alienation of them are causes of boys' later delinquency. (W152)

### Parent-Child Relations (Consensus)

The greater the value disagreement between parents and child, the more likely is delinquent behavior on the part of the child. (N063)

### Parent-Child Relations (Criticism)

A significant relationship is found between attitudes toward parental appearance and delinquent behavior, with more delinquent behavior among adolescents who are most critical of parental appearance. (N052)

### Parent-Child Relations (Evaluation)

Nondelinquents are more satisfied than are delinquents with their relations with their parents; this distinction is greater for girls than for boys. (M205)

Adolescents with favorable attitudes toward the personalities of their parents commit less delinquent behavior. (N052)

There is a positive relationship between more delinquent behavior among adolescents and critical attitude of parental appearance, particularly of the father. (N057)

The implications of lower status associated with poor appearance of the father are more significant for boys than for girls. (N057)

The more critical the child toward the appearance of his parents, the more likely he is to show delinquent behavior, particularly in the case of the boy's evaluation of the father's appearance. (N063)

The more critical the child toward the disposition of his parents, the more likely he is to show delinquent behavior. (N063)

### Parent-Child Relations (Favoritism)

Juvenile delinquency is more likely among youngsters who feel their parents discriminated against them in favor of another sibling.

### Parent-Child Relations (Financial)

There is a curvilinear relationship between financial partiality and generosity on the part of the parents and delinquent behavior in the child. (N063)

### Parent-Child Relations (Gratification)

There is a negative correlation between extent of need satisfaction through parental behavior and delinquent behavior in the child. (N063)

### Parent-Child Relations (Help)

Parents of boys who are frequent juvenile offenders are more likely to be indifferent to efforts to help the boys than are parents of boys who have one offense.

### Parent-Child Relations (Indifference)

Parents who are casual or indifferent to their child are more likely than those who are concerned with the child's well-being to produce a delinquent. (S226)

### Parent-Child Relations (Interaction)

Delinquents tend to spend less time at home than do nondelinquents. (W152)

### Parent-Child Relations (Preference)

If the child fails to win the parents' preferential affection by performing a model role, he will revert to delinquent behavior. (B033)

### Parent-Child Relations (Rebellion)

Juvenile delinquents are less submissive and more defiant toward parental authority than are nondelinquents.

### Parent-Child Relations (Recreation)

Parents of boys who are frequent juvenile offenders are less likely to take part in recreation with the boys than are parents of boys who have one offense.

### Parent-Child Relations (Rejection)

If the child feels rejected he may engage in disapproved behavior in an attempt to achieve an adequate place in the family through drawing attention to himself. (B033)

The child who was unwanted by his parents is more likely than the wanted child to become delinquent. (B238)

Parental rejection is a factor predisposing toward unsocialized aggressive behavior (which is defined as showing assaultive tendencies, starting fights, cruelty, defiance of authority, inadequate guilt feelings, etc.). (J024)

Maternal rejection is more important than paternal rejection in the development of unsocialized aggressive behavior. (J024)

The data support the hypothesis that rejection of parents by children is related to delinquent behavior; when both parent and child reject one another, delinquent behavior is still more likely. (N052)

There is a correlation between a child's rejection of the parents and delinquency in the child. (N063)

There is a correlation between parental rejection and delinquency in the child. (N063)

Fathers of delinquents are more likely than mothers to be rejecting. (O033)

Juvenile delinquent boys are more likely to feel rejected by both parents than are nondelinquents. (S229)

### Parent-Child Relations (Sadism)
Severe delinquency is frequently associated with parental sadism. (B291)

### Parent Loss
The earlier the age at separation from the parents, the higher the frequency of running away (from reform school). (S182)

There is no significant correlation for girls between the ages at which they are separated from their parents and number of court offenses. (S182)

The child who is made to fear the loss of a parent (through death, abandonment) is more likely than the child who feels secure about his parents to become delinquent. (S226)

### Parental-Role Behavior
There is a positive relationship between unethical parental behavior and delinquent adolescent behavior. (N057)

A son's delinquency correlates with inadequate supervision by the mother and with overstrict discipline by the father, independently of employment/nonemployment of the mother. (S265)

### Paternal/Maternal-Role Behavior
The father's participation in recreational activities is more significant than the mother's participation in establishing the basis for nondelinquent behavior in adolescents. (N057)

The father's behavior is more likely to be related to delinquent behavior of the child than is the mother's. (N063)

### Paternal Role (Discipline)
Discipline by the father was more common among the recidivist delinquent group than among a matched group of college freshmen.

### Paternal Role (Housekeeping)
A home in which the father assists with the housekeeping is less likely to produce delinquent children than the home in which the father refuses to do so. (N057)

### Paternal-Role Model
Nondelinquents accept the father as a role model more than delinquents do.

### Personality Development of Parents
Parents with unresolved pregenital conflicts (lack of proper introjection of parental attitudes toward authority during Oedipal phase) unconsciously advocate delinquency and therefore are more likely than others to produce delinquent children. (R110)

### Personality of Parents
Both frequency of loss of temper and of becoming emotionally upset are positively related to delinquent behavior. Loss of temper by the parent is primarily related to delinquent behavior of the child of the opposite sex. (N052)

Cheerfulness in parents is negatively associated with delinquency in adolescents, particularly for the mother. (N057)

Moodiness in parents (especially the father) is positively related to delinquency in adolescents. (N057)

Loss of temper by parents is positively related to delinquency in adolescents (especially the child of opposite sex). (N057)

Parents' tendency to become emotionally upset is positively related to delinquency in adolescents. (N057)

Nervousness in mothers is more significantly related to delinquency in adolescents than is nervousness in fathers. (N057)

The more cheerful the parents, the less likely it is that the child will show delinquent behavior. (N063)

The more nervous, irritable, and difficult to please is the parent, the more likely it is that the child will manifest delinquent behavior. (N063)

### Personality Problems of Mother
There is a correlation between the delinquent behavior of the son and the unconscious desires of his parents, particularly the destructive impulses of the mother. (W152)

### Personality Problems of Parents
A son's delinquency and a mother's sporadic employment both correlate with and are caused by the emotionally disturbed and antisocial characteristics of the parents. (S265)

### Power Structure of Family
Dominance of the mother in family affairs appears to be associated with delinquency in boys.

Homes in which the mother is dominant and where the father is tyrannical (alcoholic, brutal) are more likely than others to produce a delinquent child. (B238)

Bossing of the father by the mother shows no relationship to delinquency, but frequent bossing by the father is associated with delinquent behavior in girls. (N057)

There is no correlation between dominance by the mother and delinquency in the child, but dominance by the father is related to delinquency in girls. (N063)

### Premarital Sex Relations
Delinquent boys are more active with respect to pre- and postmarital sexual activity than are nondelinquents. (W152)

### Psychotherapy
Treatment of juvenile delinquents is more likely to be successful if the parents are included in the treatment process. (R110)

### Recreation
The more favorable the adolescent's attitude toward family recreation, the less likely it is that he will show delinquent behavior. (N063)

The greater the frequency of family recreation, the less likely it is that the child will show delinquent behavior. (N063)

### Religion of Father
The religious affiliation of the father and the degree of his religiosity have no significant relation to the delinquent behavior of the child (Cambridge-Somerville Study). (M194)

### Religiosity
Families in which parents and children attend church regularly are less likely to produce delinquents than are families in which members do not. (N057)

### Religiosity of Mother
If the mother is a devoted Catholic, the child is less likely to become a delinquent than if the mother attends church irregularly or not at all. (M194)

### Religious Behavior of Parents
Knowledge of religion imputed to the parent, religious rapport, and frequency of discussion of religious matters with parents are all associated with decreasing delinquent behavior. (N052)

### Scapegoating
When a parent displaces emotion meant for his spouse onto one of the children, he is likely to jeopardize the child's feeling of membership within the family which may lead to delinquency. (S226)

### Self-Conception
Families of juvenile delinquents have less self-respect than do families of nondelinquents. (S210)

### Self-Conception of Family
Low self-respect of the family contributes indirectly to delinquency by contributing to the traits of impracticality and lack of self-criticism.

### Sex Status
Daughters of employed mothers are more likely to show delinquent behavior than are sons. (N063)

### Sexual Behavior of Parents
Children who witness parental sexuality (which stimulates fear and aggression in the child) are more likely to become delinquent than are others. (B238)

### Sibling Relations
Boys who are stubborn or impractical are more likely to become delinquent if they are not accepted by siblings.

### Sibling Relations (Conflict)
Delinquents tend to have less conflict with their siblings than do nondelinquents and to associate with them less. (W152)

### Sibling Structure
Juvenile delinquents with nondelinquent brothers are likely to be less serious offenders than are those whose brothers are delinquent. (N059)

### Size of Family
Children from large families are more likely to be delinquent than are children from small families.

Juvenile delinquency is directly correlated with family size (in distressed areas). (I007)

The delinquent gang member usually comes from a family of several children. (J024)

Boys from smaller families are less likely to become delinquent than are boys from larger families. (N057)

There is no relationship between delinquency in girls and the size of the family. (N057)

### Social Adjustment of Parents
There is a correlation between antisocial and unethical behavior by parents and delinquent behavior in the child. (N063)

### Social Control
In a society where there are strict family controls on its members' autonomy, delinquent (or potentially delinquent) subcommunities tend to emerge. (P056)

### Social Mobility Aspirations
Families of juvenile delinquents are less ambitious to improve either their own status or their children's status than are families of nondelinquents. (S210)

### Surrogate Parent
Substitute parents do not contribute to any of the criminogenic traits.

A child's delinquency is dependent on the supervision he gets, regardless of whether the mother supervises him. (M058)

Juvenile delinquents are more likely to have parental surrogates than nondelinquents. (S210)

### Unemployment
Juvenile delinquents are more likely to come from families where there is greater unemployment among the parents than are nondelinquents. (S210)

### Urban/Rural
Rural families are less likely than urban families to produce delinquent children. (N057)

Employed mothers in rural areas are more likely to have delinquent children than are those in urban areas. (N063)

There is a correlation between urban residence and delinquency in the boy, but not in the girl. (N063)

### Value Conflict (Parents/Peers)
Juvenile delinquency is associated with a conflict between the expectations of the family and those of the gang. (B033)

### Values (Family/Society)
Organized types of delinquent groups usually arise when there is a lack of harmony and compatibility between the main values of the family and its authority structure on the one hand and the actual community and its values and authority structure on the other. (E086)

### Values (Filial Piety)
Juvenile delinquency is rare where filial piety is a central value. (B033)

## JUVENILE DELINQUENCY, AGE AT
### X    Child-Rearing Practices (Neglect)
The more neglecting the attitude of parents toward the child, the more likely it is that he will become delinquent at an early age rather than at a late age. (M194)

### X    Mother-Child Relations (Affection)
Among children who become delinquent at a late age (after the seventeenth year), more are likely to have an affectionate rather than an aggressive relationship with their mothers. (M194)

## JUVENILE DELINQUENCY (AGGRESSIVE)
### X    Dependency
Aggressive delinquency is caused primarily by the disruption of the child's dependency relationship with his parents. (B246)

## JUVENILE DELINQUENCY BY CLASS
### X    Child-Rearing Practices (Neglect)
There is a correlation between parental neglect and delinquency, but less so in the lower classes than in the higher. (S219)

## JUVENILE DELINQUENCY BY SEX STATUS
### X    Broken Home
Female juvenile delinquents are more likely than are male delinquents to come from broken homes. (M009)

### Child-Rearing Practices (Consistency)
There is a correlation between inconsistency of discipline by mothers and delinquent behavior in girls, but not in boys. (N063)

### Employment of Mother
Since direct control is more effective over girls than over boys, there is a closer relationship between employment of the mother and delinquent behavior in girls than in boys. (N057)

### Geographic Mobility
The greater the geographic mobility of the father, the more likely is delinquency in the girl, but not in the boy. (N063)

### Maternal Role, Attitude Toward
Nondelinquent girls are more likely than delinquent girls to describe their mothers as liking child rearing; this distinction does not hold for delinquent and nondelinquent boys. (M205)

## JUVENILE DELINQUENCY (CRIME AGAINST A PERSON)
### X    Child-Rearing Practices (Punishment)
If the parents use punitive or lax means of discipline, the child is more likely to commit crimes against a person than if the parents use love-oriented techniques without punitiveness. (M194)

## JUVENILE DELINQUENCY (HELP)
### X    Parent-Child Relations
Parents of boys who are frequent juvenile offenders are more likely to be indifferent to efforts to help the boys than are parents of boys who have one offense.

## JUVENILE DELINQUENCY/MENTAL ILLNESS
### X    Child-Rearing Practices (Supervision)
The parents of delinquents are more likely than the parents of psychotics and normals to fail to supervise their children or to repudiate them. (O033)

## JUVENILE DELINQUENCY/NEUROSIS
### X    Behavior Problems of Family
Unfavorable conditions (alcoholism, epilepsy, psychosis, criminality) occur more frequently in the family histories of delinquents than in those of neurotics. (B238)

### Breast Feeding
A greater number of delinquent children than neurotic children have not been breast fed. (B214)

### Breast Feeding, Duration of
Neurotic children tend to have been breast fed for longer periods than have delinquent children. (B214)

### Broken Home
A greater number of delinquent than neurotic children come from broken homes. (B214)

### Child-Rearing Practices (Consistency)
A greater number of delinquent than of neurotic children experienced inconsistent discipline in the home. (B214)

### Child-Rearing Practices (Discipline)
A greater number of neurotic children than of delinquent children experience normal discipline. (B214)

Neurotic children (neurosis measured by phobias, anxiety, obsessions) are more likely than are delinquent children to have experienced normal discipline, but are also more likely to have received overstrict discipline, while delinquent children are more likely to have received inconsistent discipline. (B238)

### Child-Rearing Practices (Strictness)
More neurotic children than delinquent (acting out) children have received overstrict discipline. (A069)

### Disorganization of Family
Delinquent children are more likely than neurotics to have undergone a series of changes of home and maternal care (neurosis measured by phobias, anxiety level, obsessions, etc.) (B238)

### Father Absence
Interruptions in the father-child relationship occur more frequently in delinquent than in neurotic children. (B214)

### Father-Child Relations
Disturbed emotional relationships between father and child occur more frequently in delinquent than in neurotic children. (B214)

### Institutional Care
Delinquents are more likely than neurotics (measured by phobias, anxiety, obsessions) to have lived part of their lives in institutions, children's homes, etc. (B238)

### Marital Adjustment
Disturbed emotional relationships occur more frequently between the parents of delinquent children than between the parents of neurotic children. (B214)

### Mother-Child Relations
Disturbed emotional relationships between mother and child occur more frequently in delinquent than in neurotic children. (B214)

### Neurosis of Parents
Parents of neurotic children show neurotic tendencies more frequently than do parents of delinquents. (B214)

### Parent-Child Relations
Delinquent children are more likely than neurotic children (phobic reactions, anxiety level) to have emotionally disturbed relationships with their parents. (B238)

### Parent-Child Relations (Affect)
Although delinquents are as conscious of parental rejection as are neurotics, they are less likely to recognize their own hostile feelings toward their parents (i.e., they are more detached and less deeply involved in family relationships than are neurotics). (W145)

### Parent-Child Relations (Deception)
Delinquent children are more likely to have been deceived as to their true parentage than are neurotic children. (B214)

### Personality of Parents
Parents of delinquent children tend to show antisocial and morally unstable tendencies more frequently than do parents of neurotic children. (B214)

### Personality Problems of Parents
The parents of delinquent children show antisocial or morally unstable tendencies more frequently than do the parents of neurotic children (neurosis measured by phobias, anxiety symptoms, etc.). (B238)

### Sibling Relations
There is no significant difference in the frequency with which disturbed relationships occur among delinquent, as compared with neurotic, children (as measured by phobic behavior, anxiety level). (B238)

### Size of Family
Delinquent children come from larger families than do neurotic children. (B214)

## JUVENILE DELINQUENCY (PROPERTY CRIMES)
### X   Child-Rearing Practices (Neglect)
If both parents have a neglecting attitude toward the child, it is more likely that the child will commit property crimes than any other kinds of crimes. (M194)

## JUVENILE DELINQUENCY (RECIDIVISM)
### X   Broken Home
Broken homes are more characteristic of repeated juvenile offenders than of first offenders. (M009)

## JUVENILE DELINQUENCY (REFORM)
### X   Child-Rearing Practices (Punishment)
If the parents use erratic and nonpunitive disciplinary methods, the delinquent child will reform earlier (before his twenty-third year) than if the parents use punitive methods. (M194)

### Mother-Child Relations (Affection)
Among juvenile delinquents, those who have loving mothers are likely to reform earlier (before their twenty-third year) than are those with a nonloving mother. (M194)

### Paternal-Role Model
If the father provides a negative role model for the child, (e.g., involving a criminal record), the delinquent child is more likely to reform later (after his twenty-third year) than if the father provides a positive role model. (M194)

## JUVENILE DELINQUENCY (RUNNING AWAY)
### X   Aggression
Delinquent children who run away are more likely to have parents who display physical aggression in the home than are delinquent children who do not run away. (F093)

### Parent-Child Relations (Rejection)
Rejection by parents is more common among children (delinquent) who run away than among children (delinquent) who do not run away. (F093)

### Parent-Child Relations (Separation)
Delinquent children who run away from home are much more likely to have histories of parent-child separation than are delinquent children who do not run away from home. (F093)

### Sexual Behavior of Parents
Delinquent children who run away are more likely to have parents who display open sexual activity in the home than are delinquent children who do not run away. (F093)

### Surrogate Parent
Delinquent boys who run away are much more likely to have step-parents or adoptive parents than are delinquent boys who do not run away. (F093)

## JUVENILE DELINQUENCY (SEX OFFENSES AND DRUNKENNESS)
### X   Child-Rearing Practices (Punishment)
It is more likely that lax or erratically punitive methods of discipline will result in sex crimes and drunkenness by the child than in any other kinds of crimes. (M194)

## JUVENILE DELINQUENCY (TRAFFIC OFFENSES)
### X   Child-Rearing Practices (Punishment)
If the parents use punitive methods of discipline rather than other methods, the child is more likely to commit traffic offenses than other types of crimes. (M194)

# K

**KIN/FRIENDS    X  Divorce, Attitude Toward**
For both the husband and wife, their family members
are more likely to disapprove of the divorce than are
their respective friends. (G157)

Both the husband's and wife's kin are less likely to be
indifferent about the divorce than are friends. (G157)

**KIN-GROUP    X  Incest Taboo**
In the absence of any type of consanguineal kin-group,
either unilinear or bilateral, there is little tendency to
extend primary incest taboos beyond secondary relatives. (M019)

**KIN-GROUP, IMPORTANCE OF    X  Age Group**
When families and kin-groups are almost self-sufficient
social units (as in segmentary societies), age-groups do
not occur. (E086)

**Avoidance Relationship**
The establishment of an avoidance relationship with certain kinsmen tends to reinforce the importance of the
kin-group. (K076)

**Husband-Wife Relations (Intimacy)**
When kin-groups play an important role in a social system, objective status and obligations to other kin, not
subjective sentiments, tend to characterize the marriage
relationship. (P012)

**Incest Taboo**
The distance to which incest taboos are extended to
kin-groups is correlated with the social importance of
those kin-groups. (M019)

**Mate Selection (Free Choice)**
Arranged marriages tend to be found in kinship systems
where the newly married couple is incorporated into a
larger kin-group. (P012)

**Religion (Sacrifice)**
Important kin units will tend to be made more salient by
the organization of communal sacrifices. (K050)

**KIN NETWORK    X  Class**
The higher the socioeconomic stratum, the more extended and tightly organized is the network of kin relations. (G134)

**KIN/NONKIN    X  Adultery, Attitude Toward**
Censure of adultery will tend to be stronger when it
involves members of the same clan. The contrary is also
asserted. (H074)

When a husband and an adulterer are members of the
same clan, the husband is less likely to be permitted to
take action against the offender. (H074)

When the husband and adulterer are of the same clan,
the act is not likely to be punished. (H138)

**Cohesion of Group**
Solidarity among kin is more easily maintained than in
other groups (i.e., occupational or neighborhood peer
groups), since the boundaries are clearer. (P083)

**Cohesion of Kin-Group**
Boundary-maintaining systems composed of consanguineal kinsmen lead to stronger feelings of closeness
among members than do boundary-maintaining systems
composed of nonconsanguineal kinsmen. (C093)

**Corporate Kin-Group**
Where kinship is extended and becomes the basis for
corporate group membership, it will drastically limit the
degree to which major roles may be successfully assigned on nonkinship bases. (F073)

**Friendship (Closeness)**
The closer the families' friends, the more likely they are
to be kin members than nonkin members. (Z008)

**Isolation of Nuclear Family**
The greater the isolation of the nuclear family in society,
the greater the sharpness of status differences between
family members and nonfamily members. (P062)

**Size of Family**
There is an association between reduction in average
family size (characteristic of modern society as compared to traditional society) and increase in sharpness of
status differences between family members and nonfamily members. (P062)

**Social Control**
Institutional controls of behavior are stronger in consanguineal boundary-maintaining systems than in nonconsanguineal boundary-maintaining systems. (C093)

**Social Network**
Informal group association occurs more frequently
among relatives than among friends, neighbors, or co-
workers. (A002)

Kinfold are more likely than any other group to be the
major group about whom people build their visiting
relationships. (H018)

**KIN/NONKIN INTERACTION    X  Class**
In the United States' lower-middle and middle-middle
classes, the frequency of relations with the collateral and
affinal network is lower than the frequency of relations
with the occupational peer group and the neighborhood. (P083)

**Consensus**
The members of a family show higher consensus on
attitudes than do the members of any artificially composed group. (D061)

There is no difference in the degree of consensus between family, on the one hand, and artificially composed groups, on the other. (D061)

Emotional interaction is less likely to lead to agreement
in the family setting than in groups of strangers, and
instrumental interaction is more likely to produce agreement in a family setting than it is among strangers. (L180)

### Emotional/Instrumental
Emotionality increases satisfaction among family members and decreases satisfaction in stranger interaction, while instrumentality increases satisfaction in stranger interaction and decreases it in family interaction. (L180)

### Maternal-Role Behavior
Younger women (nonmothers) are less apt to share task and emotional behavior when they are in a family situation than are older women (mothers) and are more apt to do so when they are with strangers. (L180)

### Sex-Role Definition
Interaction in family groups will result in a more distinct sex-role differentiation when outsiders are present than when the family members are by themselves. (L180)

## KIN/NONKIN RELATIONS
### X    Cohesion of Family
The cohesiveness of the family is directly correlated with the exclusiveness of its role as a unit of mutual aid. (L064)

### Husband-Wife Relations (Egalitarianism)
There is more equality of relationship between husband and wife (shared interests, joint organization) with a low degree of extrafamilial social contacts. (B209)

### Husband-Wife Relations (Shared Activities)
Where statuses of relative-friend-workmate are filled by the same people, the activities of the spouses tend to become separated. (G012)

### Social Network
The more highly connected the social network to which a couple belongs (i.e., its members see one another independently of the couple), the greater the expectation that the wife has many relationships with their relatives and the husband with their friends. (B268)

### Subsistence Pattern (Preindustrial)
In preindustrial societies the unit of mutual aid tends to be a kin unit. (F049)

## KIN/NONKIN TIES
### X    Social Relations, Closeness of
Consanguinity, per se, produces stronger feelings of closeness among individuals than any other type of relationship. (C093)

## KIN RELATIONS
### Class
Controlling for family size, there appears to be no significant correlation between social class and active maintenance of kin relations. (R084)

### Grandparents
The maintenance of the link with the different branches of the male line is more likely if the paternal grandfather is still alive. (H233)

### Maternal Overprotectiveness
Maternal overprotection is associated with frequent interference in the family by relatives.

### Mental Illness (Schizophrenia)
Female relatives of male schizophrenics do not differ from the female relatives of persons with other (nonorganic) mental illnesses in the degree of possessiveness they feel toward the afflicted person. (F099)

### Prostitution
Prostitutes tend to be detribalized women who have been cut off from their families. (D051)

### Residence
The spouse who has been forced to change residence at marriage is more likely to be strongly linked with his or her family of procreation than is the spouse who has not changed residence. (W115)

### Surrogate Mother
The extent to which an available kin-group aids in infant care is more a function of the interpersonal relationships and kinship ties of particular individuals than of the number of potential mother substitutes in the group as a whole. (M216)

## KIN RELATIONS (AFFECT)
### X    Kin Terminology (Classificatory)
A kin term will tend to be extended to the other kinsmen toward whom the individual shares a similar affective attitude. (L058)

## KIN RELATIONS (CLOSENESS)
### X    Genealogical Proximity/Interaction
The strength of children's affective ties with kin varies more directly with frequency of interaction than with genealogical proximity. (M054)

### Generation
The relationship between kinsmen of widely separated generations such as grandparents-grandchildren tends to be characterized by affection and indulgence. (N030)

### Inheritance
The relationship between kinsmen who are not involved in the same line of inheritance tends to be warm and indulgent. (F073)

### Kin Relations (Interaction)/Genealogical Proximity
The strength of children's affective ties with kin varies more directly with frequency of interaction than with genealogical proximity. (M054)

### Kin Terminology
Kinship terminology will tend to be used in place of the personal names when the speaker regards his relatives with a special affection. (B054)

The selection of a kin term among alternates tends to be directly correlated with the degree of intimacy of the relationship, rank, sex, and age of the kinsman. (B083)

### Kin Ties (Fictive)
Obligations to relatives of fictive kinsmen will vary directly with the closeness of the relatives to the fictive kinsmen. (E051)

### Legal Status
The character of a relationship between kinsmen tends to be more affectionate when neither is in a position of authority or legal superiority. (G055)

### Sex Status
Pairs of sisters are emotionally closer to one another than are pairs of brothers; pairs of girl cousins are closer than boy cousins.

Among older persons (50 years and up) who live by themselves, men are as likely as women to be cut off from intimate contact with kin and thus to lose the role of kinsman. (C116)

Among older persons (50 years and up), women are more likely than men to keep closer touch with both siblings and children. (C116)

## KIN RELATIONS (COOPERATION)
### X   Kin Ties (Fictive)
Patterns of cooperation between fictive kinsmen tend to occur only when the individuals are already consanguineally or affinally related. (A029)

### Residence
The degree of cooperation between kinsmen will be directly affected by their residential proximity. (M131)

## KIN RELATIONS (DEPENDENCY)
### X   Child-Rearing Practices (Kin)
When the discipline and control of the child are in the hands of other relatives as well as of the parents, the pattern of interaction among kinsmen will be characterized by mutual dependence. (H021)

### Emotional Problems of Child
Parents of emotionally disturbed children (of Italian and Irish-American backgrounds) are more likely than are parents of normal children to have conflicts concerning independence from the extended family. (V031)

### Parent-Child Relations (Authority)
When the discipline and control of the child are exclusively in the hands of the parents, patterns of interaction between kinsmen will tend to be characterized by individualism or self-reliance, not by mutual dependence. (H021)

## KIN RELATIONS (HOSTILITY)   X   Segmentation
Lineage fission is more likely to be complete when the break between member groups is accompanied by a situation of "extreme bitterness." (S283)

## KIN RELATIONS, IMPORTANCE OF
### X   Kin Ties (Fictive)
When kin relations are an important framework for social relations, the migrant will tend to establish fictive kin relations in the area in which he settles. (G063)

## KIN RELATIONS (INTENSITY)
### X   Size of Kin-Group
The fewer available relatives an old person has, the more intense is his relationship with them. (T009)

## KIN RELATIONS (INTERACTION)   X   Age
Among older persons (50 years and up), there is no relationship between age and amount of contact with intimate kin. (C116)

### Clan, Importance of
The importance of clan membership is directly correlated with the frequency of contact with clan members. (H088)

### Class
Blue collar migrants have more contact with their relatives than do white collar migrants. (J033)

Upper-class persons tend to visit their extended family more often than do lower-class persons. (S265)

### Conformity
The upper-class child has more contacts with extended kin; this prevents him from accepting deviant peer-group goals. (C086)

### Economic Cooperation
Frequency of contact is closely correlated with frequency of help between relatives. (G033)

### Exogamy
The greater the intensity and frequency of interaction with relatives, the more likely are exogamous prohibitions (U.S.). (C131)

### Genealogical Proximity
The frequency of visits between family members will be directly proportional to the closeness of kinship. (B033)

### Generation
When older persons (50 years and up) do not have children living close to them and thus available for social interaction, they are more likely to substitute as intimates collateral kin (i.e., of their own age) rather than ascending or descending kin. (C116)

### Geographic Mobility
Migrants show no fewer kinship contacts than natives do. (J034)

The greater the geographical mobility of a family, the less contact it will have with its extended kin. (L181)

Kin who have moved are less apt to visit extended family than are those who have not. (S265)

### Geographic Mobility (Urban/Rural)
Rural migrants interact more with kin than do urban migrants. (J034)

### Kin-Role Behavior
When two types of kin do not come into contact very often, no definite system of conduct is observed. (H222)

Role behavior appropriate to classificatory kin terminology tends to be correlated with the closeness of kinsmen and the opportunity for interaction with them. (N030)

### Kin-Role Definition
The specificity of the behavioral patterns associated with a kin role is directly correlated with the frequency of contact between kinsmen. (B110)

Activation of the rights and duties of a kin role is directly correlated with the frequency of contact with relevant kinsmen. (S124)

### Kin Terminology (Classificatory)
Classificatory terminology is more likely to occur when there is less interaction between kinsmen. (H147)

### Kin Ties
A wide lateral extension of kinship permits a greater freedom of choice in the maintenance of kinship ties through social contacts. (G033)

### Kin Ties (Maternal/Paternal)
The rate of interaction with kin is greater for relatives on the maternal than on the paternal side. (R084)

### Life Cycle
Family relations are more likely to be reactivated in the last stage of a person's life than in his occupational phase. (R120)

### Nuclear Family, Importance of
A widespread set of relationships with relatives seems to involve the splitting of the elementary family. (G116)

### Occupation
Loosely knit family friendship networks (i.e., a low frequency of interaction among family units) are more often found among professional families. (G156)

## Rank

Kinsmen of similar rank are more likely than those of dissimilar rank to be in frequent social contact. (G033)

For housewives, as social rank increases, so does contact with relatives. (R084)

## Residence

There is a correlation between proximity of residence of related kin and the amount of interaction within the extended family.

Geographical distance does not reduce contact between kin unless the degree of kinship is also very distant. (G033)

Only when the degree of kinship is remote does geographical distance influence contact. (G033)

### Residence/Geographic Proximity

The intimacy of the relationship between kinsmen is determined by residential rather than by consanguineal proximity. (S120)

### Residence/Lineage

Members of related lineages who live in adjacent villages tend to see more of each other than they do of people belonging to unrelated lineages who live equally near to them. (W115)

### Residence (Neolocal)

The establishment of patterns of neolocal residence tends to result in the restriction of interaction with kinsmen. (V017)

### Sex Status

Women tend to spend more time with their kin than do men. (G033)

### Size of Family

As the size of the nuclear family increases, relationships with secondary kin decrease. (R084)

### Social Mobility

The kin interaction rate of upwardly mobile families is greater than that of the families in their class of origin, but less than that of the families in their class of achievement. (R084)

Frequency of contact with relatives is likely to decrease if the individual moves into another social class. (T106)

### Stress

Family relations are more apt to be reactivated in times of strain, illness, and economic stress than at other times. (R117)

### Witchcraft

Withcraft aggression against kinsmen will be directly correlated with the frequency of contact between the individuals. (M099)

## KIN RELATIONS (INTERACTION)/GENEALOGICAL PROXIMITY
### X   Kin Relations (Closeness)

The strength of children's affective ties with kin varies more directly with frequency of interaction than with genealogical proximity. (M054)

## KIN RELATIONS (RECIPROCITY)
### X   Stability of Kinship System

The stability of a kinship system is correlated with reciprocity in kin interaction. (N030)

## KIN RELATIONS (SECURITY)
### X   Extended Family

Highly structured, rigid, tradition-determined personal communities such as the joint family of India and China or the rigid patrilineal systems of Africa, offer a higher degree of reliance or security for their members. (H026)

## KIN RELATIONS (SIBLING/CHILDREN)    X   Age

Persons between the ages of 50 and 70 are more likely to identify siblings and other collateral kin as intimates; those over 70 are more likely to choose their children as intimates. (C116)

## KIN ROLE    X   Economic Rank

When alternate kin roles present themselves, the selection will tend to be determined by the economic rank of the kinsmen. (F037)

## KIN-ROLE BEHAVIOR
### X   Economic Dependence

Kin obligations tend to be increasingly evaded with the introduction of an economy which permits economic independence. (F059)

### Genealogical Proximity

Adherence to a kin role is directly correlated with the genealogical proximity of the kinsmen. (H137)

Behavior toward classificatory kinsmen will conform more closely with the rules for that term, the closer the genealogical proximity between the individuals in the relationship. (H138)

### Kin Relations (Interaction)

When two types of kin do not come into contact very often, no definite system of conduct is observed. (H222)

Role behavior appropriate to classificatory kin terminology tends to be correlated with the closeness of kinsmen and the opportunity for interaction with them. (N030)

### Kin Terminology

When the behavioral role is in conflict with the kinship term, it is the terminological pattern which is revised. (G061)

The kinship term will tend to be used in addressing kinsmen when the speaker desires to elicit appropriate kin behavior. (H038)

The extension of terminology tends to be accompanied by the extension of the behavioral patterns associated with the kin role. (N030)

A kinship status which retains its behavioral importance will be resistant to pressures toward being classified with all other members of that generation. (V017)

### Residence

Conformity with kinship obligations is more likely to occur if the kinsmen live nearby. (B145)

Activation of descent-line privileges is directly correlated with length of residence. (D085)

Adherence to kinship obligations will tend to be prolonged only if the kinsman remains residentially propinquitous. (F068)

Deviance from lineage norms tends to be directly correlated with the spatial dispersion of the lineage members. (F073)

### Size of Community
The evasion of kinship obligations is rarer in a small, permanent, and homogeneous community. (S153)

### Size of Family
The smaller the size of the nuclear family, the greater the fulfillment of kin obligations. (R084)

### Stability of Extended Family
Fission of the extended family is more likely to occur if members of the kin unit receive differential treatment. (H086)

### Urbanization
Adherence to traditional kin roles is inversely correlated with the degree of urbanization. (B111)

### KIN-ROLE DEFINITION      X Acculturation
Kinship obligations tend to weaken under conditions of acculturation. (E067)

### Adoption
Adoption is less common where the transmission of lineage obligations is less important. (G028)

### Age Group
The conflict between kinship and age-grade allegiances will be more intense in societies where the age-grade is the major determinant of status. (E037)

### Analogy
Kin roles tend to be extended to all individuals who stand in a comparable relationship to classificatory kinsmen. (R069)

### Ancestors
The character of relations (e.g., resentment, fear) between kinsmen will tend to be projected into the society's conception of dead ancestors. (K050)

### Avoidance Relationship
Societies with a high degree of structuring of kinship patterns (unilineality, unilocality, exogamy) are more prone to kin avoidance. (S079)

### Child-Rearing Values (Dependency)
Individuals are not expected to assume responsibility for the actions of other persons in societies organized around the value of "sociological independence" (i.e., in which the individuals are anchored in and identify with the nuclear family); individuals are required to assume the responsibility for their lineage or clan-mates in societies organized around the value of "sociological interdependence" (i.e., in societies in which individuals are anchored in and identify with the wider kin-group). (C093)

### Cohesion of Kin-Group
The more obligations there are among kinsmen, the greater the solidarity there is between kinsmen. (B209)

### Extended Family (Bilateral)
With an increasing importance of the bilateral extended family in the economic sphere, other functions formerly assumed by clan members will tend also to be transferred to members of this unit. (L031)

### Joint Family/Nuclear Family
There will be more nepotism in an industrialized social system where the joint family, rather than the nuclear family, prevails. (N069)

### Kin Relations (Interaction)
The specificity of the behavioral patterns associated with a kin role is directly correlated with the frequency of contact between kinsmen. (B110)

Activation of the rights and duties of a kin role is directly correlated with the frequency of contact with the relevant kinsmen. (S124)

### Kin Terminology
Where few special duties exist between relatives in a society, there will exist few words serving to denote relationship. (B203)

When a kin position acquires increasing importance within the kinship structure, he will tend to be terminologically differentiated. (C068)

A failure to differentiate terminologically the husband and wife relationship reflects an identity of their obligation to kinsmen. (F046)

A failure to identify a kinsman or generation terminologically is an indication of the social unimportance of the relationship. (F049)

When the position of a particular kinsman is distinctive, the position will tend to be given a special kinship term. (H055)

The persistence of a kin term is directly correlated with the social importance of the relationship which it expresses. (M042)

Kinship terms are used with irregularity when there is a lack of differentiated behavior for different relatives. (M245)

The omission of kinship terminology as a form of address tends to occur when the relationship between kinsmen is informal. (S060)

Kin roles of special importance will tend to be terminologically differentiated. (S106)

Kin terminology will tend to be used when the speaker desires to emphasize the obligations of the kin relationship. (W098)

### Kin Terminology (Classificatory)
In societies having a classificatory system of relationship, terms which are used to denote relationship are also used as terms of address. (B203)

The kin role associated with a specific kin position tends to be extended to all classificatory kinsmen bearing the same term. (R069)

Classificatory terminology will tend to be employed when the kin relationship is functionally nonsignificant, so that it is not important to make distinctions between kinsmen. (V017)

### Marriage Payment
When bride price is given to the lineage of the wife's family, rights over the wife's domestic and procreative services will tend to be retained by the lineage of the husband after his death. (L041)

### Mate Selection
Marriages between near kinsmen will be more censured if the new in-law relationships require adjustment of old kin roles. (F037)

### Preferential Marriage

When actual marriages deviate from a preferential marriage pattern, they will tend to be treated as though they were actually in accordance with the rule. (L058)

### Rank

The explicitness of the behavior associated with a kin role will be directly correlated with the importance of the kinsmen in the social structure. (R066)

### Residence

When a lineage group is dispersed, rights and obligations tend to be vested in the matrilineal group as such and not in particular segments. (C090)

Behavioral patterns between kinsmen tend to be correlated with the residential alignment of kinsmen. (F039)

The extension of nuclear family-role behavior to other kinsmen tends to occur only when the kinsmen are residentially propinquitous. (H164)

The greater the degree of lineage dispersion, the narrower is the recognized range of lineage kinship behavior with the total system. (M168)

### Size of Household

The larger the household the more rules there will be specifying the frequency and type of role interaction among members. (G156)

### Size of Kin-Group

When major unilineal groups of larger scale occur, it is found that with respect to the transmission of rights and duties, the more specific the claim or obligation, the narrower the segment of the lineage involved. (F033)

### Size of Kin Unit

The smallest segments of a kinship system tend to emphasize economic activities, the median segments tend to emphasize political activities, and the largest segments tend to emphasize religious activities. (B217)

### Social Control

Family influence and control are weakened when other institutions take on the educational, recreational, and hygienic functions of the family. (A013)

### Urbanization

The degree of urbanization is directly correlated with an increased ambiguity in behavior toward kinsmen. (L064)

## KIN TERMINOLOGY
### X  Affinal Relations (Interaction)

Failure to differentiate terminologically between the husband and wife may reflect an ambilateral pattern of residence and the high frequency of interaction with both groups of affinals. (F046)

### Affinal-Role Definition

The formal character of the relationship between affinals is reflected in the selection of kin terms of address. (B083)

The terminological equation of affinals with consanguineals may be directly correlated with their acceptance of consanguineal roles upon marriage. (F046)

### Age

Informal variants of kinship terms tend to be used more by children than by adults. (B083)

Where relative age is of significance in structuring social

relations, this distinction will be found in the kinship terminology. (B111)

Formal variants of the kinship term tend to be used more as the individual becomes older. (S050)

### Age of Unilineal Descent

The proportion of unilineal features found in the terminology will be directly correlated with the age of the unilineal descent pattern. (L061)

### Authority Structure of Family

A tendency to use personal names rather than kinship terms reflects the weakening of the hierarchial structure of the family. (B083)

Asymmetrical relations of authority between the male members of an extended family creates asymmetry in the kinship terminological system. (G028)

### Clan

Crow and Omaha terminologies are associated with unilineal societies with a well-developed clan system. (L061)

Members of the same marriage clan will tend to address each other by sibling terminology. (S095)

### Class

Members of the lower class tend to use informal variants more frequently than do members of higher social classes. (B083)

The restriction of kin ties to encompass only members of the immediate nuclear family tends to occur among members of the lowest classes in urban areas. (G056)

### Cohesion of Clan

Paralleling the decline of the clan system is the decline in knowledge and use of kinship terminology. (L031)

### Coincidence

When marriage to a cross-cousin is the preferential form, a woman's husband's father and her father's sister's husband will tend to be terminologically equated. (E018)

### Descent (Bilateral)

There is a positive correlation between lineal terminology and bilateral descent. (D057)

The extension of sibling terms to both cross- and parallel-cousins indicates a change in the direcion of bilaterality. (M077)

### Descent (Patrilineal)

When a patrilineal culture exerts strong pressures on a society which is matrilineal in its organization, terminological groupings tend to break down. (A021)

With the growing importance of the patriarchial family, sibling terminology tends to be extended to cross-cousins. (R034)

### Exogamy

With an increasing violation of exogamic restrictions, kin terminology tends to be abandoned. (R064)

### Exogamy/Descent (Patrilineal)

A change from merging to bifurcate-merging terminology indicates the establishment of exogamous patrilineal organizations. (F010)

### Exogamy/Residence

The importance of residence patterns as determinants of kin terminology is inversely correlated with the presence and strength of exogamic kin-groups. (L061)

### Genealogical Position

If a given relative does not fall within the range of attributes of his genealogical placement, the kin term of address directed toward him tends to reflect his deviation, that is, to reflect his actual status in the household or in a hypothetical normative household. (N012)

### Generation

The omission of kin terms is more likely to occur with relatives of a younger generation. (C049)

### Incest Taboo

Kinship terms which apply to members of the nuclear family tend to be extended to all kinsmen who fall under the incest taboo. (L058)

The asymmetrical extension of incest taboos fosters the development of Crow-Omaha terminology. (L061)

Restrictions against sexual relations will tend to be extended to kinsmen who are terminologically equated with actual siblings. (T039)

When marriages between prohibited (but distant) kinsmen occur, there tends to be an adjustment of kinship terminology to make the union socially acceptable. (T039)

### Inheritance

Inheritance rules will be reflected in the kinship terminology. (M058)

### Isolation of Nuclear Family

The isolated nuclear family tends to be associated with kinship terminology of the lineal type. (M019)

### Kin Relations (Closeness)

Kinship terminology will tend to be used in place of the personal name when the speaker regards his relative with a special affection. (B054)

The selection of a kin term among alternates tends to be directly correlated with the degree of intimacy of the relationship, rank, sex, and age of the kinsman. (B083)

### Kin-Role Behavior

When the behavioral role is in conflict with the kinship term, it is the terminological pattern which is revised. (G061)

The kinship term will tend to be used in addressing kinsmen when the speaker desires to elicit appropriate kin behavior. (H038)

The extension of kin terminology tends to be accompanied by the extension of the behavioral patterns associated with the kin role. (N030)

A kinship status which retains its behavioral importance will be resistant to pressures toward being classified with all other members of that generation. (V017)

### Kin-Role Definition

Where few special duties exist between relatives in a society, there will exist few words serving to denote relationship. (B203)

When a kin position acquires increasing importance within the kinship structure, he will tend to be terminologically differentiated. (C068)

A failure to differentiate terminologically the husband and wife relationship reflects an identity of their obligation to kinsmen. (F046)

A failure to identify a kinsman or generation terminologically is an indication of the social unimportance of the relationship. (F049)

When the position of a particular kinsman is distinctive, the position will tend to be given a special kinship term. (H055)

The persistence of a kin term is directly correlated with the social importance of the relationship which it expresses. (M042)

Kinship terms are used with irregularity when there is a lack of differentiated behavior for different relatives. (M245)

The omission of kinship terminology as a form of address tends to occur when the relationship between kinsmen is informal. (S060)

Kin roles of special importance will tend to be terminologically differentiated. (S106)

Kin terminology will tend to be used when the speaker desires to emphasize the obligations of the kin relationship. (W098)

### Kin Ties

When there is a major realignment in the kinship system the terminological adjustment will first occur among kinsmen who are of greatest importance to ego. (L060)

### Kin Ties (Fictive)

When fictive kinship terms are used, the terms used will tend to be those of low affective content. (L057)

### Kinship, Importance of

The social importance of a kin relationship will be reflected in the number of terms which may be used to describe the relationship. (G053)

### Marriage Class System (Two-Section)

There is likely to be a negative correlation between two-section systems and Crow or Omaha types of kin terminology. (M234)

### Nuclear Family

Revisions of kinship terminology tend to be restricted within the nuclear family. (F046)

### Parental-Role Behavior

The presence of a single alternate term for parents indicates patterns of behavioral similarity between father and mother. (F046)

### Paternal/Maternal Role

When only one parent is designated by two terms according to sex of speaker, it tends to be the father. (F046)

### Preferential Marriage

When the sororate and marriage to wife's brother's daughter are both preferred marriage forms, wife's sister and wife's brother's daughter will tend to be terminologically equated. (A020)

When a preferential marriage pattern is established, potential mates tend to include those who are terminologically equated with the preferred kinsmen. (L060)

When the preferred mate is always a consanguineal relative, special affinal terms for preferred mate tend to be absent. (M019)

Preferential marriage with the wife's brother's daughter will produce the Omaha type of terminology for cross-cousins. (M019)

Rules of preferential marriage with a mother's brother's widow will produce kinship terminology of the Crow type. (M019)

### Preferential Marriage (Connubium)
A unilineal three-generational cycling of kin terminology arises from a circulation of spouses among three sibs. (L058)

### Preferential Marriage (Cross-Cousin)
A symmetrical cross-cousin marriage pattern is negatively associated with a cognatic terminology or society. (N067)

When marriage with a cross-cousin is the preferred form, cross-cousins tend to be terminologically distinguished from parallel-cousins and from the siblings of ego. (S106)

### Preferential Marriage (Exchange)
When the normal mode of marriage is by the exchange of sisters, the same kinship term tends to be applied to mother's brother's wife and father's sister, to wife's brother's wife and sister, and to wife's brother's daughter and sister's daughter. (M019)

### Rank
Kinship terms, rather than personal names, are used when the speaker desires to show deference to his relatives. (B054)

Kinship terms, rather than personal names, will tend to be used when the speaker desires to show deference to his relatives. (B054)

Kinsmen of equal rank are more likely to use informal than formal variants of kinship terms. (B083)

The kinship designation tends to be omitted when the speaker is of equal status or superior to the hearer. (S050)

### Rank of Husband/Wife
The relative status of the husband and wife will tend to be reflected in terms with which they address one another. (B083)

### Rank of Wives
Status distinction between wives in a polygynous family will tend to be reflected in the kinship terminology. (S124)

### Residence
A radical shift in residence patterns may weaken or destroy the unilineal organization, thereby causing changes in kinship nomenclature. (L061)

Kinship nomenclature tends to be directly conditioned by the rules of residence which define the kin unit. (L061)

### Residence (Avunculocal)
In the presence of avunculocal residence, terms for primary relatives tend to be extended within the same generation to their collateral relatives through females. (M019)

### Residence (Neolocal)
Neolocal residence tends to encourage the development of a lineal terminology. (V017)

### Sex-Role Definition
Changes in sex-role definitions will tend to be accompanied by a new descriptive vocabulary. (E026)

There will tend to be an omission of sex distinction within a kin term if the sex roles are not fully differentiated within the kin type. (F046)

### Sex Status
The selection of an informal variant for the terms of address for mother is more likely to occur among sons than among daughters. (B083)

Females tend to use the more formal variants of kinship terminology more frequently; males use informal variants more frequently. (N012)

The formal variant of a kinship term is more likely to be used with the parent of the same sex than with the parent of the opposite sex. (S050)

### Sibling Relations
Societies which emphasize the sibling relationship are more likely to make distinctions of age and sex in their sibling terminology. (M235)

### Sibling-Role Definition
Siblings of both sexes tend to be merged terminologically if they share the same obligations in relation to their family. (F046)

### Size of Community
Kinship terminology is more likely to be adhered to rigidly when the community is large in size. (B147)

### Size of Household
The larger the household the greater the differentiation of kinship terms. (G156)

### Stability of Extended Family
The inaccurate application of kin terminology is indicative of the disintegration of the extended family. (C049)

### Stability of Kinship Structure
Kinship terminology tends to be inconsistently applied with the deterioration of the kinship structure. (R034)

### Urbanization
The degree of urbanization tends to be directly correlated with a diminution in the use of kinship terminology. (L064)

## KIN TERMINOLOGY (ASYMMETRICAL CROSS-COUSIN)
### X   Preferential Marriage (Exchange)
Asymmetrical cross-cousin terminology is incompatible with sister-exchange marriage. (L060)

## KIN TERMINOLOGY (BIFURCATE COLLATERAL)
### X   Isolation of Nuclear Family
Bifurcate collateral terminology functions to reinforce the isolation of the nuclear family from collateral nuclear family. (S060)

### Polygyny (Nonsororal)
Nonsororal polygyny operates to produce bifurcate collateral terminology. (M019)

### Polygyny/Residence (Patrilocal)
The occasional appearance of bifurcate collateral terminology in normal or neolocal Eskimo society presumably reflects former polygyny and patrilocal residence. (M019)

### Residence (Patrilocal)

Patrilocal and matri-patrilocal residence (because of their association with nonsororal polygyny) tend to be accompanied by kinship terminology of the bifurcate collateral type. (M019)

### Stratification

Bifurcate collateral terminology tends to occur in societies with systems of ranked lineages. (K049)

## KIN TERMINOLOGY (BIFURCATE MERGING)
### X Clan

Clans, whether matrilocal, patrilocal, or avunculocal in type, tend to be associated with bifurcate merging terminology. (M019)

### Clan (Patrilineal/Matrilineal)

Bifurcate merging terminology tends to be associated with clan systems of either a patrilineal or matrilineal character. (W050)

### Descent (Matrilineal)

Over 70 per cent of all matrilineal systems for which there is information have either Crow or Iroquois cousin terms. (A048)

### Descent (Unilateral)

Bifurcate merging terminology tends to be found in societies which have rigid groupings of kinsmen based on unilateral descent. (S106)

### Descent (Unilineal)

Bifurcate merging terminology develops with the introduction of the sib system. (L039)

Bifurcate merging terminology tends to be associated with exogamous unilineal groups. (M047)

When the emphasis is upon unilineal descent, kinship terminology will tend to distinguish between the lineal and collateral kinsmen. (O023)

Bifurcate merging terminology is generally associated with a pattern of unilinear descent. (W067)

### Exogamy

Bifurcate merging terminology tends to be associated with exogamous unilinear groups. (M047)

### Marriage Class System

With the adoption of a section system, the kinship terminology will tend to be bifurcate merging in character. (E065)

### Moiety

Moieties are very widely associated with bifurcate merging terminology. (M019)

### Polygyny (Sororal)

Sororal polygyny operates to produce bifurcate merging terminology. (M019)

### Preferential Marriage (Cross-Cousin)

Bifurcate merging terminology tends to be found in societies where a cross-cousin is the preferred marriage partner. (H047)

### Preferential Marriage (Levirate)

Preferential levirate marriages may operate to minimize the criterion of collaterality and thus produce kinship terminology of the so-called bifurcate merging type. (M019)

### Preferential Marriage (Levirate-Sororate)

Bifurcate merging terminology tends to result from the institutionalization of certain rules of preferential mating, especially the levirate and sororate. (M047)

Bifurcate merging terminology tends to be associated with certain rules of preferential mating, especially the levirate and sororate. (M047)

### Preferential Marriage (Sororate)

The classification of father's brother with father and mother's sister with mother reflects the occurrence of the sororate. (A021)

## KIN TERMINOLOGY (BILATERAL)
### X Subsistence Pattern (Hunting)

In simple hunting economies, kinship terminology tends to bilateral. (N027)

## KIN TERMINOLOGY (CLASSIFICATORY)
### X Analogy

When ego's classificatory kinsmen stand in a given relationship to one another, ego is more likely to use a classificatory terminology for them which is comparable to their relationship to one another (e.g., if ego calls his father's brothers "father," he calls their children "brother and sister"). (H104)

### Clan

The classificatory system of relationship is connected with the social divisions known as "clans." (R123)

Classificatory terminology and the clan system tend to evolve together. (S098)

### Coincidence

Mother's sister's husband and mother's brother's daughter's husband will be terminologically equated with father or father's brother when the levirate and cross-generation marriage with wife's brother occurs. (F010)

When ego can trace a kinship connection to some relative in two different ways, the two types of bonds tend to be ignored and the relative tends to be called by the same term. (M019)

The equivalence of mother's brother and father's sister's son is a function of their possible identity under conditions of avuncular marriage. (M020)

When avuncular marriage operates in conjunction with a cross-cousin marriage, mother's mother and father's sister tend to be subsumed under the same term. (M020)

Under conditions of fraternal polyandry, brothers of a husband will tend to be called father by his children. (S068)

When two kin roles coincide in the same individual, classificatory terminology tends to occur. (S093)

Father's sister's daughter will tend to be terminologically equated with her mother in a dual organization, since they may both be considered potential wives. (S097)

### Descent (Patriarchy)

The emergence of a patriarchal family will result in the abandonment of a classificatory system of relationships. (R034)

### Descent (Unilineal)

When unilineal kin structure is strong, members of the same clan may be terminologically equated. (M042)

### Divorce Adjustment
Divorce will be less disruptive in societies with classificatory terminology. (R071)

### Incest Taboo
Incest taboos tend to be extended to all kinsmen who are terminologically equated with members of the nuclear family. (O016)

### Joking Relationship
Joking relationships tend to be extended to all classificatory kinsmen of the relatives in question. (R052)

### Kin Relations (Affect)
A kin term will tend to be extended to the other kinsmen toward whom the individual shares a similar affective attitude. (L058)

### Kin Relations (Interaction)
Classificatory terminology is more likely to occur where there is less interaction between kinsmen. (H147)

### Kin-Role Definition
In societies having a classificatory system of relationship, terms which are used to denote relationship are also used as terms of address. (B203)

The kin role associated with a specific kin position tends to be extended to all classificatory kinsmen bearing the same term. (R069)

Classificatory terminology will tend to be employed when the kin relationship is functionally nonsignificant, so that it is not important to make distinctions between kinsmen. (V017)

### Kinship, Importance of
When membership in a kin-group is of preeminent importance in defining social relations, members of the same group may be terminologically equated. (L060)

When lineage affiliation is important, all members of the lineage will be terminologically equated with the relative closest to ego who represents that lineage. (M082)

### Moiety
Classificatory terminology which reflects the coincidence of affinal and consanguineal kinsmen tends to occur when the society has a moiety organization. (S098)

### Moiety System
There is a correlation between the classificatory system of kinship terminology and the organization of societies into clans or moieties. (R069)

Classificatory terminology which reflects the coincidence of affinal and consanguineal kinsmen tends to occur when the society has a moiety organization. (S098)

### Polygyny (Sororal)
Under sororal polygyny, terms for ego's primary relatives tend to be extended within the same sex and generation to their collateral relatives through females. (M019)

### Preferential Marriage
When the actual kinsman is not available for the preferential marriage pattern, classificatory equivalents tend to be substituted. (L058)

The coincidence of kin type resulting from a preferential marriage pattern, such as exchange marriage, will result in classificatory terminology. (S098)

### Preferential Marriage (Levirate)
The classification of father's brother with father and mother's sister with mother reflects levirate marriage practices. (A021)

There is a correlation between the custom of the levirate and classificatory systems of terminology. (R069)

### Residence
Collateral relatives of the first ascending generation tend to be merged if neither set shares a common residence with ego. (H164)

When two kin statuses are brought together as close neighbors or actual housemates, they are more likely to be designated by a single classificatory term. (M019)

### Role Definition in Family
When kin terms of the nuclear family are extended to other kinsmen, the behavior toward these classificatory kinsmen will tend to be modeled on the behavioral pattern associated with the relevant member of the nuclear family. (S098)

### Stability of Clan
With the decline of the clan system and the parallel decline in the knowledge and use of kinship terminology, classificatory terms tend to be used in place of former descriptive or specific terms. (L031)

### Urbanization
The abandonment of the use of kinship terminology for classificatory kinsmen is directly correlated with the degree of urbanization. (S122)

## KIN TERMINOLOGY (COLLATERAL)
### X Independence of Nuclear Family
With the emergence of the nuclear family as the basic subsistence unit, a trend toward collaterality will develop and the basic Eskimo system will arise. (V017)

### Stability of Clan
The disintegration of the clan system is reflected in the loss of kinship terminology for collateral relatives. (B107)

## KIN TERMINOLOGY (EXTENSION)
### X Endogamous Demes
When the community structure is that of an endogamous deme, sibling terms tend to be extended to both cross- and parallel-cousins. (M019)

## KIN TERMINOLOGY (FICTIVE)
### X Friendship (Closeness)
Use or nonuse of kin terms when addressing friends and acquaintances is correlated with the degree of intimacy of the relationship. (N012)

### Industrialization
The fictive use of kinship terminology tends to be abandoned in the context of industrialization. (B083)

## KIN TERMINOLOGY (GENERATION)
### X Art (Design Motifs)
Kinship systems which merge alternate generations (Crow) will tend to use alternating patterns as design motifs. (B304)

Kinship systems with generational terminology (Hawaiian) will tend to use horizontal segmentary patterns as design motifs. (B304)

#### Cohesion of Clan
When the clan organization of a society is strong, generational distinctions will tend to be overridden in the kinship terminology. (M042)

#### Descent (Bilateral)
When the emphasis is on bilateral descent, terminology will be generational. (O023)

#### Descent (Matrilineal)
In the presence of exogamous matrilineages, matrisibs, or matrimoieties, kinship terms for father's sister tend to be extended to father's sister's daughter and those for brother's daughter to mother's brother's daughter. (M019)

#### Descent (Patrilineal)
In the presence of exogamous patrilineages, patrisibs, or patrimoieties, kinship terms for mother's sister tend to be extended to mother's brother's daughter and those for sister's daughter to father's sister's daughter. (M019)

#### Descent (Unilineal)
When a society tries to combine patrilineal and matrilineal terminologies, a generational system is likely to emerge. (B201)

Generation- or Polynesian-type kinship systems tend to occur in societies which are without unilineal descent groups. (L039)

When unilineal kin-groups are highly developed, generational distinctions will tend to be omitted in the kinship terminology. (P016)

#### Kindred
Bilateral kindred tend to be associated with kinship terminology of the generational type. (M019)

#### Moiety
Generational terminology is incompatible with the moiety or sectional systems. (E032)

#### Preferential Marriage (Cross-Cousin)
The need for an alternating exchange relationship in a patrilateral system requires that a lineal descent group must be clearly divided into generations of marriageable men and women. (N072)

#### Preferential Marriage (Junior)
The terminological equivalence of alternate generations of kinsmen is intimately linked with the junior marriage pattern. (M130)

#### Preferential Marriage (Second Cross-Cousins)
A three-generation rotation of unilineal kin terms may result if the preferential marriage pattern is that between second cross-cousins. (L058)

#### Residence (Bilocal)
Bilocal residence tends to be associated with kinship terminology of the generation type. (M019)

#### Stability of Kin-Group
Generational terminology tends to be found in societies in which kin-groupings are characterized by flexibility and plasticity. (S106)

#### Structure of Family
When generational terminology is employed, family structure tends to be dispersed and amorphous. (H062)

## KIN TERMINOLOGY (IROQUOIS)
#### X   Cohesion of Lineage
Weak unilineal descent groups are associated with Iroquois terminology. (C126)

## KIN TERMINOLOGY (MERGING)        X   Descent
Matrilineal systems are more likely than patrilineal ones to have a merging rather than a collateralizing terminology. (A048)

#### Descent (Matrilineal/Patrilineal)
Matrilineal systems are more likely than patrilineal ones to have merging rather than collateralizing terminology. (A048)

#### Economic Role
The terminological merging of son and daughter under a single term for child will be favored by conditions of economic equality in their obligation. (F046)

#### Marriage Class System
When the kinship is of the vertical type (i.e., merging of all members of clan regardless of generation), the resistance to sections is very strong. (E107)

## KIN TERMINOLOGY (OMAHA)
#### X   Age of Patrilineal Descent
The occurrence of Omaha systems of terminology indicates that the pattern of patrilineal descent is of great age. (L061)

#### Avunculate
The development of the avunculate in patrilineal societies is associated with the development of Omaha terminology. (L061)

## KIN TERMINOLOGY (SIBLINGS)
#### X   Descent (Patrilineal)
Terminological distinctions between half and full siblings will not occur when the patrilineal principle is strong. (R054)

## KIN TERMINOLOGY (SYMMETRICAL CROSS-COUSIN)        X   Moiety
The application of the same term to father's sister's son and to mother's brother's son is evidence for the earlier existence of a moiety system. (R034)

## KIN TERMINOLOGY (UNILINEAL)
#### X   Social Structure, Rigidity of
Lineage terminology systems tend to be associated with a rigid social structure. (S080)

## KIN TIES        X   Adoption
In societies in which the survival rate is low, adoption reinforces existing kinship bonds by "filling the gap" within the extended family. (D082)

#### Clan
The range of acknowledged kinship ties will tend to be extended by institutions such as clans. (M137)

#### Class
Kinship ties are geographically more extended toward the higher social strata. (Q001)

Family ties (among peasant and lower-class groups) tend to persist more than among upper classes in a situation of social change (family reforms). (T073)

#### Cohesion of Community
The solidarity of a community tends to be reinforced if the members of the village are bound by kinship ties. (G056)

### Cohesion of Family

Widespread sets of relationships with relatives are correlated with splitting of the elementary family. (G012)

There is no demonstrated relation between family closeness and number of consanguineal relatives. (R084)

### Conflict in Kin-Group

A failure to sever the ties of the wife to her natal group in a patrilineal and patrilocal society will engender serious tensions both within and between kin-groups. (N008)

### Death Rate

Where the mortality rate is high, the importance of consanguineal relationships tends to be less. (L063)

### Division of Labor

Kin ties tend to be of greatest importance in societies which lack patterns of economic specialization. (L072)

### Economic Cooperation

The extension or maintenance of kinship ties between spatially separated units is directly correlated with the presence of patterns of economic interdependence. (S159)

### Economic Dependence

Kinship ties will tend to disintegrate with the development of patterns of economic independence. (N046)

### Economic Pattern (Money)

The adoption of a cash economy will tend to narrow the range of kinship relationship to a smaller number of close bilateral kin. (G056)

### Economic Rank

A vertical extension of kinship ties tends to be directly correlated with the economic status of the lineage. (T039)

### Exogamy (Informal)

Exogamy is more apt to be extended further by people who identify relatives as their best friends than by people who report nonrelatives as their best friends. (C131)

### Geographic Mobility

Migratory patterns tend to be determined by where affinal and consanguineal kin outside the village are located. (G063)

Ties with relatives outside the immediate nuclear family are more affected by geographical separation in the lower than in the middle class. (R084)

### Husband-Wife Relations (Intimacy)

The husband-wife relationship will tend to be characterized by an attitude of reserve if the allegiance of the husband lies primarily with his extended family. (S115)

### Incest Taboo

Incest taboos are more likely to be extended to consanguineal than to affinal kin. (M019)

If kinship affiliation is realigned, incest taboos will be altered in harmony with this change. (V017)

### Industrialization

The range of kin ties is inversely correlated with the degree of industrialization. (B082)

### Kin Relations (Interaction)

A wide lateral extension of kinship permits a greater freedom of choice in the maintenance of kinship ties through social contacts. (G033)

### Kin Terminology

When there is a major structural realignment in the kinship system the terminological adjustment will first occur among kinsmen who are of greatest importance to ego. (L060)

### Mental Illness of Child (Schizophrenia)

Schizophrenia is more likely in a child whose parents (either or both) have remained primarily attached to their parents or siblings. (F097)

### Political Structure (Centralization)

The attenuation of kin ties tends to occur in a politically centralized society. (L072)

### Population

The attenuation of kin ties tends to occur under conditions of high population density. (L072)

### Preferential Marriage

The range of acknowledged kinship will tend to be wider if preferential marriage patterns with specific kinsmen exist. (M137)

### Preferential Marriage (Cross-Cousin)

Marriage between cross-cousins serves to reinforce existing but weakening kin ties. (T039)

### Residence

Kin-groups which are not localized are likely to contain fewer generations and to have weaker kin ties. (C052)

The maintenance of the link with the different branches of the male line is more likely if the young man has stayed near his father. (H233)

### Residence (Matrilocal)

When an uxorilocal marriage occurs in a generally patrilocal society, the children of this union tend to affiliate themselves with their mother's lineage. (T039)

### Sibling Rank

The equivalence of siblings (both male and female) creates a wide lateral extension of the kinship system. (G028)

### Social Control

As the effective range of kinship narrows, the responsibility of the kinship group for social control correspondingly diminishes. (E015)

### Social Mobility

Kinship ties are geographically more extended toward the higher social strata. (Q001)

### Social Network

There is a positive relationship between aid from family members and the divorcée's claim that she has some or many opportunities to meet people. (G157)

### Social Structure (Heterogeneity)

The attenuation of kin ties tends to occur in societies which have high degrees of cultural and social heterogeneity. (L072)

### Stability of Clan

The disintegration of the clan organization tends to accompany the weakening of kin ties. (G072)

### Stratification

The development of stratification is facilitated by the weakening of kin ties. (G031)

### Stratification of Lineages
Manipulation of descent affiliation tends to be found in societies which have stratified unilineal descent groups. (F039)

### Subsistence Pattern (Agriculture)
The persistence of kinship ties tends to be directly correlated with an agricultural economy. (T039)

### Urban/Rural
The attenuation of kin ties tends to occur in urban areas. (L072)

### Urbanization
The greater the degree of urbanization, the smaller the kinship range. (G033)

The weakening of kin ties is directly correlated with the degree of urbanization. (M076)

### Values (Achievement)
When the dominant social values center on achievement and not on ascription, the range of kinship extensions will be narrow. (S050)

### Values (Individualism)
When a high value is placed on individualism, the range within which kinship is extended will be narrow. (S050)

### Voluntary Organizations
Mutual-aid societies tend to arise in situations where bonds between kinsmen are weak. (M076)

### Voluntary Organizations (Tribal)
The establishment of tribal unions in urban areas reinforces the migrant's attachment to his native town and lineage. (L030)

## KIN TIES (BILATERAL)
### X   Employment of Women
The employment of women reinforces the trend toward bilateralism. (P083)

## KIN TIES (CONSANGUINEAL/AFFINAL)
### X   Avoidance Relationship
Very few consanguineal kin relationships are characterized by avoidance; when they do occur they are between same-generation cross-sex kin. (S189)

## KIN TIES (FICTIVE)      X   Age
The establishment of fictive kin bonds of brotherhood tends to be between men of the same age level. (O018)

### Clan
The institutionalization of fictive kin ties will be inhibited by the existence of a clan system. (F049)

### Class
Among members of the upper class, the establishment of fictive kin ties tends to occur with kinsmen rather than with nonkinsmen. (F049)

Deterioration of patterns of fictive kinship is most likely to occur among the economically mobile upper and middle classes and the industrial wage-earning working class. (M080)

The higher one's social class, the smaller the likelihood of being addressed by a stranger as a kinsmen. (N012)

### Cohesion of Community
Community solidarity will be enhanced by the extension of fictive kin ties to nonkinsmen within the area. (M080)

### Cohesion of Extended Family
The extension of the kinship unit by fictive ties with nonkinsmen tends to occur in societies where the extended family is weak. (L064)

### Cohesion of Kin-Group
When fictive kinship ties are established between individuals who are already consanguineal kinsmen, the alliance serves to reinforce preexisting bonds. (A029)

The institutionalization of fictive kin ties tends to occur in societies where kin units are weak or absent. (F049)

### Cohesion of Soceity
The institutionalization of patterns of fictive kinship strengthens intercommunity relations. (M080)

In a society marked by ethnic and linguistic diversity, the extension of kinship bonds to nonkinsmen serves as an important cohesive factor. (O018)

### Conflict
The extension of fictive kin ties will increase the potentiality of friction in intergroup relations. (W075)

### Conflict Between Kin-Groups
The extension of kin bonds to nonkinsmen increases the instability and potentialities for conflict between kin-groups. (W075)

### Economic Pattern (Feudal)
The economic organization of a feudal society tends to be particularly conducive to the institutionalization of fictive kin relations. (F049)

### Economic Role of Family
The deterioration of patterns of fictive kinship are most extreme in areas where the family no longer forms the primary unit of production. (M080)

### Geographic Mobility
The establishment of fictive kin ties with individuals in other districts facilitates physical mobility. (F049)

### Incest Taboo
Incest taboos tend to be extended to individuals with whom a bond of fictive kinship has been established. (L064)

### Industrialization
With the development of industrialization, formalized fictive kin-groups have declined in number, size, and importance. (N012)

### Kin Relations (Closeness)
Obligations to relatives of fictive kinsmen will vary directly with the closeness of the relatives to the fictive kinsmen. (E051)

### Kin Relations (Cooperation)
Patterns of cooperation between fictive kinsmen tend to occur only when the individuals are already consanguineally or affinally related. (A029)

### Kin Relations, Importance of
When kin relations are an important framework for social relations, the migrant will tend to establish fictive kin relations in the area in which he settles. (G063)

### Kin Terminology
When fictive kinship terms are used, the terms used will tend to be those of low affective content. (L057)

## Kinship, Importance of
In societies where kinship ties form the major framework for social relations, fictive kin ties tend to be instituted for nonkinsmen who attach themselves to the residential group. (W075)

### Political Structure
The importance of fictive kinship ties increases with the growth of the state and its formal institutions. (M080)

### Religion (Role of Deities)
The extension of fictive kin ties on an interclass basis may lead to a conception of the diety and his relationship to the worshipper as that of patron and client. (W075)

### Residence
The greater the distance at which a fictive kinsman resides, the more likely it is that the relationship is based on economic or political motives than on friendship. (E051)

When the relationship of fictive kinsmen is one of respect, individuals who are neither neighbors nor relatives tend to be chosen so that intimacy and quarrels can be avoided. (L064)

Where peripheral kin in a community cannot assume familial obligations because they do not live close by, neighbors tend to act as surrogates in assuming such obligations. (M054)

### Size and Stability of Kin-Group
The institutionalization of fictive kin ties will tend to occur when the corporate groups based on kinship are small and unstable. (T045)

### Social Mobility
The extent to which fictive kin ties are established between individuals of different socioeconomic classes is indicative of the degree of socioeconomic mobility. (F049)

Under conditions of social mobility, fictive kin ties tend to be established between a member of a lower class and one of a higher class. (M080)

When the community is homogeneous with high stability and low mobility, fictive kin ties tend to be established between members of the same community. (M080)

### Social Structure (Homogeneity)
Patterns of fictive kinship function most effectively in societies which are of homogeneous character. (A029)

### Stability of Society
The institutionalization of a fictive kin relationship serves to promote social stability both within—and between—classes and ethnic groups. (F049)

### Stratification
A vertical extension of fictive kin ties tends to occur when social relationships between two defined sociocultural strata or classes become closer. (M080)

### Urbanization
A decrease in the importance of the fictive kinship relationship is directly correlated with the degree of urbanization. (A029)

In urban areas fictive kinship relationships tend to be established with friends rather than with relatives. (A029)

When the urban population is largely immigrant, unstable, and socially heterogeneous, fictive kin-groups tend to arise as a substitute for actual kinship ties. (L030)

## KIN TIES, IMPORTANCE OF     X     Economic Level
When a family is marginal economically, kin ties are important for the survival of the group. (O006)

## KIN TIES (MATERNAL)          X     Marital Stability
When marital relations are unstable and primarily consensual, a strong emphasis is placed upon the maternal kin. (S102)

## KIN TIES (MATERNAL/PATERNAL)
### X     Kin Relations (Interaction)
The rate of interaction with kin is greater for relatives on the maternal than on the paternal side. (R084)

## KIN TIES OF HUSBAND/WIFE
### X     Cohesion of Lineage
Where the solidarity of the lineages of the husband and wife are so strong as to minimize the demands each spouse could make on the other, one marriage partner (usually the wife) must sever connections with his or her natal group. (Z003)

## KINDRED                      X     Descent (Bilateral)
A characteristic of bilateral societies is the formation of temporary kindred-based action groups. (F127)

### Endogamy
Kindred groupings are more likely to be endogamous than exogamous. (G156)

### Kin Terminology (Generation)
Bilateral kindred tend to be associated wtih kinship terminology of the generational type. (M019)

### Property (Individual)
Where conditions are favorable to the individual ownership of land, the bilateral kindred will replace the unilinear kin-group. (G029)

### Values
By reinforcing the marital tie in such a way that concubinage was not a legitimate outlet for sexual needs and repudiation for barrenness was no longer the husband's prerogative, Christianity has encouraged development of bilateral kindred to the detriment of the patrilineal lineage. (P083)

## KINDRED/LINEAGE     X     Corporate Kin-Group
Kindreds are less able than lineages to act as a collectivity regarding either internal activities (e.g., owning land, administering justice) or external conflicts. (G156)

## KINSHIP                      X     Acculturation
Absorption of cultural traits is more likely if the kin structure is complex and each unit has a separate cultural identity. (M233)

### Divorce
Divorce is less likely to occur in societies with a wide web of imputed kinship. (S267)

### Economic Level
A kinship structure which permits a broad definition of potential kinship will correlate with societies with marginal economies and a wide range of interareal interaction. (H225)

### Economic Pattern
Complexity of kinship structure tends to be correlated

with the complexity of the economic organization. (F039)

### Subsistence Pattern (Agriculture)
The proliferation of forms of kinship structure will tend to follow the adoption of agriculture, with its subsequent increase in food supply. (V009)

## KINSHIP (BILATERAL)
### X   Descent (Asymmetrical)
Asymmetrical descent may develop from a unilineal pattern as a consequence of the increasing importance of the bilateral family. (S097)

### Residence
When the residence pattern is not fixed, the bilateral kin-group is more likely to be the focus of attention. (B298)

Dispersion of the town, village, or settlement and a scattering of households is associated with the development of bilaterality. (S192)

### Sibling Relations (Solidarity)
In bilateral systems, sibling solidarity in adulthood is a stronger kinship bond than other kinship bonds. (I008)

### Subsistence Pattern (Herding)
Bilateral (v. unilateral) organization is particularly well adapted to large-scale reindeer herding and difficult environments. (P082)

## KINSHIP, IMPORTANCE OF     X   Acculturation
Kinship ties beyond those of closest kin tend to be unimportant where much social and cultural assimilation occurs. (E104)

### Age-Groups
Age-grading into a corporate, integrated hierarchal organization is inversely correlated with the extent to which kinship principles and groups serve as focal points of social integration. (E102)

### Authority Structure of Family
In societies where kinship provides the basis for practically all the differentiation within the social system, males have the principal rights of authority. (S080)

### Class
A deterioration of the importance of kinship is most likely to occur in the economically mobile upper and middle classes and in the industrial wage-earning working class. (M080)

### Community Isolation
The importance of kin ties is directly correlated with the degree of isolation and size of a community. (S111)

### Economic Dependence
Where the community is economically self-sufficient, role relationships are defined by kinship. (L072)

### Economic Dependence of Women
Where property relations are male-dominated, women place a higher emphasis on kinship ties. (R118)

### Economic Level
In societies with marginal economies and simple technology, kinship bonds tend to be of primary importance in defining social relations. (B075)

### Economic Pattern
If production in a society is based on the recruitment of labor through a kinship system, production organizations tend to be permanent and diffuse in nature. (U003)

### Economic Pattern (Market)
The part played by kinship in the mechanism for ordering social life diminishes as the economic relations which are critically important for maintaining the kinship system are replaced by the impersonal relations of the market. (W056)

### Economic Pattern (Trade)
The deterioration of the importance of kin ties as a framework for social relations tends to occur with the extension of economic ties through trade. (W075)

### Geographic Mobility
Kin affiliations will decrease in importance with an increase in geographical mobility. (B142)

### Isolation of Society
When the society is small and isolated, the family will play a large part in societal institutions. (F021)

### Kin Terminology
The social importance of a kin relationship will be reflected in the number of terms which may be used to describe the relationship. (G053)

### Kin Terminology (Classificatory)
When membership in a kin-group is of preeminent importance in defining social relations, members of the same group may be terminologically equated. (L060)

When lineage affiliation is important, all members of the lineage will be terminologically equated with the relative closest to ego who represents that lineage. (M082)

### Kin Ties (Fictive)
In societies where kinship ties form the major framework for social relations, fictive kin ties tend to be instituted for nonkinsmen who attach themselves to the residential group. (W075)

### Legal Structure
The legal system will tend to be minimally developed in societies which are structured along kinship lines. (H139)

### Occupational System
As the occupational system develops and absorbs functions in the society, it must be at the expense of the relative prominence of kinship organization. (P062)

### Political Structure
In the absence of political organization on the village level, kinship assumes a primary position as the major social bond. (E015)

Kin ties are of major importance in societies which lack a centralized system of political authority. (L072)

### Population
When the size of the population unit is small, social organization tends to be along kinship lines. (M033)

### Religion (Role of Deities)
The decline in the importance of kin ties will be associated with an increased emphasis on a deity associated with nonkin relationships. (W075)

### Social Structure (Homogeneity)
Where the society is characterized by a high degree of

social and cultural homogeneity role relationships tend to be defined by kinship. (L072)

### Stratification

Kin ties are of greater importance in defining social relationships in societies without a class system. (L072)

### Technology

The more "advanced" the technology, the more importance nonkinship structures assume in the system and the less kinship dominates the social structure. (P062)

### Warfare

Kinship ties beyond those of closest kin tend to be unimportant where wars of conquest have led to widespread dispersal. (E102)

## KINSHIP STRUCTURE, STABILITY OF
### X   Residence

The development, disappearance, or change in form of an extended family and clan follows an alteration in the rule of residence and is always consistent with the new rule. (M019)

# L

## LAND

**X Age at Marriage**
Where there is frontier land available, farmers tend to marry earlier. (G156)

**Cohesion Between Lineages**
The granting of land to individuals who are members of other lineages strengthens relations between lineages. (W056)

**Cohesion of Lineage**
When the lineage has control over land, it will have greater generational depth and, therefore, greater unity and strength than those lineages which have only movables to inherit. (G028)

**Conflict**
Intracommunity conflict occurs when lineages have unequal holdings in land (unless devices are developed to redistribute land rights to persons outside the owning group). (G029)

**Corporate Kin-Group**
Corporate kin landholding maintains kin ties. (F017)

**Marriage Chances**
When land is allocated directly by the village rather than through kin-groups, the percentage of adults married will be lower. (V025)

**Polyandry**
Polyandrous marriage is related to the scarcity of land and its low productivity. (B033)

**Residence**
The dispersal of kinsmen is more likely to occur when the kin-group does not have corporate ownership of land. (T039)

**Residence (Ambilocal)**
Patterns of ambilocal residence tend to arise in areas where there is an equal population pressure among land-owning kin-groups. (R054)

**Residence (Matrilocal)**
When there is a shortage of land controlled by the matrilineage, men will tend to reside with the lineage of their wives. (F019)

**Residence (Patrilocal)**
In matrilineal societies, patrilocal residence is more likely to occur if the settlement pattern permits ready access to the land of both lineages. (E108)

**Residence (Unilocal)**
Where land is abundant, unilocal residence rules develop. (G029)

Patterns of unilocal residence tend to deteriorate under conditions of land shortage. (R054)

**Stability of Family**
The stability of the farm family during a crisis is directly correlated with the degree of its attachment to the land. (B033)

**Stability of Kin-Group**
Descent groups are more likely to be stable and increase in size if membership gives rights to land as well as social status. (N071)

**Stability of Lineage**
A change in the direction of more individual forms of land holding would undoubtedly weaken the lineage system. (F073)

The persistence of a lineage as a corporate unit is directly correlated with its retention of control over land. (K058)

**Subsistence Pattern (Hunting)**
An economy based on nonmigratory animals encourages family ownership of territory. (S077)

**Subsistence Pattern (Hunting and Gathering)**
When the economy is on the level of hunting and food gathering, ownership of the land tends to be ascribed to the sib rather than to the individual family or person. (S072)

## LAND ALLOCATION

**X Inheritance (Unilineal)**
When the allocation of land, under patterns of unilinear inheritance, is no longer viewed as equitable, nonunilinear inheritance patterns will be adopted. (G029)

## LAND, AMOUNT OF

**X Polygyny**
An increase in the scarcity of land leads to fragmentation of holdings, which is conducive to a pattern of polygynous marriage. (W082)

## LAND CONSOLIDATION

**X Conflict**
Conflicts between larger kin units are less likely to occur if the land holdings of these units are not consolidated. (B299)

## LANGUAGE

**X Intermarriage (Ethnic)**
The rate of intermarriage tends to be higher when the ethnic groups in question share a common language. (L045)

## LEADERSHIP

**X Child-Rearing Practices (Giving Reasons)**
There is a positive relationship for boys and a negative relationship for girls between principled discipline by parents (reasoning with the child and apologizing for unfair treatment) and leadership abilities in the child (based on teachers' ratings of influence in group activities). (B250)

**Child-Rearing Practices (Punishment)**
Children who perceive themselves as autonomous and their parents as coercive (punishing) tend to be more active as leaders in their peer groups than others do. (H235)

**Cohesion of Family**
Members of integrated families are more likely to hold formal leadership positions in outside groups than are members from nonintegrated families. (S217)

### Parent-Child Relations (Affection)
There is a positive relationship for sons and a negative relationship for daughters between parental affection and leadership abilities in the child (based on teachers' ratings of influence in group activities). (B250)

### Parent-Child Relations (Companionship)
There is a positive relationship for sons and a negative relationship for daughters between parental companionship and leadership in the child (based on teachers' ratings of influence in group activities). (B250)

### Parent-Child Relations (Nurturance)
There is a positive relationship for sons and a negative relationship for daughters between parental nurturance and leadership abilities in the child (based on teachers' ratings of influence in group activities). (B250)

### Parent-Child Relations (Rejection)
Parental rejection and neglect are negatively related to leadership in the child (based on teachers' ratings of influence in group activities). This is especially true of the parent of the same sex as the child. (B250)

### Power Structure of Family
A home in which one parent is the principal disciplinarian is more likely to produce children with a sense of responsibility and leadership than is a home in which both parents are equally dominant. (B273)

### Sibling Structure (Age Difference)
The greater the age difference between siblings, the higher the child tends to be rated in leadership. (K149)

### Stability of Extended Family
The fission of a large extended family will tend to be inhibited if the leader is a person of character and experience. (A033)

## LEGAL RESPONSIBILITY
### X   Avoidance Relationship
In societies where children are subjected to extrusion from the household or brother-sister avoidance during the first stage of puberty (8-10 years), the concept of joint liability is found (i.e., liability falls on the members of an individual's descent group if the offender cannot be apprehended or meet his legal liability); in societies where neither extrusion nor brother-sister avoidance is found during the first stage of puberty, the concept of individual liability is found (i.e., the individual alone is held responsible for his acts). (C093)

### Genealogical Proximity
When the clan as a collectivity is responsible for the actions of its members, retaliatory action will tend to be taken against kinsmen who are most closely related to the defendent. (G039)

### Residence (Extrusion)
In societies where children are subjected to extrusion from the household or to brother-sister avoidance during the first stage of puberty (8 to 10 years), the concept of joint liability is found (i.e., liability falls on the members of an individual's descent group if the offender cannot be apprehended or meet his legal liability); in societies where neither extrusion nor brother-sister avoidance is found during the first stage of puberty, the concept of individual liability is found (i.e., the individual alone is held responsible and punished for his acts). (C093)

### Social Structure
Societies which are organized around the anchorage and identification of the individual in the wider kin-group have legal systems based on the principle of joint liability (i.e., if an offender cannot be apprehended or meet his legal liability, his liability falls on the members of his descent group); societies organized around the anchorage and identification of the individual in the nuclear family have legal systems based on the principle of several liability (i.e., the individual alone is held responsible and punished for his acts). (C093)

### Socialization, Agents of
In societies in which the children are brought up by their parents as well as by members of the children's descent group, the conception of joint liability will be found (i.e., liability falls on the members of an individual's descent group if the offender cannot be apprehended or meet his legal liability); in societies in which the children are brought up by their parents plus *nonmembers* of the children's descent group, the concept of several liability will be found (i.e., the individual alone is held responsible and punished for his acts). (C093)

## LEGAL STATUS   X   Authority Structure
The more closely associated a person (e.g., father) is to the status possessing the most jural authority (e.g., grandfather) in a hierarchy, the less likely he is to have an informal and equal relationship with his own subordinates in the hierarchy. (A009)

### Kin Relations (Closeness)
The character of a relationship between kinsmen tends to be more affectionate when neither is in a position of authority or legal superiority. (G055)

### Marriage Chances
A larger proportion of the population is likely to remain unmarried where there is equality of status between the sexes and where women have full jural rights without marriage. (N065)

### Monogamy
The status of the husband and wife is more likely to be equal when the marriage pattern is that of monogamy. (S123)

### Residence (Neolocal)
The legal statuses of husband and wife are more likely to be equal when the pattern of residence is neolocal. (S123)

## LEGAL STATUS OF WIFE   X   Class
The higher the class, the greater is the legal protection of the wife's financial needs. (G156)

### Divorce
Greater legal protection of the wife's financial needs increases the likelihood that she will seek a divorce. (G156)

### Preferential Marriage (Bilateral Cross-Cousin)
Bilateral cross-cousin marriage will occur in societies in which jural authority over a female is vested in the woman herself or is split between her matri- and patri-kin. (C126)

### Property Rights
The legal prerogatives of a woman will tend to be greater if she retains economic claims on the property of her natal family. (M063)

## LEGAL STATUS OF WOMEN
### X   Economic Dependence of Women
An increase in the economic independence of women will tend to be accompanied by an increase in their legal prerogatives. (O023)

### Rank of Women
Societies which grant women the rights to initiate divorce and to remarry in widowhood also grant them a higher rank (relative to men) than do societies which do not grant these rights. (G028)

### Stability of Family Structure
The breakdown of the family structure is reflected in an increase in litigation over women. (L079)

## LEGAL STRUCTURE          X   Cohesion of Family
Strong family relations are more likely to occur where the family is strongly supported by law. (F092)

### Divorce
Greater access to the legal agencies of the society that grant divorces is associated with higher divorce rates. (G156)

### Kinship, Importance of
The legal system will tend to be minimally developed in societies which are structured along kinship lines. (H139)

## LEGAL TIES               X   Conflict Among Kin
There is more likely to be tension between relatives when their relationship implies jural responsibilities. (F087)

## LIFE CYCLE               X   Employment of Wife
Family life cycle correlates more closely with the variations in working than does age. (L002)

### Kin Relations (Interaction)
Family relations are more likely to be reactivated in the last stage of a persons's life than in his occupational phase. (R120)

### Parent-Child Relations (Conflict)
Conflict between parents and child is partially a function of their being at different points in their life cycles and thus viewing differently many kinds of problems and opportunities. (G156)

## LINEAGE                  X   Divorce
Divorce becomes even more frequent in areas where lineages are weak or absent. (F073)

### Exogamy
In societies where lineages are found, marriage patterns will tend to be exogamous rather than endogamous. (G156)

### Fertility
The emphasis upon a high birth rate will be directly correlated with the strength of the lineage system. (F069)

### Political Structure
Lineage organization receives the highest degree of elaboration in societies which have a segmentary political structure. (F020)

### Population
The formation of a unilineal kin unit is associated with an increase in population. (S120)

### Preferential Marriage (Father's Brother's Daughter)
The institutionalization of father's brother's daughter marriage is associated with lineage organizations which are highly developed. (B087)

### Property
The development of lineage organization tends to be correlated with the presence of heritable land or livestock. (F020)

### Residence
Planned villages with wards tend to be associated with multilineage political units. (H147)

### Subsistence Pattern (Agriculture)
Almost all the tribes with a clan or gentile organization are agriculturists. (L128)

## LINEAGE COMMUNITIES              X   Descent
Monolineage communities are likely to be rarer in matrilineal than in patrilineal systems. Monolineage includes demes, agamous communities, exogamous barrios, wards, hamlets, and localized lineages. (A048)

## LINEAGE DEPTH              X   Community
Where the frequency of fissioning is such as to produce lineages of shallow depth and narrow span, the tendency for the village to become a kin-group is inhibited. (S283)

### Descent (Dual)
A limited depth of the unilineal descent group tends to occur in systems of dual descent. (G062)

## LINEAGE, IMPORTANCE OF
### X   Descent (Patrilineal/Matrilineal)
When family and lineage are nearly equal as principles of local organization, the merging of patrilineal and matrilineal kin as joint members of a single genealogical generation is more likely. (T080)

### Gerontocracy
One aspect of the declining influence of the lineage would appear to be a decline in the authority and respect granted older men. (F073)

### Husband-Wife Relations (Closeness)
The weakness of the husband-wife bond correlates with a strong lineage principle. (E101)

### Political Succession
When political offices are established as an achieved status, the importance of lineage status will be reduced. (S123)

### Polygyny
Fear of dying without an heir is one of the factors behind the polygynous system of marriage. (K158)

### Preferential Marriage (Levirate/Sororate)
The sororate and levirate are associated with greater social importnce of the clan or lineage. (S192)

### Rank
The importance of the lineage as a unit of social organization is directly correlated with social rank. (G101)

## LINEAGE/NUCLEAR FAMILY     X   Identification
Since a lineage is an indissoluble unit, it provides a more permanent sense of identification for the individual than does the nuclear family, which is dissoluble. (C093)

# LINEAGE RIGHTS
### X    Cohesion Between Lineages
The solidarity of bonds between lineages tends to be strengthened if the prerogatives which they possess are similar. (L070)

## LINEAGE TIES    X    Economic Pattern (Collective)
With a change from a collective economy to one based on individual activity, there is a loosening of the lineal and collateral bonds within the society. (H062)

### Husband-Wife Relations
When ties between lineage members are emphasized, bonds between the husband and wife are correspondingly of minimal importance. (H043)

### Marital Stability
When the allegiance to unilineal groups is paramount, marriage tends to be unstable. (B060)

Marital stability is inversely correlated with the importance of lineage ties. (F073)

### Nuclear Family, Importance of
The degree to which lineage affiliation is emphasized will be inversely correlated with the degree to which the nuclear family is emphasized. (S060)

### Political Role of Lineage
When lineage affiliations are politically important, lineage membership will tend to be more rigorously defined. (L065)

### Rank of Lineage
Ancient lineage affiliations with a more powerful lineage are more likely to be revived if the status of a lineage is low. (E047)

### Residence
Lineage affiliation will tend to be manipulated if the residence pattern has been violated. (F068)

The importance of lineage ties is directly correlated with the localization of the lineage. (F073)

Patterns of residence within a village tend to be determined by lineage affiliation. (R033)

### Size of Lineage
The retention of lineage identity tends to be directly correlated with its size. (E047)

### Warfare
Warfare between lineages tends to result in the realignment of lineage affiliations. (G031)

## LINEAGE TIES OF WIFE    X    Marital Stability
The complete legal identification of a wife with the lineage of her husband tends to result in marital stability. (F062)

When the lineage affiliation of the wife remains with her natal lineage after marriage, the lineage structure tends to undermine the stability of the marriage. (F062)

## LINEAGES, NUMBER OF
### X    Endogamy (Community)
When the village is composed of two or more lineages or clans, marriage is usually endogamous as to village. (W054)

## LONG HOUSE    X    Descent (Unilineal)
Long houses tend to be associated with a social organization which is unilineal in character. (L049)

# LOSS OF FAMILY MEMBER
### X    Emotional Adjustment
The greater the number of losses that have occurred before, the more likely it is that the loss of a member of the immediate family will be severely felt. (T091)

The longer it takes to secure a substitute, the more likely it is that the loss of a member of the immediate family will be severely felt. (T091)

The more recent the loss of a member of a person's immediate family, the more severe will be its psychological effects. (T091)

The older the member of the immediate family who has been lost, the more severe the psychological effects will be for the survivors. (T091)

The younger the person, the more severely will he be affected by the loss of a member of the immediate family. (T091)

### Extended/Nuclear Family
Death or absence of one of the adults more seriously impairs the effectiveness of the nuclear family than of the extended family. (G156)

### Marital Adjustment
The greater the person's loss of family members during childhood, the less likely is he to make a satisfactory adjustment to marriage. (T093)

### Mate Selection
Children from families which have lost (physically or psychologically) a member are more likely than those which have not to make unwise marriage decisions. (T089)

### Personality Development
The effects of the final loss (physically or psychologically) of a family member will be more severe the earlier in a person's life it occurs. (T089)

### Sex Composition of Family
The greater the imbalance of the sexes resulting from the final loss (either psychologically or physically) of a family member, the more severe will be the effects of that loss. (T089)

### Size of Family
The smaller the family, the more severe the effects of the final loss (either psychologically or physically) of a family member. (T089)

### Stability of Family
The effects of the final loss (either psychologically or physically) of a family member will be more severe if similar losses have occurred before. (T089)

The effects of the final loss (either psychologically or physically) of a family member will be more severe the longer it takes for the family to find a substitute. (T089)

### Surrogate Mother
There is a curvilinear relationship between the severity of losses suffered by women in their immediate families and the decision and ability to take on the occupation of "foster mother" for orphans. (T094)

## LOSS OF FATHER/MOTHER    X    Social Adjustment
After the age of five years, the loss of the father is more likely to have a detrimental effect on the social adjustment of the child than is the loss of the mother; before

five years, the loss of the mother has more effect. (H206)

## LOVE X Age at Marriage

The younger the individual when marriage is arranged, the lower the likelihood of a love relationship developing outside of the marriage bond. (G156)

### Child-Rearing Practices (Control)

The greater the freedom allotted to adolescents, the greater the likelihood that they will fall in love. (G156)

### Class

The role of romantic love in originating marriage is less in the upper classes. (P083)

### Courtship (Chaperonage)

The stricter the chaperonage system, the more able is the society to prevent love relationships from developing. (G156)

### Dependency

Love relationships during adolescence or young adult years help to reduce dependence on the family. (G156)

### Mate Selection

Decline of arranged marriages in a society is associated with an increase in love as a prominent factor in mate selection. (G156)

In a system where marriages are not prearranged, social patterns exist to motivate young persons to marry for love. (G156)

The more able a society is to prevent love from developing, the more able it is to control who marries whom. (G156)

### Mate Selection (Free Choice)

Love is likely to be an important criterion of mate selection if cultural conditions encourage premarital interaction between men and women in order to provide the opportunity for testing out personalities of a variety of potential mates. (W148)

Love is likely to be an important criterion of mate selection if cultural conditions stipulate that the choice of mates must be voluntary (i.e., not arranged by persons other than the marriage partners) and bilateral (i.e., both man and woman must possess at least the power of veto). (W148)

### Preferential Marriage

The narrower the specifications of which statuses can be legitimately linked in the marriage bond, the more able the society is to control love relationships. (G156)

### Sex Ratio

In a polygynous society, the short supply of eligible females may give rise to an idealization of sentimental love. (M067)

### Urbanization

The absence of strong primary group attachments among men in modern society has led to the modern ideal of marriage as a love match. (S030)

## LOVE MAGIC X Child-Rearing Practices (Sex)

Love magic is associated with a high sexual socialization anxiety (that is, childhood training emphasizes deprivation and punishment with respect to sex, producing adult anxieties). (H222)

### Mate Selection (Free Choice)

Love magic is likely to be absent when there is a puritanical sex code and the elders arrange all marriages. (H222)

### Sex Norms/Mate Selection (Free Choice)

Love magic is likely to be absent when there is a puritanical sex code and the elders arrange all marriages. (H222)

### Sex Relations

The elaboration of magical means for persuading a member of the opposite sex to engage in coital activity is less developed among people who use direct solicitation.

### Sex Status

Among the lower classes, women are more apt to resort to the use of magic to keep a man; men are more apt to resort to magic to get rid of women with whom they are living or to whom they are married. (R124)

# M

**MAGIC (SPIRITS)          X   Rank of Women**
If the rank of women is low, they are more likely to appear as male spirits. (F043)

**MANAGEMENT (FAMILY-BASED)      X   Property**
Familial and custodial organizations are more likely to be headed by manager-proprietors; contractual or voluntary organizations involve corporate proprietorship. (U003)

**MARGINAL STATUS**
                    **X   Mental Illness (Manic-Depressive)**
Manic-depressives are more likely to come from families who are in minority groups (social, economic, ethnic, or religious). (S181)

**Personality Problems of Child**
Children raised in a dissonant social context (where 25 per cent or less are of the same religion or ethnicity) are more likely to manifest symptoms of emotional disturbance than are children raised in a mixed or consonant social context. (R092)

**Scapegoating**
When parents have a marginal status in a community, they tend to discharge unresolved tensions by making a child the focus of their hostility. (B204)

**Social Change**
The individuals who are the initial acceptors of innovation tend to be those with marginal or ill-defined familial status. (R004)

**MARGINAL STATUS OF CHILD**
                                **X   Intermarriage**
The children of intermarriages are more likely to lack adequate identification and to have marginal status than are the children of homogamous parents. (B012)

**MARITAL ADJUSTMENT           X   Abortion**
There is an inverse relation between abortion and the marital adjustment of wives. (K161)

**Achievement**
If (as in the lower class) the husband is not expected to be an economic success, marital satisfaction is not affected by his failure to achieve it. (G014)

**Adjustment of Child**
A correlation exists between marriage adjustment and the child's adjustment. (F094)

**Adultery**
Marital conflict is likely to characterize most relationships when extramarital relations are prevalent. (H074)

There is a direct relation between fidelity and marital adjustment. (K161)

There is no difference between those who are highly satisfied with their marriages and those who are not, regarding whether or not they have been involved in extramarital sexual and/or emotional relationships. (N062)

**Adultery (Fantasy)**
The lower a person's marital satisfaction (as measured by Anselm Strauss's Marital Satisfaction Scale), the more likely is he to have fantasy involvements in extramarital relationships. (N062)

**Affinal Relations**
Marital adjustment is more likely when the engaged couple like their future fathers-in-law and mothers-in-law very much. (B033)

There is a direct relation between favorable relations with in-laws and marital adjustment. (K161)

Couples who are approved by the respective in-laws before marriage are more likely to be adjusted in marriage than are couples who are not approved. (L004)

**Age**
Marital problems as well as feelings of inadequacy progressively decrease with age. (G126)

There is no relationship between age and the reported level of marital happiness. (G126)

There is no relationship between age and the types of problems reported in the marital relationship. (G126)

**Age at Marriage**
An early age at marriage is predictive of marital unhappiness. (B033)

Marital happiness is directly related to early age at marriage. (B033)

**Age Difference**
The greater the age difference between spouses, the more likely it is that serious conflict will develop within the marriage. (T109)

**Age of Husband/Wife**
Marriage is most likely to be successful if the spouses are of the same age or if the wife is younger than the husband. (S244)

**Alcoholism**
The more a husband's alcoholism provides unconscious gratification for both partners, the more resistant to change are both the alcoholism and the marital conflict which it generates. (B225)

**Alcoholism of Child**
The greater the degree of parental conflict, the more likely the child will become an alcoholic. (M195)

**Alcoholism of Husband**
There is a correlation between alcoholism of the husband and intense marital conflict. (M195)

**Authoritarianism**
There is greater marital maladjustment (measured by the Burgess-Cottrell Marriage Adjustment Schedule) among authoritarian than among democratic families. (K113)

### Authority Structure of Family
Marital adjustment is positively associated with equality of authority in the family. (C023)

### Autoeroticism
There is no evidence that restraint against female masturbation is favorable to marital adjustment. (K161)

### Beauty of Women
There is a direct relation between the physical attractiveness of women and marital adjustment. (K161)

### Behavior Problems
Unsatisfactory relations between adults in the home is correlated with maladjusted behavior of the child, both at home and at school. (C117)

### Behavior Problems (Running Away)
Disturbed marital relations are associated with running away from home in girls. (R102)

### Bereavement
Orphans are less likely to have favorable marital adjustments than are people from backgrounds with one or both parents living. (K161)

### Birth Control
Couples who are able to control fertility according to their desires have a higher marital adjustment. (F002)

Marital-role tension is not related to the ability to estimate successfully future family size. (F002)

### Broken Home
Among married persons, those who were reared in divorced homes are more likely to feel inadequacies in their present marital relationship and to admit to problems in their marriages than are those from families in which one or both parents have died or from families that remained intact. (G126)

### Child-Rearing Practices (Discipline)
There is a direct relation between mild, firm childhood discipline and marital adjustment. (K161)

The type of home discipline which most tends to be associated with marital happiness is that which is described as "firm," not "harsh." (T079)

### Child-Rearing Practices (Punishment)
Parents who employ ridicule as a means of discipline are less likely to be well adjusted to each other than are those who do not. (B243)

### Child-Rearing Practices (Sex Role)
The child is more likely to learn, and to be rewarded for, sex-appropriate behavior in families characterized by interparental harmony. (P064)

### Child-Rearing Values (Punishment)
The father's approval of the use of physical punishment correlates with marital conflict. (N053)

### Childhood (Emotional Security)
Satisfactory marital adjustment is more likely when both partners experienced emotionally secure childhoods than it is when one or both partners recall an insecure childhood. (P086)

### Children
The number of children in the family does *not* affect marital tension. (F002)

### Children, Evaluation of
Husbands who feel that children are an aid to college achievement have higher marital adjustment scores than husbands who feel that children disturb college achievement (U.S.). (C003)

### Children, Number of
There is no direct correlation between the presence or absence of children or the number of children and marital happiness (I007)

### Class
There is a positive correlation between socioeconomic class and marital satisfaction scores. (G134)

Lower-class paranoid schizophrenics see their parents as more ill-suited for each other than do middle-class paranoid schizophrenics. (L155)

Marital adjustment of spouses varies directly with their social class. (R011)

Marital adjustment does not have any association with the social class of the spouse's parents, except that the lower-lower class has poorer adjustment than do the other classes. (R011)

### Class and Employment
Working-class-working-wife group has more husband-wife disagreements than do other groups. (H175)

### Conformity
Marital adjustment is associated with a high degree of conventional behavior. (B033)

### Courtship
There is a direct relation between conflict-free engagement and marital adjustment. (K161)

### Courtship, Duration of
The longer the courtship and engagement, the more likely it is that the marriage will be well adjusted. (C134)

### Criminality
There is a correlation between parental conflict and criminal behavior of the son. (M195)

### Criminality/Alcoholism
An attitude of indifference (rather than of either affection or conflict) between the parents is most likely to produce criminal behavior in the son, but is least likely to create alcoholism. (M195)

### Dating
The more successful youth are in the competitive area of dating, the less prepared they may be for marital adjustment. (S219)

Cultures that approve of dating do not necessarily produce young people that are better adjusted socially or able to make more satisfactory choices of their marriage partners. (M185)

### Death of Mother
Men who have lost mothers have oral problems and express in their marital relationships unusual dependency and hostility. (A070)

### Dependency
Couples who plan to be independent of their parents have a greater chance for marital success. (B244)

### Divorce
Divorced men are more likely to have had better adjust-

ment during the early years of marriage than are men who remain married. (P071)

Divorced women have less satisfactory marital adjustment during the early years of marriage than do women who remain married. (P071)

### Duration of Marriage
The better the marital adjustment during the early stages of marriage, the greater the chance for marital success. (M185)

The longer the length of the marriage, the poorer the marital adjustment. (P086)

### Economic Role of Husband
The husband's economic role (e.g., a combination of length of time in position, regularity of employment, amount of income, and amount of savings) is not related to his marital happiness rating. (G157)

### Economic Security
There is a greater degree of marital adjustment among couples with security as indicated by savings, lack of indebtedness, and insurance than among couples without this security. (W005)

### Education
The higher the educational level, the greater the individual's chance for marital success. (B244)

College-educated husbands who feel that college attendance aids marital adjustment have a higher marital adjustment score than do husbands who feel that it disturbs marital adjustment. (C003)

The higher the educational level, the more likely are persons to report feelings of inadequacies and marital problems. (G126)

When age is controlled, the relationship between high educational level and greater marital problems reported does not exist. (G126)

A positive relationship exists between the educational level of husband and wife and marital happiness. (G157)

Wives, but not husbands, are less happy if they have more education than their spouses. (G157)

Men tend to be happier if they are more educated than their wives; wives are slightly less happy if they have equal education. (G157)

The higher the educational backgrounds of blue collar workers, the more involved they are emotionally in their marriages. (K089)

### Education Difference Between Husband-Wife
Wives with husbands who have superior education make higher happiness scores than wives who are superior to their husbands in education. (C023)

### Education of Husband-Wife
Marital adjustment is more likely when both the husband and wife are college graduates and have had postgraduate or professional training. (B033)

Equality in education is conducive to better marital adjustment. (G157)

The higher the education, the better the marital adjustment. (O001)

### Education of Wife
If the wife's education exceeds that of the husband's by three or more years, a great amount of conflict is apt to arise in the family. (B033)

Marital happiness is greater among couples where the wife has more than a high-school education than where the wife has less than a high-school education. (B033)

### Elopement
Marital adjustment is negatively correlated with elopement. (C023)

### Emotional Adjustment
Marital adjustment is more likely when the husband and wife are emotionally stable. (B033)

### Emotional Problems
Emotional disturbance of married couples tends to be directly correlated with an attitude of severe disappointment of each partner with each other and with the marriage. (V028)

### Emotional Problems of Child
Parents who devaluate one another are more likely to have emotionally disturbed children than are parents who do not. (M200)

Emotionally disturbed children are more likely than relatively healthy children to come from families in which the marriage relationship of the parents is disturbed. (V028)

### Empathy
The more empathy from her husband the wife receives in her emotional problems, the more successful is the marriage. (S279)

When confronted with hypothetical family situations in which husband and wife must deal with role conflict, couples whose marriages were "in trouble" were less likely than those whose marriage were "not in trouble" to choose solutions which involved taking the role of the other and were characterized by less sympathy and agreement on a course of action to take. (S279)

There is no significant relationship found between empathy (defined as "taking the role of another with sufficient accuracy so that one can predict his response") and marital adjustment (Locke, Sabagh, and Thomes). (S279)

Couples who deal with conflict by remaining ignorant of each other's plans tend to be better adjusted than those who do not. (S279)

Marital happiness increases with an individual's ability to predict accurately the spouse's reactions to situations. (T092)

Marital happiness increases when self-perception and the spouse's perception are congruent. (T092)

### Employment of Mother
Employment of the mother does not change the general level of happiness in the marriage. (G156)

Employment of the mother increases the frequency of marital conflict. (G156)

There is no relationship in lower-class families between the employment of the mother and conflict between husband and wife. (M211)

Regardless of class, nonemployed mothers are more

likely to have well-adjusted marriage relationships. (N058)

Employment/nonemployment of the mother does not correlate with the extent of her sexual and marital adjustment. (S265)

Health status, marital, sexual, and emotional adjustment, and number and seriousness of child problems do not correlate with employment or nonemployment of the mother. (S265)

Employed mothers are more likely to report quarrelling in the family, to have lived apart from their husbands, and to have considered divorce. (S265)

### Employment of Wife

Couples in which the wife does not work or only works part time are likely to be better adjusted than are couples in which the wife works full time.

If the wife wants to work but does not, her level of marital adjustment will be lower. (G156)

Size of family does not affect the fact that nonemployed women have better-adjusted marriages than employed women. (N058, N063)

Women who have remarried after divorce, annulment, or widowhood are likely to have more successful marriages if they are employed than if they are not. (N058, N063)

The failure to segregate lines of achievement will result in competition for status between husband and wife which may be disruptive of the solidarity of the marriage. (P012)

Marital satisfaction is independent of whether or not the wife works. (S257)

### Employment of Wife, Attitude Toward

In families where the wife works, the husband's disapproval of her working is related to a lower level of marital adjustment. (G156)

### Employment (Regularity)

Regularity of the husband's employment is positively related to marital adjustment. (G157)

### Engagement, Duration of

The longer the period of acquaintance in courtship and engagement, the higher the probability of a successful marriage. (B033)

Long engagement periods are correlated with reports of marital happiness. (G156)

### Father-Son Relations (Affection)

Marriages generally need less dominant-submissive adjustment when the male has had close affectionate ties with his father. (T092)

### Father-Son Relations (Closeness of)

The husband's close attachment to his father in family of orientation is correlated with reports of marital happiness in family of procreation. (G156)

### Father-Son Relations (Evaluation)

Marital happiness is directly related to the congruence between the husband's self-perception and his perception of his father. (T092)

### Fertility

Doubts concerning marital adjustment may lead to not having children. (B244)

### Fertility Values

The higher the marital satisfaction of the two partners, the larger the number of children preferred.

### Friendship

Marital adjustment is more likely to occur when the husband and wife have many friends in common. (B033)

Persons who have had many friends, both male and female, are more likely to have marital success. (B244)

### Happiness

A spouse's general happiness is more closely related to satisfaction with the social-emotional aspects of a marriage relationship than with the tasks and decisions in marriage or the husband's work. (L173)

### Happiness in Childhood

There is a direct correlation between marital adjustment and the spouse's degree of happiness in childhood. (B033)

### Health

Marital adjustment is associated with good health in the husband and wife. (B033)

### Homogamy

There is a positive association between marital adjustment and a similarity in the family backgrounds of the husband and wife. (B033)

### Homogamy (Class)

Marital adjustment is higher in same-class than in cross-class marriages. (C023)

Marital adjustment tends to vary directly with the closeness of the social class of one spouse to the social class of the other spouse. (R011)

There is no association between marital adjustment and the closeness of the social class of the parents of one spouse to the social class of the parents of the other spouse. (R011)

Marital adjustment varies directly with the closeness of the social class of the parents of one spouse to the social class of the parents of the other spouse. (R011)

### Homogamy (Cultural)

People with similar cultural backgrounds have fewer marital-adjustment problems than do people with different cultural backgrounds. (B033)

### Homogamy (Ethnic/Religious)

There is a direct relation between ethnic and religious similarity and marital adjustment. (K161)

### Homogamy (Personality)

Marital happiness is a function of similarity in personality. (C023)

### Household Composition

The greater the number of adults other than husband and wife residing in the home, the more likely is disharmony between marital partners. (C117)

When other adults than the parents live in the home, the fewer the outside interests of the former, the greater the conflict between the latter. (C117)

## Husband-Wife Relations
The success of the marriage will depend upon the satisfaction of the fundamental personality needs like love, affection, self-fulfillment, and prestige. (B033)

### Husband-Wife Relations (Affection)
There is a direct relation between expressions of affection and marital adjustment. (K161)

Decline of agreement on affectional activity in the marital relationship is highly associated with a decline in marital adjustment. (P071)

### Husband-Wife Relations (Consensus)
The greater the disagreement on domestic values, the lower the marital integration of the couple. (F116)

Marital satisfaction tends to be directly correlated with a common definition of interest between the husband and wife. (G050)

Couples who have shared attitudes toward activities are more likely to have better marital adjustment than are couples who do not have shared attitudes toward activities. (L004)

Couples who are well adjusted are more likely to have congruent perceptions of each other than are maladjusted couples. (L152)

### Husband-Wife Relations (Dependency)
Marital adjustment is better where the wife feels greater dependency on the husband than the husband does on the wife. (P071)

### Husband-Wife Relations (Disagreements)
Couples who settle disagreements by compromise rather than by one or the other giving in have a better chance for marital success. (B244)

### Husband-Wife Relations (Egalitarianism)
The relationship between well-adjusted mates is more likely than that between poorly adjusted mates to be one of equality. (L004)

### Husband-Wife Relations (Emotional Interdependence)
Happily married couples have a higher degree of emotional interdependence than unhappily married couples do. (B033)

### Husband-Wife Relations (Evaluation)
Couples who are well adjusted are more likely to have congruent perceptions of each other than are maladjusted couples. (L152)

Happily married couples exhibit less realism in their personality appraisals than do unhappily married couples. (T092)

Marital happiness increases with the perceived similarity between self and spouse. (T092)

Marital happiness is not directly related to the wife's self-perception and the husband's perception of the wife. (T092)

### Husband-Wife Relations (Interaction)
The degree of physical separation between husband and wife is directly correlated with emotional disturbance. (V028)

### Husband-Wife Relations (Power)
Husbands are more likely to be adjusted to the marriage if they submit to the domination of the wife and grant her deference and respect; wives are more likely to be adjusted if they defer to the husband's judgment and expect less deference and respect from their husbands. (T092)

### Husband-Wife Relations (Shared Activities)
Couples who enjoy sharing the same activities have a greater chance of marital success. (B244)

The degree of leisure activities shared after marriage is not highly related to the degree of disenchantment felt in the marital relationship. (P071)

### Husband-Wife Relations (Shared Interests)
There is a direct relation between a community of interest (in terms of joint participation in outside activities, mutual friends, agreement on social values, and agreement on family values) and marital adjustment. (K161)

### Husband-Wife Relations (Speaking Patterns)
If one spouse needs little social stimulus to begin talking, while the other needs a greater stimulus and also perceives the former spouse's voice as irritating, the happiness score of the couple is likely to be low.

### Husband-Wife Relations (Understanding)
The more responding and understanding the husband is about his wife's emotional problems, the higher is the wife's satisfaction with the marriage life.

### Identification of Mother with Daughter
Mothers who have a high degree of identification with their daughters tend to view their marriages more positively than do mothers who fail to identify with their daughters. (H218)

### Identification with Like-Sex Parent
Men who are satisfied with their marriages are likely to identify more strongly with their fathers than are men who are unsatisfied with their marriages. (L140)

### Identification with Parents
The greater the conflict between the parents, the more likely it is that the resolution of the Oedipal conflict through identification with the same-sex parent will be impeded.

### Income
Wives from very-low-income families or from very-high-income families tend to be more satisfied with their marriages, as compared with wives from middle-income families.

Marital adjustment is associated with a moderate income at marriage, rather than with a low or high income. (B033)

Insufficient income is the most frequent source of marital conflict among both husbands and wives. (B033)

Excluding wives who hold professional jobs, there is no relationship between income and marital happiness for either spouse. (G157)

Feeling that one's income is adequate is positively related to marital adjustment. (G157)

The lower the income of a family, the more likely it is that the marriage will be unhappy. (K089)

### Income, Attitude Toward
Unhappy men more often consider it essential or desirable that the wife be financially independent of the husband and more often believe that marriage should be

postponed until income is adequate to prevent serious skimping. (T074)

### Institutional Care
Among Catholic parents, marital adjustment is not related to whether the retarded child is living at home or is institutionalized. (J027)

Among Protestant and Jewish families, lower level of marital adjustment is related to the retarded child living at home rather than being institutionalized. (J027)

### Interaction in Family
Marital success is more likely when the couples have grown up in a harmonious and understanding family environment. (C023)

### Interaction in Family (Intimacy)
Marital adjustment is positively associated with intimacy of association within the family. (C023)

### Intermarriage (Racial)
Marital happiness is lower for intermarriages than for marriages of the same race and/or religion. (B033)

### Intermarriage (Religious)
Mixed-faith marriages are associated with a slightly lower level of marital satisfaction than are nonmixed marriages. (B300)

### I.Q.
Marital adjustment is higher when one spouse perceives the other's mental ability as equal to that of his or her own. (B033)

### Juvenile Delinquency
If the husband and the wife have an incompatible marriage relationship, the child is more likely to become delinquent.

Among the predictors of nondelinquent behavior, the happiness of the marriage has greater predictive power than whether the parents have remarried or whether the child is living with both or only one. (N057)

A home in which the insecurities of the parents cause them to quarrel severely is more likely to produce delinquent children than the home in which normal disagreements are worked out among the members. (S226)

### Juvenile Delinquency/Neurosis
Disturbed emotional relationships occur more frequently between the parents of delinquent children than between the parents of neurotic children. (B214)

### Loss of Family Member
The greater the person's loss of family members during childhood, the less likely is he to make a satisfactory adjustment to marriage. (T093)

### Marital Adjustment of Parents
Persons who have parents whose marriages were happy are more likely to report happiness in their marriage relationships. (G156)

Persons who are happily married are more likely than divorced persons to rate the marriages of their parents as happy. (L012)

### Marital Stability
Widespread marital instability tends to result in a situation of conflict and mutual distrust between husband and wife. (G094)

The greater the need satisfaction in marriage, the greater the likelihood of marital stability. (G134)

### Marital Status
Marital adjustment is higher when the parents of the husband and wife are not divorced or separated. (B033)

The widowed are more successful than the divorced in remarriage. (B286)

### Marriage, Approval of
Marital adjustment is higher when the marriage has been approved by both parents. (B033)

Persons whose marriage was approved by friends and parents are more likely to have marital success. (B244)

There is a direct relation between approval of the marriage by peers and marital adjustment. (K161)

### Marriage, Attitude Toward
There is a direct relation between a high aspiration level for marriage and subsequent disillusionment. (K161)

There is a relationship between the marital happiness of parents and their children's attitudes toward marriage. (S279)

### Marriage Ceremony, Type of
Marital adjustment is higher when the husband and wife have been married by a minister or priest. (B033)

People married at home, at church, or at the minister's home are likely to have better marital adjustment than are people married by a justice of the peace. (L012)

### Maternal Role
Women's greater disenchantment during the middle years of marriage is partly a function of the birth of a child. (P071)

In emotionally disturbed marriages, the management of the children tends to be exclusively handled by the wife. (V028)

### Maternal Role, Attitude Toward
When the marriage is a happy one, the wife is more likely to see the children as a source of satisfaction to her.

### Maternal-Role Behavior
The greater the integration of the marriage, the greater the role of the mother as mediator between father and child, reinforcing the norms of the former. (F094)

### Mental Illness
Mental illness tends to be correlated with marital dissatisfaction on the part of the patient's mother. (L118)

### Mental Illness of Child, Adjustment to
Couples who are unhappily married are less likely than those who are happily married to accept or cope well with the psychotic child. (C109)

### Mental Illness of Child (Schizophrenia)
The greater the marital conflict, as well as the disturbance of the individual parent, the more likely it is that the child will be schizophrenic. (F110)

Schizophrenic children are somewhat less likely than normals to view their parents as getting along very well; they are about as likely as normals to view their parents as getting along fairly well. (K114)

The "infantile" adolescent schizophrenics are more likely to come from unhappy families in which the parents became mistrustful of each other early in their marriage and showed no capacity for flexible cooperation. (S208)

### Mental Illness of Child (Schizophrenia/Neurosis)
Schizophrenic children are more likely than neurotic children to have parents who are incompatible and emotionally disturbed. (M197)

### Mental Illness (Schizophrenia)
Mothers of schizophrenics are more likely than mothers of neurotics or of normals to have negative attitudes toward their marriages, particularly toward the sexual aspect, which they tend to find repulsive. (M218)

### Mental Retardation
The presence of a retarded child is associated with increased problems in parents' marital adjustment. (J027)

### Mother-Child Relations
When the immature mother can stabilize her own emotional functioning and anxiety level through caring for her schizophrenic child, the father can establish a less anxious relationship with the mother. (B297)

The greater the integration of role relations in the marriage, the greater the integration of the mother-child relationship. (F094)

### Mother-Child Relations (Acceptance)
There is a correlation between the mother's marriage adjustment and her acceptance of her child. (F094)

### Mother-Child Relations (Affection)
Among white collar families, a favorable view of the parents' marriage by the child is positively related to maternal affection. (H201)

Among blue collar families, a favorable view of the parents' marriage is negatively related to maternal affection. (H201)

### Mother-Child Relations (Conflict)
An important factor in determining whether or not a marriage will be a happy one is whether or not there was an absence of conflict with the mother in the husband's and wife's childhoods. (B270)

### Mother-Child Relations (Rejection/Hostility)
Unsatisfactory marital relations which cause the mother to contemplate returning to work may lead to rejection and hostility displayed toward the child. (G128)

### Neurosis
Neuroticism is correlated with poor marital adjustment among women, but not among men (Cornell Medical Index of Neurosis). (P086)

### Nonkin Relations
There is a direct relation between friendships outside the family and memberships in organizations and marital adjustment. (K161)

### Nonkin Ties
The less happily married a woman is, the more likely she is to have confidants outside the family. (K089)

### Occupation
There is no relationship between the occupation of the husband at the time of marriage and marital adjustment. (G157)

Professional and semiprofessional persons are more likely to have higher marital-adjustment scores. (G157)

Men's greater disenchantment during the early years of

marriage is partly a function of the reality of the occupational commitment. (P071)

There is a greater degree of marital adjustment among couples where the husbands are in white collar, professional, or executive occupations than where they are in manual occupations. (W004)

### Occupational Achievement
There is an inverse relation between the occupational success of women and successful marital adjustment. (K161)

### Oedipal Complex
Women who are satisfied with their marriages are likely to perceive a greater similarity between their husbands and their fathers than are women unsatisfied with their marriages. (L140)

### Ordinal Position
Children in middle ordinal positions will, in general, adjust better to the problems of courtship and marriage than will younger or older siblings, but these last two may be more intensely happy if they make the right choices. (T089)

The duplication of early (incestuous) relationships with siblings in marriage is more likely for "middle" children than for oldest or youngest. (T091)

Early sibling relationships which are not duplicated in the individual's marriage are more likely to interfere with marital adjustment in the case of "middle" children than in that of the oldest or youngest. (T091)

### Parent-Child Relations
There is a correlation between unsatisfactory relations between parents and unsatisfactory relations between parents and child. (C117)

Satisfactory parent-child relations is a more important factor in the marital adjustment of democratic families than of authoritarian families. (K113)

The more satisfactory the parent-child relationship, the better the marital adjustment of the children. (K113)

### Parent-Child Relations (Closeness)
There is a direct relation between attachment to parents and successful marital adjustment. (K161)

The lower the success of the parental relationship (measured by parents' self-appraisals of marital happiness), the less close the child-parent relationship. (L137)

Children who are closer to their fathers are more likely to view their parents' marriage as happier than are children who are closer to their mothers. (L137)

The closer the child-parent relationship, the more likely is the child to perceive the parents' relationship as happy. (L137)

The closer the child is to both parents rather than to one, the more likely he will be to view his parents' marriage as a happy one. (L137)

### Parent-Child Relations (Conflict)
Marital adjustment is associated with the absence of conflict in the relationship of the husband and wife with their respective parents. (B033)

The happier men and women rate their parents' marriages, the less likely are they to report conflicts with either of their parents. (K113)

### Parent-Child Relations (Control)
There is less correlation between expression of dominating or controlling attitudes toward children and other family satisfactions for the father than for the mother. (N053)

### Parent-Child Relations (Evaluation)
The greater the parents' mutual satisfaction, the greater their satisfaction with their children. (F094)

### Parent-Child Relations (Hostility)
A child is apt to become the focus of parental hostility when parents do not resolve tensions between themselves in other ways. (B204)

### Parent-Child Relations (Interaction)
Emotionally disturbed marriages tend to be characterized by a minimal amount of common contact with the children. (V028)

### Parent-Child Relations (Preference)
For younger children there is no correlation between the quality of the marriage and the child's attitudes toward the parents. With older children, however, the less adequate the marriage, the more likely it is that the mother will be preferred over the father. (L150)

### Parent-Child Relations (Rejection)
Parental rejection of children is associated with these family characteristics: one parent regards the other as clearly inferior, there is greater neglect of marital responsibilities, and a greater likelihood of marital infidelity.

There is an association between marital conflict and nonacceptance of the child. (R100)

### Parental Role, Attitude Toward
Marital adjustment is associated with the desire of both the husband and wife to have children. (B033)

There is a direct relation between the desire for children and marital adjustment. (K161)

Marital conflict correlates with the father's attitudes of rejection of family life, justification of quarreling, and a rejection of interaction with the child. (N053)

### Peer Relations
There is no relationship between marital adjustment and the child's relations with his peers for either authoritarian or democratic families. (K113)

### Personality
The greater the psychological insight of the individual, the more likely it is that he will choose an appropriate spouse and have a successful marriage.

Persons who are easygoing, have a modest sense of self-respect, and a sense of duty and honor have a better chance for marital success than do persons who are ambitious, moody, dominating, and nervous. (B244)

### Personality (Adaptability)
Adaptability is associated with marital adjustment and success. (B033)

### Personality Adjustment
Loss of marital adjustment is not associated with loss of personal adjustment. (P071)

### Personality (Altruism)
There is no relationship between altruism and marital adjustment. (S279)

### Personality of Father/Husband (Similarity)
Marital happiness is directly related to the congruence between the wife's perception of her husband and her perception of her father. (T092)

### Personality of Husband (Fantasy)
Unhappy husbands more often report a liking for activities usually considered adventurous or spectacular. There is a greater tendency on the part of unhappy men to compensate for their lesser self-confidence or their failure to command response by fantasies feeding the desire for recognition. Unhappy men also daydream more than do happy husbands. (T074)

### Personality of Husband/Wife
Marital success is correlated with the temperamental compatibility of the husband and wife. (B033)

### Personality of Spouse
There is a direct relation between the degree of knowledge of a spouse's personality and marital adjustment. (K161)

Marital satisfaction (measured by Locke and Terman Marital Adjustment Scales) is significantly related to description of spouse as a responsible, generous, cooperative, moderately dominant, and conventional person. (L154)

Marital dissatisfaction (measured by Locke and Terman Marital Adjustment Scales) is significantly related to perception of spouse as having extreme or intense qualities, being skeptical, distrustful, blunt, aggressive, and either too dictatorial or too passive. (L154)

### Personality of Wife (Acceptance of Others)
Marital happiness of both husbands and wives is related to the wives' acceptance of others. (E099)

### Personality Problems
Unsatisfactory relations between adults in the home are correlated with symptoms of maladjustment in both mothers and fathers. (C117)

### Personality Problems of Child
The more that the child is forced into inappropriate roles by conflict between his parents, the more likely it is that he will develop psychological disturbances.

### Physical Appearance of Husband/Wife
The higher the rating of the husband on physical appearance (i.e., attractiveness), the better the marital adjustment. This hypothesis is also denied. (K012)

The higher the rating of the wife on physical appearance, the better the marital adjustment. (K012)

Couples in which wives have higher ratings on physical appearance (i.e., are better looking) than their husbands have better marital adjustment than do couples in which wives do not have higher ratings on physical appearance than their husbands. (K012)

When there is a difference between husband and wife in rating on physical appearance, the smaller the difference, the better the marital adjustment. (K012)

### Polygyny
Mormon men take a second wife when their first marriage has been inadequate or unsuccessful. (B033)

### Power Structure of Family
Democratic marital relations are directly related to marital adjustment. (K161)

In marriages where there is low satisfaction, husbands are more apt to feel they have less influence in decision making than when marriages are highly satisfying. (L173)

Couples who make more decisions jointly (e.g., pertaining to money, child rearing, coping with crises) are more likely to be better adjusted in marriage. (P086)

Relationships which are male dominated are more likely to receive poor marital adjustment ratings than are those which are female dominated or those which are in "equilibrium." (P086)

Good marital adjustment is more likely to occur where spouse relations are equalitarian; when either spouse is dominant in the relationship, adjustment is likely to be poor. (S279)

### Pregnancy Anxiety
Women who were highly anxious during pregnancy evidence more marital conflict than do those who were not as anxious during pregnancy. (D067)

### Pregnancy, Attitude Toward
A happy reaction to their conceiving is more likely among wives who rate their marriages as happy than among those who rate their marriages as less than happy or unhappy. (P003)

### Pregnancy, Sexual Desire During
Those husbands and wives who had more sexual desire during pregnancy than before pregnancy were happier than either those who had the same degree of desire or less desire. (A significant reduction in sex desire of most respondents as pregnancy progressed was reported.) (L013)

### Premarital Acquaintance
There is a direct correlation between marital adjustment and the length of premarital acquaintance. (B033)

### Premarital Pregnancy
There is no association between premarital conception and marital adjustment. (P086)

### Premarital Sex Relations
Marital happiness is greater among couples who had no premarital sexual relationships than among couples who had premarital sexual relationships. (B033)

Those husbands and wives who were either virgins at marriage or had had intercourse only with their future spouses tend to have higher mean happiness scores than do the other groups. (T079)

### Property
There is a direct correlation between marital adjustment and home ownership and insurance. (B033)

### Rank of Family
Persons who come from a family that is respected in the community are more likely to have marital success. (B244)

### Religion
Marital adjustment is associated with the membership of both the husband and wife in the same church. (B033)

### Religion (Church Membership)
Marital satisfaction is directly related to being affiliated with a church. (B001)

### Religiosity
Marital satisfaction is directly related to church attendance. (B001)

Those who are happily married tend to be highly religious. (B033)

Religious wives experiencing low sexual satisfaction will have greater marital satisfaction than will nonreligious wives. (W001)

Sexual drive held constant, religiously oriented women are more apt to feel highly satisfied with their marriages than are nonreligious women. (W155)

### Religiosity of Women
Religious women accept more easily the frustrations in their marital lives that would lead nonreligious women to overt counteraggression. (P083)

### Remarriage
There is an inverse relation between men having been divorced prior to this marriage and marital adjustment in the succeeding marriage. (K161)

### Residence
Premarital residential propinquity will tend to be correlated with marital adjustment in societies where interdistrict relations are characterized by hostility. (B088)

Couples who plan to live in a small or suburban community rather than in a metropolitan city have a greater chance for marital success. (B244)

### Role Behavior
Couples are more apt to agree on expected success in joint task performance when they are highly satisfied with their marriages than when they are less satisfied. (L173)

Couples with low satisfaction in marriage are just as apt to perform well in joint tasks as are couples highly satisfied with their marriages. (L173)

### Role Behavior of Husband-Wife
Spouses who see each other as fulfilling an expressive (warm and emotionally comforting) role tend to be better adjusted in marriage than do those who do not. (K153)

Marital conflict tends to occur when there is a failure to conform to the ideal roles of the husband and wife. (L048)

There is a correlation between marital satisfaction and the individual's playing the role he expects and the spouse's playing the role expected of him, regardless of the content of the roles. (T092)

There is a correlation between marital satisfaction and the degree to which the husband conforms to his wife's role expectations of him, but not the wife's conformity to the husband's expectations. (T092)

### Role Definition
The degree of marital integration varies directly with the degree to which the husband values the socioemotional aspects of interaction. (T092)

### Role Definition in Family
Joint recreation and joint participation in activities by all family members brings a high degree of satisfaction with family life.

The greater the tension (lack of coordination) in the

system of roles, the lower the marital integration of the couple. (F116)

Salience of family-related responses (Kuhn Twenty Statements Test) tends to be higher among wives whose marital adjustment is good than among those with poor marital adjustment. (S279)

Couples who were well adjusted were more likely than maladjusted couples to use "consensual (references to groups) rather than subconsensual (evaluative and qualifying references to self)" responses to the Kuhn Twenty Statements Test (Buerkle). (S279)

### Role Definition of Husband-Wife

Acute tensions occur in polygynous families when the partners lack behavioral expectations for defining a multiple-mate situation. (B033)

Problems of courtship and marriage are reduced to a minimum when the roles of expected behavior are sharply defined. (B033)

Where husbands and wives have widely divergent conceptions of the behavior expected of each other, crises are almost certain to arise. (B033)

Marital strain is likely to be reduced when the partners lower their expectations of emotional performance and comply with minimal role obligations. (G134)

Divorced couples exhibit a greater disparity in their attitudes toward the roles of the husband and wife in marriage than do married couples. (J002)

There is a correlation between marital satisfaction and the congruence of the couple's attitudes toward the roles of husband and wife in marriage. (T092)

There is no relationship between marital-role agreement and marital satisfaction. (T092)

### Role Definition of Husband-Wife (Rigidity)

Emotionally disturbed marriages tend to be characterized by a rigid differentiation of husband and wife roles. (V028)

### Role Definition of Kin/Nonkin

Marital conflict is more likely to occur if the expectations of friends and relatives are not congruent with those of the couple. (B033)

### Role Model

A daughter who sees her mother's life as being favorably changed by marriage is more likely to choose her mother as an adult-role model. (H201)

### Scapegoating

The greater the extent to which a child is a symbol of the unresolved problem(s) in his family, the more likely it is that the parents will displace their conflicts from each other onto the child. (V033)

### Scholastic Achievement

As measured by the PARI, fathers of daughters who do well academically are more likely to report marital conflicts in the family than are fathers of daughters who are poor academically. (S230)

### Scholastic Adjustment

Mothers of children with school phobias tend to lack emotional support and fulfillment in their marital relationships. (E095)

Children who drop out of high school are less likely to

have successful marriages than are those who continue in school. (H189)

### Self-Conception

The lower the marital adjustment, the more likely are the individuals to define themselves in subjective terms (i.e., happy, moody, bored) than according to structural designations (i.e., student, girl, Baptist, etc.). (B295)

The stronger the individual's feeling that he is inadequate in the marital relationship, the more likely is he to perceive problems in the marriage. (G126)

A woman who evaluates her marriage as unhappy is more likely to dream of herself and her husband, or other couples, in unpleasant situations. (H232)

Well-adjusted couples are more likely to be characterized by congruence of self-image and ideal self than are maladjusted couples. (L152)

Well-adjusted spouses are likely to have greater congruence between ideal self-images and images of their spouses. (L152)

For men, congruence between self-image and image of one's father is associated with good marital adjustment, but no such relationship exists for women in relation to their mothers. (L152)

The more congruent the self-conceptions of subjects and the conceptions of them held by their spouses, the greater the marital satisfaction. (S279)

A marriage is more likely to be successful if both partners have highly favorable self-perceptions. (T092)

There is a correlation between marital compatibility and favorable self-perceptions and the even more favorable evaluation by the spouse. (T092)

Marital satisfaction is correlated with the congruence of the husband's ideal and self-concepts. (T092)

Marital satisfaction is correlated with the congruence of the husband's self-concept and his concept of his father. (T092)

Marital satisfaction is correlated with the congruence of the wives' concepts of their husbands and their concepts of their fathers. (T092)

The greater the degree of conformity of the husband's self-perception to the self-perception of other males, the more likely it is that his marriage will be happy. (T092)

Satisfaction in marriage is correlated with the congruence of the husband's self-conception and that held of him by the wife, but not with conceptions of wives as a group. (T092)

### Self-Conception of Wife

The more supportive the wife views herself to be, the more likely it is that the marriage will be well adjusted. (K153)

Unsatisfactorily married women tend to think of themselves as less cooperative and responsible than their mothers. (L140)

### Self/Parent Conceptions

For men, congruence between self-image and image of one's father is associated with good marital adjustment, but no such relationship exists for women in relation to their mothers. (L152)

### Sex Attitudes
Marital adjustment is higher when the attitude of the couple toward sex is that of interest and pleasant anticipation. (B033)

There is a direct relation between a moderately favorable attitude toward sexual relations and marital satisfaction. (K161)

### Sex Drive
Regardless of religion, those women with low sex drives are more likely to be highly satisfied with their marriages than are those with high sex drives. (W155)

### Sex Education
Marital adjustment is higher when the sources of sexual information have been parents and teachers. (B033)

Persons who received sex information from their parents in a context of understanding and affirmation are more likely to achieve marital success. (B244)

There is a direct relation between adequate sex information and later successful marital adjustment. (K161)

Affectional inhibitions in the parents will tend to be correlated with a failure to educate their children in matters of sex. (T106)

### Sex Relations
The higher the marital adjustment, the more frequent is sexual intercourse. (C134)

### Sex Relations (Petting)
There is a direct relation between the restraint of petting and marital adjustment. (K161)

### Sex-Role Definition
Marital adjustment is associated with the absence of conflict over the role definitions of the husband and wife. (B033)

When the husband has equalitarian role attitudes and the female has traditional role attitudes, marital adjustment is higher. (K161)

### Sex-Role Definition (Consensus)
The less agreement there is between husband and wife concerning the definition and relative importance of the husband's marital roles, the more poorly adjusted is the marriage. (H195)

There is no significant relationship between marital adjustment and lack of agreement between husband and wife concerning the definition and relative importance of the wife's marital roles. (H195)

### Sex Status
Among those who feel inadequate in the marital relationship, men are more likely to feel self-blame than are women. (G126)

Women tend to report more personal problems and greater unhappiness in the marital situation than men do; both sexes report feelings of inadequacy. (G126)

Women are more dependent upon a successful marriage for their adjustment to living than are men. (G156)

Women are more likely than men to complain about their marriages. (G156)

Men suffer greater marital disenchantment in the early years than women do; women experience greater disen-

chantment than men do during the middle years of marriage. (P071)

Men's greater disenchantment during the early years of marriage is partially a function of their tendency to romanticize the relationship more than women do. (P071)

A man is more likely than a woman to complain of a deficit in tension reduction in marriage; this is due to the fact that the wife has, in her children, a source of socialized regression which is not as available to him. (P083)

### Sexual Adjustment
Sexual satisfaction is more likely in happy than in unhappy marriages.

Sex adjustment has a lower association with marital happiness than do other factors such as affection, consensus, and specific satisfactions. (B033)

There is a positive relation between marital happiness and sexual adjustment, but it varies inversely with education. (K089)

There is a direct relation between an enjoyable first sexual experience and marital adjustment. (K161)

There is a direct relation between sexual compatibility (in terms of similar sex drives, early appearance of orgasm, adequacy of sex technique) and marital adjustment. (K161)

Marital discord and disruption result most frequently from quarrels over sexual matters. (S090)

Sexual gratification will have less of an effect on marital satisfaction for religiously oriented married couples; low gratification will contribute less to dissatisfaction than it would for the nonreligious and high gratification will increase satisfaction less. (W155)

Religiosity has no effect on whether or not low sexual enjoyment affects marital satisfaction. (W155)

### Sexual Adjustment of Wife
There is relatively little association between wives' marital success scores and their sexual adjustment. (B033)

### Sexual Deviance
There is no evidence to indicate any relation between earlier deviant sexual behavior, sex play, or homosexual activity and successful marital adjustment. (K161)

### Sexual Interest
Marital adjustment is associated with an equality or near equality of the strength of interest of the husband and wife in sex. (B033)

### Sibling Relations
The closer the marriage partners duplicate in their own marriage the sibling relations they experienced in their own respective families, the greater the chance for marital success. (T109)

### Sibling Relations (Affection)
The less adequate the marriage, the more likely it is that the child will have positive feelings for all his siblings rather than disliking a particular one as is the case where the marriage is good. (L150)

### Sibling Relations (Conflict)
Conflict between adults in the family is correlated with unsatisfactory relations between the child and his siblings. (C117)

### Sibling Status
Marital adjustment is higher when the husband and wife are not only children. (B033)

### Sibling Status, Complementarity of
Persons whose sibling statuses, in their respective families of orientation, were complementary to one another with reference to relative seniority of rank and sex roles will adjust better in marriage to one another than will those with noncomplementary statuses. (T089)

Because of the complete lack of sex and rank complementarity, the poorest possible mate for the oldest brother of brother(s) would be the oldest sister of sister(s). (T089)

### Sibling Structure
The greater the number of siblings of the spouse, the more difficult it will be for him to adjust to having only one spouse. (T091)

### Sibling Structure (Sex)
Persons coming from like-sexed sibling configurations are less likely to be able to adjust to their marriage partners than are those from cross-sexed configurations. (T093)

### Size of Family
Marital adjustment is inversely related to family size. (C003)

### Sleeping Arrangements
A low happiness score is seen to be reliably associated with occupancy of separate rooms. (T079)

### Social Adjustment of Family
Conflict and maladjustment between the family and the community are causes of marital conflict. (V033)

### Social Mobility
Marital success is greater when there is little or no social mobility than when there is a great deal of social mobility. (C023)

A distribution of significantly lower scores on marital adjustment is shown by the spouses who are downwardly mobile (i.e., those who have moved downward relative to their parents), compared to all spouses taken together. (R011)

If both spouses are upwardly mobile, marital adjustment is more likely for couples with simliar class backgrounds than for those of dissimilar class backgrounds (tendency not statistically proved). (R011)

If neither spouse is socially mobile or if one spouse is upwardly mobile, marital adjustment will be better for couples with similar backgrounds than for those of dissimilar class backgrounds. (R011)

If one or both spouses are downwardly mobile, marital adjustment is equally poor for those with similar and those with dissimilar class backgrounds. (R011)

### Social Network
Sociable couples are more likely to be adjusted in marriage than are unsociable couples. (L004)

There is no relationship between the husband's social activity and marital adjustment; but in poorly rated marriages, spouses shared fewer activities and the social activities of the wives were significantly reduced. (P086)

### Superego Formation
There is no significant difference between those who are high in marital satisfaction and those who are low (measured on the Strauss Scale of Marital Satisfaction) regarding their strength of conscience (as measured by the Psychopathic Deviate Scale of the Minnesota Multiphasic Personality Inventory). (N062)

### Surrogate Parent, Adjustment to
The successful adjustment of the adopted child to a new home is less likely if there is marital conflict between the foster parents. (T086)

### Values
There is a correlation between marital adjustment and the parents' rejection of adolescent social institutions. (S219)

### Values of Husband-Wife
In emotionally disturbed marriages, the husband will tend to be more traditionally oriented than will the wife. (V028)

### Values (Romanticism)
Unhappy wives value more highly than do happy wives the attitudes, activities, and situations that appear to subserve the romantic quest. They more often prefer a dance to a play and to economize on anything else rather than on clothes. They consider that personal happiness is the paramount objective in marriage, daydream frequently, and like people who are emotional. They prefer a vivacious mate to a quiet one. (T074)

### Voluntary Organizations
Marital success is directly correlated with the degree of participation of the husband and wife in such voluntary organizations as the church or the school. (B033)

### Witchcraft
Aggression as manifest in accusations of witchcraft against affinal kinsmen will tend to occur among individuals who are dissatisfied with their marital statuses. (T059)

### Work Attitudes of Mother
The mother's satisfaction with working is positively related to the general level of marital satisfaction. (G156)

## MARITAL ADJUSTMENT OF CHILD
### X   Marital Adjustment of Parents
The most significant association of any childhood familial factor with marital accord or discord is that of the happiness of the marriages of the parents of the husband and wife. (B270)

## MARITAL ADJUSTMENT OF HUSBAND
### X   Adultery, Attitude Toward
Happy husbands, more often than the unhappy, believe that it is essential for an ideal marriage that both husband and wife be absolutely faithful to each other in sex matters. (T074)

### Child-Rearing Practices (Sex)
Favorable parental attitudes in response to the child's curiosity about sex are associated with the marital adjustment of husbands. (T079)

### Husband-Wife Relations (Cooperation)
Husbands who express a high level of need satisfaction are better able to cooperate with their wives in problem

solving than are husbands who express a low level of need satisfaction.

### Husband-Wife Relations (Egalitarianism)
More unhappy than happy husbands believe it essential or very desirable that the husband "wear the pants" and that he be as old as the wife. They stress the importance of the husband's being the intellectual superior and dislike women who are more clever than themselves. (T074)

### Husband-Wife Relations (Shared Activities)
Happy husbands more often think it is essential or very desirable that mates take their vacations together; the unhappy more often think it is undesirable. (T074)

### Mate Selection
Men who marry women bearing a physical resemblance to their mothers are more likely to be happy than are men who marry women who do not resemble their mothers. (T092)

### Neurosis
Happily married husbands are less neurotic than are unhappily married husbands. (T074)

### Paternal-Role Definition
Happy husbands are more likely than unhappy husbands to consider it essential for an ideal marriage that the husband take an active interest in the discipline and training of the child. (T074)

### Personality Adjustment (Fantasy)
More unhappy than happy husbands prefer a dance to a play and more of them like movies, which presumably carry a factor of vicarious romantic satisfaction. The fact that more unhappy men like to spend money on clothing and also that more of them habitually daydream is pertinent in this connection. (T074)

### Personality (Cooperativeness)
Happy husbands show a greater positive attitude of cooperation than do unhappy husbands. When given orders, happy husbands enter enthusiastically into the situation and carry out the program. They have no aversion to asking advice and like carrying out the program of a respected superior. More happy husbands stress the importance of the wife's equality with the husband and reject the slogan that the husband should "wear the pants." (T074)

### Personality of Husband
Unhappy husbands are much more defensive, oversensitive, and contentious than are happy husbands. (T047)

Happy husbands are more likely to take initiative and responsibility than are unhappy husbands. Unhappy husbands are more likely to say that they are carefree, do not worry about possible misfortunes, and that people do not come to them for advice. (T074)

### Personality of Husband (Self-Confidence)
Happily married husbands have greater self-confidence and show less diffidence in social situations than do unhappily married husbands. Happy husbands are more likely than unhappy husbands to liven up a group on a dull day or to take the lead in enlivening a dull party. Unhappy husbands more often prefer listening to a story to telling one, are unable to play their best against a superior opponent, and dislike full-dress affairs. (T074)

### Personality of Husband (Sympathy)
Unhappy husbands, more often than happy husbands, disregard the feelings of others when accomplishing an end that is important to themselves, are more often considered to be critical of others, and are more likely to upbraid a workman who fails to have his work done on time. (T074)

### Power Structure of Family
Well-adjusted husbands are more likely than others to grant their wives greater deference and respect and to submit to wife domination. (T092)

### Premarital Sex Relations, Attitude Toward
Happy husbands, more often than the unhappy, believe that the husband should not have had intercourse with any other woman before marriage and that young people should be trained not to indulge in "petting" and "spooning." (T074)

### Sex Attitudes
Unhappy husbands, more often than the happy, consider it essential for the ideal marriage that the husband and wife be well mated sexually. (T074)

### Sex Norms (Double Standard)
Happy men, more often than the unhappy, believe that the same standard of sexual morality should apply to both husband and wife. (T074)

### Work Adjustment
Happy husbands are more methodical and painstaking in their work; they more often report that they drive themselves steadily, plan their work in detail, and enjoy occupations demanding meticulous accuracy. (T074)

## MARITAL ADJUSTMENT OF MOTHER
### X Cognitive Development
Children whose mothers have had happy childhoods and are satisfied with marriage rate higher on Rorschach tests in intellectual vigor and energy than do children whose mothers had unhappy childhoods and are not satisfied with marriage. (A071)

### Personality Development of Child
Children whose mothers have had happy childhoods and whose mothers are satisfied by their marriages rate higher on Rorschach tests in emotional freedom and freedom from conflict than do children whose mothers had unhappy childhoods and whose mothers are not satisfied with their marriages. (A071)

## MARITAL ADJUSTMENT OF PARENTS
### X Adultery, Attitude Toward
The more happily married a person's parents were, the more highly he disapproves of extramarital relations. (C124)

### Aggression
Parents of aggressive boys are more likely to have a disrupted marital relationship than are parents of normals. (B243)

### Alcoholism of Son
Alcoholism is more likely to occur if the mother manipulates the son in response to a perceived indifference of her husband toward her marriage. (C122)

### Dating, Parental Approval
The happier the parents are in their marriage, the less likely it is that they will oppose dating by their children. (S219)

#### Deviance of Son
Mothers of nondeviant boys as compared with mothers of deviant boys report a higher degree of spousal adjustment. (W137)

#### Foster Home, Adjustment to
Children who fail to establish stable relationships in foster homes are more likely than children who do to have had parents whose relationship was tense, causing emotional rejection of the child. (W145)

#### Martial Adjustment
Persons who have parents whose marriages were happy are more likely to report happiness in their marriage relationships. (G156)

Persons who are happily married are more likely than divorced persons to rate the marriages of their parents as happy. (L012)

#### Marital Adjustment of Child
The most significant association of any childhood familial factor with marital accord or discord is that of the happiness of the marriages of the parents of the husband and wife. (B270)

#### Marriage, Attitude Toward
A child's conception of marriage as a desirable goal may be challenged and his enthusiasm for marriage diminished insofar as the relationship of his parents is seen by the child as fraught with conflict and unhappiness. (W003)

Attitudes of both men and women toward marriage are directly correlated with their conception of the happiness of their parents' relationships. (W003)

#### Mate Selection (Free Choice)
Parents are most likely to interfere and try to influence the courtship patterns of their children when their own marriages have been unsuccessful. (C023)

#### Mental Illness of Child (Autism)
Autism is more likely to occur if there are marital difficulties between the parents during the vulnerable developmental period. (S188)

#### Mental Illness (Schizophrenia)
Schizophrenia tends to be directly associated with unsatisfactory marital adjustments on the part of the patient's parents. (T105)

#### Parent-Child Relations (Closeness)
The less happy the rating of parents' marriage, the greater the likelihood the children will have a stronger attachment to the mother than to the father. (L137)

The greater the parental happiness reported, the greater the degree of emotional attachment to each parent. (L137)

#### Peer Relations
Among white collar families, a positive view of his parents' marriage by the child is related to satisfactory peer relations, but among blue-collar families, a positive view of his parents' marriage by the child is related to unsatisfactory relations. (H201)

#### Scholastic Adjustment (Phobia)
Children with school phobias are likely to come from families characterized by a great deal of spousal conflict, although divorce and separation are not likely. (C115)

#### Sexual Deviance
Families of sexual deviants are more likely than are families of "normal" boys to be characterized by frequent overt conflicts between the parents. (M209)

## MARITAL ADJUSTMENT OF SON
#### X   Personality of Father
Unsatisfactorily married men believe that their fathers are more dominant and less loving than themselves. (L140)

## MARITAL ADJUSTMENT OF WIFE
#### X   Child-Rearing Attitudes (Discipline)
Happy wives more often consider it essential that children be held to a strict discipline than do unhappy wives. (T074)

#### Class
The higher the husband's social status, the more likely is the wife to value the marriage as highly satisfactory. (R011)

#### Economic Attitudes
Unhappy wives more often regard it as essential for an ideal marriage that the wife should be allowed a definite budget, more often insist that the wife should not be financially dependent on her husband, and more often believe that marriage should be postponed until income is comfortable. (T074)

#### Extramarital Relations, Attitude Toward
More happy wives than unhappy wives believe it undesirable for husband and wife to have had sex relations with each other before marriage, consider it essential that the wife be a virgin at marriage, and consider it essential that both spouses be faithful after marriage. (T074)

#### Husband-Wife Relations (Evaluation)
Wives who express a high satisfaction of their needs in marriage tend to describe their husbands in more favorable terms than do wives whose need satisfaction is low.

#### Husband-Wife Relations (Shared Activities)
Unhappy wives more often say that it is undesirable for spouses to take their vacations together; happy wives think it is desirable. (T074)

#### Neurosis
Responses commonly regarded as indicative of neurotic tendency are much more frequently given by unhappy wives than by happy wives. (T074)

#### Personality (Emotional Stability)
Unhappy wives more often than happy wives report that their feelings alternate between happiness and sadness without apparent reason, that they are often in a state of excitement or feel grouchy, and that useless thoughts keep coming into their minds to bother them. (T074)

#### Personality of Wife (Dominance)
Unhappy wives, as opposed to happy wives, tend to be more dominant and try to get their own way in their relations with men. (T074)

#### Personality of Wife (Ego-Withdrawal)
Unhappy wives more often than the happy say they face their troubles alone without seeking help, are more willing to take a chance alone in a situation of doubtful outcome, prefer to be alone at a time of emotional stress, and prefer making hurried decisions alone. (T074)

#### Personality of Wife (Kindness)
Happy wives show more evidence of kindly, cooperative, and charitable attitudes than do the unhappy and more often expect these attitudes from others. They more often report that they avoid saying things which

might hurt the feelings of others, that they are approachable, that they like old people, and that they like such activities as teaching children or contributing to charities. In contrast, unhappy wives are much more often considered critical of others and more often admit that they disregard the feelings of others when accomplishing ends important to themselves. (T074)

### Personality (Restless Striving)
Unhappy wives tend to have a greater drive toward activity than do happy wives. They also prefer to belong to many societies rather than to few and prefer work that involves change from place to place rather than work in one location. (T074)

### Personality (Self-Confidence)
Happy wives have more self-confidence than unhappy wives do, even in situations that have nothing to do with the marriage. Moreover, unhappy wives more often say that they lack self-confidence, get "rattled" easily, make excuses when caught in a mistake, and rewrite their letters before mailing them. They are more prone than happy wives to be affected by praise or blame of many people, to suffer from injured feelings, to refuse to take the lead in enlivening a dull party, and to be discouraged when the opinions of others differ from their own. (T074)

### Personality (Thrift)
Happy wives are distinguished to a higher degree than are unhappy wives by attitudes of thrift; they express more desire to save money, greater dislike of the gambling attitude, and greater dislike of occupations or occasions that are conceivably contributory to this attitude. (T074)

### Political Attitudes
In religion, politics, and moral views, happy wives have a greater majority of conservatives within their ranks than do unhappy wives. More unhappy than happy wives dislike conservative people and more of them believe that the current social order is so unjust that revolution will be necessary. More of the unhappy wives believe that religions do as much harm as good, more of them dislike Bible study, and fewer of them consider it essential that children have religious instruction (U.S.). (T074)

### Power Structure of Family
The more equal the balance of power between the marital partners, the higher the satisfaction expressed by the wife with marital intimacy.

Well-adjusted wives are more likely than others to expect less deference and respect from their husbands and to defer to their husbands' judgment. (T092)

### Urban/Rural
Wives in urban areas show higher satisfaction with marital love than do wives in rural areas.

### Work Adjustment
Happily married women tend to be more meticulous and persevering in their attitude toward work and to show greater liking for work requiring such traits than do unhappy wives. Happy wives more often drive themselves steadily in their work, whereas unhappy wives more often report that they work by fits and starts. (T074)

## MARITAL ADJUSTMENT OF WORKING MOTHERS        X   Occupation of Husband
The difference in marital adjustment scores between working and nonworking mothers tends to be smallest among women whose husbands are in professional and managerial occupations. (S257)

## MARITAL STABILITY        X   Acculturation
There is no correlation between the degree of individual acculturation and marital instability. The contrary is also asserted. (F062)

### Affinal Relations
Marital stability in patrilineal societies is directly correlated with the degree of identification of the wife to her husband's lineage. (F073)

### Affinal Ties
Marital stability is directly correlated with the strength of the bonds between affinal kinsmen. (K065)

### Age Difference
Marital stability tends to be greater when husband and wife are of approximately the same age. (T058)

### Age of Husband
The stability of the marriage is directly correlated with the age of the husband. (F073)

### Authority Structure of Family
Where there is a lack of marital stability, parental authority is weakened. (T073)

### Avoidance Relationship
Rules of avoidance between kinsmen tend to be relaxed with the persistence of the marriage and the advent of children. (E039)

### Childbirth
Marital stability is likely to increase with the birth of the first child. (E042)

### Children
Marriage is more likely to be stable if there are children. (B191)

Among those who have been divorced, there is an association between marital stability and having children. (P059)

### Children, Evaluation of
Marital stability will tend to be greater if children are valued. (H164)

### Class
Marital stability is lower among the lower classes. (G156)

### Cohesion of Family
The cohesiveness of the family is directly correlated with the stability of the marriage pattern. (L064)

### Cohesion of Kin-Group
A lack of solidarity among members of a unilateral group appears to be correlated with easy divorces, remarriages, and frequent extramarital liaisons. (H021)

### Cohesion of Lineage
The corporateness of lineages fostered the stability of endogamous unions. (S158)

### Concubinage
Marriages will tend to be more stable if concubinage is institutionalized. (B191)

### Dependency of Women
The stability of the marriage tends to decrease with an increase in the independence of women. (D031)

### Descent
Societies in which the system of descent is matrilineal tend to be characterized by greater marital instability than patrilineal societies. (L039)

### Descent (Patrilineal)
Marital stability is directly correlated with patrilineal descent. (F062)

### Economic Dependence of Women
Marital instability increases with an increasing economic independence of women. (B110)

### Economic Rank
The stability of the marriage is directly correlated with the economic status of the husband and wife. (M086)

### Economic Rank of Husband-Wife
Marital stability is more likely to characterize marriages in which both the family of the husband and wife are of high economic status. (B108)

### Economic Rank of Men and Women
Changes in the relative economic positions of men and women contribute to the instability of relations between husbands and wives. (O029)

### Economic Role of Husband-Wife
Marital stability is directly correlated with the stability of the economic role of the husband and wife. (W082)

### Employment
In the initiation of economic crisis (unemployment), the necessity of considering the children first and of facing new problems increases the stability between the husband and wife. (B207)

### Endogamy
The selection of a mate from within the kin-group is conducive to marital stability. (H165)

### Endogamy (Community)
Marital stability is more likely to occur where shifts at marriage occur only within the community and do not dislocate the husband and wife from relatives and friends. (A072)

### Endogamy (Village)
Marital stability is more likely to occur when marriages are arranged within the village. (B302)

### Fertility
The stability of a marriage is directly correlated with the fertility of the wife. (H165)

Women married once have more children than do women married two or more times. (N051)

A low birth rate is directly correlated with marital instability. (W091)

### Geographic Mobility
When geographical mobility is high, so is marital instability. (C090)

Patterns of labor migration tend to undermine the stability of marriage. (K065)

Marital breakup is more likely to occur among refugees than among nonrefugees (L001)

Wife stealing tends to increase in situations of labor migration. (S266)

Women are less likely to be tolerant of marital unhappiness in situations where patterns of labor migration provide options for mobility. (S266)

### Husband-Wife Relations (Affection)
In societies in which there are no expectations of intensive emotional attachments between husband and wife, marriages will tend to be more stable. (G138)

### Husband-Wife Relations (Consensus)
Where husband and wife do not share the same values, there is a higher probability of breakup than among those who share the same values. (L116)

### Husband-Wife Relations (Dependency)
The less the husband and wife depend on each other, the greater are their chances of splitting up. (L116)

### Independence of Women
The stability of marriage tends to decrease with an increase in the independence of women. (D031)

### Industrialization
Marital stability tends to be inversely correlated with the degree of industrialization. (D031)

### Isolation of Nuclear Family
The emergence of a nuclear family which is independent of a larger kin unit tends to be conducive to greater marital stability. (L064)

### Kin Ties (Maternal)
When marital relations are unstable and primarily consensual, a strong emphasis is placed upon the maternal kin. (S102)

### Lineage Ties
When the allegiance to unilineal groups is paramount, marriage tends to be unstable. (B060)

Marital stability is inversely correlated with the importance of lineage ties. (F073)

### Lineage Ties of Wife
The complete legal identification of a wife with the lineage of her husband tends to result in marital stability. (F062)

When the lineage affiliation of the wife remains with her natal lineage after marriage, the lineage structure tends to undermine the stability of the marriage. (F062)

### Marital Adjustment
Widespread marital instability tends to result in a situation of conflict and mutual distrust between husband and wife. (G094)

The greater the need satisfaction in marriage, the greater the likelihood of marital stability. (G134)

### Marital Stability, Expectations of
Even where a mate does not live up to the expectations of the other or up to his conception of his role in marriage, the marriage is more likely to survive if one or both expect the marriage to be permanent. (B033)

### Marriage Ceremony
Marriages are less likely to be stable if the ceremony is simple and inexpensive. (S267)

### Marriage Chances
In societies in which spouses have the option of alternative marital partners, marital stability is low. (L116)

### Marriage Payment
The amount of the marriage payment will be reduced when there are other factors to reinforce marital stability. (B032)

Marriage stability is greater where there has been marriage payment. (L113)

As a general rule, the greater the number of kinsmen who contribute to the marriage payment, or who share in receiving it, the greater is the security of marriage. (R087)

The stability of the marriage tends to be correlated with the amount which is paid as bride price. (V010)

### Mate Selection (Free Choice)
The stability of a marriage tends to be higher if the selection of a mate is the responsibility of the family rather than of the individual. (L079)

### Mate Selection (Near Kin)
Marriage with near kinsmen is more likely than marriage with strangers to insure the stability of the marriage. (S140)

### Mother Absence
There is a significant correlation between a childhood history of early maternal deprivation (below the age of six and for at least six months' duration) and broken marriages later in life. (E093)

### Occupation of Wife
Employment of the mother in a secure, bureaucratic context is less likely to lead to marital instability than is her employment in an entrepreneurial and competitive context. (S265)

### Parent-Child Relations (Closeness)
The persistence of strong ties between the wife and her parents tends to occur in situations of marital instability. (W056)

### Parental-Role Behavior
The greater the instability of domestic unions, consensual or legal, the less likely is the fulfillment of parental roles. (S211)

### Personality Adjustment
The more mature and personally well adjusted a person is, the more likely he is to build a stable marriage. (C134)

### Personality (Complementary Needs)
Marital stability is more likely if the partners have heterogamous (complementary, rather than similar) psychological needs and are from similar social backgrounds. (G134)

### Polygyny
Polygynous unions are less stable than monogamous marriages. (D055)

### Preferential Marriage
Marriages formed under preferential marriage patterns are more likely to be stable. (S267)

### Preferential Marriage (Exchange)
Marriage by exchange serves to increase the stability of the marriage. (M109)

### Preferential Marriage (Near Kin)
Marital stability is more likely to occur if the preferential marriage partner is a close kinsman. (S153)

### Property
Marital stability is closely correlated with home ownership. (F078)

### Race
Separations are more numerous among nonwhite than among white. (B033)

### Race (Urbanization)
Separation and widowhood are more likely in urban Negro families than in the rest of the population (U.S.). (L124)

### Rank of Women
Marital stability is inversely correlated with the status of women. (B302)

The status of women is directly correlated with the degree of marital stability. (H103)

### Religion
Marital breakup is no more likely to occur in areas with a large number of Catholics than in areas with few Catholics. (L001)

There is a curvilinear relationship between the predominance of a religion in a particular area and marital breakup among members of the religion. (L001)

Areas in which a particular religion is almost completely predominant, or just barely a majority, are likely to have less marital breakup among the members of the religion than are areas where the predominance of the religion is between the extremes cited. (L001)

### Religion (Christianity)
There is no direct correlation between Christianity and marital stability. (F062)

### Remarriage
Unions between previously married people are less stable. (S267)

### Residence
Marital stability is more likely to occur in communities with dense, rather than dispersed, patterns of residence. (A072)

Where a woman remains in her natal home, the marriage bond is fragile and the divorce rate is high. (G116)

The greater the instability of marriage and other mating forms, the more likely it is that persons will withdraw into domestic isolation or live with siblings. (S211)

Marital stability will be higher if kinsmen live nearby. (S266)

### Role Definition of Husband-Wife
In societies in which the emotional relationship between husband and wife is not relevant to the definition of their marital obligations, emotional conflicts and tensions are less likely to be disruptive. (G138)

The greater the complementarity of roles between husband and wife, the greater will be the stability of their marriage. (S075)

### Role Definition of Husband-Wife (Affection)
Where affection is not institutionally expected in a marriage, its absence will not produce active antagonisms which may lead to the dissolution of the marriage ties. (T106)

### Sex Ratio
Marital stability tends to be undermined where there is a scarcity of women and a competition for wives. (W056)

### Size of City
Marital breakup is not related to the size of cities. (L001)

### Size of Lineage
Marriages are less stable in larger lineage groups. (F062)

### Social Adjustment
A problem in relating to others, stemming from inadequate identification with the female role (as measured by an ambivalent response toward Rorschach Plate III), is more likely to be displayed by divorced than by married women.

### Social Change
The separation rate will tend to rise under conditions of social change or instability (F062)

The greater the amount of social change in any given period, the greater is the amount of marital disharmony. (G134)

### Social Mobility
People who marry more than once are less likely to rise occupationally. (G011)

### Socialization, Effectiveness of
An unstable marital relationship will impair the role coordination which is necessary for effective child rearing. (S205)

### Stability of Lineage
Marital stability will tend to be undermined by the deterioration of the lineage structure. (F062)

### Urban/Rural
Marital breakup is more likely to occur in urban areas than in rural areas. (L001)

In the anonymity of an urban environment, the facility with which any type of mating relationship can be established or terminated is largely responsible for the instability of domestic unions. (S211)

### Urbanization
Marital stability tends to decrease in situations of increasing urbanization. (F055)

The degree of marital instability tends to be directly correlated with the extent of urbanization. (H103)

### Values (Marital Stability)
Where the value emphasis on marital stability is high, marital stability tends to be high. (L116)

## MARITAL STABILITY, EXPECTATIONS OF
### X  Marital Stability
Even where a mate does not live up to the expectations of the other or up to his conception of his role in marriage, the marriage is more likely to survive if one or both expect the marriage to be permanent. (B033)

## MARITAL STABILITY (POLYGYNY/MONOGAMY)
### X  Economic Conditions
Economic pressures are more likely to lead to marital instability in the polygamous family than in the monogamous family. (M198)

## MARITAL STATUS    X  Abortion
Abortions are as likely to be performed upon married as upon unmarried women. (E092)

### Adultery
Belief in the prevalence of adultery is greater among single persons than among married persons. (C132)

### Age at Remarriage
Age at remarriage is associated with previous marital status: the divorced marry earlier; the widowed, later. (C010)

### Age Difference
A greater age difference is found between individuals who marry individuals of a different marital status than themselves and individuals who marry people of their own marital status (unless both have been married before). (H013)

Husbands are much older than wives when one or both have been married before than when neither has been married before. (H013)

### Age-Group Identification
Identification as being old is greater among widowed people than among married people. This hypothesis is also denied. (P002)

### Avoidance Relationship
The avoidance relationship between siblings of the opposite sex is relaxed after the marriage of the girl. (G055)

### Class
Consensual and casual unions are more common toward the lower social strata. (C024)

Remarried persons are more likely to be found in a somewhat lower class strata than are those who stay married. (G157)

### Divorce
The probability of divorce rises with each successive marriage. (M013)

### Divorce Adjustment
Divorcées who have some friends divorced or divorcing are slightly more likely to have few emotional problems in divorce than are those who have no friends divorced or divorcing. (G157)

### Economic Conditions, Adjustment to
Family groups meet economic crisis more effectively than do single, unattached, or widowed men and women. (F078)

### Economic Role of Wife
The percentage of unmarried adults will tend to be higher if the role of wife is not of economic importance. (H164)

### Emotional Adjustment
Among young adults, those who are single tend to be better adjusted emotionally than those who are married; this difference evens out, however, with age. (M232)

### Empathy
There is more empathy between married pairs than between favorite dates. (S279)

### Friendship
Middle-class couples are less likely to establish close shared friendships subsequent to marriage than they are to establish friendships separately prior to marriage. (B317)

Married men and women are more likely to turn to other people in times of unhappiness or for help than are nonmarried people. (G126)

The intensity of friendship is a function of age and marital status. (R006)

Remarried people are more likely to have family friends with whom they do not have as much in common (income, faith, origin, and kin) than are people who have intact families. (Z008)

### Friendship Choice
Families are more likely to avoid social relations with remarried families in which both parents have remarried or in which the woman only has remarried; when fathers only have remarried, avoidance is not as great. (Z008)

### Friendship (Closeness)
Remarried friends are more likely to be reported as being less intimate family friends than are friends with nondisrupted families. (Z008)

### Genealogical Ties, Knowledge of
Married persons tend to have a greater depth and breadth than the unmarried in the range of their known genealogical ties. (G033)

### Geographic Mobility
The widowed and divorced are more migratory than are the married. (F008)

A higher proportion of out-migrants are married than of the population in the cities they left. (F008)

In-migrants have a higher proportion married than has the total population. (F008)

Negro out-migrants have a lower percentage married than the Negro population of the cities from which they come. Immigrants have a higher proportion married than the total population. (F008)

### Health and Personality Adjustment
There is a correlation between mental and physical health and marriage. (M219)

### Homicide
The married are more likely to commit murder than are the single. (S078)

### Incest Taboo
The reaction to incest will be far more severe if either of the individuals is married. (H052)

### Intermarriage (Racial and Ethnic)
Those intermarrying are more likely to have been previously divorced than are couples intramarrying. (B311)

### Marital Adjustment
Marital adjustment is higher when the parents of the husband and wife are not divorced or separated. (B033)

The widowed are more successful than the divorced in remarriage. (B286)

### Marriage, Attitude Toward
In a society with high illegitimacy rates, children whose parents are legally married are more likely to wish to be married themselves than are illegitimate children. (B245)

### Mate Selection
People are more likely to marry people of the same marital status as themselves than are people of different marital statuses. (B008)

### Maternal-Role Definition
Ambiguity of the role of mother tends to increase (in order) with respect to the marital statuses of 1) widow-mother, 2) wife-mother, and 3) divorcée-mother. (G015)

### Mental Illness
Mental illness is more prevalent among divorced persons than among the widowed, among the widowed more than among the single, and among the single more than among married persons. (A006)

Mental illness is more prevalent among widowed Negroes than among divorced Negroes, but more prevalent among divorced whites than among widowed whites. (A006)

Variability in the incidence of mental illness by marital status is greater among males than among females (i.e., females are more likely than males to have the lowest incidence in mental illness among married, then the single, then the widowed, and, finally, the highest incidence among the divorced. (A006)

Among New York Negroes, mental disorders are more likely among the single than among the married, but this ratio decreases with age and the relationship is reversed among men over 50 years of age. (M219)

There is a correlation between widowhood and mental disorders among men, but not among women. (M219)

Separation and divorce are more highly correlated with mental disease among women than they are among men. (M219)

### Mental Illness (Alcoholic Psychosis)
Alcoholic psychoses are more likely among the widowed, separated, and divorced than among the married or single. (M219)

### Mental Illness by Race
Mental illness is more prevalent among widowed Negroes than among divorced Negroes, but more prevalent among divorced whites than among widowed whites. (A006)

### Mental Illness (Cerebral Arteriosclerosis and Senile Psychosis)
Psychoses with cerebral arteriosclerosis or senile psychoses are more likely among widowed men and among single women than among other marital categories. (M219)

### Mental Illness (Hospitalization)
Married persons are less likely to be admitted to mental hospitals than are single persons; single persons less likely than widowed; and widowed less likely than divorced persons. (A006)

Married mental patients, regardless of sex, are more likely than unmarried patients to remain in the community after release from the hospital. (F124)

Married persons tend to be more rapidly discharged from mental institutions than do the single. (N056)

There is no correlation between marital status of the mental patient and frequency or date of readmission to the hospital. (N056)

The widowed and divorced occupy an intermediate position between the single and the married with regard to incidence of mental illness and duration of stay in mental institutions. (N056)

### Mental Illness (Manic-Depressive and Dementia Praecox)
Dementia praecox and manic-depressive psychoses are more likely among the single than among the married. (M219)

### Mental Illness (Paresis)
Among New York Negroes, the incidence of general paresis does not correlate with marital status, with the exception of a high incidence for widowers. (M219)

### Mental Illness (Schizophrenia)
Married schizophrenics are more likely to have achieved a high level of personality integration in the premorbid period than are single people (thus accounting for more rapid recovery from schizophrenia). (F104)

### Mental Illness (Schizophrenia), Recovery from
People who are married recover from schizophrenia more rapidly than do those who are single. (F104)

### Mental Illness (Social Adjustment)
The level of recovery from mental illness of those who were released from mental hospitals is highest among those who were married, followed by those whose marriages were broken by separation, divorce, or death, and least among single persons. (A006)

### Neurosis
In New York state, divorced and separated persons have a higher hospital admission rate for psychoneuroses than do widowed persons. (M189)

In New York state, unmarried persons have a higher hospital admission rate for psychoneuroses than do married persons. (M189)

### Personality Adjustment
Widowed people are more likely to have a lower level of personality adjustment than do married people; controlling for age does not make a difference. (G126)

### Personality Adjustment (Ego Strength)
Persons who marry show greater feelings of ego deficiency than do persons who remain single. (M232)

### Personality Adjustment (Happiness)
Married people are happier than are those engaged to be married, who are happier than those never yet engaged, who are happier than those people with broken and unreplaced engagements, who are, in turn, happier than married people on the verge of divorce, the latter being the least happy of all the groups. (C023)

The widowed are more likely to have greater feelings of unhappiness than are single persons. (The difference is greater for males than for females.) (G126)

### Personality Adjustment (Worry)
Married people are more likely to report worries than are unmarried people. (The difference is greater for women than for men.) (G126)

Widows and widowers report worrying "all the time" more frequently than do single persons. (The difference is greater for males than for females.) (G126)

### Personality (Ego Strength)
Other things being equal (sex, age, intelligence, position in the family, nationality, father's occupation, community, and amount of education), persons who marry

demonstrate greater feelings of ego deficiency than persons who remain single. (M010)

### Personality Problems
Single women are less likely to have felt they were about to have a nervous breakdown than are divorced, separated, or widowed women; single men do not differ from other men in this respect. (G126)

Divorced and separated women report having felt an impending nervous breakdown more often than do men and women in other marital and nonmarital statuses. (G126)

### Physical Disability of Husband
Among men who have been physically disabled, the proportion of those who remain married exceeds those who are divorced or separated at all educational levels. (N060)

### Race
The white population has a somewhat higher proportion of marriages that are first marriages than does the non-white population. (C010)

### Remarriage
A divorced parent with children will remarry sooner than will a widowed parent with children. (B286)

### Residence
Married old people in industrially developed areas are more apt to live alone with their spouses than with other family as well or with other nonkin; nonmarried old people in industrially developed areas are as apt to live with their children or with other relatives as they are to live alone (Vienna). (R120)

Unmarried older people tend to live nearer their siblings than do married older people. (T009)

### Sex Norms
Sexual acts (outside marriage) by and with married individuals are punished more than are sexual acts by and with unmarried individuals. (B006)

### Sex-Role Definition
Divorced couples exhibit greater disagreement as to the roles of husband and wife in marriage than do married couples. (T092)

### Sibling Relations (Interaction Rate)
Unmarried older people tend to have more frequent contact with their siblings than do married older people (T009)

### Suicide
Marital statuses may be ranked in this order by suicide rate: married, single, widowed, and divorced; differences are greater for men than for women. (K024)

Suicide rate of married persons correlates more highly with business cycles than does the suicide rate of single persons. (S078)

The divorced have a higher suicide rate than do the widowed of the same age and sex. (S078)

### Suicide, Attempted
Unsuccessful suicide attempts are more likely to occur among married than among single, divorced, or widowed persons. (W125)

### Urban/Rural
The proportion of single and unattached people is greater in urban areas. (B033)

The percentage of people married is greater in urban areas than in rural areas. (H001)

## MARITAL STATUS (FEMALE)
### X   Employment of Mother
Compared with mothers who do not work, employed mothers are more likely to be widowed, divorced, or separated. (S265)

### Employment of Wife
Women married once and living with their husbands are less likely to be in the labor force than are women who have remarried. (G011)

The proportion of women married for the first time in the labor force declines with the duration of marriage, while there is little difference between the labor-force participation rates for the several durations of marriage up to ten years for those living with the second or subsequent husband. (G011)

### Employment of Women
Divorced and widowed women are more likely to work than are married women. (Y047)

### Employment of Women, Attitude Toward
Favorable attitudes toward women working tend to change to unfavorable attitudes when women are married and have children. (G015)

Single women are less likely than married women to see their employment as important for their sense of self-worth. (S257)

### Fertility
Divorced women who remarry bear fewer children than do those who were never divorced. (F101)

### Friendship
Divorcées who have different friends during the separation and divorce period than those during the marriage are more likely to rate their new friends as better or the same as their marriage friends. (G157)

Divorcées who keep their marriage friends during the separation and divorce period are slightly more likely than those with different friends to have no divorced friends but one or more divorcing friends. (G157)

### Illegitimacy
Divorced women are more likely to have illegitimate children than are the unmarried. (O027)

### Marriage Payment
Marriage payments will be highest when a wife has not been previously married. (B107)

## MARITAL STATUS (MALE)              X   Adultery
Seduction of wives of polygynists is frequent where there is a scarcity of unmarried girls in relation to the number of bachelors. (W128)

### Authority Structure of Family
The authority of the wife in the family increases upon the death of her husband. (C022)

### Education
Among American men 35 to 64 years old, those with either low or high educational levels are more likely to be married or to have been married than are those with average levels of education. (H203)

### Illegitimacy (Adoption)
The unwed mother whose child is by a man who is married, rather than unmarried, is more likely to keep her child. (J020)

### Income
Married men living with their first wives have a slightly higher median income than do those living with their second or subsequent wives. (G011)

During the initial ten years of first marriage, there is a gradual increase in income of the husband. There is also an increase for husbands married more than once, but the increase is not as appreciable. (G011)

### Income (Savings)
Men who are married and separated from their wives tend to save more of their income than do unmarried men or men whose wives are with them. (W079)

### Name Changing
Compared to the total Los Angeles population, single males constituted a significantly higher proportion of petitioners for name changes among the non-Jewish, and married males constituted a significantly higher proportion of petitioners for name changes among the Jewish. (B010)

Married men constituted a significantly higher proportion of the Jewish male petitioners for name changes than of the non-Jewish petitioners. (B010)

### Preferential Marriage (Levirate)
The practice of the leviratic union is more likely to occur if the husband's brother is a bachelor. (W067)

### Subsistence Pattern (Nomadic/Agricultural)
There is a higher proportion of single males in agricultural than in nomadic communities. (L073)

## MARITAL STATUS OF CHILD
### X   Parent-Child Relations (Authority)
Among children from the dominant social group, the single are less likely to accept parental authority than are the married. Among low-status children, the single are more likely to accept parental authority. (K121)

## MARRIAGE                           X   Mate Selection
Consensual cohabitation is less likely than either matchmaking by third parties or romantic love to act as a precipitant of marriage. (B245)

### Premarital Pregnancy
Couples who are in love tend to marry sooner when premarital pregnancy occurs than are couples who are not in love. (C125)

The greater the incidence of premarital pregnancy in society, the less social pressure there will be toward hasty marriage or subsequent divorce. (C135)

### Premarital Sex Relations
Among women there is a correlation between premarital sexual activity and nearness to marriage. (E092)

### Sexual Interest
The interest of neurotics in sexual activity decreases with adulthood and marriage. (M197)

### Social Control
Marriage lowers the rate of sexual competition among men and is thus a force for social order. (P083)

## MARRIAGE, APPROVAL OF          X   Divorce
Disapproval of the marriage by friends or kin is associated with a higher propensity for divorce. (G156)

### Divorce Process
Prior approval or disapproval of the marriage by friends or kin is unrelated to the length of time taken by the couple between a serious consideration to divorce and filing suit. (G157)

### Engagement, Duration of
Among couples who divorce, the proportion of family members who expressed approval prior to the marriage (both of the husband's and wife's family members) increases among those with a longer engagement period. (G157)

Among divorced couples, the proportion of friends (of both the husband and wife) who approved prior to the marriage increases among those who had a longer engagement. (G157)

### Marital Adjustment
Marital adjustment is higher when the marriage has been approved by both parents. (B033)

Persons whose marriage was approved by friends and parents are more likely to have marital success. (B244)

There is a direct relation between approval of the marriage by peers and marital adjustment. (K161)

### Social Network of Husband/Wife
The divorcée's family members are more likely to have expressed disapproval prior to the marriage than are her husband's family members. (G157)

The divorcée's friends are more likely to have expressed mild or strong disapproval prior to the marriage than are the husband's friends. (G157)

Both the divorcée's family and her husband's family had more definitive opinions prior to the marriage than did their respective friends, who were more likely to have been indifferent. (G157)

## MARRIAGE, ATTITUDE TOWARD
### X   Achievement Motivation
The higher the individual's achievement motivation, the less likely is he to place a high priority on marriage. (B245)

### Age
Pressures toward marriage increase with a person's increasing age. This relationship is also asserted to be curvilinear. (G015)

### Class
Middle-class and upper-class marriages are likely to be more oriented toward the child or family as a whole than are lower-class marriages, which tend to be more oriented toward the compatibility of the husband and wife, with less concern for responsibility for the children. (C121)

### Consensual Union
Where consensual unions are common, the punishments for entering them are less severe and the rewards for marrying are not as great. (G151)

### Dating
Divorcées with positive attitudes toward love and marriage are more likely to claim they have dating opportunities to meet people than are those with negative attitudes. (G157)

### Divorce
Where the possession of a household is fundamental to status, men and women are less likely to divorce unless provocation is great. (C090)

### Divorce of Parents
The attitude of women toward marriage is favorable even if their parents were divorced. (W003)

### Education
The higher the education level, the more likely a person will consider "psychic congeniality" and similar traits as important in marital adjustment. (K089)

### Education of Women
There is an inverse relation between the educational level of women and their desire for marriage. (K161)

### Engagement, Duration of
Long engagement periods are associated wth a complex of attitudes indicative of a more serious commitment to marriage in general. (G157)

### Father-Child Relations (Closeness)
The closer the child with the father (and correspondingly distant with the mother), the greater is his doubt about his chances for a successful marriage. (L137)

### Marital Adjustment
There is a direct relation between a high aspiration level for marriage and subsequent disillusionment. (K161)

There is a relationship between the marital happiness of parents and their children's attitudes toward marriage. (S279)

### Marital Adjustment of Parents
A child's conception of marriage as a desirable goal may be challenged and his enthusiasm for marriage diminished insofar as the relationship of his parents is seen by the child as fraught with conflict and unhappiness. (W003)

Attitudes of both men and women toward marriage are directly correlated with their conception of the happiness of their parents' relationship. (W003)

### Marital Status
In a society with high illegitimacy rates, children whose parents are legally married are more likely to wish to be married themselves than are illegitimate children. (B245)

### Marriage Chances
The percentage marrying will tend to be lower if marriage does not confer higher status. (H164)

### Marriage Payment
When marriage is viewed as conferring advantages on the husband and his family, the institution of bride wealth is more likely to occur. (W082)

### Parent-Child Relations (Closeness)
The closer the child is with both parents, the fewer are his doubts about his chances of a successful marriage. (L137)

### Peer Relations

Expectation of time of marriage does not correlate with peer-group popularity, but the less popular the child, the more likely it is that he will not desire marriage or any children at all. (R111)

### Personality Adjustment

The immature or not so well-adjusted person may find a greater appeal in marriage than the mature, well-adjusted person. (M010)

### Sex Status

Regardless of degree of parental happiness in marriage, females generally have more favorable attitudes toward marriage than males do. (S279)

## MARRIAGE CEREMONY          X   Age of Wife

Civil ceremonies are more frequent among younger than among older brides. (C128)

### Birth Spacing

The time interval between marriage and the birth of the first child is longer for couples having religious wedding ceremonies than for couples having civil wedding ceremonies. (C019)

### Class of Husband

Civil marriages are inversely related to the status levels of the grooms. (C128)

### Desertion

Couples involved in desertion cases are more likely to have had a civil wedding ceremony. (K010)

### Divorce

Couples having a nonreligious wedding ceremony are more likely to get divorced than are couples who have a religious wedding. (C005)

Among fertile marriages the divorce rate is higher for the civil marriages than for church marriages (Denmark). (C124)

### Illegitimacy and Premarital Conception

Premarital conception and illegitimacy are more likely to occur among couples having a civil ceremony than among those who have a church ceremony. (Denmark). (C129)

### Intermarriage (Race)

Civil, rather than religious, wedding ceremonies are more frequent in interracial marriages. (G001)

### Intermarriage (Religious)

Civil ceremonies are more frequent among interfaith marriages than among religiously endogamous marriages. (C128)

### Marital Stability

Marriages are less likely to be stable if the ceremony is simple and inexpensive. (S267)

### Occupational Rank

A rough association exists between occupational level and the proportion of couples getting married by religious ceremony among native whites. A discernible pattern for nonwhites fails to emerge. (K010)

### Premarital Pregnancy

Civil marriages are associated with higher incidence of premarital pregnancies than are church marriages. (M243)

## MARRIAGE CEREMONY, EXPENSE OF
####    X   Age at Marriage

A higher age at marriage is observed in societies in which the expense of the marriage ceremony is high. (F121)

## MARRIAGE CEREMONY, TYPE OF
####    X   Marital Adjustment

Marital adjustment is higher when the husband and wife have been married by a minister or priest. (B033)

People married at home, at church, or at the minister's home are likely to have better marital adjustment than are people married by a justice of the peace. (L012)

## MARRIAGE CHANCES          X   Age at Marriage

The younger the average age at marriage, the higher the proportion of the population who will eventually marry. (K161)

### Clan Affiliation

More nonagnatic clan members tend to marry only once, and later, than do agnatic clan members. (R054)

### Class

The higher the social rank of the woman, the more likely she is to remain unmarried. (H222)

### Dependency

Where dependence of both male and female children upon the mother is encouraged, it is more likely that both men and women will prefer relying upon and residing with their families of origin to the responsibilities of marriage. (B245)

### Economic Rank

Since the married state requires a particular minimum standard of living, the poorer one is, the less likely is he to marry. (B245)

### Education

Females with a lower educational level are more likely to marry than are females with a higher educational level. (H001)

### Extended Family

When the extended family is the most important source of support and solidarity in a society, it is more likely that all family members are interdependent in regard to their marriage chances. (P083)

### Father Absence

Sons reared in homes where the father is absent are less likely to move toward courtship and marriage than are sons from intact families, except where the father's absence occurred after the boy reached eighth grade. (S219)

### Fertility Values

A higher percentage of all women will eventually marry in societies in which fertility is stressed. (M127)

### Income

Among American males 35 to 64 years old, the higher the present income, the more likely the man is to be married or to have been married. (H203)

### Inheritance (Single Heir)

In single-heir inheritance systems, the brothers and sisters of the owner tended to remain unmarried. (H066)

### I.Q.

Persons with lower intelligence ratings are less likely to get married. (H222)

The offspring of parents with low intelligence ratings are less likely to marry or to produce children than are those of parents with average or high intelligence ratings. (H231)

### Land

When land is allocated directly by the village rather than through kin-groups, the percentage of adults married will be lower. (V025)

### Legal Status

A larger proportion of the population is likely to remain unmarried where there is equality of status between the sexes and where women have full jural rights without marriage. (N065)

### Marital Stability

In societies in which spouses have the option of alternative marital partners, marital stability is low. (L116)

### Marriage, Attitude Toward

The percentage marrying will tend to be lower if marriage does not confer higher status. (H164)

### Mate Selection (Free Choice)

The smaller the number of potential spouses available to the young person, the more able is a society to control who marries whom. (G156)

In societies in which family members are interdependent in regard to their marriage chances, marriage is more likely to be a problem of corporate action requiring centralized decision powers for the corporate group. (P083)

When the marriage-market position of any one nuclear family is related to the extended family position, the final authority on the desirability of a given match is more likely to rest with the political authority of the extended family. (P083)

### Mental Illness (Schizophrenia)

Schizophrenic individuals are less likely to marry than are normals. (B285)

Among hospitalized schizophrenics, females are more likely than males to be married. (R122)

### Mental Illness (Schizophrenia/Neurosis)

Male schizophrenics are less likely to marry than are neurotics; female schizophrenics tend to marry later than do neurotics. (M197)

### Occupational Achievement

The greater the success of a man in his career, the less likely he is to seek need gratification from marriage. (M232)

### Polyandry

The institution of polyandry tends to result in a lower percentage of women married. (G055)

### Power Structure of Family

Among schizophrenics, those from father-dominated families are more likely to be married than are those from mother-dominated families. (F117)

### Prostitution

Prostitution will tend to flourish when the percentage of men married is low. (H088)

### Religion

Second-generation American Catholics are more likely to marry than are second-generation Americans of other religions. (H203)

### Residence

The number of marriages to persons residing at a given distance immediately preceding marriage is directly proportional to the number of potential spouses living at that distance and inversely proportional to the number living at shorter distances. (C123)

The percentage of grooms marrying brides living at a given distance is proportional to the number of brides at that distance and inversely proportional to the distance. (C123)

Decrease in the likelihood of marrying is more strongly related to an increase in distance between potential spouses than to a decline in the number of potential spouses at any given distance. (C123)

### Role Definition

The high percentage of bachelors and spinsters is correlated with specific role definitions for bachelors and for spinsters. (N065)

### Scholastic Achievement

The greater the academic achievement of the man, the less likely he is to marry. (M232)

### Sex Ratio

Women are more dependent for marriage upon a favorable sex ratio than are men. (C023)

The higher the sex ratio in the population, the lower the percentage of poor males who ever marry. (F082)

### Sex-Role Definition

A larger proportion of the population is likely to remain unmarried where a virtual interchangeability of work roles makes it possible and feasible for a man or woman to live alone. (N065)

### Sex Status

Toward the upper educational and occupational strata, a higher proportion of men than of women marry, while toward the lower strata a higher proportion of women than of men marry. (G157)

Females are less likely than males to marry mental patients. (F124)

Schizophrenic females are more likely to marry than are schizophrenic males. (R103)

### Sibling Structure (Twins)

Identical twins are more likely than fraternal twins (because they identify so closely) to delay marriage and perhaps not to be married at all. (T089)

### Social Mobility Aspirations
The greater the desire of a second-generation American to attain a high socioeconomic class, the less likely he is to ever marry. (H203)

### Urban/Rural
In urban areas there has been a greater increase in the percentage of people ever married than in rural areas. (H001)

### Values
Among Western nations, the more that people come to believe in the benefits of companionship with the opposite sex, the higher the percentage eventually marrying.

## MARRIAGE CHANCES (MALE/FEMALE)
### X   Mental Illness (Schizophrenia)
More female schizophrenics are married than male because the female plays a more passive role in courting and does not need the aggressiveness and confidence which, among schizophrenics, is uncommon. (F104)

## MARRIAGE CHANCES OF WOMEN
### X   Prostitution
With the institutionalization of prostitution, a relatively large number of unmarried women will remain unmarried. (C045)

## MARRIAGE CLASS SYSTEM
### X   Cohesion of Society
A shift from a four-section to a six-section system creates a wider sphere of social solidarity by expanding the sphere of kinship relations. (L060)

### Descent
The development of a six-class marriage system from a simple dual organization tends to occur as a result of the recognition of patrilineal as well as matrilineal descent. (S095)

### Descent (Asymmetrical)
The adoption of asymmetrical descent will divide a society with a moiety organization into a six-class marriage system. (S098)

### Descent (Bilateral)
A marriage class system is more likely to arise with the adoption of bilateral descent. (S097)

### Descent (Unilineal)
A marriage class system can only emerge if one of the lines recognized in bilateral descent is dominant. (S098)

### Generational Emphasis
The marriage class system tends to be correlated with an emphasis on generational levels. (E066)

### Kin Terminology (Bifurcate Merging)
With the adoption of a section system, the kinship terminology will tend to be bifurcate merging in character. (E065)

### Kin Terminology (Merging)
When the kinship system is of the vertical type (i.e., merging of all members of clan regardless of generation), the resistance to sections is very strong. (E107)

### Moiety System
The division of a group into moieties precedes the development of a marriage class system. (R034)

### Moiety System (Cross-Cousin Marriage)
A six-class marriage system will arise from a dual organization with matrilineal descent and the marriage of cross-cousins. (S095)

### Polygyny
A high rate of polygyny increases the difficulty of observance of restrictions associated with a marriage class system. (E032)

### Preferential Marriage
An institutionalized pattern of marriage with mother's brother's wife tends to be incompatible with a system of matrimonial classes. (D026)

Marriage with a mother's brother's widow is incompatible with a four- or eight-class marriage system. (S095)

## MARRIAGE CLASS SYSTEM (DOUBLE DESCENT)
### X   Preferential Marriage (Exchange)
In addition to the simultaneous occurrence of both matrilineal and patrilineal kin-groups, marriage by sister exchange must also occur if a double descent class system is to develop. (M045)

## MARRIAGE CLASS SYSTEM (EIGHT)
### X   Incest Taboo
The eight-class marriage system develops when incest taboos are extended to both cross-cousins. (L060)

## MARRIAGE CLASS SYSTEM (SIX)
### X   Incest Taboo
The development of a six-class system tends to result from an asymmetrical extension of incest taboos to only one of the first cross-cousins. (L060)

## MARRIAGE CLASS SYSTEM (TWO-SECTION)
### X   Kin Terminology
There is likely to be a negative correlation between two-section systems and Crow or Omaha types of kin terminology. (M234)

### Preferential Marriage (Cross-Cousin)
A two-section marriage class system will be found in conjunction with patterns of cross-cousin marriage. (M234)

## MARRIAGE COUNSELING   X   Divorce Process
Couples who take a longer time between a serious consideration to divorce and filing suit are more likely to seek marriage counseling. (G157)

### Religion
Catholics are more likely than Protestants to seek marriage counseling. (G157)

## MARRIAGE (FIRST)
### X   Mate Selection (Free Choice)
First marriages are more likely to be arranged by the parents of the bride and groom. (M085)

## MARRIAGE, GOAL OF                    X   Class
The higher the class, the more willing the family is to subordinate tension reduction to other functions of marriage (such as representation and socialization) and to duties to uphold the dominant mores concerning the "sanctity" of marriage. (P083)

### Divorce
When the major function of marriage is alliance of two lineages, the husband is likely to be more hesitant about

initiating divorce for fear of alienating his wife's lineage. (P083)

### Sex Status
The primary motivation focus in marriage for women is the parent-child relationship; for men it is possession of the woman. (P083)

### MARRIAGE, GOAL OF (FERTILITY)     X   Warfare
In societies where warfare is frequent, marriage is more eagerly sought as a means of increasing fighting forces and replacing losses; where warfare is less frequent, this incentive for marriage is lacking. (C091)

### MARRIAGE, GOAL OF (TENSION MANAGEMENT)   X   Mate Selection (Free Choice)
The more important is tension management in the marriage, the more likely it is that marriage will be determined by free courtship. (P083)

### MARRIAGE, INTERGENERATIONAL
### X   Descent (Matrilineal)
### X   Age Difference
As matrilineal groups become weaker, there tends to be less disapproval of marriage between generations. (C090)

### Population
With a decrease in population, intergenerational marriages will tend to increase. (M137)

### MARRIAGE ORDER     X   Age Difference
In polygyny the difference in age between a man and each successive wife increases. (S174)

### Authority Structure of Family
In the polygamous family, the greater the seniority of the wife, the greater her authority in the family. (M198)

### Homogamy (Class)
Class endogamy is less likely to be observed in second marriages. (T054)

### MARRIAGE ORDER OF WIFE
### X   Duration of Marriage
The duration of marriage for divorced women is shorter for secondary wives. (B012)

### Rank of Wife
The status of the wife tends to be directly correlated with the order in which she was married. (W082)

### MARRIAGE PATTERN (WOMAN)
### X   Heir, Absence of
Woman-marriage (a woman marrying a woman) is more likely to occur when there is no male heir in a household. (L091)

### MARRIAGE PAYMENT
### X   Affinal Relations (Conflict)
Affinal conflict will be particularly intense if the husband has failed to pay the bride price. (S090)

### Affinal Ties
The institution of bride-wealth at marriage strengthens the affinal relationship. (S081)

### Age at Marriage
The age at marriage varies in direct relationship to the price of bride wealth. (B035)

The age of males at marriage tends to rise with the inflation of bride-wealth rates. (L026)

Men will tend to marry later in societies in which marriage payment is institutionalized. (O030)

With an increase in the amount of the marriage payment, there will be a corresponding decrease in the age of women at marriage. (T054)

### Class
In societies where there are marriage exchanges (e.g., bride price or dowry systems), the economic exchanges between the bride's family and the groom's family are more likely to approach equality toward the upper strata than toward the lower strata. (G156)

### Cohesion of Kin-Group
Marriage payment serves to reinforce the bonds between kinsmen. (H107)

### Descent
Bride price will be higher in patrilineal than in matrilineal societies. (G156)

### Descent (Matrilineal/Patrilineal)
The amount of the marriage payment tends to be higher in patrilineal than in matrilineal societies. (L101)

### Divorce
There is an inverse correlation between the divorce rate in a society and the prevalence of dowry or marriage payment. (G134)

The higher the divorce rate in a society, the smaller the size of the bride price or dowry. (G156)

The possibility of divorce is inversely correlated with the amount of the marriage payment. (S158)

### Economic Dependence
Economic independence is inhibited by the familial debt which the bride-price system creates. (V010)

### Economic Dependence of Women
Marriage without bride price is associated with the increasing economic independence of women. (L129)

### Economic Level
Where the economy does not permit the accumulation of property, marriage payments will be in services rather than in goods. (W080)

### Economic Rank
The number of relatives involved in an exchange of gifts at marriage will be directly correlated with the status of the families of the bride and groom. (H134)

### Education of Husband
The desirability of an education in the husband produces a pattern of marriage payments by the bride's family. (M081)

### Education of Wife
The size of the marriage payment is directly correlated with the educational level of the wife. (W082)

### Endogamy (Clan)
With a breakdown in the pattern of endogamous marriage in the clan, the size of the marriage payment will increase. (H165)

### Exogamy
The violation of exogamic restrictions will tend to be severely censured if the marriage results in an inequitable adjustment in the marriage payment. (W097)

### Fertility
The size of marriage payment is directly correlated with the number of years of potential fertility in the woman. (H165)

### Genealogical Proximity of Husband/Wife
The amount paid as marriage payment is inversely correlated with the closeness of the kin relationship between husband and wife. (B032)

### Groom Service
If groom service is given, the amount of the bride price will tend to be reduced. (H130)

### Husband-Wife Relations (Closeness)
The greater the extent to which marriage becomes a personal bond between the partners rather than an expression of the wider kinship network, the less the amount which will be paid as the bride price or dowry. (G134)

### Husband-Wife Relations (Power)
The dowry gives a woman economic leverage in her relations vis-à-vis the husband. (K154)

### Kin-Role Definition
When bride price is given to the lineage of the wife's family, rights over the wife's domestic and procreative services will tend to be retained by the lineage of the husband after his death. (L041)

### Marital Stability
The amount of the marriage payment will be reduced when there are other factors to reinforce marital stability. (B032)

Marriage stability is greater where there has been marriage payment. (L113)

As a general rule, the greater the number of kinsmen who contribute to the marriage payment or who share in receiving it, the greater is the security of the marriage. (R087)

The stability of the marriage tends to be correlated with the amount which is paid as bride price. (V010)

### Marital Status (Female)
Marriage payment will be highest when a wife has not been previously married. (B107)

### Marriage, Attitude Toward
When marriage is viewed as conferring advantages on the husband and his family, the institution of bride wealth is more likely to occur. (W082)

### Marriage Rate
The marriage rate varies inversely with the rate of bride price. (B035)

### Mate Selection (Free Choice)
Only in societies which legitimate parental arrangements of marriage will marriage exchanges such as bride price or dowry systems be found. (G156)

The influence which parents exercise in the selection of a mate is directly correlated with their responsibility for the marriage payment. (H164)

There is no correlation between the amount of bride wealth paid and the amount of freedom allowed the individual in choosing a mate. (P025)

As marriages based on mutual choice become more frequent, the importance of the dowry or bride price decreases. (P083)

### Mate Selection (Love)
The greater the role love plays in mate selection, the less important marriage exchanges such as bride price or dowry systems become. (G156)

### Polygyny
Where polygyny is stressed, the size of the marriage payment tends to be large. (O023)

### Preferential Marriage (Avuncular)
Avuncular marriage tends to be associated with a period of bride service followed by permanent patrilocality. (M020)

### Preferential Marriage (Cross-Cousin)
Patterns of marriage payment are unlikely to develop in societies where cross-cousin marriage is the preferential marriage form. (B111)

### Preferential Marriage (Exchange)
Marriage payment will tend to be instituted where the exchange of girls cannot be arranged. (W102)

### Property (Moveable)
Marriage payment will only occur in those societies in which moveable property can be accumulated. (E055)

### Rank
The amount of the marriage payment is directly correlated with the status of the family of the bride. (T069)

### Rank of Affines
A substantial bride price, composed of objects having only ritual and symbolic value, implies both high rank and equality of rank between wife-givers and wife-receivers. If the dowry is made up of consumer goods, the wife-givers have a lower rank than the wife-receivers do. (L051)

### Rank of Husband/Wife
If the status of the husband and wife is unequal, the marriage payment is likely to be high. (E055)

### Rank of Wife
The status of the wife is directly correlated with the size of her marriage payments. (K066)

### Residence (Matrilocal)
Matrilocal residence and a high bride price are negatively associated. (L103)

### Residence (Patrilocal)
Marriage payment tends to occur in societies in which residence is patrilocal. (C060)

When residence rules remove the bride from her home, some form of marriage payment ordinarily accompanies marriage. (M019)

Change from matrilineal, avunculocal system to patrilocal residence tends to result from either an increase in bride price or the adoption of preferential marriage by the exchange of sisters. (M171)

### Sexual Aggression
There is a direct correlation between expected bride-wealth demand and the incidence of rape. (L026)

### Social Integration
Since bride prices are not often the kind of property that can be secured easily outside the social system, in soci-

eties where the custom of bride price prevails, preparation for marriage stimulates a greater commitment of the family to the community values and a greater amount of interaction with other families. (P083)

## MARRIAGE PAYMENT (BRIDE SERVICE)
### X   Economic Rank of Parents
Bride service as a substitute for bride payment is most commonly contracted by men whose parents are dead, separated, or unwilling to shoulder the financial burden of the bride price. (S090)

## MARRIAGE PAYMENT (GROOM SERVICE)
### X   Economic Rank
If a man is of lower economic status, he is more likely to substitute groom service for bride price. (B107)

### Economic Rank of Husband
The duration of groom service is likely to be shortened if the prospective bridegroom is rich and the prospective bride comes from a poor family. (B223)

## MARRIAGE RATE
### X   Communication (Intercommunity)
A decline in the marriage rate tends to be correlated with decreased intervillage communication; the latter reduces the number of potential mates available to those of a marriageable age. (B043)

### Crisis (Social)
Great social disturbance or upheaval will cause a drop in the marriage rate. (C001)

### Economic Conditions
During depressions marriages are likely to decrease at a greater rate than during nondepression periods. (C023)

There is a direct relation between the marriage rate and prosperity and an inverse relation between marriage rate and economic decline. (K161)

Marriages tend to occur during periods when the food supply is abundant. (S099)

### Geographic Mobility
The emigration of large numbers of people of marriageable age will cause a drop in the marriage rate. (C001)

Once they have migrated, migrants have an especially high marriage rate. (H001)

### Marriage Payment
The marriage rate varies inversely with rises in the bride price. (B035)

### Remarriage Rate
Age-specific remarriage rates are generally much higher, age for age, than are age-specific first-marriage rates. (C010)

### Warfare
There is a direct relation between the outbreak of war and a rise in the marriage rate. (K161)

There is a direct relation between the termination of a war and a sharp rise in the marriage rate. (K161)

### Work
When the work schedule calls for the least amount of work or for vacations, there will be the greatest number of marriages. (C001)

## MARRIAGE SYSTEM (CIRCULAR)
### X   Preferential Marriage (Cross-Cousin)
A circular marriage system will result from a matrilateral cross-cousin marriage rule when the total society is made up of defined marriage classes, each of which is exogamous, but which are as a totality endogamous. (S026)

### Stratification
When circular marriage systems in practice fail to conform to the model, class differences will tend to develop. (L051)

## MARRIAGE SYSTEM (CONNUBIUM)
### X   Preferential Marriage (Cross-Cousin)
The establishment of a preferential marriage pattern with a matrilateral cross-cousin will tend to result in the circulation of women through the society in connubial cycles. (N023)

## MATE SELECTION   X   Acquaintanceship, Type of
Marriage is more likely for couples who meet at one or the other's home than for those who meet at work. (C002)

More couples marry who meet through their parents or relatives (while living close by) than couples who meet through school or college acquaintances. (C002)

### Affinal Ties
When affinal bonds are important, marriages subsequent to the initial marriage will tend to be contracted with the same family. (S068)

When marriages are contracted between people who live in different villages, they will tend to occur between communities which are already related by existing marriage alliances. (T039)

### Age
Mate selection tends to occur between individuals of the same generation and of similar age. (E055)

### Age of Male
The range of eligible women is greater, the older the male. (S153)

### Class
Similar social backgrounds increase the likelihood that a couple will marry one another. (G134)

Where marriage is viewed as an exchange, equivalence of social rank is likely to be the rule between contracting families. (P083)

### Cohesion of Kin-Group
When the continuity of the kinship unit is stressed, marriage will tend to be arranged by the family head and to be based on economic and social rank. (B033)

### Community
Residentially propinquitous mate selection is higher if the neighborhood is self-sufficient (i.e., in terms of shopping areas, schools, churches, recreation centers, and places of work). (K020)

Mate selection tends to occur between members of the same community. (M080)

Segregation of an identifiable group of people increases

the likelihood of residentially propinquitous marriages. (K020)

### Dating

College students tend to stress the same factors in selecting dates as in selecting mates. (C023)

### Descent

The more important the descent system for social placement, the more likely is mate selection to be regulated and not left to the whims of young people. (G156)

### Disorganization of Family

Individuals from emotionally disturbed childhood homes do not necessarily tend to marry persons with similar backgrounds. (P086)

### Divorce

Divorce is infrequent in the extended Chinese family since romance is sacrificed to prudential consideration and social status. (B033)

The more important are emotional relationships in themselves as the grounds for mate selection in marriage, the higher the divorce rate will be. (D080)

### Divorce, Ease of

When subjective factors are culturally prescribed as the basis of mate selection, a correlated easy system of divorce tends to occur. (S076)

### Education

When educational level of the groom varies directly with the educational level of the bride, then religion is controlled for. (H014)

### Endogamy (Community)

Unless there are specific rules of local exogamy, most marriages will take place between members of the same community. (M071)

### Fecundity

Men are less likely to wish to marry a sterile woman than a fecund one. (B245)

### Genealogical Proximity

People tend to select sex and marriage partners in direct proportion to the nearness of their actual or conventional kinship. (M019)

### Generation

When there is a significant discrepancy in the generational level of the husband and wife, the factors in mate selection will tend to be of an economic character. (E069)

Mate selection tends to occur between two individuals who are of the same generation. (F037)

### Homogamy (Class)

When religion is controlled for, the class of the residential area in which the bride lives varies directly with the class of the residential area in which the groom lives. (H014)

### I.Q.

Husbands and wives tend to be of the same intelligence level. (W148)

### Joint Family

Arranged marriages, preventing the conjugal bond from becoming too strong and threatening to break the household into nuclear family units, are associated with joint family systems. (G156)

### Kin-Role Definition

Marriages between near kinsmen will be more censured if the new in-law relationships require adjustment of old kin roles. (F037)

### Loss of Family Member

Children from families which have lost (physically or psychologically) a member are more likely than those which have not to make unwise marriage decisions. (T089)

### Love

Decline of arranged marriages in a society is associated with an increase in love as a prominent factor in mate selection. (G156)

In a system where marriages are not prearranged, social patterns exist to motivate young persons to marry for love. (G156)

The more able a society is to prevent love from developing, the more able it is to control who marries whom. (G156)

### Marital Adjustment of Husband

Men who marry women bearing a physical resemblance to their mothers are more likely to be happy than are men who marry women who do not resemble their mothers. (T092)

### Marital Status

People are more likely to marry people of the same marital status as themselves than people of different marital statuses. (B008)

### Marriage

Consensual cohabitation is less likely than either matchmaking by third parties or romantic love to act as a precipitant of marriage. (B245)

### Mental Illness (Schizophrenia)

The schizophrenic is likely to seek in his spouse a reincarnation of infantile aspects of early love objects. (M197)

There is a correlation between first-cousin marriage and schizophrenia in the offspring. (F105)

### Mental Illness (Schizophrenia/Neurosis)

Schizophrenics are more likely to marry persons who resemble their parents of the opposite sex than are neurotics. (M197)

### Moiety System

The institution of a moiety organization tends to discourage marriage between distant members of the same kin unit. (E032)

### Mother-Son Relations

Where his relationship with his mother as a child was not satisfying, the man may seek a girl with characteristics quite different from his mother, but establish with her the kind of relationship which he desired as a child. (B033)

### Nationality

There is a high correlation between mate selection and similarity of nationality. (C103)

### Nativity

Individuals tend to marry persons of like nativity. (S015)

## Neurosis

Neurotics are more likely to marry neurotics than they are to marry "normal" people. (T092)

## Occupation

Mate selection on the basis of occupation is more likely to be endogamous than exogamous. (C008)

Sons of fathers in any given occupational strata are more likely to be married to daughters of fathers in the same strata than to those in any other single stratum. (C008)

Men and women marry people who are in the same or allied occupations more often than can be explained by chance alone. (S012)

## Ordinal Position

The only child is more likely than others to seek a mate like his father or mother. (T089)

## Parent-Child Relations (Control)

Subtle directives expressing attitudes and values on the part of parents concerning their children's selection of a mate are more apt to be effective influences than are more obvious measures (arranged activities or threats). (J035)

## Parent/Spouse, Similarity of

Physical resemblance between the mate and a parent is not as frequent or as marked as are resemblances in attitude and temperament. (C023)

## Peer Relations

The earlier the selection of one's mate, the greater the dependence of boy-girl pairs upon each other and the decrease of interaction within each sex. (M188)

## Personality

A man who is industrious and shy will tend to seek as a mate a physically attractive and vivacious girl. (B217)

People are more willing to compromise in mate selection in the area of physical appearance than they are with respect to desired personality traits. (C023)

Persons with similar personality traits, such as self-confidence, insight, empathy, and emotional stability, are more apt to marry than are persons with dissimilar traits. (J035)

One falls in love with a particular person because that loved one represents a perfection which the lover has striven unsuccessfully to attain. (W148)

## Personality (Complementary Needs)

If a man and a woman remain together for a long period of courtship despite their having a low value consensus, they probably have a high degree of need complementarity. (B002)

If a man and a woman show a high degree of need complementarity, then it is more probable that their relationship will progress toward a permanent union. (B002)

Individuals are more likely to fall in love with others whose personality needs are complementary (e.g., need for dominance and need to submit) than with those whose needs are similar. (B002)

Those couples whose need patterns are complementary are no more likely to fall in love than are those whose need patterns are similar. (B002)

In mate selection, the need pattern of each spouse is more likely to be complementary than similar to the need pattern of the other spouse. (G156)

The tendency for an individual to select a spouse unlike himself in total emotional makeup exceeds the tendency for him to select a spouse like himself in that respect. (K011)

There is no relationship between mate selection and satisfaction of complementary needs. (T092)

## Personality (Complementary Traits)

Assertive persons tend to marry receptive persons. (W148)

If a person is highly nurturant, it is probable that he will marry someone who is highly receptive and relatively nonnurturant. (W148)

If a person is highly dominant, it is probable that he will marry someone who is highly submissive and relatively nondominant. (W148)

## Personality (Maturity)

People choose spouses who have identical levels of immaturity, but who have opposite defense mechanisms. (B297)

## Personality Problems

People tend to choose partners who share similar personality conflicts. (B204)

There is a tendency for narcissistic (self-loving) persons to marry anaclitic (dependent) persons. (W148)

## Personality Problems (Neurosis)

Among neurotics there tends to be a complementariness of neuroses between spouses. (W148)

## Personality Problems (Oral)

Women with unresolved oral conflicts tend to marry passive and feminine-oriented men. (R099)

## Polygyny (Sororal)

When the first wife has an important role in the selection of subsequent mates the pattern of polygyny will tend to be sororal. (S153)

## Rank of Clan

Mate selection tends to occur between clans of approximately the same status. (B112)

## Religion

There is a high correlation between mate selection and similarity of religion. (C103)

## Residence

The majority of marriages will be between local descent groups. (L051)

Most marriages and sexual liaisons tend to take place between residents of the same community in all societies where the community is not regularly a clan or an endogamous gene. (M019)

Individuals tend to marry members of adjacent communities. (O005)

Residential propinquity is a factor in the mate selection when the husband and wife are not kinsmen. (S121)

## Residence/Occupation

The higher a man ranged on the occupational scale, the greater the distance in standard city blocks between his home and the home of his future mate. (K013)

### Role Behavior in Family

Persons who assume the parental role in marital relations usually do not explore the field of eligible spouses very widely. (W148)

Husbands who assume the role of son in marriage usually do not explore the field of eligible spouses very widely. (W148)

### Sex-Role Definition

When the dominant position of the male is emphasized, men will tend to seek as mates women of lower economic and educational status in order to reinforce the disparity between the sex roles. (L064)

### Sex Status

Teen-aged males and females are in fairly close agreement on the criteria that the other person must meet before they will make or accept a date (e.g., the other person should be physically and mentally fit, dependable, etc.). However, they differed in certain respects: males stressed being a good cook and housekeeper, physical attractiveness, and nonuse of tobacco; females stressed importance of a good financial prospect, moderation re intimacy, parental approval, and consideration toward others (U.S.). (C012)

Females tend to be more objective than males in selecting a mate because their position in society is dependent on the male. (S076)

### Sibling Status

Single children are more likely than are persons with siblings to look for a father or mother in a potential spouse and are less likely to look for a peer. (T091)

### Size of Community

The probability of two persons marrying each other when they live in different population groupings (i.e., different towns) tends to increase with the number of persons available (i.e., the size of the population groupings) when distance between the population groupings is held constant. (E010)

### Stratification

The greater the emphasis on a sharp delimitation of rank in a society, the more likely will hypogamy be disapproved. (M167)

### Value Consensus

If a man and a woman have a high degree of value consensus, then it is more probable that they will progress toward a permanent union.

### Values

People tend to marry those who share a common culture interest and value. (B033)

### Voluntary Organizations

Fraternity men and sorority women tended to marry each other more often than can be accounted for by chance alone. (S012)

Fraternity and sorority members married spouses with no college education less than half as often as did other college men and women. (S012)

## MATE SELECTION (CLASS)     X   Race

There is a greater likelihood of the reinforcement of social-class homogamy when different racial elements in a society occupy markedly different positions of social rank. (B029)

## MATE SELECTION (COMPLEMENTARITY)
### X   Neurosis

Marriages of persons with neurotic tendencies are more likely than marriages of normals to involve complementary needs. (B293)

## MATE SELECTION (COMPLEMENTARITY/HOMOGAMY)
### X   Age at Marriage

The younger the person, the less likely is mate selection to be based mainly on complementary needs, but rather on similar sociopsychological background factors, resulting from his more limited associations. (B293)

## MATE SELECTION (DISORGANIZATION)
### X   Household Composition

The greater the disorganization of mating relations, the greater the incidence of domestic units consisting of single mothers with their children and/or their grandchildren. (S211)

## MATE SELECTION (ECONOMIC MOTIVES)
### X   Age Difference

When there is a significant disparity between the ages of the husband and wife, economic factors tend to be dominant in the selection of a mate. (T069)

## MATE SELECTION (EDUCATION)     X   Sex Status

Women are more likely to eliminate from consideration as marriage partners individuals of different educational status than are men. (B033)

## MATE SELECTION (FREE CHOICE)
### X   Acculturation

With acculturation the choice of a mate becomes increasingly independent of family opinion. (A034)

### Age

Marriages are more likely to be arranged by the parents when the couple is young. (M085)

### Age at Marriage

Men are more likely to marry late in order to maximize their position in the marriage market when families rather than peer groups control unmarried girls (thus assuring the man in his late twenties or early thirties access to desirable girls). (P083)

### Authority Structure of Family

Increased freedom in mate selection is associated with reduced control by family elders. (G156)

The more powerful the older persons are in a society, the more likely they are to have a voice in mate selection. (K152)

When there are strong patterns of authority within an extended family structure, the choice of marriage partner tends to be arranged by the parents. (S043)

### Class

Where parents are in control of marriage arrangement, social standing, economic status, and financial return are the major considerations in mate selection. (B033)

European patterns of individual choice in marriage tend to be more common among the poorer groups. (G056)

The higher the social rank of the family, the less freedom allowed in courtship. (G156)

Parental influence tends to be greater in the selection of a mate toward the upper classes. (R062)

### Courtship
With the decline of parental control over marriage, courtship on the part of young people becomes the approved preliminary to engagement and marriage. (B033)

Where there is free mate choice, it is usually preceded by courtship. (S189)

### Descent (Unilineal)/Extended Family
There is a decided, though imperfect, tendency for marriage to be either arranged or by parents' consent when either unilineal kin-groups or frequent extended family households are present. (S189)

### Divorce
As the elders and kin lose their control over marriage, the divorce rate increases. (H062)

### Economic Dependence
With increasing economic independence of the individual, the selection of the mate tends to be an individual rather than a family decision. (R038)

### Economic Dependence of Children
When children become economically independent, an increasing percentage of marriages are contracted without parental consent. (H032)

### Economic Pattern (Migrant Labor)
Under conditions of labor migration, women have far greater power and independence in marriage negotiations. (K065)

### Economic Rank
The marriages of the more wealthy families tend to be arranged by the parental groups. (E015)

### Elopement
Elopement is likely to occur when parents disregard the wishes of the child in choice of a spouse. (B181)

Elopement tends to occur when there is a serious discrepancy between the criteria of the parents and of the child for mate selection. (S043)

Where mate selection is largely the consequence of parental decision, patterns of elopement are likely to occur. (T107)

### Intermarriage
A culture which has the concept of individualism in mate choice as embedded in a "romantic complex" is more likely to have more intermarriage than is a culture without such a concept. (B012)

### Kin-Group, Importance of
Arranged marriages tend to be found in kinship systems where the newly married couple is incorporated into a larger kin-group. (P012)

### Love
Love is likely to be an important criterion of mate selection if cultural conditions encourage premarital interaction between men and women in order to provide the opportunity for testing out personalities of a variety of potential mates. (W148)

Love is likely to be an important criterion of mate selection if cultural conditions stipulate that the choice of mates must be voluntary (i.e., not arranged by persons other than the marriage partners) and bilateral (i.e., both man and woman must possess at least the power of veto). (W148)

### Love Magic
Love magic is likely to be absent when there is a puritanical sex code and the elders arrange all marriages. (H222)

### Marital Adjustment of Parents
Parents are most likely to interfere and try to influence the courtship patterns of their children when their own marriages have been unsuccessful. (C023)

### Marital Stability
The stability of a marriage tends to be higher if the selection of a mate is the responsibility of the family rather than of the individual. (L079)

### Marriage Chances
The smaller the number of potential spouses available to the young person, the more able is a society to control who marries whom. (G156)

In societies in which family members are interdependent in regard to their marriage chances, marriage is more likely to be a problem of corporate action requiring centralized decision powers for the corporate group. (P083)

When the marriage-market position of any one nuclear family is related to the extended family position, the final authority on the desirability of a given match is more likely to rest with the political authority of the extended family. (P083)

### Marriage (First)
First marriages are more likely to be arranged by the parents of the bride and groom. (M085)

### Marriage, Goal of (Tension Management)
The more important is tension management in the marriage, the more likely marriage will be determined by free courtship. (P083)

### Marriage Payment
Only in societies which legitimate parental arrangements of marriage will marriage exchanges such as bride price or dowry systems be found. (G156)

The influence which parents exercise in the selection of a mate is directly correlated with their responsibility for the marriage payment. (H164)

There is no correlation between the amount of bride wealth paid and the amount of freedom allowed the individual in choosing a mate. (P025)

As marriages based on mutual choice become more frequent, the importance of the dowry or bride price decreases. (P083)

### Mate Selection (Near Kin)
Marriage with near kinsmen is associated with the importance of parental opinion in the selection of a mate. (S140)

### Mental Illness (Schizophrenia)
Mental illness tends to be correlated with a parental marriage which was imposed upon the wife by the patient's maternal grandmother. (L118)

### Parent-Child Relations (Control)
Mate selection will tend to be controlled by parents when premarital social contacts are sharply restricted. (R035)

With the weakening of parental control, the individual

tends to make his choice of mate independent of his parents' wishes. (S134)

### Paternal/Maternal Role Behavior
Mothers tend to exert more pressure than fathers do in controlling the child's selection of a mate. (B033)

### Peer Relations
Where parents wish to control the marriage of their daughter, her peer-group activities are likely to be restricted. (P083)

### Rank
The degree of parental influence in mate selection is directly correlated with the status of the boy or girl. (W105)

### Residence (Matrilocal)
With matrilocal residence in force, parents tend to exert strong control over marriage choice of the daughter since they will become dependent upon the daughter and son-in-law in later life. (O027)

### Sex Ratio
The parental arrangement of marriages will tend to occur when there is a scarcity of women. (L100)

### Sex Status
Parental pressure to control the selection of a mate is greater when the child is a daughter. (B033)

### Social Chance
Closed systems of mate selection are more apt to exist in societies where there is less social and technological change. (J035)

### Social Mobility
Closed systems of mate selection are more apt to exist in societies with little vertical social mobility than in societies with more vertical social mobility. (J035)

### Stratification
Closed systems of mate selection are more apt to exist in societies with less status differentiation. (J035)

### Urbanization
Parental control of marriage is more likely to occur in the fringe area than in the central city. (J003)

An increase in the degree of urbanization tends to be correlated with the weakening of control of parents in the process of mate selection. (M050)

### Values (Familism)
As the force of traditional familial mores weakens, the intellectually emancipated begin, in increasing numbers, to demand the control of arranging their own marriages. (B033)

### Values (Individualism)
The more that individualism is stressed in a society, the more likely it is that an individual will make his own choice of spouse. (K152)

### Warfare
Warfare and the attendant intermixture of people of different clans tend to result in a wide choice permitted in selecting a wife. (S092)

## MATE SELECTION (INTELLIGENCE)
### X  Employment of Wife, Attitude Toward
Men who prefer women of equal intelligence are less likely to object to a woman having a career than are men who prefer women of lower intelligence than themselves. (H190)

### Personality (Self-Confidence)
Men who desire females of equal intelligence have greater self-confidence than those who do not. (H190)

### Sex-Role Adjustment
The greater the man's feelings of inadequacy in his sex role, the more likely is he to be attracted to a woman of lower intelligence than himself. (H190)

### Sex-Role Definition
Men who prefer women of equal intelligence are more tolerant of their personal likes and dislikes than are men who prefer women of lower or higher mental ability. (H190)

## MATE SELECTION (KIN)
### X  Sexual Permissiveness
Kinsmen who stand in a relationship of potential marriage partners are generally permitted to treat each other with sexual freedom. (W070)

### Size of Ethnic Group
When the size of the ethnic group is small, there is a greater likelihood of the existence of previous kin ties between people who marry. (F037)

## MATE SELECTION (LOVE)
### X  Husband-Wife Relations (Dependency)
As men become potentially less dependent upon women for home management and cooking (due to the availability of services such as restaurants, laundries, etc.), affectional ties have become a more important factor in the decision to marry. (P083)

### Independence of Nuclear Family
Love as an essential factor in mate selection is most likely to be found in societies where the nuclear family unit is relatively independent of the larger kinship group. (G156)

### Interaction in Family (Affection)
Patterns of marriage based on romantic love are more likely to occur in societies in which the family pattern is characterized by affectional frustration than in societies in which the family relationship is a warm one. (T106)

### Marriage Payment
The greater the role love plays in mate selection, the less important marriage exchanges such as bride price or dowry system become. (G156)

### Parent-Child Relations (Closeness)
Mate selection based on romantic love tends to be found in societies where the parent-child relationship is strong. (G156)

## MATE SELECTION (NEAR KIN)    X  Class
Among the upper classes, marriage with near kin is more likely than among the lower classes. (S140)

### Marital Stability
Marriage with near kinsmen is more likely than marriage with strangers to insure the stability of the marriage. (S140)

### Mate Selection (Free Choice)
Marriage with near kinsmen is associated with the importance of parental opinion in the selection of a mate. (S140)

### Polygyny
There is a definite correlation between polygyny and the incidence of marriage with near kin. (S140)

## MATE SELECTION (RELIGION)    X  Sex Status
Women are more likely than men to eliminate from consideration as marriage partners individuals of different faiths. (B033)

## MATE SELECTION (REMARRIAGE)
### X  Clan Affiliation
In remarriage, men are more likely to select a wife who is of the same clan as the first wife. (C039)

## MATE SELECTION (RESIDENCE)    X  Age
Residential propinquity as a factor in mate selection is greater among the very young and the very old than among the middle age groups. (C023)

### Community
Residentially propinquitous mate selection is higher if the neighborhood is self-sufficient (i.e., in terms of shopping areas, schools, churches, recreation centers, and places of work). (K020)

Segregation of an identifiable group of people increases the likelihood of residentially propinquitous marriages. (K020)

### Education of Husband
There is *no* relationship between educational level of prospective husbands and their choice of a mate living near their homes. (C002)

### Income
Individuals with low incomes are likely to be more propinquitous in their mate selection than are individuals with high incomes. (K020)

### Intermarriage (Religious)
A higher proportion of Catholic men who marry non-Catholic women marry propinquitously than of Catholic women who marry non-Catholic men. (Propinquitous marriage: bride and groom live within a radius of 20 blocks.) (S016)

### Occupation
Men in the professional and managerial categories are less affected by residential propinquity in selecting a spouse than are those in unskilled jobs. (C002)

Males in skilled occupations select spouses closer to their homes than do men in the clerical and sales group. (C002)

### Occupational Rank
Residential propinquity, as a factor in mate selection, is less prevalent among the professional strata than among any other occupational strata. (F009)

Occupational rank of the groom does not vary inversely with the degree of residential propinquity of groom and bride. (S012)

Occupational rank of the groom does vary inversely with the degree of residential propinquity of the groom and bride. (S012)

### Parent-Child Relations (Control)
Residential propinquity will cease to be a factor in mate selection as parental control weakens. (S121)

### Peer Relations
As the individual's degree of acceptance in the neighborhood peer group increases, so does the likelihood of residentially propinquitous mate selection. (K020)

### Population
As population density increases, so does the likelihood of residentially propinquitous mate selection. (K020)

### Race
Residential propinquity in mate selection is more characteristic of Negroes than of whites. (G020)

### Religion
The Protestant is more likely to marry someone who lives within eight standard city blocks of him than is the Catholic. (C002)

### Social Mobility Aspirations
As the mobility aspirations of individuals increase, the likelihood of residentially propinquitous mate selection decreases. (K020)

## MATERNAL DEPRIVATION
### X  Child-Rearing Practices (Neglect)
Children who suffered early maternal deprivation are likely to grow up to subject their own children to similar neglect. (B270)

### Cognitive Development
Children deprived of their mothers have an impaired ability to relate to other people and to think abstractly, and generally have an impaired ego and superego development. (B270)

### Criminality
There is a significant correlation between a childhood history of early maternal deprivation (below the age of six and for at least six months' duration) and a criminal record in later life. (E093)

### Personality of Child (Antisocial)
Maternal deprivation causes anxieties to arise in deprived children over the unsatisfactory parent-child relationship that predispose children to respond in an antisocial way to later stresses. (B270)

### Scholastic Adjustment
Children who are deprived of adequate mothering during infancy are more likely in later years to be unable to concentrate in school. (P068)

### Scholastic Adjustment (Reading)
Children with reading disabilities are more likely than those with no difficulty in reading to have had disturbed and deprived relationships with their mothers. (S225)

### Social Development
Children deprived of their mothers have an impaired ability to relate to other people, to think abstractly, and generally have an impaired ego and superego development.

### Social Mobility Aspirations
Females aspiring toward upward social mobility are no more likely than are female nonaspirants to perceive their relationships with their mothers as depriving. (R101)

## MATERNAL OVERPROTECTIVENESS
### X  Achievement Aspirations of Mother
Maternal overprotectiveness is likely to occur if the mother has been thwarted in her educational or career ambitions. (L163)

### Achievement Motivation
Overprotective mothers tend to have fewer children

with high achievement motivation than do dominant mothers. (R097)

### Age at Pregnancy
Maternal overprotectiveness tends to be directly correlated with the age of the mother at the birth of the first child. (L162)

### Aggression
Overindulgence on the part of the mother is correlated with aggressive and egocentric behavior in the child. (B033)

### Alcoholism
Maternal overprotection and pampering of the child are causes of alcoholism in later life. (M195)

Maternal overprotection of the child is not related to alcoholism in later life. (M195)

### Anxiety
Overprotective and infantilizing behavior on the part of the mother toward the child tends to foster chronic anxiety in the child. (R113)

### Anxiety Dreams
Falling dreams will tend to occur in cases of marked maternal overprotectiveness. (H216)

### Aspiration Level of Mother
Maternal overprotectiveness is likely to occur if the mother has been thwarted in her educational or career ambitions. (L163)

### Autoeroticism
Maternal overprotection does not affect patterns of masturbation in the child. (L161)

### Behavior Problems
Overprotected children are more likely to be disobedient, impudent, to exhibit temper tantrums, and to make excessive demands on others. (B033)

### Breast Feeding, Duration of
There is a correlation between maternal overprotection and length of time the infant is breast fed. (A063)

Overprotected children have a significantly longer breast-feeding time than do nonoverprotected children. (L117)

If maternal overprotection is the result of a compensatory reaction to feelings of rejection, it will not result in extended breast feeding. (L162)

### Child-Rearing Practices (Responsibility)
The mother's experience of premature responsibilities early in life is a cause of overprotection of her child. (B272)

### Childhood
Extreme deprivation in the mother's childhood is a cause of later overprotectiveness toward her own child. (B272)

The mother's experience of harsh realities early in life is associated with her later overprotectiveness toward her child. (B272)

### Childhood Experience
The mother's experience of harsh realities early in life is a cause of her later overprotectiveness toward her child. (B272)

### Class
The higher the social status of the mother, the more likely she is to be overprotective toward the child. (H183)

Male schizophrenics from the middle class are more likely to have overprotective mothers than are those from the lower class. (M197)

### Cognitive Development
Maternal overprotection is associated with acceleration and interest in reading and with arithmetic retardation.

### Cognitive Development (Verbal)
Maternal overprotection is associated with a favorable rate of verbal development in the child. (B257)

### Conformity
For boys, maternal overprotection between ages 4 and 7 is positively related to their conformity to parental demands during adolescence. (K115)

### Criminality
There is a negative correlation between maternal overprotection and criminality. (M164)

### Death of Parents
Death of the mother's parents during childhood is a cause of her later overprotectiveness toward her child. (B272)

### Dependency
Maternal overprotection tends to be directly correlated with an inhibition of patterns of independence in the child. (L163)

Maternal overprotectiveness tends to be correlated with an early/premature assumption of family responsibility (whether through death of parent or poverty). (L163)

### Drug Addiction
Mothers of drug addicts tend to be overprotective, controlling, and indulgent. (F090)

### Education of Mother
There is no relationship between maternal overprotection and the educational level of the mother. (K115)

### Emotional Problems of Mother
There is a correlation between affect hunger in the mother and her overprotection of the child. (B272)

### Employment of Mother (Regularity)
Women who are overprotective tend to have stable patterns of employment. (L163)

### Father Absence
In families where the father is away from the home for extended periods of time, the mother is more likely to overprotect her children. (G156)

Wives (of Norwegian sailors) whose husbands were absent for extended periods of time exceeded matched mothers whose husbands were not absent in being overprotective and stressing obedience and politeness (not happiness or self-realization). (M181)

### Father-Son Relations
In families characterized by maternal overprotection, the father-son relationship is one of indifference or impatience, though not overtly one of hostility. (L163)

### Grandmother-Grandchild Relations (Indulgence)
Overprotective mothers tend to be reinforced by the indulgent attitudes of grandmothers. (L163)

### Husband-Wife Relations (Shared Activities)
Parents of overprotected children share significantly fewer social activities together than do those of nonoverprotected children. (L117)

Overprotective mothers tend to share little common social life with their husbands. (L163)

### Illness of Child
Death-threatening illness in the child is a cause of maternal overprotection. (B272)

### Kin Relations
Maternal overprotection is associated with frequent interference in the family by relatives.

### Maternal-Role Behavior
Maternal overprotectiveness tends to be associated with early patterns of mothering during childhood. (L163)

### Mental Illness of Child (Schizophrenia)
Mothers of schizophrenic children tend to infantilize them with overprotection and extension of the period of dependency.

### Mental Illness (Schizophrenia)
Overprotection of the child by the mother is an essential factor in the formation of schizophrenia in the child. (B285)

Poor premorbid schizophrenics (poor general functioning before onset of illness) perceive their mothers as having been more overprotecting than do good premorbid schizophrenics or normal subjects. (G127)

Schizophrenics are more likely to come from families where there is maternal overprotection and where fathers are nondominant and/or indifferent figures. (H207)

Mothers of schizophrenics tend to be overprotective and sometimes rejecting, domineering, and aggressive. (S187)

### Mental Illness (Schizophrenia/Neurosis)
Maternal overprotection is more likely in the early background of the neurotic than in that of the schizophrenic. (M218)

Mothers of schizophrenics are likely to be more overprotective and "smothering" than are mothers of neurotics. (S187)

### Mother-Child Relations (Affection)
Maternal overprotection is directly correlated with patterns of defective maternal love on the part of the maternal grandmother. (L163)

### Mother-Child Relations (Intimacy)
Maternal overprotection tends to be correlated with an extension of early intimacy contacts (e.g., sleeping together). (L164)

### Neurosis
Overprotective and infantilizing behavior on the part of the mother tends to foster such neurotic anxiety symptoms as delusions, obsessions, phobias, etc., in the child. (R113)

### Parent-Child Relations (Affection)
Mothers of overprotected children are more likely than mothers of nonoverprotected children to have experienced a marked lack of parental affection and of childhood play. (L117)

### Parent-Daughter Relations (Deprivation)
Extreme deprivation in the mother's childhood is a cause of later overprotectiveness toward her own child.

### Parent Loss
Maternal overprotection is more likely to occur if one or both of the woman's parents have died during her childhood. (L163)

### Paternal Role
An overwhelming proportion of fathers of overprotected children played little or no authoritative role in the life of the child. (L117)

### Paternal Role (Discipline)
In families in which the mother is overprotective, the father will assume a passive disciplinary role, either voluntarily or under pressure by the mother. (L163)

### Peer Relations
Children subject to maternal overprotection tend to have difficulty in their relationships with peers. (L161)

Maternal overprotection tends to be directly correlated with patterns of deprivation of childhood play when the mother was a girl. (L163)

### Personality (Neatness)
Children of overindulging mothers are more likely to be careless, while children of domineering mothers will tend to be neat and careful. (L161)

### Personality of Child
Children whose mothers are *indulgently* overprotective will tend to be rebellious and aggressive; those whose mothers are *dominatingly* overprotective will be submissive and dependent. (L163)

### Personality of Child (Competitiveness)
Children whose mothers are overly protective and infantilizing in their behavior toward them are not likely to be overly competitive with siblings or with others. (R113)

### Personality of Child (Maturity)
Overprotective and infantilizing behavior on the part of the mother tends to foster general immaturity in the child. (R113)

### Personality of Child (Nightmares)
Children whose mothers are overly protective and infantilizing in their behavior toward the child tend to have frequent nightmares. (R113)

### Personality of Child (Submissiveness)
The more overprotective the mother, the more likely is the child to be submissive.

### Personality of Mother
Overprotective mothers will tend to be responsible, stable, aggressive women. (L163)

Mothers who tend to express their sadistic domination of their children as overprotectiveness tend themselves to be infantile and egocentric. (R115)

### Personality Problems (Affect Hunger)
There is a correlation between affect hunger in the mother and her overprotection of the child. (B272)

### Personality Problems of Child
Overprotection by the mother will lead to dominating, yielding, submissive, or effeminate behavior in the child. (B033)

### Power Structure of Family
Maternal overprotectiveness and paternal dominance are mutually exclusive. (L163)

### Pregnancy Anxiety
Maternal overprotection is directly correlated with anxiety as to the successful termination of the pregnancy. (L163)

### Pregnancy, Attitude Toward
A long period of waiting for the birth of a child is a cause of maternal overprotectiveness toward the child. (B272)

### Recreation
The maternally overprotected child is more likely to be interested in reading and less likely to be interested in sports.

Chilren who are subject to maternal overprotection tend to have passive recreational habits and to display a notable lack of interest in sports. (L161)

### Scholastic Adjustment
The maternally overprotected child is less likely to have special school problems.

### Sex-Role Behavior
Maternal overprotectiveness is not likely to occur in women who stress their femininity. (L163)

### Sexual Adjustment
Marital sexual incompatibility is a cause of maternal overprotection of the child. (B272)

### Sexual Aggression
Sexual aggressiveness is less likely to occur where maternal overprotectiveness was manifested as dominance rather than as indulgence. (L164)

### Sexual Deviance
Maternal overprotectiveness tends to result in an increased sexual drive toward the mother which manifests itself in flight from the mother and impulsive heterosexuality, impotence, or homosexuality. (L161)

### Social Adjustment
Maternal overprotectiveness tends to be negatively correlated with adjustment on the part of the child to his peers. (L162)

### Social Relations of Parents
Maternal overprotection is associated with a lesser amount of social life of the parent.

### Work Attitudes of Mother
If the mother is satisfied with her employment outside the home, she tends to feel guilty about it and as a consequence she is overprotective toward the child. (H183)

### Work Behavior of Mother
Strong degrees of responsibility, independence, and stability in work are causes of maternal overprotection of the child. (B272)

## MATERNAL ROLE
### X   Child-Rearing Practices (Consistency)
Mothers who are the primary caretakers of their babies tend to be inconsistent concerning rules about aggressive behavior and other rules. (M216)

### Class
Mothers of lower-class mental patients are more likely than mothers of middle-class mental patients to have almost sole responsibility for family affairs, have little time for the patients, and have difficulty maintaining order in the household. (M061)

Working-class mothers are more likely to have sole responsibility for family affairs, have less time for their children, and have more difficulty in maintaining order in the home than are middle-class mothers. (M197)

### Employment of Mother
Women with children are most likely to be in the labor force when all the children are in school. (G156)

### Identification with Child
The less that the mother has developed the passive aims essential to the maternal role, the less likely it is that she will be able to identify with the child's needs or to respond to his demands without feeling a threat to her own ego. (B272)

### Identification with Parents
The degree to which females feel they are like their mothers is more dependent on the extent to which the mother meets the child's concept of ideal mother than is the case among males. (J032)

### Incest (Father-Daughter)
Families in which father-daughter incest occurs are apt to be characterized by the daughters' assumption of the mother role when the mothers have deserted the family. (K091)

### Interaction in Family (Affection)
When no other adult woman in the household has a role similar to that of the mother, the average intensity of affective involvement in family relations is likely to be high (U.S.). (P012)

### Marital Adjustment
Women's greater disenchantment during the middle years of marriage is partly a function of the birth of a child. (P071)

In emotionally disturbed marriages, the management of the children tends to be exclusively handled by the wife. (V028)

### Mother-Child Relations (Affection)
Patterns of passive, demanding love are more likely to develop when the mother assumes both the supportive and the disciplinary role. (W154)

### Polygyny
The mother is more important to her children in a polygynous than in a monogamous marriage. (R030)

### Sex-Role Identification
Mothers of boys who have weak sex-role identification are more likely than those whose sons have strong sex-role identification to have taken the major role in disciplining the child. (L142)

### Superego Formation
Male subjects will rank higher on attitudinal measures of self-blame if they perceive the principal disciplinarian role in the family as being played by the mother rather than by the father. (H015)

Individuals reporting that they blame themselves and not others are more likely to perceive the mother as the principal disciplinarian in the family. (H067)

# MATERNAL-ROLE ADJUSTMENT
### X  Employment of Mother
Employment or nonemployment of the mother does not correlate with adjustment to children; however, unemployed mothers were more likely to desire children and to feel nervous due to their children. (S265)

Working mothers, more frequently than nonworking mothers, express anxiety about their role as mother (significant at 5 per cent level). (Y050)

Among dissatisfied (with role) mothers, those who work are less likely to have problems of control of child, emotional satisfaction, or adequacy of mothering. (Y050)

### Employment of Mother, Attitude Toward
Mothers who do not work and do not wish to do so are more likely to be satisfied mothers and to be more successful in child-rearing practices than are mothers who are nonworking because of a "duty to mothering." (Y050)

### Employment of Mother, Duration of
While employment of the mother initially produces poorer adjustment to children, the longer the duration of employment, the better the adjustment. (S265)

### Filicide
Conscious feelings on the part of the mother of inability to bring up the child may lead to filicide. (T085)

### Oedipal Complex
If masochistic impulses (which are derived from, and are a defense against, incestuous wishes toward her father) are only partially relinquished by the mother, she is more likely to feel inadequate in the maternal role and to express her anxiety in periodic outbursts of a sadomasochistic nature against her children. (B272)

### Personality Problems (Castration Complex)
The more severe the girl's castration complex, the less likely it is that she will be able to accept the passive aims essential to the maternal role. (B272)

### Pregnancy Anxiety
High anxiety during pregnancy is related to dissatisfaction with the maternal role. (D067)

### Surrogate Mother
When their infants are six months of age, mothers who have been the only caretaking figure for their infants are more self-confident in and are more likely to minimize the difficulties associated with child rearing than are mothers who have provided other mother figures for their infants. (C107)

When the child is six years of age, mothers who have reared the child themselves feel more self-confident in their handling of the child and in ordinary child-rearing problems than do mothers of children who have been reared by more than one mother figure (i.e., a nurse, grandparent, friend of mother, older sister of the child). (C124)

# MATERNAL-ROLE ADJUSTMENT/SIZE OF FAMILY          X  Employment of Mother
Employed mothers are more likely than nonemployed mothers to be well adjusted to children in small, but not in large, families. (S265)

# MATERNAL ROLE, ATTITUDE TOWARD
### X  Age at Marriage
Mothers who enjoy looking after their babies tend to have married younger than mothers who do not enjoy caring for their babies. (N051)

### Broken Home
Broken homes are associated with unwillingness on the part of the mother to accept the responsibility of the child. (K120)

### Child-Rearing Practices (Control/Nurturance)
Mothers who are high in control and low in nurturance are perceived by both sons and daughters as more rejecting of the homemaking role. (H196)

### Child-Rearing Practices (Rewards)
Mothers who frequently use praise or tangible rewards in child rearing express greater satisfaction with being mothers and wives than do those who use these techniques less frequently (U.S.). (S191)

### Child-Rearing Practices (Sleeping)
Rejection of the mother role is associated with rigid practices regarding the sleeping patterns of children, overabsorption in the mother role being associated with overpermissive practices regarding sleeping patterns of the child. (K113)

### Class
Middle-class mothers are less sure about the adequacy of their maternal-role performance than are upper- or lower-class mothers. (S280)

### Criminality
There is a correlation between the mother's ambivalence toward her familial role and criminal behavior in the son. (M195)

### Identification with Parents
Identification is positively related to the mother's commitment to her parental role. (R098)

### Illegitimacy
Unwed pregnant women express less desire for pregnancy and less maternal feeling than married pregnant women do. (C099)

Unwed pregnant women exhibit more depression and withdrawal and see the maternal role as being less important than (married) primigravida do. (C099)

### Juvenile Delinquency, by Sex Status
Nondelinquent girls are more likely than delinquent girls to describe their mothers as liking child rearing. This distinction does not hold for delinquent and nondelinquent boys. (M205)

### Marital Adjustment
When the marriage is a happy one, the wife is more likely to see the children as a source of satisfaction to her.

### Mental Illness of Child (Schizophrenia)
Compared to parents of children with adjustment reactions, conduct disturbances, and sociopathic symptoms, the mothers of schizophrenics are more likely to reject the homemaking role. (Z011)

### Mother-Child Relations (Tolerance)
Mothers who are unsatisfied with parenthood are more likely than other women to lack tolerance for their children's behavior. (G126)

### Paternal-Role, Attitude Toward
The intensity of the urge toward motherhood in a given

society is a function of the male attitude toward fatherhood. (D071)

### Pregnancy, Attitude Toward
Women who have a negative attitude toward pregnancy are more likely to have fewer motherly attitudes. (N051)

### Sex Attitudes
Women who feel positive toward caring for their babies tend to have positive feelings about intercourse. (N051)

### Sex-Role Adjustment
Women who dislike caring for their newborn babies are also more likely to dislike other aspects of their female biological role. (N051)

### Social Mobility Aspirations
Mothers with aspirations for upward mobility are less sure about the adequacy of their maternal-role performance than are nonaspiring mothers. (S280)

### Social Network of Husband–Wife
The more dispersed the couple's social network (i.e., its members do not see one another independently of the couple), the more likely it is that the wife will feel some dissatisfaction with the maternal role. (B267)

**MATERNAL-ROLE BEHAVIOR    X   Age of Child**
There is no relationship between age of the infant and maternal behavior (sensitivity, consistency, or frequency of maternal acts). (B272)

### Age of Mother
There is no direct correlation between maternal behavior and the age of the mother. (L165)

### Alcoholism
Mothers who resent their role in the family, as expressed by assuming the role of a martyr or by neglecting the home, are more likely to have alcoholic sons than are mothers who play passive, active, or dictatorial roles in the home. (M195)

### Behavior Problems
Children who have been frustrated in early suckling and "mothering" give up sucking later and less spontaneously.

### Breast Feeding
Whether or not breast feeding is continued is directly related to the amount of maternalness exhibited in the first few days of breast feeding. (P063)

### Breast Feeding, Duration of
Maternal behavior is positively correlated with a preference for breast feeding for five months or longer. (L165)

### Child-Rearing Practices (Aggression)
The greater the proportion of time the mother spends in child care (children aged 7–10), the more likely is she to reward the child for peer-directed aggression. (M216)

### Child-Rearing Practices (Clarity)
The greater the proportion of time the mother spends in child care (children aged 7–10), the more likely is she to communicate rules clearly to the child. (M216)

### Child-Rearing Practices (Control)
The more time the mother allocates to the care of older children (10 years plus), the less likely is she to use manipulative gifts and privileges to control the child. (M216)

### Child-Rearing Practices (Sex Role)
To the degree that the social-emotional leader (the mother) upholds the family value system, she can socialize her daughter in the sex role considered appropriate to that system. (F094)

### Dependency
The emotional dependence of the children on the mother will be increased if she serves as an intermediary between father and children. (H082)

### Emotional Adjustment of Mother
The amount of time spent in care of younger children (3–6 years of age) is not related to the emotional stability of the mother. (M216)

The greater the amount of time spent in care of older children (7–10 years of age), the higher the emotional instability of the mother. (M216)

### Employment of Mother
Lower-class working mothers are less likely to feel the need to compensate for their absence from the home than are middle-class mothers. (G156)

Employment of the mother is related to undue impatience on her part, neglect of the children, loss of discipline, loneliness of the children, and their inadequate socialization. (S265)

The working mother is less motherly than is the nonworking mother. (Y050)

### Father-Child Relations
Maternal mediation is more disruptive of father-child relationships in a nuclear than in a paternalistic society. (S216)

### Fecundity
Maternal behavior (e.g., following adoption of a child) may induce physiological changes favorable to conception in women previously sterile. This proposition is also denied. (P083)

### Happiness in Childhood
There is no direct correlation between maternal behavior and the mother's happiness in childhood. (L165)

### Health of Child
Absence of sufficient mothering is associated with gastrointestinal disorders in the child. (P072)

### Juvenile Delinquency
There is no relationship between excessively clean housekeeping (or the reverse) by the mother and delinquent behavior of the children. (N057)

### Kin/Nonkin Interaction
Younger women (nonmothers) are less apt to share task and emotional behavior when they are in a family situation than are older women (mothers) and are more apt to do so when they are with strangers. (L180)

### Marital Adjustment
The greater the integration of the marriage, the greater the role of the mother as mediator between father and child, reinforcing the norms of the former. (F094)

### Maternal Overprotectiveness
Maternal overprotectiveness tends to be associated with early patterns of mothering during childhood. (L163)

### Menstruation, Age at

There is no direct correlation between maternal behavior and age at menarche. (L165)

### Menstruation, Attitude Toward

Women who complain about menstruation are more likely to be unmotherly. (N051)

### Menstruation, Length of

Maternal behavior is directly correlated with a pattern of menstrual flow of more than five days. (L165)

### Mental Illness of Mother

The more acute the mental illness, the more likely that mothering will be affected by it. (S203)

### Mental Illness (Schizophrenia)

Mothers of schizophrenics want to be perfect parents and many perceive themselves to be perfect. (K093)

### Mental Problems (Cerebral Palsy)

Mothers of children with cerebral palsy score significantly higher on the PARI scales of Seclusiveness, Strictness, Intrusiveness, Acceleration, Encouraging, Verbalization, Equalitarianism, Comradeship, and Sharing; mothers of normal children score significantly higher on Marital Conflict, Irritability, Rejection of Homemaking Role, and Avoidance of Communication. (S249)

### Mental Retardation of Mother

There is no relationship between intelligence ratings of mentally retarded mothers and their ability to provide satisfactory child care. (B307)

### Mother-Child Relations (Gratification)

There is a correlation between the maternal-role behavior corresponding to that phase of the child's development most gratifying to the mother and the maternal role to which she may regress when confronted with frustration in later phases of the child's development. (M203)

### Mother-Child Relations (Need Gratification)

The more the mother is warm and loving and the more continuous her influence in daily routine and total lifespan, the more likely she is to be a source of safety and need gratification to the child. (P068)

### Mother-Child Relations (Phallic)

The mother's ability to imbue the child with phallic attributes and to accept herself a passive role is correlated with and determines her own capacity for psychologically normal maternal behavior. (B272)

### Oedipal Complex

If the mother defends herself against persistent masochistic impulses (which are derived from and are a defense against early incestuous wishes toward the father) by the mechanism of reaction formation, she is more likely to take a predominantly active and aggressive maternal role and to assign the rejected passive role to the child. (B272)

If the mother defends herself against persisting masochistic impulses (which are derived from and are a defense against early incestuous wishes toward the father) by the mechanism of "identification with the aggressor," she is more likely to adopt an active and aggressive maternal role and to discharge her sadistic impulses upon the child. (B272)

### Ordinal Position

There is no direct correlation between maternal behavior and the ordinal position of the child. (L165)

### Parent-Child Relations (Preference)

There is no direct correlation between maternal behavior and the mother's preference for one or the other parent during her childhood. (L165)

### Paternal-Role Behavior

As the wife becomes more involved in the mother role, the husband becomes a marginal member of the family (becomes increasingly alienated from the family and family decisions).

### Personality Problems of Child

Compared to mothers of normal children, the mothers of maladjusted children are less likely to accelerate development of the child, to reject the homemaking role, and are more likely to be secluded. (Z011)

### Personality Problems of Child (Stuttering)

The stuttering child produces in the mother feelings of helplessness, incompetency in her maternal role, reactive anger, and fear of disciplining the child. (W136)

### Self-Conception (Maternal)

Maternal behavior is positively correlated with a self-image of strong maternality. (L165)

### Sex Status of Child

There is no direct correlation between maternal behavior and the sex of the mother's child. (L165)

### Size of Family

The fewer the number of living children, the greater the ability of the mentally retarded mother to provide adequate child care. (B307)

### Superego Formation

A deep sense of guilt in a child is directly correlated with a mother who emphasizes her personal sacrifice to the interests of her family. (V029)

### Surrogate Mother

The more persons available to aid in care of older children (ages 7–10), the less time the mother will spend in caring for her offspring. This relationship does not hold for infants (cross-cultural). (M216)

## MATERNAL-ROLE DEFINITION
### X Affinal Relations (Conflict)

Conflicts between mother-in-law and daughter-in-law are more frequent than between mother-in-law and son-in-law. (B033)

### Class

The higher the socioeconomic class, the more likely it is that the wife will stress the activity of maintaining personal relationships over that of routine housekeeping. (S276)

Upper- and middle-class mothers are less likely to accept the "service" aspects of the maternal role than are lower-class mothers. (S280)

The aspect of the maternal role most likely stressed among lower-class mothers is caring for physical needs; among middle-class mothers it is development of character and morality; and among upper-class mothers it is handling social and emotional needs. (S280)

### Cohesion of Family
When no other adult woman has a role similar to that of the mother, the average intensity of affective involvement in relations within the family is likely to be high. (P012)

### Marital Status
Ambiguity of the role of mother tends to increase (in order) with respect to the marital statuses of 1) widow-mother, 2) wife-mother, and 3) divorcée-mother. (G015)

### Mental Illness (Schizophrenia)
Mothers of schizophrenics tend to set up perfectionist goals for their roles as mothers. (T105)

### Parent-Child Relations (Equalitarianism)
In a culture where the parent-child relationship is defined as equalitarian and friendly, there is little pressure during later years to terminate or change the quality of the maternal role. (C116)

### Social Mobility Aspirations
Mothers striving for upward mobility are less likely to accept the "service" aspects of the maternal role than are mothers more content with their social statuses. (S280)

## MATERNAL ROLE (DISCIPLINE)
### X     Ordinal Position
The mother plays a greater role in caretaking and discipline of the youngest child than of other children, regardless of family size. (S191)

## MATING FORMS          X     Remarriage
The greater the extent to which extraresidential union, consensual cohabitation, and marriage proceed as a typical sequence, the lesss likely is the resumption of consensual cohabitation by widows or widowers. (S211)

### Residence
Relatives and children of the wife of a male head-of-family account for a larger proportion of the family size when extraresidential mating is common. (S211)

### Urban/Rural
Urbanization or urban residence does not cause changes in the sequence of mating forms. (S211)

## MEN'S SOCIETIES      X   Economic Cooperation
Men's societies tend to occur in communities of moderate size where economic cooperation is a stable pattern. (M067)

### Residence (Matrilocal/Patrilocal)
Men's societies appear more frequently among patrilocal societies than in matrilocal ones. (M067)

### Social Structure (Differentiation)
Men's societies tend to occur in societies which are simple and relatively undifferentiated. (M067)

## MENSTRUAL TABOO     X   Castration Anxiety
Extensiveness of menstrual taboos in a society is associated with intensity and frequency of castration anxiety among men. (S079)

### Child-Rearing Practices (Obedience)
When menstrual taboos are extensive in the society there is severe punishment for disobedience and very strict obedience demands are made on children. (S079)

### Child-Rearing Practices (Punishment)
In a society that gives great importance to physical punishment as a technique of child discipline, menstrual taboos are likely to be extensive. (S079)

### Child-Rearing Practices (Sex)
Severe sexual training is associated with elaborate menstrual taboos. (S079)

### Descent
There is no correlation between the extensiveness of menstrual taboos and the various rules of descent and residence (e.g., matrilineality, patrilineality, etc.). (S079)

### Economic Role of Women
There is no correlation between extensiveness of menstrual taboos and the importance of the woman's contribution to the subsistence of the economy. (S079)

### Menstruation, Isolation During
Societies with menstrual huts tend to have taboos on sexual intercourse between husband and menstruating wife. (S189)

### Paternal Role (Discipline)
When menstrual taboos are extensive in the society, the father is expected to be the main disciplinarian. (S079)

### Sex Taboo (Postpartum)
There is a correlation between a prolonged postpartum sex taboo and elaborate menstrual taboos. (W127)

### Surrogate Parent
When the mother shares nurturance with other people in the first few years of the child's life, the society is *less* likely to have extensive menstrual taboos. (S079)

## MENSTRUAL TABOO (COOKING)
### X     Menstruation, Isolation During
Societies with menstrual huts have menstrual cooking taboos. (Wife may not cook for husband when menstruating.) (S189)

## MENSTRUATION, AGE AT
### X     Maternal-Role Behavior
There is no direct correlation between maternal behavior and age at menarche. (L165)

## MENSTRUATION, ATTITUDE TOWARD
### X     Maternal-Role Behavior
Women who complain about menstruation are more likely to be unmotherly. (N051)

## MENSTRUATION, ISOLATION DURING
### X     Menstrual Taboo
Societies with menstrual huts tend to have taboos on sexual intercourse between husband and menstruating wife. (S189)

### Menstrual Taboo (Cooking)
Societies with menstrual huts have menstrual cooking taboos. (Wife may not cook for husband when menstruating.) (S189)

## MENSTRUATION, LENGTH OF
### X     Maternal-Role Behavior
Maternal behavior is directly correlated with a pattern of menstrual flow of more than five days. (L165)

## MENTAL DEFICIENCY          X   Broken Home
Among disturbed children, mental deficiency is associated with normal, rather than broken, homes. (H198)

### Pregnancy (Stress)

Mothers who experience emotional stress during pregnancy are more likely than others to give birth to infants who suffer from mental impairment. (S227)

## MENTAL DEFICIENCY, ATTITUDE TOWARD
### X  Class

The class of the family is directly correlated with the degree to which the mental defective is defined as abnormal. (P065)

## MENTAL ILLNESS        X   Age at Marriage

Mental illness is more likely to occur among those who have had an early marriage. (L122)

### Child-Rearing Attitudes (Authoritarianism)

Mothers of psychiatric patients are more likely to have authoritarian and controlling attitudes than are mothers of normals. (T097)

### Child-Rearing Attitudes (Strictness)

Mothers of psychiatric patients are less likely to have strict child-rearing attitudes than are mothers of normals. (T097)

### Child-Rearing Practices (Achievement Demands)

Mental illness tends to be directly correlated with maternal emphasis on high performance for the child. (L126)

### Child-Rearing Practices (Discipline)

There is no correlation between psychosis and the father's methods of discipline. (M164)

### Child-Rearing Practices (Giving Reasons)
### X   Paternal/Maternal-Role Behavior

Fathers of psychotic children are more likely than mothers to explain the rationale of parental discipline. (D064)

### Child-Rearing Practices (Punishment)

Excessive maternal control and punishment after puberty tends to be directly correlated with mental illness. (S187)

### Childbirth

There is no positive correlation between psychosis and the conditions of the child's birth. (M164)

### Class

The psychopathological processes of antisocial character disorders appear to be the same regardless of the economic or social status of the family. (B310)

The severity and frequency of any particular type of psychopathology are greater in the lower classes than in the upper. (B310)

Social status is negatively correlated with mental illness, regardless of a person's marital status (single, married, divorced, etc.). (H222)

### Cohesion of Family

Where there is mental disorganization within a family based on a pattern of pseudomutuality, family members attempt to preserve the family's autonomy. (W021)

### Death

Psychologically disturbed patients have in common an appreciably greater incidence of bereavement in childhood than that obtaining among Americans in general. (A070)

### Death of Like-Sex Parent

Mental illness tends to be directly correlated with the death of the parent of the same sex. (S187)

### Death of Parent

There is no relationship between losing the parent by death and mental disorders in the child. (P072)

There is a definite correlation between the death of a parent and mental illness. (S187)

### Death of Sibling

Mental illness appears to be correlated with the death of a sibling of the patient. (S187)

### Dependency

An exclusive emotional dependency on the mother tends to be directly correlated with mental illness. (L118)

### Dependency on Father

Mental illness in women is directly correlated with a strong dependency on and preoccupation with the father during the early years. (F085)

### Emotional Problems of Mother

Mental illness is directly correlated with a family environment in which the mother is emotionally disturbed. (F085)

### Employment of Mother

Mothers who are not employed are more likely to be psychotic than are mothers who are employed. (S275)

### Ethnicity

More siblings of Jewish than of Protestant background are likely to be mentally ill if it is the mother who is mentally disturbed, suggesting that Jewish mothers have more effect on their children. (S187)

### Father Absence

Mental illness among females is more likely to occur if the father is absent from the family. (S187)

### Father-Child Relations

Mental illness is more likely to occur if the father resents the intrusion of the child. (L123)

### Father-Child Relations (Rejection)

Mental illness tends to be associated with a cruel and rejecting father. (S187)

### Father-Daughter Relations (Consistency)

Mental illness is more likely to occur when the allegiance of the daughter is with the father, particularly if inconsistent, rather than with the mother. (L123)

### Geographic Mobility

There is no relationship between residential mobility and mental illness in a family member. (F107)

If a member of the family is mentally ill, particularly if he is a husband, the family is more likely to move to a new residence. (F107)

There is no relationship between having a former mental patient in the home and residential mobility of families. (F124)

### Homosexuality

There is no positive correlation between psychosis and homosexual tendencies. (M164)

### Household Composition

Mental illness is less likely to occur where the residential unit is the extended family. (T110)

### Husband-Wife Relations (Closeness)
When the parents are close and have a high emotional investment in each other, the patient improves; conversely, when the parents are "emotionally divorced," the patient regresses. (B315)

### Husband-Wife Relations (Conflict)
Mental illness tends to be correlated with conflict between parents. (L119)

### Identification of Mother with Child
There is a high degree of correlation between mental illness and the failure of the mother of the patient to identify with the patient. (H218)

### Identification with Mother
Mental illness is directly correlated with a primary emphasis upon the mother and her family, rather than upon the father. (F085)

### Illegitimacy
Unwed mothers are more likely to have psychopathological problems prior to pregnancy than are married mothers. (L135)

### Marital Adjustment
Mental illness tends to be correlated with marital dissatisfaction on the part of the patient's mother. (L118)

### Marital Status
Mental illness is more prevalent among divorced persons than among the widowed, among the widowed more than among the single, and among the single more than among married persons. (A006)

Mental illness is more prevelant among widowed Negroes than among divorced Negroes, but more prevalent among divorced whites than among widowed whites. (A006)

Variability in the incidence of mental illness by marital status is greater among males than among females (i.e., females are more likely than males to have the lowest incidence in mental illness among the married, then the single, then the widowed, and, finally, the highest incidence, among the divorced. (A006)

Among New York Negroes, mental disorders are more likely among the single than among the married, but this ratio decreases with age and the relationship is reversed among men over 50 years of age. (M219)

There is a correlation between widowhood and mental disorders among men, but not among women. (M219)

Separation and divorce are more highly correlated with mental disease among women than they are among men. (M219)

### Mental Illness of Spouse
Spouses of mental patients are more likely to suffer from mental illness themselves than are spouses of normal people. (K159)

There is no evidence to support the idea of assortative mating among schizophrenics. (K159)

### Mother-Child Relations (Affect)
Emotional alienation from the mother will tend to produce overt manifestations of mental illness. (L125)

### Mother-Child Relations (Attachment)
Mental illness is directly correlated with an exclusive attachment to the mother. (S187)

### Mother-Child Relations (Hostility)
Mental illness tends to be correlated with hostile behavior during feeding. (L118)

### Mother-Son Relations (Affection)
Mothers of prepsychotics tend to have actively affectionate relationships with their sons. (M164)

### Mother-Son Relations (Control)
Mothers of prepsychotic sons tend to overcontrol their children more than other mothers do. (M164)

### Mother-Son Relations (Possessiveness)
Mothers of schizophrenic sons are not more possessive of them than are the mothers of sons having other nonorganic mental disorders. (F099)

### Ordinal Position
Earlier-born children are more susceptible to mental diseases than are later-born children. (M197)

Ordinal positions which permit an exclusive concern of the parents with the child are conducive to mental illness. (M197)

In the middle class, youngest boys and oldest girls are more likely than others to be mentally disturbed. (M197)

In the lower class, the oldest boy is more likely than others to become mentally disturbed. (M197)

### Parent-Child Relations
The combination of a smothering mother with either a passive father or an absent father is especially likely to produce psychosis in the son. (M164)

### Parent-Child Relations (Filial Piety)
Mental illness is less likely to occur where filial piety is emphasized. (T110)

### Parent-Child Relations (Rejection)
Parents are more likely to have rejected than to have overprotected the mentally ill individual during childhood. (S187)

### Parent Loss
When subjective factors (recalled unfavorable attitudes and/or treatment of child by the parents) and objective factors (any kind of physical separation) are viewed together, the relationship between subjective factors and subsequent tendencies toward mental disturbance holds only in cases where physical separation also occurred. (C121)

Mental illness of the parents is a significant cause of deprivation among patients suffering from dementia praecox and manic-depressive psychosis. (O034)

There is no significant relationship between either the age at which deprivation occurred or the parent was lost and the subsequent mental health or mental illness of the child. (O034)

The incidence of various types of psychiatric abnormalities is almost identical among the siblings of both deprived and nondeprived patients. (O034)

The incidence of dementia praecox is unrelated to known external stresses or deprivations. (O034)

### Parental-Role Definition/Behavior
Mental illness is more likely to occur where there is a discrepancy between the parental behavior and the socially defined role of parent. (L123)

#### Paternal Role
In the families of middle-class mentally ill patients, the father's role tended to be ambiguous in the home. (M061)

Mentally ill middle-class patients are more likely (than are lower-class patients) to question their fathers' masculinity and authority. (M061)

#### Personality (Emotional Stability)
When members of a family are undergoing therapy, it is a frequent occurrence that as one member gets better the other gets worse. (A052)

#### Personality of Mother
Mental illness is directly correlated with a family environment in which the mother is an isolated, paranoid woman and is excessively preoccupied with events within the family. (F085)

Mothers of mentally ill persons tend to be perfectionistic, narcissistic, immature, frigid, emotionally detached, frightened by body contact, and capable of functioning satisfactorily only on an intellectual level. (S187)

Mothers of the mentally ill tend to be "stiff and bitter" and inclined to anxiety, uncertainty, and obsessions. (S187)

#### Personality of Mother (Eccentricity)
Mothers of prepsychotics tend to be more eccentric than do mothers of nonprepsychotics. (M164)

#### Personality of Mother (Perfectionism)
The mothers of middle-class mentally ill patients tend to have been rigid perfectionists. (M061)

#### Personality of Parents (Projection)
Mental illness tends to be correlated with an environment in which an inordinate amount of projection by a parent is used and condoned. (J019)

#### Personality Problems of Father (Paranoia)
Mental illness is more likely to occur if the father has delusions of paranoid grandiosity. (L123)

#### Power Structure of Family
Mental illness is directly correlated with a family environment in which the mother is dominant. (M164)

Mental illness is more likely to occur if the father is strict and the mother overprotective. (M165)

#### Residence with Kin
There are more adult mental patients living in parental-family settings than would be expected on the basis of the family settings of the general population. (F124)

#### Scapegoating
Mental illness is most likely to occur in those individuals who are the focus for intrafamilial hostility. (J019)

#### Sexual Behavior of Mother
There is no positive correlation between the mother's sexual behavior and psychosis. (M164)

#### Sibling Rivalry
Mental illness is more likely to occur if the individual's siblings are perceived to be more successful. (M165)

#### Sibling Structure
When characteristics involving sibship (e.g., number, sex, and spacing) are investigated for deviations from homogeneity among seven diagnostic groups of psychiatric patients, the only significant finding is that there is an increased frequency of patients with paranoid schizophrenia among patients having a sibling less than two years older than themselves and an increased frequency of sociopathic personality and other personality disorders among those having a sibling less than two years younger than themselves. (G155)

#### Sibling Structure (Ordinal Position and Sex)
In the middle class youngest boys and oldest girls are more likely than others to be mentally disturbed. (M197)

In the lower class the oldest boy is more likely than others to become mentally disturbed. (M197)

#### Size of Household
There is no relationship between changes in household size and mental illness or hospitalization of a family member. (F124)

#### Social Isolation
Mental illness is directly correlated with a failure to establish relationships outside of the immediate family situation. (F085)

#### Social Mobility Aspirations
Parents of middle-class mentally ill patients tended to exhibit social-status-striving behavior and patients tended to behave in a like manner. (M061)

#### Social Mobility Aspirations of Mother
In middle-class families of the mentally ill, mothers tended to have had frustrated mobility aspirations and were ambitious for the patients' social advancement. (M061)

#### Social Network of Parents
There is a negative correlation between mental illness and the number of individuals perceived as important to the parents or to one parent. (L126)

#### Values (Sex Role)
In the families of mentally ill middle-class patients, the value of equality of the sexes tends to be strongly held. (M061)

#### Weaning
Mental illness tends to be directly correlated with hostile behavior during feeding and with premature or cruel weaning. (L118)

### MENTAL ILLNESS (ALCOHOLIC PSYCHOSIS)
#### X   Marital Status
Alcoholic psychoses are more likely among the widowed, separated, and divorced than among the married or single. (M219)

### MENTAL ILLNESS, ATTITUDE TOWARD
#### X   Age of Kin
The younger the relatives of a mental patient are, the more likely they are to consider mental illness an acquired, curable sickness, which is treatable by hospitalization. (F109)

#### Geographic Mobility
Among homeowners, relatives' feelings of stigma, due to a family member being a mental patient, are correlated with residential mobility. Among renters, this association holds only for the middle class (as opposed to the lower class). This correlation among middle-class renters is increased if the patient occupies the kin role of "son" and if his posthospital occupational and social performance is poor. (F107)

Families who feel stigma due to a relative's being a mental patient are less likely to be satisfied with their present dwelling unit. (F107)

### Mental Illness of Child (Schizophrenia)

The mother of the schizophrenic is more likely than the mother of the neurotic to regard the child as having been "normal" until his illness and to ascribe the illness directly to loneliness or to sexual problems. (M218)

### Mental Illness (Social Adjustment)

There is no relationship between relatives' feelings of stigma regarding the mental patient and the patient's success or failure in remaining in the community. (F124)

Relatives of successful patients with high social and occupational performance levels are least likely to express feelings of stigma; but relatives of patients with low levels of performance are as likely to express feelings of stigma as are relatives of failures (those rehospitalized). (F124)

Patients who perform at high levels socially and occupationally are more likely than those with low levels of performance to have families who have an environmental view of the causes of mental illness. (F124)

Patients who perform at high levels socially and occupationally are more likely than those with low levels of performance to have families with favorable attitudes toward mental hospitals. (F124)

Patients who perform at high levels socially and occupationally are more likely than those with low performance levels to have families who believe that mental illness does not basically change a person. (F124)

Patients who perform at a high level socially and occupationally are more likely to have families who believe that mental patients can be normal and healthy again. (F124)

Patients who perform at high levels socially and occupationally are more likely than those performing at low levels to have relatives who believe that patients are not to blame for their condition. (F124)

Patients who succeed in remaining in the community are more likely to have relatives who believe that patients are not to blame for their condition than are those who were rehospitalized. (F124)

Attitudinal responses of family members regarding mental illness are correlated with the patient's condition when he returns to his family as well as to the duration and frequency of hospitalization. (F124)

The higher the level of familial expectations regarding the former mental patient, the higher the level of the patient's performance. (S245)

### Parent/Spouse

Mental illness and resultant behavioral deviations are more likely to be tolerated by parents than by the marital partner. (S245)

### Personality of Relatives

Relatives of mental patients who have low expectations regarding posthospital performance tend to be more anomic, authoritarian, frustrated, rigid, and withdrawn than are those with high expectations. (S245)

## MENTAL ILLNESS (AUTISM)
### X Disorganization of Family

Autism is more likely to occur as a reaction to a disturbed family environment when the disturbance occurs during the period in which the mother is the primary object to the child (i.e., from six months to three years). (S188)

### Personality of Father (Compulsiveness)

Autism is more likely to occur if the father exhibits compulsive behavior during the vulnerable developmental period. (S188)

### Sibling Structure (Age Difference)

Autism is more likely to occur if another sibling is born during the vulnerable developmental period. (S188)

## MENTAL ILLNESS BY RACE    X Marital Status

Mental illness is more prevalent among widowed Negroes than among divorced Negroes, but more prevalent among divorced whites than among widowed whites. (A006)

## MENTAL ILLNESS (CATATONIA)
### X Child-Rearing Practices (Consistency)

Catatonia is more likely to occur in a family environment in which the dominant parent exercises authority inconsistently and regards the children as responsible. (S187)

### Parent-Child Relations (Dominance)

Parents of catatonic patients tend to impose their own wills upon the patients when they are children. (S187)

## MENTAL ILLNESS (CEREBRAL ARTERIOSCLEROSIS AND SENILE PSYCHOSIS)
### X Marital Status

Psychoses with cerebral arteriosclerosis or senile psychoses are more likely among widowed men and among single women than among other marital categories. (M219)

## MENTAL ILLNESS, FAMILY ADJUSTMENT TO
### X Psychotherapy

The greater the accommodation of a family for a disturbed member, the less the likelihood that he will come to psychiatric attention. (S206)

## MENTAL ILLNESS (HOSPITALIZATION)  X Class

Families of low social status are likely to leave a psychotic member of the family in a mental institution for a longer period of years than are families of high social status. (H222)

### Household Composition

There is no significant difference in the type of family setting of mental patients with low levels of social and vocational performance who succeed in remaining in the community and those who return to the hospital. (F124)

### Marital Status

Married persons are less likely to be admitted to mental hospitals than are single persons; single persons less likely than widowed; and widowed less likely than divorced persons. (A006)

Married mental patients, regardless of sex, are more likely than unmarried patients to remain in the community after release from the hospital. (F124)

Married persons tend to be more rapidly discharged from mental institutions than do the single. (N056)

There is no correlation between marital status of the mental patient and frequency or date of readmission to the hospital. (N056)

The widowed and divorced occupy an intermediate position between the single and the married with regard to incidence of mental illness and duration of stay in mental institutions. (N056)

### Role Definition in Family
Among mental patients whose posthospital social and vocational performances were low, those whose primary role in the family was that of child were more likely to stay out of the hospital than were those whose primary role was that of spouse. (F124)

Family members influence instrumental performance; married men have higher levels of instrumental performance than do single men living with parents, because wives have higher expectations than parents do. This factor does not, however, explain rates of rehospitalization. (F124)

Differential demands of family account for the fact that patients from conjugal families return to the hospital more frequently than do those from parental families. (F124)

## MENTAL ILLNESS IN FAMILY
### X   Parent-Child Relations (Preference)
Children in "sick" families are more likely to prefer the mother over the father than are those in healthier families, who like both parents nearly equally.

### Sibling Relations
Children from "sicker" families are more likely to withdraw from involvement with their siblings than are those from healthier families. (L150)

## MENTAL ILLNESS IN PARENTS' FAMILIES
### X   Juvenile Delinquency
If the family of orientation of the parents has been affected by such mental diseases as psychoses, psychoneuroses, epilepsies, sex inversions, etc., the child is more likely to become a juvenile delinquent. (G144)

If the family of orientation of the mother has been affected by more mental diseases than has the family of orientation of the father, then the child is more likely to become a juvenile delinquent. (G144)

## MENTAL ILLNESS (MANIC-DEPRESSIVE)
### X   Authority Structure of Family
Manic-depressives are likely to come from families in which there are a number of authority figures. (C092)

### Child-Rearing Practices (Authority)
Manic-depressives tend to come from families in which standards of authority are poorly expressed, yet in which strict and conventional behavior is stressed. (C092)

### Child-Rearing Practices (Demands)
Excessively high parental demands (which lead to resentment of the parents, introjection of a conflicting parent- and self-image, and dependence on external sources of self-esteem) is a cause of manic-depression in the child. (P078)

### Child-Rearing Practices (Indulgence)
Manic-depressives tend to have been overindulged in childhood. (C092)

### Interaction in Family (Emotional Intensity)
Manic-depressives tend to come from families in which the internal relations are intense and in which there is a sense of isolation from the world. (S181)

### Marginal Status
Manic-depressives are more likely to come from families which are in minority groups (social, economic, ethnic, or religious). (S181)

### Mother-Child Relations
A manic-depressive character is more likely to develop if the mother's reaction to the rebelliousness of early childhood is harsh and punishing. (C092)

The manic-depressive child is more likely than the normal child to view the mother as the moral authority in the family and his attitude toward her is likely to be unloving, but fearful and desirous of approval. (G022)

Manic-depressive patients are likely to have had an early history of "injurious maternal influence." (W154)

### Nonkin Relations
Manic-depressives are more likely to come from families in which there is considerable anxiety expressed about family relations with nonfamily members. (S181)

### Occupational Achievement of Father
Fathers of manic-depressives are most likely to be defined occupationally as failures. (C092)

### Parent-Child Relations
Manic-depressives come from families in which there has been a serious disturbance in the early parent-child relationship. (C092)

### Parent-Child Relations (Affection)
Manic-depressives are more likely to regard their fathers with greater affection than their mothers. (C092)

### Parent-Child Relations (Indulgence)
Manic-depressives tend to have been overindulged in childhood. (C092)

### Personality of Mother (Ambitiousness)
Manic-depressives are more likely to come from families in which the mothers are intensely ambitious. (C092)

### Power Structure of Family
Among manic-depressives, the mother is more likely to be the dominant parent. (G022)

### Sibling Rivalry
A home in which there is sibling rivalry is more likely than other homes to produce manic-depressive children. (W143)

### Social Isolation of Family
Families of manic-depressive patients tend to be set apart in some way from their environment; in some cases it is because of a minority-group status, in others because of financial reverses, in still others because of some aberrant behavior by a member of the family group. (G022)

### Social Mobility Aspirations of Parents
Manic-depressives are more likely to come from families in which the chief interest in the child is in his potential usefulness in improving the family's position or in meeting the parents' prestige needs. (C092)

### Surrogate Parent
Manic-depressives are more likely to come from families in which multiple parental figures share responsibilities for guidance of the infant and child. (G022)

## MENTAL ILLNESS (MANIC-DEPRESSIVE AND DEMENTIA PRAECOX)    X   Marital Status
Dementia praecox and manic-depressive psychoses are more likely among the single than among the married. (M219)

## MENTAL ILLNESS MANIC-DEPRESSIVE/SCHIZOPHRENIC)
### X   Paternal/Maternal Role
The mothers of manic-depressive patients tend to be more reliable than the fathers; this is not true of the parents of schizophrenic patients. (G022)

## MENTAL ILLNESS, MOTHER'S RESPONSE TO
### X   Class
Lower-class mothers of mentally ill children tend to be overprotective, whereas upper- and middle-class mothers tend to reject the schizophrenic child. (S187)

## MENTAL ILLNESS/NEUROSIS
### X   Cohesion of Family
The families of neurotic patients are more likely than those of mentally ill patients to be closely knit. (M061)

### Paternal Role
Fathers of lower-class schizophrenics tend to show less interest in household affairs than do fathers of neurotics. (M061)

The fathers of neurotic patients are more likely than those of mentally ill patients to display an interest in the patients' rearing and activities. (M061)

### Rank of Father
The families of neurotic patients are more likely than those of mentally ill patients to have fathers who are successful in the community. (M061)

### Surrogate Parent
The families of neurotic patients are more likely than those of mentally ill patients to have elder relatives available as surrogates if the parrents cannot devote enough time to patients. (M061)

## MENTAL ILLNESS OF CHILD
### X   Child-Rearing Attitudes
Girls with incipient psychopathology are more likely to attribute deviant child-rearing attitudes to their mothers than are normal girls. (H185)

### Child-Rearing Attitudes (Democratic)
There is no correlation between the extent to which the mother has democratic child-rearing attitudes and the mental health of the child. (T097)

### Child-Rearing Practices (Consistency)
There is a correlation between the consistency of the parents' expectations of the behavior of the child and the child's mental health. (F116)

Inconsistency of demands and prohibitions, inconsistency in rewards and punishments, and overrigidity tend to break a child's defenses, weaken the ego or superego structure, or bring about fixation at a narcissistic level. (L120)

Alternation between understimulation and overstimulation may be directly correlated with mental illness in the child. (S188)

### Child-Rearing Practices (Dependency)
There is a greater possibility of mental illness if the child is encouraged to be excessively dependent on his mother. (M164)

### Child-Rearing Practices (Discipline)
Parents tend to discipline normal siblings more rationally than psychotic children. (D064)

Mothers of prepsychotics are likely to be either punitive or entirely lax in their discipline. (M164)

### Child-Rearing Practices (Punishment)
Parents tend to discipline psychotic children more severely than they do normal children. (D064)

### Childbirth (Anxiety)
Mental illness in the child is associated with maternal anxiety at the time of birth. (L126)

### Conflict in Family
Mentally disturbed children tend to appear in families in which they are involved in conflict or in disequilibrium between the parents. (S075)

### Father Absence
The absence of the father may be less detrimental to mental health than his presence if he is too aloof or depised by the mother. (L123)

### Father Absence/Personality (Passivity)
Fathers of prepsychotic children tend to be passive or absent from the home. (M164)

### Father-Child Relations (Rejection)
Fathers of prepsychotics tend to be rejecting toward the child. (M164)

### Father-Son Relations (Hostility)
Mental illness is more likely to occur in males when the hostility of the father is turned against the child. (L123)

### Husband-Wife Relations (Conflict)
Mental illness of offspring is associated with a family enviroment in which there is open conflict between the parents. (F085)

### Identification of Mother with Child
Mental disturbances in the child are more likely to occur when the mother identifies the child exclusively with herself than when she identifies the child with both parents. (H218)

### Mental Illness of Mother
There is no significant relationship between the duration of mental illness in the mother and the degree of psychopathology in the child. (S203)

### Mental Illness of Parent
There is no correlation between psychosis in a parent and mental illness in the child. (B285)

When the dominant parent is mentally disturbed, mental illness is likely to occur. (L119)

Mental illness of offspring is directly correlated with mental illness of parent. (L119)

Mental illness in a child is more likely if a parent is mentally disordered and the mother dominant. (M164)

### Mother Absence
Children deprived of their mothers for more than eight

months of the first year are more likely than are normals to show severe psychiatric disturbances. (B270)

Mental illness induced by lack of maternal care during a period of at least two and one-half years does not seem to be relieved by the initiation of maternal care. (B270)

The absence of the mother is one of the prime causes of mental illness in children hospitalized before the age of two. (S277)

### Mother-Child Relations (Ambivalence)
Preschizophrenic children are likely to have an extremely strong and ambivalent bond to their mothers. (S187)

### Mother-Child Relations (Isolation)
Mental illness tends to be directly correlated with attempts by the mother to inhibit contacts with peers. (L126)

### Mother-Child Relations (Rejection)
There is no correlation between hostility and rejection on the part of the mother and mental illness in the child. (T097)

### Parent-Child Relations
Parents understand more of the behavior and mental life of normal siblings than of psychotic children. (D064)

### Parent-Child Relations (Affect)
Parents are more emotionally driven and impulsive (rather than rational) toward psychotic children than toward their siblings. (D064)

Parents are more emotionally involved with psychotic children than with their siblings. (D064)

Sick children tend to be more highly and more positively involved with the cross-sex parent than are healthier children. (L150)

### Parent-Child Relations (Affection)
Parents are more consistently affective (affectionateness, rapport, direction of criticism) toward normal siblings than toward psychotic children. (D064)

### Parent-Child Relations (Conflict)
There is more disciplinary friction between parents and psychotic children than between parents and their normal children. (D064)

### Parent-Child Relations (Indulgence)
Parents are more likely to be more solicitous and responsive in their attitudes toward their psychotic children than toward their other children. (D064)

### Parent-Child Relations (Oedipal)
Unconscious reversal of the Oedipal situation by the parent is correlated with the onset of psychosis. (H192)

### Parent-Child Relations (Rejection)
Parents reject the psychotic child more than do his siblings, both as a member of the family and as an individual. (D064)

### Parent Loss
In the lower class, "total deprivation" (complete loss of parent) is a more important determinant of subsequent mental disorder in the child than it is in the middle or upper classes; whereas "partial physical deprivation" (parents sick or mother working) is a more important

determinant of subsequent disorder than is total deprivation in the middle and upper classes. (C121)

### Paternal/Maternal Role
The mother is no more important than the father in the etiology of mental illness in the child. (F110)

### Paternal/Maternal-Role Behavior
Mothers are more likely than fathers to be more anxious, impulsive, and overprotective toward their psychotic children. (D064)

### Paternal-Role Behavior
Mental illness is directly correlated with a failure of the father to participate in the care and raising of the psychotic child. (F085)

### Personality of Parents
Mental illness is less likely to develop if the emotional difficulties of the mother can be counterbalanced by a stable father. (L123)

Parents of mentally ill children are more likely to be rigid, self-deceiving, and immature than are parents of normal children. (S187)

### Personality of Parents (Passivity)
Fathers of psychotic children are more passive than are mothers. (D064)

### Pregnancy, Attitude Toward
There appears to be no direct correlation between whether or not the mother desired the child and the development of a later psychosis. (R115)

### Sex Anxiety of Mother
There is no positive correlation between psychosis of the child and sexual anxiety in the mother. (M164)

### Sex-Role Model
There is a greater possibility of mental illness if the child is deprived of a male model. (M164)

### Social Isolation
Mental illness is more likely to occur among children whose extrafamilial activities are severely restricted. (L126)

## MENTAL ILLNESS OF CHILD, ADJUSTMENT TO
### X  Marital Adjustment
Couples who are unhappily married are less likely than those who are happily married to accept or cope well with the psychotic child. (C109)

### Ordinal Position
When parents are well adjusted in a marriage, the ordinal position of the psychotic child is relatively unimportant as a factor in their adjustment (i.e., to the illness). (C109)

## MENTAL ILLNESS OF CHILD (AUTISM)
### X  Illness of Parent
Autism is more likely to occur if a parent becomes ill during the vulnerable developmental period. (S188)

### Marital Adjustment of Parents
Autism is more likely to occur if there are marital difficulties between the parents during the vulnerable developmental period. (S188)

### Mother-Child Relations
Autism is directly correlated with a disturbed mother-child relationship. (S188)

### Mother-Child Relations (Closeness)
Autism occurs in young children who have not had a close, almost symbiotic, relationship with their mothers as infants. (S213)

### Parent-Child Relations
Autism is directly correlated with a disturbed parent-child relationship. (S188)

### Parent-Child Relations (Rejection)
Since parents of autistic children are more likely to be rejecting and overintellectual rather than outgoing and warm, the children fail to develop appropriate ego strength. (C109)

### Personality of Mother
Autistic children are likely to have mothers who are mechanistic and who respond perfunctorily, rather than warmly, to the child. (D070)

Mothers of autistic children are likely to be overly intellectual in outlook (i.e., are more likely to seek gratification from intellectual rather than from interpersonal sources). (D070)

Autism is more likely to occur if the mother is remote, unempathic, and compulsive. (S188)

### Personality Problems of Mother (Depression)
Autism is more likely to occur if the mother becomes severely depressed during the vulnerable developmental period. (S188)

## MENTAL ILLNESS OF CHILD (PSYCHOSIS)
### X   Identification with Parent
The prevention of normal ego development and identification processes through the Oedipal complex (due to maladjustment on the part of the parent) causes psychosis in the child. (B285)

## MENTAL ILLNESS OF CHILD (SCHIZOPHRENIA)
### X   Abortion
The frequency of previous stillbirths and abortions is much higher among mothers of schizophrenic children than among mothers of nonschizophrenics. (T108)

### Child-Rearing Attitudes
Although the mothers of schizophrenic and normal children do not differ in their attitudes toward child-rearing practices, schizophrenic children perceive their mothers as holding more deviant attitudes than do normal children. (G127)

The pathological child-rearing attitudes of mothers of schizophrenic children are a reaction to the child's disorder rather than a cause of it. (K096)

The more pathological the parental attitudes, the more severe the type of schizophrenia in the child. (W147)

### Child-Rearing Attitudes (Overpossessiveness)
Mothers of schizophrenic children tend to be more "overpossessive" (as measured by the PARI) in their child-rearing attitudes than do mothers of normal children. (S249)

### Child-Rearing Attitudes (Rigidity)
Parents of schizophrenics tend to have rigid attitudes regarding acceptable behavior. (K093)

### Child-Rearing Practices (Punishment)
Fathers of schizophrenics and of schizoids are more likely to use punishment than are fathers of children with adjustment reactions, conduct disturbances, and sociopathic symptoms. (Z011)

### Death of Parent
There is a correlation between the loss of one or both parents and the development of schizophrenia in the child. (B308)

### Dependency
The relationship between the schizophrenic child and his parents tends to be one of intense emotional dependency. (G022)

The mother of the schizophrenic is more likely than the mother of the neurotic (and the normal) to describe the child as being dependent upon her, but is less likely to disapprove of such behavior. (M218)

### Dyadic Relations in Family
Family "skews," where one dyadic relationship within it dominates family life at the expense of the needs of other members, are a cause of schizophrenia in the child. (F097)

### Father Absence
There is no relationship between the incidence of schizophrenic reactions in the child and the absence of the father during the child's first 20 years. (L144)

### Father-Child Relations
Schizophrenic children are less likely to view their fathers as dominating than are normal children. There is no difference between normal and schizophrenic children and their perceived paternal strictness and restrictiveness of children's behavior. (K114)

### Homogamy (Personality)
The parents of schizophrenic children tend to marry individuals with a defense structure that is similar to their own. (K107)

### Husband-Wife Relations
Schizophrenia in children correlates with family situations where one spouse gratifies rather than combats the other's narcisstic needs. (L114)

### Husband-Wife Relations (Conflict)
Parents of schizophrenic children who have made good premorbid adjustment show less conflict (lack of cooperation and compromise) than do parents of schizophrenics who have made poor premorbid adjustment. (F117)

### Husband-Wife Relations (Dependency)
Schizophrenia in children correlates with family situations in which the husband-wife relationship was one of neurotic dependency. (L114)

### Husband-Wife Relations (Dominance)
Schizophrenia in children correlates with family situations in which wives are dominant and castrating in their relationships with their husbands. (L114)

### Husband-Wife Relations (Evaluation)
The ego weakness of a schizophrenic child is correlated with the depreciated images for identification presented by the devaluation of one parent by the other. (L114)

Schizophrenia in the child correlates with the mother's distrust and a lack of confidence in her husband. (L114)

### Identification
Presentation to the child of irreconcilable role models for identification is a cause of schizophrenia in the child. (F097)

### Identification of Parents

Schizophrenia in children tends to appear in families where parents still identify with their parental homes. (L114)

### Incest

There is a correlation between a fear of or preoccupation with incest and schizophrenia in the child.

### Kin Ties

Schizophrenia is more likely in a child whose parents (either or both) have remained primarily attached to their parents or siblings. (F097)

### Marital Adjustment

The greater the marital conflict as well as the disturbance of the individual parent, the more likely it is that the child will be schizophrenic. (F110)

Schizophrenic children are somewhat less likely than normals to view their parents as getting along very well; they are about as likely as normals to view their parents as getting along fairly well. (K114)

The "infantile" adolescent schizophrenics are more likely to come from unhappy families in which the parents become mistrustful of each other early in their marriage and show no capacity for flexible cooperation. (S208)

### Maternal Overprotectiveness

Mothers of schizophrenic children tend to infantilize them with overprotection and extension of the period of dependency.

### Maternal Role, Attitude Toward

Compared to parents of children with adjustment reactions, conduct disturbances, and sociopathic symptoms, the mothers of schizophrenics and schizoids are more likely to reject the homemaking role. (Z011)

### Mental Illness, Attitude Toward

The mother of the schizophrenic is more likely than the mother of the neurotic to regard the child as having been "normal" until his illness and to ascribe the illness directly to loneliness or to sexual problems. (M218)

### Mental Illness of Parent (Schizophrenia)

Schizophrenia is more likely in children from schizophrenic families than in those from average backgrounds. (B285)

### Mother-Child Relations

If a mother can relate to her infant only as an extension of herself, she will damage the development of the child's ego and schizophrenic ego impairment will become evident in the second, third, and fourth years of the child's life. (A061)

Confusion of identity in the child, due to a disturbed mother-child relationship, is a cause of schizophrenia in the child. (D086)

Schizophrenic children tend to have mothers who confuse the children's needs with their own needs projected onto the children and who fail to recognize ego boundaries between themselves and the children. (L121)

### Mother-Child Relations (Affect)

Schizophrenia is more likely to occur when the infant is forced to expend all its capacity for dealing with the external world on its relationship with its mother. (S258)

### Mother-Child Relations (Affection)

The inability of the mother to love her child during early infancy is the cause of schizophrenia in the child. (M218)

In the lower class, there is a correlation between lack of maternal affection and schizophrenia in the child; in the middle class, the correlation is between schizophrenia and maternal overprotectiveness and overambitiousness for the child. (P078)

### Mother-Child Relations (Ambivalence)

Mothers of schizophrenic children are more likely than are others to have ambivalent attitudes toward their children (devotion and detachment). (B284)

### Mother-Child Relations (Approval)

While both schizophrenic and neurotic children, compared to normals, tend to show obsessive concern with cleanliness, the mothers of neurotics were less acceptant of such behavior than were the mothers of schizophrenics. (M218)

While both schizophrenic and neurotic children (compared to normals) tend to be undemonstrative and withdrawn, the mothers of schizophrenics are more likely to approve of such behavior than are mothers of neurotics. (M218)

### Mother-Child Relations (Attachment)

Mothers of schizophrenics, as compared with mothers of normals, are excessively devoted or attached. (H186)

### Mother-Child Relations (Communication)

Recurring sequences of conflicting messages ("double binds") proceeding from the mother to the child are a cause of schizophrenia in the latter. (F100)

The communications from mother to schizophrenic child are more likely than others to be incongruent (emotion contradicts verbal communication). (H187)

### Mother-Child Relations (Consistency)

A combination of maternal attitudes which foster dependency on the one hand and stress independence and assertion on the other is a cause of schizophrenia in the child. (D073)

A child is likely to be schizophrenic if his mother is alternately compassionate and rejecting. (S213)

### Mother-Child Relations (Oral)

Disturbances in the early mother-child relationship (oral phase of development) are necessary, but not sufficient, conditions for the development of schizophrenia in the child. (L139)

### Mother-Child Relations (Possessiveness)

If the mother is overly possessive, the child is more likely to become schizophrenic. (F119)

### Mother-Child Relations (Rejection)

Severe and unqualified rejection by the mother is probably not correlated with schizophrenia in the child. (L123)

### Mother-Child Relations (Understanding)

Perplexity (inability to deal adequately with the child's gratification needs) on the part of the mother leads to schizophrenia in the child. (M237)

Schizophrenic children with no organic disturbances have mothers who show a greater degree of perplexity (inability to deal adequately with the children's gratification needs) than do schizophrenic children with organic (neurological) problems. (M237)

### Parent-Child Relations
The parents of the schizophrenic child are more likely to treat him as a projection of their own ungratified needs rather than to deal with his own unmet needs. (B242)

There is no single familial syndrome which accounts for the etiology of childhood schizophrenia. (B284)

### Parent-Child Relations (Affection)
Parents of preschizophrenic patients exhibited less affection and had less contact with their children than did parents of normal children. (H241)

Schizophrenia in the child is correlated with parents' tendency to compete for his loyalty and affection. (L114)

### Parent-Child Relations (Differential Treatment)
Schizophrenic children tend to have parents who have regarded them as different and as requiring differential treatment from birth. (K093)

### Parent-Child Relations (Overprotectiveness/Rejection)
Rejection by one or both parents is more likely to be an antecedent of schizophrenia in the child than is parental overprotection. (W147)

### Parent-Child Relations (Rejection)
Ego weakness of a schizophrenic child is correlated with introjection of parental rejection of the child in process of early identification with a parent. (L114)

### Paternal Role
Schizophrenia in children correlates with low prestige of the husband in the family. (L114)

There is a correlation between the absence of a strong paternal figure in the home and schizophrenia in the child. (M218)

### Personality of Father (Sociability)
Fathers of preschizophrenic patients were less gregarious than were fathers of normal children. (H241)

### Personality of Mother
Mothers likely to produce schizophrenic children tend to be of three types: the overly demanding, hostile, but superficially sweet and polite mother; the docile, submissive mother, who cooperates to absurd limits, who is perfectionistic and sensitive to slights and who dominates through dependence; and the overtly rejecting mother. (B219)

The schizophrenogenic mother tends to be unusually Machiavellian in relationships, viewing other people as existing only to serve her own ends and consequently manipulating and exploiting them. (B219)

Compared to normal children, schizophrenics tend to perceive their mothers as relatively cold, controlling, and authoritarian, but are similar with regard to their perception of the mother's democratic attitudes or rejection of the homemaking role. (H185)

Mothers of schizophrenics tend to be more sensitive to the opinions of others than do average mothers. (T105)

### Personality of Mother (Needs)
If the emotional needs of the mothering one are met by the schizophrenic child, the chances of another child becoming mentally ill are lowered. (S208)

### Personality of Parents
The core of the defense structure (i.e., fear of annihilation) of parents of schizophrenic children is the same, regardless of socioeconomic class. (K107)

Unstable and domineering parents are more likely than others to rear schizophrenic children. (W143)

### Personality Problems of Parents
In almost all cases of childhood schizophrenia, both parents are severely disturbed people. (E089)

### Power Structure of Family
Families of schizophrenic children are more likely to show greater dominance by one parent over the other than are families of nonschizophrenic offspring. (F117)

Schizophrenic children who view their mothers as strong authority figures are more likely to view their fathers as weak authority figures than are schizophrenics who view their mothers as weak authority figures. (K114)

Schizophrenia in children correlates with family environments in which the wife excludes the husband from leadership and decision making. (L114)

Adolescent schizophrenics with "childish" reactions lived in a family structure with "a high degree of imbalance in leadership." Their fathers had more ego strength and appeared to be more capable of leadership, in most instances, than did their mothers, but they did not exercise leadership. (S208)

### Self-Conception of Father
There is no difference between schizophrenic and normal children and the degree to which they view their fathers as being certain of themselves. (K114)

### Self-Conception of Mother
Schizophrenic children are more likely to view their mothers as being sure of themselves than are normal children. (K114)

### Social Isolation of Family
Families estranged from the community are more likely to produce schizophrenic children than are others. (W143)

### Surrogate Parent
There is a positive relationship between the remoteness of the child-rearer(s) from the status of natural parents and the incidence of schizophrenic reactions in the child. (L144)

## MENTAL ILLNESS OF CHILD (SCHIZOPHRENIA/ NEUROSIS)     X Breast Feeding
Mothers of schizophrenic children are more likely to breast feed (the patients) than are mothers of neurotics.

### Conformity
Schizophrenics are more likely than neurotic children to submit to the demands of the parents and community. (M197)

### Disorganization of Family
In the lower class, more schizophrenic than neurotic

children were reared in a family atmosphere of physical tension and disorganization. (M197)

#### Employment of Child
In the lower class, schizophrenic children are more likely to be required to contribute to the family income than are neurotics. (M197)

#### Marital Adjustment
Schizophrenic children are more likely than neurotic children to have parents who are incompatible and emotionally disturbed. (M197)

### MENTAL ILLNESS OF HUSBAND
#### X   Mental Illness of Wife
The incidence of mental illness among the spouses of psychiatric patients is greater than among the general population. (K105)

### MENTAL ILLNESS OF MOTHER
#### X   Maternal-Role Behavior
The more acute the mental illness, the more likely that mothering will be affected by it. (S203)

#### Mental Illness of Child
There is no significant relationship between the duration of mental illness in the mother and degree of psychopathology in the child. (S203)

#### Mental Retardation of Child
Mentally retarded children are more likely than normals to have mothers who suffered from serious psychiatric disability during the period when the child was 6 to 18 months old. If there is no such period of psychopathology at the birth of other children in the same family, the chance of mental retardation is low. (G141)

#### Pregnancy, Attitude Toward
There is no correlation among schizophrenic, neurotic, or normal women with regard to planning or not planning pregnancy or to the number of unfavorable symptoms during pregnancy. (P080)

### MENTAL ILLNESS OF MOTHER/DAUGHTER
#### X   Identification with Mother
The greater the extent to which the daughter identifies with her mother, the more likely it is that psychosis in the mother will lead to psychosis in the daughter. (H192)

#### Ordinal Position
Psychotic breakdown in the mother is most likely to lead to psychotic breakdown in the oldest daughter, as opposed to girls in other ordinal positions. (H192)

### MENTAL ILLNESS OF PARENT   X   Age of Child
Delayed parental reaction to a trauma in his childhood is more likely to occur when the child of the disturbed parent reaches the age at which the parent had the traumatic episode. (H246)

#### Juvenile Delinquency
Although the mothers of delinquents do not differ (with respect to psychiatric diagnosis) from the mothers of psychotics and of normals, the fathers of delinquents are more likely to be sociopathic than are those of the other two groups. (O033)

#### Mental Illness of Child
Mental illness of offspring is directly correlated with mental illness of a parent. (B285)

There is no correlation between psychosis in a parent and mental illness in the child. (B285)

When the dominant parent is mentally disturbed, mental illness is likely to occur. (L119)

Mental illness in a child is more likely if a parent is mentally disordered and the mother dominant. (M164)

#### Mental Illness (Schizophrenia)
Schizophrenic patients tend to have parents who displayed psychopathology at the descriptive clinical level (mood disorder, severe neurotic symptoms, alcoholism, and psychotic illness). (M061)

#### Mental Retardation
Confinement to contact with a defective or schizophrenic parent is a cause of mental and emotional retardation in the child. (B285)

#### Sex Status of Child
Delayed parental reaction to a trauma in his own childhood is more likely to occur if his child is of the same sex as the disturbed parent. (H246)

### MENTAL ILLNESS OF PARENT (PSYCHOSIS)
#### X   Behavior Problems (By Sex)
Daughters of parents with affective (other than schizophrenic) psychoses are more likely to develop behavior problems than are sons. (B285)

### MENTAL ILLNESS OF PARENT (SCHIZOPHRENIA)
#### X   Behavior Problems
Schizophrenia in the parent may be a cause of behavior problems in the child where there is a close mother-child relationship when the child is under the age of ten or a close father-son relationship when the son is in the Oedipal phase or is under the age of six. (B285)

Schizophrenia in the mother is more likely than schizophrenia in the father to produce behavior problems in the child. (B285)

Parents with psychoses other than schizophrenia are less likely to have children who suffer from behavior problems than are schizophrenic parents. (B285)

The child of schizophrenic parents is more likely than the child of parents with other mental or behavioral disturbances to develop behavior problems before puberty. (B285)

#### Mental Illness of Child (Schizophrenia)
Schizophrenia is more likely in children from schizophrenic families than in those from average backgrounds. (B285)

#### Personality and Social Adjustment of Child
Children of schizophrenic parents are more likely to be mentally and/or socially maladjusted than are children of normals. (B285)

### MENTAL ILLNESS OF SON   X   Sex-Role Model
Mental illness tends to be directly correlated with the failure of the father to provide a male model. (L123)

### MENTAL ILLNESS OF SPOUSE
#### X   Duration of Marriage
Mental illness among the spouses of chronically ill mental patients increases with the number of years of marriage. (K159)

#### Mental Illness
Spouses of mental patients are more likely to suffer from mental illness themselves than are spouses of normal people. (K159)

There is no evidence to support the idea of assortative mating among schizophrenics. (K159)

## MENTAL ILLNESS OF WIFE
### X   Mental Illness of Husband
The incidence of mental illness among the spouses of psychiatric patients is greater than among the general population. (K105)

## MENTAL ILLNESS (PARANOIA)
### X   Authority Structure of Family
Paranoid tendencies are more likely to develop when parental authority is erratic. (S187)

### Child-Rearing Practices (Consistency)
Paranoia is more likely to occur in families in which the dominant parent expects complete obedience, yet exercises authority erratically. (S187)

### Father-Child Relations (Evaluation)
Paranoia is directly correlated with a perception of the father as weak and ineffectual. (N050)

### Homosexuality
Patients who are paranoid tend also to have homosexual tendencies. (N050)

### Mother-Child Relations
Paranoid patients tend to have mothers who accuse them of bad intentions rather than criticize them for their actions. (S187)

### Mother-Child Relations (Intensity)
Paranoia is more likely to occur when the relationship with the mother has been close and intense. (N050)

### Occupational Rank of Father/Son
Paranoia is more likely to occur when the father of the patient is of a lower occupational rank than the patient. (N050)

### Ordinal Position
Paranoia is more likely to occur among the oldest members of a group of siblings. (N050)

### Parent-Child Relations
Mental illness is directly correlated with the importance of the child to his parents. (N050)

### Social Mobility of Son
Paranoia is more likely to occur when the father of the patient is of a lower occupational rank than the patient. (N050)

## MENTAL ILLNESS (PARESIS)    Marital Status
Among New York Negroes, the incidence of general paresis does not correlate with marital status, with the exception of a high incidence for widowers. (M219)

## MENTAL ILLNESS/PERSONALITY PROBLEMS OF CHILD    X   Emotional Problems of Parent
Parents of schizophrenic and neurotic children tend to show less emotional disturbance than do parents of acting-out and psychosomatic children. (L144)

## MENTAL ILLNESS (PSYCHOSIS/NEUROSIS)
### X   Illegitimacy (Adoption)
Psychotic unwed mothers are more possessive of their babies than are neurotic unwed mothers. (Y048)

## MENTAL ILLNESS, RECOVERY FROM
### X   Emotional Problems of Spouse
A patient is less likely to respond to therapy if his or her spouse is also subject to serious emotional problems. (M228)

### Interaction in Family
Any improvement attained by the mental patient during therapy would be temporary unless his family also changed in a constructive direction. (F083)

## MENTAL ILLNESS (SCHIZOPHRENIA)
### X   Age Difference
Mothers of schizophrenics are more likely than are mothers of neurotics or of normals to have married men considerably older than themselves. (M218)

### Aggression of Mother
Schizophrenia tends to be directly correlated with a pattern of concealed maternal aggressiveness. (N061)

### Anxiety of Mother
Schizophrenia tends to be associated with a pattern of concealed tension and anxiety in the mother. (T105)

### Anxiety of Parents
Schizophrenic patients will tend to have parents who are afraid of any intense emotions, whether of love, anger, envy, or jealousy. (S259)

### Aspiration Level
Parents of normals have higher aspiration levels than do parents of neurotics or schizophrenics. (F110)

Schizophrenia tends to be correlated with strong feelings of ambition on the part of the mother for the patient and her tendency to live vicariously through the patient. (N061)

### Authority Structure of Family
The family of the schizophrenic is more likely than others to have a continuous flow of denials of its members' statements. (H187)

### Broken Home
Mothers of schizophrenics are more likely than those of neurotics or of normals to come from homes broken by separation, divorce, or death. (M218)

There is a higher incidence of divorce, separation, and desertion among parents of schizophrenics than among those of the control group ("normals"). (O034)

### Child-Rearing Attitudes (Dependency)
Mental illness is directly correlated with the hostility of the mother toward any initiative or independence on the part of the daughter. (L118)

### Child-Rearing Attitudes (Evaluation)
"Poor" premorbid schizophrenics (those with poor general functioning before the onset of illness) perceive their parents' child-rearing attitudes as being more deviant than do "good" premorbid schizophrenics, who in turn perceive these attitudes as being more deviant than do normal subjects. (G127)

### Child-Rearing Attitudes (Need Gratification)
Mothers of schizophrenic children are more likely than others to have restrictive attitudes regarding the gratification of the child's physical and psychological needs. (B284)

### Child-Rearing Attitudes (Restrictiveness)
If the mother expresses restrictive attitudes about child rearing, it is more likely that her son will become a schizophrenic. (B227)

### Child-Rearing Practices (Acceleration)
A significantly greater number of schizophrenic daughters than of normal ones believed that their mothers tried to accelerate their development during their childhood. (H186)

### Child-Rearing Practices (Aggression)
A significantly greater number of schizophrenic daughters than of normal ones believed that their mothers attempted to suppress the daughters' aggression during their childhood. (H186)

Schizophrenia tends to be directly correlated with a maternal pattern of ignoring the patient's anger. (N061)

### Child-Rearing Practices (Autoeroticism)
Schizophrenia is directly associated with a punitive and prohibitive attitude toward masturbation on the part of the mother. (T105)

### Child-Rearing Practices (Control)
Schizophrenics report having been subjected to greater parental control than do nonschizophrenics. (L155)

### Child-Rearing Practices (Dependency)
The failure of the parents to educate toward and facilitate emancipation of the children from the family is a cause of schizophrenia in the child. (F097)

A significantly larger number of schizophrenic daughters than of normal ones believe their mothers attempted to break their wills during childhood. (H186)

More schizophrenic daughters than normal ones believe that their mothers fostered the daughter's dependency on them during childhood. (H186)

Schizophrenia tends to be correlated with a continuing expectation, on the part of the mother, of obedience and dependence during adolescence. (L126)

### Child-Rearing Practices (Friendship)
Schizophrenia is directly correlated with the inhibition of friendships by the mother. (L118)

### Child-Rearing Practices (Isolation)
A significantly greater number of schizophrenic daughters than of normal ones believed their mothers attempted to exclude outside influences during their childhood. (H186)

### Child-Rearing Practices (Obedience)
Where strict obedience is emphasized in socialization, mental illness will tend to be manifest in paranoid schizophrenia. (S187)

### Child-Rearing Practices (Punishment)
Fathers of white schizophrenics are more likely than fathers of normals to administer brutal and erratic discipline and may also encourage the development of aim-inhibited hostility and a masochistic orientation toward father-symbols in later life. (B221)

Persons who have been subjected to parental trauma are more likely than others to become schizophrenic. (J019)

### Child-Rearing Practices (Restrictiveness)
Mothers of schizophrenics are more restrictive than are mothers of normals. (H186)

### Child-Rearing Practices (Sex)
Parents of normals are more likely to be acceptant of sexual expression than are parents of schizophrenics. (F110)

A significantly greater number of schizophrenic daughters than of normal ones believed that their mothers attempted to suppress the daughters' sex life during their childhood. (H186)

Mental illness is correlated with the instillation by the mother of an attitude of fear and hatred toward the opposite sex. (L118)

Mothers of schizophrenics tend to discourage the child's interest in the opposite sex. (M218)

Parents of schizophrenics are more likely than parents of others to instill deep feelings of guilt concerning masturbation and relationships with the opposite sex. (W143)

### Cohesion of Family
The more cohesive and centripetal the family structure, the more likely is the schizophrenic to manifest a symbiotic rather than an isolate pattern of interaction. (P077)

Schizophrenics tend to come from families in which the maintenance of intense intrafamily relationships assumes greater importance than the preservation of individual identity. (W124)

### Conflict in Family
Female schizophrenics are more likely to conflict with their mothers and to participate in intrafamilial conflict than are schizophrenic males. (B279)

Conflict in the home of female schizophrenics tends to center around parental disapproval of her extra familial interests and behavior; in the case of male schizophrenics, it is more likely to center around instrumental problems, such as his failure to find regular employment. (B279)

### Death of Maternal Grandfather
Mental illness tends to be correlated with an early death of the maternal grandfather. (L118)

### Death of Mother
Schizophrenic women who are more seriously ill are more likely to have experienced the deaths of their mothers at an early age (1–5 years) than are schizophrenic women who are not as seriously ill. (H226)

### Death of Parent
Schizophrenic women are more likely to have lost either or both of their parents by death at an earlier age than are normals. (H226)

There is no difference between schizophrenic and nonschizophrenic males and the age at which they experienced the death of one or both parents. (H226)

There is a correlation between the loss of one or both parents and the development of schizophrenia in the child. (B308)

### Dependency
Fathers of schizophrenics are more likely to be dependent on their mothers than are fathers of normals. (K125)

Schizophrenia tends to be directly correlated with an intense emotional relationship and strong dependency with the mother. (L126)

Schizophrenics reveal greater dependency upon parents than do nonschizophrenics. (L155)

Schizophrenia is correlated with dependency of the patient on her mother. (N061)

### Dependency of Mother
The ego weakness of a schizophrenic tends to be correlated with a parent-child relationship in which the mother is dependent upon the child for fulfillment. (L114)

Schizophrenia tends to be directly correlated with patterns of dependence of the patient's mother on the patient's maternal grandmother. (N061)

### Disorganization of Family
Schizophrenics tend to be from a disturbed family environment. (L123)

A high proportion of schizophrenics come from disorganized family environments (death, divorce, separation, psychosis, neurosis, alcoholism). (S187)

### Father Absence
Most fathers of aggressive, acting-out, "childish" schizophrenic adolescents began their participation in the life of the family after the mother-child relationship had developed during the father's absence (and, hence, were treated by the children as intruders). (S208)

### Father-Child Relations (Dominance)
Schizophrenia tends to be associated with a pattern of sadistic domination in the father's relationship with the child. (R115)

### Father-Child Relations (Jealousy)
Schizophrenia is likely to be associated with a paternal pattern of dependency on the mother, which manifests itself as aggressiveness and jealousy toward the children as competitors for her attention. (R115)

### Father-Child Relations (Rejection)
Fathers of schizophrenics are more likely to be rejecting than are fathers of normals. (K125)

Schizophrenia tends to be directly correlated with a father who is cruel and rejecting. (L123)

### Father-Child Relations (Sex)
Schizophrenia tends to be correlated with a fear of erotic interest in the father. (N061)

### Father-Son Relations (Rejection)
Good premorbid schizophrenics (good general functioning before onset of illness) perceive their fathers as having been more rejecting than do poor premorbid schizophrenics or normal subjects. (G127)

### Feeding (Demand)
There is a direct correlation between the rigidity of the mother in establishing a feeding schedule and the subsequent appearance of schizophrenia. (T105)

### Fertility
Married schizophrenic individuals tend to have fewer children than do normals. (B285)

### Husband-Wife Relations (Conflict)
There is more likely to be a high degree of marital conflict between the parents of the male schizophrenic than there is between the parents of the female. (B279)

Parents of schizophrenics are more likely to relate to each other with greater conflict and hostility than are parents of nonschizophrenics. (F117)

### Husband-Wife Relations (Evaluation)
Mothers of schizophrenic sons more often deprecate their husbands as desirable models for their sons than do mothers of normals. (K093)

Mothers of schizophrenics are more likely than are mothers of neurotics or normals to regard their husbands as having been weak, ineffectual, or remote. (M218)

Mothers of schizophrenics are more likely than those of neurotics or of normals to regard their husbands as weak, lacking ambition and drive, and avoiding responsibility in the home. (M218)

Schizophrenia among females is directly correlated with the constant deprecation of the patient's father by her mother. (N061)

### Husband-Wife Relations (Power)
There is more vying for dominance between the parents of poor premorbid schizophrenics (poor general functioning before onset of illness) than in the interaction of parents of normal subjects. (G127)

### Identification
For men there is a *negative* correlation between identification with the father, mother, and "most people," in that order, and a tendency to schizophrenia. (R103)

Among females, there is a correlation between identification with the mother and all types of abnormal trends. (R103)

### Interaction in Family
There is no relationship between the voluntary choice of living away from one's family and the development of schizophrenia, but there is an association between involuntary lack of family life (because of death, sterility, etc.) and schizophrenia. (H202)

There is no correlation between family environment and schizophrenia. (M164)

Within the families of persons who later develop acute schizophrenia episodes, those relations which are openly acknowledged as acceptable have a quality of intense and enduring pseudomutuality. (W021)

Family disorganization (schizophrenic) is correlated with an absence of spontaneity, novelty, humor, and zest in participation together. (W021)

Members of schizophrenic families tend to use intermediaries in interacting with other family members. (W021)

### Kin Relations
Female relatives of male schizophrenics do not differ from the female relatives of persons with other (nonorganic) mental illnesses in the degree of possessiveness they feel toward the afflicted person. (F099)

### Marital Adjustment
Mothers of schizophrenics are more likely than mothers of neurotics or of normals to have negative attitudes toward their marriages, particularly toward the sexual aspect, which they tend to find repulsive. (M218)

### Marital Adjustment of Parents
Schizophrenia tends to be directly associated with unsatisfactory marital adjustments on the part of the patient's parents. (T105)

### Marital Status

Married schizophrenics are more likely to have achieved a high level of personality integration in the premorbid period than are single people (thus accounting for more rapid recovery from schizophrenia). (F104)

### Marriage Chances

Schizophrenic individuals are less likely to marry than are normals. (B285)

Among hospitalized schizophrenics, females are more likely than males to be married. (R122)

### Marriage Chances (Male/Female)

More female schizophrenics are married than male because the female plays a more passive role in courting and does not need the aggressiveness and confidence which, among schizophrenics, is uncommon. (F104)

### Mate Selection

There is a correlation between first-cousin marriage and schizophrenia in the offspring. (F105)

The schizophrenic is likely to seek in his spouse a reincarnation of infantile aspects of early love objects. (M197)

### Mate Selection (Free Choice)

Mental illness tends to be correlated with a parental marriage which was imposed upon the wife by the patient's maternal grandmother. (L118)

### Maternal Overprotectiveness

Overprotection of the child by the mother is an essential factor in the formation of schizophrenia in the child. (B285)

Poor premorbid schizophrenics (poor general functioning before onset of illness) perceive their mothers as having been more overprotecting than do good premorbid schizophrenics or normal subjects. (G127)

Schizophrenics are more likely to come from families where there is maternal overprotection and where fathers are nondominant and/or indifferent figures. (H207)

Mothers of schizophrenics tend to be overprotective and sometimes rejecting, domineering, and aggressive. (S187)

### Maternal-Role Behavior

Mothers of schizophrenics want to be perfect parents and many perceive themselves to be perfect. (K093)

### Maternal-Role Definition

Mothers of schizophrenics tend to set up perfectionist goals for their roles as mothers. (T105)

### Mental Illness of Parent

Schizophrenic patients tend to have parents who displayed psychopathology at the descriptive clinical level (mood disorder, severe neurotic symptoms, alcoholism, and psychotic illness). (M061)

### Mother Absence

There is no significant correlation between early maternal deprivation (below the age of six and for at least six months' duration) and the later incidence of schizophrenia. (E093)

There is no relationship between the incidence of schizophrenic reactions in the child and the absence of the mother during the child's first 20 years. (L144)

There is no relationship between the incidence of schizophrenic reactions in the child and the absence of the mother during the child's first six years. (L144)

### Mother-Child Relations (Affection)

Mothers of schizophrenics tend to love the child not only excessively, but also conditionally. (M218)

### Mother-Child Relations (Communication)

A significantly greater number of schizophrenic daughters than of normal ones believed that their mothers tried to avoid communicating with them during their childhoods. (H186)

### Mother-Child Relations (Dominance)

A significantly greater number of schizophrenic daughters than normals believed that their mothers were overly intrusive during their childhoods. (H186)

### Mother-Child Relations (Interaction)

A significantly larger number of schizophrenic daughters than of normal ones believed that their mothers secluded themselves from the daughters during the daughters' childhoods. (H186)

### Mother-Child Relations (Rejection)

Schizophrenic mothers are more likely to use covert than overt methods of rejection and domination. (B284)

Schizophrenia is directly correlated with anxieties resulting from an early maternal rejection. (N061)

Mothers of schizophrenics will tend to be more covertly than overtly rejecting. (S187)

The schizophrenogenic mother is hateful and rejecting toward her child only to cover her truly loving, but confused maternal instincts. (S213)

### Mother-Child Relations (Seductiveness)

Schizophrenia tends to be correlated with seductive attitudes on the part of the patient's mother. (N061)

### Mother-Daughter Relations

A significantly greater number of schizophrenic daughters than of normal ones believed that their mothers were trying to dominate them during their childhoods. (H186)

A significantly greater number of schizophrenic daughters than of normal ones believed their mothers attempted to deify themselves during the daughters' childhoods. (H186)

A significantly greater number of schizophrenic daughters than normal ones believed their mothers strove for martyrdom during the daughters' childhoods. (H186)

### Mother-Daughter Relations (Intimacy)

Mental illness tends to be directly correlated with an unusually high degree of intimacy between mother and daughter. (L118)

### Mother Loss

Schizophrenic men do not differ significantly from men without schizophrenia on the variable, mean age at mother loss. (H176)

### Nonkin-Role Behavior

In schizophrenic-family social organization there tends to be secrecy about roles which move in extrafamilial directions. (W021)

### Oedipal Complex

Schizophrenics reveal more evidence of Oedipal conflict than do normal persons. (L155)

Schizophrenia will not occur when the Oedipal constellation has developed. (S258)

### Ordinal Position

"Childish" (aggressive, acting-out) schizophrenic adolescents tend to be the oldest of several siblings, who are regarded as undependable and tend to lose their birthrights to more dutiful conforming younger siblings. (S208)

Adolescent schizophrenics of a "preadolescent" type (rebellious, delinquent, irresponsible) tend to be either the oldest or the only child. (S208)

There seems to be no direct correlation between the ordinal position of the individual and the development of schizophrenia. (T105)

### Ordinal Position/Sex Status

The child who is isolated within the family by birth order or sex is more likely than others to become schizophrenic. (W143)

### Parent-Child Relations

There is no single familial syndrome which accounts for the etiology of childhood schizophrenia. (B284)

Since the schizophrenic child has remained in a symbiotic relationship with his mother, it is more likely that he, rather than other children, will react to events such as separation from parents or birth of a sibling with rage and panic. (B284)

The source of illness of good premorbid schizophrenics (good functioning before onset of illness) is more likely to be the strong element of punishment inherent in the dominating attitudes of the father; whereas the source of illness of poor premorbid schizophrenics is more likely to be estrangement due to the overprotectiveness of the mother. (G127)

Schizophrenics tend to have had aberrant relationships with their parents, in which 1) mothers rejected or overprotected them, 2) fathers displayed little affection for them, 3) parents displayed little interest in them, and 4) patients and their siblings were left on their own with little concern shown by their parents. (M061)

Schizophrenic adolescents with a "juvenile" reaction (neurotic, somatic symptoms) behaved in Oedipal fashion, acting as though they expected and feared retaliation from the fathers for the closeness they had with the mothers. (S208)

### Parent-Child Relations (Affect)

Schizophrenics are more likely to have a less-emotional relationship with the more stable of their parents. (M061)

### Parent-Child Relations (Authority) X Sex Status

There is less variation in the character of parental authority with the sex of the child among schizophrenics than among normals. (S187)

### Parent-Child Relations (Beliefs)

Fathers of schizophrenics are more likely than are mothers to show identification with the child in the area of beliefs and to project their beliefs onto the child; mothers are more likely to exhibit awareness of the actual beliefs of the patient. (K125)

Parents of acute cases of schizophrenia are more likely to be identified with and to be aware of their son's beliefs and are less likely to project upon the patient than are parents of schizophrenics who are chronically ill. (K125)

### Parent-Child Relations (Closeness) X Sex Status

Among schizophrenic children who view their mothers as the dominant authority figure, females are more likely to report feeling closer to their fathers than to their mothers and males to report feeling closer to their mothers than to their fathers. (K114)

### Parent-Child Relations (Communication)

A breakdown in perception of reality due to parental distortions in the communication process is a cause of schizophrenia. (M218)

### Parent-Child Relations (Dominance)

Schizophrenics are more likely to perceive their parents as dominating, while normals are more likely to have a multifaceted view (i.e., dominating, ignoring, overprotecting). (G127)

### Parent-Child Relations (Interest)

Fathers of schizophrenics are less likely to be interested in the patient than are mothers. (K125)

### Parent-Child Relations (Overprotectiveness)

Parents of schizophrenics tend to be overprotective. (K093)

Schizophrenic patients are likely to perceive their parents as overprotective. (M164)

### Parent-Child Relations (Overprotectiveness/Dominance)

The most predominant undesirable relationship with the parents recorded in a study of schizophrenics, as contrasted with nonpyschiatric patients, was that of overprotection and dominance. (S247)

### Parent-Child Relations (Preference) X Sex Status

Among schizophrenic children who do not report maternal domination in the family, both males and females are more likely to report preference for their mothers than for their fathers. (K114)

### Parent-Child Relations (Rejection)

Schizophrenics see parental figures as cold or rejecting. (H186)

Schizophrenia is more likely to occur where the parent of the same sex is distant and rejecting, while the parent of the opposite sex exhibits a high degree of identification. (S260)

### Parent Loss

Schizophrenic women have lost parents at a significantly earlier age than have women without schizophrenia. (H176)

It is probably *who* replaces a lost parent which determines the development of schizophrenia, rather than the loss itself. Loss of mother is most conducive to the development of schizophrenia. Replacement of the mother is more important than replacement of the father. (H176)

The incidence of parental deprivation is not higher among schizophrenic patients than among normal subjects or among patients suffering from other types of psychoses. (O034)

There is a correlation between loss of one or both parents, by death or separation, and schizophrenia in the child. (W147)

Schizrophrenics are more likely to have experienced the loss of a mother than of a father. (W147)

There is a correlation between loss of the same-sex parent and schizophrenia in the child. (W147)

Loss of the father is more likely to be an antecedent factor to schizophrenia in the child than is loss of the mother. (W147)

Parental loss is more likely to have occurred in the case of male schizophrenics than in the case of female schizophrenics. (W147)

There is no relationship between age at which a parent was lost by death or separation and schizophrenia in the child. (W147)

### Parental Image
Parents of normals are more likely than parents of neurotics or of schizophrenics to have definite images of parental figures. (F110)

### Parental Role
Parents (of schizophrenic children) who demonstrate a lack of spontaneity and pleasure are less likely than parents who show appropriate satisfaction to function adequately (with respect to communication between marital partners, the mother's decisiveness, interest in physical environment, direction, and organization). (B240)

### Parental-Role Behavior
Families of children with behavior disorders or schizophrenia caused by organic damage are more likely than families of children with psychogenic schizophrenia to function better (with respect to care, interest in physical environment, communication between marital partners, mother's decisiveness, and appropriate satisfaction with self and children). (B240)

### Paternal Role
Fathers of schizophrenic children are more likely than others to be withdrawn and ineffectual. (B284)

Most fathers of this "preadolescent" type of schizophrenic adolescent (rebellious, delinquent, irresponsible) seem to abound in "goodness" in civic life and are active leaders in business; at home, however, they tend to be passive-aggressive critics. (S208)

### Personality of Father
Fathers of female schizophrenics frequently are in severe conflict with their wives, are paranoid, and are eager to gain the support of their daughters. (L123)

Schizophrenia tends to be correlated with perception of the father as a weak, effeminate person. (N061)

### Personality of Grandparents
There is a direct correlation between schizophrenia (female) and a maternal grandmother with a domineering and overprotective personality and a maternal grandfather with a passive personality. (L118)

### Personality of Mother (Irritability)
A significantly greater number of schizophrenic daughters than of normals believed that their mothers were irritable during their childhoods. (H186)

### Personality of Mother (Warmth)
Mothers of schizophrenics will tend to be cold and rigorous. (S187)

### Personality of Parents
Parents of good premorbid (general adjustment before onset of psychosis) schizophrenics have more mature defensive structures (isolation, undoing, and displacement) than do parents of poor premorbid schizophrenics (whose defensive structures are denial and projection). (B262)

Fathers of schizophrenics are more likely to be sadistic and domineering than are fathers of normals; they are also more likely to have masochistic wives. (K125)

Schizophrenia is directly correlated with a cold, sadistic mother and a passive father. (L123)

Schizophrenics tend to have cruel fathers and overprotective mothers. (L123)

### Personality of Parents (Expressiveness)
Schizophrenia is more likely to occur when the parents repress spontaneous emotional responses. (S186)

### Personality of Parents (Other Directedness)
Parents of schizophrenics tend to be extremely sensitive to the opinions of others. (K093)

### Personality Problems of Mother
Mothers of schizophrenics are more likely to regard the environment as hostile and to show conflicting needs. (H207)

### Personality Problems of Mother (Psychosexual, Obsessive)
Mothers of schizophrenics tend to be psychosexually maladjusted and "obsessive-compulsive" in the areas of cleanliness and propriety. (M218)

### Personality Problems of Parents
Though schizophrenics tend to have parents who manifest psychopathological symptoms, the latter do not tend to exhibit the same symptoms of disturbances. (M061)

### Personality Problems of Parents (Fears)
Parents of normals are more likely than parents of schizophrenics to report a major fear that they would like to eliminate. (F110)

Parents of neurotics are more likely than are parents of schizophrenics to acknowledge a major destructive consequence of the loss of self-control. (F110)

### Personality Problems of Parents (Narcissism)
Schizophrenia tends to be correlated with parental narcissism. (R115)

### Power Structure of Family
Male schizophrenics who related well to other people and who had normal sexual contacts before the onset of their disorders are more likely to come from families in which the father was dominant, while those who were relative isolates and who had no normal sexual contacts before their disorders are more likely to come from families in which the mother was dominant. (B228)

Among schizophrenics, good premorbid adjustment is associated with father dominance; poor premorbid adjustment, with mother dominance. (F117)

Schizophrenic children are more likely to come from mother-dominated rather than from father-dominated families. (F117)

There is more paternal dominance in the interaction of the parents of "good" premorbid schizophrenics (good general functioning before onset of illness) than in the interactions of parents of poor premorbid schizophrenics. (G127)

Paranoid schizophrenics are more likely to view their mothers as strong authority figures and their fathers as weak authority figures than are catatonic schizophrenics. (K114)

Schizophrenia (female) tends to be directly correlated with an aggressive, dominating mother and a passive father. (L118)

Schizophrenic patients are likely to have come from family backgrounds in which the mother has a strong authority role and the father has a weak authority role. (M060)

### Residence
There is no relationship between the voluntary choice of living away from one's family and the development of schizophrenia, but there is an association between involuntary lack of family (because of death, sterility, etc.) and schizophrenia. (H202)

### Residence with Parents
Mental illness is more likely to occur among adult children living with their parents. (K093)

### Role Behavior in Family
Schizophrenic personality tends to emerge where the family fosters paralogic ideation, untenable emotional needs, and contradictory models for identification which cannot be integrated. (U.S.). (L114)

### Role Definition in Family
In the families of persons who later develop schizophrenia, intensity and duration of pseudomutuality lead to the development of shared family mechanisms by which deviations from the family-role structure are excluded from recognition or are delusionally reinterpreted. (W021)

There is a correlation between schizophrenia in family members and a pervasive familial subculture of myths, legends, and ideology which stress the consequences of deviation from a limited number of fixed, engulfing family roles. (W021)

### Role in Family
A correlation exists between the development of schizophrenic personality and shifts in the occupancy of family roles. (W021)

### Role Structure of Family
In schizophrenic family organization, there is a tendency for inappropriate role structures to be justified. (W021)

In families of persons who later develop schizophrenia, intensity and duration of pseudomutuality lead to the development of shared family mechanisms by which deviations from the family-role structure are excluded from recognition or are delusionally reinterpreted. (W021)

Schizophrenics tend to come from families in which there is a limited number of engulfing roles. (W124)

### Role Structure of Family (Rigidity)
Schizophrenics tend to come from families which have a more rigid role structure than is found in families of normal children. (W124)

### Self-Conception of Father
Schizophrenia tends to be correlated with fathers who have an exalted self-image. (S187)

### Sex Attitudes of Mother
Schizophrenia tends to be directly correlated with a maternal attitude of hypocrisy toward sex. (N061)

### Sex-Role Definition
There is a correlation between sex-role confusion in the child and schizophrenia.

### Sex Status
### X   Fertility
Married schizophrenic females tend to have more children than do their male counterparts. (R103)

### Sex Status
### X   Marriage Chances
Schizophrenic females are more likely to marry than are schizophrenic males. (R103)

### Sex Status
### X   Parent-Child Relations
### (Overprotectiveness/Rejection)
A background of parental overprotection and/or rejection is more likely in the case of male schizophrenics than in that of females. (W147)

The parental overprotection and/or rejection antecedent to schizophrenia does not vary with respect to same- or cross-sex parent. (W147)

### Sex Status
### X   Personality of Mother
The differences between mothers of schizophrenics and those of normal children do not correlate with sex of the child. (H207)

### Sexual Adjustment
A study of the life histories of normals and of schizophrenics shows that schizophrenics are rated twice as frequently as normals as enjoying good sexual outlets. (S247)

### Sibling Relations
In the families of schizophrenics, siblings tended to look after the patients and to punish them. (M061)

Schizophrenic patients tend to have resented the authority of their siblings who cared for them. (M061)

### Sibling Rivalry
Schizophrenia tends to be correlated with maternal patterns of aggravating sibling rivalry. (N061)

Schizophrenic adolescents with a "juvenile" reaction (neurotic, somatic symptoms) tend to come from families characterized by intensive sibling rivalry. (S208)

### Sibling Structure (Age Difference)
There is no relationship between schizophrenia and the age gaps between siblings. (L144)

### Sibling Structure (Twins)

Schizophrenia is no more likely in twins than in non-twins. (D068)

Schizophrenia is no more likely among monozygotic than among dizygotic twins. (D068)

### Size of Family

There seems to be no direct correlation between the number of siblings and the development of schizophrenia. (T105)

The larger the family, the higher the likelihood of schizophrenia. (W147)

### Size of Family of Mother

Mothers of schizophrenics tend to have come from large families. (T105)

### Social Network of Mother

Mothers of schizophrenics frequently have little or no social life because they feel they should always be available when the child wants them. (K093)

### Toilet Training

Mothers of schizophrenics are more likely to repress all memory of the toilet-training period than are mothers of neurotics or of normals. (M218)

Schizophrenia tends to be directly associated with an artificial acceleration of the toilet-training program by the mother. (T105)

### Value Conflict (Peers/Parents)

Schizophrenic adolescents are more likely than others to be confronted with peer-group values which are contradictory with parental attitudes. (W143)

## MENTAL ILLNESS (SCHIZOPHRENIA/ AGGRESSION)
### X Class

Lower-class paranoid schizophrenics are less likely to verbalize their symptoms and are more likely to manifest them through hostile acts than are middle-class paranoid schizophrenics. (L155)

## MENTAL ILLNESS (SCHIZOPHRENIA/MANIC-DEPRESSIVE)
### X Residence with Family

Schizophrenics are more likely than manic-depressives to live away from their families. (H202)

## MENTAL ILLNESS (SCHIZOPHRENIA/NEUROSIS)
### X Achievement Demands

Schizophrenics are under greater parental pressure to become successful than are neurotics. (M197)

### Birth Control

There is no correlation between schizophrenic, neurotic, or normal women with regard to planning or not planning pregnancy or to the number of unfavorable symptoms during pregnancy. (P080)

### Breast Feeding, Duration of

Mothers of schizophrenics are more likely to breast feed for a short period (six weeks or less) than mothers of neurotics.

### Child-Rearing Attitudes (Authoritarianism)

Mothers of schizophrenics are more likely than mothers of neurotics or of normals to have controlling and authoritarian attitudes toward rearing the child. (M218)

### Child-Rearing Practices (Affection/Control)

More parents of schizophrenics than of neurotics withheld their affection to control the patient's behavior. (M061)

### Child-Rearing Practices (Consistency)

In the lower class, more parents of schizophrenics than of neurotics are inconsistent in their use of discipline. (M197)

### Child-Rearing Practices (Perfectionism/Compliance)

Mothers of schizophrenics are more likely to be rigid perfectionists who stress disciplinary compliance than are mothers of neurotics. (M061)

### Child-Rearing Practices (Punishment)

In the middle class, more parents of schizophrenics than of neurotics use the technique of withdrawal of affection to control the child's behavior. (M197)

### Childbirth Problems

Mothers of schizophrenics are more likely to have had difficulties associated with parturition than are mothers of neurotics.

### Conformity

Schizophrenics rebel less against the authority of their parents than do neurotics. Schizophrenics are more likely to have complied with their parents' demands, not only in childhood, but even during adolescence, when neurotics (in both middle and lower classes) were attempting to establish their independence. (M061)

Significantly more schizophrenics than neurotics (holding class constant) tend to have had lifelong patterns of submissive behavior—conformity to standards of home and community. (M061)

### Emotional Adjustment of Parents

Parents of normals are more likely to be well adjusted emotionally than are parents of neurotics or of schizophrenics. (F110)

Parents of normals are less likely to be rigid than are parents of schizophrenics or of neurotics. (F110)

### Father Absence

Schizophrenic and neurotic persons are more likely to have suffered the loss of their fathers during childhood than are normals. (M218)

### Father-Child Relations (Authority/Sex Role)

More schizophrenic than neurotic patients questioned their fathers' masculinity and authority. (M061)

### Father-Child Relations (Closeness)

Fathers of lower-class schizophrenics tend to be regarded as more distant and punitive persons than fathers of neurotics. (M061)

### Father-Child Relations (Warmth)

In the lower class, more fathers of schizophrenics than of neurotics were regarded by the children as distant and punitive persons. (M197)

### Husband-Wife Relations (Communication)

Parents of normals are more likely than are parents of neurotics or of schizophrenics to be high in the clarity and quantity of their communication with each other. (F110)

Parents of neurotics are more likely than are parents of

schizophrenics to be communicative and unambiguous with each other. (F110)

### Husband-Wife Relations (Conflict)
Fathers of lower-class schizophrenics tend to quarrel and fight more with their wives than do fathers of neurotics. (M061)

In the lower class, more fathers of schizophrenics quarrel and fight with their wives than do fathers of neurotics. (M197)

### Husband-Wife Relations (Consensus)
Parents of normals and of neurotics are more likely than are parents of schizophrenics to be in agreement in their views. (F110)

### Husband-Wife Relations (Hostility)
Parents of schizophrenics are more likely to report hostility toward their spouses than are parents of normals or of neurotics. (F110)

### Identification with Parent
Schizophrenics have greater problems of identification with a parental figure than do neurotics. (M197)

### Marriage Chances
Male schizophrenics are less likely to marry than are neurotics; female schizophrenics tend to marry later than do neurotics. (M197)

### Mate Selection
Schizophrenics are more likely to marry persons who resemble their parents of the opposite sex than are neurotics. (M197)

### Maternal Overprotectiveness
Maternal overprotection is more likely in the early background of the neurotic than in that of the schizophrenic. (M218)

Mothers of schizophrenics are likely to be more overprotective and "smothering" than are mothers of neurotics. (S187)

### Mother Absence
Schizophrenic females are more likely to have been permanently separated from their mothers before the age of six than are neurotic females. (B308)

### Mother-Child Relations
Mothers of neurotics are more likely than are mothers of schizophrenics or of normals to emphasize the infant's physical attractiveness. (M218)

### Mother-Child Relations (Affection)
The mothers of schizophrenics are less likely to display warmth or affection for the child than are mothers of neurotics. (M197)

### Mother-Child Relations (Approval)
While both schizophrenic and neurotic children (compared to normals) tend to show an obsessive concern with cleanliness, the mothers of neurotics were less acceptant of such behavior than were the mothers of schizophrenics. (M218)

### Mother-Child Relations (Concern)
In the lower class, mothers of schizophrenics tend to show less concern for the child's personality development than do mothers of neurotics. (M197)

### Mother-Child Relations (Interaction)
In the lower class, the mothers of schizophrenics are less likely to spend time with them than are mothers of neurotics. (M197)

### Mother-Child Relations (Rejection)
In the lower class, schizophrenics are more likely to be rejected by their mothers than are neurotics. (M197)

### Parent-Child Relations (Affect)
In the lower class, more parents of schizophrenics than of neurotics express few positive feelings toward the child. (M197)

### Parent-Child Relations (Rebellion)
Neurotic girls are much more likely than schizophrenics to rebel against their parents' restrictions concerning their heterosexual activities. (M197)

### Paternal Role
In the lower class, fathers of schizophrenics have less interest in household affairs than do fathers of neurotics. (M197)

### Personality of Father (Violence)
In the lower class, more fathers of schizophrenics than of neurotics are likely to be physically violent. (M197)

### Personality of Mother (Withdrawal)
Mothers of schizophrenics are more likely than are mothers of neurotics or of normals to be emotionally and socially withdrawn, with their adult interests centered narrowly on the family. (M128)

### Personality Problems of Mother
Mothers of neurotics are more likely than are mothers of schizophrenics to recognize their own personal inadequacies and are less likely to project them outwards or to be aggressive against the male sex. (M218)

Mothers of neurotics are less likely to be mentally stable than are mothers of schizophrenics. (M218)

Mothers of schizophrenics are more likely than are mothers of neurotics or of normals to have a distorted perception of reality and a negative and emotionally restricted view of the environment, as revealed by Rorschach testing. (M218)

There is a correlation between the Rorschach responses of neurotics and of schizophrenics and the responses of their mothers. (M218)

Mothers of neurotics are more likely than are mothers of schizophrenics or of normals to show emotional immaturity and anxiety (in Rorschach testing). (M218)

### Personality Problems of Mother (Nervousness/Fears)
Mothers of neurotics are more likely than are mothers of schizophrenics or of normals to describe themselves as being nervous and subject to fears and phobias during their childhoods. (M218)

### Power Structure of Family
Mothers of schizophrenic patients have more power in the family than do mothers of neurotics. (M061)

In the middle class more schizophrenic than neurotic patients question their fathers' masculinity and authority. (M197)

### Sibling Relations
In the lower class, schizophrenic children are more likely to resent siblings' authority and to have few positive relationships with their brothers and sisters than are neurotic children. (M197)

### Sibling Relations (Power)

Significantly more schizophrenic than neurotic patients are unable to fill their roles in the sibling power structure, regardless of their birth order. (M061)

Schizophrenics are less likely than neurotic children to be able to fulfill their roles in the sibling power structure, regardless of their birth order. (M197)

### Sibling Structure

Schizophrenic children are more likely to be taken care of by their siblings than are neurotic children. (M197)

### Social Adjustment of Parents

Parents of normals are more likely to be socially well adjusted than are parents of neurotics or of schizophrenics. (F110)

### Social Isolation

In the lower class, schizophrenics are more likely than neurotics to be isolated from social contacts due to household responsibilities. (M197)

### Social Mobility Aspirations of Mother

Mothers of schizophrenics are more likely than are mothers of neurotics to have frustrated mobility aspirations and to be ambitious for the patient's social advancement. (M061)

## MENTAL ILLNESS (SCHIZOPHRENIA), RECOVERY FROM
### X   Marital Status

People who are married recover from schizophrenia more rapidly than do those who are single. (F104)

### Psychotherapy

The more a schizophrenic child in treatment shows signs of recovery, the greater is the likelihood that the parents' defense system will be threatened and that they will try to withdraw him from treatment. (K095)

### Sex Status

Divorced or separated schizophrenic males are more likely to recover than are divorced or separated females. (F104)

## MENTAL ILLNESS (SCHIZOTHYMIA)
### X   Child-Rearing Practices (Severity)

Severe child-rearing practices in the oral, sex, dependence, and aggression areas are associated with schizothymia.

## MENTAL ILLNESS (SOCIAL ADJUSTMENT)
### X   Class

The higher the social class of his family, the higher the level of posthospital social and work performance of the mental patient. (F124)

There is no relationship between social class of the family and the mental patient's success or failure in remaining in the community. (F124)

Lower-class patients are less likely to return to their families after discharge from psychiatric institutions than are those from middle-class families. (R083)

### Household Composition

The greater the extent to which the family is of the same, rather than of ascending or descending generation, the lower the level of posthospital performance of the mental patient. (S245)

### Income

The greater the income of the family, the higher the posthospital performance of the mental patient. (S245)

### I.Q. of Kin

There is no relationship between intelligence (as measured by the Borgatta-Corsini "Quick Word Test") of the mental patient's family and the patient's success or failure in remaining in the community. (F124)

The higher the relatives' intelligence (Borgatta-Corsini "Quick Word Test"), the higher the former mental patient's level of social and occupational performance is likely to be. (F124)

Patients with low levels of social and vocational performance who succeed in remaining in the community have family members with significantly lower intelligence scores (Borgatta-Corsini "Quick Word Test") than do patients who are rehospitalized. (F124)

### Marital Status

The level of recovery from mental illness of those who were released from mental hospitals is highest among those who were married, followed by those whose marriages were broken by separation, divorce, or death, and least among single persons. (A006)

### Mental Illness, Attitude Toward

There is no relationship between relatives' feelings of stigma regarding the mental patient and the patient's success or failure in remaining in the community. (F124)

Relatives of successful patients with high social and occupational performance levels are least likely to express feelings of stigma, but relatives of patients with low levels of performance are as likely to express feelings of stigma as are relatives of failures (those rehospitalized). (F124)

Patients who perform at high levels socially and occupationally are more likely than those with low levels of performance to have families who have an environmental view of the causes of mental illness. (F124)

Patients who perform at high levels socially and occupationally are more likely than those with low levels of performance to have families with favorable attitudes toward mental hospitals. (F124)

Patients who perform at high levels socially and occupationally are more likely than those with low performance levels to have families who believe that mental illness does not basically change a person. (F124)

Patients who perform at a high level socially and occupationally are more likely to have families who believe that mental patients can be normal and healthy again. (F124)

Patients who perform at high levels socially and occupationally are more likely than those performing at low levels to have relatives who believe that patients are not to blame for their condition. (F124)

Patients who succeed in remaining in the community are more likely to have relatives who believe that patients are not to blame for their condition than are those who were rehospitalized. (F124)

Attitudinal responses of family members regarding mental illness are correlated with the patient's condition when he returns to his family as well as to the duration and frequency of hospitalization. (F124)

The higher the level of familial expectations regarding the former mental patient, the higher the level of the patient's performance. (S245)

### Parent-Child Relations

The more favorable the memory a patient has of his same-sex parent, the better his adjustment and prognosis are likely to be. (V034)

### Personality of Female Relative

Mental patients with low levels of posthospital social and work performance are more likely than those with high levels of performance to be living with female relatives who are "atypical" in personality (i.e., more authoritarian, anomic, frustrated, rigid, and withdrawn than relatives of high performers). (F124)

### Personality of Kin

Formerly hospitalized mental patients who live with female relatives described as atypical in personality (being authoritarian, anomic, frustrated, rigid, and withdrawn) are likely to be less steadily employed and participate in fewer social activities than do those who live with "normal" female relatives. (F098)

There are no significant personality differences between relatives of mental patients who were rehospitalized and of those who succeeded in remaining in the community (Srole's Authoritarianism, Anomia, Frustration, Rigidity, and Withdrawal scales). (F124)

Relatives of patients performing at high levels occupationally and socially are more likely than are relatives of low-level performers to respond to personality scales in ways that "reflect the ideal stereotype of the dominant society." (F124)

Relatives of patients whose responses on five personality scales reflect the "ideal stereotypes of the dominant society" are more likely than those who do not to impose higher demands for instrumental performance on the released mental patient. (F124)

Autism (Brim Scale) in relatives' personality scores is related to low levels of social and occupational performance of male mental patients. (F124)

Cycloid thinking (Brim Scale) in relatives is related to a low level of social and occupational performance of female mental patients. (F124)

Self-sufficiency (Brim Scale) in relatives is related to higher levels of social and occupational performance of both male and female mental patients. (F124)

Emotionality (Brim Scale) in relatives is related to low levels of social and occupational performance of female mental patients, but this is not true of males. (F124)

Nervousness (Brim Scale) of relatives is related to low levels of social and occupational performance of female mental patients, but it is not related to performance of males. (F124)

High social and occupational performance of males is related to responses of low persistence (Brim Scale) from their relatives, but the opposite is the case for female patients. (F124)

Impulsiveness (Brim Scale) in relatives is related to low levels of occupational and social performance of female mental patients, but it is not related to performance of males. (F124)

Social and vocational performance levels of mental patients are more likely to be high when their family members have personality characteristics which indicate competence in handling interpersonal relationships. (F124)

There is a relationship between family members' inhibition scores and patients' posthospital social and vocational performances (Srole and Brim combined Authoritarianism, Rigidity, and Intelligence scales). (F124)

There is a correlation between relatives' depression scores and mental patients' posthospital and vocational performance levels (Srole and Brim combined Cycloid Thinking, Frustration, and Autism Scales). (F124)

Mental patients who remain in their communities in spite of unsatisfactory social adjustment tend to have female relatives who are anomic, authoritarian, frustrated, rigid, and withdrawn. (S245)

### Religion

This study failed to replicate the findings of a previous study that mental patients in Catholic families were less likely to perform at high levels socially or occupationally after release from the hospital than were those from Protestant or Jewish families. (F124)

### Residence

Formerly hospitalized mental patients who reside with their parents tend to be less steadily employed and to participate in fewer social activities than do those who reside with their conjugal families. (F098)

### Residence with Kin

Posthospital social and vocational performance is higher among mental patients living in conjugal family settings or living alone than it is among those living with their parental or sibling families. (F124)

Mental patients living in sibling families tend to have higher levels of social and vocational performance than do those living in parental families. (F124)

### Role Definition in Family

Patients whose posthospital social and work performance is low are more likely to live with relatives who do not expect them to work or to participate in social activities as soon after release from the hospital as do relatives of patients with high performance. (F124)

The hypothesis that conjugal families would be less likely than parental families to tolerate low occupational and social performance on the part of the former mental patient is not supported by the data. (F124)

The mental patient who, after release from the hospital, is identified as the chief breadwinner, is more likely to show a high level of social and work performance. (F124)

The fewer the full-time workers in the family, the more likely the released mental patient is to perform at a high level occupationally and socially. (F124)

There is no relationship between the number of full-time workers in the family and whether or not the mental patient succeeds in remaining in the community. (F124)

There is no relationship between the family's expectations regarding the mental patient's posthospital social and vocational performance and the patient's success or failure in remaining in the community. (F124)

High levels of social and occupational performance of mental patients are most likely to occur in families in which the relatives expect and insist upon a high level of performance by the patient at the time he leaves the hospital. (F124)

The data do not support the notion that high demands by the family, when not met, drive the patient back to the hospital. (F124)

If the family makes limited demands upon the patient, he is more likely to remain insulated in his family setting than he is to return to the hospital, regardless of inadequate performance. (F124)

When expectations of family members are studied over time, high performance is more likely to be maintained when expectations remain high. (F124)

### Role in Family
In general, the higher the performance level expected of the posthospital mental patient, the higher the level of his performance. (F124)

Relatives of patients whose family role is that of son have lower expectations of posthospital performance than do relatives of patients whose family role is that of husband.

### Sex Composition of Family
The greater the number of males in the family, the lower the level of posthospital performance of the mental patient. (S245)

### Sex Composition of Household
There is no relationship between level of posthospital social and vocational performance and the number of female relatives in the household of the former mental patient. (F124)

Low-level posthospital social and work performance is associated with the availability of other males in the household to supplement or replace the patient as breadwinner. (F124)

### Size of Family
The larger the size of the family, the lower the level of posthospital performance of the mental patient. (S245)

### Social Isolation of Mental Patient
Patients who perform at low levels occupationally and socially are more likely to be found in families whose members reported that this was the only place the patient could live than are patients who perform at high levels. (F124)

The absence of an alternative living situation for the former mental patient may make him less sensitive to demands of the family and the family less demanding of the patient than if the patient were able to move elsewhere. (F124)

### Status in Family (Husband/Son)
Mental patients who make satisfactory social readjustments are more likely to occupy the kin role of husband than that of son. (S245)

Relatives of mental patients whose familial role is that of "son" tend to have lower expectations regarding their posthospital performances than do relatives of patients whose familial role is that of "husband." (S245)

### Values
There is no relationship between a mental patient's success or failure in remaining in the community and scores of relatives on scales designed to measure value orientations (Brim Scales). (F124)

Fatalism, reflectiveness, animism, and belief in single action, as indicated in responses of family members to value scales (Brim Scales), are related to low social and vocational performance of the former mental patient. (F124)

## MENTAL PROBLEMS   X   Child-Rearing Attitudes
Mothers of schizophrenic children showed less pathological child-rearing attitudes than did the mothers of brain-damaged and retarded children; mothers of both groups of ill children manifest more pathological child-rearing attitudes than do mothers of normal children. (K096)

Mothers of "normals" are less certain regarding their attitudes toward various child-rearing practices than are mothers of mongols and of psychotic children. (P075)

### Child-Rearing Practices (Strictness)
Mothers of mongoloids are stricter than are mothers of psychotics, who are less strict than are mothers of normal children. (P075)

### Class
Family members of low social status are less likely to be aware of psychological problems of self and others than are family members of higher social status. (H222)

### Institutional Care
Institutionalized children are more likely than those raised in a family to develop psychiatric disturbances and to become asocial, delinquent, feeble-minded, psychotic, or problem children. (S201)

### Mother-Child Relations (Rejection)
Mothers of psychotics and mongoloids are no more rejecting than are mothers of normal children. (P075)

### Parent-Child Relations
Child rearing which does not provide the child with concrete, deep relationships with significant adults increases the likelihood that the child will develop a pathological split between emotional and intellectual functioning. (D059)

### Personality of Mother
Mothers of schizophrenic children are no more likely than mothers of brain-injured children to display pathological attitudes (as measured by the PARI). (J027)

## MENTAL PROBLEMS (CEREBRAL PALSY)
### X   Maternal-Role Behavior
Mothers of children with cerebral palsy score significantly higher on the PARI scales of Seclusiveness, Strictness, Intrusiveness, Acceleration, Encouraging, Verbalization, Equalitarianism, Comradeship, and Sharing; mothers of normal children score significantly higher on Marital Conflict, Irritability, Rejection of Homemaking Role, and Avoidance of Communication. (S249)

## MENTAL RETARDATION     X   Age Difference
Among disturbed children, the older their parents are, the greater the mental deficiency, especially for mothers 30 years of age or older at the time of conception. (H198)

### Birth Control
The more severe the retardation, the less able is the individual to carry out effective contraception. (B307)

### Child-Rearing Practices (Responsibility)
If one child in a family is mentally retarded, the oldest child is often made to play the role of parental surrogate.

### Fertility
The more severe the retardation, the lower the birth rates among mentally retarded persons. This proposition is also denied. (B307)

### Guilt
The more guilty the mother feels for bearing a retarded child, the less she accepts the child. (Z006)

### Institutional Care
### X   Marital Adjustment
Among Catholic parents, marital adjustment is not related to whether the retarded child is living at home or is institutionalized. (J027)

Among Protestant and Jewish families, lower level of marital adjustment is related to the retarded child living at home rather than being institutionalized. (J027)

### Marital Adjustment
The presence of a retarded child is associated with increased problems in parents' marital adjustment. (J027)

### Mental Illness of Parent
Confinement to contact with a defective or schizophrenic parent is a cause of mental and emotional retardation in the child. (B285)

### Mother Absence
There is a direct relation between early deprivation of maternal care and physical, social, and intellectual retardation. (B270)

### Ordinal Position
Mental deficiency among disturbed children is more frequent among intermediate and youngest children than among oldest children. (H198)

### Parent-Child Relations (Evaluation)
Parents of handicapped (retarded) children are more likely than parents of nonhandicapped children to show an autistic distortion in their perception of their children. (Z009)

### Personality Adjustment of Sibling
The presence of a retarded sibling is more likely to have an adverse effect on normal female than male siblings. (J027)

### Personality Adjustment of Sibling
### X   Ordinal Position
Younger siblings are more likely to be adversely affected by their retarded siblings than are older siblings. (J027)

### Religion
Catholic mothers are more acceptant of their retarded children than are non-Catholic mothers. The contrary is also asserted. (Z006)

Catholic and Protestant mothers of retarded children are equally accepting of their retarded children. (J027)

### Sibling Relations
### X   Institutional Care
Living arrangements (home or institutional) for retarded children are not related to sibling adjustment. (J027)

### Sibling Role
Retarded children are more likely to assume the role of the youngest child, regardless of their actual sibling position. (J027)

### Social Adjustment
The oldest child in a family with a retarded child is more likely to have poor adjustment than are the other children.

### Values
Boys who interact with a retarded sibling on a daily basis are likely to stress material aspects of future plans, such as success in business, while those who do not interact with a retarded sibling will stress such things as marital happiness.

Girls who interact with a retarded sibling are more likely to stress an ideal life of "giving"—making a contribution to society—while those who do not interact with their retarded sibling stress social acceptability and friendliness.

## MENTAL RETARDATION (DEPENDENCY)
### X   Sibling Relations
Dependent retarded children produce adverse sibling adjustments. (J027)

## MENTAL RETARDATION OF CHILD
### X   Mental Illness of Mother
Mentally retarded children are more likely than normals to have mothers who suffered from serious psychiatric disability during the period when the child was 6 to 18 months old. If there is no such period of psychopathology at the birth of other children in the same family, the chance of mental retardation is low. (G141)

## MENTAL RETARDATION OF MOTHER
### X   Maternal-Role Behavior
There is no relationship between intelligence ratings of mentally retarded mothers and their ability to provide satisfactory child care. (B307)

### Size of Family
### X   Maternal-Role Behavior
The fewer the number of living children, the greater the ability of the mentally retarded mother to provide adequate child care. (B307)

## MOBILITY ASPIRATION
### X   Paternal Role Definition
A high-status husband, who is already established socially and economically, has more time to spend around his home, as compared with the "struggling to get ahead" man, who spends all his available time trying to achieve his goals.

The tendency for the established high-status man to be more family oriented is suggested also in the fact that high-status suburban husbands do a great deal around the home. The man who struggles to get ahead does so at the expense of family participation.

## MOBILITY ASPIRATION OF CHILD
### X   Education of Mother/Father
The child is more likely to have mobility ambitions if the mother's educational level is higher than the father's than if her educational level is less than or equal to his. (T096)

If the mother's educational level is higher than that of

the father, the child's mobility aspirational level is higher. (T096)

## MOIETY                                    X  Incest
When the community is divided into two exogamous groups, the rate of incest will be high. (O011)

### Kin Terminology (Bifurcate Merging)
Moieties are very widely associated with bifurcate merging terminology. (M019)

### Kin Terminology (Classificatory)
Classificatory terminology which reflects the coincidence of affinal and consanguineal kinsmen tends to occur when the society has a moiety organization. (S098)

### Kin Terminology (Generation)
Generational terminology is incompatible with the moiety or sectional systems. (E032)

### Kin Terminology (Symmetrical Cross-Cousin)
The application of the same term to father's sister's son and to mother's brother's son is evidence for the earlier existence of a moiety system. (R034)

### Preferential Marriage (Cross-Cousin)
Patterns of preferential cross-cousin marriage tend to be associated with a moiety organization. (H077)

A pattern of matrilateral cross-cousin marriage is required when there are only two diffierent kinds of local groups and indirect exchange. (L062)

Given a system based on exogamous matrimoieties, if residence becomes avunculocal, a subsidiary system of matrilines (implying marriage with the daughters of the matrilateral female cross-cousins only) is likely to occur. (L178)

### Preferential Marriage (Intergenerational)
Marriage into an adjoining generation may occur under a moiety system. (R036)

### Preferential Marriage (Levirate)
The institutionalized pattern of marriage with a mother's brother's widow is common in a moiety organization. (S095)

### Rank of Linage
Lineage ranking is less likely to occur in societies with a moiety system. (N066)

## MOIETY SYSTEM        X  Descent (Asymmetrical)
Asymmetrical descent is associated frequently with moiety organization. (S097)

### Descent (Matrilineal)
The moiety system tends to occur in association with matrilineal descent. (G060)

Matrimoieties are found to occur in societies which have had matrilineal descent for a long time. (M019)

### Descent (Unilineal)
The unlineal affiliation of the moiety structure will tend to be consonant with patterns of affiliation on the lineage level. (E032)

A moiety system precedes the development of unilineal kin-groups or sibs. (L040)

### Endogamy (Community)
A moiety system tends to encourage community endogamy. (O005)

### Gerontocracy
Matrilineal moiety system tends to occur in association with a pattern of gerontocracy. (S097)

### Kin Terminology (Classificatory)
There is a correlation between the classificatory system of kinship; terminology and the organization of societies into clans of moieties. (R069)

Classificatory terminology which reflects the coincidence of affinal and consanguineal kinsmen tends to occur when the society has a moiety organization. (S098)

### Marriage Class System
The division of a group into moieties precedes the development of a marriage class system. (R034)

### Mate Selection
The institution of a moiety organization tends to discourage marriage between distant members of the same kin unit. (E032)

### Population
The increase in the size of population aggregates is sufficient to account for the appearance of sib and moieties. (O006)

### Preferential Marriage (Cross-Cousin)
Cross-cousin marriage tends to emerge as a consequence of a dual organization of the society. (G060)

### Preferential Marriage (Exchange)
Where there are moieties, there are, at least terminologically, patterns of exchange marriage. (A021)

### Preferential Marriage (Mother's Brother's Wife)
A simple moiety organization will tend to occur in response to the development of a mother's brother's wife marriage. (D026)

### Preferential Marriage (Second-Cousin)
Second-cousin marriage tends to characterize societies with moiety systems. (E063)

### Stratification
Lineage ranking is less likely to occur in societies with a moiety system. (N066)

The appearance of stratification among tribes without a sib structure tends to inhibit the development of sibs and moieties. (O006)

## MOIETY SYSTEM (CROSS-COUSIN MARRIAGE)
### X  Marriage Class System
A six-class marriage system will arise from a dual organization with matrilineal descent and the marriage of cross-cousins. (S095)

## MOIETY SYSTEM (MATRILINEAL)
### X  Descent (Double)
Given a system based on exogamous matrimoieties, if residence becomes patrilocal, a double descent system of matrimoieties and patrisibs will occur. (L178)

### Father-Child Relations
Bonds linking the individual with his father are more important in matrilineal societies which lack a moiety structure. (L070)

## MONEY, CHILD'S KNOWLEDGE OF
### X  Child-Rearing Practices (Economic)
Children's knowledge of the use of money correlates with the parents' permitting them to experience the use

of money and with the parents' wise handling of the family income. (M182)

Children's knowledge of the use of money does not correlate with their parents' giving them an allowance, permitting them to earn money, or using money to reward or punish their behavior. (M182)

## MONOGAMY                         X  Abortion
### X  Sex Taboo (Postpregnancy)
Married women are more likely to give the sex drive priority over the maternal impulse and thus resort to abortion in societies where there are taboos on coitus during pregnancy and lactation and where monogamy prevails. (D071)

### Cohesion of Family
Ties of affection within the nuclear family will tend to be stronger in monogamous than in polygamous unions. (A034)

### Cohesion of Lineage
The predominance of monogamous marriages in matrilineal societies which have previously been polygynous and polyandrous will tend to result in the weakening of matrilineal bonds. (G056)

### Economic Pattern
Monogamy tends to occur where simple economic patterns characterize a society. (K090)

### Economic Pattern (Private Property)
Where the economic pattern is one in which property is held privately, the mode of marriage tends to be monogamy. (E087)

### Fertility
The birth rate tends to be higher among monogamous than among polygamous unions. (P034)

### Husband-Wife Relations (Intimacy)
Monogamy through personal choice is likely to permit a higher level of intimacy in marriage than is polygyny. (P083)

### Inheritance (Matrilineal)
Where matrilineal descent and matrilocal residence are coupled with female ownership and control of agricultural land and houses, exclusive monogamy is likely to occur. (D057)

### Legal Status
The status of the husband and wife is more likely to be equal when the marriage pattern is that of monogamy. (S123)

### Mother-Child Household
In monogamous societies there is a small proportion of mother-child households. (S079)

### Parent-Child Relations (Hostility)
### X  Sex Taboo (Postpregnancy)
There is a relationship between unconscious parental hostility toward the unborn child (as a motive for abortion) and taboos on coitus during pregnancy and lactation in monogamous societies. (D071)

### Polygyny, Economic Importance of
Monogamy tends to be resisted if polygyny plays a vital role in the economy. (A030).

### Power Structure of Family
When patterns of monogamous marriage supplant traditional polygynous forms, the status of the wife tends to be one of equality rather than of subordination. (F035)

### Property (Collective)
As the economic pattern is transformed to collective property, the monogamous family tends to occur less frequently. (E087)

### Prostitution
Prostitution is correlated with monogamy. (E087)

### Residence (Matrilocal)
Matrilocal residence and service to the father-in-law are associated with monogamy. (W157)

### Residence (Neolocal)
Any factor which promotes monogamy will also favor neolocal residence. (M109)

### Resources
Pressures toward monogamy are greater where the bargaining position of women in society is stronger. (P083)

### Sex Ratio
Monogamy tends to appear where the sex ratio is not disturbed. (K090)

### Sex Taboo (Postpartum)
In monogamous societies the postpartum sex taboo is of short duration or does not exist at all. (S079)

### Sex Taboo (Postpregnancy)
With an increase in the percentage of monogamous marriages, the postpregnancy sex taboo is increasingly disregarded. (L113)

## MONOGAMY, ATTITUDE TOWARD
### X  Sex Status
Women tend to be more sympathetic to monogamy as the pattern of marriage than men do. (P034)

## MONOGAMY/POLYANDRY      X  Acculturation
Wherever modern European culture has penetrated and modified indigenous culture, polyandry is giving way to monogamy. (M048)

## MORAL BELIEFS      X  Child-Rearing Practices
Parental possessiveness and dominance are positively correlated with the child's acceptance of beliefs in immanent justice, moral realism, retribution, and severe punishment; the tendency of parents to ignore the child is negatively correlated with such beliefs. (J021)

The tendency of the parents to ignore the child should be positively correlated with the child's acceptance of belief in communicable responsibility (guilt by association); parental possessiveness and dominance should be negatively correlated with the child's acceptance of such beliefs. (J021)

### Parental/Maternal Role
During the adolescent years, fathers have greater influence on the son's moral views than on the daughter's; mothers have equal amounts of moral influence on children of both sexes. (J026)

### Peer Group/Parents
The acceptance of the idea of guilt by association is usually learned from the peer group, as opposed to parents. (J021)

## MORAL BELIEFS OF CHILD     X     Authoritarianism

Authoritarian families are more likely than others to have children who exhibit immature moral judgment, especially in the areas of immanent justice and belief in the efficacy of extreme punishment. (B275)

### Child-Rearing Practices (Permissiveness)

As parental constraint decreases, the child's belief in immanent justice, moral realism, retribution, and severe punishment tends to decline. (J021)

### Occupation of Parents

Parental occupation correlates most significantly with the child's beliefs concerning moral realism, retribution, and severe punishment. (J021)

### Parent-Child Relations (Rejection)

The more a child rejects and deprecates his parents, the greater the likelihood that he will experience a loss of moral orientation. (T099)

### Personality of Parents (Extremism)

Parents who more frequently take extreme points of view tend to have children who believe in immanent justice, moral realism, retribution, severe punishment, and communicable responsibility. (J021)

## MORALITY RATES     X     Fertility Values

Greater effort is expended to inculcate fertility values in high morality societies. (G156)

## MOTHER ABSENCE     X     Adjustment of Child

In children under five years of age, children who had intimate and happy relations with their mothers and were then deprived of them suffered more from the loss than did children who never knew their mothers. (B270)

### Age of Child

Since the child is able to differentiate an object from the love afforded by that object (because of developed ego), he will react to separation from the mother with grief and mourning; the infant whose ego is undifferentiated from the mother will react with anxiety. (B255)

### Anxiety

Since the death instinct operates in the child as the fear of annihilation, the separation of the child from his mother induces neurotic anxiety as the expression of this instinct in addition to the apprehension that the infant has destroyed (by his sadistic impulses) his mother (the persecutory object). (B255)

### Behavior Problems

Children who are separated from their mothers or from adequate mother substitutes are likely to develop such autoerotic habits as finger-sucking, other sucking activities with tongue, lips, and mouth, rocking and other rhythmical movements, head-knocking, and (among older children) masturbation.

Children who are deprived of mothers before they are six months old demonstrate behavior which is characterized, generally, by unresponsiveness; they are immobile, quiet, and listless. (B270)

Children separated from their mothers are more likely to exhibit regressive tendencies than are children not separated. (B270)

### Behavior Problems (Nonoral Eroticism)

Separation from the mother is a cause of rocking, fecal play, and other nonoral autoeroticism in the infant. (B272)

### Behavior Problems (Passivity/Hyperactivity)

Separation from the mother is a cause of the infant's loss of interest in the outside world, manifested in either passivity or hyperactivity. (B272)

### Cognitive Development

Children deprived of their mothers at birth are consistently less vocal from the age of six months than are children not so deprived. (B270)

Children separated from their mothers show less interest and reactivity as early as the eighth to twelfth weeks than do children not separated from their mothers. (B270)

The longer the child is deprived of mother or mother surrogate, the lower his intelligence level becomes (as measured on the Development Quotient Scale). (B270)

### Cognitive Development (Abstract Thinking)

Children who have been deprived of their mothers during their early years exhibit a deficiency or a lag in the capacity for abstract thinking. (C106)

### Cognitive Development (Time)

Maternally deprived children are less advanced or mature in their concept of time than are maternally nondeprived children. (C106)

### Emotional Problems of Child

If the mother is absent during infancy and, consequently, the child receives care from numerous persons instead of mainly one, the child develops problems of personal adjustment. (G121)

### Identification with Parents

Identification is related to the length, timing, and predictability of the mother's separation from the child. (R098)

### Infant Mortality

The absence of the mother during the first year is directly related to the increase in infant mortality. (S277)

### I.Q.

Children deprived of their mothers during the first year experience a large drop in intelligence (as measured by the Development Quotient Scale) between the ages of 4 and 12 months. (B270)

### Juvenile Delinquency

There is no correlation between frequency and length of separation from the mother and delinquency in the son. (N059)

Prolonged separation of a child from his mother in the first five years of life is a cause of delinquency in later life. (N059)

Juvenile delinquents who have spent part of their childhood separated from their families are more likely to commit further offenses than are those who were reared at home. (N059)

There is a correlation between the frequency of separation from the mother in early childhood and the seriousness of delinquency in the boy. (N059)

The child who has been separated from his mother (during the first three years of life) is more likely to become delinquent than are children of the same family who were not separated. (S226)

Mothers of delinquents tend to spend less time in the home than do mothers of nondelinquents. (W152)

Separation from the mother during the first five years of the infant's life is a major cause of delinquency. (Y047)

### Marital Stability

There is a significant correlation between a childhood history of early maternal deprivation (below the age of six and for at least six months' duration) and broken marriages later in life. (E093)

### Mental Illness of Child

Children deprived of their mothers for more than eight months of the first year are more likely than are normals to show severe psychiatric disturbances. (B270)

Mental illness induced by lack of maternal care during a period of at least two and one-half years does not seem to be relieved by the initiation of maternal care. (B270)

The absence of the mother is one of the prime causes of mental illness in children hospitalized before the age of two. (S277)

### Mental Illness (Schizophrenia)

There is no significant correlation between early maternal deprivation (below the age of six and for at least six months' duration) and later incidence of schizophrenia. (E093)

There is no relationship between the incidence of schizophrenic reactions in the child and the absence of the mother during the child's first 20 years. (L144)

There is no relationship between the incidence of schizophrenic reactions in the child and the absence of the mother during the child's first six years. (L144)

### Mental Illness (Schizophrenia/Neurosis)

Schizophrenic females are more likely to have been permanently separated from their mothers before the age of six than are neurotic females. (B308)

### Mental Retardation

There is a direct relation between early deprivation of maternal care and physical, social, and intellectual retardation. (B207)

### Mother-Child Relations

The better the mother-child relationship preceding separation, the more severe the immediate reactions of the child. (Y045)

The better the mother-child relationship, the better the adjustment of the child to the separation. (Y045)

### Mother-Child Relations (Closeness)

Among children over the age of five, the closer the relationship between mother and child, the greater the child's toleration of separation. (B270)

### Motor Development

The process of learning to walk is stimulated by the security offered by the mother as well as by the incentive to reach her as she calls. (S277)

Deprivation of perceptual phenomena and small radius of possible movement can be compensated for by the presence of adequate mother-child relations. (S277)

### Personality Adjustment

If the infant is under six months of age, the absence of the natural mother does not have any effect on the psychological and social well-being of the infant. (O033)

### Personality Development

Children deprived of their mothers have an impaired ability to relate to other people, to think abstractly, and generally have an impaired ego and superego development.

### Personality Problems

Partial maternal deprivation causes feelings of guilt and depression to arise in the deprived child, who has feelings of revenge for having been deprived. (B270)

### Personality Problems (Depression)

A separation of three or four months from the mother is a cause of severe "anaclitic" depression in the infant. (B272)

### Personality Problems of Child

Separation from the mother is a cause of several disturbed reactions in the child: emotional protest, search for a substitute, withdrawal from adults and from social interaction, denial of the mother image, and an attempt to transfer attachment to a substitute. (Y045)

### Physical Development

Children who have been deprived of their mothers before they are six months old fail to gain weight properly, even though they eat a diet which is adequate. (B270)

Separation from the mother is more likely to lead to retardation of physical growth than is disease. (B270)

### Social Adjustment

Complete maternal deprivation can produce a child who is unable to have stable relationships with other people. (B270)

Completely depriving a young child of his mother or mother surrogate is directly related to an increase in the inability to make relationships with other people. (B270)

Children deprived of their mothers from birth appear generally to be asocial, while children who have been deprived of maternal care and also have had some significant period without deprivation tend to be more antisocial. (B270)

Early maternal deprivation (below the age of six and for at least six months' duration) is significantly related to the later development of sociopathic personality, especially in the failure to adjust to society in the spheres of marriage, work, and relationship to law and order. (E093)

### Social Adjustment of Child

Children separated from their mothers for long periods of time during the early years are more likely to show only superficial reactions to other people and to have no real affection. (B270)

### Speech Problems

Maternal deprivation is more likely to retard the ability to speak than it is to retard neuromuscular activity. (B270)

### Surrogate Mother

The effects of maternal deprivation are less marked if the mother surrogate is someone the child knew before mother deprivation than if the mother surrogate is someone unknown to him. (B270)

#### Work Adjustment

There is a significant correlation between a childhood history of early maternal deprivation (below the age of six and for at least six months' duration) and a poor work record later in life. (E093)

## MOTHER-CHILD HOUSEHOLD
#### X   Husband-Wife Relations (Intensity)

Where a high percentage of the households in the society is made up of mother and child, the husband-wife relationship is less intense. (S079)

#### Monogamy

In monogamous societies there is a small proportion of mother-child households. (S079)

#### Mother-Child Relations (Hostility)

In matriarchal families which are characterized by coresidence of mother and daughter, daughters accept gratifications from mothers and suppress all feelings of hostility toward them.

#### Residence (Extrusion)

In societies with a high percentage of mother-child households, boys are likely to move away from home at adolescence. (S079)

#### Surrogate Mother

Infant care by older children is a function of the autonomy of mother-child households peculiar to polygamous societies, where each wife has her own living unit. (M216)

#### Weaning

In societies with a high frequency of mother-child households, the average age at weaning is later. (S079)

## MOTHER-CHILD RELATIONS     X   Aggression

Fantasy aggression by children (measured by doll play) is increased when the mother is present. (L147)

#### Behavior Problems

Genital play by the infant is related to a satisfactory relationship with the mother.

#### Breast Feeding

The more sensitive, consistent, and attentive the mother is relative to the child, the more likely she is to breast feed the infant. (B272)

#### Child-Rearing Values

The attitude of the mother toward her mentally ill child (babying, indulgence) will directly reflect the cultural definition of the mother-child relationship. (S187)

#### Cognitive Development

A strong mother-child or mother-surrogate relationship established through a certain rhythm of stimulation, gratification, and deprivation is correlated with the capacity of the child to differentiate the environment and with the manipulation of symbols in order to secure ends valued by the mother-child relationship. (P083)

#### Conflict in Family

The mother is more likely to attempt to shield the child from the effects of conflict in the home than are other adults in the home. (C117)

#### Dating

Divorcées who give more attention to their children are less likely to become steady daters. (G157)

Mothers are more likely to encourage their daughters to date than they are their sons. (K161)

#### Economic Security

Financial stress is negatively associated with positive mother-child interaction during preadolescence. (S273)

#### Emotional Problems of Mother

Negative emotional states (dullness, gloominess, unresponsiveness) in the mother are negatively associated with positive mother-child interaction during preadolescence. (S273)

#### Employment of Mother

Employment that serves ego needs of the mother improves the parent-child relationship. (G128)

If the mother is employed outside the home, she is more likely to develop a strenuous and irritable relationship with the child. (H183)

Full-time employment of mothers of children under three years of age leads to an inadequate development of the mother-child relationship. (Y047)

#### Employment of Mother, Attitude Toward

The greater the mother's guilt concerning her employment (feeling she is neglecting the child), the less satisfactory will the parent-child relationship be. (G127)

#### Health of Child

There is a correlation between three-month colic in the infant and anxious overpermissiveness on the part of the mother. (B272)

Neurodermatitis in the infant is related to maternal hostility in the garb of anxiety. (B272)

Hypermotility in the infant is related to the mother's oscillation between pampering and hostility. (B272)

#### Health of Mother

Poor physical health of the mother is negatively associated with positive mother-child relations during preadolescence. (S273)

#### Identification with Mother

There is a negative relationship between a mother's projection of fears and preferences onto the child and the child's identification with the mother. (C114)

#### I.Q.

Mothers of children of average intelligence tend to be more dominating, more ignoring, and more possessive than the mothers of gifted children. (H199)

#### I.Q. of Mother

There is a positive correlation between the mother's intelligence and positive preadolescent mother-child interaction. (S273)

#### Juvenile Delinquency/Neurosis

Disturbed emotional relationships between mother and child occur more frequently in delinquent than in neurotic children. (B214)

#### Marital Adjustment

When the immature mother can stabilize her own emotional functioning and anxiety level through caring for her schizophrenic child, the father can establish a less anxious relationship with the mother. (B297)

The greater the integration of role relations in the marriage, the greater the integration of the mother-child relationship. (F094)

## Mental Illness (Manic-Depressive)

A manic-depressive character is more likely to develop if the mother's reaction to the rebelliousness of early childhood is harsh and punishing. (C092)

The manic-depressive child is more likely than the normal child to view the mother as the moral authority in the family and his attitude toward her is likely to be unloving, but fearful and desirous of approval. (G022)

Manic-depressive patients are likely to have had an early history of "injurious maternal influence". (W154)

## Mental Illness of Child (Autism)

Autism is directly correlated with a disturbed mother-child relationship. (S188)

## Mental Illness of Child (Schizophrenia)

If a mother can relate to her infant only as an extension of herself, she will damage the development of the child's ego and schizophrenic ego impairment will become evident in the second, third, and fourth years of the child's life. (A061)

Confusion of identity in the child, due to a disturbed mother-child relationship, is a cause of schizophrenia in the child. (D068)

Schizophrenic children tend to have mothers who confuse the children's needs with their own needs projected onto the children and who fail to recognize ego boundaries between themselves and the children. (L121)

## Mental Illness (Paranoia)

Paranoid patients tend to have mothers who accuse them of bad intentions rather than criticize them for their actions. (S187)

## Mental Illness (Schizophrenia/Neurosis)

Mothers of neurotics are more likely than are mothers of schizophrenics or of normals to emphasize the infant's physical attractiveness. (M218)

## Mother Absence

The better the mother-child relationship preceding separation, the more severe the immediate reactions of the child. (Y045)

The better the mother-child relationship, the better the adjustment of the child to the separation. (Y045)

## Mother-Daughter Relations (Rejection)

A woman's rejection of her own mother may inhibit her maternal feelings relative to her own children. (T085)

## Motor Development

A strong mother-child relationship established through a certain rhythm of stimulation, gratification, and deprivation facilitates the relative desensualization of the body and the use of the body as a tool. (P083)

## Neurosis

There is no relationship between a particular kind of maternal attitude and a specific emotional disorder in the child.

## Neurosis (Anorexia)

The mother who identifies her child with a dead sibling or a parent toward whom she has entertained death wishes is more likely to produce anorectic children (extreme loss of weight, lack of appetite, low respiration) than is the mother who does not so identify her child. (F102)

## Personality (Isolation)

In order to be "alone" (to enjoy being either physically or emotionally separate from others), one must have spent time as an infant and in early childhood in the presence of one's mother without specifically interacting with her. (W141)

## Personality Problems (Stuttering)

The lower the mother's level of anxiety concerning his speech and the lower the level of irritation at his aggressive behavior, the better chance of improvement has the stuttering child. (W136)

## Pregnancy, Attitude Toward

The more favorable the attitude of the mother toward pregnancy, the more positive the relationship between mother and infant at the early stages of childhood. (B283)

## Scholastic Achievement

Mothers of children who are high scholastic achievers are more dominant and ignoring of their children than are the mothers of low scholastic achievers. (H199)

## Scholastic Adjustment

The child develops a phobia against attending school, not due to fear of such attendance, but because of anxiety about separation from a parent. (E095)

Mothers of children with school phobias tend to have disturbed relationships with dominating and overprotecting mothers or mothers-in-law. (E095)

## Self-Conception

Children who report that their mothers know all or most of their friends have higher self-esteem than do those who report that their mothers know some or none of their friends. (R129)

The positive association between the child's self-esteem and the mother's knowledge of his friends holds regardless of whether the child (in childhood) confided in the mother, in someone else, or in no one. (R129)

The positive association between the child's self-esteem and the mother's knowledge of his friends holds regardless of whether he currently sides with the mother, the father, or both equally in parental disagreements. (R129)

The positive association between the child's self-esteem and the mother's knowledge of his friends holds regardless of whether the mother was friendly or not friendly toward his friends. (R129)

Simple interest in the child (indicated by knowledge of the child's friends) may be more important than parental pleasantness or unpleasantness for the level of self-esteem in the child. (R129)

## Self-Conception of Child

There is a correlation between continuity of mothering and a sense of continuity of self in the child. (Y045)

## Sex Status

Mothers tend to feel more assured with girl babies than they do with boy babies. (B272)

There is no relationship between the sex of the infant and maternal behavior (sensitivity, consistency, or frequency of maternal acts). (B272)

## Socialization, Agents of

Boys are more likely to show positive attitudes toward the mother when the parents *are not* the main socializing agents that when they are; girls show no difference in this respect. (R089)

## MOTHER-CHILD RELATIONS (ACCEPTANCE)
### X   Child-Rearing Practices (Consistency)
Mothers who are consistent in their discipline are more accepting of their children than are mothers who are inconsistent (U.S.). (S191)

### Education of Mother
The mother's educational level is not related to maternal acceptance. (K115)

### Education of Wife
Mothers who are highly educated tend to be more accepting of their children than do mothers with less education. (K115)

### Marital Adjustment
There is a correlation between the mother's marriage adjustment and her acceptance of her child. (F094)

### Occupation of Father
Mothers whose husbands are businessmen or semi-professionals tend to be more accepting of their children than do mothers whose husbands are in other occupational categories.

### Personality of Child (Stress)
The mother's acceptance of the child is positively related to the infant's capacity to cope with stress. (Y042)

### Superego Formation
The mother's acceptance of the child and high conscience of the child are associated. (Evidence is stronger for boys than for girls.) (S191)

## MOTHER-CHILD RELATIONS (AFFECT)
### X   Behavioral Development
The mother's emotional involvement with the child is positively related to the infant's development of exploratory and manipulative behavior. (Y042)

### Death Rate
Child mortality rates are positively associated with absence of emotional interchange with the mother. (S209)

### Mental Illness
Emotional alienation from the mother will tend to produce overt manifestations of mental illness. (L125)

### Mental Illness of Child (Schizophrenia)
Schizophrenia is more likely to occur when the infant is forced to expend all its capacity for dealing with the external world on its relationship with its mother. (S258)

### Oedipal Complex
If the masochistic impulses (which are derived from and are a defense against incestuous wishes toward her father) are repressed by the mother, she is less likely to be able to extend herself emotionally to the child. (B272)

### Personality of Child (Stress)
The mother's emotional involvement with the child is positively related to the infant's capacity to cope with stress. (Y042)

### Personality Problems of Child
Absence of emotional interchange between mother and child (as found in foundling homes) produces apathetic and hyperexcitable children. (S209)

### Personality Problems of Parents
The psychopathic and unstable parent who is the cause of child neglect is often the grown-up affectionless child who is a typical product of maternal deprivation. (B270)

### Physical Adjustment
Lack of affective mother-child relations is a cause of head-rolling, body-rolling, and other hyperkinetic manifestations.

### Sex Status
Fathers, rather than mothers, are more likely to show high emotional involvement with their mothers. (B297)

### Surrogate Mother
At one year of age, children reared in families where the mothering is provided by one person display greater affect in interaction with their mothers than do children reared in families where the mothering is provided by more than one person (i.e., nurse, grandparent, mother's friend, or older sister of child). (C124)

## MOTHER-CHILD RELATIONS (AFFECTION)
### X   Age of Child
There is a positive and significant relationship between the degree of love that mothers show their infants and the degree of love shown to the same child during preadolescence. (S273)

### Age of Mother
There is no difference between younger (20–39 years old) and older (40 years old or older) mothers regarding their willingness to display affection to their children. (R097)

### Aggression of Mother
Due to a process of sublimation, there is a correlation between the mother's aggressive instincts and the extent of her tenderness for her infant. (B272)

### Alcoholism
Alcoholism is associated with the child's having a definitely expressed and disproportionately greater love for his mother than for his father. (D078)

### Authority Structure of Family
When the mother is remembered as a strong authority figure, her grown children, when parents themselves, tend to recall her less often as being highly affectionate. (B297)

### Autoeroticism
Autoerotic activity tends to be positively correlated with positive maternal affect. (H216)

Infants of ambivalent mothers tend to have characteristic rocking movements; infants of warm, consistent, and emotionally balanced mothers tend to have more frequently genital-oriented motor activity. (H216)

### Behavior Development
Affectional interchange between mother and child is positively related to the infant's development of exploratory and manipulative behavior. (Y042)

### Breast Feeding
Because of the physical closeness with the mother, breast feeding is more conducive than is bottle feeding to gratifying the child's affective needs. (Y042)

### Child-Rearing Practices (Achievement)
Maternal rewards for children's achievement efforts do

not correlate with expression of maternal affection. (C118)

### Child-Rearing Practices (Consistency)
Mothers who are consistent in their discipline are more affectionate in their relations with their children than are mothers who are inconsistent (U.S.). (S191)

### Child-Rearing Practices (Punishment)
If a child acquires his original affection for his mother under conditions which contained considerable punishment, then the child's love for his mother will persist, despite much discouragement, punishment, evidence of dislike, etc. (M187)

### Child-Rearing Practices (Reward)
Mothers who frequently use praise or tangible rewards in child rearing are warmer and more affectionate with their children than are mothers who do not use these techniques (so frequently) (U.S.). (S191)

### Childbirth Attitude
Women who feel that childbirth is hard are less likely to express physical affection for their children. (N051)

### Children, Number of
Greater concern and affection during nursing are more common among mothers who have had more than one child. (P063)

### Class
Middle-class mothers are more responsive to their babies' crying than are working-class mothers. (W002)

There is no significant difference between middle-class and working-class mothers in the amount of fun they have in taking care of their babies. (W002)

There is no significant difference between middle-class and working-class mothers in their warmth or demonstrativeness. (W002)

### Cognitive Development
The development of a sense of time in the child is dependent upon his experiencing time directly, in relation to maternal love and gratification. (Y045)

### Dependency
There is no relationship between whether or not the child has been frustrated in his affective relationship with the mother during infancy and his later dependency (at age five) (U.S.). (S191)

### Ego Development of Child
The infant who is exposed to a mother whose emotional investment is ambivalent and/or unpredictable will be more likely to have an arrested ego development. (H216)

### Employment of Mother
The degree of affection of the adolescent for the mother does not correlate with employment/nonemployment of the mother. (S265)

### Homosexuality
There is a correlation between lack of maternal affection and lesbianism in the daughter. (R104)

Mothers of male homosexuals are more likely to have withheld love, friendliness, and affection than are other mothers. (U004)

### Identification
The more emotionally remote the mother (and the weaker the daughter's attachment to her), the less likely it is that the daughter will be able to identify with a strong maternal figure who can both love and educate the child. (B272)

Identification is positively associated with the spontaneity with which the mother expresses affection. (R098)

### Juvenile Delinquency
If the child has a nonaffectionate relationship with his mother and is consulted frequently by a social worker, he will less often become delinquent than will a child with an affectionate mother. (M194)

### Juvenile Delinquency, Age at
Among children who become delinquent at a late age (after the seventeenth year), more are likely to have an affectionate rather than an aggressive relationship with their mothers. (M194)

### Juvenile Delinquency (Reform)
Among juvenile delinquents, those who have loving mothers are likely to reform earlier (before their twenty-third year) than are those with nonloving mothers. (M194)

### Marital Adjustment
Among white collar families, a favorable view of the parents' marriage by the child is positively related to maternal affection. (H201)

Among blue collar families, a favorable view of the parents' marriage is negatively related to maternal affection. (H201)

### Maternal Overprotectiveness
Maternal overprotection is directly correlated with patterns of defective maternal love on the part of the maternal grandmother. (L163)

### Maternal Role
Patterns of passive, demanding love are more likely to develop when the mother assumes both the supportive and disciplinary role. (W154)

### Mental Illness of Child (Schizophrenia)
The inability of the mother to love her child during early infancy is a cause of schizophrenia in the child. (M218)

In the lower class, there is a correlation between lack of maternal affection and schizophrenia in the child; in the middle class, the correlation is between schizophrenia and maternal overprotectiveness and overambitiousness for the child. (P078)

### Mental Illness (Schizophrenia)
Mothers of schizophrenics tend to love the child not only excessively, but also conditionally. (M218)

### Mental Illness (Schizophrenia/Neurosis)
The mothers of schizophrenics are less likely to display warmth or affection for the child than are mothers of neurotics. (M197)

### Mother-Child Relations (Aggression)
The more aggressive the mother's attitude toward the child, the less is her display of affection toward them. (C100)

### Mother-Child Relations (Authority)
There is a negative relationship between authority and affection in the children's perceptions of their mothers. (B297)

### Mother-Child Relations (Dominance)
If a mother is affectionate, her children will not be as submissive to her as if she is hostile. (C124)

### Motor Development
Babies who lack adequate affective mothering are more likely to have poor muscular development than are those who do not.

Bodily tonus is less developed among infants who have had inadequate affective mothering than among those who have not.

### Personality Adjustment of Mother
High personal adjustment of the mother (esteem for husband, self-esteem, satisfaction with current life situation) is associated with warmth toward her child (U.S.). (S191)

### Personality (Expressiveness)
Lack of satisfactory affective mothering impairs the infant's ability to communicate and express feeling.

### Personality of Child (Stress)
Affectional interchange between mother and infant is positively related to the infant's capacity to cope with stress. (Y042)

### Personality Problems of Child
Absence of an affectionate mother-child relationship (in children up to nine months of age) produces infantile behavior in the child (i.e., screaming, kicking, bed-wetting, soiling, clinging, etc.). (S202)

### Personality Problems of Mother (Oral)
A mother with unresolved oral conflicts tends to attempt to find a solution with her children by becoming demanding of them, rather than affectionate. (R099)

### Power Structure of Family
Persons who had close affectional ties to their mothers in childhood are more likely to assume equalitarian roles in marriage.

### Psychosomatic Illness
If the child suffers from deprivation of maternal care, maternal stimulation, and maternal love along with physical deprivation in his first year, he is likely to suffer from psychosomatic problems. (S201)

### Self-Conception of Mother
The higher the mother's self-evaluation, the more likely is she to have a consistently affectionate relationship with her child. (M186)

### Social Adjustment
Absence of mother love leads to maladjustment in adult responsibilities. (G127)

### Social Development
A high level of affection and emotional expression by the mother is related to the development of outgoing social behavior in the infant. (Y042)

### Work Attitudes of Mother
Mothers with positive attitudes toward their work are more likely to be affectionate toward the child than are mothers who dislike their work. (S265)

## MOTHER-CHILD RELATIONS (AGGRESSION)
### X  Mother-Child Relations (Affection)
The more aggressive the mother's attitude toward the child, the less is her display of affection toward him. (C100)

## MOTHER-CHILD RELATIONS (AMBIVALENCE)
### X  Mental Illness of Child
Preschizophrenic children are likely to have an extremely strong and ambivalent bond to their mothers. (S187)

### Mental Illness of Child (Schizophrenia)
Mothers of schizophrenic children are more likely than others are to have ambivalent attitudes toward their children (devotion and detachment). (B284)

### Scholastic Adjustment
Mothers of school phobics are more likely than those of normals to have strong feelings of both love and hostility toward their children. (D065)

## MOTHER-CHILD RELATIONS (ANXIETY)
### X  Ego Development of Child
When the dominant feeling of the parent toward the child is one of anxiety, empathized anxiety for the parent will keep the child from advancing beyond the infantile sense of union with the mother to a mature awareness of the self as a separate individual. (S259)

## MOTHER-CHILD RELATIONS (APPROVAL)
### X  Mental Illness of Child (Schizophrenia)
While both schizophrenic and neurotic children (compared to normals) tend to be undemonstrative and withdrawn, the mothers of schizophrenics are more likely to approve of such behavior than are the mothers of neurotics. (M218)

### Mental Illness (Schizophrenia/Neurosis)
While both schizophrenic and neurotic children (compared to normals) tend to show an obsessive concern with cleanliness, the mothers of neurotics were less acceptant of such behavior than were the mothers of schizophrenics. (M218)

## MOTHER-CHILD RELATIONS (ATTACHMENT)
### X  Mental Illness
Mental Illness is directly correlated with an exclusive attachment to the mother. (S187)

### Mental Illness of Child (Schizophrenia)
Mothers of schizophrenics, as compared with mothers of normals, are excessively devoted or attached. (H186)

### Sex-Role Identification
The more intense the girl's attachment to her mother (and the more difficult to surrender the mother as a love object), the more likely it is that she will adopt a reactive contempt for the female sex and identify with the father, rather than choose him as a love object. (B272)

## MOTHER-CHILD RELATIONS (AUTHORITY)
### X  Mother-Child Relations (Affection)
There is a negative relationship between authority and affection in children's perceptions of their mothers. (B297)

## MOTHER-CHILD RELATIONS (AWARENESS)
### X  Identification with Mother
There is a positive relationship between the mother's awareness of the child and identification of the child with the mother (higher for girls than for boys). (C114)

## MOTHER-CHILD RELATIONS (BIOLOGICAL)
### X  Personality of Mother (Sublimation)
The further removed a maternal activity is from biologic functions, the more likely it is that the masochistic impulses (derived from early incestuous wishes toward the

father) of the mother will be capable of sublimation. (B272)

## MOTHER-CHILD RELATIONS (CLOSENESS)
### X    Authority Structure of Family
When the mother stands in a relationship of intimacy and confidence to her children, it is difficult for her to perform disciplinary functions. (R030)

### Class
Middle-class mental patients show a greater involvement with their mothers than do lower-class mental patients. (R127)

### Husband-Wife Relations (Closeness)
The more "husband centered" the mother is, the less child centered she is, as indicated by physical closeness, sleeping together with the children, etc. (S079)

### Husband-Wife Relations (Egalitarianism)
Where both husband and wife were attached to their respective mothers, the relationship between husband and wife is more likely to be equalitarian than not. (L014)

### Juvenile Delinquency
Nondelinquent girls are more likely to talk over problems with their mothers than are delinquent girls; this distinction does not hold for delinquent and nondelinquent boys. (M205)

### Mental Illness of Child (Autism)
Autism occurs in young children who have not had a close, almost symbiotic, relationship with their mothers as infants. (S213)

### Mother Absence
Among children over the age of five, the closer the relationship between mother and child, the greater the child's toleration of separation. (B270)

### Surrogate Parent
If a child is cared for by a number of familiar adults instead of being in the exclusive care of the mother, the affectional relationship between mother and child will be less intense. (M058)

### Work Attitudes of Mother
Working mothers who like to work are more likely to feel a strong attachment to their children. (G156)

## MOTHER-CHILD RELATIONS (COMMUNICATION)    X    Aggression Anxiety
Inadequate verbal communication between mother and child produces, in the stuttering child, displaced aggression anxiety upon siblings or other relatives and fear of losing mother. (W136)

### Mental Illness of Child (Schizophrenia)
Recurring sequences of conflicting messages ("double binds") proceeding from the mother to the child are a cause of schizophrenia in the latter. (F100)

The communications from mother to schizophrenic child are more likely than others to be incongruent (emotions contradict verbal communications). (H187)

### Mental Illness (Schizophrenia)
A significantly greater number of schizophrenic daughters than of normal ones believed that their mothers tried to avoid communicating with them during their childhoods. (H186)

## MOTHER-CHILD RELATIONS (COMPLIANCE)
### X    Conformity
Social compliance (frequency and alacrity with which children accede to demands and suggestions) of the child with his mother is associated with social compliance with his peers. (C102)

## MOTHER-CHILD RELATIONS (CONCERN)
### X    Mental Illness (Schizophrenia/Neurosis)
In the lower class, mothers of schizophrenics tend to show less concern for the child's personality development than do mothers of neurotics. (M197)

### Surrogate Mother
When their infants are six months of age, mothers who have been the only caretaking agent for their infants express more concern for the well-being of their babies than do mothers who have provided other maternal figures for their infants. (C107)

## MOTHER-CHILD RELATIONS (CONFLICT)
### X    Child-Rearing Practices (Control/Awareness)
Low awareness and high control of the child are associated with greater conflict between mother and child. (C114)

### Marital Adjustment
An important factor in determining whether or not a marriage will be a happy one is whether or not there was an absence of conflict with the mother in the husband's and wife's childhoods. (B270)

### Mother-Child Relations (Empathy)
Mothers who are less able to state correctly the child's preferences, ambitions, and fears, but attempt to maintain high control, are most likely to be involved in parent-child conflict.

### Work Attitudes of Mother
The child of the mother who likes to work is less likely to assert himself against her. (G156)

## MOTHER-CHILD RELATIONS (CONFORMITY)
### X    Conformity
Social compliance (frequency and alacrity with which children accede to demands and suggestions) of the child with his mother is associated with the child's compliance toward other adults. (C102)

Within various age levels, social compliance (frequency and alacrity with which children accede to demands and suggestions) of the child with his mother is associated with social compliance with his peers. (C102)

## MOTHER-CHILD RELATIONS (CONSISTENCY)
### X    Adjustment of Child (Social and Physical)
Mood shifts in mothers characterized by alternating moods of hostility-overprotectiveness toward their children are positively associated with a diminished capacity on the part of the children to relate themselves to humans or to manipulate inanimate objects. (S209)

### Alcoholism
The more alternating and inconsistent the mother is in her affections, the more likely it is that alcoholism will develop in the son. (M195)

### Behavior Problems
Inconsistency in maternal emotions toward the child is a cause of the infant's turning back upon himself, as manifested by his rocking himself, playing with his feces, etc. (B272)

### Behavior Problems (Crying)

The amount of crying by the infant is positively related to maternal anxiety and inconsistency in attention to the infant. (B272)

### Child-Rearing Practices (Dependency)

Mothers who unwillingly accede to their children's demands for excessive dependency will be more inconsistent in the treatment of their children than will mothers who willingly accede or do not accede to their children's excessive dependency demands. (S202)

### Dependency/Aggression

Children whose mothers vacillate between nurturance and rejection are more likely to become overdependent rather than aggressive. (B243)

### Emotional Problems of Child

The mother who alternates in overindulgence and rejection of her child is more likely than is the mother who is consistent in her attitudes to produce a child who is unhappy at home and intensely homesick when away from it. (S226)

### Juvenile Delinquency

Delinquents are more likely than others to have had inconsistent interaction with their mothers. (B238)

### Mental Illness of Child (Schizophrenia)

A combination of maternal attitudes which foster dependency on the one hand and stress independence and assertion on the other is a cause of schizophrenia in the child. (D073)

A child is likely to be schizophrenic if his mother is alternately compassionate and rejecting. (S213)

### Personality of Child (Anxiety)

When a period of affectional demonstrativeness from the mother is followed by emotional aloofness, the personality of the child will reflect a deep-seated anxiety and a feeling of insecurity toward the world. (H054)

### Social Adjustment of Child (Social and Physical)

Mood shifts in mothers, characterized by alternating moods of hostility-overprotectiveness toward their children, are positively associated with a diminished capacity on the part of the children to relate themselves to human beings or to manipulate inanimate objects. (S209)

## MOTHER-CHILD RELATIONS (CONTROL)
### X Age of Child

There is a positive, though not significant, relationship between the amount of autonomy or control mothers exhibit toward their infants and the amount of autonomy or control exhibited toward the same child during preadolescence. (S273)

### Personality of Mother (Dominance)

A highly dominant mother is more likely to use severe control in her behavior toward the child. (C100)

Stated desire by the mother to dominate others is not positively associated with coercive maternal behavior practices. (C100)

### Sex Status of Child

Mothers tend to exert greater control over their daughters than over their sons. (A060)

## MOTHER-CHILD RELATIONS (DEMANDS)
### X Scholastic Achievement

The mother who makes impossible demands upon her children for attention (through hysteria, depression) is more likely than the child-centered mother to produce children who under-achieve at school. (S226)

## MOTHER-CHILD RELATIONS (DEMOCRACY)
### X I.Q.

Democratic attitudes are more characteristic of mothers of children with high, rather than low, I.Q.'s. (E102)

## MOTHER-CHILD RELATIONS (DEPENDENCY)
### X Education of Wife

The higher the education of the wife, the less dependent she is on her children.

## MOTHER-CHILD RELATIONS (DOMINANCE)
### X Mental Illness (Schizophrenia)

A significantly greater number of schizophrenic daughters than normals believed that their mothers were overly intrusive during their childhoods. (H186)

### Mother-Child Relations (Affection)

If a mother is affectionate, her children will not be as submissive to her as if she is hostile. (C124)

### Parent-Child Relations of Husband (Favoritism)

Husbands of maternally dominant mothers tend to have been favorite sons or obedient sons of dominant mothers or fathers. (L163)

### Scholastic Achievement

Mothers of children who are high achievers (in junior high school) are more dominating than are mothers of low achievers. (T090)

## MOTHER-CHILD RELATIONS (EMPATHY)
### X Identification

The mother who is better able to state correctly her child's preferences, ambitions, and fears is also more likely to feel the same way herself. This correlation between awareness and identification is higher between girl and mother than between boy and mother.

### Identification with Parents

Identification is associated with the mother's ability to empathize with the child or her capacity for direct sensitivity to his needs. (R098)

### Mother-Child Relations (Conflict)

Mothers who are less able to state correctly the child's preferences, ambitions, and fears, but attempt to maintain high control, are most likely to be involved in parent-child conflict.

### Projection

Mothers who are correct in their abilities to predict the preferences, ambitions, and fears of their children are least likely to impute incorrectly their own attitudes to the children (that is, they do not project).

## MOTHER-CHILD RELATIONS (EVALUATION)
### X Personality of Mother (Friendliness)

The mother's own perceived friendly relations with others correlate with her perception of her child as friendly to others, even though the actual friendliness of her child is not so related.

### Self-Conception

A mother who rates herself highly in terms of several selected family-attitude variables does not rate her husband and child as highly as the husband with a high self-rating rates his wife and child. (B237)

### Self-Conception of Mother
If, in terms of several selected family-attitude variables, a mother rates herself highly, she also rates her husband and child highly. (B237)

### Status in Family
Adolescent girls are more likely than their mothers to have favorable evaluations of the mother-child relationship. (M201)

## MOTHER-CHILD RELATIONS (FAVORITISM)
### X     Class
Girls from upper middle-class homes are more likely to attribute preference for a male child to the mother than are girls from the lower classes. (H181)

## MOTHER-CHILD RELATIONS (FEEDING)
### X     Personality of Child (Mastery)
The more satisfactory the feeding experience for the child, the greater his interest in and concentration upon the mastery of objects is likely to be. (B272)

## MOTHER-CHILD RELATIONS (FRUSTRATION)
### X     Personality of Child (Stress)
The greater the infant's frustration in the mother-child relationship, the less able is the infant to cope with stress situations. (Y042)

## MOTHER-CHILD RELATIONS (GRATIFICATION)
### X     Dependency of Mother
There is a negative relationship between the mother's prenatal dependency needs and postnatal dependency on her infant for need gratification. (C124)

### Maternal-Role Behavior
There is a correlation between the maternal-role behavior corresponding to that phase of the child's development most gratifying to the mother and the maternal role to which she may regress when confronted with frustration in later phases of the child's development. (M203)

## MOTHER-CHILD RELATIONS (HOSTILITY)
### X     Age of Mother
Younger mothers are more likely than older mothers to express an underlying feeling of hostility toward children. (S191)

### Child-Rearing Practices (Consistency)
Disobedience and hostility of the child are associated with lack of consistency in the child-rearing practices of the mother. (R113)

### Child-Rearing Practices (Criticism)
Children whose mothers are excessively critical and depreciative are likely to be disobedient and hostile. (R113)

### Child-Rearing Practices (Favoritism)
Children whose mothers show marked preference for the child's sibling tend to be hostile and disobedient. (R113)

### Child-Rearing Practices (Power)
The mother's assertion of unqualified power in reaction to the child's noncompliance is not caused by the hostility and rebelliousness of the child, but, rather, produces these characteristics. (H182)

### Child-Rearing Practices (Punishment)
Children whose mothers are excessively punitive are more likely to be disobedient with hostility. (R113)

### Education of Mother
The older and less educated the mother, the more severely hostile she will be toward her children. (S229)

### Father Absence
When the father is absent for long periods of time, the children are more likely to express hostility toward the mother.

### Institutional Care
If a baby is institutionalized for long periods, he will show a hostile reaction to the mother on his return to her. (B270)

### Mental Illness
Mental illness tends to be correlated with hostile behavior during feeding. (L118)

### Mother-Child Household
In "matriarchal" families which are characterized by coresidence of mother and daughter, daughters accept gratifications from mothers and suppress all feelings of hostility toward them.

### Personality of Child (Dominance)
The more hostile and punitive the mother, the greater the tendency of the child to be dominant (rather than submissive). (B232)

### Personality of Child (Hostility)
Hostile mothers are more likely than those who are not hostile to produce children who are covertly hostile. (F103)

### Pregnancy Anxiety
High anxiety during pregnancy is related to maternal hostility in child rearing. (D067)

### Superego Formation
Since the development of the conscience is dependent upon a mutually affectionate relationship between mother and child, hostile mothers are more likely than those who are not hostile to produce children with poor conscience development. (F103)

### Work Attitudes
If the mother is dissatisfied with her employment outside the home, she shows assertive behavior toward the child and, consequently, the child is hostile toward the mother. (H183)

## MOTHER-CHILD RELATIONS (IDEALIZATION)
### X     Class
Lower-class paranoid schizophrenics express greater idealization of their mothers than do middle-class paranoid schizophrenics. (L155)

## MOTHER-CHILD RELATIONS (INDULGENCE)
### X     Motor Development
Children who were overindulged by their parents are more likely to lack skill in muscular endeavors than are children who were not overprotected. (L146)

### Oedipal Complex
If the masochistic impulses (which are derived from and are a defense against incestuous wishes toward the father) persist in the mother, she is more likely to act them out by submitting her own ego to that of the child's and by being excessively indulgent. (B272)

### Scholastic Adjustment
"School phobia" (refusal to attend school) is associated

with maternal overindulgence and close mother-child relations. (L143)

### Sexual Gratification, Freedom in
Gratification of sexual impulses is more likely to occur in individuals who have been subject to maternal indulgence. (L161)

## MOTHER-CHILD RELATIONS (INTENSITY)
### X Husband-Wife Relations (Intensity)
The more "husband centered" the mother is, the less child centered she is, as indicated by physical closeness, sleeping together with children, etc. (S079)

### Mental Illness (Paranoia)
Paranoia is more likely to occur when the relationship with the mother has been close and intense. (N050)

## MOTHER-CHILD RELATIONS (INTERACTION)
### X Class
Lower-class working mothers are less likely to allocate particular time periods to spend with their children or to organize activities with them than are middle-class working mothers. (G156)

The mothers of lower-class mentally ill patients tend to spend less time with them than do those of middle-class patients. (M061)

### Conformity
The degree of attention a child receives from its mother tends to be inversely correlated with the degree of conformity of the child. (H217)

### Death Rate
### X Mother-Child Relations (Affect)
Child mortality rates are positively associated with absence of emotional interchange with the mother. (S209)

### Employment of Mother
Working lowers the interaction of the mother with the child. (Y050)

### Health
Babies who have not had adequate contact with their mothers exhibit a refusal to breast feed, loss of appetite, failure to assimilate food, and rigidity of body muscles.

### Mental Illness (Schizophrenia)
A significantly larger number of schizophrenic daughters than of normal ones believed that their mothers secluded themselves from the daughters during the daughters' childhoods. (H186)

### Mental Illness (Schizophrenia/Neurosis)
In the lower class, the mothers of schizophrenics are less likely to spend time with them than are mothers of neurotics. (M197)

### Mother-Child Relations (Warmth)
The warmer the mother in the mother-child relationship, the more time she will spend with her child simply for pleasure. (M186)

### Personality Problems
Babies who have not had adequate contact with their mothers are more likely to develop depressive and regressive states of motionlessness resembling stupor.

### Personality Problems of Child
Frustration of a child's desire to cling to or to follow his mother is more likely than the presence or absence of breast feeding to cause mental disturbance. (B239)

### Surrogate Mother
When their infants are six months of age, mothers who have been the only caretaking agent for their infants are more active and playful with their babies than are mothers who have provided other maternal figures for their infants. (C107)

In a clinical situation, among one-year-old infants, mothers who have reared their children themselves display greater interaction, both verbal and physical, with their children than do mothers of children who are being reared in families where the mothering is provided by more than one person (i.e., nurse, grandparent, friend of mother, older sister of child). (C124)

## MOTHER-CHILD RELATIONS (INTEREST)
### X Class
The mothers of lower-class mentally ill patients tend to show less concern for their children's personality development than do mothers of middle-class patients. (M061)

### Feeding
There is a correlation between the mother's interest in the child and the amount of affection and concern displayed during nursing. (P063)

### I.Q.
Lack of maternal interest is negatively correlated with the child's performance on the Picture Completion and the Picture Arrangement Test (WISC). (M213)

## MOTHER-CHILD RELATIONS (INTIMACY)
### X Maternal Overprotectiveness
Maternal overprotection tends to be correlated with an extension of early intimate contacts (e.g., sleeping together). (L164)

## MOTHER-CHILD RELATIONS (IRRITATION)
### X Pregnancy Anxiety
Mothers who were highly anxious during pregnancy evidence more irritable relations with their infants than do those who were not as anxious during pregnancy. (D067)

## MOTHER-CHILD RELATIONS (ISOLATION)
### X Mental Illness of Child
Mental illness tends to be directly correlated with attempts by the mother to inhibit contacts with peers. (L126)

## MOTHER-CHILD RELATIONS (NEED GRATIFICATION)    X Maternal-Role Behavior
The more the mother is warm and loving and the more continuous her influence in daily routine and total lifespan, the more likely she is to be a source of safety and need gratification to the child. (P068)

## MOTHER-CHILD RELATIONS (NURTURANCE)
### X Mother-Child Relations (Protectiveness)
If the mother expresses verbally a strong nurturance attitude toward the child, she is also highly protective toward the child. (C100)

### Personality Problems of Child
Children who are deprived of adequate mothering during infancy are more likely to have no emotional response to situations where it is normal and also to exhibit deceit and evasion and to steal. (P068)

### Prenatal Stimulation
If an infant receives high amounts of stimulation during the prenatal period, it requires high amounts of postnatal mothering. (O033)

### Social Adjustment
Children who are deprived of adequate mothering during infancy are more likely in later childhood to make superficial relationships with friends, accompanied by little ability to care for people. (P068)

## MOTHER-CHILD RELATIONS (OEDIPAL)
### X   Identification with Mother
The greater the identification of the woman with a psychotic mother, the more likely she is to project onto the child her former relationship with her mother, unconsciously reversing the Oedipal situation. (H192)

## MOTHER-CHILD RELATIONS (ORAL)
### X   Mental Illness of Child (Schizophrenia)
Disturbances in the early mother-child relationship (oral phase of development) are necessary, but not sufficient, conditions for the development of schizophrenia in the child. (L139)

## MOTHER-CHILD RELATIONS (PERMISSIVENESS)
### X   Dependency
The greater the permissiveness and support on the part of the mother in relation to the child, the greater the child's dependency upon and diffuse attachment to the mother. (B234)

## MOTHER-CHILD RELATIONS (PHALLIC)
### X   Maternal-Role Behavior
The mother's ability to imbue the child with phallic attributes and to accept herself a passive role is correlated with and determines her own capacity for psychologically normal maternal behavior. (B272)

## MOTHER-CHILD RELATIONS (PHYSICAL CONTACT)
### X   Body Image
A disturbance of the body image will result from a deficiency in the physical contact (touching, looking, kinesthetic experience) between mother and child. (B241)

### Surrogate Mother
When their infants are six months of age, mothers who have been the only caretaking figure for their infants are more sensuous in touching and handling their babies than are mothers who have provided other maternal figures for their infants. (C107)

## MOTHER-CHILD RELATIONS (POSSESSIVENESS)
### X   Dependency
Overpossessiveness on the part of the mother, characteristic of schizophrenogenic mothers, may actually be only the manifestation of her dependency on the child as her surrogate mother figure. (S213)

### Education of Mother
Maternal possessiveness is negatively correlated with education of the mother. (S187)

### Mental Illness of Child (Schizophrenia)
If the mother is overly possessive, the child is more likely to become schizophrenic. (F119)

## MOTHER-CHILD RELATIONS (POWER)
### X   Sex-Role Adjustment
There is a correlation between feelings of sex-role inadequacy in the woman and her perception of the maternal figure as a malevolent power. (B309)

### Sex Status
Daughters tend to be the objects of power assertion of mothers more than sons do. (H180)

## MOTHER-CHILD RELATIONS (PROTECTIVENESS)
### X   Aggression of Mother
By a process of sublimation, there is a correlation between the mother's aggressive instincts and the extent of her protective activity on behalf of her infant. (B272)

### Mother-Child Relations (Nurturance)
If the mother expresses verbally a strong nurturance attitude toward the child, she is also highly protective toward the child. (C100)

### Personality of Mother (Protectiveness)
The more autonomous the mother, the less protective she will be toward the child. (C100)

## MOTHER-CHILD RELATIONS (REJECTION)
### X   Aggression
Children having mothers who are cold, distant, and neglectful tend toward aggressive, acting out behavior, such as lying and general destructiveness. (R113)

### Alcoholism
There is a correlation between maternal rejection and alcoholism in the son when the father is present. (M195)

### Anxiety
If the mother consistently reacts with disapproval to the infant's need for tenderness, he will react with anxiety. (B255)

### Behavior Problems (Lying/Stealing)
Children whose mothers overtly reject and dislike them are more likely to lie and engage in solitary stealing. (R113)

### Breast Feeding
There is a correlation between maternal rejection of the child and the practice of bottle feeding the child. (A063)

There is no correlation between maternal rejection and the practice of bottle feeding the infant. (A063)

### Breast Feeding, Duration of
Mothers who breast feed the infant for one month or less tend to be rejecting; those who breast feed for 12 months or more tend to be overprotective. (B272)

### Broken Home
Broken homes are associated with mothers who are likely to resent and reject their children. (K120)

### Child-Rearing Practices (Punishment)
Mothers who show signs of rejection are more likely to use physical punishment even though they consider it ineffective than are mothers who fully accept their children. (S191)

### Child-Rearing Values (Punishment)
Among mothers who spank their children frequently, those who consider it ineffective are more rejecting than those who consider it effective (U.S.). (S191)

### Childbirth Problems
There is a correlation between birth difficulties and rejection of the child by the mother.

### Dependency
Mothers showing some child rejection had more dependent children than did those who showed no rejection. (S191)

### Father-Child Relations
Maternal rejection in early life is directly correlated with subsequent attitudes of disappointment toward the father. (N061)

### Husband-Wife Relations (Evaluation)
Maternal rejection in early life is directly correlated with a perception of the husband as inadequate. (N061)

### Juvenile Delinquency
Mothers of delinquents do not differ from mothers of normal children with respect to hostility toward or rejection of the child. (M208)

### Mental Illness of Child
There is no correlation between hostility and rejection on the part of the mother and mental illness in the child. (T097)

### Mental Illness of Child (Schizophrenia)
Severe and unqualified rejection by the mother is probably not correlated with schizophrenia in the child. (L123)

### Mental Illness (Schizophrenia)
Schizophrenic mothers are more likely to use covert than overt methods of rejection and domination. (B284)

Schizophrenia is directly correlated with anxieties resulting from an early maternal rejection. (N061)

Mothers of schizophrenics will tend to be more covertly than overtly rejecting. (S187)

The schizophrenogenic mother is hateful and rejecting toward her child only to cover her truly loving but confused maternal intincts. (S213)

### Mental Illness (Schizophrenia/Neurosis)
In the lower class, schizophrenics are more likely to be rejected by their mothers than are neurotics. (M197)

### Mental Problems
Mothers of psychotics and mongols are not more rejecting than are mothers of normal children. (P075)

### Neurosis of Mother
Neurotic disturbance in the mother seems to be unrelated to the severity of her rejection of her disturbed child. (S188)

### Personality Problems (Masochism)
Maternal rejection is a cause of the development of masochism in the child. (L134)

### Personality Problems of Child
If the mother's rejection of the child is specific (directly related to the child), the potential for pathogenic effects on the child is greater than if her rejection is nonspecific (transferred to the child from another source). (L134)

### Scholastic Adjustment
Children with school phobias are likely to have mothers who reject them. (S239)

### Self-Conception of Child
If a child's mother has expressed feelings of rejection of him, he will react with a corresponding feeling of self-rejection and self-deprecation. (C104)

### Self-Conception of Mother
Mothers of schizophrenics are hateful and rejecting toward their children because of events in their own childhoods which left them insecure about their ability to love. (S213)

### Sex Status
Among middle-class schizophrenic children, girls are more likely to be rejected by their mothers than are boys. (M197)

### Sexual Interest of Child
The child of a rejecting mother is likely to be generally preoccupied with sex. (S079)

### Sociopathic Personality
Rejection and other maternal behavior do not appear as important in determining sociopathic personality as in other psychiatric illnesses. (O032)

### Weaning
The more rejecting the mother is of the child, the earlier she is likely to discontinue breast feeding.

## MOTHER-CHILD RELATIONS (REJECTION/ HOSTILITY)          X   Marital Adjustment
Unsatisfactory marital relations which cause the mother to contemplate returning to work may lead to rejection and hostility displayed toward the child. (G127)

## MOTHER-CHILD RELATIONS (RESPONSIVENESS)          X   Bed-Wetting
There is no relationship between degree of responsiveness of the mother to the child's crying and duration of bed-wetting (U.S.). (S191)

### Dependency
There is no relationship between how responsive the mother is to her child's crying and the child's dependency on the mother. (S191)

## MOTHER-CHILD RELATIONS (RESTRICTIVENESS)          X   Sex Status
Girls are more likely than boys to perceive their mothers as overcircumscribing their freedom. (K101)

## MOTHER-CHILD RELATIONS (SADOMASOCHISTIC)          X   Sexual Adjustment
The more the mother's genital experience is focused on childbirth, the more likely she is to perceive her relationship with her children in its sadomasochistic aspects. (M203)

## MOTHER-CHILD RELATIONS (SEDUCTIVENESS)          X   Anxiety (Nightmares)
Children whose mothers are overly seductive in their behavior toward them are likely to have frequent nightmares. (R113)

### Behavior Problems (Nail-Biting)
Children whose mothers are overly seductive in their behavior toward them are likely to have a nail-biting problem. (R113)

### Mental Illness (Schizophrenia)
Schizophrenia tends to be correlated with seductive attitudes on the part of the patient's mother. (N061)

### Personality of Child (Maturity)
Children whose mothers are overly seductive in their behavior toward them tend to be generally immature. (R113)

## MOTHER-CHILD RELATIONS (SEX)
          X   Father Absence
Children who are raised in homes in which there is no father or father surrogate during the first six years of their lives tend to have mothers who are more sexually

attached to them than do children in normal homes. (S079)

### Mother-Child Relations (Warmth)
The cold and rejecting mother is less likely to be a sex object to the child. (S079)

## MOTHER-CHILD RELATIONS (SEXUAL INTEREST)
### X   Sex Taboo (Postpartum)
A long duration of postpartum sex taboo increases the likelihood of the mother being sexually arousing to her children. (S079)

A long duration of the postpartum sex taboo is associated with greater sexual interest on the part of the mother in her child. (S079)

## MOTHER-CHILD RELATIONS (SEXUALITY)
### X   Sexual Adjustment of Mother
The greater the sexual dissatisfaction of the mother, the earlier does she arouse sexuality and intense emotional states in the child. (B272)

## MOTHER-CHILD RELATIONS (SUCCORANCE)
### X   Class
As opposed to lower-class mothers whose husbands have entrepreneurial jobs, middle-class mothers (entrepreneurial) are less likely to give immediate attention to babies who cry when nothing serious is wrong with them. (M062)

## MOTHER-CHILD RELATIONS (TOLERANCE)
### X   Maternal Role, Attitude Toward
Mothers who are unsatisfied with parenthood are more likely than other women to lack tolerance for their children's behavior. (G126)

### Surrogate Mother
When their infants are one year old, mothers who have been the only caretaking agent for their infants are more tolerant of irritating behavior from their babies than are mothers who have provided other maternal figures for their infants. (C107)

## MOTHER-CHILD RELATIONS
### (UNDERSTANDING)   X   Employment of Mother
Mothers who have had jobs in the past are more likely to devote more effort to the understanding of their children's problems than are either presently working mothers or unemployed mothers.

### Mental Illness of Child (Schizophrenia)
Perplexity (inability to deal adequately with the child's gratification needs) on the part of the mother leads to schizophrenia in the child. (M237)

Schizophrenic children with no organic disturbances have mothers who show a greater degree of perplexity (inability to deal adequately with the children's gratification needs) than do schizophrenic children with organic (neurological) problems. (M237)

## MOTHER-CHILD RELATIONS (WARMTH)
### X   Age of Mother
The older the mother, the warmer she is toward her infant child, except when the child is a first one. (S191)

### Aggression
The less warm the mother is to the child, the more likely it is that the child will be aggressive. (B243)

### Autoeroticism
Children of warm and loving mothers are more likely to engage in masturbation than are children of cold and rejecting mothers. (S079)

### Bed Wetting
Severe training leads to late bed wetting if the mother is cold, but not if she is warm. (S191)

### Breast Feeding
There is no relationship between degree of warmth displayed toward the child in infancy and the mother's decision to breast feed or not to breast feed her child (U.S.). (S191)

### Child-Rearing Practices (Aggression)
The mother's warmth and her permissiveness toward aggression are not associated (U.S.). (S191)

### Child-Rearing Practices (Consensus)
Mothers who report agreement with spouse about child-rearing practices are more likely to be warm, accepting, and nonpunitive toward their sons than are those who report disagreement. (B243)

### Child-Rearing Practices (Consistency)
Mothers who are inconsistent in their discipline because of concern for the child (e.g., child is sick, mother doesn't want to hurt the child, etc.) are warmer with their children than are mothers who are inconsistent because of self-concern (e.g., mother is too busy, too tired, forgets to punish the child, the situation is too public, etc.) (U.S.). (S191)

### Child-Rearing Practices (Dependency)
Mothers who are accepting of dependency behavior in their children are more likely to be warmer to their children than are mothers who are not accepting. (S191)

### Child-Rearing Practices (Giving Reasons)
Mothers who have a warm relationship with their children are more likely to use praise and reasoning rather than punishment as a means of control than are mothers who do not have warm mother-child relations. (M186)

### Child-Rearing Practices (Sex)
Mothers who are not permissive regarding their children's sexual behavior tend to be more emotionally cold toward their children than do mothers who are permissive in the areas of sexual behavior (U.S.). (S191)

### Class
When mothers of the same educational level but different socioeconomic rank are compared, we find that middle-class mothers are more affectionately warm toward their children and less likely to display rejection (U.S.). (S191)

Among Irish families, social class and warmth of the mother toward the child are not associated. (S191)

### Cognitive Development
Children whose mothers are highly accepting and show great warmth toward their children are higher in intellectual originality than are children whose mothers are rejecting. (A071)

### Criminality
Normal persons are more likely to characterize their mothers as being warm and understanding than are habitual criminals. (C105)

### Dependency
There is no relationship between the warmth shown by the mother toward the infant and later (age five) dependent behavior by the child. (S191)

### Employment of Mother
If the mother is employed outside the home, she is likely to be less frustrated and more capable of warm interaction with the child. (H183)

### Feeding (Demand)
The mother's lack of warmth and scheduled feeding are associated. (S191)

### Feeding Problems
There is a positive relationship between mothers who display little warmth toward their children and child feeding problems (e.g., prolonged periods of loss of appetite, etc.) (U.S.). (S191)

### Household Composition
There is a curvilinear relationship between the number of adults residing in the family and the maternal warmth displayed toward the child, a few additional adults tending to produce conditions favorable to warmth and a larger number tending to produce less emotional expressiveness (cross-cultural). (M216)

### I.Q.
Positive, warm attitudes are more characteristic of mothers of children with high, rather than low, I.Q. (E102)

### Mother-Child Relations (Interaction)
The warmer the mother in the mother-child relationship, the more time she will spend with her child simply for pleasure. (M186)

### Mother-Child Relations (Sex)
The cold and rejecting mother is less likely to be a sex object to the child. (S079)

### Ordinal Position
Mothers are warmer with older boys than they are with younger boys; they are warmer with younger girls than with older girls. (M216)

Youngest children receive more maternal warmth than do middle children, who receive more warmth than oldest children. (M216)

Ordinal position and warmth of the mother toward the child are not associated. (S191)

### Personality Development of Child
Children whose mothers are highly accepting and whose mothers show great warmth toward them are higher in emotional spontaneity and total emotional freedom than are children whose mothers are rejecting. (A071)

### Pregnancy, Attitude Toward
The more delighted the mother over becoming pregnant, the greater the warmth displayed toward the child after his birth. (S191)

The mother's attitude toward pregnancy forecasts only slightly the warmth she will show toward her child after it is born. The forecast is even poorer for her warmth five years later. (S191)

### Residence
There is a curvilinear relationship between maternal warmth and privacy of living arrangements. The warmest mothers are the ones with intermediate privacy (single-family dwellings with neighbors, friends, and relatives nearby). (M216)

Mothers tend to be lower on maternal warmth when the child has several close cousins nearby than when the child has few such cousins in close proximity. (M216)

### Residence (Privacy)
There is a curvilinear relationship between maternal warmth and privacy of living arrangements. The warmest mothers are the ones with intermediate privacy (single-family dwellings with neighbors, friends, and relatives in close proximity). (M216)

### Sex Status
Mothers usually act more warmly toward girl babies than toward boy babies. (S191)

### Sex Status of Child
At kindergarten age, sex of child and mother's warmth toward child are not associated, but in infancy, mothers are slightly more affectionately demonstrative with baby girls than with baby boys. (S191)

### Sibling Structure
The larger the number of siblings in the family, the lower the amount of maternal warmth displayed to each individual child. (M216)

Mothers are warmest to a new child when there is a sizable age gap between this child and the next older sibling. (S191)

### Sibling Structure (Sex)
If the mother already has boys only, she tends to be relatively cold toward the new baby boy, but the sex of older children makes no difference in her attitude toward a new baby girl. The mother is just as warm, whether she has boys already, or girls, or both. (S191)

### Social Development of Child
Children of warm mothers mature more rapidly in their social behavior than do those of cold mothers. (S191)

### Socialization, Effectiveness of
The mother's warmth is not correlated with resistance to temptation in boys, but it is negatively correlated with such resistance in girls. (G120)

### Superego Formation
If a child has a warm, intimate, and continuous relationship with his mother (or with a permanent mother surrogate), the emotions of anxiety and guilt will develop in a moderate and organized way. (B270)

Guilt responses in children are positively related to the mother's warmth. (G120)

The more warm and loving the mother, the stronger the conscience produced in the child. (K103)

Warmth of the mother increases the rapidity of conscience development (U.S.). (S191)

### Surrogate Mother
The presence of kin in the family who can aid the mother in child care and who are not disruptive allows the mother to display greater warmth to her children than if she is their sole custodian. (M216)

### Toilet Training
The more severe the mother in toilet training, the lower the warmth felt for her child (U.S.). (S191)

Severe toilet training increases the amount of upset in children whose mothers are relatively cold and undemonstrative. (S191)

## MOTHER-DAUGHTER RELATIONS
### X Affinal Relations
The greater the emphasis on the tie between the mother and daughter, the more likely there is to be tension between the husband and his mother-in-law. (P062)

### Class
The urban lower class is more likely than other segments of the population to stress the kinship tie between mother and daughter. (P062)

### Descent (Bilateral)
The mother-daughter relation tends to be especially close in bilateral descent systems. (P062)

### Identification of Mother with Daughter
Mothers who have a high degree of identification with their daughters tended themselves to have a better relationship with their own mothers. (H218)

### Mental Illness (Schizophrenia)
A significantly greater number of schizophrenic daughters than normal ones believed that their mothers were trying to dominate them during their childhoods. (H186)

A significantly greater number of schizophrenic daughters than normal ones believed their mothers attempted to deify themselves during the daughters' childhoods. (H186)

A significantly greater number of schizophrenic daughters than normal ones believed their mothers strove for martyrdom during the daughters' childhoods. (H186)

## MOTHER-DAUGHTER RELATIONS (AFFECTION)
### X Behavior Problems (Running Away)
Among girls, deprivation of maternal love is associated with running away from home. (R102)

### Identification with Mother
Daughters are more likely to identify strongly with their mothers if they perceive them as nurturant, affectional, rewarding, and warm. (M206)

## MOTHER-DAUGHTER RELATIONS (AGGRESSION)    X Scholastic Achievement
As measured by the PARI, mothers of daughters who are poor academically are less tolerant of aggressive behavior in their daughters than are mothers of daughters who do well academically. (S230)

## MOTHER-DAUGHTER RELATIONS (AUTHORITY)
### X Father-Daughter Relations (Authority)
When one parent is highly authoritative toward the daughter, the other parent is not. (B260)

## MOTHER-DAUGHTER RELATIONS (COMMUNICATION)
### X Identification of Mother with Daughter
A high degree of identification of the mother with the daughter is directly correlated with ease on the part of the daughter of communicating emotions, fantasies, and dreams. (H218)

A high degree of identification of the mother with the daughter is directly correlated with an ease on the part of the daughter of communicating anger toward her mother. (H218)

## MOTHER-DAUGHTER RELATIONS (CONFLICT)
### X Father-Daughter Relations (Conflict)
At puberty mother-daughter conflicts are more likely than father-daughter conflicts in the family. (L148)

From the ages of 11 to 17, the amount of conflict or disharmony between the mother and the daughter is almost exactly complementary to that between father and daughter (i.e., an increase in one will be accompanied by a decrease in the other). (L148)

## MOTHER-DAUGHTER RELATIONS (CONTROL)
### X Identification
High maternal identification in daughters is associated with perception of the mother as high in control. (H196)

### Identification with Mother
Perception of the mother as high in control and low in nurturance is associated with high maternal identification in daughters. (H196)

## MOTHER-DAUGHTER RELATIONS (DISCIPLINE)
### X Personality of Child (Responsibility)
There is a positive association between responsibility of the daughter and the son (based on teachers' ratings of dependability in fulfilling obligations) and discipline and authority from the mother. (B250)

## MOTHER-DAUGHTER RELATIONS (DOMINANCE)    X Scholastic Achievement
Mothers of daughters who are poor academic achievers are more likely to be dominant (as measured by the PARI) than are mothers of academic achievers. (S230)

## MOTHER-DAUGHTER RELATIONS (HOSTILITY)
### X Scholastic Achievement
Mothers of daughters who are poor academically are more fearful of their own hostility (as measured by the PARI) than are mothers of daughters who do well academically. (S230)

## MOTHER-DAUGHTER RELATIONS (INTERACTION)
### X Father-Daughter Relations (Interaction)
At puberty there is more interaction, both harmonious and disharmonious, between mothers and daughters than between fathers and daughters. (L148)

## MOTHER-DAUGHTER RELATIONS (INTEREST/CONTROL)
### X Employment of Mother
Daughters of mothers who are employed are no more likely to feel that their mothers have less control over or interest in them than do daughters of mothers who are not employed. (Y047)

## MOTHER-DAUGHTER RELATIONS (INTIMACY)
### X Mental Illness (Schizophrenia)
Mental illness tends to be directly correlated with an unusually high degree of intimacy between mother and daughter. (L118)

## MOTHER-DAUGHTER RELATIONS (MATERNAL ROLE)    X Behavior Problems (Running Away)
Subtle pressure by the mother on the daughter to take over the maternal role is associated with the daughter's running away from home. (R102)

## MOTHER-DAUGHTER RELATIONS (POWER)
### X Sex-Role Identification of Daughter
Daughters who are high in sex-role identification are more likely to perceive their mothers as being powerful than are daughters who are low in sex-role identification. (M206)

## MOTHER-DAUGHTER RELATIONS (PUNISHMENT)
### X    Sex-Role Identification of Daughter
There is no difference between daughters who are high and those who are low in sex-role identification regarding their perception of their mothers as punitive and threatening. (M206)

## MOTHER-DAUGHTER RELATIONS (REJECTION)
### X    Incest (Father-Daughter)
Girls who have had sexual relations with their fathers tend to view their mothers as cruel, unjust, and depriving. (K119)

### Mother-Child Relations
A woman's rejection of her own mother may inhibit her maternal feelings relative to her own children. (T085)

## MOTHER-DAUGHTER RELATIONS (RESPECT)
### X    Scholastic Achievement
Mothers of daughters who are poor academic achievers are more likely to need the respect of their daughters (as measured by the PARI) than are mothers of daughters who do well academically. (S230)

## MOTHER-DAUGHTER RELATIONS (RESTRICTIVENESS)
### X    Identification with Mother
Girls who perceived their mothers as overcircumscribing their freedom are less likely to identify with their mothers than are those who did not so perceive their mothers. (A060)

## MOTHER-INFANT SLEEPING ARRANGEMENTS
### X    Polygyny
Polygyny is the variable most strongly associated with exclusive mother-infant sleeping arrangements. (W127)

## MOTHER LOSS
### X    Mental Illness (Schizophrenia)
Schizophrenic men do not differ significantly from men without schizophrenia on the variable, mean age at mother loss. (H176)

## MOTHER-SON RELATIONS    X    Affinal Relations
The more a mother-in-law is like a man's loved mother or unlike a disliked mother, the closer are relations between husband and mother-in-law likely to be. (K161)

### Descent (Matrilineal)
Where the mother-son tie is given prominence, the kinship structure tends to be patrilineal, patrilocal, and, generally, patriarchal. (H172)

### Homosexuality
Male homosexuals are more likely than heterosexual males to have suitor-like relationships with their mothers (i.e., bringing them gifts, taking them out as one would a girl friend). (W140)

### Mate Selection
Where his relationship with his mother as a child was not satisfying, the man may seek a girl with characteristics quite different from his mother, but establish with her the kind of relationship which he desired as a child. (B033)

### Political Structure
If the mother-son tie is of great importance, multiple national states are found. (H172)

### Religion
Catholic males report closer similarity to their mothers and approve more conforming, nurturant, and acquiescent behavior than do Jewish males (Leary's Interpersonal Check List). (H180)

### Religion (Role of Deities)
If the mother-son tie is emphasized, the religious system has many gods, basically more feminine than masculine. (H172)

### Religion (Supernatural Reliance)
Reliance on the supernatural is found where the mother-son relationship tends to have primary importance over other relationships. (H172)

### Sex Attitudes of Son
The separation of tenderness and sexuality in men is a result of the projection of the image of the loved and honored mother of the Oedipal phase, on the one hand, and, on the other, the image of the mother of the pre-Oedipal phase (with the hostility that a boy may have felt) onto the sexual partner. (G145)

### Sex Taboo (Postpartum)
A strong incestuous bond between mother and son is more likely to be established in societies with a prolonged postpartum sex taboo. (W127)

## MOTHER-SON RELATIONS (ACCEPTANCE)
### X    Dependency
There is a positive relationship between maternal acceptance during ages 2–7 and dependency upon the mother during the son's adolescent years. (K115)

## MOTHER-SON RELATIONS (ACHIEVEMENT)
### X    Alcoholism of Son
Alcoholism is correlated with a compulsive concern with ambition for the son on the part of the mother. (C122)

## MOTHER-SON RELATIONS (AFFECTION)
### X    Achievement
Among mothers with strong achievement needs, the greater the son's achievement, the greater the affectional warmth displayed by the mother. (B275)

### Aggression
There is no relationship between aggression in the boy and the amount of affection shown him by his mother. (B243)

Aggressive boys (perhaps due to dependency anxiety) are more likely than normals to avoid demonstrations of affection by the mother by the time they are adolescents. (B243)

### Behavior Problems
Adolescent boys showing behavior problems are more likely than normal boys to perceive their mothers to be more permissive and loving than their fathers. (V038)

### Child-Rearing Practices (Rewards)
Mothers who provide material rewards for their sons are more likely to show warmth for them. (B243)

### Conformity
There is a positive relationship between maternal affection during the son's early years (2–7) and his conformity to parental demands during adolescence. (K115)

### Dependency
Maternal affection during the son's early years (2–7) is positively associated with his dependency upon the mother during the adolescent years. (K115)

### Employment of Mother
Working mothers in lower-class families do not differ from nonworking mothers in the affection given their sons. (M211)

### Father-Son Relations (Affection)
The strength of the transferred attachment to the father is in direct proportion to the strength of the earlier attachment to the mother. (D076)

### Identification with Father
If the mother remains the focus of affection and reward-giving, father-son identification will be seriously retarded. (P064)

### Mental Illness
Mothers of prepsychotics tend to have actively affectionate relationships with their sons. (M164)

## MOTHER-SON RELATIONS (CLOSENESS)
### X Dependency
The greater boys' attachment to "mother figures," the higher their (reputed) dependence. (C098)

### Initiation Rites
There is a strong correlation between tribal initiations and cultures having strong mother-son ties (i.e., long nursing, common sleeping). (D057)

## MOTHER-SON RELATIONS (CONTROL)
### X Identification with Cross-Sex Parent
The more the mother is perceived as controlling, the greater the son's maternal identification. (H196)

### Identification with Mother
There is no relationship between the son's perception of the degree of control his mother exerts on his freedom and the strength of his identification with her. (A060)

### Mental Illness
Mothers of prepsychotic sons tend to overcontrol their children more than other mothers do. (M164)

## MOTHER-SON RELATIONS (EVALUATION)
### X Employment of Mother
There is no relationship in low-class families between the employment of the mother and the evaluation by her son of the mother-son relationship. (M211)

## MOTHER-SON RELATIONS (HOSTILITY)
### X Alcoholism
Alcoholism tends to be correlated with a pattern of masked hostility on the part of the mother. (C122)

### Child-Rearing Practices (Punishment)
Mothers of aggressive boys who had frequently spanked their sons tended to be hostile toward their sons. (B213)

### Incest (Father-Son)
When father-son incest occurs, it is usually looked upon with a dim view on the part of the mother and sometimes with an attitude of hostility. (Z008)

## MOTHER-SON RELATIONS (IDEALIZATION)
### X Homosexuality
Homosexuality is more common among boys who overidealize their mothers.

## MOTHER-SON RELATIONS (INDULGENCE)
### X Achievement Motivation
Indulgent and ever-forgiving mothers are not associated with high achievement motivation. (G156)

## MOTHER-SON RELATIONS (NEGLECT)
### X Juvenile Delinquency
The more neglecting is the behavior of the mother toward the son, the more likely it is that the child will exhibit more severe delinquent behavior. (M194)

## MOTHER-SON RELATIONS (NURTURANCE/CONTROL)
### X Identification with Mother
Perception of the mother as both high in control and nurturance is associated with high maternal identification in sons. (H196)

## MOTHER-SON RELATIONS (POSSESSIVENESS)
### X Class
The higher the family's socioeconomic class, the less likely it is that the mother will be overly possessive. (F119)

### Education of Mother
If the mother of a schizophrenic son has been educated beyond grammar school, she is likely to feel less possessive toward her son than if she is less well educated. (F099)

The more educated the mother of a schizophrenic boy, the less likely it is that she will be overly possessive. (F119)

### Homosexuality
The more possessive the mother, the more likely is homosexuality in the son. (R104)

### Mental Illness
Mothers of schizophrenic sons are not more possessive of them than are the mothers of sons having other nonorganic mental disorders. (F099)

## MOTHER-SON RELATIONS (PROTECTIVENESS)
### X Employment of Mother
Among stable homes (no conflict, criminality, or social deviance), nonworking mothers are more likely to be protective of their sons than are working mothers. (M211)

## MOTHER-SON RELATIONS (REJECTION)
### X Achievement Motivation
Mothers of boys with high achievement motivation tend to be more rejecting than do mothers of boys with low achievement motivation. (R098)

### Criminality
There is a correlation between maternal rejection and criminality in the son, particularly when the father is absent. (M195)

### Husband-Wife Relations (Warmth)
Aggressive boys whose mothers lack warmth for their husbands are more likely to feel rejected by their mothers than are those whose mothers more positive attitudes toward their husbands. (B243)

### Sex-Role Identification
The stronger the masculine identification of the boy, the more likely it is that he will have experienced less maternal rejection, more maternal nurturance, and less punishment for dependency. (M183)

## MOTHER-SON RELATIONS (REWARDS)
### X   Husband-Wife Relations (Warmth)
Mothers who praised their sons tended to display a high degree of warmth for their husbands. (B213)

## MOTHER-SON RELATIONS (RIDICULE)
### X   Child-Rearing Practices (Punishment)
Mothers of aggressive boys who had frequently spanked their sons tended to ridicule them. (B213)

## MOTHER-SON RELATIONS (SELF-IDEAL)
### X   Anxiety of Son
There is a correlation between the degree of discrepancy between the boy's self-perception and his mother's ideal for him and the degree of his manifest anxiety. (S225)

## MOTHER-SON RELATIONS (SEX)
### X   Castration Anxiety
The intensity and frequency of castration anxiety is associated with an intense sexual tie of the boy with the mother. (S079)

### Homosexuality
Concern with homosexuality may be a defense against strong erotic attachment to the mother. (N050)

### Sex Anxiety
The greater the intensity of the sexual tie between son and mother, the higher the level of anxiety about sex in the adult male. (S079)

### Sex Taboo (Postpartum)
In societies with a long duration of the postpartum sex taboo, the intensity of sex attraction between the son and the mother is higher. (S079)

## MOTHER-SON RELATIONS (WARMTH)
### X   Achievement Motivation
Warm mother-son relations are not associated with high achievement motivation. (G156)

The relationship between mothers and sons with high achievement motivation tends to be warmer than is the relationship between mothers and sons with low achievement motivation. (R098)

### Criminality
Criminal rates tend to be higher among boys whose mothers do not display maternal warmth. (M199)

## MOTOR ADJUSTMENT
### X   Child-Rearing Practices (Maturity Demands)
There is a negative relationship between the father's expecting overly mature behavior on the part of the child and the child's motor development. (R100)

## MOTOR DEVELOPMENT          X   Breast Feeding
Given the same environment, breast-fed infants are slightly less advanced in body development than are bottle-fed infants.

### Child Rearing (Collective)
There is no relationship between the development of motor processes and communal rearing of children. (S214)

### Child-Rearing Practices
Among Negroes, the less the parents push the child to develop motor functions (sitting, creeping, standing, walking), the more quickly will the child develop them. (W133)

### Child-Rearing Practices (Exploration)
Among Negroes, children who are discouraged from reaching out toward objects and other persons have a lower rate of motor development (sitting, creeping, standing, walking) rate than do children who are encouraged to do so. (W133)

### Child-Rearing Practices (Permissiveness)
Among Negroes, children from homes that are more permissive, rather than punishing, about nonapproved habits (thumb-sucking, hair-pulling, etc.) show more advanced motor development (sitting, creeping, standing, walking). (W133)

### Child-Rearing Practices (Restrictiveness)
Among Negroes, children who are not restricted to a specific area, but are allowed to move freely around the home, are more advanced in motor development (creeping, sitting, standing, walking) than are children who are restricted to a particular area. (W133)

### Institutional Care
There is a correlation between institutionalization and retardation and disturbance in the motor functions of the child. (Y045)

There is a correlation between institutionalization and a lowered activity level in the child. (Y045)

Institutionalization of the child results in initial hyperactivity, followed by a depression in the level of activity. (Y045)

### Mother Absence
The process of learning to walk is stimulated by the security offered by the mother as well as by the incentive to reach her as she calls. (S277)

Deprivation of perceptual phenomena and small radius of possible movement can be compensated for by the presence of adequate mother-child relations. (S277)

### Mother-Child Relations
A strong mother-child relationship established through a certain rhythm of stimulation, gratification, and deprivation facilitates the relative desensualization of the body and the use of the body as a tool. (P083)

### Mother-Child Relations (Affection)
Babies who lack adequate affective mothering are more likely to have poorer muscular development than are those who do not.

Bodily tonus is less developed among infants who have had inadequate affective mothering than among those who have not.

### Mother-Child Relations (Indulgence)
Children who were overindulged by their parents are more likely to lack skill in muscular endeavors than are children who were not overprotected. (L146)

### Pregnancy Anxiety
Infants of mothers who were highly anxious during pregnancy have lower scores on the motor aspects of the Bayley Mental Scale than do infants of mothers who were not as anxious during pregnancy. (D067)

### Surrogate Mother
At one year of age, infants reared in families where the mothering is provided by one person are more active

than infants reared in families where the mothering is provided by more than one person (i.e., a nurse, grandparent, mother's friend, or older sister of child). (C124)

## MOTOR DEVELOPMENT OF CHILD    X    Feeding
The more satisfactory the feeding experience for the infant, the greater his confidence in bodily movement is likely to be. (B272)

## MUSICAL STYLE                    X    Rank of Women
When women are secluded, owned, and exploited, the musical style will be characterized by high-pitched strident singing. (L025)

The bass song style is linked with equality of status for women. (L025)

Where women are made into chattels, the musical style tends to have a high degree of emotional content. (L025)

**Sexual Permissiveness**
The bass song style is associated with a permissive attitude toward sex. (L025)

## MYTHS        X    Child-Rearing Practices (Trauma)
There is a correlation between those aspects of child rearing which are typically traumatic for the infant in a given society and the sorts of problem situations which recur in the myths of that people. (K111)

# N

## NAME CHANGING         X   Ethnicity
A greater proportion of Jewish females than of non-Jewish females may retain their husband's name after divorce (U.S.). (B010)

### Marital Status (Male)
Compared to the total Los Angeles population, single males constituted a significantly higher proportion of petitioners for name changes among the non-Jewish and married males constituted a significantly higher proportion of petitioners for name changes among the Jewish. (B010)

Married men constituted a significantly higher proportion of the Jewish male petitioners than of the non-Jewish petitioners. (B010)

## NAMING OF CHILD       X   Role Definition
The choice of name for a child will reflect the parents' expectations regarding the role the child is to play. (W124)

## NATIONALISM     X   Isolation of Nuclear Family
There is a correlation between the rise of nationalism and the isolation of the nuclear family. (P083)

## NATIONALITY
### X   Child-Rearing Practices (Punishment)
American mothers tend to be more permissive and less punitive than do English mothers. (L169)

### Mate Selection
There is a high correlation between mate selection and similarity of nationality. (C103)

## NATIVITY           X   Mate Selection
Individuals tend to marry persons of like nativity. (S015)

## NEIGHBORHOOD RELATIONS
### X   Extended Family Ties
Extensive family connections are relatively incompatible with integration of the nuclear family into the neighborhood. (P083)

## NEUROSIS                  X   Age
Older unmarried mothers are generally more neurotic than are young unmarried mothers. (Y048)

### Broken Home
Divorce, separation, and desertion as causes of deprivation occur more frequently in the parents of psychopathic personalities and psychoneurotics than among parents of psychotics or of "normals." (O034)

### Child-Rearing (Collective)
Among collectively reared (on kibbutzim) children, neurosis is a result of specific parent-child interaction rather than of the conditions of collective education. (G124)

### Child-Rearing Practices
Children whose parents are indulgent, repressive, or inconsistent toward them are more likely to develop emotional disturbances.

There is no statistical support for the hypothesis that mothers of neurotic children are more restrictive than mothers of normal children.

### Child-Rearing Practices (Authority)
Arbitrary imposition of authority within the family of orientation correlates with neurosis in the child. (G020)

### Child-Rearing Practices (Finger-Sucking)
Harsh preventative measures for finger-sucking are correlated with neurosis in children (France). (F097)

### Child-Rearing Practices (Sex)
There is a positive relationship between the severity and punitiveness of her family and group's attitudes toward sex and the degree to which the unwed mother reacts neurotically to herself and her baby. (Y048)

### Class
The higher the unmarried mother's socioeconomic status, the more disturbed she is. (Y048)

### Death of Father
There is no difference between male psychoneurotics and normals or between women psychoneurotics and normals and the ages at which they have experienced the deaths of their fathers. (H226)

### Death of Mother
Psychoneurotics are more likely than are normal children to have experienced the deaths of their mothers while they were between the ages of one and five. (H226)

### Duration of Marriage
There is no association between duration of marriage and degree of complementarity of neurosis among married couples. (P086)

### Emotional Adjustment of Parents
The greater the emotional maladjustment of the individual parent, the more likely it is that the child will be neurotic. (F110)

### Employment of Mother
Mothers who are employed are more likely to be neurotic than are mothers who are not employed. (S275)

### Identification
Where children do not identify with parents as a result of cultural and class differences between them, they do not feel guilt or hostility at their negative feelings toward the parents and thus do not develop neuroses as a result. (G020)

### Identification with Cross-Sex Parent
Persons with neuroses tend to identify themselves with the parent of the opposite sex. (L145)

### Marital Adjustment
Neuroticism is correlated with poor marital adjustment among women, but not among men (Cornell Medical Index of Neurosis). (P086)

### Marital Adjustment of Husband
Happily married husbands are less neurotic than unhappily married husbands. (T074)

### Marital Adjustment of Wife
Responses commonly regarded as indicative of neurotic tendency are much more frequently given by unhappy wives than by happy wives. (T074)

### Marital Status
In New York state, divorced and separated persons have a higher hospital admission rate for psychoneuroses than do widowed persons. (M189)

In New York state, unmarried persons have a higher hospital admission rate for psychoneuroses than do married persons. (M189)

### Mate Selection
Neurotics are more likely to marry neurotics than they are to marry "normal" people. (T092)

### Mate Selection (Complementarity)
Marriages of persons with neurotic tendencies are more likely than marriages of normals to involve complementary needs. (B293)

### Maternal Overprotectiveness
Overprotective and infantilizing behavior on the part of the mother tends to foster such neurotic anxiety symptoms as delusions, obsessions, phobias, etc., in the child. (R113)

### Mother-Child Relations
There is no relationship between a particular kind of maternal attitude and a specific emotional disorder in the child.

### Parent-Child Relations (Authority)
The child's defeat in his fight against parental authority for freedom, spontaneity, and self-image development is the core of neurosis. (G020)

If parental authority is arbitrary, but is not an attack on the child's personality (less concerned with motivation than with behavioral conformity), neurosis is less likely. (G020)

### Parent-Child Relations (Hostility)
Parents of normals are more likely to report hostility toward their sons and toward their own parents than are the parents of neurotics. (F110)

### Parent Loss
The incidence of parental deprivation is higher among psychoneurotic and psychopathic personalities than among psychotics and "normals." (O034)

### Personality of Mother
Mothers of neurotics tend to be highly tentative persons, pervaded by guilt and worry, and in constant need of reassurance. (B219)

### Personality of Parents
Compared to mothers of younger maladjusted children, mothers of maladjusted adolescents are more likely to have the characteristics of authoritarianism, strictness, approval of activity, inconsiderateness of husband, ascendance; fathers are likely to have the characteristics of marital conflict, seclusiveness, inconsiderateness of wife (PARI). (Z011)

### Power Structure of Family
In male-dominated marriages the neurosis rate is high in both partners, but the neurosis rate is low among husbands in female-dominated marriages (Cornell Medical Index of Neurosis). (P086)

### Pregnancy
Neuroticism and autonomic overactivity often occur in infants whose mothers underwent severe emotional stress during pregnancy. (T088)

### Pregnancy, Attitude Toward
Women who are neurotic are more likely to be affected adversely by their pregnancies. (L135)

### Sex Status
There is a higher rate of "minimal neurosis" among women than among men. (P086)

## NEUROSIS (ACTING-OUT)
### X    Parent-Child Relations
Children who come from homes in which the mother is permissive and the father is aloof and/or hostile are more likely than others to become acting-out neurotics. (W143)

## NEUROSIS (ANOREXIA)
### X    Mother-Child Relations
The mother who identifies her child with a dead sibling or a parent toward whom she has entertained death wishes is more likely to produce anorectic children (extreme loss of weight, lack of appetite, low respiration) than is the mother who does not so identify her child. (F102)

## NEUROSIS/BEHAVIOR PROBLEMS OF CHILD
### X    Occupation of Father
There is no significant correlation between the father's occupation or family income and the diagnosis of the child as neurotic or acting-out. (A069)

## NEUROSIS (GASTRIC)    X    Age Difference
Gastric neurosis in married men is directly correlated with a higher-than-average proportion of marriages to older women. (F113)

### Child-Rearing Practices (Dependency)
Gastric neurosis is directly correlated with a premature emphasis by the parents on independence. (F113)

### Ordinal Position
Gastric neurosis is more likely to occur among oldest or only children. (F113)

## NEUROSIS (HYSTERIA)
### X    Parent-Child Relations (Affection)
Despite the nature of an individual's inherited tendencies, he will not develop hysteria unless he is subjected to situations during childhood causing him to crave affection. (B270)

### Rank of Women
In societies in which the female suffers many disadvantages and lower self-esteem, hysteria will be more common among females. (P058)

## NEUROSIS IN FAMILY    X    Anxiety
Within neurotic families, members tend to exhibit similar kinds of anxieties. (F077)

## NEUROSIS OF CHILD    X    Alcoholism of Parent
Children of alcoholics are more likely to be neurotic and alcoholic themselves.

## NEUROSIS OF MOTHER    X    Alcoholism
The mother of the alcoholic is likely to be neurotic—the unsatisfied, masochistic woman escaping the feminine role and exhibiting martyred or shrewish attitudes. (C122)

#### Mother-Child Relations (Rejection)
Neurotic disturbance in the mother seems to be unrelated to the severity of her counterrejection of her disturbed child. (S188)

#### Sex Attitudes of Mother
Mothers of neurotics are more likely than mothers of normals to devalue the importance of the sexual aspect of their marriages. (M218)

## NEUROSIS OF PARENTS
X    Juvenile Delinquency/Neurosis
Parents of neurotic children show neurotic tendencies more frequently than do parents of delinquents. (B214)

## NEUROSIS OF SPOUSE    X    Childhood
There is an association between the childhood emotional experience of one spouse and the C.M.I. (Cornell Medical Index of Neurosis) score of the other. (P086)

## NEUROSIS OF WIFE (INVALIDISM)
X    Dependency of Husband
When the dependency of the husband is expressed in a pattern of sadistic domination, the wife will frequently adopt symptoms of neurotic invalidism as an escape. (R115)

## NEUROSIS/PSYCHOPATHY
X    Alcoholism of Parent
Children from families with an alcoholic parent are more likely to be neurotic than psychotic. (B285)

## NONKIN ACTIVITIES    X    Cohesion of Family
The higher the degree of family cohesion, the greater the participation in organized activity outside the family. The reverse is also asserted. (S217)

## NONKIN RELATIONS    X    Acculturation
When there is a differential participation of the members of a family in the dominant institutions, members will vary greatly from one another in their degree of acculturation. (B042)

#### Cohesion of Family
As marriage becomes a more effective source of solidarity and tension reduction, there is less demand for such experiences in extrafamilial-role participations; hence, the primary character of kin networks and of other peer groups declines and they become relations of entertainment, rather than of mutual support, and can be left or entered more easily. (P083)

#### Descent (Unilineal)
A weak form of unilineal system and economic, political, and religious institutions not based on kinship are correlated. (B301)

#### Marital Adjustment
There is a direct relation between friendships outside the family and memberships in organizations and marital adjustment. (K161)

#### Mental Illness (Manic-Depressive)
Manic-depressives are more likely to come from families in which there is considerable anxiety expressed about family relations with nonfamily members. (S181)

#### Size of Family
Individuals are more likely to seek contacts outside the family if the family unit is small in size. (I007)

#### Stability of Kin-Group
Since the groups based on kinship are "small and unstable," the need for extrakinship alliances is understandable. (C094)

## NONKIN RELATIONS (CONFLICT)
X    Cohesion of Family
The solidarity of the family will be reinforced by conflict in extrafamilial relations. (S064)

## NONKIN RELATIONS (HOSTILITY)
X    Scapegoating
Where the family is unable to manifest hostilities it feels toward the outside, it tends to direct these hostilities against a family-member scapegoat. (B204)

## NONKIN-ROLE BEHAVIOR (SECRECY ABOUT)
X    Mental Illness (Schizophrenia)
In schizophrenic-family social organization there tends to be secrecy about roles which move in extrafamilial directions. (W021)

## NONKIN/SPOUSE    X    Political Attitudes
Young voters are more likely to agree with their spouses than with friends on the choice of political party and still more than with fellow workers. (M056)

## NONKIN TIES    X    Marital Adjustment
The less happily married a woman is, the more likely she is to have confidants outside the family. (K089)

#### Size of Kin-Group
As the size of the kin-group decreases, neighborhood bonds increase in importance. (H164)

## NUCLEAR/EXTENDED FAMILY    X    Death Rate
Nuclear families are more common in societies with low mortality; joint households, in societies with high mortality. (C090)

## NUCLEAR FAMILY    X    Cohesion of Community
The formation of families of procreation is likely to weaken the primary group characteristics of the "bund" type of collective and disrupt its unity (Israel). (T013)

#### Economic Pattern (Wage Labor)
The system of wage labor and the existence of a small nuclear family are associated. (G112)

#### Economic Rank
The nuclear family pattern tends to be associated with a lower socioeconomic status. (L066)

#### Geographic Mobility
The nuclear family is common where geographical mobility and individual independence are found. (C090)

#### Industrialization
The restriction of kinship obligations to the nuclear family tends to accompany industrialization. (F055)

There is no relationship between industrialization and percentage of nuclear families. (G113)

With the rise of industrialization, the nuclear family is displacing the extended family and has come to be the dominant form in urban areas. (N012)

#### Kin Terminology
Revisions of kinship terminology tend to be resisted within the nuclear family. (F046)

### Revolution

The nuclear family is more likely to be distended under conditions of revolutionary fervor and of charismatic group formation.

### Social Welfare

A predominance of small family units in a society is associated with a greater abundance of social agencies to take care of the disabled, ill, and aged. (G156)

### Subsistence Pattern (Agriculture)

In simple agricultural economies, the minimal economic group is generally the biological family. (F049)

### Urbanization

There is no relationship between urbanization and the percentage of nuclear families. (G113)

### Witchcraft

Witchcraft beliefs are incompatible with the emergence of the family of parents and children as the important group at the expense of extended kindship groupings. (G116)

## NUCLEAR FAMILY, IMPORTANCE OF
### X  Divorce

High divorce rates are more likely in social systems in which the strains attributable to the relative importance of the nuclear family and the marital relationship are great. (P062)

### Divorce Adjustment

Divorce tends to be more disruptive with an increase in the structural importance of the nuclear family. (G015)

### Economic Pattern (Money)

With the adoption of a money economy, the conjugal relationship in matrilineal tribes has been strengthened and the conjugal or parental family has emerged as the key group. (G056)

### Kin Relations (Interaction)

A widespread set of relationships with relatives seems to involve the splitting of the elementary family. (G116)

### Lineage Ties

The degree to which lineage affiliation is emphasized will be inversely correlated with the degree to which the nuclear family is emphasized. (S060)

### Property Ownership

In matrilineal societies, where women own property, the nuclear family is relatively insignificant. (D057)

### Residence

The nuclear family tends to be of less importance when the residence pattern is that of an extended family unit. (W067)

### Residence (Separate)

The importance of the nuclear family will be emphasized if it is residentially segregated, not a part of a larger kin-group. (S153)

### Size of Community

The nuclear family will tend to have greater importance as a social unit when the community is small in size. (B147)

### Tensions in Family/Personality

As the importance of the nuclear family and the marital relationship increases in a social system, the strains on these institutions and on their members as personalities increase. (P062)

## NUCLEAR/STEM FAMILY
### X  Personality of Mother (Stability)

Residence in a stem family is associated with greater emotional stability of the mother than is residence in a nuclear isolated family. (M216)

# O

**OBESITY**             **X Breast Feeding**
Obesity in the child is correlated with inadequate breast feeding and prolonged bottle feeding. (B272)

**Parent-Child Relations**
Obesity in the child is correlated with the use of the child by the parents as an object whose function it is to fulfill parental needs and to compensate for the parents' failures and frustrations in their own lives. (B218)

**Parent-Child Relations (Overprotectiveness)**
Obesity tends to be correlated with a parental environment of overprotectiveness and oversolicitousness. (F114)

**Parent-Child Relations (Rejection)**
Obesity is correlated with parental dissatisfaction with the sex of the child. (B218)

**Sex-Role Identification**
Obesity tends to be associated with a severe confusion in sexual identification. (B218)

**OCCUPATION**          **X Age at Marriage**
In general, the men in occupations requiring the acquisition of more financial resources or the pursuit of more specialized training tend to delay their first marriage more than men in most other occupations. (G012)

**Authority Structure of Family**
The professional group is more favorable to the notion of equal authority for husband and wife within the family than is any other occupational group. (F009)

**Birth Spacing**
The interval from marriage to the birth of the first child varies directly with position on the occupational scale; laborers and farmers have a shorter interval than do professional groups. (C019)

**Child-Rearing Attitudes (Sex Role)**
Mothers whose husbands have entrepreneurial jobs (as opposed to mothers whose husbands have bureaucratic jobs) more often state that, among adolescents, males should perform activities traditionally associated with their sex (washing the family car) and girls should also perform activities traditionally associated with their sex (making beds). (M062)

**Child-Rearing Practices (Dependency)**
Middle-class mothers whose husbands' occupations are in the entrepreneurial category are more likely to train their children to take a more active and independent approach to the world than are mothers whose husbands' occupations are in the bureaucratic category. (B273)

Homes in which the husband is self-employed are more likely to emphasize the development of independence and mastery in their children than are homes in which the husband is employed in a large organization, particularly within the middle class. (B273)

**Child-Rearing Practices (Permissiveness)**
Mothers whose husbands have bureaucratic jobs are more likely to be permissive in their child-rearing practices than are those whose husbands have entrepreneurial jobs. (J030)

**Child-Rearing Practices (Punishment)**
Middle-class mothers whose husbands have entrepreneurial jobs are significantly more likely than mothers of similar social status whose husbands have bureaucratic jobs to use symbolic rather than direct punishments in disciplining their children. (M062)

Middle-class mothers whose husbands have entrepreneurial jobs are more likely than are middle-class mothers whose husbands have bureaucratic jobs to use harsh means to stop a child from sucking a part of his body. (M062)

**Child-Rearing Practices (Self-Control)**
Middle-class mothers whose husbands' occupations are of an entrepreneurial nature are more likely than are mothers whose husbands' occupations are of a bureaucratic nature to emphasize their children's development of strong self-control. (M062)

**Child-Rearing Practices (Sex)**
Middle-class mothers whose husbands have entrepreneurial jobs are more likely than are mothers of the same class whose husbands have bureaucratic jobs to say that they took measures to stop a child who touched his sex organs. (M062)

**Child-Rearing Values (Adjustment/Independence)**
Mothers whose husbands have bureaucratic jobs are more likely to aim for the adjustment of their children to their social groups, whereas mothers whose husbands have entrepreneurial jobs are more likely to endeavor to foster independence in their children. (J030)

**Child-Rearing Values (Conformity)**
If the father has an entrepreneurial position, the parents try to inculcate self-reliance; if the father's position is bureaucratic, the parents attempt to inculcate accommodative values. (B273)

**Child-Rearing Values (Permissiveness)**
When couples are classed as "bureaucratic" (the breadwinner works in a large bureaucracy) or "entrepreneurial" (the breadwinner has a business of his own), the former are more permissive in their child-rearing values. (A053)

**Conformity**
The more that the individual's occupation puts him in a position of public prominence, the greater is the conformity demanded of him in his family life. (F106)

**Divorce**
There is no relationship between the occupation of the husband and the likelihood of divorce among unhappily married couples.

Unskilled occupational groups have a higher divorce rate than do skilled or professional groups. (C005)

Divorce is more prevalent among unskilled or semi-skilled occupational groups than among professional, proprietary, clerical, and sales occupational groups. (G002)

Within any given class position, specific occupations may have high or low divorce rates. (G134)

Actors, musicians, commercial travelers, and doctors have the greatest overrepresentation in divorce, although no discernible socioeconomic pattern emerges when the divorce ratios are arranged by major occupational categories. (K010)

### Divorce, Attitude Toward
The professional group is more liberal than any other occupational strata in its attitudes toward divorce laws. (F009)

### Homogamy
Homogamous marriages are less prevalent in professional strata than in any other strata. (F009)

### Illegitimacy
Illegitimate children are less likely to obtain satisfactory jobs. (G156)

Girls who are employed in the field of housework are more likely to have illegitimate children than are those in other occupations. (N055)

### Illegitimacy and Premarital Conception
Premarital illegitimacy and conception are more likely to occur among laborers than among other occupational groups. (C129)

### Illegitimacy, Attitude Toward
Pastors and physicians are more likely and social workers and public health nurses are less likely to favor marriage, as opposed to adoption, as a solution to premarital pregnancy. (S224)

### Independence of Nuclear Family
The independence of the nuclear family is directly correlated with the independence of occupation from the kin roles. (G112)

### Kin Relations (Interaction)
Loosely knit family friendship networks (i.e., a low frequency of interaction among family units) are more often found among professional families. (G156)

### Marital Adjustment
There is no relationship between the occupation of the husband at the time of marriage and marital adjustment. (G157)

Professional and semiprofessional persons are more likely to have higher marital-adjustment scores. (G157)

Men's greater disenchantment during the early years of marriage is partly a function of the reality of the occupational commitment. (P071)

There is a greater degree of marital adjustment among couples where the husbands are in white collar, professional, or executive occupations than where they are in manual occupations. (W004)

### Mate Selection
Mate selection on the basis of occupation is more likely to be endogamous than exogamous. (C008)

Sons of fathers in any given occupational strata are more likely to be married to daughters of fathers in the same strata than to those in any other single stratum. (C008)

Men and women marry people who are in the same or allied occupations more often than can be explained by chance alone. (S012)

### Mate Selection (Residence)
Men in the professional and managerial categories are less affected by residential propinquity in selecting a spouse than are those in unskilled jobs. (C002)

Males in skilled occupations select spouses closer to their homes than do men in the clerical and sales group. (C002)

### Parent-Child Relations (Affection)
Children whose fathers work in an academic capacity may be less inclined to view parental behavior as a threat to withdraw affection than are children of fathers in a nonacademic capacity. (G117)

### Parent-Child Relations (Authoritarian/Democratic)
Families where the father is connected with the academic world have more democratic parent-child relations; families with fathers whose occupations are outside of the academic world have more authoritarian parent-child relations. (G117)

### Personality of Mother (Anomie)
There is no significant correlation between the father's occupation or family income and the mother's classification according to the Srole Anomie Scale. (A069)

### Premarital Pregnancy
Premarital pregnancy rates will be higher among laboring groups than among farmers and among farmers than among professional people. (C004)

### Sex Behavior of Child
Middle-class mothers whose husbands have entrepreneurial jobs are more likely than are mothers of the same social class whose husbands have bureaucratic jobs to declare that their children did not touch their sex organs. (M062)

### Sex-Role Definition of Child
Children of fathers who have entrepreneurial jobs are more likely than are children of fathers who have bureaucratic jobs to have a clearly differentiated conception of sex roles. (J030)

### Sexual Disability of Husband (Divorce)
Among men who have been physically disabled, those who have remained married are more likely to be in managerial-professional occupations than are those who are divorced or separated. (N060)

### Size of Household
There is no correlation between size of household and occupation. (A001)

The higher the occupational level, the larger the household. (A001)

### Stability of Family
The night shift is probably less favorable to family stability than is the day shift. (P083)

The occupational lives of the waitress, the furniture mover, and the trucker are probably not favorable to family stability. (P083)

### Toilet Training

Middle-class mothers whose husbands have entrepreneurial jobs are significantly more likely than are mothers of similar social status whose husbands have bureaucratic jobs to begin urinary training of their youngsters before they are 11 months old. (M062)

Mothers whose husbands have entrepreneurial jobs are more likely than are mothers whose husbands have bureaucratic jobs to begin bowel training of their youngsters before they are ten months old. (M062)

Parents of clerical groups begin daily bladder training appreciably later than do working-class parents, but not significantly later than do professional groups (U.S.). (M180)

### Urbanization

Urbanization tends to result in a weakening of emphasis upon hereditary specialization within the caste system. (P022)

### Values (Extended/Nuclear Family)

Men who espouse nuclear family norms are more likely to hold white collar jobs; those who espouse extended family norms are more likely to have blue collar jobs. (J025)

## OCCUPATION-EDUCATION OF FATHER
### X  Occupational Aspirations of Son

The son of a lower white collar father (small business, clerical work) who has less than a high-school education is as likely to have occupational aspirations that are lower as those that are higher than his father's occupational status. (E102)

## OCCUPATION, FATHER'S ATTITUDE TOWARD
### X  Occupation of Father, Attitude Toward

Among blue collar families, there is a high correlation between the feelings of the father about his work and the feelings his family has about his work. (D005)

## OCCUPATION (HUSBAND ABSENCE)
### X  Divorce

There is a higher rate of divorce and marital unhappiness in occupations requiring travel away from home. (B033)

## OCCUPATION (NONAGRICULTURAL)
### X  Geographic Mobility

The geographical dispersion of kinsmen tends to be directly correlated with nonagricultural occupations. (T039)

## OCCUPATION OF FATHER
### X  Achievement Motivation

There is no association between the father's occupation and the child's level of achievement motivation. (C101)

### Anxiety

Children whose fathers are of professional status have lower anxiety scores (as measured by the Test Anxiety Scale) than do children whose fathers are nonprofessionals. (A062)

### Child-Rearing Practices

The occupation of the father does not correlate with the mother's child-rearing practices. (S265)

### Child-Rearing Practices (Dependency)

Among blue collar boys, there is a slight positive relationship between the degree of dissatisfaction expressed by the son concerning his father's occupation and paternal independence training. (E102)

Among white collar boys, there is a slight negative relationship between the son's dissatisfaction with his father's occupation and paternal independence training. (E102)

### Conformity

Children whose fathers are in white collar occupations are more likely to be conformists than are children whose fathers are in blue collar occupations. (E102)

### Deviance of Son

The father's occupation (white or blue collar) is not related to whether or not the boy exhibits deviant behavior. (W151)

### Education of Son

Among blue collar boys, there is a strong positive relationship between the degree of dissatisfaction expressed by the son concerning his father's occupation and the adolescent's college aspirations. (E102)

Among white collar sons, there is a slight negative relationship between the son's dissatisfaction with his father's occupation and parental insistence on college. (E102)

### Educational Aspirations

Among blue collar boys, there is a slight positive relationship between the degree of their dissatisfaction about their fathers' occupations, and their parents' insistence on a college education. (E102)

### I.Q.

There is no relationship between mental development of the preschool Negro child and the occupation of the father. (H191)

### Juvenile Delinquency

More delinquents come from families where the father is unskilled or has slight skills than from families where the father is semiskilled or skilled. (S210)

### Mother-Child Relations (Acceptance)

Mothers whose husbands are businessmen or semiprofessionals tend to be more accepting of their children than do mothers whose husbands are in other occupational categories.

### Neurosis/Behavior Problems of Child

There is no significant correlation between the father's occupation or family income and the diagnosis of the child as neurotic or acting out. (A069)

### Occupational Aspirations of Son

Dissatisfaction with the father's job is associated with high occupational aspirations in the son; a higher evaluation of the father's job is associated with sons who desire a similar occupational level. This relationship is stronger among lower-class than among middle-class sons. (E102)

### Occupational Choice

Sons of farmers are more likely to follow the occupation of their fathers than are sons of unskilled industrial workers. (B033)

The more traditional (in the family) is the father's occupation, the closer the correspondence between the son's vocational interests and the father's occupation. (C110)

### Personality Adjustment of Child (Frustration Tolerance)

University children (fathers working in an academic capacity) may develop a higher frustration tolerance than nonuniversity children. (G117)

### Personality Adjustment of Child (Inconsistency)

Children with fathers working in an academic capacity may be more able to accept occasional inconsistencies from their parents than children whose fathers are in an nonacademic capacity. (G117)

### Personality Adjustment of Child (Rebellion)

Children whose fathers work in an academic capacity may feel greater freedom to rebel when they have a definite disposition to do so than children whose fathers are in a nonacademic capacity. (G117)

### Personality of Child (Expressiveness)

Among children whose fathers' occupations are nonacademic, there may be a greater allowance and acceptance of expressions of emotion than among children whose fathers have academic jobs. (G117)

### Scholastic Achievement of Child

College students whose fathers hold professional or managerial positions are less likely to drop out of college than are students whose fathers work in other occupations. (A067)

### Self-Conception of Child

Students whose fathers are in highly authoritarian occupations (armed forces, police, detective, sheriff, bailiff) and whose stock in trade is the use of physical violence for the control of physical violence had unusually low self-esteem. (R129)

### Social Mobility Aspirations of Child

Upwardly mobile aspirations among lower-class youths are accompanied by rejection of the paternal occupational role. (E102)

### Social Mobility Aspirations of Daughter

There is no relationship between the father's occupation and the mobility aspirations of the daughter. (R101)

### Social Mobility Aspirations of Son

Sons of fathers with manual occupations have higher mobility aspirations than do sons of nonmanual fathers. (R101)

## OCCUPATION OF FATHER, ATTITUDE TOWARD
### X Occupation, Father's Attitude Toward

Among blue collar families, there is a high correlation between the feelings of the father about his work and the feelings his family has about his work. (D005)

## OCCUPATION OF HUSBAND
### X Child-Rearing Attitudes (Dependency)

Mothers whose husbands have entrepreneurial jobs are more likely than are mothers whose husbands have bureaucratic jobs to say that children should be put on their own as soon as possible to solve their own problems. (M062)

### Divorce Process

The occupation of the husband is unrelated to the length of time taken between a serious consideration of divorce and the filing of the suit. (G157)

### Feeding (Demand)

Middle-class mothers whose husbands have entrepreneurial jobs are significantly more likely than are mothers of similar social status whose husbands have bureaucratic jobs to feed babies on schedule. (M062)

### Marital Adjustment of Working Mothers

The difference in marital adjustment scores between working and nonworking mothers tends to be smallest among women whose husbands are in professional and managerial occupations. (S257)

### Sex-Role Definition

Husbands who have the most joint role relationships with their wives tend to be professional or semiprofessional (in contrast with husbands in manual occupations). (B209)

### Surrogate Mother, Attitude Toward

Mothers whose husbands have entrepreneurial jobs are more likely than mothers whose husbands have bureaucratic jobs to feel it is desirable, for the mother's sake, that a child frequently be left at home with a competent woman while the mother shops. (M026)

## OCCUPATION OF HUSBAND/WIFE
### X Social Mobility

The more equal the wife's occupation is to that of her husband the smaller part she plays in her husband's occupational mobility.

## OCCUPATION OF MATERNAL GRANDMOTHER
### X Incest (Father-Daughter)

In families where father-daughter incest occurs, the maternal grandmothers are apt to be employed in menial positions (domestics, waitresses). (K091)

## OCCUPATION OF MOTHER
### X Authoritarianism of Mother

If a mother holds an entrepreneurial job, she is more likely to be authoritarian than if she holds a bureaucratic job. (J022)

### Child-Rearing Values (Dependency)

Mothers with a profession tend to stress the importance of self-sufficiency for their children more than do nonprofessional mothers.

### Creativity/I.Q. of Child

The mothers of highly intelligent (Binet) children are more likely to be full-time housewives than are mothers of highly creative (Guilford-Cattell) children. (G132)

### Personality Problems of Child

There is no significant correlation between the mother's occupational activity and the nature of her child's problem. (A069)

### Sex-Role Definition

Mothers in entrepreneurial occupations are more likely than those in bureaucratic jobs to differentiate highly between boys' and girls' sex roles. (J022)

## OCCUPATION OF PARENTS
### X Child-Rearing Practices (Aggression)

There is no difference among occupational classes regarding punishment of children for aggression against parents. (E097)

### Child-Rearing Practices (Punishment)

The relative frequency of physical and psychological punishment is not related to the parent's occupation. (E097)

### Moral Beliefs of Child

Parental occupation correlates most significantly with the child's beliefs concerning moral realism, retribution, and severe punishment. (J021)

## OCCUPATION OF WIFE        X   Marital Stability

Employment of the mother in a secure, bureaucratic context is less likely to lead to marital instability than is her employment in an entrepreneurial and competitive context. (S265)

## OCCUPATIONAL ACHIEVEMENT
### X   Homogamy (Caste)

Women who marry into a lower caste usually marry occupationally successful males (U.S.). (G156)

### Marital Adjustment

There is an inverse relation between the occupational success of women and successful marital adjustment. (K161)

### Marriage Chances

The greater the success of a man in his career, the less likely he is to seek need gratification from marriage. (M232)

## OCCUPATIONAL ACHIEVEMENT OF CHILD
### X   Child-Rearing Practices (Restrictiveness)

Occupational failure is more likely to occur where there has been parental interference with the child's techniques for satisfaction and crippling restraints or disapproval. (H220)

## OCCUPATIONAL ACHIEVEMENT OF FATHER
### X   Mental Illness (Manic-Depressive)

Fathers of manic-depressives are most likely to be defined occupationally as failures. (C092)

## OCCUPATIONAL ASPIRATIONS
### X   Achievement Motivation

Mothers of sons with high achievement motivation have higher occupational aspirations for their sons than do mothers of those low in achievement motivation. (M246)

### Child-Rearing (Collective)

Kibbutz children identify fewer long-range occupational goals than do nonkibbutz children (on Rorschach tests). (R096)

### Cohesion of Family

Students who have high occupational aspirations are less concerned with maintaining family ties via physical closeness (i.e., they are more likely to leave the family for some time, moving around the country to facilitate occupational advancement) than are students who have lower occupational aspirations. (E102)

### Parent-Child Relations (Closeness)

Students who have high occupational aspirations report less attachment to their parents than do students with lower occupational aspirations. (E102)

### Parent-Child Relations (Favoritism)

Students who have high occupational aspirations are more likely to report parental favoritism toward some child in the family than are students with lower occupational aspirations. (E102)

### Reference Group (Family)

Boys whose reference group is the immediate family are more likely to plan to go to college or to obtain permanent, salaried employment than to plan to loaf, to go into farming, to go into the army, or to work part-time. (R111)

## OCCUPATIONAL ASPIRATIONS OF CHILD
### X   Child-Rearing Practices of Father (Punishment)

Students with high occupational aspirations are more fearful of paternal punishment than are students with lower occupational aspirations. (E102)

### Father-Child Relations (Closeness)

Students who have high occupational aspirations confide less in their fathers than do students with lower occupational aspirations. (E102)

## OCCUPATIONAL ASPIRATIONS OF PARENTS
### X   Educational Aspirations

Parents of college-oriented sons are more likely to hold middle-class occupational aspirations for their sons than are parents of noncollege-oriented sons. (E102)

## OCCUPATIONAL ASPIRATIONS OF SON
### X   Child-Rearing Practices of Father (Dependency)

High paternal independence training is associated with high occupational aspirations on the part of the son regardless of the father's occupation. (E102)

### Economic Rank

Economic responsibility forcing the oldest sons of lower-class families into early entrance into the labor market, effectively indoctrinating them into manual-type jobs, is a factor contributing to low occupational aspirations of oldest sons of lower-class families. (E102)

### Education of Father

Boys with fathers who have less than a high-school education are more likely to aspire to occupations that are higher than to occupations that are lower than those of their fathers. (E102)

Occupational aspirations of the son are positively related to the father's educational level, regardless of the father's occupation (unskilled labor to professional-managerial group). (E102)

### Education of Son

Boys who have college-oriented parents are more likely to have high occupational aspirations than are those who do not, regardless of their evaluation of their fathers' occupations. (E102)

### Father-Son Relations (Affection)

Among boys who are independent in decision making, there is no relationship between paternal love and occupational aspirations of the sons. (E102)

Among boys who are reared permissively by their fathers, high paternal love is more likely than low paternal love to be associated with high occupational aspirations in the sons. (E102)

### Father-Son Relations (Affection/Power)

Among boys who are dependent in decision making, high paternal love is associated with high occupational aspirations, more so under the condition of permissive paternal power than of autocratic paternal power. (E102)

### Father-Son Relations (Dependency)

Sons of autocratic fathers are less likely than are those whose fathers allow and encourage independent decision making to have high occupational aspirations. (E102)

### Occupation-Education of Father
The sons of a lower white collar father (small business, clerical work) who has less than a high-school education is as likely to have occupational aspirations that are lower as those that are higher than his father's occupational status. (E102)

### Occupation of Father
Dissatisfaction with the father's job is associated with high occupational aspirations in the son; higher evaluation of the father's job is associated with sons who desire a similar occupational level. This relationship is stronger among lower-class than among middle-class sons. (E102)

### Occupational Rank of Father
The higher the status of the father's occupation (unskilled labor to professional work), the more likely is the son to have managerial or professional aspirations. (E102)

### Ordinal Position
Firstborn middle-class sons are slightly more likely than later-born sons to have high occupational aspirations. The reverse is true for lower-class boys. (E102)

### Parent-Child Relations (Consensus)
Excluding low blue collar workers, at all occupational levels there is a positive relationship between the son's acceptance of the values and advice of his parents and his level of occupational aspiration. (E102)

### Parent-Child Relations (Respect)
Among lower-class sons, there is very little relation between the level of occupational aspirations and the degree of parental respect they receive for their ideas and opinions. (E102)

There is a positive relationship between parental respect for the ideas and opinions of the son and the level of his occupational aspirations. (E102)

### Size of Family
Boys from small families are slightly more likely to have professional-managerial aspirations than are those from large families, regardless of the father's occupational level (professional-managerial to unskilled labor). (E102)

## OCCUPATIONAL ASPIRATIONS OF SON /OCCUPATIONAL RANK OF FATHER
### X   Education of Father
The strength of the positive relationship between the father's educational level and the son's occupational aspirations weakens as the level of the father's occupation decreases (professional-managerial to unskilled labor). (E102)

## OCCUPATIONAL CHOICE
### X   Authority Structure of Family
Secular contact is positively associated with the increase in the son's freedom to choose an occupation. (T001)

### Father-Son Relations (Closeness)
The closer the emotional bond between the father and son, the closer the correspondence between the son's vocational interests and the father's occupations. (C110)

### Housing
When children grow up in crowded living space (family), they are less likely to want to follow the occupations of their fathers. (P061)

### Identification with Parents
The greater the degree of identification with either or both parents, the more likely is the child to develop vocational interests which are appropriately sex-typed (according to popular stereotype), depending on the parent with whom the child identifies. (C110)

The degree of the son's identification with the father significantly corresponds with the similarity of vocational interests of the son and the father's occupation. This relationship holds for mothers and daughters, but not significantly. (C110)

### Inheritance (Primogeniture)
When primogeniture is the established pattern of inheritance, other children will tend to seek nonagricultural occupations. (B082)

### Occupation of Father
Sons of farmers are more likely to follow the occupation of their fathers than are sons of unskilled industrial workers. (B033)

The more traditional (in the family) is the father's occupation, the closer is the correspondence between the son's vocational interests and the father's occupation. (C110)

### Occupational Rank of Father
The higher the status of the father's occupation, the closer the correspondence between the son's vocational interests and the father's occupation. (C110)

### Ordinal Position
In two-sibling families, firstborn girls are more likely to choose teaching as a prospective occupation than are later-born girls. (S221)

In two-sibling families, firstborn males are more likely to select psychology, public administration and accounting as prospective occupations than are later-born males. (S221)

In two-son families, the second-born male is more likely than the first to choose an occupation which involves an "application of physical power to persons, animals, and other living things" (e.g., physician, dentist, farmer, policeman, veterinarian, etc.) than are individuals from families with other two-sibling arrangements. (S221)

In two-girl families, the second-born girl is more likely than the firstborn to choose the occupations of social work, law, and YMCA secretary. (S221)

In two-sibling families, a boy with a younger sister is more likely to choose occupations that are technically creative (e.g., psychology, physics, mathematics, engineering, etc.) than are individuals from other family structures. (S221)

### Parent-Child Relations (Rejection)
There is a correlation between the accepting/rejecting nature of parental attitudes experienced during childhood and the adult choice of a person-oriented/object-oriented occupation. (G135)

There is no correlation between parental attitudes and selection of occupation in adult life. (G135)

### Power Structure of Family
Reaction to the overpowering by the mother and older sister or by the father and older brother leads to the choice of occupations which involve some power or

authority over other persons, animals, or living things by second-born siblings of families with two same-sex children. (S221)

### Sex-Role Identification
For sons, high identification with the father leads to vocational interests which are considered more "masculine." (C110)

For sons, mixed-sex identification leads to vocational interests which combine what are considered "masculine" and "feminine" characteristics. (C110)

For sons, cross-sex identification leads to vocational interests which are considered more "feminine" in nature. (C110)

For sons, low father and/or low mother identification leads to vocational interests which are considered "feminine" in nature. (C110)

### Sibling Structure (Sex)
In two-sibling families, girls with an older brother are more likely to choose economic types of occupations (life insurance, buyer, etc.) than are girls without an older brother. (S221)

In two-sibling families where both are boys, they are more likely to choose conventional economic types of occupations (e.g., sales manager, buyer, production manager, life insurance, etc.) than are children in other types of sibling structures. (S221)

In two-sibling families, the females of two-girl families are more likely to choose conventional feminine occupations (e.g., general office work, stenography, secretary, etc.) than are girls with a brother. (S221)

In two-sibling families where the children are of opposite sex, they are more likely to choose creative occupations (e.g., artist, composer, author, architect, etc.) than are individuals of families with two same-sex siblings. (S221)

## OCCUPATIONAL CHOICE (MIGRANT LABOR)
### X  Conflict in Family
The selection of migrant labor as an occupation is indicative of tensions and conflicts within the family. (F060)

## OCCUPATIONAL DISCRIMINATION
### X  Intermarriage (Racial)
In interracial marriages, the Negro spouse seems to be less subject to economic sanctions in his occupation than is the white spouse. (G001)

## OCCUPATIONAL HETEROGENEITY OF HOUSEHOLDS
### X  Income
The function of occupational heterogeneity of agricultural households in Yugoslavia is to cover the deficit in income of the agricultural holding. (B031)

### Size of Family
As family size increases, in agricultural households, the occupational heterogeneity of its members increases (relationship holds up to ten family members; afterwards there is no relation between increased family size and increased occupational heterogeneity). (B031)

## OCCUPATIONAL INTERESTS
### X  Identification with Mother
The more closely the boy identifies with his mother, the

more mature his vocational interests are likely to be (Strong Vocational Interest Blank). (S254)

The hypothesis that the identification between mother and son the higher the son's scores on the occupational level was not supported by the results (Strong Vocational Interest Blank). (S254)

The more completely the son identifies with his mother, the more likely he is to develop strong primary interest patterns. (S254)

There is apparently no relationship between congruence of the son's interests and his occupational preference and the degree of mother-son identification. (S254)

The more closely the boy identifies with his mother, the more masculine his interests tend to be. (S254)

Boys who rejected interests in masculine areas were likely to accept more fully their mothers' perception of them as their own perception than were boys who rejected interests in feminine areas. (S254)

## OCCUPATIONAL RANK
### X  Age Difference
Age differences between husbands and wives show no definite pattern in relation to level of occupation. (G012)

### Authority Structure of Family
The amount of paternal authority is greater among the higher occupational groups than among the lower occupational groups. (K030)

### Birth Control
The lower the occupational status, the less common is the use of contraception. (F101)

### Child-Rearing Attitudes (Authoritarianism)
The higher the occupational level of the husband, the less authoritarian and controlling the maternal attitudes. (Z011)

### Desertion
Comparing the occupational distribution of males in the general population and of deserting husbands broken down by race, the following occurs: among both whites and Negroes, the upper occupational classes are underrepresented in desertions; for the whites the *bottom three* occupational classes (when combined) are slightly overrepresented in desertions, while among Negroes, these classes are slightly underrepresented. (K010)

Desertion cases among nonwhites are concentrated in the lower occupational classes, but are not concentrated in the lower occupational classes among whites (i.e., there is no substantial justification for referring to desertion as the "poor man's divorce"). (K010)

### Desertion by Previously Divorced
The proportion of desertion cases which involve previous divorce experience varies directly with occupational level among native white persons. (K010)

### Divorce
There is a rough inverse association between frequency of divorce and occupational level. (K010)

### Divorce/Desertion
When the occupational distribution of Philadelphia desertion cases is compared to that of the Philadelphia divorce sample, a surprising degree of similarity is evident. (K010)

### Economic Attitudes

Where social contact among wives and families of members cuts across occupational rank of a corporation, the pressures from families are more likely to support the attitudes of management than where such contact occurs primarily "horizontally" in the hierarchy. (M166)

### Employment of Women, Attitude Toward

The professional group is more equalitarian in its views on the propriety of employment of married women than is any other occupational stratum. (F009)

### Fertility

While there was an inverse relationship between fertility and occupational status during the early part of the twentieth century, it seems that in the future there will be a direct relationship between fertility and occupational status. (W022)

### Homogamy (Class)

The higher the occupational stratum of the male, the more commonly he marries down; the lower the occupational level of the male, the more frequently he marries up. (C008)

### Homogamy (Occupation)

Intraoccupational endogamy is greater in the lower occupational strata than among the higher occupational strata. (C008)

### Marriage Ceremony

A rough association exists between occupational level and the proportion of couples getting married by religious ceremony among native whites. A discernible pattern for nonwhites fails to emerge. (K010)

### Mate Selection (Residence)

Residential propinquity as a factor in mate selection is less prevalent among the professional strata than among any other occupational strata. (F009)

Occupational rank of the groom does not vary inversely with the degree of residential propinquity of groom and bride. (S012)

Occupational rank of the groom does vary inversely with the degree of residential propinquity of groom and bride. (S012)

### Power Structure of Family

There is no significant difference in the dominance of husband and wife in family decisions, as between professors and skilled workers.

### Premarital Pregnancy

Among whites, but not Negroes, the higher the occupational rank, the lower the incidence of premarital pregnancy. (M243)

### Premarital Sex Relations

The lower the occupational rank of a male, the earlier he is likely to begin premarital sexual relations. (K160)

The lower the occupational status of a male, the more frequently he is likely to have premarital sexual relations. (K160)

### Social Mobility Aspirations

The lower the occupational level of the husband and wife, the lower their mobility aspirations.

### Social Network

Dicorcées from upper occupational strata are no more likely than those from lower strata to have divorced persons in their friendship circles. (G157)

## OCCUPATIONAL RANK OF DIVORCÉE
### X    Friendship

The higher the occupational group of the divorcée, the more likely is she to maintain marriage friends during the separation and divorce period. (G157)

## OCCUPATIONAL RANK OF FATHER
### X    Aggression

The higher the rank of the father's occupation, the higher is the rate of aggression in the child. (E097)

### Education of Father
### X    Occupational Aspirations of Son/Occupational Rank of Father

The strength of the positive relationship between the father's educational level and the son's occupational aspirations weakens as the level of the father's occupation decreases (professional-managerial to unskilled labor). (E102)

### Homogamy (Class)

Sons of upper occupational-level fathers are more likely to marry down than up; sons of lower-level fathers are more likely to marry up than down. (C008)

### I.Q.

There is a correlation between the occupational level of the father and the intelligence of the child. (B282)

### Occupational Aspirations of Son

The higher the status of the father's occupation (unskilled labor to professional work), the more likely is the son to have managerial or professional aspirations. (E102)

### Occupational Choice

The higher the status of the father's occupation, the closer the correspondence between the son's vocational interests and the father's occupation. (C110)

### Personality Adjustment of Child

The higher the prestige of the father's occupation, the better adjusted the child (as measured by the Rogers Test of Personality Adjustment) and the lower the child's sense of inferiority. (B251)

## OCCUPATIONAL RANK OF FATHER/SON
### Mental Illness (Paranoia)

Paranoia is more likely to occur when the father of the patient is of a lower occupational rank than the patient. (N050)

## OCCUPATIONAL RANK OF HUSBAND
### X    Divorce Adjustment

Divorcées whose husbands have middle- or upper-class occupations are slightly more likely than those of husbands with lower-class occupations to experience difficult emotional problems in divorce. (G157)

### Divorce, Initiation of

Wives of men in high-status occupations are slightly less likely to make the first suggestion to divorce; the husbands are slightly more likely to make the first suggestion. (G157)

### Fertility (Real/Ideal)

If the husband's occupational level is craftsman or higher, the wife tends to consider as ideal more children than she intends to have; at the lower occupational levels, this relationship is reversed. (Y046)

### Power Structure of Family
The higher the husband's occupational prestige, the greater his voice in marital decisions. (G156)

### Rank of Family
The husband/father's occupational status is correlated with the status of his family within the community. (P062)

## OCCUPATIONAL RANK OF MOTHER
### X   Death Rate
The higher the occupational level of the mother, the lower the death rate of the children. (S265)

### Juvenile Delinquency
Mothers of delinquents tend to hold lower-level jobs than do mothers of nondelinquents. (W152)

## OCCUPATIONAL RANK OF MOTHER/FATHER
### X   Homosexuality
The greater the occupational prestige of the wife outside the home, relative to the man, the more likely is homosexuality in the son. (R104)

## OCCUPATIONAL RANK OF PARENTS
### X   Creativity of Child
There is no relationship between parental occupational level and the degree of creativity of the child. (R109)

## OCCUPATIONAL RANK OF SURROGATE FATHER                                            X   I.Q.
Children with higher I.Q. are more likely to have been adopted by fathers in higher-ranking occupations than are those with lower I.Q. (H242)

## OCCUPATIONAL RANK OF WIFE
### X   Intermarriage (Racial)
Negro men marrying white women tend to marry white women with low occupational status rather than high occupational status. (G003)

### Role Definition of Wife
Wives with very low occupational status, as well as wives without jobs, rate highly their housework contributions, while they downgrade interference with the husband's career.

## OCCUPATIONAL RANK, PREMARITAL
### X   Employment of Wife
If a woman performed in an occupation previous to her marriage which required high educational achievement or specialized training, she is likely either to take outside employment or to consider it. (W150)

## OCCUPATIONAL ROLE, ECONOMIC IMPORTANCE OF                                  X   Sex Status
Men tend to assume the occupational role which is of greatest importance to the economy. (S120)

## OCCUPATIONAL STABILITY OF FATHER
### X   Incest (Father-Daughter)
Fathers who have had sexual relations with their daughters have histories of occupational instability and irresponsibility. (K119)

## OCCUPATIONAL SYSTEM
### X   Kinship, Importance of
As the occupational system develops and absorbs functions in the society, it must be at the expense of the relative prominence of kinship organization. (P062)

## OEDIPAL COMPLEX
### X   Child-Rearing Practices (Affection)
The Oedipal complex is less likely to occur in societies in which the infant is treated gently and affectionately. (D057)

### Descent (Matrilineal)
The Oedipal complex is less likely to occur in societies with matrilocal residence and matrilineal descent. (D057)

### Descent (Matrilineal)/Paternity, Ignorance of
In societies characterized by both matrilineal descent and ignorance of physiological paternity, the Oedipal complex will not occur. (M226)

### Descent (Matrilineal/Patrilineal)
The Oedipal complex develops in early infancy in matrilineal as well as in patrilineal societies. (G055)

In a patriarchal society, the Oedipal conflict involves the desire of the son to murder the father and marry the mother, whereas in matrilineal society, it is the wish to murder the maternal uncle and to marry the sister. (M173)

### Extended Family
The Oedipal complex is less likely to occur in societies in which there is an extended family pattern. (D057)

### Father Absence
The fantasy image of an absent father (both idealized and sadistic) reinforces the inverted Oedipal complex in boys. (L170)

Sons who are separated from their fathers during the Oedipal period show greater Oedipal intensity during early adult years than do sons who did not experience separation. (L170)

### Isolation of Family
The appearance of the Oedipal complex is directly correlated with the degree of isolation of the family unit. (M226)

### Marital Adjustment
Women who are satisfied with their marriages are likely to perceive a greater similarity between their husbands and their fathers than are women unsatisfied with their marriages. (L140)

### Maternal-Role Adjustment
If masochistic impulses (which are derived from, and are a defense against, incestuous wishes toward her father) are only partially relinquished by the mother, she is more likely to feel inadequate in the maternal role and to express her anxiety in periodic outbursts of a sadomasochistic nature against her children. (B272)

### Maternal-Role Behavior
If the mother defends herself against persistent masochistic impulses (which are derived from and are a defense against early incestuous wishes toward the father) by the mechanism of reaction formation, she is more likely to take a predominantly active and aggressive maternal role and to assign the rejected passive role to her child. (B272)

If the mother defends herself against persisting masochistic impulses (which are derived from and are a defense against early incestuous wishes toward the father) by the mechanism of "identification with the aggressor," she is more likely to adopt an active and aggressive maternal role and to discharge her sadistic impulses upon the child. (B272)

### Mental Illness (Schizophrenia)
Schizophrenics reveal more evidence of Oedipal conflict than do normal persons. (L155)

Schizophrenia will not occur when the Oedipal constellation has developed. (S258)

### Mother-Child Relations (Affect)
If the masochistic impulses (which are derived from and are a defense against incestuous wishes toward her father) are repressed by the mother, she is less likely to be able to extend herself emotionally to the child. (B272)

### Mother-Child Relations (Indulgence)
If the masochistic impulses (which are derived from and a defense against incestuous wishes toward the father) persist in the mother, she is more likely to act them out by submitting her own ego to that of the child's and by being excessively indulgent. (B272)

### Parent-Child Relations
The Oedipal complex will not arise in families in which the relationship between parent and child is "happy." (M226)

### Parent-Child Relations (Authority)
The child's fight with the parental authority that prohibits his normal sexual activity, not the incestuous wishes of the child, is the major cause of the Oedipal complex.

### Polygyny
Males in polygynous societies are more likely to have strong Oedipal fears. (S189)

### Religion (Role of Deities)
The Oedipal complex is less likely to occur in societies in which discipline is transferred to supernatural sources. (D057)

### Sex-Role Behavior
To be able successfully to assume socially accepted adult sex roles it is more important for the boy to give up his Oedipal ties than for the girl to relinquish strong attachments to her father. (G156)

### Sex Taboo (Postpartum)
A long duration of the postpartum sex taboo intensifies the Oedipal complex. (S079)

### Size of Family
The appearance of the Oedipal complex is inversely correlated with family size. (M226)

### Toilet Training
The development of the Oedipal complex is directly correlated with rigidity in toilet training. (M226)

### Weaning
The development of the Oedipal complex is directly correlated with rigidity in weaning. (M226)

## OPPORTUNITY STRUCTURE
### X   Sex Status of Household Head
A higher percentage of women-headed households is found in a social-status system in which the lower-class father can achieve no superior rank. (A051)

### Social Mobility
The more able upper-class family members are in preventing lower-class children from obtaining access to

skills and education, the more able they will be in retaining their status position. (G156)

The greater the accessibility of the opportunity structure to family members of the lower ranks, the more difficult it becomes for upper-class families to maintain their position. (G156)

### Stability of Extended Family
The better able it is to offer adequate opportunity to the younger generation, the greater the stability of the extended family household. (G156)

## ORAL PROBLEMS     X   Alcoholism
Oral fixation, produced by overindulgence or frustration during the oral stage of development, is associated with alcoholism. (M195)

## ORDINAL POSITION
### X   Accident-Proneness of Child
Later-born children are more likely than earlier-born children to be accident-prone. (K122)

### Achievement
There is no relationship between the child's ordinal position and his level of achievement. (S218)

Under really frightening conditions, firstborn individuals will be less effective than will later-born individuals. (S263)

Later-born flyers tend to be more effective fighter pilots than do firstborn flyers. (S263)

### Achievement Motivation
In the United States, firstborn children are likely to have higher achievement motivation than are later-born children. (M246)

In India and Japan, later-born children tend to have higher achievement motivation than do firstborn children. (M246)

Last-born children in large families tend to have lower achievement motivation than do earlier-born children in large families. (R106)

Last-born children in small families tend to have higher achievement motivation than do earlier-born children. (R106)

### Achievement Values
Only and oldest sons are more likely than are intermediate and youngest sons to have values similar to their mothers' regarding achievement. (R097)

### Adult-Child Relations
Early-born children tend to be more adult oriented than later-born children. (R106)

### Adult-Child Relations (Approval)
Second-born children are more responsive to adult approval than are firstborns, only if there is a two-to-four-year difference in age between siblings. (K098)

### Adult/Peer Relations
The first child in a family is more commonly adult-oriented, while the second child is more likely to be peer-oriented. (F084)

### Age at Marriage
There is no relation between a man's age at marriage and his sibling position. (T092)

### Aggression

Older siblings are less likely than younger or only children to display aggressive actions. (S228)

Frequency of use of parents as agents of aggression in doll play does not vary with ordinal position of the boy; only male children are more likely to use the boy doll and younger brothers the girl doll, as agents of aggression than are the older brothers. (S228)

The mother, boy, and baby dolls are less likely to be used as objects of aggression by older brothers than they are by younger or only boys. (S228)

There is no correlation between dolls used as objects or agents of aggression and ordinal position of the girl. (S228)

### Alcoholism

In families where the parents are alcoholics, younger siblings are more likely than older siblings to become alcoholics. (G125)

The relationship between birth order and alcoholism disappears when parental loss is controlled; hence, birth rank, as an independent variable, has no place in the etiology of alcoholism. (L159)

There are significantly more last-born than first- or middle-born children among alcoholics. (L159)

### Anxiety

The later born the child, the less anxious and fearful he is likely to become in an anxiety-producing situation. (S263)

Communicating with others has less effect on the anxiety level of later-born subjects than on firstborns. This proposition is also denied. (S263)

The simple physical presence of others is more likely to reduce the anxiety level of firstborn and only children than is the case for later-born children. (S263)

Firstborn children are more anxious than are later-born children. (T095)

### Anxiety (Weaning)

Older children are more likely to experience anxiety in the weaning and nursing situations than are middle or younger children. (S202)

### Aspiration Level

There is no relationship between ambition level and sibling position when family size is held constant. (T095)

### Behavior Problems

Habit disorder among disturbed children is found among only and oldest children, but not among middle children. (H198)

### Behavior Problems (Cheating)

Cheating is more common among firstborn children than among any other sibling position. (H215)

### Breast Feeding

Among families that have more than two children, older children are more likely to have been breast fed than are younger children (U.S.). (S191)

The later the birth rank of a child, the less likely it is that he will be breast-fed; if he is, the period of breast feeding will be short. (S263)

### Breast Feeding, Duration of

There is no significant correlation between the length of breast feeding and the ordinal position of the child. (L162)

Only children tend to be weaned earlier than first children of multichildren families. (L162)

Mid-children tend to be breast-fed longer than either younger or older children. (L162)

Among larger families (more than two children) where the children have been breast fed, the duration of breast feeding is shorter for older children than for younger children (U.S.). (S191)

### Child-Rearing Anxiety

Early-born children are treated with more anxiety than are later-born children. (R106)

### Child-Rearing Practices

Mothers tend to show greater relaxation in their child-rearing behavior, especially in their feeding practices, with their second and later children than with the first. (B272)

Parents discipline the first-born child more and are less consistent and more permissive in their behavior toward him than is the case for later-born children. (S263)

Firstborn children are more likely to be overprotected than later-born children. (S263)

### Child-Rearing Practices (Acceleration)

Mothers tend to accelerate the socialization training of the last-born child to the level of the elder siblings in order to be finished with child care. (R106)

### Child-Rearing Practices (Affection)

There is more disciplinary friction between the mother and the first child than with his sibling(s). (L160)

### Child-Rearing Practices (Aggression)

Older children are given more freedom in quarreling with siblings than are later children. In two-child families, the older child is also permitted more leeway in fighting with neighborhood children (U.S.). (S191)

There is no association between the ordinal position of siblings and permissiveness for parent-directed aggression (U.S.). (S191)

### Child-Rearing Practices (Attention)

First children receive greater attention than do later children. (B252)

### Child-Rearing Practices (Authoritarianism)

No relationship exists between maternal authoritarian child control and the birth order of the children. (H200)

### Child-Rearing Practices (Chores)

Older and middle children are assigned more tasks than are younger children. (S191)

### Child-Rearing Practices (Discipline)

First children are more likely than later children to be exposed to psychological discipline. (B252)

### Child-Rearing Practices (Indulgence)

Last-born children in large families are more likely to be pampered and overindulged than are earlier-born children. (R106)

### Child-Rearing Practices (Nurturance)
Second and later children receive less nurturance at bedtime from mothers than do first and only children. (S014)

### Child-Rearing Practices (Permissiveness)
Parents tend to be more permissive and relaxed in their treatment of second children than they are in relation to the firstborn child. (F084)

### Child-Rearing Practices (Punishment)
In two-child families, there is no association between ordinal position and the use of physical punishment. (S191)

Only and oldest children have suffered significantly more physical punishment and deprivation of privileges. (S191)

### Child-Rearing Practices (Responsibility)
The firstborn child is given more responsibility than is the younger child regardless of sex, but firstborn girls are given more responsibility than are firstborn boys. (K149)

### Child-Rearing Practices (Restrictiveness/Warmth)
Parents tend to handle first children with more interference, more restrictiveness, and less warmth than they handle second children. (D064)

### Child-Rearing Practices (Sibling Conflicts)
Mothers are more permissive of oldest than of middle or younger children's quarreling with siblings. (S191)

### Conformity
There is no relationship between sibling birth order and the child's tendency to conform (measured by Davis's Compliant-Defiant Instrument). (S233)

Firstborn and only children are more influencable or more likely to conform than are later-born children. (S263)

### Criminality
Habitual criminals are less likely than normal persons to have been the oldest child. (C105)

### Dependency
First children are more likely to end up anxious and dependent than are later children, who tend to be more aggressive and self-confident. (B252)

A firstborn child is more vulnerable to the loss of his parent's love than are subsequently born children. (C104)

The correlation between being a first or only child and dependency behavior in the preschool situation is caused by the less permissive scheduling of feeding, nursing, and weaning received by the first and only children. (S014)

Older children are more dependent on their parents than are middle or younger children. (S202)

Only children are more dependent than firstborn children. (S263)

In an ambiguous situation, early-born persons are more likely than later-born persons to seek other people as a means of evaluation and when with others are more likely to rely on others in evaluating their own opinions and emotional states. (S263)

### Education
Firstborn children in two-child families are more likely than their siblings to attend college, regardless of the sex of the second-born child. (A073)

### Educational Aspiration
Parents are more likely to insist that their oldest child attend college, holding class constant. (E102)

Firstborn children are more likely than later-born children to have college aspirations. (E102)

Among lower-class adolescents, those who have no siblings are much more likely to be college oriented than are those who are the oldest child in large families. (E102)

### Emotional Problems of Child
Middle children, ranging from next to oldest to next to youngest, tend to have more emotional problems than do children who are oldest or youngest. (B283)

### Employment of Mother, Adjustment to
The last-born child is more likely to suffer maladjustment as a result of the employment of his mother than are the children at other age spacings. (R108)

### Feeding (Demand)
Second and later children are treated more permissively in scheduling of feeding than are first or only children and also more permissively in aspects of infant nursing and weaning. (S014)

### Friendship Choice
Firstborns are more likely to concentrate their choice of interpersonal preferences on fewer persons than are later-born children. (S232)

As firstborns are more dependent than later-born children, they are more likely to choose their friends on the basis of what other persons will think of them, rather than according to their own personal needs. (S232)

Firstborns are more likely to choose popular persons for friends than are later-born children. (S232)

### Friendship Choice (Age)
Firstborns are more likely to prefer playmates younger than themselves than are second-born children, but this is less true, the greater the age disparity between siblings. (K094)

### Geographic Mobility
The individuals who migrate tend to be younger sons within the family. (A022)

### Identification
In general, children are more likely to identify with or be more involved with those in the family above them in the age hierarchy than with those below them (firstborn children with parents, second-born children with older siblings, etc.). (K149)

Firstborn and only children have less of a tendency to identify with other people having similar character traits than do later-born children. (S278)

### Incest (Brother-Sister)
Brother participants in incestuous relations are usually older than their sisters. (W123)

### Incest (Father-Daughter)
In the cases of father-daughter incest, the father usually selected the eldest daughter in the home as his first

incest partner, but also tried to initiate incest with the other accessible daughters. (W123)

### I.Q.
The firstborn child is more likely to be high in intelligence than are children in other ordinal positions. (B282)

The oldest child and the "baby of the family" receive disproportionate amounts of parental attention and both have average higher I.Q. scores than do middle-born siblings. (L115)

There is no relationship between the ordinal position of the child and his intelligence. (S218)

### Juvenile Delinquency
Only children and youngest children (supposedly the spoiled or favored ones) are less likely to be delinquent than are children of other birth ranks. (B238)

Only children are less likely than children who have siblings to be recidivists. (B238)

There is no correlation between birth order and delinquency. (B238)

If the child holds a middle ordinal position among the children of the family, it is more likely that he will become delinquent than if he holds any other ordinal position. (M194)

Oldest and only children show less delinquent behavior than do intermediate children. (N052)

Since intermediate sons (as opposed to eldest) prefer achievement through leadership of a group (peers) rather than through individual activity, they are more prone to delinquency than are their older brothers. (S226)

### Marital Adjustment
Children in middle ordinal positions will, in general, adjust better to the problems of courtship and marriage than will younger or older siblings, but these last two may be more intensely happy if they make the right choices. (T089)

The duplication of early (incestuous) relationships with siblings in marriage is more likely for "middle" children than for oldest or youngest. (T091)

Early sibling relationships which are not duplicated in the individual's marriage are more likely to interfere with marital adjustment in the case of "middle" children than in that of the oldest or youngest. (T091)

### Mate Selection
The only child is more likely than others to seek a mate like his father or mother. (T089)

### Maternal-Role Behavior
There is no direct correlation between maternal behavior and the ordinal position of the child. (L165)

### Maternal Role (Discipline)
The mother plays a greater role in caretaking and discipline of the youngest child than of other children, regardless of family size. (S191)

### Mental Illness
Earlier-born children are more susceptible to mental diseases than are later-born children. (M197)

Ordinal positions which permit an exclusive concern of the parents with the child are conducive to mental illness. (F085)

In the middle class, youngest boys and oldest girls are more likely than others to be mentally disturbed. (M197)

In the lower class, the oldest boy is more likely than others to become mentally disturbed. (M197)

### Mental Illness of Child, Adjustment to
When parents are well adjusted in a marriage, the ordinal position of the psychotic child is relatively unimportant as a factor in their adjustment (i.e., to the illness). (C109)

### Mental Illness of Mother/Daughter
Psychotic breakdown in the mother is most likely to lead to psychotic breakdown in the oldest daughter, as opposed to girls in other ordinal positions. (H192)

### Mental Illness (Paranoia)
Paranoia is more likely to occur among the oldest member of a group of siblings. (N050)

### Mental Illness (Schizophrenia)
"Childish" (aggressive, acting-out) schizophrenic adolescents tend to be the oldest of several siblings, who are regarded as undependable and tend to lose their birthrights to more dutiful, conforming younger siblings. (S208)

Adolescent schizophrenics of a "preadolescent" type (rebellious, delinquent, irresponsible) tend to be either the oldest or the only child. (S208)

There seems to be no direct correlation between the ordinal position of the individual and the development of schizophrenia. (T105)

### Mental Retardation
Mental deficiency among disturbed children is more frequent among intermediate and youngest children than among oldest children. (H198)

### Mother-Child Relations (Warmth)
Mothers are warmer with older boys than they are with younger boys; they are warmer with younger girls than with older girls. (M216)

Youngest children receive more maternal warmth than middle children, who receive more warmth than oldest children do. (M216)

Ordinal position and warmth of the mother toward the child are not associated (U.S.). (S191)

### Neurosis (Gastric)
Gastric neurosis is more likely to occur among oldest or only children. (F113)

### Occupational Aspirations of Son
Firstborn middle-class sons are slightly more likely than those born later to have high occupational aspirations. The reverse is true for lower-class boys. (E102)

### Occupational Choice
In two-sibling families, firstborn girls are more likely to choose teaching as a prospective occupation than are later-born girls. (S221)

In two-sibling families, firstborn males are more likely to select psychology, public administration, and accounting as prospective occupations than are later-born males. (S221)

In two-son families, the second-born male is more likely than the first to choose an occupation which involves an "application of physical power to persons, animals, and other living things" (e.g., physician, dentist, farmer, policeman, veterinarian, etc.) than are individuals from families with other two-sibling arrangements. (S221)

In two-girl families, the second-born girl is more likely than the firstborn to choose occupations of social work, law, and YMCA secretary. (S221)

In two-sibling families, a boy with a younger sister is more likely to choose occupations that are technically creative (e.g., psychology, physics, mathematics, engineering, etc.) than are individuals from other family structures. (S221)

### Parent-Child Relations (Affect)
The first child experiences a more child-centered atmosphere, but this declines after the second child. (L146)

The first child is taught "to do right," as against the parental expression of natural affection.

The first child, at first, has a more intense emotional relationship with the parents, but this later declines; the later children experience a more stable intensity of emotion from the parents. (L146)

Parents are more child centered and intense in raising their first child than subsequent children. (L146)

### Parent-Child Relations (Affection)
The first child tends to be treated with more indulgence and affection than later children. (L064)

The first child, as compared to the second and, to a lesser extent, the second child, as compared to the third, is likely to receive less emotional warmth and to experience more restriction and coercion from the parents, particularly during the preschool years. (L160)

The first child has a less-stable emotional environment than does the second; parental behavior toward the first child changes systematically in the direction of reduced interaction, resulting in decreasing affectionateness and rapport between them as the child grows older, but systematic changes in the treatment of the second child do not occur. (L160)

### Parent-Child Relations (Aggression)
Only and oldest children were "a little more aggressive" toward parents than were middle and youngest children. (S191)

### Parent-Child Relations (Attention)
Early-born children tend to command more of their parents' attention than do later-born children. (R106)

### Parent-Child Relations (Conflict)
Tension is likely to be sharpest with the oldest children since they have gone farthest along the road of social and economic maturity and so symbolize the filial generation more completely. (F087)

### Parent-Child Relations (Favoritism)
Girls are more likely than boys to report a younger brother rather than a younger sister to be both the mother's and the father's favorite child. (R129)

### Parent-Child Relations (Warmth)
In two-child families there is no difference between the children in the amount of parental warmth shown to them. (S191)

### Paternal/Maternal Role
There is a tendency for fathers to participate more in the rearing of first children than of later ones, regardless of sex. (S191)

With only children, mothers assume chief disciplinarian control for daughters, fathers for sons. (S191)

### Peer Relations
The only child from the higher economic strata is more likely to be rejected by his peers than is the only child at the middle or low economic levels. (F108)

### Peer Relations
Firstborn children are less popular among their peers than are later-born children. (S232)

### Personality
When spacing is from two to four years, firstborns tend to alibi more than do second-born children. (K104)

When spacing is over four years or under two years, girls with a younger sister are likely to be more vacillating than are girls with an older sister. (K104)

Firstborns are more likely to be curious and responsible than are second-born children, even more so if the sibling is of the opposite sex. (K126)

Firstborn girls and second-born boys with an older sister are more likely to procrastinate. (K126)

### Personality Adjustment of Sibling
Younger siblings are more likely to be adversely affected by their retarded siblings than are older siblings. (J027)

### Personality (Affiliation Tendency)
The earlier the birth rank, the greater the number of organizations to which college students belong. (S263)

### Personality (Affiliative Need)
Firstborn children show stronger affiliative tendencies than do later-born children. (D066)

Under anxiety-arousing conditions, firstborn and only children are more likely to want to be with other people than are later-born children. (S263)

In an anxiety-producing situation, firstborn and only children are much more likely than later-born individuals to seek the company of others. (S263)

The later born the child, the less likely he is to respond to anxiety by seeking company. (S263)

When anxiety level is held constant (when only truly anxious subjects are considered), firstborn and only children are more likely than later-born subjects to seek the company of others. (S263)

Firstborn subjects from both small and large families are more likely than later-born persons to respond to anxiety by seeking company. (S263)

### Personality (Anger)
Firstborn females tend to have a greater tendency to anger than do second-born females, particularly at the four-to-six-year spacing. (K104)

When spacing is under two years, second-born males tend to have a greater tendency to anger than do firstborn males; this is reversed if the spacing is from two to four years. (K104)

### Personality (Competitiveness)
Firstborn children tend to be more competitive than do later-born children. (R106)

### Personality (Dominance)
When the sibling is less than two years younger, firstborn girls have more initiative and are more dominant than are boys. (K126)

### Personality (Empathy)
Later-born persons empathize and identify more with others than do firstborn or only children. (S237)

Later-born persons tend to measure their abilities against the standards of others more than do firstborn or only children. (S237)

### Personality (Other-Orientation)
Girls who are middle children are more "internally oriented" than are those who are either the youngest or the oldest in the family. (S252)

Girls who are only children are more "other-oriented" than are those who have older siblings. (S252)

### Personality (Pain Tolerance)
Firstborn and only children do not withstand pain as well as later-born children do. This hypothesis is also rejected. (S263)

### Personality (Placebo)
The hypothesis that firstborn and only children, being more anxious, would be more responsive to placebos was not supported by the findings of this experimental study. (G137)

### Personality (Self-Confidence)
The older child in a sibling pair is more likely to be self-confident than is the younger. (K104)

### Personality (Sensitivity)
The eldest child will tend to be more adult-oriented and sensitive than will the second child. (F084)

### Personality (Shyness)
First children are more likely to be shy and second children to be friendly. (F084)

### Personality (Social Influence)
A later-born person's behavior (as measured by his performance on a counting task) is more likely to be influenced by interaction with another person than is the performance of the firstborn or only child. (S234)

Since firstborn females receive earlier and more significant training in independence (in relation to sex role or care for later-born siblings) than do firstborn males, they develop greater need achievement and eventually a greater resistance to social influence. (S235)

### Psychosomatic Illness
More patients suffering from hyperthyroidism and asthma are firstborns or eldest than middle or youngest children in the family. (P081)

### Psychotherapy
Disturbed firstborns are more likely to seek and accept psychotherapy and to remain in treatment longer than are later-born persons. (S263)

### Scapegoating
Where scapegoating is thought to relieve parental conflict, the oldest child is most often chosen to fulfill this role. (B204)

### Scholastic Achievement
A working-class boy has a greater chance of entering an upper school if he is an elder or eldest child. (L115)

Middle children are less likely to go to college. (L115)

### Scholastic Adjustment
Only and second-born children have the smallest proportion of school difficulties; youngest children are more likely to have a greater number of school difficulties.

Sons who are leaders in school and who conform to school expectations are more likely to be elder or only children; those who exhibit deviant behavior in school are more likely to be youngest and intermediate children. (W151)

### Scholastic Motivation
Among lower-class adolescents, youngest children are higher in academic motivation than are firstborns. (E102)

Among middle-class adolescents, oldest children are higher in academic motivation than are children who are youngest. (E102)

The firstborn child is higher in academic motivation than is the youngest, regardless of family size. (E102)

Middle children are lower in academic motivation than are oldest siblings. (E102)

### Scholastic Motivation by Class
The oldest child in middle-class families is higher in academic motivation than is the oldest child in lower-class families. (E102)

### Self-Conception
There is no clear relationship between birth order and self-esteem. (R129)

### Sex-Role Identification
If the age difference between two sisters is not very great, the older sister will develop the more feminine attributes and the younger will develop more bisexual attributes. (B318)

Birth order is irrelevant to the age at which sex-role preferences are acquired. (H197)

### Sibling Relations (Affection/Aggression)
Older siblings exhibit predominant feelings of love for younger ones, while younger siblings exhibit predominant feelings of aggression for older ones. (B321)

### Sibling Relations (Conflict)
Middle and younger children quarrel more with siblings than do oldest children. (S191)

### Sibling Relations (Leadership)
The firstborn child is more likely to become a leader of his siblings than are children in other positions. (C104)

### Sibling Rivalry
Degree of sibling association is a more significant determinant of rivalry and hostility for second-born children than it is for firstborn children. (K149)

### Size of Family X Anxiety
The difference in anxiety level between first- and later-born children is greater in small families than it is in large families. (S263)

### Superego Formation

Only and oldest children had more strongly developed consciences (U.S.). (S191)

### Surrogate Parents, Adjustment to

The firstborn child is more likely to suffer maladjustment as a result of placement with stepparents or guardians than are children at other age spacings. (R108)

### Warfare

Men who undertake the initiative in undertaking raids tend to be younger brothers who lack the status and prerogatives of an elder brother. (S117)

### Weaning

Middle and younger children are weaned earlier than older children. (S191)

Oldest children were weaned latest and showed greatest emotional upset at weaning. (S191)

## ORDINAL POSITION, IMPORTANCE OF
### X  Genealogy, Importance of

The existence of this mechanism (i.e., genealogy) is correlated with a form of social structure where the attainment or possession of rank, power, and religious privilege is bound up with the fact of seniority by birth. (F086)

## ORDINAL POSITION (OF ALCOHOLICS)
### X  Parent Loss

Loss of a parent was more frequent among last-born alcoholics than among those of first or middle rank. (L159)

## ORDINAL POSITION OF MOTHER
### X  Child-Rearing Practices (Power)

Mothers who have been younger children tend to find it difficult to set limits to the power of an older child. (H217)

## ORDINAL POSITION OF WIFE
### X  Power Structure of Family

The husband is more likely than not to be more dominant than the wife where the wife was an only child or the youngest child in her family. (L014)

The wife is more likely than not to be more dominant than the husband where the wife was the oldest child or the middle child in her family. (L014)

## ORDINAL POSITION/SEX STATUS
### X  Mental Illness (Schizophrenia)

The child who is isolated within the family by birth order or sex is more likely than others to become schizophrenic. (W143)

# P

**PARENT ABSENCE**  X **Autoeroticism**
Children faced with the absence of parents may turn, for alternate satisfaction, to autoerotic devices. (H239)

**Behavior Problems**
Children faced with the absence of parents may develop regressive patterns, such as loss of sphincter control. (H239)

**Personality Problems of Child**
Children who are completely deprived of parental relationships are much more likely to develop personality disorders than are children from homes where the parents are negligent and rejecting, no matter how emphasized these characteristics might be. (B270)

**PARENT-CHILD RELATIONS**  X **Age**
There is no relationship between the age of married offspring and their adjustment to their parents. (S011)

**Age of Mother**
Of wives with children, the older wives tend to be better adjusted to their own parents; while among wives without children, the younger tend to be better adjusted to their own parents. (S011)

**Anxiety**
The greater the anxiety in the child (provoked by the confusion of his parents), the more likely it is to be displaced away from the disturbed relationship and into a phobia of an object. (C119)

**Aspiration Level**
Young people with high occupational aspirations are more likely to have experienced unsatisfactory interpersonal relationships with their parents than are students with lower levels of aspiration. (R117)

**Behavior Problems**
If the mother is maladjusted and the father adopts ineffectual disciplinary methods, the child is likely to develop social-conduct problems. (P070)

**Broken Home**
The success of the parent-child relations is not necessarily contingent upon whether the home is broken or unbroken (but rather on the degree of adjustment between the child and parents). (B286)

The adjustment of adolescents to parents is likely to be poorer in broken homes than in unbroken homes. (N010)

**Child-Rearing Practices**
The behavior of parents toward their children is not significantly correlated with their remembered relationship with their own parents. (B297)

**Child-Rearing Practices, Evaluation of**
The more favorable the adolescent's attitude toward the freedom and responsibility allotted him by the parents, the more likely it is that he will have a positive attitude toward other areas of family adjustment. (N063)

**Child-Rearing Practices (Punishment)**
Parents who treat their children casually punish their children less for misdemeanors than do parents who do not treat their children casually. (S010)

**Class**
The higher the class, the more likely are the parents to treat the child as an individual rather than as a part of a collectivity (Indochina). (D065)

Adjustment of adolescents to parents varies directly with socioeconomic level when the fact that the home is broken or unbroken is held constant. The association, however, is stronger in unbroken homes. This relationship also holds when farm-nonfarm residence is held constant. (N010)

In an achievement-oriented society, the lowest classes give less support to the family socialization functions; in lower-class families, extrafamilial-role participations by the children are likely to lead to disenchantment with their parents. (P083)

**Conformity**
Children who are opposite-sex allied (i.e., join parent in family conflict) are more conforming to what is expected of them than are children who are same-sex allied. (B263)

**Dependency**
The adjustment of married offspring to their parents is directly related to the dependence of married offspring on their parents. (S011)

**Duration of Marriage**
The longer the marriage, the greater the convergence of parental attitudes and behaviors toward the children. (B232)

There is no correlation between adjustment of married offspring to their parents and number of years married. (S011)

**Empathy**
The greater the role-taking accuracy of adult children vis-à-vis (in relation to) their parents, the better the adjustment to these parents. (S279)

For tradition-oriented, dependent parents whose attitudes conflict with those of their children role-taking accuracy vis-à-vis their children is inversely related to adjustment. (S279)

**Homosexuality**
Neurotic homosexual males are more likely to have had unsatisfactory father-son relations and overintense mother-son relations than are heterosexual neurotic males. (W140)

**Husband-Wife Relations (Power)**
When there is dominance of one spouse, rather than equalitarian relations in marital situations, the father and mother are equally likely to be dominant in parental situations. (B323)

### Identification with Parents
The more the parents meet the needs of the child and teach him the things he wants to learn, the more likely is the child to attempt to emulate the parents. (C093)

### Illegitimacy (Adoption)
Unwed mothers who give up their children have better relations with their parents than do unwed mothers who keep their children. (J020)

### Intermarriage
The poorer the parent-child relations, the more likely the child will intermarry. (H240)

### Juvenile Delinquency
Delinquent boys of preadolescent age (modal age 11) are more likely to have poor family relations than are older boys (modal age 15). (F093)

Of two siblings who grew up within the same environment, the one who had a good relationship with one of the parents is less likely to become delinquent than is the other. (B238)

Juvenile delinquency is more closely linked with disturbed parent-child relationships than with more remote environmental factors. (F093)

The data provide more support for the belief that during adolescence juvenile-delinquent behavior is more closely related to the attitude of the child toward the parent than to that of the parent toward the child. (N052)

### Juvenile Delinquency (Help)
Parents of boys who are frequent juvenile offenders are more likely to be indifferent to efforts to help the boys than are parents of boys who have one offense.

### Juvenile Delinquency/Neurosis
Delinquent children are more likely than neurotic children (phobic reactions, anxiety level) to have emotionally disturbed relationships with their parents. (B238)

### Marital Adjustment
There is a correlation between unsatisfactory relations between parents and unsatisfactory relations between parents and child. (C117)

Satisfactory parent-child relations are a more important factor in the marital adjustment of democratic families than in that of authoritarian families. (K113)

The more satisfactory the parent-child relationship, the better the marital adjustment of the children. (K113)

### Mental Illness
The combination of a smothering mother with either a passive father or an absent father is especially likely to produce psychosis in the son. (M164)

### Mental Illness (Manic-Depressive)
Manic-depressives come from families in which there has been a serious disturbance in the early parent-child relationship. (C092)

### Mental Illness of Child
Parents understand more of the behavior and mental life of normal siblings than of psychotic children. (D064)

### Mental Illness of Child (Autism)
Autism is directly correlated with a disturbed parent-child relationship. (S188)

### Mental Illness of Child (Schizophrenia)
The parents of the schizophrenic child are more likely to treat him as a projection of their own ungratified needs, rather than to deal with his own unmet needs. (B242)

There is no single familial syndrome which accounts for the etiology of childhood schizophrenia. (B284)

### Mental Illness (Paranoia)
Mental illness is directly correlated with the importance of the child to his parents. (N050)

### Mental Illness (Schizophrenia)
There is no single familial syndrome which accounts for the etiology of childhood schizophrenia. (B284)

Since the schizophrenic child has remained in a symbiotic relationship with his mother, it is more likely that he, rather than other children, will react to events such as separation from parents or birth of a sibling with rage and panic. (B284)

The source of illness of good premorbid schizophrenics (good functioning before onset of illness) is more likely to be the strong element of punishment inherent in the dominating attitudes of the father; whereas the source of illness of poor premorbid schizophrenics is more likely to be estrangement due to the overprotectiveness of the mother. (G127)

Schizophrenics tend to have aberrant relationships with their parents in which 1) mothers rejected or overprotected them, 2) fathers displayed little affection for them, 3) parents displayed little interest in them, and 4) patients and their siblings were left on their own with little concern shown by their parents. (M061)

Schizophrenic adolescents with a "juvenile" reaction (neurotic, somatic symptoms) behaved in Oedipal fashion, acting as though they expected and feared retaliation from the fathers for the closeness they had with the mothers. (S208)

### Mental Illness (Social Adjustment)
The more favorable the memory a patient has of his same-sex parent, the better his adjustment and prognosis are likely to be. (V034)

### Mental Problems
Child rearing which does not provide the child with concrete, deep relationships with significant adults increases the likelihood that the child will develop a pathological split between emotional and intellectual functioning. (D059)

### Neurosis (Acting-Out)
Children who come from homes in which the mother is permissive and the father is aloof and/or hostile are more likely than others to become acting-out neurotics. (W143)

### Obesity
Obesity in the child is correlated with the use of the child by the parents as an object whose function it is to fulfill parental needs and to compensate the parents' failures and frustrations in their own lives. (B218)

### Oedipal Complex
The Oedipal complex will not arise in families in which the relationship between parent and child is "happy." (M226)

### Parent-Child Relations (Interaction)
Parents who treat their children casually spend less time with their children than do parents who do not treat their children casually. (S010)

### Parental-Role Adjustment
The degree of satisfaction felt in the parental role is not related to the types of problems experienced in relations with the child nor to the types of inadequacies felt by the parents in dealing with the child. (G126)

### Parenthood
Better adjustment to their mothers tends to be found among husbands and wives with children than among those without children. (S011)

### Personality Adjustment of Son
Both normal and disturbed soldiers tend to have more idealized memories of their mothers' behavior toward them than they have of their fathers' (i.e., for mothers, but not for fathers, both groups endorse positively, rather than negatively, toned statements of the RPBI). (V034)

### Physical Activity
Children who are opposite-sex allied (i.e., join parent in family conflict) are more physically active than children who are same-sex allied. (B263)

### Political Relations with Dependent Colonies
The attitudes of nations toward their respective colonies are extensions of the character of their parent-child relationships. (H081)

### Power Structure of Family
Girls raised in families controlled by the mother have more flexible attitudes concerning parent-child relations than do girls from father-dominated families.

### Psychopathy of Child
Abnormal or disrupted parent-child relationships are a cause of psychotic behavior problems in the child. (B285)

### Race Attitudes
Prejudiced persons are more likely than unprejudiced persons to express feelings of victimization by the parents. (A061)

### Remarriage
The longer the period after marriage in which one parent exerts the influence, the greater the disruption for the child when remarriage occurs. (B286)

### Role Conflict of Parents
The greater the parental conflict between familial and outside roles, the greater the extent to which the parents compete to dominate the wills of the children. (F106)

### Self-Conception
A child's feelings about himself are more closely related to the character of his relationships with his parents (parental expectations, strictness, favoritism, and identification with parents) than they are to experiences shared with parents (mobility, parent employment, marital status of parents, and size of family). (S279)

### Sex-Role Identification
The boy's sex typing of interests correlates more with his interaction with his father than with his mother. (M183)

### Size of Family
Adolescents in small families are more likely to have better relations with their parents than are adolescents in large families. (E100)

Adjustment of adolescents to parents varies inversely with the size of the family. (N010)

### Social Adjustment
The more satisfactory the parent-child relations, the more able is the child to relate well with his peers. (K113)

### Social Adjustment of Child
There is no measurable relationship between parental attitudes toward children and the personal and social adjustment of the children. (C098)

The attitudes a child has toward his parents are correlated with those toward many other individuals. (C098)

A positive attitude toward the parent of the same sex is likely to facilitate a child's peer-group adjustment at the preadolescent age level. (C098)

A positive attitude toward only the parent of the opposite sex is likely to hinder the child's peer-group adjustment at the preadolescent age level. (C098)

### Social Mobility
Mobile women are more likely to have experienced unsatisfactory relationships with their parents than are nonmobile women. (R117)

### Stepparent
The presence of a stepparent in the home diminishes the level of adjustment of the children to the remaining natural parent. (B286)

### Superego Formation
The greater association of sons with fathers (who are instrumentally oriented) correlates with their tendency to develop a principled and objective (situation-oriented) superego; the greater subjection of girls to withdrawal of love by mothers correlates with their tendency to develop a superego focused upon interpersonal matters rather than upon broader issues. (B234)

Children who are opposite-sex allied (i.e., join the parent in family conflict) are more blame-accepting than are children who are same-sex allied. (B263)

### Surrogate Parent-Child Relations
Because a child is identified with his real parents he prefers these, no matter how rejecting, negligent, or mistreating, to any foster-parents, regardless of how adequate the foster-parents might be. (B270)

### Urban/Rural
Adolescents who live in the city are better adjusted to their parents than are adolescents who live on a farm (U.S.). (N010)

### Value Consensus
The greater the consensus in the family on domestic values, the greater the parents' satisfaction with their daughter's performance. (F094)

### Values
Parental values have their chief effect by the way they modify relationships between parents and children rather than by directly modifying the belief system of the child. (M060)

### Values (Individualism)

Parents in an individualistic competitive society find children more of a burden than do parents in a kin-oriented society where relatives share childcare more. (F069)

### Witchcraft

When the parent-child relationship is regarded as untrustworthy, children will tend to be primary suspects for witchcraft. (L109)

## PARENT-CHILD RELATIONS (ACCEPTANCE)
### X   Child-Rearing Attitudes

As measured by the PARI, Stanford-Binet, and Q-Sort Personality Tests, there is little relationship between various parental attitudes toward child rearing and parental acceptance of the child.

### Juvenile Delinquency

Juvenile delinquents have stronger feelings of not being recognized and appreciated and are more resentful toward their parents than are nondelinquents.

Where the parents have an accepting attitude toward the child, there is no correlation between parental scolding and withdrawal of love and delinquent behavior in the child. (N063)

### Parent-Child Relations (Authoritarianism)

For mothers, strong authoritarian-control attitudes are negatively related to acceptance of the child; for fathers, democratic attitudes are positively related to child acceptance (as measured by the PARI, Stanford-Binet, and Q-Sort Personality Tests).

### Personality of Child

There is an association between acceptance by parents of their children and the following personality characteristics in the children: greater sociability, friendliness, loyalty, emotional stability, cheerfulness, dependability.

### Sex Status

Mothers tend to be more accepting of their children than fathers.

### Social Adjustment

Parental acceptance increases the likelihood that a child will develop a generally positive set of feelings toward others. (H212)

## PARENT-CHILD RELATIONS (ADVICE)
### X   Juvenile Delinquency

There is a negative relationship between delinquent behavior and the frequency with which adolescents consult their parents as to future occupations (this is particularly significant for girls). (N057)

There is a positive correlation between the amount of parental advice received and delinquency in the girl and between advice from the father and delinquency in the boy. There is an inverse curvilinear relationship between the amount of advice received from the mother and the son's delinquency. (N063)

There is a curvilinear realtionship between the frequency with which girls consult their fathers about sex and their degree of rapport about dating and delinquent behavior in the girl. (N063)

The amount of parental help and rapport with the child concerning scholastic problems or the future occupation reduces delinquent behavior in the girl, but not in the boy. (N063)

## PARENT-CHILD RELATIONS (AFFECT)
### X   Child-Rearing Practices (Deception)

When lying and deception play an important role in child training, the child will tend to withdraw psychologically from his parents. (L064)

### Empathy

A child with parents who differ in the amount and kind of affect they display is likely to be more sensitive to parental affect than is a child whose parents are similar in these characteristics. (R098)

### Environmental Problems

When the family moves from a home context to a less familiar one, the social-emotional response of the father will become more negative; conversely, the social-emotional response of the mother will become more positive. (O035)

When the family moves from a home context to a less familiar one, there will be proportionally fewer positive social-emotional responses between father and son than between father and daughter; conversely, there will be a higher proportion of positive social-emotional responses between mothers and male children than between mothers and their daughters. (O035)

### Esthetic Development

In Alorese society, a stifled emotional capacity resulting from lack of emotional ties between parents and child during childhood lessens esthetic development. (M202)

### Grandparent-Grandchild Relations

The more ego is emotionally involved in his own family of orientation, the more likely he is to extend this involvement to the family of orientation of his parents. (R084)

### Juvenile Delinquency

Severe delinquency tends to occur where the parent is withdrawn emotionally in his relationships with his children. (B291)

Juvenile delinquents are more likely to be emotionally deprived than are nondelinquents since they experience greater indifference, more actual hostility, less affection, and greater feelings of not being cared for by their parents. (S210)

### Juvenile Delinquency/Neurosis

Although delinquents are as conscious of parental rejection as are neurotics, they are less likely to recognize their own hostile feelings toward their parents (i.e., they are more detached and less deeply involved in family relationships than are neurotics). (W145)

### Mental Illness of Child

Parents are more emotionally driven and impulsive (rather than rational) toward psychotic children than toward their siblings. (D064)

Parents are more emotionally involved with psychotic children than with their siblings. (D064)

Sick children tend to be more highly and more positively involved with the cross-sex parent than are healthier children. (L150)

### Mental Illness (Schizophrenia)

Schizophrenics are more likely to have a less-emotional relationship with the more stable of their parents. (M061)

### Mental Illness (Schizophrenia/Neurosis)
In the lower class, more parents of schizophrenics than of neurotics express few positive feelings toward the child. (M197)

### Ordinal Position
The first child experiences a more child-centered atmosphere, but this declines after the second child. (L146)

The first child is taught "to do right," as against the parental expression of natural affection.

The first child, at first, has a more intense emotional relationship with the parents, but this later declines; the later children experience a more stable intensity of emotion from the parents. (L146)

Parents are more child centered and intense in raising their first child than their subsequent children. (L146)

### Parent-Child Relations (Affection)
The more affectionate the parents are to their children, the more highly involved (emotionally) they will be with them. For mothers, this relationship holds for both sons and daughters; for fathers, it holds only for sons. (B297)

### Parent-Child Relations (Affection/Authority)
Fathers report high emotional involvement with their fathers when they are remembered as high in authority; mothers report high emotional involvement with both parents when either is remembered as highly affectionate. (B297)

### Paternal/Maternal Role
Mothers and fathers are equally likely to become emotionally involved with their children. (B297)

### Personality Development
The greater the emphasis on the sadomasochistic aspects of the motives of the anal phase, the more likely it is that the relations between parent and child will be highly personal and emotional, rather than centering around more impersonal concerns, such as cleanliness, neatness, etc. (M203)

### Personality of Child (Dependency)
Early and severe emotional deprivation decreases dependency strivings in the child. (M221)

### Self-Conception
### X Parent-Child Relations (Indifference)
Exceptional indifference on the part of either or both parents is associated with low self-esteem in the child. (R129)

Contrary to the original hypothesis, it is not the punitive response of parents to poor grades that is most closely related to low self-esteem, but the indifference; those who report indifferent parental responses have lower self-esteem than do those who report punitive responses as well as lower than those who report supportive responses. (R129)

The association between parental indifference and children's self-esteem is not an artifact of social class, religion, sex, or small town/city environment; it is not a question of whether the parents were strict with the child or whether he felt the punishment they gave was deserved or undeserved. (R129)

Students who felt a lack of parental interest, but who felt that the punishment they received in childhood was deserved, had lower self-esteem than did those who

reported their parents to be interested, but who felt their punishment in childhood was generally undeserved. (R129)

### Self-Conception of Child
An indifferent attitude in parents toward their children is more likely than punitiveness to produce low self-esteem in the child. (R128)

### Self-Conception of Parents
When the parents lack a conception of self, a lack of emotional commitment to children results, which is reflected in infrequent nonintensive interaction with them. (B040)

### Sex-Role Definition
Male-child households will exhibit the highest level of positiveness in the father-son relationship when fathers and sons both hold subordinate-role positions in the society; likewise, female-child households show the highest level of positiveness in mother-daughter relationships in an unfamiliar context when both the mother and daughter assume subordinate-role positions. (O035)

### Sex Status
Among fathers, but not mothers, strong emotional involvement with one parent tends to exclude strong emotional involvement with the other. (B297)

Girls react to their parents with a pleasant feeling-tone more frequently than boys do. (G117)

### Social Mobility
Business executives with lower-class backgrounds are more likely to have had an emotionally depriving family setting during childhood than are executives from higher-class backgrounds. (R117)

### Social Mobility/Scholastic Achievement
Emotionally impoverished parent-child relations are related more to extreme vertical and geographic mobility than to high scholastic achievement or high achievement motivation in general. (E102)

### Social Network
Limited social relations with nonfamily or extended family members may lead to a heightening of the child's emotional relations with his parents.

## PARENT-CHILD RELATIONS (AFFECTION)
### X Adult-Role Behavior
The response patterns of relationships established in childhood appear to determine the expression of affection in adult life. (B270)

### Age
The younger problem son is likely to perceive both parents to be more loving and controlling than the older problem son perceives them to be. (V038)

### Age of Child
The younger the children, the higher their affection for their parents. (B286)

### Aggression
Parents of aggressive boys demonstrate less warmth and affection toward their sons than do the parents of normal children. (B246)

The more the child perceives his parents as being nurturing and gratifying, the more likely he will be to learn and practice control of aggressive behavior. (K103)

### Aggression Anxiety
Since a mutually affectionate relationship between parent and child fosters the development of conscience in the child, parents who are affectionate are more likely than those who are not to produce adolescents with high fantasy-aggression anxiety. (C133)

### Anxiety
A rise in affectional frustration will be accompanied by a corresponding anxiety toward frustration from this source. (T106)

### Authoritarianism
Authoritarianism of parents does not correlate with the intensity of affection between parents and child. (H209)

### Behavior Problems
If the child fails to obtain favorable attention (affection) from his parents, he will engage in destructive activity. (B033)

### Child-Rearing Practices (Control)
Parental use of threat that God will punish the child for deviant behavior is associated with low affectivity between parents and child. (N055)

### Child-Rearing Practices (Giving Reasons)
The more likely parents are to provide explanations for their rules, the more likely their adolescents are to have a strong attraction for their parents. (E105)

### Class
Parent-child relations are more ambivalent (greater threat of withdrawal of affection) in middle than in lower classes. (W143)

Middle-class children are more likely to identify success with parental affection than are lower-class children. (W143)

### Cohesion of Family
There is a correlation between closeness of family life and fondness for both parents on the part of the child, particularly, fondness for the mother on the part of sons. (R116)

### Conformity
There is a correlation between the degree of affection the child has for the parents and the degree to which the child conforms to parental values. (N063)

The need to retain whatever warmth may exist in situations of affective insecurity will tend to lead, in the child, to an attempt to exercise control and to conform to the ideals of the parents. (T106)

### Criminality
Among adult criminals, more have had nonloving parents than any other type. (M194)

Boys whose parents are loving tend not to become criminals. (M199)

### Economic Importance of Parents
The affection of children varies directly with their parents' effectiveness as good providers. (W056)

### Education
There is no relationship between parental education and the degree of affection shown to the children. (B250)

### Husband-Wife Relations (Affection)
Feelings of inadequacy and insecurity and inferiority on the part of either parent or frustration in the affectional relationship may lead to compensation through a struggle for attention and affection from the child. (B033)

A child can love both parents if his parents love one another; a child is forced to side with one parent against the other if the parents hate one another. (L134)

### Identification with Like-Sex Parent
The higher the affection of girls for their mothers, the closer both real and perceived identification will be. (G153)

There is no evidence that higher affection of boys for their fathers leads to closer perceived or real identification. (G153)

### Identification with Parents
In single-parent situations, one condition for being loved by the parent who is present is some type (actual or fantasy) of identification with the absent parent.

The identification of the child with the parents correlates with his love for them, not with the degree to which they are sexual objects for him (this object choice follows only as a secondary result). (B234)

The degree of identification of the child with the parent correlates with the degree to which the parent is a loved or prestigeful person. (B234)

The more frequent the expression of warmth and affection, the greater is the identification of the child with the parent. (H208)

The more positive the attitudes and feelings of the child toward the parent, the more likely he is to consider himself to be similar to his parents. (J032)

### Juvenile Delinquency
A lower proportion of mothers than of fathers of delinquents are not closely attached to their sons. (B243)

The closer and more affectionate the relationship between parents and child, the less likely it is that the child will become delinquent. (B243)

Lack of adequate affectional dependency relationships with parents is a cause of delinquency in the child. (B243)

The more the parents provide affection and a feeling of belongingness and establish rapport with the child, the less is the likelihood that the child will engage in delinquent behavior. (M178)

### Leadership
There is a positive relationship for sons and a negative relationship for daughters between parental affection and leadership abilities in the child (based on teachers' ratings of influence in group activities). (B250)

### Maternal Overprotectiveness
Mothers of overprotected children are more likely than are mothers of nonoverprotected children to have experienced a marked lack of parental affection and of childhood play. (L117)

### Mental Illness (Manic-Depressive)
Manic-depressives are more likely to regard their fathers with greater affection than their mothers. (C092)

### Mental Illness of Child
Parents are more consistently affective (affectionateness, rapport, direction of criticism) toward normal siblings than toward psychotic children. (D064)

### Mental Illness of Child (Schizophrenia)

Parents of preschizophrenic patients exhibited less affection and had less contact with their children than did parents of normal children. (H241)

Schizophrenia in the child is correlated with parents' tendency to compete for his loyalty and affection. (L114)

### Neurosis (Hysteria)

Despite the nature of an individual's inherited tendencies, he will not develop hysteria unless he is subjected to situations during childhood causing him to crave affection. (B270)

### Occupation

Children whose fathers work in an academic capacity may be less inclined to view parental behavior as a threat to withdraw affection than are children of fathers in a nonacademic capacity. (G117)

### Ordinal Position

The first child tends to be treated with more indulgence and affection than later children. (L064)

The first child, as compared to the second and, to a lesser extent, the second child, as compared to the third, is likely to receive less emotional warmth and to experience more restriction and coercion from the parents, particularly during the preschool years. (L160)

The first child has a less-stable emotional environment than does the second; parental behavior toward the first child changes systematically in the direction of reduced interaction, resulting in decreasing affectionateness and rapport between them as the child grows older, but systematic changes in treatment of the second child do not occur. (L160)

### Parent-Child Relations (Affect)

The more affectionate the parents are to their children, the more highly involved (emotionally) they will be with them. For mothers, this relationship holds for both sons and daughters; for fathers, it holds only for sons. (B297)

### Parent-Child Relations (Authority)

Children more often misperceive parental affection than they do parental authority. (B260)

The greater the degree to which family relationships are concerned with authority, the less the affection between parents and children. (S279)

### Parent-Child Relations (Evaluation)

The larger the discrepancy between actual (rated) traits for parents and the subjects' ideals for parents, the less the child tends to like the parents. (J032)

Among males, positive feelings toward the mother are more independent of the degree to which she meets her child's concept of ideal mother than is the case among females. (J032)

### Parent-Child Relations (Power)

Adolescents perceiving their parents as using coercive rather than legitimate power over them are less apt to be highly attracted to their parents. (E105)

### Parental-Role Definition

Where there is mutual agreement that each spouse shall have a high degree of independence from the home, it is likely that relations between them and their children will be of a bargaining nature, each competing for affection and power. (F106)

The greater the commitment of the parents to the family, the more likely it is that they are gratified by affectionate relationships with their children. (F106)

### Patental/Maternal Role

Children perceive no difference in the frequency with which fathers and mothers are highly affectionate. (B260)

Mothers and fathers are equally likely to offer high affection to their children. (B297)

Both boys and girls perceive their mothers as more affectionate, nurturing and loving than their fathers. (D069)

### Peer Relations

Children who rate their parents as very dominant and low in affection toward them were judged least favorably by their classmates.

### Personality Development

Insofar as a child lacks attentive love, it is more likely that its development will be delayed or retarded. (M203)

### Personality of Child (Hostility)

Parents who are not affectionate toward their children are more likely than those who are to produce overtly hostile adolescents, regardless of the degree of authoritarian control exerted. (C113)

### Scholastic Achievement

Among college students, felt lack of parental love is associated with high achievement. (D065)

### Sex Relations

The son's attachment to the mother is likely to inhibit his heterosexual activity, but the daughter's attachment to the father stimulates such activity. (S219)

### Sex-Role Identification

Children are more likely to develop appropriate sex-role preferences if they perceive their like-sex parent as rewarding, nurturing and affectionate. (M225)

Both boys and girls are more likely to develop appropriate sex-role preferences if encouraged by the father. (M225)

### Sex Status

Mothers are more likely to remember their fathers as highly affectionate; fathers are more likely to recall their mothers as highly affectionate. (B297)

Children view their parents as relatively more affectionate with a child of the opposite sex and more strict with a child of the same sex. (H180)

Males are more likely to express dislike of parents than are females. (R116)

The parent-child relationship will tend to be more affectionate and less strict when the parent and child are of the opposite sex. (W104)

### Sexual Adjustment

A sexual barrier between parents increases the likelihood that one of them will seek compensatory love from a child and treat the child seductively. (L134)

### Sibling Relations (Affection)

During childhood and adolescence, the degree of affection between siblings is less than that between mother and child, but greater than other family ties. (I018)

### Social Adjustment
There is a correlation between the degree of continuous affection received from a parent figure in the early years of infancy and the ability to establish adequate interpersonal relationships in later life, including relationships with parent substitutes. (T086)

### Socialization, Agents of
Children whose parents are not their main socializing agents are more likely to show clearly positive attitudes toward their families than are children whose parents are the main socializing agents. (R089)

### Sociopathic Personality
There is no relationship between cold and withdrawn parental behavior and the development of sociopathic personality in the child. (O033)

### Superego Formation
The greater the parent's expression of affection, the greater the degree of guilt in five-year-old children. (H208)

An affectionate relationship between the parents and the child is needed for the development of conscience. (M194)

### Toilet Training
The child's acceptance of the demands of toilet training is not related to his desire for the love and approval of his parents. (B224)

### Weaning
When parents are extremely fond of children and indulgent toward them, weaning occurs at a late period. (D025)

## PARENT-CHILD RELATIONS (AFFECTION/ AGGRESSION)
### X     Child-Rearing Values (Democratic)
The child from the democratic, egalitarian home is more likely to have a genuine, personalized love for his parents and less repressed hostility and aggression. (M203)

## PARENT-CHILD RELATIONS (AFFECTION/AUTHORITY)
### X     Parent-Child Relations (Affect)
Fathers report high emotional involvement with their fathers when they are remembered as high in authority; mothers report high emotional involvement with their parents when either was remembered as highly affectionate. (B297)

## PARENT-CHILD RELATIONS (AFFECTION/NEGLECT)     X     Juvenile Delinquency
If both parents are neglecting in their behavior toward the child, the child is more likely to become delinquent than if only one parent is neglecting and the other loving. (M194)

If the mother is neglecting toward the child and the father is loving, the child is more likely to become delinquent than if the mother is loving and the father is neglecting. (M194)

## PARENT-CHILD RELATIONS (AFFECTION/PRAISE)     X     Sex Status
Among adolescents, girls are more likely than boys to get affection and praise for its own sake (rather than as a reward). (B250)

## PARENT-CHILD RELATIONS (AGGRESSION)
### X     Aggression
Aggressive boys are more likely than normals to manifest indirect aggression against their fathers, but the two groups do not differ with respect to their mothers. (B243)

Aggressive boys are slightly more likely to be physically aggressive toward their mothers than are normals, but there is no difference between the two groups with respect to their fathers. (B243)

There is no relationship between the aggressiveness of the boy and the amount of verbal aggression he displays toward his parents. (B243)

### Ordinal Position
Only the oldest children were "a little more aggressive" toward parents than were middle and youngest children. (S191)

## PARENT-CHILD RELATIONS (AGREEMENT)
### X     Sex Status
Agreement between the parent and a child of the opposite sex increases as the child becomes increasingly involved in courtship. Between mother and daughter disagreement increases, whereas there is no change in the father-son relationship. (H229)

Both mothers and fathers are more likely to report disagreement with their same-sex offspring than they are with their opposite-sex offspring, although with advancing courtship, parents report declining disagreement with their opposite-sex offspring. (H229)

Parents' alienation from their son increases with advancing courtship, but declines for their daughter. (H229)

## PARENT-CHILD RELATIONS (AID)
### Duration of Marriage
The longer a child is married, the less likely are the parents to give financial assistance. (A066)

### Residence
The closer the parents live to their married child, the more likely are they to offer services (help in sickness, babysitting, childbirth, etc.). (A066)

## PARENT-CHILD RELATIONS (ALLEGIANCE)
### X     Conflict in Family
In case of conflict, the child tends to show more allegiance to the mother, the father, and the other adult resident in the home, in that order. (C117)

## PARENT-CHILD RELATIONS (AMBIVALENCE)
### X     Age of Child
Preadolescents display more ambivalence toward their parents than do younger children. (W135)

### Bigotry
Bigoted people tend to show more ambivalence toward their parents than do nonbigoted people. (M247)

### Child Rearing (Collective)
The reduction in the socializing duties of the Israeli parents on the collectives has reduced the ambivalence (hostility-love) of the parent-child relationship by permitting the parent to give love without thwarting the child as much as in the standard type of family. (T087)

### Ethnicity

Jewish patients are likely to have affiliative tendencies toward their fathers and withdrawal and ambivalent hostile-affiliative tendencies toward their mothers; Italian patients are likely to withdraw from both their fathers and mothers; among the Irish, the males tend to withdraw from their fathers and to have ambivalent attitudes toward their mothers, but the girls, on the other hand, have affiliative tendencies toward their fathers and, like the males, have ambivalent attitudes toward their mothers. (S187)

### Human Sacrifice

Human sacrifice is more likely to occur in societies in which there is an ambivalence in the parent-child relationship. (W154)

### Parental Role

Ambivalence toward the parent is likely to be greater if he or she assumes both the supportive and disciplinary role. (W154)

### Superego Formation

The greater the intensity of both love and hate in the parent and in the child who identifies with him, the more likely is the child to develop an extreme, self-punishing superego. (B234)

## PARENT-CHILD RELATIONS (ANGER)
### X Aggression

Aggressive boys are more likely than nonaggressive boys to perceive parent-child interaction as characterized by anger. (K103)

## PARENT-CHILD RELATIONS (ANXIETY)
### X Autoeroticism

Masturbation appears to be an attempt to flood the body with pleasurable stimulation in order to ward off the painful anxieties of the child-parent relationship. (C088)

### Homosexuality

Homosexuality is more likely to occur where the anxiety-inducing parent is of the opposite sex. (S258)

### Personality Problems (Somatic)

Felt or actual loss of parental attention or anxiety in the parent–child relationship may lead the child to seek attention by somatic functions (retention of feces, vomiting, and breath-holding).

### Religion (Role of Deities)

Societies with predominantly aggressive deities (accompanied by more hurt and pain and less nurturance in infancy) are more likely to produce anxiety on the part of the parents for the child's future welfare than are societies with benevolent deities (accompanied by nurturant child-rearing practices). (L141)

### Sex Status

Both male and female schizophrenics are less anxious in dealing with the father than with the mother. (S258)

## PARENT-CHILD RELATIONS (APPROVAL)
### X Courtship (Interracial)

Among interracial couples, the usual courtship activities do not take place in the home because of certain disapproval of their parents. (G001)

### Juvenile Delinquency

Delinquent adolescents are more likely to have difficulty in pleasing their fathers than their mothers. (N057)

### Scholastic Achievement

If the parents are approving, interested, and understanding toward the child, the child is likely to be a highly successful student, while domineering and overrestrictive parents are likely to have children who are unsuccessful students. (M174)

### Sex Status

Parents are more approving and understanding of boys than of girls. (C114)

Mothers are more likely to approve of and understand their sons rather than their daughters to a greater extent than fathers are. (C114)

## PARENT-CHILD RELATIONS (ATTACHMENT)
### X Affinal Relations

Strong attachment between an adult son and his mother is rarer than attachment between an adult daughter and her mother; hence structural protection against mother-in-law trouble from the groom's side is not as strong as it is in dealing with the wife's mother. (P083)

### Aspiration Level

Students who have high ambitions (as measured by the Reissman Scale of Ambition) express less attachment to their parents than do those who do not have high ambitions. (T095)

## PARENT-CHILD RELATIONS (ATTENTION)
### X Ordinal Position

Early-born children tend to command more of their parents' attention than later-born children. (R106)

### Social Mobility Aspirations

The more concerned the parents are with the social mobility of their children, the more likely they are to give inordinate attention to the only boy. (R129)

## PARENT-CHILD RELATIONS (AUTHORITARIAN/DEMOCRATIC)
### X Occupation

Families where the father is connected with the academic world have more democratic parent-child relations; families with fathers who occupations are outside of the academic world have more authoritarian parent-child relations. (G117)

## PARENT-CHILD RELATIONS (AUTHORITARIANISM)
### X Achievement Motivation

Mothers of boys high in achievement motivation display more authoritarianism toward their sons than do mothers of those low in achievement motivation. (M246)

Fathers of boys high in achievement motivation show less dominating or authoritarian behavior toward the son than do fathers of those low in achievement motivation. (M246)

### Parent-Child Relations (Acceptance)

For mothers, strong authoritarian-control attitudes are negatively related to acceptance of the child; for fathers, democratic attitudes are positively related to child acceptance (as measured by the PARI, Stanford-Binet, and Q-Sort Personality Tests).

### Race

Negro families tend to have more authoritarian parent-child relations than do white families. (G117)

### Religion

Controlling for family size, Catholic parents are more likely to be autocratic or authoritarian in relating to their children than are Protestant parents. (E100)

## PARENT-CHILD RELATIONS (AUTHORITY)
### X  Economic Dependence

The authority of parents tends to be directly correlated with the continuing economic dependence of their children. (L064)

### Education

Both mother and father lose influence as the children undertake school education. (H032)

### Education of Child

Among children from the dominant social group, the lower their educational level, the less likely it is that they will be acceptant of parental authority. Among children from subordinate groups, the greater the extent of their education, the more likely they are to reject parental authority. (K121)

### Identification with Parents

High identification is associated with fairly strong assumption and enactment of authority by one or both parents. (R098)

### Kin Relations (Dependency)

When the discipline and control of the child are exclusively in the hands of the parents, patterns of interaction between kinsmen will tend to be characterized by individualism or self-reliance, not by mutual dependence. (H021)

### Marital Status of Child

Among children from the dominant social group, the single are less likely to accept parental authority than are the married. Among low-status children, the single are more likely to accept parental authority. (K121)

### Neurosis

The child's defeat in his fight against parental authority for freedom, spontaneity, and self-image development is the core of neurosis.

If parental authority is arbitrary, but is not an attack on the child's personality (less concerned with motivation than with behavioral conformity), neurosis is less likely. (G020)

### Oedipal Complex

The child's fight with the parental authority that prohibits his normal sexual activity, not the incestuous wishes of the child, is the major cause of the Oedipal complex.

### Parent-Child Relations (Affection)

Children more often misperceive parental affection than they do parental authority. (B260)

The greater the degree to which family relationships are concerned with authority, the less the affection between parents and children. (S279)

### Race Attitudes

Prejudiced persons are more likely to submit to parental authority or to rebel capriciously than are the unprejudiced, who are more likely to manifest a position of principled independence. (A061)

### Rank of Ethnic Group

Children from ethnic groups of low status in countries where the norm of equality is affirmed are no more likely to reject their parents and parental authority than are children from a dominant group.

### Religious Beliefs

If the child has a strong belief in God, his demands for perfection and omnipotence in his parents decrease; thus, the authority of the parent declines slowly, rather than suddenly, with the discovery that the parental idols have feet of clay. (P083)

### Sex Status

Fathers are more likely to remember their mothers rather than their fathers as strong sources of authority. (B297)

Mothers and fathers both remember authority being exerted by one parent rather than by both. (B297)

There is less variation in the character of parental authority with the sex of the child among schizophrenics than among normals. (S187)

### Social Isolation

The greater the ecological and social isolation of a subordinate social group, the more likely it is that the children will be acceptant of parental authority and standards. (K121)

### Superego Formation

The greater the guilt feelings the parents can instill within the child, the more readily will he succumb to their authority.

## PARENT-CHILD RELATIONS (BELIEFS)
### X  Mental Illness (Schizophrenia)

Fathers of schizophrenics are more likely than are mothers to show identification with the child in the area of beliefs and to project their beliefs onto the child; mothers are more likely to exhibit awareness of the actual beliefs of the patient. (K125)

Parents of acute cases of schizophrenia are more likely to be identified with and to be aware of their son's beliefs and are less likely to project upon the patient than are parents of schizophrenics who are chronically ill. (K125)

## PARENT-CHILD RELATIONS, CHILD'S PERCEPTION OF
### X  Parent-Child Relations, Parental Perception of

The parental perception of the parent-child relationship does not correlate with the child's perception. (S250)

## PARENT-CHILD RELATIONS (CLOSENESS)
### X  Achievement Motivation

Close emotional ties between parent and child produce lower achievement motivation (college students) than does the suppression of immediate emotional response. (D065)

### Authority Structure of Family

When there is a great discrepancy in the relative authority in the husband and wife, the relationship of the wife to the children will be more intimate than that of the authoritarian father to the child, which is one of respect and avoidance. (L064)

### Behavior Problems (Lying)

There is a positive relationship between parents who are cold, distant, and neglectful and lying in the child. (R100)

### Cohesion of Lineage

The relationship between the child and his parent who is not relevant to the lineage structure will be weaker if lineage affiliation is stressed. (C056)

### Conformity

More detached parent-child relations may produce a child who has less concern for social conformity. (Y047)

### Courtship

Close attachment between mother and son is related to slow courtship progress in the son. The closer the female is to her father, the more advanced she is in courtship progress. (J026)

### Creativity

The more creative research chemists tend to report a greater isolation from parents in early adolescence. (M060)

### Employment of Mother

Children of working mothers who provide substitute care have more detached parent-child relations than do those of mothers who do not work and remain with the child. (Y047)

### Husband-Wife Relations (Role Conflict)

The stronger the ties of a husband to his parents, the greater is the likelihood that role conflicts will develop over his position as son-in-law and husband. (K089)

### Illegitimacy

Unwed mothers tended to be closer to their parents during childhood and more distant from them during adolescence than did single, never-pregnant females. (V027)

### Marital Adjustment

There is a direct relation between attachment to parents and successful marital adjustment. (K161)

The lower the success of the parental relationship (measured by parents' self-appraisals of marital happiness), the less close the child-parent relationship. (L137)

Children who are closer to their fathers are more likely to view their parents' marriage as happier than are children who are closer to their mothers. (L137)

The closer the child-parent relationship, the more likely is the child to perceive the parents' relationship as happy. (L137)

The closer the child is to both parents, rather than to one, the more likely he will be to view his parents' marriage as a happy one. (L137)

### Marital Adjustment of Parents

The less happy the rating of parents' marriage, the greater the likelihood the children will have a stronger attachment to the mother than to the father. (L137)

The greater the parental happiness reported, the greater the degree of emotional attachment to each parent. (L137)

### Marital Stability

The persistence of strong ties between the wife and her parents tends to occur in situations of marital instability. (W056)

### Marriage, Attitude Toward

The closer the child is with both parents, the fewer his doubts about his chances of a successful marriage. (L137)

### Mate Selection (Love)

Mate selection based on romantic love tends to be found in societies where the parent-child relationship is strong. (G156)

### Occupational Aspirations

Students who have high occupational aspirations report less attachment to their parents than do students with lower occupational aspirations. (E102)

### Parent-Child Relations, Stability of

If the parent-child relationship is strong, initially, the strength of the relationship tends to persist. (Z001)

### Parental-Role Behavior

The relationship between parent and child will be stronger if the parent plays a dominant role in the socialization of the child. (H137)

### Peer Relations

The more inclined the parents are to ignore the child, the freer the child is to interact with peers. (J021)

### Personality (Expressiveness)

Girls who are higher in expressive rather than in instrumental personality traits are more likely to report being closer with their fathers than with their mothers. (J026)

### Personality (Other-Orientation)

Girls who feel equally close to both parents are more other-oriented than are those who feel close to neither. (S252)

### Power Structure of Family

The closer the parent-child relationship, the more likely is the child to perceive his parents as being equal in dominance. (L137)

The closer a child feels to one parent (correspondingly, feeling distant from the other), the more likely he is to view the family as dominated by the parent he feels distant toward. (L137)

Where the family authority pattern is that of a dominant mother and a weak father, female schizophrenics will be closer to the fathers and male schizophrenics will be closer to the mothers. (S187)

### Premarital Sex Relations

The closer the parent-child relationship, the more likely is the child to be chaste before marriage. (L137)

Children who have close relations with their fathers and distant relations with their mothers are more likely to be nonvirgins than are children who are distant from their fathers and close to their mothers or distant from both. (L137)

### Residence (Extrusion)

In societies that practice neither extrusion nor brother-sister avoidance, the parents will alter their relationship to their children during the first stage of puberty by becoming slightly distant, setting new limits, imposing new expectations, and giving them new nicknames. (C093)

### Retirement

Retired parents tend to evaluate close parent-child relations more highly than employed parents do. (S220)

### Self-Conception
The closer the parent-child relationship, the higher the child's self-evaluation (self-evaluation of personality and personal attractiveness). (L137)

### Sex Education
The closer the parent-child relationship, the more likely is the child to receive sex information from his parents than from other sources. (L137)

Children who have close relations with their fathers and distant relations with their mothers are less likely to receive sex information from their parents than are children who are distant from their fathers and close to their mothers or distant from both parents. (L137)

### Sex Status
The conclusion of the infancy period is associated with the boy becoming more emotionally attached to his mother, while the daughter becomes more attached to her father. (G156)

Among schizophrenic children who view their mothers as the dominant authority figure, females are more likely to report feeling closer to their fathers than to their mothers and males to report feeling closer to their mothers than to their fathers. (K114)

Both males and females feel closer to their mothers than to their fathers. (L137)

There is no association between sex and closeness felt to the parent of the opposite sex. (L137)

Women feel closer to their parents than men do. (L137)

When parents have only one married child, the married son has just as close a relationship to them as the married daughter does; if there are married children of more than one sex, a married daughter has a closer relationship to her parents than a married son does. (S269)

Females are more likely to be more attached to their parents than males are. (W006)

### Sibling Relations
Where the parent-child relationship is a weak one, siblings become more important to the child. (P060)

### Sibling Structure (Age Difference)
The further apart in age are the siblings, the closer their relationships to their parents rather than to one another. (K149)

### Social Adjustment
The closer the child-parent relationship, the greater the child's confidence in associating with the opposite sex. (L137)

The closer the parent-child relationship, the less difficulty the child will have in making friendships with the opposite sex during early adolescence. (L137)

The closer women are with their fathers and correspondingly distant with their mothers, the greater their problems in establishing relationships with the opposite sex during adolescence. (L137)

### Social Mobility
Children who have experienced upward occupational mobility tend to keep closer relationships with their retired parents than do less successful children. (S220)

### Socialization, Effectiveness of
The more the child is exposed to his parents and, consequently, free from intervening structural ties, the more able are the parents to impose their personalities on the child. (C093)

### PARENT-CHILD RELATIONS (COMMUNICATION)    X    Homogamy (Values)
The higher the degree of contact (living with and communication among) between children and parents, the more likely are the children to select mates who have the same values found in their parental homes. (C103)

### Juvenile Delinquency
Recurring sequences of conflicting messages ("split double-binds") proceeding from the mother and father, respectively, are a cause of delinquent behavior in the child. (F100)

### Mental Illness (Schizophrenia)
A breakdown in perception of reality due to parental distortions in the communication process is a cause of schizophrenia. (M218)

### Parent-Child Relations (Hostility)
Hostility and misunderstandings are likely to result from limited communication of a nonreciprocal, as well as of a reciprocal, nature, as is characteristic of relationships between the autocratic parent and his offspring. (E100)

### Parent-Child Relations (Interaction)
In democratic homes, the lower the parent-child interaction, the more lethargic and spasmodic is the verbal exchange between the parents and child.

### Paternal/Maternal Role
Middle- and lower-class mothers discuss education with their children more often than do fathers of similar class positions; this does not hold for middle-class Negro parents. (B256)

### Personality Problems (Stuttering)
Inability on the part of an adult family member to adjust his level of communication to that of a child who is not yet capable of adequate verbalization can produce stuttering in the child. (W136)

### Scholastic Achievement of Son
Boys who are under achievers are more likely than those who are high achievers to describe their families as commonly sharing personal ideas and thoughts. (E102)

### Scholastic Adjustment
School phobia in the child is due to the ambivalent feelings and the contradictory verbal and behavioral cues of the parents. (E095)

### Self-Conception
Students who rarely or never participated in family mealtime conversations or who felt that family members were not interested in what they had to say are considerably more likely than others to have low self-esteem. (R129)

### PARENT-CHILD RELATIONS (COMMUNICATION/REJECTION)    X    Employment of Mother
Daughters of working mothers are more likely than those of nonworking mothers to feel that their parents disapproved of them, that their fathers rejected them and that they disapproved of their fathers, that there was

a lack of communication with their parents, and that homelife was not happy. (S265)

## PARENT-CHILD RELATIONS (COMPANIONSHIP)
### X   Leadership
There is a positive relationship for sons and a negative relationship for daughters between parental companionship and leadership in the child (based on teachers' ratings of influence in group activities). (B250)

### Parent-Child Relations (Preference)
The preference of the child tends to be for the parent who is most companionable and least censorious. Of the two factors, companionship seems the more weighty. (B033)

## PARENT-CHILD RELATIONS (COMPANIONSHIP/PROTECTION)
### X   Sex Status
Among adolescents, girls are more likely than boys to get parental protection and companionship for its own sake (rather than as a reward). (B250)

## PARENT-CHILD RELATIONS (COMPETITION)
### X   Environmental Problems
When the external situation is unfamiliar, so that the adaptive role of the family takes primacy, an adolescent son will be more apt to compete with his father than when the family is operating under familiar conditions and integrative behavior is more characteristic; conversely, in a familiar context (integrative), an adolescent daughter is more apt to compete with her mother than she is in an unfamiliar (adaptive) setting. (O035)

## PARENT-CHILD RELATIONS (COMPLEMENTARITY)
### X   Identification with Parent
The greater the complementarity of relations between parent and child, the less likely is the child's identification with the parent as a role model. (G120)

## PARENT-CHILD RELATIONS (CONCERN)
### X   Education
The higher the educational level of the parents, the more concern they are likely to feel about their relationships with children. (K089)

## PARENT-CHILD RELATIONS (CONFLICT)
### X   Age of Child
Conflict of daughter with father increases through adolescence, but her conflict with the mother decreases. (S219)

### Ascription/Achievement
The less the choices of life (e.g., education, occupation, marriage) are settled beforehand by ascription, the greater the degree of parent-youth conflict. (D058)

### Authority Structure of Family
There is no relationship between the degree of parent-child conflict and the type of family authority pattern. (B249)

The degree of friction which characterizes the parent-child relationship is directly correlated with the degree of authority of the parent over the child. (W098)

### Child-Rearing Attitudes
There is no relationship between parental child-rearing attitudes and the degree of conflict they had experienced with their parents during their adolescence. (B249)

### Child-Rearing Practices (Consistency)
Where discipline is inconsistent, parent-child conflict is more likely. (B249)

### Child-Rearing Practices (Discipline)
If discipline is consistent and fair, teen-agers are less likely to describe their adolescence as conflictual. (B249)

### Child-Rearing Practices (Restrictiveness)
The more severe the parental restriction upon the child, the more likely is parent-child conflict. (B249)

### Class
Tension between parents and children in the lower middle class is expressed more mildly than between parents and children in the lower class. (M061)

The expression of tension between parents and children in the lower middle class is more verbal, with violence being condemned; while in the lower class, tension is less verbally expressed. (M061)

### Cohesion of Family
Conflict and tension between the adolescent and his family are correlated with the intensity of the bonds between family members. (W113)

### Dependency (Social/Economic)
The more that adolescents withdraw socially from their families, but remain physically dependent, the more likely is parent-youth conflict. (S219)

### Economic Cooperation
Parent-child conflict is at a minimum in rural areas because farming requires the common cooperation of all members of the family and there is a common interest in family property. (B033)

### Education
There is no relationship between parental education and the degree of parent-child conflict. (B249)

### Education (Family/Nonfamily)
The more education is in the hands of extrafamilial authorities, the greater is the parent-youth conflict. (D058)

### Emotional Problems
There is a correlation between emotional disturbance in the child and his involvement in a conflict situation between his parents; the former never occurs without the latter.

### Extended Kin Ties
In Western society, a small number of kin present who can act as buffers increases the potential for conflict between parents and children. (G156)

### Husband-Wife Relations (Power)
The husband is more likely than not to be dominant over the wife where the husband had conflict with his father and the wife did not have conflict with her father. (L014)

The husband is more likely than not to be dominant over the wife where the husband had conflict with his mother and the wife did not have conflict with her mother. (L014)

The relationship between husband and wife is more likely than not to be equalitarian where neither the husband nor the wife had conflict with their mothers and where *their* parents did not conflict with one another. (L014)

The wife is more likely than not to be dominant over the husband where the wife had conflict with her mother and the husband did not have conflict with his mother. (L014)

### Immigrant/Nonimmigrant
The immigrant family undergoes the most rapid rate of social change in any society and therefore has the greatest amount of parent-youth conflict. (D058)

### Initiation Rites
The absence of transitional rituals and the prolongation of dependence of youth are causes of (American) parent-youth conflict. (S219)

### Juvenile Delinquency
Delinquents tend to have less conflict with their parents than do non-delinquents since their parents, although concerned, are permissive. (W152)

Conflict with parents and alienation of them are causes of boys' later delinquency. (W152)

### Life Cycle
Conflict between parents and child is partially a function of their being at different points in their life cycles and thus viewing differently many kinds of problems and opportunities. (G156)

### Marital Adjustment
Marital adjustment is associated with the absence of conflict in the relationship of the husband and wife with their respective parents. (B033)

The happier men and women rate their parents' marriages, the less likely are they to report conflicts with either of their parents. (K113)

### Mental Illness of Child
There is more disciplinary friction between parents and psychotic children than between parents and their normal children. (D064)

### Ordinal Position
Tension is likely to be sharpest with the oldest children since they have gone farthest along the road of social and economic maturity and so symbolize the filial generation more completely. (F087)

### Parent-Child Relations (Control)
The less explicit the steps from relative dominance to relative emancipation from parental authority, the greater the conflict between parents and children. (D058)

### Parent-Child Relations (Sex)
A greater preoccupation of the parents with the sex lives of their children increases the potential for conflict between parents and children. (G156)

### Personality Development of Child (Maturity)
The less consistent the degree of maturation of the child in various spheres (legal, economic, religious, intellectual), the greater the conflict between parents and youths. (D058)

### Power Structure of Family
The spouse who is more dominant in the marriage relationship tends to have greater conflict with the children than does the spouse who takes the more equalitarian or submissive role. (K113)

### Race
Negro children have more compliant attitudes regarding parent-child conflicts than do white children, who have attitudes reflecting more active opposition or constructive solutions. (G117)

### Scholastic Adjustment (Reading)
If there is great antagonism on the part of a child to a parent and the parent constantly stresses success in reading, the child is more likely to develop a reading disability in rebellion against the parent than is the child who can resist more openly. (S225)

### Sibling Structure
There is no relation between the amount of parent-teenager conflict in a family and the number of older siblings. (B249)

There is no relation between the amount of conflict between teen-agers and their parents and the number of younger siblings in the family. (B249)

There is no relationship between the degree of parent-child conflict and the number of relative age of siblings. (B249)

### Size of Town
There is no relationship between the degree of parent-child conflict and the size of the town in which the family lives. (B249)

### Social Change
The greater the differences between the society within which the parents grew up and that within which the child grows up, the greater the potential for conflict between parent and child. (G156)

### Surrogate/Natural Parents
Children living with both their natural parents have attitudes regarding conflict with parents that are more emotional, less compliant, and more suggestive of a constructive solution than have children not living with their natural parents. (G117)

### Values
Serious conflict between parents and children arises when the standards of the family differ markedly from those which the child meets outside the home. (B033)

### Values/Behavior of Parents
The greater the adolescent's perception of inconsistencies between the values and the actual behavior of his parents, the more likely it is that he will come into conflict with his parents on ideological grounds. (S219)

## PARENT-CHILD RELATIONS (CONSENSUS)
### X Education
The more formal education required by specialization, the greater the conflict in values between parents and youths. (D058)

### Juvenile Delinquency
The greater the value disagreement between parents and child, the more likely is delinquent behavior on the part of the child. (N063)

### Occupational Aspirations of Son
Excluding low blue collar workers, at all occupational levels there is a positive relationship between the son's acceptance of the values and advice of his parents and his level of occupational aspiration. (E102)

### Social Change, Rate of
The more rapid the rate of social change, the greater the conflict between parents and children over norms. (D058)

## PARENT-CHILD RELATIONS (CONSISTENCY)
### X   Size of Family
Parents fluctuate more in their overprotectiveness toward the psychotic child, as compared with the normal sibling, as the size of the family increases; although in most other attitudes (warmth, control), there is no such relationship. (D064)

## PARENT-CHILD RELATIONS (CONTROL)
### X   Acculturation
An increase in acculturation correlates with the weakening of parental control. (S135)

### Child-Rearing Practices (Punishment)
Corporal punishment in the discipline of children will tend to be used more when the parents can exercise a high degree of control over the children. (S064)

### Class
The more social benefits a family has to offer, the more able it will be to control the actions of its children. (G156)

Parental affection is a more powerful instrument of control in mental patients of the middle classes than of the lower classes. (M061)

### Conformity
When the parental conception of the child's role in the community is widely different from that approved by the adolescent's group, rebellious behavior will result in direct proportion to the degree to which the parents intervene. (B033)

### Dependency
The greater the child's need for parental approval, the greater his acceptance of parental limitation upon the free exercise of his will. (A059)

### Economic Dependence
The degree of effective discipline over a boy decreases as his earnings increase. (C024)

### Elopement
The rate of elopement tends to increase with a reduction in the strength of family control. (H062)

### Illegitimacy
The rate of illegitimate birth is directly correlated with the weakening of parental control. (K065)

### Initiation Rites
The age at which male initiation rites are undertaken is directly correlated with the strength of parental control over their offspring. (C146)

### Marital Adjustment
There is less correlation between expression of dominating or controlling attitudes toward children and other family satisfactions for the father than for the mother. (N053)

### Mate Selection
Subtle directives expressing attitudes and values on the part of parents concerning their children's selection of mates are more apt to be effective influences than are more obvious measures (arranged activities or threats). (J035)

### Mate Selection (Free Choice)
Mate selection will tend to be controlled by parents when premarital contact is sharply restricted. (R035)

With the weakening of parental control, the individual tends to make his choice of mate independent of his parents' wishes. (S134)

### Mate Selection (Residence)
Residential propinquity will cease to be a factor in mate selection as parental control weakens. (S121)

### Parent-Child Relations (Conflict)
The less explicit the steps from relative dominance to relative emancipation from parental authority, the greater the conflict between parents and children. (D058)

### Parent-Child Relations (Financial Help)
The economic support of parents by the children is directly correlated with the ability of the parents to maintain their position of authority within the family structure. (W082)

### Parent-Child Relations (Interaction)
When the child spends most of his time around the home, parental control is greater. (B033)

### Peer Relations
The effect of family expectation is more pronounced when the adolescent is isolated from his peer group. (B033)

Where family controls on the individual are rigid, peer groups provide a source of tension reduction. (P056)

### Political Attitudes
Highest conformity to parental values is found among the young people subject to moderate parental control. (M056)

When young people, at the lower SES level, change away from the political preferences of their parents, the change is at least partly motivated by revolt against overstrict control. (M056)

### Power Structure of Family
Persons who reacted negatively to discipline imposed by their parents, especially their mothers, are more likely to assume dominant roles in marriage. (S279)

### Rank
The more successful upper-class families are in forcing their children to hew to upper-class standards, the better able they are to maintain their class status. (G156)

### Television
The child exercises more control than his parents over both the amount of his viewing time and the selection of program content. (H178)

### Urban/Rural
The rural child is under greater parental control than is the urban child. (B033)

### Values (Secular)
As a culture becomes progressively secularized, parental control becomes lessened. (C086)

## PARENT-CHILD RELATIONS (CRITICISM)
### X   Courtship and Dating Status
Married or engaged males are more critical of their parents than are men dating one particular girl more than others; there is no difference in how much girls criticize

their parents according to whether they are dating or married or engaged. (H228)

### Courtship Status
Age held constant, males who have been engaged (excluding those who are married) are more independent (are more critical) of their parents than are those who have not; for girls, there is no difference in their independence, engaged or not. (H228)

### Creativity/Intelligence of Children
The parents of highly intelligent children are more critical of their children and of the school than are parents of highly creative children. (G114)

### Dating
Males who are dating are more likely to criticize their parents than are nondating males; girls not dating are just as likely to criticize their parents as are girls who are dating. (H228)

Age held constant, males who have gone steady are more independent of (criticize more) their parents than do those who have not; there is no such difference for females. (H228)

### I.Q./Creativity of Child
Parents of highly intelligent children (Binet) are more likely to be critical of reports concerning their child's performance in school than are the parents of highly creative children (Guilford-Cattell). (G132)

### Juvenile Delinquency
A significant relationship is found between attitudes toward parental appearance and delinquent behavior, with more delinquent behavior among adolescents who are most critical of parental appearance. (N052)

### Personality (Responsibility)
The lower the adolescent's responsibility rating (based on teachers' ratings of dependability in fulfilling obligations), the more likely he is to describe his parents as complaining about and ridiculing him. (B250)

The lower the adolescent's responsibility rating (based on teachers' ratings of dependability in fulfilling obligations), the more likely he is to see his parents as comparing him unfavorably with other children. (B250)

## PARENT-CHILD RELATIONS (DECEPTION)
### X Juvenile Delinquency/Neurosis
Delinquent children are more likely to have been deceived as to their true parentage than are neurotic children. (B214)

## PARENT-CHILD RELATIONS (DEMOCRATIC)
### X Age of Child
In families of older (high-school) youths, adolescents are more apt to view their parents' relations with them as democratic than as autocratic or permissive. (B323)

## PARENT-CHILD RELATIONS (DIFFERENTIAL TREATMENT)
### X Mental Illness of Child (Schizophrenia)
Schizophrenic children tend to have parents who have regarded them as different and as requiring differential treatment from birth. (K093)

### Paternal/Maternal Role
Fathers are more likely than mothers to treat children of the two sexes differently. (B250)

## PARENT-CHILD RELATIONS (DISCIPLINE)
### X Husband-Wife Relations (Power)
The husband is more likely than not to be dominant over the wife where the husband disliked the discipline given to him by his parents and the wife did not mind discipline given to her by her parents. (L014)

The wife is more likely than not to be dominant over the husband where the husband did not mind the discipline given to him by his parents and the wife disliked the discipline given to her by her parents. (L014)

The wife is more likely than not to be dominant over the husband where the discipline given to her by her parents was such that she had her own way. (L014)

## PARENT-CHILD RELATIONS (DOMINANCE)
### X Achievement Motivation
Fathers of sons with low achievement motivation more frequently made decisions pertaining to the son's expected activities and performances than did fathers of boys high in achievement motivation. (M246)

Dominating behavior does not inhibit the development of achievement motivation if it comes from the mother, but only if it comes from the father. (M246)

### Age of Child
Older children are more likely than younger children to view the parent of the same sex as more dominant and punitive. (K116)

### Alcoholism
Alcoholism is associated with the domineering but idealized mother and a stern, autocratic father whom one fears as a child. (D078)

### Authoritarianism
Preschool children who exhibit authoritarian behavior tend to have parents who are dominant and possessive toward their children.

### Mental Illness (Catatonia)
Parents of catatonic patients tend to impose their own wills upon the patients when they are children. (S187)

### Mental Illness (Schizophrenia)
Schizophrenics are more likely to perceive their parents as dominating, while normals are more likely to have a multifaceted view (i.e., dominating, ignoring, overprotecting). (G127)

### Parent-Child Relations (Hostility)
There is no relationship between overly dominant parents and excessive hostility on the part of the child. (R100)

### Parent-Child Relations (Obedience)
There is no relationship between overly dominant parents and excessive disobedience on the part of the child. (R100)

### Personality of Child (Submissiveness)
A dominating parent will tend to induce submission in the child. (B033)

## PARENT-CHILD RELATIONS (EGALITARIANISM)
### X Class
The higher the class of the parents, the more equalitarian and acceptant they are with their children. (M180)

### Personality Adjustment

Among high-school students who are high achievers in mathematics, the higher the personality maladjustment (Rotter Incomplete Sentence Blank), the more negative and autocratic the family relationships (Kell-Hoeflin Incomplete Sentence Blank). (K148)

### Power Structure of Family

When marital relations are equalitarian, there is more likelihood that roles in the other two areas of power relations (i.e., parental and child-rearing) will be congruent with the conjugal, that is, be "equalitarian" and "democratic," respectively; when a husband is dominant in marital relations, there is somewhat less likelihood of husband "dominance" and father "autocracy" in the other two areas; and when a wife is dominant in the marital relationship, there is the least probability of corresponding wife dominance and mother autocracy in parental and child-rearing relations. (B323)

## PARENT-CHILD RELATIONS (EGALITARIANISM/ DEPENDENCY)    X  Social Mobility Aspirations

Children who are upward aspirers are more likely to prefer equalitarian rather than dependent relations with their parents than are children who do not have mobility aspirations. (E102)

## PARENT-CHILD RELATIONS (EMPLOYMENT)
### X  Class

Upper middle-class children are more likely than lower middle- and working-class children to judge the work of their parents as pleasant. (H222)

### Employment of Mother

Girls with working mothers are more likely to feel that their mothers like to work than do those whose mothers do not work. (H222)

Children of working mothers are more likely to perceive their fathers as feeling unhappy or uncomfortable about going to work and leaving their children behind than are children of nonworking mothers. (H222)

### Sex Status

Boys are more likely than girls to perceive their fathers as feeling unhappy or uncomfortable about going to work and leaving a child behind. (H222)

Boys are much more likely than girls to perceive fathers as possibly having negative feelings toward their work. (H222)

### Sex Status of Child

Boys tend to perceive the father as feeling more positive about leaving his wife for work than do girls. (H222)

There is no difference between sons and daughters regarding their perception of mothers' attitudes toward their work. (H222)

## PARENT-CHILD RELATIONS (EQUALITARIANISM)
### X  Maternal-Role Definition

In a culture where the parent-child relationship is defined as equalitarian and friendly, there is little pressure during later years to terminate or change the quality of the maternal role. (C116)

## PARENT-CHILD RELATIONS (EVALUATION)
### X  Achievement Motivation

Among male college students, the higher the achievement score (measured by TAT), the more likely they are to view their parents as unfriendly, unhelpful, and unsuccessful. (M060)

Striving for achievement is more frequent among boys who perceive their relationship with their parents as unsatisfying. (M060)

Strong achievement motivation tends to develop when parents indicate a high evaluation of their child's competence to do a task well. (R106)

### Affinal Relations

In disturbed families, where the spouse is critical of his own parents, his marital partner tends to be friendly toward them. (B204)

### Aggression

Aggressive adolescent boys give more unfavorable pictures of their fathers than of their mothers. (B213)

### Anxiety

Parents of children with low anxiety view their children more favorably (based on personality ratings) than do parents of children with high anxiety. (D072)

Mothers do not evaluate their children any differently on personality checklists, whether the children have high or low anxiety. (D072)

Fathers of low-anxiety children evaluate them more favorably (on personality checklists) than do fathers of high-anxiety children. (D072)

Parents of boys with low anxiety are more likely to evaluate them as more mature, better leaders, and more generous and affectionate than are parents of boys with high anxiety. (D072)

Parents of girls with low anxiety are more likely to evaluate them as relaxed and adaptable than are parents of girls with high anxiety. (D072)

Parents of high-anxiety girls are more likely to see them as more ambitious than are parents of low-anxiety girls. (D072)

### Aspiration Level

If the child is overvalued by his parents, his aspirational level will be above realistic expectations of success. (A059)

### Authoritarianism

The greater the person's authoritarianism, the lower his evaluation of his parents. (C107)

### Child-Rearing Practices (Punishment)

The more gratifying to the child is his relationship with his parents, the more likely it is that he will respond to psychological techniques of discipline. (B236)

### Conformity

The more conforming the child to group opinion, the more likely is he to have an idealized perception of his parents; the more able the child is to make independent judgments, the more balanced (praise and criticism) is his perception of his parents. (M184)

### Dependency

The more overvalued the child is by his parents, the greater will be the child's dependency on external rather than intrinsic criteria as sources for his self-esteem. (A059)

### Emotional Adjustment
Parents of emotionally disturbed children are more likely to devaluate their children than are parents of normals. (M200)

### Husband-Wife Relations (Role Conflict)
In families where the degree of consensus between husband and wife on domestic values is low, there is no relationship between the extent of role tension in the marriage and the amount of disagreement between the parents as to whether they are satisfied with specific activities of the child. (F116)

### Juvenile Delinquency
Nondelinquents are more satisfied than are delinquents with their relations with their parents; this distinction is greater for girls than for boys. (M205)

Adolescents with favorable attitudes toward the personalities of their parents commit less delinquent behavior. (N052)

There is a positive relationship between more delinquent behavior among adolescents and critical attitude of parental appearance, particularly of the father. (N057)

The implications of lower status associated with poor appearance of the father are more significant for boys than for girls. (N057)

The more critical the child is toward the appearance of his parents, the more likely he is to show delinquent behavior, particularly in the case of a boy's evaluation of the father's appearance. (N063)

The more critical the child is toward the disposition of his parents, the more likely he is to show delinquent behavior. (N063)

### Marital Adjustment
The greater the parents' mutual satisfaction, the greater their satisfaction with their children. (F094)

### Mental Retardation
Parents of handicapped (retarded) children are more likely than parents of nonhandicapped children to show an autistic distortion in their perception of their children. (Z009)

### Parent-Child Relations (Affection)
The larger the discrepancy between actual (rated) traits for parents and the subjects' ideals for parents, the less the child tends to like the parents. (J032)

Among males, positive feelings toward the mother are more independent of the degree to which she meets her child's concept of ideal mother than is the case among females. (J032)

### Personality Adjustment
Neuropsychiatric patients are more likely than normal adults to give relatively unfavorable reports of the behavior of the same-sex parent with whom they should be most strongly identified. (V034)

### Personality Adjustment of Child
Parents are likely to see their children as less well adjusted personally (measured by responses to the California Test of Personality, Form B) than the children see themselves. (V034)

### Personality Problems
The more severe the psychopathology of the son, the more unfavorable his memories of his parents' behavior; the less pathological and more socially competent the son, the more favorable his RPBI memories of his parents. (V034)

### Race Attitudes
Prejudiced persons are more likely to perceive their parents in terms of conventional idealizations than are unprejudiced persons. (A061)

Unprejudiced persons are more likely to express genuine positive feelings toward their parents than are prejudiced persons. (A061)

### Scholastic Adjustment
The higher the student's evaluation of his parents, the higher the academic level at which he will perform. (C107)

### Sex Status
There is no substantiating evidence for the proposition that daughters tend to rate their fathers higher on the Parent Evaluation Scale than they do their mothers or that sons tend to rate their mothers higher; both daughters and sons tend to rate their mothers higher.

Boys are more likely to be critical of and less satisfied with their home conditions and relations with their parents than girls are. (H174)

### Social Adjustment of Child
Parents are likely to see their children as better adjusted socially (as measured by responses on the California Test of Personality, Form B) than the children see themselves.

### Social/Individual Adjustment
Parents are more likely to agree with their children's self-ratings when discussing social adjustment than when discussing individual adjustment (as measured by the California Test of Personality, Form B).

### Value Consensus
Children who have a high evaluation of their parents (Parent Evaluation Scale) tend to be in close agreement with their parents' ideology.

## PARENT-CHILD RELATIONS (FAVORITISM)
### X Aspiration Level
"High" aspirers define their parents as showing more favoritism toward some child in the family than do "low" aspirers. (D001)

### Illegitimacy
Unwed mothers tended to be favored more by their fathers than by their mothers. (V027)

### Juvenile Delinquency
Juvenile delinquency is more likely among youngsters who feel their parents discriminated against them in favor of another sibling.

### Occupational Aspirations
Students who have high occupational aspirations are more likely to report parental favoritism toward some child in the family than are students with lower occupational aspirations. (E102)

### Ordinal Position
Girls are more likely than boys to report a younger

brother rather than a younger sister to be both the mother's and the father's favorite child. (R129)

### Sibling Rivalry
Sibling rivalry is likely to be greater between children of the same sex than between those of opposite sexes because parents are more likely to make invidious comparisons between and give unequal affection and approval to children of the same sex. (R129)

### Social Adjustment
The parents of adolescents who are accepted by their peers are less likely to show favoritism within the family than are the parents of adolescents who are rejected by their peers. (F108)

### Social Mobility of Daughter
Parental favoritism of some child in the family is associated with upwardly mobile daughters. (E102)

## PARENT-CHILD RELATIONS (FEAR)
### X   Child-Rearing Practices (Punishment)
Children are more likely to fear punishment by parents who have a preconceived notion of the amount of punishment that is needed and proceed to administer it without much regard for the child's protestations than by parents who spank the child until he cries.

Physical punishment increases the child's fear of and decreases his love of the parent. (B232)

### Identification with Father by Sex Status
The greater the young boy's fear of the punitive, castrating father, the more complete the resolution of the Oedipal complex and the development of identification. With girls, however, since they are already "castrated," there is low fear of the "aggressor" and, thus, low identification with the father and low superego formation. (B234)

## PARENT-CHILD RELATIONS (FILIAL PIETY)
### X   Mental Illness
Mental illness is less likely to occur where filial piety is emphasized. (T110)

## PARENT-CHILD RELATIONS (FINANCIAL)
### X   Juvenile Delinquency
There is a curvilinear relationship between financial partiality and generosity on the part of the parents and delinquent behavior in the child. (N063)

## PARENT-CHILD RELATIONS (FINANCIAL HELP)
### X   Achievement
Children who have been successful in their occupations tend to give their retired parents more financial assistance than do less successful children. (S220)

### Age at Marriage
The younger the age at marital contraction, the more likely are couples to seek financial assistance from their parents. (I005)

### Income
As the income of parents increases, the amount of financial assistance given to children increases. (S220)

### Parent-Child Relations (Control)
The economic support of parents by the children is directly correlated with the ability of the parents to maintain their position of authority within the family structure. (W082)

### Religion
Among Jews, children who are less orthodox in their religious beliefs than their aged parents are more likely to give financial aid to them then are children who have the same religious identification. (G119)

There is no significant association between the religious affiliation of children (Orthodox, Conservative, Reform Jews, and no religion or non-Jews) and the giving of financial aid to their aged parents. (G119)

### Residence
There is no relationship between residential propinquity of parents and married child and financial assistance given by the parents to the married child. (A066)

### Retirement
Old parents who are retired desire financial assistance in preference to affection from their children more often than do old parents who are still employed. (S220)

### Sex Status
Married daughters are more likely to receive financial assistance from their parents than are married sons. (A066)

### Social Mobility
There is no significant relationship between social mobility and giving financial aid to aged parents. (G119)

## PARENT-CHILD RELATIONS (FORMALITY)
### X   Authority Structure of Family
Parental authority tends to be greater if the relationship between the parent and child is of a formal character. (R030)

## PARENT-CHILD RELATIONS (FRUSTRATION)
### X   Aggression
The more frustrated the child in his relations with his parents, the greater his need to display some form of aggression.

### Behavior Problems (Thumb-Sucking)
Thumb-sucking is the result of frustration, in general, rather than of frustration in the area of feeding.

### Identification with Parent
A child is more apt to identify with the parent with whom he has experienced more serious frustration. (U004)

### Personality of Child (Needs)
Absence of extreme frustration is associated with the child's ability to defer gratification. (B275)

### Role Behavior of Parent-Child
When the role experiences and the patterns of parent-child interaction are ambiguous, frustration is produced in both parents and child. (B040)

## PARENT-CHILD RELATIONS (GENEROSITY)
### X   Status in Family
Adolescents are more likely to perceive their parents as being more generous than the parents feel themselves to be. (M201)

## PARENT-CHILD RELATIONS (GRATIFICATION)
### X   Identification with Father
Boys who are highly identified with their fathers perceive a greater differential between their parents' reward value than do boys who are less identified with their fathers. (P076)

### Juvenile Delinquency
There is a negative correlation between extent of need satisfaction through parental behavior and delinquent behavior in the child. (N063)

## PARENT-CHILD RELATIONS (GUILT)
### X Dependency
The greater the guilt felt by the child when he is striving for independence in conflict with his parental allegiances, the less likely he is to emancipate himself from dependency on his parents. (A059)

### Social Mobility Pressures
Parental pressure for social mobility on the part of the child tends later to produce shame and guilt in the child about his parents' social status. (M197)

### Socialization, Agents of
The less guilt the child experiences in repudiating parental loyalties, the more able is he to accept values from other persons. (A059)

## PARENT-CHILD RELATIONS (GUILT/ANXIETY)
### X Personality Adjustment of Child
The greater the parents' anxiety, guilt, and insecurity in their relations with their children, the less likely are the children to develop security and confidence in themselves. (E096)

## PARENT-CHILD RELATIONS (HARSHNESS)
### X Aggression
The harsher the parents are in their relations with their children, the more likely the children are to aggress in return against the parents themselves.

### Aspiration Level
Adolescent boys with high aspirations are less apt to perceive their parents as harsh than are those with lower aspirations. (R117)

## PARENT-CHILD RELATIONS (HELP)    X Class
Parental financial assistance is more likely to be given to middle-class than to working-class children. (A066)

Parental assistance (babysitting, help in sickness and childbirth, etc.) are more likely to be given to working-class children than to middle-class children. (A066)

### Extended Kin Ties
Among working-class families, parental assistance (especially in the form of such services as babysitting and help during illness and childbirth) is more likely to be given by the wife's parents than by the husband's parents. (A066)

Among middle-class families, parental assistance to married children is as likely to be given by the wife's parents as by the husband's. (A066)

The wife's parents are more likely to give indirect financial aid, (nonreciprocal gifts) rather than cash loans (so as not to usurp the son-in-law's position as provider) than are the son's parents. (A066)

### Intermarriage
It is just as likely that parental help will be extended to children who have intermarried (religion, class, education level, ethnic descent) as to those who have married people of their own cultural backgrounds. (S002)

### Juvenile Delinquency
Parents of boys who are frequent juvenile offenders are more likely to be indifferent to efforts to help the boys than are parents of boys who have one offense.

## PARENT-CHILD RELATIONS (HOSTILITY)
### X Aggression
Children are more likely to express aggression when parental behavior toward them has been hostile and to express submissive behavior when the parental relationship has been protective and warm. (B243)

Aggressive boys do not differ from normals with respect to amount of hostility felt toward their mothers, but they tend to feel more hostility toward their fathers than do normals. (B243)

Aggressive boys are more likely to have feelings of hostility (as measured by the TAT) toward their fathers than are normals, but the two groups do not differ with respect to their mothers. (B243)

The more aggressive the child, the more hostile and less gratifying he will perceive his parents to be. (K103)

### Anxiety
Anxiety in the child may lead to hostile behavior toward the parents. (T086)

### Authority Structure of Family
The greater the authority of the parents, the more likely they are to repress their hostility and project it onto the child. (M203)

The less the authority of the parents, the more likely that the child will project his hostility onto the parents. (M203)

### Autoeroticism
There is a correlation between the extent to which a boy masturbates and his hostility toward his parents. (B243)

### Bed Wetting
Prolonged years of enuresis of childhood indicates hostility toward parents. (B283)

### Behavior Problems
Children who exhibit conduct problems are more likely to have parents who exhibit more hostility toward them than are children who do not have such problems. (S242)

### Child-Rearing Practices, Evaluation of
The greater the hostility of the child to parental discipline, the more likely he is to be hostile in other areas of parent-child interaction. (N063)

### Class
Lower-class paranoids are more likely to deny any hostility toward their parents than are middle-class paranoids. (S187)

### Dependency Anxiety
Dependency anxiety in girls correlates with parental hostility, especially the father's, but parallel relations for boys are largely insignificant. (B232)

### Marital Adjustment
A child is apt to become the focus of parental hostility when parents do not resolve tensions between themselves in other ways. (B204)

### Neurosis
Parents of normals are more likely to report hostility toward their sons and toward their own parents than are the parents of neurotics. (F110)

### Parent-Child Relations (Communication)
Hostility and misunderstandings are likely to result from limited communication of a nonreciprocal, as well as of a reciprocal, nature, as is characteristic of relationships between the autocratic parent and his offspring. (E100)

### Parent-Child Relations (Dominance)
There is no relationship between overly dominant parents and excessive hostility on the part of the child. (R100)

### Parent-Child Relations (Rejection)
Boys who felt rejected by their parents tended to be both hostile toward their parents and lacking in warmth for them. (B213)

There is a correlation between parental rejection of the child and hostility in the child toward the parents, although this may be either repressed or overt. (T086)

### Parent Loss
Traumatic deprivation during childhood (physical impairment, loss of a parent) may lead to the introjection of the parental figure and the projection upon it of the individual's aggressive hostility. (B278)

### Personality/Behavioral Problems
Those children who exhibit both behavioral and personality problems at home and at school are likely to have very hostile and punitive fathers, but relatively less hostile mothers; children with only behavioral problems tend to have fathers who are relatively less hostile and mothers who are relatively more hostile. (B232)

### Personality of Child (Hostility)
The greater the general hostility of the parent toward the child, the more likely the genesis of hostility in the child. (B232)

### Personality of Daughter (Dominance)
The more the father's hostility exceeds the mother's, the less the tendency for the daughter to become dominant (v. submissive). (B232)

### Personality Problems
Hostile-withdrawing behavior in the child tends to correlate with the degree of the father's hostility, physical punishment, and strictness; while anxious, tense, nervous behavior is associated with the degree of both the mother's and the father's hostility and physical punishment. (B232)

### Polygyny
Polygyny reduces parental counter-Oedipal hostilities toward the unborn when there are taboos on coitus after pregnancy; the hostility is greater when there is ideal polygyny but actual monogamy. (D071)

### Scapegoating
If parents' most serious unresolved problems are with persons of a given sex, a child chosen to represent family conflict will be of that sex. (B204)

The greater the extent to which the parents displace their difficulties onto the child, the more likely it is that lesser, secondary difficulties will arise (hostility against the parents from the child and community disapproval). (V033)

### Sex Status
Girls are more likely than boys to see their fathers, rather than their mothers, as hostile.

### Sex Taboo (Postpregnancy)
There is a relationship between unconscious parental hostility toward the unborn child (as a motive for abortion) and taboo on coitus during pregnancy and lactation in monogamous societies. (D071)

### Social Mobility Aspirations
Adolescents who have upward mobility aspirations show less hostility toward their parents than others do. (D077)

## PARENT-CHILD RELATIONS (INDIFFERENCE)
### X    Juvenile Delinquency
Parents who are casual or indifferent to their child are more likely than those who are concerned with the child's well-being to produce a delinquent. (S226)

### Self-Conception
Exceptional indifference on the part of either or both parents is associated with low self-esteem in the child. (R129)

Contrary to the original hypothesis, it is not the punitive response of parents to poor grades that is most closely related to low self-esteem, but the indifference; those who report indifferent parental responses have lower self-esteem than do those who report punitive responses as well as lower than those who report supportive responses. (R129)

The association between parental indifference and children's self-esteem is not an artifact of social class, religion, sex, or small town/city environment; it is not a question of whether the parents were strict with the child or whether he felt the punishment they gave was deserved or undeserved. (R129)

Students who felt a lack of parental interest, but who felt that the punishment they received in childhood was deserved, had lower self-esteem than did those who reported their parents to be interested, but who felt their punishment in childhood was generally undeserved. (R129)

## PARENT-CHILD RELATIONS (INDULGENCE)
### X    Education
The lower the parents' educational level, the more indulgent they are of their children. (B250)

### Mental Illness (Manic-Depressive)
Manic-depressives tend to have been overindulged in childhood. (C092)

### Mental Illness of Child
Parents are more likely to be more solicitous and responsive in their attitudes toward their psychotic children than toward their other children. (D064)

### Suicide
The suicide rate is higher among people who, as children, were "overpampered."

### Weaning
When parents are extremely fond of children and indulgent toward them, weaning occurs at a late period. (D025)

## PARENT-CHILD RELATIONS (INTERACTION)
### X    Acculturation
The greater the degree of acculturation, the less frequent and less intense is the interaction initiated by the parents. (B040)

### Aggression

In democratic homes, high parent-child interaction produces more aggression in the child than low parent-child interaction. (B266)

### Aspiration Level

Boys with high aspirations are more likely to have participated in shared activities with their parents than are boys with lower aspirations. (R117)

### Behavior Problems

If interaction between children and their parents is frustrated by the parents, maladaptive behavior (aggression, overdemanding, withdrawal, etc.) is likely to develop. (W137)

### Child-Rearing Practices (Permissiveness)

Promoting the child's independence is a characteristic of parents who participate in much activity with the child. Such parents also tend to be permissive in early feeding and toilet-training procedures, but to punish for misbehavior. (S010)

### Child-Rearing Practices (Punishment)

Punishing children for misbehavior is a characteristic of parents who are permissive in early feeding practices. Such parents also tend to participate in much activity with the child and to treat him casually. (S010)

### Class

Social withdrawal of adolescents from their families, as measured by leisure time spent away from the home, is greater in the lower class than in the middle class. (S219)

### Cohesion of Culture

The frequency and intensity of interaction between parents and children tends to be reduced with cultural disintegration. (B040)

### Conformity

In homes characterized by a high level of parental explanation of family decisions, high parent-child interaction produces greater nonconformity in the child than does low parent-child interaction. (B266)

### Duration of Marriage

The longer a wife has been married, the less frequently she will see her parents. (K089)

### Education

The lower the educational level of the parents, the less time they spend with their children. (B250)

### Employment of Mother

When mothers work, the contact between older parents and grown children is greater. (B312)

### Husband/Wife
### X  Husband-Wife Relations (Interaction)

Wives are more likely than husbands to see their parents two or three times a week; husbands are more likely to see their parents weekly or monthly. (W006)

### Identification

The degree to which the foster child identifies with his natural parents is correlated with, and dependent upon, the extent of his contact with them. (W149)

### Juvenile Delinquency

Delinquents tend to spend less time at home than do nondelinquents. (W152)

### Marital Adjustment

Emotionally disturbed marriages tend to be characterized by a minimal amount of common contact with the children. (V028)

### Parent-Child Relations

Parents who treat their children casually spend less time with their children than do parents who do not treat their children casually. (S010)

### Parent-Child-Relations (Communication)

In democratic homes, the lower the parent-child interaction, the more lethargic and spasmodic is the verbal exchange between the parents and child.

### Parent-Child Relations (Control)

When the child spends most of his time around the home, parental control is greater. (B033)

### Personality (Cruelty)

In democratic homes, high parent-child interaction produces a greater tendency for cruelty in the child than does low parent-child interaction.

### Personality (Curiosity)

In democratic homes, high parent-child interaction produces greater curiosity in the child than does low parent-child interaction. (B266)

### Personality (Emotionality)

In democratic homes, high parent-child interaction produces greater emotional excitability in the child than does low parent-child interaction.

In democratic homes, high parent-child interaction produces greater intensity of emotional response in the child than does low parent-child interaction. (B266)

### Personality (Impatience)

In democratic homes, high parent-child interaction produces greater impatience in the child than does low parent-child interaction.

### Personality of Child (Competitiveness)

In democratic homes, high parent-child interaction produces greater competitiveness in the child than does low parent-child interaction. (B266)

### Personality Problems/Social Adjustment

Among nursery-school children, those who have experienced a high level of parent-child interaction have the problem of management of hostility; children who have experienced a low level of parent-child interaction have the problem of achieving a satisfactory degree of social interaction.

### Personality (Quarrelsomeness)

In democratic homes, high parent-child interaction produces greater quarrelsomeness in the child than does low parent-child interaction. (B266)

### Personality (Responsibility)

The lower the adolescent's responsibility rating (based on teachers' ratings of his dependability in fulfilling obligations), the more likely is he to describe his parents as spending little time with him and avoiding his company. (B250)

### Personality (Security)

Children in foster homes are more secure if their parents are allowed to make occasional visits than if such visits do not occur. (B270)

### Scholastic Adjustment
Children from homes where there is a high level of parent-child interaction have a higher level of activity participation in nursery school than do children from homes where there is a low level of parent-child interaction. (B266)

### Sex Status
There is a tendency for each parent to interact relatively more with a child of the same sex. (This holds for American society; it is less so for German society.) (D063)

### Sibling Relations (Interaction)
Older men and women (50 years and up) visit their children or are visited by them significantly more often than they visit their siblings or other intimates. (C116)

## PARENT-CHILD RELATIONS (INTEREST)
### X   Mental Illness (Schizophrenia)
Fathers of schizophrenics are less likely to be interested in the patient than are mothers. (K125)

## PARENT-CHILD RELATIONS (INTIMACY)
### X   Parental Role (Discipline)
The parent who has the disciplinary role is less likely to have an intimate relationship with his or her children. (S153)

### Polygyny
The relationship of the mother to her children, in the polygamous family, is more intimate than that of the father to his children. (M041)

### Sex Status
Males are more intimately related to their fathers; females, to their mothers (seventh-twelfth-grade age-groups). (B286)

The relationship of parent to child is more likely to be intimate if they are of the same sex. (C023)

## PARENT-CHILD RELATIONS (NURTURANCE)
### X   Cognitive Development
Withdrawal of nurturance (support and affection) has greater association with effective performance on learning tasks than does consistent nurturance because the child is motivated to gain the assurance of the parents. (H184)

### Identification with Parents
The greater the degree of affectional nurturance and indulgence received by the child, the less likely it is that he will identify with the parent and internalize his values. (B243)

### Leadership
There is a positive relationship for sons and a negative relationship for daughters between parental nurturance and leadership abilities in the child (based on teachers' ratings of influence in group activities.) (B250)

### Personality (Apathy)
The lack of early mothering and affectionate nurturance, such as obtains for children raised in institutions, is correlated with and produces apathetic and nondependent personalities in later childhood. (K111)

### Religion (Role of Deities)
Nurturant parents or parental substitutes are more consistently found in societies with aggressive rather than benevolent deities. (L141)

## PARENT-CHILD RELATIONS (NURTURANCE/CONTROL)
### X   Sex Status
Boys are more likely than girls to judge whether one parent is more nurturant and controlling. (J026)

## PARENT-CHILD RELATIONS (OBEDIENCE)
### X   Aggression
Parents of aggressive adolescent boys report much more resistance to their discipline than do parents of control boys. (B213)

Nonaggressive boys are more likely than aggressive boys to obey their mothers rather than their fathers. (K103)

### Child-Rearing Practices (Kin)
The greater the contol of adults other than parents over the child (especially maternal grandmother), the less amenable is the child likely to be. (C117)

### Class
Middle-class children are more obedient of parental authority than are lower-class children. (S210)

## PARENT-CHILD RELATIONS (OEDIPAL)
### X   Mental Illness of Child
Unconscious reversal of the Oedipal situation by the parent is correlated with the onset of psychosis. (H192)

### Sexual Adjustment
According to the Oedipal hypothesis, the relationship of the child to the cross-sex parent determines his later heterosexual adjustment. (L133)

### Parent-Child Relations (Dominance)
There is no relationship between overly dominant parents and excessive disobedience on the part of the child. (R100)

## PARENT-CHILD RELATIONS OF HUSBAND (FAVORITISM)
### X   Mother-Child Relations (Dominance)
Husbands of maternally dominant mothers tend to have been favorite sons or obedient sons of dominant mothers or fathers. (L163)

## PARENT-CHILD RELATIONS (OVERPROTECTIVENESS)
### X   Education
The lower the parents' educational level, the more overprotective they are of their children. (B250)

### Mental Illness (Schizophrenia)
Parents of schizophrenics tend to be overprotective. (K093)

Schizophrenic patients are likely to perceive their parents as overprotective. (M164)

### Obesity
Obesity tends to be correlated with a parental environment of overprotectiveness and oversolicitousness. (F114)

## PARENT-CHILD RELATIONS (OVERPROTECTIVENESS/DOMINANCE)
### X   Mental Illness (Schizophrenia)
The most predominant undesirable relationship with the parents recorded in a study of schizophrenics, as contrasted with nonpsychiatric patients, was that of overprotection and dominance. (S247)

## PARENT-CHILD RELATIONS (OVERPROTECTIVENESS/REJECTION)
### X   Mental Illness of Child (Schizophrenia)
Rejection by one or both parents is more likely to be an

antecedent of schizophrenia in the child than is parental overprotection. (W147)

### Sex Status

A background of parental overprotection and/or rejection is more likely in the case of male schizophrenics than in that of females. (W147)

The parental overprotection and/or rejection antecedent to schizophrenia does not vary with respect to same or cross-sex parent. (W147)

## PARENT-CHILD RELATIONS, PARENTAL PERCEPTION OF
### X  Parent-Child Relations, Child's Perception of

The parental perception of the parent-child relationship does not correlate with the child's perception. (S250)

## PARENT-CHILD RELATIONS (PERMISSIVENESS)
### X  Age of Child

In families of older (high-school) youths, adolescents are more apt to view their parents' relations with them as democratic than as autocratic or permissive. (B323)

### Parental Role

When both roles in the child's rearing, the allowing and the forbidding, are united in one person, the two dangerous extremes of spoiling and repression are much harder to avoid. (W154)

### Personality Problems

A home characterized by excessive permissiveness and lack of restraint by the parents is more likely than others to produce the self-centered type of child. (W143)

### Power Structure of Family

Adolescents perceiving their mothers as dominant in both family and child-rearing practices are less likely to describe them as autocratic in dealing with them than they are to view them as equalitarian; and if they are older (high school, as opposed to junior high), they are more likely to view them as permissive or equalitarian than as autocratic. (B323)

In a wife-dominated (marital relations) home, older (high-school) boys and girls are as likely to perceive their fathers as autocratic as they are to perceive them as permissive or democratic; while in child rearing, younger (junior-high-school) adolescents are more than twice as likely to report autocratic fathers as they are permissive fathers. (B323)

In families where conjugal relations are equalitarian, adolescents are more apt to report their parents as either democratic or permissive in parent-child relations and less likely to say they are autocratic. This is less likely to be true in lower-class families. (B323)

When a wife is either dominant in the conjugal relationship or shares power with her husband, adolescents are more likely to perceive her as authoritarian than as either equalitarian or permissive in parent-child relations. (B323)

In middle-class homes where the father is the head of the family and the mother is the authority figure in child rearing, the mother is less likely to be viewed as autocratic than as democratic or permissive. (B323)

## PARENT-CHILD RELATIONS (PHYSICAL ABUSE)
### X  Aggression

Parents who severely abuse their children are more likely than others to react with hostility and with either physical or emotional attacks toward outsiders who are viewed as causing a family crisis. (Y043)

## PARENT-CHILD RELATIONS (POWER)
### X  Conformity

Adolescents who feel that their parents use coercive rather than legitimate measures in exerting their power are less likely to conform to rules of conduct when their parents are absent than are other adolescents. (E105)

### Husband-Wife Relations (Power)

The greater the spouse's residue of resentment from a power struggle, the greater is the likelihood that it will be expressed by the assertion of power over the children. (H213)

### Parent-Child Relations (Affection)

Adolescents perceiving their parents as using coercive rather than legitimate power over them are less apt to be highly attracted to their parents. (E105)

## PARENT-CHILD RELATIONS (PREFERENCE)
### X  Age of Child

The older the child, the more likely he will be to prefer one parent to the other. (B286)

As children grow older (five to nine years of age) there is an increase in mother preference and a decrease in father preference. (G117)

Children of all ages prefer their mothers to their fathers, except five-year-old girls, who prefer their fathers. (G117)

### Behavior Problems

Problem children are more likely to like parents of the opposite sex than are nonproblem children. (G117)

### Economic Role of Child

Each parent will tend to prefer, among his or her children, those who may later be expected to relieve his or her economic burden. (A030)

### Father-Child Relations (Interest)

The less interest the father has in the children, the more likely they are to prefer the mother. (L150)

### Juvenile Delinquency

If the child fails to win the parents' preferential affection by performing a model role, he will revert to delinquent behavior. (B033)

### Marital Adjustment

For younger children there is no correlation between the quality of the marriage and the child's attitudes toward the parents. With older children, however, the less adequate the marriage, the more likely it is that the mother will be preferred over the father. (L150)

### Maternal-Role Behavior

There is no direct correlation between maternal behavior and the mother's preference for one or the other parent during her childhood. (L165)

### Mental Illness in Family

Children in "sick" families are more likely to prefer the mother over the father than are those in healthier families, who like both parents nearly equally.

### Parent-Child Relations (Companionship)

The preference of the child tends to be for the parent who is most companionable and least censorious. Of the two factors, companionship seems the more weighty. (B033)

### Paternal Role (Economic)

The less adequate the father as a provider, the more likely it is that the daughter will be hostile toward him and prefer the mother and that the son will be less involved with him. (L150)

### Race Attitudes

Prejudiced men are less likely than unprejudiced to express a greater attachment for the mother than for the father and are more likely to repress feminine traits in their own behavior. (A061)

### Sex Status

Mothers are more preferred than fathers by both girls and boys; but a higher percentage of boys than of girls prefer their mothers, while a higher percentage of girls than of boys prefer their fathers. (W013)

Boys are more reluctant to criticize their mothers than their fathers.

Among five-to-eight-year-olds, boys more often express favorable reactions toward their mothers than toward their fathers; girls more often express favorable reactions toward their fathers than toward their mothers. (G117)

Both boys and girls prefer their mothers to their fathers. (G117)

Among schizophrenic children who do not report maternal domination in the family, both males and females are more likely to report preference for their mothers than for their fathers. (K114)

Irrespective of the sex of the subject, a higher proportion of subjects who express a preference for one or the other parent prefer the mother to the father. (W013)

Of those subjects who express a preference for one parent, males tend to prefer their mothers in greater proportion than do females; females tend to prefer their fathers in greater proportion than do males. (W013)

### Sex Status of Child

Girls are more likely to express a preference for one parent than are boys. (B286)

### Sex Status of Parent

In a high-school sample, children are more likely to prefer their fathers than their mothers. (C107)

In a college sample, children have a slight tendency to prefer their mothers over their fathers. (C107)

A higher proportion of both sexes profess no preference for either parent than profess preference for either the father or the mother. (W013)

### Stepchildren/Children

Stepchildren are more likely to express a preference for one parent or the other than are those children who live with both real parents. (B286)

## PARENT-CHILD RELATIONS (PROTECTIVE/ DEMOCRATIC)          X  I.Q.

The lower the I.Q. of the child, the more likely it is that the parents will be protective in their attitude toward

him; the higher the I.Q., the more likely that the mother will have democratic attitudes. (B259)

## PARENT-CHILD RELATIONS (PUNISHMENT)
### X  Institutional Care

Children who are deprived from their parents and are taken to institutions tend to regard the motive of this deprivation as being a punishment. (B270)

### Sex Status

Boys place a greater emphasis than girls upon curbing their activities to avoid parental punishment. (W138)

## PARENT-CHILD RELATIONS (PUNISHMENT/CONTROL)
### X  Superego Formation

Children who think mainly of whether an immoral act will be detected and punished are more likely to see their parents as being punitively assertive and controlling than are children who evaluate immoral behavior in terms of their own internal standards of right or wrong. (B275)

## PARENT-CHILD RELATIONS (REBELLION)
### X  Class

Lower-class mentally ill patients and their siblings tend to rebel against parental control more than do middle-class patients. (M061)

### Education

The more highly educated the parents, the more likely are their children to express opposition to parental authority. (B250)

### Employment of Mother

Children are less likely to be reported as rebellious by working mothers (of high-school background) than by nonworking mothers. (Y050)

### Identification with Family Roles

The less the parents identify with the cardinal role of family membership, the more likely is a revolt by the children during adolescence. (F106)

### Juvenile Delinquency

Juvenile delinquents are less submissive and more defiant toward parental authority than are nondelinquents.

### Mental Illness (Schizophrenia/Neurosis)

Neurotic girls are much more likely than schizophrenics to rebel against their parents' restrictions concerning their heterosexual activities. (M197)

### Physical Development

The later the physical maturation of the boy, the more likely it is that he will have rebellious attitudes toward his parents. (M172)

### Scapegoating

Repression of rebellious feelings against their fathers may cause married adults to release their aggressions against the weaker partner and children. (S219)

## PARENT-CHILD RELATIONS (RECREATION)
### X  Juvenile Delinquency

Parents of boys who are frequent juvenile offenders are less likely to take part in recreation with the boys than are parents of boys who have one offense.

### Social Mobility Aspirations

Boys who aspire upward are more likely to share leisure activities with parents (and to come from warm permissive family backgrounds). (L115)

# PARENT-CHILD RELATIONS (REJECTION)
## X    Achievement Aspiration
Persons having high achievement orientation tend to perceive their childhoods as unhappy and their relationships with their parents as involving emotional rejection. (S205)

## Achievement Motivation
Among male college students, the higher the achievement score (measured by T.A.T.), the more likely they are to perceive their parents, particularly their fathers, as rejecting.

The more rejected the child is by his parents (accompanied by a reduction in self-esteem and a turning to extrinsic sources for a sense of self-accomplishment), the greater will the child's desire for achievement be ego-motivated. (A059)

Persons having high achievement orientation tend to perceive their childhoods as unhappy and their relationships with their parents as involving emotional rejection. (S205)

## Age at Marriage
Girls who marry in their teens are more likely to have had unsatisfactory family relations (i.e., see their parents as nonloving, nonaccepting, find little satisfaction in their roles at home, rebel against their parents, etc.) than those who do not marry in their teens. (M231)

## Age of Child
Parents are more likely to reject their boys when they become adolescent than to reject them when they are small children. (M217)

## Aggression
(Reputed) aggression in boys is correlated with their rejection of one or both parent figures. (C098)

Children's aggression, in which the child shows violence, cruelty, malicious mischief, and open defiance of authority, correlates with parental rejection. (S183)

## Alcoholism
Alcoholics are more likely than nonalcholics to have rejected their parents, particularly their mothers, during childhood. (M195)

## Anxiety
There is a correlation between parental rejection and anxiety in the child. (T086)

## Aspiration Level
The more the child is rejected by his parents (consequently suffering a reduction in self-esteem), the more likely is his development of an aspirational level that is far in excess of realistic considerations. (A059)

People with high levels of aspiration are more likely to have had feelings of not being wanted by their parents when they were children than are people with low levels of aspiration. (D001)

Students who are high aspirers (as measured by Reissman Ambition Scale) are more likely to feel rejected by their parents than are those who are not high aspirers. (T095)

## Autoeroticism
There is no correlation between parental rejection of the son and the extent to which the boy masturbates. (B243)

## Bed Wetting
Neglected and/or rejected children are more likely than overprotected children to become enuretic. (B238)

## Behavior Problems
Those who are rejected by their parents show excessive activity and restlessness, make trouble in school, lack sustained application, and often show delinquent behavior.

Children who exhibit conduct problems are more likely to have parents who reject them more than do parents of nonproblem children. (S242)

## Child-Rearing Practices (Affection)
In the later years of childhood, the use of withdrawal of love as a method of discipline is correlated with parental rejection of the boy. (B243)

## Child-Rearing Practices (Consistency)
In broken homes inconsistent discipline is associated with rejection of the child. (K120)

## Child-Rearing Practices (Permissiveness)
Adolescents who have autocratic or laissez-faire and ignoring parents are more likely to report that they have felt unwanted. (E100)

Child-rearing structures which permit considerable participation in self-direction are least likely to provoke feelings of rejection in the adolescent. (E100)

## Child-Rearing Practices (Punishment)
There is a correlation between the use of deprivation of privileges as a method of discipline and an attitude of rejection and punitiveness toward the child on the part of the parents. (B243)

Parents who use ridicule as a technique of discipline are more likely to be rejecting of their sons than are those who do not. (B243)

Parents who use nagging and scolding as a means of discipline are more likely to be rejecting of the son than are those who do not. (B243)

## Class
Lower-class paranoid schizophrenics experience more feelings of rejection from their parents, particularly from their fathers, than do middle-class paranoid schizophrenics. (L155)

Children from lower-status families are more likely to reject their families than are children from higher-status backgrounds. (S274)

## Class Consciousness of Child
Among working-class elementary-school children, those who exhibit concern about their social status are more likely to reject their parents than are those who are not status conscious. (E102)

## Cognitive Development (Reading)
Rejected children are more likely to score low on reading ability.

## Criminality
There is a direct correlation between criminality and a family background in which the mother is rejecting and neglecting and the father is aggressive. (M164)

## Education
The lower the educational level of the parents, the more rejecting they are of their children. (B250)

### Emotional Problems

Dissociative behavior is more likely to result from conformity as an attempt to avoid parental rejection than from other types of internalization of parental attitudes. (W143)

### Ethnocentrism

Ethnocentric children are more likely to have parents who ignore them.

### Foster Home, Adjustment to

Children who failed to establish stable relationships in foster homes relate more stories of loneliness, rejection, and desertion of the child than do those who did establish them. They also lack a sense of family relationship. (W145)

### Homosexuality

Homosexuality is more likely to develop if the child perceives that his sex was a disappointment to his parents. (T104)

### Husband-Wife Relations (Jealousy)

The aversion of the husband or wife to children is more likely when the spouse wishes to maintain the monopoly of the love of the spouse or fears that a rival may displace him (or her). (B033)

### Identification with Family Roles

The less the parents identify with the cardinal role of family membership, the more likely it is that they will be rejected by their children. (F106)

### Identification with Like-Sex Parent

Rejection by the parent of the opposite sex tends to result in a strong identification with the parent of the same sex. (F085)

### Juvenile Delinquency

If the child feels rejected he may engage in disapproved behavior in an attempt to achieve an adequate place in the family through drawing attention to himself. (B033)

The child who was unwanted by his parents is more likely than the wanted child to become delinquent. (B238)

Parental rejection is a factor predisposing toward unsocialized aggressive behavior (which is defined as showing assaultive tendencies, starting fights, cruelty, defiance of authority, inadequate guilt feelings, etc.). (J024)

Maternal rejection is more important than paternal rejection in the development of unsocialized aggressive behavior. (J024)

The data support the hypothesis that rejection of parents by children is related to delinquent behavior; when both parent and child reject one another, delinquent behavior is still more likely. (N052)

There is a correlation between a child's rejection of the parents and delinquency in the child. (N063)

There is a correlation between parental rejection and delinquency in the child. (N063)

Fathers of delinquents are more likely than mothers to be rejecting. (O033)

Juvenile delinquent boys are more likely to feel rejected by both parents than are nondelinquents. (S229)

### Juvenile Delinquency (Running Away)

Rejection by parents is more common among children (delinquent) who run away than among children (delinquent) who do not run away. (F093)

### Leadership

Parental rejection and neglect are negatively related to leadership in the child (based on teachers' ratings on influence in group activities). This is especially true of the parent of the same sex as the child. (B250)

### Marital Adjustment

Parental rejection of children is associated with these family characteristics: one parent regards the other as clearly inferior, there is greater neglect of marital responsibilities, and a greater likelihood of marital infidelity.

There is an association between marital conflict and nonacceptance of the child. (R100)

### Mental Illness

Parents are more likely to have rejected than to have overprotected the mentally ill individual during childhood. (S187)

### Mental Illness of Child

Parents reject the psychotic child more than do his siblings, both as a member of the family and as an individual. (D064)

### Mental Illness of Child (Autism)

Since parents of autistic children are more likely to be rejecting and overintellectual rather than outgoing and warm, the children fail to develop appropriate ego strength. (C109)

### Mental Illness of Child (Schizophrenia)

Ego weakness of a schizophrenic child is correlated with introjection of parental rejection of the child in process of early identification with a parent. (L114)

### Mental Illness (Schizophrenia)

Schizophrenics see parental figures as cold or rejecting. (H186)

Schizophrenia is more likely to occur where the parent of the same sex is distant and rejecting, while the parent of the opposite sex exhibits a high degree of identification. (S260)

### Moral Beliefs of Child

The more a child rejects and deprecates his parents, the greater is the likelihood that he will experience a loss of moral orientation. (T099)

### Obesity

Obesity is correlated with parental dissatisfaction with the sex of the child. (B218)

### Occupational Choice

There is a correlation between the accepting/rejecting nature of parental attitudes experienced during childhood and the adult choice of a person-oriented/object-oriented occupation. (G135)

There is no correlation between parental attitudes and selection of occupation in adult life. (G135)

### Parent-Child Relations (Hostility)

Boys who felt rejected by their parents tended to be both hostile toward their parents and lacking in warmth for them. (B213)

There is a correlation between parental rejection of the child and hostility in the child toward the parents, although this may be either repressed or overt. (T086)

### Paternal/Maternal Role

Mothers tend to reject their children more than fathers do.

Sociopathic patients report behavior that could be regarded as rejection more frequently for fathers than for mothers. (O032)

### Personality (Cruelty)

Rejection of the child by his parents may lead to cruelty in the child in later years. (T085)

### Personality Problems of Child

Punishing and rejecting parents tend to produce fear, hostility, overaggressiveness, distrust, irresponsibility, and other antisocial behavior in the child. (D062)

### Personality (Responsibility)

Parental rejection and neglect are negatively related to responsibility in the child (based on teachers' ratings of dependability in fulfilling obligations). (B250)

### Physical Development

The later the physical maturation of the boy, the more likely it is that he will perceive his parents as highly dominating and rejecting. (M172)

### Political Attitudes

Radical political opinions are more common among people who felt that their parents rejected them as children.

### Power Structure of Family

Perceived maternal dominance is positively related to adolescent rejection of parents. (E102)

### Recidivism

Habitual criminals tend to have had rejecting parents. (M199)

### Scholastic Achievement

Adolescents who are doubtful of their own acceptance by their family seek a more secure status by means of academic (over) achievement. (M060)

### Scholastic Adjustment

The mother of a child with school phobia tends to react to the child's striving for independence and self-gratification with feelings of personal rejection and hostility. (E095)

Parental rejection is not related to "school phobia" (i.e., refusal to attend school) in the child. (L143)

### Self-Conception of Child

The more rejected the child is by his parents, the less able he is to develop self-esteem. (A059)

If the father rejects the child, the child will not become self-rejecting; if the mother rejects the child, it is likely that the child will become self-rejecting. (C112)

### Self-Conception of Parent

Parents who are self-rejecting are more likely to reject their children than are parents who are not self-rejecting (rejection measured in therapy interviews). (C112)

### Sex Status

Girls are more likely to feel rejected by their parents than boys are. (B286)

Girls report fathers are more rejecting, neglecting, and ignoring than mothers are to a greater degree than boys do. (D069)

### Sex Status of Child

Daughters show more evidence of being unwanted by their parents than sons do. (W013)

### Sibling Rivalry

The rejection of the child by its parents at the birth of a new baby leads to the manifestation of intense hostility and rivalry directed against the new arrival. (B033)

### Social Adjustment

The greater the rejection of the child by his parents, the more likely will the child be to isolate himself emotionally from others. (A059)

Parental rejection of the child may cause the child to fear rejection from others and inhibit his establishment of adequate relationships with others. (T086)

### Social Adjustment of Child

Personality maladjustment (in the child, resulting from the child-parent relationship) tends to be generalized in the child's relationship with others (e.g., consistently rejecting and punishing parents produce fear in the child who, in turn, generalizes this fear to other parental figures). (D062)

### Sociopathic Personality

Failure to supervise, repudiation by the parent, and desertion are more common among patients with sociopathic behavior disorder, than among those with other diseases and with those with no disease. Nonsupport and negligence are more common among parents of those diagnosed sociopathic personalities, as compared with parents of the no-disease group, but not among parents of patients with other psychiatric diseases. (O032)

There is an association between rejection by the parent and development of sociopathic personality in the child. (O032)

Lack of parental love and interest and excessive leniency are not related to the later development of sociopathic personality in the child. (O032)

### Stepparent-Child Relations

The more the child rejects the parent who is gone, the more steadily will he adjust to a new parent; the greater the idealization of the parent out of the home, the greater the barrier against accepting a new parent. (B286)

## PARENT-CHILD RELATIONS (RESENTMENT)
### X   Aggression

Hyperaggressive adolescents are more likely than "normals" to resent whatever demands their parents make on them. (B275)

## PARENT-CHILD RELATIONS (RESPECT)
### X   Occupational Aspirations of Son

Among lower-class sons, there is very little relation between the level of occupational aspirations and the degree of parental respect they receive for their ideas and opinions. (E102)

There is a positive relationship between parental respect for the ideas and opinions of the son and the level of his occupational aspirations. (E102)

## PARENT-CHILD RELATIONS (SADISM)
### X   Juvenile Delinquency
Severe delinquency is frequently associated with parental sadism. (B291)

## PARENT-CHILD RELATIONS (SATISFACTION)
### X   Husband-Wife Relations (Role Conflict)
In families in which the degree of consensus between husband and wife on domestic values is high, the extent of role tension in the marriage varies directly with the amount of disagreement between the parents on satisfaction with specific activities of the child. (F116)

### Value Consensus
In families in which the role tension of husband and wife is low, the degree of consensus on domestic values between husband and wife correlates with their agreement on satisfaction with specific activities of their child. (F116)

In families in which the role tension of husband and wife is high, there is no relationship between the degree of the couple's consensus on domestic values and the amount of agreement between them on satisfaction with specific activities of their child. (F116)

## PARENT-CHILD RELATIONS (SECURITY)
### X   Personality Problems
If a child between the ages of five and eight has a secure parental relationship, he is much less likely to develop serious and permanent personality disorders than if his relationship is an insecure one. (B270)

## PARENT-CHILD RELATIONS (SEPARATION)
### X   Emotional Problems of Child
The more intensive the separation of child from parent (as in a residential as opposed to a day nursery), the greater the emotional imbalance of the child. (S265)

Parents (of Italian- and Irish-American background) of emotionally disturbed children are more likely than those of normal children to contrive physical separations through family routines (working hours, recreation). (V031)

### Juvenile Delinquency (Running Away)
Delinquent children who run away from home are much more likely to have histories of parent-child separation than are delinquent children who do not run away from home. (F093)

### Surrogate Parent
Children with many parental figures are more able to tolerate separation because they trust more people than do children with fewer parental figures.

## PARENT-CHILD RELATIONS (SEX)
### X   Parent-Child Relations (Conflict)
A great preoccupation of the parents with the sex lives of the children increases the potential for conflict between parents and children. (G156)

### Personality
Disruption of libidinous relations to the parents is a causal factor in changing the personality of stepchildren. (B286)

## PARENT-CHILD RELATIONS (SEX PREFERENCE)
### X   Sex Status of Parent
Regardless of the sex of the parent, a higher proportion of parents who show a preference for children of one sex or the other prefers males over females. (W013)

Of those parents who express a preference for children of one sex or the other, fathers tend to prefer their daughters in greater proportion than do mothers; mothers tend to prefer their sons in greater proportion than do fathers. (W013)

Preferences of fathers tend to be more evenly distributed between sons and daughters than are the preferences of mothers. (W013)

### Sibling Status
Parents tend to prefer male, as opposed to female, children as their only or first child. (H181)

## PARENT-CHILD RELATIONS, STABILITY OF
### X   Parent-Child Relations (Closeness)
If the parent-child relationship is strong initially, the strength of the relationship tends to persist. (Z001)

## PARENT-CHILD RELATIONS (SUPPORT)
### X   Age of Child
In adolescence the child is less likely to turn to his parents for help and support than to other adults or peers. (J023)

### Aspiration Level
Male adolescents who are given high aspirational encouragement from parents are more apt to possess higher levels of ambition than are those given low parental motivation. (B313)

## PARENT-CHILD RELATIONS (VALUE CONSENSUS)
### X   Parent-Child Relations (Warmth)
The greater the warmth and acceptance the college student shows for his parents, the more likely it is that his ideological system will be similar to that of his parents. (C107)

## PARENT-CHILD RELATIONS (WARMTH)
### X   Achievement Motivation
Parents of sons with high achievement motivation give more psychological support and display more warmth or generally positive affection toward the sons in an achievement situation than do parents of boys with low achievement motivation. (M246)

### Adult-Role Behavior
The greater the degree of parental warmth, the more likely it is that the rule-enforcing behavior (either restrictive or permissive) of an individual will resemble that of his parents. (M179)

### Child-Rearing Practices (Giving Reasons)
There is a correlation between parental use of reasoning as a technique of control and parental attitudes of warmth, nurturance, and acceptance. (B243)

### Child-Rearing Practices (Punishment)
Spanking is most effective if applied by the parent who is warmer toward the child. (S191)

### Identification with Parents
There is a curvilinear relationship between parental warmth and the extent of the child's identification. (B243)

Identification of preschool children with parents correlates with the mother's warmth and acceptance and her use of loss of love as a means of control and, for boys, with acceptance by the father. (M183)

Frustration resulting from absence of parental love,

warmth, and support is associated with positional identification (identification without adoption of specific characteristics of the model) as against personal identification. (S240)

### Incest (Father-Daughter)
Where father-daughter incest occurs, the father is apt to have had little warmth or understanding from his own parents. (K091)

### Ordinal Position
In two-child families there is no difference between the children in the amount of parental warmth shown to them. (S191)

### Parent-Child Relations (Value Consensus)
The greater the warmth and acceptance the college student shows for his parents, the more likely it is that his ideological system will be similar to that of his parents. (C107)

### Paternal/Maternal Role
The father is more likely than the mother to be warm and solicitous with his daughters. (B250)

There is no significant difference in parental warmth between mothers and fathers of disturbed children. (P067)

The mother, as opposed to the father, is the chief source of warmth and affection for the child in the home. (P067)

### Personality Adjustment of Child
Children reared without a warm and affectionate parent-child relationship (e.g., in an orphanage) tend to acquire attitudes of distrust and defensiveness. (D062)

### Personality of Child (Ego-Strength)
The degree of parental emotional warmth and support is negatively correlated with ego weakness and introversion in the child. (S221)

### Power Structure of Family
The adolescent perceives one of his parents as his principal source of support most often when he sees the parent as sharing leadership responsibility with his spouse in marital and parental relations, next most often when the spouse is perceived as dominating in these areas, and least often when the parent is seen as dominant. (B323)

In wife-dominated families, adolescents do not think of their parents as supportive as often as in equalitarian or in husband-dominated families. (B323)

Whichever parent is perceived as the child-rearing authority is also more likely to be viewed as supportive. (B323)

### Scholastic Achievement of Daughter
Parents of daughters with high college achievement records were less indifferent to their daughters than were parents of low college achievers (as measured on the Teahan Ignoring Subscale). (T103)

### Sex-Role Model
Warm relations with the like-sex parent are associated with like-sex adult-role model choice by the children. (H201)

### Size of Family
Parent-child relations are warmer in small families than in large families. (E102)

### Social Adjustment
The degree of parental emotional warmth and support is negatively correlated with social withdrawal in the child. (S221)

### Socialization, Effectiveness of
Children whose parents are warm and nurturant are more likely to resist temptation than are those whose parents are not. (G120)

## PARENT-DAUGHTER RELATIONS
### X   Affinal Relations
The husband's adjustment to in-laws is independent of the wife's adjustment to her parents. (S011)

## PARENT-DAUGHTER RELATIONS (CLOSENESS)
### X   Employment of Mother
Daughters of working mothers do not feel as close to their parents as do daughters of mothers who do not work. (Y047)

## PARENT-DAUGHTER RELATIONS
### (DEPRIVATION)  X   Maternal Overprotectiveness
Extreme deprivation in the mother's childhood is a cause of later overprotectiveness toward her own child. (B272)

Maternal overprotection is more likely to occur if one or both of the woman's parents have died during her childhood. (L163)

## PARENT-DAUGHTER RELATIONS (REJECTION)
### X   Social Mobility of Daughter
Among middle-class, unmarried, mobile career women, a higher proportion have experienced partial rejection by parents who showed favoritism for a sibling, more than among the nonmobile women in the sample. (L115)

## PARENT LOSS                         X   Alcoholism
Loss of a parent in early childhood is more frequently a factor in the history of female than of male alcoholics. (L159)

Since female alcoholics are more likely than males to have lost a parent in early childhood and are thus more prone to psychotic disturbance, their prognosis is less favorable than that of male alcoholics. (L159)

### Behavior Problems
Children suddenly faced with the absence of parents will try to rectify the situation by seeking the return of the parents through finding an adult substitute. (H239)

### Cognitive Development
Children reared without normal parental relationships demonstrate a deficient time sense. (G128)

Children reared without normal parental relationships demonstrate a meagerness of imagination. (G128)

### Emotional Problems of Child
In children over one year of age, separation from family members causes physical as well as emotional problems, particularly increased dependency needs and regression in learned skills (e.g., feeding self, walking, speaking, and bladder control).

### I.Q.
Children who are raised without parents or adequate parent surrogates yield a significantly lower score on the Stanford-Binet I.Q. Test than do normal children. (B270)

### Juvenile Delinquency
The earlier the age at separation from the parents, the higher the frequency of running away (from reform school). (S182)

There is no significant correlation for girls between the ages at which they are separated from their parents and number of court offenses. (S182)

The child who is made to fear the loss of parents (through death, abandonment) is more likely than is the child who feels secure about his parents to become delinquent. (S226)

### Maternal Overprotectiveness
Maternal overprotection is more likely to occur if one or both of the woman's parents have died during her childhood. (L163)

### Mental Illness
When subjective factors (recalled unfavorable attitudes and/or treatment of the child by the parents) and objective factors (any kind of physical separation) are viewed together, the relationship between subjective factors and subsequent tendencies toward mental disturbance holds only in cases where physical separation also occurred. (C121)

Mental illness of the parents is a significant cause of deprivation among patients suffering from dementia praecox and manic-depressive psychosis. (O034)

There is no significant relationship between either the age at which deprivation occurred or the parent was lost and the subsequent mental health or mental illness of the child. (O034)

The incidence of various types of psychiatric abnormalities is almost identical among the siblings of both deprived and nondeprived patients. (O034)

The incidence of dementia praecox is unrelated to known external stresses or deprivation. (O034)

### Mental Illness of Child
In the lower class, "total deprivation" (complete loss of parent) is a more important determinant of subsequent mental disorder in the child than it is in the middle or upper classes; whereas "partial physical deprivation" (parents sick or mother working) is a more important determinant of subsequent disorder than is total deprivation in the middle and upper classes. (C121)

### Mental Illness (Schizophrenia)
Schizophrenic women have lost parents at a significantly earlier age than have women without schizophrenia. (H176)

It is probably *who* replaces a lost parent which determines the development of schizophrenia, rather than the loss itself. Loss of the mother is most conducive to the development of schizophrenia; replacement of the mother is more important than replacement of the father. (H176)

The incidence of parental deprivation is not higher among schizophrenic patients than among normal subjects or among patients suffering from other types of psychosis. (O034)

There is a correlation between loss of one or both parents by death or separation and schizophrenia in the child. (W147)

Schizophrenics are more likely to have experienced the loss of a mother than of a father. (W147)

There is a correlation between loss of the same-sex parent and schizophrenia in the child. (W147)

Loss of the father is more likely to be an antecedent factor to schizophrenia in the child than is loss of the mother. (W147)

Parental loss is more likely to have occurred in the case of male schizophrenics than in the case of female schizophrenics. (W147)

There is no relationship between age at which a parent was lost by death or separation and schizophrenia in the child. (W147)

### Neurosis
The incidence of parental deprivation is higher among psychoneurotic and psychopathic personalities than among psychotics and "normals." (O034)

### Ordinal Position (of Alcoholics)
Loss of a parent was more frequent among last-born alcoholics than among those of first or middle rank. (L159)

### Parent-Child Relations (Hostility)
Traumatic deprivation during childhood (physical impairment, loss of a parent) may lead to the introjection of the parental figure and the projection upon it of the individual's aggressive hostility. (B278)

### Peer Relations
Adolescents from homes where one parent is deceased are more likely to strive for attention from the opposite sex than are adolescents from families where both parents are living.

Separation of the child from his parents or parental substitutes leads the child to closer associations with other children.

### Personality Adjustment
Minnesota Multiphase Personality Inventory data on a subsample were classified into subgroups according to age and type of parent loss and were compared with a sample of the general clinic population. No significant group differences were obtained. (A070)

The older a child at the time of the death of the mother, the less serious personality damage is likely to be done. (K161)

### Personality of Child (Dependency)
Children reared without normal parental relationships develop clinging dependence upon appropriate figures in later life. (G128)

### Personality Problems
Children reared without normal parental relationships develop an exaggerated interest in the self. (G128)

### Personality Problems (Apathy)
Children reared without normal parental relationships develop qualities of resignation and apathy. (G128)

### Personality Problems (Conflict)
Children between the ages of three and five who are deprived of their parents and are not provided with adequate parent surrogates suffer acute internal conflict as a result of having developed excessive desires for affection and excessive desires for revenge. (B270)

### Personality Problems of Child

Children who experience loss of a parent during childhood are more likely to develop psychiatric illness or character defects in later life than are children who have not been separated from a parent. (B269)

Loss of a parent during one of the first five years of the child's life is more likely to cause psychopathology in later life than is parental loss after the age of five. (B269)

Loss of the mother during the first five years of the child's life is a more significant factor in subsequent psychopathology of the child than is loss of the father. (B269)

After the child reaches the age of five and until early adolescence, death of the father is as likely to be an antecedent of psychopathology in the child as is death of the mother. (B269)

The incidence of parental loss is significantly higher among female than among male sociopaths; among neurotics and controls no sex differential was found. (G140)

There is no significant difference in frequency of parental loss among neurotics and controls. (G140)

### Physical Development

If a child suffers the deprivation of one or both parents, he will not grow (physically) as much as if he had both parents. (B270)

### Psychosomatic Illness

Among children whose families have been broken by death, there is no relationship between religion and likelihood of the child to have many psychosomatic symptoms. (R129)

### Scholastic Adjustment

Children who are removed from their parents while they are between the ages of 5 and 16 are less able to concentrate on schoolwork than are children with normal parent relationships. (B270)

"School phobia" (refusal to attend school), is not associated with absence of either parent during the child's early years. (L143)

### Social Adjustment

Children between the ages of 3 and 5 who are deprived of their parents and not provided with adequate parent surrogates demonstrate unfavorable social attitudes as a result of having developed desires for affection and desires for revenge. (B270)

### Social Adjustment of Child

Separated boys, especially those separated early in life, demonstrate poorer adjustment than do the non-separated on the General Adjustment Rating. (S182)

### Sociopathic Personality

Among those who suffered parental loss, a much higher proportion of sociopaths than of neurotics were deprived before the age of five. (G140)

Sociopaths are much more likely to have suffered parental loss than are neurotics or controls. (G140)

### Suicide

Attempted suicides are more likely to have suffered the loss of a parent before the age of 15 than are nonsuicides. (G154)

Attempted suicides who had lost one or more parents had lost the parent(s) at an earlier age than had nonsuicides who had also lost one or more parents. (G154)

The suicide rate among adult orphans is higher than among people with parents living. (S078)

### Superego Formation

Separation of the child from his parents or from satisfactory parental substitutes leads to a lessening in ego strength or to incompletely developed superego. (B270)

Children who are deprived of their parents and are not provided with adequate parent surrogates suffer greatly impaired ego and superego development if this deprivation takes place for long periods before the child is two years old. (B270)

Children who are deprived of their parents and are not provided with adequate parent surrogates after the ages of three, four, or five do not suffer the same degree of impairment of ego and superego formation as do children who undergo the same type of deprivation at earlier ages. (B270)

### PARENT/PEER RELATIONS          X   Illegitimacy

As compared with single, never-pregnant females, all the unwed mothers reported that they were influenced more favorably by their mothers during childhood and by their peers during high school. (V027)

### Social Mobility Aspirations

A higher percentage of the working-class boys with aspirations and of the ambitious middle-class boys than of the unamibitious middle-class or of the nonaspiring working-class boys had been advised by one or both parents to enter the professions. (S077)

When parents advise high aspirations and the peer group does not, a higher percentage of both working-class and middle-class boys aspire to high-status occupations than when the peer group does and parents do not. (S077)

### PARENT-SON RELATIONS
#### X   Father-Son Relations (Affection)

Sons who have received insufficient paternal affection are more likely to feel unjustly treated by their parents than are sons who have received adequate paternal affection. (M204)

### PARENT-SON RELATIONS (AFFECTION)
#### X   Father-Son Relations (Affection)

Sons who have received insufficient paternal affection are less likely to feel loved by their parents than are sons who have received adequate paternal affection. (M204)

### Scholastic Achievement

Boys who are under achievers are more likely than boys who are high achievers to describe their parents as approving, trusting, and affectionate. (E102)

### PARENT-SON RELATIONS (CONTROL)
#### X   Scholastic Achievement

Boys who are under achievers are more likely than high achievers to describe their parents as nonpressuring, nonrestrictive, and noncoercive. (E102)

### PARENT-SON RELATIONS (DEPRIVATION)
#### X   Social Mobility Aspirations

There is no relationship between mobility aspirations of males and their perception of their relations with their parents as being depriving. (R101)

## PARENT-SON RELATIONS (WARMTH)
### X    Peer Relations
Warm father-son relations are related to satisfactory peer relations (i.e., outgoing peer-group behavior, initiation of friendship, influence in peer relations, and low use of physical force). Warm mother-son relations are not related to satisfactory peer relations. (H201)

### Personality of Child (Self-Confidence)
Among boys, warm father-son relations are associated with a high degree of self-confidence in the son regarding his abilities; warm mother-son relations are associated with a low degree of self-confidence regarding abilities. (H201)

## PARENT/SPOUSE
### X    Mental Illness, Attitude Toward
Mental illness and resultant behavioral deviations are more likely to be tolerated by parents than by the marital partner. (S245)

## PARENT/SPOUSE, SIMILARITY OF
### X    Mate Selection
Physical resemblance between the mate and a parent is not as frequent or as marked as are resemblances in attitude and temperament. (C023)

## PARENTAL ATTITUDES
### X    Parental Attitudes, Perception of
College students are likely to have attitudes closer to their perceptions of their parents' attitudes than to their parents' actual attitudes (as measured by the California F-Scale). (W144)

### Personality Problems of Child
Parental attitudes (PARI) have no significant relationship with the symptom type of the maladjusted child or with the maladjustment or normalcy of the child. (Z011)

## PARENTAL ATTITUDES (CONSENSUS)
### X    Behavior Problems
Adolescent boys who show behavior problems are more likely than normal boys to perceive disparities between the attitudes and behavior of their two parents. (V038)

## PARENTAL ATTITUDES, PERCEPTION OF
### X    Parental Attitudes
College students are likely to have attitudes closer to their perceptions of their parents' attitudes than to their parents' actual attitudes (as measured by the California F-Scale). (W144)

### Sex Status
Female college students are more aware than male students of their parents' attitudes (parents' responses to California F-Scale compared to students' views of parental responses). (W144)

## PARENTAL IMAGE
### X    Mental Illness (Schizophrenia)
Parents of normals are more likely than are parents of neurotics or of schizophrenics to have definite images of parental figures. (F110)

## PARENTAL ROLE    X    Age of Child
With increasing age, children increasingly attribute dominance and punitive characteristics to the same-sex parent. (H180)

### Child-Rearing Practices (Dependency)
Children are likely to report their cross-sex parents as allowing more autonomy than their same-sex parents. (D069)

### Conformity
When the mother is nurturant and nondisciplining and the father is disciplining and nonnurturant, the child will be likely to violate cultural norms when authority forces are absent. (S216)

### Dependency
There is a correlation between the degree of parental independence from family life and the degree of independence of the child from the family. (F106)

### Grandparent-Grandchild Relations (Closeness)
Closeness between grandparent and grandchild can occur only when the grandparent has given up his or her parental role, thus being disassociated from family and authority. (C116)

### Husband-Wife Relations (Closeness)
Marital ties that result from mutual dependency are strongest during the time of child rearing; marital ties that result from similarity are strongest when there are no children or after the children are grown. (C116)

### Identification
The child identifies with the parent who is the source of its most severe frustrations.

### Mental Illness (Schizophrenia)
Parents (of schizophrenic children) who demonstrate a lack of spontaneity and pleasure are less likely than are parents who show appropriate satisfaction to function adequately (with respect to communication between marital partners, the mother's decisiveness, interest in physical environment, direction, and organization). (B240)

### Parent-Child Relations (Ambivalence)
Ambivalence toward a parent is likely to be greater if he or she assumes both the supportive and disciplinary role. (W154)

### Parent-Child Relations (Permissiveness)
When both roles in the child's rearing, the allowing and the forbidding, are united in one person, the two dangerous extremes of spoiling and repression are much harder to avoid. (W154)

### Religion (Role of Deities)
Conceptions of supernatural beings correspond to and are projections of the child's parental (or parent-surrogate) images. (S036)

### Sex-Role Identification
The greater uniformity of the mother role, compared to the masculine occupational role, makes more likely the direct emulation of the mother by the girl than of the father by the son. (B234)

## PARENTAL-ROLE ADJUSTMENT    X    Abortion
There is a low correlation between the abortion of the first child and the parents' reluctance to grow up. (D071)

### Adult-Child-Role Definition
The greater the emphasis on the status disparity between adult and child, the more difficult will be the adjustment to adult status upon entering the status of parent. (D071)

### Age
The older the person, the less likely is he to report feelings of inadequacy in the parental role. (G126)

### Broken Home
Among those who are married, persons coming from families in which there has been divorce, separation, or a death of one or both parents are more likely to mention their children as the most positive aspect of their marriage than are those who were raised in families that remained intact. (G126)

### Child-Rearing Attitudes
Parents who report greater feelings of adequacy in the parental role are more likely than are parents who feel more inadequate to identify physical care or material problems as sources of concern in child rearing. (G126)

### Education
The higher the educational level, the more likely are persons to feel inadequate concerning their lack of tolerance for the child's behavior; women are more likely to express this inadequacy than are men. (G126)

The higher the educational level, the more likely are persons to feel inadequate in the affective child-parent relationship; men are more likely to express these affective difficulties than are women. (G126)

### Identification with Parent
Failure of the parents to provide adequately for the child leads to serious problems of satisfactory identification of the child with a parental figure. (M197)

Identification is positively related to the parents' self-esteem and confidence in child rearing. (R098)

### I.Q./Creativity
Parents of highly intelligent children (Binet) are more likely to be satisfied with their own child-rearing practices than are the parents of highly creative children (Guilford-Cattell). (G132)

### Parent-Child Relations
The degree of satisfaction felt in the parental role is not related to the types of problems experienced in relations with the child nor to the types of inadequacies felt by the parent in dealing with the child. (G126)

### Parental-Role Definition
Parents who see themselves in a traditional parental role tend to find positive satisfactions in children; those who evaluate their adequacy in terms of newer parental roles (e.g., interpersonal warmth or tolerance) tend to express negative or neutral parental satisfaction. (G126)

### Parental-Role Satisfaction
There is no association between the degree of satisfaction with parenthood and different kinds of expressed parental inadequacies. (G126)

### Parenthood, Attitude Toward
The greater the denial of feelings of inadequacy in the parental role, the more likely, in general, is the parent to have a lower degree of introspection about parenthood. (G126)

### Personality of Child
Parents who experienced neglect, deprivation, or rejection by their parents in their youth are likely to be deficient in the capacity to care for their children and, consequently, to produce children who mature into persons much like themselves. (B270)

### Sex Status
Women are more likely than men, at some time, to feel inadequate as parents. (G126)

Men tend to feel inadequate because of not spending enough time with their children; women tend to feel inadequate because of exasperation and loss of temper with the child. (G126)

There is no difference between men and women in their degree of felt inadequacy about emotional relations with their children or about tolerance. (G126)

### Sex Status of Parent
Among those persons who are satisfied with the parental role, men are more likely to feel inadequacies pertaining to physical material provision for the child; women are more likely to feel inadequacies related to the parent-child affective relationship. (G126)

### Size of Family
There is no relationship between family size and feelings of inadequacy in the parental role. (G126)

## PARENTAL ROLE, ATTITUDE TOWARD
### X Marital Adjustment
Marital adjustment is associated with the desire of both the husband and wife to have children. (B033)

There is a direct relation between the desire for children and marital adjustment. (K161)

Marital conflict correlates with the father's attitudes of rejection of family life, justification of quarreling, and a rejection of interaction with the child. (N053)

### Sex Status
Men are more likely to emphasize parental satisfactions that come from influencing their children or satisfactions involving achievement, ambitions, and accomplishments; women are more likely to emphasize satisfactions derived from increased love, affection, and companionship with the child. (G126)

## PARENTAL-ROLE BEHAVIOR    X Age of Child
The older the child, the more likely are the parents to share the responsibility of disciplining the child and of guiding the child's play activities. (G133)

### Employment of Mother
Entertaining the child in the late afternoon is more likely to be shared by both parents when the wife is employed full time than when she is a full-time homemaker. (G133)

Staying home with the children during part of the weekend is more likely to be shared when the wife is a full-time homemaker than if she is employed full time. (G133)

### Incest
The failure of a parent to fulfill his normal role may cause an incestuous link to develop between the child of his own sex and the other parent or to cause homosexuality in the child.

### Juvenile Delinquency
There is a positive relationship between unethical parental behavior and delinquent adolescent behavior. (N057)

A son's delinquency correlates with inadequate supervision by the mother and with overstrict discipline by the father, independently of employment/nonemployment of the mother. (S265)

### Kin Terminology
The presence of a single, alternate term for parents indicates patterns of behavioral similarity between the father and mother. (F046)

### Marital Stability
The greater the instability of domestic unions, consensual or legal, the less likely is the fulfillment of parental roles. (S211)

### Mental Illness (Schizophrenia)
Families of children with behavior disorders or schizophrenia caused by organic damage are more likely than are families of children with psychogenic schizophrenia to function better (with respect to care, interest in physical environment, communication between marital partners, mother's decisiveness, and appropriate satisfaction with self and children). (B240)

### Parent-Child Relations (Closeness)
The relationship between parent and child will be stronger if the parent plays a prominant role in the socialization of the child. (H137)

### Psychosomatic Illness
Inversion or imbalance in parental roles is a cause of duodenal ulceration in the child. (P078)

### Superego Formation
The contradictory patterns of maternal indulgence and stern paternal severity are more likely than other family constellations to produce distortion in the superego (conscience) of the delinquent child. (B238)

The internalization of moral behavior is likely to be greater when socialization and nurturance are combined in one agent (parents or peer group) than when the two functions are relatively separate. (L158)

The greater the extent to which nurturance and discipline are combined in the same parent, the greater the likelihood of value internalization. (S216)

### PARENTAL-ROLE DEFINITION        X    Class
Upper-class parents tend to recognize their absolute rank vis-à-vis their children more than do middle-class parents. (C086)

### Identification with Parents
The larger the discrepancy between subjects' ratings of actual v. ideal traits of their parents, the less similar to the parents the subjects rate themselves to be; subjects tend to identify only with those parental traits which they admire or wish to emulate. (J032)

### Isolation of Nuclear Family
Parenthood assumes more significance for the emotional balance of the parents themselves, as well as for the socialization of their children, in social structures in which the nuclear family is relatively isolated than is the case in systems in which solidarity with extended kin is more pronounced. (P062)

### Parent-Child Relations (Affection)
Where there is mutual agreement that each spouse shall have a high degree of independence from the home, it is likely that relations between them and their children will be of a bargaining nature, each competing for affection and power. (F106)

The greater the commitment of the parents to the family, the more likely it is that they are gratified by affectionate relationships with their children. (F106)

### Parental-Role Adjustment
Parents who see themselves in a traditional parental role tend to find positive satisfactions in children; those who evaluate their adequacy in terms of newer parental roles (e.g., interpersonal warmth or tolerance) tend to express negative or neutral parental satisfaction. (G126)

### Power Structure of Family
Schizophrenic males are more likely to choose as a role model the parent who dominates family decisions; schizophrenic females, to choose the nondominant parent. (H201)

### Role-Definition of Child
The hypothesis that the parent will prescribe for the child the reciprocal of the prescriptions that he holds for his own (parental) role is not confirmed. (M191)

### Stratification, Basis of
Stratification systems based on ascription are associated with parental amassing of an inheritance to provide for the child, while in a stratification system based on achievement, responsibility for the child is associated with affording him an adequate education. (G156)

### PARENTAL-ROLE DEFINITION/BEHAVIOR
### X    Mental Illness
Mental illness is more likely to occur where there is a discrepancy between the parental behavior and the socially defined role of parent. (L123)

### PARENTAL ROLE (DISCIPLINE)
### X    Child-Rearing Practices (Punishment)
Whichever parent is stricter tends to be the chief disciplinarian in the family. (S246)

### Parent-Child Relations (Intimacy)
The parent who has the disciplinary role is less likely to have an intimate relationship with his or her children. (S153)

### Sex-Role Identification
Parents of boys who have weak sex-role identification are more likely than are those whose sons have strong sex-role identification to have taken an equal part in disciplining the child. (L142)

### Superego Formation
Males who perceive their mothers as playing the principal disciplinary role in the family will rank higher on attitudinal measures of self-blame than males who perceive their fathers as playing the principal disciplinary role. (H067)

The development of conscience is facilitated if the child is disciplined by the same-sex parent. (S191)

### PARENTAL-ROLE MODEL
### X    Superego Formation
Manifestation of guilt in the child correlates with the model provided by the parents (e.g., confession, reparation). (G120)

### PARENTAL-ROLE SATISFACTION
### X    Parental-Role Adjustment
There is no association between the degree of satisfaction with parenthood and different kinds of expressed parental inadequacies. (G126)

## PARENTHOOD                                    X Adoption
Negro parents who have already had a child of their own through means other than the social agency are less likely to complete the adoption process than Negro parents who never had a child before. (This does not hold true for white parents.) (F117)

### Divorce
The shorter the interval between marriage and birth of the first child, the less likely it is that the marriage will end in divorce. This assertion is also denied. (D083)

### Empathy
Married offspring with children are more likely to appreciate the problems and difficulties of their own parents than are those without children. (S011)

### Parent-Child Relations
Better adjustment to their mothers tends to be found among husbands and wives with children than among those without children. (S011)

### Paternal Role
Male attitudes toward fatherhood are determined by the prestige obtained from fathering a child. (D071)

### Suicide
Parents have a lower suicide rate than nonparents. (S078)

## PARENTHOOD, ATTITUDE TOWARD
### X Parental-Role Adjustment
The greater the denial of feelings of inadequacy in the parental role, the more likely (in general) is the parent to have a lower degree of introspection about parenthood. (G126)

### Sex Status
Women express more negative feelings about parenthood than men do. (G126)

Women are more likely than men to view children as essential to their growth as persons, to their stability and maturity, and to the focusing of their lives. (G126)

## PARENTS/PEER GROUP                        X Conformity
A significant correlation exists between the attitude of the adolescent toward the use of kosher meat and the attitude of his membership groups (i.e., parents and peer group). (R010)

There is a tendency for adolescents to agree more closely with their peer groups than with their parents in their attitudes toward the use of kosher meat. (R010)

## PATERNAL/MATERNAL ROLE
### X Achievement Demands
Adolescents are more likely to view the mother as demanding achievement than they are the father. (B250)

### Aggression
Nonaggressive boys are more likely than aggressive boys to perceive their mothers, rather than their fathers, as punishing them. (K103)

In middle-class families, mothers tend to be more frequent targets of aggression by children than are fathers. (N049)

### Aggression/Guilt
Families in which the mother is the main source of love and the father the primary disciplinary agent are associated with aggressiveness in the child; families in which the mother is the primary agent of both discipline and love are associated with repression and intrapunitiveness in the child. (H201)

### Authoritarianism
Fathers of disturbed children are likely to be more authoritarian than mothers. (P067)

### Child-Rearing Practices (Achievement Demands)
Mothers are more likely than fathers to pressure children for achievement. (B273)

### Child-Rearing Practices (Aggression)
Mothers are more permissive of sons' aggression toward themselves than fathers are. (B243)

Middle-class mothers are more likely to place strong prohibitions on overt aggression than are fathers (U.S.). (K103)

### Child-Rearing Practices (Control)
Mothers are seen by both boys and girls to be more indirect in their control of children than are fathers. (D069)

Mothers tend to show much greater concern with the children's television viewing than do fathers. (H178)

### Child-Rearing Practices (Occupational Choice)
Middle-class mothers, white and Negro, are more likely to attempt to influence their children's occupational choice than are middle-class fathers. This does not hold for lower-class parents, white or Negro. (B256)

### Child-Rearing Practices (Permissiveness)
Children at all ages perceive mothers as more permissive or equalitarian in the child-rearing relationship than are fathers; fathers are more likely to be thought of as dominant. (E100)

### Child-Rearing Practices (Punishment)
Mothers tend to employ "love-oriented" techniques (i.e., threat of withdrawal of affection); fathers rely on more direct methods (e.g., physical punishment), but only in relation to the boy. (B273)

### Child-Rearing Practices (Sex)
Fathers are more permissive toward adolescent heterosexual behavior than are mothers. (B243)

Middle-class mothers are more permissive of the sexual activities of their children than are middle-class fathers. (L003)

Lower-class fathers are more permissive of the sexual activities of their children than are lower-class mothers. (L003)

### Child-Rearing Practices (Sex Role)
Fathers are more likely than mothers to treat children of the two sexes differently. (B273)

### Child-Rearing Practices (Strictness)
Subjects who say that the father is strict also claim that the father is the principal disciplinarian in the family. Those who report the father as mild in discipline say that the mother is the principal disciplinarian. (S078)

### Child-Rearing Values (Control)
Mothers are more likely to suggest coercive methods of control of children than are fathers. (J029)

Mothers are more likely to vacillate between mild and severe methods of control than are fathers. (J029)

### Conformity

Those viewing the mother as a disciplinarian are more likely to reveal a discrepancy between what they think they should do and what they say they actually would do than are those viewing the father as a disciplinarian. (H067)

### Environmental Problems

In an unfamiliar context, where adaptive behavior is most characteristic of the family, the father's role will be more highly active than the mother's; the converse is true in the familiar setting of the home, where integrative behavior predominates. (O035)

### Filicide

Mothers are more likely to commit filicide than fathers are. (T085)

### Kin Terminology

When only one parent is designated by two terms according to sex of speaker, it tends to be the father. (F046)

### Mental Illness (Manic-Depressive/Schizophrenia)

The mothers of the manic-depressive patients tend to be more reliable than do the fathers; this is not true of the parents of schizophrenic patients. (G022)

### Mental Illness of Child

The mother is no more important than the father in the etiology of mental illness in the child. (F110)

### Moral Beliefs

During the adolescent years fathers have greater influence on the son's moral views than on the daughter's; mothers have equal amounts of moral influence on children of both sexes. (J026)

### Ordinal Position

There is a tendency for fathers to participate more in the rearing of first children than of later ones, regardless of sex. (S191)

With only children, mothers assume chief disciplinarian control for daughters, fathers for sons. (S191)

### Parent-Child Relations (Affect)

Mothers and fathers are equally likely to become emotionally involved with their children. (B297)

### Parent-Child Relations (Affection)

Children perceive no difference in the frequency with which fathers and mothers are highly affectionate. (B260)

Mothers and fathers are equally likely to offer high affection to their children. (B297)

Both boys and girls perceive their mothers as more affectionate, nurturing, and loving than they do their fathers. (D069)

### Parent-Child Relations (Communication)

Middle- and lower-class mothers discuss education with their children more often than do fathers of similar class positions; this does not hold for middle-class Negro parents. (B256)

### Parent-Child Relations (Differential Treatment)

Fathers are more likely than mothers to treat children of the two sexes differently. (B250)

### Parent-Child Relations (Rejection)

Mothers tend to reject their children more than fathers do.

Sociopathic patients report behavior that could be regarded as rejection more frequently for fathers than for mothers. (O032)

### Parent-Child Relations (Warmth)

The father is more likely than the mother to be warm and solicitous with his daughters. (B250)

There is no significant difference in parental warmth between mothers and fathers of disturbed children. (P067)

The mother, as opposed to the father, is the chief source of warmth and affection for the child in the home. (P067)

### Personality of Sons (Masculinity)

Among boys, high and low masculinity groups (measured by the It Scale for Children) are not differentiated by descriptions of the mother, while they significantly differentiate on variables related to descriptions of the father. (J026)

### Social Adjustment

While the role of the mother is more crucial than that of the father for the development of the child's character, the role of the father is more important for the child's social adaptation. (H206)

### Therapy

Mothers are more likely than fathers to make (mental health) clinic contacts because fathers frequently fear the loss of domination of the family. (R110)

## PATERNAL/MATERNAL-ROLE BEHAVIOR
##                          X   Authoritarianism

Fathers of disturbed children are likely to be more authoritarian than mothers. (P067)

### Child-Rearing Practices (Education)

Among both lower and middle classes, mothers are much more directive than fathers in specifying the kind of school their children should attend. This holds for both Negroes and whites. (B256)

Fathers tend to be more nondirective in their advice on education than mothers are. (B297)

### Child-Rearing Practices (Giving Reasons)

Fathers of psychotic children are more likely than mothers are to explain the rationale of parental discipline. (D064)

### Child-Rearing Practices (Punishment)

The child feels punishment by the like-sex parent (as opposed to the cross-sex parent) to be more severe. (B232)

### Juvenile Delinquency

The father's participation in recreational activities is more significant than is the mother's participation in establishing the basis for nondelinquent behavior in adolescents. (N057)

The father's behavior is more likely to be related to delinquent behavior of the child than is the mother's. (N063)

## Mate Selection (Free Choice)

Mothers tend to exert more pressure than fathers do in controlling the child's selection of a mate. (B033)

## Mental Illness of Child

Mothers are more likely than fathers to be more anxious, impulsive, and overprotective toward psychotic children. (D064)

## Sex-Role Definition

Fathers differentiate their roles toward opposite-sex children, giving expressive support to daughters and instrumental support to sons; mothers do not differentiate their roles toward opposite-sex children, giving expressive support to both daughters and sons. (J026)

## PATERNAL/MATERNAL-ROLE DEFINITION
### X   Child-Rearing Practices (Punishment)

In families where both parents are warm toward the child, spanking is more effective where the father, rather than the mother, is the disciplinarian (U.S.). (S191)

### Sex Status

Refusal of the mother to accept social responsibility for the child is considered more "unnatural," a more serious violation of role obligations than is refusal on the part of the father. (G156)

### Social Relations of Child

The more the child interacts with people before the age of six, the more he tends to impute punitiveness to the father role and nurturance to the mother role. (K097)

## PATERNAL/MATERNAL ROLE (DISCIPLINE)
### X   Sex Status of Child

Boys are more likely than girls to see the father rather than the mother as the primary disciplinary agent. (H201)

While mothers discipline children of both sexes equally, fathers are more likely to discipline boys than they are girls. (J026)

### Superego Formation

Males who perceive the mother as playing the principal disciplinary role in the family will rank higher on attitudinal measures of self-blame than will males who perceive the father as playing the principal disciplinary role. (H067)

## PATERNAL ROLE     X  Descent (Matrilineal)

In matrilineal societies the father is more likely to share in the care of the children. (W154)

Because the status of the father is unstable in matrilineal societies, he must validate his position through his contribution to the everyday life of the household group. (Z001)

### Economic Conditions

Where there is insecurity in jobs for men, the father is more apt to hold a position of marginality in the family. (S080)

### Employment of Mother

There is a greater opportunity for the father to play a strong role with his children where the mother in the family also works. (M058)

### Homosexuality

Homosexuality is less likely to occur if the father has a strong position in the family. (W126)

## Identification with Father

For sons, high father identification is associated with high involvement by the father in child-rearing activities. (R098)

## Maternal Overprotectiveness

An overwhelming proportion of fathers of overprotected children played little or no authoritative role in the life of the child. (L117)

## Mental Illness

In the families of middle-class mentally ill patients, the father's role tended to be ambiguous in the home. (M061)

Mentally ill middle-class patients are more likely (than lower-class patients) to question their fathers' masculinity and authority. (M061)

## Mental Illness/Neurosis

Fathers of lower-class schizophrenics tend to show less interest in household affairs than do fathers of neurotics. (M061)

The fathers of neurotic patients are more likely than those of mentally ill patients to display an interest in the patients' rearing and activities. (M061)

## Mental Illness of Child (Schizophrenia)

Schizophrenia in children correlates with low prestige of the husband in the family. (L114)

There is a correlation between the absence of a strong paternal figure in the home and schizophrenia in the child. (M218)

## Mental Illness (Schizophrenia)

Fathers of schizophrenic children are more likely than others to be withdrawn and ineffectual. (B284)

Most fathers of this "preadolescent" type of schizophrenic adolescent (rebellious, delinquent, irresponsible) seem to abound in "goodness" in civic life and are active leaders in business; at home, however, they tend to be passive-aggressive critics. (S208)

## Mental Illness (Schizophrenia/Neurosis)

In the lower class, fathers of schizophrenics have less interest in household affairs than do fathers of neurotics. (M197)

## Parenthood

Male attitudes toward fatherhood are determined by the prestige obtained from fathering a child. (D071)

## Race Attitudes

The prejudiced woman is more likely than the unprejudiced woman to stress her father's role as the provider for the family; the unprejudiced woman is more likely to stress the intellectual and esthetic aspects of her father's character. (A061)

## Religion (Role of Deities)

The role of the Supreme Deity will be similar to the authority of the father. (H060)

## Residence

In matrilineal societies the father's area of action tends to be less where the woman, after marriage, resides with her brother and her husband comes to live or visit in their house. (G012)

In matrilineal societies, where the husband takes his wife to his home, the husband's role as father is more important (even if the children succeed to the brother-in-law). (G012)

### Role Conflict
Where contradictory demands for the mother's allegiance are made by her husband and her mother, there is a tendency for the husband to withdraw from participation in family activities, particularly in the area of child care and control. (C117)

### Scholastic Motivation of Son
For boys, high paternal involvement in child rearing is a much more important factor for high academic motivation than is husband *v.* wife dominance in general family leadership. (E102)

In families where a father is head of the household, paternal dominance or lack of involvement in child rearing is associated with low academic motivation in sons, while a more supervisory role by the father in child rearing is associated with high academic motivation in sons. (E102)

### Sex-Role Definition
Male personality elements will be maximized in families where the father occupies the role of leader. (S205)

### Superego Formation
The greater the severity of the father in his relationship to his son, the greater will be the severity of the superego in the son's personality in its domination over the ego. (S078)

Fathers of low-guilt boys play a larger role in discipline than do fathers of high-guilt boys. (S078)

## PATERNAL-ROLE ADJUSTMENT
### X   Authority Structure of Family
Fathers tend to be less secure in their role as disciplinarian as mothers take on greater responsibility and authority in the family. (M201)

### Sex-Role Adjustment
A man's functioning as a father will be impaired to whatever extent he feels threatened, insecure, and anxious about his adequacy in any of his several significant masculine roles. (L134)

## PATERNAL ROLE, ATTITUDE TOWARD
### X   Economic Role of Children
Male attitudes are more favorable toward fatherhood when the economic utility of children in the society is high. (D071)

### Marital Adjustment
### X   Parental Role, Attitude Toward
Marital conflict correlates with the father's attitudes of rejection of family life, justification of quarreling, and a rejection of interaction with the child. (N053)

### Maternal Role, Attitude Toward
The intensity of the urge toward motherhood in a given society is a function of the male attitude toward fatherhood. (D071)

## PATERNAL ROLE (AUTHORITY)
### X   Father-Daughter Relations (Alienation)
Abdication of the father from his authority role results in his daughter's emotional alienation. (B297)

## PATERNAL-ROLE BEHAVIOR        X   Class
Fathers of lower-class mental patients are more likely than fathers of middle-class mental patients to have

been feared; they were also generally uninvolved in family affairs. (M061)

The fathers of mentally ill lower-class patients tend to display less interest in household affairs than do the fathers of middle-class patients. (M061)

### Incest (Brother-Sister)
At the onset of brother-sister incest, the father was absent from, subordinate in, or indifferent to the family; or he was incapacitated, old and weak, overworked or concerned with earning a living; or he may have been completely concerned with nonfamily matters. (W123)

### Incest (Father-Daughter)
The incestuous father is more likely than the typical father to maintain his power by threats rather than by his financial contribution. (W123)

The incestuous father is more likely than the typical father to exploit his family by retaining authority but shifting responsibilities to family members. (W123)

### Maternal-Role Behavior
As the wife becomes more involved in the mother role, the husband becomes a marginal member of the family (becomes increasingly alienated from the family and family decisions).

### Mental Illness of Child
Mental illness is directly correlated with a failure of the father to participate in the care and raising of the psychotic child. (F085)

### Sex-Role Identification
Since the father of the good premorbid schizophrenic (good functioning before the onset of illness) acts in a more assertive manner and maintains a more masculine role within the family than does the father of the poor premorbid schizophrenic, it is more likely that the former serves as a more effective model for male identification for his son. (G127)

## PATERNAL ROLE (CHILD REARING)
### X   Sex Composition of Family
A father is more often involved in child rearing when all of the children in the family are boys than when there are children of both sexes or only girls. (B322)

## PATERNAL-ROLE DEFINITION
### X   Aggression Anxiety
The greater the amount of the father's participation in child rearing, the greater the aggression anxiety which develops in girls. (S246)

### Class
Fathers are more apt to hold positions of marginality of role in the family in the lower classes than in the middle class. (S080)

### Father-Child Relations (Authority)
The greater the child's conception of an ideal father approximates his actual father, the more successful will the father be in establishing authority.

### Marital Adjustment of Husband
Happy husbands are more likely than unhappy husbands to consider it essential for an ideal marriage that the husband take an active interest in the discipline and training of the child. (T074)

### Mobility Aspiration
A high-status husband, who is already established socially and economically, has more time to spend around his home, as compared with the "struggling to get ahead" man, who spends all his available time trying to achieve his goals.

The tendency for the established high-status man to be more family oriented is suggested also in the fact that high-status suburban husbands do a great deal around the home. The man who struggles to get ahead does so at the expense of family participation.

### Political Structure
As authority of the father becomes personal, state intervention becomes more likely. (T016)

As the legitimacy of the father's authority decreases—owing to the lesser importance of the clan for the family—the state increases its control over paternal authority. (T016)

### Warfare
In military societies, where a large proportion of the male population are soldiers, there will be institutionalized deterrents to the formation of attachments between the father and other members of a nuclear family. (G056)

## PATERNAL ROLE (DISCIPLINE)     X     Age of Child
The older the child, the greater is the importance of discipline by the father. (H208)

### Aggression
If the father is the chief disciplinarian of a five-year-old boy, the boy is more likely to exhibit self-aggression at age 12. (S246)

### Child-Rearing Practices (Kin)
The greater the control of adults other than parents (particularly the maternal grandmother) over the child, the more likely it is that the father will use severe punishment in handling the child. (C117)

### Joking Relationship
The joking relationship between alternate generations will occur only in the absence of a joint family organization and in systems where the father is the disciplinarian of the family. (D034)

### Juvenile Delinquency
Discipline by the father was more common among the recidivist delinquent group than among a matched group of college freshmen.

### Maternal Overprotectiveness
In families in which the mother is overprotective, the father will assume a passive disciplinary role, either voluntarily or under pressure by the mother. (L163)

### Menstrual Taboos
When menstrual taboos are extensive in the society, the father is expected to be the main disciplinarian. (S079)

### Size of Family
Fathers are more likely to control and discipline children, the larger the family size. (B322)

## PATERNAL ROLE (ECONOMIC)
### X     Parent-Child Relations (Preference)
The less adequate the father as a provider, the more likely it is that the daughter will be hostile toward him and will prefer the mother and that the son will be less involved with him. (L150)

### Paternal Role, Importance of
The relative importance of the father will tend to increase in matrilineal societies as he assumes financial responsibility for his children. (M050)

### Sibling Relations
If the father is relatively adequate as a provider, younger boys tend to be most involved with an older sister, both negatively and positively; if the father is less adequate, they tend to have as their strongest relationship a hostile one with a brother. Where the father is adequate, older boys are most involved with a younger brother, toward whom they are warm; if the father is less adequate, the relationship is more likely to be a very positive or negative one with a much younger sister. (L150)

Girls with more adequate fathers are more likely to be involved with their siblings, particularly with an older brother, than are those whose fathers are not. If the father is inadequate, young girls tend to dislike their siblings, while feeling that their siblings like them, and to be most involved with a much older sibling. (L150)

## PATERNAL ROLE (HOUSEKEEPING)
### X     Juvenile Delinquency
A home in which the father assists with the housekeeping is less likely to produce delinquent children than is a home in which the father refuses to do so. (N057)

## PATERNAL ROLE, IMPORTANCE OF
### X     Paternal Role (Economic)
The relative importance of the father will tend to increase in matrilineal societies as he assumes financial responsibility for his children. (M050)

### Residence
In matrilineal societies there is considerable variation in the degree to which the father's role is stressed. It tends to be less so where the woman, after marriage, resides with her brother and her husband comes to live in their house. (G116)

## PATERNAL-ROLE MODEL
### X     Achievement Motivation
Having a highly successful father as a role model is negatively related to high achievement motivation in the son. (G156)

### Identification with Father
The more available the father is as a role model, the higher is the son's identification with his father. (R098)

### Juvenile Delinquency
Nondelinquents accept the father as a role model more readily than do delinquents.

### Juvenile Delinquency (Reform)
If the father provides a negative role model for the child (e.g., involving a criminal record), the delinquent child is more likely to reform later (after his twenty-third year) than if the father provides a positive role model. (M194)

## PATERNAL ROLE/POWER STRUCTURE OF FAMILY     X     Scholastic Motivation of Son
For boys, high paternal involvement in child rearing is a much more salient factor for high academic motivation than is husband v. wife dominance in general family leadership. (E102)

## PATERNAL ROLE (STRICTNESS)
### X Employment of Mother
Mothers with college backgrounds more often report the father as the less strict parent when these mothers work than when they do not. (Y051)

Mothers with high-school backgrounds more often report the father as the stricter parent when these mothers work than when they do not. (Y051)

## PATERNITY, IGNORANCE OF
### X Descent (Matrilineal)
Ignorance about the role of the male in procreation is more likely to occur in matrilineal societies. (W154)

## PEER GROUP/PARENTS          X Moral Beliefs
The acceptance of the idea of guilt by association is usually learned from the peer group, as opposed to parents. (J021)

## PEER RELATIONS          X Achievement Demands
The mother's concern with the child's achievement is related to the child's being victimized or teased in his relationships with peers. (R113)

### Athletics
The fathers of adolescent boys who are accepted by their peers are more likely to be interested in athletic activities than are the fathers of boys who are rejected by their peers. (F108)

### Authoritarianism
Children from democratic homes tend to be more popular among their peers than do children from authoritarian homes. (K113)

### Broken Home
Adolescent girls from reconstituted families are more likely than those from broken and unbroken families to maintain better relations with their classmates. (B276)

There is no difference between adolescents from unbroken homes and those from broken and reconstituted homes regarding their popularity among classmates. (B276)

Adolescent boys from unbroken families are more likely to report a greater number of school friends than are adolescent boys from broken and reconstituted families. (B276)

### Child-Rearing Practices
Peer-dependent children (who seek dependent rewards from their peers but avoid close relationships with adults) tend to be raised in family environments characterized by lack of supervision and restriction, low parental demands, emotionally indifferent parents, punitive or lax discipline, and encouragement of masculine behavior. (M221)

### Child-Rearing Practices (Democratic)
Children from democratic homes (parents who encourage free experimentation by their children) are more involved in peer-centered activities than are children from nondemocratic families. (B287)

Children from democratic homes (parents who encourage free experimentation by their children) are more likely to be in a favored position (successful in bossing and having high group status) in the peer groups to which they belong. (B287)

### Child-Rearing Practices (Giving Reasons)
The child raised in a home in which parents consult with the child about regulations and attempt to explain discipline is more successful in leadership than is the child raised in an authoritarian home. (L146)

### Child-Rearing Practices (Permissiveness)
The more permissively the child is raised, the more likely it is that he will be responsive to the *mores* of his peers rather than to those of adults. (M188)

### Child-Rearing Practices (Punishment)
Children who perceive themselves as autonomous and their parents as coercive (punishing) are more actively friendly with their peers than are others. (H205)

Children who perceive themselves as autonomous and their parents as coercive (punishing) tend to be more active than others as leaders in their peer groups. (H205)

### Child-Rearing Practices (Rewards)
There is a positive relationship for boys and a negative relationship for girls between affective rewards for good behavior and leadership abilities in the child (based on teachers' ratings of influence in group activities). (B250)

### Child-Rearing Practices (Sex Role)
Greater parental punishment for boys than for girls for opposite sex behavior leads to stronger feelings of hostility among boys toward girls than among girls toward boys. (L141)

### Cohesion of Family
Family solidarity is weakened as the peer group gains in importance in the life of a child. (C087)

### Conformity
The rejection of familial authority is more likely to occur if the child finds support for his rebellion in his peer group. (A013)

The greater the strength of the adolescent clique or gang, the greater the possibility of opposition to or evasion of parental authority and sanctions. (S219)

### Dependency
Adolescent peer groups, by representing nonfamily norms, aid in reducing the child's dependence on his family. (G156)

The more involved an adolescent becomes with his peer group, the more he is emancipated from his parents. (H228)

Children who perceive themselves as autonomous and their parents as coercive (punishing) are more actively friendly with their peers than are others. (H205)

The higher the popularity of the child among peers, the less dependent he is on his parents. (M176)

The greater the commitment of the adolescent to the peer group, the less dependent he/she is likely to be upon his/her family. (P083)

### Descent (Bilineal)
More intense adolescent peer-group life is likely to be found in societies having bilineal descent and neolocal residence than in a patrilineal, patrilocal system. (P083)

### Economic Rank
Adolescents at the middle economic level whose mothers work are more likely to be rejected by their peers than are those at low or high economic levels. (F108)

### Employment of Mother
Adolescents at the middle economic level whose mothers work are more likely to be rejected by their peers than are those at low or high economic levels. (F108)

As regards peer-group adjustment, adolescents whose mothers have worked when they were young show no difference from adolescents whose mothers did not work. (Y047)

### Father Absence
Compared with girls and with boys whose fathers are absent from home, only boys whose fathers are present choose same-sex playmates more often.

Boys whose fathers are away from the home for a length of time are less well adjusted among peers than are boys whose fathers are present regularly. This is not so for girls. (G156)

### Identification with Cross-Sex Parent
Boys who perceive themselves as more like their fathers than their mothers are perceived more favorably by their peers; girls who see themselves as more like their mothers than their fathers are viewed less favorably by their peers. (J026)

### Identification with Like-Sex Parent
Children who have established a sex identification with the like-sex parent tend to prefer the company of members of their own sex. (R126)

### Identification with Parent
If the child's identification with his parent is based upon the support given by the parent, he will be less dependent upon peer-group approval than if the identification is with nonsupporting parents. (C114)

### Interaction in Family (Intimacy)
The less intimate the family life, the less likely is the child to be popular among his peers. (R111)

### Marital Adjustment
There is no relationship between marital adjustment and the child's relations with his peers for either authoritarian or for democratic families. (K113)

### Marital Adjustment of Parents
Among white collar families, a positive view of his parents' marriage by the child is related to satisfactory peer relations; but among blue collar families, a positive view of his parents' marriage by the child is related to unsatisfactory peer relations. (H201)

### Marriage, Attitude Toward
Expectation of time of marriage does not correlate with peer-group popularity; but the less popular the child, the more likely it is that he will not desire marriage or any children at all. (R111)

### Mate Selection
The earlier the selection of one's mate, the greater the dependence of boy-girl pairs upon each other and the decrease of interaction within each sex group. (M188)

### Mate Selection (Free Choice)
Where parents wish to control the marriage of their daughter, her peer-group activities are likely to be restricted. (P083)

### Mate Selection (Residence)
As the individual's degree of acceptance in the neighborhood peer group increases, so does the likelihood of residentially propinquitous mate selection. (K020)

Residentially propinquitous mate selection increases with the individual's degree of acceptance in the neighborhood peer group. (K020)

### Maternal Overprotectiveness
Children subject to maternal overprotection tend to have difficulty in their relationships with peers. (L161)

Maternal overprotection tends to be directly correlated with patterns of deprivation of childhood play when the mother was a girl. (L163)

### Ordinal Position
The only child from higher economic strata is more likely to be rejected by his peers than is the only child at the middle or low economic levels. (S220)

Firstborn children are less popular among their peers than are later-born children. (S232)

### Parent-Child Relations (Affection)
Children who rate their parents as very dominant and low in affection toward them were judged least favorably by their classmates.

### Parent-Child Relations (Closeness)
The more inclined the parents are to ignore the child, the freer the child is to interact with peers. (J021)

### Parent-Child Relations (Control)
The effect of family expectation is more pronounced when the adolescent is isolated from his peer group. (B033)

Where family controls on the individual are rigid, peer groups provide a source of tension reduction. (P056)

### Parent Loss
Adolescents from homes where one parent is deceased are more likely to strive for attention from the opposite sex than are adolescents from families where both parents are living.

Separation of the child from his parents or from parental substitutes leads the child to closer associations with other children.

### Parent-Son Relations (Warmth)
Warm father-son relations are related to satisfactory peer relations (i.e., outgoing peer-group behavior, initiation of friendship, influence in peer relations, and low use of physical force). Warm mother-son relations are not related to satisfactory peer relations. (H201)

### Peer Relations (Interaction)
There is no correlation between the frequency of association with the sibling's friends and the quality of treatment received from them. (K094)

### Political Interest of Child
"Peer-oriented" youth are less interested in politics and less desirous of being interested than are "parent-oriented" youth. (H244)

### Power Structure of Family
Mother-dominated homes are associated with sons who show a greater dislike for girls in their peer relations. (H201)

### Scholastic Adjustment
The parents of adolescent boys who are accepted by their peers are more likely to be satisfied with their sons'

adjustments in school than are the parents of boys who are rejected by their peers. (F108)

### Self-Conception
The self-esteem of boys who are younger children in a family of mostly girls is relatively impervious to the extent to which they participate actively in high-school social activities; in general, the more active the boy is in social activities, the higher is his self-esteem. (R129)

In general, boys who consider themselves to be peer-group leaders have higher self-esteem than do those who do not, but boys who are younger children in a family of mostly girls tend to have high self-esteem even if they do not consider themselves to be leaders. (R129)

### Sex Status
Girls are more likely than boys to choose opposite-sex playmates.

Among teenagers, sons are more likely to seek their social activities outside of the home than are daughters. (D079)

Girls are more likely than boys to find their siblings' associates accepting and cooperative. (K094)

### Sibling Structure
Second-born girls with older brothers are likely to favor male playmates more than are girls with older sisters or girls with younger brothers. (K149)

### Sibling Structure (Age)
The younger sibling is more likely to feel ill-treated by his sibling's friends than is the older sibling. (K094)

### Sibling Structure (Age Difference)
The greater the age disparity between siblings, the lower the frequency of association with siblings' friends. (K094)

The greater the age difference between siblings, the more likely the child is to become involved with peers; the smaller the age difference, the more they tend to be involved with each other. (K149)

The greater the difference in age between boys (except those having an older sister), the more sociable and socially acceptable they tend to be (i.e., better leaders, more friendly to peers, more popular, and more competitive); this trend does not exist among girls. (K149)

As the age difference between siblings increases, the firstborn child has less association with his sibling and their playmate groups tend to overlap less; the overlap in playmate groups and degree of association with the younger sibling decreases more rapidly with spacing among siblings of the opposite sex and decreases most slowly among girls with younger sisters. (K149)

### Sibling Structure (Sex)
When age disparity between siblings is less than four years, children are more likely to play with their sister's friends than with their brother's friends; boys, however, prefer friends of their older brother to those of their older sister. (K094)

When siblings are of opposite sex, it is more likely that the child will feel ill-treated by the sibling's friends. (K094)

When their sibling is male, firstborns are more likely to prefer male friends than are second borns; when their sibling is female, the reverse obtains as to male preference. (K094)

## PEER RELATIONS (INTERACTION)
#### X    Peer Relations
There is no correlation between the frequency of association with a sibling's friends and the quality of treatment received from them. (K094)

## PENIS ENVY                    X    Descent (Patrilineal)
Penis envy is associated with patterns of patrilineal descent and will not occur in matrilineal societies. (F112)

#### Sex-Role Definition
Ambivalence toward the sex role in women is likely to manifest itself as penis envy. (W154)

## PERSONALITY                    X    Marital Adjustment
The greater the psychological insight of the individual, the more likely it is that he will choose an appropriate spouse and have a successful marriage.

Persons who are easygoing, have a modest sense of self-respect, and a sense of duty and honor have a better chance for marital success than do persons who are ambitious, moody, dominating, and nervous. (B244)

#### Mate Selection
A man who is industrious and shy will tend to seek as a mate a physically attractive and vivacious girl. (B217)

People are more willing to compromise in mate selection in the area of physical appearance than they are with respect to desired personality traits. (C023)

Persons with similar personality traits, such as self-confidence, insight, empathy, and emotional stability, are more apt to marry than are persons with dissimilar traits. (J035)

One falls in love with a particular person because that loved one represents a perfection which the lower has striven unsuccessfully to attain. (W148)

#### Ordinal Position
When spacing is from two to four years, firstborns tend to alibi more than do second-born children. (K104)

When spacing is over four years or under two years, girls with a younger sister are likely to be more vacillating than are girls with an older sister. (K104)

Firstborns are more likely to be curious and responsible than are second-born children, even more so if the sibling is of the opposite sex. (K126)

Firstborn girls and second-born boys with an older sister are more likely to procrastinate. (K126)

#### Parent-Child Relations (Sex)
Disruption of libidinous relations to the parents is a causal factor in changing the personality of stepchildren. (B286)

#### Pregnancies, Number of
Among married women, primigravida tend to be more dependent, insecure, and fearful than do multigravida. (C099)

#### Sibling Structure
At the two-to-four-year spacing, firstborn boys are more likely to respond indirectly to fear and frustration than are second-born boys and girls with an older sister are more likely to respond indirectly than are girls with a younger sister. (K104)

### Sibling Structure (Age Difference)

The greater the sibling age disparity, the more active the boy will be. (K104)

The greater the disparity in age, the more likely is the manifestation of indirectness in response to fear and frustration by girls with a brother. (K104)

The greater the age differences among the children in a family, the more likely it is that the personality traits of groups at different ordinal positions are more reflections of parent-child relations than of direct sibling interactions. (K104)

### Sibling Structure (Sex)

At the two-to-four-year spacing, children with a cross-sex sibling are more likely to be cheerful than are those with a same-sex sibling. (K104)

At the two-to-four-year spacing, girls with a cross-sex sibling show more finality in their decisions than do those with a same-sex sibling; when the sibling is over four years older, children in like-sex pairs are less vacillating than are those in cross-sex pairs. (K104)

When sibling spacing is under two years, second-born girls tend to be more cheerful than boys. (K104)

### Size of Family

The greater the number of children, particularly from four up, mothers of maladjusted children are likely to score higher on authoritarianism, encouraging verbalization, excluding outside influence, deification, and suppression of sex; fathers are likely to score higher on irresponsibility, suppression of sex, and change of orientation (PARI). (Z011)

## PERSONALITY (ADAPTABILITY)
### X   Marital Adjustment

Adaptability is associated with marital adjustment. (B033)

## PERSONALITY ADJUSTMENT     X   Age-Groups

The age-grade, by providing the adolescent with a well-ordered predictable scheme of roles and relationships, lessens adolescent tension. (N008)

### Authoritarianism

Democratic parents are no more likely to have better-adjusted children than are authoritarian parents.

### Broken Home

Adolescents from broken homes are no more likely to show personality maladjustments (Minnesota Personality Test) than are adolescents from broken and reconstituted families. (B276)

### Child-Rearing Practices (Dependency)

Fathers of maladjusted children are less likely to report marital conflict and to force independence in the children than are fathers of normal children. (Z011)

### Childbirth

Mothers of prematurely born infants are more likely than others to react to birth in a disordered manner. (K108)

### Class

Middle-class child-rearing practices are more likely than are lower-class child-rearing practices to cause frustration and anxiety that inhibit good mental health in later years.

### Husband-Wife Relations (Egalitarianism)

Egalitarian spousal relationship is associated with boys who are well integrated into the family system and are relatively free of anxiety. (S205)

### Identification of Mother with Daughter

There is a direct correlation between the degree of identification with the daughter and the perception of the daughter as well adjusted. (H218)

Mothers are more likely to rate daughters with whom they identify as better adjusted than other siblings. (H218)

### Identification with Father

Boys who identify with their fathers are more likely to make better social and emotional adjustment (as measured by teacher ratings) than are those who do not. (P076)

### Identification with Like/Cross-Sex Parent

For both males and females, failure to identify with the father is more closely associated with trends toward abnormality than is failure to identify with the mother. (J026)

In boys, a high degree of self-concept modeling after the father is associated with high personality adjustment; in girls, a high degree of self-concept modeling after the mother is not associated with high personality adjustment. (J026)

### Identification with Parents

Nonneurotic persons do not usually identify with one parent rather than the other. (L145)

Personal identification with both parents is associated with general psychological health. (S240)

### Marital Adjustment

Loss of marital adjustment is not associated with loss of personal adjustment. (P071)

### Marital Stability

The more mature and personally well adjusted a person is, the more likely he is to build a stable marriage. (C134)

### Marital Status

Widowed people are more likely to have a lower level of personality adjustment than are married people; controlling for age does not make a difference. (G126)

### Marriage, Attitude Toward

The immature or not so well-adjusted person may find a greater appeal in marriage than may the mature and well-adjusted person. (M010)

### Mother Absence

If the infant is under six months of age, the absence of the natural mother does not have any effect on the psychological and social well-being of the infant. (O033)

### Parent-Child Relations (Egalitarianism)

Among high-school students who are high achievers in mathematics, the higher the personality maladjustment (Rotter Incomplete Sentence Blank), the more negative and autocratic the family relationship (Kell-Hoeflin Incomplete Sentence Blank). (K148)

### Parent-Child Relations (Evaluation)

Neuropsychiatric patients are more likely than normal adults to give relatively unfavorable reports of the behavior of the same-sex parent with whom they should be most strongly identified. (V034)

### Parent Loss
Minnesota Multiphase Personality Inventory data on a subsample were classified into subgroups according to age and type of parent loss and were compared with a sample of the general clinic population. No significant group differences were obtained. (A070)

The older a child at the time of the death of the mother, the less serious personality damage is likely to be done. (K161)

### Power Structure of Family
When the mother is dominant the sons are likely to be tense and rejecting. (S205)

The role-differentiated type of equalitarian family (autonomous) is more likely to produce sons who are the best socialized for smooth internal familial adjustment and for achievement roles external to the family. (S205)

### Role Definition in Family
Role differentiation in families with loosely knit social networks (friends of the couple are not friends of one another) is associated with poor emotional adjustment of the children in the family. (S216)

### Toilet Training
Exceptionally early toilet training leads to childhood personality disturbances. (F097)

### Weaning
Children who are weaned gradually show stronger feelings of belonging than do children who are abruptly weaned (as measured by the California Test of Personality). (S200)

There is no association between children who are weaned gradually and children who are weaned abruptly and their personality adjustment (i.e., finger-sucking, nail-biting, stuttering, eating difficulties, slowness and bashfulness in talking). (S200)

## PERSONALITY ADJUSTMENT (EGO STRENGTH)
### X  Marital Status
Persons who marry show greater feelings of ego deficiency than do persons who remain single. (M232)

## PERSONALITY ADJUSTMENT (FANTASY)
### X  Marital Adjustment of Husband
More unhappy than happy husbands prefer a dance to a play and more of them like movies, which presumably carry a factor of vicarious romantic satisfaction. The fact that more unhappy men like to spend money on clothing and also that more of them habitually daydream is pertinent in this connection. (T074)

## PERSONALITY ADJUSTMENT (HAPPINESS)
### X  Broken Home
Persons reared in divorced or separated homes are more likely to report feeling greater present unhappiness than are persons who were reared in homes where both or one parent died or persons from homes where the family was intact. (G126)

Among married persons, those who have come from divorced families are more likely to report unhappiness than are those who are from either families that remained intact or from families in which one or both parents died. (G126)

### Marital Status
Married people are happier than those engaged to be married, who are happier than those never yet engaged, who are happier than those people with broken and unreplaced engagements, who are, in turn, happier than married people on the verge of divorce, the latter being the least happy of all the groups. (C023)

The widowed are more likely to have greater feelings of unhappiness than are single persons. (The difference is greater for males than for females.) (G126)

## PERSONALITY ADJUSTMENT (NERVOUSNESS)
### X  Breast Feeding
There is no relationship between bottle or breast feeding and the degree of nervousness in the child. (S200)

## PERSONALITY ADJUSTMENT OF AGED
### X  Residence with Kin
Low morale among elderly persons (75 and over) is associated with their living with intimate kinsmen. (C116)

## PERSONALITY ADJUSTMENT OF CHILD
### X  Broken Home
Children whose mothers were widowed when they were relatively young tend to be somewhat better adjusted than do children whose mothers were divorced when they were young. (R129)

### Child-Rearing Attitudes (Consensus)
There is a curvilinear relationship between the amount of discrepancy between the parents in their role prescriptions for the child and the child's consequent conflict and maladjustment.

### Cohesion of Family
A complete home, mother, father, and children are necessary for the development of a balanced and socially adjusted personality in the child. (S210)

### Education of Parents
There is a low correlation between low personality adjustment in the child (as measured by the Rogers Test of Personality Adjustment) and the mother's and father's educational level, but those whose fathers have had postgraduate education have the lowest scores. (B251)

### Employment of Mother
Maternal employment during various periods of the child's life (less than 4 years, 4 to 6 years, less than 7 years) has no relationship to the child's personality adjustment (as measured by the Minnesota Test of Personality). (B294)

### Feeding
Children who were not held by the mother during feedings tend to show lower personal and social adjustment than do those who were. (B272)

### Feeding (Demand)
There is no relationship between different types of feeding, demand schedules, and weaning and the personal and social adjustment of the child. (B272)

There is no relationship between the feeding of infants on a regular or a demand schedule and their level of personality adjustment (as measured by the California Test of Personality or the Ford Modification of the Haggerty-Olson-Wickman Behavior Rating Scale). (S200)

### Occupational Rank of Father
The higher the prestige of the father's occupation, the better adjusted the child (as measured by the Rogers Test of Personality Adjustment) and the lower the child's sense of inferiority. (B251)

**Parent-Child Relations (Evaluation)**
Parents are likely to see their children as less well adjusted personally (measured by responses to the California Test of Personality, Form B) than the children see themselves. (V034)

**Parent-Child Relations (Guilt/Anxiety)**
The greater the parents' anxiety, guilt, and insecurity in their relations with their children, the less likely are the children to develop security and confidence in themselves. (E096)

**Parent-Child Relations (Warmth)**
Children reared without a warm and affectionate parent-child relationship (e.g., in an orphanage) tend to acquire attitudes of distrust and defensiveness. (D062)

**Personality of Father (Punitiveness)**
If the father is cold, maladjusted, and punitive, then the child tends to be maladjusted. (P070)

**Personality Problems of Parents**
Fathers of maladjusted children tend to be weak, ineffectual, and psychosomatic; mothers are more likely to act out their conflicts in verbal and overt behavior. (L144)

**Power Structure of Family**
Where a mother is dominant in the conjugal child-rearing and parent-adolescent relations, the family environment is more likely than not to create conflicts for the child. (B323)

**Size of Family**
Personality adjustment of children is more successful in a small family than in a larger family. (I008)

**Sleeping Arrangement**
There is no significant difference in personality adjustment between children who slept with their mothers during infancy and those who did not. (K161)

**Urban/Rural**
The average level of personality adjustment is higher among farm children than among those living in city homes. (B033)

## PERSONALITY ADJUSTMENT OF CHILD (BELONGING) X Feeding (Demand)
Children who are fed on a demand schedule rather than on a regular feeding schedule have stronger feelings of not belonging (as measured by the California Test of Personality). (S200)

## PERSONALITY ADJUSTMENT OF CHILD (FRUSTRATION TOLERANCE) X Occupation of Father
University children (fathers working in an academic capacity) may develop a higher frustration tolerance than nonuniversity children. (G117)

## PERSONALITY ADJUSTMENT OF CHILD (HOSTILITY) X Parent-Child Relations (Hostility) X Personality of Child (Hostility)
The greater the general hostility of the parent toward the child, the more likely the genesis of hostility in the child. (B232)

## PERSONALITY ADJUSTMENT OF CHILD (INCONSISTENCY) X Occupation of Father
Children with fathers working in an academic capacity may be more able to accept occasional inconsistencies from their parents than children whose fathers are in a nonacademic capacity. (G117)

## PERSONALITY ADJUSTMENT OF CHILD (ORAL) X Feeding (Demand)
Children fed on a demand schedule have no more "oral symptoms" (i.e., finger-sucking, nail-biting, stuttering, eating difficulties, bashfulness, or slowness in talking) than do children fed on a regular feeding schedule. (S200)

## PERSONALITY ADJUSTMENT OF CHILD (REBELLION) X Occupation of Father
Children whose fathers work in an academic capacity may feel greater freedom to rebel when they have a definite disposition to do so than children whose fathers are in a nonacademic capacity. (G117)

## PERSONALITY ADJUSTMENT OF DAUGHTER X Education of Parents
The level of parental education is not significantly related to the personality adjustment of daughters. (B247)

## PERSONALITY ADJUSTMENT OF FATHER/ MOTHER X Personality Problems of Child
The adjustment of the father is more crucial in determining personality problems in the child than is the adjustment of the mother. (B259)

## PERSONALITY ADJUSTMENT OF MOTHER X Mother-Child Relations (Affection)
High personal adjustment of the mother (esteem for husband, self-esteem, satisfaction with current life situation) is associated with warmth toward her child (U.S.). (S191)

## PERSONALITY ADJUSTMENT OF PARENTS X Child-Rearing Practices (Authoritarianism)
Authoritarian discipline correlates less with the developmental needs of the child than with the insecurity and irrationality of the parents. (M203)

## PERSONALITY ADJUSTMENT OF SIBLING X Mental Retardation
The presence of a retarded sibling is more likely to have an adverse effect on normal female than male siblings. (J027)

**Ordinal Position**
Younger siblings are more likely to be adversely affected by their retarded siblings than are older siblings. (J027)

## PERSONALITY ADJUSTMENT OF SON X Father-Son Relations (Hostility)
Normal subjects (soldiers) are likely to regard their fathers' behavior toward them more favorably than are neuropsychiatric subjects, who tend to recall their fathers as hostile and rejecting (Schaefer's Report of Parental Behavior Inventory—RPBI). (V034)

**Father-Son Relations (Strictness)**
Withdrawal from an extremely punitive and harsh father may favor, rather than retard, personality adjustment in the son. (M204)

**Parent-Child Relations**
Both normal and disturbed soldiers tend to have more idealized memories of their mothers' behavior toward them than they have of their fathers' (i.e., for mothers, but not for fathers, both groups endorse positively,

rather than negatively, toned statements of the RPBI). (V034)

## PERSONALITY ADJUSTMENT OF WIFE
### X Personality (Similarity)
There is no difference in personality adjustment (MMPI) between wives who perceive similarities between themselves and their husbands and those who perceive themselves as different from their husbands. (K124)

## PERSONALITY ADJUSTMENT (ORAL)
### X Weaning
There is no relationship between children who are weaned abruptly and children who are weaned gradually and their oral adjustment (i.e., finger-sucking, stuttering, eating difficulties, slowness and bashfulness in talking). (S200)

## PERSONALITY ADJUSTMENT (WORRY)
### X Marital Status
Married people are more likely to report worries than are unmarried people. (The difference is greater for women than for men.) (G126)

Widows and widowers report worrying "all the time" more frequently than do single persons. (The difference is greater for males than for females.) (G126)

### Sex Status
Among divorced and separated persons, women report worrying "all the time" much more frequently than do men. (G126)

## PERSONALITY (AFFILIATION TENDENCY)
### X Ordinal Position
The earlier the birth rank, the greater the number of organizations to which college students belong. (S263)

## PERSONALITY (AFFILIATIVE NEED)
### X Ordinal Position
Firstborn children show stronger affiliative tendencies than do later-born children. (D066)

Under anxiety-arousing conditions, firstborn and only children are more likely to want to be with other people than are later-born children. (S263)

In an anxiety-producing situation, firstborn and only children are much more likely than later-born individuals to seek the company of others. (S263)

The later born the child, the less likely he is to respond to anxiety by seeking company. (S263)

When anxiety level is held constant (when only truly anxious subjects are considered), firstborn and only children are more likely than later-born subjects to seek the company of others. (S263)

Firstborn subjects from both small and large families are more likely than later-born persons to respond to anxiety by seeking company. (S263)

### Size of Family
Both firstborn and later-born individuals in large families are less likely than their counterparts in small families to seek company when they are anxious. (S263)

There is less difference in affiliative response to anxiety between firstborn and later-born children in large families than in small families. (S263)

## PERSONALITY (AGGRESSION)      X Income
Poor management of family income is associated with the delinquency linked traits of destructiveness, destructive-sadistic trends, extroversion of action, lack of conscientiousness, and receptive trends.

## PERSONALITY (ALTRUISM)
### X Marital Adjustment
There is no relationship between altruism and marital adjustment. (S279)

## PERSONALITY (AMBITION/AGGRESSION)
### X Sibling Structure
The girl with a younger brother is more likely to be aggressive and ambitious than is the girl with an older brother. (K126)

## PERSONALITY AND SOCIAL ADJUSTMENT OF CHILD
### X Mental Illness of Parents (Schizophrenia)
Children of schizophrenic parents are more likely to be mentally and/or socially maladjusted than are children of normals. (B285)

## PERSONALITY (ANGER)      X Ordinal Position
Firstborn females tend to have a greater tendency to anger than do second-born females, particularly at the four-to-six-year spacing. (K104)

When spacing is under two years, second-born males tend to have a greater tendency to anger than do firstborn males; this is reversed if the spacing is from two to four years. (K104)

### Sibling Structure (Sex)
Boys show a greater tendency to anger than girls do, except where spacing is under two years, when a girl with a brother shows a stronger tendency than does a boy with a brother. (K104)

## PERSONALITY (APATHY)
### X Parent-Child Relations (Nurturance)
The lack of early mothering and affectionate nurturance, such as obtains for children raised in institutions, is correlated with and produces apathetic and non-dependent personalities in later childhood. (K111)

## PERSONALITY/BEHAVIORAL PROBLEMS
### X Parent-Child Relations (Hostility)
Those children who exhibit both behavioral and personality problems at home and at school are likely to have very hostile and punitive fathers, but relatively less hostile mothers; children with only behavioral problems tend to have fathers who are relatively less hostile and mothers who are relatively more hostile. (B232)

## PERSONALITY (COMPETITIVENESS)
### X Ordinal Position
Firstborn children tend to be more competitive than do later-born children. (R106)

### Sibling Structure (Age Difference)
As the age difference between siblings increases, competitiveness increases in firstborns with male siblings. (K149)

### Sibling Structure (Sex)
Girls with younger sisters are less competitive than boys with younger sisters. (K149)

## PERSONALITY (COMPLEMENTARY NEEDS)
### X  Courtship
Need complementarity is more operative at a late than at an early stage of a romantic relationship. (K109)

### Duration of Marriage
Couples who are married longer (at least 10 years) are more likely than are couples married for shorter periods of time to have complementary need patterns. (M190)

### Husband-Wife Relations (Decisions)
The husband is more likely to accept the decisions of his wife if there is a high degree of similarity between the husband's need for succorance and the wife's need to be nurturant (nurturance and succorance measured by a forced-choice questionnaire constructed by the authors). (K118)

### Marital Stability
Marital stability is more likely if the partners have heterogamous (complementary rather than similar) psychological needs and are from similar social backgrounds. (G134)

### Mate Selection
If a man and a woman remain together for a long period of courtship despite their having a low value consensus, they probably have a high degree of need complementarity. (B002)

If a man and a woman show a high degree of need complementarity, then it is more probable that their relationship will progress toward a permanent union. (B002)

Individuals are more likely to fall in love with others whose personality needs are complementary (e.g., need for dominance and need to submit) than with those whose needs are similar. (B002)

Those couples whose need patterns are complementary are no more likely to fall in love than are those whose need patterns are similar. (B002)

In mate selection the need pattern of each spouse is more likely to be complementary, rather than similar, to the need pattern of the other spouse. (G156)

The tendency of an individual to select a spouse unlike himself in total emotional makeup exceeds the tendency for him to select a spouse like himself in that respect. (K011)

There is no relationship between mate selection and satisfaction of complementary needs. (T092)

## PERSONALITY (COMPLEMENTARY TRAITS)
### X  Mate Selection
Assertive persons tend to marry receptive persons. (W148)

If a person is highly nurturant, it is probable that the person will marry someone who is highly receptive and relatively nonnurturant. (W148)

If a person is highly dominant, it is probable that the person will marry someone who is highly submissive and relatively nondominant. (W148)

## PERSONALITY (COMPULSIVENESS)
### X  Toilet Training
Compulsive character is largely the product of severity or cruelty in treatment during the period of cleanliness training. (L166)

## PERSONALITY (COOPERATIVENESS)
### X  Marital Adjustment of Husband
Happy husbands show a greater positive attitude of cooperation than do unhappy husbands. When given orders, happy husbands enter enthusiastically into the situation and carry out the program. They have no aversion to asking advice and like carrying out the program of a respected superior. More happy husbands stress the importance of the wife's equality with the husband and reject the slogan that the husband should "wear the pants." (T074)

## PERSONALITY (CRUELTY)
### X  Parent-Child Relations (Interaction)
In democratic homes, high parent-child interaction produces a greater tendency to cruelty in the child than does low parent-child interaction.

### Parent-Child Relations (Rejection)
Rejection of the child by his parents may lead to cruelty in the child in later years. (T085)

## PERSONALITY (CURIOSITY)
### X  Parent-Child Relations (Interaction)
In democratic homes, high parent-child interaction produces greater curiosity in the child than does low parent-child interaction. (B266)

## PERSONALITY DEVELOPMENT
### X  Breast Feeding
Generous suckling and later weaning lead to generosity, optimism, and cooperative peaceful behavior; ungenerous suckling and early weaning lead to arrogance, aggression, impatience, suspicion, competitiveness, quarrelsomeness, and nostalgic sadness.

### Breast Feeding, Duration of
There is no association between the duration of breast feeding and childhood personality development. (S200)

### Child-Rearing Practices
No significant and consistent one-to-one relationships have been found between child-care practices in the first and second year and later personality development. (C124)

### Child-Rearing Practices (Genital Manipulation)
A focus on the genital stage of development is more likely to occur when genital manipulation is used as a means of quieting the infant. (S261)

### Child-Rearing Practices (Overstimulation)
Maternal overstimulation of the sensory organs of the child contributes to inadequate ego growth and possibly psychosis. (B324)

### Interaction in Family
Reciprocal exchange between family members (both nuclear and extended) and the child is responsible for the child's development of a sense of self. (C093)

### Loss of Family Member
The effects of the final loss (physically or psychologically) of a family member will be more severe the earlier in a person's life it occurs. (T089)

### Mother Absence
Children who are deprived of their mothers have an impaired ability to relate to other people, to think abstractly, and generally have an impaired ego and superego development.

### Parent-Child Relations (Affect)
The greater the emphasis on the sadomasochistic aspects of the motives of the anal phase, the more likely it is that the relations between parent and child will be highly personal and emotional rather than centering around more impersonal concerns, such as cleanliness, neatness, etc. (M203)

### Parent-Child Relations (Affection)
Insofar as a child lacks attentive love, it is more likely that its development will be delayed or retarded. (M203)

### Role Behavior in Family
Inability of an individual to perform in a variety of role relationships (characteristic of the schizophrenic) may be a result of being raised in a family structure which did not permit the operation and observance of all possible role relationships. (L121)

## PERSONALITY DEVELOPMENT (AFFECT)
### X   Surrogate Mother
Interrupted affective relationships with more than one mother figure, not allowing a satisfactory growth of mutual emotional ties, develops in the child, in later years, an affectionless character. (R100)

## PERSONALITY DEVELOPMENT (MATURITY)
### X   Child-Rearing Practices (Maturity Demands)
There is no relationship between mothers who expect overly mature behavior from their children and the child's remaining immature (as measured by general immaturity, enuresis, and reluctance to go to school). (R100)

## PERSONALITY DEVELOPMENT OF CHILD
### X   Child-Rearing Practices (Maturity Demands)
Children whose mothers encourage their maturation are higher in emotional stability, total emotional freedom, group identification, and freedom from conflict than are children whose mothers encourage infantile behavior. (A071)

### Child-Rearing Practices (Rigidity)
Children whose mothers are flexible in their use of authority are higher in assertiveness and high frustration tolerance than are children whose mothers are rigid in their use of authority. (A071)

### Marital Adjustment of Mother
Children whose mothers have had happy childhoods and whose mothers are satisfied by their marriages rate higher on Rorschach tests in emotional freedom and freedom from conflict than do children whose mothers had unhappy childhoods and whose mothers are not satisfied with their marriages. (A071)

### Mother-Child Relations (Warmth)
Children whose mothers are highly accepting and whose mothers show great warmth toward them are higher in emotional spontaneity and in total emotional freedom than are children whose mothers are rejecting. (A071)

### Personality of Parents
Because unconscious parental attitudes are less understood and more difficult to revise by children, they are more effective in influencing children than are overt expressions. (W143)

## PERSONALITY DEVELOPMENT OF CHILD (EGO STRENGTH)
### X   Personality Problems of Mother (Oral)
Mothers with unresolved oral needs are likely to have children characterized by weak ego development. (R099)

## PERSONALITY DEVELOPMENT OF CHILD (MATURITY)
### X   Parent-Child Relations (Conflict)
The less consistent the degree of maturation of the child in various spheres (legal, economic, religious, intellectual), the greater the conflict between parents and youths. (D058)

## PERSONALITY DEVELOPMENT OF PARENTS
### X   Child-Rearing Practices (Nurturance)
If a person suffers from an oral character disorder (is childish, impulse-ridden), he will give inconsistent nurture to his children when they are young and will be unable to help them with their problems of development. (R110)

### Child-Rearing Practices (Rewards and Punishment)
Parents who have anal character disorders (fixation at toilet-training and language-learning stages of development) are more likely than others to use the giving and withholding of favors as a way of training their children. (R110)

### Juvenile Delinquency
Parents with unresolved pregenital conflicts (lack of proper introjection of parental attitudes toward authority during the Oedipal phase) unconsciously advocate delinquency and therefore are more likely than others to produce delinquent children. (R110)

### Therapy
Since parents who are fixated at the phallic-urethral level of psychosexual development have a competitive orientation and ability to direct their energies, they are less likely than others to appeal to social agencies voluntarily. (R110)

## PERSONALITY (DISTRUST)
### X   Child-Rearing Practices (Consistency)
Inconsistent maternal behavior and communication lead to a basic feeling of mistrust in the child.

## PERSONALITY (DOMINANCE)
### X   Ordinal Position
When the sibling is less than two years younger, firstborn girls have more initiative and are more dominant than are boys. (K126)

## PERSONALITY (DRIVE)
### X   Child-Rearing Practices (Frustration)
Frustration in the child resulting from child-rearing practices, increases the child's general drive level.

## PERSONALITY (EGO CONTROL)
### X   Identification with Mother
Among college females, degree of ego control (containment of impulse) is positively related to degree of maternal identification, overcontrollers manifesting stronger identification than undercontrollers. (B258)

## PERSONALITY (EGO RESILIENCY)
### X   Identification with Mother
Among college females, degree of ego resiliency (capacity to adapt under the strain of new environmental demands) is unrelated to degree of maternal identification. (B258)

## PERSONALITY (EGO STRENGTH)
### X   Age at Marriage
People with feelings of ego deficiency marry earlier than do those who feel more adequate. (B293)

### Child-Rearing Practices (Permissiveness)
There is a correlation between early permissiveness and susceptibility to external social sanctions. (V029)

### Identification of Mother with Daughter
A high degree of emotional security or ego strength is directly correlated with a conscious acknowledgment on the part of the mother of a personality resemblance with her daughter. (H218)

### Illegitimacy (Adoption)
Unmarried mothers who keep their children, in comparison with those who surrender their children, tend to be lower in ego strength or stability and to be more submissive. (J020)

### Marital Status
Other things being equal (sex, age, intelligence, position in the family, nationality, father's occupation, community, and amount of education), persons who marry demonstrate greater feelings of ego deficiency than persons who remain single. (M010)

### Race Attitudes
The reaction of the Negro child to prejudice is more directly related to the amount of ego strength he has acquired from family attitudes than to the presence or absence of legal segregation in his area. (M229)

## PERSONALITY (EGOCENTRICITY)
### X   Sex Relations
Sexual promiscuity tends to be associated with an egocentric personality. (H219)

## PERSONALITY (EMOTION)     X   Dependency
The more that the child's dependence is extended to the family as a whole, as opposed to his parents, the less emotional commitment he is likely to have to his marriage (when adult) or to any other single relationship. (M198)

## PERSONALITY (EMOTIONAL STABILITY)
### X   Age at Marriage
Girls who marry in their teens are more emotionally unstable than those who do not. (M231)

### Marital Adjustment of Wife
Unhappy wives, more often than happy wives, report that their feelings alternate between happiness and sadness without apparent reason, that they are often in a state of excitement or feel grouchy, and that useless thoughts keep coming into their minds to bother them. (T074)

### Mental Illness
When members of a family are undergoing therapy, it is a frequent occurrence that as one member gets better the other gets worse. (A052)

## PERSONALITY (EMOTIONALITY)
### X   Parent-Child Relations (Interaction)
In democratic homes, high parent-child interaction produces greater emotional excitability in the child than does low parent-child interaction. (B266)

In democratic homes, high parent-child interaction produces greater intensity of emotional response in the child than does low parent-child interaction.

## PERSONALITY (EMPATHY)     X   Ordinal Position
Later-born persons empathize and identify more with others than do firstborn persons or only children. (S237)

Later-born persons tend to measure their abilities against the standards of others more than do firstborn persons or only children. (S237)

## PERSONALITY (ENTHUSIASM)
### X   Sibling Structure
The personality of a boy does not vary with the fact that he has an older brother or that he is firstborn with a younger brother, except that a boy with a much older brother is more likely to be enthusiastic. (K126)

## PERSONALITY (EXCITABILITY)
### X   Child-Rearing Practices (Punishment)
The use of physical punishment by the parents is positively associated with children who are restless and excitable. (R100)

## PERSONALITY (EXPRESSIVENESS)
### X   Mother-Child Relations (Affection)
Lack of satisfactory affective mothering impairs the infant's ability to communicate and to express feeling.

### Parent-Child Relations (Closeness)
Girls who are higher in expressive rather than in instrumental personality traits are more likely to report being closer with their fathers than with their mothers. (J026)

## PERSONALITY (FEAR)     X   Anxiety
There is a correlation between the degree of fear of others (persons and spirits) typical for a culture and the degree of anxiety typically produced by socialization in that culture. (W142)

## PERSONALITY (GUILT)
### X   Child-Rearing Practices (Punishment)
The greater the punishment (and inhibition) of extrapunitive aggression, the more likely is self-aggressive or intropunitive behavior. (K111)

## PERSONALITY (HOSTILITY)
### X   Sibling Structure (Age Difference)
The greater the age difference between siblings, the greater the hostility of the firstborn male. (K149)

## PERSONALITY (IDENTITY)
### X   Interaction in Family (Inconsistency)
Since strong identification is primary for the development of a child's identity, families with inconsistencies in intrafamilial relationships are more likely than others to produce children with disturbances in identity. (B241)

## PERSONALITY (IMPATIENCE)
### X   Parent-Child Relations (Interaction)
In democratic homes, high parent-child interaction produces greater impatience in the child than does low parent-child interaction.

## PERSONALITY (INHIBITION)
### X   Child-Rearing Practices (Punishment)
There is a correlation between maternal punitiveness and generalized inhibition in the child. (K111)

## PERSONALITY (INTROVERSION)
### X   Child-Rearing Practices (Demands)
Inhibitory demands and discipline by the parents are negatively correlated with introversion in the child. (S221)

## PERSONALITY (ISOLATION)
### X    Mother-Child Relations
In order to be "alone" (to enjoy being either physically or emotionally separate from others), one must have spent time as an infant and in early childhood in the presence of one's mother without specifically interacting with her. (W141)

## PERSONALITY (MASCULINITY)
### X    Sibling Structure (Sex)
In two-sibling families where both sibs are males, they tend to score higher on the Rosenberg-Sutton-Smith Masculinity Scale than do boys without a brother. (S221)

## PERSONALITY (MATURITY)    X    Mate Selection
People choose spouses who have identical levels of immaturity, but who have opposite defense mechanisms. (B297)

### Size of Family
Children from large families will develop a more objective and mature attitude toward their environment. (I007)

## PERSONALITY (MOTHERLINESS)
### X    Breast Feeding
The psychosomatic state of motherliness is correlated with and depends upon the mother's breast feeding of the child. (B272)

## PERSONALITY (NEATNESS)
### X    Maternal Overprotectiveness
Children of overindulging mothers are more likely to be careless, while children of domineering mothers will tend to be neat and careful. (L161)

## PERSONALITY (OBSESSIONS)
### X    Child-Rearing Practices (Rules)
Parents who follow fixed rules for living, thus developing a sense of ritual in the child, are more likely to have children who develop obsessional habits (an attachment to a particular object, insistence of certain ways of doing things, etc). (F097)

## PERSONALITY OF CHILD
### X    Child-Rearing Practices (Sex/Aggression)
Children from homes in which sexuality and aggression are denied are more likely than are children from homes in which these realities are recognized to have distortions of and uncertainties about their own perceptions of family situations. (S212)

### Father Absence
When the father is absent (as in sailor families), the mother is the source of the male child's main frustrations and his personality is likely to be either passive-feminine or phallic-narcissistic.

### Maternal Overprotectiveness
Children whose mothers are *indulgently* overprotective will tend to be rebellious and aggressive; those whose mothers are *dominatingly* overprotective will be submissive and dependent. (L163)

### Parent-Child Relations (Acceptance)
There is an association between acceptance by parents of their children and the following personality characteristics in the children: greater sociability, friendliness, loyalty, emotional stability, cheerfulness, dependability.

### Parental-Role Adjustment
Parents who experienced neglect, deprivation, or rejection by their parents in their youth are likely to be deficient in the capacity to care for their children and, consequently, to produce children who mature into persons much like themselves. (B270)

### Personality of Mother
There is an inverse correlation between dependency, conformity, and cooperation of the mother and the child. (R113)

Children who are bullying, domineering, aggressive, and overly competitive with other children tend to have mothers with parallel problems serving as models for them. (R113)

Children who are hostile and disobedient tend to have aggressive mothers who serve as models for the pathology in their children. (R113)

Children who have nail-biting and thumb-sucking problems are likely to have mothers who have a parallel problem (superego conflict). (R113)

### Personality of Parents
Children tend to imitate parental defense mechanisms. (B220)

Fathers and mothers are more similar to each other (MMPI scores) than to their children. (S241)

### Surrogate Parent
Nervous, anxious children are best placed in quiet conventional types of homes, while active, aggressive children are best in free and easy homes with companions. (B270)

### Toilet Training
Severity of anal training is associated with compulsivity and rigidity of control (as measured by the Cattell Personality Test).

Severe anal training is associated with lower sociability.

## PERSONALITY OF CHILD (ACTIVITY DRIVE)
### X    Identification with Parent
The greater the strength of an exploratory or activity drive in the child, the more likely it is that he will emulate the behavior of a parent who is active in the manipulation of the environment, even without direct reinforcement. (B234)

## PERSONALITY OF CHILD (AGGRESSION)
### X    Achievement Values
There is a positive association between high achievement-oriented homes and resulting aggressive, tense, domineering, and cruel personality traits in children. (B252)

### Work Attitudes of Mother
Children of mothers with positive attitudes toward their work are less likely to be assertive, effective, or hostile in their social relations than are children whose mothers dislike their work. (S265)

## PERSONALITY OF CHILD (AGGRESSION/GUILT)
### X    Child-Rearing Practices (Power)
Direct power-assertive disciplinary techniques are associated with aggression in the child and "softer" disciplinary techniques with repression and guilt. (H201)

## PERSONALITY OF CHILD (ANAL CHARACTER)
### X Achievement Motivation
The greater the mother's need for achievement, the more likely she is to have children with an anal character.

### Child-Rearing Practices (Rigidity)
Anal character in the child is positively related to the rigidity of the mother in child rearing.

## PERSONALITY OF CHILD (ANTI-SOCIAL)
### X Maternal Deprivation
Maternal deprivation causes anxieties to arise in deprived children over the unsatisfactory parent-child relationship that predispose children to respond in an antisocial way to later stresses. (B270)

## PERSONALITY OF CHILD (ANXIETY)
### X Mother-Child Relations (Consistency)
When a period of affectional demonstrativeness from the mother is followed by emotional aloofness, the personality of the child will reflect a deep-seated anxiety and a feeling of insecurity toward the world. (H054)

## PERSONALITY OF CHILD (AUTHORITARIANISM)
### X Child-Rearing Practices (Authoritarianism)
Authoritarian control by the father correlates with the child's attitudes of deification of the parent, devotion to the father role, the child's adjustment to the present situation, the father's suppression of aggression and sex, fostering of dependency, and the use of punishment. (N053)

### Conformity
The more authoritarian and "self-rejecting" the Jewish individual is, the less is his deviation from his parents' ethocentric ideology, despite exposure to the liberalizing atmosphere of college. (H244)

## PERSONALITY OF CHILD (COMPETITIVENESS)
### X Authority Structure of Family
Children who are overly competitive with siblings tend to come from families in which there are conflicting authority figures. (R113)

### Child-Rearing Practices (Favoritism)
A child whose mother shows a marked preference for a sibling tends to be overly competitive with siblings and with other children. (R113)

### Maternal Overprotectiveness
Children whose mothers are overly protective and infantilizing in their behavior toward them are not likely to be overly competitive with siblings or with others. (R113)

### Parent-Child Relations (Interaction)
In democratic homes, high parent-child interaction produces greater competitiveness in the child than does low parent-child interaction. (B266)

## PERSONALITY OF CHILD (CONFLICT)
### X Role Conflict of Parents
The greater the parental conflict between familial and outside roles, the more likely it is that the child internalizes conflicting standards. (F106)

## PERSONALITY OF CHILD (CONSIDERATION FOR OTHERS)
### X Child-Rearing Practices (Power)
In a high power-assertive context, the child is likely to develop consideration for others based solely on fear of punishment. (H212)

Children raised in homes in which power was not used arbitrarily are likely to develop consideration for others if either love-oriented or other-oriented discipline is used. (H212)

The development of consideration for others by children raised in homes in which power was not used arbitrarily is independent of the type of discipline used. (H212)

## PERSONALITY OF CHILD (CURIOSITY)
### X Child-Rearing Practices (Clarity)
Among homes characterized by a high level of parental explanation of family decisions, explicit behavior restrictions produce a child who has restricted curiosity. (B266)

### Child-Rearing Practices (Giving Reasons)
Children from families characterized by a high level of explanation by the parents of family decisions are more curious than are children from homes where there is not much explanation of family decisions. (B266)

## PERSONALITY OF CHILD (DEPENDENCY)
### X Child-Rearing Practices (Consistency)
Mothers of overdependent children tend to be less consistent in their interaction with their children than do mothers in the control group. (S204)

Consistency of mother-child interactions is unrelated to the development of autonomy in the infant. (Y042)

### Parent-Child Relations (Affect)
Early and severe emotional deprivation decreases dependency strivings in the child. (M221)

### Parent Loss
Children reared without normal parental relationships develop clinging dependence upon appropriate figures in later life. (G128)

## PERSONALITY OF CHILD (DEPRESSION)
### X Child-Rearing Practices (Favoritism)
A child who is depressed and discouraged tends to have a mother who shows preference for the child's sibling. (R113)

### Personality of Mother
Children whose mothers have similar personality problems are less likely to be depressed. (R113)

### Power Structure of Family
Children coming from families in which there is conflict over authority are likely to be depressed and discouraged. (R113)

### Surrogate Mother
Children who are cared for by adults other than the mother for a significant proportion of the time are more likely to appear depressed and discouraged. (R113)

## PERSONALITY OF CHILD (DISOBEDIENCE)
### X Power Structure of Family
A family situation in which there are conflicting authorities tends to be associated with disobedience and hostility in the child. (R113)

## PERSONALITY OF CHILD (DOMINANCE)
### X Mother-Child Relations (Hostility)
The more hostile and punitive the mother, the greater the tendency of the child to be dominant (rather than submissive). (B232)

## PERSONALITY OF CHILD (EGO STRENGTH)
### X    Child-Rearing Practices (Demands)
Inhibitory demands and discipline by the parents are correlated with ego weakness in the child. (S221)

### Child-Rearing Practices (Permissiveness)
There is a correlation between parental tolerance and ego strength in the child. (S221)

### Identification with Parents
The weaker the child's ego, the more it resorts to identification with parents and other adult figures in its adjustment to the adult world.

### Parent-Child Relations (Warmth)
The degree of parental emotional warmth and support is negatively correlated with ego weakness and introversion in the child. (S221)

## PERSONALITY OF CHILD (EMOTIONAL MATURITY)    X    Breast Feeding, Duration of
There is a correlation between months of breast feeding and the emotional maturity of the child. (B272)

### Feeding (Demand)
There is a correlation between degree of self-regulation of food intake and the emotional maturity of the child. (B272)

## PERSONALITY OF CHILD (EMOTIONALITY)
### X    Surrogate Mother
At one year of age, infants from families where child care is provided by the mother only show more emotional responses (crying and smiling) than do infants from families where child care is provided by more than one mother figure. (C107)

## PERSONALITY OF CHILD (EXPRESSIVENESS)
### X    Occupation of Father
Among children whose fathers' occupations are nonacademic, there may be a greater allowance and acceptance of expression of emotion than among children whose fathers have academic jobs. (G117)

## PERSONALITY OF CHILD (EXTROVERSION)
### X    Size of Family
Extroversion should be more predominant than introversion among children of the small family. (I007)

## PERSONALITY OF CHILD (FEAR)
### X    Child-Rearing Practices (Clarity)
In homes where there is a high level of parental explanation of family decisions, the more explicit the behavioral restrictions, the more fearful the child. (B266)

### Child-Rearing Practices (Giving Reasons)
Children from homes where there is a high level of explanation by the parents of family decisions are more fearless than are children from homes where there is not much explanation of family decisions. (B266)

### Surrogate Mother
Among children of mothers who work, those whose mothers have provided a succession of different mother substitutes have more fears than do those whose mothers have provided more stable arrangements. (Y047)

## PERSONALITY OF CHILD (GUILT)
### X    Aggression
The less able the child is to display aggression against his parents, the more likely is he to become intropunitive.

## PERSONALITY OF CHILD (HOSTILITY)
### X    Child-Rearing Practices (Authoritarianism)
Parents who control their children in an authoritarian manner are more likely than those who rationally discipline their children to produce adolescents with high fantasy-hostility. (C113)

If parents are affectionate toward their children, then the degree of overt hostility expressed by adolescents will be positively related to the authoritarian control by their parents. (C113)

### Child-Rearing Practices (Permissiveness)
Children having mothers who are overly permissive are likely to be hostile and disobedient. (R113)

### Child-Rearing Practices (Power)
As the child's dependence on his parents decreases, the parents' unqualified power assertion is less likely to result in hostility, power assertiveness, and resistance to influence on the part of the child. (H182)

### Mother-Child Relations (Hostility)
Hostile mothers are more likely than those who are not hostile to produce children who are covertly hostile. (F103)

### Parent-Child Relations (Affection)
Parents who are not affectionate toward their children are more likely than those who are affectionate to produce overtly hostile adolescents, regardless of the degree of authoritarian control exerted. (C113)

### Parent–Child Relations (Hostility)
The greater the general hostility of the parent toward the child, the more likely the genesis of hostility in the child. (B232)

### Personality of Mother (Rigidity)
Since a mother's rigidity tends to produce anxiety (which inhibits aggressive action) and submission in her child, mothers who are rigid are more likely than those who are not rigid to produce children who are covertly hostile. (F103)

## PERSONALITY OF CHILD (IMPULSIVENESS)
### X    Child-Rearing Practices (Demands)
Inhibitory parental demands and discipline are correlated with impulsivity in the child. (S221)

### Personality of Mother
Submissive, uncertain, and anxious mothers tend to have children who are impulsive and uncontrolled. (B219)

## PERSONALITY OF CHILD (INHIBITION)
### X    Personality Problems of Mother (Masochism)
Masochistic behavior by the mother tends to produce extreme self-inhibition in the child. (S281)

## PERSONALITY OF CHILD (INTROVERSION)
### X    Cohesion of Family
The greater the familial involvement of the parents, the less likely is introversion in the child. (S221)

## PERSONALITY OF CHILD (IRRITABILITY)
### X    Surrogate Mother
At six months of age, infants reared in families where the mothering is provided by one person are less irritable than are infants reared in families where the mothering is provided by more than one person (i.e., nurse, grandparent, mother's friend, or older sister of the child). (C124)

## PERSONALITY OF CHILD (LONELINESS)
### X Surrogate Parent
Children who are reared by several parent surrogates (rather than by one or both parents or by merely one surrogate) are more likely than others to develop feelings of isolation and loneliness. (W143)

## PERSONALITY OF CHILD (MASTERY)
### X Mother-Child Relations (Feeding)
The more satisfactory the feeding experience for the child, the greater his interest in and concentration upon the mastery of objects is likely to be. (B272)

## PERSONALITY OF CHILD (MATURITY)
### X Father Absence
The absence of the father from the home (separation or divorce) is associated with greater immaturity in the son. (L171)

There is a direct relationship between the absence of a father from the home and a child's preference for immediate rather than delayed gratification (an indicatory of level of maturity). (M207)

The absence of the father will not affect the maturity of the children of a delayed-reward culture, such as Grenada (characterized by trust in economic affairs, i.e., long-term payments), as it does the children of an "immediate-reward culture." (M207)

Norwegian girls maintain greater maturity than boys do after the absence of the father from the home; this difference is not manifest in the Caribbean culture. (M207)

Absence of the father leads to immaturity in the young child, but not in the child over 11. (M207)

### Maternal Overprotectiveness
Overprotective and infantilizing behavior on the part of the mother tends to foster general immaturity in the child. (R113)

### Mother-Child Relations (Seductiveness)
Children whose mothers are overly seductive in their behavior toward them tend to be generally immature. (R113)

## PERSONALITY OF CHILD (NEEDS)
### X Father Absence
Boys whose fathers are absent from the family are less inclined to postpone gratification of their needs than are those whose fathers are at home. (B275)

### Parent-Child Relations (Frustration)
Absence of extreme frustration is associated with the child's ability to defer gratification. (B275)

## PERSONALITY OF CHILD (NEGATIVISM)
### X Child-Rearing Practices (Clarity)
Among homes characterized by a high level of parental explanation of family decisions, the more explicit the behavior restrictions, the less negative the children are. (B266)

## PERSONALITY OF CHILD (NERVOUSNESS/ANXIETY)
### X Power Structure of Family
Perceived maternal dominance is positively related to signs of nervousness and anxiety in adolescents. (E102)

## PERSONALITY OF CHILD (NIGHTMARES)
### X Authority Structure of Family
Children who have nightmares are likely to come from families in which there are conflicting authority figures. (R113)

### Maternal Overprotectiveness
Children whose mothers are overly protective and infantilizing in their behavior toward them tend to have frequent nightmares. (R113)

## PERSONALITY OF CHILD (OBEDIENCE)
### X Child-Rearing Practices (Sex Role)
Because of sex-typed child-rearing practices, girls tend to be more obedient and cooperative than boys. (B252)

## PERSONALITY OF CHILD (OTHER-ORIENTATION)
### X Power Structure of Family
Girls who perceive their mothers to be the more dominant are more other-oriented than are those who perceive both their parents to be equally dominant. (S252)

## PERSONALITY OF CHILD (PESSIMISM)
### X Child-Rearing Practices (Nurturance)
Mothers who are not nurturant are more likely to produce pessimistic children than are mothers who respond helpfully and fulfill children's needs. (F103)

## PERSONALITY OF CHILD (PLANFULNESS)
### X Child-Rearing Practices (Clarity)
Among homes characterized by a high level of explanation by the parents of family decisions, the more explicit the behavior restrictions, the less planful the child. (B266)

### Child-Rearing Practices (Giving Reasons)
Children from homes characterized by a high level of explanation by the parents of family decisions are more planful than are children from homes where there is not much explanation of family decisions. (B266)

## PERSONALITY OF CHILD (PSEUDOMATURITY)
### X Father Absence
When the father is absent for long periods of time, children are likely to develop a facade of maturity.

## PERSONALITY OF CHILD (PUNITIVENESS)
### X Child-Rearing Practices (Punishment)
Parents who are punitive are likely to have children who are also punitive [children's punitiveness measured by the Problem Situations Test (PST)]. (L149)

## PERSONALITY OF CHILD (QUIETNESS)
### X Child-Rearing Practices (Clarity)
Among homes characterized by a high level of parental explanation of family decisions, explicit behavioral restrictions produce a quiet child. (B266)

## PERSONALITY OF CHILD (RESPONSIBILITY)
### X Authority Structure of Family
The more equal the parental authority, the lower the child's ratings for responsible behavior. (B250)

### Cohesion of Family
There is a correlation between the strength of family ties of the child (college student) and the extent to which he assumes responsible adult roles. (R116)

### Mother-Child Relations (Discipline)
There is a positive association between responsibility of the daughter and the son (based on teachers' ratings of

dependability in fulfilling obligations) and discipline and authority from the mother. (B250)

## PERSONALITY OF CHILD (RESTLESS/EXCITABLE)
### X   Authority Structure of Family
Children who are restless and excitable tend to come from families in which there are conflicting authority figures. (R113)

### Child-Rearing Practices (Criticism)
Children whose mothers are excessively critical and depreciative of them tend to be restless and excitable. (R113)

### Child-Rearing Practices (Favoritism)
Children whose mothers show a marked preference for a sibling are likely to be restless and excitable. (R113)

## PERSONALITY OF CHILD (RIGIDITY)
### X   Personality of Parents (Rigidity)
If the parents score high in rigidity/flexibility measurements, the child will also score high; and if the parents score low, then the child will also score low. (A055)

There is no significant relationship between parents' amd child's rigidity/flexibility measurements. (A055)

## PERSONALITY OF CHILD (SECURITY)
### X   Breast Feeding, Duration of
Persons who were never breast fed or who were breast fed for over one year, show more security than do those who were breast fed for intermediate periods. (B272)

## PERSONALITY OF CHILD (SELF-ASSERTIVENESS)
### X   Surrogate Mother
Children of working mothers who have provided substitute care are more self-assertive than are children of mothers who do not work and who remain with their children. (Y047)

## PERSONALITY OF CHILD (SELF-CONCEPTION)
### X   Parent-Child Relations (Communication)
### X   Self-Conception
Students who rarely or never participated in family mealtime conversations or who felt that family members were not interested in what they had to say are considerably more likely than others to have low self-esteem. (R129)

## PERSONALITY OF CHILD (SELF-CONFIDENCE)
### X   Child-Rearing Practices (Democratic)
When parents seldom explain their rules to children, children of democratic parents are more apt to express self-confidence than are children of autocratic or permissive parents. (E105)

### Parent-Son Relations (Warmth)
Among boys, warm father-son relations are associated with a high degree of self-confidence in the son regarding his abilities; warm mother-son relations are associated with a low degree of self-confidence regarding abilities. (H201)

## PERSONALITY OF CHILD (SELF-CONTROL)
### X   Identification with Like-Sex Parent
The more a girl takes her mother as a role model, the greater is the degree of impulse control that she will manifest. (B288)

## PERSONALITY OF CHILD (SELF-ESTEEM)
### X   Age of Mother
Children whose mothers were relatively young when they were widowed are less likely to have high self-

esteem than those whose mothers were older when widowed. (R129)

### Bereavement/Remarriage
Children whose parents were separated by death are likely to have as high self-esteem as those from intact families if the widowed parent does not remarry. (R129)

### Religion
Catholic children of divorced parents are more likely than Catholics and Jews from intact families to have low self-esteem, but divorce makes no difference in level of self-esteem among Protestant families. (R129)

Among children whose families have been broken by death, there is no relationship between religion and low self-esteem. (R129)

Among Catholics and Protestants, differences in levels of self-esteem between only boys and girls are much smaller than is the case among Jewish children. (R129)

## PERSONALITY OF CHILD (SHYNESS)
### X   Child-Rearing Practices (Control)
Children whose mothers are rigidly dominating and controlling tend to be shy. (R113)

### Father-Child Relations (Closeness)
There is a positive relationship between fathers who are cold, distant and neglectful and shyness in the child. (R100)

## PERSONALITY OF CHILD (SOCIABILITY)
### X   Child-Rearing Practices (Punishment)
Girls who received a great deal of "interaction type of discipline" (parental reasoning, being spanked, punished by having to aid in household tasks) develop a greater interest in being with people when they become adults than do girls who received noninteraction discipline (told to leave the room, prevented from being with friends, etc. ) during childhood; this is not true for boys. (H191)

### Surrogate Parent
Persons reared by multiple parental figures are more social than those reared by one or two parents. (W158)

## PERSONALITY OF CHILD (SPEECH DEFECTS)
### X   Child-Rearing Practices (Responsibility)
Children who are given too many responsibilities by their mothers are more likely to develop speech defects. (R113)

## PERSONALITY OF CHILD (STABILITY)
### X   Surrogate Mother
Having many good (constant) mothers leads to stable personality development in the child.

## PERSONALITY OF CHILD (STRESS)
### X   Child-Rearing Practices (Adaptation)
The extent to which the mother adapts the experiences and materials to the infant's individual capacities is positively related to the infant's capacity to cope with stress. (Y042)

### Child-Rearing Practices (Consistency)
There is a low but positive relationship between maternal consistency and the infant's ability to cope with stress situations. (Y042)

### Child-Rearing Practices (Physical Contact)
The amount and quality of physical contact between mother and child are positively related to the infant's capacity to handle stress. (Y042)

### Mother-Child Relations (Acceptance)
The mother's acceptance of the child is positively related to the infant's capacity to cope with stress. (Y042)

### Mother-Child Relations (Affect)
The mother's emotional involvement with the child is positively related to the infant's capacity to cope with stress. (Y042)

### Mother-Child Relations (Affection)
Affectional interchange between mother and infant is positively related to the infant's capacity to cope with stress. (Y042)

### Mother-Child Relations (Frustration)
The greater the infant's frustration in the mother-child relationship, the less able is the infant to cope with stress situations. (Y042)

### Surrogate Mother
Whether the infant is cared for predominantly by the mother or by other persons is not related to his capacity to cope with stress situations. (Y042)

## PERSONALITY OF CHILD (STUBBORNNESS)
### X   Child-Rearing Practices (Rigidity)
There is no relationship between the mother's rigidity in child rearing and stubbornness in the child.

## PERSONALITY OF CHILD (SUBMISSIVENESS)
### X   Child-Rearing Practices (Nurturance)
The less nurturant the mother, the more submissive the child.

### Child-Rearing Practices (Rigidity)
There is no relationship between the mother's rigidity in child rearing and submissiveness in the child.

### Maternal Overprotectiveness
The more overprotective the mother, the more likely is the child to be submissive.

### Parent-Child Relations (Dominance)
A dominating parent will tend to induce submission in the child. (B033)

## PERSONALITY OF CHILD (TENACITY)
### X   Child-Rearing Practices (Clarity)
Among homes characterized by a high level of explanation by the parents of family decisions, the more explicit the behavior restrictions, the less tenacious the child. (B266)

## PERSONALITY OF CHILD (TIMIDITY)
### X   Child-Rearing Practices (Sex Role)
Because of sex-typed child-rearing practices, girls tend to be more timid and sensitive to rejection than boys. (B252)

## PERSONALITY OF CHILD (WITHDRAWAL)
### X   Achievement Demands
Children whose mothers are very concerned with the children's achievement tend to be withdrawn and seclusive and are likely to indulge in daydreaming to a great degree. (R113)

### Child-Rearing Practices (Criticism)
Children whose mothers are excessively critical and depreciative tend to be shy, seclusive, and withdrawn and to daydream a great deal. (R113)

### Surrogate Mother
Children who are cared for by an adult other than the mother for a significant proportion of the time are likely to be withdrawn and seclusive and to indulge in daydreaming to a great degree. (R113)

## PERSONALITY OF DAUGHTER
### X   Personality of Parents
More significant correlations were obtained between the MMPI scores of mothers and daughters than between those of fathers and daughters. (S241)

## PERSONALITY OF DAUGHTER (DOMINANCE)
### X   Identification with Cross-Sex Parent
Girls who rank high in dominance show stronger identification with their fathers than with their mothers. (R126)

### Parent-Child Relations (Hostility)
The more the father's hostility exceeds the mother's, the less is the tendency for the daughter to become dominant (v. submissive). (B232)

## PERSONALITY OF DAUGHTER (EXPRESSIVENESS/INSTRUMENTAL)
### X   Father-Child Relations (Closeness)
Expressive personality traits in the daughter are associated with perception of the father as attentive and protective; instrumental personality traits are associated with perception of the father as cold, distant, and critical. (J026)

### Personality of Mother
Whether the girl is more expressive or instrumental in her personality orientation is not related to her perceptions of her mother. (J026)

## PERSONALITY OF FATHER     X   Aggression
A child who is judged by his parents as aggressive, uncontrolled, and hard to discipline is likely to have a father (as judged by either the father *himself* or by the mother) who is cold and aloof, severe and authoritarian, tense, immature, prone to anger, disorganized, and unsuccessful. (B237)

### Child-Rearing Attitudes (Permissiveness)
Fathers who express permissive child-rearing attitudes are more likely to be self-reliant, ascendant, rebellious toward authority figures, persuasive, counteractive, and sarcastic. (B227)

### Child-Rearing Attitudes (Restrictiveness)
Fathers who are more restrictive in their attitudes toward child rearing tend to be constricted, submissive, suggestible individuals with little self-assurance; fathers who are more permissive tend to be more self-reliant, ascendant, and to function effectively (Q-Sort Personality Evaluations). (S249)

### Child-Rearing Practices (Control)
The more the father tends to internalize conflict (MMPI IR Score), the more likely the son is to perceive the mother to be "controlling" and "hostile controlling." (V038)

### Child-Rearing Practices (Restrictiveness)
Restrictive fathers are more likely to be submissive, suggestible, conforming, indecisive, ineffectual, and overcontrolled. (B227)

#### Criminality
Normal persons are more likely than habitual criminals to have fathers characterized as successful and respected, strict, strong, and demonstrating leadership. (C105)

#### Dependency
Pervasively dependent boys (who seek dependent relationships in an indiscriminate manner) tend to be raised in family environments characterized by dominant fathers, by paternal neuroses, grandiosity, feelings of victimization, aggressiveness, and excessive drinking. (M221)

#### Marital Adjustment of Son
Unsatisfactorily married men believe that their fathers are more dominant and less loving than themselves. (L140)

#### Mental Illness (Schizophrenia)
Fathers of female schizophrenics frequently are in severe conflict with their wives, are paranoid, and are eager to gain the support of their daughters. (L123)

Schizophrenia tends to be correlated with perception of the father as a weak, effeminate person. (N061)

#### Scholastic Adjustment
The fathers of school phobics are more likely than those of normal children to be passive and ineffectual; the mothers are more likely to be dominant. (D065)

### PERSONALITY OF FATHER (ANTISOCIAL)
#### X   Father-Son Relations (Affection)
Insufficient paternal affection is associated with the son's perception of his father as unsocial or antisocial. (M204)

### PERSONALITY OF FATHER (CHANGE)
#### X   Scholastic Achievement
Fathers of daughters who are poor academically are higher on the PARI Scale of Change Orientation than are fathers of daughters who do well academically. (S230)

### PERSONALITY OF FATHER (COMPULSIVENESS)
#### X   Mental Illness (Autism)
Autism is more likely to occur if the father exhibits compulsive behavior during the vulnerable developmental period. (S188)

### PERSONALITY OF FATHER (DOMINANCE)
#### X   Scholastic Achievement of Son
Fathers of sons with high college achievement records are less dominating than are fathers of sons with low achievement records (as measured on the Teahan Dominance Subscale). (T103)

#### Social Adjustment
Fathers are more dominant in families of schizophrenic patients who were rated to have had relatively good premorbid adjustment than are fathers of patients having very poor premorbid adjustment (Phillips Scale). (F115)

### PERSONALITY OF FATHER (HOSTILITY)
#### X   Father-Child Relations (Evaluation)
The father's perceived negative feelings toward others (hostility, etc.) are correlated with his perceptions of the child as hostile toward others, even though the actual hostility of the child is not so related.

### PERSONALITY OF FATHER/HUSBAND
#### (SIMILARITY)        X   Marital Adjustment
Marital happiness is directly related to the congruence between the wife's perception of her husband and her perception of her father. (T092)

### PERSONALITY OF FATHER (IRRESPONSIBILITY)
#### X   Scholastic Achievement
As measured by the PARI, fathers of sons who are poor academically are more likely to be irresponsible than are fathers of sons who do well academically. (S230)

### PERSONALITY OF FATHER (MASCULINITY)
#### X   Sex-Role Identification of Daughter
Strong sex-role identification in the daughter is associated with fathers who are high in masculine interests and attitudes (measured by the California Psychological Inventory). (M206)

#### Sex-Role Identification of Son
Fathers who are high on masculine interests and attitudes (measured by the California Psychological Inventory) are no more likely than those who are lower on the scale to foster strong sex-role identification in their sons. (M206)

### PERSONALITY OF FATHER/MOTHER
#### X   Illegitimacy
The personalities of the unmarried mother and father are more likely to be of similar neurotic structure than of different neurotic structure (i.e., equally irresponsible, dependent, and hostile to opposite sex). (Y048)

### PERSONALITY OF FATHER (PUNITIVENESS)
#### X   Personality Adjustment of Child
If the father is cold, maladjusted, and punitive, then the child tends to be maladjusted. (P070)

### PERSONALITY OF FATHER (SELF-ACCEPTANCE)
#### X   Sex-Role Identification
There is no relationship between the father's self-acceptance and the strength of the son's or daughter's appropriate sex-role identification. (M206)

### PERSONALITY OF FATHER (SELF-CONFIDENCE)
#### X   Child-Rearing Practices (Restrictiveness)
Restrictive child rearing by the father is positively associated with his being submissive and having little self-assurance in situations outside of the home. (R100)

### PERSONALITY OF FATHER (SOCIABILITY)
#### X   Mental Illness of Child (Schizophrenia)
Fathers of preschizophrenic patients were less gregarious than were fathers of normal children. (H241)

### PERSONALITY OF FATHER (VIOLENCE)
#### X   Mental Illness (Schizophrenia/Neurosis)
In the lower class, more fathers of schizophrenics than of neurotics are likely to be physically violent. (M197)

### PERSONALITY OF FATHER (WITHDRAWAL)
#### X   Personality of Son (Withdrawal)
A child whose personality exhibits general social withdrawal is likely to have a father with the same characteristics. (B237)

### PERSONALITY OF FEMALE RELATIVE
#### X   Mental Illness (Social Adjustment)
Mental patients with low levels of posthospital social and work performance are more likely than those with high levels of performance to be living with female relatives who are "atypical" in personality (i.e., more au-

thoritarian, anomic, frustrated, rigid, and withdrawn than relatives of high performers). (F124)

## PERSONALITY OF FIRSTBORN MALES
### X   Sibling Structure (Age Difference)
The wider the spacing between siblings, the higher are boys with younger siblings rated in social attitudes. (K149)

The greater the age difference between siblings, the less dependent, more dominant, more aggressive, and more hostile are boys with younger sisters. (K149)

## PERSONALITY OF GIRL (MASCULINITY)
### X   Sibling Structure
Girls with a brother tend to develop more feminine characteristics than do girls with a sister, who rather tend to develop more masculine characteristics. (S233)

## PERSONALITY OF GRANDPARENTS
### X   Mental Illness (Schizophrenia)
There is a direct correlation between schizophrenia (female) and a maternal grandmother with a domineering and overprotective personality and a maternal grandfather with a passive personality. (L118)

## PERSONALITY OF HUSBAND
### X   Husband-Wife Relations (Wife Beating)
Husbands who beat their wives tend to be more passive, indecisive, and sexually inadequate than are other husbands. (S253)

### Marital Adjustment of Husband
Unhappy husbands are much more defensive, oversensitive, and contentious than are happy husbands. (T074)

Happy husbands are more likely to take initiative and responsibility than are unhappy husbands. Unhappy husbands are more likely to say that they are carefree, do not worry about possible misfortunes, and that people do not come to them for advice. (T074)

## PERSONALITY OF HUSBAND (FANTASY)
### X   Marital Adjustment
Unhappy husbands more often report a liking for activities usually considered adventurous or spectacular. There is a greater tendency on the part of unhappy men to compensate for their lesser self-confidence or their failure to command response by fantasies feeding the desire for recognition. Unhappy men also daydream more than happy husbands do. (T074)

## PERSONALITY OF HUSBAND (HOSTILITY)
### X   Personality of Wife (Hostility)
The higher the husband's score on concern with negative/passive relations (complaints, resentment, etc), the higher the wife's score.

## PERSONALITY OF HUSBAND (SELF-CONFIDENCE)
### X   Marital Adjustment of Husband
Happily married husbands have greater self-confidence and show less diffidence in social situations than do unhappily married husbands. Happy husbands are more likely than unhappy husbands to liven up a group on a dull day or to take the lead in enlivening a dull party. Unhappy husbands more often prefer listening to a story to telling one, are unable to play their best against a superior opponent, and dislike full-dress affairs. (T074)

## PERSONALITY OF HUSBAND (SIMILARITY)
### X   Husband-Wife Relations (Evaluation)
Wives who perceive a high degree of similarity between themselves and their husbands and those who do not are equally likely to see their husbands as having desirable social traits. (K124)

## PERSONALITY OF HUSBAND (SYMPATHY)
### X   Marital Adjustment of Husband
Unhappy husbands, more often than happy husbands, disregard the feelings of others when accomplishing an end that is important to themselves, are more often considered to be critical of others, and are more likely to upbraid a workman who fails to have his work done on time. (T074)

## PERSONALITY OF HUSBAND/WIFE
### X   Duration of Marriage
There is a correlation between degree of similarity in psychological complexity of marital partners, as measured by the number of "human movement" responses to Rorschach tests, and the duration of the marriage.

There is a correlation between complementarity of personality traits of marital partners, as measured by the quality of "human movement" responses to Rorschach tests, and the duration of marriage.

Interaction between husbands and wives leads to assimilation of roles and both tend to grow more alike through time. (B216)

There is no evidence that spouses grow more alike in terms of interests, attitudes, temperament, and intellectual abilities as the length of marriage increases. (N073)

### Marital Adjustment
Marital success is correlated with the temperamental compatibility of the husband and wife. (B033)

### Role Behavior
Lack of personality "fit" between marital partners may be a cause of breakdown in role performance by one of them. (R105)

## PERSONALITY OF HUSBAND/WIFE (AUTHORITY)
### X   Husband-Wife Relations (Power)
Where the husband is not rebellious toward authority and the wife is rebellious toward authority, the wife is more likely than not to be more dominant than the husband. (L014)

## PERSONALITY OF HUSBAND/WIFE (SIMILARITY)
### X   Homogamy
Psychological similarity between marital partners is less likely than is sociocultural similarity. (T092)

## PERSONALITY OF KIN
### X   Mental Illness (Social Adjustment)
Formerly hospitalized mental patients who live with female relatives described as atypical in personality (being authoritarian, anomic, frustrated, rigid, and withdrawn) are likely to be less steadily employed and to participate in fewer social activities than are those who live with "normal" female relatives. (F098)

Social and vocational performance levels of mental patients are more likely to be high when their family members have personality characteristics which indicate competence in handling interpersonal relationships. (F124)

There is a relationship between family members' inhibition scores and patients' posthospital social and vocational performances (Srole and Brim combined Authoritarianism, Rigidity, and Intelligence Scales). (F124)

There is a correlation between relatives' depression scores and mental patients' posthospital social and vocational performance levels (Srole and Brim combined Cycloid Thinking, Frustration, and Autism Scales). (F124)

Mental patients who remain in their communities in spite of unsatisfactory social adjustment tend to have female relatives who are anomic, authoritarian, frustrated, rigid, and withdrawn. (S245)

There are no significant personality differences between relatives of mental patients who were rehospitalized and of those who succeeded in remaining in the community (Srole's Authoritarian, Anomia, Frustration, Rigidity, and Withdrawal Scales). (F124)

Relatives of patients performing at high levels occupationally and socially are more likely than are relatives of low-level performers to respond to the personality scales in ways that "reflect the ideal stereotype of the dominant society." (F124)

Relatives of patients whose responses on five personality scales reflect the "ideal stereotypes of the dominant society" are more likely than those who do not to impose higher demands for instrumental performance on the released mental patient. (F124)

Autism (Brim Scale) in relatives' personality scores is related to low levels of social and occupational performance of male mental patients. (F124)

Cycloid Thinking (Brim Scale) in relatives is related to a low level of social and occupational performance of female mental patients. (F124)

Self-sufficiency (Brim Scale) in relatives is related to higher levels of social and occupational performance of both male and female mental patients. (F124)

Emotionality (Brim Scale) in relatives is related to low levels of social and occupational performance of female mental patients, but this is not true of males. (F124)

Nervousness (Brim Scale) of relatives is related to low levels of social and occupational performance of female mental patients, but it is not related to performance of males. (F124)

High social and occupational performance of males is related to responses of low persistence (Brim Scale) from their relatives, but the opposite is the case for female patients. (F124)

Impulsiveness (Brim Scale) in relatives is related to low levels of occupational and social performance of female mental patients, but it is not related to performance of males. (F124)

### Role Definition in Family
Relatives who are less authoritarian, anomic, and frustrated have higher expectations of performance from mental patients. (F124)

Among female patients, expectations are correlated only with type of family, not with the personality traits of the kin. (F124)

## PERSONALITY OF MATERNAL GRANDMOTHER
### X Incest (Father-Daughter)
In families where father-daughter incest occurs, the maternal grandmothers were apt to be stern, demanding, controlling, cold, and hostile, rejecting their daughters and pampering their sons. (K091)

## PERSONALITY OF MEN (LEADERSHIP)
### X Polygyny
Polygyny is likely to create a large supply of men committed to community roles requiring a high degree of skill and responsibility, (e.g., priesthood, war leadership, estate management, and headship of lineages). (P083)

## PERSONALITY OF MOTHER        X Alcoholism
Alcoholism tends to be correlated with a serious frustration of ego needs on the part of the mother. (C122)

### Behavior Problems
A child who is a conduct problem is likely to have a mother whose personality (as estimated by her or her husband) demonstrates rejection, withdrawal, nervousness, inconsistency, and irritable aggressiveness. (B237)

### Child-Rearing Practices (Consistency)
Inconsistent disciplining of the child is correlated with the mother's view of discipline as a proof of her hostility (accompanied by guilt). (R091)

### Child-Rearing Practices (Permissiveness)
Permissive mothers tend to be extroverted and nonneurotic. Punitive mothers tend to be introverted and neurotic.

### Employment of Mother
There is no difference between married working and nonworking mothers with respect to sociability (as measured by the Gordon Personal Profile), responsibility, or ascendancy. (G127)

### Feeding
The feeding techniques employed by the mother are determined by her own personality rather than by the activity level or other characteristics of the infant. (B272)

### Maternal Overprotectiveness
Overprotective mothers will tend to be responsible, stable, aggressive women. (L163)

Mothers who tend to express their sadistic domination of their children as overprotectiveness tend themselves to be infantile and egocentric. (R115)

### Mental Illness
Mental illness is directly correlated with a family environment in which the mother is an isolated, paranoid woman, and is excessively preoccupied with events within the family. (F085)

Mothers of mentally ill persons tend to be perfectionistic, narcissistic, immature, frigid, emotionally detached, frightened by body contact, and capable of functioning satisfactorily only on an intellectual level. (S187)

Mothers of the mentally ill tend to be "stiff and bitter" and inclined to anxiety, uncertainty, and obsessions. (S187)

### Mental Illness of Child (Autism)
Autistic children are likely to have mothers who are mechanistic and who respond perfunctorily rather than warmly, to the child. (D070)

Mothers of autistic children are likely to be overly intellectual in outlook (i.e., are more likely to seek gratification from intellectual rather than from interpersonal sources). (D070)

Autism is more likely to occur if the mother is remote, unempathetic, and compulsive. (S188)

### Mental Illness of Child (Schizophrenia)
Mothers likely to produce schizophrenic children tend to be of three types: the overly demanding, hostile, but superficially sweet and polite mother; the docile, submissive mother, who cooperates to absurd limits, who is perfectionistic and sensitive to slights and who dominates through dependence; and the overly rejecting mother. (B219)

The schizophrenogenic mother tends to be unusually Machiavellian in relationships, viewing other people as existing only to serve her own ends and, consequently, manipulating and exploiting them. (B219)

Compared to normal children, schizophrenics tend to perceive their mothers as relatively cold, controlling, and authoritarian, but are similar with regard to their perception of the mother's democratic attitudes or rejection of the homemaking role. (H185)

Mothers of schizophrenics tend to be more sensitive to the opinions of others than average mothers. (T105)

### Mental Problems
Mothers of schizophrenic children are no more likely than are mothers of brain-injured children to display pathological attitudes (as measured by the PARI). (J027)

### Neurosis
Mothers of neurotics tend to be highly tentative persons, pervaded by guilt and worry, and in constant need of reassurance. (B219)

### Personality of Child
There is an inverse correlation between dependency, conformity, and cooperation of the mother and the child. (R113)

Children who are bullying, domineering, aggressive, and overly competitive with other children tend to have mothers with parallel problems serving as models for them. (R113)

Children who are hostile and disobedient tend to have aggressive mothers who serve as models for the pathology in their children. (R113)

Children who have nail-biting and thumb-sucking problems are likely to have mothers who have a parallel problem (superego conflict). (R113)

### Personality of Child (Depression)
Children whose mothers have similar personality problems are less likely to be depressed. (R113)

### Personality of Child (Impulsiveness)
Submissive, uncertain, and anxious mothers tend to have children who are impulsive and uncontrolled. (B219)

### Personality of Daughter (Expressiveness)
Whether the girl is more expressive or instrumental in her personality orientation is not related to her perceptions of her mother. (J026)

### Personality Problems of Child
Among daughters who see their mothers as authoritarian and controlling, the more dominant, independent, outgoing, and change-seeking is the daughter's personality, the more likely is she to have psychological difficulties. (H177)

### Personality Problems of Child (Masochism)
Mothers of morally masochistic children are more likely than are mothers of normal children to labor under a wide disparity between ego ideal and actual behavior (particularly in relation to sexual behavior, i.e., alternation between repression and acting out of impulses). (B281)

### Race Attitudes
Prejudiced men are more likely than unprejudiced men to perceive their mothers as self-sacrificing and moralistic. (A061)

Unprejudiced men are more likely than prejudiced men to perceive their mothers as warm, sociable, and esthetic. (A061)

Unprejudiced women are more likely than are prejudiced women to perceive their mothers as warm and lovable. (A061)

Prejudiced women are more likely than unprejudiced women to perceive their mothers as dominant, moralistic, and socially successful. (A061)

### Retarded/Cerebral-Palsied Children
As measured by the PARI, the personality configurations of mothers with retarded children differ very little from those with cerebral-palsied children. (J027)

### Schizophrenic/Brain-Injured Children
Mothers of schizophrenic children are no more likely than are mothers of brain-injured children to display pathological attitudes (as measured by the PARI). (J027)

### Sex Status
The differences between mothers of schizophrenics and of normal children do not correlate with sex of the child. (H207)

### Social Adjustment of Child
There is a greater correlation between the mother's total character structure and the child's social and psychological adjustment than there is with child-rearing practices. (B230)

### Surrogate Mother
Mothers who rear their children themselves are less hostile, dominant, and dependent in interpersonal relations than are mothers who provide maternal substitutes for their children (i.e., nurses, grandparents, older sister of child, friends, grandparents of child). (C124)

## PERSONALITY OF MOTHER (AMBITIOUSNESS)
### X Mental Illness (Manic-Depressive)
Manic-depressives are more likely to come from families in which the mothers are intensely ambitious. (C092)

## PERSONALITY OF MOTHER (ANOMIE)
### X Child-Rearing Attitudes (Consensus)
Anomic mothers tend significantly to be in disagreement with their husbands' view on discipline; nonanomic mothers report that they and their husbands were agreed. (A069)

#### Child-Rearing Practices (Consistency)
Anomic mothers tend significantly to be inconsistent in their child-rearing practices; whereas nonanomic mothers tend to be consistent. (A069)

#### Child-Rearing Practices (Punishment)
There is a significant tendency for anomic mothers to be lenient in their child-rearing practices and for nonanomic mothers to be harsh. (A069)

Anomic mothers reported that they tended to discipline their children according to their own moods, tempers, or whims: whereas nonanomic mothers tended not to let their moods influence their punishment practices. (A069)

#### Child-Rearing Practices (Scheduling)
Nonanomic mothers tend significantly to schedule their children; anomoic mothers seldom maintain scheduling. (A069)

#### Occupation
There is no significant correlation between the father's occupation or family income and the mother's classification according to the Srole Anomie Scale. (A069)

#### Personality Problems of Child (Neurosis/Acting Out)
Anomic mothers tend to have children whose problematic behavior is diagnosed as acting out and nonanomic mothers tend to have children whose problematic behavior is diagnosed as neurotic. (A069)

### PERSONALITY OF MOTHER (AUTONOMY)
#### X Mother-Child Relations (Protectiveness)
The more autonomous the mother, the less protective she will be toward the child. (C100)

### PERSONALITY OF MOTHER (COMPETITIVENESS)
#### X Achievement Motivation
Mothers of boys with high achievement motivation tend to be more competitive than do mothers of boys with low achievement motivation. (R097)

### PERSONALITY OF MOTHER (DECISIVENESS)
#### X Weaning
The greater the mother's indecisiveness, the more gentle her weaning of the child. (S191)

### PERSONALITY OF MOTHER (DOMINANCE)
#### X Achievement Motivation
Mothers of boys with high achievement motivation tend to stress the achievement training of their sons rather than independent training. (R097)

Mothers of boys with high achievement motivation tend to be more dominant and demanding than do mothers of boys with low achievement motivation. (R097)

#### Identification with Father
The more dominant the mother, the less strongly the boy tends to identify with the father. (P064)

#### Mother-Child Relations (Control)
A highly dominant mother is more likely to use severe control in her behavior toward the child. (C100)

Stated desire by the mother to dominate others is not positively associated with coercive maternal behavior practices. (C100)

#### Scholastic Achievement of Daughter
Mothers of daughters with low college achievement

records are more dominating than their daughters are. (T103)

Mothers of daughters with high college achievement records do not differ from their daughters in dominance. (T103)

#### Sex-Role Identification
A strong mother contributes to the failure of her son to develop a strong masculine feeling.

There is no support for the hypothesis that strong mothers contribute to a lack of masculine feeling.

### PERSONALITY OF MOTHER (ECCENTRICITY)
#### X Mental Illness
Mothers of prepsychotics tend to be more eccentric than do mothers of nonprepsychotics. (M164)

### PERSONALITY OF MOTHER (EMOTIONAL CONTROL)
#### X Residence
Mothers who live in multiple-family dwellings are more emotionally controlled, being less warm and less hostile, than are mothers who reside in single-family dwellings. (M216)

### PERSONALITY OF MOTHER (EMOTIONAL STABILITY)
#### X Household Composition
A mother tends to be more emotionally unstable when the only man living in the household is her husband than when other men are present. (M216)

#### Sex-Role Definition
Maternal emotional stability is not related to the degree to which mothers have responsibilities other than child training, particularly those which take them away from home. (M216)

#### Size of Family
The greater the number of children the mother must care for, the greater her emotional instability. (M216)

### PERSONALITY OF MOTHER (EXTROVERSION)
#### X Child-Rearing Practices (Punishment)
Extroverted mothers are less punitive toward their children than are introverted mothers. (L169)

### PERSONALITY OF MOTHER/FATHER (CONTROL)
#### X Personality of Son/Daughter (Control)
The degree of psychological control (inhibition/expressiveness) of parents, particularly that of the mother, is correlated with that of the son. (L151)

There is no relationship between the daughter's psychological control and that of the mother; it is, however, negatively correlated with that of the father. (L151)

### PERSONALITY OF MOTHER (FEMININITY)
#### X Sex-Role Identification
Boys who identify more with their fathers perceive their mothers as being more feminine than do boys who identify less with their fathers. (B274)

#### Sex-Role Identification of Daughter
There is no relationship between the mother's femininity (measured by the California Psychological Inventory) and the daughter's sex-role identification. (M206)

### PERSONALITY OF MOTHER (FRIENDLINESS)
#### X Mother-Child Relations (Evaluation)
The mother's own perceived friendly relations with others correlate with her perception of her child as friendly to others, even though the actual friendliness of her child is not so related.

## PERSONALITY OF MOTHER (HOSTILITY)
### X   Aggression

Since resentment is easily converted into aggressive action, particularly when encouraged (frequently hostile mothers direct a child's aggression toward other adults), mothers who are hostile are more likely to produce children who are overtly aggressive than are those who are not hostile. (F103)

### Illegitimacy (Adoption)

Controlling for father domination in the parental home, the unwed mother with strong hostile feelings toward the father of her child is more likely than is the less hostile unwed mother to keep her baby as a weapon against the man. (Y048)

## PERSONALITY OF MOTHER (INSECURITY)
### X   Alcoholism

Alcoholism tends to be associated with a high degree of maternal insecurity. (C122)

### Broken Home

Broken homes are associated with insecurity in the mother. (K120)

## PERSONALITY OF MOTHER (IRRITABILITY)
### X . Mental Illness (Schizophrenia)

A significantly greater number of schizophrenic daughters than of normals believed that their mothers were irritable during their childhoods. (H186)

## PERSONALITY OF MOTHER (MASCULINITY)
### X   Identification with Father

There is a negative relationship between a mother's masculinity and a son's identification with his father. (P076)

### Illegitimacy

There is no correlation between the female's masculine personality traits and having illegitimate children. (N055)

## PERSONALITY OF MOTHER (NEEDS)
### X   Mental Illness of Child (Schizophrenia)

If the emotional needs of the mothering one are met by the schizophrenic child, the chances of another child becoming mentally ill are lowered. (S208)

## PERSONALITY OF MOTHER (ORAL)
### X   Behavior Problems

The male children of mothers who attempt to resolve oral conflicts by acting seductively and demanding with them develop greatly exacerbated Oedipal tensions which, in turn, are compensated for by aggressive and destructive acting out. (R099)

## PERSONALITY OF MOTHER (PERFECTIONISM)
### X   Mental Illness

The mothers of middle-class mentally ill patients tend to have been rigid perfectionists. (M061)

## PERSONALITY OF MOTHER (RIGIDITY)
### X   Personality of Child (Hostility)

Since a mother's rigidity tends to produce anxiety (which inhibits aggressive action) and submission in her child, mothers who are rigid are more likely than those who are not to produce children who are covertly hostile. (F103)

## PERSONALITY OF MOTHER (SATISFACTION)
### X   Aggression

Mothers who are not satisfied with their present situations (frequency of mention of things they would rather be doing) report more aggressive children than mothers who are satisfied with their present situations (U.S.). (S191)

### Cohesion of Family

There is a correlation between the closeness of family life (as reported by college students) and the degree to which the mother is satisfied with her life. (R116)

## PERSONALITY OF MOTHER (SECLUSIVENESS)
### X   Scholastic Achievement

As measured by the PARI, mothers of sons who do well academically are less likely to be seclusive than are mothers of sons who are poor academically. (S230)

## PERSONALITY OF MOTHER (SELF-ACCEPTANCE)
### X   Sex-Role Identification of Daughter

There is a positive relationship between the mother's self-acceptance and strong sex-role identification in daughters. (M206)

## PERSONALITY OF MOTHER (SEPARATION ANXIETY)     X   Personality Problems of Child (Separation Anxiety)

Correlated with a child's separation anxiety (which gives rise to personality problems on his part) is the mother's own separation anxiety with respect to the incomplete separation from and dependence on her own mother which is reactivated in her relations with her child. (S183)

## PERSONALITY OF MOTHER (STABILITY)
### X   Nuclear/Stem Family

Residence in a stem family is associated with greater emotional stability of the mother than is residence in a nuclear isolated family. (M216)

## PERSONALITY OF MOTHER (SUBLIMATION)
### X   Mother-Child Relations (Biological)

The further removed a maternal activity is from biologic functions, the more likely it is that the masochistic impulses (derived from early incestuous wishes toward the father) of the mother will be capable of sublimation. (B272)

## PERSONALITY OF MOTHER (WARMTH)
### X   Dependency

Warmth of the mother and dependency of the child are not associated. (S191)

### Mental Illness (Schizophrenia)

Mothers of schizophrenics will tend to be cold and rigorous. (S187)

## PERSONALITY OF MOTHER (WITHDRAWAL)
### X   Mental Illness (Schizophrenia/Neurosis)

Mothers of schizophrenics are more likely than are mothers of neurotics or of normals to be emotionally and socially withdrawn, with their adult interests centered narrowly on the family. (M218)

## PERSONALITY OF PARENTS     X   Alcoholism

Alcoholism is more likely among people who had a stern, autocratic father and an overprotective mother.

Among upper-class parents of alcoholics, mothers are more likely to be overindulgent and overprotective and fathers to lack affection, be domineering, and overly severe than are parents of nonalcoholic offspring. (B261)

### Bigotry

Parents of bigoted children do not exhibit any specific personality characteristics to differentiate them from the parents of nonbigoted children. (M247)

### Child-Rearing Practices (Democratic)

A democratic approach to child rearing by the mother is correlated with her inactivity and masculinity of interests. (B259)

A democratic approach to child rearing in the father has a greater element of permissiveness than does such an approach in the mother. (B259)

### Child-Rearing Practices (Neglect)

In families where the children are seriously neglected, either parent, but mostly the mother, has a personality which is characterized by temperamental instability and incapability to adopt an abstract attitude. (B270)

### Disorganization of Family

Parents (of schizophrenic children) who lack direction and organization are less likely than are parents who are well ordered to function adequately (with respect to communication between marital partners, the mother's decisiveness, her appropriate satisfaction with self and children, interest in physical environment). (B240)

### Juvenile Delinquency

Both frequency of loss of temper and of becoming emotionally upset are positively related to delinquent behavior of the child of the opposite sex. (N052)

Cheerfulness in parents is negatively associated with delinquency in adolescents, particularly for the mother. (N057)

Moodiness in parents (especially the father) is positively related to delinquency in adolescents. (N057)

Loss of temper by parents is positively related to delinquency in adolescents (especially the child of the opposite sex). (N057)

Parents' tendencies to become emotionally upset are positively related to delinquency in adolescents. (N057)

Nervousness in mothers is more significantly related to delinquency in adolescents than is nervousness in fathers. (N057)

The more cheerful the parents, the less likely it is that the child will show delinquent behavior. (N063)

The more nervous, irritable, and difficult to please is the parent, the more likely it is that the child will manifest delinquent behavior. (N063)

### Juvenile Delinquency/Neurosis

Parents of delinquent children tend to show antisocial and morally unstable tendencies more frequently than do parents of neurotic children. (B214)

### Mental Illness of Child

Mental illness is less likely to develop if the emotional difficulties of the mother can be counterbalanced by a stable father. (L123)

Parents of mentally ill children are more likely to be rigid, self-deceiving, and immature than are parents of normal children. (S187)

### Mental Illness of Child (Schizophrenia)

The core of the defense structure (i.e., fear of annihila-

tion) of parents of schizophrenic children is the same, regardless of socioeconomic class. (K107)

Unstable and domineering parents are more likely than others to rear schizophrenic children. (W143)

### Mental Illness (Schizophrenia)

Parents of good premorbid (general adjustment before onset of psychosis) schizophrenics have more mature defensive structures (isolation, undoing, and displacement) than do parents of poor premorbid schizophrenics (whose defensive structures are denial and projection). (B262)

Fathers of schizophrenics are more likely to be sadistic and domineering than are fathers of normals; they are also more likely to have masochistic wives. (K125)

Schizophrenia is directly correlated with a cold, sadistic mother and a passive father. (L123)

Schizophrenics tend to have cruel fathers and overprotective mothers. (L123)

### Neurosis

Compared to mothers of younger maladjusted children, mothers of maladjusted adolescents are more likely to have the characteristics of authoritarianism, strictness, approval of activity, inconsiderateness of husband, ascendance; fathers are likely to have the characteristics of marital conflict, seclusiveness, inconsiderateness of wife (PARI). (Z011)

### Personality Development of Child

Because unconscious parental attitudes are less understood and are more difficult to revise by children, they are more effective in influencing children than are overt expressions. (W143)

### Personality of Child

Children tend to imitate parental defense mechanisms. (B220)

Fathers and mothers are more similar to each other (MMPI scores) than to their children. (S241)

### Personality of Daughter

More significant correlations were obtained between the MMPI scores of mothers and daughters than between those of fathers and daughters. (S241)

### Personality of Son

More significant correlations were obtained between the MMPI scores of fathers and sons than between those of mothers and sons. (S241)

### Personality Problems

Families of children with eating difficulties (Jewish) tended to be characterized by discord—the mothers being immature, domineering, punitive, and devaluating of the father and the father being ineffectual, either submissive or erratic, and self-indulgent. (S183)

### Values

Good character traits valued by the child agree with his perception of the traits by the parents, although he is more likely himself to be (and to perceive his parents as being) gratification-oriented than he is to attribute this value to his parents. (R111)

## PERSONALITY OF PARENTS (AGGRESSION)
### X Adultery

Among parents of children who are severely abused (beaten, tortured, etc.), it is the aggressive parent who is most likely to be also sexually promiscuous and unfaithful to his or her spouse. (Y043)

## PERSONALITY OF PARENTS/CHILD (SIMILARITY)
### X Self-Conception
Conflict in self-perception is more likely when the child perceives himself as different from his parents. (W158)

## PERSONALITY OF PARENTS (COMPETITIVENESS)
### X Achievement Motivation
Parents of boys with a high achievement motivation tend to be more competitive than do parents of boys with low achievement motivation. (R106)

## PERSONALITY OF PARENTS (DOMINANCE)
### X Identification with Parent
American boys tend to identify with the more aggressive and dominant parent, whether it be the father or the mother. (H211)

American girls tend to identify with the mother, regardless of the personality traits of the parents. (H211)

## PERSONALITY OF PARENTS (EXPRESSIVENESS)
### X Mental Illness (Schizophrenia)
Schizophrenia is more likely to occur when the parents repress spontaneous emotional responses. (S186)

## PERSONALITY OF PARENTS (EXTREMISM)
### X Moral Beliefs of Child
Parents who more frequently take extreme points of view tend to have children who believe in immanent justice, moral realism, retribution, severe punishment, and communicable responsibility. (J021)

## PERSONALITY OF PARENTS (INSECURITY)
### X Creativity/I.Q. of Child
Parents of highly intelligent children (Binet) are more likely to have feelings of insecurity than are the parents of highly creative children (Guilford-Cattell). (G132)

### I.Q./Creativity of Children
The parents of highly intelligent children have experienced more insecurity than have the parents of highly creative children. (G114)

Parents of highly intelligent children (Binet) are more likely to have feelings of insecurity than are the parents of highly creative children (Guilford-Cattell). (G132)

## PERSONALITY OF PARENTS (MATURITY)
### X Alcoholism
Parents of alcoholics are more likely to be emotionally immature than are parents of nonalcoholics. (B261)

## PERSONALITY OF PARENTS (OTHER-DIRECTEDNESS)
### X Child-Rearing Values (Consistency)
Parents whose character structures are "other-directed" are more likely than "inner-directed" parents to have contradictory sets of beliefs about the requirements of child rearing. (C096)

### Child-Rearing Values (Dependency)
Other-directedness in parents (measured by Kassarjian's I-Q Social Preference Scale) is positively correlated with beliefs fostering dependency in the child. (C111)

### Child-Rearing Values (Permissiveness)
Other-directedness in parents (measured by Kassarjian's I-Q Social Preference Scale) is positively correlated with the tendency to believe in permissive child rearing. (C111)

### Child-Rearing Values (Strictness)
Other-directedness in parents (measured by Kassarjian's I-Q Social Preference Scale) is positively correlated with the belief in strictness in child rearing. (C111)

### Mental Illness (Schizophrenia)
Parents of schizophrenics tend to be extremely sensitive to the opinions of others. (K093)

## PERSONALITY OF PARENTS (PASSIVITY)
### X Mental Illness of Child
Fathers of psychotic children are more passive than are mothers. (D064)

## PERSONALITY OF PARENTS (POWER)
### X Sex Status of Child
Both males and females rate their mothers as being lower in the potency factor than their fathers (measured by Osgood's Semantic Scale). (J026)

There is no difference between males and females in their potency ratings of their mothers (measured by Osgood's Semantic Scale). (J026)

Males are more likely than females to rate their fathers as higher in potency (measured by Osgood's Semantic Scale). (J026)

## PERSONALITY OF PARENTS (PROJECTION)
### X Mental Illness
Mental illness tends to be correlated with an environment in which an inordinate amount of projection by a parent is used and condoned. (J019)

## PERSONALITY OF PARENTS (RIGIDITY)
### X Personality of Child (Rigidity)
If the parents score high in rigidity/flexibility measurements, the child will also score high; and if the parents score low, then the child will also score low. (A055)

There is no significant relationship between parents' and child's rigidity/flexibility measurements. (A055)

## PERSONALITY OF PARENTS (STABILITY)
### X Adult Role
Physical and emotional steadiness of the parents is necessary for preparing the child for reciprocal adult relationships. (C093)

### Juvenile Delinquency
### X Personality of Parents
Both frequency of loss of temper and of becoming emotionally upset are positively related to delinquent behavior. Loss of temper by the parent is primarily related to delinquent behavior of the child of the opposite sex. (N052)

## PERSONALITY OF PARENTS (TOLERANCE OF AMBIGUITY) X Child-Rearing Values
Parenst who are intolerant of ambiguity (as measured by Adorno's E-Scale) tend to view their children in subordinate and restricted roles. (K117)

## PERSONALITY OF RELATIVES
### X Mental Illness, Attitudes Toward
Relatives of mental patients who have low expectations regarding posthospital performance tend to be more anomic, authoritarian, frustrated, rigid, and withdrawn than are those with high expectations. (S245)

## PERSONALITY OF SON
### X Child-Rearing Practices (Control)
The higher the son's psychopathology (MMPI), the more likely he is to perceive the mother to be "controlling" and "physically controlling." (V038)

### Father-Son Relations (Affection)

Sons who have received insufficient paternal affection are more unhappy and less calm than are those who have received adequate paternal affection. (M204)

Sons who have received insufficient paternal affection are more likely to feel dominated by a hostile, unfriendly, and controlling environment than are sons who have received adequate paternal affection. (M204)

### Personality of Parents

More significant correlations were obtained between the MMPI scores of fathers and sons than between those of mothers and sons. (S241)

### Power Structure of Family

Mother-dominated homes are associated with aggressive, impulsive, and unfriendly personality traits in sons. (H201)

## PERSONALITY OF SON (AUTONOMY)
### X   Power Structure of Family

When the father has most power in the family, the son tends to believe more in "fate" and less in leaving home. (M060)

## PERSONALITY OF SON/DAUGHTER (CONTROL)
### X   Personality of Mother/Father (Control)

The degree of psychological control (inhibition/expressiveness) of parents, particularly that of the mother, is correlated with that of the son. (L151)

There is no relationship between the daughter's psychological control and that of the mother; it is, however, negatively correlated with that of the father. (L151)

## PERSONALITY OF SON (GUILT)
### X   Child-Rearing Practices (Punishment)

Mothers of "high-guilt" boys more frequently use love-oriented techniques of punishment, while mothers of "low-guilt" boys are more likely to use physical punishment. (S078)

## PERSONALITY OF SON (HOSTILITY)
### X   Father-Son Relations (Affection)

Sons who have received insufficient paternal affection have more hostile attitudes toward others than do sons who have received adequate paternal affection. (M204)

## PERSONALTY OF SON (MASCULINITY)
### X   Identification with Father

The degree of father identification is correlated with masculinity of attitude. (P064)

### Paternal/Maternal Role

Among boys, high and low masculinity groups (measured by the It Scale for Children) are more differentiated by descriptions of the mother, while they significantly differentiate on variables related to descriptions of the father. (J026)

## PERSONALITY OF SON (OPTIMISM)
### X   Father-Son Relations

Poor father-son relations tend to produce in the son a pessimistic outlook on the future of the social order. (L179)

## PERSONALITY OF SON (POWER)
### X   Father-Son Relations (Affection)

Sons who have received insufficient paternal affection have a greater need to control and manipulate others than do sons who have received adequate paternal affection. (M204)

## PERSONALITY OF SON (REALISM)
### X   Father-Son Relations (Dominance)

Sons who view themselves as highly dependent on and dominated by their fathers have a more realistic view of the world; those who do not feel dominated or dependent are more likely to be afraid of or to avoid facing reality. (M204)

## PERSONALITY OF SON (RESPONSIBILITY)
### X   Child-Rearing Practices of Father

There is a positive relationship between responsibility in the son (based on teachers' ratings of dependability in fulfilling obligations) and discipline and authority from the father. (B250)

## PERSONALITY OF SON (SELF-CONFIDENCE)
### X   Power Structure of Family

Boys from families where there is equality between the parents in family affairs exhibit greater self-confidence (a belief in the control of one's destiny) than do those from wife-dominated or husband-dominated families. (E102)

Self-confidence in boys (a belief in the control of one's destiny) is more characteristic of boys from wife-dominant than from husband-dominant families. (E102)

## PERSONALITY OF SON (WITHDRAWAL)
### X   Personality of Father (Withdrawal)

A child whose personality exhibits general social withdrawal is likely to have a father with the same characteristics. (B237)

## PERSONALITY OF SPOUSE
### X   Marital Adjustment

There is a direct relation between the degree of knowledge of a spouse's personality and marital adjustment. (K161)

Marital satisfaction (measured by Locke and Terman Marital Adjustment Scales) is significantly related to description of spouse as a responsible, generous, cooperative, moderately dominant, and conventional person. (L154)

Marital dissatisfaction (measured by Locke and Terman Marital Adjustment Scales) is significantly related to perception of spouse as having extreme or intense qualities, being skeptical, distrustful, blunt, aggressive, and either too dictatorial or too passive. (L154)

## PERSONALITY OF SPOUSE (HOSTILITY)
### X   Husband-Wife Relations (Power)

The more dominant spouse is usually the more overtly hostile spouse. (W148)

## PERSONALITY OF WIFE
### X   Husband-Wife Relations (Wife Beating)

Wives whose husbands beat them are likely to be more aggressive, masculine, frigid, and masochistic than are other wives. (S253)

### Intermarriage (Racial), Attitude Toward

The Negro community tends to accept the white wife if her personal qualities are such as would make a Negro acceptable. (G001)

## PERSONALITY OF WIFE (ACCEPTANCE OF OTHERS)
### X   Marital Adjustment

Marital happiness of both husbands and wives is related to the wives' acceptance of others. (E099)

## PERSONALITY OF WIFE (DOMINANCE)
### X   Marital Adjustment of Wife
Unhappy wives, as opposed to happy wives, tend to be more dominant and try to get their own way in their relations with men. (T074)

## PERSONALITY OF WIFE (EGO WITHDRAWAL)
### X   Marital Adjustment of Wife
Unhappy wives, more often than the happy, say they face their troubles alone without seeking help, are more willing to take a chance alone in a situation of doubtful outcome, prefer to be alone at time of emotional stress, and prefer making hurried decisions alone. (T074)

## PERSONALITY OF WIFE (EMOTIONAL STABILITY)
### X   Husband-Wife Relations (Communication)
The higher the communication between the married couple, the more stable the emotional equilibrium of the wife. (L173)

## PERSONALITY OF WIFE (HOSTILITY)
### X   Personality of Husband (Hostility)
The higher the husband's score on concern with negative/passive relations (complaints, resentment, etc.), the higher the wife's score.

## PERSONALITY OF WIFE (KINDNESS)
### X   Marital Adjustment of Wife
Happy wives show more evidence of kindly, cooperative, and charitable attitudes than do the unhappy and more often expect these attitudes from others. They more often report that they avoid saying things which might hurt the feelings of others, that they are approachable, that they like old people, and that they like such activities as teaching children or contributing to charities. In contrast, unhappy wives are much more often considered critical of others and more often admit that they disregard the feelings of others when accomplishing ends important to themselves. (T074)

## PERSONALITY (OTHER-ORIENTATION)
### X   Ordinal Position
Girls who are middle children are more "internally oriented" than are those who are either the youngest or the oldest in the family. (S252)

Girls who are only children are more "other-oriented" than are those who have older siblings. (S252)

### Parent-Child Relations (Closeness)
Girls who feel equally close to both parents are more other-oriented than are those who feel close to neither. (S252)

## PERSONALITY (PAIN TOLERANCE)
### X   Ordinal Position
Firstborn and only children do not withstand pain as well as later-born children do. This hypothesis is also rejected. (S263)

## PERSONALITY (PERMISSIVENESS)
### X   Adultery, Attitude Toward
The less permissive an individual is, the less likely he is to approve of adultery. (C124)

## PERSONALITY (PLACEBO)   X   Ordinal Position
The hypothesis that firstborn and only children, being more anxious, would be more responsive to placebos was not supported by the findings of this experimental study. (G137)

## PERSONALITY (POWER MOTIVATION)
### X   Sibling Structure
There is no significant relationship between an individual's power motivation (i.e., his urge to dominate others in order to use them as agents for fulfilling his own goals) and either his number of siblings or his ordinal position among his siblings. (V031)

## PERSONALITY PROBLEMS     X   Adultery
Infidelity and promiscuity tend to be an "acting out" of neurotic conflict.

### Authority Structure of Family (Paternalistic)
Loss of the paternalistic family (with its emphasis on authority, responsibility, and emotional attachments), accompanied by increased freedom for the individual and lack of adequate substitution of new structures and values that were provided for by the paternalistic home, is the major cause of neurotic personality disorders. (B244)

### Behavior Problems (Feeding)
Unsatisfied tension in the mother or the infant is a primary cause of feeding disturbance. (B272)

The greater the anxiety of the mother, the more likely it is that her flow of milk for the infant is established slowly or not at all. (B272)

### Breast Feeding
There is no relationship between the type or the degree of mental disturbance which a child develops and the fact of having been breast or bottle fed. (B239)

### Child-Rearing Attitudes (Pathological)
Mothers are more likely to be pathological in their child-rearing attitudes if the child is not normal. (S187)

### Child-Rearing Practices (Consensus)
There is a positive relationship between parental conflict about authority over the child and children who are frequently discouraged, depressed, restless, and excitable. (R100)

### Child-Rearing Practices (Consistency)
Inconsistent disciplining on the part of the mother is significantly associated with the following problems evidenced in the child: 1) disobedience, with hostile component; 2) temper; 3) overly competitive with siblings; 4) restless, excitable; 5) bullying, aggressive, domineering; 6) sleep disturbance; 7) disobedience, milder; 8) stealing; 9) frequent nightmares; 10) truancy from school (possible trend). (R091)

### Child-Rearing Practices (Dependency)
Children who are denied the autonomy of free choice are more likely to become obsessed by repetitive acts or to become sticklers for exactness.

### Child-Rearing Practices (Maturity Demands)
There is a negative relationship between fathers who expect overly mature behavior on the part of the child and child-personality problems characterized by delusions, obsessions, and withdrawal. (R100)

### Child-Rearing Practices (Punishment)
There is a curvilinear relationship between parental hostility and physical punishment and personality problems in the child (in the home). (B232)

Father's hostility and physical punishment are positively related to hostile withdrawal by girls at both home and school; by boys only at home. (B232)

The more that psychological "love-oriented" techniques of discipline are used upon the child, the more likely he is to become anxious, dependent, and sensitive to rejection. (B236)

### Child-Rearing Practices (Restrictiveness)

Overinhibited behavior, characterized by seclusiveness, shyness, and apathy in children, correlates with repressive overcontrol in the parents. (S182)

### Class

The lower the social class of the unwed mother, the more likely she is to be psychologically disturbed. The contrary is also asserted. (S224)

### Illegitimacy

Unmarried mothers tend to be more neurotic and more extroverted than do married mothers (as measured by the Maudsley Personality Inventory). (E094)

### Institutional Care

Children who are raised from early infancy in institutions without adequate parent surrogates and who consequently develop personality disorders will not have these disorders cured by later community and foster-family experiences. (B270)

Children who are raised from early infancy in institutions without adequate parent surrogates do not develop normal patterns of anxiety and self-inhibition. (B270)

### Interaction in Family

When one member of a family suffers from a chronic symptomatology, the patterns of interaction within the family become stereotyped and communication becomes impoverished. (B242)

### Marital Adjustment

Unsatisfactory relations between adults in the home are correlated with symptoms of maladjustment in both mothers and fathers. (C117)

### Marital Status

Single women are less likely to have felt they were about to have a nervous breakdown than are divorced, separated, or widowed women; single men do not differ from other men in this respect. (G126)

Divorced and separated women report having felt an impending nervous breakdown more often than do men and women in other marital and nonmarital statuses. (G126)

### Mate Selection

People tend to choose partners who share similar personality conflicts. (B204)

There is a tendency for narcissistic (self-loving) persons to marry anaclitic (dependent) persons. (W148)

### Mother Absence

Partial maternal deprivation causes feelings of guilt and depression to arise in the deprived child, who has feelings of revenge for having been deprived. (B270)

### Mother-Child Relations (Interaction)

Babies who have not had adequate contact with their mothers are more likely to develop depressive and regressive states of motionlessness resembling stupor.

### Parent-Child Relations (Evaluation)

The more severe the psychopathology of the son, the more unfavorable his memories of his parents' behavior; the less pathological and more socially competent the son, the more favorable his PRBI memories of his parents. (V034)

### Parent-Child Relations (Hostility)

Hostile-withdrawing behavior in the child tends to correlate with the degree of the father's hostility, physical punishment, and strictness; while anxious, tense, nervous behavior is associated with the degree of both the mother's and the father's hostiliy and physical punishment. (B232)

### Parent-Child Relations (Permissiveness)

A home characterized by excessive permissiveness and lack of restraint by the parents is more likely than others to produce the self-centered type of child. (W143)

### Parent-Child Relations (Security)

If a child between the ages of five and eight has a secure parental relationship, he is much less likely to develop serious and permanent personality disorders than if his relationship is an insecure one. (B270)

### Parent Loss

Children reared without normal parental relationships develop an exaggerated interest in the self. (G128)

### Personality of Parents

Families of children with eating difficulties (Jewish) tended to be characterized by discord—the mothers being immature, domineering, punitive, and devaluating of the father and the father being ineffectual, either submissive or erratic, and self-indulgent. (S183)

### Religion

Among the mentally ill, the mother of the patient tends to be more disturbed if the patient is Jewish; the father is the more disturbed parent if the patient is Protestant. (S187)

### Sex Status

Women, in general, whether married or unmarried, are more likely to feel they are about to have a nervous breakdown than are men. This difference is reduced when considering only single men and women. (G126)

### Sibling Structure

Among males, the younger sibling is more likely to have nervous habits or to indulge in them more frequently than is the older; the reverse is true of females. (K104)

When spacing is over four years, children from cross-sex sibling pairs tend to have more nervous habits or to show them more frequently. (K104)

### Sibling Structure (Age and Sex)

If firstborn and spaced under two years, the children with a cross-sex sibling recover more slowly and less adequately from emotional upsets than do those with same-sex siblings. At the two-to-four-year spacing, the reverse is true. (K104)

### Sibling Structure (Age Difference)

When sibling spacing is under two years, second-born

children recover from emotional upsets faster and more thoroughly than do firstborn children. (K104)

Among firstborn children, the greater the sibling age disparity, the more rapid the recovery from emotional upsets; among second-born children, the reverse is true. (K104)

### Sibling Structure (Sex)
When spacing is over four years, children from cross-sex sibling pairs tend to have more nervous habits or to show them more frequently. (K104)

### Surrogate Mother
There is no relationship between multiple mothering and personality problems in the child. (Y045)

### Surrogate Parent
There is a correlation between living with stepparents or guardians and nervousness and aggressive behavior in the child. (R108)

### Toilet Training
Too rigid or too early toilet training will lead to thumb-sucking, whining, demanding, hostility, willfulness, and pretended autonomy.

## PERSONALITY PROBLEMS (AFFECT HUNGER)
### X Maternal Overprotectiveness
There is a correlation between affect hunger in the mother and her overprotection of the child. (B272)

## PERSONALITY PROBLEMS (ANALITY)
### X Sibling Structure (Twins)
Twinship decreases the correlation between achievement strivings and anal behavior manifestations. (B224)

## PERSONALITY PROBLEMS (ANTISOCIAL/AGGRESSION)
### X Child-Rearing Practices (Punishment)
The parents of aggressive antisocial boys discipline more punitively than do the parents of aggressive "social" boys. (M210)

## PERSONALITY PROBLEMS (ANXIETY)
### X Broken Home
Women reared in families where one or both parents have died or in divorced families show greater physical and psychological anxiety than do women from families that have remained intact. (G126)

## PERSONALITY PROBLEMS (APATHY)
### X Parent Loss
Children reared without normal parental relationships develop qualities of resignation and apathy. (G128)

## PERSONALITY PROBLEMS (CASTRATION COMPLEX)
### X Maternal-Role Adjustment
The more severe the girl's castration complex, the less likely it is that she will be able to accept the passive aims essential to the maternal role. (B272)

## PERSONALITY PROBLEMS (CONFLICT)
### X Parent Loss
Children between the ages of three and five who are deprived of their parents and are not provided with adequate parent surrogates suffer acute internal conflict as a result of having developed excessive desires for affection and excessive desires for revenge. (B270)

## PERSONALITY PROBLEMS/DELINQUENCY
### X Employment of Mother, Regularity of
Delinquent sons of irregularly employed mothers are more likely to have emotional conflicts and are more

likely to be truants at ten years of age or younger; nondelinquent sons of regularly employed mothers are more likely to manifest hostility. (S265)

## PERSONALITY PROBLEMS (DEPRESSION)
### X Child-Rearing Practices (Punishment)
The use of physical punishment by the father is positively associated with a child who is frequently depressed and discouraged. (R100)

### Institutional Care
The behavior of babies which are taken from their mothers and institutionalized at the age of six to nine months is very often a deep unresponsive depression. (B270)

### Mother Absence
A separation of three or four months from the mother is a cause of severe "anaclitic" depression in the infant. (B272)

## PERSONALITY PROBLEMS (EMOTIONAL INSECURITY)
### X Dependency
The more that a child's dependency is extended to his family as a whole, as opposed to his parents, the more likely he is to be emotionally insecure. (M198)

## PERSONALITY PROBLEMS (HOSTILITY)
### X Conformity
The more automatic and unquestioning the child's acceptance of parental authority, the more likely the unconscious accumulation of repressed resentment and hostility. (M203)

## PERSONALITY PROBLEMS IN FAMILY
### X Psychosomatic Illness (Colitis)
The incidence and severity of ulcerative colitis is correlated with psychological and psychosomatic disorders in the patient's family. (P078)

## PERSONALITY PROBLEMS (INHIBITION)
### X Child-Rearing Practices (Control)
Overinhibited behavior, characterized by seclusiveness, shyness, and apathy in children, correlates with repressive overcontrol in the parents. (S183)

## PERSONALITY PROBLEMS (MASOCHISM)
### X Mother-Child Relations (Rejection)
Maternal rejection is a cause of the development of masochism in the child. (L134)

## PERSONALITY PROBLEMS (NERVOUS BREAKDOWN)
### X Broken Home
Persons reared in divorced homes are more likely to report having felt at some time they were about to have a nervous breakdown than are persons from intact families or from families where one parent has died. (G126)

## PERSONALITY PROBLEMS (NERVOUSNESS)
### X Surrogate Mother
Among children of mothers who work, those whose mothers have provided a succession of different mother substitutes are more nervous than are those whose mothers have provided more stable arrangements. (Y047)

## PERSONALITY PROBLEMS (NEUROSIS)
### X Mate Selection
Among neurotics there tends to be a complementariness of neuroses between spouses. (W148)

## PERSONALITY PROBLEMS (NEUROSIS/ACTING OUT)
### X Child-Rearing Practices (Punishment)
Mothers or parents of neurotic children had a tendency

to repress their children's developmental instinctual drives, whereas mothers of acting-out children did not; mothers or parents of neurotic children had a tendency to punish their children socially, whereas anomic mothers did not. (A069)

## PERSONALITY PROBLEMS OF ADOLESCENTS
### X   Illegitimacy
The unwed adolescent mother is more likely to have become pregnant as a result of the emotional problems in her life than because of ignorance or lack of adult self-control. (Y048)

## PERSONALITY PROBLEMS OF CHILD
### X   Acculturation
If parents attempt to assimilate new cultural values too rapidly, they will project their role conflicts onto the child in an attempt to work out the discrepancies between new and old roles, resulting in emotional disturbances of the child. (B242)

### Anxiety of Parents
Parental anxiety about certain developmental stages in the child overstimulates or understimulates the child and may produce the same problem in the child as the parents have. (A069)

### Authoritarianism
Parents who have an authoritarian ideology tend to be dominant and possessive of their children and these traits are associated with the development of social and psychological problems (criminality, neuroses, psychoses). (K117)

### Breast Feeding
Maternal anxiety about breast feeding is a cause of irritability and excitability in the child. (B272)

### Child-Rearing Attitudes (Democratic)
There is no tendency for young daughters with incipient psychopathology to attribute more democratic attitudes that are viewed as deviant to their mothers than normal daughters do. (H177)

### Cohesion of Family
If a child is not allowed to develop a sense of belonging to the family because of the lack of affection among members, he is more likely than the child who is accepted to become psychopathic. (S226)

### Conflict in Family
Emotionally disturbed children are more likely to be involved in parental conflicts than are "normal" children. (S185)

### Emotional Adjustment of Mother
Child problems correlate more with the mother's emotional adjustment than with her occupational status. (S265)

The number and seriousness of child problems do not correlate with employment/nonemployment of the mother, but with the mother's emotional adjustment. (S265)

### Employment of Mother
Health status, marital, sexual, and emotional adjustment, and number and seriousness of child problems do not correlate with employment or nonemployment of the mother. (S265)

### Family-Community Relations
When there is a sufficient integration of the family into community organizations, the children are less likely to develop emotional problems. (B290)

### Father Absence
When the father is absent from the home, there is greater likelihood that the child will become alcoholic, homosexual, or totalitarian. (M181)

### Father-Child Relations (Hostility)
The greater the hostility of the father, the greater the incidence of personality problems (shy, anxious, withdrawn) in the child. (B232)

### Father-Child Relations (Warmth)
If the father adopts an autocratic attitude and lacks a warm parental concern, the child develops personality problems. (P070)

### Geographic Mobility
There is no relationship between the number of residences of families of disturbed children and those of normal children. (P074)

### Incest
The severity of reaction (psychopathology) to incest is of the same intensity whether girls have relations with a father or with a father substitute. (K091)

### Institutional Care
If a baby is institutionalized for a long period, when he is returned to his mother he will show an excessive demandingness toward the mother or substitute mother, in which intense possessiveness is combined with intolerance of frustration, acute jealousy, and violent temper tantrums. (B270)

The personality disorders developed by a child who has been raised from early infancy in an institution cannot be ameliorated by providing a parent surrogate if the surrogate is not provided before age two and one-half years. (B270)

Children who are raised in institutions for the first three years of their lives without parental care or adequate parental surrogates, are hyperactive, restless, unable to concentrate, unmanageable, and generally demonstrate lack of normal capacity for inhibition, as compared with normal children. (G128)

### Marginal Status
Children raised in a dissonant social context (where 25 per cent or less are of same religion or ethnicity) are more likely to manifest symptoms of emotional disturbance than are children raised in a mixed or consonant social context. (R092)

### Marital Adjustment
The more that the child is forced into inappropriate roles by conflict between his parents, the more likely it is that he will develop psychological disturbances.

### Maternal Overprotectiveness
Overprotection by the mother will lead to dominating, yielding, submissive, or effeminate behavior in the child. (B033)

### Maternal-Role Behavior
Compared to mothers of normal children, the mothers of maladjusted children are less likely to accelerate development of the child, to reject the homemaking role, and are more likely to be secluded. (Z011)

### Mother Absence
Separation from the mother is a cause of several disturbed reactions in the child: emotional protest, search for a substitute, withdrawal from adults and social interaction, denial of the mother image, and an attempt to transfer attachment to a substitute. (Y045)

### Mother-Child Relations (Affect)
Absence of emotional interchange between mother and child (as found in foundling homes) produces apathetic and hyper-excitable children. (S209)

### Mother-Child Relations (Affection)
Absence of an affectionate mother-child relationship (in children up to nine months of age) produces infantile behavior in the child (i.e., screaming, kicking, bed-wetting, soiling, clinging, etc.). (S202)

### Mother-Child Relations (Interaction)
Frustration of a child's desire to cling to or follow his mother is more likely than is the presence or absence of breast feeding to cause mental disturbance. (B239)

### Mother-Child Relations (Nurturance)
Children who are deprived of adequate mothering during infancy are more likely to have no emotional response to situations where it is normal and also to exhibit deceit and evasion and to steal. (P068)

### Mother-Child Relations (Rejection)
If the mother's rejection of the child is specific (directly related to the child) the potential for pathogenic effects on the child is greater than if her rejection is nonspecific (transferred to the child from another source). (L134)

### Occupation of Mother
There is no significant correlation between the mother's occupational activity and the nature of her child's problem. (A069)

### Parent Absence
Children who are completely deprived of parental relationships are much more likely to develop personality disorders than are children from homes where the parents are negligent and rejecting, no matter how emphasized these characteristics might be. (B270)

### Parent-Child Relations (Rejection)
Punishing and rejecting parents tend to produce fear, hostility, overaggressiveness, distrust, irresponsibility, and other antisocial behavior in the child. (D062)

### Parent Loss
Children who experience loss of a parent during childhood are more likely to develop psychiatric illness or character defects in later life than are children who have not been separated from a parent. (B269)

Loss of a parent during one of the first five years of the child's life is more likely to cause psychopathology in later life than is parental loss after the age of five. (B269)

Loss of the mother during the first five years of the child's life is a more significant factor in subsequent psychopathology of the child than is loss of the father. (B269)

After the child reaches the age of five and until early adolescence, death of the father is as likely to be an antecedent of psychopathology in the child as is death of the mother. (B269)

The incidence of parental loss is significantly higher among female than among male sociopaths; among neurotics and controls no sex differential was found. (G140)

There is no significant difference in frequency of parental loss among neurotics and controls. (G140)

### Parental Attitudes
Parental attitudes (PARI) have no significant relationship with the symptom type of the maladjusted child or with the maladjustment or normalcy of the child. (Z011)

### Personality Adjustment of Father/Mother
The adjustment of the father is more crucial in determining personality problems in the child than is the adjustment of the mother. (B259)

### Personality of Mother
Among daughters who see their mothers as authoritarian and controlling, the more dominant, independent, outgoing, and change-seeking is the daughter's personality, the more likely is she to have psychological difficulties. (H177)

### Personality Problems of Mother
The more a mother is preoccupied with the expression of love, warmth, affection, and help during therapy, the less her child in therapy is able to discuss such needs. (C104)

### Pregnancy
There is no correlation between symptom formation during pregnancy and the later development of emotional disturbance in the child. (P080)

### Sex-Role Definition
Parents (of Italian- and Irish-American background) of emotionally disturbed children are more likely than those of normal children to make a rigid differentiation between husband and wife roles. (V031)

### Sex Status of Absent Parent
There is no relationship between the sex of the absent parent and the type of personality disorder which develops in the child. (G140)

### Surrogate Parent
Apart from the possibility of an increased tendency to enuresis on the part of adopted girls, there is no difference in symptomatology between children adopted early and those brought up mainly by their own parents. (H242)

Personality and behavioral problems in the child correlate more with the quality of home environmental factors, such as the personality of the mother, marital discord, and standards of child care, than with home care v. nursery care. (S265)

## PERSONALITY PROBLEMS OF CHILD (ACTING OUT)    X    Child-Rearing Attitudes
Attitudes of mothers of disturbed children do not correlate with the child's being an "acting-out" or an "internalizing" symptom type. Fathers of "internalizers" are more likely to favor nonpunishment and express affection. (Z011)

### Child-Rearing Practices (Consistency)
Extreme inconsistency with "periods of overgratification of early instinctual drives alternated with severe frustration of these drives" is the cause of antisocial acting out in the child. (A069)

## PERSONALITY PROBLEMS OF CHILD
### (DEFENSIVENESS)     X  Employment of Mother
Sons of employed mothers are more likely to be defensive than are those of nonemployed mothers. (S265)

## PERSONALITY PROBLEMS OF CHILD
### (DEPRESSION)
#### X  Child-Rearing Practices (Control)
Controlling and inflexible child rearing on the part of fathers is positively associated with frequent depression and discouragement in children. (R100)

## PERSONALITY PROBLEMS OF CHILD
### (FRUSTRATION)    X  Social Mobility Pressures
There is a correlation between the parents' pressure upon the child to be socially mobile and frustration in the child. (M197)

## PERSONALITY PROBLEMS OF CHILD
### (MASOCHISM)
#### X  Child-Rearing Practices (Consistency)
Mothers who not only overstimulate aggressive and sexual drives in their children, but who also give promises of acceptance (love) when severely disciplining them (pain), are more likely than are mothers who discipline normally to produce children who have morally masochistic egos. (B281)

#### Child-Rearing Practices (Control)
The mothers of morally masochistic children are more likely to be overcontrolling (directly or indirectly, through attacks of family members aimed at lowering self-esteem) than are the mothers of normal children. (B281)

#### Personality of Mother
Mothers of morally masochistic children are more likely than are mothers of normal children to labor under a wide disparity between ego ideal and actual behavior (particularly in relation to sexual behavior, i.e., alternation between repression and acting out of impulses). (B281)

## PERSONALITY PROBLEMS OF CHILD
### (NERVOUSNESS)     X  Surrogate Mother
Among children of mothers who work, those whose mothers have provided a succession of different mother substitutes are more nervous than are those whose mothers have provided more stable arrangements. (Y047)

## PERSONALITY PROBLEMS OF CHILD
### (NEUROSIS/ACTING OUT)
#### X  Personality of Mother (Anomie)
Anomic mothers tend to have children whose problematic behavior is diagnosed as acting out and nonanomic mothers tend to have children whose problematic behavior is diagnosed as neurotic. (A069)

## PERSONALITY PROBLEMS OF CHILD (ORAL)
### X  Father Absence
When the father is absent from the home, boys are more apt to exhibit oral regression (thumb-sucking, nail-biting, smoking). (M181)

## PERSONALITY PROBLEMS OF CHILD
### (SEPARATION ANXIETY)
#### X  Personality of Mother (Separation Anxiety)
Correlated with a child's separation anxiety (which gives rise to personality problems on his part) is the mother's own separation anxiety with respect to the incomplete separation from and dependence on her own mother,

which is reactivated in her relations with her child. (S183)

## PERSONALITY PROBLEMS OF CHILD (STRESS)
### X  Social Mobility Pressures
Parents who pressure the child to be socially mobile, but who are financially unable to provide him with the higher education he desires cause emotional stress in the child. (M197)

## PERSONALITY PROBLEMS OF CHILD
### (STUTTERING)    X  Maternal-Role Behavior
The stuttering child produces, in the mother, feelings of helplessness, incompetency in her maternal role, reactive anger, and fear of disciplining the child. (W136)

## PERSONALITY PROBLEMS OF CHILD
### (WITHDRAWAL)     X  Employment of Mother
There is a correlation between the employment of the mother and withdrawing behavior in the child. (R108)

## PERSONALITY PROBLEMS OF FATHER
### X  Criminality
Deviant reactions to crises (aggressive or escapist) by the father are correlated with criminality in the son. (M195)

#### Geographic Mobility
There is no difference between fathers of disturbed children and fathers of normal children regarding their acceptance of residential change. (P074)

## PERSONALITY PROBLEMS OF FATHER
### (PARANOIA)    X  Mental Illness
Mental illness is more likely to occur if the father has delusions of paranoid grandiosity. (L123)

## PERSONALITY PROBLEMS OF HUSBAND/WIFE
### X  Alcoholism
Alcoholic husbands are more poorly adjusted than their wives (MMPI), particularly tending to act out in an antisocial manner. In nonalcoholic but conflicting couples, the reverse is true, but to a lesser extent. (B225)

## PERSONALITY PROBLEMS OF INFANT
### X  Pregnancy
Mothers who experienced emotional stress during pregnancy are more likely than are mothers who did not to have infants with motivational defects. (S227)

## PERSONALITY PROBLEMS OF MOTHER
### X  Criminality
Habitual criminals are much more likely to have suspicious and neurotic mothers than are normal persons. (C105)

Mothers who react unrealistically to crises through aggression, desertion, or escapism are more likely to have criminal sons than are those who respond realistically. (M195)

#### Geographic Mobility
Mothers of normal children are more likely to accept residential change than are mothers of disturbed children. (P074)

#### Juvenile Delinquency
There is a correlation between the delinquent behavior of the son and the unconscious desires of his parents, particularly the destructive impulses of the mother. (W152)

### Mental Illness (Schizophrenia)

Mothers of schizophrenics are more likely to regard the environment as hostile and to show conflicting needs. (H207)

### Mental Illness (Schizophrenia/Neurosis)

Mothers of neurotics are more likely than are mothers of schizophrenics to recognize their own personal inadequacies and are less likely to project them outwards or to be aggressive against the male sex. (M218)

Mothers of neurotics are less likely to be mentally stable than are mothers of schizophrenics. (M218)

Mothers of schizophrenics are more likely than are mothers of neurotics or of normals to have a distorted perception of reality and a negative and emotionally restricted view of the environment, as revealed by Rorschach testing. (M218)

There is a correlation between the Rorschach responses of neurotics and schizophrenics and the responses of their mothers. (M218)

Mothers of neurotics are more likely than are mothers of schizophrenics or of normals to show emotional immaturity and anxiety (in Rorschach testing). (M218)

### Personality Problems of Child

The more a mother is preoccupied with the expression of love, warmth, affection, and help during therapy, the less her child in therapy is able to discuss such needs. (C104)

### Pregnancy

The greater the severity of the prior psychological disturbances of the woman, the more likely it is that severe problems will emerge with the condition of gestation. (B280)

### Scholastic Adjustment

The mothers of school-phobic children are more likely than are the mothers of normal children to be immature and dependent on the maternal grandmother. (D065)

### Surrogate Parent

Children who fail to establish stable relationships in foster homes are more likely than are children who do to have mothers who have suffered nervous breakdowns. (W145)

## PERSONALITY PROBLEMS OF MOTHER (ANXIETY/AMBIVALENCE)
### X    Scholastic Adjustment

Mothers of children with school phobias tend to be highly anxious and ambivalent in their feelings toward others. (E095)

## PERSONALITY PROBLEMS OF MOTHER (DEPRESSION)
### X    Mental Illness of Child (Autism)

Autism is more likely to occur if the mother becomes severely depressed during the vulnerable developmental period. (S188)

## PERSONALITY PROBLEMS OF MOTHER (MASOCHISM)
### X    Personality of Child (Inhibition)

Masochistic behavior by the mother tends to produce extreme self-inhibition in the child. (S281)

## PERSONALITY PROBLEMS OF MOTHER (NERVOUSNESS/FEARS)
### X    Mental Illness (Schizophrenia/Neurosis)

Mothers of neurotics are more likely than are mothers of schizophrenics or of normals to describe themselves as being nervous and subject to fears and phobias during their childhoods. (M218)

## PERSONALITY PROBLEMS OF MOTHER (NEUROSIS)
### X    Alcoholism
### X    Neurosis of Mother

The mother of the alcoholic is more likely to be neurotic—the unsatisfied masochistic woman escaping the feminine role and exhibiting martyred or shrewish attitudes. (C122)

## PERSONALITY PROBLEMS OF MOTHER (ORAL)
### X    Mother-Child Relations (Affection)

A mother with unresolved oral conflicts tends to attempt to find a solution with her children by becoming demanding of them, rather than affectionate. (R099)

### Personality Development of Child (Ego Strength)

Mothers with unresolved oral needs are likely to have children characterized by weak ego development. (R099)

### Scholastic Achievement of Child

Children with learning problems are more likely to have mothers with excessive oral needs (dependency) and hostility directed toward their children than are those who do not have difficulty in learning. (S223)

## PERSONALITY PROBLEMS OF MOTHER (ORAL/ANAL)
### X    Breast Feeding

Women who prefer to bottle feed their children are more likely to show oral eroticism, oral sadism, and anal expulsiveness than are those who prefer breast feeding. (A063)

## PERSONALITY PROBLEMS OF MOTHER (PENIS ENVY)
### X    Breast Feeding

Women who choose to breast feed rather than bottle feed their children are more likely to manifest penis envy. (A063)

## PERSONALITY PROBLEMS OF MOTHER (PERFECTIONISM)
### X    Scholastic Adjustment of Child

The mothers of school-phobic children are more likely than are the mothers of normal children to be perfectionistic, having idealized pictures of what good mothers should be. (D065)

## PERSONALITY PROBLEMS OF MOTHER (PSYCHOSEXUAL/OBSESSIVE)
### X    Mental Illness (Schizophrenia)

Mothers of schizophrenics tend to be psychosexually maladjusted and "obsessive-compulsive" in the areas of cleanliness and propriety. (M218)

## PERSONALITY PROBLEMS OF MOTHER (UNREALISTIC ATTITUDES)    X    Illness of Child

Mothers of cerebral-palsied children do not exhibit more unrealistic attitudes than do mothers of normal children. (B320)

## PERSONALITY PROBLEMS OF PARENTS
### X    Alcoholism

Parents who reactions to crises are escapist, rather than

realistic or aggressive, are more likely to have sons who become alcoholics. (M195)

### X    Behavior Problems (Acting Out)
There is a correlation between parents' unresolved unconscious needs and the behavior of their acting-out children. (K151)

### Emotional Adjustment of Child
There is a correlation between emotional problems in the child and psychopathology in the parent. (M200)

### Employment of Mother (Regularity)
A son's delinquency and a mother's sporadic employment both correlate with and are caused by the emotionally disturbed and antisocial characteristics of the parents. (S265)

### Juvenile Delinquency
A son's delinquency and a mother's sporadic employment both correlate with and are caused by the emotionally disturbed and antisocial characteristics of the parents. (S265)

### Juvenile Delinquency/Neurosis
The parents of delinquent children show antisocial or morally unstable tendencies more frequently than do the parents of neurotic children (neurosis measured by phobias, anxiety symptoms, etc.). (B238)

### Mental Illness of Child (Schizophrenia)
In almost all cases of childhood schizophrenia, both parents are severely disturbed people. (E089)

### Mental Illness (Schizophrenia)
Though schizophrenics tend to have parents who manifest psychopathic symptoms, the latter do not tend to exhibit the same symptoms of disturbance. (M061)

### Mother-Child Relations (Affect)
The psychopathic and unstable parent who is the cause of child neglect is often the grown-up affectionless child who is a typical product of maternal deprivation. (B270)

### Personality Adjustment of Child
Fathers of maladjusted children tend to be weak, ineffectual, and psychosomatic; mothers are more likely to act out their conflicts in verbal and overt behavior. (L144)

### Scholastic Adjustment
Children with school phobias are likely to come from families in which the parents are characterized by either psychosis or neurosis. (S239)

## PERSONALITY PROBLEMS OF PARENTS (FEARS)
### X    Mental Illness (Schizophrenia)
Parents of normals are more likely than are parents of schizophrenics to report a major fear that they would like to eliminate. (F110)

Parents of neurotics are more likely than are parents of schizophrenics to acknowledge a major destructive consequence of the loss of self-control. (F110)

## PERSONALITY PROBLEMS OF PARENTS (NARCISSISM)    X    Mental Illness (Schizophrenia)
Schizophrenia tends to be correlated with parental narcissism. (R115)

## PERSONALITY PROBLEMS OF WIFE
### X    Alcoholism
Alcoholism in the husband is correlated with feelings of inadequacy and a need for dominance in the wife.

### Alcoholism of Husband
When the husband stops drinking (alcoholism), the wife is apt to develop a more severe personal pathology than she had while the husband was an alcoholic. (B225)

Wives of alcoholics showed fewer symptoms of mental disturbance when their husbands were sober than when they were drinking. (H238)

## PERSONALITY PROBLEMS OF WOMEN (SOCIOCULTURAL STRESS)    X    Fecundity
Amenorrhea, spontaneous abortion, and infertility have been shown to be associated with personal disorder that originates in sociocultural stress. (H024)

## PERSONALITY PROBLEMS (ORAL)
### X    Child-Rearing Practices (Oral Frustration)
The greater the amount of oral frustration in infancy, the more likely the incidence of oral fixation in later years. (B224)

### Mate Selection
Women with unresolved oral conflicts tend to marry passive and feminine-oriented men. (R099)

### Weaning
The greater the oral indulgence of the infant (in the form of late weaning), the more likely is the incidence of oral frustration and oral fixation in the child. (B224)

## PERSONALITY PROBLEMS (ORALITY/ANALITY/DEPENDENCY)
### X    Sibling Structure (Twins)
Twinship decreases the correlations between dependency and oral behavior and between dependency and anal behavior. (B224)

## PERSONALITY PROBLEMS/SOCIAL ADJUSTMENT
### X    Parent-Child Relations (Interaction)
Among nursery-school children, those who have experienced a high level of parent-child interaction have the problem of management of hostility; children who have experienced a low level of parent-child interaction have the problem of achieving a satisfactory degree of social interaction.

## PERSONALITY PROBLEMS (SOMATIC)
### X    Parent-Child Relations (Anxiety)
Felt or actual loss of parental attention or anxiety in the parent-child relationship may lead the child to seek attention by somatic functions (retention of feces, vomiting, and breath-holding).

## PERSONALITY PROBLEMS (SPEECH)
### X    Institutional Care
Children who are reared from early infancy in institutions and then placed in foster homes are much more likely to develop speech disabilities than are children who are placed in foster homes directly in early infancy. (B270)

## PERSONALITY PROBLEMS (STUTTERING)
### X    Mother-Child Relations
The lower the mother's level of anxiety concerning his speech and the lower the level of irritation at his aggressive behavior, the better chance of improvement has the stuttering child. (W136)

### Parent-Child Relations (Communication)
Inability on the part of an adult family member to adjust his level of communication to that of a child who is not

yet capable of adequate verbalization can produce stuttering in the child. (W136)

## PERSONALITY (QUARRELSOMENESS)
### X    Parent-Child Relations (Interaction)
In democratic homes, high parent-child interaction produces greater quarrelsomeness in the child than does low parent-child interaction. (B266)

## PERSONALITY (RESPONSIBILITY)
### X    Parent-Child Relations (Criticism)
The lower the adolescent's responsibility rating (based on teachers' ratings of dependability in fulfilling obligations), the more likely he is to describe his parents as complaining about him and ridiculing him. (B250)

The lower the adolescent's responsibility rating (based on teachers' ratings of dependability in fulfilling obligations), the more likely he is to see his parents as comparing him unfavorably with other children. (B250)

### Parent-Child Relations (Interaction)
The lower the adolescent's responsibility rating (based on teachers' ratings of his dependability in fulfilling obligations), the more likely he is to describe his parents as spending little time with him and avoiding his company. (B250)

### Parent-Child Relations (Rejection)
Parental rejection and neglect are negatively related to responsibility in the child (based on teachers' ratings of dependability in fulfilling obligations). (B250)

## PERSONALITY (RESTLESS STRIVING)
### X    Marital Adjustment of Wife
Unhappy wives tend to have a greater drive toward activity than do happy wives. They also prefer to belong to many societies rather than to a few and prefer work that involves change from place to place rather than work in one location. (T074)

## PERSONALITY (SECURITY)     X    Breast Feeding
There is no relationship between breast feeding in infancy and security in college students.

### Parent-Child Relations (Interaction)
Children in foster homes are more secure if their parents are allowed to make occasional visits than if such visits do not occur. (B270)

### Sibling Structure
The greater the number of siblings, the less the sense of security a child has. (I008)

## PERSONALITY (SELF-CONFIDENCE)
### X    Child-Rearing Practices (Clarity)
Adults who came from more-structured homes with clear standards have greater self-confidence than do those from less-structured homes. (L172)

### Marital Adjustment of Wife
Happy wives have more self-confidence than unhappy wives do, even in situations that have nothing to do with the marriage. Moreover, unhappy wives more often say that they lack self-confidence, get "rattled" easily, make excuses when caught in a mistake, and rewrite their letters before mailing them. They are more prone than happy wives to be affected by praise or blame of many people, to suffer from injured feelings, to refuse to take the lead in enlivening a dull party, and to be discouraged when the opinions of others differ from their own. (T074)

### Mate Selection
Men who desire females of equal intelligence have greater self-confidence than those who do not. (H190)

### Ordinal Position
The older child in a sibling pair is more likely to be self-confident than is the younger. (K104)

### Sibling Structure (Age and Sex)
The correlation of sibling age disparity and self-confidence is linear for boys with a brother, curvilinear for boys with a sister, and inversely curvilinear for girls with an older sister. (K104)

### Sibling Structure (Sex)
At the two-to-four-year spacing, children with cross-sex siblings tend to be more self-confident than do those with same-sex siblings. (K104)

When sibling spacing is under two years, girls tend to be more self-confident than boys do. (K104)

## PERSONALITY (SENSITIVITY)
### X    Ordinal Position
The eldest child will tend to be more adult-oriented and sensitive than will the second child. (F084)

### Sibling Structure (Sex)
The child with a brother tends to be more sensitive than the one with a sister. (K104)

## PERSONALITY (SHYNESS)     X    Ordinal Position
First children are more likely to be shy and second children to be friendly. (F084)

## PERSONALITY (SIMILARITY)
### X    Personality Adjustment of Wife
There is no difference in personality adjustment (MMPI) between wives who perceive similarities between themselves and their husbands and those who perceive themselves as different from their husbands. (K124)

### Self-Conception of Wife
Among wives, perceived similarity between self and spouse is related to favorable self-perception. (K124)

## PERSONALITY (SOCIAL INFLUENCE)
### X    Ordinal Position
A later-born persons's behavior (as measured by his performance on a counting task) is more likely to be influenced by interaction with another person than is the performance of the firstborn person or only child. (S234)

Since firstborn females receive earlier and more significant training in independence (in relation to sex role or care for later-born siblings) than do firstborn males, they develop greater need achievement and eventually a greater resistance to social influence. (S235)

## PERSONALITY (SOCIAL INTERESTS)
### X    Sex Status
Parents believe that their girls are more interested in other persons than are their boys. (G130)

## PERSONALITY (STRESS)
### X    Cohesion of Family, Change in
When strong affective ties have been formed between members of the family, situational pressures which force their modification will impose important strains upon the individual. (P012)

### Dependency
The greater the man's emotional dependence on his mother, the lower his resistance to psychological stress.

## PERSONALITY (TENACITY/AGGRESSION)
### X   Sibling Structure (Sex)
A girl with a younger or older brother with a two-to-four-year spacing is more likely (since her competitiveness will be aroused) to be aggressive and tenacious than will the girl with a similarly spaced sister. (K126)

A boy with a brother at least four years older than himself will be more aggressive, enthusiastic, ambitious, tenacious, and possessed of more interests than will a boy with a similarly older sister. (K126)

Within a two-to-four-year spacing, the child will be more aggressive, curious, and enthusiastic when his sibling is of the opposite, rather than of the same, sex, except in the case of a boy with an older sister. (K126)

## PERSONALITY (THRIFT)
### X   Marital Adjustment of Wife
Happy wives are distinguished to a higher degree than are unhappy wives by attitudes of thrift. They express more desire to save money, greater dislike of the gambling attitude, and greater dislike of occupations or occasions that are conceivably contributory to this attitude. (T074)

## PHYSICAL ACTIVITY   X   Parent-Child Relations
Children who are opposite-sex allied (i.e., join parent in family conflict) are more physically active than are children who are same-sex allied. (B263)

## PHYSICAL ADJUSTMENT
### X   Mother-Child Relations (Affect)
Lack of affective mother-child relations is a cause of head-rolling, body-rolling, and other hyperkinetic manifestations.

## PHYSICAL APPEARANCE OF HUSBAND/WIFE
### X   Marital Adjustment
Couples in which wives have higher ratings on physical appearance (i.e., are better looking) than their husbands have better marital adjustment than do couples in which wives do not have higher ratings on physical appearance than their husbands. (K012)

When there is a difference between the husband and wife in rating on physical appearance, the smaller the difference, the better the marital adjustment. (K012)

The higher the rating of the husband on physical appearance (i.e., attractiveness), the better the marital adjustment. This hypothesis is also denied. (K012)

The higher the rating of the wife on physical appearance, the better the marital adjustment. (K012)

## PHYSICAL DEVELOPMENT          X   Conformity
In the upper and middle classes, the later the maturation of the boy, the less likely he is to conform; in the lower classes, the later the maturation, the greater the conformity. With girls from the upper classes, the earlier the maturation, the greater the conformity. (T100)

### Institutional Care
The longer an infant is institutionalized, the lower his Development Quotient, as measured by the Hetzer-Wolf Baby Test, becomes. (B270)

### Mother Absence
Children who have been deprived of their mothers before they are six months old fail to gain weight properly even though they eat a diet which is adequate. (B270)

Separation from the mother is more likely to lead to retardation of physical growth than is disease. (B270)

### Parent-Child Relations (Rebellion)
The later the physical maturation of the boy, the more likely it is that he will have rebellious attitudes toward his parents. (M172)

### Parent-Child Relations (Rejection)
The later the physical maturation of the boy, the more likely it is that he will perceive his parents as highly dominating and rejecting. (M172)

### Parent Loss
If a child suffers the deprivation of one or both parents, he will not grow (physically) as much as if he had both parents. (B270)

### Pregnancy
Mothers who experience emotional stress during pregnancy are more likely than others to give birth to infants who suffer from physical impairment. (S227)

## PHYSICAL DISABILITY OF HUSBAND
### X   Marital Status
Among men who have been physically disabled, the proportion of those who remain married exceeds those who are divorced or separated at all educational levels. (N060)

## POLITICAL ACTIVITY          X   Role in Family
Individuals who are active in political and other social organizations are more likely to have family members who are also active participants. (H244)

Within families there is a somewhat higher correlation between the degree of political and social activity of husbands and wives than between parents and children. (H244)

Politically active individuals are more likely to come from families where several members are politically active than from families in which only one member is active. (H244)

### Sex Status
Male children are somewhat less likely than female children to resemble parents closely in extent of membership in political and social organizations. (H244)

For female children the resemblance with the mother in extent of social and political participation is much greater than to the father. (H244)

## POLITICAL AFFILIATION          X   Social Mobility
Upwardly mobile children whose parents are Democrats are more likely to become Republican than are those who have not been mobile. (H244)

## POLITICAL AFFILIATION OF CHILD
### X   Child-Rearing Practices (Control)
The relationship between degree of parental control and conformity to the parents' politics is curvilinear; highest conformity occurs where control was moderate, less conformity where control was weak, and least among those subject to the strictest parental control. (H244)

## Political Affiliation of Parents

Children of families in which no clear directives as to political preference come from the parents are more likely to be uncommitted or, perhaps, committed to being uncommitted, than are children whose parents have strong party ties. (H244)

Children of families who transmit the clear directive that they are independents are more likely to become independents themselves than are children of partisan parents. (H244)

Children of parents who clearly identify themselves as independents are more likely to be influenced by other considerations (as opposed to family influence) in party preference than are children of clearly partisan parents. (H244)

Parental influence is stronger in the transmission of party preference than it is in transmission of political ideology. (H244)

When the mother and the father disagree on choices of political party, the child is more apt to follow the mother's preference. (M056)

### Political Interest of Parents

Individuals who recall nothing about their parents' political views are less likely than are those who do to form party attachments. (H244)

### Voting Behavior

Individuals from families in which neither parent voted are more likely not to form any party attachments. (H244)

## POLITICAL AFFILIATION OF PARENTS
### X    Political Affiliation of Child

Children of families in which no clear directives as to political preference come from the parents are more likely to be uncommitted or, perhaps, committed to being uncommitted, than are children whose parents have strong party ties. (H244)

Children of families who transmit the clear directive that they are independents are more likely to become independents themselves than are children of partisan parents. (H244)

Children of parents who clearly identify themselves as independents are more likely to be influenced by other considerations (as opposed to family influence) in party preference than are children of clearly partisan parents. (H244)

Parental influence is stronger in the transmission of party preference than it is in transmission of political ideology. (H244)

When the mother and the father disagree on their choices of political party, the child is more apt to follow the mother's preference. (M056)

## POLITICAL AND ECONOMIC ROLE OF EXTENDED FAMILY
### X    Stability of Extended Family

The disintegration of the extended family will occur with the loss of its political and economic function. (O023)

## POLITICAL ATTITUDES    X    Age of Child

Parental influence on their children's political sentiments is less as the children grow older and influences from other agencies (school, peers) assume more relative importance. (H244)

### Class

Since overtly expressed opposition to political regimes by parents varies *inversely* with class level, parent-youth solidarity in terms of political conflict also varies inversely with social-class level. (G019)

### Husband/Wife

Husband and wife are likely to have similar political attitudes. (B265)

The correlation between one spouse's political attitudes and his or her perception of the other spouse's attitudes is greater than the actual attitude correlation. (B265)

### Marital Adjustment of Wife

In religion, politics, and moral views, happy wives have a greater majority of conservatives within their ranks than do unhappy wives. More unhappy than happy wives dislike conservative people and more of them believe that the current social order is so unjust that revolution will be necessary. More of the unhappy wives believe that religions do as much harm as good, more of them dislike Bible study, and fewer of them consider it essential that children have religious instruction (U.S.). (T074)

### Nonkin/Spouse

Young voters are more likely to agree with their spouses than with their friends on the choice of political party, and still more than with fellow workers. (M065)

### Parent-Child Relations (Control)

Highest conformity to parental political values is found among the young people subject to moderate parental control. (M056)

When young people, at the lower SES level, change away from the political preferences of their parents, the change is at least partly motivated by revolt against overstrict control. (M056)

### Parent-Child Relations (Rejection)

Radical political opinions are more common among people who felt that their parents rejected them as children.

### Political Interest of Parents

The effects of parental-training methods on political conformity seem greatest when the parents have a high level of interest in politics. (M056)

### Sex Status

Daughters are more likely than sons to have political attitudes which resemble those of their parents. (H244)

## POLITICAL ATTITUDES (CONSENSUS)
### X    Husband/Wife

Husbands and wives tend to share the same political preferences and attitudes. (W148)

## POLITICAL ATTITUDES (CONSERVATISM)
### X    Child-Rearing Attitudes (Restrictiveness)

If the family has restrictive child-rearing attitudes, the child is more likely to develop conservative political opinions. (B227)

## POLITICAL ATTITUDES OF CHILD
### X    Family/Nonfamily

The political atmosphere in an area is more likely to reduce parental influence on the political attitudes and behavior of the child when parents have deviant or minority opinions. (H244)

## POLITICAL CENTRALIZATION    X    Clan Structure
Centralized political authority tends to inhibit or curtail extensive development of a segmentary clan system. (F089)

### Descent (Matrilineal)
Matrilineages are not found in societies where central political organizations are not based on kinship. (G156)

### Religion (Ancestor Cult)
The more centralized type of political organization is correlated with a somewhat more well-defined ancestor cult. (H172)

### Stability of Lineage
A wider system of unilineal grouping will atrophy following the establishment of political centralization. (F033)

## POLITICAL DISCUSSIONS    X    Husband/Wife
The wife is more likely than the husband to discuss political matters with her spouse and to be aware of his opinions. (H244)

### Sex Status
Women are more likely than men to discuss politics with family members more often than with friends or co-workers, whereas the reverse is true of men. (H244)

## POLITICAL EXPANSION
### X    Residence (Patrilocal)
Patrilocal residence is encouraged in situations of political expansion. (M019)

## POLITICAL IMPORTANCE OF CLAN
### X    Cohesion of Clan
The disintegration of the clan structure is directly correlated with its loss of traditional political, judicial, and economic functions. (W082)

### Exogamy
When clans are politically important, exogamy is customary. (M168)

### Religion
The political functions of the clan tend to be immediately lost upon conversion to Islam. (G072)

### Segmentation
The absence of clan political or territorial functions is consistent with the lack of a high degree of segmentation. (C094)

## POLITICAL IMPORTANCE OF LINEAGE
### X    Genealogy
The absence of political functions in a lineage correlates with the absence of genealogical structure. (S087)

## POLITICAL INFLUENCE
### X    Extended/Nuclear Family
The extended family has a greater potential for commanding political influence than has the nuclear family. (G156)

## POLITICAL INTEGRATION
### X    Child-Rearing Practices
The use of bogeymen to scare children into conformity

is likely where physical punishment is little used and where there is a low level of political integration. (A053)

### Descent (Double)
A system of double descent is conducive to a pattern of politically independent villages. (H245)

Double descent functions to increase the degree of political integration between communities. (R069)

### Residence (Matrilocal)
A relatively low level of political integration is a precondition of matrilocal residence. (M019)

## POLITICAL INTEREST    X    Political Interest of Kin
An individual's level of interest in an election is more likely to be high if the level of interest of another family member is high than if it is low. (H244)

## POLITICAL INTEREST OF CHILD
### X    Peer Relations
"Peer-oriented" youth are less interested in politics and less desirous of being interested than are "parents-oriented" youth. (H244)

## POLITICAL INTEREST OF KIN
### X    Political Interest
An individual's level of interest in an election is more likely to be high if the level of interest of another family member is high than if it is low. (H244)

## POLITICAL INTEREST OF PARENTS
### X    Political Affiliation of Child
Individuals who recall nothing about their parents' political views are less likely than those who do to form party attachments. (H244)

### Political Attitudes
The effects of parental-training methods of political conformity seem greatest when the parents have a high level of interest in politics. (M056)

## POLITICAL INTEREST OF SON
### X    Father-Son Relations
Poor father-son relations tend to produce low political information and interest in the son. (L179)

## POLITICAL OPINION
### X    Child-Rearing Practices (Restrictiveness)
Parents who are less restrictive in their child-rearing practices (approving of free expression of a child's desires) are more radical in their political opinions. (S249)

## POLITICAL POWER    X    Intermarriage (Clan)
The consolidation of political power will be implemented by the intermarriage of ranking clans. (O034)

### Size of Clan
The political power of a clan is directly correlated with the number of its male members. (W082)

### Size of Family
The size of a family is directly correlated with the significance of its political role in the lineage. (L066)

### Size of Lineage
The political importance of a lineage tends to be directly correlated with its size. (L070)

## POLITICAL RANK    X    Exogamy
Exogamic restrictions are more likely to be violated if the individual is of high political status. (L109)

### Polygyny
There is a direct correlation between political rank and

the number of polygynous marriages a man contracts. (H058)

### Residence
Residence patterns are more likely to be violated if there are kinsmen of inappropriate status, yet politically powerful, with whom the individual wishes to affiliate. (L109)

## POLITICAL RANK OF FAMILY    X    Size of Family
The political status of the family tends to be directly correlated with its size. (K049)

## POLITICAL RANK OF HUSBAND
### X    Residence (Matrilocal)
Patterns of matrilocal residence are more likely to be violated if the husband is of high political status. (M125)

## POLITICAL RANK OF LINEAGE
### X    Economic Rank of Lineage
The political importance of a lineage tends to be directly correlated with its economic status. (L070)

## POLITICAL REBELLION
### X    Role Definition in Family (Dependency)
In a society where it is common that family controls on the individual are so strong as to limit severely his autonomy, political rebellion acts as a form of tension release for aggression against the family. (P056)

## POLITICAL RELATIONS    X    Intermarriage
Peaceful relations between adjacent tribes are more likely to be maintained if there is a pattern of intermarriage between the groups. (E080)

Intermarriage between different tribal groups tends to strengthen their political relations. (K060)

### Intermarriage (Community)
Political relations between communities are more likely to be hostile if there is no pattern of intermarriage between the villages. (T069)

The incidence of intermarriage will tend to be high between communities which maintain peaceful political relations. (T069)

### Intermarriage (Ethnic)
When patterns of intermarriage exist between two tribes, the character of their political relationship will tend to be cooperative. (B058)

### Sex-Role Definition
The constant, easy, brutalitarian dominance of the male over the female has a direct influence upon the attitude of the nation toward weaker, hence "inferior," peoples. (L166)

## POLITICAL RELATIONS WITH DEPENDENT COLONIES    X    Parent-Child Relations
The attitudes of nations toward their respective colonies are extensions of the characters of their parent-child relationships. (H081)

## POLITICAL ROLE OF CLAN    X    Acculturation
The political functions of the clan tend to be lost with acculturation. (W080)

### Age-Groups
The political importance of the clan structure is inversely correlated with the political importance of the age-set system. (B126)

### Genealogical Ties, Knowledge of
There is a positive correlation between the political function of a clan system and the occurrence of a genealogical structure. (E043)

## POLITICAL ROLE OF DESCENT GROUP
### X    Descent (Matrilineal)
The matrlineal descent group tends to disintegrate upon the loss of its political functions. (G056)

## POLITICAL ROLE OF EXTENDED FAMILY
### X    Cohesion of Extended Family
As extended family relationships have begun to lose their political and career meanings, the possibility of family ties based more upon affection and less upon obligation is increased. (P083)

### Stability of Extended Family
The loss of the political function has a more disintegrative effect on the extended family than does the loss of the economic function. (O023)

## POLITICAL ROLE OF KIN-GROUP
### X    Age-Groups
The extent of corporate organization of age-groups is negatively correlated with the performance by kinship groups of basic political and ritual tasks. (E086)

The greater the exclusion of kinship groups from basic political and ritual tasks and from territorial rights, the greater the degree of age-group hierarchy. (E086)

The greater the exclusion of kinship groups from basic political and ritual tasks and from territorial rights, the greater the degree of regulation of behavior by age-groups. (E086)

Where kinship groups do not perform basic political and ritual tasks and do not have territorial rights, there is a greater degree of corporate organization of the age-groups. (E086)

## POLITICAL ROLE OF LINEAGE
### X    Genealogical Depth
Long genealogies are more likely to be found in those systems where corporate lineages provide the central political framework of the total structure and where there is no specialized authority outside the lineage. (M168)

### Lineage Ties
When lineage affiliations are politically important, lineage membership will tend to be more rigorously defined. (L065)

## POLITICAL SOLIDARITY    X    Genealogical Ties
The political solidarity between communities will be increased if they share a common genealogical history. (R063)

### Homogamy
Political unity tends to be solidified by a system of hypergamous marriages. (M032)

## POLITICAL STABILITY    X    Corporate Kin-Group
The coexistence in a society of corporate lineages with political institutions of the state type makes for strains and instability. (F073)

### Preferential Marriage (Cross-Cousin)
Matrilateral alliance reduces fissive pressures in a segmentary society. (N072)

## POLITICAL STRUCTURE          X   Acculturation
Societies in which tensions exist between a state political structure and a corporate lineage organization will tend to be more susceptible to acculturation. (F073)

### Authority Structure of Family
Patterns of authority within the family structure tend to be extended into the political sphere. (B107)

The relationship of the child and father will tend to reflect the pattern of authority found in the political structure. (M029)

Where the state is democratic or nonexistent, kin relations are fairly nondeferential and "democratic." Where the state has been autocratic for a long period of time, kin relationships tend to be autocratic too. (S189)

### Child-Rearing Practices (Obedience)
Severity of obedience training is associated with the number of levels of political organization above the community level. (A053)

### Corporate Kin-Group
With the development of a state organization, the corporate function of unilinear kin-groups tends to diminish. (F039)

The emergence of the state structure is inhibited by the principle of group corporateness, which is manifest in the lineage group structure. (S087)

### Descent (Bilateral)
The flexibility of the bilateral structure mitigates against the development of extensive sociopolitical groupings of kin, since as circumstances change, alliances are dissolved. (P082)

There is an association between the political division of the nation into nonlocalized, widely dispersed sectors and strong bilateral emphasis. (S195)

### Descent (Double)
In societies characterized by dual descent, the political significance of one descent group will tend to be undercut by the fact that, in many contexts, affiliation with the other group will be relevant. (H245)

### Descent (Matriliny)
When bureaucratic political structures arise, matriliny tends to disappear. (A048)

### Descent (Unilineal)
The development of a unilineal kin structure tends to be inhibited by the establishment of centralized political authority. (F033)

Unilateral descent groups tend to be eliminated when political organization is highly developed. (L110)

### Father-Son Relations, Importance of
Where the father-son tie is central, overall national states with centralized governments exist; submission to parental authority is consistent with similar ties with the wider government. (H172)

### Geographic Mobility
A lineage structure which constitutes a single pyramidal system will be associated with a continual migration and spatial movement of the component groups. (M168)

### Inheritance
A monopolistic extension of political control will be facilitated by instituting political offices of a hereditary character. (W075)

### Kin Ties (Fictive)
The importance of fictive kinship ties increases with the growth of the state and its formal institutions. (M080)

### Kinship, Importance of
In the absence of political organization on the village level, kinship assumes a primary position as the major social bond. (E015)

Kin ties are of major importance in societies which lack a centralized system of political authority. (L072)

### Lineage
Lineage organization receives the highest degree of elaboration in societies which have a segmentary political structure. (F020)

### Mother-Son Relations
If the mother-son tie is of great importance, multiple national states are found. (H172)

### Paternal-Role Definition
As authority of the father becomes personal, state intervention becomes more likely. (T016)

As the legitimacy of the father's authority decreases—due to the lesser importance of the clan for the family—the state increases its control over paternal authority. (T016)

### Polygyny
In societies where economic institutions allow high economic rewards for executive capacity, polygyny is especially likely to occur if family ties are the only effective means of mobilizing effective political support. (P083)

### Residence
Planned villages with wards tend to be associated with multilineage political units. (H147)

The hamlet pattern of settlement tends to be correlated with local political units which are multilineage in character (Melanesia). (H147)

Localized kin-groups are associated with clan or lineage as the nucleus for a formal political structure with permanent authority. (K154)

Lineages are more likely to be autonomous and free of any centralized control if they are dispersed. (W080)

### Segmentation
There is an association between the extent of the internal differentiation of a lineage and the extent to which political roles are attached to segments of different depths. (H245)

The segmentary lineage structure is the product of a segmentary political structure and unilineal descent groupings. (S087)

### Sex-Role Definition
The distribution of women as gifts and tribute occurs in highly stratified societies where specific political institutions for insuring tribute have not yet fully evolved. (S271)

### Subsistence Pattern
When the technological pattern is not sufficiently productive or permanent of locale to support large concentrations of population or stable settlement, the sociopolitical organization will remain basically along kinship lines. (M033)

### Technology (Irrigation)

The development of a system of irrigation will tend to be accompanied by a shift from lineage-based units to politically autonomous organizations. (D086)

## POLITICAL STRUCTURE (BAND)
### X   Genealogical Depth

Shallow-depth lineages may be found in societies in which the political unit is a wandering band or horde composed of only a few families. (M168)

## POLITICAL STRUCTURE (BUREAUCRATIC)
### X   Corporate Kin-Group

One of the major obstacles to the establishment of a bureaucratic structure is the kinship system with corporate patrilineages. (F073)

## POLITICAL STRUCTURE (CENTRALIZATION)
### X   Descent (Patrilineal)

A social structure based on an association of exogamous corporate patrilineal descent groups is not likely to remain organized in a permanent political system unless it is subject to some form of overriding centralized government. (F120)

### Kin Ties

The attenuation of kin ties tends to occur in a politically centralized society. (L072)

## POLITICAL STRUCTURE (EGALITARIANISM)
### X   Genealogy, Importance of

Stress on ancestry will serve to divide the community if its political values are egalitarian. (G150)

## POLITICAL STRUCTURE (FEUDALISM)
### X   Homogamy

Patterns of hypogamy tend to occur in feudal societies. (L101)

### Preferential Marriage (Cross-Cousin)

Matrilateral cross-cousin marriage, in the absence of a moiety system, is correlated with a political structure of a somewhat feudal type. (N066)

## POLITICAL STRUCTURE (SEGMENTARY)
### X   Age Groups

Within segmentary societies, age-groups are not likely to occur. (E086)

## POLITICAL SUCCESSION
### X   Cohesion of Lineage

When political offices are established as achieved statuses, lineage solidarity is weakened. (S123)

### Descent

There is a highly significant association between lateral succession to the headman's position and matriliny and lineal succession and patriliny. (A048)

### Lineage, Importance of

When political offices are established as achieved status, the importance of lineage status will be reduced. (S123)

### Residence

Retention of lineage political rights tends to be jeopardized if the individual fails to conform to the residence pattern. (W078)

### Stratification

When political offices are established as achieved statuses, a pattern of ranking within the lineage tends to emerge. (S123)

## POLITICAL TIES, STRENGTH OF
### X   Endogamy (Community)

Political alliances beyond the community deteriorate as marriages are increasingly concluded within the same sib or village. (P008)

## POLYANDRY
### X   Descent (Matrilineal)

Polyandry is associated with matrilineality. (B205)

### Division of Labor by Sex

Polyandry is associated with the sexual division of labor in which the woman makes a very small contribution to family subsistence. (B205)

### Economic Cooperation

Polyandry often occurs where some economic advantage accrues to the participating males (e.g., land shortage, mutual help in hunting or fishing). (S189)

### Economic Level

Polyandry is associated with low economic production, forcing brothers to work cooperatively for survival. (B205)

Polyandry is more likely to occur in societies where poverty is so great that a single man cannot support a wife and children with any degree of reliability. (P083)

### Economic Role of Women

Conditions in which women play a role of equal importance in the economy and have equal rights to property are conducive to polyandry. (S068)

### Group Marriage

Polyandry is usually associated with group marriage and vice versa. (S189)

### Housing

The appearance of polyandry may be correlated with heavy demands for housing construction. (V025)

### Infanticide (Female)

Polyandry may be the result of a scarcity of women due to the practice of female infanticide. (M019)

### Land

Polyandrous marriage is related to the scarcity of land and its low productivity. (B033)

### Marriage Chances

The institution of polyandry tends to result in a lower percentage of women married. (G055)

### Polygyny

Polygyny may be regarded as a partial cause of polyandry. (D057)

### Preferential Marriage (Levirate)

Polyandry tends to develop out of an institutionalized pattern for leviratic unions. (S068)

### Property

Fraternal polyandry is associated with family systems in which both men and women have property rights, especially a dowry. (B205)

### Sex Ratio

Polyandry is associated with a surplus of men in the marriageable ages. The shortage may result from selling women, female infanticide, or neglect of female children. (B205)

### Sexual Permissiveness

One characteristic of polyandrous societies is general sexual freedom. (S189)

### Sibling Relations

Polyandry is associated with the equivalence of brothers in all transactions, including the ritual. That is, any brother is equivalent to any other brother. If one brother marries, the other brothers have sexual rights to his wife as well. (B205)

### Sibling Relations (Conflict)

Polyandry reduces potential hostility between brothers. (B205)

### Sibling Structure (Male Equivalence)

An emphasis on fraternal equivalence creates conditions conducive to polyandry. (M048)

### Social Structure

An egalitarian social structure and a situation in which the sexes have equal status within the family are conducive to polyandry. (S068)

### Stability of Family

Polyandry permits the husband to be absent for a long period of time, while maintaining the security of wife and family. A brother can protect a common wife or may even move into the household. (B205)

### Warfare

The custom of combined polyandrous and polygynous unions tends to be associated with a military society. (G055)

The institution of polyandry is particularly compatible with the society in which the primary occupational category is military. (G056)

## POLYANDRY (FRATERNAL)

### X   Cohesion of Extended Family (Patrilineal)

Fraternal polyandry functions to reinforce the solidarity of the patrilineal extended family. (G056)

### Sibling Relations (Solidarity)

The solidarity of male siblings is enhanced if they have legitimate claims to each other's wives. (G055)

### Size of Extended Family (Patrilineal)

Fraternal polyandry functions to restrict the size of the patrilineal extended family. (G056)

## POLYANDRY/POLYGYNY

### X   Descent (Matrilineal)

The combined custom of polyandrous and polygynous unions are consistent with a strong matrilineal system. (G055)

## POLYGYNY                                X   Acculturation

Acculturation is accompanied by less approval of polygyny. (J009)

Polygyny tends to be abandoned with the adoption of Christianity. (V021)

### Achievement Motivation

Low achievement motivation is more likely in cultures characterized by some form of polygyny than it is in monogamous cultures. (M246)

### Adultery

Extramarital intercourse is more frequent in polygynous households. (D055)

### Age

In polygynous societies there is a positive correlation between increasing age and a higher percentage of men in polygynous marriages. (B012)

### Age at Betrothal

Where polygyny is widely practiced, women will tend to be betrothed at an earlier age. (T058)

### Age at Marriage

Early marriages for females and late marriages for males are associated with societies where polygyny is the ideal. (G156)

### Authority Structure of Family

The husband in the polygynous family tends to be more aloof and surrounded by greater authority than does the husband of the monogamous family. (M041)

### Child-Rearing Practices (Dependency)

In societies with a high percentage of polygynous households, the young child's dependency demands are indulged and rewarded. (S079)

### Child-Rearing Practices (Sex)

Severity of sex training is greater in polygynous societies. (W127)

### Child-Rearing Practices (Sex Role)

Polygynous societies tend to have larger sex differences in socialization practices than do monogamous societies. (B264)

### Class

In societies where polygyny is practiced, the higher the man's social or economic position, the more likely is he to have more than one wife. (G156)

### Climate

Some form of polygyny is more likely to be found in hot climates than in more temperate climates. (M246)

### Competition for Women

Where polygyny is stressed, competition for women will be high. (O023)

### Concubinage

An increase in the number of concubines is directly correlated with the decrease in the number of polygynous unions. (S135)

### Conflict Between Generations

Where polygyny is the ideal, there is a strong potential conflict between different generations. (E086)

### Conflict Between Wives

The relationship between co-wives will tend to be more amicable, the more closely related they are. (H128)

### Descent (Patrilineal)

Polygyny tends to be associated with patrilineal organization. (F010)

### Desertion by Women

Desertion by the woman is more likely to occur when the husband acquires a second wife. (W108)

### Divorce

The rate of divorce tends to be higher in polygynous marriages. (B012)

When divorce is easy the stimulus to polygyny, which might otherwise come from the desire for issue, is not great. (B298)

### Economic Dependence

With the introduction of an economy which permits economic independence, the age at which a male may contract a polygynous union is younger. (W082)

### Economic Importance of Women
Polygynous unions tend to be more highly valued as a marriage form if the role of the woman has more economic importance. (W056)

### Economic Level
Polygyny tends to be encouraged when other opportunities for investment are limited. (G013)

A higher incidence of polygyny tends to accompany an increase in the economic level. (S096)

### Economic Pattern
Polygyny among the rich and powerful is more likely to occur in societies in which economic institutions allow high economic rewards for executive capacity (if agriculture or husbandry is extensive and private property well institutionalized). (P083)

### Economic Pattern (Money)
Polygyny tends to be abandoned with the institution of a money economy and wage labor. (W056)

### Economic Rank
Where economic power is less effectively secured by political power, polygyny will make the consolidation of large families estates more difficult because of fragmentation caused by the large number of heirs. (P083)

Polygyny is generally confined to men of high economic status. (T041)

The number of wives a man acquires in a polygynous union is directly correlated with his wealth. (W081)

### Economic Role of Women
Polygyny is more likely to occur where the role of the woman is of greater economic importance. (S153)

### Elopement
In polygynous societies, where it is difficult for a man to marry at an early age, the incidence of elopement is high. (W056)

### Father-Child Relations (Hostility)
There is a correlation between polygyny and the reduction of hostile paternal feelings toward the unborn. (D071)

### Father-Child Relations (Intensity)
The father-child relationship will be less intense in polygynous families. (K061)

### Fertility
Polygyny has the effect of lowering reproduction. (D055)

A decrease in the birth rate tends to accompany the repression of polygyny. The contrary is also asserted. (H135)

Husbands of barren women are likely to take additional wives. (L110)

Polygyny yields greater fertility in societies in which there are more marriageable women than men; where the sex ratio is nearly 1:1, the marriage form more likely to assure the greatest fertility is monogamy. (P083)

### Fertility Values
Polygyny tends to be associated with a strong emphasis upon a large number of children. (O023)

### Geographic Mobility
There seems to be no direct correlation between polygyny and labor migration. (S266)

### Gerontocracy
When the political structure is gerontocratic in nature, polygyny tends to be concentrated among older men. (F073)

### Homogamy
A class system associates hypergamy with polygyny. (V030)

### Husband-Wife Relations (Closeness)
The ties between husband and wife are less strong in a polygynous family. (K157)

### Husband-Wife Relations, Importance of
Polygyny, of any variety, is negatively associated with an emphasis on the husband-wife tie. (H172)

### Identification with Siblings
There is likely to be more mutual identification between sons of a monogamous couple than between sons of different mothers. (P083)

### Illegitimacy, Attitude Toward
With the prohibition of polygyny, the attitude toward illegitimacy becomes more lenient. (S134)

### Incest Taboo
The emphasis on the incest taboo is stronger where older men are permitted to take another young wife (instead of helping their younger brothers or sons to marry). (E086)

### Intermarriage
Intertribal marriage may be correlated with the practice of polygyny. (B167)

### Land, Amount of
An increase in the scarcity of land leads to fragmentation of holdings, which is conducive to a pattern of polygynous marriage. (W082)

### Lineage, Importance of
Fear of dying without an heir is one of the factors behind the polygynous system of marriage. (K158)

### Marital Adjustment
Mormon men take second wives when their first marriage has been inadequate or unsuccessful. (B033)

### Marital Stability
Polygynous unions are less stable than are monogamous marriages. (D055)

### Marriage Class System
A high rate of polygyny increases the difficulty of observance of restrictions associated with a marriage class system. (E032)

### Marriage Payment
Where polygyny is stressed, the size of the marriage payment tends to be larger. (O023)

### Mate Selection (Near Kin)
There is a definite correlation between polygyny and the incidence of marriage with near kin. (S140)

### Maternal Role
The mother is more important to her children in a polygynous than in a monogamous marriage. (R030)

### Mother-Infant Sleeping Arrangements
Polygyny is the variable most strongly associated with exclusive mother-infant sleeping arrangements. (W127)

### Oedipal Complex
Males in polygynous societies are more likely to have strong Oedipal fears. (S189)

### Parent-Child Relations (Hostility)
Polygyny reduces parental counter-Oedipal hostilities toward the unborn when there are taboos on coitus after pregnancy; the hostility is greater when there is ideal polygyny but actual monogamy. (D071)

### Parent-Child Relations (Intimacy)
The relationship of the mother to her children in the polygynous family is more intimate than that of the father to his children. (M041)

### Personality of Men (Leadership)
Polygyny is likely to create a large supply of men committed to community roles requiring a high degree of skill and responsibility (e.g., priesthood, war leadership, estate management, and headship of lineages). (P083)

### Political Rank
There is a direct correlation between political rank and the number of polygynous marriages a man contracts. (H058)

### Political Structure
In societies where economic institutions allow high economic rewards for executive capacity, polygyny is especially likely to occur if family ties are the only effective means of mobilizing effective political support. (P083)

### Polyandry
Polygyny may be regarded as a partial cause of polyandry. (D057)

### Property
Polygyny tends to occur in a patrilineal society where the economy permits the accumulation of personal property. (B033)

### Rank of Women
The increasing status of women tends to lead to a breakdown in polygynous patterns. (L079)

### Religion (Christianity)
The abandonment of polygynous practices is directly correlated with the strength of missionary pressure. (H058)

### Residence (Matrilocal)
The introduction of matrilocal residence is opposed by polygyny. (M019)

### Residence (Patrilocal)
Polygyny is particularly congenial to patrilocal residence. Hence, anything that favors polygyny also favors the development of patrilocal residence. (M019)

### Sex Ratio
The prevalence of polygyny will be directly correlated with the sex ratio. (B081)

Polygyny is more apt to be censured when there is a shortage of marriageable women. (V024)

### Sex Status
Men are more likely than women to desire several mates. (P083)

### Sex Taboo
Sex taboos are more common in polygynous societies. (O027)

Polygyny will tend to be institutionalized where there are major taboos against sexual intercourse during pregnancy and in the postnatal period. (V021)

### Sex Taboo (Postpartum)
In societies that have a high proportion of polygynous marriages, a long postpartum sex taboo is found. (S079)

### Sibling Relations (Solidarity)
In the polygynous family, siblings are united more through their relationship with their mother than with their father. (M198)

### Sibling Rivalry
Sibling rivalry is greater in polygynous families. (L133)

### Size of Kin-Group
The size of the residential kin-group will tend to decrease with a decrease in polygyny. (H164)

### Subsistence Pattern (Pastoral)
The prevalence of polygyny is directly correlated with the distribution of cattle. (S096)

### Superego Formation
Polygynous societies are low in guilt orientation since guilt is derived from identification with the male rather than the female role. (W127)

### Urbanization
Polygyny tends to be abandoned under the conditions of urban life. (K066)

### Warfare
Polygyny is more likely to occur where warfare is important. (W129)

### Weaning
In societies with a high percentage of polygynous households, the age at weaning is likely to be higher. (S079)

### Witchcraft
Sorcery is more common in polygynous societies, both sororal and nonsororal. (S189)

## POLYGYNY, ATTITUDE TOWARD
### X      Economic Level
Unless the food supply is precarious, the first wife may consider the presence of another wife to be of advantage. (S098)

## POLYGYNY, ECONOMIC IMPORTANCE OF
### X      Monogamy
Monogamy tends to be resisted if polygyny plays a vital role in the economy. (A030)

## POLYGYNY (NONSORORAL)
### X      Cohesion of Patrilineal Group
Nonsororal polygyny tends to reinforce the solidarity of the male members of the patrilineal group. (G028)

### Kin Terminology (Bifurcate Collateral)
Nonsororal polygyny operates to produce bifurcate collateral terminology. (M019)

### Residence (Matrilocal)
Nonsororal polygyny is incompatible with matrilocal residence. (W105)

### Residence (Patrilocal)

Nonsororal polygyny tends to occur in the presence of patrilocal residence and patrilineal descent. (M019)

## POLYGYNY, NUMBER OF WIVES    X Adultery

Under polygyny, wives are more likely to commit adultery if they are in a household with many wives. (C057)

### Conflict Between Wives

The amount of friction in a polygynous family is directly correlated with the number of wives. (A030)

### Father-Child Relations (Intimacy)

The greater the number of wives the father has, the less likely he is to be intimate with his children. (M198)

## POLYGYNY (RANKING OF WIVES)
### X Inheritance

Owing to polygyny and the associated practice of ranking wives, disputes about the succession are almost inevitable. (S196)

## POLYGYNY/RESIDENCE (PATRILOCAL)
### X Kin Terminology (Bifurcate Collateral)

The occasional appearance of bifurcate collateral terminology in normal or neolocal Eskimo society presumably reflects former polygyny and patrilocal residence. (M019)

## POLYGYNY (SORORAL)
### X Affinal-Role Obligations

The institutionalization of sororal polygyny may be manipulated by parents to induce their son-in-law to observe his affinal obligations (i.e., rewarding him for good behavior by letting him marry the second sister). (H049)

### Child-Rearing Practices (Indulgence)

Societies with sororal polygyny (in which co-wives customarily are sisters), as compared with other forms of marriage, are more likely to be indulgent in the initial care of the infant and less severe in subsequent socialization. (W142)

### Conflict Between Wives

There is likely to be less conflict between co-wives when polygyny is sororal. (H139)

### Kin Terminology (Bifurcate Merging)

Sororal polygyny operates to produce bifurcate merging terminology. (M019)

### Kin Terminology (Classificatory)

Under sororal polygyny, terms for ego's primary relatives tend to be extended within the same sex and generation to their collateral relatives through females. (M019)

### Mate Selection

When the first wife has an important role in the selection of subsequent mates, the pattern of polygyny will tend to be sororal. (S153)

### Residence

Co-wives regularly reside in the same dwelling if they are sisters, but occupy separate habitations if they are unrelated. (M019)

### Residence (Matrilocal)

Sororal polygyny tends to be associated with matrilocal residence. (M019)

## POLYGYNY (SORORAL/NONSORORAL)
### X Weaning

Societies with sororal polygyny are significantly less severe in weaning their children than are societies with nonsororal polygyny. (W127)

## POPULATION    X Acculturation

Apathy, due to loss of old customs in the process of acculturation, leads to extension of the practice of abortion and to a decrease in population. (B081)

When social disintegration characterizes a cultural contact situation, depopulation tends to occur. (E080)

### Clan

The appearance of the clan organization tends to be correlated with an increase in the density and the size of the population. (G045)

### Cohesion of Kin-Group

A decline in population will tend to encourage the consolidation of kinship segments which have previously separated. (W031)

### Corporate Kin-Group

With an increase in the size of the population aggregate, it becomes necessary to identify and classify groups rather than individuals, so that corporate descent groups are formed. (O006)

### Descent (Unilineal)

Nonunilineal descent groups are more likely to occur than are unilinear descent groups where the population fluctuates and expands irregularly. (B327)

### Exogamy

Exogamic restrictions tend to be violated with a decrease in population. (E068)

### Extended/Nuclear Family

Family autonomy tends to increase with an increase in population pressure. (S158)

### Genealogical Depth

With a decrease in population, the depth of genealogies is reduced. (K081)

### Incest Taboo

A population decrease tends to result in the diminution of exogamy and incest taboos. (P008)

### Inheritance (Equal Division)

Equal division of inheritance tends to increase population growth. (H006)

Any given increase in productivity, under a system of equal division of inheritance, tends to exhaust itself in an increase in population and to accelerate the process of division. (H066)

### Kin Ties

The attenuation of kin ties tends to occur under conditions of high population density. (L072)

### Kinship, Importance of

When the size of the population unit is small, social organization tends to be along kinship lines. (M033)

### Lineage

The formation of a unilineal kin unit is associated with an increase in population. (S120)

### Marriage, Intergenerational

With a decrease in population, intergenerational marriages will tend to increase. (M137)

#### Mate Selection (Residence)
As population density increases, so does the likelihood of residentially propinquitous mate selection. (K020)

#### Moiety
The increase in the size of population aggregates is sufficient to account for the appearance of sib and moieties. (O006)

#### Preferential Marriage
Preferential marriage patterns tend to be abandoned with a decrease in population. (G097)

#### Segmentary Structure
The emergence of a segmentary structure is to be expected where an increase of population and concomitant territorial expansion occur with the retention of patterns of interaction between members of the derivative communities. (F033)

#### Segmentation
The segmentation of unilinear groups tends to occur with the expansion of population. (K029)

With an increase in the size of the population aggregate, a homogeneous kinship society tends to segment into unilateral kinship groups. (O006)

#### Sex Ratio
A progressive surplusage of males is unfavorable to an increase of population. (W109)

#### Sexual Permissiveness
The lack of population limitation through sex mores is associated with a society whose size of population hovers near the minimum for survival. (W156)

#### Stability of Clan
The fission of clans or other unilinear kin-groups tends to occur with population expansion. (M020)

#### Stability of Extended Family
With an increase in population and pressure upon the land for other resources available for economic exploitation, extended families commonly split, sending off branches which migrate and settle elsewhere. (M019)

#### Stability of Kin-Group
An increase in population may result in the deterioration of the kin-group. (F069)

#### Stability of Kinship Structure
The kinship structure will tend to deteriorate with a decrease in population. (R067)

#### Stability of Lineage
A decline in population tends to result in the disintegration of the lineage structure. (L045)

An increase in the size of population aggregate may result in a revision of the inner structure of lineage segments. (O006)

The process of lineage fission tends to accelerate with an increase in population. (W056)

## POPULATION CONTROL          X   Industrialization
"Primitive" societies are more likely to use abortion and infanticide as methods of controlling the population; industrial societies use postponement of marriage, denial of marriage, and birth control. (P083)

## POPULATION DENSITY          X   Economic Level
Improvement in the resource base or improvement in the method of exploitation usually means an increase in population density and the appearance of larger bands or villages. (O006)

#### Preferential Marriage
Specificity of preferential marriage patterns tends to be correlated with situations of low population density. (R069)

#### Stratification
The development of social classes is correlated with an increase in the density of the population. (M033)

#### Structure of Family
Where population density is low (one to the square mile or less), the normal form of the family is the simple patrilineal family, with families drawn together in bands or hordes. (K090)

## POWER          X   Role Definition in Family
Instrumental leadership of a family member is associated with power for that partner.

## POWER/AUTHORITY STRUCTURE OF FAMILY
####          X   Role Definition in Family
The more important the decision or task faced by the family, the greater the likelihood that the exercise of power will correspond to the authority structure based on sex and age. (S207)

## POWER OF KIN-GROUP     X   Size of Kin-Group
The power of a localized lineage segment will be directly correlated with its size. (B134)

## POWER STRUCTURE          X   Resources
The balance of power will be on the side of that partner who contributes the greater resources to the marriage. (P083)

## POWER STRUCTURE OF FAMILIES WITH MENTALLY ILL MEMBERS          X   Class
Three clusters of interpersonal relations and child-rearing practices were found among *middle-class* parents more than among lower-class parents of mental patients: 1) the mother played a more dominant role in the family power structure as well as in the child-rearing process; 2) the father participated more in family life than in the lower class, but the children questioned his masculinity; and 3) parental control of children was primarily verbal, but was more effective than that in the lower class. (M061)

## POWER STRUCTURE OF FAMILY
####          X   Acculturation
The acculturation of matrilineal tribes tends to result in an increase in the power of the father within the family. (E046)

#### Achievement
In joint family systems, when a man has made a fortune by his own skill and has invested it in property other than farming land, he will tend to be reluctant to allow other members of the family to interfere in its management. (M021)

The more responsible and skillful the man is in extrafamilial roles, the greater is the effective superiority of the husband in family decision making. (P083)

Families with a conflict in the power structure have sons with low levels of performance and with low achievement motivation. (S205)

The equalitarian family is associated with ineffective socialization for achievement roles. (S205)

### Achievement Motivation
In families where the authority structure is more evenly dispersed, granting the mothers considerable power, the sons are more likely to be high achievement seekers. (G156)

Families where the fathers tend to dominate are not associated with high achievement motivation. (G156)

Mothers of boys with high achievement motivation tend to be more dominant than do mothers of boys with low achievement motivation. (R106)

In societies that have institutionalized male dominance, the father whose dominance is so great that a son generalizes from his low intrafamilial potency to the world at large may have a low achievement orientation. (S205)

### Achievement Values
The more the father believes in achievement values, the less his son's power is. (M060)

### Age of Child
Older (high-school) adolescents are more likely to perceive the father as dominant in family matters; younger (junior-high-school) adolescents are more likely to say there is equality between the parents. (B323)

The perception of the father or mother as dominant will decrease with age for both sexes; there will be a shift from seeing a single parent as dominant to seeing both parents as equal (U.S.). (H180)

### Aggression
Nonaggressive boys are more likely than aggressive boys to perceive the mother as being the boss of the family. (K103)

### Alcoholism
Alcoholics are more likely than others to have indulgent, overprotective mothers and domineering, inconsistently severe fathers.

The alcoholic father is more likely to play a passive and dependent role in his family than a dominant one. (M195)

### Alcoholism/Criminality
Boys from families in which the father is dominant are more likely to become criminal than alcoholic. (M195)

### Authority Structure of Family
The greater the importance of the decision to be made, the greater the correspondence between the authority structure of the family and the amount of power actually exercised. (S190)

### Child-Rearing Attitudes (Flexibility)
Parents reared in families in which the mother had more control than the father are more likely to show flexibility in their child-rearing attitudes than are those from families with other control patterns. (B249)

### Child-Rearing Practices (Dependency)
Low independence training is associated with parental autocracy. (E102)

### Childhood (Emotional Security)
Men who dominate in the marriage relationship are more likely to have experienced an emotionally insecure childhood. (P086)

### Chores
Couples who stress the importance of joint decision making also share child care and housework. (B209)

### Class
Familial relations between members of the lower class tend to be both more egalitarian and more intimate. (B083)

Middle-class adolescents are more apt to report their fathers as dominant in conjugal and child-rearing relations than are lower-class adolescents; lower-class adolescents are more apt to report their mothers as dominant in these areas. (B323)

Lower-class families are more likely to be matriarchies than are families of other classes. (C134)

Lower-class families are more likely to be patriarchal than are families of other classes. (C134)

The higher the social class, the greater the man's influence in the family. (G156)

Middle-class children are more likely to view their fathers as more powerful than are children from lower socioeconomic strata. (H180)

The higher the social rank of families, the less the power of the sons and the greater the power of the fathers. (M060)

The mother's power in decision making does seem to be influenced by class status. (M060)

### Cognitive Beliefs
The less the mother and son are dominated by the father in the power area, the greater the disposition of both to believe that the world can be rationally mastered and that a son should risk separation from his family. (M060)

### Cohesion of Family
Strong ties between parents and children tend to reduce effective leadership in the family. (B202)

### Conformity
As structural asymmetry increases in parent-child relations toward either autocratic or permissive control, parents' efforts at explanation of their rules are more necessary to make children obey. (E105)

### Dependency of Son
The less the mother and son are dominated by the father in the power area, the greater the disposition of both to believe that the world can be rationally mastered and that a son should risk separation from his family. (M060)

### Descent (Matrilineal/Patrilineal)
Control over the husband's authority is of greater importance for the matrilineage than for the patrilineage. (G156)

### Division of Labor by Sex
When the wife is the one who has the greater power in the family, she is also the one who carries most of the household labor.

### Dyadic Relations
If two family members have a relation of high dominance-high submission, each will be more apt to be either highly dominant or highly submissive to other group members than less so; and dyadic relationships among these other family members will also be characterized by high dominance-high submissiveness. (C124)

If an older family member has a low dominance toward a younger family member, the younger member will have a low submission score. (C124)

If an older family member has high dominance toward a younger family member, the younger family member will have a high submissiveness toward the older family member (the exception is where the older family member is the mother and the younger member is the child). (C124)

All the dyadic relationships in a family tend to have the same, rather than varying, ratios of dominance to submission. (C124)

### Economic Dependence
The more economically independent children and parents are of each other when children grow up, the more dominant the child becomes in the family. (B311)

Independence from parental control will tend to accompany economic independence. (H103)

### Economic Dependence of Wife
The control of the husband over the wife will tend to be weakened if the wife is economically independent. (F073)

### Economic Pattern (Money)
With the introduction of a money economy and the subsequent financial independence of sons, the position of the father is weakened by the removal of the special economic control. (R005)

### Economic Rank
Paternal power increases with an increase in the income level of the family. (K030)

### Economic Rank of Father
In matrilineal societies, the degree of control of the father over his sons is directly correlated with his wealth. (W132)

### Economic Role
When the economic position of the father is insecure (e.g., in times of unemployment), he loses the legitimation of his authority and tends to become increasingly arbitrary. (B207)

### Economic Role of Family
The influence of the mother in the family increases as the family becomes less of a production unit and more of an income-earning unit. (B031)

### Economic Role of Wife
When women control strategic resources, they will tend to have, within the nuclear family, more influence than their husbands. (H032)

When the wife is of economic importance, the relationship between husband and wife will tend to be more equal. (O023)

### Education
The greater the education of the spouse, the larger his share in marital decision making will be.

### Education of Child
Maternal authority is a more important factor in the education of the children in the family than is paternal authority. (K030)

### Education of Husband
The amount of paternal power is greater among husbands with medium educational levels than among husbands with either low or high educational levels. (K030)

The higher the educational level of the husband, the less power he exerts in the family. (K089)

### Employment
The partner who works more has more power. This is true, not only for working wives v. nonworking wives, but also even reflects the number of hours the husband works.

### Employment of Mother
The husband is more likely to be dominant in decision making if the wife is employed than if she is not. The contrary is also reported. (M215)

### Employment of Wife
No significant differences appear in the dominance in family decisions as between the employed wife and the nonemployed wife. (B208)

"Husband-dominated" families tend to become more egalitarian as a result of the wife's working outside the home. (B208)

The wife's ability to influence family decisions increases more when she works among the lower than among the upper strata. (G156)

### Employment of Women
As women seek employment outside the family, a shift in the power pattern from one single dominant head to control by consensus occurs. (B033)

### Father-Child Relations (Permissiveness)
Where the father is seen as dominant in family and child-rearing decisions, adolescents are more likely to view their fathers as autocratic than they are to view them as permissive or equalitarian. (B323)

### Friendship Choice (Sex)
Among schizophrenics, those from father-dominated families are more likely to have friends of both sexes than are those from mother-dominated families, who are more likely to be social isolates. (F117)

### Geographic Mobility
Urban migration tends to weaken parental control. (F060)

When the younger members of the family are absent because of migration to town for work, there tends to be a shift in the balance of power from the oldest to the middle generation. (G028)

### Homosexuality
Men who were reared in families where the father was weak (or absent) and the mother was the dominant figure are more inclined toward homosexuality. (W140)

### Husband-Wife Relations (Conflict)
Where there is a shift in the marital authority pattern, domestic quarrels are more frequent. (S171)

### Identification
The child is more likely to identify with the person he conceives as most powerful (i.e., the parent who most effectively controls his rewards and punishments). (A060)

### Identification with Parent
The similarity of a child's behavior to that of his parents is independent of the sex of the parent exercising power in the family. (M179)

### Illegitimacy
Unwed mothers are more likely to have been raised in homes in which one parent, particularly the mother, dominated than in one in which both parents were active participants. (Y048)

Unwed mothers are more likely than married mothers to have had possessive mothers and passive fathers. (Y048)

### Illegitimacy (Adoption)
Compared to unwed mothers who released their children for adoption, unwed mothers who kept their children came from unhappy and mother-dominated homes. (V027)

Unwed mothers from mother-dominated homes are more likely to have stronger attachments to their babies (i.e., desire to take them home) than are unwed mothers from father-dominated homes. (Y048)

### Incest (Brother–Sister)
In families where there was brother-sister incest, the father did not have the dominant position that he had in father-daughter incest families. (W123)

### Incest (Mother-Son)
In families where mother-son incest occurred, the mother was dominant, while the father was absent or subordinate. (W123)

### Income
The higher the husband's income, the less power he exerts in his family. (K089)

### Independence of Wife
The legal protection of women's property rights, the capacity to mobilize kin for assistance, and decreasing pressures against adultery make the wife under 45 a "potential prize in the seduction game" and thus decrease her dependency upon her husband for status. (P083)

### Industrialization
Rebellion of women against their subordinate position in marriage accompanies industrialization and the actual or potential economic independence of women. (B033)

### Inheritance
The maintenance of parental control tends to be correlated with patterns of delayed inheritance. (L064)

Maiden aunts, bachelor uncles, and childless couples have special powers within the family where the inheritance pattern allows for testimentary freedom. (P060)

### Isolation of Nuclear Family
When the nuclear family is isolated, there is a concomitant shift in the mother's status within the family to a position of centrality. (C024)

### Juvenile Delinquency
Dominance of the mother in family affairs appears to be associated with delinquency in boys.

Homes in which the mothers are dominant and the fathers are tyrannical (alcoholic, brutal) are more likely than others to produce delinquent children. (B238)

Bossing of the father by the mother shows no relationship to delinquency, but frequent bossing by the father is associated with delinquent behavior in girls. (N057)

There is no correlation between dominance by the mother and delinquency in the child, but dominance by the father is related to delinquency in girls. (N063)

### Leadership
A home in which one parent is the principal disciplinarian is more likely to produce children with a sense of responsibilty and leadership than is a home in which both parents are equally dominant. (B273)

### Marital Adjustment
Democratic marital relations are directly related to marital adjustment. (K161)

In marriages where there is low satisfaction, husbands are more apt to feel they have less influence in decision making than when marriages are highly satisfying. (L173)

Couples who make more decisions jointly (e.g., pertaining to money, child rearing, coping with crises) are more likely to be better adjusted in marriage. (P086)

Relationships which are male dominated are more likely to receive poor marital-adjustment ratings than are those which are female dominated or those which are in "equilibrium." (P086)

Good marital adjustment is more likely to occur where spouse relations are equalitarian; when either spouse is dominant in the relationship, adjustment is likely to be poor. (S279)

### Marital Adjustment of Husband
Well-adjusted husbands are more likely than others to grant their wives greater deference and respect and to submit to wife domination. (T092)

### Marital Adjustment of Wife
The more equal the balance of power between the marital partners, the higher the satisfaction expressed by the wife with marital intimacy.

Well-adjusted wives are more likely than others to expect less deference and respect from their husbands and to defer to their husbands' judgments. (T092)

### Marriage Chances
Among schizophrenics, those from father-dominated families are more likely to be married than are those from mother-dominated families. (F117)

### Maternal Overprotectiveness
Maternal overprotectiveness and paternal dominance are mutually exclusive. (L163)

### Mental Illness
Mental illness is directly correlated with a family environment in which the mother is dominant. (M164)

Mental illness is more likely to occur if the father is strict and the mother overprotective. (M165)

### Mental Illness (Manic-Depressive)
Among manic-depressives, the mother is more likely to be the dominant parent. (G022)

### Mental Illness of Child (Schizophrenia)
Families of schizophrenic children are more likely to show greater dominance by one parent over the other than are families of nonschizophrenic offspring. (F117)

Schizophrenic children who view their mothers as

strong authority figures are more likely to view their fathers as weak authority figures than are schizophrenics who view their mothers as weak authority figures. (K114)

Schizophrenia in children correlates with family environments in which the wife excludes the husband from leadership and decision making. (L114)

Adolescent schizophrenics with "childish" reactions lived in a family structure with "a high degree of imbalance in leadership." Their fathers had more ego strength than their mothers did and appeared to be more capable of leadership in most instances, but they did not exercise leadership. (S208)

### Mental Illness (Schizophrenia)
Male schizophrenics who related well to other people and who had normal sexual contacts before the onset of their disorders are more likely to come from families in which the father was dominant, while those who were relative isolates and who had no normal sexual contacts before their disorders are more likely to come from families in which the mother was dominant. (B228)

Among schizophrenics, good premorbid adjustment is associated with father dominance; poor premorbid adjustment, with mother dominance. (F117)

Schizophrenic children are more likely to come from mother-dominated rather than from father-dominated families. (F117)

There is more paternal dominance in the interaction of the parents of "good" premorbid schizophrenics (good general functioning before onset of illness) than in the interactions of parents of poor premorbid schizophrenics. (G127)

Paranoid schizophrenics are more likely to view their mothers as strong authority figures and their fathers as weak authority figures than are catatonic schizophrenics. (K114)

Schizophrenia (female) tends to be directly correlated with an aggressive, dominating mother and a passive father. (L118)

Schizophrenic patients are likely to come from family backgrounds in which the mother has a strong authority role and the father has a weak authority role. (M060)

### Mental Illness (Schizophrenia/Neurosis)
Mothers of schizophrenic patients have more power in the family than do mothers of neurotics. (M061)

In the middle class more schizophrenic than neurotic patients question their fathers' masculinity and authority. (M197)

### Monogamy
When patterns of monogamous marriage supplant traditional polygynous forms, the status of the wife tends to be one of equality rather than of subordination. (F035)

### Mother-Child Relations (Affection)
Persons who had close affectional ties with their mothers in childhood are more likely to assume equalitarian roles in marriage.

### Neurosis
In male-dominated marriages the neurosis rate is high in both partners, but the neurosis rate is low among hus-

bands in female-dominated marriages (Cornell Medical Index of Neurosis). (P086)

### Occupational Choice
Reaction to the overpowering by the mother and older sister or by the father and older brother leads to the choice of occupations which involve some power or authority over other persons, animals, or living things by second-born siblings of families with two same-sex children. (S221)

### Occupational Rank
There is no significant difference in the dominance of the husband or wife in family decisions, as between professors and skilled workers.

### Occupational Rank of Husband
The higher the husband's occupational prestige, the greater his voice in marital decisions. (G156)

### Ordinal Position of Wife
The husband is more likely than not to be more dominant than the wife where the wife was an only child or the youngest child in her family. (L014)

The wife is more likely than not to be more dominant than the husband where the wife was the oldest child or the middle child in her family. (L014)

### Parent-Child Relations
Girls raised in families controlled by the mother have more flexible attitudes concerning parent-child relations than do girls from father-dominated families.

### Parent-Child Relations (Closeness)
The closer the parent-child relationship, the more likely is the child to perceive his parents as being equal in dominance. (L137)

The closer a child feels to one parent (correspondingly feeling distant from the other), the more likely he is to view the family as dominated by the parent he feels distant toward. (L137)

Where the family authority pattern is that of a dominant mother and a weak father, female schizophrenics will be closer to the fathers and male schizophrenics will be closer to the mothers. (S187)

### Parent-Child Relations (Conflict)
The spouse who is more dominant in the marriage relationship tends to have greater conflict with the children than does the spouse who takes the more equalitarian or submissive role. (K113)

### Parent-Child Relations (Control)
Persons who reacted negatively to discipline imposed by their parents, especially by their mothers, are more likely to assume dominant roles in marriage. (S279)

### Parent-Child Relations (Egalitarianism)
When marital relations are equalitarian, there is more likelihood that roles in the other two areas of power relations (i.e., parental and child-rearing) will be congruent with the conjugal, that is, be "equalitarian" and "democratic," respectively; when a husband is dominant in marital relations, there is somewhat less likelihood of husband "dominance" and father "autocracy" in the other two areas; and when a wife is dominant in the marital relationship, there is the least probability of corresponding wife dominance and mother autocracy in parental and child-rearing relations. (B323)

### Parent-Child Relations (Permissiveness)

Adolescents perceiving their mothers as dominant in both family and child-rearing practices are less likely to describe them as autocratic in dealing with them than they are to view them as equalitarian; and if they are older (high school, as opposed to junior high), they are more likely to view them as permissive or equalitarian than as autocratic. (B323)

In a wife-dominated (marital relations) home, older (high-school) boys and girls are as likely to perceive their fathers as autocratic as they are to perceive them as permissive or democratic; while in child rearing, younger (junior-high-school) adolescents are more than twice as likely to report autocratic fathers as they are to report permissive fathers. (B323)

In families where conjugal relations are equalitarian, adolescents are more apt to report their parents as either democratic or permissive in parent-child relations and less likely to say they are autocratic. This is less likely to be true in lower-class families. (B323)

When a wife is either dominant in the conjugal relationship or shares power with her husband, adolescents are more likely to perceive her as authoritarian than as either equalitarian or permissive in parent-child relations. (B323)

In middle-class homes where the father is the head of the family and the mother is the authority figure in child rearing, the mother is less likely to be viewed as autocratic than as democratic or permissive. (B323)

### Parent-Child Relations (Rejection)

Perceived maternal dominance is positively related to adolescent rejection of parents. (E102)

### Parent-Child Relations (Warmth)

The adolescent perceives one of his parents as his principal source of support most often when he sees the parent as sharing leadership responsibility with his spouse in marital and parental relations, next most often when the spouse is perceived as dominating in these areas, and least often when the parent is seen as dominant. (B323)

In wife-dominated families, adolescents do not think of their parents as supportive as often as in equalitarian or husband-dominated families. (B323)

Whichever parent is perceived as the child-rearing authority, is also more likely to be viewed as supportive. (B323)

### Parental-Role Definition

Schizophrenic males are more likely to choose as a role model the parent who dominates family decisions; schizophrenic females, to choose the nondominant parent. (H201)

### Peer Relations

Mother-dominated homes are associated with sons who show a greater dislike for girls in their peer relations. (H201)

### Personality Adjustment

When the mother is dominant the sons are likely to be tense and rejecting. (S205)

The role-differentiated type of equalitarian family (autonomous) is more likely to produce sons who are the best socialized for smooth internal familial adjustment and for achievement roles external to the family. (S205)

### Personality Adjustment of Child

Where a mother is dominant in the conjugal child-rearing and parent-adolescent relations, the family environment is more likely than not to create conflicts for the child. (B323)

### Personality of Child (Depression)

Children coming from families in which there is conflict over authority are likely to be depressed and discouraged. (R113)

### Personality of Child (Disobedience/Hostility)

A family situation in which there are conflicting authorities tends to be associated with disobedience and hostility in the child. (R113)

### Personality of Child (Nervousness/Anxiety)

Perceived maternal dominance is positively related to signs of nervousness and anxiety in adolescents. (E102)

### Personality of Child (Other-Orientation)

Girls who perceive their mothers to be the more dominant are more other-oriented than are those who perceive their parents to be equally dominant. (S252)

### Personality of Son

Mother-dominated homes are associated with aggressive, impulsive, and unfriendly personality traits in sons. (H201)

### Personality of Son (Autonomy)

When the father has the most power in the family, the son tends to believe more in "fate" and less in leaving home. (M060)

### Personality of Son (Self-Confidence)

Boys from families where there is equality between the parents in family affairs exhibit greater self-confidence (a belief in the control of one's destiny) than do those from wife-dominant or husband-dominant families. (E102)

Self-confidence in boys (belief in the control of one's destiny) is more characteristic of boys from wife-dominant than from husband-dominant families. (E102)

### Power Structure of Family (Parental)

If the mother and father grew up in the same type of authority pattern, they reproduce the same authority pattern in their own family (e.g., both matricentric or both patricentric).

If the mother and father were reared in families with differing authority patterns, their own authority pattern in the family they found is different, either egalitarian or balance-of-power relationship.

### Race

No significant differences appear in the dominance patterns in family decisions of Negroes, as against whites.

The Negro husband, compared with the white husband, has less power within his family.

### Race Attitudes

Prejudiced persons are more likely than unprejudiced persons to perceive one of the parents as being dominant in the family, particularly the same-sex parent. (A061)

Unprejudiced persons are more likely than prejudiced

persons to perceive the family structure as equalitarian or as oriented toward a loving mother. (A061)

### Rank
The higher the social rank of a spouse, the more power he is likely to have in the family. (K089)

### Rank of Wife's Family
The privileges a woman has are directly correlated with the prestige of her family of orientation. (B032)

### Religion
Husband dominance tends to be more common in Catholic than in Protestant families (controlling for social class). (E100)

### Religion/Size of Family
Religious affiliation and size of family have independent effects upon the power that both parents and the adolescent wield in the child-rearing process; the combined effect of both factors (Catholicism and large size of family) substantially increases the likelihood of parental dominance. (E100)

### Residence
Suburban families are more husband dominant at every status level than are their urban peers.

### Residence (Neolocal)
Neolocality is associated with reduced control by family elders. (G156)

### Resources
At the highest-class levels, in status groups where graceful living rather than male achievement is the basis for supremacy, the wife, in directing many of the representative functions of the family, develops a level of skill and responsibility that enhances her position in the family relative to her husband. (P083)

### Role Definition in Family
Considering the family as a triad of roles: High Status Authority (HSA), Low Status Subordinate (LSS), and High Status Friend (HSF), a power alliance in competition for any of the system's resources and benefits is more apt to occur between LSS and HSF than between HSA and HSF or HSA and LSS.

Viewing the family as a triad of roles: High Status Authority (HSA), Lower Status Subordinate (LSS), and High Status Friend (HSF), if one parent plays an instrumental role vis-à-vis his children (HSA and LSS, respectively), in the presence of his spouse, the latter will tend to react in the role of High Status Friend toward the children, rather than to duplicate the HSA role.

The degree of dominance exhibited by one family member is determined more by family-role definitions than it is by more personal factors particular to the individual or to the person with whom he is interacting. (C124)

### Scholastic Achievement
Equalitarian husband-wife relations are more strongly related to academic achievement in the child than are wife-dominant, husband-dominant, or conflicting conjugal power structures. (E102)

### Scholastic Motivation
Wife dominated families are more apt to produce poorly motivated boys academically than are equalitarian or husband-dominated families. (B323)

In families where either the husband or wife is domi-

nant, adolescents with autocratic fathers in child rearing are less motivated academically than are either those with permissive or with democratic fathers. (B323)

Academic motivation among adolescent boys and older (high-school) adolescent girls is strongest when their fathers are perceived as family heads. (B323)

Girls are much more likely than boys to have high academic motivation if the family structure is equalitarian rather than wife or husband dominant. (E102)

Congruence in parental power is more related to high academic motivation in the child than is incongruence. (E102)

Which parent has greater power in child rearing has less effect than does use of explanation and reasoning on high academic motivation in the child. (E102)

### Scholastic Motivation of Child
The father's involvement in child rearing has a greater effect on high academic motivation in the child than does the husband-wife power structure. (E102)

### Self-Conception
Conflict in self-perception is more likely where the male child perceives the mother as the dominant figure in the family, with reference to authority, affection, and role model. (W158)

### Sex-Role Definition
Sons from mother-dominated families are more likely than others to see girls as more powerful than boys. (H201)

Sons from mother-dominated homes, where the father's attitudes favor male dominance, are more likely to view boys as more powerful than girls. (H201)

### Sex-Role Identification
In homes where the mother is dominant in the marital relations, the children are more likely to choose the opposite-sex parent as an adult-role model. (The relationship is stronger for boys than for girls.) (H201)

### Sex-Role Identification of Child
Husband dominance in the marital relationship is associated with like-sex adult-role model choice by the children. (H201)

### Sex Status
Boys are more likely than girls to see their fathers as dominant in both conjugal and parental relations, while girls are more likely than boys to see their mothers as dominant in both areas. (B323)

Husbands are more likely to claim that wives have greater influence; wives claim that both have the same influence (U.S.). (H175)

Little difference exists between boys' and girls' perceptions of parental discipline and power among children in the first three grades of school; boys report slightly more frequently than girls that the mother is the "boss" in the house. (H180)

### Sibling Structure (Sex)
Older middle-class girls are more likely to have highly dominant parents when they have sisters only; lower-class older girls are most likely to have dominant parents if they have brothers. (E100)

### Size of Family

Family size is inversely related to democracy in family life. (B005)

With the exception of Catholic mothers, parents in large families are more likely to exercise considerable power in child rearing than are parents in smaller families. (E100)

The larger the family, the more internal organization develops and the more likely it is that one or more persons in the family will be dominant. (I008)

As family groups enlarge from three to four to five members, power within the family tends to shift from the wife to the husband to the oldest child, when measured by the number of contributions of each member of the family (of initiated interaction). (S207)

### Social Network

Importance of joint decision making by husbands and wives increases with the looseness of family networks (i.e., the friends of the wife and husband are not friends of one another). (B210)

### Stability of Extended Family

Power rivalries within the extended family group tend to accelerate the process of fissioning within the nuclear unit. (W031)

### Stability of Family

An equalitarian family, in which both husband and wife attempt to play a dominant role, is associated with lack of effective socialization for internal stability of the family. (S205)

### Urban/Rural

Dominance of the father is more common in rural families than is dominance of the mother; dominance of the mother is more frequent in city families than is dominance of the father. (B033)

### Urbanization

Urbanization results in the weakening of parental control. (F055)

### Values

Where the middle-class values predominate (self-reliance, personal autonomy, and the belief in the superiority of the future in contrast to the past), the isolated nuclear family with comparatively egalitarian structure has higher prestige than does the patrilinear extended family of the upper class. (P083)

### Voluntary Organizations

A wife who participates in organizations outside the home has more power in the family decision making than does a wife who does not do so; activity in a formal organization provides the wife with a resource analogous to the husband's success on the job.

### Witchcraft

When the role of the wife is one of extreme subordination to her husband, her aggression is more likely to manifest itself in indirect methods (e.g., witchcraft). (L064)

## POWER STRUCTURE OF FAMILY (PARENTAL)
### X  Power Structure of Family

If the mother and father grew up in the same type of authority pattern, they reproduce the same authority pattern in their own family (e.g., both matricentric or both patricentric).

If the mother and father were reared in families with differing authority patterns, their own authority pattern in the family they found is different, either egalitarian or balance-of-power relationship.

## POWER STRUCTURE OF FAMILY (VIOLENCE)
### X  Education of Husband

The lower the educational level of the husband, the more likely he is to resort to physical punishment in order to impose his will in the family. (K089)

## POWER STRUCTURE OF FAMILY (WIFE DOMINANCE)
### X  Homosexuality

The greater the authority of the mother in the home, relative to the father, the more likely is homosexuality in the son. (R104)

## POWER STRUCTURE OF FILIAL FAMILY
### X  Power Structure of Parental Family

Authority patterns of parental families tend to be perpetuated in the families of the children. (C023)

## POWER STRUCTURE OF LINEAGE
### X  Slavery (Pawnship)

In societies with the institution of pawnship, lineage and clan elders tend to exercise greater control over their members. (D081)

## POWER STRUCTURE OF PARENTAL FAMILY
### X  Power Structure of Filial Family

Authority patterns of parental families tend to be perpetuated in the families of the children. (C023)

## PREFERENTIAL MARRIAGE    X  Acculturation

Marriage regulations tend to deteriorate under conditions of acculturation. (E067)

### Affinal Ties

When one or more marriage alliances have been established with a certain clan, there is a preference for further marriages with the same clan. (C039)

### Class

A preferential marriage pattern is more likely to be adopted if it is associated with a group which is prestigious. (C060)

### Cohesion of Kin-Group

The solidarity of the kin structure is directly correlated with the specificity of the relationship which is designated as the preferred marriage form. (N023)

### Coincidence

When the preferential marriage patterns of the levirate and of a woman to her husband's sister's son are practiced simultaneously, husband's brother and husband's sister's son will tend to be terminologically equated. (A020)

### Descent

Asymmetrical patterns of marriage require neither unilinear descent groups nor any particular rule of lineal descent. (N067)

### Descent (Asymmetrical)

When a descent pattern is asymmetrical, patterns of cross-cousin marriage must also be asymmetrical. (S097)

### Descent (Unilineal)

Ethnographic reports indicate a high correlation of the matrilateral preference in patrilineal societies; the patrilateral preference is usually recorded in societies following matrilineal descent. (L176)

### Geographical Mobility
Preferential marriage patterns will tend to be modified under conditions of high physical mobility. (E060)

### Infant Betrothal
Infant betrothal is more likely to exist where preferential marriage patterns occur. (G097)

### Kin-Role Definitions
When actual marriages deviate from a preferential marriage pattern, they will tend to be treated as though they were actually in accordance with the rule. (L058)

### Kin Terminology
When the sororate and marriage to wife's brother's daughter are both preferred marriage forms, wife's sister and wife's brother's daughter will tend to be terminologically equated. (A020)

When a preferential marriage pattern is established, potential mates tend to include those who are terminologically equated with the preferred kinsman. (L060)

When the preferred mate is always a consanguineal relative, special affinal terms for preferred mate tend to be absent. (M019)

Preferential marriage with the wife's brother's daughter will produce the Omaha type of terminology for cross-cousins. (M019)

Rules of preferential marriage with a mother's brother's widow will produce kinship terminology of the Crow type. (M019)

### Kin Terminology (Classificatory)
When the actual kinsman is not available for the preferential marriage pattern, classificatory equivalents tend to be substituted. (L058)

The coincidence of kin type resulting from a preferential marriage pattern, such as exchange marriage, will result in classificatory terminology. (S098)

### Kin Ties
The range of acknowledged kinship will tend to be wider if preferential marriage patterns with specific kinsmen exist. (M137)

### Love
The narrower the specifications of which statuses can be legitimately linked in the marriage bond, the more able the society is to control love relationships. (G156)

### Marital Stability
Marriages formed under preferential marriage patterns are more likely to be stable. (S267)

### Marriage Class System
An institutionalized pattern of marriage with mother's brother's wife tends to be incompatible with a system of matrimonial classes. (D026)

Marriage with a mother's brother's widow is incompatible with a four- or eight-class marriage system. (S095)

### Population
Preferential marriage patterns tend to be abandoned with a decrease in population. (G097)

### Population Density
Specificity of preferential marriage patterns tends to be correlated with situations of low population density. (R069)

### Premarital Sex Relations
Privileged relationships within which sexual intercourse is permitted before marriage commonly reveal a close connection with preferential mating. (M019)

### Property
When the retention of property in the kin line is desired, preferential marriage patterns between consanguineals will tend to be instituted. (L058)

### Rank of Lineage
Where the marriage chain is genuinely circular, the marriage rule does not imply any absolute difference of economic, political, or ritual status between the intermarrying groups. (L177)

### Rank of Wife
The status of the wife will be higher if her marriage conforms to the preferential marriage pattern. (K062)

### Residence
Establishment of affinal affiliations between clans tends to result in the localization of the clans. (C039)

### Sex Ratio
When there is a shortage of women, kin relationships will tend to be adjusted to permit otherwise prohibited women to become eligible as marriage partners. (E066)

Preferential marriage patterns tend to be violated when the sex ratio is uneven. (G095)

### Size of Clan
The larger the clan, the greater the likelihood of there being a pattern of preferential marriage with its members. (C039)

### Stratification
Systems of asymmetrical marriage exchange tend to create distinctions of status inequality since direct reciprocity in kind is never practiced. (L176)

### Warfare
Under conditions of warfare, preferential marriage patterns, such as cross-cousin marriage, tend to occur less frequently. (F010)

## PREFERENTIAL MARRIAGE (ASYMMETRICAL)
### X  Stratification
Asymmetrical marriage systems arise in societies which possess either status differentiation or differences in the distribution of economic resources. (S026)

## PREFERENTIAL MARRIAGE (ASYMMETRICAL CROSS-COUSIN)     X  Descent (Unilineal)
Cross-cousin marriage, if it is to be instituted in a unilineal kinship system, must be asymmetrical in its character. (T018)

### Incest Taboo
The transformation of systems of bilateral first-cross-cousin marriage into systems of asymmetrical first-cross-cousin marriage tends to be associated with an extension of incest taboos. (L061)

### Subsistence Pattern (Nomadic)
When the economic pattern shifts from a stable and restricted range for hunting and gathering to a wider pattern of movement, a preference for mother's brother's daughter marriage is likely to develop with a concomitant prohibition on marriage with father's sister's daughter. (E107)

## PREFERENTIAL MARRIAGE (AVUNCULAR)
### X   Marriage Payment
Avuncular marriage tends to be associated with a period of bride service followed by permanent patrilocality. (M020)

### Residence (Patrilocal)
With the change from patrilocality to matrilocality, avuncular marriage patterns will disappear. (M020)

## PREFERENTIAL MARRIAGE (BILATERAL CROSS-COUSIN)      X   Legal Status of Wife
Bilateral cross-cousin marriage will occur in societies in which jural authority over a female is vested in the woman herself or is split between her matri- and patri-kin. (C126)

## PREFERENTIAL MARRIAGE (CONNUBIUM)
### X   Kin Terminology
A unilineal three-generational cycling of kin terminology arises from a circulation of spouses among three sibs. (L058)

## PREFERENTIAL MARRIAGE (CROSS-COUSIN)
### X   Affinal Relations (Conflict)
The institution of cross-cousin marriage as a preferential pattern will tend to reduce affinal conflicts. (G056)

In a patrilineal system, when the cross-cousin marriage is between father's sister's son and mother's brother's daughter (v. father's sister's daughter), there is less friction between mother-in-law and daughter-in-law. (H043)

### Affinal Relations (Respect)
Under a patrilineal system, respect is paid to affines who have married a female relative, so that matrilateral rather than patrilateral cross-cousin marriage is preferred (Brahman). (G028)

### Authority Structure
The type of cross-cousin marriage which occurs will be directly correlated with the relative who exercises control over the allocation of a female as a wife (i.e., patrilateral—Fa Si Hu; matrilateral—Mo Bro; avuncular—Mo BroW: Bro). (C126)

### Authority Structure of Family
When marriage is allowed or preferred with Mo Bro Da but forbidden or disapproved of with Fa Si Da the jural authority over a young man before marriage will be vested in his father or in his father's lineage. (M023)

### Avoidance Relationship
Avoidance relations form part of the cross-cousin marriage and sib complex. (L039)

### Class
The decline in the adherence to preferential marriage patterns tends to occur more commonly among the middle class than among members of the lower class. (P023)

### Cohesion of Family
Cross-cousin marriage to the mother's brother's daughter reinforces the cohesion of the families of these siblings. (L046)

### Cohesion of Kin-Group
The institutionalization of cross-cousin marriage strengthens the integration of the kin-group. (H062)

Matrilineal cross-cousin marriage tends to destroy the solidarity of the patrilineal group. (W065)

Patrilineal cross-cousin marriage tends to reinforce the solidarity of a patrilineal group. (W065)

### Composition of Family
Patrilateral cross-cousin marriage is most likely to occur in a matrilineal society if the father has no nephews. (G055)

### Corporate Kin-Group
Since the central feature of any patrilateral system must be the alternation of exchange, the descent group cannot be a corporate group because its solidarity is destroyed by the separation of successive generations by opposed interests and statuses. (N072)

### Descent
Matrilineal societies have a higher incidence of symmetrical cross-cousin marriage than do patrilineal societies. (C124)

Where the preferential marriage pattern is that of cross-cousin marriage, descent will be traced in two lines. (E065)

Preferential unilateral cross-cousin marriage can only arise in unilateral societies. (N067)

There is no association between the rule of descent and laterality of prescription. (N072)

Cross-cousin marriage is the result of the conflict between patrilineal and matrilineal principles. (S093)

### Descent (Bilateral)
Symmetrical cross-cousin marriage is more likely to be found in bilateral societies. (C124)

When descent is bilateral, marriage with cross-cousins tends to be prohibited. (O023)

### Descent (Matrilineal/Patrilineal)
Matrilateral cross-cousin marriage is more likely to take place in patrilineal societies; patrilateral cross-cousin marriage is more likely to take place in matrilineal societies. (C093)

### Descent (Unilineal)
Matrilateral cross-cousin marriage in association with matrilineages or patrilineal cross-cousin marriage with patrilineages does not appear to produce symmetric exchanges of women. (L176)

Cross-cousin marriage tends to be associated with systems of unilineal descent. (S098)

### Divorce
Matrilineal cross-cousin marriage in a matrilineal society will tend to occur if the parents of the man are divorced. (G055)

### Incest Taboo
Cross-cousin marriage will not occur if there is an extension of incest taboos to members of the father's lineage as well as to the matrilineal sib. (M082)

### Infant Betrothal
Infant betrothal is correlated with cross-cousin marriage. (M241)

### Kin Terminology
A symmetrical cross-cousin marriage pattern is negatively associated with a cognatic terminology or society. (N067)

When marriage with a cross-cousin is the preferred form, cross-cousins tend to be terminologically distinguished from parallel-cousins and from the siblings of ego. (S106)

### Kin Terminology (Bifurcate Merging)
Bifurcate merging terminology tends to be found in societies where a cross-cousin is the preferred marriage partner. (H047)

### Kin Terminology (Generation)
The need for an alternating exchange relationship in a patrilateral system requires that a lineal descent group must be clearly divided into generations of marriageable men and women. (N072)

### Kin Ties
Marriage between cross-cousins serves to reinforce existing but weakening kin ties. (T039)

### Marriage Class System (Two-Section)
A two-section marriage class system will be found in conjunction with patterns of cross-cousin marriage. (M234)

### Marriage Payment
Patterns of marriage payment are unlikely to develop in societies where cross-cousin marriage is the preferential marriage form. (B111)

### Marriage System (Circular)
A circular marriage system will result from a matrilateral cross-cousin marriage rule when the total society is made up of defined marriage classes, each of which is exogamous, but which are as a totality endogamous. (S026)

### Marriage System (Connubium)
The establishment of a preferential marriage pattern with a matrilateral cross-cousin will tend to result in the circulation of women through the society in connubial cycles. (N023)

### Moiety
Patterns of preferential cross-cousin marriage tend to be associated with a moiety organization. (H077)

A pattern of matrilateral cross-cousin marriage is required when there are only two different kinds of local groups and indirect exchange. (L062)

### Moiety System
Cross-cousin marriage tends to emerge as a consequence of a dual organization of society. (G060)

Given a system based on exogamous matrimoieties, if residence becomes avunculocal, a subsidiary system of matrilines (implying marriage with the daughters of the matrilateral female cross-cousins only) is likely to occur. (L178)

### Political Stability
Matrilateral alliance reduces fissive pressures in a segmentary society. (N072)

### Political Structure (Feudalism)
Matrilateral cross-cousin marriage in the absence of a moiety system is correlated with a political structure of a somewhat feudal type. (N066)

### Preferential Marriage (Exchange)
Patrilateral cross-cousin marriage can be derived from a system with direct exchange. (L062)

### Preferential Marriage (Granddaughter)
The occurrence of granddaughter marriage tends to be closely associated with cross-cousin marriage. (S093)

### Preferential Marriage (Mother's Brother's Wife)
With the development of marriage with the mother's brother's widow and with the mother's brother's dauther's daughter, cross-cousin marriage with the mother's brother's daughter becomes impossible. (S097)

### Rank
When marriage into a family of comparable rank is stressed, cross-cousin marriage tends to occur, although it may not be the preferential form of marriage. (L039)

### Religion (Totemism)
The prohibition of cross-cousin marriage may be correlated with the social totemism of the region and to some extent is an effect of the latter. (E065)

### Residence
Cross-cousin marriage tends to occur when the mother's brother or the father's sister resides in a different community. (T039)

### Sexual Permissiveness
Permissive sex relationships between crosss-cousins tend to occur in societies with cross-cousin marriage. (S189)

### Size of Kin-Group
In cross-cousin marriage, larger-sized kinship groups are associated with treating distant cousins as "equivalent" and appropriate marriage partners for young people. (G156)

## PREFERENTIAL MARRIAGE (EXCHANGE)
### X Adultery
Extramarital relations are more likely to occur when the marriage has been contracted as the second phase of an exchange of women. (T064)

### Cohesion of Kin-Group
The institutionalization of exchange marriage functions to strengthen the kin ties between families. (G053)

### Descent (Asymmetrical)
Exchange of sisters as wives is prohibited by a descent system which is bilateral for one sex and unilateral for the other. (S097)

### Economic Rank
Exchange marriage is more likely to occur between members of families which are of low economic status. (H105)

### Husband-Wife Relations (Aggression)
The exchange of siblings in marriage acts as a deterrent to mistreatment by the husband or wife. (C035)

### Kin Terminology
When the normal mode of marriage is by the exchange of sisters, the same kinship term tends to be applied to mother's brother's wife and father's sister, to wife's brother's wife and sister, and to wife's brother's daughter and sister's daughter. (M019)

### Kin Terminology (Asymmetrical Cross-Cousin)
Asymmetrical cross-cousin terminology is incompatible with sister-exchange marriage. (L060)

### Marital Stability
Marriage by exchange serves to increase the stability of the marriage. (M109)

### Marriage Class System (Double Descent)
In addition to the simultaneous occurrence of both matrilineal and patrilineal kin-groups, marriage by sister exchange must also occur if a double descent class system is to develop. (M045)

### Marriage Payment
Marriage payment will tend to be instituted where the exchange of girls cannot be arranged. (W102)

### Moiety
Where there are moieties, there are, at least terminologically, patterns of exchange marriage. (A021)

### Preferential Marriage (Cross-Cousin)
Patrilateral cross-cousin marriage can be derived from a system with direct exchange. (L062)

### Rank of Women
Exchange marriage as a preferential pattern tends to be abandoned with the rise in the status of women. (M105)

### Residence (Patrilocal)
Modification of a matrilineal or avunculocal system involving a shift to patrilocal residence may occur as a result of two innovations: either an increase in the bride price or the adoption of preferential marriage by the exchange of sisters. (M171)

## PREFERENTIAL MARRIAGE (FATHER'S BROTHER'S DAUGHTER)          X   Lineage
The institutionalization of father's brother's daughter marriage is associated with lineage organizations which are highly developed. (B087)

## PREFERENTIAL MARRIAGE (FATHER'S SISTER'S DAUGHTER)          X   Cohesion of Kin-Group
Preferential marriage with the father's sister's daughter reinforces the solidarity of the kin-group, inasmuch as the cycle of exchange involves only two generations. (N023)

## PREFERENTIAL MARRIAGE (FIRST-COUSIN)          X   Cohesion of Kin-Group
The establishment of patterns of preferential marriage with the first cousin functions to reinforce the solidarity of the kin-group. (W098)

## PREFERENTIAL MARRIAGE (GRANDDAUGHTER)          X   Descent (Matrilineal)
Marriage with the granddaughter is incompatible with matrilineal descent. (S093)

### Preferential Marriage (Cross-Cousin)
The occurrence of granddaughter marriage tends to be closely associated with cross-cousin marriage. (S093)

## PREFERENTIAL MARRIAGE (GRANDSON)          X   Sex-Role Definition
Grandson-marriage is contingent upon the recognition of women as inheritable property. (S093)

## PREFERENTIAL MARRIAGE (INTERGENERATIONAL)          X   Moiety
Marriage into an adjoining generation may occur under a moiety system. (R036)

## PREFERENTIAL MARRIAGE (JUNIOR)          X   Kin Terminology (Generation)
The terminological equivalence of alternate generations of kinsmen is intimately linked with the junior marriage pattern. (M130)

## PREFERENTIAL MARRIAGE (LEVIRATE)          X   Age of Wife
Remarriage of the widow under the levirate is less likely to occur if the wife is at an advanced age. (S158)

### Bereavement
The levirate tends to minimize the disruptive consequences of the death of a husband. (R069)

### Descent (Patrilineal)
The institution of the levirate is an indication of the strength of the patrilineal organization. (K049)

### Economic Security
Claims to the widow of a deceased brother will not necessarily be activated if the woman has a grown son old enough to support her. (S096)

### Fertility
The levirate is less likely to be enforced if the wife has borne children. (T054)

### Kin Terminology (Bifurcate Merging)
Preferential levirate marriages may operate to minimize the criterion of collaterality and thus produce kinship terminology of the so-called bifurcate merging type. (M019)

### Kin Terminology (Classificatory)
The classification of father's brother with father and mother's sister with mother reflects levirate marriage practices. (A021)

There is a correlation between the custom of the levirate and classificatory systems of terminology. (R069)

### Marital Status (Male)
The practice of the leviratic union is more likely to occur if the husband's brother is a bachelor. (W067)

### Moiety
The institutionalized pattern of marriage with a mother's brother's widow is common in a moiety organization. (S095)

### Polyandry
Polyandry tends to develop out of an institutionalized pattern for leviratic unions. (S068)

### Preferential Marriage (Sororate)
The levirate and sororate tend to be correlated. (E055)

### Religion (Christianity)
The practice of the levirate tends to be abandoned with the adoption of Christianity. (S121)

### Sexual Permissiveness
Permissive sex relationships between a boy and his brother's wife are more likely to occur in societies with the levirate. (S189)

### Sibling Relations (Cohesion)
The institution of levirate tends to reinforce the cohesion of male siblings. (W082)

### Sibling Relations (Solidarity)
Where bonds between siblings are strong, the levirate tends to occur. (R069)

### Sibling Rivalry
The rule that uterine brothers should not inherit one another's wives reduces jealousy over potential claims. (C090)

## PREFERENTIAL MARRIAGE (LEVIRATE/SORORATE)    X  Affinal Ties
The levirate and sororate will tend to occur in a society which stresses the importance of retaining affinal bonds. (L039)

### Divorce
Divorce is less likely to occur in societies where the levirate and sororate have been instituted. (S158)

### Kin Terminology (Bifurcate Merging)
Bifurcate merging terminology tends to result from the institutionalization of certain rules of preferential mating, especially the levirate and sororate. (M047)

Bifurcate merging terminology tends to be associated with certain rules of preferential mating, especially the levirate and sororate. (M047)

### Lineage, Importance of
The sororate and levirate are associated with greater social importance of the clan or lineage. (S192)

### Stability of Family
The elementary family tends to be much more stable under the sororate and levirate since the death of any one member does not disrupt the equilibrium of the family structure. (W129)

## PREFERENTIAL MARRIAGE (MARRIAGE GROUP)    X  Exogamy
Where marriage groups are precisely defined, the reaction to the violation of exogamic restrictions will be more severe. (C079)

## PREFERENTIAL MARRIAGE (MOTHER'S BROTHER'S WIFE)    X  Moiety System
A simple moiety organization will tend to occur in response to the development of a mother's brother's wife marriage. (D026)

### Preferential Marriage (Cross-Cousin)
With the development of marriage with the mother's brother's widow and with the mother's brother's daughter's daughter, cross-cousin marriage with the mother's brother's daughter becomes impossible. (S097)

## PREFERENTIAL MARRIAGE (NEAR KIN)    X  Marital Stability
Marital stability is more likely to occur if the preferential marriage partner is a close kinsman. (S153)

## PREFERENTIAL MARRIAGE (PARALLEL-COUSIN)    X  Cohesion of Clan
Preferential marriage patterns which entail clan endogamy will tend to decline with the deterioration of the clan organization. (H165)

### Cohesion of Kin-Group
Parallel-cousin marriage is an effective factor in inhibiting the formation of a corporate kin-group on higher levels of segmentation. (M023)

### Ethnocentrism
Parallel-cousin marriage tends to be instituted in societies which emphasize ethnic exclusiveness. (G072)

### Heir, Absence of
In patrilineal societies in which there is no direct male heir, daughters are more likely to be married to male kinsmen of their lineage. (R118)

### Property
The preferential marriage pattern of parallel-cousin marriage will tend to be institutionalized where the retention of lineage property is stressed. (M095)

### Size of Clan
The incidence of parallel-cousin marriage is directly correlated with the size of the localized clan segment. (H165)

## PREFERENTIAL MARRIAGE (PARALLEL-CROSS-COUSIN)    X  Urban/Rural
Patterns of preferential marriage tend to deteriorate in an urban context. (P023)

## PREFERENTIAL MARRIAGE, RESTRICTIVENESS OF    X  Adultery
When the preferential marriage pattern is highly restricted, the incidence of extramarital relationships will tend to be high. (K062)

### Desertion by Wives
When the preferential marriage pattern is highly restrictive in character, the incidence of desertion by wives will tend to be high. (K062)

### Elopment
When a preferential marriage pattern is severely restrictive, the incidence of elopement will tend to be high. (K062)

## PREFERENTIAL MARRIAGE (SECOND-COUSIN)    X  Descent (Four Lines)
When the preferential marriage pattern is that of second-cousin, descent will be traced through four lines. (E065)

### Moiety System
Second-cousin marriage tends to characterize societies with moiety systems. (E063)

## PREFERENTIAL MARRIAGE (SECOND-CROSS-COUSIN)    X  Kin Terminology (Generation)
A three-generation rotation of unilineal kin terms may result if the preferential marriage pattern is that between second-cross-cousins. (L058)

## PREFERENTIAL MARRIAGE (SECONDARY MARRIAGE)    X  Joking Relationship
When preferential mating with siblings-in-law of the opposite sex is prescribed, the patterned behavior toward such relatives tends to be characterized by license. (M019)

## PREFERENTIAL MARRIAGE (SORORATE)    X  Kin Terminology (Bifurcate Merging)
The classification of father's brother with father and mother's sister with mother reflects the occurrence of the sororate. (A021)

### Preferential Marriage (Levirate)
The levirate and sororate tend to be correlated. (E055)

### Sexual Permissiveness
Sex relationships between a girl and her sister's husband are likely to be permitted in societies with the sororate. (S189)

## PREFERENTIAL MARRIAGE, VIOLATION OF    X  Conflict in Kin-Group
Patrilineal cross-cousin marriage in a matrilineal society

is more likely to occur if the man has quarreled with the leader of his matrilineage. (G055, G057)

## PREGNANCIES, NUMBER OF
### X Death Rate (Fetal)
The fetal death rate rises up to the fourth pregnancy and is irregularly lower after that. (F101)

### Personality
Among married women, primigravida tend to be more dependent, insecure, and fearful than multigravida. (C099)

### Pregnancy, Attitude Toward
Women in first pregnancy express greater fears for the coming baby and less irritability and indicate a greater degree of marital happiness than do women experiencing later pregnancies. (C099)

### Psychosomatic Illness
Previous experience with pregnancy is indeterminate relative to psychosomatic symptoms. (C099)

## PREGNANCY
### X Illegitimacy
Unwed mothers conceive in a shorter period of time than married mothers do. This hypothesis is also denied. (Y048)

Unwed mothers are less likely to miscarry than married mothers are. This hypothesis is also denied. (Y048)

Unwed mothers are less likely to experience prenatal nausea than married mothers are. This hypothesis is also denied. (Y048)

Unwed mothers have fewer complications and difficulty in giving birth than married mothers do. This hypothesis is also denied. (Y048)

### Neurosis
Neuroticism and autonomic overactivity often occur in infants whose mothers underwent severe emotional stress during pregnancy. (T088)

### Personality Problems of Child
There is no correlation between symptom formation during pregnancy and the later development of emotional disturbance in the child. (P080)

### Personality Problems of Infant
Mothers who experienced emotional stress during pregnancy are more likely than mothers who did not to have infants with motivational defects. (S227)

### Personality Problems of Mother
The greater the severity of the prior psychological disturbances of the woman, the more likely it is that severe problems will emerge with the condition of gestation. (B280)

### Physical Development
Mothers who experience emotional stress during pregnancy are more likely than others to give birth to infants who suffer from physical impairment. (S227)

### Psychosomatic Illness
All women (regardless of marital status of previous birth experience) show a highly significant increase, with pregnancy, in psychosomatic anxiety. (C099)

### Scholastic Achievement of Child
Mothers who experienced emotional stress during pregnancy are likely to give birth to infants who suffer from general impairment (mental and physical), which in turn predisposes them to lower school achievement during childhood. (S227)

### Sex-Role Identification
Men's ambivalence toward the sex role is likely to manifest itself as envy of childbearing. (W154)

### Sexual Adjustment
More people feel that pregnancy has no effect on their sexual adjustment than feel it has either an unfavorable or favorable effect. (L013)

## PREGNANCY, ACCIDENTAL
### X Fertility
The proportion of accidental pregnancies increases with the number of children the mother has. (F101)

## PREGNANCY ANXIETY
### X Child-Rearing Attitudes (Authoritarianism)
Mothers who were highly anxious during pregnancy have more authoritarian attitudes toward child rearing than do mothers who were not as anxious during pregnancy. (D067)

### Child-Rearing Practices (Authoritarianism)
The higher the anxiety level of the mother during pregnancy, the greater the likelihood that she will be overcontrolling and authoritarian in her child-rearing practices. (D075)

### Child-Rearing Practices (Control)
High anxiety during pregnancy is related to high maternal control in child rearing. (D067)

### Cognitive Development
Infants of mothers who were highly anxious during pregnancy have lower scores on the Bayley Mental Scale than do infants of mothers who were not as anxious during pregnancy. (D067)

### Emotional Adjustment of Child
Infants whose mothers were highly anxious during pregnancy exhibit lower emotional adjustment than do infants of mothers who were not as anxious during pregnancy. (D067)

### Marital Adjustment
Women who were highly anxious during pregnancy evidence more marital conflict than do those who were not as anxious during pregnancy. (D067)

### Maternal Overprotectiveness
Maternal overprotection is directly correlated with anxiety as to the successful termination of the pregnancy. (L163)

### Maternal-Role Adjustment
High anxiety during pregnancy is related to dissatisfaction with the maternal role. (D067)

### Mother-Child Relations (Hostility)
High anxiety during pregnancy is related to maternal hostility in child rearing. (D067)

### Mother-Child Relations (Irritation)
Mothers who were highly anxious during pregnancy evidence more irritable relations with their infants than do those who were not as anxious during pregnancy. (D067)

### Motor Development
Infants of mothers who were highly anxious during pregnancy have lower scores on the motor aspects of the Bayley Mental Scale than do infants of mothers who were not as anxious during pregnancy. (D067)

## PREGNANCY ANXIETY (PSYCHOSOMATIC)
### X Illegitimacy
Unwed pregnant women express less psychosomatic anxiety than do multigravida (married). (C099)

## PREGNANCY, ATTITUDE TOWARD    X Age
Age of mother and her attitude toward pregnancy are not associated (U.S.). (S191)

### Aggression
There is no relationship between the mother's attitude on becoming pregnant and the amount of reported aggression from her children. (S191)

### Behavior Problems
Mothers who are greatly concerned about hurting their unborn children during pregnancy tend to have babies who behave abnormally (in terms of crying, sleeping, fussing, etc.) during the first five days after birth. (F096)

Mothers whose babies behave abnormally in the first five days after birth either wanted their pregnancies very much or very much did not want the pregnancies. (F096)

### Birth Spacing
The greater the time between the previous and the new pregnancy, the greater was the proportion of mothers who were "delighted." (S191)

### Breast Feeding
There is no relationship between how happy the mother was on becoming pregnant and her decision to breast feed or not to breast feed the child (U.S.). (S191)

### Breast Feeding, Duration of
Children who are "wanted" tend to be nursed longer than children who are not wanted. (L162)

### Child-Rearing Attitudes
Pregnant women who regard their condition as an illness are more likely to express retaliatory child-rearing attitudes than those women who accept pregnancy as a natural development, regardless of social status. (R107)

### Child-Rearing Practices (Consistency)
Mothers who are inconsistent in their discipline because of concern for the child (e.g., child is sick, mother does not want to hurt the child, etc.) were happier on becoming pregnant than were mothers who are inconsistent because of self-concern (e.g., mother is too busy, too tired, forgets to punish the child, the situation is too public, etc.) (U.S.). (S191)

### Chores
The mothers who feel most tied down by their household duties tend to be the ones who were unhappy over pregnancy. (S191)

### Class
There is an inverse relationship between a woman's social status and her perception of pregnancy as an illness. (R107)

Middle-class mothers tend to be more pleased about the advent of a new child than do lower-class mothers (U.S.). (S191)

### Class, Attitude Toward
The socially unstable woman (dissatisfied with her social position) is more likely than the socially stable woman to view pregnancy as an illness, as troubling, and as dangerous. (R107)

### Employment of Mother
Mothers who do not work are not more pleased over pregnancy than are mothers who work (no matter whether they work only before marriage, before and after marriage, or after the birth of the child). (S191)

Previous work experience of the mother does not correlate with her acceptance of pregnancy or the mother role. (S265)

### Husband-Wife Relations (Affection)
The stronger the wife's esteem and affection for her husband, the happier she is about pregnancy. (S191)

### Husband-Wife Relations (Emotional Support)
The greater the amount of emotional support on the part of the husband, the less is the wife disturbed psychologically during pregnancy. (L135)

### Identification with Wife
It is more likely that husbands whose sexual desires lessen during the pregnancy of their wives identify with their wives and their wives experience more than do husbands whose sexual desires do not lessen. (L013)

### Marital Adjustment
A happy reaction to conception is more likely among wives who rate their marriages as happy than among those who rate their marriages as less than happy or unhappy. (P003)

### Maternal Overprotectiveness
A long period of waiting for the birth of a child is a cause of maternal overprotectiveness toward the child. (B272)

### Maternal Role, Attitude Toward
Women who have negative attitudes toward pregnancy are more likely to have fewer motherly attitudes. (N051)

### Mental Illness of Child
There appears to be no direct correlation between whether or not the mother desired the child and the development of a later psychosis. (R115)

### Mental Illness of Mother
There is no correlation among schizophrenic, neurotic, or normal women with regard to planning or not planning pregnancy or to the number of unfavorable symptoms during pregnancy. (P080)

### Mother-Child Relations
The more favorable the attitude of the mother toward pregnancy, the more positive the relationship between mother and infant at the early stages of childhood. (B283)

### Mother-Child Relations (Warmth)
The more delighted the mother over becoming pregnant, the greater the warmth displayed toward the child after his birth. (S191)

The mother's attitude toward pregnancy forecasts only slightly the warmth she will show toward her child after it is born. The forecast is even poorer for her warmth five years later. (S191)

### Neurosis
Women who are neurotic are more likely to be affected adversely by their pregnancies. (L135)

### Pregnancies, Number of
Women in first pregnancy express greater fears for the coming baby and less irritability and indicate a greater

degree of marital happiness than do women experiencing later pregnancies. (C099)

### Self-Conception of Mother
Mothers who showed comparatively low self-esteem at the time the child was 5 or 6 years old tend to be the same mothers who did not want the child in the first place. (S191)

The higher the mother's self-esteem, the more likely she will be to want the child when becoming pregnant (U.S.). (S191)

### Sex Status of Existing Children
The mother tends to be happier about a new pregnancy if her existing children are girls rather than boys only, or both boys and girls. (S191)

### Sex Taboo (Postpregnancy)
There is a correlation between the unconscious fear of superfetation and the custom of proscribing coitus during pregnancy (and lactation). (D071)

### Size of Family
The greater the number of previous pregnancies, the more likely it is that the most recent pregnancy is unwanted. (F101)

### Twins
There is a correlation between the unconscious fear of superfetation and the custom of fearing and/or killing children who are twins. (D071)

### Work Attitudes of Mother
Among the working-class mothers, attitudes toward work make little difference in the acceptance of pregnancy (U.S.). (S191)

Upper middle-class mothers who enjoy outside work are more likely to enjoy pregnancy than are those who are indifferent to outside work (U.S.). (S191)

## PREGNANCY, ATTITUDE TOWARD/CLASS
### X    Child-Rearing Attitudes
Parental attitudes toward pregnancy are more closely related to child-rearing attitudes than is class. (R107)

## PREGNANCY (EMOTIONAL PROBLEMS)
### X    Health of Child
Emotional disturbance in the mother during pregnancy is associated with gastrointestinal disorders in the infant. This hypothesis is also denied. (P072)

## PREGNANCY, PLANNED/UNPLANNED
### X    Behavior Problems
There is no relationship between abnormal behavior among newborn babies and whether or not the pregnancy had been planned. (F096)

### Education
There is no correlation between college attendance and the planning of pregnancy. This hypothesis is also denied. (P080)

### Pregnancy, Unfavorable Symptoms During
Mothers who planned their pregnancies are likely to report fewer symptoms during pregnancy than are mothers who became pregnant unintentionally. (P080)

## PREGNANCY, SEXUAL DESIRE DURING
### X    Marital Adjustment
Those husbands and wives who had more sexual desire during pregnancy than before pregnancy were happier than either those who had the same degree of desire or

less desire. (A significant reduction in sex desire of most respondents as pregnancy progressed was reported.) (L013)

## PREGNANCY (STRESS)    X    Institutional Care
Mothers who experience emotional stress during pregnancy are more likely than others to give birth to infants who are later placed in institutions (thus compounding the effect of physical and mental impairment from being born of such mothers). (S227)

### Mental Deficiency
Mothers who experience emotional stress during pregnancy are more likely than others to give birth to infants who suffer from mental impairment. (S227)

## PREGNANCY, TIMING OF    X    Birth Control
Couples who are early postmarital conceivers tend to have a higher number of unplanned pregnancies than do those who conceive later in the marriage. (C125)

### Divorce
The longer the couple waits after pregnancy to marry, the greater the chances they will divorce. (C125)

Of the premaritally pregnant who do divorce, divorce occurs earlier than among the couples who were not premaritally pregnant. (C125)

Within marriage, those who conceive very early have a higher divorce rate than those who conceive later. (C125)

Divorce rates and interval to first birth are negatively related. (C125)

## PREGNANCY, UNFAVORABLE SYMPTOMS DURING    X    Pregnancy, Planned/Unplanned
Mothers who planned their pregnancies are likely to report fewer symptoms during pregnancy than are mothers who became pregnant unintentionally. (P080)

## PREMARITAL ACQUAINTANCE
### X    Marital Adjustment
There is a direct correlation between marital adjustment and the length of premarital acquaintance. (B033)

## PREMARITAL CHASTITY
### X    Subsistence Pattern (Pastoral)
In societies with a pastoral economy and a patriarchal extended family structure, the premarital chastity of women is stressed. (P024)

## PREMARITAL PREGNANCY    X    Abortion
Premarital pregnancy that ends before marriage is much more likely to result in abortion than in miscarriage or birth. (E092)

### Age at Marriage
Premarital illegitimacy and conception are more apt to occur among very early and very late marriages. (C129)

### Birth Spacing
Where there is premarital conception, the interval between the first and second child is greater than when the first child is conceived after marriage (Denmark). (C124)

### Breast Feeding
Premarital pregnancy is more likely among those who prefer to bottle feed their children than among those who prefer breast feeding. (A063)

### Childhood (Emotional Security)
There is no relationship between premarital conception and recall of an emotionally insecure childhood. (P086)

### Divorce

Proneness to divorce among couples who are in love when premarital pregnancy occurs is lower than when premarital pregnancy is not associated with a love relationship. (C124)

In marriages where the first child is conceived premaritally (and born in wedlock) the length of the interval between conception and marriage is negatively related to divorce rate. (C124)

Marriages with premarital conception are more likely to end in divorce than are marriages with postmarital conception of the first child, except where both spouses married young (Denmark). (C129)

### Economic Conditions

A higher percentage of first births is conceived before marriage during a depression. (C023)

### Engagement, Duration of

Premarital pregnancy cases are associated with a short or nonexistent engagement period. (M243)

### Intermarriage (Religious)

Higher premarital pregnancy rates are found among mixed marriages than among homogamous religious marriages. (M243)

### Marital Adjustment

There is no association between premarital conception and marital adjustment. (P086)

### Marriage

Couples who are in love tend to marry sooner when premarital pregnancy occurs than do couples who are not in love. (C125)

The greater the incidence of premarital pregnancy in the society, the less social pressure there will be toward hasty marriage or subsequent divorce. (C135)

### Marriage Ceremony

Civil marriages are associated with a higher incidence of premarital pregnancies than are church marriages. (M243)

### Occupation

Premarital pregnancy rates will be higher among laboring groups than among farmers and among farmers than among professional people. (C004)

### Occupational Rank

Among whites, but not among Negroes, the higher the occupational rank, the lower the incidence of premarital pregnancy. (M243)

### Privacy

Premarital conceptions will occur in that season of the year when couples can attain the greatest amount of privacy. (C001)

### Religion

Catholics are no more likely than Protestants to have a higher incidence of premarital pregnancy. (M243)

Jews tend to have the lowest premarital pregnancy rates. (M243)

### Sexual Permissiveness

The greater the permissiveness of the society toward premarital sex, the greater will be the incidence of premarital pregnancy. (C135)

### Urbanization

The percentage of premarital pregnancy is higher for metropolitan cities than for smaller urban communities. (M243)

## PREMARITAL PREGNANCY, ATTITUDE TOWARD
### X    Economic Exchange

The greater the disruption of the socioeconomic system of reciprocal gifts and services caused by illegitimate births, the more likely it is that premarital pregnancy will be condemned. (D071)

## PREMARITAL PREGNANCY/DIVORCE
### X    Sexual Permissiveness

The more permissive the society regarding premarital sex relations, the less likely it is that premarital pregnancy will be associated with divorce. (C135)

## PREMARITAL PREGNANCY/MARRIAGE
### X    Sexual Permissiveness

The more permissive the society regarding premarital sex relations, the less likely it is that premarital pregnancy will lead to a hurried marriage. (C135)

## PREMARITAL SEX RELATIONS    X    Abortion

Where premarital sex relations are relatively institutionalized, it is more likely that the unwed mother aborts; where such relations are informally accepted, abortion of a resultant pregnancy is less likely. (D071)

### Adultery

Extramarital relations are more likely to occur if sexual relations are practiced before marriage. (B191)

### Age at Marriage

When marriage regulations force most men to remain bachelors until well into their thirties, the rate of seduction will be high. (H034)

The later the age of marriage, the higher the incidence of premarital sexual relations. (P052)

A decline in the incidence and risks of sex relations is likely to increase the average age at marriage and decrease the range of marriage age, especially reducing teen-age marriages. (P083)

### Aggression

Aggressive boys are more likely to engage in premarital intercourse than are normals. (B243)

### Birth Control

As birth-control knowledge becomes more generalized, exploitative premarital sex behavior as a late adolescent pattern is likely to decline. (P083)

### Child-Rearing Practices (Authoritarianism)

The more authoritarian the parents are in rearing the girl, particularly with regard to her sex behavior, the more likely it is that she may indulge in premarital sex out of rebellion and hostility against the parents. (B245)

If the parents impose authoritarian restrictions upon the girl but fail to make her aware of their reasons for doing so, it is more likely that the girl's restraint against premarital intercourse will break down when she is not under direct supervision. (B245)

### Child-Rearing Practices (Restrictiveness)

The more fully the parents insulate the girl from social contacts, the less likely it is that the contact she does have with men will lead to an orderly courtship and marriage. (B245)

### Class

Premarital intercourse is more likely to occur between people of the same social class than across class lines; when class lines are crossed, premarital intercourse is most likely between males of a higher and females of a lower social class. (E092)

In Western countries premarital sexual intercourse begins at an earlier age among men in the lower strata. (G156)

The preservation of premarital chastity will tend to be of greater concern to members of the upper class. (R040)

There is an inverse correlation between class and premarital sexual activity for men, but not for women. (S219)

### Courtship

A preoccupation with premarital sexual relations tends to occur when the demographic situation limits the availability of eligible persons. (S037)

### Dating

Early steady dating is associated with a decline in the dalliance pattern (i.e., exploitative premarital sex behavior). (P083)

### Economic Pattern (Labor)

When the pattern of economic activity permits the women and young unmarried men to work singly in the same general area, the rate of seduction will be high. (H034)

### Education

The higher the educational level, the less likely is premarital sexual intercourse. (E092)

The lower the education, the earlier a male is likely to begin acquiring sexual experience. (K160)

The lower the education of males, the more frequently they are likely to have premarital sexual relations. (K160)

### Educational Aspirations

The higher the educational aspirations of boys, the older they are likely to be before first engaging in sexual intercourse. (C134)

### Engagement, Stability of

Premarital sexual intercourse strengthens the relations of the engaged couple. (C023)

### Fecundity

Prepubertal sexual relations may result in sterility. (W109)

### Fertility

The more unstable are premarital sexual unions, the less fertile is the woman likely to be. (B245)

### Honeymoon

Couples who have had premarital sex relations are less likely to take a wedding trip than are those who have not. (P083)

### Initiation Rites

In societies that bring up their children for anchorage and identification in the wider kin-group, there is no relationship between the presence or absence of initiation ceremonies and prohibition or permission of premarital sexual relations. (C093)

### Juvenile Delinquency

Delinquent boys are more active with respect to pre- and postmarital sexual relations than are nondelinquents. (W152)

### Marital Adjustment

Marital happiness is greater among couples who had no premarital sexual relationships than it is among couples who had premarital sexual relationships. (B033)

Those husbands and wives who were either virgins at marriage or had had intercourse only with their future spouses tend to have higher mean happiness scores than do the other groups. (T079)

### Marriage

Among women there is a correlation between premarital sexual activity and nearness to marriage. (E092)

### Occupational Rank

The lower the occupational rank of a male, the earlier he is likely to begin premarital sexual relations. (K160)

The lower the occupational status of a male, the more frequently he is likely to have premarital sexual relations. (K160)

### Parent-Child Relations (Closeness)

The closer the parent-child relationship, the more likely is the child to be chaste before marriage. (L137)

Children who have close relations with their fathers and distant relations with their mothers are more likely to be nonvirgins than are children who are distant from their fathers and close to their mothers or distant from both. (L137)

### Preferential Marriage

Privileged relationships within which sexual intercourse is permitted before marriage commonly reveal a close connection with preferential mating. (M019)

### Premarital Sex Relations, Attitude Toward

The more permissive the society regarding premarital sex relations, the less likely it is that men will be more promiscuous in their premarital sex behavior than women. (B222)

The more permissive the society regarding premarital sex relations, the more likely it is that "desire" will be given as the reason for initial premarital coitus. (B222)

The more permissive the society regarding premarital sex relations, the more likely it is that persons will have a pleasant reaction to first coitus on the following day. (B222)

The greater the degree of sexual freedom customarily condemned short of the ultimate in intimacy, the less often is this extreme reached. (B222)

Approval of premarital intimacy (necking, petting, coitus) correlates with the incidence of premarital intimacy. (C095)

### Race

Premarital sexual intercourse is more likely among Negro than among white females. (E092)

### Religion

The use of a virgin in ceremonial roles is more likely to occur in societies where premarital chastity is valued. (D057)

### Religiosity

The more devout a person (as represented by frequent or infrequent church attendance), the less likely he is to engage in premarital sexual relations. (K160)

### Residence

The more the child, during pre- or early adolescence, is transferred from the home of his parents to that of other relatives or friends, the more likely it is that prohibitions against premarital intercourse will break down. (B245)

### Sex Attitudes

When there is no stigma attached to premarital relations or reproduction, sexual intercourse will be regarded as a natural and enjoyable act. (H084)

### Sex Composition of Household

The fewer men there are residing in the home able to protect the daughter, the more likely it is that the daughter will be sexually exploited. (B245)

### Sex Status

Females are more likely than males to have their first coital experience with a steady date or a fiancé. (C023)

Males tend to start coitus at an earlier age than females. (C023)

Males tend to have more premarital sex partners than females. (C023)

Males are more likely than females to give "desire" as their reason for initial coitus. (C023)

A higher percentage of females than of males confine their sexual activities outside marriage to necking and petting. (C023)

Females are more likely than males to confine sexual activity to others of the same social class, while males are more likely than females to have sexual activities with lower-class persons. (C023)

Males are more likely to have premarital sexual intercourse than are females. (C023)

Premarital sexual activity of females is correlated more highly with going steady or being in love than is that of males. (E092)

Women are more likely than men to be monogamous in their premarital sexual intercourse relationships. (E092)

### Sexual Adjustment

There is no association between sexual adjustment in marriage and premarital sexual experience. (C023)

The greater the degree of satisfaction in premarital sex activities, the less likely is frigidity or other sexual maladjustment in marriage. (S219)

### Sexual Permissiveness

The more sexually permissive the attitudes in a society, the more likely is premarital coitus. (C132)

The more permissive the culture with regard to premarital sexual intimacy, the higher the incidence of such intimacy occurring and the lower the negative effects from occurrences. (C132)

### Social Control

The greater the occupational mobility of family or in society (and the lower the control of the community), the more likely it is that girls will be exploited in premarital intercourse. (B245)

### Sterility

There is no relationship between the fear of sterility and premarital sex relations. (B245)

### Urban/Rural

The urban male and the urban female after age 20 are more likely to practice premarital petting and coitus than are their rural counterparts. (E092)

### Values (Marriage)

Even if marriage is the only approved relation between male and female, the later the approved age of marriage in the society, the more likely it is that premarital intercourse will occur. (B245)

### Warfare

Warfare is likely to result in a marked increase in premarital promiscuity. (G139)

## PREMARITAL SEX RELATIONS, AGE AT

#### X Fertility

The earlier the age at which the woman is first exposed to intercourse, the more fertile she is likely to be. (B245)

## PREMARITAL SEX RELATIONS, ATTITUDE TOWARD
#### X Adultery

Adultery is less frequent where premarital sexual relations are freely accepted. (H074)

### Adultery, Attitude Toward

There is no correlation between cultural permissiveness toward premarital sexual intercourse and permissiveness toward adulterous relations after marriage. (E092)

### Affinal Ties

Where affinal ties confer important rights to land and other resources, premarital sexual freedom is more likely to be restricted. (V036)

### Descent (Patrilineal)

Premarital relations are less likely to be tolerated in patrilineal societies. (F073)

### Drinking

Excessive drinking in a society and premarital sexual freedom tend to be associated. (K046)

### Illegitimacy

Premarital relations are more likely to be condoned if the girl does not become pregnant. (W105)

The rate of the illegitimate births tends to be inversely correlated with the severity of censure of premarital relations. (L053)

### Infant Betrothal

There is a greater control over the premarital sexual activity of a girl if she has been betrothed in infancy. (E080)

### Marital Adjustment of Husband

Happy husbands, more often than the unhappy, believe that the husband should not have had intercourse with any other woman before marriage and that young people should be trained not to indulge in "petting" and "spooning." (T074)

### Premarital Sex Relations

The more permissive the society regarding premarital sex relations, the less likely it is that men will be more promiscuous in their premarital sex behavior than women. (B222)

The more permissive the society regarding premarital

sex relations, the more likely it is that "desire" will be given as the reason for initial premarital coitus. (B222)

The more permissive the society regarding premarital sex relations, the more likely it is that persons will have a pleasant reaction to first coitus on the following day. (B222)

The greater the degree of sexual freedom customarily condemned, short of the ultimate in intimacy, the less often is this extreme reached. (B222)

Approval of premarital intimacy (necking, petting, coitus) correlates with the incidence of premarital intimacy. (C095)

### Sex Status
Teen-age girls are more conservative about necking and petting behavior than are teen-age boys. (C012)

Teen-age girls are more likely to disapprove of kissing on the first date than to approve of it. (C012)

Teen-age girls are more likely to feel that intimate petting should be delayed until after marriage than to feel it should take place before marriage. (C012)

A higher percentage of males than of females approve of premarital coitus. (C095)

## PREMARITAL SEX RELATIONS (DALLIANCE)
### X    Child-Rearing Attitudes (Sex)
Exploitative premarital sex behavior, as a later adolescent pattern, is likely to decline as parental opposition to premarital sex relations declines. (P083)

## PRENATAL STIMULATION
### X    Mother-Child Relations (Nurturance)
If an infant receives high amounts of stimulation during the prenatal period, it requires high amounts of postnatal mothering. (O033)

## PRIVACY    X    Adultery
Extramarital relations are less likely to occur if the social situation does not permit privacy. (M085)

### Premarital Pregnancy
Premarital conceptions will occur in that season of the year when couples can attain the greatest amount of privacy. (C001)

### Sexual Aggression
A high rate of sexual offenses tends to be correlated with the opportunity for privacy which the potential sex offender has. (L026)

## PROJECTION
### X    Mother-Child Relations (Empathy)
Mothers who are correct in their abilities to predict the preferences, ambitions, and fears of their children are least likely to impute incorrectly their own attitudes to the children (that is, they do not project).

## PROPERTY    X    Adoption
Patterns of adoption are not likely to occur in marginal hunting and gathering societies where there is little property. (M085)

### Ancestors
When there are no family property holdings to inherit or defend there is no pattern of binding new family unity to an ancestral tradition. (O002)

### Authority Structure of Family
If adult married children remain in their parents' homes, one of the parents is more likely to be considered head of the household than the son or son-in-law; if they start their own household and invite the parents in, they are most likely to be the household heads. (B312)

When land is owned jointly by patrilineal extended families, the authority of men over their wives, younger brothers, and sons is strengthened. (G028)

A high correlation exists between ownership or direct tenancy of the homestead and its headship. This control tends also to be rested in the dominant and senior member of the group. (S211)

### Child-Rearing Practices (Punishment)
The nurturing person is less likely to inflict pain on the infant in societies where the property is owned by the women than in societies where it is not. (L141)

### Cohesion of Family
The unity of the extended family tends to be maintained if the father retains control of all property possessed by the group as long as he lives. (G013)

### Cohesion of Kin-Group
The greater the control of disposable wealth, the greater is the tendency for the kin unit to maintain its cohesion. (F029)

### Corporate Kin-Group
Individual ownership tends to increase with the deterioration of the corporate character of the clan structure. (W103)

### Descent
As property becomes more movable and more easily transformed into money terms, the importance of the unilinear descent system declines. (P083)

As the individual's physical control over property is more protected by law and the state rather than by relatives, the importance of the unilinear descent system declines. (P083)

### Descent/Residence
There is a correlation between the sex which will own the houses and the type of descent and residence pattern. (L043)

### Divorce Arrangements
For all occupational classes, the divorcing couple are much more likely to split the property when there is more of it. (G157)

### Economic Role of Women
When women have the exclusive agricultural role, property rights to land tend to be matrilineal. (B133)

### Endogamy
Disputes over property reinforce endogamy within the kin-group. (R034)

### Endogamy (Clan)
Marriage to a man of an appropriate lineage will tend to be instituted if the desire is to retain control over valuable properties within that lineage. (B108)

### Extended Family
The extended family tends to develop where immovable property constitutes a major form of wealth. (M019)

### Fertility
Fertility rates are higher among couples who own their own homes than among those who rent. (R119)

### Geographic Mobility
Where property rights exist mainly in agricultural land and hereditary occupations, mobility will tend to be minimized. (G149)

### Intermarriage (Class)
When intermarriage of localized lineages of different social class occurs, the general tendency is the transfer of economic wealth from the lower class to the upper (i.e., hypergamy is more likely). (L051)

### Lineage
The development of lineage organization tends to be correlated with the presence of heritable land or livestock. (F020)

### Management (Family-Based)
Familial and custodial organizations are more likely to be headed by manager-proprietor; contractual or voluntary organizations involve corporate proprietorship. (U003)

### Marital Adjustment
There is a direct correlation between marital adjustment and home ownership and insurance. (B033)

### Marital Stability
Marital stability is closely correlated with home ownership. (F078)

### Polyandry
Fraternal polyandry is associated with family systems in which both women and men have property rights, especially a dowry. (B205)

### Polygyny
Polygyny tends to occur in patrilineal society where the economy permits the accumulation of personal property. (B033)

### Preferential Marriage
When the retention of certain property in the kin line is desired, preferential marriage patterns between consanguineals will tend to be instituted. (L058)

### Preferential Marriage (Parallel-Cousin)
The preferential marriage pattern of parallel-cousin marriage will tend to be institutionalized where the retention of lineage property is stressed. (M095)

### Rank
Status within the family is directly correlated with control of strategic resources. (H028)

### Rank of Husband
When women have control of the house and of the strategic resources, the status of the husband tends to be low. (L059)

### Religion (Ritual Importance of Women)
Women's importance in ritual varies directly with the absoluteness of feminine house ownership and strength of clan. (M037)

### Residence
Matrilocal residence tends to be favored in the absence of movable property which is of economic significance (e.g., herds). (M019)

### Residence (Matrilocal)
When the ownership of the house and land is by women, residence tends to be matrilocal. (L036)

### Residence (Patrilocal)
The development of any form of movable property or wealth will tend to promote patrilocal residence. (M019)

### Segmentation
The accumulation of individual property tends to accelerate the process of lineage segmentation. (G056)

### Size of Family
Among families at the middle and upper rental-value levels, there is likely to be a larger number of children in homeowning families than in tenant families. (C009)

Among families at lower rental-value levels, there is likely to be a larger number of children in tenant families than in homeowning families. (C009)

### Size of Kin-Group
Increase in personal wealth provides incentive to narrow the size of the group with a claim upon it to a few immediate kinsmen. (C090)

Smaller segments of unilineal kin-groups are more likely to be property owning than the larger groups. (S189)

### Stability of Extended Family
When an equitable divsion of family property between sons would result in an area of land too small to support a conjugal family, the sons will tend to reman together in a single household after the death of their father. (A013)

The extended family will tend to remain intact as an economic and social unit if it retains control of village land. (G028)

### Stability of Family
Family organization tends to be fairly stable when the members hold their land as property. (A014)

### PROPERTY (COLLECTIVE)     X   Monogamy
As the economic pattern is transformed to collective property, the monogamous family tends to occur less frequently. (E087)

### PROPERTY, DIVISION OF
#### X   Economic Conditions
Fission of family land is more likely to occur during periods of economic pressure. (L066)

#### Size of Lineage
When a reduction in the size in the effective lineage occurs, the fragmentation of land also occurs. (T017)

### PROPERTY EXCHANGE AT MARRIAGE
#### X   Husband-Wife Relations (Aggression)
The exchange of property between families at the time of marriage acts as a deterrent to subsequent injury of either spouse. (G035)

### PROPERTY (INDIVIDUAL)
#### X   Authority Structure of Lineage
The authority of the lineage head is undermined with the increasing importance of individually owned property. (W090)

#### Independence of Nuclear Family
The development of patterns of individual ownership of land is directly correlated with the emergence of the

parental family as a domestic group and an economically autonomous unit. (G156)

### Kindred
Where conditions are favorable to the individual ownership of land, the bilateral kindred will replace the unilinear kin-group. (G029)

## PROPERTY (MOVABLE)    X   Marriage Payment
Marriage payment will only occur in those societies in which movable property can be accumulated. (E055)

## PROPERTY OWNERSHIP
### X   Nuclear Family, Importance of
In matrilineal societies, where women own property, the nuclear family is relatively insignificant. (D057)

## PROPERTY OWNERSHIP (CORPORATE)
### X   Joint Family
The corporate ownership of landed estates tends to stabilize and strengthen the joint family. (M021)

## PROPERTY (PATRILINEAL)
### X   Residence (Matrilocal)
When patrilineal property is restricted to personal possessions which are destroyed or buried with the body upon death, the transition to matrilocal residence is not difficult to effect. (M020)

## PROPERTY RIGHTS    X   Avoidance Relationship
Avoidance patterns between siblings are more likely to occur when property rights are fluid. (M235)

### Genealogical Ties, Knowledge of
Ancestral connections are more likely to be remembered if rights in property or in offices that are valued are attached to the lineage. (M168)

### Genealogy, Importance of
Genealogy is more important when kin ties confer land rights. (G150)

### Legal Status of Wife
The legal prerogatives of a woman will tend to be greater if she retains economic claims on the property of her natal family. (M063)

### Rank of Wife
The status of the wife will be directly correlated with her property rights. (W082)

### Rank of Women
When women have no rights over land, their position in the family is low and inferior. (H171)

## PROSTITUTION    X   Age at Marriage
Postponement of men's marriage is more likely to occur where some form of prostitution or common-law arrangement with lower-class girls is possible. (P083)

### Bachelorhood
The demand for prostitutes' services declines with a decline in the bachelor population. (P083)

### Birth Control
When the pattern of marriage is monogamous, extended restriction against sexual relations between husband and wife as a method of birth control will tend to lead to prostitution. (P034)

### Divorce
The greater the institutionalized bonds against divorce, the higher the incidence of prostitution. (K161)

### Economic Pattern (Migrant Labor)
The separation of husbands from their wives and families, as migrants to urban areas, tends to be associated with a high incidence of prostitution in the urban areas. (I004)

### Husband-Wife Relations
A relationship between the need for a peer type of interaction with women and the development of a class of sophisticated prostitutes of the geisha variety occurs when the wives are made incapable of such interaction by the limitation of their experience and their formal education. (P083)

The demand for prostitutes' services has declined with the inclusion of the beauty parlor in the working-class wife's budget. (P083)

### Kin Relations
Prostitutes tend to be detribalized women who have been cut off from their families. (D051)

### Marriage Chances
Prostitution will tend to flourish when the percentage of men married is low. (H088)

### Marriage Chances of Women
With the institutionalization of prostitution, a relatively large number of unmarried women will remain unmarried. (C045)

### Monogamy
Prostitution is correlated with monogamy. (E087)

### Sex Norms
The demand for prostitutes' services has declined with the decline of the Victorian respect for frigidity in wives. (P083)

The demand for prostitutes' services has declined with the greater sexual accessibility of unmarried women. (P083)

### Sexual Behavior
The development of prostitution will diminish the social importance of the sexual act within the kinship system. (S153)

## PROTECTION    X   Cohesion of Kin-Group
When individuals are no longer dependent upon their kinsmen for personal security, the kin unit will tend to break down. (O013)

## PSYCHOPATHY    X   Socialization
Children who lack the opportunity to internalize the values of parent figures are more likely than others to become psychopaths. (W143)

## PSYCHOPATHY OF CHILD    X   Dependency
Disruption of the dependency relationship with the mother is a cause of psychopathic behavior in the child. (B243)

### Parent-Child Relations
Abnormal or disrupted parent-child relationships are a cause of psychopathic behavior problems in the child. (B285)

## PSYCHOSOMATIC ILLNESS    X   Broken Home
There is no relationship between the severity and frequency of psychosomatic symptoms of children from broken and those from unbroken homes. (N057)

Among children whose families have been broken by

death, there is no relationship between religion and the liklihood of the child to have many psychomatic symptoms. Catholics and Jews are no more likely than Protestants to have many psychosomatic symptoms. (R129)

#### Divorce
Children whose parents are divorced are more likely than those from intact families to report psychosomatic symptoms. (R129)

Catholics and Jews whose parents are divorced are more likely than those from intact families to have psychosomatic symptoms, but this is less true of Protestants. (R129)

#### Mother-Child Relations (Affection)
If the child suffers from deprivation of maternal care, maternal stimulation, and maternal love, along with physical deprivation in his first year, he is likely to suffer from psychosomatic problems. (S201)

#### Ordinal Position
More patients suffering from hyperthyroidism and asthma are firstborns or eldest than are middle or youngest children in the family. (P081)

#### Parent Loss
Among children whose families have been broken by death, there is no relationship between religion and likelihood of child to have many psychosomatic symptoms. (R129)

#### Parental-Role Behavior
Inversion or imbalance in parental roles is a cause of duodenal ulceration in the child. (P078)

#### Pregnancies, Number of
Previous experience with pregnancy is indeterminate relative to psychosomatic symptoms. (C099)

#### Pregnancy
All women (regardless of marital status of previous birth experience) show a highly significant increase, with pregnancy, in psychosomatic anxiety. (C099)

#### Religion
Catholics and Jews whose parents are divorced are more likely than are those from intact families to have psychosomatic symptoms, but this is less true of Protestants. (R129)

### PSYCHOSOMATIC ILLNESS (COLITIS)
#### X Personality Problems in Family
The incidence and severity of ulcerative colitis is correlated with psychological and psychosomatic disorders in the patient's family. (P078)

### PSYCHOSOMATIC ILLNESS OF CHILD
#### X Age of Mother
The younger the mother at the time of divorce, the more likely the children are to have many psychosomatic symptoms. (R129)

Children whose mothers were relatively young when they were widowed are more likely to show psychosomatic symptoms of anxiety. (R129)

#### Alcoholism in Family
Children from alcoholic families have more psychosomatic illnesses than do children from nonalcoholic families. (D078)

#### Illness of Parents (Dyspepsia)
Gastric neurosis in the child tends to be correlated with patterns of dyspepsia in the parents. (F113)

#### Remarriage
Children of divorce, whose mothers remarried, are more likely to have many psychosomatic symptoms than are children whose mothers did not remarry. (R129)

### PSYCHOTHERAPY      X Juvenile Delinquency
Treatment of juvenile delinquents is more likely to be successful if the parents are included in the treatment process. (R110)

#### Mental Illness, Family Adjustment to
The greater the accommodation of a family for a disturbed member, the less is the likelihood that he will come to psychiatric attention. (S206)

#### Mental Illness (Schizophrenia), Recovery from
The more a schizophrenic child in treatment shows signs of recovery, the greater is the likelihood that the parents' defense system will be threatened and that they will try to withdraw him from treatment. (K095)

#### Ordinal Position
Disturbed firstborns are more likely to seek and accept psychotherapy and to remain in treatment longer than are later-born persons. (S263)

### PSYCHOTHERAPY, ATTITUDE TOWARD
#### X Class
Middle-class families are more likely to acknowledge mental illness in their members and to support therapeutic treatment than are lower-class families. (M197)

### PSYCHOTHERAPY OF MOTHER
#### X Child-Rearing Practices (Consistency)
Therapy that focuses on alleviating guilt in mothers in regard to placing and enforcing reasonable restrictions on their children is the most effective measure of producing more consistent disciplinary measures by the mothers. (R091)

### PUBERTY      X Avoidance Relationship
The activation of an avoidance relationship between siblings tends to occur at adolescence. (S098)

#### Identification with Parents
During the first stage of puberty (8 to 10 years of age), society is more able to interfere with and weaken the child's identification with his parents, thus implanting its values and attitudes, than during the later stage of puberty. (C093)

#### Initiation Rites
Initiation ceremonies will be more severe and, consequently, effective when observed during the first stage of puberty (8 to 10 years of age) than during the second stage (after 10), as the child is more susceptible to societal influences. (C093)

More societies will take formal and explicit steps (e.g., initiation ceremonies) during the first stage of puberty (8 to 10 years of age) than during the second stage of puberty (emergence of secondary sex traits). (C093)

### PUBERTY CEREMONIES (MALE)
#### X Social Structure (Matriliny)
Male puberty ceremonies are less likely to occur in matrilineal societies. (W154)

# R

## RACE

### X Abortion
Premarital pregnancy is more likely to be terminated by induced abortion among white than it is among Negro families. (E092).

### Adoption
Negro parents who apply for adoption are more likely to prefer a child of their own coloring than a child who is much darker or lighter. (F117).

Negro couples are less likely to adopt a child than white couples, with the exception of the lower classes, where the negro adoption rate exceeds that of whites. (F118)

### Adoption, Age at
Negro couples tend to apply for adoption at a later age than white couples. (F118)

### Adoption (Sex Preference)
White couples indicate a high preference for a male child when applying for adoption; Negro couples indicate a high preference for a female child. (F117)

### Age at Marriage
A larger percentage of Negro brides than of white brides are below 19 years of age. (C010)

There is no significant difference between white and Negro grooms and the proportion marrying under 20 years of age. (C010)

Between the ages of 20 and 30 there is a smaller proportion of Negro grooms than of white grooms (U.S.). (C010)

### Authority Structure of Family
In the middle and upper class in America, there is no relationship between racial origin and the structure of authority in the family. (M215)

Negro professors are less likely to be dominant in the family as regards decisions about purchases and living standards, than are white professors. (M215)

### Broken Home
There is a higher percentage of broken homes among Negroes than among whites. (S210)

### Child-Rearing Practices (Change)
Child-rearing practices change more slowly among Negroes than among whites (U.S.). (L124)

### Child-Rearing Practices (Punishment)
Among lower-class families, fathers of Negro children tend to discipline their children more than do white fathers. (G117)

### Desertion
Desertion is more likely to occur among Negroes than among whites. (M001)

### Disorganization of Family
Family disorganization is more likely to occur among Negroes than among whites. (T002)

### Divorce
Divorce rates have been and currently are higher among nonwhites than among whites (U.S.). (G156)

Among people who are charged with desertion, divorce rates are higher for whites than for Negroes. (K010)

### Divorce Complaints
Negro divorcées are no more likely than white divorcées to charge that personality conflicts were a cause of divorce. (G157)

Negro divorcées are more likely than white divorcées to claim that value conflicts were a cause of divorce. (G157)

### Divorce Process
Whites from rural backgrounds take slightly more time between decisions to divorce and filing suits than do Negroes from the same backgrounds. (G157)

Negroes from small towns take considerably longer than do whites between decisions to divorce and filing suits. (G157)

Urban Negroes take about the same amount of time as do urban whites from serious decisions to divorce to actual filings of the suits. (G157)

### Duration of Marriage
Negroes are slightly more likely to have longer durations of marriage than are whites. (G157)

Among urban populations, Negroes are likely to have shorter durations of marriage than are whites. (G157)

Negro marriages ending in divorce are likely to have lasted longer than are white marriages ending in divorce. (K003)

### Educational Aspirations
Negro mothers are more likely to have unrealistic educational goals for their children than are white mothers. (L124)

### Employment of Mother
More Negro mothers than white mothers are in the labor force. (H018)

### Employment of Wife
Negro wives are more often employed outside the home than are white wives.

### Father-Child Relations (Interaction)
Among the lower classes, fathers of Negro children spend less time teaching and playing with their children than do white fathers. (G117)

### Feeding
Negro parents are more permissive than are white parents in feeding their children. This proposition is also denied.

### Feeding/Toilet Training
White mothers are more likely to be rigorous in the handling of feeding and weaning of their infants; Negro mothers, in the handling of toilet training. (B272)

### Fertility
More Negro families than white families are childless. This proposition is also denied. (H018)

### Illegitimacy (Adoption)
Negro unmarried mothers tend to keep their babies more than do white unmarried mothers. (J020)

### Illegitimacy, Attitude Toward
Negroes, as compared with other segments of American society, do not as strongly disapprove the having of children out of wedlock. (J020)

### Income of Divorcée
There is no difference between white and Negro divorcées who have remarried in the amount of income available for weekly expenses; among the not-remarried, white divorcées have a good deal more money for expenses than Negro divorcées. (G157)

### Intermarriage (Racial)
The initial acceptance of racial intermarriage tends to be correlated with the presence of more than two racial types. (D018)

### Marital Stability
Separations are more common among nonwhite than among white. (B033)

### Marital Status
The white population has a somewhat higher proportion of marriages that are first marriages than does the nonwhite population. (C010)

### Mate Selection (Class)
There is a greater likelihood for the reinforcement of social-class homogamy when different racial elements in a society occupy markedly different positions of social rank. (B029)

### Mate Selection (Residence)
Residential propinquity in mate selection is more characteristic of Negroes than of whites. (K020)

### Parent-Child Relations (Authoritarianism)
Negro families tend to have more authoritarian parent-child relations than do white families. (G117)

### Parent-Child Relations (Conflict)
Negro children have more compliant attitudes regarding parent-child conflicts than do white children, who have attitudes reflecting more active opposition or constructive solutions. (G117)

### Power Structure of Family
No significant differences appear in the dominance patterns in family decisions of Negroes as against whites.

The Negro husband, compared with the white husband, has less power within his family.

### Premarital Sex Relations
Premarital sexual intercourse is more likely among Negro than among white females. (E92)

### Remarriage
Remarriage is found more often among Negroes than among whites. (G011)

Negroes tend to move into a remarriage more rapidly than do whites; over time this difference diminishes. (G157)

There are no differences between Negro and white divorcées regarding the degree of satisfaction with the second marriage—the majority claiming greater satisfaction. (G157)

### Remarriage Rate
Remarriage rates for whites are about the same as for Negroes. (G157)

### Residence
In urban Negro families, children under 18 are less likely to live with their parents than are those in other families; in rural Negro families, the reverse is true (U.S.). (L124)

### Size of Family
The range of family size is much greater among Negro families than among white families. (H018)

Negro households are larger than white households (U.S.). (L124)

### Socialization, Agents of
Factors external to the family are more likely to play roles in the socialization of the Negro child than of the white child (U.S.). (L124)

### Weaning
Negro parents are more permissive in weaning their children than are white parents. This proposition is also denied.

## RACE ATTITUDES
### X  Child-Rearing Practices (Consensus)
The greater the perceived discrepancy between the parents in discouraging the child from playing with Negroes, the more prejudiced is the child. (B226)

### Child-Rearing Practices (Friendship)
The less the parents discourage their children from playing with Negro children, while not finding pleasure in letting them choose their own friends, the more ambivalent the parents are in their own racial attitudes. (B226)

Children who say that their parents have prohibited them from playing with Negroes have a higher prejudice rating than do children who say their parents did not discourage them from playing with Negroes. (B226)

Parents who are pleased with their children playing with Negroes have children who are less prejudiced than do parents who discourage interracial playmates. (B226)

Parents who have used spoken prohibitions against their children playing with Negroes produce greater racial prejudice in their children than do parents who use more subtle forms of discouragement. (B226)

### Child-Rearing Practices (Punishment)
Prejudiced persons are more likely than unprejudiced persons to report harsh and threatening parental discipline during their childhoods caused by infringement of rules rather than of principles. (A061)

### Cohesion of Family
Prejudiced persons are more likely than unprejudiced persons to have an "ingroup orientation" toward their family, manifested in a preoccupation with the family's status and prestige. (A061)

### Dependency
Prejudiced persons are more likely than unprejudiced persons to perceive their dependencies on their parents as materialistic and utilitarian rather than as based on the need for love and affection. (A061)

### Father-Child Relations (Affection)
Prejudiced males are more likely than unprejudiced males to perceive their fathers as being remote and stern, as opposed to mild and affectionate. (A061)

### Parent-Child Relations
Prejudiced persons are more likely than unprejudiced persons to express feelings of victimization by the parents. (A061)

### Parent-Child Relations (Authority)
Prejudiced persons are more likely to submit to parental authority or to rebel capriciously than are the unprejudiced, who are more likely to manifest a position of principled independence. (A061)

### Parent-Child Relations (Evaluation)
Prejudiced persons are more likely to perceive their parents in terms of conventional idealizations than are unprejudiced persons. (A061)

Unprejudiced persons are more likely to express genuine positive feelings toward their parents than are prejudiced persons. (A061)

### Parent-Child Relations (Preference)
Prejudiced men are less likely than unprejudiced men to express a greater attachment for the mother than for the father and are more likely to repress feminine traits in their own behavior. (A061)

### Parental Role
The prejudiced woman is more likely than the unprejudiced to stress her father's role as the provider for the family; the unprejudiced woman is more likely to stress the intellectual and esthetic aspects of her father's character. (A061)

### Personality (Ego Strength)
The reaction of the Negro child to prejudice is more directly related to the amount of ego strength he has acquired from family attitudes than to the presence or absence of legal segregation in his area. (M229)

### Personality of Mother
Prejudiced men are more likely than unprejudiced men to perceive their mothers as self-sacrificing and moralistic. (A061)

Unprejudiced men are more likely than prejudiced men to perceive their mothers are sociable, intellectual, and esthetic. (A061)

Unprejudiced women are more likely than prejudiced women to perceive their mothers as warm and lovable. (A061)

Prejudiced women are more likely than unprejudiced women to perceive their mothers as dominant, moralistic, and socially successful. (A061)

### Power Structure of Family
Prejudiced persons are more likely than unprejudiced persons to perceive one of their parents as being dominant in the family, particularly the same-sex parent. (A061)

Unprejudiced persons are more likely than prejudiced persons to perceive the family structure as equalitarian or as oriented toward a loving mother. (A061)

### Race Attitudes of Parents
Children's attitudes toward Negroes are related less to contact with Negroes and more to parents' attitudes toward Negroes. (M222)

### Sex Status
Among children who say their parents have not discouraged them from playing with Negro children, boys are less prejudiced than girls. (B226)

Among children who say their parents have prohibited them from playing with Negroes, there is no association between sex and degree of prejudice. (B226)

### Sibling Relations
Prejudiced persons are more likely than unprejudiced persons to idealize their siblings and are less likely to give a realistic appraisal of or to manifest genuine affect toward siblings. (A061)

### Socialization, Effectiveness of
Due to inadequate identification with the parents, prejudiced persons are less likely to internalize values and standards than are unprejudiced persons. (A061)

## RACE ATTITUDES OF PARENTS
### X   Race Attitudes
Children's attitudes toward Negroes are related less to contact with Negroes and more to parents' attitudes toward Negroes. (M222)

## RACE/CLASS
### X   Child-Rearing Practices (Severity/Consistency)
The degree of severity and consistency of child rearing is correlated more with class than with race. (B272)

## RACE (CLASS)
### X   Child-Rearing Practices (Control)
Middle-class Negro girls are expected to remain closer to home than are middle-class white girls.

### Child-Rearing Practices (Responsibility)
In both middle and lower classes, Negro parents train their girls for responsibility in household tasks at an earlier age than do white parents.

### Toilet Training
In both the middle and lower classes, Negro parents are stricter than white parents in toilet training their children.

## RACE (URBANIZATION)
### X   Household Composition
Urban Negro families are more likely than the rest of the population to have women as heads (U.S.). (L124)

### Illegitimacy
Illegitimacy is more likely among urban Negro families than among the rest of the population (U.S.). (L124)

### Marital Stability
Separation and widowhood are more likely in urban Negro families than in the rest of the population (U.S.). (L124)

## RANK         X   Adultery, Attitude Toward
Extramarital relations are more likely to be tolerated if the status of the man is high. (W104)

### Avoidance Relationship
Avoidance patterns are more likely to occur between kinsmen in direct competition for social rank. (M235)

### Cohesion of Kin-Group
The higher the rank, the greater the tendency of the larger kin unit to maintain its cohesion. (F029)

### Engagement, Duration of
The length of engagement is directly correlated with the status of the engaged couple. (H128)

### Engagement, Stability of
Engagements between individuals of high status will tend to be more stable. (B181)

### Fertility
Social prestige and authority in societies based on kinship principles are correlated with the relative fertility of individuals and families. (T080)

### Genealogical Ties, Knowledge of
The range of genealogical knowledge will be directly correlated with the social status of the individual. (D125)

### Genealogy, Importance of
Genealogies are more likely to be stressed among individuals of high status. (T069)

### Illegitimacy
Commitment to the norm of legitimacy will be greater among the strata or kin lines which enjoy a higher prestige. (G151)

### Incest Taboo
The reaction to incest may be less severe if the offending couple is of high status. (C079)

### Inheritance
Inheritance rights will be more clearly defined among families of higher status. (B183)

### Kin Relations (Interaction)
Kinsmen of similar rank are more likely than those of dissimilar rank to be in frequent social contact. (G033)

For housewives, as social rank increases, so does contact with relatives. (R084)

### Kin-Role Definition
The explicitness of the behavior associated with a kin role will be directly correlated with the importance of the kinsmen in the social structure. (R066)

### Kin Terminology
Kinship terms, rather than personal names, are used when the speaker desires to show deference to his relatives. (B054)

Kinship terms, rather than personal names, will tend to be used, when the speaker desires to show deference to his relatives. (B054)

Kinsmen of equal rank are more likely to use informal than formal variants of kinship terms. (B083)

The kinship designation tends to be omitted when the speaker is of equal status or superior to the hearer. (S050)

### Lineage, Importance of
The importance of the lineage as a unit of social organization is directly correlated with social rank. (G101)

### Marriage Payment
The amount of the marriage payment is directly correlated with the status of the family of the bride. (T069)

### Mate Selection (Free Choice)
The degree of parental influence in mate selection is directly correlated with the status of the boy or girl. (W105)

### Parent-Child Relations (Control)
The more successful upper-class families are in forcing their children to hew to upper-class standards, the better able they are to maintain their class status. (G156)

### Power Structure of Family
The higher the social rank of a spouse, the more power he is likely to have in the family. (K089)

### Preferential Marriage (Cross-Cousin)
When marriage into a family of comparable rank is stressed, cross-cousin marriage tends to occur, although it may not be the preferential form of marriage. (L039)

### Property
Status within the family is directly correlated with control of strategic resources. (H028)

### Residence
Residence patterns are more likely to be violated when the spouse who does not determine the place of residence is of high status. (H137)

### Segmentation
Lineages will tend to subdivide if they contain several prominent men. (M169)

### Sexual Aggression
Sexual aggressors are more likely to have a lower social status than are the sexually offended, when compared with the social-status relationship between nonaggressors and nonoffended. (K018)

### Size of Kin-Group
The ability of a man to attract kinsmen who live near him is directly correlated with his status. (C060)

### Social Network
The social rank of the individual will be directly correlated with the range of social and economic ties which he establishes beyond his immediate family. (W064)

### Value Conflict (Family/Economic)
Low social status is likely to accompany greater conflict between family values and values of economic success, while high social status is more apt to be found in conjunction with less conflict between family values and values of economic success. (J033)

### Values (Extended/Nuclear Family)
Those with high social rank are more apt to prefer the nuclear family values than are those with low social rank, who are more likely to prefer extended family values. (J033)

### RANK OF AFFINES          X   Avoidance Relationship
Avoidance relationships tend to be established between affinals who are of unequal status. (S153)

### Marriage Payment
A substantial bride price, composed of objects having only ritual and symbolic value, implies both high rank and equality of rank between wife-givers and wife-receivers. If the dowry is made up of consumer goods, the wife-givers have a lower rank than the wife-receivers. (L051)

### RANK OF CHILD          X   Inheritance
The rank of the child in the family will be directly correlated with his or her eligibility for the inheritance of family property. (W082)

### RANK OF CLAN
### X   Economic Importance of Clan
The persistence of economic function is greatest in clans with a higher ranking in the hierarchy of power and prestige. (F039)

### Economic Rank of Clan
The status of a clan will be directly correlated with its economic position. (T065)

### Mate Selection
Mate selection tends to occur between clans of approximately the same status. (B112)

### Residence
Clans of high status are more likely to be located at the center of the community. (W075)

### Size of Clan
Clans of high status, inasmuch as they are able to acquire more wives, will be larger in size. (E103)

The prestige of the clan tends to be directly correlated with its size. (M051)

## RANK OF DESCENT GROUP
### X    Genealogical Depth
The genealogical depth of the lineage (which is significant to ego) will be greater than that of the lineages of other relatives. (N012)

## RANK OF DIVORCÉE    X    Divorce, Initiation of
The lower the social status of the (female) divorcée in the society, the less likely are women to initiate divorce. (S115)

## RANK OF ETHNIC GROUP
### X    Education of Child
### Parent-Child Relations (Authority)
Among children from the dominant social group, the lower their educational level, the less likely it is that they will be acceptant of parental authority. Among children from subordinate groups, the greater the extent of their education, the more likely they are to reject parental authority. (K121)

### Endogamy (Ethnic)
The rate of ethnic endogamy tends to be high when the status of the ethnic group is low. (S102)

### Identification with Parents
In a society committed to the principle of status achievement, a child tends to identify less with parents who are in a less-esteemed ethnic group. (C086)

### Intermarriage (Ethnic)
When there is a discrepancy in the social status of two ethnic groups, the rate of intermarriage will be low. (T013)

### X    Marital Status of Child
### Parent-Child Relations (Authority)
Among children from the dominant social group, the single are less likely to accept parental authority than are the married. Among low-status children, the single are more likely to accept parental authority. (K121)

### Parent-Child Relations (Authority)
Children from ethnic groups of low status, in countries where the norm of equality is affirmed, are no more likely to reject their parents and parental authority than are children from a dominant group. (K121)

### X    Social Isolation
### Parent-Child Relations (Authority)
The greater the ecological and social isolation of a subordinate social group, the more likely it is that the children will be acceptant of parental authority and standards. (K121)

## RANK OF FAMILY    X    Infant Betrothal
Infant betrothal is more likely to occur among families of high status. (H138)

### Marital Adjustment
Persons who come from a family that is respected in the community are more likely to have marital success. (B244)

### Occupational Rank of Husband
The husband/father's occupational status is correlated with the status of his family within the community. (P062)

## RANK OF FATHER    X    Mental Illness/Neurosis
The families of neurotic patients are more likely than those of mentally ill patients to have fathers who are successful in the community. (M061)

### Residence (Matrilocal)
Patterns of matrilocal residence are more likely to be infringed if the father is wealthy or of high political status. (C056)

## RANK OF HUSBAND    X    Adoption of Husband
Men who are adopted into the families of their wives tend to be of lower status. (H082)

### Adultery, Attitude Toward
Reprisals against adultery are more severe if the husband's social rank is high. (B201)

### Descent (Matrilineal)
When the descent system is matrilineal, the status of the husband tends to be subordinate. (Y001)

### Endogamy
The censure of the wife by the community at the infringement of rules of caste endogamy will be less severe if the husband is of a higher status. (P020)

### Property
When women have control of the house and of the strategic resources, the status of the husband tends to be low. (L059)

### Remarriage
Remarriage of the widow is less likely to occur if the status of the deceased husband was high. (W098)

### Residence (Matrilocal)
When residence is matrilocal the husband's position will be subordinate to the other males in the extended family household. (H032)

### Residence (Patrilocal)
The violation of patterns of patrilocal residence is more likely to occur if the husband is of low status. (S115)

## RANK OF HUSBAND/ADULTERER
### X    Adultery, Attitude Toward
The action taken by a husband against the adulterer will vary with the relative rank of the individuals concerned. (T069)

## RANK OF HUSBAND/WIFE    X    Kin Terminology
The relative status of the husband and wife will tend to be reflected in the terms with which they address one another. (B083)

### Marriage Payment
If the status of the husband and wife is unequal, the marriage payment is likely to be high. (E055)

### Rank of Man/Woman
The relative rank of male and female in the society is likely to be paralleled by their relative rank within the family. (C090)

### Subsistence Pattern (Pastoral)
Inequality between husband and wife is more common in pastoral societies. (H165)

### Cohesion of Kin-Group
Allegiance to specific sections of the kin-group will tend to be directly correlated with their social rank. (G038)

More distant kin bonds will be remembered and exercised if they are links to important kin-groups and outstanding individuals. (K045)

## RANK OF KIN-GROUP
### X　Stability of Kin-Group
Fission is more likely to occur among kin-groups of high status. (S140)

## RANK OF KINSMEN　　X　Joking Relationship
The joking relationship tends to obtain between kinsmen who are not in a superordinate-subordinate relationship. (D034)

A joking relationship is more likely between kinsmen who are of equal status. (L070)

## RANK OF LINEAGE　　X　Economic Rank
The rank of a lineage will be directly correlated with its economic status. (S158)

### Genealogical Depth
The rank of the lineage will be directly correlated with the depth of its genealogy. (F039)

### Genealogy, Importance of
When the relative collateral rank of a lineage defines the social status of the individual, genealogies will assume a place of great importance in the society. (K049)

### Intermarriage
The rank of a lineage will be determined by the extent to which it intermarries with superior groups. (S158)

### Lineage Ties
Ancient lineage affiliations with a more powerful lineage are more likely to be revived if the status of a lineage is low. (E047)

### Moiety
Lineage ranking is less likely to occur in societies with a moiety system. (N066)

### Preferential Marriage
Where the marriage chain is genuinely circular, the marriage rule does not imply any absolute difference of economic, political, or ritual status between the intermarrying groups. (L177)

### Residence, Length of
The rank of a lineage will tend to be higher if its members have lived longer in the villages. (S158)

## RANK OF MAN/WOMAN
### X　Rank of Husband/Wife
The relative rank of male and female in the society is likely to be paralleled by their relative rank within the family. (C090)

## RANK OF MEN　　　　X　Acculturation
The status of male will tend to be accorded greater importance under European acculturative pressures. (S120)

### Residence (Avunculocal)
Avunculocal residence develops out of a prior matrilocal residence in response to the strengthening of the status of men. (F019)

A change in culture or in the conditions of life which significantly enhances the status importance and influence of men will tend to result in avunculocal residence in societies where the rule of descent is matrilineal. (M019)

### Residence (Patrilocal)
Patrilocal residence seems to be promoted by any change in culture or the conditions of life which significantly enhances the status importance and influence of men in relation to the opposite sex. (M019)

## RANK OF MEN/WOMEN　　　　X　Descent
The rule of descent is only indirectly correlated with the ranked status of the sexes (insofar as the rule is connected with the mode of residence). (L110)

## RANK OF MINORITIES
### X　Intermarriage (Racial and Ethnic)
The greater the rise in social rank of a minority, the greater the rate of racial and ethnic intermarriage. (B311)

## RANK OF PARENTAL GROUP　　　X　Residence
Residential affiliation will be affected by the relative social status of the parental groups. (G029)

## RANK OF WIFE　　　　X　Acculturation
As the group becomes acculturated, the status of the wife becomes more egalitarian. (S051)

### Age of Child
As the wife grows old and becomes the mother of adult sons and daughters, her social position improves. (W082)

### Children, Evaluation of
Where children are highly valued, the status of the wife is directly correlated with her fertility. (D040)

### Divorce
Divorce is less likely to occur if the status of the wife is high. (R040)

### Marriage Order
The status of the wife tends to be directly correlated with the order in which she was married. (W082)

### Marriage Payment
The status of the wife is directly correlated with the size of her marriage payments. (K066)

### Preferential Marriage
The status of the wife will be higher if her marriage conforms to the preferential marriage pattern. (K062)

### Property Rights
The status of the wife will be directly correlated with her property rights. (W082)

## RANK OF WIFE'S FAMILY
### X　Power Structure of Family
The privileges a woman has are directly correlated with the prestige of her family of orientation. (B032)

## RANK OF WIVES　　X　Conflict Between Wives
Overt conflict between wives will tend to occur between wives who are of the same age and level of seniority. (B054)

## Kin Terminology

Status distinction between wives in a polygynous family will tend to be reflected in the kinship terminology. (S124)

## Residence (Patrilocal)

The status of wives in a polygynous marriage is more likely to be equal if the residence pattern is virilocal. (W105)

## RANK OF WOMEN          X   Abortion

The abortion rate will rise with the increasing independence of women. (H111)

## Acculturation

When the woman commands the central position and authority in the family, the ethnic group will tend to be resistant toward acculturation. (B055)

## Age-Groups

The low status of women relative to men is partly a result of the age-village organization. (W128)

## Age of Male Child

In patrilineal societies, the status of a woman tends to be directly correlated with the age of her son. (F073)

## Age of Women

The status of women is directly correlated with their age. (L079)

## Competition Among Wives

In polygynous societies the acute competition among a man's various wives for the position of favorite decreases the status of women in relation to men. (W128)

## Descent (Bilateral)

The status of women tends to be higher in bilateral than in patrilineal societies. (K060)

## Descent (Matrilineal)

In matrilineal societies women tend to occupy a relatively high, if unofficial, status in the society. (M069)

## Descent (Patrilineal)

The status of women in a society with a strong patrilineal organization tends to be low. (K049)

## Desertion

Desertion is more likely to occur where women are regarded by wives as occupying subordinate status. (S266)

## Division of Labor by Sex

The status of women is more likely to be high where there is not a rigid sexual division of labor. (W081)

## Divorce, Age at

A woman is more likely to initiate divorce when she reaches old age when her status as an elderly woman independent of her marital status is high. (G142)

## Economic Dependence of Women

When women are economically independent, their rank will tend to be equal to that of men. (G028)

## Endogamy (Community)

Village endogamy strengthens the status of women. (P008)

## Fertility

The rank of women tends to be directly correlated with their fertility. (H139)

## Homosexuality, Attitude Toward

Societies in which homosexuality is less disapproved are more likely to hold women in low esteem. (C091)

## Husband-Wife Relations (Power)

In an informal decision-making situation in which the husband and wife disagree on a number of decisions, the proportion of decisions finally won by the wife will vary directly with the power position of the wife vis-à-vis the husband as defined by the culture. (S013)

## Inheritance

Where women inherit and transmit property equally with men, their status will tend to be equal to that of the men. (P011)

## Initiation Rites

When the status of women is inferior to that of men, they will tend to be excluded from the initiation rites of the males and fail to have initiation rites of their own. (J007)

## Legal Status of Women

Societies which grant women the rights to initiate divorce and to remarry in widowhood also grant them a higher rank (relative to men) than do societies which do not grant these rights. (G028)

## Magic (Spirits)

If the rank of women is low, they are more likely to appear as male spirits. (F043)

## Marital Stability

Marital stability is inversely correlated with the status of women. (B302)

The status of women is directly correlated with the degree of marital stability. (H103)

## Musical Style

When women are secluded, owned, and exploited, the musical style will be characterized by high-pitched, strident singing. (L025)

The bass song style is linked with equality of status for women. (L025)

Where women are made into chattels, the musical style tends to have a high degree of emotional content. (L025)

## Neurosis (Hysteria)

In societies in which the female suffers many disadvantages and lower self-esteem, hysteria will be more common among females. (P058)

## Polygyny

The increasing status of women tends to lead to a breakdown in polygynous patterns. (L079)

## Preferential Marriage (Exchange)

Exchange marriage as a preferential pattern tends to be abandoned with the rise in the status of women. (M105)

## Property Rights

When women have no rights over land, their position in the family is low and inferior. (H171)

## Religion (Christianity)

The status of women tends to improve in families which have adopted Christianity. (W082)

## Religion (Islam)

The adoption of Islam tends to result in the lowering of the status of women. (C057)

### Reproduction
When the mother is thought to have the exclusive role in procreation her rank is higher. (M241)

### Residence (Bilocal)
Under sedentary conditions of life, bilocal residence tends to be associated with an approximate equality in status of the two sexes, especially with regard to the ownership and inheritance of property and privileges. (M019)

### Residence (Matrilocal)
Matrilocal residence tends to be associated with a high status of women. (M019)

The rank of women tends to be higher under patterns of matrilocal residence. (S098)

### Sex Ratio
The scarcity of women—and consequent competition for them as wives—enhances the status of women. (W056)

### Sex-Role Definition
Where the activities of women are restricted to household duties, their status tends to be low. (S115)

Where there is a marked social segregation of the sexes, the status of women will tend to be low. (S153)

When there is a marked separation of masculine and feminine interests, the status of women tends to be low. (W097)

### Sexual Permissiveness
A high position of women is associated with sexual permissiveness. (M238)

### Sibling Rank
When the status of women is almost equal to that of their husbands, their social equivalence and unity with their brothers will also be more strongly emphasized. (G028)

### Subsistence Pattern (Agricultural)
The status of women in agricultural societies tends to be high as a result of the economic importance of their social role. (L082)

### Subsistence Pattern (Hunting)
In societies with hunting economies, the status of the women will tend to be low. (L082)

### Subsistence Pattern (Pastoral)
The status of women in pastoral societies tends to be low. (P024)

### Values (Individualism)
An increase in individualism results in a rise in women's position. (F069)

In matrilineal societies, increasing individualism should produce a lowering of women's positions. (F069)

### Warfare
There is an association between the cessation of warfare and a rise in the status of women. (O030)

### RANKING IN LINEAGE          X   Segmentation
Fission is more likely to occur when there is ranking within the lineage structure. (C091)

### RANKING OF LINEAGES
#### X   Genealogy, Adjustment of
The manipulation of genealogy tends to occur in societies with a ranked lineage system. (E028)

### Segmentation
The presence of a rank lineage system inhibits the development of a segmentary lineage structure. (L076)

### Stratification
A system of ranked lineages provides a basis for the emergence of social stratification. (K049)

### READING HABITS OF FAMILY
#### X   Creativity/I.Q. of Child
Families of highly intelligent children (Binet) are more likely to subscribe to many magazines than are the families of highly creative children (Guilford-Cattell). (G132)

### RECIDIVISM
#### X   Parent-Child Relations (Rejection)
Habitual criminals tend to have had rejecting parents. (M199)

### RECREATION          X   Child-Rearing Practices (Nurturance/Dependency)
Games of physical skill seem to be positively associated with low permissiveness and high conflict over nurturance and self-reliant behavior. (R003)

### Child-Rearing Practices (Permissiveness)
The presence of games of strategy is positively associated with low permissiveness in child training, high severity of bowel training, and high reward for obedient behavior. (R003)

### Children
Recreational activities of married couples tend to become more differentiated after the birth of children. (B209)

### Class
Family and kinship play a more important role in providing for companionship and recreational needs among urban working-class people than among urban people at a high social rank. (D010)

Children of middle-class parents take out physical and sexual drives in ritualized forms (e.g., sports competition) more than lower-class children do. (R127)

### Divorce
Divorce is less apt to occur where the husband has the alternative companionship of male friends in recreational activities. (D083)

Where there are opportunities for outdoor recreation, the divorce rate will be lower. (D083)

### Juvenile Delinquency
The more favorable the adolescent's attitude toward family recreation, the less likely it is that he will show delinquent behavior. (N063)

The greater the frequency of family recreation, the less likely it is that the child will show delinquent behavior. (N063)

### Maternal Overprotectiveness
The maternally overprotected child is more likely to be interested in reading and less likely to be interested in sports.

Children who are subject to maternal overprotection tend to have passive recreational habits and to display a notable lack of interest in sports. (L161)

### Scholastic Achievement of Son
Boys who are under achievers are more likely than higher achievers to describe their families as sharing recreational activities. (E102)

### Size of Family
Small families engage in more activities together than do large families. (E102)

## RECREATION OF DAUGHTER
### X   Employment of Mother
Adolescent daughters of lower-class working mothers report fewer leisure-time activities than do those of middle-class working mothers. (G156)

Among middle-class adolescent daughters, those whose mothers work tend to engage in a great deal of organized and unorganized leisure activities. (G156)

## REFERENCE GROUP    X   Cohesion of Family
Conflicting reference groups for various members of the family tend to lead to mutual alienation from the family. (B202)

### Size of Family
The larger the family, the more likely it is that children will choose organized groups rather than school chums as their reference groups. (R111)

### Values (Familism)
Girls are more likely to have as their goal being a good family member if their reference group is an organized group, but are more likely to expect praise from their parents for this attribute if their reference group is their school friends. (R111)

## REFERENCE GROUP (FAMILY)
### X   Occupational Aspirations
Boys whose reference group is the immediate family are more likely to plan to go to college or to obtain permanent, salaried employment than to plan to loaf, to go into farming, to go into the army, or to work part time. (R111)

## RELIGION    X   Aggression
There is no relationship between a parent's religious affiliation and antisocial or socialized aggression of the son. (M210)

### Artificial Insemination, Attitude Toward
Roman Catholics are more likely to disapprove of artificial insemination, regardless of whether the donor is the husband or anonymous, than are persons with other religious affiliations. (V035)

### Authoritarianism
In small families, Catholic parents are more likely than are Protestant parents to be either autocratic or authoritarian. (E100)

### Authority Structure of Family
Protestant children are more likely than Catholic children to see authority as residing in either the father or mother rather than being equally distributed between the parents. (H180)

The amount of paternal authority does not vary significantly between Catholic and Protestant families. (K030)

### Authority Structure of Family (Patriarchal)
Indigenous patterns of patriarchal authority facilitates a conversion to Christianity. (F060)

### Birth Control
The use of contraceptives is lower for Catholics than for Protestants and lower for Protestants than for Jews. (F101)

There is no correlation between religious affiliation and the planning of pregnancy. (P080)

### Child-Rearing Attitudes
Catholic parents are more likely than Protestant parents to value filial obedience. (E102)

### Child-Rearing Attitudes (Dependency)
There is no significant difference between Protestant and Catholic mothers' attitudes toward independence training in social settings where Catholics have moved away from more traditional Catholic attitudes. (M246)

### Child-Rearing Practices (Authoritarianism/Democratic)
Catholic and Protestant parents are similar in the control they exercise over their younger sons and daughters; only Catholic and Protestant fathers (not mothers) differ in relating to their older adolescents. Protestant fathers tend to be democratic, equalitarian, or permissive in rearing their older children, and proportionally more Catholic fathers tend to be either autocratic or authoritarian. (E100)

### Child-Rearing Practices (Control)
Parental affiliation with traditional churches (i.e., those that deny the competence of the actor and exalt the direct control of man's affairs by God) is associated with use of the threat, as a means of control, that God will punish the child. (N055)

### Child-Rearing Practices (Curiosity/Autonomy)
Protestant parents are more likely than Catholic parents to encourage curiosity and personal autonomy on the part of their children. (E102)

### Child-Rearing Practices (Dependency)
Catholic parents tend to begin independence training at a later date in the development of their children than do Protestant parents. (E100)

Protestant mothers stress independence and mastery in child rearing earlier than do Catholic mothers. (M246)

### Child-Rearing Practices (Discipline)
Protestant mothers are more likely to use symbolic sanctions for discipline, as opposed to physical punishment, while Catholic mothers are more likely to use physical sanction. (V037)

### Child-Rearing Practices (Restrictiveness)
Catholic fathers, but not Catholic mothers, tend to increase their control and restrictiveness as their children become older; this tendency is reversed among Protestant fathers. (E100)

Catholic mothers are more likely to be restrictive than are Protestant mothers. (V037)

### Child-Rearing Practices (Rewards)
Catholic mothers are more likely to use material rewards for good behavior than are Protestant mothers. (V037)

### Child-Rearing Values
Protestant parents are more likely than Catholic parents to stress the importance of knowledge. (M246)

### Child-Rearing Values (Dependency)

Protestant parents are more likely than Catholic parents to believe that children should be by themselves, away from their parents, and are often better when they are on their own. (M246)

Protestant parents are more likely than Catholic parents to stress the importance of an individual's finding out things on his own. (M246)

There is no significant difference between Protestant and Catholic mothers' attitudes toward independence training in social settings where Catholics have moved away from more traditional Catholic attitudes. (M246)

### Class

Religion is a more potent factor in the family life of the working-class family than in the business-class or university family. (B033)

### Cohesion of Family

Catholic families are more strongly integrated than are non-Catholic families. (Z006)

### Cohesion of Kin-Group

Kin bonds tend to be weaker if members of the family do not share the same religious affiliation. (H164)

### Dating

Catholic divorcées are less likely to date than are Protestant divorcées. (G157)

### Desertion

Desertion cases are more likely to be among Catholics than among other religious groups. (G156)

The fact that in desertion cases Catholics are overrepresented may be due to differential reporting rates between Catholics and non-Catholics. (K010)

The fact that the Catholic Church does not recognize divorce may be one factor in the overrepresentation of Catholics in desertion cases. (K010)

The overrepresentation of Catholics in desertion cases may be due to marital conflicts which stem from differing nationality backgrounds. (K010)

The overrepresentation of Catholics in desertion cases is only partially explained by the fact that a greater proportion of Catholics are found in the lower occupational classes than are other religious groups. (K010)

### Divorce

Catholics are less likely to get divorced than non-Catholics. (C023)

Among marriages of mixed faiths the divorce rate is highest when the husband is Catholic and the wife Protestant. (G156)

Marriages between persons without religious affiliations have the highest divorce rates, followed by persons of interfaith marriages. (G156)

When both husband and wife are of the same religion, few differences in divorce rates exist among Catholics, Protestants, and Jews. (G156)

When both spouses are of the same religious affiliation, their proneness to divorce is lower. (G156)

Divorce is more likely among Protestants than Jews and among Jews more than Catholics. (M001)

### Divorce Adjustment

Catholic divorcées are slightly more likely to experience difficult emotional problems during divorce than are Protestant divorcées. (G157)

### Divorce Agreements

There is no difference between Protestant and Catholic husbands regarding the keeping of divorce agreements, although husbands with no religious affiliation are less likely to keep their agreements. (G157)

### Divorce, Attitude Toward

The wife's and husband's religious affiliation is unrelated to the degree of approval/disapproval expressed by her or his kin and friends. (G157)

### Divorce Complaints

Divorcées of Protestant husbands are more likely than are divorcées of Catholic husbands to complain that personality conflicts were a cause of divorce. (G157)

Protestant divorcées are no more likely than Catholic divorcées to claim that personality conflicts were a cause of divorce. (G157)

Divorcées from mixed-faith marriages are no more likely than those from like-faith marriages to claim that personality conflicts were a cause of divorce. (G157)

Divorcées of Protestant husbands are more likely than are divorcées of Catholic husbands to claim that value conflicts were a cause of divorce. (G157)

Protestant divorcées are more likely than are Catholic divorcées to claim that value conflicts were a cause of divorce. (G157)

### Divorce Decision

The stability of the final decision to divorce is not associated with either the husband's or the wife's religious affiliation. (G157)

### Divorce, Initiation of

The religious affiliation of the wife is unrelated to who first suggests a divorce. (G157)

Among Catholic and Protestant divorcées, Catholic divorcées who rarely attend church are most likely to claim that they were the first to suggest a divorce. (G157)

### Divorce Process

The wife's or husband's religious affiliation is unrelated to the time taken between a serious consideration of divorce and filing suit. (G157)

Frequency of church attendance by the wife is unrelated to the length of time taken between a serious consideration of divorce and filing suit. (G157)

### Educational Aspirations

The importance of parental stress on college for the educational aspirations of their children reduces, but does not destroy, the effect of religious affiliation on college plans. Jews remain, at every stress level, the highest, followed by Protestants and then Catholics. (B291)

Jewish parents, followed by Protestant and Catholic parents, place the greatest emphasis on a college education for their children. (E102)

In the lower classes, Protestant youths are more likely to have positive attitudes regarding school and to feel certain about completing high school than are Catholic youths, regardless of the size of their families. (E102)

Among college-oriented youths, Catholic youths are less likely to have parents who insist on college than are Protestant youths. (E102)

Among large lower-class families, Catholic parents are more likely to stress college for older sons than are Protestant parents. (E102)

### Engagement, Stability of
Engagements between persons of different religious affiliations are more likely to be broken than are those of persons of like faith. (G157)

### Father-Child Relations (Authoritarianism)
Autocratic and authoritarian fathers are most likely to be found in large Catholic families, particularly in relation to older adolescents. (E100)

### Father-Son Relations, Importance of
Societies in which the father-son relationship is stressed will tend to be polytheistic. (H172)

### Fecundity
Catholics are more likely to have impairments to fecundity than are Protestants. (F101)

### Fertility
Protestants are more likely than Catholics to have no children and Catholics are more likely to have a large number of children than are Protestants. This proposition is also denied. (B033)

The proportion of childless couples is highest for Protestant-Catholic mixed marriages and lowest for the Catholic couple. (B033)

### Friendship
Protestant divorcées are as likely as Catholic divorcées and those of other religious faiths to maintain the friends they had during the marriage while the separation and divorce are taking place. (G157)

### Handicapped Child, Response to
Among mothers of cerebral-palsied children, Catholic mothers are more guilty, unrealistic, and withdrawn than are Protestant and Jewish mothers. (J027)

Catholic mothers of handicapped children have more pathological attitudes than do Protestant and Jewish mothers. (J027)

Among mothers of cerebral-palsied children, Protestant mothers are less anxious than are Catholic or Jewish mothers. (J027)

### Homogamy
Jews are most likely to marry endogamously, followed by Catholics and lastly by Protestants. (G156)

Persons who marry outside of their own religions are less convinced believers in the religion to which they ostensibly belong. (G156)

### Husband-Wife Relations (Conflict)
In marriages of mixed faiths, a Catholic wife is likely to tolerate more conflict than is a Protestant wife before initiating a divorce. (G156)

### Illegitimacy (Adoption)
Catholic unmarried mothers are less likely to give up their children than are mothers with other religious affiliations. (J020)

### Independence of Women
Women will tend to become more independent with the adoption of Christianity. (H103)

### Intermarriage
Intermarriage is most frequent among Protestants, less among Catholics, and least among Jews. (B244)

### Intermarriage (Ethnic)
It is more likely that interethnic intermarriage will take place among Protestants than among Catholics, and among Catholics than among Jews. (H014)

### Intermarriage (Religious)
Intermarriage is more likely to take place among Catholics than among Protestants. (C006)

In interfaith marriages the child is more likely to be brought up in the faith of the mother than in that of the father. This is less true of Catholics and Jews than of Protestants. (C134)

In mixed marriages the most common tendency seems to be that the children, especially the daughters, follow the faith of the mother. (L010)

### Marital Adjustment
Marital adjustment is associated with the membership of both husband and wife in the same church. (B033)

### Marital Adjustment X Institutional Care
Among Catholic parents, marital adjustment is not related to whether the retarded child is living at home or is institutionalized. (J027)

Among Protestant and Jewish families, lower level of marital adjustment is related to the retarded child living at home rather than being institutionalized. (J027)

### Marital Stability
Marital breakup is no more likely to occur in areas with a large amount of Catholics than in areas with few Catholics. (L001)

There is a curvilinear relationship between the predominance of a religion in a particular area and marital breakup among members of the religion. (L001)

Areas in which a particular religion is almost completely dominant or just barely a majority are likely to have less marital breakup among the members of the religion than are areas where the predominance of the religion is between the extremes cited. (L001)

### Marriage Chances
Second-generation American Catholics are more likely to marry than are second-generation Americans of other religions. (H203)

### Marriage Counseling
Catholics are more likely than Protestants to seek marriage counseling. (G157)

### Mate Selection
There is a high correlation between mate selection and similarity of religion. (C103)

### Mate Selection (Residence)
The Protestant is more likely to marry someone who lives within eight standard city blocks of him than is the Catholic. (C002)

### Mental Illness (Social Adjustment)
This study failed to replicate the findings of a previous study that mental patients in Catholic families were less

likely to perform at high levels socially or occupationally after release from the hospital than were those from Protestant or Jewish families. (F124)

### Mental Retardation
Catholic mothers are more acceptant of their retarded children than are non-Catholic mothers. The contrary is also asserted. (Z006)

Catholic and Protestant mothers are equally accepting of their retarded children. (J027)

### Mother-Son Relations
Catholic males report closer similarity to their mothers and approve more conforming, nurturant, and acquiescent behavior than do Jewish males (Leary's Interpersonal Check List). (H180)

### Parent-Child Relations (Authoritarianism)
Controlling for family size, Catholic parents are more likely to be autocratic or authoritarian in relating to their children than are Protestant parents. (E100)

### Parent-Child Relations (Financial Help)
Among Jews, children who are less orthodox in their religious beliefs than their aged parents are more likely to give financial aid to them than are children who have the same religious identification. (G119)

There is no significant association between the religious affiliation of children (Orthodox, Conservative, or Reform Jews and no religion or non-Jews) and the giving of financial aid to their aged parents. (G119)

### Personality of Child (Self-Esteem)
Catholic children of divorced parents are more likely than Catholics and Jews from intact families to have low self-esteem, but divorce makes no difference in level of self-esteem among Protestant families. (R129)

Among children whose families have been broken by death, there is no relationship between religion and low self-esteem. (R129)

Among Catholics and Protestants, differences in levels of self-esteem between only boys and girls are much smaller than is the case among Jewish children. (R129)

### Personality Problems
Among the mentally ill, the mother of the patient tends to be more disturbed if the patient is Jewish; the father is the more disturbed parent if the patient is Protestant. (S187)

### Political Importance of Clan
The political functions of the clan tend to be immediately lost upon conversion to Islam. (G072)

### Power Structure of Family
Husband dominance tends to be more common in Catholic than in Protestant families (controlling for social class). (E100)

### Premarital Pregnancy
Catholics are no more likely than Protestants to have higher incidences of premarital pregnancy. (M243)

Jews tend to have the lowest premarital pregnancy rates. (M243)

### Premarital Sex Relations
The use of a virgin in ceremonial roles is more likely to occur in societies where premarital chastity is valued. (D057)

### Psychosomatic Illness
Catholics and Jews whose parents are divorced are more likely than are those from intact families to have psychosomatic symptoms, but this is less true of Protestants. (R129)

### Psychosomatic Illness X Broken Home
Among children whose families have been broken by death, there is no relationship between religion and the likelihood of the child to have many psychosomatic symptoms. Catholics and Jews are no more likely than Protestants to have many psychosomatic symptoms. (R129)

### Religious Self-Expectations
The likelihood that adolescents' religious self-expectations will increase is greater as parental religious expectations increase. (R002)

### Religious Training of Child
Among marriages of mixed faiths, Catholic or Jewish fathers are more likely to insist that the child be raised in the Catholic or Jewish faith than are Protestant fathers to insist that the child be reared as a Protestant. (G156)

### Remarriage
Controlling for the time lapse since the divorce, Protestant divorcées are more likely to remarry than are Catholic divorcées. (G157)

Though religious affiliation does not affect the general pattern of greater satisfaction with the second marriage, Catholic divorcées who have remarried are slightly more inclined than are Protestant divorcées to say that the second marriage is much better. (G157)

### Scholastic Motivation
Among large lower-class families, Catholic adolescents are higher in academic motivation than are Protestant adolescents. (E102)

### Sexual Disability of Husband (Divorce)
In marriages where the husband has been physically disabled, Catholics are no more likely than Protestants to be divorced or separated and Jews are less likely to be divorced than are Gentiles. (N060)

### Size of Family
Within the same social strata, Catholic parents tend to have larger families than Protestant parents do. (E100)

Catholics make more revisions in the desired number of children than Protestants do. (F101)

A wife's religion is more likely to determine the size of the family than is the husband's. (F101)

### Stability of Extended Family
Conversion to Islam tends to result in the weakening of the extended family. (G072)

### Stability of Family
The influence of religion is a significant factor in the stabilization of the family. (B033)

### Sterilization
Protestant wives are more likely than Catholic wives to have operations for the prevention of conception. (F101)

# RELIGION (ANCESTOR CULT)
### X Children, Evaluation of
The importance of children will tend to be stressed in

societies which have institutionalized an ancestor cult. (F058)

#### Cohesion of Clan
Clan unity will tend to be reinforced by the institutionalization of an ancestral cult. (B111)

#### Descent (Unilineal)
The composition of the ancestor cult group will reflect the patterns of unilineal descent. (R023)

#### Economic Dependence
The ancestor cult tends to deteriorate under conditions of economic independence. (W092)

#### Political Centralization
The more centralized type of political organization is correlated with a somewhat more well-defined ancestor cult. (H172)

#### Residence
The ancestral cult is usually connected with the main cult of the society, particularly in settled communities where there can be permanent association with grave sites. (M168)

#### Stability of Family
An ancestor cult has a stabilizing influence on the family unit. (K092)

### RELIGION (ANCESTOR WORSHIP)    X    Adoption
Adoption will tend to be stressed in societies which have ancestor worship. (L088)

#### Authority Structure of Family
Ancestor worship serves to reinforce authority of elders and of the oldest male. (H164)

#### Clan, Importance of
Ancestor worship tends to reinforce the importance of clan affiliation. (H164)

#### Cohesion of Family
With the weakening of ancestor worship, family solidarity tends to deteriorate. (H103)

#### Cohesion of Kin-Group
Ancestor worship reinforces the solidarity of the kin-group. (R023)

#### Cohesion of Lineage
The ancestor cult increases the sense of group identification and group solidarity among members of the lineage. (W115)

#### Descent (Matrilineal/Patrilineal)
Ancestor worship serves to reinforce the distinction between paternal and maternal kin-groups. (H164)

#### Subsistence Pattern (Pastoral)
Ancestor worship tends to be associated with pastoral economies. (H164)

### RELIGION (BELIEFS)
#### X    Child-Rearing Practices (Conformity)
The greater the extent to which rewards are contingent upon conformity to parental demands, the greater the degree to which supernatural nurturance is thought to be contingent upon obedience to supernatural demands. (S036)

### RELIGION (CHANGE)
#### X    Intermarriage (Religious)
Spouses are as likely in mixed marriages to change from Catholicism to Protestantism as from Protestantism to Catholicism. (L010)

### RELIGION (CHRISTIANITY)
#### X    Authority Structure of Family
With the adoption of Christianity, a family authority structure becomes increasingly egalitarian. (B122)

Christianity will tend to weaken the authority of the extended family leader inasmuch as his office rests upon supernatural sanction. (O023)

#### Avoidance Relationship
Avoidance taboos are less likely to be respected among Christians. (H164)

#### Cohesion of Clan
When a matrilineal society is subject to Christian missionary pressure toward patrilineality, the clan structure disintegrates. (E016)

#### Descent
Matrilineal societies will tend to be more resistant to the acceptance of Christianity than will patrilineal societies. (H060)

#### Inheritance (Matrilineal)
Under missionary pressure, patterns of inheritance will tend to shift from matrilineal to patrilineal. (M031)

#### Marital Stability
There is no direct correlation between Christianity and marital stability. (F062)

#### Polygyny
The abandonment of polygynous practices is directly correlated with the strength of missionary pressure. (H058)

#### Preferential Marriage (Levirate)
The practice of the levirate tends to be abandoned with the adoption of Christianity. (S121)

#### Rank of Women
The status of women tends to improve in families which have adopted Christianity. (W082)

#### Residence (Neolocal)
The development of a separate household arrangement tends to be stimulated by the pressure of European missionaries. (V017)

### RELIGION (CHURCH MEMBERSHIP)
#### X    Marital Adjustment
Marital satisfaction is directly related to being affiliated with a church. (B001)

### RELIGION (CLAN CEREMONIES)
#### X    Cohesion of Clan
The occurrence of ceremonies on the clan level will function to reinforce the unity of the clan. (M046)

### RELIGION/CLASS    X    Intermarriage
Class intermarriage is as likely to take place as is religious intermarriage. (M015)

### RELIGION (CONVERSION)    X    Cohesion of Clan
Clan cohesion tends to deteriorate with the conversion of its members to nonindigenous religions. (S099)

### RELIGION/EDUCATION    X    Birth Control
When the rhythm method is the only method of family limitation used, it is inversely related to education for Catholics and directly related for Protestants. (F101)

#### Size of Family

Among Catholics there is a direct relationship between education and a positive attitude toward large family size, while there is an inverse relationship among Protestants. (F101)

### RELIGION (ISLAM)    X    Rank of Women

The adoption of Islam tends to result in the lowering of the status of women. (C057)

### RELIGION (KIN-BASED)
#### X    Economic Pattern (Trade)

The abandonment of religious elements that relate directly to kinship or to kin units is directly correlated with an extension and centralization of trade. (W075)

### RELIGION (MATERNAL DEITIES)
#### X    Cannibalism

Cannibalism tends to be associated with matrilineal fertility cults. (W154)

#### Human Sacrifice

Human sacrifice tends to be associated with matrilineal fertility cults. (W154)

#### Religious Anxiety

Religious anxiety is likely to be greater in societies which stress maternal gods. (W154)

### RELIGION OF CHILD    X    Religion of Parents

If the parents differ in degree of religiosity, children are likely to be similar to the parent whose views are closest to the dominant middle-class religious type (modern, liberal Christianity). (P073)

When the parents hold different religious beliefs (along the continuum: fundamentalism—atheism), children are more likely to hold beliefs similar to the mother than to the father. (P073)

### RELIGION OF FATHER    X    Juvenile Delinquency

The religious affiliation of the father and the degree of his religiosity have no significant relation to the delinquent behavior of the child (Cambride-Somerville Study). (M194)

### RELIGION OF HUSBAND/WIFE    X    Divorce

Divorce is more likely to occur among Catholic husbands married to Protestant wives than among Catholic wives married to Protestant husbands. (C006)

### RELIGION OF PARENTS    X    Religion of Child

If the parents differ in degree of religiosity, children are likely to be similar to the parent whose views are closest to the dominant middle-class religious type (modern, liberal Christianity). (P073)

When the parents hold different religious beliefs (along the continuum: fundamentalism—atheism), children are more likely to hold beliefs similar to the mother than to the father. (P073)

### RELIGION (RITUAL)
#### X    Child-Rearing Practices (Dependency)

Where infant dependency needs are anticipated and satisfied *prior* to their expression, supernatural nurturance is more likely to be believed to be contigent upon and evoked by compulsive rituals. (S036)

The greater the initial satisfaction of dependency, the greater the degree to which supernatural nurturance is thought to be contingent upon the employment of compulsive ritual. (S036)

#### Cohesion of Kin-Group

The persistence of the kin-group tends to be associated with its continued importance as a ritual unit. (K045)

#### Stability of Kin-Group

A disintegration of kinship units tends to accompany the destruction of ceremonial life. (B049)

### RELIGION (RITUAL IMPORTANCE OF WOMEN)
#### X    Property

Women's importance in ritual varies directly with the absoluteness of feminine house ownership and strength of clan. (M037)

### RELIGION (RITUAL OBJECTS)    X    Descent

The custodianship or control of scared objects by either men or women is correlated with a corresponding male or female descent line. (M037)

### RELIGION (ROLE OF DEITIES)    X    Anxiety

Societies with predominantly aggressive deities (accompanied by more hurt and pain and less nurturance in infancy) are more likely to produce anxiety in the child than are societies with predominantly benevolent deities (accompanied by considerable nruturance and less pain in infancy). (L141)

#### Authority Structure of Family

The role of the deity will tend to parallel that of the father in the family authority structure. (H084)

#### Child-Rearing Practices (Consistency)

The greater the inconsistency in socialization (that is, the same behavior may be both rewarded and punished), the greater the degree to which supernatural punishment is viewed as occurring arbitrarily, not contingent on good or bad behavior. (S036)

#### Child-Rearing Practices (Dependency)

Where child-rearing practices emphasize independence training, deities are likely to be aggressive rather than benevolent. (L141)

The greater the initial satisfaction of infant dependency needs as soon as they are manifested and the lower the socialization anxiety of dependence, the greater the degree to which supernatural nurturance is contingent upon propitiatory rituals (i.e., the gods give help even if not solicited and help is not contingent on obedience). (S036)

Gods are thought to be more aggressive in societies where boys are subject to strong pressure for self-reliance and independence. (W127)

The belief in aggressive gods requires child training which stresses independence and self-reliance to prepare the child for coping with a hostile world as an adult. (W127)

#### Child-Rearing Practices (Discipline)

The type of punishment by the deity for a breach of religious norms will be similar to discipline patterns within the family system of the society. (H060)

#### Child-Rearing Practices (Indulgence)

Societies with indulgent child-rearing practices have more benevolent deities in the cultural belief system; societies having less indulgent child-rearing practices have more aggressive deities. (L141)—

Societies in which infants are treated indulgently will

perceive gods as benevolent; where indulgence is low, gods will be perceived as aggressive. (W127)

### Child-Rearing Practices (Punishment)
If the nurturing agents (parents, etc.) of the society do not use pain as a control stimulus during infancy, benevolent deities are more common in the belief system. (L141)

Societies with aggressive deities and high pain in the treatment of infants are more likely to have capricious gods than are societies with benevolent deities and low pain in the treatment of infants. (L141)

The severity of parental punishment for disobedience is paralled by supernatural punishment for disobedience of supernatural demands. (S036)

### Descent (Matrilineal)
Cults of the Great Mother are more likely to be found in societies with strong matrilineal emphases. (W154)

### Oedipal Complex
The Oedipal complex is less likely to occur in societies in which discipline is transferred to supernatural sources. (D057)

### Kin Ties (Fictive)
The extension of fictive kin ties on an interclass basis may lead to a conception of the deity and his relationship to the worshipper as that of patron and client. (W075)

### Kinship, Importance of
The decline in the importance of kin ties will be associated with an increased emphasis on a deity associated with nonkin relationships. (W075)

### Mother-Son Relations
If the mother-son tie is emphasized, the religious system has many gods basically more feminine than masculine. (H172)

### Parent-Child Relations (Anxiety)
Societies with predominantly aggressive deities (accompanied by more hurt and pain and less nurturance in infancy) are more likely to produce anxiety on the part of the parents for the child's future welfare than are societies with benevolent deities (accompanied by nurturant child-rearing practices). (L141)

### Parent-Child Relations (Nurturance)
Nurturant parents or parental substitutes are more consistently found in societies with aggressive rather than benevolent deities. (L141)

### Parental Role
Conceptions of supernatural beings correspond to and are projections of the child's parental (or parent-surrogate) images. (S036)

### Paternal Role
The role of the Supreme Deity will be similar to the authority of the father. (H060)

### Socialization, Age of
The earlier the age of socialization, the greater the degree to which supernatural punishment is viewed as not contingent on good behavior. (S036)

## RELIGION (SACRIFICE)
### X   Kin-Group, Importance of
Important kin units will tend to be made more salient by the organization of communal sacrifices. (K050)

## RELIGION/SIZE OF FAMILY
### X   Education of Child
As family size increases, Catholic parents are more likely than Protestant parents to insist on college education for their children. (E102)

### Power Structure of Family
Religious affiliation and size of family have independent effects upon the power that both parents and the adolescent wield in the child-rearing process; the combined effect of both factors (Catholicism and large family size) substantially increases the likelihood of parental dominance. (E100)

## RELIGION (SUPERNATURAL RELIANCE)
### X   Mother-Son Relations
Reliance on the supernatural is found where the mother-son relationship tends to have primary importance over other relationships. (H172)

## RELIGION (TOTEMISM)   X   Conflict in Lineage
There is a positive correlation between sib totemism and intralineage conflict. (F015)

### Dependency
An intense childhood conflict over dependence on the mother appears to be a predisposing, but not sufficient, cause for the development of totemism in a society. (F015)

### Exogamy
Totemic belief is associated with groups that are not specifically exogamous. (G045)

### Preferential Marriage (Cross-Cousin)
The prohibition of cross-cousin marriage may be correlated with the social totemism of the region and to some extent is an effect of the latter. (E065)

## RELIGIOSITY   X   Age at Marriage
Persons who marry at an early age (under 18 years) are less likely to be active in religious activities than are those who marry later.

### Alcoholism
Strong adherance to Catholicism by the mother correlates negatively with alcoholism in the son. (M195)

### Birth Control
The closer the attachment to the Catholic Church, the greater the tendency to avoid contraception, while the closer attachment of Protestants to the church results in a greater use of contraception. (F101)

### Child-Rearing Practices
There is no relationship between strong religious belief and the kinds of child-rearing practices to which a child has been subjected. (B254)

### Dependency
There is no relationship between strong religious beliefs and dependence on the father. (B254)

### Divorce
Catholic divorcées who attend church infrequently following the divorce are likely to claim that they attended more frequently during the marriage. (G157)

Unhappily married couples who are not very religious are more likely to be divorced than are those who are devout. (G157)

### Divorce Decision
For both Protestants and Catholics stable divorce deci-

sions are found among those who are the most devout. (G157)

Among devout divorcées, the devout Catholic is highly stable in her decision to divorce whether or not the husband first suggested the divorce; the devout Protestant is unstable in her divorce decision if it was not the husband who first suggested the divorce. (G157)

The stability of the divorce decision is lowest for those Catholics who attended church most frequently during the marriage and began attending infrequently after the divorce. (G157)

### Divorce, Initiation of
Those Catholics who attend church less frequently are more likely than those who attend with greater frequency to be the first to suggest a divorce. (G157)

### Duration of Marriage
For Catholics, a higher frequency of church attendance increases the mean duration of marriage; for Protestants, a higher frequency of church attendance slightly decreases the duration of marriage. (G157)

### Emotional Problems of Child
In families with regular church attendance, children are less likely to develop emotional problems. (B290)

### Illegitimacy
Unwed mothers and their parents are less likely to attend church as frequently as are the single, never-pregnant girls and their parents. (V027)

### Juvenile Delinquency
Families in which parents and children attend church regularly are less likely to produce delinquents than are families in which members do not. (N057)

### Marital Adjustment
Marital satisfaction is directly related to church attendance. (B001)

Those who are happily married tend to be highly religious. (B033)

Religious wives experiencing low sexual satisfaction will have greater marital satisfaction than will nonreligious wives. (W001)

Sexual drive held constant, religiously oriented women are more apt to feel highly satisfied with their marriages than are nonreligious women. (W155)

### Premarital Sex Relations
The more devout a person (as represented by frequent or infrequent church attendance), the less likely he is to engage in premarital sexual relations. (K160)

### Sexual Activity
Active church members have lower frequencies of sexual outlets than do nonactive church members. (C023)

### Sexual Adjustment
Married couples who are religiously oriented are less apt to associate sexual gratification with marital satisfaction than are nonreligious couples. (W155)

### Sexual Aggression
Religious girls are less likely to report sexually aggressive experiences. (K001)

Girls who regularly attend church are no less likely to have had episodes of sexual aggression than are girls who do not attend church. (K018)

### Social Mobility
Upward social mobility is associated with a reduction in degree of religiosity. (G119)

## RELIGIOSITY OF CHILD
### X   Religious Beliefs of Parents
Children are more likely to have a similar degree of religiosity if both parents hold the same religious ideology (on a continuum from fundamentalism to atheism) than if the parents differ. (P073)

## RELIGIOSITY OF CHILD/PARENTS
### X   Religious Beliefs of Parents
Children are likely to have the same degree of religiosity as their parents if their parents' views conform to the middle-class dominant norms (modern, liberal Christianity). (P073)

## RELIGIOSITY OF HUSBAND–WIFE
### X   Sex Relations
Sexual intercourse in marriage decreases in frequency with increase in religious participation. (C023)

## RELIGIOSITY OF MOTHER
### X   Juvenile Delinquency
If the mother is a devoted Catholic, the child is less likely to become a delinquent than if the mother attends church irregularly or not at all. (M194)

## RELIGIOSITY OF PARENTS          X   Intermarriage
The weaker the ties of parents to religions, the more likely the child is to intermarry. (H240)

## RELIGIOSITY OF WIFE
### X   Husband-Wife Relations (Companionship)
The more constant the religious attendance by the wife (especially if it is more frequent than the husband's), the higher she values companionship with the husband.

## RELIGIOSITY OF WOMEN
### X   Marital Adjustment
Religious women accept more easily the frustrations in their marital lives that would lead nonreligious women to overt counteraggression. (P083)

## RELIGIOUS AFFILIATION          X   Birth Control
Catholic women married to Protestant men practice birth control more than do Protestant women married to Catholic men and both types practice birth control more than when both spouses are Catholic or Protestant. (L010)

## RELIGIOUS ANXIETY
### X   Religion (Maternal Deities)
Religious anxiety is likely to be greater in societies which stress maternal gods. (W154)

## RELIGIOUS BEHAVIOR OF PARENTS
### X   Juvenile Delinquency
Knowledge of religion imputed to the parent, religious rapport, and frequency of discussion of religious matters with parents are all associated with decreasing delinquent behavior. (N052)

## RELIGIOUS BELIEFS
### X   Parent-Child Relations (Authority)
If the child has a strong belief in God, his demands for perfection and omnipotence in his parents decrease; thus, the authority of the parent declines slowly, rather than suddenly, with the discovery that the parental idols have feet of clay. (P083)

## Sex Status
In cross-faith marriages, men abandon their faiths more readily than women. (Z008)

## Surrogate Parent
The supernatural world of upper-class children will be that of the peasant class since upper-class children are reared by servants who are members of the peasant class. (B048)

## RELIGIOUS BELIEFS OF PARENTS
### X  Religiosity of Child
Children are more likely to have a similar degree of religiosity if both parents hold the same religious ideology (on a continuum from fundamentalism to atheism) than if the parents differ. (P073)

### Religiosity of Child/Parent
Children are likely to have the same degree of religiosity as their parents if their parents' views conform to the middle-class dominant norms (modern, liberal Christianity). (P073)

## RELIGIOUS ROLE OF KIN-GROUP
### X  Age-Groups
The degree of corporate organization of age-groups is negatively correlated with the performance by kinship groups of basic political and ritual tasks. (E086)

## RELIGIOUS SELF-EXPECTATIONS    X  Religion
The likelihood that adolescents' religious self-expectations will increase is greater as parental religious expectations increase. (R002)

## RELIGIOUS TRAINING OF CHILD    X  Religion
Among marriages of mixed faiths, Catholic or Jewish fathers are more likely to insist that the child be raised in the Catholic or Jewish faith than are Protestant fathers to insist that the child be reared as a Protestant. (G156)

## REMARRIAGE    X  Adjustment of Child
Regarding their children's adjustment, divorcées who are remarried are more likely to claim satisfaction with the "way things are" than are those who are not remarried. (G157)

The longer the child has been in an intact family the more difficult it is for him to adjust to a new marriage after the former has been dissolved. (R129)

### Age at Marriage
Because norms regarding the age range of a potential spouse grant men more liberty in marrying someone younger, widowers are more likely to remarry than are widows. (G156)

The percentage of marriages that are remarriages varies directly with age. (H013)

### Alcoholism of Son
There is no correlation between the number of the mother's marriages and alcoholism in the son. (M195)

### Anxiety
Children of broken homes are likely to show more anxiety if the parent remarries than if he (she) does not. (R129)

### Celibacy
Because norms approving celibacy are never strict for men, widowers are more likely to remarry than are widows. (G156)

## Child Support
Divorcées who are remarried are slightly more likely than those who are not remarried to report that their husbands resented child-support payments. (G157)

If the husband does not resent the child-support payments, the remarriage of his ex-wife does not affect the continuity of his payments. If the husband does resent the child-support payments, remarriage of his ex-wife is associated with less continuity of child-support payments. (G157)

Remarriage of the divorcée is associated with less continuity of child-support payments by the ex-husband. (G157)

## Children
Widowed or divorced women with children are more likely than those with no children to remarry quickly or not at all. (G011)

## Dating
There is a positive relationship between the divorcée's desire to remarry and her dating frequency. (G157)

When the divorcée desires to remarry, there is a high positive relationship between opportunities to meet people and dating frequency; when the divorcée does not wish to remarry, a low positive relationship is found between social opportunities and dating frequency. (G157)

When there are no social opportunities reported, the relationship between the divorcée's desire to remarry and the frequency with which she dates is positive, but low. (G157)

Controlling for the time lapse since the divorce, there is a positive relationship between the divorcée's having a steady date and her claim that there is someone among her male friends that she would consider a potential spouse. (G157)

## Divorce
Divorced persons are more likely to remarry than to remain not married. (C023)

A high divorce rate in any culture will be accompanied by a high remarriage rate. (G015)

The divorce rate increases with successive marriages. (L024)

## Divorce Adjustment
Divorcées who experience their greatest periods of loneliness during either the separation period or when the decree is granted are more likely than those who experience loneliness during other periods of the divorce procedure to remarry soon after the divorce. (G157)

## Divorce, Attitude Toward
Censure expressed toward the status of the divorced woman acts to push her toward remarriage. (G015)

The ambiguity of status of the divorced woman and her lesser social approval push her toward remarriage. (G015)

Divorcées who remarried earlier are slightly more likely to report social discrimination against them because of their status as divorced. (G157)

A larger proportion of divorcées is likely to claim that

there is someone among their male friends that they might consider marrying if their friends or kin approved or felt indifferent toward the divorce than if they originally disapproved of the divorce. (G157)

### Divorce Complaints
The divorcée's complaints of the husband's staying away, drinking, being with "the boys," and gambling are associated with claims that the experience of the first marriage had made the second earlier. (G157)

### Divorce, Initiation of
Controlling for the time lapse since the divorce, divorcées who claim that their husbands were the first to suggest divorce are less likely to be remarried than when the suggestion was the divorcées or mutual. (G157)

### Divorce Process
Divorcées who take a longer time between a serious consideration to divorce and filing suit are more likely to remarry soon after the divorce. (G157)

### Divorce/Widowhood
Divorced persons are much more likely to remarry than are those who have been widowed. (M242)

### Economic Pattern (Wage Labor)
With the introduction of a wage economy, a man is no longer compelled to remarry after the death of his wife, since the wife's services are no longer indispensible. (W082)

### Education
Remarriage is more likely to take place among highly educated men than among poorly educated men. (O001)

### Education of Divorcée
College-educated divorcées move into a new marriage more slowly than do those divorcées with a high-school or grammar-school education. (G157)

### Employment of Mother
Remarriage is negatively associated with jobholding of the divorcée-mother. (G157)

Remarried divorcées (mothers) are less likely to expect to work than are those who have not remarried. (G157)

### Extra-Marital Relations
Divorcées who are in love with another man during the marriage are more likely to remarry soon after the divorce than are those who are not in love with another man. (G157)

### Father–Child Relations
With remarriage or with increasing time since the divorce, the proportion of divorcées wanting the children to see their fathers more decreases, while the proportion wanting them to see him less increases. (G157)

### Fertility Values
There will be a high rate of remarriage in societies which stress the importance of fertility. (M127)

### Friendship
Divorcées who have a circle of close friends are more likely to claim that there is someone among their male friends that they would consider marrying than are divorcées who do not have friends and those who are not finding friends. (G157)

### Husband-Wife Relations
Divorcées who feel negative or loving attitudes toward their ex-husbands are less likely to claim there is a potential spouse among their male friends than are those who feel friendly or indifferent toward their ex-husbands. (G157)

### Income of Divorcee
Remarried divorcées are more likely to claim they have enough money with which to meet expenses than are those who are not remarried. (G157)

The difference between divorcées with one or two children being more likely to claim enough to meet expenses than those with three or more children declines among those who have remarried. (G157)

Remarried divorcées have higher income expectations than do those not remarried. (G157)

Remarriage is negatively associated with the divorcée feeling that she is economically worse off at present than during the marriage. (G157)

Remarried divorcées are more likely than those who have not remarried to feel that at present they are economically better off than during the marriage. (G157)

Remarried divorcées who have stayed at the same income level are more likely than those who have not remarried to report that they have enough with which to meet expenses. (G157)

Divorcées who are not married are much more likely than those who are married to claim that they wish their income might be steadier or both steadier and larger. (G157)

Remarried divorcés are much more likely than those who are not remarried to claim that one area of improvement since the divorce is the economic. (G157)

### Marital Adjustment
There is an inverse relation between men having been divorced prior to this marriage and marital adjustment in the succeeding marriage. (K161)

### Marital Stability
Unions between previously married people are less stable. (S267)

### Marital Status
A divorced parent with children will remarry sooner than will a widowed parent with children. (B286)

### Mating Forms
The greater the extent to which extraresidential union, consensual cohabitation, and marriage proceed as a typical sequence, the less likely is the resumption of consensual cohabitation by widows or widowers. (S211)

### Parent-Child Relations
The longer the period after marriage in which one parent exerts the influence, the greater the disruption for the child when remarriage occurs. (B286)

### Psychosomatic Illness of Child
Children of divorce, whose mothers remarried, are more likely to have many psychosomatic symptoms than are children whose mothers did not remarry. (R129)

### Race
Remarriage is found more often among Negroes than among whites. (G011)

Negroes tend to move into a remarriage more rapidly than whites do; over time this difference diminishes. (G157)

There are no differences between Negro and white divorcées regarding the degree of satisfaction with the second marriage—the majority claiming greater satisfaction. (G157)

### Rank of Husband
Remarriage of the widow is less likely to occur if the status of the deceased husband was high. (W098)

### Religion
Controlling for the time lapse since the divorce, Protestant divorcées are more likely to remarry than are Catholic divorcées. (G157)

Though religious affiliation does not affect the general pattern of greater satisfaction with the second marriage, Catholic divorcées who have remarried are slightly more inclined than are Protestant divorcées to say that the second marriage is much better. (G157)

### Remarriage of Husband
The divorcée is least likely to feel unhappy at the idea of her ex-husband's remarriage if she has already remarried while he has not remarried and most unhappy if he has remarried and she has not. (G157)

### Residence
A man marrying for the first time and living with his spouse is more likely to double up with relatives or others during the initial two years of his marriage than is a man marrying for the second or subsequent time during the corresponding period of his remarriage. (G011)

### Self-Conception
Children whose divorced mothers or widowed parents remarried tend to have lower self-esteem than do those whose parents did not remarry. (R129)

Children whose parents were separated by death are likely to have as high self-esteem as those from intact families, provided the widowed parent does not remarry. (R129)

The older the child when the family is broken, the more likely he is to have low self-esteem if the mother remarries. (R129)

### Separation
Time lapse since separation does not affect the general pattern of greater satisfaction among divorcées with the second marriage. (G157)

### Sex Status
Among men recently married and living on farms, remarriage is more common than among women recently married and living on farms. (G011)

### Size of Family
Divorcée-mothers with more children are more likely to remarry soon after the divorce. (G157)

### Social Opportunities
Divorcées who claim opportunities to meet people are more likely to feel there is someone among their male friends they would consider marrying than are divorcées who claim no opportunities. (G157)

### REMARRIAGE CHANCES          X   Size of Family
Divorcée-mothers with more children are slightly more likely to consider remarriage to one of their close male friends. (G157)

### REMARRIAGE, COMPARISON WITH FIRST
#### X   Age of Divorcée
Age of the divorcée does not affect the general pattern of greater satisfaction with the second marriage. (G157)

### REMARRIAGE OF HUSBAND        X   Remarriage
The divorcée is least likely to feel unhappy at the idea of her ex-husband's remarriage if she has already remarried while he has not remarried and most unhappy if he has remarried and she has not. (G157)

### REMARRIAGE RATE              X   Marriage Rates
Age-specific remarriage rates are generally higher, age for age, than are age-specific first-marriage rates. (C010)

### Race
Remarriage rates for whites are about the same as for Negroes. (G157)

### Sex Status
At most ages the age-specific remarriage rates for men are much higher than those for women. (C010)

### Size of Family
The more children in the family, the higher the remarriage rate following divorce. (G157)

### RENT                        X   Fertility
Average monthly rent is inversely related to fertility. (D006)

### Size of Family
The larger the proportion of total income going for rent, the smaller the family is likely to be. (C009)

### REPRODUCTION                X   Rank of Women
When the mother is thought to have the exclusive role in preocreation her rank is higher. (M241)

### RESIDENCE                   X   Acculturation
A sedentary, localized, village settlement pattern permits greater resistance to acculturation than does one of a seminomadic food-gathering character. (E021)

When families live in small, scattered, unstable settlements, the degree of acculturation tends to be low. (S046)

### Achievement Motivation
There is no association between family residence (inner and outer industrial and inner and outer residential suburbs) and the child's level of achievement orientation. (C101)

### Adultery, Attitude Toward
Adultery is viewed as a more serious offense when the offender lives close by. (W128)

### Affinal Relations
Parents-in-law and children-in-law are emotionally closer if the children-in-law's own parents have died or if they live at some distance away. (T087).

### Affinal Ties
Affinal obligations are more likely to be maintained if the affines live nearby. (M129)

### Age-Groups

The importance of the age-grade system is inversely correlated with the localization of kin-groups. (E037)

Age-group organizations are more likely to be adopted and retained in societies in which the community pattern is multiclan and endogamous rather than single-clan and exogamous for descent groups are the central focus of loyalty in the latter. (L175)

### Age of Lineage

Patrilineages of recent origin are more often confined to a particular locality than others are. (G022)

### Age of Married Persons

Young couples are more likely to live with one set of parents for a while than are older couples. (G156)

### Authority Structure of Family

The missionary compound system is apt to undermine the family, more especially the respect for and authority of parents. (E080)

### Avoidance Relationship

When a strong avoidance relationship is established between relatives, the kinsmen involved are more likely to avoid common residence. (H062)

### Avuncular Relationship

An avuncular relationship between ego and the maternal uncle tends to be correlated with physical proximity between the intermarrying lineages. (F010)

### Child-Rearing Practices (Praise/Punishment)

Mothers who raise their children in multiple-family dwellings are more sparing in their use of both praise and punishment than are mothers who raise their children in single-family dwellings. (M216)

### Clan

The emergence of a clan structure tends to occur with an increase in the regularity of the residence pattern. (S120)

Clan formation requires some factor (such as war or tribal movements) which makes for dislocation of bands and concentration of them in large multiband communities. (S194)

### Class

The tendency for residential propinquity to operate in mate selection is greater among the lower socioeconomic groups than among the higher ones. (C023)

Old people are more apt to live with other generations of their family when they are of the middle class than when they are of other classes (Vienna). (R120)

### Cohesion of Clan

A greater emphasis on territorial ties is associated with the breakdown of the clan structure. (E016)

The solidarity of the clan structure is inversely correlated with emphasis on territorial ties. (E016)

The strength of ties between clan members is directly correlated with the residential localization of the clan. (F039)

### Cohesion of Community

When the pattern of settlement is dispersed, there is a low social articulation of families within the settlement. (M025)

### Cohesion of Family

Family networks are more closely knit when relatives and friends live in close proximity. (B210)

Stronger sibling and parental family roles are found in the urban-fringe family than in the central-city family. (J003)

### Cohesion of Kin-Group

Common residence will reinforce the cohesion of the kin-group. (F030)

Kinship bonds tend to be weakened if kinsmen are not residentially propinquitous. (H164)

The solidarity of a kin-group is directly correlated with its degree of localization. (H165)

### Cohesion of Lineage

Unilineal units will be weakened if the residence pattern fails to reinforce their membership. (D034)

### Community

An unplanned settlement pattern will tend to occur only where there is no localization of the lineage. (H147)

### Conflict

Conflict within a village or between villages is more likely to occur where the village is composed of a few localized lineages than were lineage members are dispersed throughout the village. (H234)

### Conflict Between Clans

Conflict between clans is more likely to occur if the clans live nearby. (M129)

### Conflict Between Lineages

Hostility tends to be more intense between lineages if they are of different territorial affiliation. (L070)

### Conflict Between Lineages

Hostility tends to be more intense between lineages if they are of different territorial affiliation. (L070)

### Conflict in Clan

The geographical separation of subclans tends to indicate the presence of friction between the groups. (M129)

### Conflict in Family

Separation of family members, one from another, is more likely to lead to family conflict than if the family remains together. (C023)

### Cooperation

Since the ties among male residents under uxorilocality are not based on kinship but on propinquity, they cooperate less among themselves than do males under virilocality. (T080)

### Corporate Kin-Group

The corporate character of a clan or large-scale lineage is directly correlated with the localization of the group. (L051)

### Courtship, Duration of

Throughout the period of the courtship, the degree of residential propinquity remains for the most part unaltered. (C002)

### Dating

Dating partners, like marriage partners, are more likely to live nearby than farther away. (C002)

### Descent

Localized lineages appear to be stronger among matrilocal than among patrilocal societies. (A072)

When a choice of descent may be made among alternatives, residence with a group frequently serves as either a contingent of final factor in fixing present affiliation and that of descendents. (D011)

Variation in residence is closely related to descent group affiliation. (F029)

When the settlement pattern is that of the scattered band, the development of a lineage organization tends to be inhibited. (S046)

### Descent (Bilateral)

Where residence patterns are flexible, bilateral descent tends to occur. (O030)

Dispersion of the town, village, or settlement and a scattering of households are associated with the development of bilaterality. (S192)

### Descent (Patrilineal/Matrilineal)

When there is a simultaneous occurrence of both patrilineal and matrilineal kin-groups, one will tend to be localized and the other non-localized. (M045)

### Descent (Unilineal)

The development of a unilinear kin-group is contingent upon the consistency of residence pattern. (G049)

Postnuptial residence patterns will generally conform to clan descent. (L049)

Clans and extended families disappear with all residence changes except that of avunculocal rule. (M019)

When the residence pattern is consistently matrilocal or patrilocal there will be a tendency for unilineal kin-groups to form. (S065)

### Division of Labor By Sex

The sexual division of labor is not correlated with residence after marriage. (A071)

### Divorce

Areas where lineages have been dispersed have higher divorce rates than do those where lineages are intact. (F073)

Where there is alternating residence accompanied by brother-sister solidarity, the divorce rate between spouses is high. (F076)

### Divorce Process

When marriage duration is over 15 years, there is no difference between rural, small-town, and urban wives regarding the time taken between a serious consideration of divorce and the filing of suit. (G157)

### Economic Conditions

In societies governed by matrilineal descent, wide-span local matrilineages are more likely to exist where access to land or to other valuable natural resources is limited. (T080)

### Economic Cooperation

Where there is no need for families to consolidate for economic cooperation, the localization of lineages tends to be inhibited. (P026)

### Economic Level

Above a minimal level of economic adjustment, a greater degree of variance in the relationship between residence rule and economic organization occurs. (A072)

### Economic Rank

When the husband's wife's family is poor, residence is more likely to be matrilocal; if both are wealthy, it is likely to be bilocal. (G013)

Patterns of matrilocal residence will be violated if the husband's lineage has greater holdings in land. (G065)

Violation of normal residence prescriptions is more likely when it may improve economic status. (L110)

### Economic Role of Kin-Group

Where dispersed homesteads and localized lineages occur, there is a tendency for work groups to be made up of consanguineal relatives; where the pattern is that of the concentrated village, lineages are of less importance and mutual assistance groups are as often composed of friends, neighbors, or affinal relatives as of consanguineal kin. (A072)

### Economy

Neolocal rules of residence are associated with systems that tend to isolate or emphasize the individual or the nuclear family: monogamy, the growth of territorial states, the development of private property, individual enterprise in the economic sphere, personal freedom in choice of marital partners, and individual migration. (P083)

### Endogamy (Clan)

Clan endogamy tends to be directly correlated with the localization of the kinship unit. (H165)

### Exogamy

Doubt about the correctness of a union tends to be reduced if the bride and bridegroom do not belong to the same residential group. (E084)

Exogamic restrictions are more likely to be infringed if the families concerned are not residentially propinquitous. (G097)

Adherence to exogamic restrictions is of greater importance when the kinsmen are of the same community. (H128)

### Exogamy (Community)

When community exogamy prohibits marriage between residents of the same community, preferred sex and marriage partners will be found to be residents of nearby communities. (M019)

### Exogamy (Village)

Patterns of village exogamy are directly correlated with territorial stabilization of kin-groups. (B302)

Village exogamy is the consequence of territorial stabilization of kin-groups. (G149)

### Extended Family Ties

The greater the dispersal of the extended family, the more likely is a conflict between the ties of kinship and marriage. (M198)

There is no correlation between the dispersal of the extended family and the strengthening of the ties of marriage. (M198)

### Fertility

The percentage of poor housing is directly related to fertility. (D006)

Fertility is likely to be higher among families living in the urban fringe areas than among urban families. (J003)

### Friendship Choice

People in newer cities are more likely to avoid friendships with broken families than are those from older cities. (Z008)

### Genealogical Depth

Where lineages are tied with specific land tracts, they are likely to have genealogies of great depth. (T080)

### Genealogical Proximity

There is a relationship between neighborhoods and kinship; the closer the kinship relation, the closer their proximity to each other in residence. (K050)

Residential propinquity tends to be directly correlated with the consanguineal proximity of the kinsmen. (L077)

### Genealogical Ties, Knowledge of

When the kinship system is of a bilateral character, the child's knowledge of his father's or his mother's branch will depend upon his place of residence. (H062)

### Genealogy, Importance of

A lack of interest in genealogical relations is associated with the settlement pattern of dispersal and recongregation. (D056)

### Gerontocracy

The greater frequency of elderly men living alone is an index of the general decline in their prestige and authority. (F073)

The position of older men appears to decline where local lineages have been physically dispersed. (F073)

### Homogamy

The smaller the hometown, the less likely girls are to marry heterogamously. (K150)

### Housing

The more available housing is, the less frequently will aged parents live with any of their grown children. (B312)

### Husband/Wife

When it is necessary for either the husband or wife to change his or her residential community at marriage, it is more usually the woman rather than the man who changes domicile. (M019)

### Husband-Wife Relations, Importance of

High importance of the husband-wife tie is associated with a kinship structure that is patrilineal, patrilocal, or neolocal. (H172)

### Illegitimacy

Illegitimate children are more likely to remain in the care of their mothers, their mothers' kin, or to live with their siblings; legitimate children are more likely to remain in their fathers' care. (S211)

### Incest Taboo

The modification of incest rules will tend to be followed by changes in the residence pattern. (P008)

The extension of incest taboos to other kinsmen beyond the nuclear family is most likely to occur among those who share a common residence with the nuclear group. (S098)

### Income

The larger the older parents' income is, the more willing are grown children to have them in the same household. (B312)

### Inheritance

When residence is patrilocal, the inheritance of economic privileges will tend to be patrilineal. (G038)

Patterns of residence will tend to be consonant with the prevailing inheritance pattern. (H129)

Avuncular inheritance will tend to be resented if the nephew does not reside with his uncle. (K049)

Patterns of descent and inheritance tend to reflect residence patterns. (T039)

The grouping of kinsmen tends to correlate with patterns of land inheritance. (T039)

Inheritance of land tends to be directly correlated with residential propinquity to the land-owning kin-group. (T039)

### Inheritance (Unilineal)

The emergence of unilineal rules of inheritance tends to be directly correlated with the stabilization of the residence pattern. (L063)

### Initiation Rites/Couvade

Initiation rites are more frequently found in societies with exclusive mother-infant sleeping arrangements and patrilocal residence, whereas the couvade is more frequent in societies with exclusive sleeping and matrilocal residence. (W127)

### Interaction among Kin

Only when the degree of kinship is remote does geographical distance influence contact. (G033)

### Interaction with Family (Intimacy)

The desire to avoid intimate family relationships is a cause of the tendency of schizophrenics to move into the central areas of big cities. (H202)

### Intermarriage (Ethnic)

The rate of intermarriage will be higher among members of the ethnic groups who reside at the periphery of the group's territory. (M046)

### Joking Relationship

Joking relationships will tend to be abandoned if the relatives in question are coresidents. (W115)

### Kin Relations

The spouse who has been forced to change residence at marriage is more likely to be strongly linked with his or her family of procreation than is the spouse who has not changed residence. (W115)

### Kin Relations (Cooperation)

The degree of cooperation between kinsmen will be directly associated with their residential proximity. (M131)

### Kin Relations (Interaction)

Geographical distance does not reduce contact between kin unless the degree of kinship is also very distant. (G033)

There is a correlation between proximity of residence of related kin and the amount of interaction within the extended family.

Only when the degree of kinship is remote does geographical distance influence contact. (G033)

### Kin-Role Behavior

Conformity with kinship obligations is more likely to occur if the kinsmen live nearby. (B145)

Activation of descent-line privileges is directly correlated with length of residence. (D085)

Adherence to kinship obligations will tend to be prolonged only if the kinsman remains residentially propinquitous. (F068)

Deviance from lineage norms tends to be directly correlated with the spatial dispersion of the lineage members. (F073)

### Kin-Role Definition

When a lineage group is dispersed, rights and obligations tend to be vested in the matrilineal groups as such and not in particular segments. (C090)

Behavioral patterns between kinsmen tend to be correlated with the residential alignment of kinsmen. (F039)

The extension of nuclear family-role behavior to other kinsmen tends to occur only when the kinsmen are residentially propinquitous. (H164)

The greater the degree of lineage dispersion, the narrower is the recognized range of lineage kinship behavior within the total system. (M168)

### Kin Terminology

A radical shift in residence patterns may weaken or destroy the unilineal organization, thereby causing changes in kinship nomenclature. (L061)

Kinship nomenclature tends to be directly conditioned by the rules of residence which define the kin unit. (L061)

### Kin Terminology (Classificatory)

Collateral relatives of the first ascending generation tend to be merged if neither set shares a common residence with ego. (H164)

When two kin statuses are brought together as close neighbors or actual housemates, they are more likely to be designated by a single classificatory term. (M019)

### Kin Ties

Kin-groups which are not localized are likely to contain fewer generations and to have weaker kin ties. (C052)

The maintenance of the link with the different branches of the male line is more likely if the young man has stayed near his father. (H233)

### Kin Ties (Fictive)

The greater the distance at which a fictive kinsman resides, the more likely it is that the relationship is based on economic or political motives rather than on friendship. (E051)

When the relationship of fictive kinsmen is one of respect, individuals who are neither neighbors nor relatives tend to be chosen so that intimacy and quarrels can be avoided. (L064)

Where peripheral kin in a community cannot assume familial obligations because they do not live close by, neighbors tend to act as surrogates in assuming such obligations. (M054)

### Kinship (Bilateral)

When the residence pattern is not fixed, the bilateral kin-group is more likely to be the focus of attention. (B298)

Dispersion of the town, village, or settlement and a scattering of households is associated with the development of bilaterality. (S192)

### Kinship Structure, Stability of

The development, disappearance, or change in form of an extended family and clan follows an alteration in the rule of residence and is always consistent with the new rule. (M019)

### Land

The dispersal of kinsmen is more likely to occur when the kin-group does not have corporate ownership of land. (T039)

### Lineage

Planned villages with wards tend to be associated with multilineage political units. (H147)

### Lineage Ties

Lineage affiliation will tend to be manipulated if the residence pattern has been violated. (F068)

The importance of lineage ties is directly correlated with the localization of the lineage. (F073)

Patterns of residence within a village tend to be determined by lineage affiliation. (R033)

### Marital Adjustment

Premarital residential propinquity will tend to be correlated with marital adjustment in societies where inter-district relations are characterized by hostility. (B088)

Couples who plan to live in a small or suburban community rather than in a metropolitan city have a greater chance for marital success. (B244)

### Marital Stability

Marital stability is more likely to occur in communities with dense, rather than dispersed, patterns of residence. (A072)

Where a woman remains in her natal home, the marriage bond is fragile and the divorce rate is high. (G116)

The greater the instability of marriage and other mating forms, the more likely it is that persons will withdraw into domestic isolation or live with siblings. (S211)

Marital stability will be higher if kinsmen live nearby. (S266)

### Marital Status

Married old people in industrially developed areas are more apt to live alone with their spouses than with other family as well or with other nonkin; nonmarried old people in industrially developed areas are as apt to live with their children or with other relatives as they are to live alone (Vienna). (R120)

Unmarried older people tend to live nearer their siblings than do married older people. (T009)

### Marriage Chances

The number of marriages to persons residing at a given distance immediately preceding marriage is directly proportional to the number of potential spouses living at that distance and inversely proportional to the number living at shorter distances. (C123)

The percentage of grooms marrying brides living at a

given distance is proportional to the number of brides at that distance and inversely proportional to the distance. (C123)

Decrease in the liklihood of marrying is more strongly related to an increase in distance between potential spouses than to a decline in the number of potential spouses at any given distance. (C123)

### Mate Selection
The majority of marriages will be between local descent groups. (L051)

Most marriages and sexual liasions tend to take place between residents of the same community in all societies where the community is not regularly a clan or an endogamous gene. (M019)

Individuals tend to marry members of adjacent communities. (O005)

Residential propinquity is a factor in the mate selection when the husband and wife are not kinsmen. (S121)

### Mating Forms
Relatives and children of the wife of a male head-of-family account for a larger proportion of the total family size when extraresidential mating is common. (S211)

### Mental Illness (Schizophrenia)
There is no relationship between the voluntary choice of living away from one's family and the development of schizophrenia, but there is an association between involuntary lack of family (because of death, sterility, etc.) and schizophrenia. (H202)

### Mental Illness (Social Adjustment)
Formerly hospitalized mental patients who reside with their parents tend to be less steadily employed and to participate in fewer social activities than do those who reside with their conjugal families. (F098)

### Mother-Child Relations (Warmth)
There is a curvilinear relationship between maternal warmth and privacy of living arrangements. The warmest mothers are the ones with intermediate privacy (single-family dwellings with neighbors, friends, and relatives nearby). (M216)

Mothers tend to be lower on maternal warmth when the child has several close cousins nearby than when the child has few such cousins in close proximity. (M216)

### Nuclear Family, Importance of
The nuclear family tends to be of less importance when the residence pattern is that of an extended family unit. (W067)

### Parent-Child Relations (Aid)
The closer the parents live to their married child, the more likely are they to offer services (help in sickness, babysitting, childbirth, etc.). (A066)

### Parent-Child Relations (Financial Help)
There is no relationship between residential propinquity of parents and married child and financial assistance given by the parents to the married child. (A066)

### Paternal Role
In matrilineal societies the father's area of action tends to be less where the woman, after marriage, resides with her brother and her husband comes to live or visit in their house. (G012)

In matrilineal societies, where the husband takes his wife to his home, the husband's role as father is more important (even if the children succeed to the brother-in-law). (G012)

### Paternal Role, Importance of
In matrilineal societies there is considerable variation in the degree to which the father's role is stressed. It tends to be less so where the woman, after marriage, resides with her brother and her husband comes to live in their house. (G116)

### Personality of Mother (Emotional Control)
Mothers who live in multiple-family dwellings are more emotionally controlled, being less warm and less hostile, than are mothers who reside in single-family dwellings. (M216)

### Political Rank
Residence patterns are more likely to be violated if there are kinsmen of inappropriate status, yet politically powerful, with whom the individual wishes to affiliate. (L109)

### Political Structure
Planned villages with wards tend to be associated with multilineage political units. (H147)

The hamlet pattern of settlement tends to be correlated with local political units which are multilineage in character (Melanasia). (H147)

Localized kin-groups are associated with clan or lineage as the nucleus for a formal political structure with permanent authority. (K154)

Lineages are more likely to be autonomous and free of any centralized control if they are dispersed. (W080)

### Political Succession
Retention of lineage political rights tends to be jeopardized if the individual fails to conform to the residence pattern. (W078)

### Polygyny (Sororal)
Co-wives regularly reside in the same dwelling if they are sisters, but occupy separate habitations if they are unrelated. (M109)

### Power Structure of Family
Suburban families are more husband dominant at every status level than are their urban peers.

### Preferential Marriage
Establishment of affinal affiliations between clans tends to result in the localization of the clans. (C039)

### Preferential Marriage (Cross-Cousin)
Cross-cousin marriage tends to occur when the mother's brother or the father's sister resides in a different community. (T039)

### Premarital Sex Relations
The more the child, during pre- or early adolescence, is transferred from the home of his parents to that of other relatives or friends, the more likely it is that prohibitions against premarital intercourse will break down. (B245)

### Property
Matrilocal residence tends to be favored in the absence of movable property which is of economic significance (e.g., herds). (M019)

## Race

In urban Negro families, children under 18 are less likely to live with their parents than are those in other families; in rural Negro families, the reverse is true (U.S.). (L124)

## Rank

Residence patterns are more likely to be violated when the spouse who does not determine the place of residence is of high status. (H137)

## Rank of Clan

Clans of high status are more likely to be located at the center of the community. (W075)

## Rank of Parental Group

Residential affiliation will be affected by the relative social status of the parental groups. (G029)

## Religion (Ancestor Cult)

The ancestral cult is usually connected with the main cult of the society, particularly in settled communities where there can be permanent association with grave sites. (M168)

## Remarriage

A man marrying for the first time and living with his spouse is more likely to double up with relatives or others during the initial two years of his marriage than is a man marrying for the second or subsequent time during the corresponding period of his remarriage. (G011)

## Residence (Avunculocal)

A concentrated village facilitates avunculocal residence. (F019)

## Residence (Matrilocal)

Matrilocal residence tends to be associated with patterns of dispersed homesteads. (A072)

## Role Definition

Behavioral patterns between kinsmen tend to be correlated with the residential alignment of kinsmen. (F039)

## Segementation

When the settlement pattern is that of a compact territorially segregated community, size of the clan and the number of its component basic lineages are restricted. (F033)

The segmentation of the lineage group tends to occur with the localization on agricultural sites. (K029)

The segmentation of local groups and lineages is likely to occur as a response to settled residence. (M168)

## Sex Composition of Family

When a family is without daughters in a matrilineal society, the unmarried men may remain at home. (S078)

## Sex Preference

A definite preference for children of one sex will be correlated with the prevailing rule of unilocal residence. (W070)

## Sex-Role Definition

Families with high degrees of role segregation by sex tend to live in homogeneous areas of low population turnover, whereas families with predominantly shared role relationships tend to live in heterogeneous areas of high population turnover. (B209)

## Sex Status

Among older (50 years and up) widowed persons, men are as likely as women to live by themselves (U.S.). (C116)

When the out-marrying spouse is a man, he will rarely move far from home. (S189)

Married daughters' initial residences are not likely to be as far from their parents as those of married sons. (S269)

## Sibling Relations (Solidarity)

Patterns of common residence will tend to reinforce the strength of the sibling relationship. (G053)

## Size of Clan

The degree of localization of the clan varies inversely with its size. (B050)

When the settlement pattern is that of compact, territorially segregated communities, there is a restriction on an increase in the size of the clan. (F033)

## Size of Joint Family

The size of a joint family will depend upon the type of housing available. (M021)

## Social Control

The control of the community over a family is greater when residence is stable rather than transient. (B033)

A unilineal group can play an effective role as agent of social control only when it is localized. (G062)

As a nonlocalized group, the matriclan can play little part in the main system of social control. (G062)

## Social Mobility

Lineages will tend to be dispersed in societies with high degrees of social mobility. (G101)

## Social Network

Closely knit networks (i.e., the members are friends of one another, not only through the husband or wife) are most likely to develop when husband and wife, together with their friends, neighbors, and relatives, have grown up in the same local area and have continued to live there after marriage. (B209)

If the husband has an occupation where his colleagues tend also to be his neighbors, it is more likely that he and his wife have an interconnected network of social contacts; if not, they are likely to have a more dispersed network (i.e., those in it do not see one another independently of the husband and wife). (B267)

The more homogeneous and stable the neighborhood in which the couple live, the more likely it is that they will have an interconnected network of social contacts (i.e., those in the network see one another independently of the husband and wife). (B267)

The greater the extent to which a couple's friends and relatives live in the same local area as they do, the more likely it is that the couple's social network is interconnected (i.e., those in the network see one another independently of the husband and wife). (B268)

## Stability of Extended Family

The proportion of individuals living alone is indicative of the weakness of the extended family pattern. (L064)

### Stability of Kinship Structure

The development, disappearance, or change in form of an extended family and clan follows an alteration in the rule of residence and is always consistent with the new rule. (M019)

### Stability of Lineage

In a matrilocal society the residence pattern will tend to be patrilocal rather than matrilocal when the lineage of the wife approaches extinction. (M082)

### Subsistence Pattern (Agriculture)

There is a direct correlation between matrilocal residence and a multicrop subsistence agriculture and between patrilocal residence and an economy based upon a single major crop. (A072)

### Subsistence Pattern (Hunting and Gathering)

In societies where the economy is marginal hunting-gathering, the residence pattern tends to be flexible. (M079)

### Subsistence Pattern (Production)

The residence rule tends to reflect the method of production which characterizes the economic pattern. (K046)

### Warfare

War tends to result in the residential disruption of previously localized kin-groups. (B064)

The localization of the clan will tend to deteriorate with the prohibition of warfare by European administrators. (B156)

Violence within a society seems noticeably absent where the vengeance group (subclan or lineage) is not a territorial unit. (H245)

Where residence is largely determined by agnatic descent and not open to choice, the motives for preserving the peace of the settlement are greater. (H245)

For patterns of feuding to occur, lineages must be localized and preserve their structural continuity. (P026)

Residence patterns will tend to be more flexible under conditions of prolonged warfare. (R054)

### Witchcraft

Hostility against kinsmen as manifest in accusations of witchcraft is more likely to occur among kinsmen who are close neighbors. (S140)

Where co-wives live in adjacent houses, preoccupation with sorcery is greater than where the co-wives live miles apart. (W127)

### RESIDENCE (AMBILOCAL)     X Land

Patterns of ambilocal residence tend to arise in areas where there is an equal population pressure among land-owning kin-groups. (R054)

### RESIDENCE (AMITALOCAL)
#### X Descent (Patrilineal)

Amitalocal residence patterns require prior rules of patrilineal descent. (G052)

### RESIDENCE (AVUNCULOCAL)
#### X Descent (Matrilineal)

The pattern of avunculocal residence requires a prior rule of matrilineal descent. (G052)

### Kin Termininology

In the presence of avunculocal residence, terms for primary relatives tend to be extended within the same generation to their collateral relatives through females. (M019)

### Rank of Men

Avunculocal residence develops out of a prior matrilocal residence in response to the strengthening of the status of men. (F019)

A change in culture or in the conditions of life which significantly enhances the status importance and influence of men will tend to result in avunculocal residence in societies where the rule of descent is matrilineal. (M019)

### Residence

A concentrated village facilitates avunculocal residence. (F019)

### Residence (Matrilocal)

Avunculocal residence can develop only from a prior matrilocal rule. (M019)

### RESIDENCE (BILOCAL)
#### X Avoidance Relationship

Societies with a bilocal rule of residence have a low severity of kin avoidance. (S079)

### Cohesion of Lineage

Anything which lessens the strength of unilinear bonds favors bilocal residence, provided that the factors that militate against neolocal residence must also be present (e.g., large, multifamily dwellings and collective rather than individual enterprise). (M019)

### Descent (Unilineal)

Where bilocal residence persists or where tendencies to unilocality do not go too far descent remains nonunilinear. (G029)

The unilinear kin-groups tend to disappear as a consequence of the adoption of bilocal or neolocal residence. (M019)

### Economic Rank of Parents

Residential affiliation under patterns of bilocal residence tend to be based upon the relative economic status of the parents of the husband and wife. (B111)

### Geographic Mobility

The adoption of a migratory life in unstable bands seems particularly conducive to a bilocal rule of residence. (M019)

### Kin Terminology (Generation)

Bilocal residence tends to be associated with kinship terminology of the generation type. (M019)

### Rank of Women

Under sedentary conditions of life, bilocal residence tends to be associated with an approximate equality in status of the two sexes, especially with regard to the ownership and inheritance of property and privileges. (M019)

### Subsistence Pattern (Hunting)

Bilocal residence tends to characterize societies with simple hunting economies. (L063)

## RESIDENCE, CHANGE IN
### X   Economic Dependence
A modification of residence patterns may occur when the deviant desires to establish a pattern of economic dependency with more affluent members of his kin-group. (G039)

## RESIDENCE (EXTRUSION)
### X   Child-Rearing Values (Dependency)
Children who are being brought up for "sociological interdependence," anchorage, and identification in the *wider kin-group* will experience physical disruption or discontinuity in their relations with the nuclear family through extrusion or brother–sister avoidance during the first stage of puberty (eight to ten years); whereas children who are brought up for "sociological independence," anchorage, and identification in the *nuclear* family will experience physical continuity without disruption in their nuclear family relations during the first stage of puberty. (C093)

### Legal Responsibility
In societies where children are subjected to extrusion from the household or to brother-sister avoidance during the first stage of puberty (eight to ten years), the concept of joint liability is found (i.e., liability falls on the members of an individual's descent group if the offender cannot be apprehended or meet his legal liability), in societies where neither extrusion nor brother–sister avoidance is found during the first stage of puberty, the concept of individual liability is found (i.e., the individual alone is held responsible and punished for his acts). (C093)

### Mother-Child Household
In societies with a high percentage of mother-child households, boys are likely to move away from home at adolescence. (S079)

### Parent-Child Relations (Closeness)
In societies that practice neither extrusion nor brother–sister avoidance, the parents will alter their relationship to their children during the first stage of puberty by becoming slightly distant, setting new limits, imposing new expectations, and giving them new nicknames. (C093)

### Sex Taboo (Postpartum)
In societies with long durations of postpartum sex taboo, boys are likely to move away from home upon reaching puberty. (S079)

## RESIDENCE/GEOGRAPHIC PROXIMITY
### X   Kin Relations (Interaction)
The intimacy of the relationship between kinsmen is determined by residential rather than by consanguineal proximity. (S120)

## RESIDENCE INHERITANCE
### X   Descent (Matrilineal)
Consistent matrilocal residence and matrilineal property interests tend to produce a matrilineal descent group. (L110)

## RESIDENCE, LENGTH OF          X   Rank of Lineage
The rank of a lineage will tend to be high if its members have lived longer in the village. (S158)

## RESIDENCE/LINEAGE
### X   Kin Relations (Interaction)
Members of related lineages who live in adjacent villages tend to see more of each other than they do of people belonging to unrelated lineages who live equally near to them. (W115)

## RESIDENCE (LONGHOUSE)          X   Stratification
Stratification is unlikely to occur in societies where the longhouse is the community settlement. (M248)

## RESIDENCE (MATRILOCAL)          X   Acculturation
The deterioration of patterns of matrilocal residence tends to be directly correlated with the degree of acculturation. (B093)

### Avoidance Relationship
An association exists between the parent-in-law taboo and matrilocal residence. (L128)

### Descent (Matrilineal)
Matrilineal descent tends to occur in societies in which the pattern of residence is matrilocal. (H043)

### Divorce
In matrilineal societies, where a woman remains in her natal home (after marriage), the marriage bond is fragile and the divorce rate is high. (G012)

### Economic Pattern
Seasonal wage work reinforces a matrilocal residence pattern. (P083)

### Economic Pattern (Money)
With the adoption of a cash economy there is a shift away from matrilocality. (H032)

### Economic Rank of Wife
In a patrilocal society, matrilocal residence is more likely to occur if the family of the wife is wealthy. (L074)

### Economic Role of Women
Matrilocal residence tends to be associated with the woman's control of the production and ownership of land. (M019)

When economic pressures increase the importance of maintaining the integrity and continuity of the female household work crew, matrilocal residence will tend to occur. (M020)

Among sedentary groups where property is significant and women are the prime cultivators, matrilocal residence is favored. (O006)

### Endogamy (Community)
There is an association between matrilocal residence in sedentary communities and local endogamy. (M019)

### Geographic Mobility
Matrilocal residence tends to occur only among the larger more stable tribes. (O006)

### Heir, Absence of
In a patrilocal society, when the family of the bride is without male heirs the residence after marriage is more likely to be matrilocal. (S059)

### Inheritance (Matrilineal)
Matrilineal inheritance of land will tend to produce a change in residence toward matrilocality (unless the village is composed of several lineages). (W054)

### Kin Ties

When an uxorilocal marriage occurs in a generally patrilocal society, the children of this union tend to affiliate themselves with their mother's lineage. (T039)

### Land

When there is a shortage of land controlled by the matrilineage, men will tend to reside with the lineage of their wives. (F019)

### Marriage Payment

Matrilocal residence and a high bride price are negatively associated. (L103)

### Mate Selection (Free Choice)

With matrilocal residence in force, parents tend to exert strong control over marriage choice of the daughter since they will become dependent upon the daughter and son-in-law in later life. (O027)

### Monogamy

Matrilocal residence and service to the father-in-law are associated with monogamy. (W157)

### Political Integration

A relatively low level of political integration is a precondition of matrilocal residence. (M019)

### Political Rank of Husband

Patterns of matrilocal residence are more likely to be violated if the husband is of high political status. (M125)

### Polygyny

The introduction of matrilocal residence is opposed by polygyny. (M019)

### Polygyny (Nonsororal)

Nonsororal polygyny is incompatible with matrilocal residence. (W105)

### Polygyny (Sororal)

Sororal polygyny tends to be associated with matrilocal residence. (M019)

### Property

When the ownership of the house and land is by women, residence tends to be matrilocal. (L036)

### Property (Patrilineal)

When patrilineal property is restricted to personal possessions which are destroyed or buried with the body upon death, the transition to matrilocal residence is not difficult to effect. (M020)

### Rank of Father

Patterns of matrilocal residence are more likely to be infringed if the father is wealthy or of high political status. (C056)

### Rank of Husband

When residence is matrilocal the husband's position will be subordinate to the other males in the extended family household. (H032)

### Rank of Women

Matrilocal residence tends to be associated with a high status of women. (M019)

The rank of women tends to be higher under patterns of matrilocal residence. (S098)

### Residence

Matrilocal residence tends to be associated with patterns of dispersed homesteads. (A072)

### Residence (Avunculocal)

Avunculocal residence can develop only from a prior matrilocal rule. (M019)

### Sibling Structure

Uxorilocal residence tends to occur when the husband has a number of male siblings. (L063)

### Warfare

In societies with patterns of local warfare, temporary matrilocal residence arises to protect the wife against vengeance by her husband's group. (K156)

Relative peacefulness is a factor that favors matrilocal residence. (M019)

## RESIDENCE (MATRILOCAL/OTHER)
### X   Initiation Rites

In matrilocal societies, female initiation rites announce the change in status when a girl marries; in other societies, her moving away from home announces the change in status. (C093)

## RESIDENCE (MATRILOCAL/PATRILOCAL)
### X   Men's Societies

Men's societies appear more frequently among patrilocal societies than in matrilocal ones. (M067)

### Residence (Village)

Settlement patterns of matrilocal cultures are more likely to be that of dispersed homesteads; patrilocal, as well as avunculocal, cultures display a trend toward concentrated villages. (A072)

## RESIDENCE (MEN'S HOUSE)
### X   Authority Structure of Family

When men are residentially separated from their wives, their control over women is less. (M067)

## RESIDENCE (NEOLOCAL)          X   Acculturation

The adoption of patterns of neolocal residence tends to accompany acculturation. (N030)

### Authority Structure of Family

With the establishment of neolocal residence, it is difficult for the older members of the family to exercise authority. (C035)

### Cohesion of Kin-Group

The disintegration of ethnic and extended family bonds will be manifest in a trend toward single-family households. (S090)

### Conflict in Kin-Group

Neolocal residence in a society which is characterized by unilocal patterns will tend to be the result of conflict within the kin unit. (M070)

### Descent (Bilateral)

Neolocal residence is normally associated with bilateral descent. (M019)

A change to neolocal residence from any form of unilocal residence will ultimately result in bilateral descent. (M019)

### Disintegration of Kin-Group

Any influence which tends to undermine or inhibit large local aggregations of kinsmen will create conditions favorable to neolocal residence. (M019)

### Economic Dependence

Economic individualism in its various manifestations (e.g., private property or individual enterprise in the economic sphere) facilitates the establishment of independent households by married couples. (M019)

As the productivity of the male has increased and as he has been able to include his own family in his work arrangement, the neolocal trend has been greatly stimulated. (V017)

### Education of Women
The self-sufficiency fostered by a higher level of education in the wife tends to produce pressures toward neolocal residence. (M081)

### Exogamy
When a marriage infringes exogamic restrictions, the couple will tend to establish neolocal residence. (C075)

### Geographic Mobility
Individual migration, as a consequence of overpopulation or developing organization, facilitates the establishment of independent households by married couples. (M019)

### Inheritance
A modification in inheritance rules, such as the replacement of primogeniture by the division of an estate among a number of heirs, will tend to favor neolocal residence. (M019)

### Isolation of Nuclear Family
Neolocal rules of residence are associated with systems that tend to isolate or emphasize the individual or the nuclear family (monogamy, the growth of territorial states, the development of private property, individual enterprise in the economic sphere, personal freedom in choice of marital partners, and individual migration). (P083)

### Kin Relations (Interaction)
The establishment of patterns of neolocal residence tends to result in the restriction of interaction with kinsmen. (V017)

### Kin Terminology
Neolocal residence tends to encourage the development of a lineal terminology. (V017)

### Legal Status
The legal statuses of husband and wife are more likely to be equal when the pattern of residence is neolocal. (S123)

### Monogamy
Any factor which promotes monogamy will also favor neolocal residence. (M019)

### Power Structure of Family
Neolocality is associated with reduced control by family elders. (G156)

### Religion (Christianity)
The development of a separate household arrangement tends to be stimulated by the pressure of European missionaries. (V017)

### Stability of Kin-Group
Kin-groups will tend to disintegrate as conditions come to favor neolocal residence. (G029)

Any influence which tends to undermine or inhibit large local aggregations of kinsmen will create conditions favorable to neolocal residence. (M019)

### Subsistence Pattern (Nomadic)
The residential unit of the husband, wife, and their dependents is more frequent in nomadic than in sedentary life. (L073)

### Superego Formation
Persons from societies with neolocal rules of residence for families have weaker superegos (less patient responsibility for illness) than do those reared in families from societies with matrilocal or patrilocal rules of residence. (W142)

### Values (Individualism)
When the culture places an emphasis upon competitive individualism, the individual nuclear family will be the basic unit of kinship organization. (V016)

## RESIDENCE/OCCUPATION     X     Mate Selection
The higher a man ranged on the occupational scale, the greater the distance in standard city blocks between his home and the home of his future mate. (K013)

## RESIDENCE (OWNED/RENTED)
### X     Stability of Family
Homeowner families are more stable than are tenant families. (C009)

## RESIDENCE (PATRILOCAL)
### X     Affinal Relations (Conflict)
Under uxorilocal residence, the friction and conflict inherent in affinal relationships will, if the society is patrilineal, tend to result in virilocal residence. (D008)

### Avoidance Relationship
There is a close association between the patrilocal rule of residence and the avoidance of the son's wife. (S079)

### Descent (Matrilineal)
If local circumstances do not favor avunculocal residence, a matrilineal society under strong patrilocal pressure, is likely to adopt patrilocal residence without giving up its matrilineal lineages, sibs, or moieties. (M019)

Matrilineal kin-groups tend to disappear or cease to be exogamous when patrilocal residence is adopted. (M019)

### Descent (Patrilineal)
When a society shifts to regular patrilocal residence, the group automatically becomes patrilineal. (G029)

### Divorce
In matrilineal societies where the woman moves out of her natal family in order to produce children for her husband's line, the woman's bonds to her husband tend to be strong and the divorce rate is low. (G012)

### Economic Pattern
Patrilocal residence rules are more likely to occur in any system in which the status of men is greatly superior to that of women (e.g., where there is a pastoral economy, polygyny, the development of movable property which can be accumulated in quantity—herds, slaves, money). (P083)

### Economic Role of Men
Patrilocal residence is promoted by any modification in the basic economy whereby masculine activity in the sex division of labor comes to yield the principle means of a subsistence. (M019)

### Inheritance (Matrilineal)
When there are several lineages within the village, it is possible to maintain patterns of patrilocal residence, although the inheritance of the land is matrilineal. (W054)

### Kin Terminology (Bifurcate Collateral)
Patrilocal and matri-patrilocal residence (because of their association with nonsororal polygyny) tend to be accompanied by kinship terminology of the bifurcate collateral type. (M019)

### Land
In matrilineal societies patrilocal residence is more likely to occur if the settlement pattern permits ready access to the land of both lineages. (E108)

### Marriage Payment
Marriage payment tends to occur in societies in which residence is patrilocal. (C060)

When residence rules remove the bride from her home, some form of marriage payment ordinarily accompanies marriage. (M019)

Change from matrilineal, avunculocal system to patrilocal residence tends to result from either an increase in bride price or the adoption of preferential marriage by the exchange of sisters. (M171)

### Political Expansion
Patrilocal residence is encouraged in situations of political expansion. (M019)

### Polygyny
Polygyny is particularly congenial to patrilocal residence. Hence, anything that favors polygyny also favors the development of patrilocal residence. (M019)

### Polygyny (Nonsororal)
Nonsororal polygyny tends to occur in the presence of patrilocal residence and patrilineal descent. (M019)

### Preferential Marriage (Avuncular)
With the change from patrilocality to matrilocality, avuncular marriage patterns will disappear. (M020)

### Preferential Marriage (Exchange)
Modification of a matrilineal or avunculocal system involving a shift to patrilocal residence may occur as a result of two innovations: either an increase in the bride price or the adoption of preferential marriage by the exchange of sisters. (M171)

### Property
The development of any form of movable property or wealth will tend to promote patrilocal residence. (M019)

### Rank of Husband
The violation of patterns of patrilocal residence is more likely to occur if the husband is of low status. (S115)

### Rank of Men
Patrilocal residence seems to be promoted by any change in culture or the conditions of life which significantly enhances the status importance and influence of men in relation to the opposite sex. (M019)

### Rank of Wives
The status of wives in a polygynous marriage is more likely to be equal if the residence pattern is virilocal. (W105)

### Sibling Relations
Virilocal residence within a matrilocal society is associated with a close cohesion of the uterine sibling group. (T080)

### Sibling Structure (Sex)
Patrilocal residence is most likely to occur in societies with patterns of matrilocal residence when the husband is without female siblings. (B108)

The violation of patterns of patrilocal residence may occur if the wife is without male siblings. (L071)

### Size of Lineage
When the number of men in the matrilineage is small, a man who is a member of the lineage will encourage his son to remain with him in patrilocal residence. (F019)

### Size of Matrilineal Group
Virilocal marriage reduces the span of the effective matrilineal unit to the matricentric family. (T080)

### Slavery
The institution of slavery in a society encourages patrilocal residence. (M019)

### Subsistence Pattern (Hunting)
Patrilocal residence tends to occur among hunters and gatherers if a tribe moves into an area where game is plentiful and dependable so that the subsistance comes to depend primarily upon the chase rather than upon the collecting activities of the women. (M019)

Hunting bands with strong lineages as the predominant economic group will be found to be associated with patrilocal residence. (O006)

### Subsistence Pattern (Pastoral)
The adoption of a pastoral economy has usually resulted in patrilocal residence. (M019)

### Subsistence Pattern (Plough Agriculture)
Where men supplant women as tillers of the soil, often in consequence of harnessing their domestic animals to the plough, patrilocal residence almost invariably occurs. (M019)

### Warfare
When warfare becomes an important activity in a society, patrilocal residence begins to occur. (M019)

## RESIDENCE (PATRILOCAL/MATRILOCAL)
### X   Economic Rank of Parental Group
Residential affiliation will tend to be with the parental group which has the largest landholding. (G029)

## RESIDENCE (PATRILOCAL /NEOLOCAL)
### X   Husband-Wife Relations (Power)
The dominant position of a husband over his wife is easier to maintain when the residence pattern is patrilocal rather than neolocal. (L064)

## RESIDENCE (PRIVACY)
### X   Mother-Child Relations (Warmth)
There is a curvilinear relationship between maternal warmth and privacy of living arrangements. The warmest mothers are the ones with intermediate privacy (single-family dwellings with neighbors, friends, and relatives in close proximity). (M216)

## RESIDENCE (SEGREGATION OF SEXES)
### X   Age at Marriage
In societies with separate residences for girls, the age of marriage will be later. (W128)

## RESIDENCE (SEPARATE)
**X   Nuclear Family, Importance of**
The importance of the nuclear family will be emphasized if it is residentially segregated, not a part of a larger kin-group. (S153)

## RESIDENCE (UNILOCAL)
**X   Community (Unilineage)**
Unilocal residence rules will tend to be more rigid in unilineal communities. (F010)

**Descent (Unilineal)**
Unilocal residential groupings tend to give rise to unilineal descent groups based on the same principle. (L061)

A fixed rule of residence whereby all men or all women after marriage continue to reside with or near their own linear relatives of the same sex is conducive to a unilinear rather than bilateral descent. (M019)

A stable unilocal residence pattern is especially influential in the development of unilineal descent groups. (M045)

**Endogamy (Community)**
Conformity to patterns of unilocal residence tends to be directly correlated with the stability of patterns of community endogamy. (L063)

**Land**
Where land is abundant, unilocal residence rules develop. (G029)

Patterns of unilocal residence tend to deteriorate under conditions of land shortage. (R054)

**Subsistence Pattern (Hunting)**
When the economic pattern of a society is that of a marginal hunting economy, ideal patterns of unilocal residence are frequently violated. (L063)

## RESIDENCE (URBAN)          X   Fertility
Among Protestants (only) there is an inverse relationship between city size and fertility rate. (F101)

## RESIDENCE (URBAN/RURAL)     X   Birth Control
People with farm backgrounds are less likely than others to control fertility. (F101)

People living in metropolitan areas are more likely than others to adopt appliance methods of family limitation and less likely to adopt either rhythm or withdrawal methods. (F101)

**Fertility**
The birth rate is higher on farms than elsewhere. (F101)

## RESIDENCE (UXORILOCAL)   X   Economic Rank
Uxorilocal residence is more likely to occur when the husband is of low economic status. (T039)

**Endogamy (Community)**
When residence is uxorilocal, the community will tend to be endogamous. (H147)

**Endogamy (Tribal)**
When the residential pattern is uxorilocal, marriage will tend to be within the political unit. (M032)

## RESIDENCE (VILLAGE)
**X   Residence (Matrilocal/Patrilocal)**
Settlement patterns of matrilocal cultures are more likely to be that of dispersed homesteads; patrilocal, as well as avunculocal, cultures display a trend toward concentrated villages. (A072)

## RESIDENCE (VIRILOCAL)
**X   Avuncular Relationship**
When residence is virilocal in a matrilineal society, the transference of hostile wishes on the part of the male from the father to the mother's brother is less completely carried out. (G055)

**Economic Role of Men**
When men play the major role in agricultural activities, the residence patterns tend to be virilocal. (G055)

**Generational Emphasis**
Virilocal residence in a matrilocal society is associated with organization by genealogical generation within the village. (T080)

**Geographic Mobility**
There is a relationship between virilocal residence in a matrilocal society and a high rate of individual mobility. (T080)

**Husband-Wife Relations**
Other things being equal, a wife will reside with her husband if he (or whoever has jural authority over him) has unrestricted rights over her sexual and economic services. (F074)

## RESIDENCE WITH CHILD       X   Urban/Rural
Co-residence of aged parents with middle-aged children is less apt to occur in urban areas than it is in rural areas. (B312)

## RESIDENCE WITH FAMILY
**X   Mental Illness**
**(Schizophrenia/Manic-Depressive)**
Schizophrenics are more likely than manic-depressives to live away from their families. (H202)

## RESIDENCE WITH KIN          X   Mental Illness
There are more adult mental patients living in parental-family settings than would be expected on the basis of the family settings of the general population. (F124)

**Mental Illness (Social Adjustment)**
Posthospital social and vocational performance is higher among mental patients living in conjugal-family settings or living alone than it is among those living with their parental or sibling families. (F124)

Mental patients living in sibling families tend to have higher levels of social and vocational performance than do those living in parental families. (F124)

**Personality Adjustment of Aged**
Low morale among elderly persons (75 and over) is associated with their living with intimate kinsmen. (C116)

**Sex Status of Mental Patient**
Male mental patients are more likely than female mental patients to be living in parental rather than conjugal family settings. (F124)

Female mental patients are more likely to live with their siblings than are male patients. (F124)

## RESIDENCE WITH PARENTS          X   Class
There is no significant relationship between the social class of the children and living with their aged parents or in independent households. (G119)

**Intermarriage (Religious)**
Single people living with their parents tend to marry

someone of their own religion more often than do single people living away from their parents. (C134)

#### Mental Illness (Schizophrenia)
Mental illness is more likely to occur among adult children living with their parents. (K093)

#### Social Mobility
There is no significant relationship between social-class mobility of children and living with their aged parents or in independent households. (G119)

### RESIDENTIAL SEGREGATION
#### X  Sex-Role Definition
The residential segregation of men is most likely to occur in societies where there is a rigorous dichotomy in sex roles. (R033)

### RESIDENTIAL STABILITY   X  Cohesion of Family
The more integrated the family, the longer its residence in the tribal community. (S217)

### RESOURCES              X  Division of Labor
Task allocation is determined by whether or not the family member is already skillful at a certain task.

#### Monogamy
Pressures toward monogamy are greater where the bargaining position of women in society is stronger. (P083)

#### Power Structure
The balance of power will be on the side of that partner who contributes the greater resources to the marriage. (P083)

#### Power Structure of Family
At the highest-class levels, in status groups where graceful living rather than male achievement is the basis for supremacy, the wife, in directing many of the representative functions of the family, develops a level of skill and responsibility that enhances her position in the family relative to her husband. (P083)

### RESOURCES OF WIFE
#### X  Authority Structure of Marriage
When the wife gains increasing resources in the family, patriarchal role definitions will weaken. (P083)

### RETARDED/CEREBRAL-PALSIED CHILDREN
#### X  Personality of Mother
As measured by the PARI, the personality configurations of mothers with retarded children differ very little from those with cerebral-palsied children. (J027)

### RETIREMENT
#### X  Parent-Child Relations (Closeness)
Retired parents tend to evaluate close parent-child relations more highly than employed parents do. (S220)

#### Parent-Child Relations (Financial Help)
Old parents who are retired desire financial assistance in preference to affection from their children more often than do old parents who are still employed. (S220)

#### Parent-Child Relations (Financial Help)
#### X  Achievement
Children who have been successful in their occupations tend to give their retired parents more financial assistance than do less-successful children. (S220)

### REVOLUTION              X  Nuclear Family
The nuclear family is more likely to be distended under conditions of revolutionary fervor and of charismatic group formation.

#### Social Mobility
The more successful upper-class families are in protecting themselves from the infiltration of lower-class members into their ranks, the more likely are those below to rebel. (G156)

### RITUAL                  X  Cohesion of Lineage
Lineage solidarity tends to be reinforced by the institution of specific ceremonies or rituals which involve all members of the social unit. (M072)

### RITUAL IN FAMILY                        X  Class
As one moves upward in the social scale, family rituals increase in number, variety, richness, and willing cooperation by individual family members. (B004)

#### Cohesion of Family
Family ritual increases pride in family. (B206)

#### Conflict in Family
Family tension and discord result from different attitudes about ritual among members of a family. (B206)

Rituals in family living reduce stress and strain in the family. (B206)

#### Interaction in Family (Interests)
Families in which the members share common interests tend to develop family rituals. (B206)

#### Size of Family
The larger the family, the more numerous and rich the family rituals. (B004)

#### Stability of Family
Parents who think of their family as stable are the most likely to initiate and continue family ritual. (B206)

### RITUAL IN KIN-GROUP
#### X  Cohesion of Kin-Group
Common ritual will tend to reinforce the cohesiveness of the kin-group. (F026)

### ROLE ADJUSTMENT            X  Sibling Status
Children who occupy special positions (only child, youngest, one of a sex) are more likely than other children to have difficulties in role stabilization in later life. (Z007)

### ROLE BEHAVIOR                           X  Class
Socialization processes operate so that those socialized in upper-class families will tend to assume more "parental" roles toward most others, whereas those socialized in families at lower levels tend to assume more "child" roles. (P062)

#### Conflict in Family
Instrumental discrepancy (i.e., the lack of the physical and practical prerequisites necessary for role performance), whether fortuitous or consciously or unconsciously motivated, is a cause of conflict in the family.

#### Husband/Wife
The husband is more likely than the wife to be less interested in the home and to be more easily attracted to activities outside of it. (G157)

The husband is more likely than the wife to be involved in activities outside of the home that have an emotional overtone (e.g., drinking, club behavior with "the boys," extreme dedication to an occupational task, etc.). (G157)

### Marital Adjustment

Couples are more apt to agree on expected success in joint task performance when they are highly satisfied with their marriages than when they are less satisfied. (L173)

Couples with low satisfaction in marriage are just as apt to perform well in joint tasks as are couples highly satisfied with their marriages. (L173)

### Personality of Husband and Wife

Lack of personality "fit" between marital partners may be a cause of breakdown in role performance by one of them. (R105)

## ROLE BEHAVIOR IN FAMILY
### X   Economic Role of Husband-Wife

Where both husband and wife work and are financially independent, there is much less familism and much more individualism in the members of the family. (B033)

### Identification with Family Roles

The greater the extent to which the parents identify with the cardinal role of family membership, the more likely they are to be able to exchange roles occasionally without confusion. (F106)

### Isolation of Nuclear Family

The isolation of the nuclear family is conditional upon the capacity of the marriage to provide stimulation and tension reduction on the peer level rather than merely on the more regressive levels of husband's omnipotence and mother-child symbiosis. (P083)

### Mate Selection

Persons who assume the parental role in marital relations usually do not explore the field of eligible spouses very widely. (W148)

Husbands who assume the role of son in marriage usually do not explore the field of eligible spouses very widely. (W148)

### Mental Illness (Schizophrenia)

Schizophrenic personality tends to emerge where the family fosters paralogic ideation, untenable emotional needs, and contradictory models for identification which cannot be integrated. (L114)

### Personality Development

Inability of an individual to perform in a variety of role relationships (characteristic of the schizophrenic) may be a result of being raised in a family structure which did not permit the operation and observance of all possible role relationships. (L121)

### Role Definition in Family

Lack of family consensus on norms pertaining to role performance is a cause of breakdown in role performance by any of its members. (R105)

### Sex Status

Women are much more likely than men to be the agents of and to initiate the familistic trend in collective settlements. (T013)

Wives are more likely to conform to husbands' expectations than are the husbands to the wives' expectations. (T092)

### Social Mobility

There are no differences between mobile and nonmobile white collar men in such indices of "familism" as number of offspring, housing status, age at marriage, and duration of childlessness. Men from lower-class origins were as family-oriented as were men from white collar backgrounds (in the modern "bureaucratic" era as contrasted with the former "entrepreneurial" era). (L115)

## ROLE BEHAVIOR OF HUSBAND
### X   Role Behavior of Wife

There is a correlation between the degree to which the husband and wife, respectively, deviate from the modal rank order of role performance in their subculture. (H204)

There is no relationship between the degree to which the husband and wife, respectively, deviate from the other's role expectations of him (her). (H204)

## ROLE BEHAVIOR OF HUSBAND–WIFE
### X   Duration of Marriage

The greater the length of the marriage, the more accurately can one marital partner assume the role of the other. (T092)

### Employment of Wife

The task of managing the family's money matters is less likely to be shared if the wife is employed full time than if she is not, the wife then being more likely to take over financial matters. (G133)

### Marital Adjustment

Spouses who see each other as fulfilling an expressive (warm and emotionally comforting) role tend to be better adjusted in marriage than do those who do not. (K153)

Marital conflict tends to occur when there is a failure to conform to the ideal roles of the husband and wife. (L048)

There is a correlation between marital satisfaction and the individual's playing the role he expects and the spouse's playing the role expected of him, regardless of the content of the roles. (T092)

There is a correlation between marital satisfaction and the degree to which the husband conforms to his wife's role expectations of him, but not the wife's conformity to the husband's expectations. (T092)

### Role Definition

Wives tend to conform more to their husbands' role expectations than husbands do to wives' expectations. (T092)

## ROLE BEHAVIOR OF PARENT-CHILD
### X   Parent-Child Relations (Frustration)

When the role experiences and the patterns of parent-child interaction are ambiguous, frustration is produced in both parents and child. (B040)

## ROLE BEHAVIOR OF WIFE        X   Age of Wife

Young wives are apt to play a strong encouraging role for their husbands as compared with the wives in their forties who are more "collaborators" with their husbands, and the older wives who concentrate mainly on housework.

### Role Behavior of Husband

There is a correlation between the degree to which the husband and wife, respectively, deviate from the modal rank order of role performance in their subculture. (H204)

There is no relationship between the degree to which the husband and wife, respectively, deviate from the other's role expectations of him (her). (H204)

## ROLE CONFLICT        X    Acculturation
When one spouse is more acculturated than the other, role conflict is greater for the husband. (S039)

### Age-Groups
Age-groups arise when the role dispositions of the family are incompatible with those of the total social structure. (E102)

### Dependency of Parents
When aged parents experience the role reversal of moving from independency to material dependency on their children, both parents and children experience role conflict. (G119)

### Husband-Wife Relations (Conflict)
Conflict in the parent between his familial and outside roles is correlated with discord between the parents, each trying to coerce and dominate the other and increase his own personal freedom. (F106)

### Independence of Nuclear Family
Where the society approves the independence of the conjugal unit but does not make this possible for the aged, role conflict for both the aged parents and their children is likely to occur. (G119)

### Paternal Role
Where contradictory demands for the mother's allegiance are made by her husband and by her mother, there is a tendency for the husband to withdraw from participation in family activities, particularly in the area of child care and control. (C117)

## ROLE CONFLICT IN FAMILY    X   Economic Role
Where the economic activities of the individual are not important, conflicting claims within the family for his services will be minimal. (S037)

## ROLE CONFLICT OF PARENTS
### X   Parent-Child Relations
The greater the parental conflict between familial and outside roles, the greater the extent to which the parents compete to dominate the wills of the children. (F106)

### Personality of Child (Conflict)
The greater the parental conflict between familial and outside roles, the more likely it is that the child internalizes conflicting standards. (F106)

## ROLE DEFINITION      X   Conflict in Family
Inadequate familiarity with required roles is a cause of conflict in the family, as, for instance, is common between adolescents and parents, between parents after the birth of the first child, and so on.

The segmentalization of an individual's activity in the urban situation increases the tension within the family. (B033)

### Industrialization
Increased concern with the definition and enactment of family obligations is associated with societies undergoing industrialization. (G156)

### Interaction in Family
The greater the parental commitment to the family, the more likely it is that each person's role outside the home will be shared by the others in the family and the less likely that outside roles will be allowed to compete with family obligations. (F106)

### Marital Adjustment
The degree of marital integration varies directly with the degree to which the husband values the socioemotional aspects of interaction. (T092)

### Marriage Chances
The high percentage of bachelors and spinsters is correlated with specific role definitions for bachelors and for spinsters. (N065)

### Naming of Child
The choice of name for a child will reflect the parents' expectations regarding the role the child is to play. (W124)

### Residence
Behvioral patterns between kinsmen tend to be correlated with the residential alignment of kinsmen. (F039)

### Role Behavior of Husband/Wife
Wives tend to conform more to their husbands' role expectations than husbands do to wives' expectations. (T092)

### Self-Conception
If the mother wishes the child to be like his father, then the child's concept of his ideal self will also resemble his father. (W158)

### Self-Image of Family
Where family norms are not rigorously defined, people tend to assume that the behavior in their own families is normatively approved. (B210)

### Social Network
The more interconnected a couple's social network (i.e., its members associate with one another), the more likely it is that the wife's obligations to her mother and to her husband will come into conflict. (B268)

### Stability of Kin-Group
An explicit definition of role, combined with a complex system of interrelated sanctions, will serve to insure the maintenance of standards of performance between kinsmen and the stability of the kinship unit. (P012)

## ROLE DEFINITION IN FAMILY
### X   Age Difference
Cognitive discrepancy in role behavior between family members is a function of age discrepancy. (S075)

### Authority Structure of Family
Decisions are more likely to be made jointly by both husband and wife when the activity concerned is within the household than when the activity is outside the household.

Loss of autocracy in the family structure leads to an increase in comradeship within the family group.

### Class
Considering the family as a triad of roles—High Status Authority (HSA), Low Status Subordinate (LSS), and High Status Friend (HSF)—the lower-class parent is more likely to play the role of HSA to a child of the same sex than is a middle-class parent, while in the middle class, a parent is more apt to play both roles, regardless of the child's sex.

## Economic Role of Nuclear Family

With the diminishing importance of the nuclear household as a producing unit, it becomes more important emotionally. (C090)

## Hospitalization

Among mental patients whose posthospital social and vocational performance was low, those whose primary role in the family was that of child were more likely to stay out of the hospital than were those whose primary role was that of spouse. (F124)

Family members influence instrumental performance; married men must meet higher levels of instrumental performance than must single men living with parents because wives have higher expectations than parents do. This factor does not, however, explain rates of rehospitalization. (F124)

Differential demands of family account for the fact that patients from conjugal families return to the hospital more frequently than do those from parental families. (F124)

## Interaction in Family

Disruption of usual family activity and continuity is associated with a tendency toward role de-differentiation within the family. (S216)

## Isolation of Nuclear Family

The greater the isolation of the conjugal unit, the greater the number of functions, such as care for the sick and aged, which are taken over by nonfamily institutions. (C134)

## Kin Terminology (Classificatory)

When kin terms of the nuclear family are extended to other kinsmen, the behavior toward these classificatory kinsmen will tend to be modeled on the behavioral pattern associated with the relevant member of the nuclear family. (S098)

## Marital Adjustment

Joint recreation and joint participation in acitivites by all family members brings a high degree of satisfaction with family life.

The greater the tension (lack of coordination) in the system of roles, the lower the marital integration of the couple. (F116)

Salience of family-related responses (Kuhn Twenty Statements Test) tends to be higher among wives whose marital adjustment is good than among those with poor marital adjustment. (S279)

Couples who were well adjusted were more likely than maladjusted couples to use "consensual (references to groups) rather than subconsensual (evaluative and qualifying references to self)" responses to the Kuhn Twenty Statements Test (Buerkle). (S279)

## Mental Illness (Hospitalization)

Among mental patients whose posthospital social and vocational performances were low, those whose primary role in the family was that of child were more likely to stay out of the hospital than were those whose primary role was that of spouse. (F124)

Family members influence instrumental performance; married men have higher levels of instrumental performance than do single men living with parents, because wives have higher expectations than parents do. This factor does not, however, explain rates of rehospitalization. (F124)

Differential demands of family account for the fact that patients from conjugal families return to the hospital more frequently than do those from parental families. (F124)

## Mental Illness (Schizophrenia)

In the families of persons who later develop schizophrenia, intensity and duration of pseudomutuality leads to the development of shared family mechanisms by which deviations from the family-role structure are excluded from recognition or are delusionally reinterpreted. (W021)

There is a correlation between schizophrenia in family members and a pervasive familial subculture of myths, legends, and ideology which stress the consequences of deviation from a limited number of fixed, engulfing family roles. (W021)

## Mental Illness (Social Adjustment)

Patients whose posthospital social and work performance is low are more likely to live with relatives who do not expect them to work or to participate in social activities as soon after release from the hospital as do relatives of patients with high performance. (F124)

The hypothesis that conjugal families would be less likely than parental families to tolerate low occupational and social performance on the part of the former mental patient is not supported by the data. (F124)

The mental patient who, after release from the hospital, is identified as the chief breadwinner, is more likely to show a high level of social and work performance. (F124)

The fewer the full-time workers in the family, the more likely the released mental patient is to perform at a high level occupationally and socially. (F124)

There is no relationship between the number of full-time workers in the family and whether or not the mental patient succeeds in remaining in the community. (F124)

There is no relationship between the family's expectations regarding the mental patient's posthospital social and vocational performance and the patient's success or failure in remaining in the community. (F124)

High levels of social and occupational performance of mental patients are most likely to occur in families in which the relatives expect and insist upon a high level of performance by the patient at the time he leaves the hospital. (F124)

The data do not support the notion that high demands by the family, when not met, drive the patient back to the hospital. (F124)

If the family makes limited demands upon the patient, he is more likely to remain insulated in his family setting than he is to return to the hospital, regardless of inadequate performance. (F124)

When expectations of family members are studied over time, high performance is more likely to be maintained when expectations remain high. (F124)

## Personality Adjustment

Role differentiation in families with loosely knit social networks (friends of husband and wife are not friends of one another) is associated with poor emotional adjustment of the children in the family. (S216)

### Personality of Kin
Relatives who are less authoritarian, anomic, and frustrated have higher expectations of performance from mental patients. (F124)

Among female patients, expectations are correlated only with type of family, not with the personality traits of the kin. (F124)

### Power
Instrumental leadership of a family member is associated with power for that partner.

### Power/Authority Structure of Family
The more important the decision or task faced by the family, the greater the likelihood that the exercise of power will correspond to the authority structure based on sex and age. (S207)

### Power Structure of Family
Considering the family as a triad of roles, High Status Authority (HSA), Low Status Subordinate (LSS), and High Status Friend (HSF), a power alliance in competition for any of the system's resources and benefits is more apt to occur between LSS and HSF than between HSA and HSF or HSA and LSS.

Viewing the family as a triad of roles, High Status Authority (HSA), Low Status Subordinate (LSS), and High Status Friend (HSF), if one parent plays an instrumental role vis-à-vis his children (HSA and LSS, respectively) in the presence of his spouse, the latter will tend to react in the role of High Status Friend toward the children rather than to duplicate the HSA role.

The degree of dominance exhibited by one family member is determined more by family-role definitions than it is by more personal factors, particularly to the individual or to the person with whom he is interacting. (C124)

### Role Behavior in Family
Lack of family consensus on norms pertaining to role performance is a cause of breakdown in role performance by any of its members. (R105)

### Sex-Role Definition
As the children become less of a burden and more of a resource, role differentiation between husband and wife increases.

### Sex-Role Definition in Society
The degree to which conjugal roles are segregated is correlated with and a reflection of the degree to which the sexes are segregated in the larger society. (F106)

### Sibling Relations (Solidarity)
The solidarity of male siblings is inversely related to the strength of the claims of members of the nuclear family on each brother. (G055)

### Size of Family
There is great specialization of functions within the family as family units become smaller and more dependent upon goods and services from the outside. (A047)

The larger the family, the greater the specialization of roles and functions of individual members. (B004)

Role specialization increases with size of family. (E100)

### Social Mobility
In the suburbs, upwardly mobile men do not have fewer children than do nonmobile men; there may be a slight inverse association. (L115)

White collar men with several children have higher levels of aspiration than do those with few children. (L115)

There are no differences between mobile and nonmobile white collar men in such indices of "familism" as number of offspring, housing status, age at marriage, and duration of childlessness. Men from lower-class origins were as family-oriented as were men from white collar backgrounds (in the modern "bureaucratic" era as contrasted with the former "entrepreneurial" era). (L115)

### Social Network
Lower-class families with closely knit networks (that is, where friends, relatives, and neighbors all tend to know each other) are more likely to differentiate clearly between instrumental and expressive roles, while a middle-class family with loosely knit networks would not be as apt to show such a differentiation. (B268)

### Stability of Family
If one parent assumes the High Status Authority role vis-à-vis the child (Low Status Subordinate) and the other spouse does not take the role of High Status Friend, tension within the family will increase unless the High Status Friend role is filled by statuses outside the family (i.e., clergyman or psychiatrist).

If one parent takes the role of High Status Authority and the other takes the role of High Status Friend, tension develops in the triad relationship with Low Status Subordinate (because the husband and wife relationship must remain positive for the marriage to survive).

Looking at the family in terms of the triad of roles, High Status Authority, Low Status Subordinate, and High Status Friend, the amount of tension produced by the interaction between a given High Status Authority and a given Low Status Subordinate is directly proportional to the difference in status between the High Status Authority and the Low Status Subordinate.

There is more balance in the family system where the relationship between High Status Authority and High Status Friend is negative.

If the relationship between High Status Friend and Low Status Subordinate in a family remains positive, pressure is likely to be exerted to change the relationship of High Status Authority and Low Status Subordinate from negative to positive, creating a sentimental congruence in which all relationships are positive.

If, in a family, the relationship between High Status Authority and the Low Status Subordinate remains negative, pressure is exerted to change the relationship from High Status Friend and Low Status Subordinate from positive to negative, creating a sentimental congruence in which one negative relationship is balanced by another.

### Status in Family
Mothers and fathers are more likely than not to evaluate similarly the role performance of family members. (M201)

Mothers and their adolescent children are more likely to

be in agreement in their evaluation of family-role performances than are fathers and adolescents. (M201)

### Tension Management

Considering the family as a triad of roles, High Status Authority (HSA), Low Status Subordinate (LSS), and High Status Friend (HSF), to insure a tension balance within a given actor, the family system is more apt to be set up so that actors play the role of HSA in one subsystem and HSF in another subsystem than to restrict an actor to one of these roles exclusively.

Viewing the family as a triad of roles, High Status Authority (HSA), Low Status Subordinate (LSS), and High Status Friend (HSF), where one parent plays an instrumental role (HSA) vis-à-vis a child (LSS) in the presence of the other spouse the situation will be a more relaxed one if the latter assumes a role of High Status Friend than if he assumes a more instrumental role.

## ROLE DEFINITION IN FAMILY (DEPENDENCY)
### X   Political Rebellion

In a society where it is common that family controls on the individual are so strong as to limit severely his autonomy, political rebellion acts as a form of tension release for aggression against the family. (P056)

## ROLE DEFINITION OF CHILD
### X   Parental-Role Definition

The hypothesis that the parent will prescribe for the child the reciprocal of the prescriptions which he holds for his own (parental) role is not confirmed. (M191)

## ROLE DEFINITION OF HUSBAND–WIFE
### X   Class

Lower-class husbands are less likely than middle-class husbands to share housekeeping tasks. (G157)

The higher the social class, the more likely husband and wife are to agree on the importance of social-emotional behavior. (L173)

### Cohesion of Family

Family adjustment is more likely to occur when the husband and wife have a congruence of economic expectations and roles. (B033)

### Cohesion of Kin-Group

Couples with closely knit kin networks (its members are in interaction with one another) tend to define more rigorously the roles of husbands and wives than do couples with loosely knit kin networks. (B210)

### Divorce

Differing opinions between husband and wife regarding their marital-role obligations are associated with a greater proneness to divorce. (G156)

### Duration of Marriage

Consensus of couples regarding marital roles is correlated with length of marriage. (T092)

### Husband-Wife Relations (Role Strain)

Deviation of husband or wife from the modal rank order of role performances in their subculture is correlated with the degree of role strain (nonfulfillment of role expectations of spouse) they experience. (H204)

The degree to which the husband's or wife's rank ordering of role expectations of the other spouse corresponds with the modal rank order of role expectations of the other spouse in their subculture is not related to the degree of role strain in their relationsip. (H204)

The degree of the husband's deviation from the modal rank order of role performance in that subculture is correlated with the degree of role strain experienced by the wife; a similar association is not found for deviation by the wife. (H204)

The degree of role strain experienced by the husband or wife is correlated with the degree of deviation of the other spouse from his or her modal rank ordering of role expectations of him (her). (H204)

### Industrialization/Urbanization

Industrialization and urbanization do not lead to a reduction in marital-role specialization. (S205)

### Marital Adjustment

Acute tensions occur in polygynous families when the partners lack behavioral expectations for defining a multiple-mate situation. (B033)

Problems of courtship and marriage are reduced to a minimum when the roles of expected behavior are sharply defined. (B033)

Where husbands and wives have widely divergent conceptions of the behavior expected of each other, crises are almost certain to arise. (B033)

Marital strain is likely to be reduced when the partners lower their expectations of emotional performance and comply with minimal role obligations. (G134)

Divorced couples exhibit a greater disparity in their attitudes toward the roles of the husband and wife in marriage than do married couples. (J002)

There is a correlation between marital satisfaction and the congruence of the couple's attitudes toward the roles of husband and wife in marriage. (T092)

There is no relationship between marital-role agreement and marital satisfaction. (T092)

### Marital Stability

In societies in which the emotional relationship between husband and wife is not relevant to the definition of their marital obligations, emotional conflicts and tensions are less likely to be disruptive. (G138)

The greater the complementarity of roles between husband and wife, the greater will be the stability of their marriage. (S075)

### Self-Conception

If a spouse deviates in behavior from the evaluative rankings of role performance in his or her subculture, he or she is more likely to experience role strain (feeling that he or she is failing role expectations).

If a spouse evaluates the role expectations of the other spouse differently than does the subculture in which he or she lives, there is no effect on the role strain in their relationship (feeling of not living up to role expectations).

If the husband deviates in behavior from the evaluative rankings of role performance in his subculture, the wife is more likely to feel role strain; by contrast, there is no correlation between her deviation in this respect and his feeling of role strain.

### Sex-Role Definition of Child

The more that the child perceives the division of expressive-instrumental functions between mother and father, the more likely is the child to differentiate the parents with respect to sex. (B234)

### Sex Status
Significantly more conservative attitudes toward the marital roles of husband and wives are found among males than among females. (J002)

Wives are more likely to value the socioemotional aspects of interaction than are husbands. (T092)

### Social Network
The greater the extent to which a couple belongs to a highly interconnected social network (friends of husband and wife are each other's friends) from which they can draw help, the more likely it is that the conjugal roles are rigidly segregated. (B268)

The more dispersed a couple's network of social contacts (i.e., its members do not see one another independently of the couple), the more likely they are to be uncertain about the norms pertaining to the rights and duties of the husband and wife. (B268)

Couples with loosely knit social networks (i.e., friends of husband and wife are not friends of one another) are more likely to develop less differentiated role definitions and activity than are couples with closely knit social networks. (S216)

## ROLE DEFINITION OF HUSBAND-WIFE (AFFECTION)    X Marital Stability
Where affection is not institutionally expected in a marriage, its absence will not produce active antagonisms which may lead to the dissolution of the marriage ties. (T106)

## ROLE DEFINITION OF HUSBAND–WIFE (RIGIDITY)    X Marital Adjustmen
Emotionally disturbed marriages tend to be character ized by a rigid differentiation of husband and wife roles (V028)

## ROLE DEFINITION OF KIN/NONKIN    X Marital Adjustment
Marital conflict is more likely to occur if the expectations of friends and relatives are not congruous with those of the couple. (B033)

## ROLE DEFINITION OF WIFE    X Class
The higher the socioeconomic class, the higher the social rewards for wives' participation in voluntary organizations. (S276)

The higher the socioeconomic class, the less likely is the role of "wife" defined in such a way as to conflict with membership in voluntary organizations. (S276)

The higher the socioeconomic class, the less is the importance attached by the wife to her familial roles. (S276)

### Employment of Wife
When wives work they change toward equalitarian authority expectations. (B208)

On the average, husbands of working wives change toward equalitarian authority expectations. (B208)

### Occupational Rank of Wife
Wives with very low occupational status, as well as wives without jobs, rate highly their housework contributions, while they downgrade interference with the husband's career.

## ROLE DEFINITIONS, FLEXIBILITY OF    X Isolation of Nuclear Family
A greater flexibility of kin role is tolerated when residence pattern is that of the isolated nuclear family. (F050)

## ROLE IN FAMILY    X Father-Son Relations (Affection)
Sons who have received insufficient paternal affection are less likely to give affection and support to their own families than are sons who have received adequate paternal affection. (M204)

### Mental Illness (Schizophrenia)
A correlation exists between the development of schizophrenic personality and shifts in the occupancy of family roles. (W021)

### Mental Illness (Social Adjustment)
In general, the higher the performance level expected of the posthospital mental patient, the higher the level of his performance. (F124)

Relatives of patients whose family role is that of son have lower expectations of posthospital performance than do relatives of patients whose family role is that of husband. (F124)

### Political Activity
Individuals who are active in political and other social organizations are more likely to have family members who are also active participants. (H244)

Within families, there is a somewhat higher correlation between the degree of political and social activity of husbands and wives than between parents and children. (H244)

Politically active individuals are more likely to come from families where several members are politically active than from families in which only one member is active. (H244)

### Social Adjustment, Premorbid
Schizophrenic patients having relatively good premorbid adjustment "play a more assertive role and enjoy more freedom" within the family than do patients with poor premorbid adjustment (Phillips Scale). (F115)

## ROLE MODEL    X Husband-Wife Relations
There is a positive association between daughters who perceive their parents as actively concerned with one another and the daughters' choice of their mothers as their adult-role models. (H201)

### Husband-Wife Relations (Conflict)
Children who report high parental disagreement are more likely to avoid choosing either parent as a role model, more often choosing peers. (H201)

### Marital Adjustment
A daughter who sees her mother's life as being favorably changed by marriage is more likely to choose her mother as an adult-role model. (H201)

## ROLE OF MOTHER    X Adult-Child Relations (Indulgence)
In societies where mothers have few economic responsibilities and are little involved in the ceremonial life of the tribe, there tends to be more indulgence with infants. (W127)

## ROLE STRUCTURE OF FAMILY
### X   Mental Illness (Schizophrenia)

In schizophrenic family organization, there is a tendency for inappropriate role structures to be justified. (W021)

In families of persons who later develop schizophrenia, intensity and duration of pseudomutuality leads to the development of shared family mechanisms by which deviations from the family-role structure are excluded from recognition or are delusionally reinterpreted. (W021)

Schizophrenics tend to come from families in which there is a limited number of engulfing roles. (W124)

## ROLE STRUCTURE OF FAMILY (RIGIDITY)
### X   Mental Illness (Schizophrenia)

Schizophrenics tend to come from families which have more rigid role structures than are found in families of normal children. (W124)

# S

## SCAPEGOATING   X   Behavior Problems of Child
If parents relieve their conflict by having a child perform the scapegoat role, the child is socialized to the role by the use of inconsistent pressures and will not learn the role of a well-behaved child. (B204)

### Cognitive Development
Where family anxiety and problems require the use of a scapegoat for relief and no child is an appropriate symbol, the child's cognitive distortion ensues to permit the scapegoating. (B204)

### Cohesion of Family
The greater the extent to which the parents displace their difficulties onto the child, the more likely it is that the stability and solidarity of the family will be maintained. (V033)

### Conflict in Family
Where anxiety and problems exist in a family, the child with physical peculiarities is most apt to become the focus of family problems. (B204)

### Emotional Problems
The greater the extent to which the parents displace their difficulties onto the child, the more likely it is that the child will become emotionally maladjusted. (V033)

### Husband-Wife Relations (Conflict)
The child selected as the object of parental hostility in a disturbed family is the one that best symbolizes the conflicts between the parents. (B204)

### Husband-Wife Relations (Intimacy)
In disturbed families, solidarity of the marriage increases with scapegoating of a child. (B204)

### Incest
In the father-daughter and brother-sister type of incest, the female participant is usually estranged from the family. The mother tends to condone, at least outwardly, the behavior of the husband and son. (W123)

### Juvenile Delinquency
When a parent displaces emotion meant for his spouse onto one of the children, he is likely to jeopardize the child's feeling of membership within the family, which may lead to delinquency. (S226)

### Marginal Status
Where parents have a marginal status in a community, they tend to discharge unresolved tensions by making a child the focus of their hostility. (B204)

### Marital Adjustment
The greater the extent to which a child is a symbol of the unresolved problem(s) in his family, the more likely it is that the parents will displace their conflicts from each other onto the child. (V033)

### Mental Illness
Mental illness is most likely to occur in those individuals who are the focus for intrafamilial hostility. (J019)

### Nonkin Relations (Hostility)
Where the family is unable to manifest hostilities it feels toward the outside, it tends to direct these hostilities against a family-member scapegoat. (B204)

### Ordinal Position
Where scapegoating is thought to relieve parental conflict, the oldest child is most often chosen to fulfill this role. (B204)

### Parent-Child Relations (Hostility)
If parents' most serious unresolved problems are with persons of a given sex, a child chosen to represent family conflict will be of that sex. (B204)

The greater the extent to which the parents displace their difficulties onto the child, the more likely it is that lesser, secondary difficulties will arise (hostility against the parents from the child and community disapproval). (V033)

### Parent-Child Relations (Rebellion)
Repression of rebellious feelings against their fathers may cause married adults to release their aggressions against the weaker partner and children. (S219)

### Sibling Relations (Conflict)
Where parental conflicts stem from conflict with their own siblings, they direct their hostility toward the child in the same ordinal position as the sibling which caused their conflict. (B204)

## SCAPEGOATING (INTRAFAMILY)
### X   Cohesion of Family
Scapegoating within a family system tends to reinforce its solidarity. (B204)

## SCHOLASTIC ACHIEVEMENT       X   Aggression
Parents of normal children have higher expectations for their sons' school achievement than do the parents of aggressive boys (both groups of boys matched for I.Q.). (B213)

### Artificial Insemination, Attitude Toward
The greater the academic achievement of the college student, the more likely he is to accept artificial insemination. (V035)

The greater the academic achievement of the college student, the less likely he is to accept artificial insemination. (V035)

### Aspiration Level
Children who drop out of high school are more likely to have parents who are indifferent to their school attendance than are those who do not drop out. (H189)

### Broken Home
There is no difference between adolescents from unbroken homes and those from broken and reconstituted homes regarding their mean school-grade point average. (B276)

### Child-Rearing Attitudes
Mothers of high achieving students are more likely to have dominating child-rearing attitudes than are mothers of low achievers. (D074)

Mothers of high achieving students are more likely to have ignoring attitudes toward the child than are mothers of low achievers, attitudes which imply high restrictions on the child in the home. (D074)

Mothers of high achieving students tend to have more punitive attitudes with respect to child rearing than do those of low achievers. (D074)

### Child-Rearing Practices (Achievement Demands)
Low scholastic achievers are more likely than high scholastic achievers to report strong parental demands for achievement. (E102)

Parental achievement demands are not related to the child's scholastic performance, regardless of the parents' social class. (E102)

Regardless of the child's academic motivation, parental achievement demands are negatively related to the child's scholastic attainment. (E102)

Parental scholastic achievement demands have little effect in keeping the child in school. (E102)

### X    Child-Rearing Practices (Achievement Demands)
### Scholastic Motivation
Parental achievement demands have a greater effect on increasing the child's academic motivation among low scholastic achievers than among high scholastic achievers. (E102)

### Child-Rearing Practices (Demands)
Parents of children with high academic achievement make more specific and more clearly defined demands upon their children than do parents of under achievers. (S256)

### Child-Rearing Practices (Dependency)
There is a positive relationship between the severity of independence training and high achievement among college students. (D065)

Parents of children with high academic achievement records showed significantly more interest in fostering the independence of their children than did parents of under achievers. (S256)

### Child-Rearing Practices (Giving Reasons)
Parental explanation of policies, when accompanied by autocratic control, is more apt to produce low academic achievement than high achievement. (E105)

### Child-Rearing Practices (Indulgence)
The indulgence of children by their kinsmen tends to retard the process of education. (B075)

### Child-Rearing Practices (Punishment)
Children who perceive themselves as autonomous and their parents as coercive (punishing) tend to do better academically than others. (H205)

### Child-Rearing Practices (Severity)
Among college students, perceived severity of upbringing is associated with high achievement. (D065)

### Child-Rearing Practices (Sex)
Mothers who are nonpermissive regarding sexual behavior expect their children to do better in school than do mothers who are more permissive in this area. (M186)

### Child-Rearing Practices (Strictness)
Mothers of children who are high achievers (in junior high school) are stricter disciplinarians than are those of low achievers. (T090)

### Child-Rearing Practices (Submission)
If a child is called on consistently to submit or to sacrifice for others his scholastic problems will be greater than those of children reared in a normal home. (S212)

### Child-Rearing Values (Agreement)
If the parents disagree between themselves on the behavior standards of the child, the child is likely to be an unsuccessful student. (M174)

### Dependency
High-school dropouts are more likely to be dependent children who are unwilling to assume any self-responsibility than are those who remain in school. This is more so for boys than for girls. (E102)

Children who perceive themselves as autonomous and their parents as coercive (punishing) tend to do better academically than others. (H205)

Mothers of daughters who are poor academic achievers are more likely to need the dependency of their daughters (as measured by the PARI) than are mothers of academic achievers. (S230)

### Disorganization of Family
High-school dropouts are more likely than graduates to come from unstable, impoverished home environments. (E102)

### Educational Aspiration
Low achieving adolescents who are exposed to conditions that generate and facilitate upward mobility (middle-class status, college-educated fathers who are active in independence training, and parents who insist on their children going to college) are as likely as are high achieving adolescents who are not exposed to such conditions to plan definitely to attend college. (E102)

### Family-School Relations
Families who support the school are more likely to facilitate the performance of their children. (P083)

### Father-Daughter Relations (Affection)
As measured by the PARI, fathers of daughters who do poorly academically are more likely to avoid expressions of affection than are fathers of daughters who do well academically. (S230)

### Father-Son Relations
Boys with primary neurotic learning inhibitions (poor learning not associated with other behavior or personality problems) are likely to have fathers who see them as competitors for their mothers' affection and who, therefore, deprecate their achievements. (G143)

### Foster-Home/Institutional Care
Children raised in foster homes achieve better in school than do children raised in institutions. (P068)

### Marital Adjustment
As measured by the PARI, fathers of daughters who do well academically are more likely to report marital conflicts in the family than are fathers of daughters who do poorly academically. (S230)

### Marriage Chances
The greater the academic achievement of the man, the less likely he is to marry. (M232)

### Mother-Child Relations
Mothers of children who are high scholastic achievers are more dominant and ignoring of their children than are the mothers of low scholastic achievers. (H199)

### Mother-Child Relations (Demands)
The mother who makes impossible demands upon her children for attention (through hysteria, depression) is more likely than the child-centered mother to produce children who under-achieve at school. (S226)

### Mother-Child Relations (Dominance)
Mothers of children who are high achievers (in junior high school) are more dominanting than are mothers of low achievers. (T090)

### Mother-Daughter Relations (Aggression)
As measured by the PARI, mothers of daughters who do poorly academically are less tolerant of aggressive behavior in their daughters than are mothers of daughters who do well academically. (S230)

### Mother-Daughter Relations (Dominance)
Mothers of daughters who are poor academic achievers are more likely to be dominant (as measured by the PARI) than are mothers of academic achievers. (S230)

### Mother-Daughter Relations (Hostility)
Mothers of daughters who are poor academically are more fearful of their own hostility (as measured by the PARI) than are mothers of daughters who do well academically. (S230)

### Mother-Daughter Relations (Respect)
Mothers of daughters who are poor academic achievers are more likely to need the respect of their daughters (as measured by the PARI) than are mothers of daughters who do well academically. (S230)

### Ordinal Position
A working-class boy has a greater chance of entering an upper school if he is an elder or eldest child. (L115)

Middle children are less likely to go to college. (L115)

### Parent-Child Relations (Affection)
Among college students, felt lack of parental love is associated with high achievement. (D065)

### Parent-Child Relations (Approval)
If the parents are approving, interested, and understanding toward the child, the child is likely to be a highly successful student, while domineering and overrestrictive parents are likely to have children who are unsuccessful students. (M174)

### Parent-Child Relations (Rejection)
Adolescents who are doubtful of their own acceptance by their family seek a more secure status by means of academic (over) achievement. (M060)

### Parent-Son Relations (Affection)
Boys who are under achievers are more likely than boys who are high achievers to describe their parents as approving, trusting, and affectionate. (E102)

### Parent-Son Relations (Control)
Boys who are under achievers are more likely than boys who are high achievers to describe their parents as nonpressuring, nonrestrictive, and noncoercive. (E102)

### Personality of Father (Change)
Fathers of daughters who are poor academically are higher on the PARI Scale of Change Orientation than are fathers of daughters who do well academically. (S230)

### Personality of Father (Irresponsibility)
As measured by the PARI, fathers of sons who do poorly academically are more likely to be irresponsible than are fathers of sons who do well academically. (S230)

### Personality of Mother (Seclusiveness)
As measured by the PARI, mothers of sons who do well academically are less likely to be seclusive than are mothers of sons who do poorly academically. (S230)

### Power Structure of Family
Equalitarian husband-wife relations are more strongly related to academic achievement in the child than are wife-dominant, husband-dominant, or conflicting conjugal power structures. (E102)

### Scholastic Achievement (Parental)
Children who have reading disabilities are more likely than those who do not to have parents who had learning difficulties. (S225)

### Self-Conception of Father
Boys with primary neurotic learning inhibitions (poor learning, not associated with behavior or personality problems) are likely to have fathers who see themselves as inadequate occupationally—as failures. (G143)

### Self-Conception of Mother
Boys with primary neurotic learning inhibitions (poor learning, not associated with other behavior or personality problems) are likely to have mothers with overly masculine self-images, who prevent their development of scholastic achievement in order to protect their own distorted self-images. (G143)

### Sex-Role Identification
Boys with primary neurotic learning inhibitions (poor learning, not associated with other behavior or personality problems) are likely to have mothers with overly masculine self-images, who prevent their development of scholastic achievement in order to protect their own distorted self-images. (G143)

### Sexual Permissiveness
As measured on the PARI, parents of children who do well academically are less likely to suppress sexuality than are parents of children who do poorly academically. (S230)

### Sibling Structure
Boys who are younger children in a family of mostly girls have lower grades than other boys. (R120)

### Size of Family
The larger the family, the lower the scholastic achievement of adolescent boys. (E102)

Size of family has no relationship to continuation in school for those with higher status or class position. (L115)

Children from larger families are more likely to drop out

of school than are equally intelligent students from smaller families (Britain). (T095)

### Toilet Training

The more severe the mother is in toilet training the child, the more likely is she to expect the child to do well in school (U.S.). (S191)

### SCHOLASTIC ACHIEVEMENT BY SEX STATUS OF CHILD    X    Child-Rearing Practices (Dependency)

High independence training by parents is associated with high scholastic achievement in adolescents; the relationship is stronger for boys than for girls. (E102)

### SCHOLASTIC ACHIEVEMENT OF CHILD
### X    Child-Rearing Practices (Authoritarian/Restrictiveness)

Mothers of high achievers are more authoritarian and restrictive in the handling of their children than are mothers of low achievers. (E102)

### Child-Rearing Practices (School Work)

High scholastic achievement in adolescents is associated with parents who emphasize the importance of being studious and with their being more vigilant and critical regarding the adolescent's school work. (E102)

### Education of Father

College students whose fathers did not obtain a college degree are more likely to drop out of college than are students whose fathers did obtain a degree. (A067)

### Education of Mother

College students whose mothers did not obtain a college degree are more likely to drop out of college than are students whose mothers did obtain a degree. (A067)

### Employment of Mother

There is no correlation between maternal employment and educational competence (grade average) of the child. (S265)

Children of working mothers are likely to have lower intellectual performance in school than are children whose mothers do not work. (S265)

### Occupation of Father

College students whose fathers hold professional or managerial positions are less likely to drop out of college than are students whose fathers work in other occupations. (A067)

### Personality Problems of Mother (Oral)

Children with learning problems are more likely to have mothers with excessive oral needs (dependency) and hostility directed toward their children than are those who do not have difficulty in learning. (S223)

### Pregnancy

Mothers who experienced emotional stress during pregnancy are likely to give birth to infants who suffer from general impairment (mental and physical) which in turn predisposes them to lower school achievement during childhood. (S227)

### SCHOLASTIC ACHIEVEMENT OF DAUGHTER
### X    Parent-Child Relations (Warmth)

Parents of daughters with high college achievement records were less indifferent to their daughters than were parents of low college achievers (as measured on the Teahan Ignoring Subscale). (T103)

### Personality of Mother (Dominance)

Mothers of daughters with low college achievement records are more dominating than their daughters are. (T013)

Mothers of daughters with high college achievement records do not differ from their daughters in dominance. (T103)

### SCHOLASTIC ACHIEVEMENT OF SON
### X    Parent-Child Relations (Communication)

Boys who are under achievers are more likely than those who are high achievers to describe their families as commonly sharing personal ideas and thoughts. (E102)

### Personality of Father (Dominance)

Fathers of sons with high college achievement records are less dominating than are fathers of sons with low achievement records (as measured on the Teahan Dominance Subscale). (T103)

### Recreation

Boys who are under achievers are more likely than high achievers to describe their families as sharing recreational activities. (E102)

### SCHOLASTIC ACHIEVEMENT (PARENTAL)
### X    Scholastic Achievement

Children who have reading disabilities are more likely than those who do not to have parents who had learning difficulties. (S225)

### SCHOLASTIC ACHIEVEMENT (READING)
### X    Toilet Training/Feeding

Children who have reading disabilities are more likely than those who do not to have experienced feeding and toilet-training periods. (S225)

### SCHOLASTIC ADJUSTMENT
### X    Achievement Motivation

Children who drop out from high school are more likely to have parents who are indifferent to their school attendance than are those who do not drop out. (H189)

### Broken Home

Adolescent girls from reconstituted families are more likely than those from broken and unbroken families to have positive attitudes regarding school. (B276)

Adolescent girls from reconstituted families are more likely than those from broken and unbroken families to maintain better relationships with their teachers. (B276)

There is no difference between adolescents from unbroken homes and those from broken and reconstituted homes regarding their degree of participation in school activities. (B276)

There is no difference between adolescents from unbroken homes and those from broken and reconstituted homes regarding their attitudes toward school. (B276)

Adolescents from unbroken homes are less likely to be absent from school than are those from broken and reconstituted homes. (B276)

### Child-Rearing Practices (Consensus)

There is no relationship between discrepancy between personal attitudes (measured by the PARI, ATE, and Q-Sort Personality Tests) and the child's first-grade school adjustment and popularity.

#### Child-Rearing Practices (Consistency)

Children with school phobias are likely to have parents who discipline inconsistently, being sometimes lenient and other times punitive. (C115)

#### Child-Rearing Practices (Criticism)

Children whose mothers are excessively critical and depreciative of them tend to be reluctant or fearful toward school. (R113)

#### Child-Rearing Practices (Dependency)

Youths with parents who are very active in independence training are much more likely than are those with inactive parents to have positive attitudes concerning school. (E102)

#### Conflict in Family

The greater the conflict between family members, especially if one (father, mother, or child) is dominant, the greater the likelihood that the child will refuse to go to school. (K106)

#### Death

School phobics are more likely than normal children to have experienced death or the threat of death (relative to self or family) prior to school attendance. (D065)

#### Dependency

School phobics are less likely than normal children to be socially mature and relatively independent from their mothers. (D065)

#### Dependency of Father

Girls with school phobias are likely to have fathers with strong dependency needs. (C115)

#### Employment of Mother

Sons of working mothers are no more likely than are sons of nonworking mothers to exhibit deviant behavior in school, to be leaders in school, or to conform to school expectations. (W151)

#### Geographic Mobility

Among sons, low geographical mobility of the family is significantly related to leadership in school and conformity to school expectations. (W151)

#### Marital Adjustment

Mothers of children with school phobias tend to lack emotional support and fulfillment in their marital relationships. (E095)

Children who drop out of high school are less likely to have successful marriages than are those who continue in school. (H189)

#### Maternal Deprivation

Children who are deprived of adequate mothering during infancy are more likely in later years to be unable to concentrate in school. (P068)

#### Maternal Overprotectiveness

The maternally overprotected child is less likely to have special school problems.

#### Mother-Child Relations

The child develops a phobia against attending school, not due to fear of such attendance, but because of anxiety about separation from a parent. (E095)

Mothers of children with school phobias tend to have disturbed relationships with dominating and overprotecting mothers or mothers-in-law. (E095)

#### Mother-Child Relations (Ambivalence)

Mothers of school phobics are more likely than those of normals to have strong feelings of both love and hostility toward their children. (D065)

#### Mother-Child Relations (Indulgence)

"School phobia" (refusal to attend school) is associated with maternal overindulgence and close mother-child relations. (L143)

#### Mother-Child Relations (Rejection)

Children with school phobias are likely to have mothers who reject them. (S239)

#### Ordinal Position

Only and second-born children have the smallest proportion of school difficulties; youngest children are more likely to have a greater number of school difficulties.

Sons who are leaders in school and who conform to school expectations are more likely to be elder or only children; those who exhibit deviant behavior in school are more likely to be youngest and intermediate children. (W151)

#### Parent-Child Relations (Communication)

School phobia in the child is due to the ambivalent feelings and the contradictory verbal and behavioral cues of the parents. (E095)

#### Parent-Child Relations (Evaluation)

The higher the student's evaluation of his parents, the higher the academic level at which he will perform. (C107)

#### Parent-Child Relations (Interaction)

Children from homes where there is a high level of parent-child interaction have a higher level of activity participation in nursery school than do children from homes where there is a low level of parent-child interaction. (B266)

#### Parent-Child Relations (Rejection)

The mother of a child with school phobia tends to react to the child's striving for independence and self-gratification with feelings of personal rejection and hostility. (E095)

Parental rejection is not related to "school phobia" (i.e., refusal to attend school) in the child. (L143)

#### Parent Loss

Children who are removed from their parents while they are between the ages of 5 and 16 are less able to concentrate on schoolwork than are children with normal parent relationships. (B270)

"School phobia" (refusal to attend school) is not associated with absence of either parent during the child's early years. (L143)

#### Peer Relations

The parents of adolescent boys who are accepted by their peers are more likely to be satisfied with their sons' adjustments in school than are the parents of boys who are rejected by their peers. (F108)

#### Personality of Father

The fathers of school phobics are more likely than those of normal children to be passive and ineffectual; the mothers are more likely to be dominant. (D065)

### Personality Problems of Mother

The mothers of school-phobic children are more likely than are the mothers of normal children to be immature and dependent on the maternal grandmother. (D065)

### Personality Problems of Mother (Anxiety/Ambivalence)

Mothers of children with school phobias tend to be highly anxious and ambivalent in their feelings toward others. (E095)

### Personality Problems of Parents

Children with school phobias are likely to come from families in which the parents are characterized by either psychosis or neurosis. (S239)

### Sex-Role Identification

Men who identify with their fathers will be better adjusted in college than those who identify with their mothers. (H194)

Women who identify with their mothers will be less well adjusted in college than will those who identify with their fathers. (H194)

### Sex-Role Identification of Father

Fathers of school-phobic children are more likely than others to have problems concerning their sexual identification. (C115)

### Sibling Rivalry

A child with school phobia is more likely than others to have a sibling who is preferred by his parents. (S239)

### Size of Family

Sons of small families (three or fewer siblings) are no more likely than are those of large families to exhibit deviant behavior in school, to be leaders in school, or to conform to school expectations. (W151)

## SCHOLASTIC ADJUSTMENT OF CHILD
### X   Cohesion of Family

The closer the student's ties to his family, the better his adjustment to the campus community. (R116)

### Employment of Mother

Maternal employment during various periods of the child's life (less than 4 years, 4 to 6 years, less than 7 years) is unrelated to the child's adjustment in school (as measured by the Otis Quick-Scoring Form, the Stanford Achievement Test, and the Iowa Test of Educational Development). (B294)

### Father Absence

Absence of an adult male in the home is correlated with academic failure in the child. (R108)

### Personality Problems of Mother (Perfectionism)

The mothers of school-phobic children are more likely than are the mothers of normal children to be perfectionists, having idealized pictures of what good mothers should be. (D065)

## SCHOLASTIC ADJUSTMENT (PHOBIA)
### X   Marital Adjustment of Parents

Children with school phobias are likely to come from families characterized by a great deal of spousal conflict, although divorce and separation are not likely. (C115)

## SCHOLASTIC ADJUSTMENT (READING)
### X   Child-Rearing Practices (Aggression)

If a child has not been allowed the expression of aggression, he is more likely than the child who has been allowed such expression to develop a reading disability. (S225)

### Feeding Problems

Children with reading disabilities are more likely than children who have no difficulty reading to have had uncomfortable experiences in the oral stage of development (particularly when being fed). (S225)

### Maternal Deprivation

Children with reading disabilities are more likely than those with no difficulty in reading to have had disturbed and deprived relationships with their mothers. (S225)

### Parent-Child Relations (Conflict)

If there is great antagonism on the part of a child toward a parent and the parent constantly stresses success in reading, the child is more likely to develop a reading disability in rebellion against the parent than is the child who can resist more openly. (S225)

### Sex Status

Since boys have more difficulty in learning to suppress aggressive drives (which impede learning) than girls do, they are more likely to develop reading difficulties. (S225)

### Sibling Rivalry

Children with reading disabilities are more likely than those without to have manifested severe sibling rivalry. (S225)

## SCHOLASTIC ASPIRATION
### X   Child-Rearing Practices (Dependency)

Adolescent college orientation is more related to parental independence training than to parental expectations concerning posthigh-school education. (E102)

## SCHOLASTIC/CREATIVE ACHIEVEMENT
### X   Authoritarianism

Parents of academic achievers are more authoritarian in their values and attitudes than are parents of creative adolescents. (E102)

## SCHOLASTIC MOTIVATION
### X   Child-Rearing Practices (Achievement Demands)

Parental achievement demands have a greater effect on increasing the child's academic motivation among low scholastic achievers than among high scholastic achievers. (E102)

### Child-Rearing Practices (Giving Reasons)/Power Structure of Family

Which parent has greater power in child rearing has less effect than use of explanation and reasoning on high academic motivation in the child. (E102)

### Education of Father/Mother

The father's educational level has a stronger effect on the adolescent's academic motivation than does the mother's educational attainment. (E102)

### Education of Parents

The greater the parents' educational attainment, the higher the adolescent's academic motivation, regardless of social class. (E102)

There is a positive relationship between parents' educational level and academic motivation in the adolescent, regardless of the degree of parental independence training. (E102)

### Ordinal Position

Among lower-class adolescents, youngest children are higher in academic motivation than are firstborns. (E102)

Among middle-class adolescents, oldest children are higher in academic motivation than are children who are youngest. (E102)

The firstborn child is higher in academic motivation than is the youngest, regardless of family size. (E102)

Middle children are lower in academic motivation than are oldest siblings. (E102)

### Power Structure of Family

Wife-dominated families are more apt to produce poorly motivated boys academically than are equalitarian or husband-dominated families. (B323)

In families where either the husband or wife is dominant, adolescents with autocratic fathers in child rearing are less motivated academically than are either those with permissive or with democratic fathers. (B323)

Academic motivation among adolescent boys and older (high-school) adolescent girls is strongest when their fathers are perceived as family head. (B323)

Girls are much more likely than boys to have high academic motivation if the family structure is equalitarian rather than wife or husband dominant. (E102)

Congruence in parental power is more related to high academic motivation in the child than is incongruence. (E102)

Which parent has greater power in child rearing has less effect than does use of explanation and reasoning on high academic motivation in the child. (E102)

### Religion

Among large lower-class families, Catholic adolescents are higher in academic motivation than are Protestant adolescents. (E102)

## SCHOLASTIC MOTIVATION BY CLASS
### X   Ordinal Position

The oldest child in middle-class families is higher in academic motivation than is the oldest child in lower-class families. (E102)

### Size of Family

Among high achieving adolescents, small family size has a greater effect on high academic motivation among lower-class than among middle-class adolescents. (E102)

## SCHOLASTIC MOTIVATION OF CHILD
### X   Child-Rearing Practices (Dependency)

Participation of both parents in independence training is associated with high academic motivation in the child. (E102)

### Child-Rearing Practices (Dependency/Achievement Demands)

Independence training has a much greater effect than do parental achievement demands on the child's academic motivation. (E102)

Among children with high scholastic records, parental achievement demands lead to high academic motivation only when accompanied by active independence training. (E102)

Among children with low scholastic records, parental achievement demands are more important than is independence training in leading to high academic motivation. (E102)

### Child-Rearing Practices (Dependency)/Education of Parents

High independence training has as great or greater an effect than does parental educational level on academic motivation in the adolescent. (E102)

### Child-Rearing Practices of Father (Autocratic/Democratic)

Academic motivation in the child increases as paternal power in child rearing decreases from autocratic to more democratic in form. (E102)

### Child-Rearing Practices of Father (Democratic)

High academic motivation in the child is strongly related to democratic child-rearing practices by the father. (E102)

### Child-Rearing Practices of Father (Dependency)

High paternal involvement in independence training is associated with high academic motivation in adolescents of both sexes. (E102)

### Child-Rearing Practices (Restrictiveness)

Among children with high scholastic records, those with low academic motivation are more apt to be reared restrictively and punitively than are those with high academic motivation. (E102)

### Education of Parents/Class

Educational level of parents has a greater effect on high academic motivation in the child than does social class. (E102)

### Educational Aspirations of Parents

Parental expectations regarding the adolescent's continuing his posthigh-school education have little influence on the adolescent's academic motivation. (E102)

Among adolescents who are not college-oriented, those whose parents have college ambitions for them are higher in academic motivation than are those whose parents do not. (E102)

### Power Structure of Family

The father's involvement in child rearing has a greater effect on high academic motivation in the child than does husband-wife power structure. (E102)

## SCHOLASTIC MOTIVATION OF CHILD BY CLASS
### X   Child-Rearing Practices (Dependency)

High independence training has a greater effect on high academic motivation among middle-class than among lower-class youths. (E102)

## SCHOLASTIC MOTIVATION OF CHILD
## BY SEX STATUS                    X   Size of Family

Among high achieving adolescents, the larger the family size, the greater the sex difference regarding academic motivation, girls being more motivated than boys. (E102)

## SCHOLASTIC MOTIVATION OF DAUGHTER
### X   Child-Rearing Practices (Control/Giving Reasons)

High parental power (parents who are either autocratic or authoritarian) combined with parental explanation of rules and discipline is associated with low academic motivation in girls. (E102)

## SCHOLASTIC MOTIVATION OF SON
### X   Child-Rearing Practices (Control/Giving Reasons)
High parental control (parents who are either autocratic or authoritarian) combined with parental explanation of rules and discipline is associated with high academic motivation in sons. (E102)

### Paternal Role
For boys, high paternal involvement in child rearing is a much more important factor for high academic motivation than is husband v. wife dominance in general family leadership. (E102)

In families where a father is head of the household, paternal dominance or lack of involvement in child rearing is associated with low academic motivation in sons, while a more supervisory role by the father in child rearing is associated with high academic motivation in sons. (E102)

## SCHOOL ATTENDANCE
### X   Child-Rearing Practices (Permissiveness)
There is a positive relationship between the mother's general permissiveness and the regularity with which the child attends school. (M216)

## SCHOOL SYSTEM          X   Dependency
An impersonal school system, by representing norms that are different from those found in the family, helps to reduce the child's dependence on his family. (G156)

## SEASON OF YEAR          X   Sexual Aggression
A high prevalence of male sex aggression occurs in the fall and in the spring. (K001)

Male sex aggression of less offensiveness is concentrated in the fall. (K001)

Male sex aggression of greater offensiveness is concentrated in the spring. (K001)

Sexual aggression at the most intimate levels of eroticism is more likely to take place during the spring and summer than during the fall and winter. (K018)

## SECRET SOCIETIES          X   Descent (Patrilineal)
Secret societies will tend to be of greater importance when the social structure is patrilineal. (C077)

### Economic Role of Women
Men's secret societies are more likely to occur in matrilineal societies, in response to the women's position of economic dominance. (W154)

## SECTION SYSTEM          X   Descent (Unilineal)
Two-section systems do not require descent groups or a particular rule of lineal descent. (N067)

## SEGMENTARY STRUCTURE
### X   Community Isolation
The development of a segmentary structure tends to be inhibited by a settlement pattern of self-sufficient communities. (F033)

### Descent (Double)
Double descent inhibits the emergence of segmentary lineages. (S087)

### Population
The emergence of a segmentary structure is to be expected where an increase of population and concomitant territorial expansion occur with the retention of patterns of interaction between members of the derivative communities. (F033)

### Territorial Expansion
The development of a segmentary structure is inhibited by the existence of physical or human barriers to territorial expansion. (F033)

## SEGMENTATION          X   Cohesion of Kin-Group
When migrating kin-groups maintain cohesion through patterns of continued interaction, the establishment of a segmentary structure is to be expected. (F033)

### Conflict in Clan
Clan fission is associated with intraclan hostility. (R054)

### Conflict in Lineage
Lineage segmentation tends to be directly correlated with internal dissension within the lineage group. (G056)

### Descent (Double)
Double descent patterns appear to be incompatible with the recognition of many levels of lineage segmentation. (H245)

### Descent (Lineage)
The lines of fission within a clan will follow the lineage affiliations of the clan members. (R054)

### Descent (Unilineal)
When patterns of unilinear descent are associated with lineage endogamy, the production of discrete kin-groups will not occur. (M023)

### Economic Level
The segmentation of local groups and lineages is, in part, a response to the pressures of the presence of heritable wealth. (M168)

Lineage segmentation will tend to occur when economic resources of the area are inadequate to support the population. (T020)

### Exogamy
The violation of regulations of clan exogamy serves as an index of impending clan fission. (M129)

The clan tends to lose its exogamous character with successive divisions within the unit. (R034)

The violation of exogamic restrictions within the lineage is indicative of an approaching lineage segmentation. (T059)

### Geographic Mobility
Migration, as a consequence of land shortage, is an important stimulus to fission. (W056)

### Kin Relations (Hostility)
Lineage fission is more likely to be complete when the break between member groups is accompanied by a situation of "extreme bitterness." (S283)

### Political Importance of Clan
The absence of clan political or territorial functions is consistent with the lack of a high degree of segmentation. (C094)

### Political Structure
There is an association between the extent of the internal differentiation of a lineage and the extent to which political roles are attached to segments of different depths. (H245)

The segmentary lineage structure is the product of a

segmentary political structure and unilineal descent groupings. (S087)

### Population

The segmentation of unilinear groups tends to occur with the expansion of population. (K029)

With an increase in the size of the population aggregate, a homogeneous kinship society tends to segment into unilateral kinship groups. (O006)

### Property

The accumulation of individual property tends to accelerate the process of lineage segmentation. (G056)

### Rank

Lineages will tend to subdivide if they contain several prominent men. (M169)

### Ranking in Lineage

Fission is more likely to occur when there is ranking within the lineage structure. (C091)

### Ranking of Lineages

The presence of a rank lineage system inhibits the development of a segmentary lineage structure. (L076)

### Residence

When the settlement pattern is that of a compact territorially segregated community, size of the clan and the number of their component basic lineages are restricted. (F033)

The segmentation of the lineage group tends to occur with the localization on agricultural sites. (K029)

The segmentation of local groups and lineages is likely to occur as a response to settled residence. (M168)

### Sibling Rank

When there is a formal disparity in status between elder and younger brothers, fission of the lineage is more likely to occur. (R004)

### Size of Kin-Group

An increase in size is likely to result in the subdivision of a kin-group. (N034)

### Size of Lineage

Delay in the segmentation of the lineage may occur if the unit is small in size. (F030)

### Stability of Social Structure

The limits of lineage segmentation are set by the condition of stability in the social structure. (S087)

### Subsistence Pattern (Pastoral)

The recurrent search for grazing lands of the pastoral economy tends to separate and scatter the lineage residential group. (G022)

### Warfare

Inter- and intra-tribal wars and raids tend to separate and scatter the lineage residential group. (G022)

## SEGMENTATION OF JOINT FAMILY          X   Conflict in Family

Hostility between wives of siblings is a major factor in the fission of the joint family. (M081)

## SELF-AGGRESSION OF CHILD   X   Size of Family

If there is only one boy in a family, he is less likely to be self-aggressive than if there are two or more. (S246)

## SELF-CONCEPTION          X   Age of Child

There is no clear relationship between the age of the child at time of divorce and his present level of self-esteem. (R129)

Among children who were very young at the time of divorce, those who had older mothers are more likely to have high self-esteem than those who had very young mothers. (R129)

### Aggression

Mothers perceive themselves to be more intropunitive than their children perceive them to be. (M177)

### Broken Home

Children of divorced or separated parents are more likely than are children of intact families to have low self-esteem. (R129)

Children whose parents are separated are as likely as children of intact families to have high self-esteem, but are less likely to have medium self-esteem and are more likely to have low self-esteem. (R129)

Children whose parents have been separated by death do not differ from those intact families in terms of self-esteem. (R129)

### Death of Mother/Father

Self-esteem of the child whose parents have been separated by death is somewhat lower if the mother has died than if the father has died. (R129)

### Emotional Adjustment

Parents of emotionally disturbed children are more likely to emphasize aggressive, distrustful, or dependent behavioral traits in describing self, spouse, and child than are parents of normals, who tend to emphasize managerial, competitive behavior. (M200)

Parents of emotionally disturbed children are more likely to show rejection of themselves and their interpersonal behavior than are parents of normals. (M200)

### Evaluation of Family Members

If a father rates himself favorably on several family attitude variables, he also rates his wife and child favorably. (B237)

### Father-Child Relations (Interest)

Paternal interest is not strongly related to self-esteem in children, except for the extreme group who reported that the father knew none of their friends; this group is distinctly more likely to have low self-esteem than those whose fathers knew most of their friends. (R129)

### Generational Emphasis

Institutionally imposed generational separateness is necessary for the child to develop a sense of identity. (C093)

### Husband-Wife Relations (Evaluation)

The higher the approval by the one marriage partner, the higher the self-confidence created in the other partner. (T092)

Persons tend to rate themselves less favorably than they rate their spouses and less favorably than they are rated by their spouses. (T092)

### Incest (Mother-Son)

The more developed the sense of self (in mother, son, or both), the less likely is mother-son incest to occur. (C093)

### Juvenile Delinquency

Families of juvenile delinquents have less self-respect than do families of nondelinquents. (S210)

### Marital Adjustment

The lower the marital adjustment, the more likely are the individuals to define themselves in subjective terms (i.e., happy, moody, bored) than according to structural designations (i.e., student, girl, Baptist, etc.). (B295)

The stronger the individual's feeling that he is inadequate in the marital relationship, the more likely is he to perceive problems in the marriage. (G126)

A woman who evaluates her marriage as unhappy is more likely to dream of herself and her husband or of other couples in unpleasant situations. (H232)

Well-adjusted couples are more likely to be characterized by congruency of self-image and ideal self than are maladjusted couples. (L152)

Well-adjusted spouses are likely to have greater congruence between ideal self-images and images of their spouses. (L152)

For men, congruence between self-image and image of one's father is associated with good marital adjustment, but no such relationship exists for women in relation to their mothers. (L152)

The more congruent the self-conceptions of subjects and the conceptions of them held by their spouses, the greater the marital satisfaction. (S279)

A marriage is more likely to be successful if both partners have highly favorable self-perceptions. (T092)

There is a correlation between marital compatibility and favorable self-perceptions and the even more favorable evaluation by the spouse. (T092)

Marital satisfaction is correlated with the congruence of the husband's ideal and self-concepts. (T092)

Marital satisfaction is correlated with the congruence of the husband's self-concept and his concept of his father. (T092)

Marital satisfaction is correlated with the congruence of the wives' concepts of their husbands and their concepts of their fathers. (T092)

The greater the degree of conformity of the husband's self-perception to the self-perception of other males, the more likely it is that his marriage will be happy. (T092)

Satisfaction in marriage is correlated with the congruence of the husband's self-conception and that held of him by the wife, but not with conceptions of wives, as a group. (T092)

### Mother-Child Relations

Children who report that their mothers know all or most of their friends have higher self-esteem than do those who report that their mothers know some or none of their friends. (R129)

The positive association between the child's self-esteem and the mother's knowledge of his friends holds regardless of whether the child (in childhood) confided in the mother, in someone else, or in no one. (R129)

The positive association between the child's self-esteem and the mother's knowledge of his friends holds regardless of whether he currently sides with the mother, the father, or with both equally in parental disagreements. (R129)

The positive association between the child's self-esteem and the mother's knowledge of his friends holds regardless of whether the mother was friendly or not friendly toward his friends. (R129)

Simple interest in the child (indicated by knowledge of the child's friends) may be more important than parental pleasantness or unpleasantness for the level of self-esteem in the child. (R129)

### Mother-Child Relations (Evaluation)

A mother who rates herself highly in terms of several selected family-attitude variables does not rate her husband and child as highly as the husband with a high self-rating rates his wife and child. (B237)

### Ordinal Position

There is no clear relationship between birth order and self-esteem. (R129)

### Parent-Child Relations

A child's feelings about himself are more closely related to the character of his relationships with his parents (parental expectations, strictness, favoritism, and identification with parents) than they are to experiences shared with parents (mobility, parent employment, marital status of parents, and size of family). (S279)

### Parent-Child Relations (Closeness)

The closer the parent-child relationship, the higher the child's self-evaluation (self-evaluation of personality and personal attractiveness). (L137)

### Parent-Child Relations (Communication)

Students who rarely or never participate in family mealtime conversations or who feel that family members are not interested in what they have to say, are considerably more likely than others to have low self-esteem. (R129)

### Parent-Child Relations (Indifference)

Exceptional indifference on the part of either or both parents is associated with low self-esteem in the child. (R129)

Contrary to the original hypothesis, it is not the punitive response of parents to poor grades that is most closely related to low self-esteem, but the indifference; those who report indifferent parental responses have lower self-esteem than do those who report punitive responses as well as lower than those who report supportive responses. (R129)

The association between parental indifference and children's self-esteem is not an artifact of social class, religion, sex, or small town/city environment; it is not a question of whether the parents were strict with the child or whether he felt the punishment they gave was deserved or undeserved. (R129)

Students who felt a lack of parental interest but who felt that the punishment they received in childhood was deserved have lower self-esteem than did those who reported their parents to be interested but who felt their punishment in childhood was generally undeserved. (R129)

### Peer Relations

The self-esteem of boys who are younger children in a family of mostly girls is relatively impervious to the extent to which they participate actively in high-school social activities, in general, the more active the boy is in social activities, the higher is his self-esteem. (R129)

In general, boys who consider themselves to be peer-group leaders have higher self-esteem than do those who do not, but boys who are younger children in a family of mostly girls tend to have high self-esteem even if they do not consider themselves to be leaders. (R129)

### Personality of Parent/Child (Similarity)

Conflict in self-perception is more likely when the child perceives himself as different from his parents. (W158)

### Power Structure of Family

Conflict in self-perception is more likely where the male child perceives the mother as the dominant figure in the family with reference to authority, affection, and role model. (W158)

### Remarriage

Children whose divorced mothers or widowed parents remarried tend to have lower self-esteem than do those whose parents did not remarry. (R129)

Children whose parents were separated by death are likely to have as high self-esteem as are those from intact families, provided the widowed parent does not remarry. (R129)

The older the child when the family is broken, the more likely he is to have low self-esteem if the mother remarries. (R129)

### Role Definition

If the mother wishes the child to be like his father, then the child's concept of his ideal self will also resemble his father. (W158)

### Role Definition of Husband-Wife

If a spouse deviates in behavior from the evaluative rankings of role performance in his or her subculture, he or she is more likely to experience role strain (feeling that he or she is failing role expectations).

If a spouse evaluates the role expectations of the other spouse differently than does the subculture in which he or she lives, there is no effect on the role strain in their relationship (feeling of not living up to role expectations).

If the husband deviates in behavior from the evaluative rankings of role performance in his subculture, the wife is more likely to feel role strain; by contrast, there is no correlation between her deviation in this respect and his feeling of role strain.

### Sibling Structure

In general, boys who consider themselves to be peer-group leaders have higher self-esteem than do those who do not, but boys who are younger children in a family of mostly girls tend to have high self-esteem even if they do not consider themselves to be leaders. (R129)

The self-esteem of boys who are younger children in a family of mostly girls is less influenced by their grades in school than is the self-esteem of other boys. (R129)

Only children have higher self-esteem than do children who have siblings. (R129)

Males who are only children are more likely to have high self-esteem than are girls who are only children. (R129)

Among girls, only children are slightly more likely to have low self-esteem, but less likely to have intermediate self-esteem than are girls with siblings. (R129)

Among Catholics and Protestants, differences in levels of self-esteem between only boys and girls are much smaller than they are among Jewish children. (R129)

In two-child families, there is no relationship between sibling structure and self-esteem. (R129)

If the family consists mostly of boys, there is no relationship between birth order and self-esteem of the boy. (R129)

The younger boy whose older siblings are chiefly or exclusively girls is likely to have higher self-esteem than are boys who have younger female siblings. (R129)

Younger boys with older brothers are more likely to have high self-esteem than are younger boys with older sisters. (R129)

### Sibling Structure (Sex)

Among males, if the majority of children in the family are boys, self-esteem is likely to be lower than if half or less than half are boys. (R129)

For girls, there is little relationship between level of self-esteem and whether the siblings are mostly girls or boys. (R129)

### Surrogate Parent

Persons who had role-taking relationships with more significant others in early childhood are likely to have self-concepts which are more "social" and extended and more homogeneous than the self-concepts of persons exposed to few parent figures in childhood. (S279)

### Urbanization

Urbanized areas comprise an environment conducive to changes in self-identification. (B010)

## SELF-CONCEPTION (MATERNAL)

### X    Maternal-Role Behavior

Maternal behavior is positively correlated with a self-image of strong maternality. (L165)

## SELF-CONCEPTION OF CHILD

### X   Age of Mother

Children whose mothers were relatively young when they were widowed are less likely to have high self-esteem than are those whose mothers were older when widowed. (R129)

### Broken Home

The child's self-esteem (as measured by Q-Sort Personality Tests) is greater among families where both natural parents are living and together than among homes broken by divorce or death of the father. (S264)

### Child-Rearing Practices (Scholastic Achievement)

Students who report only supportive responses on the part of the parents to school grades do not differ in level of self-esteem from those who report both supportive and punitive responses. (R129)

Students who report only supportive responses as well as those who report supportive and punitive responses to school grades by the parents have higher self-esteem than do those who report only punitive responses. (R129)

Students who said that their mothers were satisfied even when their grades were average or below average had higher self-esteem than did those who reported that their mothers were dissatisfied. (R129)

Students with lowest self-esteem were not those who reported their mothers to be dissatisfied, but those who said that the mother never commented on their marks. (R129)

### Child-Rearing Values (Agreement)
If the parents disagree as to the desired characteristics of the child, then the child's self-concept will also be unstable. (W158)

### Child-Rearing Values/Role Model
The child's perception of himself correlates not with the model of his parents but with the parents' ideals for the child. (B234)

### Divorce
Catholic children of divorced parents are more likely than Catholics and Jews from intact families to have low self-esteem but divorce makes no difference in level of self-esteem among Protestant families. (R129)

### Father Absence
There is a correlation between the absence of an adult male in the home and lack of self-esteem in the child. (R108)

### Father-Child Relations (Closeness)
Adolescents who report close relationships with their fathers are more likely to have high self-esteem and stable self-images than are those who describe these relationships as more distant. (R129)

When father-son closeness is controlled, upper-class boys are more likely to have higher self-esteem than are lower-class boys but the difference between them is reduced. (R129)

### Father-Child Relations (Rejection)
If a father has expressed feelings of rejection for his child, the child will not manifest a corresponding feeling of self-rejection. (C104)

### Identification with Parents
If the child's identification with his parent is based upon the support given by the parents, he will have more self-esteem than if the identification is with nonsupporting parents. (C114)

### Mother-Child Relations
There is a correlation between continuity of mothering and a sense of self in the child. (Y045)

### Mother-Child Relations (Rejection)
If a child's mother has expressed feelings of rejection of him, he will react with a corresponding feeling of self-rejection and self-depreciation. (C104)

### Occupation of Father
Students whose fathers are in highly authoritarian occupations (armed forces, police, detective, sheriff, bailiff) and whose stock in trade is the use of physical violence for the control of physical violence had unusually low self-esteem. (R129)

### Parent-Child Relations (Affect)
An indifferent attitude in parents toward their children is more likely than punitiveness to produce low self-esteem in the child. (R128)

### Parent-Child Relations (Rejection)
The more rejected the child by his parents, the less able he is to develop self-esteem. (A059)

If the father rejects the child, the child will not become self-rejecting; if the mother rejects the child, it is likely that the child will become self-rejecting. (C112)

### Sleeping Arrangements
Exclusive mother-child sleeping arrangements coupled with patrilocal residence are strongly associated with maximum conflict in identity for the child. (B251)

## SELF-CONCEPTION OF FAMILY
### X  Juvenile Delinquency
Low self-respect of the family contributes indirectly to delinquency by contributing to the traits of impracticality and lack of self-criticism.

## SELF-CONCEPTION OF FATHER
### X  Father-Child Relations (Rejection)
A father with strong feelings of self-rejection will tend to regard his son as a model of himself and reject him proportionally. (C104)

### Mental Illness of Child (Schizophrenia)
There is no difference between schizophrenic and normal children and the degree to which they view their fathers as being certain of themselves. (K114)

### Mental Illness (Schizophrenia)
Schizophrenia tends to be correlated with fathers who have an exalted self-image. (S187)

### Scholastic Achievement
Boys with primary neurotic learning inhibitions (poor learning, not associated with behavior or personality problems) are likely to have fathers who see themselves as inadequate occupationally—as failures. (G143)

## SELF-CONCEPTION OF HUSBAND/WIFE
### X  Emotional Adjustment of Child
Agreement/disagreement between a parent's self-description and the spouse's description is not related to the emotional adjustment/maladjustment of their children.

## SELF-CONCEPTION OF MOTHER   X   Aggression
Mothers who have less self-esteem report more aggressive children than do mothers who have self-confidence (U.S.). (S191)

### Breast Feeding
There is no relation between the practice of bottle feeding and a lack of self-esteem on the part of the mother. (A063)

### Child-Rearing Practices (Consistency)
Mothers who are consistent in their discipline have greater self-esteem than do mothers who are inconsistent (U.S.). (S191)

### Child-Rearing Values (Punishment)
Among mothers who spanked their children frequently, those who thought it effective had greater self-esteem than did those who thought it ineffective (U.S.). (S191)

### Deviance
Children whose mothers have low self-esteem are more likely to become social deviants than are those whose mothers have higher self-esteem. (W137)

### Fertility Values
The higher the mother's self-evaluation, the more likely is she to want children. (M186)

### Identification of Mother with Daughter
Mothers with low evaluations of self will tend to reject identifications with their daughters if they see these undesirable traits mirrored in their daughters' activities. (H218)

### Identification with Mother
The more that the mother approves of herself as a model for her children, the more likely it is that the children will emulate characteristics of the mother. (B234)

### Mental Illness of Child (Schizophrenia)
Schizophrenic children are more likely to view their mothers as being sure of themselves than are normal children. (K114)

### Mother-Child Relations (Affection)
The higher the mother's self-evaluation, the more likely is she to have a consistently affectionate relationship with her child. (M186)

### Mother-Child Relations (Evaluation)
If, in terms of several selected family-attitude variables, a mother rates herself highly, she also rates her husband and child highly. (B237)

### Mother-Child Relations (Rejection)
Mothers of schizophrenics are hateful and rejecting toward their children because of events in their own childhoods which left them insecure about their ability to love. (S213)

### Pregnancy, Attitude Toward
Mothers who showed comparatively low self-esteem at the time the child was 5 or 6 years old tend to be the same mothers who did not want the child in the first place. (S191)

The higher the mother's self-esteem, the more likely she will be to want the child when becoming pregnant (U.S.). (S191)

### Scholastic Achievement
Boys with primary neurotic learning inhibitions (poor learning, not associated with other behavior or personality problems) are likely to have mothers with overly masculine self-images, who prevent their development of scholastic achievement in order to protect their own distorted self-images. (G143)

### Toilet Training
The more severe the mother is in toilet training the child, the more likely is she to lack self-esteem (U.S.). (S191)

## SELF-CONCEPTION OF PARENTS
### X   Parent-Child Relations (Affect)
When the parents lack a conception of self, a lack of emotional commitment to children results, which is reflected in infrequent nonintensive interaction with them. (B040)

### Parent-Child Relations (Rejection)
Parents who are self-rejecting are more likely to reject their children than are parents who are not self-rejecting (rejection measured in therapy interviews). (C112)

## SELF-CONCEPTION OF SPOUSE     X   Sex Status
Wives are more likely to agree with their husbands' self-descriptions than are husbands with their wives' self-descriptions.

## SELF-CONCEPTION OF WIFE
### X   Husband-Wife Relations (Consensus)
The higher the mother's self-esteem, the more likely is there to be general agreement between mother and father. (M186)

### Husband-Wife Relations (Evaluation)
The higher the wife's evaluation of herself (self-esteem ratings), the higher her evaluation of her husband. (M186)

### Marital Adjustment
The more supportive the wife views herself to be, the more likely it is that marriage will be well adjusted. (K153)

Unsatisfactorily married women tend to see themselves as less cooperative and responsible than their mothers. (L140)

### Personality (Similarity)
Among wives, perceived similarity between self and spouse is related to favorable self-perception. (K124)

## SELF-CONCEPTION/RELIGION   X   Bereavement
Among children whose families have been broken by death, there is no relationship between religion and low self-esteem. (R129)

## SELF-CONCEPTION (SOCIAL RELATIONS)
### X   Homosexuality
Homosexuality is more likely to occur if the individual has little self-esteem and difficulty in establishing relationships with others. (T104)

## SELF-IMAGE OF FAMILY     X   Role Definition
Where family norms are not rigorously defined, people tend to assume that the behavior in their own families is normatively approved. (B210)

## SELF/PARENT-CONCEPTIONS
### X   Marital Adjustment
For men, congruence between self-image and image of one's father is associated with good marital adjustment, but no such relationship exists for women in relation to their mothers. (L152)

## SEPARATION                    X   Children
Separation is less likely to occur if there are children. (B111)

### Friendship
The longer the time lapse since the separation, the greater the proportion of divorcées who claim they presently have a circle of friends. (G157)

### Remarriage
Time lapse since separation does not affect the general pattern of greater satisfaction among divorcées with the second marriage. (G157)

### Urban/Rural
Separations are more numerous in urban than in rural areas. (B033)

## SEX ANXIETY                    X   Drinking
Sexual anxiety is inversely correlated with an excessive use of alcohol. (K046)

### Education of Parents
Education is positively correlated with less sex anxiety in both parents. (B232)

### Father-Son Relations (Rejection)
There is a correlation between the father's sex anxiety and his rejection of the son. (B243)

### Mother-Son Relations (Sex)
The greater the intensity of the sexual tie between son and mother, the higher the level of anxiety about sex in the adult male. (S079)

### Sex Status
The sex of the dominant parent will directly affect more generalized attitudes of hostility or anxiety toward relatives of the same sex. (S187)

### Sex Taboo (Postpartum)
In societies with a long duration of the postpartum sex taboo, the society is likely to have many beliefs about the dangers inherent in sex. (S079)

### Sexual Permissiveness
Parents whose sex anxieties were low tended to be more permissive of all forms of sex behavior and also less punitive for such behavior than were parents whose anxieties about sex were high. (B213)

## SEX ANXIETY OF FATHER
### X    Father-Son Relations (Acceptance)
Fathers who are highly anxious about sex are less likely to be acceptant of their sons than are fathers who are low in sex anxiety. (B213)

### Husband-Wife Relations (Warmth)
There is a correlation between the level of the father's sex anxiety and his lack of warmth toward his wife. (B243)

Fathers who were highly anxious about sex tended to be less warm toward their wives than did fathers who were low in sex anxiety. (B213)

## SEX ANXIETY OF MOTHER          X    Alcoholism
There is no correlation between the mother's sexual anxiety and alcoholism in the son. (M195)

### Bed Wetting
High sexual anxiety of the mother is associated with late persistence of bed wetting of the child. (S191)

### Breast Feeding
There is a negative correlation between the mother's sex anxiety and the practice of breast feeding the child. (A063)

### Mental Illness of Child
There is no positive correlation between psychosis of the child and sexual anxiety in the mother. (M164)

### Sexual Deviance of Son
If the mother is sexually anxious, the son is more likely to become sexually deviant. (M209)

### Toilet Training
High sexual anxiety of the mother and early toilet training of the child are associated. (S191)

High sexual anxiety of the mother and rapid completion of toilet training of the child are associated. (S191)

## SEX ANXIETY OF PARENTS
### X    Child-Rearing Practices (Sex)
There is a correlation between the level of the parents'
sex anxiety and their punitiveness against the son's sex behavior. (B243)

## SEX ANXIETY OF SON
### X    Employment of Mother
In lower-class families, if the mother is employed, the son is more likely to have sex anxieties. (M211)

## SEX ATTITUDES          X    Illegitimacy (Adoption)
Unwed mothers who kept their children had less self-confidence and experience in heterosexual relations and more negative attitudes concerning sex than did those who released their children for adoption. (V027)

### Incest
In families where sibling incest occurs, the sex attitudes between the siblings are less inhibited than in families where father-daughter incest occurs. (W123)

### Marital Adjustment
Marital adjustment is higher when the attitude of the couple toward sex is that of interest and pleasant anticipation. (B033)

There is a direct relation between a moderately favorable attitude toward sexual relations and marital satisfaction. (K161)

### Marital Adjustment of Husband
Unhappy husbands, more often than the happy, consider it essential for the ideal marriage that the husband and wife be well mated sexually. (T074)

### Maternal Role, Attitude Toward
Women who feel positive toward caring for their babies tend to have positive feelings about intercourse. (N051)

### Premarital Sex Relations
When there is no stigma attached to premarital relations or reproduction, sexual intercourse will be regarded as a natural and enjoyable act. (H084)

## SEX ATTITUDES OF MOTHER
### X    Mental Illness (Schizophrenia)
Schizophrenia tends to be directly correlated with a maternal attitude of hypocrisy toward sex. (N061)

### Neurosis of Mother
Mothers of neurotics are more likely than mothers of normals to devalue the importance of the sexual aspect of their marriages. (M218)

## SEX ATTITUDES OF SON
### X    Mother-Child Relations
The separation of tenderness and sexuality in men is a result of the projection of the image of the loved and honored mother of the Oedipal phase, on the one hand, and on the other, of the image of the mother of the pre–Oedipal phase (with the hostility that a boy may have felt) onto the sexual partner. (G145)

## SEX BEHAVIOR OF CHILD          X    Occupation
Middle-class mothers whose husbands have entrepreneurial jobs are more likely than are mothers of the same social class whose husbands have bureaucratic jobs to declare that their children did not touch their sex organs. (M062)

## SEX COMPOSITION OF FAMILY
### X    Authoritarianism
If females rather than males are predominant among the children in the family, the mother is likely to score higher on authoritarianism, fostering dependency,

breaking the will, martyrdom, deification, inconsiderateness of husband, suppression of sex, ascendance of mother, intrusiveness, and dependency of mother (PARI). (Z011)

### Child-Rearing Practices (Aggression)
The greater the number of women residing in the extended family household, the more likely is the child to be punished for peer-directed aggression. (M216)

There is no relationship between the number of men residing in the extended family household and the severity of punishment the child receives for peer-directed aggression. (M216)

### Child-Rearing Practices (Control)
Fathers are more likely to control boys with brothers and no sisters more strictly than they are boys with sisters and no brothers. (B322)

### Child-Rearing Practices (Dependency)
Among large families, parents are less active in independence training if all their offspring are boys. (E102)

### Fertility
Parents whose first two children are both of the same sex are more likely to have a third child than are parents who have two children of opposite sexes. (F123)

### Husband-Wife Relations (Wife Beating)
Wives are less likely to tolerate beating by the husband when they have an adolescent son. (S253)

### Loss of Family Member
The greater the imbalance of the sexes resulting from the final loss (either psychologically or physically) of a family member, the more severe will be the effects of that loss. (T089)

### Mental Illness (Social Adjustment)
The greater the number of males in the family, the lower the level of posthospital performance of the mental patient. (S245)

### Paternal Role (Child Rearing)
A father is more often involved in child rearing when all of the children in the family are boys than when these are children of both sexes or only girls. (B322)

### Residence
When a family is without daughters in a matrilineal society, the unmarried men may remain at home. (S078)

## SEX COMPOSITION OF HOUSEHOLD
### X  Mental Illness (Social Adjustment)
There is no relationship between level of posthospital social and vocational performance and the number of female relatives in the household of the former mental patient. (F124)

Low-level posthospital social and work performance is associated with the availability of other males in the household to supplement or replace the patient as breadwinner. (F124)

### Premarital Sex Relations
The fewer men there are residing in the home and able to protect the daughter, the more likely it is that the daughter will be sexually exploited. (B245)

## SEX DRIVE        X  Marital Adjustment
Regardless of religion, those women with low sex drives are more likely to be highly satisfied with their marriages than are those with high sex drives. (W155)

### Sex Status
Husbands are more apt to have high sex drives than are their wives. (W155)

## SEX EDUCATION      X  Adultery, Attitude Toward
Persons indicating "friends" as their source of sex education are more likely to approve of adultery than are those obtaining their sex education from other sources. (C124)

### Authoritarianism of Mother
The more authoritarian the mother, the less likely it is that the mother will communicate with the daughter, particularly on sexual matters. (B245)

### Marital Adjustment
Marital adjustment is higher when the sources of sexual information have been parents and teachers. (B033)

Persons who received sex information from their parents, in a context of understanding and affirmation, are more likely to achieve marital success. (B244)

There is a direct relation between adequate sex information and later successful marital adjustment. (K161)

Affectional inhibitions in the parents will tend to be correlated with a failure to educate their children in matters of sex. (T106)

### Parent-Child Relations (Closeness)
The closer the parent-child relationship, the more likely is the child to receive sex information from his parents than from other sources. (L137)

Children who have close relations with their fathers and distant relations with their mothers are less likely to receive sex information from their parents than are children who are distant from their fathers and close to their mothers or distant from both parents. (L137)

### Sexual Aggression
Girls who have received sexual instruction are less likely to experience sexual aggression than are girls who have not received sexual instruction. (K018)

## SEX MAGIC              X  Sexual Permissiveness
Where sexual restrictions are minimal, sex magic will tend to be absent. (H139)

## SEX NORMS               X  Age at Marriage
A decline in the double standard is likely to increase the average age at marriage and decrease the range of marriage age, especially reducing teen-age marriages. (P083)

### Descent (Patrilineal)
There is an association between patrilineage and an emphasis on sexual fidelity in marriage. (F087)

### Marital Status
Sexual acts (outside marriage) by and with married individuals are punished more than are sexual acts by and with unmarried individuals. (B006)

### Prostitution
The demand for prostitutes' services has declined with the decline of the Victorian respect for frigidity in wives. (P083)

The demand for prostitutes' services has declined with the greater sexual accessibility of unmarried women. (P083)

**Sex Status**

Males tend to be more permissive regarding sexual matters than do females.

## SEX NORMS (DOUBLE STANDARD)
**X   Marital Adjustment of Husband**

Happy men, more often than the unhappy, believe that the same standard of sexual morality should apply to both husband and wife. (T074)

**Sex Status**

A significantly larger proportion of teen-age boys than of teen-age girls favors a single standard of sexual morality. (C012)

Females are more likely to support the double standard of sexual morality than males are, but more strongly so regarding premarital relations than regarding extramarital ones. (C124)

## SEX NORMS/MATE SELECTION (FREE CHOICE)
**X   Love Magic**

Love magic is likely to be absent when there is a puritanical sex code and the elders arrange all marriages. (H222)

## SEX NORMS (PREMARITAL CHASTITY)
**X   Age at Marriage**

The earlier the age at marriage in a society, the greater is the value placed in premarital chastity. (O031)

## SEX OF CHILDREN          **X   Size of Family**

The greater the number of children of the same sex, the greater is the desire for another child of the opposite sex. (F123)

## SEX OF KINSMEN    **X   Avoidance Relationship**

Emotional involvement appears to be greater in cross- than in like-sex sibling avoidance. (M235)

## SEX PREFERENCE                 **X   Descent**

In unilineal societies, the child whose sex insures the continuity of the lineage will tend to be preferred. (W082)

**Descent (Patrilineal)**

The emphasis on male children is directly correlated with the strength of the patrilineal organization. (K049)

**Economic Role of Child**

Parents will tend to prefer children of the sex which has the economically more productive role. (L064)

**Economic Role of Men/Women**

The preferred sex of the child will be the one that is viewed as more important economically. (W157)

**Inheritance (Patrilineal)**

When the inheritance pattern is patrilineal, boys will be more highly valued than girls. (R035)

**Residence**

A definite preference for children of one sex will be correlated with the prevailing rule of unilocal residence. (W070)

**Sex Status**

The sex of the child does not correlate with his perception of the sex of child preferred by parents. (H181)

## SEX PREFERENCE, CHILD'S PERCEPTION OF
**X   Sex Preference of Parents**

Children tend to perceive a parent as preferring children of that parent's own sex. (H181)

## SEX PREFERENCE OF PARENTS
**X   Sex Preference, Child's Perception of**

Children tend to perceive a parent as preferring children of that parent's own sex. (H181)

## SEX RATIO                          **X   Adultery**

The scarcity of women in towns militates against the fidelity of a town wife. (M170)

**Age at Marriage**

When the ratio of men to women is proportionately high, the age at marriage of men will increase, while that of women will decrease. (H116)

**Authority Structure of Family**

The sex ratio does not determine the sex to which family headship is a assigned. (S211)

**Economic Role of Men/Women**

The sex ratio in marginal societies will reflect any differential economic value of sex roles. (G143)

**Engagement, Age at**

Engagement age of women will tend to be earlier if there is a scarcity of women. (J008)

**Geographic Mobility**

The sex ratio tends to reflect the permanency of the movement of migrant laborers to industrial areas. (S127)

**Homosexuality**

Homosexual practices are more frequent where bachelors greatly outnumber unmarried girls. (W128)

**Infanticide**

The sex ratio in favor of females is not likely to be brought about by male infanticide, but usually through warfare or other hazardous masculine occupations. (L110)

**Intermarriage**

The rate of intermarriage will be correlated with the sex ratio of the group. (M227)

**Intermarriage (Racial)**

Intermarriage is more likely to take place between different racial groups where there exists an imbalanced sex ratio than among groups where there is a balanced sex ratio. (B012)

The intial acceptance of racial intermarriage tends to be correlated with the scarcity of women of the upper castes. (D018)

**Love**

In a polygynous society, the short supply of eligible females may give rise to an idealization of sentimental love. (M167)

**Marital Stability**

Marital stability tends to be undermined where there is a scarcity of women and a competition for wives. (W056)

**Marriage Chances**

Women are more dependent for marriage upon a favorable sex ratio than men are. (C023)

The higher the sex ratio in the population, the lower the percentage of poor males who ever marry. (F082)

**Mate Selection (Free Choice)**

The parental arrangement of marriages will tend to occur when there is a scarcity of women. (L100)

### Monogamy

Monogamy tends to appear where the sex ratio is not disturbed. (K090)

### Polyandry

Polyandry is associated with a surplus of men in the marriageable areas. The shortage may result from selling women, female infanticide, or neglect of female children. (B205)

### Polygyny

The prevalence of polygyny will be directly correlated with the sex ratio. (B081)

Polygyny is more apt to be censured when there is a shortage of marriageable women. (V024)

### Population

A progressive surplusage of males is unfavorable to an increase of population. (W109)

### Preferential Marriage

When there is a shortage of women, kin relationships will tend to be adjusted to permit otherwise prohibited women to become eligible as marriage partners. (E066)

Preferential marriage patterns tend to be violated when the sex ratio is uneven. (G095)

### Rank of Women

The scarcity of women—and consequent competition for them as wives—enhance the status of women. (W056)

### Sexual Interest

An oversupply of males will give rise to a preoccupation with eroticism (in literature and poetry). (M167)

### SEX RATIO BY CLASS            X   Homogamy

The more hypergamy in the society, the greater a likelihood there is of a surplus of females at the top of the status hierarchy and a scarcity at the bottom. (V030)

### SEX RATIO WITHIN CASTE        X   Homogamy

Hypergamous marriages tend to occur when there is an insufficient number of marriageable women within the caste. (N030)

### SEX RELATIONS                 X   Acculturation

When a pattern of sexual relations is established between the indigenous people and members of the donor culture, the rate of acculturation is accelerated. (S046)

### Age

Sexual intercourse in marriage decreases in frequency with age. (C023)

### Class

Frequency of sexual intercourse in marriage varies inversely with socioeconomic status. (C023)

The upper strata have a higher proportion of women who derive sexual satisfaction in marriage (U.S.). (G156)

College men who date girls of lower social class are more likely to be sexually aggressive than when they date girls from the same or upper classes. (K161)

In contrast with neurotic girls from the lower class, the sexual promiscuity of those from the middle class tends to decrease with age, due to their desire for social mobility and marriage. (M197)

Male neurotics from the middle class are more likely to be passive in their approach toward women than are those from the lower class. (M197)

### Class Values

Where the pains of low status are very high, irresponsible mating behavior and primitive masculine values are more likely to predominate. (P083)

### Economic Conditions

The frequency of sexual relations tends to be directly correlated with the abundance of the food supply. (H139)

### Education of Wife

The lower the educational level of a blue collar wife, the more likely it is that she will find sexual satisfaction in an unhappy marriage. (K089)

### Education of Women

Women with more education (married to blue collar husbands) are more likely to react to marital unhappiness with deviant sexual needs than are women of low educational backgrounds. (K089)

### Employment of Women

Husbands of women who work are more likely than are husbands of nonworking wives to admit equality of control in sexual relations.

### Love Magic

The elaboration of magical means for persuading a member of the opposite sex to engage in coital activity is less developed among people who use direct solicitation.

### Marital Adjustment

The higher the marital adjustment, the more frequent is sexual intercourse. (C134)

### Parent-Child Relations (Affection)

The son's attachment to the mother is likely to inhibit his heterosexual activity, but the daughter's attachment to the father stimulates such activity. (S219)

### Personality (Egocentricity)

Sexual promiscuity tends to be associated with an egocentric personality. (H219)

### Religiosity of Husband-Wife

Sexual intercourse in marriage decreases in frequency with increase in religious participation. (C023)

### SEX RELATIONS, IMPORTANCE OF
### X   Stratification

A formal stratified society cannot maintain itself when sex relations are considered very important. (M244)

### SEX RELATIONS (INTERCASTE)    X   Sex Status

The censure of intercaste sexual relations is greater when a high-caste woman conducts a liaison with a lower-ranking man than when a high-caste man has a liaison with a lower ranking women. (S089)

### SEX RELATIONS (PETTING)
### X   Marital Adjustment

There is a direct relation between the restraint of petting and marital adjustment. (K161)

### SEX RESTRICTIONS              X   Class

The premarital behavior of girls of higher social rank tends to be more strictly controlled than that of daughters of lower social rank. (T069)

### SEX-ROLE ADJUSTMENT           X   Adoption

Reduction in the level of anxiety concerning the female role and motherhood is a causal factor in the woman's decision to adopt a child. (B309)

### Age

The older the person is, the less likely is he or she to feel inadequate as provider or housekeeper. (G126)

### Anxiety of Mother

The higher the anxiety level in the woman, the greater the tendency for her to experience conflict with her husband and to manifest irritability toward her children. (D075)

### Dating

The more insecure the parents in their sex roles, the more likely they are to encourage the child to engage in heterosexual social activity at an early age. (R104)

### Identification with Family Roles

The greater the extent to which the parents identify with the cardinal role of family membership, the more likely they are to tolerate status differences between them. (F106)

### Mate Selection (Intelligence)

The greater the man's feelings of inadequacy in his sex role, the more likely is he to be attracted to a woman of lower intelligence than himself. (H190)

### Maternal Role, Attitude Toward

Women who dislike caring for their newborn babies are also more likely to dislike other aspects of their female biological role. (N051)

### Mother-Child Relations (Power)

There is a correlation between feelings of sex-role inadequacy in the woman and her perception of the maternal figure as a malevolent power. (B309)

### Paternal-Role Adjustment

A man's functioning as a father will be impaired to whatever extent he feels threatened, insecure, and anxious about his adequacy in any of his several significant masculine roles. (L134)

### Sex Status

The girl is more likely to experience dissatisfaction in accepting her appropriate sex role than is the boy in accepting his. (B277)

Although the boy is more likely than the girl to prefer his appropriate sex model, since he experiences less exposure, he may have more difficulty in the actual process of identification. (B277)

A man is more likely to feel inadequate about his central role as provider than a woman is about her main role as housekeeper. (G126)

Among college-educated persons, women are more likely to feel inadequate concerning their main role as housekeeper than men do about their main role as provider. (G126)

### Sterility

Anxiety concerning the female role and motherhood is a cause of sterility in women. (B309)

## SEX-ROLE ADJUSTMENT OF MOTHER
### X    Breast Feeding

There is a correlation between maternal psychosexual and sex-role adjustment and the desire and ability to breast feed the child. (A063)

Women who prefer bottle feeding are more likely than are those who prefer breast feeding to manifest sex-role dissatisfaction. (A063)

## SEX-ROLE BEHAVIOR    X    Economic Conditions

A depression in our society changes the role of the father more than that of any other member, for his status and position in the family rests more on his occupational level and income than does that of other members. (B033)

### Employment of Mother

Working mothers participate less in household tasks and their husbands participate more; they have less control over household activities and are less likely to endorse the traditional sex-role ideology than are mothers who stay at home. (S265)

### Father Absence

Boys who are reared in homes in which there is no father or father surrogate for the first six years of their lives tend to be more effeminate than do boys raised in normal homes. (B216)

In families where the father is absent, male children are slower to develop sex-role patterns than in families where the father is present. (B216)

There is a strong association between father absence and sons who behave like girls both in fantasy and overt behavior. (B251)

Father absence is associated with exaggerated masculine behavior on the part of the son. (B251)

When the father is absent from the home, resources for dependency are limited and therefore the child is both more dependent on the limited resources and more resentful of the dependency because of the limited satisfaction involved. He is thus both feminine in his dependency and aggressive in his reaction against this dependency. (M181)

### Father-Son Relations (Warmth)

Acquisition of male sex-role traits (father-role playing, identification with the father, and masculinity of attitudes) are positively correlated with a warm and rewarding father–son relationship. (B216)

### Husband-Wife Relations

In social-emotional behavior, husband and wife within the same marriage tend to be more alike than they are like other husbands and wives (across marriages). (L173)

### Identification with Like/Cross-Sex Parent

Identification with the same-sex parent is correlated with normal adult sex-role behavior. (B277)

Identification with the cross-sex parent is a cause of inverted adult sex-role behavior. (B277)

A confused identification with both parents is a cause of neurotic adult sex-role behavior. (B277)

Excessive identification with the cross-sex parent in childhood is a cause of homosexuality in the adult. (B277)

### Identification with Like-Sex Parent

Feminine behavior is more closely related to imitation of the mother than masculine behavior is to imitation of the father. (H210)

### Maternal Overprotectiveness
Maternal overprotectiveness is not likely to occur in women who stress their femininity. (L163)

### Oedipal Complex
To be able successfully to assume socially accepted adult sex roles, it is more important for the boy to give up his Oedipal ties than for the girl to relinquish strong attachments to her father. (G156)

### Sex-Role Identification
Preschool children who imitate their like-sex parents are more likely to show more appropriate sex typing than are those who imitate the opposite-sex parents. (H179)

The stronger the child's identification with the like-sex parent, the more adequate his sex typing. (M183)

### Sex Status
Although male and female college students do not differ in their perceptions of their fathers' masculinity, they do differ in relation to their perceptions of their mothers' femininity (i.e., the male students perceive their mothers as being more feminine than females do). (B274)

Since fathers emphasize sex-typed differences between boys and girls more than mothers do, it is likely that boys will show more sex-appropriate behavior than girls will (through internalization of parental values). (G130)

### Superego Formation
The practice of roles of the parent of the same sex is associated with the development of conscience. (S191)

## SEX-ROLE BEHAVIOR OF FATHER
### X   Identification with Father
Boys whose fathers stress masculine behavior are more likely to identify with their fathers than are those whose fathers do not stress such behavior. (B243)

## SEX ROLE, CHILD'S PERCEPTION OF
### X   Employment of Mother
### Sex-Role Definition
(Among children 5–11 years of age) sons of working mothers are more likely than are daughters of working mothers to perceive the woman's role as involving employment outside of the home. (H236)

## SEX-ROLE DEFINITION
### X   Acculturation Anxiety
Acculturative anxiety is less likely to occur if there is a continuity of sex role between the traditional and acculturated situation (e.g., women are likely to play the same roles even in a situation of acculturation). (S039)

### Achievement Motivation
In societies which institutionalize male dominance, a male role model is necessary for achievement orientation. (S205)

### Achievement Values
In achievement-oriented cultures, there is greater role differentiation between men and women. (M060)

### Age of Child
The younger the children in a family where the mother works, the more likely it is that she will be faced with role conflict over working. (K089)

### Child-Rearing Practices (Neglect)
The ambiguity of the roles of the adult male and female is likely to result in the neglect of the children. (B040)

### Child-Rearing Practices (Sex Role)
Mothers who are most strongly inclined to differentiate sex roles place higher demands upon girls than upon boys for table manners, being neat and orderly, and instant obedience. (S191)

### Class
In families of high socioeconomic rank, both sexes participate together in leisure-time activities more, while in families of low socioeconomic status, sex-segregated patterns are more common. (G157)

Marital roles are more likely to be allocated by "traditional" sex standards among the lower class. (G157)

Children (5–11 years old) from lower middle-class and working-class homes are more likely to perceive the male role as involving nontraditional domestic activity than are children from upper middle-class homes. This is more so for boys than for girls. (H236)

Among lower occupational groups children appear to differentiate sex roles earlier and to a greater extent, leaving a smaller area of behavior permissible to both sexes, than among middle socioeconomic groups. (J022)

In middle-class families, mothers' and fathers' roles are not as sharply differentiated as in working-class families. (K089)

The lower the social class, the less likely a woman is to feel any role conflict between her position as housewife and the possible position as career woman. (K089)

Middle-class mothers have generally the same conceptions for their boys as for their girls regarding traits they consider desirable; working-class mothers are more likely to regard dependability, being a good student, and ambition as desirable for boys, but happiness, good manners, cleanliness, and neatness as more desirable for girls. (K110)

Boys from the lower classes are more likely to attribute nontraditional domestic roles to men than are boys from upper middle-class homes. (S265)

### Cohesion of Family
The greater the integration of the family, the greater the encouragement of role specialization by sex of child. (F094)

Parental-role differentiation is associated with decreased emotional intensity and increased psychological distance among family members. (S216)

### Dating
Adolescents believe that mothers know more about dating than fathers. (N057)

Adolescents believe that parents of the opposite sex know less about dating than parents of the same sex (as the adolescent). (N057)

### Descent
Patrilineal societies usually exaggerate the physiological importance of the father; matrilineal societies, the role of the mother. (H233)

### Descent (Matrilineal)
The extension of female behavior into sectors commonly defined as male is more likely to occur in matrilineal societies. (W154)

### Descent (Patrilineal)

The belief that women are dangerous as peers, either because of their excessive sexuality or because of their inherent perversity, is associated with patrilinear descent patterns. (P083)

The conception of women as property tends to be associated with a patrilineal descent system. (S093)

### Duration of Marriage

With the passage of years in the marriage, there is an increasing role differentiation between husband and wife.

### Education

The lower the educational level, the more traditional are couples' ideas about sex concerns and about the rights of men to silence and to protection from women's affairs. (K089)

The higher the educational level, the less clear is the role differentiation of spouses in marriage. (K089)

### Education of Wife

The higher the educational level of wives, the less favorable they look upon housework. (K089)

The higher the educational level of wives, the greater their satisfaction with the position of homemaker. (K089)

The higher the educational level of wives, the more likely they are to be defensive about their desire to work. (K089)

### Emotional Adjustment of Child

In nuclear families, the greater the degree of parental-role differentiation, the poorer the emotional adjustment of the child. (S216)

### Employment of Women

In lower-class groups where women are also gainfully employed, male authority is more likely to be based upon superiority in strength. (P083)

Children of working mothers are more likely to attribute work roles to women than are those of nonworking mothers. (S265)

If a woman's husband accepts an obligation for child care and household chores, then she is likely either to take outside employment or to consider it. (W150)

### Extended Kin Relations

The more segregated the family's conjugal roles, the more likely it is that each spouse can call on practical help from same-sex kin. (F106)

### Father Absence

Absence of the father from the home is a cause of delay or distortion in the sex-typing process in the son. (S228)

### Father-Son Relations

The more masculine the sex typing of the adolescent boy, the more likely it is that he will perceive his relationship with his father as favorable. (M220)

There is no correlation between the degree of masculinity of the adolescent boy and the nature of his relationship with his father. (M220)

### Homogamy

In hypogamous marriages where women marry men of inferior status, they will tend to reject the usual subordinate position. (H079)

### Homosexuality

Homosexuality is more to be expected in a society in which the relations between men and women are placed in a sharp contrast (in which men, from their early childhood, are almost exclusively in the company of men and women in the company of women). (T107)

### Husband-Wife Relations (Authority)

When there is a pronounced polarity of roles between the husband and wife, most marriages will tend to show come conflict over the question of authority. (L064)

### Husband-Wife Relations (Closeness)

Lack of husband-wife role differentiation is positively associated with conjugal solidarity. (S216)

### Husband-Wife Relations (Conflict)

Marital conflict will be reduced by specialization of sex role and activity. (S216)

### Husband-Wife Relations (Intimacy)

Where there is segregation of sexes in everyday life and interests, the husband-wife relationship is likely to be less intimate. (K157)

### Identification with Cross-Sex Parent

Cross-sex parental identification facilitates the adoption of appropriate sex role in the child. (S240)

### Identification with Parents

Appropriate sex typing and high conscience development correlate with each other and correlate with (and result from) the process of parental identification. (M183)

### Initiation Rites

Puberty rites for girls will tend to occur only in those societies in which the women play an important overt part in the society. (M038)

### Isolation of Nuclear Family

Differentiation between the roles of the parents on the basis of sex becomes more significant for the socialization process and the complementarity of roles within marriage accentuated in social systems characterized by comparative isolation of the nuclear family than is the case in systems in which solidarity with extended kin is more pronounced. (P062)

### Joint Family

Segregation of the sexes before and after marriage is associated with the joint family system, due to the fact that it prevents the possibility of strong male-female liaisons from forming that would threaten the solidarity of the male lineage. (G156)

### Kin/Nonkin Interaction

Interaction in family groups will result in a more distinct sex-role differentiation when outsiders are present than when the family members are by themselves. (L180)

### Kin Terminology

Changes in sex-role definitions will tend to be accompanied by a new descriptive vocabulary. (E026)

There will tend to be an omission of sex distinctions with a kin term if the sex roles are not fully differentiated within the kin type. (F046)

### Marital Adjustment

Marital adjustment is associated with the absence of conflict over the role definitions of the husband and wife. (B033)

When the husband has equalitarian role attitudes and the female has traditional role attitudes, marital adjustment is higher. (K161)

### Marital Status
Divorced couples exhibit greater disagreement as to the roles of husband and wife in marriage than do married couples. (T092)

### Marriage Chances
A larger proportion of the population is likely to remain unmarried where a virtual interchangeability of work roles makes it possible and feasible for a man or woman to live alone. (N065)

### Mate Selection
When the dominant position of the male is emphasized, men will tend to seek as mates women of lower economic and educational status in order to reinforce the disparity between the sex roles. (L064)

### Mate Selection (Intelligence)
Men who prefer women of equal intelligence are more tolerant of their personal likes and dislikes than are men who prefer women of lower or higher mental ability. (H190)

### Mental Illness (Schizophrenia)
There is a correlation between sex-role confusion in the child and schizophrenia.

### Occupation of Husband
Husbands who have the most joint role relationships with their wives tend to be professional or semiprofessional people (in contrast with husbands in manual occupations). (B209)

### Occupation of Mother
Mothers in entrepreneurial occupations are more likely than those in bureaucratic jobs to differentiate highly between boys' and girls' sex roles. ( J022)

### Parent-Child Relations (Affect)
Male-child households will exhibit the highest level of positiveness in the father-son relationship when fathers and sons hold subordinate role positions in the society; likewise, female-child households show the highest level of positiveness in mother-daughter relationships in an unfamiliar context when both the mother and daughter assume subordinate role positions. (O035)

### Paternal/Maternal-Role Behavior
Fathers differentiate their roles toward opposite-sex children, giving expressive support to daughters and instrumental support to sons; mothers do not differentiate their roles toward opposite-sex children, giving expressive support to both daughters and sons. ( J026)

### Paternal Role
Male personality elements will be maximized in families where the father occupies the role of leader. (S205)

### Penis Envy
Ambivalence toward the sex role in women is likely to manifest itself as penis envy. (W154)

### Personality of mother (Emotional Stability)
Maternal emotional stability is not related to the degree to which mothers have responsibilities other than child training, particularly those which take them away from home. (M216)

### Personality Problems of Child
Parents (of Italian- and Irish-American background) of emotionally disturbed children are more likely than are those of normal children to make a rigid differentiation between husband and wife roles. (V031)

### Political Relations
The constant, easy brutalitarian dominance of the male over the female has a direct influence upon the attitude of the nation toward weaker, hence "inferior," peoples. (L166)

### Political Structure
The distribution of women as gifts and tribute occurs in highly stratified societies where specific political institutions for insuring tribute have not yet fully evolved. (S271)

### Power Structure of Family
Sons from mother-dominated families are more likely than others to see girls as more powerful than boys. (H201)

Sons from mother-dominated homes, where the fathers' attitudes favor male dominance, are more likely to view boys as more powerful than girls. (H201)

### Preferential Marriage (Grandson)
Grandson-marriage is contingent upon the recognition of women as inheritable property. (S093)

### Rank of Women
Where the activities of women are restricted to household duties, their status tends to be low. (S115)

Where there is a marked social segregation of the sexes, the status of women will tend to be low. (S153)

When there is a marked separation of masculine and feminine interests, the status of women tends to be low. (W097)

### Residence
Families with high degrees of role segregation by sex tend to live in homogeneous areas of low population turnover, whereas families with predominantly joint role relationships tend to live in heterogeneous areas of high population turnover. (B209)

### Residential Segregation
The residential segregation of men is most likely to occur in societies where there is a rigorous dichotomy in sex roles. (R033)

### Role Definition in Family
As the children become less of a burden and more of a resource, role differentiation between husband and wife increases.

### Sex-Role Identification
The sharper is the cultural distinction between the sex roles of husband and wife, the higher a child will tend to score on the Draw-a-Person Test.

### Sex Status
Parental roles (i.e., association of nurturance with the mother and control with the father), are more sharply discriminated by boys than by girls. (E098)

Wives are in greater agreement concerning the definition of their roles as wives and mothers than are husbands concerning the definition of their roles as husbands and fathers. (H195)

Wives live up to their husbands' expectations of them as wives and mothers to a greater extent than husbands live up to their wives' expectations of them as husbands and fathers. (H195)

Spouses who agree on the definition and relative importance of the wife's marital roles also tend to agree on the definition and relative importance of the husband's marital roles. (H195)

(Among children 5–11 years of age) sons of working mothers are more likely than are daughters of working mothers to perceive the woman's role as involving employment outside of the home. (H236)

Boys have a negative reaction to women's work, but there is no corresponding negative reaction among girls to men's work. (R126)

### Size of Family
Differential training of boys and girls is more likely to occur in large families where a high degree of cooperation is required. (W127)

### Stability of Family Structure
The faster the rate of change in family patterns and models, the greater the ambivalence toward the position of women in the family. (K099)

### Status in Family
Daughters perceive the average woman to be more traditional ("other-oriented") than do either of their parents. (S252)

Mothers perceive the average woman to be more traditional than do fathers. (S252)

Daughters perceive men's ideal woman to be significantly more traditional than their fathers' conceptions of the ideal woman. (S252)

Daughters' perceptions of their mothers' expectations in the feminine role are close to both their mothers' self-conceptions and their mothers' ideal self-conceptions. (S252)

### Stratification
The less differentiation of women also retards class formation. (M170)

### Subsistence Pattern
Where animal foods and wild-plant foods are balanced in rank, sexual dominance is less likely to occur. (D057)

### Suffrage, Feminine
The extension of suffrage to women is associated with the development of the egalitarian family; by guaranteeing the separate identity of women outside of marriage, it makes marriage closer to a free contract. (P083)

### Values (Femininity)
The increased sex-role differentiation associated with relative isolation of the nuclear family in society is related to increased emphasis on overt, specifically feminine, attractiveness, with strong erotic overtones. (P062)

### Warfare
In military societies, where a large proportion of the male population is organized for warfare, the role of men in the family structure will be peripheral. (G056)

## SEX-ROLE DEFINITION (CONSENSUS)
### X    Marital Adjustment
The less agreement there is between husband and wife concerning the definition and relative importance of the husband's marital roles, the more poorly adjusted is the marriage. (H195)

There is no significant relationship between marital adjustment and lack of agreement between husband and wife concerning the definition and relative importance of the wife's marital roles. (H195)

## SEX-ROLE DEFINITION (EGALITARIANISM)
### X    Daughter/Wife
Men are likely to hold more egalitarian views about the role of their daughters in society than about the role of their wives. (K099)

## SEX-ROLE DEFINITION (INCONSISTENCY)
### X    Father-Son Relations (Ambivalence)
A changing male image, in which the child is adored yet the image of the father is despotic and godlike, will tend to result in an ambivalent attitude of love and hatred, submissiveness and defiance on the part of the male child toward his father. (T107)

## SEX-ROLE DEFINITION IN SOCIETY
### X    Role Definition in Family
The degree to which conjugal roles are segregated is correlated with and a reflection of the degree to which the sexes are segregated in the larger society. (F106)

## SEX-ROLE DEFINITION (INSTRUMENTAL/EXPRESSIVE)
### X    Husband/Wife
Husbands tend to have the instrumental ideal role and wives the expressive ideal role when spouses are asked to describe the "ideal mate." (K153)

## SEX-ROLE DEFINITION OF CHILD
### X    Occupation
Children of fathers who have entrepreneurial jobs are more likely than are children of fathers who have bureaucratic jobs to have a clearly differentiated conception of sex roles. (J030)

### Role Definition of Husband-Wife
The more that the child perceives the division of expressive-instrumental functions between mother and father, the more likely is the child to differentiate the parents with respect to sex. (B234)

## SEX-ROLE DEFINITION OF DAUGHTER
### X    Employment of Mother
Daughters of nonworking mothers are more likely to perceive themselves as "housewives" when they grow up than are daughters of working mothers. (H222)

Daughters of working mothers are more likely than are daughters of nonworking mothers to say that they plan to continue working after marriage. (H222)

Girls whose mothers do not work are more likely to sex-type various behaviours than girls whose mothers are employed. (H224)

Girls whose mothers are employed are less likely to sex-type various behaviors than are adults; those whose mothers do not work are more likely to sex-type behaviors than are adults. (H224)

The mother's working outside the house or not working has no influence on the daughter's conception of the feminine role. (S252)

## SEX-ROLE DEFINITION (POWER)
### X　Age of Child
The older the child is, the more he tends to discriminate male, but not female, sex and age roles by reference to their power. (E090)

The older the child, the less is the father's sex role perceived as more powerful than the mother's sex role. (E090)

## SEX-ROLE IDENTIFICATION　　X　Age of Child
Within the younger ages, identification with the controlling role of the father becomes stronger among boys, but a similar sex-type age trend is not found among girls. (E098)

Compared with younger subjects, older subjects have stronger tendencies to imitate the like-sex, rather than the opposite-sex, parent. (H179)

Frequency of like-sex imitation is not significantly greater with older children. (H179)

### Alcoholism
There is a correlation between alcoholism in men and their earlier rejection of their paternal model. (M195)

### Anxiety
Because boys experience greater anxiety than girls due to their transition from a mother tie to father identification, boys are less likely to emulate their fathers directly than are girls to emulate their mothers directly. (B234)

### Child-Rearing Practices (Permissiveness)
The more permissive the parents, the more likely it is that the boy will develop strong masculine identification. (M183)

### Child-Rearing Practices (Sex Role)
Greater parental punishment for boys than for girls for incorrect sex-role behavior leads to greater anxiety among males than among females regarding sex-role identification. (L141)

Boys' being more likely to be punished for and to repress opposite-sex-role behavior leads to the following types of identifications where there exists a discrepancy between sex-role preference and sex-role identification: boys are more likely to show same-sex preference, while having underlying opposite-sex role identifications; females will show opposite-sex preference, while having underlying same-sex role identification. (L141)

Greater parental punishment for boys than for girls for opposite-sex behavior may lead to repression, rather than an unlearning, of opposite-sex role behavior in boys. (L141)

### Class
Lower-class children develop strong preference patterns for sex-role differentiation at an earlier age than do middle-class children. (H197)

### Cohesion of Family
The lower the family's integration, the more likely it is that girls will react to criticism about the performance of social-emotional, but not instrumental, behavior. (F094)

The lower the integration of the family, the greater the possibility that boys are aware of parental criticism of their performance of instrumental behavior but perceive no definite pattern with respect to socioemotional activities. (F094)

### Death of Father
Men who have lost their fathers in childhood have difficulties in masculine identification. (A070)

When the father dies and the mother is unaffectionate and deviant in her behavior toward her sons, sex-role identification instability (both feminine and aggressive tendencies) is much more common than when the mother is affectionate and nondeviant. (M181)

### Division of Labor by Sex
The stronger the masculine identification of the boy, the more likely it is that his home is marked by a flexible division of labor between mother and father and fewer rules regarding duties. (M183)

### Father Absence
When the father is absent for long periods of time, the boy is more likely to develop a feminine sex identification.

Father absence is associated with cross-sex identification. (B251)

When the father is absent from the home, there is a greater likelihood that boys will have an unstable sex-role identification (by manifesting both feminine and aggressive behavior). (M181)

When the father is absent, male children are likely to develop feminine components in their personalities. (M181)

When the father dies, greater sex-role identification instability (manifestation of both feminine and aggressive tendencies) develops in boys than when the father absents himself from the family. (M181)

### Father Absence, Age of Child at
When the father is absent from the home and the mother is affectionate and nondeviant in her behavior toward the son, the middle childhood period (ages 6–12) is most susceptible to the development of sex-role identification instability (both feminine and aggressive tendencies). (M181)

When the father is absent from the home and the mother is deviant in her behavior and not affectionate to her son, the age of the child at the time of father absence is not important in the development of sex-role identification instability (both feminine and aggressive tendencies). (M181)

### Father-Son Relations (Affection)
If a father is warm, affectionate, and rewarding, the son is likely to develop strong masculine attitudes and to identify with his father. (M204)

### Father-Son Relations (Interaction)
The greater the interaction between father and son and the more active the role taken by the father in his son's upbringing, the stronger the masculine identification of the boy. (M183)

### Father-Son Relations (Punishment/Reward)
The more masculine and father-identified the boy, the more likely he is to perceive the father as both highly rewarding and highly punitive. (M183)

### Identification with Father
The more the child (male and female) internalizes a reciprocal role relationship with the father, the more

likely he or she is to develop an appropriate sex-role orientation. (J031)

### Identification with Like-Sex Parent
Children learn their proper sex roles through identification with their like-sex parents, if these parents represent the appropriate sex-role models. (R126)

### Interaction in Family
The more harmonious the *total* family relationship, the more likely it is that the appropriate sex modeling will occur. (P064)

### Maternal Role
Mothers of boys who have weak sex-role identification are more likely than those whose sons have strong sex-role identification to have taken the major role in disciplining the child. (L142)

### Mother-Child Relations (Attachment)
The more intense the girl's attachment to her mother (and the more difficult to surrender the mother as a love object), the more likely it is that she will adopt a reactive contempt for the female sex and identify with the father, rather than choosing him as a love object. (B272)

### Mother-Son Relations (Rejection)
The stronger the masculine identification of the boy, the more likely it is that he will have experienced less maternal rejection, more maternal nurturance, and less punishment for dependency. (M183)

### Obesity
Obesity tends to be associated with a severe confusion in sexual identification. (B218)

### Occupational Choice
For sons, high identification with the father leads to vocational interests which are more considered more "masculine." (C110)

For sons, mixed-sex identification leads to vocational interests which combine what are considered "masculine" and "feminine" characteristics. (C110)

For sons, mixed-sex identification leads to vocational interests which combine what are considered "masculine" and "feminine" characteristics. (C110)

For sons, cross-sex identification leads to vocational interests which are considered more "feminine" in nature. (C110)

For sons, low father and/or low mother identification leads to vocational interests which are considered "feminine" in nature. (C110)

### Ordinal Position
If the age difference between two sisters is not very great, the older sister will develop the more feminine attributes and the younger will develop more bisexual attributes. (B318)

Birth order is irrelevant to the age at which sex-role preferences are acquired. (H197)

### Parent-Child Relations
The boy's sex typing of interests correlates more with his interaction with his father than with his mother. (M183)

### Parent-Child Relations (Affection)
Children are more likely to develop appropriate sex-role preferences if they perceive their like-sex parents as rewarding, nurturing, and affectionate. (M225)

Both boys and girls are more likely to develop appropriate sex-role preferences if encouraged by the father. (M225)

### Parental Role
The greater uniformity of the mother role, compared to the masculine occupational role, makes more likely the direct emulation of the mother by the girl than of the father by the son. (B234)

### Parental Role (Discipline)
Parents of boys who have weak sex-role identification are more likely than those whose sons have strong sex-role identification to have taken an equal part in disciplining the child. (L142)

### Paternal-Role Behavior
Since the father of the good premorbid schizophrenic (good functioning before the onset of illness) acts in a more assertive manner and maintains a more masculine role within the family than does the father of the poor premorbid schizophrenic, it is more likely that the former serves as a more effective model for male identification for his son. (G127)

### Personality of Father (Self-Acceptance)
There is no relationship between the father's self-acceptance and the strength of the son's or daughter's appropriate sex-role identification. (M206)

### Personality of Mother (Dominance)
A strong mother contributes to the failure of her son to develop a strong masculine feeling.

There is no support for the hypothesis that strong mothers contribute to a lack of masculine feeling.

### Personality of Mother (Femininity)
Boys who identify more with their fathers perceive their mothers as being more feminine than do boys who identify less with their fathers. (B274)

### Power Structure of Family
In homes where the mother is dominant in the marital relations, the children are more likely to choose the opposite-sex parent as an adult-role model. (The relationship is stronger for boys than for girls.) (H201)

### Pregnancy
Men's ambivalence toward the sex role is likely to manifest itself as envy of childbearing. (W154)

### Scholastic Achievement
Boys with primary neurotic learning inhibitions (poor learning, not associated with other behavior or personality problems) are likely to have mothers with overly masculine self-images, who prevent their development of scholastic achievement in order to protect their own distorted self-images. (G143)

### Scholastic Adjustment
Men who identify with their fathers will be better adjusted in college than will those who identify with their mothers. (H194)

Women who identify with their mothers will be less well adjusted in college than will those who identify with their fathers. (H194)

### Sex-Role Behavior
Preschool children who imitate their like-sex parents are more likely to show more appropriate sex typing than are those who imitate the opposite-sex parents. (H179)

The stronger the child's identification with the like-sex parent, the more adequate his sex typing. (M183)

## Sex-Role Definition

The sharper the cultural distinction between the sex roles of husband and wife, the higher a child will tend to score on the Draw-a-Person Test.

## Sex-Role Model

Absence of readily available sex-role models leads to greater difficulty in males than in females in achieving sex-role identification. (L141)

## Sex Status

It is not true that the mother is the first identification model for both boys and girls or that boys later switch to the father as the main model. (E098)

Feminine behavior is more closely related to imitation of the mother than masculine behavior is to imitation of the father. (H210)

Feminine-role identification is learned in the context of a close personal relationship with the mother; masculine-role identification is learned from identification with cultural stereotypes of the masculine role derived from many contexts. (L138)

Girls have an easier time than boys do taking on appropriate sex-typed adult roles because they need not shift from identification with the mother to identification with the father (U.S.). (S191)

## Sexual Adjustment

The greater the parents' doubts concerning their own masculinity or femininity, the more likely are they to cause disturbances in the child (perversion, exhibitionism, peeping at others, impotence, etc.). (B244)

## Sibling Rivalry

Sex-role identification conflict is a more significant determinant of rivalry and hostility for firstborn children than it is for second-born children. (K149)

## Sibling Structure

A boy reared with older brothers is more likely to accept the masculine traits of his culture than is a boy reared with older sisters. (G156)

In families where there are only two children, a boy and a girl, each will tend to assimilate the traits of the opposite sex. (G156)

The greater the age difference between siblings, the greater the sex identification conflict for firstborn children. (K149)

Having like-sex siblings tends to enhance self-sex preference or identification; having opposite-sex siblings is likely to decrease self-sex preference. (R114)

Contrary to the assimilation of roles hypothesis (Brim), in three-child families, a boy having two sisters is highly masculine and anxious (due to sex-role conflict); the same is not true of girls having two brothers. (R114)

In three-child families, firstborn girls and nonfirstborn boys are least likely to have sex-identification conflicts; in a two-child family, the second-born child with a sibling of the same sex is least likely to have such problems. (R114)

## Sibling Structure (Age and Sex)

The greater the age difference between siblings, the greater the sex-identification conflict among second-born children with older siblings of the opposite sex, compared to those with siblings of the same sex; boys with older sisters have the most conflict and girls with older sisters have the least. (K149)

## Sibling Structure (Age Difference)

The greater the age difference between siblings, the greater the self-identification conflict for all firstborn children. (K149)

## Sibling Structure (Sex)

When a child begins differentiating between father and mother sex roles, he is aided in this differentiation if he has a sibling of the opposite sex. (B216)

If a child has a sibling of the opposite sex, he will tend to assimilate traits of the opposite sex. (B216)

A child who has siblings of the opposite sex has more traits appropriate to the opposite sex than does a child with siblings of only the same sex. (B216)

Firstborn children with siblings of the same sex have less sex-identification conflict than do those with younger siblings of the opposite sex; the boy with a younger brother has somewhat more conflict than does the girl with a younger sister and the girl with a younger brother may have somewhat less conflict than may the boy with a younger sister. (K149)

Having like-sex siblings tends to enhance self-sex preference or identification; having opposite-sex siblings is likely to decrease self-sex preference. (R114)

Contrary to the assimilation of roles hypothesis (Brim), in three-child families, a boy having two sisters is highly masculine and anxious (due to sex-role conflict); the same is not true of girls having two brothers. (R114)

Girls with a brother are more likely to develop feminine-role identification than are girls with a sister. (S251)

Children from families in which there are opposite-sex siblings are more likely to have attitudes that are less conforming to their sex identification than are children from families in which there are no opposite-sex siblings. (T095)

## Sleep Arrangements

Societies where the mother and father sleep together produce children whose main identification is with the adult role itself, rather than like- or cross-sex identification. (B251)

## Superego Formation

There is a correlation between degree of masculinity of young boys and their degree of conscience development. (M220)

## SEX-ROLE IDENTIFICATION OF CHILD
### X   Child-Rearing Attitudes (Authoritarianism)

The more authoritarian the mother's attitudes relative to children, the greater their imitation of like-sex parent. (H179)

### Child-Rearing Practices (Sex Role)
### X   Sex-Role Identification

Greater parental punishment for boys than for girls for incorrect sex-role behavior leads to greater anxiety among males than among females regarding sex-role identification. (L141)

### Identification with Like-Sex Parent
Imitation of the like-sex parent is more important to the development of femininity in girls than it is to the development of masculinity in boys. (H179)

### Power Structure of Family
Husband dominance in the marital relationship is associated with like-sex adult-role model choice by the children. (H201)

### Sex-Role Identification of Parents
There is a correlation between sex-role confusion in the parents and sex-role confusion in the child.

## SEX-ROLE IDENTIFICATION OF DAUGHTER
### X   Child-Rearing Practices (Punishment)
Low sex-role identification in daughters is associated with maternal use of withdrawal of love as a disciplinary technique. (M206)

### Child-Rearing Practices (Sex Role)
Strong sex-role identification in the daughter is not associated with maternal encouragement of participation in feminine activities. (M206)

Strong sex-role identification in the daughter is positively associated with paternal encouragement of the daughter's participation in feminine activities. (M206)

### Incest (Father-Daughter)
Girls who have had sexual relations with their fathers indicate poor sexual identification when tested on the Draw-a-Man Test. (K119)

### Mother-Daughter Relations (Power)
Daughters who are high in sex-role identification are more likely to perceive their mothers as being powerful than are daughters who are low in sex-role identification. (M206)

### Mother-Daughter Relations (Punishment)
There is no difference between daughters who are high and those who are low in sex-role identification regarding their perception of their mothers as punitive and threatening. (M206)

### Personality of Father (Masculinity)
Strong sex-role identification in the daughter is associated with fathers who are high in masculine interests and attitudes (measured by the California Psychological Inventory). (M206)

### Personality of Mother (Femininity)
There is no relationship between the mother's femininity (measured by the California-Psychological Inventory) and the daughter's sex-role identification. (M206)

### Personality of Mother (Self-Acceptance)
There is a positive relationship between the mother's self-acceptance and strong sex-role identification in the daughter. (M206)

## SEX-ROLE IDENTIFICATION OF FATHER
### X   Scholastic Adjustment
Fathers of school-phobic children are more likely than are others to have problems concerning their sexual identification. (C115)

## SEX-ROLE IDENTIFICATION OF PARENTS
### X   Sex-Role Identification of Child
There is a correlation between sex-role confusion in the parents and sex-role confusion in the child.

## SEX-ROLE IDENTIFICATION OF SON
### X   Child-Rearing Practices (Sex Role)
Parental encouragement of the son's participation in masculine activities is not related to the son's sex-role identification. (M206)

### Personality of Father (Masculinity)
Fathers who are high on masculine interests and attitudes (measured by the California Psychological Inventory) are no more likely than are those who are lower on the scale to foster strong sex-role identification in their sons. (M206)

## SEX-ROLE MODEL          X   Drug Addiction
Most heroin addicts come from families where there is a lack of model for the male role. (F090)

### Homosexuality
The less adequate the father as a masculine sex model, the more likely is homosexuality in the son. (R104)

### Mental Illness of Child
There is a greater possibility of mental illness if the child is deprived of a male model. (M164)

### Mental Illness of Son
Mental illness tends to be directly correlated with the failure of the father to provide a male model. (L123)

### Parent-Child Relations (Warmth)
Warm relations with the like-sex parent are associated with like-sex adult-role-model choice by the child. (H201)

### Sex-Role Identification
Absence of readily available sex-role models leads to greater difficulty in males than in females in achieving sex-role identification. (L141)

## SEX-ROLE MODEL OF SON
### X   Ethnicity of Mother/Father
The father's ethnic background has greater significance for the formation of the son's role model than the mother's ethnic background. (E091)

## SEX STATUS          X   Acculturation
Boys are more likely than girls to identify with Europeans and to emulate them. (P009)

### Acculturation Anxiety
Men tend to exhibit greater acculturative anxiety (than women) since the disruption created in rapid culture change affects them more directly. (S039)

### Affinal Relations
People have a closer relationship with their children-in-law if they have no child of the same sex. (T087)

### Affinal Relations (Conflict)
Females are more likely to complain about their in-laws than are males. (C023)

### Aggression
Among preschool-aged children, boys exhibit more (doll play) aggression than girls toward the father; while there is no difference between boys and girls regarding the amount of aggressi on displayed toward the mother. (J026)

Boys rate higher in aggression toward the father and in self-rated aggression than girls do. (L136)

The frequency of aggression in doll play is greater for boys than for girls. (L157)

Since girls retain their initial mother identification, while boys usually shift theirs to their father, girls, at age five, are more likely to display prosocial aggression and boys to display antisocial aggression. There is an increase in both sexes of prosocial behavior during the ages five to eight (U.S.). (S191)

Boys are more likely than girls to make the father and boy child the objects of aggression in doll play; girls are more likely to employ the girl and baby doll as objects of aggression. (S228)

Boys and girls do not differ in the amount of aggression directed against the mother doll. (S228)

Girls are more likely to direct aggression against the boy doll than are boys against the girl doll. (S228)

Boys are more aggressive than girls in doll play, being more likely to use physical violence, aggression involving imaginary figures, an aggression against impersonal objects. They do not differ from girls with respect to the amount of aggression involving no bodily injury. (S228)

### Alcoholism, Attitude Toward
Women are more likely to be sympathetic to the alcoholic husband than are men to an alcoholic wife.

### Artificial Insemination, Attitude Toward
Women are more likely than men to accept artificial insemination in cases where the husband is the donor. (V035)

Women are less likely than men to accept artificial insemination in cases when the donor is other than the husband. (V035)

### Authority Structure of Family
Both sons and daughters perceive mothers more often than fathers as exercising strong authority in the home. (B260)

More sons than daughters perceive their fathers as having a strong role of authority in the family. (B260)

Among teen-agers, sons are more likely than daughters to feel they have little or no voice in family affairs. (D079)

Men are more likely to view their fathers as having exercised moderate authority over them and women are more likely to view their fathers as having exercised little or no authority. (K114)

Female, as compared with male, heads of families are more preoccupied with household affairs and are less influential in the unit's external relations. (S211)

### Avoidance Relationship
Avoidance relationships will tend to be more severe if the affinal kinsman is of the opposite sex. (H165)

Like-sex sibling avoidance seems to break down more rapidly than does cross-sex avoidance. (M235)

Men seldom avoid other men and women rarely avoid women. Avoidance is, first of all, characteristic of cross-sex kin relationships. (S189)

Avoidance relationships tend to characterize affinals of adjacent generations and of the opposite sex. (T065)

### Birth Control
There is little difference between the families of male university graduates and female university graduates in the spacing of the birth of the first child after marriage. (A003)

Of those couples who indicate that they were using contraceptives since the birth of their first child, significantly more wives distrusted the contraceptive method than did husbands. (L013)

### Child-Rearing Practices
Boys receive somewhat more physical punishment than girls (except for aggressive girls). (S191)

Girls are more often disciplined by love-oriented techniques. (S191)

Girls receive somewhat more praise for "good" behavior than boys. (S191)

Girls are more often subject to withdrawal of love for "bad" behavior than boys. (S191)

### Child-Rearing Practices (Achievement)
Boys are more likely to be socialized to achieve than are girls. (G156)

Fathers are more concerned about how well their sons achieve than about how well their daughters achieve. (J026)

### Child-Rearing Practices (Achievement/Conformity)
Mothers tend to stress avoidance of undesirable qualities and/or conditions for girls and to stress development and achievement for boys.

### Child-Rearing Practices (Achievement Demands)
Girls are less likely than boys to receive strong parental demands for achievement. (E102)

### Child-Rearing Practices (Affection)
Girls are exposed to more parental affection than are boys. (B252)

### Child-Rearing Practices (Aggression)
Middle-class boys are taught to respond to acts of aggression, while middle-class girls are taught to avoid such situations. (B235)

There is no relationship between the sex of the child and the severity of the mother's punishment for mother-directed aggression. (M216)

Mothers are less permissive toward aggression in girls than in boys, but only regarding aggression toward parents and toward children outside the family, not toward siblings. (S191)

Sex of child and severity of punishment for aggression are not associated, though girls get much less encouragement to fight back in their outside quarrels (U.S.). (S191)

Boys are allowed more aggression in their relations with neighborhood children than are girls (U.S.). (S191)

Boys are allowed no more freedom than girls in relation to aggression toward sibling (U.S.). (S191)

Parents are more permissive with boys than with girls regarding parent-directed aggression (U.S.). (S191)

There is no difference between boys and girls with respect to the severity of punishment for parent-directed aggression (U.S.). (S191)

### Child-Rearing Practices (Chores)
There is no relationship between the sex of the child and the degree of responsibility training received (frequency of chore performance and number of chores assigned). (M216)

### Child-Rearing Practices (Control)
Girls tend to be under more strict adult supervision than boys. (P069)

### Child-Rearing Practices (Dependency)
Boys are pushed toward self-reliance more than girls. (G156)

### Child-Rearing Practices (Dependency)
### X   Scholastic Achievement by Sex Status of Child
High independence training by parents is associated with high scholastic achievement in adolescents; the relationship is stronger for boys than for girls. (E102)

### Child-Rearing Practices (Nurturance)
Socialization of girls is more likely to emphasize nurturance than is the socialization of boys (cross-cultural). (G156)

### Child-Rearing Practices (Nurturance/Control)
With respect to nurturance and control, the mother is likely to treat children of both sexes equally, whereas the father is more likely to be more nurturing toward the daughter and more controlling toward the son. (J031)

### Child-Rearing Practices (Obedience)
Obedience is more likely to be stressed for girls than for boys. (G156)

### Child-Rearing Practices (Permissiveness)
Mothers of young children tend to be more lenient with their sons than with their daughters. (K098)

### Child-Rearing Practices (Punishment)
Physical punishment is more frequently used by parents of boys than by parents of girls. (B232)

Fathers physically punish girls less than boys. (B232)

Children are more likely to receive punishment from the parent of the same sex. (B250)

Girls are more often disciplined by "love-oriented" techniques (praise, withdrawal of love, etc.) than boys are (U.S.). (S191)

### Child-Rearing Practices (Responsibility)
Socialization of girls stresses responsibility, "being dutiful," more so than does the socialization of boys (cross-cultural). (G156)

### Child-Rearing Problems
There is no relationship between the sex of parents and the types of child-rearing problems they name as important. (G126)

### Cohesion of Family/Achievement Values
Where there are strains between family solidarity and pressures to achieve, boys in a family are more apt to feel them than are girls. (C086)

### Dating Goal
Men are less interested in marriage as a consideration in dating than women are. (B244)

### Death of Spouse
Among older persons (those over 65), women are more able successfully to adjust to widowhood than men are to widowerhood. (C116)

### Death Ritual
As the loss of the husband is usually considered to have a greater impact on the family structure, elaborate death rituals are more likely to exist for the husband than for the wife. (G156)

### Dependency
Women tend to have a greater dependency upon the family than men do. (G153)

Women are handicapped in making the psychosocial shift to the family of procreation which our culture demands because they do not become emancipated from their families of orientation to the same degree as men. (K014)

Women do not become emancipated from their families to the same degree or in the same manner as men do. (K014)

Girls are more highly dependent on their parents than boys are when both rate low in popularity among their peers. (M176)

More male than female emotionally disturbed children have intense and dependent relationships with their mothers. (M197)

Dependence on mothers is more likely among females than among males. (S011)

The finding that there are no sex differences in summary ratings of dependency is contrary to the popular belief that girls are more dependent on their mothers than boys. (S191)

Wives are more likely to be homesick for their parents than husbands. (W006)

### Dependency/Sex-Role Conflict
Among alcoholics, females are more likely than males to have a background of sex-role confusion (rather than of dependency conflict). (M195)

### Disorganization of Family
More women than men recall disturbed childhood homes. (P086)

Disturbances in the home are likely to have a greater effect on girls than on boys since the degree and length of exposure to disturbed family situations is greater for girls. (P086)

### Divorce Adjustment
Divorce affects the general adjustment of women more than that of men. (G126)

The husband is more likely to feel guilty about demanding a divorce than is the wife. (G156)

### Divorce, Initiation of
Since the husband is more involved outside of the home environment and consequently less dependent upon the marriage as his only source of personal satisfaction, he is more likely to be the one who initiates the breakup of the marriage. (G156)

### Educational Aspiration
Boys who desire to go to college are more likely to have parents who insist on such a course of action than are

college-oriented girls, regardless of family class position. (E102)

College-educated parents are much less likely to insist on college for their daughters than for their sons. (E102)

Parents expect boys to go further in school than they do girls. (S191)

### Employment of Mother X Juvenile Delinquency by Sex Status

Since direct control is more effective over girls than over boys, there is a closer relationship between employment of the mother and delinquent behavior in girls than in boys. (N057)

### Employment of Women, Attitude Toward

Women are more likely than men to favor employment for women outside the home. (D060)

### Engagement, Stability of

Men are more likely to break an engagement if they have any doubts than are women. (P071)

### Exogamy (Informal)

Women tend to try to extend informal rules of exogamy further than men do. (C131)

### Father Absence, Adjustment to

Boys are more likely to show maladjustment as a result of the absence of the father than girls are. (R108)

### Father-Child Relations (Affection)

Boys are more likely than girls to attribute affective qualities to their fathers. (H201)

### Father-Child Relations (Dating)

Fathers are more likely to oppose dating by their daughters than by their sons. (K161)

### Father-Child Relations (Hostility)

More male than female emotionally disturbed children have distant and hostile relationships with their fathers. (M197)

### Father-Child Relations (Power)

Sons tend to be the objects of fathers' power assertion more than daughters do. (H180)

### Fertility

Married schizophrenic females tend to have more children than do their male counterparts. (R103)

### Fertility Values

Males tend to stress economic motives more than females do as reasons for desiring limitations in the size of their families of procreation. (C007)

The desire for smaller families than their parents had is more likely among males than among females (Mormon). (C007)

### Friendship

A husband is more apt to exchange confidence with the female in another couple unit (husband-initiated friends) than his wife is with the other male. (B317)

With friends of a middle-class couple (both couple and single units), husbands are more likely to exchange confidences with men than with women and wives with women than with men. (B317)

### Genealogical Ties, Knowledge of

The informant will tend to have a wider knowledge of the genealogical ties of his parent of the same sex. (G033)

Women tend to have a wider knowledge of genealogical ties than men do. (G033)

### Geographic Mobility

There is a greater likelihood that widowed and divorced men will migrate away from big cities than will widowed and divorced women. (F008)

### Homicide

The rate of homicide among males is higher than among females. (S078)

### Homogamy (Class)

Among the upper strata, a greater proportion of men marry downward than do women. (G157)

Men are more likely to marry below their social status than women are. (J035)

There is greater emphasis upon women of high status marrying endogamously than upon men. (W098)

### Homogamy (Education)

Men are more apt to marry women of lower educational attainment than women are apt to marry men of lower educational attainment. (J035)

### Homogamy (I.Q.)

People who marry are more likely to be of the same I.Q. than not and if they are not, men are more likely to be the more intelligent. (J035)

### Household Composition

Male heads of households are more likely to accommodate their daughters' than their sons' children and are more likely to accommodate their daughters' illegitimate than their legitimate children. (S211)

### Husband-Wife Relations (Aggression)

Among middle-class Americans, wives are likely to show more verbal aggression than are husbands. (W148)

### Identification

Girls tend to identify with people they know personally, either inside or outside of the family; boys identify with general societal roles or with well-known persons epitomizing these roles. (W138)

### Identification with Child

Parents tend to identify more closely with babies of the same sex as themselves.

### Identification with Cross-Sex Parent

College-educated males identify with their mothers, college-educated females identify with their fathers (similarity of responses to California F-Scale). (W144)

### Identification with Like/Cross-Sex Parent

Girls are less likely to choose mothers as the principal role model than boys are to choose fathers. (E098)

### Identification with Like-Sex Parent

Girls are more likely than boys to identify with the same-sex parent.

Boys identify with their fathers much less than girls identify with their mothers. (H193)

### Identification with Parents

The child usually identifies with the parent of the same sex as the child.

## Intermarriage

Among members of the upper caste, men are more likely to violate patterns of racial endogamy than women are; but upper-caste women are more likely than men to marry downward in caste. (M227)

## Intermarriage (Racial)

Interracial marriages tend to be between aboriginal women and white men. (F063)

Negro men and white women are more likely to intermarry than are white men and Negro women. (G003)

Marriages between Negroes and whites are most likely to be caste-hypogamous, the white woman marrying a Negro man (U.S.). (G156)

## Juvenile Delinquency

Daughters of employed mothers are more likely to show delinquent behavior than are sons. (N063)

## Juvenile Delinquency (Running Away)

Delinquent girls are more likely to run away from home than are delinquent boys. (F093)

## Kin Relations (Closeness)

Pairs of sisters are emotionally closer to one another than are pairs of brothers; pairs of girl cousins are closer than boy cousins.

Among older persons (50 years and up) who live by themselves, men are as likely as women to be cut off from intimate contact with kin and thus to lose the role of kinsman. (C116)

Among older persons (50 years and up), women are more likely than men to keep closer touch with both siblings and children. (C116)

## Kin Relations (Interaction)

Women tend to spend more time with their kin than do men. (G033)

## Kin Terminology

The selection of an informal variant for the terms of address for mother is more likely to occur among sons than among daughters. (B083)

Females tend to use the more formal variants of kinship terminology more frequently, males use formal variants more frequently. (N012)

The formal variant of a kinship term is more likely to be used with the parent of the same sex than with the parent of the opposite sex. (S050)

## Love Magic

Among the lower classes, women are more apt to resort to the use of magic to keep a man; men are more apt to resort to magic to get rid of women with whom they are living or to whom they are married. (R124)

## Marital Adjustment

Among those who feel inadequate in the marital relationship, men are more likely to feel self-blame than are women. (G126)

Women tend to report more personal problems and greater unhappiness in the marital situation than do men; both sexes report feelings of inadequacy. (G126)

Women are more dependent upon a successful marriage for their adjustment to living than are men. (G156)

Women are more likely than men to complain about their marriages. (G156)

Men suffer greater marital disenchantment in the early years than women do; women experience greater disenchantment than men do during the middle years of marriage. (P071)

Men's greater disenchantment during the early years of marriage is partially a function of their tendency to romanticize the relationship more than women do. (P071)

A man is more likely than a woman to complain of a deficit in tension reduction in marriage; this is due to the fact that the wife has, in her children, a source of socialized regression which is not as available to him. (P083)

## Marriage, Attitude Toward

Regardless of degree of parental happiness in marriage, females generally have more favorable attitudes toward marriage than males do. (S279)

## Marriage Chances

Toward the upper educational and occupational strata, a higher proportion of men than of women marry; while toward the lower strata, a higher proportion of women than of men marry. (G157)

Females are less likely than males to marry mental patients. (F124)

Schizophrenic females are more likely to marry than are schizophrenic males. (R103)

## Marriage, Goal of

The primary motivation focus in marriage for women is the parent-child relationship; for men it is possession of the woman. (P083)

## Mate Selection

Teen-aged males and females are in fairly close agreement on the criteria that the other person must meet before they will make or accept a date (e.g., the other person should be physically fit and mentally fit, dependable, etc.). However, they differed in certain respects: males stressed being a good cook and housekeeper, physical attractiveness, and nonuse of tobacco; females stressed importance of good financial prospect, moderation re intimacy, parental approval, and consideration toward others (U.S.). (C012)

Females tend to be more objective than males in selecting a mate because their position in society is dependent on the male (U.S.). (S076)

## Mate Selection (Education)

Women are more likely to eliminate from consideration as marriage partners individuals of different educational status than are men. (B033)

## Mate Selection (Free Choice)

Parental pressures to control the selection of a mate are greater when the child is a daughter. (B033)

## Mate Selection (Religion)

Women are more likely than men to eliminate from consideration as marriage partners individuals of different faiths. (B033)

## Mental Illness (Schizophrenia), Recovery from

Divorced or separated schizophrenic males are more likely to recover than are divorced or separated females. (F104)

### Monogamy, Attitude Toward
Women tend to be more sympathetic to monogamy as the pattern of marriage than men do. (P034)

### Mother-Child Relations
Mothers tend to feel more assured with girl babies than they do with boy babies. (B272)

There is no relationship between the sex of the infant and maternal behavior (sensitivity, consistency, or frequency of maternal acts). (B272)

### Mother-Child Relations (Affect)
Fathers, rather than mothers, are more likely to show high emotional involvement with their mothers. (B297)

### Mother-Child Relations (Power)
Daughters tend to be the objects of power assertion of mothers more than sons do. (H180)

### Mother-Child Relations (Rejection)
Among middle-class schizophrenic children, girls are more likely to be rejected by their mothers than are boys. (M197)

### Mother-Child Relations (Restrictiveness)
Girls are more likely than boys to perceive their mothers as overcircumscribing their freedom. (K101)

### Mother-Child Relations (Warmth)
Mothers usually act more warmly toward girl babies than toward boy babies. (S191)

### Neurosis
There is a higher rate of "minimal neurosis" among women than among men. (P086)

### Occupational Role, Economic Importance of
Men tend to assume the occupational role which is of greatest importance to the economy. (S120)

### Parent-Child Relations (Acceptance)
Mothers tend to be more accepting of their children than fathers.

### Parent-Child Relations (Affect)
Among fathers, but not mothers, strong emotional involvement with one parent tends to exclude strong emotional involvement with the other. (B297)

Girls react to their parents with a pleasant feeling-tone more frequently than boys do. (G117)

### Parent-Child Relations (Affection)
Mothers are more likely to remember their fathers as highly affectionate; fathers are more likely to recall their mothers as highly affectionate. (B297)

Children view their parents as relatively more affectionate with a child of the opposite sex and more strict with a child of the same sex. (H180)

Males are more likely to express dislike of parents than are females. (R116)

The parent-child relationship will tend to be more affectionate and less strict when the parent and child are of the opposite sex. (W104)

### Parent-Child Relations (Affection/Praise)
Among adolescents, girls are more likely than boys to get affection and praise for its own sake (rather than as a reward). (B250)

### Parent-Child Relations (Agreement)
Agreement between the parent and a child of the opposite sex increases as the child becomes increasingly involved in courtship. Between mother and daughter disagreement increases, whereas there is no change in the father-son relationship. (H229)

Both mothers and fathers are more likely to report disagreement with their same-sex offspring than with their opposite-sex offspring, although with advancing courtship parents report declining disagreement with their opposite-sex offspring. (H229)

Parents' alienation from their son increases with advancing courtship, but declines for their daughter. (H229)

### Parent-Child Relations (Anxiety)
Both male and female schizophrenics are less anxious in dealing with the father than with the mother. (S258)

### Parent-Child Relations (Approval)
Parents are more approving and understanding of boys than of girls. (C114)

Mothers are more likely to approve of and understand their sons rather than their daughters to a greater extent than fathers are. (C114)

### Parent-Child Relations (Authority)
Fathers are more likely to remember their mothers rather than their fathers as strong sources of authority. (B297)

Mothers and fathers both remember authority being exerted by one parent rather than by both. (B297)

There is less variation in the character of parental authority with the sex of the child among schizophrenics than among normals. (S187)

### Parent-Child Relations (Closeness)
The conclusion of the infancy period is associated with the boy becoming more emotionally attached to his mother, while the daughter becomes more attached to her father. (G156)

Among schizophrenic children who view their mothers as the dominant authority figure, females are more likely to report feeling closer to their fathers than to their mothers and males to report feeling closer to their mothers than to their fathers. (K114)

Both males and females feel closer to their mothers than to their fathers. (L137)

There is no association between sex and closeness felt to the parent of the opposite sex. (L137)

Women feel closer to their parents than men do. (L137)

When parents have only one married child, the married son has just as close a relationship to them as the married daughter does; if there are married children of more than one sex, a married daughter has a closer relationship to her parents than a married son does. (S269)

Females are more likely to be more attached to their parents than males are. (W006)

### Parent-Child Relations (Companionship/Protection)
Among adolescents, girls are more likely than boys to get parental protection and companionship for its own sake (rather than as a reward). (B250)

### Parent-Child Relations (Employment)

Boys are more likely than girls to perceive their fathers as feeling unhappy or uncomfortable about going to work and leaving a child behind. (H224)

Boys are much more likely than girls to perceive their fathers as possibly having negative feelings toward their work. (H224)

### Parent-Child Relations (Evaluation)

There is no substantiating evidence for the proposition that daughters tend to rate their fathers higher on the Parent Evaluation Scale than they do their mothers or that sons tend to rate mothers higher; both daughters and sons tend to rate their mothers higher.

Boys are more likely to be critical and less satisfied with their home conditions and relations with their parents than girls are. (H174)

### Parent-Child Relations (Financial Help)

Married daughters are more likely to receive financial assistance from their parents than are married sons. (A066)

### Parent-Child Relations (Hostility)

Girls are more likely than boys to see their fathers rather than their mothers as hostile.

### Parent-Child Relations (Interaction)

There is a tendency for each parent to interact relatively more with a child of the same sex. (This holds for American society; it is less so for German society.) (D063)

### Parent-Child Relations (Intimacy)

The relationship of parent to child is more likely to be intimate if they are of the same sex. (C023)

Males are more intimately related to their fathers; females, to their mothers (seventh–twelfth-grade age-groups). (B286)

### Parent-Child Relations (Nurturance/Control)

Boys are more likely than girls to judge whether one parent is more nurturant and controlling. (J026)

### Parent-Child Relations (Overprotectiveness/Rejection)

A background of parental overprotection and/or rejection is more likely in male than in female schizophrenics. (W147)

The parental overprotection and/or rejection antecedent to schizophrenia does not vary with respect to same- or cross-sex parent. (W147)

### Parent-Child Relations (Preference)

Mothers are more preferred than fathers by both girls and boys; but a higher percentage of boys than of girls prefer mothers, while a higher percentage of girls than of boys prefer their fathers. (W013)

Boys are more reluctant to criticize their mothers than their fathers.

Among five-to-eight-year-olds, boys more often express favorable reactions toward their mothers than toward their fathers; girls more often express favorable reactions toward their fathers than toward their mothers. (G117)

Both boys and girls prefer their mothers to their fathers. (G117)

Among schizophrenic children who do not report maternal domination in the family, both males and females are more likely to report preference for their mothers than for their fathers. (K114)

Irrespective of the sex of the subject, a higher proportion of subjects who express a preference for one or the other parent prefer the mother than the father. (W013)

Of those subjects who express a preference for one parent, males tend to prefer their mothers in greater proportion than do females; females tend to prefer their fathers in greater proportions than do males. (W013)

### Parent-Child Relations (Punishment)

Boys place a greater emphasis than girls do upon curbing their activities to avoid parental punishment. (W138)

### Parent-Child Relations (Rejection)

Girls are more likely to feel rejected by their parents than boys are. (B286)

Girls report that fathers are more rejecting, neglecting, and ignoring than mothers are to a greater degree than boys do. (D069)

### Parental Attitudes, Perception of

Female college students are more aware than male students of their parents' attitudes (parents' responses to California F-Scale compared to students' views of parental responses). (W144)

### Parental-Role Adjustment

Women are more likely than men, at some time, to feel inadequate as parents. (G126)

Men tend to feel inadequate because of not spending enough time with their children; women tend to feel inadequate because of exasperation and loss of temper with the child. (G126)

There is no difference between men and women in their degree of felt inadequacy about emotional relations with their children or about tolerance. (G126)

### Parental Role, Attitude Toward

Men are more likely to emphasize parental satisfactions that come from influencing their children or satisfactions involving achievement, ambitions, and accomplishments; women are more likely to emphasize satisfactions derived from increased love, affection, and companionship with the child. (G126)

### Parenthood, Attitude Toward

Women express more negative feelings about parenthood than men do. (G126)

Women are more likely than men to view children as essential to their growth as persons to their stability and maturity, and to the focusing of their lives. (G126)

### Parental/Maternal-Role Definition

Refusal of the mother to accept social responsibility for the child is considered more "unnatural," a more serious violation of role obligations than is refusal on the part of the father. (G156)

### Peer Relations

Girls are more likely than boys to choose opposite-sex playmates.

Among teen-agers, sons are more likely to seek their social activities outside of the home than daughters are. (D079)

Girls are more likely than boys to find their siblings' associates accepting and cooperative. (K094)

### Personality Adjustment (Worry)
Among divorced and separated persons, women report worrying "all the time" much more frequently than do men. (G126)

### Personality of Mother
The differences between mothers of schizophrenics and those of normal children do not correlate with sex of the child. (H207)

### Personality Problems
Women, in general, whether married or unmarried, are more likely to feel they are about to have a nervous breakdown than are men. This difference is reduced when considering only single men and women. (G126)

### Personality (Social Interests)
Parents believe that their girls are more interested in other persons than are their boys. (G130)

### Political Activity
Male children are somewhat less likely than female children to resemble parents closely in extent of membership in political and social organizations. (H244)

For female children, the resemblance to the mother in extent of social and political participation is much greater than to the father. (H244)

### Political Attitudes
Daughters are more likely than sons to have political attitudes which resemble those of their parents. (H244)

### Political Discussions
Women are more likely than men to discuss politics with family members more often than with friends or co-workers, whereas the reverse is true of men. (H244)

### Polygyny
Men are more likely than women to desire several mates. (P083)

### Power Structure of Family
Boys are more likely than girls to see their fathers as dominant in both conjugal and parental relations, while girls are more likely than boys to see their mothers as dominant in both areas. (B323)

Husbands are more likely to claim that wives have greater influence; wives claim that both have the same influence (U.S.). (H175)

Little difference exists between boys' and girls' perceptions of parental discipline and power among children in the first three grades of school; boys report slightly more frequently than girls that the mother is the "boss" in the house. (H180)

### Power Structure of Family X Scholastic Motivation
Girls are much more likely than boys to have high academic motivation if the family structure is equalitarian rather than wife or husband dominant. (E102)

### Premarital Sex Relations
Females are more likely than males to have their first coital experience with a steady or a fiancé. (C023)

Males tend to start coitus at an earlier age than females. (C023)

Males tend to have more premarital sex partners than females. (C023)

Males are more likely than females to give "desire" as their reason for initial coitus. (C023)

A higher percentage of females than of males confine their sexual activities outside marriage to necking and petting. (C023)

Females are more likely than males to confine sexual activity to others of the same social class, while males are more likely than females to have sexual activity with lower-class persons. (C023)

Males are more likely to have premarital sexual intercourse than are females. (C023)

Premarital sexual activity of females is correlated more highly with going steady or being in love than is that of males. (E092)

Women are more likely than men to be monogamous in their premarital sexual intercourse relationships. (E092)

### Premarital Sex Relations, Attitude Toward
Teen-age girls are more conservative about necking and petting behavior than are teen-age boys. (C012)

Teen-age girls are more likely to disapprove of kissing on the first date than to approve of it. (C012)

Teen-age girls are more likely to feel that intimate petting should be delayed until after marriage than to feel it should take place before marriage. (C012)

A higher percentage of males than of females approve of premarital coitus. (C095)

### Race Attitudes
Among children who say their parents have not discouraged them from playing with Negro children, boys are less prejudiced than girls. (B226)

Among children who say their parents have prohibited them from playing with Negroes, there is no association between sex and degree of prejudice. (B226)

### Religious Beliefs
In cross-faith marriages, men abandon their faiths more readily than women. (Z008)

### Remarriage
Among men recently married and living on farms, remarriage is more common than among women recently married and living on farms. (G011)

### Remarriage Rates
At most ages the age-specific remarriage rates for men are much higher than those for women. (C010)

### Residence
Among older (50 years and up) widowed persons, men are as likely as women to live by themselves (U.S.). (C116)

When the out-marrying spouse is a man, he will rarely move far from home. (S189)

Married daughters' initial residences are not likely to be as far from their parents as are those of married sons. (S269)

### Role Behavior in Family
Women are much more likely than men to be the agents of and to initiate the familistic trend in collective settlements. (T013)

Wives are more likely to conform to husbands' expectations than are the husbands to the wives' expectations. (T092)

### Role Definition of Husband-Wife
Significantly more conservative attitudes toward the marital roles of husbands and wives were found among males than among females. (J002)

Wives are more likely to value the socioemotional aspects of interaction than are husbands. (T092)

### Scholastic Adjustment (Reading)
Since boys have more difficulty in learning to suppress aggressive drives (which impede learning) than girls do, they are more likely to develop reading difficulties. (S225)

### Self-Conception of Spouse
Wives are more likely to agree with their husbands' self-descriptions than are husbands with their wives' self-descriptions.

### Sex Anxiety
The sex of the dominant parent will directly affect more generalized attitudes of hostility or anxiety toward relatives of the same sex. (S187)

### Sex Drive
Husbands are more apt to have high sex drives than are their wives. (W155).

### Sex Norms
Males tend to be more permissive regarding sexual matters than do females.

### Sex Norms (Double Standard)
A significantly larger proportion of teen-age boys than of teen-age girls favors a single standard of sexual morality. (C012)

Females are more likely to support the double standard of sexual morality than males are, but more strongly so regarding premarital relations than extramarital ones. (C124)

### Sex Preference
The sex of the child does not correlate with his perception of the sex of child preferred by parents. (H181)

### Sex Relations (Intercaste)
The censure of intercaste sexual relations is greater when a high-caste woman conducts a liaison with a lower-ranking man than when a higher-caste man has a liaison with a lower-ranking woman. (S089)

### Sex-Role Adjustment
The girl is more likely to experience dissatisfaction in accepting her appropriate sex role than is the boy in accepting his. (B277)

Although the boy is more likely than the girl to prefer his appropriate sex model, since he experiences less exposure, he may have more difficulty in the actual process of identification. (B277)

A man is more likely to feel inadequate about his central role as provider than a woman is about her main role as housekeeper. (G126)

Among college-educated persons, women are more likely to feel inadequate concerning their main role as housekeeper than men do about their main role as provider. (G126)

### Sex-Role Behavior
Although male and female college students do not differ in their perception of their father's masculinity, they do differ in relation to their perception of their mother's feminity (i.e., the male students perceive their mothers as being more feminine than do the females). (B274)

Since fathers emphasize sex-typed differences between boys and girls more than mothers do, it is likely that boys will show more sex-appropriate behavior than girls will (through internalization of parental values). (G130)

### Sex-Role Definition
Parental roles (i.e., association of nurturance with the mother and control with the father) are more sharply discriminated by boys than by girls. (E098)

Wives are in greater agreement concerning the definition of their roles as wives and mothers than are husbands concerning the definition of their roles as husbands and fathers. (H195)

Wives live up to their husbands' expectations of them as wives and mothers to a greater extent than husbands live up to their wives' expectations of them as husbands and fathers. (H195)

Spouses who agree on the definition and relative importance of the wife's marital roles also tend to agree on the definition and relative importance of the husband's marital roles. (H195)

(Among children 5–11 years of age) sons of working mothers are more likely than are daughters of working mothers to perceive the woman's role as involving employment outside of the home. (H236)

Boys have a negative reaction to women's work, but there is no corresponding negative reaction among girls to men's work. (R126)

### Sex-Role Identification
It is not true that the mother is the first identification model for both boys and girls, but boys later switch to the father as the main model. (E098)

Feminine behavior is more closely related to imitation of the mother than masculine behavior is to imitation of the father. (H210)

Feminine-role identification is learned in the context of a close personal relationship with the mother; masculine-role identification is learned from identification with cultural stereotypes of the masculine role derived from many contexts. (L138)

Girls have an easier time than boys do taking on appropriate sex-typed adult roles because they need not shift from identification with the mother to identification with the father (U.S.). (S191)

### Sexual Adjustment
Satisfactory sexual relations are more important to men than to women in their evaluation of a marriage. (G156)

### Sibling Rank
The status of a male sibling tends to be higher than that of a female. (W067)

### Sibling Relations (Affection)
Siblings of the same sex are more apt to develop strong affective ties than are siblings of different sexes. (I008)

Girls are more likely than boys to be interested in and

affectionate toward any new child in the family since the new baby gives them an opportunity to rehearse their mother roles. (R129)

### Sibling Relations (Hostility)
Disturbed male children are more likely to arouse resentment and hostility from their siblings than are disturbed girls, with the exception of frequent close relationships between middle-class disturbed boys and a sister. (M197)

### Sibling Relations (Teasing)
Boys use teasing more frequently than girls do. (K149)

### Size of Family
#### X Academic Motivation of Child by Sex Status
Among high achieving adolescents, the larger the family size, the greater the sex difference regarding academic motivation, girls being more motivated than boys. (E102)

### Social Mobility
Women are more likely than men to be upwardly mobile through marriage. (C134)

Men are more likely to be downwardly mobile in marriage than are women. (C134)

Sex differences in academic motivation of adolescents are least among those children who are most exposed to conditions generating and facilitating upward mobility (i.e., middle-class status, college-educated fathers who are active in independence training, and parents who insist on their children going to college). (E102)

### Suicide
The suicide rate of males correlates more highly with business cycles than does the suicide rate of females. (S078)

The suicide rate of males is higher than that of females. (S078)

### Superego Formation
Females are more likely than males to feel guilt regarding premarital sex.

### Toilet Training
Among mothers who have greater anxieties concerning sex, those who have boys are more likely to commence toilet training at an earlier age than are those who have girls (U.S.). (S191)

### Values (Familism)
Girls are more likely than boys to place value on being a good member of the family. (R111)

### Values (Familism/Collectivism)
Compared to each other, men tend to be more collective-oriented, and women more family-oriented. (T098)

### Voting Behavior
Women are more likely than men to report that relatives influenced the formation of their votes. (H244)

## SEX STATUS OF ABSENT PARENT
#### X Personality Problems of Child
There is no relationship between sex of the absent parent and the type of personality disorder which developes in the child. (G140)

## SEX STATUS OF CHILD
#### X Breast Feeding, Duration of
There is no direct association between the length of breast feeding and the sex of the child. (L162)

### Child-Rearing Practices (Authoritarianism)
No relationship exists between authoritarian child control and the sex of the child. (H200)

### Child-Rearing Practices (Autoeroticism)
Among mothers who were most strongly inclined to differentiate sex roles, boys' mothers were more permissive about masturbation than were girls' mothers. (S191)

### Child-Rearing Practices (Discipline/Overprotectiveness)
In the lower middle class, boys are most susceptible to the ill effects of insufficient parental discipline; girls, to the detrimental influence of parental overprotection. (B273)

### Child-Rearing Practices (Punishment)
Girls are exposed to more love-oriented discipline and to less punishment than boys are. (B252)

### Child-Rearing Practices (Sex/Dependency/Aggression)
Compared to those of maladjusted males, mothers of maladjusted females score higher on suppression of sex and ascendance of mother; fathers score higher on fostering dependency, deception suppression of aggression, and suppression of sex (PARI). (Z011)

### Child-Rearing Practices (Strictness)
Parents are more lenient in disciplining children of the opposite sex than of the same sex. (B273)

### Dating, Parental Approval of
The parent is more likely to oppose dating by the cross-sex rather than by the same-sex child. (S219)

### Employment of Mother, Attitude Toward
Girls are more likely than boys to approve of their mothers' working. (S265)

### Father-Child Relations (Appreciation)
Fathers show more appreciation of their daughters than of their sons. (J026)

### Father-Child Relations (Concern)
Fathers show less concern for their daughters than for their sons. (J026)

### Father-Child Relations (Hostility)
Girls see their fathers as more punitive and hostile than do boys. (H180)

### Identification with Like/Cross-Sex Parent
Males identify more with their fathers than with their mothers; females identify equally with both parents. (J026)

### Maternal-Role Behavior
There is no direct correlation between maternal behavior and the sex of the mother's child. (L165)

### Mental Illness of Parent
Delayed parental reaction to a trauma in his own childhood is more likely to occur if the child is the same sex as the disturbed parent. (H246)

### Mother-Child Relations (Control)
Mothers tend to exert greater control over their daughters than over their sons. (A060)

### Mother-Child Relations (Warmth)
At kindergarten age, sex of child and mother's warmth toward child are not associated, but in infancy, mothers

are slightly more affectionately demonstrative with baby girls than with baby boys. (S191)

### Parent-Child Relations (Employment)
Boys tend to perceive the father as feeling more positive about leaving his wife for work than do girls. (H222)

There is no difference between sons and daughters regarding their perception of mothers' attitudes toward their work. (H222)

### Parent-Child Relations (Preference)
Girls are more likely to express a preference for one parent than are boys. (B286)

### Parent-Child Relations (Rejection)
Daughters show more evidence of being unwanted by their parents than sons do. (W013)

### Paternal/Maternal-Role Discipline
Boys are more likely than girls to see the father rather than the mother as the primary disciplinary agent. (H201)

While mothers discipline children of both sexes equally, fathers are more likely to discipline boys than girls. (J026)

### Personality of Parents (Power)
Both males and females rate their mothers as being lower on the potency factor than their fathers (measured by Osgood's Semantic Scale). (J026)

There is no difference between males and females in their potency ratings of their mothers (measured by Osgood's Semantic Scale). (J026)

Males are more likely than females to rate their fathers as higher in potency (measured by Osgood's Semantic Scale). (J026)

### Surrogate Parent
There is no relationship between the sex of the child (children 7–10 years of age) and that of the persons who serve as caretaking agents for the child. (M216)

## SEX STATUS OF EXISTING CHILDREN
### X   Pregnancy, Attitude Toward
The mother tends to be happier about a new pregnancy if her existing children are girls rather than boys only, or both boys and girls. (S191)

## SEX STATUS OF HOUSEHOLD HEAD
### X   Household Composition
Households under male heads are more likely to have a higher proportion of nonlineage to lineage kin among male members than are households under female heads. (F072)

Men are more willing to accommodate unrelated persons in their homes than they are their own illegitimate children. With women, the reverse is true. (S211)

Domestic units under female heads are more likely to contain three (or more) generations than are units under male heads. (S211)

### Opportunity Structure
A higher percentage of women-headed households is found in a social-status system in which the lower-class father can achieve no superior rank. (A051)

### Urban/Rural
Women are more likely to be heads of households in towns than in rural areas. (A051)

In urban areas the heads of Negro households are more likely to be women than men; in rural areas, men than women. (F003)

### Urbanization
A higher proportion of Negro women heads can be found in city than in rural nonfarm populations and both urban and rural nonfarm populations have a higher percentage of women heads than do rural farm areas. (B033)

## SEX STATUS OF MENTAL PATIENT
### X   Residence with Kin
Male mental patients are more likely than female mental patients to be living in parental rather than conjugal family settings. (F124)

Female mental patients are more likely to live with their siblings than are male patients. (F124)

## SEX STATUS OF PARENT
### X   Child-Rearing Practices (Behavior Problems)
There is no relationship between the sex of the parent and the measure suggested (punishment, verbal persuasion, building confidence, diverting child, obtaining outside help) for the correction of children who lie and fight. (M223)

### Child-Rearing Practices (Strictness)
Regardless of social class or education, husbands are inclined to believe that their wives are not strict enough with the children, while the wives tend to believe that their husbands are too strict. (S191)

### Child-Rearing Problems
Women are more likely to mention having difficulties in rearing their children than are men. (G126)

### Parent-Child Relations (Preference)
In a high-school sample children are more likely to prefer their fathers than their mothers. (C107)

In a college sample children have a slight tendency to prefer their mothers over their fathers. (C107)

A higher proportion of both sexes profess no preference for either parent than profess preference for either the father or the mother. (W013)

### Parent-Child Relations (Sex Preference)
Regardless of the sex of the parent, a higher proportion of parents who show a preference for children of one sex or the other prefers males over females. (W013)

Of those parents who express a preference for children of one sex or the other, fathers tend to prefer their daughters in greater proportion than do the mothers; mothers tend to prefer their sons in greater proportion than do the fathers. (W013)

Preferences of fathers tend to be more evenly distributed between sons and daughters than are the preferences of mothers. (W013)

### Parental-Role Adjustment
Among those persons who are satisfied with the parental role, men are more likely to feel inadequacies pertaining to physical material provision for the child; women are more likely to feel inadequacies related to the parent–child affective relationship. (G126)

## SEX STATUS OF SCHIZOPHRENICS     X   Fertility
Married schizophrenic females tend to have more children than do their male counterparts. (R013)

## SEX STATUS OF STEPPARENT
### X  Stepparent-Child Relations
Stepchildren adjust better to stepfathers than to stepmothers. (B286)

## SEX TABOO                    X  Adultery
Among monogamous unions, the observance of periods of restrictions against sexual relations will tend to result in males having extramarital relations. (V021)

### Polygyny
Sex taboos are more common in polygynous societies. (O027)

Polygyny will tend to be institutionalized where there are major taboos against sexual intercourse during pregnancy and in the postnatal period. (V021)

### Size of Group
The greater the number of people involved, the greater the punishment for illicit sexual behavior. (B006)

### Social Control
The greater the number of societies in which a given type of sexual behavior is tabooed, the more severe is the punishment. (B006)

## SEX TABOO (POSTPARTUM)       X  Adultery
In monogamous marriages the custom of abstention from sexual intercourse during pregnancy and before weaning tends to result in greater promiscuity. (L113)

### Avoidance Relationship
In societies with long durations of the postpartum sex taboo, avoidance of kin is common. (S079)

In societies with long durations of the postpartum sex taboo, the severity of kin avoidance will be greater (this includes mother-in-law avoidance, son's wife avoidance, brother-sister avoidance, etc.). (S079)

### Breasts
In societies with long durations of the postpartum sex taboo, a woman's breasts are less likely to be considered sexual stimuli and feeling of breasts is not part of the sexual interaction. (S079)

### Child-Rearing Practices (Sex)
Societies with long durations of postpartum sex taboo are likely also to have a rather severe sex training. (S079)

### Fertility
The longer the period of postpartum abstinence, the lower the fertility. (N054)

### Husband-Wife Relations (Intensity)
In societies having long periods of taboo against sex relations after childbirth, the intensity of the husband and wife relationship is lower. (S079)

### Initiation Rites
A long duration of the postpartum sex taboo is associated with initiation ceremonies for boys. (S079)

In societies with long durations of postpartum sex taboo, initiation ceremonies for girls are also found. (S079)

There is a strong correlation between prolonged postpartum sex taboo and male initiation rites at puberty. (W127)

### Menstrual Taboo
There is a correlation between a prolonged postpartum sex taboo and elaborate menstrual taboos. (W127)

### Monogamy
In monogamous societies, the postpartum sex taboo is of short duration or does not exist at all. (S079)

### Mother-Child Relations (Sexual Interest)
A long duration of postpartum sex taboo increases the likelihood of the mother being sexually arousing to her children. (S079)

A long duration of the postpartum sex taboo is associated with a greater sexual interest on the part of the mother in her child. (S079)

### Mother-Son Relations
A strong incestuous bond between mother and son is more likely to be established in societies with prolonged postpartum sex taboos. (W127)

### Mother-Son Relations (Sex)
In societies with long durations of the postpartum sex taboo, the intensity of sex attraction between the son and the mother is higher. (S079)

### Oedipal Complex
A long duration of the postpartum sex taboo intensifies the Oedipal complex. (S079)

### Polygyny
In societies having a high proportion of polygynous marriages, a long postpartum sex taboo is found. (S079)

### Residence (Extrusion)
In societies with long durations of postpartum sex taboo, boys are likely to move away from home upon reaching puberty. (S079)

### Sex Anxiety
In societies with long durations of the postpartum sex taboo, the society is likely to have many beliefs about the dangers inherent in sex. (S079)

### Weaning
In societies with long durations of the postpartum sex taboo the average age of weaning is later. (S079)

### Wife-Sharing
Other males (relatives or age-mates) are more likely to have sexual access to a man's wife in societies which impose prolonged continence during pregnancy and lactation. (P083)

### Witchcraft
In societies with long durations of the postpartum sex taboo, there is more fear of sorcery. (S079)

## SEX TABOO (POSTPREGNANCY)       X  Abortion
Married women are more likely to give the sex drive priority over the maternal impulse and thus resort to abortion in societies where there are taboos on coitus during pregnancy and lactation and where monogamy prevails. (D071)

### Father-Child Relations (Hostility)
The unconscious hostility of the father toward the unborn child is a cause of taboo against coitus during pregnancy. (D071)

### Fertility
Laxity in the adherence to pregnancy taboos is directly correlated with the number of children which have preceded the pregnancy. (H122)

### Monogamy
With an increase in the percentage of monogamous marriages, the postpregnancy sex taboo is increasingly disregarded. (L113)

### Parent-Child Relations (Hostility)
There is a relationship between unconscious parental hostility toward the unborn child (as a motive for abortion) and taboos on coitus during pregnancy and lactation in monogamous societies. (D071)

### Pregnancy, Attitude Toward
There is a correlation between the unconscious fear of superfetation and the custom of proscribing coitus during pregnancy (and lactation). (D071)

### SEX TABO (PREGNANCY)    X    Adultery
Restrictions against intercourse during pregnancy are likely to lead to extramarital relations when the union is monogamous. (A034)

### Child-Rearing Practices (Sex)
Severe sex training in a society is associated with prolonged sex taboo during pregnancy.

### SEXUAL ACTIVITY    X    Educational Level
Among males there is an inverse relationship between educational level and sexual activity. (C023)

### Religiosity
Active church members have lower frequencies of sexual outlets than do nonactive church members. (C023)

### SEXUAL ADJUSTMENT    X    Adultery
Married women who are least satisfied sexually by their husbands are most likely to desire extramarital sexual relations. (C132)

### Age at Marriage
There is no correlation between age at marriage and sexual adjustment. (I005)

### Aggression
The degree of satisfaction found in a sexual relationship is related to the opportunities it offers for the expression of aggression. (S037)

### Authority Structure of Family
The greater the stress the couple places on joint decision making, the greater is the importance they attach to successful sexual relations. (B267)

### Birth Control
Wives who have confidence in the contraceptive being used experience better sexual adjustment following the birth of the first child than do wives who mistrust the contraceptive being used. On the other hand, there is no significant difference in sexual adjustment between husbands who trust the contraceptive they use and those who mistrust it. (L013)

### Childbirth Attitude
Those who fear another labor and childbirth after the first pregnancy have a poorer sexual adjustment than do those who have no such fear (U.S.). (L013)

### Divorce
Sexual problems in marriage are usually related to other marital tensions and, consequently, are not a direct cause of divorce. (G156)

Complaints of sexual problems are reported by those who divorce. (G156)

### Employment of Mother
Health status, marital, sexual and emotional adjustment, and number and seriousness of child problems do not correlate with employment or nonemployment of a mother. (S265)

### Happiness
Sexual satisfaction is more related to general happiness for men than for women. (L173)

### Husband-Wife Relations (Consensus)
The greater the stress the couple places on shared interests, the greater the importance they attach to successful sexual relations. (B267)

### Identification of Mother with Daughter
Mothers who have high degrees of identification with their daughters tend to be better adjusted sexually than are mothers who do not. (H218)

### Identification with Like/Cross-Sex Parent
Among twins, the one closer to and more identified with the cross-sex parent is more likely to become homosexual and the one closer to the same-sex parent is more likely to be heterosexual. (M212)

### Marital Adjustment
Sexual satisfaction is more likely in happy than in unhappy marriages.

Sex adjustment has a lower association with marital happiness than do other factors such as affection, consensus, and specific satisfaction. (B033)

There is a positive relation between marital happiness and sexual adjustment, but it varies inversely with education. (K089)

There is a direct relation between an enjoyable first sexual experience and marital adjustment. (K161)

There is a direct relation between sexual compatibility (in terms of similar sex drives, early appearance of orgasm, adequacy of sex technique) and marital adjustment. (K161)

Marital discord and disruption result most frequently from quarrels over sexual matters. (S090)

Sexual gratification will have less of an effect on marital satisfaction for religiously oriented married couples; low gratification will contribute less to dissatisfaction than it would for the nonreligious and high gratification will increase satisfaction less. (W155)

Religiosity has no effect on whether or not low sexual enjoyment affects marital satisfaction. (W155)

### Maternal Overprotectiveness
Marital sexual incompatibility is a cause of maternal overprotection of the child. (B272)

### Mental Illness (Schizophrenia)
A study of the life histories of normals and schizophrenics shows that schizophrenics are rated twice as frequently as normals as enjoying good sexual outlets. (S247)

### Mother-Child Relations (Sadomasochistic)
The more the mother's genital experience is focused on childbirth, the more likely she is to perceive her relationship with her children in its sadomasochistic aspects. (M203)

### Parent-Child Relations (Affection)
A sexual barrier between parents increases the likelihood that one of them will seek compensatory love from a child and treat the child seductively. (L134)

### Parent-Child Relations (Oedipal)
According to the Oedipal hypothesis, the relationship of the child to the cross-sex parent determines his later heterosexual adjustment. (L133)

### Pregnancy
More people feel that pregnancy has no effect on their sexual adjustment than feel it has either an unfavorable or a favorable effect. (L013)

### Premarital Sex Relations
There is no association between sexual adjustment in marriage and premarital sexual experience. (C023)

The greater the degree of satisfaction in premarital sex activities, the less likely is frigidity or other sexual maladjustment in marriage. (S219)

### Religiosity
Married couples who are religiously oriented are less apt to associate sexual gratification with marital satisfaction than are nonreligious couples. (W155)

### Sex-Role Identification
The greater the parents' doubts concerning their own masculinity or femininity, the more likely are they to cause disturbances in the child (perversion, exhibitionism, peeping at others, frigidity, impotence, etc.). (B244)

### Sex Status
Satisfactory sexual relations are more important to men than to women in their evaluation of a marriage. (G156)

### Social Network
The more dispersed a couple's network of social contacts (i.e., their friends are not friends of one another), the greater the emphasis they will place on successful sexual relations. (B268)

## SEXUAL ADJUSTMENT OF MOTHER
### X   Mother-Child Relations (Sexuality)
The greater the sexual dissatisfaction of the mother, the earlier does she arouse sexuality and intense emotional states in the child. (B272)

## SEXUAL ADJUSTMENT OF WIFE
### X   Marital Adjustment
There is relatively little association between wives' marital success scores and their sexual adjustment. (B033)

## SEXUAL AGGRESSION     X   Age at Marriage
A high frequency of rape will tend to occur in societies where there is a strong economic or other barrier to marriage which prolongs the bachelorhood of some males into their late twenties. (L026)

### Class
Sexual aggressors when compared with the sexually offended are more likely to be still lower in rank than are nonaggressors when compared with the nonoffended. (K018)

### Dating
A correlation exists between the degree of involvement in dating relationship and the level of erotic intimacy offense. (K001)

### Dating Frequency
Dating frequency is not significantly related to proneness to sexual aggression. (K018)

### Dating Relationship
Sexual aggression, preceded by mutually acceptable sex play, is more likely to occur among couples with a durable and involved date relationship than among couples who have just begun to date. (K018)

### Economic Relations
When the assertion of individual aggression is tabooed in the sexual sphere, the hostilities generated by sexual jealousy will find their outlets in the economic relations of the group. (M048)

### I.Q. Differences Between Dating Partners
The intelligence difference between sexually aggressive males and sexually offended females is more likely to be greater than the intelligence difference between nonaggressive males and nonoffended females. (K018)

### Marriage Payment
There is a direct correlation between expected bride wealth demand and the incidence of rape. (L026)

### Maternal Overprotectiveness
Sexual aggressiveness is less likely to occur where maternal overprotectiveness was manifested as dominance rather than as indulgence. (L164)

### Privacy
A high rate of sexual offenses tends to be correlated with the opportunity for privacy which the potential sex offender has. (L026)

### Rank
Sexual aggressors are more likely to have a lower social status than are the sexually offended, when compared with the social-status relationship between nonaggressors and nonoffended. (K018)

### Religiosity
Religious girls are less likely to have sexually aggressive experiences. (K001)

Girls who regularly attend church are no less likely to have experienced episodes of sexual aggression than are girls who do not attend church. (K018)

### Season of Year
A high prevalence of male sex aggression occurs in the fall and in the spring. (K001)

Male sex aggression of lesser offensiveness is concentrated in the fall. (K001)

Male sex aggression of greater offensiveness is concentrated in the spring. (K001)

Sexual aggression at the most intimate levels of eroticism is more likely to take place during the spring and summer than during the fall and winter. (K018)

### Sex Education
Girls who have received sexual instruction are less likely to experience sexual aggression than are girls who have not received sexual instruction. (K018)

### Sexual Restrictions
A high frequency of rape will tend to occur in societies where formal restrictions on the nonmarital sexual relations of females are severe and where physical segregation of the sexes does not occur. (L026)

### Sibling Structure (Age and Sex)
Girls who have elder male siblings are less likely to experience sexual aggression than are girls who do not have elder male siblings. (K018)

### Social Network
When premarital contact is severely restricted, the incidence of sexual aggression will tend to be high. (T041)

## SEXUAL ANTAGONISM          X  Witchcraft
In societies where there is a sharp antagonism between the sexes, witchcraft is more likely to be attributed to the subordinate sex. (N015)

## SEXUAL BEHAVIOR          X  Class
Men from lower educational and occupational levels find sexual outlets with members of the opposite sex at earlier ages than do those from higher socioeconomic levels. (K102)

### Education
Men with a grade-school education are more likely to have had premarital sexual experiences, to have extramarital relations after marriage, and around the age of 40 to limit their sexual relations to their spouses; men with a college education are more likely to be virginal when married, to refrain from extramarital contacts in the early years of marriage, and to have extramarital relations around the age of 35–40. (B244)

### Prostitution
The development of prostitution will diminish the social importance of the sexual act within the kinship system. (S153)

## SEXUAL BEHAVIOR OF MOTHER
### X  Mental Illness
There is no positive correlation between the mother's sexual behavior and psychosis. (M164)

## SEXUAL BEHAVIOR OF PARENTS
### X  Juvenile Delinquency
Children who witness parental sexuality (which stimulates fear and aggression in the child) are more likely to become delinquent than are others. (B238)

### Juvenile Delinquency (Running Away)
Delinquent children who run away are more likely to have parents who display open sexual activity in the home than are delinquent children who do not run away. (F093)

## SEXUAL BEHAVIOR OF WOMEN
### X  Incest Taboo
The low sexual excitability of women is probably a factor in permitting the incest taboo to be elaborated. (P083)

## SEXUAL DEVIANCE          X  Adultery of Father
Fathers of sexually deviant (perverted) boys are more likely to have sexual relations outside their marriage than are fathers of "normal" boys. (M209)

### Alcoholism
There is a correlation between sexual deviance in the family, as expressed in incest or illegitimacy, and later alcoholism in the child. (M195)

### Authoritarianism of Mother
If the mother is authoritarian, the son is more likely to become a sexual deviant. (M209)

### Child-Rearing Practices (Dependency)
The mothers of sexually deviant boys foster more dependency than do mothers of "normal" boys. (M209)

### Child-Rearing Practices (Punishment)
Fathers of sexual deviants are more likely to use physical punishment than are fathers of "normal" boys. (M209)

### Criminality
There is a correlation between sexual deviance in the family (illegitimacy or incest) and later criminal behavior in the son. (M195)

### Marital Adjustment
There is no evidence to indicate any relation between earlier deviant sexual behavior, sex play, or homosexual activity and successful marital adjustment. (K161)

### Marital Adjustment of Parents
Families of sexual deviants are more likely than are families of "normal" boys to be characterized by frequent overt conflicts between the parents. (M209)

### Maternal Overprotectiveness
Maternal overprotectiveness tends to result in an increased sexual drive toward the mother which manifests itself in flight from the mother and impulsive heterosexuality, impotence, or homosexuality. (L161)

### Warfare
There is a direct relation between war and the increase of deviant sexual behavior and prostitution. (K161)

## SEXUAL DEVIANCE OF SON
### X  Sex Anxiety of Mother
If the mother is sexually anxious, the son is more likely to become sexually deviant. (M209)

## SEXUAL DISABILITY OF HUSBAND, AGE AT
### X  Divorce
The earlier the age (25 years or younger) at which the spouse is physically disabled, the more likely is he to be divorced or separated. (N060)

## SEXUAL DISABILITY OF HUSBAND (DIVORCE)
### X  Education
Among men who have been physically disabled the proportion of those who remain married exceeds those who are divorced or separated at all educational levels. (N060)

### Income
Among men who have been physically disabled, those who have remained married are more likely to have higher incomes than are those who are divorced or separated. (N060)

### Occupation
Among men who have been physically disabled, those who have remained married are more likely to be in managerial-professional occupations than are those who are divorced or separated. (N060)

### Religion
In marriages where the husband has been physically disabled, Catholics are no more likely than Protestants to be divorced or separated; Jews are less likely to be divorced than Gentiles are. (N060)

### Size of Family
Among men who have been physically disabled, those who are married have a greater number of children than do those who are divorced or separated. (N060)

## SEXUAL FANTASIES
### X   Child-Rearing Practices (Sex)
When sex training in the society is severe, unconscious sexual fantasies will be numerous. (S079)

## SEXUAL GRATIFICATION, FREEDOM IN
### X   Mother-Child Relations (Indulgence)
Gratification of sexual impulses is more likely to occur in individuals who have been subject to maternal indulgence. (L161)

## SEXUAL INTEREST
### X   Age at Marriage/Premarital Relations
Institutionalized preoccupation with sex is more likely to occur in societies in which the age at marriage is late and premarital sexual relations are discouraged. (S262)

### Father-Son Relations (Affection)
Sons who have received sufficient paternal affection are more able to extend affection to members of the opposite sex than are sons who have received insufficient paternal affection. (M204)

Sons who have received sufficient paternal affection show a greater interest in the opposite sex than do sons who have received insufficient paternal affection. (M204)

### Identification with Father
High paternal identification is associated with strong heterosexual interests in the son. (M204)

### Marital Adjustment
Marital adjustment is associated with an equality or near equality of the strength of interest of the husband and wife in sex. (B033)

### Marriage
The interest of neurotics in sexual activity decreases with adulthood and marriage. (M197)

### Sex Ratio
An oversupply of males will give rise to a preoccupation with eroticism (in literature and poetry). (M167)

## SEXUAL INTEREST OF CHILD
### X   Child-Rearing Practices (Sex)
The mother's own sexual stimulation of her children is one determinant of the degree and intensity of the child's preoccupation with sex. (S079)

### Mother-Child Relations (Rejection)
The child of a rejecting mother is less likely to be generally preoccupied with sex. (S079)

## SEXUAL INTEREST OF WOMEN
### X   Economic Role of Women
With a decrease in the importance of the economic duties of women, they will tend to become increasingly preoccupied with sex. (B171)

## SEXUAL PERMISSIVENESS
### X   Dating Relationship
The more permissive the society regarding premarital sex relations, the more likely it is that those who experience premarital coitus with their steady or fiancé(e) will be satisfied with the relationship.

### Divorce
The more permissive the sex norms of a culture, the lower the divorce rate differential between premarital and postmarital pregnancies. (C125)

### Economic Level
Sexual restrictions will tend to be minimal in societies where the food supply is inadequate. (H139)

### Homosexuality, Overtness of
Overtness of homosexuality will be directly correlated with overtness of general sexual expression. (S187)

### Illegitimacy, Attitude Toward
With the increasing acceptance of illegitimate birth, restrictions on adolescent girls after puberty tend to be relaxed. (C055)

### Incest
Incest is less likely to occur if sexual relations are only minimally restricted. (H139)

### Incest (Father-Daughter)
When father-daughter incest is tolerated or not resisted in the family, the sexual norms of the family are permissive. (W123)

### Mate Selection (Kin)
Kinsmen who stand in a relationship of potential marriage partners are generally permitted to treat each other with sexual freedom. (W070)

### Musical Style
The bass song style is associated with a permissive attitude toward sex. (L025)

### Parent-Child Relations (Sex)
A greater preoccupation of the parents with the sex lives of their children increases the potential for conflict between parents and children. (G156)

### Polyandry
One characteristic of polyandrous societies is general sexual freedom. (S189)

### Population
The lack of population limitation through sex mores is associated with a society whose size of population hovers near the minimum for survival. (W156)

### Preferential Marriage (Cross-Cousin)
Permissive sex relationships between cross-cousins tend to occur in societies with cross-cousin marriage. (S189)

### Preferential Marriage (Levirate)
Permissive sex relationships between a boy and his brother's wife are more likely to occur in societies with the levirate. (S189)

### Preferential Marriage (Sororate)
Sex relationships between a girl and her sister's husband are likely to be permitted in societies with the sororate. (S189)

### Premarital Pregnancy
The greater the permissiveness of the society toward premarital sex, the greater will be the incidence of premarital pregnancy. (C135)

### Premarital Pregnancy/Divorce
The more permissive the society regarding premarital sex relations, the less likely it is that premarital pregnancy will be associated with divorce. (C135)

### Premarital Pregnancy/Marriage
The more permissive the society regarding premarital sex relations, the less likely it is that premarital pregnancy will lead to a hurried marriage. (C135)

### Premarital Sex Relations
The more sexually permissive the attitudes in a society, the more likely is premarital coitus. (C132)

The more permissive the culture with regard to premarital sexual intimacy, the higher the incidence of such intimacy occurring and the lower the negative effects from occurrences. (C132)

### Rank of Women
A high position of women is associated with sexual permissiveness. (M238)

### Scholastic Achievement
As measured on the PARI, parents of children who do well academically are less likely to suppress sexuality than are parents of children who are poor academically. (S230)

### Sex Anxiety
Parents whose sex anxieties were low tended to be more permissive of all forms of sex behavior and also less punitive for such behavior than did parents whose anxieties about sex were high. (B213)

### Sex Magic
Where sexual restrictions are minimal, sex magic will tend to be absent. (H139)

### Stability of Family System
Greater freedom in sexual relations threatens breakdown of the family system. (S171)

### Warfare
There is a greater need for the stringent regulation of sexual behavior in a society which emphasizes war and the extension of its territories. (R040)

## SEXUAL PROBLEMS (OF ADOLESCENTS)
### X Child Rearing (Collective)
Adolescents raised in kibbutzim have fewer problems concerning heterosexual activities and sexual problems have generally less salience for them than adolescents raised in families. (R096)

## SEXUAL RELATIONSHIP (POTENTIAL)
### X Joking Relationship
The joking relationship tends to obtain between relatives standing in a potential sexual relationship to each other. (M019)

## SEXUAL RESTRICTIONS
### X Avoidance Relationship
Avoidance relationships will tend to obtain between kinsmen who are prohibited as sexual partners. (M120)

### Divorce
The more restrictive the sex norms of a culture, the lower the divorce rate differential between early and late postmarital conceivers. (C125)

### Sexual Aggression
A high frequency of rape will tend to occur in societies where formal restrictions on the nonmarital sexual relations of females are severe and where physical segregation of the sexes does not occur. (L026)

### Size of Community
There is less likelihood that stringent sexual regulations will be found in a small isolated community than in a large one. (R040)

### Size of Lineage
When the lineage is small in size, sexual relations with the waves of lineage members will be prohibited. (A032)

## SEXUAL RESTRICTIONS, POST PUBERTAL
### X Autoeroticism
When there is sexual freedom of childhood and the more or less enforced repression after puberty, masturbation is fairly common. (H223)

## SIBLING GROUP　X Cohesion of Community
Under conditions of conflict, the independence of the uterine sibling group tends to jeopardize the cohesion and continuity of villages. (T080)

## SIBLING RANK　X Authority Structure of Family
A distinction will be made between siblings in terms of their order of birth if the family authority structure expresses a hierarchy of privilege and responsibility. (K045)

### Descent (Segmentary Lineage)
The segmentary lineage system rests upon the equivalence of male siblings. (L076)

### Inheritance
The equality of status of siblings will tend to be reflected in the inheritance pattern. (F073)

### Kin Ties
The equivalence of siblings (both male and female) creates a wide lateral extension of the kinship system. (G028)

### Rank of Women
When the status of women is almost equal to that of their husbands, their social equivalence and unity with their brothers will also be more strongly emphasized. (G028)

### Segmentation
When there is a formal disparity in status between elder and younger brothers, fission of the lineage is more likely to occur. (R004)

### Sex Status
The status of a male sibling tends to be higher than that of a female. (W067)

### Sibling Relations (Power)
A strong emphasis on the differential status of brothers according to age and on superordination and subordination between them accompanies a lesser emphasis on their equivalence vis-à-vis the rest of society. (G028)

### Sibling Relations (Solidarity)
The solidarity of the sibling group will be increased if there are rank differentials between the siblings. (H165)

### Sibling Rivalry
Where there is a formal disparity in status between elder and younger brothers, sibling rivalry is likely to occur. The contrary is also asserted. (R004)

### Size of Lineage
The emphasis on seniority by birth order will tend to inhibit the depth and span of the agnatic group. (S123)

### Social Structure (Differentiation)
The social equivalence of siblings is more likely to be found in societies with simple social structures. (R069)

## SIBLING RELATIONS     X   Age Difference
A large age disparity between marriage partners may offset their lack of experience in complementary sibling statuses when they were young, thereby allowing a successful marriage relationship. (T089)

### Class
Lower-class mental patients are less likely than middle-class mental patients to have had rewarding relationships with their siblings. (M061)

Lower-class children are more likely to have negative feelings toward their siblings than are those from the middle class. (M197)

### Criminality
There is significantly less interaction and support among brothers and sisters of the family of a habitual criminal than among those of a normal person. (C105)

### Descent (Patrilineal)
When residence and inheritance patterns are patrilocal and patrilineal, the relationship between male siblings will be the strongest tie in and the dominant element of the kinship structure. (G053)

### Father-Child Relations (Interest)
The greater the paternal interest in the children, the more likely they are to express ambivalent feelings toward their siblings. (L150)

### Institutional Care
Living arrangements (home or institutional) for retarded children are not related to sibling adjustment. (J027)

### Juvenile Delinquency
Boys who are stubborn or impractical are more likely to become delinquent if they are not accepted by their siblings.

### Juvenile Delinquency/Neurosis
There is no significant difference in the frequency with which disturbed sibling relationships occur among delinquent, as compared with neurotic, children (as measured by phobic behavior, anxiety level). (B238)

### Kin Terminology
Societies which emphasize the sibling relationship are more likely to make distinctions of age and sex in their sibling terminology. (M235)

### Marital Adjustment
The closer the marriage partners duplicate in their own marriage the sibling relations they experienced in their own respective families, the greater the chance for marital success. (T109)

### Mental Illness in Family
Children from "sicker" families are more likely to withdraw from involvement with their siblings than are those from healthier families. (L150)

### Mental Illness (Schizophrenia)
In the families of schizophrenics, siblings tended to look after the patients and to punish them. (M061)

Schizophrenic patients tend to have resented the authority of their siblings who cared for them. (M061)

### Mental Illness (Schizophrenia/Neurosis)
In the lower class, schizophrenic children are more likely to resent siblings' authority and to have fewer positive relationships with their brothers and sisters than are neurotic children. (M197)

### Mental Retardation (Dependency)
Dependent retarded children produce adverse sibling adjustments. (J027)

### Parent-Child Relations (Closeness)
Where the parent-child relationship is a weak one, siblings become more important to the child. (P060)

### Paternal Role (Economic)
If the father is relatively adequate as a provider, younger boys tend to be most involved with an older sister, both negatively and positively; if the father is less adequate, they tend to have as their strongest relationship a hostile one with a brother. Where the father is adequate, older boys are most involved with a younger brother, toward whom they are warm; if the father is less adequate, the relationship is more likely to be a very positive or negative one with a much younger sister. (L150)

Girls with more adequate fathers are more likely to be involved with their siblings, particularly with an older brother, than are those whose fathers are not. If the father is inadequate, young girls tend to dislike their siblings, while feeling that their siblings like them, and to be most involved with a much older sibling. (L150)

### Polyandry
Polyandry is associated with the equivalence of brothers in all transactions, including the ritual. That is, any brother is equivalent to any other brother. If one brother marries, the other brothers have sexual rights to his wife as well. (B205)

### Race Attitudes
Prejudiced persons are more likely than unprejudiced persons to idealize their siblings and are less likely to give a realistic appraisal of or to manifest genuine affect toward siblings. (A061)

### Residence (Patrilocal)
Virilocal residence within a matrilocal society is associated with a close cohesion of the uterine sibling group. (T080)

### Sibling Structure (Age Difference)
Girls with younger brothers are likely to have more trouble managing the younger siblings than are girls with younger sisters. For the former, the difficulties seem to increase as the age difference between siblings increases; but for the latter, the difficulties are most pronounced when the age difference between them is two to four years ("middle spacing"). (K149)

## SIBLING RELATIONS (AFFECTION)
    X   Alcoholism
Alcoholics are more likely than nonalcoholics to have been cool or indifferent toward their siblings during childhood. (M195)

### Marital Adjustment
The less adequate the marriage, the more likely it is that the child will have positive feelings for all his siblings rather than disliking a particular one as is the case where the marriage is good. (L150)

### Parent-Child Relations (Affection)
During childhood and adolescence, the degree of affection between siblings is less than that between mother and child, but greater than other family ties. (I008)

### Sex Status

Siblings of the same sex are more apt to develop strong affective ties than are siblings of different sexes. (I008)

Girls are more likely than boys to be interested in and affectionate toward any new child in the family since the new baby gives them an opportunity to rehearse their mother roles. (R129)

### Sibling Structure (Authority)

The degree of affection between siblings tends to be correlated inversely with authority. (S043)

## SIBLING RELATIONS (AFFECTION/AGGRESSION)
### X   Ordinal Position

Older siblings exhibit predominant feelings of love for younger ones, while younger siblings exhibit predominant feelings of aggression for older ones. (B321)

## SIBLING RELATIONS (AUTHORITY)     X   Class

Lower-class mentally ill patients tend to have resented their siblings' supervision and authority during childhood more than middle-class patients did. (M061)

## SIBLING RELATIONS (COHESION)
### X   Preferential Marriage (Levirate)

The institution of levirate tends to reinforce the cohesion of male siblings. (W082)

## SIBLING RELATIONS (CONFLICT)
### X   Age at Marriage

Girls who marry in their teens are more likely to report extensive quarreling with their siblings than are those who do not. (M231)

### Aspiration Level

There is no significant difference in the degree of sibling conflict between people who have high levels of aspiration and those who have low levels of aspiration. (D001)

There is no significant relationship between the level of aspiration and the degree of sibling conflict in childhood. (D001)

### Child-Rearing Practices (Clarity)

Among homes characterized by high levels of parental explanation of family decisions, the more explicit the behavior restrictions, the less quarrelsome the children. (B266)

### Division of Labor in Family

Status differentials in the type of labor will frequently be a source of conflict between siblings. (R012)

### Inheritance

Conflict arises among male siblings when only one gets the inheritance (magic) and where primogeniture may be set aside. (F076)

### Juvenile Delinquency

Delinquents tend to have less conflict with their siblings than do nondelinquents and to associate with them less. (W152)

### Marital Adjustment

Conflict between adults in the family is correlated with unsatisfactory relations between the child and his siblings. (C117)

### Ordinal Position

Middle and younger children quarrel more with siblings than do oldest children. (S191)

### Polyandry

Polyandry reduces potential hostility between brothers. (B205)

### Scapegoating

Where parental conflicts stem from conflict with their own siblings, they direct their hostility toward the child in the same ordinal position as the sibling which caused their conflict. (B204)

### Sibling Structure (Sex)

Tension and conflict between siblings are more likely to occur if they are male. (V020)

## SIBLING RELATIONS (FORMALITY)
### X   Sibling Structure (Age Difference)

The greater the age difference between two siblings, the greater the formality of their relationship. (F015)

### Values (Individualism)

When the emphasis is upon individually achieved status, the relations between lineage mates and siblings close in age are more formal than are relations between those with a greater age difference. (F015)

## SIBLING RELATIONS (HOSTILITY)
### X   Authority Structure of Family (Asymmetrical)

When asymmetrical relationships characterize the authority structure of the family, brothers near in age and of similar status in the extended family tend to be covertly hostile to each other. (G028)

### Sex Status

Disturbed male children are more likely to arouse resentment and hostility from their siblings than are disturbed girls, with the exception of frequent close relationships between middle-class disturbed boys and a sister. (M197)

## SIBLING RELATIONS (INTERACTION)
### X   Interaction in Family

If other family members interact frequently with the children, the children will not interact as often with each other; if they are ignored by other family members, they will interact more often. (C124)

### Parent-Child Relations (Interaction)

Older men and women (50 years and up) visit their children or are visited by them significantly more often than they visit their siblings or other intimates. (C116)

## SIBLING RELATIONS (INTERACTION RATE)
### X   Marital Status

Unmarried older people tend to have more frequent contact with their siblings than do married older people. (T009)

## SIBLING RELATIONS (LEADERSHIP)
### X   Ordinal Position

The firstborn child is more likely to become a leader of his siblings than are children in other positions. (C104)

## SIBLING RELATIONS (POWER)
### X   Mental Illness (Schizophrenia/Neurosis)

Significantly more schizophrenic than neurotic patients are unable to fill their roles in the sibling power structure, regardless of their birth order. (M061)

Schizophrenic children are less likely than neurotic children to be able to fulfill their roles in the sibling power structure, regardless of their birth order. (M197)

### Sibling Rank

A strong emphasis on the differential status of brothers according to age and on superordination and subordination between them accompanies a lesser emphasis on their equivalence vis-à-vis the rest of society. (G028)

## SIBLING RELATIONS (SOLIDARITY)
### X   Authority Structure of Family

When the relationship of men within the family is one of authority and subordination, little emphasis is placed upon the solidarity of peers. (G028)

### Authority Structure of Family (Matrilineal)

In matrilineal societies, men are less likely to quarrel with their sisters since this weakens their authority over the next generation. (C090)

### Avoidance Relationship

A mild avoidance relationship between brother and sister will tend to enhance the solidarity of the pair. (S060)

### Divorce

When the sibling group constitutes a unity, the divorce rate is high. (T080)

### Economic Dependence

When siblings are economically independent of the extended family, the equivalence and solidarity of peers is stressed. (G028)

### Economic Dependence of Siblings

The solidarity of siblings will be directly correlated with their degree of economic interdependence. (W082)

### Husband-Wife Relations (Intimacy)

When there is sister-brother solidarity, husband-wife solidarity is low. (F076)

### Kinship (Bilateral)

In bilateral systems, sibling solidarity in adulthood is a stronger kinship bond than are other kinship bonds. (I008)

### Polyandry (Fraternal)

The solidarity of male siblings is enhanced if they have legitimate claims to each other's wives. (G055)

### Polygyny

In the polygynous family, siblings are united more through their relationship with their mother than with their father. (M198)

### Preferential Marriage (Levirate)

Where bonds between siblings are strong, the levirate tends to occur. (R069)

### Residence

Patterns of common residence will tend to reinforce the strength of the sibling relationship. (G053)

### Role Definition in Family

The solidarity of male siblings is inversely related to the strength of the claims of members of the nuclear family on each brother. (G055)

### Sibling Rank

The solidarity of the sibling group will be increased if there are rank differentials between the siblings. (H165)

### Sibling Structure (Age Difference)

The smaller the age difference between siblings, the more likely it is that they will be inseparable as adults. (T089)

### Sibling Ties (Uterine)

Bonds between siblings tend to be stronger if the siblings are children of the same mother. (F022)

### Stability of Lineage

The stability of the lineage system is directly correlated with the solidarity of the siblings. (W056)

### Values (Cooperation)

Sibling solidarity will be emphasized in societies in which kin-groups and their cooperative functions are valued. (F069)

## SIBLING RELATIONS (TEASING)          X   Sex Status

Boys use teasing more frequently than girls do. (K149)

### Sibling Structure (Age Difference)

The greater the age difference between siblings, the more likely they are to tease each other. (K149)

## SIBLING RELATIONS (WARMTH)          X   Class

Lower-class mentally ill patients tend to have had fewer positive relationships with their brothers and sisters than did middle-class patients. (M061)

### Size of Family

The smaller the family size, the warmer the relations among the siblings. (E102)

## SIBLING RIVALRY          X   Age Difference

The greater the age difference, the less the rivalry between siblings. (C090)

### Birth Control

There is a correlation between parental identification with the child and regression to early attitudes of sibling rivalry and the practice of the spacing of births by abortion. (D071)

### Breast Feeding

Women who choose to bottle feed their children are more likely to report sibling rivalry than are those who breast feed. (A063)

### Child-Rearing Practices (Consistency)

The outstanding cause of sibling rivalry is the lack of consistency in discipline. (B033)

The child who is overly competitive with siblings is likely to have a mother who is inconsistent in her child-rearing practices. (R113)

### Child-Rearing Practices (Criticism)

Children whose mothers are excessively critical and depreciative tend to be overly competitive with siblings. (R113)

### Child-Rearing Practices (Responsibility)

Children who are given too many responsibilities at home by the mother (household chores, caring for younger siblings) tend to be overly competitive with siblings and to display bullying, domineering, and aggressive behavior. (R113)

### Conflict Between Wives

There is an association between sibling rivalry and rivalry between co-wives. (L133)

### Death Rate

If the death rate is low, strong competition between sons of a polygynous father (which can degenerate into fratricidal warfare) is likely to occur. (P083)

### Employment of Mother
If, in lower-class families, the mother is employed, sibling rivalry is less likely to be evident. (M211)

### Father-Son Relations (Subordination)
Explicit and almost institutionalized sibling rivalry is, in a sense, a corollary to the stern subordination-superordination relationship which obtains between fathers and sons. (F073)

### Illegitimacy
Children within the family who are illegitimate are subject to even greater sibling rivalry pressures. (C024)

### Inheritance
The character of the inheritance pattern may create a situation of intense rivalry between siblings. (S090)

### Inheritance (Primogeniture)
Where primogeniture is the basis for inheritance but where it may be set aside, jealousy among brothers is likely to result. (F092)

### Mental Illness
Mental illness is more likely to occur if the individual's siblings are perceived to be more successful. (M165)

### Mental Illness (Manic-Depressive)
A home in which there is sibling rivalry is more likely than other homes to produce manic-depressive children. (W143)

### Mental Illness (Schizophrenia)
Schizophrenia tends to be correlated with maternal patterns of aggravating sibling rivalry. (N061)

Schizophrenic adolescents with a "juvenile" reaction (neurotic, somatic symptoms) tend to come from families characterized by intensive sibling rivalry. (S208)

### Ordinal Position
Degree of sibling association is a more significant determinant of rivalry and hostility for second-born children than it is for firstborn children. (K149)

### Parent-Child Relations (Favoritism)
Sibling rivalry is likely to be greater between children of the same sex than between those of opposite sexes because parents are more likely to make invidious comparisons between and give unequal affection and approval to children of the same sex. (R129)

### Parent-Child Relations (Rejection)
The rejection of the child by its parents at the birth of a new baby leads to the manifestation of intense hostility and rivalry directed against the new arrival. (B033)

### Polygyny
Sibling rivalry is greater in polygynous families. (L133)

### Preferential Marriage (Levirate)
The rule that uterine brothers should not inherit one another's wives reduces jealousy over potential claims. (C090)

### Scholastic Adjustment
A child with school phobia is more likely than others to have a sibling who is preferred by his parents. (S239)

### Scholastic Adjustment (Reading)
Children with reading disabilities are more likely than those without to have manifested severe sibling rivalry. (S225)

### Sex-Role Identification
Sex-role identification conflict is a more significant determinant of rivalry and hostility for firstborn children than it is for second-born children. (K149)

### Sibling Rank
Where there is a formal disparity in status between elder and younger brothers, sibling rivalry is likely to occur. The contrary is also asserted. (R004)

### Sibling Structure
Sibling rivalry is likely to be more intense where there are many sons. (W056)

### Sibling Structure (Age and Sex)
Girls with younger siblings tend to be very jealous and, compared to firstborn boys, their attitudes change little with spacing. (K149)

### Sibling Structure (Age Difference)
Sibling rivalry is most likely to occur when the older child is between 18 months and three years old at the birth of the younger sibling. (B033)

The siblings closest to each other in birth order are most antagonistic, with a proportionate decrease in hostility as the distance between them increases. (C024)

Sibling rivalry is most likely to occur when the older sibling is from one to four years older than the baby. (D025)

There is much more stress in relations between siblings when the age difference between them is two to four years than at closer or wider spacing. (K149)

The smaller the age difference between siblings, the more severe their conflicts will be. (T089)

### Sibling Structure (Sex)
If siblings are opposite in sex, firstborn children tend to be more rivalrous and hostile; the reverse is true for second-born children when the sibling is of the opposite sex. (K149)

### Size of Family
There is a steady decrease in sibling jealousy with an increase in the number of children in a family. (B033)

Small middle-class families tend to have more sibling rivalry than do other types of families. (R106)

### Values (Individualism)
Sibling relationships tend to be more competitive in individualistic societies. (F069)

### SIBLING ROLE    X    Mental Retardation
Retarded children are more likely to assume the role of the youngest child, regardless of their actual sibling position. (J027)

### SIBLING ROLE DEFINITION    X    Kin Terminology
Siblings of both sexes tend to be merged terminologically if they share the same obligation in relation to their family. (F046)

### SIBLING STATUS    X    Affinal Relations (Conflict)
Conflicts between parents-in-law and children-in-law are more likely when the husband or wife is an only child. (B033)

### Age at Marriage
Only sons tend to marry early. (H165)

### Aggression

Aggressive children are more likely to be only children than are nonaggressive children. (S229)

### Anxiety

Only children tend to be less fearful and anxious than do firstborn children. (S263)

### Bed Wetting

Prolonged bed wetting is no more common in families where the child has younger brothers and sisters than where the child does not (U.S.). (S191)

### Child-Rearing Practices (Indulgence and Anxiety)

Regardless of the sex of the child, the longer the child rmains the only child in the family, probably the more indulged and possibly the more anxiously reared he will be. (K149)

### Children, Desire for

Only children are more likely than others to want no children. (T089)

### Dependency of Child

The mothers of only children reported more dependent behavior than did the mothers of children with siblings. (S191)

### Fertility Values

Single children are less likely than are persons with siblings to be content without children of their own. (T091)

### Friendship

Older persons (in their seventies) with siblings are more likely to describe their friends in terms of specific activities undertaken together while those without siblings use diffuse descriptions of their friends; friendship is a quasi-kinship relation for many older people. (C116)

### Identification with Parents

The "only" child is likely to be more strongly identified with his parents than are children of other sibling statuses. (L157)

### Marital Adjustment

Marital adjustment is higher when the husband and wife are not only children. (B033)

### Mate Selection

Single children are more likely than are persons with siblings to look for a father or mother in a potential spouse and are less likely to look for a peer. (T091)

### Parent-Child Relations (Sex Preference)

Parents tend to prefer male, as opposed to female, children as their only or first child. (H181)

### Role Adjustment

Children who occupy special positions (only child, youngest, one of a sex) are more likely than other children to have difficulties in role stabilization in later life. (Z007)

## SIBLING STATUS, COMPLEMENTARITY OF
### X Marital Adjustment

Persons whose sibling statuses in their respective families of orientation were complementary to one another with reference to relative seniority of rank and sex roles will adjust better in marriage to one another than will those with noncomplementary statuses. (T089)

Because of the complete lack of sex and rank complementarity, the poorest possible mate for the oldest brother of brother(s) would be the oldest sister of sister(s). (T089)

## SIBLING STRUCTURE
### X Adoption, Adjustment to

The successful adjustment of the adopted child to a new home is less likely when children of the foster-parents are present, but is more likely if his own siblings or another foster-child is present. (T086)

### Adult-Child Relations (Friendliness)

Girls having a sibling two years older or younger were more friendly to adults than were a parallel group of boys. (K098)

### Anxiety

In three-child families, firstborn girls and nonfirstborn boys are least likely to be anxious and to have sex identification conflicts; in a two-child family, the second-born child with a sibling of the same sex is least likely to have such problems. (R114)

### Child-Rearing Practices (Aggression)

There is no relationship between the number of siblings in the family and the severity of punishment for mother-directed aggression by the child. (M216)

The greater the number of siblings in the family, the more severe the punishment for peer-directed aggression. (M216)

### Child-Rearing Practices (Chores)

The greater the number of younger siblings a child has, the more likely is the mother to emphasize his responsibility training (frequency and variety of chores assigned). (M216)

There is no relationship between the number of siblings in the family and the degree of emphasis the mother places on responsibility training (frequency and variety of chores assigned). (M216)

### Emotional Adjustment of Child

There is a positive relationship between birth of a sibling while the child is in his second year and greater emotional maladjustment of the child. (K113)

### Health

Health estimates for firstborns from opposite-sibling pairs tend to be better than those for second-born children; the reverse obtains for children from same-sex sibling pairs. (K104)

When spacing is under four years, the health estimates for firstborns with a cross-sex sibling are better than those for firstborns with a same-sex sibling; when spacing is under two years, second-born children with a same-sex sibling are judged healthier than those with cross-sex siblings. (K104)

### I.Q.

There is a slight tendency for Negro preschool children with high mental abilities to have relatively fewer siblings. (H191)

### Juvenile Delinquency

Juvenile delinquents with nondelinquent brothers are likely to be less serious offenders than are those whose brothers are delinquent. (N059)

### Marital Adjustment

The greater the number of siblings of the spouse, the more difficult it will be for him to adjust to having only one spouse. (T091)

### Mental Illness

When characteristics involving sibship (e.g., number, sex, and spacing) are investigated for deviations from homogeneity among seven diagnostic groups of psychiatric patients, the only significant finding is that there is an increased frequency of patients with paranoid schizophrenia among patients having a sibling less than two years older than themselves and an increased frequency of sociopathic personality and other personality disorders among those having a sibling less than two years younger than themselves. (G155)

### Mental Illness (Schizophrenia/Neurosis)

Schizophrenic children are more likely to be taken care of by their siblings than are neurotic children. (M197)

### Mother-Child Relations (Warmth)

Mothers are warmest to a new child when there is a sizable age gap between this child and the next older sibling. (S191)

The larger the number of siblings in the family, the lower the amount of maternal warmth displayed to each individual child. (M216)

### Parent-Child Relations (Conflict)

There is no relationship between the amount of parent-teen-ager conflict in a family and the number of older siblings. (B249)

There is no relationship between the amount of conflict between teen-agers and their parents and the number of younger siblings in the family. (B249)

There is no relationship between the degree of parent-child conflict and the number or relative age of siblings. (B249)

### Peer Relations

Second-born girls with older brothers are likely to favor male playmates more than are girls with older sisters or girls with younger brothers. (K149)

### Personality

At the two-to-four-year spacing, firstborn boys are more likely to respond indirectly to fear and frustration than are the second-born boys; girls with an older sister are more likely to respond indirectly than are girls with a younger sister. (K104)

### Personality (Ambition/Aggression)

The girl with a younger brother is more likely to be aggressive and ambitious than is the girl with an older brother. (K126)

### Personality (Enthusiasm)

The personality of a boy does not vary with the fact that he has an older brother or that he is the firstborn with a younger brother, except that a boy with a much older brother is more likely to be enthusiastic. (K126)

### Personality (Power Motivation)

There is no significant relationship between an individual's power motivation (i.e., his urge to dominate others in order to use them as agents for fulfilling his own goals) and either his number of siblings or his ordinal position among his siblings. (V031)

### Personality Problems

Among males, the younger sibling is more likely to have nervous habits or to indulge in them more frequently than is the older; the reverse is true of females. (K104)

When spacing is over four years, children from cross-sex sibling pairs tend to have more nervous habits or to show them more frequently. (K104)

### Personality (Security)

The greater the number of siblings, the less the sense of security a child has. (I008)

### Residence (Matrilocal)

Uxorilocal residence tends to occur when the husband has a number of male siblings. (L063)

### Scholastic Achievement

Boys who are younger children in a family of mostly girls have lower grades than other boys. (R129)

### Self-Conception

The self-esteem of boys who are younger children in a family of mostly girls is less influenced by their grades in school than is the self-esteem of other boys. (R129)

Only children have higher self-esteem than do children who have siblings. (R129)

There is no clear relationship between birth order and self-esteem. (R129)

Males who are only children are more likely to have high self-esteem than are girls who are only children. (R129)

Among girls, only children are slightly more likely to have low self-esteem, but less likely to have intermediate self-esteem than are girls with siblings. (R129)

Among Catholics and Protestants, differences in levels of self-esteem between only boys and girls are much smaller than is the case among Jewish children. (R129)

In two-child families, there is no relationship between sibling structure and self-esteem. (R129)

If the family consists mostly of boys, there is no relationship between birth order and self-esteem of the boy. (R129)

The younger boy whose older siblings are chiefly or exclusively girls is likely to have higher self-esteem than are boys who have younger female siblings. (R129)

Younger boys with older brothers are more likely to have high self-esteem than are younger boys with older sisters. (R129)

In general, boys who consider themselves to be peer-group leaders have higher self-esteem than do those who do not, but boys who are younger children in a family of mostly girls tend to have high self-esteem even if they do not consider themselves to be leaders. (R129)

### Sex-Role Identification

A boy reared with older brothers is more likely to accept the masculine traits of his culture than is a boy reared with older sisters. (G156)

In families where there are only two children, a boy and a girl, each will tend to assimilate the traits of the opposite sex. (G156)

The greater the age difference between siblings, the greater the sex identification conflict for first-born children. (K149)

Having like-sex siblings tends to enhance self-sex preference or identification; having opposite-sex siblings is likely to decrease self-sex preference. (R114)

Contrary to the assimilation of roles hypothesis (Brim), in three-child families, a boy having two sisters is highly masculine and anxious (due to sex-role conflict); the same is not true of girls having two brothers. (R114)

In three-child families, firstborn girls and nonfirstborn boys are least likely to have sex-identification conflicts; in a two-child family, the second-born child with a sibling of the same sex is least likely to have such problems. (R114)

### Sibling Rivalry
Sibling rivalry is likely to be more intense where there are many sons. (W056)

## SIBLING STRUCTURE (AGE)        X    Peer Relations
The younger sibling is more likely to feel ill-treated by his sibling's friends than is the older sibling. (K094)

## SIBLING STRUCTURE (AGE AND SEX)
### X   Adult-Child Relations (Friendliness)
Among boys with siblings close to them in age, those with an older sister are more friendly to adults than those with an older brother. When the sibling is younger the pattern is reversed. (K098)

### Identification
As the age difference between siblings increases, identification of the older with the younger is highest and decreases most slowly among girls with younger sisters; it is not quite as high among boys with younger brothers and decreases slowly; it decreases more rapidly with spacing among boys with younger sisters and most rapidly of all among girls with younger brothers. (K149)

Among like-sex siblings, the greater the age difference between siblings, the greater the desire of the younger to have the assets and advantages of the older; the conscious desire of the younger to become the older sibling decreases more slowly with spacing among girls with an older brother than among boys with an older sister. (K149)

### Personality Problems
If firstborn and spaced under two years, children with a cross-sex sibling recover more slowly and less adequately from emotional upsets than do those with a same-sex sibling; at the two-to-four-year spacing, the reverse is true. (K104)

### Personality (Self-Confidence)
The correlation of sibling age disparity and self-confidence is linear for boys with a brother, curvilinear for boys with a sister, and inversely curvilinear for girls with an older sister. (K104)

### Sex-Role Identification
The greater the age difference between siblings, the greater the sex-identification conflict among second-born children with older siblings of the opposite sex compared to those with siblings of the same sex; boys with older sisters have the most conflict and girls with older sisters have the least. (K149)

### Sexual Aggression
Girls who have elder male siblings are less likely to experience sexual aggression than are girls who do not have elder male siblings. (K018)

### Sibling Rivalry
Girls with younger siblings tend to be very jealous and, compared to firstborn boys, their attitudes change little with spacing. (K149)

## SIBLING STRUCTURE (AGE DIFFERENCE)
### X   Achievement
There is no relationship between age intervals between siblings and their levels of achievement. (S218)

### Adult-Child Relations
Firstborn children with a brother two to four years younger are less friendly, less obedient, and less responsive to adults than are those with a brother four to six years younger. (K098)

The greater the age difference between siblings, the more adult-oriented is the firstborn child. (K149)

The less the age difference between siblings the more likely the firstborn child is to be more adult-oriented than is his younger sibling. (K149)

### Adult-Child Relations (Friendliness)
Second-born males are likely to be low in friendliness to adults if they have a sibling who is less than two years older, but are likely to be more friendly to adults if the sibling is more than two years older. (K098)

### Child-Rearing Practices
The greater the age difference between siblings, the more the firstborn child is "stimulated and instructed" by adults, regardless of the sex of the child. (K149)

### Child-Rearing Practices (Democratic)
The closer the children in age, the more likely it is that the mother will treat them more rationally, democratically, and with more understanding. (L160)

### Child-Rearing Practices (Indulgence)
The wider the spacing between siblings, the more relaxed the mother is and the more attention she devotes to the second-born child compared to the firstborn; the second-born male with an older sister is the most indulged. (K149)

### Child-Rearing Practices (Responsibility)
The boy with a younger brother is given more responsibility than the younger sibling when the spacing is close than is the boy with a younger sister. (K149)

As the age difference between siblings increases, girls have much more responsibility relative to the younger sibling than boys do. (K149)

### Cognitive Development
The number of interests of a child increases as the age difference between himself and his siblings increases. (K126)

### Identification with Sibling
Among like-sex siblings, the greater the age difference between siblings, the greater the desire of the younger to have the assets and advantages of the older; the conscious desire of the younger to become the older sibling decreases more slowly with spacing among girls with an older brother than among boys with an older sister. (K149)

Among second-born children, the closer the spacing between siblings, the stronger the identification with the older sibling. (K149)

### I.Q.

The greater the age interval between siblings, the greater their intelligence is likely to be. (A065)

There is no relationship between age intervals between siblings and their levels of I.Q. (S128)

### Leadership

The greater the age difference between siblings, the higher the child tends to be rated in leadership. (K149)

### Mental Illness (Autism)

Autism is more likely to occur if another sibling is born during the vulnerable developmental period. (S188)

### Mental Illness (Schizophrenia)

There is no relationship between schizophrenia and the age gaps between siblings. (L144)

### Parent-Child Relations (Closeness)

The further apart in age are the siblings, the closer their relationships to their parents rather than to one another. (K149)

### Peer Relations

The greater the age disparity between siblings, the lower the frequency of association with the sibling's friends. (K094)

The greater the age difference between siblings, the more likely the child is to become involved with peers; the smaller the age difference, the more they tend to be involved with each other. (K149)

The greater the difference in age between boys (except those having an older sister), the more sociable and socially acceptable they tend to be (i.e., better leaders, more friendly to peers, more popular, and more competitive); this trend does not exist among girls. (K149)

As the age difference between siblings increases, the firstborn child has less association with his siblings and their playmate groups tend to overlap less; the overlap in playmate groups and degree of association with the younger sibling decreases more rapidly with spacing among siblings of the opposite sex and decreases most slowly among girls with younger sisters. (K149)

### Personality

The greater the sibling age disparity, the more active the boy will be. (K104)

The greater the disparity in age, the more likely is the manifestation of indirectness in response to fear and frustration by girls with a brother. (K104)

The greater the age differences among the children in a family, the more likely it is that the personality traits of groups at different ordinal positions are more reflections of parent-child relations than of direct sibling interaction. (K104)

### Personality (Competitiveness)

As the age difference between siblings increases, competitiveness increases in firstborn children and second-born children with male siblings. (K149)

### Personality (Hostility)

The greater the age difference between siblings, the greater the hostility of the firstborn male. (K149)

### Personality of Firstborn Males

The wider the spacing between siblings, the higher are boys with younger siblings rated in social attitudes. (K149)

The greater the age difference between siblings, the less dependent, more dominant, more aggressive, and more hostile are boys with younger sisters. (K149)

### Personality Problems

When sibling spacing is under two years, second-born children recover from emotional upsets faster and more thoroughly than do firstborn children. (K104)

Among firstborn children, the greater the sibling age disparity, the more rapid the recovery from emotional upsets; among second-born children, the reverse is true. (K104)

### Sex-Role Identification

The greater the age difference between siblings, the greater the sex-identification conflict for all firstborn children. (K149)

### Sibling Relations

Girls with younger brothers are likely to have more trouble managing the younger sibling than are girls with younger sisters. For the former, the difficulties seem to increase as the age difference between siblings increases; but for the latter, the difficulties are most pronounced when the age difference between them is two to four years ("middle spacing"). (K149)

### Sibling Relations (Formality)

The greater the age difference between two siblings, the greater the formality of their relationship. (F015)

### Sibling Relations (Solidarity)

The smaller the age difference between siblings, the more likely that they will be inseparable as adults. (T089)

### Sibling Relations (Teasing)

The greater the age difference between siblings, the more likely they are to tease each other. (K149)

### Sibling Rivalry

Sibling rivalry is most likely to occur when the older child is between 18 months and three years old at the birth of the younger sibling. (B033)

The siblings closest to each other in birth order are most antagonistic, with a proportionate decrease in hostility as the distance between them increases. (C024)

Sibling rivalry is most likely to occur when the older sibling is from one to four years older than the baby. (D025)

There is much more stress in relations between siblings when the age difference between them is two to four years than at closer or wider spacing. (K149)

The smaller the age difference between siblings, the more severe their conflicts will be. (T089)

### Social Adjustment ("Skill")

The greater the age difference between siblings, the more the second child is "outclassed in skill and wisdom" by the older sibling. (K149)

## SIBLING STRUCTURE (AUTHORITY)
### X   Sibling Relations (Affection)

The degree of affection between siblings tends to be correlated inversely with authority. (S043)

## SIBLING STRUCTURE (MALE EQUIVALENCE)
### X   Polyandry

An emphasis on fraternal equivalence creates conditions conducive to polyandry. (M048)

## SIBLING STRUCTURE
## (MONOZYGOTIC/DIZYGOTIC TWINS)
**X  Homosexuality**

Homosexuality of both twins is more likely among monozygotic than among dizygotic twins. (M202)

## SIBLING STRUCTURE (ORDINAL POSITION
## AND SEX)          X  Mental Illness

In the middle class youngest boys and oldest girls are more likely than others to be mentally disturbed. (M197)

In the lower class the oldest boy is more likely than others to become mentally disturbed. (M197)

## SIBLING STRUCTURE (SEX)          X Achievement

Children with male siblings are more likely to be high in achievement than are those with female siblings. (S218)

### Achievement Motivation

There is no relationship between the individual's achievement motivation and the sex of his siblings, holding family size constant. (T095)

### Adult-Child Relations

Firstborn girls tend to be more adult-oriented than boys, regardless of the sex of their younger sibling. (K149)

### Adult-Child Relations (Friendliness)

Girls with a younger brother are more friendly to adults than are girls with a younger sister. (K098)

Girls with a younger brother (up to six years younger) are more friendly to adults and more responsive to adult sympathy and approval than are boys with a younger brother. (K098)

### Anxiety

Only male children are more anxious; only female children are less anxious than are children with other sibling sets. (R114)

In two-child families, the older child with a younger sibling of the same sex is more anxious and the older child with a younger sibling of the opposite sex is less anxious than is the norm. (R114)

In three-child families, firstborn children with siblings of the opposite sex are highly anxious; those with siblings of the same sex are low on anxiety. (R114)

### Child-Rearing Practices (Control)

Girls with brothers are more apt to experience external behavior-control methods than are girls with sisters and no brothers. (B322)

In middle-class families, the high-school-aged girl with brothers but no sisters has greatest influence in self-direction; the girl with all sisters has the least. (E100)

### Conformity

Children with male siblings have a greater tendency to conform than do children with female siblings (measured by Davis's Compliant-Defiant Instrument). (S233)

### Dependency

A boy with a much older sister is likely to be more withdrawn and dependent than is a boy with a much older brother. (K149)

### Education

Second-born children are more likely to attend college if the firstborn child is male. (A073)

### Friendship Choice (Age)

A child with a sister is more likely to prefer a younger child as a playmate than is a child with a brother. (K094)

When spacing is over four years, children from cross-sex pairs are more likely to prefer younger friends than are those from like-sex pairs. (K094)

### Friendship Choice (Sex)

The greater the age disparity between siblings, the more likely it is that the child prefers friends of the same sex. (K094)

Children from cross-sex pairs are more likely to prefer friends of the opposite sex or to be indifferent to the sex of a friend than are children of same-sex pairs. (K094)

When the age disparity between siblings is over two years, firstborns with a sister are more likely to be indifferent to the sex of a playmate than are those with a brother; for second-born children, the reverse obtains. (K094)

### Identification with Cross-Sex Parent

Having a favored sibling of the opposite sex may often aid cross-sex parental identification. (R126)

### Identification with Sibling

Among second-born children, identification with the older sibling is stronger when siblings are the same sex than it is when they are of opposite sexes (probably strongest for the girl with an older sister and weakest for the boy with an older sister). (K149)

### I.Q.

Children with male siblings are more likely to be high in intelligence than are those with female siblings. (S218)

### Marital Adjustment

Persons coming from like-sex sibling configurations are less likely to be able to adjust to their marriage partners than are those from cross-sex configurations. (T093)

### Mother-Child Relations (Warmth)

If the mother already has boys only, she tends to be relatively cold toward the new baby boy, but the sex of older children makes no difference in her attitude to a new baby girl. The mother is just as warm, whether she has boys already, or girls, or both. (S191)

### Occupational Choice

In two-sibling families, girls with an older brother are more likely to choose economic types of occupations (life insurance, buyer, etc.) than are girls without an older brother. (S221)

In two-sibling families where both are boys, they are more likely to choose conventional economic types of occupations (e.g., sales manager, buyer, production manager, life insurance, etc.) than are children in other types of sibling structures. (S221)

In two-sibling families, the females of two-girl families are more likely to choose conventional feminine occupations (e.g., general office work, stenography, secretary, etc.) than are girls with a brother. (S221)

In two-sibling families where the children are of opposite sex, they are more likely to choose creative occupations (e.g., artist, composer, author, architect, etc.) than are individuals of families with two same-sex siblings. (S221)

### Peer Relations

When age disparity between siblings is less than four years, children are more likely to play with their sister's friends than with their brother's friends; boys, however, prefer friends of their older brother to those of their older sister. (K094)

When siblings are of opposite sex, it is more likely that the child will feel ill-treated by the sibling's friends. (K094)

### Peer Relations (Friendship Choice)

When their sibling is male, firstborns are more likely to prefer male friends than are second-born children; when their sibling is female, the reverse obtains as to male preference. (K094)

### Personality

As the two-to-four-year spacing, children with a cross-sex sibling are more likely to be cheerful than are those with a same-sex sibling. (K104)

At the two-to-four-year spacing, girls with a cross-sex sibling show more finality in their decisions than do those with a same-sex sibling; when the sibling is over four years older, children in like-sex pairs are less vacillating than are those in cross-sex pairs. (K104)

When sibling spacing is under two years, second-born girls tend to be more cheerful than boys. (K104)

### Personality (Anger)

Boys show a greater tendency to anger than girls, except where spacing is under two years, when a girl with a brother shows a stronger tendency than does a boy with a brother. (K104)

### Personality (Competitiveness)

Girls with younger sisters are less competitive than boys with younger sisters. (K149)

### Personality (Masculinity)

In two-sibling families where both sibs are males, they tend to score higher on the Rosenberg–Sutton–Smith Masculinity Scale than do boys without a brother. (S221)

### Personality of Girl (Masculinity)

Girls with a brother tend to develop more feminine characteristics than do girls with a sister, who rather tend to develop more masculine characteristics. (S233)

### Personality Problems

When spacing is over four years, children from cross-sex sibling pairs tend to have more nervous habits or to show them more frequently. (K104)

### Personality (Self-Confidence)

At the two-to-four-year spacing, children with cross-sex siblings tend to be more self-confident than do those with a same-sex sibling. (K104)

When sibling spacing is under two years, girls tend to be more self-confident than boys do. (K104)

### Personality (Sensitivity)

The child with a brother tends to be more sensitive than does one with a sister. (K104)

### Personality (Tenacity/Aggression)

A girl with a younger or older brother within a two-to-four-year spacing (since her competitiveness and tenacious will be aroused) is more likely to be aggressive and tenacious than is the girl with a similarly spaced sister. (K126)

A boy with a brother at least four years older than himself will be more aggressive, enthusiastic, ambitious, tenacious, and possessed of more interests than will a boy with a similarly older sister. (K126)

Within a two-to-four-year spacing, the child will be more aggressive, curious, and enthusiastic when his sibling is of the opposite rather than of the same sex, except in the case of a boy with an older sister. (K126)

### Power Structure of Family

Older, middle–class girls are more likely to have highly dominant parents when they have sisters only; lower–class older girls are most likely to have dominant parents if they have brothers. (E100)

### Residence (Patrilocal)

Patrilocal residence is most likely to occur in societies with patterns of matrilocal residence when the husband is without female siblings. (B108)

The violation of patterns of patrilocal residence may occur if the wife is without male siblings. (L071)

### Self-Conception

Among males, if the majority of children in the family are boys, self-esteem is likely to be lower than if half or less than half are boys. (R129)

For girls, there is little relationship between level of self-esteem and whether the siblings are mostly girls or boys. (R129)

### Sex-Role Identification

When a child begins differentiating between father and mother sex roles, he is aided in this differentiation if he has a sibling of the opposite sex. (B216)

If a child has a sibling of the opposite sex, he will tend to assimilate traits of the opposite sex. (B216)

A child who has a sibling of the opposite sex has more traits appropriate to the opposite sex than does a child with a sibling of only the same sex. (B216)

Firstborn children with siblings of the same sex have less sex-identification conflict than do those with younger siblings of the opposite sex; the boy with a younger brother has somewhat more conflict than does the girl with a younger sister and the girl with a younger brother may have somewhat less conflict than may the boy with a younger sister. (K149)

Having like-sex siblings tends to enhance self-sex preference or identification; having opposite-sex siblings is likely to decrease self-sex preference. (R114)

Contrary to the assimilation of roles hypothesis (Brim), in three-child families, a boy having two sisters is highly masculine and anxious (due to sex-role conflict); the same is not true of girls having two brothers. (R114)

Girls with a brother are more likely to develop feminine-role identification than are girls with a sister. (S251)

Children from families in which there are opposite-sex siblings are more likely to have attitudes that are less conforming to their sex identification than are children from families in which there are no opposite-sex siblings. (T095)

### Sibling Relations (Conflict)

Tension and conflict between siblings are more likely to occur if they are male. (V020)

### Sibling Rivalry
If siblings are opposite in sex, firstborn children tend to be more rivalrous and hostile; the reverse is true for second-born children when the sibling is of the opposite sex. (K149)

### Social Adjustment
At the two-to-four-year spacing, the child with a same-sex sibling is more likely to be apprehensive in social situations than is one with a cross-sex sibling. (K104)

When sibling spacing is under two years, boys are more likely to be apprehensive in social situations than girls are. (K104)

Children who have siblings of their own sex only have more problems establishing heterosexual relations (up to and including marriage) than do children who have siblings of the opposite sex. (T089)

### Social Adjustment (Cooperativeness)
Among firstborns with siblings of the opposite sex, boys tend to be more uncooperative than girls do. (K149)

## SIBLING STRUCTURE (TWINS)
### X    Achievement Motivation
Twinship decreases the correlation between achievement strivings and oral behavior manifestations.

### I.Q.
Twins tend to have a lower average intelligence than the total population. (A065)

### Marriage Chances
Identical twins are more likely than fraternal twins (because they identify so closely) to delay marriage and perhaps not to be married at all. (T089)

### Mental Illness (Schizophrenia)
Schizophrenia is no more likely in twins than in non-twins. (D068)

Schizophrenia is no more likely among monozygotic than among dizygotic twins. (D068)

### Personality Problems (Anality)
Twinship decreases the correlation between achievement strivings and anal behavior manifestations. (B224)

### Personality Problems (Orality/Anality/Dependency)
Twinship decreases the correlations between dependency and oral behavior and between dependency and anal behavior. (B224)

## SIBLING TIES
### X    Extended Family, Disintegration of
Fission of the extended family tends to be resisted if the brothers are uterine rather than half-siblings. (W056)

## SIBLING TIES (UTERINE)
### X    Sibling Relations (Solidarity)
Bonds between siblings tend to be stronger if the siblings are children of the same mother. (F022)

## SIBLINGS, NUMBER OF
### X    Cohesion of Kin-Group
The incidence of partition exhibits a tendency to a progressive decrease as the size of the sibling group progressively increases. (F075)

## SIZE AND STABILITY OF KIN-GROUP
### X    Kin Ties (Fictive)
The institutionalization of fictive kin ties will tend to occur when the corporate groups based on kinship are small and unstable. (T045)

## SIZE OF CITY    X    Marital Stability
Marital breakup is not related to the size of cities. (L001)

## SIZE OF CLAN    X    Community Isolation
Compact settlement in autonomous communities is associated with restriction on the increase in the size of the clan and the number of its component basic lineages. (F089)

### Exogamy
Breaches of clan exogamy tend to occur in the clan of the greatest numerical strength. (L031)

### Political Power
The political power of a clan is directly correlated with the number of its male members. (W082)

### Preferential Marriage
The larger the clan, the greater the likelihood of there being a pattern of preferential marriage with its members. (C039)

### Preferential Marriage (Parallel-Cousin)
The incidence of parallel-cousin marriage is directly correlated with the size of the localized clan segment. (H165)

### Rank of Clan
Clans of high status, inasmuch as they are able to acquire more wives, will be larger in size. (E103)

The prestige of the clan tends to be directly correlated with its size. (M051)

### Residence
The degree of localization of the clan varies inversely with its size. (B050)

When the settlement pattern is that of compact, territorially segregated communities, there is a restriction on an increase in the size of the clan. (F033)

### Territorial Expansion
Formation of large segmented clans seems to depend upon maintaining social continuity over a widening series of territorial entities which, in turn, depends upon considerable physical mobility and facilities for continued territorial expansion. (F089)

## SIZE OF COMMUNITY    X    Descent
When the community is small, the development of a larger consanguineal unit is inhibited. (S120)

### Descent (Unilineal)
Unilineal kin-groups emerge with a minimal threshold of population size and stability. (F033)

The formation of unilineal kin-groups is directly correlated with the size of the community. (W056)

### Endogamy (Community)
Community endogamy tends to be correlated with the stabilization of community membership. (L063)

### Exogamy (Community)
In general, the smaller the residential ethnic or religious group unit, the greater the proportion of marriages contracted with spouses outside the unit. (B073)

Community exogamy is usually found in small communities, most of whose members are genetically related. (D057)

### Fertility
As village size increases, fertility decreases. (D006)

### Husband-Wife Relations (Interaction)
The rate of interaction between husbands and wives will tend to be higher if the community is small in size. (H165)

### Kin-Role Behavior
The evasion of kinship obligations is rarer in a small, permanent, and homogenous community. (S153)

### Kin Terminology
Kinship terminology is more likely to be adhered to rigidly when the community is large in size. (B147)

### Mate Selection
The probability of two persons marrying each other when they live in different population groupings (i.e., different towns) tends to increase with the number of persons available (i.e., the size of the population groupings) when distance between the population groupings is held constant. (E010)

### Nuclear Family, Importance of
The nuclear family will tend to have greater importance as a social unit when the community is small in size. (B147)

### Sexual Restrictions
There is less likelihood that stringent sexual regulations will be found in a small isolated community than in a large one. (R040)

## SIZE OF ETHNIC GROUP    X    Mate Selection (Kin)
When the size of the ethnic group is small, there is a greater likelihood of the existence of previous kin ties between people who marry. (F037)

### Social Structure (Differentiation)
The elaboration of the social structure will be directly correlated with the size of the ethnic group. (S121)

## SIZE OF EXTENDED FAMILY    X    Class
The size of the extended family tends to vary directly with its economic position and status. (H052)

The extended family tends to be smaller in the lower classes and larger in the higher classes. (H172)

### Stability of Extended Family
Fission of the extended family is more likely to occur if the unit is large in size. (G072)

The fission of the extended family, after the death of its head, will be delayed if the group is small in size. (S041)

## SIZE OF EXTENDED FAMILY (PATRILINEAL)
### X    Polyandry (Fraternal)
Fraternal polyandry functions to restrict the size of the patrilineal extended family. (G056)

## SIZE OF FAMILY
### X    Academic Motivation of Child by Class
Among high achieving adolescents, small family size has a greater effect on high academic motivation among lower-class than among middle-class adolescents. (E102)

### Academic Motivation of Child by Sex Status
Among high achieving adolescents, the larger the family size, the greater the sex difference regarding academic motivation, girls being more motivated than boys. (E102)

### Accident-Proneness of Child
Children who are accident-prone come from larger families than do normal children. (K122)

### Acculturation
A reduction in the size of the family tends to accompany acculturation. (M081)

### Achievement
Proportionally more of the most effective fighter pilots (aces) are from large families; more pilots from small families are nonaces. (S263)

### Achievement Motivation
Family size is negatively related to achievement motivation in the child. (E102)

The larger the size of the family, the lower the achievement motivation of the sons. (R083)

In lower-class families achievement motivation decreases as family size increases. (R106)

### Achievement Values
There is a curvilinear relationship between family size and value similarity between mother and son regarding achievement; value similarity is highest in medium-sized families and lowest in small and large families. (R097)

### Alcoholism
Since later-born children tend to be less welcome and less often breast-fed (and both patterns frustrate their dependency needs), large families (i.e., with more later-borns) are likely to produce a greater number of alcoholics than are small families. (S236)

### Anxiety
The larger the family, the less anxious the children are likely to be. (R114)

Subjects from large families are less anxious than are subjects from small families. (S263)

The difference in anxiety level between first- and later-born children is greater in small families than it is in large families. (S263)

### Anxiety of Mother
The smaller the number of children born to the mother, the higher her anxiety about their health. (R112)

### Aspiration Level
Parents in small families are more likely to have higher aspirations for their children than are parents in large families. (R106)

Boys from large families are less likely to have high ambitions than are boys from smaller families. This relationship does not apply for females. (T095)

Students from small families are more likely to have higher educational than material ambitions; students from large families, higher material than educational ambitions. (T095)

### Authoritarianism of Father
Fathers in small families, particularly in the middle class, tend to be less authoritarian than do fathers in large families. (R106)

### Birth Control
The smaller the family, the more likely it is to have been planned. (F101)

### Child Development

There is no relationship between family size and the mother's correct recollection of the children's developmental record (i.e., age of weaning, walking, toilet training, health record). (M236)

### Child-Rearing Attitudes

The disparity between parental attitudes (discipline, control) toward psychotic children and normal siblings decreases with increasing size of family. (D064)

### Child-Rearing Practices

Child neglect is no greater in large families than in small. (B270)

Parents in small families spend more time and effort on each child than in large families. (R106)

### Child-Rearing Practices (Achievement Demands)

Parents in small families tend to place a greater stress upon the personal achievement of their children than do parents in large families. (R106)

### Child-Rearing Practices (Authoritarianism)

No relationship exists between maternal authoritarian child control and the number of children in the family. (H200)

### Child-Rearing Practices (Control)

The larger the family, the more likely are the parents to use external rather than internal controls. (B322)

Middle-class parents with boys and lower-class parents with girls are more likely to use strict controls of their children as family size increases than are middle-class parents with no boys and lower-class parents with no girls. (B322)

### Child-Rearing Practices (Dependency)

In general, parents who have larger numbers of children living at home are more likely to prevent their adolescents from making their own decisions. This is more frequently the case among parents of younger boys and is least frequent among mothers and fathers of high-school-aged boys. (E100)

Parents with large families are less active in independence training than are parents with small families. (E102)

There is a curvilinear relationship between age of independence training and family size: mothers of medium-sized families train their children earlier than do those of large or small families. (R097)

Parents in small families tend to place greater emphasis on urging their children to be self-reliant in situations where they compete with standards of excellence. (R106)

### Child-Rearing Practices (Discipline)

Children in large families are more likely to be disciplined for the sake of family harmony than are children in small families. (R106)

### Child-Rearing Practices (Indulgence)

The larger the family, the more likely is the younger child to be indulged (U.S.). (S191)

The infant is likely to be treated more indulgently in large extended families where there are many persons to care for the infant. (W127)

### Child-Rearing Practices (Neglect)

Child neglect is no greater in large families than in small. (B270)

### Child-Rearing Practices (Permissiveness)

The larger the family, the more permissive are the parents in child rearing. (B007)

### Child-Rearing Practices (Punishment)

There is a curvilinear relationship between use of psychological punishment and family size; mothers of medium-sized families are more likely to use psychological punishment than are mothers of small or large families. (R097)

### Child-Rearing Problems

The larger the family, the more likely are parents to mention having child-rearing problems. (G126)

### Chores

Couples with no children share a greater number of household tasks than do those with children. (G133)

### Class

The frequency of the large family decreases with rising rental or educational status. (B033)

The higher the social class, the smaller the size of the family is likely to be. The contrary is also asserted for some non-Western countries. (C134)

Among couples with no unplanned pregnancies, there is a direct relationship between socioeconomic status and family size. (W022)

There is little difference in the average family size between the various social classes. The contrary is also asserted. (W023)

### Cohesion of Family

The larger the family, the greater the emphasis on the group rather than on the individual. (I007)

Emotional relationships among family members will tend to be more diffuse and stable with an increase in family size. (I007)

Affective relationships between family members are more likely to persist when the family is small in size. (I007)

Members of large families tend to be more interdependent with each other than do members of small families. The reverse is also asserted. (R106)

The larger the size of the nuclear family, the greater the amount of time and effort given to the family. (S217)

### Competition

Life in a small family is more competitive than is life in a large family. (R106)

### Conflict in Family

The smaller the family size, the more intense the feeling between its members and, hence, the more conflict between them. (D058)

### Consensus in Family

The larger the family, the greater the degree of consensus. (I007)

### Dating During Marriage

Among divorced couples, the greater the number of children, the lower the frequency with which the couple "dated" during the marriage. (G157)

### Dependency
Children in large families tend to be more self-reliant than children in small families. (R106)

### Deviance, Tolerance of
Larger families can accommodate a serious problem child or a psychotic with less emotional disruption than can the small nuclear family. (A047)

### Divorce
Marriages with few or no children have a higher divorce rate than others. (F101)

### Divorce Adjustment
Divorcées experiencing difficult emotional problems are more likely to have two or more children than one child. (G157)

### Divorce Arrangements
There is no relationship between the number of children and the type of property division (split of property, all property going to either husband or wife) made by divorcing couples. (G157)

### Divorce Decision
The stability of the final decision to divorce is not related to the number of children in the family. (G157)

### Divorce Process
The larger the family (up to three children), the longer the interval between a serious consideration of divorce and filing suit. (G157)

### Duration of Marriage
The number of children involved in a divorce is less likely to alter the average duration of marriage among urban marriages than among rural marriages. (G157)

### Dyadic Relations (Interaction)
Dyads in a large family are more likely to have a low rate of interaction than are dyads in a small family. (C124)

### Dyadic Relations (Interaction Rate)
Dyads in a large family are more likely to have a low rate of interaction than are dyads in a small family. (C124)

### Economic Conditions
The small patriarchal family will supersede the large patriarchal family when economic conditions make it a more efficient industrial instrument. (B033)

Couples who start their families early in periods of prosperity do not necessarily have a much larger completed family, especially if the period of prosperity is shortly followed by a period of depression. Conversely, couples who, in periods of depression, postpone starting their families have some tendency to make up this deficit later in life if economic conditions change before they are too old. Thus, periods of depression or of prosperity have to extend over a number of years before they materially affect the total reproduction of a generation. (W012)

### Economic Rank
The size of the joint family will depend upon the size of the family estate. (M021)

### Education of Divorcée
Among divorcées, the lower the educational level, the larger the family size. (G157)

### Education of Mother/Father
Family size shows a greater negative correlation with the educational level of the mother than with that of the father. (A065)

### Education of Wife
Farm families in which the wife's schooling was from none to six years have fewer children than do farm families in which the wife has seven or more years of schooling. (K016)

### Educational Aspiration
Only children are more likely to anticipate education beyond the high-school level than are adolescents from families with six or more children. (E102)

Insofar as the chances of attending college are concerned, a larger number of children in the family is a greater hindrance for lower-class than for middle-class youths. (E102)

### Emotional Problems of Child
Children in large families tend to have more emotional problems than do children in small families. (B283)

### Employment
Employed men have more children than do unemployed men; employed women have fewer children than do unemployed women. (B244)

### Employment of Mother
Mothers in large families are more likely to be employed than are mothers in small families. (N057)

Employed mothers are more likely to have smaller families. (S265)

### Employment of Mother, Attitude Toward
The more children a woman has, the more she sees her job as simply an economic necessity. (R121)

### Employment of Women, Attitude Toward
As the number of children increases, the economic need for the mother to be employed outside the family increases; but at the same time, the necessity that she stay at home becomes more acute. (R093)

### Father-Child Relations (Authoritarianism)
Lower-class fathers are more likely to establish autocratic or authoritarian relationships with their sons and daughters regardless of the size of the family. (E100)

### Fertility Values
Students are more likely to want smaller families than the families from which they come. (C007)

The difference in the desired size of students' families of procreation and their families of orientation increases as the actual size of the family of orientation increases. (C007)

The more children they already have, the less delighted the parents are likely to be with the prospect of having another child. (S263)

### Friendship
The more children in the family, the more likely is the divorcée to maintain marriage friends during the separation and divorce period. (G157)

### Geographic Mobility
The larger the family, the more likely it is to move. (F107)

### Husband-Wife Relations (Support)
As family groups increase in size from three to four to five, there is decreasing likelihood that there will be mutual support in the husband-wife dyad. (S207)

### Illegitimacy (Adoption)
Unwed mothers who keep their children have a higher mean number of siblings and half-siblings than do unwed mothers who release their children for adoption. (V027)

### Income
There is a positive correlation between amount of income and number of children in the family. (B244)

Farm families with a low income have fewer children than do farm families with a high income. (K016)

### Income Allocation
Family size is inversely related to the proportion of income spent for rent. (C009)

### Income, Attitude Toward
When there is a large number of children born in a family, the satisfaction with the standard of living tends to be lower; when the children number from one to three, the satisfaction with the family standard of living tends to be higher.

### Independence of Women
A restriction of family size tends to be associated with a position of greater freedom and independence for women. (S064)

### Industrialization
Increasing industrialization is correlated with decreasing family size. (K100)

### Interaction in Family
Dyads with low interaction rates are more frequent in large families than in small families. (C124)

In large families with low dominance rates, time will be scarce and it is therefore less likely that all dyads will have the same interaction rate; but in small families and in high dominance large families, the rate is more likely to be the same. (C124)

### Interaction in Family (Closeness)
Adolescents from small families have better relations with their parents and other siblings than those from larger families. (I008)

### Interaction in Family (Intimacy)
An inverse curvilinear relationship exists between size of family and intimacy of family life. (R111)

### I.Q.
The fewer the number of children, the greater the intelligence of the child. (B282)

The intelligence of an individual is positively correlated with the number of offspring he produces. (B305)

The intelligence of an individual is negatively correlated with the size of the family from which the individual comes. (B305)

Within each occupational class, children from smaller families have higher I.Q. scores on the average than do children from larger families. (L115)

### I.Q. of Parents
The lower the intelligence of the parents, the larger the average family size. (H231)

There is a curvilinear relationship between intelligence of parents and family size; parents with the highest and lowest intelligence ratings have the highest reproductive rates. (H231)

### Juvenile Delinquency
Children from large families are more likely to be delinquent than are children from small families.

Juvenile delinquency is directly correlated with family size (in distressed areas). (I007)

The delinquent gang member usually comes from a family of several children. (J024)

Boys from smaller families are less likely to become delinquent than are boys from larger families. (N057)

There is no relationship between delinquency in girls and the size of the family. (N057)

### Juvenile Delinquency/Neurosis
Delinquent children come from larger families than do neurotic children. (B214)

### Kin/Nonkin
There is an association between reduction in average family size (characteristic of modern society as compared to traditional society) and increase in sharpness of status differences between family members and nonfamily members. (P062)

### Kin Relations (Interaction)
As the size of the nuclear family increases, relationships with secondary kin decreases. (R084)

### Kin-Role Behavior
The smaller the size of the nuclear family, the greater the fulfillment of kin obligations. (R084)

### Loss of Family Member
The smaller the family, the more severe the effects of the final loss (either psychologically or physically) of a family member. (T089)

### Marital Adjustment
Marital adjustment is inversely related to family size. (C003)

### Maternal-Role Behavior
The fewer the number of living children, the greater the ability of the mentally retarded mother to provide adequate child care. (B307)

### Mental Illness (Schizophrenia)
There seems to be no direct correlation between the number of siblings and the development of schizophrenia. (T105)

The larger the family, the higher the likelihood of schizophrenia. (W147)

### Mental Illness (Social Adjustment)
The larger the size of the family, the lower the level of posthospital performance of the mental patient. (S245)

### Nonkin Relations
Individuals are more likely to seek contacts outside the family if the family unit is small in size. (I007)

### Occupational Aspiration of Son
Boys from small families are slightly more likely to have professional-managerial aspirations than are those from large families, regardless of the father's occupational level (professional-managerial to unskilled labor). (E102)

### Occupational Heterogeneity of Households

As family size increases, in agricultural households, the occupational heterogeneity of its members increases (relationship holds up to ten family members; afterwards there is no relation between increased family size and increased occupational heterogeneity). (B031)

### Oedipal Complex

The appearance of the Oedipal complex is inversely correlated with family size. (M226)

### Parent-Child Relations

Adolescents in small families are more likely to have better relations with their parents than are adolescents in large families. (E100)

Adjustment of adolescents to parents varies inversely with the size of the family. (N010)

### Parent-Child Relations (Consistency)

Parents fluctuate more in their overprotectiveness toward the psychotic child, as compared with the normal sibling, as the size of the family increases; although in most other attitudes (warmth, control), there is no such relationship. (D064)

### Parent-Child Relations (Warmth)

Parent-child relations are warmer in small families than in large families. (E102)

### Parental-Role Adjustment

There is no relationship between family size and feelings of inadequacy in the parental role. (G126)

### Paternal Role (Discipline)

Fathers are more likely to control and discipline children, the larger the family size. (B322)

### Personality

The greater the number of children, particularly from four up, mothers of maladjusted children are likely to score higher on authoritarianism, encouraging verbalization, excluding outside influences, deification, and suppression of sex; fathers are likely to score higher on irresponsibility, suppression of sex, and change of orientation (PARI). (Z011)

### Personality Adjustment of Child

Personality adjustment of children is more successful in a small family than in a larger family. (I008)

### Personality (Affiliative Need)

Both firstborn and later-born individuals in large families are less likely than are their counterparts in small families to seek company when they are anxious. (S263)

There is less difference in affiliative responses to anxiety between firstborn and later-born children in large families than in small families. (S263)

### Personality of Child (Extroversion)

Extroversion should be more predominant than introversion among children of the small family. (I007)

### Personality of Mother (Emotional Stability)

The greater the number of children the mother must care for, the greater her emotional instability. (M216)

### Personality (Warmth)

Children from large families will develop a more objective and mature attitude toward their environment. (I007)

### Political Power

The size of a family is directly correlated with the significance of its political role in the lineage. (L066)

### Political Rank of Family

The political status of the family tends to be directly correlated with its size. (K049)

### Power Structure of Family

Family size is inversely related to democracy in family life. (B005)

With the exception of Catholic mothers, parents in large families are more likely to exercise considerable power in child rearing than are parents in smaller families. (E100)

The larger the family, the more internal organization develops and the more likely it is that one or more persons in the family will be dominant. (I008)

As family groups enlarge from three to four to five members, power within the family tends to shift from the wife to the husband to the oldest child, when measured by the number of contributions of each member of the family (of initiated interaction). (S207)

### Pregnancy, Attitude Toward

The greater the number of previous pregnancies, the more likely it is that the most recent pregnancy is unwanted. (F101)

### Property

Among families at the middle and upper rental-value levels, there is likely to be a larger number of children in homeowning families than in tenant families. (C009)

Among families at lower rental-value levels, there is likely to be a larger number of children in tenant families than in homeowning families. (C009)

### Race

The range of family size is much greater among Negro families than among white families. (H018)

Negro households are larger than white households (U.S.). (L124)

### Recreation

Small families engage in more activities together than do large families. (E102)

### Reference Group

The larger the family, the more likely it is that children will choose organized groups rather than school chums as their reference groups. (R111)

### Religion

Within the same social strata, Catholic parents tend to have larger families than do Protestant parents. (E100)

Catholics make more revisions in the desired number of children than Protestants do. (F101)

A wife's religion is more likely to determine the size of the family than is the husband's. (F101)

### Religion/Education

Among Catholics, there is a direct relationship between education and a positive attitude toward large family size, while there is an inverse relationship among Protestants. (F101)

### Remarriage
Divorcée mothers with more children are more likely to remarry soon after the divorce. (G157)

### Remarriage Chances
Divorcées with more children are slightly more likely to consider remarriage to one of their close male friends. (G157)

### Remarriage Rate
The more children in the family, the higher the remarriage rate following divorce. (G157)

### Rent
The larger the proportion of total income going for rent, the smaller the family is likely to be. (C009)

### Ritual in Family
The larger the family, the more numerous and rich the family rituals. (B004)

### Role Definition in Family
There is greater specialization of functions within the family as family units become smaller and more dependent upon goods and services from the outside. (A047)

The larger the family, the greater the specialization of roles and functions of individual members. (B004)

Role specialization increases with size of family. (E100)

### Scholastic Achievement
The larger the family, the lower the scholastic achievement of adolescent boys. (E102)

Size of family has no relationship to continuation in school for those with higher status of class position. (L115)

Children from larger families are more likely to drop out of school than are equally intelligent students from smaller families (Britain). (T095)

### Scholastic Adjustment
Sons of small families (three or fewer siblings) are no more likely than are those of large families to exhibit deviant behavior in school, to be leaders in school, or to conform to school expectations. (W151)

### Scholastic Motivation by Class
Among high achieving adolescents, small family size has a greater effect on high academic motivation among lower-class than among middle-class adolescents. (E102)

### Scholastic Motivation of Child by Sex Status
Among high achieving adolescents, the larger the family size, the greater the sex difference regarding academic motivation, girls being more motivated than boys are. (E102)

### Self-Aggression of Child
If there is only one boy in a family, he is less likely to be self-aggressive than if there are two or more. (S246)

### Sex of Children
The greater the number of children of the same sex, the greater is the desire for another child of the opposite sex. (F123)

### Sex-Role Definition
Differential training of boys and girls is more likely to occur in large families where a high degree of cooperation is required. (W127)

### Sexual Disability of Husband (Divorce)
Among men who have been physically disabled, those who are married have a greater number of children than do those who are divorced or separated. (N060)

### Sibling Relations (Warmth)
The smaller the family size, the warmer the relations among the siblings. (E102)

### Sibling Rivalry
There is a steady decrease in sibling jealousy with an increase in the number of children in a family. (B033)

Small middle-class families tend to have more sibling rivalry than do other types of families. (R102)

### Social Adjustment
Children who are reared in large families are less likely to fear strangers than are only children. (B004)

### Social Mobility
The greater the social mobility of a family, the smaller the size of the family. (A065)

Patterns of social mobility are likely to be associated with a family unit which is small in size. (T106)

An emphasis on class mobility is likely to result in a reduction of family size in urban areas. (T106)

### Social Mobility Aspirations
A restriction in the size of the family tends to occur among couples who have aspirations toward social mobility. (S064)

The larger the family, the lower the mobility aspirations of the children. (T096)

### Social Mobility/Occupational Aspirations of Son
Family size has a greater effect on actual occupational mobility than on occupational aspirations, larger families having greater limitations for the actualization of high occupational aspirations. (E102)

### Social Structure (Differentiation)
The smaller size of the family unit is correlated with increased specialization of the roles and functions in society at large. (A047)

### Socialization, Effectiveness of
The number of children in the family correlates with the adequate socialization of the child. (M203)

### Structure of Family
The larger the family, the more internal organization develops. (I008)

### Surrogate Mother, Evaluation of
The divorcée is more likely to claim that substitute child care is excellent if there are fewer children in the family. (G157)

### Technology
There is a positive correlation between family size and the type of animal traction used in ploughing. (B031)

Family size decreases as oxen are replaced by horses and the latter by cows as animals used in ploughing (Yugoslavia). (B031)

### Urban/Rural
The average size of the rural family is larger than that of the urban family. (B033)

Among divorced wives, those from rural backgrounds tend to have more children than do those from urban backgrounds. (G157)

Farm families that live near cities are smaller than those that live far from cities. (K016)

### Urban/Suburban
There are a larger number of children in suburban families than in city families. (C009)

### Urbanization
There is no significant change in family size attendant on urbanization. (A065)

There is a direct relation between the degree of urbanization (urban, suburban, rural) of a family and that family's size. (C134)

## SIZE OF FAMILY BY CLASS
### X  Achievement Motivation
Small family size is more important in determining high achievement motivation in youngest males than is high social class. (R106)

### I.Q.
The larger the family (number of siblings), the lower the intelligence level of the child; this relationship declines at the higher socioeconomic levels and may even be reversed. (A065)

## SIZE OF FAMILY OF MOTHER
### X  Mental Illness (Schizophrenia)
Mothers of schizophrenics tend to have come from large families. (T105)

## SIZE OF FAMILY/RELIGION
### X  Education of Child
### Religion/Size of Family
As family size increases, Catholic parents are more likely than Protestant parents to insist on a college education for their children. (E102)

## SIZE OF FAMILY UNIT
### X  Economic Independence of Child
When the size of the family unit of consumption is small, economic independence tends to be fostered in the child. (H164)

### Economic Pattern (Mercantile)
Merchant communities are likely to have larger family units than others are. (T072)

## SIZE OF GROUP                    X  Exogamy
Out-marriages increase as the percentage of the population in each group decreases. (G156)

### Intermarriage
The rate of intermarriage with other groups will be negatively correlated with the size of the group. (M227)

### Sex Taboo
The greater the number of people involved, the greater the punishment for illicit sexual behavior. (B006)

## SIZE OF HOUSEHOLD
### X  Authority Structure of Family
The larger the household, the greater the differentiation of formal authority. (G156)

The larger the household, the more likely it is that it will have a male head. (S211)

### Conflict
The larger the household, the greater the potential for conflict among its peers. (G156)

### Economic Structure of Family
The larger the household, the greater the differentiation of economic roles. (G156)

### Husband-Wife Relations (Closeness)
The strength of the relationship between husband and wife is inversely correlated with the size of the household. (H164)

When the household size in the society becomes smaller, the relationship between a man and wife becomes closer. (H227)

### Kin-Role Definition
The larger the household the more rules there will be specifying the frequency and type of role interaction among members. (G156)

### Kin Terminology
The larger the household the greater the differentiation of kinship terms. (G156)

### Mental Illness
There is no relationship between changes in household size and mental illness or hospitalization of a family member. (F124)

### Occupation
There is no correlation between size of household and occupation. (A001)

The higher the occupational level, the larger the household. (A001)

### Social Welfare
Public assistance increases the likelihood that the aged will be kept within the kin residence, thus increasing the size of the residential unit.

### Subsistence Pattern (Pastoral/Agricultural)
The number of people in the household will be higher in pastoral than in agricultural areas. (L073)

### Value Consensus
The larger the household, the higher the consensus among members regarding what is right and wrong. (G156)

## SIZE OF JOINT FAMILY            X  Residence
The size of a joint family will depend upon the type of housing available. (M021)

## SIZE OF KIN-GROUP               X  Aggression
The smaller the kin-group, the greater the tendency for the aggressor alone to be held responsible for his act. (S086)

### Cohesion of Kin-Group
The cohesion of the kin-group is inversely correlated with its size. (H074)

### Cohesion of Lineage
The ambiguity of the lineage unit is inversely correlated with the size of the exogamic unit. (L065)

### Conflict in Kin-Group
In the process of expansion, conflict among the members increases. (F121)

### Corporate Kin-Group
Smaller segments of unilineal kin-groups are more likely to engage in continuous corporate enterprise than are larger groups. (S189)

### Economic Cooperation
Patterns of economic cooperation between kinsmen tend to be directly correlated with the size of the kingroup. (W056)

### Economic Dependence
When the size of the kin-group is small, economic independence is fostered. (H164)

### Economic Pattern
The scale of the kin-group is related to the ecological situation and the form of economic cooperation involved. (F033)

### Economic Rank of Kin-Group
The size of the kin-group will be directly correlated with its economic status. (M131)

### Exogamy
Exogamous restrictions tend to relax as the kin unit increases in size. (A033)

The smaller the kinship group, the more likely it is to be exogamous. (G156)

Prescriptions against marriage with certain kinsmen are more likely to be violated if the size of the group is small. (L041)

The degree to which exogamic restrictions are extended is inversely correlated with the size of the kin-group. (M131)

### Genealogical Ties, Knowledge of
Although the depth and breadth of genealogical knowledge increases with age, this increase is greater the larger the size of ego's kin-group during adolescence. (G033)

### Kin Relations (Intensity)
The fewer available relatives an old person has, the more intense is his relationship with them. (T009)

### Kin-Role Definition
Where major unilineal groups of larger scale occur, it is found that with respect to the transmission of rights and duties, the more specific the claim or obligation, the narrower the segment of the lineage involved. (F033)

### Nonkin Ties
As the size of the kin-group decreases, neighborhood bonds increase in importance. (H164)

### Polygyny
The size of the residential kin-group will tend to decrease with a decrease in polygyny. (H164)

### Power of Kin-Group
The power of a localized lineage segment will be directly correlated with its size. (B134)

### Preferential Marriage (Cross-Cousin)
In cross-cousin marriage, larger-sized kinship groups are associated with treating distant cousins as "equivalent" and appropriate marriage partners for young people. (G156)

### Property
Increase in personal wealth provides an incentive to narrow the size of the group with a claim upon it to a few immediate kinsmen. (C090)

Smaller segments of unilineal kin-groups are more likely to be property owning than are the larger groups. (S189)

### Rank
The ability of a man to attract kinsmen who live near him is directly correlated with his status. (C060)

### Segmentation
An increase in size is likely to result in the subdivision of a kin-group. (N034)

### Stability of Kin-Group
The stability of the kin-group is directly correlated with its size. (H165)

The formation of larger kin-groups under a pattern of bilateral descent tends to result in a highly unstable social group. (S097)

### Warfare
Larger kin and local residential units tend to fragment into households under conditions of internecine warfare. (B041)

The size of the kin-group will tend to decrease when political conditions are peaceful. (H164)

## SIZE OF KIN NETWORK          X          Class
The higher the social class, the more extended the family structure. (P083)

### Divorce Adjustment
Divorce will have a less disruptive effect when the number of the child's kin is large. (H141)

## SIZE OF KIN SUBGROUPS          X          Conflict
Smaller segments of unilineal kin-groups are more likely to be the feuding units than are larger groups. (S189)

## SIZE OF KIN UNIT          X          Kin-Role Definition
The smallest segments of a kinship system tend to emphasize economic activities; the median segments tend to emphasize political activities; and the largest segments tend to emphasize religious activities. (B217)

## SIZE OF LINEAGE          X          Cohesion of Lineage
The degree of lineage cohesiveness tends to be directly correlated with its size. (L066)

### Descent (Unilineal)
Conformity with the rules of lineality is more likely to occur if the lineage is large in size. (B147)

### Endogamy
The unilineal group will be larger when the boundaries of the endogamous unit are wide. (G056)

### Exogamy
When the lineage is large, exogamous restrictions will be confined more to preventing the actual marriage of individuals than to attempting to prohibit illicit sexual relations. (A032)

The ability to enforce exogamic restrictions is inversely correlated with the size of the lineage. (S032)

### Lineage Ties
The retention of lineage identity tends to be directly correlated with its size. (E047)

### Marital Stability
Marriages are less stable in larger lineage groups. (F062)

### Political Power
The political importance of a lineage tends to be directly correlated with its size. (L070)

### Property, Division of

When a reduction in the size of the effective lineage occurs, the fragmentation of land also occurs. (T017)

### Residence (Patrilocal)

When the number of men in the matrilineage is small, a man who is a member of the lineage will encourage his son to remain with him in patrilocal residence. (F019)

### Segmentation

Delay in the segmentation of the lineage may occur if the unit is small in size. (W030)

### Sexual Restrictions

When the lineage is small in size, sexual relations with the wives of lineage members will be prohibited. (A032)

### Sibling Rank

The emphasis on seniority by birth order will tend to inhibit the depth and span of the agnatic group. (S123)

## SIZE OF MATRILINEAL GROUP
### X Residence (Patrilocal)

Virilocal marriage reduces the span of the effective matrilineal unit to the matricentric family. (T080)

## SIZE OF MOIETY    X Cohesion of Moiety

An increase in size of prosperous moieties leads to a weakening of kinship feelings among its members. (L110)

## SIZE OF NUCLEAR FAMILY
### X Stability of Kin-Group

Stability of the kin-group decreases with size of family nucleus. (F082)

## SIZE OF RELIGIOUS GROUP
### X Intermarriage (Religion)

The rate of intermarriages between Catholics and non-Catholics varies inversely with the proportion of Catholics in the total population (provided that ethnic and/or social rank differences do not prevent occupational and social contacts). (T010)

## SIZE OF TOWN
### X Parent-Child Relations (Conflict)

There is no relationship between the degree of parent-child conflict and the size of the town in which the family lives. (B249)

## SIZE OF VILLAGE    X Descent (Double)

A system of double descent tends to result in villages of very large size. (H245)

## SLAVERY    X Authority Structure of Family

Household slavery is more likely to occur among groups where autocratic control is generalized to family (or extended family) organization. (S069)

### Child-Rearing Practices (Obedience)

The institution of slavery tends to promote child-rearing practices stressing obedience and responsibility rather than achievement. (M246)

### Residence (Patrilocal)

The institution of slavery in a society encourages patrilocal residence. (M019)

## SLAVERY/MARRIAGE OF WAR CAPTIVES
### X Economic Level

With the development of an economic surplus sufficient to support specialized groups, war captives can be incorporated into the tribe as slaves rather than as husbands and wives. (O006)

## SLAVERY (PAWNSHIP)    X Age at Marriage

The institution of pawnship is likely to be associated with a later age of marriage for men and an earlier age of marriage for women. (D081)

### Corporate Kin-Group

The development of a system of property in pawns and slaves tends to encourage the development of corporate descent groups. (D081)

### Power Structure of Lineage

In societies with the institution of pawnship, lineage and clan elders tend to exercise greater control over their members. (D081)

### Stability of Lineage

Systems of pawnship are correlated with greater control by lineage and clan elders and, consequently, with greater lineage stability. (D081)

## SLEEPING ARRANGEMENTS    X Class

There is an inverse correlation between the closeness of sleeping arrangements and class. (M230)

### Cohesion of Family

It seems highly probable that affection and degree of integration within the family are greatest among the lower class where there is a greater intimacy of sleeping arrangements. (M230)

### Couvade

There is a strong association between the practice of couvade and exclusive mother-child sleeping arrangements. (B251)

### Husband-Wife Relations (Closeness)

It would seem highly probable that a husband and wife occupying the same bed are, on the whole, likely to be closer to each other than are a husband and wife who occupy separate beds or separate bedrooms. (M230)

### Identification with Mother

Exclusive mother-child sleeping arrangements, coupled with matrilocal residence, are strongly associated with maximum feminine identification in the child. (B251)

There is a strong association between exclusive mother-child sleeping arrangements and primary feminine identification during infancy. (B251)

### Marital Adjustment

A low happiness score is seen to be reliably associated with occupancy of separate rooms. (T079)

### Personality Adjustment of Child

There is no significant difference in personality adjustment between children who slept with their mothers during infancy and those who did not. (K161)

### Self-Conception of Child

Exclusive mother-child sleeping arrangements, coupled with patrilocal residence, are strongly associated with maximum conflict in identity for the child. (B251)

### Sex-Role Identification

Societies where the mother and father sleep together produce children whose main identification is with the adult role itself rather than like- or cross-sex identification. (B251)

### Totemism

Totemism is correlated with exclusive mother-infant sleeping arrangements. (W127)

## SLEEPING ARRANGEMENTS (MOTHER-INFANT)
### X    Initiation Rites
Male initiation rites at puberty are correlated with exclusive mother-infant sleeping arrangements. (W127)

## SLEEPING ARRANGEMENTS OF HUSBAND-WIFE
### X    Divorce
The divorce rate in the various social classes is highest in the separate-bedroom class and lowest in the double-bed class. (M230)

## SOCIAL ACCEPTANCE
### X    Child-Rearing Practices (Control)
#### Income
Adolescents from families of higher-income strata who are accepted by their peers are granted more personal freedom by their families than are those at the middle and low economic levels. (F108)

## SOCIAL ADJUSTMENT
### X    Adolescent Role, Definition of
If the transition from childhood to adult status is controlled, adolescent problem behavior will be absent. (B033)

#### Age at Marriage
There is a correlation between social maladjustment and early marriage (under 18 years of age). (H189)

#### Authoritarianism
Children from democratic homes tend to be socially more outgoing then those from authoritarian homes. (K113)

#### Broken Home
Men from broken homes are less likely to show successful social adaptation than are those from intact homes. (H206)

Asocial behavior is more likely on the part of men from broken homes than men from intact homes. (H206)

#### Child-Rearing Practices (Social Behavior)
If the parents evaluate unfavorably the social behavior and achievements of the child and often punish him for failure to meet parental standards, the child is likely to develop anxiety in confronting social situations (e.g., in front of an audience, in performing a test); this is not true if the parents evaluate favorably, but punish the child infrequently. (P066)

#### Disorganization of Family
Disorganization in the family (malfunctioning of its expressive roles, i.e., interpersonal relations) causes malfunctioning in roles outside of the family system. (G122)

#### Family/Friends
Aid from friends is more highly associated with the divorcée's claims of having many or some opportunities to meet people than is aid from family members. (G157)

Divorcées who have help from both friends and family claim the most opportunities to meet people, followed by those who had help from either friends or family members, and lastly by those who had no help from either. (G157)

#### Friendship
Divorcées who have a new set of friends are slightly more likely to have more opportunities to meet people than are those who maintain their marriage friends. (G157)

Divorcées who receive help from married friends are more likely to have social opportunities than are those who receive help from a new circle of friends. (G157)

#### Illegitimacy (Adoption)
Unwed mothers who give up their children get along better with their friends than do unwed mothers who keep their children. (J020)

#### Institutional Care
Children who are reared in institutions from early infancy and then placed in foster homes are much less able to establish social relationships than are children who are placed in foster homes directly in early infancy. (B270)

A higher percentage of children raised from early infancy in institutions and then placed in foster homes is socially maladjusted than children raised in their own homes in infancy and later placed in foster homes. (B270)

Children who are raised in institutions without parental care or adequate parental surrogates are less socially mature than are normal children. (G128)

#### Loss of Father/Mother
After the age of five years, the loss of the father is more likely to have a detrimental effect on the social adjustment of the child than is the loss of the mother; before five years, the loss of the mother has more effect. (H206)

#### Marital Stability
A problem in relating to others, stemming from inadequate identification with the female role (as measured by an ambivalent response toward Rorschach plate III), is more likely to be displayed by divorced than by married women.

#### Maternal Overprotectiveness
Maternal overprotection tends to be negatively correlated with adjustment on the part of the child to his peers. (L162)

#### Mental Retardation
The oldest child in a family with a retarded child is more likely to have poor adjustment than are the other children.

#### Mother Absence
Complete maternal deprivation can produce a child who is unable to have stable relationships with other people. (B270)

Completely depriving a young child of his mother or mother surrogate is directly related to an increase in the inability to make relationships with other people. (B270)

Children deprived of their mothers from birth appear generally to be asocial, while children who have been deprived of maternal care and also have had some significant period without deprivation tend to be more antisocial. (B270)

Early maternal deprivation (below the age of six and for at least six months' duration) is significantly related to the later development of sociopathic personality, especially in the failure to adjust to society in the spheres of marriage, work, and relationship to law and order. (E093)

### Mother-Child Relations (Affection)
Absence of mother love leads to maladjustment in adult responsibilities. (G127)

### Mother-Child Relations (Nurturance)
Children who are deprived of adequate mothering during infancy are more likely in later childhood to make superficial relationships with friends, accompanied by little ability to care for people. (P068)

### Parent-Child Relations
The more satisfactory the parent-child relations, the more able is the child to relate well with his peers. (K113)

### Parent-Child Relations (Acceptance)
Parental acceptance increases the likelihood that a child will develop a generally positive set of feelings toward others. (H212)

### Parent-Child Relations (Affection)
There is a correlation between the degree of continuous affection received from a parent figure in the early years of infancy and the ability to establish adequate interpersonal relationships in later life, including relationships with parent substitutes. (T086)

### Parent-Child Relations (Closeness)
The closer the child-parent relationship, the greater the child's confidence in associating with the opposite sex. (L137)

The closer the parent-child relationship, the less difficulty the child will have in making friendships with the opposite sex during early adolescence. (L137)

The closer women are with their fathers and correspondingly distant with their mothers, the greater their problems in establishing relationships with the opposite sex during adolescence. (L137)

### Parent-Child Relations (Favoritism)
The parents of adolescents who are accepted by their peers are less likely to show favoritism within the family than are the parents of adolescents who are rejected by their peers. (F108)

### Parent-Child Relations (Rejection)
The greater the rejection of the child by his parents, the more likely will the child be to isolate himself emotionally from others. (A059)

Parental rejection of the child may cause the child to fear rejection from others and to inhibit his establishment of adequate relationships with others. (T086)

### Parent-Child Relations (Warmth)
The degree of parental emotional warmth and support is negatively correlated with social withdrawal in the child. (S221)

### Parent Loss
Children between the ages of 3 and 5 who are deprived of their parents and not provided with adequate parent surrogates demonstrate unfavorable social attitudes as a result of having developed desires for affection and desires for revenge. (B270)

### Paternal/Maternal Role
While the role of the mother is more crucial than that of the father for the development of the child's character, the role of the father is more important for the child's social adaptation. (H206)

### Personality of Father (Dominance)
Fathers are more dominant in families of schizophrenic patients who were rated to have had relatively good premorbid adjustment than in families of patients rated to have had very poor premorbid adjustment (Phillips Scale). (F115)

### Sibling Structure (Sex)
At the two-to-four-year spacing, the child with a same-sex sibling is more likely to be apprehensive in social situations than is one with a cross-sex sibling. (K104)

When sibling spacing is under two years, boys are more likely to be apprehensive in social situations than girls are. (K104)

Children who have siblings of their own sex only have more problems establishing heterosexual relations (up to and including marriage) than do children who have siblings of the opposite sex. (T089)

### Size of Family
Children who are reared in large families are less likely to fear strangers than are only children. (B004)

### Surrogate Mother
At one year of age, infants reared in families where the mothering is provided by one person are better able to relate with other people than are infants reared in families where the mothering is provided by more than one person (i.e., nurse, grandparent, mother's friend, or older sister of child). (C124)

Whether the infant was cared for predominantly by the mother or by other persons is not related to development of outgoing social behavior. (Y042)

### Weaning
There is no association between children who are weaned gradually and children who are weaned abruptly and their social adjustment (as measured by the California Personality Test and teacher's ratings on the Ford Modification of the Haggerty–Olson–Wickman Behavior Rating Scale). (S200)

## SOCIAL ADJUSTMENT (AFTER HOSPITALIZATION)
### X    Economic Role of Mental Patient
Formerly hospitalized mental patients who live with parents and are neither steadily employed nor active socially are not the only potential economic heads of the household, while those who are steadily employed and who do have social activities are usually the only potential sources of economic support in the family. (F098)

## SOCIAL ADJUSTMENT (COOPERATIVENESS)
### X    Sibling Structure (Sex)
Among firstborns with siblings of the opposite sex, boys tend to be more uncooperative than girls do. (K149)

## SOCIAL ADJUSTMENT OF CHILD
### X    Child Rearing (Collective)
Rorschach tests show no difference between kibbutz-reared and nonkibbutz-reared adolescent children in overall social adjustment. (R096)

### Child-Rearing Practices (Flexibility)
If parents are more flexible in problematic child-rearing situations (if they can change behavior, roles, and attitudes), children are more likely to be socially competent. (T102)

### Child-Rearing Practices (Giving Reasons)

Children raised in a home in which parents consult with them about regulations and attempt to explain discipline are more socially outgoing and active in both a hostile and a friendly way than children raised in an authoritarian home. (L146)

### Child-Rearing Practices (Restrictiveness)

The less autocratic, restrictive, and severe the parents, the greater is the likelihood that the child will be socially well adjusted in his peer group. (M178)

### Conflict in Family

The less the tension in family relationships (parent-parent and parent-child), the greater the likelihood that the child will be socially well adjusted within his peer group. (M178)

### Feeding, Attitude Toward

The more satisfactory the feeding experience for the infant, the more mature his social responsiveness is likely to be (B272)

### Feeding (Demand)

There is no relationship between the feeding of infants on a regular or a demand schedule and their level of social adjustment (as measured by the California Test of Personality or the Ford Modification of the Haggerty–Olson–Wickman Behavior Rating Scale). (S200)

### Foster Homes/Institutional Care

Children raised in foster homes are socially more mature and better able to establish relationships than are children raised in institutions. (P068)

### Institutional Care

Institutionalization of the child may cause him to seek affection insatiably and to be indiscriminately sociable. (Y045)

Institutionalization of the child may be a cause of inadequate social discrimination on his part, with regard to both different persons and different kinds of emotional expression. (Y045)

### Mother Absence

Children separated from their mothers for long periods of time during the early years are more likely to show only superficial reactions to other people and to have no real affection. (B270)

### Parent-Child Relations

There is no measurable relationship between parental attitudes toward children and the personal and social adjustment of the children. (C098)

The attitudes a child has toward his parents are correlated with those toward many other individuals. (C098)

A positive attitude toward the parent of the same sex is likely to facilitate a child's peer-group adjustment at the preadolescent age level. (C098)

A positive attitude toward only the parent of the opposite sex is likely to hinder the child's peer-group adjustment at the preadolescent age level. (C098)

### Parent-Child Relations (Evaluation)

Parents are likely to see their children as better adjusted socially (as measured by responses on the California Test of Personality, Form B) than the children see themselves.

### Parent-Child Relations (Rejection)

Personality maladjustment (in the child, resulting from the child–parent relationship) tends to be generalized in the child's relationship with others (e.g., consistently rejecting and punishing parents produce fear in the child who, in turn, generalizes this fear to other parental figures). (D062)

### Parent Loss

Separated boys, especially those separated early in life, demonstrate poorer adjustment than do the non-separated on the General Adjustment Rating. (S182)

### Personality of Mother

There is a greater correlation between the mother's total character structure and the child's social and psychological adjustment than with child-rearing practices. (B230)

### Social Adjustment of Father

Fathers who show great antisocial behavior are likely to have a disproportionately high number of children with antisocial behavior. (R125)

### Surrogate Parents

Child-switching (sending the child, at some period, to live with different kin) is associated with a better adaptation by the child into the larger community. (G156)

## SOCIAL ADJUSTMENT OF CHILD (SOCIAL AND PHYSICAL)
### X   Mother-Child Relations (Consistency)

Mood shifts in mothers, characterized by alternating moods of hostility-overprotectiveness toward their children, are positively associated with a diminished capacity on the part of the children to relate themselves to human beings or to manipulate inanimate objects. (S209)

## SOCIAL ADJUSTMENT OF FAMILY
### X   Marital Adjustment

Conflict and maladjustment between the family and the community are causes of marital conflict. (V033)

## SOCIAL ADJUSTMENT OF FATHER
### X   Social Adjustment of Child

Fathers who show great antisocial behavior are likely to have a disproportionately high number of children with antisocial behavior. (R125)

## SOCIAL ADJUSTMENT OF MOTHER
### X   Illness of Child

Mothers of cerebral-palsied children do not exhibit any greater tendency to withdraw from social contact than do mothers of normal children. (B320)

## SOCIAL ADJUSTMENT OF PARENTS
### X   Juvenile Delinquency

There is a correlation between antisocial and unethical behavior by parents and delinquent behavior in the child. (N063)

### Mental Illness (Schizophrenia/Neurosis)

Parents of normals are more likely to be socially well adjusted than are parents of neurotics or of schizophrenics. (F110)

## SOCIAL ADJUSTMENT OF SON
### X   Father-Son Relations (Affection)

Sons whose relations with their fathers are characterized by insufficient paternal affection are less adjusted socially than are sons who have received adequate paternal affection. (M204)

## SOCIAL ADJUSTMENT OF WIFE  X  Urban/Rural
Wives in urban areas express much higher satisfaction with their social lives than do wives in rural areas.

## SOCIAL ADJUSTMENT, PREMORBID
### X  Conflict in Family
There is more interpersonal conflict in families of schizophrenic patients with poor premorbid adjustment than in families with good adjustment (Phillips Scale). (F115)

A greater proportion of the conflict that arises in families of schizophrenics with poor, as compared to good, premorbid adjustment is due to conflict between the parents rather than between parents and son (Phillips Scale). (F115)

Schizophrenics with good premorbid adjustment have less conflict with their parents than do patients with poor adjustment (Phillips Scale). (F115)

Schizophrenics with poor premorbid adjustment have more difficulty with mother cues than with father cues on visual discrimination test's, whereas patients with good premorbid adjustment are more disturbed by father cues. (F115)

### Role in Family
Schizophrenic patients having relatively good premorbid adjustment play a more assertive role and enjoy more freedom within the family than do patients with poor premorbid adjustment (Phillips Scale). (F115)

## SOCIAL ADJUSTMENT ("SKILL")
### X  Sibling Structure (Age Difference)
The greater the age difference between siblings, the more the second child is "outclassed in skill and wisdom" by the older sibling. (K149)

## SOCIAL CHANGE
### X  Economic Pattern (Household)
When the major unit of economic production and consumption is the household, receptivity to innovation is limited. (N013)

### Extended/Nuclear Family Ties
With social class held constant, men who most accept the value of change are also most likely to support the nuclear form of intergeneration relationship (i.e., no necessary geographical propinquity, occupational involvement, nepotism, or hierarchical authority structure). (J033)

### Marginal Status
The individuals who are the initial acceptors of innovation tend to be those with marginal or ill-defined familial status. (R004)

### Marital Stability
The separation rate will tend to rise under conditions of social change or instability. (F062)

The greater the amount of social change in any given period, the greater is the amount of marital disharmony. (G134)

### Mate Selection (Free Choice)
Closed systems of mate selection are more apt to exist in societies where there is less social and technological change. (J035)

### Parent-Child Relations (Conflict)
The greater the differences between the society within which the parents grow up and that within which the child grows up, the greater the potential for conflict between parent and child. (G156)

### Social Control
In periods of rapid social change, the state is more likely to permit divorce, common law marriage, promiscuous sexuality, and private aggression in order to maximize control of the production of work and of the weapons of mass warfare.

## SOCIAL CHANGE, ATTITUDE TOWARD
### X  Values (Extended/Nuclear Family)
Men who espouse nuclear family norms are most likely to be accepting of change. Those who espouse modified-extended family norms are in the middle and those who advocate extended family norms are least likely to be accepting of change. (J025)

## SOCIAL CHANGE, RATE OF
### X  Identification with Parents
The more rapid the rate of social change, the less likely it is that the child will perceive his parents as appropriate models of behavior. (M188)

### Parent-Child Relations (Consensus)
The more rapid the rate of social change, the greater the conflict between parents and children over norms. (D058)

## SOCIAL CONTROL
### X  Adultery/Premarital Sex Relations
Adultery is punished more by primitive societies than is intercourse with one's own betrothed. (B006)

### Disorganization of Family
Family disintegration occurs when there is a tolerance of individual variation. (B033)

Family disintegration occurs where there is an absence of techniques to compel an erring member to abide by the norms of public opinion. (B033)

### Economic Pattern (Wage Labor)
When men become more dependent on income from labor abroad and less on lineage land, they free themselves more from lineage control. (F088)

### Incest Taboo
Incest which violates the strongest group norms is subject to stronger sanctions than is other incest. (F076)

### Independence of Nuclear Family
The greater the independence of the nuclear family from the wider kinship network, the less able are both to exert control over one another. (G156)

### Juvenile Delinquency
In a society where there are strict family controls on its members' autonomy, delinquent (or potentially delinquent) subcommunities tend to emerge. (P056)

### Kin/Nonkin
Institutional controls of behavior are stronger in consanguineal boundary-maintaining systems than in nonconsanguineal boundary-maintaining systems. (C093)

### Kin-Role Definition
Family influence and control are weakened when other institutions take on the educational, recreational, and hygienic functions of the family. (A013)

**Kin Ties**

As the effective range of kinship narrows, the responsibility of the kinship group for social control correspondingly diminishes. (E015)

**Marriage**

Marriage lowers the rate of sexual competition among men and is thus a force for social order. (P083)

**Premarital Sex Relations**

The greater the occupational mobility of family or in society (and the lower the control of the community), the more likely it is that girls will be exploited in premarital intercourse. (B245)

**Residence**

The control of the community over a family is greater when residence is stable rather than transient. (B033)

A unilineal group can play an effective role as agent of social control only when it is localized. (G062)

As a nonlocalized group, the matriclan can play little part in the main system of social control. (G062)

**Sex Taboo**

The greater the number of societies in which a given type of sexual behavior is tabooed, the more severe is the punishment. (B006)

**Social Change**

In periods of rapid social change, the state is more likely to permit divorce, common law marriage, promiscuous sexuality, and private aggression in order to maximize control of the production of work and of the weapons of mass warfare.

**Social Mobility**

The different types of mobility (residential, personal, vertical, ideational) all tend to free the members of the family from its control, thus individualizing them.

The more able upper-class families are in protecting their inept members from open competition within the society at large, the more able they will be to retain their rank (but the greater the likelihood they will be displaced by violence). (G156)

**Stability of Family**

Family instability occurs in an area where social control is reduced to a minimum and individual self-expression is increased to a maximum. (B033)

**Urbanization**

The degree of urbanization is inversely correlated with the extent to which kinship institutions are effective in social control. (W034)

## SOCIAL DEVELOPMENT
### X   Child-Rearing Practices (Social Stimulation)

Direct efforts by the mother to elicit social responses in the infant are moderately related to actual outgoing social behavior in the infant. (Y042)

**Maternal Deprivation**

Children deprived of their mothers have an impaired ability to relate to other people and to think abstractly and, generally, have an impaired ego and superego development.

**Mother-Child Relations (Affection)**

A high level of affection and emotional expression by the mother is related to the development of outgoing social behavior in the infant. (Y042)

## SOCIAL DEVELOPMENT OF CHILD
### X   Mother-Child Relations (Warmth)

Children of warm mothers mature more rapidly in their social behavior than do those of cold mothers. (S191)

## SOCIAL DISORGANIZATION    X   Exogamy

With the development of a situation of social disorganization, exogamic restrictions will tend to be violated. (M137)

**Illegitimacy**

Illegitimacy is directly related to social disorganization.

**Illegitimacy, Attitude Toward**

The amount of social disruption caused by illegitimacy is correlated with the degree of social disapproval of illegitimacy. (G156)

## SOCIAL DISORGANIZATION RATE
### X   Illegitimacy Rate

Social disorganization is directly correlated with illegitimacy. (S003)

## SOCIAL DISTANCE    X   Intermarriage

The following exogamous marriages are ranked in the amount of social disapproval they incur (from greatest to least) as follows: (1) interracial marriages, (2) internationality, interclass, and interfaith marriages, (3) intereducational group marriages, (4) interregional marriages (U.S.). (J035)

**Intermarriage (Racial and Ethnic)**

The greater the rate of decreasing social distance between racial and ethnic groups, the greater the rate of their intermarriage. (B311)

## SOCIAL EVOLUTION    X   Clan

Clan organization occurs in societies which represent an intermediate level of social evolution. (W076)

## SOCIAL/INDIVIDUAL ADJUSTMENT
### X   Parent-Child Relations (Evaluation)

Parents are more likely to agree with their children's self-ratings when discussing social adjustment than when discussing individual adjustment (as measured by the California Test of Personality, Form B).

## SOCIAL INTEGRATION    X   Marriage Payment

Since bride prices are not often the kind of property that can be secured easily outside the social system, in societies where the custom of bride price prevails, preparation for marriage stimulates a greater commitment of the family to the community values and a greater amount of interaction with other families. (P083)

## SOCIAL INTERACTION    X   Class

The lower the social class of a family, the less likely it is that it will entertain friends at home. (K089)

**Intermarriage**

Intermarriage between groups will be directly correlated with the frequency of intergroup interaction.

## SOCIAL ISOLATION    X   Conformity

A home which isolates a child socially is more likely than others to produce a child who conforms with the opinions of others. (J024)

**Mental Illness**

Mental illness is directly correlated with a failure to establish relationships outside of the immediate family situation. (F085)

### Mental Illness of Child
Mental illness is more likely to occur among children whose extrafamilial activities are severely restricted. (L126)

### Mental Illness (Schizophrenia/Neurosis)
In the lower class, schizophrenics are more likely than neurotics to be isolated from social contacts due to household responsibilities. (M197)

### Parent-Child Relations (Authority)
The greater the ecological and social isolation of a subordinate social group, the more likely it is that the children will be acceptant of parental authority and standards. (K121)

## SOCIAL ISOLATION OF FAMILY
### X   Mental Illness (Manic-Depressive)
Families of manic-depressive patients tend to be set apart in some way from their environment, in some cases it is because of a minority-group status, in others because of financial reverses, in still others because of some aberrant behavior by a member of the family group. (G022)

### Mental Illness of Child (Schizophrenia)
Families estranged from the community are more likely to produce schizophrenic children than others are. (W143)

## SOCIAL ISOLATION OF MENTAL PATIENT
### X   Mental Illness (Social Adjustment)
Patients who perform at low levels occupationally and socially are more likely to be found in families whose members reported that this was the only place the patient could live than are patients who perform at high levels. (F124)

The absence of an alternative living situation for the former mental patient may make him less sensitive to demands of the family and the family less demanding of the patient than if the patient were able to move elsewhere. (F124)

## SOCIAL ISOLATION OF WOMEN    X   Class
The economic importance of women of the lower class inhibits the pattern of social isolation that is found among members of the upper class. (G072)

### Economic Role of Women
The social isolation of women tends to be directly correlated with the lack of importance of their economic role. (G072)

### Husband-Wife Relations (Intimacy)
Isolation of women from the community, by reducing the value of their conversation, is likely to make intimacy between husband and wife more difficult. (P083)

## SOCIAL MOBILITY    X   Acculturation
There is a positive relationship between the acculturation of an ethnic group and its social mobility. (S051)

### Age at Marriage
The upwardly mobile tend to defer marriage (in Sweden until about age 30); those who marry before 25 have a lower chance of an ascending career.

Those who marry into a higher social class are likely to marry late, while early marriage is associated with marrying into a lower status group (England).

### Cohesion of Family
The strengthening of the family results in a restriction of social mobility and the reinforcement of social-class lines. (B033)

The general effect of upward or downward social mobility of a family member is the weakening of kinship and family ties (especially for males). (B033)

Families that are socially mobile, upward or downward, are most likely to exhibit signs of disunity than are families that are socially stable in their class patterns. (C134)

Social mobility is facilitated by weakened affective bonds between family members. (T106)

### Cohesion of Joint Family
Social mobility of one of the males, if accompanied by a reluctance to share his greater wealth, leads to a decrease in the solidarity of the joint family. (G156)

### Competition
Intraclass competition among upper-class families lessens the likelihood that any given family will maintain its status over the generations. (G156)

### Descent (Bilateral)
Bilateral descent is more likely to characterize societies with high degrees of social mobility. (G101)

### Divorce
An increase in the divorce rate is correlated with a higher rate of social mobility. (T106)

### Extended Family
Extended family systems tend to restrict the geographical and occupational mobility of males. (P083)

### Extended Family Ties
Mobile persons have patterns of extended family relations more closely correlated to their former status than to that of the class they move toward. (S272)

The degree of extended family orientation tends to increase as the head of the household engages more and more in higher-status occupations. (S272)

### Fertility
Very low or high fertility in an upper-class family is a factor that may contribute to loss of rank. (G156)

In the suburbs, upwardly mobile men do not have fewer children than do nonmobile men; there may be a slight inverse association. (L115)

Rapid social mobility in a society is associated with low fertility. (R119)

### Fertility Values
When a major shift takes place in the prestige level of the husband's job, the wife wants fewer children.

### Happiness in Childhood
The upward mobile business leader tends to come from an impoverished home with a spiritually bleak and physically depressed family atmosphere and with an inadequate, unreliable father.

### Homogamy (Religious)
The socially mobile become increasingly heterogamous in selection of boyfriends in terms of religion, while the socially nonmobile become increasingly homogamous in terms of religion. (K150)

### Identification with Parents

Children who identify with and accept the values of their parents are more likely to continue in the parents' trend of social mobility; children who rebel against their parents' values and who have accompanying ambivalent parental identification are more likely to exhibit a reversal from their parents' social mobility pattern.

### Intermarriage

Intermarriage is less likely to be disruptive in societies where patterns of mobility permit a movement from the families of orientation. (M227)

### Intermarriage (Class)

Interclass unions are more likely to occur in societies in which social mobility is stressed. (M227)

### Intermarriage (Ethnic)

Ethnic intermarriage will increase as the amount of social mobility of an ethnic group increases. (B029)

### Isolation of Nuclear Family

Where the nuclear family is a relatively isolated unit, occupational mobility is normal. (S080)

### Kin Relations (Interaction)

The kin interaction rate of upwardly mobile families is greater than is that of the families in their class of origin, but less than that of the families in their class of achievement. (R084)

Frequency of contact with relatives is likely to decrease if the individual moves into another social class. (T106)

### Kin Ties

Kinship ties are geographically more extended toward the higher social strata. (Q001)

### Kin Ties (Fictive)

The extent to which fictive kin ties are established between individuals of different socioeconomic classes is indicative of the degree of socioeconomic mobility. (F049)

Under conditions of social mobility, fictive ties tend to be established between a member of a lower class and one of a higher class. (M080)

When the community is homogeneous, with high stability and low mobility, fictive kin ties tend to be established between members of the same community. (M080)

Marital success is greater when there is little or no social mobility than when there is a great deal of social mobility. (C023)

A distribution of significantly lower scores on marital adjustment is shown by the spouses who are downwardly mobile (i.e., those who have moved downward relative to their parents), compared to all spouses taken together. (R011)

If both spouses are upwardly mobile, marital adjustment is more likely for couples with similar class backgrounds than for those with dissimilar class backgrounds (tendency not statistically proved). (R011)

If neither spouse is socially mobile or if one spouse is upwardly mobile, marital adjustment will be better for couples with similar class backgrounds than for those of dissimilar class backgrounds. (R011)

If one or both spouses are downwardly mobile, marital adjustment is equally poor for those with similar and those with dissimilar class backgrounds. (R011)

### Marital Stability

People who marry more than once are less likely to rise occupationally. (G011)

### Mate Selection (Free Choice)

Closed systems of mate selection are more apt to exist in societies with little vertical social mobility than in societies with more vertical social mobility. (J035)

### Mate Selection (Residence)

As the mobility aspirations of individuals increase, the likelihood of residentially propinquitous mate selection decreases. (K020)

### Occupation of Husband/Wife

The more equal the wife's occupation is to that of her husband, the smaller part she plays in her husband's occupational mobility.

### Opportunity Structure

The more able upper-class family members are in preventing lower-class children from obtaining access to skills and education, the more able they will be in retaining their status position. (G156)

The greater the accessibility of the opportunity structure to family members of the lower ranks, the more difficult it becomes for upper-class families to maintain their position. (G156)

### Parent-Child Relations

Mobile women are more likely to have experienced unsatisfactory relationships with their parents than are nonmobile women. (R117)

### Parent-Child Relations (Affect)

Business executives with lower-class backgrounds are more likely to have had emotionally depriving family settings during childhood than are executives from higher-class backgrounds. (R117)

### Parent-Child Relations (Closeness)

Children who have experienced upward occupational mobility tend to keep closer relationships with their retired parents than do less successful children. (S220)

### Parent-Child Relations (Financial Help)

There is no significant relationship between social mobility and giving financial aid to aged parents. (G119)

### Parent-Daughter Relations (Rejection)

Among middle-class unmarried mobile career women, a higher proportion have experienced partial rejection by parents who showed favoritism for a sibling than among the mobile women in the sample.

### Political Affiliation

Upwardly mobile children whose parents are Democrats are more likely to become Republican than are those who have not been mobile. (H244)

### Religiosity

Upward social mobility is associated with a reduction in degree of religiosity. (G119)

### Residence

Lineages will tend to be dispersed in societies with high degrees of social mobility. (G101)

### Residence with Parents

There is no significant relationship between social-class mobility of children and living with their aged parents or in independent households. (G119)

### Revolution

The more successful upper-class families are in protecting themselves from the infiltration of lower-class members into their ranks, the more likely are those below to rebel. (G156)

### Role Behavior in Family

There are no differences between mobile and nonmobile white collar men in such indices of "familism" as number of offspring, housing status, age at marriage, and duration of childlessness. Men from lower-class origins were as family-oriented as were men from white collar backgrounds (in the modern "bureaucratic" era as contrasted with the former "entrepreneurial" era). (L115)

### Role Definition in Family

In the suburbs, upwardly mobile men do not have fewer children than nonmobile men do; there may be a slight inverse association. (L115)

White collar men with several children have higher levels of aspiration than do those with few children. (L115)

There are no differences between mobile and nonmobile white collar men in such indices of "familism" as number of offspring, housing status, age at marriage, and duration of childlessness. Men from lower-class origins were as family-oriented as were men from white collar backgrounds (in the modern "bureaucratic" era as contrasted with the former "entrepreneurial" era). (L115)

### Sex Status

Women are more likely than men to be upwardly mobile through marriage. (C134)

Men are more likely to be downwardly mobile in marriage than are women. (C134)

Sex differences in academic motivation of adolescents are least among those children who are most exposed to conditions generating and facilitating upward mobility (i.e., middle-class status, college-educated fathers who are active in independence training, and parents who insist on their children going to college). (E102)

### Size of Family

The greater the social mobility of a family, the smaller the size of the family. (A065)

Patterns of social mobility are likely to be associated with a family unit which is small in size. (T106)

An emphasis on class mobility is likely to result in a reduction of family size in urban areas. (T106)

### Social Control

The different types of mobility (residential, personal, vertical, ideational) all tend to free the members of the family from its control, thus individualizing them. (B033)

The more able upper-class families are in protecting their inept members from open competition within the society at large, the more able they will be to retain their rank (but the greater the likelihood they will be displaced by violence). (G156)

### Social Control
### X   Premarital Sex Relations

The greater the occupational mobility of family or in society (and the lower the control of the community), the more likely it is that girls will be exploited in premarital intercourse. (B245)

### Stability of Kin-Group

The disintegration of kinship units tends to occur when the economic pattern necessitates social and spatial mobility. (G056)

### Stability of Kinship Structure

Disintegration of the kinship system tends to occur when the economic patterns necessitate social and spatial mobility. (G056)

### Stratification

The movement of families from one class to another is not necessarily associated with a change in the existing system of stratification in a society. (G156)

### Stratification, Basis of

A society based upon competitive achievement is associated with high downward mobility of upper-class families. (G156)

When the class structure of society is based upon extended family ties, marriage is more likely to be the crucial determinant of social mobility. (P083)

### Structure of Family

With an increase in social mobility, matrilineal societies will tend to revise their family structure to that of a small bilateral family. (G056)

## SOCIAL MOBILITY ASPIRATIONS
### X   Child-Rearing Practices (Control)

Parental leniency is associated with children who are upward aspirers. (E102)

### Child-Rearing Practices (Punishment)

Adolescents who have upward mobility aspirations are more likely than those with downward aspirations to have received psychological rather than physical punishment as children. (D077)

Parental leniency is associated with children who are upward aspirers. (E102)

Parents of upward aspirers use more verbal and less physical discipline than do parents of children who do not have mobility aspirations. (E102)

### Chores

The higher the occupational mobility desired by the husband, the less the time spent in household-task performance.

### Dependency

Children who are upward aspirers are more independent of their parents regarding judgments and behavior than are children who are not upward aspirers. (E102)

### Fertility

Lowered social mobility aspirations lead to higher fertility. (W022)

### Homogamy (Occupation)

When the wife's family occupies a higher occupational level than the husband's he adopts high mobility aspirations in order to reach that same level.

### Husband-Wife Relations (Communication)
Husbands with high mobility aspirations, as compared with nonmobile husbands, communicate more extensively with their wives about their work experiences.

### Identification with Family
Children who are upward aspirers are more conscious of the differences between themselves and their families than are children who are not upward aspirers. (E102)

### Identification with Family/Nonfamily Member
Adolescents with upward mobility aspirations are less likely than others to choose an "ideal" adult to emulate from within their own families. (D077)

### Interaction in Family
Lower satisfaction with family relationships is positively and significantly related to the willingness to sacrifice to attain a higher-level occupation. (M060)

### Interaction with Family (Leisure)
Adolescents with upward mobility aspirations are likely to spend more time than are other adolescents in leisure activities with their families. (D077)

### Intermarriage
Intermarriage is more likely to take place where a drive toward upward social mobility is present than where it is absent. (B012)

### Juvenile Delinquency
Families of juvenile delinquents are less ambitious to improve either their own status or their children's status than are families of nondelinquents. (S210)

### Marriage Chances
The greater the desire of a second-generation American to attain a high socioeconomic class, the less likely he is to ever marry. (H203)

### Maternal Deprivation
Females aspiring toward upward mobility are no more likely than are female nonaspirants to perceive their relationships with their mothers as depriving. (R101)

### Maternal Role, Attitude Toward
Mothers with aspirations for upward mobility are less sure about the adequacy of their maternal-role performances than are nonaspiring mothers. (S280)

### Maternal-Role Definition
Mothers striving for upward mobility are less likely to accept the "service" aspects of the maternal role than are mothers more content with their social statuses. (S280)

### Mental Illness
Parents of middle-class mentally ill patients tend to exhibit social-status-striving behavior, and patients tend to behave in a like manner. (M061)

### Occupational Rank
The lower the occupational level of the husband or wife, the lower their mobility aspirations.

### Parent-Child Relations (Attention)
The more concerned the parents are with the social mobility of their children, the more likely they are to give inordinate attention to the only boy. (R129)

### Parent-Child Relations (Egalitarianism/Dependency)
Children who are upward aspirers are more likely to prefer equalitarian rather than dependent relations with their parents than are children who do not have mobility aspirations. (E102)

### Parent-Child Relations (Hostility)
Adolescents who have upward mobility aspirations show less hostility toward their parents than others do. (D077)

### Parent-Child Relations (Recreation)
Boys who aspire upward are more likely to share leisure activities with parents (and to come from warm, permissive family backgrounds). (L115)

### Parent/Peer Relations
A higher percentage of the working-class boys with aspirations and of the ambitious middle-class boys than of the unambitious middle-class or the nonaspiring working-class boys had been advised by one or both parents to enter the professions. (S077)

When parents advise high aspirations and the peer group does not, a higher percentage of both working-class and middle-class boys aspire to high-status occupations than when the peer group does and parents do not. (S077)

### Parent-Son Relations (Deprivation)
There is no relationship between mobility aspirations of males and their perception of their relationship with their parents as being depriving. (R101)

### Paternal-Role Definition X Mobility Aspiration
A high-status husband, who is already established socially and economically, has more time to spend around his home as compared with the "struggling to get ahead" man, who spends all his available time trying to achieve his goals.

The tendency for the established high-status man to be more family oriented is suggested also in the fact that high-status suburban husbands do a good deal around home. The man who struggles to get ahead does so at the expense of family participation.

### Size of Family
A restriction in the size of the family tends to occur among couples who have aspirations toward social mobility. (S064)

The larger the family, the lower the mobility aspirations of the children. (T096)

## SOCIAL MOBILITY ASPIRATIONS (OCCUPATION) X Homogamy
When the wife's family occupies a higher occupational level than does the husband's, he adopts high mobility aspirations in order to reach that same level.

## SOCIAL MOBILITY ASPIRATIONS OF CHILD X Education of Father
The higher the level of education of the father, the higher the level of mobility aspiration in the child. (T095)

### Education of Mother/Father X Mobility Aspiration of Child
The child is more likely to have mobility ambitions if the mother's educational level is higher than is the father's than if her educational level is less than or equal to his. (T096)

If the mother's educational level is higher than that of the father, the child's mobility aspirational level is higher. (T096)

**Occupation of Father**

Upwardly mobile aspirations among lower-class youths are accompanied by rejection of the paternal occupational role. (E102)

## SOCIAL MOBILITY ASPIRATIONS OF DAUGHTER        X   Father-Daughter Relations

Female mobility aspirants are more likely than are female nonaspirants to perceive their relationship with their fathers as depriving. (R101)

**Occupation of Father**

There is no relationship between the father's occupation and mobility aspirations of the daughter. (R101)

## SOCIAL MOBILITY ASPIRATIONS OF MOTHER        X   Mental Illness

In middle-class families of the mentally ill, mothers tended to have had frustrated mobility aspirations and were ambitious for the patients' social advancement. (M061)

**Mental Illness (Schizophrenia/Neurosis)**

Mothers of schizophrenics are more likely than are mothers of neurotics to have frustrated mobility aspirations and to be ambitious for the patients' social advancement. (M061)

## SOCIAL MOBILITY ASPIRATIONS OF PARENTS        X   Mental Illness (Manic-Depressive)

Manic-depressives are more likely to come from families in which the chief interest in the child is in his potential usefulness in improving the family's position or in meeting the parents' prestige needs. (C092)

## SOCIAL MOBILITY ASPIRATIONS OF SON        X   Occupation of Father

Sons of fathers with manual occupations have higher mobility aspirations than do sons of nonmanual fathers. (R101)

**Social Mobility Attitudes of Parents**

Among working-class families, there is a high positive relationship between the parents' attitudes concerning achievement-mobility and the sons' consequent achievement-mobility aspirations. (E102)

## SOCIAL MOBILITY ATTITUDES OF PARENTS        X   Social Mobility Aspirations of Son

Among working class-families, there is a high positive relationship between the parents' attitudes concerning achievement-mobility and the sons' consequent achievement-mobility aspirations. (E102)

## SOCIAL MOBILITY/OCCUPATION ASPIRATIONS OF SON        X   Size of Family

Family size has a greater effect on actual occupational mobility than on occupational aspirations, larger families having greater limitations for the actualization of high occupational aspirations. (E102)

## SOCIAL MOBILITY OF CHILDREN        X   Cohesion of Family

Family solidarity is not adversely affected by the upward social mobility of the family's children. (S220)

## SOCIAL MOBILITY OF DAUGHTER        X   Parent-Child Relations (Favoritism)

Parental favoritism of some child in the family is associated with upwardly mobile daughters. (E102)

## SOCIAL MOBILITY OF MOTHER        X   Child-Rearing Practices (Aggression)

Upwardly mobile mothers are more punitive with regard to aggression by their children than are nonmobile mothers. (S014)

**Feeding (Demand)**

There is a correlation between the use of self-demand feeding by mothers and upward mobility of mothers. (S014)

## SOCIAL MOBILITY OF SON        X   Mental Illness (Paranoia)

Paranoia is more likely to occur when the father of the patient is of a lower occupational rank than the patient. (N050)

**Work Attitudes of Father**

Paternal dissatisfaction with job is positively related to having an upwardly mobile son. (E102)

## SOCIAL MOBILITY OF WOMEN        X   Extended Family Ties

Mobile women have a weaker orientation to their extended family than do stable ones. (S272)

## SOCIAL MOBILITY PRESSURES        X   Identification with Parents

Parental pressure for social mobility on the part of the child tends later to disrupt the identification of the child with parental figures and to produce a basic emotional insecurity in the child. (M197)

**Parent-Child Relations (Guilt)**

Parental pressure for social mobility on the part of the child tends later to produce shame and guilt in the child about his parents' social status. (M197)

**Personality Problems of Child (Frustration)**

There is a correlation between the parents' pressure upon the child to be socially mobile and frustration in the child. (M197)

**Personality Problems of Child (Stress)**

Parents who pressure the child to be socially mobile, but who are financially unable to provide him with the higher education he desires cause emotional stress in the child. (M197)

## SOCIAL MOBILITY/SCHOLASTIC ACHIEVEMENT        X   Parent-Child Relations (Affect)

Emotionally impoverished parent-child relations are related more to extreme vertical and geographic mobility than to high scholastic achievement or to high achievement motivation in general. (E102)

## SOCIAL MOBILITY WITHIN FAMILY        X   Age-Groups

Age-groups occur when the structure of the family or descent group blocks the younger members from attaining social status within the family. (E102)

## SOCIAL NETWORK        X   Authority Structure of Family

The more dispersed a couple's network of social contacts, the more likely they are to stress the importance of joint decision making by husband and wife. (B268)

**Child-Rearing Practices (Permissiveness)**

Parents whose chief source of guidance is their relations with their contemporaries will be much more permissive in their child-rearing practices than will parents whose chief identifications are not with other people.

### Child-Rearing Values (Popularity)
Parents whose chief source of guidance is their relations with their contemporaries will place a much greater emphasis on their child's popularity within his peer group than will parents whose chief identifications are with other people.

### Class
The lower the couple's social class, the more likely it is that they have a relatively interconnected set of social contacts (i.e., their friends are in social relations with one another). (B267)

### Community Homogeneity
Tightly knit family friendship networks (i.e., a high frequency of interaction among family units) are more often found in communities that are homogeneous. (G156)

### Community Stability
Tightly knit family friendship networks (i.e., a high frequency of interaction among family units) are more often found in neighborhoods exhibiting a great deal of stability. (G156)

### Division of Labor by Sex
Husband and wife are more likely to divide responsibilities according to traditional sex roles when they reside in a tightly knit friendship network (i.e., a high frequency of interaction among family units) than in a loosely knit friendship network. (G156)

### Education
The higher the level of education of the family, the more likely it is that it has a relatively dispersed set of social contacts. (B267)

The higher the education of a couple, the less likely it is that social contacts with friends and neighbors will decrease as the marriage progresses. (K089)

### Geographic Mobility
Where there has been residential stability and husbands and wives continue to live in the same local area in which they have grown up, women tend to associate with women and men tend to associate with men. (B209)

The greater the family's physical mobility, the more likely it is that its network of social contacts is dispersed. (B267)

### Homogamy
The more opportunities a girl has to meet eligible marriage partners, the more likely she is to make a homogamous marriage. (K150)

### Husband-Wife Relations
The husband is more likely to see his friends independently of his wife when they reside in a closely knit friendship network (i.e., a high frequency of interaction among family units) than in a loosely knit friendship network. (G156)

The more married couples can count on an outside network of friends for aid, the less often they will have to turn to one another for help. (G156)

### Husband-Wife Relations (Compatibility)
When a high value is put on the compatibility of husband and wife, their extrafamilial contacts are more likely to be shared. (B209)

### Husband-Wife Relations (Consensus)
The more interconnected a couple's social network, the more likely it is that there will be consensus on family norms. (B268)

### Husband-Wife Relations (Emotional Intensity)
The more interconnected the couple's network of social contacts, the less intense is their emotional investment in the conjugal relationship. (B267)

### Husband-Wife Relations, Importance of
The more dispersed the couple's network of social contacts (i.e., its members do not see one another independently of the couple), the greater the stress placed upon conjugal privacy and the primacy of the conjugal relationship over all external ties. (B267)

### Husband-Wife Relations (Interaction)
Husband and wife tend to spend more time apart when residing in a family friendship network which is tightly knit (i.e., a high frequency of interaction among family units) than in one which is loosely knit. (G156)

### Husband-Wife Relations (Shared Activities)
Where relatives, neighbors, friends, and workmates tend to be the same people, the activities of spouses become separated. (G116)

Couples who belong to highly connected social networks (i.e., its members see one another independently of the couple) are less likely to stress shared interests and joint recreation. (B268)

### Illegitimacy
The unwed mother is more likely than the average mother to have lacked normal social and romantic contacts. (Y048)

### Interaction in Family
The more intraconjugal interaction is idealized and stressed, the more tense are relations between conjugal units likely to be. (C134)

### Interaction in Family (Emotional Intensity)
The more dispersed the activities of the family outside the home, the more intense are the feelings between the members of the family. (D058)

### Kin/Nonkin
Informal group association occurs more frequently among relatives than among friends, neighbors, or co-workers. (A002)

Kinfolk are more likely than any other group to be the major group about whom people build their visiting relationships. (H018)

### Kin/Nonkin Relations
The more highly connected the social network to which a couple belongs (i.e., its members see one another independently of the couple), the greater the expectation that the wife has many relationships with their relatives and the husband with their friends. (B268)

### Kin Ties
There is a positive relationship between aid from family members and the divorcée's claim that she has some or many opportunities to meet people. (G157)

### Marital Adjustment
Sociable couples are more likely to be adjusted in marriage than are unsociable couples. (L004)

There is no relationship between the husband's social

activity and marital adjustment; but in poorly rated marriages, spouses shared fewer activities and the social activities of the wives were significantly reduced. (P086)

### Occupational Rank
Divorcées from upper occupational strata are no more likely than are those from lower strata to have divorced persons in their friendship circles. (G157)

### Parent-Child Relations (Affect)
Limited social relations with nonfamily or extended family members may lead to a heightening of the child's emotional relations with his parents.

### Power Structure of Family
Importance of joint decisionmaking by husbands and wives increases with the looseness of family networks (i.e., the friends of the wife and husband are not friends of one another). (B210)

### Rank
The social rank of the individual will be directly correlated with the range of social and economic ties which he establishes beyond his immediate family. (W064)

### Residence
Closely knit networks (i.e., the members are friends of one another, not only through the husband or wife) are most likely to develop when husband and wife, together with their friends, neighbors, and relatives, have grown up in the same local area and have continued to live there after marriage. (B209)

The greater the extent to which a couple's friends and relatives live in the same local area as they do, the more likely it is that the couple's social network is interconnected (i.e., those in the network see one another independently of the couple). (B268)

If the husband has an occupation where his colleagues tend also to be his neighbors, it is more likely that the couple has an interconnected network of social contacts; if not, they are likely to have a more dispersed network (i.e., those in it do not see one another independently of the couple). (B267)

The more homogeneous and stable the neighborhood in which the couple lives, the more likely it is that they will have an interconnected network of social contacts (i.e., those in the network see one another independently of the couple). (B267)

### Role Definition
The more interconnected a couple's social network (i.e., its members associate with one another), the more likely it is that the wive's obligations to her mother and to her husband will come into conflict. (B268)

### Role Definition in Family
Lower-class families with closely-knit networks (that is, where friends, relatives, and neighbors all tend to know each other) are more likely to differentiate clearly between instrumental and expressive roles, while a middle-class family with loosely-knit networks would not be as apt to show such a differentiation. (B268)

### Role Definition of Husband/Wife
The greater the extent to which a couple belongs to a highly interconnected social network (i.e., its members see one another independently of the couple from which they can draw help, the more likely it is that the conjugal roles are rigidly segregated. (B268)

The more dispersed a couple's network of social contacts (i.e., its members do not see one another independently of the couple), the more likely they are to be uncertain about the norms pertaining to the rights and duties of the husband and wife. (B268)

Couples with loosely-knit social networks (i.e., friends of husband and wife are not friends of one another) are more likely to develop less differentiated role definitions and activity than are couples with closely knit social networks. (S216)

### Sexual Adjustment
The more dispersed a couple's network of social contacts (i.e., its members do not see one another independently of the couple), the greater the emphasis they will place on successful sexual relations. (B268)

### Sexual Aggression
When premarital contact is severely restricted, the incidence of sexual aggression will tend to be high. (T041)

### Superego Formation
Internalization of parental values is more necessary for social control in a society characterized by loosely knit than by closely knit social networks (tight network means that the friends of the husband and wife are friends of one another). (S216)

## SOCIAL NETWORK OF HUSBAND/WIFE
### X   Divorce, Attitude Toward
The wife's friends and family are much more likely to feel strong approval of the divorce than are the husband's friends, but this does not hold for mild approval. (G157)

### Marriage, Approval of
The divorcée's family members are more likely to have expressed disapproval prior to the marriage than are her husband's family members. (G157)

The divorcé's friends are more likely to have expressed mild or strong disapproval prior to the marriage than are the husband's friends. (G157)

Both the divorcée's family and her husband's family had more definitive opinions prior to the marriage than did their respective friends, who were more likely to have been indifferent. (G157)

### Maternal Role, Attitude Toward
The more dispersed the couple's social network (i.e., its members do not see one another independently of the couple), the more likely it is that the wife will feel some dissatisfaction with the maternal role. (B267)

## SOCIAL NETWORK OF MOTHER
### X   Mental Illness (Schizophrenia)
Mothers of schizophrenics frequently have little or no social life because they feel they should always be available when the child wants them. (K093)

## SOCIAL NETWORK OF PARENTS
### X   Child-Rearing Practices
The more dispersed a couple's network of social contacts, the more likely they are to be self-conscious about methods of bringing up their children. (B268)

### Mental Illness
There is a negative correlation between mental illness and the number of individuals perceived as important to the parents or to one parent. (L126)

## SOCIAL OPPORTUNITIES        X  Dating
Divorcées who receive help from both friends and family in meeting people have a higher dating frequency than do those who receive help from either friends or family, followed by those who receive help from neither group. (G157)

When the divorcée both wishes to remarry and claims many opportunities to meet people, her frequency of dating is maximized. (G157)

### Remarriage
Divorcées who claim opportunities to meet people are more likely to feel there is someone among their male friends they would consider marrying than do divorcées who claim no opportunities. (G157)

## SOCIAL RELATIONS, CLOSENESS OF
### X  Kin/NonKin Ties
Consanguinity, per se, produces stronger feelings of closeness among individuals than any other type of relationship. (C093)

## SOCIAL RELATIONS OF CHILD
### X  Paternal/Maternal-Role Definition
The more the child interacts with people before the age of six, the more he tends to impute punitiveness to the father role and nurturance to the mother. (K097)

## SOCIAL RELATIONS OF PARENTS
### X  Maternal Overprotectiveness
Maternal overprotection is associated with a lesser amount of social life of the parent.

## SOCIAL STRUCTURE        X  Abortion
Societies in which abortion is culturally imposed, especially punitively, tend to be those which lack alternative outlets for neurotic tensions and anxieties. (D071)

### Economic Level
When the economic pattern is not sufficiently productive or permanent of locale to support large concentrations of population or stable settlement, the sociopolitical organization will remain basically along kinship lines. (M033)

### Economic Pattern
The organization of a society on a suprafamilial level occurs as a direct response to a change in the economic pattern. (S111)

### Incest Taboo
The extension of incest taboos is correlated either with an increase in complexity of social structure or with a higher degree of integration. (L130)

### Inheritance
Differences in inheritance systems tend to cause changes in social and economic structures. (H066)

### Legal Responsibility
Societies which are organized around the anchorage and identification of the individual in the wider kin-group have legal systems based on the principle of joint liability (i.e., if an offender cannot be apprehended or meet his legal liability, his liability falls on the members of his descent group); societies organized around the anchorage and identification of the individual in the nuclear family have legal systems based on the principle of several liability (i.e., the individual alone is held responsible and punished for his acts). (C093)

### Polyandry
An egalitarian social structure and a situation in which the sexes have equal status within the family are conducive to polyandry. (S068)

### Subsistence Pattern (Agriculture)
When the economic level is that of an isolated farming community, the family tends to be the fundamental social grouping in the society. (W055)

## SOCIAL STRUCTURE (DIFFERENTIATION)
### X  Conflict in Adolescence
The extent to which adolescence is a period of tension and conflict is directly correlated with the structural complexity of the society. (W113)

### Economic Level
Where a stable food supply permits the establishment of good-sized permanent communities, an elaboration of the social structure occurs. (M033)

### Functions of Family
The loss of the family's function is correlated with the increased specialization of the roles and functions in the society at large. (A047)

### Men's Societies
Men's societies tend to occur in societies which are simple and relatively undifferentiated. (M067)

### Sibling Rank
The social equivalence of siblings is more likely to be found in societies with simple social structures. (R069)

### Size of Ethnic Group
The elaboration of the social structure will be directly correlated with the size of the ethnic group. (S121)

### Size of Family
The smaller size of the family unit is correlated with increased specialization of the roles and functions in society at large. (A047)

## SOCIAL STRUCTURE (HETEROGENEITY)
### X  Kin Ties
The attenuation of kin ties tends to occur in societies which have high degrees of cultural and social heterogeneity. (L072)

## SOCIAL STRUCTURE (HOMOGENEITY)
### X  Divorce
Cultural homogeneity of the population appears to be correlated with a low divorce rate, while heterogeneity seems to be associated with a high rate. (B033)

### Kin Ties (Fictive)
Patterns of fictive kinship function most effectively in societies which are of homogeneous character. (A029)

### Kinship, Importance of
Where the society is characterized by a high degree of social and cultural homogeneity role relationships tend to be defined by kinship. (L072)

## SOCIAL STRUCTURE (KIN-BASED)
### X  Industrialization
Family-centered social organizations tend to disintegrate with industrialization and mobility and with the economic independence of women. (B033)

## SOCIAL STRUCTURE (MATRILINY)
### X  Puberty Ceremonies (Male)
Male puberty ceremonies are less likely to occur in matrilineal societies. (W154)

## SOCIAL STRUCTURE, RIGIDITY OF
### X   Kin Terminology (Unilineal)
Lineage terminology systems tend to be associated with rigid social structures. (S080)

## SOCIAL V. ECONOMIC RANK    X   Conformity
The "social" component of socioeconomic status (i.e., parental education) shows a stronger inverse correlation with boys' compliance with authority than does the economic component (Berkeley Social Rating Scale). (T100)

## SOCIAL WELFARE
### X   Emotional Problems of Child
Children with emotional problems are more likely to belong to families which receive public financial assistance. (B290)

### Nuclear Family
A predominance of small family units in a society is associated with a greater abundance of social agencies to take care of the disabled, ill, and aged. (G156)

### Size of Household
Public assistance increases the likelihood that the aged will be kept within the kin residence, thus increasing the size of the residential unit.

## SOCIALIZATION    X   Psychopathy
Children who lack the opportunity to internalize the values of parent-figures are more likely than others to become psychopaths. (W143)

### Superego Formation
There is a negative correlation between the age at which conscious socialization is begun and the strength of guilt feelings. (W142)

## SOCIALIZATION, AGE OF
### X   Religion, Role of Deities
The earlier the age of socialization, the greater the degree to which supernatural punishment is viewed as not contingent on good behavior. (S036)

### Socialization, Severity of
The earlier the age at which conscious socialization begins, the more severe the socialization. (W142)

## SOCIALIZATION, AGENTS OF
### X   Cohesion of Family
Collective responsibility for education and socialization welds the various relationships of the family firmly together. (M019)

### Father-Child Relations
Girls are more likely to show positive attitudes toward the father when the parents *are* the main socializing agents than when they are not. Boys show no differences in this respect. (R089)

### Legal Responsibility
In societies in which the children are brought up by their parents as well as by members of the children's descent group, the conception of joint liability will be found (i.e., liability falls on the members of an individual's descent group if the offender cannot be apprehended or meet his legal liability); in societies in which the children are brought up by their parents plus *nonmembers* of the children's descent group, the concept of several liability

will be found (i.e., the individual alone is held responsible and punished for his acts). (C093)

### Mother-Child Relations
Boys are more likely to show positive attitudes toward the mother when the parents *are not* the main socializing agents than when they are. Girls show no differences in this respect. (R089)

### Parent-Child Relations (Affection)
Children whose parents are not their main socializing agents are more likely to show clearly positive attitudes toward their families than are children whose parents are the main socializing agents. (R089)

### Parent-Child Relations (Guilt)
The less guilt the child experiences in repudiating parental loyalties, the more able is he to accept values from other persons. (A059)

### Race
Factors external to the family are more likely to play roles in the socialization of the Negro child than of the white child (U.S.). (L124)

### Superego Formation
There is a low positive correlation between the importance of parents in the society, as opposed to nonrelatives and specialists, as agents of socialization of the child and the development of guilt feelings, as measured by the patient's responsibility for his illness. (W142)

### Therapeutic Practices
The degree of importance of the parents, as opposed to other persons, as agents of socialization is not related to the extent to which a society employs intropunitive therapy (bloodletting, sacrifice) for illness. (K111)

## SOCIALIZATION ANXIETY    X   Art
There is a correlation between the degree of socialization anxiety characteristic of a society and the complexity of design of that society's art. (K111)

### Illness, Explanation of
In any society, the greater the customary anxiety concerning socialization in any area of behavior, the more likely it is that illness will be thought to be associated with that area. (W142)

### Superego Formation
The higher the average degree of socialization anxiety in any society, the greater the development of guilt feelings (as measured by the patient's feeling of responsibility for his own physical illness). (W142)

## SOCIALIZATION, EFFECTIVENESS OF
### X   Child-Rearing Practices
The greater the use of the socializing techniques which appeal to forces internal to the child's need system, the greater the internalization of moral standards. (H208)

The more frequent the use of external coercive devices, the more likely the child is to develop a moral orientation based upon fear of authority. (H208)

### Child-Rearing Practices (Aggression)
Resistance to temptation by the child is not correlated with severity toward control of aggression by parents. (G120)

### Child-Rearing Practices (Authoritarianism)
The rigidity and superficiality of authoritarian rules of discipline make less likely their internalization by the child. (M203)

### Child-Rearing Practices (Clarity)
The more explicit the standards, the more likely it is that the child will internalize the values of the socializing agent. (A058)

### Child-Rearing Practices (Consistency)
Child training is more easily attained when parental demands toward children are consistent. (M058)

Effective socialization of the child is correlated with orderly, consistent, patient behavior on the part of the parent. (M203)

### Child-Rearing Practices (Control)
Closer supervision and home ties in girls produce a greater consciousness of the status and values held by the family than is found in boys. (P069)

### Child-Rearing Practices (Demands)
The higher the level of demands and restrictions imposed by parents upon children, the more likely it is that the children will resist temptation. (G120)

### Child-Rearing Practices (Nurturance/Clarity)
Given a minimal level of nurturance, effectiveness of socialization is not increased by additional nurturance but is produced by increasing explicitness of standards. (M183)

### Child-Rearing Practices (Obedience)
The higher the level of obedience enforced by parents upon children, the more likely it is that the children will resist temptation. (G120)

Effective socialization of the child is more likely if automatic obedience, rather than positive rewards or reasoning, is stressed by parents. (M203)

### Child-Rearing Practices (Power)
The greater the use of unqualified power by the parent, the less likely is the child's internalization of controls and the more likely is his compliance on the basis of expediency or fear. (H182)

### Child-Rearing Practices (Punishment)
The disciplinary technique of denying love is more likely than physical punishment to keep the child oriented toward parental socialization goals. (G120)

Nonphysical discipline tends to be less effective in child training than physical discipline. (M058)

### Child-Rearing Practices (Restrictiveness)
If the parents are restrictive, the child is more likely to internalize parental values and more likely to resist temptation. (G118)

### Child-Rearing Practices (Severity)
A curvilinear relationship exists between the severity of demands and restrictions made by parents upon the child and the adequacy of socialization of the child. (M203)

### Child-Rearing Practices (Sex)
The higher the pressure by parents on children against overt sexual behavior, the more likely it is that the children will resist temptation. (G120)

### Extended/Nuclear Family
The Western family, particularly the American (nuclear) family, should be more effective in the functions of early socialization and tension reduction than should classical Western families or families found in pre-industrial and-/or nonliterate societies. (P083)

### Father-Son Relations (Warmth)
The warmer and more rewarding the total father-son relationship, the greater the likelihood of internalization and acceptance of parental values. (S216)

### Generational Emphasis
The adequate learning of social roles requires that there not be a confusion of the generations between parents and children (e.g., a father who acts as the son of his wife).

### Husband-Wife Relations (Communication)
Defective communication between the mother and father is likely to lessen the child's opportunity to learn to internalize the respective role systems in the family. (L121)

### Identification/Child-Rearing Practices
The child's imitation of the parental model correlates not with identification with (internalization of) parents' attitudes, but with the process of learning through differential reinforcement of his behavior. (B234)

### Identification with Adult Kin
The more the child identifies with adult relatives, the more the child acquires the desired roles and goals of his society. (G044)

### Identification with Like-Sex Parent
Conscience development (effectiveness of socialization) in the child is not necessarily associated with intensity of identification with the same-sex parent. (K103)

### Identification with Parents
Children who identify with the parent are more likely to accept the parent's moral, cognitive, and expressive standards, and thus the standards of the larger society. (B234)

### Marital Stability
An unstable marital relationship will impair the role coordination which is necessary for effective child rearing. (S205)

### Mother-Child Relations (Warmth)
The mother's warmth is not correlated with resistance to temptation in boys, but it is negatively correlated with such resistance in girls. (G120)

### Parent-Child Relations (Closeness)
The more the child is exposed to his parents and, consequently, free from intervening structural ties, the more able are the parents to impose their personalities on the child. (C093)

### Parent-Child Relations (Warmth)
Children whose parents are warm and nurturant are more likely to resist temptation than are those whose parents are not. (G120)

### Race Attitudes
Due to inadequate indentification with the parents, prejudiced persons are less likely to internalize values and standards than are unprejudiced persons. (A061)

### Size of Family
The number of children in the family correlates with the adequate socialization of the child. (M203)

### Value Commitment of Parents
The greater the internalization of values on the part of the parents, the more likely the effective socialization of the child. (M203)

### Weaning
Resistance to temptation correlates with severity of weaning in boys, but not in girls. (G120)

## SOCIALIZATION (GRATIFICATION)
### X   Therapeutic Practices
The more that custom prescribes progressive satisfaction of the child in any system of behavior, the more likely it is that customary therapeutic practices relative to illness will include an activity characteristic of that system. (W142)

## SOCIALIZATION OF CHILD
### X   Extended/Nuclear Family
The socialization of children takes longer in a nuclear family system than in an extended kin network system. (P062)

## SOCIALIZATION, SEVERITY OF      X   Anxiety
There is a correlation between the severity of socialization imposed upon the child in any system of behavior and the degree of anxiety and concern regarding that system in later life (Negative fixation). (W142)

### Socialization, Age of
The earlier the age at which conscious socialization begins, the more severe the socialization. (W142)

## SOCIOPATHIC PERSONALITY
### X   Child-Rearing Practices (Punishment)
Parents of those with sociopathic personalities use harsh discipline significantly *less* frequently than do parents of normals, but parents of the former do not differ from parents of individuals with other disorders. (O032)

### Child-Rearing Practices (Supervision)
There is a correlation between lack of maternal supervision and the development of sociopathic personality in the child. (O032)

### Divorce
It is more likely that boys with sociopathic personalities have parents who are divorced (or have been divorced before marrying) than boys with no mental problems or boys with other mental problems. (O032)

### Father-Son Relations (Physical Abuse)
Physical abuse by the father is not related to the development of sociopathic personality in the son. (O032)

### Mother-Child Relations (Rejection)
Rejection and other maternal behavior do not appear as important in determining sociopathic personality as in other psychiatric illnesses. (O032)

### Parent-Child Relations (Affection)
There is no relationship between cold and withdrawn parental behavior and the development of sociopathic personality in the child. (O033)

### Parent-Child Relations (Rejection)
Failure to supervise, repudiation by the parent, and desertion are more common among patients with sociopathic behavior disorder than among those with other diseases and those with no disease. Nonsupport and negligence are more common among parents of those diagnosed sociopathic personalities than among parents of the no-disease group, but not among parents of patients with other psychiatric diseases. (O032)

There is an association between rejection by the parent and development of sociopathic personality in the child. (O032)

Lack of parental love and interest and excessive leniency are not related to the later development of sociopathic personality in the child. (O032)

### Parent Loss
Among those who suffered parental loss, a much higher proportion of sociopaths than of neurotics were deprived before the age of five. (G140)

Sociopaths are much more likely to have suffered parental loss than are neurotics or controls. (G140)

## SOCIOPATHIC PERSONALITY OF CHILD
### X   Sociopathic Personality of Father
Patients with sociopathic problems were more likely to have sociopathic fathers than nonsociopathic fathers. (O032)

## SOCIOPATHIC PERSONALITY OF FATHER
### X   Sociopathic Personality of Child
Patients with sociopathic problems were more likely to have sociopathic fathers than nonsociopathic fathers. (O032)

## SOCIOPATHIC PERSONALITY OF SON
### X   Desertion by Father
There is a correlation between desertion by the father and sociopathic personality in the son. (O032)

### Father-Son Relations (Warmth)
There is a negative correlation between coldness on the part of the father and sociopathic personality in the son. (O032)

## SPEECH DEVELOPMENT      X   Breast Feeding
There is no relationship between the age at which a child learns to talk and bottle or breast feeding. (S200)

### Identification
There is a correlation between the presence of an adult identification model and the development of language in the child. (Y045)

### Institutional Care
The aspect of behavior of institutionalized babies which is most adversely affected is speech, with the ability to express being more retarded than is the ability to understand. (B270)

## SPEECH PROBLEMS      X   Authoritarianism
Children with articulation problems are more likely to view their parents as authoritarian than are children without articulation problems. (F095)

### Mother Absence
Maternal deprivation is more likely to retard the ability to speak than it is to retard neuromuscular activity. (B270)

### Toilet Training
Children with articulation problems are more likely to have been toilet trained at an earlier age than are children without articulation problems. (F095)

### Weaning

Children with articulation problems are more likely to have been weaned at an earlier age than are children without articulation problems. (F095)

## SPIRITUAL BEINGS
### X   Child-Rearing Practices (Aggression)

Societies with severe training in the control of aggression and which also believe that spirits cause illness are more likely to classify the spirits as animal rather than human. (W127)

## STABILITY OF CLAN      X   Functions of Clan

The disintegration of the clan structure is directly correlated with its loss of traditional political, judicial, and economic functions. (W082)

### Kin Terminology (Classificatory)

With the decline of the clan system and the parallel decline in the knowledge and use of kinship terminology, classificatory terms tend to be used in place of former descriptive or specific terms. (L031)

### Kin Terminology (Collateral)

The disintegration of the clan system is reflected in the loss of kinship terminology for collateral relatives. (B107)

### Kin Ties

The disintegration of the clan organization tends to accompany the weakening of kin ties. (G072)

### Population

The fission of clans or other unilinear kin-groups tends to occur with population expansion. (M020)

## STABILITY OF COMMUNITY
### X   Descent/Residence

In unilineally organized societies in which the mode of postmarital residence is not the same as is the mode of reckoning descent, local groupings in such societies will be unstable. (T080)

## STABILITY OF EXTENDED FAMILY
### X   Acculturation

The disintegration of the extended family is directly correlated with the degree of acculturation. (B093)

### Cohesion of Kin-Group

With the breakup of the extended family, a weakening of kinship ties in general will occur. (G072)

### Conflict in Kin-Group

Conflict within the extended family will tend to lead to its fission. (P029)

### Death of Father

Fission of the extended family is not likely to occur until the death of the father. (G072)

### Descent/Residence

When residence and descent patterns are not congruent the extended family will tend to break up upon the death of the head. (M050)

### Economic Conditions

The fission of an extended family tends to be directly correlated with economic pressures. (B086)

Adverse economic conditions will tend to hasten the fissioning of the extended family group. (W031)

### Economic Cooperation

The differentials in labor power that each family supplies to the common household are a major cause of fission of the extended family household. (R012)

### Economic Dependence

The disintegration of the extended family is directly correlated with the increasing economic independence of the individual. (O023)

### Economic Dependence of Children

Division of the extended family is more likely if the son is financially independent. (H052)

### Economic Pattern (Mercantile)

Under the impact of change from a feudal to a mercantile economic system, the patrilocal extended family is disintegrating as a permanent residential unit. (G028)

### Economic Pattern (Wage Labor)

Wage labor and opportunity for work outside the village may in themselves cause the breakdown of the extended family. (R012)

### Economic Rank

The larger the amount of land or other wealth to support it, the greater the stability of the extended family household. (G156)

When the father of an extended family is landless or extremely poor, fission of the extended family is more likely to occur. (R012)

### Housing (Urban)

The housing facilities of the urban community tend to result in the physical dislocation of the extended family. (A013)

### Inheritance

Where siblings receive an unequal proportion of family estate, there is a greater tendency for the extended family to divide. (A033)

When the system of inheritance designates an equal share for all sons, fission of the extended family is inevitable when the holdings in land are too small to support each of the sons independently. (R012)

### Inheritance (Primogeniture)

Primogeniture, as a mode of inheritance, tends to produce fission within the extended family. (S090)

### Kin-Role Behavior

Fission of the extended family is more likely to occur if members of the kin unit receive differential treatment. (H086)

### Kin Terminology

The inaccurate application of kin terminology is indicative of the disintegration of the extended family. (C049)

### Leadership

The fission of a large extended family will tend to be inhibited if the leader is a person of character and experience. (A033)

### Opportunity Structure

The better able it is to offer adequate opportunity to the younger generation, the greater the stability of the extended family household. (G156)

### Political and Economic Role of Extended Family

The disintegration of the extended family will occur with the loss of its political and economic function. (O023)

### Political Role of Extended Family
The loss of the political function has a more disintegrative effect on the extended family than does the loss of the economic function. (O023)

### Population
With an increase in population and pressure upon the land or other resources available for economic exploitation, extended families commonly split, sending off branches which migrate and settle elsewhere. (M019)

### Power Structure of Family
Power rivalries within the extended family group tend to accelerate the process of fissioning within the nuclear unit. (W031)

### Property
When an equitable division of family property between sons would result in an area of land too small to support a conjugal family, the sons will tend to remain together in a single household after the death of their father. (A013)

The extended family will tend to remain intact as an economic and social unit if it retains control of village land. (G028)

### Religion
Conversion to Islam tends to result in the weakening of the extended family. (G072)

### Residence
The proportion of individuals living alone is indicative of the weakness of the extended family pattern. (L064)

### Sibling Ties
Fission of the extended family tends to be resisted if the brothers are uterine rather than half-siblings. (W056)

### Size of Extended Family
Fission of the extended family is more likely to occur if the unit is large in size. (G072)

The fission of the extended family after the death of its head will be delayed if the group is small in size. (S041)

### Urbanization
Urban migration with industrialization is a second major factor involved in the disorganization of the Chinese extended family. (B033)

## STABILITY OF EXTENDED FAMILY (PATRILINEAL) X Values
Cultures which stress the virtue of harmony, balance, the cult of the esthetic, and a respect for the world as it is are more congenial to the stability of the patrilinear extended family. (P083)

## STABILITY OF FAMILY     X Acculturation
Families which are marginal to both unacculturated and acculturated groups tend to be restless, unsatisfied, unpredictable, and psychologically unstable. (B034)

### Acculturation Anxiety
Acculturative anxiety resulting from the contact situation tends to result in an unstable family structure. (S090)

### Authority Structure of Family
The authoritarian family structure is more likely to be stable when the children and the wife accept the authority position of the father than when they do not accept paternal authority as legitimate. (K030)

### Descent (Matrilineal)
In matrilineal systems wives and children belong to another descent group than that of the husband-father and this leads to some degree of instability in the household, for a woman is not bound to her husband by his control over her children. (C090)

### Economic Role of Men/Women
Instability of the family is likely to occur when either the male or female plays a disproportionate role in the economy. (W154)

### Fertility
Fertility decreases as family instability increases. (D055)

### Geographic Mobility
The family tends to be extremely unstable where the population is mobile (in the sense that it has no roots more than a generation deep in a given place). (A014)

### Inheritance
The stability of the family is more likely to be preserved if the father is not permitted to leave his property to his favorite. (H124)

### Land
The stability of the farm family during a crisis is directly correlated with the degree of its attachment to the land. (B033)

### Loss of Family Member
The effects of the final loss (either psychologically or physically) of a family member will be more severe if similar losses have occurred before. (T089)

The effects of the final loss (either psychologically or physically) of a family member will be more severe the longer it takes for the family to find a substitute. (T089)

### Occupation
The night shift is probably less favorable to family stability than is the day shift. (P083)

The occupational lives of the waitress, the furniture mover, and the trucker are probably not favorable to family stability. (P083)

### Polyandry
Polyandry permits the husband to be absent for a long period of time while maintaining the security of wife and family. A brother can protect a common wife or may even move into the household. (B205)

### Power Structure of Family
An equalitarian family, in which both husband and wife attempt to play a dominant role, is associated with lack of effective socialization for internal stability of the family. (S205)

### Preferential Marriage (Levirate/Sororate)
The elementary family tends to be much more stable under the sororate and levirate since the death of any one member does not disrupt the equilibrium of the family structure. (W129)

### Property
Family organization tends to be fairly stable when the members hold their land as property. (A014)

### Religion
The influence of religion is a significant factor in the stabilization of the family. (B033)

### Religion (Ancestor Cult)
An ancestor cult has a stabilizing influence on the family unit. (K092)

### Residence (Owned/Rented)
Homeowner families are more stable than are tenant families. (C009)

### Ritual in Family
Parents who think of their family as stable are the most likely to initiate and continue family ritual. (B206)

### Role Definition in Family
If one parent assumes the High Status Authority role vis-à-vis the child (Low Status Subordinate) and the other spouse does not take the role of High Status Friend, tension within the family will increase unless the High Status Friend role is filled by statuses outside the family (i.e., clergyman or psychiatrist).

If one parent takes the role of High Status Authority and the other takes the role of High Status Friend, tension develops in the triad relationship with Low Status Subordinate (because the husband-wife relationship must remain positive for the marriage to survive).

Looking at the family in terms of the triad of roles, High Status Authority, Low Status Subordinate and High Status Friend, the amount of tension produced by the interaction between a given High Status Authority and a given Low Status Subordinate is directly proportional to the difference in status between the High Status Authority and the Low Status Subordinate.

There is more balance in the family system where the relationship between High Status Authority and High Status Friend is negative.

If the relationship between High Status Friend and Low Status Subordinate in a family remains positive, pressure is likely to be exerted to change the relationship of High Status Authority and Low Status Subordinate from negative to positive, creating a sentimental congruence in which all relationships are positive.

If, in a family, the relationship between High Status Authority and the Low Status Subordinate remains negative, pressure is exerted to change the relationship from High Status Friend and Low Status Subordinate from positive to negative, creating a sentimental congruence in which one negative relationship is balanced by another.

### Social Control
Family instability occurs in an area where social control is reduced to a minimum and individual self-expression is increased to a maximum. (B033)

### Structure of Family
Among members of the lower class, a female-centered consanguinous household is more stable than is either a consensual or a legal union. (R124)

### Urban/Rural
Family instability is more likely among urban population than among rural population. (L024)

### Urbanization
The stability of the rural family decreases with the increase in urban influences. (B033)

The degree of urbanization tends to be inversely correlated with the stability of the elementary family. (L064)

### Values (Individualism)
Individualism is incompatible with the survival of the family.

## STABILITY OF FAMILY STATUS   X   Urban/Rural
The economic and social conditions of rural life place more of a premium on continuity of occupation and status from generation to generation than do urban conditions. (P012)

## STABILITY OF FAMILY STRUCTURE
### X   Acculturation
Cultural assimilation tends to be accelerated when familial institutions are changed. (S046)

Cultural features which are associated with the family tend to be more resistant to acculturation. (S111)

### Authority Structure of Family
The greater the structural stability of the family, the more likely it is that headship and dominance (formal and real leadership) coincide. (S211)

### Class
Changes in family norms and behavior are less prevalent in the elite than in the rank and file. (T013)

### Ecological Conditions
The patriarchal family structure tends to deteriorate when the geographical environment permits family self-sufficiency. (N014)

### Legal Status of Women
The breakdown of the family structure is reflected in an increase in litigation over women. (L079)

### Sex-Role Definition
The faster the rate of change in family patterns and models, the greater the ambivalence toward the position of women in the family. (K099)

### Urban/Rural
Changes in the family structure are occurring more rapidly in cities than in villages. (B033)

### Urbanization
Traditional patterns of family life and marriage tend to disintegrate under urban pressures. (H107)

## STABILITY OF FAMILY SYSTEM   X   Acculturation
The disintegration of the family system is accelerated by the adoption of external cultural values. (B043)

Acculturation tends to result in the breakdown of the traditional family system. (S135)

Cultural assimilation tends to be accelerated when familial institutions are changed. (S046)

### Sexual Permissiveness
Greater freedom in sexual relations threatens breakdown of the family system. (S171)

### Stability of Family Unit
Rates of instability in family units may vary independently of rates of instability in the family system. (G134)

## STABILITY OF FAMILY UNIT
### X   Stability of Family System
Rates of instability in family units may vary independently of rates of instability in the family system. (G134)

## STABILITY OF JOINT FAMILY     X   Acculturation
The joint family structure tends to deteriorate with increasing acculturation. (M081)

### Geographic Mobility
The breakdown of joint families tends to occur in the urban context as a consequence of the demands of physical mobility in an industrial labor force. (M021)

The joint family tends to break down when migration and settlement in a new area is by individuals and not by large blocks of patrilineal relatives. (M021)

### Housing (Urban)
The joint family tends to disappear in urban areas as a consequence of housing conditions. (M021)

### Property Ownership (Corporate)
The corporate ownership of landed estates tends to stabilize and strengthen the joint family. (M021)

### Values (Traditional)
The joint family tends to disappear when the ideology which supports it is undermined. (M021)

## STABILITY OF KIN-GROUP
### X   Conflict in Kin-Group
Fission within the kin-group tends to result as a consequence of internal conflict. (P020)

### Descent
The importance of descent is directly correlated with the stability of the kin-group. (S098)

### Descent (Bilateral)
In bilateral descent systems, there is no enduring kinship-group structure. (S080)

### Economic Rank
The stability of the kin-group is directly correlated with its economic status. (H165)

### Exogamy
The stability of the kin-group tends to be reinforced by patterns of group exogamy. (M137)

### Genealogy, Importance of
Genealogies will tend to have greater importance when the group is mobile and expanding. (B147)

### Geographic Mobility
The disintegration of the kinship groupings tends to be accelerated with migration. (B064)

### Inheritance
The rigidity or stability of inheritance patterns tends to be contingent upon the stability of the social grouping. (G038)

### Kin Terminology (Generation)
Generational terminology tends to be found in societies in which kin groupings are characterized by flexibility and plasticity. (S106)

### Land Ownership
Descent groups are more likely to be stable and increase in size if membership gives rights to land as well as to social status. (N071)

### Non-Kin Relations
Since the groups based on kinship are "small and unstable" the need for extrakinship alliances is understandable. (C094)

### Population
An increase in population may result in the deterioration of the kin-group. (F069)

### Rank of Kin-Group
Fission is more likely to occur among kin-groups of high status. (S140)

### Religion (Ritual)
A disintegration of kinship units tends to accompany the destruction of ceremonial life. (B049)

### Residence (Neolocal)
Kin-groups will tend to disintegrate as conditions come to favor neolocal residence. (G029)

Any influence which tends to undermine or inhibit large local aggregations of kinsmen will create conditions favorable to neolocal residence. (M019)

### Role Definition
An explicit definition of role, combined with a complex system of interrelated sanctions, will serve to insure the maintenance of standards of performance between kinsmen and the stability of the kinship unit. (P012)

### Size of Kin-Group
The stability of the kin-group is directly correlated with its size. (H165)

The formation of larger kin-groups under a pattern of bilateral descent tends to result in a highly unstable social group. (S097)

### Size of Nuclear Family
Stability of the kin-group decreases with size of family nucleus. (F082)

### Social Mobility
The disintegration of kinship units tends to occur when the economic pattern necessitates social and spatial mobility. (G056)

### Stratification
A necessary corollary of the class-structure social system is a breakdown, at least in part, of organization on a clan or familial basis. (S048)

### Subsistence Pattern (Agriculture)
The stability of residential descent groups will increase with the adoption of an agricultural pattern which focuses on a stable crop. (S282)

### Warfare
Under conditions of warfare, kinship alignments and local groupings tend to be unstable. (F010)

## STABILITY OF KIN STRUCTURE
### X   Descent-Residence, Consistency of
The degree of social stability is directly correlated with the congruity between descent and residence patterns. (H112)

## STABILITY OF KINSHIP STRUCTURE
### X   Acculturation
The kinship structure tends to disintegrate with increasing acculturation. (P044)

### Age at Marriage
Changes in the kinship structure tend to be retarded if there is a long span between generations (i.e., men marry late). (T058)

### Exogamy
The kinship structure tends to disintegrate with the violation of exogamic restrictions. (R067)

### Geographic Mobility
The structure of the kinship system will be weakened by the migration of men to other areas as laborers. (W056)

### Intermarriage (Ethnic)
The disintegration of the traditional kinship system is directly correlated with an increase in the rate of intermarriage. (H062)

The adoption of elements of the kinship structure of another group is more likely to occur when there is a high incidence of intermarriage between ethnic groups. (H080)

### Kin Terminology
Kinship terminology tends to be inconsistently applied with the deterioration of the kinship structure. (R034)

### Population
The kinship structure will tend to deteriorate with a decrease in population. (R067)

### Residence
The development, disappearance, or change in form of an extended family and clan follows an alteration in the rule of residence and is always consistent with the new rule. (M019)

### Social Mobility
Disintegration of the kinship system tends to occur when the economic patterns necessitate social and spatial mobility. (G056)

## STABILITY OF KINSHIP SYSTEM
### X   Kin Relations (Reciprocity)
The stability of a kinship system is correlated with reciprocity in kin interaction. (N030)

## STABILITY OF LINEAGE          X   Adoption
When the maintenance of lineal continuity is stressed, the rate of adoption will tend to be higher. (W043)

### Descent (Bilateral)
Bilateral descent undermines lineage stability. (G013)

### Descent (Symmetrical)
In societies which possess a segmented lineage system, the possibility of one of the segments decreasing in size is guarded against by rules of some form of symmetry; the symmetrical arrangement ensures at least a social permanence as great for one segment as for another. (H037)

### Economic Conditions
Adverse economic pressures will tend to undermine the persistence of a lineage system. (W056)

### Economic Pattern
The persistence of the lineage structure tends to be directly correlated with the stability and retention of the traditional economic pattern. (G056)

### Economic Pattern (Money)
The extent of the disintegration of the traditional lineage system depends on the degree of absorption of the inhabitants into the modern economy of cash crops, cash wages, and urban occupations. (G056)

### Exogamy (Lineage)
When a lineage lacks exogamy and has a bilateral kinship system of the Hawaiian type, it is less likely to endure. (G013)

### Generational Emphasis
Where genealogical generation is stressed as a principle of local organization, lineage structure is likely to be unstable. (T080)

### Geographic Mobility
Residential mobility will tend to result in the disintegration of the lineage structure. (F062)

### Land
A change in the direction of more individual forms of land holding would undoubtedly weaken the lineage system. (F073)

The persistence of a lineage as a corporate unit is directly correlated with its retention of control over land. (K058)

### Marital Stability
Marital stability will tend to be undermined by the deterioration of the lineage structure. (F062)

### Political Centralization
A wider system of unilineal grouping will atrophy following the establishment of political centralization. (F033)

### Population
A decline in population tends to result in the disintegration of the lineage structure. (L045)

An increase in the size of population aggregate may result in a revision of the inner structure of lineage segments. (O006)

The process of lineage fission tends to accelerate with an increase in population. (W056)

### Residence
In a matrilocal society the residence pattern will tend to be patrilocal rather than matrilocal when the lineage of the wife approaches extinction. (M082)

### Sibling Relations (Solidarity)
The stability of the lineage system is directly correlated with the solidarity of the siblings. (W056)

### Slavery (Pawnship)
Systems of pawnship are correlated with greater control by lineage and clan elders and, consequently, with greater lineage stability. (D081)

### Stratification
The breakdown of the lineage system appears to be directly correlated with the increasing heterogeneity in occupation and in wealth within each group. (G056)

### Subsistence Pattern
In societies with a marginal subsistence pattern, the unilineal structure of the lineage will tend to be more flexible. (B147)

## STABILITY OF MATRILINEAL ORGANIZATION
### X   Economic Level
The most unstable type of matrilineal system may be found in neolocal or avunculocal peasant societies with an economic surplus that can be converted either into permanent wealth or differential living standards. (C090)

## STABILITY OF POLYGYNOUS FAMILY  X  Death
The polygynous household in a matrilineal society is likely to disperse after the death of the husband since wives and children never become part of the husband's descent group, nor are there common property interests to hold them together over time. (C090)

## STABILITY OF SOCIAL STRUCTURE
### X  Segmentation
The limits of lineage segmentation are set by the conditions of stability in the social structure. (S087)

## STABILITY OF SOCIETY           X  Exogamy
Exogamy leads to social stability under these conditions: when there is an accepted mode of regulating descent and a classificatory system of kinship.

### Kin Ties (Fictive)
The institutionalization of a fictive kin relationship serves to promote social stability both within—and between—classes and ethnic groups. (F049)

## STATUS IN FAMILY               X  Empathy
Following marriage, sons have better insight into their fathers' attitudes than daughters have into their mothers' attitudes; while before marriage, daughters have better insight into their mothers' attitudes than sons have into their fathers'. (H229)

At the dating, engagement, and courtship stages, mothers are more apt to have better insight (i.e., better able to predict responses) into their daughters' attitudes than fathers have into their sons' attitudes. (H229)

Boys' insight into partners' attitudes during the engagement and marriage periods are better than insights into their parents' attitudes. (H229)

Dating girls have more insight into their mothers' attitudes than they do into those of their partners, but engaged and married girls understand their partners' attitudes better than they do their mothers'. (H229)

Engaged and married girls are better understood by fiancés and husbands than by parents. (H229)

Parental insight into boys' attitudes is never, in any stage of courtship, as acute as is that of their sons' partners. (H229)

### Father-Son Relations (Conflict)
When the status of the married son within the extended family is ambiguous, the father-son relationship tends to be characterized by conflict and tension. (B107)

### Mother-Child Relations (Evaluation)
Adolescent girls are more likely than their mothers to have favorable evaluations of the mother-child relationship. (M201)

### Parent-Child Relations (Generosity)
Adolescents are more likely to perceive their parents as being more generous than the parents feel themselves to be. (M201)

### Role Definition in Family
Mothers and fathers are more likely than not to evaluate similarly the role performance of family members. (M201)

Mothers and their adolescent children are more likely to be in agreement in their evaluation of family-role performances than are fathers and adolescents. (M201)

### Sex-Role Definition
Daughters perceive the average woman to be more traditional ("other-oriented") than do either of their parents. (S252)

Mothers perceive the average woman to be more traditional than do fathers. (S252)

Daughters perceive men's ideal woman to be significantly more traditional than their fathers' conceptions of the ideal woman. (S252)

Daughters' perceptions of their mothers' expectations in the feminine role are close to both their mothers' self-conceptions and their mothers' ideal self-conceptions. (S252)

## STATUS IN FAMILY (HUSBAND/SON)
### X  Mental Illness (Social Adjustment)
Mental patients who make satisfactory social readjustments are more likely to occupy the kin role of husband than that of son. (S245)

Relatives of mental patients whose familial role is that of "son" tend to have lower expectations regarding their posthospital performances than do relatives of patients whose familial role is that of "husband". (S245)

## STATUS OF DIVORCÉE             X  Divorce
The divorce rate is likely to be higher in a society in which there is social recognition of the role of divorced women. (G142)

## STATUS OF WOMEN                X  Divorce
Divorce will be rare if the women are believed to be invested with special supernatural powers. (M069)

## STEM FAMILY                    X  Industrialization
As industrialization advances, conjugal family organization replaces the stem family organization. (G112)

## STEPCHILDREN/CHILDREN
### X  Parent-Child Relations (Preference)
Stepchildren are more likely to express a preference for one parent or the other than are those children who live with both real parents. (B286)

## STEPMOTHER, ATTITUDE TOWARD
### X  Cohesion of Family
Prejudice against the entrance of a stepmother into the family produces tension in the family. (B286)

## STEPPARENT            X  Parent-Child Relations
The presence of a stepparent in the home diminishes the level of adjustment of the children to the remaining natural parent. (B286)

## STEPPARENT-CHILD RELATIONS          X  Age
The younger the children and parents, the more readily they will adjust to step-relationships. (B286)

### Broken Home (Death/Divorce)
Children who have lost a parent by death will adjust better to a stepparent than will children from divorced homes. (B286)

### Parent-Child Relations (Rejection)
The more the child rejects the parent who is gone, the more readily will he adjust to a new parent; the greater the idealization of the parent out of the home, the greater the barrier against accepting a new parent. (B286)

### Sex Status of Stepparent
Stepchildren adjust better to stepfathers than to step-mothers. (B286)

## STEPPARENT/NATURAL PARENT
### X   Adjustment of Child
The adjustment of a stepchild to stepparents is more difficult than the adjustment of a child to his real parents. (B286)

### Identification with Parents
Children living with natural parents are more likely to emulate their parents than are children living with a stepparent. (B286)

## STERILITY                          X Adoption
Adoption is most likely to occur when the married couple is sterile. (D025)

### Adoption, Success of
The success of adoption is higher among infertile couples to the degree that they have adjusted to their infertility. (L153)

### Adultery, Attitude Toward
When a man is impotent or sterile, he is more likely to condone or even to encourage the extramarital relations of his wife. (H066)

### Divorce
Divorce is more likely to occur if the wife is barren. (S090)

### Premarital Sex Relations
There is no relationship between the fear of sterility and premarital sex relations. (B245)

### Sex-Role Adjustment
Anxiety concerning the female role and motherhood is a cause of sterility in women. (B309)

## STERILITY, ADJUSTMENT TO        X Adoption
The success of adoption among infertile couples depends mainly on their having adjusted to their infertility. (L153)

## STERILITY, ATTRIBUTION OF
### X  Descent (Patrilineal)
Patrilineal tribes tend to attribute sterility to the man rather than to the woman. (T081)

## STERILIZATION                     X Class
Operations for sterilization are more frequent among the lower-income groups than among the higher-income groups. (F101)

### Education
There is an inverse relationship between the educational level and frequency of operations for sterilization. (F101)

### Religion
Protestant wives are more likely than Catholic wives to have operations for the prevention of conception. (F101)

## STRATIFICATION                    X Age-Groups
Age-groups arise where social status depends to some extent on individual achievement and is not entirely based on membership in kinship or other hereditary groups. (E086)

### Age of Betrothal
Given a relatively homogeneous level of riches or poverty in a society, there will be an absence of child betrothal practices. (F076)

### Cohesion of Clan
Clan structure tends to disintegrate with the emergence of class stratification. (B098)

### Descent
Matrilineal systems tend to have hereditary rather than complex stratification systems to a greater degree than is the case for patrilineal and bilateral systems. (A048)

### Descent (Patrilineal)
Stratification tends to result in the development of patrilineal descent. (T068)

### Descent (Unilineal)
The appearance of social stratification in a sib-structured tribe tends to weaken the social importance of the sib structure. (O006)

Unilineal computation of status tends to blur lines of stratification. (T069)

### Economic Role of Kin-Group
There is a corresponding relation between the decline of economic function of the kin-group and the rise of stratification. (F039)

### Endogamy (Class)
The more rigid the stratification, the more stringent the restrictions enforcing class endogamy. (D018)

### Endogamy (Community)
Community endogamy tends to support an egalitarian social structure. (F014)

### Functions of Kin-Group
Although other functions are lost with the rise of stratification, unilineal kin-groups tend to retain those which are associated with religious ritual. (F039)

### Geographic Mobility
Geographical mobility is a major factor in the disruption of a stable class system. (F014)

The cleavage of lineages into social classes tends to occur with migration. (K049)

### Inheritance
An inheritance pattern which involves the subdivision of the estate facilitates the economic differentiation of descent lines. (S123)

### Kin Terminology (Bifurcate Collateral)
Bifurcate collateral terminology tends to occur in societies with systems of ranked lineages. (K049)

### Kin Ties
The development of stratification is facilitated by the weakening of kin ties. (G031)

### Kin Ties (Fictive)
A vertical extension of fictive kin ties tends to occur when social relationships between two defined socio-cultural strata or classes become closer. (M080)

### Kinship, Importance of
Kin ties are of greater importance in defining social relationships in societies without a class system. (L072)

### Marriage System (Circular)
When circular marriage systems in practice fail to conform to the model, class differences will tend to develop. (L051)

### Mate Selection
The greater the emphasis on a sharp delimitation of rank in a society, the more likely will hypogamy be disapproved. (M167)

### Mate Selection (Free Choice)
Closed systems of mate selection are more apt to exist in societies with less status differentiation. (J035)

### Moiety System
Lineage ranking is less likely to occur in societies with a moiety system. (M066)

The appearance of stratification among tribes without a sib structure tends to inhibit the development of sibs and moieties. (O006)

### Political Succession
When political offices are established as achieved statuses, a pattern of ranking within the lineage tends to emerge. (S123)

### Population Density
The development of social classes is correlated with an increase in the density of population. (M033)

### Preferential Marriage
Systems of asymmetrical marriage exchange tend to create distinctions of status inequality since direct reciprocity in kind is never practiced. (L176)

### Preferential Marriage (Asymmetrical)
Asymmetrical marriage systems arise in societies which possess either status differentiation or differences in the distribution of economic resources. (S026)

### Ranking of Lineages
A system of ranked lineages provides a basis for the emergence of social stratification. (K049)

### Residence (Longhouse)
Stratification is unlikely to occur in societies where the longhouse is the community settlement. (M248)

### Sex Relations, Importance of
A formal stratified society cannot maintain itself when sex relations are considered very important. (M244)

### Sex-Role Definition
The lesser differentiation of women also retards class formation. (M170)

### Social Mobility
The movement of families from one class to another is not necessarily associated with a change in the existing system of stratification in a society. (G156)

### Stability of Kin-Group
A necessary corollary of the class-structured social system is a breakdown, at least in part, of organization on a clan or familial basis. (S048)

### Stability of Lineage
The breakdown of the lineage system appears to be directly correlated with the increasing heterogeneity in occupation and wealth within each subcaste. (G056)

### Subsistence Pattern (Agricultural/Pastoral)
The clan structure will be of an equalitarian character in societies whose economic pattern is that of migratory agriculture or pastoralism. (F039)

### Warfare
The cleavage of a lineage into classes tends to occur under the impact of war. (K049)

## STRATIFICATION, BASIS OF    X  Age-Groups
Age-groups occur in those societies in which social status depends on individual achievement and is not entirely based on membership in kinship or other hereditary groups. (E102)

### Authority Structure of Family
Where the statification system is based on individual achievement, high authority of the elders is difficult to maintain. (G156)

A job-based stratification system greatly reduces the authority of family elders, while a land-based stratification system is associated with the maintenance of both real and symbolic authority of the elders. (G156)

### Homogamy (Caste)
Hypergamy may be found in caste systems only when the basis of stratification is nonracial. (D018)

### Identification with Parents
A child tends to identify less with parents who are in a subordinate class position, in a society committed to the principle of upward mobility. (C086)

### Parental-Role Definition
Stratification systems based on ascription are associated with parental amassing of an inheritance to provide for the child, while in a stratification system based on achievement, responsibility for the child is associated with affording him an adequate education. (G156)

### Social Mobility
A society based upon competitive achievement is associated with high downward mobility of upper-class families. (G156)

When the class structure of society is based upon extended family ties, marriage is more likely to be the crucial determinant of social mobility. (P083)

### Urbanization
Kinship is more likely to be the basis of adult status in the fringe area than in the central city. (J003)

## STRATIFICATION OF LINEAGES    X  Kin Ties
Manipulation of descent affiliation tends to be found in societies which have stratified unilineal descent groups. (F039)

## STRESS    X  Kin Relations (Interaction)
Family relations are more apt to be reactivated in times of strain, illness, and economic stress than at other times. (R120)

## STRUCTURE OF FAMILY
### X  Economic Conditions
The family structure will change in response to changes in economic conditions. (W082)

### Father-Son Relations
Where the father-son axis is emphasized, the basic kin unit is the patrilineal extended family. (H172)

### Geographic Mobility
With an increase in physical mobility, the matrilineal family structure will tend to revise into a small bilateral family. (G056)

### Husband-Wife Relations (Intimacy)
The lower the level of interaction and intimacy between husband and wife, the less likely is the development of a strong conjugal system. (P083)

### Kin Terminology (Generation)
When generational terminology is employed, family structure tends to be dispersed and amorphous. (H062)

### Population Density
Where population density is low (one to the square mile or less), the normal form of the family is the simple patrilineal family, with families drawn together in bands or hordes. (K090)

### Size of Family
The larger the family, the more internal organization develops. (I008)

### Social Mobility
With an increase in social mobility, matrilineal societies will tend to revise their family structure to that of a small bilateral family. (G056)

### Stability of Family
Among members of the lower class, a female-centered consanguinous household is more stable than is either a consensual or a legal one. (R124)

### Subsistence Pattern
Where livelihood depends on intimate knowledge of the country, the natural form of the family is the patrilineal family drawn together in bands or hordes. (K090)

### Subsistence Pattern (Nomadic)
The earlier, more rigid matrilineal scheme seems to have changed into the more plastic matrideme as a result of nomadic life. (D057)

### Witchcraft
Sorcery is seen as a major cause of illness in 93 per cent of the societies with polygynous households, 60 per cent of the societies with mother–child households, 53 per cent of the societies with extended family households, and only 36 per cent of the societies with nuclear households. (W127)

## STRUCTURE OF FAMILY, CHANGES IN
### X   Intermarriage
Intermarriage tends to intensify changes in family organization in a culture-contact situation. (S053)

## SUBSISTENCE PATTERN
### X   Avoidance Relationship
Avoidance patterns are more likely to occur in marginal societies where people must live in small and isolated groups for long periods of time under conditions of extreme hardship. (M235)

### Child-Rearing Practices (Achievement/Conformity)
Compliance training is associated with high-food-accumulation economies (e.g., herding); achievement training is associated with low-food-accumulation economies (e.g., hunting and fishing). (M246)

### Child-Rearing Practices (Sex Role)
In societies where large animals are hunted, where grain rather than root crops are grown, where large or milking animals are kept, where fishing is unimportant or absent, or where settlement is nomadic rather than sedentary, large differences in training of the sexes is likely to occur. (W127)

### Clan
A society based upon a clan structure is better adapted to a subsistence than to a moneyed economy. (H064)

### Descent
The descent pattern of a society is unrelated to the means of subsistence. (G056)

### Descent (Matrilineal)
Matriliny disappears when the subsistence base shifts to one primarily dependent on movable property (e.g., domesticates) which can be controlled by individual men. (A048)

Matrilineal systems are strikingly infrequent in those areas of the world where the plough is used, where there is intensive wet-rice agriculture, or where there are extensive irrigation works coordinated and maintained by supracommunity organizations. (A048)

### Descent (Unilineal)
Poverty of habitat and of productive technology tends to inhibit the development of unilineal descent groups. (F020)

There is a universal tendency under conditions of small-scale production by domestic units for the development of unilineal kin-groups. (F033)

### Endogamy (Community)
Patterns of community endogamy tend to be correlated with a marginal subsistence economy and a scarcity of land. (W069)

### Fertility
The more sedentary life associated with gardening or fishing economies causes an increase in fertility. (T082)

### Political Structure
When the technological pattern is not sufficiently productive or permanent of locale to support large concentrations of population or stable settlement, the sociopolitical organization will remain basically along kinship lines. (M033)

### Sex-Role Definition
Where animal foods and wild plant foods are balanced in rank, sexual dominance is less likely to occur. (D057)

### Stability of Lineage
In societies with marginal subsistence patterns, the unilineal structure of the lineage will tend to be more flexible. (B147)

### Structure of Family
Where livelihood depends on intimate knowledge of the country, the natural form of the family is the patrilineal family drawn together in bands or hordes. (K090)

## SUBSISTENCE PATTERN (AGRICULTURAL)
### X   Cohesion of Lineage
The importance of unilineal affiliation tends to be stressed more strongly in agricultural societies. (W056)

### Descent (Matrilineal)

The matriarchate is closely linked with a subsistence system in which a hunting or shepherd people passes over to a stage of more intensive agriculture. (L108)

Matrilineal descent tends to be correlated with an economy based on intensive farming. (N017)

Matrilineal descent is not exclusively associated with an agricultural economy. (N017)

### Extended Family

The persistence of the extended family depends upon the population being rooted to the soil and isolated from divergent patterns of behavior. (B033)

### Extended Family, Importance of

When the economy is that of sedentary agriculture, the extended family tends to be emphasized. (E008)

### Extended/Nuclear Family

Extended families are associated with areas of spatially separated agriculture, while nuclear families tend to be associated with areas of localized agricultural systems. (A072)

### Kin Ties

The persistence of kinship ties tends to be directly correlated with an agricultural economy. (T039)

### Kinship

The proliferation of forms of kinship structure will tend to follow the adoption of agriculture with its subsequent increase in food supply. (V009)

### Lineage

Almost all the tribes with a clan or gentile organization are agriculturalists. (L128)

### Nuclear Family

In simple agricultural economies, the minimal economic group is generally the biological family. (F049)

### Rank of Women

The status of women in agricultural societies tends to be high as a result of the economic importance of their social role. (L082)

### Residence

There is a direct correlation between matrilocal residence and a multicrop subsistence agriculture and between patrilocal residence and an economy based upon a single major crop. (A072)

### Social Structure

When the economic level is that of an isolated farming community, the family tends to be the fundamental social grouping in the society. (W055)

### Stability of Kin-Group

The stability of residential descent groups will increase with the adoption of an agricultural pattern which focuses on a stable crop. (S282)

### SUBSISTENCE PATTERN (AGRICULTURAL/PASTORAL)     X   Stratification

The clan structure will be of an equalitarian character in societies whose economic pattern is that of migratory agriculture or pastoralism. (F039)

### SUBSISTENCE PATTERN (HERDING)     X   Kinship (Bilateral)

Bilateral (v. unilateral) organization is particularly well adapted to large-scale reindeer herding and difficult environments. (P082)

## SUBSISTENCE PATTERN (HORTICULTURAL)
### X   Clan

Clan systems are associated with an economy based on horticulture. (G045)

### Descent (Matrilineal)

Matrilineal systems are overrepresented in the horticultural areas. (A048)

Matrilineages are most likely to be found in societies where women play important roles in food production (e.g., societies based upon gardening). (G156)

### Economic Importance of Family

When the economic pattern is that of horticulture, the family will tend to be the major unit of economic activity. (O023)

## SUBSISTENCE PATTERN (HUNTING)
### X   Descent (Ambilateral)

In societies with simple hunting economies, descent tends to be ambilateral. (N027)

### Kin Terminology (Bilateral)

In simple hunting economies, kinship terminology tends to be bilateral. (N027)

### Land

An economy based on nonmigratory animals encourages family ownership of territory. (S077)

### Rank of Women

In societies with hunting economies, the status of the women will tend to be low. (L082)

### Residence (Bilocal)

Bilocal residence tends to characterize societies with simple hunting economies. (L063)

### Residence (Patrilocal)

Patrilocal residence tends to occur among hunters and gatherers if a tribe moves into an area where game is plentiful and dependable so that the subsistence comes to depend primarily upon the chase rather than upon the collecting activities of the women. (M019)

Hunting bands with strong lineages as the predominant economic group will be found to be associated with patrilocal residence. (O006)

### Residence (Unilocal)

When the economic pattern of a society is that of a marginal hunting economy, ideal patterns of unilocal residence are frequently violated. (L063)

### SUBSISTENCE PATTERN (HUNTING AND GATHERING)     X   Breast Feeding, Duration of

The wild food products collected by women (in societies with hunting and gathering economies) do not provide sufficient suitable food for young children, thus the time of nursing is prolonged and, consequently, intervals between births become greater. (T082)

### Descent (Bilateral)

Societies with marginal techniques of hunting and gathering tend to be characterized by bilateral descent. (S119)

### Land

When the economy is on the level of hunting and food gathering, ownership of the land tends to be ascribed to the sib rather than to the individual family or person. (S072)

### Residence

In societies where the economy is marginal hunting-gathering, the residence pattern tends to be flexible. (M079)

## SUBSISTENCE PATTERN (NOMADIC)
### X   Cohesion of Family

Nomadic tribes are likely to develop strong family and family group ties. (B223)

### Infanticide

Deformed infants are more frequently killed in nomadic areas. (D057)

### Preferential Marriage (Asymmetrical Cross-Cousin)

When the economic pattern shifts from a stable and restricted range for hunting and gathering to a wider pattern of movement, a preference for mother's brother's daughter marriage is likely to develop with a concomitant prohibition on marriage with father's sister's daughter. (E107)

### Residence (Neolocal)

The residential unit of the husband, wife, and their dependents is more frequent in nomadic than in sedentary life. (L073)

### Structure of Family

The earlier, more rigid matrilineal scheme seems to have changed into the more plastic matrideme as a result of nomadic life. (D057)

## SUBSISTENCE PATTERN (NOMADIC/AGRICULTURAL)
### X   Marital Status (Male)

There is a higher proportion of single males in agricultural than in nomadic communities. (L073)

## SUBSISTENCE PATTERN (PASTORAL)
### X   Descent (Patrilineal)

Societies with pastoral economies tend to be patrilineal. (R045)

### Economic Importance of Women

In societies with pastoral economies, women assume little importance in the economic structure. (P024)

### Exogamy

Societies with pastoral economies tend to develop an exogamous clan structure. (M069)

### Extended Family

Pastoral economics are more likely to be characterized by an extended family structure. (M069)

The extended family structure tends to be associated with pastoral economies. (P024)

### Polygyny

The prevalence of polygyny is directly correlated with the distribution of cattle. (S096)

### Premarital Chastity

In societies with pastoral economies and patriarchal extended family structures, the premarital chastity of women is stressed. (P024)

### Rank of Husband/Wife

Inequality between husband and wife is more common in pastoral societies. (H165)

### Rank of Women

The status of women in pastoral societies tends to be low. (P024)

### Religion (Ancestor Worship)

Ancestor worship tends to be associated with pastoral economies. (H164)

### Residence (Patrilocal)

The adoption of a pastoral economy has usually resulted in patrilocal residence. (M019)

### Segmentation

The recurrent search for grazing lands of the pastoral economy tends to separate and scatter the lineage residential group. (G022)

## SUBSISTENCE PATTERN (PASTORAL/AGRICULTURAL)   X   Clan Structure

The clan structure will be of an egalitarian character in societies whose economic pattern is that of migratory agriculture or pastoralism. (F039)

### Size of Household

The number of people in the household will be higher in pastoral than in agricultural areas. (L073)

## SUBSISTENCE PATTERN (PLOUGH AGRICULTURE)   X   Residence (Patrilocal)

Where men supplant women as tillers of the soil, often in consequence of harnessing their domestic animals to the plough, patrilocal residence almost invariably occurs. (M019)

## SUBSISTENCE PATTERN (PREINDUSTRIAL)
### X   Kin/Nonkin Relations

In preindustrial societies the unit of mutual aid tends to be a kin unit. (F049)

## SUBSISTENCE PATTERN (PRODUCTION)
### X   Residence

The residence rule tends to reflect the method of production which characterizes the economic pattern. (K046)

## SUFFRAGE, FEMININE     X   Sex-Role Definition

The extension of suffrage to women is associated with the development of the egalitarian family; by guaranteeing the separate identity of women outside of marriage, it makes marriage closer to a free contract. (P083)

## SUICIDE     X   Authority Structure of Family

Suicide in young people is more likely to be associated with extreme subordination to authority of the older generation than with any other cause. (S025)

### Conflict in Family

Suicide may be resorted to because of acute conflict within the family or because it is the only symptom which will be recognized as such by the family. (P078)

### Marital Status

Marital statuses may be ranked in this order by suicide rate: married, single, widowed, and divorced; differences are greater for men than for women. (K024)

Suicide rate of married persons correlates more highly with business cycles than does the suicide rate of single persons. (S078)

The divorced have a higher suicide rate than do the widowed of the same age and sex. (S078)

### Parent-Child Relations (Indulgence)
Suicide rate is higher among people who, as children, were "overpampered."

### Parent Loss
Attempted suicides are more likely to have suffered the loss of a parent before the age of 15 than are nonsuicides. (G154)

Attempted suicides who had lost one or more parents had lost the parent(s) at an earlier age than had nonsuicides who had also lost one or more parents. (G154)

The suicide rate among adult orphans is higher than that among people with parents living. (S078)

### Parenthood
Parents have a lower suicide rate than nonparents. (S078)

### Sex Status
The suicide rate of males correlates more highly with business cycles than does the suicide rate of females. (S078)

The suicide rate of males is higher than that of females. (S078)

## SUICIDE, ATTEMPTED        X  Marital Status
Unsuccessful suicide attempts are more likely to occur among married than among the single, divorced, or widowed. (W125)

## SUICIDE/HOMICIDE        X  Superego Formation
When the individual internalizes or accepts harsh parental demands and discipline, he has a higher psychological probability of suicide and a lower probability of homicide. (S078)

## SUPEREGO FORMATION                X  Adultery
Low strength of conscience (as measured by the Psychopathic Deviate Scale of the Minnesota Multiphasic Personality Inventory) is positively associated with extramarital sexual involvements. (N062)

There are no significant differences between persons having high strength of conscience and those having low conscience strength (measured by the Psychopathic Deviate Scale of the Minnesota Multiphasic Personality Inventory) with regard to either emotional (nonsexual) or fantasy extramarital involvements. (N062)

### Child-Rearing Practices (Affection)
Parents' use of withdrawal of love as a method of discipline is correlated with the degree of the child's conscience development *only when* the mother is relatively warm and affectionate. (B243)

The positive relationship between maternal use of withdrawal of love and internalization of moral standards in the child holds only if the mother-child relationship is characterized by warmth. (B275)

Love-oriented techniques of discipline and "high conscience" in five-year-old children are associated. (S191)

### Child-Rearing Practices (Aggression)
High guilt in the child correlates with severity toward control of aggression by parents. (G120)

The longer parents inhibit a child from expressing his aggression, the greater the severity of the child's superego. (G145)

### Child-Rearing Practices (Consistency)
Mothers who are not firm (unable to disapprove consistently) are more likely than are those who are firm to produce children lacking in conscience development. (F103)

### Child-Rearing Practices (Criticism)
The greater the effectiveness of parental criticism, the more complete the formation of an ego ideal and of conscience in the child. (B234)

### Child-Rearing Practices (Demands)
Parents or parental surrogates who care enough to set limits and make demands are necessary for the development of conscience in the child. (C093)

### Child-Rearing Practices (Discipline)
The child's sense of guilt about aggression correlates with parents' use of psychological discipline. (A054)

### Child-Rearing Practices (Giving Reasons)
The use of reasoning as a technique of control is associated with the development of conscience in the son as indicated by guilt feelings about aggression toward parents, teachers, and peers. (B243)

### Child-Rearing Practices (Kin)
There is a low positive correlation between the importance of relatives (other than parents), as opposed to unrelated persons, as agents of socialization of the child and the development of guilt feelings as measured by the patient's feeling of responsibility for his illness. (W142)

### Child-Rearing Practices (Nurturance)
There is no relationship between degree of initial nurturance of the child and development of guilt feelings as measured by the patient's feeling of responsibility for his illness. (W142)

### Child-Rearing Practices (Punishment)
Mothers who use less authority and less strictness are more likely to have children who have low degrees of guilt, but the 24-hour-a-day disciplinarian supported by the father develops a high guilt pattern.

The parent who produces a high level of guilt uses scolding, deprivation, ostracism, and creates hurt feelings in the child; parents who produce fear in the child use spanking and hitting more.

Children with low guilt are more likely to have parents who use a less love-oriented child-rearing technique (reasoning, praise, or deprivation).

Less indulgence or greater severity of weaning is associated with high guilt in the child.

Guilt in children correlates with psychological discipline in the middle class but not in the working class. (G120)

Resistance to temptation and reactions of guilt are correlated with psychological (*v.* physical) techniques of discipline. (G120)

There is no relationship between parental use of withdrawal of love as a method of discipline and the development of conscience in the child. (N063)

There is a low positive correlation between the use of love-oriented techniques of punishment by parents and the development of guilt feelings, as measured by the patient's feeling of responsibility for his own physical illness. (W142)

　　　SUPEREGO FORMATION

### Child-Rearing Practices (Punishment/Reward)
Children whose parents employ both rewards and punishments have a more greatly developed sense of conscience than do children whose parents employ only rewards. (R106)

### Child-Rearing Practices (Sex)
Societies with early training in modesty and the inhibition of heterosexual play tend to have a high guilt orientation. (W127)

### Child-Rearing Practices (Sex Role)
Because of sex-typed child-rearing practices, at comparable age levels, girls tend to be "better socialized" than boys. (B252)

### Class
There is no correlation between social class and the guilt of the child about disobedience or aggression. (A054)

### Father-Daughter Relations (Rejection)
There is no association between the father's rejection or acceptance of his daughter and the daughter's level of conscience development (U.S.). (S191)

### Father-Son Relations (Rejection)
Boys who have fathers who are rejecting have lower conscience development than do boys of accepting fathers (U.S.). (S191)

### Homosexuality
Homosexuality is likely to be repressed or overt to the extent that the superego is stern or weak. (T104)

### Household Composition
There is more guilt orientation in nuclear households than in mother–child households. (W127)

### Identification with Father/Mother
Children who identify with their fathers are more likely to be guilt oriented than are children who identify with their mothers. (W127)

### Identification with Like-Sex Parent
The development of conscience in the child correlates with the extent to which the like-sex parent is available as an object of identification. (G120)

### Identification with Parents
The greater the extent to which a child identifies with an aggressive, punitive parent, the greater his hostility toward himself and toward his environment at large and the less likely is the formation of superego and guilt feelings. (B234)

The greater the identification of the child with the parent, the more he imitates, not the model of his parent, but that of the parent's superego. (B234)

Since early socialization tends to produce stronger identification, it also results in guilt over contravening parental values. (W127)

### Marital Adjustment
There is no significant difference between those who are high in marital satisfaction and those who are low (measured on the Strauss Scale of Marital Satisfaction) regarding their strength of conscience (as measured by the Psychopathic Deviate Scale of the Minnesota Multiphasic Personality Inventory). (N062)

### Maternal Role
Male subjects will rank higher on attitudinal measures of self-blame if they perceive the principal disciplinarian role in the family as being played by the mother rather than by the father. (H015)

Individuals reporting that they blame themselves and not others are more likely to perceive the mother as the principal disciplinarian in the family. (H067)

### Maternal-Role Behavior
A deep sense of guilt in a child is directly correlated with a mother who emphasizes her personal sacrifice to the interests of her family. (V029)

### Mother-Child Relations (Acceptance)
The mother's acceptance of the child and high conscience of the child are associated. (Evidence is stronger for boys than for girls.) (S191)

### Mother-Child Relations (Hostility)
Since the development of the conscience is dependent upon a mutually affectionate relationship between mother and child, hostile mothers are more likely than are those who are not hostile to produce children with poor conscience development. (F103)

### Mother-Child Relations (Warmth)
If a child has a warm, intimate and continuous relationship with his mother (or with a permanent mother surrogate), the emotions of anxiety and guilt will develop in a moderate and organized way. (B270)

Guilt responses in children are positively related to the mother's warmth. (G120)

The more warm and loving the mother, the stronger the conscience produced in the child. (K103)

Warmth of mother increases the rapidity of conscience development (U.S.). (S191)

### Ordinal Position
Only and oldest children had more strongly developed consciences (U.S.). (S191)

### Parent-Child Relations
The greater association of sons with fathers (who are instrumentally oriented) correlates with their tendency to develop a principled and objective (situation-oriented) superego; the greater subjection of girls to withdrawal of love by mothers correlates with their tendency to develop a superego focused upon interpersonal matters rather than upon broader issues. (B234)

Children who are opposite-sex allied (i.e., join the parent in family conflict) are more blame-accepting than are children who are same-sex allied. (B263)

### Parent-Child Relations (Affection)
The greater the parent's expression of affection, the greater the degree of guilt in five-year-old children. (H208)

An affectionate relationship between the parents and the child is needed for the development of conscience. (M194)

### Parent-Child Relations (Ambivalence)
The greater the intensity of both love and hate in the parent and in the child who identifies with him, the more likely is the child to develop an extreme, self-punishing superego. (B234)

### Parent-Child Relations (Authority)
The greater the guilt feelings the parents can instill within the child, the more readily will he succumb to their authority.

### Parent-Child Relations (Punishment/Control)

Children who think mainly of whether an immoral act will be detected and punished are more likely to see their parents as being punitively assertive and controlling than are children who evaluate immoral behavior in terms of their own internal standards of right or wrong. (B275)

### Parent Loss

Separation of the child from his parents or from satisfactory parental substitutes leads to a lessening in ego-strength or incompletely developed superego.

Children who are deprived of their parents and are not provided with adequate parent surrogates suffer greatly impaired ego and superego development if this deprivation takes place for long periods before the child is two years old. (B270)

Children who are deprived of their parents and are not provided with adequate parent surrogates after the ages of three, four, or five do not suffer the same degree of impairment of ego and superego formation as do children who undergo the same type of deprivation at earlier ages. (B270)

### Parental-Role Behavior

The contradictory patterns of maternal indulgence and stern paternal severity are more likely than are other family constellations to produce distortion in the superego (conscience) of the delinquent child. (B238)

The internalization of moral behavior is likely to be greater when socialization and nurturance are combined in one agent (parents or peer group) than when the two functions are relatively separate. (L158)

The greater the extent to which nurturance and discipline are combined in the same parent, the greater the likelihood of value internalization. (S216)

### Parental Role (Discipline)

Males who perceive their mothers as playing the principal disciplinary role in the family will rank higher on attitudinal measures of self-blame than males who perceive their fathers as playing the principal disciplinary role. (H067)

The development of conscience is facilitated if the child is disciplined by the same-sex parent. (S191)

### Parental-Role Model

Manifestation of guilt in the child correlates with the model provided by the parents (e.g., confession, reparation). (G120)

### Paternal/Maternal Role (Discipline)

Males who perceive the mother as playing the principal disciplinary role in the family will rank higher on attitudinal measures of self-blame than will males who perceive the father as playing the principal disciplinary role. (H067)

### Paternal Role

The greater the severity of the father in his relation to his son, the greater will be the severity of the superego in the son's personality in its domination over the ego. (S078)

Fathers of low-guilt boys play a larger role in discipline than do fathers of high-guilt boys. (S078)

### Polygyny

Polygynous societies are low in guilt orientation since guilt is derived from identification with the male rather than with the female role. (W127)

### Residence (Neolocal)

Persons from societies with neolocal rules of residence for families have weaker superegos (less patient responsibility for illness) than do those reared in families from societies with matrilocal or patrilocal rules of residence. (W142)

### Sex-Role Behavior

The practice of roles of parent of the same sex is associated with the development of conscience. (S191)

### Sex-Role Identification

There is a correlation between degree of masculinity of young boys and their degree of conscience development. (M220)

### Sex Status

Females are more likely than males to feel guilt regarding premarital sex.

### Social Network

Internalization of parental values is more necessary for social control in a society characterized by loosely knit than by closely knit social networks (tight network means that the friends of the husband and wife are friends of one another). (S216)

### Socialization

There is a negative correlation between the age at which conscious socialization is begun and the strength of guilt feelings. (W142)

### Socialization, Agents of

There is a low positive correlation between the importance of parents in the society, as opposed to nonrelatives and specialists, as agents of socialization of the child and the development of guilt feelings, as measured by the patient's responsibility for his illness. (W142)

### Socialization Anxiety

The higher the average degree of socialization anxiety in any society, the greater the development of guilt feelings, as measured by the patient's responsibility for physical illness. (W142)

### Suicide/Homicide

When the individual internalizes or accepts harsh parental demands and discipline, he has a higher psychological probability of suicide and a lower probability of homicide. (S078)

### Toilet Training

There is no relationship between the age of toilet training and projective systems which reflect guilt. (W127)

### Weaning

Societies with early weaning tend to have high guilt orientations. (W127)

### Weaning/Toilet Training

Guilt of the child about disobedience of the mother correlates with late weaning and toilet training. (A054)

The child's sense of guilt about aggression correlates with early weaning and toilet training. (A054)

The earlier and/or more severe the weaning and toilet training, the greater the degree of guilt and superego strength. (G120)

# SURROGATE MOTHER

## X  Achievement Aspirations

When their infants are six months of age, mothers who have been the only caretaking figure for their infants have higher achievement aspirations for their children than do mothers who have provided other maternal figures for their infants. (C107)

When the child is six months of age, mothers who have reared the child themselves have higher achievement expectations for the child than do mothers of children who have been reared by more than one mother figure (i.e., nurse, grandparent, friend of mother, older sister of child). (C124)

## Achievement Motivation

Mothers who rear their children themselves are less likely to have achievement fantasies characterized by personal failure than are mothers who provide maternal substitutes for their children (nurses, grandparents, older sister of the child, and friends). (C124)

## Adjustment of Child

The adverse effects of institutionalization on babies are lessened if there is a mother surrogate in the institution. (B270)

## Anxiety

Children who are cared for by someone other than the mother for a significant proportion of the time are likely to have neurotic anxiety symptoms such as phobias and to tend to act peculiarly. (R113)

## Aspiration Level

When their infants are six months of age, mothers who have been the only caretaking figure for their infants have higher achievement aspirations for their children than have mothers who have provided other maternal figures for their infants. (C107)

When the child is six months of age, mothers who have reared the child themselves have higher achievement expectations for the child than have mothers of children who have been reared by more than one mother figure, i.e., a nurse, grandparent, friend of mother, older sister of child. (C124)

## Behavior Problems

The older the infant (3–7 months), the more severe the disturbances (sleeping, eating, apathy, I.Q., loss of abilities, excessive crying, and blunted social responsiveness) resulting from a change in mother figures. (Y042)

## Child-Rearing Practices (Achievement)

When their infants are one year of age, mothers who have provided other caretaking figures for their babies are more concerned with their achievement than are mothers who have been the only maternal figure for their infants. (C107)

## Cognitive Development

Whether the infant is cared for predominantly by the mother or by other persons is not related to his intellectual development. (Y042)

## Dependency

When their infants are one year of age, mothers who have been the only caretaking agent for their infants are more dependent on the child for their own need gratification than are mothers who have provided other maternal figures for their infants. (C107)

At one year of age, children are more emotionally dependent on their mothers in families where the mothering is provided by one person than in families where it is provided by more than one person (i.e., nurse, grandparent, mother's friend, and older sister of child). (C124)

Among children of mothers who work, those whose mothers have provided a succession of different mother substitutes are more dependent than are those whose mothers have provided more stable arrangements. (Y047)

## Kin Relations

The extent to which an available kin-group aids in infant care is more a function of the interpersonal relationships and kinship ties of particular individuals than of the number of potential mother substitutes in the group as a whole. (M216)

## Loss of Family Member

There is a curvilinear relationship between the severity of losses suffered by women in their immediate families and the decision and ability to take on the occupation of "foster-mother" for orphans. (T094)

## Maternal-Role Adjustment

When their infants are six months of age, mothers who have been the only caretaking figure for their infants are more self-confident in and are more likely to minimize the difficulties associated with child rearing than are mothers who have provided other mother figures for their infants. (C107)

When the child is six years of age, mothers who have reared the child themselves feel more self-confident in their handling of the child and ordinary child-rearing problems than do mothers of children who have been reared by more than one mother figure (i.e., nurse, grandparent, friend of mother, older sister of child). (C124)

## Maternal-Role Behavior

The more persons available to aid in care of older children (ages 7–10), the less time the mother will spend in caring for her offspring. This relationship does not hold for infants (cross-cultural). (M216)

## Mother Absence

The effects of maternal deprivation are less marked if the mother surrogate is someone the child knew before mother deprivation than if the mother surrogate is someone unknown to him. (B270)

## Mother-Child Household

Infant care by older children is a function of the autonomy of mother-child households peculiar to polygamous societies, where each wife has her own living unit. (M216)

## Mother-Child Relations (Affect)

At one year of age, children reared in families where the mothering is provided by one person display greater affect in interaction with their mothers than do children reared in families where the mothering is provided by more than one person (i.e., nurse, grandparent, mother's friend, or older sister of child). (C124)

## Mother-Child Relations (Concern)

When their infants are six months of age, mothers who have been the only caretaking agent for their infants express more concern for the well-being of their babies than do mothers who have provided other maternal figures for their infants. (C107)

### Mother-Child Relations (Interaction)
When their infants are six months of age, mothers who have been the only caretaking agent for their infants are more active and playful with their babies than are mothers who have provided other maternal figures for their infants. (C107)

In a clinical situation, among one-year-old infants, mothers who have reared their children themselves display greater interaction, both verbal and physical, with their children than do mothers of children who are being reared in families where the mothering is provided by more than one person (i.e., nurse, grandparent, friend of mother, older sister of child). (C124)

### Mother-Child Relations (Physical Contact)
When their infants are six months of age, mothers who have been the only caretaking figure for their infants are more sensuous in touching and handling their babies than are mothers who have provided other maternal figures for their infants. (C107)

### Mother-Child Relations (Tolerance)
When their infants are one year old, mothers who have been the only caretaking agent for their infants are more tolerant of irritating behavior from their babies than are mothers who have provided other maternal figures for their infants. (C107)

### Mother-Child Relations (Warmth)
The presence of kin in the family who can aid the mother in child care and who are not disruptive allows the mother to display greater warmth to her children than if she is their sole custodian. (M216)

### Motor Development
At one year of age, infants reared in families where the mothering is provided by one person are more active than are infants reared in families where the mothering is provided by more than one person (i.e., nurse, grandparent, mother's friend, or older sister of child). (C124)

### Personality Development (Affect)
Interrupted affective relationships with more than one mother figure, not allowing a satisfactory growth of mutual emotional ties, develops in the child, in later years, an affectionless character.

### Personality of Child (Depression)
Children who are cared for by adults other than the mother for a significant proportion of the time are likely to appear depressed and discouraged. (R113)

### Personality of Child (Emotionality)
At one year of age, infants from families where child care is provided by the mother only show more emotional responses (crying and smiling) than do infants from families where child care is provided by more than one mother figure. (C107)

### Personality of Child (Fear)
Among children of mothers who work, those whose mothers have provided a succession of different mother substitutes have more fears than do those whose mothers have provided more stable arrangements. (Y047)

### Personality of Child (Irritability)
At six months of age, infants reared in families where the mothering is provided by one person are less irritable

than are infants reared in families where the mothering is provided by more than one person (i.e., nurse, grandparent, mother's friend, or older sister of child). (C124)

### Personality of Child (Self-Assertiveness)
Children of working mothers who have provided substitute care are more self-assertive than are children of mothers who do not work and remain with their children. (Y047)

### Personality of Child (Stability)
Having many good (constant) mothers leads to stable personality development in the child.

### Personality of Child (Stress)
Whether the infant is cared for predominantly by the mother or by other persons is not related to his capacity to cope with stress situations. (Y042)

### Personality of Child (Withdrawal)
Children who are cared for by an adult other than the mother for a significant proportion of the time are likely to be withdrawn and seclusive and to indulge in daydreaming to a great degree. (R113)

### Personality of Mother
Mothers who rear their children themselves are less hostile, dominant, and dependent in interpersonal relations than are mothers who provide maternal substitutes for their children (i.e., nurses, grandparents, older sister of child, friends). (C124)

### Personality Problems
There is no relationship between multiple mothering and personality problems in the child. (Y045)

### Personality Problems (Nervousness)
Among children of mothers who work, those whose mothers have provided a succession of different mother substitutes are more nervous than are those whose mothers have provided more stable arrangements. (Y047)

### Social Adjustment
At one year of age, infants reared in families where the mothering is provided by one person are better able to relate with other people than are infants reared in families where the mothering is provided by more than one person (i.e., nurse, grandparent, mother's friend, or older sister of child). (C124)

Whether the infant was cared for predominantly by the mother or by other persons is not related to development of outgoing social behavior. (Y042)

## SURROGATE MOTHER, ATTITUDE TOWARD
### X  Occupation of Husband
Mothers whose husbands have entrepreneurial jobs are more likely than mothers whose husbands have bureaucratic jobs to feel it is desirable for the mother's sake that a child frequently be left at home with a competent woman while the mother shops. (M062)

## SURROGATE MOTHER-CHILD RELATIONS (AFFECTION)
### X  Surrogate Parents, Adjustment To
The successful adjustment of the adopted child to a new home is less likely if the foster-mother is unaffectionate. (T086)

## SURROGATE MOTHER-CHILD RELATIONS (ATTENTION)    X  Cognitive Development
Children receiving all the attention of a foster-mother are significantly accelerated in mental development

compared with those children who have to share the attention of the surrogate mother with others. (B270)

## SURROGATE MOTHER, EVALUATION OF
### X    Age of Child
The divorcée is more likely to claim that substitute child care is excellent if the children are younger than if they are older. (G157)

### Dating
Whether or not the divorcée is dating frequently, she is as likely to believe that substitute child care is excellent. (G157)

### Size of Family
The divorcée is more likely to claim that substitute child care is excellent if there are fewer children in the family. (G157)

## SURROGATE/NATURAL PARENTS
### X    Behavior Problems
Children adopted after the age of six months are more likely to exhibit antisocial tendencies than are children raised by their own parents. (H243)

### Child-Rearing Practices (Consistency)
Since parent substitutes (nurses, teachers) are more objective toward the child than parents are, they are more likely to institute basic disciplines with less frustration on the part of the child. (S214)

### Child-Rearing Practices (Rigidity)
Surrogate parents are more likely to be rigid in their attitudes and expectations toward children than are natural parents. (H243)

### Parent-Child Relations (Conflict)
Children living with both their natural parents have attitudes regarding conflict with parents that are more emotional, less compliant, and more suggestive of a constructive solution than have children not living with their natural parents. (G117)

## SURROGATE PARENT    X    Adjustment of Child
A child tends to adjust better to a parental surrogate when the surrogate's behavior is similar to that of his real parent. (M058)

The successful adjustment of the adopted child to a new home is less likely if one or both of the foster-parents are emotionally disturbed. (T086)

### Divorce Adjustment
The consequences of divorce will be less disruptive if the kinship is classificatory in character. (G093)

### Identification with Family
There is no relationship between identification with mainly one family and the age at which the child enters foster placement. (W149)

The greater the proportion of the child's lifetime spent in the present foster home, the more likely is the child to identify with his foster-parents. (W149)

### Juvenile Delinquency
Substitute parents do not contribute to any of the criminogenic traits.

A child's delinquency is dependent on the supervision he gets, regardless of whether the mother supervises him. (M058)

Juvenile delinquents are more likely to have parental surrogates than are nondelinquents. (S210)

### Juvenile Delinquency (Running Away)
Delinquent boys who run away are much more likely to have stepparents or adoptive parents than are delinquent boys who do not run away. (F093)

### Menstrual Taboo
When the mother shares nurturance with other people in the first few years of the child's life, the society is *less* likely to have extensive menstrual taboos. (S079)

### Mental Illness (Manic-Depressive)
Manic-depressives are more likely to come from families in which multiple parental figures share responsibilities for guidance of the infant and child. (G022)

### Mental Illness/Neurosis
The families of neurotic patients are more likely than those of mentally ill patients to have elder relatives available as surrogates if the parents cannot devote enough time to patients. (M061)

### Mental Illness of Child (Schizophrenia)
There is a positive relationship between the remoteness of the child-rearer(s) from the status of natural parents and the incidence of schizophrenic reactions in the child. (L144)

### Mother-Child Relations (Closeness)
If a child is cared for by a number of familiar adults instead of being in the exclusive care of the mother, the affectional relationship between mother and child will be less intense. (M058)

### Parent-Child Relations (Separation)
Children with many parental figures are more able to tolerate separation because they trust more people than do children with fewer parental figures.

### Personality of Child
Nervous, anxious children are best placed in quiet, conventional types of homes; while active, aggressive children are best in free and easy homes with companions. (B270)

### Personality of Child (Loneliness)
Children who are reared by several parent surrogates (rather than by one or both parents or merely by one surrogate) are more likely than others to develop feelings of isolation and loneliness. (W143)

### Personality of Child (Sociability)
Persons reared by multiple parental figures are more social than those reared by one or two parents. (W158)

### Personality Problems
There is a correlation between living with stepparents or guardians and nervousness and aggressive behavior in the child. (R108)

### Personality Problems of Child
Apart from the possibility of an increased tendency to enuresis on the part of adopted girls, there is no difference in symptomatology between children adopted early and those brought up mainly by their own parents. (H242)

Personality and behavioral problems in the child correlate more with the quality of home environmental factors, such as the personality of the mother, marital discord, and standards of child care, than with home care *v.* nursery care. (S265)

### Personality Problems of Mother
Children who fail to establish stable relationships in foster homes are more likely than are children who do to have mothers who have suffered nervous breakdowns. (W145)

### Religious Beliefs
The supernatural world of upper-class children will be that of the peasant class since upper-class children are reared by servants who are members of the peasant class. (B048)

### Self-Conception
Persons who had role-taking relationships with more significant others in early childhood are likely to have self-concepts which are more "social" and extended and more homogeneous than the self-concepts of persons exposed to few parent figures in childhood. (S279)

### Sex Status of Child
There is no relationship between the sex of the child (children 7–10 years of age) and the persons who serve as caretaking agents for the child. (M216)

### Social Adjustment of Child
Child-switching (sending the child at some period to live with different kinfolk) is associated with a better adaptation by the child into the larger community. (G156)

## SURROGATE PARENT, ADJUSTMENT TO
### X     Age
The younger the child, the more likely it is that he will make a satisfactory adjustment to living with stepparents and guardians. (R108)

The younger the child, the more likely is discontinuity of parent surrogates to result in feelings of insecurity on the part of the child. (S214)

### Age of Child
Very young and grown children assimilate a new parent more easily than do adolescent children. (B286)

The younger the adopted child is when he enters his new home, the more likely it is that he will successfully adjust to the situation. (T086)

### Child-Rearing Practices (Achievement Demands)
A child of low intelligence is more likely to become adjusted to a foster home if the parents do not have high expectations concerning the intellectual achievement of the child. (T086)

### Marital Adjustment
The successful adjustment of the adopted child to a new home is less likely if there is marital conflict between the foster parents. (T086)

### Ordinal Position
The firstborn child is more likely to suffer maladjustment as a result of placement with stepparents or guardians than are children at other age spacings. (T108)

### Surrogate Mother-Child Relations (Affection)
The successful adjustment of the adopted child to a new home is less likely if the foster-mother is unaffectionate. (T086)

### Surrogate Parent, Attitude Toward
The likelihood of success in foster-home care is increased when the child and his parents are both in agreement with the placement made for the child. (B270)

## SURROGATE PARENT, ATTITUDE TOWARD
### X     Surrogate Parent, Adjustment to
The likelihood of success in foster-home care is increased when the child and his parents are both in agreement with the placement made for the child. (B270)

## SURROGATE PARENT-CHILD RELATIONS
### X     Parent-Child Relations
Because a child is identified with his real parents he prefers these, no matter how rejecting, negligent, or mistreating, to any foster-parents, regardless of how adequate the foster-parents might be. (B270)

## SURROGATE SIBLINGS     X     Adjustment of Child
Foster-home care is likely to succeed if a child is placed with a child of the same age but opposite sex as the foster-child. (B270)

Foster-home care is more likely to be successful if there are other children in the home, especially if these are the siblings of the foster-child. (B270)

Foster-home care is more likely to be successful if there is a difference of four years or more in either direction between the foster-child and the foster-parents' own child of the same sex. (B270)

# T

## TECHNOLOGY
### X Child-Rearing Practices (Permissiveness)
There is a negative correlation between the level of technological development of a society and permissiveness of the child-rearing practices. (L168)

### Child-Rearing Practices (Sex Role)
Societies will be characterized by greater differentiation of socialization by sex if their economies value strength and motor skills which are typically masculine. (B264)

### Cohesion of Family
With the existence of modern means of communication, relations between kin are likely to be stronger and more frequent than they were in the past. (P083)

### Descent (Bilateral)
Bilateral organizations may also occur in societies which have rankings and considerable material wealth if the women are permitted equal access to strategic resources. (B060)

### Descent (Unilineal)
Unilineal descent groups are not of significance among peoples who live in small groups, depend upon a rudimentary technology, and have little durable property. (B045)

### Division of Labor, by Sex
Division of labor by sex is greater in agriculture, merchandising, and laboring specialties than in industrial communities where women often work along with men. (T072)

### Intermarriage (Ethnic)
The rate of intermarriage will tend to be restricted if the technological pattern of the cultures in contact are diverse. (H036)

### Kinship, Importance of
The more "advanced" the technology, the more importance nonkinship structures assume in the system and the less kinship dominates the social structure. (P062)

### Size of Family
There is a correlation between family size and the type of animal traction used in ploughing. (B031)

Family size decreases as oxen are replaced by horses and the latter by cows as animals used in ploughing (Yugoslavia). (B031)

## TECHNOLOGY (IRRIGATION)
### X Political Structure
The development of a system of irrigation will tend to be accompanied by a shift from lineage-based units to politically autonomous organizations. (D086)

## TELEVISION  X  Parent-Child Relations (Control)
The child exercises more control than his parents over both amount of his viewing time and selection of program content. (H178)

## TENSION MANAGEMENT
### X Employment of Women
As competition pressures increase and the need for women employed in "expressive" occupations (secretaries, nurses, teachers, etc.), where their function is partly that of tension reduction, increases, the tension-reduction burden on the nuclear family is likely to decrease. (P083)

### Role Definition in Family
Considering the family as a triad of roles, High Status Authority (HSA), Low Status Subordinate (LSS), and High Status Friend (HSF), to ensure a tension balance within a given actor, the family system is more apt to be set up so that actors play the role of HSA in one subsystem and HSF in another subsystem than to restrict an actor to one of these roles exclusively.

Viewing the family as a triad of roles, High Status Authority (HSA), Lower Status Subordinate (LSS), and High Status Friend (HSF), where one parent plays an instrumental role (HSA) vis-à-vis a child (LSS) in the presence of the other spouse the situation will be a more relaxed one if the latter assumes a role of High Status Friend than if he assumes a more instrumental role.

## TENSIONS IN FAMILY/PERSONALITY
### X Nuclear Family, Importance of
As the importance of the nuclear family and the marital relationship increases in a social system, the strains on these institutions and on their members as personalities increase. (P062)

## TERRITORIAL EXPANSION
### X Functions of Kin-Group
As territorial units grow larger and stronger, kinship groupings will become more simple, more vague, and increasingly limited in function. (B064)

### Segmentary Structure
The development of a segmentary structure is inhibited by the existence of physical or human barriers to territorial expansion. (F033)

### Size of Clan
Formation of large segmented clans seems to depend upon maintaining social continuity over a widening series of territorial entities which, in turn, depends upon considerable physical mobility and facilities for continued territorial expansion. (F089)

## THEFT    X  Child-Rearing Practices (Indulgence)
A high frequency of theft is found in societies with severe weaning and low indulgence of infants. (W127)

### Child-Rearing Practices (Obedience/Dependency)
Theft is more frequent in societies which severely punish older children for disobedience, irresponsibility, lack of self-reliance, and lack of achievement. (W127)

### Weaning
There is an association between a high frequency of theft in society and low infant indulgence and severe weaning. (W127)

# THERAPEUTIC PRACTICES

### X   Aggression Anxiety

The degree of anxiety generated by the socialization of aggression in the child is inversely correlated with the degree to which a society utilizes punitive measures against the child. (K111)

The degree of anxiety generated by the socialization of aggression in the child (the degree to which punishment for aggression has led to inhibitions of aggression responses and consequent intropunitive or self-aggression) is correlated with the extent to which the society employs sacrifice as a therapeutic practice. (K111)

The degree of anxiety generated by the socialization of aggression in the child is correlated with the extent to which the society employs bloodletting as a therapeutic practice. (K111)

### Child-Rearing Practices (Aggression)

Cultures that permit little aggressive behavior in small children tend to be more concerned with health matters, e.g., the use of various therapies and explanations for illness. (P084)

### Child-Rearing Practices (Dependency)

The age of socialization of independence behavior is correlated with the amount of patient activity during illness. (K111)

Initial indulgence of the drive for dependence on the mother, a child-training antecedent of guilt, is not related to the extent to which a society employs intropunitive therapy (bloodletting, sacrifice) for illness. (K111)

### Child-Rearing Practices (Punishment)

The degree of importance of love-oriented techniques of punishment is not related to the extent to which a society employs intropunitive therapy (bloodletting, sacrifice) for illness. (K111)

### Child-Rearing Practices (Sex)

Societies with severe sex training tend to believe that abstention from sexual intercourse by the patient would have a therapeutic effect on his illness. (W127)

### Socialization (Gratification)

The more that custom prescribes progressive satisfaction of the child in any system of behavior, the more likely that customary therapeutic practices relative to illness will include an activity characteristic of that system. (W142)

### Socialization, Agents of

The degree of importance of the parents, as opposed to other persons, as agents of socialization is not related to the extent to which a society employs intropunitive therapy (bloodletting, sacrifice) for illness. (K111)

### Toilet Training

Anal avoidance (e.g., involving washing or cleansing, adherence to cleanliness taboos, or the retention of feces) tends to be used as a therapeutic practice in societies which stress severe toilet training. (W127)

# THERAPY    X   Parental/Maternal Role

Mothers are more likely than fathers to make (mental health) clinic contacts because fathers frequently fear the loss of domination of the family. (R110)

### Personality Development of Parent

Since parents who are fixated at the phallic-urethral level of psychosexual development have a competitive-orientation and ability to direct their energies, they are less likely than others to appeal to social agencies voluntarily. (R110)

# TOILET TRAINING    X   Child-Rearing Anxiety

The more severe the mother is in toilet training the child, the more likely is she to be highly anxious concerning child rearing (U.S.). (S191)

### Child-Rearing Practices (Aggression)

The more severe the parents are in toilet training the child, the less likely are they to tolerate aggressive behavior by the child directed against them and the more likely are they to punish parent-directed aggression (U.S.). (S191)

Mothers who are permissive regarding the child's parent-directed aggression are less severe in toilet training than are nonpermissive mothers (U.S.). (S191)

### Child-Rearing Practices (Cleanliness)

Early toilet training is no more effective in teaching the child cleanliness habits than is later toilet training.

### Child-Rearing Practices (Dependency)

Cultures that begin toilet training early begin independence training later; cultures that begin independence training early are late in toilet training. (P084)

### Child-Rearing Practices (Household Rules)

The more severe the mother is in toilet training the child, the greater the demands on the child for conformity with household rules (table manners, neatness, orderliness, and care of house and furniture) (U.S.). (S191)

### Child-Rearing Practices (Indulgence)

When parents are particularly fond of and indulgent toward children, training in sphincter control will occur at a late age. (D025)

### Child-Rearing Practices (Orderliness)

Mothers who are severe in toilet training are more demanding regarding orderliness (U.S.). (S191)

### Child-Rearing Practices (Punishment)

The more severe the mother is in toilet training the child, the more likely is she (in other areas of child training) to use physical punishment, deprive the child of privileges, and avoid using reason in handling the child (U.S.). (S191)

### Child-Rearing Practices (Sex)

The more severe the parents are in toilet training the child, the less permissive they are about the child's sex behavior (i.e., modesty, masturbation, social sex play) (U.S.). (S191)

Mothers who are not permissive regarding their children's sexual behavior are more severe in their toilet training than are mothers who are permissive regarding sex (U.S.). (S191)

### Child-Rearing Practices (Sleeping)

There is no relationship between the mother's severity in toilet training and her strictness regarding the child's bedtime rules (U.S.). (S191)

### Class

Lower-class mothers are more severe in toilet training

than are middle-class mothers. This hypothesis is also denied. (H011)

Toilet training is begun earlier in the middle class than in the lower class (Chicago). (L003)

Toilet training is completed earlier in the lower class than in the middle class (Boston). (L003)

There is no significant difference between the middle class and the lower class in the time when toilet training is begun or completed. (L003)

Middle-class mothers whose husbands have entrepreneurial jobs are more likely than lower-class mothers (entrepreneurial) to begin bowel training when the infant is nine months old or even earlier. (M062)

Working-class mothers are quicker and more severe in toilet training than are middle-class mothers (but begin training no earlier). (S191)

Lower-class Negro parents are more likely to toilet train their babies after 12 months; upper-class Negro parents, to toilet train their babies before 12 months. (W133)

### Class/Education
Better-educated mothers, regardless of socioeconomic level, and middle-class mothers, regardless of educational level, are somewhat less severe in toilet training than are lesser-educated working-class mothers (U.S.). (S191)

### Dependency
Severity of toilet training is not related to dependency in the child. (B224)

### Education
The more highly educated the parents, the more likely are they to have toilet-training problems with their children.

### Education of Mother
Regardless of socioeconomic level, better-educated mothers toilet trained their children earlier. (S191)

### Ethnicity (Italian/Jewish)
Italian mothers tend to be more severe than Jewish mothers in toilet training their children. (M060)

### Feeding Problems
There is a positive relationship between severe toilet training and feeding problems (e.g., prolonged periods of appetite loss, etc.) in the child (U.S.). (S191)

### Husband-Wife Relations (Evaluation)
The more severe the mother is in toilet training the child, the lower her esteem for her husband (U.S.). (S191)

### Husband-Wife Relations (Warmth)
The more severe the mother in toilet training, the lower the warmth felt for her husband (U.S.). (S191)

### Illness, Explanation of
There does not seem to be any correlation between severity of toilet training and anal explanations of illness. (W127)

### Mental Illness (Schizophrenia)
Mothers of schizophrenics are more likely to repress all memory of the toilet-training period than are mothers of neurotics or of normals. (M218)

Schizophrenia tends to be directly associated with an artificial acceleration of the toilet-training program by the mother. (T105)

### Mother-Child Relations (Warmth)
The more severe the mother in toilet training, the lower the warmth felt for her child (U.S.). (S191)

Severe toilet training increases the amount of upset in children whose mothers are relatively cold and undemonstrative. (S191)

### Occupation
Middle-class mothers whose husbands have entrepreneurial jobs are significantly more likely than are mothers of similar social status whose husbands have bureaucratic jobs to begin urinary training of their youngsters before they are 11 months old. (M062)

Mothers whose husbands have entrepreneurial jobs are more likely than mothers whose husbands have bureaucratic jobs to begin bowel training of their youngsters before they are 10 months old. (M062)

Parents of clerical groups begin daily bladder training appreciably later than working-class parents, but not significantly later than professional groups (U.S.). (M180)

### Oedipal Complex
The development of the Oedipal complex is directly correlated with rigidity in toilet training. (M226)

### Parent-Child Relations (Affection)
The child's acceptance of the demands of toilet training is not related to his desire for the love and approval of his parents. (B224)

### Personality Adjustment
Exceptionally earlier toilet training leads to childhood personality disturbances. (F097)

### Personality (Compulsiveness)
Compulsive character is largely the product of severity or cruelty in treatment during the period of cleanliness training. (L166)

### Personality of Child
Severity of anal training is associated with compulsivity and rigidity of control (as measured by the Cattell Personality Test).

Severe anal training is associated with lower sociability.

### Personality Problems
Too rigid or too early toilet training will lead to thumbsucking, whining, demanding, hostility, willfulness, and pretended autonomy.

### Race (Class)
In both the middle and lower classes, Negro parents are stricter than are white parents in toilet training their children.

### Scholastic Achievement
The more severe the mother is in toilet training the child, the more likely is she to expect the child to do well in school (U.S.). (S191)

### Self-Conception of Mother
The more severe the mother is in toilet training the child, the more likely is she to lack self-esteem (U.S.). (S191)

### Sex Anxiety of Mother
High sexual anxiety of the mother and early toilet training of the child are associated. (S191)

High sexual anxiety of the mother and rapid completion of toilet training of the child are associated. (S191)

### Sex Status

Among mothers who have greater anxieties concerning sex, those who have boys are more likely to commence toilet training at an earlier age than are those who have girls (U.S.). (S191)

### Speech Problems

Children with articulation problems are more likely to have been toilet trained at an earlier age than are children without articulation problems. (F095)

### Superego Formation

There is no relationship between the age of toilet training and projective systems which reflect guilt. (W127)

### Therapeutic Practices

Anal avoidance (e.g., involving washing or cleansing, the adherence to cleanliness, or the retention of feces) tends to be used as a therapeutic practice in societies which stress severe toilet training. (W127)

### Urban/Rural

Urban working-class parents and better-educated parents commence toilet training at an earlier age than do country parents (France). (F097)

## TOILET TRAINING, COMPLETION OF
### X  Toilet Training, Severity of

There is no relationship between the severity of toilet training (scolding and punishing, taking child to toilet frequently, etc.) and the length of time it takes to complete toilet training. (S191)

## TOILET TRAINING/FEEDING
### X  Scholastic Achievement (Reading)

Children who have reading disabilities are more likely than are those who do not to have experienced disturbed feeding and toilet-training periods. (S225)

## TOILET TRAINING, SEVERITY OF
### X  Toilet Training, Completion of

There is no relationship between the severity of toilet training (scolding and punishing, taking the child to toilet frequently, etc.) and the length of time it takes to complete toilet training. (S191)

## TOTEMISM    X  Sleeping Arrangements

Totemism is correlated with exclusive mother-infant sleeping arrangements. (W127)

## TRADE UNION ATTITUDES OF FAMILY
### X  Trade Union Participation

Individuals from families with attitudes favorable to unions will tend to participate in union activities more than will others. (M166)

## TRADE UNION PARTICIPATION
### X  Trade Union Attitudes of Family

Individuals from families with attitudes favorable to unions will tend to participate in union activities more than will others. (M166)

## TWINS    X  Pregnancy, Attitude Toward

There is a correlation between the unconscious fear of superfetation, and the custom of fearing and/or killing children who are twins. (D071)

# U

**UNEMPLOYMENT**          **X Illegitimacy**
Illegitimacy is directly related to unemployment. (S003)

### Juvenile Delinquency
Juvenile delinquents are more likely to come from families where there is greater unemployment among the parents than are nondelinquents. (S210)

**URBAN/NONURBAN**      **X Duration of Marriage**
Among couples who have divorced, those with nonurban backgrounds have longer marriage durations than do those with urban backgrounds. (G157)

**URBAN/RURAL**             **X Adultery**
Belief in the prevalence of adultery is greater among those living in urban areas than in rural areas (France). (C123)

The rate of extramarital relations tends to be higher in urban than in rural areas. (E026)

### Age at Marriage
Rural men and women marry at an earlier age than do city young people. The contrary is also asserted. (B033)

### Authority Structure of Family
Decisions concerning family activities are more often made jointly by both spouses in an urban environment than in a rural environment.

### Child-Rearing Attitudes (Rigidity)
Parents who were reared on farms are more likely to be rigid in their child-rearing attitudes than are others. (B249)

### Child-Rearing Practices (Competence)
Mothers from urban areas are more likely to be knowledgable in infant care and in their interpretation of infant behavior than are mothers from rural areas. (B272)

### Child-Rearing Practices (Control)
Rural parents tend to exert greater control over their children than do urban parents. (W144)

### Child-Rearing Values (Rigidity)
Girls raised in rural areas are more likely to face inflexible rules about adolescent behavior and parental control than are girls raised in urban environments.

### Cohesion of Family
Rural background is correlated with family integration. There is no correlation between these two variables. (S217)

### Conformity with Kin-Role
Obligations toward kinsmen are more likely to be neglected in urban areas. (G083)

### Disorganization of Family
Family disorganization is more likely to occur among urban families than among rural families. (T002)

### Divorce
Countries that are rural typically have lower divorce rates than do those that are predominantly urban. (B033)

Divorce is positively related to urban residence. (C005)

In Western countries, rural people tend to have lower divorce rates than do urban dwellers. (G156)

### Divorce Adjustment
Divorcées from rural backgrounds are more likely to experience difficult emotional problems during the divorce than are divorcées from urban backgrounds. (G157)

### Divorce Complaints
Divorcées from urban backgrounds are more likely to complain about their husbands' personalities as causes of divorce than are divorcées from rural backgrounds. (G157)

Divorcées from rural backgrounds are slightly more likely to complain that their husbands were too authoritarian than are those from urban backgrounds. (G157)

Among divorcées, urban wives married to urban husbands are most likely to complain that personality conflicts were the cause of divorce, followed by rural–urban marriage combinations, and lastly by rural wives who were married to rural husbands. (G157)

Divorcées from rural backgrounds are slightly more likely to claim nonsupport as a cause of divorce than are divorcées from urban backgrounds. (G157)

Husbands of rural background are slightly more likely than those of urban background to have their ex-wives claim nonsupport as a cause of divorce. (G157)

Rural divorcées who were married to urban husbands are least likely to complain that nonsupport was a cause of their divorce, followed by urban divorcées who were married to urban husbands, next by urban divorcées who were married to rural husbands, and lastly by rural divorcées who were married to rural husbands. (G157)

Divorcées from rural backgrounds are slightly more likely to complain that their husbands' neglect of homelife was a cause of their divorces. (G157)

Rural divorcées who were married to urban husbands are most likely to complain that their husbands' neglect of homelife was a cause of divorce, followed by the urban divorcées who were married to urban husbands, and lastly by both the urban divorcées married to rural husbands and the rural divorcées married to rural husbands. (G157)

Rural divorcées who were married to rural husbands are most likely to claim that value conflicts were a cause of divorce, followed by rural divorcées married to urban husbands, next by urban divorcées married to rural husbands, and lastly by urban divorcées married to urban husbands. (G157)

### Divorce Decision

Stability of the final decision to divorce is unrelated to whether the couples are from rural or urban backgrounds. (G157)

### Divorce Process

Couples from rural backgrounds take a longer time between a serious consideration of divorce and the actual filings of the suits than do couples from urban backgrounds. (G157)

### Duration of Marriage

Of those marriages which are terminated, urban couples have a shorter duration of marriage. (M167)

### Economic Dependence of Family

Farm families are economically self-sufficient to a much greater extent than are urban families. (B033)

### Employment of Mother

Employed mothers are more likely to have urban residence than are mothers who do not work. (S265)

### Extended Family

Rural families have a wider generational span than do urban families. (B033)

### Fertility

Fertility rates tend to be higher in rural areas. (I007)

### Fertility Values

Urban wives value the chance to have children as one of the most valuable parts of marriage, while rural wives tend to do so less.

### Geographic Mobility

Farm families are more stable in residence than are urban families. (B033)

### Homogamy

For a girl, urban origins are more likely to result in a heterogamous marriage than are nonurban origins. (K150)

### Husband-Wife Relations (Communication)

Wives in urban areas tend to communicate their emotional problems with their husbands less than do wives in rural areas.

### Husband-Wife Relations (Companionship)

Rural wives rate higher the companionship with their husbands (being deprived of close contact with other women) than do urban wives.

### Husband-Wife Relations (Complaints)

Divorcées from urban backgrounds are more likely to complain about their husbands' personalities as causes of divorce than are divorcées from rural backgrounds. (G157)

Divorcées from rural backgrounds are slightly more likely to complain that their husbands were too authoritarian than are those from urban backgrounds. (G157)

Among divorcées, urban wives married to urban husbands are most likely to complain that personality conflicts were the cause of divorce, followed by rural-urban marriage combinations, and lastly by rural wives married to rural husbands. (G157)

Divorcées from rural backgrounds are slightly more likely to claim nonsupport as a cause of divorce than are divorcées from urban backgrounds. (G157)

Husbands of rural background are slightly more likely than are those of urban background to have their ex-wives claim nonsupport as a cause of divorce. (G157)

### Husband-Wife Relations (Power)

Urban wives are less submissive to their husbands than are rural wives. (H164)

### Identification with Mother

Children from rural homes are more likely to identify with their mothers than are those from urban homes. (A060)

### Illegitimacy

The rate of illegitimacy is higher in urban than in rural areas. (K065)

### Income, Allocation of

In rural families, personal appearance is sacrificed for other needs and wants to a greater extent than in the city family. (B033)

### Independence of Nuclear Family

Urban families tend to be more highly individuated (differentiated, autonomous) than do rural families. (B267)

### Intermarriage

The partners in intermarriages are more likely to be of urban background than of rural background. (G003)

### Intermarriage (Religious)

There is no relation between urban or rural background and interfaith marriage. (H240)

### Joint Family

The joint family structure is today more characteristic of rural than of urban families. (M081)

### Juvenile Delinquency

Rural families are less likely than are urban families to produce delinquent children. (N057)

There is a correlation between urban residence and delinquency in the boy, but not in the girl. (N063)

Employed mothers in rural areas are more likely to have delinquent children than are those in urban areas. (N063)

### Kin Ties

The attenuation of kin ties tends to occur in urban areas. (L072)

### Marital Adjustment of Wife

Wives in urban areas show higher satisfaction with marital love than do wives in rural areas.

### Marital Stability

Marital breakup is more likely to occur in urban areas than in rural areas. (L001)

In the anonymity of an urban environment, the facility with which any type of mating relationship can be established or terminated is largely responsible for the instability of domestic unions. (S211)

### Marital Status

The proportion of single and unattached people is greater in urban areas. (B033)

The percentage of people married is greater in urban areas than in rural areas. (H001)

### Marriage Chances

In urban areas there has been a greater increase in the percentage of people ever married than in rural areas. (H001)

### Mating Forms

Urbanization or urban residence does not cause changes in the sequence of mating forms. (S211)

### Parent-Child Relations

Adolescents who live in the city are better adjusted to their parents than are adolescents who live on a farm (U.S.). (N010)

### Parent-Child Relations (Control)

The rural child is under greater parental control than is the urban child. (B033)

### Personality Adjustment of Children

The average level of personality adjustment is higher among farm children than among those living in city homes. (B033)

### Power Structure of Family

Dominance of the father is more common in rural families than is dominance of the mother; dominance of the mother is more frequent in city families than is dominance of the father. (B033)

### Preferential Marriage (Parallel Cross-Cousin)

Patterns of preferential marriage tend to deteriorate in an urban context. (P023)

### Premarital Sex Relations

The urban male and the urban female of age 20 are more likely to practice premarital petting and coitus than are their rural counterparts. (E092)

### Residence with Child

Co-residence of aged parents with middle-aged children is less apt to occur in urban areas than it is in rural areas. (B312)

### Separation

Separations are more numerous in urban than in rural areas. (B033)

### Sex Status of Household Head

Women are more likely to be heads of households in towns than in rural areas. (A051)

In urban areas the heads of Negro households are more likely to be women than men; in rural areas, men than women. (F003)

### Size of Family

The average size of the rural family is larger than that of the urban family. (B033)

Among divorced wives, those from rural backgrounds tend to have more children than do those from urban backgrounds. (G157)

Farm families which live near cities are smaller than those which live *far* from cities. (K016)

### Social Adjustment of Wife

Wives in urban areas express much higher satisfaction with their social lives than do wives in rural areas.

### Stability of Family

Family instability is more likely among urban population than among rural population. (L024)

### Stability of Family Status

The economic and social conditions of rural life placed more of a premium on continuity of occupation and status from generation to generation than do urban conditions. (P012)

### Stability of Family Structure

Changes in the family structure are occurring more rapidly in cities than in villages. (B033)

### Toilet Training

Urban working-class parents and better-educated parents commence toilet training at an earlier age than do country parents (France). (F097)

### Value Conflict (Family/Economic)

Rural residents are more likely than urban residents or those with high social or educational status to feel that the values of economic success conflict with family values. (J033)

### Values (Extended/Nuclear Family)

Those living in urban settings are more apt to prefer nuclear family values and those living in rural areas are more inclined to extended family values. (J033)

### Weaning

In France, weaning takes place later among country children than among town children. (F097)

**URBAN/SUBURBAN          X  Size of Family**

There are a larger number of children in suburban families than in city families. (C009)

**URBANIZATION          X  Adultery**

Urban conditions tend to increase the incidence of extramarital relations. (G058)

### Age at Marriage

The more urbanized the society, the later the average age at marriage. (S219)

### Age-Groups

The extent of urbanization is inversely correlated with the persistence of the traditional age-grade system. (N016)

### Authority Structure of Family

There is a correlation between increasing urbanism and the decline of paternal authority. (C134)

Under urban conditions, with an expanding universe of social contacts, a shift of authority will occur from hereditary elders to new income-getting elites and from mother's brother to father. (F029)

Under urban pressures, there is a tendency for the father's authority and responsibility in matrilineal societies to increase rapidly over that of the mother's brother. (M050)

Urbanization is correlated with a decline in manifestations of both patriarchal and matriarchal authority. (R088)

### Cohesion of Family

There is no evidence that increased urbanization of a family leads to the disintegration of the family. (C134)

### Cohesion of Kin-Group

Where urban populations are ethnically homogeneous, there is no evidence that city life tends to weaken kinship bonds. (B306)

### Divorce
There is a direct relation between urbanization and divorce. (K161)

### Economic Dependence
With the dispersion of the children to the city for education and nonfarm occupations, the farm family declines as a self-sustaining unit. (B033)

### Economic Dependence of Women
The economic independence of Negro women is highest in the city, second in the rural nonfarm, and least in the rural farm. (B033)

### Elopement
The incidence of elopement tends to be directly correlated with the degree of urbanization. (L064)

### Exogamy
Traditional prohibitions against marriage between individuals with the same surname tends to be infringed in urban areas. (F035)

### Fertility
Fertility is inversely related to degree of urbanization. (D006)

### Fertility Values
The more urbanized the population, the smaller the number of children it prefers.

### Husband-Wife Relations (Intensity)
When families move to towns (away from kin), the conjugal bond tends to become more intense. (G012)

### Illegitimacy
The rate of illegitimacy is directly correlated with the degree of urbanization. (H164)

### Isolation of Nuclear Family
The degree of urbanization is directly correlated with an increasing proportion of independent nuclear families. (L064)

### Kin-Role Behavior
Adherence to traditional kin roles is inversely correlated with the degree of urbanization. (B111)

### Kin-Role Definition
The degree of urbanization is directly correlated with an increased ambiguity in behavior toward kinsmen. (L064)

### Kin Terminology
The degree of urbanization tends to be directly correlated with a diminution in the application of kinship terminology. (L064)

### Kin Terminology (Classificatory)
The abandonment of the use of kinship terminology for classificatory kinsmen is directly correlated with the degree of urbanization. (S122)

### Kin Ties
The greater the degree of urbanization, the smaller the kinship range. (G033)

The weakening of kin ties is directly correlated with the degree of urbanization. (M076)

### Kin Ties (Fictive)
A decrease in the importance of the fictive kinship relationship is directly correlated with the degree of urbanization. (A029)

In urban areas fictive kinship relationships tend to be established with friends rather than with relatives. (A029)

When the urban population is largely immigrant, unstable, and socially heterogeneous, fictional groups tend to arise as a substitute for actual kinship ties. (L030)

### Love
The absence of strong primary group attachments among men in modern urban society has led to the modern ideal of marriage as a love match. (S030)

### Marital Stability
Marital stability tends to decrease in situations of increasing urbanization. (F055)

The degree of marital instability tends to be directly correlated with the extent of urbanization. (H103)

### Mate Selection (Free Choice)
Parental control of marriage is no more likely to occur in the fringe area than in the central city. (J003)

An increase in the degree of urbanization tends to be correlated with the weakening of control of parents in the process of mate selection. (M050)

### Nuclear Family
There is no relationship between urbanization and the percentage of nuclear families. (G113)

### Occupation
Urbanization tends to result in a weakening of emphasis upon hereditary specialization within the caste system. (P022)

### Polygyny
Polygyny tends to be abandoned under the conditions of urban life. (K066)

### Power Structure of Family
Urbanization tends to result in the weakening of parental control. (F055)

### Premarital Pregnancy
The percentage of premarital pregnancy is higher for metropolitan cities than for smaller urban communities. (M243)

### Self-Conception
Urbanized areas comprise an environment conducive to changes in self-identification.

### Sex Status of Household Head
A higher proportion of Negro women heads can be found in city than in rural nonfarm populations and both urban and rural nonfarm populations have a higher percentage of women heads than do rural farm areas. (B033)

### Size of Family
There is no significant change in family size attendant on urbanization. (A065)

There is a direct relation between the degree of urbanization (urban, suburban, rural) of a family and that family's size. (C134)

### Social Control
The degree of urbanization is inversely correlated with the extent to which kinship institutions are effective in social control. (W034)

### Stability of Extended Family
Urban migration with industrialization is a second major factor involved in the disorganization of the Chinese extended family. (B033)

### Stability of Family
The degree of urbanization tends to be inversely correlated with the stability of the elementary family. (L064)

The stability of the rural family decreases with the increase in urban influences. (B033)

### Stability of Family Structure
Traditional patterns of family life and marriage tend to disintegrate under urban pressures. (H107)

### Stratification, Basis of
Kinship is more likely to be the basis of adult status in the fringe area than in the central city. (J003)

### Values (Familism)
The secularizing effects of urbanism on family values will be least on those values most central to the traditional family structure. (T001)

## URBANIZATION/INDUSTRIALIZATION
### X    Divorce
Urbanization and industrialization do not necessarily increase the divorce rates. (G134)

# V

## VALUE COMMITMENT OF PARENTS
### X Socialization, Effectiveness of
The greater the internalization of values on the part of the parents, the more likely is the effective socialization of the child. (M203)

## VALUE CONFLICT
### X Emotional Problems of Child
Although the parents (of Italian- and Irish-American backgrounds) of emotionally disturbed children have congruent unconscious value orientations, they are more likely than are the parents of normal children to have severe conflicts concerning new and old values, the mother appearing to be more progressive. (V031)

### Husband-Wife Relations (Conflict)
Conflict in cultural value orientations is a cause of marital conflict. (V033)

### Isolation of Family
Where there is a conflict between familial and community values, the parents may keep the children isolated from all but formal contact with the social environment outside the home. (B033)

## VALUE CONFLICT (FAMILY/ECONOMIC)
### X Education
Low educational level is likely to accompany greater conflict between family values and values of economic success, while higher educational level is more apt to be found in conjunction with less conflict between family values and values of economic success. (J033)

### Rank
Low social status is likely to accompany greater conflict between family values and values of economic success, while high social status is more apt to be found in conjunction with less conflict between family values and values of economic success. (J033)

### Urban/Rural
Rural residents are more likely than urban residents or those with high social or educational status to feel that the values of economic success conflict with family values. (J033)

### Values (Extended/Nuclear Family)
Men who espouse nuclear family norms are least likely to see a conflict between family ties and economic success values. Those who advocate modified extended family norms are in the middle of this measure and those who advocate extended family norms are most likely to see a conflict between family ties and economic success values. (J025)

Those who support an extended family norm are more likely to see a conflict between values of economic success and family values, while those espousing norms of a modified extended family have less conflict; those holding norms favoring nuclear families find the least conflict between family values and values of economic success. (J033)

## VALUE CONFLICT (PARENTS/PEERS)
### X Juvenile Delinquency
Juvenile delinquency is associated with a conflict between the expectations of the family and those of the gang. (B033)

### Mental Illness (Schizophrenia)
Schizophrenic adolescents are more likely than others to be confronted with peer-group values which are contradictory with parental attitudes. (W143)

## VALUE CONSENSUS
### X Cohesion of Family
If family members accept the legitimacy of external institutions and have a differential commitment to them, family solidarity is reduced. (B202)

### Courtship
Value consensus is more crucial at an early stage than at a later stage in a romantic relationship. (K109)

### Mate Selection
If a man and a woman have a high degree of value consensus, then it is more probable that they will progress toward a permanent union.

### Parent-Child Relations
The greater the consensus in the family on domestic values, the greater the parents' satisfaction with their daughter's performance. (F094)

### Parent-Child Relations (Evaluation)
Children who have a high evaluation of their parents (Parent Evaluation Scale) tend to be in close agreement with their parents' ideology.

### Parent-Child Relations (Satisfaction)
In families in which the role tension of husband and wife is low, the degree of consensus on domestic values between husband and wife correlates with their agreement whether they are satisfied with specific activities of their child. (F116)

In families in which the role tension of husband and wife is high, there is no relationship between the degree of the couple's consensus on domestic values and the amount of agreement between them on satisfaction with specific activities of their child. (F116)

### Size of Household
The larger the household, the higher the consensus among members regarding what is right and wrong. (G156)

## VALUES
### X Acculturation
When the orientation of the parents toward the donor culture is positive, the degree of acculturation will be higher. (B043)

### Age-Groups
In any society in which the larger societal norms are very different from those within the family, some type of age-group (e.g., adolescent peer groups) will arise to bridge the necessary transition between the two. (G156)

### Authority Structure of Family
Lack of consistent authority in the home tends to result in serious disturbance in the (manic-depressive) child's value system. (C092)

### Breast Feeding
There is a correlation between the practice of unlimited breast feeding of the infant and the norm of generosity in the larger society. (K111)

### Child-Rearing Practices
Child-rearing practices are related less to general cultural attitudes toward children than to values specific to each system or area of behavior. (W142)

### Child-Rearing Practices (Control)
There is only a low association between mothers' concern about television program content (relative to their children) and their exercise of control over programs viewed. (H178)

### Child-Rearing Values
A transition in the larger culture from repression to tolerance of basic impulses results in a similar transition in child-rearing values. (M203)

### Child-Rearing Values (Mate Selection/Occupation)
The greater a culture's emphasis on scholarship and learning, the more likely it is that parents will guide their children into intellectual careers or into marriages with intellectuals. (M203)

### Conflict between Generations
The adoption of new standards and definitions of behavior by the younger generation will be a source of intergenerational conflict in the family and community. (B042)

### Conflict in Family
When differential and contradictory values prevail in a culture, family conflict will tend to arise where family members have internalized this conflict. (S075)

### Conformity (Peers/Parents)
Adolescent girls are more inclined to follow peers' advice than parents' advice in choices deriving meaning from the peer society and more likely to favor parents' opinion than peers' in choices deriving meaning from the larger society in which there are status positions to which one can aspire as an adult. (B292)

Adolescents are more given to peer conformity in making choices in areas where social values are changing rapidly and parental conformity where social values are relatively stable. (B292)

Adolescents are more disposed to peer conformity in making choices with immediate consequences and parental conformity for choices with emphasis on long-term effect. (B292)

### Dating
There is a parallelism between the norms of competition and success prevalent in the larger American society and the norms which govern dating behavior. (S219)

### Education
The lower the educational background, the more likely a person is to believe patriarchy is the proper power structure for the family. (K089)

### Employment of Mother
Mothers with jobs tend to believe that frustration is a basic part of life more than mothers without employment.

### Employment of Wife
Employment of the wife-mother increases the likelihood that both husband and wife will have an egalitarian rather than patriarchal ideology about family life. (B231)

### Exogamy (Community)
When the marriage pattern is that of community exogamy, cultural variation between villages tends to be reduced. (L066)

### Fertility/Death Rate
In a society whose values are based upon individual initiative in coping with problems, the birth and death rates tend to be more balanced than in societies characterized by other types of individual adaptation.

In societies characterized by individuals whose actions are guided by their relations with their contemporaries, both birth and death rates are more likely to decline than in societies characterized by other types of individual adaptation.

### Homogamy (Cultural)
In most societies, preferred mates are found to be fellow citizens who do not exhibit significant cultural differences. (M019)

### Husband-Wife Relations (Egalitarianism)
In societies which emphasize vertical superordination-subordination relationships, egalitarian relationships between husband and wife are less common. (P083)

### Illegitimacy (Adoption)
The greater the recognition by the unwed mother that surrendering the child is the norm, the more likely is she to conform and thus give up the child. (J020)

### Intermarriage (Ethnic)
Intermarriage is more likely to take place among heterogeneous groups that have developed social proximity (i.e., similar standards of living, similar social-class position, etc.) than among heterogeneous groups that have not developed social proximity. (B012)

The rate of intermarriage will be higher when the cultures of the ethnic groups are similar. (L045)

### Kindred
By reinforcing the marital tie in such a way that concubinage was not a legitimate outlet for sexual needs and repudiation for barrenness was no longer the husband's prerogative, Christianity has encouraged development of bilateral kindred to the detriment of the patrilineal lineage. (P083)

### Marital Adjustment
There is a correlation between marital adjustment and the parents' rejection of adolescent social institutions. (S219)

### Marriage Chances
Among Western nations, the more that people come to believe in the benefits of companionship with the opposite sex, the higher the percentage eventually marrying.

### Mate Selection
People tend to marry those who share a common culture interest and value. (B033)

### Mental Illness (Social Adjustment)
There is no relationship between a mental patient's success or failure in remaining in the community and scores of relatives on scales designed to measure value orientation (Brim Scales). (F124)

Fatalism, reflectiveness, animism, and belief in single action, as indicated in responses of family members to value scales (Brim Scales), are related to low social and vocational performance of the former mental patient. (F124)

### Mental Retardation
Boys who interact with a retarded sibling on a daily basis are likely to stress material aspects of future plans, such as success in business; while those who do not interact with a retarded sibling stress such things as marital happiness.

Girls who interact with a retarded sibling are more likely to stress an ideal life of "giving"—making a contribution to society—while those who do not interact with their retarded sibling stress social acceptability and friendliness.

### Parent-Child Relations
Parental values have their chief effect by the way they modify relationships between parents and children rather than by directly modifying the belief system of the child. (M060)

### Parent-Child Relations (Conflict)
Serious conflict between parents and children arises when the standards of the family differ markedly from those which the child meets outside the home. (B033)

### Personality of Parents
Good character traits valued by the child agree with his perception of the traits valued by the parents, although he is more likely himself to be (and to perceive his parents as being) gratification-oriented than he is to attribute this value to his parents. (R111)

### Power Structure of Family
Where the middle-class values predominate (self-reliance, personal autonomy, and the belief in the superiority of the future in contrast to the past), the isolated nuclear family with comparatively egalitarian structure has higher prestige than does the patrilinear extended family of the upper class. (P083)

### Stability of Extended Family (Patrilineal)
Cultures which stress the virtue of harmony, balance, the cult of the esthetic, and a respect for the world as it is are more congenial to the stability of the patrilinear extended family. (P083)

## VALUES (ACHIEVEMENT)
### X Child-Rearing Practices (Affection)
There is a positive relationship between the mother's use of love-oriented discipline techniques and similar achievement values in mother and son. (R097)

### Kin Ties
When the dominant social values center on achievement and not on ascription, the range of kinship extensions will be narrow. (S050)

## VALUES (AUTHORITY)     X Age
During adolescence increasing age correlates with increasingly similar attitudes toward authority in the home and authority outside it (school and peer situations). (T100)

## VALUES/BEHAVIOR OF PARENTS
### X Parent–Child Relations (Conflict)
The greater the adolescent's perception of inconsistencies between the values and the actual behavior of his parents, the more likely it is that he will come into conflict with his parents on ideological grounds. (S219)

## VALUES (COOPERATION)
### X Cohesion of Extended Family
Extended family kinship relations will be reinforced by an emphasis on cooperation in the value system of the society. (V016)

### Sibling Relations (Solidarity)
Sibling solidarity will be emphasized in societies in which kin-groups and their cooperative functions are valued. (F069)

## VALUES (DEMOCRATIC)
### X Intermarriage (Class)
Interclass marriages are more likely to occur in societies which stress democratic values. (M227)

## VALUES (EGALITARIANISM)     X Achievement
Because there is more egalitarian bias in American than in British values, it has been more difficult for American upper-class families to claim a superiority of breed that would give them a recognized quasi-monopoly on high achievement (something that the English gentry has maintained). (P083)

## VALUES (EXTENDED/NUCLEAR FAMILY)
### X Education
Those highly educated are more apt to prefer the nuclear family, while the less highly educated prefer the extended family. (J033)

### Geographic Mobility
Those living further from the location of their homes during their early teen years are more likely to espouse nuclear family norms, while those living near their early homes are more likely to espouse extended family norms. (J033)

### Occupation
Men who espouse nuclear family norms are more likely to hold white collar jobs; those who espouse extended family norms are more likely to have blue collar jobs. (J025)

### Rank
Those with high social rank are more apt to prefer the nuclear family values than are those with low social rank, who are more likely to prefer extended family values. (J033)

### Social Change, Attitudes Toward
Men who espouse nuclear family norms are most likely to be accepting of change. Those who espouse modified extended family norms are in the middle and those who advocate extended family norms are least likely to be accepting of change. (J025)

### Urban/Rural
Those living in urban settings are more apt to prefer nuclear family values and those living in rural areas are more inclined to extended family values. (J033)

### Value Conflict (Family/Economic)

Men who espouse nuclear family norms are least likely to see a conflict between family ties and ecomomic success values. Those who advocate modified extended family norms are in the middle of this measure and those who advocate extended family norms are most likely to see a conflict between family ties and economic success values. (J025)

Those who support an extended family norm are more likely to see a conflict between values of economic success and family values, while those espousing norms of a modified extended family have less conflict; those holding norms favoring nuclear families find the least conflict between family values and values of economic success. (J033)

### VALUES (FAMILISM)  X Class

Middle-class and upper-class marriages are likely to be more oriented toward the child or family as a whole than are lower-class marriages; the latter tend to be more oriented toward the compatibility of the husband and wife and show less concern about responsibility for the children. (C121)

Middle-class men are more likely to be work oriented and to reject both strong family ties in general and strong ties with their fathers; this is in contrast with men from upper-class families who are less oriented toward work as a field of accomplishment, have stronger positive family feelings, and respect their fathers more. (L115)

### Cohesion of Family

The preservation of traditional family values increases family unity. (B033)

### Economic Cooperation

When the system of land tenure requires the economic cooperation of the family, the values which unify the family will be of a familial nature. (B033)

Familism is reinforced by the rural labor pattern when farming is a common occupation of the family with all members participating in it cooperatively. (B033)

### Economic Dependence

When the family is a self-sufficient unit family solidarity and the values of stability, continuity, and security are stressed. (B033)

### Family-School Relations

Families are less likely to support the school if the inner culture of the family is very divergent from the culture of the school. (P083)

### Mate Selection (Free Choice)

As the force of traditional familial mores weakens, the intellectually emancipated begin in increasing numbers to demand the control of arranging their own marriages. (B033)

### Reference Group

Girls are more likely to have as their goal being a good family member if their reference group is an organized group, but are more likely to expect praise from their parents for this attribute if their reference group is their school friends. (R111)

### Sex Status

Girls are more likely than boys to place value on being a good member of the family. (R111)

### Urbanization

The secularizing effects of urbanism on family values will be least on those values most central to the traditional family structure. (T001)

### VALUES (FAMILISM/COLLECTIVISM)  X Sex Status

Compared to each other, men tend to be more collective oriented and women more family oriented. (T098)

### VALUES (FAMILY)  X Class

The difference in familial attitudes between lower-class normals and paranoid schizophrenics is less than that between middle-class normals and paranoid schizophrenics. (L155)

### VALUES (FAMILY/SOCIETY)  X Juvenile Delinquency

Organized types of delinquent groups usually arise when there is a lack of harmony and compatibility between the main values of the family and its authority structure on the one hand and the actual community and its values and authority structure on the other. (E086)

### VALUES (FEMININITY)  X Sex-Role Definition

The increased sex-role differentiation associated with relative isolation of the nuclear family in society is related to increased emphasis on overt, specifically feminine, attractiveness, with strong erotic overtones. (P062)

### VALUES (FILIAL PIETY)  X Juvenile Delinquency

Juvenile delinquency is rare where filial piety is a central value. (B033)

### VALUES (INDIVIDUALISM)  X Cohesion of Family

Individualism serves to separate the individual from his family and to weaken the relationship between family members. (B033)

Where the societal value system stresses individualism, family solidarity will be weakened. (S076)

### Descent (Unilineal)

Individualism may become an increasingly important value in situations where two patterns of unilinear descent are in conflict. (F069)

### Fertility

The birth rate tends to be inversely correlated with the emphasis of the society on individualism. (F069)

### Fertility Values

The greater the concern for the future growth and continuity of the collectivity, the more likely it is that large families will be felt desirable. (T098)

The greater the emphasis put on the value of individualism, the less likely it is that large families will be considered desirable. (T098)

### Husband-Wife Relations, Importance of

Marital relationships tend to be more important and more highly valued in societies which are individualistic in their orientation. (F069)

Where the husband-wife relationship is dominant, self-reliance will be stressed. (H172)

### Kin Ties
When a high value is placed on individualism, the range within which kinship is extended will be narrow. (S050)

### Mate Selection (Free Choice)
The more that individualism is stressed in a society, the more likely it is that an individual will make his own choice of spouse. (K152)

### Nuclear Family, Isolation of
There is a relationship between value systems oriented to achievement and individualism and the growing isolation of the nuclear family. (P083)

### Parent-Child Relations
Parents in an individualistic competitive society find children more of a burden than do parents in a kin-oriented society where relatives share childcare more. (F069)

### Rank of Women
An increase in individualism results in a rise in women's position. (F069)

In matrilineal societies increasing individualism should produce a lowering of women's positions. (F069)

### Residence (Neolocal)
When the culture places an emphasis upon competitive individualism, the individual nuclear family will be the basic unit of kinship organization. (V016)

### Sibling Relations (Formality)
When the emphasis is upon individually achieved status, the relations between lineage mates and siblings close in age are more formal than are relations between those with a greater age difference. (F015)

### Sibling Rivalry
Sibling relationships tend to be more competitive in individualistic societies. (F069)

### Stability of Family
Individualism is incompatible with the survival of the family.

## VALUES (INDIVIDUALISM/COOPERATION)
### X Child-Rearing Practices (Dependency)
A society emphasizing individualistic achievement would begin by inculcating in the children a belief in their own competence, while a society emphasizing group cooperation and authority of leaders or parents would inculcate in the children a belief in their own dependence on more competent seniors. (F069)

## VALUES (MARITAL STABILITY)
### X Marital Stability
Where the value emphasis on marital stability is high, marital stability tends to be high. (L116)

## VALUES (MARRIAGE)   X Division of Labor
The more differentiated are jobs in the society in the economic sphere, the more important is mutual emotional support between spouses. (D080)

The more differentiated are jobs in the society, the more emphasis is placed on marriage for love and the less emphasis on economic advancement and social standing. (D080)

### Intermarriage (Class)
Interclass marriages are more likely to occur in societies in which romantic love is emphasized as a basis for marriage. (M227)

### Premarital Sex Relations
Even if marriage is the only approved relationship between male and female, the later the approved age of marriage in the society, the more likely it is that premarital intercourse will occur. (B245)

## VALUES OF HUSBAND–WIFE
### X Marital Adjustment
In emotionally disturbed marriages, the husband will tend to be more traditionally oriented than will the wife. (V028)

## VALUES (PATERNITY)   X Descent (Matrilineal)
In a matrilineal system there is less concern (than in a patrilineal system) with the identity of the biological father as long as the mother is married. (G156)

### Illegitimacy, Attitude Toward
Societal attitudes toward illegitimacy of children from adulterous unions vary with societal value on physiological and/or sociological paternity. (D054)

## VALUES (ROMANTICISM)
### X Marital Adjustment
Unhappy wives value more highly than do happy wives the attitudes, activities, and situations that appear to subserve the romantic quest. They more often prefer a dance to a play and economize on anything else rather than on clothes. They consider that personal happiness is the paramount objective in marriage, daydream frequently, and like people who are emotional. They prefer a vivacious mate to a quiet one. (T074)

## VALUES (SECULAR)   X Divorce
There is a direct relation between societal secularization and divorce. (K161)

### Parent-Child Relations (Control)
As a culture becomes progressively secularized, parental control becomes lessened. (C086)

## VALUES (SEX ROLE)   X Fertility Values
The more egalitarian the ideology with respect to sex differentiation, the less likely it is that large families will be considered desirable. (T098)

### Mental Illness
In the families of mentally ill middle-class patients, the value of equality of the sexes tends to be strongly held. (M061)

## VALUES (TRADITIONAL)   X Cohesion of Family
The more a society's values and institutions are based on obedience to tradition, the more dependent are its members on the family and kin-groups.

### Stability of Joint Family
The joint family tends to disappear when the ideology which supports it is undermined. (M021)

## VOLUNTARY ORGANIZATIONS   X Class
The higher the socioeconomic class, the higher the social rewards for wives' participation in voluntary organizations. (S243)

The higher the socioeconomic class, the less likely is the role of "wife" defined in such a way as to conflict with membership in voluntary organizations. (S243)

The higher the socioeconomic class, the less importance attached by the wife to her familial roles for purposes of her self-definition (compared with outside activity). (S243)

### Husband-Wife Relations (Companionship)
When both husband and wife participate jointly in organizations, the companionship experienced is greater than that of joint participation in leisure-time activities.

### Kin Ties
Mutual-aid societies tend to arise in situations where bonds between kinsmen are weak. (M076)

### Marital Adjustment
Marital success is directly correlated with the degree of participation of the husband and wife in such voluntary organizations as the church or the school. (B033)

### Mate Selection
Fraternity men and sorority women tended to marry each other more often than can be accounted for by chance alone. (S012)

Fraternity and sorority members married spouses with no college education less than half as often as did other college men and women. (S012)

### Power Structure of Family
A wife who participates in organizations outside the home has more power in the family decision making than does a wife who does not do so. Activity in a formal organization provides the wife with a resource analogous to the husband's success on the job.

## VOLUNTARY ORGANIZATIONS (TRIBAL)
### X Kin Ties
The establishment of tribal unions in urban areas reinforces the migrant's attachment to his native town and lineage. (L030)

## VOTING
### X Age of Child
Agreement between the voting patterns of parents and child decreases as the age of the child increases. (H244)

## VOTING BEHAVIOR
### X Political Affiliation of Child
Individuals from families in which neither parent voted are more likely not to form any party attachments. (H244)

### Sex Status
Women are more likely than men to report that relatives influenced the formation of their votes. (H244)

# W

## WARFARE

Men will tend to marry later in societies where warfare is an institutionalized pattern. (O030)

### Cohesion of Clan
Warfare is associated with the deterioration of the clan structure. (R054)

Localized warfare tends to reinforce the cohesion of the clan. (S099)

### Cohesion of Extended Family
Bonds of the extended family tend to weaken under conditions of general peace. (L093)

### Cohesion of Family
Warfare will tend to accentuate the importance of the family as a unit and to strengthen, among its members, a sense of family responsibility. (G139)

### Cohesion of Lineage
When patterns of interlineage warfare are abandoned, the solidarity of the lineage is diminished. (W056)

### Community (Multilineage)
Under the pressure of warfare, multilineage settlements tend to break up into the several lineages of which they are composed. (F010)

### Descent (Bilateral)
A bilateral society has better opportunities for the formation of large-scale fighting forces than does a society with a highly segmented unilineal descent system and no form of centralized authority. (F127)

### Descent (Patrilineal)
Warfare and the enhancement of the male role in regard to warfare tends to strengthen the patrilineal organization of the society. (F010)

### Disorganization of Family
Family disorganization increases with the acceleration of social changes during wartime or preparation for war. (B033)

### Divorce
In wartime divorces are likely to increase at a greater rate than in peacetime. (C023)

Countries that were mobilized during the war show a greater increase in divorce rate than do neighboring countries that did not mobilize. (Z008)

### Divorce, Grounds for
In societies in which the emphasis is upon warfare, sterility is likely to be a ground for divorce. (T107)

In societies in which the emphasis is upon warfare, the failure to have male children is likely to be a ground for divorce. (T107)

### Endogamy (Community)
Under conditions of continuous intervillage warfare communities will tend to be endogamous. (W031)

## X   Age at Marriage

### Engagement, Duration of
Length of betrothal is likely to be sharply reduced during periods of warfare. (G139)

### Fertility Values
Children are more greatly desired when warfare is common. (F092)

### Illegitimacy
In wartime illegitimacy is likely to increase at a greater rate than during peacetime. (C023)

### Intermarriage (Political)
A tribe which is not sure of its martial standing and general security may seek alliances through intermarriage with stronger tribes. (C091)

### Kinship, Importance of
Kinship ties beyond those of closest kin tend to be unimportant where wars of conquest have led to widespread dispersal. (E102)

### Lineage Ties
Warfare between lineages tends to result in the realignment of lineage affiliations. (G031)

### Marriage, Goals of (Fertility)
In societies where warfare is frequent, marriage is more eagerly sought as a means of increasing fighting forces and replacing losses; where warfare is less frequent, this incentive for marriage is lacking. (C091)

### Marriage Rate
There is a direct relation between the outbreak of war and a rise in the marriage rate. (K161)

There is a direct relation between the termination of a war and a sharp rise in the marriage rate. (K161)

### Mate Selection (Free Choice)
Warfare and the attendant intermixture of people of different clans tend to result in a wide choice permitted in selecting a wife. (S092)

### Ordinal Position
Men who undertake the initiative in undertaking raids tend to be younger brothers who lack the status and prerogatives of an elder brother. (S117)

### Paternal-Role Definition
In military societies, where a large proportion of the male population are soldiers, there will be institutionalized deterrents to the formation of attachments between the father and other members of a nuclear family. (G056)

### Polyandry
The custom of combined polyandrous and polygynous unions tends to be associated with a military society. (G055)

The institution of polyandry is particularly compatible with the society in which the primary occupational category is military. (G056)

### Polygyny
Polygyny is more likely to occur where warfare is important. (W129)

### Preferential Marriage
Under conditions of warfare, preferential marriage patterns, such as cross-cousin marriage, tend to occur less frequently. (F010)

### Premarital Sex Relations
Warfare is likely to result in a marked increase in premarital promiscuity. (G139)

### Rank of Women
There is an association between the cessation of warfare and a rise in the status of women. (O030)

### Residence
War tends to result in the residential disruption of previously localized kin-groups. (B064)

The localization of the clan will tend to deteriorate with the prohibition of warfare by European administrators. (B156)

Violence within a society seems noticeably absent where the vengeance group (subclan or lineage) is not a territorial unit. (H245)

Where residence is largely determined by agnatic descent and not open to choice, the motives for preserving the peace of the settlement are greater. (H245)

For patterns of feuding to occur, lineages must be localized and preserve their structural continuity. (P026)

Residence patterns will tend to be more flexible under conditions of prolonged warfare. (R054)

### Residence (Matrilocal)
In societies with patterns of local warfare, temporary matrilocal residence arises to protect the wife against vengeance by her husband's group. (K156)

Relative peacefulness is a factor that favors matrilocal residence. (M019)

### Residence (Patrilocal)
When warfare becomes an important activity in a society, patrilocal residence begins to occur. (M019)

### Segmentation
Inter- and intratribal wars and raids tend to separate and scatter the lineage residential group. (G022)

### Sex-Role Definition
In military societies, where a large proportion of the male population is organized for warfare, the role of men in the family structure will be peripheral. (G056)

### Sexual Deviance
There is a direct relation between war and the increase of deviant sexual behavior and prostitution. (K161)

### Sexual Permissiveness
There is a greater need for the stringent regulation of sexual behavior in a society which emphasizes war and the extension of its territories. (R040)

### Size of Kin-Group
Larger kin and local residential units tend to fragment into households under conditions of internecine warfare. (B041)

The size of the kin-group will tend to decrease when political conditions are peaceful. (H164)

### Stability of Kin-Group
Under conditions of warfare, kinship alignments and local groupings tend to be unstable. (F010)

### Stratification
The cleavage of a lineage into classes tends to occur under the impact of war. (K049)

### WEANING                         X Alcoholism
Alcoholism is associated with a pattern of indulgence in feeding followed by a traumatic period at weaning. (C122)

### Bed Wetting
There is no relationship between the duration of bed wetting and severity of weaning (U.S.). (S191)

### Behavior Problems (Crying)
Mothers whose babies cry a good deal are gentler in their weaning methods than are mothers of placid babies (U.S.). (S191)

### Behavior Problems (Finger-Sucking)
Too-early weaning may lead to finger-sucking. (F097)

### Behavior Problems (Thumb-Sucking)
There is no significant difference between early- and late-weaned children regarding the duration and severity of thumb-sucking. (Y042)

### Class
Lower-class children have a significantly higher median age at completion of weaning than do middle-class children. This hypothesis is also denied. (H011)

Upper middle-class mothers expect their children to be weaned at an earlier age than do lower-class mothers (Indonesia). (T084)

Lower-class Negro parents are more likely to bottle-wean their babies after 12 months; upper-class Negro parents are more likely to bottle-wean their babies before 12 months. (W133)

### Dependency
There is no relationship between the age at which the child begins weaning, the duration of weaning, or the age at which weaning is completed and the child's dependency (at age 5) on his mother. (S191)

The more severe the infant's weaning, the more likely it is that he will be dependent as a child. (S238)

### Dependency of Child
Severity of weaning and dependency of child are not associated. (S191)

### Emotional Adjustment
Children who are weaned late have more severe reactions to weaning than do children who are weaned early. (Y042)

### Emotional Adjustment of Child
Late-weaned infants show more weaning frustration than do early-weaned infants. (B272)

The child's frustration by weaning is associated with late weaning (longer practice in sucking), severe methods, and indecisiveness during weaning. (S191)

### Emotional Problems
Early weaning is likely to be more traumatic for the child than is later weaning. (B272)

There is no relationship between age of weaning and emotional disturbances in the child. (B272)

### Emotional Problems of Child
The greater the preparation for weaning and the more gradually the mother makes the shift, the lower the frustration experienced by the child during the transition. (S191)

The more consistent the mother is in her weaning practices, the less uncertainty produced in the child and, consequently, the lower his frustration experienced during the transition. (S191)

The longer the duration of weaning, the greater the frustration produced in the child. (S191)

### Feeding Problems
There is no relationship between the age at which weaning was started and feeding problems (e.g., prolonged periods of appetite loss, etc.) (U.S.). (S191)

### Illness, Explanation of
The severity of weaning is strongly correlated with oral explanations for illness (e.g., poisoned food or magic spells). (W127)

### Mental Illness
Mental illness tends to be directly correlated with hostile behavior during feeding and with premature or cruel weaning. (L118)

### Mother-Child Household
In societies with a high frequency of mother-child households, the average age at weaning is later. (S079)

### Mother-Child Relations (Rejection)
The more rejecting the mother is of the child, the earlier she is likely to discontinue breast feeding.

### Oedipal Complex
The development of the Oedipal complex is directly correlated with rigidity in weaning. (M226)

### Ordinal Position
Middle and younger children are weaned earlier than older children. (S191)

Oldest children were weaned latest and showed greatest emotional upset at weaning. (S191)

### Parent-Child Relations (Affection)
When parents are extremely fond of children and indulgent toward them, weaning occurs at a late period. (D025)

### Parent-Child Relations (Indulgence)
When parents are extremely fond of children and indulgent toward them, weaning occurs at a late period. (D025)

### Personality Adjustment
Children who are weaned gradually show stronger feelings of belonging than do children who are abruptly weaned (as measured by the California Test of Personality). (S200)

There is no association between children who are weaned gradually and children who are weaned abruptly and their personality adjustment (i.e., finger-sucking, nail-biting, stuttering, eating difficulties, slowness and bashfulness in talking). (S200)

### Personality Adjustment (Oral)
There is no relationship between children who are weaned abruptly and children who are weaned gradu-

ally and their oral adjustment (i.e., finger-sucking, nail-biting, stuttering, eating difficulties, slowness and bashfulness in talking). (S200)

### Personality of Mother (Decisiveness)
The greater the mother's indecisiveness, the more gentle her weaning of the child. (S191)

### Personality Problems (Oral)
The greater the oral indulgence of the infant (in the form of late weaning), the more likely is the incidence of oral frustration and oral fixation in the child. (B224)

### Polygyny
In societies with a high percentage of polygynous households, the age at weaning is likely to be higher. (S079)

### Polygyny (Sororal/Nonsororal)
Societies with sororal polygyny are significantly less severe in weaning their children than are societies with nonsororal polygyny. (W127)

### Race
Negro parents are more permissive in weaning their children than are white parents. This proposition is also denied.

### Sex Taboo (Postpartum)
In societies with long durations of the postpartum sex taboo the average age of weaning is later. (S079)

### Social Adjustment
There is no association between children who are weaned gradually and children who are weaned abruptly and their social adjustment (as measured by the California Personality Test and teachers' ratings on the Ford Modification of the Haggerty-Olson-Wickman Behavior Rating Scale). (S200)

### Socialization, Effectiveness of
Resistance to temptation correlates with severity of weaning the boys, but not in girls. (G120)

### Speech Problems
Children with articulation problems are more likely to have been weaned at an earlier age than are children without articulation problems. (F095)

### Superego Formation
Societies with early weaning tend to have a high guilt orientation. (W127)

### Theft
There is an association between a high frequency of theft in society and low infant indulgence and severe weaning. (W127)

### Urban/Rural
In France, weaning takes place later among country children than among town children. (F097)

## WEANING/FEEDING
### X Behavior Problems (Thumb-Sucking)
The earlier the child is weaned and the less frequently the child is fed, the more likely he is to suck his thumb.

## WEANING/TOILET TRAINING    X Dependency
There is no relationship between severity or age at onset of weaning and toilet training and dependency in the child. (B272)

### Superego Formation

Guilt of the child about disobedience of the mother correlates with late weaning and toilet training. (A054)

The child's sense of guilt about aggression correlates with early weaning and toilet training. (A054)

The earlier and/or more severe the weaning and toilet training, the greater the degree of guilt and superego strength. (G120)

## WIDOWHOOD                              X  Divorce

Divorces among remarried persons who have been widowed are no more likely than are divorces among primary marriages. (M242)

## WIFE INHERITANCE                        X  Adultery

The possibility of seduction is increased by the custom by which a son may inherit his father's wives. (E102)

### Incest

The likelihood that a man will seduce his father's wives is increased by the custom of permitting a son to inherit his father's wives. (E086)

## WIFE SHARING          X  Sex Taboo (Postpartum)

Other males (relatives of age-mates) are more likely to have sexual access to a man's wife in societies which impose prolonged continence during pregnancy and lactation. (P083)

## WITCHCRAFT                     X  Affinal Relations

Suspicion of the use of witchcraft by wives is directly correlated with a negative attitude toward affinal relatives. (L109)

### Age

Accusations of witchcraft are more likely to be directed against persons likely to feel the resentment and anxieties of mature ages and the frustrations springing from envy of youth. (N015)

### Child-Rearing Practices (Aggression/Sex)

Sorcery is used to explain illness more often in societies where children are punished severely, either for sex or aggression, than in other societies. (W127)

### Cohesion of Society

The moral disintegration of society is indexed by accusation of witchcraft against fathers by sons. (G012)

### Conflict Between Wives

Sorcery is more likely to occur in societies which maximize jealousy between co-wives. (W127)

### Joking Relationship

Accusations of witchcraft as manifestations of aggression are unlikely to occur between kinsmen who stand in a joking relationship. (T059)

### Kin Relations (Interaction)

Witchcraft aggression against kinsmen will be directly correlated with the frequency of contact between the individuals. (M099)

### Marital Adjustment

Aggression as manifest in accusations of witchcraft against affinal kinsmen will tend to occur among individuals who are dissatisfied with their marital statuses. (T059)

### Nuclear Family

Witchcraft beliefs are incompatible with the emergence of the family of parents and children as the important group at the expense of extended kinship groupings. (G116)

### Parent-Child Relations

When the parent-child relationship is regarded as untrustworthy, children will tend to be primary suspects for witchcraft. (L109)

### Polygyny

Sorcery is more common in polygynous societies, both sororal and nonsororal. (S189)

### Power Structure of Family

When the role of the wife is one of extreme subordination to her husband, her aggression is more likely to manifest itself in indirect methods (e.g., witchcraft). (L064)

### Residence

Hostility against kinsmen as manifest in accusations of witchcraft is more likely to occur among kinsmen who are close neighbors. (S140)

Where co-wives live in adjacent houses preoccupation with sorcery is greater than where the co-wives live miles apart. (W127)

### Sex Taboo (Postpartum)

In societies with long durations of the postpartum sex taboo, there is more fear of sorcery. (S079)

### Sexual Antagonism

In societies where there is a sharp antagonism between the sexes, witchcraft is more likely to be attributed to the subordinate sex. (N015)

### Structure of Family

Sorcery is seen as a major cause of illness in 93 per cent of the societies with polygynous households, 60 per cent of the societies with mother-child households, 53 per cent of the societies with extended family households, and only 36 per cent of the societies with nuclear households. (W127)

## WORK                              X  Marriage Rate

When the work schedule calls for the least amount of work or for vacations, there will be the greatest number of marriages. (C001)

## WORK ADJUSTMENT               X  Age at Marriage

Those who marry at an early age (under 18 years) are less likely to make a successful adjustment to their work than are those who marry later.

### Marital Adjustment of Husbands

Happy husbands are more methodical and painstaking in their work. They more often report that they drive themselves steadily, plan their work in detail, and enjoy occupations demanding meticulous accuracy. (T074)

### Marital Adjustment of Wife

Happily married women tend to be more meticulous and persevering in their attitude toward work and show greater liking for work requiring such traits than do unhappy wives. Happy wives more often drive themselves steadily in their work, whereas unhappy wives more often report that they work by fits and starts. (T074)

### Mother Absence

There is a significant correlation between a childhood history of early maternal deprivation (below the age of six and for at least six months' duration) and a poor work record later in life. (E093)

## WORK ATTITUDES                    X    Class
The higher the class, the greater the personal satisfaction derived by the mother from working.

## WORK ATTITUDES OF CHILD
### X    Employment of Mother
Children of nonworking mothers are more likely to perceive work as having unpleasant connotations for women than are children of working mothers. (H236)

Children of working mothers are more likely than are children of nonworking mothers to perceive work as having unpleasant connotations for men. (H236)

## WORK ATTITUDES OF FATHER
### X    Social Mobility of Son
Paternal dissatisfaction with job is positively related to having an upwardly mobile son. (E102)

## WORK ATTITUDES OF MOTHER
### X    Child-Rearing Practices
If mothers work and prefer to do so, or do not work and prefer not to work, working or not working makes little difference in their child-rearing behavior. (Y050)

### Child-Rearing Practices (Chores)
Mothers who enjoy their jobs are less likely to give additional responsibilities to their children than are mothers who are not as fond of their work. (Y047)

### Child-Rearing Practices (Discipline/Chores)
Mothers with positive attitudes toward their work are more likely to use milder discipline and to demand less sharing of household tasks than are mothers who dislike their work. (S265)

### Child-Rearing Practices (Indulgence)
Mothers who like their jobs are more likely to be indulgent toward their children than are mothers who are not as satisfied with their jobs. (Y047)

### X    Chores
Working mothers who like to work are less likely to shoulder their children with household tasks. (G156)

### Employment of Mother, Evaluation of
### X    Child-Rearing Practices (Consistency)
Among working mothers there is more inconsistency in child rearing among mothers who are dissatisfied with their employment than among the satisfied mothers. (Y050)

### Employment of Mother (Satisfaction)
### X    Child-Rearing Practices (Consistency)
Among nonworking mothers clarity on limit setting is more characteristic of the mothers satisfied with not working. Dissatisfied mothers show more inconsistency between principles and practices. Control is an "issue" between mother and child for dissatisfied mothers. Lack of emotional satisfaction in relationships with the child is more frequent among dissatisfied than among satisfied mothers. High confidence in the mother role is more common among satisfied mothers. In general, mothering is inferior. (Y051)

### Employment of Women
There is a significant relationship between the mother's work orientation (i.e., attitudes toward work and work history) and the daughter's decision to spend a good portion of her life in paid employment. (S231)

### Marital Adjustment
The mother's satisfaction with working is positively related to the general level of marital satisfaction. (G156)

### Maternal Overprotectiveness
If the mother is satisfied with her employment outside the home, she tends to feel guilty about it and as a consequence she is overprotective toward the child. (H183)

### Mother-Child Relations (Affection)
Mothers with positive attitudes toward their work are more likely to be affectionate toward their children than are mothers who dislike their work. (S265)

### Mother-Child Relations (Closeness)
Working mothers who like to work are more likely to feel strong attachments to their children. (G156)

### Mother-Child Relations (Conflict)
The child of the mother who likes to work is less likely to assert himself against her. (G156)

### Mother-Child Relations (Hostility)
If the mother is dissatisfied with her employment outside the home, she shows assertive behavior toward the child and, consequently, the child is hostile toward the mother. (H183)

### Personality of Child (Aggression)
Children of mothers with positive attitudes toward their work are less likely to be assertive, effective, or hostile in their social relations than are children whose mothers dislike their work. (S265)

### Pregnancy Attitude
Among the working-class mothers, attitudes toward work make little difference in the acceptance of pregnancy (U.S.). (S191)

Upper middle-class mothers who enjoy outside work are more likely to enjoy pregnancy than are those who are indifferent to outside work (U.S.). (S191)

## WORK BEHAVIOR OF MOTHER
### X    Maternal Overprotectiveness
Strong degrees of responsibility, independence, and stability in work are causes of maternal overprotection of the child. (B272)

# BIBLIOGRAPHY

# BIBLIOGRAPHY

As noted in the Introduction, each proposition in this inventory is followed by a code number, e.g., S035. This number informs the reader that the proposition was enunciated by an author whose last name begins with "S" and appears in the publication marked by that code number in the following bibliography. Thus, the bibliography is an alphabetical listing only by reference to the first letter of the author's name.

However, the publication may well not be the first to have enunciated that proposition. Indeed, in sociology it is often impossible to know who was the first. The article or book listed here is simply the one where we located the proposition.

Next, the publication listed here may also not be the best, the most reliable. The bibliography does not, then, represent a selection of the publications we have decided are the best in the field. They are simply the ones in which we located a given proposition. Of course, the expert will nevertheless recognize in this listing a high percentage of the articles and books that the field recognizes as excellent.

We also noted in the Introduction that some propositions will not be marked by a code number. We suppose that the reader may often locate such propositions by looking for them in related sources, or sources dealing with related variables. We trust that these recording errors will not cause the searcher much trouble.

(A001) Armstrong, Lincoln, and Hirabayashi, Gordan K. "Social Differentiation in Selected Lebanese Villages." *American Sociological Review* 21 (1956): 425–434.

(A002) Axelrod, Morris. "Urban Structure and Social Participation." *American Sociological Review* 21 (1956): 13–18.

(A003) Anderson, W. A. "The Spacing of Births in the Families of University Graduates." *American Journal of Sociology* 53 (1947–1948): 23–33.

(A006) Adler, Leta McKinney. "The Relationship of Marital Status to Incidence of a Recovery from Mental Illness." *Social Forces* 32, No. 2 (December 1953): 185–194.

(A009) Apple, Dorian. "The Social Structure of Grandparenthood." *The American Anthropologist* 58 (1956): 656–663.

(A010) Anderson, Robert T. "The Danish and Dutch Settlement on Amager Island: Four Hundred Years of Socio-Cultural Interaction." *American Anthropologist* 60 (1958): 683–701.

(A013) Adams, John Boman. "Culture and Conflict in an Egyptian Village." *American Anthropologist* 59 (1957): 225–235.

(A014) Adams, Richard N. "Cultural Components of Central America." *American Anthropologist* 58 (1956): 881–907.

(A020) Aginsky, B. W. "The Mechanics of Kinship." *American Anthropologist* 37 (1935): 450–457.

(A021) Aginsky, B. W. "Time Levels in Societal Analysis." *American Anthropologist* 41 (1939): 416–432.

(A022) Aginsky, B. W., and Hiroa, Kte Rangi. "Interacting Forces in the Maori Family." *American Anthropologist* 42 (1940): 195–210.

(A023) Adair, John, and Vogt, Evon. "Navaho and Zuni Veterans: A Study of Contrasting Modes of Culture Change." *American Anthropologist* 51 (1949): 547–561.

(A025) Albrecht, Andrew C. "French–Indian Relations at Natchez." *American Anthropologist* 48 (1946): 321–354.

(A029) Anderson, Gallatin. "Il Comparaggio: The Italian God-Parenthood Complex." *Southwest Journal of Anthropology* 13 (1957): 32–53.

(A030) Ames, David W. "The Economic Base of Wolof Polygyny." *Southwest Journal of Anthropology* 11 (1955): 390–403.

(A032) Ardener, E. W. "Lineage and Locality Among the Mba-Ise Ibo." *Africa* 29 (1959): 113–133.

(A033) Ardener, E. W. "The Kinship Terminology of a Group of Southern Ibo." *Africa* 24 (1954): 85–99.

(A034) Amoo, J. W. A. "The Effect of Western Influence on Akan Marriage." *Africa* 16 (1946): 228–237.

(A040) Allard, Elizabeth. "Animistic Beliefs and Rites in the Malay Archipelago." *Oceania* 16 (1945–1946): 87–108.

(A042) Ashley-Montagu, M. F. "Infertility of the Unmarried in Primitive Societies." *Oceania* 8 (1937–1938): 15–26.

(A046) Berle, David F., and Naegele, Kaspar D. "Middle Class Fathers' Occupational Role and Attitudes Toward Children." In *Modern Introduction to the Family,* edited by Norman W. Bell and Ezra F. Vogel. Glencoe, Ill.: The Free Press, 1960, pp. 126–136.

(A047) Aubert, Vilhelm. "Legal Justice and Mental Health." *Psychiatry* 21 (1958): 101–113.

(A048) Aberle, David F. "Matrilineal Descent in Cross-Cultural Perspective." In *Matrilineal Kinship,* edited by David M. Schneider and Kathleen Gough. Berkeley: University of California Press, 1961.

(A049) Aldous, Joan, and Kell, Leone. "A Partial Test of Some Theories of Identification." *Marriage and Family Living* 23–24 (1961–1962): 15–19.

(A050) Arensberg, Conrad M., and Kimball, Solon T. *Family and Community in Ireland.* Cambridge: Harvard University Press, 1940.

(A051) Adams, Richard N. "An Inquiry into the Nature of the Family." In *Essays in the Science of Culture,* edited by Gertrude E. Dole and Robert L. Carniero. New York: T. Y. Crowell, 1960.

(A052) Ackerman, Nathan W. "Interpersonal Disturbances in the Family." *Psychiatry* 17 (1954): 359–368.

(A053) Aberle, David F. "Culture and Socialization." In *Psychological Anthropology,* edited by Francis L. K. Hsu. Homewood, Ill.: Dorsey Press, 1961.

(A054) Allinsmith, W. "Conscience and Conflict: The Moral Force in Personality." *Child Development* 28 (December 1957): 469–476.

(A055) Asher, J. W. "Comment on 'The Relationship Between Rigidity–Flexibility in Children and Their Parents.'" *Child Development* 32, No. 3 (1961): 507–508.

(A056) Ainsworth, Leonard H., and Ainsworth, Mary D. "Acculturation in East Africa: Attitudes Toward Parents, Teachers and Education." *Journal of Social Psychology* 57 (1962): 409–415.

(A057) Adams, Elsie B., and Sarason, Irwin G. "Relation Between Anxiety in Children and Their Parents." *Child Development* 34, No. 1 (1963): 237–246.

(A058) Aronfreed, Justin, Cutick, Robert A., and Fagen, Stanley A. "Cognitive Structure, Punishment and Nurturance in the Experimental Induction of Self-Criticism." *Child Development* 34, No. 2 (1963): 281–294.

(A059) Ausubel, David P. "Ego Development and the Learning Process." *Child Development* 20 (December 1949): 173–190.

(A060) Aldous, Joan, and Kell, Leone. "A Partial Test of Some Theories of Identification." *Marriage and Family Living* 23 (February 1961): 15–19.

(A061) Adorno, T., *et al. The Authoritarian Personality.* New York: Harper Bros., 1950.

(A061) Abbate, Grace McLean, Dunaeff, Dorothe, and Fenichel, Carl. "A Pilot Study of Schizophrenic Children in a Non-Residential School." *American Journal of Orthopsychiatry* 27 (January 1957): 107–116.

(A062) Adams, Elsie B., and Sarason, Irwin G. "Relation Between Anxiety in Children and Their Parents." *Child Development* 34 (1963): 237–246.

(A063) Adams, A. "Choice of Infant Feeding as a Function of Maternal Personality." *Journal of Consulting Psychology* 23, No. 2 (1959): 143–146.

(A065) Aldous, Joan. "Urbanization, the Extended Family, and Kinship Ties in West Africa." *Social Forces* 41 (October 1962): 6–12.

(A065) Anastasi, A. "Intelligence and Family Size." *Psychological Bulletin* 53 (1956): 187–209.

(A066) Adams, Bert N. "Structural Factors Affecting Parental Aid to Married Children." *Journal of Marriage and the Family* 26 (August 1964): 327–331.

(A067) Astin, Alexander W. "Personal and Environmental Factors Associated with College Dropouts Among High Aptitude Students." *Journal of Educational Psychology* 55 (August 1964): 219–227.

(A069) Adams, L. J. "Mothers' Anomic Attitudes and Childhood Disorders." *Smith College Studies in Social Work* 33, No. 1 (1962): 19–40.

(A070) Archibald, H. C., Bell, D., Miller, C., and Tuddenham, R. "Bereavement in Childhood and Adult Psychiatric Disturbance." *Psychosomatic Medicine* 24, No. 4 (1962): 343–351.

(A071) Altman, Charlotte H. "Relationships Between Maternal Attitudes and Child Personality Structure." *American Journal of Orthopsychiatry* 28 (January 1958): 160–169.

(A072) Alkire, William H. "Cultural Adaptation in the Caroline Islands." *Polynesia* 69 (1960): 123–150.

(A073) Altus, William D. "College Attendance and Sex of the Sibling." *Psychological Reports* 15 (1964): 46.

(B001) Burchinal, Lee G. "Marital Satisfaction and Religious Behavior." *American Sociological Review* 2, No. 3 (1957): 306–310.

(B002) Bowerman, Charles E., and Day, Barbara R. "A Test of the Theory of Complementary Needs as Applied to Couples During Courtship." *American Sociological Review* 21 (1956): 603–665.

(B003) Blau, Zena Smith. "Changes in Status and Age Identification." *American Sociological Review* 21 (1956): 198–203.

(B004) Bossard, James H. S., and Bell, Eleanor S. "Ritual in Family Living." *American Sociological Review* 14 (1949): 463–469.

(B005) Bossard, James H. S., and Sanger, Winogene Pratt. "The Large Family System: A Research Report." *American Sociological Review* 17 (1952): 3–9.

(B006) Brown, Julia. "A Comparative Study of Deviations from Sexual Mores." *American Sociological Review* 17 (1952): 135–146.

(B007) Blood, Robert O. "A Situational Approach to the Study of Permissiveness in Child Rearing." *American Sociological Review* 18 (1953): 84–87.

(B008) Bowerman, Charles E. "Assortative Mating by Previous Marital Status, Seattle, 1939–1946." *American Sociological Review* 18 (1953): 170–177.

(B010) Broom, Leonard, Beem, Helen P., and Harris, Virginia. "Characteristics of 1,107 Petitioners for Change of Name." *American Sociological Review* 20 (1955): 33–39.

(B011) Biesanz, John, and Smith, Luke M. "Adjustment of Interethnic Marriages on the Isthmus of Panama." *American Sociological Review* 16 (1951): 819–822.

(B012) Barron, Milton L. "Research on Intermarriage: A Survey of Accomplishments and Prospects." *American Journal of Sociology* 57 (1951): 249–255.

(B013) Brown, James S. "Social Class, Intermarriage, and Church Membership in a Kentucky Community." *American Journal of Sociology* 57 (1951): 232–242.

(B014) Bend, Emil. "Marriage Offers in a Yiddish Newspaper—1935 and 1950." *American Journal of Sociology* 58 (1952): 60–66.

(B029) Broom, Leonard. "Intermarriage and Mobility in Hawaii." In *Transactions of the Third World Congress of Sociology,* Vol. 3, *Changes in Class Structure,* 277–282. London: International Sociological Association, 1956.

(B031) Bicanic, Rudolf. "Occupational Heterogeneity of Peasant Families in the Period of Accelerated Industrialism." In *Transactions of the Third World Congress of Sociology,* Vol. 4, *Changes in the Family,* 80–96.

London: International Sociological Association, 1956.

(B032) Brown, G. Gordon. "Bride-Wealth Among the Hehe." *Africa* 5 (1932): 145–157.

(B033) Burgess, Ernest W., and Locke, Harvey J. *The Family*. 2nd ed. New York: American Book Company, 1953.

(B034) Bruner, Edward M. "Primary Group Experience and the Processes of Acculturation." *American Anthropologist* 58 (1956): 605–623.

(B035) Barnett, H. G. "Peace and Progress in New Guinea." *American Anthropologist* 61 (1959): 1013–1019.

(B037) Barry, Herbert, III, Child, Irving, and Baton, Margaret K. "The Relation of Child Training to Subsistent Economy." *American Anthropologist* 61 (1959): 51–53.

(B038) Bushnell, John. "La Virgen de Guadalupe as Surrogate Mother in San Juan Atzingo." *American Anthropologist* 60 (1958): 261–265.

(B040) Boggs, Stephen T. "Culture Change and the Personality of Ojibwa Children." *American Anthropologist* 60 (1958): 47–68.

(B041) Burridge, Kenelm O. L. "Disputing in Tangu." *American Anthropologist* 59 (1957): 763–780.

(B042) Broom, Leonard, and Kitsuse, John R. "The Validation of Acculturation: A Condition to Ethnic Assimilation." *American Anthropologist* 57 (1955): 44–48.

(B043) Berreman, Gerald D. "Inquiry into Community Integration on an Aleutian Village." *American Anthropologist* 57 (1955): 49–59.

(B045) Berndt, Ronald M. "Murngin (Wulamba) Social Organization." *American Anthropologist* 57 (1955): 84–106.

(B048) Bourguignon, Erika E. "Dream and Dream Interpretation in Haiti." *American Anthropologist* 56 (1954): 262–268.

(B049) Brunner, Edward M. "Two Processes of Change in Mandan–Hidtsa Kinship Terminology." *American Anthropologist* 57 (1955): 840–850.

(B050) Barth, Frederik. "Ecologic Relationships of Ethnic Groups in Swat, North Pakistan." *American Anthropologist* 58 (1956): 1079–1089.

(B053) Brown, C. Gordon, and Barnett, James H. "Social Organization and Social Structure." *American Anthropologist* 34 (1932): 31–36.

(B054) Bascom, William R. "The Principle of Seniority in the Social Structure of the Yoruba." *American Anthropologist* 44 (1942): 37–46.

(B055) Bonos, Arlene Helen. "Romany Rye of Philadelphia." *American Anthropologist* 44 (1942): 257–274.

(B056) Bell, Norman W., and Vogel, Ezra F., eds. "The Emotionally Disturbed Child as the Family Scapegoat." *Modern Introduction to the Family*. Glencoe, Ill.: The Free Press, 1960, pp. 282–397.

(B058) Barton, R. F. "Reflection in Two Kinship Terms of the Transition to Endogamy." *American Anthropologist* 43 (1941): 540–549.

(B059) Belo, Jane. "A Study of a Balinese Family." *American Anthropologist* 38 (1936): 12–31.

(B060) Benedict, Ruth. "Marital Property Rights in Bilateral Society." *American Anthropologist* 38 (1936): 368–373.

(B063) Beals, Ralph L. "Unilateral Organizations in Mexico." *American Anthropologist* 34 (1932): 267–275.

(B064) Burrows, Edwin G. "Breed and Border in Polynesia." *American Anthropologist* 41 (1939): 1–21.

(B065) Bloom, Leonard. "The Cherokee Clan: A Study in Acculturation." *American Anthropologist* 41 (1939): 266–268.

(B066) Brant, Charles S. "On Joking Relationships." *American Anthropologist* 50 (1948): 160–162.

(B067) Barnett, H. G. "Culture Processes." *American Anthropologist* 42 (1940): 21–48.

(B073) Barnes, J. A. "Measures of Divorce Frequency in Simple Societies." *Journal of the Royal Anthropological Institute* 79 (1949): 37–62.

(B075) Brown, Elizabeth Fisher. "Hehe Grandmothers." *Journal of the Royal Anthropological Institute* 65 (1935): 83–96.

(B076) Brelsford, Vernon. "The History and Customs of the Basala." *Journal of the Royal Anthropological Institute* 65 (1935): 205–215.

(B081) Baker, John R. "Depopulation in Espiritu Santo, New Hebrides." *Journal of the Royal Anthropological Institute* 57 (1928): 279–303.

(B082) Barnes, J. A. "Land Rights and Kinship in Two Bremnes Hamlets." *Journal of the Royal Anthropological Institute* 87 (1957): 31–56.

(B083) Befu, Harumi, and Norbeck, Edward. "Japanese Usages of Terms of Relationships." *Southwest Journal of Anthropology* 14 (1958): 66–86.

(B085) Barnouw, Victor. "Eastern Nepalese Marriage Customs and Kinship Organization." *Southwest Journal of Anthropology* 11 (1955): 15–30.

(B086) Bacon, Elizabeth E. "Types of Pastoral Nomadism in Central and Southwest Asia." *Southwest Journal of Anthropology* 10 (1954): 44–68.

(B087) Barth, Frederik. "Father's Brother's Daughter's Marriage in Kurdistan." *Southwest Journal of Anthropology* 10 (1954): 164–171.

(B088) Berndt, Catherine H. "Socio-Cultural Change in the Eastern Central Highlands of New Guinea." *Southwest Journal of Anthropology* 9 (1953): 112–138.

(B092) Baer, Phillip, and Baer, Mary. "Notes on the Lacandon Marriage." *Southwest Journal of Anthropology* 5 (1949): 101–106.

(B093) Bruner, Edward M. "Cultural Transmission and Cultural Change." *Southwest Journal of Anthropology* 12 (1956): 191–199.

(B098) Becker, Howard. "In Defense of Morgan's 'Grecian Gens': Ancient Kinship and Stratification," *Southwest Journal of Anthropology* 6 (1950): 309–339.

(B107) Bunzel, Ruth. "Chichicastenango: A Guatemalan Village." Publication of *The American Ethnological Society* No. 22 (New York, 1952).

(B108) Bowers, Alfred W. *Mandan Social and Ceremonial Organization*. Chicago: University of Chicago Press, 1950.

(B110) Beattie, J. H. M. "Nyoro Marriage and Affinity." *Africa* 28 (1958): 1–22.

(B111) Bruwer, J. P. Van S. "Matrilineal Kinship Among the Kunda." *Africa* 28 (1958): 207–224.

(B111) Brant, Charles S. "Mi Mi Khaing Burmese Kinship and the Life Cycle: An Outline." *Southwest Journal of Anthropology* 7 (1951): 437–454.

(B112) Burrows, Edwin G. "Some Value to Ethos on Ifaluk Atoll." *Southwest Journal of Anthropology* 8 (1952): 13–35.

(B113) Bassir, Olumbe. "Marriage Rites Among the Aku (Yoruba) of Freetown." *Africa* 24 (1954): 251–256.

(B116) Brown, Paula. "Patterns of Authority in West Africa." *Africa* 21 (1951): 261–278.

(B118) Bartlett, F. C. "Psychological Methods for the Study of 'Hard' and 'Soft' Features of Culture." *Africa* 16 (1946): 145–155.

(B122) Bertho, J. "Le Problème du Mariage Chrétien en Afrique Occidentale Française." *Africa* 17 (1947): 252 –259.

(B126) Bernardi, B. "The Age-System of the Nilo-Hamitic People." *Africa* 22 (1952): 316–332.

(B128) Beemer, Hilda. "The Development of the Military Organization in Swaziland." *Africa* 10 (1937): 176–205.

(B133) Baumann, Hermann. "The Division of Work According to Sex in African Hoe Culture." *Africa* 1 (1928): 289–319.

(B134) Beattie, J. H. M. "Nyoro Kinship." *Africa* 27 (1957): 317–340.

(B142) Burridge, Kenelm O. L. "Descent in Tangu." *Oceania* 28 (1957–1958): 85–99.

(B145) Burridge, Kenelm O. L. "Adoption in Tangu." *Oceania* 29 (1958–1959): 185–199.

(B147) The Bureau for Native Affairs, Hollandia, Netherlands New Guinea. "Anthropological Research in Netherlands New Guinea Since 1950." *Oceania* 29 (1958–1959): 132–163.

(B148) Berndt, Ronald M. "Influence of European Culture on Australian Aborigines." *Oceania* 21 (1950–1951): 229–235.

(B150) Belshaw, Cyril S. "Recent History of Mekeo Society." *Oceania* 22 (1951–1952): 1–23.

(B151) Berndt, Catherine H., and Berndt, Ronald M. "An Oenpewlli Monologue: Culture Contacts." *Oceania* 22 (1951–1952): 24–52.

(B156) Berndt, Ronald M. "Kamano, Jape, Usurufa and Fore Kinship of the Eastern Highlands of New Guinea: A Preliminary Account." *Oceania* 25 (1954–1955): 23 –53.

(B157) Berndt, Ronald M. "Kamano, Jape, Usurufa and Fore Kinship of the Eastern Highlands of New Guinea: A Preliminary Account." *Oceania* 25 (1954–1955): 156–187.

(B158) Bell, F. L. S. "The Place of Food in the Social Life of the Tanga." *Oceania* 19 (1948–1949): 51–75.

(B162) Bogefi, George. "Santa Isabel, Solomon Islands." *Oceania* 18 (1947–1948): 327–357.

(B166) Berndt, Ronald M., and Berndt, Catherine H. "A Preliminary Report of Field Work in the Ooldea Region, Western South Australia." *Oceania* 13 (1942–1943): 51–70.

(B167) Berndt, Ronald M., and Berndt, Catherine H. "A Preliminary Report of Field Work in the Ooldea Region, Western South Australia." *Oceania* 13 (1942–1943): 143–169.

(B171) Berndt, Ronald M., and Berndt, Catherine H. "A Preliminary Report on Field Work in the Ooldea Region, Western South Australia." *Oceania* 14 (1943–1944): 124–158.

(B174) Berndt, Ronald M., and Berndt, Catherine H. "A Preliminary Report of Field Work in the Ooldea Region, Western South Australia." *Oceania* 12 (1941–1942): 308–330.

(B178) Bell, F. L. S. "Death in Tanga." *Oceania* 7 (1936 –1937): 316–339.

(B180) Bell, F. L. S. "The Avoidance Situation in Tanga." *Oceania* 6 (1935–1936): 175–198.

(B181) Bell, F. L. S. "Courtship and Marriage Among the Tanga." *Oceania* 8 (1937–1938): 403–418.

(B182) Bell, F. L. S. "Report on Field Work in Tanga." *Oceania* 4 (1933–1934): 290–309.

(B183) Bell, F. L. S. "A Functional Interpretation of Inheritance and Succession in Central Polynesia." *Oceania* 3 (1932–1933): 167–206.

(B184) Blackwood, Beatrice. "Report on Field Work in Buka and Bougainville." *Oceania* 2 (1931–1932): 199 –219.

(B185) Bateson, Gregory. "Social Structure of the Iatmul People of the Sepik River." *Oceania* 2 (1931–1932): 245–291.

(B187) Bell, F. L. S. "Warfare Among the Tanga." *Oceania* 5 (1934–1935): 253–279.

(B190) Burridge, Kenelm O. L. "Friendship in Tangu." *Oceania* 27 (1956–1957): 177–189.

(B191) Barton, R. F. *The Kalingas*. Chicago: University of Chicago Press, 1949.

(B193) Barton, R. F. "Ifugao Law." University of California Publications in *American Archeology and Ethnology* 15, No. 1 (1919).

(B201) Barnes, J. A. *Politics in a Changing Society*. London: Oxford University Press, 1954.

(B202) Bell, Norman W., and Vogel, Ezra F., eds. *Modern Introduction to the Family*. Glencoe, Ill.: The Free Press, 1960.

(B203) Brown, A. R. *The Andaman Islanders*. Cambridge: University Press, 1922.

(B205) Berreman, Gerald D. "Pahari Polyandry: A Comparison." *American Anthropologist* 64 (February 1962): 60–75.

(B206) Bossard, James H. S., and Boll, Eleanor S. "Family Ritual and Family Integration." In *Modern Introduction to the Family*, edited by Norman W. Bell and Ezra F. Vogel. Glencoe, Ill.: The Free Press, 1960, pp. 429 –434.

(B207) Bakke, E. Wight. "The Cycle of Adjustment to Unemployment." In *Modern Introduction to the Family*, edited by Norman W. Bell and Ezra F. Vogel. Glencoe, Ill.: The Free Press, 1960, pp. 112–125.

(B208) Blood, Robert O., Jr., and Hamblin, Robert L. "The Effects of the Wife's Employment on the Family Power Structure." In *Modern Introduction to the Family*, edited by Norman W. Bell and Ezra F. Vogel. Glencoe, Ill.: The Free Press, 1960, pp. 137–142.

(B209) Bott, Elizabeth. "Conjugal Roles and Social Networks." In *Modern Introduction to the Family*, edited by Norman W. Bell and Ezra F. Vogel. Glencoe, Ill.: The Free Press, 1960, pp. 248–257.

(B210) Bott, Elizabeth. "Norms and Ideology: The Normal Family." In *Modern Introduction to the Family*, edited by Norman W. Bell and Ezra F. Vogel. Glencoe, Ill.: The Free Press, 1960, pp. 435–452.

(B211) Bettelheim, Bruno, and Sylvester, Emmy. "Parental Occupations and Children's Symptoms." In *Modern Introduction to the Family*, edited by Norman W. Bell and Ezra F. Vogel. Glencoe, Ill.: The Free Press, 1960, pp. 499–509.

(B212) Bieber, Irving, *et al. Homosexuality: A Psychoanalytical Approach*. New York: Basic Books, 1962.

(B213) Bandura, Albert, and Walters, Richard H. *Adolescent Aggression*. New York: Ronald Press, 1959.

(B216) Brim, Orville G., Jr. "Family Structure and Role-Sex Learning by Children." In *Modern Introduction to the Family*, edited by Norman W. Bell and Ezra F. Vogel. Glencoe, Ill.: The Free Press, 1960, pp. 482–496.

(B217) Bird, H. Waldo, and Martin, Peter A. "Further Consideration of the 'Cold, Sick' Husband." *Psychiatry* 22 (1959): 250–254.

(B218) Bruch, Hilde. "Developmental Obesity and Schizophrenia." *Psychiatry* 21 (1958): 65–70.

(B219) Block, Jeanne, Patterson, Virginia, Block, Jack, and Jackson, Don D. "A Study of the Parents of Schizophrenic and Neurotic Children." *Psychiatry* 21 (1958): 387–397.

(B220) Beckett, Peter G. S., *et al.* "The Significance of Exogenous Traumata in the Genesis of Schizophrenia." *Psychiatry* 19 (1956): 137–142.

(B221) Brody, Eugene B. "Social Conflict and Schizophrenic Behavior in Young Adult Negro Males." *Psychiatry* 24 (1961): 337–346.

(B222) Briggs, Lloyd Cabot. *Tribes of the Sahara.* Cambridge: Harvard University Press, 1960.

(B223) Bogaras, Waldemar. "The Chuckchee." Memoir of *The American Museum of Natural History* 7 (1909).

(B224) Beller, E. "Dependency and Autonomous Achievement Striving Related to Orality and Anality in Early Childhood." *Child Development* 28 (September 1957): 287–315.

(B225) Ballard, Robert G. "The Interrelatedness of Alcoholism and Marital Conflict: 3. The Interaction Between Marital Conflict and Alcoholism as Seen Through MMPI's of Marriage Partners." *American Journal of Orthopsychiatry* 29 (July 1959): 528–546.

(B226) Bird, Charles, Monachesi, Elio D., and Burdick, Harvey. "Studies of Group Tensions: III. The Effect of Parental Discouragement of Play Activities upon the Attitudes of White Children Toward Negroes." *Child Development* 23 (December 1952): 295–306.

(B227) Block, Jack. "Personality Characteristics Associated with Fathers' Attitudes Toward Child-Rearing." *Child Development* 26 (March 1955): 41–48.

(B228) Baxten, James C., and Becker, Joseph. "Anxiety and Avoidance Behavior in Schizophrenics in Response to Parental Figures." *Journal of Abnormal and Social Psychology* 64 (June 1962): 432–437.

(B229) Brown, A. W., and Hunt, R. G. "Relations Between Nursery School Attendance and Teachers' Ratings of Some Aspects of Children's Adjustment in Kindergarten." *Child Development* 32, No. 3 (1961): 585–596.

(B230) Behrens, Marjorie J. "Child Rearing and the Character Structure of the Mother." *Child Development* 25 (September 1954): 225–238.

(B231) Buric, Olivera. "Attitudes Regarding the Status of Women in Yugoslavia." *International Social Science Journal* 14, No. 3 (1962): 166–174.

(B232) Becker, W., *et al.* "Relations of Factors Derived from Parent-Interview Ratings to Behavior Problems of Five-Year-Olds." *Child Development* 33 (1962): 509–535.

(B233) Baugh, Verner S., and Carpenter, B. L. "A Comparison of Delinquents and Non-Delinquents." *Journal of Social Psychology* 56 (February 1962): 73–78.

(B234) Bronfenbrenner, U. "Freudian Theories of Identification and Their Derivatives." *Child Development* 31 (1960): 15–40.

(B235) Boehm, Lenore, and Nass, Martin. "Social Class Differences in Conscience Development." *Child Development* 33 (1962): 565–574.

(B236) Bronfenbrenner, U. "The Changing American Child." In *Values and Ideals of American Youth,* edited by Eli Ginzberg. New York: Columbia University Press, 1961, pp. 71–84.

(B237) Becker, Wesley C. "The Relationship of Factors in Parental Ratings of Self and Each Other to the Behavior of Kindergarten Children as Rated by Mothers, Fathers and Teachers." *Journal of Consulting Psychology* 24 (December 1960): 507–527.

(B238) Bennett, I. *Delinquent and Neurotic Children:*

*A Comparative Study.* New York: Basic Books, 1959.

(B239) Bowlby, John. "The Nature of the Child's Tie to His Mother." *International Journal of Psychoanalysis* 39 (September–October 1958): 350–373.

(B240) Behrens, Marjorie L., and Goldfarb, William. "A Study of Patterns of Interaction of Families of Schizophrenic Children in Residential Treatment." *American Journal of Orthopsychiatry* 28 (April 1958): 300–312.

(B241) Beres, David, Gale, Conrad, and Oppenheimer, Lila. "Disturbances of Identity Function in Childhood: Psychiatric and Psychological Observations." *American Journal of Orthopsychiatry* 30 (April 1960): 369–381.

(B242) Bell, John E. "Recent Advances in Family Group Therapy." *Journal of Child Psychology and Psychiatry* 3 (January–March 1962): 1–15.

(B243) Bandura, Albert, and Walters, Richard H. *Adolescent Aggression.* New York: Ronald Press, 1959.

(B244) Bee, Lawrence S. *Marriage and Family Relations.* New York: Harper and Brothers, 1959.

(B245) Blake, J. *Family Structure in Jamaica.* Glencoe, Ill.: The Free Press, 1961.

(B246) Bandura, Albert, and Walters, Richard H. "Dependency Conflicts in Aggressive Delinquents." *Journal of Social Issues* 14 No. 3 (1958): 52–65.

(B247) Burchinal, Lee G. "Social Status, Measured Intelligence, Achievement, and Personality Adjustment of Rural Iowa Girls." *Sociometry* 22 (March 1959): 75–80.

(B248) Bock, Edwin A., and Burchinal, Lee G. "Social Status, Heterosexual Relations, and Expected Ages of Marriage." *The Journal of Genetic Psychology* 101 (1962): 43–51.

(B249) Bath, J., and Lewis, E. "Attitudes of Young Female Adults Toward Some Areas of Parent-Adolescent Conflict." *The Journal of Genetic Psychology* 100 (1962): 241–253.

(B250) Bronfenbrenner, U. "Some Familial Antecedents of Responsibility and Leadership in Adolescents." In *Leadership and Interpersonal Behavior,* edited by Luigi Petrullo and Bernhard M. Bass. New York: Holt, Rinehart and Winston, 1961, pp. 239–271.

(B251) Burchinal, Lee G., Gardner, Bruce, and Hawkes, Glenn R. "Children's Personality Adjustment and the Socioeconomic Status of Their Families." *Journal of Genetic Psychology* 92 (June 1958): 149–159.

(B251) Burton, Roger V., and Whiting, John W. M. "The Absent Father and Cross-Sex Identity." *Merrill–Palmer Quarterly* 7 (April 1961): 85–95.

(B252) Bronfenbrenner, U. "The Changing American Child: A Speculative Analysis." *Merrill–Palmer Quarterly* 7 (April 1961): 73–83.

(B253) Barnes, Marion J. "The Working-Through Process in Dealing with Anxiety Around Adoption." *American Journal of Orthopsychiatry* 23 (July 1955): 605–620.

(B254) Brown, L. B. "Religious Belief and Reports of Childhood Experiences." *Psychological Reports* 10 (February 1962): 269–270.

(B255) Bowlby, John. "Separation Anxiety: A Critical Review of the Literature." *Journal of Child Psychology and Psychiatry* 1 (February 1961): 251–269.

(B256) Bennett, William S., and Gist, Noel P. "Class and Family Influences on Student Aspirations." *Social Forces* 43 (December 1964): 167–173.

(B257) Bing, Elizabeth. "Effect of Child Rearing Practices on Development of Differential Cognitive Abilities." *Child Development* 34 (1963): 631–648.

(B258) Block, Jack, and Turula, Emily. "Identification, Ego

Control, and Adjustment." *Child Development* 34 (1963): 945–953.

(B259) Becker, W., *et al.* "Factors in Parental Behavior and Personality as Related to Problem Behavior in Children." *Journal of Consulting Psychiatry* 23, No. 2 (1959): 107–118.

(B260) Bronson, Wanda C., Katten, Edith S., and Livson, Norman. "Patterns of Abnormal and Social Psychology." *Journal of Abnormal and Social Psychology* 58 (March 1959): 143–152.

(B261) Bullock, Samuel, and Mudd, Emily H. "The Interrelatedness of Alcoholism and Marital Conflict." *American Journal of Orthopsychiatry* 29 (July 1959): 519–527.

(B262) Baxter, James C., Becker, Joseph, and Hooks, Walter. "Defensive Style in the Families of Schizophrenics and Controls." *Journal of Abnormal and Social Psychology* 66 (May 1963): 512–518.

(B263) Bennett, Edward M., and Johannsen, Dorothea E. "Some Psychodynamic Aspects of Felt Parental Alliance in Young Children." *Journal of Abnormal and Social Psychology* 49 (July 1954): 463–466.

(B264) Barry, Herbert, Bacon, Margaret K., and Child, Irvin L. "A Cross-Cultural Survey of Some Sex Differences in Socialization." *Journal of Abnormal and Social Psychology* 55 (November 1957): 327–332.

(B265) Byrne, Donn, and Blaylock, Barbara. "Similarity and Assumed Similarity of Attitudes Between Husbands and Wives." *Journal of Abnormal and Social Psychology* 67 (December 1963): 636–640.

(B266) Baldwin, Alfred L. "Socialization and the Parent-Child Relationship." In *Studies in Motivation,* edited by David C. McClelland. New York: Appleton-Century-Crofts, Inc., 1955, pp. 297–307.

(B267) Bott, E. "Urban Families: Conjugal Roles and Social Networks." *Human Relations* 8 (1955): 345–384.

(B268) Bott, E. "Urban Families: The Norms of Conjugal Roles." *Human Relations* 9 (1957): 325–342.

(B269) Bowlby, John. "The Adolf Meyer Lecture: Childhood Mourning and Its Implications for Psychiatry." *American Journal of Psychiatry* 118 (December 1961): 481–498.

(B270) Bowlby, John, *Maternal Care and Mental Health.* Geneva: World Health Organization, 1952.

(B272) Brody, S. *Patterns of Mothering.* New York: International Universities Press, 1956.

(B273) Bronfenbrenner, U. "The Changing American Child: A Speculative Analysis." *Social Issues* 17 (1961): 6–18.

(B274) Beier, Ernest G., and Ratzeburg, Fred. "The Parental Identification of Male and Female College Students." *Journal of Abnormal and Social Psychology* 48 (April 1953): 569–572.

(B275) Berkowitz, Leonard. *The Development of Motives and Values in the Child.* New York, London: Basic Books, 1964.

(B276) Burchinal, Lee G. "Characteristics of Adolescents from Unbroken, Broken and Reconstituted Families." *Journal of Marriage and Family Living* 26 (February 1964): 44–51.

(B277) Brown, D. "Sex-Role Preference in Young Children." *Psychological Monographs* 70, No. 14 (1956): 1–19.

(B278) Bychowski, G. "Some Aspects of Masochistic Involvement." *American Psychoanalytic Association: Journal* 7 (1959): 248–273.

(B279) Baxter, J., *et al.* Conflict Patterns in the Families of Schizophrenics." *Journal of Nervous and Mental Disease* 135 (1962): 419–424.

(B280) Bibring, G. "Some Considerations of the Psychological Processes in Pregnancy." *The Psychoanalytic Study of the Child* 14 (1959): 113–121.

(B281) Bromberg, Norbert. "Maternal Influences in the Development of Moral Masochism." *American Journal of Orthopsychiatry* 25 (October 1955): 802–812.

(B282) Barbe, W. "A Study of the Family Background of the Gifted." *Journal of Educational Psychology* 47 (1956): 302–309.

(B283) Baker, J. W., and Holzworth, A. "Social Histories of Successful and Unsuccessful Children." *Child Development* 32 (1961): 135–149.

(B284) Ballak, L. *Schizophrenia: A Review Syndrome.* New York: Logos Press, 1958.

(B285) Bender, L. "Behavior Problems in the Children of Psychotic and Criminal Parents." *Genetic Psychology Monographs* 19 (1937): 229–339.

(B286) Bowerman, Charles, and Irish, Donald. "Some Relationships of Stepchildren to Their Parents." *Marriage and Family Living* 24 (May 1962): 113–121.

(B287) Baldwin, Alfred L. "The Effect of Home Environment on Nursery School Behavior." *Child Development* 20 (June 1949): 49–61.

(B288) Block, Jack, and Turula, Emily. "Identification, Ego Control, and Adjustment." *Child Development* 34 (December 1963): 945–953.

(B289) Bing, Elizabeth. "Effect of Child Rearing Practices on Development of Differential Cognitive Abilities." *Child Development* 34 (September 1963): 631–648.

(B290) Baker, J. W., and Holzworth, A. "Social Histories of Successful and Unsuccessful Children." *Child Development* 32 (1961): 135–149.

(B291) Bloch, Donal A. "The Delinquent Integration." *Psychiatry* 15 (1952): 297–303.

(B291) Bordua, D. "Educational Aspirations and Parental Stress on College." *Social Forces* 39 (1960): 262–269.

(B292) Brittain, Clay V. "Adolescent Choices and Parent-Peer Cross-Pressures." *American Sociological Review* 28 (June 1963): 385–391.

(B293) Bolton, Charles D. "Mate Selection as the Development of a Relationship." *Marriage and Family Living* 23 (August 1961): 234–240.

(B294) Burchinal, Lee G., and Rossman, Jack E. "Relations among Maternal Employment Indices and Developmental Characteristics of Children." *Marriage and Family Living* 23 (November 1961): 334–340.

(B295) Buerkle, J. V. "Self Attitudes and Marital Adjustment." *Merril–Palmer Quarterly* 6 (January 1960): 114–123.

(B296) Buerkle, J. W., and Badgley, R. "Couple Role-Taking: The Yale Marital Interaction Battery." *Marriage and Family Living* 21 (1959): 53–58.

(B297) Bronson, Wanda C., Katten, Edith S., and Livson, Norman. "Patterns of Authority and Affection in Two Generations." *Journal of Abnormal and Social Psychology* 58 (March 1959): 143–152.

(B298) Beaglehole, Ernest, and Beaglehole, Pearl. "Ethnology of Pukapuka." *Bishop Museum Bulletin* 150 (1938).

(B299) Brown, Paula. "Chimbu Tribes: Political Organization in the Eastern Highlands of New Guinea." *Southwest Journal of Anthropology* 16 (1960): 22–35.

(B300) Bresler, Jack B. "The Relation of Population Fertility Levels to Ethnic Group Background." *Eugenics Quarterly* 8 (1961): 12–22.

(B301) Befu, Harumi. "Classification of Unilineal-Bilateral Societies." *Southwest Journal of Anthropology* 19 (1963): 335–355.

(B302) Berreman, Gerald D. "Village Exogamy in Northernmost India." *Southwest Journal of Anthropology* 18 (1962): 55–58.

(B303) Beteille, A. "A Brief Note on the Role of Cross-Cutting Alliances in Segmentary Political Systems." *Man* 233 (1960): 181–182.

(B304) Buchler, I. R. "Cubical and Tri-Dimensional Block Models of Crow Kinship Structure." *Man* 3 (1964): 6–8.

(B305) Bejema, Carl Jay. "Estimation of the Direction and Intensity of Natural Selection in Relation to Human Intelligence by Means of the Intrinsic Rate of Natural Increase." *Eugenics Quarterly* 10 (1963): 175–187.

(B306) Bascom, William. "Yoruba Urbanism: A Summary." *Man* 253 (1958): 190–191.

(B307) Bass, Medora Steedman. "Marriage, Parenthood and Prevention of Pregnancy for the Mentally Deficient." *Eugenics Quarterly* 11 (1964): 96–111.

(B308) Berg, M., and Cohen, V. "Early Separation from the Mother in Schizophrenia." *Journal of Nervous and Mental Disease* 128 (1959): 365–369.

(B309) Blum, L. "Sterility and the Magic Power of the Maternal Figure." *Journal of Nervous and Mental Diseases* 128 (1959): 401–408.

(B310) Berman, Sidney. "Anti-Social Character Disorder: Its Etiology and Relationship to Delinquency." *American Journal of Orthopsychiatry* 29 (July 1959): 612–621.

(B311) Burma, John H. "Interethnic Marriage in Los Angeles, 1948–1959." *Social Forces* 42 (December 1963): 156–165.

(B312) Baumert, Gerhard. "Changes in the Family and the Position of Older Persons in Germany." *International Journal of Comparative Sociology* 1 (1960): 202–210.

(B313) Bell, Gerald D. "Processes in the Formation of Adolescent Aspirations." *Social Forces* 42 (December 1963): 179–186.

(B314) Burchinal, Lee G., and Chancellor, Loren E. "Survival Rate Among Religiously Homogamous and Interreligious Marriages." *Social Forces* 41 (May 1963): 353–362.

(B315) Bowen, Murray. "A Family Concept of Schizophrenia." In *The Etiology of Schizophrenia,* edited by Don D. Jackson. New York: Basic Books, 1960, pp. 346–372.

(B316) Bennett, William S., Jr., and Gist, Noel P. "Class and Family Influences on Student Aspirations." *Social Forces* 43 (December 1964): 167–173.

(B317) Babchuk, Nicholas, and Bates, Alan P. "The Primary Relations of Middle Class Couples: A Study in Male Dominance." *American Sociological Review* 28 (June 1963): 377–385.

(B318) Balint, Michael, "The Younger Sister and Prince Charming." *International Journal of Psychoanalysis* 44 (1963): 226–227.

(B319) Blumenfeld, Warren S. "Note on the Relationship of Political Preference Between Generations Within a Household." *Psychological Reports* 15 (1964): 976.

(B320) Boles, Glen. "Personality Factors in Mothers of Cerebral Palsied Children." *Genetic Psychology Monographs* 59 (1959): 159–218.

(B321) Bene, Eva. "Family Relations as Experienced by Psychologically Disturbed Children." *British Journal of Medical Psychology* 32 (1959): 226–231.

(B322) Bowerman, Charles E., and Elder, Glen H., Jr. "Family Structure and Child Rearing Patterns: Effect of Family Size and Sex Composition." *American Sociological Review* 28 (December 1963): 891–905.

(B323) Bowerman, Charles E., and Elder, Glen H., Jr. "Variations in Adolescent Perception of Family Power Structure." *American Sociological Review* 29 (August 1964): 551–567.

(B324) Boyer, L. Bryce. "On Maternal Overstimulation and Ego Defects." *Psychoanalytic Study of the Child* 11 (1956): 236–255.

(B327) Brown, Paula. "Non-Agnates among the Patrilineal Chimbu." *Polynesia* 71 (1962): 57–69.

(C001) Chambliss, Rollin. "Contributions of the Vital Statistics of Finland to the Study of Factors That Induce Marriage." *American Sociological Review* 22 (February 1957): 38–48.

(C002) Clarke, Alfred C. "An Examination of the Operation of Residential Propinquity as a Factor in Mate Selection." *American Sociological Review* 17 (1952): 17–22.

(C003) Christensen, Harold T., and Philbrick, Robert E. "Family Size as a Factor in the Marital Adjustments of College Couples." *American Sociological Review* 17 (1952): 306–312.

(C004) Christensen, Harold T. "Studies in Child Spacing: I—Premarital Pregnancy as Measured by the Spacing of the First Birth from Marriage." *American Sociological Review* 18 (1953): 53–59.

(C005) Christensen, Harold T., and Meissner, Hanna H. "Studies in Child Spacing: III—Premarital Pregnancy as a Factor in Divorce." *American Sociological Review* 18 (1953): 641–644.

(C006) Chancellor, Loren E., and Monahan, Thomas P. "Religious Preference and Interreligious Mixtures in Marriages and Divorces in Iowa." *American Journal of Sociology* 61 (1955): 233–239.

(C007) Christensen, Harold T. "Mormon Fertility: A Survey of Student Opinion." *American Journal of Sociology* 53 (1948): 270–275.

(C008) Centers, Richard. "Marital Selection and Occupational Strata." *American Journal of Sociology* 54 (1949): 530–535.

(C009) Cohen, Lillian. "Family Characteristics of Homeowners." *American Journal of Sociology* 55 (1950): 565–571.

(C010) Carter, Hugh, Glick, Paul C., and Lewit, Sarah. "Some Demographic Characteristics of Recently Married Persons: Comparisons of Registration Data and Sample Survey Data." *American Sociological Review* 20 (1955): 165–172.

(C011) Caplow, Theodore. "Home Ownership and Location Preferences in a Minneapolis Sample." *American Sociological Reveiw* 13 (1948): 725–730.

(C012) Christensen, Harold T. "Dating Behavior as Evaluated by High School Students." *American Journal of Sociology* 57 (1952): 580–586.

(C019) Christensen, Harold T., and Bowden, Olive P. "Studies in Child Spacing: II—The Time Interval Between Marriage of Parents and Birth of Their First Child, Tippecanoe County, Indiana." *Social Forces* 31 (1953): 346–351.

(C022) Coughlin, Richard J. "The Position of Women in Vietnam." In *Southeast Asian Studies, Cultural Report Series.* New Haven: Yale University, 1950. (Mimeo.)

(C023) Christensen, Harold T. *Marriage Analysis,* 2nd ed. New York: Ronald Press, 1958.

(C024) Cohen, Yehudi A. "Structure and Function: Family Organization and Socialization in a Jamaican Community." *American Anthropologist* 58 (1956): 664–686.

(C029) Collier, John. "Photography in Anthropology." *American Anthropologist* 59 (1957): 843–859.

(C035) Collins, June McCormick. "An Interpretation of Skagit Intra-Group Conflicts During Acculturation." *American Anthropologist* 54 (1952): 347–355.

(C036) Chen, T. S., and Shryock, J. K. "Chinese Relationship Terms." *American Anthropologist* 34 (1932): 623–659.

(C038) Carr, Malcolm, Spencer, Catherine, and Woolley, Doriane. "Navaho Clans and Marriage at Pueblo Alto." *American Anthropologist* 41 (1939): 245–260.

(C045) Culwick, A. T. "A Method of Studying Changes in Primitive Marriage." *Journal of the Royal Anthropological Institute* 65 (1935): 185–194.

(C046) Crosse-Upcott, A. R. W. "Male Circumcision Among the Nginbo." *Journal of the Royal Anthropological Institute* 89 (1959): 169–188.

(C047) Crosby, K. H. "Polygamy in Mende Country." *Africa* 10 (1937): 249–264.

(C048) Cappannari, Stephen Z. "Marriage in Malabar." *Southwest Journal of Anthropology* 9 (1953): 263–267.

(C049) Cheng, Elizabeth. "Some Features of the Kinship Terminology Used in New York's Chinatown." *Southwest Journal of Anthropology* 8 (1952): 97–107.

(C052) Colson, Elizabeth. "Rain-Shrines of the Plateau Tonga of Northern Rhodesia." *Africa* 18 (1948): 272–283.

(C055) Culwick, G. M. "New Ways or Old in the Treatment of Adolescent African Girls." *Africa* 12 (1939): 425–432.

(C056) De Cleene, N. "La famille dans l'organisation sociale du Mayombe." *Africa* 10 (1937): 1–15.

(C060) Culwick, A. T., and Culwick, G. M. "The Function of Bride-Wealth in Ubena of the Rivers." *Africa* 7 (1934): 140–159.

(C065) Colson, Elizabeth. "Social Control and Vengeance in Plateau Tonga Society." *Africa* 23 (1953): 199–212.

(C068) Capell, A., and Lester, R. H. "Kinship in Fiji." *Oceania* 16 (1945–1946): 109–143.

(C070) Capell, A., and Lester, R. H. "Kinship in Fiji." *Oceania* 16 (1945–1946): 297–318.

(C075) Capell, A., and Lester, R. H. "Kinship in Fiji." *Oceania* 15 (1944–1945): 171–200.

(C077) Corlette, Ewan A. C. "Notes on the Natives of the New Hebrides." *Oceania* 6 (1935–1936): 48–65.

(C079) Corlette, Ewan A. C. "Notes on the Natives of the New Hebrides." *Oceania* 5 (1934–1935): 474–487.

(C081) Calley, Malcolm. "Economic Life of Mixed-Blood Communities in Northern New South Wales." *Oceania* 26 (1955–1956): 200–213.

(C086) Cousins, Albert N. "The Failure of Solidarity." In *Modern Introduction to the Family*, edited by Norman W. Bell and Ezra F. Vogel. Glencoe, Ill.: The Free Press, 1960, pp. 403–416.

(C088) Cohen, Yehudi A. "Character Formation and Social Structure in a Jamaican Community." *Psychiatry* 18 (1955), 275–296.

(C089) Cohn, Melvin L. "Social Class and Parent-Child Relationships: An Interpretation." *American Journal of Sociology* 68 (January 1963): 471–480.

(C090) Colson, Elizabeth. *Marriage and the Family Among the Plateau Tonga.* Manchester: Manchester University Press, 1958.

(C091) Coon, Carleton S. *Tribes of the Rif.* Harvard African Studies, LX (1931).

(C092) Cohen, Mabel Blake, Baker, Grace, Cohen, Robert A. Fromm-Reichmann, Frieda, and Weigert, Edith V. "An Intensive Study of 12 Cases of Manic-Depressive Psychosis." *Psychiatry* 17 (1954): 103.

(C093) Cohen, Yehudi A. *The Transition from Childhood to Adolescence.* Chicago: Aldine, 1964.

(C094) Cunnison, Ian. *The Luapula Peoples of Northern Rhodesia.* Manchester: Manchester University Press, 1959.

(C095) Christensen, Harold T., and Carpenter, George. "Timing Patterns in the Development of Sexual Intimacy: An Attitudinal Report on Three Modern Western Societies." *Marriage and Family Living* 24 (1962): 30–35.

(C096) Centers, Richard, and Centers, Louise. "Social Character Types and Beliefs About Child-Rearing." *Child Development* 34 (1963): 69–78.

(C097) Costin, Frank. "Effects of Child Psychology on Students' Perceptions of Their Parents' Attitudes Toward Parent-Child Relationships." *Child Development* 34, No. 1 (1963): 227–236.

(C098) Cox, F. N. "An Assessment of Children's Attitudes Towards Parent Figures." *Child Development* 33 (1962): 821–830.

(C099) Clifford, E. "Expressed Attitudes in Pregnancy of Unwed Women and Married Primigravida and Multigravida." *Child Development* 33 (1962): 945-951.

(C100) Crandall, V. J., and Preston, A. "Verbally Expressed Needs and Overt Maternal Behaviors." *Child Development* 32 (1962): 261–270.

(C101) Cox, F. N. "An Assessment of the Achievement Behavior System in Children." *Child Development* 33 (1962): 907–916.

(C102) Crandall, Vaughn J., Orleans, Sonya, Preston, Anne, and Rabson, Alice. "The Development of Social Compliance in Young Children." *Child Development* 29 (1958): 429–443.

(C103) Coombs, Robert H. "Reinforcement of Values in the Parental Home as a Factor in Mate Selection." *Marriage and Family Living* 24 (May 1962): 155–157.

(C104) Chance, Erika. *Families in Treatment.* New York: Basic Books, 1959.

(C105) Cline, Victor B., and Wangro, Arthur S. "Life History Correlates of Delinquent and Psychopathic Behavior." *Journal of Clinical Psychology* 15 (July 1959): 266–269.

(C106) Chambers, Juanita. "Maternal Deprivation and the Concept of Time." *American Journal of Orthopsychiatry* 31 (April 1959): 406–419.

(C107) Cooper, J., and Lewis, J. "Parent Evaluation as Related to Social Ideology and Academic Achievement." *The Journal of Genetic Psychology* 101 (1962): 135–143.

(C107) Caldwell, Bette M., and Hersher, Leonard. "Mother-Infant Interaction During the First Year of Life." *Merrill–Palmer Quarterly* 10 (April 1964): 119–128.

(C108) Caplan, Gerald. "Patterns of Parental Response to the Crisis of Premature Birth." *Psychiatry* 23 (November 1960): 365–374.

(C109) Creak, Mildred, and Ini, Sylvia. "Families of Psychotic Children." *Journal of Child Psychology and Psychiatry* 1 (June 1960): 156–175.

(C110) Crites, John O. "Parental Identification in Relation to Vocational Interest Development." *Journal of Educational Psychology* 53 (December 1962): 262–270.

(C111) Centers, Richard, and Centers, Louise. "Social Character Types and Beliefs About Child Rearing." *Child Development* 34 (1963): 69–78.

(C112) Chance, Erika. "Measuring Pathogenic Family Relationships." *International Journal of Social Psychiatry* 4 (1958): 10–17.

(C113) Chorost, Sherwood B. "Parental Child-Rearing Attitudes and Their Correlates in Adolescent Hostility." *Genetic Psychology Monographs* 66 (1962): 49–90.

(C114) Carlson, Rae. "Identification and Personality Structure in Preadolescents." *Journal of Abnormal and Social Psychology* 67 (December 1963): 566–573.

(C114) Cass, Loretta Kekeisen. "An Investigation of Parent-Child Relationships in Terms of Awareness, Identification, Projection and Control." *American Journal of Orthopsychiatry* 22 (April 1952): 305–313.

(C115) Choi, Elizabeth H. "Father-Daughter Relationships in School Phobia." *Smith College Studies in Social Work* 31 (February 1961): 152–178.

(C116) Cumming, Elaine, and Henry, William E. *Growing Old: The Process of Disengagement.* New York: Basic Books, 1961.

(C117) Clark, A., and van Sommers, P. "Contradictory Demands in Family Relations and Adjustment to School and Home." *Human Relations* 14 (1961): 97–111.

(C118) Crandall, V., Preston, A., and Rabson, A. "Maternal Reactions and the Development of Independence and Achievement Behavior in Young Children." *Child Development* 31 (1960): 243–251.

(C119) Cohn, H. "Phobias in Children." *Psychoanalysis and Psychoanalytic Review* 6, No. 3 (1959): 65–84.

(C120) Cowan, Phillip A., and Walters, Richard H. "Studies of Reinforcement of Aggression: I—Effects of Scheduling." *Child Development* 34 (September 1963): 543–551.

(C121) Cobliner, W. Godfrey. "Social Factors in Mental Disorders: A Contribution to the Etiology of Mental Illness." *Genetic Psychology Monographs* 67 (February 1963): 151–215.

(C122) Chassell, Joseph. "Family Constellation in the Etiology of Essential Alcoholism." *Psychiatry* 1 (1938): 473–503.

(C123) Catton, William R., Jr., and Smircich, R. J. "A Comparison of Mathematical Models for the Effect of Residential Propinquity on Mate-Selection." *American Sociological Review* 29 (August 1964): 522–529.

(C124) Cancian, Francesca M. "Interaction Patterns in Zinacanteco Families." *American Sociological Review* 29 (August 1964): 540–550.

(C125) Christensen, Harold T. "Timing of First Pregnancy as a Factor in Divorce: Cross-Cultural Analysis." *Eugenics Quarterly* 10 (1963): 119–130.

(C126) Coult, Allan D. "The Determinants of Differential Cross-Cousin Marriage." *Man* 47 (1962): 34–37.

(C127) Chess, Stella, Thomas, Alexander, and Birch, Herbert. "Characteristics of the Individual Child's Behavioral Responses to the Environment." *American Journal of Orthopsychiatry* 29 (October 1959): 791–802.

(C128) Chancellor, Loren E., and Burchinal, Lee G. "Relations Among Inter-Religious Marriages, Migratory Marriages and Civil Weddings in Iowa." *Eugenics Quarterly* 9 (1962): 75–83.

(C129) Christensen, Harold T. "Selected Aspects of Child Spacing in Denmark." *Acta Sociologica* 4, Fasc. 2 (1959): 35–45.

(C130) Christensen, Harold T. "A Cross-Cultural Comparison of Attitudes Toward Marital Infidelity." *International Journal of Comparative Sociology* 3 (1962): 124–137.

(C131) Coult, Allan D., and Havenstein, Robert W. "Exogamy and American Kinship." *Social Forces* 43 (December 1964): 174–180.

(C132) Christensen, Harold T. "A Cross-Cultural Comparison of Attitudes Toward Marital Infidelity." *International Journal of Comparative Sociology* 3 (1962): 124–137.

(C133) Caldwell, Betty, Hersher, Leonard, Lipton, Earle L., Richmond, Julius, Stern, George A., Eddy, Evelyn, Drachman, Robert, and Rothman, Albert. "Mother-Infant Interaction in Monomatric and Polymatric Families." *American Journal of Orthopsychiatry* 33 (July 1963): 653–664.

(C134) Cavan, Ruth S. *The American Family.* New York: Thomas Y. Crowell Co., 1963.

(C135) Christensen, Harold T. "Cultural Relativism and Premarital Sex Norms." *American Sociological Review* 25 (1960): 31–39.

(D001) Dynes, Russell R., Clarke, Alfred C., and Dimitz, Simon. "Levels of Occupational Aspiration: Some Aspects of Family Experience as a Variable." *American Sociological Review* 21 (1956): 212–215.

(D005) Dyer, William G. "The Interlocking of Work and Family Social Systems Among Lower Occupational Families." *Social Forces* 34 (1956): 230–233.

(D006) Duncan, Otis Dudley. "Fertility of the Village Population in Pennsylvania, 1940." *Social Forces* 28 (1950): 304–309.

(D007) Dumarest, André. *La Formation des Classes Sociales en Pays Annamite* (The Formation of the Social Classes in the Annamese Country). Lyon: P. Ferreol, 1935.

(D008) Dunning, R. W. "Rules of Residence and Ecology Among the Northern Ojibwa." *American Anthropologist* 61 (1959): 806–816.

(D010) Dotson, Floyd. "Patterns of Voluntary Association Among Urban Working Class Families." *American Sociological Review* 16 (1951): 687–693.

(D011) Davenport, William. "Non-Unilinear Descent and Descent Groups." *American Anthropologist* 61 (1959): 557–572.

(D012) Dorjahn, Vernon R. "Fertility, Polygyny and Their Interrelation in Temne Society." *American Anthropologist* 60 (1958): 838–860.

(D013) Donoghue, John B. "An Eta Community in Japan: The Social Persistence of Outcast Groups." *American Anthropologist* 59 (1957): 1000–1017.

(D017) Dozier, Edward P. "Comment." *American Anthropologist* 56 (1954): 680–683.

(D018) Davis, Kingsley. "Intermarriage in Caste Societies." *American Anthropologist* 43 (1941): 376–395.

(D024) Dozier, B. "Resistance to Acculturation and Assimilation in an Indian Pueblo." *American Anthropologist* 53 (1951): 56–65.

(D025) Djamour, D. Judith. "Adoption of Children Among Singapore Malaysians." *Journal of the Royal Anthropological Institute* 82 (1952): 159–168.

(D026) Deacon, A. Bernard. "A Regulation of Marriage in Ambrym." *Journal of the Royal Anthropological Institute* 67 (1927): 325–342.

(D027) Deacon, A. Bernard. "Notes on Some Islands of the New Hebrides." *Journal of the Royal Anthropological Institute* 59 (1929): 461–515.

(D029) Davies, Rodger P. "Syrian Arabic Kinship Terms." *Southwest Journal of Anthropology* 5 (1949): 244–252.

(D031) Davidson, J. "Protestant Missions and Marriages in the Belgian Congo." *Africa* 18 (1948): 120–128.

(D034) Douglas, Mary. "Alternate Generations Among the Lele of the Kasai, Southwest Congo." *Africa* 22 (1952): 59–65.

(D040) Driberg, J. H. "The Status of Women Among the Nilotics and Nilo-Hamitics." *Africa* 5 (1932): 404–421.

(D047) Durrad, W. J. "Notes on the Torres Islands." *Oceania* 11 (1940–1941): 75–109.

(D051) Dundas, Charles. "Native Laws of Some Bantu Tribes of East Africa." *Journal of the Royal Anthropological Institute* 51 (1921): 217–278.

(D054) Davis, Kingsley. "Legitimacy and the Incest Taboo." In *Modern Introduction to the Family,* edited by Norman W. Bell and Ezra F. Vogel. Glencoe, Ill.: The Free Press, 1960, pp. 398–402.

(D055) Dorjahn, Vernon R. "The Factor and Polygyny in African Demography." In *Continuity and Change in African Cultures,* edited by William R. Bascom and Melville J. Herskovits. Chicago: University of Chicago Press, 1958.

(D056) Douglas, Mary. "The Pattern of Residence Among the Lele." In *Cultures and Societies of Africa,* edited by Simon Ottenberg and Phoebe Ottenberg. New York: Random House, 1960.

(D057) Driver, H. *Indians of North America.* Chicago: University of Chicago Press, 1961.

(D058) Davis, Kingsley. "The Sociology of Parent-Youth Conflict." Reprinted in *Family: Its Structure and Functions,* edited by R. L. Coser. New York: St. Martin's Press, 1964, 455–471.

(D059) Diamond, Stanley. "Collective Child-Rearing: The Kibbutz." Reprinted in *Family: Its Structure and Functions,* edited by R. L. Coser. New York: St. Martin's Press, 1964, 426–432.

(D060) De Lauwe, M. J. Chombart. "The Status of Women in French Urban Society." *International Social Science Journal* 14, No. 3 (1962): 26–65.

(D061) Dentler, R. A. "Socioeconomic Versus Family Membership Status as Sources of Family Attitude Consensus." *Child Development* 32 (1961): 249–254.

(D062) Davitz, Joel. "Contributions of Research with Children to a Theory of Maladjustment." *Child Development* 29 (March 1958): 4–7.

(D063) Devereux, Edward C., Jr., Bronfenbrenner, U., and Suci, George J. "Patterns of Parent Behavior in the United States of America and the Federal Republic of Germany: A Cross-National Comparison." *International Social Science Journal* 14, No. 3 (1962): 488–506.

(D064) Donnelly, Ellen M. "The Quantitative Analysis of Parents' Behavior Toward Psychotic Children and Their Siblings." *Genetic Psychological Monographs* 62 (1960): 331–376.

(D065) Danziger, Kurt. "Parental Demands and Social Class in Java, Indonesia." *Journal of Social Psychology* 51 (1960): 75–86.

(D065) Davidson, Susannah. "School Phobia as a Manifestation of Family Disturbance: Its Structure and Treatment." *Journal of Child Psychology and Psychiatry* 1 (February 1961): 270–287.

(D067) Davids, Anthony, Holden, Raymond H., and Gray, Gloria B. "Maternal Anxiety During Pregnancy and Adequacy of Mother and Child Adjustment Eight Months Following Pregnancy." *Child Development* 34 (December 1963): 993–1002.

(D068) Rosenthal, D. "Confusion of Identity and the Frequency of Schizophrenia in Twins." *Archives of General Psychiatry* 3 (1960): 297–304.

(D069) Droppleman, Leo F., and Schaefer, Earl S. "Boys' and Girls' Reports of Maternal and Paternal Behavior." *Journal of Abnormal and Social Psychology* 67 (December 1963): 648–654.

(D070) Despert, J. Louise. "Some Considerations Relating to the Genesis of Autistic Behavior in Children." *American Journal of Orthopsychiatry* 21 (April 1951): 335–347.

(D071) Devereux, G. *A Study of Abortion in Primitive Societies.* New York: Julian Press, 1955.

(D072) Davidson, K. S., Sarason, S. B., Lighthall, F. F., Waite, R. R., and Sarnoff, J. "Differences Between Mothers' and Fathers' Ratings of Low Anxious and High Anxious Children." *Child Development* 29 (March 1958): 155–160.

(D073) Dworin, J., and Wyant, O. "Authoritarian Patterns in the Mothers of Schizophrenics." *Journal of Clinical Psychology* 13 (1957): 332–338.

(D074) Drews, E., and Teahan, J. "Parental Attitudes and Academic Achievement." *Journal of Clinical Psychology* 13 (1957): 328–332.

(D075) Davids, Anthony, Holden, Raymond H., and Gray, Gloria B. "Maternal Anxiety During Pregnancy and Adequacy of Mother and Child Adjustment Eight Months Following Childbirth." *Child Development* 34 (December 1963): 993–1002.

(D076) Dooley, Lucile, "The Genesis of Psychological Sex Differences." *Psychiatry* 1 (1938): 181–195.

(D077) Douvan, Elizabeth, and Adelson, Joseph. "The Psychodynamics of Social Mobility in Adolescent Boys." *Journal of Abnormal and Social Psychology* 56 (January 1958): 31–44.

(D078) Day, Barbara R. "Alcoholism and the Family." *Marriage and Family Living* 23 (August 1961): 253–258.

(D079) Duvall, Evelyn Milis. "Research Findings." *Marriage and Family Living* 23 (February 1961): 49–50.

(D080) Dennis, Norman. "Secondary Group Relationship and the Pre-eminence of the Family." *International Journal of Comparative Sociology* 3 (1962): 80–90.

(D081) Douglas, Mary. "Matriliny and Pawnship in Central Africa." *Africa* 34 (1964): 301–313.

(D082) Dunning, R. W. "A Note on Adoption Among the Southampton Island Eskimo." *Man* 62, No. 259 (1962): 163–167.

(D083) Day, Lincoln H. "Patterns of Divorce in Australia and the United States." *American Sociological Review* 29 (August 1964): 509–522.

(D084) Du Toit, Brian M. "Filiation and Affiliation Among the Gadsup." *Oceania* 31 (1964).

(D085) Douglas, Mary. "Blood-Debts and Clientship Among the Lele." *Journal of the Royal Anthropological Institute* 90 (1960): 1–28.

(D086) Dozier, Edward P. "The Pueblos of the Southwestern United States." *Journal of the Royal Anthropological Institute* 90 (1960): 146–160.

(E004) Eisenstadt, F. N. "Primitive Political Systems: A Preliminary Comparative Analysis." *American Anthropologist* 61 (1959): 200–220.

(E005) Edmonson, Munroe F. "Kinship Terms and Kinship Concepts." *American Anthropologist* 59 (1957): 393–433.

(E008) Ellis, Florence Hawley. "Comments." *American Anthropologist* 56 (1954): 678–680.

(E010) Ellsworth, John S., Jr. "The Relationship of Population Density to Residential Propinquity as a Factor in Marriage Selection." *American Sociological Review* 13 (1948): 444–448.

(E014) Eggan, Dorothy. "The General Problem of Hopi Adjustment." *American Anthropologist* 45 (1943): 357–373.

(E015) Eggan, Fred. "Some Aspects of Culture Change in the Northern Philippines." *American Anthropologist* 43 (1941): 11–18.

(E016) Eggan, Fred. "Historical Changes in the Choctaw Kinship System." *American Anthropologist* 39 (1937): 34–52.

(E018) Eggan, Fred. "Kinship Systems and Class-Cousin Marriage." *American Anthropologist* 36 (1934): 188–202.

(E019) Embree, John F. "Crisis and Local Kin Groups Among the Japanese Farmers of Kona, Hawaii." *American Anthropologist* 41 (1939): 400–407.

(E021) Elkin, A. P. "Reaction and Interaction: A Food-Gathering People and European Settlement in Australia." *American Anthropologist* 53 (1951): 164–186.

(E028) Evans-Pritchard, E. E. "The Origin of the Ruling Clan of the Azande." *Southwest Journal of Anthropology* 13 (1957): 322–343.

(E030) Eggan, Dorothy. "Instruction and Affect in Hopi Cultural Continuity." *Southwest Journal of Anthropology* 12 (1956): 347–370.

(E032) Elkin, A. P. "The Complexity of Social Organization in Arnhem Land." *Southwest Journal of Anthropology* 6 (1950): 1–20.

(E036) Elmendorf, William W. "Twana Kinship Terminology." *Southwest Journal of Anthropology* 2 (1946): 420–432.

(E037) Eisenstadt, S. N. "African Age Groups." *Africa* 24 (1954): 100–113.

(E038) Evans-Pritchard, E. E. "Some Features and Forms of Nuer Sacrifices." *Africa* 21 (1951): 112–121.

(E039) Evans-Pritchard, E. E. "Marriage Customs of the Luo of Kenya." *Africa* 20 (1950): 132–142.

(E040) Evans-Pritchard, E. E. "Nuer Marriage Ceremonies." *Africa* 18 (1948): 29–40.

(E042) Evans-Pritchard, E. E. "Nuer Bridewealth." *Africa* 16 (1946): 247–257.

(E043) Evans-Pritchard, E. E. "The Political Structure of the Nandi-Speaking People of Kenya." *Africa* 13 (1940): 260–267.

(E046) Estermann, C. "Coutumes des Mbali du Sud d'Angola." *Africa* 12 (1939): 74–86.

(E047) Evans-Pritchard, E. E. "Nuer Time-Reckoning." *Africa* 12 (1939): 189–216.

(E048) Evans-Pritchard, E. E. "Witchcraft." *Africa* 8 (1935): 417–422.

(E050) Estermann, P. C. "La tribu Kwanyama en face de la civilisation Européenne." *Africa* 7 (1934): 431–443.

(E051) Evans-Pritchard, E. E. "Azande Blood-Brotherhood." *Africa* 6 (1933): 369–401.

(E060) Elkin, A. P., Berndt, R. M., and Berndt, C. H. "Social Organization of Arnhem Land." *Oceania* 21 (1950–1951): 253–301.

(E063) Elkin, A. P. "Kinship in South Australia." *Oceania* 10 (1939–1940): 196–234.

(E064) Elkin, A. P. "Kinship in South Australia." *Oceania* 10 (1939–1940): 295–349.

(E065) Elkin, A. P. "Kinship in South Australia." *Oceania* 10 (1939–1940): 369–388.

(E066) Elkin, A. P. "Kinship in South Australia." *Oceania* 9 (1938–1939): 41–78.

(E067) Elkin, A. P. "Native Education, with Special Reference to the Australian Aborigines." *Oceania* 7 (1936–1937): 459–500.

(E068) Elkin, A. P. "Civilized Aborigines and Native Culture." *Oceania* 6 (1935–1936): 117–146.

(E069) Elkin, A. P. "Kinship in South Australia." *Oceania* 8 (1937–1938): 419–452.

(E071) Elkin, A. P. "Studies in Australian Totemism: Sub-Section, Section and Moiety Totemism." *Oceania* 4 (1933–1934): 65–90.

(E076) Elkin, A. P. "The Social Organization of South Australian Tribes." *Oceania* 2 (1931–1932): 44–73.

(E078) Elkin, A. P. "Social Organization in the Kimberley Division, Northwestern Australia." *Oceania* 2 (1931–1932): 296–333.

(E079) Elkin, A. P. "Notes on the Social Organization of the Worimi, a Kattang-Speaking People." *Oceania* 2 (1931–1932): 359–363.

(E080) Elkin, A. P. "Anthropology and the Future of the Australian Aborigines." *Oceania* 5 (1934–1935): 1–18.

(E082) Elkin, A. P. "Delayed Exchange in Wabag Sub-District, Central Highlands of New Guinea, with Notes on the Social Organization." *Oceania* 23 (1952–1953): 161–201.

(E083) Eggan, Fred. "The Hopi and the Lineage Principle." In *Social Structure,* edited by Meyer Fortes. Oxford: Clarendon Press, 1949.

(E084) Evans-Pritchard, E. E. "Nuer Rules of Exogamy and Incest." In *African Systems of Kinship and Marriage,* edited by A. R. Radcliffe-Brown and C. Daryll Forde. London: Oxford University Press, 1950.

(E086) Eisenstadt, S. N. *From Generation to Generation.* Glencoe, Ill.: The Free Press, 1956.

(E087) Engels, Frederick. "The Transformation of the Family." In *Modern Introduction to the Family,* edited by Norman W. Bell and Ezra F. Vogel. Glencoe, Ill.: The Free Press, 1960, pp. 52–54.

(E089) Esman, Aaron H., M.D., Kohn, Martin, and Nyman, Lawrence. "2. The Family of the 'Schizophrenic' Child." *American Journal of Orthopsychiatry* 29 (July 1959): 455–459.

(E090) Emmerich, Walter. "Family Role Concepts of Children Ages Six to Ten." *Child Development* 32, No. 4 (1961): 609–624.

(E091) Eron, Leonard D., Banta, T. J., Walder, Leopold O., and Laulicht, J. H. "Comparison of Data Obtained from Mothers and Fathers on Child-Rearing Practices and Their Relation to Child Aggression." *Child Development* 32, No. 3 (1961): 457–472.

(E092) Ehrmann, W. "Changing Sexual Mores." In *Values and Ideals of American Youth,* edited by Eli Ginzberg. New York: Columbia University Press, 1961, pp. 53–70.

(E093) Earle, A. M., and Earle, B. V. "Early Maternal Deprivation and Later Psychiatric Illness." *American Journal of Orthopsychiatry* 31 (January 1961): 181–186.

(E093) Eron, Leonard D., Walder, Leopold O., Toigo, Romolo, and Lefkowitz, Monroe M. "Social Class, Parental Punishment for Aggression, and Child Aggression." *Child Development* 34, No. 4 (December 1963): 849–867.

(E094) Eysenck, S. B. G., and Eysenck, H. J. "Rigidity as a Function of Introversion and Neuroticism: A Study of

Unmarried Mothers." *International Journal of Social Psychiatry* 8 (1962): 180–184.

(E095) Eisenberg, L. "School Phobia: A Study in the Communication of Anxiety." *American Journal of Psychiatry* 114 (1958): 712–718.

(E096) Escalona, Sibylle. "A Commentary upon Some Recent Changes in Child Rearing Practices." *Child Development* 20 (September 1949): 157–163.

(E097) Eron, Leonard D., Walder, Leopold O., Toigo, Romolo, and Lefkowitz, Monroe M. "Social Class, Parental Punishment for Aggression, and Child Aggression." *Child Development* 34, No. 4 (December 1963): 849–867.

(E098) Emmerich, Walter, "Parental Identification in Young Children." *Genetic Psychology Monographs* 60 (November 1959): 257–308.

(E099) Eastman, Daniel. "Self Acceptance and Marital Happiness." *Journal of Consulting Psychology* 22 (April 1958): 95–99.

(E100) Elder, G. H. "Structural Variations in the Child Rearing Relationship." *Sociometry* 25, No. 3 (1962): 241–262.

(E101) Eggan, Fred. "The Hopi and the Lineage Principle." In *Social Structure,* edited by Meyer Fortes. Oxford: Clarendon Press, 1949.

(E102) Elder, Glen H., Jr. *Adolescent Achievement and Mobility Aspirations.* Chapel Hill: Institute for Research in Social Science, 1962.

(E103) Evans-Pritchard, E. E. "The Distribution of Zande Clans in the Sudan." *Man* 59, No. 24 (1959): 21–25.

(E104) Evans-Pritchard, E. E. "Zande Clans and Settlements." *Man* 213 (1960): 169–172.

(E105) Elder, Glen H., Jr. "Parental Power Legitimation and Its Effect on the Adolescent." *Sociometry* 26 (1963): 50–65.

(E106) Eysenck, H. J. "The Inheritance of Extraversion-Introversion." *Acta Psychologica* 12 (1956): 95–110.

(E107) Elkin, A. P. "Rethinking Anthropology: A Review." *Oceania* 34 (1963–1964): 81–107.

(E108) Epstein, A. L. "Variation and Social Structure: Local Organization on the Island of Matupit, New Britain." *Oceania* 31 (1964): 1–25.

(F001) Flittie, Edwin G. "Fertility and Mortality in the Rocky Mountain West." *American Sociological Review* 22, No. 2 (1957): 189–193.

(F002) Farber, Bernard, and Blackman, Leonard S. "Marital Role Tensions and Number and Sex of Children." *American Sociological Review* 21 (1956): 596–601.

(F003) Frazier, E. Franklin. "Ethnic Family Patterns: The Negro Family in the United States." *American Journal of Sociology* 53 (1948): 435–438.

(F008) Folger, John, and Rowan, John. "Migration and Marital Status in Ten Southeastern Cities." *Social Forces* 32, No. 2 (December 1953): 178–185.

(F009) Foote, Nelson N. "Matching of Husband and Wife in Phases of Development." In *Transactions of the Third World Congress of Sociology,* Vol. 4, *Changes in the Family,* 24–34. London: International Sociological Association, 1956.

(F010) Faron, Louis P. "Araucanian Patri-Organization and the Omaha System." *The American Anthropologist* 58 (1956): 435–456.

(F012) Fridel, Ernestine. "The Role of Kinship in the Transmission of National Culture in Rural Villages in Mainland Greece." *American Anthropologist* 61 (1959): 30–38.

(F014) Freed, Stanley A. "Suggestive Type Societies in Acculturation Studies." *American Anthropologist* 59 (1957): 55–68.

(F015) Fischer, J. L. "Totemism on Truk and Ponape." *American Anthropologist* 59 (1957): 250–265.

(F016) Fallers, Lloyd. "The Predicament of the Modern African Chief: An Instance from Uganda." *American Anthropologist* 57 (1955): 290–305.

(F019) Fischer, J. L. "Avunculocal Residence on Losap." *American Anthropologist* 57 (1955): 1025–1032.

(F020) Fortes, Meyer. "The Structure of Unilineal Descent Groups." *American Anthropologist* 55 (1953): 17–41.

(F021) Foster, George M. "What Is Folk Culture?" *American Anthropologist* 55 (1953): 159–173.

(F022) Foster, George M. "The Geographical, Linguistic and Cultural Position of the Popoluca of Vera Cruz." *American Anthropologist* 45 (1943): 531–546.

(F023) Feng, H. Y. "Teknonymy as a Formative Factor in the Chinese Kinship System." *American Anthropologist* 38 (1936): 59–66.

(F025) Fortune, R. W. "Arapesh Warfare." *American Anthropologist* 41 (1939): 22–41.

(F026) Forde, C. Daryll. "Kinship in Umor–Double Unilateral Organization–Bantu Society." *American Anthropologist* 41 (1939): 523–553.

(F030) Furer-Haimendorf, Christoph von. "Elements of Newar Social Structure." *Journal of the Royal Anthropological Institute* 86, Part 2 (1956): 15–38.

(F032) Firth, Raymond. "Social Organization and Social Change." *Journal of the Royal Anthropological Institute* 84 (1954): 1–20.

(F033) Forde, C. Daryll. "Fission and Accretion in the Patrilineal Clans of a Semi-Bantu Community in Nigeria." *Journal of the Royal Anthropological Institute* 68 (1938): 311–338.

(F033) Forde, C. Daryll. "The Integration of Anthropological Studies." *Journal of the Royal Anthropological Institute* 78 (1948): 1–10.

(F034) Firth, Raymond. "Religious Beliefs and Personal Adjustments." *Journal of the Royal Anthropological Institute* 78 (1948): 25–43.

(F035) Freedman, M. "Colonial Law and Chinese Society." *Journal of the Royal Anthropological Institute* 80 (1950): 79–126.

(F037) Firth, Raymond. "Marriage and the Classificatory System of Relationship." *Journal of the Royal Anthropological Institute* 60 (1930): 235–268.

(F039) Firth, Raymond. "Some Principles of Social Organization." *Journal of the Royal Anthropological Institute* 85 (1955): 1–18.

(F039) Fried, Morton H. "The Classification of Corporate Unilineal Descent Groups." *Journal of the Royal Anthropological Institute* 89 (1959): 1–29.

(F040) Forde, C. Daryll. "Fission and Accretion in the Patrilineal Clans of a Semi-Bantu Community in Southern Nigeria." *Journal of the Royal Anthropological Institute* 68 (1938): 311–338.

(F042) Forde, C. Daryll. "Spirits, Witches and Sorcerers in the Supernatural Economy of the Yako." *Journal of the Royal Anthropological Institute* 88 (1958): 165–178.

(F043) Firth, Raymond. "Problems and Assumptions in an Anthropological Study of Religion." *Journal of the Royal Anthropological Institute* 89 (1959): 129–148.

(F045) Filipovic, Mils. "Vicarious Paternity Among Serbs and Croats." *Southwest Journal of Anthropology* 14 (1958): 156–167.

(F046) Fischer, J. L. "A Note on Terminology for Primary

Kin." *Southwest Journal of Anthropology* 15 (1959): 348–354.

(F049) Foster, George M. "Cofradia and Compadrazgo in Spain and Spanish America." *Southwest Journal of Anthropology* 9 (1953): 1–28.

(F050) Fried, Jacob. "A Relation of Ideal Norms to Actual Behavior in Tarahumara Society." *Southwest Journal of Anthropology* 9 (1953): 286–295.

(F051) Foster, George M. "Sierra Popoluca Kinship Terminology and its Wider Relationships." *Southwest Journal of Anthropology* 5 (1949): 330–344.

(F052) Flannery, Regina, and Cooper, John M. "Social Mechanism in Gros Ventre Gambling." *Southwest Journal of Anthropology* 2 (1946): 391–419.

(F055) Firth, Raymond. "Social Problems and Research in British West Africa." *Africa* 17 (1947): 77–92.

(F058) Fortes, Meyer. "Social and Psychological Aspects of Education in Taleland." *Supplement to Africa* 11, No. 4 (1938).

(F059) Forde, C. Daryll. "Government in Umor." *Africa* 12 (1939): 129–152.

(F060) Fortes, Meyer. "Culture Contact as a Dynamic Process." *Africa* 9 (1936): 24–55.

(F061) Fortes, Meyer, and Fortes, S. L. "Food in the Domestic Economy of the Tallensi." *Africa* 9 (1936): 237–296.

(F062) Fallers, Lloyd A. "Some Determinants of Marriage Stability in Busoga: A Reformulation of Gluckman's Hypothesis." *Africa* 27 (1957): 106–123.

(F063) Fink, Ruth A. "The Caste Barrier—An Obstacle to the Assimilation of Part-Aborigines in Northwest South Wales." *Oceania* 28 (1957–1958): 100–110.

(F065) Fortune, R. F. "Manus Religion." *Oceania* 2 (1931–1932): 74–108.

(F066) Fry, H. K. "Kinship in Western Central Australia." *Oceania* 4 (1933–1934): 472–478.

(F068) Firth, Raymond. "A Note on Descent Groups in Polynesia." *Man* 57 (1957): 4–8.

(F069) Fischer, L. "Folk Tales, Social Structure, and Environment in Two Polynesian Outliers." *Polynesia* 67 (1958): 11–36.

(F072) Fortes, Meyer. "Time and Social Structure: An Ashanti Case Study." In *Social Structure,* edited by Meyer Fortes. Oxford: Clarendon Press, 1949.

(F073) Fallers, Lloyd A. *Bantu Bureaucracy.* Cambridge: W. Heffer & Sons, Ltd., 1965.

(F074) Fortes, Meyer. Introduction. In *The Developmental Cycle in Domestic Groups,* Cambridge Papers in Social Anthropology, No. 1. Cambridge: Cambridge University Press, 1958.

(F075) Freeman, J. D. "The Family System of the Iban of Borneo." In *The Developmental Cycle in Domestic Groups,* Cambridge Papers in Social Anthropology. Cambridge: Cambridge University Press, 1958, 15–62.

(F077) Fisher, Seymour, and Mendell, David. "Communication of Neurotic Patterns Over Two and Three Generations." In *Modern Introduction to the Family,* edited by Norman W. Bell and Ezra F. Vogel. Glencoe, Ill.: The Free Press, 1960, pp. 616–622.

(F078) Frazier, E. Franklin. "The Impact of Urban Civilization upon Negro Family Life." In *Modern Introduction to the Family,* edited by Norman W. Bell and Ezra F. Vogel. Glencoe, Ill.: The Free Press, 1960, pp. 101–111.

(F079) Fox, J. R. "Sibling Incest." *British Journal of Sociology* 13 (June 1962): 128–150.

(F080) Forde, C. Daryll., (ed.), *African Worlds.* London: Oxford University Press, 1954.

(F081) Freedman, Alfred, Helme, William, Havel, Joan, Eustis, Marjorie, Riley, Conrad, and Langford, William S. *Family Adjustment to the Brain-Damaged Child,* 555–562.

(F082) Fei, Hsiao-Tung. *Peasant Life in China.* London: Kegan, Paul, Trench, Trubner & Co., Ltd., 1939, pp. 52–53.

(F083) Fisher, Seymour, and Mendell, David. "The Spread of Psychotherapeutic Effects from the Patient to His Family Group." *Psychiatry* 21 (1958): 133–140.

(F084) Fisher, Seymour, and Mendell, David. "Communication of Neurotic Patterns Over Two and Three Generations." *Psychiatry* 19 (1956): 41–46.

(F085) Freedman, David A. "On Women Who Hate Their Husbands." *Psychiatry* 24 (1961): 228–237.

(F086) Firth, Raymond. *We the Tikopia.* London: George Allen and Unwin, Ltd., 1936.

(F087) Fortes, Meyer. *The Web of Kinship Among the Tallensi.* International African Institute. New York: Oxford University Press, 1949.

(F088) Firth, Raymond. *Social Change in Tikopia.* London: George Allen and Unwin, Ltd., 1959.

(F089) Forde, C. Daryll. "The Anthropological Approach in Social Science." In *Readings in Social Anthropology,* edited by Morton H. Fried. New York: Thomas Y. Crowell, 1968.

(F090) Fort, Joel P., Jr. "Heroin Addiction Among Young Men." *Psychiatry* 17 (1954): 251–259.

(F092) Fortune, R. F. *Sorcerers of Dobu.* London: Geo. Routledge and Sons, 1932.

(F093) Foster, R. M. "Interpsychic and Environmental Factors in Running Away from Home." *American Journal of Orthopsychiatry* 32 (1962): 486–491.

(F094) Farber, B. "Marital Integration as a Factor in Parent-Child Relations." *Child Development* 33 (March–December 1962): 1–14.

(F095) Fitzsimons, Ruth. "Developmental, Psychosocial and Educational Factors in Children with Nonorganic Articulation Problems." *Child Development* 29 (December 1958): 482–489.

(F096) Ferreira, Antonio J. "The Pregnant Woman's Emotional Attitude and Its Reflection on the Newborn." *American Journal of Orthopsychiatry* 30 (July 1960): 553–561.

(F097) Favez-Boutonier, Juliette. "Child Development Patterns in France." In *Mental Health and Infant Development,* edited by Kenneth Snoddy. New York: Basic Books, 1956, pp. 15–24.

(F097) Fleck, S. "Family Dynamics and Origin of Schizophrenia." *Psychosomatic Medicine* 22, No. 5 (1960): 333–344.

(F098) Freeman, Howard E., and Simmons, Ozzie G. "The Social Integration of Former Mental Patients." *International Journal of Social Psychiatry* 4 (1959): 264–271.

(F099) Freeman, Howard E., Simmons, Ozzie G., and Bergen, Bernhard J. "Possessiveness as a Characteristic of Mothers of Schizophrenics." *Journal of Abnormal and Social Psychology* 58 (March 1959): 171–173.

(F100) Ferreira, A. "The 'Double-Bind' and Delinquent Behavior." *Archives of General Psychiatry* 3 (1960): 359–367.

(F101) Freedman, R., Whelpton, P., and Campbell, A. *Family Planning, Sterility and Population Growth.* New York: McGraw-Hill, 1959.

(F102) Falstein, Eugene I., M. D., Feinstein, Sherman C., M. D., and Judas, Ilse, M. S. "Anorexia Nervosa in the

Male Child." *American Journal of Orthopsychiatry* 56 (October 1956): 751–772.

(F103) Finney, Joseph C. "Some Maternal Influences on Children's Personality and Character." *Genetic Psychology Monographs* 63–64 (May 1961): 199–278.

(F104) Farina, Amerigo, Garmezy, Norman, and Barry, Herbert. "Relationship of Marital Status to Incidence and Prognosis of Schizophrenia." *Journal of Abnormal and Social Psychology* 67 (December 1963): 624–630.

(F105) Field, M. J. "Mental Disorder in Rural Ghana." *Journal of Mental Science* 104 (1958): 1043–1051.

(F106) Fallding, H. "The Family and the Idea of the Cardinal Role." Human Relations 14 (1961): 329–350.

(F107) Freeman, H., *et al.* "Residential Mobility Inclinations Among Families of Mental Patients." *Social Forces* 38 (1960): 320–324.

(F108) Feinberg, Mortimer R. "Relation of Background Experience to Social Acceptance." *Journal of Abnormal and Social Psychology* 48 (February 1953): 206–214.

(F109) Freeman, Howard E. "Attitudes Toward Mental Illness Among Relatives of Former Patients." *American Sociological Review* 26 (February 1961): 59–66.

(F110) Fisher, S., *et al.* "Parents of Schizophrenics, Neurotics and Normals." *AMA Archives of General Psychiatry* 1 (August 1959): 149–166.

(F111) Fiedler, F., and Hoffman, E. "Age, Sex and Religious Background as Determinants of Interpersonal Perception Among Dutch Children." *Acta Psychologica* 20, No. 3 (1962): 185–195.

(F112) Fromm-Reichmann, Frieda. "Recent Advances in Psychoanalytic Therapy." *Psychiatry* 4 (1941): 161–164.

(F113) Farber, Leslie H., and Micon, Leonard. "Gastric Neurosis in a Military Service." *Psychiatry* 8 (1945): 343–361.

(F114) Finesinger, Jacob E. "The Needs of Youth." *Psychiatry* 7 (1944): 45–57.

(F115) Farina, Amerigo, and Dunham, Richard M. "Measurement of Family Relationships and Their Effects." *Archives of General Psychiatry* 9 (July 1963): 64–73.

(F116) Farber, B., and McHale, J. "Marital Integration and Parents' Agreement on Satisfaction with Their Child's Behavior." *Marriage and Family Living* 21 (1959): 65–69.

(F117) Farina, Amerigo. "Patterns of Role Dominance and Conflict in Parents of Schizophrenic Patients." *Journal of Abnormal and Social Psychology* 61 (July 1960): 31–38.

(F118) Fanshel, David. *Negro Adoption.* New York: Child Welfare League of America, 1957.

(F119) Freeman, Howard E., Simmons, Ozzie G., and Bergen, Bernard J. "Possessiveness as a Characteristic of Mothers of Schizophrenics." *Journal of Abnormal and Social Psychology* 58 (March 1959): 171–173.

(F120) Fortes, Meyer. "Descent, Filiation and Affinity: A Rejoinder to Dr. Leach." *Man* 59, No. 309 (1959): 193–197; No. 331, 206–212.

(F121) Fei, Hsiao-Tung. *Peasant Life in China.* New York: E. P. Dutton and Co., 1939.

(F122) Freedman, Maurice. "A Note on Social Organization in a Rural Area of Greater Djakarta." *Man* 60, No. 119 (1960): 82–84.

(F123) Freedman, Deborah, Freedman, Ronald, and Whelpton, Pascal K. "Size of Family and Preference for Children of Each Sex." *American Journal of Sociology* 66 (1960): 141–146.

(F124) Freeman, Howard E., and Simmons, Ozzie G. *The Mental Patient Comes Home.* New York: John Wiley and Sons, 1963.

(F126) Faron, Leslie C. "The Dakota-Omaha Continuum in Mapuche Society." *Journal of the Royal Anthropological Institute* 91 (1961): 11–22.

(F127) Freeman, J. D. "On the Concept of Kindred." *Journal of the Royal Anthropological Institute* 91 (1961): 192–220.

(G001) Goldman, Joseph. "Patterns of Negro-White Intermarriage." *American Sociological Review* 19 (1954): 144–147.

(G002) Goode, William J. "Economic Factors and Marital Stability." *American Sociological Review* 16 (1951): 802–812.

(G003) Goldman, Joseph. "Characteristics of the Negro-White Intermarried in Philadelphia." *American Sociological Review* 18 (1953): 177–183.

(G007) Gourou, Pierre. *Les paysans du delta Tonkinois. Étude de géographie humaine.* Paris: Publication de l'École Française d'Extrême-Orient, Vol. XXVII, Éditions d'Art et d'Histoire, 1936. (Translated from the French for the *Human Relations Area Files* by Richard R. Miller.)

(G008) de Gentile-Duquesne, Pierre. *La situation juridique de la femme Annamite* (The Legal Status of the Annamese Woman). Paris: Jouve et Compagne, 1925. (Translated from the French for the *Human Relations Area Files* by Louis Rossi.)

(G010) Geiger, Kent. "Deprivation and Solidarity in the Soviet Urban Family." *American Sociological Review* 20 (1955): 57–68.

(G011) Glick, Paul C. "First Marriages and Remarriages." *American Sociological Review* 14 (1949): 726–734.

(G012) Glick, Paul C., and Landau, Emanuel. "Age as a Factor in Marriage." *American Sociological Review* 15 (1950): 517–529.

(G013) Goldman, Irving. "The Abolition of Polynesian Societies." In *Culture and History,* edited by Stanley Diamond. New York: Columbia University Press, 1960, pp. 687–712.

(G013) Gray, Robert S. "Sonjo Bride Price and the Question of African 'Wife Purchase.'" *American Anthropologist* 62 (1960): 34–57.

(G014) Green, Arnold W. "The 'Cult of Personality' and Sexual Relations." In *Modern Introduction to the Family,* edited by Norman W. Bell and Ezra F. Vogel. Glencoe, Ill.: The Free Press, 1960, pp. 608–615.

(G015) Goode, William J. "Pressures to Remarry: Institutionalized Patterns Affecting the Divorced." In *Modern Introduction to the Family,* edited by Norman W. Bell and Ezra F. Vogel. Glencoe, Ill.: The Free Press, 1960, pp. 316–326.

(G019) Geiger, Kent. "Changing Political Attitudes in Totalitarian Society: A Case Study of the Role of the Family." In *Modern Introduction to the Family,* edited by Norman W. Bell and Ezra F. Vogel. Glencoe, Ill.: The Free Press, 1960, pp. 173–188.

(G019) Gumpert, John Jay. "Dialect Differences and Social Stratification in a North Indian Village." *American Anthropologist* 60 (1958): 668–682.

(G020) Goldstein, Sidney. "Changing Patterns of Fertility in Norristown, Pennsylvania, 1920–1950." *Social Forces* 34 (1955): 72–77.

(G020) Green, Arnold W. "The Middle-Class Male Child and Neurosis." In *Modern Introduction to the Family,* edited by Norman W. Bell and Ezra F. Vogel. Glencoe, Ill.: The Free Press, 1960, pp. 563–572.

(G021) Griffin, Mary E., Johnson, Adelaide M., and Litin, Edward. In *Modern Introduction to the Family,* edited by Norman W. Bell and Ezra F. Vogel. Glencoe, Ill.: The Free Press, 1960, pp. 623–635.

(G022) Gibson, Gordon D. "Double Descent and Its Correlate Among the Herero of Ngamiland." *American Anthropologist* 58 (1956): 109–139.

(G022) Gibson, Robert W. "The Family Background and Early Life Experiences of the Manic-Depressive Patient." *Psychiatry* 21 (February 1958): 71–90.

(G026) Gould, Harold A. "The Implications of Technological Change for Folk and Scientific Medicine." *American Anthropologist* 59 (1957): 507–516.

(G027) Giertz, Clifford. "Ritual and Social Change: A Javanese Example." *American Anthropologist* 59 (1957): 32–54.

(G028) Gough, E. Kathleen. "Brahman Kinship in a Tamil Village." *American Anthropologist* 58 (1956): 826–853.

(G029) Goodenough, Ward H. "A Problem in Malayo-Polynesian Social Organization." *American Anthropologist* 57 (1955): 71–83.

(G031) Goldman, Irving. "Status Rivalry and Cultural Evolution in Polynesia." *American Anthropologist* 57 (1955): 680–697.

(G033) Garigue, Philip. "French Canadian Kinship and Urban Life." *American Anthropologist* 58 (1956): 1090–1101.

(G034) Gulick, John. "The Lebanese Village: An Introduction." *American Anthropologist* 55 (1953): 367–372.

(G038) Goldman, Irving. The Alkatcho Carrier: Historical Background of Crest Prerogatives." *American Anthropologist* 43 (1941): 396–418.

(G039) Gayton, A. H. "Yokuts and Western Monosocial Organization." *American Anthropologist* 47 (1945): 409–426.

(G039) Goodwin, Grenville. "The Characteristics and Function of Clan in a Southern Athapascan Culture." *American Anthropologist* 39 (1937): 394–407.

(G041) Garth, Thomas R., Jr. "Emphasis on Industriousness Among the Atsugewi." *American Anthropologist* 47 (1945): 554–566.

(G043) Gladwin, Thomas. "Comanche Kin Behavior." *American Anthropologist* 50 (1948): 72–94.

(G044) Green, Arnold W. "Culture, Normality and Personality Conflict." *American Anthropologist* 50 (1948): 225–237.

(G045) Goldschmidt, Walter. "Social Organization in Native California and the Origins of Clans." *American Anthropologist* 50 (1948): 444–456.

(G046) Gifford, Edward Winslow. "A Problem in Kinship Terminology." *American Anthropologist* 42 (1940): 190–194.

(G049) Goldschmidt, Walter. "Ethics and the Structure of Society: An Ethnological Contribution to the Sociology of Knowledge." *American Anthropologist* 53 (1951): 506–534.

(G050) Goodenough, Ward H. "Premarital Freedom on Truk: Theory and Practice." *American Anthropologist* 51 (1949): 615–620.

(G052) Goodenough, Ward H. "Amitalocal Residence." *American Anthropologist* 53 (1951): 427–429.

(G053) Garth, Thomas R., Jr. "Kinship Terminology, Marriage Practices, and Behavior Toward Kin Among the Atsugewi." *American Anthropologist* 46 (1944): 348–361.

(G056) Gough, E. Kathleen. "Changing Kinship Usages in the Setting of Political and Economic Change Among the Nayars of Malabar." *Journal of the Royal Anthropological Institute* 82 (1952): 71–88.

(G057) Gulliver, P. H. "The Age-Set Organization of the Jie Tribe." *Journal of the Royal Anthropological Institute* 83 (1953): 147–168.

(G058) Groves, Murray. "Dancing in Poreporena." *Journal of the Royal Anthropological Institute* 84 (1954): 75–90.

(G059) Griffith, J. B. "Glimpses of a Niaka Tribe (Waduruma)." *Journal of the Royal Anthropological Institute* 65 (1935): 267–296.

(G060) Ghurye, Govind S. "Dual Organization in India." *Journal of the Royal Anthropological Institute* 53 (1923): 79–91.

(G061) Goodenough, Ward H. "Componential Analysis and the Study of Meaning." *Language* 32 (1956): 195–216.

(G062) Goody, Jack. "Fields of Social Control Among the Lodagaba." *Journal of the Royal Anthropological Institute* 87 (1957): 75–104.

(G063) Gould, Harold A. "The Hindu Jajmani System: A Case of Economic Particularism." *Southwest Journal of Anthropology* 14 (1958): 428–437.

(G064) Goodenough, Ward H. "Ethnographic Notes on the Mae People of New Guinea Western Highlands." *Southwest Journal of Anthropology* 9 (1953): 29–44.

(G065) Goodenough, Ward H. "Residence Rules." *Southwest Journal of Anthropology* 12 (1956): 22–37.

(G071) Gunda, Bela. "Work and Cult Among the Hungarian Peasants." *Southwest Journal of Anthropology* 3 (1947): 147–163.

(G072) Greenberg, Joseph H. "Islam and Clan Organization Among the Hausa." *Southwest Journal of Anthropology* 3 (1947): 193–211.

(G079) Gulliver, P. H. "The Karamojong Cluster." *Africa* 22 (1952): 1–22.

(G080) Grebert, F., and Keller, J. P. "La famille Galoase et son évolution désirée par la jeunesse." *Africa* 10 (1937): 329–334.

(G087) Goody, Jack. "The Mother's Brother and the Sister's Son in West Africa." *Journal of the Royal Anthropological Institute* 89 (1959): 61–88.

(G089) Gray, Robert F. "Positional Succession Among the Wambugwe." *Africa* 23 (1953): 223–243.

(G090) Gluckman, Max. "The Village Headsman in British Central Africa." *Africa* 19 (1949): 89–94.

(G093) Geddes, W. R. "Acceleration of Social Change in a Fijian Community." *Oceania* 16 (1945–1946): 1–14.

(G094) Groves, William C. "Tabar Today: Present Day Conditions in Tatau Village." *Oceania* 6 (1935–1936): 147–157.

(G095) Groves, William C. "Report on Field Work in New Ireland." *Oceania* 3 (1932–1933): 325–361.

(G097) Groves, William C. "Tabar Today: A Study of a Melanesian Community in Contact with Alien Non-Primitive Cultural Forces." *Oceania* 5 (1934–1935): 224–240.

(G098) Groves, William C. "Tabar Today: A Study of a Melanesian Community in Contact with Alien Non-Primitive Cultural Influences." *Oceania* 5 (1934–1935): 346–360.

(G101) Goldman, Irving. "Variations in Polynesian Social Organization." *Polynesia* 66 (1957): 374–390.

(G105) Grimble, Arthur. "From Birth to Death in the Gilbert Islands." *Journal of the Royal Anthropological Institute* 51 (1921): 25–54.

(G107) Gifford, Edward Winslow. "Miwok Lineages and

the Political Unit in Aboriginal California." *American Anthropologist* 27 (1925): 389–401.

(G108) Gifford, Edward Winslow. "Tongan Society." *Bishop Museum Bulletin* 61 (1929).

(G110) Gillin, John. "Ethos and Cultural Aspects of Personality." In *Tax*, pp. 193–212.

(G111) Goody, Jack. "The Fission of Domestic Groups Among the Lodagaba." In *The Developmental Cycle in Domestic Groups,* edited by Jack Goody. Cambridge Papers in Social Anthropology Series. Cambridge: Cambridge University Press, 1958.

(G112) de Gonzalez, N. L. Solien. "Family Organization in Five Types of Migratory Wage Labor." *American Anthropologist* 63 (December 1961): 1266–1268.

(G112) Greenfield, Sidney M. "Industrialization and the Family in Sociological Theory." *American Journal of Sociology* 67 (1961–1962): 312–322.

(G113) Garfield, Viola E. "Historical Aspects of Tlingit Clans in Angoon Alaska." *American Anthropologist* 49 (1947): 438–452.

(G113) Greenfield, Sidney M. "Industrialization and the Family in Sociological Theory." *American Journal of Sociology* 67 (November 1961): 312–322.

(G114) Gough, E. Kathleen. "Female Initiation Rites on the Malabar Coast." *Journal of the Royal Anthropological Institute* 85 (1955): 45–80.

(G115) Gluckman, Max. "The Lozi of Barotseland." In *Seven Tribes of British Central Africa,* edited by Elizabeth Colson and Max Gluckman. New York: Humanities Press, 1959.

(G116) Gluckman, Max. *Custom and Conflict.* Glencoe, Ill.: The Free Press, 1959.

(G117) Grace, Harry, and Lohmann, Joan Jenkins. "Children's Reactions to Stories Depicting Parent-Child Conflict Situations." *Child Development* 23 (March 1952): 61–74.

(G118) Grinder, R. E. "New Techniques for Research in Children's Temptation Behavior." *Child Development* 32, No. 4 (1961): 679–688.

(G119) Glasser, Paul, and Glasser, Lois. "Role Reversal and Conflict Between Aged Parents and Their Children." *Marriage and Family Living* 24 (1962): 46–51.

(G120) Grinder, R. E. "Parental Child-Rearing Practices, Conscience, and Resistance to Temptation of Sixth-Grade Children." *Child Development* 33 (1962): 803–820.

(G121) Gardner, D. B., Hawkes, G. R., and Burchinal, L. G. "Noncontinuous Mothering in Infancy and Development in Later Childhood." *Child Development* 32 (1961): 225–234.

(G122) Geismar, L. L., LaSorte, M. A., and Ayres, B. "Measuring Family Disorganization." *Marriage and Family Living* 24 (February 1962): 51–56.

(G123) Glueck, Sheldon, and Glueck, Eleanor T. "Family Life and Delinquency." In *The Problem of Delinquency,* edited by Sheldon Glueck. Boston: Houghton Mifflin Co., 1959, pp. 136–138.

(G124) Golan, Samuel. "Behavior Research in Collective Settlements in Israel." *American Journal of Orthopsychiatry* 28 (July 1958): 549–564.

(G125) Gregory, Ian. "Family Data Concerning the Hypothesis of Hereditary Predisposition Toward Alcoholism." *British Journal of Psychiatry* 106 (October 1960): 1068–1072.

(G126) Gurin, Gerald, Veroff, Joseph, and Feld, Shelia. *Americans View Their Mental Health.* New York: Basic Books, 1960.

(G127) Garnezy, Norman, Clarke, Alan R., and Stockner,

Carol. "Child Rearing Attitudes of Mothers and Fathers as Reported by Schizophrenic and Normal Patients." *Journal of Abnormal and Social Psychology* 63 (July 1961): 176–182.

(G128) Goldfarb, William. "Emotional and Intellectual Consequences of Psychologic Deprivation in Infancy: A Reevaluation." In *Psychopathology of Childhood,* edited by Paul H. Hoch and Joseph Zubin. New York and London: Grune & Stratton, 1955, pp. 105–119.

(G128) Greenberg, H., Straight, B., Hassenger, W., and Raska, W. "Personality and Attitudinal Differences Between Employed and Unemployed Married Women." *Journal of Social Psychology* 53 (1961): 87–96.

(G129) Gordon, J. "Relationships Among Mothers' Achievement, Independence Training Attitudes, and Handicapped Children's Performance." *Journal of Consulting Psychology* 23, No. 3 (1959): 207–212.

(G130) Goodenough, Evelyn W. "Interest in Persons as an Aspect of Sex Difference in the Early Years." *Genetic Psychology Monographs* 55 (1957): 287–323.

(G131) Gilmore, H. "Differential Sex Ratios of Young Children in New Orleans." *Social Forces* 38 (1960): 230–240.

(G132) Getzels, Jacob W., and Jackson, Philip W. "Family Environment and Cognitive Style: A Study of the Sources of Highly Intelligent and of Highly Creative Adolescents." *American Sociological Review* 26 (June 1961): 351–359.

(G133) Geiken, Karem F. "Expectations Concerning Husband-Wife Responsibilities in the Home." *Journal of Marriage and Family Living* 26 (August 1964): 349–352.

(G134) Goode, William J. "Marital Satisfaction and Instability: A Cross-Cultural Class Analysis of Divorce Rates." *International Social Science Journal* 14, No. 3 (1962): 507–526.

(G135) Grigg, A. "Childhood Experience with Parental Attitudes: A Test of Roe's Hypothesis." *Journal of Counseling Psychology* 6, No. 2 (1959): 153–155.

(G136) Gump, P. V., and Kounin, J. S. "Milieu Influences in Children's Concepts of Misconduct." *Child Development* 32, No. 4 (1961): 711–720.

(G137) Gelfand, Sidney. "The Relationship of Birth Order to Pain Tolerance." *Journal of Clinical Psychology* 19 (July 1963): 406.

(G138) Green, Arnold W. "The 'Cult of Personality' and Sexual Relations." *Psychiatry* 4 (1941): 343–348.

(G139) Gentile, Felix M. "The Effects of the War upon the Family and Its Members." *Psychiatry* 6 (1943): 37–45.

(G140) Greer, Steven. "Study of Parental Loss in Neurotics and Sociopaths." *Archives of General Psychiatry* 11 (August 1964): 177–180.

(G141) Goshen, Charles E. "Mental Retardation and Neurotic Maternal Attitudes." *Archives of General Psychiatry* 9 (August 1963): 168–174.

(G142) Goody, Esther N. "Conjugal Separation and Divorce Among the Gonja of Northern Ghana." In *Marriage in Tribal Societies,* edited by Meyer Fortes. Cambridge: Cambridge University Press, 1962, pp. 14–54.

(G143) Galdston, M. G., Hurwitz, I., Prentice, N. M., and Sperry, B. M. "Fathers of Sons with Primary Neurotic Learning Inhibitions." *American Journal of Orthopsychiatry* 32 (1962): 462–472.

(G144) Glueck, Sheldon, and Glueck, Eleanor T. *Delinquents in the Making.* New York: Harper & Bros., 1952.

(G145) Glatzner, Henriette T. "Clinical Aspects of Adult

Therapy: Notes on the Preoedipal Phantasy." *American Journal of Orthopsychiatry* 29 (April 1959): 383 –390.

(G146) Gamble, David P. "The Temne Family in a Modern Town (Lunsar) in Sierra Leone." *Africa* 23 (1963): 209–226.

(G147) Gould, Harold A. "A Further Note on Village Exogamy in North India." *Southwest Journal of Anthropology* 17 (1961): 297–300.

(G148) de Gonzalez, Nancie L. Solien. "Some Aspects of Child-Bearing and Child-Rearing in a Guatemalan Ladino Community." *Southwest Journal of Anthropology* 19 (1963): 411–423.

(G149) Gould, Harold A. "The Micro-Demography of Marriages in a North Indian Area." *Southwest Journal of Anthropology* 16 (1960): 476–491.

(G150) Geddes, W. R. *The Land Dayaks of Sarawak.* London: H. M.'s Stationary Office, 1954.

(G151) Goode, William J. "Illegitimacy in the Caribbean Social Structure." *American Sociological Review* 25 (1960): 21–30.

(G153) Gray, Susan W., and Klaus, Rupert. "The Assessment of Parental Identification." *Genetic Psychology Monographs* 54 (1956): 87–114.

(G154) Greer, Steven. "The Relation Between Parental Loss and Attempted Suicide: A Control Study." *British Journal of Psychiatry* 110 (September 1964): 698–705.

(G155) Gregory, Ian. "Selected Personal and Family Data on 400 Psychiatric In-Patients." *American Journal of Psychiatry* 119 (November 1962): 397–403.

(G156) Goode, William J. *The Family.* Englewood Cliffs, N.J.: Prentice-Hall, 1964.

(G157) Goode, William J. *Women in Divorce.* Glencoe, Ill.: The Free Press, 1956.

(H001) Hajnal, John. "Differential Changes in Marriage Patterns" (London School of Economics). *American Sociological Review* 19 (1954).

(H008) Hunt, Chester L., and Coller, Richard W. "Intermarriage and Cultural Change: A Study of Philippine-American Marriages." *Social Forces* 35 (1957): 223–230.

(H010) Hawley, Amos H. "Rural Fertility in Central Luzon." *American Sociological Review* 20 (1955): 21–27.

(H011) Havighurst, Robert J., and Davis, Allison. "A Comparison of the Chicago and Harvard Studies of Social Class Differences in Child Rearing." *American Sociological Review* 20 (1955): 438–442.

(H012) Hollingshead, August B. "Class and Kinship in a Middle Western Community." *American Sociological Review* 14 (1949): 469–475.

(H013) Hollingshead, August B. "Age Relationships and Marriage." *American Sociological Review* 16 (1951): 492–499.

(H014) Hollingshead, August B. "Cultural Factors in the Selection of Marriage Mates." *American Sociological Review* 15 (1950): 619–627.

(H015) Henry, Andrew F. "Family Role Structure and Self Blame." *Social Forces* 35 (1956): 34–38.

(H017) Hofstee, E. W., and Kooy, G. A. "Traditional Household and Neighborhood Group: Survivals of the Genealogical-Territorial Societal Patterns in Eastern Parts of the Netherlands." In *Transactions of the Third World Congress of Sociology*, Vol. 4, *Changes in the Family*, 75–79. London: International Sociological Association, 1956.

(H018) Hill, Reuben. "Family Patterns in the Changing South." In *Transactions of the Third World Congress of Sociology*, Vol. 4, *Changes in the Family*, 127–145. London: International Sociological Association, 1956.

(H019) Hickerson, Harold. "The Feast of the Dead Among the Seventeenth Century Algonkians of the Upper Great Lakes." *American Anthropologist* 62 (1960): 81–107.

(H020) Harper, Edward C. "Two Systems of Economic Exchange in Village India." *American Anthropologist* 61 (1959): 760–778.

(H021) Hsu, Francis L. K. "Structure, Function, Content and Process." *American Anthropologist* 61 (1959): 790–805.

(H022) Hori, Ichiro. "Japanese Folk-Beliefs." *American Anthropologist* 61 (1959): 405–424.

(H023) Harris, Marvin. "The Economy Has No Surplus?" *American Anthropologist* 61 (1959): 185–199.

(H024) Henry, Jules. "Culture, Personality and Evolution." *American Anthropologist* 61 (1959): 221–226.

(H025) Hughes, Charles Campbell. "An Eskimo Deviance from the 'Eskimo' Type of Social Organization." *American Anthropologist* 60 (1958): 1140–1147.

(H026) Henry, Jules. "The Personal Community and Its Invariant Property." *American Anthropologist* 60 (1958): 827–831.

(H028) Harris, Grace. "Possession 'Hysteria' in a Kenya Tribe." *American Anthropologist* 59 (1957): 1046–1066.

(H030) Henriques, Fernando. "Color Values in Jamaican Society." *British Journal of Sociology* 2 (1951): 115–121.

(H031) Honigmann, John J., and Carrera, Richard N. "Cross-Cultural Use of Machover's Figure Drawing Test." *American Anthropologist* 59 (1957): 650–654.

(H032) Hamamsy, Laila Shukry. "The Role of Women in a Changing Navaho Society." *American Anthropologist* 59 (1957): 101–111.

(H034) Hart, C. W. M. "The Sons of Turimpi." *American Anthropologist* 56 (1954): 242–261.

(H036) Honigmann, John J. "Inter-Cultural Relations at Great Whale River." *American Anthropologist* 54 (1952): 510–522.

(H037) Hart, C. W. M. "A Reconsideration of the Natchez Social Structure." *American Anthropologist* 45 (1943): 374–386.

(H038) Hsu, Francis L. K. "The Differential Functions of Relationship Terms." *American Anthropologist* 44 (1942): 248–256.

(H043) Hsu, Francis L. K. "Observations on Cross-Cousin Marriage in China." *American Anthropologist* 47 (1945): 83–103.

(H047) Hallowell, A. Irving. "Kinship Terms and Cross-Cousin Marriage of the Mantagnais-Naskapi and the Cree." *American Anthropologist* 34 (1932): 171–199.

(H049) Hoebel, E. Adamson. "Comanche and Hekandika Shoshone Relationship Terms." *American Anthropologist* 41 (1939): 440–457.

(H052) Hsu, Francis L. K. "The Problems of Incest Tabu in a North China Village." *American Anthropologist* 42 (1940): 122–135.

(H055) Hawley, Florence. "Keresan Patterns of Kinship and Social Organization." *American Anthropologist* 52 (1950): 499–512.

(H058) Hallowell, A. Irving. "The Incidence, Character and Decline of Polygyny Among the Lake Winnipeg

Cree and Saulteaux." *American Anthropologist* 40 (1938): 235–256.

(H060) Hawley, Florence. "The Role of Pueblo Social Organization in the Dissemination of Catholicism." *American Anthropologist* 48 (1946): 407–415.

(H061) Hu, Hsien Chin. "The Chinese Concept of 'Face.'" *American Anthropologist* 46 (1944): 45–64.

(H062) Hassrick, Royal B. "Teton-Dakota Kinship Systems." *American Anthropologist* 46 (1944): 338–347.

(H063) Howell, P. P. "Some Observations on Divorce Among the Nuer." *Journal of the Royal Anthropological Institute,* 83 (1953): 136–147.

(H064) Hutton, J. H. "Problems of Reconstruction in the Assam Hills." *Journal of the Royal Anthropological Institute* 75 (1945): 1–8.

(H066): Habakkuk, H. J. "Family Structure and Economic Change in Nineteenth-Century Europe." In *Modern Introduction to the Family,* edited by Norman W. Bell and Ezra F. Vogel. Glencoe, Ill.: The Free Press, 1960, pp. 163–172.

(H066) Hodgson, A. G. O. "Notes on the Achewa and Angoni of the Dowa District of the Niassaland Protectorate." *Journal of the Royal Anthropological Institute* 63 (1933): 123–164.

(H067) Henry, Andrew F. "Family Role Structure and Self-Blame." In *Modern Introduction to the Family,* edited by Norman W. Bell and Ezra F. Vogel. Ill.: The Free Press, 1960, pp. 538–543.

(H072) Huntingford, G. W. B. "Modern Hunters: Some Accounts of the Kamelilo-Kapchepkendi Dorobo of Kenya Colony." *Journal of the Royal Anthropological Institute* 59 (1929): 333–378.

(H074) Hogbin, H. Ian. "Social Reaction to Crime: Law and Morals in the Schouten Island, New Guinea." *Journal of the Royal Anthropological Institute* 68 (1938): 223–262.

(H076) Hulse, Frederick F. "Blood Type and Mating Patterns Among Northwest Coast Indians." *Southwest Journal of Anthropology* 11 (1955): 93–104.

(H077) Hohenthal, W. D., and McCorkle, Thomas. "The Problem of Aboriginal Persistence." *Southwest Journal of Anthropology* 11 (1955): 288–300.

(H079) Humphrey, Norman Daymond. "Social Stratification in a Mexican Town." *Southwest Journal of Anthropology* 5 (1949): 138–146.

(H080) Hawley, Florence. "Big Kivas, Little Kivas and Moiety Houses in Historical Reconstruction." *Southwest Journal of Anthropology* 6 (1950): 286–302.

(H081) Hsu, Francis L. K. "Anthropology or Psychiatry: A Definition of Objectives and Their Implications." *Southwest Journal of Anthropology* 8 (1952): 227–250.

(H084) Hawley, Florence, and Senter, Donovan. "Group-Design Behaviorist Pattern in Two Acculturating Groups." *Southwest Journal of Anthropology* 2 (1946): 133–161.

(H086) Harris, Marvin. "Labor Immigration Among the Mocambique Thonga: Cultural and Political Factors." *Africa* 29 (1959): 50–66.

(H088) Hauser, André. "Les exploitations mécanisées du Moyen Congo Français." *Africa* 24 (1954): 114–129.

(H089) Horton, W. R. G. "The Ohu System of Slavery in a Northern Ibo Village-Group." *Africa* 24 (1954): 311–336.

(H090) De Heusch, Luc. "Éléments de Potlatch chez les Hamba." *Africa* 24 (1954): 337–348.

(H097) Herskovits, Melville J. "A Note on 'Woman Marriage' in Dahomey." *Africa* 10 (1937): 335–341.

(H103) Hunter, Monica. "The Effect of Contact with Europeans on the Status of Pondo Women." *Africa* 6 (1933): 259–276.

(H104) Hoernle, A. W. "An Outline of the Native Conception of Education in Africa." *Africa* 4 (1931): 145–163.

(H105) Herskovits, Melville J. "Some Aspects of Dahomean Ethnology." *Africa* 5 (1932): 266–296.

(H106) Herskovits, Melville J. "The Culture Areas of Africa." *Africa* 3 (1930): 59–77.

(H107) Hutchinson, Bertram. "Some Social Consequences of 19th Century Missionary Activity Among the South African Bantu." *Africa* 27 (1957): 160–177.

(H110) Howell, P. P. "Observations on the Shilluk of the Upper Nile." *Africa* 23 (1953): 94–109.

(H111) Holas, B. "Décès d'une femme guerze." *Africa* 23 (1953): 145–155.

(H112) Hogbin, H. Ian, and Wedgwood, Camilla H. "Local Grouping in Melanesia." *Oceania* 24 (1953–1954): 58–76.

(H116) Hogbin, H. Ian. "Sex and Marriage in Busama, Northeastern New Guinea." *Oceania* 17 (1946–1947): 119–138.

(H117) Hogbin, H. Ian. "Sex and Marriage in Busama, Northeastern New Guinea." *Oceania* 17 (1946–1947): 225–247.

(H122) Hogbin, H. Ian. "A New Guinea Infancy from Conception to Weaning in Wogeo." *Oceania* 13 (1942–1943): 285–309.

(H124) Hogbin, H. Ian. "The Father Chooses His Heir: A Family Dispute Over Succession in Wogeo, New Guinea," *Oceania* 11 (1940–1941): 1–39.

(H126) Hogbin, H. Ian. "Native Land Tenure in New Guinea." *Oceania* 10 (1939–1940): 113–165.

(H128) Hogbin, H. Ian. "Marriage in Wogeo, New Guinea." *Oceania* 15 (1944–1945): 325–352.

(H129) Hogbin, H. Ian. "Mana." *Oceania* 6 (1935–1936): 241–274.

(H130) Hogbin, H. Ian. "The Hill People of Northeastern Guadalcanal." *Oceania* 8 (1937–1938): 62–89.

(H133) Hogbin, H. Ian. "Culture Change in the Solomon Islands: Report of Field Work in Guadalcanal and Malaita." *Oceania* 4 (1933–1934): 233–267.

(H134) Hogbin, H. Ian. "Polynesian Ceremonial Gift Exchanges." *Oceania* 3 (1932–1933): 13–39.

(H135) Hogbin, H. Ian. "The Causes of Depopulation." *Oceania* 3 (1932–1933): 93–94.

(H137) Hogbin, H. Ian. "The Social Organization of Ontong Java." *Oceania* 1 (1930–1931): 399–425.

(H138) Hogbin, H. Ian. "Native Culture of Wogeo: Report of Field Work in New Guinea." *Oceania* 5 (1934–1935): 308–337.

(H139) Holmberg, Allan R. *Nomads of the Long Bow: The Siriono of Eastern Bolivia.* Washington: Smithsonian Institute, Institute of Social Anthropology, Publication No. 10, 1950.

(H141) Holmes, Lowell D. 'Ta'u: Stability and Change in a Samoan Village." *Polynesia* 66 (1957): 301–338.

(H147) Hogbin, H. Ian, and Wedgwood, Camilla H. "Local Grouping in Melanesia." *Oceania* 23 (1952–1953): 241–276.

(H149) Hogbin, H. Ian. "Polynesian Colonies in Melanesia." *Polynesia* 49 (1940): 39–68.

(H157) Herskovits, Melville J., and Herskovits, Frances S. *Trinidad Village.* New York: Alfred A. Knopf, 1947.

(H164) Hunter, Monica. *Reaction to Conquest.* London: Oxford University Press, 1936.

(H165) Hopen, C. Edward. *The Pastoral Fulbe Family in Gwandu.* London: Oxford University Press, 1958.

(H168) Henry, Jules. "Family Structure and the Transmission of Neurotic Behavior." *American Journal of Orthopsychiatry* 21 (1951): 800–818.

(H169) Henry, Jules, and Warson, Samuel. "Family Structure and Psychic Development." *American Journal of Orthopsychiatry* 21 (1951): 59–73.

(H170) Honigmann, John J. "Witch-Fear in Post-Contact Kaska Society." *American Anthropologist* 49 (147): 222–243.

(H171) Fei, Hsiao-Tung, and Chang, Chih-I. *Earthbound China.* Chicago: University of Chicago Press, 1945.

(H172) Hsu, Francis L. K. "Kinship and Ways of Life: An Exploration." In *Psychological Anthropology,* edited by Francis L. K. Hsu. Homewood, Ill.: Dorsey Press, 1961.

(H173) Honzik, M. "Developmental Studies of Parent-Child Resemblance in Intelligence." *Child Development* 28 (June 1957): 203–228.

(H174) Hawkes, G., *et al.* "Pre-Adolescents' Views of Some of Their Relations with Their Parents." *Child Development* 28 (December 1957): 393–399.

(H175) Heer, David. "Husband and Wife Perceptions of Family Power Structure." *Marriage and Family Living* 24 (1962): 56–68.

(H176) Hilgard, Josephine R., and Newman, Martha F. "Early Parental Deprivation as a Functional Factor in the Etiology of Schizophrenia and Alcoholism." *American Journal of Orthopsychiatry* 32 (1962): 298–299.

(H177) Heilbrun, Alfred B., Jr., and McKinley, Roger. "Perception of Maternal Child-Rearing Attitudes, Personality of the Perceiver, and Incipient Psychopathology." *Child Development* 33 (1962): 73–83.

(H178) Hess, R., and Goldman, H. "Parents' Views of the Effect of Television on Their Children." *Child Development* 33 (1962): 411–426.

(H179) Hartup, William. "Some Correlates of Parental Imitation in Young Children." *Child Development* 33 (1962): 85–96.

(H180) Hess, R., and Torney, J. "Religion, Age and Sex in Children's Perceptions of Family Authority." *Child Development* 33 (1962): 781–789.

(H181) Hartley, R., *et al.* "Children's Perceptions and Expressions of Sex Preference." *Child Development* 33 (1962): 221–227.

(H182) Hoffman, Martin L. "Power Assertion by the Parent and Its Impact on the Child." *Child Development* 31 (1960): 129–143.

(H183) Hoffman, Lois Wladis. "Effects of Maternal Employment on the Child." *Child Development* 32 (1961): 187–197.

(H184) Hartup, William. "Nurturance and Nurturance Withdrawal in Relation to the Dependency Behavior of Preschool Children." *Child Development* 29 (June 1958): 191–201.

(H185) Heilbrun, Alfred B., Jr., and McKinley, Roger. "Perception of Maternal Child-Rearing Attitudes, Personality of the Perceiver, and Incipient Psychopathology." *Child Development* 33 (1962): 73–83.

(H186) Heilbrun, Alfred B., Jr. "Perception of Maternal Child Rearing Attitudes in Schizophrenics." *Journal of Consulting Psychology* 2 (April 1960): 169–173.

(H187) Haley, Jay. "Direct Study of Child-Parent Interactions: Observation of the Family of the Schizophrenic." *American Journal of Orthopsychiatry* 30 (July 1960): 460–467.

(H188) Hilgard, Josephine R., Newman, Martha F., and Fisk, Fern. "Strength of Adult Ego Following Childhood Bereavement." *American Journal of Orthopsychiatry.* 30 (October 1960): 788–798.

(H189) Havighurst, R., *et al. Growing Up in River City.* New York: John Wiley & Sons, 1962.

(H190) Havron, M. D., Nordlie, P. G., and Cofer, Charles N. "Measurement of Attitudes by a Simple Word Association Technique." *Journal of Social Psychology* 46 (1957): 81–89.

(H191) Hammer, Max. "The Relationship Between Recalled Type of Discipline in Childhood and Adult Interpersonal Behavior." *Merrill–Palmer Quarterly* 10 (April 1964): 143–145.

(H191) Horton, C., and Crump, E. "Growth and Development XL. Descriptive Analysis of the Backgrounds of 76 Negro Children." *Journal of Genetic Psychology* 100 (1962): 255–265.

(H192) Hilgard, Josephine R., and Fisk, Fern. "Disruption of Adult Ego Identity as Related to Childhood Loss of a Mother Through Hospitalization for Psychosis." *Journal of Nervous and Mental Diseases* 131 (1960): 47–57.

(H193) Hartley, Ruth E. "Sex-Role Pressures and the Socialization of the Male Child." *Psychological Reports* 5 (September 1959): 457–468.

(H194) Heilbrun, Alfred B. "Parental Identification and College Adjustment." *Psychological Reports* 10 (June 1962): 853–854.

(H195) Hurvitz, Nathan. "The Marital Roles Inventory and the Measurement of Marital Adjustment." *Journal of Clinical Psychology* 16 (October 1960): 377–380.

(H196) Heilbrun, Alfred B., Jr., and Hall, Charles. "Resource Mediation in Childhood and Identification." *Journal of Child Psychology and Psychiatry* 5 (1964): 139–149.

(H197) Hartup, Willard W., and Zook, Elsie A. "Sex-Role Preferences in Three- and Four-Year-Old Children." *Journal of Consulting Psychology* 24 (December 1960): 420–426.

(H198) Hunt, Raymond G., Roach, Jack L., and Gurrslin, Orville. "Socialpsychiatric Complaints of Disturbed Children." *Journal of Consulting Psychology* 24 (April 1960): 194.

(H199) Hurley, John R. "Maternal Attitudes and Child's Intelligence." *Clinical Psychology* 15 (July 1959): 291–292.

(H200) Hart, I. "Maternal Child-Rearing Practices and Authoritarian Ideology." *Journal of Abnormal and Social Psychology* 55 (September 1957): 232–237.

(H201) Hoffman, Lois Wladis. "The Father's Role in the Family and the Child's Peer Group Adjustment." *Merrill–Palmer Quarterly* 7 (April 1961): 97–105.

(H202) Hare, E. "Family Setting and the Urban Distribution of Schizophrenia." *Journal of Mental Science* 102 (1956): 753–760.

(H203) Heer, David M. "The Marital Status of Second-Generation Americans." *American Sociological Review* 26 (February 1961): 233–241.

(H204) Hurvitz, Nathan. "The Measurement of Marital Strain." *American Journal of Sociology* 65 (1959–1960): 610–615.

(H205) Hoffman, Lois Wladis, Rosen, Sidney, and Lippit, Ronald. "Parental Coerciveness, Child Autonomy, and Child's Role at School." *Sociometry* 23 (March 1960): 15–22.

(H206) Hjelholt, G. "The Neglected Parent." *Acta Psychologica* 14 (1958): 347–352.

(H207) Horowitz, F., and Lovell, L. "Attitudes of Mothers of Female Schizophrenics." *Child Development* 31 (1960): 299–305.

(H208) Hoffman, Martin L. "Child Rearing Practices and Moral Development: Generalizations from Empirical Research." *Child Development* 34, No. 2 (1963): 295 –318.

(H209) Harris, D., *et al.* "Children's Ethnic Attitudes: II. Relationship to Parental Beliefs Concerning Child Training." *Child Development* 21 (September 1950): 169–181.

(H210) Hartup, Willard W. "Some Correlates of Parental Imitation in Young Children." *Child Development* 33 (1962): 85–95.

(H211) Hetherington, E. Mavis, and Brackbill, Y. "Etiology and Covariation of Obstinacy, Orderliness and Parsimony in Young Children." *Child Development* 34, No. 4 (December 1963): 919–943.

(H212) Hoffman, Martin L. "Parent Discipline and the Child's Consideration for Others." *Child Development* 34, No. 3 (September 1963): 573–588.

(H213) Hoffman, Martin L. "Personality, Family Structure, and Social Class as Antecedents of Parental Power Assertion." *Child Development* 34 (December 1963): 869–884.

(H214) Honzik, Marjorie P. "A Sex Difference in the Age of Onset of the Parent-Child Resemblance in Intelligence." *Journal of Educational Psychology* 54 (October 1963): 231–237.

(H215) Hetherington, E. Mavis, and Feldman, Solomon E. "College Cheating as a Function of Subject and Situational Variables." *Journal of Educational Psychology* 55 (August 1964): 212–218.

(H216) Harris, Irving D. "Characterological Significance of the Typical Anxiety Dreams." *Psychiatry* 14 (1951): 279–294.

(H217) Hilgard, Josephine R. "Sibling Rivalry and Social Heredity." *Psychiatry* 14 (1951): 375–385.

(H218) Harris, Irving D. "On Recognition of Resemblance." *Psychiatry* 16 (1953): 355–364.

(H219) Honigman, John J. "Cultural Dynamics of Sex." *Psychiatry* 10 (1947): 37–56.

(H220) Hadley, Ernest E. "Unrecognized Antagonisms Complicating Business Enterprise." *Psychiatry* 1 (1938): 13–31.

(H221) Harris, Irving, D. "Observations Concerning Typical Anxiety Dreams." *Psychiatry* 11 (1948): 301 –309.

(H222) Hollingshead, A. B. *Social Class and Mental Illness.* New York: John Wiley & Sons, 1958.

(H223) Hogbin, H. Ian. "The Sexual Life of the Natives of Ontong Java." *Polynesia* 40 (1931): 23–34.

(H224) Hartley, R. "Sex-Role Concepts Among Elementary-School Age Girls." *Marriage and Family Living* 21 (1959): 59–64.

(H225) Heinrich, Albert. "Structural Features of Northwestern Alaskan Eskimo Kinship." *Southwest Journal of Anthropology* 16 (1960): 110–126.

(H226) Hilgard, Josephine R., and Newman, Martha F. "Early Parental Deprivation as a Functional Factor in the Etiology of Schizophrenia and Alcoholism." *American Journal of Orthopsychiatry* 33 (April 1963): 409–420.

(H227) Halpern, Joel. *A Serbian Village.* New York: Columbia University Press, 1956.

(H228) Hobart, Charles W. "Emancipation from Parents and Courtship in Adolescents." *Pacific Sociological Review* (Spring 1958): 25–29.

(H230) Harris, Grace. "Taita Bridewealth and Affinal Relationships." In *Marriage in Tribal Societies,* edited by Meyer Fortes. Cambridge: Cambridge University Press, 1962, pp. 55–87.

(H231) Higgins, J. V., Reed, Elizabeth W., and Reed, S. C. "Intelligence and Family Size: A Paradox Resolved." *Eugenics Quarterly* 9 (1962): 84–90.

(H232) Hall, Calvin S. "A Cognitive Theory of Dream Symbols." In *Studies in Motivation,* edited by David C. McClelland. New York: Appleton-Century-Crofts, Inc., pp. 30–43.

(H233) Hogbin, H. Ian. *Transformation Scene.* London: Routledge and Kegan Paul, 1951.

(H234) Harris, Rosemary. "The Influence of Ecological Factors and External Relations on the Mbembe Tribes of Southeast Nigeria." *Africa* 32 (1962): 38–52.

(H235) Hoffman, Lois Wladis, Rosen, Sidney, and Lippitt, Ronald. "Parental Coerciveness, Child Autonomy, and Child's Role at School." *Sociometry* 23 (March 1960): 15–22.

(H236) Hartley, Ruth E. "Children's Concept of Male and Female Roles." *Merrill–Palmer Quarterly* 6 (1960): 83 –91.

(H237) Hogbin, H. Ian. *Law and Order in Polynesia.* Hamden: The Shoestring Press, 1961.

(H238) Haberman, Paul W. "Psychological Test Score Changes for Wives of Alcoholics During Periods of Drinking and Sobriety." *Journal of Clinical Psychology* 20 (1964): 230–232.

(H239) Heincke, Christoph M. "Some Effects of Separating Two-Year-Old Children from Their Parents: A Comparative Study." *Human Relations* 9 (1956): 105 –176.

(H240) Heiss, Jerold S. "Premarital Characteristics of the Religiously Intermarried in an Urban Area." *American Sociological Review* 25 (1960): 47–55.

(H241) Horner, Robert F. "Important Stimulus Variables in the Early Family Relationships of Schizophrenic Patients." *Journal of Clinical Psychology* 20 (1964): 344 –346.

(H242) Humphrey, Michael, and Ounsted, Christopher. "Adoptive Families Referred for Psychiatric Advice." *British Journal of Psychiatry* 109 (September 1963): 599–608.

(H243) Humphrey, Michael, and Ounsted, Christopher. "Adoptive Families Referred for Psychiatric Advice." *British Journal of Psychiatry* 110 (July 1964): 549– 555.

(H244) Hyman, Herbert H. *Political Socialization: A Study in the Psychology of Political Behavior.* Glencoe, Ill.: The Free Press, 1959.

(H245) Harris, Rosemary. "The Political Significance of Double Unilineal Descent." *Journal of Royal Anthropological Institute* 92 (1962): 86–101.

(H246) Hilgard, Josephine R. "Anniversary Reactions in Parents Precipitated by Children." *Psychiatry* 16 (1953): 73–80.

(I004) Ibbotson, Percy. "Urbanization in Southern Rhodesia." *Africa* 16 (1946): 73–82.

(I005) Inselberg, Rachel. "Marital Problems and Satisfaction in High School Marriages." *Marriage and Family Living* 24 (February 1962): 71–77.

(I006) Inselberg, Rachel. "The Causation and Manifestations of Emotional Behavior in Filipino Children." *Child Development* 29 (June 1958): 249–254.

(I007) Israeli, Nathan. "Population Trends and the Family." *Psychiatry* 4 (1941): 349–359.

(I008) Irish, Donald P. "Sibling Interaction: A Neglected Aspect in Family Life Research." *Social Forces* 42 (December 1964): 279–288.

(J001) Jansen, Luther T. "Measuring Family Solidarity." *American Sociological Review* 17 (1952): 727–733.

(J002) Jacobson, Alver Hilding. "Conflict of Attitudes Toward the Roles of the Husband and Wife in Marriage." *American Sociological Review* 17 (1952): 146 –150.

(J003) Jaco, E. Gartly, and Belknap, Ivan. "Is a New Family Form Emerging in the Urban Fringe?" *American Sociological Review* 18 (1953): 551–557.

(J007) Junod, Henri A. "La seconde école de circoncision chez les Ba-Kahaha du Nord du Transvaal." *Journal of the Royal Anthropological Institute* 59 (1929): 131– 147.

(J008) Jaenen, Cornelius J. "The Galla or Oromo of East Africa." *Southwest Journal of Anthropology* 12 (1956): 171–190.

(J009) Jahoda, Gustav. "Love, Marriage and Social Change: Letters to the Advice Column of a West African Newspaper." *Africa* 29 (1959): 127–160.

(J010) Jacobson, Paul H. "Differentials in Divorce by Duration of Marriage and Size of Family." *American Sociological Review* 15 (1950): 235–244.

(J019) Johnson, Adelaide M., Griffin, Mary E., Watson, E. Jane, and Beckett, Peter G. S. "Observations on Ego Functions in Schizophrenia." *Psychiatry* 19 (1956): 143–148.

(J020) Jones, Wyatt C., Meyer, Henry J., and Borgatta, Edgar F. "Social and Psychological Factors in Status Decisions of Unmarried Mothers." *Marriage and Family Living* 24 (August 1962): 224–230.

(J021) Johnson, R. C. "A Study of Children's Moral Judgments." *Child Development* 33 (March–December 1962): 327–354.

(J022) Johnson, R. C., Johnson, C., and Martin, L. "Authoritarianism, Occupation, and Sex Role Differentiation of Children." *Child Development* 32 (1961): 271 –276.

(J023) Josselyn, I. "The Older Adolescent." In *Values and Ideals of American Youth,* edited by Eli Ginzberg. New York: Columbia University Press, 1961, pp. 27– 35.

(J024) Jants, Irving L. "Personality and Susceptibility to Persuasion." In *Communication and Persuasion,* edited by C. I. Hovland, Irving L. Jants, and Harold H. Kelley. New Haven: Yale University Press, 1959, pp. 174–212.

(J024) Jenkins, Richard L. "Motivation and Frustration in Delinquency." *American Journal of Orthopsychiatry* 27 (July 1957): 528–537.

(J025) Johnson, Cyrus M., and Kerckhoff, Alan C. "Family Norms, Social Position, and the Value of Change." *Social Forces* 43 (December 1964): 149–156.

(J026) Johnson, Miriam M. "Sex Role Learning in the Nuclear Family." *Child Development* 34 (1963): 319 –333.

(J027) Jordan, Thomas E. "Research on the Handicapped Child and the Family." *Merrill–Palmer Quarterly* 8 (October 1962): 243–255.

(J029) Jackson, P. "Verbal Solutions to Parent-Child Problems." *Child Development* 27 (September 1956): 339 –349.

(J030) Johnson, Ronald C. "Occupational Type and 'Traditional' Family Ideology." *Child Development* 34 (June 1963): 509–512.

(J030) Johnson, Miriam M. "Sex Role Learning in the Nuclear Family." *Child Development* 34 (June 1963): 319–333.

(J032) Jourard, Sidney M. "Identification, Parent-Cathexis, and Self-Esteem." *Journal of Consulting Psychology* 21 (October 1957): 375–380.

(J033) Johnson, Cyrus M., and Kerckhoff, Alan C. "Family Norms, Social Position, and the Value of Change." *Social Forces* 43 (December 1964): 149–156.

(J034) Jitodai, Ted T. "Migration and Kinship Contacts." *Pacific Sociological Review* 6 (Fall 1963): 49–55.

(J035) Jacobsohn, Peter, and Matheny, Adam P., Jr. "Mate Selection in Open Marriage Systems." *International Journal of Comparative Sociology* 3 (1962): 98 –114.

(K001) Kirkpatrick, Clifford, and Kanin, Eugene. "Male Sex Aggression on a University Campus." *American Sociological Review* 22, No. 1 (1957): 52–58.

(K002) Kephart, William M. "The Duration of Marriage." *American Sociological Review* 19 (1954): 287– 295.

(K003) Kephart, William M., and Monahan, Thomas P. "Desertion and Divorce in Philadelphia." *American Sociological Review* 17 (1952): 719–727.

(K004) Kitagawa, Evelyn M. "Differential Fertility in Chicago, 1920–1940." *American Journal of Sociology* 58 (1953): 481–492.

(K010) Kephart, William M. "Occupational Level and Marital Disruption." *American Sociological Review* 20 (1955): 456–465.

(K011) Ktsanes, Thomas. "Mate Selection on the Basis of Personality Type: A Study Utilizing an Empirical Typology of Personality." *American Sociological Review* 20 (1955): 547–551.

(K012) Kirkpatrick, Clifford, and Cotton, J. "Physical Attractiveness, Age and Marital Adjustment." *American Sociological Review* 16 (1951): 81–86.

(K013) Koller, Marvin R. "Residential Propinquity of White Mates at Marriage in Relation to Age and Occupation of Males, Columbus, Ohio, 1938 and 1946." *American Sociological Review* 13 (1948): 613–616.

(K014) Komarovsky, Mirra. "Functional Analysis of Sex Roles." *American Sociological Review* 15 (1950): 508 –516.

(K015) Kennedy, Runy Jo Reeves. "Single or Triple Melting-Pot? Intermarriage in New Haven, 1870–1950." *American Journal of Sociology* 58 (1952): 56–59.

(K016) Keyfitz, Nathan. "A Factorial Arrangement of Comparisons of Family Size." *American Journal of Sociology* 58 (1953): 470–480.

(K018) Kanin, Eugene J. "Male Aggression in Dating Courtship Relations." *American Journal of Sociology* 63 (1957): 197–204.

(K019) Kumura, Yukiko. "War Brides in Hawaii and Their In-Laws." *American Journal of Sociology* 63 (1957): 70–76.

(K020) Kerckhoff, Alan C. "Notes and Comments on the Meaning of Residential Propinquity as a Factor in Mate Selection." *Social Forces* 34 (1956): 207–213.

(K021) Kanin, Eugene J. "Value Conflicts in Catholic Device-Contraceptive Usage." *Social Forces* 34 (1957): 238–243.

(K024) König, René. "Changes in the Western Family." In *Transactions of the Third World Congress of Sociology,* Vol. 4, *Changes in the Family,* 63–74. London: International Sociological Association, 1956.

(K027) Krader, Lawrence. "Recent Studies of the Russian

Peasant." *American Anthropologist* 58 (1956): 715–720.

(K028) Krader, Lawrence. "A Nativistic Movement in Western Siberia." *American Anthropologist* 58 (1956): 282–292.

(K029) Kaut, Charles R. "Western Apache Clan and Phratry Organization." *American Anthropologist* 58 (1956): 140–146.

(K030) König, René. "Family and Authority: The German Father in 1955." *Sociological Review* 5 (New Series) No. 1 (1957): 107–127.

(K039) Kelly, William H. "Cocopa Gentes." *American Anthropologist* 44 (1942): 675–691.

(K045) Keesing, Felix M. "Some Notes on Bontok Social Organization, Northern Philippines." *American Anthropologist* 51 (1949): 578–601.

(K046) Kobben, André J. "New Ways of Presenting an Old Idea: The Statistical Method in Social Anthropology." *Journal of the Royal Anthropological Institute* 82 (1952): 129–146.

(K048) Kroeber, A. L. "Basic and Secondary Patterns of Social Structure." *Journal of the Royal Anthropological Institute* 68 (1938): 299–309.

(K049) Krader, Lawrence. "Principles and Structures in the Organization of the Asiatic Steppe-Pastoralist." *Southwest Journal of Anthroplogy* 11 (1955): 67–92.

(K050) Krader, Lawrence. "Buryat Religion and Society." *Southwest Journal of Anthropology* 10 (1954): 322–351.

(K058) Kaberry, Phyllis M. "Land Tenure Among the Nsaw of the British Cameroons." *Africa* 20 (1950): 307–323.

(K060) Krige, Eileen Jensen. "The Place of the Northeastern Transvaal Sotho in the South Bantu Complex." *Africa* 11 (1938): 265–293.

(K061) Knopf, O. L'Enfant chez les Senoufos de la Côte d'Ivoire." *Africa* 11 (1938): 482–492.

(K062) Krige, J. D. "The Significance of Cattle Exchanges in Lovedu Social Structure." *Africa* 12 (1939): 393–424.

(K065) Krige, Eileen Jensen. "Changing Conditions in Marital Relations and Parental Duties Among Urbanized Natives." *Africa* 9 (1936): 1–23.

(K066) Kayamba, H. M. T. "The Modern Life of the East African Natives." *Africa* 5 (1932): 50–59.

(K067) Kirchhoff, Paul. "Kinship Organization." *Africa* 5 (1932): 184–191.

(K070) Kaberry, Phyllis M. "Law and Political Organization in the Abelam Tribe, New Guinea." *Oceania* 12 (1941–1942): 79–95.

(K071) Kaberry, Phyllis M. "Law and Political Organization in the Abelam Tribe, New Guinea." *Oceania* 12 (1941–1942): 209–225.

(K073) Kaberry, Phyllis M. "The Abelam Tribe, Sepik District, New Guinea." *Oceania* 11 (1940–1941): 233–258.

(K076) Kaberry, Phyllis M. "Subsections in the East and South Kimberley Tribes of Northwest Australia." *Oceania* 7 (1936–1937): 436–458.

(K078) Keesing, Felix M. "The Taupo System of Samoa: A Study of Institutional Change." *Oceania* 8 (1937–1938): 1–14.

(K081) Kaberry, Phyllis M. "The Forrest Riber and Lyne Riber Tribes of Northwest Australia." *Oceania* 5 (1934–1935): 408–436.

(K082) Kelly, C. Tennant. "Tribes on Cherburg Settlement, Queensland." *Oceania* 5 (1934–1935): 461–473.

(K087) Kluckhohn, Florence Rockwood. "Variations in the Basic Values of Family Systems." In *Modern Introduction to the Family,* edited by Norman W. Bell and Ezra F. Vogel. Glencoe, Ill.: The Free Press, 1960, pp. 304–315.

(K088) Komarovsky, Mirra. *Blue-Collar Marriage.* New York: Random House, 1962.

(K090) Kluckhohn, Clyde. "Variations in the Human Family." In *Modern Introduction to the Family,* edited by Norman W. Bell and Ezra F. Vogel. Glencoe, Ill.: The Free Press, 1960, pp. 45–51.

(K091) Kaufman, Irving, Peck, Alice L., and Tagiuri, Consuelo K. "The Family Constellation and Overt Incestuous Relations Between Father and Daughter." In *Modern Introduction to the Family,* edited by Norman W. Bell and Ezra F. Vogel. Glencoe, Ill.: The Free Press, 1960, pp. 544–554.

(K092) Keesing, Felix M. *The South Seas in the Modern World.* New York: John Day Co., 1941.

(K093) Kahn, Shirley W., and Prestwood, A. Rodney. "Group Therapy of Parents as an Adjunct to the Treatment of Schizophrenic Patients." *Psychiatry* 17 (1954): 177.

(K094) Koch, H. "The Relation in Young Children Between Characteristics of Their Playmates and Certain Attributes of Their Siblings." *Child Development* 28 (June 1957): 175–202.

(K095) Kaufman, Irving, Frank, Thomas, Heims, Lora, Herrick, Joan, and Willer, Lee. "Parents of Schizophrenic Children: 3. Four Type of Defense in Mothers and Fathers of Schizophrenic Children." *American Journal of Orthopsychiatry* 29 (July 1959): 460–472.

(K096) Klebanoff, Lewis B. "1. Parental Attitudes of Mothers of Schizophrenic, Brain-Injured and Retarded, and Normal Children." *American Journal of Orthopsychiatry* 29 (July 1959): 445–454.

(K097) Kaga, J., Hosken, B., and Watson, S. "Child's Symbolic Conceptualization of Parents." *Child Development* 32 No. 4 (1961): 625–636.

(K098) Koch, Helen L. "The Relation of Certain Family Constellation Characteristics and the Attitudes of Children Toward Adults." *Child Development* 26 (March 1955): 13–40.

(K099) Klowkowska, Antonia. "General Attitudes Towards the Respective Roles and the Equality of the Two Sexes and Towards Children." *International Social Science Journal* 14, No. 3 (1962): 66–80.

(K100) Kharchev, A. G. "Problems of the Family and Their Study in the USSR." *International Social Science Journal* 14, No. 3 (1962): 539–550.

(K101) Kell, L., and Aldous, J. "The Relation Between Mother's Child-Rearing Ideologies and Their Children's Perceptions of Maternal Control." *Child Development* 31 (1960): 145–156.

(K102) Kanous, Lawrence, Daugherty, Robert, and Cohn, Thomas. "Relations Between Hetersosexual Friendship Choices and Socioeconomic Level." *Child Development* 33 (1962): 251–255.

(K103) Kagan, Jerome. "Socialization of Aggression and the Perception of Parents in Fantasy." *Child Development* 29 (1958): 311–319.

(K104) Koch, H. "Some Emotional Attitudes of the Young Child in Relation to Characteristics of His Sibling." *Child Development* 27 (December 1956): 393–426.

(K105) Kreitman, Norman. "Mental Disorder in Married Couples." *Journal of Mental Science* 108 (July 1962): 438–446.

(K106) Kahn, Jack H., and Nursten, Jean P. "School Refusal: A Comprehensive View of School Phobia and Other Failures of School Attendance." *American Journal of Orthopsychiatry* 32 (1962): 707–718.

(K107) Kaufman, Irving, Frank, Thomas, Hemis, Lora, Herrick, Jean, Reiser, David, and Willer, Lee. "Treatment Implications of a New Classification of Parents of Schizophrenic Children." *American Journal of Psychiatry* 116 (April 1960): 920–924.

(K108) Kapland, David M., and Mason, Edward A. "Maternal Reactions to Premature Birth Viewed as an Acute Emotional Disorder." *American Journal of Orthopsychiatry* 30 (July 1960): 539–552.

(K109) Kerckhoff, Alan C., and Davis, Keith E. "Value Consensus and Need Complementarity in Mate Selection." *American Sociological Review* 27 (June 1962): 295–303.

(K110) Kohn, Melvin L. "Social Class and Parental Values." *American Journal of Sociology* 64 (January 1959): 337–351.

(K111) Kiev, A. "Primitive Therapy: A Cross-Cultural Study of the Relationship Between Child Training and Therapeutic Practices Related to Illness." *The Psychoanalytic Study of Society* 1 (1960): 185–217.

(K112) Kenkel, William F. "Dominance, Persistence, Self-Confidence, and Spousal Roles in Decision Making." *Journal of Social Psychiatry* 54 (1961): 349–358.

(K113) Kauffman, J. Howard. "Interpersonal Relations in the Traditional and Emergent Families Among Midwest Mennonites." *Marriage and Family Living* 23 (August 1961): 247–252.

(K114) Klatskin, Ethelyn H., Jackson, Edith B., and Wilkin, Louise C. "The Influence of Degree of Flexibility in Maternal Child Care Practices on Early Child Behavior." *American Journal of Orthopsychiatry* 26 (January 1956): 79–93.

(K114) Kohn, Melvin L., and Clausen, John A. "Parental Authority Behavior and Schizophrenia." *American Journal of Orthopsychiatry* 26 (April 1956): 297–313.

(K115) Kagan, Jerome, and Freeman, Marion. "Relation of Childhood Intelligence, Maternal Behaviors, and Social Class to Behavior During Adolescence." *Child Development* 34, No. 4 (December, 1963): 899–911.

(K116) Kagan, Jerome. "The Child's Perception of the Parent." *Journal of Abnormal and Social Psychology* 53 (September 1956): 257–258.

(K117) Kates, Solis L., and Diab, Lutfy N. "Authoritarian Ideology and Attitudes on Parent-Child Relationships." *Journal of Abnormal and Social Psychology* 51 (July 1955): 13–16.

(K118) Katz, Irwin, Cohen, Melvin, and Castiglione, Lawrence. "Effect of One Type of Need Complementarity on Marriage Partners' Conformity to One Another's Judgments." *Journal of Abnormal and Social Psychology* 67 (July 1963): 8–14.

(K119) Kaufman, Irving, Peck, Alice L., and Tagiuri, Consuelo K. "The Family Constellation and Overt Incestuous Relations Between Father and Daughter." *American Journal of Orthopsychiatry* 24 (April 1954): 266–277.

(K120) Koch, Margaret Body. "Anxiety in Preschool Children from Broken Homes." *Merrill–Palmer Quarterly* 7 (October 1961): 225–232.

(K121) Katz, E., and Zloczower, A. "Ethnic Continuity in an Israeli Town, I. Relations with Parents." *Human Relations* 14 (1961): 293–308.

(K122) Krall, Vita. "Personality Characteristics of Accident Repeating Children." *Journal of Abnormal and Social Psychology* 48 (January 1953): 99–107.

(K123) Kotlar, Sally L. "Instrumental and Expressive Marital Roles." *Sociology and Social Research* 46 (January 1962): 186–194.

(K124) Kogan, Kate L., and Jackson, Joan K. "Perceptions of Self and Spouse: Some Contaminating Factors." *Journal of Marriage and the Family* 26 (February 1964): 60–64.

(K125) Krinsky, L. "Personal Beliefs of Schizophrenics and Their Parents." *The Journal of Psychology* 53 (1962): 287–297.

(K126) Koch, H. "Children's Work Attitudes and Sibling Characteristics." *Child Development* 27 (September 1956): 289–310.

(K127) Kagan, Jerome, and Freeman, Marion. "Relation of Childhood Intelligence, Maternal Behaviors, and Social Class to Behavior During Adolescence." *Child Development* 34, No. 4 (December 1963): 899–911.

(K148) Kennedy, Wallace A., and Willcut, Herman. "Youth-Parent Relations of Mathematically-Gifted Adolescents." *Journal of Clinical Psychology* 19 (July 1963): 400–402.

(K149) Koch, Helen. "Attitudes of Young Children Toward Their Peers as Related to Certain Characteristics of Their Siblings." *Psychological Monographs* 70, Whole No. 426 (1956): 1–41.

(K150) Kerckhoff, Alan C. "Patterns of Homogamy and the Field of Eligibles." *Social Forces* 43 (December 1964): 289–297.

(K151) Kiernan, Irene, and Porter, Margaret E. "A Study of Behavior-Disorder Correlations Between Parents and Children." *American Journal of Orthopsychiatry* 33 (April 1963): 539–541.

(K152) Karlsson, Georg. "On Mate Selection." *International Journal of Comparative Sociology* 3 (1962): 91–97.

(K153) Kotlar, Sally L. "Instrumental and Expressive Marital Roles." *Sociology and Social Research* 46 (January 1962): 186–194.

(K154) Klima, George. "Jural Relations Between the Sexes Among the Barabaig." *Africa* 34 (1964): 9–20.

(K155) Klein, Viola. "Married Women in Employment." *International Journal of Comparative Sociology* 1 (1960): 254–261.

(K156) Keesing, Felix M. "The Isneg: Shifting Cultivators of the Northern Philippines." *Southwest Journal of Anthropology* 18 (1962): 1–19.

(K157) Krige, E. J., and Krige, J. D. *Realm of a Rain Queen.* Oxford: Oxford University Press, 1943.

(K158) Kenyatta, Jomo. *Facing Mount Kenya.* London: Secker and Warburg, 1938.

(K159) Kreitman, Norman. "The Patient's Spouse." *British Journal of Psychiatry* 110 (March 1964): 159–173.

(K160) Kenkel, William F. *The Family in Perspective.* New York: Appleton-Century-Crofts, Inc., 1960.

(K161) Kirkpatrick, Clifford. *The Family as Process and Institution.* New York: Ronald Press, 1955.

(K162) Kay, Paul. "Aspects of Social Structure in a Tahitian Urban Neighborhood." *Polynesia* 72 (1963): 325–371.

(L001) Litwak, Eugene. "Group Pressure and Family Breakup: A Study of German Communities." *American Journal of Sociology* 61 (1956): 345–354.

(L002) Lansing, John B., and Kish, Leslie. "Family Life Cycle as an Independent Variable." *American Sociological Review* 22, No. 5 (1957): 512–519.

(L003) Littman, Richard A., Moore, Robert C. A., and Pierce-Jones, John. "Social Class Differences in Child

Rearing: A Third Community for Comparison with Chicago and Newton." *American Sociological Review* 22, No. 6 (1957): 694–704.

(L004) Locke, Harvey J., and Karlsson, Georg. "Marital Adjustment and Prediction in Sweden and the United States." *American Sociological Review* 17 (1952): 10–17.

(L005) Locke, Harvey J., and Snowbarger, Vernon A. "Marital Adjustment and Prediction in Sweden." *American Journal of Sociology* 60 (1954): 51–53.

(L006) Locke, Harvey J., and Mackeprang, Muriel. "Marital Adjustment and the Employed Wife." *American Journal of Sociology* 54 (1949): 536–538.

(L010) Landis, Judson T. "Marriages of Mixed and Non-Mixed Religious Faith." *American Sociological Review* 14 (1949): 401–407.

(L011) Lowrie, Samuel H. "Dating Theories and Student Responses." *American Sociological Review* 16 (1951): 334–340.

(L012) Locke, Harvey J. "Predicting Marital Adjustment by Comparing a Divorced and a Happily Married Group." *American Sociological Review* 12 (1947): 187–191.

(L013) Landis, Judson T., Poffenberger, Thomas, and Poffenberger, Shirley. "The Effects of First Pregnancy upon the Sexual Adjustment of 212 Couples." *American Sociological Review* 15 (1950): 766–772.

(L014) Lu, Yi-chuang. "Predicting Roles in Marriage." *American Journal of Sociology* 58 (1952): 51–55.

(L018) Leslie, Gerald, Christensen, Harold T., and Pearman, Glenn L. "Studies in Child Spacing: IV. The Time Interval Separating All Children in Completed Families of Purdue University Graduates." *Social Forces* 34 (1955): 77–82.

(L019) Landis, Judson T. "The Pattern of Divorce in Three Generations." *Social Forces* 34 (1956): 213–216.

(L024) Landis, Judson T. "Some Aspects of Family Instability in the United States." In *Transactions of the Third World Congress of Sociology,* Vol. 4, *Changes in the Family,* 174–179. London: International Sociological Association, 1956.

(L025) Lomax, Alan. "Folk Song Style." *American Anthropologist* 61 (1959): 927–954.

(L026) Levine, Robert A. "Gusii Sex Offenses: A Study in Social Control." *American Anthropologist* 61 (1959): 955–990.

(L027) Levy, M. J., Jr., and Fallers, L. A. "The Family: Some Comparative Consideration." *American Anthropologist* 61 (1959): 647–651.

(L029) Lange, Charles H. "Acculturation in the Context of Selective New and Old World Peasant Cultures." *American Anthropologist* 59 (1957): 1067–1071.

(L030) Little, Kenneth, L. "The Role of Voluntary Association in West African Urbanization." *American Anthropologist* 59 (1957): 579–596.

(L031) Lange, Charles H. "The Role of Economics in Cochiti Pueblo Culture Change." *American Anthropologist* 55 (1953): 674–694.

(L035) Lewis, Oscar. "Manly-Hearted Women Among the North Piegan." *American Anthropologist* 43 (1941): 173–187.

(L036) Lowie, Robert H. "A Note on the Northern Ge Tribes of Brazil." *American Anthropologist* 43 (1941): 188–196.

(L039) Loeb, Edwin M. "Patrilineal and Matrilineal Organization in Sumatra." *American Anthropologist* 36 (1934): 26–36.

(L040) Lowie, Robert H. "Some Moot Problems in Social Organization." *American Anthropologist* 36 (1934): 321–330.

(L041) Loeb, Edwin M. "Patrilineal and Matrilineal Organization in Sumatra: The Batak and the Minangkabau." *American Anthropologist* 35 (1933): 16–50.

(L043) Lowie, Robert H. "American Culture History." *American Anthropologist* 42 (1940): 409–428.

(L045) Lessa, William A. "Ultihi and the Other Natives' Outer World." *American Anthropologist* 52 (1950): 27–52.

(L046) Levi-Strauss, Claude. "Language and the Analysis of Social Laws." *American Anthropologist* 53 (1951): 155–163.

(L048) Lewis, Oscar. "Husband and Wife in a Mexican Village: A Study of Role Conflict." *American Anthropologist* 51 (1949): 602–610.

(L049) Loeb, Edwin M., and Broek, Jan. O. M. "Social Organization and the Longhouse in Southeast Asia." *American Anthropologist* 49 (1947): 414–425.

(L051) Leach, E. R. "The Structural Implications of Matrilateral Cross-Cousin Marriage." *Journal of the Royal Anthropological Institute* 81 (1951): 23–55.

(L053) Leakey, L. S. B. "The Kikuyu Problem of the Initiation of Girls." *Journal of the Royal Anthropological Institute* 61 (1931): 277–285.

(L055) Latchan, Richard E. "The Totemism of the Ancient Andean Peoples." *Journal of the Royal Anthropological Institute* 57 (1927): 55–87.

(L056) Leakey, L. S. B. "Some Notes on the Masai of Kenya Colonies." *Journal of the Royal Anthropological Institute* 60 (1930): 185–209.

(L057) Leach, E. R. "Jinghpaw Kinship Terminology." *Journal of the Royal Anthropological Institute* 75 (1945): 59–72.

(L058) Lounsbery, Floyd G. "A Semantic Analysis of the Pawnee Kinship Usage." *Language* 32 (1956): 158–194.

(L059) Lange, Charles H. "The Keresan Component of Southwestern Pueblo Culture, Southwest." *Southwest Journal of Anthropology* 14 (1958): 34–50.

(L060) Lane, Robert, and Lane, Barbara. "The Evolution of Ambrym Kinship." *Southwest Journal of Anthropology* 14 (1958): 107–135.

(L061) Lane, Robert, and Lane, Barbara. "On the Development of Dakota-Iroquois and Crow-Omaha Kinship Terminology." *Southwest Journal of Anthropology* 15 (1959): 254–265.

(L062) Livingstone, Frank B. "A Formal Analysis of Prescriptive Marriage Systems Among the Australian Aborigines." *Southwest Journal of Anthropology* 16 (1959): 361–372.

(L063) Leacock, Eleanor. "Matrilocality in a Simple Hunting Economy (Montagnais-Naskapi)." *Southwest Journal of Anthropology* 11 (1955): 31–47.

(L064) Lewis, Oscar. *Life in a Mexican Village: Tepoztlan Restudied.* Urbana, Ill.: University of Illinois Press, 1961.

(L065) Lloyd, P. C. "The Traditional Political System of the Yoruba." *Southwest Journal of Anthropology* 10 (1954): 366–384.

(L066) Lewis, Oscar. *Village Life in Northern India.* Urbana, Ill.: University of Illinois Press, 1958.

(L068) Lowie, Robert H. "Alleged Kiowa-Crow Affinities." *Southwest Journal of Anthropology* 9 (1953): 357–368.

(L070) De Laguna, Frederica. "Some Dynamic Forces in Tlingit Society." *Southwest Journal of Anthropology* 8 (1952): 1–12.

(L071) Levi-Strauss, Claude. "Kinship Systems of Three Chittagong Hill Tribes (Pakistan)." *Southwest Journal of Anthropology* 8 (1952): 40–51.

(L072) Lesser, Alexander. "Evolution in Social Anthropology." *Southwest Journal of Anthropology* 8 (1952): 134–146.

(L073) Li, An-che. "Dege: A Study of Tibetan Population." *Southwest Journal of Anthropology* 3 (1947): 279–293.

(L074) Lowie, Robert H. "A Note on Lapp Culture History." *Southwest Journal of Anthropology* 1 (1945): 447–454.

(L076) Lienhardt. Godfrey. "Anuak Village Headsmen." *Africa* 28 (1958): 23–36.

(L077) Lewis, I. M. "Modern Political Movement in Somaliland." *Africa* 28 (1958): 244–261.

(L079) Little, Kenneth L. "The Changing Position of Women in the Sierra Leone Protectorate." *Africa* 18 (1948):.1–17.

(L080) Laydevant, F. "La coutume du Hlonepho." *Africa* 16 (1946): 83–91.

(L082) Labouret, Henri. "Situation matérielle, morale et coutumière de la femme dans l'ouest Afrique." *Africa* 13 (1940): 79–124.

(L088) Lugard, Lord. "Slavery in All Its Forms." *Africa* 6 (1933): 1–14.

(L091) Lestrade, G. P. "Some Notes on the Political Organization of the Vendea-Speaking Tribes." *Africa* 3 (1930): 306–322.

(L093) Labouret, Henri. "Le coton et l'indigène." *Africa* 1 (1928): 320–337.

(L099) Lommel, Andreas. "Modern Culture Influences on the Aborigines." *Oceania* 21 (1950–1951): 14–24.

(L100) Lester, R. H. "Betrothal and Marriage Customs of Mbau, Fiji." *Oceania* 10 (1939–1940): 273–285.

(L101) Leach, E. R. "Aspects of Bride-Wealth and Marriage Stability Among the Kachin and Lakher." *Man* 57 (1957): 50–55.

(L103) Loeb, Edwin M. "Mentawei Social Organization." *American Anthropologist* 30 (1928): 408–433.

(L108) Lutz, H. F. "Kinship in Babylonia, Assyria and Egypt." *American Anthropologist* 26 (1924): 435–453.

(L109) Leach, E. R. "Concerning Trobriand Clans and the Kinship Category 'Tabu.'" In *The Developmental Cycle in Domestic Groups.* Cambridge: Cambridge University Press, 1958, pp. 120–145.

(L110) Lowie, Robert H. *Social Organization.* New York: Rinehart and Co., 1948.

(L111) Lowie, Robert H. *The Crow Indians.* New York: Farrar and Rinehart, 1935.

(L112) Lewis, I. M. *Peoples of the Horn of Africa.* London: International African Institute, 1955.

(L113) Lawrence, J. C. D. *The Iteso.* Oxford: Oxford University Press, 1957.

(L114) Lidz, Theodore, Cornelison, Alice R., Flick, Stephen, and Terry, Dorothy. "Schism and Skew in the Families of Schizophrenics." In *Modern Introduction to the Family,* edited by Norman W. Bell and Ezra F. Vogel. Glencoe, Ill.: The Free Press, 1960, pp. 595–601.

(L115) Lipset, Seymour Martin, and Bendix, Reinhard. *Social Mobility in Industrial Society.* Berkeley: University of California Press, 1960.

(L116) Litwak, Eugene. "Divorce Law as Social Control." In *Modern Introduction to the Family,* edited by Norman W. Bell and Ezra F. Vogel. Glencoe, Ill.: The Free Press, 1960, 208–217.

(L117) Levy, David M. *Maternal Overprotection.* New York: Columbia University Press, 1943.

(L118) Lyeketsos, George C. "On the Formation of Mother-Daughter Symbiotic Relationship Patterns in Schizophrenia." *Psychiatry* 22 (1959): 161–166.

(L119) Lidz, Theodore. "Schizophrenia and the Family." *Psychiatry* 21 (1958): 21–27.

(L120) Lowrey, L. G. "Psychopathic Behavior in Infants and Children: A Critical Survey of the Existing Concepts." *American Journal of Orthopsychiatry* 21 (1951): 223–272.

(L121) Lennard, Henry L., Beaulieu, Maurice R., and Embre, Nolan. *Characteristics of Interaction Patterns in Families with a Schizophrenic Child.* Mimeo, 1963.

(L122) Linch, Albert. "Certain Cultural Influences on a Group of Clinic Patients." *Psychiatry* 21 (1958): 301–305.

(L123) Lidz, Theodore, Cornelison, Alice R., Fleck, Stephen, and Terry, Dorothy. "The Intrafamilial Environment of the Schizophrenic Patient: 1. The Father." *Psychiatry* 20 (1957): 329–342.

(L124) Leighton, Alexander H. "Psychiatric Disorder and Social Environment." *Psychiatry* 18 (1955): 367–383.

(L125) Limentani, Davide. "Symbiotic Identification in Schizophrenia." *Psychiatry* 19 (1956): 231–236.

(L126) Lu, Yi-Chuang. "Mother-Child Role Relationships in Schizophrenia." *Psychiatry* 24 (1961): 133–142.

(L127) Little, K. L. *The Mende of Sierra Leone: A West African People in Transition.* London: Routledge & Kegan Paul, 1951.

(L128) Lowie, Robert H. *Lowie's Selected Papers in Anthropology,* edited by Cora Du Bois. Berkeley: University of California Press, 1960.

(L129) Lystand, Robert A. "Marriage and Kinship Among the Ashanti and Agni." In *Continuity and Change in African Cultures,* edited by William R. Bascom and Melville J. Herskovits. Chicago: University of Chicago Press, 1958.

(L130) Lane, Barbara S. "Varieties of Cross-Cousin Marriage and Incest Taboos: Structure and Causality." In *Essays in the Science of Culture,* edited by Gertrude E. Dole and Robert L. Caniero. New York: T. Y. Crowell, 1960.

(L132) Lewis, H. "The Changing Negro Family." In *The Nation's Children,* edited by Eli Ginzberg, pp. 108–137. New York: Columbia University Press, 1960.

(L133) Levine, Robert A. "Africa." In *Psychological Anthropology,* edited by Francis L. K. Hsu. Homewood, Ill.: Dorsey Press, 1961.

(L134) Ackerman, Nathan W. *The Psychodynamics of Family Life.* New York: Basic Books, 1958.

(L135) Loesch, J. G., and Greenberg, N. H. "Some Specific Areas of Conflicts Observed During Pregnancy: A Comparative Study of Married and Unmarried Pregnant Women." *American Journal of Orthopsychiatry* 32 (1962): 624–636.

(L136) Lansky, L. M., Grandall, V. J., Kaga, J., and Baker, C. T. "Sex Differences in Aggression and Its Correlates in Middle-Class Adolescents." *Child Development* 32 (1961): 45–50.

(L137) Landis, Judson. "A Re-Examination of the Role of the Father as an Index of Family Integration." *Marriage and Family Living* 24 (May 1962): 122–128.

(L138) Lynn, David. "Sex Role and Parental Identification." *Child Development* 33 (1962): 155–163.

(L139) Lidz, Theodore, and Fleck, Stephen. "Schizophrenia, Human Integration, and the Role of the Family."

In *The Etiology of Schizophrenia,* edited by Don D. Jackson. New York: Basic Books, 1960.

(L140) Luckey, Eleanore Braun. "Marital Satisfaction and Parent Concepts." *Journal of Consulting Psychology* 24 (June 1960): 195–204.

(L141) Lambert, William W., Triandis, Leigh Minturn, and Wolf, Margery. "Some Correlates of Beliefs in the Malevolence and Benevolence of Supernatural Beings: A Cross-Societal Study." *Journal of Abnormal and Social Psychology* 58 (1959): 162–169.

(L141) Lynn, David B. "Divergent Feedback and Sex-Role Identification in Boys and Men." *Merrill–Palmer Quarterly* 10 (January 1964): 17–23.

(L142) Lefkowitz, Monroe M. "Some Relationships Between Sex Role Preference of Children and Other Parent and Child Variables." *Psychological Reports* 10 (February 1962): 43–53.

(L143) Leventhal, Theodore, and Sills, Malcolm. "Self-Image in School Phobia." *American Journal of Orthopsychiatry* 34, No. 4 (1964): 685–695.

(L144) Liverant, S. "MMPI Differences Between Parents of Disturbed and Nondisturbed Children." *Journal of Consulting Psychology* 23, No. 3 (1959): 256–260.

(L144) Lucas, Leon. "Family Influences and Schizophrenic Reaction." *American Journal of Orthopsychiatry* 34, No. 3 (1964): 527–535.

(L145) Luria, Zella. "A Semantic Analysis of a Normal and a Neurotic Therapy Group." *Journal of Abnormal and Social Psychology* 58 (September 1959): 216–220.

(L146) Laske, Joan K. "Parent-Child Relationships: Report from the Fels Research Institute." *American Journal of Orthopsychiatry* 22 (April 1952): 300–304.

(L147) Levin, Harry, and Turgeon, Valerie F. "The Influence of the Mother's Presence on Children's Doll Play Aggression." *Journal of Abnormal and Social Psychology* 55 (November 1957): 304–308.

(L148) Liccione, John V. "The Changing Family Relationships of Adolescent Girls." *Journal of Abnormal and Social Psychology* 51 (November 1955): 421–426.

(L149) Lyle, William H., and Levitt, Eugene E. "Punitiveness, Authoritarianism, and Parental Discipline of Grade School Children." *Journal of Abnormal and Social Psychology* 51 (July 1955): 42–46.

(L150) Linton, H., *et al.* "Reactions of Children Within Family Groups as Measured by the Bene-Anthony Tests." *Journal of Mental Science* 107 (1961): 308–325.

(L151) Luft, J. "Psychological Control Patterns Within Families." *Journal of Consulting Psychology* 21 (1957): 206.

(L152) Luckey, Eleanore Braun. "Perceptual Congruence of Self and Family Concepts as Related to Marital Interaction." *Sociometry* 24 (September 1961): 234–250.

(L153) Lustig, Hanna Lowe. "The Infertility Problem in Adoption." *Smith College Studies in Social Work* 30 (June 1960): 235–251.

(L154) Luckey, Eleanore Braun. "Marital Satisfaction and Personality Correlates of Spouse." *Journal of Marriage and Family Living* 26 (May 1964): 217–222.

(L155) Lane, Robert C., and Singer, J. L. "Familial Attitudes in Paranoid Schizophrenics and Normals from Two Socioeconomic Classes." *Journal of Abnormal and Social Psychology* 59 (November 1959): 328–339.

(L156) Lynn, David B., and Sawrey, William L. "The Effects of Father-Absence on Norwegian Boys and Girls." *Journal of Abnormal and Social Psychology* 59 (September 1959): 258–262.

(L157) Levin, H., and Sears, R. "Identification with Parents as a Determinant of Doll Play Aggression." *Child Development* 27 (June 1956): 135–153.

(L158) Luria, Zella, Goldwasser, Miriam, and Goldwasser, Adena. "Response to Transgression in Stories by Israeli Children." *Child Development* 34, No. 2 (1963): 271–280.

(L159) De Lint, Jan E. E. "Alcoholism, Birth Rank, and Parental Deprivation." *American Journal of Psychiatry* 120 (May 1964): 1062–1065.

(L160) Lasko, Joan Kalhorn. "Parent Behavior Toward First and Second Children." *Genetic Psychology Monographs* 49 (February 1954): 97–137.

(L161) Levy, David M. "Maternal Overprotection." *Psychiatry* 4 (1941): 393–438.

(L162) Levy, David M. "Maternal Overprotection." *Psychiatry* 2 (1939): 99–128.

(L163) Levy, David M. "Maternal Overprotection." *Psychiatry* 2 (1939): 563–597.

(L164) Levy, David M. "Maternal Overprotection." *Psychiatry* 1 (1938): 561–591.

(L165) Levy, David M. and Hess, Audrey. "Problems in Determining Maternal Attitudes Toward Newborn Infants." *Psychiatry* 15 (1952): 273–286.

(L166) La Barre, Weston. "Some Observations on Character Structure in the Orient." *Psychiatry* 8 (1945): 319–342.

(L167) La Barre, Weston. "Some Observations on Character Structure in the Orient." *Psychiatry* 9 (1946): 215–237.

(L168) Levin, A. J. "The Oedipus Myth in History and Psychiatry." *Psychiatry* 11 (1948): 283–299.

(L169) Lynn, R., and Gordon, I. E. "Maternal Attitudes to Child Socialization: Some Social and National Differences." *British Journal of Social and Clinical Psychology* 1, No. 1 (1962): 52–55.

(L170) Leichty, Mary M. "The Effect of Father-Absence During Early Childhood upon the Oedipal Situation as Reflected in Young Adults." *Merrill–Palmer Quarterly* 6 (July 1960): 212–217.

(L171) Lynn, David B. "The Husband-Father Role in the Family." *Marriage and Family Living* 23 (August 1961): 295–296.

(L172) LeShan, Lawrence, and LeShan, Eda J. "Some Recent Trends in Social Science Research Relevant to Parent Education." *Marriage and Family Living* 23 (February 1961): 31–37.

(L173) Levinger, George. "Task and Social Behavior in Marriage." *Sociometry* 27 (1964): 433–448.

(L174) Leach, E. R. *Political Systems of Highland Burma.* Cambridge: Harvard University Press, 1954.

(L175) LeVine, Robert A., and Sangree, Walter H. "The Diffusion of Age-Group Organization in East Africa." *Africa* 32 (1962): 97–110.

(L176) Lane, Barbara S. "Structural Contrasts Between Symmetric and Asymmetric Marriage Systems." *Southwest Journal of Anthropology* 17 (1961): 49–55.

(L177) Leach, Edmund. "Asymmetric Marriage Rules, Status Difference, and Direct Reciprocity: Comments on an Alleged Fallacy." *Southwest Journal of Anthropology* 17 (1961): 343–351.

(L178) Loffler, Lorenz G. "The Development of the Ambrym and Pentecost Kinship Systems." *Southwest Journal of Anthropology* 16 (1960): 442–462.

(L179) Lane, Robert E. "Fathers and Sons: Foundations of Political Belief." *American Sociological Review* 24 (1959): 502–511.

(L180) Leik, Robert K. "Instrumentality and Emotionality

in Family Interaction." *Sociometry* 26 (1963): 131–145.

(L181) Litwak, Eugene. "Geographic Mobility and Extended Family Cohesion." *American Sociological Review* 25 (1960): 385–394.

(L182) Luckey, Eleanore Braun. "Perceptual Congruence of Self and Family Concepts as Related to Marital Interaction." *Sociometry* 24 (September 1961): 234–250.


(M001) Monahan, Thomas P., and Kephart, William M. "Divorce and Desertion by Religious and Mixed Religious Groups." *American Journal of Sociology* 59 (1954): 454–465.

(M009) Monahan, Thomas P. "Family Status and the Delinquent Child: A Reappraisal and Some New Findings." *Social Forces* 35 (1957): 250–258.

(M010) Martinson, Floyd M. "Ego Deficiency as a Factor in Marriage." *American Sociological Review* 20 (1955): 161–164.

(M011) Monahan, Thomas P. "Is Childlessness Related to Family Stability?" *American Sociological Review* 20 (1955): 446–456.

(M012) Mukherjee, Ramakrishna. "The Economic Structure and Social Life in Six Villages of Bengal." *American Sociological Review* 14 (1949): 415–425.

(M013) Monahan, Thomas P. "How Stable Are Remarriages?" *American Journal of Sociology* 58 (November 1952): 280–288.

(M014) Marches, Joseph R., and Turbeville, Gus. "The Effect of Residential Propinquity on Marriage Selection." *American Journal of Sociology* 58 (1953): 592–595.

(M015) Marcson, Simon. "A Theory of Intermarriage and Assimilation." *Social Forces* 29 (1950): 75–78.

(M016) Monahan, Thomas P. "Does Age at Marriage Matter in Divorce?" *Social Forces* 32, No. 1 (October 1953): 81–87.

(M019) Murdock, George T. *Social Structure.* New York: The MacMillan Co., 1949.

(M020) Murphy, Robert F. "Matrilocality and Patrilineality in Munburutu Society." *American Anthropologist* 58 (1956): 414–434.

(M021) Morris, H. F. "The Indian Family in Uganda." *American Anthropologist* 61 (1959): 779–789.

(M023) Murphy, Robert F., and Kasden, Leonard. The Structure of Parallel Cousin Marriage." *American Anthroplogist* 61 (1959): 17–29.

(M025) Mayer, Adrian C. "Associations in Fiji Indian Rural Society." *American Anthropologist* 58 (1956): 79–108.

(M026) Mischel, Walter. "Psychological Aspects of Spirit Possession." *American Anthropologist* 60 (1958): 249–260.

(M027) Murphy, Robert F. "Inter Group Hostility and Social Cohesion." *American Anthropologist* 59 (1957): 1018–1035.

(M029) Miller, Walter B. "Two Concepts of Authority." *American Anthropologist* 57 (1955): 271–289.

(M031) Mead, Margaret. "The Swaddling Hypothesis: Its Reception." *American Anthropologist* 56 (1954): 395–409.

(M032) Miller, Eric J. "Caste and Territory in Malabar." *American Anthropologist* 56 (1954): 410–420.

(M033) Meggers, Betty J. "Environmental Limitations on the Development of Culture." *American Anthropologist* 56 (1954): 801–824.

(M034) Millon, René S. "Trade, Tree Cultivation, and the Development of Private Property in Land." *American Anthropologist* 57 (1955): 698–712.

(M037) Marcson, Simon. "Some Methodological Consequences of Correlational Analysis in Anthropology." *American Anthropologist* 45 (1943): 588–601.

(M038) Miner, Horace. "Songhoi Circumcision." *American Anthropologist* 44 (1942): 621–637.

(M042) Murdock, George Peter. "Kinship and Social Behavior Among the Haida." *American Anthropologist* 36 (1934): 365–388.

(M043) Mead, Margaret. "More Comprehensive Field Methods." *American Anthropologist* 35 (1933): 1–15.

(M045) Murdock, George Peter. "Double Descent." *American Anthropologist* 42 (1940): 555–561.

(M046) Mercier, Paul. "The Social Role of Circumcision Among the Besorube." *American Anthropologist* 53 (1951): 326–337.

(M047) Murdock, George Peter. "Birfurcate Merging; A Test of Five Theories." *American Anthropologist* 49 (1947): 56–68.

(M048) Mandelbaum, David G. "Polyandry in Kota Society." *American Anthropologist* 40 (1938): 574–583.

(M050) Mair, Lucy P. "Marriage and Family in the Dedza District of Nyasaland." *Journal of the Royal Anthropological Institute* 81 (1951): 103–119.

(M051) Mills, J. P. "The Mishmis of the Lohit Valley, Assam." *Journal of the Royal Anthropological Institute* 82 (1952): 1–12.

(M054) Michel, Andrée Vielle. "Kinship Relations and Relationships of Proximity in French Working-Class Households." In *Modern Introduction to the Family,* edited by Norman W. Bell and Ezra F. Vogel. Glencoe, Ill.: The Free Press, 1960, 287–294.

(M056) Maccoby, Eleanor E., Matthews, Richard E. and Morton, Anton S. "The Family and the Political Behavior of Youth." In *Modern Introduction to the Family,* edited by Norman W. Bell and Ezra F. Vogel. Glencoe, Ill.: The Free Press, 1960, pp. 189–200.

(M058) Maccoby, Eleanor E. "Effects upon Children of Their Mothers' Outside Employment." In *Modern Introduction to the Family,* edited by Norman W. Bell and Ezra F. Vogel. Glencoe, Ill.: The Free Press, 1960, pp. 521–537.

(M058) Mead, Margaret. "A Two Relationship System." *Journal of the Royal Anthropological Institute* 67 (1937): 279–304.

(M059) Malcolm, L. W. G. "Notes on Birth, Marriage and Death Ceremony on the Egap Tribe, Central Cameroon." *Journal of the Royal Anthropological Institute* 53 (1923): 388–401.

(M060) McClelland, David C., Baldwin, Alfred L., Bronfenbrenner, Urie, and Strodtbeck, Fred L. *Talent and Society.* Princeton: D. Van Nostrand Company, Inc., 1958.

(M061) Myers, Jerome K., and Roberts, Bertram H. (eds.). *Family and Class Dynamics in Mental Illness.* New York: John Wiley and Sons, 1959.

(M062) Miller, Daniel R., and Swanson, Guy E. *The Changing American Parent.* New York: John Wiley & Sons, 1958.

(M063) Mead, Margaret. "The Role of the Individual in Samoan Culture." *Journal of the Royal Anthropological Institute* 58 (1928): 481–495.

(M066) Mayer, Adrian C. "The Dominant Paths in a Region of Central India." *Southwest Journal of Anthropology* 14 (1958): 407–427.

(M067) Murphy, Robert F. "Social Structure and Sex Antagonism." *Southwest Journal of Anthropology* 15 (1959): 87–98.

(M069) Merriam, Alan P. "The Concept of Culture Applied to the Belgian Congo." *Southwest Journal of Anthropology* 15 (1959): 374–395.

(M070) Miles, F. W. "Maya Settlement Patterns: A Problem for Ethnology and Archaeology." *Southwest Journal of Anthropology* 13 (1957): 239–248.

(M071) Murdock, George Peter. "Changing Emphasis in Social Structure." *Southwest Journal of Anthropology* 11 (1955): 361–370.

(M072) McClellan, Catharine. "The Interrelation of Social Structure with Northern Tlingit Ceremonialism." *Southwest Journal of Anthropology* 10 (1954): 75–96.

(M075) Mayer, Adrian C. "Some Hierarchical Aspects of Caste." *Southwest Journal of Anthropology* 12 (1956): 117–144.

(M076) Miller, Beatrice D. "Ganye and Kidu: Two Formalized Systems of Mutual Aid Among the Tibetans." *Southwest Journal of Anthropology* 12 (1956): 157–170.

(M077) Mickey, Barbara H. "Acoma Kinship Terms." *Southwest Journal of Anthropology* 12 (1956): 249–256.

(M079) Murdock, David P. "South American Culture Areas." *Southwest Journal of Anthropology* 7 (1951): 416–436.

(M080) Mintz, Sidney W., and Wolf, Eric R. "An Analysis of Ritual Co-Parenthood (Compadrazgo)." *Southwest Journal of Anthropology* 6 (1950): 341–368.

(M081) Mandelbaum, David G. "The Family in India." *Southwest Journal of Anthropology* 4 (1948): 123–139.

(M082) Murdock, George P., and Goodenough, Ward H. "Social Organization of Truk." *Southwest Journal of Anthropology* 3 (1947): 331–359.

(M084) Mitchell, J. Clyde, and Epstein, A. L. "Occupational Prestige and Social Status Among Urban Africans in Northern Rhodesia." *Africa* 29 (1959): 22–40.

(M085) Marshall, Lorna. "Marriage: Kung Bushmen." *Africa* 29 (1959): 335–365.

(M086) Mitchell, Sir Philip. "The Survey of African Marriage and Family Life." *Africa* 24 (1954): 149–156.

(M092) Mercier, P. "Le consentement au mariage et son évolution chez les Betammadibe." *Africa* 20 (1950): 219–229.

(M095) Matthews, Z. K. "Marriage Customs Among the Barolong." *Africa* 13 (1940): 1–24.

(M099) Marwick, M. G. "The Social Context of Tewa Witch Belief." *Africa* 22 (1952): 97–119.

(M102) Meekel, H. Scudden. "Social Administration of the Kru." *Africa* 10 (1937): 75–96.

(M105) Meek, C. K. "Marriage by Exchange in Nigeria." *Africa* 9 (1936): 64–74.

(M109) Meek, C. K. "The Kulu in Northern Nigeria." *Africa* 7 (1934): 257–269.

(M114) Mair, L. P. "Native Land Tenure in East Africa." *Africa* 4 (1931): 314–329.

(M120) Marshall, Lorna. "The Kin Terminology System of the Kung Bushmen." *Africa* 27 (1957): 1–25.

(M122) Maquet, Jacques J. "Les groupes de parente du Rwanda ancien." *Africa* 23 (1953): 25–29.

(M124) Matson, J. N. "Testate Succession in Ashanti." *Africa* 23 (1953): 224–232.

(M125) Mitchell, J. C. "The Yao of Southern Nyasaland." *Africa* 19 (1949): 94–100.

(M126) Maquet, Jacques J. "The Modern Evolution of African Populations in the Belgian Congo." *Africa* 19 (1949): 265–272.

(M127) Mitchell, J. Clyde. "An Estimate of Fertility in Some Yao Hamlets in Liwonde District of Southern Nyasaland." *Africa* 19 (1949): 293–308.

(M128) Meggitt, M. J. "The Ipili of the Porgera Valley, Western Highlands District, Territory of New Guinea." *Oceania* 28 (1957–1958): 31–55.

(M129) Meggitt, M. J. "The Enga of the New Guinea Highlands: Some Preliminary Observations." *Oceania* 28 (1957–1958): 253–330.

(M130) McConnel, Ursula H. "Junior Marriage Systems: A Comparative Survey." *Oceania* 21 (1950–1951): 107–145.

(M131) Mayer, Adrian C. "Fiji Indians Kin-Group: An Aspect of Change in an Immigrant Society." *Oceania* 24 (1953–1954): 161–171.

(M136) McConnel, Ursula H. "Social Organization of the Tribes of Cape York Peninsula, North Queensland." *Oceania* 10 (1939–1940): 434–455.

(M137) McConnel, Ursula, H. "The Wik-Munkan and Allied Tribes of Cape York Peninsula, North Queensland." *Oceania* 4 (1933–1934): 310–356.

(M144) Meggitt, M. J. "The Valleys of the Upper Wage and Lai Rivers, Western Highlands, New Guinea." *Oceania* 27 (1956–1957): 90–135.

(M150) Mears, W. G. A. "The Educated Native in Bantu Communal Life." In *Western Civilization and the Natives of South Africa,* edited by Isaac Schapera. New York: Humanities Press, 1967.

(M163) Miller, Derek H. "Family Interaction in the Therapy of Adolescent Patients." *Psychiatry* 21 (1958): 277–284.

(M164) McCord, William, Porta, Judith, and McCord, Joan. "The Familial Genesis of Psychosis." *Psychiatry* 25 (1962): 60–71.

(M165) Meyer, Joachim-Ernst. "Depersonalization in Adolescence." *Psychiatry* 24 (1961): 360–375.

(M166) March, James G., and Simon, Herbert A. *Organizations.* New York: John Wiley & Sons, 1958.

(M167) Moller, Herbert. "The Social Causation of the Courtly Love Complex." *Comparative Studies in Society and History* 1 (1958–1959): 137–163.

(M168) Middleton, John, and Trait, David. *Tribes Without Rulers.* London: Routledge and Kegan Paul, 1958.

(M169) Maquet, Jacques J. *The Premise of Inequality in Ruanda.* Published for the National African Institute. London: Oxford University Press, 1961.

(M170) McCall, Daniel F. "Dynamics of Urbanization in Africa." In *Cultures and Socieites of Africa,* edited by Simon and Phoebe Ottenberg. New York: Random House, 1960.

(M171) Murdock, George Peter. *Africa.* New York: McGraw-Hill Book Co., 1959.

(M172) Mussen, Paul, and Jones, M. "Self Conceptions, Motivations, and Interpersonal Attitudes of Late- and Early-Maturing Boys." *Child Development* 28 (June 1957): 243–256.

(M173) Malinowski, Bronislaw. "Sex and Repression." Reprinted in *Family: Its Structure and Functions,* edited by R. L. Coser. New York: St. Martin's Press, 1964, pp. 449–454.

(M174) Morrow, W. R., and Wilson, R. C. "Family Relations of Bright High-Achieving and Under-Achieving High School Boys." *Child Development* 32, No. 3 (1961): 501–510.

(M175) Medinnus, Gene R. "Q-Sort Descriptions of Five-Year-Old Children by Their Parents." *Child Development* 32, No. 3 (1961): 473–489.

(M176) McCandless, Boyd R., Bilous, C. B., and Bennett,

H. L. "Peer Popularity and Dependence on Adults in Preschool-Age Socialization." *Child Development* 32, No. 3 (1961): 511–518.

(M177) Morgan, P., and Grier, E. "The Direction of Aggression in the Mother-Child Punishment Situation." *Child Development* 27 (December 1956): 447–457.

(M178) Mummery, Dorothy V. "Family Backgrounds of Assertive and Non-Assertive Children." *Child Development* 25 (March 1954): 63–80.

(M179) Maccoby, Eleanor E. "The Taking of Adult Roles in Middle Childhood." *Journal of Abnormal and Social Psychology* 63, No. 3 (1961): 493–503.

(M180) Mehlman, B., et al. "Child-Rearing Practices in Kent, Ohio." *Child Development* 33 (1962): 391–401.

(M181) McCord, Joan, McCord, William, and Thurber, Emily. "Some Effects of Paternal Absence on Male Children." *Journal of Abnormal and Social Psychology* 64 (May 1964): 361–369.

(M182) Marshall, H., and Magruder, L. "Relations Between Parent Money Education Practices and Children's Knowledge and Use of Money." *Child Development* 31 (1960): 253–284.

(M183) Mussen, Paul and Distler, L. "Child-Rearing Antecedents of Masculine Identification in Boys." *Child Development* 31 (1960): 80–100.

(M184) Mussen, Paul, and Kagan, Jerome. "Group Conformity and Perceptions of Parents." *Child Development* 29 (March 1958): 57–60.

(M185) Mace, David. "Some Reflections on the American Family." *Marriage and Family Living* 24 (May 1962): 109–112.

(M186) Milton, G. A. "A Factor Analytic Study of Child-Rearing Behaviors." *Child Development* 29 (1958): 381–392.

(M187) McClelland, David C. "The Importance of Early Learning in the Formation of Motives." In *Motives in Fantasy, Action, and Society: A Method of Assessment and Study,* edited by John W. Atkinson. Princeton: D. Van Nostrand Company, Inc., 1958, pp. 437–452.

(M188) Mead, Margaret. "The Young Adult." In *Values and Ideals of American Youth,* edited by Eli Ginzberg. New York: Columbia University Press, 1961, pp, 37–51.

(M189) Malzberg, Benjamin. "A Statistical Study of First Admissions with Psychoneuroses in New York State, 1949–1951." *American Journal of Psychiatry* 116 (August 1959): 152–157.

(M190) Murstein, Bernard I. "The Complementary Need Hypothesis in Newlyweds and Middle-Aged Married Couples." *Journal of Abnormal and Social Psychology* 63 (July 1961): 194–197.

(M191) Medinnus, Gene R. "The Relation Between Parental Prescriptions for Child and Parent Roles." *The Journal of Social Psychology* 60 (June 1963): 101–106.

(M192) Maas, Henry S., and Engler, Richard E. *Children in Need of Parents.* New York: Columbia University Press, 1959.

(M193) Markham, Sylvia. "A Comparative Evaluation of Psychotic and Nonpsychotic Reactions to Childbirth." *American Journal of Orthopsychiatry* 31 (1961): 565–578.

(M194) McCord, William, McCord, Joan, and Zola, I. K. *Origins of Crime.* New York: Columbia University Press, 1959.

(M195) McCord, William, and McCord, Joan. *Origins of Alcoholism.* Stanford: Stanford University Press, 1960.

(M196) Monahan, Thomas P. "Broken Homes by Age of Delinquent Children." *Journal of Social Psychology* 51 (1960): 387–397.

(M197) Myers, J., and Roberts, B. *Family and Class Dynamics in Mental Illness.* New York: John Wiley and Sons, 1959.

(M198) Marris, R. *Family and Social Change in an African City.* Evanston, Ill.: Northwestern University Press, 1962.

(M199) McCord, Joan, and McCord, William. "The Effects of Parental Role Model on Criminality." *Journal of Social Issues* 14, No. 3 (1958): 66–75.

(M200) McDonald, R. "Intrafamilial Conflict and Emotional Disturbance." *The Journal of Genetic Psychology* 101 (1962): 201–208.

(M201) Marina, Ramon Fernandez, Sierra, Eduardo D. Maldonado, and Trent, Richard D. "Three Basic Themes in Mexican and Puerto Rican Family Values." *Journal of Social Psychology* 46 (November 1958): 167–182.

(M201) Maxwell, Patricia Henderson, Connor, Ruth, and Walters, James. "Family Member Perceptions of Parent Role Performance." *Merrill–Palmer Quarterly* 7 (January 1961): 31–37.

(M202) McClelland, David C. (ed.) *Studies in Motivation.* New York: Appleton-Century-Crofts, Inc., 1955, 278–286.

(M203) Mead, Margaret, and Wolfenstein, M. *Childhood in Contemporary Cultures.* Chicago: University of Chicago Press, 1955.

(M204) Mussen, Paul, Young, H. Boutoutline, Gaddini, R., and Morante, L. "The Influence of Father-Son Relationships on Adolescent Personality and Attitudes." *Journal of Child Psychology and Psychiatry* 4 (1963): 3–16.

(M205) Morris, Ruth. "Female Delinquency and Relational Problems." *Social Forces* 43 (October 1964): 82–89.

(M206) Mussen, Paul, and Rutherford, Eldred. "Parent-Child Relations and Parental Personality in Relation to Young Children's Sex-Role Preferences." *Child Development* 34 (1963): 589–607.

(M207) Mischel, Walter. "Father-Absence and Delay of Gratification: Cross-Cultural Comparisons." *Journal of Abnormal and Social Psychology* 63 (July 1961): 116–124.

(M208) Madoff, J. "The Attitudes of Mothers of Juvenile Delinquents Toward Child Rearing." *Journal of Consulting Psychology* 23, No: 6 (1959): 518–520.

(M209) McCord, William, McCord, Joan, and Verden, Paul. "Family Relationships and Sexual Deviance in Lower-Class Adolescents." *International Journal of Social Psychiatry* 8 (1962): 165–179.

(M210) McCord, Joan, McCord, William, and Howard, Alan. "Family Interaction as Antecedent to the Direction of Male Aggressiveness." *Journal of Abnormal and Social Psychology* 66 (March 1963): 239–242.

(M211) McCord, Joan, McCord, William, and Thurber, Emily. "Effects of Maternal Employment on Lower-Class Boys." *Journal of Abnormal and Social Psychology* 67 (August 1963): 177–182.

(M212) Mesnikoff, A., et al. "Intrafamilial Determinants of Divergent Sexual Behavior in Twins." *American Journal of Psychiatry* 119 (1963): 732–738.

(M213) Maxwell, A. "Discrepancies Between the Pattern of Abilities for Normal and Neurotic Children." *Journal of Mental Science* 107 (1961): 300–307.

(M214) Marsten, B., and Coleman, J. "Specificity of Attitudes Toward Paternal and Non-Parental Authority Figures." *Journal of Individual Psychology* 17 (1961): 96–101.

(M215) Middleton, R., and Putney, S. "Dominance in Decisions in the Family: Race and Class Differences." *American Journal of Sociology* 65 (1959–1960): 605–609.

(M216) Minturn, Leigh, and Lambert, William W. *Mothers of Six Cultures.* New York: John Wiley and Sons, Inc., 1964.

(M217) McCord, Joan, and McCord, William. "Cultural Stereotypes and the Validity of Interviews for Research in Child Development." *Child Development* 32 (1961): 171–185.

(M218) McGhie, A. "A Comparative Study of the Mother-Child Relationship in Schizophrenia." *British Journal of Medical Psychology* 34 (1961): 195–221.

(M219) Malzberg, B. "Marital Status and Mental Disease Among Negroes in New York State." *The Journal of Nervous and Mental Disease* 123 (1956): 457–465.

(M220) Mussen, Paul. "Some Antecedents and Consequents of Masculine Sex-Typing in Adolescent Boys." *Psychological Monographs* 76, No. 2 (1961): 1–24.

(M221) McCord, William, McCord, Joan, and Verden, Paul. "Familial and Behavioral Correlates of Dependency in Male Children." *Child Development* 33 (March–December 1962): 313–326.

(M222) Mosher, D., and Scodel, A. "Relationships Between Ethnocentrism in Children and the Ethnocentrism and Authoritarian Rearing Practices of Their Mothers." *Child Development* 31 (1960): 369–376.

(M223) Murray, David C. "An Investigation of One Town's Opinion Relative to the Problems of Child Guidance." *Child Development* 20 (June 1949): 79–100.

(M224) McCandless, Boyd R. "Psychosocial Development of Personality." *Child Development* 20 (September 1949): 123–129.

(M225) Mussen, Paul, and Rutherford, Eldred. "Parent-Child Relations and Parental Personality in Relation to Young Children's Sex-Role Preferences." *Child Development* 34 (September 1963): 589–607.

(M226) Montagu, M. F. Ashley. "Nescience, Science and Psychoanalysis." *Psychiatry* 4 (1941): 45–60.

(M227) Merton, Robert K. "Intermarriage and the Social Structure: Fact and Theory." *Psychiatry* 4 (1941): 361–374.

(M228) Martin, Peter A., and Bird, H. Waldo. "An Approach to the Psychotherapy of Marriage Partners." *Psychiatry* 16 (1953): 123–127.

(M229) Miller, Esther. "Some Hypotheses Concerning the Influence of Segregation of Negro Personality Development." *Psychiatry* 16 (1953): 291–297.

(M230) Montagu, M. F. Ashley. "Some Factors in Family Cohesion." *Psychiatry* 7 (1944): 349–352.

(M231) Moss, J. Joel, and Gingles, Ruby. "Teen-Age Marriage: The Teacher's Challenge." *Marriage and Family Living* 23 (May 1961): 187–190.

(M232) Martinson, F. "Ego Deficiency as a Factor in Marriage: A Male Sample." *Marriage and Family Living* 21 (1959): 48–52.

(M233) Mead, Margaret. "The Mountain Arapesh." *Anthropological Papers of the American Museum of Natural History* 36 (1938).

(M234) Maybury-Lewis, David, "Parallel Descent and the Apinaye Anomaly." *Southwest Journal of Anthropology* 16 (1960): 191–216.

(M235) McClellan, Catharine. "Avoidance Between Siblings of the Same Sex in Northwestern North America." *Southwest Journal of Anthropology* 17 (1961): 103–124.

(M236) Mednick, Sarnoff A., and Shaffer, John B. P. "Mothers' Retrospective Reports in Child Rearing Research." *American Journal of Orthopsychiatry* 33 (April 1963): 457–461.

(M237) Meyers, Donald I., and Goldfarb, William. "Studies of Perplexity in Mothers of Schizophrenic Children." *American Journal of Orthopsychiatry* 31 (1961): 551–564.

(M238) Malinowski, Bronislaw. *The Argonauts of the Western Pacific.* New York: Dutton and Co., 1953.

(M239) Macleod, William Christie. "On the Significance of Matrilineal Chieftainship." *American Anthropologist* 31 (1921): 495–524.

(M240) Mair, Lucy. *An African People in the 20th Century.* New York: George Routledge and Sons, 1934.

(M241) Malinowski, Bronislaw. *The Sexual Life of Savages in (Northwestern) Melanesia.* New York: Harcourt, Brace and World, 1929.

(M242) Mohanan, Thomas P. "The Changing Nature and Instability of Remarriages." *Eugenics Quarterly* 5 (1958): 75–85.

(M243) Mohanan, Thomas P. "Premarital Pregnancy in the United States: A Critical Review and Some New Findings." *Eugenics Quarterly* 7 (1960): 133–147.

(M244) Mead, Margaret. "Social Organization of Manua." *Bishop Museum Bulletin* 76 (1930).

(M245) Mead, Margaret. "The Mountain Arapesh." *Anthropological Papers of the American Museum of Natural History* 40 (1947).

(M246) McClelland, David C. *The Achieving Society.* Princeton: D. Van Nostrand Company, Inc., 1961.

(M247) McCord, William, McCord, Joan, and Howard, Alan. "Early Family Experiences and Bigotry." *American Sociological Review* 25 (1960): 717–722.

(M248) Miles, Douglas. "The Ngadju Longhouse." *Oceania* 31 (1964): 45–57.

(N006) Nakane, Chie. "Changes in Matrilineal Families in Assam" (Institute for Oriental Culture, University of Tokyo). In *Transactions of the Third World Congress of Sociology,* Vol. 4, *Changes in the Family,* 231–235. London: Internation Sociological Association, 1956.

(N008) Nadel, S. F. "Two Nuba Religions: An Essay in Comparison." *American Anthropologist* 57 (1955): 661–679.

(N010) Nye, F. Ivan. "Adolescent-Parent Adjustment: Socioeconomic Level as a Variable." *American Sociological Review* 16 (1951): 341–349.

(N011) Norbeck, Edward, and Befu, Harumi. "Informal Fictive Kinship in Japan." *American Anthropologist* 60 (1958): 102–117.

(N013) Nash, Manning. "The Multiple Society in Economic Development: Mexico and Guatemala." *American Anthropologist* 59 (1957): 825–833.

(N014) Newell, W. H. "Family Quarrels in a North Malayan Teochiu Chinese Vegetable-Growing Community." *American Anthropologist* 59 (1957): 266–277.

(N015) Nadel, S. F. "Witchcraft in Four African Societies: An Essay in Comparison." *American Anthropologist* 54 (1952): 18–29.

(N016) Norbeck, Edward. "Age-Grading in Japan." *American Anthropologist* 55 (1953): 373–384.

(N017) Nimuendaju, Christ, and Lowie, Robert H. "The

Dual Organization of the Ramko Kamekra (Canella) of Northern Brazil." *American Anthropologist* 39 (1937): 565–582.

(N020) Newell, W. H. "The Brahman and Caste Exogamy in North India." *Journal of the Royal Anthropological Institute* 85 (1955): 101–110.

(N023) Needham, Rodney. "The Formal Analysis of Prescriptive Patrilateral Cross-Cousin Marriage." *Southwest Journal of Anthropology* 14 (1958): 199–219.

(N024) Needham, Rodney. "Vaiphei Social Structure." *Southwest Journal of Anthropology* 15 (1959): 396–406.

(N026) Needham, Rodney. "Siriono and Penan: A Test of Some Hypotheses." *Southwest Journal of Anthropology* 10 (1954): 228–232.

(N027) Needham, Rodney. "The System of Teknonyms and Death-Names of the Penan." *Southwest Journal of Anthropology* 10 (1954): 416–431.

(N028) Nagai, Michio, and Bennett, John W. "A Summary and Analysis of 'The Familial Structure of Japanese Society' by Takeyoshi Kawashima." *Southwest Journal of Anthropology* 9 (1953): 239–250.

(N030) Nett, Betty R. "Historical Changes in the Osage Kinship System." *Southwest Journal of Anthropology* 8 (1952): 164–181.

(N034) Nadel, S. F. "Land Tenure on the Eritrean Plateau." *Africa* 16 (1946): 1–22.

(N041) Nilles, John. "The Kuman of the Chimbu Region, Central Highlands, New Guinea." *Oceania* 21 (1950–1951: 25–65.

(N045) Nilles, J. "Natives of the Bismarck Mountains, New Guinea." *Oceania* 15 (1944–1945): 1–18.

(N046) Nayacakalou, R. R. "The Fijian System of Kinship of Marriage." *Polynesia* 66 (1957): 44–59.

(N048) Nayacakalou, R. R. "The Fijian System of Kinship and Marriage." *Polynesia* 64 (1955): 44–55.

(N049) Naegele, Kaspar D. "Some Problems in the Study of Hostility and Aggression in Middle-Class American Families." In *Modern Introduction to the Family,* edited by Norman W. Bell and Ezra F. Vogel. Glencoe, Ill.: The Free Press, 1960, pp. 417–428.

(N050) Novey, Samuel. "The Out-Patient Treatment of Borderline Paranoia States." *Psychiatry* 23 (1960): 357–364.

(N051) Newton, Niles. *Maternal Emotions.* New York: Paul B. Hoeber, Inc., 1955.

(N052) Nye, F. Ivan. *Family Relationships and Delinquent Behavior.* New York: John Wiley and Sons, 1958.

(N053) Nichols, R. "A Factor Analysis of Parental Attitudes of Fathers." *Child Development* 33 (1962): 791–802.

(N054) Nag, Moni. "Factors Affecting Human Fertility in Nonindustrial Societies: A Cross-Cultural Study." *Yale University Publications in Anthropology* 66 (1963).

(N055) Nottingham, R. "A Psychological Study of Forty Unmarried Mothers." *Genetic Psychology Monographs* 19 (May 1937): 155–228.

(N055) Nunn, Clyde Z. "Child-Control Through a 'Coalition with God.'" *Child Development* 35, No. 3 (1964): 417–432.

(N056) Norris, V. "A Statistical Study of the Influence of Marriage on the Hospital Care of the Mentally Sick." *Journal of Mental Science* 102 (1956): 467–486.

(N057) Nye, F. Ivan. *Family Relationships and Delinquent Behavior.* New York: John Wiley and Sons, 1958.

(N058) Nye, F. Ivan. "Maternal Employment and Marital Interaction: Some Contingent Conditions." *Social Forces* 40 (December 1961): 113–119.

(N059) Naess, S. "Mother-Separation and Delinquency." *British Journal of Criminology* 2, No. 4 (1962): 361–374.

(N060) Nagi, Saad Z., and Clark, Donovan L. "Factors in Marital Adjustment After Disability." *Journal of Marriage and the Family* 26 (May 1964): 215–216.

(N061) Noble, Douglas. "Hysterical Manifestations in Schizophrenic Illness." *Psychiatry* 14 (1951): 153–160.

(N062) Neubeck, Gerhard, and Schletzer, Vera M. "A Study of Extra-Marital Relationships." *Marriage and Family Living* 24 (August 1962): 279–284.

(N063) Nye, F. Ivan. *Family Relationships and Delinquent Behavior.* New York: John Wiley and Sons, 1958.

(N064) Needham, Rodney. "An Analytical Note on the Structure of Siriono Society." *Southwest Journal of Anthropology* 17 (1961): 239–255.

(N065) Nash, June, and Nash, Manning. "Marriage, Family and Population Growth in Upper Burma." *Southwest Journal of Anthropology* 19 (1963): 251–266.

(N066) Nakane, Chie. "Cross-Cousin Marriage Among the Garo of Assam." *Man* 2 (1958): 7–12.

(N067) Needham, Rodney. "Descent, Category, and Alliance in Siriono Society." *Southwest Journal of Anthropology* 20 (1964): 229–240.

(N068) Nye, F. Ivan. "Employment Status and Recreational Behavior of Mothers." *Pacific Sociological Review* 1 (Fall 1958): 69–72.

(N069) Nimkoff, M. F. "Is the Joint Family an Obstacle to Industrialization?" *International Journal of Comparative Sociology* 1 (1960): 109–118.

(N070) Needham, Rodney. "Some Disputed Points in the Study of Prescriptive Alliance." *Southwest Journal of Anthropology* 19 (1963): 186–207.

(N071) Nayacakalou, R. R. "Land Tenure and Social Organization in Western Samoa." *Polynesia* 69 (1960): 104–122.

(N072) Needham, Rodney. *Structure and Sentiment.* Chicago: University of Chicago Press, 1962.

(N073) Nielsen, Johannes. "Mental Disorders in Married Couples (Assortative Mating)." *British Journal of Psychiatry* 110 (September 1964): 683–697.

(N074) Needham, Rodney. "The Wikmunkan Mother's Brother: Inference and Evidence." *Polynesia* 72 (1963): 139–151.

(O001) Ogburn, William F. "Education, Income, and Family Unity." *American Journal of Sociology* 53 (1948): 474–476.

(O002) Opler, Morris Edward. "Component, Assemblage, and Theme in Cultural Integration and Differentiation." *American Anthropologist* 61 (1959): 955–964.

(O005) Oliver, Douglas L., and Howells, W. W. "Micro-Evolution: Cultural Elements in Physical Variation." *American Anthropologist* 59 (1957): 965–976.

(O006) Oberg, Kalervo. "Types of Social Structure Among the Lowland Tribes of South and Central America." *American Anthropologist* 57 (1955): 472–487.

(O007) Opler, Morris Edward, and Singh, Rudra Datt. "Two Villages of Eastern Uttar Pradesh (U.P.), India: An Analysis of Similarities and Differences." *American Anthropologist* 54 (1952): 179–190.

(O008) Opler, Morris Edward. "Apache Data Concerning the Relation of Kinship Terminology to Social Classification." *American Anthropologist* 39 (1937): 201–212.

(O011) Oberg, Kalervo. "Crime and Punishment in Tlingit Society." *American Anthropologist* 36 (1934): 145–156.

(O012) Osgood, Cornelius. "Tamaina Culture." *American Anthropologist* 35 (1933): 695–717.

(O013) Oberg, Kalervo. "Terena Social Organization and Law." *American Anthropologist* 50 (1948): 283–291.

(O015) Ottenberg, Simon. "Igo Oracles and Intergroup Relations." *Southwest Journal of Anthropology* 14 (1958): 295–317.

(O016) Olmsted, D. L. "Tequislatec Kinship Terminology." *Southwest Journal of Anthropology* 14 (1958): 449–453.

(O017) Epstein, A. L. "Linguistic Innovation and Culture on the Copperbelt, Northern Rhodesia." *Southwest Journal of Anthropology* 15 (1959): 235–253.

(O018) Okada, Ferdinand E. "Ritual Brotherhood: A Cohesive Factor in Nepalese Society." *Southwest Journal of Anthropology* 13 (1957): 212–222.

(O020) Oberg, Kalervo. "The Bacairi of Northern Matto Grosso." *Southwest Journal of Anthropology* 4 (1948): 305–319.

(O021) Opler, Morris Edward. "Reaction to Death Among the Mescalero Apache." *Southwest Journal of Anthropology* 2 (1946): 454–467.

(O023) Oberg, Kalervo. "Kinship Organization of the Banyankole." *Africa* 11 (1938): 129–159.

(O027) Opler, Morris Edward. *Apache Life-Way.* Chicago: University of Chicago Press, 1941.

(O028) Opler, Morris Edward. "Rule and Practice in the Behavior Between Jicarilla Apache Affinal Relatives." *American Anthropologist* 49 (1947): 453–462.

(O029) Ottenberg, Phoebe V. "The Changing Economic Position of Women Among the Afikpo Ibo." In *Continuity and Change in African Cultures,* edited by William R. Bascom and Melville J. Herskovits. Chicago: University of Chicago Press, 1958.

(O030) Ottenberg, Simon, and Ottenberg, Phoebe V. *Cultures and Societies of Africa.* New York: Random House, 1960.

(O031) Opler, Morris Edward. *Apache Life-Way.* Chicago: University of Chicago Press, 1941.

(O032) O'Neal, Patricia, Robins, Lee N., King, Lucy J., and Schaefer, Jeanette. "Parental Deviance and the Genesis of Sociopathic Personality." *American Journal of Psychiatry* 118 (1962): 1114–1124.

(O033) O'Neal, Patricia, Robins, Lee N., King, Lucy J., and Schaefer, Jeanette. "Parental Deviance and the Genesis of Sociopathic Personality." *American Journal of Psychiatry* 118 (June 1962): 1114–1124.

(O033) Ourth, L., and Brown, K. B. "Inadequate Mothering and Disturbance in Neonatal Period." *Child Development* 32 (1961): 285–295.

(O034) Oltman, Jane E., McGarry, John J., and Friedman, Samuel. "Parental Deprivation and the 'Broken Home' in Dementia Praecox and Other Mental Disorders." *American Journal of Psychiatry* 108 (March 1952): 685–694.

(O035) O'Rourke, John F. "Field and Laboratory: The Decision-Making Behavior of Family Groups in Two Experimental Conditions." *Sociometry* 26 (1963): 422–435.

(P001) Psathas, George. "Ethnicity, Social Class, and Adolescent Independence from Parental Control." *American Sociological Review* 22, No. 4 (1957): 415–423.

(P002) Phillips, Bernard S. "A Role Theory Approach to Adjustment in Old Age." *American Sociological Review* 22, No. 2 (1957): 212–217.

(P003) Poffenberger, Shirley, Poffenberger, Thomas, and Landis, Judson T. "Intent Toward Conception and the Pregnancy Experience." *American Sociological Review* 17 (1952): 616–620.

(P004) Pusic, Eugen. "The Family in the Process of Social Change in Yugoslavia" (University of Zagreb). *Sociological Review* 5 (New Series) (1957): 207–224.

(P008) Pospisil, Leopold. "Social Change and Primitive Law: Consequences of a Papuan Legal Case." *American Anthropologist* 60 (1958): 832–837.

(P009) Powdermaker, Hortense. "Social Change Through Imagery and Values of Teenage Africans in Northern Rhodesia." *American Anthropologist* 58 (1956): 783–813.

(P010) Provinse, John. "The American Indian in Transition." *American Anthropologist* 56 (1954): 388–394.

(P012) Parsons, Talcott. "The Kinship System of the Contemporary United States." *American Anthropologist* 45 (1943): 22–38.

(P013) Priokofjew, G. "Proto-Asiatic Elements in Ostyak-Samoyed Culture." *American Anthropologist* 35 (1933): 131–133.

(P016) Parsons, Elsie Clews. "The Kinship Nomenclature of the Pueblo Indians." *American Anthropologist* 34 (1932): 277–389.

(P020) Pocock, David F. "Inclusion and Exclusion: A Process in the Caste System of Gujerat." *Southwest Journal of Anthropology* 13 (1957): 19–31.

(P022) Pocock, David F. " 'Difference' in East Africa: A Study of Caste and Religion in Modern Indian Society." *Southwest Journal of Anthropology* 13 (1957): 289–300.

(P023) Patai, Raphael. "Cousin-Right in Middle Eastern Marriage." *Southwest Journal of Anthropology* 11 (1955): 371–390.

(P024) Patai, Raphael. "Nomadism: Middle Eastern and Central Asia." *Southwest Journal of Anthropology* 7 (1951): 401–414.

(P025) Pearsall, Marion. "Distributional Variation of Bride-Wealth in the East African Cattle Area." *Southwest Journal of Anthropology* 3 (1947): 15–31.

(P026) Peristiany, J. G. "Pokot Sanctions and Structure." *Africa* 24 (1954): 17–25.

(P029) Prins, A. H. J. "An Outline of the Descent System of the Teita, Northeastern Bantu Tribe." *Africa* 20 (1950): 26–37.

(P034) Parrinder, E. G. S. "Christian Marriage in French West Africa." *Africa* 17 (1947): 260–268.

(P035) Paulme, Denise. "Parenté à plaisanteries et alliance par le sang en Afrique Occidentale." *Africa* 12 (1939): 433–444.

(P044) Piddington, Marjorie, and Piddington, Ralph. "Report of Field Work in Northwestern Australia." *Oceania* 2 (1931–1932): 342–358.

(P050) Pitt-Rivers, G. L. F. "Aua Island: Ethnographical and Sociological Features of a South Sea Pagan Society." *Journal of the Royal Anthropological Institute* 55 (1925): 425–438.

(P052) Parsons, Elsie Clews. *Mitla, Town of the Souls.* Chicago: University of Chicago Press, 1936.

(P056) Pitts, Jessie. "The Family and Peer Groups." In *Modern Introduction to the Family,* edited by Norman W. Bell and Ezra F. Vogel. Glencoe, Ill.: The Free Press, 1960, pp. 266–286.

(P057) Parsons, Talcott, and Fox, René C. "Illness, Therapy, and the Modern American Family." In *Modern Introduction to the Family*, edited by Norman W. Bell and Ezra F. Vogel. Glencoe, Ill.: The Free Press, 1960, pp. 347–360.

(P058) Parker, Seymour. "Eskimo Psychopathology in the Context of Eskimo Personality and Culture." *American Anthropologist* 64 (February 1962): 76–96.

(P059) Parsons, Talcott. "The Stability of the American Family System." In *Modern Introduction to the Family*, edited by Norman W. Bell and Ezra F. Vogel. Glencoe, Ill.: The Free Press, 1960, pp. 93–97.

(P060) Pitts, Jesse. "The Family and Peer Groups." In *Modern Introduction to the Family*, edited by Norman W. Bell and Ezra F. Vogel. Glencoe, Ill.: The Free Press, 1960, pp. 266–286.

(P061) Plant, James S. "Family Living Space and Personality Development." In *Modern Introduction to the Family*, edited by Norman W. Bell and Ezra F. Vogel. Glencoe, Ill.: The Free Press, 1960, pp. 510–520.

(P062) Parsons, Talcott, and Bales Robert F. (in collaboration with James Olds, Morris Zelditch, Jr., and Philip E. Slater). *Family: Socialization and Interaction Process*. Glencoe, Ill.: The Free Press, 1955.

(P063) Potter, Howard W., and Klein, Henriette R. "On Nursing Behavior." *Psychiatry* 20 (1957): 39–46.

(P064) Payne, Donald E., and Mussen, Paul H. "Parent-Child Relations and Father Identification Among Adolescent Boys." *Journal of Abnormal and Social Psychology* 52 (1956): 358–362.

(P065) Perry, Stewart E. "Some Theoretic Problems of Mental Deficiency and Their Action Implications." *Psychiatry* 17 (1954): 45–73.

(P066) Paivio, A., Baldwin, A. L., and Berger, S. M. "Measurement of Children's Sensitivity to Audiences." *Child Development* 32, No. 4 (1961): 721–730.

(P067) Platt, H., Jurgenson, G., and Chorost, S. "Comparison of Child-Rearing Attitudes of Mothers and Fathers of Emotionally Disturbed Adolescents." *Child Development* 33 (1962): 117–122.

(P068) Pease, Damaris, and Gardner, Bruce. "Research on the Effects of Non-Continuous Mothering." *Child Development* 29 (March 1958): 141–147.

(P069) Phelps, Harold, and Horrocks, John. "Factors Influencing Informal Groups of Adolescents." *Child Development* 29 (March 1958): 69–86.

(P070) Peterson, D. R., Becker, W. C., Shoemaker, D. J., Luria, Z., and Hellmer, L. A. "Child Behavior Problems and Parental Attitudes." *Child Development* 32 (1961): 151–162.

(P071) Pineo, Peter C. "Disenchantment in the Later Years of Marriage." *Marriage and Family Living* 23 (February 1961): 3–11.

(P072) Peturddon, E. "A Study of Parental Deprivation and Illness in 291 Psychiatric Patients." *International Journal of Social Psychiatry* 7 (1961): 97–105.

(P072) Pinneau, Samuel R., and Hopper, Harold E. "The Relationship Between Incidences of Specific Gastro-Intestinal Reactions of the Infant and Psychological Characteristics of the Mother." *Journal of Genetic Psychology* 93 (September 1958): 3–13.

(P073) Putney, Snell, and Middleton, Russell. "Rebellion, Conformity and Parental Religious Ideologies." *Sociometry* 24 (June 1961): 125–135.

(P074) Pedersen, Frank A., and Sullivan, Eugene. "Relationships Among Geographical Mobility, Parental Attitudes and Emotional Disturbances in Children." *American Journal of Orthopsychiatry* 34, No. 3 (1964): 575–580.

(P075) Pitfield, M., and Oppenheim, Ann. "Child Rearing Attitudes of Mothers of Psychotic Children." *Journal of Child Psychology and Psychiatry* 5 (1964): 51–57.

(P076) Payne, Donald E., and Mussen, Paul H. "Parent-Child Relations and Father Identification Among Adolescent Boys." *Journal of Abnormal and Social Psychology* 52 (May 1956): 358–362.

(P077) Parsons, A. "Family Dynamics in South Italian Schizophrenics." *Archives of General Psychiatry* 3 (1960): 507.

(P078) Post, F., and Wardle, J. "Family Neurosis and Family Psychosis." *Journal of Mental Science* 108 (1962): 147–158.

(P080) Patterson, V., *et al.* "The Relation Between Intention to Conceive and Symptoms During Pregnancy." *Psychosomatic Medicine* 22, No. 5 (1960): 373–376.

(P081) Pilot, Martin L., and Kormos, Harry R. "Ordinal Position in Asthma and Hyperthyroidism." *Archives of General Psychiatry* 11 (August 1964): 181–184.

(P082) Pehrson, Robert N. "The Bilateral Network of Social Relations in Konkama Lapp District." *University of Indiana, Slavic and East European Series* 5 (1957).

(P083) Pitts, Jesse R. "The Structural-Functional Approach." In *Handbook of Marriage and the Family*, edited by Harold T. Christianson. Chicago: Rand McNally and Co., 1964, pp. 51–124.

(P084) Prothro, W. Terry. "Patterns of Permissiveness Among Preliterate Peoples." *Journal of Abnormal and Social Psychology* 61 (July 1960): 151–154.

(P085) Paul, Lois, and Paul, Benjamin D. "Changing Marriage Patterns in a Highland Guatemalan Community." *Southwest Journal of Anthropology* 19 (1963): 131–148.

(P086) Pond, D. A., Ryle, A., and Hamilton, Madge. "Marriage and Neurosis in a Working-Class Population." *British Journal of Psychiatry* 109 (September 1963): 592–598.

(P087) Pospisal, Leopold. "Kapauku Papuans and Their Kinship Organization." *Oceania* 30 (1959–1960): 188–205.

(Q001) Quain, Buell. *Fijian Village*. Chicago: University of Chicago Press, 1948.

(Q002) Query, J. Neale. "Pre-Morbid Adjustment and Family Structure: A Comparison of Selected Rural and Urban Schizophrenic Men." *Journal of Nervous and Mental Disease* 133 (1961). 333–338.

(R001) Ramsey, Charles E., and Nelson, Lowry. "Change in Values and Attitudes Toward the Family." *American Sociological Review* 21 (1956): 605–609.

(R002) Rosen, Bernard C. "The Reference Group Approach to the Parental Factor in Attitude and Behavior Formation." *Social Forces* 34 (1955): 137–144.

(R003) Roberts, John M., Arth, Malcolm J., and Bush, Robert R. "Games in Culture." *American Anthropologist* 61 (1959): 597–605.

(R004) Read, K. E. "Leadership and Consensus in a New Guinea Society." *American Anthropologist* 61 (1959): 425–436.

(R005) Reining, Conrad C. "The Role of Money in the Zamde Economy." *American Anthropologist* 61 (1959): 39–43.

(R006) Reina, Ruben E. "Two Patterns of Friendship in a

Guatemalan Community." *American Anthropologist* 61 (1959): 44–50.

(R010) Rosen, Bernard C. "Conflicting Group Membership: A Study of Parent-Peer Group Cross-Pressures." *American Sociological Review* 20 (1955): 155–161.

(R011) Roth, Julius, and Peck, Robert F. "Social Class and Social Mobility Factors Related to Marital Adjustment." *American Sociological Review* 16 (1951): 478–487.

(R012) Rosenfeld, Henry. "Processes of Structural Change Within the Arab Village Extended Family." *American Anthropologist* 60 (1958): 1127–1139.

(R013) Romney, A. Kimball, and Epling, Philip J. "A Simplified Model of Kariera Kinship." *American Anthropologist* 60 (1958): 59–75.

(R017) Radcliffe-Brown, A. R. "White's View of the Science of Culture." *American Anthropologist* 51 (1949): 503–512.

(R021) Radcliffe-Brown, A. R. "The Comparative Method in Social Anthropology." *Journal of the Royal Anthropological Institute* 81 (1951): 15–22.

(R023) Radcliffe-Brown, A. R. "Religion and Society." *Journal of the Royal Anthropological Institute* 75 (1945): 33–43.

(R024) Raglan., F. R. S., Lord. "Incest and Exogamy." *Journal of the Royal Anthropological Institute* 61 (1931): 167–180.

(R026) Radcliffe-Brown, A. R. "Notes on the Social Organization of Australian Tribes." *Journal of the Royal Anthropological Institute* 53 (1923): 424–447.

(R027) Radcliffe-Brown, A. R. "A Regulation of Marriage in Anbrym." *Journal of the Royal Anthropological Institute* 67 (1927): 343–348.

(R030) Raum, O. F. "Some Aspects of Indigenous Education Among the Chaga." *Journal of the Royal Anthropological Institute* 68 (1938): 209–221.

(R031) Roberts, J. A. Fraser. "The Unborn Child." *Journal of the Royal Anthropological Institute* 89 (1959): 117–127.

(R033) Read, K. E. "Cultures of the Central Highlands, New Guinea." *Southwest Journal of Anthropology* 10 (1954): 1–43.

(R034) Ruhemann, Barbara. "The Relationship Terms of Some Hill Tribes of Burma and Assam." *Southwest Journal of Anthropology* 4 (1948): 155–198.

(R035) Radin, Paul. "Japanese Ceremonies and Festivals in California." *Southwest Journal of Anthropology* 2 (1946): 152–179.

(R036) Ruhemann, Barbara. "A Method for Analysing Classificatory Relationship Systems." *Southwest Journal of Anthropology* 1 (1945): 531–576.

(R038) Robin, J. "L'évolution du mariage coutumier chez les musulmans du Senegal." *Africa* 17 (1947): 192–201.

(R039) Radcliffe-Brown, A. R. "On Joking Relationships." *Africa* 13 (1940): 195–210.

(R040) Read, Margaret. "The Moral Code of the Ngoni and Their Former Military State." *Africa* 11 (1938): 1–24.

(R045) Read, Margaret. "Tradition and Prestige Among the Ngoni." *Africa* 9 (1936): 453–484.

(R052) Radcliffe-Brown, A. R. "A Further Note on Joking Relationships." *Africa* 19 (1949): 133–140.

(R053) Ryan, D'Arcy. "Names and Naming in Mendi." *Oceania* 29 (1958–1959): 109–116.

(R054) Ryan, D'Arcy. "Clan Formation in the Mendi Valley." *Oceania* 29 (1958–1959): 257–289.

(R056) Russell, T. "The Fataleka of Malaita." *Oceania* 21 (1950–1951): 1–13.

(R057) Reay, Marie. "Mixed Blood Marriage in Northwestern New South Wales." *Oceania* 22 (1951–1952): 116–129.

(R060) Read, K. E. "Morality and the Concept of the Person Among the Gahuku-Gama." *Oceania* 25 (1954–1955): 233–282.

(R062) Reay, Marie, and Sitlington, Grace. "Class and Status in a Mixed-Blood Community (Moree, N. S. W.)." *Oceania* 18 (1947–1948): 179–207.

(R063) Read, K. E. "Social Organization in the Markham Valley, New Guinea." *Oceania* 17 (1946–1947): 93–118.

(R064) Reay, Marie. "A Half-Caste Aboriginal Community in Northwestern New South Wales." *Oceania* 15 (1944–1945): 296–323.

(R065) Repa, T. W. "Depopulation in New Zealand." *Oceania* 3 (1932–1933): 227–234.

(R066) Radcliffe-Brown, A. R. "The Social Organization of Australian Tribes." *Oceania* 1 (1930–1931): 34–63.

(R067) Radcliffe-Brown, A. R. "The Social Organization of Australian Tribes." *Oceania* 1 (1930–1931): 206–246.

(R069) Radcliffe-Brown A. R. "The Social Organization of Australian Tribes." *Oceania* 1 (1930–1931): 426–456.

(R071) Raven-Hart, R. "A Village in the Yasawas (Fiji)." *Polynesia* 65 (1956); 95–154.

(R076) Reay, Marie. "Native Thought in Rural New South Wales." *Oceania* 20 (1949–1950): 89–118.

(R077) Read, K. E. "The Political System of the Ngara Wapum." *Oceania* 20 (1949–1950): 185–223.

(R081) Rosenthal, Maurice J., M.D. "The Syndrome of the Inconsistent Mother." *American Journal of Orthopsychiatry* 32 (1962): 637–644.

(R082) Rapport, Rhona. "The Family and Psychiatric Treatment." *Psychiatry* 23 (1960): 53–62.

(R083) Rosengren, William R. "The Hospital Careers of Lower and Middle Class Psychiatric Patients." *Psychiatry* 25 (1962): 16–22.

(R085) Richards, Audrey I. (ed.). *Economic Development and Tribal Change.* Cambridge: W. Heffer and Sons (n.d.).

(R086) Richards, Audrey I. *Hunger and Work in a Savage Tribe.* Glencoe, Ill.: The Free Press, 1948.

(R086) Richards, Audrey I. *Land, Labour and Diet in Northern Rhodesia.* Published for International African Institute. London: Oxford University Press, 1939.

(R087) Richards, Audrey I. *Hunger and Work in a Savage Tribe.* Glencoe, Ill.: The Free Press, 1948.

(R088) Redfield, Robert. *The Folk Culture of Yucatan.* Chicago: University of Chicago Press, 1941.

(R089) Rabin, A. I. "Attitudes of Kibbutz Children to Family and Parents." *American Journal of Orthopsychiatry* 29 (January 1959): 172–179.

(R090) Rapp, Don W. "Child-Rearing Attitudes of Mothers in Germany and the United States." *Child Development* 32, No. 4 (1961): 669–678.

(R091) Rosenthal, Maurice J. "The Syndrome of the Inconsistent Mother." *American Journal of Orthopsychiatry* 32 (July 1962): 637–644.

(R092) Rosenberg, Morris. "The Dissonant Religious Context and Emotional Disturbance." *American Journal of Sociology* 68 (July 1962): 1–10.

(R093) Rosenmayr, Leopold. "The Austrian Woman." *International Social Science Journal* 14, No. 3 (1962): 157–165.

(R094) Rapaport, David. "Behavior Research in Collective Settlements in Israel." *American Journal of Orthopsychiatry* 28 (July 1958): 587–597.

(R095) Rabin, A. I. "Behavior Research in Collective Settlements in Israel." *American Journal of Orthopsychiatry* 28 (July 1958): 577–584.

(R096) Rabin, A. I. "Culture-Components as a Significant Factor in Child Development: Two Kibbutz Adolescents." *American Journal of Orthopsychiatry* 31 (1961): 493–504.

(R097) Rosen, Bernard C. "Family Structure and Value Transmission." *Merrill–Palmer Quarterly* 10 (January 1964): 59–76.

(R097) Rosen, Bernard C. "Socialization and Achievement Motivation in Brazil." *American Sociological Review* 27 (October 1962): 612–624.

(R098) Rau, Lucy. "Parental Antecedents of Identification." *Merrill–Palmer Quarterly* 6 (January 1960): 77–82.

(R098) Rosen, Bernard C., and D'Andrade, Rou. "The Psychosocial Origins of Achievement Motivation." *Sociometry* 22 (September 1959): 185–218.

(R099) Rexford, Eveoleen N., and van Amerongen, Suzanne Taets. "The Influence of Unsolved Maternal Oral Conflicts upon Impulsive Acting Out in Young Children." *American Journal of Orthopsychiatry* 27 (January 1957): 75–87.

(R100) Rosenthal, Maurice J., Ni, Ernest, Finkelstein, Melville, and Berkwits, Gloria. "Father-Child Relationships and Children's Problems." *Archives of General Psychology* 7 (November 1962): 360–375.

(R101) Rushing, William A. "Adolescent-Parent Relationship and Mobility Aspirations. *Social Forces* 43 (December 1964): 157–166.

(R102) Robey, Aames, Rosenthal, Richard, Snell, John, and Lee, Rita. "The Runaway Girl." *American Journal of Orthopsychiatry* 34, No. 4 (1964): 762–767.

(R103) Rosenthal, D. "Familial Concordance by Sex with Respect to Schizophrenia." *Psychological Bulletin* 59 (1962): 401–421.

(R105) Rapoport, R., and Rosow, I. "An Approach to Family Relationships and Role Performance." *Human Relations* 10 (1957): 209–221.

(R106) Rosen, Bernard C. "Family Structure and Achievement Motivation." *American Sociological Review* 26 (August 1961): 574–585.

(R107) Rosengren, William A. "Social Status, Attitudes Toward Pregnancy and Child Rearing Attitudes." *Social Forces* 41 (December 1962): 127–134.

(R108) Rouman, J. "School Children's Problems as Related to Parental Factors." *Journal of Educational Research* 50 (1956): 105–112.

(R109) Rivlin, L. "Creativity and the Self-Attitudes and Sociability of High School Students." *Journal of Educational Psychology* 50 (1959): 147–152.

(R110) Reiner, B. S. *Character Disorders in Parents of Delinquents.* New York: Family Service Association of America, 1959.

(R111) Rose, A. "Reference Groups of Rural High School Youth." *Child Development* 27 (September 1956): 351–363.

(R112) Robertson, William O. "An Investigation of Maternal Concerns by Mail Survey." *Child Development* 32, No. 3 (1961): 423–426.

(R113) Rosenthal, M. J., Ni, E., Finkelstein, Melville, and Robertson, R. E. "A Study of Mother-Child Relationships in the Emotional Disorders of Children." *Genetic Psychology Monographs* 60 (August 1959): 65–116.

(R114) Rosenberg, B. G., and Sutton-Smith, B. "Ordinal Position and Sex-Role Identification." *Genetic Psychology Monographs* 70 (November 1964): 297–328.

(R115) Reichard, Suzanne, and Tillman, Carl. "Patterns of Parent-Child Relationships in Schizophrenia." *Psychiatry* 13 (1950): 247–257.

(R116) Rose, A. "Acceptance of Adult Roles and Separation from Family." *Marriage and Family Living* 21 (1959): 120–216.

(R117) Rushing, William A. "Adolescent-Parent Relationship and Mobility Aspirations." *Social Forces* 43 (December 1964): 157–166.

(R118) Rosenfeld, Henry. "On Determinants of the Status of Arab Village Women." *Man* 95 (1960): 66–70.

(R119) Rosenthal, Erich. "Jewish Fertility in the United States." *Eugenics Quarterly* 8 (1961): 198–217.

(R120) Rosenmayr, Leopold, and Kockeis, Eva. "Propositions for a Sociological Theory of Aging and the Family." *International Social Science Journal* 15 (1963): 410–426.

(R121) Rosenmayr, Leopold. "Selected Problems of the Family in Urban and Rural Austria." *International Journal of Comparative Sociology* 1 (1960): 89–102.

(R122) Rainer, John, and Firchein, I. Lester. "Mating and Fertility Patterns in Families with Early Total Deafness." *Eugenics Quarterly* 6 (1959): 117–127.

(R123) Radcliffe-Brown, A. R. *The Andaman Islanders.* Glencoe, Ill.: The Free Press, 1948.

(R124) Rosenthau, Celia Stopnicka. "Lower Class Family Organization on the Caribbean Coast of Colombia." *Pacific Sociological Review* 3 (Spring 1960): 12–17.

(R125) Robins, Lee N., Gyman, Harry, and O'Neal, Patricia. "The Interaction of Social Class and Deviant Behavior." *American Sociological Review* 27 (August 1962): 480–492.

(R126) Rabban, Meyer. "Sex-Role Identification in Young Children in Two Diverse Social Groups." *Genetic Psychology Monographs* 42 (1950): 81–158.

(R127) Rainwater, Lee. "A Study of the Personality Differences Between Middle and Lower Class Adolescents; The Szondi Test in Culture-Personality Research." *Genetic Psychology Monographs* 54 (1956): 3–86.

(R128) Rosenberg, Morris. "Parental Interest and Children's Self-Conceptions." *Sociometry* 26 (1963): 35–49.

(R129) Rosenberg, Morris. *Society and the Adolescent Self-Image.* Princeton: Princeton University Press, 1965.

(S001) Stoodley, Bartlett H. "Normative Attitudes of Filipino Youth as Compared with German and American Youth." *American Sociological Review* 22, No. 5 (October 1957): 553–561.

(S002) Sussman, Marvin B. "The Help Pattern in the Middle Class Family." *American Sociological Review* 18 (1953): 22–28.

(S003) Schmitt, Robert C. "Illegitimate Birth Rates in an Atypical Community." *American Journal of Sociology* 61 (1956): 476–477.

(S004) Schnepp, Gerald J., and Yui, Agnes Masako. "Cultural and Marital Adjustment of Japanese War Brides." *American Journal of Sociology* 61 (1955): 48–50.

(S010) Sewell, William H., Mussen, Paul H., and Harris, Chester W. "Relationships Among Child Training Practices." *American Sociological Review* 20 (1955): 137–148.

(S011) Stryker, Sheldon. "The Adjustment of Married Offspring to Their Parents." *American Sociological Review* 20 (1955): 149–154.

(S012) Sundal, A. Philip, and McCormick, Thomas C. "Age at Marriage and Mate Selection: Madison, Wisconsin, 1937–1943." *American Sociological Review* 16 (1951): 37–48.

(S013) Strodtbeck, F. L. "Husband-Wife Interaction Over Revealed Differences." *American Sociological Review* 16 (1951): 468–473.

(S014) Sears, Robert R. "Ordinal Position in the Family as a Psychological Variable." *American Sociological Review* 15 (1950): 397–401.

(S015) Schwartz, Shepard. "Mate Selection Among New York City's Chinese Males, 1931–1938." *American Journal of Sociology* 56 (1951): 562–568.

(S016) Schnepp, Gerald J., and Roberts, Louis A. "Residential Propinquity and Mate Selection on a Parish Basis." *American Journal of Sociology* 58 (1952): 45–50.

(S022) Shaw, Lulie A. "Impressions of Family Life in a London Suburb (Studies of a General Practice IV) (University of Bristol). *Sociological Review* 2 (New Series), No. 2 (1954): 179–194.

(S025) Smolski, T. "Quelques données statistiques sur le suicide au Vietnam (Some Statistical Data on Suicide in Vietnam)." *Dan Viet Nam: Le Peuple Vietnamien*, No. 111: 55–59. Hanoi: École Française d'Extrême-Orient, 1949, *Human Relations Area Files.*

(S026) Salisbury, Richard F. "Asymmetrical Marriage Systems." *American Anthropologist* 58 (1956): 639–655.

(S027) Slobodchin, Richard. "Some Social Functions of Kutchin Anxiety." *American Anthropologist* 62 (1960): 122–133.

(S028) Slater, Marian Kreiselman. "The Ecological Factors in the Origin of Incest." *American Anthropologist* 61 (1959): 1042–1059.

(S030) Slaughter, C. "Modern Marriage and the Roles of the Sexes" (University of Leeds). *Sociological Review* 4 (New Series), No. 2 (1956): 213–221.

(S031) Stark, W. "Peasant Society and the Origins of Romantic Love" (University of Manchester). *Sociological Review*. 1 (New Series), No. 2 (1953): 83–92.

(S032) Solien, Nancie L. "The Non-Unilinear Descent Group in the Carribean and Central America." *American Anthropologist* 61 (1959): 578–583.

(S033) Srinivas, M. N. "The Dominant Caste in Rampura." *American Anthropologist* 61 (1959): 1–15.

(S036) Spiro, Melford E., and D'Andrade, Roy G. "A Cross-Cultural Study of Some Supernatural Beliefs." *American Anthropologist* 60 (1958): 456–466.

(S037) Schwartz, Marc J. "Sexuality and Aggression on Romonum, Truk." *American Anthropologist* 60 (1958): 467–486.

(S039) Spindler, Louise, and Spindler, George. "Male and Female Adaptation in Cultural Change." *American Anthropologist* 60 (1958): 217–233.

(S040) Schneider, David M. "Political Organization, Supernatural Sanction and the Punishment for Incest on Yap." *American Anthropologist* 59 (1957): 791–800.

(S041) Sahlins, Marshall D. "Land Use and the Extended Family in Moala, Fiji." *American Anthropologist* 59 (1957): 449–462.

(S043) Stoodley, Bartlett H. "Some Aspects of Tagalog Family Structure." *American Anthropologist* 59 (1957): 236–249.

(S046) Service, Elman R. "Indian-European Relations in Colonial Latin America." *American Anthropologist* 57 (1955): 411–426.

(S048) Sears, William H. "The Socio-Political Organization of Pre-Columbian Cultures on the Gulf Coastal Plain." *American Anthropologist* 56 (1944): 339–346.

(S049) Spiro, Melford E. "Is the Family Universal?" *American Anthropologist* 56 (1954): 839–846.

(S050) Schneider, David M., and Homans, George C. "Kinship Terminology and the American Kinship System." *American Anthropologist* 57 (1955): 1194–1208.

(S051) Spiro, Melford E. "The Acculturation of American Ethnic Groups." *American Anthropologist* 57 (1955): 1240–1252.

(S052) The Social Science Research Council Summer Seminar on Acculturation, 1953. "Acculturation: An Exploratory Formulation." *American Anthropologist* 56 (1954): 973–1002.

(S053) Spicer, Edward H. "Spanish-Indian Acculturation in the Southwest." *American Anthropologist* 56 (1954): 663–684.

(S057) Schull, William J. "The Effect of Christianity on Consanguinity in Nagasaki." *American Anthropologist* 55 (1953): 74–88.

(S059) Shimkin, D. B., and San Juan, Pedro. "Culture and the World View: A Method of Analysis Applied to Rural Russia." *American Anthropologist* 55 (1953): 329–348.

(S060) Schneider, David M. "Yap Kinship Terminology and Kin Groups." *American Anthropologist* 55 (1953): 215–236.

(S063) Speck, S. G., and Schaeffer, C. E. "Catawba Kinship and Social Organization with a Résumé of Tutelo Kinship Terms." *American Anthropologist* 44 (1942): 555–575.

(S065) Smith, Marian W. "The Coast Salish of Puget Sound." *American Anthropologist* 43 (1941): 197–211.

(S068) Steward, Julian H. "Shoshoni Polyandry." *American Anthropologist* 38 (1936): 561–664.

(S069) Siegel, Bernard J. "Some Methodological Considerations for a Comparative Study of Slavery." *American Anthropologist* 47 (1945): 357–392.

(S070) Speck, Frank G. "Siouan Tribes of the Carolinas as Known from Catawba, Tutelo, and Documentary Sources." *American Anthropologist* 37 (1935): 201–225.

(S072) Schmidt, W. "The Position of Women with Regard to Property in Primitive Society." *American Anthropologist* 37 (1935): 244–256.

(S075) Spiegel, John. "The Resolution of Role-Conflict Within the Family." In *Modern Introduction to the Family,* edited by Norman W. Bell and Ezra F. Vogel. Glencoe, Ill.: The Free Press, 1960, pp. 361–381.

(S076) Sirjanki, John. "Cultural Configurations in the American Family." In *Modern Introduction to the Family,* edited by Norman W. Bell and Ezra F. Vogel. Glencoe, Ill.: The Free Press, 1960, pp. 295–303.

(S077) Simpson, Richard L. "Parental Influence, Anticipatory Socialization, and Social Mobility." *American Sociological Review* 27 (August 1962): 517–522.

(S077) Speck, Frank G., and Eiseley, Loren C. "The Significance of Hunting Territory Systems of the Algonkinkians in Social Theory." *American Anthropologist* 41 (1943): 269–280.

(S078) Short, James F., and Henry, Andrew F. *Suicide and Homicide.* Glencoe, Ill.: The Free Press, 1954.

(S078) Spencer, Robert F., and Barrett, F. A. "Note on a Bachelor House in the South China Area." *American Anthropologist* 50 (1948): 463–478.

(S078) Swanton, John R. "Some Neglected Data Bearing

on Cheyenne, Chippewa, and Dakota History."
*American Anthropologist* 32 (1930): 156–190.

(S079) Stephens, William N. *The Oedipus Complex.*
Glencoe, Ill.: The Free Press, 1962.

(S080) Smith, Raymond T. "Community Status and
Family Structure in British Guiana." In *Modern Introduction to The Family,* edited by Norman W. Bell and
Ezra F. Vogel. Glencoe, Ill.: The Free Press, 1960, pp.
258–265.

(S080) Spoehr, Alexander. "Observations on the Study of
Kinship." *American Anthropologist* 52 (1950): 1–
15.

(S081) Seligman, Brenda. "The Problem of Incest and
Exogamy: A Restatement." *American Anthropologist*
52 (1950): 305–316.

(S085) Smith, Marian W. "Village Notes from Bengal."
*American Anthropologist* 48 (1946): 574–582.

(S087) Smith, M. G. "On Segmentary Lineage Systems."
*Journal of the Royal Anthropological Institute* 86,
Part ii (1956): 39–80.

(S089) Stevenson, H. N. C. "Status Evaluation in the
Hindu Caste System." *Journal of the Royal Anthropological Institute* 84 (1954): 45–65.

(S090) Siegel, Morris. "Effects of Culture Contacts on the
Form of the Family in a Guatemalan Village." *Journal
of the Royal Anthropological Institute* 72 (1942): 55
–68.

(S092) Stevenson, H. N. C. "Feasting and Meat Division
Among the Zahau Chins of Burma." *Journal of the
Royal Anthropological Institute* 67 (1937): 15–32.

(S093) Seligman, Brenda Z. "Maritan Gerontocracy in
Africa." *Journal of the Royal Anthropological Institute* 54 (1923): 231–250.

(S095) Seligman, Brenda Z. "Bilateral Descent and the
Formation of Marriage Classes." *Journal of the Royal
Anthropological Institute* 67 (1927): 349–375.

(S096) Seligman, C. G., and Seligman, Brenda Z. "The
Bari." *Journal of the Royal Anthropological Institute*
58 (1928): 409–479.

(S097) Seligman, Brenda Z. "Asymmetry in Descent, with
Special Reference to Pentecost." *Journal of the Royal
Anthropological Institute* 58 (1928): 533–558.

(S098) Seligman, Brenda Z. "Incest and Descent: Their
Influence on Social Organization." *Journal of the
Royal Anthropological Institute* 69 (1927): 231–272.

(S099) Stenning, Derrick J. "Transhumance, Migratory
Drift, Migration: Patterns of Pastoral Fulani Nomadism." *Journal of the Royal Anthropological Institute*
87 (1957): 57–73.

(S100) Schapera, I. "Christianity and the Tswana." *Journal of the Royal Anthropological Institute* 88 (1958):
1–9.

(S102) Solien, Nancie L. "West Indian Characteristics of
the Black Carib." *Southwest Journal of Anthropology*
15 (1951): 300–307.

(S104) Sjoberg, Andrée F. "Lipan Apache Culture in Historical Perspective." *Southwest Journal of Anthropology* 9 (1953): 76–98.

(S106) Spoehr, Alexander. "The Generation Type Kinship
System in the Marshall and Gilbert Islands." *Southwest
Journal of Anthropology* 5 (1949): 107–116.

(S111) Steward, Julian H. "Levels of Socio-Cultural Integration: An Operational Concept." *Southwest Journal
of Anthropology* 7 (1951): 374–390.

(S115) Sun, E-Tu Zen. "Results of Culture Contacts in
Two Mongol-Chinese Communities." *Southwest Journal of Anthropology* 8 (1952): 183–210.

(S116) Spencer, Robert E. "The Arabian Matriarchate: An

Old Controversy." *Southwest Journal of Anthropology* 8 (1952): 478–502.

(S117) Swadesh, Morris. "Motivations in Nootka Warfare." *Southwest Journal of Anthropology* 4 (1948):
76–93.

(S118) Siegel, Bernard J. "Currents of Anthropological
Theory and Value Concepts." *Southwest Journal of
Anthropology* 4 (1948): 199–210.

(S119) Steward, Julian H. "American Culture History in
the Light of South America." *Southwest Journal of
Anthropology* 3 (1947): 85–107.

(S120) Service, Elman. "Recent Observations on Hazasu-
pai Land Tenure." *Southwest Journal of Anthropology*
3 (1947): 360–366.

(S121) Schapera, I. "Some Features in the Social Organization of the Tloka (Bechuland Protectorate)." *Southwest Journal of Anthropology* 2 (1946): 16–47.

(S122) Spencer, Robert F. "The Annamese Kinship System." *Southwest Journal of Anthropology* 1 (1945):
284–310.

(S123) Smith, M. G. "The Hausa System of Social Status."
*Africa* 29 (1959): 239–252.

(S124) Schwab, William B. "The Terminology of Kinship
and Marriage Among the Yoruba." *Africa* 28 (1958).

(S127) Stent, G. E. "Migrancy and Urbanization in the
Union of South Africa." *Africa* 18 (1948): 161–183.

(S131) Schapera, I. "Field Methods in the Study of Modern Culture Contact." *Africa* 8 (1935): 315–328.

(S134) Schapera, I. "Premarital Pregnancy and Native
Opinions." *Africa* 6 (1933): 59–89.

(S135) Schapera, I. "The Bakxatla Baxakxafela." *Africa* 6
(1933): 402–414.

(S137) Spagnolo, L. M. "Some Notes on the Initiation of
Young Men and Girls in the Bara Tribes." *Africa* 5
(1932): 393–403.

(S140) Schapera, I. "Marriage of Near Kin Among the
Tswana." *Africa* 27 (1957): 139–159.

(S141) Smith, M. G. "Secondary Marriage in Northern
Nigeria." *Africa* 23 (1953): 298–323.

(S144) Stanner, W. E. H. "Continuity and Schism in an
African Tribe: A Review." *Oceania* 29 (1958–1959):
208–217.

(S147) Stanner, W. E. H. "Murinbata Kinship and Totemism." *Oceania* 7 (1936–1937): 186–216.

(S148) Stanner, W. E. H. "Aboriginal Modes of Address
and Reference in the Northwest of the Northern Territory." *Oceania* (1936–1937): 300–315.

(S152) Stanner, W. E. H. "Ceremonial Economics of the
Mulluk and Madngella Tribes of the Daly River, North
Australia." *Oceania* 4 (1933–1934): 156–175.

(S153) Sharp, Lauriston. "The Social Organization of the
Yir-Yoront Tribe, Cape York Peninsula." *Oceania* 4
(1933–1934): 404–431.

(S156) Stanner, W. E. H. "The Daly River Tribes: A Report of Field Work in North Australia." *Oceania* 3
(1932–1933): 377–405.

(S158) Stenning, Derrick J. *Savannah Nomads.* London:
The Oxford University Press, 1959.

(S159) Sahlins, Marshall D. "Differentiation by Adaptation in Polynesian Societies." *Polynesia* 66 (1957): 291
–300.

(S161) Schapera, I. "The Tswana Conception of Incest."
In *Social Structure,* edited by Meyer Fortes. Oxford:
Clarendon Press, 1949.

(S166) Sanderson, Meredith. "Relationships Among the
Wayao." *Journal of the Royal Anthropological Institute* 50 (1920): 369–376.

(S171) Schapera, I. *Western Civilization and the Natives*

*of South Africa.* London: Geo. Routledge and Sons, 1934.

(S174) Stenning, Derrick J. "Household Liability Among the Pastoral Fulani." In *The Developmental Cycle in Domestic Groups,* edited by Jack Goody. London: The Cambridge University Press, 1958, pp. 92–119.

(S181) Smith, Joseph H. "The Metaphor of the Manic-Depressive." *Psychiatry* 23 (1960): 375–383.

(S182) Sklarew, Bruce H. "The Relationship of Early Separation from Parents to Differences in Adjustment in Adolescent Boys and Girls." *Psychiatry* 22 (1959): 399–405.

(S183) Spiegel, John P., and Bell, Norman W. "The Family of the Psychiatric Patient." In *American Handbook of Psychiatry,* Volume I, edited by Silvano Arieti. New York: Basic Books, Inc., 1959, pp. 114–149.

(S184) Silber, Earle, Perry, Stewart E., and Bloch, Donald A. "Patterns of Parent-Child Interaction in a Disaster." *Psychiatry* 21 (1958): 159–167.

(S185) Spiegel, John P. "The Resolution of Role Conflict Within the Family." *Psychiatry* 20 (1957): 1–16.

(S186) Surek, S. A., and Berlin, I. N. "Elements of Psychotherapeutics with the Schizophrenic Child and His Parents." *Psychiatry* 19 (1956): 1–9.

(S187) Sanua, Victor D. "Sociocultural Factors in Families of Schizophrenics." *Psychiatry* 24 (1961): 246–265.

(S188) Sarvis, Mary A., and Gracia, Blanche. "Etiological Variables in Autism." *Psychiatry* 24 (1961): 307–317.

(S189) Stephens, William N. *The Family in Cross-Cultural Perspective.* New York: Holt, Rinehart & Winston, 1963.

(S190) Schapera, I. "The Sin of Cain." *Journal of the Royal Anthropological Institute* 85 (1955): 33–43.

(S191) Sears, Robert R., Maccoby, E., and Levin, H. *Patterns of Child Rearing.* New York: Harper and Row, 1957.

(S192) Spoehr, Alexander. *Changing Kinship Systems.* Chicago: Field Museum of Natural History, Anthropological Series, 33, No. 4 (1947).

(S193) Southall, A. W. and Gutkind, P. C. W. "Townsmen in the Making, East African Studies." East African Institute of Social Research, 9 (1957).

(S194) Steward, Julian H. *Theory of Culture Change.* Urbana: University of Illinois Press, 1955.

(S195) Southan, Aidan. *Alur Society.* Cambridge: W. Heffer and Sons, Ltd. 1953.

(S196) Schapera, I. *Government and Politics in Tribal Societies.* London: Watts, 1956.

(S197) Schapera, I. *Bantu-Speaking Tribes of South Africa.* London: Routledge and Kegan Paul, 1937.

(S200) Sewell, William H., and Mussen, Paul H. "The Effects of Feeding, Weaning and Scheduling Procedures on Childhood Adjustment and the Formation of Oral Symptoms." *Child Development* 23 (June 1952): 185–191.

(S201) Spitz, Rene A. "Hospitalism." In *The Family: Its Structure and Functions,* edited by R. L. Coser. New York: St. Martin's Press, 1964, pp. 399–425.

(S202) Stendler, Celia Burns. "Critical Periods in Socialization and Overdependency." *Child Development* 23 (March 1952): 3–12.

(S203) Sessex, J. N., Gassman, F., and Raffel, S. C. "Care of Children at Home with Severely Disturbed Parents." *American Journal of Orthopsychiatry* 32 (1962): 266–267.

(S204) Stendler, Celia Burns. "Possible Causes of Overdependency in Young Children." *Child Development* 25 (June 1954): 125–146.

(S205) Strauss, Murray. "Conjugal Power Structure and Adolescent Personality." *Marriage and Family Living* 24 (1962): 17–25.

(S206) Sampson, Harold, Messinger, Sheldon L., and Towne, Robert D. "Family Processes and Becoming a Mental Patient." *American Journal of Sociology* 68 (July 1962): 88–96.

(S207) Scott, Frances Gillespie. "Family Group Structure and Patterns of Social Interaction." *American Journal of Sociology* 68 (September 1962): 214–228.

(S208) Serrano, A. C., McDonald, E. C., Goolishian, H. A., MacGregor, R., and Ritchie, A. M. "Adolescent Maladjustment and Family Dynamics." *American Journal of Psychiatry* 118, No. 10 (1962): 897–901.

(S209) Spitz, Rene A. "The Role of Ecological Factors in Emotional Development in Infancy." *Child Development* 20 (September 1949): 145–150.

(S210) Shulman, Harry M. "The Family and Juvenile Delinquency." In *The Problem of Delinquency,* edited by Sheldon Glueck. Boston: Houghton Mifflin Co., 1959, pp. 128–136.

(S211) Smith, M. G. *West Indian Family Structure.* Seattle: University of Washington Press, 1962.

(S212) Sperry, Bessie, Staver, Nancy, Reiner, Beatrice S., and Ulrich, David. "Renunciation and Denial in Learning Difficulties." *American Journal of Orthopsychiatry* 28 (January 1958): 89–111.

(S213) Searles, Harold F. "Positive Feelings in the Relationship Between the Schizophrenic and His Mother." *International Journal of Psychoanalysis* 39 (November–December 1958): 569–586.

(S214) Spiro, M. E. *Children of the Kibbutz.* Cambridge: Harvard University Press, 1958.

(S216) Slater, Philip E. "Parental Role Differentiation." *American Journal of Sociology* 67 (1961–1962): 296–311.

(S217) Sebald, Hans, and Andrews, Wade H. "Family Integration and Related Factors in a Rural Fringe Population." *Marriage and Family Living* 23–24 (1961–1962): 347–351.

(S218) Schoonover, S. "The Relationship of Intelligence and Achievement to Birth Order, Sex of Sibling, and Age Interval." *Journal of Educational Psychology* 50 (1959): 143–146.

(S219) Smith, Ernest. *American Youth Culture.* Glencoe, Ill.: The Free Press, 1962.

(S220) Streib, Gordon F. "Family Patterns in Retirement." *Journal of Social Issues* 14, No. 2 (1958): 46–60.

(S221) Slater, P. "Parental Behavior and the Personality of the Child." *The Journal of Genetic Psychology* 101 (1962): 53–68.

(S221) Smith, B., Roberts, J., and Rosenberg, B. "Sibling Associations and Role Involvement." *Merrill–Palmer Quarterly* 10 (January 1964): 25–38.

(S222) Stubblefield, Robert L. "Children's Emotional Problems Aggravated by Family Moves." *American Journal of Orthopsychiatry* 25 (January 1955): 120–126.

(S223) Staver, Nancy. "The Child's Learning Difficulty as Related to the Emotional Problem of the Mother." *American Journal of Orthopsychiatry* 23 (January 1953): 131–141.

(S224) Strand, G., and Larson, W. "Five Professions View the Unmarried Parent." *International Journal of Social Psychiatry* 6 (1960): 269–276.

(S225) Silverman, Jerome S., Fite, Margaretta W., and Mosher, Margaret M. "Learning Problems: I. Clinical Findings in Reading Disability Children—Special Cases of Intellectual Inhibition." *American Journal of Orthopsychiatry* 29 (April 1959): 298–314.

(S225) Stewart, L. "Manifest Anxiety and Mother-Son Identification." *Journal of Clinical Psychology* 14 (1958): 382–384.

(S226) Stott, D. H. *Unsettled Children and Their Families.* London: University of London Press, Ltd., 1956.

(S227) Stott, D. H. "Abnormal Mothering as a Cause of Mental Subnormality–I. A Critique of Some Classic Studies of Maternal Deprivation in the Light of Possible Congenital Factors." *Journal of Child Psychology and Psychiatry* 3 (April–June 1962): 79–91.

(S228) Sears, P. "Doll Play Aggression in Normal Young Children: Influence of Sex, Age, Sibling Status, Father's Absence." *Psychological Monographs* 65, No. 6 (1951): 1–42.

(S229) Sloane, R. B., Davidson, P., Holland, L., and Payne, R. W. "Aggression and Effects of Upbringing in Normal Students." *Archives of General Psychology* 7 (November 1962): 374–384.

(S230) Shaw, Merville, and Dutton, Bert E. "The Use of the Parent Attitude Research Inventory with the Parents of Bright Academic Underachievers." *Journal of Educational Psychology* 53, No. 5 (October 1962): 203–208.

(S231) Siegel, Alberta Engvall, and Curtis, Elizabeth Ann. "Familial Correlates of Orientation Toward Future Employment Among College Women." *Journal of Educational Psychology* 54 (February 1963): 33–37.

(S232) Schachter, Stanley. "Birth Order and Sociometric Choice." *Journal of Abnormal and Social Psychology* 68, No. 4 (1964): 453–456.

(S233) Schmuck, Richard. "Sex of Sibling, Birth Order Position, and Female Dispositions to Conform in Two-Child Families." *Child Development* 34 (1963): 913–918.

(S234) Stotland, Ezra, and Cottrell, Nickolas B. "Similarity of Performance as Influenced by Interaction, Self-Esteem, and Birth Order." *Journal of Abnormal and Social Psychology* 64 (March 1962): 183–191.

(S235) Sampson, Edward E. "Birth Order, Need Achievement, and Conformity." *Journal of Abnormal and Social Psychology* 64 (February 1962): 155–159.

(S236) Smart, Reginald G. "Alcoholism, Birth Order, and Family Size." *Journal of Abnormal and Social Psychology* 66 (January 1963): 17–23.

(S237) Stotland, Ezra, and Walsh, James A. "Birth Order and an Experimental Study of Empathy." *Journal of Abnormal and Social Psychology* 66 (June 1963): 610–614.

(S238) Sears, R. R., Whiting, J. W. M., Nowlis, V., and Sears, P. S. "Some Child-Rearing Antecedents of Aggression and Dependency in Young Children." *Genetic Psychology Monographs* 47 (1953): 135–234.

(S239) Suttenfield, Virginia. "School Phobia: A Study of Five Cases." *American Journal of Orthopsychiatry* 24 (April 1954): 368–380.

(S240) Slater, Philip E. "Toward a Dualistic Theory of Identification." *Merrill–Palmer Quarterly* 7 (April 1961): 113–126.

(S241) Sopchak, Andrew I. "Spearman Correlations Between MMPI Scores of College Students and Their Parents." *Journal of Consulting Psychology* 22, No. 3 (1958): 207–209.

(S242) Schulman, Robert E., Shoemaker, Donald J., and Moelis, Irvin. "Laboratory Measurement of Parental Behavior." *Journal of Consulting Psychology* 26 (April 1962): 109–114.

(S243) Slater, C. "Class Differences in Definition of Role and Membership in Voluntary Associations and Among Urban Married Women." *American Journal of Sociology* 65 (1959–1960): 616–619.

(S244) Schmitt, Robert C. "Age Differences in Marriage and Divorce in Hawaii." *Sociology and Social Research* 44 (March–April 1960): 266–268.

(S245) Simmons, O., and Freeman, H. "Familial Expectations and Posthospital Performance of Mental Patients." *Human Relations* 12 (1959): 233–242.

(S246) Sears, Robert R. "Relation of Early Socialization Experiences to Aggression in Middle Childhood." *Journal of Abnormal and Social Psychology* 63 (November 1961): 466–492.

(S247) Schofield, William, and Balian, Lucy. "A Comparative Study of the Personal Histories of Schizophrenic and Nonpsychiatric Patients." *Journal of Abnormal and Social Psychology* 59 (September 1959): 216–225.

(S248) Sears, R. "Relation of Fantasy Aggression to Interpersonal Aggression." *Child Development* 21 (March 1950): 5–6.

(S249) Schaefer, Earl, and Bell, Richard. "Development of a Parental Attitude Research Instrument." *Child Development* 29 (September 1958): 339–358.

(S250) Serot, N. M., and Teevan, R. C. "Perception of the Parent-Child Relationship and Its Relation to Child Adjustment." *Child Development* 32 (1961): 373–378.

(S251) Schmuck, Richard. "Sex of Sibling, Birth Order Position, and Female Dispositions to Conform in Two-Child Families." *Child Development* 34 (December 1963): 913–918.

(S252) Steinmann, Anne. "A Study of the Concept of the Feminine Role of 51 Middle-Class American Families." *Genetic Psychology Monographs* 67 (May 1963): 275–352.

(S253) Snell, John E., Rosenwald, Richard J., and Robey, Ames. "The Wifebeater's Wife." *Archives of General Psychiatry* 11 (August 1964): 107–112.

(S254) Stewart, Lawrence H. "Mother-Son Identification and Vocational Interest." *Genetic Psychology Monographs* 60 (August 1959): 31–63.

(S255) Siegel, Alberta Engvall, and Curtis, Elizabeth Ann. "Familial Correlates of Orientation Toward Future Employment Among College Women." *Journal of Educational Psychology* 54 (1963): 33–37.

(S256) Shaw, Merville C. "Note on Parent Attitudes Toward Independence Training and the Academic Achievement of Their Children." *Journal of Educational Psychology* 55 (December 1964): 371–374.

(S257) Siegel, Alberta Engvall, and Hass, Miriam Bushkoff. "The Working Mother: A Review of Research." *Child Development* (September 1963): 513–542.

(S258) Szalita-Pemow, Alberta. "Remarks on Pathogenesis and Treatment of Schizophrenia." *Psychiatry* 14 (1951): 295–300.

(S259) Searles, Harold F. "Data Concerning Certain Manifestations of Incorporation." *Psychiatry* 14 (1951): 397–413.

(S260) Standish, Christopher T., Mann, James, and Menzer, Doris. "Some Aspects of the Psychopathology of Schizophrenia." *Psychiatry* 13 (1950): 439–445.

(S261) Silverberg, William V. "The Personal Basis and Social Significance of Passive Male Homosexuality." *Psychiatry* 1 (1938): 41–53.

(S262) Sullivan, Harry Stack. "Developmental Syndromes." *Psychiatry* 3 (1940): 28–42.

(S263) Schachter, Stanley. *The Psychology of Affiliation: Experimental Studies of the Sources of Gregariousness.* Stanford: Stanford University Press, 1959.

(S264) Simmons, Roberta Kiefere, and Lamberth, Edwin L. "Q Sort Technique as a Means of Determining the Relation of Family Structure to Self-Concept." *Marriage and Family Living* 23 (May 1961): 183–184.

(S265) Stoltz, L. "Effects of Maternal Employment on Children." *Child Development* 31 (1960): 749–782.

(S266) Skinner, Elliott P. "Labour Migration and Its Relationship to Sociocultural Change in Mossi Society." *Africa* 30 (1960): 375–401.

(S267) Swift, M. G. "A Note on the Durability of Malay Marriages." *Man* 208 (1958): 155–159.

(S268) Solien, Nancie L. "Changes in Black Carib Kinship Terminology." *Southwest Journal of Anthropology* 16 (1960): 144–159.

(S269) Sweetser, Dorian Apple. "Asymmetry in Intergenerational Family Relationships." *Social Forces* 41 (May 1963): 346–352.

(S270) Sharma, K. N. "Occupational Mobility of Castes in a North Indian Village." *Southwest Journal of Anthropology* 17 (1961): 146–164.

(S271) Skinner, E. P. "The Mossi Poqsoire." *Man* 28 (1960): 20–23.

(S272) Stuckert, Robert P. "Occupational Mobility and Family Relationships." *Social Forces* 41 (March 1963): 301–307.

(S273) Schaeffer, Earl S., and Bayley, Nancy. "Consistency of Maternal Behavior from Infancy to Preadolescence." *Journal of Abnormal and Social Psychology* 61 (July 1960): 1–6.

(S274) Sewell, William H., and Hallee, A. O. "Factors in the Relationship Between Social Status and the Personality Adjustment of the Child." *American Sociological Review* 24 (1959): 511–520.

(S275) Sharp, Lawrence J. "Employment Status of Mothers and Some Aspects of Mental Illness." *American Sociological Review* 25 (1960): 714–717.

(S276) Slater, C. "Class Differences in Definition of Role and Membership in Voluntary Associations and Among Urban Married Women." *American Journal of Sociology* 65 (1959–1960): 616–619.

(S277) Spitz, Rene A. "Hospitalism: An Inquiry into the Genesis of Psychiatric Conditions in Early Childhood." *Psychoanalytic Study of the Child* 1 (1945): 53–74.

(S278) Stotland, Ezra, and Dunn, Robert E. "Identification, Oppositeness, Authoritarianism, Self-Esteem, and Birth Order." *Psychological Monographs* 76 (1961): 528.

(S279) Stryker, Sheldon. "The Interactional and Situational Approaches." In *Handbook of Marriage and the Family,* edited by Harold T. Christensen. Chicago: Rand McNally Co., 1964, pp. 125–170.

(S280) Swinehart, James W. "Socio-Economic Level, Status Aspirations and Maternal Role." *American Sociological Review* 28 (June 1963): 391–399.

(S281) Szasz, Thomas S. "The Communication of Distress Between Child and Parent." *British Journal of Medical Psychology* 32 (1959): 161–170.

(S282) Scheffler, H. W. "Choiseul Island Descent Groups." *Polynesia* 72 (1963): 177–187.

(S283) Schneider, David M. "Double Descent on Yap." *Polynesia* 71 (1962): 1–24.

(S284) Schapera, I. "Kinship and Politics in Tswana History." *Journal of the Royal Anthropological Institute* 93 (1963): 159–173.

(T001) Tambiah, S. J., and Ryan, Bryce. "Secularization of Family Values in Ceylon." *American Sociological Review* 22, No. 3 (1957): 292–297.

(T002) Toby, Jackson. "The Differential Impact of Family Disorganization." *American Sociological Review* 22, No. 5 (1957): 505–512.

(T009) Townsend, Peter. "The Family Life of Old People: An Investigation in East London." *Sociological Review* 3 (New Series), No. 2 (1955): 175–195.

(T010) Thomas, John L. "The Factor of Religion in the Selection of Marriage Mates." *American Sociological Review* 16 (1951).

(T011) Thompson, Warren S. "Differentials in Fertility and Levels of Living in the Rural Population of the United States." *American Sociological Review* 13 (1948): 516–534.

(T012) Thomas, John L. "Religious Training in the Roman Catholic Family." *American Journal of Sociology* 57 (1951): 178–183.

(T013) Talmon-Garber, Y. "The Family in Collective Settlements." In *Transactions of the Third World Congress of Sociology,* Vol. 4, *Changes in the Family,* 116–126. London: International Sociological Association, 1956.

(T015) Tanc, Nezahat (University of Istanbul). "Note sur la famille Turque et le taux de suicides des gens mariés." In *Transactions of the Third World Congress of Sociology,* Vol. 4, *Changes in the Family,* 113–115. London: International Sociological Association, 1956.

(T016) Tran-Van-Trai. *La Famille Patriarcole Anamite.* Paris: P. Lapagesse, 1942. (Translated from the French for the *Human Relations Area Files* by C. A. Messner.)

(T017) Tugby, Donald J. "The Social Function of Mahr in Upper Mandailing, Sumatra." *American Anthropologist* 61 (1959): 631–640.

(T018) Titiev, Mischa. "The Importance of Faith in Primitive Kinship." *American Anthropologst* 58 (1956): 854–865.

(T026) Thomson, Donald F. "The Joking Relationship and Organized Obscenity in North Queensland." *American Anthropologist* 37 (1935): 460–490.

(T035) Thomas, Bertram. "Anthropological Observations in South Arabia." *Journal of the Royal Anthropological Institute* 62 (1932): 83–103.

(T039) Tambiah, S. J. "The Structure of Kinship and Its Relationship to Land Possession and Residence in Pata Bumbara, Central Ceylon." *Journal of the Royal Anthropological Institute* 88 (1958): 21–44.

(T041) Taylor, Douglas. "Kinship and Social Structure of the Island Carib." *Southwest Journal of Anthropology* 2 (1946): 180–212.

(T045) Tew, Mary. "A Further Note on Funeral Friendship." *Africa* 21 (1951): 122–124.

(T046) Tait, David. "An Analytical Commentary on the Social Structure of the Dogon." *Africa* 20 (1950): 175–199.

(T054) Torday, E. "The Principles of Bantu Marriage." *Africa* 2 (1929): 255–290.

(T055) Thurnwald, Richard. "Social Systems of Africa." *Africa* 2 (1929): 352–380.

(T058) Tait, David. "The Family, Household, and Minor Lineage of the Konkomba." *Africa* 26 (1956): 219–249.

(T059) Tait, David. "The Family, Household and Minor Lineage of the Konkomba, Part II." *Africa* 26 (1956): 332–342.

(T061) Tait, David. "The Political System of Konkomba." *Africa* 23 (1953): 213–223.

(T064) Thomas, K. H. "Notes on the Natives of the Vanimo Coast, New Guinea." *Oceania* 12 (1941–1942): 163–186.

(T065) Trevitt, J. W. "Notes on the Social Organization of Northeast Gazelle Peninsula, New Britain." *Oceania* 10 (1939–1940): 350–359.

(T067) Todd, J. A. "Report on Research Work in Southwest New Britain, Territory of New Guinea." *Oceania* 5 (1934–1935): 80–101.

(T068) Thurnwald, Richard C. "Pigs and Currency in Buin: Observations About Primitive Standards of Value and Economics." *Oceania* 5 (1934–1935): 119–141.

(T069) Thurnwald, Hilde. "Woman's Status in Buin Society." *Oceania* 5 (1934–1935): 142–170.

(T071) Todd, J. A. "Native Offenses and European Law in Southwest New Britain." *Oceania* 5 (1934–1935): 437–460.

(T072) Tax, Sol. "Economy and Technology." In *Heritage.* Glencoe, Ill.: The Free Press, 1952, pp. 43–65.

(T073) Timasheff, Nicholas S. "The Attempt to Abolish the Family in Russia." In *Modern Introduction to the Family,* edited by Norman W. Bell and Ezra F. Vogel. Glencoe, Ill.: The Free Press, 1960, pp. 55–63.

(T079) Terman, Lewis M. *Psychological Factors in Marital Happiness.* New York: McGraw-Hill Co., 1938.

(T080) Turner, V. W. *Schism and Continuity in an African Society.* Manchester: Manchester University Press, 1957.

(T081) Thurnwald, Richard C. *Black and White in East Africa.* London: Routledge and Sons, 1935.

(T082) Thurnwald, Richard C. *Economics in Primitive Societies.* London: Oxford University Press, 1932.

(T084) Thomas, R. Murray, and Surachmad, Winarno. "Social-Class Differences in Mothers' Expectations for Children in Indonesia." *Journal of Social Psychology* 57 (1962): 303–307.

(T085) Tuteur, Werner, and Glotzer, Jacob. "Murdering Mothers." *American Journal of Psychiatry* 116 (November 1959): 447–452.

(T086) Trasler, G. *In Place of Parents: A Study of Foster Care.* New York: The Humanities Press, 1960.

(T087) Townsend, Peter. *The Family Life of Old People.* Baltimore: Penguine, 1963.

(T088) Thompson, William R. "Early Environment: Its Importance for Later Behavior." In *Psychopathology of Childhood,* edited by Paul H. Hoch and Joseph Zubin. New York and London: Grune and Stratton, 1955, pp. 120–139.

(T088) Tyler, F., *et al.* "Relationships Among Motivations of Parents and Their Children." *The Journal of Genetic Psychology* 101 (1962): 69–81.

(T089) Toman, Walter. *Family Constellation.* New York: Springer Publishing Co., 1961.

(T090) Teahan, John E. "Parental Attitudes and College Success." *Journal of Educational Psychology* 54, No. 2 (April 1963): 104–109.

(T091) Toman, W. "Family Constellation as a Character and Marriage Determinant." *International Journal of Psychoanalysis* 40 (1959): 316–319.

(T092) Tharp, B. "Psychological Patterning in Marriage." *Psychological Bulletin* 60 (1963): 97–117.

(T093) Toman, W. "Family Constellations of the Partners of Divorced and Married Couples." *Journal of Individual Psychology* 18 (1962): 48–51.

(T094) Toman, W. "Family Constellations as a Basic Personality Determinant." *Journal of Individual Psychology* 15 (1959): 199–211.

(T095) Turner, Ralph H. "Some Family Determinants of Ambition." *Sociology and Social Research* 46 (July 1962): 397–411.

(T096) Turner, Ralph H. "Some Family Determinants of Ambition." *Sociology and Social Research* 46 (July 1962): 397–411.

(T097) Tolor, A., and Rafferty, W. "The Attitudes of Mothers of Hospitalized Patients." *Journal of Nervous and Mental Disease* 136 (1963): 76–81.

(T098) Talmon-Garber, Y. "Social Structure and Family Size." *Human Relations* 12 (1959): 121–146.

(T099) Talmon-Garber, Y. "Social Change and Family Structure." *International Social Science Journal* 14, No. 3 (1962): 468–487.

(T100) Tuma, E., and Livson, N. "Family Socioeconomic Status and Adolescent Attitudes to Authority." *Child Development* 31 (1960): 387–399.

(T101) Trapp, Philip, and Kausler, Donald. "Dominance Attitudes in Parents and Adult Avoidance Behavior in Young Children." *Child Development* 29 (December 1958): 507–513.

(T102) Tallman, Irving. "Adaptability: A Problem Solving Approach to Assessing Child Rearing Practices." *Child Development* 32, No. 4 (1961): 651–668.

(T103) Teahan, John E. "Parental Attitudes and College Success." *Journal of Educational Psychology* 54 (April 1963): 104–109.

(T104) Thompson, Clara. "Changing Concepts of Homosexuality in Psychoanalysis." *Psychiatry* 10 (1947): 183–189.

(T105) Tietze, Trude. "A Study of Mothers of Schizophrenic Patients." *Psychiatry* 12 (1949): 55–65.

(T106) Thorner, Isidor. "Sociological Aspects of Affectional Frustration." *Psychiatry* 6 (1943): 157–173.

(T107) Tomasic, Dinko. "Personality Development of Dinaric Warriors." *Psychiatry* 8 (1945): 449–493.

(T108) Terris, Milton, Lapouse, Rema, and Monk, Mary. "The Relation of Prematurity and Previous Fetal Loss to Childhood Schizophrenia." *American Journal of Psychiatry* 121 (November 1964): 476–481.

(T109) Toman, Walter. "Large Age Differences Among Spouses and Their Family Constellations." *Psychological Reports* 13 (August 1963): 386.

(T110) Tsung-Yi, Lin. "A Study of the Incidence of Mental Disorder in Chinese and Other Cultures." *Psychiatry* 16 (1953): 313–336.

(U002) Underwood, Francis F. R. W., and Honigmann, Irma. "A Comparison of Socialization and Personality in Two Simple Societies." *American Anthropologist* 49 (1947): 557–577.

(U003) Udy, Stanley H. *Organization of Work.* New Haven: Human Relations Area Files Press, 1959.

(U004) Ullman, Paul S. "Parental Participation in Child-Rearing Practices as Evaluated by Male Social Deviants." *Pacific Sociological Review* 3 (Fall 1960): 89–95.

(V001) Vernon, Glen M., and Stewart, Robert L. "Empathy as a Process in the Dating Situation." *American Sociological Review* 22, No. 1 (1957): 48–52.

(V002) Vincent, Clark E. "The Unwed Mother and Sampling Bias." *American Sociological Review* 19 (1954): 562–567.

(V008) Vu, Cong Hoe. *Du suicide dans la société Annamite* (Suicide in Annamese Society). Hanoi: Imprimerie Tonkinoise, 1937. (Translated from the French for the *Human Relation Area Files* by Charles Messner.)

(V009) Vogt, Evon V. "On the Concepts of Structure and

Process in Cultural Anthropology." *American Anthropologist* 62 (1960): 18–33.

(V010) Van Baal, Erring J. "Acculturation." *American Anthropologist* 62 (1960): 108–121.

(V016) Vogt, Evon V. "American Sub-Cultural Continua, as Exemplified by the Mormons and Texans." *American Anthropologist* 57 (1955): 1163–1172.

(V017) Voget, Fred. "Kinship Changes at Caughnawaga." *American Anthropologist* 55 (1953): 385–394.

(V019) Voget, Fred. "Acculturation at Caughnawaga: A Note on the Native-Modified Group." *American Anthropologist* 53 (1951): 220–231.

(V020) Vansina, J. "La famille nucléare chez les Bushoong." *Africa* 28 (1958): 95–108.

(V021) VanWing, J. "La polygamie au Congo Belge." *Africa* 17 (1947): 93–102.

(V024) Vial, L. G. "Some Statistical Aspects of Population in the Morobe District, New Guinea." *Oceania* 8 (1937–1938): 383–397.

(V025) Vayda, A. P. "Love in the South Seas." *Polynesia* 67 (1958): 78–80.

(V027) Vincent, Clark E. *Unmarried Mothers.* Glencoe, Ill.: The Free Press, 1961.

(V028) Vogel, Ezra F. "The Marital Relationship of Parents of Emotionally Disturbed Children: Polarization and Isolation." *Psychiatry* 23 (1960): 1–12.

(V029) De Vos, George. "The Relation of Guilt Toward Parents to Achievement and Arranged Marriage Among the Japanese." *Psychiatry* 23 (1960): 287–301.

(V030) Van Den Berghe, Pierre L. "Hypergamy, Hypergenation, and Miscegenation." *Human Relations* 13 (1960): 83–91.

(V031) Veroff, Joseph. "Development and Validation of a Projective Measure of Power Motivation." In *Motives in Fantasy, Action, and Society: A Method of Assessment and Study,* edited by John W. Atkinson. Princeton: D. Van Nostrand Co., 1958, pp. 105–116.

(V031) Vogel, Ezra F. "The Marital Relationship of Parents of Emotionally Disturbed Children: Polarization and Isolation." *Psychiatry* 23 (February 1960): 1–12.

(V032) Van Der Veen, F., Huebner, B., Jorgens, Barbara, and Neja, P., Jr. "Relationships Between the Parents' Concept of the Family and Family Adjustment." *American Journal of Orthopsychiatry* 34, No. 1: 45–55.

(V033) Vogel, Ezra F., and Bell, Norman W. "The Emotionally Disturbed Child as a Family Scapegoat." *Psychoanalysis and the Psychoanalytic Review* 47, No. 2 (1960): 21–42.

(V034) Vogel, William, *et al.* "Relationships Between Memories of Their Parents' Behavior and Psychodiagnosis in Psychiatrically Disturbed Soldiers." *Journal of Consulting Psychology* 28 (April 1964): 126–132.

(V035) Vernon, G., and Boadway, J. "Attitudes Toward Artificial Insemination and Some Variables Associated Therewith." *Marriage and Family Living* 21 (1959): 43–47.

(V036) Vayda, A. P. "Love in Polynesian Atolls." *Man,* 61, No. 242 (1961): 204–205.

(V037) Veroff, Joseph, Feld, Sheila, and Gurin, Gerald. "Achievement Motivation and Religious Background." *American Sociological Review* 27 (1962): 205–217.

(V038) Vogel, William, and Lauterbach, Carl G. "Relationships Between Normal and Disturbed Sons' Percepts of Their Parents' Behavior, and Personality Attributes of the Parents and Sons." *Journal of Clinical Psychology* 19 (January 1963): 52–56.

(W001) Wallin, Paul. "Religiosity, Sexual Gratification and Marital Satisfaction." *American Sociological Review* 22, No. 3 (1957): 300–305.

(W002) White, Martha Sturm. "Social Class, Child Rearing Practices, and Child Behavior." *American Sociological Review* 22, No. 6 (December 1957): 704–712.

(W003) Wallin, Paul. "Marital Happiness of Parents and Their Children's Attitude to Marriage." *American Sociological Review* 19 (1954): 20–23.

(W004) Williamson, Robert C. "Socio-Economic Factors and Marital Adjustment in an Urban Setting." *American Sociological Review* 19 (1954): 213–216.

(W005) Winch, Robert F., Ktsanes, Thomas, and Ktsanes, Virginia. "The Theory of Complementary Needs in Mate Selection: An Analytic and Descriptive Study." *American Sociological Review* 19 (1954): 241–249.

(W006) Wallin, Paul. "Sex Differences in Attitudes to 'In-Laws': A Test of Theory." *American Journal of Sociology* 59 (1954): 466–469.

(W010) Winch, Robert F. "The Theory of Complementary Needs in Mate-Selection: A Test of One Kind of Complementariness." *American Sociological Review* 20 (1955): 52–56.

(W011) Winch, Robert F. "The Theory of Complementary Needs in Mate-Selection: Final Results on the Test of the General Hypothesis." *American Sociological Review* 20 (1955): 552–555.

(W012) Woofter, T. J. "Factors Sustaining the Birth Rate." *American Sociological Review* 14 (1949): 357–366.

(W013) Winch, Robert F. "Further Data and Observations on the Oedipus Hypothesis: The Consequence of an Inadequate Hypothesis." *American Sociological Review* 16 (1951): 784–795.

(W021) Wynne, Lyman C., Ryckoff, Irving M., Day, Juliana, and Hirsch, Stanley I. "Pseudo-Mutuality in the Family Relations of Schizophrenics." In Norman W. Bell and Ezra F. Vogel, *The Family.* New York: The Free Press (1968), pp. 628–649.

(W022) Westoff, Charles F. "Social Change and Fertility in the United States: Theory and Research." In *Transactions of the Third World Congress of Sociology,* Vol. 4, *Changes in the Family,* 41–49. London: International Sociological Association, 1956.

(W023) Willoughby, Gertrude. "The Working Class Family in England." In *Transactions of the Third World Congress of Sociology,* Vol. 4, *Changes in the Family,* 155–160. London: International Sociological Association, 1956.

(W027) Wike, Joyce. "Problems in Fur Trades Analysis: The Northwest Coast." *American Anthropologist* 60 (1958): 1086–1101.

(W031) White, Raymond C. "The Luiseno Theory of 'Knowledge.'" *American Anthropologist* 59 (1957): 1–19.

(W034) Wagley, Charles, and Harris, Marvin. "A Typology of Latin American Sub-Cultures." *American Anthropologist* 57 (1955): 428–451.

(W035) Wolf, Eric R. "Type of Latin American Peasantry: A Preliminary Discussion." *American Anthropologist* 57 (1955): 252–271.

(W037) Wilson, Monica. "Nyakyusa Ritual and Symbolism." *American Anthropologist* 56 (1954): 228–241.

(W041) Wolf, Eric R. "Affect of Group Relations in a Complex Society." *American Anthropologist* 58 (1956): 1065–1078.

(W043) Weckler, J. E. "Adoption on Mokil." *American Anthropologist* 55 (1953): 555–568.

(W045) Williams, S. E. "Group Sentiment and Primitive

Justice." *American Anthropologist* 43 (1941): 523–539.

(W047) Woods, Carter A. "A Criticism of Wissler's North American Culture Areas." *American Anthropologist* 36 (1934): 517–523.

(W049) Warner, William Lloyd. "Morphology and Function of the Australian Language of Kinship." *American Anthropologist* 33 (1931): 172–198.

(W050) White, Leslie A. "A Problem in Kinship Terminology." *American Anthropologist* 41 (1939): 566–573.

(W052) Warner, William Lloyd. "Morphology and Functions of the Australian Murngin Types of Kinship." *American Anthropologist* 32 (1930): 207–256.

(W054) Wallace, Anthony F. C. "Mentaweian Social Organization." *American Anthropologist* 53 (1951): 370–375.

(W055) Whyte, William Foote. "The Sicilian Peasant Society." *American Anthropologist* 46 (1944): 65–74.

(W056) Worsley, P. M. "The Kinship System of the Tallensi: A Reevaluation." *Journal of the Royal Anthropological Institute* 86 (1956): 37–75.

(W058) Wilson, Monica. "Nyakusua Age-Villages." *Journal of the Royal Anthropological Institute* 79 (1949): 21–26.

(W059) Williams, F. E. "The Reminiscences of Ahuia Ova." *Journal of the Royal Anthropological Institute* 69 (1939): 11–44.

(W062) Williams, S. E. "Sex Affiliation and Its Implications." *Journal of the Royal Anthropological Institute* 62 (1932): 51–81.

(W064) Wedgwood, Camilla H. "Death and Social Status in Melanesia." *Journal of the Royal Anthropological Institute* 57 (1927): 377–397.

(W065) Wilson-Hassedon, J. R. "Ethnological Notes on the Shuwalbe Group of the Borroro Fulani in the Kurafi District of Keffi Emirate, Northern Nigeria." *Journal of the Royal Anthropological Institute* 57 (1927): 275–293.

(W067 or W069) Wilbert, Johannes. "Kinship and Social Organization of the Kekuana and Boajiro." *Southwest Journal of Anthropology* 14 (1958): 51–60.

(W069) Wolf, Eric R. "Closed Corporate Peasant Communities in Meso America and Central Java." *Southwest Journal of Anthropology* 13 (1957): 1–18.

(W070) Wilbert, Johannes. "Notes on Guahibo Kinship and Social Organization." *Southwest Journal of Anthropology* 13 (1957): 88–98.

(W071) Wallace, Anthony S. C. "Political Organization and Land Tenure Among the Northeastern Indians, 1600–1830." *Southwest Journal of Anthropology* 13 (1957): 301–321.

(W073) Wagley, Charles. "Economics of a Guatemalan Village." *Memoirs of the American Anthropological Association* 58 (1941).

(W075) Wolf, Eric R. "The Social Organization of Mecca and the Origins of Islam." *Southwest Journal of Anthropology* 7 (1951): 329–356.

(W076) White, Leslie A. "Evolutionary Stages, Progress, and the Evaluation of Cultures." *Southwest Journal of Anthropology* 3 (1947): 165–192.

(W078) Wilks, Ivor. "Akwamu and Otublohum: An 18th Century Akan Marriage Arrangement." *Africa* 29 (1959): 391–404.

(W079) Warmington, W. A. "Saving and Indebtedness Among Cameroon Plantation Workers." *Africa* 28 (1958): 329–343.

(W080) Whiteley, Wilfred. "Modern Local Government Among the Makua." *Africa* 24 (1954): 349–458.

(W081) Wilson, Godfrey. "Anthropology as a Public Service." *Africa* 13 (1940): 43–61.

(W082) Wagner, Gunther. "The Changing Family Among the Bantu Kavirondo." Supplement to *Africa* 12, No. 1 (1939).

(W083) Wilson, Godfrey. "Introduction to Nyakyusa Law." *Africa* 10 (1937): 16–36.

(W084) Wilson, Godfrey. "An African Morality." *Africa* 9 (1936): 75–99.

(W085) Wagner, Gunther. "The Study of Culture Contacts and the Determination of Policy." *Africa* 9 (1936): 317–331.

(W090) Ward, Barbara E. "Some Observations on Religious Cults in Ashanti." *Africa* 26 (1956): 47–61.

(W091) White, C. M. N. "Conservatism and Modern Adaptation in Luvale Female Puberty Ritual." *Africa* 23 (1953): 15–21.

(W092) White, C. M. N. "Stratification and Modern Changes in an Ancestral Cult." *Africa* 19 (1949): 324–331.

(W093) Wedgwood, Camilla H. "Manam Kinship." *Oceania* 29 (1958–1959): 239–256.

(W097) Williams, F. E. "Natives of Lake Kutubu, Papua." *Oceania* 11 (1940–1941): 259–294.

(W098) Wedgwood, Camilla H. "The Life of Children in Manam." *Oceania* 9 (1938–1939): 1–29.

(W100) Whiting, John W. M., and Reed, Stephen W. "Kwoma Culture." *Oceania* 9 (1938–1939): 170–216.

(W102) Williams, F. E. "Mission Influence Amongst the Keveri of Southeast Papua." *Oceania* 15 (1944–1945): 89–141.

(W103) Wedgwood, Camilla H. "Report on Research Work in Nauru Island, Central Pacific." *Oceania* 7 (1936–1937): 1–33.

(W104) Wedgwood, Camilla H. "Women in Manam." *Oceania* 7 (1936–1937): 401–428.

(W105) Wedgwood, Camilla H. "Report on Research Work in Nauru Island, Central Pacific." *Oceania* 6 (1935–1936): 359–391.

(W106) Wedgwood, Camilla H. "Women in Manam." *Oceania* 8 (1937–1938): 170–192.

(W108) Wedgwood, Camilla H. "Report on Research in Manam Island, Mandated Territory of New Guinea." *Oceania* 4 (1933–1934): 373–403.

(W109) Williams, F. E. "Depopulation and Administration." *Oceania* 3 (1932–1933): 218–226.

(W113) Wedgwood, Camilla H. "A Review of 'Coming of Age in Samoa' by Margaret Mead." *Oceania* 1 (1930–1931): 123–125.

(W114) Warner, W. Lloyd. "Murngin Warfare." *Oceania* 1 (1930–1931): 457–494.

(W115) Winter, Edward H. *Bwamba: A Structural-Functional Analysis of a Patrilineal Society.* Cambridge: W. Heffer and Sons, Ltd., 1959.

(W117) Winiata, Maharaia. "Leadership in Pre-European Maori Society." *Polynesia* 65 (1956): 212–231.

(W123) Weinberg, S. Kirson. *Incest Behavior.* New York: Citadel Press, 1955.

(W124) Wynne, Lyman C., Ryckoff, Irving M., Day, Julianna, and Hirsch, Stanley I. "Pseudo-Mutuality in the Family Relations of Schizophrenics." *Psychiatry* 21 (1958): 205–220.

(W125) Weiss, James M. A. "The Gamble with Death in Attempted Suicide." *Psychiatry* 20 (1957): 17–25.

(W126) Wohl, R. Richard, and Trosman, Harry. "A Retrospect of Freud's 'Leonardo.'" *Psychiatry* 18 (1955): 27–39.

(W127) Whiting, John W. M. "Socialization Process and

Personality." In *Psychological Anthropology,* edited by Francis L. K. Hsu. Homewood, Ill.: Dorsey Press, 1961.

(W128) Wilson, Monica. *Good Company.* London: Oxford University Press, 1951.

(W129) Warner, W. Lloyd. *A Black Civilization.* New York: Harper and Brothers, 1937.

(W130) Wagner, Gunther. *The Bantu of North Kavirondo.* Published for the International African Institute. London: Oxford University Press, 1949.

(W131) White, Leslie A. *The Evolution of Culture.* New York: McGraw-Hill, 1959.

(W132) Watson, William. *Tribal Cohesion in a Money Economy.* Manchester: Manchester University Press, 1958.

(W133) Williams, Judith R., and Scott, Roland B. "Growth and Development of Negro Infants: IV. Motor Development and Its Relationship to Child Rearing Practices in Two Groups of Negro Infants." *Child Development* 24 (June 1953): 103–121.

(W134) Wenar, Charles. "The Reliability of Mothers' Histories." *Child Development* 32, No. 3 (1961): 491–500.

(W135) Wattenberg, E. W. "Ten-Year-Old Boys in Trouble." *Child Development* 28 (March 1957): 43–46.

(W136) Wyatt, Gertrude, and Herzan, Helen. "Therapy with Stuttering Children and Their Mothers." *American Journal of Orthopsychiatry* 32 (1962): 148–151.

(W137) Winder, C. L., and Rau, Lucy. "Parental Attitudes Associated with Social Deviance in Preadolescent Boys." *Journal of Abnormal and Social Psychology* 64 (June 1962): 418–424.

(W138) Winker, James B. "Age Trends and Sex Differences in Wishes, Identifications, Activities and Fears of Children." *Child Development* 20 (December 1949): 191–200.

(W139) Winterbottom, Marian R. "The Relations of Need for Achievement to Learning Experiences in Independence and Mastery." In *Motives in Fantasy, Action, and Society: A Method of Assessment and Study,* edited by John W. Atkinson. Princeton: D. Van Nostrand Company, 1958, pp. 453–478.

(W140) West, D. J. "Parental Figures in the Genesis of Male Homosexuality." *International Journal of Social Psychiatry* 5 (Autumn 1959): 85–97.

(W141) Winnicott, D. W. "The Capacity to Be Alone." *International Journal of Psychoanalysis* 39 (September–October 1958): 416–420.

(W142) Whiting, J., and Child, I. *Child Training and Personality: A Cross-Cultural Study.* New Haven: Yale University Press, 1953.

(W143) Weinberg, S. Kirson. *Society and Personality Disorders.* New York: Prentice-Hall, Inc., 1952.

(W144) Werner, Emmy. "Milieu Difference in Social Competence." *Journal of Genetic Psychology* 91 (1957): 239–249.

(W144) Williams, Eugene I., Jr., and Williams, Carl D. "Relationships Between Authoritarian Attitudes of College Students, Estimation of Parents' Attitudes, and Acute Parental Attitudes." *Journal of Social Psychology* 61 (1963): 43–48.

(W145) Williams, Jessie M. "Children Who Break Down in Foster Homes: A Psychological Study of Patterns of Personality Growth in Grossly Deprived Children." *Journal of Child Psychology and Psychiatry* 2 (June 1961): 5–20.

(W146) Weatherley, Donald. "Maternal Response to Childhood Aggression and Subsequent Anti-Semitism." *Journal of Abnormal and Social Psychology* 66 (February 1963): 183–185.

(W147) Wahl, C. "Some Antecedent Factors in the Family Histories of 392 Schizophrenics." *American Journal of Psychiatry* 110 (1954): 668–674.

(W148) Winch, Robert F. *Mate Selection: A Study of Complementary Needs.* New York: Harper and Brothers, 1958.

(W149) Weinstein, E. "Family Identification of Foster Children." *Social Forces* 38 (1959): 58–61.

(W150) Weil, Mildred W. "An Analysis of the Factors Influencing Married Women's Actual or Planned Work Participation." *American Sociological Review* 26 (January 1961): 91–96.

(W151) Weinberg, Carl. "Family Background and Deviance or Conformity to School Expectations." *Journal of Marriage and Family Living* 26 (February 1964): 89–91.

(W152) Wirt, R., and Briggs, P. "Personality and Environmental Factors in the Development of Delinquency." *Psychological Monographs* 73, No. 15 (1959): 1–47.

(W153) Woods, P., Glavin, K., and Kettle, C. "A Mother-Daughter Comparison on Selected Aspects of Child Rearing in a High Socioeconomic Group." *Child Development* 31 (1960): 121–128.

(W154) Weigert-Vowinkel, Edith. "The Cult and Mythology of the Magna Mater from the Standpoint of Psychoanalysis." *Psychiatry* 1 (1938): 347–378.

(W155) Wallin, Paul, and Clark, Alexander L. "Religiosity, Sexual Gratification, and Marital Satisfaction in the Middle Years of Marriage." *Social Forces* 42 (December 1964): 303–309.

(W156) Weyer, E. M. *The Eskimos.* New Haven: Yale University Press, 1932.

(W157) Wagley, Charles, and Galvas, Edwards. *The Tenetehara Indians of Brazil.* New York: Columbia University Press, 1949.

(W158) Wechsler, Henry, and Funkenstein, Daniel H. "The Family as a Determinant of Conflict in Self-Perception." *Psychological Reports* 7 (1960): 143–149.

(Y001) Young, Rev. T. Cullen. "Tribal Inter-Mixture in Northern Nyasaland." *Journal of the Royal Anthropological Institute* 63: 1–18.

(Y002) Young, T. Cullen. "A Good Village." *Africa* 7 (1934): 89–96.

(Y003) Young, Michael. "Distribution of Income Within the Family." *British Journal of Sociology* 3 (1952): 305–321.

(Y004) Yang, Martin C. *A Chinese Village.* New York: Columbia University Press, 1945.

(Y042) Yarrow, Leon J. "The Relationship Between Nutritive Sucking Experiences in Infancy and Non-Nutritive Sucking in Childhood." *Journal of Genetic Psychology* 84 (1954): 149–162.

(Y042) Yarrow, Leon J. "Research in Dimensions of Early Maternal Care." *Merrill–Palmer Quarterly* 9 (April 1963): 101–114.

(Y043) Young, Leontine. *Wednesday's Children.* New York: McGraw-Hill, 1964.

(Y045) Yarrow, L. "Maternal Deprivation." *Psychological Bulletin* 58 (1961): 459–490.

(Y046) Yeracaris, C. "Differentials in the Relationship Between Values and Practices in Fertility." *Social Forces* 38 (1959): 153–158.

(Y047) Yudkin, Simon, and Holme, Anthea. *Working Mothers and Their Children.* London: Michael Joseph, Ltd., 1963.

(Y048) Young, Leontine. *Out of Wedlock.* New York: McGraw-Hill, 1954.

(Y049) Yeracaris, Constantine A. "Differentials in Ideal Family Size: Buffalo, 1956." *Sociology and Social Research* 44 (September–October 1959): 8–11.

(Y050) Talmon-Garber, Y. "Social Structure and Family Size." *Human Relations* 12 (1959): 121–146.

(Y051) Yarrow, M. R., Scott, P., de Leeuw, L., and Heinig, C. "Child-Rearing in Families of Working and Non-working Mothers." *Sociometry* 25 (1962): 122–140.

(Y053) Yalman, Nur. "On the Purity of Women in the Castes of Ceylon and Malabar." *Journal of the Royal Anthropological Institute* 93 (1963): 25–58.

(Z001) Zelditch, Morris, Jr. "Role Differentiation in the Nuclear Family: A Comparative Study." In *Modern Introduction to the Family,* edited by Norman W. Bell and Ezra F. Vogel. Glencoe, Ill.: The Free Press, 1960, pp. 329–338.

(Z003) Zelditch, Morris, Jr. "The Typical Marriage Preferences of the Ramah Navaho." *American Anthropologist* 61 (1959): 470–491.

(Z006) Zuk, G. H., Miller, R. L., Bartram, J. B., and Kling, F. "Maternal Acceptance of Retarded Children: A Questionnaire Study of Attitudes and Religious Background." *Child Development* 32, No. 3 (1961): 525–540.

(Z007) Ziegler, Frederic J., Imboden, John B., and Mayer, Eugene. "Contemporary Conversion Symptomatology: A Clinical Study." *American Journal of Psychiatry* 110 (April 1960): 901–910.

(Z008) Zimmerman, Charles C., and Cervantes, Lucius F. *Successful American Families.* New York: Pageant Press, 1960.

(Z009) Zuk, G. "Autistic Distortions in Parents of Retarded Children." *Journal of Consulting Psychology* 23, No. 2 (1959): 171–176.

(Z010) Zunich, Michael. "The Relation Between Parental Attitudes Toward Child Rearing and Child Behavior." *Journal of Consulting Psychology* 26 (April 1962): 197.

(Z011) Zuckerman, M., *et al.* "The Parental Attitudes of Parents of Child Guidance Cases." *Child Development* 31 (1960): 401–417.